D1208544

HANDBOOK OF THE BIRDS OF THE WORLD

Volume 7

Jacamars *to* Woodpeckers

Lynx Edicions

BirdLife
INTERNATIONAL

HANDBOOK OF THE BIRDS OF THE WORLD

Volume 7

Jacamars *to* Woodpeckers

Josep del Hoyo
Andrew Elliott
Jordi Sargatal

David Christie
Nigel Collar
Errol Fuller
Jennifer Horne
Tadeu de Melo-Júnior

Pamela Rasmussen
Lester Short
Joe Tobias
Hans Winkler
Thomas Züchner

Colour Plates by

Hilary Burn
Clive Byers
John Cox
Errol Fuller
Al Gilbert

Ren Hathway
Mark Hulme
Julian Hume
Àngels Jutglar
Francesc Jutglar
Ian Lewington

Dave Nurney
Chris Rose
Brian Small
Ian Willis
Tim Worfolk

Consultant for Systematics
and Nomenclature

Walter J. Bock

Consultant for Status
and Conservation

Nigel J. Collar

Lynx Edicions

Barcelona

Recommended citation:
del Hoyo, J., Elliott, A. & Sargatal, J. eds. (2002). *Handbook of the Birds of the World*. Vol. 7. Jacamars to Woodpeckers.
Lynx Edicions, Barcelona.

Citation to individual contributions recommended in the following format:
Rasmussen, P.C. & Collar, N.J. (2002). Family Bucconidae (Puffbirds). Pp. 102-138 in:
del Hoyo, J., Elliott, A. & Sargatal, J. eds. (2002). *Handbook of the Birds of the World*. Vol. 7. Jacamars to Woodpeckers.
Lynx Edicions, Barcelona.

© **Copyright Lynx Edicions 2002**

All rights reserved. No part of this book may be reproduced or transmitted in any form or by any means, electronic or
mechanical, including photocopy, recording or any information retrieval system without the prior written permission of the
copyright holders.

Printed on paper manufactured by Sappi in a totally acid-free watersystem.

Colour reproductions by *Edifilm, S.A.* Barcelona
Printed and bound in Barcelona by *Grafos, S.A. Arte sobre papel*
Dipòsit Legal: B-3238-2002
ISBN: 84-87334-37-7

OVERSIZE
QL
673
.H265
1992
vol. 7

0012924292

cl

Authors of Volume 7

D. A. Christie
Assistant Editor of British Birds *and freelance ornithologist, Southampton, England*

Dr N. J. Collar
Research Fellow, BirdLife International, Cambridge, England.

E. Fuller
Tunbridge Wells, England.

J. F. M. Horne
Senior Research Fellow, National Museums of Kenya, Nairobi, Kenya.

T. A. de Melo-Júnior
Department of Vertebrate Zoology, Universidade Franca, Franca, São Paulo, Brazil.

Dr P. C. Rasmussen
Michigan State University Museum, East Lansing, Michigan, USA.

Professor L. L. Short
Lamont Curator Emeritus, American Museum of Natural History, New York, USA;
and Senior Research Associate, National Museums of Kenya, Nairobi, Kenya.

Dr J. A. Tobias
Freelance ornithologist, Cambridge, England.

Professor H. Winkler
Konrad Lorenz Institute of Ethology, Austrian Academy of Sciences, Vienna, Austria.

T. Züchner
Alexander Koenig Research Institute and Zoological Museum, Bonn, Germany.

UWEC McIntyre Library

JUN 0 6 2002

___ Claire, WI

Editorial Council

Ramón Mascort
(President)

Josep del Hoyo
Ramón Mascort Brugarolas
Carmen Pascual
Pilar Ruiz-Olalla
Jordi Sargatal

Assistant to Editors

Nicole Wirtz

Correction of Texts

David Christie

Alan Elliott	*Anna Motis*
Heather Elliott	*Jaume Orta*
Julian Hughes	*Joe Tobias*
Francesc Jutglar	*Bruno Walther*
Jeffrey Marks	*Mike Wilson*

Documentation

Teresa Pardo
Marta Fenollar

Design

Josep del Hoyo
Xavier Ruiz

Production

Xavier Ruiz

Administration

Pilar Ruiz-Olalla
Ramon Mascort Brugarolas
Esther Curpián
Gemma López
Teresa Bassas
Francesc Capdevila
Conchi García
Olga González
Sílvia Trota

CONTENTS

LIST OF PLATES

Foreword

Extinct Birds

The subject of recent extinctions is one that seems, increasingly, to be a part of popular culture. Today the words Great Auk (*Pinguinus impennis*), moa (Dinornithidae), Thylacine or Tasmanian Wolf (*Thylacinus cynocephalus*), Quagga (*Equus quagga*) and, of course, Dodo (*Raphus cucullatus*) are names with which many people are familiar. Yet, while the subject has always held an intrinsic fascination, it is one that comparatively few have cared to pursue – until recently. Now, the increasing vigour of the conservation movement, combined with the new vogue for popular science, has brought with it a fresh awareness of, and enthusiasm for, the subject.

It is not difficult to see why. First, there is the mystery – and mystery exerts a great influence over the human psyche. Yet, paradoxically, recently extinct creatures are accessible in a way that animals known only from the fossil record are not. They sometimes seem almost touchable but, of course, this is only an illusion. In reality, they remain as elusive as those species that passed away aeons ago.

Recent extinctions have a major advantage over those from the deep past: they offer the possibility that we may learn something significant from their example. Perhaps if we listen to these woeful stories we may be able to find a way to prevent similar tragedies from occurring in the future. Or, perhaps not!

Then, also, there is the tantalizing possibility of rediscovery. While there may be no chance of finding a *Tyrannosaurus* lurking is some jungle fastness, who can say with certainty that Pink-headed Ducks (*Rhodonessa caryophyllacea*) do not still survive in an Indian wilderness? There have been numerous examples of rediscovery and, doubtless, there will be others.

It has become traditional to regard 1600 as an approximate cut-off date from which to determine recently extinct bird species. Lionel Walter Rothschild's pioneering work of 1907 began this trend, since which time the date of 1600 has been adopted by several other writers, including the present one. The date is not quite as arbitrarily chosen as it may seem. The year 1600 represents a date heralding a period at which relatively reliable records began to accumulate; before this time it is generally impossible to make realistic sense of the few records that exist. The date also largely eliminates fossil birds or most birds known only from skeletal material. Such a subject is a vast and complex one and totally beyond the scope of a work such as this. For various technical and practical reasons it is impossible to put an exact figure on the number of bird species that have become extinct during the last 400 years. Obviously, any number may have passed away without leaving any trace at all. Concerning those of which we have certain knowledge, most authors would agree that there are something between 80 and 100, depending on how one interprets evidence. Sadly, this number is likely to increase dramatically during the next few years.

At many practical levels the subject of recent extinctions is a difficult one, for how can these be accurately and consistently defined? First comes the very complex question, "How do you know it is extinct?" In many cases – the Dodo, for instance – it is obvious: a very large, conspicuous bird restricted to a relatively small island could certainly not survive unnoticed. In others the issue is rather more difficult to resolve. From the ranks of the world's bird species it is possible to select a considerable number that might be extinct. But on the other hand, they might not be!

Figure 1. Egg of Aepyornis maximus, *life-size; some eggs were even larger.*

[Photo: Errol Fuller]

In order to help the reader in comparing this foreword with the main body of the HBW texts, normal HBW usage has been adopted in the taxonomy and in the choice of vernacular names. Also, the criteria followed throughout HBW have likewise been applied here in the decisions as to which forms are included and which omitted. The editors are extremely grateful to Errol Fuller for very kindly agreeing to adapt his own preferred usage in all three aspects. See also editors' Introduction to Volume 7, page 69.

One well-known definition states that any creature not seen for a period of 50 years may be regarded as extinct. Unfortunately, however, such a definition – understandable and persuasive though it may be – is unworkable from any realistic point of view. Patterns of decline, remoteness of terrain occupied, recent changes to the environment and a whole variety of other elements may be relevant in this or that particular instance. There are a number of bird species that went missing for upwards of 50 years and then returned from seeming oblivion, notably the Forest Owlet (*Athene blewitti*) and the New Caledonian Owlet-nightjar (*Aegotheles savesi*) "absent" for 113 years and 118 years respectively, and even more recently Bruijn's Brush-turkey (*Aepypodius bruijnii*), rediscovered on the remote and almost inaccessible New Guinean island of Waigeo. Yet there are others that have been seen in the last decade or two that could now categorically be considered extinct.

Rarity is a peculiar thing. Some species can stay rare for decades, or even centuries, without actually dropping into the doleful condition of extinction. Others become extinct in much more dramatic style.

The celebrated case of the Takahe (*Porphyrio mantelli*) of New Zealand provides a perfect example. Known from just four specimens taken during the nineteenth century, the species "vanished" for a period of 50 years before being rediscovered during 1948. Since this time the species has limped on in extreme rarity and managed to survive into the twenty-first century. This might be compared with the famous downfall of the Passenger Pigeon (*Ectopistes migratorius*), which at the start of the nineteenth century was possibly amongst the most numerous birds on Earth. In the space of two or three decades numbers plummeted from many, many millions to just a handful of individuals, and during 1914 the last individual of all died in her cage at the Cincinnati Zoo.

What does all this mean? Simply that, while there may be guidelines to govern the nature of extinction, there are no hard and fast universal rules. Each case must be judged on its own merits.

This introduction to the subject features only those birds that can claim without doubt the title of extinct. Other, more controversial, cases are reviewed in brief.

Another great difficulty that surrounds extinct birds concerns the definition of a species. As so many of these creatures are poorly known it is by no means certain that some of them had actually passed the boundary at which they could be regarded as full species. This might particularly be the case where a form is known only from skeletal remains, but even with more substantial evidence there may still be controversy over definitions, as indeed is apparent with the differing taxonomic views regarding even common and well-known taxa. One authority might define an extinct form as simply a subspecies, while others may see it as a full and legitimate species. The Norfolk Kaka (*Nestor* (*meridionalis*) *productus*) and the Guadalupe Caracara (*Polyborus* (*plancus*) *lutosus*) are good examples. Both hover rather uneasily at the junction where full species meet subspecies, and either can be fairly defined in either way.

Then there is the matter of mystery species and others that might be termed "hypothetical". A surprisingly large number of species have been described from just a single specimen with no other similar bird ever turning up. Sharpe's Rail (*Gallirallus sharpei*), for instance, was described from a single specimen that was purchased by the Leiden Museum during 1865 and came from an unknown source. Since that time no comparable specimen has come to light. Is the bird a freak or is it an otherwise unknown – but legitimate and presumably extinct – species? Probably it is the latter, but no-one knows for sure.

"Hypothetical" birds come into a related but slightly different category. These are forms that have been described from early travellers' tales or descriptions. The desire to name new species seems so great that many ornithologists (who should have known better) have succumbed to temptation and named birds on evidence that is totally unsatisfactory and against the rules of scientific nomenclature. Perhaps the most famous case of this kind is that of the White Dodo (*Raphus solitarius*) of Reunion. There is a very, very small amount of evidence that such a bird may once have existed but absolutely no hard proof of any kind. Many other "hypothetical" bird species have been proposed but, while their stories may be fascinating, none of these have any real place in a serious list of extinct birds.

It may be worth briefly remarking on another category of disappearing species, namely those classified by BirdLife International as "Extinct in the Wild", at present numbering just three species, the Alagoas Curassow (*Mitu mitu*), the Guam Rail (*Gallirallus owstoni*) and the Socorro Dove (*Zenaida graysoni*). Sadly, it is very likely that within just a few years quite a number of other species may join this group. The prime candidate must be Spix's Macaw (*Cyanopsitta spixii*), with a wild population of only a single bird from 1990 until it disappeared in 2001, but with at least 60 birds (probably all closely related) currently held by aviculturalists. By definition, all such species survive in captivity, and the chances of their eventual reintroduction to their natural range should not be discounted, so they remain outwith the strict scope of this foreword.

All these considerations mean that no-one can come up with a definitive extinct list that is totally satisfactory to everyone else. Even the birds featured here are at some variance with the list given in the present author's recent (2001) book *Extinct Birds*. In order to ensure continuity and conformity with HBW, certain eliminations and additions have been made. Most notably, several species covered in *Extinct Birds* have been excluded from this foreword because they have already received full treatment in the main body of HBW, with individual species account, illustration and map; most of these were, perhaps optimistically, listed as "Almost certainly Extinct". These variations should be regarded in the spirit in which such determinations must necessarily be made. No decisions on what is extinct or what is not, what represents a subspecies and what does not, should be regarded as graven in stone. All such things change according to current knowledge and attitude. The information given here represents a good and honest guess at the truth – but it should never be considered as an absolute truth.

Reasons for recent extinctions are, of course, many and various but most are due to human intervention. Hunting and shooting, though the most obvious kind of destructive processes, are not – at the species level – necessarily the most devastating. Destroying habitats and/or altering them have caused immense damage. The problems caused by complete destruction of habitat are obvious, but alteration, in the form of altering land use or introducing alien species, is similarly critical and both of these are among the main factors that destroy bird populations and ultimately lead to extinctions.

The geography of recently extinct birds is a particularly revealing one. By and large such extinctions come from islands rather than from the major land masses. Although there are a number of spectacular exceptions – and this number is likely to increase in the coming decades – it is on oceanic islands and island groups that the major casualties have occurred. Thus, the Hawaiian Islands, the Mascarenes, New Zealand and the islands south of Japan are all among the great theatres of extinction.

Clearly, if a species' habitat is demolished or radically altered, sooner or later that species will inevitably vanish along with the environment. With many island birds being endemics, it must follow that a species lost from its island home is a species lost entirely. Many, many island forms are already gone and many more are today under threat; there is little doubt that true island insularity hugely increases any species' vulnerability.

At a less dramatic level, local populations of otherwise flourishing species are often wiped out when a marsh is drained or a forest chopped down. If the species is plentiful elsewhere, its loss in one particular place may well pass unnoticed. Even subtle interference can sometimes have the same result and such subtle interventions can take many forms. The results of the random (or sometimes highly organized) introduction of predators to predator-free places are obvious but the introduction of animals with no predatory intent can cause equal chaos. Competition for limited territory or an ecological niche is one obvious area of concern. Equally insidious are the possibility of introduced disease, the spread of alien plants pushing out the natural flora, or the introduction of poisons.

There is a tendency to think that the creation of reserves might provide a convenient solution. Unfortunately this setting aside of portions of land does not necessarily work. When environments become fragmented, it is often not possible to foresee the ultimate consequences of such fragmentation.

The birds featured here are listed in an order conforming to the general arrangement of HBW. A short preface for each major bird group that is currently affected by extinction is included to facilitate some discussion of controversial or problematical forms.

Concerning many extinct species virtually nothing is known; about others there is a considerable body of information. If basic ornithological information is not given in any particular case, it may be assumed that this is because such information remains unknown.

A computation has recently been made (for BirdLife International's book *Threatened Birds of the World*, 2000) that one in eight of the world's bird species (around 1200 species) are at risk of extinction during the next 100 years. No-one should assume, therefore, that extinct species are irrelevant. They are not things that are gone and best forgotten. Rather, they should be seen as something to illuminate the future. And that future will be much drabber, should we not look at these pictures from history and learn from them.

RATITES

The celebrated nineteenth century ornithologist Alfred Newton defined the ratites as:

> That division of the Class Aves whose sternum developing no "keel" resembles a raft or flat-bottomed boat.

This is, then, a rather loose assemblage of creatures but from it can be selected a number of the largest birds known to us. Among living ratites are the Ostrich (Struthionidae), the rheas (Rheidae), the cassowaries (Casuariidae) and the Emu (Dromaiidae), and the much smaller and different-looking kiwis (Apterygidae). Among extinct groups are the elephantbirds (Aepyornithidae) and the moas (Dinornithidae).

The origins of these rather un-birdlike birds are unclear and how each of the distinct groups relate to one another – if at all – is a matter of some controversy.

The major areas of mystery concerning the ratites can be summed up in two questions. Did the various ratite orders evolve separately or are they all derived from a common ancestral stock? Was this ancestral stock – or these stocks – made up from true flying birds, or were these prehistoric creatures that never actually acquired the power of flight?

As far as the second question is concerned, it can be said that the extinct moas show no vestige of a wing. In simplistic terms they are the most perfect of bipeds, their forelimbs having vanished without trace. Notwithstanding this curious fact, it seems most likely that the ancestors of the birds now called ratites could all fly perfectly well and that they gradually lost the power in much the same way, and for much the same reasons, as other flightless birds.

Figure 2. Richard Owen photographed alongside the skeleton of a moa, in about 1865. In his right hand, he holds Rule's Bone.

The question of common ancestry is, perhaps, rather more contentious. Although most of the ratites show some overall similarity in general appearance, this may be entirely due to the factor known as convergent evolution. In other words, these creatures may have grown to look alike simply because they share similarities in their lifestyles.

Traditionally, the five extant ratite families have been awarded four or five separate orders, but in recent years there has been an increasing tendency to lump them all in a single order, Struthioniformes, with the different groupings being reduced to four suborders, the families Casuariidae and Dromaiidae being placed in the same suborder. How this affects the extinct Aepyornithidae and Dinornithidae, each traditionally placed in its own separate order too, is not always discussed, but the general consensus of opinion is that they too are probably most usefully placed in this all-enveloping Struthioniformes.

Ratites have certainly been very successful in many parts of the world and Africa, Asia, South America and Australia have all been occupied. So too have smaller land masses: New Zealand, Madagascar, New Guinea and many of the islands that make up Indonesia. Yet despite this evident success, the ratites have been in general decline during the age of man. There is, for instance, no doubt that until comparatively recently Ostriches occurred in many places where they can no longer be found. They have vanished from many parts of Africa, from Asia, and from Arabia, where the last individuals may have died during the 1940's or, perhaps, during the 1960's. There is evidence that Ostriches once lived in parts of southern Russia. Whether the birds that inhabited all these places belonged to just a single species or whether there were, in fact, several different kinds, is difficult to determine.

Similarly, it is difficult to determine exactly which ratite species have become extinct since 1600. For the purposes of this work four species have been selected, an elephantbird and three moas, although in each of these cases there is doubt over the actual date of extinction, and some might consider that these birds were gone before 1600. Each of the four is known only from skeletal remains, skin or egg fragments, and in some cases complete eggs. Curiously, the eggs of moas are excessively rare whereas their bones are relatively common; the reverse is the case with the elephantbirds and their eggs turn up far more frequently than their bones.

Two other forms are sometimes listed as recently extinct species. These are dwarf emus from Kangaroo and King Islands, off the south coast of Australia, known from skeletal remains and a single stuffed specimen now in Paris. Although there is no doubt that these two island forms are now extinct, both having vanished during the early years of the nineteenth century, there is uncertainty over whether either had passed the point at which it could be considered specifically distinct from their extant relative on the mainland, the Emu (*Dromaius novaehollandiae*).

There has been a certain amount of sloppiness over the way in which scientific names for these forms have been changed. The Kangaroo Island birds are now usually listed as *Dromaius novaehollandiae baudinianus* (formerly *D. n. diemenianus*) and those from King Island as *D. n. ater* (previously *minor*). There is, in fact, no certainty over which specimens came from which island, and, as a result, the switch to these names from older ones may not be justified. The controversy over this is still raging (see Greenway, 1958, Jouanin, 1959, Fuller, 2000a) so no hard and fast determination can be made.

Another rather distinct form was the Tasmanian Emu (*Dromaius novaehollandiae diemenensis*) but, like *D. n. baudinianus* and *D. n. ater*, it had probably not evolved into a species that could be regarded as separate from the Emu of the Australian mainland. This Tasmanian population became extinct during the middle years of the nineteenth century.

AEPYORNITHIDAE

Great Elephantbird   *Aepyornis maximus*

Aepyornis maximus
I. Geoffroy Saint-Hilaire, 1851
Ann. Sci. Nat. Zool. **Ser. 3, no. 14**: 209.

The Great Elephantbird of Madagascar holds the distinction of having laid the largest egg known to man, in fact the largest of single-celled objects. This extraordinary egg is far bigger than that laid by any known dinosaur or any other giant reptile and is thought to have given rise to Arab tales of the "roc".

Nothing is known of the bird's habits and even its exact appearance in life is unknown; it is assumed that it looked something like an enormous Emu. Standing some 3 m high, this was an incredibly ponderous and heavy bird and in terms of sheer weight it is the largest bird ever known to have lived.

There appear to have been several related species occupying the island of Madagascar and this particular one – the largest – seems to have been the last to become

16

extinct. The testimony of the first French Governor of Madagascar, Étienne de Flacourt, seems to indicate that individuals still survived in the 1650's. He mentioned a large bird that laid an egg similar to that of an Ostrich. Sadly for Monsieur de Flacourt, he was killed by Algerian pirates on his way back to France without further elaborating on his story.

The gigantic eggs of the bird, as big as an American football or a rugby ball, are still found from time to time in Madagascar and fragments of them are common at certain localities. Although virtually complete skeletons exist, bones seem to be much, much rarer than eggs.

DINORNITHIDAE

Slender Moa   *Dinornis torosus*

Because the original fauna of New Zealand contained no mammals, these islands were often called "The Land of Birds". Such a title has long been inappropriate, as introduced mammals now rule the land in much the same way as they do elsewhere – but for aeons birds represented the dominant lifeform. Quite why mammals were originally excluded from this corner of the planet is one of the mysteries of prehistory, but excluded they certainly were. In the land now known as New Zealand, birds adapted to fill many of the niches more familiarly occupied by mammals.

The most spectacular of these creatures were the birds now known as moas. There were a number of species and argument rages today over just how many. Some authorities put the figure as low as 10, others identify 30 or 40; such controversy is typical of the kind of difficulty experienced when ornithologists try to make sense of osteological material and have little else to go on. In the case of the moas there are some skin and feather fragments as well as a very few eggs and egg pieces, but these remains are tantalizing and reveal little of significance.

The largest of the moas, *Dinornis giganteus*, was the tallest known bird ever and it raised its head, upon a long serpentine neck, to the extraordinary height of around 4 m. Although not as hugely ponderous as the Madagascan Great Elephantbird, this was a considerably taller creature and presumably it must have been an awe-inspiring sight.

The evidence suggests that this particular species was probably gone by 1600 but it seems probable that a smaller – but still gigantic – relative, *Dinornis torosus*, survived after this date.

There is, in fact, much controversy over the date at which the last of the moas became extinct. Some argue that this was at a comparatively antique time, others suggest the extinction was much more recent.

Dinornis torosus Hutton, 1891
New Zealand J. Sci. **1(6)**: 2476.

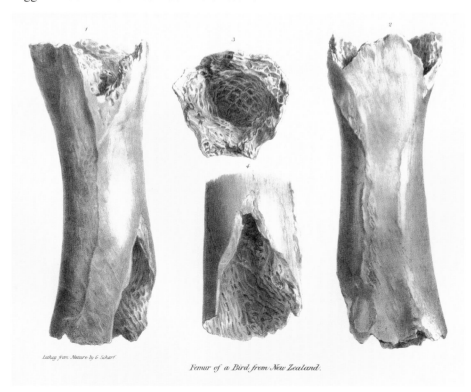

Figure 3. Rule's Bone.
This fragment, brought and shown to Richard Owen by John Rule, is the article which led to Owen's sensational deduction that large ostrich-like birds had once inhabited New Zealand, and indeed might still do so.
Lithograph by G. Scharf, 1842.

Lithog from Nature by G. Scharf.

Femur of a Bird from New Zealand.

A fragment of bone from *Dinornis torosus* seems to have been the first moa relic to come to the attention of ornithologists. This was in 1839 when the celebrated comparative anatomist Richard Owen stuck his neck out and made his famous announcement that there had lived in New Zealand – or even perhaps at that time still lived – a gigantic bird similar to an Ostrich. Owen based this deduction on a very small fragment of bone that had been brought to him for identification by a Dr John Rule. Despite the unpleasant things that are often said of him, Owen was certainly not lacking in courage: had he been proved wrong, his reputation, and indeed his whole career, would have been in tatters. However, only a short time after his sensational announcement, solid proof, in the form of skeletons, came to light and proved his deductions to have been accurate.

Bones of *D. torosus* have been found at widely scattered localities on New Zealand's South Island. Their comparative rareness in swamp deposits suggests that the species may have preferred hill country. Some of the tops of the skulls of this species show deep pits in the surface and this may indicate that birds carried crests.

Greater Broad-billed Moa *Euryapteryx gravis*

Dinornis gravis Owen, 1870
Trans. Zool. Soc. London **7**: 123.

There were several moas belonging to the genus *Euryapteryx* and these are distinguished from other moas by their broad, round-tipped beaks. Species have been described from both the South Island of New Zealand and the North. *Euryapteryx gravis* seems to have been the most widespread of these, and it has left its remains scattered throughout New Zealand. Although it was rather smaller than birds belonging to the genus *Dinornis*, it was nonetheless a very large and bulky creature. Its bones are said to be those that are most commonly found in Polynesian kitchen middens, so there is little doubt that this bird was often eaten by man.

At what date this supply of meat ran out is not known and it is possible that the species was extinct before 1600. On the other hand, birds of this species may have been the creatures referred to by ancient Maoris when they recalled moa hunts that took place during the last half of the eighteenth century. These intriguing stories have long fascinated researchers and they centre around the reminiscences of aged warriors who told their tales of long ago during the middle years of the nineteenth century. Whether these old men were simply enjoying being the centre of attention or whether there was some substance in their stories is a matter of speculation.

Lesser Megalapteryx *Megalapteryx didinus*

Dinornis didinus Owen, 1883
Trans. Zool Soc. London **11**: 257.

Although gigantic by bird standards, this creature was diminutive in comparison to other moas, standing little more than a metre tall. It may have been restricted only to the South Island.

It seems quite likely that the species survived to a later date than any other, and it may have been extant during the early nineteenth century; there are even those who hope that it survives still in some remote mountain fastness of New Zealand's fiordland. Its small size and the wild terrain it occupied may have combined to enable it to survive when the lines of its larger relatives failed.

There are several relics of this species that have survived in a remarkably good state of preservation. Dried heads and necks with ligaments and flesh attached have been found and so too have feathers and mummified feet. Such finds come from the province of Otago and they make it clear that the species was feathered right down to the toes. The feathers show an open structure, lacking barbicles and presenting a rather hair-like appearance. They are greyish-brown in colour, some with a rufous tinge and some tipped with white.

Sir George Grey, at one stage Prime Minister of New Zealand, was once told at Preservation Inlet, South Island, of the recent capture and killing of a small moa out of a drove of six or seven. This incident is supposed to have happened around 1868. Did it really occur, or is it just a story?

PODICIPEDIFORMES

This group of birds may or may not contain extinct species but it certainly contains several that are under grave threat of extinction. The most seriously threatened is the Atitlan Grebe (*Podilymbus gigas*), and it now seems highly likely that this form is actually extinct. In Volume 1 of HBW, the species was listed as Almost Certainly Extinct; several years later the "almost" can probably be removed. However, since the genes of this creature may still exist, there may be an argument for retaining it on the list of living creatures for a while longer.

Affected by habitat degradation, the introduction of an alien, predatory fish and the arrival of a closely related species with which it hybridized, the species – in its purest sense – seems no longer to be extant.

The Atitlan Grebe was always restricted to a single lake in Guatemala, where it adapted to the prevailing conditions by becoming flightless and isolating itself from its close relative, the widespread Pied-billed Grebe (*Podilymbus podiceps*). In essence this was simply an outsize version of the Pied-billed, and it was probably always vulnerable to the threat of hybridization with that species. This seems to be the factor that finally led to the loss of Lake Atitlan's grebe, an event that probably took place around 1990. The possibility that a few pure-bred examples of the species still exist cannot be completely excluded, of course, although it seems very doubtful. For more on this species and the cases of the probably extinct Rusty Grebe (*Tachybaptus rufolavatus*) and Colombian Grebe (*Podiceps andinus*), see HBW 1, pages 185-194.

PROCELLARIIFORMES

This group, containing the albatrosses, shearwaters and petrels, includes many threatened species but only one seems to be extinct.

HYDROBATIDAE

Guadalupe Storm-petrel   *Oceanodroma macrodactyla*

The island of Guadalupe lies off the coast of Baja California, some 320 km southwest of San Diego. It should not be confused with Guadeloupe in the West Indies. Guadalupe of the Pacific was once a home to several forms that are now extinct; these were mainly subspecies of more widespread birds.

A distinct species of storm-petrel once lived here, a species that nested in burrows carved out of the soft soil beneath trees on the steep north-eastern ridges of this small island. The population was probably never large but there is no reason to suppose that it was anything but thriving until cats and goats were introduced to the island. Cats are known to have infested the nesting areas and, presumably, it was this agency that brought about the destruction of the petrels. Apart from the fact that breeding began in March and continued until May, with a single white egg being laid, nothing of significance is known of the species. It seems to have become extinct during the years immediately preceding World War I.

Oceanodroma macrodactyla W. E. Bryant, 1887
Bull. Calif. Acad. Sci. **2**: 450.

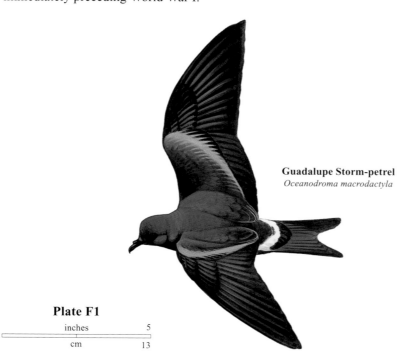

Guadalupe Storm-petrel
Oceanodroma macrodactyla

Plate F1

inches	5
cm	13

PELECANIFORMES

One member of this order can confidently be listed as extinct, but there is one other rather mysterious form that may be. This is a bird known as Kenyon's Shag (*Phalacrocorax kenyoni*). It is identified from just three specimens from Amchitka Island, in the Aleutian Archipelago of the north Pacific, collected during the late 1950's and preserved as skeletons. The external appearance of this bird is unknown. So too is its relationship to other cormorants, and it has even been suggested that these may merely have been outsize individuals of the extant Red-faced Cormorant (*Phalacrocorax urile*), a species that is still common in this same area. It is not even known if the form *kenyoni* still survives, so this is truly a mystery bird.

PHALACROCORACIDAE

Spectacled Cormorant   *Phalacrocorax perspicillatus*

Phalacrocorax perspicillatus Pallas, 1811
Zoographia Russo-Asiat. **2**: 305.

The spectacular Spectacled Cormorant is a particularly striking member of the list of extinct birds. Discovered on Bering Island during 1741 by the celebrated naturalist George Wilhelm Steller, the species was exterminated in little more than a century. At the time of its discovery this large cormorant was common, although its range was very

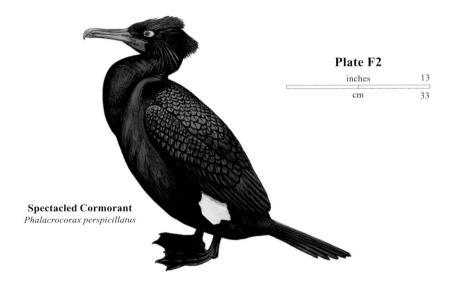

Plate F2

| inches | 13 |
| cm | 33 |

Spectacled Cormorant
Phalacrocorax perspicillatus

limited. In addition to Bering Island, it was also found on the nearby Commander Islands, and it probably lived on other islands of the Aleutian Archipelago in the north Pacific. Its general unwariness, its suitability for the pot and its small wings that rendered it almost flightless, combined to make this bird an obvious target for man.

There are very few specimens in existence and nothing of significance is known of the bird in life.

CICONIIFORMES

There are several seriously threatened birds in this order but only one full species is known to have become extinct during the last 400 years.

ARDEIDAE

Rodrigues Night-heron   *Nycticorax megacephalus*

Ardea megacephala Milne-Edwards, 1874
Ann. Sci. Nat. Zool. **Ser. 5, no. 19**: 10.

During 1691 a small band of Huguenots, fleeing from religious persecution in France, ended up marooned for around two years on the Mascarene island of Rodrigues, far out in the Indian Ocean. Their leader was one François Leguat, and this gentleman made notes on the things he saw during his stay on the island, notes that included detailed observations of the birds he encountered. Years later, after his return to Europe, Leguat's notes were published in book form (simultaneously, in both English and French) and his book was called *A New Voyage to the East Indies* (1708). This splendid little volume provides primary source material for a number of extinct species, including the present one.

Leguat describes a powerfully built and pugnacious heron that had almost lost the power of flight but had developed strong legs that enabled it to move very quickly.

In their loneliness (there were no women with the small band!), Leguat and his followers found some small solace in the companionship of some endemic geckos, which they shook down from the trees. These little creatures, which were themselves to become extinct around the time of World War I, were surprisingly tame and the Huguenots often allowed them to feed from their own table. So bold and aggressive were the herons, however, that Leguat and his friends had great difficulty in protecting their little pets from the marauding birds.

Despite their bullying manner, the night-herons died out at an unknown date during the eighteenth century. There is a fleeting mention of them in a document that dates from around 1725 but nothing more recent is recorded of the living bird.

During the 1870's bones were found on Rodrigues that confirm the earlier written reports and suggest that this species was derived from a night-heron, but nothing more is known of it.

ANSERIFORMES

The waterfowl – the swans, geese and ducks – have always been enormously attractive to man. Like parrots, they are comparatively easy to domesticate and they have been bred in captivity, or semi-captivity, for many centuries. Ducks, geese and swans have been used for food, sport and also simply for decorative purposes.

Many kinds have been seriously affected by changing patterns of land use, habitat alteration and wetland drainage. Many species have declined drastically and four are now regarded as extinct and discussed below, although there is still some hope that two of them might conceivably still hang on in remote parts of their ranges.

One other species, the Chatham Swan (*Cygnus sumnerensis*), sometimes occurs on lists of recently extinct birds but there is no real evidence to show when this creature died out. Known only from bones, it may well have become extinct long before 1600. Another species that is sometimes listed as recently extinct is *Sarkidiornis mauritiana* from Mauritius but, like the Chatham Swan, there is little to suggest that this creature lived on into recent historical times, and again it is known only from bones.

Were it not for the fact that many kinds of waterfowl can be successfully bred in captivity, there would have been several additional extinctions, and some very notable conservation success stories concern waterfowl. Perhaps the most famous is that of the Néné or Hawaiian Goose (*Branta sandvicensis*). The population of this striking goose was long in decline and by the early 1950's it had plummeted to around 30 individuals. With numbers at this low level the prospects of the species' survival looked bleak. At various times during the nineteenth century and early years of the twentieth (and also in several places) it had proved possible to breed Nénés under captive conditions and so one last effort was made to save the species at the famous waterfowl reserve at Slimbridge, England. The operation was an enormous success and numbers steadily increased. There are now hundreds of Nénés in existence and captive colonies can be seen in many parts of the world. The species has also been reintroduced to its native Hawaiian Islands where around a thousand individuals probably survive. There is no reason to suppose that its future is anything but secure.

Another Hawaiian species or subspecies that survives thanks largely to captive breeding is the Laysan Duck (*Anas (platyrhynchos) laysanensis*). It is recorded that numbers once dropped as low as seven individuals and during the 1930's the tiny surviving population was alleged to contain just a single female. Somehow this form survived, and a captive breeding programme was started in 1958. Many birds have been successfully bred in captivity and populations of Laysan Ducks now exist in a number of waterfowl collections. Unfortunately, some of these populations may no longer be pure.

A form that has caused considerable confusion is the one known as the Marianas Duck ("*Anas oustaleti*") and there is no general agreement about the true nature of this creature. It comes from the Pacific islands of Guam, Tinian and Saipan and there are two distinct colour morphs, one of which resembles a Mallard (*Anas platyrhynchos*), the other looking rather like a Pacific Black Duck (*Anas superciliosa*). Because of this resemblance and also because of the extreme isolation of the islands on which it occurs, it seems likely that the population is the result of hybridization. Probably, individuals of the two commoner species arrived on the islands, naturally or with human assistance, and, because of the unusual circumstances, interbred. A viable hybrid population was established and some authorities consider that the colony represents the evolution of a species through the mechanism of hybridization. Unfortunately, this evolutionary experiment – assuming that this is what it is – seems to be coming to an end. The isolated colony is now very close to extinction; indeed, perhaps it is already gone.

ANATIDAE

Crested Shelduck   *Tadorna cristata*

Pseudotadorna cristata Kuroda, 1917.
Tori **1**: 1.

Only a very few specimens of this striking duck are in existence, and virtually nothing is known of it in life. Even the limits of its original range are a matter of speculation; there is an assumption that it bred in eastern Siberia and migrated to Korea and Japan, but this may be incorrect. It is not even certain that it is extinct, although hopes for its continuing survival are probably forlorn.

The most recently obtained specimen was taken in 1916 but a number of much later sightings are claimed, including a reported observation in southern China as late as 1990. Such unsubstantiated sightings should be taken with caution, but as long as tracts of potentially suitable habitat remain in unsurveyed areas, hope lives on.

Although the earliest known specimen was taken near Vladivostock during 1877, the Crested Shelduck was not recognized as a species until 1917 when the Japanese ornithologist Nagamichi Kuroda formally described it. Prior to this the form had been regarded as a hybrid between the Ruddy Shelduck (*Tadorna ferruginea*) and the Falcated Duck (*Anas falcata*).

Despite the fact that this is now such a mysterious bird, it seems that it was well known historically to both the Japanese and the Chinese and it is said to be depicted on a number of antique artefacts.

Pink-headed Duck   *Rhodonessa caryophyllacea*

Anas caryophyllacea Latham, 1790
Index Orn. **2**: 866.

There is a certain amount of controversy over whether or not the Pink-headed Duck of north-eastern India still survives. Probably it does not, but there are those who believe it might and every few years or so an expedition goes in search of it. Thus far none of these expeditions has proved successful.

This was a shy and wary bird that sometimes emitted a wheezy whistle and was always difficult to flush. Its rather secretive nature is one of the factors that encourages the optimists. Against this it might be said that individuals were found without too much difficulty during the nineteenth century and early years of the twentieth, yet none has been seen in the wild since the 1930's.

On the water – where the birds spent most of the hot day – individuals showed a rather peculiar, stiff-necked posture and a strange triangular patch was evident on the top of the head. Despite some reports to the contrary, they seem to have been capable divers and were probably omnivorous feeders. Small groups sometimes gathered, particularly during the cooler months, and typically these groups consisted of six to eight birds, although sometimes the groups were considerably larger. The birds were rarely seen in the air and descriptions of their mode of flight are mildly contradictory: one report suggests that it was rapid and powerful, while another maintains it was light and easy.

Pink-headed Ducks bred in April and May and they built circular nests from dry grass and feathers. The eggs – white or faintly yellowish in colour – were almost spherical in shape and the clutch numbered between five and ten. The species was recorded from Assam, Manipur, Bengal, Bihar, Myanmar and Orissa.

Curiously, the last Pink-headed Duck of all may have died in England, thousands of miles from its native home. A number of captive individuals were kept in a private collection at Foxwarren Park, Surrey, and a rumour suggests that a male bird may have survived until 1945.

Labrador Duck   *Camptorhynchus labradorius*

Anas labradoria J. F. Gmelin, 1789
Syst. Nat. **1(2)**: 537.

The Labrador Duck is one of the most mysterious of North American birds. It was always uncommon, shy and wary and for these reasons seems to have been little affected by shooting.

Plate F3

inches   8

cm   20

Crested Shelduck
Tadorna cristata
♀
♂

Pink-headed Duck
Rhodonessa caryophyllacea
♀
♂

Labrador Duck
Camptorhynchus labradorius
♂   ♀

Auckland Merganser
Mergus australis
♂

Reasons for its extinction are unknown but one school of thought suggests that it was a very specialized feeder unable to cope with the vast changes to the environment that came about as a result of European settlement. This idea is, perhaps, supported by the slightly aberrant development of the bill which shows a curious softness around the edges.

The species occupied the eastern seaboard of North America where it seems to have ranged from Labrador, in which area it may have spent the summer months, down to Chesapeake Bay. Nesting grounds were never reliably located; they may have been in Labrador or on islands in the Gulf of St Lawrence. Several eggs exist that are attributed to the species, but all are of doubtful provenance.

Labrador Ducks seem to have declined rapidly after 1840 and the last sighting of the species dates from the 1870's. A specimen was apparently taken from Long Island waters during 1875 and another individual was allegedly shot near Elmira, New York, during 1878.

Auckland Merganser   *Mergus australis*

The Auckland Islands lie some 320 km south of New Zealand and this rather forlorn group was once home to a species of merganser that, while not entirely flightless, showed a marked reduction in wing size compared with its relatives. As often happens when birds develop in evolutionary backwaters (i.e. areas without mammalian predators), the adults begin to resemble the immature stages of their relatives and this is just what was happening in the case of this merganser. Similarly, and typically, its chicks were showing none of the distinctive patterning shown in related species.

Mergus australis Hombron and Jacquinot, 1841
Ann. Sci. Nat. Zool. **16**: 320.

The Auckland Merganser was first discovered in 1840 during a French exploratory visit to New Zealand waters. Two French corvettes, *L'Astrolabe* and *La Zelée*, arrived at the rarely visited and remote Auckland Islands, and some of the crew collected specimens. A Lieutenant Charles Jacquinot obtained a merganser and published a description of it, jointly, with ship's surgeon, Jacques Hombron. No further examples were spotted for 30 years or so, but then the species was seen on a number of occasions until the year 1902, after which time it vanished.

The most extraordinary aspect relating to this species lies, perhaps, in its range. Five kinds of merganser exist north of the equator, a sixth inhabits parts of Brazil but none – other than this one – occurs anywhere near the Auckland Islands. Bones found in Polynesian kitchen middens indicate that the species once occurred on the main islands of New Zealand.

The reasons for its extinction are unknown, although some reports suggest that individuals were prone to hide among rocks when pressed, rather than take to the water and dive like their European counterparts. Such a defensive strategy obviously did not work well against man and the predatory mammals he introduced.

FALCONIFORMES

The birds of prey are, of course, well known as being among the most persecuted of the world's birds, yet, despite the fact that many are seriously threatened, none can be categorically listed as recently extinct.

One form that might qualify as an extinct species is the Guadalupe Caracara (*Polyborus plancus lutosus*). There is no doubt that the form is extinct, as no individual has been seen since the year 1900, but what is in doubt is the bird's taxonomic status. This is one of those creatures that hovers close to the border of what defines a full species and what defines a subspecies. Some authorities (including the present writer, 2001) have regarded it as a species in its own right, while others relegate it – with equal justice – to subspecific rank, considering it simply an island subspecies of the Crested Caracara (*Polyborus plancus*).

Irrespective of the taxonomic view taken, this bird is one of those that disappeared as a direct result of human persecution. Exasperatingly, the last individuals on record were a flock of eleven birds, of which the scientific collector Rollo Beck shot nine. There were no further records (see HBW 2, page 242)

GALLIFORMES

In addition to the single species from this order that is definitely extinct, another may well be, and a third provides one of ornithology's little mysteries.

The species that may well be extinct is the Himalayan Quail (*Ophrysia superciliosa*), last reliably recorded during the nineteenth century. Inhabiting the undergrowth of steep Himalayan slopes at around 1650-2100 m, this quail has repeatedly been the object of speculation with regard to its possible continued existence, but, despite a number of claimed sightings, no convincing proof has emerged. Nevertheless, the difficulty of the terrain it inhabits means that the optimists continue to believe in its possible survival (see HBW 2, page 513).

The mystery bird is the Double-banded Argus (*Argus (argus) bipunctatus*). This form is known from a single feather found at an unknown location at some time before 1871. This feather, although similar to those of the two known species of argus pheasant, is markedly different to that carried by either. Does it come from a freak? Does it come from a distinct species? Is that species extinct? No-one knows.

PHASIANIDAE

New Zealand Quail   *Coturnix novaezelandiae*

Coturnix novae-zelandiae
Quoy and Gaimard, 1830
Voy. 'Astrolabe', Zool. **1**: 242.

It is difficult to account for the disappearance of the New Zealand Quail. A closely related, possibly conspecific, Australian species, the Stubble Quail (*Coturnix pectoralis*), flourishes in its homeland, yet the New Zealand birds failed to survive the coming of Europeans.

Plate F4

inches 3
cm 8

New Zealand Quail
Coturnix novaezelandiae

♂   ♀

The species seems to have been common on the grass-covered downs of New Zealand's South Island until the mid-nineteenth century, but then, suddenly, its numbers plunged and within two decades it was all but gone. The factors responsible for this decline are unknown. Introduced mammalian predators, overhunting (presumably the birds provided the kind of "sport" that colonists were used to in their old homes), the burning off of land, or an unknown – and introduced – avian disease are all reasons that have been speculatively put forward.

The latest specimens were taken during the late 1860's and individuals were, apparently, seen up to the mid-1870's. After this they vanished.

GRUIFORMES

This large and varied order includes the rails, a group of birds which has suffered a large number of extinctions, a fact that can be accounted for by the tendency of birds of this kind to disperse at random. Rails are particularly prone to colonize oceanic islands, diversify, and then lose the power of flight. Such a tendency makes them particularly vulnerable when their safe, island paradises become safe no longer, when they are invaded by mammalian predators.

Eleven extinct species are recognized here, although differing taxonomic views can lead to rather different lists. To these eleven may be added the Bar-winged Rail (*Nesoclopeus poecilopterus*), a Fijian species not reliably recorded since 1890, and the Kosrae Crake (*Porzana monasa*), from the Caroline Islands, not recorded since at least the mid-nineteenth century; both have already been covered by HBW 3, pages 161 and 189. Another supposed member of this latter genus, Miller's or the Tahiti Crake (*Porzana nigra*), is often listed as an extinct species but in reality this should be considered a hypothetical form (see Walters, 1988, and Fuller, 2000a). Also deserving of mention is the Mascarene Coot (*Fulica newtoni*), not included in the list herein, as there is no hard evidence that it survived until 1600, although there are seventeenth century reports of it from both Reunion and Mauritius. The difficult case of Sharpe's Rail (*Gallirallus sharpei*) has already been mentioned (see page 12).

RALLIDAE

Mauritian Red Rail   *Aphanapteryx bonasia*

Scattered among the seventeenth century written accounts and illustrations that relate to the celebrated Dodo are descriptions and pictures of a flightless bird of a rather different kind. These pictures show a creature that in overall shape and appearance looks something like a kiwi. A long, down-curved beak, rather hair-like plumage and stout legs all add to this impression. The bird in question bore no genuine relationship to the kiwis, however. It was a rail and, like the Dodo, it came from the island of Mauritius.

Like its more famous fellow, the Mauritian Red Rail or Red Hen failed to survive the coming of Europeans by more than a few decades. The Dutch arrived on Mauri-

Apterornis bonasia Sélys Longchamps, 1848
Rev. Zool.: 292.

tius, with devastating effect, during 1598, and it is highly doubtful if there were any red "hens" left a century later.

Peter Mundy, an English traveller who penned fascinating reminiscences of his exploits, described the species as:

> A Mauritius henne, a Fowle as bigge as our English hennes...of which we got only one. It hath a long, Crooked sharpe pointed bill. Feathered all over, butte on their wings they are soe Few and smalle that they cannot with them raise themselves From the ground...They bee very good Meat, and are also Cloven footed, soe that they can Neyther Fly nor Swymme.

Mundy was recalling events of 1638 and the fact that he and his companions got only a single individual surely indicates that the species was already rare. Earlier accounts suggest that the birds gathered in flocks and were fatally attracted to the colour red. By means of a piece of red material they could be induced to approach and then, of course, they were caught.

Leguat's Rail | *Aphanapteryx leguati*

Erythromachus leguati Milne-Edwards, 1874
Ann. Sci. Nat. Zool. **Ser. 5, no. 19**: 15.

The Huguenot refugee François Leguat discovered a relative of the Mauritian Red Rail during his two-year sojourn on the island of Rodrigues:

> Our Wood-hens are fat all the year round and of a most delicate taste. Their colour is always of a bright grey, and there is very little difference in the plumage between the two sexes. They hide their nests so well that we could not find them out and consequently did not taste their eggs. They have a red list about their eyes, their beaks are straight and pointed, near two inches long, and red also. They cannot fly, their fat makes them too heavy for it. If you offer them anything that's red, they are so angry they will fly at you and catch it out of your hand, and in the heat of the combat we had an opportunity to take them with ease.

It is curious to note how this last piece of information conforms to the reported behaviour of the Mauritius Red Rail.

An anonymous manuscript – alleged to have been written by a marooned sailor named Tafforet – dating from around 1725, described a creature that could not fly, was armed with a heavy beak, made a continual whistling, fed on tortoise eggs (Rodrigues was once home to a now extinct species of giant tortoise) and was a powerful runner.

Since no subsequent visitor to Rodrigues mentions any such creature it may be assumed that these birds became extinct soon after 1725.

In 1874 bones were found in a Rodrigues cave and these appear to correspond with the early accounts; they constituted the material on which Alphonse Milne-Edwards based his formal description of this species. Additional skeletal finds have subsequently been made.

Wake Rail | *Gallirallus wakensis*

Hypotaenidia wakensis Rothschild, 1903
Bull. Brit. Orn. Club **13**: 78.

The Wake Rail has acquired the grim celebrity of having been eaten out of existence by hungry Japanese soldiers during World War II. Unable to fly, these rails could scuttle about their island home quickly, but despite their agility any efforts to escape would have been no match for the concerted efforts of a few peckish men. Before World War II the rails were plentiful but by the time the Japanese garrison left Wake Island in 1945 there were none left.

Remote Wake Island is situated far out in the Pacific, hundreds of kilometres from the Hawaiian group. Despite its extreme isolation, rails something like today's Buff-banded Rail (*Gallirallus philippensis*) managed to colonize it at some period in the distant past, and from this ancestral stock the form developed that has become known as the Wake Rail. Over generations the size became smaller, the plumage lost its brightness and the wings became rudimentary. As Wake is small, low and scrub-covered, the rails probably had to make use of any food source that came their way; molluscs, insects and other invertebrates are likely to have provided the basic diet.

Other than the fact that breeding was observed to take place in July and August, and that individuals made the low chattering and clucking that is typical for a rail, nothing of substance is known of this species.

Mauritian Red Rail
Aphanapteryx bonasia

Wake Rail
Gallirallus wakensis

Chatham Rail
Gallirallus modestus

Tahiti Rail
Gallirallus pacificus

Dieffenbach's Rail
Gallirallus dieffenbachii

Laysan Crake
Porzana palmeri

Hawaiian Crake

*Porzana sandwichensis
sandwichensis*

*Porzana sandwichensis
millsi*

White Gallinule
Porphyrio albus

Samoan Moorhen
Gallinula pacifica

Plate F5

inches 5

cm 13

Tahiti Rail
Gallirallus pacificus

Rallus pacificus J. F. Gmelin, 1789
Syst. Nat. **1(2)**: 717.

The Tahitian Red-billed or Tahiti Rail is known only from a painting that survives today in the collection of the Natural History Museum, London. This painting was produced by Georg Forster, one of the naturalists who sailed with Captain James Cook on his second epic voyage around the world during the 1770's. Forster's credentials are impeccable, so there need be no doubt that he saw just such a bird as that depicted.

The individual that served as a model for his picture was found on Tahiti, where it was known as *tevea*, *oomnaa* or *eboonaa*. No-one knows why it became extinct – or when – but it seems likely that this was connected with the introduction of cats and rats to the island.

Dieffenbach's Rail
Gallirallus dieffenbachii

Rallus dieffenbachii G. R. Gray, 1843
Trav. New Zealand **2**: 197.

The remote Chatham Islands lie way to the south of New Zealand and here, in isolation, two species seem to have developed from an ancestral stock that resembled the Buff-banded Rail. The less evolved of these is Dieffenbach's Rail, and this form seems to have developed from a comparatively recent invasion of the ancestral birds. Indeed there is some doubt as to whether or not this form had actually passed beyond the stage at which it could be regarded as just a subspecies. Apart from some minor plumage differences, it sports a sharply downturned beak and this is clearly an adaptation to the conditions prevailing on the island.

Nothing is known of the bird in life. It is known from just a single specimen collected during the 1840's and now in the collection of the Natural History Museum, London.

Chatham Rail
Gallirallus modestus

Rallus modestus Hutton, 1872
Ibis **Ser. 3, no. 2**: 247.

This species seems to provide a fairly typical example of the way in which rails develop on isolated islands. It is assumed that this is another form that has evolved from an ancestral stock resembling the Buff-banded Rail, but in this case the evolution was rather more advanced than in others.

Following the arrival of this ancestral stock, the birds diversified over aeons, assumed a neotenous appearance (adults began to resemble juveniles), lost the power of flight, and their plumage began to assume a rather hair-like appearance. All these developments enabled the birds to make maximum use of the rather limited resources available on the Chatham Islands, by cutting down on what were, for them, unnecessary and costly forms of energy expenditure, but, of course, they rendered them horribly vulnerable if, and when, the situation changed. The coming of man and his introduction of mammals, either intentional or not, caused just such a change.

The species seems to have been on several islands of the Chatham group – Chatham Island itself, Pitt Island and Mangere – but it is from Mangere that the majority of surviving specimens come, and this seems to have been the last stronghold. From here the birds vanished around 1900. By this time much of the land had been burned off, sheep were grazing and cats had overrun the island.

All that is known of the species is that it nested in burrows or in hollow trees, ate insects and laid a creamy-white egg.

Ascension Rail
Atlantisea elpenor

Atlantisea elpenor Olson, 1973
Smithsonian Contrib. Zool. **152**: 7.

The evidence for the former existence of a small rail on Ascension Island is of two kinds. First, bones from a rail have been found on the island and, second, there exists a seventeenth century written account of just such a creature. This account was written by the much travelled Englishman Peter Mundy, the same man who also penned an account of the extinct rail of Mauritius. Mundy's descriptions are always reliable and in this case he also provided a crude but explicit drawing of the birds he saw. He wrote:

> Alsoe halfe a dozen of a strange kind of fowle, much bigger than our Sterlings...colour grey or dappled, white and blacke feathers intermixed, eies red like rubies, wings very imperfitt, such as wherewith they cannot raise themselves from the ground. They were taken running, in which they are exceeding swift, helping themselves a little with their wings...It was more than ordinary dainety meat, relishing like a roasting pigge.

Figure 4. Ascension Rail sketched by Peter Mundy, who visited the island in 1656.

Nothing more is known of the species. Why and when it became extinct are also matters completely shrouded in mystery.

28

Laysan Crake   *Porzana palmeri*

Laysan is a tiny coral island around 1280 km to the north-east of Hawaii, and one of its few inhabitants was a small species of rail. Because it is so remote, the island was infrequently visited but, nevertheless, there are several good accounts of the bird in life. These consistently tell of how bold the tiny creatures were, hunting for flies between the feet of men, or entering huts and other buildings in search of food. All kinds of insects and their larvae were eaten and the rails would often squabble with Laysan Finches (*Telespyza cantans*) over the broken eggs of noddies and terns (Sternidae). Scraps were taken from the carcasses of dead seabirds, and vegetable matter was also consumed. In short, no food resource was neglected.

The Laysan Crake was flightless, but birds could move with incredible swiftness and agility when attacked by frigatebirds (*Fregata*) and other larger seabirds. The call was described as a warbling and chattering, and there was a peculiar evening chorus that began soon after darkness fell and lasted for just a few seconds. The birds all started their chorus in unison and then all fell silent together. The sound produced was said to be like a handful of marbles being thrown onto a glass roof and then descending in a series of bounds.

Breeding occurred between April and July. A nest was made of grass and leaves, and this material was arched over to make a roof with an entrance at the side.

During the 1890's these little birds were common but then rabbits and guineapigs were introduced to the island, and the habitat deteriorated. By 1925 the vegetation was gone, and Laysan was a desert. During this year two rails were seen, but by 1936 there were certainly none left. The species was not quite extinct, however. During 1891 a few individuals had been transferred to Eastern Island in the Midway Atoll, and here the small population flourished. By the start of World War II the birds were common. Then, alas, a US Navy landing craft drifted ashore bringing with it an accidental invasion of rats. Within two years the last Laysan Crakes were gone.

Porzanula palmeri Frohawk, 1892
Ann. and Mag. Nat. Hist. **9**: 247.

Hawaiian Crake   *Porzana sandwichensis*

A small species of rail once inhabited the main island of Hawaii and perhaps some other Hawaiian islands. A handful of specimens exist in the museums of the world but these have in themselves caused some controversy. Two of them are rather paler in colour than the rest, giving rise to the idea that there may have been two species rather than one. This claimed second species is herein tentatively treated as a separate race, *millsi*. On the other hand the general consensus of informed opinion is that the paler individuals may simply be immatures.

Apart from the probability that these birds were extinct by the end of the nineteenth century, nothing is known of them.

Rallus sandwichensis J. F. Gmelin, 1789
Syst. Nat. **1(2)**: 717.

P. s. millsi (Dole, 1878)
Hawaiian Alm. Ann. **1879**: 54.

Samoan Moorhen   *Gallinula pacifica*

There seem to be eleven specimens of this species in the world's museums, the first collected during 1869 and the last perhaps a mere five years later. Since then the species has never more been located.

Little is known of it other than that it inhabited the Samoan island of Savaii. It was called the *puna'e* by the local inhabitants, it was probably flightless (or almost so), and it had exceptionally large eyes, from which fact it has been deduced that it was nocturnal or crepuscular in habit.

The reasons for its extinction are unknown but, presumably, introduced predators will have played some part.

Pareudiastes pacifica Hartlaub and Finsch, 1871
Proc. Zool. Soc. London **1871**: 25.

White Gallinule   *Porphyrio albus*

When British ships belonging to what was known as the First Fleet were dispatched under Governor Phillip to Australia during the late 1780's, their task was to found a penal colony to which British felons could be transported. Much of interest surrounds this rather unpleasant endeavour and one of the by-products of the epic journey was a great upsurge in knowledge concerning Australian natural history.

One of the creatures that was brought to attention as a result of the expedition was a rather strange and albinistic swamphen that occurred on Lord Howe Island, a small and isolated piece of land lying some 480 km off the eastern coast of Australia. These birds were white, or mostly so, and considerably larger and heavier than ordinary swamphens and they had comparatively formidable bills. In fact, they seem to have been evolving independently into an entity that was reminiscent of New Zealand's Takahe (*Porphyrio mantelli*).

Fulica alba Shaw, 1790
In: White's *J. Voy. New South Wales*: 235.

Unfortunately for the birds, men who visited the island were easily able to kill them with sticks and this fact alone makes it highly likely that they were flightless. Just two specimens of the White Gallinule (or Lord Howe Swamphen) are in existence today, one in Vienna, the other in Liverpool.

Once man began to visit their island home regularly, the species' days were numbered, and it seems to have survived for only a few decades after the coming of the First Fleet.

CHARADRIIFORMES

The Charadriiformes comprise a diverse group containing waders, gulls and auks. In addition to the three species discussed below, there are two others that are often listed as extinct, and may well be so, though herein the possibility of their survival is given the benefit of the doubt. These are the Javanese Wattled Lapwing (*Vanellus macropterus*), last definitely recorded in 1939, and the Eskimo Curlew (*Numenius borealis*) for which sightings are occasionally claimed right up to the present time, but which, if extant, could probably only number a handful of individuals (see HBW 3, pages 418 and 503).

SCOLOPACIDAE

White-winged Sandpiper   *Prosobonia leucoptera*

Ellis's Sandpiper   *Prosobonia ellisi*

Tringa leucoptera J. F. Gmelin, 1789
Syst. Nat. **1(2)**: 678.

Prosobonia ellisi Sharpe, 1906
Bull. Brit. Orn. Club **16**: 86.

Whether there was one extinct species of sandpiper occupying the Pacific islands of Tahiti and Moorea or whether there were, in fact, two remains something of an enigma. The naturalists who actually saw the birds in life and handled fresh specimens were convinced that there was only one, but more recent commentators have produced reasonable arguments that there were two: a form from Tahiti (*leucoptera*) with a more sandy-coloured breast; and another from Moorea (*ellisi*), with more reddish underparts. No definitive solution to this problem is possible.

Although there were once several specimens in existence, only one (an example now in Leiden) survives today. This is one of the more sandy-coloured individuals. The species was only ever seen by naturalists who sailed with Cook and one of them, Georg Forster, painted a picture of a Moorea bird showing the more reddish breast. It is on the basis of this painting that the form *ellisi* is named.

Clearly the birds – whether there was once species or two – became extinct at an early date. Other than the fact that Forster found it close to small brooks, nothing is known of it in life.

White-winged Sandpiper
Prosobonia leucoptera

Ellis's Sandpiper
Prosobonia ellisi

Plate F6

inches   3

cm   8

ALCIDAE

Great Auk

Pinguinus impennis

Alca impennis Linnaeus, 1758
Syst. Nat. **10**: 130.

The Great Auk is one of the true stars of extinction. Its story rises and falls like a Greek tragedy. This was a creature that had evolved perfectly to take advantage of a particular ecological niche but its very adaptation rendered it totally incapable of withstanding the depredations of man. It is probably true to say that the species was doomed from the prehistoric day when man first invented the boat. Use of boats enabled men to visit lonely islands and skerries, to round capes and headlands and reach otherwise inaccessible stretches of coast, and thus to pursue Great Auks to their final refuges.

The weakness in the Great Auk's lifestyle lay in the fact that it had lost the power of flight, and when it waddled clumsily ashore to breed in large colonies on islands of the North Atlantic it was totally vulnerable to a predator as ruthless and inventive as man. In addition, its large size made it a natural target. For ten months of each year Great Auks lived at sea, and it was only the necessity of breeding that brought them ashore for a few brief and doom-laden weeks.

First, Great Auks were driven back from all their most accessible breeding haunts. Then they were steadily forced back into even more remote areas. By the start of the eighteenth century they bred only on a few far-flung islands, each of which was difficult to land upon. The greatest of the breeding colonies appears to have been at Funk Island, off the coast of Newfoundland, and here the birds assembled in vast numbers during the months of May and June. Unfortunately for the auks the island lay near to the end of a long stretch of open water on the sea route from Europe to America. Hungry sailors feasted on the defenceless creatures and discovered that not only did they provide a handy food source, but also their feathers and the oil from their bodies were very useful commodities. By the late eighteenth century this vast colony had been wiped out and for all practical purposes the Great Auk bred only on a few islands off the coast of Iceland. On one of these in particular, the species seemed safe. This was an island known as the Geirfuglasker (which loosely translated means "Great Auk island"). The birds were safe here simply because the prevailing currents were so fierce and unpredictable that the island was almost impossible to land upon. While the species was wiped out elsewhere, the stronghold on the Geirfuglasker still held out. Then, catastrophe befell. A submarine volcanic explosion during the winter of 1830 caused the Geirfuglasker to sink beneath the surface of the waves never to reappear. When the few surviving Great Auks returned to their breeding rock and found it gone, they were forced to choose another site. This they did and they selected the infamous island of Eldey, a great rock that held one major disadvantage: although difficult to land upon, such a feat was by no means impossible. And land man did. In the first raid upon the island 24 birds were caught. A year or so later 13 were obtained. Each successive raid brought a dwindling haul until in June of 1844 just two individuals – a male and a female – were killed. None was ever seen again.

Plate F7

Great Auk
Pinguinus impennis

*A Last Stand.
Great Auks in the mist
by Errol Fuller.*

The story of the killing of these supposedly "last" two birds has acquired almost legendary status and it occurs in many variants. All of these variants derive from the notes of two Victorian ornithologists, John Wolley and Alfred Newton, who recorded the tale after conducting extensive interviews with the Icelanders who actually participated in the event. Their notes show that on either 2nd or 3rd June an eight-oared fishing boat left the Icelandic mainland and made for the island of Eldey. Here, three of the crew struggled ashore and spotted two Great Auks among hundreds of smaller seabirds. They pursued the pair, caught them both and strangled them. The men returned to the boat and with great difficulty managed to scramble back into it. Once safely back on the mainland the leader of the raiding party took the road to the Icelandic capital Reykjavik, where he hoped to sell the birds. On the road it seems that he met, by chance, a trader with an interest in Great Auks – and the dead birds were sold on the spot. Curiously, the skins themselves vanished and no-one knows for certain what became of them (there is, however, some evidence to show that they might be the specimens now in Los Angeles and Brussels), although the internal organs of these two birds, preserved in spirits are now at the Zoological Museum in Copenhagen.

After its extinction, the surviving relics of the Great Auk – in the form of eggs and stuffed birds – became highly sought after. Through the second half of the nineteenth century, and afterwards, such items changed hands for large sums of money. In 1890 a stuffed bird would have cost around £400 (the price of four or five ordinary-sized houses) and an egg only slightly less.

Although the species has acquired a sort of cult status, surprisingly little is known of it in life. We know it was flightless, that it lived in and around the waters of the North Atlantic and must therefore have preyed on fish and other oceanic creatures. We know it laid a large pyriform egg, that it came ashore – helplessly – to breed for a few weeks each year, and that it spent the rest of its time at sea. The rest is speculation.

COLUMBIFORMES

The pigeons as a whole have been badly affected by extinction. The reasons for this are probably those that apply broadly in the cases of other badly affected groups, the rails and the parrots. Each of these groups shows a marked tendency to disperse to oceanic islands where the species that evolve show a terrible vulnerability to changing conditions.

In addition to the two members of the extinct family Raphidae, and the seven species of Columbidae covered below, two other pigeon species may well be extinct but are not included here as there is a faint possibility that they may still survive. These are the Red-moustached Fruit-dove (*Ptilinopus mercierii*) from the Marquesas Islands in the Pacific and the Choiseul Pigeon (*Microgoura meeki*) of the Solomon Islands; the last definite records of these two were, respectively, some 80 and 100 years ago. Both have already been covered (see HBW 4, pages 187 and 216).

RAPHIDAE

Rodrigues Solitaire   *Pezophaps solitaria*

Didus solitarius J. F. Gmelin, 1789
Syst. Nat. **1(2)**: 728.

The island of Rodrigues, far out in the Indian Ocean, is one of the Mascarene group and here a dodo-like species evolved from an ancestral pigeon stock. This species has become known as the Rodrigues Solitaire.

The Huguenot refugee François Leguat, whose name occurs so regularly in the stories of extinct birds, took a particular liking to this species and it is from his account that most information concerning it is derived.

Leguat was marooned on Rodrigues during 1691 and stayed for around two years. He and his small band of followers became entranced by the strange bird they found there and Leguat penned a number of observations of the Solitaire. One of these constitutes the first recorded observation of territorial behaviour in birds:

> All the while they are sitting...or bringing up their young one, which is not able to provide for its self in several Months, they will not suffer any other Bird of their Species to come within 200 yards round of the Place; but what is very singular, is that Males will never drive away the Females; only when he perceives one he makes a noise with his wings to call [his] Female, and she drives the unwelcome Stranger away, not

leaving it till 'tis without her Bounds. The Female do's the same as the Males, whom she leaves to the Male.

The only other early authority for the birds of Rodrigues is an anonymous author, usually thought to have been a marooned sailor by the name of Tafforet, who wrote a document that has come to be known as the *Relation de l'Île Rodrigue*. A translation of the part of this document that relates to the Solitaire reads:

> The Solitary...weighs...40 or 50 pounds. They have a very big head, with a...frontlet, as if of black velvet. Their feathers are neither feathers nor fur...of a light grey colour, with a little black on their backs. Strutting proudly about...they preen their plumage...and keep themselves very clean...[They] run with quickness among the rocks, where a man, however agile, can hardly catch them...They do not fly at all, having no feathers to their wings but they flap them and make a great noise...I have never seen but one little one alone with them, and if anyone tried to approach it, they would bite him severely. These birds live on seeds and leaves of trees.

Confirmation of the one-time existence of this creature comes from bones found in caves on Rodrigues. Complete skeletons have been assembled and these show that there was an extraordinary divergence in the size of the sexes with the males being much bigger. The bones also confirm some anatomical details that were mentioned by Leguat.

The remarks in the *Relation* indicate that the birds were still plentiful during the 1720's, and the document is thought to date from around 1725. However, at some time soon afterwards, they seem to have declined rapidly. During 1761 the Abbé Pingré arrived on the island with the intention of viewing the Transit of Venus. He arrived in time to see the heavenly wonder but not, it seems, in time to see the Solitaire. If the species still existed at this time it was so rare that it stood at the very brink of extinction.

Solitaires seem to have been tasty birds and it can only be assumed that settlers who arrived on Rodrigues during the eighteenth century ate them out of existence.

Dodo   *Raphus cucullatus*

The Dodo is probably the most powerful of all icons of extinction. "Dead as a Dodo" is an expression familiar to almost everybody in the English-speaking world. The name is unforgettable and so too is the bird's appearance, an appearance made memorable through the paintings of Roelandt Savery and their many derivatives, chiefly, perhaps, John Tenniel's illustrations for Lewis Carroll's *Alice's Adventures in Wonderland*. On the Dodo's home island of Mauritius the image of the bird is everywhere – on crockery, T-shirts, sweets and all kinds of ornamental souvenir ware.

More has been written about the Dodo than about any other extinct bird, but the reader should beware. Dodo literature is studded with inaccuracies and ludicrous theories, and despite the flood of words almost nothing is known of the bird in life.

Dutch mariners arrived on the Dodo's home island of Mauritius during September of 1598. We have no way of knowing how the species was faring before this but we do know that the arrival of the Dutch meant doom for the Dodo. Within 40 years of Dutch arrival the Dodo was virtually extinct, unable to withstand the joint assaults of man and the mammals he introduced – pigs, rats and monkeys, creatures that may not have threatened the adult birds but certainly threatened the young and the eggs. The existing seventeenth century reports become very thin on the ground after 1640 and even more so do original pictures. Indeed, after 1638 all Dodo images are derivations of earlier ones. The Dodo may have been in existence for several more decades but as a species it was a spent force from around this time.

There is no doubt that hungry sailors visiting Mauritius played a large part in the extermination of the Dodo and a very considerable proportion of the sparse contemporary literature concerns the edibility of the bird. Apparently, the flesh was rather tough and not particularly good to eat so whenever possible the men turned their attention to smaller, tastier birds. The Dodo held one big advantage for them, however. Being large and flightless, it was easy to locate and catch.

Although it interacted with man for such a short period of time, this exotic creature quickly gained some celebrity. A few living individuals reached Europe; several ornithologists have tried to calculate the number, but the evidence is flimsy and we have no real idea of how many there were. Also, the Dutch seem to have taken live birds to India and Indonesia. It has even been suggested that Dodos were taken to Japan but there is no proper proof of this.

Figure 5. Rodrigues Solitaire by François Leguat, from his 1708 book A New Voyage to the East Indies.

Struthio cucullatus Linnaeus, 1758
Syst. Nat. **10**: 155.

*Figure 6. Dodo.
A hand-coloured lithograph,
based on a 1626 painting
by Roelandt Savery.*

The actual natural history of the Dodo is shrouded in mystery. How it used its curious beak, what it ate, even what parts of Mauritius it inhabited are all matters of debate. Almost certainly the species lived on fruits, nuts and other vegetable matter that it found on the forest floor but the records seem to indicate that it occurred only in certain areas. Woods close to the shore were probably a favoured habitat. It certainly seems unlikely that the birds inhabited the entire island. Had this been the case, the extinction could not have happened so rapidly.

Despite the early date of disappearance, the Dodo has left a number of physical relics behind. First, there are bones. With just a few exceptions these come from a small area of swamp known as the Mare aux Songes, close to the southern coast of Mauritius. From this material several complete skeletons have been assembled and these confirm the impression (gained from seventeenth century pictures and writings) that this was a large and heavy bird. It does seem, however, that it may not have been quite so bulky and clumsy as previously supposed and probably adopted a rather upright stance.

The most famous Dodo relics of all are a head and a foot that were once part of an entire stuffed bird. The body of this specimen was destroyed long ago but the head and foot were preserved and they are kept today at the University Museum of Zoology, Oxford.

Many people leave museums convinced that they have seen a stuffed Dodo. They have not, for there are none in existence. What they have seen are carefully constructed models made from the feathers of other birds.

The best description of the Dodo in life comes from the pen of an English courtier named Thomas Herbert who visited Mauritius in 1628 during a round trip to Persia:

> Her body is round and fat...her visage darts forth melancholy, as sensible of Nature's injurie in framing so great a body to be guided with complementall wings, so small and impotent, that they serve only to prove her bird. The halfe of her head is naked seeming couered with a fine vaile, her bill is crooked downwards, in midst is the trill [nostril], from which part to the end tis of a light green, mixed with pale yellow tincture; her eyes are small and like to Diamonds, round and rowling, her clothing downy feathers, her train three plumes, short and inproportionable, her legs suiting to her body, her pounces sharp, her appetite strong and greedy.

The actual date of extinction is a matter of some doubt. Although the Dodo was on its last legs as a functioning species by 1640, there is little doubt that individuals lingered for some time afterwards. The last record has traditionally been regarded as a mention made by one Benjamin Harry who was writing in 1681. Following a visit to Mauritius, Harry compiled a list of the island's products and Dodos were included in this list. It is by no means certain, however, that Harry actually saw these birds. He may merely have been compiling a list of items that he knew had come from the island. Anthony Cheke (1987), who has conducted much research on the ornithological history of the Mascarenes, believes that the last Dodo observation was made by a certain Volquard Iversen and relates to the year 1662. Iversen was marooned on Mauritius for several months and claimed to have encountered Dodos on a small offshore island to which he waded at low tide. Even this record may not stand up to scrutiny, however. Some evidence suggests that the name Dodo was transferred to the Mauritius Red Rail during the second half of the seventeenth century, and Iversen's record may perhaps result from confusion over terminology.

COLUMBIDAE

Bonin Woodpigeon   *Columba versicolor*

The avifaunas of several islands to the south of Japan have been badly depleted, and one of these island groups, the Bonins (Ogasawara), has lost several distinct forms.

Columba versicolor Kittlitz, 1832
Kupfer. Nat. Vog. **1**: 5.

One of these was the Bonin Pigeon, a large, dark bird that was discovered in 1827 during the exploratory voyage of *HMS Blossom*. It seems to have survived until around 1890, the last known specimen being collected during 1889. The bird's general unwariness and the implication that it showed no fear of man doubtless contributed to its downfall. Very little is known of its habits but it seems likely that it required well-wooded territory where it probably fed upon fruit, seeds and buds. The species is known to have inhabited Peel Island (Chichijima) and Nkondo-shima and it probably lived on other islands of the Bonin group.

There seem to be only three specimens of the species in existence. One belongs to the Natural History Museum, London, a second is in St Petersburg and the third is in Frankfurt.

Ryukyu Woodpigeon   *Columba jouyi*

This species, closely related to the last, occurred on the Ryukyu and Daito Islands, another of the island groups to the south of Japan. It was last recorded on the Daito Islands during 1936. Although certainly extinct on Okinawa where it was last seen in 1904, the species may possibly cling to existence on some of the smaller islands. Like its relative it appears to have required heavily forested country.

Columba jouyi Stejneger, 1887
Amer. Nat. **21**: 583.

Nothing is known of the bird in life and reasons for its disappearance are unclear.

Passenger Pigeon   *Ectopistes migratorius*

The celebrated Passenger Pigeon has, perhaps, the most extraordinary story of any extinct bird. It may once have been the most numerous bird on Earth, and at the start of the nineteenth century vast flocks of this species blackened American skies. Yet during the course of 100 years the tremendous numbers dwindled until just a handful of birds remained. The last individual of all, a female named Martha, died in her cage at the Cincinnati Zoological Gardens at 1:00 p.m. on 1st September 1914.

Columba migratoria Linnaeus, 1766
Syst. Nat. **12**: 285.

Early descriptions of the massed flights of the Passenger Pigeon are remarkable. In 1759 a certain Peter Kalm wrote:

> In the spring of 1749...there came from the north an incredible number of these pigeons to Pennsylvania and New Jersey. Their number, while in flight, extended 3 or 4 English miles in length, and more than one such mile in breadth, and they flew so closely together that the sky and the sun were obscured by them, the daylight becoming sensibly diminished by their shadows.
> The big as well as the little trees...sometimes covering a distance of 7 English miles, became so filled with them that hardly a twig or a branch could be seen which they did not cover...when they alighted on the trees their weight was so heavy that not only big limbs and branches were broken straight off, but less firmly rooted trees broke down completely under the load. The ground below the trees where they had spent the night was entirely covered with their dung, which lay in great heaps.

During the 1830's John James Audubon penned his famous account:

> The air was literally filled with pigeons, the light of noonday was obscured as by an eclipse; the dung fell in spots not unlike melting flakes of snow...pigeons were still passing in undiminished numbers and continued to do so for three days in succession.

Bonin Woodpigeon
Columba versicolor

Ryukyu Woodpigeon
Columba jouyi

Passenger Pigeon
Ectopistes migratorius

♀   ♂

Liverpool Pigeon
Caloenas maculata

Tanna Ground-dove
Gallicolumba ferruginea

Mauritius Blue-pigeon
Alectroenas nitidissima

Plate F8

inches   5
cm   13

These vast and spectacular flights rendered the Passenger Pigeon vulnerable in a quite remarkable way. So easy was it to shoot the birds that one simply had to point a rifle skywards and repeatedly pull the trigger. Hunting competitions were organized and for one of these it is known that a haul of more than 30,000 dead birds was necessary to claim a prize. With many hands turned against it there is little wonder that Passenger Pigeon numbers began to fall drastically.

However, it is simply not possible to shoot such a numerous species out of existence. It seems that there were additional factors and that these factors centered around the species' need to operate in such vast groups. The birds moved around nomadically, looking for rich crops of beechmast, acorns or chestnuts, and when an exceptionally good site was located the birds were attracted in huge numbers. The forests were steadily depleted, however, and so good crops became fewer and farther between. To compound this, so many thousands of pigeons were shot that their scouting capacity dropped, making it even more difficult for them to locate adequate food supplies. Once numbers had fallen below a certain level, even though that level may have been incredibly high, the Passenger Pigeon was doomed as a species. Clearly this was a creature that could only survive in huge numbers. The critical figure may have been a million individuals, it may have been twenty million; we shall never know. But at some point during the mid-nineteenth century, the figure was passed and from that moment onwards the species was spiralling downwards to extinction. The decline became apparent during the 1870's. At the start of this decade the flocks seemed as healthy as ever, but by its end the ranks were noticeably thinned and by the end of the century the species was virtually gone from the wild, leaving only a few individuals in captivity. It seems that the decline was accelerated too by an outbreak of Newcastle disease, a paramyxoviral disease that attacks the digestive tract and nervous system, and is known to affect domestic poultry as well as many species of wild bird.

The Passenger Pigeon was quite unlike most other pigeons. Its body was beautifully streamlined, with a small head and long, pointed wings and tail. This body design allowed the bird to fly with great swiftness and agility. When wheeling, dropping or rising in the air, the beautiful, yet subtly marked, plumage would flash spectacularly in the sun.

Naturally, such enormous numbers had a marked effect on the vegetation. The birds ate acorns and nuts of all kinds as well as fruit, grain, insects and other invertebrates.

When they nested they did so in colossal colonies and sometimes these extended for many kilometres. Nesting sites of 65 km were recorded and it is estimated that 16 km by 5 km were characteristic. The nest was flimsily made from twigs, and one white egg was laid. The peak breeding period occurred in April and May, although breeding could take place at any time between March and September. Both parents helped with the incubation, and the single chick was cared for by the adults until it was around two weeks old. Then, suddenly, the old birds would depart leaving the fat chick abandoned and crying in the nest. After a while the baby bird would drop to the ground and a day or two later it would take to the air and leave.

Liverpool Pigeon   *Caloenas maculata*

Two hundred years ago there were two specimens of this species in existence. Now there is just one. No-one knows where it came from or when it was collected, although this was certainly at some time during the last half of the eighteenth century. The specimen is now in the collection of the Liverpool Museum, and it has been there since 1851, when it was bequeathed to the people of Liverpool by Edward Stanley the 13th Earl of Derby.

Columba maculata J. F. Gmelin, 1789
Syst. Nat. **1(2)**: 780.

Stanley was one of the great collectors of the nineteenth century, a period that is rightly celebrated for the collecting zeal that inspired so many rich men. Not only did he collect preserved birds and other animals, he also collected live ones, and the menagerie he put together in the grounds of his home, Knowsley Hall, became famous throughout Europe. The Earl collected hundreds of pictures and albums of pictures relating to natural history and commissioned the famous artist Edward Lear to paint portraits of the animals in his menagerie. He assembled a magnificent library and acquired two copies of what is now the world's most valuable illustrated book, Audubon's *Birds of America* (a copy of this work recently changed hands for £8,000,000), one of which he promptly cut up to make a scrapbook featuring pictures of "birds of the world"!

Considering its antiquity, his specimen of the Liverpool Pigeon is in a remarkably fresh state of preservation. In appearance, the bird shows affinity to the widespread Nicobar Pigeon (*Caloenas nicobarica*), but notwithstanding the similarity it is clearly distinct. For reasons that are not entirely clear, the specimen has been overlooked by many commentators and there has been a tendency among those who do know of its existence to regard it as a freak. Few of these have actually seen it, however.

It is assumed that the specimen was brought back from an expedition to the South Pacific and that the species inhabited a Pacific island – but this is just a guess. Obviously, nothing is known of the living bird.

Tanna Ground-dove   *Gallicolumba ferruginea*

The Tanna Ground-dove is known today from just a single, rather crude, painting by Georg Forster that was produced during Captain Cook's second voyage around the world. This painting is in the Forster portfolio at the Natural History Museum, London, and in the margin the following words are inscribed:

Gallicolumba ferruginea J. R. Forster, 1844
Descr. Anim.: 265. (Published posthumously).

Tanna, female, 17th August 1774.

Nothing more is known of the species. A specimen of it did once exist although this, like the species itself, vanished long ago. Concerning the events of 17th August Georg Forster's father, Johann Reinhold, made this spare record:

I went ashore, we shot a new pigeon and got a few plants.

The island of Tanna is one of the islands of Vanuatu, and for many years it had an ugly reputation on account of the ferocity of the native inhabitants. For this reason it was seldom visited during the nineteenth century, and at some time during that period the native pigeon seems to have passed away.

Mauritius Blue-pigeon   *Alectroenas nitidissima*

Columba nitidissima Scopoli, 1786
Deliciae Florae Faunae Insubricae **2**: 93.

When the first Dutch mariners landed on Mauritius, they were hungry after weeks at sea on meager rations. Naturally, they caught Dodos and ate them. Soon, however, they tired of the rather tough meat on these easily caught creatures and turned their attentions to smaller, tastier birds. Among those that they mentioned particularly were small pigeons and these seemed to provide a welcome alternative to the cloying flesh of the Dodos. A remarkable pair of illustrations drawn in Mauritius and dating from 1601 show a dead individual of the species. It is in the journal, or log, of one of the first Dutch ships to visit Mauritius and, although anonymous, the pictures are brilliantly and expressively rendered. This journal is now kept at the Rijksarchiv in the Hague and it relates to the voyage of the ship *Gelderland*.

Despite the existence of the journal, almost two hundred years were to pass before the species was formally described and brought to zoological attention. In 1782 Pierre Sonnerat mentioned a specimen of the bird that he had collected in 1774, during his extensive travels to the East. However, as he did not adhere to the Linnaean principle of scientific naming, it was left to Giovanni Antonio Scopoli some four years later to give it its scientific name.

This striking pigeon, with strange wax-like, elongated head and neck feathers, is now represented in the world's museums by just three specimens, one in Mauritius itself, one in Paris and one in Edinburgh. The living bird, with its peculiar headdress and beautiful colouring, must have been a remarkable sight, contrasting markedly with the three dingy, antiquated stuffed examples that survive. These specimens date from the last part of the eighteenth century and the first decades of the nineteenth, the most recent having been collected in 1826. Soon after this date the species seems to have become extinct. Given the early disappearance of so many Mauritian birds it is perhaps surprising that this pigeon lasted so long.

Julien Desjardins, a specimen dealer who spent many years on Mauritius and who received the 1826 specimen, provided the only information of the bird in life. He described how it lived alone near riverbanks and fed on fruit and freshwater molluscs.

Rodrigues Pigeon   *Alectroenas rodericana*

Columba rodericana Milne-Edwards, 1874
Ann. Sci. Nat. Zool. **Ser. 5, no. 19**: 14.

This species is known from bones discovered on Rodrigues during the 1870's and described by Alphonse Milne-Edwards, the celebrated expert on fossil birds at the Paris museum. Milne-Edwards described the species primarily on the evidence of a sternum, and chose to assign it to the genus *Columba*, whereas later researchers have shown an inclination to place it in the genus *Alectroenas*, alongside the extinct pigeon of Mauritius *Alectroenas nitidissima*. Either designation may be correct.

This is another of those rather mysterious birds that seem to have been observed in life by the Huguenot refugee François Leguat. He wrote:

> The pigeons here are somewhat less than our own [European pigeons] and all of a slate colour, fat and good. They perch and build their nests upon trees; they are easily taken being so tame, that we have had fifty about our table to pick up the melon seeds which we threw them, and they lik'd mightily...they never built their nests in the Isle, but in the little Islets that are near it. We suppos'd 'twas to avoid the persecution of the rats, of which there are vast numbers in this Island.

Presumably this description can be correlated with the evidence of the bones. Leguat's account clearly indicates two factors that contributed to the species' extinction – tameness and the depredations of rats.

PSITTACIFORMES

A great many parrots are threatened with extinction or are in serious decline. Partly this is due to the vulnerability of island forms, for many parrots are inhabitants of small islands, but partly, and paradoxically, it is due to their great popularity. For

Norfolk Kaka
Nestor productus

Black-fronted Parakeet
Cyanoramphus zealandicus

Raiatea Parakeet
Cyanoramphus ulietanus

♂ ♀
Newton's Parakeet
Psittacula exsul

Cuban Macaw
Ara tricolor

Carolina Parakeet
Conuropsis carolinensis

Mascarene Parrot
Mascarinus mascarinus

Plate F9

inches 4
cm 10

centuries man has been unable to resist the temptation to interfere with populations, move them about and keep individuals as pets.

Nine extinct species are dealt with herein. Two others have already been considered "Almost certainly Extinct" in HBW, and so are not covered here, although elsewhere they have been listed by the present author as extinct (see Fuller, 2000a). These are the Paradise Parrot (*Psephotus pulcherrimus*) and the Glaucous Macaw (*Anodorhynchus glaucus*). There is much negative evidence to show that both are extinct, but perhaps there remains a very small chance that they survive (HBW 4, pages 382 and 419).

The names of a number of what can only be termed "hypothetical" parrot species sometimes occur on lists of the extinct. Among these are several amazons and macaws alleged to come from the West Indies that were described by nineteenth and twentieth century ornithologists on the basis of written reports made by travellers in earlier centuries. The problems with these reports are twofold. First, they are usually vague; second, parrots have been moved around so much by humans that a sighting of an unexpected parrot on one island need not signify a new species. These names cannot, therefore, be accepted as valid.

PSITTACIDAE

Norfolk Kaka
Nestor productus

Nestor productus Gould, 1836
Proc. Zool. Soc. London **1836**: 19.

This is one of these forms that can be interpreted either as a subspecies or as a full species in its own right. In this particular case interpretation is a subjective commodity and each of the interpretations has its merits.

The Kaka (*Nestor meridionalis*) is a relatively well-known representative of the New Zealand avifauna, widely distributed, although nowhere plentiful, on both main islands and on a number of smaller offshore islands. It is a fairly stocky parrot of medium size with striking but quite variable plumage.

Until around the middle of the nineteenth century a closely related bird occurred on Norfolk Island and its close neighbour Phillip Island, both of which lie in the Tasman Sea almost half way between New Zealand and Australia. The plumage of the Norfolk and Phillip Island birds is somewhat different to those from New Zealand, but it seems quite likely that the two could have interbred, had they come into contact. However, the two forms have acquired a fairly separate identity in ornithological literature and if museum specimens are compared it is quite easy to tell them apart – even without reference to locality data.

All birds on Norfolk Island were badly affected by the establishment of penal settlements for criminals transported from Britain. These were founded during the last decade or so of the eighteenth century and they were used during the first few decades of the nineteenth. There is no doubt that convicts and early settlers entirely disrupted the peace and tranquility of the island and the large, brightly coloured parrots would have made a very tempting target. Norfolk Kakas were probably caught primarily for food but there is no doubt that they were also taken as pets. The famous ornithological writer John Gould saw one in Sydney during his visit in the late 1830's and the last individual of all may well have been a bird that died in its cage in London in 1851, or soon after.

Almost nothing is known of the bird in the wild. Apparently it nested in holes in trees and laid up to four eggs. It frequented the rocks and the tree tops, was very tame, as might be expected in an island form, and was seen feeding on blossoms. The population seems to have been prone to a strange deformity of the beak.

As far as is known these parrots were first extirpated on Norfolk Island, and held out for a little longer on Phillip.

Raiatea Parakeet
Cyanoramphus ulietanus

Psittacus ulietanus J. F. Gmelin, 1788
Syst. Nat. **1(1)**: 328.

This is another of the species known only from the records and specimens brought back by those who sailed with Cook on his three exploratory voyages around the world.

There is some doubt over which particular expedition encountered this bird, but it seems likely that the encounter took place when naturalists of the third voyage called at Raiatea (then called Ulietea) in the Society Islands of the South Pacific, during November 1777. At least two specimens were collected and these are now in the Natural History Museum, London and the Naturhistorisches Museum, Vienna.

Nothing is known of the species, nor can any realistic reasons be advanced for its extinction which, presumably, took place soon after Cook's last voyage, for the birds were never encountered again. Perhaps they were unable to withstand the attacks of introduced mammals or maybe man's meddling with parrots was a factor.

Black-fronted Parakeet   *Cyanoramphus zealandicus*

Like the Raiatea Parakeet, this was another inhabitant of the Society Islands, but as far as is known this particular species was restricted to Tahiti.

Both species are closely related to the well known *Cyanoramphus* parakeets of New Zealand but they are physically separated from these by 3220 km of open sea. Probably, they had quite similar lifestyles although this cannot be confirmed as there are no records concerning the two extinct species.

Again like the Raiatea Parakeet, this species was first brought to light by naturalists who sailed with Cook, although in this particular case it was also recorded by a few later visitors.

A painting by Sydney Parkinson, made during Cook's first voyage, is kept at the Natural History Museum, London, and there are also a handful of specimens in existence – one in London, two in Liverpool, one in Paris and one in Perpignan.

The last record of the species dates from 1844, but nothing is recorded of the bird in life.

Psittacus zealandicus Latham, 1790
Index. Orn. **1**: 102.

Newton's Parakeet   *Psittacula exsul*

A greyish-blue parakeet belonging to the familiar ring-necked group once lived on the Mascarene island of Rodrigues. Curiously, it survived for much longer than most of the endemic bird species of the island. Certainly, individuals were still alive during the 1870's, although it is clear that all were gone soon after that.

Little is known of the species but it seems that the two early chroniclers of the birds of Rodrigues, François Leguat and the anonymous author who is usually considered to be a certain Monsieur Tafforet, both saw this species and made observations of it. Certainly, both authors mention parakeets. One complication of these early reports is that Leguat mentioned seeing green as well as blue parakeets. There may have been different colour morphs of the species or the two colours might be explained by the occasional arrival of storm-blown individuals belonging to the more familiar *Psittacula* species. Possibly, such individuals could interbreed with the endemic birds. In addition to these complicating factors, there is skeletal evidence to show that more than one parakeet species once inhabited the island.

Leguat and his followers saw birds – presumably Newton's Parakeets – feeding on the nuts of an olive-like tree, and they taught some of these parakeets to speak, surely an indication of just how tame such birds were. Apparently they became bi-lingual; they could speak in both French and Flemish! When Leguat and his little band of followers fled the island they took a parakeet with them on their voyage to Mauritius.

Although the species was obviously common during the period of Leguat's visit (1691), it was rare by the nineteenth century. Just two specimens are known and both are in the collection of the University Museum of Zoology, Cambridge. Both were collected during the 1870's, the last on 14th August 1875.

The reasons for extinction are unknown, but it is likely that the bird's original tameness and the infestation of the island by mammals were primary causes.

Palaeornis exsul A. Newton, 1872
Ibis **Ser. 3, no. 2**: 33.

Mascarene Parrot   *Mascarinus mascarinus*

Like the preceding species, just two specimens of this striking, middle-sized parrot exist. One is in Paris, the other in Vienna. Both probably date from the last years of the eighteenth century or the early years of the nineteenth. A record of an individual surviving in a European aviary until 1834 (see Hahn, 1841) is now considered to be false.

Very little is known of the species other than the fact that its home was the Mascarene island of Reunion. Why it vanished and when is not known but it can be assumed that it became extinct during the first decades of the nineteenth century.

Psittacus mascarin. Linnaeus, 1771
Mantissa: 524.

Broad-billed Parrot   *Lophopsittacus mauritianus*

Pictures drawn by Dutch explorers visiting the island of Mauritius during the early seventeenth century clearly show a rather strange and aberrant parrot, and these pictures can be correlated with bones found on the island. The bones, like the pictures and a few contemporary written descriptions, indicate the former existence of a large-headed parrot.

Apart from the fact that such a bird once existed, little can be meaningfully said of it. It certainly still lived during the early seventeenth century, but it probably became extinct not long afterwards. It may have lasted until the last decades of the seventeenth century or it may have been lost well before this.

Psittacus mauritianus Owen, 1866
Ibis **Ser. 2, no. 2**: 168.

Plate F10

Broad-billed Parrot
Lophopsittacus mauritianus

Broad-billed Parrots on Mauritius. The exact appearance of this species is unknown, but skeletal remains and early accounts permit a degree of confidence in this reconstruction by Julian Hume. Also pictured are Mauritius Parakeets (Psittacula echo), *currently listed as Critically Endangered.*

Rodrigues Parrot — *Necropsittacus rodericanus*

Psittacus rodericanus Milne-Edwards, 1867
Ann. Sci. Nat. Zool. **Ser. 5, no. 8**: 151.

A parrot comparable in size to a large cockatoo with an outsize beak once inhabited the island of Rodrigues. An almost complete skull of this creature has been found and this relic can be matched with an account in the anonymous document – written around 1725 – known as the *Relation de l'Île Rodrigue*. This account describes a long-tailed parrot with a large head. The writer suggests that the species was green in colour and lived on islets to the south of the main island. Probably it had been penned back to these refuges on account of the incursions of rats. To find water the parrots had to fly across to the main island of Rodrigues itself, surely an indication that the islets would not have been the birds' first and original choice as a home. Individuals were seen eating small black seeds from a tree that smelled of lemons.

Probably the species became extinct during the late eighteenth century.

Cuban Macaw — *Ara tricolor*

Psittacula tricolor Bechstein, 1811
Allgem. Ueb. Vög. **4**: 64.

This distinctive and beautiful macaw, around a third smaller in size than its largest relatives, was an inhabitant of the island of Cuba.

The most recent record of a living bird comes from La Vega, close to the Zapata Swamp, where an individual was killed during 1864. It is thought that a few birds survived for a decade or two after this date, but there is no actual proof of this. Presumably, the species' decline was due to human interference: the taking of birds for food or their capture as pets.

Although it has a very distinctive identity, almost nothing is known of the species in life. It is assumed that its habits were similar to those of its more familiar, extant relatives.

Attempts have been made to create artificial Cuban Macaws by selectively breeding their near relatives. Some parrot fanciers have claimed that a degree of success has been achieved but the word of many parrot breeders is notoriously unreliable – and in any case such created creatures would have little, if any, real connection with the actual species.

Carolina Parakeet — *Conuropsis carolinensis*

Psittacus carolinensis Linnaeus, 1758
Syst. Nat. **10**: 97.

C. c. ludovicianus (J. F. Gmelin, 1788)
Syst. Nat. **1(1)**: 347.

The Carolina Parakeet, like its compatriot the Passenger Pigeon, declined from vast numbers to just a few individuals within the period of a century. This was once considered a pest species, with communal feeding habits, that ranged across the southern and eastern USA. It ruined orchards, wrecked corn fields, destroyed grain stocks and thereby aroused the anger of man. The species seems to have had few defensive skills. When individuals were shot, their companions would fly squawking above the dead or wounded and eventually they would settle among their downed fellows. Naturally, they then made easy targets themselves.

A parrot having the capability of inhabiting the USA is in itself something of a peculiarity, and there are surprising records of this species flying over snow-covered fields. In the years of its abundance the species liked forested lowland and showed a preference for land close to water. It lived mostly among buttonwood, cypress or sycamore and roosted in hollow stumps into which individuals would crowd and cluster together. At dawn the birds would flock to the top branches of the trees and then they stayed quiet for much of the day. Late afternoon and early evening would see great bursts of activity. When the birds decided to eat they would fly swiftly down to the chosen feeding area and arrive in a blaze of colour.

As far as breeding is concerned, there are conflicting descriptions. Some records tell of several parakeets laying their eggs together in tree holes, while others indicate that fragile nests were made from twigs and that these were sited in the forks of branches.

Two races of the species are commonly recognized, the nominate form and a western subspecies named *ludovicianus*. These two races are rather poorly distinguished, however.

Through much of the nineteenth century the Carolina Parakeet was a particularly common bird. Even as late as the 1880's it could be found in some numbers. Yet soon after this the species could hardly be found in the wild at all.

As the century drew to its close, a few individuals still survived in captivity, most particularly a group in the same Cincinnati Zoo that provided a home to the last Passenger Pigeon. The very last Carolina Parakeets were a pair named Lady Jane and Incas, and by 1917 these two birds had been cage-mates for something like 32 years. Then, Lady Jane died, leaving Incas the sole representative of the species. He survived, alone, for just a few months until February 1918, when he died in his cage surrounded by his keepers. They were in unanimous agreement: their bird had died of grief. His little body was frozen in a block of ice and sent for preservation to the Smithsonian Institution in Washington but, curiously, it never arrived or, if it did, it was stolen. Perhaps this hardly matters; there are several hundred specimens of this species in the world's museums.

There are several alleged late records dating from the 1920's and 1930's that supposedly relate to Carolina Parakeets still surviving in the wild, but these are probably bogus.

CUCULIFORMES

Delalande's or the Snail-eating Coua (*Coua delalandei*), a large, ground-dwelling cuckoo-like bird from Madagascar is almost certainly extinct, and has already been covered thus in HBW (see HBW 4, page 581). It has not been definitely recorded since 1834 but partly because rumours of its continuing existence circulated during the 1920's, there has been reluctance in some quarters to add the species to the ranks of the extinct.

STRIGIFORMES

The Laughing Owl (*Sceloglaux albifacies*) of New Zealand is usually considered to be extinct but for the purposes of HBW the optimistic view has been taken that there is still a remote chance of its survival (see HBW 5, page 239). It has not been reliably recorded since the early decades of the twentieth century, however, and more recent reports are probably false.

It seems clear that at least two now-extinct owl species occupied the Mascarenes during recent historical times, but only one of these has left definitive specimen material behind, and is discussed below. The other has come to be known as *Otus commersoni*. A fairly detailed description of this creature was made by the naturalist/dealer Julien Desjardins, who saw a dead specimen during 1836, and there is a drawing of what seems to be the same species made by one Philippe Sanguin de Jossigny around 1770. This was a largish owl with ear tufts that inhabited the island of Mauritius. Since there is no remaining specimen material of any kind, it is impossible to assign this form to any particular owl group. Other claimed owl species from the Mascarenes were named as *Bubo leguati*, *Strix sauzieri* and *Strix newtoni*, but these forms must be considered even more hypothetical.

Figure 7. Otus commersoni, *as drawn by Philippe Sanguin de Jossingny around 1770.*

STRIGIDAE

Rodrigues Little Owl
Athene murivora

Athene murivora Milne-Edwards, 1874
Ann. Sci. Nat. Zool. **Ser. 5, no. 19**: 13.

The anonymous author of the *Relation de l'Île Rodrigue* (c. 1725) mentions a small owl that preyed on little birds and lizards and could be heard calling in fine weather.

This brief account is often correlated with some fairly fragmentary skeletal material that was found on the island around a century and a half later. This correlation is, of course, a little tenuous but it is by no means unreasonable.

The skeletal remains were assigned to the genus *Athene* by the celebrated French comparative anatomist Alphonse Milne-Edwards who, during the last decades of the nineteenth century was the leading expert in fossil and sub-fossil birds. Unfortunately, his suggestion that the remains could be assigned to *Athene* may not be correct. First, the remains by no means represent a complete specimen. Second, the *Athene* species with which Milne-Edwards compared the Rodrigues material has more recently been reassigned to the genus *Ninox*. This highlights the difficulty of making judgements when assessing incomplete skeletal material. What the evidence of the bones does show is that this species had legs of particular strength and length for an owl of this rather small stature. It can be deduced, therefore, that it was more terrestrial than most owls.

The reasons for its extinction are unknown, as too is the time of this event.

CAPRIMULGIFORMES

The Jamaican Poorwill (*Siphonorhis americana*), not definitely recorded since the 1860's, is often treated as extinct, but the secretive nature of nightjars, in conjunction with recent observations of "unidentifiable" nightjars in remoter parts of the island, give some cause for hope to persist (see HBW 5, page 344). Optimists take heart from the recent rediscovery of the New Caledonian Owlet-nightjar (*Aegotheles savesi*), not definitely recorded since 1880 (or perhaps 1915) until rediscovered in 1998.

APODIFORMES

Although the hummingbirds (Trochilidae) make up a rather homogeneous family, their classification is a very complex matter. Just a small part of the problem is that there are a great many taxa described from single or few specimens of doubtful provenance, a number of which have subsequently been reclassified as hybrids or aberrant individuals. One of the problems with describing a species from just a single individual is that it can be so easy to misunderstand the true nature of that example.

One such case is that of a form recently described as the Bogota Sunangel (*Heliangelus zusii*), on the basis of a specimen that was purchased in Bogotá, Colombia, in 1909 and is now in Philadelphia. Many hummingbird specialists are not inclined to accept it as a valid species, reckoning it probably to be a hybrid, though there is much dispute as to its claimed parentage! Another poorly known form sometimes listed as a threatened species, but recently reported to be probably of hybrid origin, is the Tachira Emerald (*Amazilia* (*Polyerata*) *distans*). In such cases, taxonomic difficulties override the debate as to whether or not such forms are extinct. One apparently extinct form has, however, received somewhat more widespread acceptance as a valid species.

TROCHILIDAE

Brace's Emerald
Chlorostilbon bracei

Sporadinus Bracei Lawrence, 1877
Ann. New York Acad. Sci. **1**: 50.

Although there is indeed fairly general acceptance of Brace's Emerald as a valid species, the same doubts hang about it as in the aforementioned cases, and the present author considers it to be a rather poorly established species. However, a number of hummingbird experts have spoken in its favour and in line with the designations of these specialists it is included here.

In fact, there is very little that can be meaningfully said of it (see HBW 5, page 533). The single known specimen was collected in July 1877 and was apparently

Brace's Emerald
Chlorostilbon bracei

Plate F11

inches   1

cm   3

found on New Providence in the Bahamas. No such bird had ever been seen there before, and there is a reasonable possibility that it may have been a wind-blown vagrant. There has been an attempt to correlate fossil remains found on the island with the preserved skin, but any attempt to make proper sense of tiny hummingbird bones amongst the mass of valid taxa described is really perhaps asking too much.

CORACIIFORMES

The large and diverse order Coraciiformes includes the kingfishers (Alcedinidae), and in this family is a very poorly known form that may constitute an extinct species. This is a bird rather similar to the Micronesian Kingfisher (*Todiramphus cinnamominus*) and known as the Ryukyu Kingfisher (*Todiramphus* (*c.*) *miyakoensis*) after the islands to the south of Japan that it presumably inhabited. Unfortunately, it is one of those creatures known only from a single specimen, taken in 1887, and this extreme limitation makes interpretation difficult, especially as the bill colour is not known. It is probably either an extinct species or an extinct subspecies; either interpretation has its merits. However, there is also some doubt as to whether it might have been brought to the islands by chance vagrancy or through human intervention, or indeed that it might be a mislabelled specimen, so any systematist is in a difficult position in trying to decide. An interesting, if rather sad, related case is that of the nominate race of the Micronesian Kingfisher, endemic to the island of Guam: it is now probably extinct in the wild there, although it still survives in captivity.

PICIFORMES

There are two species in this order that are probably extinct, although optimists still express hope for their survival. These are the Imperial Woodpecker (*Campephilus imperialis*) and its celebrated relative the Ivory-billed Woodpecker (*Campephilus principalis*). Both are dealt with elsewhere in this volume (see page 534).

PASSERIFORMES

As might be expected, an order as vast as the Passeriformes contains quite a number of extinct species. In all, 26 are covered herein. In addition there are two species that are often regarded as extinct and that in all probability are. These are the Bush Wren (*Xenicus longipes*) and the Aldabra Brush-warbler (*Nesillas aldabrana*). Despite relatively recent records of each, in 1972 and 1983 respectively, there is only a remote chance that either survives. Both species will be fully covered in HBW in due course.

Several other species hover around the very brink of extinction. Gurney's Pitta (*Pitta gurneyi*) is one such species and, despite great conservation efforts over the last

15 years, it could be gone by the time this volume is published. So too could the Po'o'uli (*Melamprosops phaeosoma*), a species that at the time of writing seems to have only three surviving representatives, all of which are males! Another Hawaiian bird for which there is very little hope is the Molokai Creeper (*Paroreomyza flammea*), last recorded in 1963 and probably now extinct.

On the brighter side, the Four-coloured Flowerpecker (*Dicaeum quadricolor*), once confidently considered extinct, was recently rediscovered, but its hold on survival is very tenuous and it could vanish at any time. Similarly, the Sao Tome Grosbeak (*Neospiza concolor*), not recorded since 1888 until rediscovered in 1991, is presumed to survive with only a tiny population that urgently needs safeguarding.

ACANTHISITTIDAE

Stephens Wren   *Xenicus lyalli*

Traversia lyalli Rothschild, 1894
Bull. Brit. Orn. Club **4**: 10.

Although so tiny in size the Stephens Wren was an altogether remarkable creature. It may have had the smallest natural range of any known bird. It may have been the only flightless passerine. It may have been the only creature discovered and then exterminated by a single animal – a lighthouse keeper's cat.

During 1894 this single domesticated predator brought to its owner a series of tiny corpses. These grisly little events occurred on the small island of Stephens lying in the Cook Straits, the channel that separates New Zealand's North Island from the South. The lighthouse keeper in question – a Mr Lyall, after whom the species is scientifically named – was something of an amateur ornithologist. He preserved the specimens and, realizing that the birds might be rather unusual, passed them on to a dealer. Soon the majority of them were shipped to Europe where most were bought by Walter Rothschild, the celebrated natural-history collector, who was then busy assembling his wonderful museum at Tring in Hertfordshire, England. Thus, *Xenicus lyalli* became known to science. By the time its existence was broadcast to the world, via the ornithological journal *Ibis*, the species was already extinct. The cat had stopped bringing in dead specimens and the birds were never seen again. It seems likely that forest clearance for the construction of the lighthouse, in 1894, may also have made a significant contribution to the bird's demise.

The only human observation of Stephens Wrens was made by the lighthouse keeper himself. He saw the birds twice, both times in the evening. Disturbed from holes among the rocks, they ran fast in the dusk, like mice. They never tried to take to the air and this suggestion of flightlessness is borne out by the poorly developed wings which indicate weak flight at best.

Skeletal remains of what seems to have been a flightless wren have been found on the New Zealand mainland. Some writers believe that this proves that Stephens Wrens were once widespread in New Zealand and that the birds discovered during 1894 were simply a relict population, but it seems far more likely that the skeletal remains come from a similar but quite separate creature. There are a number of objections to the case for the Stephens Wren being associated with the mainland skeletal remains. First, what material were the bones compared with? Second, how did a wren that was flightless, or almost so, manage to reach Stephens Island?

Sir Walter Buller (1905), the great chronicler of New Zealand birds, quoted from a correspondent of *The Canterbury Press* who had written the following:

And we certainly think that it would be as well if the Marine Department, in sending lighthouse keepers to isolated islands where interest-

Plate F12

inches   2
cm   5

Stephens Wren
Xenicus lyalli

ing specimens of native birds are known or believed to exist, were to see that they are not allowed to take any cats with them, even if mouse-traps have to be furnished at the cost of the state.

TURDIDAE

Bay Thrush

Turdus ulietensis

This is another of those species known today only from a painting by Georg Forster. This painting, now in the Forster portfolio at the Natural History Museum, London, was produced on 1st June 1774 at Raiatea in the South Pacific, and according to an inscription it shows a female.

Turdus ulietensis J. F. Gmelin, 1789
Syst. Nat. **1(2)**: 815.

Although no actual specimen is in existence, there was one once, and presumably this was the bird from which the picture was painted. The ornithological writer John Latham saw it in the collection of Sir Joseph Banks and wrote a description of it for his book *General Synopsis of Birds* (1781-1785), giving it the name "Bay Thrush". Latham was a pioneering ornithologist, but headstrong, and in his early works he simply gave common English names to the birds he described, deliberately ignoring the fast-gaining Linnaean system of scientific naming. By the time he realized his mistake, he was too late: the lapse had left the field open for Johann Friedrich Gmelin, who in the meantime had produced his own book *Systema Naturae* (1788-1789), just a few years after Latham's. Gmelin attached scientific names to many of the birds that Latham had originally described and, because of this, it is Gmelin's name that is associated with so many of Latham's original descriptions.

Naturally, a species represented in such a flimsy manner as is the Bay Thrush is bound to be surrounded by mystery – and this the Bay Thrush most certainly is. Most importantly, it is by no means sure that the species was actually a thrush. Georg Forster and his father Johann Reinhold were efficient naturalists who sailed with Cook, but when they saw this creature they were rather uncertain of its affinities and described it as a thrush with some degree of reluctance. A particularly un-thrushlike feature was a notch in the bill.

Whatever its precise relationships, this bird seems to have been a valid and distinct species. The reasons for its extinction are entirely unknown but this event must have happened soon after the visit of Cook and the Forsters for no other naturalist ever mentioned seeing the species.

The Forsters themselves gave a few fleeting details about the bird in life. They said it had a soft, fluting voice and lived among thickets in valleys. Apart from these bare facts, nothing is known of the species.

Plate F13

inches 3
cm 8

Grand Cayman Thrush
Turdus ravidus

Kittlitz's Thrush
Zoothera terrestris

Grand Cayman Thrush

Turdus ravidus

The Grand Cayman Thrush became extinct towards the middle of the twentieth century, but considering the comparative lateness of this date very little is known of it. One of the few things on record is a description of its song, which was apparently rather weak and hesitant, more, perhaps, a subdued warbling than a melodic triumph.

Mimocichla ravida Cory, 1886
Auk **3**: 499.

As the name indicates, the species came only from the island of Grand Cayman, in the West Indies, where it inhabited dense woodland. It was closely related to a widespread West Indian species, the Red-legged Thrush (*Turdus plumbeus*).

The Grand Cayman birds were large and beautiful grey thrushes that first came to public attention during 1886, when C. B. Cory described the species. He found it to be common on the island, but its decline was to be rapid. By the outbreak of World War I, it was rare and could only be found in remote areas of woodland. No specimens were taken after this time and the last recorded sighting occurred before the start of World War II. Destruction of habitat was probably a key factor in the species' disappearance, as it seemed to need areas of dense woodland.

The last stronghold appears to have been at the eastern end of the island. Severe hurricanes during the years 1932 and 1944 are thought to have played some role in the final destruction of the species.

Kittlitz's Thrush   *Zoothera terrestris*

Turdus terrestris Kittlitz, 1830
Mém. Acad. Imp. Sci. St. Pétersb. **1**: 244-245.

The name of Baron Friedrich Heinrich von Kittlitz is associated with the stories of several extinct birds. During the late 1820's he explored a number of Pacific islands during a round-the-world expedition on a Russian corvette called the *Senjawin*.

In June 1829 Kittlitz landed on Peel Island (Chichi-jima), the largest island in the Bonin group (Ogasawara-shoto). Kittlitz was one of only a very few Europeans to see the Bonins in something approaching their pristine state. Within a few years of his visit, the original ecosystem had been shattered. Just two years after he left, a group of American, British and Polynesian colonists arrived and settled. Then whalers began to call and started to use the Bonins as a suitable place to replenish their stores and careen their vessels. Rats arrived and the devastation of the endemic birdlife was horrendous.

Kittlitz made his landing place at a spot called Port Lloyd that had been visited and named just a year before by a British expedition under the command of a Captain Beechey in *HMS Blossom*. Surprisingly, Kittlitz found a seemingly common bird that the British had entirely overlooked, the handsome ground thrush that now bears his name. During his short stay, Kittlitz saw this bird quite often but no later naturalist ever did. He sailed away, apparently taking four specimens with him, and the bird was never seen again. His specimens are today divided between the museums of Frankfurt, St Petersburg, Leiden and Vienna.

Whether Kittlitz's Thrush occupied other islands in the Bonin group is not known.

ZOSTEROPIDAE

Robust White-eye   *Zosterops strenuus*

Zosterops strenua Gould, 1855
Proc. Zool. Soc. London **1855**: 166.

So impressed was he by the comparatively large size of this species, for a white-eye, that the famous nineteenth century ornithologist and writer John Gould felt inclined to give this bird the common name of "Robust Zosterops", and this same sensation is perhaps recalled somewhat in the scientific name that he gave it. Gould had developed a considerable interest in the avifauna of Australia and published his celebrated book *The Birds of Australia* between the years 1840 and 1848. It was later, while he was undertaking research for a *Supplement* to this work, that he became aware of this particular species.

The species was endemic to the island of Lord Howe, a tiny piece of land, 11 km long by 1·6 km wide, that lies far out in the Tasman Sea between Australia and New Zealand. During the mid-nineteenth century, when the bird was first identified, it was

Plate F14

inches 2
cm 5

Robust White-eye
Zosterops strenuus

found to be common, and the population stayed healthy for the next 60 years or so. Then in 1918, an incident occurred that proved fatal for many of the birds of Lord Howe. A ship, the *SS Makambo*, was accidentally grounded at a site known as Ned's Beach. Black rats (*Rattus rattus*) left the stricken vessel and poured ashore – and the consequences were disasterous. In a very short space of time the white-eyes were gone. A search made just ten years later could find no trace of them.

There are a few records concerning the habits of the species. When it was common it was regarded as something of a pest. It was destructive to fruit and crops, and was even said to suck the eggs of other bird species! Its own eggs were laid during November and December. They were blue and, typically, the clutch consisted of two or three. The nest was cup-shaped and made from rootlets and grasses with a soft lining of disintegrated leaves and other suitable materials.

Curiously, another kind of white-eye lived on tiny Lord Howe. This was a race of the widespread Silvereye (*Zosterops lateralis*), and to distinguish the larger birds belonging to the species *Z. strenuus* local people gave them the name "big grinnels".

MELIPHAGIDAE

Kioea   *Chaetoptila angustipluma*

In terms of extinct birds the Hawaiian Islands are one of the world's black spots. The losses at species and subspecies level have been enormous and there is no sign that this process is letting up. There are several species and races that are unlikely to see out the next decade, such as the Po'o'uli, mentioned above.

Entomiza angustipluma Peale, 1848
US Expl. Exped. **8**: 147.

Many Hawaiian species are known only from skeletal material, and it is not known when such creatures died out. Perhaps it was comparatively recently, perhaps it was some way back in time. Other species are known just from small series of specimens taken by ornithological collectors during the last decade of the nineteenth century, at which time there was a great spate of scientific interest in the Hawaiian Islands. What can be said with certainty is that the coming of man entirely shattered the ecosystems of the islands. It is clear that the Polynesian arrival had a devastating effect. Although the coming of Europeans, centuries later, probably increased the pace of extinction, the real damage was already done, and the endemic avifauna consisted largely of scattered, fast-diminishing populations.

One such badly affected species was the Kioea, a large and handsome honeyeater. The species was first noticed during the visit to Hawaii of Charles Pickering and Titian Ramsay Peale as part of *The United States Exploring Expedition* of 1838-1842. At the time Peale wrote of it:

> It is very active and graceful in its motions, frequents the woody districts, and is disposed to be musical, having most of the habits of a Meliphaga [honeyeater]; they are generally found about those trees that are in flower.

Clearly Pickering and Peale experienced no great difficulty in finding individuals, but the birds were rapidly becoming rarer. In the period leading up to 1859, during which year the last known specimen was taken, a local shopkeeper with an interest in natural history, J. Mills, killed two or three individuals on wooded slopes below the crater of the volcano Kilauea. After Mills's last record, Kioeas were never seen again. Clearly, and notwithstanding the fact that Pickering and Peale located birds reasonably easily, the species was approaching extinction even as it was being discovered.

Four specimens survive today and there may never have been more. Of these, one is in Honolulu, one in New York, one in Washington and one in Cambridge, England.

Apart from the brief account given by Peale, there is almost nothing on record concerning the species' habits. Although Peale described the birds as inclined to be musical, the call was described as a loud "chuck", but this is the sum of additional knowledge.

The species is said to have been an inhabitant of the high plateau between the mountains and the edge of the forest but whether or not this kind of area was representative of the original range cannot be said. Although the Kioea was only ever located on the island of Hawaii, fossil evidence shows that the species was also once present on Oahu and Maui, and it was also claimed to have occurred on Molokai.

Hawaii 'O'o   *Moho nobilis*

The ancient kings and princes of Hawaii chose this unfortunate creature to be their "royal" bird. As is so often the case when monarchs choose, being the "chosen" one

Gracula nobilis Merrem, 1786
Av. Rar. Icon. Descr. **1**: 7.

does not necessarily confer safety – and it definitely did not in this case. The honour merely meant that 'O'os were expected to provide plumes for the famous robes, capes and helmets that are today so prized by ethnologists, but which were once an integral part of the whole culture of pre-European Hawaii. The downfall of the 'O'o lay in the beautiful tufts of yellow feathers that grew below the wings and on the lower abdomen. These were ripped from the living bird and then woven into a bed of coarse netting; gradually, after the unwilling input of many hundreds of individuals, the cloak began to take shape.

After the feathers were stolen from the bird, those who had trapped it were supposed to let it go. Whether or not they did is something of an open question. 'O'os fried in their own fat were, apparently, a great delicacy and it is hard to imagine hungry Hawaiians passing up the chance of a tasty morsel, particularly as any chance of being caught defying the law would presumably be remote. Even if the plumes were carefully removed and the bird released there is no guarantee that it would be capable of surviving, for the shock alone might be sufficient to cause death, but perhaps it could.

The species was first scientifically discovered by naturalists who sailed with Cook on his third voyage around the world. Cook himself did not survive this expedition and was killed at Kealakakua Bay, Hawaii, during February 1779. The voyage itself was completed, however, and when the ships eventually arrived in England specimens of *Moho nobilis* were among the treasures brought back. John Latham in his *General Synopsis of Birds* (1781-1785) described the "Yellow-tufted Bee-eater" from these specimens.

Although the species must once have been common on Hawaii, by the time of the coming of Europeans it was in decline and no European observer described it as anything but shy and wary. No wonder! It was seen to take nectar from flowers but it also

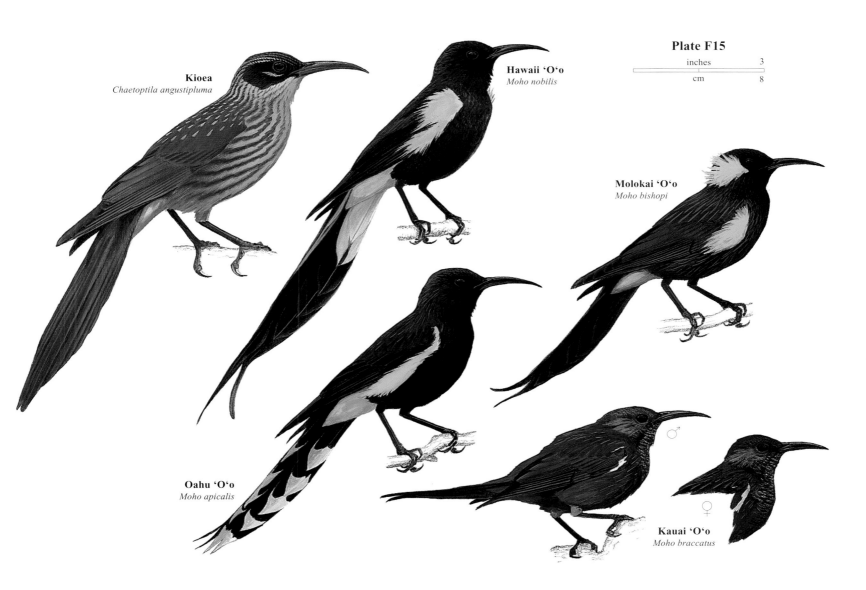

Kioea
Chaetoptila angustipluma

Hawaii 'O'o
Moho nobilis

Plate F15

inches   3

cm   8

Molokai 'O'o
Moho bishopi

Oahu 'O'o
Moho apicalis

Kauai 'O'o
Moho braccatus

tucked into bananas, as well as insects and their larvae. In flight it showed a dipping action and the wings moved so rapidly that they made a continuous buzzing sound. These birds frequented the topmost branches of the trees and, perhaps as a result of this preference, the nest and eggs were never found, although an experienced ornithologist, R. C. L. Perkins, did see young individuals that were recently out of the nest.

The call was harsh and clear, and from it the name 'O'o is derived. Since there is often confusion, it might be added that the pronunciation of this name should be in the form of two o's separated by a glottal stop, "oh-oh", rather than "oooww".

The records indicate that the species was once widespread over the whole island of Hawaii, as it was evidently able to live at quite high altitudes.

Hunting for plumes obviously depleted numbers, but other factors probably also played a part in bringing about its extinction. Perhaps some kind of avian disease carried to Hawaii by an introduced species was partly responsible or maybe it was just the general breakdown of the ecosystem that was responsible for the species' disappearance.

The last genuine report of the Hawaii 'O'o probably concerns an individual heard singing on the slopes of the volcano Mauna Loa around the year 1934.

Oahu 'O'o   *Moho apicalis*

The main islands of Hawaii each had their own distinctive species of 'O'o. All are closely related but their respective island isolations led to certain clear differences.

Moho apicalis Gould, 1861
Proc. Zool. Soc. London **1860**: 381.

The Oahu 'O'o was distinguished chiefly by its strikingly marked black and white tail. Like its relative on Hawaii it sported yellow flank plumes and undertail-coverts.

This was probably the first of the 'o'os to become extinct. A certain Herr Deppe, about whom virtually nothing is known, collected a series of specimens during 1837 from the hills behind Honolulu. Never again was the species encountered or, if it was, no-one ever mentioned it. Specimens do exist for which there is no provenance noted, so it is possible that a later collector found the species. Three that are known to have been taken by Deppe are in the museums of Berlin, Vienna and New York, but in addition to these there is a second specimen in New York, two examples in London, one in Paris, and one in Cambridge, Massachusetts.

Nothing is known of the living bird.

Molokai 'O'o   *Moho bishopi*

The 'o'o that inhabited the island of Molokai was discovered rather later than the others but it was known to science as an extant species for only a very short period.

Acrulocercus bishopi Rothschild, 1893
Bull. Brit. Orn. Club **1**: 41.

Towards the end of the nineteenth century there was a sudden surge of interest in the birds of Hawaii, and several teams of collectors ranged over the islands in search of specimens. It is a curious fact that a number of Hawaiian birds are known solely from this period. Clearly the species in question were all at the point of extinction when they were discovered, and were it not for the collecting zeal that inspired these Hawaiian expeditions during the 1880's and 1890's, their existence and passing would probably have gone entirely unnoticed by the world of ornithology. Two beautifully illustrated books resulted from the collections made at this time, *Aves Hawaiiensis* (1890-1899) by S. B. Wilson and A. H. Evans and *The Avifauna of Laysan and the Neighbouring Islands* (1893-1900) by Walter Rothschild, and it is from the words and pictures contained in these books that almost all knowledge of certain lost species is derived.

The Molokai 'O'o provides just such a case. Described in 1893 by Walter Rothschild from specimens procured by men in his pay, it was gone by the early years of the twentieth century, the last definite record coming from the year 1904. A few later sightings were claimed but these may or may not be reliable.

Curiously, and remarkably, the species was reported from the nearby island of Maui during 1981 but this claimed sighting is almost certainly a misidentification. Nevertheless, there is some evidence to show that the species did once inhabit Maui. A certain H. W. Henshaw, who was a very reliable observer, reported seeing an individual during June, 1901.

Virtually nothing is known of the species in life. It differed from the two previous species by showing bright yellow cheek tufts and by carrying a tail with much less white on it.

Kauai 'O'o   *Moho braccatus*

The fourth species 'o'o clung to survival for much longer than the others. It was also the most divergent of the four. Whereas the other three are very similar looking crea-

Moho braccatus Cassin, 1855
Proc. Acad. Nat. Sci. Philadelphia **7**: 440.

tures that show their close affinity quite clearly, the Kauai 'O'o was comparatively aberrant. By no means so flashy in appearance, it was an altogether more sober-looking bird. Clearly, it was taking a rather different evolutionary path on its home island which is farther west and a little more remote than the other 'o'o islands.

It was probably this very remoteness that enabled the species to survive longer than its relatives, and, although it was extremely rare from the beginning of the twentieth century, a few individuals held out until the 1980's. Their stronghold was a wild place known as the Alaka'i Swamp, a wet montane plateau broken up by ravines.

This area acquired something of a worldwide celebrity as a natural refuge for endangered birds and several rare species and races clung to existence here and nowhere else. Although it provided a sanctuary of sorts for many years, the Alaka'i Swamp was not in itself enough to save the Kauai 'O'o. The small colony that had established itself there dwindled slowly until by 1981 it seemed that just a pair survived. The female of this pair disappeared during 1983 as a result of the devastation caused by Hurricane Iwa. The male continued to be seen until 1985. A rather evocative photograph of this individual exists. It was taken by Hawaiian bird expert H. Douglas Pratt and shows the bird sheltering forlornly in the branches of a tree. The flute-like call of this bird may have been heard during 1987 but the bird itself was never seen again.

Although the Kauai 'O'o managed to linger on until comparatively recently, its main decline was remarkably rapid. George Munro, a man who spent much of a very long life studying Hawaiian birds, recorded that in 1891 the species was common and occurred from sea-level right up to the mountain tops. In 1899 he left the island and did not return for 29 years, but when he did finally go back, he failed to see or hear a single individual.

CALLAEATIDAE

Huia
Heteralocha acutirostris

Neomorpha acutirostris Gould, 1837
Synop. Birds Australia **1**: pl. 11.

Perhaps the most celebrated of extinct passerines is the Huia (pronounced hoo-ee-ah). This strange, funereal-looking creature fascinated all of those who came into contact with it. First, it caught the imagination of the Maoris, who accorded it a special place in the natural order of things. Among the great treasures of ethnology are items known as *waka-huias*. These are intricately carved wooden boxes that the Maoris made expressly to hold the black tail feathers with white tips that characterized the Huia. To this war-like people the feathers themselves held an almost magical significance. They were worn in battle, given as tokens of friendship or respect, and mourned over in times of grief.

After the European invasion of New Zealand, the birdlife came under intense scrutiny and no species fascinated ornithologists more than the Huia. This was probably largely due to a unique peculiarity of the Huia's anatomy. The beak of the male differs markedly from that of the female. At first sight this might not seem of any particular importance but no other known bird species shows a comparable difference: although

Plate F16

inches 6
cm 15

Huia
Heteralocha acutirostris

♂   ♀

plumages may vary vastly between the sexes, beaks are always fairly similar. In the case of the Huia, however, the beak of the male is powerful and rather crow-like whereas that of the female is long, slender and down-curved. This difference was so unexpected that when specimens first reached ornithologists they were thought to constitute two separate but related species, the female being given the name *acutirostris* and the male *crassirostris*.

What was the reason for this divergence? The answer to this question has to be that pairs co-operated in feeding. If two birds could tap different food sources then the territory that they needed to occupy would be smaller. Perhaps the great wonder is why such a useful-seeming adaptation is not commoner. It could, of course, be argued that the very fact of the Huia's extinction indicates that the strategy does not really work.

The male Huia could use its chunky beak to break up rotting branches or trunks, leaving the female free to come along behind and use her long, slender bill to probe into the distressed material for insects and their larvae. A favourite food item was, apparently, the huhu, a large plump grub of the nocturnal beetle *Prionoplus reticularis*; another was the weta (*Hemideina megacephala*).

As might be expected in pairs of birds that are so dependant on each other, extreme distress was shown by any individual that lost its mate. There are several accounts that detail the behaviour of birds whose mate had been shot. Instead of flying off at the sound of the gunfire, the survivor would stay and search for its downed fellow. Doubtless, this kind of unwariness was one of the prime reasons for the species' extinction. Probably it fell prey to four-legged mammalian predators as easily as it fell prey to man.

The range of the Huia was always rather restricted. It seems to have occurred only on New Zealand's North Island – although there are one or two indications that it may have been present at the very north of the South Island. Even on the North Island only certain areas seem to have suited it. The famous chronicler of New Zealand birds Sir Walter Buller commented on the fact that in winter Huias needed to descend from any mountainous territory occupied, in order to avoid the extremes of cold. Probably it was this liking for warmth that prevented Huias from successfully inhabiting the rather cooler South Island.

Largely thanks to the works of Buller, a body of information exists on the lifestyle of this bird. The call was as the name; Huia is simply a phonetic rendering of it. It was described as soft and fluting and altogether haunting. The species laid 2-4 greyish eggs that were marked with brown and purplish spots and blotches, and breeding occurred during the Southern Hemisphere summer, chiefly around the month of November.

There is no doubt that the species' general demeanour rendered it ripe for extinction, but other factors probably played a part. Chief among these is the fact that large areas of the North Island became cultivated or were given over to grazing, so the woodland that formed the Huia's natural habitat became ever more fragmented. The last fully accepted sighting of living Huias dates from the year 1907, but it is almost certain that a few birds lingered on after this date.

The best description of the bird in life comes from the pen of Buller (1887-88):

> The Huia never leaves the shade of the forest. It moves along the ground, or from tree to tree, with surprising celerity by a series of bounds or jumps. In its flight it never rises, like other birds, above the tree-tops, except in the depths of the woods, when it happens to fly from one high tree to another...They are generally met with in pairs, but sometimes a party of four or more are found consorting together...this species builds its nest in hollow trees, forming it of dry grass, leaves and the withered stems of herbaceous plants, carefully twined together in a circular form, and lined with softer material of a similar kind.

TURNAGRIDAE

Piopio *Turnagra capensis*

The Piopio, or New Zealand Thrush, may have been two species rather than one. Two quite distinct kinds existed, and they are usually regarded as races of the same species: nominate *capensis* of the South Island; and race *tanagra* of the North Island. There are good reasons for supposing that they should be treated as separate species. First, the plumages are very different. Second, the structure of the beak is not quite the

Tanagra capensis Sparrman, 1787
Mus. Carlsonianum **2**: 45.

T. c. tanagra (Schlegel, 1865)
Nederlandsch Tijdschrift Dierkunde **3**: 190.

Plate F17

inches   3
cm   8

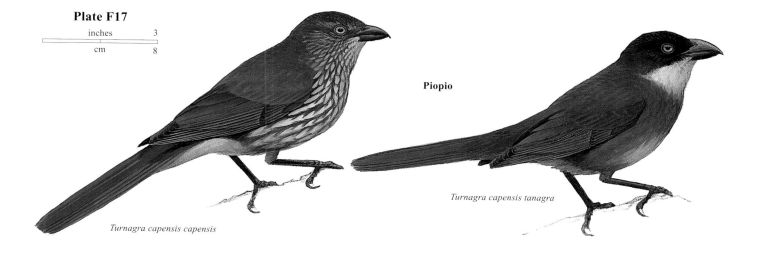

Piopio

Turnagra capensis tanagra

Turnagra capensis capensis

same, being considerably heavier and stouter in North Island birds. Third, each had a clearly definable and isolated geographical range, so they had no scope for interbreeding. It is perhaps the extreme rarity of specimens from the North Island that has prevented this idea from being investigated further. A third suggested race, *minor*, identified from specimens taken from tiny Stephens Island, a short distance offshore from the South Island in the Cook Straits, is only doubtfully distinct from the South Island form.

Just as the question of species is somewhat doubtful, so too is the bird's place in any systematic list. There is no general agreement as to where this creature's relationships lie and it has been associated with various passerine groups. Certainly it is not a thrush. This term was used simply as a comforter for early settlers in New Zealand who were anxious to see in the new land anything that could remind them of their old homes. Thus, there are New Zealand robins, New Zealand crows, New Zealand wrens and New Zealand thrushes, none of which have any real connection with the species that inhabited the "old" country, but which simply bore a vague, superficial resemblance to them. Systematists have aligned the Piopio (a Maori word that is derived from the bird's call) with the whistlers and the bowerbirds. The bowerbird hypothesis is, perhaps, the more likely, but the Piopio could easily belong close to another group altogether.

In the early days of European settlement Piopios were common birds, at least on South Island. The species was able to occupy many differing types of environment from sea-level up to the higher alpine country; the preference was for wooded country close to water. Its fate was almost certainly sealed by the fact that it was so tame and confiding. Individuals would hop around doors and windows in the hope of picking up scraps of food, or drop unwarily onto the forest floor. This left them horribly vulnerable to the attacks of dogs and cats, and the species steadily succumbed. Although much later dates are sometimes given, it seems that the last reliable record of the North Island Piopio comes from the year 1902. A few South Island birds survived for rather longer but by the early years of the twentieth century this form too was realistically finished. The most recent record which has any claim to credibility comes from Lake Hauroko in 1949.

Piopios lived on a fairly wide variety of different kinds of food. They would eat insects, worms, fruit, buds, seeds, leaves and any kitchen scraps that they could get hold of. A cup-shaped nest was built in the trees from twigs and mosses, with a lining of soft grasses or down. Two white eggs, spotted and blotched with brown, were laid in December.

The musicality of the species was mentioned by Buller (1887-88). Describing a captive individual, he wrote:

> It was when I obtained a caged Piopio that I first became acquainted with its superior vocal powers...He often astonished me with the power and variety of his notes. Commencing sometimes with the loud strains of the Thrush, he would suddenly change his song to a low flute-note of exquisite sweetness; and then abruptly stopping, would give vent to a loud rasping cry, as if mimicking a pair of Australian Magpies confined in the same aviary. During the early morning he emitted at intervals a short flute-note, and when alarmed or startled uttered a sharp repeated whistle.

STURNIDAE

Kosrae Starling

Aplonis corvina

Three starlings of the genus *Aplonis* have vanished. The species from Kosrae Island, one of the Caroline group in the Pacific, is known from just a series of specimens collected by F. H. von Kittlitz in December 1827. Five skins exist today, three in St Petersburg and two in Leiden; there may be another in Frankfurt but it has not proved possible to verify this rumour. Kittlitz took both adult and immature individuals and expressed the opinion that he would not have believed these to belong to the same species had he not shot an intermediate example.

His observations reveal that the species lived on small mammals, lizards and insects. Its call was loud, and individuals were solitary in their habits. He recorded that it seemed rare at the time of his visit, and doubtless it was well on the way to extinction, as no later naturalist ever managed to locate it.

Kosrae had become a popular resort for visiting whalers, who used the island to repair their vessels and generally recuperate after their exertions. Rats were introduced and these animals quickly overran the island. They had a greatly detrimental effect on the bird populations, and doubtless their presence was a major factor in the starling's extinction.

Lamprotornis corvina Kittlitz, 1832
Kupfer. Nat. Vog. **2**: 12.

Mysterious Starling

Aplonis mavornata

This species is known from just a single skin in the collection of the Natural History Museum, London. For many years this skin was a complete mystery and its origin was entirely unknown, but thanks to some comprehensive detective work conducted

Aplonis mavornata Buller, 1887
Birds New Zealand **1**: 25.

Plate F18

inches 4
cm 10

Kosrae Starling
Aplonis corvina

Mysterious Starling
Aplonis mavornata

♂ ♀
*Aplonis fusca
fusca*

Reunion Starling
Fregilupus varius

Norfolk Starling

♂ ♀
*Aplonis fusca
hulliana*

by Storrs Olson of the Smithsonian Institution in Washington, its origin is now relatively clear.

The bird was collected by Andrew Bloxam, a naturalist who served aboard *HMS Blonde* when it sailed to Honolulu carrying the bodies of Liholiho and Kamamalu, King and Queen of Hawaii, who had died of measles during a trip to London. While in the Pacific the *Blonde* called at the Cook Islands and on the afternoon of 9th August 1825 Bloxam went ashore on the island of Mauke. Here, during a visit of no more than two hours, he shot a pigeon, a kingfisher and a starling. Nothing more is known of his unique starling. Bloxam simply stated that his bird was killed "hopping about a tree".

Norfolk Starling   *Aplonis fusca*

Aplonis fuscus Gould, 1836
Proc. Zool. Soc. London **1836**: 73.

A. f. hulliana Mathews, 1912
Nov. Zool. **18**: 451.

The third extinct member of the genus *Aplonis* inhabited the islands of Norfolk and Lord Howe. Both these Tasman Sea islands have lost several of their endemic birds and the starling vanished during the first half of the twentieth century. The species has been divided into two races, the nominate from Norfolk Island and race *hulliana* from Lord Howe.

Although the reasons for extinction on Norfolk Island are unclear, it is quite apparent why the birds vanished from Lord Howe. They were among the creatures doomed by the grounding of a ship, the *SS Makambo*, in 1918 on a stretch of shore known as Ned's Beach. Rats escaped from the vessel and quickly infested the previously rat-free island. Within just a few years the starlings were gone.

Little is on record concerning the species. In the days of its abundance it was something of a pest, often feeding on fruit and crops. The nest was loosely built in a tree hollow from twigs and grasses. The birds laid 3-5 bluish eggs, speckled and blotched with red. Lord Howe birds went locally by the name *cudgimaruk*, a name derived from the call.

Reunion Starling   *Fregilupus varius*

Upupa varia Boddaert, 1783
Table Planches Enlum: 43.

This large and rather beautiful species, also known as the Bourbon Crested Starling, was characterized by an extraordinary lace-like crest. It was an inhabitant of the Mascarene island of Reunion (formerly called Bourbon). It was known locally by the name *huppe*, which is also the French name for the Hoopoe (*Upupa epops*). It is perhaps not surprising, then, that the starling was originally placed in the Hoopoe's genus, *Upupa*.

Like so many island birds, this was a tame and confiding species. Islanders described how easily individuals could be knocked down with sticks. Despite this, the Reunion Starling survived for much longer than many other Mascarene bird species. It seems to have been relatively common right through into the early years of the nineteenth century, although by the middle years of that century it had disappeared altogether.

Nothing, apart from its appearance, is known of this species. Indeed, its taxonomic placement is also disputed, as some authors consider it to be a helmet-shrike (Prionopidae).

Rodrigues Starling   *Necropsar rodericanus*

Necropsar rodericanus Slater, 1879
Philos. Trans. **168**: 427.

The skeletal remains of a starling were found on the island of Rodrigues during the 1870's. Although there may be no connection, these bones have been associated with a brief account in the document known as the *Relation de l'Île Rodrigue*, which was probably written by a marooned sailor named Tafforet during 1725. A translation reads:

> A little bird is found which is not common...One sees it on the Islet de Mat, which is to the south of the main island, and I believe it keeps to that islet on account of the birds of prey which are on the mainland, and also to feed with more facility on the eggs of the fishing birds which feed there, for they feed on nothing else but eggs, or some turtles dead of hunger, which they...tear out of their shells. These birds are a little larger than a blackbird, and have white plumage, part of the wings and tail black, the beak yellow, as well as the feet, and make a wonderful warbling.

Whether these words should really be matched with the bones cannot be said with any degree of certainty.

FRINGILLIDAE

Bonin Grosbeak
Chaunoproctus ferreorostris

A large, spectacular grosbeak-like bird once lived on the Bonin Islands to the south of Japan. It is known from nothing more than two series of skins that were collected during the 1820's, skins that are in themselves a little puzzling. Some are rather larger than others, giving rise to the supposition that individuals may have been collected from different islands and that each island may have supported its own population.

Coccothraustes ferreorostris Vigors, 1829
Zool. J. **4**: 354.

Plate F19

| inches | 3 |
| cm | 8 |

Bonin Grosbeak
Chaunoproctus ferreorostris

All the known specimens derive from two expeditions. The first of these was the voyage of *HMS Blossom*, which vessel called at Peel Island (Chichi-jima), one of the Bonins, during June 1827. The tameness of the birds led the leader of the expedition, Captain Beechey, to assume that there had been no permanent human presence on the island. When the *Blossom* sailed away several grosbeak specimens were aboard.

Just months later F. H. von Kittlitz landed on Peel during the voyage of the Russian corvette *Senjawin*. Whether Kittlitz took birds from elsewhere is not known. His brief notes provide the only record of the bird in life. He noticed them on the forest floor, singly or in pairs, and described the call as a soft, pure and high piping.

No naturalist ever saw the grosbeak again. By the 1850's, when Peel Island was searched by members of an American naval expedition, there was no sign of it.

DREPANIDIDAE

Ula-ai-Hawane
Ciridops anna

Although it was once well known to the natives of Hawaii, by the time that Europeans began their ornithological exploration of the island, this species has virtually disappeared.

The striking red, black and silver Ula-ai-Hawane is known from just five specimens, two in New York (one of which is either an immature or a female, and shows a greenish plumage), one in Cambridge (Massachusetts), one in Honolulu and one in Tring. The first of these was taken by an amateur naturalist and shopkeeper by the name of Mills about the year 1859. The last was collected from Mount Kohala in 1892. Probably the species became extinct soon after this date, although the experienced and reliable Hawaiian ornithologist George C. Munro reckoned he might have glimpsed an individual as late as 1937.

Quite clearly, this is one of those Hawaiian species that stood at the brink of extinction even as it was being discovered to science. Native Hawaiian knowledge of the species indicated that it was once widely distributed on the island of Hawaii, although it was only ever seen close to the hawane palm.

Fringilla anna Dole, 1878
Hawaiian Alm. Ann. **1879**: 49.

Koa Finch

Rhodacanthis palmeri

Rhodacanthis palmeri Rothschild, 1892
Ann. and Mag. Nat. Hist. **Ser. 6, no. 10**: 111.

R. p. flaviceps Rothschild, 1892
Ann. and Mag. Nat. Hist. **Ser. 6, no. 10**: 111.

The Koa Finch is something of a mystery. Was it one species or was it two? Were the "Greater" and "Lesser" Koa Finches both members of the same species?

During 1891 Henry Palmer was busy collecting specimens on the Hawaiian Islands for Walter Rothschild. The enormously wealthy scion of the famous banking family was at this time frantically acquiring material for his museum at Tring, Hertfordshire, England. Nothing interested him more than rare, extinct and curious birds, and he was later to write his famous book *Extinct Birds*, 1907. Palmer had been commissioned to sail to Hawaii in search of whatever he could find. He linked up with George C. Munro, and together the two men combed Hawaii.

One of their "finds" was a series of large "finches" that they took from the koa forests in the Kona district of Hawaii. First of all it should be made clear that these were not finches at all; they were Hawaiian honeycreepers that had evolved a finch-like form, in order to exploit a vacant ecological niche. The original collectors, Palmer and Munro, were quite clear in their minds about the nature of the birds they had discovered. They felt that these creatures belonged to a single, rather variable, species, and it is worth noting that the two forms were collected on the very same trees. They then dispatched the specimens of their new bird to Rothschild.

When the preserved specimens reached Rothschild in England, he formed a different conclusion to that of his collectors, and he delightedly separated his new possessions into two groups; nothing pleased Rothschild more than to be able to name a new form! The larger individuals, with more orange heads, he assigned to a new species that he called, in honour of his collector, *Rhodacanthis palmeri*. To cover the smaller birds with heads that were rather more yellow he proposed the name *Rhodacanthis flaviceps*. Rothschild identified eight individuals that he felt belonged to this second species, two males and six females. After Palmer's original collecting success, no further specimens that could be assigned to *flaviceps* were ever taken or seen. However, the larger birds were observed again, and captured. Over a period of five years a few individuals were encountered. Then these birds vanished too. There is no record later than 1896.

Palmer's notes were bequeathed by Rothschild to the Natural History Museum, London, but, unfortunately, many of them were destroyed by tidy-minded museum workers, so we will never know exactly what was in his mind.

The argument for or against two species is a fairly basic one. Does one agree with the experienced field ornithologists who actually saw the living bird, or does one take notice instead of undoubted differences that were noticed by cabinet naturalists? It is possible that the smaller, yellower birds were immatures or first-year birds, and this idea might tidily explain why they were never encountered after 1891. There were no more immatures because the species was standing at the edge of extinction and no longer breeding properly. The last sighting of the species actually involved an observation of some very young birds but, probably, these did not live long.

The big problem with the evidence of the specimens is that is difficult to correlate it with the birds in life. Although the most extreme examples of each form appear to be rather different, there are areas of overlap between some of the other specimens. The real truth is probably unresolvable, and is simply a matter of interpretation.

Unfortunately, knowledge of the living bird in no way matches the amount that has been written concerning the supposed status of the species – or pair of species. The best description of the bird in life was given in 1903 by R. C. L. Perkins, a man who left behind some of the most evocative writings on the extinct birds of the Hawaiian Islands:

> Although spending most of its time in the tops of the loftiest koa trees, *Rhodacanthis* occasionally visits the lesser trees...chiefly for the sake of the caterpillars that feed upon them...Its chief food, however, is the green pod of the koa tree, which it swallows in large-sized pieces and its blue bill is often stained with the green juice and fragments of the pods...The song...consists of four, five or even six whistled notes, of which the latter ones are much prolonged...Although the notes are not loud, they are very clear, and...easily imitated...Were it not for this fact *Rhodacanthis*, when keeping to the leafy crowns of tall koa trees...would be most difficult to get sight of...The green plumaged young...are fed partly on fragments of koa pods.

Kona Grosbeak

Chloridops kona

Chloridops kona Wilson, 1888
Proc. Zool. Soc. London **1888**: 218.

The Hawaiian honeycreepers form one of the most striking illustrations of adaptive radiation, but, unfortunately, so many of them are extinct that the example is now historical rather than living.

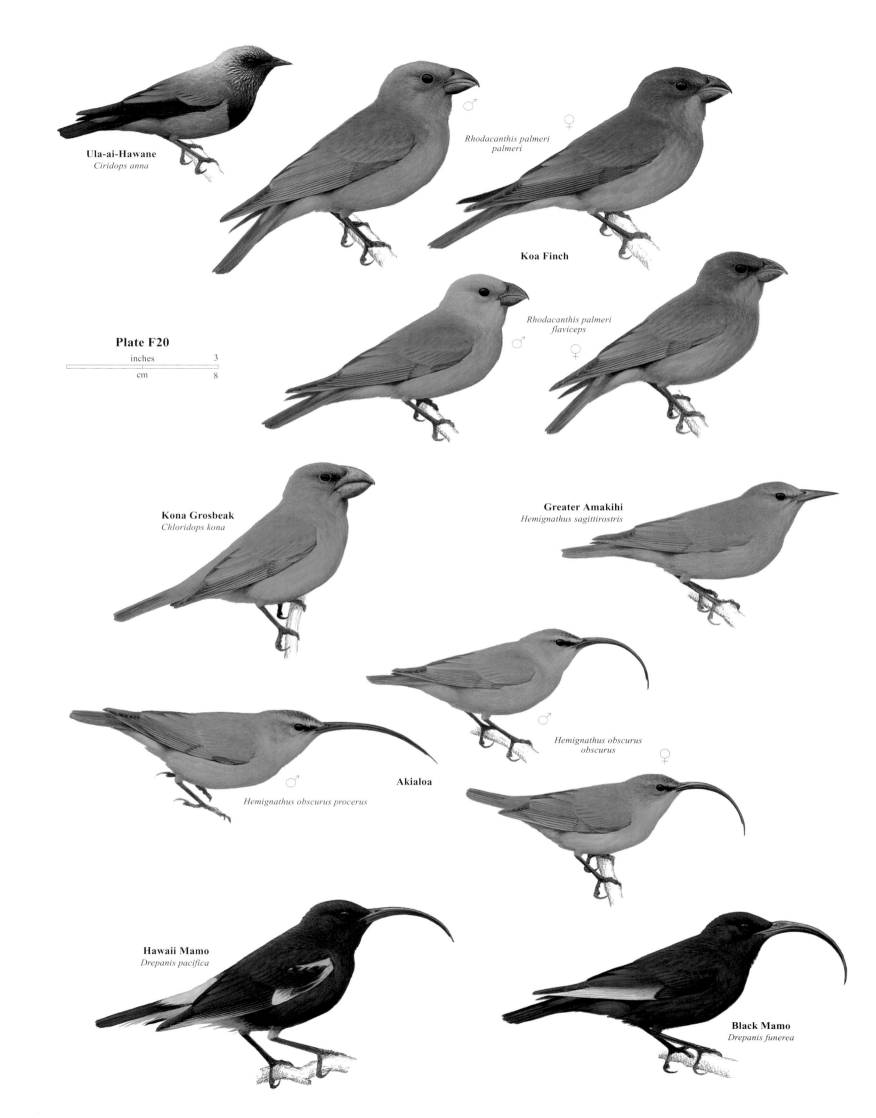

Ula-ai-Hawane
Ciridops anna

Rhodacanthis palmeri palmeri

♂ ♀

Koa Finch

Rhodacanthis palmeri flaviceps

♂ ♀

Plate F20

inches	3
cm	8

Kona Grosbeak
Chloridops kona

Greater Amakihi
Hemignathus sagittirostris

Hemignathus obscurus obscurus

♂ ♀

Akialoa

Hemignathus obscurus procerus

♂

Hawaii Mamo
Drepanis pacifica

Black Mamo
Drepanis funerea

At some point in prehistory an ancestral honeycreeper stock somehow arrived at the Hawaiian Islands and found a situation that was ripe for exploitation. Due to the remoteness of the islands there were many ecological niches that were not successfully occupied. The ancestors of the honeycreepers adapted accordingly and lifestyles were adopted that would in more normal circumstances be the prerogative of other kinds of birds. Thus, there are honeycreepers that came to resemble finches, some that developed almost parrot-like bills, still others that acquired long, slender, down-curved beaks useful for probing, and yet others with more general all-purpose beaks. This fascinating diversity has been horribly diminished by the process of extinction.

The Kona Grosbeak was a perfect example of the way in which the ancestral honeycreepers adapted. It had evolved a short and incredibly powerful bill that enabled it to exploit food types that more normally developed birds could not. Indeed, the sounds of hard seeds and nuts being split by the awesome bill of this species betrayed its presence to field collectors.

This is another bird that was best described by R. C. L. Perkins (1903). He wrote:

> It is a dull, sluggish bird, and very silent – its whole existence may be summed up in the words "to eat". Its food consists of seeds of the aaka, and as these are very minute, its whole time seems to be taken up in cracking the extremely hard shells...Its beak is nearly always dirty, with a brown substance adherent to it, which must be derived from the sandal nuts.

The species was discovered on the slopes of the famous volcano Mauna Loa in the Kona district of Hawaii during 1887. It was seen again several times during the next few years, but the last sighting occurred in 1894 and it is assumed that these birds became extinct soon after that date.

Greater Amakihi — *Hemignathus sagittirostris*

Viridonia sagittirostris Rothschild, 1892
Ann. and Mag. Nat. Hist. **Ser. 6, no. 10**: 112.

The Greater Amakihi, a rather non-descript little honeycreeper coloured olive green, was discovered by the world of ornithology during 1892 when Rothschild's collector Henry Palmer took four specimens. In December 1895 a few individuals were collected, and the species was located again during 1900. The following year it was found once more, since which time it has never been seen again.

By the time of its ornithological discovery the species was restricted to a very small part of the island of Hawaii, the dripping rainforest to either side of the Wailuku River at elevations of 300-900 m.

Whenever it was seen, this species was observed creeping along the branches of ohia trees or in the foliage. Individuals ate insects and their grubs and other invertebrates. They were also seen to feed on the nectar of the ohia flower.

The habitat that this species occupied is long gone and the area is now covered with sugar cane.

Akialoa — *Hemignathus obscurus*

Certhia obscura J. F. Gmelin, 1788
Syst. Nat. **1(1)**: 470.

H. o. lanaiensis Rothschild, 1893
Bull. Brit. Orn. Club **1**: 24.

H. o. ellisianus (G. R. Gray, 1859)
Cat. Birds Trop. Isl. Pac. Ocean: 9.

H. o. procerus Cabanis, 1889
J. Orn. **39**: 331.

Because it is so poorly known, the honeycreeper family, in particular its extinct members, arouses a certain amount of controversy. It is classified and reclassified over and over again, and drastic revisions of the family are made from time to time. Unfortunately, these revisions are, of necessity, made from specimen material rather than from any real recourse to the living birds. For this reason these revisions should be viewed with a certain degree of caution. They tend to be prone to the whims and prejudices of individuals, and also subject to the dictates of fashion.

In no case is this better exemplified than in the instance of the Akialoa. Perhaps the Akialoa constitutes one species, perhaps two, perhaps even four. It has been divided into two, a "Greater" and a "Lesser", and into four with each inhabited Hawaiian island being held to have its own species. The specimen material is very difficult to interpret, however. The forms from Lanai (*lanaiensis*) and O'ahu (*ellisianus*) are known only from very, very few specimens, so there is no real series on which to base conclusions. The other two forms, nominate *obscurus* from Hawaii and *procerus* from Kauia, are known from rather more skins, but even in these cases comparisons are clouded by various factors. The main problem is that the Akialoa was a generally variable bird and individuals of each kind show some overlap in terms of size and colour. It is possible that individuals became brighter in colour when they were breeding, although it should be said that there is no real evidence of this. Bill length is held to be a significant character, but this too is variable: there is evidence to show that towards the end of its existence as a species, the Akialoa's beak tended to be rather shorter than in earlier years. Perhaps this was because the birds were generally in poor health, and collectors who took specimens during the 1890's noticed that individuals were often covered in sores, tumours and swellings, particularly on the head and feet; or maybe the new circumstances on the islands were inhibiting proper growth.

The most sensible way forward is, perhaps, to regard the Akialoa as a single species with four races. Bearing in mind the paucity of specimen material available, no other course seems meaningful.

However they may be interpreted, the birds that are known as Akialoas were among the most intriguing of the honeycreepers. The extraordinarily delicate beak is in complete contrast to the shorter, stumpy bills of the Koa Finch and the Kona Grosbeak. The lower mandible was often considerably shorter than the upper, and with this strange device individuals were able to suck nectar from the flowers of ohias and lobelias, and they could also probe into cavities for insects and their larvae. R. C. L. Perkins noticed them clinging to tree trunks like "true" creepers when they were feeding.

While it is known that there were Akialoas on Hawaii, O'ahu, Lanai and Kauai, it is quite possible that birds were present on other islands. It is surprising to find, for instance, that they were never reported from Molokai and Maui. Perhaps they vanished from these islands at a comparatively early date. It is likely that the Akialoas from Oahu became extinct around 1840, although there are claimed records, made by experienced ornithologists, of possible sightings made during the late 1930's. The Lanai and Hawaii populations disappeared around 1900, but Kauai birds held out for much longer. Their stronghold was the same Alaka'i Swamp that was home to the last Kauai 'O'os. A few individuals were still in existence during the early 1960's but the last record of them seems to date from 1967.

The obvious frailty of the Akialoa reflects the fragility of the honeycreepers as a whole. In addition to all the other factors that depleted them, the danger that the mosquito posed cannot be overstated. Once this insect arrived in the Hawaiian Islands, birds that lived at lower altitudes were seriously affected by the bites of these creatures. Even those species living at altitudes that were unattractive to mosquitoes could be vulnerable. Sometimes they would descend to lower levels to ride out the effects of hurricanes, and then the bites could prove fatal. Captive birds that have been brought down from altitude have been observed to die within minutes of sustaining a bite.

Hawaii Mamo   *Drepanis pacifica*

The Hawaii Mamo suffered in the same way and for the same reason as the Hawaii 'O'o. The rich yellow feathers of the uppertail- and undertail-coverts attracted the attention of the kings and princes of Hawaii, and these feathers were used in the making of ceremonial cloaks and other artifacts. The most famous cloak of all, that of Kamehameha I was made from the feathers of an extraordinary number of birds. An estimate has been made that 80,000 individuals were used before the garment could be brought to completion.

Certhia pacifica J. F. Gmelin, 1788
Syst. Nat. **1(1)**: 470.

The Hawaii Mamo was one of the first Hawaiian birds to come to the attention of Europeans and specimens were brought back from the Pacific to England by the naturalists who participated in James Cook's third voyage. Surprisingly little is known of it, however. The birds fed on nectar, particularly from the flowers of arborescent lobelias, but they are thought also to have eaten insects. The call was described as a single, long, rather mournful and haunting note.

The species was only ever noticed on the island of Hawaii and it was last seen during 1898.

Black Mamo   *Drepanis funerea*

A bird very closely related to the Hawaii Mamo once lived on the island of Molokai. Here it was discovered by R. C. L. Perkins at an altitude of 1525 metres during June 1893. What is known of the species comes largely from Perkins's account.

Drepanis funerea A. Newton, 1894
Proc. Zool. Soc. London **1893**: 690.

Individuals were only ever seen low down in the underbrush. Dangerously, for a creature that spent its time close to the ground, the birds were rather tame, and Perkins found it easy to observe them at close quarters. He believed that they fed exclusively on nectar, and he wrote:

> I saw three adult males of this bird in one low bush passing from flower to flower and spending only a few seconds over each...Even those flowers which were at a height of no more than a foot from the ground were carefully explored. The crown of the head of each of these birds was plentifully encrusted...with the sticky white or purplish-white pollen of the lobelias and gave them a singular appearance...they will sit quietly

preening their feathers when they have a very comical appearance, much stretching of the neck being necessary to enable them to reach the fore parts of the body with the tip of their long beaks.

Following Perkins's discovery of the species, it was found on several more occasions, but was last seen in June 1907. There is no real chance that it could have survived as the habitat in which it lived has been virtually destroyed.

PARULIDAE

Bachman's Warbler   *Vermivora bachmanii*

Sylvia Bachmanii Audubon, 1833
Birds Amer. **2**: pl. 185.

This tiny species divided its time between the south-eastern USA and Cuba, where it wintered. It was first identified by the Reverend John Bachman, a close personal friend of the famous painter and writer John James Audubon. Bachman was a resident of Charleston, and in July 1833 he found, in a local swamp, a small yellow and black bird that he did not recognize. He sent it on to Audubon for formal identification and the famous ornithologist quickly realized that it was something entirely new. Audubon, quite naturally, gave the species his friend's name.

For a period of more than 50 years after that nothing further was heard of the new creature. Then, in 1886, a hunter by the name of Charles Galbraith shot a bird he had never seen before, just north of New Orleans. The next year he shot six more of the same birds, and during the following year he killed no less than 31. At this point he decided to have his mysterious specimens identified. They proved to be Bachman's Warblers.

A year later, in March 1889, on a single day 21 warblers of the species struck a lighthouse on the Florida Keys. Just three years later a hunter killed 50 individuals on Florida's Suwannee River.

Through the first half of the twentieth century it proved possible to locate Bachman's Warblers from time to time, but then the observations proved much less frequent. By the 1980's the species was probably extinct, although, given its tendency to disappear, there is a faint chance that it might still survive.

Although Bachman's Warblers were always surrounded by a certain amount of mystery, their nests were found on a number of occasions. These were built low down in dense patches of bramble, situated along forested river courses.

Reasons for the species' extinction are unclear. The effect of hurricanes, changing land use, and the fragmentation of suitable territory have all been proposed as factors. Another suggestion is that the species was coming into increasing contact with the parasitic Brown-headed Cowbird (*Molothrus ater*), due to extensive forest clearance, and that the encroachments of this bird proved irresistible.

Plate F21

inches	2
cm	5

Bachman's Warbler
Vermivora bachmanii

♂   ♀

Hypothetical Species and Mystery Birds

No account of the world's recently extinct birds can be quite complete without some mention of "hypothetical" extinct species and "mystery" birds. The names of such creatures frequently litter the lists of extinct species and create endless confusion.

Hypothetical species can be defined as birds that have been scientifically named, mainly by nineteenth and twentieth century ornithologists, on the basis of early traveller's tales or antique paintings, and of which no specimen material exists. The problems associated with such names are self-evident. First, they contravene the rules of zoological nomenclature by being too vague. Second, there is no actual proof that the described creatures ever existed, or that they were what they seemed to be. The names may be founded upon mistakes, misunderstandings or even plain old-fashioned lies.

Mystery birds are seemingly distinct kinds that are known from just a single specimen, or a very small number of specimens, that, for a variety of reasons, may not be exactly what they seem to be.

Although the two categories are obviously related, it is easiest to discuss them separately.

It is a surprising fact that so many hypothetical species have been named (by ornithologists who should have known better!), and that they have gained a significant place in ornithological literature – but such is the case.

Most are forms resurrected from the accounts of travellers from the seventeenth or eighteenth centuries, and given formal, albeit invalid, scientific identities by more modern writers. The problems with such accounts are several. First, they may have been – and usually were – written by men with no real background in natural history. Second, they may have been based on hearsay. Third, the accounts may be flimsy and superficial in the extreme. Fourth, there was often a tendency among early travel writers to fill up the pages of their books with accounts of creatures that were entirely, or partly, fanciful. The fourth category obviously speaks for itself and needs no further discussion. Similarly, the problems with the second and third categories are perfectly apparent. A more complex set of problems is posed by the first. When men have no knowledge of natural history (or even when they do), they are likely to misinterpret what they see. A description of a new creature may be entirely truthful in spirit, yet still be absolutely misleading in effect. Perhaps the observer saw something that was new to him but was otherwise well known. Perhaps he casually mentioned a crow when the bird he had seen was actually a starling, and the words get in the way of the truth. Sometimes, the description may be entirely inaccurate.

Early paintings of birds that cannot be precisely aligned with any known species are also problematical. To take a picture, even when painted by an artist of talent, at face value, is often unrealistic. The problem here is one of intention. There is often no way of knowing whether an artist was trying to produce a true likeness, whether his intention was simply decorative, or whether it lay somewhere between the two. There

Figure 8. White Dodo. Chromolithograph based on painting by F. W. Frohawk.

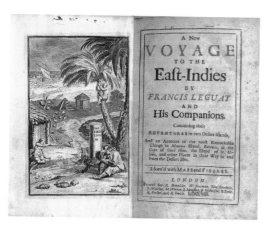

Figure 9. The opening pages of François Leguat's 1708 book, A New Voyage to the East Indies, *in which he supplies much of the very scant information that is known about several extinct Mascarene forms.*

is also the matter of technique. Many of the pictures on which names have been based were drawn by men with little or no skill. Yet, nuances of detail on such pictures have been taken absolutely seriously by some ornithologists when, quite clearly, such details may simply be the result of inadequate drawing ability. These pictures may be charming and curious, and they may show something of genuine interest. On the other hand they may not! When scientific names are proposed solely on the basis of such pictures these names should be regarded as invalid.

The inclusion of several species known today only from the paintings of Georg Forster, who was by no means an efficient technician, may seem to contravene these ideas, but it should be borne in mind that Forster's pictures were originally backed up by specimen material. Unfortunately, in the cases in question, that material has not survived.

The best known of all hypothetical species is the so-called White Dodo of Reunion. The evidence that such a creature existed is flimsy in the extreme yet many ill-judged words have been written about it (including some by the present author), and it was given the technical name *Raphus solitarius*. Two accounts from the early seventeenth century suggest that there may have been a creature that looked something like a White Dodo on Reunion, but these are far too vague to enable the building of any kind of sensible hypothesis. Another strand of evidence concerns a well-known series of seventeenth century Dutch paintings by Pieter Holsteyn (later copied by another painter named Pieter Witthoos) that show a White Dodo. Unfortunately, however, there is absolutely nothing to link these pictures to Reunion. Nor is there anything to show that the model for the pictures was anything other than an albinistic Dodo of the more ordinary kind. Similarly, because we know nothing of the intention of the original artist, it is quite fair to suppose that he made his Dodo white simply because he wanted to. What can be said with some certainty is this: had a Dodo-like bird evolved independently on the island of Reunion, it would have looked radically different from its relative on Mauritius, rather than looking just like a regular Dodo that had been bleached. It would necessarily have developed in a different direction, in much the same way as did the dodo-like solitaire of the island of Rodrigues. This creature, while showing many dodoesque features, has a number of entirely independent ones – and this is only to be expected of a flightless creature evolving independently on a separate island. It is quite possible that a relative of the Dodo did actually live on Reunion, but there is not one scrap of hard evidence to show this.

Another hypothetical species that has acquired almost equal celebrity has come to be known as Leguat's Giant (*Leguatia gigantea*). This is a bird that the Huguenot refugee François Leguat claimed to have seen on Mauritius during the 1690's. His description makes it clear that this was a slender, very tall creature. As Leguat was generally a very truthful recorder it may be assumed that he really did see something, but just what that something was is difficult to say. The likelihood is that he may have seen a flamingo and that he was entirely unfamiliar with such a creature.

The list of hypothetical species is fairly endless, and by and large such mythical birds are properly beyond the scope of this work.

The problems associated with mystery birds are equally difficult to resolve. If a bird is known from just a single specimen or just a very small number of specimens, there can be all kinds of difficulty involved in assessing the correct position. This is especially so if the bird was never observed properly in the wild. The possibility that such birds may be simply freaks or perhaps hybrids between better-known species cannot be discounted. Naturally, if birds turn up just once and then many years pass without anything similar being found, there is always the possibility that the species – if species it truly is – has become extinct.

There are, in fact, a surprisingly large number of birds known from only very limited specimen material. The family of birds-of-paradise (Paradisaeidae), for instance, contains more than 20 mysterious forms known only from excessively rare and isolated specimens. These are generally considered to be hybrids between some of the better-known kinds, but some may not be.

Ultimately, such decisions are often based on individual prejudices, as the actual hard evidence is not sufficient to build a proper determination.

The case of the Lanai Hookbill (*Dysmorodrepanis munroi*), a honeycreeper from the Hawaiian island of Lanai, provides a good example. It may be a "good" species and, if it is, it is almost certainly extinct. On the other hand, it may be a freak. Just a single example of this creature is known and this was collected during 1913 by George C. Munro, whose name so often occurs in accounts of Hawaiian birds. The specimen shows a very distinct but rather peculiar arrangement of the beak and experts interpret this in two contrasting ways: some argue that the beak's peculiar nature is the sure

64

mark of a freak; others suggest that it is a clear and distinct indication of a "good" species.

In some respects similar is the case of Townsend's Bunting (*Spiza townsendi*). This is a form described by the celebrated John James Audubon from a unique specimen taken in Pennsylvania. No similar bird has ever come to light, but, since the specimen shows some relationship to the Dickcissel (*Spiza americana*), the form is usually relegated to the status of freak or hybrid.

Ross's Plover (*Thinornis rossi*), a strange shorebird from New Zealand waters was described from a single specimen taken in 1840, during the exploratory voyage of the British vessels *Erebus* and *Terror*. Usually, it is regarded as an aberrant, perhaps young, individual of the Shore Plover (*Thinornis novaeseelandiae*), itself a very rare bird. It may or may not be. Similarly, Cooper's Sandpiper (*Calidris cooperi*), collected during the nineteenth century on Long Island, New York, might be a "good" species, although nowadays the general consensus is that it is a hybrid of the Curlew Sandpiper (*Calidris ferruginea*) and the Sharp-tailed Sandpiper (*Calidris acuminata*).

The big problem with all these forms (and there are a considerable number of them) is that we shall simply never know what they really were.

To these forms can be added many that are simply known from fragmentary bone material. For the purposes of a work like this there is little point in pursuing such insufficient yet tantalizing material. Such a pursuit leads to endless list-making, argument and counter-argument. Those recently extinct creatures that we know from clearcut specimen material are tantalizing and mysterious enough in themselves and, most regrettably, it seems inevitable that, unless conservation action is given full institutional backing right away, there will soon be many more well-known, and not so well-known, names to add to the ranks of the extinct.

Errol Fuller

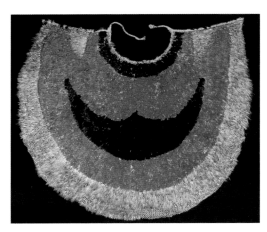

Figure 10. Cape made from the feathers of Hawaiian birds. This island group is one of the hot spots of avian extinction.

References cited

Amadon, D. (1947). An estimated weight of the largest known bird. *Condor* **49(4)**: 159-164.

Amadon, D. (1950). The Hawaiian honeycreepers. *Bull. Amer. Mus. Nat. Hist.* **95**: 155-262.

Andersen, J.C. (1926). *Bird Song and New Zealand Song Birds*. Whitcombe & Tombs, Auckland, New Zealand.

Anderson, A. (1989). *Prodigious Birds*. Cambridge University Press, Cambridge.

Anon. (1789). *The Voyage of Governor Phillip to Botany Bay*. John Stockdale, London.

Anon. (1891). *Relation de l'Île Rodrigues*. Hakluyt Society, London.

Archey, G. (1941). The moa. *Bull. Auckland Inst. & Mus.* **1**: 5-101.

Audubon, J.J. (1827-1838). *The Birds of America*. 4 Vols. Edinburgh.

Audubon, J.J. (1831-1839). *Ornithological Biography*. 5 Vols. A & C Black, Edinburgh.

Austin, O.L. & Singer, A. (1963). *Birds of the World*. Hamlyn, London.

Bailey, A.M. (1956). *Birds of Midway and Laysan Islands*. Denver Museum of Natural History Pictorial **12**, Denver, Colorado.

Baker, R. (1951). *The Avifauna of Micronesia*. University of Kansas Museum of Natural History, Lawrence, Kansas.

Baldwin, P. (1949). The life history of the Laysan Rail. *Condor* **51(1)**: 14-21.

Barbour, T. (1943). *Cuban Ornithology*. Memoirs of the Nuttall Ornithological Club **9**, Cambridge, Massachusetts. 144 pp.

Bárðarson, H. (1986). *Birds of Iceland*. Published privately, Reykjavik.

Beattie, H. (1954). *The Moa*. Otago Daily Times, Otago, New Zealand.

Bechstein, A. (1811). *Kurze Uebers*.

Beechey, F. (1839). *The Zoology of Captain Beechey's Voyage to the Pacific*. London.

Benson, C.W. & Penny, M.J. (1968). A new species of warbler from the Aldabra Atoll. *Bull. Brit. Orn. Club* **88(6)**: 102-108.

Berger, A. (1972). *Hawaiian Birdlife*. University of Hawaii Press, Honolulu.

Berlioz, J. (1935). Notice sur les specimens naturalisés d'oiseaux éteint. *Arch. Mus. Hist. Nat., Paris* **6**: 485-495.

Berlioz, J. (1946). Oiseaux de la Réunion. *Faune de l'Empire Français* **55**: 1-81.

Blanford, W. (1898). *The Fauna of British India*. Taylor & Francis, London.

Blasius, W. (1884). Zur Geschichte der Ueberreste von *Alca impennis*. *J. Orn.* **4**: 58-176.

Boddaert, P. (1783). *Planches Enluminees*. Paris.

Bonaparte, C.L. & Schlegel, H. (1850). *Monographie des Loxiens*. Paris.

Bond, J. (1936). *Birds of the West Indies*. Academy of Natural Sciences, Philadelphia.

Bontekoe, V. (1646). *Iovrnael ofte Gedenckwaerdige beschrijvinghe vande Oost-Indische*. Hoorn, Netherlands.

Bouillard, M. (1875). Relation de l'Île Rodrigues. *Proc. Zool. Soc. London* **1875**: 39-42.

Brewster, W. (1889a). Present status of the Wild Pigeon. *Auk* **6**: 285-291.

Brewster, W. (1889b). Nesting habits of the Carolina Parakeet. *Auk* **6**: 336-337.

Brown, T. (1836). *Works* (Wilkin edition). Vols. 1-2. London.

Brush, A. (1976). Waterfowl feather proteins. *J. Zool.* **179**: 467-498.

Bry, T. & Bry, J. (1601). *Variorum Novigationis*. Amsterdam.

Bryan, W.A. (1901). *A Key to the Birds of the Hawaiian Group*. Bishop Museum, Honolulu.

Bryan, W.A. (1908). Some birds of Molokai. *Occas. Pap. Bishop Mus., Honolulu* **4**: 133-176.

Bryant, W.E. (1887). Additions to the ornithology of Guadalupe. *Bull. Calif. Acad. Sci.* **6**: 269-318.

Bucknill, J. (1924). The disappearance of the Pink-headed Duck. *Ibis* **Ser. 11, no. 6**: 146-151.

Buick, T. (1931). *The Mystery of the Moa*. Thomas Avery, New Plymouth, New Zealand.

Buick, T. (1936). *The Discovery of* Dinornis. Thomas Avery, New Plymouth, New Zealand.

Buick, T. (1937). *The Moa-hunters of New Zealand*. Thomas Avery, New Plymouth, New Zealand.

Buller, W.L. (1872-1873). *A History of the Birds of New Zealand*. Van Voorst, London.

Buller, W.L. (1882). *Manual of the Birds of New Zealand*. Colonial Museum, Wellington.

Buller, W.L. (1887-1888). *A History of the Birds of New Zealand*. 2 Vols. Published privately, London.

Buller, W.L. (1895). Stephen Island Wren. *Ibis* **Ser. 7, no. 1**: 236.

Buller, W.L. (1904). The Laughing Owl. *Ibis* **Ser. 8, no. 4**: 639.

Buller, W.L. (1905). *Supplement to The Birds of New Zealand*. 2 Vols. Published privately, London.

Burton, P.J.K. (1974). Anatomy of the head and neck of the Huia. *Bull. Brit. Mus. (Nat. Hist.) Zool.* **27**: 1-48.

Byron, Lord (1827). *Voyage of HMS Blonde to the Sandwich Islands*. J. Murray, London.

Caldwell, J. (1876). Notes on the zoology of Rodríguez. *Proc. Zool. Soc. London* **1875**: 644-647.

Carré, M. (1669). *Voyage des Indes Orientales*. Paris.

Cassin, J. (1855). The 'o'o of Kauia. *Proc. Acad. Nat. Sci. Philadelphia* **7**: 440.

Cauche, F. (1651). *Relations Véritables et Curieuses de l'Île de Madagascar et Brésil*. Paris.

Chilton, C. ed. (1909). *The Sub-antarctic Islands of New Zealand*. Philosophical Institution of Canterbury, Canterbury, UK.

Chisholm, A. (1922). *Mateship with Birds*. Whitcombe & Tombs, Melbourne.

Clark, A. (1905). Lesser Antilles macaws. *Auk* **22**: 266-273.

Clark, A. (1908). The macaw of Dominica. *Auk* **25**: 309-311.

Cokinos, C. (2000). *Hope is the Thing with Feathers*. Tarcher/Putnam, New York.

Colenso, W. (1843). Some enormous fossil bones lately found in New Zealand. *Tasmanian J. Sci.* **2**: 31-105.

Collar, N.J. & Stuart, S.N. (1985). *Threatened Birds of Africa and Related Islands*. The ICBP/IUCN Red Data Book. Part 1. 3rd edition. ICBP & IUCN, Cambridge.

Collar, N.J., Crosby, M.J. & Stattersfield, A.J. (1994). *Birds to Watch 2: the World List of Threatened Birds*. BirdLife Conservation Series **4**. BirdLife International, Cambridge.

Collar, N.J., Gonzaga, L.P., Krabbe, N., Madroño, A., Naranjo, L.G., Parker, T.A. & Wege, D.C. (1992). *Threatened Birds of the Americas*. The ICBP/IUCN Red Data Book. Part 2. 3rd edition. ICBP, Cambridge.

Cory, C. (1886). A thrush from Grand Cayman Island. *Auk* **4**: 94.

Cracraft, J. (1976). The species of moa. *Smithsonian Contrib. Paleobiol.* **27**: 189-205.

Daubenton, E. (1765-1781). *Planches Enluminée*. London.

Day, D. (1981). *The Doomsday Book of Animals*. Ebury Press, London.

De Vis, C. (1884). The moa in Australia. *Proc. Roy. Soc. Queensland* **1**: 23-28.

Delacour, J. & Scott, P. (1954-1964). *The Waterfowl of the World*. 4 Vols. Country Life, London.

Des Murs, M. (1849). *Iconographie Ornithologique*. Paris.

Diamond, A.W. ed. (1987). *Studies of Mascarene Island Birds*. Cambridge University Press, Cambridge.

Dickerman, R.W. (1965). The Slender-billed Grackle. *Auk* **82(2)**: 268.

Dill, H. & Bryan, W.A. (1912). Report of an expedition to Laysan Island in 1911. *US Biol. Survey Bull.* **42**: 1-30.

Dole, S.B. (1878). List of Birds of the Hawaiian Islands. Pp. 41-58 in: Thrum, T. (1878). *Hawaiian Almanac and Annual, 1879*. Honolulu.

Du Tertre, J. (1667). *Histoire Générale des Antilles Habitées par les François*. Paris.

Dubois, "Le Sieur" (1674). *Les Voyages Faits par Le Sieur D.B. aux Îsles Dauphine ou Madagascar et Bourbon ou Macarenne, és années 1669, 1670, 1671, 1672*. Paris.

Duff, R. (1949). Moas and Man. *Antiquity* **23**: 172-179.

Dumont D'Urville, J.S.C. (1830-1835). *Voyage de Découvertes de l'Astrolabe Exécuté par Ordre du Roi, Pendant les Années 1826, 1827, 1828 et 1829, sous le Commandement de M. J. Dumont D'Urville*. 4 Vols. J. Tastu, Paris.

Dumont D'Urville, J.S.C. (1842-1854). *Voyage au Pole Sud et dans l'Océanie sur les Corvettes l'Astrolabe et la Zelée; Exécuté par Ordre du Roi Pendant les Années 1837, 1838, 1839 et 1840 sous le Commandement de M. J. Dumont D'Urville*. 7 Vols. Paris.

Dutcher, W. (1891). The Labrador Duck. *Auk* **8**: 301-16.

Finn, F. (1915). *Indian Sporting Birds*. F. Edwards, London.

Finsch, O. (1881). Ornithological letters from the Pacific. *Ibis* **Ser. 4, no. 5**: 102-114.

Finsch, O. & Hartlaub, G. (1867). *Beitrag zur Fauna Centralpolynesiens*. Halle, Germany.

Fisher, H. & Baldwin, P. (1945). A recent trip to Midway. *Elepaio* **6**: 11-16.

Fisher, H. & Baldwin, P. (1946). War and the birds of Midway Atoll. *Condor* **48(1)**: 3-15.

Fisher, J., Simon, N. & Vincent, J. (1969). *The Red Book*. Collins, London.

Fisher, W. (1906). Birds of Laysan and the Leeward Islands. *Bull. US Fish Commission* **23(3)**: 767-807.

de Flacourt, É. (1658). *Histoire de la Grande Isle Madagascar*. Paris.

Fleming, C. & Lodge, G. (1983). *George Edward Lodge, Unpublished Bird Paintings*. Michael Joseph, London.

Fleming, J. (1915). On the Piopio. *Proc. Biol. Soc. Washington* **28**: 121.

Forbes, H. (1893). Birds inhabiting the Chatham Islands. *Ibis* **Ser. 6, no. 5**: 521-545.

Forshaw, J. & Cooper, W. (1978). *Parrots of the World*. Collins, London.

von Frauenfeld, G. (1868). *Neu Aufgefundene Abbildung des Dronte*. Wien.

French, J. (1919). *The Passenger Pigeon in Pennsylvania*. Altoona Tribune Co., Altoona, Pennsylvania.

Frith, C.B. & Beehler, B.M. (1998). *The Birds of Paradise*. Oxford University Press, Oxford.

Frohawk, F. (1892). Description of a new species of rail from Laysan Island. *Ann. and Mag. Nat. Hist.* **9**: 247-249.

Fuller, E. (1995). *The Lost Birds of Paradise*. Swan Hill, Shrewsbury, UK.

Fuller, E. (2000a). *Extinct Birds*. Oxford University Press, Oxford.

Fuller, E. (2000b). *The Great Auk*. Published privately, Southborough, Kent.

Galbreath, R. (1989). *Walter Buller, the Reluctant Conservationist*. GP Books, Wellington.

Garrod, A.H. (1875). On the form of the lower larynx in certain species of ducks. *Proc. Zool. Soc. London* **1875**: 151-156.

Gaskell, J. (2000). *Who Killed the Great Auk?* Oxford University Press, Oxford.

Geoffroy St. Hilaire, I. (1850). Notice sur des ossements et des oeufs trouves a Madagascar dans des alluvious modernes, et provenant d'un oiseau gigantesque. *Ann. Sci. Nat.* **Ser. 3, no. 14**: 206-216.

Gmelin, J.F. (1789). *Systema Naturae*. Leipzig.

Godman, F.C. (1907-1910). *A Monograph of the Petrels*. Witherby, London.

Gosse, P. (1847). *The Birds of Jamaica*. Van Voorst, London.

Gould, J. (1837). *A Synopsis of the Birds of Australia and Adjacent Islands*. London.

Gould, J. (1840-1848). *The Birds of Australia*. 7 Vols. Published privately, London.

Gould, J. (1843-1844). *The Zoology of the Voyage of HMS Sulphur*. London.

Gould, J. (1855). Lord Howe Island White-eye. *Proc. Zool. Soc. London* **1855**: 166.

Gould, J. (1860). Description of a new species of hornbill from western Africa. *Proc. Zool. Soc. London* **1860**: 380.

Gould, J. (1932-1937). *The Birds of Europe*. 5 Vols. Published privately, London.

Grandidier, A. (1876-1885). *Histoire Physique, Naturelle et Politique de Madagascar*. Paris.

Gray, G. (1843). [Laughing Owl]. Page 197 in: Dieffenbach, E. (1843). *Travels in New Zealand*. Vol. 2. John Murray, London.

Gray, G. (1862). List of the birds of New Zealand. *Ibis* **Ser. 1, no. 4**: 214.

Gray, J. (1846-1850). *Gleanings from the Menagerie and Aviary at Knowsley Hall*. Knowsley, UK.

Greenway, J. (1958). *Extinct and Vanishing Birds of the World*. American Committee for International Wildlife Protection Special Publication **13**. New York.

Grieve, S. (1885). *The Great Auk or Garefowl*. Published privately, Edinburgh.

Groen, H. (1966). *Australian Parakeets*. Published privately, Haren.

Gundlach, J. (1876). *Contribución a la Ornitología Cubana*. Habana.

Günther, A. & Newton, E. (1879). Extinct birds of Rodríguez. *Phil. Trans. Roy. Soc.* **168**: 423-437.

Hachisuka, M. (1937a). Kuina mundyi. *Bull. Brit. Orn. Club* **57**: 156.

Hachisuka, M. (1937b). Revisional note on the didine birds of Réunion. *Proc. Biol. Soc. Washington* **1**: 69-72.

Hachisuka, M. (1953). *The Dodo and Kindred Birds*. Witherby, London.

Hadden, F. (1941). Midway Islands. *Hawaiian Planters' Record* **45**: 179-221.

Hahn, C. (1841). *Ornithologischer Atlas*. Nurenberg.

Hahn, P. (1963). *Where is that Vanished Bird?* Royal Ontario Museum, Toronto.

Halliday, T. (1978). *Vanishing Birds*. London.

Harrison, M. (1970). The Orange-fronted Parakeet. *Notornis* **17**: 115-125.

Harry, B. (1681). A coppey of Mr. Benj. Harry's Journall when he was chief mate of the shippe *Berkley Castle*, 1679. *British Mus. Additional Manuscript* **3668**: 11D.

Hartert, E. (1927). Types of birds in the Tring Museum. *Nov. Zool.* **34**: 1-38.

Hartlaub, G. (1893). Vier seltene Rallen. *Abh. Naturwiss. ver. Bremen* **12**: 389-402.

Hartlaub, G. & Finsch, O. (1871). The Samoan Wood Rail. *Proc. Zool. Soc. London* **1871**: 25.

Hasbrouck, E. (1891). The Carolina Parakeet. *Auk* **8**: 369-370.

Henshaw, H. (1900). Introduction of foreign birds into the Hawaiian Islands with notes on some of the introduced species. Pp. 132-142 in: Thrum, T. (1900). *Hawaiian Almanac and Annual, 1901*. Honolulu.

Henshaw, H. (1901). Complete list of the birds of the Hawaiian Possessions, with notes on their habits. Pp. 54-106 in: Thrum, T. (1901). *Hawaiian Almanac and Annual, 1902*. Honolulu.

Henshaw, H. (1902). Complete list of the birds of the Hawaiian Possessions, with notes on their habits. Pp. 73-117 in: Thrum, T. (1902). *Hawaiian Almanac and Annual, 1903*. Honolulu.

Henshaw, H. (1903). Complete list of the birds of the Hawaiian Possessions, with notes on their habits. Pp. 113-145 in: Thrum, T. (1903). *Hawaiian Almanac and Annual, 1904*. Honolulu.

Herbert, T. (1634). *A Relation of some Yeares' Travaile, begunne Anno 1626 into Afrique and the Greater Asia, Especially the Territories of the Persian Monarchie, and some Parts of the Oriental Indies and Isles Adiacent*. London.

Hindwood, K.A. (1940). The birds of Lord Howe Island. *Emu* **40**: 1-86.

Hoare, M. ed. (1982). *The Resolution Journal of J. R. Forster*. Hakluyt Society, London.

Hombron, J. & Jacquinot, H. (1841). A description of the Auckland Islands Merganser. *Ann. Sci. Nat. Zool.* **16**: 320.

Howard, R. & Moore, A. (1980). *A Complete Checklist of the Birds of the World*. Oxford University Press, Oxford.

von Hugel, Baron (1875). A new specimen of the Auckland Islands Merganser. *Ibis* **Ser. 3, no. 5**: 392.

Hull, A. (1909). The birds of Lord Howe and Norfolk islands. *Proc. Linn. Soc. New South Wales* **34**: 636-693.

Hume, A.O. & Marshall, C. (1879-1881). *The Game Birds of India, Burma and Ceylon*. 3 Vols. A. Acton, Calcutta.

Hutton, F. (1872). Notes on some birds from the Chatham Islands, collected by H. H. Travers esq.; with descriptions of two new species. *Ibis* **Ser. 3, no. 2**: 243-250.

Hutton, F. (1891). On the classification of the moas. *New Zealand J. Sci.* **1(6)**: 2476-2479.

Jehl, J.R. (1972). On the cold trail of an extinct parrot. *Pacific Discovery* **25**: 24-29.

Jerdon, T. (1864). *Birds of India*. Calcutta.

Jouanin, C. (1959). Les emeus de l'Expedition Baudin. *Oiseau et RFO* **29**: 169-203.

Kalm, P. (1759). A description of wild pigeons which visit the southern English colonies in North America certain years in incredible multitudes. (Reprinted in *Auk* **28**: 53-66, 1911).

Kear, J. & Scarlett, R. (1970). Auckland Islands Merganser. *Wildfowl* **21**: 78-86.

King, W. ed. (1981). *Endangered Birds of the World*. Smithsonian Institution Press and ICBP, Washington, D.C.

Kittlitz, F.H. von (1830). Kittlitz Thrush. *Mem. Acad. Sci. St. Petersburg* **1**: 245.

Kittlitz, F.H. von (1832-1833). *Kupfertafeln zur Naturgeschichte der Vogel*. Frankfurt am Mai.

Kittlitz, F.H. von (1858). *Denkwürdigkeiten eier Reise nach dem Russichen Amerika, nach Micronesien*. Gotha, Germany.

Knox, A.G. & Walters, M.P. (1994). *Extinct and Endangered Birds in the Collections of the Natural History Museum*. British Ornithologists' Club Occasional Publications **1**. 292 pp.

Kuroda, N. (1917). [Crested Shelduck]. *Tori* **1**: 1. In Japanese.

Kuroda, N. (1924). [On a third specimen of a rare species *Pseudotadorna cristata* Kuroda]. *Tori* **4(18)**: 171-180. In Japanese.

Kuroda, N. (1925). *A Contribution to the Knowledge of the Avifauna of the Riukiu Islands*. Tokyo.

LaBastille, A. (1990). *Mama Poc*. W.W. Norton & Co., New York.

Labat, J. (1742). *Nouveau Voyage aux Isles de l'Amerique*. Paris.

Latham, J. (1781-1785). *A General Synopsis of Birds*. 3 Vols. London.

Latham, J. (1787). *Supplement to the General Synopsis of Birds*. London.

Latham, J. (1790). *Indian Ornithology*. London.

Laycock, G. (1969). The last parakeet. *Audubon* **71**: 21-25.

Leguat, F. (1708a). *Voyages et Avantures en Deux Isles Désertes des Indes Orientales*. Paris.

Leguat, F. (1708b). *A New Voyage to the East Indies*. London.

Lendon, A. (1973). *Australian Parrots in Field and Aviary*. Angus & Robertson, Sydney.

Lever, C. (1985). *Naturalized Mammals of the World*. Longman, Harlow.

Lichtenstein, M.H.K. ed. (1844). *Descriptions Animalium quae in Itinere ad Maris Australis Terras*. Berlin Academy, Berlin.

Linnaeus, C. (1758). *Systema Naturae*. Stockholm.

Lysaght, A. (1953). A rail from Tonga. *Bull. Brit. Orn. Club* **73**: 74-75.

Medway, D. (1979). Some ornithological results of Cook's third voyage. *J. Soc. Bibl. Nat. Hist.* **9**: 315-351.

Mees, G.F. (1964). Twee Exemplaren van *Aplonis corvina* in Leiden. *Ardea* **52**: 190-193.

Mees, G.F. (1977). *Pareudiastes pacifica*. *Zool. Med.* **50**: 230-242.

Merrem, B. (1786). *Avium Rariorum et Minus Cognitarum Icones et Descriptiones Collectae e Germanicus Latinae Factae*. Leipzig.

Mershon, W. (1907). *The Passenger Pigeon*. Outing Publishing Co., New York.

Meyer de Schauensee, R. (1957). On some avian types, principally Gould's, in the collection of the Academy. *Proc. Acad. Nat. Sci. Philadelphia* **109**: 123-146.

Michelant, M. ed. (1865). *Voyage de Jacques Cartier au Canada en 1534*. Paris.

Milne-Edwards, A. (1866-1873). *Recherches sur la Faune Ornithologique Étiente des îles Mascareignes et de Madagascar*. Paris.

Milne-Edwards, A. (1869). *Aphanapteryx imperialis*. *Ibis* **Ser. 2, no. 5**: 256-275.

Milne-Edwards, A. (1874). Recherches sur la faune ancienne des Iles Mascareignes. *Ann. Sci. Nat. Zool.* **Ser. 5, no. 19**: 1-31.

Milne-Edwards A. & Oustalet, E. (1893). Notice sur quelques espèces d'oiseaux ... étient. Pp. 190-252 in: *Centenaire de la Fondation du Musée d'Histoire Naturelle, Paris*.

Mundy, P. See Temple & Anstey (1919-1936).

Munro, G. (1944). *Birds of Hawaii*. Tuttle, Honolulu.

van Neck, J. (1601). *Het Tweede Boek*. Middleburg.

Newton, A. (1861). Abstract of J. Wolley's researches in Iceland respecting the Garefowl or Great Auk. *Ibis* **Ser. 1, no. 3**: 374-399.

Newton, A. (1872). On an undescribed bird from the island of Rodrigues. *Ibis* **Ser. 3, no. 2**: 30-34.

Newton, A. (1875). Note on *Palaeornis exsul*. *Ibis* **Ser. 3, no. 5**: 342.

Newton, A. (1893). On a new species of *Drepanis* discovered by Mr. R. C. L. Perkins. *Proc. Zool. Soc. London* **1893**: 690.

Newton, A. & Gadow, H.F. (1893). On additional bones of the dodo and other extinct birds. *Trans. Zool. Soc. London* **7**: 281-302.

Newton, A. & Newton, E. (1868). On the osteology of the solitaire. *Phil. Trans. Roy. Soc.* **1869**: 327-362.

Newton, A. & Newton, E. (1876). On the Psittaci of the Mascarene Islands. *Ibis* **Ser. 3, no. 6**: 281-289.

Newton, E. (1861). Ornithological notes from Mauritius. *Ibis* **Ser. 1, no. 3**: 270-277.

Oliver, W. (1949). *The Moas of New Zealand and Australia*. Bulletin of the Dominion Museum **15**. 196 pp.

Oliver, W. (1955). *New Zealand Birds*. A.H. & A.W. Reed, Wellington.

Olson, S.L. (1973). Evolution of the rails of the South Atlantic islands. *Smithsonian Contrib. Zool.* **152**: 7.

Olson, S.L. (1977). A synopsis of the fossil Rallidae. Pp. 339-373 in: Ripley, S. (1977). *Rails of the World*. Boston.

Olson, S.L. (1986). An early account of some birds from Mauke. *Notornis* **33**: 197-208.

Olson, S.L. (1999). Kona Grosbeak (*Chloridops kona*), Greater Koa-Finch (*Rhodacanthis palmeri*), Lesser Koa-Finch (*Rhodacanthis flaviceps*). No. **424** in: Poole, A.F. & Gill, F.B. eds. (1996). *The Birds of North America*. Vol. 11. Academy of Natural Sciences & American Ornithologists' Union, Philadelphia & Washington, D.C.

Oudemans, A. (1917). *Dodo-studien*. Johannes Muller, Amsterdam.

Oustalet, E. (1896). *Faune des Îles Mascareignes*. Annales des Sciences Naturelles Zoologie **3**. 129 pp.

Owen, R. (1839). Exhibited bone of an unknown stuthious bird from New Zealand. *Proc. Zool. Soc. London* **7**: 169-171.

Owen, R. (1866a). *Memoir on the Dodo*. London.

Owen, R. (1866b). [*Lophopsittacus mauritianus*]. *Ibis* **Ser. 2, no. 2**: 168-171.

Owen, R. (1870). On *Dinornis*. Part XIV. *Trans. Zool. Soc. London* **7**: 123-150.

Owen, R. (1879). *Memoirs on the Extinct Wingless Birds of New Zealand*. 2 Vols. London.

Owen, R. (1883). On *Dinornis*. Part XXIV. *Trans. Zool Soc. London* **11**: 257.

Pallas, P.S. (1811). *Zoographia Russo-Asiatica*. Vol. 2.

Parker, T. (1893). On the presence of a crest in certain species of moa. *Trans. New Zealand Inst.* **25**: 3-6.

Peale, T. (1848). *United States Exploring Expedition*. Philadelphia.

von Pelzeln, A. (1860). Norfolk Island Kaka. *Sitz. Mathem., Naturwiss. Klasse Acad. Wissen. Wien* **41(15)**: 319-332.

von Pelzeln, A. (1873). On the birds in the Imperial collection at Vienna obtained from the Leverian Mus. *Ibis* **Ser. 3, no. 3**: 105-124.

Perkins, R.C.L. (1893). The Koa Finch. *Ibis* **Ser. 6, no. 5**: 103.

Perkins, R.C.L. (1903). Vertebrata. Pp. 365-466 in: *Fauna Hawaiiensis*. Vol. 1. Cambridge University Press.

Peters, J.L. (1931-1986). *Check-list of Birds of the World*. 15 Vols. Museum of Comparative Zoology, Harvard University Press, Cambridge, Massachusetts.

Phillipps, W. (1963). *The Book of the Huia*. Whitcombe & Tombs, Christchurch, New Zealand.

Phillips, J. (1922-1926). *A Natural History of the Ducks*. Houghton Mifflin, Boston.

Piveteau, J. (1945). Étude sur l'*Aphanapteryx. Annales de Paléontologie* **31**: 31-37.

Polack, J. (1838). *New Zealand*. London.

Potts, T. (1870-1874). On the birds of New Zealand. *Trans. Proc. New Zealand Inst.* **2-6**.

Pratt, H.D. (1979). *A Systematic Analysis of the Endemic Avifauna of the Hawaiian Islands*. University of Michigan, Ann Arbor, Michigan.

Pratt, H.D., Bruner, P. & Berrett, D. (1987). *A Field Guide to the Birds of Hawaii and the Tropical Pacific*. Princeton University Press, Princeton, New Jersey.

Quammen, D. (1996). *The Song of the Dodo*. Hutchinson, London.

Quoy, J. & Gaimard, J. (1830). *Voyage de l'Astrolabe*. Paris.

Richardson, J. (1844-1875). *The Zoology of the Voyage of HMS Erebus and Terror*. London.

Rothschild, L.W. (1892). Description of seven new species of birds from the Sandwich Islands. *Ann. and Mag. Nat. Hist.* **Ser. 6, no. 10**: 108-112.

Rothschild, L.W. (1893-1900). *The Birds of Laysan and the Neighbouring Islands*. 2 Vols. R.H. Porter, London.

Rothschild, L.W. (1894). A new species from Stephens Island. *Bull. Brit. Orn. Club* **4**: 19.

Rothschild, L.W. (1903). *Rallus wakensis. Bull. Brit. Orn. Club* **13**: 78.

Rothschild, L.W. (1907a). *Extinct Birds*. Hutchinson, London.

Rothschild, L.W. (1907b). On extinct and vanishing birds. Pp. 191-217 in: *Proceedings of the 4th International Ornithological Congress, London*. Dulau, London.

Rothschild, M. (1983). *Dear Lord Rothschild*. Hutchinson, London.

Rowley, G. (1875-1878). *Ornithological Miscellany*. 3 Vols. Trübner, London.

Schorger, A. (1955). *The Passenger Pigeon*. University of Wisconsin, Madison, Wisconsin.

Scopoli, G.A. (1786-1788). *Deliciae Florae et Faunae Insubricae*.

Seebohm, H. (1890). Birds of the Bonin Islands. *Ibis* **Ser. 6, no. 2**: 95-108.

Sélys Longchamps, E. (1848). [*Aphanapteryx bonasia*]. *Rev. Zool.*: 292.

Sharpe, R.B. (1906). A note on the White-winged Sandpiper. *Bull. Brit. Orn. Club* **16**: 86.

Slater, P. (1978). *Rare and Vanishing Australian Birds*. Rigby, Sydney.

Sonnerat, P. (1782). *Voyage aux Indes Orientales*. 2 Vols. Paris.

Sparrman, A. (1787). [*Turnagra capensis*]. *Mus. Carlsonianum* **2**: 45.

Stattersfield, A.J. & Capper, D.R. eds. (2000). *Threatened Birds of the World*. Lynx Edicions & BirdLife International, Barcelona & Cambridge.

Stejneger, L. (1887). Description of a new species of Fruit Pigeon (*Janthoenas jonyi*) from the Liu Kiu Islands, Japan. *Amer. Naturalist* **21**: 583.

Stresemann, E. (1930). Welche Paradiesvogelarten der Literature sind Hybriden Ursprungs? *Nov. Zool.* **36**: 3-13.

Stresemann, E. (1949). Birds collected in the North Pacific area during Capt. James Cook's last voyage (1778-1779). *Ibis* **91**: 244-255.

Stresemann, E. (1950). Birds collected during Capt. James Cook's last expedition (1776-1780). *Auk* **67(1)**: 66-88.

Strickland, H. & Melville, A. (1848). *The Dodo and its Kindred*. London.

Stuart Baker, E.C. (1908). *Indian Ducks and their Allies*. Bombay Natural History Society, London.

Tatton, J. (1625). Voyages of Castleton. Pp. 533-534 in: *Purchas's Pilgrimage*. London.

Taylor, R. (1873). An account of the first discovery of moa remains. *Trans. New Zealand Inst.* **5**: 97-101.

Temple, R. & Anstley, L. eds. (1919-1936). *The Travels of Peter Mundy in Europe and Asia, 1608-1667*. Haklyut Society, London.

Uchida, S. (1917). [On *Pseudotadorna cristata*]. *Tori* **2(6)**: 6-8. In Japanese.

Vigors, N. (1828). Article XLVII. Sketches in ornithology, etc. by N. A. Vigors. *Zool. J.* **4**: 345-358.

Wagler, J. (1829). *Isis von Oken* **22**: col. 738.

Walters, M. (1988). Probable validity of *Rallus nigra* Miller, an extinct species from Tahiti. *Notornis* **35**: 265.

Wetmore, A. (1925). Bird life among lava rock. *Natl. Geogr.* **48**: 76-108.

Wetmore, A. (1937). Cuban Red Macaw. *J. Agric. Univ. Puerto Rico* **21**: 12.

Wheaton, J. (1882). *Report on the Birds of Ohio*. Ohio Geological Survey **4**. 442 pp.

White, J. (1790). *Journal of a Voyage to New South Wales*. Debretts, London.

Wilson, S. (1888). On *Chloridops*, a new generic form of Fringillidae from the island of Hawaii. *Proc. Zool. Soc. London* **1888**: 218.

Wilson, S. & Evans, A. (1890-1899). *Aves Hawaiiensis*. R.H. Porter, London.

Wood, J. (1871). [*Argusianus bipunctatus*]. *Ann. and Mag. Nat. Hist.* **Ser. 4, no. 8**: 67.

The previous volume was accompanied by a poll aimed at establishing the preferences of the majority of readers with reference to how the remainder of the HBW series should proceed. The question was essentially whether we should continue our recent trend of longer, fuller texts, more photos, and more extensive coverage of subspecific variation on more plates, resulting in a few more volumes than previously envisaged, or take a step backwards from these possible excesses and aim for levels of coverage closer to those used at the start of the series, and thus stick to the previously projected 12 volumes (See Introduction to Volume 6). We were particularly keen that our readers should participate actively in the overall planning of the rest of the series, as you, the users, are in the best position to judge collectively what the best course may be.

The results of the poll have been quite revealing. The number of replies received, alone, is worth mention –almost 3000 from over 40 countries. Such a large response seems to be a good indication that the matter caught the interest of many readers. A remarkable total of 93% of those who answered the poll indicated that they were in favour of the option of dealing with the species in greater detail, whereas only 7% stated they would prefer the series be kept at 12 volumes—indeed, many of these kindly expressed their intention to continue to support the project even in the event that the series were to be extended. Given that the option chosen by the vast majority of our readers coincides with the one that we, the editors, also prefer, it is now established that the series will definitively be extended to a total of 16 volumes, so that there will be enough space to deal comprehensively with the ever-increasing volume of information available and also to illustrate the species extensively by means of both plates and photos. We are convinced that the overall results of this decision will be clearly more useful, and also a richer celebration of the enormous variety present in Class Aves. The HBW website (http://www.hbw.com) provides more details of the poll results.

Turning to the present volume, we are delighted to be able to start it with a foreword dedicated to one of the subjects most frequently requested by our readers: extinct birds. To cover this topic comprehensively, we always felt that a good deal of space would be needed, especially as we wanted this to be a highly illustrated foreword; to this end we felt that Volume 7 was ideal for the purpose. For this huge subject, we have been fortunate indeed to be able to count on the expert authorship of Errol Fuller, who has recently published a second, revised edition of his spectacular *Extinct Birds*, as well as producing recent monographs on two of the most evocative of extinct bird species, the Great Auk (*Pinguinus impennis*) and the Dodo (*Raphus cucullatus*).

Because so little is known about so many extinct forms, there are often considerable doubts as to their taxonomic status. In many cases, there is even some doubt as to whether they really are extinct, or might survive in small numbers in some remote area. All in all, we felt that it would be rather confusing for readers if such doubtful cases differed in treatment from the versions already adopted in HBW to date, and we are particularly grateful to the author for kindly adapting his own preferred list, that of *Extinct Birds*, to fit the HBW version, in all cases. One of the major omissions from his list comprises a series of species already covered in HBW (most of them listed as "Almost certainly Extinct"), each with its own species account, map and illustration. It seemed pointless to waste available space by repeating the material on each of these species, even though a realist would probably have to admit that the chances of the continued survival of some of them must be very close to nil.

We particularly wanted to maintain HBW standards of extensive illustration, and to this end a series of plates was specially commissioned to depict all the recently extinct bird species whose appearance in life is sufficiently known. Of course, in this matter too there were borderline decisions, including two that were particularly notable for the similarity of their cases: the Tanna Ground-dove (*Gallicolumba ferruginea*) and the Bay Thrush (*Turdus ulietensis*) are each known merely by a single painting by the same person, but, while the former was considered to allow just enough certainty to permit its illustration, the latter presented too many areas of uncertainty, so no illustration was attempted.

Each species in the foreword has its original name placed alongside, together with the other relevant details of its original description. In contrast, and as in the main body of HBW texts, subspecies are listed using only their currently accepted names, with the describer and year of publication following, with or without brackets depending on the original genus, in accordance with ICZN norms. In this foreword, all references of scientific descriptions are listed immediately after the basic details of their respective descriptions.

This concluding non-passerine volume is accompanied by a practical plastic-coated index of the groups covered in the first seven volumes, allowing even a novice on birds quickly to locate any of the families in this first part of the series. Although most readers will already be reasonably familiar with the traditional taxonomic sequence followed by HBW, we believe that the existence of several other sequences, some varying drastically from the traditional one, could raise some doubts as to where exactly a certain family is covered in the HBW series; it is hoped that the index will prove handy for rapid clarification. There are two ways of using the index. On one side, there is a visual scheme in taxonomic sequence, in which each non-passerine family is symbolized by one of its most representative members, followed by the volume and the page number on which the corresponding family section starts. On the other side of the index there is an alphabetical list of the scientific and English names of all of the orders and families covered in Volumes 1-7, as well as the English names of all species groups included in the families. For example, in order to find out where the family Hawks & Eagles is covered, the reader can look it up under Accipitridae, baza, buzzard, chanting-goshawk, cuckoo-hawk, eagle, fish-eagle, fishing-eagle, hawk, honey-buzzard, kite, sea-eagle, serpent-eagle, snake-eagle, vulture, etc. Additional scientific ranks, such as suborders and subfamilies, are not included, as they would be of very limited use in such a reference system. Logically, an index of all of the passerines will be included in the last volume of the series.

The sources of French, German and Spanish names have been the same as in previous volumes, with Normand David and Peter Barthel once again kindly helping out in any doubtful cases with the French and German names, respectively. The latest group of Spanish names was published in *Ardeola* **48(1)**: 107-110.

Acknowledgements

As in previous volumes, we owe a great debt to many museums, and those working there. Chief amongst these are the British Museum of Natural History at Tring (Robert Prys-Jones, Michael Walters, Mark Adams, Cyril Walker, Effie Warr, Alison Harding), the American Museum of Natural History in New York (Joel Cracraft, George Barrowclough, Mary LeCroy, Paul Sweet, Shannon Kenney, Peter Capainolo, Terry Chesser, Maria Rios), the Louisiana State University Museum of Natural Science (Van Remsen, Steve Cardiff, Donna Dittmann, Mario Cohn-Haft, Dan Lane, Alexandre Aleixo, Jason Weckstein, Rob Faucett, John O'Neill) and the Smithsonian Institution, National Museum of Natural History in Washington (James Dean, Gary Graves, Pam Rasmussen, Richard Zusi). Also of great assistance have been the Field Museum in

Chicago (David Willard, Shannon Hackett), the Kenya Natural History Museum (Leon Bennun, George Amutete, Kuria), the Colección Phelps de Venezuela (Miguel Lentino, Margarita Martínez, Clemencia Rodner, Robin Restall), the Delaware Museum of Natural History (Gene Hess), the Museum of Comparative Zoology in Harvard (Alison Pirie, Peter Alden, Jeremiah Trimble), the National Museums of Scotland in Edinburgh (Bob McGowan), the Natuurhistorisch Museum at Leiden (René Dekker, Martien van Oijen), Liverpool Museum (Tony Parker), the Departamento de Zoologia of the Universidade de São Paulo (Luís Fábio Silveira) and the Academy of Natural Sciences at Philadelphia (Nate Rice).

We are similarly indebted to a whole host of libraries, which time and again come to our rescue. Yet again, the contribution made by Effie Warr and Alison Harding of the British Museum of Natural History at Tring has been immense. We are very grateful too to the Museu de Zoologia of Barcelona (María Ángeles Iglesias), the Sociedad Española de Ornitología in Madrid (Blas Molina) and the Estación Biológica de Doñana (José Cabot). Our warm thanks are also due to Gustaf Aulén, Raül Aymí (Grup Català d'Anellament), Juliane Diller (Ornithological Society of Bavaria), Yeser Elmas and John Rose (Natural History Museum, London), John C. Fisher (Western Foundation of Vertebrate Zoology), Diego Giraldo-Canas (*Caldasia*), Juan Carlos Guix, Janet Hinshaw (University of Michigan), Fritz Hirt (SVS International Operations, Switzerland), Hans Källander (*J. Avian Biology*), Kanitha Kasina-Ubol (Siam Society), Chichiro Kikuchi (*Birder*, Japan), Blaise Mulhauser (Muséum d'Histoire Naturelle, Neuchâtel), Jevgeni Shergalin, Jeremy Speck (BirdLife UK), Oscar A. Spitznagel (Aves Argentinas/Asociación Ornitológica del Plata), Ante Strand (Swedish Ornithological Society) and Xu Weishu (China Ornithological Society).

For assistance with many assorted doubts connected with nomenclature and scientific descriptions, we are once again very grateful to Alan Knox, and also to Murray Bruce, Normand David, Edward Dickinson, Miguel Lentino, Flávio Lima and Michael Walters. We should also like to mention Alan P. Peterson's excellent web on Zoological Nomenclature, which has helped us out on many occasions.

The texts have benefited notably through the input of referees and the addition of much material, often unpublished. We should like to thank all who have contributed, particularly Nick Athanas, Judy Davis, Geoffrey Field, Al Gilbert, Michael S. Husak, Andy Kratter, Dan Lane, Juan Mazar-Barnett, John O' Neill and Pam Rasmussen. Robert Ridgely once again very kindly reviewed all the maps of South American species, making notable improvements in many cases. We are also very grateful to Jeff Price for checking and commenting on both the maps and the Status and Conservation sections for all the North American species.

Liberal access to Guy Tudor's own personal collection of reference photos has again been a major boon, and we are very grateful to him for his continued support. We have again benefited greatly from our agreements with VIREO at the Academy of Natural Sciences in Philadelphia (Doug Wechsler), and with the National Sound Archive of the British Library (Richard Ranft). Our grateful thanks also to David Ascanio, Mario Cohn-Haft and Barry Walker, for help with particular bird calls.

The various authors and artists involved in the present volume would like to thank Mark Adams, Dean Amadon, Allison V. Andor, J. Phillip Angle, John C. Arvin, the late Luis Baptista, Eustace Barnes, George Barrowclough, John Bate, Ernest Baurenfeind, William Belton, Christine Blake, Walter J. Bock, Cordula Bracker, Pat Brunauer, Greg Budney, Phil Burton, Scott Cannop, Steve Cardiff, Juan Manuel Carrión B., Marcelo Carvalho, J. C. Chebez, Lisa Choegyal, Mario Cohn-Haft, Nigel Collar, Peter Colston, Paul Coopmans, Tim Crowe, J.C. Daniels, René Dekker, Jared M. Diamond, Tony Diamond, Bob Dowsett, Françoise Dowsett-Lemaire, Siegfried Eck, Renate van den Elzen, Christian Érard, Patricia Escalante-Pliego, Alan Feduccia, John Fitzpatrick, Jon Fjeldså, Bruce Forrester, Irma Franke, Dawn and Clifford Frith, Anita Gamauf, Kimball Garrett, Cecilia and Nathan Gichuki, Frank B. Gill, Derek Goodwin, the late Mary Lou Goodwin, Shannon Hackett, Jürgen Haffer, Bill Hardy, Ed N. Harrison, Sebastian K. Herzog, Gene K. Hess, Nancy Hilgert de Benevides, Heinrich Hoerschelmann, Elizabeth Höfling, Julian Hume, S. A. Hussain, C. W. Hustler, Hussain Isack, Lois Jammes, Jerry Jennings, Ned K. Johnson, Leo Joseph, Stuart Keith, Lloyd Kiff, Ben King, Guy Kirwan, Claus König, Dan Lane, Scott Lanyon, Wesley E. Lanyon, Mary LeCroy, Miguel Lentino, Richard Liversidge, Huw Lloyd, Nancy Lopez de Kochalka, Michel Louette, Sue Luck, Joe Marshall, Mary Jo MacConnell, Sjoerd Mayer, Juan Mazar Barnett, Klaus Michalek, Sandra Bos Mikich, Marie-Yvonne and Gérard Morel, Gene Morton, David Moyer, Jorge R. Navas, Alvaro José Negret, David Newbitt, F.C. Novaes, Storrs Olson, John O'Neill, David C. Oren, Fernando Pacheco, Robin Panza, Ken Parkes, Bob Payne, Ray Paynter, Chris Perrins, D. Stefan Peters, Town Peterson, Roberto Philips, Derek Pomeroy, Pilai Poonswad, Robert Prys-Jones, Richard

Ranff, Pamela S. Rasmussen, Josef Reichholf, Van Remsen, David Ricalde, Robert Ridgely, Mark Robbins, Scott Robinson, Clemencia Rodner, Francisco Sagot, Paul Salaman, Pedro Scherer-Neto, Thomas Schulenberg, Herbert G. Shifter, K. L. Schuchmann, Lucia Severinghaus, Fred Sibley, Dick Sloss, Karl Somadikarta, Barbara and David Snow, Gary Stiles, Bob Stjernstedt, Morten Strange, Paul Sweet, Dante M. Teixeira, Christopher W. Thompson, Russell Thorstrom, Emil Urban, John-Pierre Vande weghe, Paulo Vanzolini, Jacques Vieillard, François Vuilleumier, Amy Weibel, David R. Wells, Bret Whitney, David Willard, Hans Winkler, Christopher Witt, Hafiz S. A. Yahya and Richard Zusi, and the Academy of Natural Sciences of Philadelphia, the American Museum of Natural History, the Bombay Natural History Society, the British Museum (Natural History) at Tring, the California Academy of Sciences, the Carnegie Museum of Natural History, the Colección Phelps de Venezuela, the Museo Nacional de Historia Natural in La Paz, the Collection of Cornell University, the Dickey Collection of the University of California, the Divisão de Museu de Historia Natural at Curitiba (Brazil), the Durban Natural Science Museum, the Field Museum of Natural History in Chicago, the Edward Grey Institute of Field Ornithology, the Institut Royal des Sciences Naturelles de Belgique, the Koninklijk Museum voor Midden-Africa at Tervuren, the Los Angeles County Museum of Natural History, the Moore Collection of Occidental University in Los Angeles, the Musée d'Histoire Naturelle at La Chaux de Fonds (Switzerland), the Musée d'Histoire Naturelle in Paris, the Museo de Ciencias Naturales in Cali, the Museo de Historia Naturel Javier Prado in Lima, the Museo de Historia Natural Noel Kempf Mercado in Santa Cruz (Bolivia), the Museo de Historia Natural de Paraguay, the Museo de la Universidad Nacional in Bogotá, the Museu Nacional de Brasil in Rio de Janeiro, the Museu Paraense Emilio Goeldi in Belém (Brazil), the Museu de Zoologia at Universidade de São Paulo, the Museum of Comparative Zoology, the National Museum of Natural History (Smithsonian Institution) in Washington, the Museum of Natural Sciences at Louisiana State University, the Museum of Vertebrate Zoology of University of California, the Museum und Forschungsinstitut Alexander Koenig in Bonn, the Museum Zoologicum Bogoriense in Bogor (Java), the National Museum in Bulawayo, the National Museums of Kenya, and the Vienna Natural History Museum.

Santiago Guallar again provided useful help with some of the bibliography sections. Many, many thanks to all those who helped us in a wide variety of ways, and especially to Yolanda Aguayo, Maria Josep de Andrés, Elisa Badia, Dolors Buxó, Juan Antonio Cantí, Cam Christie, Xavier Fosch, Fortunato Frias, Ricard Gutiérrez, Rosa Llinàs, Isabel Martínez, Rafael Martínez, Albert Martínez-Vilalta, Eva Muñoz, María Teresa Obiols, Jim and Mary Ramsay, Olga Rius, Javier Rodríguez, César Ruiz, Eloi Ruiz-Olalla, Arantxa Sánchez and Aurea Vilalta.

We are very grateful to Julian Hume and Errol Fuller for their kind permission to use their plates in the foreword. Errol Fuller also generously supplied all of the archival material used in his foreword. Finally, we are delighted to be able to close our acknowledgement section once again with our warm thanks to Toni Llobet for producing the illustration that graces the back cover of the volume.

Order GALBULIFORMES

Galbuliformes

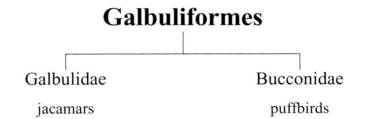

Galbulidae   Bucconidae

jacamars   puffbirds

Class AVES
Order GALBULIFORMES
Family GALBULIDAE (JACAMARS)

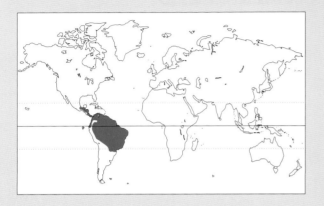

- Small to medium-sized slender perching birds with small feet, rounded wings, and very long bill used to catch insects in flight; plumage varies from brightly coloured and iridescent to fairly dull.
- 14-34 cm.

- Neotropical.
- Wooded, mostly lowland habitats.
- 5 genera, 18 species, 37 taxa.
- 2 species threatened; none extinct since 1600.

Systematics

Given their relatively obtrusive behaviour and conspicuous coloration, it is perhaps not surprising that 17 of the 18 jacamar species have been known for at least 100 years, and most for far longer than that. Indeed, the only more recent taxon that currently stands as a full species, the Purus Jacamar (*Galbalcyrhynchus purusianus*), was described in 1904 after specimens had masqueraded for many years as females of the White-eared Jacamar (*Galbalcyrhynchus leucotis*). Before the mid-1700's, and even long after then, the jacamars had been confused with the kingfishers (Alcedinidae). A separate genus was first applied to the jacamars in 1760, by Brisson, who gave them the name *Galbula*, a classical term the legitimate proprietor of which is believed to be the Golden Oriole (*Oriolus oriolus*). It may be of incidental interest to note that, although the name *Galbula* had been used earlier by Möhring, in 1752, Brisson is the only pre-Linnean author whose generic names are recognized when they are additional to those of Linnaeus himself. The jacamars were finally divided into a separate family, the Galbulidae, by Bonaparte, in 1850, although it was then placed between the trogons (Trogonidae) and the kingfishers. This family designation still stands today.

This link between jacamars and kingfishers is a feature of early ornithological writings. In 1743, the Paradise Jacamar (*Galbula dea*) was given the name "Swallow-tailed Kingfisher", and over a century later the superficial similarites between these two groups still led to their being associated taxonomically. The first three jacamars described, in 1758, 1766 and 1776, respectively, were allocated to the kingfisher genus *Alcedo*. In 1847, G. R. Gray classified the jacamars as the fourth subfamily of his "Alcedinidae", and in 1852 Cassin perpetuated this link by including the Galbulidae as a subfamily of the "Halcyonidae", where it was stranded incongruously between two groups of Asian forest kingfishers, the "Dacelininae" (*sic*) and the "Tanysipterinae". In 1840, following an investigation of the feather tracts of birds, a study known as pterylography, C. L. Nitzsch arranged the jacamars alongside another outwardly similar group, the bee-eaters (Meropidae), together with the motmots (Momotidae) and the rollers (Coraciidae), a course that may have prompted Reichenbach to include jacamars within his "Meropinae" in 1852. After a multitude of other taxonomic arrangements, the ordinal placement of the jacamars remains a source of debate and confusion.

Convincing evidence connects the Galbulidae and the puffbird family Bucconidae as sister taxa, despite past inconsistencies in the broader systematic placement of the two families.

Together they form the clade Galbulae, a treatment that has been almost universally adopted for some 250 years (see page 103). Notwithstanding this close association, few authorities would dispute the fact that the Galbulidae and the Bucconidae represent separate families. Most obviously, the jacamars have a bill that is conspicuously longer, straighter and thinner than that of the puffbirds, their plumage is usually so much sleeker, brighter and glossier, and they have a more slender shape and a noticeably smaller head than do the Bucconidae. Galbulids differ further from bucconids in many minor features of bone, muscle and feather design. For example, while both families possess an aftershaft on the contour feathers, there are constant differences between them in the structure of this feature: the aftershaft of puffbirds is a simple group of barbs, whereas that of jacamars is a single shaft that is subdivided. These two structures are apparently homologous and thus, along with many other minor differences between the bucconids and the galbulids, tend to support their close relationship rather than undermine it. While the anatomy and life-history strategy of puffbirds are almost certainly more primitive, no living bucconid appears likely to be a precursor or ancestor of jacamars. Although the Swallow-winged Puffbird (*Chelidoptera tenebrosa*) has a foraging strategy which resembles that of jacamars, this similarity is evidently superficial and due to convergence.

Following A. Wetmore's classification, these two groups, combined as the Galbulae, have traditionally been treated as a suborder of the Piciformes, with the other families of that order combined in the suborder Pici, but whether this accurately reflects evolutionary history remains to be resolved. Although cladistic analysis of skeletal and muscular morphology has suggested monophyly of the Piciformes, this view is by no means universally held. The Galbulae and the Pici have been unified largely on the basis of a complex derived morphology of the hind limb, in particular the arrangement of the digital flexor tendons, associated with zygodactyly. Nevertheless, an alternative viewpoint holds that this feature is doubtfully homologous in the Galbulae and the Pici and, moreover, that no other features unequivocally corroborate the hypothesis of monophyly. To some researchers, the skeletal, muscular and tendinal anatomy of zygodactyly differs between these two groups, the difference being perhaps as great as that which separates them from the parrots (Psittaciformes) and the cuckoos (Cuculiformes). This suggests that the zygodactylous condition evolved independently along different pathways, with similar functional results. If this is the case, it tends not to prove any close relationship between the Galbulae and other piciform families.

The four species of Brachygalba *form a superspecies of rather short-tailed jacamars that range from eastern Panama to Bolivia and southern Brazil. In addition to their shortened tail feathers, they have short wings and a highly reduced inner hind toe. With seven accepted races, the Brown Jacamar is the most variable species in the genus. However, two of these races were initially combined into a separate species, while another, known from only a single specimen, might be anything from a separate species to merely an aberrant individual of another race, so a detailed revision is required.*

[Brachygalba lugubris melanosterna, Serra dos Carajás, Pará, Brazil. Photo: Luiz Claudio Marigo]

Indeed, separation of the Galbulae and the Pici has often been proposed. In 1880, W. A. Forbes, on the basis of several morphological features, singled out the trogons, bee-eaters, rollers and cuckoo-rollers (Leptosomidae) as potential relatives, adding that "it is amongst these that the nearest living allies of the Jacamars and consequently the Puff-birds must be found". More recently, a considerable body of evidence has been compiled which indicates that jacamars are not piciforms at all, and should be moved to the Coraciiformes. P. J. K. Burton analysed the foraging behaviour and morphology of the Galbulae, concluding that in almost every aspect of feeding-apparatus structure they share important characters with the typical Coraciiformes and virtually none with the Piciformes. These shared characters include a desmognathous palate, and similarities in mandibular musculature, tongue design and cranial osteology. In addition, the lacrimal-ectethmoid bone complex is well developed in the Galbulae but highly reduced in other piciform families, a feature which the latter have in common with the Passeriformes, and the coracoid of the Galbulae is similar to that found in the Coraciiformes. Analysis of egg-white proteins suggested that the Galbulae might, after all, prove to be closer to the kingfishers than to the piciforms. The list of anomalies is extensive: galbulids and bucconids both have a naked oil gland, in contrast to the tufted gland of other piciforms; their incubation period is long for piciforms, but similar to that of burrow-nesting Coraciiformes; their skulls are characteristically similar in design; and the tongue bears a distinctive median groove on the dorsal surface that is absent in all other apparently related families.

While electrophoretic analysis of 20 protein-coding loci supported the grouping of the Galbulidae with the Bucconidae as sister groups, it suggested that the Piciformes were polyphyletic. Indeed, it showed the genetic distance between the Galbulae and a coraciiform, the Blue-crowned Motmot (*Momotus momota*), to be considerably smaller than that between the Pici families and the motmot. It has even been suggested that the Galbulae derive from ancient stock not far removed from that which gave rise to the Old World rollers, and even to the cuckoo-rollers of Madagascar and the Comoros, perhaps not too far-fetched a notion given other faunal similarities between those unusual Afrotropical islands and the Neotropics.

In view of the continuing controversy, it is often argued that retention of the Galbulae as a suborder of the Piciformes is not quite satisfactory. Indeed, C. G. Sibley advocated that a separate order, Galbuliformes, should be erected to accommodate the uniqueness of the Galbulidae and the Bucconidae as a group. Such an arrangement highlights their divergence, and avoids placing them too close to either the Piciformes or the Coraciiformes. Herein it has been considered the best option available on current evidence. It must be stressed, however, that further work is essential to clarify the true relationships of all these groups.

The resemblance of the New World jacamars to the Old World bee-eaters, in both their morphology and their behaviour, has often been noted. Although the taxonomic relationship between coraciiform and traditional piciform families is controversial, it appears that bee-eaters and jacamars are, at best, distant relatives. Both families nevertheless contain a good proportion of smallish, brightly plumaged birds, often extensively green in colour, with a long, pointed bill and short legs. Both are energetic, are vocal and have gregarious tendencies. Moreover, they exhibit remarkable similarities in breeding biology: both are cavity-nesters, their eggs are similar in colour, shape and size, they have long incubation and short nestling periods, and they show a lack of nest sanitation. Furthermore, an absence of a distinct juvenile plumage is a feature common to both families. This situation can perhaps best be explained by convergent evolution resulting from the considerable ecological congruence between the two groups; their diets and foraging techniques are in some cases almost identical.

The members of the Galbulidae are, for the most part, remarkably uniform in structure and behaviour, the only exceptions being the notably divergent genera *Galbalcyrhynchus* and *Jacamerops*. The latter was formerly considered sufficiently distinct to be separated in a subfamily as the Jacameropinae, although this subdivision is no longer regarded as acceptable. Most other jacamar species are only weakly differentiated, a fact that indicates a fairly recent radiation of the family at species level, and probably even at genus level, from very few ancestors in the Pleistocene period.

According to the taxonomic view that currently finds favour, there are five genera of jacamars. The genus *Urogalba* was previously used for the Paradise Jacamar, and *Psilipornis* for the Yellow-billed Jacamar (*Galbula albirostris*), but both have since been subsumed by *Galbula*, which, with ten species, is the most diverse jacamar genus. The next most diverse is *Brachygalba*,

The New World Galbulidae, such as the White-chinned Jacamar, and the Old World Meropidae, or bee-eaters, are somewhat similar in shape and structure, often with brightly coloured plumage, and with a sharply pointed bill and short legs. Moreover, both groups contain species that excavate nesting cavities in vertical banks and forage primarily on aerial insects. These similarities result from convergence, because genetic and morphological data indicate that jacamars are only distantly related to bee-eaters and other coraciiform families.

[Galbula tombacea tombacea, Amacayacu National Park, Amazonas, Colombia. Photo: Otto Pfister]

containing four species. Otherwise, *Galbalcyrhynchus* consists of two closely related taxa and, finally, there are two monotypic genera, *Jacamerops* and *Jacamaralcyon*. Members of the genus *Brachygalba*, sometimes referred to as "short-tailed jacamars", are smaller than those of the genus *Galbula*, with shorter wings and tail and a slightly shorter bill. They also possess a greatly reduced inner hind toe, such that only one hind toe is often visible in the field. Despite its obvious similarities to *Brachygalba*, the Atlantic Forest genus *Jacamaralcyon* seems worthy of retention owing to its unique toe morphology, its longer tail, its plumage colour and its elongated head feathers. Close ecological similarities between the two groups are, however, evident in south-east Brazil: there is no overlap zone between the Three-toed Jacamar (*Jacamaralcyon tridactyla*) and the Brown Jacamar (*Brachygalba lugubris*) where their ranges meet, or at least did so until recently, in the state of São Paulo.

It is convenient to separate these genera into eight zoogeographic groups, five of which are superspecies complexes containing two or more allopatric or parapatric relatives. Geographical isolation is maintained in some cases by natural barriers. For example, the Green-tailed Jacamar (*Galbula galbula*) and the south Amazonian form *rufoviridis* of the Rufous-tailed Jacamar (*Galbula ruficauda*) are separated by the Amazon itself and the lower River Tapajós. In some cases, however, similar species occupy adjoining areas without any natural barrier separating them. Thus, the White-chinned Jacamar (*Galbula tombacea*) and the Bluish-fronted Jacamar (*Galbula cyanescens*) are closely related species living in the upper Amazon; although they occupy adjacent ranges, they are, however, parapatric and have never been recorded interbreeding. The two examples given here involve members of the "Green-tailed Jacamar superspecies", an assortment of five morphologically similar, predominantly bright green and rufous species that also includes the Coppery-chested Jacamar (*Galbula pastazae*). Fifteen of the 18 jacamar species fit neatly into such superspecies groupings, while the remaining three species are monotypic. Incidentally, a large proportion of other Neotropical groups, such as the manakins (Pipridae) and the toucans (Ramphastidae), can be similarly arranged in groups of superspecies.

An analysis of the distribution of superspecies-members in the jacamars, among other families, led J. Haffer to propose the theory that speciation had occurred during periods in which populations were separated from one another. He suggested that widespread ancestors of these forms were isolated in forest refugia during arid or cold phases of the Quaternary period. Under these circumstances of restricted distributions, reproductive isolating mechanisms evolved in some cases, through random mutations and selection, and these ruled out interbreeding when secondary contact was established later, after intervening areas had been recolonized by forest habitat. In cases where isolating mechanisms were sufficiently developed to prevent interbreeding, species have remained parapatric where contact is resumed, this being a result of their overlapping ecological niches. This hypothesis, derived in part from the study of jacamar distributions, provides probably the best explanation for the speciation mechanisms that led to the current patterns of diversity observed in the Amazon Basin.

Within the Galbulidae, there remain several cases in which the taxonomic status of forms is disputed. The Purplish Jacamar (*Galbula chalcothorax*) was treated by Haffer as a subspecies of the Bronzy Jacamar (*Galbula leucogastra*). Because the two are separated geographically, and stable morphological differences exist between them, it would seem better, however, to treat these taxa as distinct species, together forming a superspecies.

A number of uncertainties surround the constituent subspecies of the Brown Jacamar. The southern form *melanosterna* was initially described as a full species, but was subsequently relegated to the rank of a subspecies of the Brown Jacamar. Nevertheless, as both it and the race *naumburgi* are divergent, and no contact zones are known between them and other races of this wide-ranging species, a reassessment of their taxonomic status would seem desirable. In addition, the form *phaeonota*, known only from the type specimen, was described as a separate species, but it, too, is now generally regarded as a subspecies of the Brown Jacamar; further research is necessary to confirm its taxonomic placement or, indeed, its validity as a taxonomic entity at all.

Another problem concerns the southern form *rufoviridis* of the Rufous-tailed Jacamar. This was long treated as a separate species, under the name of the Spot-tailed Jacamar, but this status has been retracted on the grounds of the southern taxon's general morphological similarity to other subspecies of the Ru-

The two members of the genus Galbalcyrhynchus differ from other galbulids in having a chunky body, a dagger-like bill, bright red irides, a short, squared-off tail and dark chestnut plumage. The White-eared Jacamar is nearly identical in appearance to the Purus Jacamar (Galbalcyrhynchus purusianus), the latter differing only in lacking white ear-coverts. So close is the resemblance that Purus Jacamars were initially thought to be female White-eared Jacamars! The two species occupy largely non-overlapping ranges in northern South America but come into contact along the upper River Ucayali in eastern Peru, apparently without interbreeding.

[Galbalcyrhynchus leucotis, llanos of Venezuela. Photo: Art Wolfe]

fous-tailed Jacamar. It is, however, obstructed from those races by three other, more divergent forms regularly treated as species, namely the Green-tailed, Bluish-fronted and White-chinned Jacamars. This is a situation which, when it comes to designating populations as subspecies of other taxa, is usually regarded as not permissible. The taxonomic status of *rufoviridis* is, therefore, deserving of review.

Finally, a specimen of a galbulid taken from near Zanderij, in Surinam, is apparently a hybrid between a Green-tailed Jacamar and a Bronzy Jacamar. In size it is closer to the former, while in weight and coloration it is intermediate between those two species. This is the only reported instance of hybridization in the family, and it is of added interest in view of the fact that the two putative parent species are not considered to be particularly closely related.

Morphological Aspects

Jacamars range in size from the Brown Jacamar, the smallest individuals of which are roughly 14 cm in length and weigh only 17 g, to the much larger Great Jacamar (*Jacamerops aureus*) and Paradise Jacamar. In the case of the last two, the subspecies *amazonum* of the latter reaches 34 cm in length, while the most bulky individuals of the Great Jacamar can weigh up to 76 g. Galbulids tend to have rather a small head, a long, slender bill, relatively small zygodactylous feet and, in many cases, colourful plumage.

Externally, the nostrils have a well-developed operculum, and their elliptical or sigmoidal apertures are situated towards the culmen at the base of the bill. Behind them emerge a few conspicuous forwardly directed bristles, the anterior ones in the rictal series. The posterior cranium and occipital region extends relatively far back, creating a sloping profile of the head reminiscent of the head shape of the bee-eaters. The wings of galbulids are relatively short and rounded, with ten primaries, the outermost of which is short, and twelve secondaries. The tail is often long, full and graduated, presumably an adaptation for agility in flight, although this function is mysteriously superfluous to members of the genus *Brachygalba*, which have a shorter, narrower tail, and *Galbalcyrhynchus*, with a very

short, square-ended tail. Twelve rectrices are usually present, with the outermost pair highly abbreviated. In the genera *Brachygalba* and *Jacamaralcyon*, this abbreviation is taken to its conclusion and only five pairs of rectrices remain. The primary moult follows a simple descendant, centrifugal sequence, while moult of the secondaries and the rectrices is apparently irregular. The oil gland is naked.

Osteologically, the vomer is absent and the post-orbital process is very long. There are 14 cervical and five dorsal vertebrae, and two distinct cervical ribs and five pairs of true ribs.

The visceral anatomy is characterized by a fairly muscular gizzard, the absence of a gall bladder, and a very short intestine with large capacious caeca. Galbulid flesh has a strong distasteful odour, likened to that of trogons. The tongue is quite long, being around 2·5 cm in the Rufous-tailed Jacamar, and is a thin, flat, simple structure lacking extreme modification; in other words, it is longer than the shortened tongue of the kingfishers, but shorter than the long specialized tongue of the woodpeckers (Picidae). There is apparently a suggestion of a brush-tip on the tongue of the Great Jacamar, a character shared with a puzzling assortment of species without any apparent underlying ecological basis.

The typical jacamar bill looks, as put by T. W. Sherry, "better suited to opening letters than catching insects". It is elongated and sharply pointed, somewhat like that of bee-eaters, but, in contrast to its Old World counterpart, a jacamar usually holds its bill at an oblique angle, pointing upwards, not unlike a hummingbird (Trochilidae). Two genera do not comply with this morphological format: *Galbalcyrhynchus* has a deeper, heavier, dagger-like bill reminiscent of that of kingfishers, with a strong dorsal ridge, while *Jacamerops* has a shorter, deeper, somewhat flattened and decurved bill. The typical jacamar has been likened, both in appearance and in behaviour, to a motmot or a trogon, a comparison that could never be applied to its closest relatives.

Aerial insectivores tend to have a bill of one of two types. A broad and short bill, forming a cavernous aperture when opened, is possessed by, for example, the swallows (Hirundinidae), nightjars (Caprimulgidae) and broadbills (Eurylaimidae). The second type, slender and pincer-like, is a characteristic of the New World jacamars, as well as the Old World bee-eaters. Three hypotheses have been advanced for the design of this second type of hunting instrument. First, a long bill keeps stinging or venomous insects, such as Hymenoptera, away from vulnerable portions of the face, and also provides leverage for beating prey against a perch. It has even been postulated, somewhat speculatively, that such a bill allows the predator to hold insects sufficiently far from its eyes that it can identify an individual prey and decide whether it is palatable. Secondly, given the importance of Lepidoptera and Odonata in the diet, bill morphology may be an adaptation for capturing long-winged prey. For example, a long bill could serve to reach past the obstacle of the fragile wings so that the insect's body can be grasped firmly. If it is the wings alone that are grasped, the prey frequently escapes (see Food and Feeding). Finally, and perhaps most importantly, a direct relationship exists between bill length and the linear speed at which mandible tips can move. This biomechanical fact is presumably crucial, as it means that long-billed birds should be able to capture fast-moving prey more readily than can short-billed birds. These hypotheses are not mutually exclusive, and it is likely that the various factors have operated in combination to shape the bill of jacamars.

The legs of jacamars are short and weak, with the tarsi scutellated anteriorly but smooth posteriorly. The feet are small and zygodactylous, the second and third digits pointing forwards and the first and fourth permanently reversed. The two front digits are syndactylous, being linked at the base to roughly as far as the middle of the second phalanx and thus forming a "shovel", somewhat like the three front digits of kingfishers. In both cases, this feature may perform a useful function during the excavation of nest-holes (see Breeding). The galbulids show a tendency towards digit reduction. In the genus *Brachygalba*, the first digit, or hallux, is vestigial, while in the Three-toed Jacamar, the sole member of the genus *Jacamaralcyon*, the hallux is entirely absent, the fourth digit remaining as the only hind toe. In the latter genus, the first metacarpal, equivalent to the thumb, is well developed.

The colour of galbulid soft parts is often diagnostic, but can also be confusingly variable. For example, the iris of *Galbalcyrhynchus* is coral-red, while that of the four *Brachygalba* species is sometimes red, but may also be whitish or strikingly light blue, seemingly enamelled. The Three-toed Jacamar has dark brown irides, although they are often spotted or entirely

yellowish-brown or red. It has been suggested that, in this last species at least, eye colour develops in tandem with age, but this has not yet been proven. Variability in this characteristic requires further study in order to elucidate its correlates. In contrast, the eyes of *Galbula* and *Jacamerops* are usually dark brown, sometimes paler or warmer brown, but never strikingly pale or bright. Jacamars tend to have a rather large area of bare skin in the orbital and loral region that is usually blackish, greyish or brownish, although it is also occasionally brightly coloured. In the Yellow-billed Jacamar, for example, it is conspicuously yellow, and in *Galbalcyrhynchus* it is pinkish-red. Bill coloration adheres to a similar pattern of variation: most species have a black bill, while that of the Yellow-billed Jacamar is yellow and that of *Galbalcyrhynchus* is pinkish-red. A pale bill is also found in the White-throated Jacamar (*Brachygalba albogularis*) and in some subspecies of the Brown Jacamar.

The plumage of *Galbula* and *Jacamerops* is colourful, often with rich rufous on the tail and underparts and with an iridescent or metallic sheen, chiefly of green, blue or bronze, on the upperparts and the breast. The long bill and glossy plumage prompted early naturalists to associate galbulids with kingfishers, and these brightly plumaged jacamars also recall overgrown hummingbirds in shape and coloration. Some jacamar species, however, principally those in the genus *Brachygalba* and the related *Jacamaralcyon*, are much more dull. These tend to be dark brown with white patches, and only hints of gloss and colour. The sexes of all jacamars generally display only minor dimorphism, the females often being slightly duller than the males, particularly on the abdomen, and they are most readily identified by the throat colour. Males tend to have a conspicuous patch of white on the throat that is replaced by a buffy or rufescent patch on females, a difference already apparent in the young prior to fledging. Immatures are often duller still, in addition to which they retain a distinctly shorter bill for several months after fledging. Furthermore, in species with bright soft-part coloration, the colours tend to be less bright on young birds. Apart from these differences, there is usually no distinct juvenile plumage pattern and, consequently, jacamars can be quite difficult to age.

Interestingly, immature Pale-headed Jacamars (*Brachygalba goeringi*) appear to be more colourful than their parents, espe-

Blue-necked Jacamars and Yellow-billed Jacamars (Galbula albirostris) *are closely related galbulids that are easily recognized by their striking emerald-green upperparts and extensively yellow bill. The lower mandible is completely yellow in both species, but in Blue-necked Jacamars the upper mandible ranges from completely black to mostly yellow, as in this bird. Some authors treat these taxa as a single species, but intergrades are unknown in the potential zone of overlap in eastern Peru. The specific epithet of the Yellow-billed Jacamar means "white bill," which suggests that the type specimen's bill had perhaps faded prior to examination by scientists.*

[Galbula cyanicollis, *Imperatriz, Maranhão, Brazil. Photo: Haroldo Palo, Jr.*]

All jacamars occupy wooded habitats, primarily lowland or riparian forest, and they seldom occur at elevations above 1000 m. Most species favour the edge or the canopy of the forest rather than the interior or the understorey. Pale-headed Jacamars conform with this general trend and tend to occupy the drier end of the habitat spectrum, being found at the edge of second-growth and gallery forest and in open woodland and savanna. They often perch conspicuously on bare branches, where they may be readily visible to aerial predators; this may explain their sombre plumage, an aid in camouflage.

[*Brachygalba goeringi*, Mesa de Cavacas, Guanare, Portuguesa, Venezuela. Photo: Benjamín Busto]

cially on the upperparts, where they are quite strongly glossed with green. It has been suggested that, since ontogeny generally accords with phylogeny, the bright plumage of immatures implies a bright ancestor, and that sombre plumage is a more recent adaptation. It has been speculated that ancestral *Brachygalba* might have ascended from the lower-stratum foraging niche of *Galbula* and adopted prominent perches on the treetops and open boughs of the canopy, where they perhaps proved more vulnerable to the depredations of raptors. Hence, they evolved more subtly coloured plumage as camouflage.

Habitat

The jacamar family is exclusively Neotropical, occurring from southern Mexico to southern Brazil. Records of the Rufous-tailed Jacamar from Argentina, including a lost specimen, remain unconfirmed and are, therefore, treated as provisional. Within this general range, jacamars are absent from all but a few associated islands.

Galbulids are principally arboreal, resorting to other habitats only when nesting. As a result of this, all are associated with more or less wooded habitats, 13 of the 18 species being found in the Amazon Basin and 15 occurring in Brazil. Underlying this distributional trend is the predilection of many species for lowland or riverine forest, although within this general habitat they occupy a broad variety of niches, from the understorey to the upper canopy, and from forest edge to deep forest. The presence of banks, termitaria or the exposed bases of uprooted trees for nesting is presumably vital. Most jacamars are species of low altitudes, or the nearby foothills, which they tend to ascend to 600 m, occasionally 1000 m or, rarely, 1300 m. Only the Coppery-chested Jacamar preferentially frequents higher altitudes in the submontane zone of the Andes, where its presence has been confirmed at localities lying between 600 m and 1600 m, although most often at 1000-1300 m.

Despite the marked association of all jacamars with woodland and forest, the Great and Yellow-billed Jacamars are perhaps the only galbulids regularly encountered within these habitats. Most members of the family are restricted almost exclusively to the edge or the canopy of forest. The Rufous-tailed Jacamar, for example, prefers forest borders, treefalls, streamsides and scrubby second growth near forest, although it does occur locally inside undisturbed forest. Alternatively, the Paradise Jacamar and the Bronzy Jacamar tend to perch almost solely on bare branches in the canopy, and they do so regardless of the canopy height, which may be anything from 2 m to 50 m. Unlike the puffbirds, which are notoriously unobtrusive in their behaviour, the jacamars are conspicuous by nature, which allows one to be relatively certain that the predominance of records of these birds at forest edge reflects real ecological patterns. At the same time, however, the preponderance of sightings of canopy-frequenting species at edges and gaps in forest is doubtless due in part to the greater ease with which they are detected when thus situated.

Ten species of jacamar are associated strictly with humid forest and its borders. The Rufous-tailed Jacamar, apart from its northern subspecies *melanogenia*, does not, however, fall within this category, as it also inhabits scrubby deciduous cactus-rich woodland along the Caribbean coasts of Venezuela and Colombia, wooded *llanos*, savannas, and dry *cerrado* and *caatinga* woodlands in Brazil. All *Brachygalba* and *Jacamaralcyon* species occur in highly patchy habitats and are not really linked to humid forest at all. For example, the southern race *melanosterna* of the Brown Jacamar occupies the dry central Brazilian tableland, avoiding humid habitat to the north, while the Three-toed Jacamar inhabits drier, vine-entangled woodland and forest patches in south-western Brazil, generally shunning nearby tracts of humid Atlantic Forest.

Similarly, ten species of galbulid show a preference for riverine or lacustrine vegetation in at least parts of their range. The scarce White-throated Jacamar is apparently restricted to riparian regrowth and river islands in the lowlands of eastern Brazil and Peru. The Bluish-fronted Jacamar, the Purus Jacamar and the White-eared Jacamar are often found around oxbow lakes or along Amazonian rivers, and even the widespread Rufous-tailed Jacamar shows a distinct association with riverine forest, this being especially so in the case of the subspecies *melanogenia* of Central America. In addition, many jacamar species frequent the borders or interior of the cyclically flooded forest known as *várzea*, and at least two of these, the Yellow-billed and Great Jacamars, also occur in permanently flooded forest, or *igapó*. According to H. Sick, the Blue-necked Jacamar (*Galbula cyanicollis*), along with the Green-and-rufous Kingfisher (*Chloroceryle inda*), occupies *várzea* in the Belém area of northern Brazil only when these forests are flooded twice daily by tides.

The association of jacamars with watercourses and successional habitats is reflected in the fact that, in primary forest, the distribution of the latter is related to that of the former. The course of large Amazonian rivers is in constant flux, as the waters regularly drift across their floodplains for more than 25 m each year. These constantly shifting river channels cut back forest on the outer side of meanders, leaving bare alluvial deposits in their wake. On these deposits, vegetation proceeds through a roughly 300-year sequence of relatively well-defined stages, at the end of which stands mature rainforest. In an attempt to clarify the importance of these regenerating riverine forests for birds, S. Robinson and J. Terborgh studied the dynamics of an avian community along the River Manu, in Peru. They found that Bluish-fronted Jacamars generally avoided early successional stages, characterized by, for example, monocultures of *Tessaria integrefolia*, followed by stands of the cane *Gynerium sagittatum*, and then by gap-loving trees such as *Cecropia*; populations were most dense, with 13 territories per 100 ha, in mid-successional stages with a mixed canopy and *Ficus/Cedrela* forest, and became less dense again, at three territories in 100 ha, in mature floodplain-forest. This pattern was repeated by the less abundant Purus Jacamar. These two galbulids, along with a suite of other species, were most abundant in relatively narrow bands of successional forest created by fluctuating river courses, a fact that has important implications for the assessment and conservation of bird populations.

At many Amazonian localities, between four and six species of jacamar co-exist. Most of them are remarkably similar in their dietary requirements and foraging methods, and it appears that they are able to achieve this sympatry by means of a rough partitioning of the habitat among them. For example, north of Manaus, in Brazil, the Yellow-billed Jacamar generally occupies the understorey, mid-levels and edge of primary and secondary forest. The Great Jacamar inhabits the same forests, but largely avoiding secondary formations, and most often frequenting middle levels and the lower canopy. The Paradise Jacamar, meanwhile, is a supracanopy species, foraging from emergent bare boughs high above the ground. A fourth species, the Bronzy Jacamar, tends to perch on top of second growth, scrub and lower-stature sandy forest. By foraging in different places, they minimize competition for resources. Similarly, C. H. Fry found that four galbulids living alongside each other in Minas Gerais, in south-eastern Brazil, "avoided competing by favouring different habitats"; these were the Bronzy, Brown, Paradise and Rufous-tailed Jacamars. Niche separation by habitat selection is thus one factor that allows increased jacamar diversity. Another factor is diet, one example of which is provided by the Yellow-billed Jacamar and the Great Jacamar. These two species sometimes forage at similar heights in forest, but, with their morphologically dissimilar bills, they target insects of different sizes and types and are therefore less likely to impinge on each other's success.

More often than not, however, the diet and the habitat selection of related jacamars overlap so extensively that sympatry is precluded. This is the case in upper Amazonia, where the ranges of the White-chinned Jacamar and the Bluish-fronted Jacamar meet abruptly in continuous forest; there is no overlap in the ranges of the two species, and no interbreeding between them. Where habitat is less continuous in the contact zone of related species, they may exhibit locally divergent habitat preferences. The Green-tailed Jacamar usually occupies a niche similar to that exploited by the Rufous-tailed Jacamar, and the two usually exclude each other in areas where they come into contact. In a small area of Guyana, however, they are reported to be sympatric and apparently ecologically separated, with the Green-tailed frequenting riverine habitat and hilly areas, and the Rufous-tailed Jacamar being associated with extensive isolated savannas. At the same time, it should be noted that this apparent ecological separation was questioned by G. F. Mees, who found the Green-tailed Jacamar only on inland savannas in Guyana.

The tolerance of disturbance and of man-modified habitats shown by most jacamar species is presumably a result of their preference for edge habitats. In some parts of its range the Rufous-tailed Jacamar occurs in leafy suburban gardens, and the Purus Jacamar has been seen on roadside wires in settled areas. The Three-toed Jacamar has been recorded around busy picnic spots and tiny, highly degraded woodlots (see Status and Conservation).

General Habits

The Galbulidae are almost entirely diurnal. Nevertheless, according to Sick, the Rufous-tailed Jacamar apparently forages in near-darkness on occasion, disclosing its activities by tapping prey loudly against a branch. Fifteen species, the great majority of the family, are most often encountered as singletons or pairs, and less frequently as trios or small groups, the last possibly being family parties. The remaining three, the White-eared, Purus and Three-toed Jacamars, almost always forage and apparently also breed in groups of four to six individuals, with up to ten sometimes recorded. The composition of these groups and the kinship within them are unknown. The nineteenth-century chronicles of J. Natterer, usually a scrupulously accurate observer, contain a reference to one flock of around 30 Brown Jacamars on the banks of the Rio Grande in Minas Gerais, Brazil. Whatever the reason for this unusual congregation, no similarly large gathering has been reported since. Although gregariousness is rare among jacamars, some species, such as the Yellow-billed Jacamar, frequently troop with antwren (*Myrmotherula*) flocks or follow mixed-species foraging parties in the lower storey of rainforest, and this is a habit occasionally indulged in also by, for instance, the Rufous-tailed Jacamar. Other galbulids, including the Bronzy and the Paradise Jacamars, regularly associate with mixed flocks in the canopy, and the Rufous-tailed Jacamar is again one of several species that occasionally do so.

For much of the day, jacamars habitually perch motionless between foraging flights, like the puffbirds. They sometimes remain still for long periods of time, moving only the head, but they are, nevertheless, considerably more active than puffbirds. They make much more rapid side-to-side movements of the head, hence appearing far more alert, and they tend to call and to make aerial sorties much more frequently. The head movements of the smaller galbulids, such as the Green-tailed Jacamar, tend to be much more rapid than those of the Paradise Jacamar or the Great Jacamar. One Three-toed Jacamar moved its head rapidly, at a rate of about 84 movements per minute, while looking for prey. When perching, most species appear to direct their attention obliquely upwards, holding the bill at a jaunty angle of about 45°. Paradise Jacamars tend to carry the bill at a slightly shallower angle, perhaps 20°; this is probably because they perch at greater heights, and prey animals are therefore more often level with or lower than the bird itself. At least some species, including the Great Jacamar, have the habit of about-facing rapidly, suddenly switching the direction of their view. A single perch, or cluster of perches, may be used continuously for up to an hour.

The flight of jacamars is usually swift, darting and fairly brief when chasing prey or switching perches. Long distances are sometimes covered, however, when moving between foraging patches or escaping danger, and at these times the birds fly with bursts of rapid wingbeats interspersed with sailing glides, such that their progress can appear erratic or undulating.

Little is on record regarding the comfort behaviour of the family. Head-scratching is apparently performed by the indirect method, the leg being brought over the wing. Interestingly, this is in contrast to the Bucconidae, which employ the direct method in which the leg is raised beneath the wing. The Galbulidae, as most other birds, clean the bill frequently by wiping it on a branch, although sometimes they use the feet, too. The Rufous-tailed Jacamar is often observed dust-bathing on dirt or gravel roads, but there appear to be no confirmed records of sunning by any members of this family.

Roosting takes place in burrows, at least in the case of some galbulid species. Groups of Three-toed Jacamars, for example, roost communally in burrow systems, all group-members assisting in the digging of these. The burrows are usually sited in situations similar to those used for nests, in banks 0·8-6 m high. Two such roosting cavities were 62-72 cm deep, 6-9 cm high and 6 cm wide. It is not known whether nesting by this species takes place in cavities previously used for roosting, but this is perhaps likely. It is, however, certain that Three-toed Jacamar chicks, once they have fledged, return to the nesting cavity for nocturnal roosting, sometimes accompanied by adults. Similarly, a family of two adult and four juvenile Pale-headed Jacamars used its

With its streamlined body, needle-like bill, and elongated central tail feathers, the Paradise Jacamar is distinctive enough to have warranted placement in its own genus, Urogalba, prior to being moved to its present position in Galbula. The four currently accepted races exhibit subtle differences in size and plumage coloration that may only represent variation through a cline. During the early taxonomic history of the Galbulidae, this species played a central role in the mistaken notion that jacamars were kingfishers (Alcedinidae). Indeed, as the first galbulid known to science, the Paradise Jacamar received the name "Swallow-tailed Kingfisher" in 1743, and was later placed in the kingfisher genus Alcedo by Linnaeus. From the mid-nineteenth century onwards, jacamars and puffbirds (Bucconidae) have been recognized as close relatives, and often considered to be allied to one or another family within either the Coraciiformes or the Piciformes. In the last decade or so, however, jacamars and puffbirds have increasingly been separated in their own order, Galbuliformes, based on a combination of morphological, DNA-DNA hybridization and electrophoretic studies.

[*Galbula dea amazonum*, Cristalino Jungle Lodge, Mato Grosso, Brazil. Photo: Edson Endrigo]

nest-burrow as a dormitory for at least two months after the chicks had fledged. The young tended to enter the hole around 1·5 hours before darkness fell, with the adults entering later. The dual use of the burrow by this species, and the greater number of individual birds which it must accommodate, can perhaps explain why the burrow itself is about twice as long as the nest-burrow of the Rufous-tailed Jacamar, a species that appears never to use the nest as a family roosting site after fledging. The use of nest-holes for roosting has never been recorded for the puffbirds, the single other family in the Galbuliformes, although this may be a reflection of the limited amount of field study which the Bucconidae have received. Among the Piciformes, a better-known order, it is a common habit of woodpeckers, certain barbets (Capitonidae) and toucans.

Jacamars are highly sedentary animals that defend resources within a multi-purpose territory occupied by a pair or a group. At least in the case of breeding Rufous-tailed Jacamars, these territories appear to be rather small, as foraging adults are almost always within view from the vicinity of the nest. Antagonistic interactions sometimes occur as a result of competition for mates, territories and nest-sites. Disputes between males of the Rufous-tailed Jacamar tend to involve sustained bouts of loud complex singing, sometimes with aggressive dashes by one bird towards another, but real physical contact is rare. Although the male is apparently the more aggressive, both sexes contribute to territory defence. Pairs of Rufous-tailed Jacamars, for example, have been observed co-operating in order to repel other hole-nesters from the vicinity of active nests. One instance of this was witnessed in Venezuela, where Southern Rough-winged Swallows (Stelgidopteryx ruficollis) were "violently attacked and driven off", as were Blue-crowned Motmots. The hirundine does at least occasionally breed in cavities excavated by jacamars, although it is not known whether it ever succeeds in usurping the occupants or merely uses abandoned nests. Given the formidable weapon of the jacamar's bill, the latter seems the more likely. Indeed, jacamars sometimes use the bill with some ferocity during aggressive encounters with conspecifics, as has been recorded in captivity for species of Galbula. Moreover, when two groups of Purus Jacamars, each containing five individuals, interacted aggressively at Cocha Cashu, in Peru, four of the birds were seen to lock bills and pull back and forth, while the remaining six perched and sang at close range.

Voice

Disregarding the unusual voice of the Great Jacamar, the most common jacamar vocalizations consist of single, high call notes that are often given liberally throughout the day, either from a perch or in flight, and which are audible at long range. The call of the Rufous-tailed Jacamar, for example, is a frequently repeated "peeup" or "peee", usually terminating abruptly; it is uttered by both sexes, and is sometimes repeated three to ten times in succession. A very rapid trill is also occasionally given by that species. Similar sharp foraging calls are emitted by all Galbula species for which information is available, these alternatives being described as "quep" for the Coppery-chested Jacamar, "keelip" for the White-chinned Jacamar, and so on. These calls are essentially similar throughout the genus, as is the tendency for them to be delivered in series, sometimes so rapidly that trills are produced. The smaller Brachygalba species give analogous single calls. That of the Pale-headed Jacamar is transcribed as "weet", while the call of the Dusky-backed Jacamar (Brachygalba salmoni) is written as "feet", that of the Brown Jacamar as "chewee" and the White-throated Jacamar's call as "psueet". Again, these calls are similar for all four members of the genus, but they are distinctly different in quality from Galbula calls, being weaker, thinner, and more plaintive or upslurred. Similarly, they are given in series when excited, and then develop in some cases into an insect-like trill. The call of the Three-toed Jacamar is a clipped "churr", and that of the White-eared Jacamar is a loud "kyew".

Some jacamars are remarkable among non-passerine birds for their elaborate, protracted songs. According to A. F. Skutch,

male Rufous-tailed Jacamars are capable of singing "so splendidly that few true songbirds (Oscines) could surpass them". The delivery varies in tempo, with slow drawn-out notes accelerating into melodious or chuckling trills, ascending in pitch until very high notes are reached, whereupon slow notes are resumed. This sequence is interspersed with twittering and a low, nasal "bee-bee-bee". These impressive performances can last for several minutes, but they are much less frequently heard than are the usual calls. Similar song types are also part of the vocal repertoire of Brachygalba species. A singing Pale-headed Jacamar, for example, gives the usual short call in a rapid series that accelerates in pace and ascends in tone, ending in a sharp trill. When the bird is excited, this sequence is sometimes uttered repeatedly, resulting in an undulating series of sharp crescendos, twitters and high, thin trills. At these times, the jacamar turns its body rapidly from side to side, and jerks the tail at each syllable, or flicks it up and down rhythmically, as if beating time.

The general pattern of vocalizations given by those two species is repeated, so far as is known, by all members of their respective genera. There appears to be a continuum between low-intensity calls and high-intensity peeping, trilling, twittering and tail-flicking. At the lowest intensity, a single sharp note is emitted, this being the standard foraging or contact call. This is sometimes extended into a series when the individual is excited, and, when this excitement increases still further to stimulate song, the series is either given in crescendo or is expanded to include a terminal high-pitched trill. At the far end of the spectrum is a variable and protracted medley of all different components of the repertoire; although this longer sequence is heard less frequently, it incorporates calls given singly, in level series and in ascending series, mixed with high, thin trills and extra ornamentations such as protracted notes and low buzzy notes. Jacamar vocalizations can thus be viewed as a continuous hierarchy of elements based on simple sounds, rather than the more dichotomous pattern, found among many passerines, of simple call notes on the one hand and very different complex songs on the other.

It appears that, in the genera Brachygalba and Galbula, complex songs are given only by males. They sometimes countersing at close range to each other in disputes over mates or territories, each apparently trying to match or to better the other's efforts with sheer volume and repertoire size. Group vocalizations in which both sexes take part are a feature of the more gregarious jacamars. While the song of an individual Three-toed Jacamar is a modest sequence of short, relatively weak whistles, the complex group song lasts for up to 20 seconds and involves various shrill ascending whistles, apparently uttered by up to six birds simultaneously. In groups of the White-eared Jacamar and the Purus Jacamar, the individual members also combine their vocalizations in order to increase the overall volume and complexity of the sound, especially during interactions with neighbouring groups.

The three most aberrant galbulids in terms of morphology appear also to have the most divergent vocalizations. The Great Jacamar sings at long intervals with an unusual long, high-pitched, hawk-like whistle, first rising and then falling in pitch, but it is otherwise rather silent. The White-eared Jacamar gives a prolonged rising trill, presumably the song, which is reminiscent of the voice of a woodcreeper (Dendrocolaptidae); it also utters very loud single "kyew" or "cue" calls, these accelerating into a chatter when excited. The Purus Jacamar gives a descending "peeeur" whistle and a sharp "pee".

Unlike passerines, which rarely sing before fledging, nestling Rufous-tailed Jacamars develop songs like those of the adults and can be heard trilling and calling regularly and for long periods. These vocalizations emanating from the nest are audible from some distance, at least 21 m, and the young jacamars, when they are about two weeks old, often emit them almost throughout the day. Interestingly, observations at the nest of a pair of Pale-headed Jacamars suggested that the nestlings were far less vocal, only rarely trilling when the adults appeared at the cavity entrance.

When held in the hand, jacamars produce a bill-snapping sound with the mandibles.

Of the 18 species of Galbulidae, fifteen are decidedly non-social and are typically encountered as singletons or in pairs. Larger parties, consisting of perhaps three or four individuals, often prove to be family members. Thus, this group of four Brown Jacamars may rightly consist of two parents and their progeny from the latest breeding attempt. A nineteenth-century report by a reputable observer of 30 Brown Jacamars in a flock in Minas Gerais, Brazil, is a mystery in that no such concentrations have been encountered since. Several species, including Yellow-billed (Galbula albirostris), Rufous-tailed (Galbula ruficauda), Bronzy (Galbula leucogastra) and Paradise Jacamars (Galbula dea), are known to join mixed-species foraging flocks in the forest canopy or at army ant swarms.

[Brachygalba lugubris caquetae, El Tuparro National Park, Colombia. Photos: Otto Pfister]

Food and Feeding

With the sole exception of the Great Jacamar, all jacamars are exclusively insectivorous. Their diets consist almost entirely of winged prey, caught in flight. They usually operate from temporarily favoured perches upon which they wait passively for insects to fly within range. On sighting appropriate prey, the jacamar embarks on a swift, darting flight which, once the prey is caught, with an audible click of the mandibles, switches to a sweeping glide. This is often followed by a return to the same perch, or a nearby one, where the insect is beaten and consumed. The clicking sound is all the more audible when the target is missed, and the mandibles then snap shut without obstruction. Aerial pursuits are often spectacular, aerobatic and prolonged, and at such times the jacamar is even more unwary than usual, sometimes flying within a metre of an observer.

The Paradise Jacamar tends to forage from high, exposed perches in the canopy, from which, after having sighted flying prey, it executes a dive. There is some evidence to suggest that it favours flowering trees so that it can capture the bees and beetles that visit the flowers. The dive is followed by a swift pursuit with rapid and agile changes of direction. Less frequently, foraging flights are made directly upwards towards insects flying overhead. After capturing the prey item, the bird returns to a perch with an undulating flight, changing perches after about 50% of forays. During a five-hour period of observation, foraging flights made by this species covered distances ranging from 1 m to 12 m, and were mostly 4·5-9 m; the flights were generally of short duration, lasting 1·3-5·6 seconds, with an average of 3·2 seconds. The frequency of forays was calculated at 21·8 per hour,

a considerably higher rate of foraging flights than that recorded for the Swallow-winged Puffbird, the only aerial insectivore among the bucconids.

As other jacamars tend to sit lower down in vegetation, they perhaps exhibit a greater frequency of upward flights than does the Paradise Jacamar. Further, the activity rates appear to be higher among the smaller galbulids, such as the Green-tailed Jacamar, with foraging flights perhaps twice as frequent, at around 40 per hour, although the distance and duration of flights are possibly less.

Perches selected by jacamars tend to be in rather open positions, such as bare or dead branches offering good all-round vision. The Rufous-tailed Jacamar has been reported as stationing itself above rotting fruit on the forest floor, apparently taking advantage of the numerous butterflies and dipteran flies attracted to this food source. In addition, three Purplish Jacamars encountered in eastern Ecuador were reported as all being perched on the nests of bees (Apidae), although whether they were foraging on the bees was not clear. Equally, it is conceivable that these reported nests were actually misidentified arboreal termitaria in which the jacamars were nesting, but this seems unlikely. A more plausible explanation is that jacamars occasionally position themselves near the nests of bees or social wasps (Vespidae) and harvest the regular supply of flying adults.

The usual victims of foraging forays are soft-bodied species of butterfly and moth (Lepidoptera), dragonflies (Odonata), wasps, bees and flying ants (Hymenoptera), flies (Diptera), beetles (Coleoptera), and various bugs (Hemiptera) including homopterans such as cicadas (Cicadidae). It should be noted that, while large and spectacular prey are sometimes caught, the vast majority of food items are tiny insects. Only flying individuals of prey animals are pursued, the same species being entirely ignored when they are perched on nearby vegetation. There is a single anomalous record of a female Rufous-tailed Jacamar emerging from a half-built burrow with a grub in her bill that she proceeded to eat. The only regular exception to the rule concerns the Great Jacamar, which often makes wing-whirring dashes to snatch prey from foliage, rather than catching aerial insects. The foraging behaviour of this galbulid is more akin to that of puffbirds, trogons and motmots.

Of several hundred pursuits by Rufous-tailed Jacamars observed in Costa Rica, about 40% resulted in the insect's escape. This often happens because the bird grasps a butterfly's wings, rather than any substantial part of the insect's body. Indeed, one of the commonest forms of damage to the wings recorded on living butterflies in Costa Rica was apparently the unique snips made by jacamars, resembling the marks left by a forceps-like instrument. After a successful foray, the jacamar beats the prey item against a branch or other hard perch to kill it, and to break off the wings or more resistant chitinous parts, before swallowing the food, although such treatment is not necessary for small soft-bodied dipterans. Favoured perches of jacamars can thus be identified by the brilliant carpet of butterfly wings littering the ground below. Even though the wings of large-winged prey are usually knocked off before consumption, butterflies are sometimes swallowed, or carried to the nestlings, with the wings still attached. The amount of beating delivered to each food item is generally in direct proportion to the size and toughness of the individual prey, but it is often less than that carried out by other insectivores. Indeed, galbulids regularly consume social wasps without beating them at all, which suggests that the jacamars may have some immunity to the stings of vespids. Moreover, in five hours of observation of foraging Paradise Jacamars, the wiping of wasps back and forth against a branch to devenom them, a practice frequently undertaken by bee-eaters, was observed only once.

So far as is known, all jacamar species regularly regurgitate pellets containing the indigestible chitinous parts of insects. Analysis of these pellets can sometimes help to determine the kinds of prey animals being eaten by these birds.

The proportions of different prey types selected by jacamars vary among species, and apparently even within species accord-ing to site and season. In Mato Grosso, in south-central Brazil, the diet of breeding Rufous-tailed Jacamars, as calculated by pellet analysis and the contents of nestlings' gizzards, report-edly comprised 86% Hymenoptera, 10% Coleoptera, 2% Odonata, 1·2% Lepidoptera, and tiny proportions of Hemiptera and Orthoptera. A study of the same species in Central America, however, revealed that Odonata and Lepidoptera predominated in the diet. How might these differences arise? From observa-tions in Costa Rica, Sherry reported that Lepidoptera and Odonata were frequently recorded in the diet of breeding birds, but were less commonly taken outside that season, and it has been postu-lated that large-bodied insects are favoured during the breeding period because they are easy to transport to nestlings. Other fieldworkers repeatedly recount that small insects are certainly eaten immediately, rather than being carried to the brood. When nestlings are only four days old, they have been seen to be given dragonfly bodies as long as the chicks themselves. This prefer-ence for provisioning large items is not surprising when one re-alizes that prey items are brought one at a time to nestlings, a strategy unlike that of passerines, which often return from for-ays with the beak crammed full of items. Nevertheless, it should be borne in mind that dietary information derived from nest watches will probably exaggerate the proportion of butterflies and dragonflies in the diet, as such items, being large, are more easily identifiable.

Although this notion of a preference for larger insects when breeding is contradicted by the Brazilian data, and also by the fact that large quantities of euglossine bees have been found at some burrows in Central America, it could be that at least some of the items identified in those instances involved food regur-gitated by adults rather than fed to nestlings. It is also possible that Lepidoptera, because of their more digestible body parts, are less frequently identified in pellet remains, although their wing scales might be conspicuous. While differences in study methods could therefore underlie apparent differences in diet, variation in dietary preference doubtless reflects differences in prey abundance between separate sites, as well as between sea-sons and between habitats. For example, stomachs of Yellow-billed Jacamars from near Manaus, in Brazil, examined by M. Cohn-Haft, usually contained no winged termites (Isoptera), but at times some were completely packed with them. This sug-

Jacamars catch insects in aerial sallies launched from an exposed perch. They feed almost exclusively on flying insects and will ignore suitable prey types that are present on nearby vegetation or on the ground. The feeding ecology of the Rufous-tailed Jacamar has been well studied in several parts of its range. This individual has captured a large dragonfly and beaten it against a branch to render it immobile and also to remove its wings before swallowing it. Along with butterflies and moths, dragonflies make up the bulk of this species' diet in Central America, especially during the breeding season.

[*Galbula ruficauda melanogenia*, Corcovado National Park, Costa Rica. Photo: Doug Wechsler/ VIREO]

gests that, when a hatch occurs, the resultant abundant food source is harvested enthusiastically.

Lepidoptera species are not randomly selected. Jacamars appear to target butterflies which have a bulky abdomen, such as skippers (Hesperiidae), and they are capable of capturing very large Neotropical butterflies, such as those in the genera *Morpho*, *Caligo* and *Papilio*. The relationship between abdomen size of butterflies and the dietary preferences of jacamars is, however, somewhat circular, as palatable butterflies tend to have much larger flight muscles than do unpalatable species, a characteristic that enables them to escape from predators more efficiently. In other words, their relative body size is perhaps a result of predation pressure rather than a cause of it.

A more intractable relationship concerns the avoidance of noxious prey. Many butterflies contain toxins or other repellent substances, usually derived from host plants, which render them unpalatable. Research has shown that galbulids are adept at quickly recognizing a surprisingly large number of unpalatable species, presumably through experience of their foul flavour coupled with their characteristic vivid markings. In Costa Rica, the Rufous-tailed Jacamar has been recorded as catching and then rejecting many unpalatable butterflies, including, among others, *Battus polydamas*, *Catagramma buguba*, *Eueides lybia*, *Nessaea aglaura* and *Perrhybris pyrrha*. Most frequently, these species are able to escape after brief detention in the jacamar's bill, reaping the benefit of their noxious nature, and they are thereafter usually ignored by this galbulid. The relative safety experienced by these insects is increased the more distinctive they are, and most of them have therefore evolved aposematic coloration; in other words, they have acquired extremely bright and distinctive patterns which help jacamars to identify these lepidopterans before attacking them. These distinctive patterns are mimicked in their turn by palatable butterflies in response to the selective pressure of jacamar foraging behaviour: those individuals most resembling aposematically coloured species receive the same benefits as do the latter, resulting, after many generations, in identical lookalikes. In general, palatable butterflies fly rapidly and erratically, while those with aposematic patterning fly more slowly and directly. This situation probably develops partly as a signalling system by which jacamars recognize noxious prey, although non-noxious mimics tend to fly like their models rather than like their relatives, but also partly through relaxed predation pressure on such butterflies. In effect, jacamars in Costa Rica targeted almost exclusively those butterflies that were the most cryptic and the most difficult to catch. As one of the few animal groups to specialize in the hunting of butterflies in flight, the Galbulidae are quite possibly the most powerful factor driving the evolution of these fantastically accurate mimicry complexes so often observed in Neotropical butterflies.

Much interesting research into this system has been conducted by P. Chai in Costa Rica, involving both wild and captive Rufous-tailed Jacamars. The birds generally attacked palatable butterflies rapidly, especially when they were hungry. Unpalatable species tended to be ignored unless the jacamars were deprived of food for a few hours, after which time their reluctance to take noxious prey diminished. One palatable species, *Consul fabius*, has an upperwing pattern that almost exactly mimics the coloration of the noxious *Heliconius ismenius*, and an underwing pattern that closely resembles a dead leaf. Its appearance in flight is determined by its upperwings, and these are consequently designed to deter jacamars by masquerading as the wings of a poisonous insect. At the same time, as *Consul fabius* is totally safe from jacamars when perched, but is then vulnerable to countless other watchful insectivores, adaptive forces have operated to maximize crypsis rather than aposematic coloration when the insect is resting.

Analysis of the stomach contents of the White-eared Jacamar, a species with a relatively short, robust, dagger-like bill, has revealed that it feeds primarily on wasps and bees. This is quite surprising in view of its bill morphology, which was assumed by Burton to denote a preference for large or hard-bodied prey. The Great Jacamar is much more sluggish than its relatives, tending to remain motionless on its mid-level perch in forest for several minutes at a time, and then making a short

Jacamars feed on a wide variety of insects, most of which are apparently small, soft-bodied species. Typical prey items include butterflies and moths (Lepidoptera), bees, wasps and flying ants (Hymenoptera), dragonflies (Odonata), beetles (Coleoptera), flies (Diptera), and winged termites (Isoptera). Results of feeding studies may vary depending on the techniques employed by researchers. For example, a small prey item, like that caught by this Rufous-tailed Jacamar, might be eaten immediately rather than transported to the nest, and would thus be missed during a nest watch. Similarly, soft-bodied prey types that are easily digested whole might well be underestimated in studies based on pellet analysis.

[*Galbula ruficauda melanogenia*, Braulio Carrillo National Park, Costa Rica. Photo: Kevin Schafer]

sally, more often than not ending in a move to a different perch. As this large galbulid tends to glean prey that is perched on leaves, rather than taking flying insects, it has a slightly broader, shorter bill than that possessed by most other jacamars. This is thought to be a secondary character, as in all other details of its feeding-apparatus morphology this species closely resembles other galbulids (see Morphological Aspects). The Great Jacamar is one of very few galbulids known to consume non-insect prey, having been recorded taking spiders and even small reptiles, such as lizards, on occasion.

Different members of the family have responded to competition with other jacamar species by occupying ecologically separate foraging niches that allow them to live in sympatry. In general, predominantly bright green species, such as the Rufous-tailed Jacamar, hunt at low levels on forest edges and, to a lesser extent, within forest. The Paradise Jacamar and the Brown Jacamar, meanwhile, exploit the space above the canopy, perching on emergent boughs and dead branches at the tops of trees. Between these strata lies the mid-storey, and this is occupied by species such as the Great Jacamar. In some places, this niche separation allows several species of jacamar to co-exist in the same forest (see Habitat).

Breeding

The study of breeding systems of Neotropical birds remains in its infancy for most groups, and the jacamars are no exception. Much of what is known of the breeding behaviour of the Galbulidae is due to the patient endeavour and careful observation of Skutch, who spent many hours sitting concealed near nests of the Rufous-tailed Jacamar, recording the visits of adults and the development of their progeny.

Jacamars usually breed as socially monogamous pairs, although some species apparently breed in co-operative groups of three to five individuals, and perhaps more. While *Galbula* species are generally monogamous, there is an unusual report of one female and two male Green-tailed Jacamars co-operating to build

Owing to toxins obtained from their food plants, many butterflies are unpalatable to birds. Rufous-tailed Jacamars, and perhaps other galbulids as well, recognize noxious species and modify their prey choice accordingly. They have been seen seizing and then quickly rejecting several species of toxic butterfly, which often escape with only minor injuries and subsequently are ignored by the birds. Noxious species tend to be brightly coloured and to fly more slowly and less erratically than do tasty species. Palatable mimics enjoy the same lack of attention from jacamars that is afforded to toxic species.

[Galbula ruficauda rufoviridis, Caratinga, Brazil. Photo: Janet Gorski]

a nest, suggesting that the mating system of these birds can occasionally be more complex. The Three-toed Jacamar is more habitually gregarious and may well form small breeding colonies, with up to 20 holes having been recorded in some earth banks. This species builds multiple-use burrows, catering for both roosting and breeding, and single individuals regularly participate in the digging of several burrows, although interpretation of this is complicated by the fact that nest-tunnels often have multiple entrances. Moreover, some burrows are constructed by more than two individuals, up to seven having been recorded in one case, although this might have involved a roosting cavity, and nonparent group-members apparently help to feed fledglings. In another group-living species, the Purus Jacamar, six individuals excavated a presumed nest-cavity in an arboreal termitary in Peru, but it was not discovered how many contributed to parental care. These two species, along with the White-eared Jacamar, are the most social members of the family, and further study is required to clarify the nature of their breeding systems. Certainly, if Three-toed Jacamars were indeed proved to breed colonially and cooperatively, with helpers at the nest, another remarkable behavioural link would be established with the bee-eaters, several species of which, such as the much-studied White-fronted Bee-eater (*Merops bullockoides*), have this social system.

The breeding season of galbulids is variable throughout the Neotropics, presumably according to patterns of rainfall and prey abundance. While it might be predicted that the timing of nesting should be synchronized with the onset of rains, and thus the emergence of many flying insects, this is not always the case. The Three-toed Jacamar appears to breed in south-east Brazil during the wettest period, whereas the Yellow-billed Jacamar is reported to breed in the dry season in the Guianas. Nest-building by Rufous-tailed Jacamars in Costa Rica often starts in February, in the middle of the dry season, although the rains usually arrive at the time when the nestlings are developing.

Courtship among jacamars involves bouts of singing and courtship feeding by the male, which frequently catches insects for his mate, diligently knocking off their wings before presenting them to her. During nest-building, Rufous-tailed Jacamars have been observed to perch side by side, the male bobbing his head up, down and sideways, swinging his tail up and down, and giving low squealing notes while the female trills. The two also perch alongside each other while fanning the tail and bowing together, in the manner of woodpeckers.

Jacamars breed in cavities which they dig into soft substrate. The nests of twelve species have been described. Those of seven species are known only from termitaria and those of three others only from earth banks, while the remaining two species are known to use both sites. No descriptions exist of the nests of the other six species of Galbulidae. Given the paucity of information available, it seems likely that most species will eventually be found to utilize both forms of nest-site. In all probability, however, the Paradise Jacamar nests exclusively in arboreal termitaria, as it is rarely seen below the canopy, and the Three-toed Jacamar only in earth banks, because few termitaria are large enough to accommodate colonies.

Those galbulids which excavate nest-holes in soil select vertical banks of varying size, from 30 cm to several metres in height, and usually of sand, clay or some other soft substance. In forest habitat these banks are normally situated alongside rivers, although, with the advent of trails and roads, they are often provided by the associated cuttings. More rarely, nests are sited in steep slopes or angled landslips, rather than in precipitous banks. In level forest where banks are unavailable, the Rufous-tailed Jacamar has been recorded nesting in soil lifted by the roots of a large fallen tree, provided that the attached earth is sufficiently deep. One advantage of such a site is that the gap created by the treefall is a favoured foraging habitat. Jacamars appear not to locate burrows according to the presence of concealing vegetation but, instead, to place more importance on the presence nearby of a handy perch and on an unobstructed flightpath to and from the hole. A few recorded nest-holes, including those of the Coppery-chested and the Rufous-tailed Jacamars, have been partially concealed behind overhanging vegetation, such as roots at the top of a bank. The Great Jacamar has been reported by native Amazonians to nest occasionally in rotting tree stumps, a habit which, although not unlikely, does require confirmation.

The use of arboreal and terrestrial termitaria has frequently been reported for several species of kingfisher, parrot and puffbird, among others. In level forest where banks are scarce, and also in the canopy, termitaria presumably provide a vital nest-site for jacamars, too. More surprisingly, the Rufous-tailed Jacamar has been recorded nesting in a termitarium even when a soil bank stood only a short distance away; in this case, the bank was dry and hard, and it is possible that, in such circumstances, termitaria are preferred because of their relative brittleness and ease of excavation. For some time an opposite view prevailed, its premise being that termitaria are often extremely hard and galbulid bills quite fragile, so that jacamars were in fact less likely to excavate their own nests in termitaria and more likely to utilize the cavities made by other animals. The dimensions of termitarium cavities occupied by galbulids were nevertheless suspiciously similar to jacamar holes in other sites. More recently, several species, such as the Purus, Green-tailed and Paradise Jacamars, have been directly observed as they excavated holes in termitaria, thereby establishing incontrovertibly that they are capable of performing this feat. Indeed, the Yellow-billed Jacamar, a small species with a fine bill, was watched in Surinam by G. F. Mees while it was "hacking" a hole in an arboreal termitarium. This description suggests that the bill is deceptively strong.

Nest-digging individuals use the bill to loosen soil or sand, or termitarium walls, a process during which their mandibles often become dirty while the plumage remains remarkably clean. Most debris is then removed by kicking with the small feet, which are modified into a shovel shape (see Morphological Aspects) perhaps for this very purpose, but the birds sometimes emerge from burrows with lumps of earth held between the mandibles. There is some indication that the mandibles may become damaged in the process of nest-construction. In museum collections of Three-toed Jacamars, along with a small mist-netted sample, significantly more females than males had broken bill tips, suggesting both that excavation might be undertaken more commonly by the female and that this might result in fracture of the mandible tips. It is difficult to confirm this hypothesis without empirical observations, and, moreover, gunshot is a frequent cause of bill damage in specimens. Conversely, Wetmore reported that Rufous-tailed Jacamars, despite their digging activities, exhibited a surprising lack of bill damage.

In one case, a Three-toed Jacamar was recorded with a very worn left foot, leading Sick to speculate that the species is predominantly left-footed when nest-building. More recent observations have suggested, however, that the feet are used alternately by this jacamar when clearing debris from the nest. While there is little further information on this topic, Skutch, in an account of a female Rufous-tailed Jacamar's nest-building behaviour, mentions that, in kicking earth backwards with her feet, she threw out "twin jets". This appears to imply that the feet were used simultaneously.

Both the male and the female contribute in digging, the little available information suggesting that the female performs the bulk of this task, at least in the early stages. In Central America, a female Rufous-tailed Jacamar performed almost all the digging at first, remaining in the nest-chamber for several minutes at a time; the male stood sentinel nearby, calling frequently and catching insects occasionally. After a day the male began short bouts of digging, each less than a minute in duration, and eventually he spent almost as much time in excavation work as did the female. Digging was undertaken almost throughout the day, during which time the female rarely caught food for herself. The male made up for his lower contribution to building by providing her with insects. When he caught these, he called to his mate from outside the burrow, whereupon she emerged to be fed. At first the birds came out of the hole tail first, but after a while the burrow was widened so that they could turn around inside it and emerge head first.

When completed, nest-cavities are generally long and narrow. Those of Rufous-tailed Jacamars are 29-50 cm long, 4-6 cm broad and 3·5-4·5 cm high, while a cavity of the smaller Pale-headed Jacamar measured 80 cm in length, 4 cm across and 3 cm in height. Cavities tend to be shorter when made amongst upturned roots and in termitaria, although no significant difference in dimensions has been shown. One entrance burrow made by a Rufous-tailed Jacamar in a small arboreal termitary, however, was only 6 cm long, with a full cavity length, including the nest-chamber, of 14 cm, while others, in larger terrestrial termitaria, have been up to 31 cm in length. Their dimensions are doubtless determined by the size and shape of the termitary. The longest galbulid burrow ever recorded is that of a Three-toed Jacamar, measured at 146 cm.

Burrows of the Rufous-tailed Jacamar, unless deflected by an obstruction, are usually straight, such that the nest-chamber is at least partially visible. Other burrows are reported to be curved upwards so that the chamber is invisible, as was the case with one cavity made by Coppery-chested Jacamars. It is likely that all species build both straight and curved burrows, depending on circumstances. When roots or other obstructions are met, the angle deviates, often sideways or downwards, to bypass the obstacle. In the view of some authors, jacamar burrows, or at least those of the Rufous-tailed Jacamar, are easily distinguishable from other cavities on account of the rectangular shape of the entrance, with vertical sides. There seems, however, to be no real consensus on this, and the entrances of other burrows of the same species have been described as elliptical. A few species of jacamar regularly have two or more access, or escape, routes to the nest-chamber, presumably as a defence against predation.

The time taken to complete a burrow appears to be highly variable, a fact that would seem likely to relate at least in part to the density of the substrate into which the burrow is excavated. In an example already given, a pair of Rufous-tailed Jacamars appeared almost to finish the task in three days. In contrast, a pair of Three-toed Jacamars took nearly two months to complete a burrow in a bank. One nest of the Green-tailed Jacamar was excavated by three individuals, two males and one female, each taking turns of about five minutes' duration to dig into an arboreal termitarium, usually in the afternoon; individuals not engaged in excavation usually sat close to the nest, catching insects, but not moving very far away. The burrow advanced by around 2-3 cm a day, even though work lasted for up to eight hours daily, and the entire job took about four weeks to complete. At the outset, the group worked for a total of about one hour each day, but this gradually increased to up to eight hours, while individual bouts increased from a couple of minutes to 15 minutes. The assistance of the extra male was presumably highly important. This event, incidentally, represents the only record for any *Galbula* species of more than one male at a nest.

Located at the end of the burrow, the nest-chamber is unlined, but it quickly becomes covered with the glittering chitinous parts of insects regurgitated by the incubating parents. By the time of hatching, the chamber is liberally befouled with excrement and insect parts, a situation common to many burrow-nest-

Foraging Green-tailed Jacamars perch on exposed sites in shrubby edges of tall forest, moving the head rapidly as they scan the lower and middle levels of the foliage for insects. Their diet consists mainly of Hymenoptera, Lepidoptera, Diptera, Coleoptera and Odonata. The smaller jacamars tend to be the more active foragers. Thus, Green-tailed Jacamars, of 18-22 cm, may attempt up to 40 aerial sallies per hour, whereas Paradise Jacamars (Galbula dea), which measure about 25-34 cm, attempt an average of only 22 sallies per hour.

[Galbula galbula, El Tuparro National Park, Colombia. Photo: T. McNish/VIREO]

ing birds. Jacamars sometimes clean out the nest-hole and reuse it in consecutive years.

Egg-laying by jacamars tends to take place at some time between ten days and six weeks after the completion of the burrow. The interval between the deposition of each egg is apparently two to four days. The eggs themselves are shiny, almost spherical and usually pure white, in common with those of many other hole-nesting birds, as they require no mottling or camouflage to conceal them from predators. Rarely, Rufous-tailed Jacamar eggs are lightly freckled with reddish or cinnamon spots.

The clutch generally comprises between two and four eggs, although apparent full clutches of one egg have been reported. The Rufous-tailed Jacamar follows the common pattern among birds of laying increasingly larger clutches with increasing latitude. In Guatemala the most common clutch is of four eggs, and in Rio de Janeiro province, in Brazil, this species has been recorded laying two clutches a year, each of four eggs. Closer to the equator, four out of eleven nests in Costa Rica contained two eggs, six held three and the eleventh held four; three or four eggs are reported in Venezuela, and in Trinidad and Tobago three is the commonest clutch size, with two or four more rare. At lower latitudes still, Amazonian populations, of the subspecies *rufoviridis*, are thought to lay only one egg per clutch. Replacement clutches are usually laid in the event of abandonment.

Studies of wild-living Rufous-tailed Jacamars indicate that the incubation period is quite variable, lasting between 19 and 23 days, and occasionally up to 26 days in adverse conditions. Eggs of the same species in captivity, however, have been recorded as hatching after only 18 days. This difference in the period of incubation suggests that embryo development is determined by such factors as temperature, as might be expected.

Incubation is undertaken by both sexes and is sometimes initiated before completion of the clutch. In the case of the Rufous-tailed Jacamar, the best-known member of the family, the female tends to incubate at night. The male sometimes arrives outside the burrow before sunrise and calls, whereupon the female emerges. In observations of this behaviour in Central America, the male then waited for a short period, during which he caught a few insects, having perhaps 20 minutes of daylight in which to feed; he then took over incubation at 05:30-06:00 hours, apparently later on overcast days. In some pairs, the female leaves the nest without waiting for the male to arrive. Notwithstanding the female's patience or otherwise, the two adults then proceed to incubate throughout the day in alternating bouts. At a nest watched in Guatemala, each stint tended to last for 2-2·5 hours, while for a pair in Costa Rica the duration of individual bouts of incubation was somewhat shorter, between 84 and 113 minutes. The male usually undertakes a longer bout during the late afternoon, following which the female begins her overnight session, entering the burrow a little after sunset. At each change-over there may be some calling and displaying, but the eggs are rarely left unattended for a period of more than five minutes. Incubation is normally carried out for about 95% of daylight hours, and is continuous during the hours of darkness.

Unlike the nestlings of most Piciformes, which are generally naked on hatching, those of the Rufous-tailed Jacamar hatch with a copious covering of long, whitish down. Many other non-piciform hole-nesting species, such as the parrots, the owls (Strigidae) and the swifts (Apodidae), also have very pale downy chicks, rather than the mottled camouflaged chicks of ground-nesting birds; this is presumably a result of reduced predation risk, and an adaptation that allows the adults to see the nestlings more clearly in the darkness of the cavity. Long down filaments on the chin and throat make nestling jacamars appear bearded. In common with members of the order Piciformes, however, galbulid nestlings have a strange appearance, at least initially, because the lower mandible projects distinctly beyond the upper one. Nestlings of the Rufous-tailed Jacamar hatch with the eyes closed, these forming dark protuberances on the sides of the head until they open, after about six days. At the same stage the pin-feathers emerge, with tufts of down at their tips. By the twelfth day after hatching the feathering is quite well developed, and the nestlings can already be sexed by the colour of their throat feathers. Whereas the outer and inner toes

are directed forwards when the chick hatches, on nestlings over six days old they point backwards, as on adults. Nestling jacamars often have pale yellowish legs with a prominent soft oval callus on the "heel" or tarsus. This heel pad, a feature also of young bee-eaters, kingfishers, woodpeckers, toucans and barbets, probably serves to cushion the chicks against the rough, unlined nest-chamber. Skutch reports that the pads of Rufous-tailed Jacamars are nearly smooth.

Although the chamber appears woefully unhygienic, with no attempt made by the adults to dispose of waste material, the chicks remain remarkably clean. This is partly because they usually stand erect, and do not let their plumage touch the floor or walls of the nest-chamber. Nevertheless, sufficient residue of animal matter and faeces is present to allow maggots to proliferate inside the nest-chamber. In one case, a brood of Rufous-tailed Jacamars had to vacate the nest after it was colonized by large numbers of ants, apparently attracted to the rotting faecal matter and insect parts. This exposure led to the death of the chicks. The loud vocalizations of nestling Rufous-tailed Jacamars suggest that they are not usually preyed on by animals that hunt acoustically.

When nestling Rufous-tailed Jacamars are taken from the nest, parents returning with food in the bill perch nearby and call in alarm, but they tend not to mob or to perform distraction displays. Adults, at least females, when brooding chicks, sometimes allow themselves to be touched by humans, rather than fleeing.

The majority of food items collected for the nestlings are apparently caught within 50 m of the nest, particularly those brought in by the male. Studies of Rufous-tailed Jacamars have provided some evidence to suggest that females forage farther afield, and return to nestlings with larger prey items, than do males. Skutch watched one pair of these birds for 25 hours during the six days before the two chicks fledged. He found that, of a total of 122 deliveries, the adult male provided 88 and the female 34. He concluded that "from every aspect, the male was the more industrious provider", always feeding the chicks first before dawn and tending to stay closer to the nest to forage. The total intake was 2·4 feeds per chick per hour. Skutch's observations at a nest containing four young Pale-headed Jacamars were briefer, but, around the third week after hatching, 13 visits were made by the adults in 1·5 hours; this equates to a similar hourly feeding rate of 2·2 deliveries per chick. When the nestlings are very young, the adults take food to the nest-chamber itself. After several days, however, the chicks tend to advance towards the burrow entrance until, finally, they perch sufficiently close to it that their parents need only insert a small portion of the body to deliver food items.

Rufous-tailed Jacamar nestlings apparently fledge after 20 to 26 days. They promptly acquire a plumage similar to that of adults, but are recognizable by the fact that they have a short bill. In the few cases studied, fledging has not been synchronous, with young birds often emerging a few hours, or even days, apart. Variations in the duration of the fledging period are probably determined largely by food availability. One pair in Costa Rica nested in the same burrow for two years in succession; the chicks in the first year were well developed when they fledged, at 21-22 days, whereas those in the second year fledged at 25-26 days yet were poorly developed. The second breeding attempt was made late in the season, and the abundance of butterflies and dragonflies at that time was seemingly rather low. At least in the case of young Rufous-tailed and Pale-headed Jacamars, the act of leaving the nest is accompanied by a great deal of loud vocalizing by adults and offspring alike. Young Rufous-tailed Jacamars sometimes leave the burrow before they can properly fly, although this is probably not a common occurrence. Adults and young of some species tend to roost together in the burrow after fledging, this period of communal roosting by family-members lasting for up to eight weeks. This has been shown to be so with Pale-headed Jacamars, but is apparently not the case with Rufous-tailed Jacamars, which roost separately.

One pair of Yellow-billed Jacamars in French Guiana was found to be double-brooded, excavating a new cavity for the second clutch only a short distance from the first nest. A pair of Rufous-tailed Jacamars in Costa Rica also raised two clutches,

Much of what is known about the breeding biology of galbulids comes from studies of Rufous-tailed Jacamars. Their breeding season varies widely with latitude, beginning as early as February in Central America as opposed to November or December in Brazil and Bolivia. Courting males sing to females and frequently bring them food. Paired birds may sit side by side near their uncompleted nest, the male bobbing his head in all directions, pumping his tail up and down, and emitting low squeals while the female produces a trill. Pair members will also perch next to each other while performing a mutual display of head bowing and tail fanning. Both sexes help build the nest, which consists of a tunnel dug into a vertical bank, an arboreal or terrestrial termitarium, or the dirt-laden roots of an overturned tree. The clutch of 2-4 eggs is incubated for about three weeks by both sexes, the female taking the lead at night; the young leave the nest when they are between three and four weeks old, and often two broods will be raised per year. Most of the Galbula species are thought to be socially monogamous, although several other species, most notably the Three-toed Jacamar (Jacamaralcyon tridactyla), the Purus Jacamar (Galbalcyrhynchus purusianus) and perhaps the White-eared Jacamar (Galbalcyrhynchus leucotis), are suspected of breeding co-operatively in groups of four to six birds.

[Galbula ruficauda ruficauda, llanos of Venezuela. Photo: François Gohier/ Auscape]

the second nest built about 150 m from the first. It seems reasonable to conclude that most galbulid species can be double-brooded, although this appears to be exceptional in the case of the relatively well-studied Rufous-tailed Jacamar.

Movements

All jacamars appear to be wholly sedentary. The only reported study involving uniquely marked individuals concerned two Rufous-tailed Jacamars, one of each sex. Observations showed that one of these, the female, remained a breeding resident on approximately the same territory until at least four years after initial capture. Similarly, the marked male was still present in the same location one year later.

Despite this apparently strict site-fidelity, however, long-term studies at certain localities have proven that individual jacamars may wander. These are perhaps young birds in search of territories, or those displaced by habitat loss. For example, Skutch writing of his residence at Los Cusingos, in Costa Rica, records that "at long intervals, I hear the stirring calls of a solitary jacamar, apparently a wandering male seeking a mate that he cannot find. Without one, he does not stay".

Relationship with Man

Despite the ambivalence that most jacamars show towards people, humans have in general proved to be rather fond of the jacamar. The Galbulidae have endeared themselves to man on account of several behavioural and morphological traits, among which can be listed their apparently trusting nature, their spryness and their gaudy coloration. In stark contrast to their apparently ponderous and slow-witted allies, the puffbirds, jacamars have frequently been the subject of praise. According to Skutch, jacamars possess "all the physical features that win so much admiration for hummingbirds – metallic brilliance of plumage, richness and variety of colour, abundant vitality, gracefully dashing movements". He describes them as "electrified with a high voltage".

Often equated with overgrown hummingbirds, the jacamars are again likened to that group by R. ffrench, because of their "excitable temperament and intense vitality". This vitality is an often repeated theme: even the jacamar's voice "helps create the impression of a bird keyed up to the highest pitch of excitement". Likewise, the Rufous-tailed Jacamar has been described as an "aery, gemlike bird with bright brown eyes and rapier bill". Sherry remarked that this species was one of the reasons why birdwatchers go to the Neotropics. It must be added that, in general, it is the members of the genus *Galbula* upon which these distinctions fall. Those in the genus *Brachygalba* are more modest creatures, in truth rather dull in colour. As an adjunct to their colourful activity, the jacamars are often unwary of people, allowing a close approach, especially when nesting. While this confidence is considered charming by many, it also renders the birds vulnerable to hunting.

The resemblance of the Galbulidae to hummingbirds, even if somewhat superficial, has led to the same name being applied to both groups in various portions of their range. Examples include *beija-flor* ("flower-kisser") or *chupa-flor* ("flower-sucker") in Brazil, *gorrión* in Guatemala, and *tucuso* in Venezuela. This terminology overlooks the fact that hummingbirds feed on nectar, whereas jacamars are, with a single exception, entirely insectivorous; this is the kind of mistake that native Indians, who coined the name "jacamares", usually do not make. The Great Jacamar, of course, looks nothing like a hummingbird, and it often shares local names with the motmots, such as *Juró* in Panama. In much of Amazonian Brazil, jacamars share the name *ariramba* with the kingfishers; to distinguish the former from the latter, jacamars are also given the name *bico-da-agulha*, or "needle-bill". Other colloquial names reflect the cavity-nesting behaviour of the family, as in the local name *cavadeira*, meaning "digger", for the Three-toed Jacamar in Brazil.

Charles Kingsley's account of his first meeting with a Rufous-tailed Jacamar in the shady forests of Trinidad admirably conveys the beauty of these birds. Although he unfortunately mistakes a *Morpho* butterfly for a moth, and treats the male jacamar as a female, his words aptly capture the dazzling intensity of these creatures which have thrilled so many naturalists and visitors to the Neotropics:

"And what was that second, larger flash of golden green which dashed at the moth, and back to yonder branch not ten feet off? A Jacamar – kingfisher as they miscall her here, sitting fearless of man, with the moth in her long beak. Her throat is snowy white, her underparts rich red brown. Her breast, and all her upper plumage and long tail, glitter with golden green. There is light enough in this darkness it seems."

Whether jacamars are regarded by local natives as a worthwhile supplement to their diet is not really known, but it would seem unlikely that these birds represent a valued food. The flesh of jacamars is reported to have a strong, distasteful odour, likened to that of trogons.

Status and Conservation

The majority of jacamar species occupy broad ranges in forested lowlands. Their preference for a rapidly disappearing habitat in areas where that habitat is most easily destroyed leaves them vulnerable to population declines. For many galbulids, this alarming situation is alleviated by two main factors: the occupation of an extensive range, and the predilection for forest edge. The first of those results in a resilience to habitat loss on the basis that it is difficult for humans to eradicate all the appropriate forest over a very wide area of a species' distribution. The second allows jacamars to survive, and even to thrive, in fairly broken, fragmented and disturbed habitat. All the same, even the commonest species, the Rufous-tailed Jacamar, has been reported to have disappeared from certain sites as a result of uncontrolled habitat loss and poaching, as happened in some forests in Costa Rica in the 1940's.

The response of different species to habitat destruction varies according to their ecological requirements. Research carried out by J. M. Thiollay in French Guiana revealed that the abundance of birds in the forest interior tended to decrease in response to selective logging; among these, the Yellow-billed Jacamar decreased dramatically and the Great Jacamar disappeared altogether. Meanwhile, species inhabiting the forest edge or the canopy, including the Paradise Jacamar, actually increased as a result of selective logging, although this apparent effect may have been partially an artefact of their easier detection in broken habitats.

Two species of galbulid occupy greatly restricted ranges, and both are considered globally threatened according to IUCN criteria. One is the Coppery-chested Jacamar, a scarce inhabitant of middle altitudes and forested valleys in the eastern Andes from southernmost Colombia to northernmost Peru. This species, the only jacamar restricted to the subtropical zone, is listed as Vulnerable by BirdLife International. It has been recorded at elevations ranging from 600 m to 1700 m, and is apparently most common between 1000 m and 1300 m. It has been recorded only once in Colombia since its discovery there in 1970, and the largest population undoubtedly occurs in Ecuador. At Río Bombuscaro, in the province of Zamora-Chinchipe, it is reported to be fairly common on the basis of the presence of four to six resident pairs along a section of trail 2-3 km long. This area lies within the Podocarpus National Park, which is currently the only measure providing any protection for the species. Although the Coppery-chested Jacamar has been found at several other sites and may prove to be secure, it seems to be very thinly and patchily distributed. As it is generally confiding, hunting could be a problem in some recently settled areas. Moreover, this jacamar appears to be dependent on fairly intact lower montane forest, a habitat type seriously threatened by agricultural settlement, cattle grazing, and clearance for coffee and tea cultivation. Extensive protected areas are required

Considered to have been common in the nineteenth century, the Three-toed Jacamar has declined substantially in distribution and numbers and is no longer common anywhere. At present, an estimated 250-1000 individuals occur in small patches of dry, lowland Atlantic Forest in south-eastern Brazil. They may persist in some areas of degraded habitat if native understorey has been retained, but habitat loss and subsequent range restriction continue to render the birds vulnerable to local extinction and to the negative effects of inbreeding. Currently listed as Endangered by BirdLife International, the Three-toed Jacamar is in dire need of effective conservation measures.

[*Jacamaralcyon tridactyla*, Atlantic Forest, Rio de Janeiro, Brazil. Photo: Luiz Claudio Marigo]

in this zone. Podocarpus National Park has itself in recent times been under threat from mining activities and colonization by humans, and requires focused conservation action on behalf of this species and a diverse array of threatened Andean fauna for which the area is vitally important.

The other globally threatened galbulid is the unusual Three-toed Jacamar, which is considered Endangered. It is an endemic species of the Atlantic Forest in south-eastern Brazil, although the forest which it prefers is not the moist evergreen rainforest associated with this region. It appears to favour drier scrubby woodlots, often surrounded by cultivation, and it occurs even in eucalyptus (*Eucalyptus*) woodland so long as natural understorey remains. In either habitat it requires earth banks in which to nest and roost. From the accounts of J. T. Reinhardt, one can deduce that this species was very common in Rio de Janeiro state and Minas Gerais in the nineteenth century. Since that time it seems to have undergone an inexplicable decline, having apparently disappeared from Espírito Santo, Paraná and São Paulo, and since the mid-1970's reports of its presence have come only from eastern Minas Gerais and Rio de Janeiro. In these two states this jacamar is extremely local, but is common at a few sites, although it may be somewhat under-recorded as its preferred degraded habitat is understandably unattractive to ornithologists. Fieldwork in Minas Gerais in the late 1990's confirmed early records of the species' occurrence in the region, and established its continued presence in some fragments of habitat severely disturbed by humans. Habitat loss and the collapse of roosting and nesting cavities through subsidence, especially during the rainy season, are major threats. Detailed studies of remaining populations of the Three-toed Jacamar, and the establishment of reserves in representative habitat fragments, are strongly recommended. In addition, the artificial provision and maintenance of earth banks would perhaps benefit the species, and such measures could profitably be undertaken as an experimental conservation strategy in suitable areas.

Although no other galbulids are currently considered threatened, or even near-threatened, it could be argued with some justification that two species need to be re-evaluated with regard to their conservation status. Both could be deemed to be scarce and potentially threatened with extinction. The White-throated Jacamar frequents lowland riparian habitats near the junction of

Brazil, Bolivia and Peru. It is rarely recorded, is apparently local and is quite specialized in its habitat requirements. In common with several other species, it appears to be reliant on successional habitats along Amazonian rivers. Comprehensive surveys are required to establish its exact distribution and status throughout its range, as also are effective measures to control habitat loss along the relevant Amazonian tributaries. There is an uncertain historical record of this jacamar from Jaen, in the Peruvian department of Cajamarca, far from its currently known range, suggesting that this species should be searched for in the catchment of the Río Marañón. It occurs in Tambopata Reserve, in Peru, an important area that requires effective protection.

The Dusky-backed Jacamar of Colombia and Panama appears to be relatively scarce. Its known range should be thoroughly surveyed at the earliest opportunity, in order to establish the species' true status and to assess its population trends. At the same time, it would be wise to seek suitable locations for establishing additional protected areas, with the aim of safeguarding this poorly known jacamar.

In summary, the widespread use of edge habitats by jacamars has meant that some species may have benefited substantially as a result of the destructive actions of humans. Increased fragmentation of forest in Amazonia has presumably opened up many areas to colonization by these species, and their populations may well have risen as a result. This relationship is reversed, of course, for those species which prefer intact forest, and all jacamars tend to be most common in areas where human populations are sparse. Moreover, in the face of wholesale development, deforestation and disturbance, jacamars generally disappear. It is significant that only one species, the Rufous-tailed Jacamar, is known to frequent the wooded fringes of certain towns and cities.

General Bibliography

Avise & Aquadro (1987), Bock (1992, 1994), Burton (1984), Cracraft (1968, 1981), Donatelli (1987, 1992), Fry (1970a), Haffer (1968, 1974), Lanyon & Zink (1987), Marshall (1909), Mayr (1998), Olson (1983), Peters (1948), Raikow & Cracraft (1983), Rothschild (1964), Sclater (1879-1882), Sibley (1956, 1996), Sibley & Ahlquist (1972, 1990), Sibley & Monroe (1990), Sibley *et al.* (1988), Simpson & Cracraft (1981), Skutch (1985a), Steinbacher, G. (1935), Steinbacher, J. (1937), Swierczewski (1977), Swierczewski & Raikow (1981), Todd (1943a).

PLATE 1

inches 4
cm 10

1

2

♀
♂ 3

4

ssp *melanosterna*

ssp *lugubris*

ssp *fulviventris*

5

6

7

ssp *chalcocephala*

♀
♂
ssp *albirostris*

♂

♂ ssp *ruficauda*

8

♀

10

ssp *melanogenia*
♂

ssp *pallens*
♂

ssp *rufoviridis*
♂

9

Genus *GALBALCYRHYNCHUS*
Des Murs, 1845

1. **White-eared Jacamar**
Galbalcyrhynchus leucotis

French: Jacamar oreillard   **German**: Kastanienglanzvogel   **Spanish**: Jacamará Orejiblanco
Other common names: Chestnut Jacamar (when lumped with *G. purusianus*)

Taxonomy. *Galbalcyrhynchus leucotis* Des Murs, 1845, "Santa Fé de Bogotá", Colombia; presumably = Amazon lowlands.
Forms a superspecies with *G. purusianus*. Sometimes considered conspecific, but no intermediate forms documented despite their co-existence on R Ucayali, in Peru; studies along potential zone of contact would help clarify their relationship. Monotypic.
Distribution. E of Andes in S Colombia (S from Meta), Ecuador and NE Peru (S to R Ucayali), and W Brazil along R Solimões (E to below mouth of R Purús at Caviana, opposite Manacapurú).

Descriptive notes. 18-21 cm; 44-50 g. Chunky jacamar, recalling kingfisher (Alcedinidae), looking broad-winged and short-tailed in flight. Plumage is entirely reddish-chestnut, forehead, crown, wings and tail glossed bronzy or greenish-black, with conspicuous white ear-coverts; robust bill 4·8-5·6 cm (4·1-4·5 cm from nostril), light pinkish with dark tip, sometimes looking white depending on light conditions; iris bright red; bare eyering and loral region pinkish-red; feet relatively large, pinkish-red. Immature generally paler, some fine darkish streaks on abdomen, bill shorter. VOICE. Presumed song a prolonged rising trill resembling that of a woodcreeper (Dendrocolaptidae); also occasional loud "kyew" or "cue" call, sometimes in series; vocalizations given by single bird or by small groups in concert.
Habitat. Lowland humid primary forest (*terra firme* and *várzea*) and secondary forest, mainly along borders near clearings, rivers and streams, at up to 500 m.
Food and Feeding. Insects, apparently Hymenoptera and Lepidoptera predominating; sturdiness of bill suggests that it may favour larger or harder prey than that taken by most jacamars. Forages at medium height and up to canopy, sometimes lower along edges. Perches solitarily, in pairs or small groups (up to 8), on exposed branches; darts out to feed on flying insects, often returns to same perch.
Breeding. Birds in breeding condition reported in Jun in Colombia; nest Jul in NE Peru. One nest in NE Peru was situated in arboreal termitarium 3 m above ground; 2 birds seen entering and leaving repeatedly over 2 days. No further information available.
Movements. Sedentary.
Status and Conservation. Not globally threatened. Generally common and conspicuous throughout range, e.g. particularly numerous around Limoncocha and Imuyacocha (Ecuador). No immediate threats documented, despite the ongoing destruction of lowland forest; preference for successional and edge habitats suggests good survival prospects. Occurs in several protected areas, such as Amacayacu National Park, in Colombia, and Cuyabeno Reserve, in Ecuador.
Bibliography. Best *et al.* (1997), Butler (1979), Canaday & Jost (1999), Chapman (1917, 1926), Clements & Shany (2001), Cory (1919), Cracraft (1985), Forrester (1993), Haffer (1974), Hill & Greeney (2000), Hilty & Brown (1986), Meyer de Schauensee (1949, 1952, 1982), Nicéforo & Olivares (1967), Olrog (1968), Ortiz & Carrión (1991), Parker *et al.* (1982), Ridgely & Greenfield (2001), Ridgely *et al.* (1998), Rodner *et al.* (2000), Sick (1993), Snethlage (1914), Stotz *et al.* (1996), Taczanowski (1886).

2. **Purus Jacamar**
Galbalcyrhynchus purusianus

French: Jacamar roux   **German**: Purúsglanzvogel   **Spanish**: Jacamará del Purús
Other common names: Chestnut Jacamar (when lumped with *G. leucotis*)

Taxonomy. *Galbalcyrhynchus purusianus* Goeldi, 1904, upper Rio Purús, Brazil.
Forms a superspecies with *G. leucotis*. Sometimes considered conspecific (and was initially presumed to represent female of that form), although no intermediate forms documented despite the fact that both occur on R Ucayali, in Peru; studies along potential zone of contact would help clarify their relationship. Monotypic.
Distribution. E Peru (Madre de Dios, Puno, upper R Ucayali) to W Brazil (upper R Juruá and R Purús) and N Bolivia (Beni, Pando).

Descriptive notes. 20 cm; 50 g. Forehead, crown, wings and tail dark bronzy or greenish-black; plumage otherwise chestnut; large bill 5·2-5·5 cm (4·4-4·7 cm from nostril), light pinkish, tipped dark; iris bright red; bare eyering and loral region pinkish-red; feet relatively large, pinkish-red. Differs from very similar *G. leucotis* in lacking white ear-coverts. Immature paler, bill smaller. VOICE. Call a series of loud "peeeur" whistles and a sharp "pee".
Habitat. Inhabits borders of lowland primary and secondary *terra firme* and *várzea* forest, often near rivers, oxbow lakes, swamps with *Cecropia* and palms. By R Manu, in Peru, frequents middle successional stages (mixed canopy, *Ficus/Cedrela* and transitional forest). Rarely in forest interior. In Beni, in Bolivia, has been observed perching on roadside electricity wires in settled areas.

Food and Feeding. Insects, usually wasps and bees (Hymenoptera) and termites (Isoptera); of 21 prey items recorded at Cocha Cashu, Peru, all were Hymenoptera. Also reported to catch fish in Peru, although this probably the result of confusion with kingfishers (Alcedinidae). Large bill does, however, suggest that some large prey may be taken. Groups of 1-6 forage from mid-level to canopy. Insects caught by sallying from a perch. Hymenoptera beaten thoroughly on perch before consumption.
Breeding. Hole-excavation observed in Oct in Peru. Probably co-operative breeder; groups of 4-6 sometimes sing and display together. In Peru, 6 individuals observed excavating a single burrow in a termitarium 4·7 m above ground, burrow volume 43 litres; cavity was occupied during the day, thus almost certainly a nest, although breeding not confirmed and possibility that hole functioned as a roost-site not ruled out. No further information available.
Movements. Sedentary.
Status and Conservation. Not globally threatened. Locally fairly common, but generally scarce in Peru. Occurs in Manu Biosphere Reserve, Peru. Apparently tolerates disturbed and partially man-modified habitats, and no specific threats are known.
Bibliography. Brightsmith (1999), Clements & Shany (2001), Cory (1919), Forrester (1993), Gyldenstolpe (1945a, 1945b), Haffer (1974), Meyer de Schauensee (1982), Olrog (1968), Parker *et al.* (1982), Pinto (1938b), Remsen & Traylor (1989), Robinson (1997), Robinson & Terborgh (1997), Ruschi (1979), Sick (1993), Snethlage (1914), Stotz *et al.* (1996), Terborgh *et al.* (1984), Traylor (1958).

Genus *BRACHYGALBA*   Bonaparte, 1854

3. **Dusky-backed Jacamar**
Brachygalba salmoni

French: Jacamar sombre   **German**: Salmonglanzvogel   **Spanish**: Jacamará Dorsioscuro
Other common names: Salmon's Jacamar

Taxonomy. *Brachygalba salmoni* P. L. Sclater and Salvin, 1879, Río Nechí, Antioquia, Colombia.
Forms a superspecies with *B. goeringi*, *B. lugubris* and *B. albogularis*. Isolated population in N Colombia at Carmen, in Bolívar, described as race *carmenensis* on the basis of slight differences in plumage coloration and bill shape, but these appear to fall within range of individual variation elsewhere in Colombia and Panama. Monotypic.
Distribution. E Panama (Darién) and NW Colombia (N Antioquia, S Córdoba, N Bolívar).

Descriptive notes. 16·5-18 cm; male 18·5 g, female 16 g. Male has upperparts, chest, flanks and underwing coverts dark greenish-black, somewhat glossy on chest, bluer in worn plumage; crown and, particularly, forehead dull brown, slightly glossed greenish; primaries blackish; cheeks and malar sooty-blackish; throat buffy-white or white, belly and centre of breast cinnamon; undertail-coverts cinnamon, longest bronze-green; bill 3·6-4·9 cm, slender and sometimes slightly decurved, black; iris red; feet black. Female similar but throat buff, iris dark reddish-brown. Immature has upperparts and secondaries fringed cinnamon-buff, shorter bill, grey iris. VOICE. Call a plaintive, upwardly inflected "sweet" or "feet", frequently repeated, sometimes expanded to "pe-peet", "pe-pe-pe-peet" or a longer series; probably has more complex song like *B. goeringi*.
Habitat. Shrubby edges, treefalls, trails and clearings of humid primary and secondary forest with tall trees, and along fairly open streambanks, in lowlands and hills up to 700 m.
Food and Feeding. Flying insects, including Hymenoptera (Apidae, Vespidae), Isoptera, Lepidoptera (including moths) and Coleoptera. Usually perches in pairs or small family groups on exposed horizontal branches, often in canopy, sometimes on low bushes, generally at greater heights than *Galbula ruficauda*; sallies short distances (usually less than a few m), sometimes medium or long distances, to catch insects in air. Often returns to same perch after capture.
Breeding. Birds in breeding condition in Jan-Feb in Colombia. No information on breeding behaviour; probably nests in earth bank.
Movements. Sedentary.
Status and Conservation. Not globally threatened. Restricted-range species: present in Darién Lowlands EBA and in Nechí Lowlands EBA. Reckoned to be relatively scarce in general, but locally common. In Panama, generally uncommon in Darién (rare at Cerro Pirre). Occurs in Los Katíos National Park, Colombia. Tolerates, or perhaps even prefers, a degree of habitat disturbance whereby clearings and regrowth are created. Isolated population in Bolívar, N Colombia, possibly vulnerable to habitat destruction. Surveys required in order to establish population size and trends.
Bibliography. Anon. (1998b), Bangs & Barbour (1922), Cory (1919), Cracraft (1985), Haffer (1962, 1974, 1975), Hilty & Brown (1986), Meyer de Schauensee (1949, 1950, 1982), Nicéforo & Olivares (1967), Olrog (1968), Orejuela (1985), Ridgely & Gwynne (1989), Ridgway (1914), Robbins *et al.* (1985), Rodner *et al.* (2000), Stotz *et al.* (1996), Wetmore (1968a).

4. **Pale-headed Jacamar**
Brachygalba goeringi

French: Jacamar à tête pâle   **German**: Fahlnacken-Glanzvogel   **Spanish**: Jacamará Acollarado

Taxonomy. *Brachygalba goeringi* P. L. Sclater and Salvin, 1869, near Maruria, north of Lake Valencia, at foot of Guiguc Mountains, Venezuela.
Forms a superspecies with *B. salmoni*, *B. lugubris* and *B. albogularis*. Monotypic.

On following pages: 5. Brown Jacamar (*Brachygalba lugubris*); 6. White-throated Jacamar (*Brachygalba albogularis*); 7. Three-toed Jacamar (*Jacamaralcyon tridactyla*); 8. Yellow-billed Jacamar (*Galbula albirostris*); 9. Blue-necked Jacamar (*Galbula cyanicollis*); 10. Rufous-tailed Jacamar (*Galbula ruficauda*).

Distribution. NE Colombia (Arauca, Casanare) and NW Venezuela (Lara E to Aragua, N Guárico, Barinas, Apure).

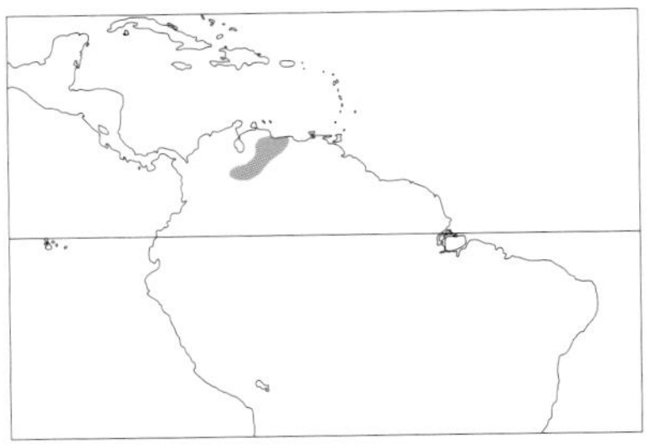

Descriptive notes. 16·5-18 cm; 16-18 g. Male has crown and upper mantle ashy-brown, rest of upperparts, tail and wings dark brown with greenish sheen, becoming bluish-black in worn plumage; pale supercilium more rufescent-brown at rear; throat buffy-white, breastband ash-brown, flanks dark brown, chestnut band across upper belly, rest of underparts white; bill 4·5-5·1 cm long (3·4-4·5 cm from nostril), slender, black; iris reddish brown; feet black. Female like male, perhaps with more extensive chestnut on belly. Immature has shorter bill, grey crown and greyish-brown nape, whiter throat, supercilium and side of head, dusky patch on cheeks and ear-coverts, brighter upperparts more strongly glossed green and fringed and tipped with ferruginous, feathers of pectoral band and flanks tipped buff or white. Voice. Thin, high "weet", sometimes in series, accelerating in pace and ascending in tone, ending in a sharp trill, this sequence sometimes given repeatedly when excited, resulting in undulating series of sharp crescendos, twitters and high thin trills, during which the body is often turned rapidly from side to side and the tail flicked up and down; also a low twittering; nestlings generally silent, but can give similar, though weaker, calls.

Habitat. Edges of deciduous, secondary and gallery forest, typically in *llanos*; also light open woodland, thickets, clearings and drier savanna, occurring up to 1100 m but usually considerably lower.

Food and Feeding. Mostly Lepidoptera and Odonata. During c. 5 hours of nest watches in Venezuela, about half of food items brought to nestlings were adult Odonata 4-5 cm long with wings detached; next most prevalent were small or medium-sized Lepidoptera, mostly skippers (Hesperiidae), usually delivered with wings attached; much rarer items were small Diptera and probably Homoptera; adults possibly consumed different items at the feeding grounds. Among butterflies, Heliconiinae are generally ignored, presumably because of their distastefulness, as are morphos (Morphinae), presumably because of their large size. Usually perches in pairs or small family groups on exposed branches emerging from canopy, or on lower shrubs, overhanging branches and roots along streambanks. Makes acrobatic darting and looping sallies from a perch to catch flying insects. In Venezuela, tends to occupy higher foraging niche than sympatric *Galbula ruficauda*, feeding almost entirely from treetops rather than the lower storey.

Breeding. Apr-May in Venezuela. One nest dug into a clay bank, burrow 90 cm above ground, 80 cm long with nest-chamber at end; 4 nestlings; after fledging, adults and offspring roosted in nest for several weeks. No information on incubation and nestling periods.

Movements. Sedentary.

Status and Conservation. Not globally threatened. Common throughout its range, although apparently local in NE Colombia. No specific threats documented so far, despite overall habitat loss in certain areas as a result of deforestation.

Bibliography. Blake (1961), Cory (1919), Haffer (1974), Hilty & Brown (1986), Meyer de Schauensee (1949, 1982), Meyer de Schauensee & Phelps (1978), Nicéforo & Olivares (1967), Olrog (1968), Rodner *et al*. (2000), Skutch (1968), Stotz *et al*. (1996), Underdown (1929).

5. Brown Jacamar

Brachygalba lugubris

French: Jacamar brun **German**: Braunbrust-Glanzvogel **Spanish**: Jacamará Pardo
Other common names: Todd's Jacamar (*phaeonota*)

Taxonomy. *Galbula lugubris* Swainson, 1838, Kanuku Mountains, Guyana.
Forms a superspecies with *B. salmoni*, *B. goeringi* and *B. albogularis*. No contact or intergradation between races is known, and potential zones of overlap merit investigation to elucidate taxonomic relationships. Race *phaeonota*, known only from the type specimen, was described as a separate species, but considered probably a form of present species; further research necessary to confirm its taxonomic placement or, indeed, its validity. Races *melanosterna* and *naumburgi* previously treated as together constituting a separate species, and their taxonomic status may require reassessment. Seven subspecies recognized.

Subspecies and Distribution.
B. l. fulviventris P. L. Sclater, 1891 - E of Andes in C Colombia (Buenavista, Villavicencio).
B. l. obscuriceps J. T. Zimmer & Phelps, Sr., 1947 - S Venezuela (upper Orinoco region, R Ocamo) and NW Brazil (upper R Padauiri, R Negro).
B. l. lugubris (Swainson, 1838) - E & S Venezuela through the Guianas to NE Brazil.
B. l. caquetae Chapman, 1917 - S Colombia E of Andes (S from Caquetá) S to E Ecuador and N Peru.
B. l. phaeonota Todd, 1943 - W Brazil, at Tonantins (on R Solimões).
B. l. naumburgi Chapman, 1931 - NE Brazil (Maranhão, Piauí).
B. l. melanosterna P. L. Sclater, 1855 - E Bolivia (Santa Cruz) and C & S Brazil (Pará S to Rondônia, Mato Grosso, Goiás, W Minas Gerais, W São Paulo).

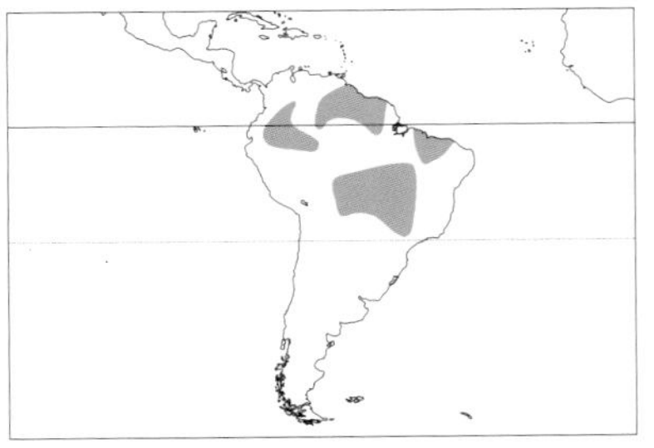

Descriptive notes. 14-18 cm; 17-23 g. Upperparts, including crown, sooty-brown, lower back darker, glossed greenish-black; diffuse pale supercilium; wings and tail blackish with slight blue sheen, absent on primaries; chin and throat whitish, breast and flanks rufescent-brown, lower breast and belly whitish or occasionally buffy, undertail-coverts rufescent-brown; bill 4-5 cm long (3·4-4·2 cm from nostril), slender, straight, generally black; iris dark brown; bare eyering blackish-brown; feet black, base of tarsi sometimes yellowish. Immature not described. Races differ from nominate in tone and intensity of colour on upperparts and breast, S races generally with yellowish bill base, paler eyes, yellow eyering: *fulviventris* has browner upperparts and breast, buffy belly; *obscuriceps* has blackish crown, dark brown upperparts and breast, rufescent-brownish or buffy rest of underparts; *caquetae* has crown tipped pale ochraceous-buff, nape, mantle and breast more rufescent, lower back to uppertail-coverts more blackish; *phaeonota* is more uniform, darker, less rufescent on upperparts, throat, breast, flanks and undertail-coverts, isolating dirty white belly, the feathers of chin and upper throat with whitish shaft streaks and rufescent tips; *naumburgi* is dark brown above, black wings and tail glossed greenish, blackish below with white throat and belly; *melanosterna* similar to previous, but proximal half or whole of lower mandible pale yellow, eyes pale blue. Voice. High, insect-like descending "tick tick tick ti ti ti ti tit t t t", terminating in stuttering trill; call a very high, sharp whistle, "hilew", rather different from *Galbula* calls, or lower "chewee".

Habitat. Canopy, edges and shrubby clearings of primary and secondary *terra firme*, *várzea* and gallery forest, rarely cloudforest, also open savanna woodland, most often on riverbanks with scattered trees and shrubs; usually in lowlands to 900 m, but records extend to 1500 m in Venezuela.

Food and Feeding. Diet includes Hymenoptera (e.g. 12-mm Apidae, Vespidae, Chrysididae), Coleoptera (e.g. 7-mm Staphylinidae, Curculionidae), Homoptera (e.g. cicadas), Diptera (e.g. Tabanidae) and Lepidoptera. Perches in pairs or small parties on exposed branches in upper canopy, less commonly down almost to ground level; often beside or over water. Sallies from perch for flying insects.

Breeding. Family with 3 juveniles in late Mar and birds in breeding condition in late May in Colombia. No further information available; presumably breeds in arboreal termitarium or in burrow dug into bank.

Movements. Sedentary.

Status and Conservation. Not globally threatened. Fairly common locally throughout much of range, including Surinam, French Guiana, and W Brazil (Rondônia); was previously considered abundant, at least seasonally, in S Brazil. Generally uncommon in E Ecuador, but numerous at Limoncocha; uncommon in N Peru. Occurs in Imataca Forest Reserve and El Dorado, Venezuela, in Amacayacu National Park, Colombia, and in Chapada dos Guimarães National Park, Brazil. Although sensitive to wholesale deforestation, its habitat requirements suggest that selective logging would not be a threat. Race *phaeonota*, known only from type locality, requires further study to clarify its conservation status.

Bibliography. Cadena *et al*. (2000), Chapman (1917, 1926, 1931), Cory (1919), Fry (1970b), Griscom & Greenway (1941), Haverschmidt & Mees (1994), Hellmayr (1929), Hilty & Brown (1986), Meyer de Schauensee (1949, 1982), Meyer de Schauensee & Phelps (1978), Naumburg (1930), Nicéforo & Olivares (1967), Parker *et al*. (1982), Phelps & Phelps (1958), Pinto (1938b), Remsen & Traylor (1989), Ridgely & Greenfield (2001), Sargeant (1994), Schubart *et al*. (1965), Sclater & Salvin (1879), Sick (1993), Snethlage (1914), Snyder (1966), Stotz, Fitzpatrick *et al*. (1996), Stotz, Lanyon *et al*. (1997), Tostain *et al*. (1992), Willard *et al*. (1991), Willis (1992), Willis & Oniki (1990), Zimmer, J.T. & Phelps (1947), Zimmer, K.J. & Hilty (1997), Zimmer, K.J. *et al*. (1997).

6. White-throated Jacamar

Brachygalba albogularis

French: Jacamar à gorge blanche **Spanish**: Jacamará Gorgiblanco
German: Weißkehl-Glanzvogel

Taxonomy. *Galbula albogularis* Spix, 1824, Pará = Rio Javarí, Brazil.
Forms a superspecies with *B. salmoni*, *B. goeringi* and *B. lugubris*. Monotypic.

Distribution. E Peru (Loreto, Madre de Dios, possibly Cajamarca), W Brazil (R Solimões, R Javarí, upper R Purús) and N Bolivia (Pando, La Paz).

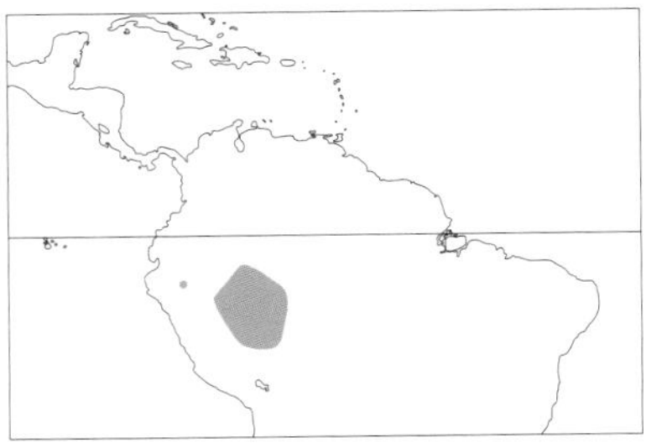

Descriptive notes. 15-16 cm. Male has throat, supercilium and side of head conspicuously white; upperparts dark brown or dull black, glossed greenish-blue; primaries and tail black, tail quite short and square; breast and belly dark brown or blackish, glossed greenish-blue, elongated chestnut patch on middle of belly; undertail-coverts blackish; bill 4-5 cm long (3·8 cm from nostril), slender, pale yellow; iris pale blue; bare facial skin yellow; feet black. Female similar, with perhaps more extensive chestnut on belly. Immature not described. Voice. Call a plaintive upslurred "psueet" or "kuweei", given infrequently.

Habitat. Edges of lowland primary forest, usually in successional habitat along rivers, e.g. young forest with *Cecropia* trees, river islands and "Zabolo" habitat.

Food and Feeding. Diet poorly known, but Lepidoptera (including *Eurema*, *Eunica*) and Hymenoptera (e.g. Vespidae) recorded. Perches quietly on exposed branches at canopy level, often shaded by large leaves. Sallies from a perch, generally 1-17 m up, to catch flying insects; foraging flights of 2-30 m reported.

Breeding. No specific information available; nest presumably in burrow in earth bank or termitarium, as in other jacamars.

Movements. Presumably sedentary.

Status and Conservation. Not globally threatened. Known from only few scattered localities. Appears to be rare, patchily distributed, and specialized in habitat requirements, although this may be a reflection more of uneven sampling effort and this species' generally inconspicuous nature rather than of its true status. Regular at Tambopata Reserve, in Peru. No immediate threats are recorded, although it is probably sensitive to destruction of riverine habitat. As very little is known about the species' ecology, distribution or status, much fieldwork is required to investigate these aspects.

Bibliography. Allen (1995), Angehr & Aucca (1997), Bronaugh (1984), Clements & Shany (2001), Cory (1919), Cracraft (1985), Donahue (1994), Forrester (1993), Foster *et al*. (1994), Griscom & Greenway (1941), Guilherme (2000, 2001), Haffer (1974), Meyer de Schauensee (1982), Olrog (1968), Parker & Remsen (1987), Parker *et al*. (1982), Pinto (1938b), Remsen & Parker (1984b), Remsen & Traylor (1989), Sick (1993), Snethlage (1914), Stotz *et al*. (1996), Whittaker & Oren (1999).

Genus *JACAMARALCYON* Lesson, 1830

7. Three-toed Jacamar

Jacamaralcyon tridactyla

French: Jacamar tridactyle **German**: Dreizehen-Glanzvogel **Spanish**: Jacamará Tridáctilo

Taxonomy. *Galbula tridactyla* Vieillot, 1817, São Paulo, Brazil.
Close to *Brachygalba*, particularly *B. lugubris*, but isolated by foot morphology, elongated head feathers and gregarious behaviour. Monotypic.
Distribution. SE Brazil (Minas Gerais, Espírito Santo, Rio de Janeiro, São Paulo, Paraná).

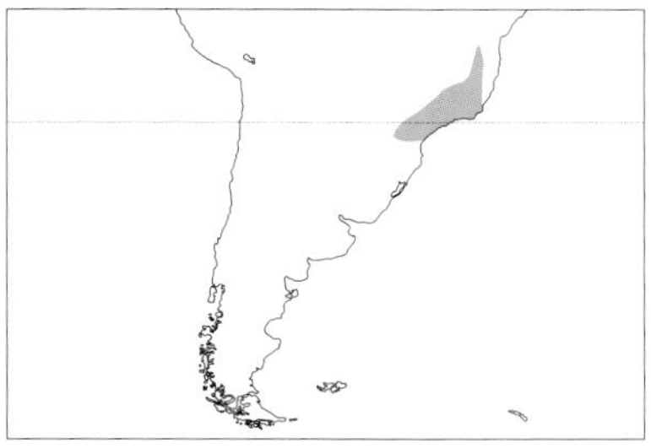

Descriptive notes. 17-20 cm; male 17·4-18·8 g, female 17·8-19·3 g. Head chestnut-brown, more blackish-brown on throat, thin golden-buff stripes on forehead, lores and throat; elongated head feathers often ruffled; back and graduated tail uniform blackish, glossed with green; central breast and belly white, sides of abdomen clear grey, undertail-coverts greyish; bill c. 4·7 cm long (3·6-3·9 cm from nostril), pointed, all black; iris dark brown, often spotted or wholly yellowish-brown or red (apparently an age-related feature); tarsus and feet blackish-grey, only 3 toes, soles yellowish. Differs from superficially similar *Brachygalba lugubris* in elongated head feathers, 3-toed foot. Immature has less evident golden stripes on head, short tail, shorter bill with white base. Voice. Song a sequence of short, relatively weak whistles; complex group song up to 20 seconds long, various shrill ascending whistles, apparently given by 2-6 individuals simultaneously; call a sharp rasping "churr", from perch or in flight.
Habitat. Semi-deciduous or gallery forest, mainly small isolated fragments only a few ha in extent, at edges or in degraded areas with bushes and scattered tall trees, usually near or along watercourses, roads and tracks where earth banks present; at 240-1100 m. Often in sites tangled with vines, or highly degraded and heavily disturbed by people, near urban areas. Sometimes tolerates eucalyptus (*Eucalyptus*) woodland where natural understorey remains, but tends to avoid intact evergreen forest.
Food and Feeding. Mainly Hymenoptera, Lepidoptera, Diptera and other small insects, including dragonflies (Odonata), termites (Isoptera), Homoptera, Hemiptera, and beetles (Coleoptera). One study showed Hymenoptera, particularly wasps, to make up the bulk of the diet; another revealed a preference for small cryptic Lepidoptera, as well as Diptera and Hymenoptera. Diet composition appears to vary seasonally with rainfall and insect abundance; capture of cicadas (Cicadidae) and flying termites, for example, is most frequent in Sept-Dec (early wet season), when these insects abound. Small groups of 2-10 individuals perch 8-15 m up, sometimes down almost to ground level, on tall trees (e.g. *Cecropia*, *Inga*, *Piptadenia*, *Eucalyptus*) or on vines, bamboo, tall grasses, wires and fences, darting into the open to catch flying prey, often close to foliage, returning more often than not to same perching area; sometimes foraging from the same perch or group of perches for at least 30 minutes. Of 173 sallies, 42 (24%) resulted in successful capture.
Breeding. Sept-Feb, at time of highest rainfall. Possibly colonial, up to 20 holes recorded in same bank; observations suggest a degree of co-operation, with groups of 5 or more. Burrow c. 6·5 cm wide at entrance, 84-146 cm long, excavated in earth bank, completion reportedly taking up to 2 months; individuals often build several holes simultaneously, with 2-7 birds/cavity. Clutch 2 eggs; incubation by at least a pair, possibly helped by others, period 19-20 days; chicks fledge after 28-30 days, thereafter visit nest-burrow for roosting, sometimes accompanied by adults; other group-members appear to help feed fledglings.
Movements. Sedentary.
Status and Conservation. ENDANGERED. Restricted-range species: present in Atlantic Forest Lowlands EBA. Historically very common. Has declined dramatically in range and numbers; recent reports only from C & S Minas Gerais and from Rio de Janeiro (R Paraiba Valley), where it is very local, but common at a few sites. Not recorded in Espírito Santo since 1940; no reports from São Paulo since mid 1970's, and no reliable records from Paraná since 1961. Estimated world population below 1000 individuals. It appears to prefer degraded woodland and tolerates a fair degree of human disturbance, but its absence from many apparently suitable sites suggests a habitat specialization that remains poorly understood. Habitat loss and collapse of roosting and nesting cavities as a result of subsidence, especially during the rainy season, are major threats. Detailed studies on remaining population and strict protection of representative fragments of habitat are recommended. In Minas Gerais, occurs in the highly disturbed Fernão Dias State Park, as well as in Caratinga Biological Station and in UFMG Ecological Station. Occurs also in several privately protected woodlots.
Bibliography. Bernardes *et al*. (1990), Bomfim & Reis (1996), Collar & Andrew (1988), Collar, Crosby & Stattersfield (1994), Collar, Gonzaga *et al*. (1992), Collar, Wege & Long (1997), Cory (1919), Cracraft (1985), Ferreira de Vasconcelos *et al*. (1999), Forrester (1993), Knox & Walters (1994), Lyons (1999), Machado & Lamas (1996), Machado *et al*. (1995), Melo-Júnior (1996, 1998, 2000, 2001b, 2001c), Meyer de Schauensee (1982), Olrog (1968), Schubart *et al*. (1965), Sick (1993, 1997), Silveira & Nobre (1998), Stattersfield & Capper (2000), Tobias *et al*. (1993), Wege & Long (1995), Willis & Oniki (1993).

Genus *GALBULA* Brisson, 1760

8. Yellow-billed Jacamar
Galbula albirostris

French: Jacamar à bec jaune **German**: Gelbschnabel-Glanzvogel **Spanish**: Jacamará Piquigualdo

Taxonomy. *Galbula albirostris* Latham, 1790, South America = Cayenne.
Forms a superspecies with *G. cyanicollis*; the two are sometimes considered conspecific, but no intergradation has been observed in zone of potential sympatry in R Ucayali Valley, NE Peru, and their populations are otherwise separated by R Amazon almost throughout its length. Race *chalcocephala* possibly a distinct species, as morphological differences from nominate race considerable and apparently constant, with no intergrades known; further studies needed in zone of potential overlap in Venezuela (upper R Orinoco) to clarify its taxonomic status. Two subspecies recognized.
Subspecies and Distribution.
G. a. albirostris Latham, 1790 - E Colombia (Mitú, Vaupés), S & E Venezuela (S of R Orinoco), the Guianas and N Brazil (N of Amazon).
G. a. chalcocephala Deville, 1849 - SE Colombia E of Andes (S of Meta), E Ecuador and W Brazil (upper R Negro) S to NE Peru (S to upper R Ucayali); possibly also S Venezuela (upper R Orinoco).

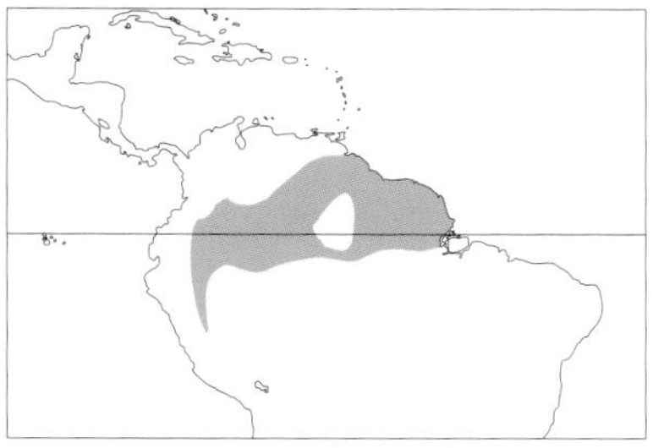

Descriptive notes. 18-21 cm; 16-24 g. Male has metallic purplish or coppery gloss on crown; rest of upperparts, including sides of head and neck, shining emerald-green; primaries dull black; tail relatively short and moderately rounded, outer rectrices brown, more cinnamon towards bases; chin buff, throat white, entire rest of underparts pale cinnamon-rufous; bill 3·5-4·3 cm long (2·8-3·4 cm from nostril), slender, pale yellow, upper mandible tipped dusky or blackish; iris dark brown; bare eyering and loral region yellow; feet yellow, black claws. Female has rufous-buff throat, as well as slightly paler underparts. Immature undescribed. Race *chalcocephala* is slightly larger (bill 3·1-3·8 cm from nostril), all or most of upper mandible dusky or black, upperparts metallic bronzy green, crown more bronzy purple, chin darker, lower underparts richer darker cinnamon-rufous. Voice. Song a high-pitched "peea peea-pee-pee-te-t-t-e'e'e'e'e'e", terminating in long rattling trill; calls a sharp "peek" and "trra", sometimes in rapid series, given by single bird or several together.
Habitat. In contrast to other jacamars, inhabits mainly interior of primary and mature secondary *terra firme*, *várzea* and *igapó* forest, most frequently at small clearings, treefall gaps, occasionally at edge. Also vine-tangled woodland, less commonly in gallery forest or sandy coastal forest. Usually below 900 m, but recorded to 1300 m in Venezuela. Generally frequents lower level to mid-level, 1-10 m above ground.
Food and Feeding. Insects, including Coleoptera (e.g. Cassididae), Hemiptera, Homoptera (e.g. Cicadidae), Diptera, and Hymenoptera including e.g. ants (Formicidae: Ponerinae), bees (Apidae), and wasps (Vespidae) 10-15 mm long. Stomachs sometimes contain large numbers of winged termites (Isoptera). Possibly also takes Lepidoptera and Odonata. Sits on open perches, typically in pairs, sallying forth from time to time to catch passing insects. Often joins mixed-species foraging flocks.
Breeding. Breeds during dry season in the Guianas, i.e. Jun-Sept in Surinam, Jul-Nov in French Guiana; at least occasionally double-brooded, as pair in French Guiana laid first clutch end Jul, followed by a second clutch in a new cavity in early Nov. Four reported nests were all excavated in arboreal termitaria 1·5-3 m above ground, these apparently often attached to the spiny bark of mature *Astrocaryum sciophilum* in French Guiana; nest possibly sometimes in earth bank, as with congeners, although so far this has not been confirmed. Clutch 2 eggs; no information on incubation and fledging periods.
Movements. Sedentary.
Status and Conservation. Not globally threatened. Uncommon in E Colombia and E Ecuador, but generally fairly common in E Peru, Amazonian Brazil, S Venezuela and the Guianas. No immediate threats are known but, since this species is more restricted to forest interior (and usually that of mature forest), it is presumably sensitive to deforestation and other types of habitat destruction. Indeed, a population in French Guiana declined dramatically in response to selective logging. Occurs in several protected areas throughout its range, e.g. Imataca Forest Reserve and El Dorado, in Venezuela, Amacayacu National Park and Tinigua National Park, in Colombia, and Cuyabeno Reserve, in Ecuador.
Bibliography. Bangs & Penard (1918), Blake (1962), Cadena *et al*. (2000), Chapman (1917, 1926), Cohn-Haft *et al*. (1997), Cory (1919), Davis (1986), Griscom & Greenway (1941), Haverschmidt & Mees (1994), Hilty & Brown (1986), Meyer de Schauensee (1949, 1982), Meyer de Schauensee & Phelps (1978), Nicéforo & Olivares (1967), Olrog (1968), Parker *et al*. (1982), Peres & Whittaker (1991), Phelps & Phelps (1958), Pinto (1938b), Reynaud (1998), Ridgely & Greenfield (2001), Sargeant (1994), Schubart *et al*. (1965), Sick (1993), Snethlage (1914), Snyder (1966), Stotz *et al*. (1996), Thiollay (1992), Thiollay & Jullien (1998), Tostain *et al*. (1992), Willard *et al*. (1991), Zimmer (1930), Zimmer & Hilty (1997).

9. Blue-necked Jacamar
Galbula cyanicollis

French: Jacamar à joues bleues **German**: Blauhals-Glanzvogel **Spanish**: Jacamará Cariazul
Other common names: Blue-cheeked/Purple-necked Jacamar

Taxonomy. *Galbula cyanicollis* Cassin, 1851, Pará, Brazil.
Forms a superspecies with *G. albirostris*; sometimes considered conspecific, but no intergradation observed in zone of potential sympatry in R Ucayali Valley, NE Peru, and their populations are otherwise separated by R Amazon almost throughout its length. Considerable geographical variation in plumage characters; upper Amazonian subpopulation possibly a separate race, or even distinct species. Monotypic.
Distribution. E Peru (S to lower R Ucayali) and Brazil S of Amazon (E to Maranhão, S to Rondônia and N Mato Grosso).

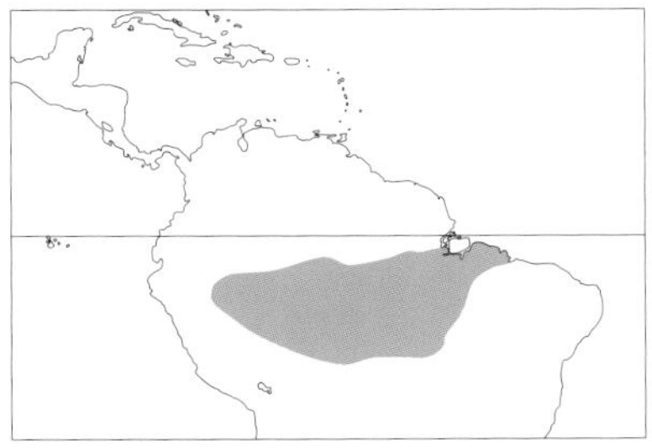

Descriptive notes. 19-22 cm; 21-26 g. Male has crown often bluish, cheeks and malar steel-blue in E (apparently varying clinally to green with only traces of blue in W birds); upperparts shining green; tail relatively short and moderately rounded, with inner pair of rectrices shining green, and remainder green-fringed rufous; underparts uniform chestnut; bill 3·9-5 cm long (3·4-4·1 cm from nostril), upper mandible usually black but considerable individual variation from all black to, rarely, all yellow, lower mandible yellow; iris dark brown; bare eyering and loral region yellow; feet yellow. Differs from *G. albirostris* in slightly larger size, bluer head, chestnut chin and throat. Female has slightly duller underparts. Immature not described. Voice. No information available, although likely to be similar to that of *G. albirostris*.
Habitat. Lower strata in interior of lowland evergreen forest, occasionally at edges; often in *várzea* forest and, indeed, where these are flooded cyclically (as in tidal areas near Belém, Brazil), seems to appear within the forest only when it is flooded. Also occurs locally in gallery forest in Brazilian *cerrado*. To 900 m.
Food and Feeding. Recorded prey Coleoptera, Hymenoptera (e.g. Ichneumonidae 15 mm long, Apidae, Formicidae) and Diptera (e.g. Brachycera). Possibly also takes Lepidoptera and Odonata. Sallies from a perch to take flying insects.

Breeding. Birds with enlarged gonads or egg in oviduct in Sept; 2 active nests found in Jun and Oct in Brazil. Nest in arboreal termitarium 1-2 m above ground. Clutch 2 eggs; no information on incubation and fledging periods.

Movements. Sedentary.

Status and Conservation. Not globally threatened. Generally common throughout range. Occurs within several protected areas, e.g. Tapajós National Park, in Brazil. Owing to its greater reliance on intact forest understorey, this species, as *G. albirostris*, is likely to be more susceptible to deforestation than are most other jacamars.

Bibliography. Clements & Shany (2001), Cory (1919), Forrester (1993), Griscom & Greenway (1941), Gyldenstolpe (1945a), Haffer (1974), Haverschmidt (1960), Ihering & Ihering (1907), Meyer de Schauensee (1982), Naumburg (1930), Oren & Parker (1997), Parker *et al*. (1982), Pinto (1935, 1938b), Ruschi (1979), Schubart *et al*. (1965), Sick (1993), da Silva (1996), da Silva *et al*. (1990), Snethlage (1914), Stotz *et al*. (1996), Zimmer *et al*. (1997).

10. **Rufous-tailed Jacamar**

Galbula ruficauda

French: Jacamar à queue rousse   **German**: Rotschwanz-Glanzvogel   **Spanish**: Jacamará Colirrufo
Other common names: Black-chinned Jacamar (*melanogenia*); Rufous-and-green/Spot-tailed Jacamar (*rufoviridis*)

Taxonomy. *Galbula ruficauda* Cuvier, 1816, Guyana.
Forms a superspecies with *G. galbula*, *G. pastazae*, *G. tombacea* and *G. cyanescens*. Race *rufoviridis* (with *heterogyna*) geographically separated from other races by *G. galbula*, *G. tombacea* and *G. cyanescens*, and long regarded as a full species; given its phenotypic similarity to other forms of present species, however, probably best treated as conspecific, pending further research. Race *melanogenia* previously considered a separate species, but this treatment confounded by limited hybridization with nominate race around Gulf of Urabá, NW Colombia; Ecuadorian and Colombian individuals tend towards smaller size and darker coloration, but differences considered insufficient for recognition of additional geographical races. Races *heterogyna*, *pallens* and *brevirostris* may form parts of clinal variation, as differences in coloration are minor. Six subspecies currently recognized.

Subspecies and Distribution.

G. r. melanogenia P. L. Sclater, 1853 - E Mexico (Veracruz, Oaxaca, Chiapas) S to W Andes of Colombia and Ecuador.
G. r. pallens Bangs, 1898 - extreme N Colombia (Santa Marta, lower Magdalena Valley) and extreme NW Venezuela (Zulia).
G. r. brevirostris Cory, 1913 - N Colombia (Norte de Santander) and NW Venezuela (around head of L Maracaibo).
G. r. ruficauda Cuvier, 1816 - C Colombia (Magdalena Valley N of Cauca, Arauca, Casanare), Venezuela (except NW & S), Trinidad and Tobago, Guyana (and very scarce E to coastal French Guiana), and N Brazil (upper R Branco, in Roraima).
G. r. rufoviridis Cabanis, 1851 - much of Brazil S of Amazon and E of R Madeira, and N Bolivia (Pando, La Paz); records from Paraguay and Argentina unconfirmed.
G. r. heterogyna Todd, 1932 - E Bolivia (Beni, Cochabamba, Santa Cruz) and SC Brazil (W Mato Grosso).

Descriptive notes. 19-25 cm; 18-28 g. Male has upperparts, including face and wing-coverts, and broad breastband shining metallic coppery green; primaries blackish; relatively long tail graduated, central pair of rectrices longest and metallic green, remainder cinnamon-rufous; chin very pale buffy; throat white (sometimes speckled green); some birds on Tobago have head glittering green with bluish gloss, back golden reddish-green, central pair of rectrices golden-orange with green shaft, pectoral band glittering reddish; belly, undertail-coverts and underwing-coverts rufous-chestnut; bill 4-5·7 cm long (3·9-5·0 cm from nostril), slender, sharp, black; iris brown; bare eyering and loral region greyish; feet yellowish-brown to greyish-flesh, black claws. Female has chin and throat cinnamon-buff, belly and underwing-coverts dark cinnamon-buff, slightly duller and paler than male. Immature has shorter bill initially tipped buff, shorter tail, duller more bronzy upperparts, broader and less clean-cut pectoral band. Race *melanogenia* has varying amount of black on chin, central 2 pairs of rectrices green; *pallens* similar but has rufous areas paler, especially in female, and narrower chestband, longer bill; *brevirostris* also paler, but with shorter bill; *rufoviridis* brighter green, has white chin, central 2 pairs of rectrices green, remainder rufous, terminal portions of outer rectrices green on outer web; *heterogyna* similar to previous but paler. VOICE. Standard song an accelerated sequence

of notes with terminal trill; prolonged song of male varies in tempo, with melodious and buzzy sections of drawn-out peeps interspersed with twittering, chuckling or ascending trills and low "bee-bee-bee"; frequently repeated call a brisk, thin, penetrating "peeup" or "peee", usually terminating abruptly, sometimes repeated 3-10 times in succession, by both sexes; also a very rapid trill.

Habitat. Wide variety of habitats, including shady borders of humid, deciduous and semi-arid formations, *terra firme*, gallery and second-growth forest, banks of creeks and streams, marshes, bamboo patches, plantations, thickets, *llanos* and savannas with scattered trees; in lowlands, locally to 900 m, rarely to 1350 m. Also interior of scrubby deciduous cactus-rich woodland along Caribbean coasts of Venezuela and Colombia, and dry *cerrado* and *caatinga* woodland in Brazil. N race *melanogenia* more strictly associated with humid habitats, preferring forested streams. Perches at lower and middle levels, frequently in shaded edge habitats, also at clearings inside forest but rarely within forest itself.

Food and Feeding. Variety of Lepidoptera, Odonata, Hymenoptera, Isoptera, Hemiptera, Orthoptera, and Coleoptera (e.g. Geotrupidae, *Bolboceras*). In Mato Grosso, Brazil, 86% of prey items were Hymenoptera, including Ichneumonidae (e.g. *Metopius*), Chalcididae, Eucharitidae, Pteromalidae, Scoliidae, Bethylidae, Formicidae (e.g. *Camponotus*, *Odontomachus*, *Messor*), Pompilidae (e.g. *Cryptochilus*), Vespidae (e.g. Eumeninae, *Apoica*, *Polybia ruficeps*, *P. fastidiosuscula*, *P. quadricincta*, *Epipona tatua*, *Agelaia vicina*, *A. multipicta*), Sphecidae (e.g. *Liris*, *Pison*, *Trypoxylon*, *Cerceris/Eucerceris*, Bembicini), Apoidea (e.g. Halictidae, *Hemisia*); 10% were beetles, including Staphylinidae, Coprinae, Elateridae, Bruchidae, Curculionidae and Scolytinae; small minority were Lepidoptera, Odonata and Hemiptera. In a study in Central America, however, Lepidoptera and Odonata made up a large proportion of the diet, at least in breeding season. During 120 hours of field observation in Costa Rica, 109 Lepidoptera were captured, including 28 Papilionidae, 49 Hesperiidae and 32 moths; butterflies included very large forms such as *Morpho*, *Papilio* and *Caligo*, smaller varieties such as Charaxinae, Satyrinae, Brassolinae, most Nymphalinae and even a few Heliconiinae; many noxious butterfly species, including Heliconiinae, were either pecked and rejected or entirely ignored. Perches singly or in pairs 1-3 m above ground, occasionally up to 10 m in low canopies, on partially exposed slender horizontal branches, from which makes aerial sallies. After capture, prey is taken to a perch and usually beaten several times against a branch to stun it, and knock off its wings, before swallowing. Observations in Goiás, Brazil, indicated that the social wasps *Polybia ignobilis*, *P. quadricincta*, *P. fastidiosuscula*, *Epipona tatua* and *Agelaia multipicta* were consumed in flight. Sometimes associates loosely with mixed-species foraging flocks.

Breeding. May-Jun in Mexico; Feb-Jul in Guatemala, Honduras, Costa Rica, Panama, Trinidad and Tobago; Apr-Jun in Venezuela; usually Jan-Apr, rarely Oct, in Colombia; Nov-Dec in Bolivia; Sept-Dec in Brazil (Minas Gerais); often double-brooded. Male regularly feeds female during courtship. Burrow excavated by both sexes, usually 20-50 cm deep but sometimes shorter, with terminal nest-cavity, in sand bank, steep bare slope, uplifted roots of fallen tree, or arboreal or terrestrial termitarium, usually 0-3 m above ground. Clutch 2-4 eggs, perhaps sometimes only 1 in Amazonia; both sexes incubate, female at night, period 19-23 days; chick hatches with copious covering of long, whitish down, lower mandible projecting beyond upper, outer and inner toes directed forwards; fledging period 19-26 days (18 days recorded in captivity), shorter in Venezuela than in Costa Rica.

Movements. Usually highly sedentary; possibly some short-distance dispersal.

Status and Conservation. Not globally threatened. Generally common and widespread. Fairly common in Mexico (Oaxaca), uncommon in Belize; common to abundant along Caribbean slope from Honduras to N Colombia, uncommon in SW Colombia (Nariño) and NW Ecuador. Nominate race was judged extremely common on Tobago in 1930's, fairly common there in 1990's, and abundant in much of Venezuela, but rare in French Guiana (possibly only a recent colonist). Race *heterogyna* is common along R Beni, in N Bolivia. Race *rufoviridis* generally common or very common in Brazil, even in highly degraded areas. While deforestation and habitat loss are the major threats, most races readily tolerate man-made habitats, in some regions being common along roadsides and in cocoa plantations. Declines reported in Costa Rica and Panama due to hunting, habitat loss and human interference, partly because of stricter habitat preferences of *melanogenia*. Recorded in many protected areas throughout its range, e.g. Carara Biological Reserve and Corcovado National Park, in Costa Rica, Guatopo National Park and Henri Pittier National Park, in Venezuela, Tayrona National Park, in Colombia, and Brasília National Park, in Brazil.

Bibliography. de Andrade (1992), dos Anjos & Schuchmann (1997), dos Anjos *et al*. (1997), Binford (1989), Bond & Meyer de Schauensee (1943), Canevari *et al*. (1991), Chai (1986a, 1986b, 1987, 1988, 1990, 1996), Chai & Srygley (1990), Cooper (1997), Descourtilz (1983), England (2000), ffrench (1991), Fogden (1993), Friedmann & Smith (1950, 1955), Friedmann *et al*. (1957), Fry (1970a, 1970b), González-García (1993), Gyldenstolpe (1945b), Haffer (1967a, 1967b, 1975, 1997c), Haverschmidt (1960), Haverschmidt & Mees (1994), Hayes (1995), Herklots (1961), Hilty & Brown (1986), Howell & Webb (1995), Land (1970), Levey & Stiles (1994), Marini *et al*. (1997), Medina (1955), Meyer de Schauensee (1949, 1982), Meyer de Schauensee & Phelps (1978), Monroe (1968), do Nascimento *et al*. (2000), Naumburg (1930), Nicéforo & Olivares (1967), Oniki & Willis (1999), Ortiz & Carrión (1991), Parker & Goerck (1997), Parrini *et al*. (1999), de la Peña (1994), Raw (1997), Ridgely & Greenfield (2001), Ridgely & Gwynne (1989), Salaman (1994), Schubart *et al*. (1965), Sherry (1983a), Sick (1993), Silveira (1998), Skutch (1937, 1963, 1968, 1983), Slud (1960, 1964), Snyder (1966), Stiles & Levey (1994), Stiles & Skutch (1989), Stotz *et al*. (1996), Tostain *et al*. (1992), Vallely & Whitman (1997), Verea & Solórzano (1998), Verea *et al*. (1999), de Vries (1994), Wetmore (1968a).

PLATE 2 ➤

11 ♂ ♀

12 ♂ ♀

13 ♂ ♀

14 ♂ ♀

15 ♂ 16 ♂ ♀

ssp *aureus* ♀ ♂

17

ssp *dea*

ssp *amazonum*

18

ssp *ridgwayi* ♂

PLATE 2

inches 4

cm 10

11. Green-tailed Jacamar
Galbula galbula

French: Jacamar vert **German**: Grünschwanz-Glanzvogel **Spanish**: Jacamará Coliverde

Taxonomy. *Alcedo Galbula* Linnaeus, 1766, Cayenne and Brazil = Cayenne.
Forms a superspecies with *G. ruficauda*, *G. pastazae*, *G. tombacea* and *G. cyanescens*. Thought to have hybridized with *G. leucogastra* in Surinam. Monotypic.
Distribution. E Colombia (Vichada, Meta), S & E Venezuela (S of R Orinoco), the Guianas and N Brazil (S to lower reaches of R Madeira and R Tapajós).

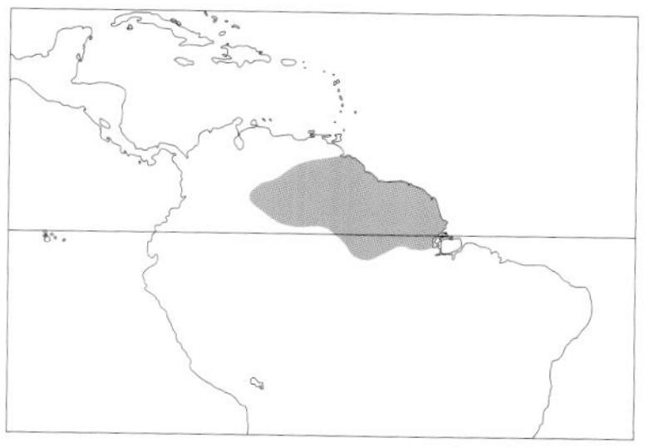

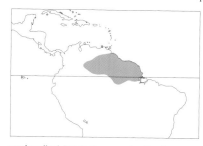

Descriptive notes. 18-22 cm; 18-29 g. Male has upperparts and chestband shining metallic coppery green, usually more bluish on crown and sides of head; primaries dull black; tail relatively short and very rounded, metallic bluish-green; chin blackish, throat white (sometimes sparsely speckled green), lower underparts and underwing-coverts rufous-chestnut; undertail dusky, tinged bluish; bill very long, 4·6-5·2 cm (3·4-4·7 cm from nostril), slender, all black; iris dark brown; bare eyering blackish-grey; feet brownish-yellow, black claws. Female similar, but has throat and chin buff, underparts slightly duller and paler. Immature not described. Voice. Song accelerating "peeo peeo peea pee-pee-pee-pee-pe-pe-pe-e-e-e-e'e'e'e", ending in sharp trill; call a frequently repeated "peep" or "peer", sometimes doubled or in series but not terminating with trill; occasionally "daw-dit-dot-dit".
Habitat. Borders (but not interior) of humid *terra firme*, *várzea*, gallery and secondary forest, mangroves, bushy marshland, coffee plantations, most often in open woodland, savanna and shrubby areas, along streams and rivers, and on lightly forested (including sandy) ridges; from coastal regions to 700 m. Perches from lower to middle levels. Occupies similar niche to that of *G. ruficauda*, and the two usually exclude each other in areas of contact; where sympatric, in small areas of Guyana and French Guiana, they are thought to be separated ecologically, present species frequenting riverine habitat and hilly areas, while the locally rarer *G. ruficauda* is associated with extensive savannas; their ranges are parapatric in S Venezuela, the former frequenting forested hills and the latter occupying adjacent dry *llanos* savanna.
Food and Feeding. Predominantly Hymenoptera (e.g. Ichneumonidae), but also Lepidoptera, Hemiptera, Diptera (Brachycera), Coleoptera (e.g. Chrysomelidae, Lamellicornia), also Odonata including damselfies (Zygoptera) and Libellulidae, *Orthemis ferruginea*, *Micrathyria*. Perches, often in pairs, on exposed branches; sallies to catch flying insects. Probably more active foraging than *G. dea*, with perhaps around 40 forays per hour, and much more rapid head movements while perched.
Breeding. Breeds in Feb-Mar in Venezuela, in May-Jun and Aug in Surinam, and in Apr and Sept in Brazil. Burrow excavated in low bank or arboreal termitarium; in Surinam, 3 individuals (2 males, 1 female) observed excavating in an arboreal termitarium 3 m above ground. No information on clutch size or on incubation and fledging periods.
Movements. Sedentary.
Status and Conservation. Not globally threatened. Generally common, at least in coastal portions of its range and in river valleys of S Venezuela (e.g. R Orinoco, R Caura, R Paragua). The commonest jacamar in coastal Surinam. Occurs in several protected areas throughout range, e.g Imataca Forest Reserve and El Dorado, in Venezuela, Voltzberg-Raleigh Falls Reserve, in Surinam, and Tapajós National Park, in Brazil.
Bibliography. Bangs & Penard (1918), Burton (1976), Cory (1919), Forrester (1993), Friedmann (1948), Griscom & Greenway (1941), Haffer (1997c), Haverschmidt & Mees (1994), Hilty & Brown (1986), Meyer de Schauensee (1982), Meyer de Schauensee & Phelps (1978), Olrog (1968), Oren & Parker (1997), Phelps & Phelps (1958), Pinto (1938b), Reynaud (1998), Ruschi (1979), Schubart *et al.* (1965), Sick (1993), Snethlage (1914), Snyder (1966), Stotz *et al.* (1996), Tostain *et al.* (1992), Zimmer & Hilty (1997).

12. Coppery-chested Jacamar
Galbula pastazae

French: Jacamar des Andes **German**: Kupferglanzvogel **Spanish**: Jacamará Cobrizo

Taxonomy. *Galbula pastazæ* Taczanowski and Berlepsch, 1885, Mapoto and Machay, Ecuador.
Forms a superspecies with *G. ruficauda*, *G. galbula*, *G. tombacea* and *G. cyanescens*; most closely related to the last two. Monotypic.
Distribution. Extreme S Colombia (El Carmen, in SE Nariño) and S along E slope of Andes in E Ecuador (to extreme S at Zumba); recorded once from extreme N Peru (R Cenepa, in Cordillera del Condor). Reported occurrence in Brazil erroneous, based on a misidentified female *G. cyanescens*.

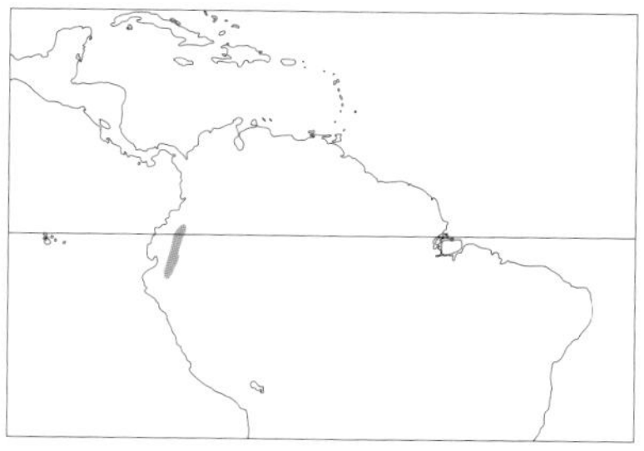

Descriptive notes. 23-24 cm; c. 31 g. Largest *Galbula*. Male has crown entirely metallic green, glossed bluish; rest of upperparts metallic bronzy green; 2 central pairs of tail feathers green, remainder coppery rufous, small green apical spot on outer rectrices; throat and chest shining green, chin and upper throat often flecked whitish, rest of underparts, including undertail, rich dark rufous; bill 4·8-5·4 cm long (4·5 cm from nostril), long, heavier than close relatives, black; iris dark brown; prominent bare yellowish-orange eyering; feet greyish. Female has distinctive dark rufous throat, less prominent eyering. Immature not described. Voice. Song is a series of notes that rises in frequency, and accelerates slightly, slowing down again for the final 2 or 3 notes, "pee pee pee pee-pee-pee-pee-pee-pe-pe-pe-pee-pee-pee-pee pee pee peee"; full song starts with several short notes, runs into rapid trill, slows to several longer notes, and ends with another trill; call is a series of loud "quep" notes, although species is often silent.
Habitat. Frequents understorey and edges of humid lower montane forest and second growth. Ranges considerably higher than all other jacamars, at 600-1700 m, most often 1000-1300 m; single reports from 2100 m and 2600 m are thought to be inaccurate, probably due to mislabelling.
Food and Feeding. Prey items found among stomach contents include fragments of insects, mainly Coleoptera and Hymenoptera. Perches for prolonged periods, individually or in loose pairs or family groups, fairly low down (usually 1-4 m) on exposed branches, from where sallies to catch flying insects. Apparently more often encountered singly in non-breeding season.
Breeding. Nov-Dec in Ecuador. Nest in earth bank; 3 nests were each 1·5-2 m up in bank 2·5 m tall created by cutting of trail through forest, 1 tunnel half-hidden by overhanging vegetation, another at least 50 cm deep and curving upwards so that nest-chamber was invisible; a nest found at 1350 m in Pastaza Valley (Ecuador) in Oct 1939, 37 cm long with entrance 5 cm in diameter, and with 2 eggs, was considered to be of *G. tombacea*, but altitude and location make it likely that it belonged to present species. Clutch size and incubation and fledging periods not recorded.
Movements. Sedentary.
Status and Conservation. VULNERABLE. Restricted-range species: present in Ecuador-Peru East Andes EBA. Only 1 record in Colombia, at Putumayo in 1993, since its discovery in that country in 1970, although area of occurrence rarely visited by ornithologists. Size of Ecuadorian population unknown; reported to be fairly common at Río Bombuscaro, in Podocarpus National Park, on basis of 4-6 pairs along a trail 2-3 km long. Threats to this park over recent years have been mining and colonization by humans and, given its importance for a wide variety of threatened Andean fauna, it requires focused conservation action. Although the species has been found at several other sites and may prove to be secure, it appears to be thinly and patchily distributed. Moreover, it appears to be dependent on fairly intact lower montane forest in the Andes, a habitat type seriously threatened by agricultural settlement, road-building, cattle grazing, and clearance for cultivation of coffee and tea. Extensive and effective protected areas are required in this zone. As it is generally confiding, hunting could be a problem in some recently settled areas.
Bibliography. Balchin & Toyne (1998), Bloch *et al.* (1991), Butler (1979), Chapman (1926), Collar, Crosby & Stattersfield (1994), Collar, Gonzaga *et al.* (1992), Collar, Wege & Long (1997), Cory (1919), Cracraft (1985), Fitzpatrick & Willard (1982), Hilty & Brown (1986), Meyer de Schauensee (1982), Olrog (1968), Poulsen & Wege (1994), Rahbek *et al.* (1995), Rasmussen *et al.* (1996), Ridgely & Greenfield (2001), Rodner *et al.* (2000), Salaman *et al.* (2002), Schulenberg & Awbrey (1997), Stattersfield & Capper (2000), Stotz *et al.* (1996), Wege & Long (1995), Williams & Tobias (1994).

13. White-chinned Jacamar
Galbula tombacea

French: Jacamar à menton blanc **Spanish**: Jacamará Barbiblanco
German: Weißkinn-Glanzvogel

Taxonomy. *Galbula tombacea* Spix, 1824, São Paulo de Olivença, Brazil.
Forms a superspecies with *G. ruficauda*, *G. galbula*, *G. pastazae* and *G. cyanescens*; most closely related to the last two. Differences between nominate race and *mentalis* possibly clinal. Two subspecies recognized.
Subspecies and Distribution.
G. t. tombacea Spix, 1824 - E of Andes in Colombia (S of Villavicencio, in Meta), NE Ecuador (Napo), NE Peru (Loreto), and W Brazil S of Amazon (E to Tonantins area).
G. t. mentalis Todd, 1943 - NW Brazil on both banks of R Solimões (E to R Negro and R Madeira).

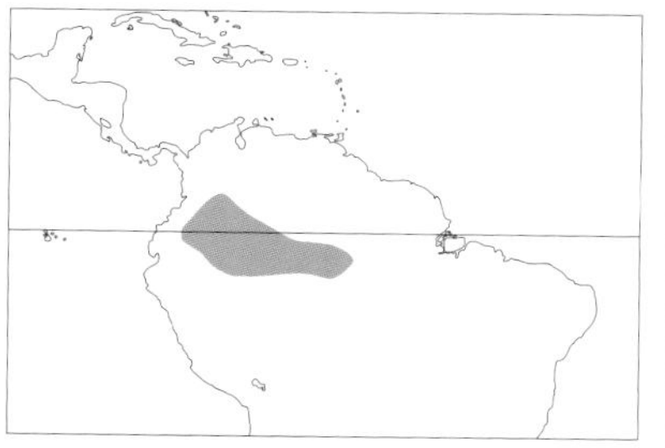

Descriptive notes. 19-23 cm; 21·5-25 g. Male has crown ash-brown with bluish gloss on hindcrown; rest of upperparts dark metallic bronzy green, primaries blackish; 2 central pairs of rectrices green, remainder rufous, outer 2 pairs with small green patches near tips; smallish white chin spot 5-7 mm across; throat and chest glittering green, rest of underparts, including underwing-coverts and undertail, rufous-chestnut; bill 4·5-5·3 cm long (3·5-4·3 cm from nostril), slender, black; iris dark brown; bare eyering and loral region greyish; feet greyish-brown. Female has belly paler ochraceous. Immature apparently undescribed. Race *mentalis* differs in larger white chin spot (8-11 mm across), upperparts glossed more coppery bronze, bluish on crown more extensive. Voice. Song an accelerating "pee-pee-pee-pee-pe-pe-pe-pe'pe'pe'pe'e'e", terminating in trill; call a sharp "keelip" or "peeup", often in series; all vocalizations reminiscent of *G. ruficauda*.
Habitat. Shrubby borders and treefalls of *terra firme*, *várzea* and gallery forest, often along rivers and streams in lowlands; up to 1200 m.
Food and Feeding. Only Hymenoptera (Vespidae, Formicidae) reported; presumably eats similar prey to that taken by *G. ruficauda*. Perches solitarily or in pairs on exposed branches 1-8 m up; sallies to catch flying insects in shrubby undergrowth and forest openings.
Breeding. No reliable information. A nest considered to be of this species, found at 1350 m in Pastaza Valley in Ecuador, in Oct 1939, was 37 cm long, 5 cm in diameter at the mouth, and contained 2 eggs; in view of altitude and location, however, likelihood that it belonged to *G. pastazae* is difficult to rule out.
Movements. Sedentary.
Status and Conservation. Not globally threatened. Widespread. Generally uncommon in Colombia and Ecuador, and rare in E Peru; common on R Urucu, in Amazonas, Brazil. Occurs in several protected areas throughout its range, e.g. Amacayacu National Park and Tinigua National Park, in Colombia. No immediate threats have been identified, although habitat loss caused by deforestation doubtless continues to reduce population size. Requires further studies on details of life history.
Bibliography. Best *et al.* (1997), Blake (1962), Butler (1979), Cadena *et al.* (2000), Chapman (1917), Clements & Shany (2001), Cory (1919), Cracraft (1985), Forrester (1993), Guilherme (2000, 2001), Haffer (1974), Hilty & Brown (1986), Meyer de Schauensee (1949, 1982), Nicéforo & Olivares (1967), Olrog (1968), Parker *et al.* (1982),

On following pages: 14. Bluish-fronted Jacamar (*Galbula cyanescens*); 15. Purplish Jacamar (*Galbula chalcothorax*); 16. Bronzy Jacamar (*Galbula leucogastra*); 17. Paradise Jacamar (*Galbula dea*); 18. Great Jacamar (*Jacamerops aureus*).

Peres & Whittaker (1991), Ridgely & Greenfield (2001), Ridgely *et al.* (1998), Rodner *et al.* (2000), Ruschi (1979), Sick (1993), Stotz *et al.* (1996), Taczanowski (1886).

14. Bluish-fronted Jacamar

Galbula cyanescens

French: Jacamar à couronne bleue **German**: Blaustirn-Glanzvogel **Spanish**: Jacamará Coroniazul
Other common names: Blue-fronted Jacamar

Taxonomy. *Galbula cyanescens* Deville, 1849, Sarayacu, River Ucayali, Peru.
Forms a superspecies with *G. ruficauda*, *G. galbula*, *G. pastazae* and *G. tombacea*; most closely related to the last two. Monotypic.
Distribution. S of Amazon in E Peru, W Brazil (E to R Madeira) and N Bolivia (S to N La Paz).

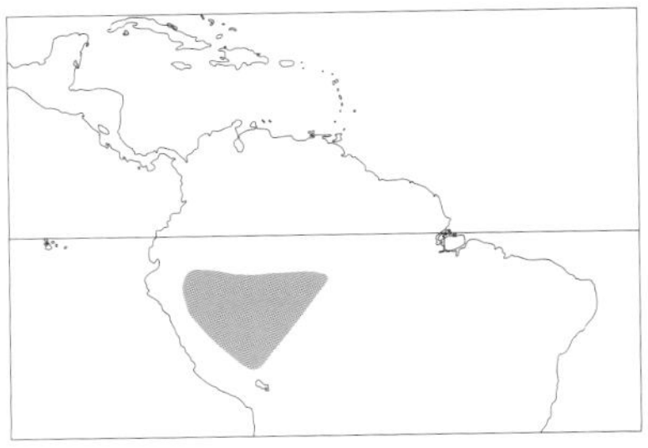

Descriptive notes. 20-23 cm; 22-26 g. Male has entire crown metallic green to bluish; upperparts metallic green, glossed bluish, sometimes coppery; primaries blackish; tail rufous, 2 central pairs of rectrices green, outer 2 pairs with small green patches near tips; chin and upper throat blackish, often freckled whitish; throat and chest green, rest of underparts, including underwing-coverts and undertail, rufous; bill 4·4-5·5 cm long, slender, black; iris dark brown; bare eyering and loral region greyish; feet greyish-brown. Differs from very similar *G. tombacea* in having green to bluish crown, smaller or non-existent white chin spot. Female as male, but with ochraceous lower breast and belly. Immature undescribed. Voice. Long series of high-pitched "kree" or "kree-ip" notes; full song an excited series of notes that accelerate to a trill, slow again to individual notes, then accelerate to a final flourish, "kip kip-kip-kipkikikrkrkrrr-kree-kree-kree-kip-kip-kikikrrrrreeuw".
Habitat. Edges of humid primary forest, gallery forest and second growth, often in streamside and lakeside vegetation, at up to 1000 m. By R Manu, in Peru, was found generally to avoid early successional stages, populations being most dense in mid-stages with mixed canopy and *Ficus/Cedrela* forest, becoming less dense again towards mature forest.
Food and Feeding. No specific taxa recorded as food, but diet thought to be similar to that of *G. ruficauda*. Perches on exposed branches at mid-levels, often 12-20 m up, but also in scrub layer; sallies to catch flying insects. Sometimes joins mixed-species flocks.
Breeding. No information available.
Movements. Sedentary.
Status and Conservation. Not globally threatened. Although poorly known, apparently common throughout its range. In Peru, density of up to 13 pairs/100 ha recorded by R Manu. Occurs in Manu National Park and Tambopata Reserve, in Peru, and in Madidi National Park, Bolivia. No specific threats recorded.
Bibliography. Allen (1995), Angehr & Aucca (1997), Bronaugh (1984), Clements & Shany (2001), Cory (1919), Cracraft (1985), Davis (1986), Donahue (1994), Forrester (1993), Foster *et al.* (1994), Gyldenstolpe (1945a), Ihering & Ihering (1907), Meyer de Schaunsee (1982), Munn (1985), Olrog (1968), Parker & Bailey (1991), Parker & Remsen (1987), Parker *et al.* (1982), Pinto (1938b), Remsen & Traylor (1989), Robinson & Terborgh (1997), Ruschi (1979), Sick (1993), Snethlage (1914), Stotz *et al.* (1996), Terborgh *et al.* (1984), Traylor (1958), Zimmer (1930).

15. Purplish Jacamar

Galbula chalcothorax

French: Jacamar violacé **German**: Purpurglanzvogel **Spanish**: Jacamará Violáceo

Taxonomy. *Galbula chalcothorax* P. L. Sclater, 1855, Quijos, Ecuador.
Forms a superspecies with *G. leucogastra*. Sometimes regarded as conspecific, but geographical isolation and apparently stable morphological differences support treatment as separate species. Monotypic.
Distribution. SE Colombia (Putumayo, Vaupés, Guainía), E Ecuador, E Peru and W Brazil (R Juruá).

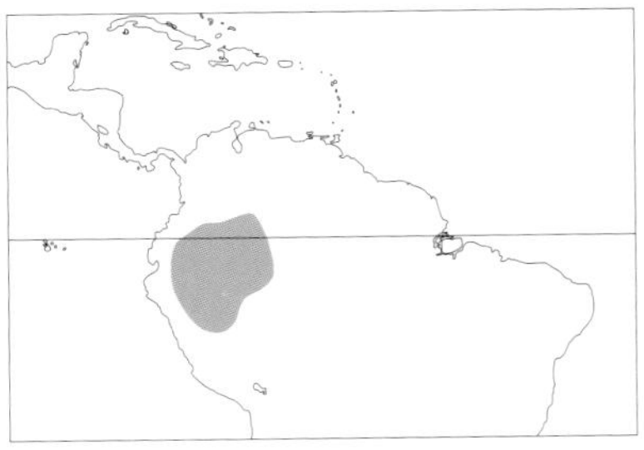

Descriptive notes. 20-23 cm; 24·5-26·5 g. Male has crown and sides of head blackish-green with bluish sheen; upperparts, including tail, and breast metallic reddish-purple or coppery red; chin black, throat white, belly blackish with feathers tipped white, especially on lower flanks and towards vent; underside of tail dusky, outer rectrices tipped and fringed whitish on inner web; underwing-coverts black; bill 4-4·8 cm long (3·2-3·7 cm from nostril), slender, all black; iris dark brown; bare eyering and loral region greyish-black; feet black. Differs from *G. leucogastra* in distinctly larger size, particularly wing length; generally shows more purplish tones. Female as male, but throat and belly yellowish-fulvous or buff. Immature undescribed. Voice. Song is rising series of inflected notes, often in pairs, "weeee weeee wi-deee wi-deee wi-deee", sometimes accelerating into trill; call "weeee", similar to that of Dusky-capped Flycatcher (*Myiarchus tuberculifer*).
Habitat. Edges, clearings, treefalls and canopy of primary and secondary *terra firme* forest, also sand-belt woodland, and often along rivers or streams; mainly below 500 m, but in Ecuador locally up to 1000 m.
Food and Feeding. No information on diet, but presumably similar to that of *G. ruficauda*. 3 specimens taken in E Ecuador were apparently all on bees' nests, but whether they were foraging on bees is not made clear. Singles, pairs or groups of 3-4 perch from low to high levels (2-10 m), sometimes on exposed canopy branches, more often in shrub layer. Sallies for flying insects. Sometimes associates with mixed-species flocks.
Breeding. No information available.
Movements. Sedentary.
Status and Conservation. Not globally threatened. Poorly known and generally uncommon. Fairly common in Ecuador along R Napo, and occurs in Cuyabeno Reserve; scarce in E Colombia, where reported from Tinigua National Park, in Meta, and Amacayacu National Park, in SE Amazonas; rare in E Peru. It is probably threatened to some extent by forest degradation and habitat loss. Further ecological studies are needed to determine its habitat requirements, status and distribution.
Bibliography. Balchin & Toyne (1998), Best *et al.* (1997), Butler (1979), Cadena *et al.* (2000), Chapman (1926), Clements & Shany (2001), Cory (1919), Cracraft (1985), Forrester (1993), Goodfellow (1902), Gyldenstolpe (1945a), Hilty & Brown (1986), Meyer de Schauensee (1982), Olrog (1968), Parker *et al.* (1982), Pearson (1975b), Ridgely & Greenfield (2001), Ridgely *et al.* (1998), Rodner *et al.* (2000), Ruschi (1979), Schulenberg & Awbrey (1997), Snethlage (1914), Stotz *et al.* (1996).

16. Bronzy Jacamar

Galbula leucogastra

French: Jacamar à ventre blanc **German**: Bronzeglanzvogel **Spanish**: Jacamará Bronceado

Taxonomy. *Galbula leucogastra* Vieillot, 1817, South America = Cayenne.
Forms a superspecies with *G. chalcothorax*. Sometimes regarded as conspecific, but geographical isolation and apparently stable morphological differences support treatment as separate species. Thought to have hybridized with *G. galbula* in Surinam. Birds from R Tapajós, Brazil, described as race *viridissima* on basis of greener plumage, but this character is difficult to assess, and colour apparently falls within range of individual variation shown elsewhere in species' range. Monotypic.
Distribution. S Venezuela (S Bolívar, Amazonas), the Guianas and Brazil (from upper R Negro and R Purús E to R Madeira and R Tapajós) S to Rondônia, Mato Grosso and N Bolivia (Pando).

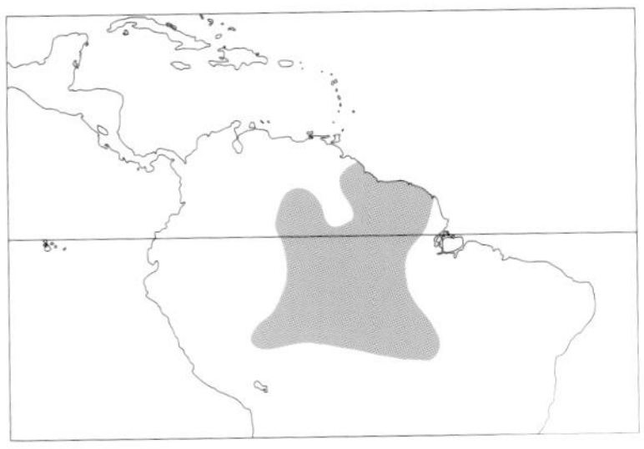

Descriptive notes. 19-22 cm; 15-18 g. A relatively small, dark jacamar. Male has crown and sides of head metallic dark greenish-blue; rest of upperparts and entire breast metallic bronzy green, sometimes with slight purplish gloss; primaries blackish; graduated tail bronze-green on upper surface, especially central pair of rectrices; chin black; throat, belly, underwing-coverts and undertail-coverts with extensive white, underside of tail dusky, outer rectrices edged and tipped white; bill 3·9-4·6 cm long (3-3·3 cm from nostril), slender, black; iris dark brown; bare eyering and loral region black; feet black. Differs from *G. chalcothorax* in distinctly smaller size, particularly wing length; generally shows brighter rufous tones. Female has throat and belly buff or ochraceous, eyering and loral region blackish-grey. Immature unknown. Voice. Song high, ascending and accelerating whistling notes, apparently similar to *G. albirostris* but ending with trill, rather than rattle; also distinctive very high-pitched, rhythmic sequence, "eww-hihi heww-heehee heww", this also described as rising series of triplets, "weeee, weep-pip-pweeeeee, weep-pip-pweeeeee, weep-pip-pweeeeee"; calls sharp and clipped.
Habitat. Edges and clearings of primary and secondary *terra firme* forest, white-sand *campinarana* in Amazonia, wooded savannas and (at least in coastal French Guiana) marshes scattered with woodlots, regularly along streams and rivers in lowlands; locally to 900 m. Occurs locally in gallery forest, dry forest and *cerrado* in Brazil, where it occupies light undergrowth and open lower canopies.
Food and Feeding. Only reported food items are Neuroptera (Mantispidae), Hymenoptera (Apidae, *Melipona*; also Chrysididae, Ichneumonidae), Diptera (Syrphidae, Asilidae), Hemiptera, Homoptera (Fulgoridae). Perhaps takes fewer Lepidoptera or Odonata than do other *Galbula* species. Perches in pairs, groups of 3 or 4, but frequently singly, from low to high levels (usually 2-10 m), on exposed canopy branches or the upper shrub layer. Sallies for flying insects, as other jacamars. Sometimes associates with mixed-species canopy flocks.
Breeding. 2 nests found, both in arboreal termitarium: in Surinam in Jul, 6 m above ground, very short entrance, nest-chamber measuring 8 cm by 8 cm, 1 nestling, fed by both adults; other in French Guiana, early May, 15 m above ground. No further data available.
Movements. Sedentary.
Status and Conservation. Not globally threatened. Appears to be uncommon throughout its range. Not uncommon in Surinam, very rare in French Guiana; in Brazil, rare N of Manaus, uncommon further south. No immediate threats are recorded, but may suffer to some extent from overall habitat loss. Several protected areas, however, exist within its range, e.g. Tapajós National Park, Brazil.
Bibliography. Bangs & Penard (1918), Cohn-Haft *et al.* (1997), Cory (1919), Forrester (1993), Fry (1970b), Griscom & Greenway (1941), Haverschmidt (1958, 1960), Haverschmidt & Mees (1994), Hindwood (1959), Meyer de Schauensee (1982), Meyer de Schauensee & Phelps (1978), Olrog (1968), Oren & Parker (1997), Parker & Remsen (1987), Phelps & Phelps (1958), Pinto (1938b), Remsen & Traylor (1989), Rodner *et al.* (2000), Sick (1993), da Silva (1996), Snethlage (1914), Snyder (1966), Stotz *et al.* (1996), Tostain *et al.* (1992), Willard *et al.* (1991), Willis & Oniki (1990), Zimmer & Hilty (1997), Zimmer *et al.* (1997).

17. Paradise Jacamar

Galbula dea

French: Jacamar à longue queue **German**: Paradiesglanzvogel **Spanish**: Jacamará Colilargo

Taxonomy. *Alcedo Dea* Linnaeus, 1758, Surinam.
Previously placed in a separate genus *Urogalba*, but this now subsumed by *Galbula*. Races described largely on the basis of differences in size and plumage tone, but these may represent only clinal variation. Four subspecies recognized.
Subspecies and Distribution.
G. d. dea (Linnaeus, 1758) - S Venezuela (upper R Orinoco), the Guianas, and Brazil N of Amazon (E of R Negro).
G. d. brunneiceps (Todd, 1943) - SE Colombia (E Guainía, Vaupés, S to Amazonas), E Ecuador, E Peru, and W Brazil (W of R Negro and, S of Amazon, between R Madeira and R Tapajós).
G. d. phainopepla (Todd, 1943) - W Brazil S of Amazon (W of R Madeira).
G. d. amazonum (P. L. Sclater, 1855) - NC Brazil (W to R Tapajós, S to N Mato Grosso) and N Bolivia (Pando, Beni, N La Paz).
Descriptive notes. 25·5-34 cm; 25-32·5 g. Slender, elongated jacamar with plumage appearing all black at a distance. Crown dark brown; rest of upperparts, including tail, glossy black with slight bluish sheen; wings metallic bluish-black, bronze-green sheen on coverts and inner remiges; rectrices

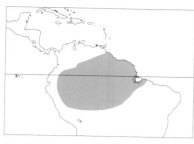

very long and narrow, particularly central pair (14-18 cm); chin blackish with brown spot, conspicuous white throat and upper breast to sides of neck, rest of underparts blackish; underwing-coverts white; bill 4·9-6·8 cm long, needle-like, black; iris dark brown; feet black, soles yellowish-brown. Immature not described. Race *brunneiceps* has longer wings, shorter tail, longer bill, crown slightly paler brown, upperparts with more bronzy greenish sheen, less bluish, wing-coverts glossed bronzy green, brown spot on chin smaller; *amazonum* larger, has slightly longer wings, longer bill, shorter tail, crown light brown with feathers tipped brownish-white, uppertail-coverts, tail and tertials bronzy to greenish, black chin less extensive, white throat more extensive; *phainopepla* is similar to previous but generally smaller and brighter, upperparts and tail more greenish, wing-coverts and tertials washed more bronzy.

Voice. Usually fairly quiet; song a well-spaced "peep peep peep peep peep peep pee pee pe pe", usually descending, becoming slightly faster and weaker towards end; call a single "pip", or "glewweh" like a distant woodcreeper (Dendrocolaptidae) or hawk (Accipitridae); also a low "ghib-ghib-rrehha".

Habitat. Humid primary and secondary *terra firme*, *várzea*, savanna forest, locally also dry forest and gallery forest along rivers and streams; usually below 500 m, but locally to 1100 m. Generally at canopy level, descending to lower levels at borders (very rarely in interior). Most often recorded at treefalls, clearings or edges.

Food and Feeding. Recorded prey items include Lepidoptera (e.g. Rhopalocera), Odonata (e.g. Libellulidae), Diptera (e.g. Tabanidae), Hymenoptera (e.g. Vespidae, Apidae; these usually the vast majority of food items), and Coleoptera (e.g. Curculionidae). Stomach contents have included spiders. Perches in singles, pairs or groups of 3 or 4. Sallies from exposed perch on outer or upper branches, sometimes as low as 1 m but usually in canopy, foraging height thus dependent on vegetation structure. Catches insects in air, often after direct stooping dive and agile chase, but sometimes after vertical upward flight; returns to a perch with undulating flight, changing perches after c. 50% of forays. In 5 hours of observation, flights occurred at rate of 21·8 per hour, ranged in distance from 1 m to 12 m (mostly 4·5-9 m), and were generally of short duration, 1·3-5·6 seconds (mean 3·2 seconds). It is unclear whether spiders are taken aerially, from webs, or from branches. Sometimes joins mixed-species flocks in canopy.

Breeding. Pair excavating nest-burrow in arboreal termitarium in May in Colombia; pairs regularly seen near high arboreal termitaria in dead trees in Surinam and French Guiana. No further information available.

Movements. Sedentary.

Status and Conservation. Not globally threatened. Generally common, but often overlooked because of its canopy-dwelling habits. Very common in sand-belt forest of Guainía and Vaupés, in Colombia; common along waterways in Guyana, where has been observed in the botanical garden of Georgetown; quite common in Surinam, French Guiana and S Venezuela, and generally common throughout Amazonia. Rare and local in E Ecuador; locally common in E Peru. No immediate threats are known, but general habitat destruction presumably continues to reduce populations. Numbers may increase in response to selective logging, as recorded in French Guiana, although this possibly a result of easier opportunity of detection. Recorded in many protected areas, e.g. Imataca Forest Reserve and El Dorado, in Venezuela, Amacayacu National Park, in Colombia, Tambopata Reserve, in Peru, and Tapajós National Park, in Brazil.

Bibliography. Allen (1995), Bangs & Penard (1918), Brace *et al.* (1997), Burton (1976), Cohn-Haft *et al.* (1997), Cory (1919), Descourtilz (1983), Donahue (1994), Fry (1970b), Griscom & Greenway (1941), Gyldenstolpe (1945a, 1945b), Haverschmidt & Mees (1994), Hilty & Brown (1986), Meyer de Schauensee (1982), Meyer de Schauensee & Phelps (1978), Olrog (1968), Oren & Parker (1997), Parker *et al.* (1982), Peres & Whittaker (1991), Phelps & Phelps (1958), Pinto (1938b), Remsen & Traylor (1989), Sargeant (1994), Sick (1993), Snyder (1966), Stotz *et al.* (1996), Thiollay (1992), Thiollay & Jullien (1998), Tostain *et al.* (1992), Willard *et al.* (1991), Zimmer & Hilty (1997), Zimmer *et al.* (1997).

Genus *JACAMEROPS* Lesson, 1830

18. Great Jacamar
Jacamerops aureus

French: Grand Jacamar   **German**: Riesenglanzvogel   **Spanish**: Jacamará Grande

Taxonomy. *Alcedo aurea* P. L. S. Müller, 1776, Berbice, Guyana.
Was formerly considered sufficiently distinct to be placed in a monotypic subfamily Jacameropinae, although this no longer considered warranted. Specific scientific name frequently spelt as *aurea*, but this incorrect as genus name is masculine. Slight variations in tone and intensity of upperpart and underpart coloration in different parts of range, but considerable overlap mitigates against naming of further geographical races. Four subspecies recognized.

Subspecies and Distribution.
J. a. penardi Bangs & Barbour, 1922 - Costa Rica (Caribbean slope), S to W Colombia (E to E Andes) and NW Ecuador (Esmeraldas).
J. a. aureus (P. L. S. Müller, 1776) - Colombia E of Andes, S Venezuela and the Guianas.
J. a. isidori Deville, 1849 - E Ecuador, E Peru, W Brazil (E to R Purús) and N Bolivia (Beni, N La Paz).
J. a. ridgwayi Todd, 1943 - lower Amazonian Brazil (E of R Negro on N bank, E of R Tapajós on S bank) S to Mato Grosso.

Descriptive notes. 25-30 cm; 57-76 g. By far the most bulky jacamar. Male has chin, sides of face and entire upperparts iridescent green, glossed with bluish on chin, forehead, crown and tail, with golden, purplish or coppery on mantle; primaries blackish; tail rather long, broad and rounded, central pair of rectrices brighter coppery bluish-green; lower throat gleaming white, rest of underparts chestnut-rufous, underside of tail dusky or blue-black; bill 4·6-5·5 cm, relatively short, stout and decurved, all black; iris dark brown or chestnut-brown; bare eyering and lores grey; feet dark horn or green-grey, claws black. Female similar, but lacks white patch on throat. Immature similar to adult female, but duller and less iridescent above with little or no coppery sheen, paler and duller below, rectrices narrowly tipped dull bronze. Race *penardi* has greener upperparts; *isidori* has paler underparts; *ridgwayi* has upperparts more purplish, chin, forehead and crown more greenish than blue, underparts darker and more amber-brown than previous race. **Voice.** Often silent; song, usually given at long intervals, a prolonged penetrating, high-pitched, hawk-like "kle-eeeeeuuuu", the preliminary clipped note abruptly shifting to long falling whistle; pairs counter-call with various soft buzzing, grating or cat-like mewing notes, sometimes doubled.

Habitat. Unbroken humid forest and well-shaded forest borders, often along streams and rivers (including *várzea* and *igapó* forest), less commonly at forest edges and in tall open second growth; also locally in gallery forest on Brazilian *cerrado*. Usually below 700 m, locally to 1100 m.

Food and Feeding. Various Hymenoptera of families Scoliidae, Vespidae (*Pachodynerus*), Apidae, Ichneumonidae and Formicidae, also Hemiptera, Homoptera, Lepidoptera, Odonata, also Coleoptera of families Buprestidae (*Chrysobothris*), Cetonidae, Chrysomelidae, Scarabeidae, Cerambycidae (*Trachyderes succinctus*). At least in Costa Rica, spiders and small lizards also taken. More sluggish than other jacamars, therefore easily overlooked; often very confiding. Perches in pairs or solitarily on slender branches or horizontal vines from mid-levels to lower canopy, usually at 4-10 m, lower at edges or gaps. Sallies to catch flying insects; tends not to return to same perch. Also gleans insects, spiders and small lizards from foliage in flight. Beats most prey against perch before swallowing. Rarely, if ever, joins mixed flocks.

Breeding. Breeds in Mar-Jun in Costa Rica, in Apr-May in W Colombia (Chocó), in Jan in Brazil (R Negro), in Oct in Peru; timing probably related to variations in wet season. Nest in arboreal termitarium 3-15 m above ground; also reported in rotting tree trunk. No information on clutch size, nor on incubation and fledging periods.

Movements. Sedentary.

Status and Conservation. Not globally threatened. Generally considered rare or uncommon, although it may often be overlooked owing to its unobtrusive canopy-dwelling nature; recorded much more frequently when voice is known. Rare to very uncommon, and apparently decreasing, in Costa Rica. Uncommon and apparently local in Panama, Colombia and Ecuador; in Panama, widespread but uncommon around Canal area, Darién and Cerro Pirre. Widespread in Guyana; not very numerous in Surinam. Apparently rare in E Peru; common in Rondônia, Brazil. Presumably adversely affected by deforestation; indeed, reported to decline substantially after selective logging in French Guiana. No immediate threats are known. Occurs in several protected areas throughout range, e.g. Imataca Forest Reserve and El Dorado, in Venezuela, Tambopata Reserve, in Peru, Tapajós National Park, in Brazil, and Madidi National Park, in Bolivia. Further studies needed to estimate population numbers.

Bibliography. Allen (1995), Blake (1962), Cadena *et al.* (2000), Chapman (1926), Descourtilz (1983), Donahue (1994), Foster *et al.* (1994), Haffer (1975), Haverschmidt & Mees (1994), Hilty & Brown (1986), Levey & Stiles (1994), Meyer de Schauensee (1949, 1950, 1952, 1982), Meyer de Schauensee & Phelps (1978), Nicéforo & Olivares (1967), Oren & Parker (1997), Ortiz & Carrión (1991), Parker & Bailey (1991), Parker *et al.* (1993), Peres & Whittaker (1991), Remsen & Traylor (1989), Ridgely & Greenfield (2001), Ridgely & Gwynne (1989), Salaman *et al.* (1999), Sargeant (1994), Schubart *et al.* (1965), Sick (1993), da Silva (1996), Slud (1960, 1964), Snyder (1966), Stiles & Levey (1994), Stiles & Skutch (1989), Stotz *et al.* (1996), Terborgh *et al.* (1984), Thiollay (1992), Thiollay & Jullien (1998), Tostain *et al.* (1992), Traylor (1958), Wetmore (1968a), Willard *et al.* (1991), Zimmer & Hilty (1997).

Class AVES
Order GALBULIFORMES
Family BUCCONIDAE (PUFFBIRDS)

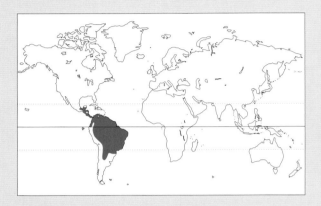

- Small to medium-sized perching birds with large head, short rounded wings, stocky body, small feet, and narrow tail; plumage soft, and drab to contrasting.
- 13-29 cm.

- Neotropical.
- Wooded, mostly lowland habitats.
- 12 genera, 35 species, 72 taxa.
- No species threatened; none extinct since 1600.

Systematics

The puffbirds have been treated in modern works as comprising, variously, 30 to 36 species, these divided among as few as seven to as many as 13 genera. Somewhat surprisingly for a group that remains relatively little known, no new species of Bucconidae have been discovered since 1925, and only four taxa that stand as full species were named after 1900. In fact, fully two-thirds of the recognized species have been known for at least 150 years, and most of the others for nearly as long. Despite this lengthy history of the majority of puffbird species, most have proven to be difficult subjects of field study, and even basic data on nesting, feeding and vocalizations are still lacking for several of them.

Several fossil species and genera were for a time placed within the Bucconidae, some having been moved there from other families in which they were originally described. The fossil *Neanis* [*Hebe*] *schucherti* was once thought to represent the earliest passeriform, in the family Rhinocryptidae, but was later recognized as a member of the Eocene "puffbird" group. Another, *Uintornis*, was first thought to be a woodpecker (Picidae), and then a cuckoo (Cuculidae), and yet another, *Botaurides*, was originally named as a heron (Ardeidae). These fossils, while closest to the Bucconidae, nevertheless differ from the modern family in a suite of characters, including a shorter mandibular symphysis, a broader manus, and several details of the distal end of the tarsometatarsus. These differences led A. Feduccia and L. D. Martin, in 1976, to place them in a new family, Primobucconidae; since then, the modern Bucconidae have been considered unrepresented in the fossil record. The Primobucconidae was said to be the dominant group of small arboreal birds in the Lower and Middle Eocene of North America, having radiated into several species and genera; at least one species was also identified from the Eocene of Britain. More recently, however, the taxa that were brought together in the Primobucconidae have been shown to belong to at least three different families, so that, after the removal of several taxa from the Primobucconidae, only one remains in that family. In a paper published in 1998, G. Mayr showed that an Eocene fossil from the famous Messel quarry in Germany has numerous similarities with the Primobucconidae, and primobucconid-like birds certainly occur both at Messel and at Quercy, in France. Small non-passerines with various degrees of zygodactyly were clearly the dominant perching birds in the Eocene of the Northern Hemisphere.

Early systematists often placed the puffbirds together with the barbets (Capitonidae), sometimes even in the same genus, and although Buffon considered the New World barbets and the puffbirds

to be related, using the name "Tamatia" for both, he believed that the Old World barbets were unrelated. In the middle of the nineteenth century, J. Cabanis and F. Heine treated the Bucconidae and the Capitonidae as separate families, and most subsequent researchers have considered these two groups to be fairly distantly related. Nevertheless, not long after Cabanis and Heine's work was published, H. Burmeister and even H. Schlegel treated the puffbirds and the barbets together, differentiating them principally on the basis of the number of rectrices which they possess. In 1850, C. L. Bonaparte recognized the barbets and the puffbirds as separate families, but confusingly reversed the family and generic names from those in subsequent usage. Numerous other early classifications united some or all of the zygodactylous groups, such as the Cuculiformes, the Piciformes, the Coraciiformes and the Trogoniformes, in various combinations, primarily or solely on

The puffbirds comprise a well-defined monophyletic assemblage, most species having a bulky head, large eyes, a robust bill, a bristly face and loose plumage. Nevertheless, agreement on generic limits within the Bucconidae has proven rather difficult. The Spotted Puffbird belongs to a controversial genus, Nystactes, which is usually merged with Bucco. The most distinctive trait of the two Nystactes species is their strongly bifid, or cleft, bill tip. Both species also have a black bill and an unbarred tail.

[*Nystactes tamatia pulmentum*, Amacayacu National Park, Colombia. Photo: Patricio Robles Gil]

The Chestnut-capped
Puffbird belongs to one of
five monospecific genera
in the Bucconidae. Placed
in the "bucconine" group
by Ridgway, it exhibits the
ancestral puffbird plumage
pattern that includes a
broad breastband, strong
facial markings and a pale
hindcollar that contrasts
with the rest of the
upperparts. It is generally
considered to be
monotypic, although some
authors treat birds from
the Río Caura region of
southern Venezuela as a
separate race, caurensis.
Like the genus Nystactes,
Argicus is often merged
with Bucco.

[Argicus macrodactylus,
Beni Biological Station,
Bolivia.
Photo: J. Hornbuckle/
VIREO]

the basis of the toe arrangement, despite the major differences between some of the groups in the form of zygodactyly involved.

Almost all authorities, beginning with H. G. Möhring in 1752, have agreed upon the sister-taxon relationship between Galbulidae (jacamars) and Bucconidae, though a few notable exceptions exist. C. L. Nitzsch, in his influential study of pterylography published in 1840, concluded that the Galbulidae possess an aftershaft, while the Bucconidae lack this, and subsequent workers accepted this uncritically as a major difference between the two groups. In 1956, however, C. G. Sibley showed that the Bucconidae do in fact have a vestigial aftershaft that is homologous to the small aftershaft of the Galbulidae.

An overwhelming number of morphological and biochemical characters link the Galbulidae and the Bucconidae, and no serious doubts have been raised as to the monophyly of the clade formed by these sister taxa, traditionally classified as the suborder Galbulae, within Piciformes. The two groups are similar in virtually all of the many osteological and myological aspects studied by J. Steinbacher, as well as in their syringeal and hyoid morphology. Characters that have been taken to be synapomorphies, or at least useful taxonomic characters shared by the two families, include the form of the tongue; the strongly desmognathous palate; the lack of ectepicondylar processes on the humeri; the conditions of the anterior iliac blades, the furcula, the sternal plate and the posterolateral processes; the possession of two carotids; the long, globose caeca; the naked, bilobed uropygial gland; the similar type of zygodactyly; and apparently derived conditions of trochlea IV. Some characters traditionally cited as diagnosing the Galbulae are not well established, and at least one, the forked spina externa, has been found to be variable and widespread. Externally, the two families share forward-directed setae surrounding the bill; eyelashes; similar pterylography; non-oscinine wing-coverts; and the same number and moult patterns of remiges and rectrices. Several biochemical studies have supported their relationship as sister taxa: first, electrophoretic studies of egg-white proteins; then an allozyme study of the Piciformes and Coraciiformes; and DNA-DNA hybridization analyses.

Nevertheless, the status of the Bucconidae and the Galbulidae as separate families has rarely been questioned, although H. Seebohm merged them in 1895, as did S. D. Ripley 50 years later. This near-consensus may be due to the fact that jacamars and puffbirds differ in several obvious external characters. Bucconids have a shorter, more curved, hooked, heavier bill, often with a bifid tip; reduced or non-existent plumage gloss; and a general chunky, large-headed shape. Internally, the two families differ in the form of the spinal cord, with Bucconidae bearing that of Piciformes and many other groups, while the type shown by Galbulidae is as that of Coraciiformes, among other groups. Moreover, bucconids differ from jacamars in having a rounded gonys; a vomer; a high keel on the palatine; six ribs; minor differences in most muscle groups and skeletal elements; several minor differences in pterylography; a posteriorly scutellate tarsus; and full, lax, earth-toned plumage.

The relationships of the Galbulae, which as a unit has enjoyed nearly universal acceptance, have nevertheless been the subject of considerable controversy. After a plethora of alternative placements, the Galbulae have in recent years most often been placed as a suborder within the order Piciformes, following A. Wetmore's classification. By far the most thorough study of the morphology of both jacamars and puffbirds was that of J. Steinbacher, published in 1937. After making comprehensive comparisons of their musculature, osteology, internal anatomy, and other aspects with those of the Capitonidae and the Picidae, Steinbacher's overwhelming conclusion was that jacamars and puffbirds are closely related, but also that jacamars are somewhat closer to barbets in many respects than are puffbirds. Steinbacher did not seriously question the tenet that all were piciforms, although, unfortunately, his comparisons with coraciiforms were extremely limited. The case for inclusion of the Galbulae in the Piciformes has been defended mainly by J. L. Cracraft and R. J. Raikow, using phylogenetic analyses of morphological characters, but it remains supported by only a few characters, mainly zygodactyly, the validity and homology of which were strongly disputed by S. L. Olson. In P. J. K. Burton's detailed study of puffbird morphology, which appeared in 1984, the view that the Bucconidae are better placed with the Coraciiformes was supported. Furthermore, it has recently been shown that one of the many characters in which the Galbulae differ strikingly from the remaining families of Wetmore's Piciformes is the lack of villi, the projections on the basalmost downy barbules of the breast feathers. Also, the Galbulae pos-

The two members of the genus Hypnelus may be conspecific, as they hybridize near Lake Maracaibo. The two forms are strongly differentiated from each other in plumage, however, the Two-banded Puffbird having two black breastbands and a pale throat, and the Russet-throated Puffbird (Hypnelus ruficollis) having a single black breastband and a rusty throat. Hybridization appears to be limited, for most specimens can be clearly assigned to one form or the other. Unless future studies in the contact zone suggest otherwise, the two taxa are probably best treated as separate species.

[Hypnelus bicinctus bicinctus, Caño Colorado, Monagas, Venezuela. Photo: Peter Boesman]

sess the primitive state for an electrophoretic marker that is derived in the remaining members of Wetmore's Piciformes; C. G. Sibley and J. E. Ahlquist have found, in multiple biochemical data sets, that relationships of the Galbulae with the rest of the Piciformes are weak at best; and in an electrophoretic study the Galbulae were sister to a motmot of the genus *Momota*, a coraciiform, followed by a picine. Sibley has long advocated treatment of the Galbulae as a separate order, Galbuliformes, and on the currently available evidence this seems to be the safest course to steer.

All bucconids are rather similar in basic shape, structure and general appearance, with the notable exception of the surprisingly martin-like Swallow-winged Puffbird (*Chelidoptera tenebrosa*). Even this aberrant form, however, would seem to be undeniably a puffbird, with quite typical bucconid internal morphology. Within the past century, no doubts have been expressed about the monophyly of the family Bucconidae. There are several clear-cut genera, which can scarcely be treated in any other manner: the nunbirds in the genus *Monasa*; the White-faced Nunbird (*Hapaloptila castanea*) in its own monospecific genus; the Swallow-winged Puffbird in *Chelidoptera*; the nunlets in *Nonnula*; the Lanceolated Monklet (*Micromonacha lanceolata*) in another monospecific genus; and the "soft-feathered" puffbirds in the genus *Malacoptila*. The remainder of the family, however, poses more difficulty in generic allocation. P. L. Sclater, in 1882, placed all the rest in the genus *Bucco*. However, too much variation exists among the 15 species involved to justify keeping all within a single genus. About three decades later, R. Ridgway included them in a subfamily Bucconinae, while recognizing differences at the generic level. More recently, G. W. Cottrell, in 1968, reverted to the inclusive genus *Bucco*, on the grounds that all but one member had a cleft-tipped bill.

The distribution within the proposed subfamily Bucconinae of the bifid bill tip nevertheless requires further comment, as recent observations differ from those of Cottrell, whose work has prompted some authors to return to Sclater's expanded genus *Bucco*. While Cottrell considered that, in the Bucconinae, all but one species, the Chestnut-capped Puffbird (*Argicus macrodactylus*), show the bifid bill tip, this feature has been found to be very pronounced in members of the genera *Hypnelus* and *Nystactes*, less so in *Notharchus*, but reduced to a slightly broadened but essentially non-bifid tip in *Nystalus* and the Collared Puffbird (*Bucco capensis*). Moreover, the bill of the Chestnut-

capped Puffbird has a pointed, definitively non-bifid tip. It should be noted that juveniles do not show a bifid tip at first, and there is some variability among adults of bifid-tipped species, this being almost certainly related to wear and replacement of the ramphotheca. The presence of the bifid bill tip seems correlated with other characters that define natural groups within the Bucconinae, and these groups should be recognized at least as subgenera, if not as full genera.

The most perplexing problem at the generic level involves the Collared Puffbird, which in bill shape and colour, as well as plumage pattern, is closer to species of *Nystalus* than to other members of an expanded genus *Bucco*. Since it is the type species of the genus and family, however, it cannot be removed from the genus *Bucco*. Resurrection of generic names in former widespread usage, until they were all placed in *Bucco* by J. L. Peters, provides an interim solution to the problem, pending further study. Thus, the genus *Argicus* can be used for the Chestnut-capped Puffbird, and the genus *Nystactes* for the Spotted Puffbird (*Nystactes tamatia*) and the Sooty-capped Puffbird (*Nystactes noanamae*). This is congruent with the bill-tip morphology and other external characters: *Bucco* and *Nystalus* have a non-bifid or very slightly bifid tip of the bill, a brightly coloured bill, and a barred tail; *Argicus* has an autapomorphic or unique plumage pattern and a fine bill tip; and *Nystactes* has a strongly bifid, all-black bill, and some distinctive plumage features. In 1936, H. von Boetticher suggested that the cleft tip of the bill, which is unique to the Bucconinae, is used as a vice, but evidence in support of this notion remains elusive.

In Ridgway's classification, the Bucconinae were distinguished from the other members of the family principally by the heavy, straight, hook-tipped bill, in most cases with a slightly to strongly bifid tip. The remaining species, all of which he grouped in Malacoptilinae, on the other hand, typically have a somewhat curved bill but lack a strong terminal hook or any suggestion of the bifid tip. While the plumage within the Bucconinae is highly variable, in general the component taxa have more contrasting colours and ornate patterns, such as a broad black breastband, a pale hindcollar, spotted upperparts, whitish underparts, and a strong facial pattern. Conversely, the Malacoptilinae exhibit mainly dark, relatively uniform plumage, with one or a few, often semi-concealed patches of contrasting colour about the face or wing that are probably used in display; in addition, they often have lengthened throat feathers. Members of the genus

Malacoptila (meaning "soft feather") have mainly pale-streaked or pale-spotted brown upperparts with a patch of contrasting colour on the breast. The smaller nunlets in *Nonnula* comprise a fairly uniform genus having mostly drab, entirely unstreaked or unspotted plumage with subtle colour patterns of brown, rufous and grey; they also have a fairly long, thin, curved bill, usually with silvery sides, and conspicuous eye-rings which are sometimes formed by brightly coloured bare skin. The nunbirds in the genus *Monasa* are strikingly different in behaviour from all other puffbirds; and morphologically, too, they form a readily diagnosed group, all having a relatively shorter, brightly coloured bill, black to dark grey plumage relieved only, if at all, by small white patches, and a longer, broad tail. Two aberrant monotypic genera are *Micromonacha*, a tiny, short-tailed, uniquely patterned bird with solidly dark upperparts, streaked underparts, and a complex undertail pattern; and *Hapaloptila*, a large, mainly bright chestnut Andean species that combines certain external features of both *Malacoptila* and *Monasa*, while its bill is "inflated" and scarcely curved, being almost hooked, and its wings are relatively long, hence the former name of "Slenderwing". The most aberrant puffbird of all, however, is clearly *Chelidoptera*, which, as its common name of Swallow-winged Puffbird implies, is highly adapted for aerial activity. It has relatively long wings, a shorter, narrow bill, sleek, tight plumage, and a short and broad tail, and Burton noted that it has an unusually large heart. Despite its apparent distinctness, it is not placed in a separate subfamily; its adaptations to a more aerial lifestyle seem to have involved primarily superficial characteristics.

Over half of the 35 species of puffbird are monotypic. By contrast, most of the wide-ranging species exhibit complex geographical variation. These are the White-necked Puffbird (*Notharchus macrorhynchos*), the White-whiskered Puffbird (*Malacoptila panamensis*), the Spotted Puffbird, the White-fronted Nunbird (*Monasa morphoeus*) and the Rusty-breasted Nunlet (*Nonnula rubecula*). In all these cases, there is long-standing disagreement as to the number and distribution of valid subspecies, and further study is needed. The subspecific nomenclature of two other bucconids seems to be especially unsettled. For the Rufous-capped Nunlet (*Nonnula ruficapilla*), the possibility of undescribed races has been mentioned in the literature; and, for the Black-streaked Puffbird (*Malacoptila fulvogularis*), at least four subspecies have been described, all of which seem likely to represent individual, seasonal and age-related variation. Further, in the case of the Spotted Puffbird, three subspecies previously considered valid probably represent intergrading, variable populations.

The possibility of an undescribed species of *Nystalus* in Brazil, based on a sight record, has been mentioned in recent literature, by C. A. Peres and A. Whittaker in 1991, but the description provided fits that of Striolated Puffbird (*Nystalus striolatus*). Another taxonomic puzzle concerns a species named by A. de W. Bertoni, in 1901, as *Microtrogon galbuloides*. Unfortunately, the describer of this did not even indicate whether a specimen was preserved; it has merely been presumed, from the inadequate description, to represent a puffbird, which on geographical grounds could be only the Rusty-breasted Nunlet, but it may not be a bucconid at all. In any case, Bertoni's collection has evidently now disintegrated, so we shall probably never know for certain the identity of this bird.

There are several cases among the Bucconidae in which the specific status of a given taxon is in question or has been disputed. These include the Semicollared Puffbird (*Malacoptila semicincta*), which has sometimes been regarded as a subspecies of the White-chested Puffbird (*Malacoptila fusca*); most authors, however, consider the several constant differences between the two, and the lack of intergradation between them, sufficient to establish the former as a full species. A less clear-cut case is that of the White-necked Puffbird, which has normally been attributed the isolated southern Brazilian population, *swainsoni*, as a subspecies. The latter is fairly distinctive, and was said by Sibley in 1996 to differ vocally, although comparative studies are needed. In addition, as the geographically nearest races of *macrorhynchos* differ greatly from *swainsoni*, and there is no possibility of overlap or intergradation, it seems better to treat the southern form as a distinct species, the Buff-bellied Puffbird (*Notharchus swainsoni*). At the same time, however, it should be noted that the nominate race of the White-necked Puffbird in the Guianan region is also distinctive in appearance and possibly in song; thus, further study of the situation is required. Another species-level problem involves the Spot-bellied Puffbird (*Nystalus maculatus*) and its southern subspecies *striatipectus*. Their specific distinctness has recently been convincingly espoused by J. M. C. da Silva, who recommended that *striatipectus* be treated as a separate species, for which the name Streak-bellied Puffbird would be appropriate. This proposal was based largely on the phylogenetic species concept; there are also several additional constant differences between adults of the two taxa, with no intermediates recorded. However, the vocalizations of the two forms

Malacoptila *puffbirds have lengthened throat feathers and lax plumage, the latter being reflected in their generic name. Most of the species are quite heavily streaked or spotted on the breast and back, a notable exception being the Rufous-necked Puffbird, which has the streaking confined to the head. White-chested Puffbirds exhibit the streaking typical of the genus but get their common name from a white breast patch that often is not visible in the field.*

[Left: *Malacoptila rufa brunnescens*, Serra dos Carajás, Pará, Brazil. Photo: Luiz Claudio Marigo.

Right: *Malacoptila fusca*, Morona-Santiago, Ecuador. Photo: Steven Holt/VIREO]

are similar, and it will be necessary to evaluate this case under the biological species concept before accepting the proposed split. A further example where uncertainty prevails concerns the Pied Puffbird (*Notharchus tectus*). This is comprised of two groups of races, one trans-Andean and one cis-Andean, which may prove to be separate species.

Two dissimilar-looking taxa that have been considered conspecific, on the basis of hybridization between them, are the Two-banded Puffbird (*Hypnelus bicinctus*) and the Russet-throated Puffbird (*Hypnelus ruficollis*). As the great majority of specimens are clearly of one form or the other, suggesting that hybridization is fairly limited, it is probably best to follow Peters in treating them as separate species, pending a thorough study that will elucidate the nature of their contact zones. Uncertainty also clouds the taxonomy of the Rusty-breasted Nunlet, which is highly variable regionally over a wide range; a revision of its disjunct component subspecies, some of which may merit the status of full species, is needed. On the other hand, the Grey-cheeked Nunlet (*Nonnula frontalis*) and the Rufous-capped Nunlet are quite similar, and have sometimes been treated as conspecific. Finally, the White-fronted Nunbird, currently treated as a single polytypic species, was earlier divided into several different species; intermediates between some of the component taxa exist, however, whence their relegation to the status of subspecies, although there are obvious differences between the disjunct northern group of races and the Amazonian and south-east Brazilian races, and further study is needed.

Morphological Aspects

The origin of the family name Bucconidae has been disputed. It has been thought to refer to the large bill, but it could also incorporate the meaning of "charlatan" or "tonto", the latter alluding to the perceived stupidity of these birds (see Relationship with Man).

All puffbirds have a relatively large head and large eyes, and a swollen-based, fairly heavy, curved and/or hooked bill. There are well-developed rictal bristles continuous with numerous setae surrounding the bill base, the anterior ones of which are for-

wardly directed, and the nostrils have a large operculum. The wings are relatively short to very short, and rounded; and the tail is short to medium-length, narrow, and graduated, though broader and longer in some *Monasa* species.

Osteologically, the quadrate has a short, broad, pointed orbital process; the medial condyle is extremely deep, ending in a rounded tubercle, with the lateral and posterior condyles merged. The postorbital process is long, curved and broad; a retroarticular process or medial brace is lacking; and there is a strong postorbital ligament. There are 14 cervical and four dorsal vertebrae, two distinct cervical ribs, and four true ribs. The visceral anatomy of the family is characterized by a capacious oesophagus, a thick-walled muscular gizzard, no gall bladder, and a short intestine with long globose caeca. Bucconids have fairly small zygodactylous feet, on which the first and fourth digits are permanently reversed. The body temperature is low to average for higher non-passerines. Interestingly, the White-eared Puffbird (*Nystalus chacuru*) has been reported to undergo periods of torpor within its burrow during cold weather.

Several species have elongate throat feathers, which may form conspicuous display features. Puffbirds have been called drab-plumaged, but most have at least one major plumage feature, such as a large white throat spot, a black chestband, or rufous on the throat or crown, that enlivens their appearance. Some have a complex plumage pattern, and several are strikingly pied and fairly glossy, or are sharply patterned in chestnut, black, brown and white. Additionally, the irides, the orbital skin and/or the bill are often brightly coloured. The plumage, bill and feet of some species of *Nystalus* may become stained during the nesting season by the soil of their burrows.

A number of species have spotting or scaling on the upperparts at all ages, which, together with the fluffy plumage, tends to give them a look of immaturity. Age-related plumage variation is, in fact, minimal in most bucconids, and some species are difficult to age except by bill characters. There are no bucconids in which the plumage pattern of the juveniles is truly different from that of the adults. Typically, juveniles have reduced, duller markings than adults; the areas which are white on adults are tinged with buff or fringed with dark on juveniles, while the dark areas are more fringed or spotted with pale col-

The five members of the genus Notharchus exhibit an impressive array of plumages with a basic theme of black and white. The strikingly plumaged White-necked Puffbird is among the largest of the bucconids and has one of the widest ranges, occurring from southern Mexico south to northern Bolivia. Geographical variation in this species is complex and not well understood, with three races currently recognized, and two other proposed ones rejected. The northern race, hyperrhynchus, differs from the the nominate in having much more white on the forehead and hindcollar and a larger bill; indeed, it may be a separate species.

[Notharchus macrorhynchos hyperrhynchus, near Esmeralda, Amazonas, Venezuela. Photo: Bruno Walther]

Washed with rufous and barred all over except on the throat, the Barred Puffbird resembles the female Fasciated Antshrike (Cymbilaimus lineatus), and the two are sometimes sympatric. It is the only bucconid thought to have colour morphs, darker rufous birds originally being listed as race "fulvidus". Puffbirds are well known for seeming lethargic, sitting motionless for long periods before making a rapid dash to snatch a prey item out of the air or from the foliage. The generic name Nystalus means "drowsy", reflecting the seemingly languid habits of the family.

[Nystalus radiatus, Río Claro, Magdalena, Colombia. Photo: Otto Pfister]

our. In those species which have bright bare-part colours, these colours are typically duller on juveniles. Variability in iris colour among presumed adults is great for some species, and studies are needed to determine what the significance of this may be.

Sexual dichromatism is almost absent among the members of this family. It occurs only in two species of *Malacoptila*, and in one of these, the Moustached Puffbird (*Malacoptila mystacalis*), the difference in appearance between males and females is minor. It has frequently been noted that female puffbirds of several species are slightly larger than the males, although this has not been tested statistically.

Only one species is thought to exhibit true colour morphs. This is the Barred Puffbird (*Nystalus radiatus*), which occurs in both light and dark rufous morphs.

In the only major moult study for the family, published in 1968, J. Haffer found that primary moult follows a simple descendant, centrifugal sequence, while moult of the secondaries and rectrices is irregular. For the nunbirds, the body moult has been reported to occur during the post-nuptial period, and to be protracted.

The flight of puffbirds is generally very fast and direct, on rapidly beating wings (see General Habits, Food and Feeding). The wings of at least one species, the White-necked Puffbird, produce a low whirring noise in flight.

It is worth mentioning the apparent physical resilience of these birds. Some puffbirds have been found to be, for birds of their size, unusually difficult to kill by thoracic compression or by shooting, individuals often reviving subsequent to apparent death. This may be attributed, at least partly, to their notably strong ribs as compared with those of jacamars of similar size. Indeed, several bucconid species have acquired colloquial names which reflect their ability to withstand being hit by stones flung by catapult or slingshot (see Relationship with Man).

As a final point of interest, preparers of specimens have noted that many puffbird species are malodorous. Indeed, representatives of all genera except *Hapaloptila* were reported as such in a recent survey. Since at least G. Shaw's writings, in 1815, it has been known that puffbirds are not especially edible, and perhaps their oft-remarked confiding and imperturbable nature (see General Habits), which has frequently allowed members of a pair or group to be shot sequentially (see Relationship with Man), is related to this circumstance. On the other hand, their unpleasant odour could simply be a result of the type of prey that they ingest, which would have a side benefit of making them undesirable as prey themselves.

Habitat

The Bucconidae are found exclusively in the Neotropics, from southern Mexico to northern Argentina. Within this region, they are absent from islands except for a very few on the continental shelf. They reach their greatest abundance and diversity in northern South America, especially in Amazonia.

Puffbirds are almost entirely arboreal except, in the case of some species, when nesting. All are therefore strongly associated with wooded habitats, and, indeed, most are intimately linked with humid tropical lowland forest. No fewer than 70% of puffbirds, a total of 25 species, occur in Brazil, and almost as many, 23, are present in the Amazon Basin. Very few puffbirds,

Measuring 13-16 cm in length, and weighing only 15-20 g, the nunlets are diminutive puffbirds. Their plumage is a sombre mix of browns, reds and greys and has no streaking or spotting. They have a relatively long, thin bill and either a white or a reddish eye-ring, the latter colour usually formed by bare skin. The Brown Nunlet has a pale rufous loral spot and is uniformly plain brownish on the crown and upperparts; the rufous colour on its underparts decreases in richness from the throat to the belly. It is a restricted-range species that inhabits the understorey of humid lowland forest in the Upper Amazon-Napo Lowlands Endemic Bird Area in Ecuador, Colombia and Peru.

[Nonnula brunnea, Zancudo Cocha, Ecuador. Photo: Doug Wechsler/ VIREO]

Sexual dichromatism is rare in puffbirds, occurring only in two Malacoptila species. In one, the Moustached Puffbird (Malacoptila mystacalis), the sexes are so similar in appearance that plumage dichromatism is generally ignored in field guides. In contrast, the sexes are noticeably different in the White-whiskered Puffbird: males have a rufous tone to the plumage, especially about the face and chest, whereas females are greyer overall and tend to be more heavily streaked on the underparts. With four accepted races, the species is widely distributed from south-east Mexico to Ecuador and Colombia. It is much less common in the northern half of its range than farther south.

[Malacoptila panamensis poliopis, near Alto Tambo, Ecuador. Photo: Steven Holt/VIREO]

however, are deep-forest species; the Black-breasted Puffbird (*Notharchus pectoralis*), the Collared Puffbird, the Black-streaked Puffbird and the Brown Nunlet (*Nonnula brunnea*) are perhaps the closest to being so. Most of the Bucconidae are birds of forest edge, tree-fall gaps and streamsides, where tangles of vegetation form at different levels up to the canopy. In such places, the birds find both the narrow horizontal perches that they require and the mix of green-leaf and dead-leaf large invertebrates that make up most of their diet. A few species appear to be associated, though not exclusively, with bamboo stands, and a few others with lake and river margins. While most are birds of lowland tropical forest and edge, several have adapted to drier, more open woodland, and at least one reaches moderate altitudes in the Andes.

This apparent habitat preference may to some extent, however, be a matter of constraint. It has been observed that *Malacoptila* puffbirds are much less common in forest east of the Andes than is the White-whiskered Puffbird in forest west of those mountains; east of the Andes, the Rufous-necked Puffbird (*Malacoptila rufa*) and the Semicollared Puffbird are more birds of forest edge, sandy woodland and swamp margins. In Honduras, by contrast, the White-whiskered Puffbird is an inhabitant of deep forest. It may be that this difference, if real, is due to a higher diversity of avian species in Amazonian forest than in Central American forest, such that *Malacoptila* species are at a disadvantage when competing for resources inside forest in the Amazon and Orinoco Basins.

Pressure limiting the puffbirds to the edge habitats may come from birds of other families, as well as from the *Monasa* nunbirds. Nunbirds are large and numerous, and may well help to exclude other Amazonian bucconids from the middle storeys of forest. Indeed, some nunbirds also do this to others of their genus. The White-fronted Nunbird is the dominant species, occupying *terra firme* forest and edge, while the Yellow-billed Nunbird (*Monasa flavirostris*) is associated with bamboo and second-growth borders, and the Black-fronted Nunbird (*Monasa nigrifrons*) is a bird of the seasonally and permanently flooded forest habitats known respectively as *várzea* and *igapó*. So clear is this habitat division between Black-fronted and White-fronted Nunbirds that the two species were once seen a few metres apart, following an ant swarm as it moved from *várzea* alongside a stream into *terra firme*. Although these two species partition habitat widely thus

in Amazonia, they have mutually exclusive ranges in south-eastern Brazil, a matter which is deserving of ecological study.

A slightly different pattern of habitat specialization is found among the members of the genus *Nonnula*. In Amazonia, the Rusty-breasted Nunlet occupies *terra firme* forest, but it also penetrates *várzea*, while in northern Amazonian Brazil the sympatric Chestnut-headed Nunlet (*Nonnula amaurocephala*) occurs in *igapó* forest, and south of the Amazon the Rufous-capped Nunlet is over much of its range a bird of riverine bamboo thickets. The River Amazon itself is the dividing line between two quite differently plumaged congeners, the White-chested and Rufous-necked Puffbirds, as it also is between the Black Nunbird (*Monasa atra*) and the Black-fronted Nunbird. In Colombia, altitudinal replacement is seen in the case of two closely related species, the White-whiskered Puffbird and the Moustached Puffbird: the former occurs in the lowlands, the latter in the lower Andes.

Several bucconids have seemingly inexplicable discontinuities of range that are not obviously correlated with habitat or competitive exclusion. Prime examples are the Brown-banded Puffbird (*Notharchus ordii*) of northern and southern Amazonia, so far not recorded from central Amazonia; the Striolated Puffbird, found in western and extreme eastern Amazonia, but nowhere in between; and the Crescent-chested Puffbird (*Malacoptila striata*), which has two widely separated populations, one near the mouth of the Amazon and the other in south-eastern Brazil.

It is worth emphasizing that the Rufous-capped Nunlet is not always an inhabitant of bamboo, and that the White-whiskered Puffbird is in some places a deep-forest bird. These facts indicate that habitat selection is relative and plastic, depending on a variety of factors, including competition from other members of the family. The habitat used by some species also varies over the course of the day. A. F. Skutch noted that White-whiskered Puffbirds come out of the forest to forage in adjoining shady pastures or other clearings, this occurring most often in the dim light of early morning or late afternoon, and in periods of wet or overcast weather.

Moreover, it is not entirely proven that so many puffbirds are genuine edge species. While the patterns revealed to date doubtless reflect real circumstances, they are unlikely to be the complete patterns. Puffbirds, because of their remarkable stillness and silence (see General Habits), are observed relatively

For all practical purposes, puffbirds make their living in trees and are closely tied to wooded habitats. Several species excavate nesting burrows below ground, but even these forage from elevated perches and thus are never far from trees. Despite their arboreal habits, however, few puffbirds are denizens of deep, unbroken forest. Rather, they seem to favour forest edges, tree-fall gaps and other clearings. Whether this apparent preference for edge habitats is based on forest structure or on some other factor remains to be determined. For example, in some Malacoptila puffbirds, the affinity for edge habitat seems to be positively correlated with the diversity of other bird species in the forest interior, raising the possibility that interspecific competition constrains puffbirds to edges. Moreover, because puffbirds are so lethargic, their apparent proclivity for open habitat may be due to the fact that they are easier to observe there than in denser habitats. Whatever habitat they occupy, puffbirds typically perch on horizontal branches while they scan for potential food items. Most species, including the Pied Puffbird, often use exposed perches. In contrast, a few species, including the Moustached Puffbird, prefer more concealed perches in dense tangles near the ground beneath the canopy of humid forest.

[Above:
Notharchus tectus tectus,
near Esmeralda,
Amazonas, Venezuela.
Photo: Bruno Walther.

Below:
Malacoptila mystacalis,
Guatopo, Venezuela.
Photo: Robin Chittenden/
FLPA]

The majority of puffbirds occupy humid lowland forest, with few species occurring at elevations above 1200 m.
A notable exception is the White-faced Nunbird, which lives at higher elevations than any other bucconid. This species is found most often on steep slopes along the edge of wet foothill forest above 1500 m, and it ascends as high as 2900 m into the cloudforest zone. This distinctively marked species, with its solid grey cap, large bill encircled by white feathers, bright chestnut underparts and long tail, is uncommon to rare throughout its range from western Colombia and Ecuador south to north-west Peru.

[*Hapaloptila castanea*, Pichincha, Ecuador.
Photo: Steven Holt/VIREO]

rarely; whether one is caught sight of or not is seemingly only a matter of chance. If, therefore, almost all the observations are made in the understorey and edges of forest, it is possible that this may in part be because birds in the canopy are simply invisible. There is at least a modest chance that some bucconid "edge specialists" also spend parts of their daily or annual cycle in the canopy, and so go largely undetected. Skutch thought that this might be true of White-whiskered Puffbirds. Furthermore, M. A. Carriker found that the White-necked Puffbird was fairly common in Costa Rica only because of the way in which the edges of a clearing filled up with birds in response to a sudden abundance of wood-boring insects in the trees that had been left to rot. Did this reveal the species to be an edge specialist, or had numbers of White-necked Puffbirds simply been drawn from other forest micro-habitats, perhaps the canopy, in which they were less visible?

One micro-habitat that may be important for many species of puffbird is standing or running water. White-whiskered Puffbirds have been found to occupy territories focused on streams, with ridges often serving as border areas. These birds tend to avoid flat summit areas altogether; indeed, one female which did take up residence in such a flat, dry area at the headwaters of a stream failed to procure a mate during her year's occupancy. This suggests that streams are crucial for reproductive capacity in this species, presumably because they promote an increase in understorey foliage and, hence, a greater biomass of appropriate food. Some 50% of all puffbird species show a preference for vegetation close to water. This is hardly surprising when one considers that these are possibly the closest ecological equivalents to the Old World forest kingfishers (Alcedinidae). In fact, they are sometimes even referred to as "kingfishers" by local people.

A handful of bucconid species have radiated into foothill and submontane forest areas. These include one species of *Nystalus*, three of *Malacoptila*, and two species in monotypic genera, the Lanceolated Monklet and, notably, the White-faced Nunbird. The last occurs from 750 m, though mostly from 1500 m, up to an altitude of 2900 m, ascending higher than any other puffbird. A small number of the Bucconidae, including all but one of the four *Nystalus* species and both of the *Hypnelus* puffbirds, have specialized in occupying drier, more open woodland habitats. Some of these, along with the anomalous Swal-

low-winged Puffbird, are the species most likely to be seen in man-modified habitats, such as the sides of railway tracks. White-eared Puffbirds often perch on telegraph wires and fences, and occur in suburban areas where trees preserve parklike conditions.

General Habits

Puffbirds get their English name from their frequent and peculiar habit of fluffing out the plumage and drawing in the large head, so that, perched on a branch, they appear almost ball-like and not much like birds at all. This behaviour may serve to disguise them from avian predators, since sitting, as they do, in exposed positions, waiting for prey to move, must have its risks. Certainly, the explanation for the obdurate stillness of puffbirds would seem to be the need not to be seen by either predator or prey. Nevertheless, foraging puffbirds commonly do not fluff their feathers.

This stillness is also a notable puffbird trait, for these birds allow an extremely close approach before flushing. The birds might fluff up their feathers and still-perch while waiting for improved hunting conditions, possibly connected with slight torpor for energy conservation. Skutch argued that puffbirds, although sitting motionless for long periods, are ever alert, and that their behaviour at the nest (see Breeding) shows what remarkably keen-sighted, wary creatures they are. Their visual powers are testified to by the astonishing ability that they show when picking prey from leaves (see Food and Feeding).

Nunbirds and nunlets tend to sit in a rather upright stance. Other puffbirds may slouch more, although still with the tail held vertically. The short legs mean that the body appears to be resting on the perch; they probably also limit these birds' mobility, although the nunbirds are capable of suddenly switching around on a branch. Usually, the only movement made by a bucconid when perched involves deliberate slow turning of the head as it watches for prey.

The one other movement commonly shown by a perched bucconid involves the tail. This tends to happen only as the bird prepares for flight, whether forced or voluntary. A White-whiskered Puffbird will nervously lift its short, narrow tail, and jerk it, motmot-like, in slow sideways movements, first to the right and

A handful of puffbirds, including three of the four species of Nystalus, are found in drier woodland, brushy grassland and savanna, and they will also regularly use disturbed habitats. The White-eared Puffbird carries this penchant to an extreme: not only does it favour wooded edges and second growth, it also occupies coffee plantations, tree-lined streets in towns, and railroad rights-of-way, where it often can be seen perched conspicuously on a telephone wire, fence wire or fencepost.

[Nystalus chacuru uncirostris, Apurímac, Peru. Photo: Günter Ziesler]

then to the left, or rotate it, before it takes wing. Two-banded Puffbirds also have this habit, swinging the tail through an arc in a series of three or four abrupt jerks, beginning out on one side and "clicking" around to the other, and then back again. At least four species of *Nonnula* and two other *Malacoptila* puffbirds show similar such movements of the tail. Nunbirds appear instead to rotate or flick the tail backwards, allowing it slowly to become reset in the vertical. In all cases, this tail-moving behaviour seems to express alarm, excitement and/or flight intention. There is also an observation of a Rusty-breasted Nunlet sitting quietly in front of observers, and repeatedly flicking one or both wings high above the back in the manner of some small flycatchers (Tyrannidae).

The flight of puffbirds is very fast and direct, on rapidly beating wings. Most flights are made either as foraging attacks or in order to change from one perch to another, but they are equally brief and darting. The more slender *Monasa* nunbirds, however, fly with a few quick wingbeats followed by a short sail, sometimes circling gracefully and unhurriedly; when returning from a sally, they glide upwards to a perch. In the air, the wings of the White-fronted Nunbird appear rather short and rounded, and the tail looks long, broad-feathered and full; in short flights through the canopy, this species is often suggestive of a jay (Corvidae). Nunbirds sometimes engage playfully in short sallying flights, ostensibly with no intention of catching prey. The most graceful bucconid in the air, however, is undoubtedly the Swallow-winged Puffbird, which is the only member of the family that has evolved to catch most, if not all, of its prey in flight. It can shape its wings for rapid upward attack, and then set them forward with open slotting in the manner of a vulture or hawk (Accipitridae) in order to stall and circle slowly, with elegant aerobatic manoeuvres; from this, it can then change again to hovering, or to a swooping, slightly undulating flight to another piece of airspace, before drifting back down to a high perch.

Perhaps not surprisingly for a family that is relatively poorly known, the roosting habits and comfort behaviour of puffbirds appear hardly ever to have been recorded. The more sociable members of the family sleep side by side on branches. When resting, these birds sink on to the branch and bring the nictitating membranes over the eyes. The Bucconidae scratch the head by the direct method, bringing the foot forward and up under the wing, but observations of preening have rarely been recorded. White-fronted Nunbirds take dust baths, and have been seen

flopped down in the grass in a sunny spot with the wings spread out, obviously sunning.

Little is known of the parasites of the Bucconidae, but several species have been found to harbour blood parasites of the genus *Haemoproteus*. A parasitic nematode of the genus *Procyrnea* (Habronematidae) has been reported from the Swallow-winged Puffbird, and a mallophagan louse *Picicola* (Philopteridae) has been found on the Crescent-chested Puffbird, the latter representing the first known non-passerine host of this mallophagan subgenus. Several Amazonian species of bucconid showed evidence of arboviruses; indeed, the presence of these insect-borne viruses was detected in 18% of all individuals sampled.

Although puffbirds sometimes remain immobile when in danger, they generally react in a more positive manner. When a puffbird becomes anxious, as when hearing the alarm call of another bird, it sleeks its plumage, presumably in readiness for rapid take-off, while at the same time angling itself forwards until the body, head and tail are more or less all in line. Often, the bird stares ahead at the source of danger, adopting an intense binocular expression that, to one observer, gave the impression of fierceness or myopia. One White-eared Puffbird reacted to an observer by pressing itself against its low branch, facing the intruder head-on, and gazing almost cross-eyed with intensity, appearing strangely rodent-like.

If they do take flight, alarmed puffbirds quickly fly into the shelter of palm clumps or other tangled vegetation in the understorey, and it seems, from some accounts, that many species habitually make use of screening greenery at the first sign of disturbance. When caught, they may feign death. Fieldworkers who net puffbirds find that the trapped birds are often docile, fluffing themselves up and opening the bill, while others will bite hard. One female puffbird, when dug out of a nest, closed her eyes as if dead. An interesting reaction to a passing vulture was given by another individual, which was reported to have swung beneath the perch until the perceived danger had passed.

The rather solitary puffbirds of deep-shade habitats, if they wander into more open situations than those in which they are normally found, appear to provoke mobbing behaviour from some passerines. This is possibly because of their superficial resemblance to owls of the genus *Glaucidium*. Black-breasted Puffbirds have been seen being violently attacked by Yellow-green Vireos

(*Vireo flavoviridis*), and there are observations of both Crescent-chested and White-whiskered Puffbirds being mobbed by a host of small birds. On one occasion, a White-whiskered Puffbird was seen being pursued, every time it flew, by Grey-capped Flycatchers (*Myiozetetes granadensis*) and several species of hummingbird (Trochilidae).

White-whiskered Puffbirds, while usually solitary, can also occur in small groups of up to a dozen individuals, and White-eared Puffbirds may at times be found in small groups of two to five birds. During most of the year, Pied Puffbirds move about in small parties of six or so. Even the seemingly solitary Lanceolated Monklet is sometimes met with in groups of up to three. Although these species are often encountered singly, family members may stay together for some time after the young fledge. Among the Bucconidae, there appears to be a correlation between the level of overall activity and the degree of sociability. As an example, Pied and Two-banded Puffbirds have been judged to be more active than some of their more solitary relatives. Within any species, however, activity levels may also vary depending on the presence or absence of offspring.

In the case of nunbirds in the genus *Monasa*, the persistence of young on the territory has been incorporated into the entire social system. These birds are group-territorial, with at least some of the offspring remaining on site in order to help to advertise and defend the territory in future breeding efforts. "Flocks" appear to be stable groups that are confined to particular home ranges or territories, each part of which they visit at regular intervals. Members of Black-fronted Nunbird groups have been seen transferring food to one another, although all birds in the group appeared to be adult. While holding prey such as a large insect 3-4 cm long, the "donor" gives a characteristic whistle, whereupon the recipient approaches and collects the item directly from the other's bill. This behaviour has also been recorded for White-fronted Nunbirds, where it was interpreted either as the feeding of older young or as indicative of adults coming into breeding condition.

Not surprisingly for such sedentary species, puffbirds appear, from the scant evidence available, to be territorial throughout the year. The territories of White-whiskered Puffbirds are roughly circular, centred on some major stream drainage and commonly bordered by ridges, and almost 300 m in diameter. During disputes, individuals of this species call while spreading the tail slightly and wagging it back and forth, either tilting it upwards or holding it tent-like in an inverse "V". They face each other at close range, with the body sleeked, carpals out and wingtips slightly lowered. They often sleek the head plumage and raise the white tufts above and to each side of the base of the bill, as well as, at times, raising normally concealed whitish spots between the tufts, so that the beak is outlined in white. They then stand high on their legs, stretch the neck, and wigwag the body back and forth, sometimes indulging also in bill-grappling. Females fluff out the streaked chest feathers conspicuously. During episodes of countersinging, the bill is pointed upwards. In the case of the Spotted Puffbird, the disputants fluff out their speckled belly feathers and the orange feathers of the throat and chest, exposing the black neckstripes.

Black-breasted Puffbirds are as aggressive intraspecifically as they are indifferent interspecifically. Territorial pairs react to each other in turn by singing loudly at intervals, mainly in the daytime rather than at dawn or dusk. When giving the song, the bird stands "as upright but level-headed as a drill sergeant", sleeking its head and body feathers, showing the white nape and black chest, and then flies at a passing conspecific while uttering a series of loud grunts.

White-fronted Nunbirds advertise their territories with many vocalizations and spectacular group singing, the latter involving co-ordinated barking or "gobbling" for up to 15 minutes at a time (see Voice). The frequency of these performances appears to increase between October and December, when a resurgence in song activity occurs in many individuals. Nunbirds stream to the location of the bird initiating the calls, and the performances trigger similar ones by nunbirds in neighbouring territories. Presumably, the displays serve both to promote internal flock co-ordination and to impress and deter neighbouring flocks.

Voice

Puffbirds are among the most silent of the birds in Neotropical forests, and only the nunbirds and *Nystalus* species could be said to produce loud calls and attractive songs. As with many forest kingfishers in Asia, a number of puffbirds tend to sing only very early and late in the day, for very short periods before dawn and after sunset. Even the more vocal species, such as the White-eared Puffbird, still give their best performances during these half-dark minutes of the day.

Even when these birds are calling, they can often appear as if they are not. The White-necked Puffbird does not open its bill, nor does its throat move, while it is vocalizing. The White-whiskered Puffbird can be equally undemonstrative. Skutch recounts

Bucconids are amongst the quietest birds in Neotropical forests, often singing only for brief periods at sunrise and sunset. Sometimes they vocalize without opening the bill, making it difficult to locate the sound, even from a short distance. Not so with this Spot-bellied Puffbird, which delivers its song with open bill. It has recently been suggested that the two races of this species may constitute two separate species, and some possible slight differences in voice have been reported, but all in all it seems that their vocalizations are rather similar. More study is required, especially in the area of probable contact in the Brazilian Pantanal.

[Nystalus maculatus, Pantanal of Brazil. Photo: Edson Endrigo]

Perched on a horizontal branch as it scrutinizes its surroundings for suitable prey, this Striolated Puffbird has adopted the standard posture of a foraging bucconid. Hunting perches usually offer unobstructed views in all directions. Attacks are initiated in a swift dash from the perch, to strike at prey that may be in the air, on the ground, among foliage, or on a tree limb or trunk, the latter assaults being termed "sally-strikes". An actively hunting bird may sit so still as to appear half-asleep, then bursting into flight with rapid wingbeats in pursuit of its quarry. Successful birds often return to the same perch to consume their catch and then resume the wait for further prey.

[*Nystalus striolatus*, Serra dos Carajás, Pará, Brazil. Photo: Luiz Claudio Marigo]

that, at a nest of this species, he heard a rapid undulatory twittering lasting for minutes on end, which he took to be the insistent begging of a recently fledged passerine. The male puffbird was all the while in plain view, but never showed any movement of the bill. It was only on a second occasion, when the calling was heard and again the male was in view, that Skutch saw "the slightest vibration of his mandibles".

The songs of puffbirds commonly consist of series of identical or near-identical high-pitched whistles, sometimes ending in trills or in a different series of notes, and sometimes rising or falling in pitch. The six *Nonnula* nunlets all have very similar songs which seem to differ in the number of notes and their length and emphasis. The Barred Puffbird makes a very human-like wolf-whistle, whereas the White-faced Nunbird utters hoots reminiscent of *Glaucidium* owls. It is the *Monasa* nunbirds that have the most developed vocabularies, doubtless a result of their group-territorial behaviour. They have loud, relatively musical songs which are often given in choruses, becoming more complex and babbling and continuing for many minutes. A few puffbirds in other genera, however, commonly deliver their songs as a duet, if not a chorus, notable among these being the White-eared Puffbird. This species is popularly known in Brazil as the *fevereiro*, meaning February, because of the sound that results from the pair-members eliding the basic "fufu" unit of their song. It is from this sound that the species' scientific name of *chacuru* is derived. To some people the noise recalls crazed laughter, thus providing another analogy with the kingfishers, this time the kookaburras (*Dacelo*), also dry-country birds.

Careful study reveals that puffbirds, despite their long silences, do have moderately extended vocabularies. The White-whiskered Puffbird utters several sounds, all weak and thin, and usually accompanied by a movement of the tail. Its commonest note is a gentle, high "tsinnnn", but it also has a protracted, slightly descending "sssssssss", a plaintive descending "tseee", and a strong and repeated, hummingbird-like descending "tsirrrr" given with the bill wide open. One of these calls may be referable to the interminable, weak, complaining notes that have been reported to be given by parents when near nestlings. On the other hand, the sound heard by Skutch on the occasion, mentioned above, when he could not tell that the bird was calling, was an altogether different one, "a rapid, undulatory twittering, some-

times almost a sizzling", which Skutch interpreted as an expression of anxiety. At an ant swarm, when behaving aggressively towards a conspecific that is not a mate, this species will displace its rival while uttering a rattling grunt, "chwiahh". Individual White-whiskered Puffbirds, when confronting each other, also grunt when simply alighting on a new perch. In one protracted dispute between two pairs, one male attacked the other with a rough whistled "seeieeee" rather than the usual grunt, while the other female attacked her counterpart with grunts.

The most elaborate vocabulary appears to belong to the White-fronted Nunbird, which has a considerable variety of clamorous, querulous calls. In a 1964 article, P. Slud identified ten different vocalizations. These included prolonged excited gabbles that can sound in parts like a police whistle; low whistles; rather smooth, sometimes rippled notes recalling the sound of a small pulley; a weak "ank-ank"; a short "how how"; a single "oo"; a trogon-like "chahring"; a low, nasal, quick "chíkara"; a full-voiced "kü-kü-kü-kü-kü-kü"; and musical nasal whining notes at different speeds. Later, E. O. Willis noted that this nunbird sometimes gives "chert" chirps before a foraging sally, and that it displaces competitors at perches by uttering rattling chirps and gurgles; one gave a "cha-a-a-a-a-a" as it displaced a conspecific. The prolonged gabbles are the song. Members of this group-territorial species converge from different directions to perch a few inches apart along a horizontal limb, where, with the neck stretched and the bill pointing upwards, the spread tail lifting and lowering, they call very loudly with the mouth wide open, excitedly and in unison, for a minute or more.

The calls of the various *Monasa* species can be so loud as to startle the observer. Some of their calls may even startle other bird species, because these nunbirds are forest "vigilantes", having well-developed alarm or anti-predator calls. Those of the Black-fronted Nunbird, for example, consist of short "too-loo-loo" gurgles, in greater alarm punctuated with a loud whistled "peer peer peer peer", which causes birds of all species to freeze. Almost exactly the same call is given by White-fronted and Black Nunbirds, in those cases sending other birds to cover. The Black-breasted Puffbird, even though it is not sociable like the *Monasa* species, also has highly developed alarm behaviour. At the appearance of a predator such as a hawk, it stands erect, puffs out its nape and body feathers, and gives a sharp, protracted, but highly ventriloquial

Bucconids feed mainly on insects, although next to nothing is known about the diet of a dozen species in the family. Various Lepidoptera, Orthoptera, Hymenoptera and Homoptera are commonly reported as prey items. Several species attend army-ant swarms or join mixed-species feeding flocks, taking advantage of food items stirred up from the ground or flushed from the vegetation as the ants or foraging flock move below and through the understorey, respectively. Spot-bellied Puffbirds often forage from low perches, attacking prey in the foliage or on the ground. They feed primarily on insects, but an individual in Brazil was observed capturing a colubrid snake.

[*Nystalus maculatus*, Pantanal of Brazil. Photo: Patricio Robles Gil]

"wheeeer" once every two to four seconds. This has a dramatic effect even on birds at ground level, which make hysterical dashes for cover and indulge in extended tail-jerking sessions.

While in the nest, young White-whiskered Puffbirds are usually silent. As with most nestling birds, however, the real or apparent sound of wingbeats near the mouth of the burrow can cause older broods to commence a high-pitched, rapid trilling. Once out of the nest, they can be as insistent as any fledglings, giving a weak scratchy note and sibilant chittering calls. Young White-fronted Nunbirds constantly utter a piping "chiv-ree", Black Nunbirds a continual "pseuh-wooh", and Black-breasted Puffbirds a persistent "wheet". The alarm calls of the Plain-brown Woodcreeper (*Dendrocincla fuliginosa*) cause young bucconids to become silent, as do those of their parents. The young nunbird, each time it gives its begging call, flashes its pale gape at the parent.

Food and Feeding

All members of the Bucconidae for which the food and feeding habits have been reported are chiefly insectivorous. One species, the Swallow-winged Puffbird, is probably exclusively so, since it appears to forage only in the air.

Apart from the Swallow-winged Puffbird, which makes fast upward dashes into airspace, and then more slowly undulates and circles back down to its perch, the hunting technique is standard throughout the family. The birds make flycatcher-type sallies from an open perch that offers good all-round vision, *Cecropia* often being favoured, and they target prey that is amid green foliage, on trunks and branches, on the ground or in the air. Attacks aimed at animals on substrates are commonly called "sally-strikes", which is very apt for the way in which it conveys something of the speed and directness of a puffbird's foraging flight pattern. After many minutes spent perched on some shaded or open branch, unathletic and immobile except for the occasional deliberate head movement, often giving the impression of being only half-awake and largely indifferent, the bird suddenly launches into a hurtling direct dash with rapidly beating wings, its body looking surprisingly slender. Having captured its quarry, often with a loud snap of the bill, it carries the prey, still alive, back to a perch, frequently the original one, where the item is

beaten and swallowed. The whole sequence is very similar to that of a foraging kingfisher. Indeed, if one seeks an explanation of why the latter family failed so signally to radiate in Neotropical forests, competitive exclusion by the Bucconidae must be high on the list of plausible reasons.

Some evidence of the speed of puffbird foraging flights has emerged during the detailed studies of Amazonian birds conducted by Willis, who has several times seen puffbirds outfly dendrocolaptines in pursuit of flushed prey at ant swarms. In one instance, a White-fronted Nunbird rapidly overtook a Buff-throated Woodcreeper (*Xiphorhynchus guttatus*) in a long chase after a flying insect, and in another a Black Nunbird passed a Plain-brown Woodcreeper pursuing a cicada (Cicadidae).

Although the nunbirds readily come to the ground for prey, aerial sallies to take flying prey appear to be commoner among, and more appropriate to, these more streamlined species, which have a longer, broader tail and a narrower bill. Inevitably, these sallies are likely at times to be rather longer-distance attacks. The sally-strikes that are the chief tactic of the chunkier, smaller-tailed species are relatively short-distance affairs, but they still involve ranges of 5-50 m and can sometimes be spectacular as the bird hits the foliage in pursuit of its prey; occasionally, however, the tactic is changed at the last moment from strike to hover-glean, depending on the substrate and the intended prey.

The large eyes, and their slightly binocular arrangement on the large head, evidently provide the bucconids with extremely high visual resolution, even in very poor light conditions. The very slightest movement made by a cryptic animal can be picked up by the bird: one observer saw a solitary ant cause an orthopteran to move a leg, which prompted a nunbird to attack. Several observers have noted how puffbirds can be active into the dusk, at a time when other diurnal birds have started roosting. The powerful twilight vision of the Bucconidae doubtless enables them to capture insects, such as moths and cicadas, which become active only as the light fades. Incidentally, there is a record of a Spotted Puffbird catching hawkmoths (Sphingidae) at a flowering plant, the only reported instance of a bucconid waiting at a fixed point to which prey will come.

Some puffbirds take advantage of "beaters" in the forest. They accompany monkey troops and flocks of caciques (*Cacicus*), they follow the daily foraging flocks of mixed bird species, the very numbers within which cause disturbances to other smaller ani-

This White-eared Puffbird has managed to catch a large orthopteran. This species routinely captures prey from the ground, taking lizards, larger insects, and wingless arthropods such as millipedes, centipedes and scorpions, and it even obtains such unlikely prey items as velvet worms (Peripatus) and crabs. Although the heart of its distribution is in central Brazil, the White-eared Puffbird ranges into northern Argentina a few degrees south of the tropic of Capricorn. It has one of the southernmost distributions of any bucconid and is reported to lower its body temperature and enter torpor during cool weather.

[Nystalus chacuru, Mato Grosso, Brazil. Photo: Doug Wechsler/ VIREO]

White-faced Nunbirds
do much of their foraging
in the canopy, gleaning
wasps, crickets,
grasshoppers, locusts and
butterfly larvae from the
vegetation. Recent
observations of more than
200 food deliveries at the
first nest known to science
revealed that 78% of
the prey were insects.
The remainder of the food
items included lizards, a
frog, nestling birds, and a
mouse, the latter two prey
categories never having
been reported previously.
In another study, a
stomach contained plant
matter identified as either
buds or fruit. Only six
species of puffbirds are
known to consume plant
parts, and the significance
of this food type in their
diet is unknown.

[*Hapaloptila castanea*,
Tandayapa Valley,
Pichincha, Ecuador.
Photo: Nicholas Athanas]

mals, and they similarly follow the army-ant swarms which do the same thing, but to animals larger than themselves, on the forest floor and in certain trees. Nunbirds sometimes move about under canopy-travelling groups of primates and flocks of oropendolas (*Psarocolius*, *Gymnostinops*) and caciques, apparently in order to seize on prey which those birds flush downwards as they move. White-fronted Nunbirds commonly travel with large mixed-species bird flocks containing caciques, woodcreepers, woodpeckers, pihas (*Lipaugus*), mourners (*Rhytipterna*, *Laniocera*) and various trogons (Trogonidae). Rufous-necked Puffbirds have been seen closely following an understorey flock of antbirds (Thamnophilidae) and tanagers (Thraupidae), and at least five other puffbirds have been noted as doing likewise. Certainly, many species of bucconid are at least occasional attenders at ant swarms, although the naturally higher-foraging species such as the White-necked and Pied Puffbirds rarely do so, as is the case with others, such as the Collared and Spotted Puffbirds, that are confined to habitats in which ant swarms are rare.

When the White-whiskered Puffbird follows swarms, it commonly perches 1-2 m up on thin branches that are about 2 cm wide, thus not so thin that they wave under the bird's weight and give away its presence. From such a perch, it makes most of its captures in sallies to the ground. The basic behaviour is probably very similar to that adopted away from ant swarms. Typically, a foraging individual sits on a branch, with the plumage fluffed out and the tail down and closed, for long periods; just before making a sally, it sleeks its feathers and leans forwards, tail in line with the body, staring in the direction of the prey. After a strike it returns to the perch, still sleeked, then fluffs itself out and assumes a vertical posture, either to wait again or, if the strike was successful, to eat its catch. If the puffbird sees a prey disappear under leaves, it may settle on the ground and swipe aside the leaves with its bill in order to make its capture, and in doing so it stands remarkably high on its legs, recalling a thrush of the genus *Turdus*.

The food of puffbirds consists of large arthropods and small reptiles and amphibians, with berries occasionally being taken by some species. Most of the diet is made up of insects, apparently chiefly Lepidoptera in the form of caterpillars and moths, and Orthoptera in the form of grasshoppers, locusts, bush-crick-

ets and crickets. Nunbirds seem best adapted to preying on Orthoptera of up to about 6 g in mass. In addition, a wide variety of other insects is eaten, including mantises (Mantidae), bugs (Hemiptera), roaches (Blattodea), cicadas, stick-insects (Phasmida), butterflies, dragonflies (Odonata) and so on. It seems that beetles (Coleoptera) are taken most often when certain species of them become numerous: there are records of puffbird stomachs being crammed with particular kinds of beetle when sudden abundances of the latter had occurred, whereas observations at ant swarms suggest that Coleoptera are rarely taken. It may be that beetles in the size-class that puffbirds target are too well armoured to be worth catching, or are too strictly nocturnal, and that smaller beetles become economical to catch only when there are enough of them in a given area to justify a diversion from the search for larger prey.

Apart from insects, the arthropod prey of puffbirds includes spiders, scorpions (Scorpiones), centipedes (Chilopoda), millipedes (Diplopoda), crabs and velvet worms (*Peripatus*). Among vertebrate prey consumed, lizards are most commonly reported, but both snakes and frogs are clearly regular in the diet of many bucconids. The massive bill of a puffbird is deeper than it is wide, generally with a powerful gripping hook tip, and the large head allows for strong jaw muscles and a wide gape. Most species have profuse rictal bristles, which presumably protect soft parts of the head from heavily armed or otherwise noxious insects. When a prey item is captured, it is held head outwards and routinely beaten on a branch until it is not only dead, but also reasonably free of toxins and sufficiently broken up to be more easily ingested. Then, it is turned in the bill and swallowed head first. A Black Nunbird was once seen catching a huge centipede which it proceeded to crush at both ends, as if it could not be sure which end was the head. When dealing with a scorpion, a Black-breasted Puffbird chews the animal's thorax until it stops moving, and then swallows the food whole. The handling time for a prey item, such as a large grasshopper caught by a nunbird, may be as long as twelve minutes.

Swallow-winged Puffbirds, since they feed on the wing, take somewhat different prey. Bees, wasps, alate termites and flying ants appear to be the staple diet of this species. These prey items are not so large as the ones taken by other puffbirds, and many seem to be swallowed in flight. Surprisingly, this conspicuous, relatively well-studied puffbird has not been reported to beat and process prey items on a branch after having captured them.

The importance of plant food in the diet of puffbirds is unknown. The berries of mistletoe (Loranthaceae) have been found in the stomach of a Spotted Puffbird, while the Lanceolated Monklet is known to take berries, and a White-faced Nunbird stomach was found to contain either fruit or buds. In addition, the White-eared Puffbird is reported to take vegetable matter. Most notably, one Russet-throated Puffbird had apparently been feeding exclusively on seeds, and birds of this species, when sampled emetically, were found to have consumed the fleshy fruits of one particular plant on a regular basis. It may be significant that two of the species mentioned here, the Lanceolated Monklet and the White-faced Nunbird, are in their own monotypic genera, and represent distinctive bucconid lineages, and that two others, the Spotted and Russet-throated Puffbirds, live in strongly seasonal habitats.

The food brought to young in the nest appears to differ little, if at all, from that taken by adults. At a nest of White-whiskered Puffbirds, mantids, moths, caterpillars and spiders, along with small *Anolis* lizards up to 12 cm long, were brought to nestlings only two days old.

After they leave the nest, young puffbirds have the habit of flying to snatch or "hover-glean" food from the bill of a parent. This is doubtless invaluable practice for independent foraging, which may not commence until a month after fledging (see Breeding).

Breeding

Puffbirds are probably monogamous. Most species breed, and perhaps live together throughout the year, as territorial pairs, but a few may have slightly more complex systems. Certainly, the nunbirds breed in co-operative groups, which appear to involve the offspring from previous years helping to defend the territory and feed the young. Swallow-winged Puffbirds tend to nest in loose, non-territorial groups, and non-parent visitors to nests have been witnessed.

Although the nests of many bucconids have not been documented, the information that does exist indicates that puffbirds nest in cavities. From the evidence available, it appears that the genera *Notharchus*, *Bucco* and *Hypnelus* are typical, but seemingly not obligate, users of arboreal termitaria, while *Nystalus*, *Monasa* and *Chelidoptera* always nest in earth tunnels; the species of *Malacoptila* and *Nonnula* are reported to use both types of site. There are also poorly documented reports of White-necked and White-whiskered Puffbirds and Rusty-breasted Nunlets nesting in holes in trees, and of White-whiskered Puffbird nests in holes in bamboo. The Russet-throated Puffbird has the apparently unique habit among the Bucconidae of taking over the mud nests of the Pale-legged Hornero (*Furnarius leucopus*), although it does this only occasionally. Sometimes, puffbirds may nest in a cavity excavated in previous years.

The timing of breeding appears, at least in the case of ground-nesting species, to coincide with the start of dry seasons. This, of course, minimizes the risk of flooding in the burrow.

A pair of Black-breasted Puffbirds, when excavating a hole in a very large black nest of the termite *Nasutitermes pilifrons*, took turns of between one minute and a quarter of an hour at the task, one bird tapping at and crunching the hard woody material while the off-duty partner stood sentinel nearby. The pair worked persistently, both morning and afternoon, for many hours a day until, after some two weeks of effort, the structure was seemingly complete. It consisted of a narrow, horizontal tunnel, about 18 cm in length and 3 cm in diameter, leading to a spacious, neatly rounded, unlined chamber in the heart of the termitary. The eggs, however, were laid only some ten days later. During the period of egg-laying, one partner stood guard in front of the nest, as occurred during the ten-day interval between the completion of the nest and the deposition of the first egg.

Similar behaviour and/or results have been recorded for other species, including the Brown-banded Puffbird and the Two-banded Puffbird. One pair of the latter dug an entrance tunnel about 8 cm across, leading backwards and upwards for nearly the entire diameter of the termite dwelling to a slightly enlarged spherical chamber about 15 cm across. There was no lining in the chamber, the egg being deposited on the debris at the bottom of the nest-cavity.

Skutch was never sure whether ground-nesting puffbirds excavated their own burrows or used pre-existing ones, and there is a report that the birds use holes dug by armadillos and pacas (*Cuniculus*). Nevertheless, two neglected old records, from 1909 and 1922, indicate that these birds do dig their own burrows, and some more recent observations confirm this fact. In 1922, J. P.

With a deep and powerfully hooked bill and strong jaw muscles, many puffbirds are capable of capturing vertebrate prey, as demonstrated by this Collared Puffbird, which has seized a small frog. This species often hunts from shaded perches in the understorey, regularly taking snakes, lizards and large insects from the forest floor. Larger prey, and those possessing weapons such as pincers or stingers, are thoroughly beaten against a branch or other hard surface before being swallowed head first. This behaviour serves not only to kill the prey item, but also to help break it up into manageable pieces and perhaps even to remove toxins.

[Bucco capensis, French Guiana. Photo: Olivier Tostain]

Nunbirds in the genus Monasa *sometimes forage on the ground and from the foliage, as shown by the orthopteran and the caterpillar captured by these Black-fronted Nunbirds. This species also associates with army ants, and sometimes follows troops of monkeys to obtain prey disturbed by the primates. However, nunbirds take more prey in flight than do most other puffbirds. This is naturally related to the fact that they are more graceful in flight, sometimes gliding and circling upwards when returning to a hunting perch. In addition, they are fully capable of rapid flight, as proven by their ability to overtake woodcreepers (Dendrocolaptidae) during pursuit of prey at army-ant swarms.* Monasa *nunbirds are rather large bucconids that depart radically in appearance, as well as in behaviour, from all other puffbirds. They have dark, mostly unmarked plumage; a short, brightly coloured bill; and a relatively long, broad tail. The body is streamlined, and they tend to perch in a more upright posture than do typical puffbirds.*

[Monasa nigrifrons nigrifrons,
Amacayacu National Park,
Colombia.
Photos: Patricio Robles Gil]

da Fonseca gave some idea of why nest construction by bucconids has so rarely been witnessed. His pair of White-eared Puffbirds was extraordinarily vigilant, the off-duty bird keeping the most careful watch and calling the digging partner out of the hole at the slightest hint of danger, both then flying away in total silence; as soon as the danger had passed, the pair returned to resume its activities, which, if uninterrupted, would last all day. In another early observation, this time involving Spot-bellied Puffbirds of the subspecies *striatipectus*, sometimes called the "Streak-bellied Puffbird", it was noted that the sharp hooked tip of the male's bill appeared to be abraded, and that this might be due to its undertaking most of the work of excavation. Digging with the bill has been confirmed for both sexes of the Crescent-chested Puffbird and both those of the White-whiskered Puffbird, although in the latter case the male takes the major role. On the other hand, Black-fronted Nunbirds were recently watched as they used their feet to dig a nest.

Ground nests are dug at an angle into flat or gently inclining ground. The smaller species of the family may construct tunnels only some 0·5 m long, whereas the larger nunbirds build burrows up to 1·5 m in length. The tunnels are straight, and terminate in a chamber which is lined with bits of leaf. At the entrance, there is a low collar or frame of leaf parts, twigs and overlying leaves which is presumably created by the birds themselves, although the behaviour has never apparently been witnessed. This frame blends with the ground, and helps to conceal the small opening in the forest floor. The Black Nunbird and its congeners make fairly large piles of leaves under which a rounded tunnel runs along the ground from one edge to the entrance of the nest-tunnel itself.

Returning to Skutch's uncertainty, one reason for it was that he never saw tailings of earth that would suggest that the birds had done their own digging, and other observers have noted the lack of such evidence even at nests of the Swallow-winged Puffbird. Such tailings do, however, appear, but it is thought that they very quickly get washed away by rain or covered by leaves; in the case of the Swallow-winged Puffbird, the earth appears to be trodden in at the lip of the entrance, forming a slight smooth dome. In any case, the birds continue to be highly vigilant at whichever site they choose. The Black-breasted Puffbirds watched by Skutch at their termitarium nest, as mentioned above, waited ten days after completing the nest before laying, one or the other member of the pair guarding the nest for much of the time. It is presumably during this period that mating occurs.

Copulation by puffbirds has rarely been witnessed. In one instance involving a pair of Black-breasted Puffbirds foraging together, the male was 0·6 m from the female when he fluffed his plumage, suddenly gave a grunting "chwah-it" three times and flew above her. She held her wings out and her tail closed and up, while he fluttered his outspread wings; the male then flew 0·6 m away again, wiped his bill rapidly, and looked about with the body rather puffed out. His mate slowly recovered to an upright posture, wiped her beak rapidly, and flew off. The male remained, fluffed himself up, and gave a loud song after a third Black-breasted Puffbird sang in the distance.

The eggs of puffbirds are white, dull to glossy, and relatively small, like those of a woodpecker. They are laid at intervals of about two days. Most puffbirds lay clutches of two to three eggs. A replacement clutch may be laid if the first is lost, but it appears that no species of bucconid rears more than one brood per year. The sexes share incubation duties. In the case of the ground-nesting White-whiskered Puffbird, the schedule is very simple. The male covers the eggs from just after midday and until dawn, and roughly an hour after he leaves the female arrives for a stint lasting five to eight hours; she, in turn, leaves the eggs uncovered for an hour or more, until the male returns for his session. The termitary-nesting Black-breasted Puffbird has a more complex incubation schedule, the mates replacing each other after much shorter periods of attendance. Since the nest-chamber of this species is less accessible to predators than is a burrow in the ground, the parents can afford to be rather less discreet in their habits.

Swallow-winged Puffbirds incubate for 15 days in total, but their different-sized young suggest that they start with the first

The Swallow-winged Puffbird has a small head, a short bill, long wings, and a short tail, and it is highly adapted for aerial activity. Perched on a bare twig atop an emergent tree, its silhouette is very martin-like. It is thought to be exclusively insectivorous, particularly favouring bees, wasps, flying ants and winged termites, and catching its prey in rapid aerial sallies from exposed perches. In general its prey items tend to be smaller than those caught by other puffbirds, and its prey is often swallowed in flight; there are no reports of this species beating its prey after capture. Its nest is a tunnel in flat ground or an earth bank, and its hatchlings are unique among puffbirds in having the skin black, rather than pink. Chicks of this and other burrow-nesting species of puffbirds are unusually mobile, being able to crawl to the entrance of the tunnel to receive food from their parents on the very day of hatching!

[*Chelidoptera tenebrosa tenebrosa.*
Above: Serra dos Carajás, Pará, Brazil.
Photo: Luiz Claudio Marigo.

Below: near Sinnamary, French Guiana.
Photo: Roland Seitre/Bios]

egg, while in other puffbirds incubation may begin with the last. The nestlings hatch blind, naked and pink, although those of the Swallow-winged are black. Despite this appearance of an altricial condition, however, they can immediately move about actively on their bed of dead leaves. This remarkable mobility, so far observed only among ground-nesting puffbirds, enables them, from day one, to crawl up the tunnel, which is often over a metre long, to the entrance to receive food from the parent, which, presumably for security reasons, never places its body farther than half-way into the tunnel. Curiously, it is the male that broods the young in the burrow, leaving only for brief periods during the first few days, whereas the female carries out all the feeding of the brood in their first week or so of life. Even after brooding has completely ceased, the female continues to take by far the greater share of provisioning. In one case, the ratio of feeds provided by female and male during a fortnight of observation was 25 to 3; in another, it was 32 to 3. In nunbirds, as many as five adults may attend a nest, but that these groups are composed of the two parents and their recent offspring can only be surmised.

The rate of food delivery to the nest varies with the size of prey items. The adults, especially the female, appear extremely sensitive to the condition of the young, bringing them food

This White-faced Nunbird
stands alongside the first
nest described for this
species, as recently as
in the year 2000.
Observations at this site
provided much new
information on the
breeding biology of the
species. The nest was a
tunnel dug into a bank
amid humid forest at an
elevation of 1900 m;
it took at least 25 days,
and possibly as long as
46 days, to construct.
Two eggs were laid in
late May, and the young
hatched in mid-June,
leaving the nest in the
latter part of July; the
precise figures that
emerged were an
incubation period of
15-18 days and a nestling
period of 37-38 days.
Both sexes shared in
nest-building, incubation,
and brood-rearing duties.

[Hapaloptila castanea,
Tandayapa Valley,
Pichincha, Ecuador.
Photo: Nicholas Athanas]

promptly when they are eager for it, but staying away for long periods if the last feed was particularly substantial. A lizard seems to satisfy a nestling's hunger for several hours.

When the nestlings are six days old, their pin-feathers are sprouting, especially on the head and wings. Two or three days later, they bristle with long, unopened feather sheaths. At ten days, the feathers begin to break through the sheath, expanding at the tips, and the eyes open; the bill is whitish. During the next two or three days the feathers develop rapidly, and at the age of 14 days the chicks are well clothed, with plumage rather similar to that of the parents. Fledging takes place at around 20 days, although the period for nunbirds is 30 days.

Predation is a major risk for puffbird eggs and nestlings, and disappearances of either have often been attributed to snakes. The safety of the earth burrow depends on several factors: its concealment; the parents' caution when visiting; the minimization of the number of visits; the silence and invisibility of the nestlings; and the absence of odour in the tunnel. Moreover, there is a remarkable phenomenon that takes place within the nest: once brooding stops at around the ninth day, and after their last feed of the day, the young retreat to the nest-chamber and throw up a screen of leaves that conceals them at night. This probably serves to deceive predators which hunt by touch or heat, such as snakes and large spiders, rather than those which hunt by sight or scent. The young also seem to have qualities which render them uninteresting to army ants. This is indicated by the fact that the ants have been seen to swarm around burrows, yet have left the occupants, and even the maggots in the nest's detritus, unharmed.

Newly fledged puffbirds sally to take proffered prey from the bill of a parent. They are usually not capable of foraging independently until at least a month after fledging. On one occasion, involving White-fronted Nunbirds, an older immature which attempted to hover-snatch food from an adult was rebuffed by the latter, which gave a bill-down display and uttered a loud screech. Nevertheless, among many bucconids, including apparently all nunbirds, there is a long period of association, and sometimes food-exchanging, between parents and offspring. Sightings of amicable trios towards the start of the breeding season suggest that the young often stay on the natal territory for the best part of a year.

Movements

The Bucconidae are highly sedentary birds, and there have been no studies that show them to undertake any real migrations. Notably, one Rufous-necked Puffbird which was ringed in June at Belém, in Brazil, was recaptured at the same site five times, in the months of July, November, March and April. Even circumstantial clues to migratory habits, such as birds entering houses at night or being killed by cats or cars in unusual areas, have never been reported for any members of this family. Only four of the southernmost species have been thought, albeit on slender evidence, to undertake migrations, and even then only in part of their ranges.

Conversely, the Two-banded Puffbird is a species which dwells in seasonal habitat, yet it has not been reported as a seasonal visitor to such habitat. On the other hand, it seems to show a curious unevenness of temporal distribution. An example of this is the fact that one museum collector spent the three years from 1944 to 1946 in a study area without once finding this species, and then, during June 1947 to May 1949, found it to be fairly common throughout that same area.

Since the Bucconidae have not reached Panama's offshore islands, they must be considered poor dispersers across open terrain and water. White-whiskered Puffbirds are territorial, and one ringed individual remained on its territory for nine years. This seems likely to be the norm for the majority of species, especially those inhabiting wetter forests, where the seasons are ill-defined. The group behaviour of nunbirds is another sign of a deep-rooted sedentariness in the family, which clearly evolved in the equatorial lowlands where food resources are largely stable throughout the year.

Relationship with Man

The most obvious and, in fact, almost the only relationship that puffbirds have with man is as the target of his abuse, and the word "stupid" has frequently been applied to members of this family. This is due mostly to the fact that perch-and-pounce feeders, in which category the puffbirds excel, tend to use their stillness between pounces as a camouflage, both to make them less

Nesting exclusively in holes that they excavate in level or gently sloping ground, Black Nunbirds time their breeding to coincide with the start of the dry season, presumably so as to minimize the chance of nest tunnels becoming flooded. Tunnels are dug at a shallow angle and may extend up to 1·5 m in length, ending in a chamber lined with bits of vegetation. Nunbirds apparently pile up leaves to form a frame around the nest entrance, which no doubt helps to conceal the nest from the view of predators, among other possible functions. Like woodpeckers (Picidae), puffbirds lay relatively small white eggs. A replacement clutch may be produced if the first clutch is lost, but no species is known to attempt a second brood in the same nesting season. Exhibiting the white lesser coverts that are the hallmark of the species, an adult carries a small lizard to the nest entrance and presumably is about to provision the brood within. Apart from lizards, Black Nunbirds take a wide variety of insects and other arthropods, most prey being obtained from a solid substrate rather than in the air. They also follow army-ant swarms and have been observed below flocks of Red-rumped Caciques (Cacicus haemorrhous), presumably looking for prey that flee as the icterids move through the canopy.

[Monasa atra, French Guiana. Photos: Olivier Tostain]

visible to potential prey and to conceal them from potential predators. In the event of an onslaught, therefore, their abiding reaction is simply to freeze. Collectors, however, regarded this highly
adaptive behaviour as the height of stupidity. In 1873, E. L.
Layard reported on a successful outing as follows:

"I subsequently obtained two more, and was struck with
their extreme stupidity. Three birds were in company on
a very high tree. I had only my little collecting gun, with
a quarter of a dram of powder and dust-shot, but, selecting the lowest, fired at him. He swung round on his twig
and hung suspended. I loaded quickly and aimed at the
next, who never moved; at the first report he fell dead,
and the third remained. I fired again, without effect; but
the next shot brought it down."

Again and again one finds them vilified for this trait. Comments such as "the most stupid birds imaginable", "a picture of
stupid lethargy", "rather dull and stupid", "stupidly watching one
until they can be almost taken in the hand", and so on, abound in
the earlier literature. Children in Venezuela call the Two-banded
Puffbird *aguantapiedra*, "stone-endurer", because it refuses to fly
when they pelt it; similarly, the White-necked Puffbird earned the
local name *cabeza piedra* from its ability to withstand being hit by
stones flung by slingshot. The Portuguese settlers of Brazil nick-
named the Crescent-chested Puffbird *João doido*, meaning "dozy
John", *doido* being the word that Portuguese settlers elsewhere in
the world applied so aptly to the Dodo (*Raphus cucullatus*).

Many other colloquial names bestowed upon puffbirds, including *João bobo*, *Durmili* and *Durmilon*, as well as scientific
ones such as *Nystalus* (drowsy) and *Ecchaunornis* (puffed-up or
arrogant bird), emphasize the perceived stupidity or laziness of
these birds, for which early explorers such as F. de Azara, as
long ago as 1805, heaped scorn upon them. Despite such widespread and long-standing ideas, there is no objective evidence
for a lack of intelligence among the members of this family, and
all are certainly capable of bursts of activity.

Nevertheless, although this physical lethargy disguises a keen
alertness, puffbirds do have a dumb-looking appearance, too:
"there is something very grotesque in the appearance of all the
Puff-birds", wrote W. Swainson. Perhaps the Amerindians knew

better. Wetmore, in a 1968 volume on the birds of Panama, reported a superstition regarding the White-whiskered Puffbird in
that country. Boys watching him skinning a specimen called it
pájaro brujero, meaning witchdoctor bird, because its call was
like the singing of the Guaymi witchdoctors.

Also in Panama, White-fronted Nunbirds were not common
in the Darién woods, but they were abundant in and around the
Indian settlements in that region. There they could be seen at any
time, dusting on a little pathway or "perched about the house almost as tame as the little paraquets". This reveals an interesting
aspect of puffbird "tameness", namely that where they remained
unpersecuted they were ready to live in such proximity to man.

The German name *Faulvogel* is still used for all the
Bucconidae with the sole exception of the *Monasa* nunbirds. Like
so many other vernacular names attached to members of this family, it means an idle or slothful bird, although it could equally be
translated as a bird that is rotten or putrid and, hence, foul-smell-
ing. It is interesting that many bucconid species have been found
by preparers of specimens to be malodorous (see Morphological
Aspects), and as long ago as 1815 Shaw noted that puffbirds are
not very edible. As a consequence, puffbirds are not sought after
for food, although Shaw mentioned that native peoples do sometimes eat them. Nor are they sought after for captivity, since their
diet of large insects, their lethargic habits, their infrequent and
unspectacular vocalizations, their relative ungracefulness and
their dull colours make them hardly suitable or attractive as pets.

Status and Conservation

No species of bucconid is threatened with global extinction, and
only one, the Sooty-capped Puffbird, is currently considered
Near-threatened. The Lanceolated Monklet and the Chestnut-
headed Nunlet were formerly placed in this latter category, but
the conservation status of both appears now to be more secure
than was previously thought. Nevertheless, all three remain extremely poorly known, and in the absence of information it would
seem wise to view their status with some precaution.

Four bucconids are species of restricted range, as defined by
BirdLife International, which means that the extent of occurrence
of each is less than 50,000 km². The Sooty-capped Puffbird is con-

The Lanceolated Monklet
was formerly classified
as Near-threatened by
BirdLife International.
It ranges from the
Caribbean slope of Costa
Rica south to western
Brazil and extreme
northern Bolivia. Often
considered to be rare
throughout much of its
range, this tiny species,
which weighs only some
20 g, is generally silent
and retiring and thus is
difficult to detect in the
middle and upper storeys
of the humid forest that it
prefers. More recent
information indicates that,
fortunately, its populations
appear to be in better
shape than was previously
thought. The species
feeds mainly on insects
and is one of only a
few puffbirds known
to eat berries.

[*Micromonacha
lanceolata*,
near Taisha,
Morona-Santiago, Ecuador.
Photo: Doug Wechsler/
VIREO]

No bucconid is classed as threatened, and only the Sooty-capped Puffbird is listed as Near-threatened. It inhabits humid lowland forest in coastal Colombia, within the Chocó Endemic Bird Area. It is common in Los Katios National Park but in recent years has been found in only one other area. Elsewhere, it has suffered from widespread habitat conversion and human encroachment associated with livestock grazing and agricultural development. On the bright side, most of the localities from which specimens are known have not been visited since the mid-1960's, so this species may be more widespread than is currently thought.

[*Nystactes noanamae*. Photo: John S. Dunning/ Ardea]

fined to the Chocó Endemic Bird Area in western Colombia, a region under threat from deforestation on a grand scale. The Semicollared Puffbird helps to define the South-east Peruvian Lowlands Endemic Bird Area, which stretches into both Brazil and Bolivia; this area remains relatively intact at present, although oil and gas extraction are becoming increasingly important in the region. The other two bucconids in this category are both nunlets of the genus *Nonnula*. The Brown Nunlet is found in the Upper Amazon-Napo Lowlands Endemic Bird Area, and the Chestnut-headed Nunlet in the Amazon Flooded Forests Endemic Bird Area.

The fact that puffbirds are often so difficult to detect may be a pointer to the likelihood that virtually all species will be found to be moderately common. Only the Sooty-capped Puffbird appears to have a sufficiently constrained distribution and to be experiencing habitat loss significant enough to warrant concern in the near term.

Within its very small range in western Colombia, the Sooty-capped Puffbird has been recorded from only two sites in recent years. At one of these, the Los Katíos National Park, it appears to be common, and it is possible that this species survives in reasonable numbers elsewhere, as few of the ten or so localities from which specimens are known have been visited by ornithologists since the mid-1960's. On the other hand, its lowland forest habitat is under severe threat from logging and conversion to agricultural uses. Plantations of bananas and oil palms (*Elaeis guineensis*) are rapidly replacing the natural forest, while cattle ranching and settlement by human populations, with their attendant developments, are an increasing threat to this species. The fact that even the Sooty-capped Puffbird has been found in non-pristine habitat may, however, be a reason for optimism.

In general, puffbirds have profited very little from human actions, but their widespread use of edge habitats means that at least some species must have benefited from the construction of roads and railways through pristine forest areas. The most obvious beneficiary is the Swallow-winged Puffbird, which may have increased its numbers as a result of new nesting and foraging sites being opened up. The White-eared Puffbird uses suburban trees, but in all likelihood the species was present in such areas long before housing developments created their mock-savanna effect, and it is therefore probably merely hanging on in these places.

Regardless of the fact that so few puffbirds have been registered as being of conservation concern, they do belong to a guild, known as the subcanopy sallying insectivores, that has been well documented as experiencing difficulties in the face of habitat

modification and loss. The use by some bucconids of edge habitats has, however, proved to be the saving grace for the species concerned. Work carried out by J. M. Thiollay in logged and unlogged forest established that larger insectivorous birds of the upper storeys, such as the Black Nunbird and the Collared and White-chested Puffbirds, declined with selective logging. By contrast, members of the family that use edge habitats or clearings with scattered trees and vine-tangles to sally-glean, including the Pied, White-necked and Swallow-winged Puffbirds, showed an increase in numbers. It is clearly important to establish the responses of other bucconids to the impact of major habitat disturbances, such as logging.

Meanwhile, a study of a very small forest island, 87 ha in extent, in lowland Ecuador revealed that puffbirds do poorly in such isolation. Several species appeared to drop out within a few years, as was the case with Pied and Barred Puffbirds, while others, in this instance the White-necked and White-whiskered Puffbirds, were so infrequently recorded that their populations were thought to be unviable. Since two of the species seen to be faring badly when their habitat is fragmented are two of the bucconids found by Thiollay to improve their status with selective logging, it would appear that there are few grounds for complacency over the status of any of the puffbirds in the long term. It is widely accepted that large areas of pristine habitat are important for the long-term conservation of biological diversity. The more this perception is put into practice in Central and South America, the greater will be the benefit to the puffbirds.

General Bibliography

Avise & Aquadro (1987), Beddard (1898), Bennett *et al.* (1986), Bock (1994), Brodkorb (1970), Brom (1990), Burmeister (1856), Burton (1984), Cabanis & Heine (1850-1851), Canaday (1996), Chandler (1916), Cottrell (1968), Cracraft (1981), Dégallier *et al.* (1992), Feduccia (1976), Feduccia & Martin (1976), Friedmann (1930b), Fürbringer (1888), Haffer (1968), Houde & Olson (1988), Lanyon & Zink (1987), Leck (1979), Mayr (1998), Nitzsch (1840), Olrog (1972), Olson (1983, 1985), Olson & Feduccia (1979), Parker & Carr (1992), Peters (1948), Pinto *et al.* (1996), Raikow & Cracraft (1983), Ripley (1945), Schlegel (1863), Sclater (1879-1882, 1891), Seebohm (1895), Sherry & McDade (1982), Sibley (1956, 1996), Sibley & Ahlquist (1972, 1990), Sibley & Monroe (1990, 1993), Sibley *et al.* (1988), Simpson & Cracraft (1981), Skutch (1969b, 1985b), Steinbacher, G. (1935), Steinbacher, J. (1937), Steullet & Deautier (1946), Swierczewski (1977), Swierczewski & Raikow (1981), Todd (1943a), Weldon & Rappole (1997), Willis (1982a, 1982b, 1982c), Woodbury (1998).

ssp *macrorhynchos*

1

ssp *hyperrhynchus*

2

3

4

5

ssp *tectus*

ssp *subtectus*

6

variants

ssp *tamatia*

7

ssp *pulmentum*

8

9

10

typical

rufous morph
"*fulvidus*"

11

12

ssp *striolatus*

ssp *torridus*

ssp *maculatus*

13

ssp *striatipectus*

PLATE 3

inches   4

cm   10

Genus *NOTHARCHUS* Cabanis & Heine, 1863

1. White-necked Puffbird
Notharchus macrorhynchos

French: Tamatia à gros bec **German**: Weißhals-Faulvogel **Spanish**: Buco Picogordo

Taxonomy. *Bucco macrorhynchos* J. F. Gmelin, 1788, Cayenne.
Forms a superspecies with *N. swainsoni*, with which usually regarded as conspecific (see page 105). Races *hyperrhynchus* and *paraensis* markedly distinct from nominate, and together may constitute a separate species. Birds from El Salvador and NW Nicaragua sometimes separated as race *cryptoleucus*, but probably indistinguishable from *hyperrhynchus*. Population of Santa Marta Mts (N Colombia) may represent a separate race; further study needed. Three subspecies currently recognized.

Subspecies and Distribution.
N. m. hyperrhynchus (P. L. Sclater, 1856) - S Mexico (Oaxaca) S to N & NE Venezuela, and S to Colombia, Ecuador, E Peru, N Bolivia and W Brazil (E to R Tapajós and S to Mato Grosso).
N. m. macrorhynchos (J. F. Gmelin, 1788) - extreme E Venezuela, the Guianas and extreme N Brazil S to the Amazon.
N. m. paraensis Sassi, 1932 - lower Amazon Valley in Brazil (Pará E of R Tapajós and into N Maranhão).

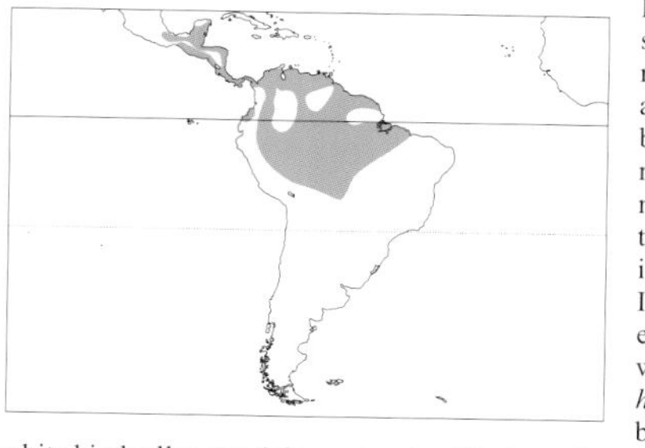

Descriptive notes. 25 cm; 81-106 g. Plumage strongly pied. Mostly glossy blue-black, narrow white forehead, white throat, sides of face and upper breast, thin white nape-collar; broad black breastband, white central abdomen, narrowly white-barred black patches on sides; narrow white edgings to feathers of upperparts; tail black with narrow white tips; bill all black; iris red, brown or straw-coloured; feet black. Immature duller black with buffy feather edgings; pectoral band may be incomplete; white areas washed buffy; iris brown. Race *hyperrhynchus* differs from nominate in much broader white forehead, larger bill, broader white hindcollar, much less extensive black patches on sides; *paraensis* similar, with bill exceptionally long. VOICE. Song a very high weak trill at variable speeds, usually descending, "ui-ui-ui... wi-di-dik wi-di-dik wi-di-dik..."; melodious and harsh calls, notably a clear nasal falling "düür".

Habitat. Occurs from ground level to canopy and in edge of humid to semi-arid formations, chiefly in second-growth woodland (often where *Cecropia* dominant) and edge habitats, open woodland and savanna, mixed woods of oak (*Quercus*) and pine (*Pinus*), clearings with scattered tall trees, abandoned plots and forest openings; also primary tropical evergreen and semi-evergreen forest, *terra firme* forest, transitional forest, flooded and swampy forest with many dead trees, landward side of mangroves, river margins, and plantations. Proximity to running water may be important. Generally found from sea-level up to 1200 m; in Venezuela reaches 1200 m N of R Orinoco, but only at 100-250 m S of it.

Food and Feeding. Insects, including Orthoptera (Locustidae), Hymenoptera (Apidae, Xylopidae), Hemiptera, Homoptera (Fulgoridae), Coleoptera (Cetonidae) and Lepidoptera; also small vertebrates, some vegetable matter. Once noted taking the large green scarab *Macraspis lucida* when it was abundant in high tree crowns. Investigates swarms of army ants. Still-hunts from high bare perch, diving at prey, which is beaten on perch before ingestion.

Breeding. Mar-May in Costa Rica; Jan-Jul in Panama; May and Sept in Colombia; Jun in Venezuela; hole excavation recorded in Jul and Aug in Brazil (Manaus). Nest in cavity, excavated by both sexes, in large arboreal termitary, or hole in tree, usually 12-15 m up, but recorded to 18 m and as low as 3 m; hole in ground and earth bank reportedly also used; pair in Brazil dug hole in termite nest in Jul, and dug third hole in same nest in Aug. Clutch size and incubation and fledging periods not documented.

Movements. Presumably resident.

Status and Conservation. Not globally threatened. Very to fairly uncommon in Mexico; now rare in El Salvador owing to clearance of lowland forest; uncommon in Honduras. In Costa Rica, occurs in Corcovado National Park and Santa Rosa National Park. Commonest puffbird in Canal Zone, Panama. Fairly common in Colombia, where occurs in Tayrona National Park. Rare to uncommon in Ecuador; present in Cotacachi-Cayapas National Park. Widespread in French Guiana, but rarer in coastal areas. Fairly common to common in Amazon region, perhaps less frequent in Bolivia (where judged rare at 2 study sites) and Peru, although sedentary habits thought to lead to underestimation of true numbers. In Peru, up to 2 pairs/km², although only 0·5 pairs/km² in *Ficus*/*Cedrela* transitional forest.

Bibliography. Alvarez del Toro (1980), Anon. (1998b), Binford (1989), Brace *et al.* (1997), Carriker (1910), Chapman (1917, 1926), Cohn-Haft *et al.* (1997), Cory (1919), Darlington (1931), Dickey & van Rossem (1938), Dugand (1947), Friedmann (1948), González-García (1993), Griscom (1932), Gyldenstolpe (1945b), Haffer (1975), Haverschmidt & Mees (1994), Henriques & Oren (1997), Hilty & Brown (1986), Howell & Webb (1995), López *et al.* (1989), Meyer de Schauensee & Phelps (1978), Monroe (1968), O'Neill & Pearson (1974), Olivares (1957), Oniki & Willis (1982), Parker, Foster *et al.* (1993), Parker, Parker & Plenge (1982), Paynter (1955), Peres & Whittaker (1991), Ridgely & Greenfield (2001), Ridgely & Gwynne (1989), Robinson & Terborgh (1997), van Rossem (1934), Sargeant (1994), Sassi (1939), Schäfer & Phelps (1954), Short (1975), Sick (1993), Slud (1960, 1964), Sneidern (1954), Stiles & Skutch (1989), Stotz *et al.* (1996), Tashian (1952), Terborgh *et al.* (1990), Thiollay (1992), Thurber *et al.* (1987), Todd (1943a), Todd & Carriker (1922), Tostain *et al.* (1992), Wetmore (1968a), Willis (1982a), Willis & Eisenmann (1979), Zimmer *et al.* (1997).

2. Buff-bellied Puffbird
Notharchus swainsoni

French: Tamatia de Swainson **German**: Swainson-Faulvogel **Spanish**: Buco de Swainson

Taxonomy. *Bucco swainsoni* G. R. Gray, 1846, Brazil.
Forms a superspecies with *N. macrorhynchos*, and usually regarded as conspecific (see page 105). Monotypic.

Distribution. SE Brazil (Espírito Santo to Santa Catarina), E Paraguay, and NE Argentina (Misiones).

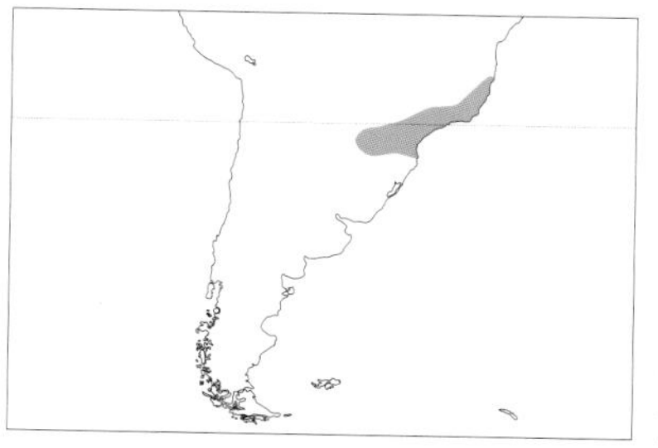

Descriptive notes. 23·5 cm. Black upperparts glossed green, feathers buffy-edged; very narrow white forehead, white throat and upper breast, greyish-white sides of face and thin nape-collar; black breastband, pale rufous abdomen, grey patches on sides; bill black; iris red, brown or straw-coloured; feet black. Differs from very similar *N. macrorhynchos* mainly in green gloss above, pale rufous belly with much more limited, greyer flank marks, greyer face and hindcollar, narrower black breastband, smaller bill. Immature duller; pectoral band may be incomplete; iris brown. VOICE. A descending sequence of whistles, varying in rhythm, "ui-ui---dibule-dibule...".

Habitat. Lowland humid forest, and logged and tall secondary forest.

Food and Feeding. Insects, including Orthoptera, Hymenoptera, Hemiptera, Coleoptera and Lepidoptera; also small vertebrates, some vegetable matter. Investigates army-ant swarms. Still-hunts from tops of tall bare trees.

Breeding. Breeds in Sept-Oct in S of range. Excavates hole in termite nest; one cavity in Paraguay was 12 m above ground. No information on clutch size, or other aspects of breeding.

Movements. Unclear; possibly a summer migrant, Sept-Mar, to Atlantic Forest in Brazilian state of São Paulo; resident in Iguazú, in extreme NE Argentina.

Status and Conservation. Not globally threatened. In Brazil, relatively rare in São Paulo state, uncommon in Paraná; frequently encountered in E Paraguay; generally rare in Argentina (Misiones), though regularly recorded in Iguazú area.

Bibliography. Aguirre & Aldrighi (1983), Aleixo & Galetti (1997), dos Anjos *et al.* (1997), Barnes *et al.* (1993), Brooks *et al.* (1993), Canevari *et al.* (1991), Chebez (1994), Cory (1919), Forrester (1993), Hayes (1995), Olrog (1968), de la Peña (1994), Pereyra (1950), Saibene *et al.* (1996), Sargeant & Wall (1996), Schmidtuz *et al.* (2001), Schubart *et al.* (1965), Short (1972b, 1975), Sick (1993).

3. Black-breasted Puffbird
Notharchus pectoralis

French: Tamatia à plastron **German**: Gürtelfaulvogel **Spanish**: Buco Pechinegro

Taxonomy. *Bucco pectoralis* G. R. Gray, 1846, no locality.
Forms a superspecies with *N. ordii*. Monotypic.

Distribution. Canal Zone of Panama E to C Colombia and S to NW Ecuador.

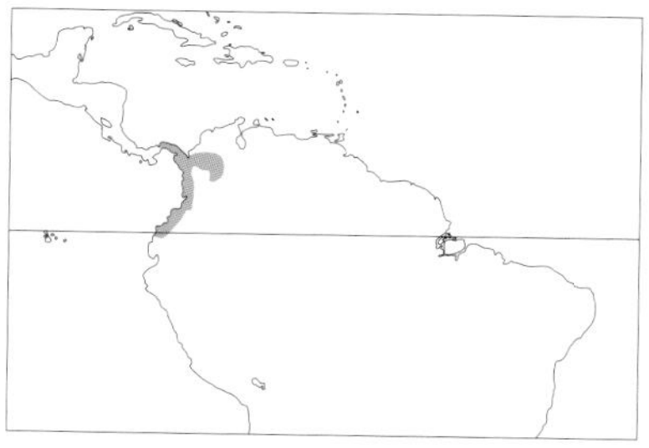

Descriptive notes. 19-23 cm; 60-69 g. Mostly glossy blue-black; white throat, separated by a broad black band from white auricular patch, narrow white nuchal collar; scapulars, wing-coverts, rump and uppertail-coverts narrowly fringed white; tail black, slightly graduated, narrowly tipped white; broad black band from breast to upper belly, lower belly whitish, sides dark grey with buffy fringes; bill all black; iris dark brown or dark red; feet blackish. Immature not described. VOICE. Song 10-30 loud "kwee" whistles followed by 3 or so lower, slower "whew" whistles ending with a few fading "wheet-whew" wolf-whistles; rasping "chah-chah-chah" in territorial disputes.

Habitat. Humid and wet lowland forest, second-growth woodland, often near running water; less frequently at forest edge, associated with heliconias and bamboo; more restricted to forest than *N. macrorhynchos*. Mainly occupies canopy foliage; much less often on exposed open perches, but drops low at army-ant swarms with some frequency. Occurs up to 1000 m.

Food and Feeding. Large centipedes (Chilopoda), millipedes (Diplopoda), scorpions (Scorpiones), spiders, roaches (Blattodea), grasshoppers or katydids (Orthoptera), mantises (Mantidae), stick-insects (Phasmida), beetles, caterpillars and lizards. Commonly follows swarms of the ant *Eciton burchelli*, which often penetrate the upper understorey and subcanopy; moves down to forage around foliose palms and rotten, liana-draped or epiphyte-laden branches. Still-hunts, diving after prey and returning to perch, where beats prey before swallowing it.

Breeding. Mar-May in NW Colombia; Mar-Jul in Panama. Nest in hole c. 18 cm deep, excavated by both sexes, in arboreal termitarium 2·3-12·5 m up in subcanopy tree. Clutch 3 eggs, but only 1-2 young observed in fledged broods; incubation by both sexes, period unknown.

Movements. Presumably resident.

Status and Conservation. Not globally threatened. Generally uncommon, but common at least locally, and habit of spending long periods motionless inside canopy probably mask its status elsewhere. Sensitive to habitat disturbance.

Bibliography. Anon. (1998b), Best *et al.* (1997), Borrero (1962), Brabourne & Chubb (1912a), Chapman (1917, 1926), Cory (1919), Eisenmann (1952), Hilty & Brown (1986), Krabbe (1991), Olivares (1957), Ridgely & Greenfield (2001), Ridgely & Gwynne (1989), Ridgely *et al.* (1998), Ridgway (1914), Rodner *et al.* (2000), Rodriguez (1982), Skutch (1948c, 1983), Stotz *et al.* (1996), Strauch (1977), Taylor (1995), Wetmore (1968a), Willis (1980, 1982a), Willis & Eisenmann (1979).

4. Brown-banded Puffbird
Notharchus ordii

French: Tamatia de Cassin **German**: Braunbinden-Faulvogel **Spanish**: Buco Pechipardo

On following pages: 5. Pied Puffbird (*Notharchus tectus*); 6. Chestnut-capped Puffbird (*Argicus macrodactylus*); 7. Spotted Puffbird (*Nystactes tamatia*); 8. Sooty-capped Puffbird (*Nystactes noanamae*); 9. Collared Puffbird (*Bucco capensis*); 10. Barred Puffbird (*Nystalus radiatus*); 11. White-eared Puffbird (*Nystalus chacuru*); 12. Striolated Puffbird (*Nystalus striolatus*); 13. Spot-bellied Puffbird (*Nystalus maculatus*).

Taxonomy. *Bucco Ordii* Cassin, 1851, Venezuela.
Forms a superspecies with *N. pectoralis*. Monotypic.
Distribution. S Venezuela (Amazonas), NW & NC Brazil (N of Amazon and in Mato Grosso), E Peru and N Bolivia; also probably E Colombia.

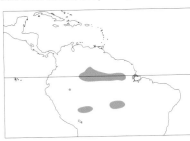

Descriptive notes. 20 cm; 51·5 g. Slightly glossy black above, narrow white forehead and hindcollar, thin black line from gape to eye; uppertail-coverts fringed white, tail one-third graduated, black with narrow white tips; face and chin to upper breast white, black band across mid-breast, passing at lower edge to olive-brown, then breaking into brown spots, these becoming black on sides; central belly and undertail-coverts white; white central band on undertail; underwing-coverts mostly black, broad white wingband on bases of remiges below; bill black; iris dark brown; feet black. Immature not described. VOICE. Song lengthy, with several clear, loud introductory whistles followed by cadenced couplets and triplets.

Habitat. Canopy and edge of rainforest, transitional forest, open stunted forest growing on white-sand soils and rock areas, also forest clearings and scrubby vegetation at edge of *terra firme* forest. 150-300 m.
Food and Feeding. Unrecorded; observation of individual making a sallying flight suggests that feeding habits, and presumably prey, probably typical of genus.
Breeding. Nest excavation in Dec and specimen with developed gonads in Feb, in Venezuela. One nest a cavity in termitarium, 4-5 m up in largely bare tree, excavated by both sexes. No information on clutch size, incubation period or fledging period.
Movements. Presumably resident.
Status and Conservation. Not globally threatened. Evidently occurs at low densities, although widely distributed throughout the upper reaches of the Orinoco and the Amazon. Uncommon in Amazonas, Brazil; present in Cristalino River Private Reserve, N Mato Grosso. Recently discovered (1990's) in NE Peru, near Iquitos, representing significant range extension; this site, in an area of white-sand soils, has subsequently been protected as Alpahuayo-Mishana Reserve. Although thought to occur in E Colombia, status there uncertain and further study required.
Bibliography. Berlepsch (1908), Clements & Shany (2001), Cory (1919), Donahue (1994), Foster *et al.* (1994), Friedmann (1948), Meyer de Schauensee & Phelps (1978), Parker & Remsen (1987), Parker *et al.* (1982), Peres & Whittaker (1991), Phelps & Phelps (1958), Remsen & Traylor (1989), Rodner *et al.* (2000), Ruschi (1979), Sick (1993), Snethlage (1914), Stotz *et al.* (1996), Willard *et al.* (1991), Zimmer & Hilty (1997), Zimmer *et al.* (1997).

5. Pied Puffbird
Notharchus tectus

French: Tamatia pie   **German**: Elsterfaulvogel   **Spanish**: Buco Pío

Taxonomy. *Bucco tectus* Boddaert, 1783, Cayenne.
Sometimes placed in genus *Bucco*. Race *subtectus* considered a distinct species by some authors. Three subspecies recognized.
Subspecies and Distribution.
N. t. subtectus (P. L. Sclater, 1860) - Caribbean Costa Rica S to W & NC Colombia and NW Ecuador.
N. t. tectus (Boddaert, 1783) - S Venezuela, the Guianas and N Amazonian Brazil (E as far as Maranhão).
N. t. picatus (P. L. Sclater, 1856) - SE Colombia, E Ecuador and E Peru to E Bolivia and WC Brazil.

Descriptive notes. 14-17 cm; 21-40 g. Mainly glossy black above and white below; dark bare patch behind eye; distinct short white line from nasal bristles to behind eye, small white spots on crown; white on some scapulars; white patches near tail base and at tail tips, distal outer webs black on most rectrices; broad black pectoral band, black flank patches lightly barred white; bill all black; eyes brown; feet black. Immature duller, browner above, white areas tinged buff, wing-coverts spotted buffy-white, rectrices paler, breastband pale-fringed; pale-tipped bill. Race *subtectus* smaller than nominate, with smaller bill, narrower pectoral band, less or no white spotting on crown, and greyer flanks vaguely barred white; *picatus* larger than nominate, darker, less white on lateral tail feathers. VOICE. Song a thin but loud, high-pitched, bat-like series of whistles, "tee-oo" or "pwee pwee pwee" in various patterns, slowing at end; call "pseee tidit, tidit-tidit", like tyrant-flycatcher (Tyrannidae), also twitters, etc.

Habitat. Inhabits tropical lowland humid evergreen forest, edges, clearings and streamsides, second growth with scattered tall trees, abandoned clearings, gallery and riverine forest, mangroves, woodland, savanna. In Costa Rica apparently confined to the tropical belt, frequenting clearings with scattered trees, plantations and pastures inside generally wooded country, and appears to avoid primary forest. In the Guianas occupies high forest, also other habitats such as coastal mangroves, plantations, sand-ridge and savanna forest, shrubby second growth, and granite vegetation in form of low, dense, vine-clad woodland. Occurs in lowlands up to 1000 m; below 300 m in Costa Rica.
Food and Feeding. Dragonflies (including Libellulidae), Orthoptera (including Locustidae), bugs (Hemiptera), butterflies and moths, bees and wasps (including Sphegidae), beetles (including Elateridae), termites (Isoptera). One stomach contained hard-shelled beetles of a single species. Forages from open or dead branch, usually high in canopy, sometimes lower down.
Breeding. Jun in Panama; Feb-Aug in Colombia; apparently around Mar in Ecuador; Sept in Surinam; Mar-May and Nov in French Guiana. Nest in hole excavated in arboreal termitarium, situated 4-25 m above ground. Clutch 2 eggs; no information available on incubation and fledging periods.
Movements. Presumably resident, but appears to move around countryside in irregular pattern, at least seasonally.

Status and Conservation. Not globally threatened. In Costa Rica, increasingly rare with deforestation. Fairly common in Panama in 1970's. Common in W Colombia, where present in Los Katíos National Park. Common in the Guianas. In Venezuela, occurs in Imataca Forest Reserve and El Dorado. Generally uncommon in C & S Amazon region, uncommon near Manaus, and apparently rare in Rondônia; fairly common in E Amazon. Apparently rare in Peru and Bolivia; occurs in Noel Kempff Mercado National Park, Bolivia.
Bibliography. Anon. (1998b), Bates *et al.* (1989), Bond (1954), Borges (1994), Brosset (1964), Chapman (1917, 1926), Cohn-Haft *et al.* (1997), Cory (1919), Davis (1986), Dubs (1992), Haffer (1959, 1975), Haffer & Borrero (1965), Haverschmidt (1948), Haverschmidt & Mees (1994), Henriques & Oren (1997), Hilty & Brown (1986), Meyer de Schauensee & Phelps (1978), O'Neill & Pearson (1974), Olivares (1957), Oren & Parker (1997), Parker, Foster *et al.* (1993), Parker, Parker & Plenge (1982), Pinto (1966), Ridgely & Greenfield (2001), Ridgely & Gwynne (1989), Ridgway (1914), Rodriguez (1982), Romero (1977), Sick (1993), Slud (1960, 1964), Snyder (1966), Stiles (1985), Stiles & Skutch (1989), Stotz & Bierregaard (1989), Stotz *et al.* (1996), Thiollay (1992), Tostain *et al.* (1992), Wetmore (1968a), Willis (1980, 1982a), Willis & Eisenmann (1979), Willis & Oniki (1990), Zimmer & Hilty (1997), Zimmer *et al.* (1997).

Genus *ARGICUS*   Cabanis & Heine, 1863

6. Chestnut-capped Puffbird
Argicus macrodactylus

French: Tamatia macrodactyle   **German**: Braunkappen-Faulvogel   **Spanish**: Buco Cabecirrojo

Taxonomy. *Cyphos macrodactylus* Spix, 1824, Fonte Boa, Brazil.
Usually placed in genus *Bucco*. Birds from R Caura region of S Venezuela often treated as race *caurensis*, but probably inseparable from other populations. Monotypic.
Distribution. S Venezuela, E Colombia and E Ecuador S to E Peru, upper Amazonian Brazil and N Bolivia.

Descriptive notes. 14-15 cm; 25 g. Crown chestnut; long narrow whitish supercilium, broader white stripe just below cheek bisecting black patch on side of face and broad collar across lower throat; chin and upper throat rufescent-white, varying in extent, elongated shafts of chin feathers recurving over bill; narrow bright orange-rufous nuchal collar; rest of upperparts dark brown, a few lighter bars on back, many on rump; light buffy-rufous scalloping on lower mantle, scapulars and wing-coverts; remiges dark brown; tail rather long, narrow, graduated about a third of its length, dark warm brown; whitish upper breast, remaining underparts mainly buffy with fine vague dusky barring except on lower belly; bill all black; iris red to brown, bare eye-ring dark grey; feet brownish-grey or greenish-grey. Immature similar, differs in having shorter bill. VOICE. Song a series of plaintive but abrupt rising notes ending in twitter, "pup pup pep pep peep peep pip pip pip piz".

Habitat. Usually found in the subcanopy, understorey and undergrowth near water at borders of humid *terra firme* and *várzea* forest, especially along *várzea* river edge and in riverine bamboo, also *igapó* and creek margins, second-growth woodland, early successional growth, riverbank forest, lake margins, transitional forest, willow (*Salix*) bars, wet shrubbery in clearings, gallery forest, palm groves; also scrubby forest away from water. Occurs from sea-level up to at least 600 m.
Food and Feeding. Large roach (Blattodea) found in one stomach. Observed once to appear at dusk to catch moths on the wing. Almost always solitary, pair members apprently not foraging together. No other information.
Breeding. Nest in hole in arboreal termitarium. No other details known.
Movements. Presumably resident.
Status and Conservation. Not globally threatened. Locally common in Venezuela, e.g. 6 heard calling simultaneously. Uncommon in Colombia and Ecuador. Uncommon generally in Peru; density of 1 pair/km² in floodplain-forest at Cocha Cashu, increasing to 19 pairs/km² in earliest successional stages; observed in Peru along Cuzco-Manu Road and at Amazonia Lodge. In Brazil, uncommon in Amazonas, at Manaus and in Rondônia.
Bibliography. Allen (1995), Angehr & Aucca (1997), Bond (1954), Bond & Meyer de Schauensee (1943), Chapman (1917, 1926), Clements & Shany (2001), Cory (1919), Donahue (1994), Goodfellow (1902), Gyldenstolpe (1945a, 1951), Hilty & Brown (1986), Meyer de Schauensee & Phelps (1978), Newman (1993), O'Neill & Pearson (1974), Parker *et al.* (1982), Peres & Whittaker (1991), Ridgely & Greenfield (2001), Ridgely *et al.* (1998), Robinson & Terborgh (1997), Rodner *et al.* (2000), Sick (1993), Stotz *et al.* (1996), Terborgh *et al.* (1990), Traylor (1958), Willard *et al.* (1991).

Genus *NYSTACTES*   Gloger, 1827

7. Spotted Puffbird
Nystactes tamatia

French: Tamatia tacheté   **German**: Fleckenfaulvogel   **Spanish**: Buco Moteado

Taxonomy. *Bucco Tamatia* J. F. Gmelin, 1788, Cayenne and Brazil.
Genus usually merged into *Bucco*. Forms a superspecies with *N. noanamae*. Several other races proposed, including *inexpectatus* (NC Brazil), *punctuliger* (C Brazil) and *interior* (SW Brazil), but these apparently represent inconstant, intergrading populations. Three subspecies currently recognized.

Subspecies and Distribution.

N. t. tamatia (J. F. Gmelin, 1788) - E Colombia (S to Vaupés) E to Venezuela, the Guianas, and S to N bank of Amazon.

N. t. pulmentum (P. L. Sclater, 1856) - SE Colombia S to E Ecuador, NE Peru, W Brazil and NE Bolivia.

N. t. hypneleus (Cabanis & Heine, 1863) - Amazonian Brazil E of R Tapajós.

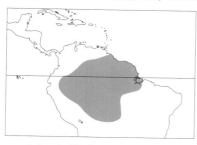

Descriptive notes. 18 cm; 33-42 g. Diffuse rufous band at base of bill to above and behind eye, changing to indistinct rufous spots on dark brown crown; poorly marked blackish line from base of bill through and below eye to upper ear-coverts, bordered below by white stripe connecting to narrow white nuchal band; triangular black patch below white cheekstripe, whitish chin with long, stiff, recurved white bristles; rufous throat to upper breast and sides of neck; upperparts dark brown as crown, with buffy scalloping on lower mantle, back and especially rump and uppertail-coverts; flight-feathers dark brown, secondaries edged buffy; tail graduated for quarter of length, dark brown with buffy edges; whitish breast to lower flanks spotted and scaled black, markings diminishing in size and number on flanks; centre of belly and undertail-coverts white with small black spots; buffy underwing-coverts and bases of undersides of flight-feathers; bill all black; iris bright red, bare eyering dark grey; feet dark grey or greenish. Immature may have barred paler throat, more chevron-like spots below, buffier lower underparts, indistinct face pattern, heavily buff-barred upperparts, buffy collar. Race *pulmentum* has very pale throat, brighter forehead, and heavier spotting; *hypneleus* larger but smaller-billed than nominate, heavier spotting below, notably across breast. VOICE. Song a series of 10-20 whistled "chyoi" notes (c. 2 per second), then a few at lower pitch and slower, ending with c. 4 inflected "pchooii, pchooii, pchooii, peejowee" whistles; faint wheezy whistles in disputes.

Habitat. Mainly found in *várzea* and *igapó* forest, humid forest borders, mature second growth, impoverished sandy savanna woodland, sand-ridge forest, gallery forest, palm groves, and marshy edges, shrubbery and bushes, often near water; rarely in deep forest. Occurs from lowlands up to 1400 m.

Food and Feeding. Caterpillars, scorpions (Scorpiones), flies (Brachycera), beetles (Carabidae, Curculionidae), Isoptera, bees; also berries of mistletoe (Loranthaceae). One bird seen catching large hawkmoths (Sphingidae) attracted to flowering shrubs at dusk. Still-hunts from low exposed perch. Sometimes follows army ants.

Breeding. Apr in Venezuela; courtship feeding in Jun in French Guiana; laying in Sept in Bolivia. Clutch 2 eggs. Other details not documented.

Movements. Presumably resident.

Status and Conservation. Not globally threatened. Uncommon in most of range, including the Guianas, Peru and most of Brazil. In Amazonas, Brazil, evidently common in one area along R Purus and on R Urucu. Occurs in Amacayacu National Park, Colombia.

Bibliography. Bates *et al.* (1992), Bierregaard (1988), Chapman (1926), Cherrie & Reichenberger (1921), Cohn-Haft *et al.* (1997), Cory (1919), Dubs (1992), Friedmann (1948), Griscom & Greenway (1941), Gyldenstolpe (1951), Haffer (1975), Haverschmidt (1977), Haverschmidt & Mees (1994), Henriques & Oren (1997), Hilty & Brown (1986), Meyer de Schauensee & Phelps (1978), Newman (1993), Parker *et al.* (1982), Peres & Whittaker (1991), Phelps & Phelps (1949), Pinto (1966), Remsen & Parker (1983), Ridgely & Greenfield (2001), Sargeant (1994), Schubart *et al.* (1965), Sick (1993), Snethlage (1914), Snyder (1966), Stotz *et al.* (1996), Todd (1943a), Tostain *et al.* (1992), Willis (1982b), Zimmer & Hilty (1997).

8. Sooty-capped Puffbird

Nystactes noanamae

French: Tamatia de Colombie **German**: Rußkappen-Faulvogel **Spanish**: Buco de Noanamá

Taxonomy. *Bucco noanamæ* Hellmayr, 1909, Noanamá, Río San Juan, Chocó, Colombia.
Genus usually merged into *Bucco*. Forms a superspecies with *N. tamatia*. Monotypic.
Distribution. Coastal W Colombia from Gulf of Urabá S to R San Juan.

Descriptive notes. 18 cm. Crown and nape blackish to greyish-black; long, prominent white supercilium becoming grey towrds rear, broad black line through and below eye and including ear-coverts; dark brown mantle; tail rather short, strongly graduated, dusky, narrowly fringed buff; white chin, lower face and throat; very broad black pectoral band; lower underparts buffy-white with black scalloping; bill all black; iris red, bare eyering dark grey; feet pale grey. Immature not described. VOICE. No information available.

Habitat. Inhabits humid and wet forest, second-growth woodland and adjacent non-forest areas (once an abandoned cocoa plantation), also scrub; keeps to lower parts of vegetation. Occurs in lowlands, up to 100 m.

Food and Feeding. Limited information available. Known to take insects. Perches for long periods on open branches, motionless and inconspicuous, before stooping on large insects in foliage of understorey.

Breeding. Pair delivering food to nest in arboreal termitarium, late Aug. No further information.

Movements. Presumably resident.

Status and Conservation. Not globally threatened. Currently considered Near-threatened. Restricted-range species: present in Chocó EBA. Generally uncommon. Common in Los Katíos National Park, in Chocó. Although recent confirmed records from just 2 sites, only few of the c. 10 localities from where this species is known (specimens collected) have been investigated since 1966. Considerable deforestation caused by logging and by conversion of forest to banana and oil palm (*Elaeis guineensis*) plantations, along with human settlement, development, cattle ranching and other land-use changes, are all regarded as significant threats.

Bibliography. Chapman (1917), Collar *et al.* (1994), Cory (1919), Haffer (1959, 1975), Hellmayr (1911), Hilty & Brown (1986), Meyer de Schauensee (1982), Nicéforo & Olivares (1967), Olrog (1968), Pearman (1993a), Rodner *et al.* (2000), Rodríguez (1982), Stattersfield & Capper (2000), Stotz *et al.* (1996).

Genus *BUCCO* Brisson, 1760

9. Collared Puffbird

Bucco capensis

French: Tamatia à collier **German**: Halsband-Faulvogel **Spanish**: Buco Musiú

Taxonomy. *Bucco capensis* Linnaeus, 1766, Cape of Good Hope; error = the Guianas.
Birds from SE Colombia to Ecuador and E Peru sometimes treated as race *dugandi*, but this form is doubtfully distinct. Monotypic.
Distribution. Amazon Basin from E Ecuador and SE Colombia E to S Venezuela, the Guianas and N Brazil (E to Belém), and S to NE Peru and N Mato Grosso.

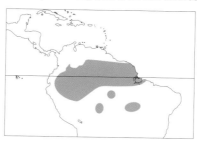

Descriptive notes. 19 cm; 46-62 g. Dark rufous above, crown to mantle, wing-coverts and tertials finely barred, rump paler rufous with fewer black bars; complete black collar around upper mantle and breast, bordered on nape and sides of neck by narrow buffy collar; primaries, primary coverts and secondaries dark brown, secondaries edged rusty; tail rather short, square-tipped, graduated for about a quarter of length, orange-chestnut narrowly banded black; chin and throat white to buffy-white; lower breast to centre of belly and undertail-coverts buffier, grading to bright orange-fulvous on lower flanks; bill variably orange to dusky upper mandible, orange lower; iris whitish, orange or vermilion, bare skin around eye orange-yellow; feet light green, orange or brown; claws entirely pale. Immature very like adult, but bill and head paler. VOICE. Song a repeated "cua-will, cua-will…"; "qu'a'a'a'al' cua-will" in response to playback of song.

Habitat. Understorey and sometimes middle storey to subcanopy of primary humid *terra firme* forest, dry hilly country, bamboo bordering rivers; also *várzea* in lower Amazon, and possibly restricted to denser patches. Lowlands to 1700 m.

Food and Feeding. Lizards, snakes and frogs, taken from the forest floor or from foliage; also beetles, orthopterans, cicadas (Cicadidae) and other large insects. Still-hunts from shaded perch. Sometimes joins mixed-species flocks; more rarely follows army ants.

Breeding. May in Venezuela; laying female in Sept in Guyana. Excavates a hole in arboreal termitarium. No information on clutch size, nor on incubation and fledging periods.

Movements. Presumably resident.

Status and Conservation. Not globally threatened. Uncommon to common in most of range. Rare to locally uncommon in Ecuador. Generally rare in Peru, though locally not uncommon, e.g. near Iquitos. In Brazil, common along R Urucu, in Amazonas, but less frequent in N Mato Grosso. Reported rarity may perhaps be simply a result of its extreme unobtrusiveness, but this species appears to be highly sensitive to habitat disturbance. Present in several protected areas, e.g. Amacayacu National Park (Colombia), Manu National Park (Peru) and Cristalino River Private Reserve (Brazil).

Bibliography. Bierregaard (1988), Chapman (1917, 1926), Cohn-Haft *et al.* (1997), Cory (1919), Dugand & Borrero (1946), Friedmann (1948), Gilliard (1949a), Griscom & Greenway (1941), Gyldenstolpe (1945a, 1951), Haverschmidt & Mees (1994), Hellmayr (1910), Henriques & Oren (1997), Hilty & Brown (1986), Maxwell (1937), Meyer de Schauensee (1951), Meyer de Schauensee & Phelps (1978), O'Neill (1969), O'Neill & Pearson (1974), Olivares (1962, 1964b), Pearson *et al.* (1977), Peres & Whittaker (1991), Phelps & Phelps (1958), Pinto (1938b, 1953), Ridgely & Greenfield (2001), Robbins *et al.* (1987), Sclater & Salvin (1873), Sick (1993), Snethlage (1914), Snyder (1966), Stotz, Fitzpatrick *et al.* (1996), Stotz, Lanyon *et al.* (1997), Thiollay (1992), Thiollay & Jullien (1998), Tostain *et al.* (1992), Traylor (1958), Willard *et al.* (1991), Willis (1982b), Zimmer *et al.* (1997).

Genus *NYSTALUS* Cabanis & Heine, 1863

10. Barred Puffbird

Nystalus radiatus

French: Tamatia barré **German**: Grünschnabel-Faulvogel **Spanish**: Buco Barrado

Taxonomy. *Bucco radiatus* P. L. Sclater, 1854, Nova Grenada = Magdalena Valley, Colombia.
May form a superspecies with *N. striolatus*. Form described as race *fulvidus* is probably only a colour morph. Monotypic.
Distribution. C Panama E to W Colombia and S to W Ecuador.

Descriptive notes. 22 cm; 63 g. Rufescent overall, with black barring; large whitish loral spot grading to pale rufous-white stripe over eye; blackish crown with dark rufous bars widest on forehead, grading to narrow, more spot-like bars near nape; upper napeband solid black, lower pale yellowish-rufous; black upper mantle broken by rufous spotting, grading to dark chestnut rear upperparts and wings with narrow black bands; primaries less regularly barred, blotchier on outer feathers; tail long, narrow, slightly graduated, chestnut with narrow black bands; chin whitish, grading to pale rufous underparts with fine blackish barring except on central abdomen; undertail-coverts brighter rufous; bill greyish-yellow to blackish; iris creamy-yellow; feet greenish-grey. Probable dark rufous morph ("*fulvidus*") deeper rufous all over, rufous line above eye indistinct. Immature has shorter bill, paler hindcollar, paler with chevron-like marks below. VOICE. Call a long, slow, ventriloquial and very human-like wolf-whistle, "phweeeeeet-weeeeeeuuuu", c. 4-5 seconds long, repeated about twice per minute.

Habitat. Lower storeys of lowland humid and wet forest borders, second-growth woodland, edges of forest trails, relatively open streamside vegetation, overgrown clearings with scattered trees, and thickets in open plains; locally in Ecuador, can regularly be seen perching on wires over agricultural land. Occurs up to 900 m, and locally up to 1500 m above Mindo (Ecuador).

Food and Feeding. Beetles, Orthoptera, large caterpillars, and small lizards. Foraging behaviour apparently not reported.

Breeding. Apparently breeds about Mar in Ecuador. No other information on breeding or reproductive biology.

Movements. Presumably resident.

Status and Conservation. Not globally threatened. Locally common in Colombia, but rarely seen. Uncommon to fairly common in Ecuador; present in Río Palenque Science Centre, and occurs along Chiriboga (Old Santo Domingo) Road.

Bibliography. Allen (1998), Angehr (2001), Best *et al.* (1997), Brosset (1964), Burton (1973), Chapman (1917, 1926), Cory (1919), Engleman (1997), Goodfellow (1902), Haffer (1967b, 1975), Hilty & Brown (1986), Kirwan & Marlow (1996), Olivares & Romero (1973), Ridgely & Greenfield (2001), Ridgely & Gwynne (1989), Ridgely *et al.* (1998), Ridgway (1914), Robbins & Ridgely (1990), Robbins *et al.* (1985), Rodner *et al.* (2000), Rodríguez (1982), Salvin & Godman (1888-1904), Stotz *et al.* (1996), Taylor (1995), Wetmore (1968a).

11. White-eared Puffbird

Nystalus chacuru

French: Tamatia chacuru **German**: Weißohr-Faulvogel **Spanish**: Buco Chacurú

Taxonomy. *Bucco chacuru* Vieillot, 1816, Paraguay.
Two subspecies recognized.

Subspecies and Distribution.
N. c. uncirostris (Stolzmann, 1926) - E Peru, NE Bolivia and adjacent Brazil.
N. c. chacuru (Vieillot, 1816) - NE, E & S Brazil, E Paraguay and NE Argentina.

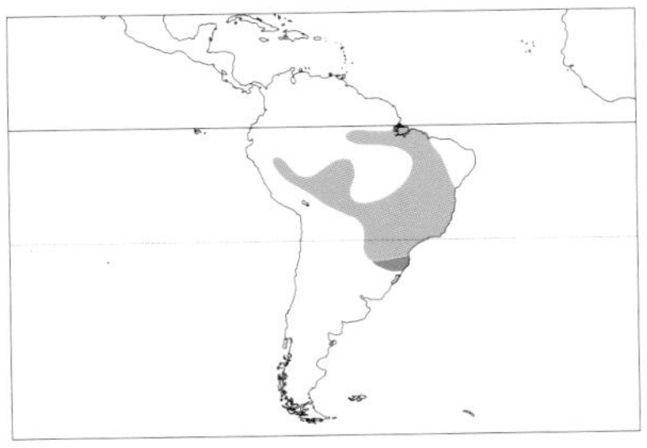

Descriptive notes. 21-22 cm; 48-64 g. White above bill, becoming narrow white crown-stripe; short pale supercilium; white upper ear-coverts, malar region and throat; large black patch mainly on lower ear-coverts connecting to black postocular line; dark brown crown variably spotted and barred dull rufous, broad white nuchal collar; mantle, dark brown rump and wings heavily dappled dark rufous, barred effect on tertials; tail medium length, slightly graduated, dark brown with narrow, widely spaced buffy bars, pale tip; whitish below, variably washed ochraceous, some narrow dark scalloping on breast, heavier on flanks; bill reddish; iris brown or greyish-green; legs and feet dusky flesh-coloured or light olive-green. Immature has duskier bill, dark barring on nuchal collar, and blackish striations on underparts. Race *uncirostris* has larger bill, whiter underparts, slightly longer wing. VOICE. Loud, whistled whinnying song of c. 8 double low/high whistles, tremulous and descending, "fufu-fofo-fufu-fofo-fufufuu…", often by pair in duet.

Habitat. Mid-stratum and edge of tropical dry forest, second growth, gallery forest, open woodland, wooded grassland, *campos*, *cerrado*, tropical savanna, scrub, clearings, pastures, open country with scattered vegetation; also cultivated fields (e.g. coffee groves) bordering railroads, tree-lined streets in rural suburbs. Perches on telephone and fence wires and posts. Sometimes hunts along well-vegetated streams, and ranges from ground level to canopy. Recorded up to 2500 m in Peru.

Food and Feeding. Arthropods, and small vertebrates such as lizards, commonly taken from the ground. Invertebrate prey includes insects caught in mid-air, often along streams, but also non-flying animals such as millipedes (Diplopoda), centipedes (Chilopoda), scorpions (Scorpiones), and even velvet worms (*Peripatus*) and crabs. Vegetable matter also reported. Still-hunts from mid-levels.

Breeding. Sept-Dec in SE Brazil; at start of rains in C Brazil. Nest-hole dug in ground or bank, occasionally in road cutting or railroad embankment. Clutch 2-4 eggs. No information on incubation and fledging periods.

Movements. Mainly resident; apparently migratory in extreme S.

Status and Conservation. Not globally threatened. Uncommon and local in Peru; uncommon in Argentina; fairly common in Bolivia. Common in parts of SE & C Brazil (e.g. Bahia, Distrito Federal), moderately so in Rio Grande do Sul, fairly common in Mato Grosso; present in several protected areas in Brazil, including Itatiaia National Park, Serra da Canastra National Park, Brasília National Park, Emas National Park and Chapada dos Guimarães National Park.

Bibliography. dos Anjos & Schuchmann (1997), Antas & Cavalcanti (1988), Azara (1802-1805), Barnes *et al.* (1993), Belton (1984), Canevari *et al.* (1991), Capper *et al.* (2000), Carriker (1935), Chubb (1910), Cory (1919), Dubs (1992), Eckelberry (1962), da Fonseca (1922), Gyldenstolpe (1945b), Hayes (1995), Hellmayr (1929), Laubmann (1930, 1939), Lourenco & Dekeyser (1976), Mitchell (1957), Oniki & Willis (1999), Parker & Bailey (1991), Parker *et al.* (1982), Pearman (1993b), de la Peña (1994), Pinto (1936, 1940, 1943, 1944a, 1944b, 1948, 1952), Pinto & Camargo (1948), Raw (1997), Remsen (1986), do Rosário (1996), Saibene *et al.* (1996), Schmitt *et al.* (1997), Schubart *et al.* (1965), Sclater & Salvin (1879), Scott & Brooke (1985), Sick (1958b, 1993), Snethlage (1927-1928), Stotz *et al.* (1996), Willis (1992), Willis & Oniki (1990, 1991).

12. Striolated Puffbird

Nystalus striolatus

French: Tamatia striolé **German**: Strichelfaulvogel **Spanish**: Buco Estriado

Taxonomy. *Bucco striolatus* Pelzeln, 1856, Dourado and Engenho do Capitão Gama, Rio Guapore, Mato Grosso, Brazil.
May form a superspecies with *N. radiatus*. Two subspecies recognized.

Subspecies and Distribution.
N. s. striolatus (Pelzeln, 1856) - upper Amazon in E Ecuador, E Peru, W & C Brazil, and N Bolivia.
N. s. torridus Bond & Meyer de Schauensee, 1940 - NC Brazil (E Pará S of Amazon).

Descriptive notes. 20 cm; 47 g. White loral spot, chin and upper throat, buffy sides of head and supercilium finely streaked dusky; dark brown crown broadly barred rufous, becoming mostly blackish at nape; broad buffy hindcollar; upper mantle blackish, dark brown rest of upperparts with buffy-

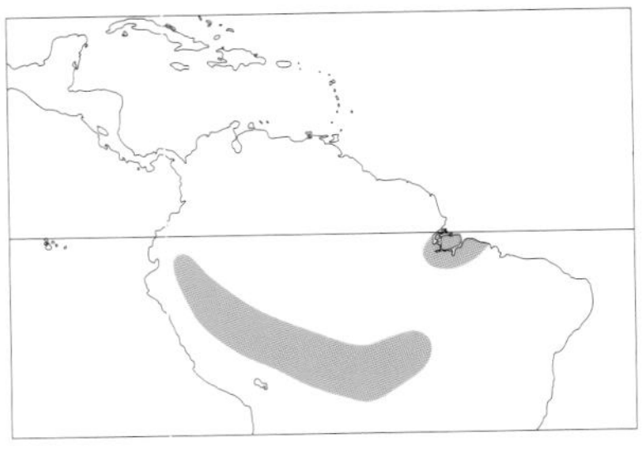

rufous spots, becoming bars towards rear; tail medium length, narrow, slightly graduated, blackish-brown with fine rufous bars; lower throat ochraceous with fine blackish streaks, grading to paler but more heavily striped breast and flanks, whiter and nearly unstreaked on central lower underparts; undertail-coverts buffier; bill olive-green, with very variable blackish-brown tip and base of lower mandible; iris pale ochre; legs brown, feet dirty green. Immature undescribed. Race *torridus* larger, duller, with broader streaking below, and larger bill. VOICE. Call a soft, sad whistle, "whip, whi-wheeu, wheeeeeuu", with distinctive cadence.

Habitat. Canopy, subcanopy and edges of humid lowland tropical forest, *terra firme* and low-lying swamp-forest, also transitional forest, forest openings, second growth, usually near water and/or clearings; also foothill forest to 1700 m in Ecuador (Cordillera de Cutucú).

Food and Feeding. No information on diet. Still-hunts from canopy, or sometimes in middle storey.

Breeding. Sept in Peru. Nest in underground cavity; 4 eggs. No other information available.

Movements. Presumably resident.

Status and Conservation. Not globally threatened. Rare to locally uncommon in Ecuador, though may be overlooked. Fairly common in Peru, where holds mean territory size of 9 ha at Cocha Cashu. Locally quite common in Brazil; frequently recorded in Cristalino River Private Reserve. Rarely recorded in Bolivia. Densities may reflect habitat preference: 5·0 territories/km² in middle successional-stage woodland (*Ficus*/*Cedrela*), 13·0 in later *Ficus*/*Cedrela* transitional forest, 7·0 in mature floodplain forest.

Bibliography. Best *et al.* (1997), Bond & Meyer de Schauensee (1940), Brace & Hornbuckle (1998), Brace *et al.* (1997), Chapman (1921b, 1926), Clements & Shany (2001), Cory (1919), Donahue (1994), Dubs (1992), Parker *et al.* (1982), Pelzeln (1867-1871), Pinto (1947), Remsen *et al.* (1986), Ridgely & Greenfield (2001), Ridgely *et al.* (1998), Robbins *et al.* (1987), Robinson & Terborgh (1997), Rodner *et al.* (2000), Sick (1993), Snethlage (1927-1928), Stotz *et al.* (1996), Taylor (1995), Terborgh *et al.* (1990), Zimmer, J.T. (1930), Zimmer, K.J. *et al.* (1997).

13. Spot-bellied Puffbird

Nystalus maculatus

French: Tamatia tamajac **German**: Fleckmantel-Faulvogel **Spanish**: Buco Durmilí
Other common names: Spot-backed Puffbird; Streak-bellied Puffbird (*striatipectus*)

Taxonomy. *Alcedo maculata* J. F. Gmelin, 1788, Brazil = Ceará.
Race *striatipectus* may be a separate species, on basis of morphology, but vocalizations apparently similar; further study required in zone of probable contact, in Pantanal. Proposed race *parvirostris* (C Brazil) not reliably separable from nominate; *pallidigula* (SW Brazil) synonymous with *striatipectus*, showing only minor, apparently clinal, differences. Two subspecies currently recognized.

Subspecies and Distribution.
N. m. maculatus (J. F. Gmelin, 1788) - NE & C Brazil (to SW Mato Grosso).
N. m. striatipectus (P. L. Sclater, 1854) - SC & SE Bolivia (Cochabamba, Chuquisaca, Santa Cruz) and SC Brazil (W Mato Grosso do Sul) S to W & C Paraguay and NW Argentina (S to Córdoba).

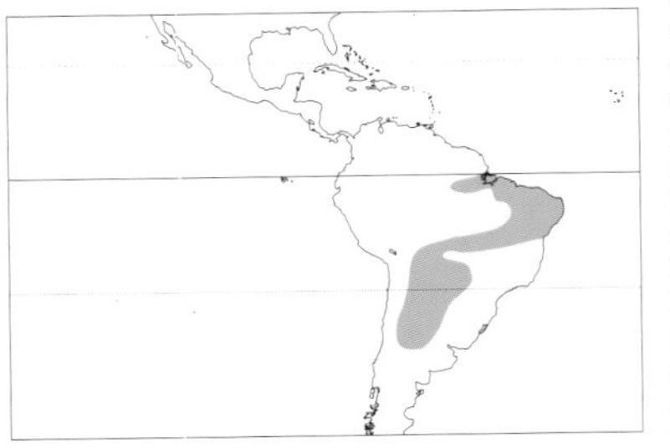

Descriptive notes. 18-19 cm; 32-38 g (nominate), 33-42 g (*striatipectus*). Off-white feathers around base of bill and face lightly marked dusky, ear-coverts more heavily streaked, postocular streak and malar even more so; buffy supercilium; dark brown crown boldly spangled buffy; pale rufous hindcollar; mantle and wing-coverts to uppertail-coverts barred and spangled buffy; tail long, narrow, slightly graduated, broadly banded black with narrow buffy bars and tip; underparts mainly white, bright orange-rufous lower throat, upper breast and sides of neck; lower breast and sides boldly spotted black, flanks streaked black; lower central underparts white, flanks and undertail-coverts buffier; bill mainly red with dusky base, culmen and tip; iris pale yellow; legs rather long, feet brownish-olive. Immature has short duskier bill, paler hindcollar and breast, underpart spotting shaped as diamonds or streaks. Race *striatipectus* has face more heavily streaked, hindcollar paler, crown spotting whiter, upperparts less spangled, tail more narrowly banded, breast more extensively but paler rufous, lower breast and upper flanks streaked rather than spotted, bill thinner, more arched, duller. VOICE. Undulating "tewre-tewtewretewtewre"; *striatipectus* also has disyllabic 3-note whistle, "tuhú tuhú tuhú", repeated at intervals; sings in duos or trios.

Habitat. Low and medium levels in the *cerrado*, *caatinga* and *campo* regions, occupying lowland and foothill semi-deciduous woodland and woodland edge, savanna and palm groves, arboreal-arbustive *caatinga*, shrubs, scrub, pastures and cultivation. In S of range (*striatipectus*), in chaco, dry subtropical forest, transitional forest, isolated woodland patches; in arid montane vegetation in Bolivia, extending above 2000 m. Perches on wires by railroads.

Food and Feeding. Chiefly insects, including caterpillars; recorded taking colubrid snake *Chironius flavolineatus* in Brazil. Still-hunts from low perches, capturing prey on ground or foliage.

Breeding. Apparently unrecorded for nominate race. Race *striatipectus* breeds in Oct in Paraguay, in Jan-Feb in Bolivia. Nest in underground cavity, lined with leaves, in earth bank or level soil. Clutch 2-3 eggs. Incubation and fledging periods not documented.

Movements. Presumably resident; possibly some seasonal wandering by nominate race in parts of EC Brazil.

Status and Conservation. Not globally threatened. Common in NE Brazil, including inside Serra da Capivara National Park, in Piauí; in 1947, described as one of the commonest birds in Pernambuco. Race *striatipectus* supposedly rare in Paraguay, but probably under-recorded; common in S Brazil; in Argentina, common in Jujuy and Salta, uncommon in Córdoba.

Bibliography. Canevari *et al.* (1991), Contino (1980), Contreras *et al.* (1990), Cory (1919), Dubs (1992), Fjeldså & Mayer (1996), Friedmann (1927), Hartert & Venturi (1909), Hayes (1995), Henriques & Oren (1997), Krabbe *et al.* (1996), López de Casenave *et al.* (1998), Medeiros-Neto *et al.* (1997), Ménégaux (1925), do Nascimento (2000), Nores *et al.* (1983), Novaes (1992), Olmos (1993), de la Peña (1994, 1997), Pereyra (1950), Pinto (1935, 1947), Pinto & Camargo (1961), Piratelli, Pereira & Siqueira (1996), Piratelli, Siqueira & Marcondes-Machado (2000), Remsen *et al.* (1986), Salvadori (1895), Sargeant & Wall (1996), Schmitt *et al.* (1997), Schubart *et al.* (1965), Short (1975, 1976), Sick (1993), da Silva (1991), Steinbacher (1962), Stotz *et al.* (1996), Todd (1943a), Tubelis & Tomás (1999), Wetmore (1926), Willis (1992), Willis & Oniki (1993).

PLATE 4 ➤

14

ssp *ruficollis*

ssp *coloratus*

ssp *decolor*

15

16

ssp *striata*

ssp *minor*

17

18

19

20

ssp *rufa*

ssp *brunnescens*

♀ ♂

ssp *panamensis*

21

22

♀

♂

ssp *magdalenae*

♀ ♂

ssp *inornata*

♂ ♀

ssp *poliopis*

23

PLATE 4

inches   4

cm   10

Genus *HYPNELUS* Cabanis & Heine, 1863

14. **Russet-throated Puffbird**
Hypnelus ruficollis

French: Tamatia à gorge rousse   **German**: Rostkehl-Faulvogel   **Spanish**: Buco Bobito

Taxonomy. *Capito ruficollis* Wagler, 1829, Mexico; error = Santa Marta, Colombia.
Forms a superspecies with *H. bicinctus*, and often considered conspecific owing to hybridization in Maracaibo region of Venezuela and in Catatumbo lowlands of Colombia; however, hybridization apparently rather limited, with most individuals belonging clearly to one or the other of these well-distinguished forms, and treatment as separate species seems the most realistic approach, pending in-depth studies. Proposed race *striaticollis* (NW Venezuela) may form part of a cline and herein included in *decolor*, but further study required. Three subspecies currently recognized.
Subspecies and Distribution.
H. r. decolor Todd & Carriker, 1922 - extreme NE Colombia (Guajira Peninsula) and NW Venezuela (Falcón).
H. r. ruficollis (Wagler, 1829) - N Colombia, and NW Venezuela W of L Maracaibo.
H. r. coloratus Ridgway, 1914 - W Venezuela (S of L Maracaibo).

Descriptive notes. 20-22 cm; 41-57 g. Head dark brown, rufescent spot over nares, rufous and white spot in front of eye, whitish cheek patch, crown spotted pale brown; partial buffy or white hindcollar; dull brown upperparts mottled greyish, notably on scapulars and tertials; wing-coverts buff-edged, rump and uppertail-coverts buffy-scaled; tail long, square-tipped, slightly graduated, dark brown with narrow pale edgings; chin white, rich rufous lower throat and upper breast, whitish breastband, broad blackish lower breastband, rest of underparts buffy-rufous with some black spots or bars on sides; bill all black; iris yellow to white; feet black or dull green. Immature has buffy scaling above and on breastband and ear-coverts, paler throat, shorter pale-tipped bill, spottier flanks, finely dark-marked sides of neck. Race *decolor* paler above, especially on cheeks, whiter lower breast and belly with less black barring on flanks; *coloratus* as nominate, but has blacker cheeks, deeper orange throat patch, and richer orange-buff underparts. VOICE. Noisy, duets with repeated rhythmic "woduk" notes in crescendo for up to 20 seconds, then diminishing, ending with only 1 bird calling; high insect-like "seeeeep" call.
Habitat. Low-lying areas in open deciduous forest and edge, tree savanna, along waterbodies, dense second growth, woodland, arid scrub with scattered trees, dry thickets.
Food and Feeding. Many beetles found in one stomach, seeds in another; diet presumably much as for other Bucconidae, but in one emetic sample invertebrates (9 species) composed 87% and fleshy fruit (1 species) 13%.
Breeding. May in Colombia. Nest in arboreal termitarium; sometimes takes over the oven-shaped nest of Pale-legged Hornero (*Furnarius leucopus*). Clutch 3 eggs. No details of incubation and fledging periods.
Movements. Presumably resident.
Status and Conservation. Not globally threatened. Common to abundant along the dry littoral open woods of Colombia; less common in heavier forest. Occurs in Salamanca National Park (Colombia) and Morrocoy National Park (Venezuela).
Bibliography. Barnes & Phelps (1940), Cory (1919), Dugand (1947), Haffer (1959, 1961, 1975), Haffer & Borrero (1965), Hilty & Brown (1986), Meyer de Schauensee & Phelps (1978), Olivares & Romero (1973), Phelps (1944), Phelps & Phelps (1958), Poulin *et al.* (1994), Ridgway (1914), Rodner *et al.* (2000), Salvin & Godman (1888-1904), Stotz *et al.* (1996), Todd & Carriker (1922), Verea & Solórzano (1998), Verea *et al.* (2000).

15. **Two-banded Puffbird**
Hypnelus bicinctus

French: Tamatia bifascié   **German**: Doppelband-Faulvogel   **Spanish**: Buco Bicinto
Other common names: Double-banded Puffbird

Taxonomy. *Tamatia bicincta* Gould, 1837, Cayenne; error = Venezuela.
Forms a superspecies with *H. ruficollis*, and commonly treated as conspecific owing to hybridization in Maracaibo region of Venezuela and in Catatumbo lowlands of Colombia; however, hybridization apparently rather limited, with most individuals belonging clearly to one or the other of these well-distinguished forms, and treatment as separate species seems the most realistic approach, pending in-depth studies. Two subspecies recognized.
Subspecies and Distribution.
H. b. bicinctus (Gould, 1837) - interior NE Colombia (in *llanos*), and N Venezuela (S to NE Bolívar and NW Amazonas).
H. b. stoicus Wetmore, 1939 - Margarita I, off N Venezuela.
Descriptive notes. 20-21 cm; 35-44 g. Head dark brown, buff from nares to eye, whitish cheek patch; partial whitish hindcollar; dull brown upperparts with whitish mottling, notably on scapulars and tertials, whitish edgings to wing-coverts; tail long, square-tipped, slightly graduated, dark brown with narrow pale edgings; chin whitish, grading to buffy-rufous underparts; two black breastbands, upper broader and joining with black patch on lower face, lower narrow and somewhat broken, thin partial black band across belly, black spots on flanks; bill all black; iris yellow, bare orbital ring blackish; feet dark grey. Differs from *H. ruficollis* in paler throat, double breastband, paler mottling above. Immature has black areas sullied with brown. Race *stoicus* slightly browner and paler above, larger bill, less marked face, upper breastband with buffy tips. VOICE. Song a rhythmic repeated "tak-ta-tóoo"; call a croaking note, surprisingly loud, sometimes given in flight.

Habitat. Occupies areas of thinly wooded tropical savanna (*llanos*), thickets, abandoned cultivation, streamside trees, and upper stages and edges of deciduous woodland, perching on thin open shaded branches under canopy. restricted to lowlands, below 500 m. Found in bushland and woods on plains and in foothills on Margarita I.
Food and Feeding. Small beetles, dragonflies and other insects found in gizzards and stomachs. Still-hunts from exposed high perch on thin branches, or shaded, mid-storey or subcanopy perch.
Breeding. May and Jun, and recent fledgling seen in Dec, in Venezuela. Excavates nest in arboreal termitarium. No information on clutch size, nor on incubation and fledging periods.
Movements. No seasonal movements recorded, although a species of seasonal habitat. Nevertheless, observed to be absent from an area for several years, then very common in that same area.
Status and Conservation. Not globally threatened. Generally common in Venezuela. Common throughout much of *llanos*, where vast areas of suitable habitat remain, and human land uses do not appear to pose any immediate threats. On Margarita I, extremely common at Ochenta in 1930's, but no recent details regarding current status.
Bibliography. Beebe (1909), Carriker (1955), Cherrie (1916), Cory (1919), Friedmann (1948), Friedmann & Smith (1950, 1955), Gines *et al.* (1953), Hilty & Brown (1986), Lowe (1907), Meyer de Schauensee (1982), Olrog (1968), Phelps & Phelps (1958), Robinson & Richmond (1895), Rodner *et al.* (2000), Schäfer & Phelps (1954), Verea *et al.* (1999), Wetmore (1939), Yepez *et al.* (1940).

Genus *MALACOPTILA* G. R. Gray, 1841

16. **Crescent-chested Puffbird**
Malacoptila striata

French: Tamatia rayé   **German**: Halbmond-Faulvogel   **Spanish**: Buco Rayado
Other common names: Striated Puffbird

Taxonomy. *Bucco striatus* Spix, 1824, Rio de Janeiro and Bahia, Brazil.
Two subspecies recognized.
Subspecies and Distribution.
M. s. minor Sassi, 1911 - NE Brazil (N Maranhão).
M. s. striata (Spix, 1824) - E & SE Brazil (S Bahia S to Santa Catarina).

Descriptive notes. 17·5-20 cm; 41-45 g. Rufescent around base of bill to above and in front of eye, moustache buffy or white; rest of head blackish, streaked buffy, continuing to blackish upperparts; dark brown uppertail-coverts tipped or scalloped rufous-brown; dark brown wings, small buffy arrow-shaped tips on coverts; tail longish, steeply graduated, dark brown; white crescent on upper breast, bordered below by broad black band; diffuse rufous area below band in centre of breast, grading to dull brown sides scalloped buffy; centre of belly whitish; bill all black; iris brown, bare orbital ring blackish; feet bluish or grey. Immature not described. Race *minor* smaller, breast brighter, lower underparts whiter. VOICE. High whistle of 10 or more notes, like a small tyrannid, "bieh, bieh, bieh…".
Habitat. Interior of humid lowland forest with abundance of fallen leaves; logged forest, second-growth forest, forest edges with grass. Usually stays low at edges of clearings, roads and other openings, more rarely moving into deeper forest. Ranges up to 2100 m.
Food and Feeding. Observed taking prey at an army-ant swarm along a dirt road. No other information.
Breeding. Apr and Oct in São Paulo state, in SE Brazil. Nest excavated in earth bank along road. Clutch size and incubation and fledging periods not documented.
Movements. Status unclear; a summer migrant, Sept-Mar, to Atlantic Forest in São Paulo state.
Status and Conservation. Not globally threatened. Little known, and no data on relative abundance. Occurs in Nova Lombardia (Augusto Ruschi) Biological Reserve and Sooretama Biological Reserve, both in Espírito Santo.
Bibliography. Aguirre & Aldrighi (1983), Aleixo & Galetti (1997), Cory (1919), Ferreira de Vasconcelos *et al.* (1999), Figueiredo & Lo (2000), Goerck (1999), Holt (1928), Machado (1996), Mallet-Rodrigues *et al.* (1997), Mitchell (1957), Oniki (1981), Oniki & Emerson (1981), Parker & Goerck (1997), Pinto (1952), do Rosário (1996), Sargeant & Wall (1996), Schubart *et al.* (1965), Scott & Brooke (1985), Sick (1993), Sick & Pabst (1968), Stotz *et al.* (1996), Venturini *et al.* (2001), Willis (1982c).

17. **White-chested Puffbird**
Malacoptila fusca

French: Tamatia brun   **German**: Weißbrust-Faulvogel   **Spanish**: Buco Pechiblanco

Taxonomy. *Bucco fuscus* J. F. Gmelin, 1788, Cayenne.
Forms a superspecies with *M. semicincta*. Birds from S Venezuela sometimes separated as race *venezuelae*, but appear indistinguishable from other populations. Monotypic.

On following pages: 18. Semicollared Puffbird (*Malacoptila semicincta*); 19. Black-streaked Puffbird (*Malacoptila fulvogularis*); 20. Rufous-necked Puffbird (*Malacoptila rufa*); 21. White-whiskered Puffbird (*Malacoptila panamensis*); 22. Moustached Puffbird (*Malacoptila mystacalis*); 23. Lanceolated Monklet (*Micromonacha lanceolata*).

Distribution. E Ecuador and SE Colombia E to S Venezuela and the Guianas and S to NE Peru and N Brazil (N of Amazon).

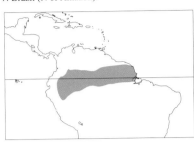

Descriptive notes. 18-19 cm; 39-45 g. Head and upperparts mostly dark brown with conspicuous buffy shaft streaks; background colour of crown blackish-brown; whitish lores, whiskers and chin; tail medium length, strongly graduated, warm brown; white patch on upper breast; streaks on lower breast grade into vaguely striped and mottled belly; flanks, centre of belly and undertail-coverts whiter; bill black on upper mandible except basal third, black on distal half of lower, rest yellow to pinkish; iris yellow or red; feet pale olive. Immature has dark brown eye, bill more yellow. VOICE. High thin "seeee", sometimes lasting 2 seconds and descending.

Habitat. From near the ground to middle storey in primary humid evergreen *terra firme* forest on well-drained soils, second-growth woodland, plantations, woodland borders, saplings along riversides, clearings with scattered trees. Generally occurs up to 750-900 m, but locally even up to 1200 m.

Food and Feeding. Large insects, notably Orthoptera (Acrididae), as well as caterpillars; also Arachnoidea (Araneida). Makes sharp sallies from perch to take prey from low branches or ground. Occasionally follows ant swarms and also mixed-species flocks. Usually solitary, but sometimes in pairs.

Breeding. No certain information. Observer close to hole in arboreal termitarium elicited alarm calls.

Movements. Presumably resident.

Status and Conservation. Not globally threatened. In Ecuador, generally uncommon but locally quite common. Uncommon in Peru and Amazon region. Apparently nowhere very common; often considered rare, but is also particularly unobtrusive, so may often be under-recorded. Occurs in Amacayacu National Park (Colombia) and in Cuyabeno Reserve (Ecuador).

Bibliography. Bierregaard (1988), Clements & Shany (2001), Cohn-Haft *et al.* (1997), Cory (1919), Dugand & Phelps (1948), Haverschmidt & Mees (1994), Hilty & Brown (1986), Meyer de Schauensee & Phelps (1978), Newman (1993), Parker *et al.* (1982), Penard & Penard (1908-1910), Phelps & Phelps (1947), Reynaud (1998), Ridgely & Greenfield (2001), Ridgely *et al.* (1998), Rodner *et al.* (2000), Sick (1993), Snyder (1966), Stotz & Bierregaard (1989), Stotz *et al.* (1996), Thiollay (1992), Thiollay & Jullien (1998), Tostain *et al.* (1992), Traylor (1951a), Willis (1982c), Zimmer (1930).

18. Semicollared Puffbird
Malacoptila semicincta

French: Tamatia à semi-collier   **German**: Halbring-Faulvogel   **Spanish**: Buco Mediocollar

Taxonomy. *Malacoptila semicincta* Todd, 1925, Hyutanahan, Rio Purús, Brazil.
Forms a superspecies with *M. fusca*. Monotypic.
Distribution. Extreme W Brazil, SE Peru and NW Bolivia.

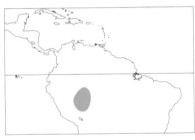

Descriptive notes. 18-19 cm; 44 g. Blackish-brown head and upperparts with conspicuous pale shaft streaks; rufous hindcollar; white lores, whiskers and chin; tail medium length, strongly graduated, brown; thin white patch on upper breast; blackish streaks on lower breast, paler and more diffuse on flanks, rest of underparts whitish; bill black on upper mandible except base, dark tip of lower, rest orange-yellow; iris dark red, white eye-ring; feet pale greenish-flesh. Differs from *M. fusca* in whiter crown streaks, rufous hindcollar, more orange bill, more extensive black on upper mandible but less on lower; darker eye, white eyering; paler feet. Immature slightly duller. VOICE. A series of thin, rather high-pitched, melancholy, descending "Fééeur" or "pseeu" whistles, each at first widely spaced, less than 1 second long, and starting on the same pitch; then dropping in pitch, "pseeu-uuu-uuu", several being given in rapid succession without pause on the same lower pitch. A second bird may simultaneously give a few higher, well-spaced whistles.

Habitat. Inhabits understorey, undergrowth and lower middle storey at edges of humid tropical lowland *terra firme* evergreen forest, and also transitional forest. Occurs form sea-level up to 1050 m.

Food and Feeding. No information available.

Breeding. No information.

Movements. Presumably resident.

Status and Conservation. Not globally threatened. Restricted-range species: present in Southeast Peruvian Lowlands EBA. Occurs in Tambopata Reserve, Peru. Has been judged to be rare, but 2-3 pairs/km² found in mature floodplain-forest at Cocha Cashu, in Peru. In Brazil, uncommon along R Urucu, in Amazonas.

Bibliography. Allen (1995), Angehr & Aucca (1997), Clements & Shany (2001), Donahue (1994), Gyldenstolpe (1945b, 1951), Meyer de Schauensee (1982), Morrone (2000), Novaes (1957), Olrog (1968), Parker *et al.* (1982), Peres & Whittaker (1991), Remsen & Traylor (1989), Robinson & Terborgh (1997), Seilern (1934), Sick (1993), Stotz *et al.* (1996), Terborgh *et al.* (1990), Todd (1925), Traylor (1951a).

19. Black-streaked Puffbird
Malacoptila fulvogularis

French: Tamatia à gorge fauve   **German**: Ockerkehl-Faulvogel   **Spanish**: Buco Listado

Taxonomy. *Malacoptila fulvogularis* P. L. Sclater, 1854, Bolivia.
May form a superspecies with *M. panamensis* and *M. mystacalis*. Previously recognized Colombian races *substriata* (Meta) and *huilae* (Huila) remain poorly known and are probably invalid. Monotypic.
Distribution. E slope of Andes from C Colombia to S Ecuador, Peru and NW Bolivia.

Descriptive notes. 19-22 cm; 65 g. Head blackish with white shaft streaks, white spot in front of eye and at base of forehead, whitish chin and whiskers; upperparts dark brown, narrow whitish shaft streaks on mantle changing to buffy triangular tips on back, and to scalloping on wing-coverts, tertial tips and rump; tail rather long, strongly graduated, square-tipped, solid brown; centre of throat to breast ochraceous, lower breast and upper belly to upper flanks strongly streaked black and white, grading to dark-mottled whitish lower belly and flanks; centre of belly and undertail-coverts dingy whitish; bill all black; iris carmine, narrow white eye-ring; feet dark. Immature not described. VOICE. Song is a very high-pitched ascending whistle, lasting under 4 seconds.

Habitat. Understorey of humid primary subtropical and montane forest and open woodland on E Andean foothill and lower slopes, at 500-2300 m; in Bolivia penetrates dry and semi-deciduous forest.

Food and Feeding. Large invertebrates recorded. Perches immobile for long periods in middle or lower storeys, periodically making sudden sallies forth to take prey from branches or leaves. Sometimes follows ant swarms and joins mixed-species feeding flocks.

Breeding. No information.

Movements. Presumably resident.

Status and Conservation. Not globally threatened. Few localities known in Colombia. Generally uncommon in Ecuador, but fairly common in R Bombuscaro area of Podocarpus National Park. Uncommon in Peru; occurs on Cuzco-Manu Road. Apparently rare in Bolivia, but occurs along La Paz-Coroico Road.

Bibliography. Best *et al.* (1997), Chapman (1926), Clements & Shany (2001), Cory (1919), Dunning (1993), Hilty & Brown (1986), Hornbuckle (1999), Meyer de Schauensee (1945, 1946a), Parker *et al.* (1982), Perry *et al.* (1997), Remsen & Traylor (1989), Ridgely & Greenfield (2001), Ridgely *et al.* (1998), Robbins *et al.* (1987), Rodner *et al.* (2000), Salaman *et al.* (1999), Stotz *et al.* (1996), Taylor (1995), Williams & Tobias (1994), Zimmer (1930).

20. Rufous-necked Puffbird
Malacoptila rufa

French: Tamatia à col roux   **German**: Goldstirn-Faulvogel   **Spanish**: Buco Cuellirrojo

Taxonomy. *Bucco rufus* Spix, 1824, "in sylvis fl. Amazonum" = São Paulo de Olivença, westernmost north Brazil.
Two subspecies recognized.
Subspecies and Distribution.
M. r. rufa (Spix, 1824) - S of Amazon from NE Peru to W Brazil (E to R Madeira) and S to E Bolivia and E Mato Grosso.
M. r. brunnescens J. T. Zimmer, 1931 - S Amazon Basin E of R Madeira (N Brazil).

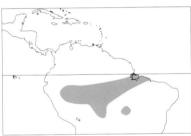

Descriptive notes. 18 cm; 36-44 g. Large rufous loral spot, dark grey crown and upper ear-coverts streaked pale; full dark rufous collar, at rear grading into rather dark brown mantle and rest of upperparts, warmer on uppertail-coverts and tail edgings; tail brown; white patch on upper breast with narrow black band below, patch of rufous-brown on lower breast grading to paler dull brown on lower underparts, whiter in centre of belly; bill dark blue-greyish on upper mandible, largely paler blue-grey on lower; iris dark brown or dark red, thin bluish orbital ring; feet olive-grey. Immature slightly paler and duller. Race *brunnescens* has stronger white streaks on darker grey crown, with paler rufous lores and forehead, and slightly less rufous upperparts. VOICE. Song a high, thin, descending, slightly modulated whistle lasting c. 1·5-3·0 seconds; call similarly high, thin, slightly descending plaintive "seeeee", c. 0·5 seconds.

Habitat. Understorey (1-10 m) of primary humid *terra firme* forest, edges, *várzea* undergrowth, *igapó*, low and vine-rich riverine forest, and *cerrado*.

Food and Feeding. No information on food, except that an individual at an ant swarm took tiny prey off a leaf. Still-hunts from low to mid-level perch, capturing prey in lower foliage. Sometimes joins mixed-species flocks, and follows army ants.

Breeding. Nest reported as tunnel 0·5 m long in ground. No other details reported.

Movements. Presumably resident.

Status and Conservation. Not globally threatened. In Brazil, common in part of Rondônia but uncommon on R Urucu, in Amazonas; rare in Mato Grosso, but frequently recorded near Alta Floresta. Rare in Peru, where has been recorded in Pacaya Samiria National Reserve. Occurs in Noel Kempff Mercado National Park, Bolivia.

Bibliography. Begazo & Valqui (1998), Clements & Shany (2001), Cory (1919), Gyldenstolpe (1951), Henriques & Oren (1997), Hilty & Brown (1986), Novaes (1970, 1976), Oren & Parker (1997), Parker *et al.* (1982), Peres & Whittaker (1991), Pinto (1947), Schönwetter (1967), Schubart *et al.* (1965), Sick (1993), da Silva (1995), da Silva *et al.* (1990), Snethlage (1914, 1935), Stotz, Fitzpatrick *et al.* (1996), Stotz, Lanyon *et al.* (1997), Willis (1982c), Zimmer, J.T. (1931), Zimmer, K.J. *et al.* (1997).

21. White-whiskered Puffbird
Malacoptila panamensis

French: Tamatia de Lafresnaye   **German**: Weißzügel-Faulvogel   **Spanish**: Buco Barbón
Other common names: Brown Puffbird

Taxonomy. *Malacoptila panamensis* Lafresnaye, 1847, Panama.
May form a superspecies with *M. fulvogularis* and *M. mystacalis*. Birds from SE Nicaragua to W Panama sometimes separated as race *fuliginosa*, but this name probably based on an aberrant bird and these populations are indistinguishable from *inornata*; birds from Pacific coast of Chocó, NW

Colombia, described as race *chocoana*, inseparable from *panamensis*. Four subspecies currently recognized.

Subspecies and Distribution.

M. p. inornata (Du Bus de Gisignies, 1847) - Caribbean slope from SE Mexico (N Chiapas, E Tabasco) to W Panama (including Bocas del Toro).

M. p. panamensis Lafresnaye, 1847 - Pacific slope from SW Costa Rica to NW Colombia.

M. p. magdalenae Todd, 1943 - Magdalena Valley (WC Colombia).

M. p. poliopis P. L. Sclater, 1862 - SW Colombia and W Ecuador.

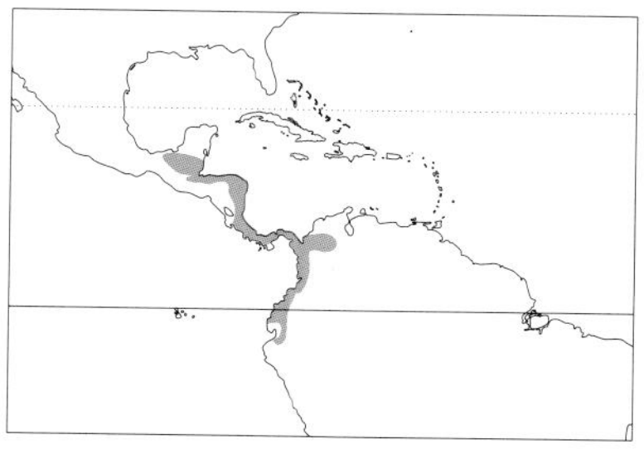

Descriptive notes. 18-21 cm; 33-46 g. Male mainly rufous, in particular on lores and on supercilium; ear-coverts long with pale rufescent shaft streaks; whitish central streak on forecrown; upperparts behind crown browner, speckled buffy; rump brighter rufous; wing dull brown with rufescent edgings; tail medium length, strongly graduated, bright rufous; elongate white malar feathers, rufescent throat and breast; lower breast to flanks streaked blackish, ground colour grading to whitish on sides and centre of belly; undertail-coverts dull buff; pale rufous inner webs of flight-feathers on underwing; bill black above, pale horn below; iris red; legs and feet bluish-grey to dull yellow-green. Female greyer overall, breast tinged ochraceous, rest of underparts more streaked. Juvenile like adult of respective sex, but shorter-billed, female breast duller. Race *inornata* male almost unstreaked and completely rufous-washed below, crown tinged grey, female less boldly marked below; *poliopis* male rather rufous overall, heavily streaked below, female darker grey above than nominate, rufous breast, more strongly streaked below; *magdalenae* somewhat less dimorphic than other races, both sexes more strongly streaked below than nominate, male darker above and on ear-coverts. Voice. Weak peep or high, thin whistles; high, faint "tsinnnn" in alarm; in territorial fights, various high-pitched squeaks and a rapidly repeated high "see-it-hee-hee" or similar phrase.

Habitat. Understorey (3-8 m) of primary humid and wet forest near treefalls, edge, older adjacent second growth, also younger forest, thicket-like tangled shaded second growth mixed with emergent trees, and wooded edges of openings with scattered trees generally; also shady pastures, cacao plantations, vine-tangled jungles, often along trails; in Honduras more a bird of interior forest. Lowlands to 900 m on Caribbean slope, to 1400 m on Pacific slope.

Food and Feeding. Large invertebrates, including scorpions (Scorpiones), spiders, roaches (Blattodea), crickets, mantids, stick-insects (Phasmida), beetles, neuropterans, caterpillars, termites, cicadas (Cicadidae), and especially large grasshoppers; also certain armour-plated terrestrial centipedes (Chilopoda) several inches long. The stomach of a gravid female was distended with insects, principally locusts. Vertebrate prey comprises small frogs, lizards and snakes, including poisonous coral snakes (Elapidae). Sallies from perch. Sometimes attends mixed flocks of small birds, or foraging swarms of army ants.

Breeding. Jul in Mexico; Apr-Jul in Nicaragua; Mar-Jul, main activity Apr-May, in Costa Rica; May-Aug in Panama, with digging noted Jan-Oct; Feb-Mar in Colombia. Nest in hole in level, slightly sloping or sometimes steeply sloping ground, usually in primary forest (once in tall secondary forest); occasionally hole in tree, bamboo stem or arboreal termitarium; sometimes same hole used in subsequent year. Clutch 2-3 eggs; incubation period unknown; nestling period 20 days.

Movements. Presumably resident.

Status and Conservation. Not globally threatened. Like many other species of tropical rainforest in Central America, it decreases rapidly from S to N, and is not really common anywhere N of Costa Rica. Very rare in Mexico; rare in Belize; rather rare in Nicaragua. Common in S Costa Rica, where the most frequently observed puffbird, most abundant in lowlands below 300 m; distinctly uncommon inside virgin forest, far more abundant in edge habitats; occurs in Caracara Biological Reserve and in Corcovado National Park, Costa Rica. Fairly common on Barro Colorado I, Panama; rare in Darién, E Panama, but common at low levels in adjacent NW Colombia. Common generally in NW Colombia, and abundant in coffee plantations. Fairly common locally in W Ecuador; present in Río Palenque Science Centre.

Bibliography. Álvarez del Toro (1980), Álvarez-López (1987), Anon. (1998b), Carriker (1910, 1955), Chapman (1917), Cory (1919), Dearborn (1907), Eisenmann (1957), González-García (1993), Haffer (1968, 1975), Hilty & Brown (1986), Howell, S.N.G. & Webb (1995), Howell, T.R. (1957), Land (1970), Meyer de Schauensee (1950), Monroe (1968), Olivares (1957), Richmond (1893), Ridgely & Greenfield (2001), Ridgely & Gwynne (1989), Ridgway (1914), Robbins *et al.* (1985), Rodríguez (1982), Russell (1964), Salaman (1994), Salvin & Godman (1888-1904), Skutch (1948c, 1958a), Slud (1960, 1964), Stiles (1985), Stiles & Skutch (1989), Stiles *et al.* (1999), Stotz *et al.* (1996), Tashian (1952), Taylor (1995), Wetmore (1968a), Willis (1980, 1982c), Willis & Eisenmann (1979).

22. **Moustached Puffbird**

Malacoptila mystacalis

French: Tamatia à moustaches **German**: Schnurrbart-Faulvogel **Spanish**: Buco Bigotudo

Taxonomy. *Monasa mystacalis* Lafresnaye, 1850, Valparaíso, Santa Marta, north Colombia. May form a superspecies with *M. fulvogularis* and *M. panamensis*. Population of SW Colombia possibly merits subspecific status, as race *pacifica*. Monotypic.

Distribution. Andes of Colombia and NW & N Venezuela.

Descriptive notes. 20-23 cm; 47-50 g. Male drab brown above; dark-bordered white area around lores and base of forehead, small blackish patch above nares, white half-ring at rear of eye; ear-coverts richer brown with pale shaft streaks; dark-surrounded white malar whiskers; chin feathers long, pale rufous; upperparts with white to buffy spots, large and in rows on wing-coverts, as narrow bars on back to uppertail-coverts; wings plain brown with narrow buffy edgings; tail longish, strongly graduated, brown with narrow buffy tips; throat to breast pale rufous, vague band of dark streaks around lower edge; lower flanks dull brown, barred and streaked whitish, central abdomen and undertail-coverts white; underwing-coverts and bases of remiges buffy; bill black, most of lower mandible bluish; iris red, dark orbital ring; feet silvery-bluish. Female generally greyer, duller brown above, more heavily marked with buff above and on ear-coverts, paler breast, more heavily marked below. Immature has shorter bill; darker, more obscurely marked overall, with little rufous below. Voice. High thin peeping, similar to congeners.

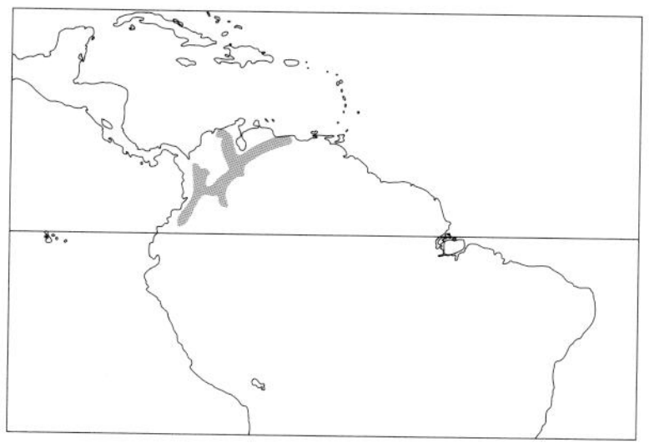

Habitat. Inhabits undergrowth, 2-6 m above ground, in dense tangled parts of humid and wet forest, often in gulleys and on slopes, also forest edge, open woodland, deciduous forest, rarely reaching the lower limits of cloudforest. Occurs at 350-2100 m.

Food and Feeding. No information available.

Breeding. Evidence suggests Feb-Sept in Colombia, May-Aug in Venezuela. Nest in hole in earth bank. Clutch size and incubation and fledging periods not known.

Movements. Presumably resident.

Status and Conservation. Not globally threatened. Uncommon in Colombia. Fairly uncommon in Venezuela; occurs in Henri Pittier National Park.

Bibliography. Chapman (1917), Cory (1919), Donegan *et al.* (1998), Gines *et al.* (1953), Hellmayr (1911), Hilty (1997), Hilty & Brown (1986), Meyer de Schauensee (1982), Meyer de Schauensee & Phelps (1978), Olrog (1968), Rodner *et al.* (2000), Salaman (1994), Schäfer & Phelps (1954), Stotz *et al.* (1996), Todd (1943a), Todd & Carriker (1922), Vélez & Velázquez (1998), Verea & Solórzano (2001), Verea *et al.* (1999), Wetmore (1939).

Genus *MICROMONACHA* P. L. Sclater, 1881

23. **Lanceolated Monklet**

Micromonacha lanceolata

French: Barbacou lancéolé **German**: Streifenfaulvogel **Spanish**: Monjilla Lanceolada

Taxonomy. *Bucco lanceolata* Deville, 1849, Pampa del Sacramento, upper Ucayali River, eastern Peru. Birds from Costa Rica to W Panama named as race *austinsmithi*, but characters weak and inconstant. Monotypic.

Distribution. Caribbean slope of Costa Rica and WC Panama; also from SW & WC Colombia S on both sides of Andes, in W to NW Ecuador and in E to NE Peru, extreme W Brazil and N Bolivia.

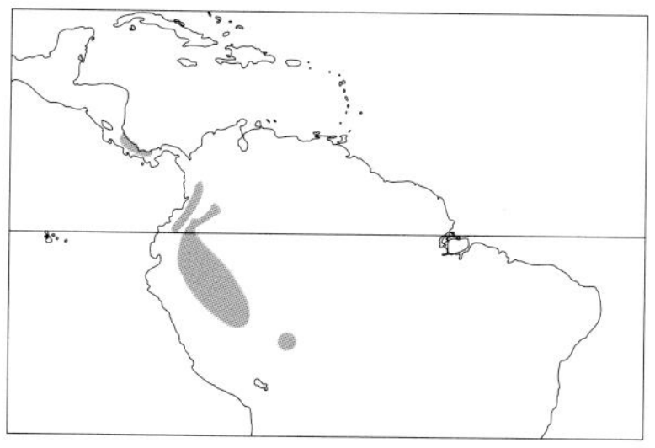

Descriptive notes. 13-15 cm; 19-22 g. Entirely dark, buffy-scaled warm brown above; profuse long recurved whitish nasal tufts and chin feathers, black-bordered white loral patch continuing across forehead, white rim at rear edge of eye; dark brown wings; tail shortish, narrow, rather graduated, brown above, grey below, with broad blackish subterminal bands and buffy tips; white underparts heavily but variably streaked black, most markedly on side of throat, with central belly plain white, undertail-coverts tinged ochraceous; buffy underwing-coverts and bases of remiges; bill black; iris brown; feet leaden, upper tarsi washed reddish-pink. Immature has less distinct face pattern, less streaking below. Voice. Rarely heard, 1-5 high, thin, plaintive rising whistles, each slightly higher than preceding one; thin, high-pitched "tsip tsip" as contact call.

Habitat. Middle and upper storeys, shady open borders, edges and natural treefall clearings in primary forest and mature second growth, even in small forest patches and shaded coffee plantations; possibly showing some link to water, as sometimes perches over small streams; also middle and upper storeys of wet primary lowland and montane evergreen forest. Occurs at 300-2100 m, mostly below 1500 m.

Food and Feeding. Feeds on insects, including cicadas and katydids; also berries. Sallies for insects from exposed perch. Sometimes follows mixed-species flocks of small birds.

Breeding. May in Costa Rica; May in Ecuador; young being fed in Dec in Bolivia. One nest found in Ecuador was an excavated tunnel, 40 cm long, in a trail embankment; entrance 6 cm high by 5 cm wide; burrow curved down to enlarged chamber, floor of which littered with leaves. Clutch 2 eggs; estimated incubation period c. 15 days; no details available on fledging period.

Movements. Presumably resident.

Status and Conservation. Not globally threatened. Formerly considered Near-threatened. Has been described as rare throughout range, but this may reflect fact that this species is difficult to detect. Rare in Costa Rica. Few records from Panama; recorded along Oleoducto Road, in W Panama. Uncommon in W Colombia and in W Ecuador. Present in Jatun Sacha Biological Station, in E Ecuador, but habitat there possibly threatened by plans to construct a road through centre of the reserve. Regular records from SE Ecuador suggest that this area may be a stronghold, but equally the species may be evenly distributed throughout range. Common on R Urucu, in Amazonas (Brazil). Generally rare and local in Peru, but regularly recorded in area of R Sucusary, near Iquitos.

Bibliography. Allen (1998b), Anon. (1998), Balchin & Toyne (1998), Cardiff (1983), Chapman (1917), Collar *et al.* (1994), Cory (1919), Davis (1986), Dwight & Griscom (1924), Fjeldså & Krabbe (1986), Freile & Endara (2000), Gandy (1994, 1995), Hilty (1977, 1997), Hilty & Brown (1986), Hornbuckle (1999), Marín *et al.* (1992), Parker *et al.* (1982), Peres & Whittaker (1991), Ridgely & Greenfield (2001), Ridgely & Gwynne (1989), Sagot (1998), Salaman (1994), Sick (1993), Slud (1964), Stiles (1985), Stiles & Skutch (1989), Stotz *et al.* (1996), Taylor (1995), Wetmore (1968a), Williams & Tobias (1994), Young *et al.* (1998).

24

ssp *rubecula*

ssp *duidae*

ssp *tapanahoniensis*

25

26

27

ssp *frontalis*

ssp *pallescens*

ssp *ruficapilla*

28

ssp *rufipectus*

29

30

31

32

33

ssp *grandior*

ssp *pallescens*

ssp *morphoeus*

34

35

ssp *tenebrosa*

ssp *brasiliensis*

PLATE 5

inches 4

cm 10

Genus *NONNULA* P. L. Sclater, 1854

24. **Rusty-breasted Nunlet**

Nonnula rubecula

French: Barbacou rufalbin   **German**: Rotkehl-Faulvogel   **Spanish**: Monjilla Macurú

Taxonomy. *Bucco rubecula* Spix, 1824, Malhada, Rio São Francisco, western Bahia, Brazil.
Forms a superspecies with *N. sclateri* and *N. brunnea*. Taxonomy uncertain and confused: listed races may involve more than one species; also some of listed races probably comprise more than one taxon (e.g. nominate race in E Brazil has plumage soft and silky, in SE of range plumage loosely webbed, in both cases numerous tonal differences from "typical" nominate); also validity of some recognized races possibly doubtful; extensive revision needed. Seven subspecies tentatively recognized.
Subspecies and Distribution.
N. r. duidae Chapman, 1914 - E Venezuela in S Amazonas (N of R Orinoco).
N. r. interfluvialis Parkes, 1970 - S Venezuela (S of R Orinoco) S to R Negro in N Brazil.
N. r. tapanahoniensis Mees, 1968 - S Guianas and N Brazil (N bank of lower Amazon).
N. r. simulatrix Parkes, 1970 - SE Colombia, and NW Brazil (between R Negro and R Amazon).
N. r. cineracea P. L. Sclater, 1881 - NE Ecuador, NE Peru, and W Brazil S of Amazon (S to Rondônia).
N. r. simplex Todd, 1937 - S bank of lower Amazon, N Brazil.
N. r. rubecula (Spix, 1824) - E & SE Brazil (Bahia and Goiás S to Paraná), E Paraguay and NE Argentina (Misiones).

Descriptive notes. 14-16 cm; 17-20 g. Whitish band from nasal tufts joining white eyering; blackish moustachial line, white chin; plain dark grey-brown upperparts and sides of head, greyer crown, slightly more rufescent uppertail-coverts and wing-coverts, secondaries edged buffy-rufescent (in E Brazil paler and greyer above, especially crown, lores rufous; in SE of range, much darker and browner overall, lores also rufous); tail square-tipped, rather graduated, dark brown (warmer brown in SE); throat to lower breast and flanks brown with rufescent tinge, abdomen grading to whitish (in E Brazil bright orange-rufous lower throat to mid-belly, paler orange flanks, white central belly and vent, silver-grey undertail); underwing-coverts buffy; bill mainly black; iris brown; feet blackish-grey or brown. Immature duller, throat to breast drab pale brown, upperparts faintly edged rufescent, bill dark with pale tip. Races vary in structure and coloration, N races having longer, narrower bill with well-curved tip and paler gonys, shorter tail with contrasting silvery edgings, whereas E Brazilian races have short, broad, straighter bill with darker gonys, longer plain tail, and races N of Amazon with rufescent lores, S of Amazon paler and duller: *tapanahoniensis* has prominent dark grey crown, cinnamon-tinged vent; *duidae* has rufous lores and chin; *simulatrix* darker-tailed than last, *interfluvialis* greyer; *simplex* drab, dark; *cineracea* paler, warmer brown underparts than last. VOICE. Song a series of "weeip, weeip, weeip" notes; repeated sharp "tick"; excited squealing in response to playback of *N. frontalis*.
Habitat. Found mainly in middle storey (but from ground level to canopy) of humid *terra firme* and (vine-bordered) *várzea* forest, and also second growth and forest edge with or without bamboo; mainly occurs in sandy-belt forest in Venezuela; occupies scattered riverine woods in SE Brazil (Paraná). Locally occurs in lowlands up to 1000 m. In upper Amazonia excluded from *igapó* forest by *N. amaurocephala*.
Food and Feeding. Large arthropods reported, including beetles, crabs and katydids (Orthoptera) up to 2·5 cm long. Sometimes joins mixed-species flocks.
Breeding. Immature seen in Nov in lower Amazon. Nest in hole in bank or in tree. No further details of nest, nor of clutch size or other aspects of breeding biology.
Movements. Presumably resident.
Status and Conservation. Not globally threatened. Widely reported as being rare, on basis of very low contact rates during fieldwork, but species is probably under-recorded owing to unobtrusive habits. Rare around Manaus (Amazon) and in SE Brazil, but in latter region variably rare to common in Paraná. Generally rare in Peru. Not uncommon around Sapucay, in Paraguay; occurs in several protected areas in that country, including Reserva Natural del Bosque Mbaracayú, La Golondrina Private Nature Reserve and Estancia Itabó Private Nature Reserve. Scarce in Argentina; occurs in Iguazú National Park. Only recently recorded in Ecuador, during 1990's, where occurs in Cuyabeno Reserve.
Bibliography. dos Anjos & Schuchmann (1997), dos Anjos *et al.* (1997), Barnes *et al.* (1993), Bierregaard (1988), Braun *et al.* (2000), Brooks *et al.* (1993), Canevari *et al.* (1991), Chapman (1914a), Chrostowski (1921), Chubb (1910), Cohn-Haft *et al.* (1997), Cory (1919), Ferreira de Vasconcelos *et al.* (1999), Friedmann (1948), Gyldenstolpe (1951), Haverschmidt & Mees (1994), Hayes (1995), Hilty & Brown (1986), Machado (1999), Marini (2001), Mees (1968), Meyer de Schauensee & Phelps (1978), Novaes (1980), Olivares (1967), Oren & Parker (1997), Parkes (1970), de la Peña (1994), Piratelli *et al.* (2000), Ridgely & Greenfield (2001), Romero (1978), do Rosário (1996), Saibene *et al.* (1996), Sick (1993), Stotz *et al.* (1996), Todd (1919, 1937, 1943a), Tostain *et al.* (1992), Whittaker & Oren (1999), Whittaker *et al.* (1995), Willard *et al.* (1991), Zimmer & Hilty (1997).

25. **Fulvous-chinned Nunlet**

Nonnula sclateri

French: Barbacou de Sclater   **German**: Gelbkinn-Faulvogel   **Spanish**: Monjilla de Sclater

Taxonomy. *Nonnula sclateri* Hellmayr, 1907, Humaythá, Rio Madeira, Brazil.

Forms a superspecies with *N. rubecula* and *N. brunnea*; sometimes treated as a race of latter. Monotypic.
Distribution. SE Peru, W Brazil S of Amazon (E to R Madeira) and N Bolivia.

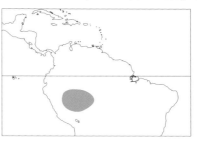

Descriptive notes. 14-15·5 cm; 15-17 g. Overall dull brown; lores rufous-brown; conspicuous grey patch below and behind eye, including ear-coverts; edgings to secondaries often buffy; chin pale rufous, grading to rufescent-brown of throat and breast; sides dull fulvous; abdomen grading to whitish in centre; undertail-coverts white; tail relatively long and narrow; bill largely black, partly grey below; iris brown, reddish eyering; legs pale brown to dark grey. Immature not described. VOICE. Song is a series of up to 30 plaintive "weeip, weeip, weeip" notes, similar to that of *N. rubecula* but with more, longer and less stressed notes.

Habitat. Occupies open understorey of humid primary and disturbed *terra firme* and *várzea* forest, and forest edge, commonly in or near bamboo thickets close to water. Restricted to lowlands.
Food and Feeding. No information on diet. May follow understorey bird flocks.
Breeding. No information.
Movements. Presumably resident.
Status and Conservation. Not globally threatened. In Peru, rare overall, but locally common at Balta. In general, very infrequently encountered in Brazil. Status in Bolivia uncertain, but available evidence suggests it to be rare.
Bibliography. Clements & Shany (2001), Cory (1919), Gyldenstolpe (1945a, 1951), Hellmayr (1910), Meyer de Schauensee (1982), Morrone (2000), Novaes (1957), O'Neill (1969), Olrog (1968), Parker & Remsen (1987), Parker *et al.* (1982), Remsen & Traylor (1989), Ruschi (1979), Sick (1993), Stotz *et al.* (1996), Todd (1943a), Whittaker & Oren (1999).

26. **Brown Nunlet**

Nonnula brunnea

French: Barbacou brun   **German**: Einfarb-Faulvogel   **Spanish**: Monjilla Canela

Taxonomy. *Nonnula brunnea* P. L. Sclater, 1881, Sarayacu, Peru.
Forms a superspecies with *N. rubecula* and *N. sclateri*; sometimes considered conspecific with the latter of these. Has at times been treated as conspecific with *N. frontalis* and *N. ruficapilla*. Monotypic.
Distribution. SC Colombia, E Ecuador and N Peru.

Descriptive notes. 14-15 cm. Buffy-rufous band from short nasal tufts to eye, narrow buffy eye-ring, dark greyish-brown ear-coverts; rest of head and upperparts dark plain brown, edges of secondaries buffy; tail slightly graduated; chin and central abdomen pale rufous, grading to dull dark rufous throat and flanks; centre of belly and undertail-coverts buffy-rufous; underwing-coverts rufous; bill mostly dark; iris dark brown; feet dark. Immature undescribed. VOICE. Song is a series of 20-25 "treeu" notes, repeated steadily, starting quietly, building up, and then fading again towards end.

Habitat. Occupies understorey to subcanopy of humid lowland *terra firme* forest, as well as cluttered second-growth woodland. In Ecuador, mainly occurs below 400 m, but locally recorded up to c. 700 m.
Food and Feeding. No information available on diet. Sometimes joins antwren (*Myrmotherula*) flocks in lower storeys.
Breeding. No information.
Movements. Presumably resident.
Status and Conservation. Not globally threatened. Restricted-range species: present in Upper Amazon-Napo Lowlands EBA. Rare to uncommon in Ecuador, being uncommon at Limoncocha; present in Cuyabeno Reserve and also at Jatun Sacha Biological Station, but habitat of latter possibly threatened by plans for construction of a road through the centre of the reserve. Rare in Peru. Little known; research required.
Bibliography. Best *et al.* (1997), Borrero (1960), Clements & Shany (2001), Cory (1919), Curson & Lowen (2000), Hilty & Brown (1986), Meyer de Schauensee (1946a, 1982), Olrog (1968), Parker *et al.* (1982), Pearson *et al.* (1977), Ridgely & Greenfield (2001), Ridgely *et al.* (1998), Rodner *et al.* (2000), Stotz *et al.* (1996), Taylor (1995).

27. **Grey-cheeked Nunlet**

Nonnula frontalis

French: Barbacou à joues grises   **German**: Grauwangen-Faulvogel   **Spanish**: Monjilla Carigrís

Taxonomy. *Malacoptila frontalis* P. L. Sclater, 1854, interior of Colombia.
Forms a superspecies with *N. ruficapilla* and *N. amaurocephala*; has at times been treated as conspecific with the former of these, and also with *N. brunnea*. Nominate race somewhat variable in colour, and is thought possibly to comprise more than one taxon; further investigation and analysis required. Race *pallescens* has on occasion been considered to belong to *N. ruficapilla*, although both geographically and morphologically they are decidedly distant. Three subspecies currently recognized.

On following pages: 28. Rufous-capped Nunlet (*Nonnula ruficapilla*); 29. Chestnut-headed Nunlet (*Nonnula amaurocephala*); 30. White-faced Nunbird (*Hapaloptila castanea*); 31. Black Nunbird (*Monasa atra*); 32. Black-fronted Nunbird (*Monasa nigrifrons*); 33. White-fronted Nunbird (*Monasa morphoeus*); 34. Yellow-billed Nunbird (*Monasa flavirostris*); 35. Swallow-winged Puffbird (*Chelidoptera tenebrosa*).

Subspecies and Distribution.
N. f. stulta Wetmore, 1953 - C Panama to extreme NW Colombia.
N. f. pallescens Todd, 1919 - Caribbean lowlands of N Colombia.
N. f. frontalis (P. L. Sclater, 1854) - interior N Colombia.

Descriptive notes. 14-15 cm; 14·5-19·5 g. Crown very dark chestnut, upperparts plain brown, rump brighter; grey lores, supercilium, and ear-coverts, thin darker eyestripe; tail graduated about a quarter length, square-tipped, dark brown, blackish near tip; chin to lower breast and flanks rufous, centre of abdomen buffy, undertail-coverts white; bill silvery-blue or grey, black on culmen and cutting edges; iris dark brown, bare orbital ring reddish; feet dull brown or greenish-grey. Immature paler, duller. Race *pallescens* has entire upperparts paler, crown very dull, throat and breast buff; *stulta* has crown very dark and dull, tail blacker except for outer feathers, rump drabber. VOICE. A plaintive, measured series of up to 20 notes, "weeip weeip, weeip...".
Habitat. Moist to humid forest, gallery forest, edge, and second-growth woodland, borders and thickets in lowlands, preferring vine-tangled and riverine woodlands, usually not deep inside unbroken humid forest; to 1000 m. Generally in lower storeys (3-12 m), but ranges up to lower canopy.
Food and Feeding. Orthopterans, caterpillars, earwigs (Dermaptera), small beetles, membracids, and spiders. Sometimes joins mixed foraging flocks of antwrens (*Myrmotherula*), small flycatchers (Tyrannidae) and others.
Breeding. Feb-Jun in Colombia, and recent fledgling seen in May. No other details.
Movements. Presumably resident.
Status and Conservation. Not globally threatened. Considered uncommon to rare in Panama. Race *pallescens* apparently rare, but may be overlooked and under-recorded; species judged to be generally fairly common in Colombia.
Bibliography. Anon. (1998b), Bangs & Barbour (1922), Cory (1919), Dugand (1947), Eisenmann (1952), Griscom (1929), Haffer (1967b, 1974, 1975), Haffer & Borrero (1965), Hilty & Brown (1986), Ridgely & Gwynne (1989), Ridgway (1914), Rodner *et al*. (2000), Rodríguez (1982), Salvin & Godman (1888-1904), Stotz *et al*. (1996), Todd & Carriker (1922), Wetmore (1953, 1968a), Willis & Eisenmann (1979).

28. Rufous-capped Nunlet
Nonnula ruficapilla

French: Barbacou à couronne rousse   **Spanish**: Monjilla Coronada
German: Rotscheitel-Faulvogel

Taxonomy. *Lypornix ruficapilla* Tschudi, 1844, Peru.
Forms a superspecies with *N. frontalis* and *N. amaurocephala*; has been treated as conspecific with former, and also with *N. brunnea*. Race *pallescens* of *N. frontalis* has on occasion been considered to belong in present species, although geographically and morphologically distant. Four subspecies currently recognized.
Subspecies and Distribution.
N. r. rufipectus Chapman, 1928 - NE Peru.
N. r. ruficapilla (Tschudi, 1844) - E Peru and W Brazil S of Amazon.
N. r. nattereri Hellmayr, 1921 - S Amazon Basin in Mato Grosso, N Bolivia and N Brazil (W Pará).
N. r. inundata Novaes, 1991 - R Tocantins, in E Pará.

Descriptive notes. 13·5-14 cm; 14-22 g. Extensive deep chestnut crown patch; entire face, nape and sides of breast cold grey; upperparts from mantle plain dull brown, more rufescent on secondary edges and uppertail-coverts; chin to breast orange-rufous, flanks paler rufous, grading to whitish central underparts and undertail-coverts; bill silvery-blue, black on culmen and cutting edges; iris dark brown, bare orbital ring reddish and swollen; feet dark brownish-grey. Immature has yellowish-brown eyelids. Race *rufipectus* brighter, especially breast, darker cap; *nattereri* duller breast, darker cap; *inundata* darker and duller still.
VOICE. A long series (13-30 notes) of sharp, clear, short, upward-inflected whistles, "fwick!-fwick!...", given at a fairly even rate of 2-3 per second, the series slightly softer and lower in pitch near beginning and end.
Habitat. Inhabits subcanopy and undergrowth in humid forest edges, *terra firme* forest, second growth, transitional forest, river margins, dense low forest along streams, and *igapó*. In most of its range species is associated with bamboo (notably river-edge bamboo thickets), but also found in habitats without bamboo; at one site in Rondônia (W Brazil) territories found along roadside forest edge with abundant viny second growth; in Peru strongly associated with *Tessaria*, the early successional floodplain-forest stage; in hilly forest often found along streambeds.
Food and Feeding. Insects found in 4 stomachs of specimens from Bolivia. No further details documented.
Breeding. No information; 4 adults collected in Jun in Bolivia, and 3 in Jun and Aug in C Brazil, were not breeding.
Movements. Presumably resident.
Status and Conservation. Not globally threatened. Described as rare or uncommon in Peru, but this is probably in part a matter of perception, and in part a question of habitat; thus, records show 19·0 territories/km² in earliest successional stage (*Tessaria*) but only 3·0 territories/km² in later stages, in backwaters, and this species is infrequent in mature forest; frequently recorded at Manu Wildlife Centre (SE Peru). Common on R Urucu, in W Amazonas, Brazil. Apparently uncommon to rare in Bolivia.
Bibliography. Aleixo *et al*. (2000), Allen (1995), Angehr & Aucca (1997), Anon. (1998b), Bates *et al*. (1989), Bond (1954), Borrero (1962), Chapman (1928a), Clements & Shany (2001), Cory (1919), Donahue (1994), Dubs (1992), Novaes (1991), Oren & Parker (1997), Parker *et al*. (1982), Robinson & Terborgh (1997), Schulenberg & Remsen (1982), Sclater & Salvin (1866), Sick (1993), da Silva *et al*. (1990), Stotz *et al*. (1996), Terborgh *et al*. (1990), Zimmer (1930), Zimmer *et al*. (1997).

29. Chestnut-headed Nunlet
Nonnula amaurocephala

French: Barbacou à face rousse   **German**: Rotkopf-Faulvogel   **Spanish**: Monjilla Cabeciparda

Taxonomy. *Nonnula amaurocephala* Chapman, 1921, Manacapurú, Rio Solimões, Brazil.
Forms a superspecies with *N. frontalis* and *N. ruficapilla*. Monotypic.
Distribution. NW Brazil N of Amazon and W of R Negro.

Descriptive notes. 14-15 cm; 15-16 g. Rather distinctive a species within its fairly uniform genus. Shows large rufous nasal tufts; entire head to upper mantle and breast to upper belly bright rufous; back, wings and tail plain dull brown, rump washed olive; abdomen grading to whitish; bill mostly black, blue-grey at base; iris red; feet lead-grey. Immature similar to adult but has brown iris. VOICE. No information available.
Habitat. Occupies understorey of shaded *igapó* forest (relatively stunted seasonally flooded blackwater woodland), where is usually observed c. 3 m above ground level, sometimes up to 7-8 m up. Apparently excluded from *terra firme* forest by *N. rubecula*, but birds seen moving through secondary growth where thick vines climbed into tree canopies and tangled in lower bushes.
Food and Feeding. Presumably chiefly invertebrates; observed making short sallying flights of 0·5-3 m.
Breeding. No information.
Movements. Presumably resident.
Status and Conservation. Not globally threatened. Formerly considered Near-threatened. Restricted-range species: present in Amazon Flooded Forests EBA. Recent information on habitat suggests that the species is relatively secure for the present: *igapó* forest is widespread within the basin of R Negro, W of the river itself, and is under little pressure; moreover, this is a quiet and immobile species, making it likely to be overlooked. Present in Jaú National Park, and has been observed at Manaus.
Bibliography. Collar *et al*. (1994), Gyldenstolpe (1945a), Meyer de Schauensee (1982), Morrone (2000), Olrog (1968), Pearman (1994b), Pinto (1938a), Ruschi (1979), Sick (1993), Stotz *et al*. (1996), Todd (1943a), Whittaker *et al*. (1995).

Genus *HAPALOPTILA*   P. L. Sclater, 1881

30. White-faced Nunbird
Hapaloptila castanea

French: Barbacou à face blanche   **German**: Diademfaulvogel   **Spanish**: Buco Cariblanco
Other common names: White-faced Nunlet

Taxonomy. *Malacoptila castanea* J. Verreaux, 1866, Santa Fé de Bogotá = Frontino, Antioquia, Colombia.
Monotypic.
Distribution. W Colombia, C Ecuador and NW Peru.

Descriptive notes. 23-25 cm; 75-84 g. Heavy whitish nasal tufts, large black-bordered white patch from base of bill right across forehead; crown grey-brown, grading to dark brown mantle and sides of face, to even darker brown on wings and tail; tail rather long, graduated for a third of length; chin and throat white, contrasting with bright chestnut rest of underparts; underwing-coverts and bases of remiges rufous; bill all black; iris red; legs and feet grey. Immature not described. VOICE. Song a series of upward-inflected single hoots, or double hoots like pygmy-owl (*Glaucidium*), sometimes extending to trill; call a mournful, downslurred "wuooooo".
Habitat. Humid and wet forest and cloudforest, edges and small clearings, on steep slopes and by ravines. In foothills, in range 750-2900 m, mostly above c. 1500 m.
Food and Feeding. Coleoptera (once many small beetles), Hymenoptera, Orthoptera, Lepidoptera (larvae); in one study, a few small insects together with plant material, either buds or fruit, found in stomachs. Food given to nestlings at nest in Ecuador was 78% insects, 8·4% other items (including lizards, nestling birds, a mouse, a frog) and 13·6 unseen and/or unidentified. Mainly forages in canopy, but active at all levels and sometimes very low down.
Breeding. Apr in Colombia; eggs laid in late May, in Ecuador. Only nest known to date, in Ecuador, was burrow dug into bank above recent landslide; tunnel 38 cm long led to chamber 23 cm long by 16 cm wide by 10 cm high; construction at least 25 days, possibly 46 days or more. At same nest: clutch 2 eggs; incubation 15-18 days; fledging 37-38 days; both adults shared duties in nest building, incubation and feeding of young.
Movements. Presumably resident.
Status and Conservation. Not globally threatened. Rare and local in parts of Colombian range; occurs in La Planada Nature Reserve. Uncommon and apparently very local in Ecuador, where thought to be absent from extensive tracts of apparently suitable habitat. Decidedly uncommon in Peru.
Bibliography. Allen (1998), Athanas & Davis (2000), Berlioz (1954), Best *et al*. (1997), Chapman (1926), Clements & Shany (2001), Cory (1919), Davies *et al*. (1994), Fjeldså & Krabbe (1990), Hilty & Brown (1986), Krabbe (1991), Miller (1963), Parker, Parker & Plenge (1982), Parker, Schulenberg *et al*. (1985), Pearman (1995), Ridgely

& Greenfield (2001), Ridgely *et al.* (1998), Rodner *et al.* (2000), Salaman (1994), Sneidern (1955), Stotz *et al.* (1996), Strewe (2000a), Taylor (1995).

Genus *MONASA* Vieillot, 1816

31. **Black Nunbird**

Monasa atra

French: Barbacou noir **German**: Mohrentrappist **Spanish**: Monja Negra
Other common names: Black Nunlet

Taxonomy. *Cuculus ater* Boddaert, 1783, Cayenne.
Forms a superspecies with *M. nigrifrons* and *M. morphoeus*. Monotypic.
Distribution. S & E Venezuela and the Guianas S to N Brazil (N of Amazon and E of R Negro); possibly also extreme E Colombia (E Vichada, E Guainía).

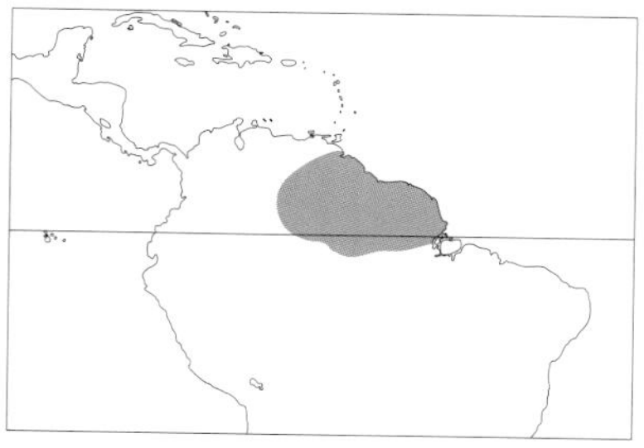

Descriptive notes. 25-29 cm; 74-104 g. Glossy blue-black above, conspicuous white lesser coverts along upper edge of wing, grading to white and then grey scalloping on median and lower coverts; tertials large and broad, edged grey; tail long and broad, rounded; throat feathers long; underparts dark grey, grading to medium grey on abdomen; underwing-coverts pale grey to whitish; bill entirely red; iris red to brown, with patch of bare blackish skin behind eye; legs and feet slate-black. Immature sootier above than adult, and browner below; apparently has darker eye (birds with medium or dark brown eyes may be non-adult). VOICE. Flute-like "whoo-doo-doo" and descending "hyoo-hoo-hoo-oo-oo"; loud "yawkl-diddl" or "quee-didada" in duet; call surprisingly loud, often uttered by several birds in company.
Habitat. Understorey to canopy of humid *terra firme*, gallery and *várzea* forest, strongly favouring areas near water, forest edge, scrub and more open situations. In one study birds were often found high in subcanopy, near huge trees, near liana-crowned trees, near palms, and at rotted stumps or on dead limbs, and regularly used tall second growth, partly cleared plantations, treefall and escarpment gaps. Lowlands to 1000 m.
Food and Feeding. Insects including Orthoptera (Locustidae), Coleoptera (Buprestidae), Malacodermata (Rutelidae), Hemiptera, Heteroptera (Coreidae), and larvae of Lepidoptera; also stick-insects (Phasmida). Scorpions (Scorpiones), spiders, large centipedes (Chilopoda) and lizards also taken. Sallies and hovers to take prey. Some insects caught on the wing, but prey more usually plucked from substrate. Follows ant swarms; sometimes moves underneath groups of Red-rumped Caciques (*Cacicus haemorrhous*) in the canopy, possibly to watch for downward-flushed prey.
Breeding. Mar-May in Venezuela; Aug-Sept in main dry season, but probably also Apr-May, in French Guiana; apparently also 2 nesting seasons per year at Manaus (N Brazil). Nest in hole in level ground. Clutch size and incubation and fledging periods not documented.
Movements. Presumably resident.
Status and Conservation. Not globally threatened. Common locally in Venezuela, and very common at Cerro de la Neblina. Perhaps scarcer in Brazilian range, but common near Manaus. Common in the Guianas, and described by one mid-20th-century explorer as "one of the most abundant non-colonial forest birds of the interior of Guyana", but also common in coastal forest and savanna areas.
Bibliography. Aguirre & Aldrighi (1983), Bierregaard (1988), Blake (1950), Borges (1994), Borges & Guilherme (2000), Cherrie (1916), Chubb (1916), Cohn-Haft *et al.* (1997), Cory (1919), Friedmann (1948), Haverschmidt & Mees (1994), Meyer de Schauensee & Phelps (1978), Parker *et al.* (1993), Phelps & Phelps (1958), Rodner *et al.* (2000), Snyder (1966), Stotz *et al.* (1996), Thiollay (1992), Thiollay & Jullien (1998), Todd (1943a), Tostain *et al.* (1992), Willard *et al.* (1991), Zimmer & Hilty (1997).

32. **Black-fronted Nunbird**

Monasa nigrifrons

French: Barbacou unicolore **German**: Schwarzstirntrappist **Spanish**: Monja Unicolor
Other common names: Black-fronted Nunlet

Taxonomy. *Bucco nigrifrons* Spix, 1824, Rio Solimões, Brazil.
Forms a superspecies with *M. atra* and *M. morphoeus*. Two subspecies recognized.
Subspecies and Distribution.
M. n. nigrifrons (Spix, 1824) - SE Colombia, E Ecuador, E Peru, and much of Brazil (E, N of Amazon, to R Negro and, S of Amazon, to Pará and Alagoas and S to E Mato Grosso do Sul and W São Paulo).
M. n. canescens Todd, 1937 - E Bolivia.

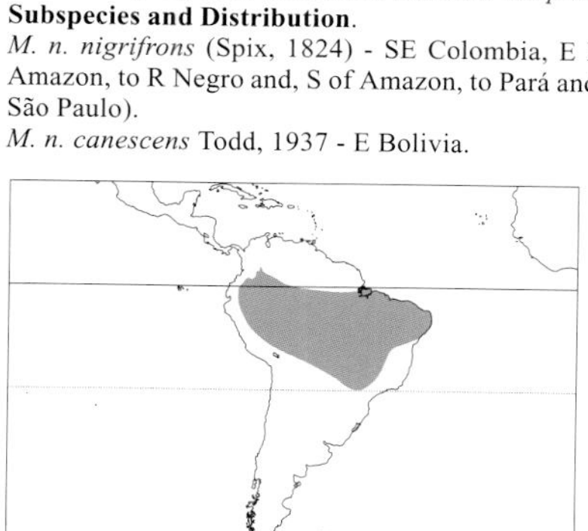

Descriptive notes. 26-29 cm; 68-98 g. All sooty-black plumage, blackest around bill, with rear part of body blue-grey, tail blue-black, underwing-coverts sooty-black; bill red; iris dark, a little area of dark bare skin behind eye; legs black. Immature dirty slate with irregular reddish markings, throat mixed with reddish. Race *canescens* slightly paler and greyer than nominate. VOICE. Song is a rapid series of melodious upslurred "clerry" or "curry" whistles, broken by occasional downslurred "turra turra" trill, often given as group chorus lasting for several minutes; call is a sporadic single dull note.

Habitat. Chiefly in low riverbank and lake-margin trees and bamboo. Unlike other nunbirds, forages low in open understorey of *várzea*, *igapó* and gallery and other riverside woodland, second-growth forest, dry deciduous and semi-deciduous woodland, palm groves of *Orbignya mertensiana* along streambeds through savanna, swampy river islands, transitional forest, and middle and late successional floodplain-forest. Absent from *terra firme* forest, which is occupied by *M. morphoeus*. Occurs up to 1000 m.
Food and Feeding. Arthropods, and small lizards; prey 1-4 cm long, mostly less than 2 cm. Most prey insects, chiefly Lepidoptera, also Orthoptera, Hemiptera and Homoptera, Hymenoptera (wasps), and others. Prey taken mostly in flight, e.g. butterflies, alate termites; also from ground, and from foliage up to 5 m up. Follows primate troops, taking prey they dislodge; also follows army ants, when recorded prey includes leaf-mimic katydids, grasshoppers, caterpillars, spiders and lizards.
Breeding. Jun and Oct in Colombia; in dry season in Peru; in lower Amazon evidence of grown young in Feb; nest excavation in May in S Brazil; female ready to lay in Jun in W Brazil (Acre). Nest in hole in bank or flat ground. Clutch 3 eggs; incubation and fledging periods not documented.
Movements. Presumably resident.
Status and Conservation. Not globally threatened. Common in Colombia and common in Ecuador. Common to abundant in Amazonian Brazil and around Pantanal. Common in Peru, where at one study site (Cocha Cashu) as many as 28 birds/km², territory size 8 ha; in most favourable habitat (mid-successional stages) as many as 22 territories/km², decreasing to 7 territories/km² in mature floodplain-forest. Fairly common to frequent in Bolivia.
Bibliography. Aguirre & Aldrighi (1983), Allen (1995), Best *et al.* (1997), Bond (1954), Brace *et al.* (1997), Bronaugh (1984), Cavalcanti (2000), Cory (1919), Donahue (1994), Dubs (1992), Dugand (1948, 1952), Goodfellow (1902), Gyldenstolpe (1945a), Hellmayr (1929), Hilty & Brown (1986), Marini (2001), de Mello & Mello (1998), de Melo & Marini (1999), Novaes (1957), O'Neill & Pearson (1974), Olivares (1962), Oniki & Willis (1999), Oren & Parker (1997), Parker *et al.* (1982), Pelzeln (1867-1871), Peres & Whittaker (1991), Perry *et al.* (1997), Pinto (1936), Pinto & Camargo (1954, 1957), Piratelli, de Mello & Mello (1998), Piratelli, Siqueira & Marcondes-Machado (2000), Ridgely & Greenfield (2001), Robinson (1997), Robinson & Terborgh (1997), Schubart *et al.* (1965), Sick (1993), Skutch (1948c, 1972), Snethlage (1914), Stotz, Fitzpatrick *et al.* (1996), Stotz, Lanyon *et al.* (1997), Taylor (1995), Teixeira *et al.* (1988), Terborgh *et al.* (1990), Todd (1937), Willis (1982b), Willis & Oniki (1990), Zimmer *et al.* (1997).

33. **White-fronted Nunbird**

Monasa morphoeus

French: Barbacou à front blanc **German**: Weißstirntrappist **Spanish**: Monja Frentiblanca
Other common names: White-fronted Nunlet

Taxonomy. *Bucco Morphoeus* Hahn and Küster, 1823, Brazil.
Forms a superspecies with *M. atra* and *M. nigrifrons*. Nominate and races *grandior* and *fidelis* have been considered three distinct species by some authors. Birds from NE Bolivia sometimes separated as race *boliviana*, but apparently indistinguishable from *peruana*. Seven subspecies currently recognized.
Subspecies and Distribution.
M. m. grandior P. L. Sclater & Salvin, 1868 - E Honduras and E Nicaragua to W Panama.
M. m. fidelis Nelson, 1912 - Caribbean E Panama and NW Colombia (E to S Córdoba).
M. m. pallescens Cassin, 1860 - SE Panama to W Colombia (S to upper R San Juan).
M. m. sclateri Ridgway, 1912 - N & C Colombia (Magdalena Valley S to N Tolima).
M. m. peruana P. L. Sclater, 1856 - E Ecuador, SE Colombia and S Venezuela S to E Peru, upper Amazonian Brazil (E to R Tapajós) and NE Bolivia.
M. m. rikeri Ridgway 1912 - Amazonian Brazil from R Tapajós E to Piauí.
M. m. morphoeus (Hahn & Küster, 1823) - E Brazil (Bahia S to Rio de Janeiro).

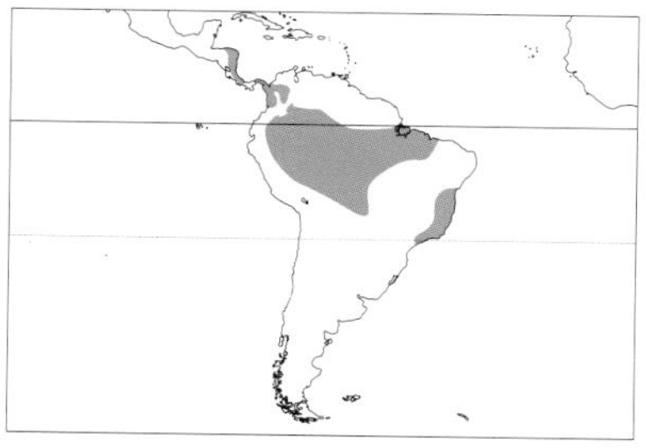

Descriptive notes. 21-29 cm; 90-101 g (Central America), 63-80 g (Venezuela), 77-87 g (E Amazon), 80-84 g (Bolivia). Dark greyish-black, greyer below, with white forehead and chin; bill orange-red; iris brown; legs black. Differs from *M. nigrifrons* in white forehead and chin, greyer body plumage, more orange-red bill. Immature buffy-rufous face, plumage tinged brownish with brownish edges to body feathers and wing-coverts, paler and duskier bill. Races differ from nominate in darkness of plumage, extent of white on face, and size, largest and with black hood, paler wings and broad purplish-glossed tail in N (S to W Colombia), smaller and darker with white chin, mostly grey neck and narrower bronzier tail in Amazonia and S: of N races, *sclateri* has black chin, little contrast between black neck and grey body, moderately pale wing-coverts, *pallescens* similar but much paler and more contrasting, with most white on forehead of any race, *fidelis* as previous but whitish chin and slightly darker body and wing-coverts, *grandior* as previous but slightly darker body and little neck/breast contrast, larger bill; in S range, *rikeri* slightly paler than nominate, *peruana* paler still. VOICE. Rather varied; common call is a blurred descending whistle with short rippling trill, "peeeur-r-r-r-r"; also a loud, mournful "how how how" and various rippling trills, churrs and rattles; group choruses of loud gobbling, barking notes, sustained for up to 20 minutes at a time, chiefly at beginning and end of day.
Habitat. Mid-levels to canopy of tall humid lowland *terra firme* and low hill-country rainforest, treefall gaps, adjoining shady semi-open areas, high trees bordering river beaches, gallery forest, transitional forest, mature floodplain-forest, also abandoned clearings with scattered trees, borders in partly deforested areas, shaded cacao plantations and uninhabited tree-scattered clearings; sometimes contiguous patches of second growth. Noted as common around Indian clearings in forest. Mostly found below 300 m, but up to 750 m in Panama (Cerro Pirre); reaches 1050 m in Peru and locally 1350 m in Ecuador (head of R Guataracu).
Food and Feeding. Bush-crickets, ground-crickets and other Orthoptera up to 6 g, also beetles, stick-insects (Phasmida), mantises (Mantidae), cicadas (Cicadidae), caterpillars, moths, small butterflies, dragonflies, spiders, large plated centipedes (Chilopoda), millipedes (Diplopoda), scorpions (Scorpiones), frogs and small lizards; also fruits of *Trichilia micrantha*. Follows army ants, foraging flocks of caciques (*Cacicus*) and oropendolas (*Psarocolius*, *Gymnostinops*), and troops of monkeys.
Breeding. Dec-May in Costa Rica; Feb-May in Colombia; newly fledged young recorded in area of lower Amazon in Jan-Feb. Nest is an oblique tunnel in level or sloping forest floor, 80-140 cm

long and 8 cm wide, the mouth surrounded by a collar of dead leaves and twigs, nest-chamber lined with leaves; attended by 3-6 adults. Clutch 2-3 eggs; incubation and fledging periods not documented.

Movements. Presumably resident.

Status and Conservation. Not globally threatened. Considered common to abundant in Costa Rica. Uncommon to locally common in Panama. Fairly common in C Colombia. Common at Cerro de la Neblina in Venezuela. Generally uncommon to fairly common in Ecuador. Common in Peru, where population density recorded was of 1 pair or group/km² in final successional stage of floodplain-forest. Common in Amazonian Brazil, and fairly common in E Brazil (Atlantic Forest). Fairly common in Bolivia.

Bibliography. Allen (1995), Anon. (1998b), Argel-de-Oliveira (1992), Bangs & Barbour (1922), Bond & Meyer de Schauensee (1943), Bronaugh (1984), Carriker (1910), Cory (1919), Davis (1972), Dubs (1992), Friedmann (1948), Gyldenstolpe (1945a, 1951), Haffer (1975), Hellmayr (1929), Henriques & Oren (1997), Hilty & Brown (1986), Meyer de Schauensee & Phelps (1978), Monroe (1968), Oren & Parker (1997), Peres & Whittaker (1991), Pinto (1947), Pinto & Camargo (1954), Ridgely & Greenfield (2001), Ridgely & Gwynne (1989), Ridgway (1914), Robinson & Terborgh (1997), Salvin & Godman (1888-1904), Sargeant & Wall (1996), Scott & Brooke (1985), Sherry (1983b), Sick (1993), da Silva & Oniki (1988), Skutch (1972), Slud (1960, 1964), Snethlage (1914), Stiles (1985), Stiles & Skutch (1989), Stiles et al. (1999), Stotz et al. (1996), Todd (1943a), Wetmore (1968a), Willard et al. (1991), Young et al. (1998), Zimmer (1930).

34. Yellow-billed Nunbird

Monasa flavirostris

French: Barbacou à bec jaune   **German**: Gelbschnabeltrappist   **Spanish**: Monja Piquigualda
Other common names: Yellow-billed Nunlet

Taxonomy. *Monasa flavirostris* Strickland, 1850, Peru.
Monotypic.
Distribution. Amazon Basin in SE Colombia and E Ecuador S through E Peru, W Brazil (E to R Negro and R Purus) and N Bolivia.

Descriptive notes. 23-25 cm; 39 g. Sooty-black overall, with lesser wing-coverts mainly white, lower underparts very dark grey; underwing-coverts white, axillaries and bases of remiges greyish; tail rather long, slightly graduated, with rectrices rather narrow for the genus, greenish-black; bill yellow, noticeably shorter than those of congeners; iris dark, bare dark skin by eye; feet blackish. Immature slightly duller black than adult, white areas somewhat sullied, culmen ridge dusky. VOICE. Song consists of full melodious lengthy phrases in choruses, typically including a frequently repeated "wheekit-wheeyk, wheekit-wheeyk...".

Habitat. Occupies subcanopy and understorey of humid forest, transitional forest, and second growth or borders at forest openings; also *terra firme* borders, second-growth woodland, and overgrown clearings with scattered trees; bamboo stands in SW Amazonia. Largely replaced inside lowland *terra firme* forest by *M. morphoeus* and in *várzea* by *M. nigrifrons*. In Colombia, mainly occurs in or near foothills, ranging up to 1400 m; in Ecuador, usually below 400 m, but locally up to 750 m.

Food and Feeding. Details of diet not recorded. Appears to forage more in air, less at substrates, than congeners, also showing stronger tendency to perch on exposed branches high up at forest edge.

Breeding. No information.

Movements. Presumably resident.

Status and Conservation. Not globally threatened. Considered to be rather local in Colombia, although observations there suggest that it is extremely easy to overlook; occurs in Amacayacu National Park. Uncommon and local in Ecuador. Rather rare in Peru, where observed at Tingo María and in the area around Iquitos. Reckoned to be comparatively rare throughout its range, but this may be due to this species' unobtrusive habits and the consequent difficulties of detecting its presence.

Bibliography. Allen (1995), Angehr & Aucca (1997), Best et al. (1997), Borrero (1960), Clements & Shany (2001), Cory (1919), Donahue (1994), Gyldenstolpe (1951), Hilty & Brown (1986), Meyer de Schauensee (1982), Olrog (1968), Parker et al. (1982), Ridgely & Greenfield (2001), Ridgely et al. (1998), Rodner et al. (2000), Ruschi (1979), Salaman et al. (1999), Sick (1993), Snethlage (1914), Stotz et al. (1996), Taylor (1995), Willis (1982b).

Genus *CHELIDOPTERA*   Gould, 1837

35. Swallow-winged Puffbird

Chelidoptera tenebrosa

French: Barbacou à croupion blanc   **German**: Schwalbenfaulvogel   **Spanish**: Buco Golondrina
Other common names: Swallow-wing

Taxonomy. *Cuculus tenebrosus* Pallas, 1782, Surinam.
Three subspecies recognized.
Subspecies and Distribution.
C. t. pallida Cory, 1913 - NW Venezuela.
C. t. tenebrosa (Pallas, 1782) - Venezuela (except NW), E Colombia and the Guianas S to E Ecuador, E Peru, Brazil (except SE) and N Bolivia.
C. t. brasiliensis P. L. Sclater, 1862 - coastal SE Brazil.

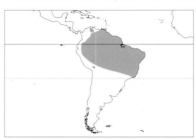

Descriptive notes. 14-15 cm; 30-41·5 g. Sooty-black overall with some bluish iridescence above; lower back to uppertail-coverts white; wings long and pointed, tertials large; tail short, square, broad, black with small pale tips when fresh; chin whitish and throat greyish, with long hair-like feathers; breast grading from black to grey, orange-chestnut band on lower underparts, white undertail-coverts; underwing-coverts and axillaries white; bill black; iris dark brown; feet dark grey or black. Immature resembles adult. Race *brasiliensis* large, more ochraceous lower underparts below whitish band, rather variable rufescent tint to rump, underwing-coverts, axillaries and undertail-coverts; *pallida* paler below, with well-marked whitish band between black breast and chestnut abdomen. VOICE. Twittering song often given in flight; calls include "tsi-tsi-tsi" and high clear "di-didi dí-didi dí-didi...".

Habitat. Optimum breeding habitat appears to be open areas with sandy soils and scattered bushes surrounded by forest, but also recorded from open tree and shrub savannas, clearings, edges of transitional forest, second-growth and deciduous forest, scrub, roadside trees, river margins, *várzea*, riverine and gallery forest in *llanos*; typically perches in riverside emergents and lake-margin trees. Lowlands, chiefly below 1000 m, rarely to 1750 m.

Food and Feeding. Takes relatively slow-moving, small to medium-sized flying insects, including Hymenoptera (Apidae, Meliponinae, Formicidae), Coleoptera (once "stink bugs", apparently referring to beetles), Homoptera (Fulgoridae), Heteroptera, Orthoptera, Isoptera, Diptera; targets termite emergences and winged ants. Captures aerial insects in rapid level or upward sorties from exposed branches. Prey usually swallowed in flight.

Breeding. Jan-Jun and Nov in Venezuela; Jul-Dec and Mar-Apr in Surinam; Aug-Nov in French Guiana. Nest in oblique tunnel dug usually in flat sandy ground, but often in earth bank, frequently near river; commonly takes advantage of man-made openings and embankments, such as airstrip, railway cutting or roadside. Clutch 1-2 eggs; incubation 15 days; fledging period not documented.

Movements. Presumably resident.

Status and Conservation. Not globally threatened. Best characterized in general as locally common, since it occurs patchily within its range, according to habitat availability. In Brazil, common in much of Amazonas, Pará and Mato Grosso, yet reported as uncommon to common in Rondônia, and noted as rare at a study plot in Manaus. Uncommon to quite common in Ecuador. Fairly common generally in Peru, but uncommon in Tambopata Reserve. Fairly common in Bolivia. Presumably benefits from opening-up of continuous forest: for example, the species was recently reported to be abundant along the Trans-Amazonian Highway by Tapajós National Park, in W Pará, Brazil, with 1-4 birds perched atop trees seemingly every few 100 m; and in Surinam it is common along the railway S from Paramaribo wherever it cuts through forest.

Bibliography. Allen (1995), Borges (1994), Burton (1976), Cherrie (1916), Cory (1919), Donahue (1994), Dubs (1992), Friedmann (1948), Friedmann & Smith (1950), Gyldenstolpe (1945a, 1951), Haverschmidt (1950), Haverschmidt & Mees (1994), Hellebrekers (1942), Hellmayr (1929), Henriques & Oren (1997), Hilty & Brown (1986), Meyer de Schauensee & Phelps (1978), Novaes & Lima (1992b), Oren & Parker (1997), Parker et al. (1982), Pearce-Higgins (2000), Peres & Whittaker (1991), Pinto (1947), Pinto & Camargo (1961), Ridgely & Greenfield (2001), Robinson (1997), Robinson & Terborgh (1997), Sargeant & Wall (1996), Schubart et al. (1965), Scott & Brooke (1985), Sick (1993), Skutch (1948c), Snethlage (1908, 1914), Snyder (1966), Stotz et al. (1996), Thiollay (1992), Tostain (1980), Tostain et al. (1992), Traylor (1958), Willis & Oniki (1990).

Order PICIFORMES

Piciformes

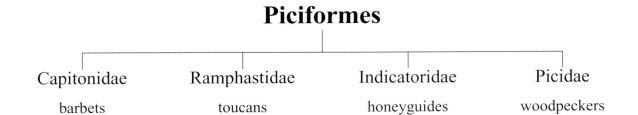

Capitonidae	Ramphastidae	Indicatoridae	Picidae
barbets	toucans	honeyguides	woodpeckers

Class AVES
Order PICIFORMES
Family CAPITONIDAE (BARBETS)

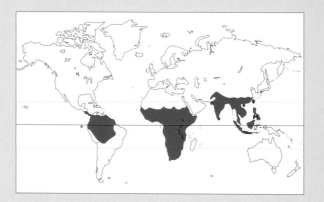

- Small to moderately large, robust arboreal birds with strong bill and sharp claws.
- 9-35 cm.

- Pantropical, with greatest diversity in Afrotropical.
- Forest, woodland and scrub.
- 13 genera, 82 species, 214 taxa.
- 1 species threatened; none extinct since 1600.

Systematics

Fossils provide little help in determining the relationships of the barbets (Capitonidae) with other avian families. Indeed, fossilized wood cavities from the Eocene, ascribed to early woodpeckers (Picidae), could have been excavated by ancestral barbets. Miocene barbets are known from Florida and, interestingly, from Europe. The genus *Capitonides* from the latter region seems very close to modern ground barbets of the African genus *Trachyphonus*, which nowadays occur only south of the Sahara.

Despite the lack of useful fossil information, it is widely agreed that the barbets are closely related to the toucans (Ramphastidae), and that both of these families are close to the honeyguides (Indicatoridae) and the woodpeckers, all four belonging in the order Piciformes. Traditionally, the jacamars (Galbulidae) and the puffbirds (Bucconidae) have been placed in this same order, although their marked differences from the remainder that have led to their frequently being partitioned off in a separate suborder, Galbulae. Current opinion, backed up by both morphological and biochemical studies, goes still further and concludes that they are almost certainly not piciform, calling instead for their isolation in a separate order, Galbuliformes; this is the arrangement adopted herein (see page 74).

The barbets are short-necked, large-headed, strong-billed and sturdy birds. They develop rapidly within the egg, hatch featherless, with the eyes closed, in a cavity nest, and then develop more slowly until they fledge. Barbets are less specialized and more generalized than are the toucans, honeyguides and woodpeckers, although sharing many features with them, notably including the zygodactyl foot and its "sehnenhalter" arrangement. Most capitonids are the epitome of the efficient frugivore, consuming much fruit, and regulating their activities around current sources of fruit.

The classification of the barbets is somewhat controversial. Some authorities treat them as a single family; others combine them all in one family together with the toucans, and still others separate them continentally at the family level, with the Neotropical barbets and the toucans then lumped in one family. The last two of these treatments are provisional, cladistic classifications that stress the points of branching of the various groups in time. It may be considered preferable to adopt an evolutionary approach, giving due consideration to the branching of the various groups, but also to their divergence. In fact, barbets are clearly identifiable as such on all continents. It is generally accepted that their close relatives, the toucans, are derived from an ancestor in common with American barbets, from which they have diverged. The toucans then evolved a suite of characters unique to them, and all are closely similar and differ from barbets, as E. Höfling has shown: toucans are toucans, not large barbets. Their divergence and speciation are therefore recognized by treating the toucans as a separate family from the Capitonidae. Aside from this matter, and the relative taxonomic rank of the included taxa, there seems no reason to dispute the classification of the barbets presented by R. O. Prum, or the arrangement and order of the family-level taxa given by Prum and, in earlier works, by E. V. Swierczewski and R. J. Raikow and by P. J. K. Burton.

The barbets are the second most numerous of the piciform families after the woodpeckers, and are considered by Burton the least specialized of these families. Seven of the 13 genera and half of the 82 species are Afrotropical and, curiously, they outnumber the woodpeckers in that region. Tropical Asia and America each have three genera, with 26 Asian species, mostly in the genus *Megalaima*, while 15 species occupy tropical America, and in both regions they are greatly outnumbered by woodpeckers. The Neotropical barbets are strictly tropical, with but two species some-

Only very few of the currently listed species of barbet remained unknown to science into the twentieth century, the last being described in 1921, until the startling discovery of the very distinctive Scarlet-belted Barbet in July 1996, on a remote range of hills in north central Peru; the species was formally described only in 2000. It is apparently fairly common at the type locality, but its known range is so tiny that the overall population is possibly small, and the species probably deserves to be treated as threatened.

[*Capito wallacei*, Cordillera Azul, Loreto, Peru. Photo: Dan Lane]

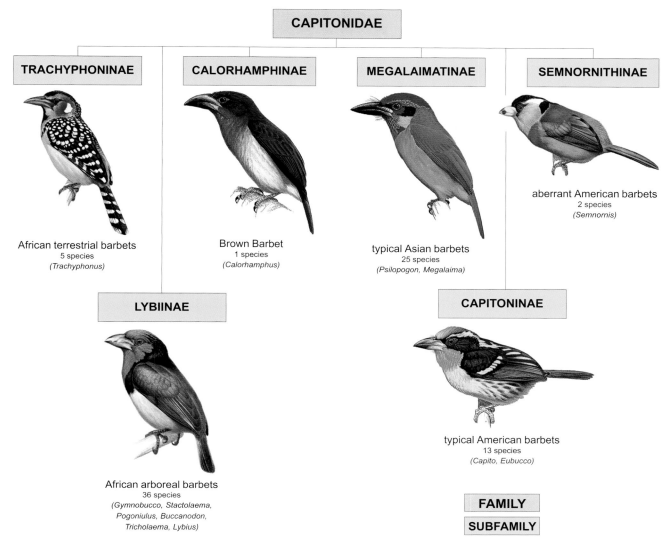

CAPITONIDAE

TRACHYPHONINAE

African terrestrial barbets
5 species
(*Trachyphonus*)

CALORHAMPHINAE

Brown Barbet
1 species
(*Calorhamphus*)

MEGALAIMATINAE

typical Asian barbets
25 species
(*Psilopogon, Megalaima*)

SEMNORNITHINAE

aberrant American barbets
2 species
(*Semnornis*)

LYBIINAE

African arboreal barbets
36 species
(*Gymnobucco, Stactolaema, Pogoniulus, Buccanodon, Tricholaema, Lybius*)

CAPITONINAE

typical American barbets
13 species
(*Capito, Eubucco*)

FAMILY

SUBFAMILY

Subdivision of the Capitonidae.

[Figure: Ian Lewington & Tim Worfolk]

Although the present treatment of the family recognizes 82 species, there are various divergent subspecies that are often considered species in their own right. One of these is "Woodward's Barbet", a race of the Green Barbet with two disjunct populations, one in Tanzania and the other in South Africa. Although this form differs from other races of Green Barbet in the intensity of yellow behind the eye and the ridged bill, it is approached morphologically by some of these races and is vocally identical to them.

[*Stactolaema olivacea woodwardi*, Ngoye Forest, Natal, South Africa. Photo: Nico Myburgh]

times reaching the temperate zone of mountains. Asian barbets penetrate temperate parts of the Himalayas, and reach the temperate edge of lowland China. Afrotropical barbets occur to near the limit of trees in mountains, and extend into temperate South Africa.

In each of the three regions in which they occur, the barbets can be seen to form a number of distinctive groups. These constitute a total of six subfamilies, which could equally be regarded as tribes. Within Africa, the distinctive Trachyphoninae contains the five species of *Trachyphonus*, and the Lybiinae includes six closely interrelated genera and 36 species. Trachyphoninae once ranged at least into Europe, and today penetrates the southern fringe of the Sahara. Uniquely plumaged with spots and yellow, red, orange, black, pink and white markings, its members include three ground barbets of open to near-desert habitats. Two species show a unique plumage dimorphism between the sexes. Ground barbets burrow into earthen banks, into termite mounds, and even vertically into level ground. Pair-members duet and, except for the Crested Barbet (*Trachyphonus vaillantii*), the male and the female sing different duet songs. The only forest-dwelling species, the Yellow-billed Barbet (*Trachyphonus purpuratus*), is a bird of dense undergrowth, also feeding on the ground. These are among the most insectivorous of barbets, but they eat fruit as well.

The Lybiinae has two genera of forest barbets, *Gymnobucco* and *Buccanodon*, but most species of the other four genera occur in woodland, bushland and scrub. The four bristle-headed, often bare-faced species of *Gymnobucco* are the most social, and the most dull-coloured, of barbets. Much of their life centres around the colony, which ranges from small to 200-pairs strong, in dead forest trees. The barely separable *Stactolaema*, differing from *Gymnobucco* in having less of a keel on the culmen and in a trend towards yellow and white in the pattern of the head, is comprised of four woodland species, green to brown or black in colour, with

calls and songs similar to those of *Gymnobucco*. Some maintain anvils at which they break up insects before feeding them to the young. All are social species, and often have helpers.

The nine small tinkerbirds of the genus *Pogoniulus* live in forest, woodland and scrubland, eating fruits that include, nota-

Most barbets are brightly coloured, and all have stout, pointed bills. Although there are notable differences in shape, size and coloration, all in all barbets are immediately recognizable as such throughout their distribution. The family occupies three continents, each of which holds two endemic subfamilies, one moderately large and one small: in South America, the larger subfamily, Capitoninae, illustrated here by the Black-spotted Barbet, and Semnornithinae, with only two species; in tropical Asia, 25 species of Megalaimatinae, here represented by the Red-throated Barbet, but only a single species in Calorhamphinae; and in Africa, the more speciose Lybiinae, including the Spot-flanked Barbet, together with the five species of Trachyphoninae. These geographical pairings of subfamilies have been treated by some recent authors as three distinct families, but there are serious problems with this course, particularly in that it is far from clear that any of the three pairings would group together taxonomically closest relatives: Semnornithinae does not appear to have any very close relatives, and shows no notable link with Capitoninae; Calorhamphinae is thought perhaps to have originated in Africa from an ancestral member of Lybiinae, and seems much closer to this subfamily than to Megalaimatinae; while Trachyphoninae is possibly of European rather than African origin, and shows no particular connection with Lybiinae.

[Above left: *Capito niger punctatus*, Morona-Santiago, Ecuador. Photo: Doug Wechsler/ VIREO.

Above right: *Megalaima mystacophanos mystacophanos*. Photo: John Wightman/ Ardea.

Below: *Tricholaema lacrymosa lacrymosa*. Photo: M. D. England/ Ardea]

Not all barbets are brightly coloured. The four species in the African genus Gymnobucco, for example, including the Grey-throated Barbet pictured here, are rather dull, with bristled heads and a tendency towards bare faces. They are also unusually social, spending much of their lives in the vicinity of colonies containing up to 200 pairs in dead forest trees.

[Gymnobucco bonapartei cinereiceps. Photo: E. & D. Hosking/ FLPA]

The Great Barbet is the largest member of the family, possessing a very bulky and unusually pale bill. Like the other twenty-three species in the Asian genus Megalaima, it is essentially green with patches of red and black. This species is less striking than most, however, with a much less complicated pattern of coloration on the head. In an interesting convergence with many of the Neotropical toucans, the undertail-coverts are red.

[Megalaima virens virens. Photo: Kenneth W. Fink]

bly, mistletoe berries, as well as insects. Spotted and striped, with patches of black, yellow, red and white, tinkerbirds are solitary and nest in pairs, excavating tiny cavities in trees for nesting and roosting. They have a broad repertoire of vocalizations, but most sing with piping or popping notes. One form, known only from its type from Zambia and previously considered a full species, with the name "*Pogoniulus makawai*", is now generally accepted as representing an odd variant of the Yellow-rumped Tinkerbird (*Pogoniulus bilineatus*). The monotypic genus *Buccanodon* shows anatomical differences from species of *Pogoniulus*, and it connects that genus with *Tricholaema*. Larger than tinkerbirds, it is a forest frugivore that congregates at fruiting trees, and its purring song is unlike those of other barbets. The six species of *Tricholaema* differ from all the above-mentioned Afrotropical genera in having a single notch and "tooth" on each maxillary tomium, and occasionally a smaller second tooth, although the White-eared Barbet (*Stactolaema leucotis*) shows tendencies towards this. One *Tricholaema* species is a forest denizen, while the others occur in woodland to near-desert scrub conditions, and in general they are not social. They have a striped head, and distinctive, loud, hooting and nasal "nyah" songs. Two species are sexually dimorphic, the Hairy-breasted Barbet (*Tricholaema hirsuta*) in the shade of yellow of the dorsal spots, and the Spot-flanked Barbet (*Tricholaema lacrymosa*) in eye colour.

The largest genus of Afrotropical barbets is *Lybius*, with twelve species falling into two groups. All have one or two strong teeth on the tomia, and the largest species possesses ridges and grooves on the bill. Only the Double-toothed Barbet (*Lybius bidentatus*) penetrates forest, where it enters the undergrowth; like its Sahelian relatives the Bearded Barbet (*Lybius dubius*) and the Black-breasted Barbet (*Lybius rolleti*), it exhibits sexual dimorphism in its white lateral patch below, this being clear white in males and spotted black in females. Related to these three are the Brown-breasted (*Lybius melanopterus*) and the Black-backed Barbets (*Lybius minor*), the females of which occasionally have spots on the sides. All five have squawky calls or "songs", or emit a trilled song. The seven remaining *Lybius* species are social, occurring mainly in groups of three to eight individuals. They sing in duets, and have elaborate, noisy greeting ceremonies that may precede a more or less intersexual duet by the primary pair. All seven are patchily coloured, often with black, white, red and yellow patterns.

Of the two tropical Asian subfamilies, the social Calorhamphinae, with its single, monotypic genus *Calorhamphus*, is dully coloured but showing some pinkish and bristle-like feathers on the crown. Somewhat resembling African *Gymnobucco* in its

keeled basal culmen, it has unique features of the palate and has facial bristles only on the chin. Like those of several other Asian barbets, its legs are reddish. It is further characterized by sexual dimorphism in bill colour and by its odd, squealing calls.

The Megalaimatinae is the other Asian subfamily, containing the monotypic genus *Psilopogon* and 24 largely green species of *Megalaima*. These exhibit features of the skull that demarcate them, and a laterally swollen base of the maxilla; the mandibular gonys shows a pronounced upward curve. The bristly feathers around the base of the bill are longer than those of any other barbets, some extending beyond the tip of the bill. *Psilopogon* is closely related to the "*virens* group" of *Megalaima*. In its hindcrown sexual marking and the "hash-mark" on its bill, as well as its very lax plumage, it displays some resemblance to American *Semnornis*. Its graduated tail and the location of facial bristles in distinct nasal tufts are other characteristics.

Megalaima is a rather uniform genus, with blue and, especially, green as important colours, these colours not being significant in the Afrotropical barbets. The two-dozen species average larger than the American or African barbets; indeed, the Great Barbet (*Megalaima virens*) is the largest of all capitonids, falling within the size range of the smaller toucanets (*Aulacorhynchus*). The Great Barbet and the almost equally large Red-vented Barbet (*Megalaima lagrandieri*) share some features, such as a tendency for tuft arrangement of facial bristles, semi-lax plumage, and aspects of head colour. The remaining *Megalaima* species can conveniently be separated into five groups. The first of these includes streaky, large barbets, namely the Brown-headed (*Megalaima zeylanica*), Lineated (*Megalaima lineata*) and White-cheeked Barbets (*Megalaima viridis*) and, probably, the Green-eared Barbet (*Megalaima faiostricta*). A group of particularly heavy-billed barbets restricted to South-east Asia comprises the Brown-throated (*Megalaima corvina*), Gold-whiskered (*Megalaima chrysopogon*), Red-crowned (*Megalaima rafflesii*), Red-throated (*Megalaima mystacophanos*) and Black-banded Barbets (*Megalaima javensis*), all showing the many-patched, colourful head pattern of the remainder of the genus. The Red-throated is the only Asian barbet with very marked sexual dimorphism in head colours, the sexes appearing like separate species. The central group of the genus contains nine moderate-sized, typical *Megalaima* species with a complex head pattern: the Yellow-fronted (*Megalaima flavifrons*), Golden-throated

The Yellow-spotted Barbet is intermediate in size and structure between another two African genera, Pogoniulus and Tricholaema. However, it shows anatomical differences from both of these groups, and its purring song is vocally unique. It is therefore classified alone in the monotypic genus Buccanodon.

[Buccanodon duchaillui. Photo: E. & D. Hosking/ FLPA]

(*Megalaima franklinii*), Black-browed (*Megalaima oorti*), Blue-throated (*Megalaima asiatica*), Moustached (*Megalaima incognita*), Mountain (*Megalaima monticola*), Yellow-crowned (*Megalaima henricii*), Flame-fronted (*Megalaima armillaris*) and Golden-naped Barbets (*Megalaima pulcherrima*). The little Blue-eared (*Megalaima australis*) and Bornean Barbets (*Megalaima eximia*) are derived from the last group. Finally, the Crimson-throated Barbet (*Megalaima rubricapillus*) and the ubiquitous Coppersmith Barbet (*Megalaima haemacephala*) are small, red-footed species with an intricate head pattern. The well-known Coppersmith is the only non-forest capitonid of tropical Asia, and is the most widely distributed, occurring from Pakistan and Sri Lanka across to China and the Philippines. The songs of all of these barbets tend to be of short phrases or single notes, or of short trills, loud and repeated over long periods, making them characteristic sounds of the tropical Asian forest. As many as seven species occur sympatrically in Malaysia, the highest degree of sympatry among any congeneric barbets.

As in the two tropical Old World regions, there are two subfamilies in the Neotropics, but with many fewer species. The Capitoninae has two genera, *Capito* of nine species and *Eubucco* of four, with several anatomical specialities; and, unlike Old World barbets and many toucans, most are strongly sexually dimorphic. Very much restricted to the tropics are the black, brown, yellow, red, orange and white species of *Capito*. Some, such as the Spot-crowned (*Capito maculicoronatus*) and the Five-coloured Barbets (*Capito quinticolor*), rather closely resemble Afrotropical species of *Tricholaema*, and the White-mantled Barbet (*Capito hypoleucus*) suggests the central African Black-backed of the genus *Lybius*, but *Capito* has no notch-tooth on the tomium. The striking Scarlet-belted Barbet (*Capito wallacei*) was discovered as recently as in 1996, on an isolated plateau in north-central Peru. The *Capito* species are essentially non-social, gathering only at fruiting trees; their songs are of low hooting or popping notes in series, sometimes as a trill in the manner of *Tricholaema* barbets. Longer-tailed *Eubucco*, the other capitonine genus, contains four smaller species, most inhabiting Andean-cordilleran slopes of Middle to northern South America; in this genus, the females are markedly different from the respective males in the colour around the head to breast, such that some females were initially described as separate species. The lowland Lemon-throated Barbet (*Eubucco richardsoni*), along with the Black-girdled (*Capito dayi*) and Cinnamon-breasted Barbets (*Capito brunneipectus*), occurs in south-western Amazonia east only to the central Amazon Basin south of the River Amazon. No barbet reaches central-eastern and south-eastern Brazil or Paraguay, and all are forest species.

The final subfamily, the Semnornithinae, with the one genus *Semnornis*, is unique among all piciform and near-piciform birds in having the bill tip pronged above, the prong fitting into a notch in the tip below. The bill is "swollen" laterally at its base, and is relatively the shortest of all barbet bills. The genus contains two montane species of southern Central America and north-western South America. Both species exhibit sexual dimorphism involving glossy black, erectile nape feathers, recalling the Asian *Psilopogon*. The dully coloured Prong-billed Barbet (*Semnornis frantzii*) and the gaudy Toucan-barbet (*Semnornis ramphastinus*) readily "bite" out nesting cavities with the special bill tip, and sing or duet in series of deep honking or popping notes.

It is curious that the larger barbets in Africa and Asia show no convergence towards the toucans. Existing American barbets are recognizably capitonids, as has been remarked upon by C. G. Sibley and J. E. Ahlquist, and by S. M. Lanyon and J. G. Hall. Toucans are not merely very large barbets, but have evolved their own unique array of characters, including those of skull, bill, tongue, tail vertebrae, feather structure, patterns of sexual dimorphism, and large, colourful bare areas of the head and a lack of rictal and chin bristles, as well as sleeping posture, predatory habits and other features. In all of these they differ more from the barbets than the various groups of barbets differ among themselves.

Finally, it is also worth noting a major stumbling-block for those who would recognize three barbet families, one for each of their continents. Of the pairs of subfamilies present on each continent, it is far from clear that any geographical pairing would link closest relatives: there is no evidence of any close relation between the Trachyphoninae and the Lybiinae; Calorhamphinae does not appear to be particularly close to Megalaimatinae, and may in fact be closer to Lybiinae; and Semnornithinae does not appear to be very closely related to Capitoninae. In consequence, a continental split into three families would seem decidedly ill-advised.

Morphological Aspects

Barbets have a stout, pointed bill that is usually shorter than the head, and is not compressed laterally, but in many cases is as

The four brightly coloured members of the genus *Eubucco* live in the forests of South and Central America, principally on the slopes of the Andean cordillera. Sexual dimorphism is generally not strongly marked in barbets, but it is particularly pronounced in this genus, as illustrated by these Versicoloured Barbets, the male above and the female below. Indeed, in the case of the Red-headed Barbet (*Eubucco bourcierii*), the male and female were initially described on consecutive pages of the same publication as separate species! The four *Eubucco* barbets have a slenderer, sharper bill than their closest relatives, the *Capito* barbets; they also show a longer tail and a different standard plumage pattern.

[*Eubucco versicolor versicolor*, Manu National Park, Peru. Photos: David Tipling/ Windrush (above); David Tipling/VIREO (below)]

wide as it is deep. The culmen curves downwards, from slightly to markedly so, and the gonys is straight or curves upwards. The edges of the bill, the tomia, are smooth to irregular; two of the African genera have a notch and one or two "teeth". The bill of all capitonids is sufficiently sturdy to allow the excavation of nesting cavities. The relatively short tongue is more or less brushy at the tip. Around the bill, there are short to very long nasal and rictal bristles, or at least chin bristles. The neck is short, to the extent that barbets often appear "neckless", the head being closely applied to the body as in the puffbirds, the rollers (Coraciidae) and the broadbills (Eurylaimidae). The short to occasionally long, rarely graduated tail has ten rectrices, and the rounded wings have ten primaries. The oil-gland is naked or tufted, with two lobes and a modest papilla. The palate, the skull, and the leg skeleton vary somewhat. The hair-like villi of the downy breast-feather barbules are relatively short and not strongly recurved. The bare skin around the orbit is small to moderate in extent, and usually not brightly or multicoloured, while in all genera but *Gymnobucco* the face and gular skin are feathered.

Certain structural features of the skull and palate, the musculature, and the rather long, thin bill are characters of the Trachyphoninae that set them apart from other barbets. These Afrotropical species also have long legs and a rather long, graduated tail. A slight to strong crest characterizes these species, which also have modest rictal bristles, as do most Afrotropical barbets except for *Gymnobucco* and some *Lybius* species. Among the Lybiinae, which also exhibit particular skull characters, a strongly ridged culmen typifies *Gymnobucco*, this feature being weaker in *Stactolaema*, and even less marked but still present in *Pogoniulus*. The last genus has a tufted oil-gland, a short tail and a short first toe. *Buccanodon* has a longer first toe and tail, and a naked oil-gland, like *Tricholaema*, but it lacks the "tooth" of the latter. Members of *Tricholaema* tend to have hair-tipped feathers on the throat to breast, as do a few species of *Lybius* and *Capito*. *Lybius* barbets are generally larger than the others, with a heavier, more toothed bill.

In Asia, the single species in the Calorhamphinae, the Brown Barbet (*Calorhamphus fuliginosus*), has particularities of palate structure, perhaps responsible for its peculiar voice, as well as a ridge on the culmen, bristles only on the chin, reddish legs, and an unswollen base of the bill. The two genera in the Megalaimatinae, *Psilopogon* and *Megalaima*, have distinct features

of the skull and an expanded base of the maxilla on both sides. Strong bristles, a basically green plumage, which is also rather soft, and harlequin-like head markings characterize these barbets. The bill in profile is doubly convex, and varies among species mainly in length and stoutness.

The American subfamily Capitoninae has characteristic skull traits, less pronounced bristles than Asian barbets, a rather short tail, smooth bill tomia, and no bulging of the bill base. *Capito* tends to have a ridge across the culmen that may be flat at its base, and the outer primary is narrow and short. *Eubucco* has a more slender bill, a broad, short outer primary, and a longer tail than *Capito*, as well as a different plumage pattern. The two distinctive barbets that make up the subfamily Semnornithinae have a very short, doubly convex bill with a pronged tip, this being possibly related to the fact that they may be more frugivorous on the whole than are the members of the subfamily Capitoninae. They share some anatomical features with certain other barbets, in addition to which they have a particularly lax plumage. Compared with the Capitoninae, the two *Semnornis* species have a longer tail that is slightly graduated, longer bristles about the bill, and nostrils that are located in grooves.

Juveniles of the barbets tend to be duller than adults, and with a more lax plumage. The patches of colour present on the adults of most species are often lacking on the juveniles, and appear only gradually. Young of the "tooth-billed" or "prong-billed" species lack those respective attributes for several months. Hatchling barbets are blind and naked, and rest on the abdomen and the two spike-scuted hypotarsi.

The moult patterns of the Capitonidae are not well known. Moult commences in the second half of the breeding season, usually with the innermost primary being shed first. The primaries are moulted outwardly; the secondaries are replaced both inwardly, from number 1, and in both directions, from secondary 7 or 8. Tail moult appears to vary greatly, even within groups, but many more data are needed for any definitive conclusions to be drawn. The most common pattern, perhaps, is for the tail feathers to be moulted from rectrix 2 or 4, both inwards towards the central one and outwards towards the outermost rectrix. In *Trachyphonus*, the tail moult may start with any feather or with two adjacent feathers, and proceed inwards from the outer feather, outwards from the inner, or in both directions, from rectrix 2, 3 or 4, or from 2 and 3, or from 3 and 4.

One of the most constant feature of barbets is the stout, relatively short, pointed bill that is not usually compressed laterally. The cutting edges of the bill vary from smooth to irregular, with the Bearded Barbet occupying the latter end of this continuum. Its mandibles are distinctly ridged and grooved and there are two strong "teeth" on the cutting edge of the upper mandible. This species lives in dry forest, open woodland and secondary growth in West Africa. As can be seen here, barbets sometimes use the tail as a prop, like the related woodpeckers, despite the fact that their tail feathers are much less tough.

[*Lybius dubius*, Gambia. Photo: Michael Gore]

Almost every patch of tall woodland in tropical Asia seems to be inhabited by one or more species of the genus Megalaima, most members of which have a striking head-pattern combining green, blue, black, yellow or red. This species, the Black-browed Barbet, lives in the Sundaic mountains where it is strongly tied to humid forest. Indeed, most of its congeners are humid forest birds, with a few preferring dry forest, and only one species, the Coppersmith Barbet (Megalaima haemacephala), tolerant of very sparsely wooded areas. Barbets are associated with forest principally because of their food supply and their nesting and roosting sites.

[Megalaima oorti oorti, Fraser's Hill, Malaysia. Photo: Morten Strange/ NHPA]

Habitat

A vital feature of habitats occupied by barbets is the presence of trees with sufficient dead wood in their branches, or dead trees or stumps, suitable for the excavation of nesting and roosting cavities. All barbets excavate such cavities and, so far as is known, roost in holes. Tropical Asian and American barbets are more or less confined to forest, mainly in the lowlands, but some species occupy lower and middle montane forest, and a few are found in temperate montane forest. These forest habitats are, for the most part, wet or humid, but some Asian barbets will at least forage in dry forest. One Asian species, the Coppersmith Barbet, is adapted for living in forest edges, woodland, scrub and gardens, and is therefore very widespread and common. Several American capitonids, particularly the Scarlet-crowned (*Capito aurovirens*) and Scarlet-hooded Barbets (*Eubucco tucinkae*), prefer dense undergrowth of river edges and islands in western Amazonia.

Afrotropical barbets are more varied in their choice of habitats. The Red-and-yellow (*Trachyphonus erythrocephalus*), Yellow-breasted (*Trachyphonus margaritatus*) and D'Arnaud's Barbets (*Trachyphonus darnaudii*) constitute the ground barbets, all three of which live in dry scrub or wooded grassland and are free of any dependence upon tree cavities, since they nest in the earth. Most of the arboreal species of other genera prefer wood-

The African barbets are more numerous, in terms of species, and less restricted to forest habitat than their Asian and South American cousins. Indeed, around half are birds of dry forest and semi-arid environments. The Red-and-yellow Barbet, for example, is most at home in the wooded savanna, rocky scrub and gardens of East Africa. Unlike most other barbets it is not constrained by the availability of tree cavities, because it nests in the ground.

[Trachyphonus erythrocephalus erythrocephalus, Tanzania. Photo: Tim Laman]

extent in upland forest or forest edge, and the remaining 21 are denizens of woodland, bushland, scrub and semi-open country. The difference in habitat preferences between the Afrotropical barbets and those in Asia and the Neotropics probably reflects the repeated fragmentation and very restricted occurrence of Afrotropical forest in the late Tertiary period, compared with the situation in tropical Asia and America.

The greatest degree of sympatry among barbets occurs in habitats in Malaysia, where up to seven species are found together, in parts of Zaire and Gabon, with up to eight or even nine species, and in western Amazonia, with three or possibly four species together. Generally, where congeneric species of barbet are concerned, the maximum number that seem capable of living sympatrically appears to be only two. The exceptions to this rule are *Gymnobucco*, with up to three species occurring together, *Pogoniulus*, with a maximum of four species, and especially *Megalaima*, with as many as five and, locally, seven co-existing species that may be separated ecologically by their foraging and feeding habitats. Sympatric species of *Megalaima* also differ appreciably from one another in size. Most congeneric barbets that are closely related do not occur in the same areas or, if they do, they are separated altitudinally, as in the cases of the Red-crowned and Gold-whiskered Barbets in Malaysia, and the Eastern Green (*Pogoniulus simplex*) and Moustached Green Tinkerbirds (*Pogoniulus leucomystax*) in East Africa. Where close relatives do meet and marginally overlap, they tend to be separated by micro-habitat and may defend territories against one another. Thus, in eastern Rwanda, the Black-collared Barbet (*Lybius torquatus*) and the Red-faced Barbet (*Lybius rubrifacies*) meet and overlap somewhat, interacting frequently, where the latter's rolling, wooded grassland habitat abuts the lakeside and riverine woodland favoured by the Black-collared Barbet.

Degradation of habitats adversely affects those barbets that prefer more wooded areas, and favours the species of more open woodland, bushland and "edge". In parts of upland Kenya, the formerly extensive highland woods and forest favoured by the Moustached Green Tinkerbird have become highly fragmented and, to a large extent, eliminated. Here, the Yellow-rumped Tinkerbird of highland-forest edge and woodland that is successful in thickets, edges of dense woods and gardens is common, but the lower-altitude Red-fronted Tinkerbird (*Pogoniulus pusillus*) that occupies bushland and open woodland has invaded

Barbets often perch in a characteristic fluffed-up posture, as adopted by this Crested Barbet, with the feathers of the upperparts and underparts partly or fully erected. This can be with the purpose of cooling down when the bird is hot; of drying out when wet; or to show off various colours during display.

[Trachyphonus vaillantii vaillantii, Kruger National Park, South Africa. Photo: Nigel Dennis/Bios]

land, although all four species of *Gymnobucco* are confined to forested habitats. The tiny tinkerbirds of the genus *Pogoniulus* inhabit forest, woodland and scrub, even in semi-deserts. The Yellow-spotted Barbet (*Buccanodon duchaillui*) is strictly a forest bird, as also is the Hairy-breasted Barbet, the latter being the only one of *Tricholaema* species occupying such habitats. Otherwise, only the Yellow-billed and Double-toothed Barbets extend into the dense understorey of forest, second growth and thickets. All told, of the 41 Afrotropical barbets, eight may be termed forest-restricted, four inhabit forest undergrowth, eight occur in woodland and to some

This Red-and-yellow Barbet is stretching its wings and erecting its neck feathers in the characteristic stance of sun-bathing birds. Barbets seem particularly fond of this activity, often spending regular periods sunning themselves early in the day, or especially after bathing or rainfall. Sun-bathing is often associated with other forms of comfort behaviour such as preening. Typically, paired birds or group members will allopreen between bouts of sunning.

[Trachyphonus erythrocephalus erythrocephalus, Olduvai Gorge, Tanzania. Photo: Mike Wilkes/ BBC Natural History Unit]

the area; although some separation by habitat remains, all three species overlap locally and can be heard singing by the stationary observer. Throughout tropical Asia, the elimination of forested areas continues; where regeneration and fragmentation occur, the barbets that are restricted to primary forest suffer fragmentation of their distribution, and only those species able to occupy patchy second growth may persist. Thus, in formerly forested Singapore, the Red-crowned Barbet, tolerant of second growth, is the only species of capitonid that remains, except for the fact that the Coppersmith Barbet, which invaded degraded forested country from northern Peninsular Malaysia within the twentieth century, had colonized Singapore by 1960, and is now the only common barbet there.

Even some barbets which are rather strictly limited to forest habitats do find and visit fruiting trees in pastures and village gardens, provided that some forest is nearby. This occurs perhaps most commonly in the Indian region, with its long history of human occupation and a tolerant attitude towards wildlife. Great, Brown-headed, Lineated and Crimson-throated Barbets may join Coppersmith Barbets at village fig trees to take ripening fruits, and they can become pests in orchards. Even in South America, Orange-fronted Barbets (*Capito squamatus*) feed in fruit trees in pastureland. Isolated trees alongside forest also attract such species as the Yellow-billed and Grey-throated Barbets (*Gymnobucco bonapartei*) in Africa, the Golden-throated in Asia, and the Black-spotted (*Capito niger*) and Prong-billed Barbets in America, the birds using the trees as nesting sites. A likely reason for this is that the trees, being isolated, are somewhat protected from arboreal snakes and mammalian predators, which cannot readily reach the nest-site directly.

Barbets have a relatively restricted vocabulary and are slow to tire of their own voice. This Blue-throated Barbet, like most others in its genus, sings with a short phrase of hollow notes, often with a more trilling introduction, and it can continue with an almost interminable rhythmical series, a familiar background sound in the forests of Asia. As these barbet species usually sing while motionless high in the tree-tops, they can be frustratingly difficult to see.

[Megalaima asiatica asiatica, Margalla Hills, Pakistan. Photo: Nigel Bean/ BBC Natural History Unit]

General Habits

Since their roosting cavities are usually excavated by the birds themselves, and are thus less subject to infestation by pests and parasites than are secondary cavities, barbets tend to rise only moderately early, and to retire rather early in the evening. Social barbets that roost in groups, such as the Red-and-yellow and Black-collared Barbets, gather to preen for a brief period shortly after they leave the hole in the morning, and then give a greeting ceremony followed by a duet. The social barbets, and even those that roost in pairs, may interact for a while, entering and leaving the roosting cavity several times, before settling in for the night. Near or at the equator, barbets may roost for eleven hours or more per day, and on rainy, cool days they may spend even longer in the cavity. Crimson-throated Barbets have been found to roost for an average of 12·5 hours daily, and the Coppersmith Barbet, which roosts singly, appears to spend an even greater part of the day roosting. Immatures that roost with their parents may return to the roost somewhat earlier than do the adults. Interactions of the occupants may prevent entry by very late-arriving young birds

The most complex vocalizations produced by barbets, and indeed any piciform birds, are given by members of the African genera Trachyphonus *and* Lybius. *These group-living species give loud choruses that initiate a synchronized duet performed by the primary pair. Calls in these species are sex-specific: this female Yellow-breasted Barbet, for example, is answering the whistled triplet of her mate with her own longer series of higher-pitched and shorter whistles.*

[Trachyphonus margaritatus somalicus, southern Danakil Desert, near Sardo, Ethiopia. Photo: Gertrud & Helmut Denzau]

While the song of the Coppersmith Barbet is one of the most familiar bird sounds in many parts of tropical Asia, it is not most popular. The rapid series of tapping "tok-tok" notes that gives this bird its vernacular name can be heard almost throughout the day, and sometimes throughout the night. So persistent and invariable is its delivery that it can drive an innocent bystander to distraction!

[*Megalaima haemacephala indica*, Keoladeo National Park, India. Photo: Manfred Pfefferle]

or helpers. One roosting hole of Prong-billed Barbets held 16 individuals on at least one occasion, and once 19.

Barbets living in more open country rest in shady bushes and trees during the heat of the day. The forest-dwelling species, however, forage for fruit all day long. The songs of barbets are often among the few that are uttered throughout the day; indeed, some capitonid species are numbered among the "brain-fever" birds, so called for the monotonous regularity with which their songs are delivered, and epitomized by certain of the cuckoos (Cuculidae). Most barbets drink water when they are able to do so, and may bathe in water-filled crevices in trees; the period

that a White-cheeked Barbet spends in a bout of bathing has been timed at up to eleven minutes. When a particular fruiting tree is laden with fruits, the movements of a barbet may be narrowly defined, between that tree and the individual bird's roosting site. During the breeding season, a pair of Moustached Green Tinkerbirds may nest and raise young on a territory less than 1 ha in size. The daily movements of other barbets, however, usually encompass much larger areas, with longer distances involved. Indeed, those species living in Sahelian Africa, such as the Yellow-breasted Barbet and Vieillot's Barbet (*Lybius vieilloti*), may forage over 1 km² or more in a day.

The complex repertoire of duet calls and group calls given by the D'Arnaud's Barbet varies racially and geographically. There are usually only two song-types given in duets by any given population, but these are not rigidly sex-specific with some individuals switching song-types. Interestingly, if one of the primary duetting pair is experimentally removed, another group member takes its place and sings the same song. These co-ordinated vocalizations probably function in maintaining group hierarchy, synchronizing breeding attempts, and mediating co-operative territory defence.

[*Trachyphonus darnaudii darnaudii*, Lake Bogoria, Kenya. Photo: Günter Ziesler]

Over anything more than very short distances, the flight of most barbets, especially that of the larger species, may be undulating, although it may vary, as, for example, when the bird is chased by a predator. The little *Pogoniulus* tinkerbirds fly in a direct line. Barbets are not particularly fast fliers, but some are faster than others. The Black-collared Barbet is speedier than *Stactolaema* species such as Anchieta's Barbet (*Stactolaema anchietae*); their relatives and nest parasites, the longer-winged honeyguides, can outfly these and other barbets.

Barbets may perch atop a bush or tree to sun themselves in the morning, and will also do so in order to dry their plumage following rains. Much preening may occur at such times. Paired birds preen one another, and some social species, such as the Brown-breasted Barbet, engage in allopreening among all members of a group. Bill-wiping is a frequent action when the birds are feeding on fruits (see Food and Feeding). Capitonids scratch the head directly, with one foot raised over a wing. Stretching movements are typical, with one leg and wing stretched on one side, then usually the other leg and wing, and then both wings, and this can be accomplished expertly by a barbet while hanging upside-down. Under hot conditions, and after vigorous activities such as chasing, barbets pant with the bill held open.

As a rule, piciforms tend to be aggressive, even belligerent, especially at food sources and around their nesting and roosting cavities. These birds' sturdy bill and stocky build, as well as their adroitness and strength in clinging and hanging to the bark, as when excavating a cavity, are probably factors relating to their pugnaciousness. Among the barbets, interspecific aggression is most evident in the breeding season, when "innocent" birds of species that are not nest-hole competitors are attacked without cause. Competition may be reflected in cases where larger barbet species have been seen to go out of their way to chase smaller barbets. In addition, Afrotropical barbets regularly, and at times for lengthy periods, become involved with honeyguides, which they recognize and may attack even outside the breeding period. Their belligerence renders them good mobbers of hawks (Accipitridae), owls (Strigidae) and terrestrial predators. Where intraspecific aggression is concerned, the non-social barbets are fiercely protective of their territories and react instantly to the presence and singing of any conspecific within a territory. These species are intolerant of others under captive conditions, and even within a pair aggression may preclude successful breeding. So-

cial barbets, too, defend home ranges or territories; those that sing in chorus and in duet tend to patrol their territorial borders, performing greeting ceremonies and responding instantly to neighbouring groups of their own species when the latter call.

During encounters, barbets use a great range of visual and auditory displays, many involving the head and bill. When an individual is faced with a prospective antagonist, the position of the head is important, a fact rarely appreciated by observers. Most capitonids have a head that is patterned, even spectacularly so in some species of *Megalaima*, *Eubucco* and *Tricholaema*, among others. As a result, signals presented with the head and bill upwards, enhancing the malar, throat and chin feathers and obscuring the crown and upper face, as opposed to downwards, emphasizing the often erected feathers of the forehead to nape and supercilia and obscuring the ventral head pattern, are important, and the bill itself covers part of the display patterning. Bill-pointing, gaping, stilted bill-wiping and bill-snapping are included among the displays of one barbet species or another. The tail is drooped or, often so in males, cocked; rarely, it is spread, as in the case of duetting D'Arnaud's Barbets. The wings may be rapidly flicked, or spread or waved, and interactions usually involve loud, rustling wing sounds in chases and when one individual supplants another. The rump feathers are sometimes spread; often partly erected, they typically extend out over the tail base, then producing a rather characteristic barbet silhouette, one which is, incidentally, also typical of a honeyguide. In some barbets, the rump is brightly coloured and shows well when fluffed. The breast feathers may be fluffed, showing off colours and particular patterns, such as the red lateral spots of some species of *Megalaima*, or the coloured hair-tipped feathers of the Black-throated Barbet (*Tricholaema melanocephala*) and the Yellow-billed Barbet. In a few cases, the flanks and sides are important, and these feathers may be spread to show colour patches, as in the Spot-crowned Barbet, emphasizing sexual markings as in the "*bidentatus* group" of *Lybius*, or simply contrasting with the dark thigh colours as in the Brown-breasted Barbet. Considering the prevalence of red undertail feathering in the toucans, it is worth noting the absence of a red undertail patch on American barbets; interestingly, such a patch is found in a few Old World species, such as the Asian Red-vented Barbet, and most notably in species of ground barbet.

Nobody could fail to be impressed with these various display patterns and colours, epitomized by the complex greeting

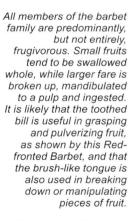

All members of the barbet family are predominantly, but not entirely, frugivorous. Small fruits tend to be swallowed whole, while larger fare is broken up, mandibulated to a pulp and ingested. It is likely that the toothed bill is useful in grasping and pulverizing fruit, as shown by this Red-fronted Barbet, and that the brush-like tongue is also used in breaking down or manipulating pieces of fruit.

[Tricholaema diademata massaica, Kenya. Photo: Michael Gore]

This Yellow-crowned Barbet is eating a forest fig (Ficus), *this fruit being its preferred item of diet. When an individual finds a rich source of food, such as one of the huge fruiting figs typical of mature Sundaic forests, it usually spends much of its time in and around the canopy of this tree. One study individual monitored over four days, ranged over an area of 7·5 ha, but spent 75% of its time at a* Ficus binnendykii *tree, and usually roosted nearby. At abundant sources of food, many barbets aggregate in substantial numbers. Up to 70 Coppersmith Barbets, for example, have been recorded in particularly suitable fruiting trees. This latter species eats a wide selection of fruit throughout its range, often preferring smaller varieties, as befits its modest size.*

[Above: *Megalaima henricii brachyrhyncha*, Gunung Palung National Park, Borneo. Photo: Tim Laman.

Below: *Megalaima haemacephala indica*, Kuala Selangor, Malaysia. Photo: Morten Strange/ NHPA]

The foraging and feeding techniques adopted by barbets are straightforward. Ripe fruits are plucked wherever they can be reached, sometimes snipped from their berth using the toothed bill, as the White-headed Barbet has undoubtedly done at this palm. Barbets' feet are strong, and when necessary the birds can cling acrobatically in various positions to reach fruit. Their neck is short and strong, a characteristic that presumably facilitates the removal of well-anchored fruit.

[*Lybius leucocephalus albicauda*, Masai Mara National Park, Kenya. Photo: Peter Craig-Cooper/ VIREO]

ceremonies of social groups of the array of duetting *Lybius* species, and of the Red-and-yellow Barbet. The position of dominance of an individual in the social hierarchy of a group is probably put forward in such intricate displays.

Competitive interplay between barbets is at its most obvious where larger species not only drive away smaller ones, but also enlarge the nesting or roosting holes of the latter, usually when these are somewhat close to their own cavities. Brown-headed Barbets enlarge and render unfit for use entrances to nests of nearby Coppersmith Barbets, and the Coppersmiths also are forced to abandon nests by Blue-throated Barbets. White-cheeked Barbets in India excavate into the nesting cavities of Crimson-throated Barbets and throw out any eggs or young that they find inside. These obvious acts suggest the existence of regular, strong competition among sympatric barbets, to the extent that it may have an influence on the particular micro-habitats used by different species, and such competition may enforce the altitudinal separation of capitonids where their ranges coincide.

Voice

Well-studied species of barbet have been shown to have a repertoire of seven to twelve calls, including the song, some of which are associated closely with visual displays. There are also non-vocal acoustic displays. Most barbets give relatively low-pitched "hoot", "hoop" or "pop" notes that may be repeated in short to long series as a song, uttered with the bill closed or nearly so. A few species, such as the Brown-breasted Barbet, utter squawks but have no apparent song. The most complex, even melodic songs are known from the genera *Trachyphonus* and *Lybius*. Many barbets sing throughout the year, and their songs provide a monotonous background sound characteristic of the habitat in which they live. Some smaller barbets, such as the tinkerbirds and the Black-throated Barbet, emit notes that are very loud for the size of the bird. There may be three or four calls restricted to the nestling and fledgling stages, and as many as four mechanical, non-vocal displays. The latter include bill-snapping, bill-wiping, bill-tapping associated with the nesting cavity, and wing-rustling by such species as Whyte's (*Stactolaema whytii*),

Anchieta's, Chaplin's (*Lybius chaplini*), White-headed (*Lybius leucocephalus*) and Red-faced Barbets.

Aggressive calls generally are noisy, and commonly include fast, chattery, squawky, honking, rattling, squeaky and grating sounds, usually repeated in short to long phrases and often compounded, as in a squeaky grating or a squeaky chatter.

It should be stressed that the full range of vocalizations of many capitonids remains unknown, this being especially true of Asian and some American species, for which the song may be all that has been reported. Particularly lacking is information on the usually softer, so-called "intimate" notes occurring during the interplay of the male and the female near the nest, and the soft interactive calls of adults and young. Additional information is required also with regard to the softer calls uttered in greeting ceremonies and the initial notes of choruses for those barbets in which they occur. For an understanding of the role of individuals and of the primary pair in choruses and greeting ceremonies, the soft notes and calls in choruses that do not lead to duets, compared with those that do initiate duets, appear to be important, and further knowledge of these would be particularly useful.

Some barbets have what appear to be alternate or secondary songs. The "pop-singing" tinkerbirds such as the Yellow-rumped have equally loud, faster pop notes in repeated trills, as do the Red-fronted and Yellow-fronted Tinkerbirds (*Pogoniulus chrysoconus*). These also give nasal, honking calls with short series of notes. In species of *Tricholaema*, there is a "hoop" song and also a "nyah" series; early in the breeding cycle, the male Red-fronted Barbet (*Tricholaema diademata*) seems to sing mainly "hoop" series as a song, sometimes answered by its mate's "nyah" "song"; later, however, a male may start with the "nyah" version, and then shift to the "hoop" version. In the Black-throated Barbet of drier, more open areas, the "hoop" song is replaced by the "kaaa" song, and the "nyah" by a "pyaw" or "ptaw" version, both noisier and harsher than in the Red-fronted Barbet, and uttered in shorter, staccato series.

The song has evolved into a faster trill of hoop-like notes in some species of *Capito* and in *Eubucco*, while in Africa it has become an even faster clicking trill in the Crested, Double-toothed and Black-backed Barbets and a purring trill in the Yellow-spot-

The Brown Barbet is an anomalous, dully coloured Asian barbet, separated in a monotypic subfamily on the basis largely of its unique palate morphology, the restriction of facial bristles to the chin, sexual dimorphism in bill colour and odd squealing vocalizations. Its diet consists largely of fruit although considerable quantities of insects are also eaten, and the stomachs of some specimens have been found to be replete with arthropods. It gathers its food, often socially, in a rather agile manner, as seen here, by hanging upside-down, tit-like, at clusters of fruit or flowers and at clumps of dead leaves. The Black-collared Barbet of Africa is also an agile and opportunistic forager, taking a wide variety of fruit, but also gleaning for insects in foliage, picking and probing along the bark of branches and twigs, or in lichen and termitaria. Like several other barbets, it has been recorded catching insects aerially by sallying out from a perch.

[Above: *Calorhamphus fuliginosus tertius*, Borneo.
Photo: Roland Seitre/Bios.

Below: *Lybius torquatus bocagei*, Chobe National Park, Botswana.
Photo: M. Watson/Ardea]

As is the case with other members of the Capitonidae, the Moustached Barbet, a species restricted to hill forest in South-east Asia, is quite often seen at flowers, probably because it sometimes drinks nectar but also because of the insect prey which can be found around inflorescences. Some species even squeeze flowers with their feet to extract the nectar.

[Megalaima incognita elbeli, Khao Yai National Park, Thailand. Photo: Mike Potts/ BBC Natural History Unit]

ted Barbet. Many Asian species of *Megalaima* have songs comprising various phrases of "tok" or "tuk" notes, the phrases being more or less species-specific. Some *Megalaima* species incorporate tiny trills into the song phrases, as do the Black-browed and Moustached Barbets; in others, a short trill may initiate the song, as in the Lineated Barbet, or there may be a separate trill song, as in the Red-crowned Barbet. The more hooping, popping or hooting songs seem ventriloquial, and may vary in volume simply as a result of the barbet turning its head as it sings.

The American barbets in general have simple hooting songs delivered at moderate speeds, in phrases, or as more or less rapid trills. The Spot-crowned Barbet is an exception, having a harsher song of "klaaak" notes. The two montane *Semnornis* species also sing simple songs of hoarse "kaw" or "awnk" notes in rapid or slow, long series, sometimes in duets. Their voices do not differ substantially from those of other barbets.

The complex, chorus-initiated duets of barbets of the genera *Trachyphonus* and *Lybius* are the most significant of capitonid and, indeed, of all piciform vocalizations. The sex-specific, different duet songs of male and female Black-billed (*Lybius guifsobalito*), Red-faced and Black-collared Barbets, which are synchronized, are melodic vocal productions, as are the equally complex, meshing songs uttered by pair-members of the three ground barbets, the Red-and-yellow, Yellow-breasted and D'Arnaud's. These songs appear to enable the primary pair to synchronize its breeding effort, to "control" the subordinate members of its social group, and to afford a co-ordinated mode of territorial maintenance throughout the year. The fact that these vocalizations evolved within the Afrotropical barbet groups, rather than among other groups, probably reflects the more open habitats, in which displaying barbets are easily visible, occupied by these non-forest genera.

In the chorus, the intricate weaving of different calls with such visual displays as swinging of the body and head, bowing, twisting and twitching or cocking of the tail, wing-flicking and wing-spreading, bill-snapping, erection of some feathers, as well as other gyrations, makes the *Trachyphonus* and *Lybius* barbets conspicuous. The barbets also turn, jump over one another, and parade before one another, and then generally freeze in place as the primary pair initiates the duet. In the ground barbets, the primary pair faces in directions appropriate to likely responses by neighbours, but the primary male and female also move to force

downwards in the bush or tree any subordinate group-member that attempts to hop upwards towards the level at which the primary pair sings its duet.

Food and Feeding

Well known as frugivorous birds, most capitonids have a mixed diet of animal and plant foods, with fruits predominating. All barbets, however, must of necessity exploit animal food when feeding the young immediately after the eggs hatch, when nutrients essential for growth and development are required. Barbets are sufficiently opportunistic as to shift to insectivory when there is a significant emergence of termites, with flying insects everywhere; it is thought very likely that poorly known barbets for which only fruits are reported as food will be found to sally for winged termites, or to pick them from leaves and branches, at times when these insects are briefly superabundant. The diets of many species are known from only few observations, and from stomach contents of specimens the collection dates of which do not cover all times of the year. An important observation that could be considered indicative of a degree of insectivory of a barbet species is its presence in the mixed-species foraging flocks of diverse insectivorous birds.

For the family as a whole, figs (*Ficus*), including strangler figs, are of major importance. In tropical Asia, several of these tree species, fruiting two or three times a year, may occur at a single site and substantially support local barbets. Plant families such as the Lauraceae, Moraceae and Melastomataceae are particularly important. Other major foods are fruits of the genera *Cecropia*, *Euterpe*, *Loranthus* and other mistletoes, *Macaranga*, *Micronia*, *Musanga*, *Ocotea*, *Prunus*, *Rauvolfia*, *Trema*, *Virola* and many others, of diverse families. Over 60 fruits of some 20 families of plants are eaten by the Toucan-barbet at one site. A few barbets gather in numbers, the Blue-eared Barbet sometimes occurring in flocks of 100 or more individuals at a single fruiting tree. The fruits exploited must be of an appropriate size for the open, extended mouth of the Capitonidae. Where there are barbet species of different sizes, the larger ones prefer larger fruits, it being more efficient to feed on these. Thus, several species of *Megalaima* of different sizes regularly occur together, as do the very heavy-billed Bearded Barbet and the smaller tooth-billed

Like many barbets, the Orange-fronted Barbet feeds at many levels in the forest, its movements governed mainly by the availability of ripe fruit. As it feeds, the indigestible remains of fruit are regurgitated, and in this way barbets play a major role in disseminating seeds away from the parent plants. The bird seen here feeding on Carludovica palmata *is a female, as evidenced by the pale scaling on the scapulars and upperwing-coverts. This species occupies a restricted range in the Chocó EBA of Pacific slope Colombia and Ecuador, where it is generally uncommon.*

[Capito squamatus, Río Palenque, Ecuador. Photo: X. Ferrer & A. de Sostoa]

Vieillot's Barbet in Sahelian Africa. The larger Black-spotted and the smaller Lemon-throated Barbet, belonging to two different genera, can also be found feeding alongside one another in South America.

Fruit stones (or pits) swallowed with a whole fruit are regurgitated. So far as is known, these stones are not left in the nest to form a carpet, as commonly occurs among the toucans. Interestingly, a barbet about to sing often regurgitates such indigestible items; playback of a barbet's song very frequently triggers regurgitation, as if the barbet were getting rid of an impediment before singing, or were moving as to seek out an "intruder". Smaller fruits are more rapidly digested, and their seeds and pits pass through the digestive system and are voided. Some tinkerbirds regurgitate sticky seeds of mistletoe berries and stick them about the tree surface next to their nest entrance, possibly to deter predators. Barbets are thus major dispersers of seeds of fruiting plants, and are thus important in maintaining the health of the ecosystems of which they are a constituent part. Plants dependent upon birds for seed dispersal may evolve larger fruits that are more likely to be digested and their seeds cast away from the tree or bush producing them. Plants have other dispersal strategies as well, these involving, for example, gradual ripening such that all fruits are not ready at once, or the location of the fruits on thin twiglets where they are difficult for individual birds to gather and eat in large numbers. Big fruits may require the barbets to take them apart: the bird has to seize a fruit, clasp it in the feet, and peck it, taking off pieces, all requiring effort and energy.

Fruits and vegetables readily eaten in cultivated orchards and plantations, and in captivity, are legion. They include apples, bananas, carrots, cherries, custard apples (*Annona*), dates, grapes and raisins, guavas, lantana berries, lettuce, mangos, melons, mulberries, papayas, pears, tomatoes, and whinberries (*Vaccinium*). In captivity, barbets also consume bread, dry and wet cereal, dogmeal, eggs, tinned and other meats, including hamburgers, milk and other foods, as well as numerous insects and dead mice. Captive Yellow-breasted Barbets survive well on a simple diet of meat and eggs. Other plant materials taken at times

by some barbets are the nectar of certain plants, such as species of *Bombax*, *Butea*, *Combretum*, *Erythrina* and *Inga*, the buds of elms (*Ulmus*), and the flower parts of rhododendrons and probably *Quararibia* and others. Black-collared Barbets tear off a piece of apple and hold it in the bill, "tonguing" it with their brush tongue until the morsel is so tiny that it is swallowed. Toucan-barbets hold tubular flowers in their feet and squeeze nectar into the bill; they also hold some berries in the bill, gradually crushing them, the juice flowing down the throat, and then tossing away the remaining berry parts. Red-crowned Barbets eat vine tendrils and thistle seeds at times.

The regularity of consumption of arthropod foods is rather questionable in that the data for many barbets consist of scattered observations. On a number of occasions, in East Africa, several pairs of *Pogoniulus*, *Tricholaema*, *Stactolaema* and *Lybius* have been watched as they worked over the bark of trees and branches, obviously gleaning and taking small insects. The Five-coloured Barbet in America and the Yellow-throated Tinkerbird (*Pogoniulus subsulphureus*) in Africa have been seen tapping into trunks of trees, and Neotropical Black-spotted Barbets forage on branches. Asian Coppersmith Barbets work on branches, tapping at times, and Red-throated Barbets tap on tree trunks, making pitted holes in the bark; the often dirty-billed Gold-whiskered Barbet pecks hard into dead wood at times, and it also may forage in arboreal termitaria. Most American barbets of the genus *Capito* eat more fruits by far than they do insects, but up to 18% of the diet of Black-spotted Barbets consists of arthropod prey, often taken from clusters of dead leaves. Observations show that *Eubucco* barbets regularly forage in dead-leaf clusters for insects and spiders; up to half the stomachs of Lemon-throated and 40% of those of Scarlet-hooded Barbets contain arthropod prey. Fully insect-laden stomachs of Brown Barbets in Asia indicate that that species does at times feed largely on insects.

Scorpions are taken by Asian and American barbets, at least. Some of the other non-insect prey known to be exploited by the Capitonidae include spiders and centipedes, eaten by some Asian and African barbets, slugs of the genus *Limax*, which are taken

Although many species of barbet in South America and Africa are quite often seen accompanying mixed-species foraging flocks, relatively few Asian barbets tend to follow flocks. They are apt to forage alone, or to congregate at fruiting trees. Up to 100 Blue-eared Barbets have been counted at a single tree in Thailand, but these are not roving flocks of barbets; they are just temporary aggregations. The forest barbets of Asia, although mostly rather similar in terms of plumage, come in a variety of different sizes. This variation, along with the differences in foraging strategies and dietary requirements that result from it, underlies the high degree of sympatry observed in some areas. In some Malaysian forests seven species of barbet, including the Blue-eared, forage alongside each other, quite often visiting the same fruiting fig (Ficus). Barbets are often the most numerous birds at these trees, usually accompanied by smaller numbers of other frugivores or omnivores such as bulbuls (Pycnonotidae), pigeons (Columbidae) and hornbills (Bucerotidae).

[Megalaima australis duvaucelii, Gunung Palung National Park, Borneo. Photo: Tim Laman]

The diminutive tinkerbirds have the smallest and finest bills in the barbet family. It is not surprising, therefore, that they tend to consume the smallest fruit. This Yellow-fronted Tinkerbird, when it is not foraging for other fruit or flycatching for a variety of insects, specializes in collecting mistletoe berries and other dainty fare in the dry woodlands of Africa.

[*Pogoniulus chrysoconus extoni*, Nylsvley, South Africa. Photo: Warwick Tarboton]

This Brown-headed Barbet is providing its offspring with food, in this case a praying mantis. Like most frugivores, barbets tend to consume a certain amount of arthropod food, but the proportion of insects caught increases greatly during the nestling and fledgling phases, presumably because there is insufficient protein available in fruit to fuel the rapid growth of tissue, feather and bone.

[*Megalaima zeylanica inornata*, India. Photo: Jagdeep Rajput/ Planet Earth]

by Green Barbets (*Stactolaema olivacea*), and snails, which are sometimes consumed by *Trachyphonus* and by one species of *Tricholaema*. Crested Barbets include some worms in their diet. Among the insects consumed at times by barbets are ants, dragonflies, cicadas, crickets, grasshoppers, locusts, cerambycid and other beetles, hornets, bees, vespid wasps, roaches, caterpillars and some flying moths, harvestmen, mantids, stick-insects, tabanid and other flies, Hemiptera, Homoptera and flying termites, as well as some termite larvae and eggs. Large and armoured insects are bashed and broken before being swallowed; for this purpose, *Stactolaema* barbets use natural "anvils", which they may partly excavate and which they keep clean. Birds' eggs and nestlings are at times eaten by ground barbets, Miombo Pied Barbets (*Tricholaema frontata*) and Lineated Barbets, and possibly other capitonids. Lizards and frogs are captured by Lineated and Brown-headed Barbets, and by Red-and-yellow Barbets, and Yellow-fronted Barbets feed geckos to their young.

The foraging methods of the Capitonidae reveal nothing out of the ordinary. Ripe fruits are plucked as and where they can be reached by the various barbets. Those species with a "tooth" or a pronged bill tip can presumably snip off fruits more readily than can some others, but all barbets, as they have a strong neck and bill, and the ability to cling and hold on to various twig and branch surfaces, manage to secure ripe fruits. The big Asian species, such as the Great Barbet, pull powerfully to the side and twist the head slightly to pluck certain figs. Most barbets are able to hawk insects, if at times inelegantly, and they do so repeatedly in situations where emerging termites are present in swarms. The specialists that forage among dead-leaf clusters reach out to or cling to the clusters, probing, pecking and even tearing at them to locate insects. The Spot-crowned Barbet is a follower of army ants that forage voraciously over the forest floor, the bird taking as prey any moths, grasshoppers or other insects that fly up, fleeing from the ants. At least ten species of American barbet, representing both subfamilies and all three genera, have been noted as participants in mixed-species foraging flocks, and many, if not most, of the Afrotropical non-social barbets will at least occasionally take part in such flocking. Rather few Asian barbets occur in mixed-species foraging flocks, but many of these are little-known canopy-dwellers that are not often observed for periods of time sufficient to allow such determination of habits.

In-depth studies of more species of barbet are required in order that a proper evaluation can be made of their preferred feeding modes and any seasonal variations in diet. The foods of too few species are known, and in many cases information is based on stomach contents, which have often been incompletely studied and are not representative of all seasons. Simply following a

Despite the high water content of fruit, barbets drink frequently. They visit pools of water on the ground, or trapped in epiphytes or tree holes, and drink by collecting water in the bill and then raising the head to allow the liquid to trickle down into the gullet. The action is well illustrated here by this Yellow-rumped Tinkerbird, one of the most widespread and common members of the genus Pogoniulus.

[Pogoniulus bilineatus bilineatus, Ndumu Game Reserve, Natal, South Africa. Photo: Peter Ginn]

few marked barbets throughout a day would yield significant rewards in terms of data-gathering.

Breeding

Breeding often takes place in the rainy season, as in the monsoon rains in much of tropical Asia. Where rains are not particularly seasonal, the breeding period may be protracted, even covering essentially the entire year, but losses of nests to cavity competitors, the predation of eggs or young, and the occurrence of second or even third broods in some barbets complicate the picture. If there is an indication of seasonality, with a wetter season and a less wet, drier one, barbets tend to breed in the drier period. In the Himalayan region and in China, breeding follows the northern temperate regime, with nesting taking place mainly in March-July. In temperate and near-temperate southern Africa the austral seasonality holds, and breeding is in September or October to February. Sahelian and sub-Sahelian barbets in the Afrotropics breed from February onwards. Non-forest areas with one to three wet/dry seasons have complex patterns that may vary with overall rainfall. Barbets breeding usually in the main rainy season may do so late in that season if rains are especially heavy, or they may breed in the second, less rainy period; they may also nest at the end of prolonged rains that occasionally obscure seasonality. Opportunistic breeding can be essential, for in drought years most barbets may fail to breed. In such areas, over many years, breeding records of, say, Red-fronted Barbets may occur in virtually every month.

Most barbets are capable of breeding at one year of age, but in the case of the larger species, and also many barbets of moderate size, this may happen rarely. The data concerning age of first breeding are sparse. In social barbets, one or more young of the year may remain as helpers in the next breeding season, when they will not breed. C. Restrepo, studying Toucan-barbets, observed that the earliest age at which the birds first bred was 18-19 months.

The availability of food (see Food and Feeding) and a good supply of suitable dead trees or branches for nesting and roosting cavities (see Habitat, General Habits) are obviously breeding prerequisites for barbets. The monogamous, non-social

species usually maintain territories with a larger home range. With suitable foods, mainly mistletoe berries, Moustached Green Tinkerbirds can breed in isolated forest patches of less than 1 ha in extent, but in forest with abutting territories they may defend an area of up to 20 ha. One problem for forest-breeding barbets is the occurrence of large fruiting trees, which act as a magnet

Like woodpeckers (Picidae), most barbets almost invariably construct their own nests and roosting holes by excavating wood to form a cavity. They do not, in general, utilize the abandoned nests of other species. By doing so, they probably reduce the risk of conferring a lethal parasite load on their offspring. This Crested Barbet is digging into a broken-ended stump, a process that is likely to take 18-30 days before completion of the cavity. As might be expected, the difficulty and length of the task is related to the softness of the substrate and to the bill morphology of the species involved.

[Trachyphonus vaillantii vaillantii, Hwange National Park, Zimbabwe. Photo: Roger de la Harpe/ Planet Earth]

The nest-holes of tinkerbirds are generally very small, and the birds will often complete them in a period of about ten days. The entrance to a tinkerbird nest is typically some 2-2·5 cm in diameter, whereas those of most other barbets tend to be around 5 cm across. As the cavity is usually bored into dead or rotten wood that has split, tinkerbird nest-holes can be remarkably deep, sometimes extending up to 1 m. The nest-hole of the Yellow-fronted Tinkerbird tends to be sited about 2-5 m above ground level.

[*Pogoniulus chrysoconus chrysoconus*, Casamance, southern Senegal. Photo: Michael Gore]

for other barbets in the surrounding areas. Such trees normally cannot be defended; feeding barbets from afar often fly to such food sources above the canopy, avoiding challenges from conspecific territorial barbets below them. Those species inhabiting more open forest, woodland and wooded grassland-scrubland habitats often have large, nebulous territories with even larger home ranges. The location of roosting holes and nesting sites can strongly influence the shape of the territory. In near-desert and Sahelian habitats, neighbouring pairs or social groups may be several kilometres apart, rarely meeting one another. Territories along streams in dry country may be linear, following the channel of a watercourse.

Forest-dwelling Afrotropical barbets have territories of 4-20 ha, the size generally being greater in secondary forest. These territory sizes seem to apply also to most tropical Asian barbets, but the bigger species of *Megalaima* are likely to have territories that are somewhat to considerably larger. In the Neotropics, the Toucan-barbet has a territory of less than 20 ha and the Black-spotted Barbet one of under 10 ha; that of the smaller Lemon-throated Barbet is 10-25 ha, and Scarlet-hooded Barbets defend territories of probably 10-20 ha in a larger home range of up to 100 ha.

Among non-forest barbets, about 10 ha is the estimated territory size for the Miombo Pied Barbet. Social Brown-breasted and White-headed Barbets occupy 5-12 ha of woodland per social group, although in more linear, streamside habitat they may occur at intervals of up to 0·5 km. The Black-collared Barbet has territories of 20-50 ha in coastal Kenya and Zambia, but its groups require 80-125 ha in South African farmlands.

Within the genus *Trachyphonus*, Yellow-billed Barbets occupy territories of about 11 ha in primary forest, but of approximately 8 ha in secondary forest in Gabon. Territories of Crested Barbets average some 21 ha in farmland and woodland. The ground barbets have greater requirements, and their territories vary. D'Arnaud's Barbets in Kenya need 20-100 ha, depending upon the habitat, while Yellow-breasted Barbets' territories are 100 ha and more in the Sahel. The third of these terrestrial species, the Red-and-yellow Barbet, has territories as large as 50 ha, but in habitat with lush streamside vegetation it can make do on as little as 4-5 ha, centred on a streambed, and feeding out from this on each side of the watercourse.

Highly social, colonially nesting species of *Gymnobucco* riddle a dead tree with their nests, up to 250 cavities of Naked-faced Barbets (*Gymnobucco calvus*) having been counted in one tree. Pairs and trios defend only the area around their nest-cavity, so that occupied nests may be as close to each other as 1-2 m. The colonies may contain nests of two or three species of *Gymnobucco*, such as Naked-faced, Bristle-nosed (*Gymnobucco peli*) and even Grey-throated Barbets. Occasionally, a pair of Yellow-billed Barbets will excavate a nesting cavity among those of the *Gymnobucco* species. These large, mixed colonies are unique among the Piciformes, whether that order be narrowly defined or broadly inclusive of the jacamars and puffbirds. Brown Barbets in Asia are social and may nest in loose colonies of up to three or four nests, and at times other capitonids nest rather close together, as with White-eared and Whyte's Barbets, but in these cases the pairs or groups forage in opposite directions, away from each other's nest.

The quality of the habitat has direct effects upon population density. In poorer habitats, the territories of barbets are larger and often not contiguous. In such situations, dispersed young birds may "establish" what prove to be ephemeral territories, and they move elsewhere to try again. Young male Yellow-crowned Barbets may be forced to occupy suboptimal territories in peatswamp-forest. Among social barbets, the quality of the habitat is reflected in the size of the social groups, with poorer habitat harbouring more pairs, rather than groups, and the groups holding three or four individuals, rather than four to seven. This is perhaps most obvious in the case of the very conspicuous Red-and-yellow Barbet. In comparatively lush wooded-bushland, the loud choruses of the group are heard, followed by duets, from several directions. In drier or more degraded rough terrain, however, choruses may not be noticed, a duet may be heard from a dry *lugga*, or ravine, and one has to strain to hear even one distant duet response: the "groups" are mainly pairs.

Although many barbets sing throughout the year, and social, duetting barbets utter duets in all months, the tempo of singing, simultaneous singing of pair-members, countersinging, and duetting increases significantly as breeding commences. More often, one sees a barbet, usually the male, cocking its tail when near its mate. Paired White-mantled and Green Barbets sing simultaneously, while males and females of the Red-fronted and

Rotten or dead wood is usually favoured by tree-nesting barbets because it is soft and easily excavated. This Red-crowned Barbet has nested in just such a location, reaping the benefits of easy excavation but running the risk of its nest-site toppling over or breaking off. The nests are sited at varying heights above the ground, sometimes as low as 1 m up for this species, their position being related to the availability of suitable substrates. Given a choice, most barbets tend to nest fairly high up in trees. Barbets do not usually line their nests with any material other than a few wood-chippings from the building phase; most chips are carried away from the nest. As we can see from this photograph, the head is often the only part of a barbet regularly visible during the breeding season, and this is perhaps one reason why so many species in the family have such striking species-specific markings centred around the bill.

[*Megalaima rafflesii*, Sime Forest, Singapore. Photo: Ong Kiem Sian]

Acacia Pied Barbets (*Tricholaema leucomelas*) sing back and forth at one another, often one "hoop"-singing and the other "nyah"-singing (see Voice). Lineated and Brown-headed Barbets increase the tempo of songs, and both males and females sing. The chorusing, social barbets go through greeting ceremonies and duets at frequent intervals at the periphery of their territories. Several species will even sing all night on moonlit nights, Red-throated and Lineated Barbets being examples.

Flight displays are part of the breeding ritual of many capitonids. The male Black-spotted Barbet, for example, flutters in flight around the female. White-eared, Whyte's, Anchieta's, Hairy-breasted, Red-fronted, White-headed, Chaplin's, Red-faced, Black-billed and Black-collared Barbets are among those species with a gliding, "floating" display-flight, performed by the male as, with wings stilted or fluttering, he comes to perch beside a female or flies to her. Male Lineated Barbets use a noisy, flopping flight when approaching the female.

Courtship feeding of the female by the male, when the former may pass back the item proffered, almost in teasing fashion, is usually an indication of breeding, yet it is remarkable how infrequently it has been observed. The behaviour occurs in all four species of *Stactolaema*, in the better-known species of *Pogoniulus*, in the Red-fronted Barbet and, among the *Lybius* species, at least in the White-headed, Black-collared, Brown-breasted, Black-backed and Double-toothed Barbets. It is exhibited also by Crested Barbets and ground barbets, by the Asian Lineated, White-cheeked, Red-throated, Flame-fronted, Blue-eared, Crimson-throated and Coppersmith Barbets, and by the American Red-headed (*Eubucco bourcierii*) and Prong-billed Barbets. It seems very probable that virtually all capitonids will be found to engage in courtship feeding. This behaviour may precede copulation. In an observation of courtship feeding by the little Yellow-rumped Tinkerbird, what was presumably the male fed 13 consecutive berries to his mate, and 32 berries in 25 minutes, indicating that a good number of fruits can be held in the oesophagus by the displaying male.

Although roosting holes may be excavated at any time of the year, the excavation of the nesting cavity is another conspicuous feature of the early breeding season. In solitary barbets, the sec-

ond member of the pair is generally evident around the "construction site" when a nest is being excavated, a process in which both male and female usually take part. The cavity, as it is dug, becomes a focal point for courtship activities, and change-over at excavating may be a part of courtship; at times, the male and female replace each other too rapidly to allow either to perform effective excavating. A few barbets are known to tap, really to "drum" in the manner of woodpeckers, at the edge of the cavity entrance. These include several species of *Stactolaema*, and the White-headed Barbet. All capitonids excavate their own nests in trees or posts, or, in the case of the ground barbets, in earthen banks or the ground, while some, such as the Brown and the Black-backed Barbets, dig into arboreal carton-ant nests. Some barbets will occasionally excavate deeper within old nesting or roosting cavities. Further, they sometimes use old woodpecker holes, and rarely they usurp a nest of another species, as did one Crested Barbet pair which took over the hole of a Rufous-necked Wryneck (*Jynx ruficollis*). The Crested Barbet at times uses nestboxes, too; other barbets could probably be induced to use such boxes, but in the tropics nestboxes are all too readily seized upon by bees, snakes and small mammals, if not by other birds.

Excavation of nests may proceed slowly or rapidly. The selected sites are usually at some height above the ground, but a shortage of suitable dead wood may cause the birds to utilize unusually low sites, or fence posts. Even standing logs and broken, hanging branches may be used at times. Smaller barbets often, or perhaps even usually, excavate on the underside of small dead branches. Soft though the tail feathers may be when compared with those of woodpeckers, the barbet, when working in this way, sometimes uses the tail as a prop, the Coppersmith Barbet being one example.

The cavity can be excavated rapidly, in as short a period as ten days in the case of Yellow-rumped Tinkerbirds. This probably reflects the rottenness of the wood, which is sometimes split or harbours a natural cavity within, explaining why a few such tinkerbird nests are as deep as 1 m, while the small Crimson-throated Barbet's nest-chamber can on rare occasions be 1·5 m from the entrance. In general, most barbets for which there are relevant data available take 18-30 days to construct the cavity. The Acacia Pied Barbet, however, can do so in eleven days, whereas the White-eared and White-headed Barbets may take up to six weeks, despite helpers assisting with the excavation. The nests of tinkerbirds have an entrance hole 2-2·5 cm in diameter, that of most barbets being about 5 cm. In the Black-collared Barbet, cavities are excavated to about 48 cm, strictly by the pair, while roosting cavities are about 13 cm deep. The nest of a pair of Black-backed Barbets, when built in a termitarium, may have a 10-cm tunnel leading to a chamber 10 cm in diameter. Usually some wood chips are left at the bottom as a lining; most of the chips produced in excavation are carried away from the nest, except at the start. The Blue-throated Barbet is reported to use a nest lining of grass, or even wool at times.

The Red-and-yellow and Yellow-breasted Barbets excavate horizontally into an earthen bank, usually to a depth of approximately 40 cm, but the latter may burrow to a depth of 1 m. The nest is in a chamber of about 10 cm diameter. D'Arnaud's Barbet digs its tunnel straight into the earth, usually beside a grass tussock, and the tunnel may be 45-90 cm deep. The nest-chamber is not at the bottom of this vertical shaft, but, rather, is excavated to one side off the main tunnel, at a point well above the bottom, allowing rainwater to enter the soil at the bottom and thus, in most cases, preventing flooding of the chamber itself.

Courtship continues during nest-building. Copulation may be preceded by courtship feeding or by allopreening sessions, or it may occur with no preliminary displays. The social barbets usually go through displays involving bowing, swinging of the body, and flipping and cocking of the tail, and flight displays may lead to copulation. In Anchieta's Barbets, grating calls are uttered, and the male glides to the female; the two bow, and the male cocks its tail and courtship-feeds its mate, before mounting her from either side. The *Tricholaema* barbets sometimes copulate with no display other than the soliciting of the female, or the male may glide in or fly over her with stiffened wings, land and cock its tail, and the two birds often swing and bob about; the female crouches,

While most of the Asian and South American barbets nest in solitary pairs, a few African species are social. Whyte's Barbet, for example, breeds in groups of up to six birds, with helpers assisting the primary pair at the nest. Little is known about the dynamics of this system, but it is likely that helpers are related to the breeding pair. In general, one group member perches almost constantly near the nest, keeping a watchful eye for predators as well as competitors for nest-holes and brood parasites.

[*Stactolaema whytii sowerbyi*, Marondera, Zimbabwe. Photo: Geoff McIlleron]

Many of the smaller barbets, such as the Coppersmith, tend to nest high in the branches of dead trees, where they are safer from the pryings of predators. While snakes, monkeys, squirrels, mustelids and raptors are known to predate the eggs or young, one of the greatest threats to the success of breeding attempts is the belligerence of other barbets. Direct competition between species in this family is evident through regular aggressive encounters, with larger species driving away smaller ones, and through the wrecking of nesting or roosting cavities. Bigger barbets achieve this by enlarging the cavities used by their smaller relatives, such that they are no longer suitable for their use.

[Megalaima haemacephala indica, Kaeng Krachan National Park, Thailand. Photo: Bernard van Elegem]

Territory size varies with species, and also within a particular species it often varies with the nature and quality of the particular habitat type occupied. In poor-quality habitat, the terrestrial Red-and-yellow Barbet may hold a territory of up to 50 ha, but where a stream makes the surrounding vegetation more abundant and productive, a pair can require only 4-5 ha, and at times the species occurs at densities of about 1 pair/200 m. This male is bringing a dragonfly to the nest. At least during the day, the male's contribution to chick feeding and incubation is greater than that of the female.

[Trachyphonus erythrocephalus erythrocephalus, Kenya. Photo: Alan Root/ Oxford Scientific Films]

waggles her wings and fluffs her feathers, and the pair copulates. Black-collared Barbets perform a greeting ceremony in which the whole group participates; the primary male cocks its tail and displays beside the primary female, and the two may touch bills and mate at one side of the group. In Crested Barbets, both sexes erect the crest, the female crouches, the two touch bills, and they then copulate. Red-and-yellow Barbets courtship-feed, and preen each other, and the male cocks its tail and raises its crest, parading before the female until she crouches, trembling, and they mate. Little is known of the behaviour of Asian barbets before and during copulation, other than the fact that courtship feeding may precede it. There may be little in the way of display because pair-bonds are long-term; in captivity, one of the pair, as breeding begins, often kills any additional conspecific caged with them. Copulation may occur twice in rapid succession, each performance lasting 6-7 seconds in the case of White-cheeked Barbets, compared with 10-12 seconds in the Afrotropical Black-backed. Among the American species, the male Black-spotted Barbet will flutter in display over its mate, land beside her, and bounce about with wings fluttering prior to mating. Male Red-headed Barbets courtship-feed, and the male then mounts and treads atop its mate, holding her nape feathers during coition. Displaying male Toucan-barbets cock the tail, fluff the throat and crown feathers, and erect the white superciliary feathers so that they flare out to the sides, before the two birds copulate.

The eggs and, therefore, the clutch sizes of the Capitonidae are incompletely known. The eggs of three-quarters of the Afrotropical species have been described, as have those of half the tropical Asian species and of just over one quarter of the Neotropical barbets. Known clutch sizes range from one to seven eggs; larger barbets, and particularly Asian barbets, tend to lay smaller clutches of two or four, but White-eared and Red-and-yellow Barbets can lay six-egg clutches. The eggs are white, more or less in the form of a long oval, and smooth to slightly rough in texture. They range in weights from approximately 1 g to 18 g, and one egg is laid each day until the clutch is completed.

The parents and any adult helpers have a brood patch, indicating that incubation is shared. Incubation commences when the last or the penultimate egg is laid. Change-overs in duties are shorter, at intervals of 10-30 minutes, in those species with helpers that incubate, as in the White-eared, White-headed and Green Barbets. Non-social barbets may take turns at up to three-hour intervals. The Flame-fronted Barbet, on returning to the nest, taps at the entrance to signal to its mate to leave. The off-duty mate often perches near the incubating parent, and Green Barbets sometimes sing together, one from within the nest, while incubating. It is not unusual for an adult barbet to sit tightly; in one instance, a nest with eggs was sawed free and carried home, where the collector found a Black-collared Barbet sitting on the clutch.

The incubation period of Afrotropical barbets is 12-19 days, and, so far as is known, that range applies to tropical Asian and American barbets as well. In cases in which the two parents do not roost in the nest together, the female seems to incubate at night, but sometimes, as with the Red-and-yellow Barbet, the male incubates more than the female during the day. In the social barbets of the Afrotropics, a "guard" sometimes perches close by the nest while another incubates inside; indeed, when the nest is first occupied by barbets, one of the adults usually remains near it. This is not only an anti-predator action, but is also necessary to protect the hole from would-be usurpers, usually secondary cavity-nesters. Moreover, the Afrotropical barbets are plagued by one or another of the nest-parasitic honeyguides, especially the Lesser Honeyguide (Indicator minor). The honeyguide may monitor the barbets' nests, try to approach them at whatever their stage, and lay in them if they are at the appropriate stage. Lesser Honeyguides will interfere with chorusing and duetting social barbets, and can disrupt a nesting attempt, thereby providing opportunities for a honeyguide to parasitize during the next nesting. In one such instance of disruption, after Lesser Honeyguide interference, two members of a group of Chaplin's Barbets chased the honeyguides, while another group-member entered the nest, carried the four eggs one by one to the entrance and systematically crushed each one, dropping them below. Any successful laying of a honeyguide egg in a barbet nest virtually ensures the destruction of the barbet's eggs or young by the hatchling honeyguide.

On hatching, the naked, blind barbets clearly exhibit the egg tooth with which they crack the shell in order to emerge. They rest in sitting posture on the spiky-scuted hypotarsal tubercles,

The open-country barbets in the genus Trachyphonus, *including the Red-and-yellow Barbet, nest in freshly made burrows dug into earth banks or termite mounds. The tunnel is generally sited 1-4 m above the surrounding lower ground, and is at least 40 cm deep. A new tunnel is excavated each year. Raising young in the group-living ground barbets is a co-operative affair. Group size in Red-and-yellow Barbets reaches eight, and even in these large groups all individuals help the primary pair to feed insects to the nestlings; it is not yet known whether or not all individuals contribute to excavating the cavity. This picture shows two males perched at the nest entrance.*

[Trachyphonus erythrocephalus erythrocephalus, *Tarangire National Park, Tanzania. Photo: Dave Richards]*

and on the abdomen. All those species that are sufficiently well known begin feeding the young on insects, or on a mix of insects and fruits. In the socially nesting species, all members of the group feed the young, which are also brooded, mainly by the parents, during cool or wet periods until the feathers appear, at about two weeks of age. Some, and perhaps most, barbets regurgitate food to the nestlings, at least initially. Feeding rates occasionally reach as high as 20 per hour, although the chicks are more usually fed six to 15 times per hour. In some barbet species, a brood-feeding adult remains in the nest until the other parent, or another individual, appears with food, as happens with Fire-tufted Barbets (*Psilopogon pyrolophus*). In social species, except those of *Gymnobucco*, "guard" barbets continue to stay around the nest, and they sometimes feed the young; in one observation, one guard hawked insects by the nest, feeding the young three times in 30 minutes. Gradually, more fruits than insects are brought to the young, but some insects continue to be fed to them, especially by species of *Stactolaema*, ground barbets and the Toucan-barbet. The adults enter the nest to feed the brood until rather late in the nestling period, often up to the last week, after which the young are fed at the entrance.

The nest-cavity remains clean throughout the season, as the barbets remove faecal material from the nest. At first this material may be eaten, but later on in the cycle it is carried away from the site and dropped, usually as a faecal sac, which is sometimes mixed with wood chips. On average, faecal sacs are removed on about every third feeding; Yellow-rumped Tinkerbirds, for example, took away twelve sacs over a period of two hours, during which they fed the young 38 times. Large pits or stones egested into the nest are also removed. Some additional excavation is occasionally carried out in order to provide more wood chips for mixing with the often loose faecal matter, as has been recorded for Prong-billed Barbets.

Snakes, monkeys, squirrels, mustelids and other predators are known to take eggs or young from barbet nests. For the smaller capitonids, however, a greater nuisance can be posed by other, larger barbets, which excavate to enlarge the nest opening, and then clear the cavity of eggs or young, as the White-cheeked Barbet does to nests of the Crimson-throated Barbet. The Plate-billed Mountain-toucan (*Andigena laminirostris*) frequently usurps the nests of Toucan-barbets. Army ants, often referred to as safari ants, are a predator on nestlings; one "army", having located the nest of a Whyte's Barbet in a tree trunk, killed and dismembered the nestlings and carried off the pieces to their own nest. Human disturbance of nests of all birds in tropical regions, and especially in Africa, where predators have for millennia followed trails of humans as a tactic for locating food, all too frequently leads to the destruction of nestlings, eggs and adults; in some areas, 90% of nests examined closely have "failed", and this makes regular visits to nests to examine their contents very risky indeed. Another source of predation, in this case certainly restricted to Africa, is the African Harrier-hawk (*Polyboroides typus*), the long legs of which have flexible joints; this raptor clings to the bark and reaches its legs far into tree cavities, from which it can extract the eggs and young of any barbets which do not nest in deep hollows. The Neotropical Crane Hawk (*Geranospiza caerulescens*), with a similar leg structure, is possibly also a predator of barbets in America. Finally, but importantly, the Afrotropical honeyguides must be considered a major cause of nest failures, since these birds almost always parasitize the nests of barbets, to the extent that every Afrotropical honeyguide represents a lost barbet clutch.

As with other piciforms, the nestling periods of barbets are rather long and the development of the chicks slow. Tiny tinkerbirds leave the nest at 17-23 days of age, whereas the larger barbets have nestling periods of 25-46 days. Examples of the latter include 28-35 days for species of *Tricholaema*, and, among *Lybius* species, 33-35 days for the Black-collared Barbet and 38-39 days for the larger Double-toothed Barbet; about 42 days for the Fire-tufted Barbet, and 35-38 days for several small to large species of tropical Asian *Megalaima*; and, in the American tropics, 34 days for the Black-spotted Barbet, 31-42 days for the Red-headed Barbet, and 43-46 days for the Toucan-barbet. One female Fire-tufted Barbet, the mate of which died when the nestlings were three weeks old, was able to raise the young successfully by herself.

Nestling barbets develop slowly, but add most of their weight towards adulthood in their first two weeks, after which progress

In pair-living barbets, such as these Brown-headed Barbets in India, change-overs at the nest during the incubation period tend to occur every three hours or so. This contrasts with the situation in the group-living barbets that switch over at the nest every 10-30 minutes. Off-duty pair members are regularly seen perching near the nest-hole, and some species of barbet occasionally counter-sing to each other, one from within the nest-hole and the other outside.

[*Megalaima zeylanica zeylanica*, Delhi Ridge Forests, Dhaula Kuan, Delhi, India. Photo: Ashok Jain/ BBC Natural History Unit]

The courtship behaviour of
the Red-fronted Tinkerbird
is poorly known, but in
many barbet species,
including some tinkerbirds,
courtship feeding is known
to play an important part.
In some cases, pair
members will pass food
items between them
almost teasingly; both
courtship feeding and
allopreening can be
precursors to copulation.
Other barbet displays tend
to involve posturing by
pair or group members,
raising of feathers to show
off the flashy crown
and head patterns, and
cocking or flicking the tail.

[Pogoniulus pusillus
pusillus,
Mkuzi Game Reserve,
Natal, South Africa.
Photo: Geoff McIlleron]

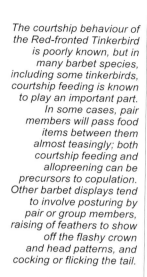

in eye, muscle and feather development is rapid, although weight gain slows and often ceases in the last week in the nest. The eyes may not open fully until nearly three weeks after hatching. Vocalizations shift gradually, the begging calls of young chicks differing, often considerably, from those of fledglings. At 27 days of age, nestling D'Arnaud's Barbets can utter duet-like notes. The well-feathered young reach the nest entrance within their last week in the nest. As the time for fledging approaches, food is often withheld by the adults, as happens with Brown-headed Barbets, and the adults may hold food conspicuously nearby, enticing the nestlings to leave the cavity. Generally, the young are led back to the nesting cavity for roosting at night. Soon thereafter, the nest is often "handed over" to the fledglings, the adults roosting elsewhere, as in the White-headed Barbet.

Subsequent care of the fledglings varies greatly, even within species, being dependent partly upon whether or not the adults begin a second brood. Fledged Coppersmith Barbets are independent at fledging or within two days of it. Adult White-cheeked Barbets feed their fledglings for just two to four days, roosting with them in the nest; the young are then cast out, and disperse from the territory by ten days of age, by which time the pair is renesting. In social barbets, the young may remain with their parents and group for up to five months or more, as in the case of Black-collared Barbets, but that species will nest up to four times in a year, and its groups rarely number more than four or five individuals, so that numbers of young must disperse. Black-throated Barbets tend to fledge only two offspring, one of which then accompanies each parent daily, the parents foraging in different directions from one another. Fledged Red-fronted Barbets remain a month or two with their parents, and are then driven from the territory. A likely reason why young barbets are able to reach independence as quickly as they do is that the parents can lead them to a fruiting tree and simply let them feed there; after a few days, the juveniles have acquired information which they can then use to locate fruits on their own, especially if nesting has taken place at a time of food abundance.

Crested Barbets in Africa sometimes nest as many as four times in a season. The young remain with the adults for a short period after fledging, and the parents then keep them from returning to the nest. As their parents renest, the young of the ex-

isting brood generally disperse from the territory. Double-brooded Asian barbets include the Great Barbet in China, which can raise three broods in Hong Kong, and the Lineated and Yellow-fronted Barbets; as these species nest strictly in pairs, the young of the first brood must of necessity become independent rather rapidly. Most American barbets are poorly known in terms of the relations between adults and young. In captivity, Black-spotted Barbets sometimes feed their young for about three weeks after fledging, while captive Red-headed Barbets renest after the first nesting, their fledglings being essentially independent. Fledgling Prong-billed Barbets, which lack the bill prong of the adult, accompany their parents back to the nest, and are fed for up to 40-45 days, until they can feed themselves readily. The Toucan-barbet, also prong-billed, raises two or, occasionally, three broods in Colombia. Its juveniles beg for up to four weeks after fledging, and do not have the notch-hook on the bill fully developed until about four months of age. The young of the first brood can act as helpers in raising a second brood.

In studies in southern Colombia, Toucan-barbets were found to raise on average about 1·4 broods per season. Those pairs breeding with helpers successfully reared to fledging an average of 1·1 clutches per year, whereas pairs without helpers fledged only 0·5 clutches per year. The mean age of dispersal of male Toucan-barbets is 10·1 months, and that of females 9 months, indicating that young helpers assisting in the following breeding season may be mainly the survivors of second and third broods of the preceding year.

The data on longevity among barbets are very sparse, and permit little in the way of meaningful comment. Captives of one small and one large species of *Megalaima* are known to have attained an age of nine years. This suggests that at least some barbets may reach ten to twelve or more years of age in the wild, which is about the same as is known for the honeyguides.

Movements

To put it simply, barbets disperse, but few exhibit any real movements, perhaps none moving 100 km or more. The greatest displacements are those made by the Himalayan species, espe-

cially the Great Barbet, which migrates downslope to the foothills and protected valleys, where it spends the winter. This barbet and others sometimes move locally, from more humid woodland to adjacent dry woodland, to forage for fruits. Other than such mini-migrations, the only movements made by capitonids are those of dispersal, although these may be over rather long distances; those of some dry-region barbets, such as along watercourses, could even be considered emigration.

Droughts can cause large-scale shifts of scrubland barbets, such as Red-fronted Tinkerbirds, into nearby hills and uplands. Dispersal-immigration by Acacia Pied Barbets into dry areas of western and south-western South Africa has occurred within the past century, coinciding with the planting of exotic trees, especially including Australian *Acacia* species, and the planting of fruit trees in formerly treeless areas. Permanent surface water is also more widespread in these areas.

Studies have shown that individual barbets at the fringes of the range regularly disperse about 10-12 km beyond the area in which they are normally found. This distance seems a rather likely one for the dispersal of most species of barbet.

Relationship with Man

There seem to be few relationships between barbets and man that do not refer directly to conservation (see Status and Conservation). Widespread in the tropics, and very vocal, these birds, as a group, are well known both to birdwatchers and to local inhabitants in general. The colourful ground barbets provide feathers for garments and ornamentation of tribes such as the Samburu and the Maasai in East Africa. Despite their relatively small size, barbets are sometimes hunted for food by children, if not by adults.

Members of the Capitonidae are not held by many aviculturalists on a worldwide basis. In some parts of their ranges, however, they are collected in some numbers to be kept as pets by local people, this practice being particularly prevalent in South American countries. The Toucan-barbet is one species possibly threatened locally by such collecting. Some Asian barbets can

be seen in rather high numbers in Singapore, Bangkok and other bird-marketing places, and some are taken in China as pets. As with many other bird species, barbets are illegally captured in Indonesia to form part of the menu of local restaurants.

In some areas of tropical Asia, and in some gardens and orchards in the Neotropics, these birds are regarded as pests because of their habit of eating, or otherwise damaging, fruits such as papayas and mangos. The Brown-headed, White-cheeked and Yellow-fronted Barbets damage and consume tomatoes, as well as other fruits, and are treated as pests in coffee plantations of India and Sri Lanka.

Status and Conservation

Currently, only one species of barbet is considered to be globally threatened, namely the White-mantled Barbet, which is listed as Endangered. Nine other capitonids are considered Near-threatened: the Afrotropical Chaplin's and Red-faced Barbets; the Asian Red-crowned, Red-throated, Black-banded and Yellow-crowned Barbets; and the Neotropical Orange-fronted and Five-coloured Barbets and Toucan-barbet. In addition, the so-called White-chested Tinkerbird, now generally treated as a variant form ("*makawai*") of the Yellow-rumped Tinkerbird (see Systematics), is listed as Data-deficient.

Although these ten species represent only a fairly small percentage of the total of 82 Capitonidae, this is not the time to be sanguine about the future prospects of tropical-forest birds. T. C. Whitmore and others, writing about tropical rainforest in the last decade of the millennium, offer no hope for the saving of major tracts of tropical Asian and most tropical African rainforests. In woodland areas of East Africa, sights that can be seen every day include the cutting of trees, destructive firewood-gathering involving the killing of living trees to be collected some time later, and the conversion to charcoal of patch after patch of remnant primary and secondary woodland. There is no mistaking the fact that the greed of humans and the inexorable pressures of expanding populations pose the most serious threat to forest and woodland barbets. That a few years still remain in which to save substantial tracts of Neotropical and some central African forest

In seasonal climates, barbets tend to nest during the rains, but where seasons are more constant the timing of breeding is diffuse and can occur virtually all year round. Most barbets can raise more than one brood in a season, while the Crested Barbet has been recorded nesting four times in a season. When their parents renest, young from previous broods tend to disperse away from the natal territory. In some cases this means young birds reaching independence and dispersing within a very few days of fledging.

[*Trachyphonus vaillantii vaillantii*, Mkuzi Game Reserve, Natal, South Africa. Photo: Leen van der Slik/ Animals Animals]

As with other piciform birds, the nestling period in barbets is protracted and the development of chicks is slow. This Acacia Pied Barbet will feed its nestlings for 32-35 days before they fledge, an enormous amount of time for a bird of its size. As cavity nests are less susceptible to predation than open or terrestrial nests, there is less advantage in nestlings becoming independent shortly after hatching. This allows barbets to produce smaller, energetically cheaper eggs, and to rear hatchlings from an earlier stage.

[*Tricholaema leucomelas leucomelas*, Western Cape, South Africa. Photo: Peter Steyn/Ardea]

Afrotropical barbets are plagued by a family of related brood-parasitic birds, the honeyguides (Indicatoridae), foremost amongst which in terms of its impact on barbet breeding success is the Lesser Honeyguide (Indicator minor). This species may monitor barbet nests, and lay in them at the appropriate stage. If the stage is too advanced, the honeyguide can disrupt the breeding attempt so that the barbets re-lay, thereby giving the brood-parasite a chance to contribute to the next clutch. Barbets are highly aware of the threat of honeyguides, chasing them away if they approach the nest-site and sometimes responding to the disturbance by crushing their own eggs. If a Lesser Honeyguide successfully lays an egg in a barbet's nest, the reproductive output of the latter is almost always eliminated, as the honeyguide chick breaks the barbet's eggs and kills its chicks. The parasite's strategy regularly meets with success: this photograph shows an adult Black-collared Barbet feeding a young Lesser Honeyguide. Reports of the tolerance of barbets to disturbance are somewhat mixed. For example, as well as the honeyguide example above, nesting barbets disturbed in captivity regularly destroy their eggs or young. In contrast, after a Black-collared Barbet nest was sawn from a tree, the nest collector found the adult bird still incubating when he returned home!

[Lybius torquatus, near Bulawayo, Zimbabwe. Photo: E. & D. Hosking/ FLPA]

Nest cavities are kept clean and hygienic by barbets throughout the breeding cycle. The adults remove faecal material, either as sacs or mixed with woodchips from the base of the nest. Indigestible fruit remains and fruit stones are also gathered up and carried away from the nest, as illustrated by this Coppersmith Barbet. In this way the Capitonidae differ from their relatives the Ramphastidae, which tend to allow a deep layer of fruit stones to gather in the cavity. Also seen here is an adult delivering pulverized and probably regurgitated food into the nestling's gape. Regurgitation is probably the main feeding technique employed by barbets, at least early in the nestling stage. In this instance, however, the nestling is quite mature, as indicated by the advanced development of its feathering, its open eyes, and the fact that it is feeding at the entrance to the cavity, something young barbets only do as they approach fledging.

[*Megalaima haemacephala indica*, Katong, Singapore Photos: Ong Kiem Sian]

The two races of the Spot-crowned Barbet occur in Panama and northern Colombia, where they are locally fairly common. Given this fact, the species is not thought to be immediately threatened. Nevertheless, very little is known about its ecological requirements and there are no estimates of its population size or rates of decline. Given its apparent dependence on forested habitat, and the lack of information regarding its status, it would seem to require research and close monitoring in order to assess the impact of rapid deforestation in its range.

[*Capito maculicoronatus rubrilateralis*, Valle, Colombia. Photo: J. Dunning/VIREO]

areas is little consolation, given the lack of political will in both developing and developed countries. Of particular concern for barbets is the intensity of the human need for dead wood, the removal of which eliminates nesting sites. Even the selective logging sometimes practised in southern Asia removes the host trees of strangling figs, and thus the figs themselves, a primary barbet food.

Pressure on barbets from the capture of birds for the cagebird market is a lesser problem made significant through even greater removal of the habitat itself. Obviously, as barbets become ever more restricted to smaller fragmented forest patches, the local capturing of them in these remnants becomes significant; and we ought to be able to stop such practices, because they are illegal in the countries in which they occur. The Toucan-barbet and the Fire-tufted Barbet are two species frequently taken for the cagebird trade.

There are some favourable practices that afford assistance to the birds. The planting of fruiting trees attracts barbets to gardens. Moreover, in India, the general antipathy towards the killing of animals, despite the depredations of barbets on fruit trees, has resulted in the presence of forest-edge species in rather open country and in city suburbs. In the Afrotropics, softwood trees, even exotics such as Australian acacias and Neotropical jacarandas, attract barbets by providing sites for roosting and nesting cavities. Such cavities of Yellow-rumped and Moustached Green Tinkerbirds, and also of Spot-flanked and White-headed Barbets, have been found in jacarandas, and it is thought almost certain that forest fragments with jacarandas beside them would attract at least Yellow-billed and Double-toothed Barbets. Nestboxes, which are known to be accepted by at least one species, the Crested Barbet, can be tried on a large scale for other barbets, especially in secondary forest and logged forest in which "firewood" has been gathered. Even though some boxes would be appropriated by other animals, it is likely that several would remain available for barbets.

To judge from the number of species of capitonid and their widespread occurrence in extant forest areas as frugivores, it is apparent that these are important agents for the dispersal of the seeds of certain forest and woodland trees. In maintaining intact forest, attention needs to be paid to the plight of these and other frugivores. There are almost no available data on their signifi-

cance for the health of such forested areas, but studies of frugivores by H. E. McClure and others suggest that the barbets may be of considerable importance.

A few open-habitat species of the Afrotropics, such as the Acacia Pied Barbet and Red-fronted Tinkerbird, have benefited from anthropogenic activities other than locally. Some non-forest barbets, the Double-toothed being an example, may have been

Sharing the subfamily Megalaimatinae with the diverse and familiar Asian genus Megalaima, *is the associated monotypic genus* Psilopogon. *This contains the Fire-tufted Barbet, with its long graduated tail and facial bristles arranged in a distinct nasal tuft. It is endemic to the Sumatra and Peninsular Malaysia EBA, where it remains common in many areas, but it is susceptible to the continuing removal of humid montane forest to supply timber and make room for agricultural expansion.*

[*Psilopogon pyrolophus*. Photo: Rob & Ann Simpson]

aided by the opening-up of forest. Furthermore, it is possible that some Sahelian species that are arboreal, such as Vieillot's and Bearded Barbets and the Yellow-fronted Tinkerbird, have gained as much through forest clearance in the south, and from the planting of some fruiting trees about homesteads, as they have lost through the felling of Sahelian trees for buildings and firewood. Overall, the three ground barbets may have increased their numbers marginally, although degradation of habitats exploited in the past may have lowered their populations, but there are no firm data to confirm this. Forest barbets have without doubt suffered loss of habitat in the Afrotropics, where forested land is still being cleared by slash-and-burn tactics. Favoured tribes are allowed to encroach upon, settle in and even entirely destroy forest "reserves"; not only does this occur with the knowledge and connivance of leading businessmen and government officials, but some parts of reserves are gifted as favours for political support by those at the highest level. It is a tragedy to see indigenous African "green" movements stifled, and their protagonists' complaints brushed aside. In Kenya, such actions are responsible for, among other things, the fragmenting of the ranges of coastal-forest Green Barbets and Eastern Green Tinkerbirds, and of woodland Black-collared Barbets of the distinctive subspecies *irroratus*.

Wars are not just human tragedies, but also affect wildlife, in most ways adversely. Virtually all recent conflicts have as causal factors the heightened competition for land. In Africa, overpopulated Rwanda has run out of space: except for three or four parks and reserves, every bit of land is under some form of human use. One consequence of the recent and well-publicized civil war there has been the overrunning of the northern half of once grand Akagera National Park that ran along most of the country's eastern border with Tanzania. Settlers moved in with large herds of cattle, cleared trees for building and firewood, burned large areas, and shot out the small to large game. That area covered about one-quarter of the world range of the Red-faced Barbet, the fate of which may now be in doubt.

So far as is known, the tropical Asian barbets have not undergone any expansion or increase in numbers, with the single exception of the non-forest Coppersmith Barbet. Some other species of *Megalaima* have perhaps been buffered by their ability to utilize second-growth forest, but removal of the primary forest which they have occupied historically must surely have prevented their populations from increasing. One can only be chilled by

what must be the terrible effects of the calamity of the fires, smoke and smog of the late 1990's as recorded by N. Brown in Sumatra and Borneo; on top of these are the as yet unknown and unreported effects upon growth and on seasonality of fruiting, and the changed ecology of the forest trees upon the fruits of which the dozen or so barbets of those islands depend. Severe smog effects have spread even over Peninsular Malaysia, where other barbets occur. Thus, the direct effects of the fires upon hundreds of thousands of hectares of forest may be but a small part of the destruction they have wrought on unburned forest; and, what is worse, clearance of forest other than by fire still continues.

Neotropical barbets appear to be under somewhat less threat, but all are forest species, mostly of moist or wet evergreen forest, a habitat that is increasingly threatened. The new road being built from Manaus, on the River Amazon in Brazil, northwards to Venezuela, with huge areas alongside it opened to slash-and-burn colonization, will bisect the northern Amazonian forest and open up far north-western Brazil to exploitive human activities of every type. Understorey species such as the Scarlet-crowned and Scarlet-hooded Barbets, adapted to shifting river-edge and island habitats, may be able to survive quite easily, but there is concern for the canopy-dwelling barbets, particularly those of restricted ranges, such as the Cinnamon-breasted Barbet.

Perhaps the one factor in the barbets' favour that puts them in a somewhat better position for survival than their larger frugivorous cousins the toucans, and others, such as the hornbills, is that the capitonids, owing to their smaller size, require smaller territories and home ranges. A 100,000-ha area of park or reserve in western Amazonia can be expected to hold 2000-4000 pairs of barbets of several species. Even larger forest parks could ensure the survival of these species. Nevertheless, the amount of illegal logging is reckoned to be about 80 % of all logging endeavours in Amazonian Brazil, and an almost exponential increase in logging during the 1990's has been documented by W. F. Laurance and others. These factors give cause to fear that all too soon a point will be reached at which relatively few large areas of protected tropical evergreen forest remain, this before there is full awareness of the need to save intact forest, and before there is sufficient knowledge of the species that require conservation action. Without the political will to make forest reserves sacrosanct and free from any fur-

Although the Banded Barbet has a rather small range, being restricted to woodlands in Ethiopia and Eritrea, it is not considered threatened, as it is locally quite common and tolerant of a fair degree of habitat degradation. As with most tropical species, however, data on its population size, ecology and threats are sparse. Further research needs to aim at providing such information for this and various other poorly known barbets.

[Lybius undatus leucogenys, Lake Langano, Ethiopia. Photo: Dick Forsman]

Both members of the aberrant subfamily Semnornithinae have a curious prong on the tip of the upper mandible that fits neatly into a notch in the lower mandible; this feature is unique amongst piciform and near-piciform birds. One of these taxa, the Prong-billed Barbet, is a restricted-range species endemic to the Costa Rica and Panama highlands EBA, a region that is suffering widespread habitat destruction, as a result of burning, logging and conversion to agricultural use.

[Semnornis frantzii, Monteverde Cloud Forest Reserve, Costa Rica. Photo: Robert Behrstock]

The Toucan-barbet is so named because it bears a superficial resemblance to some members of the Ramphastidae; in particular, the texture and colour of the plumage resembles the mountain-toucans, one species of which it lives alongside, and indeed competes with, in the humid hill forests of western Andean Colombia and Ecuador. Its population was recently estimated at c.73,000 individuals, too high for inclusion in the threatened categories at the current rate of decline. However, such is the level of forest destruction in its range, and such is the threat of trapping for the cage-bird trade, that its status might very shortly require re-evaluation; at present it is classified as Near-threatened.

[*Semnornis ramphastinus caucae*, Río Ñambí, Colombia. Photo: Patricio Robles Gil]

ther pressures to exploit them, the consequences will be both tragic and irreversible.

Only eight to ten species of barbet have ever been bred in captivity, and relatively few aviculturalists have experience in maintaining these birds in aviaries. Fortunately, there is perhaps sufficient information available to suggest that most barbets can be maintained relatively easily under appropriate conditions, and

that breeding them poses no major problems. Techniques for the captive-breeding of barbets need to be developed more fully, and broadcast to aviculturalists. Establishing small captive populations from diverse sources will be a task requiring scientific and government assistance. A limitation is the aggression displayed by barbet pairs, particularly of species of *Megalaima*, towards other conspecific individuals in their cages. Perhaps this problem would be minimal in large aviaries. All restricted-range barbets are candidates for captive-breeding. These include species under threat, such as the White-mantled Barbet and the Toucan-barbet in the Americas, and also perhaps the Five-coloured, Orange-fronted and Cinnamon-breasted Barbets in the Neotropics, the Black-banded and Brown-throated Barbets in Java, and the Mountain and Golden-naped and, possibly, the Bornean Barbet, these last three found only in Borneo. Action is needed to determine the number of existing individuals of the recently discovered Scarlet-belted Barbet, and to evaluate the potential threats to it.

The sense of urgency in these matters heightens yearly, as it becomes ever more evident that the current human generation, bridging two millennia, may have the final word on the survival of from 25% to as many as 50% of the existing avian species. What it says will echo down the years, for ever.

The Brown-throated Barbet is a rather large and dull-coloured species that lives in the mountain forests of Java. The massive devastation of lowland and hill forests on this heavily populated Indonesian island has left few patches of forest standing. Fortunately, although its range is small, this species is quite common at higher altitudes, where several areas of suitable habitat are relatively secure. For this reason it is not classed as a threatened species, pending further developments in the preservation of its remaining forests.

[*Megalaima corvina*, Java. Photo: Luis Javier Barbadillo]

General Bibliography

Avise & Aquadro (1987), Ballmann (1983), Berlioz (1937), Bock (1994), Brown (1998), Burton (1984), Cracraft (1981), England (1985), Feduccia (1999), Friedmann (1930b), Gaud & Atyeo (1996), Goodwin (1964), Gyldenstolpe (1917), Höfling (1995, 1998), Johnston (1988), Lane (1999), Lanyon & Hall (1994), Lanyon & Zink (1987), Laurance (1998), Lucas (1897), Macdonald, J.D. (1938), MacDonald, M. (1960), Marshall & Marshall (1871), Mayr & Bock (1994), McClure (1966, 1974), Miller (1915, 1924), Olson (1983, 1985, 1991), Peters, D.S. (1991), Peters, J.L. (1948), Prum (1988), Raikow & Cracraft (1983), Remsen *et al.* (1993), Restrepo & Mondragón (1998), Ripley (1945, 1946), Short (1971e, 1979, 1985b), Short & Horne (1979, 1980b, 1982a, 1984b, 1984c, 1985a, 1986a, 1987b, 1988b, 1992a, 2001), Sibley (1996), Sibley & Ahlquist (1985, 1990), Sibley & Monroe (1990, 1993), Sibley *et al.* (1988), Simpson & Cracraft (1981), Snow (1981), van Someren (1956), Stresemann & Stresemann (1966), Swierczewski (1977), Swierczewski & Raikow (1981), Verheyen (1955a, 1955b), Whitmore (1990), Yahya (1982, 1988).

PLATE 6

inches

cm

ssp *purpuratus*

ssp *togoensis*

ssp *suahelicus*

ssp *goffinii*

ssp *vaillantii*

1

2

ssp *elgonensis*

ssp *erythrocephalus*

ssp *versicolor*

3

4

ssp *shelleyi*

ssp *cinereiceps*

6

7

ssp *bonapartei*

ssp *boehmi*

ssp *calvus*

9

ssp *emini*

ssp *darnaudii*

5

8

ssp *usambiro*

ssp *vernayi*

ssp *congicus*

Subfamily TRACHYPHONINAE

Genus *TRACHYPHONUS* Ranzani, 1821

1. **Yellow-billed Barbet**

Trachyphonus purpuratus

French: Barbican pourpré **German**: Gelbschnabel-Bartvogel **Spanish**: Barbudo Piquigualdo

Taxonomy. *Trachyphonus lurpuratus* [sic] J. Verreaux and E. Verreaux, 1851, Gabon.
Often placed in monotypic genus *Trachylaemus*, but morphology, plumage, behaviour and some vocalizations similar to those of *T. vaillantii*, which thus connects present species to *T. erythrocephalus* and others. Four subspecies recognized.
Subspecies and Distribution.
T. p. goffinii (Schlegel, 1863) - Sierra Leone E to Ghana-Togo border.
T. p. togoensis (Reichenow, 1892) - extreme E Ghana to SW Nigeria.
T. p. purpuratus J. Verreaux & E. Verreaux, 1851 - SE Nigeria E to S Central African Republic, S to N Angola and C Zaire.
T. p. elgonensis Sharpe, 1891 - S Sudan and E Zaire E to W Kenya.

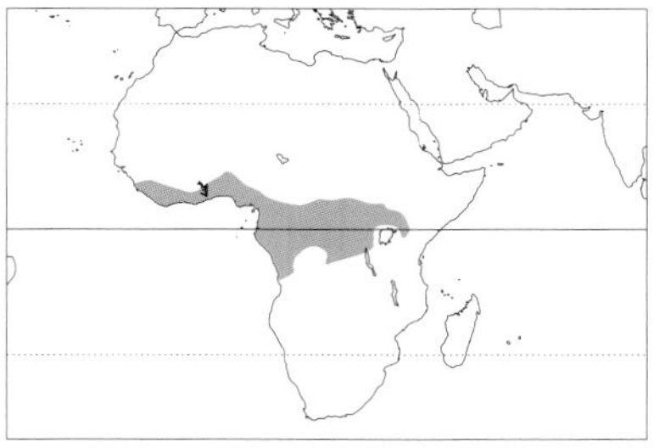

Descriptive notes. 23-24 cm; 65-100 g (mainly 75-95 g). Nominate race black, red, yellow and white, with silvery-pink throat, yellow bill and facial skin, dark eye, and white scapular mark seen when it moves; red spattered about head; tail quite long; usually spotted yellow below. Differs from similar *Lybius bidentatus* in white scapular mark, darker (less bright red) throat to breast with pink spotting, lack of red bar in wings, and yellow about belly. Immature paler, black lacks gloss, reds duller, no silver on throat. Race *elgonensis* very like nominate, but more red, less silvery, on sides of throat; *togoensis* has brighter red than others and extending to throat, silver-pink streaks broader on throat, plainer underparts, yellow tips on rump feathers, dark facial skin; *goffinii* resembles *togoensis*, but has less red head, more spots of pink (less streaky) on throat, more yellow in rump, and somewhat clearer pale yellow below. VOICE. Large repertoire; song low "hoop" notes at 1-2 per second (notes slower in race *goffinii*), in series as long as 5 minutes; duetting infrequent, and female probably utters "wa-hoop" to "wup-oop" in duet; also soft "oop" and chattery "chaa-aa" notes by pair, and in aggressive encounters; soft, irregular "oonk" notes by both of pair in greeting ceremony; soft "ooo-ooo" notes in or at nest; "eh-eh-" calls; "toc-toc" as alarm; young chatter noisily, or give rattle-like notes, and loud "yeh-eh—" when fed. Loud wing-fluttering at c. 15 beats per second in interactions.
Habitat. Lowland and lower montane forest in understorey, also riverside thickets and forest, forested swamps, old secondary forest, dense forest patches, and adjacent gardens and cultivated areas. Sea-level to 1300 m in W, to 2800 m in E (Kenya).
Food and Feeding. Arthropods, including ants and termites, larvae of various insects; also snails; and fruits of avocados, figs, and diverse species of e.g. *Beilschmiedia*, *Heisteria*, *Macaranga*, *Musanga*, *Polyalthia* and *Pycnanthus*, in Sierra Leone especially *Sterculia* fruits. Skulking forest-understorey bird, feeds mainly below 10 m, often below 5 m, to the ground; hops and bounds on ground, and up and along branches, gleaning, picking fruits; flycatches occasionally; often perches quietly.
Breeding. Oct-Mar in W; Jan-Jul in Nigeria; Aug-Jan in Cameroon, C Zaire and Angola; probably all year in Uganda and Kenya. Nests mainly or entirely in pairs; very pugnacious, especially to other barbets, able to nest successfully within large colony of *Gymnobucco bonapartei*. Duets and displays, including tail-cocking by presumed male, much bowing, erection of throat and facial feathers, wing-spreading, bill-tapping. Both adults excavate cavity in stub or dead branch, up to 30 m above ground but usually below 8 m; rarely uses old woodpecker cavity; nesting trees include *Ficus* and *Polyscias fulva*. Eggs 2-4; incubation and nestling periods unknown; chicks fed 4-14 times per hour, parents keep nest clean by removing faecal material; at least 1 young may remain with parents up to next breeding period.
Movements. Resident, and sedentary.
Status and Conservation. Not globally threatened. Densities of 8-13 pairs/km² in Gabon, where nests may be as close as 200 m; 5 pairs/km² in Liberia. Not uncommon in Sierra Leone. Requires forest with dense undergrowth; after forest clearance, often disappears when forest remnants too small or too far apart. Occurs in several protected areas, e.g. Gola Forests Reserves (Sierra Leone), Korup National Park (Cameroon), Impenetrable Forest National Park (Uganda), Kakamega Nature Reserve (Kenya) and Kibira National Park (Burundi).
Bibliography. Allport *et al.* (1989), Bannerman (1933, 1953), Bates (1930), Britton (1980), Brosset & Érard (1986), Brown & Britton (1980), Cave & Macdonald (1955), Chapin (1939), Cheke & Walsh (1996), Christy & Clarke (1994), Colston & Curry-Lindahl (1986), Dean (2000), Dowsett (1989b, 1990), Dowsett & Dowsett-Lemaire (1993), Dowsett & Forbes-Watson (1993), Elgood *et al.* (1994), Field (1999), Friedmann & Williams (1971), Fry *et al.* (1988), Gatter (1997), Grimes (1987), Lewis & Pomeroy (1989), Lippens & Wille (1976), Louette (1981b), Mackworth-Praed & Grant (1957, 1962, 1970), Nikolaus (1987), Pinto (1983), Rand *et al.* (1959), Serle (1950, 1954, 1965), Short *et al.* (1990), Snow (1978), Thiollay (1985a), Zimmerman (1972), Zimmerman *et al.* (1996).

2. **Crested Barbet**

Trachyphonus vaillantii

French: Barbican promépic **German**: Haubenbartvogel **Spanish**: Barbudo Crestado
Other common names: Levaillant's Barbet

Taxonomy. *Trachyphonus Vaillantii* Ranzani, 1821, south-east Cape Province.
Forms a link between forest-dwelling *T. purpuratus* and typical ground barbets such as group including *T. erythrocephalus* and *T. darnaudii*, being intermediate in bill morphology and some plumage features. Racial differentiation difficult to evaluate, owing to mosaic evolution (correlated with rainfall, birds being paler in more xeric areas) and individual variation; proposed race *nobilis*, known from single specimen from Botswana, now included within nominate. Two subspecies recognized.
Subspecies and Distribution.
T. v. suahelicus Reichenow, 1887 - C Angola, S & E Zaire and SW Uganda to N Tanzania, S to Zambia, N Zimbabwe, Malawi and C Mozambique.
T. v. vaillantii Ranzani, 1821 - S Angola, NE Namibia, N & E Botswana, S Zimbabwe, and from S Mozambique S to E South Africa.

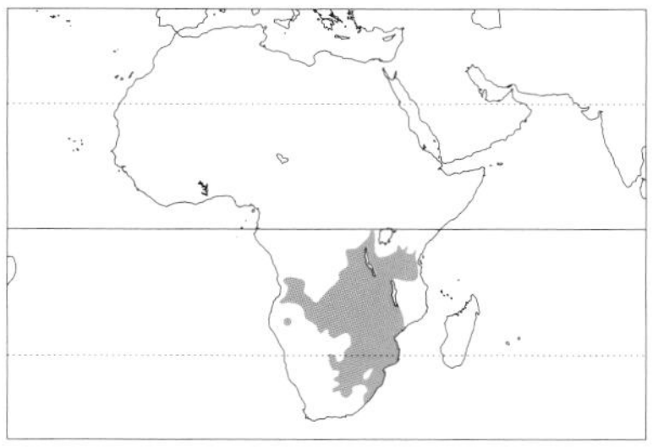

Descriptive notes. 22-23 cm; 57-85 g. Distinct crest and unique white, yellow, red and black colour pattern. Nominate race has black and white area around ear opening, yellow and red head, black crest, yellow and white marks on black back, white inner wing-covert stripe, red-tipped uppertail-coverts, white spot-bars on tail; shiny black "shield" on breast has silver-pink to white spots (variable, some have none), and red markings on yellow below. Female similar overall but generally somewhat duller and paler. Immature duller, paler, with dark bill (yellower in adult). Race *suahelicus* tends to have narrower breast shield broken up by pinkish markings, more yellow underparts, less white marks on back, more red on crown. VOICE. Distinctive trilling "di-di-di-" song with 10-17 notes per second for up to 5 minutes, resembles shorter songs of *Lybius bidentatus* and Scaly-throated and Spotted Honeyguides (*Indicator variegatus* and *I. maculatus*); pair-members loosely sing together, only parts of songs overlap ("duet"); also alarm rattle "kek-kek-kek-", much like *T. erythrocephalus*, at 10-11 per second, given also by 2-week-old young; single or double "kik" notes when adults close together, grating "a-a-a-a-" notes at 30 per second, begging "zweep", and "tirr-tirr" of nestlings are other calls. Audible bill-wiping near nest or roost apparently distinct for each pair.
Habitat. Woodland and thickets, especially where there are termite mounds, also plantations, including pines, streamside vegetation in dry areas, often amid palms (*Phoenix*); often common in *Brachystegia* and mopane (*Colophospermum mopane*) woods with termite mounds. Usually at 200-1800 m, but down to sea-level in E, and rarely to 2250 m.
Food and Feeding. Fruits and seeds, including those of guavas, figs and berries; also insects, such as grasshoppers and locusts, various beetles, wasps, roaches, termites, and larvae of numerous insects; also snails, worms; takes suet at feeders, and pirates eggs and nestlings of small birds. Hops on ground, mainly under bushes, and along branches, probes into bark crevices and lichens, tears at debris in trees or on ground, clings to and even hangs from leaves to reach insects.
Breeding. Sept-Mar in all areas; earlier, to Aug, in South Africa; up to 4 broods in a season in S. Courtship feeding and bill-touching with much duetting occur when copulating frequently. Nest usually excavated by both adults in stump, dead tree, underside of dead branch, or in sisal stalk; occasionally usurps nesting cavity of Rufous-necked Wrynecks (*Jynx ruficollis*), or uses old woodpecker hole or nestbox, or old swallow (Hirundinidae) or weaver (Ploceidae) nest; nest 1-4 m up, rarely to 18 m, entrance c. 3·8 by 6·4 cm, cavity 15-100 cm deep, deeper when renesting or using old cavity. Eggs 2-5, laid at daily intervals; female incubates at night, both parents by day, period 13-17 days; young fed 104-120 times a day, mainly on insects, adults remove faecal material; young reach entrance at c. 14 days; nestling period 17-30 or more days; juveniles stay with parents, but driven from nest (though remaining on territory) if pair renests. Nests parasitized by Lesser Honeyguide (*Indicator minor*).
Movements. Typically sedentary; may sometimes move some distance, and disperse along watercourses in arid areas.
Status and Conservation. Not globally threatened. Generally common; density can reach c. 5 pairs/100 ha in some woodland areas. Adaptable, aggressive barbet where not persecuted; some individuals are taken as cagebirds. Present in Mikumi National Park (Tanzania), South Luangwa National Park (Zambia), Vwaza Marsh and Liwonde National Parks (Malawi) and Kruger National Park (South Africa).
Bibliography. Benson & Benson (1977), Benson *et al.* (1971), Britton (1980), Brown & Britton (1980), Chapin (1939), Clancey (1964, 1974b, 1993, 1996), Dean (2000), Dowsett & Dowsett-Lemaire (1993), Dowsett & Forbes-Watson (1993), Earlé & Grobler (1987), Evans *et al.* (1994), Fry *et al.* (1988), Ginn *et al.* (1989), Harrison *et al.* (1997), Herholdt & Earlé (1987), Irwin (1981), Kopij (1998), Lewis (1982), Lippens & Wille (1976), Liversidge (1991), Mackworth-Praed & Grant (1957, 1962, 1970), Maclean (1993), McFarlane (1991), van Niekerk (1993), Parker (1999), Penry (1994), Pinto (1983), Prozesky (1966), Rushforth (1999), Rutgers & Norris (1977), Short *et al.* (1990), Snow (1978), Sohtke (1984), Stenhouse (1993), Steyn (1996), Tarboton (2001), Tarboton *et al.* (1987), Thompson (1998), Ward (1986, 1989), Zimmerman *et al.* (1996), Van Zyl (1987, 1989, 1994).

3. **Red-and-yellow Barbet**

Trachyphonus erythrocephalus

French: Barbican à tête rouge **German**: Flammenkopf-Bartvogel **Spanish**: Barbudo Cabecirrojo

Taxonomy. *Trachyphonus erythrocephalus* Cabanis, 1878, Ukamba, south-west Kenya.
Forms a superspecies with *T. margaritatus*, with which sometimes thought conspecific; both rather closely related to *T. darnaudii*, less so to *T. vaillantii*. Proposed races *gallarum* (SC Ethiopia) and *jacksoni* (S Ethiopia to NC Kenya) probably represent intergrades of races *shelleyi* and *versicolor*. Three subspecies currently recognized.
Subspecies and Distribution.
T. e. shelleyi Hartlaub, 1886 - SE Ethiopia to NW & S Somalia.
T. e. versicolor Hartlaub, 1883 - NE Uganda and SE Sudan to S & CE Ethiopia and N Kenya.
T. e. erythrocephalus Cabanis, 1878 - C Kenya to NE & NC Tanzania.
Descriptive notes. 20-23 cm; 40-75 g. Very distinctive barbet. Male nominate race has black cap and slight crest, and black throat patch; spotted and streaked red, yellow, white and black, with long, pointed orange or red bill; white "half-moon" about ear opening, surrounded by black and red; black upperparts, marked yellow and white, with red tips of uppertail-coverts; tail with large yellowish spot-bars; yellow with some spotting and marks below, and red undertail-coverts. Distinguished from *T. darnaudii* by larger size, brighter appearance, different head pattern, larger and brighter bill; from *T. margaritatus* by much more red in plumage, black and red edge to white ear-covert marks. Female red-

On following pages: 4. Yellow-breasted Barbet (*Trachyphonus margaritatus*); 5. D'Arnaud's Barbet (*Trachyphonus darnaudii*); 6. Grey-throated Barbet (*Gymnobucco bonapartei*); 7. Sladen's Barbet (*Gymnobucco sladeni*); 8. Bristle-nosed Barbet (*Gymnobucco peli*); 9. Naked-faced Barbet (*Gymnobucco calvus*).

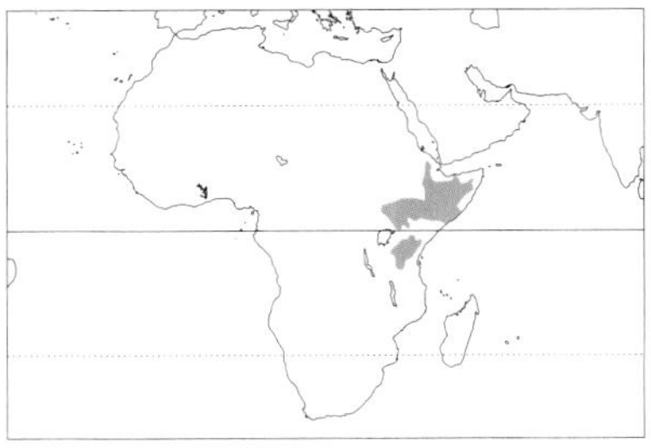

yellow on crown, rarely with a little black; more commonly has small black bib. Immature more yellow and brown, dull. Races vary mainly in brightness and intensity of colour: *versicolor* slightly smaller than nominate, with less red on head and body and none on uppertail- or undertail-coverts, rather more yellow overall; *shelleyi* considerably smaller, with even less red and orange, more yellow, belly yellow-white. VOICE. Songs "erupt" from greeting ceremony and chorus of all group-members, but only primary pair sings synchronized duet with overall sound of "red'n yell-ow" as repeated duet set; male 3 whistled notes dropping in pitch, female 3-5 higher-pitched, shorter whistles, these fitting together, at about 2 sets every 3 seconds, repeated over and over for up to 2 minutes; pre-duet chorus of "tik", "tik-it" and "chowp" notes, though birds arriving to join start with loud, rattling "kuk" series; other calls a soft "chuk" by adults coming to feed young, sharp "kik-kik-" alarm, and begging, chattery notes.

Habitat. Uneven terrain with outcrops, steep stream channels, or termite mounds in open woodland, wooded grassland, scrubland, and edges of deserts with lush streamside vegetation. Rarely to sea-level (Somalia), and up to 1820 m, occasionally 1980 m, rarely 2130 m.

Food and Feeding. Figs, other fruits and their seeds, as well as spiders, various insect larvae, beetles, mantids, grasshoppers, locusts, harvestmen, termites and ants; also eats lizards, centipedes, small birds and birds' eggs; takes all kinds of household refuse, including bread, cereal, hamburger, chicken bones, bananas, melon, in fact any food discarded by humans. Forages in group, sometimes very loosely, moving over ground, under or near bushes and trees; will search walls and roofs of buildings and probe tyres and radiators of cars for insects.

Breeding. Feb-Jul in N, also in S, where may breed Sept-Jan; mainly during and after rains. Male of group hops about primary female, male tail cocked, female's swinging, both with head feathers erect, may allopreen, male feeds mate at times; in duets, other group-members actively kept below duetting male and female. Nest dug in bank or termite mound 1-4 m from ground, tunnel 40 cm or more deep, diameter of nest-chamber c. 11·2 cm; new tunnel excavated yearly, unknown whether helpers assist in digging; territories often large, but along well-wooded stream sometimes c. 1 pair/200 m. Eggs 2-6; incubation period unknown; in captivity, male incubates, feeds young more than does female; all group-members (up to 8) feed insects and other arthropods to chicks, removing legs and wings from larger ones, feeding rate 2·5-12 times per hour; nestling period unknown; fledged young move with group, beg from all members.

Movements. Mainly sedentary, but wanders; occurs casually S to SC Tanzania, and wanders into range of *T. margaritatus* in N Somalia.

Status and Conservation. Not globally threatened. Generally common throughout range. Group size probably reflects relative health of populations. Dominant over other barbets, including *T. darnaudii* of flatter, drier country (where latter may outcompete present species), and also over woodpeckers. In some parts of range, children dig out nests; feathers used in adornment by some tribes; this species is also taken to be kept as cagebird. Present in several protected areas, e.g. Samburu Reserve, and Tsavo East and Tsavo West National Parks (Kenya), and Serengeti National Park (Tanzania).

Bibliography. Archer & Godman (1937-1961), Ash & Miskell (1983, 1998), Benson (1946), Britton (1980), Brown & Britton (1980), Cave & Macdonald (1955), Clarke (1985), Dowsett & Dowsett-Lemaire (1993), Dowsett & Forbes-Watson (1993), England (1973b), Friedmann (1930a, 1930b), Fry *et al.* (1988), Jackson & Sclater (1938), Lewis & Pomeroy (1989), Mackworth-Praed & Grant (1957), Nikolaus (1987), Reynolds (1974), de Ruiter (1997), Schmitt & Lyvere (1980), Short & Horne (1980b, 1985a), Short *et al.* (1990), Snow (1978), Stevenson & Fanshawe (2001), Zimmerman *et al.* (1996).

4. **Yellow-breasted Barbet**

Trachyphonus margaritatus

French: Barbican perlé **German**: Perlenbartvogel **Spanish**: Barbudo Perlado

Taxonomy. *Bucco margaritatus* Cretzschmar, 1826, Sennar, east-central Sudan.

Forms a superspecies with *T. erythrocephalus*, and the two are sometimes considered conspecific; both are related rather closely to *T. darnaudii*, less so to *T. vaillantii*. Validity of subdivision into races perhaps questionable; also, NE Sudan birds, described as race *kingi*, and those from C Sudan, as *berberensis*, both considered indistinguishable from nominate. Two subspecies currently recognized.

Subspecies and Distribution.

T. m. margaritatus (Cretzschmar, 1826) - E Mauritania E to Chad, C & NE Sudan, N Ethiopia, and Eritrea.

T. m. somalicus Zedlitz, 1910 - E Ethiopia and Djibouti to N Somalia.

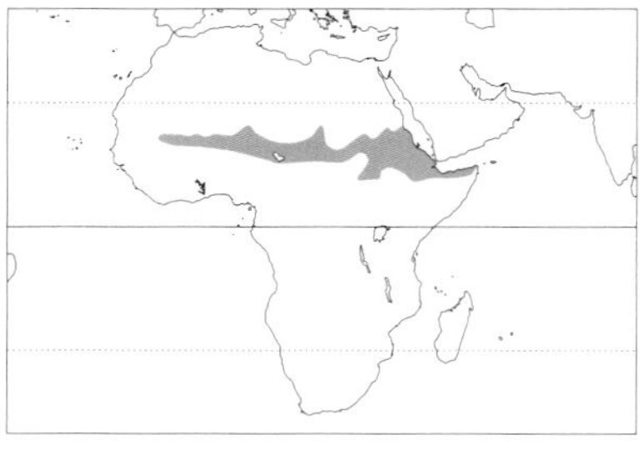

Descriptive notes. c. 21 cm; 44-64 g. Male of nominate race patterned yellow, red, white and black (fades to brown); short crest, black cap, yellow on head with some orange, white mark over ear opening, black throat patch; white spots above and white spot-bars in tail; long orange bill; whitish underparts with variable yellow wash, and yellow and orange marks on black breastband. Distinguished from very similar *T. erythrocephalus* by having plumage less orange and red, much more yellow, and by white ear-covert spot lacking black and red surroundings; differs from *T. darnaudii* in larger size, longer and brighter bill, no black spots on head. Female rather similar but lacks black throat patch. Race *somalicus* slightly paler, has whiter belly, is smaller than nominate, although freshly moulted specimens not distinguishable from latter. VOICE. Very like that of *T. erythrocephalus*, with duet "tew-choo-to,-" similar, songs slightly higher-pitched and notes a trifle faster; chorus and ceremony similar, with "chewp" and "tik" notes; also rattling call in alarm, or by barbet coming in to join chorus, and "cheh-cheh-" calls.

Habitat. Rough terrain such as along streams or wadis, in sandy *Acacia* wooded grassland, in hilly scrub, or stabilized sand dunes near coast, in irrigated gardens and around habitations, especially ruins. Sea-level to 1800 m.

Food and Feeding. Omnivorous: eats berries and fruits such as figs and *Salvadora persica*, and centipedes, grasshoppers, locusts, mantids, beetles and other insects and their larvae; probably takes eggs and young of small birds; captives survived well on diet of eggs and meat. Forages in noisy groups, on ground and in bushes and trees.

Breeding. May-Jun in all areas; also Mar and Aug-Oct in Niger, Feb-Jun in Chad, to Jul in Sudan, Feb-Nov in Ethiopia, also Feb and Apr in Somalia; possibly 2 broods per season in some places. Groups excavate tunnel in bank, cliff edge, wall, well with earthen sides, or old building, tunnel up to 1 m long and c. 5 cm in diameter, entrance within 3 m of ground; territories irregular and large, probably dictated by habitat. Eggs 3-6; no information on incubation and nestling periods, or on general breeding biology.

Movements. Largely resident, and sedentary; probably wanders somewhat at times.

Status and Conservation. Not globally threatened. Uncommon, but widespread. Considerable variety of habitats used suggest that species is secure for present. Occurs in several protected areas, e.g. Aïr et Ténére National Park (Niger), Ouadi Rimé-Ouadi Achim Reserve (Chad) and Awash National Park (Ethiopia).

Bibliography. Archer & Godman (1937-1961), Ash & Miskell (1983, 1998), Bannerman (1933, 1953), Bates (1930), Cave & Macdonald (1955), Cheesman & Sclater (1935), Dowsett & Dowsett-Lemaire (1993), Dowsett & Forbes-Watson (1993), Elgood *et al.* (1994), Fairon (1975), Friedmann (1930a), Fry *et al.* (1988), Giraudoux *et al.* (1988), Lamarche (1980, 1988), Mackworth-Praed & Grant (1938, 1957, 1970), Newby (1980), Nikolaus (1987), Rutgers & Norris (1977), Short & Horne (1985a), Smith (1957), Snow (1978), Tilahun *et al.* (1996), Urban & Brown (1971), Zinner (2001).

5. **D'Arnaud's Barbet**

Trachyphonus darnaudii

French: Barbican d'Arnaud **German**: Ohrfleck-Bartvogel **Spanish**: Barbudo Capuchino
Other common names: Maasai/Masai/Usambiro Barbet (*usambiro*)

Taxonomy. *Micropogon darnaudii* Prévost and Des Murs, 1850, Kordofan, south Sudan.

Related to the *T. margaritatus* superspecies, but not very closely. Race *usambiro* sometimes considered a full species on basis of vocal and other differences, but one of two duet roles is identical to those of other races, and *usambiro* is no more distinct than are they. Nominate includes proposed race *zedlitzi* (L Baringo, Kenya). Four subspecies normally recognized.

Subspecies and Distribution.

T. d. darnaudii (Prévost & Des Murs, 1850) - SE Sudan and SW Ethiopia S to NE Uganda and WC Kenya.

T. d. boehmi Fischer & Reichenow, 1884 - S & E Ethiopia and S Somalia S to EC & SE Kenya and NE Tanzania.

T. d. usambiro Neumann, 1908 - SW Kenya to CN Tanzania.

T. d. emini Reichenow, 1891 - NC Tanzania (E to Dar es Salaam suburbs).

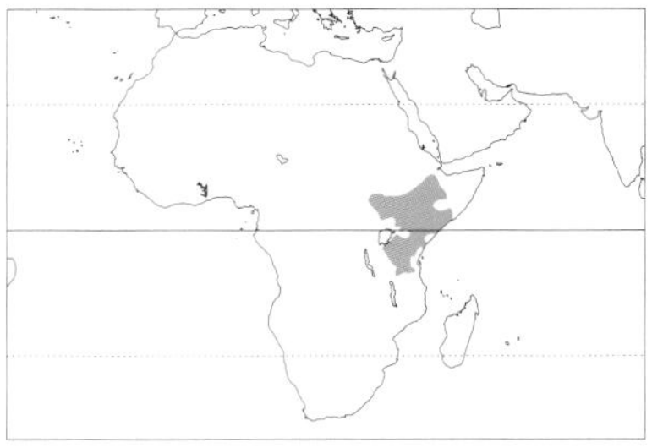

Descriptive notes. 16-19 cm; 17-39 g (*darnaudii*, *boehmi*), 32-51 g (*usambiro*, *emini*). Rather distinctive. Nominate race brown, black, yellow and orange, speckled and streaked; white spots on brown back and tail, speckled head with some orange; small black throat patch extending to upper breast, black half-band across breast, mainly yellow underparts with red vent; bill rather short, brownish. Most similar to *T. erythrocephalus* and *T. margaritatus*, but considerably smaller, with black spots on head, less orange and red in plumage, shorter and brown bill. Sexes alike. Immature duller, less yellow. Race *boehmi* has unmarked black cap, and bill often rather dark; *emini* similar but yellower, with stronger black throat patch, whiter below, yellower bill; *usambiro* has crown spots yellower, more distinct breastband, usually more dark belly bars, on average darker bill. VOICE. Complex repertoire, duet varies within and between races; 2 duet roles not absolutely assignable sexually, role A used by immatures, some of which later adopt role B of duet, single adults sing only A or B and, if recordings of one played back at different speeds, adult with other role responds at matching speed; song A usually of 1 long and 2 (or 3) shorter notes in a set; song B with different long initial note and 2 or 3 other, short notes, with first note synchronously set between first and second A notes; in race *usambiro*, A song reduced to 3-7 grating notes, B like that of other races; overall effect in most races "ker-ka-tee-too-tle,-", sets repeated for up to 3 minutes; all group-members chorus in preliminary greeting ceremony before duets; if duetter removed, replaced within 1-2 minutes by another group-member, always singing song of missing duetter, so possible that adult can switch songs from A to B or vice versa. Pre-duet notes mainly "tik-et, tik-et", also used in aggressive encounters; alarm a loud "tik" or chirp to aerial predator, repeated noisy "shreee-eek" to terrestrial predator; also hissing "ch-ch-ch" notes from pair; begging is soft "dddddd-" trill at 45 elements per second, clustered in sets of c. 0·2 seconds, repeated loud notes of same type when fed by adult; chattering call by fledged young, also by food-soliciting female. Loud bill-wiping; and wing-rustling or wing-fluttering at 15-25 beats per second by barbets flying to join group.

Habitat. Open areas, wooded grassland, open woods, bushland, degraded shrubby grassland and pasture, favouring old "manyattas" (bomas, Maasai camps) that have been abandoned; frequently forages about camps and facilities in parks. Where *T. erythrocephalus* or *T. margaritatus* present, frequents flatter areas, away from streambeds used by these larger relatives. Generally at 200-1900 m, reaches coast in Somalia; race *usambiro* and, in part, *emini* at 1600-2100 m.

Food and Feeding. Omnivorous: diverse fruits and berries, including *Grewia*, and their seeds, also insects of many kinds (ants, termites, grasshoppers, larvae and eggs of these and others). Feeds low or on ground, in loose groups, moving to nearest bush at sign of danger. Flycatches in jump-hops upwards, for termites. Birds gradually work around territory, pausing to chorus or, if response heard, to duet.

Breeding. Feb-Aug and Oct in Sudan and Ethiopia to NE Tanzania; all months but Mar and May in SW Kenya and rest of Tanzania, greatly dependent on flooding, most breeding just before or immediately after rains; gonads of all group-members somewhat enlarged throughout year. Most groups of 3 birds, sometimes as many as 5 adults. Primary pair duets with crown, facial and upperpart feathers erected, head bobbing; tail spread and that of 1 bird (often female, sometimes both) cocked and waved, or flicked closed and then spread, or both hold tail down; any group-member other than pair driven down in bush if it starts singing. Nest-tunnel dug straight into ground, often in open, sometimes beneath grass tuft, to depth of 45 cm or to 90 cm; chamber off to one side, well above bottom of shaft (avoiding flooding to some extent), lined with grass; territory c. 100 ha, patrolled by foraging group with periodic duets along borders, where any counter-duetting singers attacked by duetting pair if they come too close. Eggs 2-4; incubation and nestling periods unknown, as is role of helpers, but pair seemingly performs most of incubation and brood-feeding; fledged young follow adults, begging loudly, return early in the evening to roost in nest, leaving in late morning, also return to nest during inclement weather. Apparently only 1 or 2 young survive, and probably

remain in the group until next breeding season; captive young sing at 27 days of age. Longevity to 13 years in captivity.
Movements. Resident and sedentary, with local movements only.
Status and Conservation. Not globally threatened. Not uncommon throughout range; often common, even around villages, where frequently observed seeking food. Present in several protected areas, e.g. Samburu Reserve, and Tsavo East and Tsavo West National Parks (Kenya), and Tarangire and Serengeti National Parks (Tanzania).
Bibliography. Albrecht & Wickler (1968), Anzenberger (1974), Archer & Godman (1937-1961), Ash & Miskell (1983, 1998), Benson (1946), Britton (1980), Brown & Britton (1980), Cave & Macdonald (1955), Dowsett & Dowsett-Lemaire (1993), Dowsett & Forbes-Watson (1993), Fernald (1973), Friedmann (1930a, 1930b), Friedmann & Loveridge (1937), Fry *et al.* (1988), Kalas (1973), Lewis & Pomeroy (1989), Mackworth-Praed & Grant (1957), Nikolaus (1987), Payne (1971), Schmidl (1982), Seibt & Wickler (1977), Short & Horne (1980b, 1983b, 1984b, 1985a), Short *et al.* (1990), Snow (1978), Stevenson & Fanshawe (2001), Tyroller (1974), Ward (1972a), Wickler (1973), Wickler & Uhrig (1969), Zimmerman *et al.* (1996).

Subfamily LYBIINAE

Genus *GYMNOBUCCO* Bonaparte, 1850

6. Grey-throated Barbet

Gymnobucco bonapartei

French: Barbican à gorge grise **German**: Trauerbartvogel **Spanish**: Barbudo Gorgigrís
Other common names: Bonaparte's Barbet

Taxonomy. *Gymnobucco Bonapartei* Hartlaub, 1854, Gabon.
W populations of *cinereiceps* formerly separated as race *intermedius*. Two subspecies currently recognized.
Subspecies and Distribution.
G. b. bonapartei Hartlaub, 1854 - W Cameroon and Gabon E to SW & EC Zaire.
G. b. cinereiceps Sharpe, 1891 - Central African Republic, S Sudan and E Zaire, S to N Angola, Burundi, W Kenya and NW Tanzania.

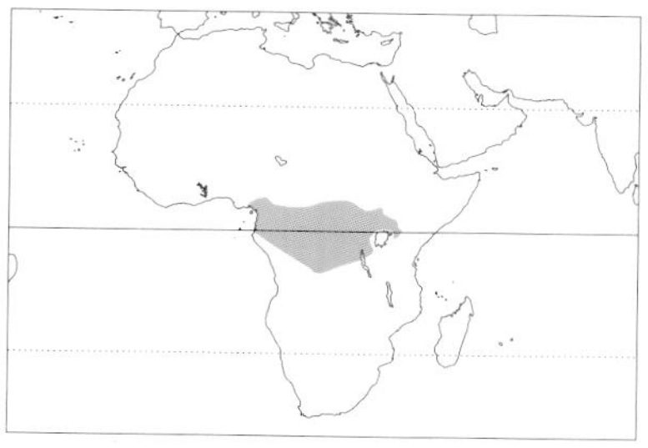

Descriptive notes. 16·5-19 cm; 45-75 g. Nominate race with forehead and forecrown greyish-black with yellowish streak-like spots, hindcrown, nape, neck sides and ear-coverts grey-brown, brownish bristly tufts about blackish bill; throat grey; body brown with buffish spots and streaks; wings and tail dark brown; eyes brown. Distinguished from congeners by combination of fully feathered head, dark bill, grey throat, darker bristly nasal tufts. Sexes alike. Immature sootier, more streaky, bill paler, nasal tufts short and soft, not bristly. Race *cinereiceps* larger, more contrasting pale spots on forehead, throat to breast paler grey, back greyer, head grey, longer nasal tufts with buff bases, eyes cream to yellow. Voice. Loud "whew", "whee-ew" or "peek"; rattling, buzzy and nasal "chaaa"; loud wing sounds.
Habitat. Primary, secondary and riverine forest, forest patches, overgrown plantations, pastures near forest, and around villages with fruiting trees. In lowlands and, towards E, up to 2450 m.
Food and Feeding. Diverse fruits and berries, such as figs, and those of *Musanga*, *Prunus*, and *Rauvolfia*; also arthropods, including stick-insects, wasps, beetles, dragonflies, grasshoppers and others, including larvae. Feeds in groups; aggressive at fruiting trees.
Breeding. Lays Jan-Aug in Cameroon, Nov-Feb in Gabon, Sept-Jul in forest area of Congo and W Zaire, Mar-Dec in S Zaire, Nov to as late as May in Sudan and Uganda, and Oct-Mar in W Kenya. Social, in small to large colonies, sometimes with other *Gymnobucco*; nests as close as 1 m. Nest in cavity in dead tree, 2 m or more up. Eggs 3-5, cared for sometimes by other group-members than the pair; incubation period not known; hatchling naked, orbit flesh-coloured, yellow bill with black tip, eyes grey-brown when opened; no information on nestling period or care of young.
Movements. Resident; dependent largely on fruiting trees, moves some distance to them.
Status and Conservation. Not globally threatened. Widespread, somewhat adaptable, and relatively abundant. Threats involve removal of dead trees, and isolation of fruiting trees from forest as habitat is opened up, but wide range and abundance within habitat indicate that it is less threatened than others of its genus. Present in Impenetrable Forest National Park (Uganda) and Kakamega Nature Reserve (Kenya).
Bibliography. Bannerman (1953), Baranga & Kalina (1991), Britton (1980), Brosset & Érard (1986), Brown & Britton (1980), Cave & Macdonald (1955), Chapin (1939), Christy & Clarke (1994), Dean (2000), Dowsett (1989b, 1990), Dowsett & Dowsett-Lemaire (1991, 1993), Dowsett & Forbes-Watson (1993), Friedmann (1978a), Friedmann & Williams (1971), Fry *et al.* (1988), Lewis & Pomeroy (1989), Lippens & Wille (1976), Louette (1981b), Mackworth-Praed & Grant (1957, 1970), Nikolaus (1987), Pinto (1983), Serle (1950, 1954), Short & Horne (1985a), Snow (1978), Stevenson & Fanshawe (2001), Taylor (1983), Zimmerman (1972), Zimmerman *et al.* (1996).

7. Sladen's Barbet

Gymnobucco sladeni

French: Barbican de Sladen **German**: Rußbartvogel **Spanish**: Barbudo de Sladen
Other common names: Zaire Barbet

Taxonomy. *Gymnobucco sladeni* Ogilvie-Grant, 1907, Mawambi, Zaire.
Forms a superspecies with *G. peli*, both also rather closely related to *G. calvus*. Monotypic.
Distribution. C & E Zaire (E to near borders of Uganda and Rwanda); reported also SW Central African Republic.
Descriptive notes. c. 17 cm. Dark brown barbet with bare face, pale tufts about bill; throat grey to brownish-grey; bill blackish. Differs from *G. bonapartei* in bare head, less streaky appearance;

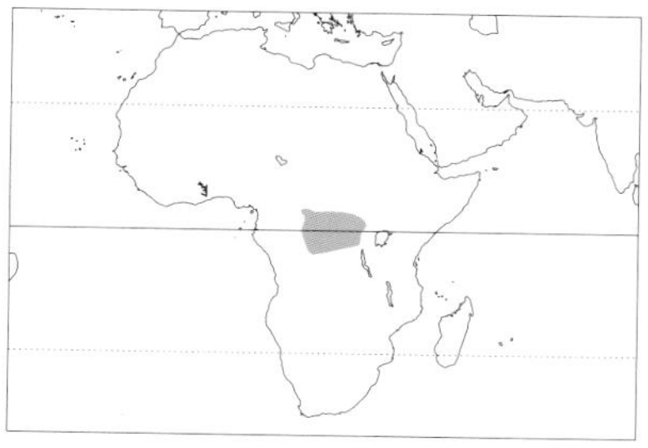

from *G. peli* in darker, less streaky plumage, dark bill. Sexes alike. Immature paler-billed, shows feathers on head, has darker tufts, paler below. Voice. Soft "pyew" notes, also rattling and chattering notes; similar to *G. peli*.
Habitat. Forest, often together with *G. bonapartei*, but details lacking.
Food and Feeding. Poorly known; feeds on *Musanga* and other fruits, and also takes insects; few details available.
Breeding. Probably lays Jan-Sept, inferred from dates of juveniles. Nest and eggs not known; associates with *G. bonapartei*, presumably nests in their colonies.
Movements. Sedentary.
Status and Conservation. Not globally threatened. Very poorly known species; even basic data are needed for this barbet, as details of distribution and habits uncertain owing to confusion with similar but much commoner *G. bonapartei*. Available data considered insufficient to establish true status; apparently uncommon at best, and potentially rare. In view of absence of information, conservation status of this species probably merits reassessment. No readily perceived threats except those that are facing all hole-nesters in forest, especially fragmentation of habitat and removal of dead trees.
Bibliography. Chapin (1939), Dowsett (1989b), Dowsett & Dowsett-Lemaire (1993), Dowsett & Forbes-Watson (1993), Fry *et al.* (1988), Germain & Cornet (1994), Lippens & Wille (1976), Mackworth-Praed & Grant (1970), Pedersen (2000), Schouteden (1962), Short & Horne (1983b, 1985a, 1988b), Snow (1978).

8. Bristle-nosed Barbet

Gymnobucco peli

French: Barbican à narines emplumées **German**: Borstenbartvogel **Spanish**: Barbudo de Pinceles

Taxonomy. *Gymnobucco Peli* Hartlaub, 1857, Dabocrom, Ghana.
Forms a superspecies with *G. sladeni*, both also rather closely related to *G. calvus*. Monotypic.
Distribution. S Sierra Leone E to S Cameroon, W Zaire and S to Gabon and Cabinda (N Angola).

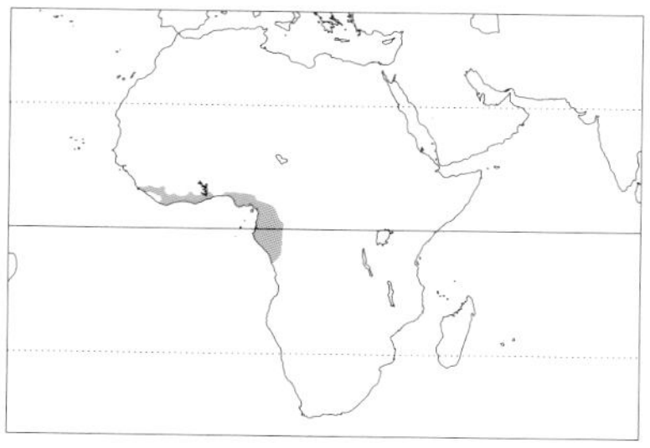

Descriptive notes. c. 17 cm; 41-63 g. Male brown, with bare blackish-grey head; pale bristly tufts around base of bill; secondaries and tertials narrowly edged yellowish; bill yellow to light brown. Distinguished from *G. bonapartei* by pale bill, bare face, and lack of grey on neck; from *G. calvus* by smaller bill, indistinct yellowish-buff edges to wing feathers, and bristly tufts above bill; from *G. sladeni* by paler, more yellow-brown coloration, more yellow on wings, paler bill. Female like male. Immature has feathered brown head, soft darker tufts about head, and darker bill than adult. Voice. Series up to 5 seconds long of soft hoots; "pyew" notes pitched higher than those of *G. calvus*; "tyee" chatters or rattles.
Habitat. Primary and dense secondary forest and nearby fruiting trees, riverine swamps in high forest, also logged forest and plantations. In lowlands to 1100 m.
Food and Feeding. Fruits and insects. Hangs in manner of tit (Paridae) to secure fruits. Feeds in fruiting trees with often more common *G. bonapartei* and, especially, *G. calvus*.
Breeding. Apparently Sept-Jan in Liberia, Nov-Dec in Ghana, May-Jun in Nigeria, most of year but especially in dry season in Cameroon, and Oct-Apr in Gabon. Nests colonially, either alone or with *G. calvus* and to lesser extent *G. bonapartei*. Nest and eggs undescribed, but holes of this species observed at 10-35 m in trees.
Movements. Resident, and sedentary.
Status and Conservation. Not globally threatened. Status uncertain. Little known, and possibly overlooked; easily confused with *G. calvus* and *G. bonapartei*; further information required, especially since it is usually less common than those 2 species; may have special requirements, as yet unidentified, so possible that any pressures on it remain to be elucidated. Favoured, at least temporarily, by forest clearance. Known to occur in Gola Forests Reserves (Sierra Leone) and Taï Forest National Park (Ivory Coast).
Bibliography. Allport *et al.* (1989), Bannerman (1933, 1953), Bates (1930), Bowden (2001), Brosset & Érard (1986), Chapin (1939), Cheke & Walsh (1996), Christy & Clarke (1994), Demey & Fishpool (1994), Dowsett (1989b), Dowsett & Dowsett-Lemaire (1991, 1993), Dowsett & Forbes-Watson (1993), Elgood *et al.* (1994), Farmer (1979), Field (1999), Fry *et al.* (1988), Gatter (1997), Grimes (1987), Lippens & Wille (1976), Louette (1981b), Mackworth-Praed & Grant (1970), Pinto (1983), Rodewald *et al.* (1994), Sargeant (1993), Serle (1950), Short & Horne (1985a), Snow (1978), Thiollay (1985a).

9. Naked-faced Barbet

Gymnobucco calvus

French: Barbican chauve **German**: Glatzenbartvogel **Spanish**: Barbudo Calvo

Taxonomy. *Bucco calvus* Lafresnaye, 1841, Ashanti, Ghana.
Apparently related rather closely to *G. sladeni* and *G. peli*. Birds from Mt Cameroon S to Gabon formerly separated from nominate, as race *major*. Three subspecies currently recognized.
Subspecies and Distribution.
G. c. calvus (Lafresnaye, 1841) - Sierra Leone E to Cameroon and Gabon.
G. c. congicus Chapin, 1932 - W Congo (Brazzaville) and W Zaire S to NW Angola.
G. c. vernayi Boulton, 1931 - WC Angolan uplands.
Descriptive notes. c. 18 cm; 47-67 g. Male nominate race with crown and face unfeathered, blackish to blue-grey; buff to dull brown bristly tufts on chin and at lateral base of lower mandible, short hair-like feathers on forehead and lores; upperparts dark brown with thin pale streaks; underparts brown to grey-brown with fine pale streaks; bill yellow to pale brownish. Differs from *G. bonapartei* in pale bill and naked face; from *G. sladeni* in less dark plumage, pale bill, paler bristle tufts; distinguished from similar *G. peli* by larger bill, deeper brown rump, darker and less conspicuous nasal tufts. Sexes alike. Immature paler, with less prominent pale shaft streaks on body, looser plumage. Race *congicus* very like nominate, but slightly larger, with broader streaks, throat paler

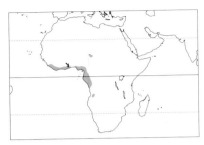

greyish-white, has small more yellowish-buff tufts also at nostrils; *vernayi* like *congicus*, but slightly darker above, still more broadly pale-streaked below with pale throat, and lacks tuft on chin of other races. VOICE. Song soft "poo" notes in series; "kyew" call longer, pitched lower than in *G. peli*; variable rattling notes, and chittering begging calls of young.

Habitat. Primary and adjacent secondary forest, into wooded grassland, and nearby plantations, farms and villages with fruiting trees. Occurs at up to 1820 m.

Food and Feeding. Eats diverse wild and cultivated fruits, including those of species of fig, *Enantia*, *Harungana*, *Musanga*, *Parinari*, *Rauvolfia*, *Trema*, papayas, and others; also feeds on arthropods, including crickets, beetles and other insects; also on nectar, such as that of *Bombax*. Feeds in manner of tit (Paridae) in foliage and along branches. Highly social at all times; nearly always in groups; quarrelsome and aggressive at food sources, chases off other barbets.

Breeding. Breeds Mar-Dec in W Africa, also Jan-Feb in Ghana and Nigeria; most of year in Cameroon, Oct-Apr in Gabon and Congo; year-round roosting in nest-holes may distort reports of apparent breeding. Colonial, often with sympatric congeners, in colonies of up to 250 pairs. Nest in cavity excavated in dead tree, at 8-40 m above ground; hole used also for roosting. Eggs 2-5, usually 3; details of incubation, fledging, feeding rates, and other information meagre, insufficient to indicate factual data.

Movements. Resident; shifts foraging sites as different fruiting trees come into fruit.

Status and Conservation. Not globally threatened. Generally common throughout range. Seems less affected by fragmenting of forest than are *G. sladeni* and *G. peli*; nevertheless, its social habits and colonial nesting mean that it requires suitable dead trees for roosting and breeding. Further research needed on breeding biology. Present in Gola Forests Reserves (Sierra Leone) and Mount Kupé National Park (Cameroon).

Bibliography. Allport *et al.* (1989), Bannerman (1933, 1953), Bates (1930), Bowden (2001), Brosset & Érard (1986), Chapin (1939), Cheke & Walsh (1996), Christy & Clarke (1994), Colston & Curry-Lindahl (1986), Dean (2000), Demey & Fishpool (1994), Dowsett (1989b), Dowsett & Dowsett-Lemaire (1991, 1993), Dowsett & Forbes-Watson (1993), Elgood *et al.* (1994), Farmer (1979), Field (1999), Fry *et al.* (1988), Gatter (1997), Grimes (1987), Lippens & Wille (1976), Louette (1981b), Mackworth-Praed & Grant (1962, 1970), Pinto (1983), Rand (1951), Rand *et al.* (1959), Serle (1950, 1954), Short & Horne (1985a), Snow (1978), Stahl (1998), Thiollay (1985a).

PLATE 7 ➤

ssp *leucotis*

ssp *kilimensis*

ssp *leucogrammica*

ssp *whytii*

ssp *sowerbyi*

ssp *buttoni*

11

ssp *stresemanni*

ssp *terminata*

ssp *anchietae*

ssp *olivacea*

13

ssp *scolopaceus*

14

ssp *woodwardi*

12

ssp *katangae*

ssp *flavisquamatus*

15

ssp *belcheri*

18

ssp *subsulphureus*

19

16

ssp *coryphaeus*

17

ssp *hildamariae*

ssp *chrysopygus*

ssp *pusillus*

21

ssp *chrysoconus*

ssp *bilineatus*

20

ssp *affinis*

22

ssp *fischeri*

ssp *extoni*

PLATE 7

ssp *leucolaimus*

ssp *xanthostictus*

inches 3

cm 8

Genus *STACTOLAEMA*

C. H. T. Marshall & G. F. L. Marshall, 1870

10. **White-eared Barbet**

Stactolaema leucotis

French: Barbican oreillard **German**: Weißohr-Bartvogel **Spanish**: Barbudo Orejiblanco

Taxonomy. *Megalæma leucotis* Sundevall, 1850, Natal.
Sometimes placed in monospecific genus *Smilorhis*. Kenyan population sometimes separated as race *kenyae*, but normally considered inseparable from *kilimensis*. In past, race *bocagei* of *Lybius torquatus* erroneously listed as a race of present species. Three subspecies normally recognized.
Subspecies and Distribution.
S. l. kilimensis (Shelley, 1889) - CE & SE Kenya to NE Tanzania.
S. l. leucogrammica (Reichenow, 1915) - highlands of C & S Tanzania.
S. l. leucotis (Sundevall, 1850) - Malawi and Mozambique S to Swaziland and Natal.

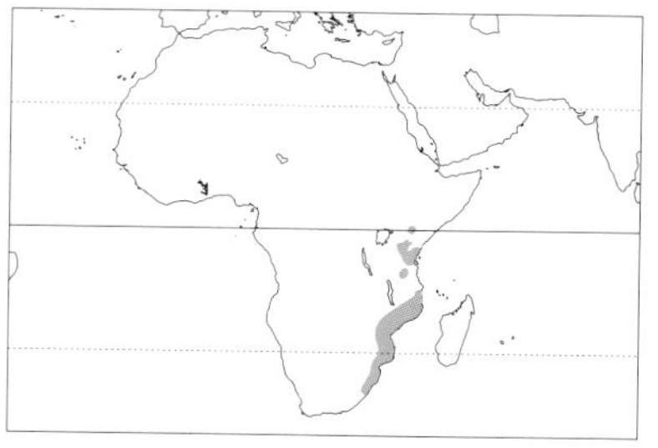

Descriptive notes. c. 18 cm; 48-63 g. Dark brown woodland barbet with white belly and dark head. Nominate race has black head with white stripe behind eye, white on rump and uppertail-coverts; bill blackish. Differs from *S. whytii* in having no white in wings, and different head pattern. Sexes alike. Immature blacker than adult. Races differ mainly in plumage darkness, and amount of white on head: *leucogrammica* with more white on head, extending also under eye, dark rump; *kilimensis* dark, with rump generally whiter than in nominate. Voice. Various harsh "skreek" calls, and "whew" calls (resembling those of *Gymnobucco*); grating, buzzy notes and trills; also taps at nest entrance, wipes bill and flutters wings noisily during encounters; nestlings give piping "wi" notes and trills.
Habitat. Moist primary and secondary forest, forest edge, also nearby gardens and plantations where fruiting trees present, and where dead trees and limbs are available for excavation. Attains elevations of up to 2600 m in N, often on forested slopes.
Food and Feeding. Diet made up of fruits, including figs, guavas, pawpaws, mangoes, juniper and other berries; insects, including hornets, wasps, roaches, dragonflies, crickets, moths, grasshoppers and locusts; and spiders. Uses special sites as "anvils" for killing and disarming insects. Gleans, works over bark, and flycatches for termites and other aerial insects. Aggressive and dominant at food sources.
Breeding. Lays Jun-Jan in all areas, in N after main rains. Social nester. Courtship feeding occurs; paired birds give flight displays. Nest 5-18 m up, in tree cavity c. 50-75 cm deep; in Kenya, area defended by group c. 8 ha. Eggs 2-6; helpers assist in incubating, period 14-18 days, also in feeding young; typically 1 barbet remains as "guard" while other adults forage, chicks fed 8-20 times an hour; nest kept clean; nestling period c. 39 days; most young that survive remain with group for a year or more.
Movements. Resident, and sedentary.
Status and Conservation. Not globally threatened. Little information on status; apparently common at least in NE Tanzania, but local and uncommon in Kenya; said to occur in Taita Hills in SE Kenya, but no confirmed records and possibly absent there. Present in Mtunzini and Umlalazi Nature Reserve (South Africa). Disappearing in some highland parts of its range in N; habitat increasingly fragmented, with dead trees being cleared away. Species should be monitored, especially as its range is discontinuous.
Bibliography. Benson & Benson (1975, 1977), Britton (1980), Brooks *et al*. (1998), Brown & Britton (1980), Clancey (1964, 1971a), Dowsett & Dowsett-Lemaire (1993), Dowsett & Forbes-Watson (1993), Earlé & Grobler (1987), Fry *et al*. (1988), Ginn *et al*. (1989), Harrison *et al*. (1997), Irwin (1981), Lewis & Pomeroy (1989), Mackworth-Praed & Grant (1957, 1962), Maclean (1993), Moreau & Moreau (1937), Oatley (1968), Priest (1934, 1948), Short & Horne (1984a, 1985a), Short *et al*. (1990), Skutch (1987), Snow (1978), Stevenson & Fanshawe (2001), Steyn (1996), Tarboton (2001), Waiyaki & Bennun (2000), Yates (1975), Zimmerman *et al*. (1996).

11. **Whyte's Barbet**

Stactolaema whytii

French: Barbican de Whyte **German**: Spiegelbartvogel **Spanish**: Barbudo Especulado
Other common names: Sowerby's Barbet (*sowerbyi*)

Taxonomy. *Smilorhis whytii* Shelley, 1893, Zomba, Malawi.
Forms a superspecies with *S. anchietae*. Six subspecies recognized.
Subspecies and Distribution.
S. w. whytii (Shelley, 1893) - SC Tanzania to Mozambique and SE Malawi.
S. w. stresemanni (Grote, 1934) - SW corner of Tanzania and adjacent NE Zambia.
S. w. terminata Clancey, 1956 - highlands around Iringa, in S Tanzania.
S. w. angoniensis (Benson, 1964) - E Zambia to SW Malawi.
S. w. sowerbyi Sharpe, 1898 - E Zimbabwe to extreme S Malawi.
S. w. buttoni (C. M. N. White, 1945) - NC Zambia; almost certainly also extreme S Zaire.
Descriptive notes. c. 19 cm; 51-62·5 g. Brown woodland barbet with white chin and 2 white wing patches. Nominate race has top of head black, spotted with white, white line below eye, yellow restricted to nasal tufts; whitish lower belly and vent. Separated from *S. leucotis* by white wing patches; from *S. anchietae* by whiter wing patches, and generally darker head with white chin. Sexes alike. Immature darker and less spotted, with yellow on head reduced. Races differ from nominate in having more yellow on head: *sowerbyi* with yellow on forehead and over eye, and as spots over crown to nape; *terminata* has yellow of crown more golden, dark central part of fore-

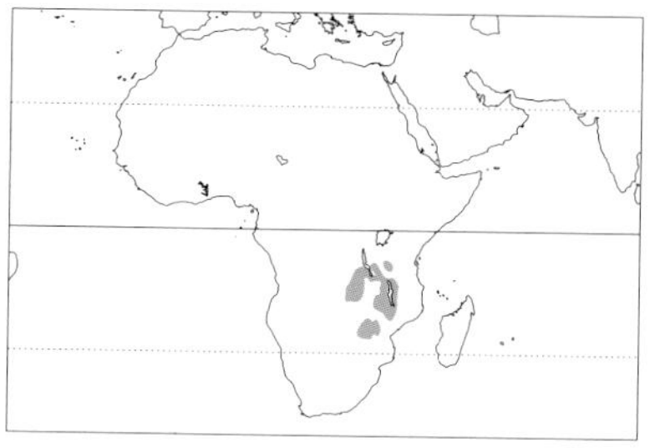

head, throat to breast black below white chin; *angoniensis* heavily marked yellow over crown, to nape; *buttoni* yellow instead of white under eye, only spotted yellow on forehead and crown, and white chin patch small; *stresemanni* fully yellow to mid-crown, more white in wings, yellower under eye. Voice. Song is soft series of "hoo" notes, 0·7-1 per second, faster than that of *S. anchietae* (these low-pitched songs like those of *Gymnobucco*), and probably by paired birds only, sometimes as duets; trill calls in chases of Lesser Honeyguide (*Indicator minor*) and *Lybius torquatus*; soft buzzy grating by adults around nest; soft "eh-eh-eeh" in courtship feeding; "yek" calls (as in *S. leucotis* and some *Gymnobucco* species) in conflicts, including with *S. anchietae* and other barbets, more "yeek"-like in persistent chasing of honeyguides; squawking, shrieking notes, longer in alarm as against snakes. Mechanical sounds include wing-fluttering at 25 beats per second in conflicts, bill-wiping at 20 per second in encounters, bill-tapping at 2-10 (rarely up to 20) per second inside or at nest entrance.
Habitat. *Brachystegia* woodland, partly cleared woods, riverside woods, and gardens, at 750-2500 m. Found in same woodland as *S. anchietae* near Ndola, in N Zambia.
Food and Feeding. Eats berries, and fruits such as figs, masuku (*Uapaca kirkiana*) and others; also insects, including ants, termites, grasshoppers, dragonflies and others. Forages in groups for fruits, even going to ground to pick them up; often forages solitarily for insects, obtained by gleaning and by flycatching. Regularly uses "anvil" to break up large insects, especially armoured ones. Probes into lichens, hangs like tit (Paridae); flies strongly and directly from site to site.
Breeding. Aug-Jan, mainly Oct-Dec. Nests in groups, with helpers, group containing up to 6 birds, nests sometimes as close together as 100 m. Courtship-feeds, displays with cocked tail, swinging and spreading of tail, bowing and swinging of body and head; in aggression within group, or against *S. anchietae*, facial and crown feathers spread, head bobbed, wings flicked, and bill-wiping. Cavity excavated at 2-20 m in dead tree, or on underside of dead branch in living tree; from completion, a "guard" barbet usually perches near it; group territory as small as 5 ha, very aggressive to all other barbets in nest area. Eggs 2-5; incubation period unknown; young fed insects at first, then gradually more fruit, until fruits are main item; up to 24 feeds per hour; nestling period c. 40 days; helpers, parents and fledged young roost in nest, young incorporated into group, with which they remain for unknown period. Nests parasitized by Lesser Honeyguide (*Indicator minor*). One nest preyed on by army ants, which killed and removed young in tiny pieces.
Movements. Resident and sedentary.
Status and Conservation. Not globally threatened. Somewhat adaptable, can exist in patches of woodland where considerable clearance has been carried out, so long as trees that are suitable for nesting and roosting remain. Nonetheless, more data needed about its specific requirements, as woodland is being cleared rapidly in many areas.
Bibliography. Benson (1964), Benson & Benson (1977), Benson *et al*. (1971), Britton (1980), Clancey (1995, 1996), Dowsett & Dowsett-Lemaire (1993), Dowsett & Forbes-Watson (1993), Fry *et al*. (1988), Ginn *et al*. (1989), Goodwin (1964), Harrison *et al*. (1997), Irwin (1981, 1998), Mackworth-Praed & Grant (1957, 1962), Maclean (1993), Marshall (1996), Newman (1996), Priest (1934, 1948), Short & Horne (1985a), Short *et al*. (1990), Sinclair *et al*. (1993, 1997), Snow (1978), Stevenson & Fanshawe (2001), Tarboton (2001).

12. **Anchieta's Barbet**

Stactolaema anchietae

French: Barbican à tête jaune **German**: Strohkopf-Bartvogel **Spanish**: Barbudo de Anchieta
Other common names: Yellow-headed Barbet

Taxonomy. *Buccanodon anchietae* Bocage, 1869, Caconda, south-west Angola.
Forms a superspecies with *S. whytii*. Three subspecies recognized.
Subspecies and Distribution.
S. a. katangae (Vincent, 1934) - NE Angola, S Zaire, and NW, NC & EC Zambia.
S. a. rex (Neumann, 1908) - WC Angola.
S. a. anchietae (Bocage, 1869) - SC Angola E to near Zambian border.

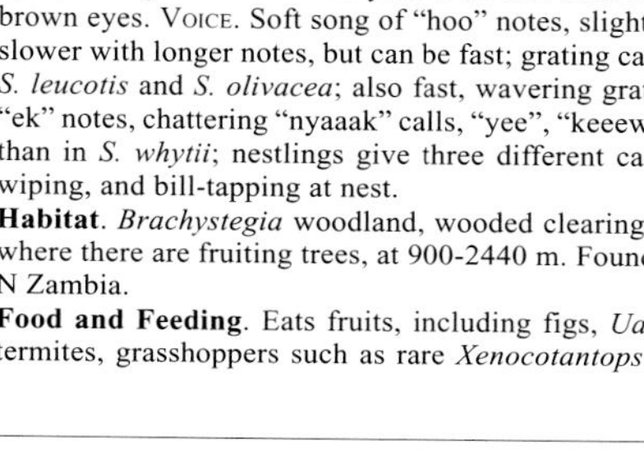

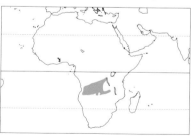

Descriptive notes. 18-19 cm; 36-54 g. Brown woodland barbet with yellow markings on head. Nominate race with pale yellow forehead, crown, face and chin, blackish-brown hindcrown and nape with fine white or yellow-white spots; white wing patch; upper breast black with yellowish streaks, lower belly whitish; dark brown eyes, black orbital skin. Distinguished from *S. whytii* by more extensive yellow, including chin, only single white wing patch. Sexes alike. Immature duller brown, has yellow in bill, and yellow orbital skin. Races weakly defined: *rex* with unspotted black hindcrown and nape, grey-brown to pale brown eyes; *katangae* shows richer yellow on face than nominate, with larger breast spots, whiter belly, brown eyes. Voice. Soft song of "hoo" notes, slightly higher-pitched than in *S. whytii* and usually slower with longer notes, but can be fast; grating calls less buzzy than those of *S. whytii*, more like *S. leucotis* and *S. olivacea*; also fast, wavering grating "aaAAAaaaa", soft "koot" and associated "ek" notes, chattering "nyaaak" calls, "yee", "keeew" and other calls; shrieks longer, lower-pitched than in *S. whytii*; nestlings give three different calls. Mechanical sounds of wing-rustling, bill-wiping, and bill-tapping at nest.
Habitat. *Brachystegia* woodland, wooded clearings, riverine woods, and edges of forest, always where there are fruiting trees, at 900-2440 m. Found in same woodland as *S. whytii* near Ndola, in N Zambia.
Food and Feeding. Eats fruits, including figs, *Uapaca kirkiana* and *U. nitida*, and others; also termites, grasshoppers such as rare *Xenocotantops parazernyi*, locusts, wasps, beetles and flies.

On following pages: 13. Green Barbet (*Stactolaema olivacea*); 14. Speckled Tinkerbird (*Pogoniulus scolopaceus*); 15. Eastern Green Tinkerbird (*Pogoniulus simplex*); 16. Moustached Green Tinkerbird (*Pogoniulus leucomystax*); 17. Western Green Tinkerbird (*Pogoniulus coryphaeus*); 18. Red-rumped Tinkerbird (*Pogoniulus atroflavus*); 19. Yellow-throated Tinkerbird (*Pogoniulus subsulphureus*); 20. Yellow-rumped Tinkerbird (*Pogoniulus bilineatus*); 21. Red-fronted Tinkerbird (*Pogoniulus pusillus*); 22. Yellow-fronted Tinkerbird (*Pogoniulus chrysoconus*).

Gleans, probes for insects, especially where mosses and lichens occur, and flycatches from perch. Special notches in branches or depressions in bark used as "anvils" to kill and dismember insects. Drinks water from lichen "cups". Flies fast and directly to fruiting trees and bushes, usually in groups. Aggressive at fruiting trees.
Breeding. Jul-Nov; in S Zaire nests in rainy season, Jan-Jun. Social, groups of up to 6 at a nest. Nest excavated at 2-10 m in stub, dead tree or dead branch, depth 25 cm or more; always 1 barbet on "guard" after excavation completed; attacks any bird close to nest, any other barbet that chances to sing nearby, and leads in mobbing predators such as mongooses (Viverridae). Eggs 2-5; incubation and nestling periods unknown; eggshells carried away from nest, as is faecal material; chicks fed 3-17 times an hour, by all group-members; adult once caught 3 insects in 30 seconds, fed them singly to nestlings. Frequently parasitized by Lesser Honeyguide (*Indicator minor*); in one observation, nestling honeyguide was fed at entrance but, as soon as it left nest, was instantly driven away 300 m and more by members of the group.
Movements. Resident and sedentary.
Status and Conservation. Not globally threatened. No reliable details on numbers, but appears to be locally common. Seems tolerant of some clearing of woodland, but dependence on dead wood and fruits suggests that monitoring is necessary.
Bibliography. Anon. (1998a), Aspinwall & Beel (1998), Benson *et al*. (1971), Chapin (1939), Clancey (1995), Dean (1974a, 2000), Dowsett & Dowsett-Lemaire (1993), Dowsett & Forbes-Watson (1993), Fry *et al*. (1988), Horne & Short (1988), Lippens & Wille (1976), Mackworth-Praed & Grant (1962, 1970), Payne (1967b), Pedersen (2000), Pinto (1983), Robertson (1998b), Short & Horne (1985a), Snow (1978), Traylor (1963).

13. Green Barbet

Stactolaema olivacea

French: Barbican olivâtre **German**: Olivbartvogel **Spanish**: Barbudo Oliváceo
Other common names: African Green Barbet, Olive Barbet; Woodward's Barbet (*woodwardi*)

Taxonomy. *Barbatula olivacea* Shelley, 1880, Rabai, south-east Kenya.
Sometimes placed in monospecific genus *Cryptolybia*, but differences in morphology, plumage and some vocalizations are minimal and generally considered quite insufficient to warrant generic separation. Race *woodwardi* sometimes treated as full species, but its features are shown to some degree in other races, and they are vocally identical. Proposed race *hylophona* included within *woodwardi*, though tending towards N races. Five subspecies recognized.
Subspecies and Distribution.
S. o. olivacea (Shelley, 1880) - SE Kenya and NE Tanzania.
S. o. howelli (Jensen & Stuart, 1982) - Udzungwe and Mahenge Mts, in C Tanzania.
S. o. rungweensis (Benson, 1948) - highlands of SW Tanzania and N Malawi.
S. o. woodwardi Shelley, 1895 - disjunctly in SE Tanzania (Rondo Plateau) and Natal (Ngoye Forest).
S. o. belcheri (W. L. Sclater, 1927) - NW Mozambique (Mt Namuli) and S Malawi (Mt Thyolo).

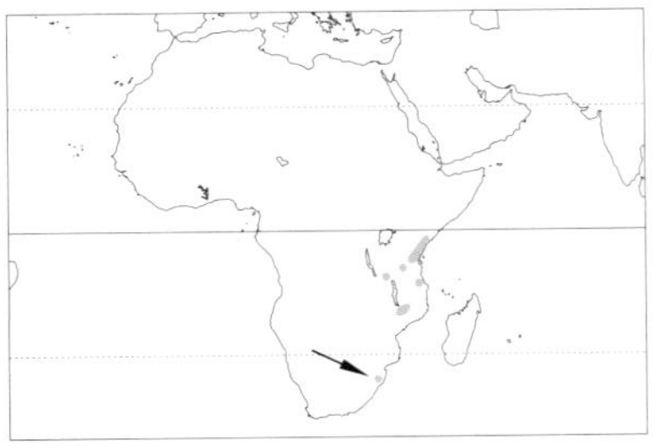

Descriptive notes. 17-18 cm; 40-60 g. Generally olive-green, unpatterned barbet. Nominate race has forehead to nape blackish-brown, ear-coverts greyer; hint of yellow-green area behind eye; eyes dull reddish. Differs from superficially similar *Pogoniulus simplex* in much larger size, lack of wing markings. Sexes alike. Immature somewhat duller than adult. Races *rungweensis* and *howelli* more bronzy (golden-green) above and darker-headed than nominate, *howelli* blackish on crown, and *rungweensis* with black to nape, buffish-olive behind eye, more greyish-olive below; *belcheri* more contrasting in colours, with greener, even yellow-green, ear-coverts, darker brownish or blackish rest of head, blackish throat and breast, darker green back; *woodwardi* green like nominate, but area behind eye more yellow and patch-like, dark forehead and lores, base of culmen more keel-like. Voice. Song up to 30 loud "chowp" notes introduced by "chuk", by either or both of pair together, occasionally as true duet; soft "ooo-ooo" series sometimes follow "chowp" songs, these slow notes resembling songs of *S. whytii* and *S. anchietae*; also squawking "shreek" calls, possibly alarm, used sometimes against honeyguides (Indicatoridae); other calls include interactive "kek", soft "ah", also grating, buzzy notes at 35-48 per second or faster; chatter and grating-churring notes from nestlings. Also bill-wiping and wing-fluttering displays.
Habitat. Wet to dry forest and dense to open woodland, and in Kenya *Brachystegia* woodland, using canopy to lower understorey, wherever fruits are found. Occurs in lowlands and hills to c. 2000 m. Interactions with other barbets suggest that those such as *S. leucotis* and *Lybius torquatus* could affect utilization of habitat.
Food and Feeding. Takes fruits such as figs, *Flagellaria guineensis* and many others, including berries of diverse types; also arthropods, including beetles, roaches, termites, moths, and the slug *Limax flavus*. Regurgitates larger fruit stones and hard insect parts. Flycatches and gleans for insects. Moves in groups of up to 6, more usually 3 or 4 when feeding. May join mixed-species foraging flocks of orioles (Oriolidae), starlings (Sturnidae), helmetshrikes (*Prionops*), flycatchers (*Muscicapa*) and drongos (Dicruridae).
Breeding. Sept-Apr generally, mainly Sept-Jan in S. Social, nests in groups of up to 8. Displays include courtship feeding, spreading of rump, face and crown feathers, and various postures; countersinging, used also against other barbets, e.g. *Lybius torquatus*. Excavates hole at 3-22 m in tree, usually on underside of dead branch of live tree but also in stub of dead tree, cavity to c. 60 cm deep, entrance c. 5 cm, nest-chamber c. 15 cm; 1 barbet "guards" hole during day. Eggs 3-6; change-overs in incubating duties at c. 30 minutes, incubation period c. 18 days; all adults feed young, c. 3 times per hour, at first insects, then mainly fruits, up to 4 figs in 1 feed; chamber may be enlarged as young grow, wood chips with faecal matter carried away by adults; nestling period c. 35 days. Post-fledging details lacking. Nests parasitized by Lesser Honeyguide (*Indicator minor*).
Movements. Resident and sedentary.
Status and Conservation. Not globally threatened. Common in coastal Kenya, where shows some adaptation to *Brachystegia* forest adjacent to wet forest; locally common in NE Tanzania, for example in E Usambaras. Suffers some pressure from other barbets, woodpeckers and honeyguides in form of nest-cavity and other competition, and brood parasitism by honeyguides. S races *belcheri* and *woodwardi* appear to be much rarer, need monitoring; other populations may remain to be discovered in C Mozambique; South African population of *woodwardi* may number only c. 1000 individuals (c. 300 pairs or groups). Continued forest clearance could place entire species under threat.
Bibliography. Barnes (2000), Belcher (1930), Benson (1948), Benson & Benson (1977), Britton (1980), Brooke (1984), Brown & Britton (1980), Chittenden *et al*. (1998), Clancey (1958c, 1964, 1979a, 1979c, 1985b, 1989b), Dowsett & Dowsett-Lemaire (1993), Dowsett & Forbes-Watson (1993), Dowsett-Lemaire & Dowsett (1987), Evans & Anderson (1992), Fry *et al*. (1988), Ginn *et al*. (1989), Harrison *et al*. (1997), Holliday & Tait (1953), Holsten *et al*. (1991), Irwin (1981), Jensen & Stuart (1982), King (1978/79), Lewis & Pomeroy (1989), Liversidge (1991), Mackworth-Praed & Grant (1957, 1962), Maclean (1993), Priest (1948), Ripley & Heinrich (1969), Schönwetter (1967), Short & Horne (1979, 1980a, 1985a), Short *et al*. (1990), Snow (1978, 1979), Tarboton (2001), Zimmerman *et al*. (1996).

Genus *POGONIULUS* Lafresnaye, 1844

14. Speckled Tinkerbird

Pogoniulus scolopaceus

French: Barbion grivelé **German**: Schuppenbartvogel **Spanish**: Barbudito Escolopáceo
Other common names: Spectacled Tinkerbird/Tinkerbarbet

Taxonomy. *Xylobucco scolopaceus* Bonaparte, 1850, Ashanti, Ghana.
No close relatives. Forms described as *aloysii* from Kenya and Uganda and *flavior* from N Angola considered synonyms of *flavisquamatus*. Three subspecies recognized.
Subspecies and Distribution.
P. s. scolopaceus (Bonaparte, 1850) - Sierra Leone and SE Guinea E to S Nigeria.
P. s. stellatus (Jardine & Fraser, 1852) - Bioko I (Fernando Póo).
P. s. flavisquamatus (J. Verreaux & E. Verreaux, 1855) - S Cameroon E to Uganda, S to N Angola and S Zaire.

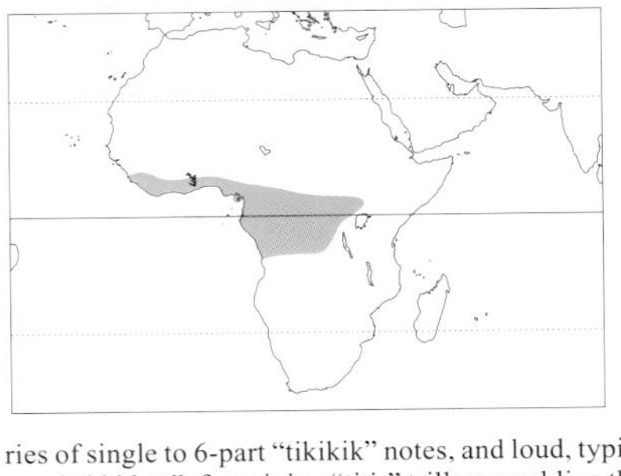

Descriptive notes. c. 12 cm; 11-18 g. Rather large for a tinkerbird, with scaly markings above. Nominate race has blackish-olive crown feathers broadly edged and tipped with yellow; upperparts blackish-grey with broad yellow fringes, rump yellower; underparts light yellow-buff with darker mottling. Sexes alike. Immature similar to adult, with markings yellower, base of bill yellow, often barred throat. Race *flavisquamatus* larger than nominate, more marked and thus darker below, crown especially darker than in other races; *stellatus* largest, more olive-green above, paler below. Voice. Variable, diverse, song-like series of single to 6-part "tikikik" notes, and loud, typically tinkerbird-like "tok-tok-"; also toad-like, nasal "bbbbttt", fast piping "titi-" trills resembling those of *P. simplex* superspecies, and loud, high-pitched "hyet" notes in series.
Habitat. Occupies primary forest at edges, in clearings, and also secondary forest and plantations of trees; requires dead wood for excavating hole; enters gardens. Occurs up to 1300 m in W Africa, up to 1800 m farther E.
Food and Feeding. Diet of fruits and arthropods (mainly insects). Fruits include those of figs, and species of *Coelocaryon*, *Heisteria*, *Macaranga*, *Rauvolfia* and others; ants, termites, beetles, flies and earwigs among insects eaten. Gleans from foliage and branches, and flycatches from perch. Forages in vines, bushes and trees, but mainly in canopy and subcanopy. May join mixed-species foraging flocks.
Breeding. Long season, or possibly renests: most months in W Africa, but especially Sept-Feb; in Apr-Jun on Bioko; in Oct-Mar in Cameroon and Gabon, Feb-Aug in Zaire, and probably Aug-Jan and May in Uganda. Breeds in pairs, sometimes trios; once 4 adults seen feeding nestlings. Nest excavated at 0·5-22 m, often higher, in dead tree, stub, even hanging dead branch; territory at least 6-8 ha in primary forest, up to c. 33 ha in secondary forest, maintained throughout year. Eggs 2-4; no data on incubation, fledging, or feeding of young, but groups or families of up to 5 roost together.
Movements. Resident and sedentary.
Status and Conservation. Not globally threatened. Widespread, and somewhat adaptable. Population in Liberia estimated at 1,200,000 pairs; estimates of 12-15 pairs/km^2 in Gabon secondary forest; common in Sierra Leone. No longer occurs in W Kenya, but may never have been common there. Present in several protected areas, e.g. Gola Forests Reserves (Sierra Leone), Korup National Park (Cameroon) and Kibale Forest National Park (Uganda).
Bibliography. Allport *et al*. (1989), Bannerman (1933, 1953), Bates (1930), Britton (1980), Brosset & Érard (1986), Brown & Britton (1980), Chapin (1939), Cheke & Walsh (1996), Christy & Clarke (1994), Colston & Curry-Lindahl (1986), Dean (2000), Dowsett (1989b), Dowsett & Dowsett-Lemaire (1993), Dowsett & Forbes-Watson (1993), Elgood *et al*. (1994), Field (1999), Fry *et al*. (1988), Gatter (1997), Germain & Cornet (1994), Grimes (1987), Lewis & Pomeroy (1989), Lippens & Wille (1976), Louette (1981b), Mackworth-Praed & Grant (1957, 1962, 1970), Pérez del Val (1996), Pérez del Val *et al*. (1994), Pinto (1983), Rand *et al*. (1959), Serle (1950, 1957, 1965), Short & Horne (1985a), Short *et al*. (1990), Snow (1978), Thiollay (1985a), Zimmerman *et al*. (1996).

15. Eastern Green Tinkerbird

Pogoniulus simplex

French: Barbion vert **German**: Schlichtbartvogel **Spanish**: Barbudito Sencillo
Other common names: Green(!)/African Green Tinkerbird/Tinkerbarbet

Taxonomy. *Barbatula simplex* Fischer and Reichenow, 1884, Pangani River, north-east Tanzania.
Forms a superspecies with *P. leucomystax* and *P. coryphaeus*, all three having in past been placed in separate genus *Viridibucco*. Birds of S Malawi and Mozambique sometimes separated as race *hylodytes*. Monotypic.
Distribution. SE Kenya (S from Arabuko-Sokoke Forest) to NE Tanzania, and S disjunctly to SE Malawi and S Mozambique (Sul do Save); also Zanzibar.
Descriptive notes. c. 9 cm; 7-10·5 g. Tiny, active green barbet lacking distinctive head markings. Both sexes olive-green above, with yellow rump; wings blackish with much yellow; underparts light olive-yellow to greyish-yellow. Differs from similar *P. leucomystax* in less dark upperparts,

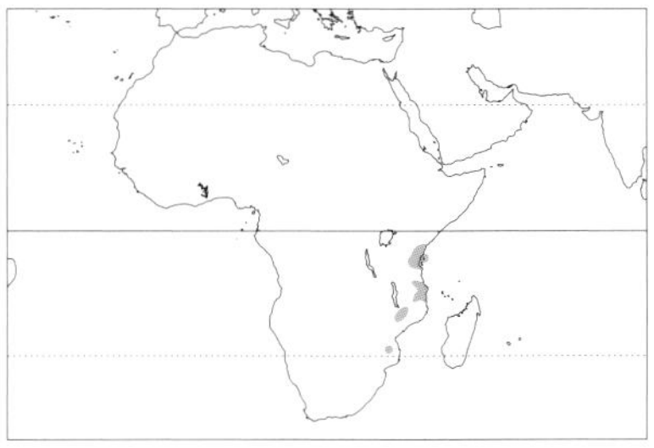

lack of white malar line; from other *Pogoniulus* species in lack of patterning. Immature with yellow basal half of bill. VOICE. Song of 2 types, a "pop-trill" very like that of sympatric race *fischeri* of *P. bilineatus* but higher-pitched, faster and shorter, and a variable piping trill, slow to fast (20-30 notes per second); also grating "ggggg", noisier long grating notes, and "prit" notes.

Habitat. Occupies dense undergrowth in primary forest, also in forest thickets and edges, as in coral rag bush; occasionally occurs in mangroves; rarely enters *Brachystegia* woods adjacent to forest. Occurs from sea-level up to 300 m in N, but up to 900 m in Usambara Mts in NE Tanzania, there overlapping with *P. leucomystax*, which generally replaces it at higher elevations; but where *P. leucomystax* is absent, as E of Rift Valley in S Malawi, present species occurs at up to 1525 m.

Food and Feeding. Diet largely unknown, but apparently mainly fruits, especially mistletoe berries (*Loranthus*); also gleans for insects. Flits about rapidly; seems to move constantly, calling as it does so. Occasionally joins mixed-species foraging flocks.

Breeding. Aug-Sept in Kenya, also Dec-Mar in Tanzania, and Oct-Dec in Zanzibar. Very little known: 1 nest with young 2 m up in thin dead tree in Kenya; sings generally below 7 m, so nests probably low; eggs and other details undescribed.

Movements. Resident and sedentary.

Status and Conservation. Not globally threatened. Uncommon and local in N of range; no details available from elsewhere. Relatively poorly known species; other populations may remain to be discovered in C Mozambique; much research required in order to uncover details of its ecology and breeding behaviour.

Bibliography. Benson & Benson (1977), Britton (1980), Clancey (1971a, 1984d, 1985b, 1996), Dowsett & Dowsett-Lemaire (1993), Dowsett & Forbes-Watson (1993), Evans & Anderson (1992), Fry *et al*. (1988), Ginn *et al*. (1989), Harrison *et al*. (1997), Holsten *et al*. (1991), Horne & Short (1988), Jackson & Sclater (1938), Lewis & Pomeroy (1989), Mackworth-Praed & Grant (1957), Maclean (1993), Mlingwa (2000), Newman (1996), Pakenham (1979), Short & Horne (1985a), Short *et al*. (1990), Sinclair *et al*. (1993, 1997), Snow (1978), Stevenson & Fanshawe (2001), Stuart & Jensen (1981), Waiyaki & Bennun (2000), Zimmerman *et al*. (1996).

16. Moustached Green Tinkerbird

Pogoniulus leucomystax

French: Barbion à moustaches **German**: Bergbartvogel **Spanish**: Barbudito Bigotudo
Other common names: Whiskered Green Tinkerbird, Moustached Tinkerbird/Tinkerbarbet

Taxonomy. *Barbatula leucomystax* Sharpe, 1892, Sotik, west Kenya.
Forms a superspecies with *P. simplex* and *P. coryphaeus*, all three having in past been placed in separate genus *Viridibucco*. Populations of present species show slight clinal increase in size towards S, but no constant geographical colour differences to warrant subspecific differentiation; birds from Chyulu Hills (Kenya) formerly separated as race *chyulu*. Monotypic.

Distribution. Extreme E Uganda (Mt Elgon) and C Kenya, S in highlands to Malawi mountains W of Rift Valley.

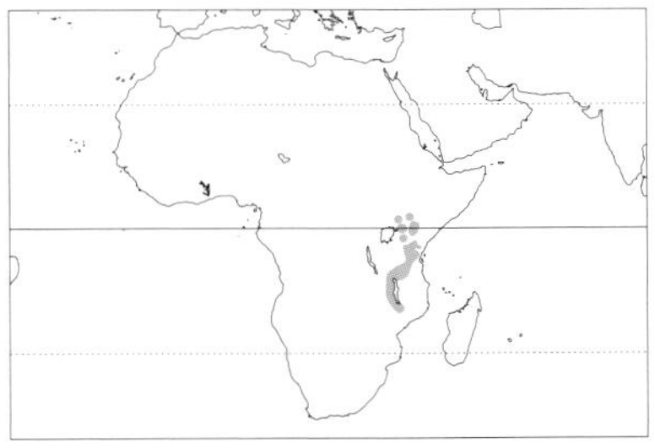

Descriptive notes. c. 9·5 cm; 8-14·5 g. Active small, green barbet. Both sexes dark olive-green above, with bright yellow rump; distinctive white malar stripe and dark lores; wings blackish with broad yellow wingbars, yellow feather edges; underparts light greyish-yellow, darker on breast. Distinguished from *P. simplex* by white malar mark, darker green crown and back. Immature has half or more of basal bill yellow. VOICE. Song, by male or female, a short to long piping trill at 6-20 notes per second, slow to faster, or tempo varying; also short, fast trills, often with varying number of notes in each set within series; other calls are sharp "pit" or "pit-it", grating "grrrr" notes, chattery "chaaaa" series, and rattling "griiiiik"; slow "ti-ti-ti-" to fast "peep-eep-" calls from nestlings.

Habitat. Generally in forest with dense undergrowth in mountains, but ranges from small remnant patches of forest to gardens and dense thickets; seems often to require presence of mistletoe (Loranthaceae) for breeding. Usually at 900-2500 m, rarely up to 3000 m, and in Usambara and Uluguru Mts, in Tanzania, down to 450 m. Known to overlap with *P. simplex* only at 450-900 m in W Usambaras, and replaces that species at higher elevations.

Food and Feeding. Eats fruits and berries, especially mistletoe berries (Loranthaceae, including *Engleriha inequilatera*); also flycatches for insects, but no details of species taken. Regurgitates fruit stones, often sticks those of mistletoe around nest entrance. Moves rapidly, feeding mainly at 2-8 m. Subordinate to *P. bilineatus* at food sources.

Breeding. May-Jun and Aug-Jan in N, thus in either of 2 rainy seasons; mainly Oct-Nov in S; in Malawi, 2 broods in a year, with 2-month interval between. Nests in pairs, but only 1 sleeps in nest at night. Nest, excavated by both adults, 3-7 m up in tree or stub, often in jacaranda in suburban areas, with entrance c. 2 cm; territories in suburban Nairobi 4-20 ha, but as small as 0·2 ha in Nyika Plateau, in Malawi; male sings just before roosting and after leaving nest in morning, as well as sporadically in bursts. Eggs 2-3; incubation period not known; both adults feed chicks, nestling period 32-34 days.

Movements. Resident; largely sedentary, with local dispersal and perhaps shifts to breeding areas (forest patches) from non-breeding locations.

Status and Conservation. Not globally threatened. The most widespread member of its superspecies, and the only one showing some adaptability. Locally common; fairly common to scarce in Kenya; less common than sympatric *P. bilineatus*; known to occur in Tsavo East and Tsavo West National Parks. On Nyika Plateau, in Malawi, 2 breeding pairs in forest patch as small as 1·2 ha, but densities lower in intact forest.

Bibliography. Aspinwall & Beel (1998), Atkins (1985), Belcher (1930), Benson & Benson (1977), Benson *et al*. (1971), Britton (1980), Brooks *et al*. (1998), Brown & Britton (1980), Clancey (1971d), Dowsett & Dowsett-Lemaire (1993), Dowsett & Forbes-Watson (1993), Dowsett-Lemaire (1983a), Fry *et al*. (1988), Horne & Short (1988), Jackson & Sclater (1938), Johnston-Stewart & Heigham (1982), Lewis & Pomeroy (1989), Mackworth-Praed & Grant (1957, 1962), Moreau & Moreau (1937), Ripley & Heinrich (1969), Short & Horne (1985a, 1988b), Snow (1978), Stevenson & Fanshawe (2001), Zimmerman *et al*. (1996).

17. Western Green Tinkerbird

Pogoniulus coryphaeus

French: Barbion montagnard **German**: Gelbrücken-Bartvogel **Spanish**: Barbudito Coronado
Other common names: Green(!)/Western Tinkerbird/Tinkerbarbet

Taxonomy. *Barbatula coryphaea* Reichenow, 1892, Buea, Mount Cameroon.
Forms a superspecies with *P. simplex* and *P. leucomystax*, all three having in past been placed in separate genus *Viridibucco*. Races poorly defined, but widely separated geographically. Three subspecies recognized.

Subspecies and Distribution.
P. c. coryphaeus (Reichenow, 1892) - E Nigeria and adjacent W Cameroon uplands.
P. c. hildamariae (W. L. Sclater, 1930) - E Zaire, SW Uganda and W Rwanda.
P. c. angolensis (Boulton, 1931) - WC Angola.

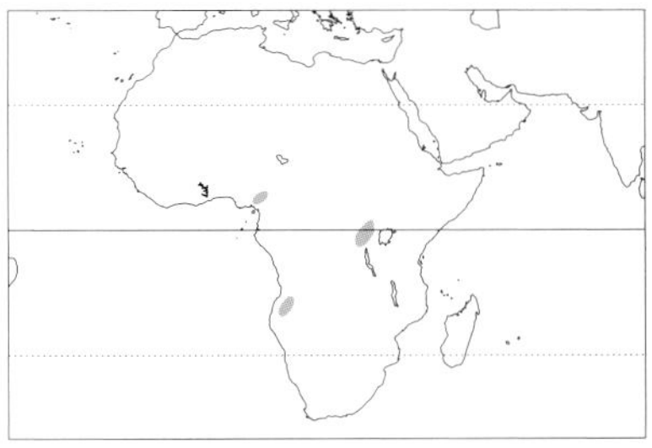

Descriptive notes. c. 9-10 cm; 8-13 g. A rather distinctive, small montane barbet. Both sexes of nominate race with broad golden-yellow band from forehead to rump, bordered black on each side; white malar stripe; wings black and gold; and greyish-olive underparts. Easily distinguished from both *P. simplex* and *P. leucomystax* by general coloration and pattern, but voice similar. Immature duller than adult, base of bill yellow. Race *hildamariae* slightly smaller, more yellow, less golden; *angolensis* still paler yellow, duller and greyer, less olive, below. VOICE. Main vocalization fast to slow piping trills in series, much like those of *P. leucomystax*, 5-12 notes per second; other calls little known.

Habitat. Usually montane forest in dense undergrowth, also edges, clearings, riverine thickets and dense secondary forest; occasionally forages into adjacent woodland and *Eucalyptus* plantations, and visits fruiting trees in the open. Occurs at 900-3030 m, mainly 1900-2500 m.

Food and Feeding. Eats fruits and berries, including figs and mistletoe berries (Loranthaceae); also beetles and probably other insects, but data are sparse. Feeds mainly 2-10 m up in trees; clings like tit (Paridae) to fruits. Moves about rapidly.

Breeding. Oct in Cameroon, Jun-Aug and Nov-Jan in E Zaire, Apr-May in Uganda, and May-Jun in Angola. Non-social breeder, strongly territorial. Nest excavated at 0·6-5 m in dead stub or small dead tree; 1 was 80 cm deep and up to 50 mm wide, with entrance hole 2 cm across and with sprouting seeds stuck around it. Eggs 3; no information on incubation and nestling periods, or on role of sexes.

Movements. Mainly resident; post-breeding downslope movement occurs, rarely down to c. 50 m, bringing it into range of several lowland tinkerbirds.

Status and Conservation. Not globally threatened. Appears to be generally uncommon and local, but no detailed data on population numbers. Little known also about its breeding biology and general ecology. Requirement for further information on this species considered of some importance, particularly in view of its small fragmented range. Present in several protected areas, e.g. Gashaka-Gumti Reserve (Nigeria), Mount Kupé National Park (Cameroon) and Impenetrable Forest National Park (Uganda).

Bibliography. Ash *et al*. (1989), Bannerman (1953), Britton (1980), Chapin (1939), Dean (2000), Dowsett (1989a, 1990), Dowsett & Dowsett-Lemaire (1993), Dowsett & Forbes-Watson (1993), Elgood *et al*. (1994), Fry *et al*. (1988), Jackson & Sclater (1938), Larison *et al*. (2000), Lippens & Wille (1976), Louette (1981b), Mackworth-Praed & Grant (1957, 1962, 1970), Pedersen (2000), Pinto (1983), Prigogine (1971), Serle (1950, 1964, 1965), Short & Horne (1985a), Short *et al*. (1990), Snow (1978), Stevenson & Fanshawe (2001), Stuart & Jensen (1986).

18. Red-rumped Tinkerbird

Pogoniulus atroflavus

French: Barbion à croupion rouge **German**: Rotbürzel-Bartvogel **Spanish**: Barbudito Culirrojo

Taxonomy. *Bucco atro-flavus* Sparrman, 1798, Sierra Leone.
Rather isolated member of genus, perhaps near to *P. bilineatus* and the superspecies formed by *P. pusillus* and *P. chrysoconus*. "*P. erythronotos*" is a synonym. Monotypic.

Distribution. Senegambia E in forested areas to S Cameroon, thence to SE Central African Republic and W Uganda, and S to Cabinda (N Angola), R Congo and CE Zaire.

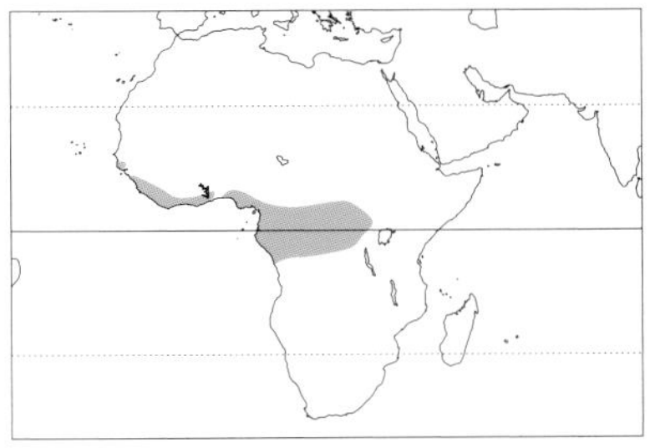

Descriptive notes. c. 12-13 cm; 14-21·5 g. Relatively large tinkerbird with distinctive pattern. Both sexes glossy black above, with yellow wingbar and red rump; side of head with 2 yellow stripes, broader malar stripe; throat yellow, rest of underparts pale greyish-olive. Distinguished from all other *Pogoniulus* by red rump. Immature duller, more sooty and less black, base of bill yellow. VOICE. Song an unbroken series of "pop" notes at 1·3 per second; also fast "bdddddt" trill series 3-4 seconds long with 29 notes per second, and higher-pitched, shorter, slower trills with notes c. 16 per second.

Habitat. Primary and secondary forest, including some mature mangrove forest, edges, adjacent clearings, forest-grassland mosaic, plantations and other cultivated areas; extends into open floodplains in S Sierra Leone. Usually below 800 m, but occasionally to 1550 m in W Africa, to 1800 m in Cameroon and to 2400 m in NE Zaire.

Food and Feeding. Eats mainly fruits, including figs, and species of *Allophyllus*, *Musanga*, *Rauvolfia* and others, especially *Loranthus*; also undetermined insects and spiders. Forages at all levels, in forest mostly in canopy.

Breeding. Nov-May and Aug in W Africa, May-Jun in Central African Republic, Jun-Feb in Uganda. Other data very sparse: territorial, sings all year, singers depress tail, erect and spread red rump feathers; presumably excavates hole in dead tree, but no details; eggs 2-3.

Movements. Resident and sedentary.

Status and Conservation. Not globally threatened. Estimated 300,000 pairs in Liberia, where density of 5-8 pairs/km²; common in Sierra Leone. Usually uncommon, however, and considered the least common lowland tinkerbird, perhaps because of competition with larger barbets and woodpeckers for nesting and roosting sites; such competition possibly more likely owing to this species' comparatively large size for a tinkerbird. Further data needed on all aspects of its biology. Present in several protected areas, e.g. Taï Forest National Park (Ivory Coast) and Korup National Park (Cameroon).

Bibliography. Allport *et al.* (1989), Bannerman (1933, 1953), Barlow *et al.* (1997), Bates (1930), Britton (1980), Brosset & Érard (1986), Chapin (1939), Chappuis (1981), Cheke & Walsh (1996), Christy & Clarke (1994), Clancey (1984c), Colston & Curry-Lindahl (1986), Dean (2000), Dowsett (1989b), Dowsett & Dowsett-Lemaire (1993), Dowsett & Forbes-Watson (1993), Elgood *et al.* (1994), Field (1999), Friedmann (1978a), Fry *et al.* (1988), Gatter (1997), Grimes (1987), Lippens & Wille (1976), Louette (1981b), Mackworth-Praed & Grant (1970), Morel & Morel (1990), Pinto (1983), Rand *et al.* (1959), Serle (1950, 1965), Short & Horne (1985a), Short *et al.* (1990), Snow (1978), Thiollay (1985a).

19. Yellow-throated Tinkerbird

Pogoniulus subsulphureus

French: Barbion à gorge jaune **German**: Gelbkehl-Bartvogel **Spanish**: Barbudito Gorgigualdo

Taxonomy. *Bucco subsulphureus* Fraser, 1843, Bioko.
Closely related to *P. bilineatus* and the superspecies formed by *P. pusillus* and *P. chrysoconus*. Three subspecies recognized.
Subspecies and Distribution.
P. s. chrysopygus (Shelley, 1889) - Sierra Leone and SE Guinea E to S Ghana.
P. s. flavimentum (J. Verreaux & E. Verreaux, 1851) - Togo E to S Central African Republic and S Uganda, and S to C Zaire.
P. s. subsulphureus (Fraser, 1843) - Bioko I (Fernando Póo).

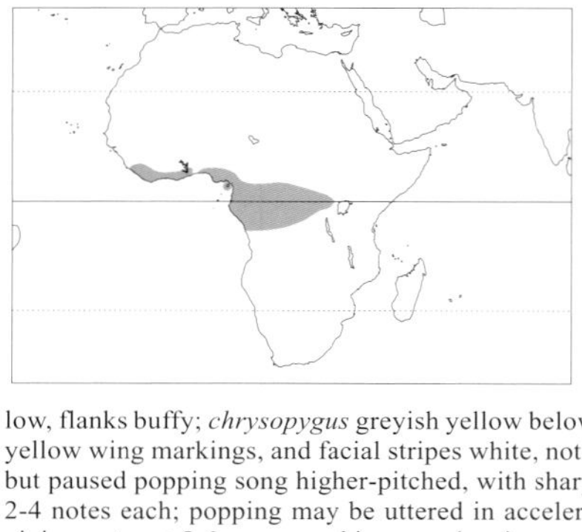

Descriptive notes. c. 9·5 cm; 7·5-13 g. Tiny, black, yellow and white tinkerbird. Both sexes with glossy blue-black crown to back; nominate race with yellow rump and yellow throat; pale yellow supercilia, thin yellow line across forehead extending into whiter moustachial stripe; flight-feathers with whitish inner webs, pale yellowish edges; underparts pale yellowish, greying at sides. Distinguished from *P. bilineatus* by smaller size, yellow throat; from *P. atroflavus* by smaller size, yellow rump. Immature duller, upperpart feathers edged yellowish, base of bill yellowish. Race *flavimentum* less grey below, more olive-yellow, flanks buffy; *chrysopygus* greyish yellow below, with whiter throat, broader and more golden-yellow wing markings, and facial stripes white, not yellow. Voice. Resembles that of *P. bilineatus*, but paused popping song higher-pitched, with sharp "pyop" as first note, song sets normally with 2-4 notes each; popping may be uttered in accelerating series for several seconds; also yipping, piping notes at 5-6 per second in paused series; and single "pyip" notes woven with multiple "yi-yi-yi" notes into varying series; nestlings give piping, tinkling notes.
Habitat. Primary and old secondary forest, streamside forest, forest borders, and submontane forest; enters gardens. Possibly excluded from more open habitats by larger *P. bilineatus*, but co-occurs with it in open forest, forest-savanna mosaic and areas of palms in parts of Sierra Leone. Occurs from sea-level to 2100 m; on Bioko generally below *P. bilineatus*, up to 800-1000 m.
Food and Feeding. Diet of diverse fruits, such as figs and species of *Allophyllus*, *Heisteria*, *Macaranga*, *Trema* and others; also takes insects from around such flowers as *Bombax*, and consumes others such as ants and termites, as well as wood-boring beetle larvae. Most foraging is in dense canopy and subcanopy above 20 m, making it difficult to observe.
Breeding. Mainly Jan-Jul but as early as Sept in Sierra Leone, Liberia and Guinea; Dec-Jan in Ivory Coast and Ghana; all year in Nigeria and probably Cameroon; Sept-Mar in Gabon, Congo and Zaire; Feb-May on Bioko; and May-Jun and Dec-Jan (following both rainy seasons) in Uganda. Nest usually at c. 4 m, few other details (but a roosting hole once only 8 cm deep in stub 5 cm thick); territory 9-10 ha in Gabon. Eggs 2-3; no information on incubation and fledging periods; chicks fed at intervals of 1-13 minutes, by both parents.
Movements. Resident and sedentary.
Status and Conservation. Not globally threatened. Together with *P. bilineatus* is a characteristic bird of forest in W & C Africa; usually appears to be less numerous than the larger *P. bilineatus* but is also mistaken for it. Estimated population in Liberia 700,000 pairs, with densities of up to 15 or more/km², and greatly outnumbers *P. bilineatus* in that country; common throughout S Sierra Leone. Also suggested to occur in SW Senegal, on basis of vocal record; this would represent significant range extension, but confirmation required. Usually requires more dense cover than *P. bilineatus*, or is physically kept from edge habitats by that species. More information is needed about its ecology and population dynamics. Present in several protected areas, e.g. Gola Forests Reserves (Sierra Leone) and Korup National Park (Cameroon).

Bibliography. Allport *et al.* (1989), Bannerman (1933, 1953), Barlow *et al.* (1997), Bates (1909), Britton (1980), Brosset & Érard (1986), Brown & Britton (1980), Chapin (1939), Chappuis (1981), Cheke & Walsh (1996), Christy & Clarke (1994), Colston & Curry-Lindahl (1986), Demey & Fishpool (1994), Dowsett (1989b), Dowsett & Dowsett-Lemaire (1993), Dowsett & Forbes-Watson (1993), Elgood *et al.* (1994), Field (1999), Fry *et al.* (1988), Gatter (1997), Grimes (1987), Lippens & Wille (1976), Louette (1981b), Mackworth-Praed & Grant (1957, 1970), Morel & Morel (1990), Pérez del Val (1996), Pérez del Val *et al.* (1994), Pinto (1983), Rand *et al.* (1959), Serle (1965), Short & Horne (1985a), Short *et al.* (1990), Snow (1978), Thiollay (1985a).

20. Yellow-rumped Tinkerbird

Pogoniulus bilineatus

French: Barbion à croupion jaune **Spanish**: Barbudito Culigualdo
German: Goldbürzel-Bartvogel
Other common names: Golden-rumped Tinkerbird/Tinkerbarbet; Lemon-rumped Tinkerbird/Tinkerbarbet (*leucolaimus*); White-chested Tinkerbird/Tinkerbarbet ("*makawai*")

Taxonomy. *Megalæma bilineata* Sundevall, 1850, Natal.
Appears to be most closely related to *P. subsulphureus* and the superspecies formed by *P. pusillus* and *P. chrysoconus*; possibly fairly close to *P. atroflavus*. Yellow-rumped races *mfumbiri*, *leucolaimus* and *poensis* have been thought to represent a separate species, *P. leucolaimus*, but they intergrade with the three golden-rumped races in E Zaire, Rwanda and Burundi; also, vocal evidence suggests that *leucolaimus* is conspecific with present species. In view of similarity and intergradation between these two groups, other described forms considered untenable: thus, *sharpei* (S Ghana), *togoensis* (Gambia to S Nigeria) and *nyansae* (W shore L Victoria) regarded as synonymous with *leucolaimus*; *urungensis* (S shore L Tanganyika) with *mfumbiri*; *alius* (C Kenya) with *jacksoni*; *pallidus* (Sokoke Forest) and *conciliator* (Uluguru Mts) with *fischeri*; and *rovumensis* (SE Tanzania), *deceptor* (E Zimbabwe), *riparium* (S Mozambique, NE South Africa) and *oreonesus* (Malawi) with nominate *bilineatus*. In addition, single specimen from NW Zambia originally described as separate species, "*P. makawai*", on basis of plumage differences and bigger bill, but now generally considered no more than aberrant individual of present species. Six subspecies recognized.
Subspecies and Distribution.
P. b. leucolaimus (J. Verreaux & E. Verreaux, 1851) - Senegambia E to S Cameroon, S Central African Republic and W Uganda, S to N Angola, and S Zaire.
P. b. poensis (Alexander, 1908) - highlands of Bioko I (Fernando Póo).
P. b. mfumbiri (Ogilvie-Grant, 1907) - SW Uganda and E Zaire to W Burundi, W Tanzania and E & NC Zambia.
P. b. jacksoni (Sharpe, 1897) - E Uganda and C Kenya S to E Burundi and N Tanzania.
P. b. fischeri (Reichenow, 1880) - coastal Kenya S to NE Tanzania; also Zanzibar, and Mafia I (off E Tanzania).
P. b. bilineatus (Sundevall, 1850) - E Zambia and S Tanzania S to E South Africa.

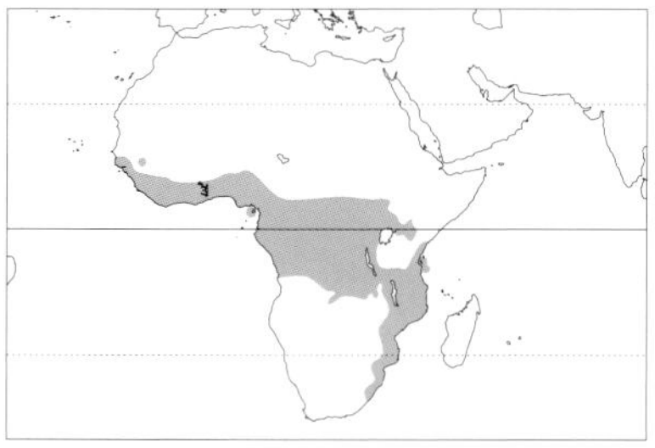

Descriptive notes. 10-12 cm; 11-18·5 g, but *fischeri* 8-12·5 g, and *leucolaimus* 7-14 g. The epitome of a tinkerbird, with contrastingly marked face, strong bill, rather short tail. Both sexes of nominate race black above, with golden rump, golden-yellow in wings; white supercilia, white line across forehead and down to neck side, white throat; underparts pale olive-yellow, more olive laterally. Distinguished from similar *P. subsulphureus* by larger size, white throat, more golden rump, from very similar white-throated race *chrysopygus* of latter also more safely by voice. Immature duller, greener, less black than adults, with yellow base of bill. Races differ mainly in coloration of pale areas of plumage, forming two groups according to rump colour: *jacksoni* and *fischeri* golden-rumped like nominate, former smaller, greyer and less olive below, and paler generally, *fischeri* very small, with whiter throat, yellower rest of underparts, larger gold rump, and becoming clinally paler to N; other three races all yellower-rumped, *mfumbiri* large and with buff on sides and flanks, *leucolaimus* small and brighter yellow, with even less olive, and *poensis* paler yellow on rump and underparts and with whiter breast. Voice. Usual song paused popping, series of "pop" notes at c. 3 per second, in sets generally of 2-6, more in some situations, first and last sets with fewest notes; N birds of race *fischeri* substitute "pop-trill" for paused popping, more S individuals of same race employ both songs; occasional nasal "honk", lacking overtones, within popping song; also pure "honk" calls in series, especially at start of and after breeding, also so-called "frog" call "driii-driii-", with burry "rrrrrk" perhaps a version of it; also "pop-op" calls in series, sharp "chip" notes, rattling "bdddddt" in interactions, common "zddddd" grating calls with elements at c. 90 per second, and begging "di-di-di-". Mechanical signals include wing-fluttering, bill-tapping at or in cavity.
Habitat. Forested highlands and lowlands, especially at edges, about clearings, in forest clumps left over after clearing, in thickets, riverine forest, moist parts of drier woods, tree plantations, and gardens. In coastal Kenya, shares forest habitat with *P. simplex*, more open wooded habitats with *P. pusillus*; in C & W Africa less often in dense forest than is smaller *P. subsulphureus*, but occurs with it and with *P. atroflavus* and *P. scolopaceus*. On Bioko, is a highland species generally occurring above *P. subsulphureus*; elsewhere, may impinge on highland *P. leucomystax* and *P. coryphaeus*. Occurs from sea-level to 1800 m in W Africa, to 2600 m in C Africa and on Bioko (where usually above 800-1000 m), to 3000 m in E Africa, c. 1600 m in Zimbabwe and 600 m in South Africa.
Food and Feeding. Fruits essential, including especially mistletoe berries (*Loranthus*, *Tieghemia*, *Sulphurea*, *Viscum*), also *Ficus*, and species of *Allophyllus*, *Clausenia*, *Ekebergia*, *Macaranga*, *Maesa*, *Ochna*, *Ocotea*, *Polyscias*, *Prunus*, *Psychotria*, *Trema* and others; insects also taken, including termites, ants, noctuid moths and other Lepidoptera, Homoptera, curculionid and galerucid beetles, among others. Discards epicarp of mistletoe berries as fruits eaten, cellulose layer is digested, pectin layer over seeds passes through digestive system and egested with seed; small berries swallowed, regurgitated in courtship feeding. Insects caught by gleaning and flycatching, even in exotic trees. Isolated fruiting trees may be defended by a single bird.
Breeding. Nov-Apr in W Africa; all year in Cameroon, Apr-Nov and Jan in Gabon, Congo and Zaire; May-Jun in Uganda; Jan-Mar and Aug in W Kenya, Mar-Jul and Sept-Jan in coastal Kenya and Tanzania, May-Aug and Nov-Feb (during and after rains) in C Kenya and EC Tanzania; Apr-May and Sept-Dec on Mafia I and Zanzibar; Oct-Jan in Angola to Zambia and Malawi, and eggs in Sept-Dec in South Africa; sometimes 2 broods in a season. Singer erects rump feathers, puffs throat, flicks tail with each note, turns head side to side in almost vertical posture; courtship feeding of up to 32 berries in 25 minutes, sometimes followed by copulation (e.g. 3 times in 25 minutes). Nest, excavated by both adults, 1-10 m up in dead tree, stump, post or dead branch; entrance diameter 2·5 cm, cavity 2·5 cm into branch, 40-100 cm deep, nest-chamber 3·5 cm by 5 cm, lined with wood chips; territory c. 4 ha. Eggs 2-5, usually 3; incubation c. 12 days, by both adults; chicks fed insects at first, later also fruit, at rates of up to 19 feeds per hour; nestlings' faecal material eaten at first by parents, later young present anal area to adult, which then carries away faecal sac, in one instance 12 sacs removed after 38 feeds in 2-hour period; fledging at 17-20 days; few data on post-fledging period, but occurrence sometimes of second brood suggests rapid independence. Up to 4 young fledge; nests parasitized by Least (*Indicator exilis*) and Scaly-throated Honeyguides (*I. variegatus*), and also recorded by Pallid Honeyguide (*I. meliphilus*); 1 tinkerbird pair enlarged cavity entrance apparently to facilitate exit of large young honeyguide.
Movements. Resident, and largely sedentary, but dispersal up to 20 km.
Status and Conservation. Not globally threatened. Form "*makawai*" officially considered Data-deficient. Widespread, and common throughout range; generally commonest tinkerbird wherever it occurs, although in Liberia far less numerous than *P. subsulphureus*. Adapts to various habitat changes. Despite searches having been carried out, "*makawai*", now thought almost certainly to be variant of present species, not recorded in the 35 years since first discovered, in 1965. Present in several protected areas, e.g. Abuko Nature Reserve (Gambia), Kakamega Nature Reserve (Kenya), Kruger National Park and Mkuzi Reserve (South Africa).

Bibliography. Anon. (1998d), Bannerman (1933, 1953), Barlow *et al.* (1997), Bennun (1991), Benson & Benson (1977), Benson & Irwin (1965a, 1965b), Benson *et al.* (1971), Britton (1980), Brosset & Érard (1986), Brown & Britton (1980), Cave & Macdonald (1955), Chapin (1939), Cheke & Walsh (1996), Christy & Clarke (1994), Clancey (1971c, 1985c), Collar & Andrew (1988), Collar & Stuart (1985), Collar *et al.* (1994), Colston & Curry-Lindahl (1986), Day (1981), Dean (2000), Dowsett (1979a, 1980, 1990), Dowsett & Dowsett-Lemaire (1980, 1993), Dowsett & Forbes-Watson (1993), Elgood *et al.* (1994), Field (1999), Friedmann (1930a, 1978a), Fry *et al.* (1988), Gatter (1997), Ginn *et al.* (1989), Goodwin (1965), Gore (1990), Grimes (1987), Harrison *et al.* (1997), Irwin (1981), Lewis

& Pomeroy (1989), Lippens & Wille (1976), Liversidge (1991), Louette (1981b), Mackworth-Praed & Grant (1957, 1962, 1970), Maclean (1993), Madge (1971), Milstein (1995), Mlingwa (2000), Pakenham (1979), Pérez del Val (1996), Pérez del Val *et al.* (1994), Pinto (1983), Pitman (1929), Prigogine (1972, 1977, 1980a, 1985), Rand *et al.* (1959), Serle (1950), Short & Horne (1985a), Short *et al.* (1990), Snow (1978), van Someren (1956), Tarboton (2001), Thiollay (1985a), Vande weghe (1980), Ward (1989), White (1953), Zimmerman (1972), Zimmerman *et al.* (1996).

21. Red-fronted Tinkerbird

Pogoniulus pusillus

French: Barbion à front rouge **German**: Feuerstirn-Bartvogel **Spanish**: Barbudito Frentirrojo
Other common names: Red-fronted Tinkerbarbet

Taxonomy. *Bucco pusillus* Dumont, 1816, Sunday River, east Cape Province.
Forms a superspecies with *P. chrysoconus*, which it meets marginally in Ethiopia and South Africa with no apparent hybridization; both are also closely related to *P. bilineatus* and *P. subsulphureus*, and perhaps fairly close to *P. atroflavus*. Populations to E and S of L Victoria formerly separated as race *eupterus*. Three subspecies currently recognized.
Subspecies and Distribution.
P. p. uropygialis (Heuglin, 1862) - Eritrea and N & C Ethiopia to N Somalia.
P. p. affinis (Reichenow, 1879) - SE Sudan, SE Ethiopia and S Somalia S to SE Tanzania.
P. p. pusillus (Dumont, 1816) - S Mozambique and E South Africa.

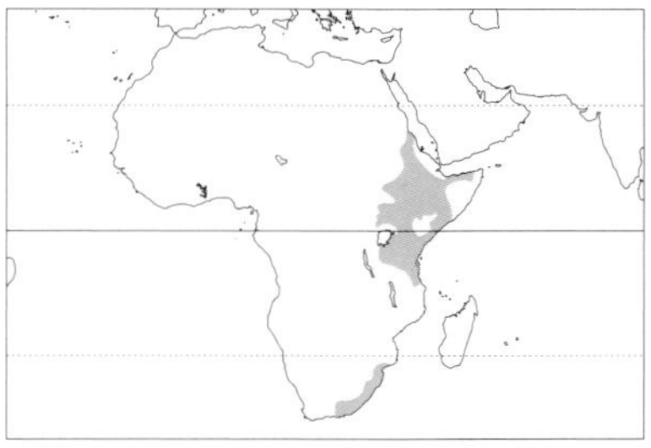

Descriptive notes. 9·5-11·5 cm; 6-12·5 g. Tiny, short-tailed tinkerbird with black, gold-yellow and white streaky and spotted pattern, and red forecrown. Both sexes of nominate race with golden wing-covert patch coalescing with golden-yellow edges to flight-feathers; yellowish streaks on back, yellow rump; throat yellow, rest of underparts light olive-greyish with yellow tinge. Distinguished from very similar *P. chrysoconus* by red forehead. Immature lacks red patch on head. Race *affinis* smaller than nominate, is less gold with more of a yellow wingbar (not patch), white-streaked rather than yellow-streaked above, with more orange-red forehead, occasional red tips to rump feathers, whiter throat; *uropygialis* close to *affinis*, but yellower streaks dorsally, still less gold in wings, and frequently shows red in rump. Voice. Song slow "pop" notes unbroken by pauses, to 20 minutes at 109-140 per minute in S Africa, generally 110-130 but also 45-200 per minute in Kenya; also trills in series, often starting with 1 note as singles, to double notes, then up to 8 notes in a set, "pip-ip-ip-ip-ip-"; low "wee" note after courtship feeding; other calls include interactive grating series with 60-180 elements per second, piping that is high-pitched and faster than comparable calls of *P. chrysoconus*, when breeding honking nasal series at c. 90 notes per minute and pitched higher than in *P. bilineatus*, and frog-like snore 0·5 seconds long with 90 elements per second. Responds equally to playback of *P. chrysoconus* voice.
Habitat. Various dry woodland, bushland, riverine bush in desert, scrubland, cut-over forest and gardens. Invades opened forest as at Arabuko-Sokoke Forest, in Kenya, where meets *P. simplex*. Occurs in more moist woods than does *P. chrysoconus* in S Africa, but in drier bushed areas than that species in Ethiopia. Strong interactions among tinkerbirds, and between this species and larger barbets such as *Tricholaema diademata*, suggest that these barbets impinge on one another. Found from sea-level to 2000 m, even 2200 m where *P. bilineatus* absent, but below 1550 m in Ethiopia.
Food and Feeding. Diverse fruits and berries, mainly mistletoe berries (Loranthaceae); also unspecified insects (including beetles) and spiders. Flies directly to food sources, keeping in denser clumps amid sparse vegetation; forages over branches and trunks at times, much as warblers (*Sylvietta*); pecks or taps to get at insects under bark.
Breeding. Feb-Sept, occasionally Oct, in N, and Oct-Dec in S. Singer erects rump, throat and red frontal feathers, flips tail at each pop; responds to countersingers with faster song, grating and displaying, swinging head, and chasing off. Nest excavated at 1-6 m in tree such as *Acacia* or *Commiphora*, usually on underside of dead branch, entrance c. 2 cm, chamber to 55 cm deep and 30-50 cm in diameter; territory up to 10 ha, territories not always abutting, nor occupied every year, defended against *P. chrysoconus* as well as own species, but can overlap with *P. bilineatus* territory and even using same songposts at different times. Eggs 2-4, usually 3; both sexes incubate, period c. 12 days, and feed nestlings as well as carry away faecal material; nestling period c. 23 days.
Movements. Some movements suggested by disappearance from some sites after breeding; in uplands numbers fluctuate from year to year.
Status and Conservation. Not globally threatened. Common in most of range; fairly common in Kenya. The commonest tinkerbird along with *P. chrysoconus* and *P. bilineatus*. More precise data on habitat requirements are needed. Present in several reserves, e.g. Awash National Park (Ethiopia), Mikumi National Park (Tanzania) and Mkuzi Reserve (South Africa).
Bibliography. Archer & Godman (1937-1961), Ash & Miskell (1998), Benson (1946), Britton (1980), Brown & Britton (1980), Cave & Macdonald (1955), Dowsett & Dowsett-Lemaire (1993), Dowsett & Forbes-Watson (1993), Friedmann (1930a, 1930b), Fry *et al.* (1988), Ginn *et al.* (1989), Harrison *et al.* (1997), Heuglin (1861), Jackson & Sclater (1938), Lewis & Pomeroy (1989), Mackworth-Praed & Grant (1957, 1962), Maclean (1993), Miskell (1989), Monadjem *et al.* (1994), Ross (1970), Schmidl (1982), Short & Horne (1985a, 1988b), Short *et al.* (1990), Skead (1944, 1945), Smith (1957), Snow (1978, 1979), Steyn (1996), Tarboton (2001), Ward (1989), Zimmerman *et al.* (1996), Zinner (2001).

22. Yellow-fronted Tinkerbird

Pogoniulus chrysoconus

French: Barbion à front jaune **German**: Gelbstirn-Bartvogel **Spanish**: Barbudito Frentigualdo
Other common names: Yellow-fronted Barbet(!)/Tinkerbarbet

Taxonomy. *Bucco chrysoconus* Temminck, 1832, Senegal.
Forms a superspecies with *P. pusillus*, overlapping very narrowly in Ethiopia and E South Africa and apparently not hybridizing; both are also closely related to *P. bilineatus* and *P. subsulphureus*, and perhaps fairly close to *P. atroflavus*. Proposed races *schubotzi* (WC Niger to SW Sudan), *zedlitzi* (E Sudan) and *centralis* (NE Zaire and Uganda) regarded as synonyms of *chrysoconus*; *schoanus* (C Ethiopia) included in *xanthostictus*; and *rhodesiae* (SW Zaire to Malawi) and *mayri* (S Zaire to NE Angola) in *extoni*. Three subspecies currently recognized.
Subspecies and Distribution.
P. c. chrysoconus (Temminck, 1832) - SW Mauritania and Senegal E to NW Ethiopia, S to N edge of forest in C Cameroon, N & NE Zaire, Burundi and NW Tanzania.
P. c. xanthostictus (Blundell & Lovat, 1899) - highlands of C & S Ethiopia.
P. c. extoni (E. L. Layard, 1871) - Angola and S Zaire E to S Tanzania, S to NC Namibia, N Botswana, Transvaal and S Mozambique.

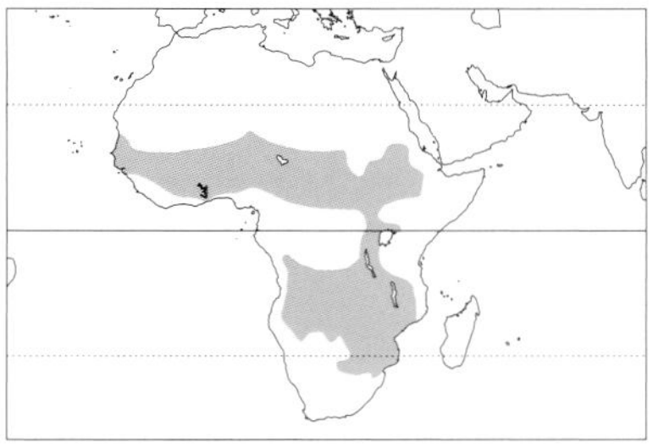

Descriptive notes. c. 10·5-12 cm; 8-20 g. Small, strong-billed, short-tailed tinkerbird with yellow-gold, black and white spotted and striped pattern, and yellow to orange forecrown. Both sexes of nominate race with fine black band above bill, golden-yellow (rarely, more orange) forecrown, hindcrown streaked white on black; yellowish-white back streaks, yellowy wing markings; lemon-yellow throat and breast. Distinguished from very similar *P. pusillus* by forecrown colour. Immature lacks yellow patch on black forehead. Race *xanthostictus* has smaller forehead patch, narrower white streaks on crown, green-yellow dorsal streaks, more gold in wings, is paler yellow with greenish tinge below; *extoni* larger, with broader black band in front of orange to gold frontal patch, and greyer underparts than N races. Voice. Nearly identical to *P. pusillus*; song long series of "pop" notes (occasional "honk" notes interjected) at 80-120 per minute for up to 11 minutes; piping trills of 5-8 notes per second for up to 20 seconds, also variable multiple piping trills each 1 second long and having 2-15 notes (either trill can switch to popping song, or used in response to latter); intermediate piping-popping calls also occur; common interactive call a grating "dddzzh", intense interactions marked by fast, very high-pitched barrage of grating calls longer and slower than in *P. pusillus*; also single "dit" notes in loose series. Loud wing-fluttering during interactions.
Habitat. Occupies dry scrub, Sahelian woodland and wooded grassland, and riverine woods; also montane evergreen forest in Ethiopia; also found around pasture and remnant forest patches. Woodlands include those with *Acacia*, *Brachystegia*, *Combretum*, *Terminalia* and other trees. Occurs from sea-level up to c. 1500 m, but up to 1800 m in Malawi, and in Ethiopia above *P. pusillus* at 1600-3000 m.
Food and Feeding. Diverse fruits, especially mistletoe berries, figs, fruits of *Uapaca nitida*; fruit stones are regurgitated. Also flycatches for diverse insects, including beetles, and gleans for their larvae in foliage and on branches at all levels. Feeds alone or in pairs; very aggressive towards other tinkerbirds and small barbets. Joins mixed-species foraging flocks.
Breeding. May-Aug and Dec in Gambia and Mali, Feb-Nov in Nigeria; Mar-Oct in Sudan, Ethiopia and Uganda; Sept-Dec in W Kenya, Mar-Jun and Oct-Nov in Zaire; Aug-Jan, also May, in Zambia, Zimbabwe, Angola and South Africa. Male sings with forehead and rump feathers erected, tail flicked in time with notes; encounters with much wing-fluttering, erected frontal patch, side-to-side swinging with head high, emphasizing throat, or head low, emphasizing forehead patch, and may cock tail. Nest excavated 2-5 m up in dead stub or branch, often on underside, in tree such as fig, frangipani, *Acacia* or *Terminalia*, entrance c. 2 cm. Eggs 2-3; incubation by both parents, for c. 12 days; both adults feed young, which egest fruit stones inside nest; nestling period c. 3 weeks.
Movements. Generally resident; some seasonal movement suspected in Nigeria.
Status and Conservation. Not globally threatened. Widespread, and common; locally common in W Kenya. Along with *P. pusillus* and *P. bilineatus* is the commonest tinkerbird. In some woodland areas, densities may reach up to 30-35 pairs/km². Seems to be fairly adaptable. Present in numerous national parks, e.g. W (Niger), Comoé (Ivory Coast), Bénoué (Cameroon), Murchison Falls and Lake Mburo (Uganda), Akagera (Rwanda), Ruvuvu (Burundi) and Mikumi (Tanzania).
Bibliography. Bannerman (1933, 1953), Barlow *et al.* (1997), Bates (1930), Benson & Benson (1977), Benson *et al.* (1971), Britton (1980), Brown & Britton (1980), Cave & Macdonald (1955), Chapin (1939), Cheke & Walsh (1996), Clancey (1974a), Cocker (2000), Curzon & Curzon (1996), Dean (1974a, 2000), Dowsett & Dowsett-Lemaire (1993), Dowsett & Forbes-Watson (1993), Elgood *et al.* (1994), Friedmann (1930a, 1930b, 1978a), Fry *et al.* (1988), Ginn *et al.* (1989), Giraudoux *et al.* (1988), Gore (1990), Grimes (1987), Harrison *et al.* (1997), Horne & Short (1988), Irwin (1981), Lewis & Pomeroy (1989), Lippens & Wille (1976), Liversidge (1991), Louette (1981b), Mackworth-Praed & Grant (1957, 1962, 1970), Maclean (1993), Milstein (1995), Monadjem *et al.* (1994), Penry (1994), Pinto (1983), Ross (1970), Short & Horne (1985a, 1988b), Short *et al.* (1990), Snow (1978, 1979), Tarboton (2001), Thiollay (1985a), Zimmerman *et al.* (1996).

PLATE 8

23

inches 3

cm 8

♂ ssp *hirsuta*

♀

ssp *angolensis* ♂

24

ssp *ansorgii* ♂

ssp *flavipunctata* ♂

♀ ssp *diademata* ♂

25

26

27

ssp *massaica* ♂

ssp *stigmatothorax*

ssp *melanocephala*

♀ ssp *lacrymosa* ♂

29

ssp *blandi*

28

ssp *radcliffei* ♂

ssp *flavibuccalis*

Genus *BUCCANODON* Hartlaub, 1857

23. **Yellow-spotted Barbet**

Buccanodon duchaillui

French: Barbican à taches jaunes **German**: Gelbfleck-Bartvogel **Spanish**: Barbudo Pintado
Other common names: (Duchaillu's) Yellow-spotted Tinkerbird/Barbet

Taxonomy. *Barbatula Duchaillui* Cassin, 1855, Moonda River, Gabon.
Genus related both to *Pogoniulus* and to *Tricholaema*; larger than former, similar in size to latter but lacks bill "teeth", and vocally distinct from both genera. No close relatives. Birds from S Congo described as race *gabriellae*, but now considered indistinguishable; populations at higher elevations are larger, but insufficient difference to warrant any racial separation. Monotypic.
Distribution. Sierra Leone and Guinea E to Ghana; and SW Nigeria E to W Kenya, and S to Cabinda (N Angola), C Zaire, W Rwanda and NW Tanzania.

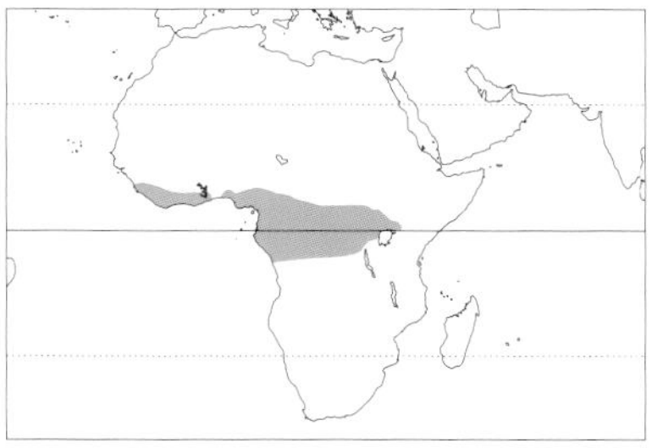

Descriptive notes. 15·5-17 cm; 37-50 g. Larger and chunkier than a tinkerbird. Both sexes glossy black, with yellow spots above and, below black upper breast, yellow and black barring to undertail area; distinctive orange-red forehead and forecrown, and yellow supercilia; orbital skin black, bill black. Immature lacks red on head, has pinkish orbital skin, and yellow bill with dark tip. Voice. Distinctive purring "brrrr--t" of up to 3 seconds, notes at 38-45 per second, in loose series to 30 minutes, up to 5 songs per minute; possibly also soft hooting song (Ivory Coast), nearly as in *Tricholaema hirsuta*; also grating calls, with nasal version, chattering "chchch" calls to 0·5 seconds, and soft "bdaa-aa-" calls, all during encounters.
Habitat. Inhabits forest, including old secondary forest, forest patches, edges, overgrown clearings and tree plantations; also in riverine forest with surrounding forest. Occurs from lowlands up to c. 2250 m.
Food and Feeding. Eats many small fruits, such as those of *Allophyllus*, *Ficus*, *Heisteria*, *Musanga* and *Vismia*, and oil palm (*Elaeis guineensis*) nuts; also insects such as termites, and snails. Clings, grasps thin branchlets, gleans fruits or insects; small figs taken at 3 per minute; occasionally flycatches. Forages at heights of 8-30 m. Sometimes congregates in groups of up to 12 at trees laden with ripe fruits, where attacked by species of *Gymnobucco*. Joins mixed-species foraging flocks.
Breeding. Aug-Apr in Liberia, Ivory Coast and Ghana; Nov-Mar and May-Jun in Nigeria; probably all year in Cameroon and Gabon (especially Jan-Sept), Feb-Sept in Zaire; Aug-Mar in Uganda and W Kenya. Singer appears as fluffy ball, tail projecting, then leans head forward, points bill down in "bow", erects head and rump feathers, sings, then resumes upright posture; responds to playback of song with rapid wing-flicking, tail-twitching, intense peering. Nest in cavity, once 15 m up, but no other information; territory c. 10 ha in Gabon. Clutch size, incubation and fledging periods, and other details of breeding, undescribed.
Movements. Resident and sedentary; moves only locally to fruiting trees.
Status and Conservation. Not globally threatened. Reasonably common; in Sierra Leone, common in E but less so in W; local and uncommon in Kenya. Estimated 300,000 pairs in Liberia, where over 10 pairs/km², and as many as 3 males singing in 16-ha forest patch. Generally, however, does not persist in small patches of forest, disappears as forest becomes fragmented. Relatively little-known species; additional information is required in relation to its habitat and breeding requirements, and its breeding biology. Occurs in several protected areas, e.g. Taï Forest National Park (Ivory Coast), Korup and Mount Kupé National Parks (Cameroon) and Kakamega Nature Reserve (Kenya).
Bibliography. Allport *et al*. (1989), Bannerman (1933, 1953), Bates (1930), Britton (1980), Brosset & Érard (1986), Brown & Britton (1980), Chapin (1939), Cheke & Walsh (1996), Christy & Clarke (1994), Colston & Curry-Lindahl (1986), Demey & Fishpool (1994), Dowsett (1989a, 1989b), Dowsett & Dowsett-Lemaire (1993), Dowsett & Forbes-Watson (1993), Elgood *et al*. (1994), Field (1999), Fry *et al*. (1988), Gartshore (1989), Gatter (1997), Grimes (1987), Horne & Short (1988), Jackson & Sclater (1938), Lewis & Pomeroy (1989), Lippens & Wille (1976), Louette (1981b), Mackworth-Praed & Grant (1957, 1970), Pinto (1983), Serle (1950, 1957, 1965), Short & Horne (1985a, 1988b), Short *et al*. (1990), Snow (1978), Thiollay (1985a), Zimmerman (1972), Zimmerman *et al*. (1996).

Genus *TRICHOLAEMA*

J. Verreaux & E. Verreaux, 1855

24. **Hairy-breasted Barbet**

Tricholaema hirsuta

French: Barbican hérissé **German**: Fleckenbartvogel **Spanish**: Barbudo Hirsuto
Other common names: Hairy-breasted Toothbill; Spot-headed Barbet (*flavipunctata*)

Taxonomy. *Pogonias hirsutus* Swainson, 1821, Ghana.
No close relatives. Exact delimitation of races difficult owing to intergradation; nominate and race *flavipunctata* hybridize over an extensive zone, roughly from Ghana to S Nigeria; proposed races *hybrida* (Niger Delta) and *chapini* (SE Cameroon E to C Zaire) considered indistinguishable from, respectively, nominate and *ansorgii*. Four subspecies currently recognized.
Subspecies and Distribution.
T. h. hirsuta (Swainson, 1821) - Sierra Leone E to SC Nigeria (Niger Delta).
T. h. flavipunctata J. Verreaux & E. Verreaux, 1855 - from at least SE Nigeria through Cameroon (except SE) to C Gabon.
T. h. ansorgii Shelley, 1895 - SE Cameroon E to W Kenya, S to E Congo, C Zaire and NW Tanzania.
T. h. angolensis Neumann, 1908 - S Gabon and S Congo S to NW Angola and S Zaire.

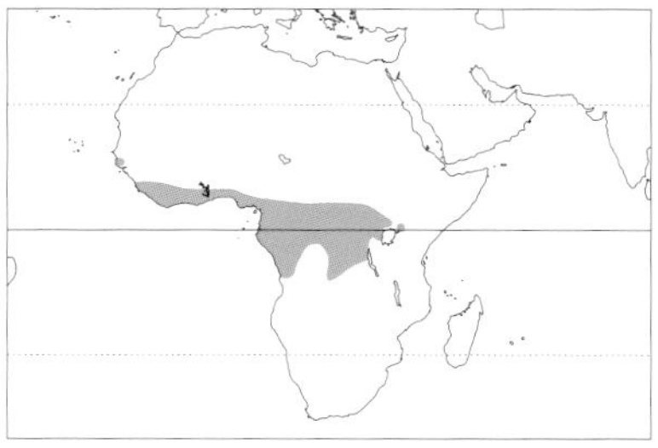

Descriptive notes. 17-18 cm; 43-63 g. Yellow, blackish and white forest barbet. Male nominate race black above with yellow spots, yellow edges to wing feathers; white superciliary and sub-moustachial marks; throat black, throat and breast feathers with hair-like tips, rest of underparts yellow with black spots. Differs from *Buccanodon duchaillui* in head pattern, no red on crown, larger bill. Female differs from male in more golden markings above, brighter tone below; white tips to feathers of chin and throat. Immature pale-billed, duller, with lax plumage, lacks adult's "tooth" on bill. Race *flavipunctata* with head spotted and lacking white stripes, browner above, brown markings below; *ansorgii* dark-headed with very narrow white facial stripes, streaked white chin and throat, yellow spots onto nape or crown, and brown-black ground colour above and markings below; *angolensis* like *flavipunctata* but browner, overall dull and not cleanly patterned, crown brownish, face with pale streaky spots, brownish-white throat with darker bars, vaguely brown markings below. Voice. Song a series of "oop" or "oork" notes at c. 1 per second for up to 20 seconds, but varies, may be short with fast notes, perhaps averages faster in nominate race; also a croaking "oo-o-o-oork", interactive grating calls, and "wuk" notes. Wipes bill audibly and flips wing during encounters.
Habitat. The most forest-adapted *Tricholaema*. Inhabits lowland primary and adjacent dense secondary forest and edges, infrequently riverine forest. Usually below 1000 m, reaching 1800 m in W Uganda.
Food and Feeding. Fruits and arthropods: eats berries, and drupes of such plants as *Ficus*, *Morinda*, *Musanga*, *Pachypodanthium*, *Pycnanthus*, *Rauvolfia*, *Solanum* and *Trema*; also beetles, lepidopteran larvae and others. Insect prey larger than that taken by *Buccanodon duchaillui*. Probes into lichens, mosses and bark crevices, hovers at times to seize insect or fruit; often smashes insect against bark to remove limbs. Feeds mainly above 20 m, sometimes lower, occasionally pursuing insects through undergrowth. At fruiting trees rarely in numbers; aggressive to smaller *Buccanodon duchaillui* and tinkerbirds, also small woodpeckers, but submissive to social *Gymnobucco bonapartei*. Sometimes joins mixed-species foraging flocks.
Breeding. Aug-Feb, possibly from Jun, in W Africa; Apr-May in Cameroon, Feb-Mar in Gabon and Congo, most months in Zaire; Feb-Jul and Sept in Uganda and W Kenya. Both sexes sing throughout year, singer spreads hair-like breast feathers apron-like, puffs throat, erects rump feathers and turns head from side to side; gliding flight displays with wings fixed. Nest and eggs inadequately described; seen at holes high in trees, and 1 nest in Sierra Leone c. 30 m up in underside of sloping branch; territory estimated at 13-20 ha in Liberia, 5-10 ha in W Kenya. Possibly parasitized by Least Honeyguide (*Indicator exilis*).
Movements. Resident and sedentary.
Status and Conservation. Not globally threatened. Population in Liberia estimated at 250,000 pairs; not uncommon but very local in Sierra Leone; rare in Kenya. Appears to be rather strictly tied to intact, large forest blocks, more so than is *Buccanodon duchaillui*. Poorly known species; study required of its ecology and breeding behaviour. Occurs in several protected areas, e.g. Gola Forests Reserves (Sierra Leone), Taï Forest National Park (Ivory Coast), Korup National Park (Cameroon) and Kakamega Nature Reserve (Kenya).
Bibliography. Allport *et al*. (1989), Bannerman (1933, 1953), Barlow *et al*. (1997), Bates (1930), Britton (1980), Brosset & Érard (1986), Cave & Macdonald (1955), Chapin (1939), Chappuis (1981), Cheke & Walsh (1996), Christy & Clarke (1994), Colston & Curry-Lindahl (1986), Dean (2000), Dowsett (1989b), Dowsett & Dowsett-Lemaire (1993), Dowsett & Forbes-Watson (1993), Elgood *et al*. (1994), Field (1999), Fry *et al*. (1988), Gartshore (1989), Gatter (1997), Grimes (1987), Jackson & Sclater (1938), Lewis & Pomeroy (1989), Lippens & Wille (1976), Louette (1981b), Mackworth-Praed & Grant (1957, 1962, 1970), Morel & Morel (1990), Pinto (1983), Serle (1950, 1965), Short & Horne (1985a), Short *et al*. (1990), Snow (1978), Thiollay (1985a), Zimmerman *et al*. (1996).

25. **Red-fronted Barbet**

Tricholaema diademata

French: Barbican à diadème **German**: Diadembartvogel **Spanish**: Barbudo Diademado

Taxonomy. *Pogonorhynchus diadematus* Heuglin, 1861, Upper White Nile, Ethiopia.
Forms a superspecies with *T. frontata* and *T. leucomelas*, and all three have in the past been considered conspecific; all respond strongly to playback of each other's song. Fairly closely related also to *T. lacrymosa*. Races weakly differentiated; birds from NE Uganda E to Mt Kenya, described as race *musta*, now considered inseparable from nominate. Two subspecies currently recognized.
Subspecies and Distribution.
T. d. diademata (Heuglin, 1861) - SE Sudan and NC Ethiopia S to SE Uganda and C Kenya.
T. d. massaica (Reichenow, 1887) - SC Kenya S to SW & C Tanzania.
Descriptive notes. 16-17 cm; 22-25 g. Small, short-tailed barbet with black, white and yellow plumage, prominent notch on bill tomia. Male of nominate race has red forehead, yellow supercilia, white throat, yellow streaks on back, yellow rump; whitish below, with few blackish spots on flanks. Distinguished from *T. leucomelas* by whitish, not black, throat and upper breast; from similar *Pogoniulus pusillus* by larger size, differences in head pattern. Female averages less red on forehead. Immature duller, with lax plumage, red on forehead smaller or lacking, no "tooth" on bill. Race *massaica* differs from nominate in having, on average, more spots or spot-streaks ventrally, though variation great. Voice. Primary song slow to fast series of up to 20 "hoop" notes, usually 4-6 per second; fast "hoop" songs by paired birds mark early breeding season; secondary song "nyah" or "yeah" notes given singly or in series at 1-1·5 per second; occasionally "nyah" notes interjected into "hoop" song; interactive, chattery, fast "yeh" notes in series; also grating "chaaa" calls, low "di-di-" notes, higher "tik-tik-" calls. Also wing-rustling.

On following pages: 26. Miombo Pied Barbet (*Tricholaema frontata*); 27. Acacia Pied Barbet (*Tricholaema leucomelas*); 28. Spot-flanked Barbet (*Tricholaema lacrymosa*); 29. Black-throated Barbet (*Tricholaema melanocephala*).

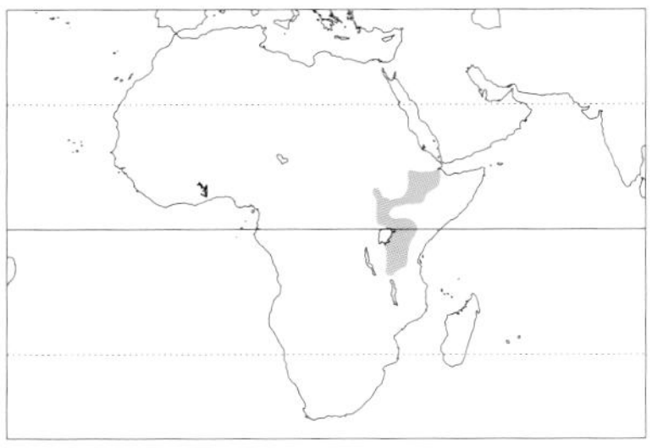

Habitat. Occupies woodland such as *Acacia* and *Combretum* woods, but also wooded grassland and pastures with bushes; generally found in drier situations than is *T. lacrymosa*, and in more moist sites than those favoured by *T. melanocephala*. Occurs at 600-2100 m.
Food and Feeding. Eats fruits such as those of *Carissa edulis*, *Euclea*, *Grewia* and others, also tendrils of vines and thistle-like seeds; in addition, in captivity, will feed on foods such as lettuce, apples and carrots; also takes insects, including termites, grasshoppers and ants, and captives accepted egg yolk, fly maggots, mealworms and locusts. Egests pellets of fruit stones, seeds and insect parts. Gleans from branches and foliage; goes to ground to take termites, and also breaks into tunnels on trees to eat them.
Breeding. Jan-Sept in most areas, also Nov-Mar in N Tanzania. Singing posture with bill pointing down, rump and throat feathers erected; crown and forehead feathers erect during encounters; aerial display by male to female, but little or no display before copulation. Nest, excavated by both adults, at 1-8 m in stub or branch of tree, euphorbia or sisal stem; territory large, with irregular borders, size uncertain. Eggs 2-4; incubation period uncertain, over 12 days, individual sessions of up to 3 hours, off-duty adult guards nest; adults tap, perhaps enlarging chamber, while incubating; chicks fed by both adults, at intervals of 5-30 minutes, nestling period c. 28 days; young leave territory c. 2 months after fledging. Nests parasitized by Lesser Honeyguide (*Indicator minor*).
Movements. Resident and sedentary.
Status and Conservation. Not globally threatened. Uncommon in Kenya and N Tanzania. Numbers seem to be stable. Species is somewhat adaptable, as it frequents degraded habitats that retain potential nesting and roosting sites. Range sometimes reported as extending to NW Somalia, but this requires confirmation. Occurs in several protected areas, e.g. Lake Nakuru National Park (Kenya) and Serengeti National Park (Tanzania).
Bibliography. Benson (1946), Britton (1980), Brown & Britton (1980), Cave & Macdonald (1955), Clancey (1984b), Dowsett & Dowsett-Lemaire (1993), Dowsett & Forbes-Watson (1993), England (1973a), Friedmann (1930a, 1930b), Friedmann & Loveridge (1937), Fry *et al.* (1988), Grant & Mackworth-Praed (1946), Jackson & Sclater (1938), Lewis & Pomeroy (1989), Mackworth-Praed & Grant (1957), Rutgers & Norris (1977), Schmidl (1982), Short & Horne (1985a, 1988b), Short *et al.* (1990), Snow (1978), van Someren (1956), Stevenson & Fanshawe (2001), Taylor (1983), Vincent (1946), Zimmerman *et al.* (1996).

26. Miombo Pied Barbet

Tricholaema frontata

French: Barbican du miombo **German**: Miombobartvogel **Spanish**: Barbudo del Miombo
Other common names: Miombo Barbet

Taxonomy. *Pogonorhynchus frontatus* Cabanis, 1880, Angola.
Forms a superspecies with *T. diademata* and *T. leucomelas*, and all three have in the past been considered conspecific; all respond strongly to playback of each other's song. Known to hybridize occasionally with *T. leucomelas* in S Zambia. Fairly closely related also to *T. lacrymosa*. Monotypic.
Distribution. S Zaire to SW Tanzania and S to C Angola, S Zambia and W Malawi.

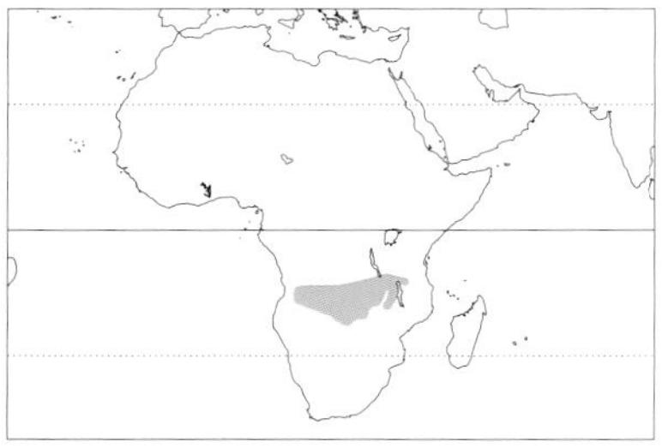

Descriptive notes. c. 16 cm; c. 25 g. Black, white and yellow barbet. Both sexes have red spot in central part of forehead, pale yellow supercilia, brown ear-coverts, brown bill, and scaly malar area; nape is spotted white, upperparts black with yellow spots; breast yellow, rest of underparts whiter, all usually with black spotting. Distinguished from *T. leucomelas* by very spotted underparts, lack of black throat patch; hybrids are intermediate. Immature lacks red on crown, has no "tooth" on bill. Voice. Primary song 6-30 "hoop" notes at c. 2 per second, songs at 3-5 per minute; secondary "nyeh" song or call, singly, or in series of up to 12 notes at 1-1·5 per second, notes shorter than in *T. diademata*; also grating calls, and "yeh" calls in interactions, and 2 calls of young when begging. Loud wing-rustling during interactions.
Habitat. Inhabits woodland, usually of *Brachystegia*; generally found in more wooded habitats than *T. diademata* and *T. leucomelas*, but occurs in some degraded woodland patches and clearings in Zambia and also patchy woods in Angola. Generally observed at 500-1100 m, but at 900-1520 m in Malawi.
Food and Feeding. Eats fruits and insects, but diet not known in detail. Certainly takes figs, and consumes some termites and beetles; possibly takes nestling birds or bird eggs. Inconspicuous, usually solitary, gleans in leaf clusters and on bark; flycatches occasionally. Drives away foraging *Pogoniulus chrysoconus*.
Breeding. Sept-Dec, rarely Jul-Mar. Male sings with throat puffed, bill down, turning head side to side. Nest 1-15 m up in dead branch, often on underside, of tree such as *Brachystegia* or *Acacia polyacantha*; hole dug horizontally to c. 7·5 cm, then vertically to as much as 30·5 cm; territory c. 10 ha. Eggs 2-3; incubation and nestling periods unknown; both adults provision young, at 2-10 feeds per hour, insects fed at first, with fruits predominating later on; adults remove faecal material regularly.
Movements. Resident and sedentary.
Status and Conservation. Not globally threatened. No data on numbers, but appears to be locally common. Populations presumably becoming more fragmented with continuing clearance of woodland. More information needed on species' ecology and breeding biology, as well as on its numerical status.
Bibliography. Anon. (1998a), Aspinwall & Beel (1998), Belcher (1930), Benson & Benson (1977), Benson *et al.* (1971), Britton (1980), Chapin (1939), Dean (2000), Dowsett & Dowsett-Lemaire (1993), Dowsett & Forbes-Watson (1993), Fry *et al.* (1988), Johnston-Stewart & Heigham (1982), Mackworth-Praed & Grant (1962, 1970), Pearson (1983), Pedersen (2000), Pinto (1983), Ripley & Heinrich (1966), Short & Horne (1985a, 1988b), Short *et al.* (1990), Snow (1978), Stevenson & Fanshawe (2001), Traylor (1960, 1965).

27. Acacia Pied Barbet

Tricholaema leucomelas

French: Barbican pie **German**: Rotstirn-Bartvogel **Spanish**: Barbudo Pío
Other common names: Pied Barbet

Taxonomy. *Bucco leucomelas* Boddaert, 1783, Cape of Good Hope.
Forms a superspecies with *T. diademata* and *T. frontata*, and the three have in the past been treated as conspecific; all respond strongly to playback of each other's song. Occasionally interbreeds with *T. frontata* in S Zambia. Fairly closely related also to *T. lacrymosa*. Species name sometimes erroneously spelt *leucomelan*, *leucomelaena* or *leucomelaina*, but original *leucomelas* must stand, as being non-Latinized Greek. Proposed race *namaqua* (W South Africa) included within *leucomelas*, *nkatiensis* (N Botswana) within *centralis*, and *zuluensis* (SE Zimbabwe S to Natal) within *affinis*. Three subspecies currently recognized.
Subspecies and Distribution.
T. l. centralis (Roberts, 1932) - Angola, extreme SW Zambia and W Zimbabwe, S to S Namibia, N Cape Province and W Natal.
T. l. affinis (Shelley, 1880) - E Zimbabwe and SW Mozambique, S to E Cape Province, E & N Lesotho and N Natal.
T. l. leucomelas (Boddaert, 1783) - C, S & SW Cape Province.

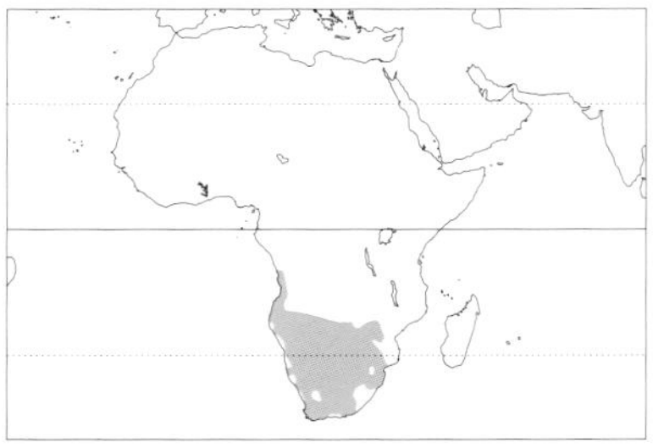

Descriptive notes. c. 17 cm; 23-45 g. Small, chunky, black, yellow and white barbet. Both sexes of nominate race with red forehead, yellow-white supercilia, and black chin, throat and upper breast; upperparts brownish-black with yellow spots and streaks, rump yellow, wings brown; belly whitish, flanks washed yellow, usually some black spots below. Distinguished from *T. diademata* and *T. frontata* by black throat and upper breast; from *Pogoniulus pusillus* additionally by larger size. Immature like adult but duller, with lax plumage, no red on head, no "tooth" on bill. Race *centralis* blacker, less brown, than nominate, often lacking ventral spots; *affinis* usually more yellowy white below than *centralis*, more spotted and even streaked black below than nominate. Voice. Main vocalizations, "hoop" and "nyah" series, nearly identical to those of *T. frontata* and *T. diademata*, with "hoop" song slightly faster than in former and slower than in *T. diademata*.
Habitat. Woodland, including *Acacia* and *Baikiaea* woods, especially where open, also streamside woods, scrubland, gardens, farms, parks, even in exotic wattle (*Acacia*) plantings; occurs in deserts and parks where suitable nesting trees present. From sea-level or, more usually, 400 m to 1500 m.
Food and Feeding. Omnivorous: takes fruits such as those of lantana and *Salvadora persica*, seeds from pods of *Sophora*, occasionally nectar; also suet from feeders; and also various grasshoppers, beetles, wasps and other insects. Forages at all levels in bushes and trees, even isolated trees; will cling or hang to reach fruits.
Breeding. As long as Sept-Jun in Angola; farther E & S mainly Aug or Sept-Jan, but Aug-Oct in far SW; sometimes nests 2-4 times in a season. Nests strictly in pairs. Displays involve spreading of forehead and throat feathers, side-to-side swinging of head and body, tail-flicking. Both adults excavate nesting cavity in tree or stump, entrance c. 4 cm, depth to 16 cm or more, base lined with wood chips; occasionally uses old nest of swallow (Hirundinidae). Eggs 1-4, average 2·9 in South Africa; incubation 14-16 days, by both parents; young fed by both adults, which keep nest clean by removal of faecal material, often mixed with wood bits; nestling period 32-35 days; fledglings can feed themselves by 6 days, independent within 2 months.
Movements. Resident, and generally sedentary.
Status and Conservation. Not globally threatened. No figures on numbers or densities available, but species appears to be common throughout much, if not all, of its range. Reasonably adaptable, and tree-planting activities have been major factor in this species' expansion of range towards SW. Occurs in several national parks, e.g. Etosha and Waterberg Plateau (Namibia), Rhodes Matopos and Hwange (Zimbabwe) and Upington to Augrabies Falls and Kruger (South Africa).
Bibliography. Benson *et al.* (1971), Clancey (1958c), Curio (1978a, 1978b), Dean (2000), Dedekind (1997), Dowsett (1989c), Dowsett & Dowsett-Lemaire (1993), Dowsett & Forbes-Watson (1993), Earlé & Grobler (1987), Fry *et al.* (1988), Ginn *et al.* (1989), Goodwin (1964), Harrison *et al.* (1997), Herholdt & Earlé (1986), Hoesch (1957), Irwin (1981), Liversidge (1991), Macdonald (1983, 1984, 1986), Mackworth-Praed & Grant (1962), Maclean (1993), Morris (1988), Parker (1999), Peck (1983), Penry (1994), Pinto (1983), Poley (1973), Priest (1934), Rutgers & Norris (1977), Short & Horne (1985a, 1988b), Snow (1978), Steyn (1996), Tarboton (2001), Tarboton *et al.* (1987), Ward (1989), Willows (1989).

28. Spot-flanked Barbet

Tricholaema lacrymosa

French: Barbican funèbre **German**: Tränenbartvogel **Spanish**: Barbudo Lacrimoso
Other common names: Spotted-flanked Barbet

Taxonomy. *Tricholaema lacrymosa* Cabanis, 1878, Athi River, central Kenya.
Closely related to *T. melanocephala*, but the two are considered not close enough to form a superspecies. Apparently quite closely affiliated also with the superspecies that includes *T. diademata*, *T. frontata* and *T. leucomelas*. Species name sometimes misspelt as *lachrymosa*. Races only weakly differentiated; proposed race *narokensis*, from Doinyo Narok (Kenya), included within nominate; birds from EC Tanzania, described as race *ruahae*, now considered inseparable from *radcliffei*. Two subspecies currently recognized.
Subspecies and Distribution.
T. l. lacrymosa Cabanis, 1878 - NE Zaire to S Sudan and C Kenya, and S to C Uganda and NE Tanzania.
T. l. radcliffei Ogilvie-Grant, 1904 - E Zaire and S Uganda to WC Kenya, S to Burundi, NE Zambia and SW Tanzania.
Descriptive notes. 13-14 cm; 18-27 g. Small black, white and yellow barbet. Male nominate race with white supercilia, blackish upperparts, brown rump with yellow streaks; wing feathers with yellow edges; chin and throat to central upper breast black, rest of underparts whitish to creamy, flanks with large black spots, undertail-coverts yellowish with black spots; eyes creamy to orange. Distinguished from *T. melanocephala* by unspotted back, spotted flanks. Female like male, except

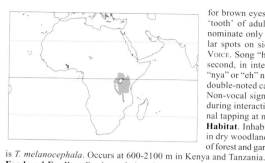

for brown eyes. Immature duller, without bill 'tooth' of adult. Race *radcliffei* differs from nominate only in having smaller, more circular spots on sides and flanks, and paler iris.
Voice. Song "hoop" notes in series at 1-2 per second, in interactions to 4 per second; also "nya" or "eh" notes in series, grating calls, low double-noted calls, and "wup" or "pop" series. Non-vocal signals include loud wing-rustling during interactions, bill-wiping, and slow signal tapping at nest.

Habitat. Inhabits wet woodland, wetter areas in dry woodland, also riverine woods, patches of forest and gardens; found in wetter areas than is *T. melanocephala*. Occurs at 600-2100 m in Kenya and Tanzania.

Food and Feeding. Feeds on fruits of many kinds, e.g. mistletoe (*Loranthus*) berries, *Ficus* and *Cordia*; also takes various types of insect, including ants and beetles; possibly also nectar. Flies rapidly from site to site, working through foliage and moving over branches and trunks, when taking insects.

Breeding. Generally Sept-May, or Jul, usually in dry period before or after rains. Usually in pairs, occasionally trios. Male cocks tail, and pair-members call and answer frequently. Nest, excavated by both adults, often on underside of dead branch, or in trunk of dead tree, 2-18 m up, cavity to c. 33 cm deep, nest-chamber 6-7·6 cm, lined with wood chips; interacts strongly with similar-sized hole-nesters, defends cavity against these. Eggs 2-4; both adults incubate and feed young; incubation and nestling periods unknown; adults sleep with young in nest at night. Probably parasitized by Lesser Honeyguide (*Indicator minor*).

Movements. Resident and sedentary.

Status and Conservation. Not globally threatened. No information on numbers or densities; locally common in Kenya and Tanzania. Where competition from larger barbets is intense, nests in thin stubs too small for those, thus indicating need for preserving dead trees and stubs for this and similar small species in woodland. Precise limits of range in S require confirmation. Occurs in several protected areas, e.g. Masai Mara Reserve (Kenya), Akagera National Park (Rwanda), Ruvuvu National Park (Burundi) and Tarangire and Ruaha National Parks (Tanzania).

Bibliography. Aspinwall (1973), Aspinwall & Beel (1998), Britton (1980), Brown & Britton (1980), Cave & Macdonald (1955), Chapin (1939), Dowsett (1989c), Dowsett & Dowsett-Lemaire (1993), Dowsett & Forbes-Watson (1993), England (1977), Friedmann (1930a, 1930b), Friedmann & Loveridge (1937), Fry *et al.* (1988), Gaugris *et al.* (1981), Goodwin (1964), Jackson & Sclater (1938), Lewis & Pomeroy (1989), Lippens & Wille (1976), Mackworth-Praed & Grant (1957, 1970), Nikolaus (1987), Ripley & Heinrich (1969), Schouteden (1966), Short & Horne (1985a, 1988b), Short *et al.* (1990), Snow (1978), Stevenson & Fanshawe (2001), Zimmerman *et al.* (1996).

29. Black-throated Barbet

Tricholaema melanocephala

French: Barbican à tête noire   **German**: Schwarzkopf-Bartvogel   **Spanish**: Barbudo Cabecinegro
Other common names: African Black-throated Barbet, Brown-throated Barbet; Yellow-cheeked Barbet (*flavibuccalis*)

Taxonomy. *Pogonias melanocephala* Cretzschmar, 1826, north Ethiopia.
Closely related to *T. lacrymosa*, but not so close as to form a superspecies. Races moderately distinctive; *flavibuccalis*, known from few NC Tanzanian specimens, sometimes considered a separate species, or a megasubspecies, though it could actually be no more than a morph. Four subspecies currently recognized.

Subspecies and Distribution.
T. m. melanocephala (Cretzschmar, 1826) - N & C Ethiopia, Djibouti and NW Somalia.
T. m. stigmatothorax Cabanis, 1878 - SE Sudan, S Ethiopia and S Somalia, S to C Tanzania.
T. m. blandi E. L. Phillips, 1897 - CN & NE Somalia.
T. m. flavibuccalis Reichenow, 1893 - NC Tanzania (Seronera region and Wembere steppes).

Descriptive notes. 12-13 cm; 17-25 g. Small black and white barbet. Both sexes of nominate race with white supercilia, glossy black above with yellow spots and streaks, wing feathers edged yellow; black chin to breast and in band to upper belly, rest of underparts white. Distinguished from *T. lacrymosa* by yellow spots above, no spots below; from various *Pogoniulus* species by somewhat larger size, black throat. Immature paler, duller, plumage lax, no bill "tooth". Race *stigmatothorax* differs from nominate in lacking gloss on black areas, with head and ventral dark areas browner, less black, and often has orange spot on lower breast; *blandi* more brown and paler than *stigmatothorax*, throat, forehead, often also on crown; *flavibuccalis* resembles nominate, but pale head stripes are yellow, centre of back to tail base yellow, and black bib ends on breast, not belly. Voice. Very vocal, large repertoire; has "kaaa" instead of "hoop" song, and "ptaa" or "ptaw" song-like call, both 3-4 notes long; simultaneous singing occurs, both birds using "kaaa" or one using "ptaw" song; harsh "nyah" calls become grating at times; also rattling calls, chatter calls, single or double "da-dit" calls; "chchchaa" to "chrrr" begging calls, shorter and louder when adult approaches. Fluttering wing sounds accompany interactions, along with grating, rattle-like chatter and "ptaw" calling.

Habitat. Very dry woodland, brushland, scrubland, including desert with some cover; in drier areas at lower elevations (to 1820 m) than *T. lacrymosa*. Where co-occurs with latter species, it is found in drier sites, whereas *T. lacrymosa* prefers areas around streamsides.

Food and Feeding. Insects, including various larvae, flies and termites; also fruits, as of *Ficus*, *Grewia*, *Salvadora* and *Sanseveria*, and buds of some *Acacia* species. Insects taken by flycatching, hovering, gleaning, and probing along bark and into flowers.

Breeding. Feb-Jun in Ethiopia, Somalia, Kenya, Tanzania; also Jul-Aug and Nov-Dec in parts of Kenya and Tanzania. Breeds in pairs, rarely in trios. Singer erects head and throat feathers, perches upright, tail down and twitching in time to notes, and turns head from side to side; interactions marked by much calling, bobbing and swinging of head and body, hair-like tips of spread black ventral feathers hanging as apron over white ones. Nesting cavity often in underside of thin, dead branch, details of nest undescribed; cavity vigorously defended against barbets and woodpeckers throughout year; territory irregular, sometimes linear such as 1 km along streambed in very dry areas. Clutch unknown, estimated at 2-3 from observations of fledged young; usually 1 juvenile seen, or 2 (1 with each parent).

Movements. Resident and sedentary.

Status and Conservation. Not globally threatened. No information on numbers, but appears at least locally common; fairly common in Kenya and Tanzania; very uncommon in NE Somalia. May benefit from degradation of more wooded habitats, and from some desertification. Present in several protected areas, e.g. Fôret du Day National Park (Djibouti) and Tsavo East and Tsavo West National Parks (Kenya).

Bibliography. Archer & Godman (1937-1961), Ash & Miskell (1983, 1998), Benson (1946), Britton (1980), Brown & Britton (1980), Cave & Macdonald (1955), Dowsett & Dowsett-Lemaire (1993), Dowsett & Forbes-Watson (1993), Érard (1976), Friedmann (1930a, 1930b), Friedmann & Loveridge (1937), Fry *et al.* (1988), Jackson & Sclater (1938), Lewis & Pomeroy (1989), Mackworth-Praed & Grant (1957), Nikolaus (1977), Short & Horne (1985a, 1988b), Short *et al.* (1990), Smith (1957), Snow (1978), Stevenson & Fanshawe (2001), Zimmerman *et al.* (1996).

ssp *salvadorii*

ssp *buchanani*

ssp *undatus*

31

ssp *vieilloti*

ssp *leucogenys*
variants

30

ssp *thiogaster*

ssp *albicauda*

ssp *senex*

32

PLATE 9

inches ——————— 3

cm ——————— 8

ssp *leucogaster*

ssp *lynesi*

33

ssp *leucocephalus*

yellow-headed
morph

variants

35

ssp *zombae*

34

ssp *torquatus*

36

ssp *irroratus*

typical

Genus *LYBIUS* Hermann, 1783

30. **Banded Barbet**

Lybius undatus

French: Barbican barré **German**: Wellenbartvogel **Spanish**: Barbudo Etíope

Taxonomy. *Pogonias undatus* Rüppell, 1837, Simien Province, central Ethiopia.
Not particularly closely related to others of genus; may represent connecting link between genera *Tricholaema* and *Lybius*. Races rather well marked for a species with small range. Proposed races *senafensis* in NE of range, *gardullensis* in W & SW, and *squamatus* in E considered untenable. Four subspecies recognized.
Subspecies and Distribution.
L. u. thiogaster Neumann, 1903 - far NE Ethiopia and Eritrea.
L. u. undatus (Rüppell, 1837) - NW to C Ethiopia.
L. u. leucogenys (Blundell & Lovat, 1899) - SC to SW Ethiopia.
L. u. salvadorii Neumann, 1903 - SE Ethiopia.

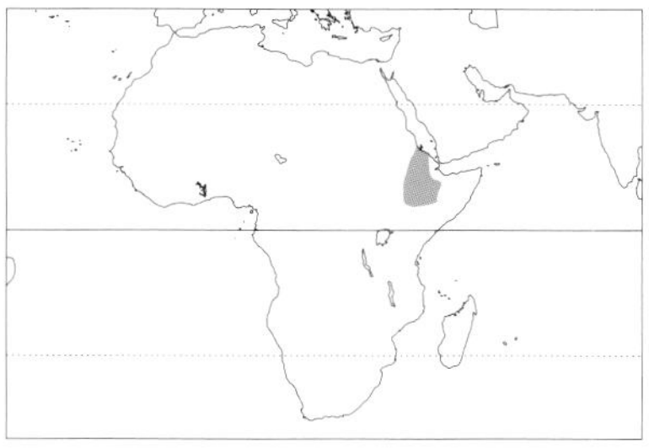

Descriptive notes. 16-17·5 cm; 35·5-42 g. Small barbet with red forehead. Both sexes of nominate race with black head, upper mantle and breast, white line behind eye, red forehead; upperparts brown-black with pale edgings, rump barred yellow; underparts below breast evenly barred blackish-brown and white. Differs from *Tricholaema* species in lacking bold head patterning and hair-tipped throat feathers. Immature much duller, lacks or has but trace of red on forehead. Race *leucogenys* has barring uneven in centre of underparts, also very variable, some individuals almost entirely black, and others with patchy white to fully white head other than forehead, also red or orange on forehead can be present also on face, chin and throat, and belly yellowish or even orangey; *salvadorii* like nominate, but wedge-shaped white marks on throat, white spots on sides of neck, wavy barring on breast to belly; *thiogaster* browner than *salvadorii*, with brown wedge-streaks on yellow-white throat, face and breast, and streaky marks from breast to belly. Voice. Only vocalizations reported are "gr-gr-grgrgr-" notes and "tock" or "took" series as song, latter resembling that of *Megalaima haemacephala*.
Habitat. Woodland, bushland, and streamside trees, at 300-3040 m.
Food and Feeding. Fruits, including figs, and insects, including beetles and cockchafers, have been noted. Flycatches for insects; moves through trees and bushes in foliage and on branches, gleaning insects and fruits, sometimes clinging upside-down, like a tit (Paridae).
Breeding. Probably Jan-Jun. Birds encountered in pairs only, likely to be territorial throughout year. Nest a cavity in branch or stub of tree, details not known. Eggs undescribed, and no information on other aspects of breeding.
Movements. Resident and sedentary.
Status and Conservation. Not globally threatened. Very poorly known, and few data on populations; thought to be commoner in S of range. Probably competes with similarly sized *L. guifsobalito* and *Tricholaema diademata*, but no available information. Further research required on population numbers, ecology and breeding behaviour.
Bibliography. Benson (1946), Cheesman & Sclater (1935), Desfayes (1975), Dowsett & Dowsett-Lemaire (1993), Dowsett & Forbes-Watson (1993), Francis & Shirihai (1999), Friedmann (1930b), Fry *et al.* (1988), Goodwin (1964), Heuglin (1861), Macdonald (1938), Mackworth-Praed & Grant (1957), Ryan (2001), Shirihai & Francis (1999), Short & Horne (1985a, 1988b), Smith (1957), Snow (1978), Tilahun *et al.* (1996), Urban (1980), Urban & Brown (1971).

31. **Vieillot's Barbet**

Lybius vieilloti

French: Barbican de Vieillot **German**: Blutbrust-Bartvogel **Spanish**: Barbudo Sangrante

Taxonomy. *Pogonius vieilloti* Leach, 1815, Ethiopia.
Not very closely related to congeners, probably closest to the group comprising *L. leucocephalus*, *L. chaplini* and *L. rubrifacies*. Races ill-defined, with some mosaic variation, and clinal variation in colour intensity. Three subspecies recognized.
Subspecies and Distribution.
L. v. buchanani Hartert, 1924 - S Mauritania and Mali E to S Chad, and S to S Sahel region (E to NC Nigeria).
L. v. rubescens (Temminck, 1823) - Sahel fringe from Gambia and Sierra Leone E to C Nigeria, N Cameroon, Central African Republic and NC Zaire, reaching coast from Ivory Coast to Nigeria.
L. v. vieilloti (Leach, 1815) - C Sudan and NW Ethiopia S to NE Zaire, S Sudan and W Ethiopia.

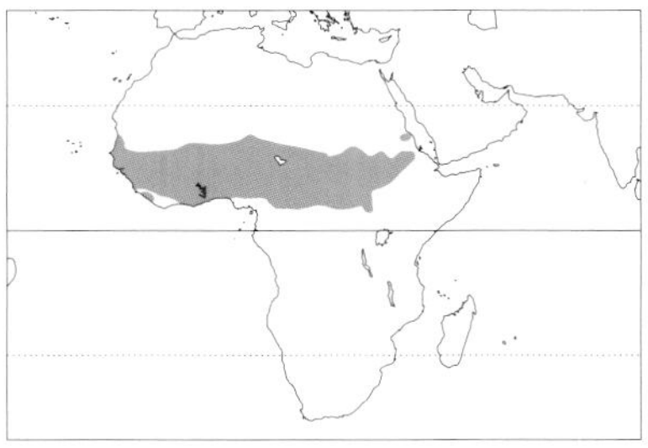

Descriptive notes. c. 16 cm; 31-43 g. Distinctive red, brown and yellow barbet with strong bill and short-tailed, dumpy appearance. Both sexes of nominate race with red head, blackish back with pale spots, yellow rump and uppertail-coverts; yellow with red spots below; notched bill blackish. Immature duller and much less red, browns greyer, bill paler without notch. Race *buchanani* paler than nominate; *rubescens* averages darker above, with red spots below larger, but very variable. Voice. Song by 1 or 2 of group an "ope-ope-" at intervals of c. 1·4 seconds, others of group chatter; noisy choruses like those of some races of *L. leucocephalus*; also snarling alarm note, soft "cwa" call and interactive "pew" call.
Habitat. Wooded grassland, forest-grassland mosaic, open woods, streamside trees, forest edges and cultivation, including plantations and gardens. Occurs from sea-level to c. 1500 m.
Food and Feeding. Eats fruits, such as those of *Ziziphus mauritiana*, gourds (*Coccinea grandis*), *Butyrospermum*, mistletoe (*Loranthus*) berries, and figs; also insects, including termites, ants and caterpillars. Feeds in groups, from ground to canopy, in foliage and along bark of branches.
Breeding. Apr-Sept generally; also later in year in W (after rains); also Jan in Liberia. Nest excavated in dead branch or stub, often in isolated tree in open, 1-8 m above ground, entrance 3-4 cm; variably sized territory defended throughout year. Eggs 2-3; incubation and fledging periods unknown, and data lacking on most aspects of breeding, including degree of help by group-members other than primary pair.
Movements. Resident; largely sedentary, but post-breeding groups sometimes move around beyond usual territory, up to 8 km.
Status and Conservation. Not globally threatened. Locally common; common in Sierra Leone; in Liberia, 20-35 pairs/km², with inselbergs cleared for agriculture holding single pairs. Loss of habitat owing to degradation and desertification perhaps offset by new areas being made available to this species by cutting and clearing of forest. Research needed on social aspects of lifestyle, as species often occurs in groups, not only in pairs. Present in several protected areas, e.g. Aïr et Ténére National Park (Niger), Ouadi Rimé-Ouadi Achim Reserve (Chad), Dinder National Park (Sudan), Comoé National Park (Ivory Coast), Falgore Reserve (Nigeria) and Bénoué National Park (Cameroon).
Bibliography. Allport *et al.* (1989), Bannerman (1933, 1953), Barlow *et al.* (1997), Bates (1930), Cave & Macdonald (1955), Chapin (1939), Cheke & Walsh (1996), Colston & Curry-Lindahl (1986), Dowsett & Dowsett-Lemaire (1993), Dowsett & Forbes-Watson (1993), Elgood *et al.* (1994), Field (1999), Friedmann (1930b), Fry *et al.* (1988), Gatter (1997), Giraudoux *et al.* (1988), Goodwin (1964), Gore (1990), Grimes (1987), Lamarche (1980), Lippens & Wille (1976), Louette (1981b), Mackworth-Praed & Grant (1957, 1970), Morel & Morel (1990), Newby (1980), Nikolaus (1987), Quantrill & Quantrill (1998), Rodwell (1996), Short & Horne (1985a), Snow (1978), Thiollay (1985a).

32. **White-headed Barbet**

Lybius leucocephalus

French: Barbican à tête blanche **German**: Weißkopf-Bartvogel **Spanish**: Barbudo Cabeciblanco
Other common names: White-bellied Barbet (*leucogaster*)

Taxonomy. *Laimodon leucocephalus* de Filippi, 1853, White Nile in extreme south Sudan.
Related to *L. chaplini* and *L. rubrifacies*, though not very closely; all three fairly close also to *L. vieilloti*. Races *albicauda* and *leucogaster* have sometimes been considered separate species; former interbreeds with other races wherever they meet, but latter is isolated geographically. Proposed race *usukumae* (SE of L Victoria) possibly recognizable: represents populations intermediate between *albicauda* or *lynesi* and nominate *leucocephalus*. Birds from N Tanzania described as race *pareensis* considered inseparable from *albicauda*. Six subspecies currently recognized.
Subspecies and Distribution.
L. l. adamauae Reichenow, 1921 - N & C Nigeria E to S Chad, W Central African Republic and NW Zaire.
L. l. leucocephalus (de Filippi, 1853) - possibly E Central African Republic, and S Sudan and NE Zaire to NW Tanzania and WC Kenya.
L. l. senex (Reichenow, 1887) - C & SC Kenya.
L. l. albicauda (Shelley, 1881) - SW & S Kenya to N Tanzania.
L. l. lynesi C. H. B. Grant & Mackworth-Praed, 1938 - C Tanzania.
L. l. leucogaster (Bocage, 1877) - highlands of SW Angola.

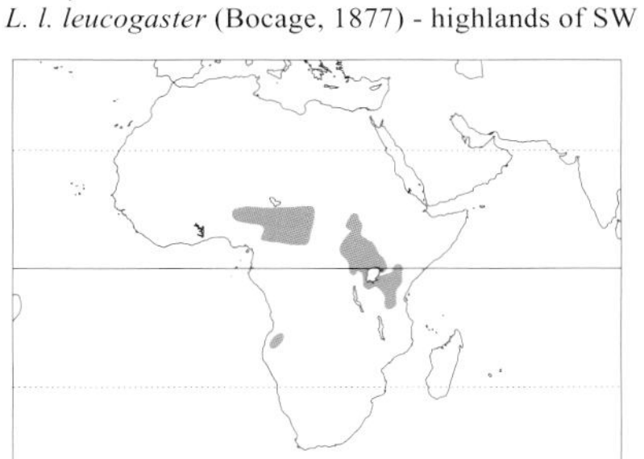

Descriptive notes. 18-19·5 cm; 45-81 g. Distinctive large-bodied, white-headed barbet with much white elsewhere in plumage. Both sexes of nominate race white, apart from blackish back and tail, brown lower breast and belly with white streaks, and blackish wings, latter spotted white; black bill with large "tooth". Immature with lax plumage, more grey or brown in white areas of adult, bill paler with "tooth" obscure or absent. Race *adamauae* like nominate, but ventral brown-black restricted to lower down belly and flanks, underwing-coverts white, spotted with black; *albicauda* with tail mainly white (very base may be brown), belly and flanks blackish-brown with white spots, underwing-coverts dull black with white streaks; *senex* all white below, wings and back more brown, with white of wing limited to scapulars; *lynesi* like *albicauda*, but less blackish-brown on belly and flanks, tail base brown-black; *leucogaster* resembles nominate and *adamauae*, but with only white in wings being on inner wing-coverts, and no black on underparts. Voice. Group "greeting ceremonies" with and without ensuing song, varying racially, with chipping, chattering usually by pair only in *senex*, noisy slower notes in *albicauda*, clearer, more melodic notes in *leucocephalus*, similar but faster and lower-pitched in *adamauae*; "duet" portion of chorus not synchronous, songs more or less simultaneous; also grating calls, low "pew" notes, chatter and rattle calls (with loud versions used against honeyguides), "kerr-rek" call, and "pzheeeeet" call. Mechanical signals are loud wing-rustling, comb-scraping like bill-wiping, and tapping or side-to-side whacking of bill against cavity entrance.
Habitat. Open woodland, streamside trees, bushland with trees, open areas with fig or other fruiting trees, cultivated areas and gardens; often near water. Usually above 600 m, to 2300 m.
Food and Feeding. Diverse fruits, including cultivated guavas and others, and figs, Cape lilac, and berries; also insects, including termites, flies, ants and others. Groups fly to fruit trees, also individually work over bark of trees and foliage, though clumsy. Opens tunnels of arboreal termites; takes dung beetles on ground at times, although usually a bird of the canopy.
Breeding. Feb-Jun in N, also Aug-Dec in Kenya (before and after rainy seasons), Sept-Feb in Angola, Dec-Mar in parts of Tanzania and Uganda, Oct-Nov in Cameroon. Nests in groups of up to 8, but pair may prevent "helpers" from roosting in nest. Elaborate greeting calls, songs, tapping at nest, courtship feeding by male, floating flight displays, bobbing, wing-flicking and other displays. Nest excavated in fig, jacaranda or other soft-wooded tree, 5-20 m up in dead branch, often on underside of branch; opening narrow; excavation slow or rapid, at times completed in c. 10 days. Eggs 2-4; incubation 15-21 days, all adults participating, change-overs frequent; hatchlings fed directly or by regurgitation, at up to 15 times per hour; nestling period unknown; fledglings quickly learn to feed themselves, adults may vacate nest and allow young to roost alone in it. Usually 2

On following pages: 33. Chaplin's Barbet (*Lybius chaplini*); 34. Red-faced Barbet (*Lybius rubrifacies*); 35. Black-billed Barbet (*Lybius guifsobalito*); 36. Black-collared Barbet (*Lybius torquatus*).

young fledge; nest parasitized by Lesser Honeyguide (*Indicator minor*), which often disrupts choruses and activities around nest, despite guarding barbet, and at times delays or disrupts breeding.
Movements. Resident; usually sedentary, but wandering occurs; vagrant to near sea-level in Kenya.
Status and Conservation. Not globally threatened. Uncommon in Nigeria; locally fairly common in Kenya and Tanzania. Relatively adaptable, nests in modified habitats so long as they still contain fruiting trees for foraging and dead limbs for nesting. Present in several protected areas, e.g. Murchison Falls National Park (Uganda), Masai Mara Reserve and Nairobi National Park (Kenya), and Tarangire National Park (Tanzania). Angolan race *leucogaster* is restricted in range, and should be monitored.
Bibliography. Bannerman (1933, 1953), Britton (1980), Brooke (1970), Brown & Britton (1980), Cave & Macdonald (1955), Chapin (1939), Dean (2000), Dowsett & Dowsett-Lemaire (1993), Dowsett & Forbes-Watson (1993), Elgood *et al*. (1994), Friedmann (1930a), Fry *et al*. (1988), Jackson & Sclater (1938), Lewis & Pomeroy (1989), Lippens & Wille (1976), Louette (1981b), Mackworth-Praed & Grant (1957, 1962, 1970), Nikolaus (1987), Pinto (1973, 1983), Short & Horne (1979, 1982b, 1983a, 1985a, 1988b), Short *et al*. (1990), Snow (1978), van Someren (1956), Stevenson & Fanshawe (2001), Zimmerman *et al*. (1996).

33. Chaplin's Barbet

Lybius chaplini

French: Barbican de Chaplin **German**: Feigenbartvogel **Spanish**: Barbudo de Chaplin

Taxonomy. *Lybius chaplini* S. R. Clarke, 1920, Kafue River, Zambia.
Related to *L. leucocephalus* and to *L. rubrifacies*, and all three fairly close also to *L. vieilloti*. Monotypic.
Distribution. SC Zambia, in area between Kafue Park and Moshi in W, E to Lusaka.

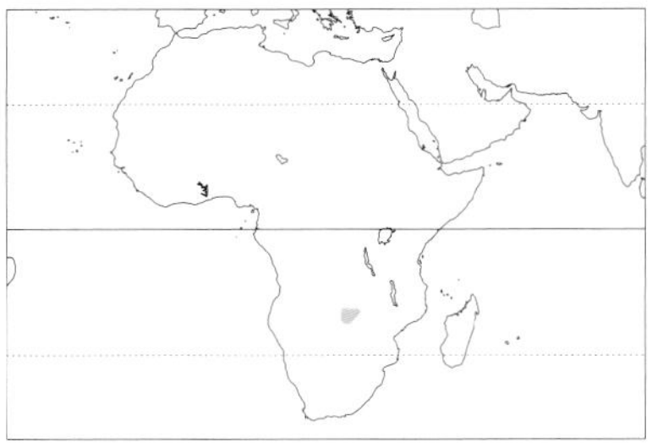

Descriptive notes. c. 19 cm; 64-75 g. Both sexes white, with blackish wings and tail, and red face; wings edged yellow; bill prominently notched. Differs from *L. leucocephalus* in having red and yellow in plumage. Immature duller, without red, and paler, bill lacking or with just trace of 'tooth'. Voice. Conspicuous greeting chorus with buzzy, grating notes, nasal "put-ut-ut-" and audible bill-snapping, sometimes leading into duet by 2, occasionally 3, of the group, the song a noisy cackle that speeds up, resembles that of *L. rubrifacies* but sets of notes less precise; also "snip-et" calls in aggression, squawking "yekka-yekawk" calls at honeyguides (*Indicator*), "chough" calls, soft "wup" notes. Bill-tapping at nest entrance during change-overs, bill-wiping and wing-flicking sounds in aggression.
Habitat. Woodland edges, pastures and open areas with scattered fruiting trees, wooded streamsides, and gardens with nearby fruit trees; almost completely restricted to areas where fig *Ficus sycomorus* is abundant.
Food and Feeding. Little known; eats figs and various fruits and berries, also undetermined insects. Gleans in foliage of (non-fruiting) bushes and trees, hops over bark of limbs, probes into mosses and debris on bark, and flycatches from perch. Groups visit fruiting trees, may cross open areas 400 m or more wide to reach these; forages up to 1 km from nest or roost.
Breeding. Aug-Nov; also reported in Feb, such late nestings possibly due to interference from Lesser Honeyguide (*Indicator minor*). Nests in groups. In greeting ceremonies, birds hop from side to side, jump over one another, wave one or both wings, bow, swing body, spread and flick tail feathers, move tail up and down or side to side, erect head feathers, and 1 bird may cock tail; *L. torquatus* pairs or groups often elicit calls and chases. Nest excavated by all group-members, at height of 3-9 m in dead tree or, more usually, branch of live tree, such as *Ficus*, or *Parinari mobola*; entrance oval, once 3·6 cm by 4 cm, cavity c. 34 cm deep, chamber in 1 case 5·4 cm by 7·5 cm; territory c. 40 ha in farmland with scattered trees and woodland patches. Eggs 2-4; details of incubation and nestling periods, and helper activities, unknown. Nest parasitized by Lesser Honeyguide; in 1 observation, while 2 group-members chased honeyguides, another member entered nest, carried the 4 barbet eggs individually to entrance, and crushed each one.
Movements. Resident and sedentary.
Status and Conservation. Not globally threatened. Currently considered Near-threatened. Locally common, but range restricted probably to only a few hundred km². Adapts to human activities and accepts man-altered habitats, so long as trees are still present for nesting, roosting and feeding; fortunately, when woodland is cleared for agriculture, fig trees are commonly left intact. However, minimum acceptable density of fig trees remains undetermined; research needed in order to establish ecological requirements, and also precise distribution. Occurs in Kafue National Park (Zambia), though present in only small numbers.
Bibliography. Anon. (1998a), Aspinwall & Beel (1998), Benson *et al*. (1971), Colebrook-Robjent & Stjernstedt (1976), Collar & Stuart (1985), Collar *et al*. (1994), Dowsett & Dowsett-Lemaire (1980, 1993), Dowsett & Forbes-Watson (1993), Fry *et al*. (1988), Horne & Short (1988), Leonard *et al*. (2001), Mackworth-Praed & Grant (1962), Short & Horne (1983b, 1985a, 1988a, 1988b), Snow (1978), Stattersfield & Capper (2000).

34. Red-faced Barbet

Lybius rubrifacies

French: Barbican à face rouge **German**: Rotgesicht-Bartvogel **Spanish**: Barbudo Carirrojo

Taxonomy. *Pogonorhynchus rubrifacies* Reichenow, 1892, Biharamulo, north-west Tanzania.
Related to *L. leucocephalus* through *L. chaplini*, the combined group also fairly close to *L. vieilloti*; also related to *L. guifsobalito* and *L. torquatus*. Distinct from all, however, in morphology; duet form nearest to that of *L. chaplini*, but songs of male and female of present species differ, as they do in *L. guifsobalito*. Monotypic.
Distribution. SW Uganda, E Rwanda and NW Tanzania.
Descriptive notes. 17·5-18·5 cm. Both sexes entirely brown-black, except for red face and yellow edges of flight-feathers; bill grey to horn-coloured. Differs from *L. guifsobalito* in having less red in plumage, no white on wing-coverts; from *L. torquatus* in all-dark body. Immature greyer, without red on head, paler bill lacks "tooth". Voice. Group greeting ceremonies with grating, "skizzy" notes, "eh" notes and chattery calls, with some bill-snapping and bill-wiping; this may lead to noisy duet of up to c. 6·5 seconds, one giving "kkaa" or "bakk" notes, the other higher-pitched "go" or "ko" notes ("ga-bakk" duet), differing from *L. leucocephalus* and *L. chaplini* in more or less synchronous, sexually different songs. Bill-wiping, bill-snapping and wing-rustling sounds in interactions.

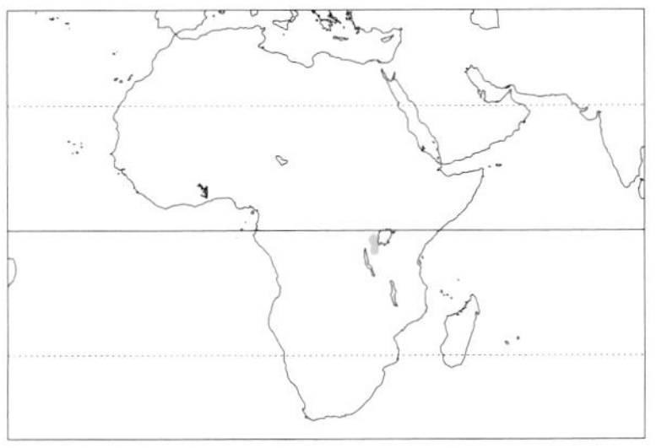

Habitat. Inhabits woodland, including *Acacia polyacantha* woods along lakes and streams, and also mixed *Albizia-Acacia-Commiphora* woodland; also occupies *Combretum-Acacia* and *Combretum-Ficus* wooded grassland, at 1140-1550 m.
Food and Feeding. Diet composed of figs and other fruits, and undetermined insects. Flycatches for insects at times, and plucks fruits from foliage of fruiting bushes and trees. Forages in groups.
Breeding. Gonadal data of specimens indicate breeding in Feb-Mar and Oct. Social, in groups of up to 7. Tail-cocking, gliding-floating flight displays, hunched posture with rump, back and facial feathers erected, bowing and swinging of body with vocalizations in greeting ceremonies and before duets. 1 cavity excavated by 2 birds at 18 m in branch of dead *Acacia polyacantha*, but possibly a roosting hole; defends variably sized territory, including against *L. torquatus* in riverine woods where co-occurring with latter, and then frequent interactions. No information on clutch size, incubation and nestling periods, and other aspects of breeding.
Movements. Resident and sedentary.
Status and Conservation. Not globally threatened. Currently considered Near-threatened. Has smallest range of any African barbet. Perhaps locally common, but total population small. Status uncertain, thought possibly vulnerable, but probably not under immediate threat. Large area of habitat where species was common in 1982 has been subjected to change as settlers poured into a major portion of Akagera National Park (E Rwanda), as a result of the civil war; roughly two-thirds of park has been lost. Habitat in Tanzania thought to be reasonably secure, but species occurs in very low densities here. More information is required about this species' biology, and on its numbers in SW Uganda and NW Tanzania. Present in Lake Mburo National Park (Uganda), Akagera National Park (Rwanda) and Ruvuvu National Park (Burundi).
Bibliography. Bennun & Njoroge (1996), Britton (1980), Collar & Stuart (1985), Collar *et al*. (1994), Dowsett & Dowsett-Lemaire (1993), Dowsett & Forbes-Watson (1993), Fry *et al*. (1988), Horne & Short (1988), Jackson & Sclater (1938), Mackworth-Praed & Grant (1957), Robertson (1997a), Schouteden (1966), Short & Horne (1983b, 1985a, 1988a, 1988b), Short, Horne & Muringo-Gichuki (1990), Short, Horne & Vande weghe (1983), Snow (1978), Stattersfield & Capper (2000), Stattersfield *et al*. (1998), Stevenson & Fanshawe (2001).

35. Black-billed Barbet

Lybius guifsobalito

French: Barbican quifsobalito **Spanish**: Barbudo Guifsobalito
German: Purpurmasken-Bartvogel

Taxonomy. *Lybius guifsobalito* Hermann, 1783, Ethiopia.
Closely related to *L. torquatus* (similar size, coloration, displays, sexual duet roles), but not so close as to form a superspecies with it, although each reacts strongly to playback of the other's voice. Also related, less closely, to *L. rubrifacies*. Birds become smaller clinally from N to S, but insufficient for racial differentiation; populations from White Nile southwards formerly separated as race *ugandae*. Monotypic.
Distribution. E Sudan, Eritrea and W & C Ethiopia, S to extreme NE Zaire, C Uganda, W Kenya and CN Tanzania; range expanding in W Kenya. Recently reported from N Cameroon, so may occur in Central African Republic.

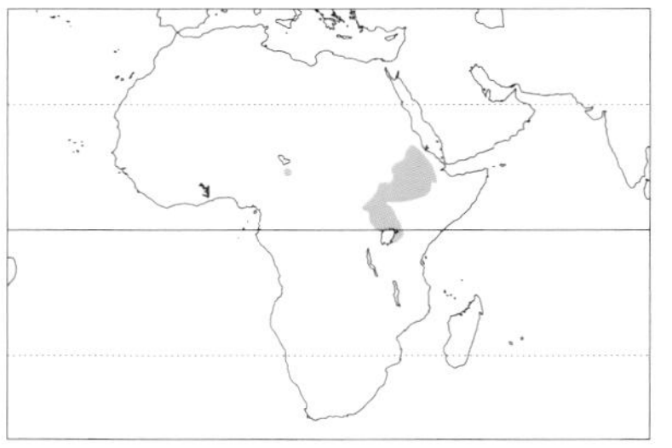

Descriptive notes. 16-18 cm; 35-57 g. Chunky, short-tailed, mostly black barbet. Both sexes with red forehead, face and throat to upper breast, mainly black body; some yellow to white on edges of flight-feathers and (when fresh) rectrices, also in wing-coverts; black bill has 1-2 "teeth". Differs from *L. torquatus* in black lower underparts. Immature duller, red areas more orange and less extensive, bill without "teeth". Voice. Complex greeting ceremonies with chattering, grating, "kek" notes, often leading to duet or occasionally 3-bird singing, with distinct sexual songs, one (male?) lower "a-poot", other higher-pitched "kik-ka", in synchrony over 3-10 seconds or more; duet similar to that of *L. torquatus* but noisier, faster; "wup-wup-" in series by lone bird, possibly location or gathering call; during encounters grating calls, "kek" notes, chatter calls, and frequent loud bill-wiping and wing-fluttering.
Habitat. Open woodland, such as *Acacia* and *Combretum-Terminalia*, bushed woods, edges of riverine forest and woods, gardens and cultivated areas with fruiting trees; even uses eucalyptus groves for singing. Occurs at 900-1600 m, up to 2200 in Ethiopia.
Food and Feeding. Berries and fruits, including figs, guavas, papayas, peppers and others, as well as ants, termites, beetles, Hemiptera and other insects. Gleans along branches and in foliage, picking fruit and insects; flycatches at intervals, extensively so when termites are flying.
Breeding. Oct-Dec, but Mar-May in Ethiopia. Groups of up to 7 perform greeting ceremonies, with bowing, tail-swinging, erection of head feathers, bill-wiping, tail-cocking; also floating flight display to perch, and wing-fluttering; 1 duetter cocks tail, partly spreads wings, as other slightly raises wings, bows and pivots to each side. Roosting cavities recorded at 5 m and 8 m, and nest presumably similar, but no details. No reliable information available on clutch size, incubation and nestling periods, and relative behaviour of pair and helpers.
Movements. Resident and sedentary.
Status and Conservation. Not globally threatened. Locally common in SE of range; probably locally common elsewhere. Seems to be reasonably adaptable; occurs in some degraded habitats, and is expanding its range in places. This species' biology, however, is little known and requires study. Present in Awash National Park (Ethiopia) and Murchison Falls National Park (Uganda).
Bibliography. van Beirs (1997), Benson (1946), Britton (1980), Britton & Britton (1971), Brown & Britton (1980), Cave & Macdonald (1955), Chapin (1939), Cheesman & Sclater (1935), Dowsett & Dowsett-Lemaire (1993), Dowsett & Forbes-Watson (1993), Friedmann (1930a, 1930b), Fry *et al*. (1988), Horne & Short (1988), Jackson & Sclater (1938), Lewis & Pomeroy (1989), Lippens & Wille (1976), Mackworth-Praed & Grant (1957, 1970), Nikolaus (1987), Payne (1967a), Robertson (1994), Short & Horne (1983b, 1985a, 1988b), Short *et al*. (1990), Smith (1957), Snow (1978), Speir (1990), Stevenson & Fanshawe (2001), Zimmerman (1967), Zimmerman *et al*. (1996), Zinner (2001).

36. Black-collared Barbet

Lybius torquatus

French: Barbican à collier   **German**: Halsband-Bartvogel   **Spanish**: Barbudo Acollarado

Taxonomy. *Bucco torquatus* Dumont, 1816, Brazil; error = Cookhouse, eastern Cape Province, South Africa.
Closest relative is *L. guifsobalito* (with similar size, coloration, displays, sexual duet roles), but the two are not so close as to form a superspecies, though they react strongly to playback of each other's voice. Also related, less closely, to *L. rubrifacies*. Race *bocagei* intergrades with *congicus* and *torquatus*, and both *vivacens* and *irroratus* intergrade with *zombae*; partly white morphs occur in at least two races (*zombae*, *irroratus*), and have been treated as races under names "*albigularis*" and "*nampunju*"; birds from W Zimbabwe described as *lucidiventris* are inseparable from *bocagei*. In past, race *bocagei* was erroneously listed as a race of *Stactolaema leucotis*. Seven subspecies recognized.

Subspecies and Distribution.

L. t. pumilio Grote, 1927 - E Zaire, S Uganda, E Rwanda and W Tanzania S to NE & E Zambia, N & W Malawi and NW Mozambique.

L. t. irroratus (Cabanis, 1878) - coastal E Kenya S to CE Tanzania.

L. t. zombae (Shelley, 1893) - SE Tanzania to SC Malawi and NE & C Mozambique.

L. t. congicus (Reichenow, 1898) - N & NC Angola E to SC Zaire and NW Zambia.

L. t. bocagei (Sousa, 1886) - S Angola and NE Namibia E to SW Zambia, N Botswana and W Zimbabwe.

L. t. vivacens Clancey, 1977 - E Zimbabwe and S Malawi to WC & SC Mozambique.

L. t. torquatus (Dumont, 1816) - SE Botswana and Transvaal E to Swaziland and E South Africa.

Descriptive notes. 17·5-19 cm; 35-48 g in N, 45-80 g in S. Common, conspicuous, vocal and social brown, black and yellow barbet. Both sexes of nominate race with red (sometimes yellow) over much of head and throat, black hindcrown, nape and mantle, with brown remaining upperparts finely vermiculated with black; black band across breast, yellow belly; large bill black with 1 or 2 "teeth". Differs from *L. rubrifacies* in yellow belly, more red in plumage, brown back; from *L. melanopterus* in yellow belly, no dark thigh patch. Immature duller, little or no red on head, brown bill paler and lacking "teeth". Race *congicus* like nominate, but separated by *bocagei*, which is yellower ventrally, with few lateral vermiculations on flanks; *pumilio* smaller, more orangey on head and breast, paler yellow belly becoming whiter on flanks; *vivacens* similar to *pumilio*, but browner above with finer vermiculations, still paler, whiter, below; *irroratus* resembles *pumilio*, but smaller, paler below, with hair-tipped red throat-breast feathers that hang over black collar; *zombae* variable, with no red on head, face rather spotted to streaked white, orange or yellow on black, underparts paler and less yellow, white-marked morphs common.

Voice. Complex, sexually discrete songs in duet, starting with greeting ceremony involving "tyaw", grating "zzzz", chatter, and "chatter-tyaw" calls that lead into synchronized "pudit" and higher, longer "tay" songs in "pudit-tay, pudit-tay" duet; duets have 2-20 sets of the 2-note forms in 2-10 seconds; also "pup" or "wup" in series, "yaaak" in alarm, and low notes. Wing-fluttering at c. 33 beats per second, and bill-tapping at or inside nest.

Habitat. Diverse open woodland to pasture habitats, avoiding deserts and forest: includes farmland, gardens, *Acacia* woodland, riverine woods, wooded grassland, and *Parinari-Pericopsis* woodland. From sea-level to 1820 m.

Food and Feeding. Grapes, guavas, figs, and fruits of *Euclea*, *Hippobromus*, *Lycium*, *Rhus*, *Royena*, *Scutia*, *Trichelia* and *Ziziphus*, among others; also ants, rose chafers, beetles, bees and other hymenopterans, and other insects. Gleans in foliage, and picks and probes along bark of twigs and on trunks of bushes and trees; works in lichens, debris and termite tunnels. Pecks out and eats seeds from dried pods of *Cassia abbreviata*. Occasionally flycatches from perch.

Breeding. Aug-Apr in most areas, also Apr-May in Rwanda and E Zaire, also Jul in last; mainly Sept-Dec S of Angola and Zimbabwe; up to 4 clutches in a season. Social, nests in group. Displays include bill-wiping, bill-pointing, bowing, bobbing, swinging of body and bill, swinging and flicking of tail, tail-cocking, wing-rustling, slow gliding display flight, with greeting ceremonies, duets and bill-tapping. Nest, excavated mainly or fully by primary pair, 0·5-6 m up in stump or dead limb or branch, often on underside, cavity to 48 cm deep, tunnel from entrance c. 8·5 cm; territory 20-50 ha in N, to 125 ha in S. Eggs 1-5, in S average clutch size 3·3; incubation, by all members of group, with guard barbet outside, period 18-19 days; nestlings fed by all group-members, reach entrance at c. 28 days, fledge in 33-35 days; young stay in group for c. 5 months, some remaining as helpers through following season. Parasitized by Lesser Honeyguide (*Indicator minor*), disruptions by which can also delay breeding.

Movements. Resident and sedentary.

Status and Conservation. Not globally threatened. Common in many parts of range; coastal race *irroratus* apparently locally fairly common, but habitat diminishing and its population probably requires monitoring. Species' aggressiveness towards other hole-nesters, and its frequent dominance over smaller barbets through interactions and even enlarging of their nesting and roosting holes, possibly renders it less vulnerable to loss of suitable breeding sites. Present in numerous protected areas, e.g. Ruvuvu National Park (Burundi), Rhodes Matopos National Park (Zimbabwe) and Kruger National Park and Mkuzi Reserve (South Africa).

Bibliography. Abell (1992), Belcher (1930), Benson & Benson (1977), Benson *et al.* (1971), Bingham (1999), Bowland (1988), Britton (1980), Brown & Britton (1980), Chapin (1939), Clancey (1956, 1971a, 1977d, 1977e, 1984a), Cooper & Groves (1969), Cyrus (1988), Dean (2000), Donnelly (1973), Dowsett & Dowsett-Lemaire (1993), Dowsett & Forbes-Watson (1993), Friedmann & Loveridge (1937), Fry *et al.* (1988), Ginn *et al.* (1989), Goodwin (1996), Harrison *et al.* (1997), Horne & Short (1988), Irwin (1981, 1996), Jackson & Sclater (1938), Lewis & Pomeroy (1989), Lippens & Wille (1976), Liversidge (1991), Mackworth-Praed & Grant (1957, 1962, 1970), Maclean (1993), Moyer (1980), Penrith (2000), Penry (1994), Pinto (1983), Rankin (1981), Rutgers & Norris (1977), Short & Horne (1979, 1982a, 1983a, 1985a, 1988b, 1992c), Short *et al.* (1990), Skead (1950), Snow (1978), Steyn (1996), Steyn & Densham (1975), Steyn & Scott (1974), Tarboton (2001), Tarboton *et al.* (1987), Vande weghe (1974), Ward (1986, 1989), Williams (1966), Zimmerman *et al.* (1996).

PLATE 10

inches 3
cm 8

PLATE 10

37. Brown-breasted Barbet

Lybius melanopterus

French: Barbican à poitrine brune   **Spanish**: Barbudo Pechipardo
German: Braunbrust-Bartvogel
Other common names: Black-winged Barbet

Taxonomy. *Pogonias (Laimodon) melanopterus* W. K. H. Peters, 1854, Mocimboa, Mozambique.
Related to *L. minor*; also to the *L. bidentatus* group, which includes that species and the superspecies formed by *L. dubius* and *L. rolleti*. Paler brown Somalian birds sometimes placed in separate race, *didymus*, but in fresh plumage they are dark, as are those from farther S, so separation not justified. Monotypic.
Distribution. Mainly coastal, from S Somalia to SC Mozambique, ranging inland along rivers, more so in S, reaching to EC Kenya, CS Tanzania and N & SE Malawi; inland populations often disjunct.
Descriptive notes. c. 19 cm; 45-61 g. Long-tailed barbet with pale bill. Male with head red, giving way to brown on breast and back, lower back mostly white; thighs blackish, conspicuous against white belly; bill light horn, with 1 or 2 "teeth". Female like male, but at least 1 female known with flank spots, suggesting sexual dimorphism. Immature duller, less red. VOICE. No song, equivalent perhaps is "nyekk" or "rrakk", singly, or up to 10 at 1 per second; sometimes

more noisy "nyaaaak"; also nasal grating "skzzzz" at c. 2 per second during encounters and prior to copulation. Loud wing-fluttering and bill-wiping during aggressive interactions.
Habitat. Inhabits forest patches and partly cut-over areas, as well as forest edges, cultivated trees, riverine forest or woods, gardens, and trees along roads of villages and city suburbs. Generally found below 600 m, but occurs up to 1700 m in both Tanzania and Malawi.
Food and Feeding. Relatively little known. Feeds on insects (including hymenopterans), and also on figs, cultivated fruits and diverse other fruits and berries. Flycatches, sometimes making 3-4 captures in a single flight; also gleans insects and fruits in foliage and along branches and twigs.
Breeding. Nov-Jun, also Aug; has 2 broods in places, in captivity breeds up to 3 times a year. Usually breeds in social groups of up to 7, sometimes including subadults from earlier brood. Much allopreening, tail-flipping and bowing among all group-members. Nest not described in detail, but 1 likely nest at 6 m in stub of broken large dead tree; apparently territorial. Clutch size unknown, but up to 3 young, possibly 4, recorded; no data on incubation, fledging, and other

aspects of breeding. Interactions with parasitic Lesser Honeyguide (*Indicator minor*) occur, sometimes delaying nesting.
Movements. Resident; largely sedentary, but may wander some distance along rivers.
Status and Conservation. Not globally threatened. No data available on numbers; groups in mixed cultivation and woodland along roads at intervals of c. 300-500 m. Breeds in Liwonde National Park (Malawi). Often very local, and uncommon, and these factors, together with disjunct nature of distribution, suggest that it may be vulnerable; precise limits of range in S still require confirmation. More information also required on species' biology. Although interfered with by *L. torquatus*, it is dominant over that species; probably affected adversely by nest parasitism by Lesser Honeyguide.
Bibliography. Archer & Godman (1937-1961), Ash & Miskell (1983, 1998), Belcher (1930), Benson & Benson (1977), Bohmke & Macek (1994), Britton (1980), Brown & Britton (1980), Cordeiro (1989), Dowsett & Dowsett-Lemaire (1993), Dowsett & Forbes-Watson (1993), Friedmann & Loveridge (1937), Fry *et al.* (1988), Jackson & Sclater (1938), Johnston-Stewart & Heigham (1982), Lane (1982), Lewis (1984), Lewis & Pomeroy (1989), Mackworth-Praed & Grant (1957, 1962), Michler (1999), Nyirenda (1992), Short & Horne (1985a, 1988b, 1992c), Short *et al.* (1990), Snow (1978), Stevenson & Fanshawe (2001), Zimmerman *et al.* (1996).

38. Black-backed Barbet
Lybius minor

French: Barbican de Levaillant **German**: Rosenbauch-Bartvogel **Spanish**: Barbudo Frentirrojo
Other common names: MacClounie's Barbet (*macclounii*)

Taxonomy. *Pogonias minor* Cuvier, 1817, north Angola.
Related both to *L. melanopterus* and to the *L. bidentatus* group, latter including that species and the superspecies formed by *L. dubius* and *L. rolleti*. Race *macclounii* considered a separate species by some, but interbreeds with nominate *minor* over a considerable area (SW Zaire to NC Angola); form sometimes referred to as "*intercedens*" is hybrid between those races. Two subspecies currently recognized.
Subspecies and Distribution.
L. m. minor (Cuvier, 1817) - S Gabon to W Zaire and S to WC Angola.
L. m. macclounii (Shelley, 1899) - NE Angola, SC Zaire, S Burundi and W Tanzania S to N & W Zambia and NW Malawi.

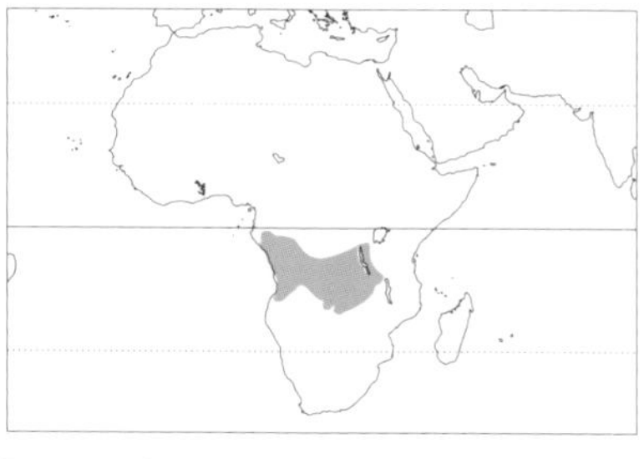

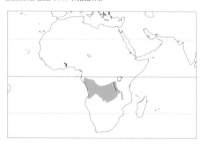

Descriptive notes. 19·5-21 cm; 40-57 g. Long-tailed, pale-billed barbet with much white in plumage. Male nominate race with red forehead and forecrown, blackish lores, rest of head brown; upperparts blackish-brown; white below, with orange-pink on belly, black thighs; bill light pinkish-grey to pale horn-grey, often tinged greenish above and pink below, with 1 or 2 "teeth"; orbital skin whitish-ochre to violet; legs pale, pinkish-flesh. Female like male, but at least two females known with spotting on flanks suggestive of sexual dimorphism. Immature duller, lacks red, has yellow in place of pink. Race *macclounii* has sides of head white, hindcrown and upperparts black, with white bands on each side of mantle meeting at mid-back to form white "V". Voice. Song of trilled buzzy notes at c. 26 per second, 1-3 seconds long, resembles those of *Trachyphonus vaillantii* and *L. bidentatus*; "krek" or "krek-ek" call like major call of *L. bidentatus*; also fast or slow grating in interactions, screeching calls used with grating, also "car" note. Other signals are bill-tapping, hard bill-wiping and wing-rustling.
Habitat. Woodland, gardens and open places with scattered trees and plantations, edges of forest, riverine vegetation, and thickets in formerly wooded country; enters pine plantations when foraging. Attracted to termite mounds and carton-ant nests.
Food and Feeding. Diet little known: fruits, berries, their seeds, also palm-nut fibres; and various flying insects and larvae, such as inchworms. Feeds from ground to canopy, in branches and foliage; plucks fruits, gleans insects, and flycatches, and hovers to take insects.
Breeding. Mainly Aug-Dec; also later, to Apr, in Gabon and Zaire, and as early as Jul in Malawi. Nests in pairs or trios. Tail-flitting, swinging of tail and body, bowing, tail-cocking and allopreening occur. Nest excavated by 2 adults, of which 1 possibly a helper, at 2-8 m in arboreal carton-ant nest, or tree stub or dead branch (e.g. of *Brachystegia* or *Syzygium guineense*), tunnel in carton-ant nest 10 cm deep and leading to 10-cm spherical chamber; readily renests in new chamber, even within 25 cm of old nest; territorial, but nests as close as 300 m, and nest defended against hole-nesters such as starlings (Sturnidae), other barbets (*L. torquatus* kept 50 m or more away), and Lesser Honeyguides (*Indicator minor*). Eggs 3-4; incubation by all adults; incubation and fledging periods unknown; fledglings follow adults, are fed entirely on fruits. Probably parasitized by Lesser Honeyguide.
Movements. Resident and sedentary.
Status and Conservation. Not globally threatened. Appears to be scarce to locally more common. Adaptable, occurs in gardens, but requires suitable nesting sites. Almost certainly suffers through nest parasitism by honeyguides. Present in Ruvuvu National Park (Burundi).
Bibliography. Anon. (1998a), Aspinwall & Beel (1998), Belcher (1930), Benson & Benson (1977), Benson & White (1957), Benson *et al.* (1971), Bouet (1961), Britton (1980), Brooke (1964), Carter *et al.* (1984), Chapin (1939), Dean (2000), Dowsett (1969), Dowsett & Dowsett-Lemaire (1980, 1993), Dowsett & Forbes-Watson (1993), Fry *et al.* (1988), Goodwin (1964), Grant & Mackworth-Praed (1942), Johnston-Stewart & Heigham (1982), Lippens & Wille (1976), Mackworth-Praed & Grant (1957, 1962, 1970), Pinto (1983), Ripley & Heinrich (1966), Short (1982a), Short & Horne (1985a), Snow (1978, 1979), Stevenson & Fanshawe (2001), Traylor (1960, 1963), Verheyen (1953).

39. Double-toothed Barbet
Lybius bidentatus

French: Barbican bidenté **German**: Doppelzahn-Bartvogel **Spanish**: Barbudo Bidentado
Other common names: Tooth-billed Barbet

Taxonomy. *Bucco bidentatus* Shaw, 1798, Nigeria.
Relationship with *L. dubius* and *L. rolleti* indicated by plumage pattern and by sexual dimorphism in flank pattern; related also, but less closely, to *L. minor* and *L. melanopterus*. Races only slightly differentiated; also, proposed races *friedmanni* from S Cameroon to Cabinda (N Angola) and *aethiops* from Ethiopia now included within *aequatorialis*. Two subspecies recognized.
Subspecies and Distribution.
L. b. bidentatus (Shaw, 1798) - Guinea-Bissau, Guinea, Sierra Leone and Liberia E to C Cameroon.
L. b. aequatorialis (Shelley, 1889) - E Cameroon E to C Ethiopia, S to NW Angola, N Zaire, Burundi and NW Tanzania.

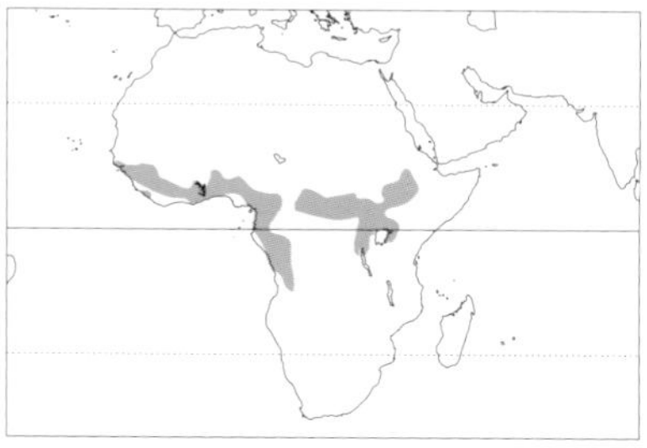

Descriptive notes. c. 23 cm; 65-91 g. Large, white-billed red and black barbet. Male nominate race glossy black above, with small white patch on lower back, narrow red wingbar; face and underparts red, with white patch between red belly and black rear flanks; yellow skin around eye, iris yellow to brownish; bill yellowish-white with 2 notches. Distinguished from *L. dubius* and *L. rolleti* by red, not black, throat and breast, and lack of distinct grooves on "double-toothed" bill. Female differs from male only in having tiny black spots or streaks on red adjacent to white flank patch. Immature duller, orbital skin and iris grey. Race *aequatorialis* with paler and narrower wingbar. Voice. Song a buzzy trill of doubled notes at 23-35 per second for up to 15 seconds; pair-members sing synchronously, usually one singing much longer than other; single to triple "krex", noisy location call, variable, like some calls of *L. melanopterus*, *L. minor* and *L. dubius*; also double "aaaaarrk" notes, "awk", "uh-uh-" sounds, all with fast mechanical clicking elements. Loud bill-snapping and bill-wiping, taps at nest entrance, and flicks wings loudly during encounters.
Habitat. Forest understorey, particularly at edges and around clearings, also secondary forest, streamside forest and woods, thickets, dense woods, trees over cultivation and gardens. Lowlands to 1800 m generally, to 2300 m in W Kenya.
Food and Feeding. Eats fruits and arthropods: avocados, figs, fruits of *Musanga*, papayas, red peppers, palm nuts; and ants, beetles, Hemiptera, emergent termites, and various larvae. Insects hunted among leaves and along bark; also flycatches occasionally to frequently. Usually forages in dense foliage below 10 m.
Breeding. Season long, perhaps all year in many areas; more often Nov-May in W Africa, also Apr-Nov in Cameroon, Gabon, Ethiopia and Angola. In pairs, with or without helpers. Displays mainly by pair, include tail movements, erection of flank feathers (showing sex), bowing, allopreening. Nest excavated mainly by pair, at 2-30 m in rotten tree stub or branch, including isolated tree near cover but in open, cavity entrance 5 cm, depth to 46 cm; nest defended against oxpeckers (*Buphagus*) and Lesser Honeyguide (*Indicator minor*). Eggs 2-4; incubation with many change-overs, period c. 13-14 days; hatchlings fed insects, later more fruit, by pair and any helpers, all of which also keep nest clean; nestling period 37-39 days; fledglings, helpers if any, and parents return nightly to roost in nest.
Movements. Resident and sedentary.
Status and Conservation. Not globally threatened. Widespread, and reasonably common almost everywhere in range; locally common in Sierra Leone; uncommon and local in Nigeria; fairly common in Kenya; rare, possibly overlooked, in Liberia, where extremely few confirmed records. Adaptable. Occurs in several protected areas, e.g. Comoé National Park (Ivory Coast), Mount Kupé National Park (Cameroon), Murchison Falls National Park (Uganda), Akagera National Park (Rwanda) and Ruvuvu National Park (Burundi).
Bibliography. Bannerman (1933, 1953), Bates (1930), Britton (1980), Brosset & Érard (1986), Brown & Britton (1980), Cave & Macdonald (1955), Chapin (1939), Cheesman & Sclater (1935), Cheke & Walsh (1996), Christy & Clarke (1994), Colebrook-Robjent (1984), Colston & Curry-Lindahl (1986), Dean (2000), Dowsett & Dowsett-Lemaire (1993), Dowsett & Forbes-Watson (1993), Elgood *et al.* (1994), England (1976), Faust (1969), Field (1999), Friedmann (1930a), Fry *et al.* (1988), Gatter (1997), Grimes (1987), Halleux (1994), Jackson & Sclater (1938), Lamarche (1980), Lewis & Pomeroy (1989), Lippens & Wille (1976), Louette (1981b), Mackworth-Praed & Grant (1957, 1962, 1970), Nikolaus (1987), Pinto (1983), Rand *et al.* (1959), Short & Horne (1985a), Short *et al.* (1990), Snow (1978), Taylor (1983), Thiollay (1985a), Zimmerman *et al.* (1996).

40. Bearded Barbet
Lybius dubius

French: Barbican à poitrine rouge **Spanish**: Barbudo Pechirrojo
German: Furchenschnabel-Bartvogel

Taxonomy. *Bucco dubius* J. F. Gmelin, 1788, Mopti, Mali.
Forms a superspecies with *L. rolleti*; both are also closely related to *L. bidentatus*. Monotypic.
Distribution. W Sahel from N Senegambia and Guinea-Bissau E to SW Chad, S to Guinea, C Ivory Coast, C Ghana, Togo and Benin, C Nigeria, C Cameroon and NW Central African Republic.

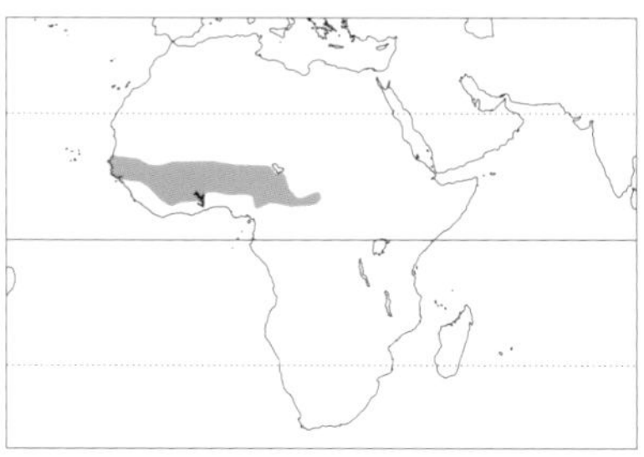

Descriptive notes. c. 25·5 cm; 80-108 g. Distinctive, large, red, black and white barbet with big yellow bill. Male glossy black above, with white patch on lower back; black hair-like feathers projecting over chin and base of bill; red cheeks and underparts with black breastband, white flank patch, black rear flanks; yellow skin around eye, yellow iris; bill yellow with 2 "teeth", and grooves. Distinguished from *L. rolleti* by yellow facial skin and eye, red on breast, bill with grooves on underside as well as on sides; from *L. bidentatus* by larger size, black breastband, bigger and more yellow bill with grooves. Female differs from male in having black spots on white flank patch. Immature like adult but duller, red areas orangey, bill duller and with grooves and "teeth" obscure or lacking. Voice. Song not known; has "krawk" or "caw" notes, noisy but less grating than in *L. bidentatus*; also whirring "hurr-hurr-" reported.
Habitat. Occurs around trees in dry areas, including in *Acacia*, baobabs (*Adansonia digitata*), figs, fruiting trees in gardens, and in thickets, open woods, abandoned farms, secondary growth, and

On following page: 41. Black-breasted Barbet (*Lybius rolleti*).

associated undergrowth, from near sea-level to c. 1500 m.

Food and Feeding. Almost unknown. Groups move from fruiting tree to fruiting tree, readily clipping fruits with powerful bill; presumably takes insects as well.

Breeding. May-Sept in W, also Dec in Niger and Ghana; Feb-Jul or to Sept farther E in Nigeria and Cameroon. Social, in groups of up to 5. Displays undescribed apart from flicking of long tail. Nest excavated at any height in dead stub or dead branch, e.g. of *Acacia* or palm; territory probably large and irregular, but data lacking. Reported to lay 2 eggs; no other information on wild-living birds; in captivity, 2 eggs, incubation at least 16 days, hatching on consecutive days, nestling period c. 40 days.

Movements. Resident and apparently sedentary.

Status and Conservation. Not globally threatened. Common in Senegambia, common in Nigeria, and thought to be at least locally common elsewhere, although no data on numbers. Clearing of trees, especially dead ones, and desertification presumably disadvantageous to this species; on other hand, planting of fruit trees and clearing of forest in S parts of range likely to favour it, although bringing it into greater sympatry and possible competition with adaptable *L. bidentatus*. Research required on species' ecology and biology. Occurs in numerous protected areas, e.g. W National Park (Niger), Saloum Delta National Park and Niokola Koba National Park (Senegal), Abuko Nature Reserve (Gambia), Comoé National Park (Ivory Coast), Falgore Reserve (Nigeria), Bénoué National Park (Cameroon) and Bamingui-Bangoran National Park (Central African Republic).

Bibliography. Bannerman (1933, 1953), Barlow *et al.* (1997), Bates (1930), Callaghan (1999), Chappius (1981), Cheke & Walsh (1996), Dowsett & Dowsett-Lemaire (1993), Dowsett & Forbes-Watson (1993), Elgood *et al.* (1994), Fry *et al.* (1988), Genz (1999), Giraudoux *et al.* (1988), Gore (1990), Grimes (1987), Helsens (1996), Lamarche (1980), Larison *et al.* (2000), Louette (1981b), Mackworth-Praed & Grant (1970), Morel & Morel (1990), Rodwell (1996), Serle (1950), Short & Horne (1985a, 1988b), Snow (1978), Thiollay (1985a), Traylor & Parelius (1967).

41. **Black-breasted Barbet**

Lybius rolleti

French: Barbican à poitrine noire   **Spanish**: Barbudo Pechinegro
          German: Schwarzbrust-Bartvogel

Taxonomy. *Pogonias Rolleti* de Filippi, 1853, Upper White Nile in extreme south Sudan. Forms a superspecies with *L. dubius*; both are closely related to *L. bidentatus*. Monotypic.

Distribution. S Chad, NE Central African Republic and S Sudan to extreme NE Zaire and N Uganda.

Descriptive notes. c. 27 cm; 96-105 g. Distinctive, large, big-billed, black, white and red barbet. Male all glossy black, except for white patch on lower back, red belly, white flank patch; black hair-like feathers around base of bill, especially out over nostrils; facial skin blue to grey, eyes brown; ivory bill "toothed" and with grooves on sides. Distinguished from *L. dubius* by all-black throat and breast, and dark eyes and facial skin; from *L. bidentatus* additionally by larger size, much heavier bill with prominent grooves. Female has small black spots on white flank patch. Immature less glossy black, browner, reds duller and more orange-red. VOICE. Almost unknown; low, harsh grating note reported, and loud fluttering wing sounds.

Habitat. E Sahelian areas with woods, thickets and scattered trees, such as trees along water-courses, also in gardens and cultivation, even at times in eucalyptus groves; at 200-1200 m or more, to as high as 2134 m in W Sudan.

Food and Feeding. Diet of fruits, including guavas, mangoes, figs and others; presumably eats insects as well. Foraging behaviour not described, nor has occurrence in groups.

Breeding. Feb-Jul, perhaps occasionally later, to Nov, in N; Sept-Dec in N Uganda. Nest excavated in tree, at up to c. 5 m. Eggs apparently 1-2; incubation and nestling periods unknown; adults carry food in bill to nestlings, remove faecal material from nest. No other information available.

Movements. Presumably resident and sedentary.

Status and Conservation. Not globally threatened. One of the least well known of all barbets; no information on numbers, probably uncommon or, perhaps, locally more common; ecology and breeding biology very poorly known. Could come under threat through desertification of habitat and removal of dead wood for fires; potentially assisted by forest clearance in S of range, but there it is subject to competition from adaptable *L. bidentatus*.

Bibliography. Bretagnolle (1993), Britton (1980), Carroll (1988), Cave & Macdonald (1955), Chapin (1939), Dowsett & Dowsett-Lemaire (1993), Dowsett & Forbes-Watson (1993), Fry *et al.* (1988), Germain (1992), Goodwin (1964), Lynes (1925), Mackworth-Praed & Grant (1957, 1970), Nikolaus (1987), Pedersen (2000), Short & Horne (1988b, 1991), Short *et al.* (1990), Snow (1978), Stevenson & Fanshawe (2001).

PLATE 11 ➤

♀
ssp *fuliginosus*
♂

42

♂
ssp *tertius*

♂
ssp *hayii*

43
♂

♀

44
ssp *virens*

ssp *marshallorum*

45
ssp *lagrandieri*

ssp *rothschildi*

46
ssp *caniceps*

ssp *zeylanica*

ssp *lineata*
pale bird   dark bird

ssp *inornata*

47

ssp *hodgsoni*
dark bird

PLATE 11

inches   4
cm   10

Subfamily CALORHAMPHINAE

Genus *CALORHAMPHUS*   Lesson, 1839

42. **Brown Barbet**
Calorhamphus fuliginosus

French: Barbu fuligineux   **German**: Braunbartvogel   **Spanish**: Barbudo Pardo

Taxonomy. *Mycropogon fuliginosus* Temminck, 1830, Pontianak, west Borneo.
Relationships unclear, and species remains very poorly known. Race *detersus* possibly inseparable from *hayii*. Four subspecies currently recognized.
Subspecies and Distribution.
C. f. detersus Deignan, 1960 - S Myanmar (extreme S Tenasserim) and adjacent peninsular Thailand (S to Trang).
C. f. hayii (J. E. Gray, 1831) - Malay Peninsula and Sumatra.
C. f. tertius Chasen & Kloss, 1929 - N Borneo.
C. f. fuliginosus (Temminck, 1830) - Borneo (except N).

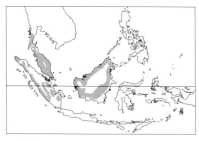

Descriptive notes. c. 17·5 cm; 38·5-47·5 g. Heavy-billed, short-tailed barbet with brown upperparts. Male nominate race with dull red to rufous-pink on throat and breast; bill black, legs and feet orange-red. Female like male, but bill brown to horn. Immature duller, lacks hair-tips to shafts of crown and throat feathers. Race *tertius* paler brown on head, rufous-pink on throat barely extends to breast, male with browner bill; *hayii* paler and duller on head and throat, with rufous-pink replaced by rusty-buff wash, and yellow tinge from breast to belly; *detersus* very like *hayii*, larger and paler, often sooty on chin. VOICE. Sibilant "pseeee" calls, usually in series; also "pseeoo" call.
Habitat. Inhabits primary lowland forest, rarely up to 1000 m in lower hill forest; also occurs in swampy forest, some secondary forest and cut-over areas with fruit trees; sometimes found in cacao plantations.
Food and Feeding. Fruits such as those of *Ficus*, and berries; seeds of fruits to 10 mm found in stomachs; also undetermined insects. Usually feeds in small groups of up to 6 or 8 individuals, in understorey to canopy, birds calling squeakily as they forage. At times moves along tree surfaces, in clusters of leaves, clinging in manner of tit (Paridae).
Breeding. Jan-Jul; Feb-Sept in Borneo. Social; up to 3 or more pairs nest in single tree or stub. Nest 1-10 m up, occasionally as high as 20 m, in stump, dead tree or branch, or in arboreal carton-ant or termite nest. Clutch 2-3; no information on incubation and fledging periods.
Movements. Resident and, so far as known, sedentary.
Status and Conservation. Not globally threatened. Fairly common to common in most of range; common in Borneo. Range of habitats used suggests some adaptability. Present in several protected areas, e.g. Khao Nor Chuchi (Thailand), Batu Punggul Forest Reserve and Gunung Mulu National Park (Peninsular Malaysia) and Kerinci-Seblat and Way Kambas National Parks (Sumatra). Research required, notably into possible taxonomic relationships.
Bibliography. Baker (1934a), Bromley (1952), Chasen (1939), Deignan (1960), Duckworth & Kelsh (1988), Holmes & Burton (1987), Jeyarajasingam & Pearson (1999), Laman *et al.* (1996), Lambert (1987, 1989a), Lekagul & Round (1991), Lim Kim Seng (1992), MacKinnon & Phillipps (1993), van Marle & Voous (1988), McClure (1966), Medway (1972), Medway & Wells (1976), Nee & Guan (1993), Riley (1938), Robinson (1928), Robinson & Chasen (1939), Robson (2000), Round (1988), Short & Horne (1991), Smythies (1986, 1999), Thompson (1966), Vowles & Vowles (1997), Wells (1985, 1999), Wells *et al.* (1978), Wilkinson, Dutson & Sheldon (1991), Wong (1986).

Subfamily MEGALAIMATINAE

Genus *PSILOPOGON*   S. Müller, 1835

43. **Fire-tufted Barbet**
Psilopogon pyrolophus

French: Barbu à collier   **German**: Rotbüschel-Bartvogel   **Spanish**: Barbudo Picofuego

Taxonomy. *Psilopogon pyrolophus* S. Müller, 1835, Sumatra.
Genus rather closely related to *Megalaima*. Monotypic.
Distribution. Mountain slopes of Peninsular Malaysia and Sumatra; recently reported extreme S Thailand.
Descriptive notes. c. 29 cm; 107-149 g (Malaysia). Largely green barbet of mountains. Male with red-tipped crown feathers, grey face, yellow throat patch bordered by black chestband; red tuft of feathers at base of bill; bill sturdy, yellow with irregular black bar in centre. Female lacks red on crown. Immature duller, greyer, sootier, nasal tuft mainly whitish. VOICE. Trilling song 3-8 seconds long, sounding like a cicada, notes shorten and increase in tempo from 1-2 to 12-14 per second, "dddzza-ddzza-" to "-zz-zz-zz"; also a whistled note, and a squeak.
Habitat. Primary and secondary forest, forest edges and patches, especially in dense foliage with vines and creepers. Mostly at 900-1500 m, locally down to 400 m, and up to 2020 m.

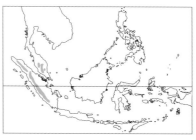

Food and Feeding. Figs and other fruits, also insects; in captivity also grapes, apples, pears, bananas, and breeding captives consumed locusts, mealworms, mice and small dead rats, all mandibulated before being fed to young. Forages in pairs or family groups, pecking and probing, also hanging in foliage to reach fruits or insects.
Breeding. Jan to mid-Sept. Breeds in pairs. Males countersing, holding body nearly horizontal, in encounters may fall to ground clasping and pecking one another. Both adults excavate cavity in dead tree or branch at 4 m or more above ground. Eggs not described, clutch probably 2; incubation period unknown; both parents feed young at first, each remaining in nest until other returns to feed; in captivity, nestling diet shifted to solely fruit at c. 1 week; nestling period c. 42 days. Fledglings fed by parents for 5-8 days after fledging, then feed independently.
Movements. Resident; sedentary, 1 bird recaptured at same site 13 months after first netted.
Status and Conservation. Not globally threatened. Restricted-range species: present in Sumatra and Peninsular Malaysia EBA. Uncommon to locally common in Peninsular Malaysia; common in Sumatra. Although appears to be under no immediate threat, clearing of slope forests in its restricted range may soon fragment populations severely. Present in several protected areas, e.g. Kerinci-Seblat National Park (Sumatra).
Bibliography. Allen (1953), Baker (1934a), Berlioz (1936), Glenister (1971), Holmes (1996), Jeyarajasingam & Pearson (1999), MacKinnon & Phillipps (1993), Madoc (1976), van Marle & Voous (1988), McClure (1964a, 1964b), Medway (1972), Medway & Wells (1976), Robinson (1909, 1911, 1928), Robinson & Chasen (1939), Robson (2000), Rutgers & Norris (1977), Seth-Smith (1929), Stattersfield *et al.* (1998), Sujatnika *et al.* (1995), Wells (1985, 1999), Wilkinson & McLeod (1984).

Genus *MEGALAIMA*   G. R. Gray, 1842

44. **Great Barbet**
Megalaima virens

French: Barbu géant   **German**: HeulBartvogel   **Spanish**: Barbudo Grande
Other common names: Giant Barbet, Giant/Great Hill Barbet, Great Himalayan/Himalayan Great Barbet

Taxonomy. *Bucco virens* Boddaert, 1783, China.
Related to *M. lagrandieri*, but not very closely. Races weakly to moderately marked; Indochinese birds, described as race *indochinensis*, now considered indistinguishable from nominate; birds of Mishmi Hills (NE Assam) formerly recognized as race *mayri*, but inseparable from *clamator*. Four subspecies currently recognized.
Subspecies and Distribution.
M. v. marshallorum (Swinhoe, 1870) - NE Pakistan and NW India E to W Nepal.
M. v. magnifica Stuart Baker, 1926 - E Nepal E to C Assam.
M. v. clamator Mayr, 1941 - NE Assam, N Myanmar, SW China (W Yunnan) and NW Thailand.
M. v. virens (Boddaert, 1783) - C Myanmar and SE China S to NC Thailand and N Vietnam.

Descriptive notes. 32-35 cm; 164-295 g. Largest barbet, with big bill. Both sexes of nominate race with entirely dark bluish head with some green tones, brown and green body streaked with yellowish below; undertail-coverts red; bill yellowish. Xanthochroic specimens occur rarely. Immature similar but duller, sootier, with pink undertail-coverts. Race *clamator* larger, bluer, darker; other two races paler brown and blue-headed with conspicuous yellow-green nape streaks, *magnifica* less marked, *marshallorum* palest with blue-violet on head and greatest amount of yellowish nape streaking. VOICE. Loud, distinctive "kee-aar" to "peeao" notes in long series, with countersinging; female may give shorter, faster notes, male slower, longer notes; also harsh "karr-r", "gyok", soft notes in short series, soft song notes, and a long, repeated querulous note by displaying paired birds. Noisy wing-rustling, especially in display.
Habitat. Forest, both deciduous and evergreen, and wooded valleys on mountain slopes; visits orchards and garden trees with fruits. Usually at 800-2400 m, but breeds down to 300 m in Himalayas, also up to 3000 m, and reaches sea-level in SE China.
Food and Feeding. Diverse fruits, especially figs, berries, wild plums, ivy berries, barberries, "medlar" and "pepul" fruits; also flower petals of rhododendrons, blossom of pear (*Pyrus sinensis*), nectar and petals of silk cotton tree (*Bombax ceiba*), and buds and catkins of trees such as *Ulmus*. Also eats ants, termites, hornets, beetles, cicadas, mantids and other insects. Hawks for insects at times, may drop on to insect from above. Outside breeding season, gathers in numbers of up to 40 at fruiting tree.
Breeding. Feb-Aug or Sept; sometimes 2 or even 3 broods in a season. Much singing and countersinging, simultaneous singing of pair; courtship displays with tail-wagging and head-bowing. Nest excavated by male and female, 3-12 m up in dead tree or branch, often on underside of latter, cavity can be 60 cm or more deep; sometimes old woodpecker hole used. Eggs 2-5, mainly 3-4, laid on wood chips at bottom of cavity; both parents incubate, feed young, enter and leave nest rapidly; incubation period 13-15 days, nestling period more than 38 days; fledged young call like adults, are effectively independent in c. 7-8 days. In captivity known to live for 13 years.
Movements. Resident, with altitudinal movements; those at elevations above c. 800 m migrate down to lower hilly areas and valleys for winter.

On following page: 45. Red-vented Barbet (*Megalaima lagrandieri*); 46. Brown-headed Barbet (*Megalaima zeylanica*); 47. Lineated Barbet (*Megalaima lineata*).

Status and Conservation. Not globally threatened. Common in N Indian Subcontinent, although very local in Pakistan; possibly still present in Bangladesh, but no recent records; common in SE Asia. Somewhat adaptable where some forest exists, as on slopes amid valley cultivation. Present in numerous protected areas across extensive range, e.g. Namdapha National Park (India), Tai Po Kau Nature Reserve (Hong Kong) and Nam Nao, Doi Inthanon and Kaeng Krachan National Parks (Thailand).
Bibliography. Ali (1962, 1977, 1996), Ali & Ripley (1983), Ali *et al.* (1996), Baker (1934a), Büngener (1990), Caldwell & Caldwell (1931), Deignan (1945), Delacour & Jabouille (1931), Dodsworth (1912), Dymond (1998), Eames & Ericson (1996), Étchécopar & Hüe (1978), Grimmett *et al.* (1998, 2000), Herklots (1954), Inskipp & Inskipp (1991), Lekagul & Round (1991), Lewthwaite (1993), MacKinnon & Phillipps (2000), Martens & Eck (1995), Morioka & Sakane (1981), Riley (1938), Ripley (1982), Roberts (1991), Robson (2000), Round (1988), Rutgers & Norris (1977), Shrestha (2000), Smythies (1986), Viney & Phillipps (1983), Vo Quy & Nguyen Cu (1995), Wells (1999), Whistler (1941), Yahya (2000), Zhao Zhengjie (1995).

45. Red-vented Barbet

Megalaima lagrandieri

French: Barbu à ventre rouge **German**: Rotsteiß-Bartvogel **Spanish**: Barbudo Ventrirrojo
Other common names: Lagrandieri's Barbet

Taxonomy. *Megalaima Lagrandieri* J. Verreaux, 1868, Baria, Cochinchina.
Possibly connects genus with *Psilopogon*, and has sometimes even been placed in latter. Allied to *M. virens*, but not particularly closely. Races not particularly well defined. Two subspecies currently recognized.
Subspecies and Distribution.
M. l. rothschildi (Delacour, 1927) - N Laos and N Vietnam.
M. l. lagrandieri J. Verreaux, 1868 - S Laos and S Vietnam.

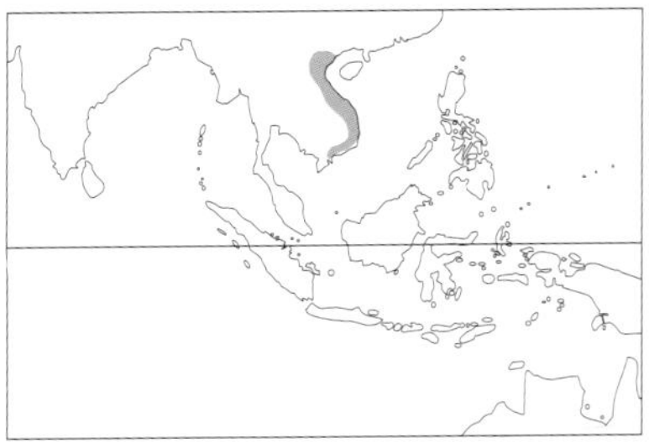

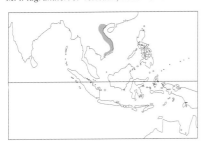

Descriptive notes. c. 29 cm. Large, green to bronzy green barbet. Both sexes of nominate race with head mostly brown, greyish on sides and throat, blue line over eye; red undertail-coverts; reddish feathers in bristly tuft at base of bill; bill large, dull, with yellowish tip and cutting edges. Immature duller, browner, with orangey tuft at bill base. Race *rothschildi* darker brown and green than nominate, shows little or no yellow mixed with red in nasal tuft. Voice. Loud song or call of "kyaa", "kyow" or "yowt" notes, singly, or in series at 30-75 notes per minute for up to 10 seconds or more; alarm "grrrik-grrrik".
Habitat. Evergreen and semi-evergreen forest; occurs in lowlands and on forested slopes and ridges, to 2100 m.
Food and Feeding. Eats fruits such as figs, and insects, but details unknown. May gather at fruiting trees more regularly than does *M. virens*.
Breeding. Data from specimens suggest season Jan-Jul. Male and female of pair probably sing together in territorial formation or maintenance; countersinging occurs. Nest, eggs, incubation period and other details of breeding undescribed.
Movements. Resident and probably sedentary.
Status and Conservation. Not globally threatened. Uncommon to common; often one of commonest barbets in its rather limited range, where it appears to be widespread. This species' ecology and biology, however, are very poorly known, and study is required to elucidate its conservation status. Present in Nam Bai Cat Tien National Park, Bach Ma National Park and Cuc Phuong National Park (Vietnam).
Bibliography. Chazee (1994), Delacour & Jabouille (1931), Duckworth *et al.* (1999), Eames (1995), Eames & Ericson (1996), Eames & Robson (1992), Eames *et al.* (1994), Goodwin (1964), Robinson & Kloss (1919b), Robson (1996a, 2000), Robson, Eames, Nguyen Cu & Truong Van La (1993a, 1994b), Robson, Eames, Wolstencroft *et al.* (1989), Stepanyan (1995), Thewlis, Duckworth *et al.* (1996), Thewlis, Timmins *et al.* (1998), Vo Quy & Nguyen Cu (1995).

46. Brown-headed Barbet

Megalaima zeylanica

French: Barbu à tête brune **German**: Braunkopf-Bartvogel **Spanish**: Barbudo Cabecipardo
Other common names: Green Barbet(!), Oriental/Great/Large Green Barbet

Taxonomy. *Bucco Zeylanicus* J. F. Gmelin, 1788, Sri Lanka.
Forms a superspecies with *M. lineata*, and in past often treated as conspecific; they are narrowly sympatric in N India and SW Nepal, but with no apparent hybridization. Possibly related also to *M. viridis* and *M. faiostricta*, but not very closely. W Himalayan birds (Kangra to Garhwal) previously recognized as race *kangrae*, but now considered inseparable from *caniceps*. Three subspecies currently recognized.
Subspecies and Distribution.
M. z. caniceps (Franklin, 1831) - SW Nepal and N India (Punjab and Uttar Pradesh S to N Maharashtra, Orissa and Bihar).
M. z. inornata Walden, 1870 - CW & SW India (Maharashtra, Goa and Karnataka).
M. z. zeylanica (J. F. Gmelin, 1788) - S India (Kerala, S Tamil Nadu) and Sri Lanka.

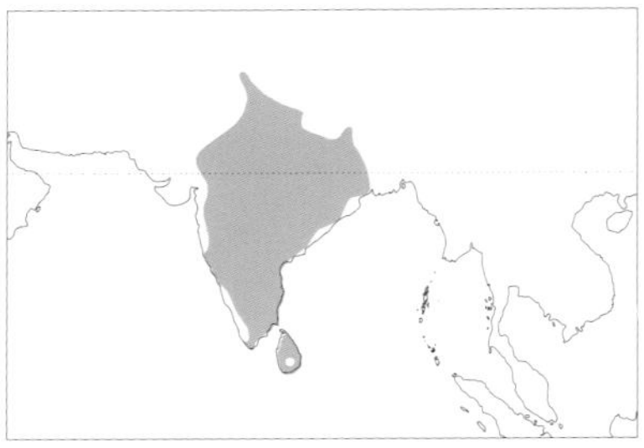

Descriptive notes. 25-28 cm; 108-140 g. Large, streaky green and brown barbet. Both sexes of nominate race with prominent pale streaks on brown head, mantle and breast; throat brown; rest of plumage green, wing-coverts with white spots; bill brown-yellow or flesh-coloured, becoming red-orange when breeding; large area of facial skin dull yellow, turning orange or red-orange when breeding; legs yellowish. Distinguished from *M. lineata* by white wing-covert spots, brown throat, narrower white streaks on foreparts, larger area of bare facial skin with dark feathering around it. Immature duller. Race *inornata* larger and paler, duller brown, but brown encroaches on mid-back and belly, streaks far less prominent, crown almost buffy; *caniceps* also large and pale, but brown restricted anteriorly as in nominate race, and streaking well defined. Voice. Song starts with trilling, then double "po-kok" or "too-kkak" notes in long or short, regular or irregular series, up to 200 notes per minute at start, slowing to 80 or 60, notes harsher than in *M. lineata*; trills also given alone; alarm of "kukk" notes, also laugh-like mobbing call; begging "karrr" notes as in *M. lineata*.
Habitat. Forest, neither very wet nor very dry, also edges, gardens and tree plantations, deciduous woods and scrubland, and even roadside trees. In New Delhi has adapted to suburban gardens and fruiting trees.
Food and Feeding. Feeds on fruits, especially figs, *Syzygium* fruits, and berries, including those of coffee, and also tomatoes and garden fruits; takes flower petals and nectar of *Bombax*, *Erythrina* and *Butea*; also takes animal food including beetles, mantids, ants, termites, and various large and small lizards. In one study in WC India, present species appeared to prefer much larger fig species (*Ficus bengalensis*, *F. mysorensis*) than did *M. haemacephala*. May gather with other barbets and frugivorous birds. Often bathes.
Breeding. Feb-Oct. Both sexes sing simultaneously, and countersing with others. Nest, excavated by both adults, at 2-15 m in tree or branch, often on underside, or in fence post, cavity to 46 cm. Eggs 2-4; incubation and nestling periods unknown; female incubates, broods young at night, both sexes incubate during day and feed young; at fledging, adults withhold food to entice young to leave nest.
Movements. Resident; makes only local movements to fruiting trees, orchards.
Status and Conservation. Not globally threatened. Locally common in much of India; locally fairly common in W Nepal; common in Sri Lanka. Aggressive and somewhat adaptable barbet. Has been reported as being a minor pest in coffee plantations, but recent work indicates the contrary, as species takes stem-boring *Xylotrechus quadripes*. Present in several protected areas, e.g. Corbett National Park (NC India) and Bellanwila-Attidiya Sanctuary (Sri Lanka).
Bibliography. Abdulali (1974), Ali (1962, 1969, 1996), Ali & Ripley (1983), Baker (1934a), Bhunya & Sultana (1983), Daniels, R.J.R. (1997), Dhindsa & Sandhu (1982), Grimmett *et al.* (1998, 2000), Harrison (1999), Henry (1998), Inskipp, C. & Inskipp (1991), Inskipp, T. *et al.* (1996), Kaul & Ansari (1981), Lamsfuss (1998), Mahabal & Lamba (1987), Majumdar *et al.* (1992), Martens & Eck (1995), Mukherjee (1952, 1953, 1995), Phillips (1978), Rand & Fleming (1957), Ripley (1982), Rutgers & Norris (1977), Saha & Dasgupta (1992), Short & Horne (1991), Shrestha (2000), Sugathan & Varghese (1996), Whistler (1941), Yahya (1980, 1988, 1991, 2000).

47. Lineated Barbet

Megalaima lineata

French: Barbu rayé **German**: Streifenbartvogel **Spanish**: Barbudo Listado
Other common names: Green Barbet(!), Grey-headed Barbet

Taxonomy. *Capito lineatus* Vieillot, 1816, Australasia; error = Java.
Forms a superspecies with *M. zeylanica*, and often treated as conspecific in past, but no apparent hybridization in the narrow area of sympatry in N India and SW Nepal. Possibly related also to *M. viridis* and *M. faiostricta*, but not very closely. Race *hodgsoni* tends towards nominate race in Peninsular Malaysia; other forms described include *rana* (Kumaon to WCNepal), *kutru* (Orissa) and *intermedia* (Myanmar to Indochina), but all now included within *hodgsoni*. Two subspecies currently recognized.
Subspecies and Distribution.
M. l. hodgsoni (Bonaparte, 1850) - NW India and Nepal E to SC China (W Yunnan), S to Orissa, Bangladesh, Manipur, S Myanmar, SC Vietnam and N Peninsular Malaysia.
M. l. lineata (Vieillot, 1816) - Java and Bali.

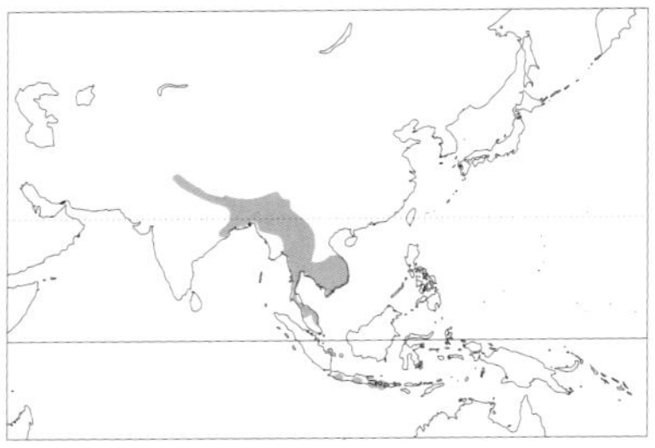

Descriptive notes. 25-30 cm; 115-205 g. Large, green and streaky barbet; individual variation in intensity of coloration. Both sexes of nominate race heavily streaked on head, upper mantle and breast, whitish streaks broader than dark brown ones; throat and chin tend to be whitish; rest of plumage green; bill yellow, pink or horn, becoming creamy pink with yellow base when breeding; yellow or gold skin around eye; legs yellow. Distinguished from *M. zeylanica* by bolder white streaking, pale throat, no wing-covert spots, smaller area of bare orbital skin. Immature duller, buffier. Race *hodgsoni* clinally larger to N and NW. Voice. Song usually with trilled introduction, then series of "poo-tok", often long, at 40-90 notes per minute, notes clearer, less noisy, and first syllable of each pair longer than in *M. zeylanica*, and songs can vary with single or triple notes mixed in; female song faster, trilled sets of notes, alone or with male; has long "hoo-hoo" series, also long trill followed by shorter ones, and several guttural and whistling notes, as well as others.
Habitat. Evergreen forest, especially at clearings and edges, also pine forest, teak, sal and deciduous forest and woodland, open secondary forest, plantations, gardens with cover, and fig and other fruiting trees along roads, even into urban areas.
Food and Feeding. Diverse fruits, especially figs, those of *Grewia*, strawberries, in captivity also bananas; flower petals and nectar from species of *Erythrina* and *Bombax* and others; larvae of various insects, termites; also frogs, nestling birds and probably bird eggs. Congregates at fruiting trees with other barbets.
Breeding. Jan-Jul in most areas; Sept-May in Malay Peninsula; Jan-Jul and Sept-Oct in Java and Bali. Territorial, sings much of year, role of female in territory defence uncertain; in aggression birds droop wings, gape, call. Both adults excavate nest-hole in dead tree or branch, even standing log, or stump, 2-12 m above ground, cavity to 50 cm deep. Eggs 2-4; both parents incubate, both feed young; incubation period c. 14-15 days; other details of nesting largely unknown.
Movements. Resident and sedentary.
Status and Conservation. Not globally threatened. Common in Nepal, fairly common locally in India, frequent in Bhutan, locally common in Bangladesh; common in SE Asia. Aggressive and adaptable species. Present in numerous protected areas, e.g. Corbett and Kaziranga National Parks (India), Chitwan National Park (Nepal), Doi Inthanon National Park (Thailand) and Nam Bai Cat Tien National Park (Vietnam).
Bibliography. Abdulali (1974), Ali (1977, 1996), Ali & Ripley (1983), Ali *et al.* (1996), Baker (1934a), Berwick (1952a, 1952b), Bromley (1949), Deignan (1945, 1963), Delacour & Jabouille (1931), Eames & Ericson (1996), Glenister (1971), Grimmett *et al.* (1998, 2000), Hellebrekers & Hoogerwerf (1967), Inskipp, C. & Inskipp (1991), Inskipp, T. *et al.* (1996), Jeyarajasingam & Pearson (1999), Lekagul & Round (1991), MacKinnon & Phillipps (1993, 2000), Madoc (1976), Martens & Eck (1995), Medway & Wells (1976), Mukherjee (1952, 1953), Riley (1938), Ripley (1982), Robinson & Chasen (1939), Robson (2000), Round (1988), Short & Horne (1991), Shrestha (2000), Smythies (1986), Stepanyan (1995), Vo Quy & Nguyen Cu (1995), Wells (1999), Whistler (1941), Xu Weishu *et al.* (1996), Yahya (1980, 1988, 2000), Zhao Zhengjie (1995).

PLATE 12 ➤

48

49

♀

♂

50

♂ ssp *chrysopogon*

♀

51

ssp *chrysopsis* ♂

52

53

ssp *ampala* ♂

♀

♂ ssp *mystacophanos* ♀

54

55

ssp *annamensis*

ssp *oorti*

57

ssp *nuchalis*

ssp *ramsayi*

ssp *franklinii* 56

ssp *auricularis*

ssp *sini*

ssp *faber*

PLATE 12

inches   4

cm   10

48. White-cheeked Barbet

Megalaima viridis

French: Barbu vert **German**: Grünbartvogel **Spanish**: Barbudo Cariblanco
Other common names: Brown-headed Barbet(!), (Indian) Little/Small Green Barbet

Taxonomy. *Bucco viridis* Boddaert, 1783, Mahé, India.
Possibly related, though not very closely, to *M. zeylanica* and *M. lineata*, also to *M. faiostricta*, and other streaky *Megalaima*. Monotypic.
Distribution. WC & SW India, from SW Madhya Pradesh (R Narbada) S to Palni, Nilgiri Hills, Bangalore area and W Tamil Nadu.

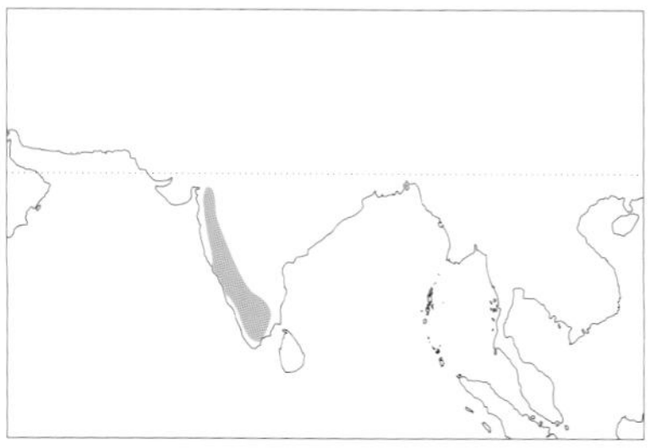

Descriptive notes. c. 23 cm; 71-90 g. Green barbet, both sexes having dark brown head with conspicuous white ear-covert patch and white line above eye; throat white, breast and neck brown with broad white streaks; facial skin dark; legs greyish. Differs from *M. zeylanica* in smaller size, and white cheek patch. Immature duller, browner or greyer, with patterns obscured. Voice. Song starts with loud trill of c. 1 second, followed by series of double "tu-kowt" notes that shorten to "t'kot", tempo varying, mainly 1-2 per second; song-like "tot-tot" singly or irregularly in alarm, aggression, also fast song notes and trills during encounters; "cheen-cheen" pre-copulatory call; begging "karr-karr-" notes, become louder as young are fed.
Habitat. Primary and secondary forest and woodland, including wet deciduous and evergreen, also parks, plantations such as coffee, and fruit trees in gardens and parks; is pest in coffee plantations and orchards. At sea-level to 1800 m, rarely 2400 m.
Food and Feeding. Banyan, pipal, other figs and fruits and berries, including those under cultivation; sips nectar; animal food, especially insects including butterflies, dragonflies, mantids, cicadas, beetles and winged termites, as well as earthworms and spiders. In one study in S India, present species preferred much larger fig species (*Ficus mysorensis*, *F. insignis*) than did *M. rubricapillus*; c. 30% of its dietary items consisted of animal food. When feeding on figs, commonly swallows the fruit whole. Takes insects and larvae in foliage and along branches and trunks; hawks for moths and winged termites; sometimes lands on ground. Sometimes gathers in parties of up to c. 20 to feed on fruits. Aggressive at fruiting trees, and in mixed feeding flocks, and also about nest.
Breeding. Dec-Jul, before heaviest monsoon rains; commonly 2 broods, second started 4-6 days after fledging of first. Nests in pairs, which persist more than 1 year. Nest excavated in c. 20 days, mainly by male, female doing some work, in dead branch, cavity entrance 5·1 cm in diameter, average depth 32·2 cm; territory is nesting tree, nests rarely 19 m apart in different trees; sometimes destroys eggs or young of *M. rubricapillus* nesting nearby. Eggs 2-4, usually 3, laid at 1-day intervals starting 3-5 days after nest completed; incubation by both parents, female incubating at night, eggs covered 75% of daytime, period 14-15 days; eggs hatch within 1 day, chicks fed by both adults, mainly insects to 5 days, switching at 5-10 days to fruits, feeding rates 9·6, 8·5 and 4·6 per hour respectively for broods of 3, 2 and 1; young brooded until day 14; nestling growth averages 2·7 g per day to 21 days, then slight loss as fed less; faecal sacs carried away 2-4 times per hour at first, later 6-7 times per hour for 3 nestlings; nestling period 36-38 days, food withheld during last 2-3 days; all young fledge on same day, are fed only 2-4 days before becoming independent, dispersing out of area in 10 days. Fledging success 75·5%; suffers predation by hawks such as Shikra (*Accipiter badius*), Brown Hawk-owl (*Ninox scutulata*) and palm squirrels (*Funambulus*).
Movements. Resident and essentially sedentary, dispersing over short distances.
Status and Conservation. Not globally threatened. Reasonably common throughout range, and adaptable. Has been reported as being a minor pest in coffee plantations, but recent work indicates the contrary, as species takes stem-boring *Xylotrechus quadripes*; also important in consuming large numbers of caterpillars of *Hyblaea puera*, a grave defoliator of teak (*Tectona grandis*). Present in several protected areas, e.g. Rajiv Gandhi (Nagarhole), Mudumalai, Periyar and Indira Gandhi National Parks (India).
Bibliography. Ali (1969, 1996), Ali & Ripley (1983), Baker (1934a, 1934b), Balachandran (1999), Berlioz (1936), Chakravarthy & Purna Chandra Tejasvi (1992), Daniels, R. J. R. (1997), Goodwin (1964), Grimmett *et al*. (1998), Jayson & Mathew (2000), Kannan (1998), Kazmierczak (2000), Mahabal & Lamba (1987), Ripley (1982), Rutgers & Norris (1977), Saha & Dasgupta (1992), Sugathan & Varghese (1996), Yahya (1980, 1987, 1988, 1991, 2000), Zacharias & Gaston (1999).

49. Green-eared Barbet

Megalaima faiostricta

French: Barbu grivelé **German**: Grünohr-Bartvogel **Spanish**: Barbudo Orejiverde
Other common names: Lineated Barbet(!)

Taxonomy. *Bucco faiostrictus* Temminck, 1831, Cochinchina.
May be related, but not very closely, to *M. zeylanica* and *M. lineata*, also to *M. viridis*, or possibly to *M. franklinii* and *M. oorti*. Species name sometimes spelt erroneously as *faiostriata*. Two subspecies recognized.
Subspecies and Distribution.
M. f. praetermissa (Kloss, 1918) - N Thailand, Laos, N Vietnam and S & SE China (S of Canton).
M. f. faiostricta (Temminck, 1831) - C & S Thailand, Cambodia and S Vietnam.
Descriptive notes. c. 24 cm. Streaky-headed, green, short-tailed barbet. Male has brownish streaks on crown and nape, green ear-coverts; malar region and throat streaked; underparts light green with often inconspicuous red or orange spot on each side of breast, variably streaked depending on plumage wear; bill mostly dark. Differs from *M. lineata* in smaller size, smaller and darker bill, green ear-coverts, all-green mantle. Female differs from male in lacking red breast spots, or sometimes in having them present but reduced to mere traces of red or orange-yellow. Immature duller, more olive. Race *praetermissa* larger, with somewhat darker head. Voice. Song a rapid series of compound "twa-ta-ta-tat" or "too-er-took" notes at c. 2·5 per second; also much slower series of single "tawt" or "toook", and a trill call.

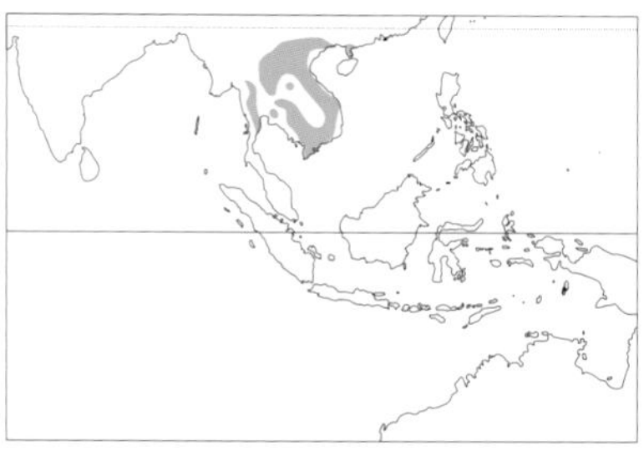

Habitat. Primary evergreen and to some extent deciduous forest, staying in canopy; most common in evergreen forest, not extending into plantations or second growth; seems not to frequent edges, or to leave forest for purpose of foraging. In lowlands to 900 m, sometimes to 1035 m.
Food and Feeding. Feeds on fruits such as figs and those of *Trema* and *Eugenia*, berries; presumably also takes some insects, but little is known.
Breeding. Feb-Jul, but timing little known. Nest excavated in dead branch or, particularly, dead standing trunk; 2 eggs reported; no information on incubation and nestling periods or on roles of parents.
Movements. Resident; sedentary in S, but in N may move more or less extensively in deciduous forest, seeking fruits.
Status and Conservation. Not globally threatened. Apparently common in Thailand and Indochina; reportedly rare in China. Seems generally difficult to locate, probably because it favours canopy of evergreen forest, where not easy to detect. Requires monitoring, and study needed of its habits, ecology and breeding biology. Present in several protected areas, including Kaeng Krachan and Khao Yai National Parks (Thailand), and Nam Bai Cat Tien National Park (Vietnam).
Bibliography. Deignan (1945, 1963), Delacour & Jabouille (1931), Duckworth (1996), Duckworth *et al*. (1999), Eames (1995), Eames & Ericson (1996), Eames *et al*. (1994), Étchécopar & Hüe (1978), Goodwin (1964), Lekagul & Round (1991), MacKinnon & Phillipps (2000), McClure (1974), Riley (1938), Robinson & Kloss (1919b), Robson (2000), Robson *et al*. (1989), Round (1988), Stepanyan (1995), Vo Quy & Nguyen Cu (1995), Xu Weishu *et al*. (1996), Zhao Zhengjie (1995).

50. Brown-throated Barbet

Megalaima corvina

French: Barbu corbin **German**: Braunkehl-Bartvogel **Spanish**: Barbudo Corvino
Other common names: Javan Barbet(!), Javan Brown-throated Barbet

Taxonomy. *Bucco corvinus* Temminck, 1831, Java.
Belongs to the group that also includes *M. chrysopogon*, *M. rafflesii*, *M. mystacophanos* and *M. javensis*. Thought by some to represent *M. chrysopogon* in Java, and this may prove to be a valid interpretation. Monotypic.
Distribution. Mountain forests of W Java.

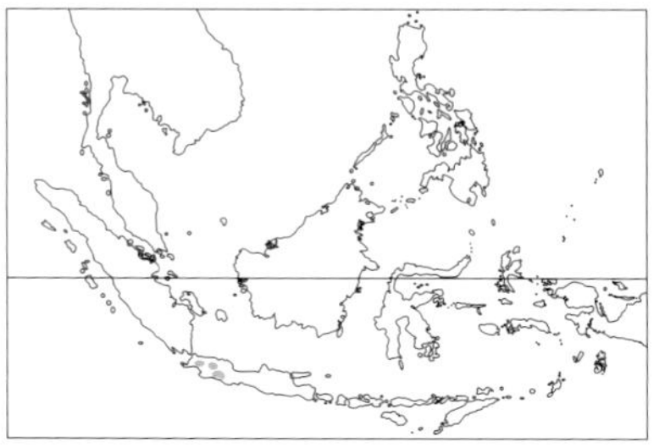

Descriptive notes. c. 27 cm; 1 male 130 g. Distinctive, large green barbet with brown head. Both sexes with unstreaked brown head, neck and upper breast, usually with yellow-gold mark on nape; green of upperparts sometimes with blue tint; bill blackish. Immature duller, bill paler. Voice. Song a series of 3- or 4-noted sounds, "too-ta-ta-toot", for c. 20 seconds, each compound note c. 0·9 seconds long; also short fast trill that may introduce song, a slow, short trill that may do likewise, and a rattly alarm note.
Habitat. Fragmented, wet mountain forest at 800-2000 m.
Food and Feeding. Diet mainly fruits, especially figs; presumably also insects at times. Feeds usually in canopy, alone or in small groups, possibly families, with other fruit-eating birds.
Breeding. Annual moult late May-Dec suggests main breeding season Jan-Jun; also Aug, and Oct reported; may be partly double-brooded. Reportedly lays 2 eggs in tree cavity, but no details, and nest and other aspects of breeding undescribed.
Movements. Presumably resident.
Status and Conservation. Not globally threatened. Restricted-range species: present in Java and Bali Forests EBA. Formerly listed as Near-threatened, but apparently quite common, at least locally, within its very small range, though no estimates available of population size or even of area of habitat remaining. Information is needed on this species' breeding biology and ecology, also on its requirements for roosting cavities, and on year-round relations of pair-members, in case action should become necessary to conserve it. Known to occur in Gunung Gede-Pangrano National Park (Java).
Bibliography. Andrew (1985, 1992), Berlioz (1936), Collar *et al*. (1994), Goodwin (1964), Hellebrekers & Hoogerwerf (1967), Hoogerwerf (1948), Kuroda (1933), MacKinnon (1988), MacKinnon & Phillipps (1993), Marshall & Marshall (1871), Nijman & Sözer (1996), Robson (1994), Sargeant (1997), Stattersfield *et al*. (1998), Sujatnika *et al*. (1995), Wells (1985).

51. Gold-whiskered Barbet

Megalaima chrysopogon

French: Barbu à joues jaunes **German**: Goldwangen-Bartvogel **Spanish**: Barbudo Carigualdo

Taxonomy. *Bucco chrysopogon* Temminck, 1824, Sumatra.
Belongs to the group that also includes *M. corvina*, *M. rafflesii*, *M. mystacophanos* and *M. javensis*. Three subspecies recognized.
Subspecies and Distribution.
M. c. laeta (Robinson & Kloss, 1918) - SW Thailand and Peninsular Malaysia; probably also extreme S Myanmar.
M. c. chrysopogon (Temminck, 1824) - Sumatra.
M. c. chrysopsis Goffin, 1863 - Borneo.
Descriptive notes. c. 30 cm; 110-215 g. Large, green barbet with heavy black bill. Male of nominate race has red forehead, yellow forecrown and red hindcrown, broad brown eyestripe, yellow malar area; greyish-white throat bordered blue at rear; orbital skin dark bluish, bill black. Female

On following pages: 52. Red-crowned Barbet (*Megalaima rafflesii*); 53. Red-throated Barbet (*Megalaima mystacophanos*); 54. Black-banded Barbet (*Megalaima javensis*); 55. Yellow-fronted Barbet (*Megalaima flavifrons*); 56. Golden-throated Barbet (*Megalaima franklinii*); 57. Black-browed Barbet (*Megalaima oorti*).

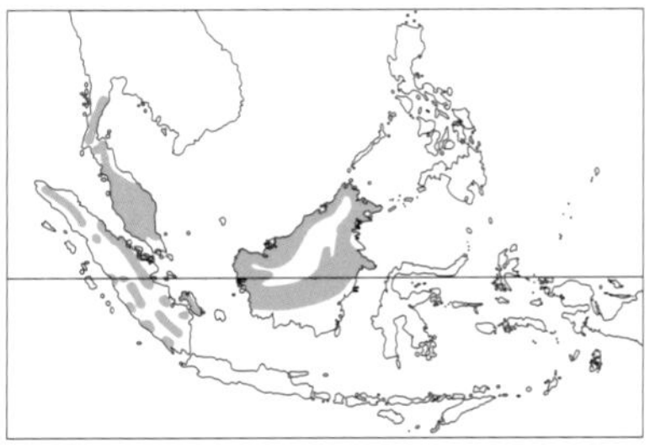

like male, sometimes with paler areas on bill. Immature duller, reds muted, bill pale horn, has cream or yellowish orbital skin. Race *laeta* has golden-yellow rather than yellow malar; *chrysopsis* resembles nominate, but has more yellow forecrown, smaller red tips on blue crown feathers, blacker band from lores to ear-coverts, occasionally red spot on each side of breast. VOICE. Song a loud, rapid, short to minutes-long series of double notes, "too-tuk", at 70-150 per minute; another song is fast, low trill of up to c. 20 seconds, but often in series that slow within and between trills; trills may lead into "too-tuk" song, notes of which closely resemble trill notes played slowly.

Habitat. Evergreen forest, swamp-forest, also tall secondary forest, and around forest clearings; also cacao plantations. Possibly some competition in lowlands with *M. rafflesii*. Occurs in lowlands, but in Borneo and Peninsular Malaysia mainly found in foothills above 250 m, especially at 750-1000 m; up to c. 1500 m.

Food and Feeding. Details little known, as this is a canopy bird. Mainly fruits such as figs and berries; probably also insects, seen pecking into dead wood. Specimens often have dirty bill, suggesting foraging or excavating cavities in arboreal carton-ant or termite nests.

Breeding. Feb-Aug, or even to Nov, possibly includes renesting. When breeding, sings through heat of day. Few records of nesting: nest excavated in dead tree or branch; eggs 2; no other information. Longevity to 9 years in captivity.

Movements. Presumably resident and sedentary.

Status and Conservation. Not globally threatened. Uncommon to common in Thailand and Peninsular Malaysia; common in Sumatra and Borneo. Knowledge of its ecology and population biology lacking, research required. If species is territorial, as is likely, its territories would probably be large, hence fragmenting of habitat could pose a risk to it. Present in several protected areas, including Khao Nor Chuchi (Thailand) and Kerinci-Seblat, Gunung Leuser and Way Kambas National Parks (Sumatra).

Bibliography. Berlioz (1936), Chasen (1934, 1939), Deignan (1963), Fogden (1970), Glenister (1971), Goodwin (1964), Holmes & Burton (1987), Jeyarajasingam & Pearson (1999), Lambert (1987, 1989a), Lekagul & Round (1991), MacKinnon & Phillipps (1993), Madoc (1976), van Marle & Voous (1988), McClure (1966), McClure & Bin Othman (1965), Medway (1972), Medway & Wells (1976), Molesworth (1955), Riley (1938), Robinson (1928), Robinson & Chasen (1939), Robson (2000), Round (1988), Smythies (1986, 1999), Thiollay (1995), Thompson (1966), Wells (1985, 1999), Wells *et al.* (1978), Wilkinson, Dutson & Sheldon (1991).

52. Red-crowned Barbet

Megalaima rafflesii

French: Barbu bigarré **German**: Vielfarben-Bartvogel **Spanish**: Barbudo Multicolor
Other common names: Many-coloured Barbet

Taxonomy. *Bucco Rafflesii* Lesson, 1839, Bangka Island, Sumatra.
Belongs to the group that also includes *M. corvina*, *M. chrysopogon*, *M. mystacophanos* and *M. javensis*; apparently related rather closely to *M. javensis* and *M. chrysopogon*. Birds from S Myanmar and Malay Peninsula described as race *malayensis*, those from Belitung I and Mendanau Is as *billitonis* and those from Borneo as *borneensis*, but no constant differences in plumage coloration or size sufficient to warrant subspecific recognition. Monotypic.

Distribution. S Myanmar (S Tenasserim) and peninsular Thailand S to Singapore, E Sumatra, Bangka and Belitung, and Borneo.

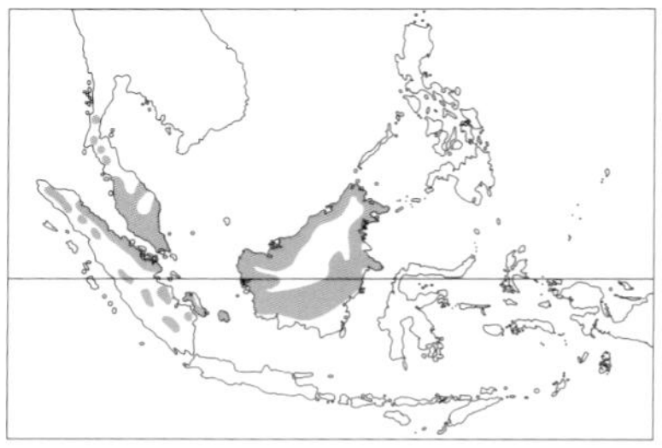

Descriptive notes. c. 26 cm; 99-150 g. Large, chunky green barbet. Both sexes have red crown, red spot below eye, red mark on side of neck, black and yellow face, as well as blue throat and broad supercilia. Distinguished from other similar barbets by combination of entirely red crown, blue line over eye and yellow face patch. Immature duller than adult, with bright colours muted, bill pale at base. VOICE. Song starts with low "took" notes at 1 per second, leading to "tuk" notes at c. 3 per second, for 5-15 seconds; some songs end in fast trill "-datttttttt"; songs repeated monotonously, 2-3 per minute.

Habitat. Inhabits primary forest, as well as old second-growth forest, *Shorea pavonina* forest, and poor-quality dipterocarp slope forest; also plantations of rubber and durian (*Durio zibethinus*). Almost strictly a lowland species, occurring only below 600 m on mainland, below 500 m in Sumatra; unusually up to 800 m but mostly below 250 m in Borneo. Possibly competes with usually more upland *M. chrysopogon*.

Food and Feeding. Little known, as forages in forest canopy. Diverse fruits, such as figs, some cultivated fruits; also insects, some dug from bark with strong bill.

Breeding. Jan-Jul; Nov-May in Sumatra. Very little known, and no data on courtship behaviour. Nest reportedly excavated at 1-5 m in tree, 1 at 4·5 m; eggs at least 2; no other information.

Movements. Resident, and sedentary so far as is known.

Status and Conservation. Not globally threatened. Currently considered Near-threatened. Known to range from scarce to locally fairly common in mainland part of range, but populations now fragmented throughout range; forest clearance has caused its disappearance from virtually all of its former haunts in Thailand, and a similar process is apparent in Malaysia; appears to be common in Sumatra and Borneo, but all primary lowland forests of the region are under imminent threat of destruction. Does show some adaptability, including occurrence as one of few barbets in urbanized Singapore. Very poorly known, however, and much research needed on its ecology and general biology, in particular to assist in assessing its conservation status. Present in several protected areas, including Khao Nor Chuchi (Thailand), Panti Forest Reserve and Bako National Park (Peninsular Malaysia), Bukit Timah Nature Reserve (Singapore) and Way Kambas National Park (Sumatra).

Bibliography. Berlioz (1936), Deignan (1963), Duckworth & Kelsh (1988), Gibson-Hill (1949a), Goodwin (1964), Holmes & Burton (1987), Jeyarajasingam & Pearson (1999), Laman *et al.* (1996), Lekagul & Round (1991), Lim Kim Seng (1992), MacKinnon & Phillipps (1993), van Marle & Voous (1988), McClure & Bin Othman (1965), Medway & Wells (1976), Mees (1986), Riley (1938), Robinson (1928), Robinson & Chasen (1939), Robson (2000), Round (1988), Smythies (1986, 1999), Stattersfield & Capper (2000), Thiollay (1995), Voous (1961), Vowles & Vowles (1997), Wells (1985, 1990, 1999), Wells *et al.* (1978), Wilkinson, Dutson & Sheldon (1991).

53. Red-throated Barbet

Megalaima mystacophanos

French: Barbu arlequin **German**: Harlekinbartvogel **Spanish**: Barbudo Arlequín
Other common names: Gaudy Barbet

Taxonomy. *Bucco mystacophanos* Temminck, 1824, Sumatra.
Belongs to the group that also includes *M. corvina*, *M. chrysopogon*, *M. rafflesii* and *M. javensis*. Forms described as *aurantiifrons* from peninsular Thailand and *humii* from Borneo now included within nominate. Two subspecies recognized.

Subspecies and Distribution.
M. m. mystacophanos (Temminck, 1824) - S Myanmar (SC Tenasserim), SW and peninsular Thailand, Peninsular Malaysia (except S), Sumatra and Borneo.
M. m. ampala (Oberholser, 1912) - Batu Is, off W Sumatra.

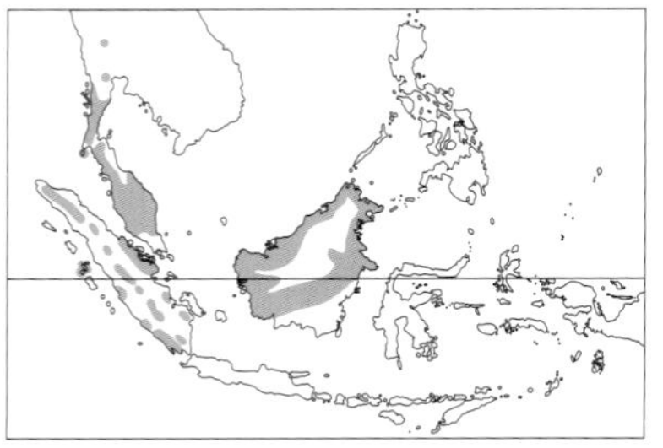

Descriptive notes. c. 23 cm; 60-95 g. Moderately large, green barbet with strongest sexual dimorphism of any Old World capitonid. Male of nominate race has yellow forehead and small yellow malar mark; red crown, loral spot, chin and throat, and mark on side of breast; blue cheek and lower throat; and black eyestripe; bill large, black. Female slightly larger than male, paler, has narrow, pale yellow forehead, pale yellow chin and throat, red loral spot, small red crown patch surrounded by blue, blue over eye and on cheek and malar, often a muted red mark at throat-breast junction, paler lower mandible. Immature pale-billed, mainly dull green and grey, bright colours muted, reds appear last; sexable c. 2 days after fledging. Race *ampala* differs from nominate in bigger bill, more square and, in female, larger red crown patch, female throat bluer. VOICE. 2 songs, both vary; one a series of single to 4 "tyuk", "tuk" or "tyowp" notes with variable pauses, some long, between sets of notes, in one case song of 4-note sets had 23 sets, 92 notes, in 36 seconds; second song fast trills in series that slow down and become shorter in each trill, may break up into notes leading to first song; males countersing using both songs; male gives low "hoot" to female in display. Sometimes uses bill-tapping signals.

Habitat. Foothill and also lowland dipterocarp forest, logged forest, second-growth forest, plantations of rubber, durian (*Durio zibethinus*) and cacao, and also visits fruiting trees in gardens and villages; mainly in canopy, descends to understorey in dense cover. Sea-level to 1060 m; mainly at low elevations, but in C Borneo commonly 750-980 m.

Food and Feeding. Mainly fruits, especially figs, also others such as durian; also insect larvae; and snails at times, e.g. in courtship feeding. Captives, when nesting, ate crickets, mealworms, maggots, waxworms and other insects. Insect larvae taken by pecking, making pits in bark; 1 individual worked 20 minutes, pecking over 4 m^2 of surface of dead stub.

Breeding. May-Jun on mainland; Nov-May and Sept in Sumatra; in Borneo reported Jun-Jul, but immatures Nov-Jun with most in Apr, so likely breeds all year. Singer flicks tail down, extends throat, keeps bill closed; in courtship feeding, male bows low to female, bill forward, calls. Nest excavated 3-6 m up in tree, or arboreal ant nest or termitarium. Eggs 2-4; in captivity, incubation period 17-18 days, nestling period 24-29 days, incubation and brood-feeding by both sexes, young independent within 1 week, then second brood started; no comparable data for wild birds. Captive female aggressive to male during nesting; in one year female killed male after eggs hatched, later killed 2 of 4 young.

Movements. Resident, and probably sedentary.

Status and Conservation. Not globally threatened. Currently considered Near-threatened. Seems to be common throughout range; no data on Batu Is race *ampala*. Appears quite adaptable. Information needed on breeding biology of wild populations. Almost all primary lowland forests within its range are under imminent threat of destruction, so its use of some forests at higher altitudes may prove decisive for its survival. Present in several protected areas, including Khao Nor Chuchi (Thailand), Batu Punggul Forest Reserve (Peninsular Malaysia) and Kerinci-Seblat National Park and Sungai Penuh Reserve (Sumatra).

Bibliography. Berlioz (1936), Chasen (1939), Deignan (1963), Duckworth & Kelsh (1988), Glenister (1971), Goodwin (1964), Holmes (1996), Holmes & Burton (1987), Jeyarajasingam & Pearson (1999), Lambert (1987, 1989a), Lekagul & Round (1991), MacKinnon & Phillipps (1993), van Marle & Voous (1988), McClure (1966), McClure & Bin Othman (1965), Medway & Wells (1976), Meyer de Schauensee (1934), Riley (1938), Ripley (1944), Robinson (1928), Robinson & Chasen (1939), Robson (2000), Roth & Michalski (1994), Round (1988), Short (1973e), Smythies (1986, 1999), Stattersfield & Capper (2000), Thiollay (1995), Thompson (1966), Wells (1985, 1990, 1999), Wells *et al.* (1978), Wilkinson, Dutson & Sheldon (1991).

54. Black-banded Barbet

Megalaima javensis

French: Barbu de Java **German**: Javabartvogel **Spanish**: Barbudo de Java
Other common names: Javan(!)/Kotorea Barbet

Taxonomy. *Bucco Javensis* Horsfield, 1821, Java.
Belongs to the group that also includes *M. corvina*, *M. chrysopogon*, *M. rafflesii* and *M. mystacophanos*; probably closest to *M. rafflesii*, having similar size and sexual monomorphism, or possibly to *M. mystacophanos*. Monotypic.

Distribution. Lowland Java and Bali.

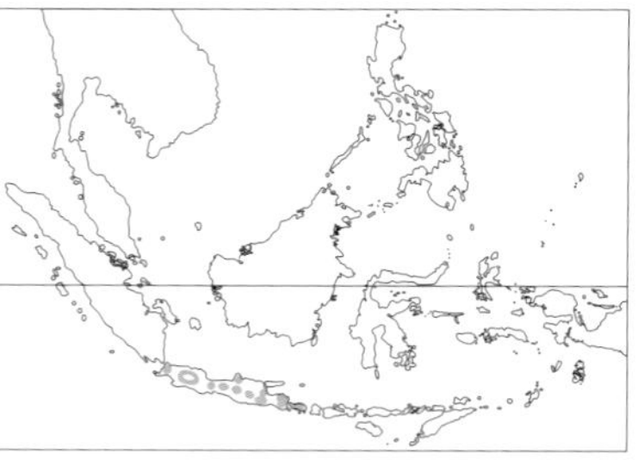

Descriptive notes. c. 26 cm; male 115 g. Large green barbet with yellow crown and black bill. Both sexes have black, blue and red head markings; black lores and eyestripe, black extending down through ear-coverts to connect with black breastband; red spot on lores, red throat, red mark on side of breast. Immature duller, bright colours muted, bill paler. VOICE. Song somewhat variable, usually accelerating series of double "too-took" notes, for 10-45 or occasionally 60 seconds, sometimes with pauses, and sometimes irregular; at times single "too" notes at 3 per second, or "tyaap" and "tap" notes that speed up; not known if both sexes sing.

Habitat. Lowland and hill forest, including teak forest, where not densely wooded, also forest patches; up to c. 1500 m.
Food and Feeding. Poorly known; fruits such as figs, and insects reported.
Breeding. Feb-Sept, and reported also in Dec, thus much of year; perhaps double-brooded. Reportedly lays 2 eggs in tree cavity, but no other details available.
Movements. Resident and sedentary.
Status and Conservation. Not globally threatened. Currently considered Near-threatened. Known to be widespread, and often common, though in a much-fragmented habitat. Lowland forests within its range have suffered intensive destruction, so occurrence of species at higher altitudes is of considerable conservation importance. Data on breeding and foraging are needed, as are population estimates and other information from Bali, where species is possibly less numerous. Sometimes trapped for cage-bird trade. Present in several protected areas, including Aas Purwo National Park (E Java).
Bibliography. Andrew (1992), van Balen (1999), Berlioz (1936), Collar & Andrew (1988), Collar *et al.* (1994), Goodwin (1964), Grantham (2000), Hellebrekers & Hoogerwerf (1967), Hoogerwerf (1948, 1969), Kuroda (1933), MacKinnon (1988), MacKinnon & Phillipps (1993), Nijman & Sözer (1996), Sargeant (1997), Stattersfield & Capper (2000), Wells (1985).

55. Yellow-fronted Barbet
Megalaima flavifrons

French: Barbu à front d'or **German**: Goldstirn-Bartvogel **Spanish**: Barbudo Frentigualdo
Other common names: Sri Lanka/Ceylon Yellow-fronted Barbet, Yellow-faced Barbet

Taxonomy. *Bucco flavifrons* Cuvier, 1816, Sri Lanka. No close relatives. Monotypic.
Distribution. Sri Lanka.

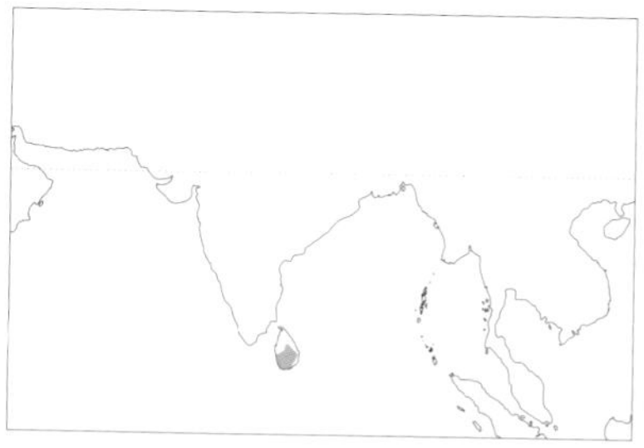

Descriptive notes. 21-22 cm; male 57-60 g. Medium-sized green barbet. Both sexes with gold forecrown and front of malar, rest of side of head blue, chin and throat blue; pale streaks on nape, pale spots on breast. Immature duller. Voice. Song somewhat variable series of double "toowo" or triple "too-ka-o" notes, often starting as fast "towowowow-", then slowing to c. 1 per second, may last 2 or more minutes; countersinging and likely simultaneous singing of pair; other calls as yet undescribed.
Habitat. Most common in SW hill forest, gardens and tree plantations; less common in wet lowland forest, and along streams in drier E; found very locally near streams in drier N. Ranges up to c. 2000 m.
Food and Feeding. Various fruits and berries, including figs, also guavas and papayas; takes some insects and small lizards.
Breeding. Probably all year, peaks Mar-May and Aug-Sept. Nest excavated in softwood tree such as *Bombax* or *Doona*, mainly at 1·8-3 m, entrance hole 5 cm, cavity excavated to c. 20 cm but if used in several years can be 60 cm or more deep. Eggs 2-3; no information on incubation and fledging periods, or on feeding rates; nestlings said to vary in size, so incubation presumably from first egg, or long intervals in laying.
Movements. Resident; probably sedentary, but in drier areas may have to leave territory to seek food.
Status and Conservation. Not globally threatened. Restricted-range species: present in Sri Lanka EBA. Generally common and adaptable. In some areas considered a pest in orchards, causing crop damage. Present in several protected areas in Sri Lanka, e.g. Bellanwila-Attidiya Sanctuary, Kelani River Forest Reserve, Ingiriya Forest Reserve and Sinharaja Forest Reserve.
Bibliography. Abdulali (1974), Ali & Ripley (1983), Baker (1934a), Berlioz (1936), Goodwin (1964), Grimmett *et al.* (1998), Harrison (1999), Henry (1998), Jones *et al.* (1998), Kazmierczak (2000), Kotagama & Fernando (1994), Lamsfuss (1998), Legge (1983), Phillips (1978), Ripley (1982), Rutgers & Norris (1977), Stattersfield *et al.* (1998), Whistler (1944), Wijesinghe (1994).

56. Golden-throated Barbet
Megalaima franklinii

French: Barbu de Franklin **German**: Goldkehl-Bartvogel **Spanish**: Barbudo de Franklin
Other common names: Gold-throated Barbet

Taxonomy. *Bucco Franklinii* Blyth, 1842, Darjeeling.
Related to *M. oorti*, being quite similar in morphology and voice; the two are possibly connected also to *M. faiostricta*. Proposed race *tonkinensis*, from N Vietnam, now considered inseparable from nominate; *trangensis* from peninsular Thailand (known from only five specimens) and *minor* from Peninsular Malaysia, both regarded as indistinguishable from *ramsayi*. Three subspecies currently recognized.
Subspecies and Distribution.
M. f. franklinii (Blyth, 1842) - WC Nepal and SE Tibet E along Himalayan slopes to N Myanmar, and S China (W & S Yunnan, SW Guangxi), S to Bangladesh (no recent records), N Thailand, N Laos and N Vietnam.
M. f. ramsayi (Walden, 1875) - C Myanmar and NW Thailand S through Malay Peninsula.
M. f. auricularis (Robinson & Kloss, 1919) - E Laos and S Vietnam.

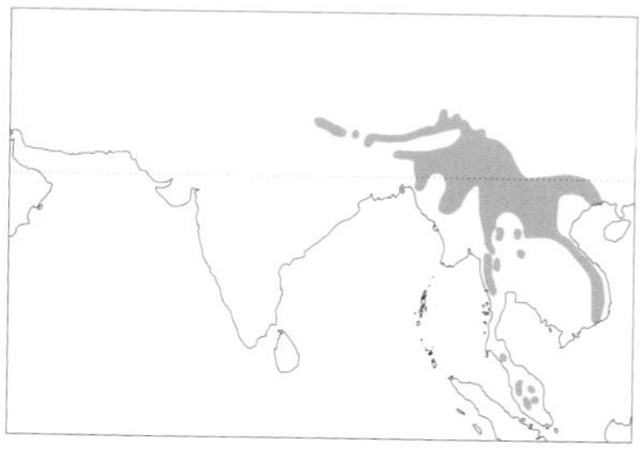

Descriptive notes. c. 22·5 cm; 50-73 g (*ramsayi*), 71-101 g (*franklinii*). Chunky green barbet often showing blue or even violet tones, especially in wings, with red on forehead and nape, golden on crown and throat. Male of nominate race has broad black eyestripe, greyish ear-coverts, deeper golden colour on upper throat, paler lower throat. Female less violet in wings. Immature duller, greener, bright colours and black muted. Race *ramsayi* has slightly narrower red forehead, duller yellow on throat, and ear-coverts and rear eyestripe streaked black and whitish; *auricularis* has red nape patch smaller, ear-coverts washed violet, entire throat deep yellow, has thin blackish line from rear of supercilia around head to form collar along junction of yellow throat and green breast. Voice. Variable song starts with trill, can continue as all-trill song, or trill followed by "tuk" notes at 1 per second or these interspersed with trills sporadically; or followed by double or triple "tu-KEE-ow", or variably "too-ka-weel", at 58-65 per minute; in latter type (Indian, Nepalese and Malaysian versions very similar), first note is soft, thus at a distance only 1or 2 elements of the compound note heard.
Habitat. Montane forest, evergreen or moist deciduous, frequently along steep ravines and broken slopes, with mosses and ferns a frequent element. Generally at 900-2200 m, rarely to 600-800 m, more often above 2200 m, and to 2700 m; usually at higher elevations than *M. oorti* and *M. asiatica*.
Food and Feeding. Mainly frugivorous, taking especially figs, various berries, such as whinberries, and guavas; arthropods occasionally noted as part of diet. Unobtrusive; feeds in middle storey and canopy, occasionally descending to understorey. Sometimes visits fruiting tree in numbers.
Breeding. Mar-Aug in most areas, Feb-May in Malaysia. Monotonous singing and countersinging, singer points bill upwards as it calls. Nest excavated by male and female at 2-6 m in rotten dead tree or stump, often leaning over stream; entrance hole less than 5 cm, short entry tunnel, then cavity downwards to c. 25 cm, nest-chamber c. 8 cm in diameter. Eggs 2-5; both parents incubate and both also feed young, but incubation and nestling periods unknown, and roles of each parent unclear; male sometimes sings near nest-hole while female incubates; no other information.
Movements. None known; some birds may move downhill from higher elevations in N of range.
Status and Conservation. Not globally threatened. Sometimes common in parts of very extensive range, but little known. Locally frequent in NW of range, and common in Bhutan; no recent records from Bangladesh, but thought that it may possibly still survive there in Chittagong Hill Tracts; common in much of SE Asia. Preference for steep, densely wooded ravines may be of benefit to its conservation. Present in several protected areas, including Doi Inthanon and Kaeng Krachan National Parks (Thailand).
Bibliography. Ali (1977), Ali & Ripley (1983), Ali *et al.* (1996), Baker (1934a), Berlioz (1936), Deignan (1945, 1963), Delacour & Jabouille (1931), Dickinson (1986), Eames (1995), Eames & Ericson (1996), Étchécopar & Hüe (1978), Glenister (1971), Grimmett *et al.* (1998, 2000), Inskipp & Inskipp (1991), Jeyarajasingam & Pearson (1999), Lekagul & Round (1991), MacKinnon & Phillipps (2000), Martens & Eck (1995), McClure (1964a, 1964b), Medway & Wells (1976), Meyer de Schauensee (1934), Morioka & Sakane (1981), Riley (1934, 1938), Ripley (1982), Robinson & Chasen (1939), Robson (2000), Robson *et al.* (1989), Round (1988), Smythies (1986), Stepanyan (1995), Vo Quy & Nguyen Cu (1995), Wells (1999), Wells *et al.* (1978), Yahya (2000), Zhao Zhengjie (1995).

57. Black-browed Barbet
Megalaima oorti

French: Barbu malais **German**: Schwarzbrauen-Bartvogel **Spanish**: Barbudo Cejinegro
Other common names: Embroidered/Malayan/Müller's Barbet; Hainan Barbet (*faber*); Taiwanese/Formosan Barbet (*nuchalis*)

Taxonomy. *Bucco Oorti* S. Müller, 1835, Sumatra.
Related to *M. franklinii*, with similar morphology and vocalizations, and both possibly connected also to *M. faiostricta*. Also probably allied to *M. asiatica* and *M. incognita* and to group that includes *M. henricii*, *M. armillaris* and *M. pulcherrima*, and has also been considered by some authors to be be close to *M. monticola*. Very well-marked races *sini* and *faber* could prove specifically distinct; *nuchalis* also sometimes thought possibly to be a distinct species, but tends to bridge differences between these two races and nominate *oorti* and *annamensis*; thus, all are considered better treated as races of present species. Five subspecies currently recognized.
Subspecies and Distribution.
M. o. nuchalis (Gould, 1863) - Taiwan.
M. o. sini (Stresemann, 1929) - S China (Guangxi).
M. o. faber (Swinhoe, 1870) - Hainan I.
M. o. annamensis (Robinson & Kloss, 1919) - S & E Laos and S Vietnam.
M. o. oorti (S. Müller, 1835) - Peninsular Malaysia and Sumatra.

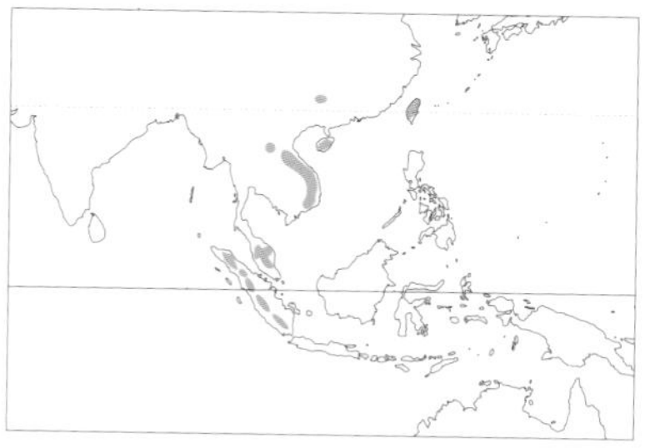

Descriptive notes. c. 21·5 cm; 62-123 g. Montane green barbet with red on forehead or lores and nape, yellow-gold throat with blue lower border, red on breast, black stripe over and behind eye and in upper malar region, blue ear-coverts. Both sexes of nominate race with only little red on nape, broadly yellow-tipped crown feathers, red on breast restricted to small lateral spot. Immature duller, with colours subdued. Races *sini* and *faber* with black crown, more red on breast, former with more red on nape sometimes extending to mantle, and some *faber* also with suggestion of red on mantle; *nuchalis* and *annamensis* intermediate between those and nominate, yellow-crowned with more red on nape than nominate, *nuchalis* with red on mantle, *annamensis* sometimes with hint of that and with broader black eyestripe and more blue on lower throat. Voice. Song a series of triple-noted phrases, "too-tuk-trrrrrk", at 65-75 phrases per minute, accent on third note, phrases sometimes with soft extra initial note or extra terminal "-ta" (vocal data reported only from Malaysia, Sumatra and Vietnam); singer turns head, giving soft-loud variation.
Habitat. Generally lower montane forest and upper dipterocarp forest in Malaysia, also pine forest and orchards and towns with fruiting trees in Sumatran highlands; subtropical and some tropical evergreen forest in China. Above 300 m in Taiwan, 600 m in Sumatra, 900 m elsewhere, to 2000 m or occasionally 2400 m; usually occurs at elevations below *M. franklinii* and above *M. henricii*.
Food and Feeding. Little known. Fruits comprise its diet, and probably takes insects when breeding, but no information available. Active in canopy and subcanopy.
Breeding. Feb-Nov in Sumatra, Mar-Jun in Malaysia, probably Feb-May in Hainan and Jun-Aug in Taiwan. Countersinging occurs in breeding period. Nest excavated at 2-10·5 m above ground in tree; 3 eggs reported in Taiwan; no further details available. A captive lived 5 years and 9 months.
Movements. Resident; upslope post-breeding movement reported in Taiwan.
Status and Conservation. Not globally threatened. Fairly common to common in most of range; common in Sumatra. Range fragmented, and clearing of forest at altitudinal levels where this species lives may place it in jeopardy; race *sini* of Yao Shan range in China may be at risk, as may be rare *faber* in Hainan, both of which occur in a limited range, and both of which could also be distinct species. Too little information available on population and breeding biology for its conservation needs to be assessed; further research required. Present in several protected areas, including Bach Ma National Park (Vietnam) and Kerinci-Seblat National Park and Sungai Penuh Reserve (Sumatra).
Bibliography. Allin & Edgar (1948), Berlioz (1936), Delacour & Jabouille (1931), Eames (1995), Eames & Ericson (1996), Ebert (1985), Étchécopar & Hüe (1978), Glenister (1971), Goodwin (1964), Hill (2001), Inskipp *et al.* (1996), Jeyarajasingam & Pearson (1999), MacKinnon & Phillipps (1993, 2000), Madoc (1976), van Marle & Voous (1988), Medway & Wells (1976), Robinson (1928), Robson (2000), Robson *et al.* (1993a), Schifter (1967), Severinghaus & Blackshaw (1976), Stepanyan (1995), Thiollay (1995), Vo Quy & Nguyen Cu (1995), Wells (1999), Xu Weishu *et al.* (1996), Zhao Zhengjie (1995).

ssp *chersonesus*

ssp *incognita*

59

ssp *elbeli*

ssp *euroa*

58

ssp *davisoni*

typical

ssp *asiatica*

"*rubescens*"
morph

60

61

62

ssp *australis*

64

ssp *orientalis*

ssp *duvaucelii*

ssp *cyanotis*

63

ssp *intermedia*

ssp *cebuensis*

65

66

ssp *haemacephala*

67

ssp *rubricapillus*

ssp *rosea*

ssp *malabarica*

ssp *indica*

PLATE 13

inches   3

cm   8

58. Blue-throated Barbet

Megalaima asiatica

French: Barbu à gorge bleue   **German**: Blauwangen-Bartvogel   **Spanish**: Barbudo Gorgiazul
Other common names: Blue-breasted/Blue-cheeked Barbet

Taxonomy. *Trogon asiaticus* Latham, 1790, Calcutta.
Closely related to *M. incognita*, and a mixed pair reported in the wild, while race *chersonesus* somewhat intermediate between the two species; also related to *M. franklinii* and *M. oorti*. Has in past been thought to form a superspecies with *M. monticola*, and was sometimes even considered conspecific, but morphological differences seem sufficient to warrant separate species status. Form described as race "*rubescens*" from S Assam and NW Myanmar is a morph of nominate *asiatica*; *laurentii*, described from Yunnan, is a synonym of *davisoni*. Three subspecies currently recognized.
Subspecies and Distribution.
M. a. asiatica (Latham, 1790) - NE Pakistan E along Himalayas to N Myanmar and S China (W Yunnan), S to Bangladesh and C Myanmar.
M. a. davisoni Hume, 1877 - SE Myanmar E to S Yunnan and N & C Vietnam.
M. a. chersonesus (Kloss & Chasen, 1927) - E peninsular Thailand.

Descriptive notes. 22-23 cm; 61-103 g. Medium-sized, short-tailed green barbet with blue throat and face. Both sexes of nominate race with black-edged red cap and forehead broken by yellowish and black or blue bands across mid-crown; eye conspicuous amid surrounding blue; sometimes has tiny black and red submoustachial spot at base of mandible; red mark on each side of upper breast. Erythristic morph ("*rubescens*") more or less red over back and even on underparts. Differs from *M. incognita* in crown pattern, and in all-blue face and throat without black bar. Immature duller, head pattern subdued. Race *davisoni* paler blue on head, female lacks red lateral breast spot; *chersonesus* has still paler blue on head, at least on throat, chin even showing yellowish, crown mostly blue with small red nape patch. VOICE. Song of 3-note phrases, "tu-ku-tuk", in variably long series, often ending in short trill; also version with 4-note phrase, "ta-tu-ku-tuk", at 90-105 phrases per minute; song much softer, less noisy, than those of *M. zeylanica* and *M. lineata*, and with 1-2 more notes per phrase; other calls not fully described.
Habitat. Primary and secondary evergreen and deciduous mountain forest, also clearings, edges, orchards, plantations, and gardens, and entering towns and cities where fruiting trees present. Near sea-level in NE India and Bangladesh; more usually 200-2000 m, rarely up to 2450 m. Normally at higher elevations than *M. incognita* where the two co-occur.
Food and Feeding. Eats figs and other fruits, and berries, also flowers of pistachio (*Pistacia integgerima*) and probably others; also many insect larvae, mantises, crickets and centipedes. Captives eat fruits, even entire dates, and vigorously pursue and eat various insects. Bashes larger animal prey against limbs before consuming them. Forages in canopy, but comes to understorey for fruits. Seems less shy than most congeners.
Breeding. Mar-Jul; also later in S and at low altitudes, where double-brooded. Countersinging and simultaneous singing of paired birds; bobbing and head-turning and tail-twitching in display, much courtship feeding. Nest excavated by both adults, at 1·5-8 m, sometimes higher, in dead tree or branch, often on underside, sometimes in tree over water; entrance large, even to 7 cm, with short tunnel inwards, then downwards to 10-30 cm or more; may use same nest for 2 years, or enlarge old woodpecker hole. Eggs 2-5, mainly 3-4; both adults incubate, eggs attended by 1 parent at all times, period c. 14 days; both parents feed young, carry away faecal sacs; nestling period not known; fledglings reported to reach independence rapidly. A captive lived for 10 years and 10 months.
Movements. Resident, and largely or entirely sedentary; possible downslope movements from highest altitudes in range.
Status and Conservation. Not globally threatened. Common almost everywhere in range; common but local in Pakistan, where possibly expanding range; common in Nepal, where densities of 2·5 singing males/km reported; common in India and Bhutan, and locally common in Bangladesh; generally common in SE Asia. Isolated race *chersonesus* sometimes considered under threat, but apparently not uncommon within very small range. An adaptable species. Present in numerous national parks, e.g. Corbett and Kaziranga (India), Chitwan (Nepal) and Nam Nao and Kaeng Krachan (Thailand).
Bibliography. Abdulali (1974), Ali (1977, 1996), Ali & Ripley (1983), Ali *et al.* (1996), Baker (1934a), Berlioz (1936), Biswas (1947), Cheng Tsohsin (1964), Deignan (1945, 1963), Delacour & Jabouille (1931), Eames & Ericson (1996), Étchécopar & Hüe (1978), Fox (1933), Goodwin (1964), Grimmett *et al.* (1998, 2000), Inskipp, C. & Inskipp (1991), Inskipp, T. *et al.* (1996), Lekagul & Round (1991), MacKinnon & Phillipps (2000), Mierow & Shrestha (1978), Norris (1950), Rand & Fleming (1957), Riley (1938), Ripley (1982), Roberts (1991), Robinson (1928), Robson (2000), Round (1988), Rutgers & Norris (1977), Schifter (1967), Shrestha (2000), Smythies (1986), Stepanyan (1995), Vo Quy & Nguyen Cu (1995), Wells (1999), Whistler (1941), Xu Weishu *et al.* (1996), Yahya (1980, 2000), Zhao Zhengjie (1995).

59. Moustached Barbet

Megalaima incognita

French: Barbu de Hume   **German**: Grünscheitel-Bartvogel   **Spanish**: Barbudo Bigotudo
Other common names: Hume's Blue-throated Barbet

Taxonomy. *Megalaima incognita* Hume, 1874, Tenasserim.
Closely related to *M. asiatica*, with mixed pairing reported in the wild; race *chersonesus* of latter somewhat intermediate between the two species. Three subspecies recognized.
Subspecies and Distribution.
M. i. incognita Hume, 1874 - S Myanmar (Tenasserim) and W Thailand.
M. i. elbeli Deignan, 1956 - NE & E Thailand, N Laos and N Vietnam.
M. i. euroa (Deignan, 1939) - SE Thailand, Cambodia, S Laos and S Vietnam.

ish-blue than in *euroa*. VOICE. Several songs or variants, main one starts with single "tuk" that shifts into double "tuk-uk" or triple "tuk-a-tuk" notes, another with triple-noted sets each ending in trill, "tuk-tuk-trrrrr"; generally short, c. 1 phrase per second for 10-12 seconds, but countersinging results in longer, more rapidly uttered songs; song notes sometimes used as single-phrase call; also long, variable trills, up to 25 seconds or more, may mark interactions.
Habitat. Evergreen monsoon forest and edges, generally at 400-1400 m, less commonly to c. 2000 m; where occurring with *M. asiatica*, is usually found at lower altitudes. Seems not to leave forest cover.
Food and Feeding. Fruits of various figs and of other trees, such as *Macaranga* and *Trema*; when breeding also insects, including cerambycid beetles and stick-insects. Insects hammered to break them into pieces, before being fed to young.
Breeding. Few data. Season Dec-Jun. Sings for 9 months of year. Cavity excavated in dead tree or branch, at 10-15 m; once in "piccolo" tree that also contained nest of *M. faiostricta*. Eggs and incubation and nestling periods undescribed; young reportedly fed mostly fruits, some insects.
Movements. Resident, and sedentary so far as is known.
Status and Conservation. Not globally threatened. Apparently fairly common to common in much of range. Little known. Strictly a forest species, living at altitudes where much clearance occurs; data therefore needed in order to monitor this barbet, and to assess its conservation status and requirements. Present in several national parks, e.g. Kaeng Krachan, Khao Yai and Nam Nao (Thailand).
Bibliography. Baker (1934a, 1934b), Berlioz (1936), Chazee (1994), Deignan (1956, 1963), Delacour & Jabouille (1931), Duckworth (1996), Duckworth *et al.* (1999), Eames & Ericson (1996), Goodwin (1964), Lekagul & Round (1991), McClure (1974), Meyer de Schauensee (1934), Riley (1938), Robson (2000), Round (1988), Smythies (1986), Stepanyan (1995), Vo Quy & Nguyen Cu (1995).

60. Mountain Barbet

Megalaima monticola

French: Barbu montagnard   **German**: Borneobartvogel   **Spanish**: Barbudo Montano

Taxonomy. *Cyanops monticola* Sharpe, 1889, Mount Kinabalu, Borneo.
Relationships unclear. Has been considered to form a superspecies with *M. asiatica*, and sometimes even thought conspecific, but differences in morphology indicate separate species status. Has also been allied by some authors to *M. oorti*. Monotypic.
Distribution. Mountains of N Borneo, from Mt Kinabalu S to Kapuas and Kayan Mts

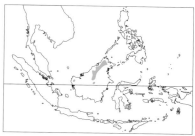

Descriptive notes. 20-22 cm; male 65-110 g, female 83-112 g. Rather small, chunky, green barbet with yellowish throat. Male has forecrown bluish-yellow, hindcrown and nape red with partial blue border, head pattern somewhat obscured by fine streaking; throat with yellowish-buff wash, more or less spotted grey and often with some blue visible at rear, red mark on each side of upper breast. Female like male, but larger. Immature duller, with orange-red hindcrown-nape patch. VOICE. Song repeated phrases of fast notes, "tu-tu-tu-tu-tuk" to faster "tu-t-t-t-tuk", variable number of notes in phrase, up to 6 phrases per second, with irregular, brief pauses; song can last for several minutes.
Habitat. Lower montane and slope dipterocarp forest, also edges, and garden and orchard fruit trees near and even in villages. Usually at 600-1200 m, uncommonly 300-1670 m; occurs at roughly same elevations as *M. eximia*; replaced by *M. henricii* at c. 600 m and lower, and by *M. pulcherrima* at c. 1320 m, with little or no overlap with them.
Food and Feeding. Diverse fruits, including "lunuk" berries and figs; probably some insects. Forages at all levels, climbing and searching on bark of trunks and stems of bushes. Joins mixed-species foraging flocks of babblers (*Stachyris*, *Yuhina*).
Breeding. Very poorly known. Data from specimens indicate season Nov-Jun. No information available on nest, eggs, incubation, nestling life, and parental roles.
Movements. Resident and probably sedentary.
Status and Conservation. Not globally threatened. Restricted-range species: present in Bornean Mountains EBA. Appears to be quite common and somewhat adaptable, but no details on numbers. Little-known species, and nothing known of its breeding biology; much research required. Known to occur in Mount Kinabalu and Gunung Mulu National Parks (Borneo).
Bibliography. Andrew (1992), Berlioz (1936), Davison (1992, 1997), Goodwin (1964), Greenway (1978), Holmes (1997), Inskipp *et al.* (1996), Jenkins & de Silva (1978), MacKinnon & Phillipps (1993), Prieme & Heegaard (1988), Robson (1998), Smythies (1999), Stattersfield *et al.* (1998), Sujatnika *et al.* (1995), Wells (1985), Wells *et al.* (1978), Wilkinson, Dutson & Sheldon (1991), Wilkinson, Dutson, Sheldon, Noor & Noor (1991).

61. Yellow-crowned Barbet

Megalaima henricii

French: Barbu à sourcils jaunes   **Spanish**: Barbudo Coronigualdo
German: Gelbscheitel-Bartvogel

On following pages: 62. Flame-fronted Barbet (*Megalaima armillaris*); 63. Golden-naped Barbet (*Megalaima pulcherrima*); 64. Blue-eared Barbet (*Megalaima australis*); 65. Bornean Barbet (*Megalaima eximia*); 66. Crimson-throated Barbet (*Megalaima rubricapillus*); 67. Coppersmith Barbet (*Megalaima haemacephala*).

Taxonomy. *Bucco henricii* Temminck, 1831, Sumatra.
Closely related to *M. armillaris* and *M. pulcherrima*, with which has sometimes been considered conspecific or to form a superspecies; all three likely also to be related to group including *M. oorti*, *M. asiatica* and *M. incognita*. Races rather poorly differentiated. Two subspecies recognized.
Subspecies and Distribution.
M. h. henricii (Temminck, 1831) - S peninsular Thailand S to Sumatra.
M. h. brachyrhyncha (Neumann, 1908) - Borneo.

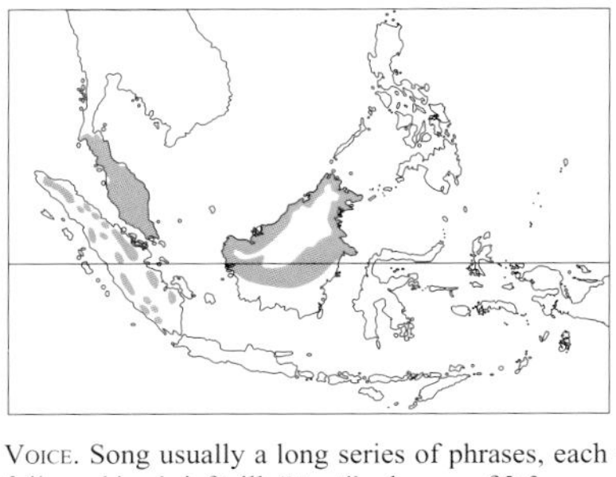

Descriptive notes. 21·5-22·5 cm; 65-83 g. Green, sturdy-billed barbet with blue throat and much yellow on crown. Both sexes of nominate race with central hindcrown blue, golden-yellow from forehead extending broadly around crown over eyes; black lores and line through eye, pale green cheeks and line over eye; narrow red band on upper neck side, red mark on each side of breast at border of throat. Immature duller, bright colours paler, only forehead yellow, and base of bill pale, greyish. Race *brachyrhyncha* smaller-billed, less bright, with blue areas more violet-blue, green of ear-coverts yellower, yellow top of head less golden. Voice. Song usually a long series of phrases, each with 2-7 "tuk" notes preceded by, or sometimes followed by, brief trill, "ttrrrt"; phrases of 2-3 seconds, may sometimes lack trill note.
Habitat. Mainly lowland dipterocarp forest, also mixed and dipterocarp hill forest; secondary as well as primary forest; low swampy forest, cacao plantations, partly logged forest. Younger males may utilize suboptimal habitats. Below 750 m, rarely to 950 m; mainly over 200 m in Sumatra; in Borneo replaced by *M. monticola* above c. 600 m, with little or no overlap; usually found below *M. oorti*.
Food and Feeding. Eats fruits, mainly figs (*Ficus*); other foods not known. An individual monitored for 4 days ranged over 7·5 ha and spent 75% of time near or at fruiting *Ficus binnendykii* tree; movements primarily from that tree to canopy of a 40-m tree in which it roosted. No other information on feeding habits.
Breeding. Data from specimens indicate season Feb-Aug. Seen at roosting or nesting holes in canopy of trees; reported to excavate nest 9 m above ground in tree. No other information.
Movements. Resident, thought to be sedentary.
Status and Conservation. Not globally threatened. Currently considered Near-threatened. Uncommon in Thailand, fairly common in Peninsular Malaysia; seemingly more common in Sumatra and Borneo, but even so not numerous there. Widespread destruction of lowland forests is prevalent throughout its range, so occurrence at higher altitudes may prove important for survival of this species; concomitant loss of fig trees is almost certainly reducing numbers. Present in several protected areas, e.g. Khao Nor Chuchi (Thailand) and Gunung Mulu National Park (Peninsular Malaysia). Information on its biology is urgently needed.
Bibliography. Berlioz (1936), Bromley (1952), Chasen (1939), Deignan (1963), Glenister (1971), Goodwin (1964), Greenway (1978), Holmes & Burton (1987), Jeyarajasingam & Pearson (1999), Lambert (1989a, 1989b), Lekagul & Round (1991), MacKinnon & Phillipps (1993), van Marle & Voous (1988), McClure (1966), Medway (1972), Medway & Wells (1976), Riley (1938), Robinson (1928), Robinson & Chasen (1939), Robson (2000), Round (1988), Smythies (1999), Stattersfield & Capper (2000), Thiollay (1995), Thompson (1966), Wells (1985, 1999), Wells *et al*. (1978), Wilkinson, Dutson & Sheldon (1991).

62. Flame-fronted Barbet

Megalaima armillaris

French: Barbu souci-col **German**: Temminckbartvogel **Spanish**: Barbudo Coroniazul
Other common names: Orange-fronted(!)/Blue-crowned Barbet

Taxonomy. *Bucco armillaris* Temminck, 1821, Java.
Closely related to *M. henricii* and *M. pulcherrima*, with all three sometimes thought to be conspecific or to form a superspecies; all are apparently related also to group including *M. oorti*, *M. asiatica* and *M. incognita*. Races not well differentiated; E Javan birds intermediate in size between those of W Java and those of Bali. Two subspecies recognized.
Subspecies and Distribution.
M. a. armillaris (Temminck, 1821) - Java.
M. a. baliensis (Rensch, 1928) - Bali.

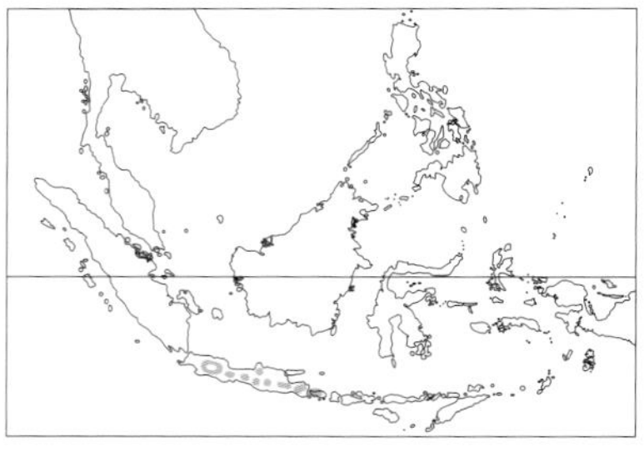

Descriptive notes. 20-21·5 cm; 63-74 g. Smallish, heavily set green barbet with stout bill, and extensive yellow to orange forehead. Both sexes of nominate race have yellowish-orange from forehead and forecrown, blue mid-crown to nape, black line through eye, black at front of malar; gold to orange mark on each side of lower neck, and golden-orange across upper breast. Immature duller, areas of yellow-orange and blue paler, smaller. Race *baliensis* slightly larger, with forehead slightly more red-orange or brown-orange, and a similar tendency on sides of neck and breast. Voice. Song a series of short trills, "t-t-t-rrrt", repeated endlessly; also single buzzy "tirrr" note.
Habitat. Primary lowland and hill forest, edges, fruiting trees in nearby gardens and plantations; found at all levels up to c. 2500 m, commonest above 600 m.
Food and Feeding. Fruits, including coffee fruits, also some insects; spiders also recorded. In captivity, nestlings eat mealworms, crickets and young mice.
Breeding. Feb-Jul, also Sept-Jan; possibly double-brooded. Courtship feeding occurs. Nest excavated high in tree; in captivity, both adults excavate cavity to 35 cm deep, completed in 1 month. Eggs 2; in captivity, incubation by both parents, period 13-15 days, female aggressive to male after hatching, young fed by both parents, 1 tapping on outside results in other leaving; hand-reared young open eyes at c. 14 days, feathers emerge at 17 days, first flight at c. 37 days. Captive pair produced 3 clutches each of 2 eggs, hand-rearing resulting in 3 healthy immatures.
Movements. Resident and sedentary.
Status and Conservation. Not globally threatened. Restricted-range species: present in Java and Bali Forests EBA. Generally not uncommon, and is the commonest barbet in Java and Bali. Appears somewhat adaptable. Information required on species' ecology and biology in the wild. Present in Gunung Gede-Pangrano National Park and, apparently rare, in Aas Purwo National Park (Java).
Bibliography. Andrew (1985, 1992), Berlioz (1936), Goodwin (1964), Grantham (2000), Hellebrekers & Hoogerwerf (1967), Hoogerwerf (1969), Kuroda (1933), MacKinnon (1988), MacKinnon & Phillipps (1993), Marshall & Marshall (1871), Mason & Jarvis (1989), Mees (1996), Nijman & Sözer (1996), Parr (1996), Sargeant (1997), Stattersfield *et al*. (1998), Sujatnika *et al*. (1995), Wells (1985).

63. Golden-naped Barbet

Megalaima pulcherrima

French: Barbu élégant **German**: Prachtbartvogel **Spanish**: Barbudo Elegante
Other common names: Golden-rumped/Kinabalu Barbet

Taxonomy. *Megalæma pulcherrima* Sharpe, 1888, Mount Kinabalu, Borneo.
Closely related to *M. henricii* and *M. armillaris*, and all three have been considered conspecific or to form a superspecies; all appear also to be related to group that includes *M. oorti*, *M. asiatica* and *M. incognita*. Monotypic.
Distribution. N Borneo mountains, from Kinabalu and Trus Madi S to Mulu and Murud.

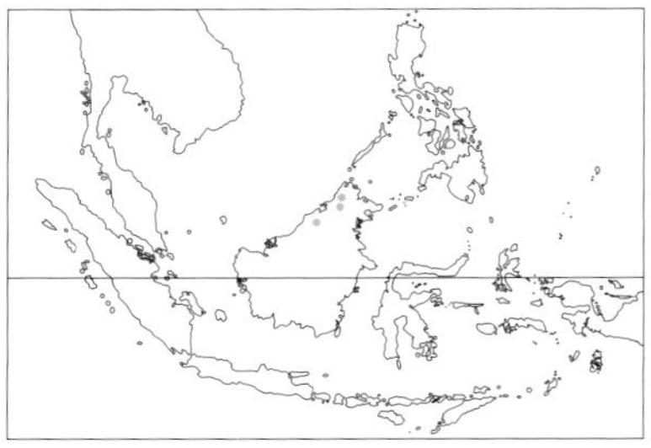

Descriptive notes. 20-21·5 cm; 55-76 g. Distinctive, strong-billed, smallish green barbet of mountains. Male with blue from forehead to hindneck, blue throat, gold patch on upper mantle at edge of hindneck; black lores to just behind eye, edged blue; face green, but green-gold over eye. Female perhaps paler gold and blue. Immature duller generally, lacking any gold. Voice. Song of 3-note phrases, "chut-chut-chtttt", variably long, at 18-25 phrases per minute, ending in 2-note phrases, "chutt-chut" or "chew-chew"; another a series of short trills, "trrrrt", or trill-note phrases, "trrr-trrr-trrrrrrr", each with 1-3 short trill notes followed by longer one; also a "twaak" call in short series.
Habitat. Montane primary and secondary forest, moss-clad forest, edges and adjacent partly cut-over areas. At 1000-3100 m; usually above 1500 m, and thus at higher levels than *M. eximia* and *M. monticola*, on Mt Mulu above latter at 1320-1650 m.
Food and Feeding. Little known. Meagre data from stomach contents indicate fruits and berries, and a "green shoot". Forages in mid-storey and canopy.
Breeding. Data from specimens indicate season Dec-Mar. No other data available.
Movements. None known; presumably resident.
Status and Conservation. Not globally threatened. Restricted-range species: present in Bornean Mountains EBA. No information on relative abundance, but appears to be rather local. Its upland forest habitat is less threatened than forest at lower elevations. Known to occur in Mount Kinabalu and Gunung Mulu National Parks (Borneo). Although species is in no immediate danger, it is very poorly known; in view of its restricted highland range, data on its ecology and biology are needed in case future action is required for its conservation.
Bibliography. Anderson *et al*. (1982), Anon. (2000), van Balen (1997), Berlioz (1936), Davison (1992), Goodwin (1964), Holmes (1997), Jenkins & de Silva (1978), MacKinnon & Phillipps (1993), Robson (1996b), Smythies (1999), Stattersfield *et al*. (1998), Strange (2000), Wells (1985), Wells *et al*. (1978).

64. Blue-eared Barbet

Megalaima australis

French: Barbu à calotte bleue **German**: Blauohr-Bartvogel **Spanish**: Barbudo Variable
Other common names: Crimson-browed/Little Barbet; Large-billed Barbet ("*robustirostris*")

Taxonomy. *Bucco australis* Horsfield, 1821, Java.
Closely related to *M. eximia*, these together comprising the so-called "*Mesobucco* group". Races and "population groups" connected by intermediates; some authors suggest race *orientalis* possibly better lumped within *cyanotis*. Birds from S Myanmar and SW and peninsular Thailand often treated as race *stuarti*, but apparently no more than intermediate form between *cyanotis* and *duvaucelii*. Other described forms include *hebereri* from Bali, considered synonymous with nominate; *borneonensis* from Borneo and *robinsoni* from S Peninsular Malaysia, synonymized with *duvaucelii*; and *invisa* from NW Thailand, synonymized with *cyanotis*. Form described from Assam as "*robustirostris*" long considered a separate species, but apparently matched by specimen from Laos, and these probably represent immature birds of present species. Six subspecies currently recognized.
Subspecies and Distribution.
M. a. cyanotis (Blyth, 1847) - SE Nepal E to E Bangladesh and NE India, S China (Yunnan), Myanmar (except N & E) and NW Thailand S to N Malay Peninsula.
M. a. orientalis (Robinson, 1915) - E Thailand, Cambodia, Laos and Vietnam.
M. a. duvaucelii (Lesson, 1830) - Peninsular Malaysia, Sumatra, Bangka and Borneo.
M. a. gigantorhina (Oberholser, 1912) - Nias I, off W Sumatra.
M. a. tanamassae (Meyer de Schauensee, 1929) - Batu Is, off W Sumatra.
M. a. australis (Horsfield, 1821) - Java and Bali.

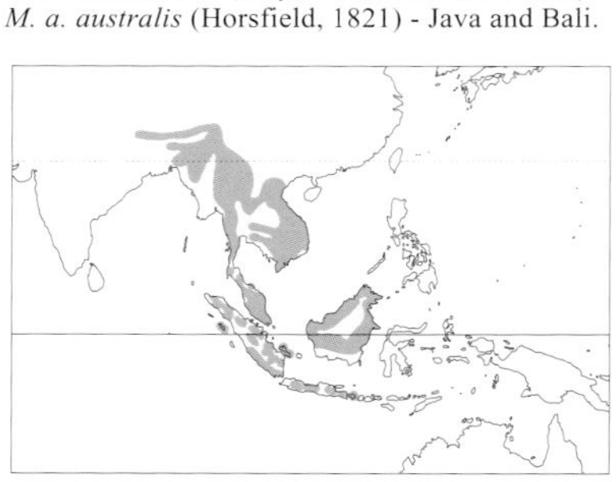

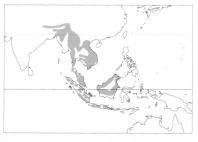

Descriptive notes. 16-17 cm; 26-39 g. Small, green, stout-billed barbet with blue crown and throat, black band between throat and breast. Both sexes of nominate race with blue forehead and crown, yellow ear-coverts and cheeks framed by black eyestripe and moustachial line, black lores; blue throat with black band below, and yellow-gold across breast. Immature duller, head mainly green, lacking pattern and bright colours, bill and orbital skin paler. Races differ mainly in detail and colours of head and breast patterns, variation complex, all lacking yellow on ear-coverts: *cyanotis* with black forehead, blue mid-crown and green hindcrown, orange-red cheek patch, blue ear-coverts with red above and below, blue throat with narrow black border, no yellow-gold on breast; *orientalis* similar, but slightly larger and paler overall, commonly with narrow red patch across upper breast; *duvaucelii* with black forehead, black ear-coverts with larger red patches above and below, red cheek patch, pale loral spot, much broader black band on upper breast, some with some red below the black. Voice. Several, variable "songs", e.g. a series of double "ta-trrrt" to "tu-tuuk" notes at 96-132 per minute, at times for minutes on end, sometimes ending in pigeon-like "ooooooo", or with single notes interspersed, or as full, single-noted song at 180 notes per minute; also so-called "police-whistle" song, a trilling but burred "ttirrr,ttirrr,-"; grating notes in encounters, irregular series of "teeow" notes, chittering or chattery notes resembling begging calls, and fast trills and series of piping notes.

Habitat. Primary forest and edges in lowlands and foothills; mainly evergreen forest, but may move into regrowing and patchy forest, and visit plantations, gardens, bamboo and deciduous forest. Generally below 1200 m, and below 1000 m in Borneo, Bali and Peninsular Malaysia, but to 1500-1600 m in parts of SE Asia and Sumatra, and to 2000 m in Java.

Food and Feeding. Fruits, including figs and others, also reportedly insects. Feeding behaviour not reported. Gathers in numbers of up to c. 100 at fruiting trees in Thailand.

Breeding. Feb-Jun in much of range; from Jan in Vietnam, Mar-Sept in Thailand, Jan-Jul in Peninsular Malaysia, and Feb-Oct in Sumatra and its islands, Java and Borneo. Sings incessantly, pair-members simultaneously; head-bobbing, side-to-side tail movement in aggressive or courtship displays; courtship-feeds fruits repeatedly before copulation. Nest excavated in dead trunk or branch, often on underside of branch, at up to 25 m, mostly at 3-12 m; may excavate in old woodpecker hole; once beneath arboreal carton-ant nest; 1 nest had entrance hole 3 cm wide, vertical tunnel 20·5 cm deep. Eggs 2-4; incubation and nestling periods, and roles of parents, undocumented.

Movements. Resident; generally territorial and sedentary, but some post-breeding movements occur to fruiting sources, including into habitats not used for breeding.

Status and Conservation. Not globally threatened. Often one of the commonest of barbets; common in SE Asia, and common in Greater Sundas; scarce and very local in Nepal, and uncommon in India; fairly common locally in Bhutan, and local in Bangladesh. Appears to be adaptable. Present in numerous protected areas, e.g. Kaziranga National Park (India), Kaeng Krachan and Khao Yai National Parks (Thailand), Nam Bai Cat Tien National Park (Vietnam) and Way Kambas National Park (Sumatra).

Bibliography. Ali (1977), Ali & Ripley (1983), Ali *et al.* (1996), Baker (1934a), Deignan (1941, 1945, 1963), Delacour & Jabouille (1931), Eames & Ericson (1996), Eames *et al.* (1994), Fleming & Traylor (1968), Glenister (1971), Grimmett *et al.* (1998), Hellebrekers & Hoogerwerf (1967), Inskipp, C. & Inskipp (1991), Inskipp, T. *et al.* (1996), Jeyarajasingam & Pearson (1999), Laman *et al.* (1996), Lambert (1989a), Lekagul & Round (1991), MacKinnon & Phillipps (1993, 2000), Madoc (1976), van Marle & Voous (1988), McClure (1966, 1974), McClure & Bin Othman (1965), Medway & Wells (1976), Mees (1996), Riley (1938), Ripley (1944, 1953, 1982), Robinson (1927, 1928), Robinson & Chasen (1939), Robson (2000), Robson *et al.* (1989), Round (1988), Smythies (1986, 1999), Stepanyan (1995), Thiollay (1995), Thompson (1966), Vo Quy & Nguyen Cu (1995), Wells (1999), Wells *et al.* (1978), Wilkinson, Dutson & Sheldon (1991), Zhao Zhengjie (1995).

65. Bornean Barbet
Megalaima eximia

French: Barbu à gorge noire **German**: Schwarzkehl-Bartvogel **Spanish**: Barbudo Eximio
Other common names: Black-chinned/Black-throated(!)/Crimson-crowned Barbet

Taxonomy. *Mesobucco eximius* Sharpe, 1892, Mount Dulit, Borneo.
Closely related to *M. australis*, the two comprising the so-called "*Mesobucco* group". Racial separation of Mt Kinabalu population uncertain, based principally on blue throat colour, but this may be indicative of subadult, and more or less matched by probable subadult specimens from elsewhere in species' range, where also some with mostly blue or mixed throat colour; also, individuals have been seen on Mt Kinabalu with black throat, as adults in rest of range; further research required. Two subspecies tentatively recognized.

Subspecies and Distribution.
M. e. cyanea (Harrisson & Hartley, 1934) - Mt Kinabalu.
M. e. eximia (Sharpe, 1892) - mountains of N, NW & C Borneo, from Trus Madi and Brassey Range SW to Poi, Penrissen and Niut, and S to Barito Ulu.

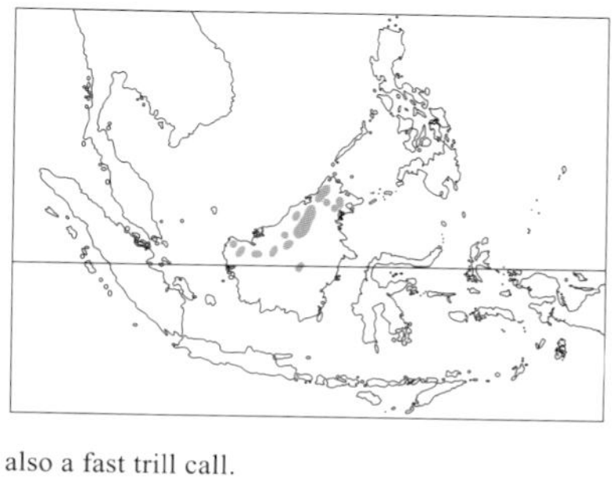

Descriptive notes. 15-16 cm. Small, strong-billed, green barbet with complex head pattern. Male nominate race with black forehead to forecrown, red hindcrown, blue line from lores over eye; yellow patch under eye; blue ear-coverts often finely margined black; red at rear of malar; black throat, red on chest. Female duller, may have blue in forehead. Immature duller, reds muted or absent, throat blue and black with some white. Race *cyanea* supposedly differs from nominate in having blue throat, blue in black of forehead and forecrown, reduced red. VOICE. Song rapid series of single "tiuk" notes at 3-6 per second, for up to 40 seconds or more; also a fast trill call.

Habitat. Wet mountain forest, keeping mostly to canopy. Most specimens from altitudes of 900-1387 m, but occurs down to 370 m in places; generally below *M. pulcherrima*, approximately at elevations of much larger *M. monticola*.

Food and Feeding. Data very meagre; figs and other fruits known to be included in diet. Generally feeds in canopy.

Breeding. Possibly May-Oct or later. Singer puffs out throat and turns head side to side. Nest and eggs undescribed, and no information on other aspects of breeding.

Movements. Resident, presumably sedentary.

Status and Conservation. Not globally threatened. Restricted-range species: present in Bornean Mountains EBA. Uncommon, and very poorly known, but occurs in more montane parts of Borneo than does either of that island's 2 other endemic montane capitonids, *M. monticola* and *M. pulcherrima*, e.g. Mount Kinabalu and Gunung Mulu National Parks. Requires further research and, in view of the little that is known about it, should probably be monitored.

Bibliography. Anderson *et al.* (1982), Andrew (1992), Berlioz (1936), Davison (1992), Gore (1968), Harrisson & Hartley (1934), Holmes (1997), Jenkins & de Silva (1978), MacKinnon & Phillipps (1993), Prieme & Heegaard (1988), Smythies (1999), Stattersfield *et al.* (1998), Sujatnika *et al.* (1995), Wells (1985), Wilkinson, Dutson & Sheldon (1991), Wilkinson, Dutson, Sheldon, Noor & Noor (1991).

66. Crimson-throated Barbet
Megalaima rubricapillus

French: Barbu à couronne rouge **German**: Malabarschmied **Spanish**: Barbudo Capirrojo
Other common names: Small Barbet; Ceylon Small/Sri Lanka Small/Crimson-fronted Barbet (*rubricapillus*)

Taxonomy. *Bucco rubricapillus* J. F. Gmelin, 1788, Sri Lanka.
Closely related to *M. haemacephala*, with which forms the so-called "*Xantholaema* group". Race *malabarica* well marked, sometimes treated as a distinct species; vocalizations, however, very similar to those of nominate. Species name formed from Latin adjectival stem and Latin noun, and must be treated as a noun in apposition, so is therefore indeclinable; modification to "*rubricapilla*" is thus unjustified. Two subspecies currently recognized.

Subspecies and Distribution.
M. r. malabarica (Blyth, 1847) - SW India (Goa S to S Kerala and W Tamil Nadu).
M. r. rubricapillus (J. F. Gmelin, 1788) - Sri Lanka.

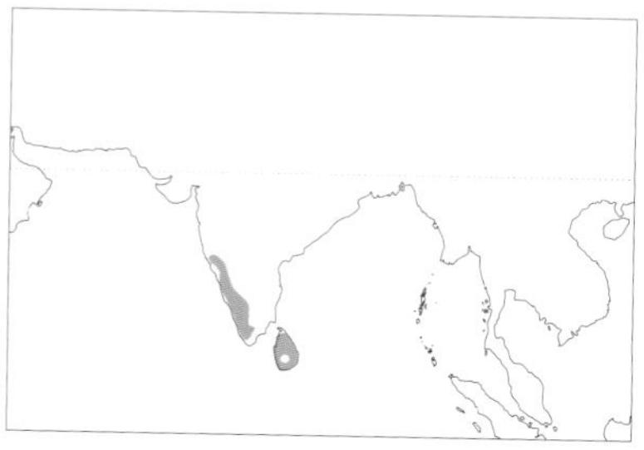

Descriptive notes. 16-17 cm; 32-42 g. Small, chunky, green barbet with reddish legs and feet. Male nominate race with red forehead, gold over and under eye, black line through eye, all bordered by posterior black band, and behind that some blue that extends around to meet blue of malar; golden-orange throat, orange-red breast marks. Female less bright orange-red on breast. Immature duller, lacking bright markings, paler on throat. Race *malabarica* larger, without gold, has red of forehead extending over forecrown and over entire face, malar and throat to breast, sometimes shows faint streaking below. VOICE. Song a series of groups of 4-12 "tok" or "ta" notes at 2-4 per second, with pause of c. 1 second between groups; nominate race usually faster, more trill-like groups, notes at c. 8 per second; variable, 3-12 notes in a group, 10-30 groups per series, the song or series lasting 30 seconds or longer, sometimes for 5 minutes or more; "cheen-cheen" during copulation, also used in interactions; soft "kwank" notes when feeding together; begging young give "kuk" notes in series, and tap inside nest-cavity.

Habitat. Inhabits evergreen forest, forest edges, plantations of fruiting trees, and remnant forest patches, extending into agricultural areas with trees, and gardens; in Sri Lanka also occurs locally along streams, in drier areas; present at up to c. 1300 m. Where range overlaps with that of *M. haemacephala*, the two tend to be separated by habitat, present species being more closely linked to forest.

Food and Feeding. Figs, such as those of banyan and bo trees, also other fruits, berries; small insects, including caterpillars, borer larvae, ants and winged termites; unidentified insects fed to young. Congregates at fruiting trees in groups of up to at least 30 individuals. In one study in S India, present species preferred much smaller fig species (*Ficus tsiela*, *F. retusa*, *F. gibbosa*) than did *M. viridis*; animal food constituted c. 20% of dietary items of present species. When feeding on figs, pecks repeatedly at the fruit rather than swallowing it whole.

Breeding. Dec-May in India, where c. 50% of pairs double-brooded; Dec-Sept in Sri Lanka. Much courtship feeding. Nest excavated by both adults, for c. 18 days, 8-20 m above ground in underside of thin branch, often below previous year's nest; average measurements 3·85 cm entrance, 17 cm depth, 7·25 cm chamber diameter, but cavity to 1·5 m in trees such as *Erythrina*, *Artocarpus*, *Poinciana*, *Shorea* and coconut; nests well apart, unusually as close as 70 m. Eggs 2-3, usually 2, laid within 3-5 days; female incubates at night, both sexes by day, change-overs with "cheen" calls, period 14-15 days; both adults feed young, regurgitate insects and fruits for c. 4 days, then shift to fruits, rate 2-4 feeds per hour, increasing to c. 13 per hour before fledging; young brooded at first, especially during rain, faecal sacs removed first hourly, later c. 5 times an hour, weight gain of chicks 1·4 g per day to 21 days, then decreases, then remains steady to fledging, at 35-37 days; adults withhold food to encourage fledging; fledglings return to nest with adults for only 2-4 days, then independent and disperse out of area; adults renest 4-6 days after fledging of first brood. Fledging success over 50 %; greatest cause of failure is attacks by *M. viridis*, which enlarges nest entrance, removes eggs or young; nest often destroyed by *M. viridis* or *M. zeylanica* if in large branch or near their nests.

Movements. Resident; mainly sedentary, some feeding outside territory, young disperse away from territory.

Status and Conservation. Not globally threatened. Common but local in Indian part of range; common in Sri Lanka in wet lowlands, more local in dry zone. Appears reasonably adaptable, at least in India: in Kerala has adapted to man-altered habitats, and is able to thrive well in plantations and in farmed areas; in Sri Lanka, habitat degradation and destruction are considered possible threats, especially where enforcement of conservation laws and protection of national parks are placed low among priorities. Present in several protected areas, e.g. Indira Gandhi and Periyar National Parks (India), and Sinharaja Forest Reserve and Uda Walawe National Park (Sri Lanka).

Bibliography. Abdulali (1974), Ali (1969, 1996), Ali & Ripley (1983), Baker (1934a), Berlioz (1936), Chakravarthy & Purna Chandra Tejasvi (1992), Daniels, R.J.R. (1997), Gokula & Vijayan (1997), Grimmett *et al.* (1998), Grubh & Ali (1970), Harrison (1999), Henry (1998), Inskipp *et al.* (1996), Kannan (1998), Kazmierczak (2000), Lamsfuss (1998), Legge (1983), Phillips (1978), Ripley (1982), Saha & Dasgupta (1992), Sugathan & Varghese (1996), Whistler (1944), Yahya (1980, 1987, 1988, 2000), Zacharias & Gaston (1999).

67. Coppersmith Barbet
Megalaima haemacephala

French: Barbu à plastron rouge **German**: Kupferschmied **Spanish**: Barbudo Calderero
Other common names: Crimson-breasted/Crimson-headed Barbet

Taxonomy. *Bucco haemacephalus* P. L. S. Müller, 1776, Philippine Islands.
Closely related to *M. rubricapillus*, with which forms the so-called "*Xantholaema* group". Forms described from peninsular India, *confusa* from NW and *lutea* from SE, synonymous with *indica*. Nine subspecies currently recognized.

Subspecies and Distribution.
M. h. indica (Latham, 1790) - NE Pakistan E to S China, S to Sri Lanka, Singapore and Vietnam.
M. h. delica (Parrot, 1907) - Sumatra.
M. h. rosea (Dumont, 1816) - Java and Bali.
M. h. haemacephala (P. L. S. Müller, 1776) - N Philippines: Luzon, Mindoro.
M. h. homochroa Dziadosz & Parkes, 1984 - Tablas, probably Romblon, possibly Masbate.
M. h. celestinoi Gilliard, 1949 - Catanduanes, Biliran, Samar, Leyte.
M. h. intermedia (Shelley, 1891) - C Philippines: Panay, Guimaras, Negros.
M. h. cebuensis Dziadosz & Parkes, 1984 - Cebu.
M. h. mindanensis Rand, 1948 - Mindanao.

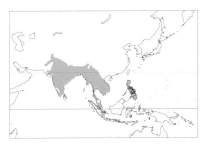

Descriptive notes. 15-17 cm; 30-53 g. Small, chunky, green barbet with streaked underparts, and reddish legs and orbital skin. Male nominate race with red forehead and forecrown, yellow above and below eye, black eyestripe and moustache, all bordered at rear by black band, with some greyish-blue behind that; chin and throat yellow, red patch on lower throat and upper breast. Female less bright red, has yellow in red breast mark. Immature lacks all red at first, is streaky onto throat, has much paler bill. Races form two basic groups: *indica*, *delica*, *celestinoi* and *mindanensis* with yellow above and below eye, and yellow chin and throat, like nominate, but these areas wholly or mainly red in *rosea*, *homochroa*, *intermedia* and *cebuensis*; within the two groups, racial differences involve shades of colour, width of breastband and black crownband and their degree of intrusion with respectively yellow and bluish, and small size differences. VOICE. Song given persistently through day, on moonlit nights, long series of "tok" or "took" or "tonk" notes, tempo varies greatly, 80-200 per minute, but usually slower and lacking pauses compared with that of *M. rubricapillus*; Nepalese and Philippine songs closely similar; song-like notes also as alarm, and in aggression; also "kuank" notes in short series when feeding together, aggressive grating notes, and young beg with "tuk-tuk-" calls.

Habitat. Edges of moist forest, drier deciduous forest, scrub and secondary forest, plantations of diverse trees, mangroves, casuarinas, gardens and fruit trees in villages and even cities, extending into wet forest clearings and areas around logging camps; often breeds along roadsides, in village gardens, or orchards. Generally below 1500 m, to 1830 m in Nepal; rarely reaches 2200-2250 m in Sumatra and Luzon. Overlaps with *M. rubricapillus*, though usually separated ecologically, present species generally occurring in more open, drier habitats.

Food and Feeding. Diverse fruits, including figs, pipal fruits, guavas, mangoes, custard-apples, berries; also crickets, beetles, mantids and various insect larvae. In one study in WC India, present species appeared to prefer much smaller fig species (*Ficus gibbosa*, *F. infectoria*, *F. religiosa*) than did *M. zeylanica*. Captives thrive on figs, grapes, lantana berries, mulberries, bananas, milk and

roaches. Feeds at all levels; hawks for flying termites and moths, and works over bark of trees for insects. Gathers at some fruiting trees in numbers of up to 70.

Breeding. Jan-Oct in Pakistan, India and Nepal, often double-brooded; generally Feb-Jul in Himalayan region; Nov-May in Sri Lanka; Feb-Jul in SE Asia and Philippines; Apr-Oct in Sumatra and Java. Much singing, puffing throat, turning and bobbing head, flicking tail; courtship feeding frequent. Nest excavated at 1·5-13 m or higher in decayed or dead tree, branch, or fence post, trees including *Erythrina*, mango, *Melia*, *Moringa*, *Pongamia*, rubber, *Bombax* and *Cochlospermum*; new cavity excavated yearly, or female may commence new cavity or enlarge old one following breeding, this then completed in breeding season; cavity entrance 3·8-5 cm, depth 15-80 cm. Eggs 2-4, usually 3; incubation by both parents, for 12-14 days; nestlings fed by both parents, brooded, faecal sacs removed from nest area, nestling period c. 35 days; at least in India fledglings independent at fledging; adults may then begin second brood; fledglings often disperse together, are attracted to other pairs still nesting and are chased away. Breeding success often affected by *M. viridis*, which may evict adults or enlarge and ruin holes.

Movements. Generally resident; possibly some migration in NW of range, in Pakistan.

Status and Conservation. Not globally threatened. Widespread and common almost throughout range, may be world's commonest barbet; uncommon in Bhutan. Adaptable non-forest species, showing preference for man-altered habitats; able to survive in variety of habitats, including in urban areas. Assisted by forest clearance and logging; since 1930's has invaded C & S Peninsular Malaysia, even colonizing heavily urbanized Singapore. Present in numerous protected areas, e.g. Keoladeo Ghana National Park (India), Nam Bai Cat Tien National Park (Vietnam), Kuala Selangor National Park (Peninsular Malaysia), Way Kambas National Park (Sumatra), Baluran National Park (Java) and Bali Barat National Park (Bali).

Bibliography. Ali (1969, 1977, 1996), Ali & Ripley (1983), Ali *et al.* (1996), Baker (1934a), Bharos (1997), Danielsen *et al.* (1994), Deignan (1945, 1963), Delacour & Jabouille (1931), Dhindsa *et al.* (1986), Dickinson *et al.* (1991), Dilger (1953), Dziadosz & Parkes (1984), Eames & Ericson (1996), Étchécopar & Hüe (1978), Gilliard (1949b), Glenister (1971), Grimmett *et al.* (1998), Harrison (1999), Hellebrekers & Hoogerwerf (1967), Holmes (1996), Inskipp & Inskipp (1991), Jeyarajasingam & Pearson (1999), Lekagul & Round (1991), MacDonald (1960), MacKinnon & Phillipps (1993, 2000), Madoc (1976), van Marle & Voous (1988), McClure (1998), Medway & Wells (1976), Mukherjee (1995), Muthukrishnan & Sundarababu (1982), Neville (1973), Phillips (1978), Rabor (1977), Rand (1948), Riley (1938), Ripley (1982), Roberts (1991), Robson (2000), Round (1988), Rutgers & Norris (1977), Smythies (1986), Stepanyan (1995), Thiollay (1995), Tooth (1901), Vo Quy & Nguyen Cu (1995), Wells (1999), Whistler (1941), Whistler & Kinnear (1935), Wingate (1953), Yahya (1980, 1988, 2000), Zhao Zhengjie (1995).

PLATE 14 ➤

68

69 ♀ ♂

70 ssp *maculicoronatus* ♂

ssp *rubrilateralis* ♂

71 ♂

72 ♀ ♀

73 ♀ ♂

ssp *amazonicus*

74 ♀

ssp *niger* ♀

ssp *punctatus* ♀

ssp *orosae* ♂

75 ♂

76 ♀

ssp *auratus* ♀

ssp *aurantiicinctus* ♀

PLATE 14

inches 3

cm 8

Subfamily CAPITONINAE
Genus *CAPITO* Vieillot, 1816

68. **Scarlet-crowned Barbet**
Capito aurovirens

French: Cabézon oranvert   **German**: Olivrücken-Bartvogel   **Spanish**: Cabezón Oliva
Other common names: Plaintive Barbet

Taxonomy. *Bucco aurovirens* Cuvier, 1829, Peru.
No apparent close relatives. Monotypic.
Distribution. SE Colombia E to NW Brazil (E to R Negro), and S through E Ecuador to CE Peru
and W Brazil (E & S to Tefe and Acre).

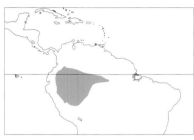

Descriptive notes. c. 19 cm; 46-75 g. Green-olive barbet with orange-yellow throat to breast, whitish chin. Male with red crown to nape, some black in olive lores, olive-green ear-coverts, lower underparts olive, grey and yellow. Female with white crown, becoming olive on hindcrown. Immature duller, greyer olive, throat yellow; crown olive, male with traces of red, female with white. VOICE. Song a series of low "ttroup" or "ttdoot" notes, effect that of frog or toad calling, some notes more hoarse, croaking, at c. 1·75 per second for up to 9 seconds; sexes sing together, one slower, croaking notes, other faster, clearer; also faster, short, more trilling "twot-twot-" at 3-4 notes per second; several calls, grating-like. Loud wing-rustling during encounters.
Habitat. Near water in seasonally flooded *várzea* forest, floodplain low forest, forest swamps, forest transitional to dryland forest, and secondary forest, using all levels from ground to canopy. Extends upwards only to 500-600 m along Andean foothills.
Food and Feeding. Berries, fruits, some insects, details unknown; captives eat beetles, earwigs, mealworms. Gleans in foliage, on branches and twigs, probes into dead leaf clusters. Uncommonly with mixed-species foraging flocks.
Breeding. Jan-May in Colombia and Ecuador; Jul-Aug, also Apr and Dec, in Peru; probably Dec onwards in Brazil. Countersinging occurs, singer twitches wings with notes, points bill downwards, turns head side to side. Nest, eggs and all other data on breeding undescribed. Longevity over 5 years in captivity.
Movements. Presumaby resident.
Status and Conservation. Not globally threatened. Overall reasonably common; common in Colombia; fairly common to common in Ecuador, and especially numerous at Limoncocha; fairly common in Peru. Adapted to shifting habitats; probably occupies many riverine islands where undisturbed. Present in several protected areas, e.g. Cuyabeno Reserve (Ecuador).
Bibliography. Berlioz (1937), Best *et al*. (1997), Bloch *et al*. (1991), Butler (1979), Chapman (1926), Clements & Shany (2001), Gyldenstolpe (1945a), Haffer (1978), Hilty & Brown (1986), Meyer de Schauensee (1949, 1964, 1966, 1982), Norris (1950), Olrog (1968), Parker *et al*. (1982), Remsen & Parker (1983, 1984a), Remsen *et al*. (1993), Ridgely & Greenfield (2001), Rodner *et al*. (2000), Rutgers & Norris (1977), Shifter (1962, 1967), Sick (1985, 1993), Stotz *et al*. (1996), Webb (1950).

69. **Scarlet-belted Barbet**
Capito wallacei

French: Cabézon du Loreto   **German**: Loretobartvogel   **Spanish**: Cabezón de Loreto
Other common names: Wallace's Scarlet-belted Barbet

Taxonomy. *Capito wallacei* O'Neill *et al*., 2000, c. 77 km WNW of Contamana, Loreto, Peru.
No very close relatives apparent; possibly closest to *C. quinticolor*, *C. hypoleucus* or *C. niger*, but further research required. Monotypic.
Distribution. NC Peru E of Andes: known only from isolated low plateau NW of Contamana, between R Huallaga and R Ucayali.

Descriptive notes. c. 19·5 cm; 65-78 g. Distinctive black, white, yellow and red barbet. Male has red cap, with red extending to middle of back, white and yellow mid-back to uppertail-coverts; white line over eye, narrow black bar on forehead, black band on lores through eye to black side of neck; malar region and throat to upper breast white, broad red breastband, lower breast to belly golden to yellow, with olive, orange or even red admixed at sides. Female differs from male only in having some white spots in black below eye, and buff to yellow or white marks forming a line on outer scapulars; 1 female with several black spots at lower edge of red breastband. Immature unknown. VOICE. Song a fast, low-pitched trill of c. 2 seconds, "tdddddd-", resembles distant woodpecker drumming at fast rate; trill suggests songs of *Eubucco* and *C. brunneipectus*; guttural call notes, "ggrrrakk", suggest those of *C. hypoleucus*.
Habitat. Montane and submontane forest, wet and moss-festooned, some of it stunted, at 1350-1500 m. Occurs above elevation at which *C. niger* is found.

Food and Feeding. Fruits and their seeds; most likely insects, as well. Occurs in mixed-species foraging flocks, at up to 10 m in trees.
Breeding. Moult and gonadal condition of Jul specimens indicate season probably Mar-May. Nest and eggs undescribed, and no other information.
Movements. Resident and sedentary.
Status and Conservation. Not globally threatened. Species' conservation status uncertain, as its discovery so recent; should probably be considered Vulnerable. Discovered only in Jul 1996, and currently known only from 1 very small and isolated area in NC Peru; has not been located in other areas of Peru, and is probably a relict of formerly larger population. Population size uncertain, but evidently small, although species is fairly common at type locality. Any human modification of habitat and any development and forest clearance in its limited range would be likely to endanger it.
Bibliography. Anon (2001), Clements & Shany (2001), Lane (2000), O'Neill *et al*. (2000), Parr (2000).

70. **Spot-crowned Barbet**
Capito maculicoronatus

French: Cabézon à calotte tachetée   **German**: Tropfenbartvogel   **Spanish**: Cabezón Pechiblanco

Taxonomy. *Capito maculicoronatus* Lawrence, 1861, Atlantic side of Isthmus of Panama.
Has been thought to form a superspecies with *C. squamatus*, but, although sharing some plumage patterns, probably not very closely related; the two are separated geographically by divergent *C. quinticolor*. Forms described as race *pirrensis* from S Panama and NW Colombia and *melas* from Caribbean E Panama now considered indistinguishable from *rubrilateralis*. Two subspecies currently recognized.
Subspecies and Distribution.
C. m. maculicoronatus Lawrence, 1861 - W Panama (Veraguas) E to Canal Zone.
C. m. rubrilateralis Chapman, 1912 - E Panama to NW Colombia (E to Antioquia and S to Valle).

Descriptive notes. 16-18 cm; 44-66 g. Black, white and yellow barbet, mainly plain black above. Male nominate race with crown spotted brown-white; white throat, white giving way to yellow, gold or golden-orange on upper breast; mid-breast to undertail white with black spots, with yellow to golden-orange area on flanks. Female entirely black on face and throat to breast. Immature duller. Race *rubrilateralis* with narrower culmen with more grooved nostrils than nominate, more white in crown, flank mark more orange, even red. VOICE. Song a series of harsh "kkaaak" notes, gradually shifting to "kkkaakkk" sounds, quality similar to voice of *Semnornis*; sometimes notes double or triple, sound like throat-clearing; sometimes two birds, possibly pair, sing together, one giving typical slow song, other using softer "kk-ggkkk" sounds. Some sounds mechanical, possibly bill-snapping.
Habitat. Inhabits wet primary lowland and hill forest, and occasionally secondary forest. Occurs from sea-level generally up to 600-900 m, sporadically up to 1000 m; rarely to 1200 m in Tacarcuna area of E Panama.
Food and Feeding. Various drupes, other fruits, berries; also insects, such as Orthoptera. Forages in mid-storey to canopy. At times follows army ants, taking fleeing insects. Occasionally groups of up to 6, perhaps families, or up to 10 at fruiting trees.
Breeding. Birds in breeding condition Dec-Apr, excavating nest in Mar, in Colombia; fledged young in early Jun in Panama. Male and two females seen at a nest. No other information.
Movements. Mostly resident, presumed to be sedentary, though possibly a short-distance migrant in places.
Status and Conservation. Not globally threatened. Uncommon to locally fairly common in Panama, where perhaps most numerous in Darién zone; fairly common in Colombia. Species' dependence on forest makes it important that information be secured on its biology, to ensure that its requirements are known, should any future conservation action become necessary.
Bibliography. Anon. (1998b), Berlioz (1937), Chapman (1917), Greenway (1978), Haffer (1975), Hellmayr (1911), Hilty (1997), Hilty & Brown (1986), Meyer de Schauensee (1949, 1964, 1966, 1982), Olrog (1968), Remsen *et al*. (1993), Ridgely & Gwynne (1989), Robbins *et al*. (1995), Rodner *et al*. (2000), Stotz *et al*. (1996), Terborgh & Winter (1982), Wetmore (1968a).

71. **Orange-fronted Barbet**
Capito squamatus

French: Cabézon à nuque blanche   **German**: Weißnacken-Bartvogel   **Spanish**: Cabezón Escamoso
Other common names: Rufous-fronted Barbet

Taxonomy. *Capito squamatus* Salvin, 1876, Santa Rita, Ecuador.
Has been thought to form a superspecies with *C. maculicoronatus*; shares some plumage patterns with that species, but probably not very closely related, and is separated geographically from it by divergent *C. quinticolor*. Possibly distantly related to *C. hypoleucus*. Monotypic.
Distribution. Extreme SW Colombia (SW Nariño) and W Ecuador (S to El Oro).
Descriptive notes. 16-18 cm; 56-64 g. Sturdy-billed, chunky, white-capped, largely black and white barbet. Male with orange to red frontal patch, white crown, variably brown nape; upperparts black, with broad, wavy white edging on tertials; yellowish-white chin to breast, rarely orangish on breast to belly, flanks usually lightly spotted black, white about lower belly and vent. Female has yellow-orange patch on forehead, fine white bars or vermiculations on black of back and wing-coverts, black chin to mid-breast. Immature duller. VOICE. Song low-pitched, very fast, soft, purring trill to c. 4 seconds; call a noisy, single or double "tyik" or "trrik"; series of these in alarm, as against snake.
Habitat. Inhabits wet lowland and hill forest, commonly ranging into secondary forest, forest edge, nearby cultivated areas, farms, orchards, plantations, and pastures with fruiting trees; will cross large open areas to reach isolated fruiting trees. Mainly occurs in areas below 800 m, but locally

---

On following pages: 72. White-mantled Barbet (*Capito hypoleucus*); 73. Black-girdled Barbet (*Capito dayi*); 74. Cinnamon-breasted Barbet (*Capito brunneipectus*); 75. Black-spotted Barbet (*Capito niger*); 76. Five-coloured Barbet (*Capito quinticolor*).

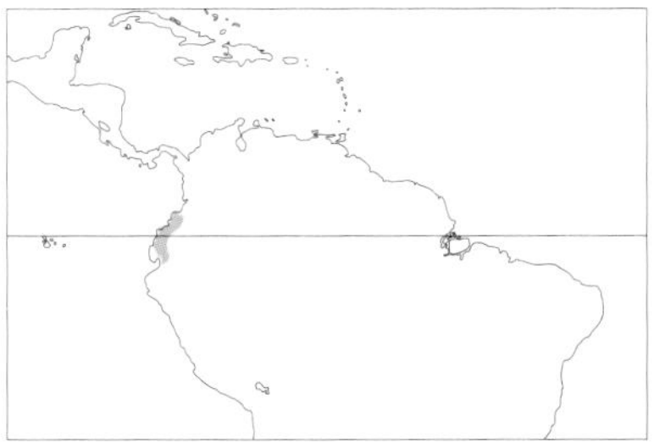

found up to 1500 m. In area of overlap with *C. quinticolor*, the two are apparently separated by habitat, present species more readily moving into forest edge, younger second growth and plantations.
Food and Feeding. Diverse fruits and berries, including *Cecropia* species and *Castilla elastica*; also beetles and probably other insects. Stomach contents contained fruit alone in 77%, rest having some arthropods. Forages at all levels in bushes and trees, mainly in pairs, egesting seeds as it feeds; probes into clusters of dead leaves for insects and spiders. Joins mixed-species foraging flocks.
Breeding. Jul-Sept, probably earlier as well. Occasionally several males sing alternately from close to a female. Nest, eggs and other aspects of breeding activities virtually unknown; reported to excavate nest high in tree; one probable cavity nest found 4 m up in dead tree, in plantation. Up to 4 young raised by captive pair.
Movements. Resident and probably sedentary.
Status and Conservation. Not globally threatened. Currently considered Near-threatened. Restricted-range species: present in Chocó EBA. One of the least well-known barbets. No information available on numbers, but species is apparently not common in general, although considered locally quite common in Ecuador. Forest destruction and human colonization are rife within its small range. Nevertheless, although it occupies a small range and is poorly known, it does seem somewhat adaptable, readily occurring in some non-forest habitats. Present in Río Palenque Science Centre (Ecuador).
Bibliography. Allen (1998), Berlioz (1937), Best *et al.* (1997), Butler (1979), Chapman (1917, 1926), Hilty & Brown (1986), Jahn *et al.* (2000), Meyer de Schauensee (1949, 1964, 1966, 1982), Olrog (1968), Ortiz & Carrión (1991), Parker & Carr (1992), Remsen *et al.* (1993), Ridgely & Greenfield (2001), Rutgers & Norris (1977), Stadler (1992), Stattersfield & Capper (2000), Stattersfield *et al.* (1998), Stotz *et al.* (1996), Strewe (2000b), Terborgh & Winter (1982), Williams & Tobias (1994).

72. White-mantled Barbet
Capito hypoleucus

French: Cabézon à manteau blanc **Spanish**: Cabezón Dorsiblanco
German: Weißmantel-Bartvogel

Taxonomy. *Capito hypoleucus* Salvin, 1897, Valdivia, Antioquia, Colombia.
Appears to be rather isolated within genus; probably related distantly to *C. squamatus*, possibly more closely to newly discovered *C. wallacei* and also to *C. dayi* and *C. brunneipectus*. Racial differences rather slight. Three subspecies currently recognized.
Subspecies and Distribution.
C. h. hypoleucus Salvin, 1897 - C Andes of NW Colombia (Bolivar to Antioquia).
C. h. carrikeri Graves, 1986 - Botero area of R Porce, in Antioquia.
C. h. extinctus Graves, 1986 - Magdalena Valley in Caldas, Cundinamarca and Tolima.

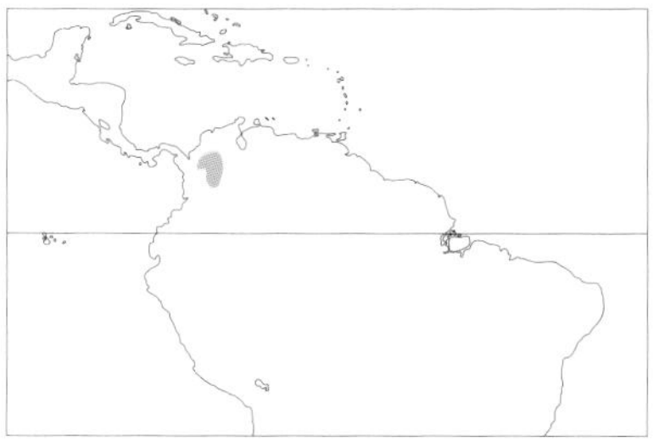

Descriptive notes. 18-19 cm. Strong-billed, rathyer chunky, black, white, brown, red and yellow barbet with yellow-horn bill. Male nominate race with red forehead and crown, black side of head; black upperparts with white nape and inverted white "V" on back; white throat and malar region, pale brown breastband, rest of underparts clear yellow-white; bill pale yellow-horn. Differs from all other *Capito* in bill colour. Female has black spot on front of white malar. Immature lacks brown breastband. Racial differences slight: *carrikeri* with more yellow in white of back and underparts than nominate; *extinctus* has somewhat browner breastband than others. VOICE. Song of 15-30 "hoop" notes that rise slightly in tempo, 3-5 seconds long; call a grating "drrrurtt", resembling that of *C. squamatus*; chattering "kek-ek" and "tteeaw" notes when several feeding in same tree. Probably also bill-wiping as display.
Habitat. Occupies fragmented lower montane moist forest, forest patches, secondary forest, cacao and coffee plantations with fruiting trees, and forest edges; occurs at 700-1600 m, unusually lower, down to 200 m.
Food and Feeding. Berries, fruits, and insects; fruits identified are of *Cupania* and *Cecropia*, and mangoes; stomachs contained "seeds" of fruits, and unidentified insects and fruits. Forages in pairs or families, but several may gather at fruiting trees up to 1 km from cover; usually in canopy. Tears apart dead-leaf clusters for insects, forages among mistletoe clumps. At times joins mixed-species foraging flocks.
Breeding. Probably Apr-Sept; seen attending nest in late Apr, and late breeding-period moult starts May. Singer "hoops" in horizontal position, bill downwards, flicks tail up and down with notes; pair-members sing as close together as 6 cm, sing simultaneously, 2 pairs sometimes countersing even in isolated fruiting tree unlikely to be within territory. Nests, eggs and other breeding details undescribed.
Movements. Resident; leaves territory to feed on fruits, but probably moves only locally.
Status and Conservation. ENDANGERED. Restricted-range species: present in Nechí Lowlands EBA. Apparently rare, but locally common; little known. Nominate race possibly extinct; *carrikeri* apparently not observed in wild since 1950. Paradoxically, *extinctus*, thought to be extinct when first described in 1986, is only race known certainly to survive: was relocated in May 1990, and several observations made since then, at a number of sites, suggest that this race is common, if local; indeed, the Serranía de las Quinchas seems to hold a healthy population, which merits further study. Within species' very small range, clearance of forest continuing, with further fragmenting of habitat and many remaining patches on steep slopes; range evidently contracting. It does, however, seem somewhat adaptable, and is by no means restricted to forest. Conservation efforts crippled by lack of knowledge of this species' breeding behaviour, roosting habits, and other ecological aspects. Recommended that protection be sought of patches of habitat as large as possible, perhaps 100 ha, with habitat corridor system connecting these, and also safeguarding of smaller patches.
Bibliography. Anon. (1996a), Chapman (1917), Collar & Andrew (1988), Collar, Crosby & Stattersfield (1994), Collar, Gonzaga *et al.* (1992), Graves (1986), Hilty (1985), Hilty & Brown (1986), Meyer de Schauensee (1949, 1964, 1966, 1982), Olrog (1968), Rodner *et al.* (2000), Schifter (1967), Stattersfield & Capper (2000), Stattersfield *et al.* (1998), Stiles *et al.* (1999), Stotz *et al.* (1996), Terborgh & Winter (1982), Wege & Long (1995).

73. Black-girdled Barbet
Capito dayi

French: Cabézon du Brésil **German**: Kehlbinden-Bartvogel **Spanish**: Cabezón Brasileño
Other common names: Day's Barbet

Taxonomy. *Capito dayi* Cherrie, 1916, Porto Velho, River Madeira, Brazil.
Possibly related to *C. hypoleucus*. Monotypic.
Distribution. Amazonian Brazil between upper R Madeira and upper R Tocantins, S to E Bolivia (NE Santa Cruz) and WC Mato Grosso.

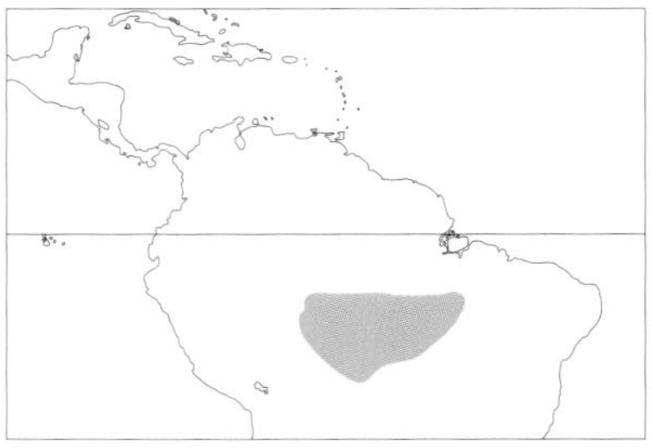

Descriptive notes. 16-17 cm; 56-74 g. Sturdy-billed black and white barbet with black "girdle" across white underparts. Male with crimson cap, white lateral marks on back, white or yellow-white tertial patch; cinnamon throat, variably barred to unmarked; hair-tipped white breast feathers, yellowish rear flanks to lower belly, red undertail-coverts; whitish bill. Female differs in having all-black crown. Immature not described. VOICE. Song a series of "hooo" or "rroh" notes at 3-6 per second for up to 10 seconds, recalls that of *C. hypoleucus* and also of Striated Antthrush (*Chamaeza nobilis*); noisy "kuk" notes at c. 2 per second, also a grating rattle.
Habitat. Lowland and lower hill slopes in moist to wet forest canopy, ranging into secondary forest with fruiting trees; also unoccupied, old cacao plantations. Reaches upper R Paraguay system at 50-550 m.
Food and Feeding. Feeds mainly on fruits, including figs, *Cecropia* fruits and others, but also takes some arthropods. Typically encountered as solitary individuals or in pairs to small groups, usually high in trees; feeds at 2-30 m, mainly at 15-25 m; forages in dead-leaf clusters. Joins mixed-species foraging flocks.
Breeding. Poorly known. Data, mainly from Amazonia and Rondonia, suggest breeding Aug-Nov, also Feb and Jun. Sings erect with tail down, bill slightly below horizontal, throat and breast feathers erected so that hair-like-tips stand out. Nest and eggs unreported.
Movements. Resident, presumably sedentary.
Status and Conservation. Not globally threatened. No precise information available on numbers. Because of its rather restricted range, and as forest habitat becomes increasingly fragmented, the status of this species should be monitored. Information required on its breeding habits and general requirements. Known to occur in Noel Kempff Mercado National Park (Bolivia).
Bibliography. Anon. (1995a), Bates *et al.* (1989), Berlioz (1937), Greenway (1978), Haffer (1978, 1987, 1993a, 1997a, 1997c), Kratter *et al.* (1992), Meyer de Schauensee (1966, 1982), Naumburg (1930), Novaes (1976), Novaes & Lima (1992a), Olrog (1968), Pearman (1994a), Remsen & Traylor (1989), Remsen *et al.* (1993), Schubart *et al.* (1965), Sick (1958a, 1985, 1993), Stotz, Fitzpatrick *et al.* (1996), Stotz, Lanyon *et al.* (1997), Zimmer *et al.* (1997).

74. Cinnamon-breasted Barbet
Capito brunneipectus

French: Cabézon à poitrine brune **German**: Zimtbrust-Bartvogel **Spanish**: Cabezón Pechipardo
Other common names: Brown-chested Barbet

Taxonomy. *Capito brunneipectus* Chapman, 1921, Villa Braga, River Tapajós, Brazil.
Was long merged in *C. niger*, but differs markedly in morphology from all races of that species, and has distinctive song; may not be related directly to *C. niger*. Monotypic.
Distribution. Brazil S of Amazon, between lower R Madeira and lower R Tapajós; S limit of range unknown.

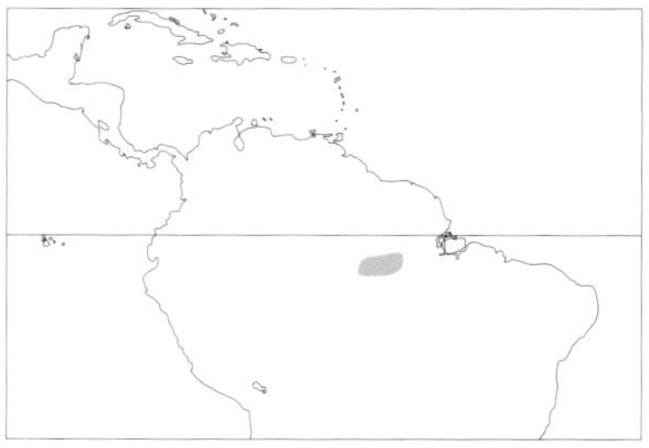

Descriptive notes. c. 18 cm; male 58 g. Chunky-billed black, cinnamon, whitish and olive to yellow barbet. Male with dull gold top of head, black patch through eye; black back with converging yellow lines; buffy yellowish-white throat, underparts streaky olive or yellow with cinnamon breastband; bill pale grey and black. Female duller than male, has more buff-yellow markings on wings, more cinnamon throat finely spotted black. Immature undescribed. VOICE. Song a rapid "hoo" trill of short notes accelerating from c. 20 to c. 40 per second, ending "brrrrrrrrt"; resembles songs of *Eubucco* and *C. wallacei*.
Habitat. Lowland wet forest, usually in canopy.
Food and Feeding. Known foods are insects and other arthropods, but few stomachs examined; presumed to eat fruits as well. Climbs vines, hops on branches and twigs. Joins mixed-species foraging flocks.
Breeding. A male with enlarged testes was found moulting in Aug, and some birds collected were completing moult Jul-Aug; thus species possibly breeds prior to Jul, perhaps as early as Mar-Apr. No other information available.
Movements. Probably resident.
Status and Conservation. Not globally threatened. Known from only few localities, namely Boim, Igarape, Villa Braga and Borba, and S limit of range currently unknown. Not rare near Boim. Species' small range, coupled with the fact that so little is known about its habitat requirements and breeding habits, suggests that it should be monitored; its conservation status possibly requires reassessment. It may be relevant that a genus of spiny tree rat (*Lonchothrix*) and a CITES-listed marmoset (*Callithrix humeralifer*) are among mammals with an almost identical distribution to this barbet's.
Bibliography. Berlioz (1937), Chapman (1921a, 1928b), Emmons (1990), Griscom & Greenway (1941), Haffer (1997c), Olrog (1968), Oren & Parker (1997), Sick (1985, 1993).

75. **Black-spotted Barbet**

Capito niger

French: Cabézon tacheté   **German**: Tupfenbartvogel   **Spanish**: Cabezón Turero
Other common names: Gilded Barbet (*auratus*)

Taxonomy. *Bucco niger* P. L. S. Müller, 1776, no locality = Cayenne.
No very close allies; possibly fairly close to *C. quinticolor*. Was long considered to include *C. brunneipectus* as race, but that species differs markedly in morphology from all races of present species, and has distinctive song; the two are perhaps not related directly. Nominate race may be specifically distinct from all others, latter then constituting a separate polytypic species, *C. auratus*, but nominate *niger* may meet other races in N Brazil (Roraima); given similarity of all forms herein included in present species, combined with individual distinctiveness of all American barbet species currently recognized, it seems best to avoid such a split until studies have been carried out in areas of possible overlap in Roraima. Many races intergrade. Other races described from NW Brazil are *transilens* (upper R Negro), considered synonymous with *nitidior*, and *novaolindae* (Nova Olinda) and *arimae* (R Purús), both treated as synonymous with *amazonicus*, possibly fitting into a cline from orange-throated *insperatus* in S towards red-throated *amazonicus* in N; birds described as race *intermedius* (WC Venezuela) inseparable from *aurantiicinctus*; forms *macintyrei* from SW Colombia and Ecuador and *conjunctus* from Peru fall within range of variation of *punctatus*. Form "*bolivianus*" known only from type specimen of unknown locality, possibly from R Beni (N Bolivia); now thought most likely to be an aberrant specimen of *insperatus*. Nine subspecies currently recognized.

Subspecies and Distribution.
C. n. aurantiicinctus Dalmas, 1900 - Venezuela in upper Orinoco region, W Bolívar and Amazonas.
C. n. niger (P. L. S. Müller, 1776) - E Venezuela, the Guianas, and NE Brazil N of Amazon.
C. n. punctatus (Lesson, 1830) - SC Colombia (from Meta) along lower E Andes to C Peru (Junín area).
C. n. nitidior Chapman, 1928 - extreme E Colombia and S Venezuela S to near Peru-Brazil border (N of Amazon) and to lower R Japura.
C. n. hypochondriacus Chapman, 1928 - N Brazil from Roraima (Maraca) S along R Branco to angle between lower R Negro and R Solimões.
C. n. auratus (Dumont, 1816) - NE Peru from mouth of R Napo S along R Amazon and R Ucayali.
C. n. amazonicus Deville & Des Murs, 1849 - W Brazil S of R Solimões from upper R Juruá and Tefe E to R Purús.
C. n. orosae Chapman, 1928 - E Peru from R Orosa E to R Javari, S to extreme W Brazil (Cruzeiro del Sol region of Acre).
C. n. insperatus Cherrie, 1916 - SE Peru, N Bolivia and W Brazil (Calama).

Descriptive notes. 16-19 cm; 41-72 g. Brightly patterned barbet, with spots or streaks below; much individual variation in richness of coloration. Male nominate race with red forehead, yellowish crown and nape, latter streaked dusky, whitish to straw-yellow supercilia; broad black band from lores back to neck side; upperparts black with yellowish line on each side of mantle, pale yellowish wingbar and tips of tertials; throat red, breast and belly yellow, flanks tinged olive with some black streaks. Female more heavily marked, pale flecking and edging above, more heavily spotted or streaked below. Immature duller. Races differ mainly in head colours and amount of markings below, falling into three groups: red-throated (*niger*, *nitidior*, *auratus*, *amazonicus*); orange-throated (*aurantiicinctus*, *hypochondriacus*, *insperatus*); and orange-throated with female spot-throated (*punctatus*); with *orosae* intermediate between *auratus* and *insperatus*. VOICE. Song of double, sometimes single, low "hoot" notes in series for 5-60 but usually 6-20 seconds, ventriloquial, 1-2 double notes per second, increasing somewhat in tempo and dropping in volume, confusable with Blue-crowned Motmot (*Momotus momota*) song and possibly with higher-pitched, more trilling, double-noted song of *Eubucco richardsoni*; call soft "trra-trra" notes.

Habitat. Lowland and low hill floodplain-forest, *terra firme* forest, riverine forest in later successional stages, second growth, edges, clearings, and gardens and plantations; reaches humid lower montane forest, and mossy elfin forest in Peru; also in palms and forest patches in some savanna areas. Replaced by *C. aurovirens* in *várzea* and undergrowth. Up to 1000 m in Brazil, to 1600 m in Venezuela, to 1700 m in Ecuador, and locally over 1500 m in Peru.

Food and Feeding. Diverse fruits, such as figs, those of *Cecropia*, *Ocotea*, *Pagama plicata*, *Guarea guara*, mangoes, form up to 80% of diet; nectar at times; also various insects, e.g. grasshoppers, locusts, and spiders eaten, can represent up c. 18% of diet. Captives accepted bananas, raisins, locusts, mealworms, and young mice. Hangs, reaches, probes, peers, seeks insects in dead-leaf clusters from a nearby perch, goes over limbs and trunks where lichens growing, may tap at bark. Usually solitary, sometimes in pairs; up to 10-15 can gather at large fruiting tree. Occasionally joins mixed-species foraging flocks, working canopy to middle or lower levels. Sometimes follows Red-throated Caracaras (*Daptrius americanus*) as they hunt for wasp nests.

Breeding. Sept-May or later, to Jul, in N & NE of range; Mar-Nov in Colombia and Ecuador; Jun or Jul to as late as Feb in Peru to Bolivia. Display involves cocking and twisting of tail, male bouncing around female, also flutter-flight displays, chases; male sings with head arched and bill down, tail flicking upwards with each note. Pair excavates cavity at 5-12 m in tree, cavity c. 20-30 cm deep. Eggs 3-4; both parents incubate, period unknown; fledging at c. 34 days.

Movements. Resident, and sedentary, no movements known.

Status and Conservation. Not globally threatened. Commonest Neotropical barbet. In Peru, 10·5 pairs/100 ha in mature forest, 15 pairs/100 ha in transition forest, and up to 20 pairs/100 ha in late successional riverside habitat. Fairly common in Colombia; fairly common to common in Ecuador; uncommon in Peru. Voices of several races unknown. An important species, providing cavities used later by other species; if this barbet comes under threat, others will also suffer.

Bibliography. Berlioz (1937), Blake (1950), Bloch *et al.* (1991), Bond & Meyer de Schauensee (1943), Brodkorb (1939b), Chapman (1917, 1921b, 1926, 1928b), Cherrie (1916), Chubb (1916), Clements & Shany (2001), Foster *et al.* (1994), Friedmann (1948), Greenway (1978), Gyldenstolpe (1945a, 1951), Haffer (1997c), Haverschmidt & Mees (1994), Hellmayr (1907a, 1907b, 1910, 1929), Hilty & Brown (1986), Karr *et al.* (1990), Krabbe (1991), Maria & Olivares (1967), Meyer de Schauensee & Phelps (1978), Moskovits *et al.* (1985), Norton (1965), Parker & Bailey (1991), Phelps & Phelps (1958), Remsen *et al.* (1993), Ridgely & Greenfield (2001), Robbins *et al.* (1987), Robinson (1997), Robinson & Terborgh (1997), Rosenberg (1997), Rutgers & Norris (1977), Schroeder (1999), Sclater & Salvin (1873), Sick (1985, 1993), Snyder (1966), Stotz *et al.* (1996), Thiollay (1992), Thiollay & Jullien (1998), Tostain *et al.* (1992), Ward (1971), Willard *et al.* (1991), Zimmer (1930).

76. **Five-coloured Barbet**

Capito quinticolor

French: Cabézon à cinq couleurs   **Spanish**: Cabezón Cincocolores
German: Fünffarben-Bartvogel

Taxonomy. *Capito quinticolor* Elliot, 1865, Colombia.
Relationships unclear, but possibly close to *C. maculicoronatus* and *C. squamatus*, and also to *C. niger*. Monotypic.

Distribution. W Colombia from C Chocó (Quibdó area) S to NW Ecuador (Esmeraldas).

Descriptive notes. 17-18 cm; 54-69 g. Rather heavy-billed barbet. Male black above, with red cap, yellow "V" on mantle, yellow wingbar and edges of tertials; white throat to breast, gold or orange on belly, with black spots on flanks. Female black above, streaked with golden-yellow, including on crown, ear-coverts and wing-coverts, markings sometimes orangey; below, spotted black on white throat and breast, more streaky gold flanks, clear yellow-gold belly. Immature not described. VOICE. Both sexes sing low-pitched, hollow, hoop trill of 3-8 seconds at c. 1·5 notes per second; also guttural "churr" call.

Habitat. Lowland wet forest, forest edges, adjacent second growth and disturbed forest, generally below c. 350 m, but locally up to c. 600 m. In area of contact with *C. squamatus*, apparently separated by habitat, present species being more closely tied to primary and mature secondary forest.

Food and Feeding. Mainly fruits; some insects. Forages in canopy to mid-level, at edges to understorey. Joins mixed-species foraging flocks at times, working through branches and foliage.

Breeding. Essentially unknown. Specimens suggest season Apr-Jul. Seen in pairs, possibly with third bird at times. Male bows, bill down, inflates throat, pumps head downwards and forwards with each note as it sings, cocks tail at times. Pair reported apparently incubating 5 m up in old woodpecker hole in tree near stream. No other information available.

Movements. Assumed to be sedentary.

Status and Conservation. Not globally threatened. Currently considered Near-threatened. Restricted-range species: present in Chocó EBA. Formerly classed as Vulnerable, but recent work shows that more forest remains in the region than had been feared. Nonetheless, species remains little known. In one study, found at linear density of 3·5 pairs/km of disturbed forest in N Ecuador. In Ecuador, first encountered only in 1990; its limited range there contains only two protected areas holding potentially suitable habitat, Cotacachi-Cayapas National Park (marginal) and Awá Ethnographic Reserve; species not yet located at either, and their effective protection seems uncertain; surveys required. Situation in Colombia apparently more encouraging, with recent records at several sites and large areas of forest remaining intact, with no immediate threats apparent. In general, and in long term, forest destruction and associated human settlement are main threats. Despite local occurrence in restricted range, species also occurs in second-growth forest and therefore not totally dependent on undisturbed habitats. Information urgently needed on its biology if it is to be monitored appropriately and effective action taken to conserve it.

Bibliography. Anon. (1996a), Berlioz (1937), Best *et al.* (1997), Chapman (1917), Collar *et al.* (1994), Hellmayr (1911), Hilty & Brown (1986), Jahn *et al.* (2000), Maria & Olivares (1967), Meyer de Schauensee (1949, 1964, 1966, 1982), Olrog (1968), Pearman (1993a), Remsen *et al.* (1993), Ridgely & Greenfield (2001), Rodner *et al.* (2000), Salaman (1994), Stattersfield & Capper (2000), Stattersfield *et al.* (1998), Stotz *et al.* (1996), Terborgh & Winter (1982).

ssp *richardsoni*

♂

♀

ssp *bourcierii*

♀

♂

78

ssp
aurantiicollis

♂

♀

77

ssp
aequatorialis

♀

♂

ssp
occidentalis

♀

ssp *nigriceps*

♂

78

♂

♀

ssp *orientalis*

79

♂

♀

ssp *versicolor*

♀

♂

80

♂

♂

ssp
steerii

♀

ssp
glaucogularis

♀

81

♀

♂

82

♂

♀

PLATE 15

Genus *EUBUCCO* Bonaparte, 1850

77. Lemon-throated Barbet
Eubucco richardsoni

French: Cabézon à poitrine d'or **German**: Goldbrust-Bartvogel **Spanish**: Cabezón Pechiamarillo

Taxonomy. *Capito richardsoni* G. R. Gray, 1846, no locality = Ecuador.
No close relatives, and the only lowland member of genus. A specimen from upper R Napo (Ecuador) represents a hybrid between nominate race of present species and race *orientalis* of *E. bourcierii*. N races with blue nape sometimes combined as "*richardsoni* group", with yellow-naped S races referred to as "*aurantiicollis* group". Form from S Colombia and N Peru described as *granadensis* considered synonymous with nominate, but possibly a valid race; birds from C Peru named as race *coccineus* now considered inseparable from *aurantiicollis*. Four subspecies currently recognized.
Subspecies and Distribution.
E. r. richardsoni (G. R. Gray, 1846) - SE Colombia (S from Meta), E Ecuador and N Peru (W of Iquitos).
E. r. nigriceps Chapman, 1928 - NE Peru from lower R Putumayo and lower R Napo, E to extreme NW Brazil (W Amazonas N of Amazon).
E. r. aurantiicollis P. L. Sclater, 1858 - E Peru from R Marañón, E to W Brazil S of Amazon (E almost to R Juruá) and S to NW Bolivia.
E. r. purusianus Gyldenstolpe, 1941 - W Brazil S of Amazon, from R Juruá E to upper R Madeira.

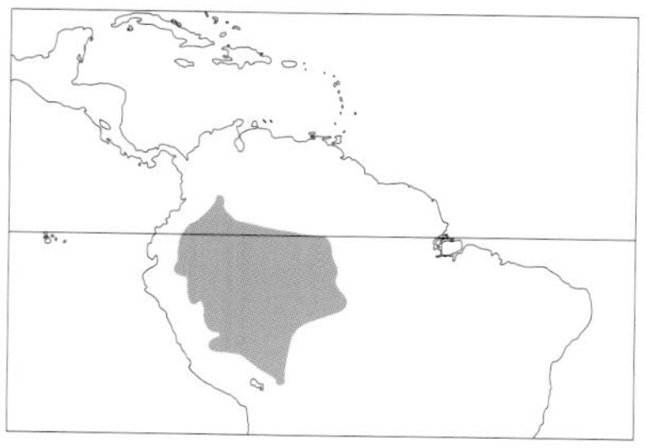

Descriptive notes. c. 15·5 cm; 24-40 g. Multi-coloured, sharp-billed, active barbet with marked sexual dimorphism. Male nominate race with red crown, blue nape, green upperparts; chin red with variable black admixed, throat yellow, breast orange-red, belly and flanks greener and streaked dark; bill greenish-horn to yellow. Female with black line above bill, grey-blue forehead becoming green on crown, black ear patch with golden superciliary continuing around rear of patch; throat bluish, breast orange-gold, lower underparts streaked on pale blue-yellow ground colour. Immature duller, shows sexual features early. Race *nigriceps* has back slightly more blue-green, male with black to maroon-black crown; *aurantiicollis* has yellow nape, more yellow or even orange in dorsal green, male with more gold or orange on throat; *purusianus* close to *aurantiicollis*, but male pinkish-red on breast, yellowish nuchal patch narrower. Voice. Song of soft double or usually triple "hoo" notes in fast, trill-like series, c. 4 compound notes per second for 1·5-5 seconds; sometimes slower, and overall slower than in other *Eubucco*.
Habitat. Generally lowland forest, also dense second growth, forest edges and clearings, and forest edge of flooded *várzea*; reaches upper tropical hill forest, rarely to 1375 m, usually below 1100 m. Numbers greater in late forest stages near rivers and lakes than in mature forest.
Food and Feeding. Fruits such as those of *Cecropia* and their seeds, also grasshoppers, locusts, spiders, less often roaches; c. 37% of food arthropods. Forages, usually alone or in pairs, in canopy to mid-levels, at 12-24 m, occasionally down to 5 m. Clings to take fruits. Over one-third of feeding spent seeking insects in dead-leaf clusters, tearing these apart; often hangs upside-down. Frequently joins mixed-species foraging flocks.
Breeding. Season probably Feb or Apr to Nov, or somewhat earlier in S. Males countersing from canopy, c. 7 songs per minute, singer bows head with notes, erects crown and nape feathers, flits tail in time with notes. Nest and eggs undescribed; territory c. 10 ha. No other information.
Movements. Probably sedentary.
Status and Conservation. Not globally threatened. Considered common in many areas; uncommon in Ecuador and Peru. Reported densities of 4-5 pairs/100 ha. Information on breeding needed in order to assess species' requirements. Probably competes with larger *Capito niger*, which often commences singing just as present species starts, causing latter to cease or to move away. Present in several protected areas, e.g. Cuyabeno Reserve (Ecuador) and Tambopata Reserve (Peru).
Bibliography. Berlioz (1937), Bloch *et al*. (1991), Borges *et al*. (2001), Butler (1979), Chapman (1917, 1926, 1928a), Clements & Shany (2001), Foster *et al*. (1994), Gyldenstolpe (1951), Haffer (1978), Hilty & Brown (1986), Krabbe (1991), María & Olivares (1967), Meyer de Schauensee (1949, 1964, 1966), Olivares (1962), Parker & Bailey (1991), Parker *et al*. (1982), Perry *et al*. (1997), Remsen & Parker (1984a), Remsen & Traylor (1989), Remsen *et al*. (1993), Ridgely & Greenfield (2001), Robinson & Terborgh (1997), Rosenberg (1997), Schulenberg & Remsen (1982), Sick (1985, 1993), Stotz *et al*. (1996), Terborgh *et al*. (1990), Traylor (1951b).

78. Red-headed Barbet
Eubucco bourcierii

French: Cabézon à tête rouge **German**: Andenbartvogel **Spanish**: Cabezón Cabecirrojo
Other common names: Flame-headed/Bourcier's Barbet

Taxonomy. *Micropogon Bourcierii* Lafresnaye, 1845, Colombia.
Original naming of species confused, with male described first and on very next page female named as "*Micropogon Hartlaubii*". Has been thought to form a superspecies with *E. tucinkae*, and even regarded as conspecific, but the two appear to be only distantly related. Probably not closely related to other members of genus, although race *orientalis* has hybridized with nominate race of *E. richardsoni* in E Ecuador. Six subspecies recognized.
Subspecies and Distribution.
E. b. salvini (Shelley, 1891) - Costa Rica and W Panama.
E. b. anomalus Griscom, 1929 - E Panama (around Cerro Pirre, Cerro Tacarcuna); probably also adjacent NW Colombia.
E. b. bourcierii (Lafresnaye, 1845) - Andes of W Venezuela disjunctly S to C Colombia (E side of C Andes, slopes of E Andes).
E. b. occidentalis Chapman, 1914 - slopes of W Andes in Colombia.
E. b. aequatorialis (Salvadori & Festa, 1900) - W Ecuador on W Andean slope and in coastal mountains.
E. b. orientalis Chapman, 1914 - E Andean slope of Ecuador, and N Peru (Cajamarca, Amazonas).

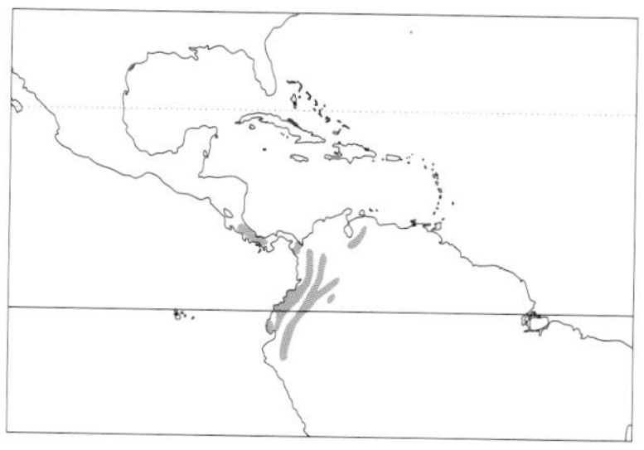

Descriptive notes. c. 16 cm; 30-45 g. Small, pale-billed, multicoloured green barbet. Male nominate race with black around base of bill, red head and neck, narrow whitish nape band, green upperparts; red on throat and upper breast fading to yellowish on belly, flanks with greenish streaks; bill yellow. Female much duller, no red, with blue ear patch bordered with black and gold at rear, greenish-yellow throat, breast golden. Immature as respective adult but duller, can be sexed at fledging, but male retains some green on head for months. Races vary mainly in extent of red on male underparts, whether to breast or to belly, with variable orange and gold at rear of red, in *aequatorialis* red ending sharply in yellow on breast; females vary in having forehead black or mixed black and blue, in extent and colour of yellow or orange behind ear-coverts, and in other minor ways. Voice. Short, fast trill song "poooddddddrrrrr", notes c. 27 per second, for c. 2 seconds, ventriloquial, inconspicuous, similar to songs of *E. versicolor* and *Capito brunneipectus*; chattery call notes; young beg squeakily. Also aggressive wing-fluttering.
Habitat. Primary forest in undergrowth, about trails and clearings, ranging into thickets and secondary forest of wet montane tropical and subtropical areas; frequently on ridges; in cloudforest. Mainly at 1000-1800 m, but also lower, to c. 400 m in Middle America and W South America, rarely down to 200 m; to c. 2400 m in Colombia, 1900 m in Ecuador, and 2100 m in Costa Rica.
Food and Feeding. Fruits, berries of *Micronia*, *Myrica*, *Ocotea* and others; at feeders and in captivity, melons, tomatoes, apples, carrots, guavas, cherries, bananas; also takes flies, earwigs, beetles, caterpillars, roaches, spiders, even scorpions. Feeds at 2-15 m. Acrobatic; gleans, hovers, and hangs; seeks out dead-leaf clusters, pecking and tearing them for arthropods. Often solitary, or in pairs, aggressive; occasionally in groups of up to 8 at fruiting trees. Joins mixed-species foraging flocks.
Breeding. Mar-Jul from Middle America S to Colombia, Ecuador and Peru; Dec-Apr in Venezuela. Singing male fluffed head and neck feathers, dropped tail below "humped" rump, in response to playback of *E. richardsoni* song. Both members of pair excavate nest, or enlarge old woodpecker hole, at c. 0·5-2·5 m in tree or stub, or occasionally in rotten fence post; nest entrance c. 3 cm, depth to c. 18 cm. Eggs 2-5; incubation period c. 15 days; hatchling fed insects at start, nestling period 31-42 days.
Movements. Some downslope post-breeding movement noted in Costa Rica and Panama, probably occurs also in Ecuador.
Status and Conservation. Not globally threatened. Often local; fairly common in Colombia; uncommon to fairly common in Ecuador; rare and local in Peru. Since this species is inconspicuous, often silent, it could be more common than is apparent. Seems to disappear when all primary forest has been removed, hence needs to be monitored. Present in several protected areas, e.g. Tapantí National Park and Guayabo National Monument (Costa Rica), and Río Ñambí Natural Reserve (Colombia).
Bibliography. Bartmann (1975), Berlioz (1937), Bloch *et al*. (1991), Chapman (1914b, 1917, 1926), Clements & Shany (2001), Ebert (1985, 1986), Faust (1969), Griscom (1929, 1935), Haffer (1987), Hellmayr (1911), Hilty (1997), Hilty & Brown (1986), Karr *et al*. (1990), Krabbe (1991), María & Olivares (1967), Meyer de Schauensee (1949, 1964, 1966), Meyer de Schauensee & Phelps (1978), Miller (1963), Parker & Carr (1992), Parker *et al*. (1982), Remsen & Parker (1984a), Remsen *et al*. (1993), Ridgely & Greenfield (2001), Ridgely & Gwynne (1989), Ridgway (1914), Robbins, Parker & Allen (1985), Robbins, Ridgely *et al*. (1987), Rutgers & Norris (1977), Salaman (1994), Schifter (1967), Slud (1964), Stiles (1983), Stiles & Skutch (1989), Stotz *et al*. (1996), Wetmore (1968a), Wheelwright *et al*. (1984), Worth (1938).

79. Scarlet-hooded Barbet
Eubucco tucinkae

French: Cabézon de Carabaya **Spanish**: Cabezón de Carabaya
German: Scharlachkopf-Bartvogel

Taxonomy. *Capito tucinkae* Seilern, 1913, Carabaya, Peru.
Has been thought to form a superspecies with *E. bourcierii*, and long considered conspecific, but appears to be very distinct species, only distantly allied to *E. bourcierii*. No close relatives within genus. Monotypic.
Distribution. E Peru from lower R Ucayali, E to W Amazonian Brazil (E to R Tejo in upper R Juruá area of Acre) and S to W Bolivia (La Paz).

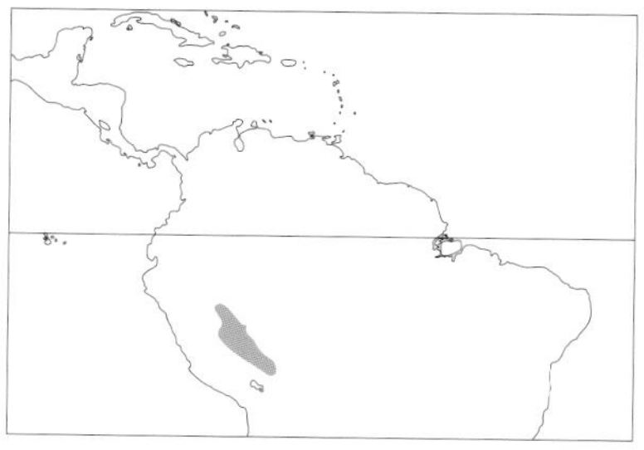

Descriptive notes. c. 17 cm; 40-44 g. Red-headed barbet with black chin, golden-yellow nuchal band, green upperparts with some red on mantle, yellow bill. Male with red throat with some yellow showing, red breaking into orange and yellow on lower breast, grey patch on sides impinging on red of breast, and olive-streaked flanks. Female has pale yellow throat, golden-orange band on breast, less orangey below. Immature undescribed. Voice. Song a fast "oop-oop-oop-" series at c. 6·5-7 notes per second for 2-4 seconds, much recalling Afrotropical *Tricholaema lacrymosa*, faster than song of *E. richardsoni*, can be given at 5 songs per minute; longer songs repeated sustainedly by male in response to playback.
Habitat. Found within c. 150 m of rivers and oxbow lakes, in "zabolo", bamboos and *Heliconia* in thick understorey beneath such trees as *Cecropia*, *Cedrela odorata*, *Nectandra*, *Acacia*, *Erythrina*, *Sapium* and *Terminalia*; also occurs in overgrown, abandoned farm gardens near rivers and on river islands. From c. 150 m to, occasionally, as high as 850 m or higher along rivers emerging from Andes.
Food and Feeding. Diverse fruits of various figs, *Coussapoa*, *Cecropia*, *Psychotria*, *Tabernaemontana*, and others, especially of Lauraceae; also flowers or nectar of *Inga*, *Quararibea* and *Combretum*; also diverse insects, such as termites, and other arthropods. Studies indicate diet c. 60% fruits, 40% arthro-

On following pages: 80. Versicoloured Barbet (*Eubucco versicolor*); 81. Prong-billed Barbet (*Semnornis frantzii*); 82. Toucan-barbet (*Semnornis ramphastinus*).

pods. Feeds at 2-11 m, gleaning and plucking fruits; systematically seeks dead-leaf clusters in bushes, vines and trees, probing and tearing at them for insects and other animals. Joins mixed-species foraging flocks of wrens (Troglodytidae), tanagers (Thraupidae) and others.
Breeding. Season possibly Jul and later in Peru. Male sings with head bowed, bill nearly touching breast. Pair excavated cavity in fig tree 1·5 m over water in Sept, nest abandoned later. No other information available.
Movements. Resident, and sedentary so far as is known.
Status and Conservation. Not globally threatened. Restricted-range species: present in Southeast Peruvian Lowlands EBA. Few data on numbers; judged to be rare in Peru. In study in Peru, maximum c. 3 pairs/100 ha in late successional *Ficus*/*Cedrela* forest along R Manu; fewer pairs in earlier and later successional stages. Possibly more common and adaptable than perceived, for its habitat is irregularly worked by ornithologists, and it is fundamentally a species of ever-changing, shifting river-edge habitat. Comparison could be made with *Capito aurovirens*, which occupies similar habitat to N & E of this species. Further data required on its breeding habits and requirements.
Bibliography. Anon. (1995a), Clements & Shany (2001), Collar, Crosby & Stattersfield (1994), Collar, Gonzaga *et al.* (1992), Foster *et al.* (1994), Haffer (1978), Meyer de Schauensee (1982), O'Neill (1969), Olrog (1968), Parker & Bailey (1991), Parker, Castillo *et al.* (1991), Parker, Parker & Plenge (1982), Remsen & Parker (1983, 1984a), Remsen *et al.* (1993), Robinson (1997), Robinson & Terborgh (1997), Stattersfield *et al.* (1998), Stotz *et al.* (1996), Terborgh, Fitzpatrick & Emmons (1984), Terborgh, Robinson *et al.* (1990), Traylor (1951b), Whittaker & Oren (1999), Williams (1995).

80. **Versicoloured Barbet**

Eubucco versicolor

French: Cabézon élégant **German**: Buntbartvogel **Spanish**: Cabezón Versicolor

Taxonomy. *Bucco versicolor* P. L. S. Müller, 1776, Maynas, Peru.
No close relatives. Races well marked, but general patterns similar; also, they interbreed, and intermediates occur. Three subspecies recognized.
Subspecies and Distribution.
E. v. steerii (P. L. Sclater, 1878) - N Peru from WC Amazonas S to N Huánuco.
E. v. glaucogularis (Tschudi, 1844) - E Huánuco S to N Cuzco.
E. v. versicolor (P. L. S. Müller, 1776) - S Peru (Cuzco, Puno) to NC Bolivia (Cochabamba).

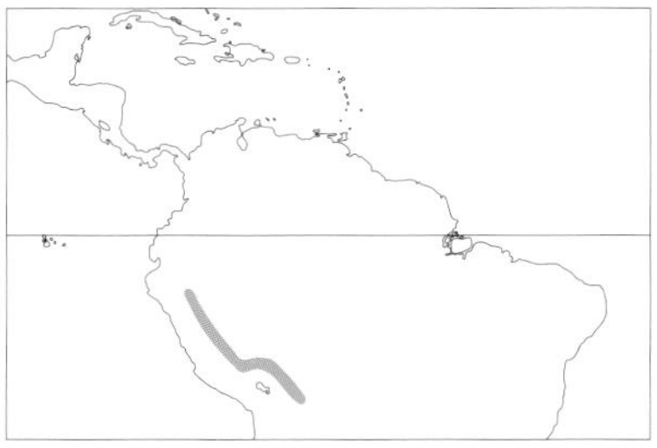

Descriptive notes. c. 16 cm; 26-41 g. Small, sturdy-billed, multicoloured barbet. Male of nominate race red-capped, with narrow black around base of bill, green to blue-green upperparts; red throat, lower throat and malar blue, blue on nape; yellow on breast, red centre of lower breast, green flank streaks; eyes red, bill yellowish. Female has blue around eye, on ear-coverts and to throat, orange-gold over eye and around rear of ear-coverts; narrow red band on breast, green-blue to blue-green on lower breast. Immature shows dull or partial colouring of adult of respective sex, eyes brown. Races differ mainly in throat and malar colours of male, and in amount and intensity of orange around ear-coverts and tone of breast colour of female: male *glaucogularis* with red upper throat, blue mid-throat, orangey lower throat, yellow malar; male *steeri* with middle and lower throat yellow, yellow malar, no breastband, female more yellow-crowned. Voice. Song a fast, low-pitched trill c. 2 seconds long at c. 30 notes per second, given 3-5 times per minute, resembles that of allopatric *E. bourcierii*, also somewhat that of *Capito brunneipectus*.
Habitat. Submontane humid forest with prominent epiphytes and mosses, also old secondary forest, less often in Bolivian dry forest; occurs at 675-2225 m, more usually at 1000-2000 m.
Food and Feeding. Diverse fruits and their seeds c. 80% of diet; also takes beetles and other arthropods, mainly by poking and tearing at clusters of dead leaves. Usually solitary or in pairs, sometimes in company of mixed feeding flocks.
Breeding. All facets essentially unknown. Data from specimens suggest season Jul-Dec. Apparently territorial in pairs; male sings regularly.
Movements. Probably sedentary.
Status and Conservation. Not globally threatened. Very little known, and virtually nothing known of its breeding habits and requirements. Considered uncommon in Peru. Conservation status may need to be reassessed in view of paucity of data; possible that distinct populations could come under threat. Race *steerii*, the most distinctive of the three subspecies, is a candidate for special monitoring.
Bibliography. Anon. (1995a), Berlepsch & Stolzmann (1906), Bond (1954), Bond & Meyer de Schauensee (1943), Chapman (1921b), Clements & Shany (2001), Davies *et al.* (1994), Hornbuckle (1999), Meyer de Schauensee (1966, 1982), Olrog (1968), Parker & Bailey (1991), Parker *et al.* (1982), Perry *et al.* (1997), Remsen & Parker (1984a), Remsen & Traylor (1989), Remsen *et al.* (1993), Stotz *et al.* (1996), Traylor (1951b), Zimmer (1930).

Subfamily SEMNORNITHINAE

Genus *SEMNORNIS* Richmond, 1900

81. **Prong-billed Barbet**

Semnornis frantzii

French: Cabézon de Frantzius **German**: Aztekenbartvogel **Spanish**: Cabezón Cocora

Taxonomy. *Tetragonops frantzii* P. L. Sclater, 1864, surrounds of San José, Costa Rica.
Relationship with *S. ramphastinus* suggested by bill morphology, but probably not very closely related. Monotypic.
Distribution. NC Costa Rica (Tilaran Range) S in mountains to W Panama (W Veraguas).

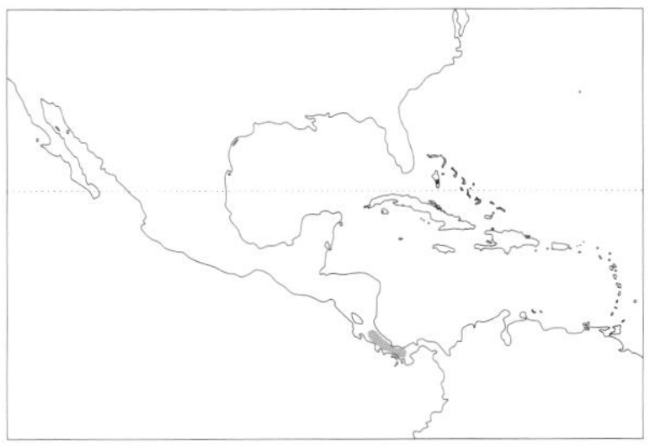

Descriptive notes. c. 18 cm; 55-72 g. Distinctive orangey brown-olive barbet with thick bill hooked and pronged. Male with black lores and chin, orange forecrown, elongated, shiny, erectile black nape feathers, brownish-olive upperparts; rest of head and down to breast dull orange, grey patch at side of breast, lower underparts olive-green, belly washed golden; orbital skin grey; bill short, thick, broad-based, grey, upper mandible with double prong, lower with small hook. Female lacks elongated black nape feathers, where tends to show grey. Immature greyer, has yellowish, larger orbital area, poorly developed bill prongs and notch. Voice. Song commonly heard, series of hollow "kaw" to "aw" notes at c. 5-6 per second for 10-50 seconds; sexes sometimes sing simultaneously, even duetting, male for longer and at lower pitch; calls include rattles, cackling alarm notes, "skurr" and "kwaaah" aggressive notes, grating, and "tchuk" calls; nestlings squeak sharply.
Habitat. Wet montane forest, edges, trees in clearings, and well-developed second growth. Extreme altitude limits 500-2740 m, mostly 1200-2200 m; in Costa Rica most common at 1500-1800 m. Roosts in group, sometimes several groups in 1 cavity, up to 19 birds in 1 hole.
Food and Feeding. Fruits from over 20 families of trees, shrubs and epiphytes, such as *Ficus*, and species of *Clusia*, *Guettarda*, *Malaviscus*, *Micronia*, *Ocotea*, *Ossaea*, *Rubus* and *Symplocarpon*, also nectar and some flowers; some insects taken, mostly when feeding young nestlings. Eats whole fruits, breaks fruits or squeezes berries, swallowing juices, discarding rest. Forages in groups of up to 5, or singly.
Breeding. Groups break up Feb-Mar, egg-laying Mar-Jun. Nests in territorial pairs, with much singing, countersinging, duetting. Cavity excavated at 3-18 m in tree. Eggs 4-5; parents roost in nest, share incubation, cover eggs over 80% of daytime, incubation period 14-15 days; both adults feed and brood chicks, remove faecal material with wood chips, excavating more to provide needed chips; nestling period unknown; fledglings roost in nest with parents, forage together in group.
Movements. None reported, presumably sedentary.
Status and Conservation. Not globally threatened. Restricted-range species: present in Costa Rica and Panama Highlands EBA. Often common in limited range, occurs in various parks and reserves in some numbers, e.g. Tapantí National Park and Monteverde Biological Reserve (Costa Rica); tame, generally confiding. No known threats.
Bibliography. Anon. (1998b), Berlioz (1937), Blake, E.R. (1958), Blake, J.G. & Loiselle (2000), Delgado (1985), Fogden (1993), Murray (1988), Nadkarni & Matelson (1989), Remsen *et al.* (1993), Ridgely & Gwynne (1989), Ridgway (1914), Skutch (1944b, 1980, 1983, 1987, 1989), Slud (1964), Stattersfield *et al.* (1998), Stiles (1983, 1985), Stiles & Skutch (1989), Stotz *et al.* (1996), Wetmore (1968a), Wheelwright *et al.* (1984), Young *et al.* (1998).

82. **Toucan-barbet**

Semnornis ramphastinus

French: Cabézon toucan **German**: Tukanbartvogel **Spanish**: Cabezón Tucán
Other common names: Toucan-billed Barbet

Taxonomy. *Tetragonops ramphastinus* Jardine, 1855, between Quito and Mount Cayambe, in east Ecuadorian Andes.
Related to *S. frantzii*, with which it shares distinctive bill morphology, but relationship not very close. Races poorly defined. Two subspecies currently recognized.
Subspecies and Distribution.
S. r. caucae Gyldenstolpe, 1941 - W Colombia on both slopes of W Andes, from Valle to Nariño.
S. r. ramphastinus (Jardine, 1855) - Andes of NW & WC Ecuador.

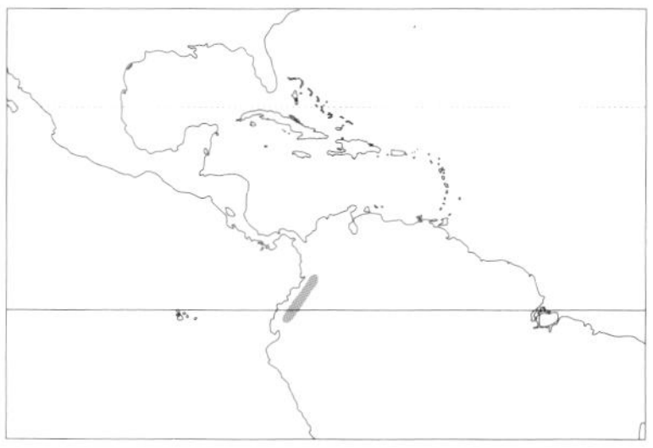

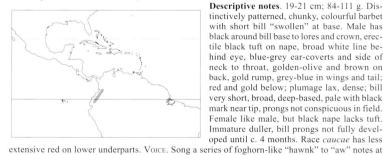

Descriptive notes. 19-21 cm; 84-111 g. Distinctively patterned, chunky, colourful barbet with short bill "swollen" at base. Male has black around bill base to lores and crown, erectile black tuft on nape, broad white line behind eye, blue-grey ear-coverts and side of neck to throat, golden-olive and brown on back, gold rump, grey-blue in wings and tail; red and gold below; plumage lax, dense; bill very short, broad, deep-based, pale with black mark near tip, prongs not conspicuous in field. Female like male, but black nape lacks tuft. Immature duller, bill prongs not fully developed until c. 4 months. Race *caucae* has less extensive red on lower underparts. Voice. Song a series of foghorn-like "hawnk" to "aw" notes at 1·5-2·5 per second for up to 3 minutes, often by pair-members simultaneously, male at lower pitch and often starting and ending "duets"; clicks bill, often in notes starting song; in addition to snapping-clicking bill sounds, gives clicking calls with bill snaps in them, "bbrripp", at 1-2 per second; also "gkaa", "caw", rattle and chatter notes, "kawk" notes, purring, and "kyak" contact notes. Wings flop and rustle noisily during interactions.
Habitat. Inhabits understorey of wet montane forest, especially at edges and in dense second growth, including low bushy secondary forest with scattered tall trees; also found in overgrown pastures, and feeds in isolated pasture trees. Mainly occurs at 1000-2000 m, but reaches 2400 m in some areas.
Food and Feeding. Fruits of at least 62 species of some 20 plant families, mostly of species found in disturbed areas, and including especially *Cecropia* and *Clusia*, but others of the Melastomataceae, Moracaceae and Guttiferae also taken; termites and other insects eaten, more so than fruits in Apr. Nestling diet c. 54% fruits, 40% insects, 6% parts of flowers, fungi and vertebrates. Forages at 1-30 m in groups of up to 6. Hops and climbs about, gleaning. Forages for c. 12 hrs of day, at up to c. 270 m from roosting site. Joins mixed-species foraging flocks of flycatchers (Tyrannidae), tanagers (Thraupidae) and warblers (Parulidae).
Breeding. Feb-Oct; sometimes 2 or even 3 broods in a season. Group often breaks up at start of breeding; c. 42% nest in pairs, remainder in trios or quartets, but breeding apparently by primary pair only. Much duetting, where species common also much countersinging; probable male cocks tail, fluffs breast, spreads white supercilia. Nest excavated low in dead tree, often *Nectandra* or *Ocotea*, average height above ground 1·5 m in tree with breast-height diameter c. 0.38 m; new cavity excavated yearly, often in same tree as in previous year; territory c. 4-11 ha in SW Colombia. Eggs probably 2-3, mean clutch size c. 1·4; any helpers share incubation, and brooding and

feeding of young; incubation period c. 15 days; fledging 43-46 days; males disperse at c. 308 days of age, females at c. 273 days, juveniles sometimes remain as helpers in following season, older helpers driven away by pair at start of breeding. Success variable: 1 or 2 young fledge in wild, mean 1·3, in captivity sometimes 3; success of first broods higher for pairs with helpers than for those without, but that of subsequent broods equal with or without; some nests lost to falling of stub, also sometimes taken over by Plate-billed Mountain-toucan (*Andigena laminirostris*). Earliest first age of breeding 1·56 years (570 days).

Movements. Resident; sedentary, dispersal averages only 0·5 km.

Status and Conservation. Not globally threatened. CITES III. Currently considered Near-threatened. Restricted-range species: present in Chocó EBA. Generally uncommon to locally common within the c. 20,000 km² area of its range; nests have been found only 270 m apart. Surveys of La Planada Nature Reserve (SW Colombia) in late 1980's, extrapolated to rest of range, suggested total numbers for entire range of c. 73,000 birds. Main problem is taking of birds for cagebird trade, as well as by local people for pets, this being a major threat in some areas; habitat loss is also a potential problem, with forest destruction rampant in most of range, but species appears to be adaptable, and where not molested occupies secondary thickets and dense growth with scattered trees around gardens. Controlling the illegal taking of birds is considered essential if this species is to be adequately protected. Present in several protected areas, e.g. La Planada Nature Reserve and Río Ñambí Natural Reserve (Colombia).

Bibliography. Allen (1998), Álvarez-López (1989), Berlioz (1937), Best *et al*. (1997), Bloch *et al*. (1991), Butler (1979), Chapman (1917, 1926), Collar & Andrew (1988), Donegan & Dávalos (1999), Fjeldså & Krabbe (1990), Gyldenstolpe (1941a), Hellmayr (1911), Hilty (1985), Hilty & Brown (1986), King (1978/79), María & Olivares (1967), Meyer de Schauensee (1949, 1964, 1966), Remsen *et al*. (1993), Renjifo *et al*. (1997), Restrepo (1990), Restrepo & Beltrán (1989), Restrepo & Mondragón (1988, 1998), Ridgely & Greenfield (2001), Rutgers & Norris (1977), Salaman (1994), Sherbourne (1996), Stattersfield & Capper (2000), Stattersfield *et al*. (1998), Stotz *et al*. (1996), Strewe (2000b), Ward (1972b), Welford (2000).

Class AVES
Order PICIFORMES
Family RAMPHASTIDAE (TOUCANS)

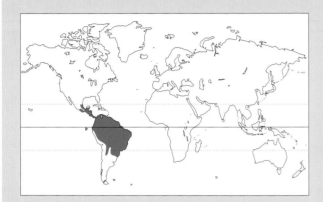

- Medium-sized to large, colourful arboreal birds with huge bill and long tail.
- 30-61 cm.

- Neotropical, with greatest diversity in Amazonia.
- Tropical forest, mostly in lowlands, but reaching temperate zone in mountains; one species ranges into woodland.
- 6 genera, 34 species, 78 taxa.
- 1 species threatened; none extinct since 1600.

Systematics

The toucans that comprise the family Ramphastidae have long intrigued biologists and travellers. Because of the uniquely serrated bill tomia, a characteristic of all toucans, and probably owing to the length of the bill, too, eighteenth-century European scientists initially thought that the toucans' diet was of fish that the birds themselves caught. Toucans are "flagship" species, well known and recognizable representatives of the Neotropical forest.

According to E. Höfling's investigations, the toucans are remarkably uniform morphologically, while S. J. H. Hackett and C. A. Lehn found that, at the genus level, the araçaris (*Pteroglossus*), for example, constitute a group of species that are genetically much alike. With more species on their single continent than the somewhat similar but unrelated hornbills (Bucerotidae) have in either the Afrotropics or tropical Asia, toucans have evolved into an ample range of medium-sized to large frugivores. Their overall uniformity, along with many unique features in which they have diverged from their original barbet-like ancestor, argues for their systematic treatment as a family apart from the closely related barbets (Capitonidae): nobody could mistake a toucan for a barbet. There is universal agreement that the toucans share an ancestor in common with the American barbets. As C. G. Sibley and J. E. Ahlquist have noted, after the toucans branched from the line that gave rise to Neotropical barbets, the latter retained a barbet morphology; in other words, it was the toucans that diverged, acquired new, "toucan" features, and then diversified, giving rise to the present array of ramphastid species. Hence, it is considered inappropriate to follow the essentially cladistic classifications that either merge all the barbets within one family along with the toucans, as did R. O. Prum, or treat the Neotropical barbets and toucans together as one family separate from the Old World barbets, as did Sibley and Ahlquist, and Sibley and B. L. Monroe. These other modes of classifying the toucans should be viewed as provisional, and limited in considering points of branching, while ignoring the divergence of the toucans from the barbets.

P. J. K. Burton, who investigated features of the feeding apparatus and skull, treated the toucans as a family, which he placed immediately after the barbets and preceding the honeyguides (Indicatoridae) and the woodpeckers (Picidae). Prum tabulated some morphological, behavioural and other natural-history features and, on the basis of their supposed or real derived states, placed all barbets and toucans in the family

Ramphastidae, preceding the Indicatoridae and the Picidae. Within the Ramphastidae, he arranged the barbets in six subfamilies, followed by a single subfamily of toucans. Sibley and Ahlquist, followed by Sibley and Monroe, studied DNA-DNA hybridization in the Piciformes, and, using these results and some morphological and other traits, came up with a piciform provisional classification in which the honeyguides and the woodpeckers are families, in that sequence, in the infraorder Picides, followed by an infraorder Ramphastides. The latter contains, first, two superfamilies, each with one family of Old World barbets, and then a third superfamily, Ramphastoidea, comprising a single family in which the Neotropical barbets

The toucans are quite uniform morphologically, with rather few taxonomic subdivisions, and the species within these tending to be quite closely related. In the current classification, the Ramphastidae are grouped into six genera, although the Curl-crested Araçari has sometimes been placed in a seventh, Beauharnaisius, *on the basis of its unique characteristics, primarily its "permed and lacquered" head feathers, and its atypical voice. This species inhabits humid forests in Amazonian Brazil and the eastern lowlands of Peru and Bolivia.*

[*Pteroglossus beauharnaesii.* Photo: Frank W. Lane/ FLPA]

The number of species recognized within the Ramphastidae varies widely depending on which taxonomic viewpoint is assumed. The 34 species recognized here include many distinct subspecies that are sometimes separated at the species level. The Channel-billed Toucan, for example, includes the forms vitellinus, culminatus, ariel and citreolaemus, four taxa that differ conspicuously in the colour of their bills and plumage, but which intergrade freely along their contact zones, producing hybrids that have themselves been described as separate taxa in the past.

[Ramphastos vitellinus citreolaemus, near Cartagena, Colombia. Photo: Art Wolfe]

are placed in one subfamily and the toucans, as the final taxon, in the subfamily Ramphastinae.

Nevertheless, it may be considered better, at least for the time being, to follow the classical arrangement of the toucans amid the barbets, honeyguides and woodpeckers, treating these in four separate families. Thus, the barbets together form the family Capitonidae, followed by the toucans as the Ramphastidae, then the honeyguides in the Indicatoridae, and ending with the woodpeckers in the family Picidae. The traits of the toucans, including their specialized features, are discussed below (see Morphological Aspects).

Fossil toucans are few, and do not go back beyond the Pleistocene. They are therefore, so far, not of much help to systematists.

The morphological uniformity within the Ramphastidae is such that the subdivision of the family into genera is considered sufficient, and recognition of a higher category such as subfamily or tribe is unwarranted. The six genera are closely interrelated, but can be characterized as follows. The green toucanets comprise the genus *Aulacorhynchus*, in which there are six species that tend to occur in montane forest, from Mexico to Bolivia. E. V. Swierczewski and R. J. Raikow used several muscle and tendon conditions to set them apart from at least the genera *Pteroglossus* and *Ramphastos*. The species of *Aulacorhynchus* are relatively small, as their vernacular name toucanet suggests, and they have a long, graduated tail and a more or less typical, long bill that is rather broader at its base than is the case with other toucans. They often have grooves in the bill surface and chestnut tips of the tail. Cytochrome studies by F. K. Barker and S. M. Lanyon suggest that *Aulacorhynchus* comprises a clade with the genera *Andigena* and *Selenidera*. *Aulacorhynchus* is morphologically and behaviourally a toucan, with no particular barbet-type features. The green toucanets are closely similar to one another, and, as P. Schwartz noted, their vocalizations are generally similar. Most are allopatric in their distribution, some replacing each other altitudinally, and all are alike sexually, except that males have a longer, usually distinctly longer, bill than that of the females. Five of the six species were illustrated by J. Gould, in 1854, in his gorgeous portrayal of the family. These

toucanets seem to fall into two groups. The Emerald Toucanet (*Aulacorhynchus prasinus*) along with the superspecies formed by the Groove-billed (*Aulacorhynchus sulcatus*) and the Chestnut-tipped Toucanets (*Aulacorhynchus derbianus*) represents one group, the other being the red-rumped group of a single superspecies comprised of the Crimson-rumped (*Aulacorhynchus haematopygus*), Yellow-browed (*Aulacorhynchus huallagae*) and Blue-banded Toucanets (*Aulacorhynchus coeruleicinctis*). Some sympatry occurs between species of the two groups, but, within either group, there is only a limited degree of range overlap between species, this being exhibited by the Emerald and Groove-billed Toucanets.

The genus *Selenidera*, also with six species, inhabits lowland forest of Amazonia and the Atlantic forest of south-east Brazil and adjacent areas, except that the Yellow-eared Toucanet (*Selenidera spectabilis*) occupies mountain forest from Honduras to north-western South America. These are, with *Aulacorhynchus*, the smallest of the toucans. They have distinctive muscle features, and exhibit sexually dimorphic plumages of a type that is all but unique within the Piciformes, being shared with a couple of araçaris. They are strictly forest toucans, and prefer forest with a well-developed middle storey. Five species have chestnut tips of the tail, and all have fluffy red undertail-coverts used in displays that closely resemble those of species of *Andigena*. Yellow, orange or tawny ear-covert tufts, and a flank patch, as well as a yellow collar, are characteristics of most of these species. The males are black about the head and foreparts, where females are rufous or chestnut to grey. Three paler-eyed species show horizontally slit-like eyes resulting from dark marks on the iris, before and behind the pupil. All of the species replace each other geographically, and J. Haffer considered all six of them to form a superspecies. The Guianan Toucan (*Selenidera culik*) of north-eastern South America and the montane Yellow-eared Toucanet, however, exhibit certain differences from the other four that would appear to set them apart. The Tawny-tufted (*Selenidera nattereri*), Gold-collared (*Selenidera reinwardtii*), Gould's (*Selenidera gouldii*) and Spot-billed Toucanets (*Selenidera maculirostris*) have nearly identical songs and accompanying displays; they replace

The seven members of the genus Ramphastos, *with piebald plumage and a huge, brightly coloured bill, epitomize the toucan that is widely popularized through art and advertising. Of these, it is the Toco Toucan that is the most familiar. This is the largest member of the family, with a loud call and an enormous bill; moreover, it is seen more frequently than other Ramphastidae across much of its range because it is not tied to forest, often living in quite open habitat near gallery or* cerrado *woodlands.*

[*Ramphastos toco albogularis*,
Iguazú National Park,
Argentina.
Photo: Günter Ziesler]

each other around north-western to south-eastern Amazonia and in the Atlantic forest region, and are treated as a superspecies. All but one of the *Selenidera* species were shown in Gould's monograph.

Andigena, the mountain-toucan group of four large, montane forest toucans, occurs along the Andes from Colombia and Venezuela to Bolivia. Its members have a dense, lax plumage and a broader-based, less deep long bill than do other large toucans. They are rather like *Selenidera* in their red undertail-coverts, displays and chestnut tipping of the graduated tail, which is, however, longer than in *Selenidera*. Instead of having a bill pattern of long horizontal marks and lateral spots as in the above genera, these flashy, dark toucans have patchy marks and bright splotches on the bill. The sexes are alike in plumage. Their loud, long songs include the longest notes of any piciform so far recorded. The Grey-breasted (*Andigena hypoglauca*), the Hooded (*Andigena cucullata*) and the Plate-billed Mountain-toucans (*Andigena laminirostris*) replace one another geographically and are thought to form a superspecies. The Black-billed Mountain-toucan (*Andigena nigrirostris*) of the northern Andes has a duller bill and overlaps somewhat with the Grey-breasted Mountain-toucan. Gould's monograph has accounts and illustrations of all four of these spectacular toucans.

Because of its rather soft, fluffy plumage, the Saffron Toucanet (*Baillonius bailloni*) was placed by Gould in the genus *Andigena*, but this is a mainly lowland toucan of the Atlantic forest region, and its nearest relationships appear to be with *Pteroglossus*. Its yellow and green plumage, unmarked except for a red rump, is not particularly *Pteroglossus*-like, nor are its red, yellow and green to brown bill and its red facial skin. In view of its evident differences from other toucans, the Saffron Toucanet is accorded its own monotypic genus. It has many vocalizations, among which the song calls to mind that of the Ivory-billed Araçari (*Pteroglossus azara*). Its graduated tail is, in relation to the bird's total size, the longest in its family. The female is more dully coloured overall than is the male, as well as having a shorter bill.

Ten species of araçari make up the genus *Pteroglossus*, characterized by "clown-like" patterns and colours. These have a long, brightly marked bill, hooked at the tip, and a long, gradu-

ated tail. Sexual dimorphism in two species resembles that exhibited by the *Selenidera* toucanets, and several more show slight aspects of this pattern in their nape and neck colours. The slit-like eye of several *Selenidera* species is suggested, or occurs fully, in three species of *Pteroglossus*. All but two of the ten species are banded yellow, red and/or black below, although the black/red breastband is reduced to a spot in two. Hard, shiny black, curly, modified head feathers distinguish the Curl-crested Araçari (*Pteroglossus beauharnaesii*). The Green (*Pteroglossus viridis*), the Lettered (*Pteroglossus inscriptus*), the Red-necked (*Pteroglossus bitorquatus*) and the Ivory-billed Araçaris seem to form a natural group of less banded, smaller species, and there appear to be no definite grounds for recognizing any superspecies among them, although the first two could possibly be close enough to be treated as such. Another species group is represented by five colourful araçaris, namely, the Collared Araçari (*Pteroglossus torquatus*), the Fiery-billed Araçari (*Pteroglossus frantzii*), the Black-necked Araçari (*Pteroglossus aracari*), the Chestnut-eared Araçari (*Pteroglossus castanotis*) and the Many-banded Araçari (*Pteroglossus pluricinctus*). Within this group, the Collared and Fiery-billed Araçaris form a superspecies, as do the Black-necked and the Chestnut-eared. All five have a nearly identical, piercing "pseeet" call given in irregular, sometimes staccato bursts. The Curl-crested Araçari stands apart from these. Generally, the araçaris are lowland-forest species, some favouring riverine situations, but they can extend into hill forest and submontane situations. They occur from Mexico to Paraguay. Gould discussed and illustrated nine of these *Pteroglossus* species, and a number of subspecies of several of them.

For most people, the seven species of the genus *Ramphastos* represent the typical, classic image of a toucan. All are black above, with a white, yellow or red throat to breast, more or less square, short tail, red undertail-coverts, and white or yellow to red uppertail-coverts. These large toucans have a deep, long, variably coloured bill. Anatomical characters are associated with the external nostrils, which, in adults, are hidden beneath the base of the bill. The facial skin and areas around the eye are brightly coloured. All have emarginated, club-shaped tips of the outer two primaries. There is no sexual dimorphism in plumage, but males

When the first specimens of toucans reached Europe in the eighteenth century it was hypothesized that their diet consisted of fish which the bird caught with its long, serrated bill. Looking at the impressive mandibles of this Green Araçari, it is easy to understand why this mistake was made, although the serrations seem to run the wrong way for capturing slippery fish! The long and curiously serrated bill and the strange feathered tongue are adaptations to frugivory, tools that allow the toucan to pluck, manipulate and consume arboreal fruit. Although it looks very heavy, the bill is in fact extremely light, being essentially hollow with thin bony struts for structural support. Pteroglossus araçaris have bills that are more distinctly hooked at the tip than in other members of the family. Their plumage is usually vividly patterned in red, yellow and black, and their tails are long and graduated.

[Pteroglossus viridis. Photo: Chuck Dresner/ DRK Photo]

usually have a longer bill. Five of the seven species, often termed the "croakers", repeat a single "eeark"-like note in short to long series. These are the Red-breasted (*Ramphastos dicolorus*), the Rainbow-billed (*Ramphastos sulfuratus*), the Choco (*Ramphastos brevis*), the Channel-billed (*Ramphastos vitellinus*) and the Toco Toucans (*Ramphastos toco*), and, according to Haffer and others, they appear to form a natural group. The White-throated Toucan (*Ramphastos tucanus*) and the Yellow-throated Toucan (*Ramphastos ambiguus*) "sing" by using yelping, phrased notes, and these two seem to represent a separate group. There exists what could be seen almost as mimicry in bill and plumage colour patterns between the groups, as demonstrated by the Choco and Yellow-throated Toucans, and the Channel-billed (in part) and White-throated Toucans. In addition, the upperparts of the Rainbow-billed and Choco Toucans, in the first group, and the Yellow-throated Toucan, in the second, are tinted maroon on black. In terms of geographical distribution, the two groups show a large degree of sympatry, whereas the species within either one of the groups do not in general overlap in range with others of the same group. The single exception is the huge Toco Toucan, the only woodland-riverine member of the genus, which overlaps with two species of its own group, the Red-breasted and Channel-billed Toucans, as well as with the White-throated Toucan. The *Ramphastos* species generally are lowland toucans of forest habitats, ranging from Mexico to Argentina, and rarely ascending to 1600-1800 m in Andean valleys. Gould treated and illustrated all seven species and major subspecies of these toucans in his 1854 monograph.

The approach to systematics of species adopted here is that of an evolutionary biologist employing the biological species concept, as discussed by D. Amadon and L. L. Short in 1992, and by Haffer in 1995 and 1997. As pointed out by D. W. Snow, this has served science well, and, indeed, it has been argued by N. J. Collar that it seems the best system when it comes to treating matters of conservation. Tactics include the utilization of data provided at points where taxa in question meet "on the ground", as well as inferences drawn from known, closely related biologi-

cal species that reveal their specific status by co-existing sympatrically without interbreeding. Hybridization with back-crossing can be regarded as a potentially positive evolutionary factor, and not as wholly negative.

Among possible incipient species that some might consider as full species are no fewer than six races of the Emerald Toucanet. The Mexican subspecies *wagleri* differs in several minor features of the bill and in the colour of the crown and forehead, but is otherwise like the nominate race, including in its voice and in the colours of its facial and orbital areas and its eye. The others are *caeruleogularis*, possibly including the form *cognatus*, of Costa Rica to northern Colombia, which has a blue-violet throat; white-throated *albivitta* of north-western South America; grey-throated *phaeolaemus*, which appears to intergrade with the races *albivitta*, *griseigularis* and *cyanolaemus*; blue-throated *cyanolaemus* of north-eastern Peru and eastern Ecuador, which seems to intergrade to the south with *atrogularis*; and the black-throated *atrogularis* and, possibly, *dimidiatus* of eastern Andean slopes in Peru to Bolivia, and nearby lowlands. All of these forms of the Emerald Toucanet share a yellow, black and chestnut bill and certain plumage features, as well as vocalizations, with other conspecific races. None is as distinct as is the subspecies *calorhynchus* of the Groove-billed Toucanet, which is sympatric with at least two races of the Emerald Toucanet, from which it differs in voice, in lacking rusty tail-tips and undertail, and in the structure, if not the colour, of its bill.

The subspecies *calorhynchus* is the only form of any species of *Aulacorhynchus*, other than races of Emerald Toucanet, to have a black and yellow bill. It is sometimes considered a full species, but Schwartz showed it to be like other races of the Groove-billed Toucanet in voice, and it intergrades with the nominate race of that species where the ranges of the two approach one another. In plumage features and in bill structure and pattern, *calorhynchus* closely resembles the other subspecies of the Groove-billed Toucanet.

The two subspecies of the Gold-collared Toucanet of western Amazonia are considered separate species by some cladists.

The epicentre of toucan diversity is Amazonia. They are characteristic birds of tall humid forests throughout much of South and Central America. Members of the genus Ramphastos, *like these* Channel-billed Toucans, *are largely confined to the canopy of lowland rainforest, most of them venturing no further than the foothills. Indeed, many are so closely adapted to continuous forest habitat that they gradually lose height when flying over long distances. This means that wide rivers pose an effective barrier to their dispersal, and the ranges of many species and subspecies in the family are divided by the Amazon or its tributaries. For the same reason, very few islands are inhabited by toucans.*

[Ramphastos vitellinus culminatus, east of River Branco, Amazonian Brazil. Photo: Nick Gordon/ BBC Natural History Unit]

As their name suggests, the four species of mountain-toucan are adapted to montane forest, and in this respect they are almost unique within the family. This Grey-breasted Mountain-toucan is pictured here in its native habitat: smaller stature epiphyte-laden cloudforest. The species often occurs in clamorous groups and has been seen up to 3650 m above sea-level. It is regularly found right at the tree-line, on the edge of open páramo.

[Andigena hypoglauca lateralis, Shintuya road, Peru. Photo: R. S. Ridgely/ VIREO]

The nominate race and the southern *langsdorffii* differ essentially in bill colours, but intergrade in the upper Ucayali and Huallaga Valleys of north-central Peru. They are otherwise almost indistinguishable, and have the same songs and accompanying displays, which are, moreover, so like those of Gould's and the Spot-billed Toucanets, as well as those of the Tawny-tufted Toucanet, that these might perhaps be treated as conspecific. The four species replace one another around Amazonia, and share in detail the colour markings used in their displays.

Among the araçaris, the two races of the Lettered Araçari, east Amazonian nominate *inscriptus* and west Amazonian *humboldti*, are sometimes treated as specifically distinct. Western *humboldti* is larger, has a somewhat different but still "inscripted" bill pattern, and has a red mouth-lining, the latter being black in the nominate race. The two seem to be vocally indistinguishable. Although separated by the Madeira River, they cross it occasionally, or "island capture" may move numbers from one side to the other; in any case, hybrids occur sporadically, and their differences seem not so great as those that exist among related, sympatric species in this group. Indeed, the form *olallae*, described from the Rio Juruá itself, and regarded initially as a full species, was found to be a presumably rare hybrid between the race *humboldti* of the Lettered Araçari and the broadly sympatric race *mariae* of the Ivory-billed Araçari. Large southern Amazonian rivers likewise separate perhaps incipient species of the Red-necked Araçari, the Tocantins River separating *bitorquatus* to the east and *reichenowi* west of it to the Tapajós River, which further separates the latter from the race *sturmii*, which occurs westwards to the Madeira River. These populations differ mainly in bill coloration, and a few other traits. Unfortunately, few series of specimens are available that might show what happens in places where they meet in, as Haffer noted, the upper reaches of these rivers; assuming that suitable habitats exist, they may meet where the rivers are narrower and less of a barrier. A few museum collections reveal that hybrids occur, as in the Cururu Valley of the upper Rio Tapajós, between the forms *reichenowi* and *sturmii*. The differences between these various populations seem not to be significant enough for them to be accorded species status. Similarly, the Ivory-billed Araçari has three subspecies which are treated by some authorities as species, and which differ essentially in bill markings, but not by very much. These are the nominate race, inhabiting the region between the lower Rio Negro and the Amazon River, *flavirostris* of north-western Amazonia, and *mariae* of south-western Amazonia. The nominate race interbreeds across the Amazon with *mariae*, and up the Rio Negro with *flavirostris*, while the latter interbreeds with *mariae* both across the Amazon-Solimões River and around the Rio Marañon in northern Peru. It seems impossible to accept these subspecies as biological species. In fact, by designating all the above races as full species one would eliminate all subspecies in these taxa.

In the "higher" *Pteroglossi*, no valid evidence of hybridization between the Black-necked and Chestnut-eared Araçaris has been found, their ranges being essentially parapatric, with only occasional, local sympatry. A single hybrid between the Many-banded and the Black-necked Araçaris is known from Carapo, on the Paragua River, Venezuela, but no real significance can be attached to this, other than noting the particularly close relationship among these three members of the "Collared Araçari group". That group also includes the Fiery-billed Araçari, which is, with some hesitation, accepted here as a full species, separate from the Collared Araçari; the two do not come into direct contact except casually, and a single hybrid is known from Aranjuez, near the Gulf of Nicoya, in Costa Rica. On the other hand, there appears to be no good reason to elevate to species status the two north-western South American forms of the Collared Araçari, *erythropygius* and *sanguineus*. These are closely similar to each other, differing only in bill colour, and a case might be made for treating the two as forming a single species, separate from the Collared, but they differ less markedly from the latter than does the Fiery-billed Araçari, and, as Haffer has clearly shown, the race *sanguineus* intergrades with the nominate race of the Collared in the region from easternmost Panama to north-western Colombia. It can be added here that *sanguineus* and *erythropygius* interbreed in south-west Colombia and north-west Ecuador; the two converge in bill pattern and colours, and examination of a series of six specimens from Gualea, in Ecuador, revealed that all were hybrids. In terms of their vocalizations, these races are alike, and resemble the nominate race of the Collared Araçari. It is worth noting that the Fiery-billed Araçari, with its fine bill serrations, strongly different bill pattern, broader, more red belly-band and, probably, longer call notes, differs more from the *torquatus* group of races than does either *sanguineus* or *erythropygius*. All of these, including the Fiery-billed, may end up being treated as conspecific when further studies have provided additional data.

Among the toucans of the genus *Ramphastos*, there are three species with distinctive subspecies that some scientists would regard as full species. The Channel-billed Toucan has four well-marked subspecies: nominate *vitellinus* of north-eastern South America north of the Amazon; *citreolaemus* of north-east Colombia to north-west Venezuela; *culminatus* of all of western Amazonia; and *ariel* of south-eastern Amazonia to south-east Brazil. All four have essentially identical vocalizations, and differ in the colours of the bill, bare parts, breast and belly. The subspecies *culminatus* interbreeds with *citreolaemus* in Venezuela, and toucans from the eastern half of the latter's range appear to be essentially all hybrids. Furthermore, *culminatus* intergrades with *vitellinus* across northern Amazonia, from Venezuela to north-central Brazil. To the south of the Amazon, *culminatus* intergrades with *ariel* along that river and between Rondônia and Bolivia, as well as, in the east, between Piauí and São Paulo, a vast area with large populations of apparent hybrids, some of which bear names, such as "*berliozi*" for *vitellinus* × *culminatus*, and "*osculans*", "*theresae*" and "*pintoi*" for *culminatus* × *ariel*. There is no allopatry of these subspecies other than that of *vitellinus* and *ariel*, which are separated by the lower Amazon; they have long interbred where they meet, and it is now quite impossible to draw geographical boundaries between them. Introgression, impeded by rivers and currently by some deforested habitats, affects even extreme populations in Peru, Roraima and Minas Gerais.

The White-throated Toucan is larger than the Channel-billed. Rivers pose less of a barrier to it, and it is more mobile. Its nominate race, which extends from eastern Amazonia to the Guianas, eastern Venezuela and northern Maranhão, includes a morph with an orange-red bill that was once considered a different species, under the name "*Ramphastos erythrorhynchus*" or "*R. aurantiirostris*". The western Amazonian race *cuvieri*, occurring from western Venezuela to the fringe of northern Bolivia, is sometimes treated as specifically distinct from the nominate race. These two, however, show fewer differences from each other than do the races of the Channel-billed Toucan, differing mainly in lateral bill colour and in the colour of the uppertail-coverts. Variably intermediate populations occur in a large area from southern Venezuela to Mato Grosso and Goias, and from the Rio Solimões and Rondônia east to Para, connecting the "pure" parental populations of the far west and the far east. The subspecies *inca* of much of central Bolivia seems to represent a semi-stabilized hybrid population that is closest to *cuvieri*, but with a chestnut-red basal patch on each side of the bill, and redder uppertail-coverts than in either of the above forms. Since intermediates constitute a huge population that both separates and connects the parental taxa, *R. tucanus* is best treated as but one biological species.

Finally, the Yellow-throated Toucan comprises three races, one of which, *swainsonii* of Honduras to north-western South America as far as south-west Ecuador, has been considered specifically distinct from nominate *ambiguus* of the eastern Andes from Colombia to Peru, despite their very close similarity. Compared with the nominate race, *swainsonii* differs in having the sides of the bill less black and more chestnut-red in colour, though sometimes black at the edges, although the black bill of the nominate race sometimes has chestnut near its base. The facial-orbital colour of *swainsonii* is yellow-green to greenish-yellow, but overlapping to a degree with nominate *ambiguus*, in which the colour is blue or pale green or yellow-green. The eyes of *swainsonii* are yellow-green to brown, but with variants showing white, or partly pure green or partly yellow eyes, whereas those of the nominate race are normally grey-brown, green-brown or blue-brown, but vary to yellow and to grey. In view of the variation in these characters, the differences may

be regarded as trivial. There also is the race *abbreviatus* of north-east Colombia and northern Venezuela, with a bill coloration like that of nominate *ambiguus*, but with the face colour as in *swainsonii*. Suggestive evidence of interbreeding between *ambiguus* and *swainsonii* is presented by old specimens from the Cauca Valley, in western Colombia, in addition to which the two forms have the same distinctive song phrases. It should be noted that the traditional separation of *ambiguus* from *swainsonii* has its basis in the fact that the Choco Toucan was for a long period regarded as a race of *R. ambiguus*, being sympatric with *swainsonii*. Only with the realization that the Choco Toucan is, in fact, a distinct species was it possible to recognize the allopatry of *ambiguus* and *swainsonii*, and their very close relationship, as Haffer has demonstrated.

Such taxa as those outlined above, through their population interactions, prove or negate their status as species either by coming to co-exist in sympatry without interbreeding, or by interbreeding with more or less free, but, of course, ecologically conditioned, gene flow. Thus, they demonstrate what they are, if habitat conditions allow them to meet. If not, then it is necessary to study aspects of their behaviour, including vocalizations, and their ecology that will allow some conclusions to be drawn as to their likely interactions were they to meet.

Morphological Aspects

The long, deep and narrow bill, usually brightly coloured, and with small to large forward-facing serrations, or "teeth", is the hallmark of all toucans. The bill is also very light, with thin bony struts making for much space and little solid substance to the structure beneath its covering, or rhamphotheca. Unlike their relatives, the barbets, the toucans have the bill culmen curving downwards at its tip, often forming a hawk-like hook, and the gonys of the mandible is straight or, more usually, curves slightly downwards along its length, and definitely curves downwards at its tip. The base of the bill has a narrow to broad, thickened area around the sides to the nostrils, often indented forwards from the rear and surrounding the nostrils in front, and then reaching on to the culmen. This vertical base line is unique to the toucans, and is usually conspicuously coloured, often in contrast to the lateral-bill and culmen colours. In species of *Ramphastos*, the line is broad and includes the base of the culmen, the external nostrils having evolved to open backwards and upwards, underneath the rear edge of the top of the bill. This basal line develops slowly and is not present in juvenile toucans; the "teeth" and the patterning of the bill also develop slowly in young toucans. The bill of the large toucans is translucent, although that of the immatures is opaque. The colour patterns of toucans' bills are complex, with broad horizontal or angled marks, vertical bands and splotches, all multicoloured and unlike the patterns of other piciform bills.

Toucans lay their eggs in a natural cavity, or one constructed previously by woodpeckers, or occasionally barbets. Although they can "excavate" pieces of rotten wood from old cavities in very rotten stubs, this is a rare occurrence. The downcurved tip of the bill does not lend itself to excavation. In those pairs of Emerald Toucanets that attempt to create a cavity, it is usually the female, with the shorter and straighter bill, that excavates (see Breeding).

Toucans have a larger area of bare skin around the orbit, extending on to the face and to the lores and even the bill, than do the barbets. The skin and the eye are visible in frontal view, and are usually brightly coloured, even patterned. The iris of several pale-eyed species, of two genera, has dark areas to the front and rear of the dark pupil, sometimes referred to as a "glitch", the whole giving the appearance of a slit-eye, a feature not found in any other piciforms. The gular area of skin is of more or less the same colour as the face. Unlike the barbets, including all those of the Neotropics, the toucans lack bristles around the base of the bill.

The ramphastid tongue is extremely long, up to 14-15 cm, and is laminated along the sides and brush-like towards the tip. The fine villi in the breast feathers of toucans were found by T.

As with other cavity-nesting birds that cannot effectively excavate wood, the availability of mature trees with natural nest-sites is of paramount importance to the striking Rainbow-billed Toucan, and all other members of the family. Suitable cavities are produced where boughs have snapped from trunks of trees or where large woodpeckers have excavated their own nests. The infrequency of such nest-sites in young trees explains the paucity of toucans in secondary regrowth or heavily logged forest. Beyond this requirement the next important limiting factor on toucan numbers and distribution is food. A good supply of fruit is essential for breeding, while spatial and seasonal variations in fruit supply underlie distinct local migrations of toucans.

[*Ramphastos sulfuratus sulfuratus*, Calakmul, Campeche, Mexico. Photo: Patricio Robles Gil]

G. Brom to be more than twice as long as those of the barbets, and longer than in all birds otherwise examined. Other anatomical features of the toucans have been discussed, and compared with those of barbets, by Short and J. F. M. Horne. Höfling found the skull, including the palate and other bones, to be very much alike in all toucans, with various features unique to the family. One structural complex found only in the Ramphastidae involves the modification of nine tail vertebrae, their processes and the spines. The rear three vertebrae are fused, and attach to the others by a fluid-bearing ball-and-socket joint, giving toucans the ability to snap the tail forwards until it touches the head; sleeping toucans appear as a ball of feathers, with the tip of the tail sticking out over the crown. No barbet or any other piciform seems to have these novel specialities, or to sleep in this posture.

In contrast to the American barbets, most of which are distinctly sexually dimorphic, the majority of toucans do not show any sexual dimorphism in plumage and bare-part colours. Moreover, those toucans, mainly species of *Selenidera* and a few of *Pteroglossus*, with plumage differences between the sexes exhibit patterns of dimorphism that are unique to the Ramphastidae and do not resemble patterns found in other piciforms. Most toucans are strongly sexually dimorphic in the length, and thereby in the profile shape, of the bill. Males often have a bill 10% or more longer than that of females. The male bill appears longer and thinner, and the female bill generally seems shorter, deeper and more block-shaped. Such differences in bill size and shape are not evident in the barbets.

In their metabolism, toucans of a number of species show a strong and deadly tendency to store iron in the body, often leading to haematosis. Known by aviculturalists for some time, this unfortunate habit somewhat restricts the fruits that can be fed to them. Toucans die readily from this disease, otherwise unknown in piciform birds.

The flight of the larger toucans is somewhat undulating, with a series of flaps alternating with glides. The smaller species beat their wings faster and fly more directly, some araçaris appearing like bustling, buzzy auklets (*Aethia*) in flight. Generally, when crossing any open areas, toucans fly across one by one, each waiting for the one ahead to get to a tree before taking off. Their flight is rather weak. Large toucans attempting to cross watercourses gradually lose height, and may not make it to the far side of wide rivers. In savannas with woodland thickets visited by toucans, one technique used by hunters is to run, chasing the toucans from wooded patch to wooded patch, until the birds are more winded than are the runners themselves; exhausted, the toucans fall to the ground and, unable to rise into the air, they are easily picked up. Toucans are alone among piciforms in that they do not display aerially.

Toucans bound and jump, leap or hop, often upwards in tree branches. They can cling to small branches, and, with the long bill, reach fruits unavailable to other fruit-eating birds. The bill is a weapon as well, used in bill-fencing "matches", probably involving dominance hierarchies in groups, but also in securing prey. The toucan is not built like a predator, but the long, hook-tipped bill is an effective device for tearing into nests and snatching out nestling birds and eggs. Some toucans regularly investigate the hanging nests of American blackbirds (Icteridae) and flycatchers (Tyrannidae), tearing into them, and removing anything edible. This predatory capability, given to toucans secondarily as a "preadaptation" following its primary fruit-acquiring function, is probably a very important factor in securing sufficient proteins as nutrients for the young at their early, fast-growing stage.

The huge bill, with its diverse markings, also intimidates other birds, not only those competing with the toucans for fruits in a fruiting tree, but also those avian species the young of which the toucans eat; the bill thereby reduces the mobbing actions of such birds. The late P. Bühler developed a related concept involving secondary use of the bill as an ultimate intimidator, following some points made by H. Sick. Bühler even viewed the highlighting and contrasting patterns of the "teeth" of some toucans as having evolved to enhance the intimidating effects. While these interesting views are respected, there are nevertheless many cases of species with otherwise well-marked "teeth" containing races in which this feature is unmarked or less marked. Further, two closely related species may differ in this character, as demonstrated by, for example, the Collared

Many toucans are usually found in noisy groups, and this is particularly true of Pteroglossus araçaris. The Lettered Araçari is typical of the genus, several individuals usually hopping conspicuously from branch to branch or following each other in single file from tree to tree. Larger gatherings of toucans have been reported at plentiful sources of fruit or during eruptive movements. The latter sometimes involve hundreds or thousands of individuals crossing waterbodies, or attempting to cross them, and moving temporarily into previously unoccupied areas.

[Pteroglossus inscriptus inscriptus, Imperatriz, Maranhão, Brazil. Photo: Haroldo Palo Jr.]

A relatively large proportion of a toucan's time is spent dedicated to various forms of comfort behaviour. These include tussling and "playing" amongst group members, as well as resting, stretching, scratching, preening and yawning. One of the reasons that this Emerald Toucanet has time available for this is that it takes up to 75 minutes to digest a large fruit. As the digestive tract can be filled in a relatively short space of time, it is often necessary for toucans to wait until digestion is completed before foraging continues.

[Aulacorhynchus prasinus caeruleogularis, Costa Rica. Photo: Michael & Patricia Fogden]

rences between males and females, the sexes do not vary in bill markings, so these do not have a sexual function. Certainly, the colours of the bill could act as a species-specific feature, and they may in some cases do so, but they do not function in this way in highly variable species the populations of which, despite having different bill colours and patterns, seem to interbreed freely.

The plumage patterns of the toucans are multicoloured and generically distinctive. All toucanets of the genus *Aulacorhynchus* are green with some blue and yellow areas; white, yellow or blue may mark the head, and the colours of the tail tips and the undertail- and uppertail-coverts relieve the general green coloration. These patterns are not found in any other avian family and, moreover, within the Ramphastidae, they are unique to this genus. The green, rusty, black and grey colours of *Selenidera* toucanets are made complex by these species' sexual dimorphism, and are further enhanced by bright rump, undertail, flank, ear-covert and other patches, as well as by the contrastingly coloured tail tips. The species of *Andigena* have general colours suggestive of *Selenidera*, but all have bronzy and grey-blue to whitish-blue in their plumage. Their undertail-coverts are red, and the area of rump and uppertail-coverts tends to be yellow; there is no sexual dimorphism. *Baillonius*, only slightly patterned, is the most uniformly coloured of the genera, resembling no other, although it shares a red rump with the araçaris of the genus *Pteroglossus*. With their black or chestnut and black hood, and their yellow underparts, the latter usually banded with red or with red, black and green, the brightly plumaged araçaris have no counterpart within the Piciformes, or among other toucans; the nape patch occasionally present in the genus suggests *Selenidera*. The large *Ramphastos* species have a black cap, upperparts, tail and belly, setting off the bright throat-breast colour with a red band at the rear, the red undertail-coverts, and the white, red or yellow rump and uppertail-coverts. These patterns, especially when added to the often fantastic bill colours and markings, and the facial and eye colours, are strictly "toucanesque".

However recently the toucans may have diverged from an ancestor which they have in common with the barbets, their array of unparalleled morphological and other characters, the

and the Fiery-billed Araçaris: the former has highly marked, outlined "teeth", while on the Fiery-billed they are smaller and non-contrasting. It would seem that ancestral toucans should have acquired visibly well-marked "teeth" when the toucan bill was evolving; these should not have to evolve *de novo* in species after species. Although there are obvious bill-size diffe-

The size and shape of the toucan's bill precludes grooming of the head except by another individual. It is perhaps for this reason that allopreening is such a frequent year-round activity for members of the family. In this pair of Yellow-throated Toucans, the longer-billed male can be seen preening the crown feathers of his shorter-billed mate.

[Ramphastos ambiguus swainsonii, northern Colombia. Photo: Art Wolfe]

number of species in the group, their ecology, and their dominant position as Neotropical frugivores are deemed sufficient reasons to accord these highly distinctive birds family status, separate from the barbets (see Systematics).

Habitat

Toucans range through forested lowlands from north-central Mexico south to western and eastern Argentina, a much greater area than that occupied by Neotropical barbets. Most are strictly forest species, and have trouble crossing rivers that are wide. One genus, *Andigena*, is confined to montane subtropical and temperate forest of the northern Andes, there reaching the tree-line. Another genus, *Aulacorhynchus*, is found essentially in montane forest, although not so high as that reached by some species of *Andigena*, and its members range into lowland forest in northern Central America, and in Peru. Emerald Toucanets sometimes occur in dry montane forest or woodland. The Collared Araçari spills into dry deciduous woodland in Costa Rica and, farther north, in Yucatán. The Toco Toucan is, however, the only ramphastid favouring open country with forest patches, savanna woodland, and forest edges along rivers, both large and small. It also ranges at times into dry upland Bolivian valleys, seeking fruits, and it courses through the Chaco woodlands, mainly along streams, and through thickets and palms of the Pantanal in Bolivia, Mato Grosso and Paraguay.

Most of the forest toucans will enter second-growth forest near primary forest, and some penetrate the *campos* along sufficiently dense riverine forest. The subtropical Atlantic forest, or remnants thereof, is home to several toucans in southern Brazil and adjacent Paraguay and Argentina. These include one essentially riverine araçari, the Chestnut-eared. Lowland-forest toucans ascend to various elevations at the foot of the Andes, in the mountains of Venezuela and the Guianas, and in south-eastern Brazil. Most reach only 1000-1200 m, but the nominate race of the Yellow-throated Toucan occurs in submontane forest at 700-2600 m along the eastern Andes, from Colombia to Peru. Lowland toucans such as the Yellow-throated and

Choco Toucans regularly forage into uplands in western Ecuador. Where the Red-breasted and Channel-billed Toucans meet in south-eastern Brazil, the former breeds in forest on mountain slopes. Although most toucans live in lowland forest, they do vary in their choice of micro-habitats; toucanets of the genus *Selenidera*, for example, prefer forest on higher ground and with a dense middle and lower storey. Even use of the habitat may vary. The big White-throated Toucans sing from exposed perches emerging above the forest, whereas the smaller Channel-billed Toucans sing from perches beneath the canopy, usually hidden from view.

A critical aspect of habitat is the availability not, as with the barbets and woodpeckers, of trees suitable for cavity excavation, but of suitable cavities themselves. The toucans, generally unable themselves to excavate (see Morphological Aspects), require pre-existing cavities for nesting and, in the case of some of the smaller species, also for roosting. Such facilities are provided by the holes of large woodpeckers, either abandoned or occupied, and large natural cavities, mostly those which sometimes form where major branching occurs, and those created by rot where large branches have broken off and fallen. One reason why second-growth forest cannot be utilized fully by toucans is the usual lack of such large cavities in new, young trees. On the other hand, trees isolated from the forest, standing in nearby pastures or on trails alongside forest, often have cavities. These are the result of exposure to the elements of a tree that was once part of the forest, and to woodpeckers seeking out such trees for their holes because they are subject to less predation from arboreal animals.

So far as is known, the greatest degree of sympatry among toucan species occurs in south-eastern Peru. There, at Tambopata Reserve or Manu National Park, one can observe the co-existence of eight species of toucan, about as many as the number of barbets occurring together in African forest. These include one species each of two genera, two species of *Ramphastos*, and four of *Pteroglossus*. The last genus involves three species, the Ivory-billed, Lettered and Chestnut-eared Araçaris, that tend to favour floodplain and river-edge forest, and the more generally distributed Curl-crested Araçari. All four may eat fruits of the same

Toucans are in general very noisy birds, most often heard delivering simple repetitive yelps, croaks or squeals. Ramphastos *species call for long periods on exposed perches, their "songs" being one of the dominant background sounds of lowland forests in South America. Although toucan repertoires seem very small, quite a variety of notes are given. The Chestnut-eared Araçari, for example, gives a series of piercing notes, or three or four whistled "weets", and also a woodpecker-like "pyee-tyee-tyee-tyet" call, the last possibly being a form of song. Toucans often cock their tails, and araçaris often twitch and cock the tail and throw the head about when calling.*

[*Pteroglossus castanotis castanotis*,
Pantanal, Brazil.
Photo: Tom Ulrich/
Oxford Scientific Films]

As with other members of
the genus Aulacorhynchus,
the closest that the
Groove-billed Toucanet
comes to singing is a slow,
monotonous series of up
to about 20 growling,
croaking or barking notes,
variable in quality. In this
genus, the members of a
pair often call together, the
male at a distinctly lower
pitch than the female, and
neighbouring pairs may
countersing in response.
At least some of these
toucanets also rattle or
clap the bill, and the
voices of some other
bird species may on
occasion be imitated.

[Aulacorhynchus sulcatus
sulcatus,
Aragua, Venezuela.
Photo: Luiz Claudio Marigo]

tree, but usually not all together; rather, one species leaves as another group of a different species arrives.

Fruiting trees are of vital importance to toucans (see Food and Feeding), and a regular supply within a limited area is essential for breeding. That fruits may not always be available, even under natural conditions with no human modification of forest, is suggested by old accounts of widespread influxes of toucans into areas around major rivers, such as the Amazon; as Sick reported, these can involve up to 1000 individuals of some species. Toucans supplement natural foods by invading fruit plantations accessible to them, often seasonally, and by making local movements, such as shifting downslope, as do some Yellow-eared and Emerald Toucanets. The Grey-breasted Mountain-toucan lives in the high Andes of north-western South America, in temperate forest that abuts treeless, open *páramo*. It is resident at these altitudes, and must secure enough fruits to be able to live there.

The large size of toucans and their need for substantial quantities of fruits preclude their expansion northwards into North America, although lack of appropriate forest habitat in the north of Mexico and the south-western USA may also be current factors of relevance. Toco Toucans extend beyond the tropics as far south as forested areas of Tucumán, in north-west Argentina, and the riverine woodland and forest of Chaco and Corrientes in the north-east of that country; in the past they probably wandered farther, even to Buenos Aires. Here, it may be lack of habitat in the *pampas* and insufficiency of fruits farther south in forest and *monte* scrub along the Andes that prevented further southward expansion.

As is the usual situation, closely related species tend not to live in the same area. This is demonstrated by the Yellow-throated and White-throated Toucans along the eastern slopes of the Andes, where the Yellow-throated occurs on mountain slopes; and, as Haffer showed, by the Choco, Rainbow-billed and Channel-billed Toucans in northern Colombia. In the Andes, the mountain-toucans are allopatric: in the north, the Black-billed Mountain-toucan, while not a member of a superspecies with the Grey-breasted Mountain-toucan, occurs generally below the latter, but the two do overlap somewhat. There may even be altitudinal replacement of species of *Aulacorhynchus* by mountain-toucans. For example, the very local Yellow-browed Toucanet in Peru occurs at 2100-2500 m, below the Grey-breasted Mountain-toucan and, incidentally, above the Emerald Toucanet; and the Hooded Mountain-toucan of the Bolivian Andes lives above 2400 m generally, and thus usually at a higher elevation than the Blue-banded Toucanet, below which live the Chestnut-tipped and Emerald Toucanets.

Amazonia is the centre of distribution of the toucans, even including the mountain-toucans and the green toucanets, most of which occur in highlands adjacent to western and north-western Amazonia. Colombia, with its great diversity of habitats, may have been the site of origin of a number of species, even of those, such as the Yellow-throated Toucan and the Yellow-eared Toucanet, which currently have their major range in Central America. Colombia is today home to 21 members of the family, 62% of all toucan species, although none is endemic to that country. Certainly, the Fiery-billed Araçari originated in Central America. So also, perhaps, did the Emerald Toucanet and the Rainbow-billed Toucan, as invaders from South America, later isolated and evolving in Central America, then re-entering South America; alternatively, they could have evolved in Colombia, and later invaded Central America. To the south-east, in the Serra do Mar subtropical forest centre in eastern Brazil, the genus and monotypic species of the Saffron Toucanet probably evolved as an ancient offshoot of an ancestor in common with *Pteroglossus*. The Red-breasted Toucan seems likely to have evolved there long ago, but the Spot-billed Toucanet is thought to have reached that region from Amazonia more recently, perhaps during a wet cycle, along rivers to the west and north, deriving from an ancestor in common with the very closely related, possibly even conspecific Gould's Toucanet. All the modern genera of toucans, with the exception of *Baillonius*, would seem to have originated in Amazonia.

No toucans or barbets appear to have reached the West Indies. The toucans are poor candidates for avian water-crossing species. The occurrence of Channel-billed Toucans on Trinidad is very likely due to the connection of Trinidad to Venezuela in the geologically recent past, rather than to over-water invasion.

General Habits

For perhaps most of the time, the majority of toucans live in groups. Exceptions are some of the green toucanets, several species of *Selenidera*, some mountain-toucans, and the Green and Lettered Araçaris. Large gatherings of some toucans occasionally occur in migratory or eruptive movements, and at large fruiting trees with many ripe fruits. Examples include flocks of up to 20 Emerald Toucanets, twelve Plate-billed Mountain-toucans, and 22 Rainbow-billed, over 20 White-throated and 20 Yellow-throated Toucans. Most toucans breed in pairs, some retiring to part of a group home range; they then form family groups, or rejoin their own social group accompanied by their young. In all probability, only some of the araçaris regularly breed in small groups of three or four individuals.

The smaller toucans appear to roost in old nesting cavities or old woodpecker holes. Guianan Toucanets kept in captivity roost alone, in separate cavities if more than one of these is available; if there is but one, the male roosts in the cavity and the female outside it. The green toucanets roost in pairs in cavities. After breeding, araçaris sometimes roost in groups, or as many as will fit into one cavity, the remainder using another. Big *Ramphastos* toucans roost in groups, clustered beside one another, on a branch of a dense tree. The cavity-roosting species may attempt to take over the roosting holes of woodpeckers, harassing them regularly.

In the heat of the day, many toucans simply sit, often in a fruiting tree, in which case they may "control" access to the fruits. Others may sleep, occasionally in the full sleeping posture with tail pulled up forwards to the head (see Morphological Aspects). The daily routine can mean early visits to the neighbourhood's fruiting trees, or more lengthy foraging trips in search of new sources of fruit. The large toucans often spend some time in calling, an activity that is sometimes repeated late in the day. In the case of araçaris roosting together, there may be much calling and displaying among group-members before they take to the roosting cavity for the night.

"Play", involving "sparring" or "duelling" with the bill, has been observed in several ramphastid species of different genera. The birds approach one another and whack their bills together, or they clasp bills and push and tug. These bouts may involve contests between members of a group relating to dominance of the individuals. Paired birds at times reinforce the pair-bond by gentle, pushing "duels". Tag-chasing around and around, with repeated supplanting, among members of a group may also be concerned with the dominance hierarchy, and, moreover, group-members sometimes "play" at throwing a fruit from one to another, the fruit presumably being finally eaten.

Activities such as "play", various interactions, and even singing and sexual behaviour, may take place during the periods of time required for the digestion of large fruits by the toucans, as N. T. Wheelwright has shown. Because some fruits can take up to 75 minutes to digest, the presence of several of these in the digestive system may preclude further consumption of fruit. The "free" time during digestion can therefore be used for various of the birds' other activities.

Comfort behaviour involves a number of different activities. Moulting toucans scratch more often than do non-moulting toucans. For the head, scratching is by the direct method, over the wing, using one leg or the other. The bill is wiped at intervals during feeding. Perhaps because of the long bill, paired adults of the large toucan species allopreen all year, and even other members of a group sometimes preen each other's face, carefully, with the tip of the immense bill. Preening is frequent, and so, too, is stretching and yawning. A Plate-billed Mountain-toucan, for example, stretches one leg down and extends the wing of the same side upwards, the tail being spread to the opposite side, and then repeats this with the other wing and leg; finally, both wings are stretched and, often, the toucan yawns. Sunning occurs especially after rain: this is performed by spreading the feathers on the side facing the sun, sometimes with the head turned over, the body draped over a branch, so that one side, including the wing, and the throat skin are in the sun. Toucans also pant, holding the bill open, and probably cool themselves by evaporation of water from

the long, brushy tongue and the mouth-lining (see Morphological Aspects). Bathing occurs, probably often, in the water that collects in arboreal crevices. All the large toucans seem to bathe, as do the well-known species of araçari, such as the Collared and Fiery-billed Araçaris. Captive mountain-toucans and Spot-billed Toucanets bathe regularly.

Despite the presence of liquids in the fruits which they consume, those toucans observed frequently are known to drink. They usually take water from a tree crevice, or that held in bromeliads. Often, the water is not "gulped"; the toucan puts its bill deep into the water, and then holds the bill only slightly above the horizontal, allowing water to trickle or flow into the oesophagus.

Aggression varies considerably among toucan species, but one can assume that the adopting of a face-on posture signifies aggression. Otherwise, a number of different stances and movements are used, depending on the species. In the green toucanets, aggressors lash the tail and cock it, lean, peer, and make side-to-side movements with the head and bill forwards. *Selenidera* toucanets raise the head and hold it up, go into a horizontal posture, and call. One female Guianan Toucanet, kept in a cage with another female, pursued the latter, forcing allopreening upon it. Gold-collared Toucanets flap the wings and thrash the tail, and spread the red feathers of the undertail-coverts. The Plate-billed Mountain-toucan bobs its head, flips its tail up and down and, similarly, erects the red undertail-coverts. Green Araçaris hold the head up and swing it from one side to the other, shake the tail from side to side, and then cock the tail and twitch it. On the other hand, Black-necked Araçaris bow, erecting the head to one side, then dropping it down to the other side, often cocking the tail forwards as far as the back. Collared Araçaris stretch the head, bow, nod, and jerk all about; a dispersing araçari trying to join a group was held by the bill, and pecked by various group-members, becoming bloodied. Curl-crested Araçaris bow very deeply up and down, jumping from perch to perch and giving "krek" calls. Aggressive Red-breasted Toucans raise the nape feathers, swing the head from side to side, and lean forwards. In conflicts, a submissive Choco Toucan erects the crown feathers and spreads the tail, while the aggressor holds the bill low, with crown feathers sleeked, and the tail closed, showing more of the white of the uppertail-coverts. In the case of Toco Toucans, the attacker directs its bill forwards, rattles, pecks forward and grabs, and bangs the bill loudly on a branch. White-throated Toucans point the bill at an opponent and switch the tail from one side to the other.

Interactions between different species of toucan are frequent in occurrence, although the smaller toucans usually keep their distance from larger ones. Emerald Toucanets sometimes chase Collared Araçaris, which may return the chase, with several group-members attacking. Collared Araçaris are aggressive towards single Choco Toucans, "buzzing" the Choco and flying at it when it is airborne. The Black-necked Araçari and other *Pteroglossus* species tend to stay well away from White-throated Toucans, as do Channel-billed Toucans. Red-breasted Toucans supplant Chestnut-eared Araçaris, and one or two of the former together can keep groups of Saffron Toucanets out of a fruiting tree. Interestingly, even though Rainbow-billed Toucans will nest close to Yellow-throated Toucans, they are frequently supplanted by the latter species at food sources. Among the araçaris, it is simply the larger or more numerous species that is dominant: for example, five Chestnut-eared Araçaris were seen to drive four Lettered Araçaris from a potential nesting cavity, the former later nesting in the cavity.

Larger toucans and araçaris are often mobbed by calling birds, and are attacked in flight by various tyrant-flycatchers. The highly predatory White-throated Toucan, when alone or in pairs, is readily mobbed by several species of tyrant-flycatcher (see Food and Feeding), and in flight the toucan may even suffer the indignity of having a flycatcher land on its back. Not surprisingly, hunting araçaris, when they skulk about in dense bushes or trees, are mobbed by various small birds. That the mobbers have reason to fear toucans is evidenced by the fact that *Selenidera* toucanets are clearly attracted to birds caught in mist-nets; they will attack and eat birds that are trapped in this way.

Toucans are primarily frugivorous, consuming a wide variety of arboreal fruits; Emerald Toucanets have been recorded eating 115-120 fruit types from around 50 families of plants. They tend to eat smaller, more carbohydrate-rich berries early in the day, later moving to high-nutrient fruits. In the dry season food supplies are scarce, and individuals need to feed for longer periods on berry-like fruits and make longer-distance forays from one food source to another. Most members of the family, however, are opportunistic omnivores. Although this Guianan Toucanet is consuming berries, it will take insects encountered while foraging; indeed, in captivity *Selenidera* toucanets can be maintained on an all-insect diet, and will actively hunt insects in their cages. Moreover, members of this genus are known to be quite carnivorous, sometimes attacking small birds trapped in mist-nets and often being mobbed by passerines.

[Above: *Aulacorhynchus prasinus caeruleogularis*, Costa Rica. Photo: Michael & Patricia Fogden.

Below: *Selenidera culik*, French Guiana. Photo: Alain Guillemot/ Bios]

Despite their rather clumsy appearance, toucans are very agile in trees and are adept at stretching acrobatically to reach food. Even the largest species, the Toco Toucan, can hang daintily to pluck small fruits with its long bill. It can twist them off by swivelling its bill and can detach them by tugging with considerable force. In their range, toucans are generally responsible for consuming the majority of fruit at major fruiting trees and are thus extremely important vectors for seed dispersal in Neotropical forest ecosystems.

[*Ramphastos toco albogularis*, Iguazú National Park, Argentina. Photo: Günter Ziesler]

On the other hand, the toucans, although kings of the frugivores at a fruiting tree, are hardly without enemies of their own, including human hunters (see Status and Conservation). Various forest eagles, hawks and eagle-owls are major predators of toucans. Ornate Hawk-eagles (*Spizaetus ornatus*), White Hawks (*Leucopternis albicollis*) and Collared Forest-falcons (*Micrastur semitorquatus*) prey on Collared Araçaris in Central America. The Ornate Hawk-eagle and the Great Horned Owl (*Bubo virginianus*) prey on Channel-billed Toucans, including those roosting on branches of trees, and in Tikal National Park, in Guatemala, the Rainbow-billed Toucan is commonly eaten by Black Hawk-eagles (*Spizaetus tyrannus*), as well as by Ornate Hawk-eagles. In some species, such as the Channel-billed Toucan, the social group will sometimes follow larger, noisier falconiform groups, particularly Red-throated Caracaras (*Daptrius americanus*), as a measure to lessen the chances of predation.

Voice

Acoustical displays are important in the Ramphastidae. The non-vocal sounds produced by toucans range from bill-tapping to bill-clattering and loud rustling of the wings during interactions. Wing-rustling is often surprisingly noisy, and is especially notable in the *Ramphastos* toucans with their emarginated outer two primaries. Although it is not apparent from their often very repetitive songs, most toucans have a large vocal repertoire. It should, however, be noted that what recordists call "small sounds" are unknown for many toucans. Indeed, what might be termed "songs" in the classic sense are not well understood in the case of some species, mainly the araçaris.

Sounds resembling bill-snapping are evident as single, mechanical sounds, and are associated with the calls of some green toucanets, the *Selenidera* toucanets, the mountain-toucans, the *Ramphastos* toucans and some araçaris. They are most obvious in the songs of the large mountain-toucans and the *Ramphastos* toucans, and can be dominant in some notes. Because some calls

with the snaps, as well as some of the rattle calls with very mechanical sounds, are uttered with the bill closed, it may be that they are produced by the tongue hitting against the inside of the bill; on the other hand, they may, indeed, be vocal. Bill-whacking in aggression is an obvious sound, the toucan hitting a branch with the bill, while loud wiping of the bill is a further aggressive activity in interactions. In addition, many toucans tap the bill rapidly against the entrance to the nesting cavity, and some do so inside the nest, effectively "drumming" in the manner of woodpeckers and some barbets.

Growling, grunting and barking notes, variable in minor detail and in their length and the tempo at which they are given, make up the often monotonous, long "songs" of the green toucanets of the genus *Aulacorhynchus*. Paired individuals may sing simultaneously, the male at a lower pitch, often stimulating countersinging by neighbouring pairs. These are typical sounds of montane forest.

Four closely related species of *Selenidera*, the Tawny-tufted, Gold-collared, Gould's and Spot-billed Toucanets, during their essentially identical visual bowing displays, utter growl-like "krowk" or "krrawk" notes more or less with each bow; these vary in tempo among the species. Of their two congeners, the Guianan Toucanet has, instead, a series of rattle-squawks, and also gives series of screams very like those of the mountain-toucans, while the song of the Yellow-eared Toucanet is, by contrast, a "tik-kit" series. Usually, the songs are uttered separately by males and females, but sometimes the sexes sing simultaneously.

The mountain-toucans utter braying series of "eeeeaah" notes, sometimes compounded with bill-snapping sounds; snaps may lead into the song. These are given with accompanying bows like those of *Selenidera* toucanets. The song notes of the Grey-breasted Mountain-toucan are the longest recorded for any piciform, up to two seconds or more in length. The Saffron Toucanet utters a "teeee-up" series, without such obvious displays as those of the two previous genera.

Araçaris vary in their calls, with songs, as such, not known for most species. Some have "kek" or rattle calls, for example the Green, Lettered and Red-necked Araçaris. The Ivory-billed

Toucans "monitor" regular fruiting trees to assess the food supply, and individuals are known to guard productive fruit sources, driving off other frugivores, even a mate. Nevertheless, their foraging requirements are not entirely met by forest fruit. Several species visit gardens or plantations to feast on fruit such as bananas and papayas, as illustrated by this Collared Araçari and Red-breasted Toucan. They dig into large fruit, returning repeatedly to the known resource, and some species drop to the ground to feed on fallen fruit. The form of Collared Araçari shown here is often treated as a separate species, the Pale-mandibled Araçari, a restricted-range near-endemic of western Ecuador; however, regular interbreeding occurs with the race sanguineus of Collared Araçari in north-western Ecuador and also in extreme south-western Colombia, suggesting that only one species is involved.

[Above: *Pteroglossus torquatus erythropygius*, Tinalandia, Ecuador.

Below: *Ramphastos dicolorus*, Itatiaia National Park, Brazil.
Photos: Kevin Schafer]

Araçari has a wailing song of "waaaa" or "traaa-at" notes in series, not unlike that of the Saffron Toucanet. All five members of the "Collared Araçari group" utter very similar, short "peeeent" or "sneeep" notes in irregular series, but they seem to have no song as such. Curl-crested Araçaris give deep "rrek" to grunting notes, the latter like those of the green toucanets; these are delivered in irregular series with intermingled bill-snapping sounds.

The big *Ramphastos* toucans can be divided vocally into two groups. The first is the croaking, honking group of five species, which utter calls in long or short, regular or irregular series. The notes have both noisy and clear elements, these being either muted or enhanced. Thus, the notes of the Red-breasted Toucan are "grrekk"-like, those of the Rainbow-billed vary from "bbrrik" to "ggrrr", and the notes of Choco Toucans sound like "tyeerp" to "tree-ak". Channel-billed Toucans usually have clearer "keee", "kerrrk" or "kee-ark" notes, and the Toco has the deepest, grunting "groomkk" sound. These vocalizations are "sung", the female's higher-pitched, sometimes clearer notes at times given simultaneously with those of the male, eliciting countersinging by other individuals. The other two *Ramphastos* species, the White-throated and Yellow-throated Toucans, sing in yelping sets of more musical notes, phrased more or less as "Dios-te-de": more like "keeow-yelp-yelp" in the White-throated, and more double-noted, "Dios, te-de, te-de", in the Yellow-throated. The numbers of yelps following the initial note of a phrase can vary. The sexes of these two species, females of which again have higher-pitched voices, sometimes sing together on exposed perches, their sounds being a dominant feature of the background ambience of Neotropical lowland forest. Most of these vocalizations are represented on a useful cassette produced by J. W. Hardy and colleagues in 1996.

The singing postures of toucans vary a great deal. That of the green toucanets is simple, the upright bird perhaps twitching its tail below the often half-erected rump feathers. Most of the *Selenidera* toucanets flare their ear-tufts and red undertail-coverts, bow deeply, with the tail usually moving downwards, and then raise the head and tail high more or less in time with the notes of the song, or the tail may be held cocked and twitched. In the Yellow-eared Toucanet, however, the head is tossed up to one side, the semi-cocked tail flopped to the opposite side, and the bird then bows, following this with a toss of the head and a switch of the tail to the opposite side. Song postures of mountain-toucans are generally like those of species of *Selenidera*. There is no described singing posture of the Saffron Toucanet, and the araçaris have no precise posture when uttering their calls, although they often switch and cock the tail, and toss the head about.

In the "croaking group" of *Ramphastos* toucans, the singer stretches the head out and up and swings it in a smooth or jerky arc from side to side, dipping but not bowing deeply. Some species drop the cocked tail with each note, and then, after five or six notes, swing the head to the other side and cock the tail again; sometimes, the head is held erect throughout and the tail is twitched. The two species comprising the "yelping group" raise the head upwards, either vertically or to the side, gradually lowering it with the notes until the posture becomes a more or less deep bow, and then swing the head upwards, or out and upwards, to the other side, the tail moving up and down with the head. The incorporation of swinging and bobbing-bowing movements is a feature of the displays of toucans, barbets, woodpeckers and some honeyguides, and is not necessarily associated with "singing".

The many other sounds made by toucans include predominantly rattling calls and bill-rattling, along with growling and grating notes, and begging notes, such as the "cha-cha-" uttered by Emerald Toucanets. Also heard are "ark" notes in interactions, soft rattling "intimate" calls such as "un", "ik", "eh", "tut", "wek", "eee", "perp", "rak" and "tweah", chatters, croaks, a piping "zneep", and a grunting "tuk" and other low calls. Araçaris and Saffron Toucanets have low purring calls. Young toucans in the nest generally utter peeping, squeaky, whining, buzzy or wailing notes in series. Collared Araçaris have a little-known "pee-yew" alarm call, and emit an aggressive "arghrr", as well as loud "pit" notes in alarm; other toucans utter "kyeek" or squeak-like alarm calls. Chestnut-eared Araçaris are known to give three or four whistled "weets", and a woodpecker-like "pyee-tyee-tyee-tyee-tyet" call, possibly a song.

Toucans augment their fruit diet with a variety of other items. Some species are known to hunt and consume small mammals; others eat lizards, sometimes hunting them co-operatively; others eat roosting bats, or frogs, toads and snakes. Some species follow army ants, normally positioning themselves close to the front edge of the column, and dropping onto or chasing insects flushed by swarm. As an indication of their carnivory, captive individuals of some species, including White-throated Toucans, are said to prefer meat to fruit, even hunting and eating small birds that enter their cages.

[*Ramphastos tucanus cuvieri*,
River Branco,
100 km north of Manaus,
Brazil.
Photo: Nick Gordon/
Ardea]

This male Toco Toucan is delivering a stolen egg to his chicks inside their cavity nest. This illustrates an important aspect of toucan foraging strategy: more than half the toucans of five genera are known to steal eggs and young from nests of other species, and it is very likely that the remainder do so at least occasionally. Some species are very bold, chasing other species (even birds of prey) from their nests to steal the contents.

[Ramphastos toco, near Das Emas National Park, Mato Grosso, Brazil. Photos: François Gohier (left); François Gohier/ Ardea (right)]

Most of the sounds made by toucans are unique to the family. Those sounds that are similar to calls of barbets also resemble those of other piciforms.

Food and Feeding

These large birds are primarily frugivorous. They seek out and "monitor" fruiting plants of a wide range of species. The fruits that they eat, although diverse, tend to be red, red and black, orange, purple, black, green, brown and yellow in colour. A single species, such as the Emerald Toucanet, will consume fruits of 115-120 species, representing about 50 families of plants. A dominant large toucan at a fruiting tree, say, the Yellow-throated Toucan at a tree of *Virola sebifera*, may take 45% of the tree's fruits, each of which yields about 825 calories. The toucans, therefore, play a very major role in the dispersal of seeds of many fruiting trees.

Important families of fruiting plants, mainly trees, are the Lauraceae, Moraceae, Cecropiaceae, Melastomataceae, Solanaceae, Myrtaceae, Clusiaceae, the palms Arecaceae, Rosaceae, Urticaceae, and many others. Of especial importance are species of *Beilschmiedia, Caesaria, Cecropia, Coussapoa, Didymoponax, Ficus, Inga, Nectandra, Neea, Ocotea,* the palms *Euterpe* and *Oenocarpus,* the peppers *Capsicum* and *Piper, Phoebe, Protium, Prunus, Rubus, Steicula* and *Virola.* The ramphastid diet thus includes berries, arils of various sizes, fruits with seeds that pass through the digestive tract, and large-stoned drupes such as avocados, the seeds or stones of which must be regurgitated, as well as large, pod-like fruits such as *Cecropia,* or *Piper* peppers, that must be held in the feet and broken open. These frugivores also eat nectar and flowers of species of *Clusia, Combretum, Erythrina, Mcclenia, Quararibea, Saurauia* and others. Captive toucans accept apples, avocados, bananas, cooked beets and carrots, blueberries, cantaloupes, watermelons and other melons, chopped cabbage and lettuce, grapes and raisins, guavas, frozen maize, papayas, peaches, pears, peas, raspberries,

and cooked zucchini. Because of these birds' propensity for storing iron (see Morphological Aspects), however, oranges and other high-iron foods are to be avoided.

Wheelwright showed that Emerald Toucanets eat smaller, more carbohydrate-rich berries early in the day, and that they monitor fruiting trees, later moving to high-nutrient fruits. Fruit availability is important. In the dry season, this toucanet has to feed for a longer period, lower down, on smaller-seeded fruits, and it has to move greater distances from one food source to another. Generally, a toucanet made feeding visits lasting two to eight minutes, took an average of two fruits totalling 26 g per visit, and took 24-70 minutes to digest the fruits; larger fruits require more regurgitation to facilitate digestion. C. M. Riley and K. G. Smith, in their study of the Emerald Toucanet, found that the sexes fed on the same fruits and used the same foraging modes; they also found that the diet shifted to about 21% animal matter when the adults were feeding nestlings.

The dispersal strategies of the plants may vary. Several toucan species feed on fruits of the palm *Oenocarpus.* As Bühler pointed out, this palm produces large-stoned fruit with little, but nourishing, flesh; the fruits ripen a few at a time, on long filamentous stalks that hang down. It is difficult for toucans to gain and maintain a perch, and so they leave after eating few fruits, thus facilitating dispersal of the seeds away from the trees. Incidentally, in addition to seeds, the legs of small passerine birds and the legs and tails of mice fed to captive Red-breasted Toucans also pass through the digestive tract.

Toucans are also opportunistic omnivores, and they need to capture insects or other animal foods for their young in the early nestling stages. Since toucans tend to breed when many small birds are nesting, opportunities are available to secure eggs and young of birds, and nearly half the toucans of five genera are known to do so. Indeed, in parts of Brazil, Red-breasted Toucans are persecuted for this habit. At least seven species eat lizards, and paired Yellow-throated Toucans will at times hunt these co-operatively. Three species of the genera *Andigena* and *Ramphastos* are known to hunt for and eat small mammals, while

This Red-breasted Toucan is caught in the act of plundering a Great Kiskadee (Pitangus sulphuratus) nest situated in the trailing branches of an Araucaria tree. In such cases, toucans prise open the nest, often ignoring the entrance, and eat the chicks or eggs. At least seven species in the family have been recorded opening the suspended nests of caciques or oropendolas (Icteridae). It is because of this predilection that toucans are often mobbed by smaller birds. The efficacy of this defence behaviour is limited, however, because of the persistence of toucans: one species was observed stealing flycatcher eggs despite being mobbed by twelve flycatchers of three species at the time!

[Ramphastos dicolorus, Rio de Janeiro, Brazil. Photo: Gustavo Banhara Marigo]

Channel-billed Toucans take roosting bats, and also eat frogs and toads. Snakes are captured and eaten by six species.

Insects are taken at least occasionally by a number of toucans, with orthopterans such as cicadas and grasshoppers the most frequent prey. Beetles, homopterans, caterpillars, flies, bees, ants and flying termites are eaten, the Toco Toucan being one of at least three ramphastids that will "fly-catch" for aerial insects. Rainbow-billed, Choco and Channel-billed Toucans follow army-ant columns, seizing insects and vertebrates flushed by the ants, while the Gold-collared Toucanet and the Grey-breasted Mountain-toucan take insects while foraging as members of mixed-species flocks. In captivity, Plate-billed Mountain-toucans and Red-breasted, Toco and White-throated Toucans systematically hunt and eat small birds that enter aviaries. Interestingly, Toco and White-throated Toucans kept as pets are said to prefer meats to fruits, and these species have been fed on a long-term basis on boiled eggs, meat, bread and a small bird per day. Captive *Selenidera* toucanets can be maintained on an all-insect diet and, indeed, will forage for insects in their cages. Centipedes and spiders are other toucan foods.

Groove-billed Toucanets are well-known nest-robbers, and several other species have been seen to indulge in this type of behaviour. Emerald Toucanets attempted to enter a barbet nest with calling young, and Yellow-throated Toucans tried to reach Collared Araçari nestlings in a cavity. At least seven toucanets, araçaris and toucans have been recorded opening the suspended nests of Yellow-rumped Caciques (*Cacicus cela*) and oropendolas to get at the contents. In a study in Manu National Park, Peru, it was found that, of 41 attacks by Chestnut-eared Araçaris on cacique colonies over a three-month period, 24% were successful. Four Lettered Araçaris regularly raided cacique nests; they also took two young from pigeon (Columbidae) nests, ate young finches (Fringillidae) from cavity nests, and were successful in obtaining eggs or young from three swallow (Hirundinidae) nests. White-throated Toucans, although being mobbed by twelve flycatchers of three species, still managed to steal eggs from a flycatcher nest, and Yellow-throated Toucans ate the young of three flycatcher species. One of those Yellow-throated Toucans even

chased a female Double-toothed Kite (*Harpagus bidentatus*) from her nest and ate the young. White-throated Toucans achieved a success rate of 36% in raids on cacique nests; and, in attempts to obtain young flycatchers from nests, their success rates were 20% for *Pitangus* flycatchers, 50% for *Myiozetetes* species, and 33% for *Megarhynchus* flycatchers. In view of the degree of nest predation by toucans, it is no surprise that they are frequently mobbed by other birds.

When foraging, toucans fly one at a time into a fruiting tree and quickly jump into positions for grasping, tugging and pulling off ripe fruits. They are very agile, the immense bill not deterring them from hanging and reaching, twisting the neck about, and seizing fruits. The length of the bill enables them to reach far from their centre of gravity, and the hook tip and jutting serrations give them certain purchase. Even Toco Toucans can hang and daintily pluck small fruits. On one occasion, a semi-tame Toco rifled the pockets of the observers, hanging upside-down as it turned out pocket-linings; pulling against the bird's tugs resulted in terrier-like shaking and fast back-and-forth twists with power. Red-breasted Toucans can keep numbers of Saffron Toucanets from a fruit tree, and Yellow-throated Toucans sometimes guard a tree, evicting any other frugivores, even a mate. The last species descends to the ground to eat fallen bananas, and Channel-billed and Toco Toucans also drop down to feed on fallen fruits, the latter making fast, 70-cm hops on the ground.

Large fruits, pods, and insects and vertebrates are held in one or both feet and broken up; in the case of a mammal or snake, the food is "mandibulated", meaning that it is worked over by the serrated "teeth" of the bill.

When hunting animal food, toucans skulk with the head held low, looking all around constantly. Working in tandem to catch a lizard, one goes after the prey bill first, while the other perches close by or flies to the other side of a tree trunk, ever ready to snatch up the reptile. Various toucans probe into epiphytes for insects or frogs. Gold-collared Toucanets carefully ply the bark of trees, along the trunk, out on to branches and in foliage, probing into debris, mosses and crevices. Like hawks

Despite the liquid content in fruit, toucans frequently drink. They usually take water trapped in tree crevices or in bromeliads, drinking by closing the bill as deeply as possible into the water, then raising it just above the horizontal so that the water trickles down the inside of the bill. It is thus possible that this Rainbow-billed Toucan is visiting this bromeliad for the purpose of seeking water, but it might also be looking for insects or frogs; toucans are known to prise open bromeliads for this purpose.

[Ramphastos sulfuratus. Photo: Carol Farneti/ Planet Earth]

(Accipitridae) and small owls (Strigidae), the toucanet gravitates towards sounds of birds in trouble, such as those trapped in mist-nets. Toucans following army ants move low above the leading edge of the ant column, peering, dropping down to pick up prey, or even chasing it.

Breeding

The mountain-toucans and the toucanets of the Andes breed mostly from January to July, or somewhat later, in the north, and from June to December farther south, in Peru and Bolivia. It is during these periods that the greatest numbers of plants are fruiting. Amazonian toucans have a long breeding season, this being possibly due in part to the occurrence of renesting. In northern Central America, the breeding season is approximately the same as that in southern North America, namely from January to July. Paraguayan, Argentine and south Brazilian toucans follow a typical austral regime, breeding usually from August to February, with some commencing earlier and a few nesting later. The widespread Channel-billed Toucan breeds from June to November in north-eastern South America, but from November to July in Venezuela, August to March in western Brazil and October to April in south-central Brazil, while some breeding takes place in most areas in the months of February to July. Such seasonality has not been evaluated with regard to the seasonality of fruits on which these toucans depend, except in the far north and south of the overall range; at those extremes, the appropriate spring-summer period is the flowering and fruiting time of the year.

Details of toucan territories and their sizes are little known, and from only few locations, and the relationship between home range and territory is poorly understood. Territories may vary seasonally, or be partitioned between the primary pair and the rest of a social group, and they are readily abandoned under adverse fruiting conditions. Often, territories are smaller in a preferred habitat, and larger elsewhere.

At Manu, in Peru, Emerald Toucanets have been found to occur at two pairs per 100 ha of successional *Ficus/Cedrela* for-

est along lakes and rivers, and at 1·5 pairs per 100 ha in mature forest. Gold-collared Toucanet pairs live mainly in mature forest, each pair having a home range of 100 ha, of which about 35 ha represent the territory. In the same area, Lettered Araçaris are found along rivers, at a density of less than one pair per 100 ha. Ivory-billed Araçaris living in the same early successional stages of riverine forest occur at two pairs per 100 ha, a pair using perhaps 20 ha of a 50-ha home range; in very late successional stages, and in mature forest, 200 ha hold just a single pair of that species. Chestnut-eared Araçaris in this riverine habitat are less common, at one pair per 200 ha, than are Lettered or Ivory-billed Araçaris. The Curl-crested Araçari, however, favours mature forest, where one pair or group uses 20-25 ha, but in riverine late successional stages it requires 50 ha or more.

The existence of suitable nesting cavities is a prerequisite for a usable territory. In the 1920's, J. Van Tyne apparently found ideal conditions on Barro Colorado Island, in Panama, for in 16 ha of mature forest there he located nests of three pairs/groups of Collared Araçaris, four pairs of Rainbow-billed Toucans and two pairs of Yellow-throated Toucans. The Plate-billed Mountain-toucan in Colombia was found to have a group home range of 8-9 ha; the pair nests alone within that range, which may be deserted by the group in poor years. In south-eastern Brazil, Saffron Toucanets appear to maintain a territory of approximately 40 ha per pair. G. R. Bourne found White-throated Toucans in groups in very large home ranges for much of the year; the primary pair defends a small territory in this range for the breeding season, and then rejoins the group, along with any young that are raised. In a study in Peru, White-throated Toucans had territories that varied from about 30 ha in late successional riverine forest to some 50 ha in mature forest; they were more numerous than Channel-billed Toucans, which occupied territories of 40-67 ha.

In those cases in which the toucans live mainly in groups, the more mature, but still non-breeding, individuals comprise "floaters" within the population. From these, a breeding toucan losing its mate would presumably select a new mate. To the extent that the groups are composed of subadult and immature individuals they are not potential breeders, and they can give the impression to the observer of a greater effective population than really exists. More needs to be learned about group composition, home-range size, and the relative availability of suitable nesting and, for some species, roosting cavities.

Breeding sociality is not common generally. Green toucanets seem to clear their territory of group-members and to breed as pairs. *Selenidera* toucans seemingly do the same, although there is a record of a nesting trio of Guianan Toucanets. Breeding mountain-toucans occur as pairs. Even among the generally social araçaris, most species breed in pairs, with trios known for the Lettered, Ivory-billed and Fiery-billed Araçaris. Red-necked, Black-necked and Curl-crested Araçaris are likely to nest in social groups of three or four individuals, and Chestnut-eared Araçaris may occasionally do so. Collared Araçaris nest in groups of up to five or six, but the primary pair keeps the others from the nest during egg-laying and incubation; after the eggs have hatched, they rejoin the parents and nestlings, roost in the nest, and feed the young. The large toucans seem to breed strictly in pairs, and in captivity, once breeding commences, they usually kill any conspecific toucan caged with them.

Although no toucans appear to breed colonially, nor do two or more females of a group seem to breed, there are numerous cases of pairs of both large and small species nesting rather close together, as happens with some barbets. These cases have not, however, been studied in any detail. It seems likely that pairs of conspecific toucans, having happened to find nesting cavities within 100 m or less of each other, then regulate their foraging and other activities in opposite directions, away from one another.

It is probably rare for a toucan, even a small one, to breed in its first year. Yearlings are likely to make up the bulk of groups cast out of territories by pairs of green toucanets and mountain-toucans. *Ramphastos* toucans may barely be adult at one year old. Avicultural information suggests that most large toucans nest successfully only when they reach three or four years of age, and, in any case, not until two years. Captive male Red-breasted Toucans first bred at 34 months and captive females at 21 months, suggesting that, under some conditions, females can breed at two years of age. If nesting cavities are at a premium, it is unlikely that young, newly formed pairs, or pairs with young replacement individuals of one or the other sex, will be able to compete with older, experienced pairs. Finding, or taking over from other hole-nesters, a suitable nesting cavity would presumably be difficult for young adults. If the suitable cavities are already taken, the available habitat would be saturated, and entry into the breeding population by younger adults would be impossible. Indeed, Plate-billed Mountain-toucan pairs, whatever their age, may not breed yearly.

Most toucans are unable to excavate a nesting cavity, although a few green toucanet pairs do so. Yet aviary experience and several field observations suggest that some excavation, by one or both pair-members, is an essential part of pair formation and maintenance, and probably important for physiological synchronization of their breeding. The normal procedure is for the toucan to find a vacant cavity or to take over one already occupied. Fiery-billed Araçaris, for example, use old or usurped cavities of the relatively large Lineated Woodpecker (*Dryocopus lineatus*) and Pale-billed Woodpecker (*Campephilus guatemalensis*). The smaller toucans may exert themselves to drive out occupants of usable cavities. Repeated attempts to usurp a cavity could interfere with the nesting woodpeckers or other birds, allowing a takeover by the toucans. Large toucans that are successful ordinarily return to the same nest early in the next breeding season, and begin clearing it and preparing it for laying. The height of the cavity often seems not to matter, the securing of a cavity being more important than is its location. Toco Toucans, for instance, even nest on or inside termite mounds on the ground, often in those where Campo Flickers (*Colaptes campestris*) have previously excavated a nest.

The Emerald Toucanet, especially the female with its shorter, straighter bill, can excavate or "bite" out wood if the wood is very rotten, and it will even use the tail, soft though it is, as a "prop". The toucanets drop the pieces of wood away from the nest. Araçaris at times tear out the rotted centres of cavities that they occupy, whether natural or woodpecker-made; they frequently use holes with very narrow entrances into which they must squeeze, as they are unable to excavate hard bark and underlying wood. Spot-billed Toucanets will also tear into well-rotted wood, and may start and complete some excavations; old woodpecker cavities are apt to be safer, in harder wood. Plate-billed Mountain-toucans do some excavation, and may on occasion have to work for six weeks or so to complete a nest, some excavating continuing during incubation. Their nests may be

Although many species of toucan spend the non-breeding season foraging in groups, breeding sociality is not common. Certainly all of the larger toucans, such as the Toco Toucan, always nest in pairs; indeed, when a breeding pair is held captive with another conspecific, the members of the pair generally kill the third bird. Even in the highly social araçaris, while the group may stay essentially integrated during the breeding season, the nesting pair will usually keep the other group members away from the nest during the egg-laying and incubation periods. After hatching the group reassembles to roost in the nest cavity and share parental care.

[*Ramphastos toco*, Brazil.
Photo: Tom Brakefield/
DRK Photo]

Although most species of toucan use only available cavities, some are capable of digging out a nest in soft substrate. The Emerald Toucanet, for example, often excavates or bites through soft rotten wood, and carries the debris away from the nest. It tends to be the female that performs this task, perhaps because her bill is shorter, straighter and thus more sturdy, but also because the female performs the greater part of nest duties. One of the other chores is that of nest sanitation, involving the removal of faecal material mixed with shreds of rotten wood.

[*Aulacorhynchus prasinus caeruleogularis*, Costa Rica. Photo: Michael & Patricia Fogden]

nearly 2 m deep. This species often excavates nesting cavities in well-rotted, perhaps over-rotted, stubs or dead trees that may fall down at any time. At other times it usurps a cavity from Toucan-barbets (*Semnornis ramphastinus*) that have chosen to carve a nest in a tree sufficiently broad to allow use by the larger toucan.

The big *Ramphastos* toucans not only clean out debris, but also tear into rotted wood at the bottom of the natural cavities that they use. Cavities used for consecutive years become deeper and deeper, to 2 m on occasion, with each year's cleaning. The nests of these species are 2-30 m or more above the ground. The toucans seem to seek out cavities with narrow entrances, but to a great extent they have to accept them wherever and however they are situated. Nest-sites are selected and visited for one to two months before they are occupied. Most end up with a lining of fruit stones up to 7 cm or more in depth. Sometimes the eggs are not laid until two weeks after the cavity is ready.

Smaller toucans may select cavities in isolated trees in pastures, as an anti-predator strategy. Once occupied, the nest is rather conspicuous, although the adults approach quietly, and often in a roundabout way. The toucans will defend the nest, and even mob certain predators, but they are wary and often watch the predator at a distance. Interestingly, Yellow-throated Toucans were seen to chase away a kinkajou (*Potos flavus*), an arboreal mammal, rattling the bill at it.

As might be expected where pair-bonds tend to be long, the courtship displays of toucans are not elaborate, and copulation can occur without prior ritual. The plumage and bare parts, the wherewithal for display, appear not to change seasonally, and are, rather, determined by age, sex and condition of the toucan. Colour patterning and markings, such as red undertail-coverts, coloured marks over the eye or on the ear-coverts, and the frontal and lateral patterns of the head and bill, are likely important, and can be shifted by movements and by erecting and lowering of the feathers. The most prevalent courtship displays are courtship feeding and allopreening, the latter especially about the face and eyes, although this can occur to an extent throughout the year in large toucans. Some species, such as the Plate-billed Mountain-toucan, courtship-feed only in the vicinity of the nest. Courtship feeding is known to occur in all genera of toucans, while delicate allopreening is most frequent in *Ramphastos*, but is also performed by green toucanets, *Selenidera*, *Baillonius* and a few araçaris.

Plate-billed Mountain-toucans display by jumping about, the male calling with tail cocked, and both sexes erecting the red undertail-coverts and the yellow-gold flank mark. During this, the moving bill and face colours are, of course, a notable feature. In Saffron Toucanets, courtship feeding is carried on to the extent that the "gifted" fruit is passed back and forth, while there is extended allopreening of the female's face by the male, and both sexes tap-drum at the nest. Very little information is available on courting araçaris; apparently, the pair-members bob and bow at one another repeatedly, a possible effect of this being that the shorter bill of the female is displayed differently from the male's against the pattern of the underparts. In Red-breasted Toucans, allopreening is carried to the point of feeding-chases of the female by her fruit-carrying mate. The male Toco Toucan cocks the tail and spreads the red undertail-coverts, leaping about the female, and in captivity the male can become too aggressive towards its mate for breeding to occur. Allopreening male White-throated Toucans softly "chew" or "nibble" on the female's face with the tips of the mandibles. During the courtship period, Yellow-throated Toucans regurgitate one fruit after another, up to five at one feeding. The male of this species, which sometimes keeps even its mate from a fruiting tree, will often come to allow her to feed in it with him, at a distance, or he may turn over the tree to her control, moving himself to another nearby.

One to five white eggs are laid by green toucanets, two to four by *Selenidera*, two or three by the Plate-billed Mountain-toucan and by *Baillonius*, two to five by araçaris, and one to five by *Ramphastos* toucans. These are laid at daily intervals, incubation commencing with the last egg in the case of the Rainbow-billed Toucan, but starting with the first egg in White-throated Toucans. Copulation continues through the laying cycle. In the Plate-billed Mountain-toucan, the female solicits and the male mounts as she crouches; he puts his head over her nape and holds her nape feathers as she partly spreads her wings and tail, copulation lasting for 15-20 seconds. In Yellow-throated Toucans, there appear to be no preliminary displays prior to copulation. Female White-throated Toucans droop the tail and body, with wings held out, and then raise the tail, whereupon the male mounts, and he may stay thrusting atop her for up to 35 seconds.

The female often incubates more than the male, and incubates at night in the cases of the well-studied Emerald Toucanet

items at once in the bill, and the oesophagus. Two feeds in an hour is perhaps the average rate. In one study, White-throated Toucans fed the chicks 1·8-6·4 times per hour, the male averaging fewer feeds; the combined hourly rate of 6·4 occurred late in the nestling period, on a day when both parents made a total of 32 feeding visits in 15 hours. Both sexes of the Plate-billed Mountain-toucan feed the brood regularly at first, but after two weeks the female, which stays closer to the nest, feeds them more often. In Channel-billed Toucans, feeds may number about 29 per day, but occasionally there is a gap in feeding of up to nine hours. Animal food items are brought more often early in the period, and mostly by males.

The nest-cavity is usually kept clean, a task carried out by both adults. Occasionally, females undertake more of this burden. In Collared Araçaris, adults were not seen to carry away faecal material until the fourth week; the chicks' droppings are perhaps eaten at first, and carried away only as the young grow larger, or, more probably, the material is carried within the bill. Wood chips are mixed with the faeces, and this may account for the excavating work performed by incubating adults, designed to produce more chips.

Fledging has rarely been observed. One Fiery-billed Araçari fledged as long as three days after others of its brood, but no comparable data are available on other species of toucan. Except in the case of some araçaris, fledglings are generally not led back to the nest. White-throated Toucans, for example, lead their fledged young to join the group within the home range, and away from the nest. In captivity, the young sometimes beg over a lengthy period, but they can feed themselves rather quickly. Crimson-rumped Toucanets feed the fledglings for about two weeks, while a young Spot-billed Toucanet was fed to some extent for 55 days. Some green toucanets and mountain-toucans raise a second brood on occasion. Plate-billed Mountain-toucans can also raise two broods, but they may not nest in some years; they feed the young of the first brood for 20 days or so, but then drive them from the territory. Young Toco Toucans soon learn to feed themselves in aviaries, where the pair may raise two broods in a season. In contrast, Fiery-billed Araçaris which lose their young, or eggs, are not known to renest in the same year. Fledged araçaris often accompany their parents and any helpers for a lengthy period, and young Lettered Araçaris may remain with their parents until the following breeding season.

Nest failures are perhaps most often due to the collapse or fall of the nesting stub or tree, which sometimes breaks off through the nest. In addition, nests can be taken over by mammals, by other large birds, even other toucans, or by reptiles, bees and other animals, and a further problem is that rainwater can flood the cavity.

Toucans suffer various degrees of predation and nest parasitism during the breeding season, and they are often taken by raptors (see General Habits). Individual hawks or falcons sometimes specialize on toucans: for example, the "extra" Collared Forest-falcon forming a trio at the nest of a pair of these raptors brought 27 Rainbow-billed Toucans to the nestling falcons in a period of ten weeks. Furthermore, monkeys such as the white-throated capuchin monkey (*Cebus capucinus*) are known to take the eggs and young of White-throated Toucans, and probably those of other ramphastids, too. Snakes, and mammalian predators such as various weasels (Mustelidae), no doubt also raid toucan nests. Moreover, young, recently fledged toucanets and araçaris, and even young fledglings of the large species of toucan, when they are not yet flying efficiently, are probably very vulnerable to adult avian predators.

Information on breeding success is virtually lacking, but it is considered doubtful whether most pairs of toucans manage to raise one young bird to independence yearly.

Although there are no data available on the longevity of toucans in the wild, these birds can live for a long time in captivity. Twenty years is probably not an unusual age. J. Jennings reported on a pair of Channel-billed Toucans, already adult when he obtained them; they bred two years later, and continued to do so, successfully, for 14 consecutive years, by which time they must have been at least 18 years old. Many of those toucans bred in captivity are eight to twelve years old. Extensive field studies of

and the Plate-billed Mountain-toucan. Both parents incubate during the day. In White-throated Toucans, the female sits at night, and, while incubating during the day, is fed on the nest by the male. Incubation stints recorded for Rainbow-billed Toucans last from four to 86 minutes, and those of Fiery-billed Araçaris are two to 102 minutes, averaging 25-28 minutes. Data on incubation period are available for eleven species, representing all genera, and these give an average of 16·3 days. The incubation period is 15-17 days in the toucanets, araçaris and mountain-toucans, and 15-18 days in *Ramphastos* species.

At hatching, the young are blind and naked, with a long neck, strongly tubercled heel pads, a misproportioned bill with the lower mandible longer than the maxilla, which bears the egg tooth, and an uptilted uropygial area at the tail base. They perch on a tripod formed by the two hypotarsal heels and the belly, with feet in the air and with upward-pointing uropygium. The rapid incubation, typical of piciforms, is followed by a long nestling period with an initial phase of fast growth lasting about two weeks, during which proteins and other nutrients are essential. At this stage, Collared Araçari pairs allow members of the social group back into the nest for roosting, and to feed the nestlings. The chick's feathers begin to appear at two weeks, the eyes begin to open in two to four weeks, and at four to five weeks the chick is well feathered. Nevertheless, in none of the toucan species are the young known to fledge before 40 days. Those of two very large toucans, the White-throated and Yellow-throated, fledge in 43 and 45 days, respectively, so size matters little. For some species, the nestling period covers a wide range: 43-52 days have been recorded for the Channel-billed Toucan, and 46-60 days, with an average of 50·3 days, for Plate-billed Mountain-toucans. Broadly, then, 40-60 days is the range of toucan nestling periods.

Toucans are generally wary and easily disturbed. In aviary conditions, Green Araçaris sometimes eat their young if disturbed; two nestlings were saved from their parents by fostering them with a pair of Spot-billed Toucanets, which raised them successfully. At first, the naked young must be brooded at cool times, as during rain. Both parents brood, the female more so in several species. Both also feed the tiny hatchlings, in some cases by regurgitation. Feeding rates are lower than those recorded for the barbets, but toucans can hold several

Toucans are often limited by nest-site availability, preferring cavities in secure locations but utilizing low or insecure sites if there is a shortage of options. If available, nests with narrow entrances are preferred; the Green Araçari, like several of its relatives, prefers disused woodpecker holes. Smaller toucans regularly position their nests in isolated trees, in agricultural land alongside forest, for example, and it is possible that thus situated they confer some protection against arboreal mammalian and reptilian predators. Nest occupants tend to mob predators that approach the nest, often clattering their bills as a sign of aggression.

[*Pteroglossus viridis*, Amazonia. Photo: E. & D. Hosking/ FLPA]

The female Emerald Toucanet, as in most toucans for which data are available, generally contributes more time to incubation than the male, and tends to incubate during the night. Taking an average of those species for which information has been gathered gives an average incubation period of 16·3 days for the family, being slightly shorter than this for the smaller toucanets and araçaris and slightly longer for the larger Ramphastos toucans. Pair-bonds in toucans are protracted and it is thus not surprising that breeding displays are modest, copulation often occurring without display as a precursor. Courtship feeding is common, however, with regurgitated fruit regularly offered by the male.

[*Aulacorhynchus prasinus caeruleogularis*, Monte Verde Cloud Forest Reserve, Costa Rica. Photo: Stephen J. Krasemann/DRK Photo]

marked individual birds are required in order to ascertain whether or not such ages are attained in the wild.

Movements

Regular migrations and long-range dispersal are little known among the toucans. Emerald and Yellow-eared Toucanets in Central America do undertake downslope movements after the breeding season, or late within that period. It is possible that these involve mainly subadult and yearling birds, and therefore perhaps only one such movement would occur in a lifetime. Information is needed on whether or not breeding adults participate in these movements, and, if they do, to what extent. Similar downslope movements are made by Andean Plate-billed Mountain-toucans, in some numbers at times, and adults may be among those "migrating".

In south-eastern Brazil and adjacent Argentina, Red-breasted Toucans and Saffron Toucanets sometimes invade plantations of fruiting trees and coffee farms in mid-winter. These species often breed on mountain slopes, and it is likely that they move to lower elevations after breeding. Whether these are truly yearly migrations or whether they occur only in certain years is not known. Chestnut-eared Araçaris may make similar displacements.

Significant eruptive movements were formerly a feature of Toco and White-throated Toucans, and possibly Channel-billed Toucans, in the region of the Amazon and Oyapuk Rivers in northern Brazil and adjacent French Guiana. These involved hundreds or, at times, even a thousand or more toucans, often during June, and at Belém, on the lower Amazon, the birds moved from south to north. Such movements possibly occur as a result of the periodic failure of whole crops of forest fruits. Little is known about these eruptions; when reaching towns, the birds were often slaughtered. Any such movements that take place nowadays should be observed and monitored, since one effect of widespread clearance of forest in Amazonia is a shift in climate, especially in rainfall, which could have wholesale impacts on fruiting trees, the size of their crop, and the seasonality of fruiting.

The normal dispersive movements of the Ramphastidae are likely to be not very great, although they could be so in the non-forest Toco Toucan. Data on dispersal are, however, minimal.

Relationship with Man

The "banana-billed" Toco and Rainbow-billed Toucans are among the most familiar of Neotropical birds to people everywhere. Indeed, toucans are among the best-known of all bird species, their general appearance making them instantly recognizable even to people whose knowledge of birds and ornithology is virtually non-existent. They are noted for their colours, and they cause amusement with their antics and the absurdly long and deep bill that they possess.

The fact that Gould devoted two editions, the second very much revised, to a monograph of the Ramphastidae, with excellent plates and a surprisingly detailed verbal account, attests to the long-term popularity of the family. At least their conspicuousness and uniqueness resulted in several species of *Ramphastos* and one araçari having been named by Linnaeus himself, in 1758, making the toucans' taxonomic debut as old as that of the woodpeckers, and older than that of the barbets and honeyguides.

Certainly, these amazing birds were long known by Amerindian tribes and by early European colonists, who hunted and captured them. Being naturally inquisitive, toucans are easily attracted by imitation of their whistles. The birds were then either eaten or maintained as pets. At least one toucanet, several araçaris and all the large *Ramphastos* toucans have suffered from man's hunting for food. Like piciforms generally, toucans are probably "good eating".

Because of their unusual appearance, toucans were, and in places still are, prized as trophies. Toco Toucans often nest in

Cavities with small entrances are generally preferred, usually those just large enough to admit the passage of the occupant. Small holes are an advantage because nests are vulnerable to predation by arboreal mammals, snakes and even other toucans; indeed, a Yellow-throated Toucan (Ramphastos ambiguus) *was observed trying to reach Collared Araçari nestlings in their nest cavity. The Collared Araçari, pictured here, lives in groups that roost together in a tree cavity until breeding commences, at which time the nesting pair will monopolize the cavity and the other group members have to roost elsewhere.*

[Pteroglossus torquatus erythrozonus, Belize. Photos: Steve Kaufman/ DRK Photo]

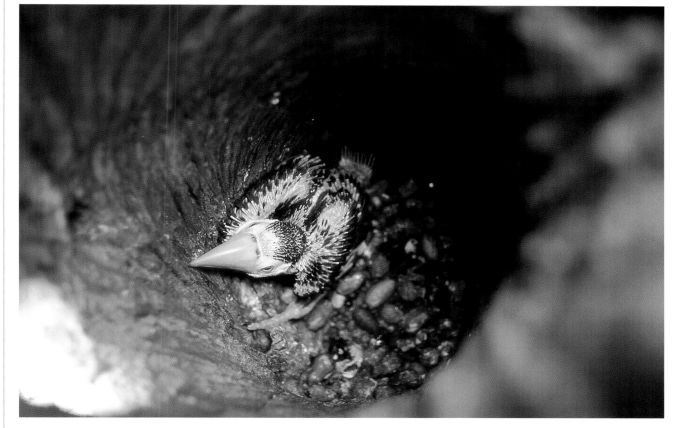

In toucans, as with most piciforms, the short incubation period is followed by a lengthy nestling stage, usually between 40 and 60 days, before fledging occurs. Like all young toucans, this nestling Toco Toucan hatched blind and naked. It stands on the callused heel pads typical of piciforms with its feet in the air, balancing on its belly, and awaiting deliveries of food from its parents. By two weeks old, the feathers have broken through; between the second and fourth weeks the eyes open; and at four to five weeks the chick is well feathered.

[*Ramphastos toco toco*, Aporé, Goiás, Brazil. Photo: Haroldo Palo Jr.]

earth banks, where they are easily captured. In some areas, the person, usually a child, who discovers the nest is deemed then to be the owner of both the nest and its occupants, and is therefore entitled to take and sell the nestlings. In former times, toucans and araçaris were so abundant that they were frequently offered for sale in the markets of large cities, such as Rio de Janeiro. Hunting of toucans is still practised today in some areas (see Status and Conservation).

The bright feathers of the toucan's plumage, especially those of the rump, were valued by many Amerindian tribes, which used them in their adornments, a practice documented as long ago as the sixteenth century. A photograph in Sick's 1993 avifauna on the birds of Brazil depicts a tribal woman's collar from the Rio Gurupi region of Maranhão; the collar itself is made from feathers from the upper breast of the Channel-billed Toucan, the insect-shaped pendant consisting of feathers from two species of cotinga (Cotinginae). In earlier times, Brazilian rulers, notably the Emperors Pedro I and II, had magnificent official robes made from the breast feathers of, primarily, Channel-billed Toucans, and it is likely that some tribal peoples used these feathers for similar purposes.

The extraordinary bill of the toucan must have intrigued numerous people over many generations, and fired their imagination. Medicinal remedies used by native peoples as a cure for a number of ailments have not infrequently included toucan parts, especially the bills, presumably ground into a powder. The efficacy of such concoctions is perhaps debatable, but the ramphastid bill is not known to contain any constituent item that could be of benefit in treating sicknesses of any kind.

Similarly, these birds' outlandish appearance has led to their being used as attention-catching and memorable logos in advertising. One advertisement for a well-known Irish stout-beer used the image of a *Ramphastos* toucan in a long-running campaign, although this has since been superseded by a more modern, *avant garde* approach to promoting the product. In that example, it was supposedly not only the toucan's eye-catching bill, but also its general black-and-white appearance, mirroring the colour of the stout, that appealed to the advertiser's designers.

It is, perhaps, not really surprising that the toucan's bizarre looks have also resulted in less favourable "motives" being attributed to it. One Brazilian legend tells how the toucan, endowed

with its enormous bill, had desires to be regarded as the king of all winged creatures. The toucan concealed itself inside a tree trunk, as indeed it would when nesting, so that only its bill was visible. Other birds, on seeing the bill and its obvious great size, were ready to accept the toucan as the king. When the toucan left the tree cavity, however, and revealed its whole self, a thrush immediately cried out "He's nothing but nose!". The toucan's cover was exposed, and it left in a demoralized state.

At times when wild fruit crops are scarce or difficult to come by, toucans often visit commercial crops and gardens with fruit trees. In some parts of Central and South America where toucan populations remain healthy, the birds can cause serious damage in orchards and other fruit-growing sites, and are regarded as pests.

Status and Conservation

As large as they are, being the largest species of the order Piciformes, the toucans are perhaps fortunate to have their centre in Amazonian South America rather than in Malaysia or Central Africa, where the survival of forest tracts is more uncertain. This is not to say that there is any reason for complacency. Toucans, since they are relatively large birds, are more thinly distributed and less abundant, and therefore require larger areas to ensure the survival of their populations than do, for example, the barbets. Illegal removal of timber, accounting for perhaps 80% or more of the logging in Amazonian Brazil, where this activity has generally increased two-fold to three-fold since 1990, heightens our concern for these essentially forest denizens. The fact that major new roads, under construction in several parts of Amazonia, carry along with them a broader band of forest clearance than would simple "rights of way" is especially alarming, because their width of over 1 km almost precludes the crossing of these sterile tongues of "progress" by toucans. There seems little doubt that forest clearance and fragmentation are now the major threats to the long-term survival of these forest frugivores, the plight of which is such that it makes them ideal "flagship", or "keystone" or "indicator", species in the efforts to preserve large, intact blocks of habitat.

The rapid provision of accurate information to human inhabitants, both adults and youngsters, of large cities and of the towns near major areas of forest removal is essential. The well-

known toucan species can be used to help demonstrate to people how forests function ecologically, and to illustrate the need for diversity, and the importance of dispersal, both of tree seeds and of toucans, to the continued existence and health of tropical forest. The Plate-billed Mountain-toucan has been used rather as a flagship species in montane southern Colombia, and the Rain-

bow-billed Toucan is a now widely known symbol of the huge upswing in conservation attitudes in Belize.

On top of the obvious threats to their habitats, the hunting of toucans continues today in parts of Central America, Amazonia and Paraguay. Amerindians of the Amazon often have cultural bases for hunting certain animals, and whole tribes may specialize on a few types of birds, such as toucans and guans (Cracidae). That hunting can be significant in reducing the numbers of toucans is suggested by the fact that village hunters killed 57 Yellow-throated Toucans in a two-week period, and by reports from Brazil of a single hunter killing 150 Black-necked Araçaris in one day. The ease with which toucans can be taken by gun is indicated by the following episode. When hunters of a group of five Lettered Araçaris killed one young bird, the others of the group circled the hunters, "mobbing" them; two more were shot, and a fourth continued calling and flying close to the hunters, who then shot and killed that one; the single remaining araçari stayed near the spot for the rest of the day, calling frequently. The calls of some toucans can be mimicked, thereby drawing the birds to the hunters. Araçaris are killed locally because of their fruit depredations, and Red-breasted Toucans are sometimes killed as predators of smaller birds, while in some places a belief in the value of toucans in medicine has accounted for the killing of Choco and Channel-billed Toucans (see Relationship with Man).

Many are also captured for the live-bird trade and as local pets. Even in modern times, some homes in Brazil and Venezuela have pet toucans, and others have realistically mounted, stuffed specimens. Most zoos and bird collections of aviculturalists in the Neotropics have toucans on display, often in fairly large numbers; all of these come from the wild, for until the 1990's there were no toucans being bred in captivity in the region. Probably more toucans are taken today as pets in areas surrounding major population centres than are hunted for food.

In fact, although only one species of Ramphastidae is currently considered globally threatened, and three are currently listed as Near-threatened, others and, in particular, certain subspecies could well come under threat very soon. The montane Yellow-browed Toucanet, with a very restricted range, is considered Endangered. The three Near-threatened species include two of the four mountain-toucans that comprise the genus *Andigena*, and the Atlantic forest Saffron Toucanet, the sole mem-

The excrement of nestlings being semi-liquid, faecal material is difficult to clear from the nest, and yet the nest is invariably kept hygienic. While both adults carry faecal material away from the nest, this sometimes appears not to happen until well after hatching. It might be that adults carry it hidden within the bill during early stages. This Gold-collared Toucanet is seen carrying faecal material mixed with wood-chips: the need for a layer of absorbant wood-chips perhaps dictates the adults' behaviour of partially excavating in cavities before nesting, and for the gradual deepening of nest-chambers after a series of breeding attempts.

[Selenidera reinwardtii langsdorffii,
Tambopata Reserve,
Peru.
Photo: Mark Jones]

Young Channel-billed Toucans fledge between 43 and 52 days after hatching, this wide variation presumably being dependent on environmental factors such as temperature and food supply. No toucan has been recorded fledging in under 40 days, and the duration of the fledging period is unrelated to species size. After fledging, young toucans usually beg for a few weeks but can feed themselves after only a few days.

[Ramphastos vitellinus culminatus,
Aguarico River, Ecuador.
Photo: Art Wolfe]

As they are so immediately recognizable to non-ornithologists, and because of their need for large tracts of relatively uninterrupted forest, toucans make ideal "flagships" for regional conservation programmes. The stunning Plate-billed Mountain-toucan, for example, has been used for some time as a logo for conservation organizations and projects in Ecuador and Colombia. This species is currently categorized as Near-threatened because it occupies a restricted range in the Andean cloudforests of those two countries, a habitat that is continually shrinking in extent because of clearance for agriculture and settlements. The species is still relatively common in many areas, however, even in quite disturbed and degraded forests, such that its population is not thought small enough to justify its being classed as threatened.

[*Andigena laminirostris*, La Planada, Colombia. Photo: Patricio Robles Gil]

ber of the genus *Baillonius*. Until recently, all four of these species, along with the other two *Andigena* species, the Hooded and Black-billed Mountain-toucans, were listed as Near-threatened.

Of the mountain-toucans, those of lower montane forest, where clearing is severe and sustained, are possibly the most directly threatened. These are the Plate-billed Mountain-toucan and perhaps one or another subspecies of the Black-billed Mountain-toucan. The latter has a restricted range as a species, to say nothing of its three subspecies. Efforts aimed at informing the local human population, together with direct attempts at conservation of the Plate-billed Mountain-toucan, are under way in Ecuador. It is hoped that more information will soon be forthcoming on the situation of the Peruvian Yellow-browed Toucanet now that guerrilla activity has lessened in the region to which it is restricted. The threat to the Saffron Toucanet in Paraguay, southeast Brazil and adjacent north-east Argentina is mainly in the form of fragmentation of its habitat in the relatively heavily human-populated areas where it exists. It is doubtful whether even the dual national parks and forest reserves around Iguazú Falls in Brazil and Argentina together hold a sufficiently large population to guarantee its survival in the short term. The human-disturbance factor may be important to the conservation of secretive, shy species such as the Saffron Toucanet. An emphasis on protection of the watershed and on flood-control is important to the conservation of all of these toucans.

Other ramphastid species not currently considered to be threatened or near-threatened may be deserving of a reassessment of their conservation status. The Tawny-tufted Toucanet has a relatively small range in northern Brazil and adjacent southern Venezuela in which it shows a preference for white-sand riverine habitat. Its habitat could be cut in two by the already approved, massive road scheme linking Manaus, in Brazil, to Venezuela, and further encroached upon by the associated opening of land to settlement. To the immediate south of that toucanet, the nominate race of the Ivory-billed Araçari has a restricted range within the wedge formed by the Rio Negro and the Amazon. It seems to prefer river-edge habitat within this range, and any major fragmenting of forest there could bring it under threat. The narrow montane range of the Yellow-eared Toucanet is highly fragmented in Central America, populations in which have no contact

with those in western Colombia and north-west Ecuador, yet forested areas continue to be cleared. The problems are exacerbated by the need for connecting corridors of forest that permit the species' downslope movements and return (see Movements). Another species to watch is the Red-breasted Toucan of southeastern South America, which lives in somewhat similar habitats to those occupied by the Saffron Toucanet. It is, however, larger, and thus probably has a smaller population that is becoming even more fragmented, in addition to which it is a shy, easily disturbed toucan.

Several subspecies could be of concern regarding potential threats to them. The Groove-billed Toucanet, restricted as a species to north-east Colombian and northern Venezuelan mountains, has a race, *erythrognathus*, confined to the north-east corner of Venezuela, where habitat is fast disappearing. It should be monitored. The central, nominate race of that species could also come under threat as the human population rises and land is cleared. Also in need of monitoring, and about which little is known, is the distinctive, isolated race *osgoodi* of the Chestnut-tipped Toucanet, the smallest member of the family and restricted to the Acary and Wilhelmina Mountains in the Guianas. An eye should be kept also on the race *abbreviatus* of the Yellow-throated Toucan, found in north-east Colombia and the mountains of northern Venezuela. This subspecies requires large forest tracts in areas where fragmentation of forest is ongoing.

As alarm bells are sounded about the conservation of rarer, possibly threatened species and races of toucans, it should be noted that the gouging-away of Amazonian forest will probably create subpopulations of many of the more common toucan species and subspecies. In the case of the Channel-billed and White-throated Toucans, middle Amazonian populations are diversely hybrid, tending more or less towards one or another of the subspecies. As these populations inevitably become fragmented with clearance of the forest in one area after the other, it seems wise to give attention to the preservation of the isolates, for they are patently adapted to the habitats that they occupy. Furthermore, the genetic potential which they represent could benefit their species, helping those species to persist. There appears no reason why concern should be expressed with regard to any genetic "impurity", against which some environmentalists tend to discriminate when dealing with primary "pure" species.

Will any toucans benefit, or are they benefiting, from current deforestation and colonization by man? The Toco Toucan, with its preference for forest edges, riverine forest and woodland, and wooded patches in savanna, may be one such species. It is probably moving into partly cleared areas of Amazonia from its riverside habitats. So long as some patchy forest and sufficient fruiting trees remain, the species and its populations could expand. On the negative side, these expanding populations will be in close human contact, and losses of nests and of young birds taken as pets will hamper the expansion. Elsewhere in its range, complete removal of forest and woodland, as in the Chaco, eliminates the species, as tiny fragmented subpopulations are exposed to intense human pressure in the form of disturbance, hunting, and the taking of nestlings. Moreover, the recent intensive use of land bordering the Paraguay River, along which Toco Toucans have long moved, has meant that, at intervals, forest, woodland and, in fact, any tree cover are now lacking for several kilometres or more. This must restrict the species' movements further, to its detriment.

It seems imperative that the capturing of toucans in the wild be considered an unlawful act. Where such laws exist, it is important that they be enforced; where they do not, the exactment of them should surely be a priority. Given the conspicuousness of toucans, particularly as their habitats become ever more fragmented, increasing numbers of local people may well desire a toucan as a pet, and bird-catchers will attempt to take these birds, legally or illegally, in order to funnel them into the lucrative trade in cagebirds. It is essential that people, and especially young people, be made aware of the threats to their local wild birds, and of the fact that these are best left in the wild. Efforts such as those in Belize, which bring whole communities into an understanding of ecological matters and instil in them a pride in their wild birds, demonstrate that progress can be made, rapidly, in halting the capture of nestling birds. To the extent that suitable veteri-

The Fiery-billed Araçari has a restricted range that falls within the South Central American Pacific Slope Endemic Bird Area of Costa Rica and Panama. Despite this, and a certain contraction of its range in Panama, the species is not considered to be of conservation concern because it remains common in certain localities and its overall numbers are thought to remain sufficiently high at present.

[*Pteroglossus frantzii*, Corcovado National Park, Costa Rica. Photo: Manfred Pfefferle]

Baillonius *is the only modern genus of toucans that appears not to have originated in Amazonia. It is erected solely for the Saffron Toucanet, an anomalous yellowish species that inhabits the Atlantic Forest of south-east Brazil, northernmost Argentina and eastern Paraguay. The swathe of forest in this region was once vast but is now broken up into shrinking fragments under constant pressure from logging and clearance for agriculture. While this species is still too widespread and numerous to be counted amongst the many threatened birds restricted to the Atlantic Forest, it may well join them if habitat destruction in this region continues.*

[*Baillonius bailloni,* Espírito Santo, Brazil. Photo: Michel Gunther/ Bios]

nary and other expertise can be brought into the local milieu, centres for the rehabilitation of toucans can assist in their conservation and in the informing of the people.

The provision of accurate, reliable information is the keystone for bird preservation. People generally should be made aware of why exotic trees are essentially worthless to birds, especially toucans. This is not to say that the planting of exotic, fast-growing trees may not be useful as a source of firewood, and for local construction, as it can reduce the loss of indigenous forest trees. Even for such purposes, however, indigenous trees are still a better choice, although more needs to be known about the planting, growth and tending of local trees. There is no question that firewood trees are essential, at least until such time as technology has provided cheap, readily available alternatives locally for heating and cooking in developing tropical countries. Zoos and botanic gardens in tropical America can help by planting fruit trees among their exhibits, attracting and helping to save toucans. A good example is the Catharine and Robert Wilson Botanical Garden, near San Vito, in south-western Costa Rica, which is now a paradise for wild toucans. Orchardists should be encouraged to plant some fruit trees "for the birds", especially on the orchard edges nearest to forest remnants. Park authorities could usefully plant fruiting trees around their headquarters and other buildings. Toucans are among many birds that come to these, and they are attractions to visitors; the birds often become tame, and observable.

It is well worth experimenting with nestboxes for use by toucans. The success in breeding toucans in aviaries, and the use of various pre-cut logs and palms and other log-boxes, indicate that the provision of nestboxes would be a positive strategy, particularly in secondary forest, forest patches and parks, and on private property. Some boxes will be used by other bird species, mammals and other animals. If designed for one or several of the local toucans, however, they could become a successful tool in improving the quality of habitats that may already provide sufficient fruits and other foods, but not enough appropriate sites for nesting.

Toucans do breed in captivity, but with certain difficulties, such as the large amount of space required by the large toucans. A captive-breeding centre for toucans has been declared by the United States Fish and Wildlife Service at the Fallbrook, California, avi-

aries run by Jennings, who has bred more species of toucan than anybody else. Some North American and European zoos, and a few private aviculturalists, have experience in breeding certain of the species. It does seem essential that the main breeding centres be established within the countries in the Neotropics where toucans occur, or formerly occurred, naturally. To this end, Jennings has helped spearhead endeavours, particularly in Brazil. It is likely that, once techniques have been "fine-tuned", many of the smaller toucans could be bred in numbers sufficient to allow their effective re-establishment in the wild, as and when this becomes necessary. In such cases, captive-bred toucans might require supplemental feeding of fruits for some time after release.

Of course, even a fine, viable captive-breeding programme is no guarantee of the long-term survival of toucans. This depends pre-eminently upon the occurrence of suitable habitat, including a sufficient diversity of fruiting trees to meet the birds' nutritional needs throughout the year. The principal requirement for the conservation of these unique and significant birds is, therefore, the preservation of their habitat.

General Bibliography

Amadon & Short (1992), Avise & Aquadro (1987), Barker & Lanyon (1996), Beltrán (1994), Bock (1994), Bourne (1974), Brom (1990), Bühler (1995a, 1996, 1997), Burton (1984), Collar (1997), Cracraft (1981), Cracraft & Prum (1988), Gaud & Atyeo (1996), de Germiny (1930a, 1930b), Gould (1854), Gyldenstolpe (1917), Hackett & Lehn (1997), Haffer (1968, 1969, 1974, 1995, 1997a), Höfling (1991, 1995, 1998), Höfling & Gasc (1984a, 1984b), Jennings (1986, 1993a), Lanyon & Zink (1987), Lucas (1897), Macquarrie *et al.* (1992), Mayr & Bock (1994), Miller (1915), Olson (1983), Peters (1948), Prum (1988), Raikow & Cracraft (1983), Remsen *et al.* (1993), Riley & Smith (1992), Robinson (1985), Robinson & Terborgh (1997), Rutgers & Norris (1977), Schulenberg & Parker (1997), Schwartz (1972), Short (1985b), Short & Horne (2001), Sibley (1996), Sibley & Ahlquist (1990), Sibley & Monroe (1990, 1993), Sibley *et al.* (1988), Simpson, B.B. & Haffer (1978), Simpson, S.F. & Cracraft (1981), Skutch (1954, 1985c), Snow (1981, 1997), Stresemann & Stresemann (1966), Swierczewski (1977), Swierczewski & Raikow (1981), Terborgh *et al.* (1990), Van Tyne (1929), Verheyen (1955a, 1955b), Wheelwright (1991), Willis (1983).

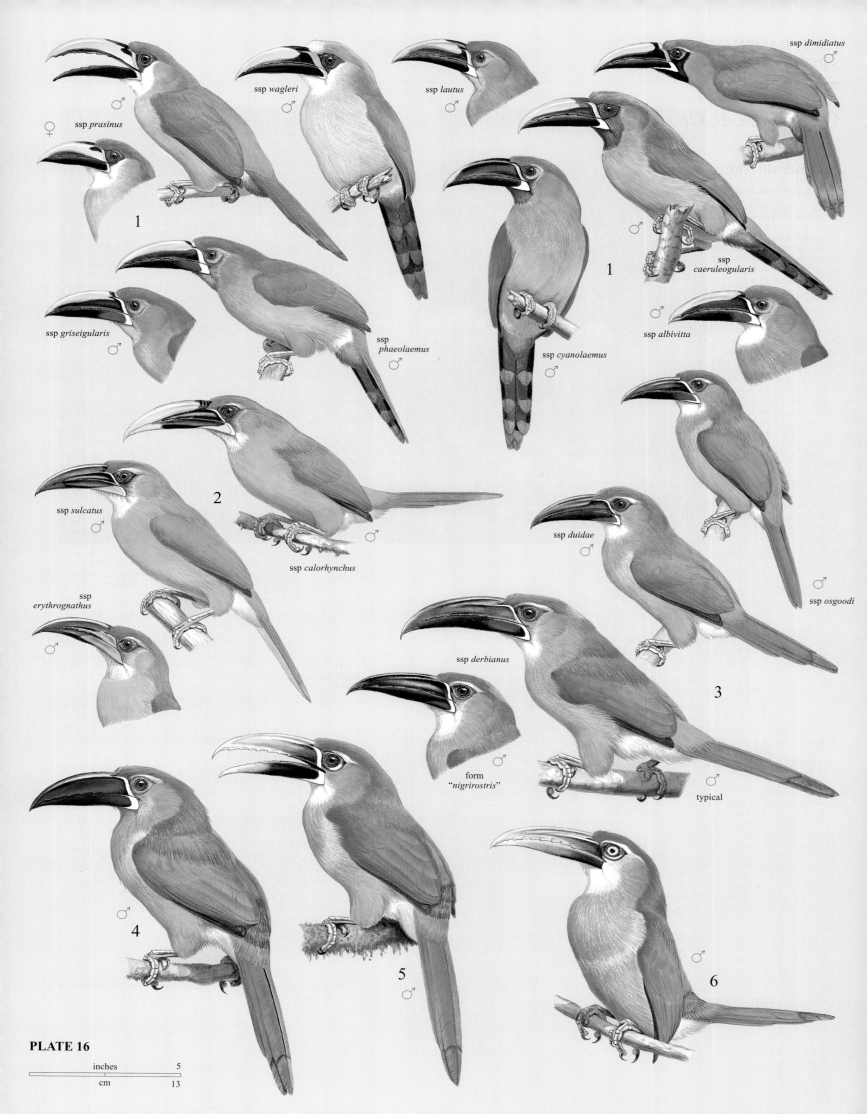

♀ ssp *prasinus*

ssp *wagleri* ♂

ssp *lautus* ♂

ssp *dimidiatus* ♂

1

ssp *caeruleogularis* ♂

1

ssp *griseigularis* ♂

ssp *phaeolaemus* ♂

ssp *albivitta* ♂

ssp *cyanolaemus* ♂

ssp *sulcatus* ♂

2

ssp *duidae* ♂

ssp *erythrognathus* ♂

ssp *calorhynchus* ♂

ssp *osgoodi* ♂

ssp *derbianus* ♂

3

form "*nigrirostris*" ♂

typical ♂

4 ♂

5 ♂

6 ♂

PLATE 16

inches 5

cm 13

Genus *AULACORHYNCHUS* Gould, 1835

1. **Emerald Toucanet**

Aulacorhynchus prasinus

French: Toucanet émeraude **German**: Laucharassari **Spanish**: Tucanete Esmeralda
Other common names: Blue-throated Toucanet (*caeruleogularis*)

Taxonomy. *Pteroglossus prasinus* Gould, 1834, Valle Real, Mexico.
Related rather closely to *A. sulcatus* (especially race *calorhynchus*), and also, less closely, to *A. derbianus*. Of the many races, several are sometimes considered to represent separate species, especially *wagleri*, *caeruleogularis*, *albivitta*, *phaeolaemus*, *cyanolaemus* and *atrogularis*; these, however, are all similar vocally, bill pattern varies relatively little, and all interbreed with each other or with other races wherever they meet; also, mosaic evolution evident among white-throated and blue-throated races. Races intergrade widely, notably *virescens* with nominate. Race *cognatus* possibly inseparable from *caeruleogularis*. Of other races proposed, *chiapensis* (SE Mexico) and *stenorhabdus* (W Guatemala, N El Salvador) considered synonymous with *virescens*, probably showing only clinal differences; *maxillaris* (Costa Rica, W Panama) with *caeruleogularis*; and *petax* (W Andes of Colombia) with *phaeolaemus*. Fourteen subspecies currently recognized.
Subspecies and Distribution.
A. p. wagleri (Sturm, 1841) - SW Mexico (Sierra Madre del Sur, in Guerrero and SW Oaxaca).
A. p. prasinus (Gould, 1834) - E Mexico (SE San Luis Potosí to N Oaxaca) S & E to Yucatán, Belize and N Guatemala.
A. p. warneri Winker, 2000 - SE Mexico (Sierra de Los Tuxtlas, in S Veracruz).
A. p. volcanius Dickey & van Rossem, 1930 - E El Salvador (San Miguel Volcano slopes).
A. p. virescens Ridgway, 1912 - SE Mexico (Chiapas) to Honduras and Nicaragua.
A. p. caeruleogularis (Gould, 1854) - Costa Rican mountains to W Panama.
A. p. cognatus (Nelson, 1912) - C & E Panama S to W Colombia (Chocó).
A. p. lautus (Bangs, 1898) - NE Colombia (Santa Marta Mts).
A. p. albivitta (Boissonneau, 1840) - W Venezuelan Andes S to Colombia (E slope of C Andes, E Andes) and E Andean slopes of Ecuador.
A. p. griseigularis Chapman, 1915 - N part of W Andes and W slope of C Andes of Colombia.
A. p. phaeolaemus (Gould, 1874) - W slope of W Andes in W Colombia, N of Patia Canyon.
A. p. cyanolaemus (Gould, 1866) - E Andean slope of S Ecuador to N Peru (La Libertad, Amazonas).
A. p. atrogularis (Sturm, 1841) - E Andean slope from N Peru to C Bolivia (W Santa Cruz).
A. p. dimidiatus (Ridgway, 1886) - hills and lowlands from E Peru to W Brazil (Acre) and N Bolivia (Pando).

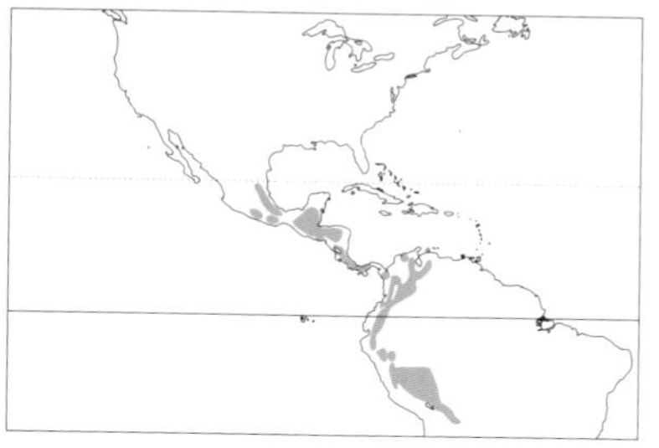

Descriptive notes. 30-37 cm; male 124-239 g, female 110-205 g (S races lighter, except *albivitta* and *phaeolaemus* as heavy as N *prasinus*). Green toucanet with black and yellow bill, sometimes with some chestnut colour at base; basal line of bill large, white to gold; tail tipped chestnut, undertail-coverts chestnut. Male of nominate race has bronze-green crown, white throat, dark grey-brown to rufous orbital skin, yellow-white basal line of bill. Differs from *A. sulcatus* in chestnut colour of tail tips and undertail-coverts. Female like male, but shorter-billed. Races vary in throat colour, colour of basal line of bill, tone of green around head and breast, and extent of black from bill base and tomia to culmen and tip of maxilla: *wagleri* like nominate, but crown yellower, breast paler with blue tinge; *albivitta* also white-throated, with white basal bill line, and more blue around eye than previous race; *warneri* has yellow wash on throat and auriculars; *caeruleogularis* and *cognatus* have blue to violet throat; *cyanolaemus* has blue throat, and almost all-black bill; *phaeolaemus* has blue-grey throat; *griseigularis* has grey throat; *atrogularis* and *dimidiatus* black-throated, *dimidiatus* also smallest of all races. Voice. Song an often prolonged series of variable barking to growling notes, from loud, hoarse "ggruk" to soft "ah" or "ek", c. 1·5 to 3 per second, notes shorter and tempo faster than in congeners; sexes at times sing together, male lower-pitched, and countersinging can result in song up to 3 or even 5 minutes long. Growl, rattled "eeaaah", other soft calls uttered singly; nestlings beg with single, later double, "cha" notes.
Habitat. Usually wet montane and submontane forest, cloudforest, edges, well-developed secondary forest, pasture with thickets, sometimes plantations and gardens, occasionally pine-oak woodland and alder woods. In Peruvian lowlands along rivers and lakes, in transitional forest, and floodplain-forest. In areas of overlap with other species of *Aulacorhynchus*, usually separated from them by altitude; locally occurs up to 3700 m, in Peru.
Food and Feeding. Fruits include lauraceous species (*Ocotea*, *Nectandra*, *Phoebe*) and solanaceous species (*Solanum*, *Cestrum*), also *Cecropia* and *Piper*; c. 120 species recorded eaten at one locality; also eats flowers or flower parts. Animal food includes beetles, grasshoppers, Homoptera, flies, caterpillars and Hymenoptera, also spiders, scorpions, bird eggs and young, lizards, snakes. Yellow plumage tints require carotenoids in diet. Regular visits to a feeding tree usually last 2-8 minutes, rarely up to 4 hours recorded; averages 26 g of fruit eaten per visit; digestion 24-70 minutes, so can consume more small fruits at once than larger ones. Sneaks through trees; enlarges cavity entrance to get at nest contents. Usually solitary when foraging, but sometimes in groups, occasionally quite large ones.
Breeding. Mar-Jul or later in Middle America, generally similar in NW South America, locally from Feb and to Nov; sometimes 2 broods. Displays with nodding, head-jerking, tail-cocking; courtship feeding may lead to copulation. Nest 2-27 m up, often at forest edge or on tree in pasture, even in utility pole, oval entrance higher than wide, to 57 cm deep; can excavate in very rotten wood, or usurps woodpecker nest if entrance in sufficiently decayed wood; much of excavating is by female, and some done as part of courtship; nest sometimes reused in subsequent years. Eggs 1-5; incubation period c. 16 days, female performing greater share; naked hatchlings brooded mostly by female, which feeds small fruits, male brings more arthropods, eggs, vertebrates; nest sanitation mainly by female, which can raise young alone; nestling period 42-45 days. Preyed on by weasels, monkeys, falcons, hawks; usually 2 young fledge.
Movements. Some evidence of downslope movement in Middle America, mainly by groups of young birds.
Status and Conservation. Not globally threatened. Locally common in parts of range. Found in moderate numbers in El Triunfo Biosphere Reserve, Chiapas, Mexico. Present in several protected areas in Costa Rica, e.g. Tapantí and Birds of Volcán Poás National Parks, Guayabo National Monument and Monteverde Biological Reserve. Uncommon to fairly common locally in Ecuador. In Peru, fairly common, with c. 2 pairs/100 ha of transitional forest, fewer in more mature forest. May be threatened locally, perhaps in particular those races with restricted ranges, as forest is generally cleared from lower mountain slopes.
Bibliography. Anon. (1995a), Binford (1989), Bond (1954), Chapman (1917, 1926), Dickey & van Rossem (1930, 1938), Fjeldså & Krabbe (1990), Foster *et al.* (1994), Hellmayr (1913), Hilty & Brown (1986), Hornbuckle (1999), Howell & Webb (1995), Jennings, J. (1977, 1981, 1995b), Krabbe (1991), Krabbe *et al.* (1997), Lowery & Dalquest (1951), María & Olivares (1967), Meyer de Schauensee (1949, 1964, 1966), Meyer de Schauensee & Phelps (1978), Miller (1963), Monroe (1968), Nadkarni & Matelson (1989), O'Neill & Gardner (1974), Parker & Bailey (1991), Parker, Schulenberg *et al.* (1985), Paynter (1955), Phelps & Phelps (1958), Remsen *et al.* (1993), Ridgely & Greenfield (2001), Ridgely & Gwynne (1989), Ridgway (1914), Riley (1986a, 1986b), Riley & Smith (1986, 1992), Robbins, Parker & Allen (1985), Robbins, Ridgely *et al.* (1987), Robinson & Terborgh (1997), Rowley (1966, 1984), Santana & Milligan (1984), Sick (1985, 1993), Skutch (1944a, 1967), Slud (1964), Stiles & Skutch (1989), Stotz *et al.* (1996), Terborgh *et al.* (1990), Thurber *et al.* (1987), Todd & Carriker (1922), Van Tyne (1935), Wagner (1944), Wenny & Levey (1998), Wetmore (1943, 1968a), Whittaker & Oren (1999), Winker (2000), Young *et al.* (1998).

2. **Groove-billed Toucanet**

Aulacorhynchus sulcatus

French: Toucanet à bec sillonné **German**: Blauzügelarassari **Spanish**: Tucanete Picosurcado
Other common names: Yellow-billed Toucanet (*calorhynchus*)

Taxonomy. *Pteroglossus sulcatus* Swainson, 1820, Venezuela.
Forms a superspecies with *A. derbianus*. Rather closely related also to *A. prasinus*, with which race *calorhynchus* overlaps somewhat. Race *calorhynchus* sometimes considered a separate species, but resembles other races vocally and intergrades with nominate. Three subspecies recognized.
Subspecies and Distribution.
A. s. calorhynchus (Gould, 1874) - NE Colombia (Santa Marta and Perijá Mts) E into W Venezuela (E to SW Lara).
A. s. sulcatus (Swainson, 1820) - N Venezuela (Falcón E to Miranda).
A. s. erythrognathus (Gould, 1874) - NE Venezuelan mountains.

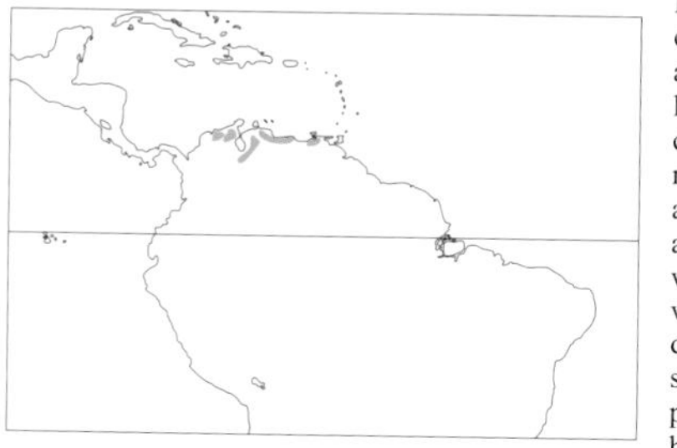

Descriptive notes. 33-37 cm; 150-200 g. Typical green toucanet, white-throated, with blue about rear of eye, undertail-coverts green-yellow, bill flat at base of culmen, grooved along culmen, mandible also grooved. Male nominate race with thin white basal line at bill, occasionally lacking; black from before eye diagonally across tomia to gonys of mandible, rest of bill wine-red to brown-red. Female slightly smaller, with shorter bill. Immature with lax plumage, duller, rectrices more pointed, has paler orbital skin, bill lacks grooves and tomial "teeth" and pattern obscured; shows evidence of spiky hypotarsal pad. Race *erythrognathus* lacks basal line of bill, black of bill reduced to near centre of mandible and tomial area, mandible orange-red near base, culmen more rounded, nostrils lower on maxilla, grooves shallower; *calorhynchus* very like nominate, including structure and pattern of bill, but white base line slightly broader and brown-red of nominate replaced by yellow distally, yellow-green near base of maxilla. Voice. Song of barking-growling notes or croaks, vary in quality, "wik-wik-" to "waak-waak-", c. 2·4 per second, in usually short series of up to c. 20 notes; sometimes notes are compound in series. Also rattles bill.
Habitat. Humid montane forest, from upper tropical to edge of temperate forest, also second growth, forest edges, nearby isolated trees, even gardens. Does not cross sizeable open areas. Usually recorded at 900-2000 m, but up to 2440 m in Colombia; in N Venezuela, occurs on wet slopes down to 400 m or lower.
Food and Feeding. Fruits, insects, eggs and young of birds; few data, but reported as frequently raiding nests of birds, and as omnivorous. Forages from understorey to canopy, alone, in pairs, or in groups; in last case, birds move in single file from spot to spot.
Breeding. Specimens indicate breeding Mar-Jul, except May-Aug in NE Venezuela. Nest, eggs, and all other aspects of breeding undocumented.
Movements. None reported.
Status and Conservation. Not globally threatened. No detailed information available on numbers, but species appears to be common generally in suitable habitat, e.g. in Henri Pittier National Park, Venezuela. Also occurs in Cueva de los Guácharos National Park, Venezuela. Biological and further ecological data required in case any of the three subspecies should eventually need to be monitored.
Bibliography. Boesman (1998), Bond *et al.* (1989), Cory (1919), Fjeldså & Krabbe (1990), Haffer (1974), Hellmayr & Seilern (1912), Hilty & Brown (1986), Meyer de Schauensee (1949, 1964, 1966, 1982), Meyer de Schauensee & Phelps (1978), Olrog (1968), Phelps & Phelps (1958), Ridgway (1914), Rodner *et al.* (2000), Röhl (1935), Schäfer & Phelps (1954), Schwartz (1972), Stotz *et al.* (1996), Todd & Carriker (1922), Verea & Solórzano (2001), Wetmore (1939).

3. **Chestnut-tipped Toucanet**

Aulacorhynchus derbianus

French: Toucanet de Derby **German**: Derbyarassari **Spanish**: Tucanete de Derby

Taxonomy. *Aulacorhynchus Derbianus* Gould, 1835, no locality = Huánuco, Peru.
Forms a superspecies with *A. sulcatus*. Also related, less closely, to *A. prasinus*. Form described from C Peru as *nigrirostris* now lumped within nominate *derbianus*. Four subspecies currently recognized.

On following pages: 4. Crimson-rumped Toucanet (*Aulacorhynchus haematopygus*); 5. Yellow-browed Toucanet (*Aulacorhynchus huallagae*); 6. Blue-banded Toucanet (*Aulacorhynchus coeruleicinctis*).

Subspecies and Distribution.
A. d. derbianus Gould, 1835 - extreme S Colombia S along E slope of Andes to C Bolivia (Cochabamba).
A. d. duidae Chapman, 1929 - mountains of S Venezuela in Amazonas and W Bolívar, and adjacent N Brazil.
A. d. whitelianus (Salvin & Godman, 1882) - mountains of S Venezuela (SE Bolívar) and N Guyana.
A. d. osgoodi Blake, 1941 - S Guyana (Acary Mts) and Surinam (Wilhelmina Mts).

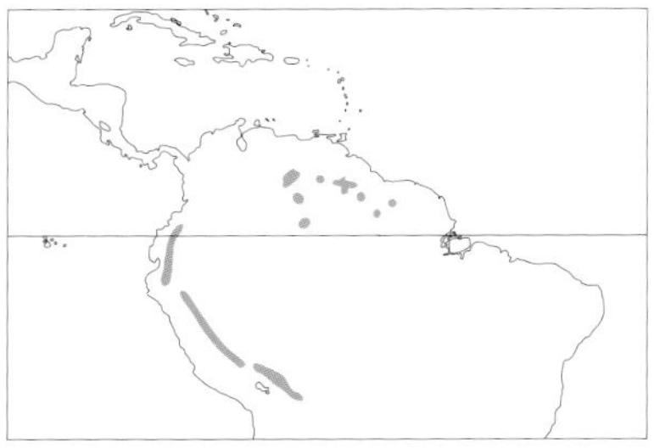

Descriptive notes. 33-41 cm; 141-262 g (*derbianus*), 117-160 g (other races). Green toucanet with grooves on maxilla only, bill tip especially hooked, base line of bill narrowly but conspicuously white, equal in width on mandible and maxilla; throat white, rump green, undertail-coverts yellow-green. Both sexes of nominate race with deep red and black bill, some individuals fully black-billed; bluish on nape, tail feathers tipped chestnut; blue under and behind brown-red orbital area. Differs from similar *A. sulcatus* in chestnut tips of tail, deep red base of mandible, lack of mandibular groove. Race *duidae* smaller than nominate, less blue on head and around eye, redder (less black) bill, smaller rusty tail tips; *whitelianus* smaller still, with smaller rusty tipping on tail; *osgoodi* smallest, lacks rusty tail tips. Voice. Song often long series of "grrrrump" to "kwuk" notes, 1·2-1·55 per second, notes longer and more evenly pitched than in *A. sulcatus*; some versions probably sexual in nature, pair-members often sing simultaneously. Also "ggg-rgg", "ngg-ngg", and rattling "bbdt-bbdt" notes. Voices of 2 smallest races not recorded.
Habitat. Usually subtropical moist montane cloudforest, to tropical high-valley forest in Bolivia; forested slopes on tepuis in Venezuela, and hilly tropical forest in Guyana and Surinam. Generally at 600-2400 m, in Andes usually 800-1600 m, in the Guianas at c. 300-800 m. In Andes usually occurs below *A. coeruleicinctis* and *A. prasinus*, but above latter in S Peru and Bolivia.
Food and Feeding. Little known. Fruits and their seeds comprise much of diet, but insects, including ants and grasshoppers, also reported. Feeds largely in canopy, often in pairs, occasionally in groups of up to c. 10.
Breeding. Data from specimens suggest breeding in May-Oct in Andes, Feb-Jul in NE of range. No other information; nest and eggs unknown, even territoriality not firmly established.
Movements. Probably sedentary.
Status and Conservation. Not globally threatened. Little known. Still common in some Andean and Venezuelan localities. Occurs in Imataca Forest Reserve and El Dorado, Venezuela. In Ecuador, generally rare to uncommon; regularly recorded in small numbers in Podocarpus National Park. Rare in Peru. Information urgently needed on subspecies *osgoodi*, potentially threatened, in small Guyana-Surinam range.
Bibliography. Anon. (1995a), Blake (1941, 1950), Bond (1954), Bond & Meyer de Schauensee (1943), Chapman (1917, 1926, 1929, 1931), Chubb (1916), Cory (1919), Dickerman & Phelps (1982), Fjeldså & Krabbe (1990), de Germiny (1930a), Greenway (1978), Haverschmidt & Mees (1994), Hilty & Brown (1986), Hornbuckle (1999), Mayr & Phelps (1967), Meyer de Schauensee (1949, 1964, 1966), Meyer de Schauensee & Phelps (1978), Morrone (2000), Parker & Bailey (1991), Parker *et al.* (1993), Phelps & Phelps (1958), Remsen (1984), Remsen *et al.* (1993), Ridgely & Greenfield (2001), Ridgway (1914), Robbins *et al.* (1987), Röhl (1935), Sick (1985, 1993), Snyder (1966), Stotz *et al.* (1996), Traylor (1951a), Willard *et al.* (1991), Zimmer (1930).

4. Crimson-rumped Toucanet
Aulacorhynchus haematopygus

French: Toucanet à croupion rouge **German**: Blutbürzelarassari **Spanish**: Tucanete Culirrojo

Taxonomy. *Pteroglossus hæmatopygus* Gould, 1835, no locality = Concordia, Antioquia, Colombia.
Forms a superspecies with *A. huallagae* and *A. coeruleicinctis*. Two subspecies recognized.
Subspecies and Distribution.
A. h. haematopygus (Gould, 1835) - Andean slopes from W Venezuela (Perijá Mts) and N & C Colombia S to SW Colombia; possibly also E slope in N Ecuador.
A. h. sexnotatus (Gould, 1868) - extreme SW Colombia and S in W Ecuador.

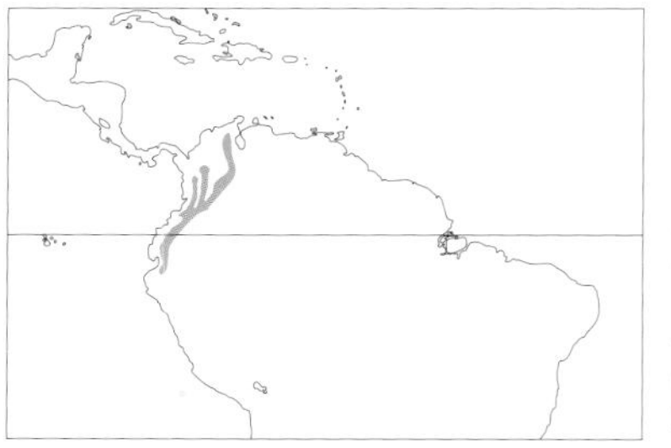

Descriptive notes. 40-45 cm; 200-232 g (*haematopygus*), 141-200 g (*sexnotatus*). Green toucanet with red rump, rather block-like brown-red and black bill flattened on culmen base, thus ridged on sides, white basal line broadening ventrally and widest at lower base of mandible. Male nominate race with bluish areas over eye, below eye, on sides of breast; throat green; central 2-3 pairs of rectrices chestnut-tipped; orbital skin orange-brown. Female shorter-billed. Immature has duller, lax plumage, with orangey rump; lacks bill "teeth", bill mainly reddish with pattern obscured, no basal bill line. Race *sexnotatus* smaller, with less blue in plumage and more red on bill. Voice. Series of variable, gruff, barking notes, "daakk" to "gggruk", to 2 minutes or longer, slower and lower-pitched than in *A. prasinus*; pair-members sing together, partly in duet, male with deeper, growl-like notes, female with clearer "drak". Also soft, long notes, rattle notes, interactive "snark" calls; loud wing sounds, especially during interactions.
Habitat. Lowland premontane to montane evergreen forest and second growth, edges, dense thickets nearby, also isolated fruit trees in pastures and gardens. Generally at 300-2200 m, occasionally to 2750 m.
Food and Feeding. Mainly fruits, such as those of *Cecropia* and lauraceous plants, palm nuts; probably also some insects and bird eggs; captives catch and eat small birds and insects inside aviaries, also dead mice when breeding. Feeds alone, in pairs or in small groups; skulks through understorey to canopy, bounding upwards in trees. Slower, less laboured flight than *Pteroglossus*. Drinks from epiphytes that hold water.
Breeding. Jan-May, as early as Nov in Ecuador and S Colombia. Much singing, calling, chasing until pair established at start of breeding; both sexes courtship-feed, allopreen, male cocks tail, erects breast feathers; singing bird points bill below horizontal, twitches tail in time with notes; switches tail about, cocks tail, assumes compressed "thin" look, drops down in attacks. Probably in most cases nest in old woodpecker hole, with rotted wood excavated out. In captivity, up to 4 eggs; female does much of the incubating, period c. 16-17 days; nestling naked, pink, fed on insects, fruits, young birds; nest kept clean by both parents; young develop slowly, feathering starts to appear before eyes open at c. 3 weeks, fully feathered except for flight-feathers at c. 6 weeks, fledging at c. 7 weeks; young probably return to roost with parents, may stay together until next breeding season.
Movements. None known.
Status and Conservation. Not globally threatened. Common in Colombia, where occurs in La Planada Nature Reserve and Río Ñambí Natural Reserve. Fairly common in Ecuador, where present in Podocarpus National Park. Seems to be adaptable, using secondary forest even in patches. Breeds successfully in captivity.
Bibliography. Allen (1998), Best *et al.* (1993), Bloch *et al.* (1991), Boesman (1998), Chapman (1917, 1926), Cory (1919), Evans & Coles (1982), Fjeldså & Krabbe (1990), de Germiny (1930a), Haffer (1974), Hilty (1997), Hilty & Brown (1986), Hughes (1988), Lantermann (1995), Maria & Olivares (1967), Meyer de Schauensee (1949, 1964, 1966), Meyer de Schauensee & Phelps (1978), Miller (1963), Parker & Carr (1992), Phelps & Phelps (1958), Remsen *et al.* (1993), Ridgely & Greenfield (2001), Ridgely *et al.* (1998), Rundel (1975), Salaman (1994), Salaman *et al.* (1999), Schlenker (2000), Schulenberg & Parker (1997), Stotz *et al.* (1996), Thompson (1980), Todd *et al.* (1973).

5. Yellow-browed Toucanet
Aulacorhynchus huallagae

French: Toucanet à sourcils jaunes **Spanish**: Tucanete del Huallaga
German: Gelbbrauenarassari

Taxonomy. *Aulacorhynchus huallagae* Carriker, 1933, Utcubamba, La Libertad, Peru.
Forms a superspecies with *A. haematopygus* and *A. coeruleicinctis*, and perhaps closer to latter. Monotypic.
Distribution. Locally in Peru (San Martín and La Libertad).

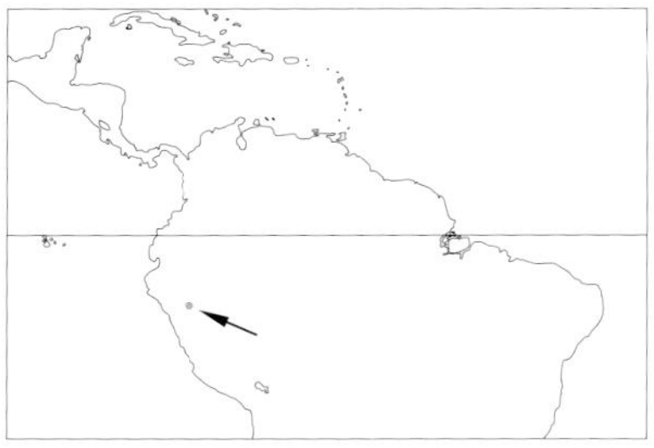

Descriptive notes. 38-44 cm; 150-278 g. Green toucanet with red rump, and black-based, ivory-tipped bill, base line of which is white, broader on mandible. Yellow superciliary mark, pale blue to yellow-white mark under eye, black orbital skin; white throat, pale blue across lower breast to sides, gold-yellow undertail-coverts; two central pairs of rectrices chestnut-tipped. Female has shorter bill. Differs from rather similar *A. coeruleicinctis* in white basal line of bill, and also distinct gold-yellow undertail patch. Voice. Variable, usually growling "gggrrowk" notes, varying in length, c. 1·2-1·6 per second; occasionally a clearer, "peet-peet-".
Habitat. Montane wet cloudforest with mosses and epiphytes, at 2125-2510 m; usually at elevations above *A. prasinus* and below *Andigena hypoglauca*.
Food and Feeding. Fruits and their seeds, some melostome fruits; probably also some insects and other animals. Probes into flower clusters of *Clusia*, a dominant tree in its habitat. Forages singly, in pairs or in small groups.
Breeding. Season includes Oct, probably early Oct, but uncertain. Adult approached playback of voice, shifted head and tail from side to side, synchronously, but in opposite directions. No other data available.
Movements. Presumably sedentary.
Status and Conservation. ENDANGERED. Restricted-range species: present in North-east Peruvian Cordilleras EBA. Until recently considered Near-threatened. Local and little-known species; in recent times, forest within its limited range has in places been taken over for growing coca, probably further reducing both range and numbers of present species. Where it does occur, it has sometimes been seen in fair numbers; new Río Abiseo National Park might hold sizeable population, although current information suggests species is very rare there; other areas where it occurs are largely unprotected. Range very small, for reasons unknown, perhaps connected to competition from other toucan species; does not appear to occupy all apparently suitable forest available within its overall range. Data on species' ecology and biology urgently needed in order to assist in plans for its monitoring.
Bibliography. Bond (1954), Carriker (1933), Clements & Shany (2001), Collar & Andrew (1988), Collar, Crosby & Stattersfield (1994), Collar, Gonzaga *et al.* (1992), Fjeldså & Krabbe (1990), Haffer (1974), Leo *et al.* (1988), Meyer de Schauensee (1966, 1982), Olrog (1968), Parker (1990), Parker, Parker & Plenge (1982), Parker, Schulenberg *et al.* (1985), Remsen *et al.* (1993), Schulenberg & Parker (1997), Stattersfield & Capper (2000), Stattersfield *et al.* (1998), Stotz *et al.* (1996), Wege & Long (1995).

6. Blue-banded Toucanet
Aulacorhynchus coeruleicinctis

French: Toucanet à ceinture bleue **German**: Grauschnabelarassari **Spanish**: Tucanete Pechiazul

Taxonomy. *Aulacorhynchus cærulei-cinctis* d'Orbigny, 1840, no locality = Yungas, Bolivia.
Forms a superspecies with *A. haematopygus* and *A. huallagae*, and possibly closer to latter. Putative race *borealis* of NC Peru (Junín) considered invalid, as appears to be based on individual, not geographical, variation. Species name often listed as *coeruleicinctus*, but original spelling, *coeruleicinctis*, must stand. Monotypic.
Distribution. C Peru (S Huánuco) on E Andean slope, including a few isolated montane areas to E, to S & SE Bolivia (Chuquisaca, Santa Cruz).

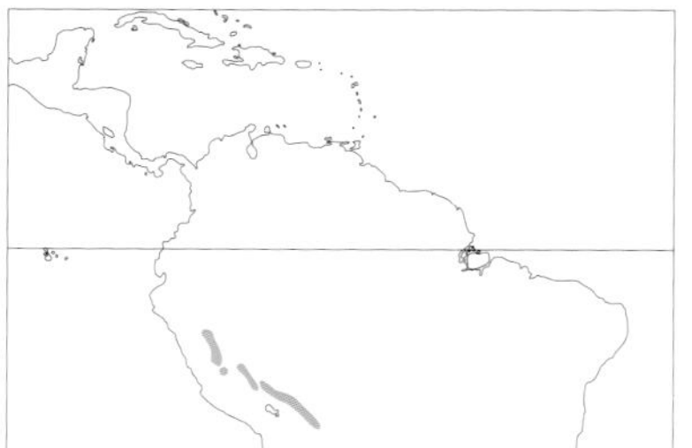

Descriptive notes. 40-44 cm; 173-257 g. Green toucanet with red rump, blue-horn bill lacking basal line. Blue and white superciliary and white throat; blue band across breast from sides, often somewhat diffuse; undertail-coverts greenish-yellow; tail with rusty chestnut tips on central feathers, rusty colour less extensive or absent on second rectrices; orbital skin dark greyish, but pale blue below eye; eyes white to yellow, sometimes brown or brown-red, no geographical pattern (e.g. brown or white in SC Peru). Differs from *A. huallagae* in having bill narrower at base, with no white line, more rigid laterally, and greener (not golden) undertail-coverts. Sexes alike. Immature duller, with lax plumage; lacks tomial serrations;

has rump and tail particularly dull. VOICE. Song a series of barking, growling, variable notes, "kunnk" to "krakk", 1-2·2 notes per second, lasting to over 1 minute; also various rattle calls, "kyak" yelps, a "kra-a-a" and "gek-ek-ek" compound notes. Functions of variants and calls unknown.

Habitat. Various forms of montane subtropical moist forest, cloudforest with dense undergrowth, reaching edge of subhumid tropical forest below and temperate forest above; recorded at 1470-3050 m, more usually 1600-2500 m.

Food and Feeding. Not known in detail. Fruits, also insects and other arthropods. Forages alone, in pairs or in small groups, from understorey to canopy.

Breeding. Data from specimens indicate season Jan-Apr, or later, in Peru, Aug-Jan in Bolivia. Nest, eggs, courtship and other aspects of breeding unknown.

Movements. No information.

Status and Conservation. Not globally threatened. No information on numbers; considered to be generally uncommon in Peru, though regularly noted near Manu Cloud Forest Lodge. Clearing of montane forest from lower levels could have adverse effect on this toucanet, although it should have noticeable impact on others such as *A. prasinus* and *A. derbianus* before this species. Studies required on its breeding biology and ecology.

Bibliography. Anon. (1995a), Bond (1954), Bond & Meyer de Schauensee (1943), Carriker (1933), Cassin (1867), Clements & Shany (2001), Fjeldså & Krabbe (1990), de Germiny (1930a), Haffer (1974), Meyer de Schauensee (1966, 1982), Olrog (1968), Parker *et al.* (1982), Remsen (1985), Remsen & Traylor (1989), Remsen *et al.* (1993), Ridgway (1914), Schulenberg & Parker (1997), Stotz *et al.* (1996), Terborgh (1972).

7

8

variant with
no white markings
on lower mandible
♂

9

ssp *langsdorffii*

♂

♀

ssp *reinwardtii*

10

♂

♀

11

♀

♂

♂

12

♀

PLATE 17

inches 4

cm 10

Genus *SELENIDERA* Gould, 1837

7. Guianan Toucanet

Selenidera culik

French: Toucanet koulik **German**: Pfefferfresser **Spanish**: Tucanete Culik

Taxonomy. *Pteroglossus Culik* Wagler, 1827, Cayenne.
Distinct from all others of genus. Although not very closely related to *S. spectabilis*, both that and present species have sometimes been thought to belong to probable superspecies formed by *S. nattereri*, *S. reinwardtii*, *S. gouldii* and *S. maculirostris*, but they differ from those four in voice and displays. Monotypic.
Distribution. Extreme SE Venezuela, the Guianas and N Brazil N of Amazon (from lower R Negro E to E Amapá).

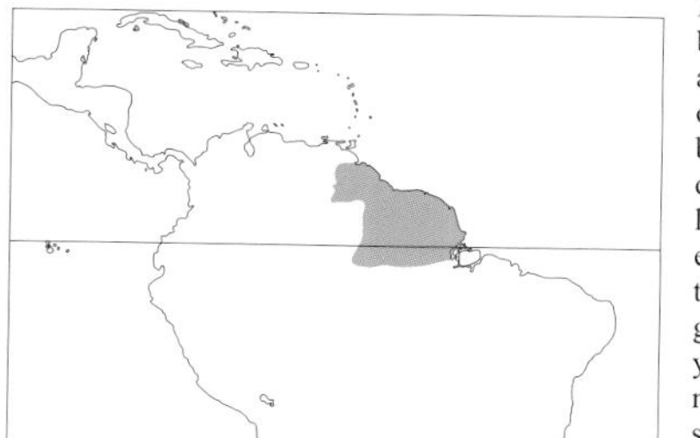

Descriptive notes. 33-35 cm; 129-165 g. Long bill red and black, upperparts green, tail green above with chestnut tips usually on all pairs of rectrices, red undertail-coverts. Male with black forehead to nape, throat and most of underparts, gold "collar" across upper mantle; large blue facial-orbital area, gold or yellow ear-tuft, black cap. Female with chestnut nape to upper back, muted yellow "collar", grey to green-grey underparts with belly green-yellow, paler blue orbital skin, shorter bill. Immature with lax plumage, duller, black areas sootier; bill less patterned, black mixed with brown. VOICE. Large repertoire, basic call rattle joined with squawk, rooster-like at times; rattles used alone aggressively, or introducing squawks; also long scream, like that of *Andigena*, perhaps an alarm call, but given in series with rattles as prelude; various soft rattles and other calls, some aggressive, others used in courtship feeding and at nest.
Habitat. Moist lowland to hill forest, and gallery forest in savannas; selectively cut forest used less than primary, undisturbed forest. Usually below 600 m; to 800-900 m in Venezuela and Surinam. Competes with woodpeckers for roosting and nesting holes.
Food and Feeding. Peppers, *Cecropia* and other fruits, including figs and palm fruits; also insects at times. Evidence for co-evolution with palm *Oenocarpus bacaba*, allowing toucanets few fruits at a time. In captivity, does well on grapes, melons, peppers, cooked beets and carrots. Feeds mainly in canopy, in pairs or small groups.
Breeding. Mar-May, or Apr-Jul in Brazil. Male courtship-feeds female, allopreens; raises head when calling or singing, sometimes directs song to sides with head up (shows sexual colours). Takes over woodpecker hole for nesting; a nest 9 m up palm tree in casava field, with 2 nestlings and 3 adults present, hence may nest socially. Eggs 2-3; no details on incubation and nestling periods, or on other aspects.
Movements. Probably sedentary.
Status and Conservation. Not globally threatened. Often common. Possible that relatively small size and formidable bill may enable this species to acquire suitable nesting cavities more readily than its larger relatives.
Bibliography. Beebe *et al*. (1917), Blake (1950, 1963), Bühler (1993, 1995b), Chubb (1916), Cohn-Haft *et al*. (1997), Cory (1919), Haffer (1974, 1978, 1987, 1991), Haverschmidt & Mees (1994), Jennings, J. (1993b, 1995b), Karr *et al*. (1990), Meyer de Schauensee (1966), Meyer de Schauensee & Phelps (1978), Morrone (2000), O'Brien (1979), Parker *et al*. (1993), Phelps & Phelps (1958), Remsen *et al*. (1993), Rodner *et al*. (2000), Sick (1985, 1993), Snyder (1966), Stotz & Bierregaard (1989), Stotz *et al*. (1996), Thiollay (1992), Tostain *et al*. (1992).

8. Tawny-tufted Toucanet

Selenidera nattereri

French: Toucanet de Natterer **German**: Nattererarassari **Spanish**: Tucanete de Natterer

Taxonomy. *Pteroglossus Nattereri* Gould, 1836, Brazil.
Probably forms a superspecies with *S. reinwardtii*, *S. gouldii* and *S. maculirostris*; *S. culik* and *S. spectabilis* have sometimes been included too, but these two appear to differ from others in voice and display behaviour. Monotypic.
Distribution. Patchily distributed along rivers, from extreme E Colombia (R Vaupés region) and S Venezuela to NW Brazil (R Solimões from Tonantins to Codajás, and N to upper R Negro); reports from Guyana and French Guiana require confirmation, as there is no evidence of occurrence in intervening areas.

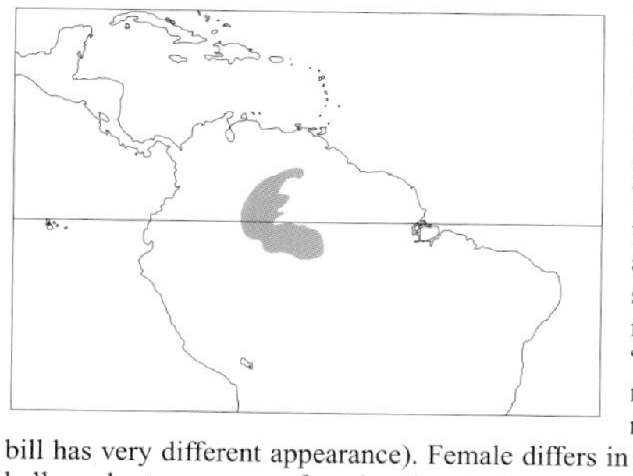

Descriptive notes. 32-33 cm; 148-165 g. Green above, with red undertail-coverts, and green tail tipped chestnut on central 3 feather pairs. Male black on head, and from chin and throat to belly, with long, "double", tawny-yellow ear-tuft, gold-yellow to rusty flank patch, golden-yellow band on upper mantle; orbital-facial skin blue to bright green-yellow, pink near lores; bill red at basal line, culmen green to lime-green, with square to angular blue patch near base of both maxilla and mandible, greenish or whitish tomial "teeth", usually white vertical lines on lower mandible (sometimes absent), rest of bill brown-red to red or greenish-horn (on dried specimens, bill has very different appearance). Female differs in chestnut crown to upper mantle, rusty chin to belly, paler tawny ear-tuft and yellow back band, green-muted flank patch, orbital-facial skin less bright. VOICE. Growl-like, croaking "ggruuukk" notes, c. 83-86 per minute, recorded calls mainly 10-15 seconds in duration; also more rattling version, "dddrik-"; other rattle calls show tendency towards those of *S. culik*.
Habitat. Forested lowlands, frequently on sandy soil, usually near streams; also low open forest.
Food and Feeding. Only fruits and fruit seeds found in stomachs; no other data.
Breeding. Almost unknown. Season suggested as Mar-May in all areas, mostly Apr-Nov. Displays, eggs, nest and all other details undocumented.
Movements. Probably sedentary.
Status and Conservation. Not globally threatened. Range is not small, but apparent patchiness of this species' occurrence gives cause for concern; reasons for presence in some areas and absence in many others uncertain. Data urgently needed on its habitat and feeding requirements, as well as on its breeding biology and behaviour.
Bibliography. Chubb (1916), Cory (1919), Friedmann (1948), Gyldenstolpe (1945a), Haffer (1974, 1978, 1991, 1997b), Hilty & Brown (1986), María & Olivares (1967), Meyer de Schauensee (1949, 1964, 1966), Meyer de Schauensee & Phelps (1978), Morrone (2000), Olivares (1964a), Parker *et al*. (1993), Pelzeln (1867-1871), Phelps & Phelps (1958), Pinto (1938a), Remsen *et al*. (1993), Rodner *et al*. (2000), Schomburgk (1848), Sick (1985, 1993), Snyder (1966), Stotz *et al*. (1996), Todd (1943b), Tostain *et al*. (1992), Willard *et al*. (1991), Zimmer & Hilty (1997).

9. Gold-collared Toucanet

Selenidera reinwardtii

French: Toucanet de Reinwardt **German**: Reinwardtarassari **Spanish**: Tucanete de Reinwardt
Other common names: Golden-collared Toucanet; Langsdorff's Toucanet (*langsdorffii*)

Taxonomy. *Pteroglossus Reinwardtii* Wagler, 1827, Brazil.
Probably forms a superspecies with *S. nattereri*, *S. gouldii* and *S. maculirostris*; *S. culik* and *S. spectabilis* have sometimes been included too, but these two appear to differ from others in voice and display behaviour. Race *langsdorffii* has sometimes been considered a separate species, but interbreeds with nominate race in N Peru (upper R Ucayali and R Huallaga), where intergrades occur. Two subspecies recognized.
Subspecies and Distribution.
S. r. reinwardtii (Wagler, 1827) - EC & SE Colombia (along Brazil border) S to E Ecuador and CN & NE Peru.
S. r. langsdorffii (Wagler, 1827) - NC & E Peru, and W Brazil (E, S of R Solimões, to R Purus and probably upper R Madeira), S to NW Bolivia (W of R Beni).

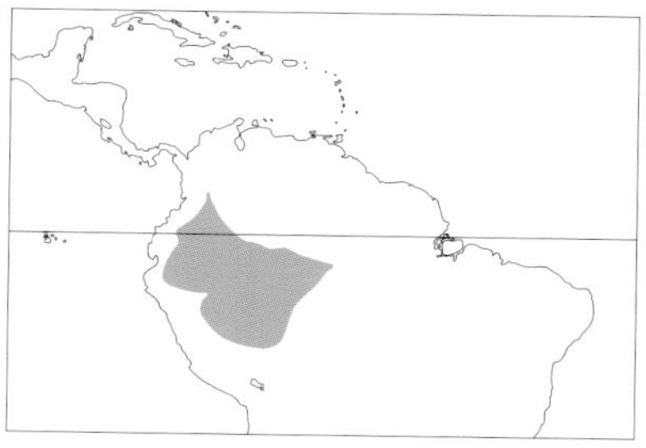

Descriptive notes. 33-35 cm; 129-178 g (*reinwardtii*), 134-200 g (*langsdorffii*). Male nominate race with black head to mantle, gold-yellow ear-tuft, and yellow band separating black from green back and tail; black below, with gold or orange-gold flank patch, red-undertail-coverts; central 2-3 pairs of rectrices tipped chestnut; bill with black basal line, black culmen expanding to all-black distal maxilla and mandible, tomial teeth black to ivory, rest of bill dull red; pale eye with darkened iris before and behind pupil, pupil appearing slit-like; orbital skin variably green, blue or yellow. Female chestnut where male black, duller ear-tuft blends with chestnut background, flank patch less gold, yellow band on upper back narrower, bill shorter. Immature with blotchy bill, no basal line, no tomial "teeth", keel at base of culmen, duller throughout, lax-plumaged, rusty-orange undertail; sexual features appear early. Race *langsdorffii* has orbital area greener, flank patch more orange, but differs mainly in bill colours: maxilla mainly black, mandible distally black, rest of sides green to grey-green, "teeth" creamy to whitish, or bill can be nearly all black, or sometimes with 2-4 vertical or angled black lines above maxillary tomia, latter suggesting pattern of *S. maculirostris*. VOICE. Song of both races a series of c. 4-14 "ggrraawk" notes at 60-85 per minute, notes longer than in *S. gouldii* and *S. maculirostris*, tempo much as in *S. maculirostris*; sexes seem to sing solo, not duetting; countersinging occurs; calls include "eh", "uh", "kik" and other softer sounds; also loud bill-wiping in aggression, loud wing sounds in interactions.
Habitat. Lowland and lower hill and mountain-slope forest, also floodplain-forest and occasionally *várzea*, but more common in dry upper areas of forest and on ridges; uses forest edges, but not secondary forest. Occurs generally up to c. 1000 m, in Ecuador sparsely up to 1200 m, in Peru reaching 1500 m rarely, and to 1300 m in NW Bolivia.
Food and Feeding. Diverse fruits, including figs, *Cecropia* fruits and many others; also some insects, and in captivity can be maintained on all-insect diet; has been captured while seeking to attack small birds in mist-nets. Forages from understorey to canopy, singly, in pairs, or in groups of up to 4 birds. Forages over bark and foliage, fly-catches inexpertly but successfully, also probes for termites. Joins mixed-species foraging flocks.
Breeding. Mar-Jul in N, Jun-Dec in Peru, Bolivia and W Brazil. Apparently territorial, mainly or entirely in pairs. Male courtship-feeds female, sometimes several fruits in succession, laying fruit across into her open bill; singer lowers tail as bows head deeply, then cocks it as head and bill lifted high, and red undertail-covert feathers erected, roughly 2-3 notes per full bow and rise. Nest in tree cavity, but unknown to what extent excavated, and nest details undescribed; used cavities seen at 2·4-4 m. Clutch size and other breeding data unreported.
Movements. Probably sedentary, and territorial throughout year.
Status and Conservation. Not globally threatened. Generally uncommon in Colombia. Uncommon to fairly common in Ecuador. Reported to be fairly common locally in Peru, but recorded density of only c. 1 pair/100 ha of forest, of which c. 35% is utilized. Occurs in Cuyabeno Reserve, Ecuador, and in Tambopata Reserve, Peru. Additional information needed regarding species' requirements for breeding. This genus is an appropriate one for designating indicator species, as the *Selenidera* toucanets are more strictly forest species than are other toucans.
Bibliography. Anon. (1995a), Bond (1954), Chapman (1917, 1921b, 1926), Clements & Shany (2001), Cory (1919), Cracraft & Prum (1988), Foster *et al*. (1994), Gyldenstolpe (1945a, 1951), Haffer (1974, 1978, 1991, 1993a, 1997b), Hilty & Brown (1986), Hornbuckle (1999), Karr *et al*. (1990), María & Olivares (1967), Meyer de Schauensee (1949, 1964, 1966), Morrone (2000), Novaes (1957), Parker & Bailey (1991), Parker & Remsen (1987), Parker *et al*. (1991), Remsen & Traylor (1989), Remsen *et al*. (1993), Ridgely & Greenfield (2001), Robinson & Terborgh (1997), Salaman *et al*. (1999), Sick (1985, 1993), Stotz *et al*. (1996), Terborgh *et al*. (1990), Traylor (1958), Zimmer (1930).

On following page: 10. Gould's Toucanet (*Selenidera gouldii*); 11. Spot-billed Toucanet (*Selenidera maculirostris*); 12. Yellow-eared Toucanet (*Selenidera spectabilis*).

10. Gould's Toucanet

Selenidera gouldii

French: Toucanet de Gould **German**: Gouldarassari **Spanish**: Tucanete de Gould

Taxonomy. *Pteroglossus Gouldii* Natterer, 1837, Pará, Brazil.
Probably forms a superspecies with *S. nattereri*, *S. reinwardtii* and *S. maculirostris*; *S. culik* and *S. spectabilis* have sometimes been included too, but these two appear to differ from others in voice and display behaviour. Closely related to *S. maculirostris*, and may be conspecific, as sometimes treated. Populations named as races *hellmayri* (NC Brazil) and *baturitensis* (NE Brazil) appear to represent clinal variation of trivial nature, size decreasing eastwards; either or both of these sometimes placed in *S. maculirostris*. Monotypic.
Distribution. C & E Brazil, S of Amazon (from R Madeira E to Maranhão and N Ceará), S to E Bolivia (R Mamoré, E Beni and NE Santa Cruz) and C Mato Grosso, there reaching tributaries of upper R Paraguay.

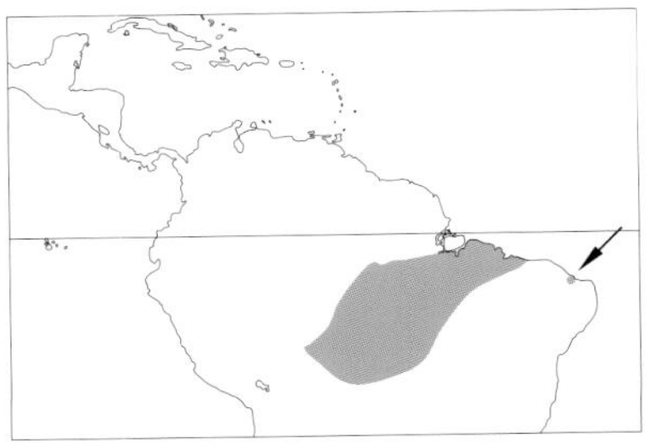

Descriptive notes. c. 33 cm; 131-209 g. Male with black head to mantle, gold-yellow ear-tuft, yellow band on upper back, green back and tail; black below, with golden flank patch, red-undertail-coverts; central 1-3 pairs of rectrices tipped chestnut; maxilla with narrow ivory base behind black patch, latter often with 3-5 vertical black lines beneath, mandible with ivory base to over half-way along and much smaller black patch below or ahead of front end of maxillary patch, one-third or more of bill tip orange-yellow, tomia ivory; yellow eye slit-like owing to darkened iris before and behind pupil; facial-orbital area green-yellow to blue. Distinguished from almost identical *S. reinwardtii* and *S. maculirostris* in bill colours. Female chestnut where male black, ear-tuft duller, flank patch more yellow, yellow band on upper back narrower, bill shorter. Immature duller, virtually lacking yellow band on back, plumage lax, bright areas of adults duller; bill lacks "teeth" and fine basal line, pattern obscure, blotchy, pale areas horn-coloured. Voice. Series of "ggrawnk" to "ggrraaw" notes, very like those of *S. reinwardtii* and *S. maculirostris*, but at slower tempo of 60-75 per minute; other calls probably also similar.
Habitat. Moist to wet tropical lowland forest, and gallery forest, especially in N *cerrado*; also palm forest, deciduous forest, some secondary forest, and thickets near forest; at times *várzea* flooded forest. Occurs on some slopes to 700 m, e.g. in Serra de Baturitá (Ceará, in NE Brazil), and to 725 m in Bolivia.
Food and Feeding. Very little known. Fruits, e.g. of the palm *Euterpe*; also, "meat" in one stomach. Forages from undergrowth to canopy, usually in pairs or in groups of up to 4.
Breeding. Season suggested as May-Sept; probably from Jun-Jul in W Brazil (Amazonas, Rondônia) and in Bolivia. No information available on nest, eggs and all other aspects; probably much as for *S. maculirostris*.
Movements. Presumably sedentary.
Status and Conservation. Not globally threatened. No information available on numbers. This species' ability to use second growth should favour it. Details of breeding and ecology are needed for possible monitoring.
Bibliography. Anon. (1995a), Bates *et al.* (1989), Beebe (1916), Cory (1919), Dubs (1992), Griscom & Greenway (1937), Gyldenstolpe (1945a), Haffer (1974, 1978, 1991, 1993a, 1997b), Hellmayr (1910), Novaes (1976), Novaes & Lima (1991), Oren & Parker (1997), Parker *et al.* (1991), Pinto & Camargo (1961), Remsen & Traylor (1989), Sick (1985, 1993), da Silva (1996), Stotz, Fitzpatrick *et al.* (1996), Stotz, Lanyon *et al.* (1997), Todd (1943b), Willis (1976), Willis & Oniki (1990), Zimmer *et al.* (1997).

11. Spot-billed Toucanet

Selenidera maculirostris

French: Toucanet à bec tacheté **German**: Fleckenarassari **Spanish**: Tucanete Piquimaculado

Taxonomy. *Pteroglossus maculirostris* M. H. K. Lichtenstein, 1823, Brazil.
Probably forms a superspecies with *S. nattereri*, *S. reinwardtii* and *S. gouldii*; *S. culik* and *S. spectabilis* have sometimes been included too, but these two appear to differ from others in voice and display behaviour. Closely related to *S. gouldii*, and possibly conspecific, as sometimes treated. Forms described as *hellmayri* (NC Brazil) and *baturitensis* (NE Brazil), apparently result only of clinal variation, usually treated as part of *S. gouldii*, but sometimes included in present species. Monotypic.
Distribution. Atlantic forest of SE Brazil (S Bahia and E Minas Gerais S to Paraná and Santa Catarina, possibly to Rio Grande do Sul), also adjacent E Paraguay and NE Argentina (Misiones).

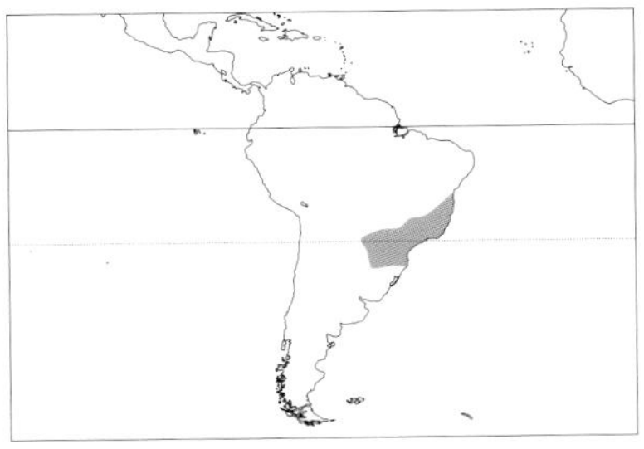

Descriptive notes. 33-37 cm; 137-193 g. Male with black head and underparts, green upperparts and tail, with gold-yellow ear-tuft, yellow hindcollar, yellow-gold flank mark, rusty thighs, red undertail-coverts, chestnut tips of central 3 pairs of rectrices; bill with fine black basal line, mainly greenish-yellow to ivory, brighter at tip, central culmen black, maxilla with 3-5 vertical black stripes (rear 1 or 2 can be isolated or dull), mandible with small anterior black mark level with or sometimes slightly forward of front maxillary stripe; eye yellow, black pupil appearing slit-like; orbital skin blue to green and yellow. Distinguished from *S. gouldii* and others of superspecies by bill pattern and colours. Female chestnut on head, more cinnamon-rufous underparts, cinnamon front of ear-tuft and flanks, bill shorter. Immature lax-plumaged, dull, without collar, bill muted in colour, without tomial "teeth"; shows black vertical maxillary marks at c. 8-9 weeks of age. Voice. Gruff, growling "ggrooaw" to "kkrowk" notes in series lasting to c. 15 seconds, at tempo of 75-90 per minute; sexes usually sing one at a time, sometimes together but usually not very close; somewhat similar notes during interactions, also low "tut" notes, rattling notes, purring low notes, bill-snapping sounds.
Habitat. Subtropical moist primary forest, selectively cut forest, nearby secondary patches, palm groves of *Euterpe edulis*; gallery forest at SE edge of the *cerrado*; also remnant patches of forest in Paraguay. Occurs to over 1000 m on mountain slopes that have forest remaining.
Food and Feeding. Fruits of *Euterpe*, *Cecropia* and others; insects and vertebrates probably also taken; in captivity eats many cultivated fruits, also captures insects in aviaries, and feeds dead young mice to nestlings. Forages in middle storey and undergrowth, even down to ground at times. Feeds singly, in pairs, or in small groups, but at one tree 19 seen with 5 *Baillonius bailloni* and other birds. Drinks from tree crevices. Often perches for extended periods; infrequently flies to isolated fruit trees in open, used by other toucans.
Breeding. Dec-Jun in N, Oct-Jan in S part of range. Most data from aviary birds. Nests in pairs, territorial. Male courtship-feeds, sometimes repeatedly, with regurgitated fruits, may give female a piece and keep rest, and pair allopreens; singer bows low, more or less in time with notes, raising head high, ear-covert tuft flared, flank patch out, undertail-coverts fluffed, tail twitched upward and sideways, to cocked position, then down, head may be held up or down for 2 notes, tail may move twice with 1 note, entire display like that of *Andigena* species. Nest probably excavated in old woodpecker hole; in captivity, both sexes excavate in rotted log with an essential chamber cut out for them. Eggs 2-3; for captives, incubation c. 15 days, both sexes in nest at night, male rattles softly when entering; nestlings fed fruits and dead mice, develop slowly, can be sexed by plumage at c. 25 days, reach 120 g at 31 days, fledging at 6-7 weeks, fed by adults until c. 55 days. One aviary pair, after its fledged young had been removed, adopted two 2-day-old *Pteroglossus viridis* and successfully raised them.
Movements. Unknown.
Status and Conservation. Not globally threatened. CITES II. Sizeable populations exist in some protected areas in Brazil, such as around Iguaçu, but locally threatened in other parts, where loss of forest has impact on species. Elsewhere in Brazil, occurs in Nova Lombardia Biological Reserve and Sooretama Biological Reserve. Present in Iguazú National Park, Argentina. Small Paraguayan populations much separated, and inbreeding probably occurs: present in that country in Estancia San Antonio Private Nature Reserve, Reserva Natural del Bosque Mbaracayú, La Golondrina Private Nature Reserve and Estancia Itabó Private Nature Reserve. Information needed on breeding biology of wild birds.
Bibliography. Belton (1984, 1994), Brooks *et al.* (1993), Buzzetti (2000), Canevari *et al.* (1991), Capper *et al.* (2000), Chebez (1994), Cory (1919), Cracraft & Prum (1988), Galetti *et al.* (1998), Guix (1995), Guix & Jover (2001), Guix *et al.* (2000), Haffer (1974, 1978, 1991, 1997b), Hayes (1995), Jennings, J. (1985b, 1995a, 1995b), Lüdicke (1960), McConnell (1991), Meyer de Schauensee (1966), Narosky & Yzurieta (1993), Parker & Goerck (1997), de la Peña (1994), Pinto (1935), do Rosário (1996), Saibene *et al.* (1996), Sick (1985, 1993), da Silva (1996), Stotz *et al.* (1996).

12. Yellow-eared Toucanet

Selenidera spectabilis

French: Toucanet à oreilles d'or **German**: Gelbohrarassari **Spanish**: Tucanete Orejigualdo

Taxonomy. *Selenidera spectabilis* Cassin, 1857, Cucuyos de Veragua, Panama.
Distinct within genus. Although not very closely related to *S. culik*, both that and present species have sometimes been thought to be part of probable superspecies formed by *S. nattereri*, *S. reinwardtii*, *S. gouldii* and *S. maculirostris*, but they differ from those four in voice and displays. Monotypic.
Distribution. N Honduras S, locally, to NW & CW Colombia and extreme NW Ecuador (Esmeraldas); apparently absent from SW Colombia.

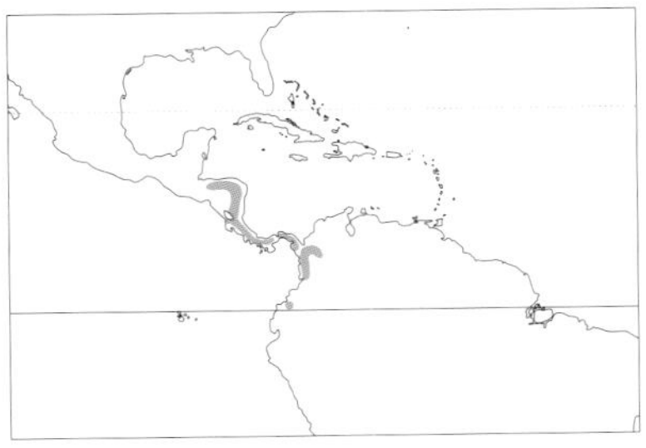

Descriptive notes. 36-38 cm; 175-245 g. Largest, most distinctive of its genus. Male with black cap to hindneck, with yellow ear-tuft, green back and uppertail-coverts, and blackish tail; below, black chin and malar to belly, yellow flank patch, chestnut thighs, red undertail-coverts; long bill with grey or black basal line, yellow (sometimes with admixed green) maxilla with olive-brown from base diminishing distally, mandible dark olive to brownish-black, tomial tips horn-coloured, mouth-lining orange-red; orbital skin blue to green and yellow. Distinguished from other *Selenidera* by larger size, bill pattern, lack of yellow collar, no chestnut tips of rectrices. Female differs from male in chestnut forehead to hindneck, no yellow ear-tuft (but black ear-coverts sometimes with yellow flecks), shorter bill. Immature duller, plumage lax, bill pattern vague and no tomial teeth; plumage shows sexual features, but black of adult male is sooty and chestnut of adult female brownish. Voice. Song a short to long series normally of double notes, "tik-ett", often with associated rattles or snapping of bill, at 1·1-1·8 notes per second; pair-members sometimes sing simultaneously; also rattling notes, both long and short, as calls, rattle possibly made by tongue inside closed bill.
Habitat. Wet forested slopes and ridges in lowlands; also forest edges, adjacent secondary forest, and fruit trees close to forest. Generally at 300-1100 m, extremes sea-level to c. 1500 m; in Honduras below 500 m.
Food and Feeding. Few observations. Diet of fruits, many arillate, such as those of *Dendropanax*, *Guateria*, *Hampea* and *Protium*; also insects, spiders, lizards. Inconspicuous; feeds in pairs or small groups, from middle storey to canopy, lower at times.
Breeding. Apr-Aug generally; perhaps earlier in Honduras, as early as Feb in Colombia, possibly earlier still in Ecuador. Singing bird bows and tosses head upwards, bill sometimes open, showing red-orange mouth, and tail flits up to one side and then other, often flipped twice with each double note. Other data essentially lacking; condition of female specimens indicates clutch size probably 2-4 eggs.
Movements. Downslope post-breeding movement into lowlands known to occur in Costa Rica and Panama, sometimes preceded by individuals gathering in groups larger than family; it is uncertain whether such movements involve most of population, or predominantly younger birds. Rare occurrence in NW Ecuador has been suggested to coincide only with very wet El Niño years; further investigation required.
Status and Conservation. Not globally threatened. Uncommon to locally fairly common in N of range. Appears to have decreased in Costa Rica, where habitat continuity possibly essential for it to thrive; occurs in that country in Braulio Carrillo National Park. Generally uncommon to rare, and local, in NW South America; rare and local in NW Ecuador, where may only occur sporadically. Should be considered for monitoring, but basic information needed regarding its biology. Not known to be kept in captivity.
Bibliography. Anon. (1998b), Best *et al.* (1997), Blake (2001), Blake & Loiselle (2000), Bond & Meyer de Schauensee (1944), Chapman (1917), Cory (1919), Gillespie (2001), Haffer (1974, 1975, 1997b), Hilty & Brown (1986), Karr *et al.* (1990), Meyer de Schauensee (1949, 1964, 1966), Monroe (1968), Norton *et al.* (1972), Remsen *et al.* (1993), Ridgely & Greenfield (2001), Ridgely & Gwynne (1989), Ridgely *et al.* (1998), Ridgway (1914), Robbins *et al.* (1985), Rodner *et al.* (2000), Slud (1964), Stiles (1983), Stiles & Levey (1994), Stiles & Skutch (1989), Stotz *et al.* (1996), West (1976), Wetmore (1968a).

PLATE 18 ➤

13

14

15

ssp *hypoglauca*
♂

ssp *lateralis*
♂

♂

♂

ssp *occidentalis*
♂

16

ssp *nigrirostris*
♂

ssp *spilorhynchus*
♂

17

♂

♀

18

♀

19

ssp *inscriptus*
♀

ssp *humboldti*
♂

♀

PLATE 18

Genus *ANDIGENA* Gould, 1851

13. Grey-breasted Mountain-toucan

Andigena hypoglauca

French: Toucan bleu **German**: Blautukan **Spanish**: Tucán Pechigris

Taxonomy. *Pteroglossus hypoglaucus* Gould, 1833; no locality = Colombia.
Forms a superspecies with *A. cucullata* and *A. laminirostris*. Races poorly differentiated, intergrading in Ecuador. Two subspecies recognized.
Subspecies and Distribution.
A. h. hypoglauca (Gould, 1833) - mountains of C & S Colombia to E Ecuador.
A. h. lateralis Chapman, 1923 - Andes of E Ecuador and Peru.

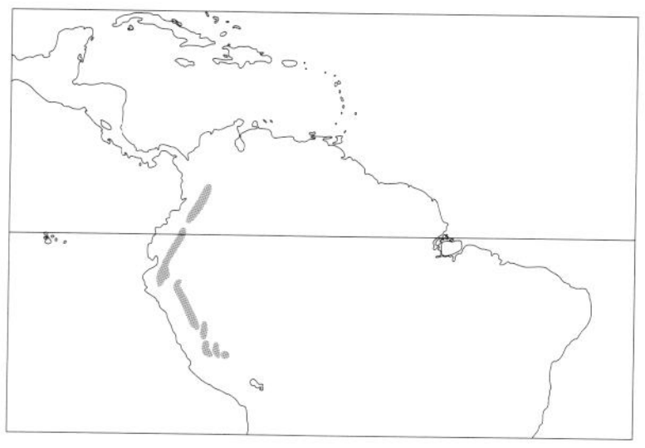

Descriptive notes. 46-48 cm; 244-370 g. Large toucan with black cap and face, grey-blue hindneck, green-tinged brown back, grey-blue to grey underparts. Male nominate race with bright yellow rump, blackish to brown-black tail with 2-3 central pairs of feathers tipped chestnut; sides and flanks somewhat pale grey-blue, thighs chestnut, undertail-coverts red; bill yellow to greenish basally, with black band near base, separated from red-orange culmen by thin oblique black line, mandible yellow with distal half black; facial skin mostly blue, with some black around brown eye. Female as male, but bill shorter. Immature duller, bright colours muted, bill brown to blackish and horn-coloured with no marks at base and without "teeth". Race *lateralis* has paler yellow rump, variable pale yellow flank patch, yellow to green eye with bluer outer ring. Voice. Song of low "gweeeeeeeat", at 1·75 to over 2 seconds the longest known piciform note, slowly repeated at 24-36 per minute, with occasional bill-whacking sounds; notes vary considerably; "wek", singly or in irregular series, aggressive and alarm notes, with or without added bill-snaps.
Habitat. Wet temperate montane forest, often in cloudforest, stunted trees at tree-line, edges and second growth. Reaches higher elevations than other toucans; at 2200-3650 m generally, occasionally lower, to 1800 m in parts of Peru and under 1700 m in Ecuador. Although locally sympatric with *A. nigrirostris*, apparently never found in same site, being replaced by that species at c. 2300-2500 m and below, but at times can probably hear each other.
Food and Feeding. Various fruits and berries, including species of *Rubus*, *Cecropia* and others; presumably animal foods fed to young, but unknown. Forages singly or in groups of up to 6, from canopy to near ground, usually quiet and not conspicuous. Can hang upside-down when feeding. May join mixed-species foraging flocks of tanagers (Thraupidae), thrushes (*Turdus*) and New World blackbirds (Icteridae).
Breeding. Dec-Feb in Colombia, Jun/Jul-Nov in Ecuador and Peru. No information on breeding behaviour, nest or eggs; possibly occupies large home range or territory.
Movements. None known.
Status and Conservation. Not globally threatened. Currently considered Near-threatened. Occurs in several protected areas, including Las Cajas National Recreation Area and Podocarpus National Park, in Ecuador. Within its range, some areas of high-altitude forest are certainly being cleared, though most of the clearance going on is at lower elevations than those occupied by this species; nonetheless, forest loss occurs throughout species' range, in some areas to severe degree, especially in Colombia; clearance in different areas for commercial and subsistence agriculture, grazing, mining activities, fuel, etc.; best preserved forest appears to be in SE Peru. Population fragmentation and inbreeding are possible problems; further information is needed on all aspects of its biology.
Bibliography. Baez *et al*. (1997), Best *et al*. (1997), Bloch *et al*. (1991), Bond (1954), Butler (1979), Chapman (1917, 1926), Clements & Shany (2001), Cory (1919), Cresswell, Hughes *et al*. (1999), Davies *et al*. (1994, 1997), Fjeldså (1987), Fjeldså & Krabbe (1990), Greenway (1978), Haffer (1974), Hilty (1985), Hilty & Brown (1986), Hornbuckle (1999), Jacobs & Walker (1999), Krabbe (1991), López *et al*. (2000), Meyer de Schauensee (1949, 1964, 1966, 1982), Olrog (1968), Ortiz & Carrión (1991), Parker, Parker & Plenge (1982), Parker, Schulenberg *et al*. (1985), Remsen (1984), Remsen *et al*. (1993), Renjifo *et al*. (1997), Ridgely & Greenfield (2001), Stattersfield & Capper (2000), Stotz *et al*. (1996), Williams & Tobias (1994).

14. Hooded Mountain-toucan

Andigena cucullata

French: Toucan à capuchon **German**: Schwarzkopftukan **Spanish**: Tucán Encapuchado

Taxonomy. *Pteroglossus cucullatus* Gould, 1846, Cocapata, Cochabamba, Bolivia.
Forms a superspecies with *A. hypoglauca* and *A. laminirostris*. Monotypic.
Distribution. Andes in SE Peru (Puno) and W & C Bolivia (La Paz to Cochabamba).

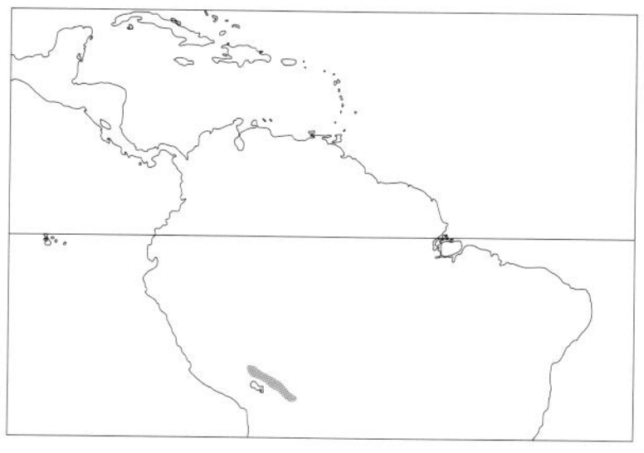

Descriptive notes. 48-50 cm; 222-380 g. Brown-backed, green-winged, blackish-tailed toucan with grey-blue collar across hindneck, black head including ear-coverts and throat; sooty-blue to blue-grey below, with rusty thighs and red undertail-coverts; facial skin shades of pale blue; bill yellow-green with black tip, mandible yellow for basal two-thirds with black spot near base. Differs from *A. hypoglauca* and *A. laminirostris* in mainly green-yellow bill, lack of yellow rump patch, no chestnut tips of tail feathers, more black on head. Female like male, but shorter bill. Immature duller, lax plumage sootier on head, greyer below, bright colours muted, rectrices more pointed; bill dull, with dark culmen and tip, mandible shows spot at base but lacks yellow behind it, no tomial "teeth". Voice. Song a slow series of "peeeeah" notes c. 1·5 seconds long, in regular to irregular series at intervals of 1-5 seconds; also series of "ik" or "tik" notes at c. 2 per second; bill-clapping with either of these calls.
Habitat. Wet temperate and uppermost subtropical forest, usually above range of most other toucans, c. 2400-3300 m, at times wandering to 2000 m, where it could meet *Aulacorhynchus coeruleicinctis*.
Food and Feeding. Fruits, species of which undetermined, but various colours of seeds and skins of different sizes in stomachs. Forages singly or in groups of up to 4, probably family parties, from canopy to understorey. Little known.
Breeding. Season estimated from Feb-Jun, perhaps earlier, to Nov. Displays, nest, eggs, and all other aspects of cycle unreported; generally calls or sings from treetops, often in morning and evening.
Movements. Possible movement down to below usual altitude, perhaps by foraging independent subadults.
Status and Conservation. Not globally threatened. Restricted-range species: present in Bolivian and Peruvian Upper Yungas EBA. Until recently considered Near-threatened. Found to be surprisingly common in late 1990's in humid montane forest near Cochabamba, in C Bolivia, where at least 10 individuals in study area of 2 km^2. Uncommon in Peru. Has small range in which pairs or groups occupy large areas, so populations may be small generally, and somewhat fragmented. Data on nesting and foraging are needed in order to provide bases for monitoring.
Bibliography. Anon. (1995a), Bond & Meyer de Schauensee (1943), Cassin (1867), Clements & Shany (2001), Collar, Crosby & Stattersfield (1994), Collar, Gonzaga *et al*. (1992), Cory (1919), Fjeldså & Krabbe (1990), de Germiny (1930a), Haffer (1974), Herzog *et al*. (1999), Meyer de Schauensee (1966, 1982), Olrog (1968), Parker *et al*. (1982), Remsen (1984, 1985), Remsen & Traylor (1989), Remsen *et al*. (1993), Stattersfield *et al*. (1998), Stotz *et al*. (1996).

15. Plate-billed Mountain-toucan

Andigena laminirostris

French: Toucan montagnard **German**: Leistenschnabeltukan **Spanish**: Tucán Piquiplano
Other common names: Plain-billed/Laminated Mountain-toucan/Hill-toucan

Taxonomy. *Andigena laminirostris* Gould, 1851, Quito, Ecuador.
Forms a superspecies with *A. hypoglauca* and *A. cucullata*. Monotypic.
Distribution. W Andes from SW Colombia (Patia Canyon, in Nariño) S to S Ecuador (S possibly as far as R Chanchan).

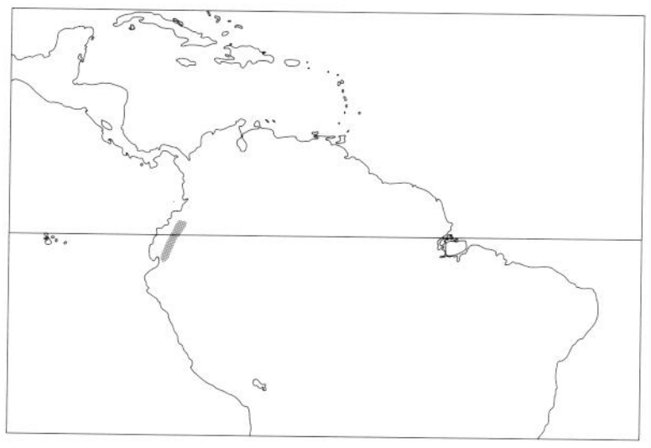

Descriptive notes. 46-51 cm; 275-355 g. Large, with black forehead to hindneck, rest of upperparts brown and green, except for pale yellow rump; tail blackish, central 2-3 pairs of rectrices tipped chestnut; blue-grey sides of neck; blue-grey chin to belly, with yellow patch on sides and flanks, chestnut thighs, red undertail-coverts; bill black, with reddish base narrow on maxilla, nearly half-way along on mandible, sides of maxilla near base covered by raised, square creamy or buffy yellow "plate"; facial skin blue above, yellow below; eye brown-red. Differs from both *A. hypoglauca* and *A. cucullata* in pattern of bill, lack of blue hindcollar. Female slightly smaller than male, differs mainly in shorter bill. Immature greyer below, browner above, grey-black bill with "plate" only hinted at by yellow area, no tomial "teeth". Voice. Song a series of loud, braying "kyeeowp" to "kyewp", 35-42 per minute, initiated by rattles, vocal or made by tongue against inside of bill, that gradually take on "eeeowp" sound and lose rattle element; rattles variable, up to 3 per second (usually 1-2), and some bill-snapping, but bill nearly to fully closed during many rattles; female at higher pitch; also squeak notes, "ddrak" possibly as contact call, "ek-ek" calls when pair-members close together; several begging calls; loud wing-flapping during interactions.
Habitat. Moist montane forest with epiphytes, mosses, bromeliads; also enters nearby secondary forest, and occurs where forest has been selectively logged. Mainly at 1300-2500 m; found occasionally down to 300 m, and rarely up to 3200 m.
Food and Feeding. Mainly fruits, in Colombia of 49 plants in 22 families; especially important are species of *Cecropia*, arecaceous palms, *Ocotea*, *Beilschmiedia*, myrtaceous trees, *Clusia*, *Ficus*, *Miconia* and *Blakea*, the first 5 of which are important in nestling diet. Although up to 98% frugivorous, c. 16% of food provided to young is animal, e.g. beetles and other insects, snails, birds and eggs, and rodents; will tear open birds' nests to get at chicks; captives prey on eggs and young of any birds caged with them. Largest fruits broken up by holding with foot and tearing with bill, others swallowed whole; most seeds pass through gut, but largest, such as avocado seed, regurgitated. Feeds in groups at height of 2-30 m, in one study mean height 15·2 m. Aggressive towards hole-nesters, especially Toucan-barbets (*Semnornis ramphastinus*), *Aulacorhynchus haematopygus* and woodpeckers.
Breeding. Mar-Oct in Colombia, Jun-Sept in Ecuador. Sometimes 2 broods, but may not breed yearly. Groups with home range break up prior to breeding, non-breeders keeping away from nest area. Often pair-members bound about, undertail-coverts erected, flank patches spread, male cocking tail; sings with bowing and bobbing of head and bill, tail flicked and cocked and lowered, undertail-coverts fluffed, very much as in species of *Selenidera*; male courtship-feeds female, latter stays close to nest, may solicit food from male, copulation 15-20 seconds in duration. Nest 6-30 m up in dead tree, stump, utility pole, often usurped from Toucan-barbet; some excavating occurs, and continues during nesting; captives excavate soft palm logs; nest entrance round to oval, c. 8 cm in diameter, depth c. 2 m. Eggs 2-3, laid c. 2 weeks after nest ready; both sexes incubate, female sits at night, incubation period c. 16-17 days; both also feed young, female tends to feed more often, feeding rate 1-2 times per hour, small items fed first, later larger fruits, male may feed more insects; most nest sanitation by female; nestlings open eyes at c. 4 weeks, fledging at 46-60 days, mainly 49-51 days; fledglings do not return to nest, fed by parents for 2-3 weeks, are chased from territory if second brood attempted. Nest predation often severe, usually only 1 or 2 young fledge.

On following pages: 16. Black-billed Mountain-toucan (*Andigena nigrirostris*); 17. Saffron Toucanet (*Baillonius bailloni*); 18. Green Araçari (*Pteroglossus viridis*); 19. Lettered Araçari (*Pteroglossus inscriptus*).

Movements. Downslope and other movements noted in Colombia, with groups of up to 25 moving to lower levels in Aug; this probably due to reduced fruit availability, as groups sometimes leave home range in poor fruiting seasons, joining other groups and wandering extensively.
Status and Conservation. Not globally threatened. Restricted-range species: present in Chocó EBA. Currently considered Near-threatened. Home range of 1 group 8·34 ha. Fairly common in La Planada Nature Reserve, Colombia. Common locally where forest remains more or less intact, but lives at altitudes at which clearing of forest is rampant; main causes of clearance include logging, cattle grazing, mining and agriculture. Also, illegally taken for captive-bird trade. Protective measures, and tighter enforcement of these by authorities, needed in all parts of range.
Bibliography. Allen (1998), Beltrán (1994), Best *et al.* (1997), Bloch *et al.* (1991), Butler (1979), Chapman (1926), Cory (1919), Fjeldså & Krabbe (1990), Hilty & Brown (1986), Meyer de Schauensee (1949, 1964, 1966, 1982), Olrog (1968), Remsen *et al.* (1993), Renjifo *et al.* (1997), Restrepo (1990), Restrepo & Mondragón (1998), Ridgely & Greenfield (2001), Ridgely *et al.* (1998), Rodner *et al.* (2000), Rundel (1975), Salaman (1994), Schlenker (2000), Shannon (1991), Stattersfield & Capper (2000), Stattersfield *et al.* (1998), Stotz *et al.* (1996), Suárez & García (1986), Terborgh & Winter (1983), Tobin & Rundel (1975).

16. Black-billed Mountain-toucan

Andigena nigrirostris

French: Toucan à bec boir **German**: Schwarzschnabeltukan **Spanish**: Tucán Piquinegro

Taxonomy. *Pteroglossus nigrirostris* Waterhouse, 1839, no locality = Subia, near La Mesa, Cundinamarca, Colombia.
Rather distinct from other *Andigena* species. Races intergrade where they meet. Three subspecies recognized.
Subspecies and Distribution.
A. n. nigrirostris (Waterhouse, 1839) - Andes of W Venezuela and E Andean slopes in Colombia.
A. n. occidentalis Chapman, 1915 - W Andes of Colombia.
A. n. spilorhynchus Gould, 1858 - C Andes and W slope of E Andes in S Colombia, and E slope in Ecuador; recently collected in extreme N Peru (Cerro Chinguela).

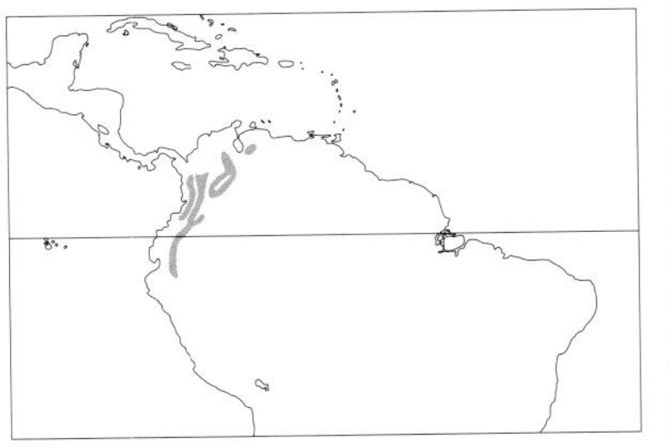

Descriptive notes. 48-51 cm; 335-367 g, 450 g (1 subadult). Black-capped mountain-toucan with bronzy upperparts, pale yellow rump, dark slate tail with chestnut tips of central 2-3 rectrices; white face and throat, grading into blue on breast, chestnut thighs, red undertail-coverts. Male nominate race with bill all black, moderately broad-based; facial skin pale blue before eye, yellow or orange behind; eye brown-red. Distinguished from *A. hypoglauca* by all-dark bill, white throat. Female shorter-billed than male. Immature duller. Races differ mainly in bill coloration: *spilorhynchus* with bill broader-based, with dark red over small area at base and along sides of maxilla; *occidentalis* has bill similarly broader, with thick red base which on culmen extends distally more than half-way along, also darker chestnut thighs. VOICE. Commonly rattling or bill-clacking sounds, rattles varying in length, at c. 25 per minute; also series of c. 3-15 nasal "gwaaak" notes, with overtones, at tempo of 25-45 per minute; variable, notes can be drawn out, or yelp-like, or mixed with rattling; also loud wing sounds during interactions.
Habitat. Moist to wet cloudforest, subtropical to temperate montane forest, thickets, bogs, cultivated areas beside forest, open areas with scattered fruiting trees. At c. 1700-2700 m; rarely down to 1200 m, and to 3245 m. Where sympatric with *A. hypoglauca*, apparently never found in same site, being replaced by that species at c. 2300-2500 m and higher; probably within hearing distance of each other at times.
Food and Feeding. Little known. Diet mainly fruits and their seeds, but also some insects, e.g. beetles; 1 stomach with beetles and no fruit remains. Feeds in pairs or family groups, mainly in canopy, which often not very high.
Breeding. Aug-Nov in W Venezuela, Mar-Aug in Colombia and probably similar or later in Ecuador. Details all but unknown, and nest and eggs unreported; supposed nest in tree cavity at c. 20 m, but no details given.
Movements. None, so far as is known.
Status and Conservation. Not globally threatened. Until recently, species was considered Near-threatened; not now listed as such, but probably still hovers around borderline. Local in much of range. Occurs in Puracé National Park, Colombia. Because it occurs below *A. hypoglauca*, and clearing of forest proceeds from lower to higher elevations, may actually be more likely to come under threat than that species; populations in Ecuador considered to be smaller than those of *A. hypoglauca*. Lack of biological information impedes monitoring of present species.
Bibliography. Best *et al.* (1997), Butler (1979), Chapman (1917, 1926), Clements & Shany (2001), Cory (1919), Fjeldså & Krabbe (1990), Greenway (1978), Haffer (1974), Hilty (1985), Hilty & Brown (1986), Krabbe (1991), López *et al* (2000), Meyer de Schauensee (1949, 1964, 1966, 1982), Meyer de Schauensee & Phelps (1978), Olivares (1963), Olrog (1968), Phelps & Phelps (1958), Rasmussen *et al.* (1996), Renjifo *et al.* (1997), Ridgely & Gaulin (1980), Ridgely & Greenfield (2001), Ridgely *et al.* (1998), Rodner *et al.* (2000), Salaman *et al.* (2000), Stotz *et al.* (1996), Vélez & Velázquez (1998).

Genus *BAILLONIUS* Cassin, 1868

17. Saffron Toucanet

Baillonius bailloni

French: Toucan de Baillon **German**: Goldtukan **Spanish**: Arasarí Banana
Other common name: Baillon's/Banana Toucan/Toucanet

Taxonomy. *Ramphastos Bailloni* Vieillot, 1819, no locality = Brazil.
Has been allied with *Andigena*, and even placed within that genus, but probably more closely related to *Pteroglossus*, though even this relationship appears to be distant. Probably a relict species, purportedly the sister taxon of *Pteroglossus*. Monotypic.
Distribution. E Brazil (Pernambuco; Bahía, Espírito Santo and adjacent Minas Gerais S to W & NE Santa Catarina and far N Rio Grande do Sul) to EC Paraguay and NE Argentina (N Misiones).

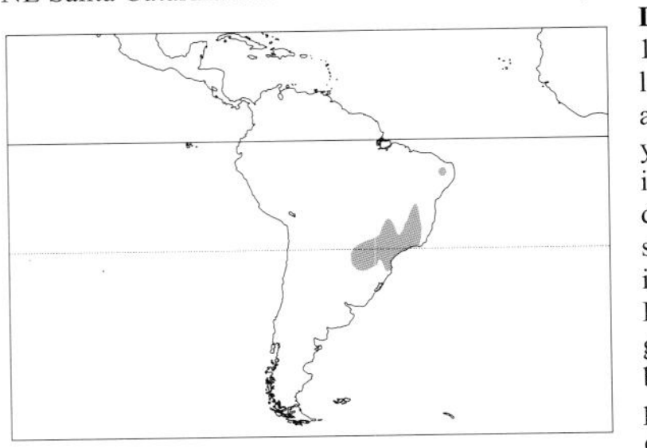

Descriptive notes. 35-39 cm; female c. 156-169 g. Highly distinctive. Male saffron-yellow, gold and olive, with rump red; culmen and most of bill horn with obvious greenish-yellow tones, red area around base narrowing to a point around middle of maxilla, with diffuse greenish to grey-blue margins; facial skin red; eye pale yellow. Female more olive, less gold and yellow, with shorter bill. Immature with lax plumage more olive and grey, rump pinkish-red, blotchy bill without basal line and tomial "teeth", rectrices more pointed, tarsi with remnant hypotarsal scutes, eye brown. VOICE. Extensive repertoire: song a series of 12-15 loud "teeee-up" notes, c. 1·75 per second; also "yeep" or "yi" notes in series, may be rattle-like, some rattles wavering and to 35 seconds or more; purring, soft "uh" or "perp" notes, low "eeeeee" notes, soft rattles or tapping at nest, rattles also in courtship feeding and aggression.
Habitat. Moist subtropical forest, generally on slopes and beside streams; also edges, and in secondary and selectively logged forest. From sea-level to 1550 m, in S usually at c. 400-600 m.
Food and Feeding. Mainly fruits, such as those of *Cecropia*, *Ficus*, *Euterpe*, *Sloanea* and *Nectandra*. Possibly eats young birds; once seen to enter woodpecker nest containing young after throwing out female woodpecker, was still in nest after 3 hours. Feeds in pairs or small groups, skulking and inconspicuous; 5 fed with 19 *Selenidera maculirostris* in fruiting palmito (*Euterpe edulis*), with other birds such as trogons (Trogonidae). Also seen with rails (Rallidae) and doves (Columbidae) on ground in ploughed field.
Breeding. Jun-Jul in far N, Dec-Apr in most of range. Details little known. Probably nests in pairs, excavating out old woodpecker hole. Male sings, also courtship-feeds female, both tap at nest entrance, allopreen; male may attempt copulation after softly allopreening facial area of female. Captive pair laid 2-3 eggs, both male and female incubated, period c. 16 days. No other information. Longevity in captivity up to 13 years and 3 months.
Movements. Probably moves to fruiting trees outside home range; possibly also some downslope movement after breeding.
Status and Conservation. Not globally threatened. CITES II. Currently considered Near-threatened. Nowhere common, but is quite inconspicuous, and numbers possibly underestimated. In hills of mainly lowland SE São Paulo, c. 5 birds/km² at altitude of 400-600 m; another study in the same area found a density of c. 12 birds/km². Main threats are cage-bird trade, hunting, and habitat loss; montane forest generally suffering less intensive destruction than lowland forests, but isolated patches of forest in N are increasingly suffering inroads from agriculture and pastoral farming. Species occurs in several protected areas in all three countries of its range: known to occur in Itatiaia and Foç do Iguaçu National Parks, in Brazil; in Estancia San Antonio Private Nature Reserve, in Reserva Natural del Bosque Mbaracayú, in La Golondrina Private Nature Reserve, and in Estancia Itabó Private Nature Reserve, all in Paraguay; and in Iguazú National Park, Argentina. Still hunted in parts of Paraguay, where often occurs in fragmented forest patches. More information required on pair and group relations, as well as data on breeding in the wild.
Bibliography. Aleixo & Galetti (1997), Belton (1984, 1994), Brooks *et al.* (1993), Canevari *et al.* (1991), Chebez (1994), Eckelberry (1964), Galetti *et al.* (1998), Giraudo & Sironi (1992), Guix (1995), Guix & Jover (2001), Guix, Mañosa *et al.* (1997), Guix, Martín *et al.* (2000), Hackett & Lehn (1997), Haffer (1974), Hayes (1995), Holt (1928), Jennings, J. (1995b), Lowen *et al.* (1996), Madroño & Esquivel (1995), Madroño, Clay *et al.* (1997), Meyer de Schauensee (1966, 1982), Narosky & Yzurieta (1993), Navas & Bó (1988), Olrog (1968), Parker & Goerck (1997), de la Peña (1994), do Rosário (1996), Saibene *et al.* (1996), Scherer-Neto (1985), Schifter (1998), Sick (1979, 1985, 1993), Stattersfield & Capper (2000), Storer (1989), Stotz *et al.* (1996), Sztolcman (1926), Tobias *et al.* (1993).

Genus *PTEROGLOSSUS* Illiger, 1811

18. Green Araçari

Pteroglossus viridis

French: Araçari vert **German**: Grünarassari **Spanish**: Arasarí verde

Taxonomy. *Ramphastos viridis* Linnaeus, 1766, Cayenne.
May form a superspecies with *P. inscriptus*. Less closely related to *P. bitorquatus*. Race *humboldti* of *P. inscriptus* treated by some authors as belonging within present species, but appears much closer to *P. inscriptus*. Monotypic.
Distribution. E Venezuela (Delta Amacuro S to E Amazonas) E through the Guianas, and S to N Brazil (S to Amazon, W to E Roraima and R Negro).

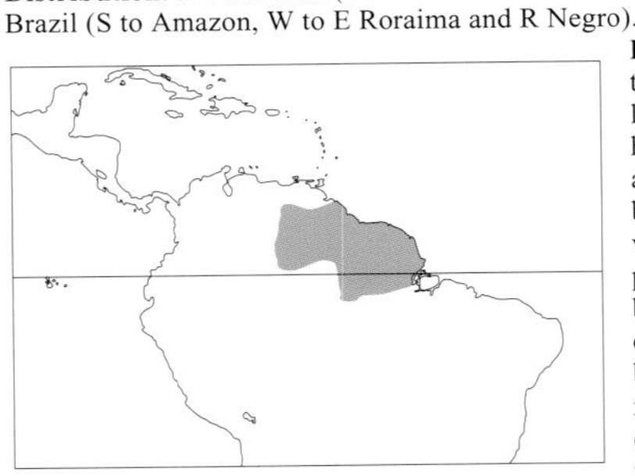

Descriptive notes. 30-39 cm; 110-162 g. Distinctive, small toucan, green above and yellow below, with red rump. Male with black head; bill yellow above, black below, with orange to red in between and at base of mandible, "teeth" ivory to white; facial skin violet-blue to greenish-yellow, with scarlet patch over and behind eye. Female shorter-billed, with chestnut to rusty head, cinnamon often showing on underparts. Immature duller, bill horn-coloured with few signs of patterning, no "teeth", more keeled; shows sexual colours early, but more cinnamon below. VOICE. Rattling "brididididit", 1-6 per second, some more rattling as "dddddt", others as "up-up-up" resembling slow motorbike; also soft chattering, purring and whining notes; calls more "voiced", less mechanical, than those of *P. inscriptus*.
Habitat. Lowland forest including sand-ridge forest, riverine forest in savanna country, tall second-growth forest, also some tree plantations, and fruiting trees isolated from but near forest; from sea-level to c. 800 m.

Food and Feeding. Mainly fruits, such as figs, and fruits of *Cecropia*, palm (*Oenocarpus*) and others, dispersing their seeds widely; captives eat mealworms, various fruits such as berries, bananas, apples, grapes, papayas, peaches, pears, maize, also carrots and peas. Forages mainly in pairs and small groups, from canopy to lower levels of understorey. Clings to hanging palm fruits; may reach fruits from upside-down position. Sometimes follows Red-throated Caracara (*Daptrius americanus*) groups through forest.

Breeding. Generally Feb-Jun; Oct-Apr near Amazon mouth. Breeds in pairs. Male courtship-feeds female, calls with tail cocked, often switching it up and down, and sideways; may feed her inside nest-cavity. Nest up to 20 m or higher, an old cavity of woodpeckers, which it excavates further; in captivity, both sexes perform some excavation. Most data from captive birds: eggs 2-4; incubation by both sexes, period c. 17 days; both adults feed young; nestling period 43-45 days; young probably remain with parents for 6 or more months. In captivity, easily disturbed by human activity, may eat or abandon young; 2 chicks 2 days old adopted and successfully reared by pair of *Selenidera maculirostris*, after latter's fledged young had been removed.

Movements. Presumed to be sedentary.

Status and Conservation. Not globally threatened. CITES II. Species' small size and its ability to use secondary forest should be positive factors in its conservation. Occurs in Imataca Forest Reserve and El Dorado, Venezuela. Almost no information on breeding biology of wild populations; study needed.

Bibliography. Beebe *et al.* (1917), Blake (1950, 1963), Bühler (1993, 1995b, 1996), Cherrie (1916), Chubb (1916), Cohn-Haft *et al.* (1997), Friedmann (1948), Haffer (1974, 1978), Haverschmidt & Mees (1994), Jennings (1993a), Karr *et al.* (1990), McConnell (1991), Meyer de Schauensee (1966), Meyer de Schauensee & Phelps (1978), Page (1988), Phelps & Phelps (1958), Remsen *et al.* (1993), Rodner *et al.* (2000), Sick (1985, 1993), Snyder (1966), Stotz & Bierregaard (1989), Stotz *et al.* (1996), Thiollay (1992), Thiollay & Jullien (1998), Tostain *et al.* (1992), Vince (1998), Zimmer & Hilty (1997).

19. Lettered Araçari
Pteroglossus inscriptus

French: Araçari de Humboldt   **German**: Schriftarassari   **Spanish**: Arasarí Marcado

Taxonomy. *Pteroglossus inscriptus* Swainson, 1822, Guyana; error = Pará, Brazil.
May form a superspecies with *P. viridis*. Less closely related to *P. bitorquatus* and *P. azara*. Race *humboldti* sometimes considered a separate species, but interbreeds sporadically with nominate race in R Madeira region; *humboldti* placed within *P. viridis* by some authors, but appears more appropriately treated with present species. Form from upper Amazonia, described as race *didymus*, now considered a synonym of *humboldti*; form described from R Juruá as "*olallae*", and initially thought to be full species, found to be hybrid between *humboldti* and *P. azara mariae*. Two subspecies recognized.

Subspecies and Distribution.
P. i. humboldti Wagler, 1827 - SE Colombia and W Brazil (E narrowly along Amazon to R Negro mouth in N, broadly E, S of Amazon, to R Madeira, crossing it occasionally in N and, more often, in S), S in lowlands E of Andes to NC Bolivia.
P. i. inscriptus Swainson, 1822 - NC Brazil S of Amazon (from R Madeira E to Maranhão, NW Piauí, S to E Bolivia, SW Mato Grosso (in upper R Paraguay drainage) and upper R Tocantins; also E Brazil in Pernambuco and E Alagoas.

Descriptive notes. 33-40 cm; 95-140 g (*inscriptus*), 111-185 g (*humboldti*). Green and yellow, with red rump, unusual bill marks. Male nominate race with black head; bill with yellow basal line, oval yellow patch with black script-like marks on maxilla and mandible, with black beyond it and be-

hind it, black mouth-lining; facial skin blue to nearly violet, with red area below and behind eye. Female shorter billed, with chestnut on face, sides of neck, malar area and throat to chin. Immature duller, bill pattern much subdued. Race *humboldti* much larger; bill with black on culmen and tip, basal line and pale area of maxilla more orange (latter still "inscripted"), mandible entirely black apart from orange-yellow base, mouth-lining red, thighs more rusty, more buff to rusty tinge at belly-breast border; in female, chestnut extends onto crown and nape. Common call a fast series of "kik" or "kek" notes, c. 3 per second, mainly to c. 5 but sometimes to 50 seconds, often variable within series, usually with 1 accented "kek-ek" per series; also rattles, "bdddddt", in short bursts, mechanical elements rapid at over 30 per second; and single "rak" notes.

Habitat. Primary lowland forest, including seasonally flooded *várzea*, forested islands, nearby secondary forest, riverine forest as at edges of Brazilian *cerrado*, dense "zabolo" cane and bamboo along streams, also palm woods, dense *cerrado* woodland; may be forced into some habitats by competition from larger, sympatric araçaris. Occasionally reaches montane subtropical forest along Andes, to 1000 m, even 1200 m.

Food and Feeding. Fruits such as those of *Ficus*, *Cecropia* and *Ocotea*; probably insects as well; also, groups prey on nestlings of some pigeons (Columbidae), finches (Fringillidae) and swallows (Hirundinidae), and perhaps also those of Yellow-rumped Cacique (*Cacicus cela*), nests of which it sometimes tears apart. Feeds mainly in groups or pairs, from canopy to subcanopy; sometimes descends to ground when following ant swarms. When *P. azara* or other araçaris arrive in groups, present species retreats from fruiting tree in fast, direct flight, each bird grasping 1 fruit on departure.

Breeding. Data from specimens indicate Dec-Jul in W of range, Aug-Mar in E. Displays, nest, eggs and other aspects all undescribed in detail. Known to enter tree cavities, 1 pair reportedly nested in lone dead *Cedrela odorata* tree standing in lakebed; a group of 4 apparently had nest usurped by 5 *P. castanotis*. Young stay with parents for extended period, perhaps beyond 1 year in some cases, if nesting in group.

Movements. Apparently sedentary.

Status and Conservation. Not globally threatened. Density in SE Peru up to 1 territory/100 ha in mixed habitat of *Ficus-Cedrela*, transitional forest and mature floodplain-forest. Fairly common in Ecuador. Occurs in Amacayacu National Park, Colombia, and in Cuyabeno Reserve, Ecuador. This species' diverse use of habitats suggests adaptability. Possibly some threats locally, as in case of isolated NE Brazilian population of Pernambuco and Alagoas. Hunted by humans, and sometimes entire group may be killed one by one. Lack of knowledge of its breeding biology would hamper any conservation efforts, if and when needed.

Bibliography. Anon. (1995a), Bates *et al.* (1989), Beebe (1916), Berlepsch (1889), Bond (1954), Borrero (1959), Cavalcanti & Marini (1993), Chapman (1917, 1926), Cory (1919), Cracraft & Prum (1988), Foster *et al.* (1994), Friedmann (1958b), Fry (1970b), de Germiny (1930a), Gyldenstolpe (1941b, 1945a, 1951), Hackett & Lehn (1997), Haffer (1974, 1978, 1987, 1993a), Hellmayr (1910, 1929), Hilty & Brown (1986), Karr *et al.* (1990), Krabbe (1991), María & Olivares (1967), Meyer de Schauensee (1949, 1964, 1966), Naumburg (1930), Olivares (1962), Pacheco & Whitney (1995), Parker & Bailey (1991), Remsen & Parker (1983), Remsen *et al.* (1993), Ridgely & Greenfield (2001), Robinson (1985, 1997), Robinson & Terborgh (1997), Sick (1985, 1993), da Silva (1996), Stotz, Fitzpatrick *et al.* (1996), Stotz, Lanyon *et al.* (1997), Terborgh *et al.* (1990), Willis (1976, 1983), Willis & Oniki (1990), Zimmer *et al.* (1997).

ssp *sturmii*

20

♂

ssp *mariae*
♂

ssp *azara*
♂

ssp *flavirostris*
♂

21

♂

ssp *reichenowi*

♀

ssp *bitorquatus*

22

♂

ssp *australis*
♂

23

ssp *castanotis*
♂

ssp *erythrozonus*
♂

25

ssp *torquatus*
♂

ssp *sanguineus*
♂

24

♂

ssp *erythropygius*
♂

26
♂

27
♂

PLATE 19

inches 5

cm 13

20. **Red-necked Araçari**

Pteroglossus bitorquatus

French: Araçari à double collier **German**: Rotnackenarassari **Spanish**: Arasarí Cuellirrojo
Other common names: Double-collared Araçari

Taxonomy. *Pteroglossus bitorquatus* Vigors, 1826, no locality = north-eastern Brazil.
Probably related more closely to *P. inscriptus* and *P. viridis* than to *P. azara*. Races *sturmii* and *reichenowi* considered by some authors to constitute two further distinct species, but they clearly share major features with nominate race, and differences between the various populations seem significant enough only for subspecific treatment; also, *sturmii* and *reichenowi* appear to hybridize, e.g. in SW Pará (Cururu Valley of upper R Tapajós) and N Mato Grosso. Three subspecies currently recognized.
Subspecies and Distribution.
P. b. sturmii Natterer, 1842 - NC Brazil S of Amazon, between R Madeira and R Tapajós, S to Rondônia, Bolivia (E Beni, NE Santa Cruz), thence E to C Mato Grosso (R Paraguay drainage, and E almost to R Xingu).
P. b. reichenowi Snethlage, 1907 - S of Amazon, between R Tapajós and R Tocantins, S to N Mato Grosso.
P. b. bitorquatus Vigors, 1826 - NE Brazil S of Amazon: Marajó I and E of R Tocantins to Maranhão.

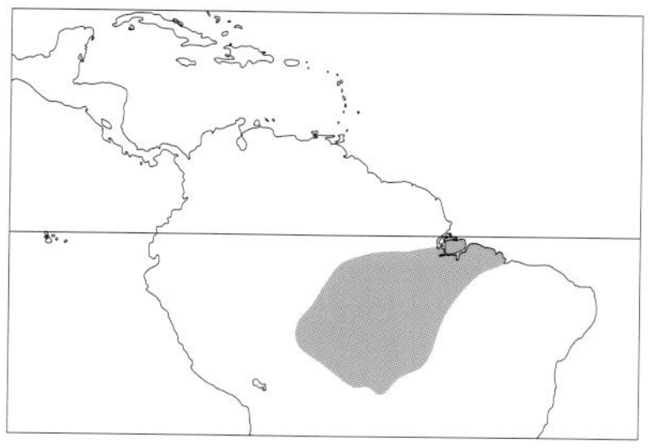

Descriptive notes. c. 36 cm; 112-117 g. Green and yellow with red rump, red nape and upper back, broad red breast patch. Male nominate race with blackish crown, dark brown ear-coverts and face to chin and throat, lower throat bordered by narrow black and yellow bands; bill with yellow, green-yellow or green-white maxilla with white and black tomial "teeth", mandible black with this colour angling upwards towards rear, setting off large white base; orbital skin blue to greenish-grey, facial skin red; eye yellow to reddish with brown marks before and behind pupil, latter thus looking slit-like. Female differs in browner crown, less black on lower throat, narrower yellow band in front of red breast, shorter bill. Immature duller, browner, more orange where adults red, plumage lax, bill lacking "teeth" and basal line and obscurely patterned horn and brown. Races differ mainly in bill coloration, and a few other traits: *reichenowi* with no yellow or only as traces in front of red breast, red of sides not reaching flanks, bill somewhat similar to nominate but black of mandible meets white base and breaks into 2-5 black spots along tomia; *sturmii* largest, has broader yellow band on breast before the red compared with nominate, maxilla with less black on tomial "teeth", mandible almost all black beyond orange-yellow basal line, tip yellow-white, eye brown. VOICE. Series of "tik" or "tek" notes, tempo c. 13 per second, usually grouped in sets of c. 6 but only brief pauses between sets; may have cadence like "revving-up" motorbike; also "ttak" or "tyat", more varied, less mechanical in clusters; also grating notes, single "ik" notes, a "tweah", and growl-like, chattery "dcheeeaah" calls.
Habitat. Inhabits lowland and hilly moist tropical forest, well-drained forest, and gallery forest where its range reaches *cerrado*; also found in dense bamboo and tree growth alongside streams and tall secondary forest. Recorded from sea-level up to c. 550 m, reaching its highest levels in Bolivia.
Food and Feeding. Very poorly known. Eats fruits of various species of fig, cinnamon and Cecropia; probably also takes some insects and vertebrates, such as nestling birds, eggs and lizards. Observed attacking a vine snake, though it is not known whether this was predation or mobbing; the snake escaped. Forages in middle storey and canopy, in pairs or groups of up to 5-6 birds.
Breeding. Virtually unknown. Specimen data suggest season Feb-Aug in much of range, later, Apr-Sept, in upper R Tapajós region, even later, Jul-Dec, in Bolivia and Mato Grosso. Nest and eggs undescribed, and no details available on behaviour; seen entering and leaving possible nesting cavity in NE Brazil (near Belem, NE Pará), in Nov.
Movements. Probably resident, with only local movements.
Status and Conservation. Not globally threatened. No details available on population numbers. Occurs in Noel Kempff Mercado National Park, Bolivia. Habitat probably being fragmented in some areas by road-building and clearance of forest. Data on breeding biology required for any conservation efforts.
Bibliography. Anon. (1995a), Bates *et al.* (1989), Beebe (1916), Cabot *et al.* (1988), Cory (1919), Cracraft & Prum (1988), Griscom & Greenway (1941), Gyldenstolpe (1941b, 1945a, 1951), Hackett & Lehn (1997), Haffer (1969, 1974, 1978, 1993a, 1993b, 1997c), Hellmayr (1910, 1929), Meyer de Schauensee (1966), Morrone (2000), Naumburg (1930), Novaes (1976), Oniki & Willis (1983), Oren & Parker (1997), Remsen *et al.* (1993), Sick (1985, 1993), da Silva (1996), Stotz, Fitzpatrick *et al.* (1996), Stotz, Lanyon *et al.* (1997), Whittaker (1996), Willis (1976), Willis & Oniki (1990), Zimmer, J.T. & Mayr (1943), Zimmer, K.J. *et al.* (1997).

21. **Ivory-billed Araçari**

Pteroglossus azara

French: Araçari d'Azara **German**: Rotkropfarassari **Spanish**: Arasarí de Azara
Other common names: Azara Araçari/Toucan; Yellow-billed Araçari (*flavirostris*); Brown-mandibled/Maria's Araçari (*mariae*)

Taxonomy. *Ramphastos Azara* Vieillot, 1819, Brazil.
Related to *P. bitorquatus* and *P. inscriptus*. Thought unlikely to be related directly to any of the "*P. torquatus* group". Races *flavirostris* and *mariae* sometimes considered to constitute two separate species, but both of these and nominate race interbreed wherever they meet: *mariae* with nominate and *flavirostris* along Amazon, and with *flavirostris* also in N Peru; *flavirostris* also interbreeds with nominate race on upper R Negro. Race *mariae* has hybridized with race *humboldti* of *P. inscriptus* in W Brazil (R Juruá), and hybrid was originally thought to be a distinct species under the name "*P. olallae*". Present species, as constituted herein, has sometimes erroneously been named *P. flavirostris*, apparently due to confusion over priority. Three subspecies currently recognized.
Subspecies and Distribution.
P. a. flavirostris Fraser, 1841 - SE Colombia, S Venezuela and NW Brazil (W of upper R Negro, S to N bank of R Solimões) to E Ecuador and NE Peru.
P. a. azara (Vieillot, 1819) - Brazil in Amazonas, between W bank of R Negro and N bank of R Solimões-Amazon.
P. a. mariae Gould, 1854 - S of Amazon, from E Peru and W Brazil (E to R Madeira), S to NC Bolivia.

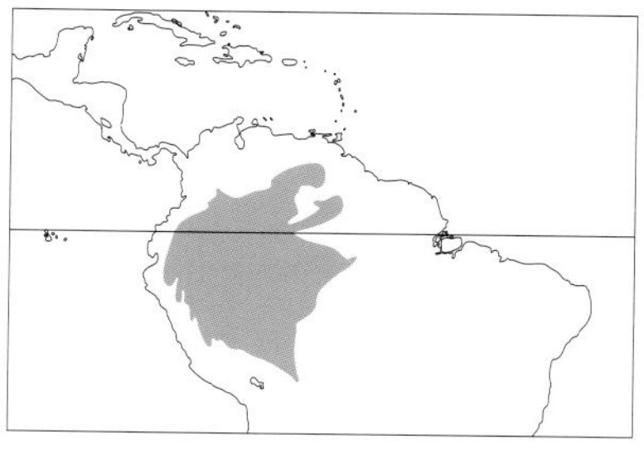

Descriptive notes. 36-45 cm; 100-200 g, mainly 120-160 g. Typical banded araçari, small and with long, mostly yellow or cream bill. Male nominate race has black cap, rest of head and throat chestnut, black band across lower throat, almost entirely maroon-red upper back to nape, red rump; broad red upper breastband, broad black lower breastband, yellow belly, thighs largely green; yellow bill with deep red to brown line on side of maxilla, broad at base, tapering to black tip, tomial "teeth" red, black and ivory; orbital area black to grey, generally surrounded by maroon to red facial skin. Female shorter-billed, with cap dark brown, narrower line of black at lower throat. Immature duller, lax-plumaged, black areas browner, reds more orangey, yellow paler, mottled, bill vaguely marked without tomial "teeth" or basal line. Races differ almost solely in bill colour: *flavirostris* has yellow to greenish-cream or ivory maxilla with orange spot below nostril, black and white "teeth", mandible yellow or ivory with tiny to long and narrow orange-brown line at centre beside tomia; *mariae* with maxilla yellow to ivory with black and white "teeth", black sometimes forming tomial line distally, mandible mainly orange-brown, tip yellow or ivory, base beyond yellow basal line sometimes with small buff area behind brown, also orbital area perhaps more narrowly slaty-grey, so red facial area larger. VOICE. Possible song a series of 2-6 wailing "twaaa-a-a" or "tweee-ee" or "traaa-at" notes, each 0·2-0·5 seconds long, up to c. 1 per second, slowing in tempo over series, sometimes with initial more squawking "treee-awk" note; series of "ttaaaaw" given at times; also voiced rattles, grunt-like contact notes, nasal "nyek", purr-like notes, "kyeek" alarm, pure rattles "bddddt", loud wing noises during interactions.
Habitat. Inhabits seasonally flooded as well as *terra firme* wet forest, in lowlands and up to lower slopes of mountains, at times reaching cloudforest; also occurs in bamboo and other riverine vegetation, gallery forest, woodland and forest along streams in savanna, secondary forest, plantations of trees, and edges. Numbers tend to be greatest in early and middle successional stages along lakes and streams, with fewer individuals in later successional stages, and fewest in latest transitional stages and in *terra firme* forest; occupation of islands and shifting rivers perhaps responsible for some apparently cross-river interbreeding of races across the Amazon-Solimões system. Mainly found below 600 m, but reaches 900 m and locally as high as 1400 m along E Andes between Ecuador and Bolivia.
Food and Feeding. Feeds on fruits of *Ficus*, *Cecropia*, *Ocotea*, *Paginea* and others; has also been observed flycatching, and arthropod remains were found in one stomach; overall, however, few details available. Usually forages in pairs and in groups of 3-5 individuals, in upper levels and canopy, but also caught in mist-nets in understorey. Flees from fruiting trees on approach of calling group of larger *P. beauharnaesii*.
Breeding. Data from specimens indicate breeding season of Dec-May in NE of range, Feb-Aug in W & SW. Courtship feeding observed in the wild; no displays otherwise reported. Nest undescribed, probably uses old woodpecker hole; seen entering a cavity 18 m up a tree. Eggs 2-3 or 4; no further information available.
Movements. Probably resident.
Status and Conservation. Not globally threatened. Fairly common in Colombia and Peru, but uncommon in Ecuador. Recorded density c. 2 pairs/100 ha in optimum habitats. Occurs in Cuyabeno Reserve, Ecuador, and in Tambopata Reserve, Peru. Varied habitats utilized and changing nature of its successional habitats suggest that species is not likely to become threatened in near future. Lack of knowledge of its breeding could hinder any conservation action, should that become necessary.
Bibliography. Anon. (1995a), Beebe *et al.* (1917), Berlepsch (1889), Bond (1954), Chapman (1926), Cherrie (1916), Clements & Shany (2001), Cory (1919), Foster *et al.* (1994), Friedmann (1948), de Germiny (1930a), Gyldenstolpe (1941b, 1945a, 1951), Hackett & Lehn (1997), Haffer (1969, 1974, 1978, 1985, 1987, 1993a), Hellmayr (1907a, 1910), Hilty & Brown (1986), Ihering (1900), Karr *et al.* (1990), María & Olivares (1967), Meyer de Schauensee (1949, 1964, 1966), Meyer de Schauensee & Phelps (1978), Moskovits *et al.* (1985), Olivares (1964a), Parker & Bailey (1991), Phelps & Phelps (1958), Remsen *et al.* (1993), Ridgely & Greenfield (2001), Robinson & Terborgh (1997), Schönwetter (1967), Sick (1985, 1993), Stotz *et al.* (1996), Terborgh *et al.* (1990), Todd (1943b), Willard *et al.* (1991), Zimmer & Hilty (1997).

22. **Black-necked Araçari**

Pteroglossus aracari

French: Araçari grigri **German**: Schwarzkehlarassari **Spanish**: Arasarí Cuellinegro
Other common name: Maximilian's/Wied's Araçari

Taxonomy. *Ramphastos Aracari* Linnaeus, 1758, Brazil.
Forms a superspecies with *P. castanotis*. Both belong to the "*P. torquatus* group", which also includes *P. pluricinctus*, *P. torquatus* and *P. frantzii*, all being closely related. Contrary to some views, probably not closely related to *P. azara*. Race *atricollis* has hybridized with *P. pluricinctus* in SE Venezuela (Carapo, R Paragua). Other described forms now considered unacceptable are *roraimae* (E Venezuela and the Guianas), synonymized with *atricollis*; *amazonicus* (NC & EC Brazil), now lumped into nominate; and *wiedii* and *formosus* (S & E Brazil), synonymized with *vergens*. Three subspecies currently recognized.
Subspecies and Distribution.
P. a. atricollis (P. L. S. Müller, 1776) - E Venezuela and the Guianas, and N Brazil S to R Amazon (W to R Negro).
P. a. aracari (Linnaeus, 1758) - disjunct populations in NC, E & SE Brazil: S of Amazon, W to R Madeira, E to Maranhão and S to NE Mato Grosso and Goiás; E Pernambuco and E Alagoas; and also Minas Gerais and Espírito Santo.

On following pages: 23. Chestnut-eared Araçari (*Pteroglossus castanotis*); 24. Many-banded Araçari (*Pteroglossus pluricinctus*); 25. Collared Araçari (*Pteroglossus torquatus*); 26. Fiery-billed Araçari (*Pteroglossus frantzii*); 27. Curl-crested Araçari (*Pteroglossus beauharnaesii*).

P. a. vergens Griscom & Greenway, 1937 - S Goiás, S Minas Gerais and Espírito Santo S to E Paraná and E Santa Catarina.

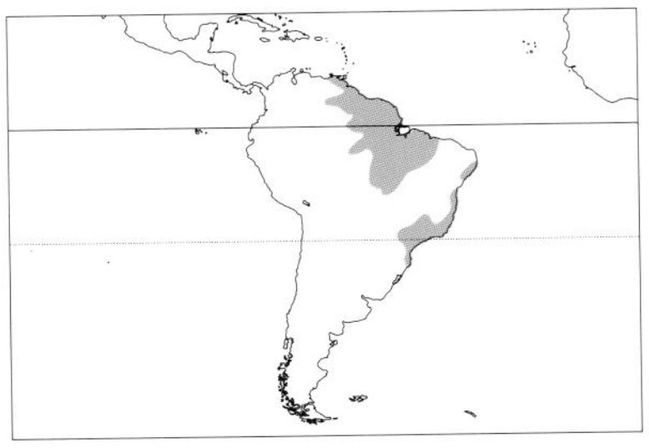

Descriptive notes. 43-46 cm; 177-325 g. Male nominate race with black head, chestnut-black ear-coverts, green above with red rump; yellow below, with broad red band across lower breast, thighs greenish; bill ivory with black culmen and mandible; facial-orbital skin blue-grey to black, eye brown. Differs from *P. castanotis* in almost entirely black head to upper breast and upper back; also, whiter, less orange-yellow, bill, less black maxilla. Female like male, but bill shorter. Immature with lax plumage, black and green areas sootier, browner, red and yellow colours paler, bill browner, duller, pattern less clear, no tomial "teeth", no ivory basal line. Race *atricollis* differs from nominate in generally broader culmen stripe, more red-brown in ear-coverts, more cinnamon-rusty thighs; *vergens* with culmen stripe only slightly broader than in nominate, black of ear-coverts and of chin and throat (except lower throat) replaced by chestnut, thus more closely resembling *P. castanotis*. Voice. Common call "tsee-eet" to "sneet", in irregular series, or regular at c. 2 per second; also used singly, sometimes as longer "tseeeeeee-it"; also rattled "bdd-dddit", produced vocally or by bill-snapping.

Habitat. Occurs in lowland wet forest, sand-ridge forest, secondary forest, some woodlands, *cerrado*, gallery forest of savannas, edges and clearings, also fruit-tree plantations (e.g. papayas), and single fruiting trees near forest. Generally found in lowlands below 500-600 m; at higher elevations in S Venezuela, it is replaced by *P. pluricinctus*; occasionally recorded up to 1000 m in SE of range.

Food and Feeding. Diverse fruits of species of *Ficus*, *Virola*, other genera of Sapotaceae, various palms including *Oenocarpus*, and others; also takes insects; captives eat a range of fruits, dog meal, chopped cabbage and lettuce, grated carrots, and mice, crickets and roaches. Feeds in groups of up to 6, occasionally more, in canopy and subcanopy; clings, turns, hangs to reach food. Captives feed also on ground, turning bill and head sideways to pick up bits of food. Avoids large *Ramphastos* toucans, watches them closely. Is an important seed-disperser of fruiting trees.

Breeding. Season Nov-Aug in most of range, but Sept-Feb in S. Breed in pairs; captive pairs coming into breeding condition kill other "group"-members caged with them. Displays include rump-fluffing, head-tossing, bowing, tail-cocking; courtship feeding occurs, male may feed incubating female. Nest situated in old woodpecker hole, with some excavating probably occurring; captives given pulpy palm log with only entrance cut out readily excavate cavity, to 10 cm by 80 cm. Eggs 2-4; incubation by both parents, 16-17 days; hatchling naked, grey, sits on hypotarsal pads and cloaca; young fed by both parents, which sometimes regurgitate items as they approach nest; fledging at c. 40 days, and family group moves away from nest; no data on subsequent parent-young relationships, observed groups are presumed to constitute single family, or extended family with previous year's young joining parents and fledged young for much of year.

Movements. Mainly resident, so far as is known.

Status and Conservation. Not globally threatened. CITES II. Widespread, and still relatively common in many areas. SE race *vergens*, living near heavily populated cities and farming areas, possibly suffering drastic fragmentation of its population. Species is hunted in places; once 150 individuals killed by 1 person in single day. Present in several protected areas, e.g. Imataca Forest Reserve and El Dorado (Venezuela), and Rio Doce State Park, Sooretama Biological Reserve and Parque Estadual da Pedra Talhada (Brazil).

Bibliography. Beebe *et al*. (1917), Blake (1950, 1963), Brabourne & Chubb (1912b), Bühler (1993, 1995b, 1996), Cherrie (1916), Chubb (1916), Cory (1919), Friedmann & Smith (1950), Fry (1970b), Griscom & Greenway (1937, 1941), Haffer (1969, 1974, 1978, 1985, 1987, 1993a, 1997c), Hackett & Lehn (1997), Haverschmidt & Mees (1994), Hellmayr (1910, 1929), Meyer de Schauensee (1966), Meyer de Schauensee & Phelps (1978), Moskovits *et al*. (1985), Novaes & Lima (1992a), Oniki & Willis (1983), Parker & Goerck (1997), Pernalete (1989), Phelps & Phelps (1958), Pinto (1935), Remsen *et al*. (1993), do Rosário (1996), Schomburgk (1848), Sick (1985, 1993), Snyder (1966), Stotz *et al*. (1996), Thiollay (1992), Tostain *et al*. (1992).

23. Chestnut-eared Araçari

Pteroglossus castanotis

French: Araçari à oreillons roux **German**: Braunohrarassari **Spanish**: Arasarí Caripardo

Taxonomy. *Pteroglossus castanotis* Gould, 1834, River Solimões, Brazil.
Forms a superspecies with *P. aracari*. Both belong to the "*P. torquatus* group", which also includes *P. pluricinctus*, *P. torquatus* and *P. frantzii*, all being closely related. Contrary to some views, probably not closely related to *P. azara*. Nominate intergrades with race *australis* in S & E of its range. Two subspecies recognized.

Subspecies and Distribution.
P. c. castanotis Gould, 1834 - S & E Colombia and W Brazil (along N bank of R Solimões-Amazon to lower R Negro), S to SE Peru and, in Brazil, to Acre and S Amazonas (extending E to R Madeira).
P. c. australis Cassin, 1867 - NC Brazil S of Amazon, E to Parintins, and S to NE & E Bolivia, E Paraguay, NE Argentina (Misiones), and SE Brazil (E to W Minas Gerais and W São Paulo, and Paraná to N Rio Grande do Sul).

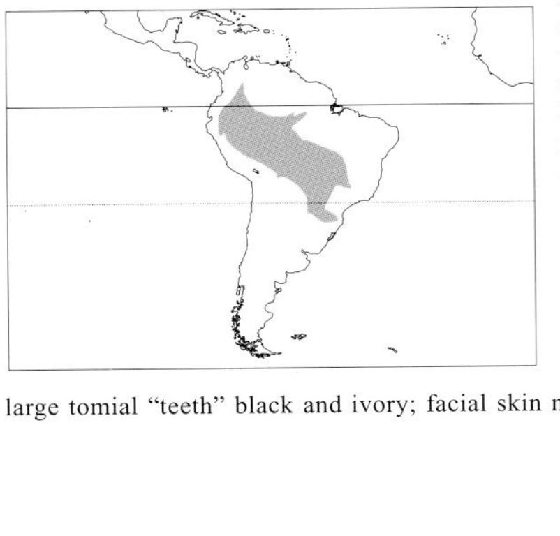

Descriptive notes. 43-47 cm; 220-310 g (slightly lighter to S). Male nominate race with black crown to nape, brown to chestnut sides of head, lower nape and upper throat, lower throat black; dark green above with red rump; underparts yellow, with red or red and chestnut-black band on lower breast-belly, often some red also on upper breast, thighs cinnamon to chestnut-black; broad-based bill with orange to yellow basal line, mandible mainly black, maxilla with broad triangular black culmen stripe and orange-yellow sides, latter narrowing from tip backwards over long black triangle pointing from base towards tip, large tomial "teeth" black and ivory; facial skin mainly blue. Female browner from crown to nape and upper throat, narrower black area of lower throat, bill shorter. Immature duller, bill pattern muted, no basal line or tomial "teeth". Race *australis* paler, rusty on nuchal area to upper throat, thighs green and rusty, red band below with rufous (not chestnut-black) admixed, base of bill with red mark ahead of orange basal band, latter more pronounced than in nominate race. Voice. Major call "sneeep" to longer "psheee-eeep", in irregular series at c. 2 per second, piercing and high-pitched; also single "tekk" call, low "eeee-eee", call with 4 whistled "weet" notes and a "pyeee-tyee-tyee-tyee-tyet."

Habitat. Shows predilection for wet forest about lakes and rivers, *várzea* flooded forest, forest islands in rivers, swampy and old stream-channel forest, gallery forest, also old secondary forest, edges, clearings, and disturbed areas; in addition, found in dense bamboo and canebrake "zabolo", *cerrado*, plantations and farms in forest, coffee plantations, and even woodland patches in *cerrado* and Pantanal. In SE Peru, tends to be commonest in middle stages of succession along rivers and lakes, being less common than either *P. inscriptus* or *P. azara* in earlier successional stages, and decidedly uncommon in primary forest. Is the only toucan species on some Amazon islands; probably under pressure of competition from congeners. Occurs mainly below 600 m, but up to 1200-1300 m in places along Andes, and up to 1000 m or more in WC & SE Brazil (Minas Gerais and Goiás).

Food and Feeding. Feeds on fruits such as those of *Cecropia*, *Coussapoa*, *Ficus*, *Ocotea* and others; at times, takes flowers and nectar, and also insects. Also hunts nestling birds and searches for eggs; in one study, species was successful in 24% of its attempts in obtaining young Yellow-rumped Caciques (*Cacicus cela*) from their colonies; also known to prey on nests of swallows (Hirundinidae), finches (Fringillidae), doves (Columbidae). Attacks and drives some *Campephilus* woodpeckers from their cavities. Forages in lower canopy down to understorey, in vines and shrubs, as well as in trees; takes fruits by reaching, even hanging upside-down. Investigates, probes crevices and tree cavities.

Breeding. Season Feb-Sept in N & W, Jun-Jan in Bolivia; Sept-Feb in SE Brazil, NE Argentina and E Paraguay. More than pair may be involved in some nestings, as very frequent in groups, uncommonly seen alone or in pairs. Rump often erected in display. Nest in old woodpecker hole, probably clears hole by excavating; in Peru, 2 nests in dead *Cedrela odorata* trees standing in lakebed; 5 birds of present species seen to drive 4 *P. inscriptus* from tree cavity, later nested in it. Eggs 2, probably up to 4; incubation and nestling periods unknown. Longevity in captivity 17 years and 9 months.

Movements. Crosses rivers, occasionally large ones; in SE, numbers gather in loose flocks, which move into fruit and other plantations as austral winter begins.

Status and Conservation. Not globally threatened. CITES II. Considered common in Colombia and Peru, uncommon to fairly common in Ecuador; probably relatively common throughout much of rest of range. Occurs in a number of protected areas, such as Iguazú National Park, Argentina, and, in Paraguay, in Estancia San Antonio Private Nature Reserve, Reserva Natural del Bosque Mbaracayú, La Golondrina Private Nature Reserve and Estancia Itabó Private Nature Reserve; also in Tambopata Reserve, Peru. Rather catholic in its use of habitats; probably more tolerant of changes, and more adaptable, than are its more forest-restricted relatives. Is still hunted by humans in parts of its range.

Bibliography. Anon. (1995a), Bates *et al*. (1989), Belton (1984, 1994), Berlepsch (1889), Bond (1954), Bond & Meyer de Schauensee (1943), Brooks *et al*. (1993), Canevari *et al*. (1991), Cavalcanti & Marini (1993), Chapman (1917, 1921b, 1926), Cory (1919), Foster *et al*. (1994), Fry (1970b), Giraudo & Sironi (1992), Griscom & Greenway (1937), Gyldenstolpe (1945a, 1951), Hackett & Lehn (1997), Haffer (1974, 1985, 1987, 1993a), Hayes (1995), Hellmayr (1910), Hilty & Brown (1986), Hornbuckle (1999), Karr *et al*. (1990), Krabbe (1991), María & Olivares (1967), Meyer de Schauensee (1949, 1964, 1966), Morales (1988), Narosky & Yzurieta (1993), Naumburg (1930), Novaes (1957), O'Brien (1979), Parker & Bailey (1991), Parker & Goerck (1997), Pearman (1993b), de la Peña (1994), Pinto (1932, 1948), Remsen & Parker (1983), Remsen *et al*. (1993), Ridgely & Greenfield (2001), Robinson (1985, 1997), Robinson & Terborgh (1997), do Rosário (1996), Schifter (1998), Short (1975), Sick (1985, 1993), Stager (1961a), Stotz *et al*. (1996), Terborgh *et al*. (1990), Traylor (1952), Willis (1976), Willis & Oniki (1990).

24. Many-banded Araçari

Pteroglossus pluricinctus

French: Araçari multibande **German**: Doppelbindenarassari **Spanish**: Arasarí Fajado

Taxonomy. *Pteroglossus pluricinctus* Gould, 1836, River Solimões, Brazil.
Belongs to the "*P. torquatus* group", which also includes *P. aracari*, *P. castanotis*, *P. torquatus* and *P. frantzii*; within this group possibly closest to *P. castanotis* and *P. aracari*. Female hybrid between present species and *P. aracari atricollis* known from SE Venezuela (Carapo, R Paragua). Monotypic.

Distribution. NE Colombia and NW & SE Venezuela S in lowlands to NE Peru (S to R Ucayali, but mostly N of R Marañón) and NW Brazil (N of R Solimões, E to N Roraima, middle R Negro and upper R Japurá).

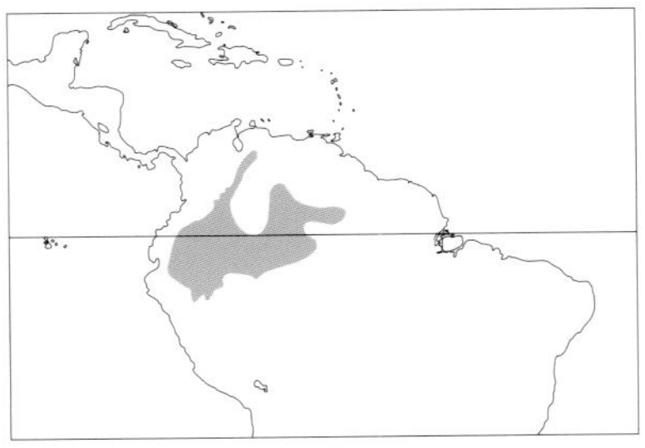

Descriptive notes. 43-46 cm; 215-302 g. Large, notably short-winged araçari with distinctively banded underparts. Male with head and throat black except for small chestnut area behind eye; dark green above, with red rump; yellow below, upper breast marked with red, and with black anterior band and black and red posterior one; thighs chestnut, green and yellow; bill with orange-yellow basal line, mandible black, maxilla orange-yellow with broad black culmen and black at base; orbital and facial skin blue-green to various shades of green; eye yellow. Differs from all other toucans in pattern of underparts. Female differs from male in shorter bill; shows less or no chestnut behind eye, and on average has broader black breastband. Immature lax-plumaged, duller overall than adults, especially yellow areas, and has green thighs; bill grey, brown, horn and black, with only a suggestion of the adult pattern, and no tomial "teeth" or basal line. Voice. Gives "seeent", "seeet" or "see-yeet" notes, often paired in loose series to fast bursts, functions unclear, but serve as contact, aggressive and alarm notes; terminal notes may be rough "bbbrt", resembling some calls of unbanded araçaris and *P. bitorquatus*.

Habitat. Mainly inhabits low, wet but not flooded primary forest, generally occurring in smaller numbers in *várzea* and gallery forest. Ranges up into wet upper tropical forest, at 500-750 m, along Andes; in S Venezuela, at higher elevations in upper valleys, replaces *P. aracari*; recorded up to 900 m.

Food and Feeding. Little known. Various fruits and some arthropod remains found in stomachs. Forages in pairs, in small groups or singly, in forest canopy.
Breeding. Estimated season Nov-Mar in Colombia and Ecuador, and Mar-Oct in Brazil, Venezuela and, probably, Peru. No information available on nest, clutch size, parental duties or any other aspects of breeding.
Movements. Probably resident.
Status and Conservation. Not globally threatened. Relatively poorly known: apparently uncommon to fairly common in Colombia and Ecuador, and fairly common in Peru; no other information available. Occurs in several protected areas, including Amacayacu National Park, Colombia, and Cuyabeno Reserve, Ecuador. Range not precisely known in some areas, e.g. in NW Brazil. Lack of information on its biology and population ecology would be serious handicaps if species comes to need any protective action.
Bibliography. Berlepsch & Hartert (1902), Blake (1961), Boesman (1998), Bond (1954), Chapman (1917, 1926), Cherrie (1916), Clements & Shany (2001), Cory (1919), Friedmann (1948), Hackett & Lehn (1997), Haffer (1967b, 1974, 1978, 1985, 1987, 1993a, 1997c), Hilty & Brown (1986), María & Olivares (1967), Meyer de Schauensee (1949, 1964, 1966), Meyer de Schauensee & Phelps (1978), Moskovits *et al*. (1985), Olivares (1962, 1964a), Phelps & Phelps (1958), Remsen *et al*. (1993), Ridgely & Greenfield (2001), Ridgely *et al*. (1998), Salaman *et al*. (1999), Sick (1985, 1993), Stotz *et al*. (1996), Zimmer & Hilty (1997).

25. Collared Araçari
Pteroglossus torquatus

French: Araçari à collier **German**: Halsbandarassari **Spanish**: Arasarí Acollarado
Other common names: Spot-breasted/Banded/Ringed/Red-rumped/Red-backed/Spot-chested Araçari; Stripe-billed Araçari (*sanguineus*); Pale-mandibled Araçari (*erythropygius*)

Taxonomy. *Ramphastos torquatus* J. F. Gmelin, 1788, Veracruz, Mexico.
Forms a superspecies with *P. frantzii*; although not in full contact, these two have hybridized, and they may be conspecific. Both belong to the "*P. torquatus* group", which also includes *P. aracari*, *P. castanotis* and *P. pluricinctus*, all these species being closely related. Southern races *sanguineus* and *erythropygius* sometimes considered to represent one or two additional species, but they interbreed to a significant extent with each other in SW Colombia and NW Ecuador, as also does *sanguineus* with nominate *torquatus* in E Panama and NW Colombia, so they are better treated as races of present species; in addition, race *nuchalis* intergrades with *sanguineus*. Birds from SE Mexico (Chiapas), described as *esperanzae*, now lumped within nominate *torquatus*; those from NW Venezuela, named as race *pectoralis*, now included in *nuchalis*. Five subspecies currently recognized.
Subspecies and Distribution.
P. t. torquatus (J. F. Gmelin, 1788) - EC Mexico S to NW corner of Colombia.
P. t. erythrozonus Ridgway, 1912 - Yucatán Peninsula, S to Belize and NE Guatemala.
P. t. nuchalis Cabanis, 1862 - NE Colombia (area of Santa Marta Mts) and mountains of N Venezuela.
P. t. sanguineus Gould, 1854 - E Panama and N & NW Colombia S to NW Ecuador.
P. t. erythropygius Gould, 1843 - W Ecuador; recently recorded in extreme N Peru (Tumbes).

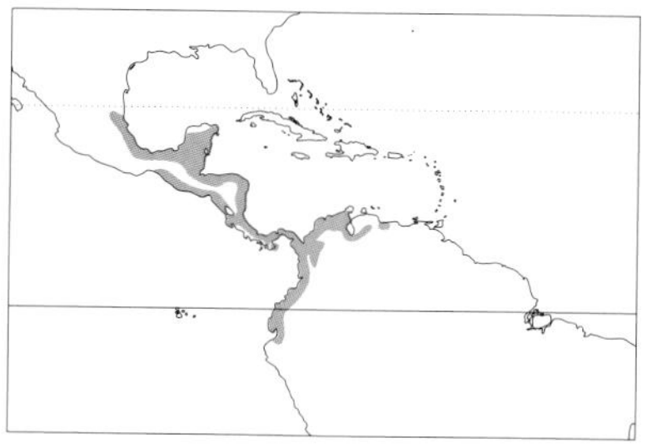

Descriptive notes. 43-48 cm; 147-198 g (*erythrozonus*), 240-310 g (*erythropygius*). Male nominate race with black head and throat, maroon-chestnut nuchal collar, dark green upperparts, red rump; yellow below, breast with red patch and black spot, belly with black and red band, flanks red, thighs rufous; bill with white basal line, black mandible, yellow-ivory maxilla black-tipped with black culmen line, orange-red area near base, and coarse, large tomial "teeth"; facial-orbital skin red and blue to slaty; eye cream or yellow. Female with nuchal collar darker than in male, with bill shorter. Immature duller than adults, with dark areas sootier, cinnamon in green areas on upperparts, reds and yellows generally paler, and breast mark larger; blotchy bill lacks tomial "teeth" and basal line, facial skin yellow-orange, eyes blue to brown or white. Race *erythrozonus* similar to nominate but much smaller, with breast spot smaller or absent; *nuchalis* with breast mark on average larger, thighs paler and cinnamon, "teeth" finer; *sanguineus* lacks chestnut nuchal mark, and has bill broader with ridges beside nostrils, tip orange-yellow, long black line on each side along tomia, "teeth" fine and inconspicuous; *erythropygius* larger but shorter-tailed, also lacks nuchal mark, bill without culmen stripe, almost entirely pale ivory-yellow, with black tip to mandible, black line along maxilla above tomia, and rather fine tomial "teeth". Voice. Major call "tseeep", high-pitched and variable, 1-3 per second in series, notes often doubled as "tis-seek"; present species reacts strongly to playback of this call, but equally to calls of *P. castanotis* and *P. aracari*; also produces rattle notes, or rattle-"tseeep" calls, soft rattles "bddddt" at nest (captives); grating "dddd", purring calls, "pee-yew" notes; alarm squeak or loud "pit" notes; aggressive "arghrr"; chatters, and other calls; makes loud wing sounds in interactions; hits nest entrance with bill, and can sound like woodpecker drum.
Habitat. Inhabits wet or moist primary forest in lowlands, in some places occurring up into subtropical cloudforest; also uses secondary forest, forest patches, gallery forest in woodland, edges, clearings, plantations of fruits, cacao and coffee, forest swamps, and mixed forest and cultivation. Generally found below 1000 m, but recorded up to 1300 m in Mexico, and up to 1500 m in W Ecuador (W Pichincha).
Food and Feeding. Feeds on fruits of species of *Caesaria*, *Ehretia*, *Ficus*, *Metopium*, *Myrica*, *Neea*, *Protium*, *Talisia*, *Trophis*, *Virola*, various palms, guavas and papayas; often regurgitates fruits and then swallows them again. Also takes eggs and young of birds, lizards, and insects; feeds insects to hatchlings. Forages in pairs, and in groups of up to five individuals, sometimes up to 15, rarely 20, mostly in canopy, but lower down in plantations. Jumps, clings, leans and hangs in order to get fruits; probes into epiphytes. Tears apart bird nests it encounters, whether occupied or not. Sometimes associates with *Ramphastos* toucans; a group was seen to attack and chase a lone *R. brevis*.
Breeding. Jan-Aug throughout range, but breeds in most months in Colombia. May nest in groups, but only 1 adult incubates and roosts in nest. Displays with swinging, bowing, jerking head about, calling, pair-members sometimes side by side, rump feathers erected; often cocks and shakes tail interactively. Nest in old woodpecker hole, especially of large *Campephilus* woodpecker, 6-30 m up, entrance to 7 cm, nest c. 16 cm deep, 12 cm wide, with thick layer of regurgitated seeds and fruit stones at bottom; nest reused if breeding successful. Eggs 2-5, commonly 3; incubation c. 16 days; after hatching, any helpers return to feed young, roost in nest; newly hatched young 8-9 g, captives double weight every 4 days, are brooded by parents and helpers, which feed insects to them for c. 1 month; nest kept clean by adults, removing faecal material; young come to entrance at c. 35 days, fledge at c. 44 days; may return to nest to roost, or family roosts in other hole. Nest predators probably include *Ramphastos ambiguus*; among other predators are raptors such as Collared Forest-falcon (*Micrastur semitorquatus*), Ornate Hawk-eagle (*Spizaetus ornatus*) and White Hawk (*Leucopternis albicollis*); dispersing araçaris may face attacks that bloody them in attempting to join new group. Has lived 12 years and 8 months in captivity.
Movements. Largely sedentary so far as known, with only local movements.
Status and Conservation. Not globally threatened. Considered to be common to fairly common in Mexico; common, even locally abundant, in Central America; common in Colombia; locally common in Ecuador, although race *erythropygius* has declined markedly as a result of extensive deforestation. In Panama, density c. 1 pair or group/5-6 ha. Could become threatened locally, and perhaps generally, with continued clearing of forest and fragmenting of distribution, but seems adaptable, using diverse habitats; becomes tame when not molested. Hunted by humans in some places. Present in several protected areas, e.g. Guayabo National Monument, Santa Rosa and Braulio Carrillo National Parks (Costa Rica), Los Katíos National Park and Río Ñambí Natural Reserve (Colombia), and Río Palenque Science Centre (Ecuador).
Bibliography. Álvarez del Toro (1980), Best *et al*. (1993), Binford (1989), Blake (2001), Bloch *et al*. (1991), Brodkorb (1939a, 1943), Brydon (1995), Chapman (1917, 1926), Dickey & van Rossem (1938), Gómez de Silva (1998), Hackett & Lehn (1997), Haffer (1967a, 1967b, 1974, 1975, 1985, 1987), Hellmayr (1911), Hilty (1997), Hilty & Brown (1986), Howe (1977, 1981), Howell, S.N.G. & Webb (1995), Howell, T.R. (1957), Jennings (1996), Kantak (1979), Karr *et al*. (1990), Kilham (1977f), Lowery & Dalquest (1951), Madrid *et al*. (1991), María & Olivares (1967), Meyer de Schauensee (1949, 1964, 1966), Meyer de Schauensee & Phelps (1978), Monroe (1968), de Montes (1989), O'Brien (1979), Olivares & Romero (1973), Parker & Carr (1992), Paynter (1955), Phelps & Phelps (1958), Pople *et al*. (1997), Rangel-Salazar & Enríquez-Rocha (1993), Remsen *et al*. (1993), Ridgely & Greenfield (2001), Ridgely & Gwynne (1989), Robbins *et al*. (1985), Rowley (1984), Rundel (1975), Salaman (1994), Santana *et al*. (1986), Schifter (1996), Schlenker (2000), Skutch (1958b, 1987, 1989), Slud (1964, 1980), Stiles (1983), Stiles & Skutch (1989), Stotz *et al*. (1996), Thorstrom *et al*. (1991), Thurber *et al*. (1987), Todd (1943b), Todd & Carriker (1922), Van Tyne (1929, 1935), Wetmore (1943, 1968a), Wetmore *et al*. (1984), Williams & Tobias (1994).

26. Fiery-billed Araçari
Pteroglossus frantzii

French: Araçari de Frantzius **German**: Feuerschnabelarassari **Spanish**: Arasarí Piquinaranja

Taxonomy. *Pteroglossus Frantzii* Cabanis, 1861, Aguacate, Costa Rica.
Forms a superspecies with *P. torquatus*; although not in full contact, these two have hybridized, and they may be conspecific. Both belong to the "*P. torquatus* group", which also includes *P. aracari*, *P. castanotis* and *P. pluricinctus*, all these species being closely related. Monotypic.
Distribution. From W Costa Rica (Gulf of Nicoya) S into Panama (W Chiriquí; formerly occurring E to Veraguas).

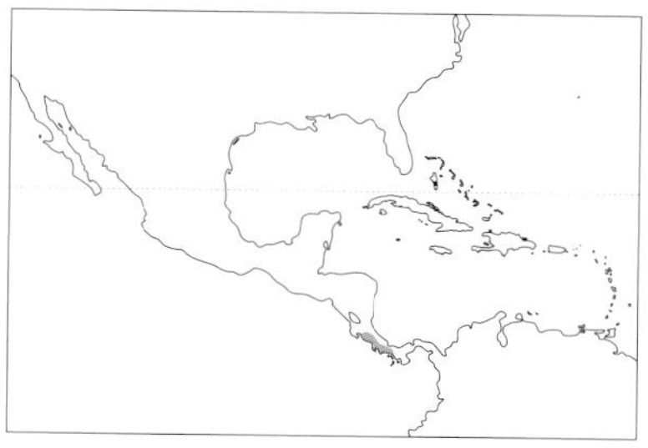

Descriptive notes. c. 45 cm; 225-280 g. Male with black head and throat, chestnut nuchal collar, blue green upperparts with red rump; yellow mixed with red below, black spot on breast, red breast-belly bar with little black; bill with ivory basal line, black mandible, mainly red maxilla with tip yellow and base greenish, black culmen, fine tomial "teeth" not conspicuous; red orbital-facial skin with black loral area. Distinguished from very similar *P. torquatus* by red maxilla with pale tip, less conspicuous "teeth", and redder band below. Female like male, but darker nuchal collar, shorter bill. Immature duller, bill pattern obscure. Voice. Calls "pseep" to "tis-sik" in series, high-pitched, probably indistinguishable from those of *P. torquatus* and essentially as in other species of the "*P. torquatus* group"; also a croaking call, and soft rattle.
Habitat. Inhabits wet lowland forest, edges, cleared areas in forest, and secondary forest; less numerous in forest of foothills and lower mountains, occurring up to 1200 m, occasionally to 1500 m or even 1800 m.
Food and Feeding. Feeds on fruits, such as those of *Cecropia*, *Dipterodendron*, *Ficus*, *Lacistema* and *Protium*, also vines such as *Souroubea*; in addition, captures insects, especially during nesting period. Takes eggs and young of such birds as doves (Columbidae) and woodpeckers; Lineated Woodpeckers (*Dryocopus lineatus*) guard nests to prevent predation and usurpation by this araçari species. Feeds in pairs or in groups of up to 10 individuals, mostly in or near canopy, but comes to low berry-bearing bushes. Holds larger fruits and pods by foot as it breaks them or eats them piecemeal.
Breeding. Season Jan-Apr, perhaps later in Panama. Mostly in pairs, occasionally in trios, thus subadults make up most groups. "Duelling" occurs, hitting bills together and holding bills; pair-members courtship-feed berries and pieces of large fruits. Uses old woodpecker nest or ejects woodpecker from newly excavated one. Eggs 2, possibly more; incubation, for unknown period, by parents and any helpers, for short to long periods, mostly shorter, average 15-27 minutes in several cases, eggs covered c. 65% of daytime; chicks are fed insects at first, then mainly fruits; nestling period unknown, two young fledged 3 days apart; newly fledged young led back to nest to roost, but may not reach nest for 1-2 nights. Nests that are situated in old cavities of trees isolated in pastures suffer high predation, or may be cut down. Probably does not breed until 2 years old or more.
Movements. Considered resident.
Status and Conservation. Not globally threatened. Restricted-range species: present in South Central American Pacific Slope EBA. Occurs in Caracara Biological Reserve and Corcovado National Park, in Costa Rica. Reasonably common in some areas, but small range, together with range contraction that has been taking place in Panama, suggest that monitoring may be needed; formerly occurred E in Panama to Veraguas and islands such as Brava, Cebaco and Gobernador Is. Studies needed of breeding within forest, of group formation, and of dispersal and movements of groups.
Bibliography. Angehr (1995), Anon. (1998b), Aparicio (1996), Blake (1958), Cory (1919), Delgado (1985), Hackett & Lehn (1997), Haffer (1974), Nadkarni & Matelson (1989), Olrog (1968), Remsen *et al*. (1993), Ridgely & Gwynne (1989), Ridgway (1914), Skutch (1969a, 1983, 1989, 1999), Slud (1964), Stattersfield *et al*. (1998), Stiles & Skutch (1989), Stotz *et al*. (1996), Wetmore (1968a).

27. Curl-crested Araçari

Pteroglossus beauharnaesii

French: Araçari de Beauharnais   **German**: Krauskopfarassari   **Spanish**: Arasarí Crespo

Taxonomy. *Pteroglossus Beauharnaesii* Wagler, 1832, Pará; error = eastern Peru.
Distinct from congeners, and in past occasionally isolated in monotypic genus or subgenus *Beauharnaisius*. Probably related to ancestor of the "*P. torquatus* group", which comprises *P. aracari*, *P. castanotis*, *P. pluricinctus*, *P. torquatus* and *P. frantzii*; recent work suggests it is unlikely to be related to *P. inscriptus* and *P. bitorquatus*. Monotypic.
Distribution. SW Amazonia S of Amazon, from N Peru (S of R Marañón) and W Brazil (E to mouth of R Madeira and, farther S, to upper R Xingu), S to N & C Bolivia (Pando, Cochabamba) and N Mato Grosso.

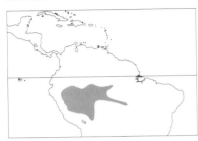

Descriptive notes. 42-46 cm; 164-280 g. Unmistakable, with relatively short bill, very long tail. Both sexes have curled, modified, shiny black feathers, like pieces of enamel, on top of head; red upper back and rump, rest of upperparts dark green; pale throat, the yellow-white feathers with shiny black spots at tips, sometimes persisting on to yellow breast, band across lower breast red with some black, belly yellow, undertail-coverts yellow but can show red; bill with basal line brown-orange, mandible ivory-coloured, becoming oranger towards tip, orangey culmen expanding distally, then yellow at tip, maxilla with maroon stripe narrowing distally on sides and with green or bluish above it, tomial "teeth" ivory-white; blue facial-orbital skin, ruby-red over and behind eye, often hidden in feathers; iris red. Female shorter-billed than male. Immature duller. VOICE. Very variable, deep "rrek" notes, soft "rrr" to hard, even grunting "grenk" notes, in series, faster or slower, some accented with bill-snapping; softer "et-et" by group before roosting; occasional piping "eet" notes; variation likely related to individual interactions in group.
Habitat. Occurs in lowland wet forest, both well-drained and swampy, forest edges and clearings, also lower hill forest; usually found below 500 m, but occasionally recorded up to c. 900 m near Andes.
Food and Feeding. Diet poorly known, mainly fruits such as figs and those of *Ocotea*; also eggs and young birds at times, perhaps when it is nesting and needs protein for young. Forages almost entirely in groups of 3-12, mainly in canopy, but to 1·2 m in bushes of clearings. Vigorously attacks and tears apart nests of Yellow-rumped Cacique (*Cacicus cela*) at times. Captives reportedly not so aggressive and predatory as are other araçaris.
Breeding. Data from specimens indicate season May-Aug, occasionally to Nov or even Feb. Probably nests in groups. Displays include deep bowing and calling, with chase-bounding. Nest and eggs, hence all associated behaviour, unknown.
Movements. Some aggregations reported along Amazon when many trees in fruit, as in Jul; presumably local or short-distance movements involved.
Status and Conservation. Not globally threatened. Relatively widespread, but not well known. Generally occupies forest at density of c. 1 bird/10-12 ha, or c. 8 birds/100 ha, but fewer occur in successional stages beside rivers and lakes in Peru. More data on this species' biology are essential, in case it becomes necessary to protect it; observations of interactions with *P. aracari* and *P. castanotis* could provide useful information. Vulnerable to human hunting activities: when one member of group is taken by hunter or predator, rest of group do not flee but all remain nearby, calling loudly. Known to occur in Tambopata Reserve (Peru).

Bibliography. Allen (1995), Anon. (1995a, 1997), Bond (1954), Brush (1967), Clements & Shany (2001), Cory (1919), Gyldenstolpe (1945a, 1951), Hackett & Lehn (1997), Haffer (1974, 1978, 1985, 1993a, 1993b, 1997c), Hellmayr (1910), Hilty & Brown (1986), Karr *et al.* (1990), Kavkova & Kralickova (1997), Meyer de Schauensee (1966), Parker & Bailey (1991), Remsen, Hyde & Chapman (1993), Remsen, Traylor & Parkes (1986), Robinson (1985), Robinson & Terborgh (1997), Rundel (1975), Sick (1985, 1993), Stotz *et al.* (1996), Terborgh *et al.* (1990), Zimmer *et al.* (1997).

PLATE 20 ➤

28

29

ssp *sulfuratus*

ssp *brevicarinatus*

30

ssp *citreolaemus*

ssp *culminatus*

31

ssp *ariel*

ssp *vitellinus*

32

ssp *tucanus*

ssp *inca*

33

ssp *ambiguus*

ssp *cuvieri*

34

ssp *swainsonii*

ssp *abbreviatus*

PLATE 20

inches 6

cm 15

Genus *RAMPHASTOS* Linnaeus, 1758

28. **Red-breasted Toucan**
Ramphastos dicolorus

French: Toucan à ventre rouge **German**: Bunttukan **Spanish**: Tucán Bicolor
Other common names: Green-billed/Keel-billed(!) Toucan

Taxonomy. *Ramphastos dicolorus* Linnaeus, 1766, Cayenne; error = south-eastern Brazil.
No very close relatives. One of the so-called "croaking group" of *Ramphastos* species, along with *R. sulfuratus*, *R. brevis*, *R. vitellinus* and *R. toco*; possibly closest to *R. sulfuratus*. Has hybridized with *R. vitellinus*. Monotypic.
Distribution. SC, CE & SE Brazil (S Tocantins, C Minas Gerais and W Espírito Santo to NC Rio Grande do Sul) to E Paraguay and N Argentina (E Chaco, Corrientes).

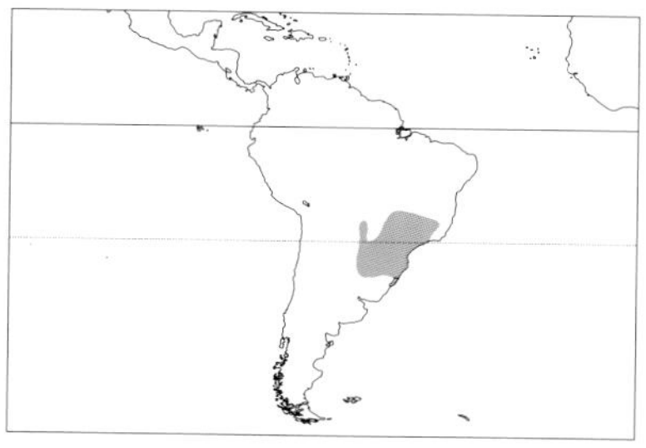

Descriptive notes. 42-48 cm; 265-400 g (averages larger towards S). Both sexes are glossy black from forehead to tail, except red uppertail-coverts; sides of face, most of bib yellow-white with central orange area; broad red area on lower breast, belly and undertail-coverts, vent and flanks black; bill with broad black basal line that projects forwards at tomia, is mainly green to green-yellow, tip yellow, tomial "teeth" ivory with red line through and above them on maxilla, some green striations from tomia upwards on maxilla; red facial skin, blue to yellow-green around eye; iris green-blue to green-yellow. Female shorter-billed than male. Immature with lax plumage, duller, especially paler in red areas, also orange and yellow paler, iris brown at first; bill with nostrils on top of base, no tomial "teeth", largely pale yellow, no red or green. Voice. Sometimes long series of noisy honking "grrekk" notes, higher-pitched than similar grunting croak of *R. toco*, noisier than in *R. vitellinus*, tempo variable, often c. 31 per minute, occasionally at 2 per second; also low "ek", "zneep", growl-like begging, bill-tapping at nest, and tongue-rattling with bill closed in aggression.
Habitat. Inhabits subtropical and tropical montane and submontane forest, also some second-growth scrub, trees in Pantanal savanna, and lowland forest at times; extends into plantations after breeding. Mainly found at 100-1500 m, but rarely up to 2070 m; may breed at higher elevations where *R. vitellinus* occurs.
Food and Feeding. Feeds on fruits, such as those of introduced *Ardiontophoenix*, *Cabralea*, *Didymopanax*, the palm *Euterpes edulis*, *Guarea*, *Morus*, *Myrciaria*, and *Syagrus*; also takes green coffee fruits and other orchard fruits; captives fed on apples, bananas, cherries, grapes, peas, raspberries, zucchini, and others. Also takes insects at times, and preys on small birds; in cages, hunts down House Sparrows (*Passer domesticus*) that have come in to eat its food. Usually in pairs or groups, occasionally gathering in parties of up to 20 individuals or more. Forages mostly in canopy, but readily drops to ground to pick up fallen fruits. Aggressive towards *Baillonius bailloni* and *Pteroglossus castanotis*, and captives are aggressive towards other birds such as woodpeckers and parrots (Psittacidae).
Breeding. Season Oct-Feb in S, Jan-Jun farther N; has been recorded laying 3 clutches in 5 months in captivity. Often in territories, usually in pairs; aggressive to conspecifics, at times to mate in captivity. Sings usually with head thrown up to one side, then other, sometimes cocks tail, does not bow; male allopreens, courtship-feeds female, tongue-rattles in crouch after her, may attempt to copulate. Excavates to enlarge hole opening, and to clear and enlarge cavity; 1 nest partly excavated in exotic plane (*Platanus*) tree; another 6 m above ground, with entrance 6·5 cm, cavity only 15 cm deep, 13 cm wide at bottom. Eggs 2-4; both adults incubate, female sometimes more, period c. 16 days; young fed insects at first, then fruits, larger ones of which are broken up by parent; in captivity, parents fed 2 dead mice or sparrows per day to nestlings, and roost with young; nestling period c. 40 days, 2 definite instances of 42 days; post-fledging behaviour in wild unknown. Known-age female bred at 21 months, male at 34 months. Longevity in captivity up to 16 years and 8 months.
Movements. Downslope movements occur, especially in S, in Jun-Jul, birds moving into plantations of fruiting trees.
Status and Conservation. Not globally threatened. Probably reasonably common in general. Occurs in various protected areas, e.g. Itatiaia National Park (Brazil), Estancia San Antonio, La Golondrina and Estancia Itabó Private Nature Reserves, and Reserva Natural del Bosque Mbaracayú (Paraguay), and Iguazú National Park (Argentina). Is still persecuted in some places as a predator of small birds and because it eats fruits in plantations; is hunted for food in other places. Should probably be monitored, as its habitat around increasingly urbanized centres is disappearing.
Bibliography. Belton (1984, 1994), Brehm (1969), Brooks *et al.* (1993), Bühl (1982), Canevari *et al.* (1991), Cory (1919), Eckelberry (1964), Galetti *et al.* (1998), Guix (1995), Guix & Jover (2001), Guix & Ruiz (1995), Haffer (1974, 1985, 1991, 1997b), Hayes (1995), Hayes *et al.* (1990), Höfling & Camargo (1993), Höfling *et al.* (1986), Holt (1928), Iwinski & Iwinski (1984), Lange (1967), Martín (2000), Maurício & Dias (1998), Meyer de Schauensee (1966), Narosky & Yzurieta (1993), Novaes (1949), de Oliveira (1985), Parker & Goerck (1997), de la Peña (1994), Remsen *et al.* (1993), do Rosário (1996), Schifter (1998), Schönwetter (1967), Short (1975), Sick (1985, 1993), da Silva (1996), Stotz *et al.* (1996), Thirkhill (1987).

29. **Rainbow-billed Toucan**
Ramphastos sulfuratus

French: Toucan à carène **German**: Fischertukan **Spanish**: Tucán Piquiverde
Other common names: Keel-billed(!)/Sulphur-breasted Toucan

Taxonomy. *Ramphastos sulfuratus* Lesson, 1830, Mexico.
Distinctive within the so-called "croaking group", which also includes *R. dicolorus*, *R. brevis*, *R. vitellinus* and *R. toco*. Not especially closely related to any other species, with nearest relatives probably *R. dicolorus* and *R. brevis*. Races weakly defined, intergrading where they meet. Two subspecies recognized.
Subspecies and Distribution.
R. s. sulfuratus Lesson, 1830 - SE Mexico (from Veracruz) S through Belize and Guatemala to Honduras.
R. s. brevicarinatus Gould, 1854 - Guatemala, Belize and Honduras S to N Colombia (R Atrato, lower R Cauca and lower R Magdalena) and extreme NW Venezuela.

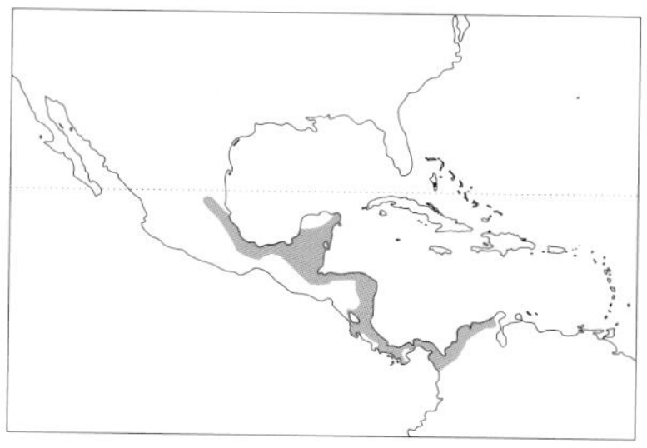

Descriptive notes. 46-51 cm; 275-550 g, male 20-50 g heavier than female. Large black, white, yellow and red toucan. Both sexes of nominate race with maroon tinge to black of head and upper back; throat to breast yellow, with narrow, often inconspicuous red band beneath; bill orange, blue and green, with red tip; facial skin yellow-green, sometimes with blue, even orange, in it; iris green to brown or yellow. Distinguished from all other toucans by bill colours. Female smaller and shorter-billed than male. Immature with duller, softer plumage, tips of rectrices more pointed, bill colours muted, bill more keeled, nostrils on top of bill, no "teeth". Race *brevicarinatus* generally smaller, with broader, but still narrow, red band behind yellow on breast. Voice. Series of variable notes, "bbrrik" to more grunting "ggrrr", grating elements slower than in other "croaking" toucans, higher-pitched than *R. toco*, female higher-pitched than male; pair may "sing" simultaneously, countersinging with other pairs; also "bbbbbdt" rattle that is vocal or made by tongue in bill, soft "nip" notes, and buzzing, squeaky, whining and wailing calls of young.
Habitat. Usually occurs in wet lowland forest, occasionally lower montane subtropical forest, extending into dry areas in forest along streams; often at edges, in old secondary forest, in larger forest patches, overgrown plantations, as of coffee; less often penetrates mangrove forest and dry deciduous forest. Visits fruiting trees in open pastures. Generally found below 800 m, in places higher; locally up to 1600 m in Colombia, 1400 m in Mexico, and 900-1300 m in other parts of Central America.
Food and Feeding. Fruits of various trees, lianas and others: e.g. of *Alchornea*, *Aristolochia*, the palm *Astrocaryum*, *Cecropia*, *Ehretia*, *Exothea*, *Ficus*, *Iriartea*, *Malmea*, *Metapodium*, *Nectandra*, *Neea*, *Ocotea*, *Phoebe*, *Poulsenia*, *Protium*, *Prunus*, *Rapanea*, *Symplocos*, *Trichilia*, *Trophis*, *Virola*, and others, including fruits over 30 mm long, swallowed whole. Also eats various beetles, cicadas, grasshoppers, ants, spiders, some lizards and snakes, and probably bird eggs. De-husks some fruits with bill; holds larger insects and vertebrates in foot, breaks them up with bill. Usually in pairs or families, sometimes in gatherings of up to 22. Forages from canopy to middle levels; comes to ground rarely, e.g. for discarded bananas. Tears open some bird nests. At times follows army-ant swarms seeking food.
Breeding. Mainly Jan-Jul. Jerks head and tail when singing; male courtship-feeds female. Nest in natural cavity 3-27 m above ground, entrance hole often very small, difficult for male to enter, cavity to c. 45 cm, at times to 2 m deep; cavity cleaned out up to 6 weeks before laying, may place green leaves into nest and remove them later; nesting trees include species of *Cupania*, *Hura* and *Inga*; nest reused in following year if breeding successful. Eggs 1-4, laid on consecutive days; incubation by both parents, for 4-86 minutes at a time, period uncertain; naked hatchling sits on abdomen and spiky hypotarsal protuberances; both parents feed young insects and fruits, also some vertebrates, and remove faecal debris; young fully feathered at c. 37 days, fledge at 42-47 days; family leaves nest area after fledging. Predation by hawk-eagles (*Spizaetus*) and Collared Forest-falcons (*Micrastur semitorquatus*) possibly significant; 1 of last species, over 10-week period, delivered 27 individuals of this toucan to nest as food for its young. Lives to at least 15 years and 7 months in captivity.
Movements. Apparently only local movements.
Status and Conservation. Not globally threatened. CITES II. Considered to be fairly common to common in Mexico; common in parts of Costa Rica and Panama, mainly on Caribbean slope; common in Colombia. Recorded density of up to 4 pairs nesting in 16 ha of forest in Panama. Survival in forest patches of different sizes requires study. Relatively tame in protected areas. Possibly under some degree of threat locally. Likely disturbance factors, including taking of young as pets in some areas, are important when considering its conservation. This species is hunted by humans in parts of its range. Present in several protected areas, e.g. Santa Rosa National Park and Guayabo National Monument (Costa Rica), and Los Katíos and Tayrona National Parks (Colombia).
Bibliography. Álvarez del Toro (1980), Berry & Coffey (1976), Binford (1989), Bond & Meyer de Schauensee (1944), Brodkorb (1943), Chapman (1917), Clinton-Eitniear (1982), Cory (1919), Eitniear (1982), Haffer (1967a, 1974, 1975, 1985, 1987), Hilty & Brown (1986), Howe (1977), Howell, S.N.G. & Webb (1995), Howell, T.R. (1957), Kantak (1979), Karr *et al.* (1990), Lowery & Dalquest (1951), Madrid *et al.* (1991), Meyer de Schauensee (1949, 1964, 1966), Meyer de Schauensee & Phelps (1978), Monroe (1968), de Montes (1989), Parker *et al.* (1994), Paynter (1955), Phelps & Phelps (1958), Remsen *et al.* (1993), Ridgely & Gwynne (1989), Ridgway (1914), Robbins *et al.* (1985), Schifter (1998), Schönwetter (1967), Schürer (1985), Schütter (2000), Sill & Sosa (1996), Skutch (1971, 1980), Slud (1964), Stiles (1983), Stiles & Levey (1994), Stiles & Skutch (1989), Stotz *et al.* (1996), Thorstrom *et al.* (1991), Todd (1943b), Todd & Carriker (1922), Van Tyne (1929, 1935), Wetmore (1943, 1968a), Willis (1983), Young *et al.* (1998).

30. **Choco Toucan**
Ramphastos brevis

French: Toucan du Choco **German**: Küstentukan **Spanish**: Tucán del Chocó

Taxonomy. *Ramphastos ambiguus brevis* Meyer de Schauensee, 1945, River Mechengue, Cauca, Colombia.
A distinctive species within the so-called "croaking group" of *Ramphastos* species, which also includes *R. dicolorus*, *R. sulfuratus*, *R. vitellinus* and *R. toco*. Probably most closely related to *R. sulfuratus*; sibling species of *R. ambiguus*, though not very closely related to it. Was long considered to be a race of *R. ambiguus*, but differs significantly in several aspects, notably voice. Monotypic.
Distribution. NW Colombia (N Chocó) S, W of Andes, to SW Ecuador (S to Manta Real).
Descriptive notes. 46-48·5 cm; 365-482 g. Both sexes with maroon tinge in black from forehead to upper back; black above, uppertail-coverts white; yellow throat and breast, narrow red band below yellow, black belly, red undertail-coverts; bill yellow above, with green on culmen and central sides meeting black of maxillary base, with grey marks above 3-5 maxillary tomial "teeth", mandible

On following pages: 31. Channel-billed Toucan (*Ramphastos vitellinus*); 32. Toco Toucan (*Ramphastos toco*); 33. White-throated Toucan (*Ramphastos tucanus*); 34. Yellow-throated Toucan (*Ramphastos ambiguus*).

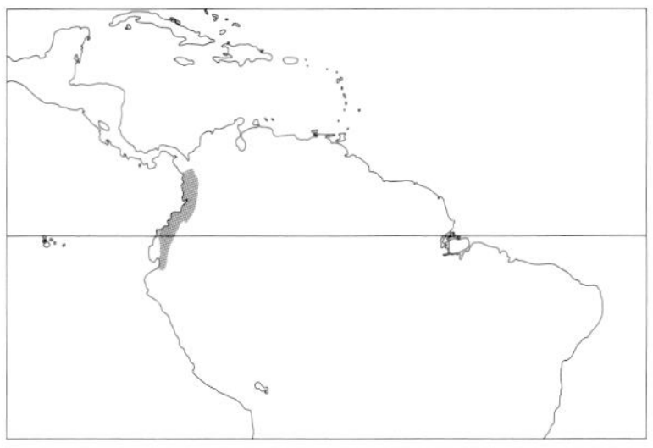

black, tip sometimes yellow; facial-orbital skin yellow-green to olive-green, shows bluish in some; iris green with yellow to grey tinge. Distinguished from very similar *R. ambiguus swainsonii* by smaller size, and voice. Female with shorter, more blocky-looking bill than male. Immature soft-plumaged, colours duller, red orangey, bill more keeled, basal line and "teeth" absent, nostrils visible on top, which is browner. VOICE. A series of croaks, "tree-aak" to "tyook" or "tyeerp", 40-55 (sometimes to 100) per minute, notes growl-like and longer at start of series, which may go on for some minutes; male deeper, more growly notes; variations include more honking version, and soft notes audible only at close range; also clacks bill, and makes grating, clapping sounds with bill closed.

Habitat. Generally inhabits lowland forest and also forest on lower Andean slopes, as well as adjacent pastures with fruiting trees or plantations. Groups or pairs wander widely, moving upslope to c. 1550 m.

Food and Feeding. Diet little known; mainly undetermined fruits in stomachs; probably takes some insects and small vertebrates. Feeds in canopy, often with *Pteroglossus torquatus*, with which it interacts, but rarely with larger *R. ambiguus*. Can turn head upside-down in feeding. Noted following raiding army ants, presumably for animal prey they disturb. Drinks from water in bromeliads.

Breeding. Poorly known. Thought to breed in Jun-Aug, probably earlier, to Jan, in W Colombia. "Singing" bird swings head upwards to one side, and across and up in an arc to other, with almost no downward or bowing motion; in conflicts, holds head low, plumage sleeked except for erected rump and undertail-covert feathers. No information available on nest, eggs, incubation or other details.

Movements. None known other than upslope, foraging movements in pairs or in groups of up to 6, rarely 14.

Status and Conservation. Not globally threatened. Restricted-range species: present in Chocó EBA. No information available on numbers. Judged to be uncommon to locally common in Ecuador, where has declined markedly due to extensive deforestation; large populations apparently persist in Esmeraldas, where much of forest remains largely intact. Occurs in Río Ñambí Nature Reserve, Colombia, and in Río Palenque Science Centre, Ecuador. May possibly become threatened by further fragmentation of habitat; patchy habitat likely to render foraging for food for young difficult; also, nest-sites may be limited, as species probably requires large, secure natural cavities. Hunted for food, and its bill is used in traditional medicinal remedies. Requires study in order to determine its requirements, and to ascertain whether its present conservation status needs to be reassessed.

Bibliography. Allen (1998), Best *et al.* (1997), Butler (1979), Chapman (1917, 1926), Cory (1919), Haffer (1967a, 1974, 1975, 1985, 1987, 1991), Hilty & Brown (1986), María & Olivares (1967), Meyer de Schauensee (1945, 1949, 1964, 1966, 1982), Parker & Carr (1992), Remsen *et al.* (1993), Ridgely & Greenfield (2001), Ridgely *et al.* (1998), Rodner *et al.* (2000), Salaman (1994), Stattersfield *et al.* (1998), Stotz *et al.* (1996), Todd (1943b), Willis (1983).

31. Channel-billed Toucan

Ramphastos vitellinus

French: Toucan ariel **German**: Dottertukan **Spanish**: Tucán Picoacanalado
Other common names: Osculated/Sulphur-and-white-breasted Toucan; Citron-throated/Orange-billed Toucan (*citreolaemus*); Yellow-ridged Toucan (*culminatus*); Ariel Toucan (*ariel*)

Taxonomy. *Ramphastos vitellinus* M. H. K. Lichtenstein, 1823, Cayenne.
One of the so-called "croaking group" of toucans, along with *R. dicolorus*, *R. sulfuratus*, *R. brevis* and *R. toco*. No very close relatives. Has hybridized with *R. dicolorus*. All four races well marked, and sometimes considered four distinct species: all four, however, interbreed to massive extent wherever they meet, forming huge hybrid populations, e.g. *culminatus* interbreeds with *citreolaemus* in NW Venezuela, with nominate *vitellinus* in S Venezuela and Brazil N of Amazon, and widely with *ariel* S of Amazon (in Amazonas, W Pará, Rondônia, Tocantins, Goiás, Piauí, NW São Paulo, and Mato Grosso); hybrids probably outnumber genetically "pure" individuals of all forms, and it proves impossible to draw strict boundaries separating races geographically. Several previously described forms now known to represent hybrids: "*berliozi*" (R Negro, N Brazil) is cross between nominate *vitellinus* and *culminatus*; and "*osculans*" (upper R Negro), "*theresae*" (NE Brazil) and "*pintoi*" (SE Brazil) are all hybrids of *culminatus* with *ariel*. Four subspecies currently recognized.

Subspecies and Distribution.
R. v. citreolaemus Gould, 1844 - CN & NE Colombia into NW Venezuela.
R. v. culminatus Gould, 1833 - NW & SW Venezuela, and Colombia E of Andes, E to C & E Brazil (W Pará, Piauí), and S to C Bolivia, Mato Grosso and SE Brazil (NW São Paulo).
R. v. vitellinus Lichtenstein, 1823 - Trinidad, and E Venezuela, the Guianas, and NE Brazil N of Amazon.
R. v. ariel Vigors, 1826 - Brazil S of Amazon, E from R Tapajós in Pará, Maranhão and Piauí, and disjunctly from E Pernambuco S to Santa Catarina.

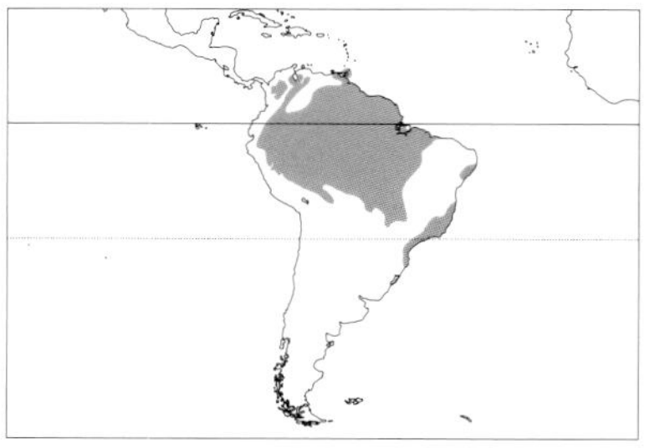

Descriptive notes. 46-56 cm; 285-455 g, female averages 10-25 g less than male. Black above and on belly, with pale throat and breast, brightly coloured uppertail-coverts, red undertail-coverts; laterally channelled bill mostly black with black basal line. Both sexes of nominate race with red uppertail-coverts, white-sided orange-centred bib, broad red breastband; bill all black but for blue patch towards base; facial skin blue, iris brown. Immature duller, lax plumage with muted reds, orange and yellow, rectrices more pointed, face paler, eyes dark, bill more keeled with diffuse patterning, nostrils atop bill, no basal line; spiky tarsal "heel". Races differ mainly in colours of bill, bare parts, underparts: *ariel* similar to nominate, but gold around base of bill and blue basal culmen spot, facial skin red, iris pale blue, bib has orange to its edge, where yellower, and red breastband very broad and extending to abdomen; *citreolaemus* has deeper bill with green-yellow culmen and orange, yellow and blue around its base, face blue, iris dark blue, bib mainly yellow-white, red breastband narrow, also pale yellow uppertail-coverts; *culminatus* generally heaviest race, has shallower bill with yellower culmen and yellow and blue base without orange, iris brown, bib almost purely white, red breastband very narrow, also gold-yellow uppertail-coverts; hybrids varyingly intermediate, with some semi-stabilization of populations of *culminatus* × *ariel* in EC Brazil. VOICE. All races have note, disyllabic, of noisy and clear elements mixed variously, "kee-ark" to "kerrrk" to "keee", singly or in series, c. 30-50 per minute; sexes sing simultaneously, female generally slower, at higher pitch than male, countersinging common; grunting to whistle-like notes less harsh than in *R. sulfuratus*, *R. toco* and *R. dicolorus*, but lacking yelping, whistled, clear quality of *R. tucanus* and *R. ambiguus*; also pure grunts, peeping calls of young; clacks bill aggressively, taps softly to loudly at nest, producing woodpecker-like drumming.

Habitat. Forested lowlands, most commonly near water, forest edge, also swamp-forest, forest clearings, riverine forest and forest patches in savannas and llanos, *cerrado* river forest, and up into wet upper tropical and at times subtropical forest to c. 1700 m; much less common in secondary, selectively cut forest, even a decade or more after cutting. Occurs below *R. dicolorus* in SE Brazil.

Food and Feeding. Palm "nuts", figs, other fruits; also insects, spiders, other arthropods, lizards and other small vertebrates, probably frogs, toads, and roosting bats; takes eggs and young of birds; and nectar or flowers of *Combretum* and *Quararibea*. In captivity, kills and eats other birds in aviary; thrives on meat such as mice, and cooked carrots, potatoes and spinach, eggs, dog food, apples, pears, bananas, papayas, grapes. Feeds in canopy to middle storey, descends to ground for fallen fruits or to prey on animals. Stalks lizards, insects; takes termites in air; tears apart bird nests for eggs and young. Joins other birds following army ants, seizing small animals disturbed by the ants. Drinks from bromeliads, holds bill open in rain. Submissive to *R. tucanus*, also less actively dominant than that species in latter's absence, often allowing other toucans to feed in same tree. Sometimes follows noisy groups of social Red-throated Caracaras (*Daptrius americanus*), as anti-predator strategy.

Breeding. Almost all populations breeding to some extent in Feb-Jul; Aug-Mar in W Brazil, Oct-Apr in SC Brazil and Nov-Jul in Venezuela; extends into Aug-Sept, even to Nov, in the Guianas, NE Brazil and Ecuador. Male courtship-feeds female; singing in canopy, rarely from open perch as does *R. tucanus*, arc-swinging of head without deep bowing, may swing tail rapidly or jerk head in all directions; in captivity, breeding male and female kill any others caged with them. Nest in natural cavity, at any height, but sites limited so can be as low as 3·5 m; small entrance preferred, once 6·5 × 5·7 cm, but diameter to 10 cm; paired birds spend much time at cavity before laying, return to previously used hole if breeding there successful; territory c. 40 ha. Eggs 2-4 (2-5 in captivity); both sexes incubate, female perhaps more than male, which may feed her in nest, incubation period 16-18 days; hatchlings fed by both parents, probably with animal food at first; 3 chicks of captive pair were fed 10 mice and c. 80 small to large arthropods daily, and sought large insects entering cage; feeding rate very variable, e.g. once in 9 hours, and 29 feeds in 1 day; nest kept clean, faecal material removed; eyes of chicks open about as feathers start to appear, at 2-3 weeks, well feathered at 7 weeks, fledge at 37-46 days, young may fledge over several days; little information on post-fledging period, but captives feed themselves by c. 60 days. Normally 2 or 3 young fledge; preyed upon by hawk-eagles (*Spizaetus*) and Great Horned Owls (*Bubo virginianus*); captive pair laid 14 clutches in 14 consecutive years. Breeding possible at 2 years, more likely successful at 3-4 years of age.

Movements. Some movement suggested, not well known; rarely erupts in large numbers.

Status and Conservation. Not globally threatened. CITES II. Appears to be reasonably common, at least locally, throughout its range; uncommon to locally common in Ecuador. In lakeside Peruvian forest 2 pairs/100 ha, but 1·5 pairs/100 ha in mature forest away from water. Occurs in several protected areas, including Asa Wright Nature Centre, in Trinidad, Imataca Forest Reserve and El Dorado, in Venezuela, Chapada dos Guimaraes National Park, Rio Doce State Park and Nova Lombardia Biological Reserve, in Brazil, Tambopata Reserve, in Peru, and Noel Kempff Mercado National Park, in Bolivia. Nesting-site requirements likely to be critical. Hybrid populations may prove genetically important in its conservation, as forest habitat becomes more fragmented. Is hunted by humans for food, also for use in medicine; formerly hunted for its feathers, which were used in official robes of Brazilian emperors.

Bibliography. Anon. (1995a), Bates *et al.* (1989), Beebe *et al.* (1917), Berlepsch (1889), Berlepsch & Hartert (1902), Blake (1950, 1961, 1963), Bloch *et al.* (1991), Bond (1954), Bond & Meyer de Schauensee (1943), Bourne (1974), Camargo (1967), Chapman (1917, 1926), Cherrie (1916), Chubb (1916), Cory (1919), ffrench (1991), Friedmann (1948), Fry (1970b), Galetti *et al.* (1998), de Germiny (1937a, 1937b), Gibbons (1992), Griscom & Greenway (1941), Guix (1995), Guix & Jover (2001), Guix & Ruiz (1995), Gyldenstolpe (1945a, 1951), Haffer (1967a, 1969, 1974, 1975, 1978, 1985, 1991, 1997a, 1997b, 1997c), Haverschmidt & Mees (1994), Hellmayr (1910, 1929, 1933), Hilty & Brown (1986), Höfling & Camargo (1993), Ihering (1900), Jennings (1979, 1993c), Karr *et al.* (1990), Krabbe (1991), Lill (1970), María & Olivares (1967), Messias *et al.* (1990), Meyer de Schauensee (1949, 1964, 1966), Meyer de Schauensee & Phelps (1978), Moskovits *et al.* (1985), Novaes (1949, 1960, 1976), Novaes & Lima (1992a), Olivares (1962), Oniki & Willis (1983), Oren & Parker (1997), Parker & Goerck (1997), Perry *et al.* (1997), Phelps & Phelps (1958), Pinto (1932, 1935, 1938a, 1948), Reiser (1905), Remsen *et al.* (1993), Ridgely & Greenfield (2001), Robbins *et al.* (1987), Robertshaw (1987), Robinson (1997), Robinson & Terborgh (1997), do Rosário (1996), Scherer-Neto & Straube (1995), Schönwetter (1967), Sick (1985, 1993), Snyder (1966), Stager (1961a), Stotz, Fitzpatrick *et al.* (1996), Stotz, Lanyon *et al.* (1997), Terborgh *et al.* (1990), Thiollay (1992), Thiollay & Jullien (1998), Todd (1943b), Tostain *et al.* (1992), de Wald (1988), Wilkinson & McLeod (1991), Willard *et al.* (1991), Willis (1983), Willis & Oniki (1990), Zimmer, J.T. (1930), Zimmer, K.J. & Hilty (1997).

32. Toco Toucan

Ramphastos toco

French: Toucan toco **German**: Riesentukan **Spanish**: Tucán Toco
Other common names: Giant Toucan

Taxonomy. *Ramphastos Toco* P. L. S. Müller, 1776, Cayenne.
Distinctive, with no very close relatives. Belongs to the so-called "croaking group" of *Ramphastos* species, which also includes *R. dicolorus*, *R. sulfuratus*, *R. brevis* and *R. vitellinus*. Race *albogularis* poorly differentiated. Two subspecies tentatively recognized.

Subspecies and Distribution.
R. t. toco P. L. S. Müller, 1776 - the Guianas and NE Brazil, S coastally to Pará, up Amazon W to Manaus, including large lower tributaries; SE Peru.
R. t. albogularis Cabanis, 1862 - Bolivia and C Brazil (Mato Grosso and Piauí) S to Argentina (Tucumán, Santa Fe) and SE Brazil (SE Rio Grande do Sul).

Descriptive notes. 55-61 cm; 500-860 g. Marginally the largest toucan, mostly black, with white bib and uppertail-coverts, red undertail-coverts. Both sexes of nominate race with fine red band behind white of throat, throat washed yellow; high-keeled bill red-orange, redder along ridge of culmen, black basal band and large black "spot" on tip of maxilla; facial skin orange, orbital skin violet, iris brown. Female almost size of male, including bill. Immature sooty-black, red and yellow colours pale, whitish orbital skin, spiky hypotarsal "heels", bill more keeled with irregular

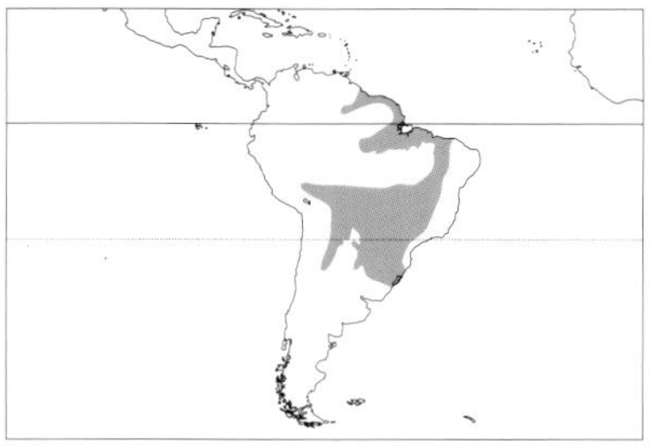

brownish markings, no tomial "teeth" or basal band; bill features develop slowly, can take nearly 1 year to acquire basal line, "teeth" and black spot. Race *albogularis* tends to have shorter bill, less yellow wash on throat, thinner red breastband, but much variation in both races. VOICE. Series of deep, grunting "groomkk" notes, singly or at c. 50 per minute; also grating call and soft notes, and loud rattling or clacking, sometimes of bill, but may use tongue inside closed bill; bangs bill against branch; much noise from wings, especially in interactions; young give "ehh-ehh-" calls.

Habitat. The only non-forest toucan. Inhabits mainly riverine and coastal edges of forest, patches of forest and palm groves in savannas, wooded islands, streamsides in Chaco and *cerrado*, scrub, plantations, orchards; occasionally suburban gardens, rarely in cities. Reaches upland Bolivian valleys, to 1750 m.

Food and Feeding. Fruits such as figs, those of *Cacos*, *Capsicum*, *Psidium*, *Steiculia*, oranges and others; regularly takes insects such as caterpillars, termites, and preys on nestling birds and eggs; captives prefer meat, regularly hunt down any small birds entering their cages. Usually forages in small groups, moving in single file, with heavy beats and glides, from site to site; perches conspicuously. Feeds in canopy, but descends to ground at times, hops c. 70 cm per bound. Agile; twists, pulls with bill and head, shaking head, can hang and turn about adeptly upside-down.

Breeding. Sept-Feb in most areas, Dec-Jun in Bolivia to W Argentina, May-Jun in NE Brazil (Piauí). Little known in wild. Mated birds tap bills frequently, allopreen, male at times spreading red undertail-coverts, cocking tail; aggression with loud rattling or bill-clapping, face-on to antagonist, approach, and attack. Some excavating of nest possibly essential; can nest in certain hollow palms, also in banks of streams and in terrestrial termite nests opened by Campo Flicker (*Colaptes campestris*); in captivity, hollow log readily used if outer hard area opened by humans. Eggs 2-4; incubation by both parents, period 17-18 days, captive male aggressive to mate at times; hatchling fed insects at first, with more and more fruits added, in captivity fed insects, mice, dog food; female may feed more than male as young develop; nest kept sanitary in early stages, later may become dirty; fledging at 43-52 days; young soon feed themselves in aviaries. Pairs can raise several broods per year in captivity. First breeding probably not until 2 or 3 years of age. Captives live to at least 15 years and 9 months.

Movements. Family groups and pairs range widely, cross large rivers and open areas; eruptions known, at least formerly, along Amazon during Jun.

Status and Conservation. Not globally threatened. CITES II. No data available on numbers; considered to be rare in Peru. Occupies large range and, since it does not require forested habitat, it may potentially spread into cleared forest areas. Occurs in various protected areas throughout its range. This species is hunted, however, and its young are taken as pets, so that it possibly needs to be monitored. Present in numerous protected areas, e.g. Serra da Canastra, Brasília and Das Emas National Parks (Brazil), Noel Kempff Mercado National Park (Bolivia), Reserva Natural del Bosque Mbaracayú, Estancia San Antonio and La Golondrina Private Nature Reserves (Paraguay), and El Rey, Calilegua and Iguazú National Parks (Argentina).

Bibliography. de Andrade (1992), Anon. (1995a), Belfort *et al.* (2000), Belton (1984, 1994), Bond & Meyer de Schauensee (1943), Brooks *et al.* (1993), Canevari *et al.* (1991), Chubb (1916), Contreras *et al.* (1990), Cory (1919), Dye & Morris (1984), Foster *et al.* (1994), Fry (1970b), Fukaya (1985), Graham *et al.* (1980), Griscom & Greenway (1941), Guix (1995), Haffer (1974), Haverschmidt & Mees (1994), Hayes (1995), Hoy (1968), Marini (2001), Meyer de Schauensee (1966), Mikich (1991), Narosky & Yzurieta (1993), Naumburg (1930), Novaes (1949), Parker & Bailey (1991), Paterson (1997), de la Peña (1994), Pinto (1948), Remsen *et al.* (1993), Rodrigues *et al.* (2000), do Rosário (1996), de Ruiter (1999), Rundel (1975), Scherer-Neto & Straube (1995), Schifter (1998), Schomburgk (1848), Schönwetter (1967), Schürer (1987), Schütter (2000), Seibels (1979), Short (1975), Sick (1985, 1993), da Silva *et al.* (1997), Snyder (1966), Stager (1961a), Stotz *et al.* (1996), Svoboda (1988), Sztolcman (1926), Tagaki & Sasaki (1980), Thiollay (1988), Todd (1943b), Tostain *et al.* (1992), Wetmore (1926), Willis & Oniki (1990).

33. White-throated Toucan

Ramphastos tucanus

French: Toucan à bec rouge **German**: Weißbrusttukan **Spanish**: Tucán Pechiblanco
Other common names: White-breasted Toucan; Cuvier's Toucan (*cuvieri*); Red-billed/Orange-billed Toucan (*tucanus*); Inca Toucan (*inca*)

Taxonomy. *Ramphastos Tucanus* Linnaeus, 1758, Surinam.
No very close relatives. Fairly close to *R. ambiguus*, but probably not forming a superspecies; together they constitute the so-called "yelping group" of toucans. Race *cuvieri* considered a separate species by some, but interbreeds with nominate over vast area; variably intermediate populations occur in large area in Brazil from R Solimões and Rondônia E to Pará, and from S Venezuela to Mato Grosso and Goiás. Race *inca* sometimes merged with *cuvieri*, with which intergrades, and *inca* appears to represent semi-stabilized hybrid population; in past, alternatively at times considered a distinct species. Forms named as "*aurantiirostris*", "*erythrorhynchus*" and "*haematorhynchus*" are merely red-billed or orange-billed variants of nominate race; other described forms are *monilis* from Guyana and *oblitus* from R Tapajós, Brazil, both now included within nominate. Three subspecies recognized.

Subspecies and Distribution.
R. t. cuvieri Wagler, 1827 - S & SW Venezuela, also SE Colombia and W Amazonian Brazil S to E Peru and N Bolivia.
R. t. tucanus Linnaeus, 1758 - E Venezuela, the Guianas, and NE Brazil E of R Negro and, S of Amazon, E of lower R Xingu in N Pará and N Maranhão.
R. t. inca Gould, 1846 - N & C Bolivia.

Descriptive notes. 53-58 cm; 515-700 g (*tucanus*), 560-830 g (*cuvieri*), 540-780 g (hybrid *tucanus* × *cuvieri*). Mainly black, large toucan with very long bill, white bib bordered by red band at rear, red undertail-coverts. Both sexes of nominate race with yellow-white uppertail-coverts; bill dark red to orangey with green-yellow culmen stripe, basal area yellow above, blue below, with narrow black basal band; red mouth-lining; facial area green-blue or blue; orbital darker, to violet; iris brown. Female shorter-billed. Immature with spiky "heel" scutes, plumage sooty rather than black, bib yellowish-white, undertail-coverts pink or orange, bill browner, culmen pattern obscure, no basal line or "teeth", facial-orbital skin grey-blue, iris blue; bill not fully adult until c. 1 year. Race *cuvieri* somewhat larger than nominate, uppertail-coverts more golden, tips sometimes orange or red, has dark area of bill blacker (but even some W birds often show red-brown near bill base); *inca* like *cuvieri*, but redder tips of uppertail-coverts, and regularly shows variably sized red-brown patch on base of dark bill, even on mandible; *inca* less variable in these traits than are highly

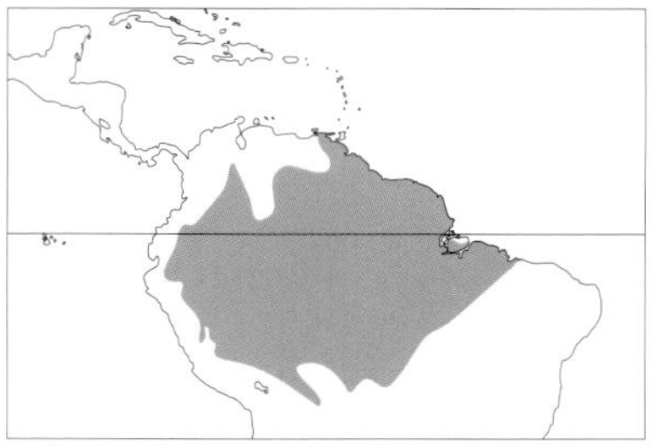

variable hybrids of *cuvieri* × *tucanus* to N & E of its range. VOICE. Song yelping "keeow-yelp-yelp-", or "Dios-te-de-", very different from repeated single croaks of *R. vitellinus*, in phrases of up to 7 "yelp" notes after longer first, notes often strung together, usually with pause between last "yelp" and the "keeow" of next phrase; female at higher pitch, using higher overtones than male, 1 female gave 67 notes to male's 83 in 1 minute; rattling, either vocal or by tongue with bill closed, often interjected among calls; rattles in series at times, loud in aggression, soft rattles between mated birds; also bill-tapping at nest, smacking of bill against branches, soft "tuk" and "took" notes, "te-te-tut-tut-" calls; from begging nestlings buzzy squeaks, later wails.

Habitat. Mainly lowland tropical forest, especially old riverbeds, late stages of successional forest and mature forest near water; forages also in earlier successional stages of streamside forest with *Cecropia* and *Ficus*; also secondary forest, forest edges and clearings, patches of forest where being cleared, dead trees in lakes, forest patches in savannas, pasture trees, plantations, gardens, mangroves, *cerrado* river forest, and occasionally city trees. Usually below 900 m, higher in parts of Andean slopes; to 1440 m in Guyana.

Food and Feeding. Diverse fruits, including those of *Astrocaryum*, *Cecropia*, *Coussapoa*, *Didymopanax*, *Ficus*, *Ocotea*, *Phytolacca*, *Protium*, *Psidium*, *Tapinia*, *Trattinickia*, *Syzygium*, *Virola*, and palms (*Euterpe*, *Oenocarpus*); also flowers and nectar of *Combretum* and *Quararibea*; also beetles, caterpillars, cicadas, termites, lizards, bird eggs and birds. Captives can prefer meat to fruits, eat various fruits, carrots, corn and peas, dogfood, myna pellets, mealworms, other insects, birds and mice; 1 survived well on bread, eggs, meat and a small bird daily. Forages in canopy, singly, in pairs, or in groups of up to 7, rarely 20. Bounds, twists, reaches, holds larger fruits in foot. Dominant over all birds at fruiting trees. Mobbed as nest predator; once took eggs of flycatcher (Tyrannidae) despite mobbing efforts of 12 flycatchers of 3 species; success rate of attacks on nests of flycatchers, doves (Columbidae) and Yellow-rumped Caciques (*Cacicus cela*) varies from 20% to 100%.

Breeding. Jan-Jul in the Guianas, Colombia, Ecuador and most of Venezuela; Feb-Sept/Oct in Bolivia and N Brazil; May-Aug in Peru and NE Venezuela; and Apr-Dec in SC Brazil. Pair leaves group, breeds in small part of group home range. Much play in groups, including bill-fencing, or "tag", supplanting one another; sings from conspicuous perch, raising bill high, gradually lowering to bow, then raising again, tail flicking up as bill raised; paired birds allopreen, especially face and orbit, may courtship-feed all year. Nest in natural cavity, at 3-20 m or more in tree such as *Caryocar*, *Eschweilera*, *Inga* or *Mora*, cavity cleared of debris some time before laying; nest entrance 6-15 cm × 12-17 cm, cavity to 1·2 m or more deep, lined with wood bits and fruit seeds; same nest used yearly if breeding successful. Eggs 2-3; incubation by both parents, either may perform most at night, diurnal shifts in one study 18-49 min, incubation period 15-16 days; hatchlings brooded often for 2 weeks, while naked, by both parents; both feed, perhaps female more than male, c. 2-7 times per hour; chick's eyes open as feathers break out, at c. 29 days; faecal material removed at intervals; young can reach entrance at c. 39 days, fledge at 48-49 days, after which family leaves nest for good; post-fledging behaviour little known. Eggs and young preyed on by white-throated capuchin monkey (*Cebus capucinus*). Probably does not breed until 2 years old or more.

Movements. Size of group's home range is large, but imprecisely known, and birds may move long distance at times, perhaps owing to failure of fruits, especially along Amazon and R Oyapuk in N Brazil; at Belém, as many as 1000 individuals recorded moving from S to N in Jun, with smaller numbers of *R. toco*.

Status and Conservation. Not globally threatened. CITES II. Common in many areas, e.g. in Peru; uncommon to locally common in Ecuador. Present in several protected areas, including Imataca Forest Reserve and El Dorado, Venezuela, and Tambopata Reserve, Peru. Because of its large size, its dependence on forest, and its importance in tree-seed dispersal, this species is a good "indicator" or "flagship" species. Availability of nesting cavities and forest clearance present conservation problems as habitats are fragmented. This toucan is also hunted by native peoples; when it holds back from attempting to cross large rivers in savanna, it is chased from one tree patch to another until unable to fly, and thus easily caught.

Bibliography. Allen (1995), Anon. (1995a), Bates *et al.* (1989), Beebe (1916), Beebe *et al.* (1917), Berlepsch (1889), Berlepsch & Hartert (1902), Blake (1961, 1963), Bloch *et al.* (1991), Bond (1954), Bond & Meyer de Schauensee (1943), Bourne (1974), Bühler (1993, 1995b), Chapman (1917, 1926), Cherrie (1916), Chubb (1916), Cory (1919), Foster *et al.* (1994), Friedmann (1948), Friedmann & Smith (1950), Greenway (1978), Griscom & Greenway (1937, 1941), Gyldenstolpe (1945a, 1951), Haffer (1974, 1978, 1987, 1991, 1993a, 1997a, 1997b, 1997c), Haverschmidt & Mees (1994), Hellmayr (1910, 1929), Hilty & Brown (1986), Jennings (1985a), Karr *et al.* (1990), Maria & Olivares (1967), Meyer de Schauensee (1964, 1966), Meyer de Schauensee & Phelps (1978), Moskovits *et al.* (1985), Naumburg (1930), Novaes (1949, 1960, 1976), Olivares (1962), Olivares & Romero (1973), Oren & Parker (1997), Parker & Bailey (1991), Phelps & Phelps (1958), Remsen *et al.* (1993), Ridgely & Greenfield (2001), Robinson (1985, 1997), Robinson & Terborgh (1997), Schlenker (2000), Schütter (2000), Schwartz (1977), Sick (1985, 1993), da Silva (1996), Skutch (1989), Snyder (1966), Stotz & Bierregaard (1989), Stotz, Fitzpatrick *et al.* (1996), Stotz, Lanyon *et al.* (1997), Terborgh *et al.* (1990), Thiollay (1992), Thiollay & Jullien (1998), Todd (1943b), Tostain *et al.* (1992), Willard *et al.* (1991), Willis (1976, 1983), Willis & Oniki (1990), Zimmer, J.T. (1930), Zimmer, K.J. & Hilty (1997), Zimmer, K.J. *et al.* (1997).

34. Yellow-throated Toucan

Ramphastos ambiguus

French: Toucan tocard **German**: Goldkehltukan **Spanish**: Tucán Pechigualdo
Other common names: Black-mandibled/Yellow-breasted Toucan; Chestnut-mandibled/Swainson's Toucan (*swainsonii*)

Taxonomy. *Ramphastos ambiguus* Swainson, 1823, no locality = Buenavista, Colombia.
No close relatives. Fairly close to *R. tucanus*, but probably not forming a superspecies; these two constitute the so-called "yelping group" of toucans. Long considered to include *R. brevis* as race, but they are now generally accepted as distinct species, with different vocalizations. Race *swainsonii* often treated as a distinct species, but resembles nominate in behaviour, voice and morphology, and they apparently interbred in former contact zone in Colombia (lower Cauca Valley); species treatment of *swainsonii* presumably based largely on its sympatry with *R. brevis*, when this form was thought to belong within present species. Other described forms include *innominatus* from Colombia, a synonym of nominate *ambiguus*, and *tocard* and *tocardus*, which are synonyms of *swainsonii*. Three subspecies recognized.

Subspecies and Distribution.

R. a. swainsonii Gould, 1833 - SE Honduras, Nicaragua and Costa Rica S to W Colombia (E to Cauca Valley, formerly middle Magdalena Valley) and S along W Andes to SW Ecuador (El Oro).
R. a. abbreviatus Cabanis, 1862 - NE Colombia, and NW & N Venezuela (E in mountains to Miranda).
R. a. ambiguus Swainson, 1823 - SW Colombia (from upper R Magdalena) S along E Andean slopes to SC Peru (Junín).

Descriptive notes. 53-56 cm; 599-746 g. Large, mainly black toucan with maroon tips of crown to upper back feathers, less so on wings and below; creamy uppertail-coverts, red undertail-coverts; yellow-gold bib ending in red breast. Both sexes of nominate race with large bill having black line around base, green-yellow on culmen broadening distally, blackish triangle on rest of maxilla and on mandible, but sometimes some chestnut near base; facial skin blue or pale green or yellow-green; iris normally grey-brown, green-brown or blue-brown, but vary to yellow or grey. Female has shorter, more block-shaped bill. Immature with sharp, pointed scutes of "heels", soft-plumaged, black sootier, less maroon tipping, yellow and red colours muted, tail feathers pointed, bill with more of keel, obscurely patterned, no "teeth" or basal band, nostrils open on top. Races vary mainly in colours of bill, facial skin and eyes, but considerable overlap: *swainsonii* with dark area of bill more red to brown, though often tending to black at edges and fore area, facial skin yellow-green or green-yellow, iris usually yellow-green to brown (variable, sometimes white, or partly pure green, or partly yellow); *abbreviatus* smaller, bill like nominate, facial skin like *swainsonii*. VOICE. Yelping phrases, repeated at length, first note longer and double, others shorter, often transcribed as "Dios, te-de, te-de", loud, double-noted character different from mainly single-noted *R. tucanus*; initial "kee-yow" usually followed by 2 shorter notes, in some phrases by 1, 3 or 4; male and female may sing together, countersing with others; also rattle sounds in aggression, a grunt, a croak; loud wing-flapping sounds.

Habitat. Forest in lowlands and lower mountain slopes, cloudforest, forest patches, edges, old secondary forest, forest clearings and swamps, riverine forest, nearby plantations, gardens with trees, golf courses. Locally to 1850 m in Middle America; *swainsonii* to 2286 m in Ecuador, other races 700-2670 m and usually above 1000 m, down to 400 m in Venezuela.

Food and Feeding. Mainly fruits, such as species of *Beilschmiedia*, *Caesearia*, *Cecropia*, *Didymopanax*, *Faramea*, *Hampea*, *Protium*, *Sorocea*, *Tetragastris*, *Trophis* and *Virola*, and palms of genus *Socratea*; flower parts of *Cecropia*; also fallen bananas in plantations; also takes various insects, including cicadas and stick-insects, hunts snakes, lizards, small birds and mammals, takes eggs and nestlings. Major disperser of some seeds, can take 45% of fruit crop at single tree. Favours canopy, but does come lower at times. Sometimes feeds in small groups, rarely gatherings of up to 20. Dominant over other frugivorous birds; 1 bird may defend whole fruiting tree against others, including mate. Audacious, sometimes hunts co-operatively; 1 took over chase of lizard from smaller *R. sulfuratus*, caught and ate lizard; another drove Double-toothed Kite (*Harpagus bidentatus*) from nest, took egg; 2 veered over squirrel monkeys (*Saimiri oerstedii*), each plucking baby from back of a monkey.

Breeding. Dec-Jul in all areas. Sings from conspicuous perch, all year, singer raises head high, gradually lowers head and bill with notes, in high-low bow, sometimes alternating rise from one side to other; male allopreens female about head, may courtship-feed her, regurgitating several fruits, female may pass food back and be fed again, or may allopreen mate. Nest in natural cavity at 5-15 m, entrance often small; occasionally nests close to *R. sulfuratus*, within 17 m. Probably 2-3 eggs; both parents incubate, feed young, defend nest from predators; no other details available. Longevity in captivity to at least 13 years and 5 months.

Movements. Moves up and down slopes in search of fruiting trees, possibly moves extensively into adjacent habitats at times.

Status and Conservation. Not globally threatened. Generally fairly common, locally common to very common. Uncommon in Peru. Uncommon to locally common in W Ecuador (*swainsonii*), where has declined markedly due to extensive deforestation, although sizeable population apparently persists in Esmeraldas, where much of forest remains largely intact; uncommon to rare and apparently very local in E Ecuador (*ambiguus*). Data on densities lacking, but in Panama 2 pairs nested in 16 ha. Does, however, require large forest tracts to sustain populations, and forest clearance and fragmentation have reduced it to point of near-extinction in some places. Occurs in Corcovado National Park and Braulio Carrillo National Park, in Costa Rica. Hunted in places, and is easily attracted by mimicked whistle of song; 57 taken by hunters of 1 village over two-week period. The fact that little is known of this species' breeding biology is a handicap to any conservation effort that might be needed.

Bibliography. Blake (2001), Blake & Loiselle (2000), Bloch *et al*. (1991), Boinski (1992), Bond (1954), Chapman (1917, 1926), Fjeldså & Krabbe (1990), Haffer (1967a, 1974, 1975, 1991, 1997a), Hellmayr (1911), Hilty (1997), Hilty & Brown (1986), Hornbuckle (1999), Howe (1977, 1981, 1983), Howell (1957, 1971), Jennings (1991, 1998), Krabbe (1991), Laughlin (1952), María & Olivares (1967), Meyer de Schauensee (1949, 1964, 1966), Meyer de Schauensee & Phelps (1978), Mindell & Black (1984), Monroe (1968), Phelps & Phelps (1958), Remsen *et al*. (1993), Ridgely & Greenfield (2001), Ridgely & Gwynne (1989), Ridgway (1914), Robbins *et al*. (1985), Salaman (1994), Schifter (1998), Schütter (2000), Skutch (1944a, 1972, 1980), Slud (1960, 1964), Stiles (1983), Stiles & Levey (1994), Stiles & Skutch (1989), Stiles *et al*. (1999), Stotz *et al*. (1996), Todd (1943b, 1947), Todd & Carriker (1922), Van Tyne (1929), Wetmore (1968a), Zimmer (1930).

Class AVES
Order PICIFORMES
Family INDICATORIDAE (HONEYGUIDES)

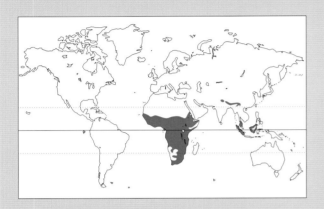

- Medium-small, rather nondescript arboreal birds with small head, short bill, nostrils often raised, and generally rather drab plumage with white outer-tail markings.
- 10-20 cm.

- Sub-Saharan Africa and southern Asia.
- Forest and woodland, including streamside trees in near-desert; from lowlands to near tree-line in mountains.
- 4 genera, 17 species, 33 taxa.
- No species threatened; none extinct since 1600.

Systematics

Despite their superficially passerine-like appearance, the 17 mainly green or olive honeyguides of the family Indicatoridae are members of the order Piciformes, allied with the other, more typical-looking piciform birds, the barbets (Capitonidae), the toucans (Ramphastidae) and the woodpeckers (Picidae). Their relationships with other groups within the Piciformes are, however, unclear. Various anatomical aspects (see Morphological Aspects) have led some authors to place the honeyguides near the barbets, whereas others have suggested that they are more closely related to the woodpeckers. P. J. K. Burton, for instance, found their structural bases for feeding to be similar to those of barbets. Through DNA-DNA hybridization studies, however, C. G. Sibley and J. E. Ahlquist concluded that the honeyguides are closer to the woodpeckers than they are to other piciforms. Nevertheless, their displays, including aerial displays, along with other aspects of their behaviour, and their vocalizations seem more like those of barbets than those of woodpeckers.

Perhaps the major point is that the Indicatoridae are distinctive, and not particularly close to one or another of the piciform families. Many of the species are poorly known, inconspicuous birds of tropical forest. The Dwarf Honeyguide (*Indicator pumilio*) was described in 1958, and the Yellow-footed Honeyguide (*Melignomon eisentrauti*) as recently as 1981, and the biology of both remains largely unknown. The mysterious Lyre-tailed Honeyguide (*Melichneutes robustus*), famed for sounds produced in its aerial display, indeed is known from some countries and large regions of Central Africa only thanks to those very sounds. Most of what is known about honeyguides comes from investigations of five or six species, and even for those the information is incomplete. There are few fossils of honeyguides, dating back only to the Pliocene of South Africa.

The Indicatoridae can be divided into two subfamilies, perhaps better thought of as tribes. These are the thin-billed Prodotiscinae, with three species of *Prodotiscus* and two species of *Melignomon*, and the heavier-billed, typical honeyguides of the subfamily Indicatorinae, comprised of the Lyre-tailed Honeyguide in *Melichneutes* and the closely related genus *Indicator* with its eleven species. So far as is known, all are nest parasites, using as hosts other Piciformes, other cavity-nesters, and several avian species that build deep or covered nests. All but one of those honeyguides for which the eggs are described lay white eggs. The exception is the Eastern Green-backed

Honeyguide (*Prodotiscus zambesiae*), which lays either white or blue eggs, the latter matching those of one host group, the white-eyes (*Zosterops*). Both that species and the Western Green-backed Honeyguide (*Prodotiscus insignis*) also have a fully white outer tail; all other honeyguides have a variable amount of dark tipping of the outer tail feathers, less prominently so in juveniles, which show more white in the tail than do adults. The Prodotiscinae have a gizzard with thicker walls than that of the Indicatorinae, and the skeletal sternum is more deeply notched. The small species of *Prodotiscus* have more rounded nostrils, softer feathers, thinner skin, and a deeper keel of the sternum than do other honeyguides, as well as only ten tail feathers, and a white patch on the border of the flanks and rump, these feathers being erectile. *Melignomon* tends towards the Indicatorinae in its thicker skin, its rougher feathering, and the fact that it possesses twelve rectrices, long slit nostrils, and a less deep sternal keel; the two species may take some honey-

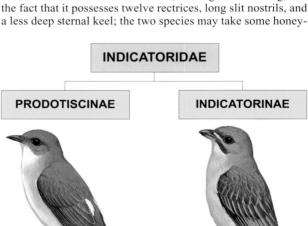

Subdivision of the Indicatoridae

[Figure: Hilary Burn]

```
INDICATORIDAE
├── PRODOTISCINAE
│   thin-billed honeyguides
│   5 species
│   (Prodotiscus, Melignomon)
│
└── INDICATORINAE
    typical honeyguides
    12 species
    (Indicator, Melichneutes)

FAMILY    SUBFAMILY
```

Taxonomic uncertainties are numerous in the family Indicatoridae. The Thick-billed Honeyguide overlaps marginally with the Lesser Honeyguide (Indicator minor), *probably interbreeding in parts of Nigeria. However, the two are ecologically separated in western Uganda, with the Thick-billed strictly confined to forest, while the Lesser inhabits more open, wooded country. They are considered to form a superspecies. The Thick-billed differs only slightly from the Lesser in being darker grey below and deeper olive-green above, with a slightly larger bill. Their voices appear to be virtually identical.*

[*Indicator conirostris.*
Photo: Eric Hosking/FLPA]

bee (*Apis*) wax, as well as deriving wax from insect coverings (see Food and Feeding).

It is likely that the Indicatorinae depend upon beeswax in their diet, at least during part of the year. The nostrils are raised with membranous sides on a stouter, broader bill, and the gizzard is thin-walled. Three species of *Indicator* are sexually dimorphic in plumage, and two others of the eleven species are sexually dimorphic in the colour of the gape. These include some of the best-known members of the family, such as the Greater Honeyguide (*Indicator indicator*), which leads humans to bees' nests (see General Habits). Males of these species sing in trills, series of double notes, or series of melodic phrases. Hosts of *Indicator* honeyguides are mainly piciform birds such as barbets and woodpeckers, but the Greater Honeyguide utilizes 40 or more hosts of a diverse range of species. The genus *Melichneutes*, closely related to *Indicator*, contains only the Lyre-tailed Honeyguide, notable for its highly modified tail: the central two tail feathers curve outwards, the long central undertail-coverts project between these lyre-shaped feathers, and the four outer pairs of rectrices are short and spiky, all these features being apparently related to the species' circling, diving flight display. Lyre-tailed Honeyguides are flat-bodied, with a deeper sternum and a barely thicker gizzard than the other honeyguides.

Most honeyguides are Afrotropical, but two species of *Indicator*, the Yellow-rumped Honeyguide (*Indicator xanthonotus*) and the Sunda Honeyguide (*Indicator archipelagicus*), occur in tropical Asia, the former along the southern Himalayas, and the latter in the Malay Peninsula, Sumatra and Borneo. It is reasonable to assume that their ancestor reached Asia from Africa, and that the two species then diverged from one another. They do not meet, and, reflecting the absence of other honeyguides in their ranges, the white in the outer tail is muted. Both show a feature otherwise shared only with the African Greater Honeyguide, namely the presence of bright yellow in the plumage: the rump patch in the case of the Yellow-rumped Honeyguide, and the "shoulder" of the male Sunda Honeyguide.

Assuming that the thick, tough skin, the upraised nostrils, and the guiding behaviour are derived features, it follows that the ancestral honeyguide was a small, barbet-like bird similar to species of *Prodotiscus*, but perhaps with a heavier bill, for excavating nesting cavities. Alternatively, the nest parasitism may have evolved very early in the family, with no recent ancestor a nest-excavator. In relation to the honeyguides' wax "predation" and the co-evolution of honeybees and honeyguides, it is significant that beeswax utilization by African honeyguides involves only one bee species of the genus *Apis*, namely *A. mellifera*; and, according to L. Garnery and colleagues, that species' ancestor probably entered Africa from the Middle East not much more than one million years ago. The thick skin and the nostril modifications of most honeyguides are not required for any purpose other than protection against the honeybee. The implication is that *Melignomon*, *Indicator* and *Melichneutes* evolved relatively recently. Wax can be obtained from colonies of sweatbees (*Trigona*), which are incapable of stinging, but such nests are less accessible to honeyguides than are those of the frequently absconding honeybee; *Trigona* nests are often in the ground, their entrances are small, and the wax may be deep inside. Thus, there are intriguing questions and puzzles regarding the evolution of the honeyguides.

Morphological Aspects

The Indicatoridae are difficult to characterize in terms of their morphology. Their characteristics become apparent only upon close observation, as the birds investigate honeybee nests, or flash the dark-tipped white outer tail in chases of or pursuits by their hosts, with which they interact frequently (see General Habits, Breeding). All honeyguides seek wax as a major food, either from the waxy covering of insects such as scale insects (Coccidae), or from the wax structures of honeybees' nests. Species favouring beeswax have a thickened skin, presumably as some protection from bee stings, although attacks by honeybee swarms are at times fatal to the honeyguides. Enzymes capable of digesting the wax seem well to be developed in the Indicatoridae, and A. R. Place and others have found similar protein substances in seabirds and various landbirds; such enzymes have so far not been found in other piciform birds.

As with many of the barbets, at least some of the species of *Indicator* have a finely fringed or brushy tongue that may be bifid, and rictal and chin bristles are present, even if short. The stronger-billed honeyguides have a notch along the sides of the bill tomia, a trait exhibited among allies only by the barbets. Hypotarsal scuted "heels" are well developed in the naked, blind young honeyguides, as are the membranous bill hooks with which they kill any of the host's young, or destroy its eggs. There are other internal morphological attributes involving the oil-gland, muscle ligaments and the skeleton. Honeyguides have a smaller head in relation to the body when compared with the large-headed barbets, toucans and woodpeckers, which also have a larger, more specialized bill.

Rather long, narrow wings give power to the thrust of the honeyguide's body in flight, and permit an array of flight displays. These nest parasites rather readily evade their hosts, and are able to outfly them in most instances. The female honeyguide may soon tire the hosts, enabling her to gain access to their nest to lay an egg. The wings have nine functional primaries and a small tenth primary, which is vestigial or absent in species of *Prodotiscus*. All genera except *Prodotiscus* have six pairs of rectrices, as do the woodpeckers; *Prodotiscus* has five pairs, as do the barbets and toucans. The outermost tail feather is mildly to considerably reduced in the larger honeyguides.

The thick skin of most honeyguides is likely to have evolved in response to bee stings. In addition, however, it preadapts the birds, affording them added protection, in confrontations with hosts, as well as in conflicts with other honeyguides at wax sources. Despite the protection provided by this thick skin, honeyguides are not immune to bee stings. An excessively bold action around a bees' nest can precipitate an attack by the venomous insects; bodies of honeyguides have been found with up to 300 or more stings, particularly about the eyes, around the base of the bill, on the legs, and indeed all over the body.

The bill is rather generalized, and is suitable for fly-catching forays, for probing in the bark of trees, and for pulling away pieces of beeswax. The rictal and chin bristles may prevent debris from insect parts and sticky wax from contaminating the feathers of the head. The legs of honeyguides differ in length from species to species, and are used by the birds in somewhat different ways while feeding on beeswax. The Scaly-throated Honeyguide (*Indicator variegatus*) crouches over wax that is of large bulk, perching and pulling; it often holds a larger piece of wax between its legs, toes clamped about the front end, with the body touching the wax. Greater Honeyguides have longer, less feathered legs; they peck from side to side in a generally upright posture, not crouching. Lesser Honeyguides (*Indicator minor*) sometimes crouch, but they do not generally clasp the wax. The more or less notched bill of adults of these species may help in freeing wax, as well as in aggressive "biting". The Greater and Scaly-throated Honeyguides, when under pressure from numbers of others at a wax source, often pick off a piece of the material and fly with it to a secluded spot; they are often chased by others, but can lift and fly with pieces as heavy as 14 g. Lesser Honeyguides and Pallid Honeyguides (*Indicator meliphilus*) rarely fly with large pieces of wax, but they do at times carry away a tiny fragment.

K. E. Stager demonstrated that the olfactory lobe of the brain is well developed in the Indicatoridae. Although olfaction may play some role in the locating of beeswax or bees' nests, it is not thought to be of great importance. Field experience indicates that bee colonies are generally known to the honeyguides of the area in question. These birds' eyesight is keen, as is their hearing; indeed, they may be able to track individual honeybees to a nest. Moreover, most honeybees' nests are located in situations previously occupied by honeybees, and hence they are regularly checked by the honeyguides, which also monitor humans and their activities. It is possible, however, that olfaction assists the birds in locating bees' nests in heavily forested areas.

The distinctive outer-tail markings of honeyguides are rather uniform among the Afrotropical species. Observations suggest that this pattern, or "flag", is a useful cue for immature honeyguides, allowing them to "tag along" after an adult, of either their own or another species, to sources of wax. Further, in all species except those of the genus *Prodotiscus*, the tail of immatures is much whiter, less dark-tipped, than that of adults. This rather constant difference in the tail pattern between adults and immatures seems to be part of the signalling system that allows immatures dominance at food sources (see General Habits).

The bare area around the eye is smaller than the corresponding naked orbital area shown by the barbets and the toucans.

The most characteristic plumage feature of most honeyguides, particularly immatures, is the strikingly white outer tail. The signal effect, further enhanced on this young, probably male, Greater Honeyguide by the white rump patch, apparently stimulates juveniles to follow others to wax sources, and human honey-hunters to stay with their "guide" (generally a female or immature). The tail pattern is also thought to play a part in the signalling system that allows immatures dominance at food sources, but it may also elicit attacks by the foster-parents on a fledgling honeyguide when the young bird's departure from the hosts' nest first reveals the pattern.

[*Indicator indicator*, Sicolo, north Kenya. Photo: John Downer/ Planet Earth]

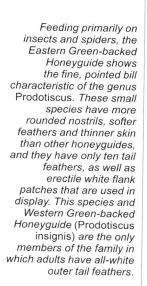

Feeding primarily on insects and spiders, the Eastern Green-backed Honeyguide shows the fine, pointed bill characteristic of the genus Prodotiscus. *These small species have more rounded nostrils, softer feathers and thinner skin than other honeyguides, and they have only ten tail feathers, as well as erectile white flank patches that are used in display. This species and Western Green-backed Honeyguide (*Prodotiscus insignis*) are the only members of the family in which adults have all-white outer tail feathers.*

[Prodotiscus zambesiae ellenbecki, Karen, Kenya. Photo: Dave Richards]

The orbital skin is thick and heavy, and not likely to be of much signal importance, except that immatures have a brighter, lighter orbital area than do adults. In immature Greater Honeyguides the orbital skin is blue, this colour extending on to the crown beneath the feathers; it is yellow in young Scaly-throated Honeyguides, and pale grey in young Lesser Honeyguides. Adults of the last species appear bigger-eyed than immatures, because the orbital area is black and is seen as part of the eye by an observer; the immature shows a small-looking dark eye, the surrounding skin being pale grey and contrasting with the eye colour.

In immatures of the Scaly-throated Honeyguide, as well as those of the Spotted Honeyguide (*Indicator maculatus*), the gape, which is used in aggression, with bill held wide open, is fully pink. In adult males it is shiny black, whereas females have a pink gape that gradually gathers grey shadow marks with age. With the striking gape colour, along with plumage markings of the crown and throat, and the colour of the orbital skin, the young of these species are dominant at food sources. The immature Greater Honeyguide has a unique yellow-gold, cream and olive-brown plumage quite different from that of adults, and indeed unlike that of any other honeyguide. These immatures instantly become "superdominant" when arriving at a bees' nest, where an individual may feed for 20-30 minutes (see General Habits). When two or more immatures appear together at a food source, the older, less juvenile bird gives way to the other or others.

Apart from those species with a wholly distinct immature plumage, such as the Greater Honeyguide, there are others with markings that are more or less indicative of immaturity, such as the Scaly-throated and Spotted Honeyguides with their barred juveniles. Otherwise, the immature plumage can be distinguished in general terms by the whiter outer tail feathers, the colour of the orbital skin, and several other features, including the more pointed tail feathers; the overall colour is often darker and greener than that of adults, and the facial and other markings are muted. For example, the loral area of the Lesser Honeyguide is white in adults, but grey in immatures, and the malar stripe is less marked in young Least (*Indicator exilis*), Dwarf, Lesser and Thick-billed Honeyguides (*Indicator conirostris*) than it is in adults of those species. Recently fledged

young honeyguides have creased, wrinkled belly skin, and the hypotarsal "heel" with spiky projections may still be evident. Remnants of the gape "wattle" at the corner juncture of the upper and lower mandibles are visible on juveniles for a period of several months after they leave the nest.

Habitat

Honeyguides are predominantly forest and woodland species of the tropics of Africa and Asia. Always bound by their need for suitable hosts, they range into montane woodland, and to the fringes of temperate woods in parts of South Africa, on high African mountains, and along the Himalayas, where Yellow-rumped Honeyguides occasionally reach the timber-line. The Greater and Lesser Honeyguides, the most broadly distributed members of the family, extend into dry woodland, and into wooded Sahelian grassland, while Scaly-throated Honeyguides occupy dense streamside thickets in near-desert areas of southern Somalia. Although Lesser Honeyguides, in particular, have invaded dry regions as their host barbets, mainly the Acacia Pied Barbet (*Tricholaema leucomelas*), have extended their ranges, barbets nevertheless occur in some arid bushland parts of Namibia, Somalia and the northern Sahel beyond the range of any honeyguide.

The planting of trees by humans is an important aspect of the dynamics of honeyguide populations. Fruiting trees are especially attractive to barbets, which are major hosts of honeyguides. In the Sahel, such trees may favour honeyguide hosts and, in consequence, the honeyguides themselves, perhaps offering a significant argument against the elimination of trees in man's never-ending quest for fuelwood. Forest clearance has benefited honeyguides of more open country, especially in West Africa, where forest species are experiencing drastic loss of habitat. In the case of the rather strictly forest-dwelling Thick-billed Honeyguide and its very close relative, the adaptable Lesser Honeyguide of open wooded habitats and edges, the latter is expanding its range throughout formerly forested, recently cleared areas, leading to its replacement of the Thick-billed.

Beeswax can be regarded as a primary source of food for most honeyguides. Afrotropical western honeybees, the source of the "Africanized", so-called "killer" bees in the Americas, abscond from nests frequently, and more often use holes with larger entrances than do European races of the species; they also migrate under certain conditions. Wax may thus become accessible directly to the honeyguides if the entrances to nests are sufficiently large. In dry regions of Africa, the honeybees sometimes migrate when conditions are severely dry; where bees' nests are in rocks or otherwise in the ground they may be inaccessible, and once bees are gone from such an area, and honey is therefore unavailable, human honey-hunting activities may cease, rendering the habitat marginal even for Greater and Lesser Honeyguides. As a result, very dry zones occupied by some xeric-adapted barbets, such as the Black-throated (*Tricholaema melanocephala*), Acacia Pied and Yellow-breasted Barbets (*Trachyphonus margaritatus*), can, at least seasonally, be devoid of honeyguides. The importance of this critical wax resource is such that its absence, or its inaccessibility, can render the habitat unsuitable for honeyguides. Under less severely arid conditions, that is, for most honeyguides in most places, insects are usually available as food, and the honeybees' activities do not force large-scale movements of the honeyguides, but they may influence the local concentrations of honeyguides and their foraging habits.

So far as is known, bearing in mind that information on fully half the species of Indicatoridae is very scant, the honeyguides exhibit their ancestral tree-cavity dependence by using hosts that are cavity-nesters. These nests can be in the ground, or in termite mounds, or carton-ant nests, if not in a tree. Since honeybees principally use tree cavities for their nests, this enforces a cavity relationship of honeyguides: most honeyguides seek beeswax, and insect prey as well, in cavities. Females, employing cavity-nesting birds as hosts, must search for and gain entrance to these cavities to lay their eggs. In a real sense, then, and unlike most barbets and woodpeckers but like almost all toucans, the honeyguides are secondary users of nest-cavities. They gain the advantage of primary cavity-nesters, including a clean nesting substrate and fewer parasites, by utilizing primary cavity-

nesters as hosts. The presence of trees suitable for nest-excavation, usually partly rotten, decayed trees or stubs, is therefore essential for the honeyguides, as well as for their hosts.

General Habits

Tough and aggressive, if inconspicuous birds, the honeyguides do not take kindly to aggression by other birds of less than large size. This perhaps reflects their thick, tough skin, but only to a degree, as all their piciform relatives are, after all, also aggressive. Faster than their hosts, which naturally react aggressively to the parasites' close approach to their nests, they are often chased by host birds; before the chase ceases, however, the honeyguides are seen to be chasing the host. At least the Lesser Honeyguide, during interactions with barbet hosts engaging in duets and group pre-duet choruses, such as the Black-collared Barbet (*Lybius torquatus*), seems to utilize its speed in following and, indeed, coming to a perch with the calling group; this causes a breakdown in the normal chorus-duetting, and possibly disrupts breeding, even resulting in renesting and thus allowing another chance for parasitism by the honeyguides.

Their aggression is vital in the gatherings of honeyguides that congregate about any beeswax source. Over 50 honeyguides of four species have been attracted to beeswax feeders in one day, with as many as 37 of them netted in that period. At a source of wax, there are more or less strongly fixed dominance hierarchies within any species. Usually immatures are dominant, followed by females, and then adult males. Of course, the relative hunger of various individuals results in some reversals. More complex are the interspecific hierarchies. In observations in Kenya, Scaly-throated Honeyguides have usually been found to be dominant over the two or three accompanying species, namely the Greater and Lesser Honeyguides and, at times, the Pallid Honeyguide. The very distinctly plumaged immature Greater Honeyguide, however, is superdominant, readily driving off all other honeyguides. Although much smaller, immature Lesser

This forest-dwelling Least Honeyguide shows the zygodactyl feet typical of honeyguides, with two toes directed forwards and two backwards. Other typical features of the family include powerful, sharp claws and rough plumage, essentially olive-green above, greyish below, with bare skin surrounding the eye, and rictal and chin bristles. Apart from visiting bees' nests, foraging Least Honeyguides have been observed moving about in the canopy, gleaning insects from leaves, making flycatching sallies, inspecting various cavities and probing in moss and lichen on branches.

[*Indicator exilis exilis*, Mann's Spring (2100 m), Mt Cameroon, Cameroon. Photo: Doug Wechsler/ VIREO]

Honeyguides are able on occasion to chase Scaly-throated and some adult Greater Honeyguides from the beeswax. As is often the case in the avian world, very aggressive, dominant honeyguides may become so occupied in attacking and chasing one another that lower-ranking species and individuals in the hierarchy may obtain the opportunity to eat some wax. Another tactic adopted by the Greater and Scaly-throated Honeyguides is to make off with a piece of wax, and to find a quiet nook where they can eat undisturbed. More often than not, however, the honeyguide carrying wax is chased in flight, and, being awkward and ungainly, is forced to drop the material, which may then become the focus of a squabble.

Although the habit of leading humans and other mammals to bees' nests is responsible for the name "honeyguide", it is believed that only the Greater Honeyguide actually "guides", and apparently guides only humans, to nests. In more than 15 years of close work with hundreds of Scaly-throated and Lesser Honeyguides, no instance has ever been found involving behaviour by those two species that could be associated with guiding. That is not to say that they, and others, including various forest honeyguides, do not attend humans; they do. Any humans making noise, as when cutting wood or building fires, act as attractants to honeyguides. The birds follow people engaged in such tasks, often approaching them closely, and even fly to tents and vehicles, which they may inspect. Their attention is often overlooked by the humans. Scaly-throated and Greater Honeyguides have a "search-flight", an unduly slow, very undulating, up-and-down, somewhat circular flight over people and their disturbances. Those species, and others, follow one another as well; when wax is found, an avian "bush telegraph" seems to draw in numbers of honeyguides. It is extremely probable that at least adult honeyguides in a given area know the location of many bee colonies. Why should they not? The bees frequently abscond, and nests are used over and over again by bee swarms for so long as the cavities remain usable.

The guiding Greater Honeyguides, the bulk of which are immatures and females, perch, not necessarily conspicuously, in the vicinity of a human being, and call repeatedly (see Voice). If no attention is paid to the bird, it may call off and on, cease after several calls, or continue for up to an hour; one individual called at intervals to the observers, as they moved about a small area, paying no heed to it, for a period of some three hours. If one follows the honeyguide for a short distance and then stops, the bird may call very frequently, move to several different perches, and may then change its direction (see also Relationship with Man). By knowing the location of bees' nests in an area, a person can readily guess to which occupied nest he or she is being guided. In one instance, a female led the observers to four separate nests in less than one hour. No special displays are associated with guiding; the repetitive, insistent calling and the frequent moves, rendered conspicuous by the spread tail and bounding, upward flight to a perch, are seen also in other contexts. Experience shows that, in the vicinity of the bees' nest, the Greater Honeyguide is silent and looks on at the humans. Honey-hunters would then build a smoky fire, and climb to the nest; traditionally, they leave a large chunk of honeycomb for the guider, but it is the opening of the nest and the moving away of the honeybees that reward the individual guider and other attentive honeyguides attracted by the activities.

Guiding is not a predictable activity. In months of working with and among honeyguides, handling Greater Honeyguides almost daily, one of the two researchers would be guided on one day, perhaps several times; several days or a week would then pass with no guiding. A more common feature was incipient guiding, whereby more or less guiding calls were uttered, but not persistently, and for only a short time before ceasing. Indeed, some immature, would-be guiders appeared not to know the mode, as they would not lead an observer away, but only called, apparently at the two people, and then disappeared. This long-term study found that encounters with "investigating" Scaly-throated Honeyguides were more frequent than were incidents of guiding by Greater Honeyguides. The Scaly-throated Honeyguides flew, usually inconspicuously, over the observers, perched nearby, watched, came to the fire, and perched on the vehicle or went inside it; the birds

Typically calling from a prominent perch, the male Greater Honeyguide is easily identified by its dark crown and throat, pale cheek patches and powerful pink bill. The main component of this species's song, often given from a traditional perch, is repeated "wit-burr", "vik-tor" or "burr-wit" sounds. This, the best-known honeyguide, is the only species that regularly guides humans to honey sources: the bird (an adult of either sex or a juvenile) draws attention by its persistent chattering calls, bobbing, tail-flirting and frequent fluttering flights between perches and towards the honey source, which it will most likely have found by using visual cues. Boran honey-hunters of Kenya traditionally use a special penetrating whistle and other sounds to keep their "guide" interested.

[Indicator indicator, Kruger National Park, Natal, South Africa. Photo: Nigel Dennis/ NHPA]

Most honeyguide species
appear to be attracted by
human activities such as
chopping wood and
making fires, and numbers
of honeyguides of various
species will gather where
humans have driven the
bees away by smoking out
the nest. The rough
plumage and thick skin of
some honeyguides may
give some defence against
bee stings, but birds can
be killed in a major assault
by a swarm. This adult
Lesser Honeyguide, with
the pale lore and dark
malar stripe found in
several species, also has
the powerful, stubby bill
typical of the genus
Indicator; this is
apparently well suited to
scraping off bits of left-
over comb.

[Indicator minor teitensis,
Athi River, Kenya.
Photo: Michael Gore]

were regularly netted by stringing a net beside the fire, the fire being a device for keeping away large mammals, as well as for boiling water for morning beverages. The disappearance of the guiding phenomenon of Greater Honeyguides in suburbs of metropolitan centres such as Nairobi, in Kenya, suggests that guiding is not a genetically deeply embedded, very highly evolved aspect of behaviour, but that it is, rather, a relatively recent "add-on" to the wax-seeking and wax-acquiring habits of this species.

Wax-eating requires water, and readily available water is a feature at most of the study sites at which there is a great deal of honeyguide activity. Those individuals seen regularly for much of a morning, and feeding frequently, appear to drink every hour or so. Most, however, show no interest in bathing, even when observing the bathing activities of other avian species.

While non-social generally, honeyguides usually come into frequent contact with others of their own species or with other species of Indicatoridae. Any beeswax source attracts small to large numbers of honeyguides, and aggressive interactions are commonplace. Away from these sites, and otherwise except when breeding, honeyguides are solitary birds. Immatures will at times approach adults without aggression, and will even perch above an active feeding site without entering into interactions. Fledglings may beg from adult conspecifics, as well as from their foster-parents or any bird resembling the fosterers. Comfort activities, especially preening of the wings and tail, are important, and are performed in the same way as in other piciforms.

Of the comparatively few displays described for the Indicatoridae, that of the Lyre-tailed Honeyguide is by far the most interesting. This species, rather than singing from a perch, employs a fantastic aerial display. After giving several introductory "pee" notes, it goes into a steep, fast dive with the modified tail feathers spread. It is presumably the air passing through these feathers that produces the "kwa-ba, kwa-ba" series of sounds that are so characteristic of the forest areas inhabited by the Lyre-tailed Honeyguide. Lest this be considered overly distinctive within the family, far less spectacular aerial displays, with sound

at considerably lower volume, are known for the Greater, Lesser, Scaly-throated and Pallid Honeyguides; and the three *Prodotiscus* species also have aerial displays during which they call, in at least two cases over their territories. The male Greater Honeyguide, either on or off the singing territory, sometimes performs a "winnowing" display-flight in which it flutters in one or more circles over a female, making wing sounds; occasionally, it mistakes an older immature of either sex for a female.

Little is known of the roosting behaviour of honeyguides. Radio-telemetry studies of male Scaly-throated Honeyguides have shown that the birds do not roost in cavities, but instead use dense trees and bushes. Territorial males may roost in one of their song trees, a dangerous ploy, perhaps, for at least one such male was killed, probably by a Verreaux's Eagle-owl (*Bubo lacteus*), in his main song tree. Most males roost within their territory or close by, although not always at the same site every night. One singer regularly roosted 5 km downstream from its singing territory. Subordinate males around a territory are more mobile. They may roost near a particular territory on one night, several kilometres away from it on the next night, and in yet another direction on the following night. At one major wax-feeding site which was not within or even near any territory, feeding birds left the area one hour or, less often, as little as half an hour before dark, presumably to reach a favourite roosting site.

Forest honeyguides fly directly or in undulating flight, and usually not very far, although they may move about rather constantly throughout the day. They do not cross large open areas. Even woodland and thicket species, such as the Scaly-throated Honeyguide, prefer to stay within or near cover, using streamside vegetation through which to move from one site to another. On the other hand, Greater, Lesser and Eastern Green-backed Honeyguides do at times fly over open areas even as wide as a kilometre or more, often undulating their flight in the manner of some barbets and woodpeckers; through even wider areas of grassland, they may perch briefly in a shrub, herb or bush, before continuing across the opening.

Beeswax constitutes an important part of the diet of the rather secretive Scaly-throated Honeyguide, although it also takes many insects by flycatching. It is capable of carrying quite large pieces of comb, and often pecks and tears at a piece wedged beneath its body and grasped with its feet. The strong bill and raised nostrils are clearly visible here. Scaly-throated Honeyguides observed feeding on wax proved to be dominant over other honeyguide species, even the larger ones.

[Indicator variegatus, Langata, Kenya. Photo: Peter Davey/ Bruce Coleman]

Voice

Songs are known for all but one of the well-studied honeyguides, the exception being the Yellow-rumped, which appears to lack a song. The songs are often musical, unlike any woodpecker vocalizations, and are delivered in barbet-like postures that include arching of the neck, bill pointing downwards, rump feathers loosely fluffed, and tail twitching slightly with the notes. In the Scaly-throated and Spotted Honeyguides, a simple, fast trill for several seconds constitutes the song. The Lesser, Thick-billed and Least Honeyguides emit a "wew" introductory note, followed by a trill that is slower than in the previous two species, while the Sunda Honeyguide sings a fast trilled song preceded by a cat-like, rising "miaaw" note. The Greater Honeyguide begins its song with a bow and a soft "peew", followed by a varied number of double notes transcribed as "Victor" or, rather, "TOR-VIK", or "Burr-wit"; this is the only honeyguide species in which the female is known occasionally to utter, aggressively, the same song as that of the male.

Among the smaller species of *Indicator*, Willcocks's (*Indicator willcocksi*) and Pallid Honeyguides sing similar songs of repetitive, triple-noted phrases, the former sounding like "wa-will-it", and the Pallid "wa-wee-it". Apart from the Brown-backed Honeyguide (*Prodotiscus regulus*), which sings a soft trill, the rest of the small honeyguides are poorly known. The songs of the Western Green-backed, Yellow-footed and Dwarf Honeyguides are unknown. The Eastern Green-backed sings, but its song has not been described, while recent recordings of Zenker's Honeyguide (*Melignomon zenkeri*) reveal its song to be a long series of slow "psee" to "pseep" notes.

There remains the Lyre-tailed Honeyguide, which, instead of a song delivered from a perch, uses an aerial display with introductory "pee" notes followed by "kwa-ba, kwa-ba" sounds (see General Habits). The latter are presumably produced by the tail feathers, and are characteristic sounds of the forest areas where this poorly known honeyguide lives.

Honeyguides have a broad repertoire of vocalizations other than song. Some have an aggressive, song-like trill or squeaks, or piping notes. The Scaly-throated Honeyguide, as an example of a reasonably well-studied indicatorid, has a variety of such sounds: a piping, whistled "wee" series uttered aggressively by males; a song-like trill but with "pyew" sounds in it, also given by males; loud chattery calls given repeatedly by females in aggression; buzzy skizz notes; a post-copulatory wavering whistled series or a floppy aerial display with "wup, wup" sounds; and three distinct calls of the young, namely chatters, yelps and wails. Loud rustling wing sounds accompany aggressive calling and chasing by this species. It is likely that the other honeyguides have a more or less equivalent repertoire of calls, and the Lesser, Greater and Pallid certainly do.

Immature Greater Honeyguides utter an aggressive "feeeer" that drives away other honeyguides in a feeding situation, this becoming an ear-splitting "pseeeeaar" from trapped birds held in the hand. In aggression, adults and older immatures of this species utter peeping to piping and chattering series of notes, often wavering in pitch, and resembling the begging calls of young Greater Honeyguides.

Similar calls to the last are also used as guiding calls. These consist of a chatter made up of "tya" notes compounded with peeps or pipes, thus double-noted, and varying in pitch. No calls have been heard from guiding Greater Honeyguides that differ from variations of the calls just described, which are emitted also by aggressively interacting, chasing Greater Honeyguides.

Food and Feeding

Beeswax, chiefly the wax of honeybees of the genus *Apis*, forms the major element of the diet of most honeyguides. Noteworthy among other foods are scale insects (Coccidae), which essentially replace beeswax in the diets of the slender-billed species of the genus *Prodotiscus*. They are also important to Zenker's

Honeyguide and, probably, to the Yellow-footed Honeyguide. All honeyguides are known to eat insects and spiders. Other than scale insects, insects are represented in the diet by honeybee eggs and larvae but few adults, aculeate Hymenoptera, sweatbees, and caterpillars, including waxworms and eggs of *Galleria* that infest beeswax, along with beetles, termites, flies, mayflies, winged and wingless ants, aphids, homopterans, hemipterans and orthopterans. Diverse spiders include those of the Thomisidae and Oxyopidae. Plant fibres and some fruits, including figs (*Ficus*), are eaten. Honeyguides are occasionally noted as taking bird eggs and nestlings, but this must be rare; they are not mobbed by other birds. Since their young are raised at least to the fledging stage by diverse host species, they eat the foods of the hosts, generally insects and fruits.

Those species using beeswax secure it wherever it is accessible and not defended vigorously by honeybees, the stings of which, in numbers, readily kill a honeyguide, despite its thickened skin. In Africa, the entrances to most bees' nests are accessible to honeyguides, especially of the smaller species. When the cavity is full to its entrance with comb, the comb may be eaten by honeyguides in the cool hours of morning, before honeybees become active. For most honeyguides, in most areas, it is the recently vacated nests that yield the resource to the birds, which squeeze in, and work over the walls of the nest and its ceiling, scraping off bits of left-over comb. The stubby bill of species of *Indicator* smaller than the Greater and Scaly-throated Honeyguides may in fact be adapted to enable them to carry out such scraping more efficiently. The Yellow-rumped Honeyguide may be forced to scrape left-over bee comb from cliff faces after giant or rock honeybees (*Apis dorsata* or *A. laboriosa*) have moved off to a new site for their open colony.

All the species of honeyguide that are moderately to well known indulge in fly-catching, in which they sally from perches after insects or spiders. Small honeyguides, such as the Pallid and the two green-backed species, hover when fly-catching, at times in front of flowers such as those of *Erythrina*, *Rubus* and *Gymnosporia*. Other insects are obtained by gleaning from the bark of tree branches and foliage, and larger honeyguides sometimes work over tree trunks. Greater Honeyguides will also on occasion follow a woodpecker, snapping up insects flushed by the creeping picid. Most honeyguides, but especially those of

the genera *Prodotiscus* and *Melignomon*, will at times join mixed-species foraging flocks of insectivorous birds. When alate termites swarm, all honeyguides abandon other foraging activities and sally for these insects. So far as is known, there are no reports of honeyguides foraging for, and eating, fruits, but stomach contents of adult specimens of, for example, the Eastern Green-backed and Lyre-tailed Honeyguides have been found to include fruits such as figs and mistletoe (*Loranthus*) berries.

Newly fledged honeyguides almost immediately commence gleaning on branches and inspecting crevices in search of food, even as they beg from their foster-parents. They follow the honeyguide "signals", the white marks on the spread outer tail, to wax sources, tagging after adults and older immatures. In very rare instances, a begging fledgling has been fed by an adult of its own species, the reported cases involving young Western Green-backed and Yellow-rumped Honeyguides.

Breeding

All honeyguide species that are sufficiently well known are brood parasites, and it is thought likely that the others also will prove to be so. Information relating to hosts, especially, is lacking for both species of *Melignomon*, for both Asian honeyguides, and for the little Dwarf and Willcocks's Honeyguides. Meagre, suggestive information regarding hosts is known for the Least, Thick-billed, Spotted and Lyre-tailed Honeyguides. Most of the available data on nest parasitism among the Indicatoridae refer to the Eastern Green-backed, Brown-backed, Lesser, Scaly-throated and Greater Honeyguides.

Breeding seasonality is clear-cut in the near-temperate Yellow-rumped Honeyguide, and in populations of Greater, Lesser and Scaly-throated Honeyguides at corresponding latitudes, all of which breed in the hemispherically equivalent spring and summer. Elsewhere, in the tropics, seasonality is far less evident. Of course, the breeding seasons of the honeyguides are attuned to those of their hosts. In addition, rainfall is a critical factor in breeding seasonality. In forests which experience an extended wet season, or where it is more or less wet all year, some individuals may have a protracted breeding period, while others may breed at one particular time of year, and others at other times; in

Watching in silence while honey-hunters gain access to a bees' nest, a honeyguide will move in to feed once they have gone; tribal peoples traditionally leave a piece of honeycomb as a reward for their "guide". Greater Honeyguides probably take a range of insects caught by flycatching and not only beeswax, but also bees, their eggs and larvae. This species's habit of perching conspicuously and flycatching, coupled with its aggressiveness, leads to frequent antagonistic encounters with a variety of other bird species.

[*Indicator indicator*, Kruger National Park, South Africa. Photo: Nigel Dennis/ NHPA]

Wax, either from honeybee nests or from the waxy coverings of certain insects, is an important food item for all honeyguides. Pallid Honeyguides and also Lesser Honeyguides (Indicator minor) rarely fly with large pieces of wax, but they more frequently carry away a small fragment. More research is required into the processes whereby the wax is digested; enzymes capable of this are well developed in the honeyguide family, while the suggested possible role of bacteria remains disputed for the present.

[Indicator meliphilus
meliphilus,
Athi River, Kenya.
Photo: P. Davey/VIREO]

unusually wet years, with rainfall extending into all months in woodland that is normally dry and wet seasonally, the honeyguides may follow the same regime. Conversely, when prolonged drought occurs, honeyguides may cease breeding activity for the year.

Most male honeyguides of the better-known species maintain a singing territory, a term considered preferable to "songpost" or "studpost", used chiefly in southern Africa. Territorial male Scaly-throated Honeyguides regularly sing from one of several trees or bushes, using certain sites and certain perches at each site. Particular sites, or trees, are sometimes used for long periods, even years, but much more often the birds shift their sites, and use different trees, so that the territory may, over time, change in shape and size. Singing territories of different males are usually not adjacent; when they are, one bird is gradually forced out. Singing male Scaly-throated Honeyguides on prime territories are usually three or more years old. Territories attract other, subordinate and younger males, some of which are transient, whereas others may be more persistent. A territory can attract up to eight or nine males at a time. The dominant, territorial male sings for long periods, and stays within his territory most of the time, thus monitoring other males and seeking mates. If he leaves the territory, a secondary male may sing tentatively, and then gradually move to occupy a singing site; such males sometimes copulate with a visiting female. Males securing a territory can hold it for as long as seven years, but most are able to do so for only one or two years. Some territories are "traditional", with examples from South Africa of singing territories of Greater Honeyguides that have persisted for decades. Young males will attempt to establish a territory where none has previously existed, but such territories are usually ephemeral. A male at a less contested, presumably poorer-quality site may be a secondary male at another male's territory, and may ultimately replace the dominant male there.

Other well-known honeyguide species more or less fit the pattern outlined above for the Scaly-throated. Greater Honeyguide territories are in more open terrain, at woodland edges, or in bushland. These territories are widely spaced and, perhaps partly for that reason, attract fewer secondary males than do those of the Scaly-throated Honeyguide. Male Yellow-rumped Honeyguides do not sing, but defend a territory at a rock face bearing colonies of the rock honeybee. In the breeding season, a territorial male challenges all conspecifics coming to "his" larder, driving off other males, and courting the females that come to the beeswax resource he controls. Subor-

dinate males tend to remain near such a territory, and may at times challenge the dominant male, as well as sneak copulations with visiting females if the territorial male is away. Should the dominant male be taken by a predator, the prime territories, at least, are taken over almost instantly by one of the secondary males; this has been found to be the case for all well-studied honeyguides. Male Brown-backed and Pallid Honeyguides at the extremes of the range, or in poor habitat, tend to initiate a territory, test it out, and then move on to sing at another site; in other words, most sing only temporarily, at various sites. Young male Lesser Honeyguides may do the same.

With the strategy of a male being to gain and hold a favourable territory, what do the females do? Breeding female Scaly-throated Honeyguides need to locate suitable feeding sites, especially for beeswax in non-lush settings. They must be able to locate host nests within a radius of travel, and they must find an accessible, suitable male with which to mate. Some females accomplish these goals within a limited area, and are rarely or never found elsewhere; presumably, these areas are optimal sites for their breeding. Other females move about much more in the breeding and non-breeding seasons. Female Scaly-throated Honeyguides seem to fight only at sources of beeswax. In contrast, at least some adult female Greater Honeyguides engage in prolonged encounters during which one or both may sing male-like songs, a phenomenon which, on current knowledge, is unique among the Indicatoridae. It is unknown whether a particular female mates with only one male, at least for one clutch, or whether all females are, as most seem to be, promiscuous, as are males.

The actual egg-laying habits of an individual are almost unknown. R. B. Payne, in his studies of specimens of Greater and Lesser Honeyguides in the well-defined breeding season of southern Africa, found the overall clutch size to be about 20 eggs, laid in distinct sets of four or five each. It is suggested that tropical honeyguides lay perhaps as many, or more, eggs, but in smaller sets of three or four. Within a set, a female lays about every second day; she therefore copulates to fertilize an egg on the day of its ovulation, and then has the next day in which to lay the egg in the nest of an appropriate host. Data are needed on other species, and from tropical populations, to test these generalizations.

Evidence exists that males, as well as females, monitor the activities and nests of their hosts. Most data relate to Lesser Honeyguides, but Scaly-throated and Spotted Honeyguides come to playback of recordings of their host woodpeckers' calls, and also to calling woodpeckers themselves, triggering aggressive interactions. Males may monitor hosts and nests with regard to the location of their own singing territory, to the occurrence of breeding by their hosts, and to the success of their presumed offspring. They sometimes also act to keep other males away from duetting barbet pairs. A strategem, if hosts already have eggs of their own, is for a male honeyguide to interfere with the hosts, interrupting and disturbing them, thereby causing nest failure and affording a new opportunity for the parasite to lay. Females, of course, monitor the hosts' nests. There is suggestive evidence that a male Lesser Honeyguide occasionally acts in concert with a female, presumably one with which he has mated, to afford her an opportunity to gain access to the hosts' nest. An intriguing report exists of two Lesser Honeyguides assisting a host pair of Acacia Pied Barbets in preventing Rüppell's Parrots (*Poicephalus rueppellii*) from usurping the barbets' nest-cavity.

The laying female may puncture or remove one or more of the host's eggs. There are many cases of Eastern Green-backed Honeyguides indulging in this behaviour, which also occurs in some Greater Honeyguides, and perhaps less often in others. The honeyguides' own eggs are elliptical, and are white; an exception is provided by some Eastern Green-backed Honeyguides that lay blue eggs, matching in colour those of the frequent host white-eyes. The female must be quick, and may take only 10-15 seconds to lay and leave. Hosts such as barbets can kill or maim a honeyguide caught in the nest, and barbets have been seen to toss and slam a honeyguide against the nest entrance before releasing it. Female honeyguides also receive rough treatment from their partner during copulation; the male clasps the hindneck feathers or even the skin, at times leaving a bare area that may be wounded. Breeding females may require a good rehabilitation period between laying sets of eggs.

In elaborating the hosts utilized by honeyguides, one has to realize that females may have insufficient time to locate a host's nest that has eggs at the appropriate stage of development. The timing of laying must be such that it will allow close synchrony of hatching of the host's clutch and the honeyguide's own egg, or earlier hatching of the latter. Some eggs may therefore be "dumped" in the nest of a non-host species. Warblers (Sylviidae), flycatchers (Muscicapidae), white-eyes and perhaps sunbirds (Nectariniidae) seem to be the preferred hosts of the small *Prodotiscus* honeyguides. These are cup-nesters, mainly species constructing deep cups or covered nests, but some cavity-nesters such as petronias (*Petronia*) and tits (*Parus*) may possibly be used. Hosts of the *Melignomon* honeyguides are unknown, but may include barbets of the genus *Gymnobucco*. Suspected hosts of small species of *Indicator* are various of the small barbets known as tinkerbirds (*Pogoniulus*); Pallid Honeyguides are known to use Yellow-rumped Tinkerbirds (*P. bilineatus*) as hosts, and may parasitize other barbets as well.

The Thick-billed Honeyguide lays in nests of the Grey-throated Barbet (*Gymnobucco bonapartei*), and probably those of others of that genus. Of the 19 or 20 hosts of the Lesser Honeyguide, the chief victims are barbets, with nine species recorded, six of which are social; the others are three or four woodpeckers and two bee-eaters (*Merops*), and, perhaps only occasionally, a kingfisher (*Halcyon*), a swallow (*Hirundo*), two starlings (Sturnidae) and the Yellow-throated Petronia (*Petronia superciliaris*). All but the swallow are cavity-nesters, the swallow building a closed mud nest. The Spotted Honeyguide is suspected of using *Gymnobucco* barbets as hosts, as is the Lyre-tailed Honeyguide. Six woodpeckers, two barbets and a tinkerbird are recorded as hosts of the Scaly-throated Honeyguide. This honeyguide, however, is too large to fit into a tinkerbird cavity and possibly "dumped" the egg, laying it through the entrance; V. G. L. van Someren reported that, remarkably, the tinkerbirds enlarged the nest-chamber and entry tunnel in order to accommodate the nestling honeyguide.

There are about 40 hosts recorded for the Greater Honeyguide. In some areas, the majority of its eggs are laid in the nests of one or two species, especially bee-eaters, kingfishers and starlings. A roller (*Coracias*), three woodhoopoes (Phoeniculidae), the Hoopoe (*Upupa epops*), four kingfishers (Alcedinidae), eight bee-eaters, three barbets, six woodpeckers, three swallows, three starlings, two thrushes (*Myrmecocichla*), two petronias, a tit and a sunbird are the known hosts, these being cavity-nesters or, in a

few cases, builders of closed nests. The number and variety of its hosts may be related to the striking sexual and age dimorphism of the Greater Honeyguide, far exceeding that of any other indicatorid species.

So far as is known, honeyguide eggs are not removed from nests by the hosts, except in cases, perhaps of "dumping", in which the honeyguide lays before the host has commenced laying. The eggs take twelve to 18 days to hatch, an incubation period that is short by comparison with that of many host species, but in fact no shorter than in other piciforms, even including toucans. The honeyguide hatches naked, blind and weak, with a well-developed egg tooth, and small, sharp, curved membranous hooks on the tips of the mandibles; it also possesses spiny hypotarsal "heels", and it sits on these and on the belly. From this point onwards, the hatchling moves its head about, clinging to and biting anything it touches, except the foster-parents. It punctures and destroys the host's eggs one by one. If any of the host's nestlings are present, they are "bitten" and lacerated, and they weaken and die, and are then removed by the parents. There are no known cases of a fosterer's own young surviving to fledging if a honeyguide is raised in the nest. The membranous bill hooks presumably break off at as early an age of seven days in species of *Prodotiscus*, but they are present for 14 days or more in larger honeyguides, which occasionally still bear one or both hooks at fledging. On occasions, two or more honeyguide eggs are laid in the same host's nest, possibly a result of "egg-dumping"; in some such cases, albeit rarely, the hatchling honeyguides, with their thick skin, fail to cause serious injury to one another, and so may be raised together successfully.

Nestling honeyguides beg loudly, and, by securing food intended for a number of the host's young, they grow rapidly, the larger species gaining up to about 2 g in weight per day. There have been suggestions that nestling Greater Honeyguides mimic the begging calls of their specific hosts, but observations have so far not found this to be the case. The young honeyguides have several calls, and these shift developmentally. Greater Honeyguides, even where favouring one particular host, nevertheless parasitize various other species, and, moreover, the young do not vary in their mouth and facial-skin colours. Nothing in the behaviour of honeyguides suggests that individuals have either genetic or imprinted host-specificity. The eyes of the nestling honeyguide open at between ten and 20 days, by which time the chick is rather well feathered. The young of the smaller species fledge at about 21 days, while larger ones leave the nest at about 35 days of age. Nestlings do not appear at the nest entrance until a few days before fledging. While at the entrance they may see and hear monitoring adult honeyguides, perhaps their own parents.

At fledging time at a barbet's nest, the appearance of the flying, emergent honeyguide confounds the foster-parents and their helpers, which may suddenly react as to the presence of an adult, by chasing the fat young honeyguide out of the territory. Whether or not the hosts react aggressively to the young honeyguide, problems usually arise rapidly. These are due partly to the young honeyguide failing to return to roost in the nest with its foster-parents, and partly to the frequently divergent foraging habits exhibited by the hosts and the honeyguide. For example, the young honeyguide's failure to follow foster-parent barbets to fruiting trees, its lack of "enthusiasm" for ground-foraging with starling fosterers, or the inability of a young honeyguide to forage in the air or to travel far to feeding sites with fostering bee-eaters must place stress on the bond between honeyguide and host.

Problems may be fewer between *Prodotiscus* honeyguide fledglings and foster-parent warblers or white-eyes, which do not return to the nest. Those host species glean for insects close by the nest, and perhaps roost with the youngster side-by-side in a bush or tree.

Fledged honeyguides spend either no time at all or up to seven days with their foster-parents. Many are probably independent within one or two days, as indeed are some young barbets.

Juvenile honeyguides of those species which exploit beeswax seem to tag along with other honeyguides, thus arriving at a food source at which they are apt to be dominant (see Morphological

All honeyguides are apparently brood parasites. Appearing at the nest entrance within only a few days of fledging, this young Lesser Honeyguide has been reared by Black-collared Barbets (Lybius torquatus). The honeyguides monitor and may even guard potential hosts and their nests, and the female honeyguide, perhaps having previously tired the nest-owners by repeated chasing, has to lay and leave quickly when a favourable opportunity arises. On hatching, after 12–18 days, the young honeyguide uses sharp mandibular hooks to puncture the hosts' eggs or fatally injure any chicks. Begging loudly, the nestling thrives on a typical barbet diet which includes fruit, but not wax, and may be brought by the barbet parents and a helper. The fledgling thus tends to be heavy on leaving the nest and may be independent within only 1–2 days. Probably to the consternation of its foster-parents, the juvenile does not return to the nest to roost as would a young barbet, but quickly begins rather to associate with other honeyguides, following them to wax sources, where immatures are dominant.

[Indicator minor minor, South Africa. Photo: E. & D. Hosking/ FLPA]

Aspects, General Habits). Furthermore, they are likely to be heavy when they leave the nest, where they have no competitors for food. This allows a period of time for them to find food before hunger becomes severe. For the first few months up to six months or more they enjoy a dominant status in their juvenile plumage, before acquiring a fully adult plumage.

Movements

Most male honeyguides in most areas remain more or less on, or near, their singing territory (see Breeding) throughout the year. Male Yellow-rumped Honeyguides dependent upon the colonies of giant or rock honeybees on rock faces may remain in or near the singing territory through the winter if the beeswax resource is plentiful. Immature and female Yellow-rumped Honeyguides are more mobile and move widely; even territorial males forage away from their territory, to as far as 10 km. Forest-dwelling honeyguides are less well known, although males of some species, such as the Spotted and the Lyre-tailed Honeyguides, sing or display more or less regularly all year. One problem in understanding these essentially tropical birds is that much of the information available on the Indicatoridae comes from the fringe of the subtropics in southern Africa, where the birds are strictly limited by strong summer-winter seasonality, a factor alien to most honeyguide populations, which do not reach such colder regions.

Almost all honeyguides are resident, spending their entire life in the area in which they were raised. Some undertake local movements, perhaps irregularly beyond a radius of 8-20 km of the natal site. Adverse conditions cause Lesser Honeyguides to gravitate to favourable sites in or near their place of origin. In a long-term study area in Kenya where there are few breeding Lesser Honeyguides, there is in most years a sudden deluge of young Lesser Honeyguides, many of them very young, such that more individuals of this species are ringed than of the more commonly breeding Scaly-throated and Greater Honeyguides. Within the breeding season, female honeyguides sometimes move up to 8 km or so, and, exceptionally, territorial males may do so in order to forage at a particular site.

Dispersal has led to the invasion by some species, especially the Lesser Honeyguide, of certain areas in south-western Africa. It is surely no coincidence that such movements have followed closely on the heels of the expansion into these areas of host Acacia Pied Barbets.

The Yellow-rumped Honeyguide is probably the most migratory member of the family, although it could hardly be termed a true migrant. Some birds apparently move upslope in the Himalayas after breeding. Likewise, some individuals, perhaps many, migrate to lower elevations in the autumn, although territorial males and some others remain around the cliffs where they breed, so long as they can glean beeswax from the abandoned colonies of rock honeybees that have moved downslope for the winter.

Of course, many honeyguide species are poorly known, and it is possible that some movements occur of which ornithologists are as yet unaware. Nevertheless, regional observers and authorities consider that most species are sedentary. Studies show that those honeyguides which have been investigated in some detail exhibit only local movements in search of food, except for the somewhat larger-scale dispersal by immatures.

Relationship with Man

The relationship between honeyguides and beeswax has been known to humans for a considerable time, and certainly to African honey-gathering tribesmen for millennia. Honeyguides have intrigued Western peoples and the Chinese for centuries with their wax-eating, their guiding behaviour and, more recently, their nest parasitism. The last seems to many to be cruel in the extreme, for every honeyguide is a "killer", representing a lost brood of some host. Rather, honeyguides should be respected as highly evolved, efficient brood parasites, and unique among birds in their near dependence on beeswax.

Thus, despite the paucity of knowledge of honeyguides, the habits of these relatively drab birds have long captured people's interest. Third-century Chinese scribes wrote of "little birds of the wax combs", this being based on second-hand reports referring to the Yellow-rumped Honeyguide of the Himalayas, a species which does not enter China. For many thousands of years, African tribespeople have noted and watched honeyguides, and followed them to bees' nests. Early religious missionaries in Africa were surprised by birds that came to altars and took pieces of wax from their beeswax candles.

Within Africa, the honeyguides have evolved investigative behaviour that involves humans, for individuals of several species of *Indicator* follow, watch and monitor human activities, especially chopping, hammering and fire-building. Early European explorers and ornithologists were intrigued by the honeyguides, especially when the birds' nest parasitism and the Greater Honeyguide's guiding behaviour came to their attention.

So far as is known, only one species, the Greater Honeyguide, has evolved the habit of leading or guiding humans to bees' nests. This behaviour allows traditional honey-hunting peoples to acquire honey more efficiently, as H. A. Isack and H. U. Reyer have shown. It has often been said that the honeyguide also guides other mammals, and particularly the ratel, or honey-badger (*Mellivora capensis*), to sources of food, presumably using much the same method as it does for humans. Although this remains a real possibility, there appears to be little real evidence to support such claims. Clearly, this is one aspect of the honeyguide's behaviour that requires further research, along with investigation into whether species other than the Greater Honeyguide lead humans in a similar way.

The honeyguide's behaviour when leading a human to a nest has already been described (see General Habits), but a further well-documented example, from Zimbabwe, is of interest. In July 1998, C. B. Cottrell encountered a female Greater Honeyguide perched 10 m away, and giving the chatter call associated with guiding. The bird, having caught the observer's attention, then flew out of sight behind a large, extensive and densely vegetated termite mound, where it chattered again, while the observer had to take a longer route around the obstruction; the bird, although unable to see the human, must have followed an appropriate route, since it reappeared alongside the observer and chattered once more. From there it flew some 30 m and settled close to a previously invisible bees' nest, thereby placing the observer in a dilemma: the nest was a commercial one, and belonged to a colleague!

There appears to have been a substantial decline in the incidence of guiding since the middle of the twentieth century, at any rate in some of the more densely populated areas. The results of a survey, initiated in 1998 by Cottrell, may shed light on this subject.

Collection of honey from wild honeybees remains locally important to people as a source of energy in the Himalayas and in parts of Africa. Even the honeycomb pieces are utilized in Africa for the making of beverages. To the extent that the comb is collected along with the honey, the impact upon honeyguides is more or less substantial (see Status and Conservation).

Status and Conservation

Honeyguides are unique among piciform birds in that so little is known about over half of the members of the family. For these, only the most basic information is available on their distribution and a few fragments of data on their habits, two species having been discovered within the past half-century. Several seem very rare, yet this may be in part due to their inconspicuousness. Indeed, the Lyre-tailed Honeyguide is known in some areas and a few countries only from the sounds produced in its remarkable aerial display (see General Habits).

Whatever factors play roles impinging adversely on honeyguides, the greatest threat by far must be the loss of suitable habitat associated with the increasing human populations in Africa and Asia. For the Yellow-rumped Honeyguide in the Himalayas, this means ever more frequent harvesting of honey

The combination of olive-brown to black-brown upperparts and golden-yellow to cream or white underparts make this juvenile Greater Honeyguide easily distinguishable from all other members of the family, including adults of its own species. Further characteristic features include the pale lores, pale bare skin around the eye and yellow-green crown. Several honeyguide species are known to drink more or less regularly, amongst them the Greater Honeyguide. This species, in particular, apparently needs to drink when feeding on wax.

[Indicator indicator, Gambia. Photo: David Hosking/ FLPA]

and the attendant destruction of the nests of rock honeybees, as documented by E. Valli and D. Summers. This over-exploitation by humans interferes with the feeding and breeding activities of this honeyguide, which has certainly become much rarer throughout most of its range during the past four decades. All of the truly forest-dependent species, such as the Spotted, Lyre-tailed and Sunda Honeyguides, are experiencing fragmentation of their habitat, this sometimes resulting in their replacement by a more open-country relative. Such has been the case with the Thick-billed Honeyguide, which has lost out to the Lesser Honeyguide.

Pressure is becoming severe on woodland honeyguides, too, both directly and indirectly. The expanding human population, ever questing firewood, eliminates dead trees and stubs used by honeyguide hosts for excavating nesting cavities; fewer cavities mean fewer nesting places for honeybees, as well. Such activities have a subtle effect on the location of singing territories by male honeyguides, probably through shifts in the location of bees' nests.

Although no species of the Indicatoridae is currently considered threatened by BirdLife International, the Yellow-footed Honeyguide is officially classified as Data-deficient. In addition, three species are classified as Near-threatened: the Dwarf Honeyguide, and the two Asian species, the Sunda and Yellow-rumped Honeyguides.

The forest-inhabiting Yellow-footed Honeyguide quite probably is threatened, but assessment of its true status is difficult since its range is incompletely known, this at a time when forest is being cleared at a staggering rate in West and Central Africa. The Lyre-tailed Honeyguide, conspicuous through its aerial displays, may possibly be threatened, or may become so shortly. So long as huge areas of lowland forest remained intact, man could arguably afford to be complacent in his lack of knowledge of such species, but this situation no longer applies. Both of these forest honeyguides, and others, urgently require study in order to acquire data on which to base methods of monitoring such species, and then measures for safeguarding them.

A further human activity having a major impact upon honeyguides is the greatly expanded practice of apiculture. As honeybees become "domesticated", and as they increasingly occupy artificial hives, the beeswax resource becomes unavailable to honeyguides. This is particularly true of suburban and near-suburban areas surrounding major and even minor cities in Africa. Nowadays, households in rural areas frequently have several

or more bee hives that they control. Honeyguides that are, naturally, attracted to artificial hives are driven away by some honey-culturers. In any event, since the surrounding areas are largely cleared, and remaining patches of natural vegetation are manicured through firewood-gathering, the effects on the structure and size of honeyguide populations are likely to be severe, although, essentially, they are unknown.

To the extent that habitat and hosts remain, it is likely that some benefits accrue to the *Prodotiscus* species through the planting of flowerbeds and the presence of some natural herbs and bushes that support scale insects, the wax covering of which is a major food resource for these honeyguides (see Food and Feeding). For the Greater Honeyguide, the most open-country member of the family, it is possible that the loss of wax that results from modern methods of apiculture is partly or even mainly offset by the widespread opening-up of formerly forested areas, which thus become accessible to this honeyguide.

So long as some honey-gathering persists in remaining natural habitat, and pastoral herd-tenders still locate and open up bees' nests, the guiding behaviour of Greater Honeyguides may survive. Perhaps it is only in very large reserves, where honey-hunting humans can co-exist with wildlife in reasonably natural situations, that we can be assured of the continuance of this unique symbiotic association.

General Bibliography

Avise & Aquadro (1987), Barnard (1998), Bennett *et al.* (1986), Bock (1994), Bowden *et al.* (1995), Brosset (1981), Burton (1984), Chapin (1958, 1962), Colston (1981), Cottrell (1998), Cracraft (1981), Cronin & Sherman (1977), Diamond (1985), Diamond & Place (1988), Forbes-Watson (1977), Friedmann (1954a, 1954b, 1955, 1958a, 1970, 1971, 1976, 1978b), Friedmann & Kern (1956), Fry (1977), Gyldenstolpe (1917), Hoesch (1957), Hussain (1978, 1988), Hussain & Ali (1983), Isack & Reyer (1989), Johnsgard (1997), Lanyon & Zink (1987), Louette (1981a), Lowe (1946), Maclean (1990), Miller (1915), Olson (1983, 1985), Payne (1984, 1989, 1992), Peters (1948), Place *et al.* (1991), Raikow & Cracraft (1983), Ranger (1955), Rothstein & Robinson (1998), Short (1985b), Short & Horne (1979, 1983a, 1985b, 1988b, 1990a, 1992a, 1992b, 1992c, 2001), Sibley (1996), Sibley & Ahlquist (1985, 1990), Sibley & Monroe (1990, 1993), Sibley *et al.* (1988), Simpson & Cracraft (1981), Skead (1950), Stager (1967), Stuart & Stuart (1999), Swierczewski (1977), Swierczewski & Raikow (1981), Valli & Summers (1988), Verheyen (1955a, 1955b), Vernon (1987a, 1987b), Wong (1984).

ssp *insignis*

ssp *flavodorsalis*

1

2

3

4

5

ssp *willcocksi*

6

7

ssp *ansorgei*

8

9

ssp *conirostris*

10

ssp *ussheri*

11

12

ssp *stictithorax*

ssp *maculatus*

13

variants

♀ ♂

ssp *xanthonotus*

14

♂

ssp *radcliffi*

15

♀ ♂

16

♂ ♀

17

♂ ♀

PLATE 21

inches 3

cm 8

Subfamily PRODOTISCINAE

Genus *PRODOTISCUS* Sundevall, 1850

1. Western Green-backed Honeyguide
Prodotiscus insignis

French: Indicateur pygmée   **German**: Liliputlaubpicker   **Spanish**: Indicador Insigne
Other common names: Cassin's (Sharp-billed)/Green-backed Honeyguide/Honeybird

Taxonomy. *Hetærodes insignis* Cassin, 1856, Moonda River, Gabon.
Forms a superspecies with *P. zambesiae*, and has been considered conspecific; the two possibly meet in Angola, where the form referred to as "*lathburyi*" appears intermediate; further study required, based on fresh material. Two subspecies recognized.
Subspecies and Distribution.
P. i. flavodorsalis Bannerman, 1923 - Sierra Leone E, probably disjunctly, to SW Nigeria.
P. i. insignis (Cassin, 1856) - SE Nigeria S to N Angola, and disjunctly E in Zaire to S Sudan and W Kenya.

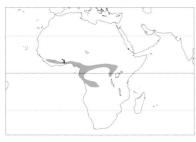

Descriptive notes. c. 10 cm; 9-13 g. Small, greenish bird with thin, flycatcher-like bill. Both sexes of nominate race various shades of green above, with erectile white patch between rump and flanks; outer tail, including tips, wholly white; olive-grey below, paler in centre. Differs from *P. zambesiae* in greener, more golden-olive upperparts, darker underparts. Immature duller, greyer, sometimes shows remnants of hypotarsal spiny "heel". Race *flavodorsalis* slightly smaller than nominate, with less olive, more yellow-green, above, and paler underparts. VOICE. Almost unknown; chattering calls reported, also weak "ski-a" or "whi-hihi" notes.
Habitat. Primary and well-developed secondary forest, riverine forest, forest edges and clearings, and large trees in coffee and other plantations. Lowlands from sea-level regularly to 1000 m; to 1500 m in Liberia (Mt Nimba), to 1100-1200 m in Zaire and Angola, and at 700-2200 m in Uganda and W Kenya.
Food and Feeding. Insects, preferentially scale insects (Coccidae) and their exudate, also wasps, caterpillars, flies, shield-bugs (Pentatomidae) and others; also spiders; occasionally fruits. Feeds in understorey and to canopy, flits from perch to perch flashing tail-tips, is an adroit fly-catcher; often takes insects at flowers of *Erythrina*, *Gymnosporia*, and other trees. Joins mixed-species foraging flocks at times.
Breeding. May in Liberia; recorded in Oct-Nov in Sierra Leone; Sept-Jan in Ghana, Cameroon, Gabon and Angola; probably Jun-Sept in Zaire; Mar-Apr in Sudan, Uganda and W Kenya. Lays in cup-nests of species such as warblers (*Apalis*), sunbirds (*Nectarinia*), probably flycatchers (Muscicapidae) and white-eyes (*Zosterops*). Eggs at least 2; no information on incubation period; 1 observed fed regularly by sunbird hosts for 8-9 days after fledging; adult of present species reported feeding a juvenile, a very rare occurrence in Indicatoridae.
Movements. Probably only local movements.
Status and Conservation. Not globally threatened. Very little known; widespread but never common, and range disjunct. Not uncommon in Sierra Leone; rare to uncommon in Liberia, where possibly overlooked; scarce in Kenya, where apparently extinct in Yala River Forest Reserve. Known to occur in Gola Forests Reserves (Sierra Leone), Taï Forest National Park (Ivory Coast), Kibale Forest National Park (Uganda), and Kakamega Nature Reserve (Kenya).
Bibliography. Allport *et al.* (1989), Bannerman (1933, 1953), Barlow *et al.* (1997), Bates (1930), Britton (1980), Brosset (1981), Brosset & Érard (1986), Chapin (1939), Cheke & Walsh (1996), Christy & Clarke (1994), Colston & Curry-Lindahl (1986), Dean (2000), Demey & Fishpool (1994), Demey *et al.* (2000), Dowsett (1989b), Dowsett & Dowsett-Lemaire (1991, 1993), Dowsett & Forbes-Watson (1993), Elgood *et al.* (1994), Field (1999), Fry *et al.* (1988), Gatter (1997), Gore (1994), Grimes (1987), Jackson & Sclater (1938), Lewis & Pomeroy (1989), Lippens & Wille (1976), Louette (1981b), Mackworth-Praed & Grant (1957, 1970), Morel & Morel (1990), Nikolaus (1987), Pinto (1983), Serle (1954, 1965), Short & Horne (1985b), Short *et al.* (1990), Snow (1978), van Someren & Cunningham-van Someren (1949), Thiollay (1985a), Zimmerman *et al.* (1996).

2. Eastern Green-backed Honeyguide
Prodotiscus zambesiae

French: Indicateur gris   **German**: Graubauch-Laubpicker   **Spanish**: Indicador del Zambeze
Other common names: Slender-billed/Eastern Honeyguide/Honeybird

Taxonomy. *Prodotiscus zambesiæ* Shelley, 1894, Zomba, Malawi.
Forms a superspecies with *P. insignis*, with which has been considered conspecific; the two may meet in Angola, where some birds possibly intermediate, including unassignable form known as "*lathburyi*"; further study required. N Tanzanian birds formerly separated as race *reichenowi*, but this is now considered a synonym of *ellenbecki*. Two subspecies recognized.
Subspecies and Distribution.
P. z. ellenbecki Erlanger, 1901 - S Ethiopia, Kenya and N Tanzania.
P. z. zambesiae Shelley, 1894 - C Angola, S Zaire and S Tanzania, S to NE Namibia, S Zimbabwe and C Mozambique.
Descriptive notes. c. 11 cm; 9-16·5 g. Both sexes of nominate race grey-green above, with erectile patch of white between rump and flanks; outer tail feathers white, including tips; grey-white underparts. Differs from very similar *P. insignis* in paler plumage, especially white belly and undertail-

coverts; distinguished from *P. regulus* by greener, less brown, back, no dusky tips on white outer tail feathers; from smaller species of *Indicator* by thin, pointed bill. Immature duller, greyer, paler than adult. Race *ellenbecki* slightly darker than nominate, more yellow-green above. VOICE. In flight display, utters "szh-szh-" (or "skee-aa", or "zzzzzzz"), dropping in pitch; also squeaky chatter; begging call of fledgling a squeaky "tz-tz-tz-".
Habitat. Inhabits forest, moist woodland, streamside forest, and also gardens; woodland includes *Baikiaea*, *Brachylaena-Croton-Olea*, and miombo (*Brachystegia*). Occurs from sea-level up to 2130 m, mostly above 300 m.
Food and Feeding. Eats scale insects (Coccidae) and their waxy exudates, also other Homoptera, Coleoptera, termites, caterpillars, other flying insects; also spiders; some fruits and seeds, e.g. of mistletoes (*Loranthus*). Reports of eating wax at bees' nests considered very unlikely, as *Prodotiscus* lacks the thick skin of wax-eating species of Indicatoridae. Drinks from birdbaths. Fly-catches frequently; also works over foliage and bark, e.g. of rose bushes with scale insects; flies often, spreading tail. Joins mixed-species foraging flocks.
Breeding. Apr-Aug and Dec-Feb in N, Aug-Feb in S, mainly in or after rainy season. Possible courtship displays over treetops with calls, 3-4 birds may fly about, tail may be fanned, one holding wings vertically when reaching another, then gliding and dropping behind; perched display involving one bowing to other with white rump-flank patch erected. Hosts include at least 3 species of white-eye (*Zosterops*), sunbird (*Nectarinia amethystina*), flycatchers (of genera *Muscicapa*, *Platysteira* and *Terpsiphone*), possibly also hole-nesting tits (*Parus*), petronias (*Petronia*) and tinkerbirds (*Pogoniulus*); female probably destroys hosts' eggs; occasionally 2 honeyguides in a nest. Eggs 2 or more; incubation period c. 12 days, nestling period c. 21 days; begging young have yellow-orange gape.
Movements. None known; possibly wanders, as often disappears from a site for long period.
Status and Conservation. Not globally threatened. Little known. Fairly common in Kenya and Tanzania. Habits indicate some adaptability, and may thrive if common hosts do so.
Bibliography. Benson & Benson (1977), Benson *et al.* (1971), Britton (1980), Chapin (1939), Clancey (1980b, 1985b, 1996), Cunningham-van Someren (1970), Dean (2000), Dowsett & Dowsett-Lemaire (1993), Dowsett & Forbes-Watson (1993), Friedmann (1930b, 1969, 1971), Fry *et al.* (1988), Ginn *et al.* (1989), Harrison *et al.* (1997), Leonard (1998b), Lewis & Pomeroy (1989), Mackworth-Praed & Grant (1957, 1962, 1970), Maclean (1993), Parkes (1994), Pinto (1983), Short & Horne (1985b), Short *et al.* (1990), Snow (1978), Stevenson & Fanshawe (2001), Steyn (1996), Tarboton (2001), Vernon (1987a, 1987b), Zimmerman *et al.* (1996).

3. Brown-backed Honeyguide
Prodotiscus regulus

French: Indicateur de Wahlberg   **German**: Wahlberglaubpicker   **Spanish**: Indicador Dorsipardo
Other common names: Wahlberg's/Sharp-billed Honeyguide/Honeybird

Taxonomy. *Prodotiscus regulus* Sundevall, 1850, Mohapoani, west Transvaal.
No very close relatives. Forms named as *peasei* and *adustoides* are synonyms of nominate; *caurinus* synonymous with *camerunensis*. Two subspecies recognized.
Subspecies and Distribution.
P. r. camerunensis Reichenow, 1921 - disjunctly from Guinea E to SE Nigeria, thence E to N Cameroon and W Central African Republic.
P. r. regulus Sundevall, 1850 - EC Sudan and SW Ethiopia S (to E of forest) to S Zaire, Angola and NE Namibia, E to Indian Ocean coast and S to E Cape Province; recorded once in NW Somalia.

Descriptive notes. 12-13·5 cm; 9·5-16 g. Grey and brown, thin-billed, flycatcher-like bird. Both sexes of nominate race grey-brown above, with dark tip of white outer tail feathers; sometimes conspicuous, erectile white patch between rump and flanks; grey-white below. Distinguished from *P. insignis* and *P. zambesiae* by browner back, dark tips to outer tail feathers; differs from other honeyguides in more pointed, thinner bill. Immature duller, lacks dark tips of white outer tail. Race *camerunensis* darker than nominate. VOICE. Song a short trill, rather like stronger song of *Indicator variegatus* and *I. maculatus*, c. 2 seconds long, from canopy; also "tsip, tseep" or single to double "zeet"; at times "zeet-zeet" at each drop in undulating flight; "tsirr-tsirrrt", and chattering call; "zzzzz" in (courtship) flight; and "tseeu, tseeu" by young bird pumping tail.
Habitat. Woodland, including *Acacia*, *Brachystegia*, *Combretum*, mopane (*Colophospermum mopane*) and other types, also wooded grassland, streamside woods and forest borders, scrub, bushland, thickets, plantations and gardens; crosses grassland to 2 km wide. Sea-level to 2000 m.
Food and Feeding. Feeds extensively on waxy scale insects (Coccidae), on mistletoe (*Loranthus*) and other plants; also insect larvae, including those of beetles, Lepidoptera and others, and aphids, flies, winged termites and other insects. Reports of its seeking and eating beeswax considered unfounded. Gleans, probes in foliage and on bark at all levels, hovers before flowers for insects; hawks aerial insects from perch. Joins mixed-species foraging flocks.
Breeding. Probably May-Sept in W Africa; Nov-Mar in Kenya and Ethiopia, and Mar, May and Oct in Zaire; Oct-Mar in S Africa. Display with erected body feathers, especially flank-rump patch, drooped wings, tail spread, head forward and "zzzz" call, other bird called "zeep" and flew, first bird followed. Hosts are warblers (including *Camaroptera*, but especially *Cisticola*), sunbird (*Nectarinia senegalensis*), and Yellow-throated Petronia (*Petronia superciliaris*); investigates old nests of swifts (Apodidae), swallows (*Hirundo*) and starlings (Sturnidae). Eggs 5-6; details of incubation and nestling periods unknown.

Movements. Probably some wandering, as irregular at some sites (e.g. in C Kenya), and sites used for singing often abandoned. Numbers appear to vary seasonally in E South Africa, with notable influxes in 1924 and 1986 suggested to be irruptions; these may be linked to sporadic records from SW Cape.

Status and Conservation. Not globally threatened. Considered probably commonest species of *Prodotiscus*, although no data on relative numbers. Rare in Liberia; local and uncommon in Kenya. Apparently expanding its range in parts of South Africa, as a result of tree planting.

Bibliography. Anon. (1998a), Ash & Miskell (1998), Baird (1979), Bannerman (1933, 1953), Benson & Benson (1977), Benson *et al.* (1971), Britton (1980), Cave & Macdonald (1955), Chapin (1939), Cheke & Walsh (1996), Clancey (1964, 1975), Colston & Curry-Lindahl (1986), Dean (2000), Demey & Fishpool (1991), Demey *et al.* (2000), Dowsett & Dowsett-Lemaire (1993), Dowsett & Forbes-Watson (1993), Earlé & Grobler (1987), Elgood *et al.* (1994), Fabian (1981), Friedmann (1930a), Fry *et al.* (1988), Gatter (1997), Ginn *et al.* (1989), Harrison *et al.* (1997), Irwin (1981), Leonard (1998b), Lewis & Pomeroy (1989), Lippens & Wille (1976), Louette (1981b), Mackworth-Praed & Grant (1957, 1962, 1970), Maclean (1971, 1993), Manson (1985), Nikolaus (1987), Penry (1976, 1994), Pinto (1983), Priest (1948), Schmidl (1982), Serle (1950, 1957), Short & Horne (1985b), Short *et al.* (1990), Skead (1951), Snow (1978), Steyn (1996), Tarboton (2001), Tarboton *et al.* (1987), Thiollay (1985a), Vernon (1974), Zimmerman *et al.* (1996).

Genus *MELIGNOMON*   Reichenow, 1898

4. Zenker's Honeyguide
Melignomon zenkeri

French: Indicateur de Zenker   **Spanish**: Indicador de Zenker
          German: Weißschwanz-Honiganzeiger

Taxonomy. *Melignomon zenkeri* Reichenow, 1898, Yaoundé, Cameroon.
Forms a superspecies with *M. eisentrauti*, which it possibly meets in Cameroon. Monotypic.
Distribution. S Cameroon E to S Central African Republic and SW Uganda, S to Gabon and N & CE Zaire.

Descriptive notes. c. 14·5 cm; female 24-25 g. Nondescript, rather dull honeyguide. Both sexes yellow-olive to brown-olive above, with dark-tipped white outer tail; olive-grey to grey-brown below, with yellow towards centre; legs usually show some yellow (with olive, green or pink); bill pointed, relatively broad, not stubby. Distinguished from *Prodotiscus* by larger size, no white patch on upperparts, larger pointed bill. Immature darker, greener than adult, legs yellower, outer tail whiter, even all white at tips. Voice. Known only from one series of songs from Cameroon, though there is a remote possibility that these songs could have been from *M. eisentrauti*, voice of which unknown. Song apparently a series of up to 32 "psee" notes, or with louder "pseep" in mid-song, c. 10-20 seconds long, drops rapidly in volume near end, like slowed song of *Prodotiscus regulus* or even *Indicator variegatus* or *I. maculatus*.
Habitat. Lowland to lower montane forest and secondary forest, including edges, and cultivated areas with some standing trees. To 1150 m in Cameroon, 1530 m in E Zaire.
Food and Feeding. Little known; scale insects (Coccidae), including pupae and cocoons, and grey wax-like items mixed with insects. Tough skin and slit-like nostrils suggest that beeswax may be eaten, as does the netting of an individual near a recently cut-out bees' nest, where *Indicator* species were present.
Breeding. Virtually unknown. Surmised to breed during Feb-Mar (end wet season through dry) in Cameroon; Jun in Central African Republic; reported in Jan-Mar and Jul-Aug (wet and dry seasons) in E Zaire; and Jul in Uganda. No information on eggs or hosts; once chased by 2 Grey-throated Barbets (*Gymnobucco bonapartei*) from perch near dead stub bearing their nests.
Movements. Presumably sedentary.
Status and Conservation. Not globally threatened. Very little known, and status uncertain. Apparent rarity possibly due to its being overlooked, since all honeyguides, even where relatively common, are rather infrequently noted by observers. More information urgently needed concerning its biology. Present in Mount Kupé National Park (Cameroon).
Bibliography. Bannerman (1933, 1953), Bates (1930), Bowden (2001), Bowden *et al.* (1995), Britton (1980), Chapin (1939), Colston (1981), Dowsett & Dowsett-Lemaire (1993), Dowsett & Forbes-Watson (1993), Dowsett-Lemaire & Dowsett (1998), Friedmann (1968, 1978a), Friedmann & Williams (1968), Fry *et al.* (1988), Lippens & Wille (1976), Louette (1981a, 1981b), Mackworth-Praed & Grant (1970), Robertson (1997b, 1998a, 1998c), Serle (1959, 1965), Smith *et al.* (1996), Snow (1978), Stevenson & Fanshawe (2001).

5. Yellow-footed Honeyguide
Melignomon eisentrauti

French: Indicateur d'Eisentraut   **Spanish**: Indicador Patiamarillo
          German: Eisentrauthoniganzeiger
Other common names: Coe's/Eisentraut's Honeyguide

Taxonomy. *Melignomon eisentrauti* Louette, 1981, near Grassfield, north-east Liberia.
Forms a superspecies with *M. zenkeri*, which it may meet in Cameroon. Monotypic.
Distribution. Sierra Leone, Liberia (Mt Nimba, Wonegizi Mts), SW Ghana and SW Cameroon; reports from Ivory Coast require confirmation.
Descriptive notes. c. 14·5 cm; 18-29 g, males average heavier. Both sexes yellowish-olive above, with dark-tipped white outer tail; grey-white below, with green-yellow about breast and belly, white undertail-coverts; mainly yellow bill and legs, variable in depth of colour. Distinguished from similar *M. zenkeri* by distinctly paler, whiter undertail-coverts contrasting with rest of underparts, yellow bill, generally yellower legs; from *Prodotiscus* by lack of white on side of rump, stronger and yellow bill, pale yellowish legs. Immature paler, yellower below, outer tail with small or no dark tips of white feathers. Voice. Unknown.

Habitat. Mainly primary forest, also adjacent secondary forest; lowlands to at least 750 m.
Food and Feeding. Feeds on insects and their seeds; probably also eats beeswax, as yellow waxy material found in stomachs. Forages in canopy up to middle heights; gleans from leaves and branches; sometimes hangs, feet upwards, to take insects. Occasionally joins mixed-species foraging flocks.
Breeding. Unknown. Data from specimens suggest breeding in Mar (possibly Nov-Jun) in Liberia, and Aug and Dec in Cameroon. Hosts possibly woodpeckers.
Movements. Presumably sedentary.

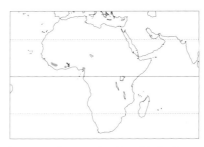

Status and Conservation. Not globally threatened. Data-deficient. Very poorly known. Rare throughout range, and habitat diminishing as forest cleared; easily overlooked, however, and possibly more common than thought. Described only in 1981, and now known from a dozen or so sites in at least 4 countries across W Africa; conceivably present, but undiscovered, in other forested parts of W Africa. Known to occur in Sapo National Park, Liberia, and in Gola Forests Reserves, Sierra Leone. Key to understanding both present species and *M. zenkeri* is their as yet unknown hosts.
Bibliography. Allport (1991), Allport *et al.* (1989), Bowden *et al.* (1995), Collar & Andrew (1988), Collar & Stuart (1985), Collar *et al.* (1994), Colston (1981), Colston & Curry-Lindahl (1986), Dickerman *et al.* (1994), Dowsett & Dowsett-Lemaire (1993), Dowsett & Forbes-Watson (1993), Dutson & Branscombe (1990), Field (1999), Fry *et al.* (1988), Gartshore (1989), Gartshore *et al.* (1995), Gatter (1997), Grimes (1987), Hockey (1997), Louette (1981a, 1981b), Macdonald (1980), Morel & Chappuis (1992), Serle (1959, 1965), Snow (1978), Stattersfield & Capper (2000), Thiollay (1985a), Vuilleumier *et al.* (1992).

Subfamily INDICATORINAE
Genus *INDICATOR*   Stephens, 1815

6. Dwarf Honeyguide
Indicator pumilio

French: Indicateur nain   **German**: Kurzschnabel-Honiganzeiger   **Spanish**: Indicador Enano
Other common names: Pygmy Honeyguide

Taxonomy. *Indicator pumilio* Chapin, 1958, Tshibati, east Zaire.
No very close relationships apparent; has been linked by some authors with *I. meliphilus*, and in past with *I. exilis*. Monotypic.
Distribution. E Zaire to SW Uganda, W Rwanda and W Burundi.

Descriptive notes. c. 12 cm; 11·5-15 g. Very small honeyguide with stubby bill. Both sexes olive, green and grey, with white mark on loral area, greenish-grey malar; brownish-olive dorsal streaks; white outer tail feathers with dark tips; pale chin streaky, green-grey throat to breast, whitish belly, flanks and undertail-coverts with some mottling or streaking. Distinguished from *I. willcocksi* by white lores, from other small *Indicator* species by less distinct malar; differs from thin-billed species of *Prodotiscus* in stubby bill. Immature has whiter outer tail, is greyer, below more streaky. Voice. A "tuutwi" call is only vocalization known; thought by some to have no song, but sound resembling song of African Emerald Cuckoo (*Chrysococcyx cupreus*) reported, thus possibly like songs of *I. willcocksi* and *I. meliphilus*.
Habitat. Highland forest of moist and dry types, as well as openings and edges, at 1840-2400 m; up to 1500 m in SW Uganda, and perhaps elsewhere.
Food and Feeding. Flies, other insects, and beeswax. Insects hawked; visits both abandoned and occupied, accessible bees' nests, feeds on beeswax placed out for other honeyguides by humans.
Breeding. Season in E Zaire probably Aug-Dec, probably also May-Jun, possibly Feb. Eggs and hosts unknown; probably parasitizes tinkerbirds (*Pogoniulus*) or small woodpeckers.
Movements. Probably sedentary.
Status and Conservation. Not globally threatened. Currently considered Near-threatened. Restricted-range species: present in Albertine Rift Mountains EBA. Apparently not uncommon at some sites, but its forest habitat is severely threatened in places. Known to occur in Kahuzi-Biega National Park, Zaire, in Nyungwe Forest Reserve, Rwanda, and in Impenetrable (Bwindi) Forest National Park, Uganda. Is very likely easily overlooked; was first discovered, in 1950's, only through the putting-out of beeswax to attract other honeyguides, a strategy rarely, if ever, used by those seeking it. More information desirable in order to assess potential threats.
Bibliography. Britton (1980), Chapin (1958, 1962), Collar & Stuart (1985), Dowsett (1985, 1990), Dowsett & Dowsett-Lemaire (1993), Dowsett & Forbes-Watson (1993), Friedmann (1963, 1969), Friedmann & Williams (1968, 1971), Fry *et al.* (1988), Greenway (1978), Keith & Twomey (1968), Lippens & Wille (1976), Mackworth-Praed & Grant (1970), Omari *et al.* (1999), Prigogine (1971, 1978, 1980b), Snow (1978), Stattersfield & Capper (2000), Stattersfield *et al.* (1998), Stevenson & Fanshawe (2001), Williams & Friedmann (1965), Zimmerman (1972).

7. Willcocks's Honeyguide
Indicator willcocksi

French: Indicateur de Willcocks   **Spanish**: Indicador de Willcocks
          German: Guineahoniganzeiger

Taxonomy. *Indicator willcocksi* Alexander, 1901, Prahou, Ghana.

May form a superspecies with *I. meliphilus*; that species is very similar in size and vocally, and responds readily to playback of present species' song. Was long confused with *I. exilis*, but differs vocally. Races poorly known; form *propinquus* from Cameroon originally thought to be a distinct species, but now considered a synonym of nominate *willcocksi*. Birds collected in N Liberia (Wonegizi) thought to be *I. exilis*, but might in fact refer to present species. Three subspecies recognized.

Subspecies and Distribution.
I. w. ansorgei C. H. B. Grant, 1915 - Guinea-Bissau.
I. w. willcocksi Alexander, 1901 - Sierre Leone E to S Nigeria, S Cameroon and W Uganda, S to Gabon and C & CE Zaire.
I. w. hutsoni Bannerman, 1928 - NC Nigeria E to S Chad and SW Sudan.

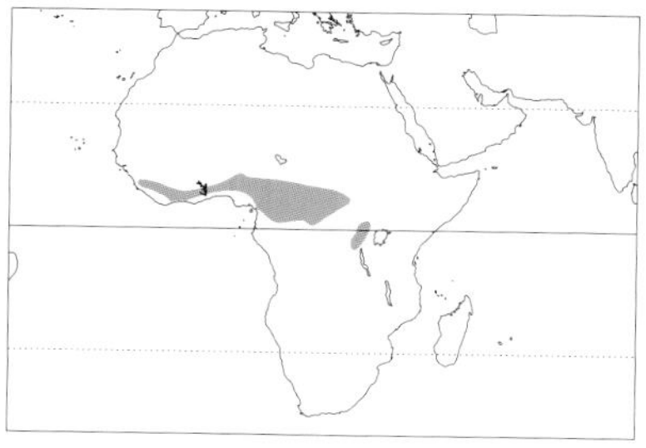

Descriptive notes. 12-13 cm; 11-20·5 g. Small, streaky, green honeyguide with stubby bill, lacking distinctive features. Both sexes of nominate race have typical honeyguide tail pattern, with distinct dark tips on white outer feathers; below, shades of olive-grey with some flank streaks, and whiter belly to undertail-coverts, E birds tending towards greyer breast. Differs from *I. exilis* in lack of dark malar and white loral mark, and less heavy flank streaks. Immature more yellow-green, less olive, above, darker on breast, tail feathers more pointed, outer tail whiter. Race *hutsoni* smaller, paler, less green, greyer, breast in particular greyer; *ansorgei* also smaller, crown greyer than back and less streaky, greyer below than *hutsoni*, sometimes trace of white loral mark. Voice. Repertoire largely unknown; song a series of 3-note phrases, "pa-will-it", last note with distinct snap as of bill-snap, closely resembles that of *I. meliphilus*, lacks characteristic initial note of *I. exilis*, *I. conirostris* and *I. minor* songs.

Habitat. Inhabits primary and tall secondary forest, riverine forest, adjacent tree plantations, mosaic of forest, shrubs and grassland, and larger patches of forest where clearing occurs; race *hutsoni* found in woodland. Mainly occurs in lowlands below 1000 m, up to 1500 m in E Zaire; recorded at 1000-1800 m in W Uganda.

Food and Feeding. Insects, including ants, termites, and larvae of Lepidoptera; also beeswax, possibly also waxy exudates of certain insects. Hawks insects; feeds in foliage and on branches, usually in canopy.

Breeding. Apr-Sept in most areas; probably also Jan-Feb in Ghana, Nigeria and Cameroon, possibly Oct in Uganda. Male apparently sings from small "territory", attracting females. Eggs and hosts unknown; Speckled Tinkerbird (*Pogoniulus scolopaceus*) is possible host, and one around nest in Uganda repeatedly attacked by this honeyguide for over 1 hour.

Movements. Sedentary, so far as known.

Status and Conservation. Not globally threatened. Not uncommon in Sierra Leone, where appears to be much commoner than *I. exilis*; uncommon in Liberia; precise distribution and status in W Africa unclear. Known to occur in Korup National Park (Cameroon) and Impenetrable Forest National Park (Uganda). May possibly be under threat W of Liberia, in Guinea-Bissau, but species is too poorly known to establish this. As with many honeyguides, biology very little understood owing to lack of observations.

Bibliography. Allport *et al.* (1989), Britton (1980), Brosset & Érard (1986), Chapin (1939, 1962), Chappuis (1981), Cheke & Walsh (1996), Christy & Clarke (1994), Colston & Curry-Lindahl (1986), Demey & Fishpool (1991, 1994), Dickerman *et al.* (1994), Dowsett & Dowsett-Lemaire (1993), Dowsett & Forbes-Watson (1993), Dowsett-Lemaire & Dowsett (1998), Elgood *et al.* (1994), Field (1999), Fishpool (1993), Fishpool *et al.* (1997), Friedmann (1969), Friedmann & Williams (1968, 1971), Fry *et al.* (1988), Gartshore (1989), Gatter (1997), Grimes (1987), Lippens & Wille (1976), Louette (1981b), Mackworth-Praed & Grant (1970), Prigogine (1971), Serle (1965), Short & Horne (1985b), Short *et al.* (1990), Snow (1978), Sørensen *et al.* (1996), Thiollay (1985a).

8. Pallid Honeyguide
Indicator meliphilus

French: Indicateur pâle **German**: Tavetahoniganzeiger **Spanish**: Indicador Pálido
Other common names: Eastern (Least) Honeyguide

Taxonomy. *Melignothes exilis meliphilus* Oberholser, 1905, Taveta, south-east Kenya.
May form a superspecies with *I. willcocksi*; closely similar in size and voice, and responds to playback of that species' song. Was long confused with *I. exilis*, but differs vocally; has been linked by some authors with *I. pumilio*. Birds from border region of SC Kenya and N Tanzania have been treated as separate species, *I. narokensis*; however, described on basis of an immature specimen which is indistinguishable from type (also an immature) of present species, so synonymous with nominate *meliphilus*. S Malawi birds, described as *appelator*, inseparable from *angolensis*. Two subspecies recognized.

Subspecies and Distribution.
I. m. meliphilus (Oberholser, 1905) - E Uganda and C Kenya S to CN & EC Tanzania; also recorded from SW Sudan (R Boro).
I. m. angolensis Monard, 1934 - C Angola E to S Zaire and S Malawi, and SE to EC Zimbabwe and C Mozambique.

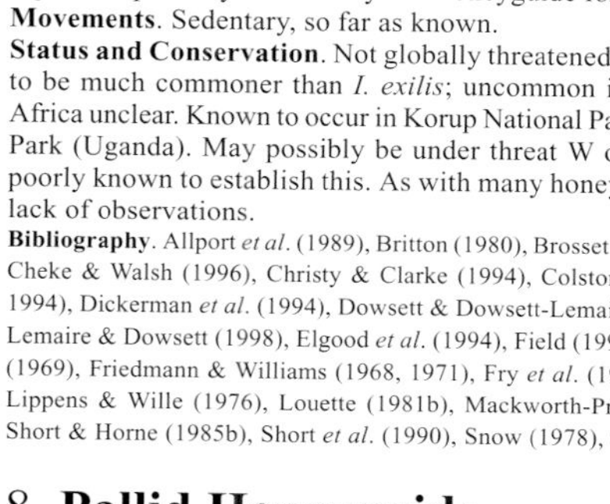

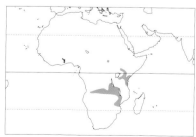

Descriptive notes. c. 13 cm; 11-18 g. Small, stubby-billed, plain-faced honeyguide. Both sexes of nominate race with grey-green crown, greenish-grey face with malar not contrasting, but with distinct white loral mark; back more olive than crown, rump more yellowish-green with only light streaking; tail with dark-tipped white outer feathers; below, yellow-grey to yellow-white or beige, greyer at sides. Differs from *I. minor* in smaller size, paler plumage, without marked malar, less streaky; from *I. exilis* in much paler plumage less strongly streaked on flanks and back, no dark malar. Immature darker, without loral mark, outer tail feathers pointed with little or no dusky tipping. Race *angolensis* slightly larger, somewhat darker green above with stronger streaks, greyer below. Voice. Song 10-25 triple-noted phrases, "a-wee-it" or "pa-wee-wit", 9-18 seconds long, starts softly, phrases of 1 or 2 notes, then louder, with final note in phrase a mechanical snap or click, song slower with slightly longer notes than that of *I. willcocksi*; in conflicts "pweet", often in series of up to 8 notes, in male-male conflicts may lead into song; also squeaks, noisy, at e.g. barbets (Capitonidae), and raspy "skeee", and "zeet-zeet" or "zit-zit" calls; chattering notes; and "prrrrrit" at *I. minor*. Also "wip, wip,-" sounds in flight display, which sometimes precedes song.

Habitat. Diverse woodland, especially streamside trees, *Brachystegia* woods, and forest edges; sea-level to c. 2000 m.

Food and Feeding. Arthropods, including winged ants (*Monomorium*), beetles, aculeate hymenopterans, hunting-spiders (Thomisidae, Oxyopidae), and reportedly fruits and flowers, latter possibly taken with insects; also wax at accessible or abandoned bees' nests. Very active forager, gleaning in leaves and on bark, sallying for insects, hovering for them, flitting about; can fly-catch in mid-song, completing song as it lands. Submissive to *I. minor*, *I. variegatus* and *I. indicator* at bees' nests, but enters nest when others fight; also cleans wax from walls of old nests. Chases, and chased by, flycatchers (Muscicapidae), drongos (Dicruridae) and barbets.

Breeding. Probably Mar-Sept in N, also Nov-Feb (perhaps depending upon rainfall in 1, 2 or 3 rainy seasons); possibly Apr and more likely Sept-Jan in S. Male sings from 2-7 or more trees in 250-500 m^2, sites sometimes ephemeral in drier habitats; winnowing flight display in circle below canopy when 2-3 birds present, probably related to breeding; many elements in aggressive displays, "fluff-gape", tail movements including cocking. Only documented host is Yellow-rumped Tinkerbird (*Pogoniulus bilineatus*); probable others are other tinkerbirds and small N race *irroratus* of Black-collared Barbet (*Lybius torquatus*); reports of Bennett's Woodpecker (*Campethera bennettii*) and White-eared Barbet (*Stactolaema leucotis*) as hosts are considered erroneous. Eggs, and incubation and fledging periods, unknown.

Movements. Certainly local movements occur, distances unknown.

Status and Conservation. Not globally threatened. Uncommon to locally common in most of range; local and uncommon in Kenya. Estimation of numbers difficult, as likely to be inconspicuous in areas where larger relatives are common.

Bibliography. Anon. (1998a), Benson & Benson (1977), Benson *et al.* (1971), Britton (1980), Carter (1978a), Chapin (1939, 1954, 1962), Clancey (1980b, 1985b), Dean (2000), Dowsett (1972a), Dowsett & Dowsett-Lemaire (1993), Dowsett & Forbes-Watson (1993), Fry *et al.* (1988), Ginn *et al.* (1989), Harrison *et al.* (1997), Irwin (1981), Irwin & Benson (1967), Jackson & Sclater (1938), Lewis & Pomeroy (1989), Lippens & Wille (1976), Mackworth-Praed & Grant (1957, 1962, 1970), Maclean (1993), Pinto (1983), Short & Horne (1979, 1985b, 1990a), Short, Horne & Chapin (1987), Short, Horne & Muringo-Gichuki (1990), Snow (1978), Steyn (1996), Tarboton (2001), Vincent (1935), Waiyaki & Bennun (2000), Zimmerman *et al.* (1996).

9. Least Honeyguide
Indicator exilis

French: Indicateur menu **German**: Barthoniganzeiger **Spanish**: Indicador Chico

Taxonomy. *Melignothes exilis* Cassin, 1856, Moonda River, Gabon.
Relationships uncertain. In the past, *I. willcocksi*, *I. meliphilus* and even *I. minor* were often confused with present species; *I. pumilio* was also on occasion linked with present species. Nominate and race *pachyrhynchus* intergrade in broad zone from E Central African Republic and SW Sudan to NE Zaire and W Uganda, where precise limits of respective ranges unclear. Form *leona*, known from a single immature bird taken near Freetown (Sierra Leone), now considered a synonym of nominate. Birds collected in N Liberia (Wonegizi) said to be very similar to *I. willcocksi ansorgei* from neighbouring Guinea-Bissau, possibly representing undescribed race of present species; alternatively, they might in fact be referable to *I. willcocksi*. Three subspecies currently recognized.

Subspecies and Distribution.
I. e. exilis (Cassin, 1856) - Senegal E to E Central African Republic and NE Zaire, S to N Angola and NW Zambia.
I. e. pachyrhynchus (Heuglin, 1864) - SW Sudan and extreme E Zaire, E to W Kenya and S to NW Tanzania, Rwanda and Burundi.
I. e. poensis Alexander, 1903 - Bioko I (Fernando Póo).

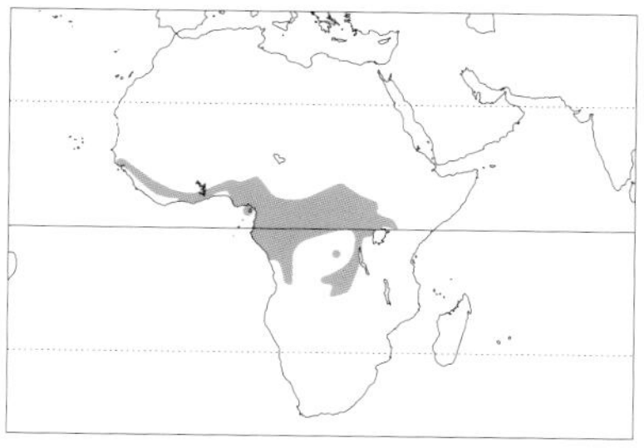

Descriptive notes. c. 14 cm; 12-23 g. Well-marked, dark honeyguide. Both sexes of nominate race with white loral area outlined darkly, distinct blackish malar stripes, dark-tipped white outer tail; breast light greyish-olive, paler on flanks and belly, dark streaks on flanks. Distinguished from very similar *I. minor* and *I. conirostris* by smaller size, and very dark, sharply outlined flank streaks. Immature very like smaller *I. willcocksi* and *I. pumilio*, but stronger flank streaks and distinct malar. Races *pachyrhynchus* and *poensis* paler than nominate, *pachyrhynchus* also larger. Voice. Song faster "wheer-wheer-" to slower "pew-pew-" series, very like those of *I. minor* and *I. conirostris* but higher-pitched; also rattly, aggressive trill, "kwiew, kwiew", and aggressive "tsa-tsa-".

Habitat. Primary and secondary forest, old clearings, forest-shrub-grassland mosaic, gallery forest, plantations with trees, and edges of forest villages. Often near bee nests in forest. From lowlands up to 2400 m; on Bioko, usually found up to 600 m, but recorded up to 1400 m.

Food and Feeding. Eats beeswax; also larvae and eggs of bees, beetles, flies and their eggs, grasshoppers, aphids, scale insects (Coccidae), leafhoppers (Homoptera), caterpillars, ants, termites, and various spiders; also some fruits. Several may gather at bees' nest where wax is accessible; spends up to 66 minutes at a time feeding. Active, sallies for flying insects, investigates cavities.

Breeding. Season often prolonged, e.g. Aug-Mar in Liberia; recorded Feb and May in Cameroon, Jan and Jun in Zaire. Territorial, defends singing territory; displays in flight. Hosts unknown, but likely barbets, e.g. tinkerbirds (*Pogoniulus*) and Grey-throated Barbet (*Gymnobucco bonapartei*). No information on eggs, or incubation and nestling periods; young probably leave foster-parents soon after fledging. Large gonads of juveniles suggest that they can breed in first year.

Movements. Probably sedentary.

Status and Conservation. Not globally threatened. Widespread, but not common; precise distribution and status in W Africa unclear. Uncommon in Sierra Leone; locally not uncommon in NW & N Liberia; local and uncommon in Kenya. Race *poensis* not rare; has adapted to cocoa and coffee plantations and other woodland areas modified by man. Known to occur in Kakamega Nature Reserve, Kenya. Appears to be somewhat adaptable, occurring in various wooded habitats. As with little-known forest species of all kinds, more information is required on its biology before any potential threats can be assessed.

Bibliography. Archer & Glen (1969), Aspinwall & Beel (1998), Bannerman (1933, 1953), Barlow *et al.* (1997), Bates (1930), Bennun & Njoroge (1999), Benson *et al.* (1971), Britton (1980), Brosset & Érard (1986), Cave &

Macdonald (1955), Chapin (1939, 1962), Chapin *et al.* (1987), Cheke & Walsh (1996), Christy & Clarke (1994), Clancey (1977c), Colston & Curry-Lindahl (1986), Dean (2000), Dickerman *et al.* (1994), Dowsett (1989b, 1990), Dowsett & Dowsett-Lemaire (1991, 1993), Dowsett & Forbes-Watson (1993), Elgood *et al.* (1994), Field (1999), Fishpool *et al.* (1997), Friedmann (1963), Friedmann & Williams (1971), Fry *et al.* (1988), Gartshore (1989), Gatter (1997), Grimes (1987), Jackson & Sclater (1938), Lewis & Pomeroy (1989), Lippens & Wille (1976), Mackworth-Praed & Grant (1957, 1962, 1970), Nikolaus (1987), Pérez del Val (1996), Pérez del Val *et al.* (1994), Pinto (1983), Prigogine (1971, 1978), Serle (1965), Short & Horne (1985b), Short *et al.* (1990), Snow (1978), Thiollay (1985a), Zimmerman (1972), Zimmerman *et al.* (1996).

10. Thick-billed Honeyguide

Indicator conirostris

French: Indicateur à gros bec **Spanish**: Indicador Picogrueso **German**: Dickschnabel-Honiganzeiger

Taxonomy. *Melignothes conirostris* Cassin, 1856, Moonda River, Gabon.
Forms a superspecies with *I. minor*; these two have often been merged, but they occur together in W Uganda without interbreeding; they may interbreed in Nigeria, but are so similar in appearance that hybrids are difficult to establish. Supposedly paler form, described as race *pallidus*, considered in part variant of nominate, although some *pallidus* treated as synonymous with race *senegalensis* of *I. minor*. Two subspecies currently recognized.
Subspecies and Distribution.
I. c. ussheri Sharpe, 1902 - SE Sierra Leone disjunctly E to S Ghana.
I. c. conirostris (Cassin, 1856) - S Nigeria E to S Central African Republic and W Kenya, S patchily to N Angola and S & CE Zaire.

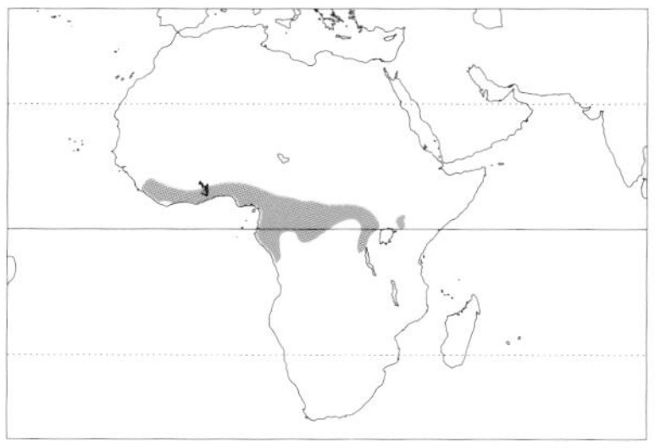

Descriptive notes. c. 15 cm; 24·5-38 g, rarely 50 g. Dark grey-olive forest honeyguide. Both sexes of nominate race with typical dark-tipped white outer tail, usually with dark malar stripes, white chin, white loral mark and variable flank streaks. Distinguished from *I. exilis* by larger size, less green plumage, white loral mark less strongly outlined in black, less dark flank streaks; from similar *I. minor* by greener, less grey upperparts, and darker underparts with streaked flanks. Immature darker, greener than adult, more white on tail, with fewer and weaker facial markings. Race *ussheri* yellower on crown and mantle, much paler below. Voice. Song a series of "wit" or "weet" notes introduced by "whew", varies in slow to fast delivery, sounds identical to that of *I. minor*; vocal repertoire poorly known, requires study.
Habitat. Lowland and submontane forest, forest-grassland mosaic, including dense secondary and riverine forest, often near bees' nests and colonies of *Gymnobucco* barbets. Rarely to 2300 m.
Food and Feeding. Eats beeswax, also some bees, including sweatbees (*Trigona*), and caterpillars, beetles, termites and other insects; young eat food of hosts, including figs (*Ficus*) and other fruits. Hawks insects in the air. Several may gather at a bees' nest, along with *I. exilis* and other honeyguides.
Breeding. Season long, at least in N & E Zaire and Cameroon; Sept-Mar in Liberia; recorded in Oct-Nov in Sierra Leone. Little known. Male with singing territory to which females come, as probably do other males. Lays in nests of Grey-throated Barbet (*Gymnobucco bonapartei*), probably also of other colonial *Gymnobucco* barbets. Eggs laid in sets of at least 4, 1 egg per nest. No other information.
Movements. Sedentary.
Status and Conservation. Not globally threatened. Common locally in Sierra Leone; uncommon in Liberia; local and uncommon in Kenya. Known to occur in Taï National Park (Ivory Coast), Mt Kupé National Park (Cameroon), La Lopé National Park (Gabon) and Kakamega Nature Reserve, Kenya. Likely to be common in extensive forest. Its range is, however, contracting and becoming fragmented with forest clearance; species is being replaced by *I. minor* at edges and in cleared areas, and thus could become threatened. Hybridization with *I. minor* could also pose a threat.
Bibliography. Allport *et al.* (1989), Bannerman (1933, 1953), Bates (1930), Bennun & Njoroge (1999), Britton (1980), Chapin (1939), Christy & Clarke (1994), Colston & Curry-Lindahl (1986), Dean (2000), Demey & Fishpool (1994), Dowsett & Dowsett-Lemaire (1993), Dowsett & Forbes-Watson (1993), Elgood *et al.* (1994), Field (1999), Friedmann (1971), Friedmann & Williams (1971), Fry *et al.* (1988), Gartshore (1989), Gatter (1997), Grimes (1987), Halleux (1994), Jackson & Sclater (1938), Lewis & Pomeroy (1989), Lippens & Wille (1976), Louette (1981b), Mackworth-Praed & Grant (1957, 1970), Pinto (1983), Prigogine (1971, 1972), Serle (1965), Short & Horne (1985b, 1992b), Snow (1978), Zimmerman (1972), Zimmerman *et al.* (1996).

11. Lesser Honeyguide

Indicator minor

French: Petit Indicateur **German**: Nasenstreif-Honiganzeiger **Spanish**: Indicador Menor

Taxonomy. *Indicator minor* Stephens, 1815, Zwartkop River, Cape Province, South Africa.
Forms a superspecies with *I. conirostris*; these two have often been merged, but they occur together in W Uganda without interbreeding; they may interbreed in Nigeria, but are so similar in appearance that hybrids are difficult to establish. In past, often confused with *I. exilis* and other small honeyguides. Several additional named races now judged untenable: *erlangeri* considered synonymous with *diadematus*; *valens* with *teitensis*; *albigularis* with nominate *minor*; and *pallidus* and *alexanderi* synonymous with *senegalensis*, although some *pallidus* are probably variant form of *I. c. conirostris*. Six subspecies currently recognized.
Subspecies and Distribution.
I. m. senegalensis Neumann, 1908 - Senegambia E to Chad and W Sudan, S to C Ivory Coast, S Nigeria, N Cameroon and N Central African Republic.
I. m. riggenbachi Zedlitz, 1915 - C Cameroon E to SW Sudan, S to NE Zaire, W Uganda and Burundi.
I. m. diadematus Rüppell, 1837 - C Sudan E to N Somalia.
I. m. teitensis Neumann, 1900 - SE Sudan E to S Somalia, S & W (around lowland forest) to C Angola, NE Namibia, Zimbabwe and C Mozambique.
I. m. damarensis (Roberts, 1928) - S Angola and N Namibia.
I. m. minor Stephens, 1815 - S Namibia, SE Botswana, and S Mozambique to South Africa.
Descriptive notes. c. 15-16 cm; 21-39 g. Both sexes of nominate race dark greyish-green above, greyer or browner when worn, with white loral spot, strong malar stripe; dark-tipped white outer tail; much paler below, light olive-grey, with only weak streaks on flanks; black orbital skin makes dark eye look large. Distinguished from smaller honeyguides by head pattern; from *I. exilis* by less black outlining of flank streaks, less black about loral spot; from *I. meliphilus* by more distinct malar stripes; distinction from *I. conirostris* difficult where they meet, but usually by paler grey breast, paler and less streaked above. Immature greener than adult, without clear markings on head, orbital skin greyer so that eye appears smaller. Races vary slightly in colour tones and size: *riggenbachi* more golden-green and more streaked above, less olive-tinged below; *senegalensis* duller than *riggenbachi*, less streaked, usually whiter breast and belly; *diadematus* duller, browner; *teitensis* somewhat yellower above, paler below; *damarensis* greyer, paler above than nominate, often tinged brown, little or no olive, also malar indistinct or absent. Voice. Song a distinct, soft "pyew" or "wee-yew" followed by fast to slow series of 10-30 (usually 13-22) "wit" (occasionally "wi-nk") notes, repeated every 10-180 seconds in bouts of up to 2 hours; aggressive, song-like, short "pwee-wee-wee-weew" to "pwee-wit-it" series; also squeaky, aggressive "ty-yeah" or "tyeek"; aggressive trills, slow "di-di-di-" to fast "tdddd-", wavering or regular in pitch; also, squeak-trill calls, chattery alarm call, soft "kish", and hard "kik" notes. Nestlings call "ty-ty-", "tyew-tyew" (or "pyee-pyee"), when fed "tyiiiiiiiii-", these respectively at c. 12, 5 and 25 per second. Mechanical sounds a wing-rustling, in display flight by male over female sounds like irregularly running motorcycle.

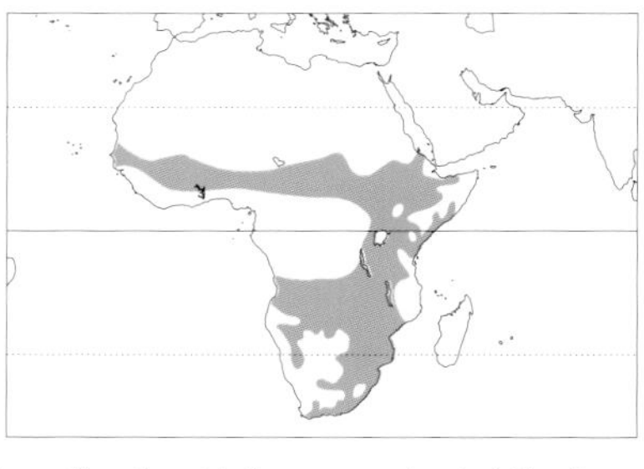

Habitat. *Acacia*, *Brachystegia* and other woodland, wooded grassland (Sahel), bushland, fragmented forest and edges, also gardens, and orchards and other plantations, including in suburbs of cities; race *senegalensis* extends S into newly cleared areas of former forest; not found inside forest. Occasionally reaches 3000 m in E Africa.
Food and Feeding. Beeswax; also hymenopterans (wasps, ants, rarely honeybees), caterpillars, termites, mayflies, and spiders; nestlings take berries and other fruits and insects fed by hosts. Searches for holes and crevices in trees and rocks, investigates fires and noises of humans, follows (does not guide) humans and other honeyguides to wax sources. Pugnacious and persistent at bees' nests; immatures dominant over adults, sometimes over larger honeyguides at wax sources. Hawks insects adeptly; works over bark and foliage of trees. Drinks, occasionally bathes.
Breeding. Recorded in all months in areas where seasons vary year to year; mainly Sept-Mar in S Africa. Male establishes singing territory, sometimes traditional site, often ephemeral in tropics, centred around 1-4 trees, sings much of day for 2-10 months in tropics, c. 6 months in S Africa; females come to territory to mate, copulations usually low in bush or tree nearby; male may perform winnowing flight display over female before copulation. Recorded hosts are 6 species of social barbet (*Stactolaema whytii*, *S. anchietae*, *S. olivacea*, *Lybius chaplini*, *L. leucocephalus* and *L. torquatus*), 3 non-social barbets (*Tricholaema diademata*, *T. leucomelas* and *Trachyphonus vaillantii*), Rufous-necked Wryneck (*Jynx ruficollis*) and other woodpeckers (*Campethera bennettii*, *C. abingoni*, probably *C. nubica*, and *Dendropicos fuscescens*), 2 bee-eaters (*Merops pusillus* and *M. oreobates*), Striped Kingfisher (*Halcyon chelicuti*), White-throated Swallow (*Hirundo albigularis*), Violet-backed Starling (*Cinnyricinclus leucogaster*), African Pied Starling (*Spreo bicolor*), and Yellow-throated Petronia (*Petronia superciliaris*); defends some host nests against other conspecifics; male sometimes assists female to enter nest. Eggs 2-4, laid in series, up to c. 20 eggs per season; incubation period 12-16 days; hatchling with bill hooks, kills host's young, or breaks eggs; fledges at c. 38 days, then chased out of the area by some barbets; fledgling does not return to nest, may not follow foster-parents, soon leaves to search cavities for beeswax. Adult longevity sometimes more than 8 years.
Movements. Some local post-breeding movements by young and adults; disperses 10 km or more.
Status and Conservation. Not globally threatened. Common in Sierra Leone; uncommon in Somalia, where no recent records from N; locally common and widespread in Kenya, Tanzania and South Africa. Highly adaptable species, with no apparent threats.
Bibliography. Archer & Godman (1937-1961), Ash & Miskell (1998), Bannerman (1933, 1953), Barlow *et al.* (1997), Bates (1930), Benson & Benson (1977), Benson *et al.* (1971), Britton (1980), Brown & Britton (1980), Cave & Macdonald (1955), Celliers (1994), Chapin (1939), Cheke & Walsh (1996), Clancey (1964, 1977a), Colebrook-Robjent (1984), Colebrook-Robjent & Stjernstedt (1976), Cunningham-van Someren (1972), Cyrus (1988), Dean (2000), Dedekind (1997), Dowsett (1990), Dowsett & Dowsett-Lemaire (1991, 1993), Dowsett & Forbes-Watson (1993), Earlé & Grobler (1987), Elgood *et al.* (1994), Field (1999), Forbes-Watson (1977), Friedmann (1930a), Friedmann & Williams (1971), Fry *et al.* (1988), Ginn *et al.* (1989), Gore (1990), Graaf (1996), Grimes (1987), Hanmer (1997), Harrison *et al.* (1997), Hoesch (1957), Horne & Short (1988), Irwin (1981), Lewis & Pomeroy (1989), Lippens & Wille (1976), Liversidge (1991), Lockwood (1981), Longrigg (1993), Louette (1981b), Mackworth-Praed & Grant (1957, 1962, 1970), Maclean (1993), van der Merwe (1986), Moyer (1980), Payne (1992), Penry (1994), Pinto (1983), Ranger (1955), Roberts (1956), Rushforth (1999), Short & Horne (1979, 1983a, 1985b, 1988a, 1990a, 1992b, 1992c), Short *et al.* (1990), Skead (1950, 1951), Snow (1978), van Someren (1956), Spottiswoode (1994), Steyn (1996), Steyn & Myburgh (1986), Steyn & Scott (1974), Tarboton (2001), Thiollay (1985a), Underhill, G.D. (1991), Underhill, G.D. & Underhill (1992a), Underhill, L.G. *et al.* (1995), Van der Merwe (1986), Winterbottom (1969), van Zijl (1994), Zimmerman *et al.* (1996).

12. Spotted Honeyguide

Indicator maculatus

French: Indicateur tacheté **German**: Tropfenbrust-Honiganzeiger **Spanish**: Indicador Moteado

Taxonomy. *Indicator maculatus* G. R. Gray, 1847, no locality = Gambia.
Forms a superspecies with *I. variegatus*, marginally overlapping in SW Sudan and W Uganda. Proposed race *feae* synonymous with nominate *maculatus*; *theresae* with *stictithorax*. E race often listed as "*stictothorax*" but original spelling, *stictithorax*, must stand. Two subspecies currently recognized.
Subspecies and Distribution.
I. m. maculatus G. R. Gray, 1847 - Gambia to Nigeria.
I. m. stictithorax Reichenow, 1877 - S Cameroon E to SW Sudan, S to N Angola (Cabinda), S & E Zaire and SW Uganda.
Descriptive notes. c. 18 cm; 42-54 g. Both sexes olive and green, with distinct pale spots on breast; dark tail has dark-tipped white outer feathers; outermost rectrices very short. Distinguished from similar *I. variegatus* by greener upperparts, less white underparts, with throat to breast more spotted, less scaly. Immature more barred and streaked, less spotted below, with whiter tail. Race *stictithorax* has paler and greener crown; more streaky on face, more olive and yellow on underparts. Voice. Little known; song a trill, slightly faster than that of *I. variegatus*, "brrrrrr" for up to 3 seconds; chattering calls; also wing sounds in flight display.

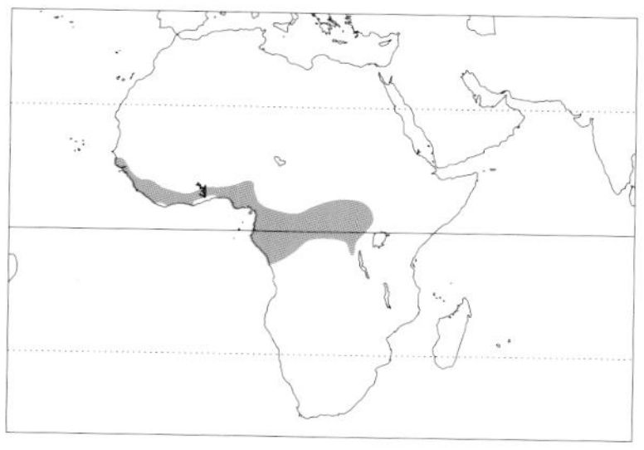

Habitat. Primary and dense secondary forest, forest clearings, riverine forest, and much-overgrown farms and plantations; mainly at middle to lower levels, below 15 m. Ranges up to 2130 m locally.
Food and Feeding. Beeswax; also feeds on insects, such as larval moths and butterflies, ants, beetles and termites, and spiders; probably also fruits; young eat foods of host. Attracted to beeswax, searches abandoned bees' nests. Forages for insects mainly in canopy, but comes down to undergrowth for beeswax. Follows humans in forest.
Breeding. Gonadal and egg data suggest long season, probably Aug-Mar in Liberia; recorded in Dec in Sierra Leone. Male in singing territory much of year, some territories maintained by same or replacement male for up to 5 years; sometimes winnowing flight display. Hosts largely unknown, suspected to include social barbets of genus *Gymnobucco*, and Buff-spotted Woodpecker (*Campethera nivosa*), latter similar in pattern to present species; Brown-eared Woodpecker (*Campethera caroli*) reported as host in Sierra Leone; in Gabon, was immediately attracted by playback of call of Golden-crowned Woodpecker (*Dendropicos xantholophus*). No other breeding information available.
Movements. Sedentary.
Status and Conservation. Not globally threatened. Rare and sporadic in Gambia, and few records in Senegal; not uncommon in parts of Sierra Leone; not uncommon in Liberia. Known to occur in Abuko Nature Reserve, Gambia, in Korup National Park, Cameroon, and in La Lopé National Park, Gabon. As a rather forest-dependent bird, it should be monitored, because forest habitat suffering clearance and fragmentation. Information on breeding and hosts essential for any conservation efforts.
Bibliography. Allport *et al*. (1989), Bannerman (1933, 1953), Barlow *et al*. (1997), Bates (1930), Britton (1980), Brosset & Érard (1986), Chapin (1939), Cheke & Walsh (1996), Christy & Clarke (1994), Colston & Curry-Lindahl (1986), Dowsett (1989b), Dowsett & Dowsett-Lemaire (1991, 1993), Dowsett & Forbes-Watson (1993), Dyer *et al*. (1986), Elgood *et al*. (1994), Field (1999), Friedmann (1978a), Friedmann & Williams (1971), Fry *et al*. (1988), Gartshore (1989), Gatter (1997), Germain & Cornet (1994), Gore (1990), Grimes (1987), Halleux (1994), Horne & Short (1988), Lippens & Wille (1976), Louette (1981b), Mackworth-Praed & Grant (1957, 1970), Morel & Morel (1990), Nikolaus (1987), Payne (1986), Pinto (1983), Sande (2000), Short & Horne (1985b, 1988b, 1992b, 1992c), Snow (1978), Thiollay (1985a), Wacher (1993), Williams (1951).

13. Scaly-throated Honeyguide
Indicator variegatus

French: Indicateur varié **German**: Strichelstirn-Honiganzeiger **Spanish**: Indicador Variegado
Other common names: Variegated Honeyguide

Taxonomy. *Indicator variegatus* Lesson, 1830, Knysna, South Africa.
Forms a superspecies with *I. maculatus*, barely overlapping with it in SW Sudan and W Uganda. Despite widespread distribution, exhibits mosaic geographical pattern of variation, as well as varying individually, seasonally and with age, rendering accurate racial subdivision impossible for present; birds from S Somalia to NE Tanzania formerly separated in race *jubaensis*. Monotypic.
Distribution. S Ethiopia and S Sudan to S Somalia, S through E Africa (W to E Rwanda and E Burundi), and from C Angola E to E Zaire and W Tanzania, S to Zambia, E Zimbabwe and E Cape Province.

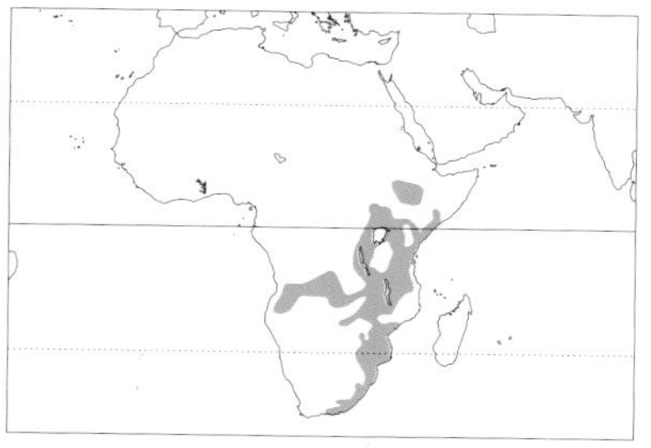

Descriptive notes. c. 18-19 cm; 34-55 g, rarely up to 61 g. Both sexes green and olive with black-tipped white outer tail pattern, very short outermost tail feathers; streaky crown and face, and rather variable scaly to streaky olive-grey and white throat and breast. Distinguished from *I. maculatus* by less green upperparts, paler underparts less spotted. Immature has spotted crown, criss-cross pattern of streaks, bars below, and nearly all-white outer tail; male becomes black-gaped, female pink-gaped with some dusky grey that increases in older females. Voice. Song a trill 0·6-4 seconds long, generally a bit slower than in *I. maculatus*, in quality churring or like policeman's whistle, soft or loud, faster or slower, occasionally croaky; alternate song 3-8 whistled pipes, during territory establishment or in interactions with other males; song-like "trill-pyew" a common, aggressive, often wavering call; females interact using aggressive chattering with gaping, in several variations; also a post-copulatory, high, whistled series; nestlings give chattery "chess" calls, yelps, and wailing calls. Wing-rustling sounds in encounters, and in "searching" flights over prospective feeding sites, humans, and other honeyguides; also "wup-wup-" sounds in display-flight.
Habitat. Diverse woodland, forest patches, riverine woods, thickets, overgrown plantations, bamboo, juniper woods, also dense streamside thickets in some dry areas. Mostly unobtrusive except at beeswax sources and where singing. Usually below c. 2200 m, rarely to 3350 m.
Food and Feeding. Beeswax eaten all year; takes bee larvae and eggs, also termites, flies, caterpillars, ants, beetles, aphids, sometimes other arthropods; nestlings eat foods of host, including fruits. Follows humans in woods, inquisitive, explores cavities; gleans along bark and limbs, visits flowers for insects; also hawks insects. Aggressive at bees' nests; females dominant over males, immatures over adults. Clasps wax between legs while eating, can carry off comb weighing up to 11 g. Drinks, bathes. Sometimes joins mixed-species foraging flocks.
Breeding. Lays in diverse seasons in tropics, mainly Aug-Feb in S Africa. Male sings from trees or bushes in territory, territory sometimes traditional, held for up to 8 years, or sometimes shifting, even within a season; in tropics sings all year, even in moult; female may breed mainly with 1 male, or visit and copulate with several; winnowing flight by male can precede or follow copulation. Known hosts include 6 species of woodpecker (*Campethera abingoni*, *C. nubica*, *Dendropicos fuscescens*, *D. griseocephalus*, *D. goertae* and *D. namaquus*), Yellow-rumped Tinkerbird (*Pogoniulus bilineatus*), Whyte's Barbet (*Stactolaema whytii*), Black-collared Barbet (*Lybius torquatus*), probably also other woodpeckers and barbets, possibly also a swift (*Apus horus*) and a petronia (*Petronia superciliaris*). Female lays eggs in series of 3-5, several series in clutch, 1 egg in each nest; incubation period c. 18 days; hatchling has bill hooks, kills host's young or destroys eggs; nestling period c. 28 days; fledgling does not return to nest, may beg indiscriminately from passing woodpeckers, and from adults of its own species; independent in 1-4 days or so. Male first breeds at 3 or more years, occasionally 2, female at 2 years. Longevity 10 or more years.
Movements. Sedentary, but regularly moves up to 10 km, even 20 km, when seeking food; disperses to 10 km or more.
Status and Conservation. Not globally threatened. Relatively common, and widespread. Uncommon in Somalia; generally uncommon in Kenya and Tanzania. Fairly common in Ngoye Forest, South Africa, perhaps in part due to strong local population of Green Barbet (*Stactolaema olivacea*), which it parasitizes. Known to occur in Impenetrable (Bwindi) Forest National Park, Uganda, in Nyungwe Forest Reserve, Rwanda, and in Mkuzi Reserve, South Africa. No known threats identified.
Bibliography. Anon. (1998a), Archer & Glen (1969), Ash & Miskell (1998), Beel (1997), Benson & Benson (1977), Britton (1980), Brown & Britton (1980), Cave & Macdonald (1955), Chapin (1939), Clancey (1964, 1977b, 1979b, 1985a), Davey (1994), Dean (2000), Dowsett (1990), Dowsett & Dowsett-Lemaire (1993), Dowsett & Forbes-Watson (1993), Dowsett-Lemaire (1983b), Friedmann (1930a), Friedmann & Williams (1971), Fry *et al*. (1988), Furlong (2000), Ginn *et al*. (1989), Harrison *et al*. (1997), Horne & Short (1988), Irwin (1981), Irwin & Benson (1967), Jackson & Sclater (1938), Lewis & Pomeroy (1989), Lippens & Wille (1976), Mackworth-Praed & Grant (1957, 1962, 1970), Maclean (1993), Ndang'ang'a & Borghesio (1999), Newby-Varty (1946), Nikolaus (1987), Payne (1986), Pinto (1983), Ranger (1955), Schultz (1991), Short & Horne (1985b, 1988b, 1990a, 1992c), Snow (1978), Steyn (1996), Tarboton (2001), Tarboton *et al*. (1987), Taylor (1983), Taylor & Taylor (1988), Thomson (1993), Zimmerman *et al*. (1996).

14. Yellow-rumped Honeyguide
Indicator xanthonotus

French: Indicateur à dos jaune **German**: Gelbbürzel-Honiganzeiger **Spanish**: Indicador Indio
Other common names: Himalayan/Indian/Orange-rumped Honeyguide

Taxonomy. *Indicator xanthonotus* Blyth, 1842, Darjeeling.
Closest relatives are probably *I. archipelagicus* and *I. indicator*. Probably derived from early Asian invasion of *Indicator* from Africa, and originating from same ancestral stock that gave rise to *I. archipelagicus*; both have bright yellow in plumage and short outer rectrix, a combination of features shared only with African *I. indicator*. Birds from NE Assam, Nagaland and Manipur to N Myanmar, described as race *fulvus*, now considered inseparable from nominate. Two subspecies currently recognized.
Subspecies and Distribution.
I. x. radcliffi Hume, 1870 - NE Pakistan (presumed extinct), and Himalayan slopes of NW India, possibly to W Nepal.
I. x. xanthonotus Blyth, 1842 - Nepal E to NE India, SE Tibet and N Myanmar.

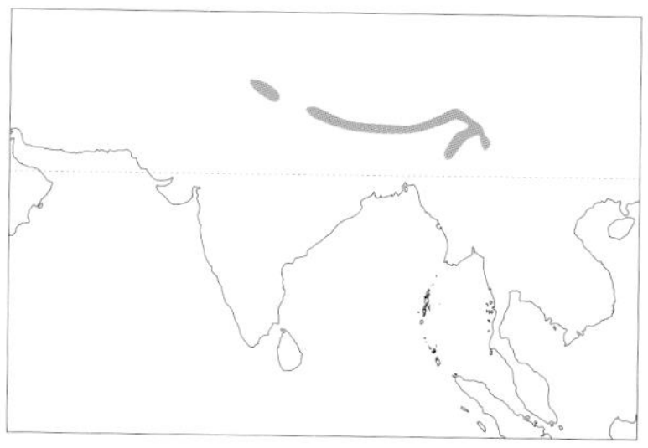

Descriptive notes. 15-16 cm; male 29-34 g, female 25-31 g. Small-headed honeyguide with bright yellow in plumage. Male nominate race greenish-grey, with yellow to gold forehead, crown and face, conspicuous yellow or orange rump patch, white on inner webs of tertials, and broad dark ventral streaks; tail appears all dark, square-ended. Female with more restricted yellow, not gold or orange-gold, on head, and yellower rump than male. Immature duller. Race *radcliffi* plainer, greyer, yellower areas less gold and orange, and reduced, vague streaking below. Voice. Little known, but apparently does not sing; calls include "weet" or "cheet", chipping notes, "tzt", and, in flight, "chaenp-chaenp".
Habitat. Rocky, wooded gorges and streams with cliffs having colonies of giant honeybee (*Apis dorsata*); usually with deciduous-coniferous forest nearby. Mainly at 1500-2300 m, but also 610-3500 m.
Food and Feeding. Beeswax a staple food; also takes insects in flight, mostly smaller than bees, though reported to take some bees. Gathers at bees' nests on rock faces, eats unguarded or exposed wax, and fallen pieces; also takes wax at abandoned nests. Groups of up to 50 may come to exposed wax source after breeding season.
Breeding. Apr-Jun. Male sets up territory along cliff face with bees' nests, drives off other males, but sometimes several males with territories if cliff extensive and has numerous bees' nests; struts, raises head, flicks wings up and down, copulates with as many as 18 females; if male absent, others take over and breed with incoming females; females visit more than one male, copulate with them. Territory sometimes defended for much of year, except when birds moulting or if numbers of young and adults seeking wax on territory become too great after breeding. Probably nest parasite, but hosts unknown. No information on eggs, incubation, nestling, or fledgling period; single report of female feeding an immature.
Movements. Some evidence for upslope, post-breeding movement, and some individuals probably migrate downslope for the winter, but few data available.
Status and Conservation. Not globally threatened. Currently considered Near-threatened. Probably extinct in Pakistan; very rare and local in India; local and uncommon in Nepal and Bhutan; rare in SE Tibet and also in N Myanmar. Conservation status perhaps merits reassessment. Lack of knowledge of this species' breeding biology, including possible hosts, and of its behaviour away from bees' nests makes it difficult to assess any threats to it; it is possible that harvesting of honey may disrupt its breeding activities in places.
Bibliography. Ali (1962, 1977), Ali & Ripley (1983), Ali *et al*. (1996), Baker (1934a), Bishop (1999a), Choudhury (2001), Cronin & Sherman (1977), Diesselhorst (1968), Fleming (1963), Fleming & Traylor (1968), Fleming *et al*. (1976), Friedmann (1976), Grimmett *et al*. (1998), Hussain (1978), Hussain & Ali (1979, 1983), Inskipp & Inskipp (1991), Poole (1995), Ripley (1982), Roberts (1991), Robson (2000), Short & Horne (1991), Smythies (1986), Stattersfield & Capper (2000), Underwood (1992).

15. Sunda Honeyguide
Indicator archipelagicus

French: Indicateur archipélagique **German**: Malaienhoniganzeiger **Spanish**: Indicador Malayo
Other common names: Malay/Malaysian Honeyguide

Taxonomy. *Indicator archipelagicus* Temminck, 1832, Pontianak, Borneo.
Closest relatives are probably *I. xanthonotus* and *I. indicator*. Thought to have derived from early Asian invasion of *Indicator* from Africa, and thus from same ancestral stock as *I. xanthonotus*; bright yellow in plumage and short outer rectrix exhibited by both Asian species, and this combination otherwise shared only with African *I. indicator*. Monotypic.

Distribution. Forest of lowland S peninsular Thailand, possibly adjacent Myanmar, and Peninsular Malaysia (except S), Sumatra and Borneo.

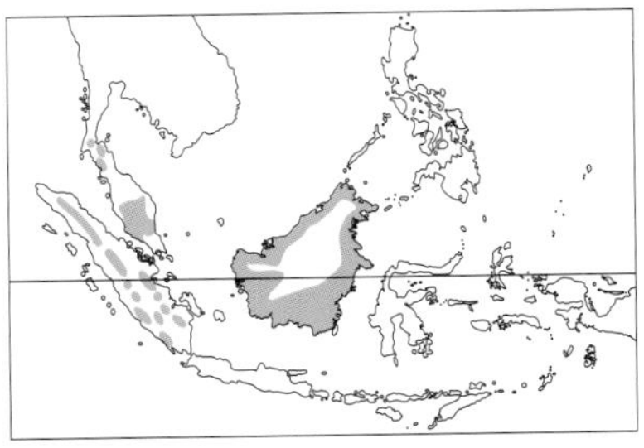

Descriptive notes. c. 16 cm; 23-38·5 g. Nondescript olive bird with pointed bill. Male dark olive-brown above, with bright yellow patch on inner leading edge of wing, some white in outer tail, often some white on rump and uppertail-coverts; white to yellow-grey below with blotchy or vaguely streaked appearance, more streaked on thighs and flanks; eye red. Female lacks yellow in wing. Immature like female, but greener above, with more white showing in rump and uppertail-coverts, more streaky or scaly below; eye brown. VOICE. Cat-like "kiaaw" given singly, or introducing trilling song lasting 1-3 (rarely 7) seconds at c. 19 elements per second; trilling-grating calls in interactions.
Habitat. Lowland dipterocarp forest, also at times adjacent cocoa plantations and gardens; associates with open-nesting honeybees (*Apis dorsata* and *A. florea*). Occurs at up to 700 m, sometimes to 900 m.
Food and Feeding. Poorly known. Eats beeswax, also insects, including some adult and larval bees; observed around bees' nests and at flowering trees with bees present. Method used to obtain wax from exposed but bee-covered plates of comb not described. May react to human presence, but does not "guide".
Breeding. Breeds Jan-Aug or Sept. Male sings from several trees in territory, stretches neck, puffs throat, may flick wings as sings. Not known if nest-parasitic, and no information on any other aspects of breeding; observations of singing suggest breeding system resembling those of Afrotropical honeyguides.
Movements. Sedentary.
Status and Conservation. Not globally threatened. Currently considered Near-threatened. Generally uncommon to rare; scarce to uncommon in Thailand and Malay Peninsula, with range contraction, now apparently absent in S Peninsular Malaysia. Known to occur in Khao Nor Chuchi (Khao Pra Bang Khram Non-Hunting Area), Thailand, in Batu Punggul Forest Reserve, Peninsular Malaysia, and in Gunung Mulu National Park, Peninsular Malaysia. Clearing of forest throughout species' range makes it imperative that information be obtained on its breeding habits, in order that any potential threats can be adequately assessed.
Bibliography. Friedmann (1976), Gibson-Hill (1949a), Glenister (1971), Gönner (2000), Harrisson (1950), Holmes (1996, 1997), Holmes & Burton (1987), Lekagul & Round (1991), MacKinnon & Phillipps (1993), van Marle & Voous (1988), Medway & Wells (1976), Payne (1986), Robinson (1928), Robinson & Chasen (1939), Robson (1988, 2000), Round (1988), Short & Horne (1991), Smythies (1999), Stattersfield & Capper (2000), Strange (2000), Wells (1974, 1985, 1999), Wilkinson, Dutson & Sheldon (1991), Wong (1984, 1986).

16. Greater Honeyguide
Indicator indicator

French: Grand Indicateur **German**: Schwarzkehl-Honiganzeiger **Spanish**: Indicador Grande
Other common names: Black-throated Honeyguide

Taxonomy. *Cuculus indicator* Sparrman, 1777, Great Fish River, Cape Province, South Africa.
Not very closely related to African congeners; perhaps closest to African *I. variegatus* and *I. minor* and Oriental *I. xanthonotus* and *I. archipelagicus*; possibly not too distant from *Melichneutes robustus*. Moderate individual, seasonal and altitudinal variation, along with mosaic pattern of geographical variation, makes racial subdivision impracticable. Monotypic.
Distribution. Sahel zone from Senegambia and S Mali across to Eritrea, S to near coast of W Africa, and S (around main forested belt) through EC Africa including E & S Zaire, much of E Africa, and from Angola, NE Namibia and N & E Botswana to Mozambique, S to Cape Province.

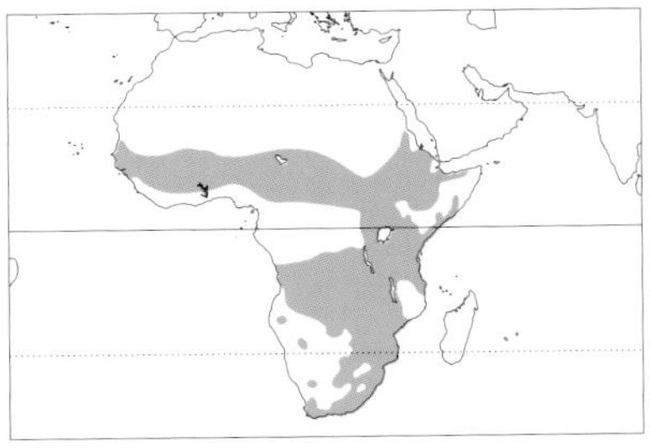

Descriptive notes. 19-20 cm; 34-62 g, mostly 40-57 g. Distinctive. Male unmistakable, brown above, with black throat, white cheeks, pink bill, yellow or golden-yellow shoulder patch, white outer-tail patches, white underparts with dark streaks on flanks; outer tail feathers short. Female duller, browner-looking, without cheek patch, has throat white (often discoloured), bill darker, pale underparts with fine flank streaks. Immature very different, olive-brown above with yellow-tipped forecrown and forehead feathers, creamy-white rump, yellow or gold on much of throat and especially breast, pearly white lower underparts lacking streaks; orbital skin blue at fledging; takes up to 1 year to gain adult plumage. VOICE. Song, usually by male, sometimes by female, soft "peew" and then series of "tor-vik" notes; loud "feee" or "feeeeer" aggressive note by immature, and by male in intense intraspecific and interspecific conflicts; also assorted piping, peeping, "tya" and noisy chattering notes that can be combined, and used variously in aggression as well as in guiding, in last case notes often doubled; chattering trills, "tya-trills" and piping with "feeer" notes may be uttered after copulation; begging calls insistent "kreeek" or "karrreeek", also variable but not host-specific. Mechanical signals include wing-rustling, bill-snapping, and "wa-da, wa-da" in aerial display by male.
Habitat. Open woods, woodland edges, bushland, streamside woods, bushes in dry areas, plantations, gardens with trees, thickets, and trees lining suburban streets; often in vicinity of bees' nests. Occurs at up to 2000 m, occasionally to 3000 m in E Africa.
Food and Feeding. Eats mainly beeswax, also grubs and eggs of honeybees, and diverse insects, including termites, winged ants, flies and others; nestling eats foods of host, including fruits. Aggressive at bees' nests, immature always superdominant; pecks at wax while standing, often carries off pieces to 10 g or more in weight. Fly-catches for insects. Leads humans to bees' nests by giving agitated chattery, piping calls; most guiders are immatures or subadults, some adults never guide; guiding behaviour very erratic, in some suburbs apparently not practised at all. Bees' nests often accessible, and frequently abandoned by bees; adults monitor several, even many, nests. Also attracted to noise of wood-chopping, and fires; follows other honeyguides. Digests wax readily, requires drinking water.
Breeding. Accords with breeding seasons of hosts; in dry areas of tropics breeds in wet seasons, in wet regions breeds in dry seasons; recorded in Apr in Sierra Leone; generally in austral spring-summer in S Africa. Male sings from one of a series of perches in singing territory, latter traditional or shifting within or between years, may give winnowing flight display in circle or ellipse over attracted female, both on territory and at feeding site. Hosts at least 1 roller (*Coracias abyssinicus*), Hoopoe (*Upupa epops*), 3 woodhoopoes (*Phoeniculus purpureus*, *Rhinopomastus cyanomelas*, *R. minor*), 4 kingfishers (*Ceyx pictus*, *Halcyon chelicuti*, *H. albiventris*, *H.leucocephala*), 8 bee-eaters (*Merops pusillus*, *M. oreobates*, *M. bullockoides*, *M. superciliosus*, *M. nubicus*, *M. hirundineus*, *M. orientalis*, *M. boehmi*), 3 barbets (*Trachyphonus vaillantii*, *Tricholaema leucomelas*, *Lybius torquatus*), 6 woodpeckers (*Jynx ruficollis*, *Campethera nubica*, *C. notata*, *C. abingoni*, *C. tullbergi*, *Dendropicos goertae*), 4 swallows (*Hirundo cucullata*, *H. semirufa*, *H. albigularis*, *Riparia cincta*), 3 starlings (*Lamprotornis chalybeus*, *L. nitens*, *Spreo bicolor*), 2 thrushes (*Myrmecocichla aethiops*, *M. formicivora*), 2 sparrows (*Passer griseus*, *Petronia superciliaris*), a tit (*Parus niger*), and a sunbird (*Nectarinia senegalensis*); other hosts likely, but may "dump" eggs, e.g. in nests of other barbets and woodpeckers, thrushes, bulbuls (Pycnonotidae), starlings and orioles (Oriolidae). Up to 20 eggs, laid in sets of up to 5, usually 1 egg per nest, frequently punctures host's eggs; incubation period unknown, short; hatchling with membranous bill hooks, lacerates and kills host's young, hooks lost in 2 or more weeks; fledges at 35-40 days, remains in trees neither returning to nest to roost nor following foster-parents; usually independent in c. 3 days. Longevity sometimes more than 12 years.
Movements. Essentially resident, but disperses to 20 km or more; regularly moves 8-10 km; juvenile disperses to 8 km or more in few days.
Status and Conservation. Not globally threatened. Fairly common, and widespread; occurs widely in the Sahel and sub-Saharan Africa, except in desert, forest and grassland; in all but desert parts of W South Africa. Probably not uncommon in Sierra Leone; status in Liberia uncertain, apparently rare; uncommon in Somalia; rather local but widespread in Kenya and N Tanzania. Reasonably adaptable in diverse habitats, and expanding into formerly forested areas. Present in numerous national parks, e.g. Murchison Falls (Uganda), Mikumi (Tanzania) and Comoé (Ivory Coast).
Bibliography. Ash & Miskell (1998), Balança & de Visscher (1997), Bannerman (1933, 1953), Barbour (1973), Barlow *et al.* (1997), Bates (1930), Benson & Benson (1977), Benson *et al.* (1971), Berruti *et al.* (1995), Bretagnolle (1993), Britton (1980), Carter (1978b), Cave & Macdonald (1955), Chapin (1939), Cheke & Walsh (1996), Chiweshe & Dale (2000), Clancey (1964), Dean (1985, 2000), Dean *et al.* (1990), Demey *et al.* (2000), Diamond & Place (1988), Dowsett (1990), Dowsett & Dowsett-Lemaire (1991, 1993), Dowsett & Forbes-Watson (1993), Dowsett-Lemarie *et al.* (1993), Dyer (1975), Earlé & Herholdt (1987), Elgood *et al.* (1994), Field (1999), Friedmann (1930a, 1930b, 1958a, 1970), Fry (1974, 1977), Fry *et al.* (1988), Ginn *et al.* (1989), Gore (1990), Grimes (1987), Haagner (1907, 1911), Hanmer (1997), Harrison *et al.* (1997), Irwin (1981), Isack (1987, 1988a, 1988b, 1998, 1999), Isack & Reyer (1989), Jubb (1966, 1968), Kingdon (1977), Lewis & Pomeroy (1989), Lippens & Wille (1976), Liversidge (1991), Mackworth-Praed & Grant (1957, 1962, 1970), Maclean (1993), Macpherson (1975), Madge & Cunningham-van Someren (1975), Ndang'ang'a & Borghesio (1999), Nikolaus (1987), Parker (1966), Payne (1986, 1992), Penry (1994), Pinto (1983), Plowes (1948), Priest (1934), Prigogine (1971), Ranger (1955), Roberts (1956), Short & Horne (1985b, 1990a, 1992c), Skead (1950, 1951), Snow (1978), Storer (1992), Tarboton (2001), Tarboton *et al.* (1987), Traylor (1963), Tucker (1975, 1976), Verheyen (1953), Wood (1940), Zimmerman *et al.* (1996).

Genus *MELICHNEUTES* Reichenow, 1910

17. Lyre-tailed Honeyguide
Melichneutes robustus

French: Indicateur à queue en lyre **Spanish**: Indicador Lira
German: Leierschwanz-Honiganzeiger

Taxonomy. *Melignomon robustus* Bates, 1909, Bitye, River Dja, Cameroon.
Closely related to *Indicator*, wherein perhaps closest to *I. indicator*, but separated generically on basis of unique tail and undertail-coverts, as well as voice and behaviour. Monotypic.
Distribution. Disjunctly from Sierra Leone and Guinea E to S Cameroon, SE Central African Republic, N Zaire and SW Uganda, S to N Angola and SC & E Zaire.

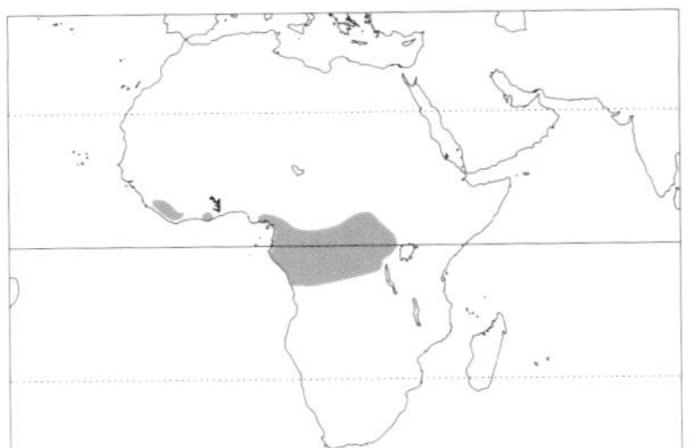

Descriptive notes. c. 18 cm; 47-61·5 g. Dull colours with unique lyre-shaped tail diagnostic. Male with outward-curling tail feathers, elongated central undertail-coverts nearly as long as longest rectrices, outermost tail feathers tiny. Distinguished from somewhat similar female *I. indicator* by slightly larger size, bronzy tinge above, distinctive tail. Female with shorter tail, but shape still distinctive. Immature darker, also with "bent" tail feathers. VOICE. In aerial display loud "pee-pee" sounds at 4-5 per second, grading into "ve-bek, ve-vek" or "kwa-ba, kwa-ba" sounds at c. 2 per second, latter apparently made by air passing through spread tail feathers, audible for 1 km; also has buzzy, chattery calls and "kutta-kutta" notes.
Habitat. Primary forest and adjacent edges, logged forest, secondary forest and plantations; attracted to bees' nests; frequents colonies of barbets of genus *Gymnobucco*. In lowlands, uncommonly to 2000 m.
Food and Feeding. Eats beeswax; also takes termites, other insects, spiders, and fig (*Ficus*) fruits. Foraging habits largely unknown.
Breeding. Season mainly inferred from aerial displays, but may display when not breeding; Oct-Dec in Sierra Leone, Nov-Apr in Liberia, Dec-Jun in most of W Africa, Sept-Nov in Nigeria and Cameroon; Dec-Mar, and more late Apr-Sept (dry season), in Gabon; Mar-Sept in Congo and Zaire. Male displays by circling upwards and diving down with wing sounds; not known if female also displays aerially. Hosts unknown, suspected are barbets of genus *Gymnobucco* and perhaps *Pogoniulus*. No information on eggs, or on other aspects of breeding.
Movements. Presumably sedentary.
Status and Conservation. Not globally threatened. Little known, and only occasionally common in and near primary forest. Distribution known partly from display sounds alone; relatively few specimens. Locally not uncommon in Sierra Leone, where 12 display-sites/km²; uncommon to not uncommon in Liberia, where 1 male/3-4 km²; display-sites c. 1 km apart in Gabon forest (1 site

1300 x 400 m). Known to occur in Taï Forest National Park, Ivory Coast, in Gola Forests Reserves, Sierra Leone, and in La Lopé National Park, Gabon. Probably rather vulnerable in places; information required on species' breeding biology and ecology.

Bibliography. Allport *et al.* (1989), Bannerman (1933, 1953), Bates (1930), Brosset & Érard (1986), Chapin (1939, 1954), Christy & Clarke (1994), Colston & Curry-Lindahl (1986), Dean (2000), Demey & Fishpool (1991), Dowsett (1989b), Dowsett & Dowsett-Lemaire (1993), Dowsett & Forbes-Watson (1993), Dranzoa (1994), Elgood *et al.* (1994), Field (1999), Friedmann (1978a, 1978b), Fry *et al.* (1988), Gatter (1997), Grimes (1987), Halleux (1994), Lippens & Wille (1976), Louette (1981b), Mackworth-Praed & Grant (1970), Pinto (1983), Prigogine (1971), Rodewald *et al.* (1994), Rougeot (1951, 1959), Serle (1957), Short & Horne (1985b), Snow (1978), Thiollay (1985a).

Class AVES
Order PICIFORMES
Family PICIDAE (WOODPECKERS)

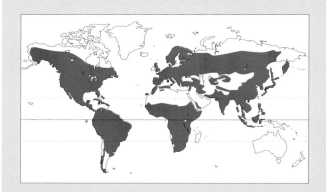

- Small to rather large birds with straight medium-length bill, short legs with four long toes, some species with only three toes; tail of most long, with strong central feathers; long tongue with barbed tip.
- 7·5-60 cm.

- Holarctic, Neotropical, Afrotropical and Oriental.
- Forest, woodland and grassland, from cold temperate zone to tropics.
- 28 genera, 216 species, 661 taxa.
- 11 species threatened; none definitely extinct since 1600.

Systematics

Fossil bones of woodpeckers are rarely found. According to S. L. Olson, the earliest examples from the Northern Hemisphere appear from the middle and late Miocene, some 16-12 million years ago and about 10 million years ago, respectively. In 2001, however, G. Mayr reported a fossil tarsometatarsus of a piciform bird from the late Oligocene of Germany, thus dating back about 25 million years. It appears similar in size and proportions to that of a modern *Dendropicos*, the Cardinal Woodpecker (*Dendropicos fuscescens*). A feather preserved in amber that was discovered on the Caribbean island of Hispaniola constitutes the oldest fossil record of a woodpecker in the New World. As reported by R. C. Laybourne and colleagues in 1994, it is at least 24 million years old, thus originating from before the onset of the Miocene, and it reveals close relationships with the extant Antillean Piculet (*Nesoctites micromegas*). Furthermore, holes found in the petrified woods of Arizona and Wyoming, which are 40-50 million years old, suggest that woodpeckers were present in the Americas at a very much earlier period.

In fact, on the basis of the DNA-DNA hybridization data obtained by C. G. Sibley and J. E. Ahlquist, one may speculate that the true woodpeckers diverged from their closest relatives at a very early stage, some 50-53 million years ago. Careful analysis of data from the mitochondrial cytochrome *b* gene and the nuclear-encoded â-fibrinogen intron 7 suggests that the piculets of the modern subfamily Picumninae diverged from the other woodpeckers 9-15 million years ago, and that the base of the Picini branch dates back to about 7·5 million years. Modern genera were probably established about five million years ago.

Piciform birds are among the oldest of all avian forms. Morphological analyses and molecular data suggest that the woodpeckers (Picidae), the honeyguides (Indicatoridae), the barbets (Capitonidae) and the toucans (Ramphastidae) descended from a common stock. Classical mophological analyses, biochemical data of proteins and DNA all support the notion that the closest relatives of the woodpeckers are the honeyguides, with which they are then linked to the barbets. Neither morphological nor molecular data supply any evidence for a close relationship with the jacamars (Galbulidae) and the puffbirds (Bucconidae), both of which have traditionally been included in the Piciformes but are now regarded as forming a separate order, the Galbuliformes. Unfortunately, all relevant analyses of morphology and molecular genetics that have been made have examined only relatively few species from each of the major groups. No study so far undertaken on these birds has

been based on a sufficiently large set of species that was properly representative of the group in terms of geographical origins and lineages. As a consequence, and because the phylogenetic relationships among woodpeckers are far from solved, as will be discussed below, it is difficult to determine precisely where the Picidae originated.

Several attempts have been made to classify the woodpeckers. None, however, has been so all-embracing and comprehensive as the monograph of L. L. Short, published in 1982, which was preceded by extensive taxonomic work on this family by that same author. Short's arrangement was adopted by Sibley and B. L. Monroe in 1990, and was also followed by H. Winkler and D. A. Christie in their 1995 monograph of the Picidae. The few DNA data available to Sibley, Ahlquist and others at the time when they conducted their genetic research into avian taxonomy had not produced any evidence conflicting with the views put forward by Short.

The system proposed by Short rests on some essential assumptions. The first of these is that specialized woodpeckers originated at several different times from more generalized ancestors. The second, and probably the most crucial one, is that the taxonomic value of external morphological and behavioural

Woodpeckers are one of the oldest avian forms, having diverged from their closest relatives as long ago as 50 million years. The largest branch of the family, with 61 species, is the Campetherini tribe, to which the Rufous-bellied Woodpecker belongs. Most members of the family are associated with trees, and representatives can be found from sea-level to high altitudes, and across every continent except Australasia, Oceania and Antarctica.

[*Dendrocopos hyperythrus hyperythrus*, Central Highlands, Bhutan. Photo: Roland Seitre/Bios]

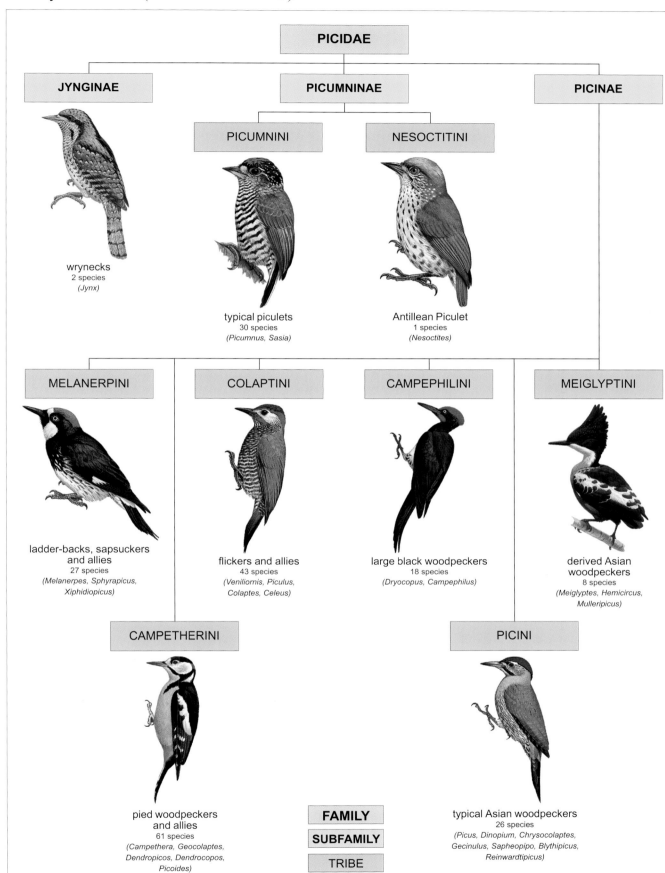

PICIDAE

JYNGINAE

PICUMNINAE

PICINAE

PICUMNINI

NESOCTITINI

wrynecks
2 species
(Jynx)

typical piculets
30 species
(Picumnus, Sasia)

Antillean Piculet
1 species
(Nesoctites)

MELANERPINI

COLAPTINI

CAMPEPHILINI

MEIGLYPTINI

ladder-backs, sapsuckers
and allies
27 species
(Melanerpes, Sphyrapicus,
Xiphidiopicus)

flickers and allies
43 species
(Veniliornis, Piculus,
Colaptes, Celeus)

large black woodpeckers
18 species
(Dryocopus, Campephilus)

derived Asian
woodpeckers
8 species
(Meiglyptes, Hemicircus,
Mulleripicus)

CAMPETHERINI

PICINI

pied woodpeckers
and allies
61 species
(Campethera, Geocolaptes,
Dendropicos, Dendrocopos,
Picoides)

FAMILY

SUBFAMILY

TRIBE

typical Asian woodpeckers
26 species
(Picus, Dinopium, Chrysocolaptes,
Gecinulus, Sapheopipo, Blythipicus,
Reinwardtipicus)

Subdivision of the Picidae

[Figure: Hilary Burn,
Ian Willis, Mark Hulme,
John Cox & Chris Rose]

data can be ascertained by careful study of the biology of the birds. Consequently, extensive field studies would allow one to discriminate between traits that are phylogenetically conservative, and hence useful as taxonomic characters, and those that are functional and thus more susceptible to convergent evolution. Anatomists have been reluctant to make such a distinction. Short was also convinced that convergence in plumage

coloration is unlikely to produce resemblance in details of colour patterns. As a case in point, he mentioned the tail coloration of South American and Asian piculets of the genus *Picumnus*. There are, however, two ways in which similar patterns can arise. One is a combination of convergence, due to similar selective forces, with parallelism, due to common ancestry and shared mechanisms of development. The other re-

Picumninae, with 31 species, and the true woodpeckers which constitute the largest subfamily, the Picinae, totalling 183 species. These three subfamilies represent deep branches in the phylogeny of the woodpeckers.

The true woodpeckers are split into six tribes. The Colaptini, containing the flickers (*Colaptes*) and allies, and the Melanerpini, which includes the *Melanerpes* species, the sapsuckers (*Sphyrapicus*) and related picids, together comprise seven genera which, with the exception of a single species, are confined to the New World. The sole exception is the colaptine Rufous Woodpecker (*Celeus brachyurus*), which lives in Asia. The Picini tribe of seven genera of "typical" Old World picids, such as the Eurasian Green Woodpecker (*Picus viridis*) and the flamebacks (*Dinopium*, *Chrysocolaptes*), occurs only in the Palearctic and Oriental Regions, while the three somewhat aberrant genera *Meiglyptes*, *Hemicircus* and *Mulleripicus* together form the tribe Meiglyptini, which is confined to southern Asia, where it is found almost exclusively within the tropics. The Campephilini includes two genera of large, mostly black or blackish woodpeckers, the "logcocks" (*Dryocopus*) and the "ivory-bills" (*Campephilus*); the latter are confined to the Americas, while the former genus is widespread in Eurasia, too. Finally, the largest tribe of all, the Campetherini group of "pied" woodpeckers and allies, occurs on all continents inhabited by the family; this is due to the fact that it contains the widespread genera *Dendrocopos* and *Picoides*, as well as the two Afrotropical genera *Campethera* and *Dendropicos*.

Short considered the Campephilini to be an offshoot of the Colaptini, while the latter tribe is thought itself to be connected with the Campetherini. The African genus *Campethera* shares many characteristics with South American *Colaptes*, *Piculus* and *Celeus*. Generally, the plumage in these two groups is often greenish and the underparts are barred or spotted, and that pattern can easily shift between bars and spots in both groups. Other details of plumage coloration, such as yellow tail shafts or malar stripes as the conveyors of sexual signals, are also shared. The greatest plumage similarities are exhibited by the young of these groups. The genera *Piculus* and *Campethera* both possess large man-

lates to the not so unlikely possibility that species of one group mimic those of another with which they are sympatric and with which they are likely to interact interspecifically. Such an argument was posited by M. L. Cody to explain the similarities between the Asian *Chrysocolaptes* and *Dinopium* and between the American *Dryocopus* and *Campephilus*.

There is no doubt that this current system poses many problems. Any changes would, of course, mean altering our views about which character states are convergent. Convergence and parallelism seem to be rather common among woodpeckers, and an analysis of molecular data may be the only method of sorting out those characters that are evidence for common ancestry. In the following paragraphs, the problems are discussed in the context of the currently accepted classification of the Picidae. Although, in the light of existing knowledge of the family, this taxonomic arrangement seems to be the most sensible one to follow, there can be little doubt that a major revision of the whole group is called for. This is indicated by several molecular studies which have been undertaken since the late 1990's. These recent investigations do not yet permit a comprehensive analysis to be carried out, but they do point out some very important findings which are worthy of further attention and discussion.

An interpretation of the correct sequence of phylogenetic events depends very much on where one places the origin of typical woodpecker features. It may be assumed that woodpecker radiation started with a rather generalized picid, one that looked and behaved like, for instance, the present-day *Melanerpes*, and that from this early non-specialist the specialists, such as *Campephilus*, derived much later. Alternatively, the "woodpecker niche" may have been first conquered by a specialist, which was the ancestor of both specialized and generalized woodpeckers. At present, a great deal more data are needed to enable one scenario to be favoured over the other.

The grouping and the gross phylogenetic relationships of the subfamilies of the Picidae seem rather clear. The two wrynecks in the subfamily Jynginae form a very distinct sister-group to the remaining woodpeckers. The latter contain two major radiations: the diminutive piculets in the subfamily

The taxonomy of the woodpeckers is complex and not well understood. The Orange-backed Woodpecker, living in the lowland forests of South-east Asia, is currently placed in a monotypic genus within the Picini tribe of predominantly Asian woodpeckers. It was previously placed in the related genus Chrysocolaptes, although it differs considerably from the latter in plumage colours, behaviour and calls. It seems likely that this handsome picid is more closely related to the Maroon and Bay Woodpeckers (Blythipicus rubiginosus and B. pyrrhotis). Further work is required to determine whether these three species would, in fact, be better combined in a single genus.

[Reinwardtipicus validus xanthopygius, West Kalimantan, Borneo. Photo: J. M. Lammertink]

The plumage differences between some picid taxa are so small that there remains uncertainty over their taxonomic status. A prime example from Africa is the Grey-headed Woodpecker, which has recently been split from the Grey Woodpecker (Dendropicos goertae), a decision by no means supported by all taxonomists. Such are the similarities in the vocalizations, plumage and behaviour of the two that field identification on the periphery of their ranges is problematic, and exacerbated by the existence of hybrids. These two species, together with the Olive Woodpecker (Dendropicos griseocephalus), form a superspecies, and all three are sometimes placed in a separate genus Mesopicos.

[Dendropicos spodocephalus rhodeogaster, Serengeti, Tanzania. Photo: Ferrero-Labat/ Auscape]

Among the polytypic woodpeckers, it is not unusual for the races to be regarded as forming two or more groups, which some taxonomists would in many cases prefer to treat as separate species. The Green-barred Woodpecker is typically divided into two intergrading groups. The "melanochloros group" contains two races which are arboreal, living in the forests and savannas of Brazil and parts of Bolivia, Paraguay and Argentina. These tend to have stronger green and yellow hues on the wings and underparts than do the more southerly races of the "melanolaimus group". The latter three, melanolaimus, nigroviridis and leucofrenatus, are generally browner above, with a white rump, have heavier black streaking on the throat, and are more terrestrial. They reside in the pampas and Chaco woodland of Bolivia, southern Brazil and Argentina, the southernmost populations being at least partially migratory. The taxonomy is complicated by the fact that members of the two different groups interbreed along the River Paraná and the River Uruguay. Many authors consider this species to form a superspecies with the Spot-breasted Woodpecker (Colaptes punctigula), which is widely distributed across northern South America. Both species, along with the Black-necked Woodpecker (Colaptes atricollis) of the Peruvian Andes, are often referred to collectively as "forest flickers"; these are sometimes placed in a separate genus Chrysoptilus, distinct from the terrestrial Colaptes flickers. To display aggression, as in this photograph, the woodpecker fans its tail feathers, directing the underside at its opponent, and flicks its wings to reveal a flash of yellow on the underside.

[Colaptes melanochloros leucofrenatus, Salado Depression, Buenos Aires, Argentina. Photo: Yves Bilat/Ardea]

Until very recently, the Eurasian Three-toed Woodpecker has been treated as conspecific with its close relative the American Three-toed Woodpecker (Picoides dorsalis), which is smaller and darker. Apart from plumage differences, however, evidence gathered from DNA analyses, as well as the considerable geographical separation of the two taxa, suggests that they should be regarded as two separate species forming a superspecies.
In addition, a number of rather distinctive races in Asia, some of them also isolated from the main range of the species, may prove to be genetically distinct. This is yet another instance in which much more research is clearly required in order to clarify the taxonomy.

[Picoides tridactylus tridactylus, Patienemi, Finland. Photo: Marc Duquet/Bios]

dibular glands, and have similar features in the tracheal and other muscles, as well as showing some similarities also to *Celeus*, and both have peculiar asymmetrical testes.

The Melanerpini, according to Short's reasoning, are derived from the same old ancestral group as the Colaptini and the Campetherini. The Meiglyptini and the Picini are more specialized woodpeckers which, like the Campephilini, are assumed to have arisen later. Their common ancestors may have been among the Campetherini, assumed to have been distributed over the whole of the Old World and to have been later replaced by their more modern phylogenetic offspring.

Recently published results of phylogenetic analyses of mitochondrial and nuclear DNA, conducted by W. S. Moore and his co-workers, have revealed some interesting data that can only partly be incorporated in the present system. Not only do these pertain to the relations among the tribes, as described above, but they also challenge the current assignment of genera to these tribes, and they may even render obsolete the present arrangement of species into genera. The most important result of these studies, and seemingly a rather robust one, is an apparent very close relationship between South American colaptine *Veniliornis* and the North American *Picoides* group, particularly the Hairy Woodpecker (*Picoides villosus*), currently placed in the Campetherini. *Veniliornis* also shares with the American *Picoides*, and with the African *Dendropicos* species, a derived anatomical condition, namely the absence of an accessory leg muscle, M. semitendinosus, that is present in most other woodpeckers. The possible taxonomic consequence would be to include *Veniliornis* in the Campetherini. The data further indicate that the ivory-bills form a clade with the melanerpine woodpeckers, whereas the *Dryocopus* species would belong to a line that includes the flickers, which themselves show some affinities with the Old World Picini. Despite the intriguing possibilities thrown up by these recent studies, there is certainly a need for DNA analyses to be carried out on more picid species, particularly Asian ones, before a new comprehensive system of woodpecker relationships and taxonomy can be built.

The two wryneck species in the genus *Jynx* probably represent an old lineage of picids that has branched off very early from the one that eventually led to the true woodpeckers. They form one superspecies with an Old World distribution. The wrynecks are cryptically coloured, with brown, grey and black patterns matching the structure of a typical bark surface. They move along branches in a rather passerine-like manner, and frequently descend to the ground. The foot is a zygodactyl, yoke-shaped, four-toed perching foot. The feathers of these sexually monomorphic birds are soft, and this is particularly true of the long tail feathers, which are more or less rounded at the tip. The short bill is somewhat curved, and pointed, with the nostrils rounded and exposed and only partly covered by feathering. The tip of the tongue is only slightly pointed and is smooth, without any barbs. Having a short, curved, pointed bill, the wrynecks cannot excavate their own nest, but they do breed in natural cavities and in old holes made by other woodpeckers.

The 31 piculets exhibit many specializations that characterize the Picidae. The feature that distinguishes them most conspicuously from other woodpeckers is the tail, which has short and only slightly pointed feathers. The plumage is soft, and is dominated by brown to greenish colours with black markings. The forehead and crown, which are more or less densely spotted and streaked, bear the signals for sexual recognition, with orange or red on males and white on most females. These tiny birds move rapidly along thin branches, and they may hammer vigorously and with persistence. In all these activities, the tail is only rarely used as a support. As with most woodpeckers, the nostrils are covered by feathers, and the bill is pointed, slightly curved on the culmen, and compressed laterally. The long tongue has a rounded tip with fine bristles. The members of this subfamily are sufficiently "woodpecker-like" to be able to excavate their own breeding holes. Their calls are not unlike those of other woodpeckers, and some species drum (see Voice). Indeed, drumming is regularly heard from several picumnines, among them the Speckled Piculet (*Picumnus innominatus*) and the two Asian species of *Sasia*, and, in the Neotropics, the White-barred (*Picumnus cirratus*) and Mottled Piculets (*Picumnus nebulosus*).

The relationships between the South American piculets and the Old World picumnines have never been thoroughly investigated. The Asian Speckled Piculet is very similar to its American congeners, with which it shares a colour pattern found in no other avian species: laterally converging white bars on the outer tail feathers and a white stripe on the central feathers. While

All 14 members of the genus Dendropicos are restricted to Africa, and most occur only in dense primary forest. As a consequence, there remain significant gaps in knowledge of their distribution and ecology, and of the relative distinctness or otherwise of various races. The race johnstoni of Elliot's Woodpecker has a much brighter plumage than that of the nominate race, and it favours the highlands of south-east Nigeria and south-west Cameroon, whereas the nominate race occupies lower altitudes in that region. The highland form is considered by some to be a separate species, but it appears to interbreed with the nominate race in Cameroon.

[Dendropicos elliotii johnstoni, Mann's Spring, Cameroon. Photo: Doug Wechsler/ VIREO]

American and Old World piculets, along with the other Asian-Neotropical relationships found among woodpeckers, which are discussed below, are certainly among the most interesting problems of avian phylogeny and biogeography.

Within the South American piculets, species limits and general taxonomy are still far from clear. Scant knowledge about the behaviour and ecology of these birds in many parts of the continent, together with considerable geographical variation within individual species and relatively frequent interbreeding, largely prevents the drawing of any firm conclusions. It is possible that these tiny woodpeckers underwent differentiation only recently, and that they are in fact all closely related and form but a few species or superspecies.

As has been shown in recent studies of the piculets of Venezuela by M. Lentino and colleagues, a greater pool of data may well change our perception of these woodpeckers in many ways. This is well illustrated by the situation regarding the picumnine *nigropunctatus*, which lives in the delta of the River Orinoco. Originally described by J. T. Zimmer and W. H. Phelps, Sr., in 1950, as a new species, *Picumnus nigropunctatus*, this very poorly known taxon was subsequently considered by Short, in 1982, to be a synonym of the subspecies *salvini* of the Golden-spangled Piculet (*Picumnus exilis*). The taxon *salvini* had been named in 1893, but with no type locality, and the single specimen had apparently been obtained in Colombia, from among skins purchased in Bogotá, the true origin of which is notoriously obscure. Unfortunately, however, very few specimens of these piculets were available at the time when Short conducted his researches, and he was able to compare only the type specimens of the two piculets; nor, it seems, did he manage to compare either with the subspecies *obsoletus* of the Scaled Piculet (*Picumnus squamulatus*). Only some years later, from 1998 onwards, were Lentino and others able to examine a relatively large series of skins of *nigropunctatus*, obtained mostly after Short's work appeared. It then became clear that the taxon exhibited several significant plumage differences from *salvini*, to the extent that to treat the two as synonymous would appear to be stretching the imagination too far. Moreover, a further twist to the tale was revealed. The form *salvini* was found to be so similar to *obsoletus* as to suggest that the two were, in fact, almost certainly referable to the same taxon. Following these careful analyses of larger sam-

many other features may be convergent owing to the diminutive size of these species, there is no obvious reason why this particular tail pattern should have evolved independently in the two groups. On the other hand, one could argue that it is very unlikely that a species which must have been separated for a very long time would not have diverged genetically to a greater extent than its present taxonomic status implies. Thus, the relationship between these geographically isolated groups of South

The two discrete racial groups of the rather dingy Brown-capped Woodpecker are frequently treated as separate species. The three races in the western "nanus group" live in the Indian Subcontinent, and have a red orbital ring but no dark malar stripe. By contrast, birds of the eastern "moluccensis group", distributed in the lower part of Peninsular Malaysia and through the Sunda Islands, have darker eyes but no orbital ring, and possess a dark malar stripe and heavier underpart streaking. At just 13 cm in length and weighing a mere 15 g, these woodpeckers are easy to overlook in the highest branches and twigs of secondary forest, plantations and parkland trees.

[Dendrocopos moluccensis nanus, Keoladeo Ghana (Bharatpur) National Park, India. Photo: Otto Pfister]

Determining the boundary line between a subspecies and a full species can be exceedingly difficult. Disputes remain over the clinal variation shown by such species as the Crimson-mantled Woodpecker, of which five races are recognized along the Andes. The photograph shows a male of the race brevirostris, which is intermediate between the northern races and the very distinct atriceps of south-eastern Peru and north Bolivia. The latter, with its black crown and duskier upperparts, could perhaps be thought a distinct species, but the existence of this intermediate race is one argument for not treating it as such.

[Piculus rivolii brevirostris, Sierra Sabanilla, Zamora-Chinchipe, Ecuador. Photo: Doug Wechsler/ VIREO]

ples, the Venezuelan researchers' suggestion that *nigropunctatus* is a genuine species, and that the type of *salvini* may well be a misidentified Scaled Piculet of the subspecies *obsoletus*, does seem an eminently sensible one.

While such stories are not so rare in avian taxonomy, they do underscore the point that much work has still to be done with regard to the systematics of the South American piculets. Similar confusion has hitherto existed, for example, in the subspecific designation within the Ochraceous Piculet (*Picumnus limae*) and between that and the Tawny Piculet (*Picumnus fulvescens*). In 1961, a new form, *saturatus*, was described from north-east Brazil, as a subspecies of the Ochraceous Piculet. Based on a single male specimen, it was distinguished from typical *limae* mainly by the intense ochre to ferruginous coloration of the underparts and neck sides. In the same year, a new species, the Tawny Piculet, was described from the same region, in this case from a female specimen. At the time, neither set of describers appeared aware of the other's discovery, which was unfortunate, since the two piculets were very similar in general plumage. Short, in his 1982 monograph, put forward the possibility that the two represented the same taxon. Meanwhile, O. M. O. Pinto, one of the original describers of *saturatus*, had stated, in 1978, that he now considered that taxon to be synonymous with *fulvescens*, which he regarded as a subspecies of *P. limae*. Pinto's conclusion had been overlooked by Short and also by later authors, including Winkler and Christie. Close examination of the specimens, along with comparison of published illustrations, does, indeed, show that the two are more or less identical in appearance, except that one is a male and the other a female; the synonymization of the two taxa seems perfectly logical. In addition, the Tawny Piculet appears not to be very much like the Ochraceous Piculet, and the relationship of the two species remains to be determined.

The merger of the single African species with two of the three Asian species in what, according to modern taxonomy, constitutes the genus *Sasia* seems to be less problematic. Nevertheless, their relationship with the other piculets remains to be studied more thoroughly. The three species of this genus possess a bare area around the eye, and they lack the white tailstripes. They are further distinguished by a very round cross-section of the upper mandible, and by having zygodactyl feet on which the first toe is

greatly reduced in the African Piculet (*Sasia africana*) and absent in the Rufous (*Sasia abnormis*) and the White-browed Piculets (*Sasia ochracea*).

By far the largest of all the Picumninae is the Antillean Piculet, which appears to be rather isolated from the other extant woodpeckers. It inhabits the Caribbean island of Hispaniola, where it, or a very similar ancestor, has lived since at least 24

One of the commoner woodpeckers in Peninsular Malaysia and the Greater Sundas, the Crimson-winged Woodpecker forms a superspecies with the Lesser Yellownape (Picus chlorolophus). In the past, it was often treated as a subspecies of the latter, which occurs at higher elevations in Malaysia and Sumatra. The two may meet at about 1000 m, although the Crimson-winged Woodpecker is only infrequently recorded at such altitudes in these areas, favouring lowland forest and plantations. There are certainly no known records of hybridization between the two species.

[Picus puniceus puniceus, near Baluran National Park, Java. Photo: Tony Tilford/ Oxford Scientific Films]

Although the Gilded Flicker is very similar to the Northern Flicker (Colaptes auratus) and, indeed, is not significantly divergent genetically from the "cafer group" of that species, it seems better to treat the two as allospecies. They appear to be segregated by their habitat preferences during the breeding season, even though they associate freely at other times of the year. Gilded Flickers live in arid scrubland and desert with large cacti, which they exploit for nesting purposes. Having excavated a hole in a live cactus, the flickers have to wait until the sap has dried before using the cavity for nesting.

[Colaptes chrysoides mearnsi,
Arizona, USA.
Photo: R. & N. Bowers/
VIREO]

The true woodpeckers assigned to the subfamily Picinae are characterized by unique features of the bill, tongue and skull, as well as by distinctive variants of the zygodactyl toe arrangement and by a specialized tail. These features and details of the moulting pattern, as well as their early development, are intimately related to the habits of these birds. These habits are typified by the foraging method, which to a greater or lesser degree includes subsurface feeding that is carried out mainly on trees, but which has in some cases changed into, or been complemented by, the digging-up of ant or termite nests on the ground (see Food and Feeding). This predominant foraging mode goes along with the birds' hole-nesting habits. Woodpeckers excavate their own nesting holes mainly into dead wood, although some ground-foraging species dig their nests into the ground (see Breeding). Woodpeckers hop bipedally along branches, and their climbing style derives from this locomotor pattern. The typical structural adaptations found in the picine woodpeckers are all connected with these habits. The central feathers of the noticeably graduated tail are strong and pointed, with especially strong shafts and vanes and with stiff barbs; they are more or less clearly curved forwards at the tip. These characteristics are most fully developed in the medium-sized to large arboreal species. The bill is usually straight, with ridges, and with a pointed or chisel-like tip. In most species, the nostrils are protected by covering feathers. The exceptionally long, extensible tongue has a barbed tip, with a high diversity of barb arrangements among species. The precise length of the tongue and the arrangement of the tongue-bones also vary greatly.

The Picinae woodpeckers are most diverse in southern Asia and in South America, but they are also widespread in the Holarctic Region and in Africa. Within this large subfamily of true woodpeckers, as already mentioned, several tribes can be recognized.

The Melanerpini comprise 27 species in three genera that are restricted to the New World. They include moderately specialized and hence very generalist and successful woodpeckers. They are able to make use of all typical woodpecker locomotory styles, and all species are excellent fliers. In fact, many melanerpines regularly cover long distances over open areas, while some are short-distance migrants and the sapsuckers are

million years before the present. Its bill is long, slightly curved and pointed. The behaviour of this odd piculet is reminiscent of that of a barbet rather than that of a woodpecker. While the Antillean Piculet certainly represents a very old stock, its relationship to other woodpecker lineages is still obscure. Until more information is available, it seems best to place it in its own tribe, the Nesoctitini.

The Andaman Islands, in the northern Indian Ocean, host a distinctive subspecies of the Fulvous-breasted Woodpecker. The noticeably pale bill, the large rounded or heart-shaped spots on the upper breast, and the prominent barring on the belly and flanks are all clearly apparent on this male. This isolated race is smaller and proportionately longer-tailed than other races, which occur from the Himalayan foothills of northern Pakistan eastwards to Java and Bali. This species is one of a handful of woodpeckers in which the females have longer wings and a longer tail than do the males, although the reason for this is not clear.

[Dendrocopos macei andamanensis,
Mount Harriet,
South Andaman,
Andaman Islands.
Photo: Ron Saldino/VIREO]

and nuts, and the occasional lizard or nestling bird. The various species either are boldly patterned in black and white with areas of red and yellow, or exhibit finer black and white horizontal barring; no clear-cut line can, however, be drawn between these two types of patterning. Sexual differences in plumage coloration are either well marked or absent, and juveniles differ from the adults more conspicuously than is the case with most woodpeckers. Sociality, living in family groups, or even in co-operative groups with complex interrelations, is widespread among the members of this tribe. In this regard, it is worth noting here that many social species of woodpecker are rather monomorphic, which is possibly an adaptation designed to reduce aggression (see Morphological Aspects, General Habits). Among the Melanerpini, however, there is no convincing relationship between the degree of sexual dimorphism and sociality, since the tribe contains completely monomorphic species, such as the Guadeloupe Woodpecker (*Melanerpes herminieri*), that are no more inclined to social living than are other species. Many melanerpine species are frugivorous, or take nuts and seeds, and the most specialized sapsucking woodpeckers are found in this tribe. Most melanerpines are not only conspicuous visually, but also striking vocally, being garrulous and loud.

The largest genus in this tribe is *Melanerpes*, containing 22 species. These were formerly split in two major groups, the "ladder-backed" *Centurus* and the boldly patterned *Melanerpes*. Between these extremes, however, many intermediate patterns occur, and the group is in all respects rather uniform, so that distinguishing several genera would not seem to be justified. Splitting would also blur the distinctiveness of the other two genera. The four species of North American sapsuckers in the genus *Sphyrapicus* are placed within this tribe because they exhibit many anatomical, behavioural and ecological similarities to *Melanerpes*. Meanwhile, there is overwhelming evidence from molecular data, too, that these birds are indeed close relatives of *Melanerpes*. They show similar colour patterns to the members of that genus, and the juvenile plumage may likewise be distinct, while sexual dimorphism is either well expressed or absent.

All *Sphyrapicus* species are more or less migratory, and the sapsucking habit is well developed. Sapsuckers show their greatest diversification along the Pacific coast of North America. An analysis of their DNA, conducted by C. Cicero and N. K. Johnson, has clarified the relationships among them, indicating that Williamson's Sapsucker (*Sphyrapicus thyroideus*) is closest to the ancestral species. The best-known of the four, the

genuine long-distance migrants. It is, therefore, not surprising that flycatching is a common foraging technique among these picids, nor that this group has successfully colonized all the major Caribbean islands, where some endemic species have also evolved. The niche breadth of these woodpeckers is further augmented by a more or less well-developed ecological and morphological sexual dimorphism, particularly on islands. The bill is long, usually pointed, and slightly to strongly curved, and can be used for excavating, for probing, and for taking fruit, acorns

No other picid exhibits such an amazing variation in plumage and size as does the Greater Flameback. This extraordinary species, which extends from western India to the Philippines, occurs as 13 races, the reddish rump being the only feature common to all. In particular, the six races in the Philippines, all smaller than the others and with red eyes, differ so much in appearance that each could be taken for a separate species. Indeed, some of these highly distinctive taxa, isolated on islands, may have evolved into full species, but DNA analysis and detailed studies of their vocalizations and ecology are required before this issue can be resolved.

[*Chrysocolaptes lucidus haematribon*, near Coto, Zambales Province, Luzon, Philippines. Photo: Doug Wechsler/ VIREO]

The two wryneck species, the only members of the Old World subfamily Jynginae, probably represent an ancient lineage of picids that branched off very early from the one that eventually led to the true woodpeckers. Although wrynecks have cryptic plumage, matching the colours of bark, they spend more time on the ground than do most woodpeckers. Some individuals of the Ethiopian race of the Rufous-necked Wryneck show extensive rufous on the underparts, as is evident in this photograph.

[*Jynx ruficollis aequatorialis*, Debre Zeyit, Ethiopia. Photo: Göran Ekström]

This photograph of a Crimson-bellied Woodpecker captures very well the position of the legs and feet when climbing. The legs are short in proportion to the size of the bird, and the feet are large and strong, with powerful, curved claws providing maximum grip, even on the smoothest of bark or, in some cases, even on telegraph poles. The fourth toe on each foot is extended to the outside of the body, counteracting the forces exerted by gravity and by the woodpecker's own pecking actions. The varied lifestyles and body size of woodpeckers, however, dictate the precise morphology. Members of the genus Campephilus are among the largest woodpeckers and need to do more than most to maintain their hold on a vertical surface. They cling to the substrate with the legs directed more outwards, and often with all toes pointing more or less forwards. A callus at the "heel" is pressed against the trunk in order to support the efforts of the claws and tail.

[Campephilus haematogaster haematogaster, Putumayo, Colombia. Photo: Luis Mazariegos]

Yellow-bellied Sapsucker (*Sphyrapicus varius*), is a widespread species. This and the Red-naped Sapsucker (*Sphyrapicus nuchalis*) sometimes hybridize in western Canada, but genetic analysis supports their status as separate species, while the Red-breasted Sapsucker (*Sphyrapicus ruber*), which also interbreeds to a limited extent with both, may be the most recently evolved member of this group.

In Cuba and its nearby islands there lives a woodpecker which has been assigned to a genus of its own. This is the Cuban Green Woodpecker (*Xiphidiopicus percussus*), a very green-looking species which, nevertheless, exhibits a colour pattern that is somewhat reminiscent of that of the sapsuckers. The latter, incidentally, migrate regularly to the Caribbean islands. The Cuban Green Woodpecker does not show some of the more derived morphological character states that are common to *Melanerpes* and *Sphyrapicus*. It lacks, for instance, a characteristic tie between certain tendons of the toes. It remains to be shown whether this indicates that this little-known species represents the remnant of an ancestral species, or whether this picid has secondarily lost these specializations again during its long, separate evolution on an island.

Within the Picinae, the largest of the six tribes is the Campetherini, comprising a great diversity of very small to medium-sized woodpeckers. It currently includes five genera, with a total of 61 species, which occur in Asia, Europe, Africa and the Americas. These picids move and behave like typical arboreal woodpeckers. They not infrequently descend to the ground, and one species has evolved into a typical ground woodpecker. The

bill is rather straight, with a pointed or chisel-like tip. The feet show the typical arrangement of arboreal woodpeckers; the first toe is of little significance, and has been lost in three of the *Picoides* species, namely the closely related and recently split Eurasian Three-toed (*Picoides tridactylus*) and American Three-toed Woodpeckers (*Picoides dorsalis*) and the similar-looking Black-backed Woodpecker (*Picoides arcticus*) of the Nearctic. The tail is moderately long, with typically strong central feathers. On most campetherine species, at least the outer tail feathers show light spots which may be fused to form large white areas.

The African genus *Campethera* contains twelve species which have the back greenish in colour. Sexual differences in coloration frequently involve the moustachial stripes and the colour of the forecrown or crown. On males, the crown is red with more or less black streaking and, in most species, there is a red moustache. Females lack the red moustache, which instead is black, or greenish-black, or spotted black and white; in addition, red on the head is restricted to the rear crown or is absent altogether, and the black crown is often spotted with white. Features related to arboreal feeding are only moderately expressed in this seemingly primitive genus. The bill is more curved than that of woodpeckers more adapted for excavating, and is therefore also mainly pointed or with only a slightly developed chisel-tip.

There has been a fair amount of confusion over the taxonomy of these Afrotropical species, some of which present real difficulties in field identification. Perhaps the greatest dilemma is that which surrounds the status of the Nubian (*Campethera*

The development of the woodpecker's tail is as crucial to its tree-climbing niche as is that of its feet. As this photograph of a Lesser Yellownape illustrates, true woodpeckers have a stiff tail, with pointed central feathers and strong barbs. The outermost rectrices are greatly reduced and probably functionless, whereas, on many picids, the central feathers are slightly curved at the tip, to allow firmer contact with the substrate. During climbing, and when the bird is alert, the tail's function is to keep the body away from the surface; only when the woodpecker is relaxed does the tail serve as an additional prop.
The lower vertebrae and the pygostyle bone are enlarged in order to provide sufficient space for the large tail muscles. It is interesting to note that the central feathers that develop on the tail of juvenile picids are shorter than those which will grow from the second calendar-year, giving the tail a graduated shape.
During the annual moult, at least in the case of the true woodpeckers, this central pair of rectrices is replaced after the other tail feathers.

[*Picus chlorolophus wellsi*, Kurunegala, Sri Lanka. Photo: T. S. de Zylva/FLPA]

nubica), Bennett's (*Campethera bennettii*) and Reichenow's Woodpeckers (*Campethera scriptoricauda*) in eastern and southern Africa. Although Sibley and Monroe recognized the three as distinct species, others have treated Reichenow's Woodpecker as a subspecies of one or the other of the first two. Indeed, Reichenow's is almost identical to the nominate race of Bennett's Woodpecker, differing only in its shorter wings, slightly smaller size and some details of the head pattern, and the two appear also to have more or less the same vocalizations. The similarities between these three picids are such that in areas where their ranges come close together, as in, for instance, Rwanda, there is disagreement over which taxon is present in some places. Further research is clearly required in this region. Although this may eventually indicate that this group involves only one or two species, the treatment of it as comprising three species may help to promote detailed studies both in the field and in the laboratory. Comparable research should also clarify the taxonomic status of the Mombasa Woodpecker (*Campethera mombassica*), some-

times lumped with the relatively widespread Golden-tailed Woodpecker (*Campethera abingoni*). In this case, however, there appear to be clear differences between the two in morphology, voice and drumming behaviour, and their treatment as separate species seems justified.

Another instance where it has been suggested that a single species should be split relates to the Green-backed Woodpecker (*Campethera cailliautii*). The western subspecies *permista* of this small but rather noisy picid is distinguished by having plain green upperparts and fully barred underparts, whereas all other races are spotted or barred above and spotted below. For some years the two forms were considered to be different species, the eastern one being referred to as the "Little Spotted Woodpecker", but the two appear to hybridize regularly across an extensive zone where they meet, from southernmost Sudan to north-west Angola.

Also wholly African are the 14 species of the genus *Dendropicos*, which also often show some greenish coloration. They seem generally to be more arboreal than the members of

A strong bill is necessary for the frequent hammering and digging activities so typical of the Picidae. The majority of woodpeckers, therefore have a long or longish bill that is fairly straight and has a broad base. In addition, the nostrils are equipped with specialized feathers to protect them from flying debris. For birdwatchers, the holes and other cavities drilled in trees provide the most visible evidence of a woodpecker's presence, especially in the case of such species as the Golden-tailed Woodpecker. This picid, although widespread across sub-Saharan Africa, is rather unobtrusive among dense trees and thickets. The greenish to brownish upperparts, usually with an element of pale barring or spotting, that characterize the genus Campethera are well shown by this female. The males of most species in this solely African genus have the entire top of the head red.

[Campethera abingoni abingoni, Kruger National Park, South Africa. Photo: Alan Wilson/Aquila]

the preceding genus, and this is reflected in the fact that they possess strong claws, and a bill that is only slightly curved. Sexual dichromatism in this genus pertains to the crown or the nape, areas which are not red on females; white frontal markings are present on females only of the Bearded Woodpecker (*Dendropicos namaquus*). As with *Campethera*, the underside may be plain, spotted, barred or streaked, and some species, notably the Fire-bellied Woodpecker (*Dendropicos pyrrhogaster*), also show extensive red coloration on the underbody. The yellow shafts of the central tail feathers are a characteristic that is common to both of these genera, and it has been used to separate them from the other brownish woodpeckers of the tribe. The yellow shafts are shared also with the African Ground Woodpecker (*Geocolaptes olivaceus*), which represents a monotypic genus having features related to its ground-foraging habits. The long and curved bill and the moderately stiff tail feathers are typical of species which forage on the ground. Compared with its arboreal relatives, the plumage colours of *Geocolaptes* are dull. It

seems most likely that the Ground Woodpecker branched off from *Campethera*. Its social behaviour probably evolved convergently with that of some of the terrestrial flickers, which also, incidentally, have flight-feathers with yellow or orange shafts.

It is worth mentioning that several authors have preferred to split the genus *Dendropicos* into three, with the Grey Woodpecker (*Dendropicos goertae*) superspecies then united with Elliot's Woodpecker (*Dendropicos elliotii*) in *Mesopicos*, and the larger and somewhat more specialized Bearded, Fire-bellied and Golden-crowned Woodpeckers (*Dendropicos xantholophus*) placed in *Thripias*. While there may be some merit in this, at least with regard to the general appearance of the taxa in question, the similarities of all are probably too great to be ignored, and merging them in a single genus, as did Short, appears to be the better option.

Within the genus *Dendropicos*, a number of issues relating to species limits still need to be resolved. In particular, the Grey-headed Woodpecker (*Dendropicos spodocephalus*) is considered

Among the common
features possessed by
the woodpeckers of the
genus Celeus are a well-
developed crest, a short
bill, and unfeathered
nostrils. The plumage
is dominated by rufous,
black, brown and cream,
or by just one or two of
those colours. In the case
of the mainly brown
species, as illustrated by
this female Pale-crested
Woodpecker, the
coloration is perhaps
related to the shady areas
of the forest in which
these picids live. Celeus
woodpeckers differ from
most others in having feet
that are not specialized for
climbing tree trunks, the
fourth toe being shorter
than the front toes. This
is probably because most
members of the genus, as
fruit-eaters, have less
need to climb vertical
trunks.

[Celeus lugubris kerri,
Bonito, Mato Grosso
do Sul, Brazil.
Photo: Edson Endrigo]

by many authors to be no more than a subspecies of the Grey Woodpecker. Although it exhibits fairly obvious plumage differences from the latter, such as a larger and brighter red patch on the underparts, the subspecies *abessinicus* of the Grey Woodpecker, which is geographically close to it in eastern Sudan and north and west Ethiopia, is intermediate in plumage. Moreover, there appear to be no differences between these two picids in their behaviour and vocalizations, and there may well be a good case for treating them as conspecific, as did Short and others.

The 34 species of pied woodpecker, lumped into one single genus *Picoides* by Short, were included by him within the Campetherini. They are widely spread over Eurasia and the Americas, while one species occurs in sub-Saharan Africa and two survived in the Palearctic enclave of northern Africa. These are arboreal, rather advanced woodpeckers of small to medium size. The bill is straight, and chisel-tipped, with strong ridges that render the feather-covered nostrils slit-like. The stiff and ventrally curved tail provides evidence of the arboreal habits of these woodpeckers. The first toe varies in length, but is usually short, and, as already mentioned, it is completely absent in three species. The plumage is patterned in black, or sometimes brown, and white. Sexual markings are found on the crown and the nape, those of the males being red or yellow, whereas the females have these areas black or brown or have the bright markings reduced in extent. In the case of some Asian species, and also the American Red-cockaded Woodpecker (*Picoides borealis*), the sexual badges are greatly reduced and are confined to small markings at the side of the crown or nape. The Red-cockaded Woodpecker is also the only species in this group that is known to be social and to be a communal breeder.

Short felt that primitive pied woodpeckers, such as the Philippine Woodpecker (*Dendrocopos maculatus*) and the Sulawesi Woodpecker (*Dendrocopos temminckii*) of Asia, show such a close resemblance to the Afrotropical *Dendropicos*, such as the Abyssinian Woodpecker (*Dendropicos abyssinicus*), that he included the whole group in the Campetherini. He also merged the former genus *Dendrocopos* with *Picoides*, which before that contained only two species, namely the Black-backed Woodpecker and the "Three-toed Woodpecker", the latter being the two three-toed picids of the Holarctic, at that time combined as one species. The loss of one toe was judged to be of minor taxonomic

significance, and not a valid generic character. The coloration, behaviour and distribution of the three-toed woodpeckers suggest a close relationship with the Nearctic and Central American Hairy Woodpecker. *Picoides*, as defined by Short, would be one of the larger bird genera, and attempts have been made to split it up into smaller units. H. Ouellet, working partly with insufficient data, did not question the close relationship between the American group and the three-toeds, but he split the other Eurasian species as *Dendrocopos*, proposing the separation of all the American species as *Picoides*. This probably does make sense. Curiously enough, in addition to the case of this analysis based on colour pattern, these two groups have never been equally represented in morphological or molecular analyses, the problem in this context being a lack of material for the Asian pied woodpeckers. Clearly, the American species form a closely knit group which is probably also monophyletic. Behaviour, vocalizations and coloration suggest that the Hairy Woodpecker, the White-headed Woodpecker (*Picoides albolarvatus*) and Strickland's Woodpecker (*Picoides stricklandi*) are close relatives, and the Red-cockaded Woodpecker appears to belong to this group, too. This grouping is also supported by DNA studies. The two South American species, the Striped Woodpecker (*Picoides lignarius*) and the Chequered Woodpecker (*Picoides mixtus*), would then form another group together with the three smaller Central and North American species, the Ladder-backed (*Picoides scalaris*), Nuttall's (*Picoides nuttallii*) and Downy Woodpeckers (*Picoides pubescens*). It is in this assemblage that molecular studies appear also to place *Veniliornis*, a genus currently included in the Colaptini.

Dividing up Short's *Picoides* further is not an easy task. To split the small Asian species from *Dendrocopos* would probably be the most sensible course. This would involve grouping the Pygmy (*Dendrocopos kizuki*), Grey-capped (*Dendrocopos canicapillus*), Brown-capped (*Dendrocopos moluccensis*), Philippine and Sulawesi Woodpeckers in a separate genus. Molecular data suggest that the three-toed woodpeckers, *arcticus*, *tridactylus* and *dorsalis*, have branched off this lineage. The medium-sized Eurasian species, such as the Great Spotted (*Dendrocopos major*) and White-backed Woodpeckers (*Dendrocopos leucotos*), seem to belong together. On the other hand, the position of the smaller Lesser Spotted Wood-

The degree of sexual dimorphism exhibited by the Picidae varies considerably, being far more marked in some species than in others. The most striking difference in plumage between the sexes is displayed by the Williamson's Sapsucker of North America. While the male, shown here, sports pied upperparts, a red throat patch and a lemon-yellow belly, the female is far less gaudy, being mostly buff with dark brown barring. For some years during the nineteenth century, the sexes were, in fact, treated as two different species. The female was first described in 1852, and the male was described five years later, in 1857, as another species of sapsucker. It was not until individuals of the two "species" were found together feeding young that scientists realized their mistake, and the male and female were then taxonomically united. Williamson's Sapsucker is, incidentally, one of the exceptionally few woodpecker species in which the adults have been documented feeding the nestlings of another species, in this case young Red-breasted Sapsuckers (Sphyrapicus ruber) in Oregon, the only US state where the two species' ranges overlap. While such behaviour, presumably a response to a strong feeding stimulus, appears to be very rare among non-passerine birds, it is not uncommon for passerines of one species to feed the nestlings or the fledged brood of another, even quite unrelated species.

[Sphyrapicus thyroideus nataliae, Rocky Mountain National Park, near Colorado, USA. Photo: S. & D. & K. Maslowski/FLPA]

pecker (*Dendrocopos minor*) remains problematic, since DNA data suggest a close relationship with the North American *pubescens* woodpeckers. Ouellet separated the Brown-backed Woodpecker (*Dendrocopos obsoletus*) by placing it with other African species in the genus *Dendropicos*. There are, however, good reasons for retaining this species with other Old World pied woodpeckers in the genus *Dendrocopos*, one of these being the coloration of the shafts. It is interesting to note that

Sibley and Monroe, in their treatise on the distribution and taxonomy of the world's birds, largely followed the classification proposed by Short for the Picidae, but they split his *Picoides* in the way suggested by Ouellet, including the latter's treatment of the Brown-backed Woodpecker. The Arabian Woodpecker (*Dendrocopos dorae*) shows many similarities to African woodpeckers and to the Asian pied woodpeckers, and its current distribution is not of much help, because it lives in an area with an avifauna in which both the Afrotropical and the Palearctic biogeographical regions are well represented. For the time being, it is probably wiser to retain it in *Dendrocopos*.

Among this array of pied woodpeckers, several taxonomic problems remain to be resolved at the species level. The Brown-capped Woodpecker, for example, may turn out to comprise a species pair. It occurs as two discrete populations, one in India and Sri Lanka and the other in Peninsular Malaysia and the Sunda Islands. Besides being separated geographically, the two groups exhibit a number of plumage differences. The Indian woodpeckers are only lightly streaked below and do not have a dark moustache, whereas the eastern ones have heavily dark-streaked underparts and a conspicuous blackish moustache; the latter also lack the red eyering shown by the western birds, which is possibly a significant difference. The South-east Asian population has been regarded by a number of authors as a separate species, the Sunda or Malaysian Pygmy Woodpecker, and further research may support this treatment.

The "Three-toed Woodpecker", in the classical conception, covers a huge Holarctic range. Recent molecular data, however, strongly urge the splitting of the North American forms as a separate species, *Picoides dorsalis*, which may also show some ecological differences from the Eurasian populations. Moreover, in Asia, the geographical isolation and distinctive coloration of the Chinese form *funebris* would probably justify its separation at the species level, and it is even possible that the isolated Alpine-Carpathian populations in Europe should be assigned species rank. In this connection, one should not be confused by the fact that A. C. Bent called the American *dorsalis* the "Alpine" Three-toed Woodpecker.

An interesting situation is presented by the Hairy Woodpecker in North and Central America. This widespread picid demonstrates spectacular clinal variation from the tropical montane part

Some members of Picidae are relatively large. In the Crimson-crested Woodpecker, a species found across the northern Neotropics, the male measures up to 38 cm in length and can weigh as much as 280 g. Even so, this is only half as heavy as the largest picids, the Ivory-billed (Campephilus principalis), *Imperial* (Campephilus imperialis) *and Great Slaty Woodpeckers* (Mulleripicus pulverulentus), *each of which can weigh 550 g or more.*

[Campephilus
melanoleucos
melanoleucos,
Hato Piñero,
llanos of Venezuela.
Photo: Kevin Schafer]

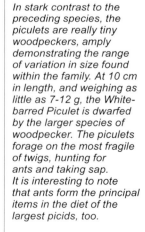

In stark contrast to the preceding species, the piculets are really tiny woodpeckers, amply demonstrating the range of variation in size found within the family. At 10 cm in length, and weighing as little as 7-12 g, the White-barred Piculet is dwarfed by the larger species of woodpecker. The piculets forage on the most fragile of twigs, hunting for ants and taking sap. It is interesting to note that ants form the principal items in the diet of the largest picids, too.

[Picumnus cirratus
cirratus,
Poços de Caldas,
Minas Gerais, Brazil.
Photo: Haroldo Palo Jr/
NHPA]

Despite having diverged from the other woodpeckers between nine and 15 million years ago, the subfamily of piculets, the Picumninae, retains many of the specializations that characterize the picids as a whole. Like the "true" woodpeckers in the subfamily Picinae, piculets have a strong bill capable of digging cavities, and a long tongue with fine bristles. Apart from their tiny size, the most obvious differences are the short tail, with only slightly pointed feathers, and the soft plumage, dominated by sombre colours. Of the 31 piculets, 27 are classified in the genus Picumnus, *found in South America but with a single species in Asia. Three others, including the two here, are combined in the genus* Sasia. *These are so short-tailed as to appear tailless. They also have a bare patch around the eye, very obvious in the African Piculet, as well as a more rounded upper mandible; as shown by the photograph of a Rufous Piculet, the first toe is more or less absent. The presence of a piculet in Africa, a continent in which the Picidae is under-represented compared with Asia and the Neotropics, is perhaps surprising. Evolving thousands of kilometres away from its congeners, the African Piculet appears to be the only member of its subfamily that avoids ants in its diet.*

[Above: *Sasia africana*, near Limbe, Cameroon. Photo: Doug Wechsler/ VIREO.

Below: *Sasia abnormis abnormis*, Danum Valley Conservation Area, Sabah, Borneo. Photo: Doug Wechsler/ VIREO]

of its range northwards to the boreal forest. Birds from the former area are small and brown-looking, while the northern populations are medium-sized and contrastingly patterned in pitch-black and dazzling white. The northernmost subspecies, *septentrionalis*, with conspicuous lines of white wing spots and pure white underparts, is markedly bigger than the plain-winged, brown-bodied form *sanctorum* from south Mexico to Panama, so much so, in fact, that the two give every appearance of belonging to different species. Nevertheless, they are connected by ten other forms of variably intermediate appearance.

The third tribe of true woodpeckers, the Colaptini, represents an almost exclusively American lineage, probably most closely related to the African members of the Campetherini. This tribe comprises four distinct genera, one of which, *Celeus*, is rather different and possibly merits higher taxonomic rank. The others are *Veniliornis*, *Piculus* and *Colaptes*. The genus *Veniliornis*, containing 13 Central and South American species, shows many similarities to the campetherine lineage, particularly to the pied woodpeckers. This has, in the past, been attributed to convergent evolution, since this genus is made up of rather arboreal species. As already discussed in some detail, a new interpretation of the phylogeny of this group may soon emerge and, when more evidence becomes available, the whole of the Campetherini and Colaptini assemblages will almost certainly have to be reshuffled taxonomically. The bill of *Veniliornis* is well adapted for excavating, as it is strong and straight, with ridges and slit-like, feather-covered nostrils. The species in this genus have green and often more or less red upperparts, a characteristic which distinguishes them from the pied woodpeckers, but is strongly reminiscent of some of the African picids. Sexual badges are revealed on the crown, which is bright red on males and dark, sometimes streaked pale olive, on females.

In the ten Central and South American woodpeckers in the genus *Piculus*, the sexual signals invariably include the malar region, and in some species the crown, sometimes conspicuously coloured in red and yellow, is also involved. Green to bronze colours predominate in the remainder of the plumage, and the shafts are yellowish to brown. These are mainly arboreal species. The bill, however, is slightly curved and rather pointed, whereas the claws are well developed. The tail, too, is moderately "arboreal-adapted", being only slightly curved ventrally. These features have led to the conclusion that this genus represents an intermediate stage between the arboreal *Veniliornis* and the more terrestrial flickers.

The flickers, combined in the genus *Colaptes*, are represented by nine species. The so-called "forest flickers", comprising the Black-necked (*Colaptes atricollis*), Spot-breasted (*Colaptes punctigula*) and Green-barred Woodpeckers (*Colaptes melanochloros*), bear a superficial resemblance to species of the preceding genus. The other six are largely or highly terrestrial,

Most woodpeckers are
sexually dimorphic in
colour, with males wearing
the more prominent sexual
badges. In broad terms,
the amount of red in the
malar region and on the
crown is the key difference
between the sexes.
The females of most
species have these parts
of the plumage dull or
blackish, as shown by this
female Scarlet-backed
Woodpecker. If the bright
colour is present on both
sexes, it usually covers a
smaller area on the
female. The Scarlet-backed
Woodpecker, found in arid
scrub along the coast from
south-west Colombia to
north Peru, is one of many
poorly known picids.
The travelling enthusiast
can still contribute much to
our understanding of these
intriguing birds.

[Veniliornis callonotus
major,
Olmos,
Lambayeque, Peru.
Photo: J. Dunning/VIREO]

and possess a long to very long, curved and pointed bill. One species, the threatened Fernandina's Flicker (*Colaptes fernandinae*) of Cuba, has the nostrils exposed and not covered by feathers. The tail is long, but is not especially stiff and curved as in arboreal woodpeckers. The feet are large, with well-developed claws, and a relatively long first toe. It is worth noting, too, that even the structure of the skull lacks the typical expression of features related to wood-working. The sexual badges of *Colaptes* are restricted to the malar region. Otherwise, the plumage is predominantly brownish in the case of the ground-dwelling species and greenish in the forest flickers. The shaft colours are yellow to orange. The flickers in general are well known for their conspicuous visual and vocal displays. The social and group behaviour of the ground-dwelling species, however, has been little investigated.

Recent molecular analyses, including of *Piculus* and *Colaptes* species, suggest, however, that these two genera cannot be upheld. It seems that the Neotropical flickers and *Piculus* may form an assemblage of closely related species that share an ancestry with the somewhat separated North American flickers. One can surmise, therefore, that *Piculus* should possibly be merged with South American *Colaptes* and that, if any generic split is to be made, it should separate the Neotropical *Colaptes-Piculus* species from the North American flickers of the *auratus* group, which were already recognized by Short as being rather different. At present, what can be stated with some degree of certainty is that the species in these two genera need to be rearranged. The North American flickers are a renowned example of interbreeding in the central-plains hybrid zone, discussed further below. The so-called "Red-shafted Flicker" and "Yellow-shafted Flicker", together with the Gilded Flicker (*Colaptes chrysoides*), were united by Short in one polymorphic and widely distributed species. These three are, however, clearly recognizable genetically, as well as ecologically.

Additional investigation should also shed light on the relationships of some of the little-known picids in the genera *Veniliornis* and *Piculus*. For example, the superspecies made up by the Rufous-winged (*Piculus simplex*), Stripe-cheeked (*Piculus callopterus*), Lita (*Piculus litae*) and White-throated Woodpeckers (*Piculus leucolaemus*) is just one case in which the currently accepted taxonomic arrangement may be found to be unsubstantiated.

Within the colaptine woodpeckers, the eleven species in the genus *Celeus* are rather distinct and probably most closely related to *Colaptes* and *Piculus*. Nevertheless, one member of the Picini tribe, the Banded Woodpecker (*Picus miniaceus*) of the Malay Peninsula and the Greater Sundas, also displays close resemblances to *Celeus*, and one could speculate that the sole Old World member of the latter genus, the Asian Rufous Woodpecker, is merely a highly convergent offshoot of the *Picus* stock. It also exhibits an anatomical resemblance to *Meiglyptes*. The main colours of *Celeus* are brown, black and cream. The various spe-

The sexual dimorphism
displayed by the Heart-
spotted Woodpecker is
unique among the Picidae
in that the female sports
the brighter colours.
The photograph shows her
creamy-white forehead
and forecrown, features
that are black on the male.
The posture of this
individual, sitting
passerine-like across a
branch high in the
treetops, is typical of the
species. Although this is a
very short-tailed picid, its
tail still has the stiffness,
the pointed central
rectrices and the strong
barbs that characterize
most members of the
family. One peculiarity
of the two Hemicircus
species, however, is the
frequent presence on
the back of a strange
resin-like substance,
the origin and function of
which remain a mystery.

[Hemicircus canente,
Goa, India.
Photo: Neil Bowman/FLPA]

Among the many endemic species on the large Caribbean island of Cuba is a woodpecker that merits a genus of its own. The male Cuban Green Woodpecker is significantly heavier than the female; indeed, males in the highlands are double the weight of lowland females. This may enable the sexes to use different techniques to exploit different sources of food, as has been shown to be so for two other Caribbean picids, the Hispaniolan and Guadeloupe Woodpeckers (Melanerpes striatus and M. herminieri). Certainly, the Cuban species' diet is variable, from large invertebrates to the eggs of other birds, including heron (Ardeidae) species.

[Xiphidiopicus percussus percussus, Zapata Swamp, Cuba. Photo: Doug Wechsler/ VIREO]

by the bill, the eye and the chin, and in one species, the Rufous-headed Woodpecker (*Celeus spectabilis*), also the sides of the crest. The male has red in these areas, whereas the female does not. Some *Celeus* species breed in the arboreal nests of social insects, and most members of this genus seem to be highly frugivorous; they will reach out a long distance from a trunk or branch to obtain fruits.

The South American species of *Celeus* have often been used as an example of the avian speciation process in Amazonia. Short grouped them according to coloration and bill shape. Recent observations indicate, however, that colours may be associated with the preferred forest stratum, the brown forms making use more of structures in the forest shade, and so they may possibly be subject to convergence. It remains to be seen, therefore, whether the Chestnut-coloured (*Celeus castaneus*), Chestnut (*Celeus elegans*), Pale-crested (*Celeus lugubris*) and Blond-crested Woodpeckers (*Celeus flavescens*) really do form a superspecies that is set apart both from the Scaly-breasted Woodpecker (*Celeus grammicus*) and Waved Woodpecker (*Celeus undatus*) assemblage and from the four other Neotropical species. In this connection, it could perhaps be significant that the Rufous-headed Woodpecker has become a bamboo specialist.

In its present composition, the tribe Campephilini holds two genera, distributed over Eurasia and the Americas. The 18 species are large picids, and are boldly coloured in black and white and a variable amount of red. Many of them possess a crest that can, in some cases, assume spectacular shapes, one example being provided by the Magellanic Woodpecker (*Campephilus magellanicus*). The members of this group are highly specialized for excavating wood, in which they chisel deep holes or pits. They forage on the trunks of large trees, and they descend to ant hills as well. Bark-scaling is a very common feeding technique.

The genus *Dryocopus* contains seven species, collectively known as the logcocks. Two of these are widely spread over the Northern Hemisphere, one in the Old World and the other in the New World. The remaining five species are found in the south-temperate, subtropical and tropical regions. Those living in South and Central America almost completely overlap in range with the eleven species of the genus *Campephilus*. The rare Helmeted Woodpecker (*Dryocopus galeatus*) seems to be a good intermediate between *Dryocopus* and *Celeus*, and hence between the Campephilini and the Colaptini. It has a slightly curved bill which

cies have a greater or lesser degree of barring, and possess a crest that is more or less well developed. The bill is not long, and in most cases is curved, while the nostrils are not covered by feathers either in the Neotropical species or in the one Asian species, whereas they are covered in the Picini. The feet also reveal that these woodpeckers are not specialized trunk-climbers and that they do little excavating. The fourth toe is shorter than or equal to the front toes in length; the first toe is short, as it is on most picids. The Asian species has the fourth toe reduced the most. Sexual dichromatism affects mainly the region enclosed

A common feature of many woodpeckers is the possession of a crest, although this tends to be most obvious on the very largest species, such as this White-bellied Woodpecker. The crest is erected both during courtship display and in aggressive postures, but it is not always instantly apparent to the human observer which message is being conveyed. The crest is frequently raised when the woodpecker alights on a perch, and is lowered only when the bird feels secure and is ready to start foraging.

[Dryocopus javensis javensis, Sumatra, Indonesia. Photo: Alain Compost/ Bios]

is narrow and pointed, and exposed nostrils, whereas the other species of the genus *Dryocopus* have a straight bill with a well-developed chisel-tip and nostrils covered by feathers. The tail feathers are long, and curved forwards ventrally, and the central pair has strong and pointed tips. The front toes and the fourth toe are of about the same length, with the first about half their length. Visual sexual differences involve the amount of red on the crown and the malar region.

Otherwise referred to as the ivory-bills, the large woodpeckers of the genus *Campephilus* are all crested, and their sexual badges are found mainly on the crown and affect the crest coloration and the malar region. The chisel-tipped bill is long and straight, with the nostrils well protected and covered by feathers. The tail is long and stiff, and curved forwards near the tip, where the feathers are strong and pointed. All the toes are long, the fourth significantly longer than the front toes. They are directed forwards when climbing, and the tarsus may then closely touch the substrate. This genus, incidentally, houses the two picids which are the most critically endangered of all woodpeckers. These are the Imperial Woodpecker (*Campephilus imperialis*) and the Ivory-billed Woodpecker (*Campephilus principalis*), both of which may well already be extinct (see Status and Conservation).

Morphological as well as molecular data suggest that this tribe is not monophyletic at all. *Campephilus* may have branched off from the basal melanerpine lineage. This genus shows some similarity in hind-limb musculature to the southern Asian flamebacks of the genus *Chrysocolaptes*, but it differs from them morphologically in many other aspects. *Dryocopus*, on the other hand, may share an ancestry with the colaptine clade, with the Helmeted Woodpecker providing a link with *Celeus*. Foot morphology, feeding habits and vocalizations, including instrumental signals, would support this interpretation, and the many similarities between these two groups of large woodpeckers could be seen as being due to convergence and, possibly, social mimicry. It remains to be shown how the Black Woodpecker (*Dryocopus martius*), which occurs across chiefly northern Eurasia, and the White-bellied Woodpecker (*Dryocopus javensis*), confined to the more southerly parts of Asia, relate to the monophyletic American *Dryocopus* species, because they, too, differ in behaviour and vocalizations. The diet of the logcocks

consists mainly of ants, whereas the *Campephilus* ivory-bills seem to forage mostly for large beetle larvae.

With seven diverse genera, the Picini represent a great Eurasian radiation of woodpeckers. Some similarities in plumage and behaviour suggest that this group shares a common ancestry with the Colaptini, particularly with *Celeus*. Convergence in the features involved may be considerable, however, and, as in other cases of woodpecker systematics, a combination of traditional methods with the techniques of molecular biology will certainly help towards a better understanding of the relationships.

Within the tribe there are two genera which each contain only one species. The first is *Reinwardtipicus*, which shows some overall similarities to *Chrysocolaptes*, but morphologically and behaviourally seems to be closer to *Blythipicus*. It was separated from the former genus by Short. Both the Bay Woodpecker (*Blythipicus pyrrhotis*) and the Maroon Woodpecker (*Blythipicus rubiginosus*) are brown to reddish-brown in colour and more or less barred on the back, this coloration being most likely an adaptation to their gloomy habitat, indicating that colour may, after all, be a less useful diagnostic character. Both also have a rather long bill that is straight and chisel-tipped, and the nostrils are protected by feathers. The tail is short and has stiff central feathers, which also are curved forwards at the tip. As with other arboreal woodpeckers, the first toe is short. The rather inconspicuous sexual markings affect the sides of the nape.

Similar features and habits characterize the other monotypic genus, *Sapheopipo*, occurring only on Okinawa, an island in the Ryukyu Archipelago in the western Pacific. Its bill is slightly curved, although chisel-tipped, and the nostrils, as those of *Blythipicus*, are covered by feathers, but the tail is longer and softer than that of the latter. The fourth toe is rather long. Males have the crown and forehead feathers tipped red, and the sides of the nape are red as well. D. Goodwin, who based his 1968 classification of the Picidae on the general appearance and coloration of museum specimens, argued that this peculiar insular species is a direct descendant of the White-backed Woodpecker, a *Dendrocopos* species which is represented on other Pacific islands of the region by some distinct subspecies. Indeed, the morphology of the Okinawa Woodpecker (*Sapheopipo noguchii*) does show some similarities to the *Dendrocopos* woodpeckers.

Many woodpeckers are adorned with a crest, the prominence of which varies according to species and, in particular, with the degree of excitement of the individual. The Celeus *species of the Neotropics are all rather obviously crested. This female Blond-crested Woodpecker, as it raises its crest in an alert or aggressive posture, reveals the elongated feathers of the nape that make up this appendage.*

[*Celeus flavescens flavescens*,
São Paulo, Brazil.
Photo: Edson Endrigo]

Several members of the genus Picus *have a scaly-looking pattern on the underparts. This is particularly well marked on the aptly named Scaly-bellied Woodpecker, which inhabits deciduous and pine forests at high altitudes on the Himalayan slopes, from Afghanistan to Darjeeling. This strong scaly appearance is produced by broad black submarginal lines on the feathers, these being clearly apparent in this photograph of a male. This noisy woodpecker frequently forages on the ground, having little option when it ventures beyond the tree-line, but it also obtains much of its insect food by pecking and hammering on trees.*

[*Picus squamatus squamatus*,
Sete, Nepal.
Photo: Otto Pfister]

Although the majority of woodpeckers are sexually dimorphic, the Picidae tend to exhibit fewer plumage and morphological differences than do birds of many other families. Furthermore, it has been suggested that, with the woodpeckers, sexual dimorphism is less marked among the social species, but there seem to be too many exceptions to this concept for it to be a likely phenomenon. For most woodpecker species, the sexes are differentiated by the colour of the malar stripe or, as in the case of the Yellow-fronted Woodpecker, the top of the head: whereas the male has the crown and nape red, the female is black in these areas. Some other features distinguish the sexes, although these are generally not discernible in the field. The most common differences are in body length and bill size. Males are usually larger, and this can often be assessed when pair-members are seen together, as in this photograph. There are, however, some exceptions: female piculets tend to be larger than the males, and the same is true of some pied woodpeckers. Sexual dimorphism is not simply a means by which the males and the females can recognize one another; it can also have ecological repercussions, with the sexes exploiting different parts of the territory when foraging, and adopting different feeding techniques. These differences are also reflected in characters of the bill, feet and tail.

[Melanerpes flavifrons, Itatiaia, Rio de Janeiro, Brazil. Photo: Edson Endrigo]

Sexual dimorphism is clearly apparent in these photographs of Cream-backed Woodpeckers and Golden-green Woodpeckers, both from South America. The former species is relatively unusual in that a large area of the female's head is red, although the male shows a great deal more of this colour. The female Golden-green Woodpecker, on the other hand, lacks red altogether, having a very different head pattern from that of her mate. The latter species also illustrates the great geographical variability found within some of the Picidae. Across its range, from east Panama to northern Argentina, it occurs in nine distinct races, the largest of which, capistratus in north-west Amazonia and polyzonus in south-east Brazil, are up to 80% heavier than the nominate race, shown here. The sexual badges can vary, too: males of the race paraensis in north-east Brazil do not have the red malar stripe exhibited by males elsewhere in the species' range. The typical colours in a woodpecker's plumage result from carotenoid pigments: astaxanthin and doradexanthin are responsible for red, while lutein, zeaxanthin and cryptoxanthin account for yellow and green colours. The so-called picofulvins are distinct picid pigments that produce the yellow colour of some species.

[Above: *Campephilus leucopogon*, Pantanal, Mato Grosso, Brazil. Photo: Haroldo Palo Jr.

Below: *Piculus chrysochloros chrysochloros*, Pantanal, Mato Grosso, Brazil. Photo: Hubert Klein/Bios]

A typical woodpecker of the subfamily Picinae has ten primaries, eleven secondaries and twelve tail feathers. The outer primary is much shorter than the others, and the outermost tail feather is greatly reduced in length, as is demonstrated in this photograph of a flying female Grey-faced Woodpecker. The characteristically bounding flight comprises a series of rapid wingbeats interspersed with brief gliding on closed wings. Some of the bigger species, however, especially the large logcocks (Dryocopus) and ivory-bills (Campephilus), have a more sustained flapping flight, not unlike that of crows (Corvidae). A similar direct flight, but with more rapid beats, is adopted by the smaller Dendrocopos and Picoides species when pursuing rivals.

[Picus canus canus, near Rosenheim, Germany. Photo: Marianne Bracht]

The largest genus of the Picini, *Picus*, includes 14 species, one of which, the Grey-faced Woodpecker (*Picus canus*), has a very wide distribution extending right across the northern Palearctic and through the Oriental Region. Ground-feeding is common among the members of this group, and ants form the typical diet. The corresponding adaptations are a straight to slightly curved and more or less pointed bill, and a long tongue. The tail is long and stiff. The fourth toe is of about the same length as the front toes, and the first toe is about half their size. The general plumage coloration is partly or mainly green, often with barring below. Sexual colour dimorphism is reflected in the crown and/or the moustachial stripe. Some *Picus* species have a conspicuous crest, as typified by the yellownapes of southern Asia.

Dark greenish colour, sexual markings on the crown, and a small crest are also the characteristics of the two *Gecinulus* species, both of which are bamboo specialists. The short bill is slightly curved, but the chisel-tip and the rather broad base indicate that these two woodpeckers frequently hammer. The nostrils are covered with feathers. The tail is soft and broad, which may be a secondary adaptation for climbing on bamboo. These picids possess three toes of about equal length.

The two remaining South Asian genera of the Picini, *Dinopium* with four species and *Chrysocolaptes* with two, are sympatric in many areas. The bill of *Dinopium* is short to moderately long, curved, and pointed to slightly chisel-tipped. It is long, straight, strongly built and chisel-tipped in *Chrysocolaptes*. The slit-like nostrils are only partly covered by feathers in *Dinopium*, but are fully concealed in *Chrysocolaptes*. The genus *Dinopium* has a tail that is fairly soft, long and somewhat curved, whereas the tail of the *Chrysocolaptes* species is much stronger, particularly in the central feathers with their stiffened and pointed tips. The fourth toe is slightly shorter than the front toes in *Dinopium*, which has a first toe that is short to very short and rudimentary and, in two species, has been lost altogether. By contrast, the two *Chrysocolaptes* species have the fourth toe long and more forward-directed, and the first toe is moderately long.

The dominant plumage colours in both genera are green, red, golden to yellow, black and white, and all six species are crested. The array of species and subspecies of these two structurally rather different genera reveal many parallels in coloration, rendering them rather similar where they exist in sympatry. Sexual colour differences pertain to the crown in both groups, and also affect the moustachial area in *Dinopium*. When examined closely, it can be seen that this particular region of the head is also differently patterned in the two genera, with the black stripes in different positions.

Besides the striking parallelism, the group poses some difficult taxonomic problems. These relate essentially to the populations that are presently included in one polymorphic species, the Greater Flameback (*Chrysocolaptes lucidus*). These populations exhibit a spectacular range of bright plumage colours, which could suggest that these mainly insular forms constitute separate species. The variation affects not only the colour of the back, which may be greenish-golden to red, but also the head and the neck, which show a variety of bold patterns of red, yellow, black and white. All populations, however, have in common a red lower back and rump. This is clearly a situation where genetic analyses could greatly improve our understanding of the taxonomy of the different forms.

Apparently old and therefore strongly differentiated and aberrant Asian woodpeckers form the Meiglyptini. Because of their rather odd shapes and colours, they do not seem to have much in common. This tribe comprises eight species, ranging in size from very small to very large, in three genera. The few characters which they share are a thin, long neck, a bulky body and a relatively small head. Some species possess fine spots on the head and neck or a contrasting white crown, plumage features that are not found in any other woodpecker.

The genus *Meiglyptes* consists of three small brown, black and white species. The short bill is curved and pointed, and the nostrils are only partly covered by feathers. The feet, with the fourth toe about as long as the front toes, are of the typical picid type. The tail, on the other hand, is somewhat aberrant, since it is rather short. Both sexes have a crest on the relatively small head. Sexual differences are restricted to a red moustachial stripe or patch on the males, which is absent on females.

United in the genus *Hemicircus* are two rather small species which are predominantly black and white in colour and, as *Meiglyptes*, are also crested. The bill is of medium length, rather straight, and chisel-tipped, indicating strong pecking habits. The tail appears even shorter than that of the preceding genus, but it is stiff and is slightly bent forwards near the tip. The fourth toe is longer than the front toes, and the first is about half the length of the fourth. The males of the Grey-and-buff Woodpecker (*Hemicircus concretus*) have much red in the crest, whereas the females show only traces of cinnamon or red. The sexual dimorphism exhibited by the other species, the Heart-spotted Woodpecker (*Hemicircus canente*), is unique among woodpeckers in that the male has a black face, crown and crest, while the female's forehead and frontal part of the crown are white.

Finally, the three species of *Mulleripicus* are medium-sized to large picids which have a rather small head on a conspicuously thin and long neck. A very slender and sparsely feathered neck is, incidentally, found also in the *Dryocopus* logcocks. The bill of the three *Mulleripicus* woodpeckers does not show the specialized features related to excavating, being long, slightly curved and only slightly chisel-tipped. The nostrils are fully covered by feathers. The long tail is bent forwards towards the tip, and is stiff. The fourth toe is shorter than or as long as the front toes, and is about twice the length of the first toe. These somewhat unusual picids have a grey to black general coloration, with the head and neck finely spotted with white. The females lack any red, whereas the males either possess a red moustache or have red colour encompassing the malar region, the forehead and the orbital area. The large size of these three woodpeckers, together with some anatomical similarities to the genus *Dryocopus*, suggested to earlier authors a close relationship between the two genera.

The biogeography of woodpeckers presents many interesting aspects and problems. It is, of course, intimately linked with the problem of the phylogeny of the group. The *Picumnus* piculets are most diverse in the Neotropics. It seems sensible, therefore, to assume that they have a Neotropical origin, which leaves the origin of the one Asian species, the Speckled Piculet, rather mysterious. There can be little doubt that the melanerpine woodpeckers represent a successful American radiation. The exact area of their origin may lie somewhere between northern South America and southern North America. The phylogeny of the Campetherini, on the other hand, poses many problems, such that their geographical origin, too, is uncertain. It seems certain that the name-giving genus *Campethera* is African and has radiated on that continent. The same can be assumed for the *Dendropicos* woodpeckers. There is no reason to doubt that the *Colaptes* and *Piculus* woodpeckers are of American origin, but the relationships between this group and *Celeus* have not yet been firmly established. The position of the Rufous Woodpecker, the sole member of *Celeus* in the Old World, where it is spread over large parts of southern Asia, clearly needs to be reanalysed as well. If the latter's position in the currently accepted system is upheld, one is left with almost exactly the same problem as that with the *Picumnus* piculets. In both cases, lowland South America may have been a secondary centre of diversification, and the relative species richness may be a misleading clue as to the ancestral area of the two groups. *Campethera* and the Colaptini probably go back to a common geographical origin, and would thus represent an example of the relationships between the tropical African and South American avifaunas. The *Campephilus* ivory-bills are clearly American, too. Much less clear, however, is the biogeography of the other large and, in many respects, similar woodpeckers currently placed together in *Dryocopus*. Even if one assumes that this genus, as it is conceived today, is monophyletic, its present distribution could be explained equally well with a Eurasian or an American origin, so long as phylogeny is not considered.

Short, in his major 1982 monograph of the group, favoured a New World origin of the Picidae. Known fossils and the high diversity of species in that part of the world could be mentioned in favour of this hypothesis, which is further supported by the fact that the primitive piculets, possibly *Campephilus* and the generalist melanerpines may all have an American origin. If one accepts this view, then the wrynecks would have invaded the Old World rather early, and without leaving a trace in the New World. The hypothesis rests on a number of suppositions, including, among other things, the current view concerning the

Many woodpeckers have a barred pattern on the wings and tail, this being particularly striking when the bird is seen in flight. As revealed by this Lesser Spotted Woodpecker leaving its hole in a dead stump, the barred effect is produced by regularly spaced rows of large, rather rounded spots on one or, often, both webs of each feather. Although competent fliers, the vast majority of picids are more or less sedentary, making only short-distance dispersive movements. Some of the normally resident species, however, occasionally undertake longer migrations. Lesser Spotted Woodpeckers living in the cold northern parts of the Palearctic, for example, sometimes turn up as far south as the Black Sea.

[*Dendrocopos minor buturlini*, Provence, France. Photo: Guy Bortolato/Bios]

The woodpecker tongue is one of the most remarkable of anatomical structures to be found among birds, enabling the family to exploit food resources beyond the reach of most other vertebrates. The key features of the tongue are its length and the specially structured tip, along with the sublingual glands, which produce a sticky fluid. Associated with this are long, specialized muscles which enable the woodpecker to extend and retract the tongue, while controlling the movements of its tip. When the special tongue muscles contract, the structure becomes stiff. The tip of the tongue of typical woodpeckers is equipped with backward-pointing barbs, arranged in single rows, loosely spaced, or in dense, brush-like rows, according to species. In some picids, such as the Black Woodpecker, the barbs are grouped in clusters of three to five. In others, they are present along the whole tip of the tongue, while in certain species, such as the Middle Spotted Woodpecker (Dendrocopos medius), they are concentrated at the extreme tip. Those picids which carry out much of their foraging on the ground have thinner and shorter barbs, a good example of this being the Eurasian Green Woodpecker. For these terrestrial foragers, the tongue functions more as an adhesive stick than as a spear, and its tip is rounded rather than pointed.

[Above: *Dryocopus martius martius*, Dachau, Germany. Photo: Alfred Limbrunner.

Below: *Picus viridis*. Photo: Kim Taylor/ Bruce Coleman]

With their numerous morphological adaptations, the Picidae are well suited not only for climbing on trunks, but also for grasping smaller branches and twigs, and for moving on flatter substrates. The Rufous-winged Woodpecker, for example, frequently forages high up in the thinner branches of trees, but also at lower levels, where it climbs up or along large limbs and trunks; it prefers the interior of forest rather than edges, the individual here having been photographed inside humid tropical forest. Similarly, the Red-crowned Woodpecker, found in deciduous habitats, forages at various heights, but prefers the middle and lower levels; it is just as capable of climbing on tree trunks as it is of grasping twigs just a few millimetres wide in the upper canopy. One species well adapted to a life spent mostly on the ground is the Eurasian Wryneck. Lacking the stiff tail of other woodpeckers and without the specialized feet, it favours more open habitats. The individual shown here, photographed while on migration through the Middle East, presents the typical view that an observer is likely to obtain of the species.

[Above left: *Piculus simplex*, Guácimo, Limón, Costa Rica. Photo: Marco Saborío]

Above right: *Melanerpes rubricapillus rubricapillus*, Venezuela. Photo: Neil Bowman/FLPA]

Below: *Jynx torquilla*, Eilat, Israel. Photo: Alan Williams/ NHPA]

phylogeny of woodpeckers, and the assumption that generalists were at the baseline of their evolution.

The Oriental Region is, however, as likely a candidate for having been the first centre of woodpecker radiation. There, the major groups are very distinctly differentiated, but they have remained largely confined to the Oriental Region. If these woodpeckers represent an old stock, one has to explain from which lineages African and New World species derived. If the Picidae originated in America, then the Asian radiation was possibly more recent, the particular lineages must have diverged substantially

in a short time, and they may have replaced woodpeckers that represented the ancestral America-derived forms.

Africa is relatively poor in woodpeckers and lacks large species. This would seem to rule out the possibility that the Picidae have originated on that continent, although similarities with some of the smaller capitonid barbets have been noticed. It should be borne in mind, however, that the particular history of Africa and its forests, which generally harbour a comparatively less diversified avifauna, may obscure old biogeographical relationships. Relatively high geomorphological stability and the presence of a rich barbet fauna may have hindered extensive radiation of woodpeckers. One could easily imagine that African ancestors of the Campetherini produced offshoots that led to a South American as well as an Asian radiation. The two groups may then have met again in North America and in north-east Asia.

The "Out of Africa" hypothesis suggested here, which should be considered as seriously as the preceding ones, posits that both the Oriental and the New World radiations are secondary, with the former being the older one.

From all that has been discussed here so far, it should be quite evident that, among the Picidae, numerous taxonomic problems remain to be resolved, at several levels. Some of these have already been mentioned above, but there are many others, particularly with respect to species limits, and involving taxa in virtually all genera. For example, the north-west African form *vaillantii* of the Eurasian Green Woodpecker is frequently treated as a separate species, the "Levaillant's Woodpecker", primarily on the basis of some plumage differences, although these are largely bridged by the Iberian subspecies *sharpei*; yet some authors consider that *sharpei*, too, merits the status of a full species. The relationship between these picids and the Japanese Woodpecker (*Picus awokera*), which is closer in appearance to *vaillantii*, as well as between those and the allopatric Scaly-bellied Woodpecker (*Picus squamatus*) of south-central Asia, has yet to be satisfactorily determined. Similar problems surround some of the South-east Asian forms of *Picus*, the field identification of which can be far from simple.

Another example concerns the small *Dendrocopos* taxon inhabiting the Sulu Islands in the Philippines. This has recently been deemed by some authors to be a distinct species, *Picoides (Dendrocopos) ramsayi*, since it differs very markedly in plumage from the Philippine Woodpecker; it has also been reported to differ vocally from populations on the other islands. While there may, therefore, be a good argument for considering *ramsayi* a full species, it would seem more prudent to conduct additional research into the situation, including further investigation of its relationship with the Sulawesi Woodpecker.

In a 2000 review of its checklist, the American Ornithologists' Union divided Strickland's Woodpecker into two species. This was based on differences in morphology, behaviour and habitat between the isolated southern populations and the birds in the rest of the range. This split may yet prove to be warranted, but there do seem to be several important similarities between the two groups, in voice and ecology, for instance. This is just one more example of the need for additional research on the taxonomy of the Picidae.

New molecular methods of analysis have revived the discussion on species concepts and, as a logical consequence, the delimitation of species. As the preceding paragraphs have shown, many of these problems are relevant to the woodpeckers. Picids which range over huge areas may be split into different species on the basis of some more or less arbitrary genetic criteria. Small insular populations are a special problem. They occur among widespread species such as the Eurasian Three-toed Woodpecker, the Great Spotted Woodpecker and the White-backed Woodpecker, and they are particularly enigmatic in South-east Asian species such as the "pygmy woodpeckers" and the Greater Flameback. The most interesting cases, however, are those in which adjacent putative species form contact zones that contain hybrids. For the woodpeckers, such zones are relatively well known and studied. They involve closely related species. Aside from these relatively common cases of hybridization, rare cases of possible hybrids between more distantly related forms have been found, as well.

Hybrids between subspecies are known among the piculets, and in the Campetherini, the Colaptini and the Picini. Included in this list is the best-known hybrid zone of all woodpeckers, namely the one which runs through North America and which separates the western and eastern forms of the Northern Flicker (*Colaptes auratus*). The western form, *cafer*, commonly referred to as the "Red-shafted Flicker", sports a black moustache and a red nape, whereas the eastern, nominate form, the "Yellow-shafted Flicker", has the red moustache but no red on the nape. The two were for a long time treated as separate species. As their colloquial names indicate, they differ also in the colour of the shafts of the wings and tail, the feathers of which, on the underside, are, furthermore, of the same colour as the shafts. These two subspecies frequently hybridize in the region where their ranges overlap, in a zone that runs from Texas and Oklahoma north to Saskatchewan and westwards through British Columbia to Alaska. The mating behaviour of the flickers in this hybrid zone, which appears to have been stable for centuries, is still puzzling.

The structure and composition of forest habitats determine the fortunes of woodpeckers. Most species thrive in primary forest, but fewer cope with the modern methods of forest management. The Middle Spotted Woodpecker inhabits temperate forest in Europe, where its requirements are such that its population density is determined by the supply of dead wood and oaks (Quercus). The rough bark of oaks harbours the small arthropods, such as beetles and caterpillars, that the species favours. Meanwhile, old trees with soft, dead parts are essential for this small-billed woodpecker to excavate a nest-cavity.

[Dendrocopos medius medius, Ruppiner Schweiz, near Berlin, Germany. Photo: Bengt Lundberg/ Bios]

The dense forests of the world's highest mountain range host several woodpeckers, the commonest of which is the Himalayan Woodpecker. This hardy species lives among extensive conifer stands and in oak (Quercus) and rhododendron (Rhododendron) mountain forest above 2000 m, at times ascending beyond the tree-line. It can also be found in mixed forest with junipers (Juniperus). For the Himalayan Woodpecker and several other picids, trees are themselves an important source of protein. These arboreal foragers, which only rarely descend to the ground, use anvils in which to break open pine cones for the seeds, an important food in winter.

[*Dendrocopos himalayensis albescens*, Dachigam National Park, Kashmir. Photo: Gertrud & Helmut Denzau]

In some parts, in the south, hybrids seem to be more viable, and no assortative mating has been documented, adults showing no clear preference for mates of their own colour type. Extensive data on a northern population of flickers, however, did show assortative mating. Hybrids can easily be scored according to plumage characters. One study demonstrated that individuals of the same colour are more likely to mate than are differently coloured ones. This remains true even when the fact that "Red-shafted Flickers" breed a little later has been taken into account. The major reason for the stability of the hybrid zone and the distinctiveness of the subspecies involved may be purely ecological, with each subspecies best adapted to its regional climate and vegetation.

Among the Picidae, it is not so unusual for hybrids to occur also between species, mainly those which are considered to be members of the same superspecies. They are found among South American piculets, as, for example, between the White-wedged Piculet (*Picumnus albosquamatus*) and subspecies of the White-barred Piculet. In the case of the Campetherini, hybrids are known between the Little Green Woodpecker (*Campethera maculosa*) and the Green-backed Woodpecker, between the Great Spotted and the White-winged Woodpeckers (*Dendrocopos leucopterus*), and between the American Ladder-backed and Nuttall's Woodpeckers. In the Neotropics, the Little Woodpecker (*Veniliornis passerinus*) and the Dot-fronted Woodpecker (*Veniliornis frontalis*) sometimes hybridize, as also do the Chestnut and Pale-crested Woodpeckers, as well as two of the logcocks, namely the Black-bodied (*Dryocopus schulzi*) and the Lineated Woodpeckers (*Dryocopus lineatus*). In Europe, hybrid pairings are occasionally reported also between the largely sympatric Grey-faced and Eurasian Green Woodpeckers.

An interesting example of interbreeding is provided by the Syrian Woodpecker (*Dendrocopos syriacus*) in the Palearctic Region. This species occasionally hybridizes with the Sind Woodpecker (*Dendrocopos assimilis*) at the south-eastern rim of its range, in Iran, and it also hybridizes now and then with the Great Spotted Woodpecker, a species that it meets more frequently since its rather recent range expansion. Dynamic range shifts are a relatively frequent cause of hybridization in the melanerpine woodpeckers, including the sapsuckers. The Golden-fronted Woodpecker (*Melanerpes aurifrons*), for example, has only re-

cently moved into Oklahoma, where it occasionally interbreeds with the Red-bellied Woodpecker (*Melanerpes carolinus*); the two seem not to interbreed, however, in Texas, where they meet in a zone that reaches from the Gulf coast northwards to Oklahoma. Red-breasted and Red-naped Sapsuckers interbreed occasionally, although they are distinctly different in coloration. Their hybridization reflects both close genetic relatedness and the secondary contact after the last glaciation.

Gene flow within species is important when it comes to maintaining genetic diversity. It relies on dispersal, and is compromised when the range of a species is very fragmented. This is the case with the Red-cockaded Woodpecker. In this species, movement between colonies is associated with reduced availability of roosting cavities, and seems to be sufficient for the exchange of genes within populations. Overall genetic diversity is, however, low, and gene flow is about adequate to counterbalance genetic drift. All the same, the population as a whole is highly fragmented, and individual populations have already attained notable genetic differentiation.

Morphological Aspects

The size range of woodpeckers is not especially noteworthy when compared with that of other non-passeriform birds, although extant species vary from as little as about 7 g in the case of the tiny piculets up to about 570 g in the largest species, such as the Great Slaty Woodpecker (*Mulleripicus pulverulentus*) and the Ivory-billed Woodpecker. This wide range of sizes permits woodpeckers to live in many different habitat types, and segregation by size may also be an important factor for the co-existence of sympatric species (see Habitat).

The typical picid's morphology features many distinct characteristics, all of which reflect the fundamental habits of these birds of excavating wood, removing bark, and probing deeply into crevices and bore holes, among other things, as well as climbing on vertical surfaces. They include a strong, mostly straight bill, a reinforced skull, a perching foot modified for climbing, and a stiffened tail. The tongue of woodpeckers has undergone many important modifications, rendering it one of the most remarkable anatomical structures to be found among birds.

The Magellanic Woodpecker is just about the largest picid in South America, where it is confined to the Andes of south Chile and adjacent parts of south-west Argentina. In this rather inhospitable climate, it flourishes in the mature forests of southern beech (Nothofagus) and cypress (Cupressus) that grow in the foothills of the Andes Mountains. Washed by heavy rains from clouds that develop over the Pacific Ocean, these forests gather luxuriant coats of mosses and lichens, in which the Magellanic Woodpecker probes for adult beetles and grubs. Despite its large size, it is able to cling skilfully, almost in the manner of a tit (Paridae), to the thinnest of branches. This imposing woodpecker, which can be seen from sea-level up to the timber-line, generally requires big trees, such as this Araucaria, in addition to which it appears to favour areas with an undergrowth of bamboo. It sometimes strays from its preferred habitat into more open woodland, and will also visit disturbed forest, but it seems to be far more at home in relatively quiet tracts of forest.

[Campephilus magellanicus, Conguillo National Park, southern Chile. Photo: Günter Ziesler]

Those woodpeckers which carry out a lot of excavating are armed with a straight bill, strengthened with longitudinal ridges, and with a chisel-like tip. The pecking action wears off the horny tip in such a manner that the tip maintains its chisel shape. The species which undertake a greater amount of probing or earth-working have a bill that is longer and slightly decurved. This makes it more appropriate for probing and for exerting biting force at the tip. Nevertheless, even the bill of the most specialized excavators is still well suited for a strong grip, thereby enabling the woodpecker to tear away pieces of wood or bark and to carry large food items, including fruits, seeds, pine cones and nuts. In other words, the adaptations for pecking do not compromise other bill actions. That fact certainly contributes much to the great behavioural and ecological versatility of the group.

A straight bill with a wide base is, on its own, far from sufficient to explain the ability of woodpeckers to hammer and dig into hard, live wood repeatedly and for lengthy periods of time. There are more highly specialized structures associated with the skeletal part of the bill and with the skull. The hinge between the foremost point of the skull and the upper mandible, or maxilla, is folded inwards. As a consequence, when the bill strikes a hard surface, the bone there experiences a tension rather than compression. The impact of the blow would normally rotate the upper jaw upwards. This potentially dangerous movement is prevented by the protruding overhanging frontal part of the skull. Because the blow produces tension, it can be counteracted by a special muscle. This action of this muscle is therefore an important means by which the shock is absorbed. Its efficiency in this is greatest when the bill is straight and when its line of action coincides with that of the muscle. Since it runs below the braincase, the latter does not experience the direct shock wave of the impact. The head moves in a straight line and, consequently, it is not subject to rotational forces on impact. The relatively small size of a woodpecker head, as compared with that of a human, also prevents destructive forces from building up when the bill decelerates at a rate of more than 1000 g. The ear is another organ that is very sensitive to mechanical shock, and woodpecker ears show some special features that may be related to the greater protection needed. The round window of the inner ear is less than half the size of that of other birds, its membrane is very thick at one end, and the columella has two basal plates instead of one.

Many of the particular morphological characteristics of the Picidae are associated with hammering. Among them are the neck muscle M. longus colli and features associated with it, such as elongated hypapophyses of vertebrae 10-15, which serve as insertion points for the neck muscle, and fused sublateral processes of vertebrae 6-10, which form gliding channels for the tendons of this muscle. The fact that highly specialized excavators occur in several different woodpecker lineages may explain why some derived character states are present in groups that are seemingly not closely related.

The nostrils of most picid species are protected by special feathers, and in the most specialized woodpeckers they are slit-like, lying under a ridge. In the two wrynecks in the genus *Jynx*, the feathering only partly covers the nostrils. A similar condition is found in the African Ground Woodpecker and in two Asian genera, *Dinopium* and *Meiglyptes*. The nostrils of the four *Dinopium* woodpeckers are close to the culmen, in contrast to the slit-like and feather-covered nostrils of the similar-looking *Chrysocolaptes* pair of picids. In the case of woodpeckers of the genus *Celeus*, and also one of the *Dryocopus* logcocks, the Helmeted Woodpecker, there are no feathers at all covering the nostrils. As a general rule, nostrils that are close to the culmen are found in ground-foraging species and in those which only rarely excavate, whereas the nostrils are far apart in species that hammer regularly and frequently.

The tongue is the most important tool for woodpeckers which probe deeply. Its length, the specially structured tip, and the associated sublingual glands, which produce a sticky fluid, determine its actions and functions. Woodpeckers can protrude and retract the tongue with ease, while at the same time being able to control the movements of its tip. For such actions, long, specialized muscles are required. These muscles insert in places very

The mature boreal forests that extend right across the northern parts of the Northern Hemisphere are inhabited by a number of woodpecker species. A typical picid of the spruce (Picea) and fir (Abies) stands of the European taiga is the Eurasian Three-toed Woodpecker, which survives well in these forests, even in the snowy conditions of winter. Farther east, in the Siberian taiga, it lives predominantly in larch (Larix) forest. When breeding, this woodpecker prefers rather dense, shady forest with plenty of dead trees and fallen timber, where beetle larvae are easier to obtain. At other times, however, it frequently moves into more open habitat, seeking out exposed parts of trees, and visiting trees that have been blown over or have fallen under the weight of snow. During these periods, this woodpecker not uncommonly occurs in concentrations at sites where food is available in good quantity. The female shown here was one of 30-40 Eurasian Three-toed Woodpeckers which gathered in more open woodland in the Oulu area of west Finland, at the top end of the Gulf of Bothnia, during the winter of 1998/99. It is interesting that in parts of eastern Europe, such as Poland, where there are larger remnants of natural forest, this species is just as likely to be found in wet ash-alder (Fraxinus-Alnus) stands or in oak-hornbeam (Quercus-Carpinus) woodland as in pure coniferous stands.

[Picoides tridactylus tridactylus, Oulu, Finland. Photo: Jari Peltomaki/ Windrush]

Big trees are an important element of the habitat for many of the Picidae, especially the bigger species. The commonest large picid of the northern Amazon Basin is the Red-necked Woodpecker, a male of which is shown here. Although more than 30 cm long, this handsome woodpecker is nevertheless dwarfed by the huge trees of the lowland rainforest. Here, these birds forage for beetle and moth larvae in the upper trunks and limbs beneath the canopy, often of the same trees in which smaller woodpeckers utilize the lower storeys. Within its exclusively South American range, which extends west to Ecuador and south to central Bolivia and the northern Mato Grosso region, this species is most commonly encountered in rainforest, terra firme *forest and* várzea *forest, but it can* also be found in cloudforest, in light second growth, and in riverine woodland in savanna regions.

[*Campephilus rubricollis rubricollis,* near Approuague River, French Guiana. Photo: Thierry Montford/ Bios]

One factor behind the success of the woodpeckers is that closely related species can exploit different resources. Nowhere is this better illustrated than in the Amazon rainforest, where the two Celeus species depicted, the Cream-coloured Woodpecker and the Ringed Woodpecker, live side-by-side. The Cream-coloured Woodpecker, one of the most brightly plumaged of the family, is found in swampy areas, along the edges of rivers and forest pools. The slightly larger Ringed Woodpecker also lives in the rainforest, but it much prefers tall trees in tall forest, where it is a far more elusive species. The fact that these two close relatives are able to co-exist in the same areas says much about the abundance of food in such habitats, where both species take fruits and seeds, as well as ants. The Cream-coloured Woodpecker, incidentally, is one of many picids which exhibit a wide degree of individual variation, as well as a number of intermediate populations which are difficult to assign to a particular subspecies. The male shown here, with extensive brown colour on the wings, has an appearance much closer to that of the race tectricialis, which intergrades with the nominate race in the area in which the photograph was taken; moreover, the nominate race is so variable that it is hardly practicable to attempt a subspecific identification.

[Above: *Celeus flavus*, Serra dos Carajás, Pará, north-east Brazil.
Photo: Luiz Claudio Marigo.

Below: *Celeus torquatus torquatus*, Las Claritas, Bolívar, south-east Venezuela.
Photo: Bernard Van Elegem]

A few woodpeckers are equally at home in coastal scrub and mangrove as in inland forest. The Streak-breasted Woodpecker, for example, inhabits broadleaved evergreen forest in the southern parts of Myanmar and adjacent Thailand, but in the south of its small range, which reaches only to the central Thai-Malay Peninsula, it is perhaps more likely to be found in coastal habitats. This female is foraging for ants on a lateral branch above the mud of a mangrove forest. Interestingly, the closely related Laced Woodpecker (Picus vittatus), *which is sometimes considered conspecific, also nests and feeds in these same coastal habitats, even where the ranges of the two overlap, in Tenasserim and western Thailand.*

*[*Picus viridanus, *Krabi Bay, south Thailand. Photo: Bernard Van Elegem]*

different from the insertion points usually found in birds. They sheath the long hyoid bones that provide the necessary stiffness of the total structure. These bones are elongated and thin towards the posterior end and, hence, are flexible. The degree of flexibility of the tongue is modulated by muscle action, so that, when the special tongue muscles contract, the structure becomes stiff. The long bones are wound around the back of the skull; they meet in the frontal region, or, in species with a very long tongue, they enter the bill at the nostril cavity. In some species, the hyoids do not enter the nostrils but are, instead, wound around the right eye. Among the American woodpeckers, this latter condition is incipient in the White-headed Woodpecker and fully developed in the Hairy Woodpecker. It is shown also by the two *Hemicircus* species of southern Asia, one of which, the Heart-spotted Woodpecker, exhibits the development of the condition most spectacularly. Not only do all of these species probe extensively, but they are also strong excavators. The adaptations for the latter activity leave no room for an extension of the hyoid horns and their muscles into the bill, hence this unique solution. In various picid species, the tongue has become shorter as a secondary adaptation. Examples of this are the sapsuckers and the White Woodpecker (*Melanerpes candidus*) of America.

Members of the subfamily Picinae, the true woodpeckers, have the tip of the tongue equipped with a few to many backward-pointing barbs. The number and the particular shape of these are rather variable among species, and reflect their functions. They are arranged in rows of single, loosely spaced barbs, as in, for example, the Neotropical *Piculus* and the Eurasian *Picus*, or in dense to brush-like rows, as in, for instance, *Campephilus*, some *Melanerpes*, *Sphyrapicus* and the Asian Rufous-bellied Woodpecker (*Dendrocopos hyperythrus*). In some cases, the barbs are grouped in clusters of three to five, a condition exhibited by species of *Picumnus*, *Campethera*, *Dendropicos*, *Dendrocopos* and *Veniliornis*, among others. They may occur along the whole tip of the tongue or be concentrated at the extreme tip. Examples of picids with barbs mainly at the very tip of the tongue include the Neotropical Golden-olive Woodpecker (*Piculus rubiginosus*) and, in Europe, the Middle Spotted Woodpecker (*Dendrocopos medius*) when compared with its more widespread congener the Great Spotted Woodpecker. The barbs become thinner and shorter in those species

which carry out much of their foraging on the ground. For these picids, the tongue functions more as an adhesive stick than as a spear, and its tip is also rounded rather than pointed.

In the head of a woodpecker, three particular types of gland can be found. The maxillary gland is usually relatively large, and is characteristic of the family. It is situated in the floor of the orbit and is easily confused with the nasal gland, located nearby. This latter gland is close to the nasal cavity in most picids. In the wrynecks and the piculets it enters the orbital region, which is reminiscent of the condition found in passerines. The largest gland, however, is the mandibular gland, without doubt the most characteristic feature of the picid glandular system. Its size may be reduced in some species, as a secondary specialization in the more habitual excavators. By contrast, species which secure their prey by using the tongue as a glue-stick possess large glands.

A particularly large oil-gland has been found in the Chestnut-coloured Woodpecker of Central America, although why this species should possess a bigger gland than do other picids is not certain. A similarly unexplained phenomenon involves two congeneric picids from the southern parts of Asia, the Heart-spotted and the Grey-and-buff Woodpeckers, on both of which a peculiar resin-like substance is not uncommonly present in the plumage of the back. Rather surprisingly, it has not been possible so far to trace the origin of this substance back to specific glands or, indeed, to any other source, and its provenance remains a mystery. Possibly associated with this is the fact that woodpeckers give off a characteristic strong, resinous odour. It has been suggested that this is connected with their food, although H. Sick maintained that the odour originated from the plumage, perhaps from oils produced by the uropygial gland, or even from the feathers themselves. Certain species, such as the Blond-crested Woodpecker and some populations of the Chestnut Woodpecker, seem to emit a more intense odour, but there seems to be no obvious explanation of why this should be so.

The legs of woodpeckers are short, with strong feet and powerful, curved claws. The tarsus and the toes are covered with well-developed, overlapping scales. The picid foot derives from the yoke arrangement, or the zygodactyl foot, found in many perching birds such as the parrots (Psittacidae), the cuckoos (Cuculidae) and the puffbirds, and in the more closely related barbets. When woodpeckers climb, however, the arrangement

*Although typically associated with trees in fairly open country, and common in plantations and in built-up areas, Syrian Woodpeckers will also take advantage of more unusual habitats. Some individuals of this opportunistic species make frequent visits in winter to reedbeds, a habitat also utilized by Great Spotted and Lesser Spotted Woodpeckers (*Dendrocopos major *and* D. minor*). The reed seeds, and invertebrates concealed within the plants' stems, can be an important factor in the survival of local populations, especially in such areas as northern Greece, where other food sources may be scarce during hard winter weather.*

[*Dendrocopos syriacus*, Tel Aviv, Israel. Photo: David Tipling/ Windrush]

of the toes takes on a different pattern, the fourth toe then being extended laterally to the outside. This enables the woodpecker to counteract the pulling forces that are exerted by gravity and by its own pecking actions. The first toe, or hallux, is not of much use in this situation and has consequently been lost in several species, including about 20% of individuals of the Himalayan Flameback (*Dinopium shorii*), all Common Flamebacks (*Dinopium javanense*) and Olive-backed Woodpeckers (*Dinopium rafflesii*) and the two *Gecinulus* species of Asia, as well as, of course, the Eurasian and the American Three-toed Woodpeckers along with the closely related Black-backed Woodpecker. The toe directed backwards may help to counteract turning moment at the foot and, together with the tail, assists in keeping the bird's body clear of the substrate. In the large ivorybills, all toes are needed in order to negotiate the substantial gravitational forces; they are all four directed forwards, and the function of the hind toe, now no longer available, is probably taken on by a special pad located at the "heel" of the tarsus of these species.

It is not only the skull and the legs that show adaptations which relate to the pecking and climbing habits of the Picidae. The rib cage, too, exhibits such particularities. The more a woodpecker species hammers for its living, the wider are its ribs. The first sternal rib is least wide in the Eurasian Wryneck (*Jynx torquilla*); that of the American Three-toed Woodpecker, when scaled with femur length, is more than five times as wide as the wryneck's.

The list of morphological adaptations for tree-climbing would be incomplete without those found in the tail. With the exception of the wrynecks and the piculets, all woodpeckers have a stiff tail with pointed central feathers and strong barbs. In many tree-climbing species, the tail is curved ventrally at the tip. It is relatively soft and broad in the bamboo-climbing *Gecinulus* species. In the three short-tailed *Meiglyptes* "buff" woodpeckers, the Buff-rumped (*Meiglyptes tristis*), Black-and-buff (*Meiglyptes jugularis*) and Buff-necked Woodpeckers (*Meiglyptes tukki*), the tail is rather soft and lacks the typical woodpecker features. It is picine-like, however, in the latter's similarly very short-tailed relatives, the black-and-white *Hemicircus* species, both of which frequently excavate. Typical modifications of the woodpecker tail include the enlarged pygostyle bone and caudal vertebrae,

enabling the powerful tail muscles to insert there. The tail itself is more or less stiff, the central feathers especially having very rigid shafts in the case of the specialized climbers. Woodpeckers possess six pairs of tail feathers, the outermost of which is greatly reduced, in some species to a tiny feather, and is probably functionless. The central rectrices show the characteristic pointed tips and are reinforced by longitudinal ridges, which strengthen the shafts, while the barbs are curved. The vanes are therefore concave, so that the tip of each central feather makes firm contact with the substrate.

When a woodpecker clings to a vertical surface, the tail and the feet act together. The tail's function during active climbing, and even when the woodpecker is stationary and alert, is to keep the body away from the tree surface. The feet provide the pull and thrust during active climbing and when the bird is at rest. Only when the woodpecker is relaxed does the tail serve as an additional prop. It is also important during hammering, because then the forces that tend to push the woodpecker away from the tree are especially strong and have therefore to be overcome by the joint action of feet and tail.

Woodpeckers ascend a tree by means of essentially bipedal hopping. A single hop consists of two phases: a power stroke, and a very brief floating in mid-air. At the beginning of the first phase, the bill points upwards in the direction of the intended movement and the woodpecker pushes itself up along the surface, keeping the front part of the body and the head close to the substrate; at the very last moment, the tail is lifted. Then, in the second phase, the grip of the feet is relaxed, the tail is held parallel to the surface, and for a split second the woodpecker is suspended in the air, without any contact with the substrate; at the same time, the feet are brought forwards in a rapid movement and they take hold of the surface, against which the tail is also once again braced. There is a continuum between this specialized vertical hop-climbing and hopping on horizontal surfaces. Interestingly, the three most specialized ground-living species, the Ground Woodpecker of South Africa and two Neotropical picids, the Andean Flicker (*Colaptes rupicola*) and the Campo Flicker (*Colaptes campestris*), walk with alternating strides.

Collectors of specimens have quite frequently remarked that the skin of woodpeckers is tough compared with that of other birds of similar size. This may be an adaptation that allows them

Throughout the world, habitats created by humans or influenced by their activities are exploited by a variety of woodpecker species. Indeed, some picids have adapted extremely well to the expansion of the human population since the nineteenth century. A good example from North America is the Red-headed Woodpecker, which is widespread in the United States east of the Rockies. Not only will this attractive picid use artificial nest-sites, such as buildings and pumps, but it also feeds in gardens throughout the year. This applies both to resident populations and to those breeding in the northern and north-western parts of the range, many of which move south-east after the breeding season. This species, the most omnivorous of the Picidae, is a frequent visitor to suburban gardens and woodlots, where it generally has easy access to a wide variety of food items. The adult shown here was feeding on cherries, one of many soft fruits consumed in large quantity by this woodpecker in the autumn. Juvenile Red-headed Woodpeckers are duller than the adults, having a brown head and some dark bars in the white wing patch. The red plumage of the head is acquired gradually, and by late winter most are very like the adults, but dark bars are often still present on the secondaries of immature birds in the ensuing spring.

[Melanerpes erythrocephalus, Marion County, Illinois, USA. Photo: Richard Day/ Oxford Scientific Films]

An arid desert is not,
at first sight, the most
obvious habitat for a
woodpecker, but a small
number of picids have
adapted to living in areas
that many bird species
would find too inhospitable.
The diminutive Ladder-
backed Woodpecker of
the south-west United
States is one such
species, being a typical
inhabitant of very arid
country and deserts.
Its southern races, which
live in northern Central
America south to
Nicaragua, are more likely
to be found in dry pine-oak
(Pinus-Quercus)
woodland, but do occur
locally in clearings in
humid forest; more
surprisingly, this rather
shy species also lives in
mangroves in El Salvador
and Honduras.
The dominant plants in the
desert habitat are cacti,
which provide a nest-site
for Ladder-backed
Woodpeckers, as well as
two sources of food:
the fruit of the cactus, and
a variety of small insects
and their larvae. These
woodpeckers also forage
among yuccas (Yucca),
as well as in low scrub
and occasionally on
the ground.

[Picoides scalaris
cactophilus,
Rio Grande Valley,
Texas, USA.
Photo: Tom Vezo]

to deal better with well-armed insects such as ants, and it is interesting to note that the Picidae share this dermal characteristic with the honeyguides, which are regularly subjected to the risk of bites and stings by Hymenoptera.

Only a few picids have body parts that are bare of feathers. Extensive areas of bare orbital skin occur in *Sasia* piculets and in some true woodpeckers, the latter being mainly melanerpines. They consist primarily of bare eyerings, which can be orange-yellowish to blackish, and which are duller and different in colour on juveniles. Often accentuated by striking plumage coloration, this bright orbital-skin colour adds to the striking facial patterns found among many melanerpine woodpeckers. The orbital rings of other species are narrow and exhibit a wide range of colours, from red in the case of some piculets to greenish and bluish in picine woodpeckers. Iris colour varies among species. In addition, it differs between juveniles and adults, changing for example from grey to whitish in some species, such as some melanerpines, and from brown to crimson in Great Spotted Woodpeckers.

The typical body feathers of woodpeckers in essence do not differ from those of other birds. A unique feature of the woodpeckers, however, is the curved or scimitar shape of the basal cells of the barbules of the contour feathers. The afterfeathers are variable in length, with a very short aftershaft. Picids are generally naked upon hatching and, moreover, they do not develop natal downs; instead, they grow a plumage of contour feathers resembling the ones found on the adults. As with other birds, the feathers are arranged in well-defined tracts of growth, the whole arrangement being referred to as pterylosis. A featherless area along the crest of the head and circular bare areas on the temples are features characteristic of woodpeckers.

Within the Picidae, the coloration of the plumage varies moderately among species and genera. Black and brown, white, red and green are the dominant colours. In most cases, the more conspicuous colours are seen on the head and neck, where sexual badges and specific juvenile colour patterns are concentrated.

Plumage colours may be adaptations to habitat characteristics, governed by intraspecific communication, or the result of social mimicry. They may be conservative in nature and be best explained in terms of a phylogenetic origin, or they may signal that the species in question is unpalatable to potential predators.

Tests of the latter hypothesis, using Great Spotted Woodpeckers, failed to corroborate it. Adaptation to habitat characteristics, whereby the bird achieves camouflage through the matching of its plumage with the background, is probably widespread, although corresponding quantitative data are lacking. The most convincing example of a cryptic pattern is certainly that of the two wrynecks. Dull and brown colours are found in species that occur deep in the shade of the forest understorey, as typified by the Bay Woodpecker in the Malay Peninsula and the Greater Sundas, and they may also be prevalent among picids that spend much time on brown-coloured bark or similarly brown substrates such as ant nests, as do various species of *Celeus*. Bright colours and stark contrasts are least conspicuous in the upper forest strata, and in open woodland. The various black-and-white patterns found for instance in the *Dendrocopos* and *Picoides* pied woodpeckers, and which are also rather common among the melanerpines, may serve as appropriate examples. Woodpeckers which frequently descend to the ground, on the other hand, are generally less brightly coloured, having the head not strongly marked, and the plumage generally dominated by brown, grey or greenish colours. In many cases, these largely terrestrial picids are barred, and have a pale, white or bright yellowish, rump that is conspicuous when the bird takes off. These birds, when seen from above, are perfectly camouflaged against their background, as demonstrated supremely by a Eurasian Green Woodpecker foraging on a grassy meadow.

Several instances exist of species of different genera showing parallel variation wherever they occur sympatrically. This is best illustrated by the case of the *Chrysocolaptes* and *Dinopium* flamebacks. Both genera contain red-backed and golden-tailed forms, and sympatric subspecies of these two different genera have the same colour of the back. All subspecies of the Black-rumped Flameback (*Dinopium benghalense*) and the Common Flameback that are sympatric with the more widespread of the two *Chrysocolaptes*, the Greater Flameback, possess the red rump of the latter. The black-rumped subspecies of the former are not sympatric with red-rumped Greater Flamebacks. The large *Dryocopus* and *Campephilus* woodpeckers, which are structurally well separated from each other and yet often strikingly similar in plumage pattern, are perhaps another example of social mimicry. There have been two different hypotheses put forward

One of only three woodpeckers that can truly be described as terrestrial, the Andean Flicker is common in the grasslands of the Andean puna, where it thrives at altitudes of up to 5000 m. These wary birds also venture into the humid shrubland of the páramo, feeding in broken, rolling country. The long bill, constituting 15% of the total length, is used to obtain larvae from deep beneath the soil surface. Andean Flickers even nest on the ground, where they dig a metre-long tunnel in an earth bank, although natural holes in rocky cliffs are also utilized. They often excavate roost-holes in the walls of abandoned native houses.

[Colaptes rupicola rupicola, Lauca National Park, north Chile. Photo: Andres Hinojosa Morya]

to explain this intriguing phenomenon. One is that competition between such pairs is intense, because the two species involved are closely related and similar in behaviour; similar plumage patterns would help to maintain interspecific territories. The species are, however, not related sufficiently closely for them to hybridize. The other hypothesis assumes "aggressive mimicry". In this case, the two different species would not match each other in strength, but, on the contrary, one species would be superior and aggressive and the other one timid. The mimicry by the latter would protect it from interference by the former, because the would-be aggressor would not dare to attack an opponent that looks like a conspecific and is likely, therefore, to be its match and to involve it in a costly fight. Scattered evidence supports the second hypothesis. In either case, if this type of resemblance concerns close relatives, parallel development of the same colour pattern is not a difficult process to conceive. These cases may become more convincing examples of convergent evolution when phylogenetic relationships have been clarified (see Systematics).

Some species are polychromatic. This means that, in a single population, various types of coloration occur. One could take as an example the *Dryocopus* woodpeckers of South America. There, the Black-bodied Woodpecker may have a white scapular stripe, but there are some individuals which lack this pattern. These forms occur close to another species of the same genus, the Lineated Woodpecker, which is represented there by the subspecies *erythrops*, and in this subspecies we find a similar polychromatism. The significance of this variation is not at all clear, but it may be related to aggressive mimicry, as discussed in the previous paragraph.

Intraspecific variation reveals the lability of certain patterns. Breast and belly spots can easily be replaced by streaks, and crown coloration, too, is variable, as also is that of the back. A ladder-like patterning as opposed to a plain-coloured back is found, for example, in subspecies of the Grey-capped Woodpecker, the White-backed Woodpecker and Strickland's Woodpecker.

The dark parts of the plumage of many campetherine species exhibit an iridescence, a phenomenon caused by regular micro-structures in the feathers. In experiments using ultraviolet spectroscopy, the wing feathers of the Great Spotted Woodpecker were found to reflect UV radiation. The red, yellow and green colours so characteristic of many woodpeckers are due to carotenoid pigments. In particular, astaxanthin and doradexanthin are responsible for red, and lutein, zeaxanthin and cryptoxanthin for yellow and green colours. The so-called picofulvins are distinct picid pigments and account for the yellow of some species.

Irrespective of the normal variation within species, occasional instances of aberrant plumage also occur within the Picidae. Perhaps the least rare of these are examples of woodpeckers with very pale or abnormally dark areas resulting from partial albinism or melanism. A less expected case involved a male Grey-faced Woodpecker in France which had the mantle, back, uppertail and upperwings very clearly dark-barred, rather than plain green; the head was typical of the local subspecies, the nominate one, but for a pronounced thin black line running from the forecrown to the hindneck, although a similar, if less obvious, line is frequently present on this subspecies.

Most species of woodpecker are sexually dimorphic in coloration, the males wearing the more prominent sexual badges. Sexual dichromatism, however, is not extremely pronounced, and in many species both sexes are colourful. One reason for this is without doubt the fact that the nesting habitat does not require special camouflage for the incubating bird. In almost all cases of sexual colour differences, it is the male that has red or, in some cases, yellow somewhere on the head; if this bright colour is present also on the female, it invariably covers a smaller area. Experiments on flickers and pied woodpeckers have demonstrated that these badges are recognized by the woodpeckers. There are several species which show only indistinct sexual markings. The males of some small picids, including the Asian Sulawesi, Brown-capped and Pygmy Woodpeckers, and some subspecies of the Grey-capped Woodpecker, are only weakly differentiated from the females. Their badges are reduced to small red spots on the

While many species of woodpecker are more often than not observed only solitarily during much of the year, this is certainly not true of all picids. Lineated Woodpeckers, for example, commonly forage in pairs throughout all months of the year, the partners keeping in frequent vocal contact as they move through the open forest in the lowlands and hills of Central America and the Amazon Basin. Despite the propensity to remain in pairs throughout the year, however, the male and female roost separately, often in holes dug into nests of tree-living termites. This is one of several species which, although wary and easily alarmed, will readily visit large isolated trees, especially dead ones, in exposed situations. The southern part of this fairly common woodpecker's range reaches Argentina, where the plumage of both sexes differs from that of populations farther north in lacking the white stripes on the scapulars.

[*Dryocopus lineatus erythrops*, Iguazú National Park, Misiones, Argentina. Photo: Bill Coster/NHPA]

edge of the crown. In North America, the co-operatively breeding Red-cockaded Woodpecker shows a very similar male head marking that is likewise difficult to detect in the field. Experiments by J. M. Hagan and J. M. Reed indicated that red colour bands artificially attached to males, and only to males, of this species had a detrimental consequence in terms of the number of young which such a male could sucessfully rear to fledging, whereas other colours did not produce the same result. One reason for this is possibly that red colour provokes more frequent or more fierce aggressive attacks from other members of the colony. The sexual markings of certain flickers are also not very conspicuous. Sometimes the male does not show any red, and is distinguished from the female only by having a black moustache, as is often the case with the Cuban Fernandina's Flicker. In the Heart-spotted Woodpecker, neither sex shows any red or yellow in the plumage: the female has the forehead and most of the crown white, while the male's forehead and forecrown are black with very fine white dots or speckles. There are several picids in which both sexes are brightly coloured red on the head, with sexual differences being minimal or non-existent. These include Lewis's Woodpecker (*Melanerpes lewis*), the Puerto Rican Woodpecker (*Melanerpes portoricensis*), the Red-headed Woodpecker (*Melanerpes erythrocephalus*) and the Red-breasted and Red-naped Sapsuckers in the New World, and the Middle Spotted Woodpecker in Europe.

So far, there has not been a satisfactory explanation for these differences in sexual dichromatism exhibited among the members of the Picidae. One suggestion is that sexual dimorphism decreases in social species, but there are too many exceptions to this concept for it to be a likely explanation. For example, the more or less territorial Guadeloupe Woodpecker is sexually monochromatic, although there are clear differences between males and females in bill length; yet on other Caribbean islands there live much more social congeners, such as the Hispaniolan Woodpecker (*Melanerpes striatus*), that are dichromatic.

In the Colaptini, the Meiglyptini and the Picini, together with African members of the Campetherini, it is frequently the malar region that bears the sexually dimorphic coloration. Females of those species either lack a malar stripe, or have the stripe broken up by spotting or streaking, or of a different colour, often lacking the red found on males. In some species of the above-mentioned groups, as well as in the piculets and, notably, the pied woodpeckers, sexual plumage differences pertain to the crown. In many instances, the crown is partially or wholly red on males, while on females the red either is absent or is reduced in extent and intensity. Looking at all these groups, there is great variation in the head pattern. The genus *Picus*, for example, displays all possible combinations of dimorphic patterns that involve the malar and the crown.

The sexes may also differ in size, and in mensural characters such as bill length. Females of *Sasia* piculets and of the Antillean Piculet are slightly larger than the males, and the female tends to be the larger in other piculets, too. Even so, there is some intraspecific variation, as exemplified by the Greyish Piculet (*Picumnus granadensis*): Short noted that, in the nominate subspecies, the male is slightly larger than the female, whereas the female is the larger in the subspecies *antioquensis*. With the exception of the Acorn Woodpecker (*Melanerpes formicivorus*) and the Grey-breasted Woodpecker (*Melanerpes hypopolius*), males of *Melanerpes* species are generally heavier and longer-billed than females, and these differences are more pronounced in insular forms. The sexes of the sapsuckers are more or less identical in terms of their size, whereas the male of the Cuban Green Woodpecker is distinctly heavier and longer-billed than the female. Among the African Campetherini, sexual differences in size and structure are negligible in the *Campethera* species, while they are manifest in several species of *Dendropicos* the males of which have a longer bill. Females of the five small Asian pied woodpeckers, the Sulawesi, Philippine, Brown-capped, Grey-capped and Pygmy Woodpeckers, along with those of the somewhat bigger Fulvous-breasted (*Dendrocopos macei*) and Stripe-breasted Woodpeckers (*Dendrocopos atratus*), tend to have longer wings and a longer tail when compared with males of the respective species, as

A few picids are highly social in their behaviour. One of these is the White Woodpecker. This highly distinctive Neotropical species is generally observed in small groups of five to eight individuals, which are sometimes accompanied by other picids, especially flickers (Colaptes). In fact, so typical is its flocking behaviour that the arrival of a chattering group of White Woodpeckers in a fruiting tree has been likened to parrots (Psittacidae) dropping from the sky. Among the Picidae, the phenomenon of group-living occurs most frequently among the tropical melanerpine species which feed on fruits and other plant material, suggesting that it may result from the clustered nature of this food source. The joint efforts of several individuals may be useful in locating fruiting trees. Moreover, as small groups cross open country in search of the next food source, the habit of flocking may also reduce the risk of predation. Although the White Woodpecker appears to be not uncommon, little else is known about the extent of its communal lifestyle, such as whether it nests semi-colonially. The complex social nature of the related Acorn Woodpecker (Melanerpes formicivorus) is far better known, since that species not only breeds in closely knit groups but also extends its group-living to the collective gathering and storage of food.

[Melanerpes candidus, Pantanal, Mato Grosso, Brazil. Photo: Haroldo Palo Jr/ NHPA]

Woodpeckers have a well-organized daily routine. Unless there are chicks in the nest which need to be fed, the level of activity is reduced in the middle of the day. At this time the birds generally rest, as this female Chilean Flicker appears to be doing in the dry scrub of southern South America. Some individuals may doze, fluffing up the plumage and creating a more huddled appearance. A resting woodpecker may intermittently stretch its gape, commonly referred to as "yawning", or remove unwanted items from its bill by vigorously shaking its head. The woodpecker usually remains in the open during the daytime, but roost-holes are sometimes used during this midday rest.

[Colaptes pitius, Puerto Natales, Chile. Photo: Isabel Martínez & Andy Elliot]

also do females of the far more widespread Old World Lesser Spotted Woodpecker. Otherwise, males of the pied species, with the exception of the Downy and Red-cockaded Woodpeckers, are slightly heavier than females, and also have a longer bill but, often, a proportionally shorter tail. Sexual size differences are weakly developed in the colaptine woodpeckers. In the Campephilini and the Picini tribes, the general pattern is that males are slightly heavier, longer-billed and proportionally short-tailed when compared with females. Of course, some variation exists among species in the extent of this dimorphism.

Of particular interest is the way in which sexual morphological differences relate to ecological differences between the sexes. This is discussed in more detail below (see Habitat).

The coloration of young woodpeckers is usually distinct from that of the adults, and this has given rise to many speculative theories. These centre mainly on the question of whether the great diversity of colour patterns found on nestling and juvenile woodpeckers comprises "primitive" or "advanced" character states. A functional explanation would seem possible, but corresponding experimental studies have not been carried out. There are several species the juveniles of which show more red on the head than do the adults. This condition is found in the well-studied Great Spotted Woodpecker and its allies, among them the Syrian Woodpecker, the immature of which in addition possesses a more or less conspicuous red breastband which the adults lack. Juveniles of both sexes of these species have the forecrown red, whereas the red sexual badge of adult males is located at the nape. A similar age-dependent condition is presented by the Maroon Woodpecker of southern Myanmar to Sumatra and Borneo. Rather intriguingly, the reverse pattern is found in the Afrotropical *Campethera* picids, the juvenile males of which have the badge only on the hindcrown or nape, while the adult males have the entire crown red or yellow. There are some other cases in which the position of the juvenile marking differs from that of the adult: the immature Red-cockaded Woodpecker, for instance, has a red patch in the centre of the crown. The juvenile coloration of some species, such as many Colaptini and some Melanerpini, Picini and *Dryocopus*, more or less matches that of the adult. In the Black Woodpecker, for example, the sexual differences appear when the nestling is ten days old, although some individuals, probably females, do not show any red at this stage.

In fact, the extent of the red on juveniles of many species, as typified by the Great Spotted Woodpecker, varies within and among nests, and what seem to be sexual differences are already visible in these early stages. Unfortunately, however, no study based on large sample sizes has yet shown whether these apparent sexual differences agree with the actual sex of all the individuals involved.

The juvenile plumage of the wrynecks does not exhibit any conspicuous marks that could serve as signals. The young of these two Old World species differ, however, in having a barred underside, a pattern that is replaced by arrowhead marks in the adult plumage.

The embryonic development of woodpeckers is shorter than that of most other birds of comparable size, while the juvenile development is slower. Wrynecks and woodpeckers are naked on hatching. The pads or flaps on the base of the lower jaw extend over the edge of the bill, and are almost completely reduced upon fledging. They are certainly organs that help in the transfer of food from the parents to the nestlings in the darkness of the hole (see Breeding). The outer edge of the "heel" of the newly hatched wryneck or woodpecker bears wart-like swellings that are shed in the early phase of the nestling's development. Feathers can be seen to develop under the skin on about the sixth day, and they break through the skin three days later.

When discussing the development of the larger flight-feathers, it is necessary to consider this in connection with the peculiar moult of the Picidae. The extent of the juvenile moult varies among species. Piculets of the genus *Picumnus* shed only the feathers of the crown after they have left the nest. *Sasia* species, on the other hand, moult the feathers of the underside, too, upon leaving the nest. All piculets, however, renew their plumage in a full first moult after they have bred for the first time. Conversely, young wrynecks and true woodpeckers replace the primaries, the tail feathers and the rest of the plumage, but do not renew the secondaries and primary coverts until later. The outer primary of juveniles is longer and wider than that of adults; in addition, the tail is shorter and is different in shape, because the feathers adjacent to the central pair remain shorter. Juveniles commence their moult with the primaries. The innermost, first primary is replaced first, and the moult then proceeds outwards; only when the sixth or seventh primary has been shed does the moult of the contour feathers begin. This moult is completed before the new outer primary has developed fully. In some species, the juvenile begins the moult when still in the nest, and some time before leaving it, which means that the first primaries are grown and then dropped without having ever been used. In these cases, therefore, the two innermost primaries remain small and thin. This pattern is developed to the greatest extreme in the Eurasian Three-toed Woodpecker, the chicks of which replace the five to seven innermost primaries before they leave the nest-hole. This is probably adaptive, since northern and montane species living in cool-temperate areas have to complete the moult before the end of the short summer season, so that they are then able to disperse or migrate. Tropical woodpeckers, in contrast to those of more temperate areas, have the innermost primary only somewhat reduced.

Tropical species lead a more sedentary life than do temperate ones, and their moult can therefore be spread over a long period. The variation in juvenile moult patterns within the genus *Picus* may serve as an instructive example. The tropical Laced Woodpecker (*Picus vittatus*) in South-east Asia has only the innermost primary reduced, whereas, in the temperate Eurasian Green Woodpecker and, even more so, in northern subspecies of the Grey-faced Woodpecker, the two innermost feathers are greatly reduced and measure only one-third or less of the corresponding adult feathers. Similar variation occurs among the pied woodpeckers. As already mentioned, the strongest reduction is found in the Eurasian Three-toed Woodpecker. Compared with that species, the juvenile innermost primaries are less reduced in the Great Spotted Woodpecker, and they are comparatively even less so in the closely related, generally more southern Syrian and Fulvous-breasted Woodpeckers. Melanerpine woodpeckers, incidentally, do not begin to shed their juvenile primaries until after they have left the nest.

Adult moult is tied in with the breeding cycle and occurs after the nesting season. Neither the wrynecks nor the true woodpeckers moult the eleven secondaries during the first moult. For those species for which data are available, there are two moult centres in the secondaries, located respectively at the first and the eighth secondary. In the genus *Colaptes*, for example, after three or four feathers have been moulted from the eighth secondary outwards on either side, moult starts at the first secondary and progresses inwards. Some deviations from the normal pattern of wing moult do, however, occur. Migratory Red-headed Woodpeckers in North America arrest the wing moult immediately after it has begun, and continue it once they arrive in the wintering areas. The related Lewis's Woodpecker completes the moult of its wings and tail early, but it does not complete the body moult until late autumn or early winter. In similar fashion, the sapsuckers terminate their juvenile moult very late in the season, such that they do not acquire adult plumage until as late as February. Of particular interest is the wing moult of the Andean Flicker, which is very variable and protracted, and therefore does not interfere greatly with its capacity for flight. This strategy is presumably crucial when one considers this open-country species' habitat utilization and vertical migration. Migratory populations of species which are partial migrants may also adapt the moult strategy to fit their behaviour. For example, large numbers of Great Spotted Woodpeckers, primarily juveniles, periodically leave the northern parts of Europe after the breeding season. Studies in Norway have shown that these migrating individuals frequently show a reduced intensity of wing and tail moult compared with non-migrants; in addition, the primary moult is sometimes arrested, just as happens with Red-headed Woodpeckers in America.

The specialized function of the picid tail requires some adaptive changes in the moult sequence, too. Species with a stiff tail that is heavily used in arboreal climbing replace the central pair of rectrices last of all. The moult begins at the second-innermost feathers and continues outwards, although some species of *Celeus* and *Dendropicos* may start the tail moult at the third-innermost pair of feathers. In analogy with the moult of the inner primaries, these feathers initially remain short on juveniles, causing the juvenile tail to have a graduated shape, as can be seen on, for example, young Black Woodpeckers and Eurasian Three-toed Woodpeckers. The tiny outermost rectrix may be shed before

the fourth. In the wrynecks and at least some individuals of the Cardinal Woodpecker, the tail is moulted in a reversed sequence, beginning with the outer feathers, and this is also the case with some picine species. From what is known of the Picumninae, the tail moult of these tiny woodpeckers does not appear to follow any regular pattern.

Habitat

The various adaptations of woodpeckers, manifest in their morphology, locomotion, and foraging and nesting habits, have developed over the course of the evolution of these birds towards a life in trees. The forests and woodlands of the world, with the exception of those of Australasia, are therefore the prime home of the family. A few picids have evolved partly ground-living habits, but they still nest in trees and live in wooded habitats. Woodpeckers which frequently feed on the ground are found among the African Campetherini, the flickers and the Picini. Even fewer species are completely terrestrial, and only three could really be so described. These are the aptly named Ground Woodpecker of South Africa, the Andean Flicker living in the mountains of that name, and the Campo Flicker of the *pampas* and savannas of South America. The vast majority of woodpeckers are, however, tied to wooded habitats, these ranging from dense tropical and boreal forests to lighter woodlands and to sparsely timbered semi-deserts. Trees offer food, protection, signalling posts and nesting sites. Numerous studies have shown that, for many species, a minimal amount of dead wood is required for a habitat to be suitable.

Tropical rainforest harbours the greatest numbers of woodpeckers. In this respect, the forests of South-east Asia and South America are the most diverse and, in both regions, as many as 13 species can be found living sympatrically within an area of about 100 ha or less. This may seem surprising when one considers the fact that woodpeckers are already highly specialized in ways that are to a greater or lesser degree similar for all species, so that it may be difficult for them to partition the habitat by developing further specializations.

As this Northern Flicker illustrates, woodpeckers use the bill to preen their body feathers and to clean the feet. A more difficult manoeuvre involves stretching a leg and foot to tend to the head, neck and bill, as this requires that the bird temporarily releases its grip on the vertical surface. Woodpeckers also maintain their plumage in prime condition by shaking the body and wings, by rubbing the face and other areas on tree bark, and by using the bill to apply preen oil to their feathers. This fatty substance, produced by the uropygial gland, is worked into the plumage with the bill, which the woodpecker then wipes clean on twigs or branches.

[Colaptes auratus auratus, Illinois, USA. Photo: R. & S. Day/VIREO]

Bathing in water is a type of maintenance behaviour that is not very often recorded for the Picidae, but it almost certainly occurs more frequently than is apparent from observations. Water-bathing is accomplished in the open, during precipitation, or in a suitable shallow pool. During rain showers, the woodpecker stretches its wings and, often, fans the tail, to take advantage of the moisture, after which it preens in the usual fashion. Both ground-loving species, such as the Eurasian Green Woodpecker, and arboreal ones bathe in this passive manner. Woodpeckers also utilize water that has collected in a depression in a tree, such as a rot hole or at the site of a fork, or on the ground. In these situations they bathe more actively, splashing themselves rapidly for a few seconds at a time, but taking frequent short breaks, alert to the danger of potential predators. Perhaps the Eurasian Green Woodpecker in the lower photograph, a male of the Iberian race sharpei, having less black on its face than the nominate race shown above, is keeping an eye on the Azure-winged Magpie (Cyanopica cyana) in the background.

[Above: Picus viridis viridis, Lorraine, France.
Photo: Regis Cavignaux/ Bios.

Below: Picus viridis sharpei, Avila, Spain.
Photo: Roger Tidman/ NHPA]

Surprisingly few woodpeckers are known to perform anting, an activity sometimes integrated with sun-bathing. One of these is the Gilded Flicker. Anting occurs among many avian species, but its function is unclear. A popular belief is that it helps to prevent the build-up of ectoparasites. Another theory is that active anting, whereby the bird rubs ants against its plumage, may be a specialized part of feeding behaviour, designed to rid the insects of their acid and render them more palatable. This seems rather unlikely in the case of picids, many of which consume a wide variety of ant species but make no attempt to treat the prey before swallowing.

[*Colaptes chrysoides mearnsi*, near Tucson, Arizona, USA. Photo: S. & D. & K. Maslowski/FLPA]

In each of his two study sites in tropical lowland rainforest in Malaysia, Short found 13 species of woodpecker. These covered the full size range that exists within the family, with the tiny Rufous Piculet at the small extreme and the Great Slaty Woodpecker at the top end. Although the size ratio among these sympatric woodpeckers did not follow a regular pattern of increase, it was evident that size differences contributed greatly to niche separation. This was particularly true for those species which engage in much pecking and excavating. The less specialized forms were not so widely separated by size, and these species exploited, in the main, an almost unlimited food source, namely ants and termites. Furthermore, the 13 picids demonstrated differences in their use of the habitat. The largest of them all, the Great Slaty Woodpecker, weighing over 400 g and with some individuals over 500 g, occupies huge territories and covers relatively long distances between its feeding sites. The latter comprise big trees, often standing alone in an open area, but also small trunks on which this woodpecker may feed not far from the ground. Although this species possesses a large bill, it carries out a great deal of gleaning and probing; when excavating, it delivers several powerful blows. It is rather restless and mobile, covering large sections of a tree in its search for food, and not remaining for long at any particular site. The second largest species in the Malaysian lowland rainforest, the White-bellied Woodpecker, weighs about half as much as the previous species and requires large foraging ranges, although these are not so extensive as those of the Great Slaty Woodpecker. It is much more of an excavator, and it forages chiefly on the dead parts of live trees, and on dead trees that have fallen or are still standing. This species may excavate deep pits, and it often stays at favoured sites for long periods of time and visits them repeatedly. Smaller than the White-bellied Woodpecker by about 80 g, the Orange-backed Woodpecker (*Reinwardtipicus validus*) forages from close to the ground up to the canopy, preferring the middle strata. There, it moves about actively yet excavates frequently, in short bursts of activity. The somewhat smaller Olive-backed Woodpecker is confined to swampy sections of the forest, where it forages mainly close to the ground, moving slowly but constantly. In these Malaysian forests, three *Picus* species are sympatric: the reddish-coloured Banded Woodpecker forages in densely vegetated, concealed sites, the Chequer-throated Woodpecker (*Picus*

mentalis) is found mainly between 3 m and 15 m above the ground, and the Crimson-winged Woodpecker (*Picus puniceus*) searches for food in the canopy. Two other congeneric species, the Buff-rumped and Buff-necked Woodpeckers, are also separated mainly by habitat use, the former foraging very actively in the canopy, while the latter often seeks food near the ground and in the understorey. Heavy understorey in tracts of dense primary and secondary forest is the principal habitat of the Maroon Woodpecker, which is well camouflaged by its brown colours; it specializes in extracting insects and their larvae from rotten trunks and fallen logs by hacking with its powerful bill. Also brown, but utilizing a much greater diversity of habitats and foraging sites, the Rufous Woodpecker may at times be observed feeding on the ground, on termite mounds, but it also moves constantly along branches and trunks. It gleans and probes, and occasionally taps. It searches among bamboo (*Bambusa*), as well as coconuts and arboreal ant nests, preferring to stay mainly in dense vegetation and in dark sites. The smallest woodpeckers in this forest ecosystem are the Grey-and-buff Woodpecker and the Rufous Piculet. They are not likely to interfere with the other woodpeckers, for they feed on small-sized substrates, nor are they likely to compete with each other, since they are well segregated by the strata which they use. The piculet forages in dense vegetation at low levels. The Grey-and-buff Woodpecker, on the other hand, explores small twigs and leaf clusters high in the canopy.

The same number of sympatric picid species was found by Winkler and others in South America, in a lowland rainforest lying at the same latitude as the Malaysian sites. Although these Neotropical woodpeckers are phylogenetically more uniform, niche separation among them follows similar principles to those demonstrated in South-east Asia. The smallest species was the Golden-spangled Piculet, weighing just 9 g, and the largest, each at about 200 g, were the Lineated, the Red-necked (*Campephilus rubricollis*) and the Crimson-crested Woodpeckers (*Campephilus melanoleucos*). Although these large species were seen feeding on the same trunk, albeit at different times, they were thought to be going for different prey, some seeking ants and termites, for example, and others taking grubs. The four *Celeus* species present in the same forest, the Ringed (*Celeus torquatus*), Scaly-breasted, Cream-coloured (*Celeus flavus*) and Chestnut Woodpeckers, are kept largely apart by the fact that each one prefers a different forest stratum from those frequented by the others. Since, in the case of these woodpeckers, frugivory is of some importance, the good food supply may further foster the co-existence of so many congeners. The bark-gleaning guild in the Neotropics also contains several species of ovenbird (Furnariidae) and woodcreeper (Dendrocolaptidae). The ability to exploit different resources despite many shared specializations no doubt contributes to the great success of the woodpeckers as a family.

The principles that are seen to operate in rainforests apply to temperate zones as well. Wherever several species of woodpecker are sympatric, and occur in the same kind of habitat, they are separated ecologically by size, foraging stratum, foraging style and food preferences. It should be noted here that foraging stratum does not signify only the height, or relative height, within the forest or in a single tree. Implicit within the term are the diameter of the trunk, limb or branch, and their angle of slant, along with the condition of the bark, all of which are important niche dimensions as well. This finer subdivision of the habitat becomes especially apparent when one considers ecological differences between sexes.

Ecological sexual dimorphism is widespread among woodpeckers. In its most simple form, the sexes may differ in the parts of the territory which they use when they are feeding nestlings. Sexual differences occur also, however, when woodpeckers forage for their own sustenance. The differences pertain to foraging height, to the use of micro-habitats as just described, and to the foraging techniques applied. These ecological differences are also reflected in mensural characters of the bill, feet and tail. Sexual differences may be most pronounced during harsh ecological conditions and can, therefore, show seasonal fluctuations. One of the species that was first studied is the Hairy Woodpecker of North and Central America. Whenever food is scarce, Hairy Woodpeckers resort to foraging for wood-boring grubs, mainly by excavating; in winter, when this habit is most common, the males excavate even more than do the females. Again, sexual differences in the foraging behaviour of the Red-bellied Woodpecker are most pronounced in winter, when males more often search trunks for arthropod food. The Golden-fronted Woodpecker, another melanerpine species with some ecological sexual dimorphism, forages mostly on medium-sized to large branches

and on trunks. Studies have demonstrated that this picid's most important feeding techniques are gleaning and searching, which together constitute 50% of its foraging actions; less common are pecking and hammering, which make up 28%, and probing in crevices and holes, which account for 13%. With this species, it is the males that peck slightly less frequently than do females, and they also forage less often on small twigs.

Sexual differences in feeding ecology are widespread also among the pied woodpeckers of the genera *Dendrocopos* and *Picoides*, as, for instance, in the Hairy Woodpecker. In the case of the Old World Great Spotted Woodpecker, these differences in foraging are very slight and are noteworthy only in winter. The sexes of the White-backed Woodpecker differ morphologically, the male having the larger bill. Males of this species hammer more strongly than do females and are more persistent in their work, in addition to which they visit both live trees and taller trees more often, and forage on larger branches. With this species, too, sexual differences are most significant in the winter, and the proportions of the foraging techniques used change with the seasons; working deeply into the timber decreases from about 20% of techniques observed in winter to about 12% in the post-breeding season. Compared with their mates, female Strickland's Woodpeckers in America forage more on twigs than on trunks and large branches, especially towards the onset of the breeding season. The sexes of the Red-cockaded Woodpecker differ minimally in their morphological measurements, but they exhibit constant foraging differences, these being most pronounced in the winter months from January to March. Males of this rare but well-studied picid use mainly the upper trunk and branches, while females tend to feed on the lower trunk. A similar difference has been found to be typical for foraging Downy Woodpeckers in winter. For this widespread Nearctic species, good observational and experimental evidence has been accumulated to indicate that sexual niche segregation is maintained by intraspecific aggression: the male keeps the female away from the crown of trees by making frequent attacks on her. In the case of the White-headed Woodpecker, which is confined to the mountains of western North America, sexual differences in foraging are most pronounced in the southern part of its range. There, females feed more on trunks, whereas males rely more on cones, particularly the huge ones of the Coulter pine (*Pinus coulteri*),

Aggression between woodpeckers is very frequent in occurrence, and is often very difficult to distinguish from courtship behaviour. In many cases, however, it is directed mostly at individuals of the same sex, as these two male Northern Flickers illustrate. During antagonistic encounters, the bill is pointed upwards and the wings are raised and flicked prior to an assault, which often involves stabbing at the opponent with the bill. Aggressive behaviour decreases during the period of incubation and brood care, which may be one factor enabling locally high breeding densities of Northern Flickers to occur, although nesting times are staggered to reduce such conflicts.

[*Colaptes auratus auratus*, Long Island, New York, USA. Photo: Tom Vezo]

In the open grasslands of
South America, two male
Campo Flickers engage
in aerial combat.
Such conflicts usually
take place close to nest-
sites, reaching a peak
around the time of egg-
laying, but they also occur
at roosts. They start with
agitated calls, followed by
wing-flicking and swinging
movements of the head
and body. If the intruder
does not withdraw,
physical combat ensues in
which the bill and the feet
are deployed as the main
weapons. Observations in
the wild, supported by
experiments using
dummies, indicate that
such fights are usually
between individuals of the
same sex, whether the
intruder is a single bird
or one of a pair.

[Colaptes campestris
campestroides,
Pantanal, Mato Grosso,
Brazil.
Photos: Roland Seitre/
Bios]

and, as with the Downy Woodpecker, this sexual separation appears to be maintained by male aggression. Circumstances seem to be reversed with the Eurasian Three-toed Woodpecker. In this species, it is the males that forage at lower levels, mainly on trunks, and prefer large trees, while the females forage higher up and have a greater niche breadth, using also relatively thin trees and branches and, in summer, more frequently exploiting live trees. Both sexes forage lower in winter but, when partners forage together at that season, females restrict their feeding to higher levels, indicating that in this instance, too, the male controls the female's foraging niche. This seems also to be the case with the Middle Spotted Woodpecker. Interestingly, in the isolated North African population *numidus* of the Great Spotted Woodpecker, the sexes exhibit a greater difference than is apparent among Central European populations, and, as with the two foregoing species, it is the females that are found mainly in the crown and that prefer thinner branches.

From these few examples, it should be clear how several different species of woodpecker, as well as the two sexes of the same species, are able to divide up their shared habitat by means of micro-habitat selection and different foraging modes. There are many similar examples throughout almost the entire world range of the family.

Whether habitat-partitioning is simply the by-product of the phylogenetic history of the individual species involved, reflecting adaptations to some past ecological conditions of resource availability, or whether it has been shaped by competitive interactions is a difficult question to answer. Negative correlations between the population densities of two potential competitors may indicate that competition is responsible, but there are alternative explanations as well. Simple habitat alteration or changes in local climate, for instance, can affect two different species in dissimilar ways. Habitat use on islands may be explained by "competitive release", or it may be the result of poor resources. At any rate, woodpeckers on islands do often exhibit such changes in habitat use. Locally, Black Woodpeckers and Grey-faced Woodpeckers have been found to show negative relationships in their population densities, with the Black Woodpecker decreasing when the Grey-faced Woodpecker was increasing. On Scandinavian islands on which the latter species was absent, however, the Black Woodpecker was observed in a wider range of habitats and at higher densities than it was on islands where both picids were present.

High population densities and flexible habitat use are also typical of many melanerpine island species. These populations expand the species' niche further by means of a greater ecological differentiation of the sexes. Thus, the best examples of ecological sexual dimorphism, relating both to morphology and to foraging behaviour, are found on islands. It has already been mentioned that the Golden-fronted Woodpecker, a mainland species, exhibits some ecological differences between the sexes. The insular Hispaniolan Woodpecker, however, displays greater sexual dimorphism, with, for instance, a difference of about 21% between males and females in bill length, while the corresponding figure for its continental relative is less than 10%. Other insular melanerpine species, such as the Guadeloupe and Puerto Rican Woodpeckers, and the peculiar Cuban Green Woodpecker, all show a morphological sexual difference of 15-19%. Parallel differences in the proportions of feeding techniques used and foraging locations exploited have also been documented for some of these species. In studies of Hispaniolan Woodpeckers, females used gleaning about 50% more than did males and they probed much less frequently, with probing accounting for 0·6% of observations of feeding, as opposed to 34% for males; and males used hammering or pecking twice as much as did females. Males of the Guadeloupe Woodpecker, too, peck more frequently than the females do. Again, these sexual differences are most pronounced during the harsh conditions of the dry season. The sexes of the Puerto Rican Woodpecker also forage in different strata and use different foraging techniques. Males peck and probe more and tend to forage in the lower and middle parts of trees; females, on the other hand, prefer to glean, and are more frequently found in the middle strata and in the canopy. The greater divergence between the sexes of insular populations is often explained as being the result of an intense intersexual competition that has not been constrained by competition from other woodpeckers.

Fire is an important factor that determines forest dynamics in many areas, and it is also, therefore, important for several woodpecker species. Trees killed by fire become easily infested by wood-boring insects, among which are some significant pest species. This is the case in the coniferous forests of the Northern Hemisphere, where American Three-toed, Black-backed and

One of the most widespread picids in North America is the Hairy Woodpecker, a female of which is shown here. This species lives in forest and woodland but also visits gardens, and is usually seen alone. A relatively sturdy woodpecker, it is dominant over all other Nearctic members of its genus apart from the slightly bigger Black-backed Woodpecker (Picoides arcticus). Its behaviour encompasses the full range of aggressive displays, while defensive posture is indicated by fully spread wings. Confrontations occur not only with other picids but also with members of other bird families, especially Common Starlings (Sturnus vulgaris), which frequently take possession of woodpecker holes.

[Picoides villosus villosus, northern Wisconsin, USA. Photo: S. Nielsen/DRK]

Hairy Woodpeckers concentrate around the sites of forest fires, a habit mirrored in the Old World by Eurasian Three-toed Woodpeckers. Even the presumably extinct Ivory-billed Woodpecker (see Status and Conservation) used burned areas. Moreover, Red-cockaded Woodpeckers may profit from fires, because such events keep the hardwood mid-storey in check and help to maintain the specific characteristics of the open pine woodland which this endangered species needs. Forest fires are often natural phenomena, occurring on a fairly regular basis. The same cannot be said of the slash-and-burn agriculture practised in many tropical countries, but even this may provide additional snags that can be used as roost-sites and even as nesting sites by several species of woodpecker.

Secondary or somewhat degraded forest can represent good woodpecker habitat. Indeed, even the fragmentation of forest may benefit certain species which prefer more open areas, the Eurasian Green Woodpecker being a good example. Even some of the large *Campephilus* ivory-bills can be seen in secondary and fragmented forest, where they seem to be attracted especially to single dead or dying trees. Such observations have in fact prompted the suggestion that the Ivory-billed Woodpecker could perhaps be saved from extinction by the killing of trees through girdling, fire or even poison, but this action, even if viable, would seem hardly likely to be effective at this late stage in the species' history (see Status and Conservation).

Bearing in mind what has just been said, it is not surprising that many picid species have become emancipated from primary natural forest. Indeed, secondary forest, orchards, coffee plantations, suburbs, gardens, and both small and large city parks are far from being the least suitable habitats for many woodpeckers. Good examples are provided by the many melanerpine species that are a typical component of the avifauna of suburbs, villages and gardens throughout much of the Americas. In Europe, it is notable that the range expansion of the Syrian Woodpecker was entirely related to the existence of man-made habitats. That species' widespread congener, the Great Spotted Woodpecker, frequents parks and gardens from Britain and north-west Africa in the west across to China and Japan in the east, and it attains its highest known breeding densities in suburban managed woodland. Similarly, in North America, the Downy Woodpecker is a typical inhabitant of suburbia, where it maintains stable populations, while its relative, Nuttall's Woodpecker, is widespread in California and thrives in wooded environments in and near human settlements. Parks may, in fact, represent optimal habitats for a number of woodpeckers, because they tend to contain old trees that would long since have been removed in managed forest. Fruits and nuts in gardens and commercial orchards can in some cases provide essential sources of food, and in the Northern Hemisphere woodpeckers are common visitors to artificial feeders and birdtables in winter.

Forest-management practices in many cases determine the quality of the habitat for woodpeckers. The species which have possibly been studied most intensively in this respect are the Red-cockaded Woodpecker in North America and the Middle Spotted Woodpecker in Europe. The misfortune of the former is that its preferred habitat is also a prime target for loggers. This species requires old pine stands in the south-eastern USA that are regularly subject to fires, which prevent hardwood from becoming dominant. The pines offer secure nest-sites because they allow the woodpeckers to maintain a constant, protective flow of resin around the nesting and roosting holes, a facility which no other trees can provide.

On the opposite side of the Atlantic Ocean, most of the central European populations of the Middle Spotted Woodpecker live in managed forests, and these remain suitable for this locally endangered species only if they retain a minimum proportion of oaks (*Quercus*). Forest or woodland without suitable, and therefore old, cavity trees can be used only for foraging, although snag management and, in a few instances, the provision of artificial snags can relieve such a situation. Several studies have demonstrated that, for woodpeckers which live in forest, the relative supply of dead branches and dead or dying trees is a reliable predictor of their occurrence and population density. Old stands are in most cases, therefore, good woodpecker habitats. Species which undertake comparatively little excavation of timber may be sensitive to factors other than dead wood alone. Thus, as has been shown in a number of studies, Middle Spotted Woodpeckers, in most parts of their range, require oak trees, with their rich insect fauna and furrowed bark, as an important forest constituent.

Small woodpeckers are able to utilize as foraging habitats not only the branches and twigs of trees, but also other parts of the vegetation. Their size permits them to exploit bushes, the stalks of herbaceous plants and, most commonly, corn, reed (*Phragmites*) and bamboo. The last occurs in the habitat of several species, although it is not clear in every case whether the woodpeckers do in fact require the presence of bamboo for their sustenance. For example, a number of picumnines, such as the Golden-spangled, White-barred and Mottled Piculets in the Neotropics, and the Speckled, Rufous and White-browed Piculets in Asia, are associated with bamboo to a certain degree, but they are not restricted to such habitats. Similarly, the small Asian Fulvous-breasted Woodpecker has been found in bamboo stands, and the southernmost subspecies of the Hairy Woodpecker frequents montane oak-bamboo forest in Central America. In South America, the Bar-bellied (*Veniliornis nigriceps*), Little and Green-barred Woodpeckers are more or less accidentally associated with bamboo, as also are the Asian Rufous, White-bellied and Black-and-buff Woodpeckers, along with the Laced Woodpecker and some other *Picus* species, and the two *Blythipicus* woodpeckers.

This tall-growing, woody-stemmed grass is, however, of greater importance for some picids. The very small Grey-and-buff and Heart-spotted Woodpeckers apparently prefer the presence of bamboo in their habitat, while the medium-sized Lesser Yellownape (*Picus chlorolophus*) seems to be closely associated with bamboo, and uses it for foraging. The Rufous-headed Woodpecker has been found to be a near-obligate bamboo specialist in south-eastern Amazonian Peru, its population density apparently constrained by the availability of nest-sites, for which it requires trees. In south-east Asia, the Bamboo Woodpecker (*Gecinulus viridis*) is, as its name implies, confined to areas with bamboo, which may comprise pure stands or consist of patches in forest. Its close relative, the Pale-headed Woodpecker (*Gecinulus grantia*), prefers bamboo beneath forest canopy, although it can also be encountered away from this specialized grass. These last two picids forage mainly by gleaning prey from the bamboo stalks as they work methodically and slowly up them.

The dry, hollow stalks of reeds, although far narrower than bamboo stems, are exploited for the arthropods which may lurk inside them. A species which has learned to take advantage of this source of food is the Lesser Spotted Woodpecker. This picid generally inhabits open woodland and similar wooded habitats in most of its range, but in some areas it visits reedbeds from time to time. In parts of Europe, the food obtained from the reeds can be an important factor in the winter survival of local populations.

Some members of the Picidae live in semi-deserts or at the edge of true deserts. The Arabian Woodpecker, for example, occurs in environments ranging from relatively lush mountain habitats to the edge of the Arabian Desert, where grazing livestock leaves hardly anything but bare sand and a few scattered acacias (*Acacia*), just sufficient for this small woodpecker to procure its food and to drill its nest-holes. Acacias are similarly exploited by the Little Grey Woodpecker (*Dendropicos elachus*), a poorly known Afrotropical species which is confined to semi-desert on the southern edge of the Sahara. The semi-deserts of North and South America are all inhabited by woodpeckers. The large cacti found in these arid parts of the New World serve as a good replacement for trees and are regularly utilized in Central America by the Ladder-backed and Gila Woodpeckers (*Melanerpes uropygialis*), which both excavate nests in the cacti and use the fruits for food.

Grassland is another treeless habitat that has in several places been conquered by woodpeckers. In Africa, species such as the Fine-spotted Woodpecker (*Campethera punctuligera*) are found in grasslands with at times widely scattered trees and patches of bare ground, and the congeneric Bennett's Woodpecker allocates most of its foraging efforts to ground-feeding, often in grassland away from wooded areas. The most extreme example in this group of woodpeckers is, however, the Ground Woodpecker, which inhabits open rocky terrain in the uplands of South Africa, occurring mostly above 1200 m and ascending as high as 2100 m. This unique terrestrial picid lives on the grassy boulder-strewn slopes and hillsides and in open grassy country with rocky ridges, as well as frequenting barren or eroded areas in the hills. Even in the south-west of its range,

where it can be found down to sea-level, it prefers similar rocky and grassy areas, such as roadsides.

The *pampas* and the *puna* grasslands of South America are inhabited by specialized flickers. In the high Andes of west-central South America, the Andean Flicker lives in open terrain and forest edge at high elevations. It is common in the grassland of the Andean *puna* zone between 2000 m and 5000 m, and it also ventures into the humid shrubland of the *páramo* and other montane scrub and woodland. Its preferred feeding grounds are grassy areas around rocky outcrops. The remarkably long bill of this colaptine is well adapted for probing and digging into the soil to obtain larvae concealed deep beneath the surface. In places where trees, cliffs, rocks or walls are lacking, buildings are used as lookouts and signalling posts. The flicker's feeding areas may be far from its nesting grounds or roost-sites, and may be situated at lower altitudes. In the lowlands of eastern South America, the Campo Flicker is another conspicuous grassland woodpecker which forages almost exclusively on the ground, searching among stones, close to decaying fallen logs and on roads. It also seeks food on termite mounds or anthills, which, as other such prominent structures as isolated trees, poles, wires, cacti and rocks, are used also as vantage points from which to survey its surroundings. This woodpecker, like its Andean congener, does use forest edge, but it never advances into the forest interior.

Highly important requisites of woodpecker habitats are sites for nesting and roosting. The Eurasian Wryneck, which is not morphologically adapted for sustained excavation of wood, uses the old holes of other woodpeckers, other natural cavities and artificial nestboxes; in eastern Asia, its nests have also been found in buildings. The species' African sibling, the Rufous-necked Wryneck (*Jynx ruficollis*), adopts the former nests of barbets or woodpeckers, or appropriates natural crevices in trees, as well as using nestboxes, hollow fence posts and holes under the eaves of houses. Most members of the family, however, construct their own nests, although there is some variation in this respect. Woodpeckers that are less inclined to excavating wood, such as the flickers, are more likely to use pre-existing holes or to make new cavities into very soft wood.

Among birds, drumming is unique to the piculets and the true woodpeckers. Contrary to suggestions in popular culture, it is not used for excavating holes but, instead, is an acoustic signal used primarily as a means of communication between partners, often in a territorial context. The head and neck are specially adapted to facilitate both drumming and frequent pecking; muscles that contract before impact act as shock-absorbers. Drumming is performed by both sexes, and both the sound produced and the frequency of rolls vary considerably according to species. The Robust Woodpecker, for instance, makes a loud double rap, one to three times per minute. Recent studies demonstrate that the drum's cadence encodes information for species recognition.

[Campephilus robustus, Iguazú National Park, Misiones, Argentina. Photo: J. & A. Calo]

Many woodpeckers are highly vocal. The majority of species produce a single short call, and a longer series of notes often with a rattling quality. The Golden-olive Woodpecker's vocalizations are fairly typical for the family. Its normal call is a single loud "deeeeh", while the long-distance communication is a protracted high trill; the liquid "woick-woick-woick" given during antagonistic encounters is a highly characteristic picid call. Woodpecker vocalizations often relate to specific activities, such as fighting, copulating, maintaining contact while foraging, and displaying. In the last two contexts, calls are particularly important for those species which do not drum.

[*Piculus rubiginosus*. Photo: M. D. England/ Ardea]

Since the typical woodpecker nest is carved into dead wood, or into trunks or branches which have soft or rotten wood at the core, trees and palms that provide corresponding resources are an essential element of the habitat for many picids. Nevertheless, a wide variety of other substrates will often suffice. For example, utility poles are frequently used for nest-building, and fence posts are perfectly acceptable as nesting sites for smaller species such as the Neotropical Red-crowned (*Melanerpes rubricapillus*) and Spot-breasted Woodpeckers, among others. Similarly, cacti are ideal tree substitutes for many of the melanerpine species. In other cases, the large nests of arboreal insects are adequate for hole-making purposes, as with the Rufous Woodpecker in Asia, the Pale-crested and Golden-green Woodpeckers (*Piculus chrysochloros*) in the Neotropics, and the Buff-spotted Woodpecker (*Campethera nivosa*) in the Afrotropics. Those species living in grassland where trees are more or less absent require no more than earth banks, termite mounds or reasonably soft ground into which to dig their burrows. The various sites used by the Picidae for nesting are discussed in more detail later (see Breeding).

Roosting sites selected by woodpeckers are similar to those used for nesting. All members of the family roost in holes and, so far as the male is concerned, the roost and the nest are in most cases one and the same place during the breeding period. While old nests are often used for roosting, or special cavities are sometimes constructed for this purpose, the requirements of a roost-site are less strict than are those of a nesting site. As a consequence, an even wider range of usage is possible, and nestboxes, buildings, arboreal termitaria and the like have been recorded, besides the usual holes excavated in wood. Outside the breeding season, single dead trees may at any one time provide shelter for several individuals of various species.

General Habits

Many woodpeckers give the impression of being solitary and aggressive birds. The widespread temperate-zone species, such as the Great Spotted Woodpecker and its North American analogue, the Hairy Woodpecker, certainly fit this picture. With such species, observers can even find it difficult to distinguish between courtship and aggression in the behavioural repertoire, because both components appear to be present during encounters between the sexes. Moreover, the partners rarely maintain contact beyond the immediate vicinity of the nest-site, and they seem to be at most only loosely in touch with each other outside the breeding season. Pair-members of other species maintain vocal contact at least during the breeding season. Examples are the Red-crowned Woodpecker, Strickland's Woodpecker, the Arabian Woodpecker, the Fine-spotted Woodpecker, the Nubian Woodpecker and the flamebacks, to name but a few. Among tropical species, contact between pair-members outside the breeding season seems to be more common.

In the tropics, there are more picid species with juveniles that stay with their parents for an extended period of time. This prolonged contact between parents and their offspring seems to be the most important foundation for group-living among members of this family. Sociality among woodpeckers not only expresses itself in the habit of individuals of foraging together in a group, but also pertains to the sharing of a communal roost. Even the piculets follow this pattern. The Olivaceous Piculet (*Picumnus olivaceus*) lives in pairs or in groups of up to five individuals. Both parents roost in the nest before egg-laying and also during incubation, which task they share, and both also feed the young. Even after these have fledged, the whole family continues to roost in the same hole for some months. If a second brood is to be attempted, the young of the first brood stay on and roost with the parents, at least until the hatching of the new clutch of eggs. Similar behaviour by Blood-coloured Woodpeckers (*Veniliornis sanguineus*) has been observed in South America. A further example is provided by the Olive Woodpecker (*Dendropicos griseocephalus*) of Africa, the female and male of which roost together in the nest during the egg and the nestling stages. If only one juvenile is produced, as is frequently the case with this species, the whole family, consisting of both parents and a single offspring, will often roost together in the former nest for several more months. It seems that this younger individual may stay on and act as a helper during the next breeding attempt.

Among the Picidae, it is the mainly subtropical and tropical melanerpine woodpeckers that exhibit the greatest tendency towards group-living. For these woodpeckers, living in a group is closely connected with communal breeding. The general pattern

Most true woodpeckers, such as this female Black-rumped Flameback, maintain contact over long distances with a rattle-like or screaming call that has a frequency of between 1 and 2·5 kHz, ensuring good sound transmission in the forest. Contact calls from one member of a pair elicit an immediate response from the partner, but such calls are also used between a pair and its neighbours. Shorter calls are given by fledged young to indicate their location to parents. Nestlings have yet different calls, most of them associated with begging, but some are alarm calls made in the presence of an intruder. Black-rumped Flameback chicks, for example, make a hissing sound, similar to that emitted by young wrynecks (Jynx).

[Dinopium benghalense benghalense, Ranthambore, India. Photo: Patricio Robles Gil]

seems to be much as that described above for the campetherine Olive Woodpecker. Thus, group-living evolves through extended contact between parents and fledglings which eventually may lead to helping and to communal roosting. As with the Olive Woodpecker, males and females of the Golden-naped Woodpecker (*Melanerpes chrysauchen*) not only share incubation according to the general pattern found among woodpeckers (see Breeding), but they also roost together in the nest. The two or three young remain in the nest for more than one month, and, when fledged, they are looked after by their parents for a further couple of months. The offspring roost with the parents until the next breeding season. If the adults begin a second brood in the same season, the young of the first brood act as helpers. Sociality seems to be even more prevalent in the closely related and highly social Yellow-tufted Woodpecker (*Melanerpes cruentatus*), which is found in pairs or in groups of three to five individuals, with occasional groups containing up to twelve birds. This species is a communal breeder, with adult helpers, and up to five individuals may share a roost.

The phenomenon of group-living and communal breeding reaches its ultimate peak of development with another *Melanerpes* species, the Acorn Woodpecker. This extensively studied picid possibly has the most complex social system of all avian species. Details of its breeding behaviour are given later (see Breeding); they follow largely the pattern described above. What makes the Acorn Woodpecker's sociality so special is the fact that the group activity is not restricted to breeding, but is also essential for the creating of the larders, or acorn stores, that are so characteristic of this species (see Food and Feeding). These "granaries" may consist of 50,000 holes, each containing a single acorn. It takes a group of woodpeckers years to create such a big resource, and it requires a group to defend and maintain it. Lewis's Woodpecker also stores acorns in autumn and winter, but, unlike the Acorn Woodpeker, it uses existing cracks only, rather than drilling special holes, and each individual, or occasionally a pair, defends its own store. Similarly, Red-headed Woodpeckers gather at sites where the acorn crop or the production of beech (*Fagus*) mast is high, but they create and defend individual stores.

Communal roosting offers some energetic advantages during the colder months of the year. For example, M. A. du Plessis and co-workers found that, during the non-breeding season, the heat loss suffered by individual Acorn Woodpeckers could be reduced by as much as 17% or more when four members of the group roosted together in the same cavity. There are also, however, some potential disadvantages involved in communal roosting. Sharing the roost with too many other individuals can be problematic, particularly when it comes to leaving in the morning. As M. T. Stanbeck observed, if two individuals try to leave the roost-hole at the same time, they can both get stuck in the exit and perish; in addition, they can thereby prevent others from leaving the roost, and these, too, will then die.

The Red-cockaded Woodpecker is another member of the family which regularly lives in groups. Again, a particular resource is an important factor in terms of determining the species' sociality, and in this case it is the availability of suitable breeding sites (see Breeding). Red-cockaded Woodpeckers possess individual roosts, and only the male stays with the nestlings during the breeding season. These roosts, however, are not very far apart from each other. Such aggregations of cavity trees used by groups of Red-cockaded Woodpeckers are termed "clusters", or colonies.

Group-living has evolved also among the terrestrial woodpeckers. Here, the critical resource seems again to be proper nestsites. The Andean Flicker and, to a lesser extent, the Campo Flicker form loose colonies, and cases of incipient coloniality have also been described for the Northern Flicker. With the last species, the staggering of nesting times allows for close proximity of nests, since it results in a reduced level of aggression during the periods of incubation and brood care. Another reason may be that ground woodpeckers are more vulnerable to predation and that they "close ranks" because of this.

Individual woodpeckers demonstrate an excellent knowledge of the whereabouts of resources in their home range. They are well aware of the location of roosts, and are therefore able to find an alternative roosting site, even in the dark, when disturbed at the primary roost, and they seem also to be well informed about the location of feeding sites. Such knowledge may also be an important resource shared by a group. Observations on the African Ground Woodpecker, for which ant nests are a critical resource, clearly hint at such a possibility. Reduction of aggressive badges (see Morphological Aspects) and various modifications in behaviour help to maintain sociality. Among the terrestrial woodpeckers, a clear tendency towards more camouflaged plum-

Many woodpeckers utter low, intimate calls as part of courtship, immediately prior to copulation and during change-overs at the nest. This reinforces the pair-bond, but is often inaudible beyond a few metres. In contrast, when two rivals meet, as have these two male Crimson-crested Woodpeckers, the calls are noticeably louder. This large species is often rather silent, but in situations such as this it utters a shrill piping "put put puttas", sometimes continuing for minutes, before chasing away the intruder or becoming embroiled in a fight with it.

[*Campephilus melanoleucos malherbii*, Santa Marta, north Colombia. Photo: Otto Pfister]

age exists. Brownish colours prevail, and there is even intraspecific co-variation between terrestrial habits and general plumage coloration. In particular, sexual badges are reduced in the ground-dwelling woodpeckers. If this has been primarily part of the change towards more protective coloration, then it may also have fostered the evolution of sociality. The group-living Red-cockaded Woodpecker is essentially monomorphic. Similarly, the colour dichromatism of the Acorn Woodpecker is not very spectacular, either, and consists of the female having black on the frontal part of the otherwise red crown, while the male's entire crown is red. As pointed out earlier (see Morphological Aspects), however, the notion that monochromatic species are likely to be social is not true in all cases.

Finding resources that are irregular in occurrence may also require joint effort. Woodpeckers often congregate in fruiting trees. Even if they had individually found such a tree, tolerance towards other birds may be advantageous at such rich food sources and could form a first stepping stone in the evolution of sociality. The Hispaniolan Woodpecker regularly forages in groups, and particularly large numbers gather on fruiting trees. The White Woodpecker, a species that is also known to form such aggregations, often visits more open places, and to reach certain foraging sites it sometimes flies long distances. Hence, individuals or small groups can be seen crossing open country. This habit may also foster group-living, because it reduces the risk of predation. Many other melanerpine species prefer open country, and their tendency to form groups may also be associated with their general habitat preferences. For example, the migratory Lewis's Woodpecker, which occurs mostly in open woodland and orchards, is markedly gregarious, and sometimes forms large flocks in autumn. Young and adults of this species keep together in migrating flocks (see Movements). On arrival at the wintering grounds, when food stores are established, the flocks break up and probably all individuals attempt to found and defend their own stores. Flickers and Great Spotted Woodpeckers also form loose groups during their long-distance movements.

The benefits of group-living are evident also in the mixed-species flocks which commonly occur both in the tropics and in the temperate zones, and which are thought to afford foraging advantages and protection from predators to their participants.

In temperate regions, mixed flocks are formed mainly in winter, during the non-breeding season. Piculets and woodpeckers frequently join such groups. The small Striped Woodpecker of southern South America, for instance, frequently associates with ovenbirds. Small woodpeckers in the Northern Hemisphere regularly participate in flocks which have tits (*Parus*) as the core species and nuthatches (*Sitta*) and other small birds as associated species. This applies especially to the Eurasian Lesser Spotted Woodpecker, to the Japanese Pygmy Woodpecker and its tropical relative the Philippine Woodpecker, and to the American Downy Woodpecker. Studies of the Downy Woodpecker have demonstrated that this picid "understands" the tits' various alarm calls and other vocalizations and that it adjusts its vigilance accordingly. It is not only the small woodpeckers that join these roving bands of birds. Medium-sized and large woodpeckers also participate in mixed-species flocks, and a melanerpine woodpecker or a *Celeus* species is a common sight, for instance, in the mixed flocks that form temporarily in a Neotropical fruiting tree. When joining insectivorous foraging flocks, however, these picids and the *Piculus* species prefer the company of other bark-foragers such as the dendrocolaptid woodcreepers, although the large Lineated Woodpecker has, nevertheless, been observed with flocks of small antwrens (Thamnophilidae). In South-east Asia, the Lesser Yellownape and other woodpeckers regularly join the motley mixed-species flocks that are common in this region, these foraging parties containing, among others, various species of babbler (Timaliidae), drongos *(Dicrurus)* and other insectivores, and jays and magpies (Corvidae). Individuals of the yellownape's congener, the more terrestrial Grey-faced Woodpecker, that live in the tropics prefer the company of other ground-foragers. Even the large Great Slaty Woodpecker is known occasionally to forage together with the almost equally big White-bellied Woodpecker and the mid-sized Greater Flameback, and on rare occasions several picids will join together to forage. In disturbed forest in Sumatra, a group of five woodpeckers, all within 10 m of each other on the horizontal plane, was made up of individuals of five different species: these were the Banded, Chequer-throated, Olive-backed, Orange-backed and Buff-necked Woodpeckers.

While these various accounts of the grouping behaviour of woodpeckers are of great interest, it would be a mistake if the impression were given that these birds are generally sociable. In most cases, they are not. Even when they join other species, they tend to stay at the periphery of the group, and conspecifics are tolerated only at some distance. There is little in their signalling behaviour that conveys any degree of "friendliness" towards others of their kind. Only in the case of the melanerpines and the Red-cockaded Woodpecker do frequent chattering and twittering vocalizations indicate a greater affability.

Woodpeckers are diurnal birds which exhibit a well-organized daily routine. They leave the roost at sunrise and begin their chores without much delay. During the breeding season, signalling behaviour, particularly drumming, reaches a peak in the morning hours. The level of general activity is reduced around the midday period, and at this time woodpeckers may doze or engage in preening and similar behaviour. Before returning to the roost for the night, they often indulge in another bout of signalling activity. Individuals, having flown to the roost-site, do not always enter the hole immediately. This is especially true of those which are not yet familiar with a certain roost, in which case they may remain in its vicinity for a lengthy period of time, usually perching at some high vantage point, from where they often call, before finally entering the roosting cavity. A number of observations and field studies indicate that females generally enter their roosts later than do males, but further investigation is required in order to determine whether this is a widespread trait among the members of this family.

The roost is an important focal location in the life of a woodpecker. It offers protection from predators and from adverse weather conditions. There is little doubt, either, that hole-roosting contributes to the high adult survival that has been found to characterize birds which excavate their own nests, all of which invariably also roost in cavities. In most woodpecker species, the male's roost becomes the nest by default. Roosting holes are sometimes visited briefly during the day, and woodpeckers may even roost there at noon. This behaviour can mislead observers, particularly in the tropics, as it can be misinterpreted as breeding behaviour.

Roost-holes may be excavated at any season. Juvenile woodpeckers which have just dispersed from the natal territory often engage in roost-construction as one of the first tasks that they carry out in their new home range. The demands on the quality of roost-sites are less stringent than those placed on nest-sites and, as mentioned earlier (see Habitat), old cavities, nestboxes and various other suitable structures are readily accepted for roosting. For most picids, the roost is the centre of life for each individual. In the case of the Red-cockaded Woodpecker, availability of suitable trees for the setting-up of roosts, as well as of nests, determines the group size. Suitable trees contain up to five holes, and hole-excavation can take weeks or even months. These clusters of cavity trees are used by individual groups of these social woodpeckers. Individuals of different species may share the same tree as a roost-site if it contains several holes. As already mentioned, most individuals can resort to an alternative site when disturbed at the main roost.

When threatened in the roost, woodpeckers try to leave it immediately if there is still some light. Otherwise, they press themselves against the bottom of the hole. Outside the cavity, when threatened by predators, they protect themselves by crouching against the substrate. The two wrynecks take advantage of the camouflage which their plumage offers them, but the others picids, as a rule, move quickly to conceal themselves behind a branch or on the other side of the trunk. When attacked, they spread the wings and use the formidable bill as a weapon. If taken in the fangs or claws of a predator, they utter piercing screams. At the nest, woodpeckers emit incessant alarm calls when a predator is close, and they will also launch attacks against it.

During periods when they are not engaged in other urgent activities, woodpeckers devote time to the maintenance of their plumage. This includes preening for the most part, and more rarely sun-bathing and water-bathing. The Picidae possess about the same repertoire of comfort movements as that described for other birds. The feathers are preened with the bill, something which requires some acrobatic actions if the bird is clinging to a vertical surface and the lower breast or the belly have to be reached. The bill is also used to groom the toes. Woodpeckers scratch the head, neck and bill both indirectly and directly, by moving the foot over the wing as well as under it, but whether this follows a

Beetle larvae are one of main sources of woodpecker food. Indeed, the Picidae are the only birds able to reach the larvae of insects that bore deep under the bark of trees, accounting for their great success in so many regions of the world. Ants or the adults and larvae of beetles dominate the diet of most woodpecker species. These soft-bodied invertebrates are especially important for nestlings, as illustrated by this male Grey Woodpecker returning to its nest-hole in a West African garden. Abundant in the diet of many picids are the large larvae of long-horned beetles (Cerambycidae), metallic wood-boring beetles (Buprestidae), bark beetles (Scolytidae), and the wood-boring caterpillars of carpenter-moths (Cossidae).

[Dendropicos goertae goertae, Banjul, Gambia. Photo: Michael Gore]

systematic pattern is not clear. Some picid species seem never to lower the wing for head-scratching; others scratch the head either by bringing one foot forward under the wing or by raising it over the lowered wing, performing the latter movement even when clinging to a vertical surface. Woodpeckers frequently rub their face on bark, a kind of behaviour known to occur also among the toucans, and they use sweeping movements of the bill to distribute the fatty substances from the uropygial gland over the plumage. They clean the bill by wiping it on twigs and bark. They also shake the body along its longitudinal axis, and shake their wings. Simultaneous stretching of the leg and wing is a particularly difficult action for birds to carry out when clinging to a vertical surface, as they have to release the grip of one foot for a while; thus, the leg is sometimes only minimally stretched or is not stretched at all. By contrast, the double wing-and-neck stretch does not conflict with clinging vertically and can, therefore, be performed according to the usual avian pattern.

Resting, dozing and sleeping woodpeckers fluff up the plumage, lending them a more round-headed and short-necked appearance. Woodpeckers also exhibit gaping and retching movements, commonly referred to as "yawning", and they remove unwanted items from the bill by means of vigorous head-shaking.

Sun-bathing woodpeckers are rather rarely observed in the field, although this comfort activity is performed fairly regularly by members of the family when kept in captivity. So far as is known, woodpeckers sun-bathe only in full sunlight. A sunning Great Spotted Woodpecker will erect the feathers of the head and body, and spread the wings and tail to their fullest extent, then exposing them to the sun's rays; in addition, it turns the head such that the cheeks collect as much sunlight as possible. A very similar posture was adopted by a wild-living Eurasian Green Woodpecker which was observed sunning as it clung to a bare branch at the top of a large beech tree: in this instance, the bird's yellow rump feathers were conspicuously fluffed up, so that they glistened brilliantly in the sunlight, and the bill was held only just perceptibly open. This sunning posture appears to be the one adopted by all woodpeckers, including the *Melanerpes* and others.

Woodpeckers occasionally take a water-bath. Puddles on the ground and water that has accumulated in a suitable depression somewhere in a tree serve as an ideal bathtub, and in these they bathe in a manner similar to that of other birds. An interesting observation concerned a female Great Spotted Woodpecker which was watched as it moved clumsily through the terminal leaf clusters of an oak tree, thrashing about in one cluster before moving on to another and repeating this behaviour. The bird's actions included brief periods of hanging upside-down while flapping, which caused much rainwater to be shed from the foliage. When the woodpecker emerged, wet and bedraggled, some seven minutes later, it shook off the excess water and proceeded to preen. The observer considered that this was an example of bathing, especially since the relatively light rain which had fallen shortly before, following a prolonged dry spell, had rapidly drained away, so that no surface puddles were present. The incident took place in south-east England in June, a period of the year during which Great Spotted Woodpeckers frequently forage among foliage in a manner very like that described (see Food and Feeding), but the tree was apparently, and rather surprisingly, more or less devoid of suitable food at the time.

Dust-bathing has been documented for only a few picid species. These are the Green-barred Woodpecker and two other *Colaptes*, namely the Northern and Campo Flickers, and also the Black Woodpecker.

Several species, covering six genera, perform active as well as passive anting. The Eurasian Wryneck, the Red-headed Woodpecker and Red-bellied Woodpeckers, the Yellow-bellied Sapsucker, the Northern and Gilded Flickers, the Scaly-breasted Woodpecker and the Eurasian Green Woodpecker have all been recorded as indulging in these activities. The function of this behaviour, which occurs among many species of bird, is not clear. It has been suggested that it may be a method of countering ectoparasites. An alternative interpretation is that it constitutes a special element of feeding behaviour whereby the birds, in rubbing the ants on the plumage, rid the insects of their acid and thus render them palatable.

The complex foraging and feeding behaviour of woodpeckers requires high cognitive skills. These can be associated with the manipulation of objects and of prey, and with spatial knowledge. The method of processing food items in anvils (see Food and Feeding) shares many characteristics with tool use. It requires that the woodpecker matches the size and shape of the object with that of the crevice in which it is placed. Even more demanding is the preparation of anvils. In addition, efficient excavation for obtaining wood-boring larvae also requires flexible adjustment to wood texture, to the type of bore holes in which the larva lives, and so forth. A knowledge of the location of re-

The diet of the critically threatened Okinawa Woodpecker is fairly typical of that of many medium-sized and large picids. This woodpecker forages mostly for large arthropods, especially beetle larvae, and spiders, but it also takes many fruits, berries and seeds when they are available. Interestingly, it has also been observed to feed a gecko to its nestlings, making it one of only a handful of woodpeckers recorded as taking reptiles or amphibians. For most picids such occurrences are probably a result of opportunism, although a species of tree-frog has been found to constitute over 10% of food items fed by Guadeloupe Woodpeckers (Melanerpes herminieri) to their chicks.

[*Sapheopipo noguchii*, Okinawa, Japan. Photo: Masakazu Kudaka]

Woodpeckers obtain their food in a number of different ways, enabling a variety of species to co-exist within the same habitat. Some, such as the Golden-fronted Woodpecker of the southern USA and Central America, hammer through the bark with a rapid series of blows, before probing and searching in the shallow pit created. Woodpeckers probably detect prey beneath the bark by using visual cues, and then make probing taps to locate a weaker point in the substrate before drilling. They may also use sound and smell to locate wood-boring beetles, but there is, as yet, no hard experimental evidence to support this theory.

[Melanerpes aurifrons aurifrons, Rio Grande Valley, Texas, USA. Photo: John Cancalosi/ Ardea]

plete locally. In a similar way, Black Woodpeckers, too, seem to possess a detailed knowledge of the whereabouts of the ant nests in their home range, and they are able to locate these even when they are buried beneath a thick cover of snow. Knowledge of many potential feeding sites, and of the times when they have been visited, is a necessity for a foraging strategy that is known as trap-lining (see Food and Feeding).

From all this, one would expect that woodpeckers are highly intelligent birds. Particular laboratory studies of this aspect are, however, restricted to Great Spotted Woodpeckers. These picids quickly learn the task of pulling several vertically stacked drawers in the correct sequence so that a nut placed in the topmost drawer will fall into the bottom one, from which it can then be retrieved. Great Spotted Woodpeckers are also able to learn to "ask for" particular food types by giving various knocking signals with the bill, in what could be thought of as a simple kind of "Morse code". In experiments, they were able to signal for a pistachio nut with one blow, for a cricket (Orthoptera) with two blows, and for a mealworm with three blows. Moreover, they could instantaneously understand that the presentation of a picture of a pistachio meant that a corresponding box containing that reward was now available as an item of food. This demonstrates an ability that clearly approaches the cognitive feats of which parrots are known to be capable. Indeed, the forebrain of a Great Spotted Woodpecker is almost as highly developed as that of a Common Raven (*Corvus corax*).

Compared with non-storers, food-storing birds, such as certain tit species and corvids, possess a relatively large hippocampus, that part of the brain which is involved in the extensive use by birds of spatial memory. These species are able to memorize thousands of food locations. Among the Picidae, however, storers and non-storers do not exhibit such clear differences in the development of the hippocampus. Hairy and Downy Woodpeckers are as well endowed in this respect as is the food-storing Red-headed Woodpecker. The latter stores its food in centralized larders and has a relatively smaller hippocampus than the Red-bellied Woodpecker, which is a "scatter-hoarder" in the same way as are tits and jays. The high values of the two *Picoides* species may, indeed, indicate that spatial skills are needed not only for scatter-hoarding, but also for other spatially difficult challenges that are frequently encountered by woodpeckers.

Woodpeckers are generally good fliers, some species being regular migrants which cover large distances between their breed-

sources is very important in a woodpecker's life. Roosts may be approached from a great distance in direct flight, and the precise location of anvils seems to be perfectly well known to a woodpecker. Circumstantial evidence suggests that individuals of the Ground Woodpecker apparently learn the exact location of anthills, which they visit on a regular basis and may even de-

On a tall, dead tree trunk in East Africa, a male Bearded Woodpecker vigorously pecks at a hole, flicking shards of wood to the ground and swallowing a grub. The bill is ideal for chiselling and excavating, tearing off bark and wood fibres, as well as for grabbing and carrying food. The second photograph captures the split-second semi-closure of the eyelid, to protect the sensitive membranes from flying wood chips. Whereas some species remain in one place for just a few seconds, Bearded Woodpeckers spend a long time at each hole, consume all that they can reach, and then fly to the next potential food source some distance away.

[Dendropicos namaquus namaquus, Lake Nakuru National Park, Kenya. Photo: Dave Richards]

In common with other
large Dryocopus and
Campephilus species,
Black Woodpeckers often
excavate huge pits in
their search for the
nests of tree-living ants.
Large chunks of bark are
removed before the bird
chisels deep, long
rectangular holes into
the tree trunk, following
the texture of the wood
fibres. Although Black
Woodpeckers can
sometimes be hard to
locate, the large gouges
in softwood trees are a
tell-tale sign of their
presence; even so,
the large foraging area
exploited by this species
means that the birds are
not necessarily close
at hand.

[Dryocopus martius
martius,
Oka Game Reserve,
near Moscow, Russia.
Photo: Roland Seitre/Bios]

ing and non-breeding quarters (see Movements). The normal active flight of the majority of species involves series of rapid wingbeats interspersed with briefer periods of gliding on closed wings, producing an efficient bounding flight that is highly characteristic of this family. Certain species, such as the melanerpines, have a somewhat straighter, less undulating flight, and the largest picids, including the logcocks and the ivory-bills in the Campephilini tribe, also fly in a more direct manner. Furthermore, the typically undulating fliers, such as the *Dendrocopos* and *Picoides* species, are capable of more sustained flapping flight in a straight line when pursuing rivals, although such chases are usually over relatively short distances. Conversely, even the really big woodpeckers can sometimes show a slightly dipping pattern when, for instance, moving across a clearing.

Voice

The sounds emitted by woodpeckers are single short calls, variably protracted series of call notes, often with a rattling quality, and screams. In addition, a variety of instrumental signals is produced. No woodpecker species has the capacity for vocal utterances that attain the musical quality of the songs of passerine birds or waders (Scolopacidae). Moreover, the vocalizations of the Picidae are not learned. The instrumental signals, notably the drumming, are quite unique in the avian world.

Analyses of the vocalizations of the widespread pied woodpeckers in the genera *Dendrocopos* and *Picoides* have yielded a repertoire of about 13 calls, which fall into seven categories. In most other cases, the vocal repertoires of woodpeckers are poorly documented, but all members of the Picidae certainly appear to have a wide range of calls. These constitute important signals in various social situations, and they carry specific messages. Although the following commentary is based mainly on studies of pied woodpeckers, it is more than likely that other picids also possess a similarly rich vocal repertoire. Indeed, further research will probably show that the calls of woodpeckers provide an excellent model for avian acoustic communication, adding an extra dimension to the knowledge that has been gained from the extensively studied songs and other vocalizations of the oscines.

All pied woodpeckers, with the possible exception of the Arabian Woodpecker, utter single notes at varying levels of excitement, from low to intense, which reveal the location of an individual. They are given at high rates by excited birds, particularly during alarm at the nest. In the case of some species, of which the Great Spotted Woodpecker is an example, these calls can be heard over a considerable distance. The single-note calls of the majority of picids comprise short clicks, generally referred to as "Kick-calls". Those of the Hairy Woodpecker and its relative Strickland's Woodpecker are rather long, and those of the Red-Cockaded Woodpecker consist of protracted "churr" calls. Churrs of similar physical structure are widespread among species of the genus *Melanerpes*.

Most pied woodpeckers and other woodpecker species, however, use rattle-like or trill-like calls, sometimes preceded by an introductory call note, as a means of maintaining contact over long distances. This can apply to the communication between the members of a pair and also to that between territorial neighbours. Pair-members may respond immediately with this call when they receive the partner's signal. Shorter versions of these signals are given also by fledged young, probably to indicate their whereabouts to the parent. Among the large species, as well as some small ones such as the Lesser Spotted Woodpecker, these signals are not so rapid as to be described as trills, but, rather, they are made up of long and, in some cases, loud series of notes. Detailed relevant studies have not yet been carried out, but it is likely that these signals are adapted to the environment. Initial analyses have already revealed that call notes are roughly within the frequency window of 1-2·5 kHz for good sound transmission in forest.

One of the larger species, the Black Woodpecker in the genus *Dryocopus*, is known to possess two very distinct types of call that are delivered in specific contexts. The one most often heard is the loud flight call, given in short series, and with a grating quality. It can be transcribed as "krükrükrükrü". The other is uttered by an individual when not moving, and is often given upon landing. It is a far-carrying "kleea", not so conspicuous as the preceding call type.

Pied woodpeckers, and probably most, if not all, other picids, possess calls the use of which is restricted to the breeding season. These calls are usually produced in more or less regular, sometimes protracted series, and they are loud and, often, squeaky and long. These vocal signals may be associated with other forms of advertisement, such as drumming and the "Flutter-aerial-display" (see Breeding). They are most similar in function to the songs of other birds, and they become very important and conspicuous among those woodpecker species which perform only little or no drumming. These vocalizations, as well as the long-distance call type mentioned above, are frequently delivered from the upper tiers of the habitat, and it seems that they are given mainly by males. The strange call of the Middle Spotted Woodpecker belongs in this category. It consists of a far-carrying slow series of nasal "gwäh" notes, and it is unlike any sound that is produced by other, sympatric woodpeckers. In an interesting analysis of 326 songs of this species which he heard in spring in three different parts of France, over a period of several years, M. Cuisin reported a rather surprising level of variation. For example, the number of syllables in the song varied from just a single "gwäh" to as many as 33, and the speed of delivery from fairly rapid to slow and laboured, while the vocal quality was sometimes clear and sometimes hoarse. In addition, he recorded a wide variation in the frequency with which songs were uttered. The vocal activity of the Middle Spotted Woodpecker is known to be reduced in situations where its population density is low, but it seems likely that, within any particular area, there is also a comparatively wide variation from year to year in the frequency of acoustic advertisement, as has been recorded for several other woodpeckers. When a species' song is so highly variable, the question arises of how easily it is recognized by potential mates and rivals of the same species. With a sedentary picid such as the Middle Spotted Woodpecker, however, it is quite probable that individuals are very familiar with the finer details of the voice of all of their congeners living in the same area.

The song of the Eurasian Wryneck may also be mentioned here. Delivered in spring, it is this species' most characteristic call. It consists of a series of up to 15 or so whistled notes, at times somewhat harsh in quality, that rise slightly in pitch; the sequence is not unlike the call of a Eurasian Hobby (*Falco subbuteo*), which is sympatric with the wryneck in most of the latter's breeding range. This advertisement is uttered incessantly, even during bright daylight, in the early part of the breeding season, and becomes less frequent, often ceasing altogether, once pair formation has taken place. This species' sole congener, the Afrotropical Rufous-necked Wryneck (*Jynx ruficollis*), has a comparable song which is used for territorial advertisement.

A wide range of vocalizations is given by woodpeckers in a variety of social, mostly more or less aggressive situations. These calls may be associated with the swinging and bowing displays demonstrated by woodpeckers in agonistic situations (see Breeding), and they are normally referred to collectively as "Wicka-calls" as an approximation of the character of the sound. Among the *Celeus* species, for instance, they have a rather nasal quality, while those of the pied and the melanerpine species are whipping sounds. The Acorn Woodpecker's most common call can be rendered as repeated "whaaka-whaaka" or "wa-ka" notes. This utterance is given when a group-member lands, flies past or takes off, and it attains high rates during territorial disputes. At full intensity, when it is sometimes accompanied by wing-spreading, it ends with a rasping "trtrtr". Similar grating or rolling sounds are delivered in synchrony with bowing displays. Other variants of this call type have a twittering quality, and are frequently given by, for example, the social Red-cockaded Woodpecker. Generally, all of these calls vary in intensity, emphasis and overall structure in apparent accordance with the motivation of the individual signaller. Prior to or during copulation, and at change-overs at the nest, woodpeckers emit low intimate calls, rich in harmonics, which are audible to a human being only at very close range.

Among the three or more different types of calls that are produced by nestling woodpeckers, the more or less constant twittering, buzzing or rasping sound is the most conspicuous one. This call reaches the peak of intensity when a food-bearing adult approaches and enters the nest-hole. There appears to be some interspecific variation with regard to the frequency of occurrence and the intensity of these begging calls during the periods between feeds. The two other types of call uttered specifically by nestlings, and which have not been recorded for adults, are soft notes emitted after relief from a stressful situation, or during such a situation, a typical example of which would be a fight with siblings. These calls probably represent short-distance signals directed at the nestmates or parents. The nestlings of wrynecks

Little is known about the diets of most piculets, especially those in South America, so that this sequence of a feeding Ochre-collared Piculet is quite remarkable. These tiny birds, less than 10 cm long, are found among tall growth, including introduced bamboo, in a relatively small region south of the Tropic of Capricorn. The photographer has captured this male as it hammers a small hole in a bamboo stem, inserts its bill, and pulls out a larva that was concealed inside. The grub is swallowed whole, the entire episode being completed in just a few seconds. The prominent ochre-coloured collar that separates this species from the closely related and otherwise very similar White-barred Piculet (Picumnus cirratus) is shown to advantage in these photographs.

[*Picumnus temminckii*, Juréia, São Paulo, Brazil. Photos: Edson Endrigo]

produce similar begging sounds; older chicks, however, when threatened in the nest, hiss in the same way as do adult wrynecks when they encounter a threat.

Woodpeckers scream or shriek when captured by a predator or handled by a human. They also emit screaming calls when in peril of "losing the battle" during fights with conspecifics. As was demonstrated by a study of the Acorn Woodpecker, however, not all individuals of a population scream in such situations.

The complexity of certain call categories and the readiness of a species to vocalize, but not the repertoire size, seem to be related to the degree of sociability. Thus, the melanerpine woodpeckers, which include the most social members of the family, are among the most vocal of all the Picidae. In contrast, solitary species such as the White-backed Woodpecker are relatively rarely heard and are very difficult to locate by their vocalizations alone. Even the conspicuously coloured and large ivory-bills in the genus *Campephilus* are likely to be detected more because of the noise which they produce while foraging than by their vocalizations. The tonal quality of long-distance signals, and the frequency with which the members of a pair exchange them, may be related to habitat structure and other ecological factors. In either case, corresponding comparative studies are, unfortunately, not available.

Most species of the subfamilies Picinae and Picumninae produce loud, rhythmic series of sounds by hammering against a resonant object, a practice known as drumming. The two wrynecks, however, do not drum. Despite popular belief among many laypersons, these instrumental signals made by the true woodpeckers and the piculets are not produced while the individual bird performs its woodwork in the context of feeding or nest-excavation. They are, therefore, true means of communication. The mechanics of drumming differ from those involved in the excavating of wood for cavities or while foraging in that the main movements are carried out by the head-and-neck system. The rapid rhythm and the time course of the individual strokes that make up a single burst of drumming are difficult to describe. In a comprehensive empirical and theoretical study that considered the mass of the head, the length of the neck muscles and their distance from the centre of the spine, and the length of the neck, M. Kaiser modelled the basic features of drumming. The predicted duration of the downstroke amounts to about 100-60% of the upstroke. Moreover, the details of the drumming signal seem to correlate with the ecology of a species. For instance, in the case of typical wood-pecking species, the rhythm or cadence accelerates as the amplitude falls; with species which obtain their food by gleaning, on the other hand, the signal slows down towards the end, or it remains uniform in rhythm and amplitude throughout the roll. Just a few of many examples to illustrate this difference are the Greater Flameback and the Acorn, Fire-bellied, Great Spotted, Nuttall's, Black-backed and Pileated Woodpeckers (*Dryocopus pileatus*), all of which forage by pecking and hammering and all of which have drumrolls that accelerate; whereas, among the gleaners, the Northern Flicker's rolls remain steady in rhythm, and those of the Downy and Ladder-backed Woodpeckers and the Buff-rumped and Buff-necked Woodpeckers decelerate. The cadence within rolls ranges from about ten to 25 beats per second. The number of drumrolls delivered per minute varies, depending on the species; it ranges from 0·3 in the case of the Rufous Woodpecker to 19 in the more widespread Lesser Spotted Woodpecker.

Both sexes drum, although the males perform this action more frequently. Some species appear to exhibit no difference between the sexes in the quality of these instrumental signals, while the females of other species give rolls that are less strongly developed than are those of the males. For instance, the drumrolls of the female Black Woodpecker are generally shorter than her mate's, and they vary more in rhythm, which is also somewhat slower. The extent of seasonal fluctuation in the frequency of drumming suggests that this activity has a close link with territorial behaviour. Signalling posts are often rather exposed and in the upper parts of trees. As a point of interest, woodpeckers often combine comfort behaviour with drumming, and they will preen during the regular pauses between individual rolls.

Drumming, when analysed quantitatively, is fairly species-specific, at least where sympatric picids are concerned, and in many cases the differences between species are perfectly detectable even to the human ear. The woodpeckers themselves, however, will not uncommonly react in a rather indiscriminate manner to drumming signals. Hence, they may react to playbacks of the tape-recorded drumming of other species, and they engage in

In general, woodpecker species which undertake substantial wood-working when foraging are rather poorly equipped to reach along a trunk or branch for surface-dwelling food. By contrast, species such as the Greater Yellownape are expert gleaners, picking ants, termites and beetles from the bark while in a perched position. Gleaners move on quickly to another feeding site after exhausting a food supply, although, since the renewal time of surface prey is short, the individual can return to the same spot regularly. Greater Yellownapes, a female of which is shown here, rarely peck or excavate, but they do prey on the young of other hole-nesting birds.

[*Picus flavinucha wrayi*, Fraser's Hill, Peninsular Malaysia. Photo: Morten Strange/ VIREO]

The largest of the Picidae known to survive in the New World, the Pileated Woodpecker favours dead or dying wood, pecking and hammering at one spot for long periods, particularly in winter, for its preferred prey of large carpenter ants (Camponotus). These photographs of a male show clearly the combination of bill and tongue in action. About half of the bill is pushed into the tree, the mandibles slightly apart to allow the tongue to extend into the hole. When the prey item is located and speared, the bill is retracted from the hole and the morsel consumed. In this instance, the tongue is first manipulating the prey against the upper mandible to facilitate the swallowing of the food.

[*Dryocopus pileatus pileatus*, Crossville, Tennessee, USA. Photos: Frank Schneidermeyer/ Oxford Scientific Films]

interspecific drumming "duels". Of course, this is not always the case. D. J. Dodenhoff and colleagues carried out a useful investigation to determine the extent to which woodpeckers exchanged drumming interspecifically, and examined the variables within drumming by which one species might recognize another. Using playback of four North American *Picoides* species, Nuttall's, White-headed, Hairy and Downy Woodpeckers, they found that individuals responded far less intensely to drumrolls of other, sympatric picids when the latter's drum cadences were dissimilar to their own; on the other hand, there was no significant difference between the behavioural reactions to drumrolls of conspecifics and the reactions to those of other species that are not sympatric when the cadences of the drumrolls were similar. The results, published in 2001, suggest that the drum's cadence encodes information for species recognition, and that, if an individual drums at a similar cadence to that of a sympatric heterospecific, then the signal may elicit the same response as that to a conspecific.

More species-specific vocal long-distance signals may be closely associated with or interspersed with drumming, as demonstrated by, for example, the Lesser Spotted Woodpecker in Eurasia and the Yellow-bellied Sapsucker in North America. In some cases, such vocalizations may partly replace drumming as a territorial advertisement, the Northern Flicker being a typical example of this, or they may even almost fully replace it, as occurs with the Middle Spotted Woodpecker. These digressions from what might be considered the norm for the respective genera are perhaps a reaction, or an adaptation, to the possible interference from other drumming species living in the same habitats.

Woodpeckers show a distinct preference for dead wood as a substrate for drumming. Thus, drumming could advertise habitat quality, since dead wood is, for most picid species, an important constituent of high-quality habitats. The evidence gathered so far, however, does not support this hypothesis. Rather, woodpeckers appear to choose particular drumming sites mainly because they produce loud and far-carrying sounds. These sites can also be artificial structures, such as metal poles, television aerials and buildings. Indeed, metal parts of buildings and such structures as sirens are not infrequently used for drumming, and

the result is a remarkably loud and startling signal. One observer in southern England who watched a Great Spotted Woodpecker hammering on a public-address system at a racecourse noted that, of the three large, conical speaker horns, the bird had selected to hammer on the metal base of the one that was pointing directly towards a rival woodpecker about 100 m away on a tree; the latter's drumming response to the exceptionally loud signal was described as sounding "pathetic" in comparison.

This drumming signal may have originated from the regular habit of carrying out woodwork on dead trees, an activity that inadvertently discloses the location of the bird and reveals the quality of the substrate on which it is working. It has probably evolved from the rather regular strokes that are produced when the woodpecker excavates a nesting or roosting hole. Taps at the hole are often given in encounters between the members of a breeding pair, and for several species of picid these constitute another, simpler instrumental signal.

Various species have developed more complex or irregular types of drumming than the simple rolls that are produced by most members of the family. Variation is especially pronounced among the melanerpine woodpeckers. The infrequent drumming of Lewis's Woodpecker consists of a weak roll followed by three or four individual taps, while the drumroll of the Red-bellied Woodpecker may be preceded by a single, discrete strike of the bill. The sapsuckers drum in a very distinctive manner. The Yellow-bellied Sapsucker produces rolls with clearly separated taps at the end and, sometimes, also at the beginning, giving a signal which sounds like "toc-toc-trrrrrrrrrr-ta-ta-toc--toc---toc". The Red-naped Sapsucker's drum is structured similarly. Likewise, the signal of Williamson's Sapsucker comprises a regular roll with several beats appended, although these terminal strikes are more widely spaced than those of the other sapsucker species. This pattern is not, however, confined to the sapsuckers. The Bearded Woodpecker in the Afrotropics also produces a drumroll with an ensuing series of four regular taps. Furthermore, the distinctive drumming of the Rufous Woodpecker in Asia has been likened to the sound emitted by a stalling engine, and is often transcribed as "bdddd-d-d--d----dt". A reversed pattern is shown by the Lineated Woodpecker, which commences with a couple

In the dense, gloomy understorey of South-east Asian evergreen forests, the strikingly bright yellow bill of the Maroon Woodpecker is often the first thing that draws the alert observer's attention to this picid's presence among the shadows. Seldom ascending more than a few metres above ground level, this species spends most of its life among the lush, tangled undergrowth, where the long pale bill, with its chisel-shaped tip, is perfectly suited to this woodpecker's foraging technique. It hammers a hole into live wood, quickly excavating a pit 2-3 cm deep and twice as long along the stem. From this pit, the bird catches beetles and other insect larvae with its sticky tongue. Maroon Woodpeckers also frequently attack rotten wood and decaying fallen logs, which they quickly break into pieces by hammering with the bill, thereby exposing larvae which can be easily snapped up.

This woodpecker, incidentally, plays a prominent role in the augury practised by the Iban people of Borneo; of seven augural bird species, two are members of the Picidae, the other being the Rufous Piculet (Sasia abnormis).

[Blythipicus rubiginosus, Mount Kinabalu, Borneo. Photos: Roland Seitre/ Bios]

Many woodpeckers obtain their food from dead or decaying wood, a typical example being the Pale-billed Woodpecker of Central America. A variety of methods is employed to remove bark from trees. The technique used by this and many other of the large species starts with a few bill blows that leave characteristic horizontal marks on the exposed wood; the bark is then levered off, and disposed of with a swift flick of the bill. Some picids, however, such as the Red-cockaded and Strickland's Woodpeckers (Picoides borealis and P. stricklandi) of North America, will use their feet to dislodge loose bark.

[Campephilus guatemalensis guatemalensis, Guanacaste, Costa Rica. Photo: Rob Curtis/VIREO]

of slow taps which are then followed by the roll. Some species produce only short double raps. One such example is the Chestnut Woodpecker, the drumming of which is a simple "dop, dop". This type of instrumental signal, however, is most typical of the ivory-bills. Thus, in the rainforests of South America, the Red-necked and the Robust Woodpeckers (*Campephilus robustus*) betray their presence by their distinctive "tok tók". In the case of another ivory-bill, the often syntopic Crimson-crested Woodpecker, the second blow is extended into a brief burst, so that the drumroll sounds like "da-drrr".

Mutual tapping, with one bird inside the hole and the other at the entrance, is typical of the Red-headed Woodpecker, as well as of some other melanerpine species such as the Jamaican Woodpecker (*Melanerpes radiolatus*), the Red-crowned and Red-bellied Woodpeckers and the Yellow-bellied Sapsucker. Double raps at the hole are also known to be part of the instrumental signals of the Pileated Woodpecker. That species' Eurasian congener, the Black Woodpecker, produces single strikes at the hole on various occasions, as when advertising a cavity and, especially, at change-overs during the periods of hole-excavation and incubation. These taps may lead to rhythmic series of blows with a delivery rate of about 80 blows per minute, even running to frantic and long series of blows at a rate of 140 per minute, and some brief fragments of drumming may be evident as well. This close relationship of the instrumental signals becomes apparent in the Guadeloupe Woodpecker, too. This species delivers short rolls and mutual tapping at the hole.

Besides drumming and tapping, other non-vocal sounds are produced by the Picidae. Most notable among these are the noises produced by the wings. The wingbeats of most woodpeckers can be heard in the flapping phase of the bounding flight. More conspicuous, and possibly of some relevance for communication, are the audible wingbeats of an excited woodpecker when searching for the location of an opponent, as has been demonstrated in playback experiments, or the wing noise of an agitated picid when it flies to its opponent or mate. The wings also produce sound during the fluttering aerial display (see Breeding). Even the tongue can produce a vibrating sound on tree surfaces, as had been noted by J. Jackson for the Red-cockaded Woodpecker, but it is not certain whether this has any functional significance.

Food and Feeding

Woodpeckers feed primarily on insects and their larvae, and other arthropods, and many of the members of this family rely to a greater or lesser extent on plant products such as nuts, fruits and tree sap. Many also take the nestlings of other hole-nesting species, but open-nesting birds are not exempt from woodpecker predation, either. The diet of nestling woodpeckers consists mainly of insects, represented chiefly by hymenopterans, beetles, hemipterans, homopterans, caterpillars, and dipteran flies. Some picids, including the Acorn, Lewis's and Jamaican Woodpeckers, the sapsuckers, and the Syrian and other pied woodpeckers, feed acorns and fruits to older broods.

Access to the larvae of wood-boring insects and to the nests and mounds of ants and termites is made possible as a result of the morphological adaptations of the Picidae (see Morphological Aspects), and this ability is also one of the reasons for the great success of the family in so many climatic regions of the world. In addition, many woodpeckers are rather omnivorous and opportunistic feeders. The American melanerpines belong in this category, but so, too, does the Great Spotted Woodpecker of Eurasia. Insular species, such as the Jamaican Woodpecker and the West Indian Woodpecker (*Melanerpes superciliaris*), are particularly flexible in their choice of food. Very frequently, there are marked seasonal differences in the diet, a good example of which is provided by the northern populations of the Great Spotted Woodpecker. This species, in the boreal part of its vast range, changes from a predominantly insect diet in the summer to one of pine or spruce (*Picea*) seeds in the winter, and in spring it supplements its diet with tree sap. Similar radical seasonal changes are observed among the sapsuckers, which for much of the time rely on the sap of trees, and among other melanerpines, including, for example, Lewis's Woodpecker and the Red-bellied Woodpecker.

The picid bill is the ideal tool for excavating food. At the same time, even the bill that is most specialized for chiselling is still suited for other tasks, such as grabbing and carrying large objects, tearing off bark and wood fibres, and pulling apart pieces of meat. Only those woodpeckers which do not undertake much excavating work possess a bill that is optimized for grasping objects or for digging; in the first case the bill is slightly curved

Fallen branches and trees are an important component of the forest ecosystem, although one that is scarce in managed modern temperate plantations. Fallen, rotten timber is visited and exploited by many woodpecker species. An excavated pit is already apparent on the side of this log, and the male Pileated Woodpecker is opening up a second, in search of the ants that comprise the bulk of its diet. Rotting wood is a transitory habitat, home to a wide variety of invertebrates, and is exploited by many bird families, none more so than the Picidae.

[Dryocopus pileatus pileatus,
Sanibel Island,
Florida, USA.
Photo: Arthur Morris/
Windrush]

and has a pointed tip, while, in the second, the digging bill is long. The action of the bill is greatly augmented by the long, barbed tongue (see Morphological Aspects) with which ants and termites can be licked up, and with which a wood-boring larva, once its tunnel has been chiselled open, can be finally speared. A further way in which the bill's range of operation is evident is in the use of cracks and other structures as anvils, a highly interesting aspect that is discussed in greater detail below.

Woodpeckers, then, are primarily insectivores, with a diet that reveals a special emphasis on wood-boring larvae and on those that hide in crevices in and under the bark of dead limbs or trunks of trees, or in the ground. The large larvae of long-horned beetles (Cerambycidae), the round-headed borers, are typical woodpecker prey. So also are the flat-headed borers, larvae of the metallic wood-boring beetles of the family Buprestidae, the larvae of the bark beetles (Scolytidae), and wood-boring caterpillars of carpenter moths (Cossidae), as well as hymenopterans, especially horntails (Siricidae). The ivory-billed woodpeckers in the genus *Campephilus* are renowned for their habit of taking very large beetle larvae, and both they and other woodpeckers also readily take adult beetles. Among the smaller picids, the White-backed Woodpecker of Eurasia is a prominent example of a specialist predator of wood-boring larvae, in this case those of long-horned beetles and carpenter moths. Not surprisingly, woodpeckers also capture and consume other insects, and spiders, which they may happen to find under or on the bark. During the warm seasons of the year, and especially when feeding young, they commonly exploit the flush of leaf-chewing caterpillars and plant-lice. Generally, the nestling's diet differs from that of the adult, and particularly from the latter's diet outside the breeding season, in being more diverse and in containing less plant material and more soft-bodied insects and insect larvae.

There is a degree of uncertainty over the way in which woodpeckers find their food when it is concealed in timber. It is probable that they detect it initially by some optical give-away signs; with some probing taps they are able to locate a hole. Field experiments have demonstrated that they readily learn to find food, such as sunflower seeds, in holes covered with tape, and many other observations indicate that woodpeckers possess an excellent knowledge of the locations of potential prey. One observer

placed mealworms in holes in a log and then plugged the holes with cork stoppers, an operation designed to prevent other birds from obtaining the food, which was intended for the local Great Spotted Woodpeckers. The plan worked: while the House Sparrows (*Passer domesticus*), Common Starlings (*Sturnus vulgaris*) and others were unable to locate the worms, the woodpeckers immediately knocked out the plugs to obtain the food. There is some speculation that a prey item may be located by the sound that it makes, but hard experimental evidence for this appears not to exist. Field experiments have also shown that woodpeckers react to smell, although, once again, there are no decisive data that would indicate that olfaction plays a role in the detecting of prey.

Ants (Formicidae) are a common food of the Picidae. The two wrynecks are ant specialists. The adults feed both themselves and their nestlings chiefly on ants, and their pupae and eggs, which they obtain from the terrestrial nests of these insects by gleaning, probing and tongue action. In fact, at least 60% of all woodpecker species are known to include ants in the diet. Perhaps surprisingly, termites (Isoptera), on the other hand, are eaten by only a few species, among them the Ground Woodpecker of South Africa. The many picids which feed on ants range from the smaller species to the largest, and the habit is particularly marked among the members of the genera *Picus*, *Dinopium*, *Gecinulus*, *Campethera*, *Geocolaptes*, *Piculus*, *Colaptes*, *Celeus*, *Dryocopus*, *Meiglyptes*, *Hemicircus* and *Mulleripicus*. Indeed, ants are the most important food for the Eurasian Green Woodpecker; and even in the diet of its less specialized relative, the Grey-faced Woodpecker, ants of the genera *Myrmica* and *Lasius*, along with termites and their brood, still prevail and can often comprise more than 90% of the stomach contents of individuals. The food taken by the threatened Red-cockaded Woodpecker includes up to 95% ants by biomass, with a clear peak in spring, when the diet of males contains on average 85% ants. The males of that species consume more ants than do the females, and ants also form an important portion of the nestling diet. That ants and termites represent an important food source for the large *Dryocopus* logcocks has been demonstrated by studies of the Pileated Woodpecker and the Black Woodpecker, but at least two other of their congeners, the Lineated and the White-bellied Woodpeckers, are also known to take many ants. The diet of the

Probing is a technique used to obtain prey that may be concealed in a crevice or hole little wider than the diameter of the bill. It is a method frequently employed by the delicately marked Fine-spotted Woodpecker when foraging in epiphytes and vine tangles, at the base of trees and oil palms (Elaeis guineensis), or on the ground. Having inserted its bill, the bird flicks out its sticky tongue, gluing small insects, especially ants, to the tip. The elongated tongue of woodpeckers means that the depth to which these birds can probe is increased substantially beyond the mandible tips.

[Campethera punctuligera punctuligera, Fajara golf course, Gambia. Photo: Gordon Langsbury]

Black Woodpecker has been found to contain 54% ants in winter and up to 97% in the milder seasons, and these insects comprise about 80-99% of the diet of nestlings of this species. These large *Dryocopus* woodpeckers target the nests of large ants living within trees. Thus, they prey on *Camponotus* ants that live and nest in the core of living pines and spruces, while the Neotropical species, such as the Lineated Woodpecker, seek out the well-armed ants of the genus *Azteca* in hollow parts of trumpet trees (*Cecropia*). Other large ant-eating and termite-eating woodpeckers are the Ashy Woodpecker (*Mulleripicus fulvus*), which is confined to the Indonesian island of Sulawesi, and the related Great Slaty Woodpecker, the biggest of all the Old World's picids, which occurs from north-west India across to south-west China and southwards to the Greater Sundas. In Central America and north-west South America, the smaller Cinnamon Woodpecker (*Celeus loricatus*) also locates ants that live symbiotically in plants, and exploits these.

Woodpeckers seem not to shy away even from rather aggressive ants. The overlapping tarsal scutes and the feathers that cover the nostrils of many species would seem to comprise the corresponding adaptations to counter the armoury of these insects. At least one species, the White Woodpecker of the Neotropics, is known to open the nests of wasps and wild bees to take the broods and the honey of these hymentopterans.

Very little is known about the diets of the piculets. For the few species for which food items have been recorded, ants appear to be by far the most important source of nutrition, although termites are also sometimes eaten and, in several cases, small beetles, spiders and other arthropods. A notable exception is the African Piculet. This species, the only picumnine present in the African continent, appears to avoid ants altogether, preferring instead to sustain itself on wood-boring beetle larvae supplemented with adult beetles and some other insects. It is also worthy of note that the largest member of this subfamily, the Antillean Piculet, feeds principally on arthropods, including ants, but also takes a reasonable quantity of fruit.

Practically all members of the Picidae for which adequate information is available ingest some plant material, and some species rely at least partly on plant products. In fact, frugivory is widespread among the woodpeckers, and fruits and berries are taken by many species. Although they rely heavily on ants and other insects, the wrynecks have been observed to feed on the berries of elder (*Sambucus*), and even the ivory-bills occasionally consume fruit, as also do two of the logcocks, the Pileated and White-bellied Woodpeckers. Nuts and the stones of fleshy fruits are frequently eaten by the pied woodpeckers, and the northern populations of the Great Spotted Woodpecker are heavily dependent on the seeds of pines and spruces. The most frugivorous group, the American genus *Melanerpes*, not only takes much fruit but also, in the case of many of its species, eats nuts and, above all, acorns, while the related sapsuckers have been observed to eat buds in spring. Although some species appear to take certain fruits merely to get at the seeds which they contain, as with the Syrian Woodpecker when it attacks apricots and prunes (see also Relationship with Man), the seeds are not the primary goal for the truly frugivorous woodpeckers. Hence, woodpeckers may be important seed-dispersers in some ecosystems.

Frugivory is apparently least common among African woodpeckers and is most common among the melanerpines and the South American *Celeus*. Woodpeckers of these last two groups may be among the most frequent visitors to Neotropical fruiting trees. They act as dispersers of seeds only when they swallow the fruits, and whether they do that depends very much on the type of fruit involved. For example, the Black-cheeked Woodpecker (*Melanerpes pucherani*) has been observed to swallow the seeds of the flacourtiaceous tree *Caesaria corymbosa*, but to strip the arils of the burseraceous *Protium* and drop the seeds under the mother tree, thus in the latter case acting as a seed thief from the plant's perspective. The Red-crowned and Golden-fronted Woodpeckers and the Campo Flicker eat fruits of cacti on a sufficiently regular basis to act as seed-dispersers for those plants. Gila Woodpeckers feed on the berries of mistletoes (*Phoradendron*) during November and December, but because they spend little time in the host plant they contribute little to the dispersal of the hemi-parasite. The Golden-naped Woodpecker is a typical example of a melanerpine woodpecker that takes much fruit. It feeds on the fruits of the bird- and bat-dispersed *Cecropia* trumpet trees, on figs, on various arillate seeds, and on bananas, oranges and palm fruits, and it also accepts these fruits at artificial feeders. *Cecropia* fruits, figs and various other plant foods make up about half of

The Yellow-crowned Woodpecker, a small species inhabiting dry, open woodland across most of the Indian Subcontinent, takes much of its food by gleaning. Moving over the bark of a tree, it plucks insects from the surface and from crevices. It also excavates bark and dead wood for subsurface larvae. This is one of a number of Old World picids that also feed on nectar, although this is a more common component in the diet of New World woodpeckers. Several of the latter take sugar water from feeders specially set up in gardens to attract hummingbirds (Trochilidae).

[Dendrocopos mahrattensis mahrattensis, Keoladeo Ghana (Bharatpur) National Park, India. Photo: Manfred Pfefferle]

the diet of the Jamaican Woodpecker and of the West Indian Woodpecker. A predilection for fruits results in some melanerpines being attracted in rather large numbers to commercial orchards of oranges, papayas, bananas and apples, where they may cause some damage (see Relationship with Man).

Many of the smaller and medium-sized Picidae feed on nectar. This behaviour has been recorded for a number of *Dendrocopos* species, among them the Brown-capped Wood-pecker, the Yellow-crowned Woodpecker (*Dendrocopos mahrattensis*), the Crimson-breasted Woodpecker (*Dendrocopos cathpharius*) and the Great Spotted Woodpecker, and several other Asian or Eurasian species, including the Lesser Yellownape, the Streak-throated Woodpecker (*Picus xanthopygaeus*), the Grey-faced Woodpecker, and the Black-rumped and Greater Flamebacks. The sipping of nectar is also not uncommon in the New World among melanerpine and *Celeus*

These photographs of Lineated Woodpeckers illustrate the capability of one species of employing very different feeding techniques. Hammering and pecking, and probing into excavations, are common foraging methods used by this woodpecker. In broad terms, males prefer larger branches than those utilized by females. In this instance, however, the female has hammered several holes in a trunk and is probing one of these for invertebrates, whereas the male, on the right, has pecked the bark from a smaller overhanging branch and is plucking insects from the exposed wood.

[Left: Dryocopus lineatus erythrops, Telêmaco Borba, Paraná, Brazil. Photo: Haroldo Palo Jr.

Right: Dryocopus lineatus lineatus, San Fernando de Apure, Venezuela. Photo: Luiz Claudio Marigo]

While some woodpeckers depend on the same type of prey throughout the year, others switch between seasons, reflecting the availability of different foods. In autumn, the Red-bellied Woodpecker takes advantage of the season's crop of soft-cased fruits, of both cultivated and wild species, especially in the northern half of its United States range. It switches in winter to seeds and nuts, which it will hoard for use when the supplies are exhausted in late winter. During the summer, this species' diet is dominated by insects, especially ants, although it also licks sap from scarred trees or from wells created by sapsuckers (Sphyrapicus).

[*Melanerpes carolinus*, Long Island, New York, USA. Photo: Tom Vezo]

woodpeckers, and a number of species will readily take sugar water from feeders, too.

Because of their ability to excavate, woodpeckers can tap another rich source of plant fluids. This is the sap that is available in the sap-transporting cells of the phloem of trees. After the dormant season, rich sap flow becomes established in the early spring, at a time when other food sources may still be poor or depleted, and thus provides vital sustenance at a critical time immediately prior to the nesting season. Many species of woodpecker cover the bark of living trees with series of regularly spaced holes from which they obtain the sugary sap. Typically, the holes, known as "sap wells", are arranged in horizontal rows, and these rows, together with those made in previous years, can extend over rather distinctly large parts of a tree. The holes are just deep enough to reach the tree's sap-transporting vessels, and secretions may appear within seconds after the woodpecker has penetrated the bark. Once sap has begun to flow, the woodpecker licks up the sugary and protein-rich fluid. Other bird species, including other woodpeckers, as well as mammals such as squirrels (Sciuridae), mice (Muridae), dormice (Gliridae) and deer (Cervidae), and various insects, also take advantage of this food source. As an added bonus, the woodpeckers readily snap up ants that are attracted to these pits to collect a share of the nutritious fluid.

For the North American Yellow-bellied Sapsucker, tree sap constitutes an important part of the nutrition. This woodpecker taps numerous deciduous and coniferous species, very commonly poplar (*Populus*), willow (*Salix*), birch (*Betula*), maple (*Acer*), hickory (*Carya*) and alder (*Alnus*), as well as pines, spruces and firs (*Abies*). Sap is tapped at all parts of a tree, on the trunk as well as in the crown. Upon its return from the wintering grounds, the sapsucker uses old sap wells or other sources of sap on bruised parts of a tree. During late summer and autumn sap and phloem form the species' staple food, and many fresh wells are made. If insect food becomes scarce for any reason, the utilization of sap may start earlier in the summer. The Red-naped Sapsucker uses sap holes throughout the year, exploiting various conifers and deciduous trees and bushes on the breeding grounds. Williamson's Sapsucker, like the other species of its genus, drinks sap from various tree species, among them the lodgepole pine (*Pinus contorta*), the alpine hemlock (*Tsuga mertensiana*), both red and white firs (*Abies magnifica*, *A. concolor*), the Jeffrey pine (*Pinus jeffreyi*) and the quaking aspen (*Populus tremuloides*).

Sap-sucking is also important for various other melanerpine species, including the Acorn, Gila, Red-bellied, White-fronted (*Melanerpes cactorum*) and Hispaniolan Woodpeckers. Acorn Woodpeckers, in order to acquire a supply of sap, drill holes 3-19 mm deep and 5-15 mm wide into live oaks; for Californian populations of this species, sap is especially important in the months of June and July. For the White-fronted Woodpecker, it figures most prominently in the diet during the dry season in the austral winter, in semi-desert conditions, when sap-feeding accounts for between 16% and 83% of the species' foraging efforts.

Contrary to the earlier beliefs of many ornithologists, amateur and professional alike, sap-sucking is by no means restricted to the New World. At least four of the pied woodpeckers, at least in some parts of their respective ranges in the Old World, all rely on sap in spring. These are the Arabian, the Rufous-bellied, the Great Spotted and the Eurasian Three-toed Woodpeckers. The importance of the nutritious sap for these species, and the exact role that it may play in their survival in the period preceding the breeding season, have not, however, been properly quantified. Its contribution to the daily energy intake and as a protein source is probably substantial. Tree sap may even be, for short periods, the key resource for survival in harsh environments, such as boreal and mountain forests, and arid habitats.

Frugivory and pecking, especially when coupled with a largely sedentary lifestyle, lead naturally to the exploitation of another rich food source, namely seeds. Indeed, it is the species of woodpecker which frequently engage in those activities that also habitually exploit seeds and nuts. The significance of this food varies geographically. Generally, it is most important in more seasonal environments, and the degree to which it is exploited varies within a species' range. The Acorn Woodpecker's staple diet consists of dried acorns, but green acorns are taken as well. Acorns make up about half of the nutriment of northern populations, for which they are the basic energy source in winter; South American populations of the species, however, are less dependent on acorns, and rarely store them. Other seeds, such as those of pines, are also taken by this woodpecker, which, furthermore, occasionally feeds older broods of nestlings with acorns. Acorns contain tannins, a fact which generally renders them less profitable for birds. Compared with jays, however, Acorn Woodpeckers fare much better with a diet that consists of acorns alone, and they are able to cope with the physiological effects of tannins. Two of the species congeners, the Red-bellied

The most frugivorous
group of all the Picidae
is the New World genus
Melanerpes. A typical
example is the Red-
crowned Woodpecker of
northern South America.
This female is feeding on
the sweet fleshy fruits
of a mango tree, but the
species is equally fond
of papayas, bananas
and various other fruits
and berries. Indeed, its
liking for fruit is such that
it often brings it into
conflict with owners of
commercial fruit
plantations, and even
gardeners may consider
this bird a nuisance
because of its fruit-eating
habits. When feeding on
fruit, the woodpecker
sometimes pierces the
skin and then pecks
small pieces in situ.
Alternatively, it will tear off
a larger chunk of the
growing fruit and fly with it
to a nearby tree, where a
crevice or crack in the
bark may be used as an
anvil to enable the bird to
pick more manageable
pieces at its leisure.
As well as consuming fruit,
many woodpeckers eat
nuts and seeds, and some
species probably play an
important role in seed
dispersal.

[*Melanerpes rubricapillus
rubricapillus,*
in *llanos* of Venezuela.
Photo: Jean-Louis le
Moigne/NHPA]

and Red-headed Woodpeckers, also regularly eat acorns and various other seeds and nuts.

The harvesting and consumption of acorns and other nuts is a practice that is restricted seasonally, and in the case of another *Melanerpes* species, Lewis's Woodpecker, it is associated with a corresponding habitat shift and migration-like movements. In Eurasia, the northern populations of the Great Spotted Woodpecker are the ones most dependent on the availability of pine or spruce seeds, or beech mast. This may also be correlated with some local movements and habitat shifts, and poor seed yields can lead to eruptive dismigration by this species (see Movements). Various studies have shown that Great Spotted Woodpeckers strip about ten pine cones of their seeds per day, and they consume a daily total of about 700-1450 seeds, weighing 11-14 g.

With the exception of the wrynecks and the piculets, most members of the Picidae are rather omnivorous, and many different types of food have been recorded in their diets. A number of species will occasionally snatch a lizard or a frog. This has been documented for the Eurasian Green Woodpecker, the Great Spotted and Pygmy Woodpeckers, the Greater Yellownape (*Picus flavinucha*), the Okinawa Woodpecker and the Afrotropical Bearded Woodpecker in the Old World, and for the Acorn, Jamaican, Red-bellied and West Indian Woodpeckers in America. In some cases, the parent may even feed these items to the young, and it is particularly noteworthy that tree-frogs of the species *Eleutherodactylus martinicensis* constitute about 10% of the prey items fed to nestlings by the Guadeloupe Woodpecker. In the Neotropics, the White Woodpecker has been observed feeding on raw meat hung up to dry, an example of the kind of opportunism that is rather widespread among the Picidae. Among the more unusual arthropod prey, scorpions (Scorpiones) are known to be taken now and then by Great Spotted and Fulvous-breasted Woodpeckers, centipedes (Chilopoda) are an occasional prey of Greater Yellownapes, and millipedes (Diplopoda) are sometimes eaten by Golden-tailed Woodpeckers. Molluscs also feature in the diets of the Picidae: for example, Great Spotted Woodpeckers have been observed to open mussels, and snails are taken by the Jamaican Woodpecker. An interesting observation concerns the collecting of small bones from raptor pellets by the Red-cockaded Woodpecker prior to egg-laying, presumably as a source of calcium. Bone fragments have also been found in the nestling food of Eurasian Three-toed Woodpeckers.

In most parts of the world in which they occur, woodpeckers are rather frequent visitors to gardens, where they will freely visit birdtables and other artificial feeders. Besides accepting a wide variety of natural foods, often placed out specially to attract these birds, they will also feed avidly on such highly nutritious items as suet. Indeed, in the more severe winter conditions in the northern parts of the world, the survival prospects of several picids can be enhanced by the provision of such food in gardens.

Woodpeckers utilize many distinct foraging techniques. The most typical are wood-excavating in its various forms, the flaking-off of bark, probing, and gleaning. With the exception of some melanerpine species, flycatching is only rarely used to obtain prey. Usually, there are clear seasonal differences in the frequency with which the various feeding techniques are employed. Costly subsurface techniques occur during the harsher conditions of the non-breeding season, when the range of foraging methods used is also at its least diverse, while gleaning and opportunistic foraging are typical of the breeding season. A further general trend is that the mobility of a woodpecker decreases with increasing body size, the result being that larger species tend to stay longer on a foraging site, and to move less frequently and more slowly.

There are many styles adopted by woodpeckers when excavating for food. In most cases, shallow pits are created, and the action consists of a combination of hammering and tearing away wood. The tiny piculets hammer small holes to gain access to the ants which burrow into thin twigs and stems. By contrast, the Black Woodpecker and other *Dryocopus* species excavate huge pits in their search for the nests of tree-living ants. Some of the distinctly chisel-billed species, such as the White-backed and Maroon Woodpeckers, prefer soft wood for their work, literally

gouging into the substrate. The Yellow-bellied Sapsucker drills shallow holes in many tree species in order to obtain sap and phloem; these holes may be arranged in vertical columns, as horizontal bands or, when on smaller branches, in spiralling bands. Among the more terrestrial picids, the well-studied Eurasian Green Woodpecker pecks funnel-shaped holes up to 12 cm deep in the ground, having first swept away moss, dead leaves, debris or snow with the bill, and it then procures its ant prey with the action of its very long tongue. Such holes, which are often exploited in lengthy and repeated visits, expose the tunnel systems of the ants, which appear en masse when disturbed by the woodpecker. When snow cover is heavy, it may dig tunnels almost 1 m long in order to reach its favoured food.

Foraging woodpeckers employ a variety of techniques to remove bark from trees. They may begin with a few tangential blows of the bill, which they then use as a lever to pry off a piece of bark. These bill blows leave characteristic horizontal marks arranged in regularly spaced rows on the exposed wood. Loose bark is simply torn off with the bill and disposed of with a swift flick of the bill. Some woodpeckers, including, among others, the Red-cockaded and Strickland's Woodpeckers of America, have been recorded as dislodging bark with their feet.

Access to concealed prey is very frequently achieved through the action of probing. The woodpecker inserts its bill into a crevice or hole in bark or exposed wood, or in epiphytes and vine tangles, or in the ground or in mud, as, for example, in mangrove stands; the same method is employed for probing in fruits and in flowers. Having inserted its bill in this way, the woodpecker then

The Celeus *woodpeckers subsist mainly on ants and termites, but most are known to feed regularly on fruit, too. This behaviour is particularly marked among the South American members of the genus. They frequently roost in fruit trees, and will ignore invertebrates completely for short periods when a fruit crop is abundant. As the photograph of a male Chestnut Woodpecker shows, the bird has no difficulty in clinging to a slender twig in order to get at the fruit, and it will remove all of the flesh down to the stone. A woodpecker will return to the same individual fruit, or to the same tree, for several days to take advantage of such easily obtainable food. Although frugivory is most common among the* Melanerpes *and* Celeus *species living in the Neotropics, it is also practised by many other members of the family. These range in size from the small Antillean Piculet* (Nesoctites micromegas) *to two of the largest of all woodpeckers, the Pileated and White-bellied Woodpeckers* (Dryocopus pileatus *and* D. javensis).

[Celeus elegans elegans, *French Guiana. Photo: Thierry Montford/ Bios]*

The Yellow-fronted
Woodpecker is one of the
Melanerpes genus that is
almost entirely dependent
on plant material for food.
It stores seeds for use in
leaner times, a habit more
usually associated with
omnivorous woodpeckers
living in seasonal climates.
Some woodpeckers
disperse the seeds of
tropical plants, although
their usefulness in this
respect is variable.
This species' relative,
the Black-cheeked
Woodpecker (Melanerpes
pucherani), for example,
swallows the seeds of the
flacourtiaceous tree
Caesaria corymbosa and
voids them later, thus
aiding their dispersal;
in the case of the
burseraceous Protium,
however, it simply drops
the seeds beneath the
tree, thus acting as a seed
thief from the plant's
perspective.

[Melanerpes flavifrons,
Iguazú National Park,
Misiones, Argentina.
Photo: Julián Alonso]

flicks out its sticky tongue so as to glue small insects, especially ants, and to spear grubs and other prey hidden deep in the substrate by means of the tongue's barbed tip. The use of the sticky and barbed tongue, which increases the range of action of the bill far beyond the mandible tips, is highly characteristic of the gleaning and probing behaviour of foraging woodpeckers. An additional point of interest is that, should a woodpecker accidentally drop an item of food, it may very occasionally open a wing slightly to prevent the food from falling to the ground; although there are few observations of this behaviour, it has been recorded for about half a dozen picid species.

Gleaning is the most common surface manoeuvre carried out by all members of the family. It is a relatively simple action in which the woodpecker, while clinging to or sitting on the substrate or perch, grabs a nearby food item. The picid anatomy allows these birds to reach a long distance with little effort. This is a great aid to frugivorous species, some of which, such as the melanerpines, are particularly skilled in reaching beneath a perch. There are, however, specific differences in just how far a woodpecker will reach sideways when on a trunk. It seems that, generally, those species which undertake a lot of woodwork are poor reachers. The Chestnut Woodpecker, for example, is very good at reaching, but does not excavate very frequently. Many members of the Picidae, particularly the smaller ones, hang upside-down to get at certain food items. During the process of foraging in this manner, a woodpecker may run along the underside of a branch, as do Middle Spotted and Arabian Woodpeckers, among others, or it may cling crosswise in a more tit-like fashion, as demonstrated by the Great Spotted, Lesser Spotted and Buff-rumped Woodpeckers.

When a tree harbours many caterpillars, this abundant source of food is eagerly exploited by some picids. In Europe, this situation coincides more or less with the period when Great Spotted Woodpeckers have just completed their breeding cycle, and from June to August both adults and juveniles of this species often take advantage of the glut of caterpillars. Moving around rather clumsily among the foliage of such trees, they hop about, and hang upside-down with wings flapping, while gleaning prey.

Woodpeckers are generally good fliers, and most are capable of covering large distances between feeding sites. In normal

circumstances, they exhibit an efficient bounding flight (see General Habits). A different mode of flight is needed, however, for aerial flycatching. This is a foraging tactic practised by several of the picids, being most pronounced among the melanerpines. Acorn Woodpeckers are expert fly-catchers, and are most active in utilizing this foraging strategy in the late hours towards dusk. They sally from a snag or fence post and catch a single insect on each flight. In spring this foraging mode is most important, often involving the whole social unit, and aerial prey is also a significant part of the diet of the nestlings. In South America, the White Woodpecker occasionally catches insects on the wing. Probably the woodpecker most specialized in flycatching, however, is another *Melanerpes* species, Lewis's Woodpecker. Both its foraging activities and its migratory behaviour (see Movements) are reflected in its overall style of flight, typified by longer phases of flapping flight and by relatively low air speed. Individuals of this species frequently sit on prominent perches, from where they spend much time in scanning the surroundings for potential prey. From these perches they sally into the air, approaching insects in a crow-like flight, with elaborate manoeuvres leading to the final capture; having successfully caught the prey, they frequently use gliding flight to return to the perch. Lewis's Woodpeckers do not take aerial prey only in single excursions; over 10% of their flycatching involves continuous flights lasting several minutes, and in which several insects may be seized. The Yellow-bellied Sapsucker, too, frequently takes prey on the wing. It sallies occasionally from an exposed perch, returning to the same post or to a different one.

Yet another skill possessed by woodpeckers, and again associated with pecking and the ability to work on hard wood, is the use of what are termed "anvils". Practically all woodpeckers which take prey that they cannot mandibulate sufficiently for ingestion carry such items to a fork, crevice or similar place in which the unwieldy item can be fixed. With the help of such an anvil, they can smash hard-cased beetles, open galls, remove the stones of fruits or prepare them for consumption, and so forth.

The use of anvils is not unique among birds, since, for instance, thrushes (Turdidae) and probably also kingfishers (Alcedinidae) smash snails on stones, but it is certainly most highly developed among the woodpeckers. Picids which rely almost to-

Fallen fruit is an easily accessible source of food for many birds and other animals. Although not a terrestrial woodpecker in the true sense, the Green-barred Woodpecker spends at least some time foraging on the ground. This is especially the case with the races inhabiting the Chaco woodland, pampas and scrub and in the southern parts of the range, which are partly terrestrial. Ants constitute by far the greater part of the diet of this Neotropical species, but it is opportunistic and will feed on berries and fruits. This male, having come across some fallen citrus fruit in the Argentine pampas, proceeds to attack it with vigour. The northern subspecies of the Green-barred Woodpecker are more arboreal in their habits, but they, too, will take advantage of fruit, whether still on trees or on the ground.

[Colaptes melanochloros leucofrenatus, Salado's Depression, Buenos Aires, Argentina. Photos: Yves Bilat]

A great many woodpeckers include nuts in their diet, one of them being the Great Spotted Woodpecker. Insects and larvae are its dominant food items in summer, while in autumn the birds switch to plant material, such as walnuts and hazelnuts.

This species, the most numerous picid in much of its Eurasian range, is an opportunistic omnivore. It has also been recorded as taking nectar, sap, scorpions, frogs and even mussels, as well as nestlings of hole-dwelling birds. Experiments show that woodpeckers readily learn to find food. Great Spotted Woodpeckers quickly removed cork stoppers from holes in a log to obtain mealworms that had been placed inside.

[Left: *Dendrocopos major pinetorum*, Black Forest, Germany. Photo: Manfred Pfefferle.

Right: *Dendrocopos major pinetorum*, The Netherlands. Photo: Jan van de Kam/ Bruce Coleman]

tally on anvils for obtaining pine and spruce seeds are the most specialized, and the best-studied species in this regard is therefore the Great Spotted Woodpecker. The most primitive types of anvil, those described above, are used by most species. In many cases, a particular anvil is utilized only once, although some woodpeckers may use one site repeatedly. A more advanced form of this behaviour is represented by the use of a number of anvils of varying sizes, with selection being made according to the object that has to be manipulated at any given time. In the most highly developed form of anvil use, the anvil is created by the woodpecker itself for that specific purpose. Great Spotted Woodpeckers concentrate their activity at one anvil which can accommodate cones of different sizes; they utilize ancillary anvils much less frequently, and mainly to open cones of a specific shape. In order to use the same anvil repeatedly, the woodpecker has to empty it before reuse. To do this, the Great Spotted Woodpecker has devised a neat method: it places the new object between its breast and the substrate, it then removes the old one, a pine cone for instance, and finally, with a few blows of the bill, it fixes the new object in the anvil for processing. Hundreds of stripped cones may lie under a heavily used anvil. This behaviour, involving the clearing-out of a site for reuse, occurs apparently only among very advanced species. So far, the Great Spotted Woodpecker is the only one which seems to carry out these actions as a regular part of anvil use; such behaviour has not been observed for related species.

During anvil use, the woodpecker wedges food or some other object into a crack in the bark, mandibulates it, leaves, visits the site again later, and sometimes then transports the item to another place. The moving of objects among different anvils is a rather common component of anvil use.

Anvils allow woodpeckers to take advantage of highly nutritional food sources that would otherwise be inaccessible to them. In its most highly evolved form, the use of anvils has all the characteristics of genuine tool-using. In this context, another kind of tool use has been observed in which a Gila Woodpecker dipped pieces of bark or seeds into a honey syrup provided at a feeder, and then fed the nutritious liquid to its fledglings.

Especially if anvils are primitive, as is the case with cracks and other suitable sites that are used opportunistically, it can often be difficult to draw a line between caching and anvil use if fragments of food are left behind. The storing of food is sometimes, therefore, not clearly separable from the use of anvils. When an anvil has not been cleaned out for reuse, the intended food, or some of it, then remains in its position, and the new item has to be placed into another crevice. Syrian Woodpeckers, for example, may fill long cracks with the opened stones of plums or with apricots. Thus, it may sometimes not be clear whether a species really caches food.

Notwithstanding these possible problems in defining caching behaviour, there are many perfectly obvious cases of food-storing among the melanerpine woodpeckers. Two types of food-storing can be recognized, known respectively as scatter-hoarding and larder-hoarding. The Red-bellied Woodpecker provides an example of the former. These woodpeckers begin to collect and store acorns, hickory nuts, hazel (*Corylus*) nuts, corn, pine seeds and various other seeds in autumn, and continue to do so into early winter; they store single food items usually in crevices, and occasionally also cache insects and fruit. Every item is placed in a different location, a food-storing strategy that is reminiscent of the caching behaviour of crows (Corvidae) and tits.

The larder-hoarding species, on the other hand, focus their storing activity on just a few sites. Red-headed Woodpeckers place larger insects in crevices or cavities as interim stores. They store many acorns, beech mast and other nuts and corn in single cracks and bark crevices during years with good mast crops, and they defend their one or few larder trees against all intruders, both of their own and of other species. Harvesting of the crop occupies most of the woodpeckers' active time in the early autumn. Items are stored in any kind of natural or man-made crevice, and holes are not excavated by the woodpecker itself; if a nut does not fit into the intended storage site, the nut is broken into pieces rather than the crevice being prepared to fit the food. Some stores are sealed with wood chips. Lewis's Woodpeckers also shell the acorns and nuts which they harvest in autumn, using several anvils for

When snow covers their foraging areas and insects are scarce, woodpeckers living in the higher latitudes of the Northern Hemisphere are often forced to change their dietary habits. Many become more dependent on cached food, or turn to the most readily available plant matter. In most cases, this means pine (Pinus) or spruce (Picea) seeds, which offer a highly nutritious source of food. This male White-backed Woodpecker demonstrates the manner in which this species uses its bill as a pair of tweezers, reaching between the scales of the cone to remove the seeds. Plant matter, including seeds, nuts and fruits, makes up only a small proportion of the diet of this woodpecker. Even in the harsh conditions of a Siberian winter, when temperatures remain below zero throughout the day for several months on end, it is more likely to obtain its food by hammering deeply into the lower trunks of small trees in search of the large wood-boring larvae of cerambycid beetles.

[Dendrocopos leucotos leucotos, northern Ussuriland, south-east Siberia, Russia. Photos: Yuri Shibnev]

Almost all woodpeckers which take large or hard items of food also make use of what are termed "anvils". These are crevices or forks in trees, or similar sites, which are readily utilized for securing nuts, fruits and large hard-cased insects, and preparing them for consumption. Most such anvils are used only once, and in some cases the woodpecker itself creates the anvil. Anvils are particularly important for certain picids which eat conifer seeds, and one species in particular, the Great Spotted Woodpecker (Dendrocopos major), has developed the behaviour further. This woodpecker repeatedly uses the same anvil, which is designed so that it can accommodate cones of different sizes. Before each use, the woodpecker has to clear out the anvil, and for this it has devised an interesting method which reveals just how advanced this species is: while holding the new cone firmly in place between its breast and the substrate, it removes and discards the old one and then, with a few bill blows, fixes the new cone in position. A single Great Spotted Woodpecker is capable of stripping up to 50 cones per day, the number depending on the species of conifer. As a result, thousands of broken cones can be found beneath a heavily used main anvil. In addition, a small number of secondary anvils may be used infrequently, primarily to process cones of a specific shape. It has been estimated that, in winter, an individual Great Spotted Woodpecker can, on a daily basis, consume up to 1700 pine seeds, or 8000 larch (Larix) seeds, or as many as 10,000 spruce (Picea) seeds.

[Anvil and pine cones, northern Finland. Photo: David Tipling/ Windrush]

Some woodpeckers are so dependent on a particular food source that they cache food to ensure a sufficient supply to see them through the winter. One of the most remarkable phenomena is the storing behaviour of the fittingly named Acorn Woodpecker. In North America, where acorns make up half or more of this species' diet, and are the staple food in the non-breeding season, the woodpeckers set up special "larders", or "granaries". Small groups of this social picid drill numerous funnel-shaped holes in a tree trunk, into each of which they push an acorn collected from nearby. These granaries can contain up to 50,000 holes, excavated over many years, and are defended by all group-members.

[*Melanerpes formicivorus*, central California, USA. Photo: Dave Maslowski]

this processing work, and they store the food in natural crevices. They may widen natural cracks for this purpose, but they do not drill individual holes for each acorn. These woodpeckers tend their stores by moving the acorns around, which inhibits fungal growth. If superabundant, insects, such as swarming carpenter ants (*Camponotus*), are also stored in cracks near the nest, from where they are later retrieved and fed to the young. Although Lewis's Woodpeckers do not defend any feeding territories, they do defend individual food caches vigorously. Competition over the mast accumulated in the stores is most intense with the Acorn Woodpecker. Only when a crop is in ample supply, as for example in almond plantations or, rather exceptionally, near corn silos, will they sometimes do without stored mast.

There is no doubt that the thousands of funnel-shaped holes produced by Acorn Woodpeckers are there for the purpose of storing acorns, and indeed this woodpecker is certainly the best-known storing species among the Picidae. Prior to storage, the acorns are collected in the trees or on the ground. Acorn Woodpecker stores are seldom very far away from oak trees. These larder-hoarding woodpeckers store acorns whole or piecemeal in crevices in bark or wood, in anthropogenic structures or amid epiphytes, but most acorns are cached in specially made holes. These densely spaced holes, with nearest-neighbour distances of about 28 mm, cover large areas of the outer surface of such trees as oaks, pines and others. Stores of this kind, which are also referred to as larders or granaries, may contain up to 40,000-50,000 holes, and it takes years for the woodpeckers to excavate all of these. The larders are tended constantly and are carefully looked after. The food-storing behaviour of this group-living species varies geographically, however, and not all Acorn Woodpecker groups possess granaries. Storing appears to be least common in the southern parts of the species' range.

Many species of woodpecker regularly prey on the nests of other birds. The picids for which this behaviour is well documented include the Greater Yellownape, the Grey-faced Woodpecker, the flickers, the *Melanerpes* species, and the *Picoides* and *Dendrocopos* pied woodpeckers The Great Spotted Woodpecker is particularly notorious for its habit of taking the eggs and nestlings not only of hole-nesters, but also of Eurasian Penduline Tits (*Remiz pendulinus*) and of species which rear their young in open nests. Even Acorn Woodpeckers will occasion-

ally steal eggs, while its close relative the Red-headed Woodpecker, one of the most omnivorous of all the Picidae, obtains the young of hole-nesting birds by widening the hole entrance. This latter species has a really wide range of prey that includes, in addition to the eggs and nestlings of both hole-nesting and open-nesting birds, a wide variety of insects such as grasshoppers, crickets, beetles and their larvae, moths, butterflies and caterpillars, and wasps, as well as earthworms, lizards and mice.

An interesting and unusual observation of predatory behaviour concerned a Cuban Green Woodpecker which was watched as it visited a heronry. The dense colony held many Snowy Egrets (*Egretta thula*) and Cattle Egrets (*Bubulcus ibis*), with scattered pairs of Tricolored Herons (*Egretta tricolor*). Although it seemed initially that the woodpecker might have been seeking insects, its main food, among the small mangrove bushes, it was eventually confirmed that it was, in fact, puncturing the egrets' eggs to reach the contents inside.

There are many overt and subtle differences in the way in which woodpeckers move while foraging. The style of locomotion may be an important means of niche separation among species, and even between the sexes (see Habitat). Generally, the most economic method would be for a woodpecker to hop upwards and to fly downwards, but many deviations from this general pattern exist. Gleaning species are agile, often moving sideways and back again on large trunks, and frequently moving downwards, while smaller species, such as the Middle Spotted and Arabian Woodpeckers, move deftly along the undersides of limbs. Clinging to terminal twigs demands a strong grip, and is therefore a feature mainly of small picids or rather powerful ones.

Similarly, there are many different ways in which a single patch of foraging habitat is used. For example, a woodpecker may spend a long time at one spot to excavate, or it may hardly stop at all while gleaning, or it may pause just briefly to work on a single site. There appear also to be differences in the likelihood that a woodpecker will return to the same site. For gleaners, renewal times of the prey are short, so that reuse of the same site poses little problem. For species that feed on solitary burrow-dwelling creatures, however, it usually pays them not to return once they have exploited the site. This foraging strategy, known as trap-lining, requires a knowledge of all or most of the sites where prey are likely to be found, as well as a good memory of when such sites have been visited. Downy Woodpeckers can be categorized as trap-liners; they have been found to return to the same spot in only two out of more than 1200 cases. The regular rounds of their home ranges made by the Ground Woodpeckers in South Africa no doubt serve a similar purpose.

Many of the Picidae forage solitarily, and this is to be expected in the case of those which seek prey that are unpredictable in occurrence. In the tropics, however, many of the gleaners not uncommonly forage in mixed flocks with other bird species, including, at times, other woodpeckers (see General Habits).

Like most other bird species, woodpeckers drink by inserting the bill into water and then raising the head and bill to allow the liquid to flow down into the gullet. Small puddles in tree forks and similar hollows constitute important arboreal sources of water, as also do many bromeliads in which water collects. In addition, woodpeckers frequently leave the trees and descend to the ground in order to drink from rainwater puddles and other freshwater sources, whether temporary or more permanent.

Breeding

Woodpeckers breed in holes carved into wood or, in the case of a few species, dug into the ground. The nest-chamber is not lined with any additional soft material other than the few wood chips and "sawdust" that may remain at the bottom of the mainly pear-shaped hole, and the eggs are white. Monogamy is the predominant breeding system among the Picidae. It is associated with a relatively high contribution by the males to nest-hole construction, nest-guarding and brood care. As a rule, the male remains in the hole with the eggs or young during the night. During the daytime, both parents are needed to incubate the eggs and raise the young. The fact that the male undertakes most of the excavating work, and also takes a large share of the parental duties, is the key for understanding the breeding and social systems of the members of this family.

Although little information is available on the territoriality of tropical species, the territorial behaviour of woodpeckers living in the temperate zones is well documented. Woodpeckers in general are territorial birds. Furthermore, they defend their territories not only during the breeding season, but throughout the rest of the year. In particular, those Northern Hemisphere species which store food (see General Habits, Food and Feeding) maintain and defend winter territories. The territories occupied and defended during the non-breeding season often differ from those maintained during the breeding period, the former frequently being associated with special resources. Red-headed Woodpeckers, for example, leave their breeding territories in autumn and migrate to areas that offer a good supply of beech mast or of oak trees (see Movements). Such shifts of habitat, with the associated territorial shifts, can occur on almost any spatial scale.

Woodpeckers advertise their presence with drumming and vocal signals. Conflicts take place close to prospective nest-sites, at roosts, or at localized resources such as food stores. Aggressive encounters are frequent at the beginning of the breeding season, and reach a peak around the time of egg-laying. These aggressive clashes involve several types of vocalization, together with wing-flicking and swinging movements of the head and body. In close combat, the bill and the feet are the main weapons, and in such circumstances the opponents may both fall to the ground in the heat of the action. Fights can involve only two individuals, more often than not of the same gender, or two pairs.

The displays of woodpeckers consist of variations of a common repertoire of movements. The courtship displays and aggressive displays of the picids have much in common, and it is not always easy to distinguish between the two types of behaviour. The basic pattern of behaviour in close encounters is exhibited by both the wrynecks and the piculets, as well as by the true woodpeckers in the subfamily Picinae. In such situations, the feathers of the crown and nape are erected, the head is extended, and the bill is directed forwards at the opponent; invariably, the display includes the spreading of the tail. At higher intensity, the displaying woodpecker often droops its wings and engages in variable kinds of swinging movements of the head and body.

For the Gila Woodpecker of North America's southern deserts, life revolves around cacti. As well as providing nesting holes, these plants are a source of invertebrates, fruit and nectar. The sipping of nectar is by no means uncommon among the melanerpine and Celeus woodpeckers, and nectar is taken at least occasionally by a number of other picids. The Gila Woodpecker is, however, the only member of the family to have been observed using a tool to obtain food. One was watched dipping pieces of bark and seeds into honey syrup at a garden feeder, and then provisioning its fledglings with the nutritious liquid.

[Melanerpes uropygialis uropygialis, Arizona Desert, USA. Photo: John Cancalosi/ BBC]

Some species do no more than swing the head laterally, with the bill held more or less upright. Most, however, perform rhythmic movements of both the head and the body. In the majority of species these involve lateral swaying, with the bill pointing directly forwards or slightly upwards and describing circles or figures-of-eight, but the display movements of the melanerpine woodpeckers are more in the vertical plane. In the case of the latter group, characteristic bowing movements are performed, and these are typically accompanied by loud calls. In contrast, the accompanying vocalizations of other picid species, which swing horizontally from side to side, are not necessarily very far-carrying.

These types of behaviour are exhibited when partners meet and also during aggressive encounters with competitors. In addition, all woodpeckers flick their wings in defence, and some of the species spread the wings widely and hold them extended in courtship, too. Wing-flicking frequently precedes an assault, which often involves an antagonist stabbing at its opponent, and finally making a supplanting attack. Observations of aggressive encounters involving a single intruder, as well as of fights between neighbouring pairs, have often revealed that opponents are attacked sex for sex, and the same results have been obtained in experiments in which dummies have been used as "rivals". Aggression is reduced during the period of brood care, which has the effect of enabling locally high breeding densities to be achieved without too much needless agitation.

Aerial displays by woodpeckers are apparently signals for the mate only. The flutter-aerial-display typically comprises a gliding flight in which the wings are held well above the back, particularly upon landing. During the course of this flight, series of drawn-out, somewhat squeaky calls are uttered. The "circle-flight" of Lewis's Woodpecker is more elaborate. The male of that species circles its nest tree in a smooth glide, with the wings extended and held at a high angle; the flight ends at the nest entrance, where the "churr" call is given. Woodpecker males possibly use aerial displays to show a prospective nest-site to the female.

Mate-feeding forms part of the courtship ritual of wrynecks, and the male sometimes continues to feed his partner even during the incubation period. Otherwise, courtship

Nectar represents an excellent source of sugar-rich protein, and is taken from a wide variety of plant species, as illustrated by the male Gila Woodpecker in this photograph and the preceding one. The agility and suppleness of the woodpecker are well demonstrated here: while clinging crosswise on a thin branch, the bird twists its head and neck through 270 degrees to reach into the hanging bell of the flower. Besides feeding on insects and their larvae, Gila Woodpeckers take both nectar and rising sap in summer, and then forage for seeds and galls in autumn and winter. An observer in Arizona noted small groups of these picids tearing the galls of Pachypsylla venusta from the leaves of a tree, before wedging each in a crack in a fence post and chiselling out the contents. Hundreds of gall cases were subsequently found littering the ground beneath the fence post.

[Melanerpes uropygialis uropygialis, Arizona Desert, USA. Photo: John Cancalosi/ BBC]

feeding is known to be practised by only few of the Picidae species. It has been observed for two of the *Dinopium* flamebacks, the Olive-backed Woodpecker and the Black-rumped Flameback, and for two *Melanerpes* species, the Guadeloupe and Hispaniolan Woodpeckers.

Among many picid species, the pair-bond, or, at least, loose contact by vocal communication and before roosting, appears to be maintained through the non-breeding season. Nevertheless, it

is not unusual for pair-members to split up for the entire period between breeding seasons, particularly when each individual defends a localized resource such as a food store (see Food and Feeding). Many individuals may maintain a cohesive relationship, but often this is not very obvious to the observer, and there is certainly a great deal of variation both within and among species.

Breeding partners not infrequently remain together over several breeding seasons, and the divorce rate is rather low. Instances of an individual mating with a different partner do occur, however, even if the previous partner is still within the same area. The high male investment in the breeding process means that polygamous matings are predisposed more towards polyandry than towards polygyny, and it may lead to a reversal in the courtship roles of the sexes. Egg production is no constraint, since woodpeckers are indeterminate egg-layers; this means that the number of eggs that a female lays is controlled by clutch size, rather than by the number which she has already produced in a given season. In a well-documented case of polyandry by the Great Spotted Woodpecker in Japan, the female laid her eggs in two different nests from which two and three nestlings eventually fledged. Her contribution to the feeding of the nestlings was about 6% and 38% of the total feeding effort at each respective nest. In Japan, males of the Great Spotted Woodpecker that breed with polyandrous females occupy territories that are intermediate in quality between those of unmated males and those of monogamous males; they also produce fewer offspring than do the latter. The success of polyandrous females is only marginally higher than that of monogamous ones. On the other hand, a study of Lesser Spotted Woodpeckers in Sweden showed that the number of young successfully reared to fledging by polyandrous females was about 40% greater than that achieved by those in monogamous pairings. Almost 10% of the females of this smaller species are polyandrously mated, and about 3% of the males exhibit multi-nest polygyny. Females of such polygynous males are, however, likely to fail in their efforts to raise a brood successfully.

One important constraint on the evolution of more diverse mating patterns among the Picidae is the male's role of nocturnal incubation and brooding. A single woodpecker would face great difficulties if attempting to raise a brood from hatching to fledging entirely on its own. Only when the nestlings no longer require brooding can one partner rear them to the flying stage,

Although several woodpecker species catch insects on the wing, the technique is probably more highly developed in the Lewis's Woodpecker of western North America than in any other member of the family. From a prominent perch, the woodpecker scans the surroundings, often for lengthy periods, looking for large insects. On sighting a suitable prey, it approaches at low speed, using a flapping flight resembling that of a crow (Corvidae); closing in on the insect, it employs elaborate twisting manoeuvres to catch the prey, before gliding back to a perch. More remarkably, this species frequently performs continuous hunting flights lasting for some minutes, during which several insects are often seized.

[*Melanerpes lewis*, Siskiyou County, California, USA. Photo: William Grenfell]

Nestling woodpeckers are generally fed on soft-bodied insects, mostly the adults and larvae of ants, bees, wasps, beetles, Lepidoptera and flies. As the chicks grow, they cope with larger prey, such as the adult moth which this male Golden-fronted Woodpecker has brought to its nest-hole in Central America. Perhaps surprisingly, some picids, including pied woodpeckers of the genera Dendrocopos and Picoides, and sapsuckers (Sphyrapicus), will also feed acorns and fruits to older broods. Fragments of bone have been found in the nestling food of Eurasian Three-toed Woodpeckers (Picoides tridactylus), perhaps supplied as a source of calcium for growing chicks.

[*Melanerpes aurifrons*, Guatemala. Photo: Stephan Bonneau/ Bios]

The most terrestrial of the Palearctic Region's true woodpeckers, the Eurasian Green Woodpecker relies on grassland ants throughout the year. Formica species are favoured in winter, and those of the genus Lasius in spring and summer. Using the bill to sweep moss, dead leaves or snow from the surface, the bird pecks funnel-shaped holes up to 12 cm deep; these holes, which are exploited repeatedly, expose the tunnel systems of the ants, which appear en masse when disturbed by the woodpecker. The bird pictured has found an exposed ant nest at the base of a tree, and snow does not prevent it from feeding. This species will dig tunnels up to a metre long through snow in order to reach ants.

[Picus viridis viridis, Siggerud, near Oslo, Norway. Photo: Pall Hermansen/ NHPA]

although, even then, without being able to compensate fully for the loss of its mate. There may, however, be extremely rare exceptions to this general rule. A highly unusual observation was made in 1999, when a solitary pair of Red-cockaded Woodpeckers, without helpers, was found to have two simultaneous nests in two separate cavity trees within a cluster (see General Habits). The male incubated and brooded and fed the young at one nest, while the female carried out all these duties at the other; a single young fledged from each nest. It is probably significant that the recorded incubation and nestling periods at both nests were several days longer than is usual for this species, in addition to which the two parents combined to feed both nestlings in the days just before the young left their respective cavities.

Genetic analyses also indicate that woodpeckers are generally monogamous. A comprehensive study of very dense populations of the Great Spotted and the Middle Spotted Woodpeckers in Europe could not find any evidence for extra-pair fertilizations. Even among the socially breeding species, the same underlying pattern of monogamy or polyandry is evident.

Ecological constraints are the most likely explanation for the evolution of co-operative breeding by woodpeckers. Together with other benefits for juveniles of staying with the enlarged family, ecological factors contribute to the maintenance of this breeding system. The two best-studied picids in this respect are the Acorn Woodpecker and the threatened Red-cockaded Woodpecker. When individuals would encounter great difficulties in attempting to find a good breeding site, either because vacancies are rare or are hard to find, or because certain risks, such as predation, are high, it may pay those individuals to stay with the family with which they were raised. The fact that the young of some tropical species, such as those of the Great Slaty Woodpecker in Asia, remain with the parents until a new breeding cycle commences is a further indication of possible constraints on dispersal and on the production of holes.

The social system of the Acorn Woodpecker has been extensively studied in recent years. It is characterized by the occurrence of a co-operative polygynandry and by the presence of non-breeding helpers recruited from the group's offspring. The system is very variable and is one of the most complex ones to be found in the avian world. Single pairs occur, as well as groups of 15 adults which contain up to ten non-breeding helpers. In all instances, there is only a single active nest at a time in the breeding territory. The whole group takes part in the job of nestling care, and all members defend the territory and the acorn stores. Because conspecific intruders are predominantly females, the breeding females are involved in territorial defence significantly more than are the males. The group-members roost either individually in adjacent holes or as small bands of several birds in one hole, engaging in brief mutual mounting prior to roosting. Within groups, dominance hierarchies are established which probably regulate access to mates and which, at least among immatures, are not sex-related. Temporary breeding pairs, without helpers, are formed by birds that disperse individually in autumn.

Groups of this species usually comprise up to four reproductively active males, which are related to each other, and one breeding female. In about 20% of groups, a second breeding female, usually a sister of the first, is present. The group's offspring of previous years are attached as helpers to those which are actively breeding. Broodmates remain at the breeding territory for up to several years.

Whether or not an individual Acorn Woodpecker stays with its family as a helper is influenced by the variation in quality of the territories available. Those woodpeckers which have hatched in high-quality territories tend to remain with the group rather than to disperse, although the data accumulated so far suggest that the lifetime fitness of these individuals is lower. Studies indicate that females disperse earlier, and two to three times farther, than do males, and that they also make greater attempts to enter another breeding group. Similarly, the chances of finding a new breeding opportunity vary between the sexes, and are better for females than for males. Reproductive vacancies caused by the death of breeders in other groups are often filled by sibling units, comprising up to two sisters and four brothers, which have dispersed together from the natal group. Many broodmates stay together for their entire lives, and share mates.

Costs can be incurred by staying with the natal group. In such situations, Acorn Woodpeckers, rather than engaging in incestuous relationships, forgo the chance of breeding for some years, thereby reducing the overall reproductive potential of the population by about 10%. Thus, relatedness to other group-members largely determines whether an Acorn Woodpecker breeds within its group. If individuals of opposite sexes are closely related, such as brother and sister, or parent and offspring, they are very unlikely to breed with each other. Incest avoidance is a powerful principle that provides a fundamental explanation of the relationships in this complex breeding system. Helpers, when with a parent or uncle/aunt of the opposite sex which hold breeding status, never breed incestuously with these relatives. On the other hand, if the female is replaced by a new, unrelated one, male helpers may achieve fertilizations. When a vacancy for one or more breeding males arises, some male helpers may on rare occasions produce offspring with their mother.

In the minority of instances in which two breeding females are present in a group, these lay their eggs together in one nest. In such cases, however, competition between the females is intense and the individuals involved partly destroy each other's eggs. They share parentage of the group's offspring equally. Paternity is much more skewed. All male helpers, so long as they are not closely related to the female, may fertilize eggs. One particular male is, however, responsible for most of the offspring, and that male is in this respect almost three times as successful as its closest competitor. All other males are able only rarely to contribute genetically to the brood. Unlike other co-operatively breeding species, the reproductively active individuals in Acorn Woodpecker groups engage in matings only with members of their own group.

Young males of the Red-cockaded Woodpecker either disperse to other areas up to 22 km away to search for a breeding opportunity, or delay their attempts at reproduction and wait for a breeding vacancy in their own group. In the case of the second strategy, they remain within the natal territory and become helpers to their parents in the next breeding cycle. These two strategies are roughly equivalent in terms of relative fitness. Most Red-cockaded Woodpecker helpers are males, which outnumber female helpers by a factor ranging variously from 10:1 to 27:1. The oldest of these males inherits the territory if the breeding male disappears, while others may become breeders in an adjacent territory. The males which disperse often remain unmated territory-holders, or establish themselves as helpers in a non-natal group, or become floaters. Females stay with the natal group in only very few cases, and they disperse farther than do males, moving up to 32 km. The risk of incest seems to be low for the Red-cockaded Woodpecker. Helpers do not fertilize the eggs that produce the brood which they help to raise. Otherwise, the rare extra-pair fertilizations that occur stem from males which do not belong to the group.

For these two co-operatively breeding, group-living woodpeckers, the benefits gained by an individual through staying with the group include the availability of suitable breeding sites, specialized food sources, such as fruiting trees, mast and anthills, and large food stores. These resources can often be difficult to find; or they may, prior to exploitation, require great investment on the part of the woodpecker, involving the establishment of a food store, hole-construction, and learning the whereabouts of feeding sites; or they are, in many cases, already occupied by other woodpeckers. In such circumstances, successful establishment by the individual after dispersal becomes exceedingly difficult. Although single woodpeckers can, of course, produce their own holes, this is by no means an activity without costs and without constraints. Appropriate nest-sites may be limited because suitable dead wood cannot be found, or hole-building may take a very long time if the wood is hard and the species' requirements are very specific. This is particularly the case for Red-cockaded Woodpeckers, which have great difficulty in

Given that ants form a major component of the diet of so many picids, it is surprising that relatively few woodpeckers regularly feed on termites.
For species such as the Streak-throated Woodpecker of the Indian subcontinent and mainland South-east Asia, however, termites figure prominently in the diet. As this male demonstrates, this species attacks termite nests on the ground. Several other picids exploit the nests of terrestrial termites, the Campo Flicker (Colaptes campestris) of South America being a good example, whereas others open up the nests of arboreal termites and use them as roost-sites or nest-sites.

[Picus xanthopygaeus, Corbett National Park, northern India. Photo: Otto Pfister]

A number of woodpecker species regularly prey on the nests of other birds, taking both the eggs and the nestlings of hole-nesters. The Great Spotted Woodpecker has, in fact, gained a somewhat notorious reputation for this kind of predatory behaviour. This male in south-east England preyed on nests of both Blue Tits and Great Tits (Parus caeruleus and P. major) and, as the photograph shows, fed the chicks to its own brood. Great Spotted Woodpeckers also deprecate open nests, in addition to which they are, at least locally, key predators of Eurasian Penduline-tits (Remiz pendulinus). The suspended pouch-like nests of the latter are easily opened up by the powerful bill of this picid.

[Dendrocopos major pinetorum, Brentwood, Essex, England. Photo: Alan Parker/FLPA]

Although invertebrates comprise the bulk of the diet of most woodpeckers, many individuals are opportunistic, especially when close to human habitation. Such opportunism is, in fact, rather typical of the White Woodpecker of the Neotropics. This female is pecking chunks from raw meat that has been hung up to dry in south Brazil. The species also opens the nests of wasps and wild bees to take both the grubs and the honey, as well as indulging in aerial flycatching. It also forages quite frequently in fruit trees, including commercial plantations, a habit which can make it an unpopular bird among local growers.

[Melanerpes candidus, Pantanal, Mato Grosso, Brazil. Photo: Regis Cavignaux/ Bios]

Co-operative breeding is probably an ancestral trait. The forming of loose colonies, as described for flickers, and the occurrence of occasional helpers among solitary and monogamous species is, therefore, not surprising. Co-operative breeding is widespread also among African barbets, and it is a strategy adopted by at least three species of the Neotropical barbet-toucan clade. In these instances, the basic mechanism is similar to the one found in the Picidae: the young of one brood help to raise those of the next brood, and males contribute a great deal, particularly to the task of incubation.

Rare instances of woodpecker pairs being helped by another, closely related species have been documented. In North America, for example, there are cases of Hairy Woodpeckers feeding Downy Woodpecker chicks and of American Three-toed Woodpeckers feeding nestlings of the Black-backed Woodpecker. In a recent observation in Oregon, a male Williamson's Sapsucker was watched as it fed the nestlings of a pair of Red-breasted Sapsuckers; interestingly, the male true parent provided fewer feeds than did the other two adults. It has been suggested that these instances of helping involve individuals that are responding to a strong feeding stimulus, a theory which is widely acknowledged as a probable explanation for the more frequent cases of passerine young being fed by non-conspecifics.

Irrespective of whether a woodpecker species breeds as single pairs or in co-operative groups, the typical picid nest is carved into dead wood, or into living branches and trunks which contain soft or rotten wood at the core. Trees, bushes and palms that provide corresponding resources are therefore essential for many picids, but these birds are able also to use a wide variety of other substrates in which to dig their nest-holes. For example, utility poles and fence posts are frequently used, the latter particularly by small species such as the Red-crowned, Heart-spotted, Ladder-backed, Smoky-brown (*Veniliornis fumigatus*) and Spot-breasted Woodpeckers. Root systems projecting from a riverbank may suf-

establishing new roost-sites and nest-sites. Analyses of extensive demographic data reveal that, for this species, the strategy of remaining with the group and acting as a helper is as successful as is that of dispersing and finding new breeding opportunities. The Red-cockaded Woodpecker, along with other co-operatively breeding picids, exhibits some morphological and behavioural features which have probably evolved as responses to group-living. Red-cockaded Woodpeckers are much more vocal than are any of their congeners, and the plumage badges which may elicit aggression (see Morphological Aspects) are tiny and can easily be concealed. Such features, and probably some others, reduce the costs of staying with the parents. For the Acorn Woodpecker, the localized resource provided by the granaries, which are the work of many individuals of this species carried out over many years (see Food and Feeding), may have been an important driving force in reducing post-natal dispersal and, consequently, promoting the strategy of group-living.

Comparative studies of the evolution of group-living and co-operative breeding among some members of the Picidae have not yet evaluated the possible role of fruits and other plant material in this process. These sources of food may foster the strategy of living in social groups by the fact that, rather than being scattered over wide areas, they occur in localized clusters. This means that joint effort is required on the part of the birds to locate fruiting trees on the one hand and, on the other, to provide sufficient food for a large number of birds. Indeed, the way in which chattering groups of White Woodpeckers reportedly drop into a fruiting tree is reminiscent more of the behaviour of parrots than of that of typical picids. The contrasting situation is presented with resources that are elusive and hard to procure, as is the case with the large larvae of wood-boring beetles; these circumstances certainly preclude any behaviour similar to that appropriate for the exploitation of localized fruiting trees.

The critical resource that drove the evolution of group-living among ground-dwelling woodpeckers seems to be that of suitable nest-sites. The Andean Flicker and, to a lesser extent, the Campo Flicker form loose colonies, with pairs concentrated in areas where there is an adequate supply of sites suitable for the excavation of burrows.

Tree sap constitutes an important source of nutrition and energy for many woodpeckers, but the four sapsucker species are the most specialized in their systematic exploitation of this resource. Sapsuckers drill neat rows of holes on mature trees, these sometimes covering a wide area of the trunk. The bird takes an occasional sip from the holes, but spends more time alert to potential competitors, and vigorously defending its wells. Even within the limited North American Pacific coastal range of the Red-breasted Sapsucker, here seen visiting its sap wells on a mountain ash (Sorbus) tree, several other species will take advantage of open wells.

[*Sphyrapicus ruber daggetti*, central California, USA. Photo: S. Maslowski/FLPA]

fice, as well. Some of the smaller Picinae species, such as the Little Woodpecker in the Neotropics, have been found to nest in bamboo, and the larger Bamboo Woodpecker regularly does so in South-east Asia, from where there is good evidence that the latter's congener, the Pale-headed Woodpecker, also occasionally excavates its nest-hole in a bamboo stem. Another Neotropical picid, the White Woodpecker, sometimes uses holes among rocks, and such versatile species as the American Red-headed Woodpecker not only breed in natural holes, but will readily nest also in buildings and in other artificial structures, including pumps.

Cacti are perfect tree substitutes for quite a few melanerpine species. Indeed, the White-fronted Woodpecker, the Hispaniolan Woodpecker, the Golden-cheeked Woodpecker (*Melanerpes chrysogenys*), the Red-crowned Woodpecker, and the Grey-breasted and Gila Woodpeckers habitually nest in cacti. Among the flickers in the genus *Colaptes*, the Gilded Flicker sites its nests most frequently high up in giant saguaro cacti (*Carnegiea gigantea*) and less commonly in cottonwood (*Populus deltoides*) and willow (*Salix*) trees. Striped Woodpeckers, too, sometimes breed in cacti, and the Ladder-backed Woodpecker, in its xeric habitat with limited numbers of suitable nest trees, uses as nest-sites not only fence posts, but also yuccas (*Yucca*), agaves (*Agave*) and large cacti. Strickland's Woodpecker will also utilize agaves.

Even the large nests of certain arboreal social insects can serve as nesting substrates for woodpeckers. In the Neotropics, the Golden-green Woodpecker frequently breeds in such structures and the Black-necked and Green-barred Woodpeckers are known to do so at least occasionally. More notably, the Asian Rufous Woodpecker regularly digs its breeding holes into the football-sized nests of tree-ants of the genus *Crematogaster* that are still occupied by the ants and their brood; this woodpecker may in the same way exploit the nests of other ants, such as *Plagiolepis* species, but it also excavates cavities in trees and stubs. In South America, the Pale-crested Woodpecker not uncommonly digs its holes into the nests of arboreal ants or termites, and so, too, does its relative the Blond-crested Woodpecker, while the Cuban Green Woodpecker also occasionally uses arboreal termitaria for its own nesting purposes. Among the African picids, the Buff-spotted Woodpecker is known to excavate its nest not only in wood, but also, and frequently, into the arboreal nests of termites or ants.

This kind of behaviour, in which the nests of social insects are exploited by birds for their own breeding attempts, is not restricted to members of the Picidae, but is shared with several other avian families; these are the parrots, the trogons (Trogonidae), the kingfishers, the jacamars and the puffbirds.

Compared with most of the Picidae, the Northern Flicker undertakes relatively little excavating work, and this may be the reason why it rather commonly chooses to breed in other, often peculiar, sites. Among these are not only fence posts, utility poles and nestboxes, which may be expected, but also such unusual sites as clothesline poles, marine breakwater pilings, cliffs of hardened silt or clay, haystacks, and a variety of suitable structures on buildings.

The small size of the piculets enables these diminutive woodpeckers to nest in a wide range of substrates. The holes of the Asian Speckled Piculet, for example, are generally located in small dead branches, in bamboo, or even in palm fronds. Slender stubs, branches and bamboo are also suitable nesting sites for the South American piculets and for the three African and Asian *Sasia* piculets.

Those woodpeckers which live in more or less treeless grasslands and which, in addition, have a bill that is of little use for hard woodworking must of necessity resort to ground burrows. One of the best examaples is the Andean Flicker, which digs its tunnel-like nest into earth banks, among cliffs and in other rocky terrain; the tunnel is about a metre long, is horizontal or slightly upward-sloping, and ends in a nest-chamber. Only rarely does this species excavate in the *Polylepis* trees that are found in the Andean highlands. Its relative, the Campo Flicker, will either use nests of the arboreal termite *Constrictotermes cypergaster* or, in treeless country, dig into the mounds of a terrestrial termite, *Cornitermes cumulans*, or into earth banks. Like its South American equivalents, the Ground Woodpecker in South Africa digs its nest-tunnels into a bank, often in a road cutting, or into the ground among rocks.

The breeding cycle commences with the selection of a nest-cavity. Although woodpeckers are primary cavity-nesters, not all species construct a new hole each year. In particular, those woodpecker species which are not so well adapted for excavation often use old holes or, more rarely, nestboxes. Nevertheless, most

The Red-naped Sapsucker breeds in aspen (Populus tremuloides) and conifer forests of the Rocky Mountains, and spends the rest of the year in the high oak (Quercus) woodlands of the arid south-west United States and Mexico. This woodpecker uses sap holes throughout the year, often exploiting pine (Pinus) trees in summer, as this male demonstrates. Each hole is cut so that the inner section holds a small quantity of sap. The holes sometimes merge into a vertical groove, into which the sapsucker places its bill and runs it upwards, sipping as it goes. Sap wells created by sapsuckers are visited by various other picids, as well as other animals. Deer, squirrels, mice and a wide variety of insects take advantage of this free source of nutrition. Among the most frequent insects to exploit sapsucker wells are ants, which are, paradoxically, a major food of many picids.

[Sphyrapicus nuchalis, Forest Road, Colorado, USA. Photo: Rob Curtis]

of the other species, as typified by the American and Eurasian Three-toed Woodpeckers, practically always construct a new hole for each breeding attempt. Both the male and the female may advertise their individual roosting sites as the future nest-site, underlining their respective preferences by drumming in the vicinity of the prospective nest-site, performing display-flights and tapping at the hole. Both sexes may, in addition, begin to create one or several new holes. Later, activities are focused at one hole, which eventually becomes the male's roost and the pair's nest. Even so, the decision may still be revised immediately before egg-laying commences. It is the primary task of the male to construct a suitable hole and then to offer it as a nest-site.

Construction of the nest is an important ingredient of pair formation. The nest is not necessarily built completely anew in each breeding season, but some cleaning and other work at the hole is almost invariably carried out. The task of constructing a new hole from scratch takes a Black Woodpecker about two weeks if excavating in soft wood and up to four weeks in hard wood. Northern Flickers, if they breed in a tree cavity at all, spend from five days to three weeks in working at a hole. That species, as other picids less endowed with carpentering abilities, only infrequently excavates a completely new nest-hole, preferring instead to adapt a natural hollow or an old hole of another woodpecker if it cannot use the existing roost of the male. The Black Woodpecker, too, prefers to excavate holes in dead trees, which would seem to be due to the fact that less effort is required to dig into dead wood. Interestingly enough, this preference appears to be accompanied by certain costs, since the fledging rate has been found to be about 10% higher in nests that are constructed in live trees. In both of these species, which represent approximately the upper and lower ranges of excavating abilities among the true woodpeckers, the male takes the major share of the work of nest-construction, particularly in the final stage.

The first step in the construction of a hole consists in the excavating of the entrance part, which may be in hard, live wood. At this stage, the female and the male sometimes participate in equal share. After a deeper tunnel has been completed, and soft wood has been reached, the nest-chamber is dug out. This is usually pear-shaped or, in some cases, mainly involving small woodpeckers and piculets, rather cylindrical, and it follows closely the structure of the trunk or limb. The nest-chamber is created by forceful pecking and the tearing-off of pieces of the substrate.

Hammering is usually more rhythmic than that performed when foraging. Initially, all the work is carried out from outside the hole. In the final stage of construction, however, a bout of work typically commences with the woodpecker entering the hole and collecting wood chips. Beakfuls of these chips are then removed from the hole, the woodpecker sticking its head out of the entrance and characteristically tossing them away with energetic sideways flings. After chips have been removed, a task which

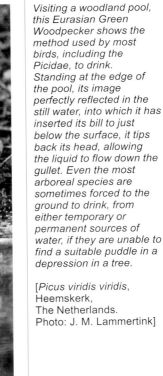

Woodpeckers drink frequently, this being especially so with those species which include pine (Pinus) seeds in their diet. Small puddles which form in tree forks, and in similar hollows in branches and trunks, are important sources of water for arboreal species. Tropical picids, such as the Hispaniolan Woodpecker, also take water that collects in the centre leaves of bromeliads, as well as using the plants as a source of insects. A female of this social woodpecker is shown here.

[Melanerpes striatus, Santo Domingo Botanical Garden, Dominican Republic. Photo: Doug Wechsler/ VIREO]

Visiting a woodland pool, this Eurasian Green Woodpecker shows the method used by most birds, including the Picidae, to drink. Standing at the edge of the pool, its image perfectly reflected in the still water, into which it has inserted its bill to just below the surface, it tips back its head, allowing the liquid to flow down the gullet. Even the most arboreal species are sometimes forced to the ground to drink, from either temporary or permanent sources of water, if they are unable to find a suitable puddle in a depression in a tree.

[Picus viridis viridis, Heemskerk, The Netherlands. Photo: J. M. Lammertink]

Their intelligence and adaptability have facilitated the success of many woodpecker species. They regularly come to gardens for food and, as this male Golden-fronted Woodpecker demonstrates, will take advantage of any suitable human structure that provides a convenient source of fresh water. In its arid habitats in the southern United States and Central America, fruits and other foods, including insects, can supply a fair amount of the liquid requirements of this and other woodpecker species, but fresh water is also a necessity. Picids accept a wide variety of natural foods, often placed out specially to attract them, and many species are also avid consumers of highly nutritious suet. This provisioning may reduce the level of mortality during severe winter conditions in northern latitudes, enabling the birds to maintain their range farther north than would otherwise be possible. Tropical woodpeckers, however, are equally prepared to take advantage of the offerings of human beings, as can be witnessed by visitors to rainforest lodges across the world.

[Melanerpes aurifrons
aurifrons,
Rio Grande Valley,
Texas, USA.
Photo: John Cancalosi/
Ardea]

Hole-construction and nest-site selection are constrained by various ecological and, at least among co-operative breeders, demographic factors. This aspect has been particularly well studied for the Acorn Woodpecker. This species' preferred, or most commonly used, nest-sites do not necessarily coincide with those that are likely to produce the highest reproductive success. The woodpeckers show a clear preference for nesting in dead limbs, although nests in live wood offer a more favourable, less variable micro-climate. Nests excavated high up in trees and those in tree species with smooth bark provide the best protection from predators. Thus, the availability within a territory of large tree species, those that offer strong limbs even at great height, and of smooth-bark tree species has a restrictive influence on nest-site selection. The feasibility of digging a hole in live wood not only depends on species-specific morphological endowment, but is also constrained by the greater effort needed to carry out such a task. Large groups are more likely to be successful when engaging in such costly activities.

These findings probably apply to all woodpeckers. When Great Spotted Woodpeckers, for example, breed as low as a half-metre above the ground in a certain location, they do so almost certainly because no suitable large trees are available. The same is true also for other and larger species.

The peculiar nesting habits of the co-operatively breeding Red-cockaded Woodpecker illustrate the role of the nest-cavity in effective protection against predation. The male of this species selects holes according to the capacity of the respective pine trees to produce a good yield of resin. Roosting and nesting Red-cockaded Woodpeckers maintain a flow of resin around the hole entrance by daily bouts of excavating at small wounds, this fresh resin having the effect of preventing rat snakes (*Elaphe*) and nest competitors from entering the hole. With this species, incidentally, both male and female of the breeding pair, as well as helpers, take part in the construction of the nest.

Woodpeckers which dig their holes into live pine wood are obliged to make the nest-chamber only in the heartwood, where it cannot be filled by resin. Similar problems are encountered by those species which excavate live cacti, among which are several *Melanerpes* woodpeckers, the Gilded Flicker and even a few *Picoides* species. These are forced to wait until the sap dries up

Courtship displays of woodpeckers feature many elements that are used also when showing aggression. The crown feathers are erected, the head raised and the wings drooped. Mate-feeding has been observed as part of the courtship ritual of only a few picid species, among them two Dinopium *species and two* Melanerpes, *but has only rarely been reported for the White-naped Woodpecker. Here, the red-crowned male of the latter has just presented his yellow-crowned mate with a beetle larva.*

[*Chrysocolaptes festivus festivus*, Ranthambore, India. Photo: Don Roberson]

can take some time and is often the only activity at the nest immediately before egg-laying, some further excavation work may follow. Chip-tossing and a few occasional pecks can sometimes still be witnessed during incubation. The floor of the nest remains covered by wood chips, and these can later become soaked with the nestlings' faeces and form sticky clods, which are then removed by the parents.

Many trees provide a hard outer "shell" and a soft "heart", the latter caused by fungal heart-rot. A broken, cut or otherwise damaged branch may be the source of decay which continues in the limb or into the main trunk. Many holes are therefore sited immediately below such an injury. Tree fungi, such as the bracket-forming polypore *Fomes*, are also associated with soft heartwood, and woodpeckers frequently select spots just below these, the "umbrella" of the body of the fungus sheltering the hole entrance. The number of sites suitable for nest-excavation is limited, and it diminishes in accordance with a decreasing ability of individual species to construct a new hole in hard wood. Wood hardness decreases from live to dead trees, and with increasing height in trees. Given all the constraints associated with a good nest-site, nest-site availability plays a key role in the life of any woodpecker species (see also Status and Conservation).

Picid holes are often at the periphery of a home range and adjacent to a more open section of the habitat. In these circumstances, there is a need for the cavity entrance to be protected to a reasonable extent, and this is apparently achieved by means of its orientation. One study of hole-entrance orientation on artificial snags revealed that the entrances of holes constructed in the summer were randomly oriented, while those of holes made in the winter months faced away from the direction of the prevailing wind. Hole-entrance diameter depends primarily on the body size of the species in question, but it is also, to some extent, dependent on temperature. The colder the outside temperature is, the narrower is the entrance and the deeper is the chamber.

Many woodpecker species construct their holes on the underside of a sloping limb, and, furthermore, some holes are located even in virtually horizontal branches, with the entrance then facing vertically downwards. A good number of species excavate their holes in rotten stubs, an action which often weakens these stubs considerably. The result is that the pair loses its hole, because wind stress causes the wood to break at the site of the hole.

All woodpeckers raise their young in a hole of some type. In the majority of cases, this is excavated in a tree or branch. The Great Slaty Woodpecker, at 50 cm long the largest Old World picid, typically nests high up, to 45 m, in the trunk of a large tree. Interestingly, this adult male, seen outside its nest-hole 28 m up in a very large, dying sal (Shorea) tree, was one of a group that included another male and a female, which together reared two young. This species' offspring often stay with the parents until a new breeding cycle begins; in this instance, a juvenile perhaps assisted with brood-rearing.

[*Mulleripicus pulverulentus pulverulentus*, East Kalimantan, Borneo. Photo: J. M. Lammertink]

While this male Golden-fronted Woodpecker has opted for a natural nest-site, many pairs of this species excavate cavities at the top of telegraph poles. Some poles can contain five or six nests and, in areas where this woodpecker is present in high densities, these can bring down telephone lines. In Texas, legal protection of the Golden-fronted Woodpecker was temporarily suspended in the twentieth century, such was the damage that its nests caused. The majority of woodpecker species usually dig their holes either in rotten wood or in trees with a softwood core, since such sites are easier to excavate. Nevertheless, live timber offers several advantages, among them a less variable micro-climate inside the hole, and better protection from potential predators, which find it more difficult to break into a hole in hard, live wood. The fledging rate among Black Woodpeckers (Dryocopus martius), for example, has been shown in some studies to be about 10% higher from nests in live wood than from those in rotten substrates.

[Melanerpes aurifrons aurifrons, Texas, USA. Photo: Tom Vezo]

before they are able to use the hole which they have created. The majority of woodpeckers, however, since they prefer to excavate the nest-chamber in the decayed softer parts of trees, do not face such problems.

In northern temperate zones, the breeding season for woodpeckers begins early in spring, with egg-laying occurring generally in April. In Europe, Black Woodpeckers sometimes commence laying in the middle of March, but most of this species' clutches are started in mid-April, which is also the time when Middle Spotted, Great Spotted and Eurasian Green Woodpeckers lay their first eggs. The Lesser Spotted Woodpecker begins slightly later, and the Grey-faced Woodpecker starts laying up to two weeks later. The Eurasian Three-toed Woodpecker breeds at higher elevations, and its egg-laying season is therefore delayed until the second half of May. Similarly, montane populations of the Great Spotted Woodpecker have a delayed breeding season compared with that of lowland populations, and their clutches are laid after those of the White-backed Woodpecker. In central Europe, the migratory Eurasian Wryneck, on its return from the African winter grounds (see Movements), starts to lay its eggs usually in the second half of May, although on rare occasions it may lay from the end of April. Besides this general pattern, actual laying dates may vary from year to year, as has been shown by U. Wiktander and his co-workers, who studied the population biology of the Lesser Spotted Woodpecker in Sweden over many years. They found that, as with many other bird species, the chances of survival of the fledged young decreased the later the laying date became.

Resource availability is certainly an important factor in determining the timing of the breeding season. In North America, late broods of the Black-backed Woodpecker, for instance, may be associated with forest fires, clutches having been initiated within a few days after the passage of a fire in the second half of June. Acorn Woodpeckers breed from April through to June, but they may also, rarely, nest in August and September. Not surprisingly, tropical species often breed at varying seasons, or throughout the entire year, depending on the locality and its particular ecological conditions. For woodpeckers, as well as other avian species, which live in the tropics, clear associations between environmental conditions and the timing of breeding have still to be elucidated.

According to the information available, woodpeckers copulate relatively frequently. They often copulate near the nest when the latter is nearly completed, and during the egg-laying phase several copulations take place each day, sometimes separated by only short intervals of 15 minutes. Females often initiate copulation. A pattern typical of many, if not all, picids is the following: while the male is near or at the nesting cavity, generally engaged in excavation work, the female will fly first to the hole and then to a favoured copulation branch, where she adopts her soliciting crouch. An interesting phenomenon is the reversed mounting which forms part of the copulatory behaviour of some *Melanerpes* species, including the Red-bellied and Lewis's Woodpeckers, and which has also been recorded for the Middle Spotted Woodpecker. In this, the female begins the sequence and mounts the male, which then proceeds to perform the copulatory act proper in the normal fashion. Reversed mounting, which also occurs after a copulation, may be an exaggerated form of soliciting by the female.

Copulations by woodpeckers take place on more or less horizontal limbs, on which the female may perch lengthwise or crosswise. The usual procedure is that the female crouches down and the male mounts her; in the case of some species, this action by the male is associated with his fluttering or hovering above the female. The act of copulation lasts for six to 16 seconds, after which the male descends gradually and, usually, flies off; both partners commonly preen afterwards. Copulation is often introduced by some activity at the hole, especially tapping or mutual tapping (see Voice), and is generally accompanied by calls that are low in both pitch and loudness. Frequently, the same location is used in consecutive matings.

It is by no means uncommon for copulations to take place some weeks before egg-laying. They are often associated with disputes with intruders, and in these cases usually happen immediately after such a clash has occurred. Regular copulation reaches a peak during the period of egg-laying, and then peters out in the course of incubation.

The eggs of the members of this family are invariably white, like those of other hole-nesting species, although they can sometimes become stained by resin, or by other substances present in the nest. There are some differences in shape, some eggs being more spherical and others more elongate, and those of some species seem to have rather thin shells. Eggs are usually laid at daily intervals until the clutch is complete. Experiments have demonstrated that woodpeckers are indeterminate layers, which means that the number of eggs that a female will lay is essentially controlled by a predetermined clutch size, and not by the number of eggs that she has already laid during any particular breeding cycle. The removal of a new egg from a nest will, therefore, cause the female to continue to lay. When clutches have been experimentally manipulated in this manner, as many as 71 eggs have been obtained from a single female Northern Flicker, 28 from a Red-headed Woodpecker, and 62 from a Eurasian Wryneck.

Compared with most secondary hole-nesters, woodpeckers have relatively small clutches. Among the Picidae themselves, those species with a high propensity for nesting in old holes tend to lay larger clutches, while the clutches of tropical species are generally smaller. For example, the Eurasian Wryneck, which nests in pre-existing holes, lays seven to ten eggs, and occasionally as many as twelve, although a large percentage of its clutches contain a far lower number. In contrast, the tiny piculets of the tropics, from what little is known of their breeding biology, appear to have a normal clutch size of just two or three eggs. Furthermore, woodpeckers living in temperate zones exhibit some latitudinal variation in clutch size, which tends to increase with greater seasonality of the habitat: in other words, the greater the difference between biomass productivity in summer and that in winter, the greater the likelihood of more eggs being laid in each clutch. In the case of Lewis's Woodpecker, for instance, the average clutch size throughout its distribution in western North America is 5·88 eggs, with the number of eggs laid by each female ranging from five, or rarely four, to nine; most clutches, however, contain six or seven eggs, and the average number per clutch in-

Construction of arboreal nest-holes begins with a circular funnel, which is fashioned into a cylindrical hole to form the entrance. The entrance hole is generally narrower in cold climates than in the tropics, and, unsurprisingly, smaller species, such as the Olive Woodpecker, create smaller holes than do larger ones. Most woodpeckers take a couple of weeks to complete a nest-cavity, although they normally give up and find a new site if they do not find softwood beneath the surface. Many picids, in particular the smaller ones, excavate a nesting hole on the underside of a sloping limb, to protect the chamber from rain or melting snow.

[*Dendropicos griseocephalus griseocephalus*, Somerset West Country Park, South Africa. Photo: J. J. Brooks/Aquila]

In contrast to the Afrotropical picid in the preceding photograph, the Robust Woodpecker of South America is a very big picid. Correspondingly, the entrance to its nesting cavity is significantly larger. A hard outer "shell" and a soft inner core, in which the pear-shaped nest-chamber is excavated, are crucial to arboreal woodpeckers. The birds probably identify trees having a soft "heart" by visual cues, such as damaged bark or the presence of fungal growth. Since a broken or damaged branch allows the main trunk or limb to decay, holes are often sited below such an injury. Tree fungi are also associated with soft heartwood, as in this instance, where the pair of Robust Woodpeckers has excavated a large hole on a tree patterned by bracket fungi. The nest-hole of many woodpeckers is often at the edge of a home range, in more open habitat, its orientation providing some protection from the weather. The entrances of holes constructed in winter usually face away from the direction of the prevailing wind, whereas those excavated in the warmer climate of summer are more randomly oriented.

[*Campephilus robustus*, Iguazú National Park, Misiones, Argentina. Photo: J. & A. Calo]

Dead wood is a key feature of the habitat of many woodpeckers, as it provides not only a source of invertebrates but also sites for nesting.
This male Greater Flameback has found an ideal location for its nest, in a tall dead tree.
This species can take up to a month to complete the construction of its nesting cavity, even with both sexes working in soft wood. As is the case with many medium-sized picids, the entrance is oval in shape and the chamber is not lined, although some of the last wood chips and flakes are usually allowed to remain on the nest-floor after excavation.

[*Chrysocolaptes lucidus guttacristatus*,
Khao Yai National Park,
Thailand.
Photo: C. B. Frith]

creases from south to north. Although nests with as few as three and even two eggs have been reported for this species, those clutches may well have been incomplete ones. Lewis's Woodpecker is, incidentally, the biggest of the *Melanerpes* species, and its clutch size, which is comparatively large for that of a picid, would seem to corroborate the suggestion that, among members of that genus at least, clutch size is correlated with body size.

Should a clutch be destroyed for any reason, the female will often lay a replacement. Otherwise, almost all woodpeckers for which sufficient information is available are generally single-brooded. Nevertheless, several *Melanerpes* species are known to be capable of rearing more than one brood in a season. The Gila Woodpecker, for example, not infrequently has two and even three broods in a season, and the Golden-fronted Woodpecker occasionally raises two broods in Texas and, rarely, up to three in Central America. Groups of Acorn Woodpeckers periodically have a second breeding season, laying in August and September, having already bred in spring; such second nestings tend to take place in years with good acorn yields and when breeding success in the preceding spring was poor. Other melanerpines which are occasionally multi-brooded include the Red-bellied Woodpecker and the Red-headed Woodpecker. Rare second broods have been recorded also for the Downy Woodpecker, the Red-cockaded Woodpecker and the Northern Flicker in America, and for the Black-rumped Flameback in the Indian Subcontinent. The Old World wrynecks, on the other hand, regularly rear more than one brood in a season. In the southern part of the Eurasian Wryneck's breeding range, about 20% of pairs start a second brood and a few attempt a third. Rufous-necked Wrynecks in Africa may be even more prolific, making up to four breeding attempts in a season; one pair successfully raised three successive broods, with periods of 14-24 days between the fledging of one brood and the laying of the next clutch.

Woodpeckers have rather short incubation periods, ranging from nine to 14 days. Incubation proper generally starts once the clutch has been completed, or a day or two before that, although brief bouts of nest attendance can sometimes be observed even before an egg has been laid. Both male and female parents have well-developed brood patches, and they share incubation duties. In the case of the Red-cockaded Woodpecker, helpers also develop small brood patches, and they, too, may incubate. The male sits on the eggs at night, and he also remains overnight in the hole with the young until the end of the nestling period. During

the day, the male and the female share incubation duties more or less equally, and no clear evidence has ever been obtained that would indicate an uneven average contribution of the sexes. During change-over, the individual arriving to take over duties sometimes announces its presence by tapping; otherwise, the partners remain silent, with only very low intimate calls sometimes audible if the two meet at close distance. This intersexual

The nesting and roosting cavities of the tiny, compact Grey-and-buff Woodpecker of South-east Asia are often close together. This male is one of four individuals of this species which roosted in adjacent holes in a dead tree, the toes of a female inside the uppermost hole being just visible. In this case, the woodpeckers are using holes made by a larger species of picid. It is not unusual among the members of this family for the male's roosting hole to become the nest-site of the pair, although that is unlikely to happen here, since the cavities are too large to be utilized by this species for breeding. Optimal nesting sites are used repeatedly by woodpeckers, often of several species, and more than one hole may be occupied at a time, especially in the tropics.

[*Hemicircus concretus sordidus*,
West Kalimantan, Borneo.
Photo: J. M. Lammertink]

Several species of the genus *Celeus regularly construct their nests in the huge tree nests of ants or, less frequently, termites. The habit is particularly well known for the Rufous Woodpecker, the sole Old World representative of the genus. This species commonly excavates a breeding cavity in the football-sized nest of arboreal ants of the genus* Crematogaster, *as this one has done in Sri Lanka. It is perfectly normal for the nest to be still occupied by the insects. Quite how the birds protect themselves from the stinging ants is not known, but they may acquire the appropriate odour during their feeding visits. The ants, however, sometimes destroy the brood if the delicate balance is disturbed from outside.*

[*Celeus brachyurus jerdonii,* Kurunegala, Sri Lanka. Photo: T. S. V. de Zylva/ FLPA]

behaviour has already begun in an earlier stage of the breeding cycle, during the period of hole-construction.

The eggs usually hatch within one and the same day, although there are occasions, as with the large Black Woodpecker, when hatching may be spread over two days. Unhatched eggs and dead nestlings are removed by the parents. Similarly, eggshells are often removed immediately, but they may also be left in the nest for several days. The chicks remain in the nest for a relatively long time, three to four weeks, which results in the combined incubation and nestling periods being similar in length to the total duration of chick development among other altricial birds of equivalent size. It has been suggested that the high fledging/ incubation ratio of 2·09, compared with about 1·23 for other altricial birds, as well as the low embryonic metabolism of the Picidae, can possibly be explained by the problems of gas exchange in the nest-chamber.

As already mentioned (see Morphological Aspects), the chicks are completely naked when they hatch, and they do not develop any down feathers. They stick closely together, forming a pyramid, in order to keep warm, and are usually brooded by the parents during the first days of their life. The parents enter the nest to feed the chicks for the better half of the nestling period, only in the later stages provisioning them at the hole entrance. As a point of interest, the sex ratio of nestlings is balanced. Although there have been some estimates that have suggested otherwise, as, for example, in the cases of the Black Woodpecker and the Red-cockaded Woodpecker, these conclusions could not stand up to closer scrutiny and analysis when large samples were used.

Melanerpine and many other woodpeckers, including the wrynecks and piculets, carry food and deliver it to the chicks in the tip of the bill. Flickers, *Dryocopus* logcocks and *Picus* species, on the other hand, regurgitate the nestling food, which they carry in the oesophagus and proventriculus. These species which feed their young by regurgitation often bring in food to the brood

at longer intervals than do other picid species. In the earlier stages, both parents share the duties of brooding and feeding. Towards the end of the nestling period, however, one of the partners, generally the female, may drop out, and appear again later only to care for some of the fledglings. Only among multi-brooded species, mainly the melanerpine woodpeckers, does the female sometimes take over most of the chores at the end of the nestling period. This is possibly in order to free the male for the preparation of the next nest-cavity, so that the next brood can be initiated without too much delay.

During the first days, the parents have to encourage the young to open the bill in order to feed them. They trigger begging behaviour by touching the base of the chick's bill. Later, the scratching noises made by the adults when approaching the nest-hole, and the darkening of the nest entrance, are sufficient to elicit intense begging, which is also stimulated by the begging of a nestmate. Begging calls can often be heard emanating from the nest-site even when no parent is at the nest. At the end of the nestling period, the young are fed at the hole entrance, and it is by no means unusual at this time to see a single begging nestling peering out of the nest-hole and calling when the parents are away. The noise made by begging woodpeckers can be audible at great distances, but there are some species-specific differences. Eurasian Green Woodpecker nestlings, for instance, call more frequently and more loudly than do those of the Grey-faced Woodpecker, and a similar comparison applies to the Great Spotted Woodpecker and the Middle Spotted Woodpecker.

There appears to be great variation among pairs, and maybe even species, as to which sex contributes the more to nest sanitation. The nestlings produce their faeces soon after having been fed, and the faeces, often mixed with material from the nest-cavity floor, are then carried away by the adults. The nests of Great Spotted Woodpeckers and Acorn Woodpeckers, for instance, remain clean right up to the very end of the nestling pe-

In landscapes where trees are scarce, cactus stems provide a good substitute. In the desert areas of the southern United States and Mexico, several melanerpine woodpeckers regularly choose such sites for nesting, including the Gila Woodpecker. The pair shown here has built its nest in a giant saguaro cactus (Carnegiea gigantea), a typical nest-site of this species. Gilded Flickers (Colaptes chrysoides) also habitually construct their nests high up in a giant saguaro. Most picids rear only one brood in a single season, but the Gila Woodpecker often produces two or even three broods.

[Melanerpes uropygialis uropygialis, Saguaro National Park, Arizona, USA. Photo: François Gohier]

riod, whereas in those of the Golden-fronted, Grey-faced and Black Woodpeckers, among others, the parents, in particular the female, cease to remove excrement, debris and other extraneous material in the last days before the young leave the hole. Faeces are seemingly often collected from the floor of the cavity and are mixed with wood dust and chips. These hole contents are important in assisting nest sanitation for species such as the sapsuckers, which have rather liquid faeces with thin or, possibly, no faecal sacs. Helpers of the Red-cockaded Woodpecker contribute as much to nest sanitation, brooding and brood-feeding as do the two parents.

Observations have revealed that nestlings of the Black Woodpecker not uncommonly die of starvation even when there is no indication of any food shortage. This may suggest the existence of sibling competition, although there could also be other factors, such as diseases and parasites, that cause mortality of this kind. Older nestlings, at least, are rather aggressive towards each other. Woodpecker chicks also direct aggressive-looking actions towards the parents, which maintain an increasingly greater distance from the growing young when feeding them.

When disturbed in the nest, the young cease begging and crouch closely to the bottom of the cavity. Nestling wrynecks, if thus alarmed, exhibit a peculiar type of behaviour involving snake-like head movements and hissing. This reaction is fully developed in adult wrynecks which are threatened while in the hole: the hissing is then accompanied by crest-raising, and the head is moved slowly towards the intruder and then suddenly retracted. This unique behaviour has been interpreted as snake mimicry. Interestingly, wrynecks surprised in the open perform rather stereotyped head movements which, again, are rather reminiscent of those of a snake, although they do not normally utter hissing sounds in these circumstances.

Fledglings, having vacated the nest, are somewhat aggressive in their demands for food, uttering loud squeaking calls as they approach the parent. It is not unusual, especially among woodpeckers in temperate zones, for the two adults to divide the brood between them, the male accompanying one or more juveniles and the female the others. The period over which the juveniles are fed by their parents, or stay with them, is unknown for most species. Juveniles of the social Red-cockaded Woodpecker are fed for up to six months after leaving the nest. In the case of this and other eminently social picids, the young remain with the group for an extended period, possibly covering several years. Among several

tropical species, too, the parents accompany the young more or less regularly for a protracted period of time, and the family-members may remain together as a unit until the parents begin the next reproductive cycle. Some woodpeckers share their roost with a fledgling, in which case only one young is produced.

Nest success, calculated as the relative number of clutches which produce at least one young, is generally high among woodpeckers, typically from more than 70% to 100%, and this relates to the fact that these birds excavate their own nests. The majority of failures is due to the eggs not hatching or to the deaths of small nestlings. When Black Woodpecker chicks die, they do so mainly within the first ten days after hatching. In a 20-year study of the Black Woodpecker in central Germany, U. Lange investigated the breeding success of this species in an area dominated by coniferous forest, but with a deciduous element of about 10%. Of 238 broods, the success of 44 was not known; of the remaining 194 broods, however, he was able to confirm that 177, or 91%, were successful. The average productivity for all nests combined was 2·71, while the successful nests produced an average of 3·04 young each. Most failures were caused by the adults deserting the nest because of cold weather. Similarly, a ten-year study of Lesser Spotted Woodpeckers in southern Sweden revealed that the most common cause of breeding failure was the abandoning of the nest, although, in this case, this was precipitated by the disappearance of one of the adults. Altogether, 34% of the breeding attempts made by these small woodpeckers were without fledging success.

Sociality influences breeding success, too. In North America, studies of the Acorn Woodpecker have demonstrated that fledging success increases with group size. Similarly, Red-cockaded Woodpecker pairs with helpers fledge 1·5 times as many young as do unassisted pairs.

Although the range of potential nest predators of woodpeckers is limited, owing to the hole-nesting habits of these birds, predation at the nest is still an important factor in the nesting success of the members of this family. Predators are usually restricted by the size of the hole entrance. As a consequence, snakes, squirrels, martens (Martes), and other birds, including even other woodpeckers, are almost certainly the most significant nest predators. New holes excavated in live trees are least subject to predation. Holes in dead trees, or holes that are used repeatedly, run a higher risk of being preyed on. As mentioned above, Red-cockaded Woodpeckers carry out daily bouts of excavation at small

Terrestrial woodpeckers, such as the Ground Woodpecker, dig burrows for nesting purposes. As an exposed vertical face is required for nesting, roadside verges are often used. The male Ground Woodpecker carries out the majority of the work of tunnel-excavation. When complete, the tunnel is about 1 m long, and at the end it contains an enlarged nest-chamber. Pairs of this species, which is confined to southern Africa, will also occupy holes in a cliff face, and will even rear their young in a suitable hollow between rocks. It is not at all uncommon for a pair to use the same nest-site for a number of successive breeding seasons. Whereas the South American ground-dwelling picids, the Campo and Andean Flickers (Colaptes campestris and C. rupicola), are semi-colonial, the Ground Woodpecker is more of a solitary breeder, even though it is often seen in small groups. Nevertheless, a helper, frequently a younger bird from the previous year's brood, often assists a breeding pair in providing food for the chicks.

[Geocolaptes olivaceus prometheus, Wakkerstroom, South Africa. Photo: Warwick Tarboton]

wounds around the hole entrance, particularly around the lower rim, in order to maintain a flow of fresh resin, which generally prevents snakes from entering the hole. Even so, this may not be effective against other potential predators, nor against certain nest competitors such as southern flying squirrels (*Glaucomys volans*). Moreover, the mesh snake traps placed at the base of trees bearing cavities made by this threatened picid can sometimes have unfortunate consequences, when the woodpecker itself becomes ensnared and dies. There is also a documented instance of a Yellow-bellied Sapsucker being caught in such a trap, which resulted in its death.

Raptors, especially hawks (*Accipiter*) and buteos (*Buteo*), are known to prey on adult and, especially, juvenile woodpeckers outside the nest-hole or roost-hole. In North America, for example, there are numerous reports of Northern Flickers being taken by diurnal birds of prey, and it is likely that most picids are at least occasional victims of such avian predators.

The ability to construct holes as nest-sites is one of the key features of woodpeckers. Cavities provide almost perfect shelters for spending the night, as well as for rearing a family. It is hardly surprising, therefore, that holes made by woodpeckers have become a central resource for the survival of many other species of bird, as well as for many mammals, including bats, and other animals, even insects. Non-excavating avian cavity-nesters are often serious competitors for woodpecker nest-sites, and frequently force the rightful owners to leave a nest and to start excavation of a new one. In most parts of the world where the Picidae are represented, starlings (Sturnidae) are among the most persistent hole-usurpers, and in Central and South America tityras (*Tityra*) and some woodcreepers are equally unyielding. All of these bird species are notorious for the constant threat that they pose to woodpecker nests and roosts, but there are many others. Araçaris (*Pteroglossus*), for example, consume the eggs or chicks of the woodpecker before taking occupation of its hole. Hence, the nest, even if it is ready to be used, cannot be left unoccupied, and a prime task of the male is, therefore, nest defence. Only the immediate nest vicinity is defended from intruders.

In addition, African woodpeckers are regularly parasitized by honeyguides. Several members of the latter family, as part of their normal breeding strategy, lay their eggs in the holes of other birds. At least nine Afrotropical picids are known to suffer from this nest parasitism. These are the Rufous-necked Wryneck, itself a secondary hole-nester, along with five or more *Campethera* species and three *Dendropicos* woodpeckers.

The many birds which rely partly or wholly on cavities made by woodpeckers include several ducks (Anatidae) and pigeons (Columbidae), parrots, owls (Strigidae), hornbills (Bucerotidae), certain crows and swifts (Apodidae), and a fair number of passerines, among them bluebirds (*Sialia*), tits and nuthatches. Indeed, the survival of parrot populations in some regions appears to be largely dependent on the existence of a healthy woodpecker population: for instance, in a study of four parrot species in an area of Atlantic rainforest in south-east Brazil, 36 of the 37 parrot nests found were in old picid holes.

During the construction or adaptation of a hole, most woodpeckers remain under immense pressure exerted by secondary hole-nesters and sympatric picid species. These may be little more than a minor nuisance, but they may also be formidable foes and incessant usurpers. In many areas, Common Starlings are the most important competitors for the holes of small woodpeckers (see Status and Conservation), although medium-sized picids are often able to cope with them rather successfully. Lewis's Woodpecker, for instance, appears to win most of its encounters with this widespread songbird, which has been deliberately or accidentally introduced not only in North America, where it has expanded considerably, but also in southern Africa and several other parts of the world outside its natural Eurasian range. A study of three species of woodpecker in Ohio, USA, in the early 1990's found that Red-bellied Woodpeckers lost 39% of their freshly excavated cavities to starlings; Northern Flickers and Red-headed Woodpeckers, however, were far more aggressive in defence, losing 14% and 15%, respectively, of their holes to the introduced starlings.

A most interesting account by A. Jha of the efforts made by another member of the starling family, the Jungle Myna (*Acridotheres fuscus*), to take over the hole of a pair of Black-rumped Flamebacks in a Calcutta garden, in east India, illustrates the aggression and persistence of these nest-usurpers. In mid-April, a woodpecker hole in a coconut tree (*Cocos nucifera*) was occupied by a pair of mynas, which had begun nest-building inside the cavity; the pair continued to collect material for a further three days, until, on the fourth day, a flameback was seen just inside the cavity entrance, having apparently taken over the

While a female Yellow-tufted Woodpecker investigates a snag, its mate makes the initial attempts at an entrance hole. Yellow-tufted Woodpeckers are communal breeders: a number of nests may be excavated in close proximity to each other in a single tree, with adults provisioning young in several of them. Co-operative breeding is most common among the members of this genus. Interestingly, a close relative of this species, the Yellow-fronted Woodpecker, has been filmed as the two members of a pair simultaneously built nest-cavities in a tree, the two holes separated from each other by no more than 40 cm.

[*Melanerpes cruentatus*, Tambopata-Candamo Reserve, Peru. Photo: Tui de Roy]

Building the nest is an important component of pair-bonding. For virtually all picids for which sufficient information is available, it is the male that undertakes the majority of the work. This pair of Ashy Woodpeckers was watched during the early and middle stages of nest-excavation. Work was carried out daily, but only during the cooler morning hours, and the male did about three-quarters of the digging. The hole was 12 m up, and faced away from the direction of the strong morning sunlight; a few metres below it was another hole, this one shallow and incomplete, which had recently been abandoned by the pair. It is rather common for members of this family to start several new holes, sometimes even completing more than one, before a final selection is made. The chosen cavity then becomes the pair's nest, and for the male, which always incubates at night, it also serves as a roost. Sometimes, at the last moment before the eggs are laid, a pair will even switch to another hole. Woodpeckers are generally monogamous, and incubation and the brooding and feeding of young are tasks shared by the two partners. A woodpecker is usually able to cope successfully with the work on its own only once the chicks are old enough for brooding to be no longer necessary.

[*Mulleripicus fulvus fulvus*, Tangkoko-Dua Saudara, north Sulawesi. Photo: Brian J. Coates/ Lynx]

Once they have made the initial funnel-shaped hole, small woodpeckers, such as this Red-headed Woodpecker of eastern North America, grip the lower rim of the entrance and forcefully peck and tear away pieces of wood, flicking them to the ground. Hammering is usually more rhythmic than when foraging. This barkless stump is a typical site for a Red-headed Woodpecker nest, the bird often starting the hole at an existing crack. This picid is one of several that face competition from other hole-nesting species, but it is vigorous in the defence of its hole, losing only 15% of its cavities to Common Starlings (Sturnus vulgaris).

[Melanerpes erythrocephalus, Alma, Marion County, Illinois, USA. Photos: Richard & Susan Day/Animals Animals]

hole. Over the following nine days, when the mynas repeatedly attempted to return to their nest, the woodpeckers chased them away and themselves entered the hole. Then, with no warning, a group of 25-30 noisy mynas appeared in the nearby trees; a few of them dashed inside the hole and forced out the incumbent flameback, while others attacked the woodpecker's mate perched outside on the trunk of the tree. In the ensuing fight, the mynas' ferocity was such that, to the observer, it seemed likely that they would kill the woodpeckers, but the intervention of a local boy caused all the birds to fly away. On the next day, the mynas were back in the hole, where they eventually reared two young. The flamebacks were not seen in the vicinity again.

Owls of many species frequently take over woodpecker holes, both old and new ones. Pygmy-owls (*Glaucidium*) make short work of the job, and can kill a woodpecker that is bold enough to resist the take-over of its hole.

From all this, it should be amply evident that woodpeckers, because of the part they play as hole-constructors in many habitats, and because of their important role in the food chain and in foraging actions, are truly keystone species in a great many of the earth's terrestrial ecosystems. This may be illustrated by an example from Peru, where a dead tree about 25 m tall was found to contain numerous woodpecker holes, six of which were simultaneously occupied by breeding birds; these comprised two pairs of *Aratinga* parakeets, one pair of tityras, one of martins (*Progne*), and two pairs of different woodpecker species, one a *Melanerpes* and the other a *Dryocopus*. There are many similar examples from all areas of the world range occupied by the Picidae.

Woodpeckers generally reach maturity in the first year of life. In many cases, they breed for the first time during the breeding season following the one in which they hatched. Members of co-operatively breeding species, however, may delay nesting themselves for several years, depending on when they obtain an opportunity to breed within the group.

For the majority of the Picidae, there is no information available on longevity or on average lifespan. Wrynecks generally live for two to ten years, while most picid species probably live for an average of two or three years. The maximum

age recorded for the Great Spotted Woodpecker is nine years, and that for the Northern Flicker is nine years and two months, while a Red-bellied Woodpecker has been known to live for twelve years and one month. A ringed Gila Woodpecker was recaptured when nearly eight years old, while American Three-toed and White-headed Woodpeckers live for at least six to eight years, and the same probably applies to the Black-backed Woodpecker and many other picids. The demography is well known only for the two best-studied social species. The Acorn Woodpecker may reach an age of at least 16 in the case of males and 15 in the case of females, and the Red-cockaded Woodpecker can live for at least twelve years. In the case of the former species, adult survival seems to be independent of age, but the sexes differ to the extent that male survivorship is positively correlated with group size.

Long-term ringing studies in Peninsular Malaysia have produced some interesting figures on the lifespan of a number of species, based on the intervals between retrapping of ringed individuals. For the Rufous Piculet, the longest interval was seven years and two months, while that for the Rufous Woodpecker was only three years. Among the Picini, the oldest Banded Woodpecker was one month short of six years, and two Laced Woodpeckers were still alive after nine years and ten years, respectively. In addition, of 35 Common Flamebacks, at least six survived for more than four years and at least three for over eight years; the oldest two were still alive after more than ten years. During these studies, a Buff-necked Woodpecker was retrapped when it had reached an age of five years and three months.

Movements

For the most part, woodpeckers are sedentary birds. Only a very small proportion of species, or, rather, populations, can be described as truly migratory. Most of the movements undertaken by picids are dispersive, and involve mainly juvenile birds, and they are probably difficult to distinguish from seasonal shifts in habitat and altitude. Some species undergo eruptive movements that are driven by food shortage. Outbreaks of budworms and similar pests, often associated with wind damage or fire, may attract certain woodpecker species from the local area, but rarely to the extent that the individuals involved travel any great distance to exploit such sources of abundant food. Most data on woodpecker movements, if they exist at all, are vague, and relevant information is either relatively scant or simply not available. The piculets, for example, are thought to be more or less completely sedentary birds. In Peninsular Malaysia, two ringed Rufous Piculets, both females, were retrapped after several years only about 800 m from where they had originally been ringed, but little else is known about the possible movements of these diminutive members of the family. In these circumstances, one cannot entirely rule out the possibility that at least some of them make local, seasonal movements.

Those woodpeckers that do migrate generally do so during the day, although these movements are seldom conspicuous and are, therefore, not well documented. Migrating woodpeckers do, however, sometimes form flocks, and it has been repeatedly noted that flocks of migrating Great Spotted Woodpeckers in north Europe also contain individuals of other picid species.

Dispersal and post-breeding nomadism are probably most pronounced among temperate species and also, possibly, among those species living in arid and semi-arid zones. In the case of tropical woodpeckers, the young, rather than dispersing from the natal territory, may stay with their parents for an extended period of time. Dispersal, or, rather, the reduced opportunities that it brings for acquiring a new breeding site, is one of the crucial aspects in the understanding of communal breeding by woodpeckers (see Breeding).

Observations of woodpeckers outside their normal breeding range are often the only indication of dispersal. For example, records of the Grey Woodpecker in west-central Mauritania, as well as in south Nigeria and coastal Ghana, are most likely to represent extreme cases of post-breeding dispersal. In Europe, the sedentary Middle Spotted Woodpecker appears intermittently outside its breeding range, as, for example, in Estonia, or in its former breeding area in southern Sweden, where its last successful nesting took place in 1980; indeed, individuals have even been seen at Sweden's famed coastal bird observatory of Falsterbo. The Eurasian Green Woodpecker, despite its signifi-

cantly larger size, exhibits juvenile dispersal mostly to distances of only 30 km, and rarely farther, although there are records of young birds moving up to about 200 km from the parental territory. One of that species' Asian congeners, the Lesser Yellownape, may be a further example of a woodpecker dispersing to areas outside the normal breeding range, as it is known to reach north-east Pakistan on occasion, presumably from its nesting areas in the Himalayan foothills of north India. Although these are a few examples of longer movements made by woodpeckers that are generally more or less sedentary, dispersal can in some cases be over greater distances. The dispersive movements undertaken by juvenile Great Spotted Woodpeckers, for instance, regularly extend over 100 km, and can cover as much as about 600 km.

As stated above, it is often not at all easy to distinguish post-breeding dispersal from seasonal movements that are made in order to escape harsh climatic conditions. In the Northern Hemisphere, some of the occasionally more notable movements that are recorded for certain species, such as the Black Woodpecker, show a peak in autumn, but there seems to be no corresponding return movement in spring, although irregular movements may occur in the latter season as well (see also Status and Conservation). In comparison, altitudinal displacements show a much clearer pattern, generally, and such movements are rather widespread among picid species. In Asia, for example, northern populations of the Grey-capped Woodpecker move to adjacent lowlands in winter, and continental populations of the related Pygmy Woodpecker behave similarly. So, too, do Brown-fronted Woodpeckers (*Dendrocopos auriceps*), Himalayan Woodpeckers (*Dendrocopos himalayensis*) and Nepalese populations of the Rufous-bellied Woodpecker, all of which breed at high altitudes. Many other pied woodpecker species of the temperate zones of Europe and North America are known to be subject to varying degrees of altitudinal movement, descending to lower levels for the winter season. Even the largely tropical Arabian Woodpecker can be found down to the Tihama lowlands in the non-breeding, winter season, while at least part of the population breeding in the Asir Mountains moves upslope in the summer months. The colaptine Dot-fronted Woodpecker, distributed at comparable latitudes in the Southern Hemisphere, in the Neotropics, also

The later stages of nest-building involve working inside the hole, which means that large quantities of wood chips and sawdust that collect on the floor of the nest-chamber have to be removed. This male Red-bellied Woodpecker, working inside an ash (Fraxinus) tree, brings wood shavings to the entrance hole and disposes of them in typical woodpecker fashion, with an energetic flick. Among many picids, copulation occurs during the period of nest-construction, reaching a peak just before and during egg-laying. The Red-bellied Woodpecker is, incidentally, one of several Melanerpes species in which reversed mounting has been observed, whereby the female mounts the male.

[*Melanerpes carolinus*, Cincinnati, Ohio. Photos: Dave Maslowski]

The way in which wood chips and flakes are removed from the inside of the nesting cavity during the process of construction is highly characteristic of the Picidae. The same method is employed by all species, from the smallest to the biggest. In these photographs, shards of wood are flung from the nest entrance by a male North American Pileated Woodpecker, one of the largest picids, and by a male White-spotted Woodpecker, a very much smaller member of the family living in South America. The technique of tossing out wood chips is essentially identical in both cases. The height at which the nest-hole is constructed varies considerably according to species. While the White-spotted Woodpecker tends to nest low down in a stub, the Pileated Woodpecker's nest is usually 6-12 m above the ground in an old tree and is sometimes as high as 30 m. Where huge rainforest trees are available, some of the larger woodpeckers nest at heights of up to 50 m.

[Above: *Dryocopus pileatus abieticola*, Rutland, Maine, USA. Photo: John E. Swedberg/ Ardea.

Below: *Veniliornis spilogaster*, Iguazú National Park, Misiones, Argentina. Photo: Julián Alonso]

As with much else about their ecology and biology, relatively little is known about the breeding habits of the diminutive piculets. The range of nesting opportunities is perhaps greater than that for larger woodpeckers, as very small trunks, branches and bamboo are all suitable sites. This White-wedged Piculet, however, has chosen a log that is in use as a fence post. From the little information available, a piculet's nest-chamber, which tends to be cylindrical rather than, as that of true woodpeckers, pear-shaped, typically contains just two or three eggs, fewer than the average clutch size of larger picids.

[Picumnus albosquamatus guttifer, Pantanal, Mato Grosso, Brazil. Photos: Xavier Ferrer & A. de Sostoa]

moves a short distance downslope outside the breeding season, and the Chestnut-coloured Woodpecker wanders into Caribbean coastal scrub and mangrove during the austral winter.

A number of *Picus* woodpeckers in Europe and Asia exhibit similar altitudinal shifts on a seasonal basis. These include certain populations of the widely distributed Grey-faced Woodpecker, which move from breeding habitats at higher elevations to more favourable lower wintering grounds, such as riparian woodland and areas of human habitation. This is essentially true also for two of that species' congeners. These are the Scaly-bellied Woodpecker, the Himalayan populations of which partly descend to lower altitudes in winter, and the Japanese Woodpecker, which likewise moves to lower habitats in severe winters. A further example among the Picini tribe is that of the Bay Woodpecker, chiefly an upland breeder, which can be recorded at low elevations outside the breeding season.

Some species that occur in dry habitats also undertake seasonal movements. The Arabian Woodpecker has already been mentioned. Populations of Bennett's Woodpecker that nest in the most arid areas of this species' African range fly short distances to more moderate climates after the breeding season, and some seasonal movements appear to be made also by the White-fronted Woodpecker in the Neotropics. It is quite likely that similar short-distance flights are undertaken by other dryland woodpeckers.

As is to be expected, medium-range seasonal movements are most marked among woodpeckers living in cool temperate habitats. Some of the species involved may also migrate over larger distances. Many of these movements are irregular and nomadic and involve only certain populations, as typified by, for example, the Grey-faced Woodpecker. Apart from local altitudinal movements, this picid is basically as sedentary as most other members of the family, but members of northern populations wander variable distances in winter, and some Scandinavian individuals occasionally perform short migrations in autumn. In America, some Acorn Woodpeckers leave the breeding areas in autumn, and those of southern Arizona and the adjacent Mexican mountains possibly fly farther south in northern Mexico. The related Red-bellied Woodpecker concentrates in favourable areas in winter, and it may then occur outside its breeding areas, while the species' northern populations, at least in really harsh winters, migrate southwards. In the case of the congeneric Red-

headed Woodpecker, however, southward migration by northern and, especially, north-western populations is of more or less regular annual occurrence, and flocks of up to several hundred individuals can be seen during this passage in the period from August to November. In winter, these woodpeckers remain in regions south and east of a line drawn approximately from south Texas north to eastern Kansas and south-east Iowa and across to Ohio and New Jersey, returning to their breeding grounds in late February and March. Occasional Red-headed Woodpeckers are seen, in winter or summer, in areas west of the breeding range, even in western Canada and California, and there are also reports of this species flying over the Gulf of Mexico in October. The Green-barred, Striped and Chequered Woodpeckers serve as examples of medium-distance migrants from the Southern Hemisphere. In the case of the first of those three picids, at least some of the southernmost populations, after breeding in northern Patagonia, migrate to northern Argentina, as also do populations from the Cordoba highlands of north-central Argentina. Southern populations of the other two species migrate to, respectively, west-central Argentina and the Mato Grosso.

In the Northern Hemisphere, northern populations of the Lesser Spotted Woodpecker of Eurasia are at least partly migratory, and that species' Nearctic analogue, the Downy Woodpecker, may also be so. In the case of the former, north European birds sometimes reach the Black Sea; the migration is often irruptive and may parallel the more striking movements of Great Spotted Woodpeckers. Although even northern and montane populations of the Downy Woodpecker have been found to be residents for the most part, a degree of movement has been observed along the Atlantic coast which could indicate that, locally, this woodpecker may be partially migratory; furthermore, in the west, some individuals have been known to reach Mexico. It has been suggested, however, that these movements, rather then representing true migration, involve dispersing individuals.

While northernmost populations of the New World Hairy Woodpecker show some unspectacular seasonal movements, those of the similarly sized Great Spotted Woodpecker in the Old World are subject to eruptive and conspicuous migrations. These periodic exoduses are triggered by poor crops of pine or spruce seeds, and they begin in late summer, after the breeding season; individuals may stray more than 3000 km, and some arrive on islands, even remote ones. Although this phenomenon occurs occasionally among this species' Far Eastern populations, it is considerably more striking in Europe, where mass emigration from Scandinavia and Russia can involve many thousands of woodpeckers. For example, in a massive eruption that took place in the autumn of 1962, numbers of Great Spotted Woodpeckers on the small south Finnish island of Säppi, in the Gulf of Bothnia, reached a peak of about 10,000 on 17th August; more recently, 2240 passed through a single site in Latvia in autumn 1999. An interesting aspect of these periodic large-scale movements, which are comprised chiefly of juveniles, is that other picids are often caught up in them. In this context, allusion has already been made to the Grey-faced and Lesser Spotted Woodpeckers, but another species deserving of mention in this regard is the White-backed Woodpecker. Some local movements aside, this attractive pied woodpecker is chiefly a resident, but its continental populations occasionally undertake eruptive southward or westward migration, sometimes in connection with similar movements by Great Spotted Woodpeckers, and relatively large numbers from Russia can then reach Finland and Sweden.

The two three-toed woodpeckers of the Holarctic Region perform eruptive migrations as well. Although mountain populations of the Eurasian species are largely sedentary, those breeding in the northern parts of the range rather frequently move south and west after breeding, sometimes in reasonably large numbers, and the Siberian subspecies *crissoleucus* regularly migrates greater distances. In eastern North America, American Three-toed Woodpeckers move south at irregular intervals, and a similar pattern of periodic migration is followed by the closely related Black-backed Woodpecker. These eruptive movements, while certainly not approaching the proportions of those exhibited by *Picoides* species in northern Europe, can at times be notable. The largest invasion of Black-backed Woodpeckers in the north-eastern USA occurred in 1974, when over 460 individuals were estimated to have arrived from their breeding areas in the boreal forest of eastern Canada. It is thought that these irregular eruptive migrations may be caused by regional population increases brought about by very favourable conditions, such as outbreaks of spruce budworm, or, conversely, they may be precipitated by a lack of suitable food in the form of wood-boring insects.

The annual movements of Lewis's Woodpeckers, which travel variable distances after breeding, do not always involve all the individuals of a population. Of particular interest, however, is that the change from living in open pine woodland during the spring and summer breeding season to spending the rest of the year in oak woodland and orchards is associated with significant changes in the diet. From being an insectivore during the breeding period, this North American woodpecker becomes a vegetarian in autumn and winter, when it feeds mainly on acorns or nuts, supplemented by fruits. In August and early September, Lewis's Woodpeckers are largely nomadic, wandering to other habitats in the mountains or visiting orchards. At this time they move around in flocks and, if suitable winter habitats are very close by, they need to travel only small distances. Only about half of the population in south-eastern Colorado leaves the breeding area, whereas the populations of Idaho, Wyoming and Montana are probably forced to migrate longer distances. The winter range is generally within the southern portions of the breeding range, northwards to Oregon and, in smaller numbers, to British Columbia, but in the south some extend outside the breeding area to as far as north-west Baja California, eastern Arizona and southern New Mexico, and, rarely, into northern Mexico. Climatic conditions and the distribution of acorn crops largely determine the winter distribution. This species' migrations can on occasion be rather spectacular, with totals of up to 2000 or more birds, in flocks ranging from two or three individuals to several tens, passing a particular place in one hour. Food supply is the most important criterion for Lewis's Woodpecker when it comes to selecting the wintering habitat, and that is why oak woodland, commercial orchards, especially of almond (*Prunus amygdalus*), walnut (*Juglans*) or hickory, and other areas with ample food supply, such as corn, are preferred.

Those populations of the Northern Flicker that breed north of a theoretical line joining the northern parts of California, Oklahoma and Virginia are migratory, although there seems to be some difference in this respect between the red-shafted form in the west and the eastern, yellow-shafted flickers. The former is certainly migratory in Alaska and western Canada, but it may be less inclined to move far from the breeding areas in its western USA range. Unlike Lewis's Woodpecker, which migrates mostly by day, flickers are chiefly nocturnal migrants. Nevertheless, they can be seen migrating during the day, too, in sometimes large flocks, flying low over the ground. Their wintering grounds are concentrated in the USA, from the south-western states through Texas to Florida, with a few extending south into northern Mexico.

In the New World, the most migratory of all the woodpeckers is the Yellow-bellied Sapsucker, which winters far south of its breeding range in Canada, the north-eastern USA and the Appalachian Mountains. This melanerpine species ranges in winter from about south Kansas, southern Ohio and Connecticut southwards through Texas and the Gulf Coast states to Mexico, and beyond through Central America to Costa Rica and, rarely, to Panama. The entire West Indies are also included in the species' winter distribution, which covers a wide variety of habitats ranging from forest and forest edge, and various semi-open habitats, pastures and clearings, to orchards and even suburban areas, as well as coastal palm groves. The Red-naped Sapsucker, confined to western North America, is less migratory than its relative, and winters from Arizona south to north-west Mexico, although a few may occasionally reach the northern parts of Central America. Its non-breeding habitats in Arizona are oak woodlands mixed with juniper (*Juniperus*) or pine, or pure oak woodland, in upland areas, whereas it normally shuns oak and pine woodland when breeding. The Red-breasted Sapsucker, breeding along the North American Pacific coast, is even less migratory than the last species, even its northern, nominate subspecies being virtually sedentary. Some do leave the breeding grounds, however, and the species winters south to northern Baja California. The fourth sapsucker, Williamson's, is almost restricted as a breeding bird to the western half of the USA, extending only a short way north into Canada and south into the Mexican mountains. It is a partial migrant, and it appears that western populations do not move so far as the eastern ones, which

With less need for camouflage against passing predators, the eggs of woodpeckers are invariably white, making them easier for the parents to see within the dark nest-chamber. Nests are unlined, apart from a bed of remaining wood chips. These are especially important in nests such as this Yellow-bellied Sapsucker's; as the liquid nestling diet results in thin or non-existent faecal sacs, droppings are mixed with the chips to facilitate their removal by the parents. The number of eggs laid is determined by optimal clutch size, not by the number already laid. A female Northern Flicker (Colaptes auratus), when her eggs were experimentally removed, continued to lay, and produced 71 eggs.

[Sphyrapicus varius, Ontario, Canada. Photo: George Peck]

Incubation, which begins within a day or two of the clutch being completed, is short, but the young stay in the nest for a relatively long time and, in some cases, remain with the parents for months after fledging. Although the male sleeps in the nest at night, incubation and brooding during the daytime are usually shared by the parents, which work in shifts. A male West Indian Woodpecker is pictured here outside the nest as his mate is about to leave; change-over is accompanied by low calls. With this species, the male does most of the brood-feeding, enabling the female to regain condition for a second clutch, which is not uncommon for this picid.

[*Melanerpes superciliaris superciliaris*, Zapata Swamp, Cuba. Photo: Doug Wechsler/ VIREO]

migrate down into Sinaloa and Durango, some even reaching as far south as Michoacán in southern Mexico. Again, this woodpecker, which breeds in coniferous forest, has somewhat different preferences in the non-breeding period, which it spends in humid to mesic habitats such as pine-oak and oak-juniper woodland. Various observations indicate that, for all four sapsucker species, the females winter farther south, and the males return to the breeding grounds earlier than do the females.

The migratory capacities of the Yellow-bellied Sapsucker are reflected in the fact that it has been recorded on at least three occasions in western Europe. There are also three records of the Northern Flicker in Europe, but in this case considerable doubt surrounds the provenance of the birds: two were almost certainly "ship-assisted" and had hitched a ride on an ocean-going vessel, while the third, a corpse, is presumed to have died while on a ship at sea.

Notwithstanding the migratory feats of some of the North American picids, it is in the Old World that the most spectacular examples of migration by woodpeckers are found. The isolated north-east Asian population of the Rufous-bellied Woodpecker in Manchuria and Ussuriland seems to be totally migratory, the birds passing through central China in autumn and spring as they commute to and from their wintering grounds in southern China. While it could be argued that this journey is rivalled by that made by some of the sapsuckers in North America, the same cannot be said about the migration of the Eurasian Wryneck. This aberrant woodpecker is a genuine long-distance migrant, making annual southward flights of 8000 km and more to its non-breeding quarters, and capable of covering a distance of over 600 km in eight days. In contrast to the true woodpeckers in the subfamily Picinae, wrynecks migrate mainly at night. All northern populations in the huge range of the species are summer visitors to those regions. The European and west Asian populations winter in the savannas and drier areas of West and Central Africa, while those breeding in eastern Asia migrate to the Indian Subcontinent and South-east Asia. Some individuals of the nominate form winter in Mediterranean countries and in south-east Iran. The less migratory wrynecks breeding in the Mediterranean region and north Africa migrate only short distances or move altitudinally. In autumn, European breeders cross the Alps in August and September and then move down through the Iberian Peninsula or the Balkans; every year at this season, some Eurasian Wrynecks from Scandinavia migrate through Britain, where they can be especially numerous during anticyclonic conditions, when they are drifted westwards by easterly winds. At least a proportion of those populations breeding in the western half of Asia probably fly over Turkey and the Arabian Peninsula. The relatively clumsy wrynecks sometimes pay a heavy toll to Eleonora's Falcons (*Falco eleonorae*), which specialize in capturing tired migrant birds as they attempt to cross the Mediterranean Sea. Many Eurasian Wrynecks do not leave Africa until April, arriving back on the breeding grounds in May.

Fewer details are known about this species' movements in eastern Asia, where migrants are recorded in Korea in September and in April and May, and occasional individuals turn up in western Alaska, but the general timing appears to parallel that observed in the western parts of the range. In Japan, wrynecks breeding on Hokkaido leave in August and September and return in late April and May; although a few appear to spend the non-breeding season in the southern part of the country, southwards from central Honshu, the great majority leave Japan after breeding.

The Eurasian Wryneck's African sibling species, the Rufous-necked Wryneck, is partially migratory in the southern parts of its range. Some individuals, after having bred in South Africa, move as far north as eastern Zaire, and migrants are recorded in February and March as they pass through north-eastern South Africa.

Relationship with Man

Probably the majority of people are able to recognize a woodpecker as such, although many non-naturalists might not be aware that the wrynecks and the piculets are also woodpeckers. With their frequently colourful plumage, their habit of tapping and drumming on wood and other surfaces, and their close association with dark cavities, the woodpeckers have long been a source of intrigue for humans. References to these fascinating and often beautiful birds can be found in legends and creeds dating right back to ancient civilizations. It is only in the African continent that this

Without a specialist bill to excavate wood, some picids depend on existing cavities for nesting. These species tend to lay larger clutches: seven eggs is not atypical for the Eurasian Wryneck, and some individuals can lay as many as twelve eggs in a single clutch. Feeding so large a brood requires dozens of foraging trips each day, both parents carrying in food and removing faeces for three weeks, at which time the young wrynecks leave the nest. Those species which excavate their own holes, the majority of the Picidae, produce smaller clutches, probably because they are not limited by the availability of nest-sites, and therefore require less reproductive effort during their lifetime. Even these, however, need to make frequent feeding visits to satisfy the demands of their young.

[Jynx torquilla tschusii, Italy.
Photo: Paolo Fioratti/
Oxford Scientific Films]

avian family appears to have had little influence on humans, but that may be because woodpeckers are, on the whole, less numerous there than they are elsewhere in their world range.

Generally, the true woodpeckers of the Picinae tribe are rather popular birds. In most parts of the world where they occur, they are welcomed as attractive and interesting creatures which enliven the local forest, woodland or gardens. A very large number of these species, representing virtually all genera, have also been kept in captivity, and many have been bred and reared successfully. Great Spotted Woodpeckers are a prime example of this, but numerous others, including lesser-known picids such as the Asian Fulvous-breasted and Black-headed Woodpeckers (*Picus erythropygius*), have been kept in aviaries.

Woodpeckers have been used as recognizable symbols in advertising, although it is difficult to find any relationship between a pecking and digging picid and an alcoholic beverage. Perhaps a clue is to be found in one of the many humorous folklore tales recounted in the Canadian province of Manitoba. The story, although not meant to be taken seriously, tells how the Yellow-bellied Sapsucker missed the official "handing-out of colours" to birds because, through constantly drinking the sap of birch trees, it had become too inebriated to attend the ceremony; the other birds, having received theirs, presented the sapsucker with a variety of colours in order to console it.

In North America, a famous cartoon feature has "Woody Woodpecker" as its main character. The bird's laughing voice is intended to represent its song, and one can, with a little imagination, accept this interpretation. On the other hand, the cartoon woodpecker's lightning-rapid drilling to create a hole, and the combination of this action with powerful bill blows, are departures from the reality of the genuine picid's behaviour, even if such fanciful ideas appeal to the viewing audience.

Woodpeckers are mentioned in poetry, too. One of the best examples is provided by the seventeenth-century poet Marvell, in which the description of the foraging behaviour of the "Hewel", a derivative of the Anglo-Saxon *hyghwhele*, the name used for

the Eurasian Green Woodpecker, demonstrates the poet's joy in accurate observation of nature:

"He walks still upright from the Root,
Meas'ring the Timber with his Foot;
And all the way, to keep it clean,
Doth from the Bark the Wood-moths glean."

Another superb example, this time referring to the varied diet of the Northern Flicker at garden feeders and in fields, comes from the pen of G. Newkirk, a dentist and poet who lived in California in the latter part of the nineteenth century. Newkirks's anthropomorphic verse gives voice to the flicker:

"And I like dessert in reason,
Just a bit of fruit in season,
But my delicacy is ants,
Stump or hill inhabitants;
Thrusting in my sticky tongue,
So I take them, old and young."

The striking vocalizations of many picids have earned them a myriad of colloquial names. In Britain, for example, the Eurasian Green Woodpecker's laughing call is reflected in countless local names, one of which, "Yaffle", is still used today by some countryfolk. By the end of the eighteenth century, this name, which may possibly have descended from Anglo-Saxon, had become the usual one for the species, and its meaning was even extended to denote the making of a woodpecker-like sound by a human. In parts of France, this species is known as "the miller's solicitor", because it announces the imminent arrival of rain and the consequent rising of water levels that will allow the mills to work. Indeed, the name "Rainbird" was applied to the Eurasian Green Woodpecker in many European languages, as in the German "*Regenvogel*", and it was similarly used for the Eurasian Wryneck, also said to be a predictor of rain. Another old German

On returning to the nest with food, woodpeckers rarely fly directly to the entrance hole. Most alight on the substrate a few centimetres to the side, or sometimes above, the entrance. Here, the male Red-necked Woodpecker takes a few seconds to check that there are no predators, either inside the cavity or on a nearby branch. He can also establish, through quiet calls, whether his partner is already attending the chicks. Once convinced that all is normal, the bird will move quickly to the entrance hole and drop inside. As the chicks develop and fill the nest-cavity, the adults bring food only to the entrance, as the Little Woodpecker in the lower photograph is doing. Prey fed to the brood increases in size as the nestlings grow. In addition, and not surprisingly, it varies in proportion to the size of the bird, as is obvious from the differences in size of the larvae being delivered by these two Neotropical species.

[Above: *Campephilus rubricollis rubricollis*, French Guiana. Photo: Olivier Tostain.

Below: *Veniliornis passerinus olivinus*, Mato Grosso, Brazil. Photo: Iany Sauvanet/Bios]

name for the wryneck, once a very common bird in the European countryside, was "*Gießvogel*", after the word *Gießen*, meaning teeming rain, but also, coincidentally, reflecting that species' song, "giaß, giaß,…". In America, early colonists from Europe invented all kinds of names for the birds that were new to them, in many cases referring to what were, to the settlers, unusual vocalizations, colours or patterns, or aspects of behaviour.

Myths and legends surrounding woodpeckers date far back in history. In the legend of Romulus and Remus, the twins who founded the city of Rome, the woodpecker, besides helping the wolf to feed the twins, also helped it to defend sacred trees. A Roman coin shows the wolf feeding the two foundlings beneath a sacred fig (*Ficus*) tree in which two woodpeckers are perched. For the Romans, the woodpeckers held a place of particular honour, and were considered to represent industry, bravery and war. The association between the woodpecker and Mars, the God of War, is a very old one, and the connection can still be seen in the scientific name of the Black Woodpecker, *martius*. It is also of interest to note that, before the systematic scientific naming of animals and plants came into force, the name "*Picus martius*" was applied to other species, in particular the Eurasian Green Woodpecker.

The woodpecker features also in Greek and Hindu mythology and legends. Like the greatest of the Greek gods, Zeus, the Hindu God Indra was said to transform himself into a woodpecker in order to pursue his amorous adventures. In Europe, a Black Woodpecker's feather was regarded as making the person who held it lucky in love.

While superstitious beliefs ascribe the ability to forecast the weather to several kinds of bird, foremost among these are the woodpeckers. Notions of woodpeckers as rain-forecasters are widespread in many parts of the world. The Guadeloupe Woodpecker's drumming was thought by some to foretell the arrival of rain. In many European countries, the call of the Eurasian Green Woodpecker, when slow, drawn out and doleful, was said to announce the imminent arrival of rain. Ancient European peoples believed that this bird was a prophet, especially of rain and storms, and that it had supernatural powers because of its association with thunder, rain and fertility. E. A. Armstrong, after examining all the various myths and legends, and the clues contained within them, concluded that a "woodpecker cult" existed in Neolithic times, when oak forest still covered extensive areas of Europe and, at the same time, humans were starting to cultivate the land. Rain is of great importance for cultivation, and the woodpecker bringing the rain would also symbolize fertility. The bright green colours of the Eurasian Green Woodpecker, and its habit of digging into the ground, would have served only to reinforce such beliefs; moreover, it has even been regarded as having inspired the invention of the plough. This species was a rain-forecaster to the druids of ancient Britain, to whom the oak tree was sacred. The woodpecker's association with oaks would naturally have led to its being regarded as having special powers.

When theistic religions and Christianity came more to the fore, a switch in emphasis appears to have taken place. The woodpecker had, it seems, acquired too high a position in life and needed to be "put in its place". This is revealed by a number of interesting tales and legends in which the woodpecker is punished for its disobedience. One story, from the Gironde region of south-western France, relates that God, after having created the earth, ordered all the birds to excavate the hollows that were destined to become seas and wetlands; the woodpecker was the only one to disobey. Later, when all the other birds had completed the work, God decreed that the woodpecker, since he had

Woodpeckers which obtain most of their food by gleaning bring a greater number of prey items to the nest in each delivery than do those which peck and hammer for food. This female Grey-capped Woodpecker is returning to her nest, in eastern Siberia, with the bill stuffed full of invertebrates. The food delivery also includes a small snail, which should provide the nestlings with a challenge. The diet of young picids is usually made up of easily digested soft-bodied insects, and includes less plant material than that of the adults.

[*Dendrocopos canicapillus doerriesi*, north Ussuriland, south-east Siberia, Russia. Photo: Yuri Shibnev]

At least 60% of all woodpecker species include ants in the diet, but the two wrynecks which constitute the subfamily Jynginae are true ant specialists. Because ants occur in great quantity in concentrated sources, these picids are able to collect the food and deliver it to the young in bulk. This is perfectly illustrated by this Rufous-necked Wryneck, which has returned to its nest-hole with a massive load of ant pupae for its chicks. Adult wrynecks feed both themselves and their nestlings on ants, including their pupae and eggs, obtained from terrestrial nests by gleaning and probing. They exploit ants of many different genera, using the sticky tongue which, unlike that of other picids, is smooth and barbless. Mate-feeding forms part of the courtship ritual of the wrynecks, and the male sometimes continues to feed his partner even during incubation.

[*Jynx ruficollis ruficollis*, near Johannesburg, South Africa. Photo: Geoff McIleron]

Woodpecker chicks hatch naked and blind. All brood-members usually hatch on the same day, and develop to fledging over the relatively long period of three to four weeks in the nest-cavity. At this very early stage, when just a couple of days old, these six young Northern Flickers respond to the returning female with urgent begging calls. Woodpeckers deliver food to their nestlings by one of two methods. Either they regurgitate it, as is the case with the flickers and two other genera, or they pass the food from the bill tip to the chick's mouth, a technique employed by the wrynecks, the piculets and many of the true woodpeckers. Visible on some of these nestlings are the pads at the base of the lower jaw, which extend over the edge of the bill. These assist the parents in the transfer of food in the darkness of the hole, and they will have disappeared almost completely by the time the chicks fledge. The clutch size of Northern Flickers varies considerably, both with timing of laying and with latitude. Clutches laid earlier in the season tend to be larger than later ones, and clutch size increases gradually from south to north. The latitudinal increase is of the order of one egg for every additional 10 degrees of latitude.

[Colaptes auratus luteus, near Dexter, Maine, USA. Photo: Dwight R. Kuhn/ DRK]

With still at least a week until their first flight, these young Pileated Woodpeckers can only lie in their natal cavity, waiting for food, and for their juvenile feathers to develop. Thin sheaths remain on the flight-feathers, although the red crown is already obvious. The coloration of some young woodpeckers differs strikingly from that of the adults, with juveniles of several species showing markings that are lost after the first moult. Young Great Spotted Woodpeckers (Dendrocopos major), for example, possess a red forecrown, whereas this part of the plumage is black on the adults of both sexes.

[Dryocopus pileatus abieticola, near Harrisburg, Pennsylvania, USA. Photo: Joe McDonald/ DRK]

been unwilling to peck at the ground, would for the rest eternity be assigned to pecking at wood, and, as he had refused to assist in the digging work, he should drink nothing but rain. That is why he is always calling "pluie pluie", the French word for rain, and always climbing upwards in order to obtain the drops falling from the sky. This tale would seem somewhat ironic if it were intended to refer to the ground-digging Eurasian Green Woodpecker, the most visible and widespread picid in the region; it would apply better to the Black Woodpecker, although that species was not present in south-west France until relatively recently.

An Estonian version of the story appears to relate more obviously to the Black Woodpecker. In this, the woodpecker refused to help in the digging because he did not wish to get his fine golden coat dirty. His vanity earned him severe punishment from the Lord, who stated that the woodpecker would henceforth wear a cloak of sooty-black and would be able to drink only from rain falling from the sky; his voice would be heard only when all the other birds were seeking shelter from approaching storms.

Other stories tell of the woodpecker's lack of charity. In Norse legend, the Lord and St Peter, hungry after having walked far, called upon a woman named Gertrude, who was baking cakes and wore a close-fitting red cap on her head. When they begged her for food, her baking efforts all produced cakes that were, she said, too big; she was unable to provide any that were small enough to be given away, so she told the visitors that they must go without. The Lord replied that, since she had so little love as to begrudge the hungry travellers a morsel of food, she was to be punished by being turned into a bird that seeks food between bark and bole and never gets a drop to drink. She was immediately transformed into a woodpecker, and flew straight up the chimney. The legend says that "Gertrude's bird" can still be seen flying around, with her red cap on her head and her body all black from the soot of the chimney. This is clearly a reference to the Black Woodpecker.

A variation of the same Scandinavian legend was given by a French priest. In this, Gertrude made her husband's life a misery, and the wretched man said that he would not go to paradise if his wife went there. One day, a poor man came to the door and asked for water, but Gertrude pushed him away with threats and abuse; the caller was Jesus Christ. Because Gertrude would not give to the poor, she was sentenced to a life of eternal wandering and insatiable thirst; furthermore, for the whole universe to know

her and her sinfulness, she would always wear a red beret on her head and would announce, with a plaintive call, the water that she would seek in a vain quest to satisfy her thirst. Gertrude was instantly transformed into a woodpecker; in this version of the story, however, she becomes a green woodpecker.

The use of woodpecker feathers in ornamentation appears not to be very common. In western North America, the finery of the Klamath Indian shamans included tiaras made of the skin of Red-headed Woodpeckers, and necklaces made of golden woodpecker feathers. The Pomo Indians of California fashioned exquisite coiled baskets studded with crests of quails (*Lophortyx*), the scalps of various woodpeckers, and hummingbird feathers. They used the red feathers of the Pileated Woodpecker primarily for currency, and only to a very limited extent for ornamentation. It seems, however, that the Acorn Woodpecker, which was abundant in California, was more heavily exploited there, and probably elsewhere in the western USA and Mexico, for its brilliant red head feathers. One full-size cape was found to be covered all over with the red crown feathers of this species, and it has been suggested that several thousand individuals may perhaps have been killed to decorate this single garment. The woodpeckers were often trapped as they emerged from the overnight roosting holes.

The same native Indians also used Acorn Woodpeckers for food, although picids in general appear not to have been utilized to any great extent for this purpose. The fact that they have a relatively tough skin and emit a strong, resinous odour (see Morphological Aspects) may have something to do with this. In the nineteenth century, European settlers in North America, as well as using flicker feathers to decorate hats, sometimes sold these woodpeckers in food markets; the roasted birds were thought by some to taste like ants, a major food of flickers. During that same period, the flesh of the Red-headed Woodpecker was described as being tough and having a strong smell of ants and other insects, which rendered it barely edible. Interestingly, the Tuaguses, a nomadic tribe inhabiting a region of the upper Yenisey, in central Siberia, believed that the flesh of the Grey-faced Woodpecker possessed special powers. The flesh was roasted, ground up and mixed with fat, and the mixture was then applied to the tribe's hunting arrows. It was claimed that any animal hit by one of these coated arrows always died.

As the chicks become older, the most robust nestlings scramble to the entrance hole, often by stretching across the nest-cavity, testing their strong toes on its opposite walls. This nestling Bennett's Woodpecker has just been fed at the nest entrance by the female parent. The chick can be identified as a male by its black malar stripe. Young females, incidentally, generally show at least some indication of the brown ear-coverts and brown chin and throat which distinguish the adult female from the male. The Bennett's Woodpecker, patchily distributed in southern Africa, where it prefers open miombo (Brachystegia) woodland, is an interesting picid. Outside the breeding season it is rather social, often being seen in small groups, which spend most of the time foraging on the ground in grassy areas. These parties frequently accompany glossy starlings (Lamprotornis) as they search for ants and termites and their nests.

[Campethera bennettii bennettii, Nylsvley, South Africa. Photo: Warwick Tarboton]

Many woodpeckers frequent the tops of trees, at least at times, and so they are close to the sun. Because of this, the bright red and yellow feathers of some species have been thought to be associated with the origin of light, the sun, and with fire. Various native peoples in America, including the Klikitat of Washington, in north-west USA, and nearby tribes in British Columbia, believed that the woodpecker was the master of fire. One of the stories of the Kutenai tribe tells how Coyote, the son-in-law of Sun, in order to assure successful hunting, traversed the savanna while wearing woodpecker feathers tied to his moccasins, lighting fires wherever he ran. In Asia, there is a similar connection between woodpeckers and fire in Malaysia; these birds were said to have given the gift of fire to the Négritos Semang, and the woodpecker thereby became a sacred bird which the Semang people will not harm. This is probably linked to a superstition in Germany, where the burning in a fireplace of wood chips from a Black Woodpecker nest is believed to bring happiness.

Superstition and witchcraft often go hand in hand. The wrynecks' peculiar movements of the head and neck when cornered (see Breeding) have, not surprisingly, earned these picids the name of "snake-bird". This behaviour has also resulted in the Eurasian Wryneck being used in witchcraft in Britain, and probably elsewhere in Europe. In order to effect the return of a faithless lover, a wryneck was captured and tied to a wheel, which was then made to revolve. It is also of interest that, in the Middle Ages, the wryneck often went by the English name of "Inyx", a name which, by the transposition of letters, a common process in the evolution of language, became the scientific name for the genus, *Jynx*. Since the wryneck could also be used in witchcraft to cast a spell on an enemy, this gave rise to the modern word "jinx", meaning a bringer of bad luck. The innocent wryneck came to the fore again in the 1990's, following the reunification of Germany, when a politically opportunistic person was referred to as a *Wendehals*; only few people, however, realized that this name, "neck-turner", was also that of a cryptically coloured woodpecker that performs strange snaking movements with its head and neck.

Supernatural powers have been attributed to woodpeckers in many ways. Since these birds seem to know their way around in forests, which are often thought of as mysterious places, where a man could easily get lost, it is not difficult to understand how they came to be regarded as guides. When the Sabines, or Picentes, of ancient Italy migrated to Picenum, or "Woodpecker Town", their chiefs were led by a woodpecker; the name Picenum was retained as a reminder of the supernatural woodpecker's good deeds. Throughout the Americas, the woodpeckers' behaviour in spending most of their time on the trunks of trees, between the earth and the sky, led to their being regarded as spatial guides. The Klikitat natives, for instance, entrusted the sapsuckers alone to create two parallel upright links to the heavens with arrows. In tropical South America, the Tacana mythology includes the story that, if a woman's husband has become lost, the tapping or drumming by a woodpecker on a clay pot belonging to the woman will help to guide him on his way.

The use of augury was formerly widespread throughout the world, and involved many diverse creatures, including the Picidae. Many different interpretations were put on the augural animal's actions. In Guadeloupe, for example, the drum of a woodpecker could not only signify rain, but also foretell that somebody would die, or that a days's hunting would not be successful. According to the Waiwai Indians of Guyana, the nature of the sound made by a woodpecker foretold the sex of an unborn child, and was linked with the sound of their own drums, which they classified in two groups: the big ones produced low notes and were female, while the small ones with higher notes were male. So, if the bird gave a whistled "swissis" the child would be a boy, but if it rapped out "tororororo" then a girl could be expected.

It is in Borneo, however, that the most renowned examples of augury are to be found. Here, the Iban, or Sea Dayaks, a polytheistic people, practised augury as what was to them a perfectly logical way of life. In Iban belief, the most important god is Singalang Burong, but he seldom reveals himself. Instead, he makes his will known through his sons-in-law, who appear in

Begging for food becomes more intense as the chicks grow. Furthermore, the parents become wary of approaching the youngster, with its increasingly large bill. This male Black Woodpecker, however, has little choice, since this is one of the species which provides food, almost always insects, by regurgitation. In the final days before fledging, the adults enter the hole far less frequently, preferring instead to drop the food from the rim of the entrance, and they no longer remove excrement and other debris from the interior of the hole. The well-developed plumage of this juvenile male suggests that fledging will occur soon. Even once the juveniles are on the wing, however, the parental duties are not over, as feeding by the male continues for up to a month. The sexual differences in this widely distributed Palearctic woodpecker appear on the plumage of the young at about ten days of age, although a small number of individuals, probably females, do not show any red on the head in the juvenile stage.

[Dryocopus martius martius,
Oulanka National Park,
Kuusamo, Finland.
Photo: H. Hautala/FLPA]

The insatiable demands for food by young woodpeckers can lead to conflict and aggression at the nest. What appear to be attacks on the parent, as shown by this young male Pileated Woodpecker, are common. Such behaviour, despite its apparent aggressive nature, is, however, simply an extension of begging behaviour, when the parent has not been so quick to supply food as the nestling had expected. Aggression does occur among siblings as they become older and more cramped in the nest, especially if food deliveries are not quite adequate. Moreover, various studies have found that in the case of the Pileated Woodpecker's Old World relative, the Black Woodpecker (Dryocopus martius), the nestlings not uncommonly die of starvation even when there appears to be plenty of food available. It is unclear whether sibling competition is responsible for this nestling mortality or whether another factor, such as disease or parasites, may be implicated.

[Dryocopus pileatus pileatus,
Shenandoah National Park,
Virginia, USA.
Photo: Rob & Ann Simpson]

Campo Flickers are one of a number of picid species which present food to nestlings by regurgitation. The adults forage for ants and termites during brood-rearing, breaking into terrestrial nests to obtain large quantities of food quickly. They carry the food in the oesophagus and proventriculus, and regurgitate it directly into the chick's mouth, even when the youngster is close to, or past, the fledging stage. Species which feed their young by this method tend to deliver food to the nest at longer intervals compared with other picid species. As well as the flickers, other woodpeckers which feed their chicks by regurgitation include the Dryocopus logcocks and the Picus species.

[Colaptes campestris campestroides, Salado's Depression, Buenos Aires, Argentina. Photos: Yves Bilat]

seven different bird forms. These comprise a kingfisher, two trogons, the Crested Jay (*Platylophus galericulatus*), the White-rumped Shama (*Copsychus malabaricus*) and, importantly, two woodpeckers: the Rufous Piculet, or *ketupong*, and the Maroon Woodpecker, *pangkas*. Significantly, the tiny piculet is the most senior of all seven augural birds, and is regarded as the guardian of man's welfare. This is perhaps less surprising when one considers that it is a common, restless and rather noisy bird around Bornean habitations, where its constant presence is taken as signifying that the piculet takes a keen interest in man's affairs. So important is the Rufous Piculet that its behaviour can determine the actions of an entire longhouse. The Maroon Woodpecker, although not so powerful an omen as the piculet, is still an augur that can have a great influence on the Iban.

Even in the middle part of the twentieth century, these beliefs were so strong that people almost feared that the birds themselves, as opposed to the god which they represented, were capable of causing harm. Whenever a Rufous Piculet or a Maroon Woodpecker was either seen or heard, great significance was attached to the event. If any of the augural birds flies from right to left across a person's path, or is heard on the right, this is a positive and powerful omen of good fortune; the reverse direction or side implies the opposite. Similarly, the bird flying in the same direction as the observer is a sign of good fortune, whereas one flying in the opposite direction is an inauspicious omen. In addition, the alarm calls of the two picids are associated with danger or are a sign of bad fortune. For example, when men are about to fell a forest to make a swidden, the alarm call of the Rufous Piculet indicates that they must abandon all work for the day and return to the longhouse; the highly inauspicious alarm call of the piculet, the senior of all augural birds, is a sure warning that, if felling continues, one of them will suffer serious injury from an axe. Nevertheless, a certain amount of freedom attaches to these omens, and the symbolism depends to a large extent on the interpretation placed on it.

A war party, on hearing the call of the Maroon Woodpecker, will welcome this as it foretells the triumphant shouts associated with the taking of an enemy head.

Although modern life, with its global methods of communication and the changing attitudes of humans, has to a great extent modified and altered the beliefs of many native peoples, there are still numerous surviving examples of how these seven birds ruled the life of the Iban people. With regard to the two picids, the following sample accounts should help to illustrate the importance that was attached to them. One afternoon in April 1950, a western anthropologist, J. D. Freeman, was conversing with a local Iban chief when a Rufous Piculet began to call close to the farmhouse in which they were sitting. The chief, named Kubu, said that he was not sure what the augury, which was heard by everybody in the house, meant, but that something was being told to the people. Later, after the evening meal, a woman of the house and her young son suddenly developed a gastric sickness: Kubu immediately announced that the *ketupong's* augury had been a warning not to eat the food, which must have been responsible for the illness. Four months after that event, in another instance, a woman who had arrived in a village after a boat journey along the river very soon died. Not long thereafter, it became known that, a short way down the river, a Maroon Woodpecker had uttered an alarm call and flown back and forth across the party's path; rather than stopping to observe the prescribed rituals, however, the party had ignored the augury and continued to paddle on to the village. The local augur, on hearing this, castigated the party's leader for having failed to take heed of the warning.

Another intriguing example, this time from the western side of the world, illustrates again how woodpeckers were thought to have special powers. In the latter part of the Middle Ages and later, it was believed that these birds knew about the magical properties of plants and their roots. Although it is not possible, from the tales told, to determine exactly which plants were involved,

The dense forests of the world's highest mountain range host several woodpeckers, the commonest of which is the Himalayan Woodpecker. This hardy species lives among extensive conifer stands and in oak (Quercus) and rhododendron (Rhododendron) mountain forest above 2000 m, at times ascending beyond the tree-line. It can also be found in mixed forest with junipers (Juniperus). For the Himalayan Woodpecker and several other picids, trees are themselves an important source of protein. These arboreal foragers, which only rarely descend to the ground, use anvils in which to break open pine cones for the seeds, an important food in winter.

[Dendrocopos himalayensis albescens, Dachigam National Park, Kashmir.
Photo: Gertrud & Helmut Denzau]

In some parts, in the south, hybrids seem to be more viable, and no assortative mating has been documented, adults showing no clear preference for mates of their own colour type. Extensive data on a northern population of flickers, however, did show assortative mating. Hybrids can easily be scored according to plumage characters. One study demonstrated that individuals of the same colour are more likely to mate than are differently coloured ones. This remains true even when the fact that "Red-shafted Flickers" breed a little later has been taken into account. The major reason for the stability of the hybrid zone and the distinctiveness of the subspecies involved may be purely ecological, with each subspecies best adapted to its regional climate and vegetation.

Among the Picidae, it is not so unusual for hybrids to occur also between species, mainly those which are considered to be members of the same superspecies. They are found among South American piculets, as, for example, between the White-wedged Piculet (*Picumnus albosquamatus*) and subspecies of the White-barred Piculet. In the case of the Campetherini, hybrids are known between the Little Green Woodpecker (*Campethera maculosa*) and the Green-backed Woodpecker, between the Great Spotted and the White-winged Woodpeckers (*Dendrocopos leucopterus*), and between the American Ladder-backed and Nuttall's Woodpeckers. In the Neotropics, the Little Woodpecker (*Veniliornis passerinus*) and the Dot-fronted Woodpecker (*Veniliornis frontalis*) sometimes hybridize, as also do the Chestnut and Pale-crested Woodpeckers, as well as two of the logcocks, namely the Black-bodied (*Dryocopus schulzi*) and the Lineated Woodpeckers (*Dryocopus lineatus*). In Europe, hybrid pairings are occasionally reported also between the largely sympatric Grey-faced and Eurasian Green Woodpeckers.

An interesting example of interbreeding is provided by the Syrian Woodpecker (*Dendrocopos syriacus*) in the Palearctic Region. This species occasionally hybridizes with the Sind Woodpecker (*Dendrocopos assimilis*) at the south-eastern rim of its range, in Iran, and it also hybridizes now and then with the Great Spotted Woodpecker, a species that it meets more frequently since its rather recent range expansion. Dynamic range shifts are a relatively frequent cause of hybridization in the melanerpine woodpeckers, including the sapsuckers. The Golden-fronted Woodpecker (*Melanerpes aurifrons*), for example, has only re-cently moved into Oklahoma, where it occasionally interbreeds with the Red-bellied Woodpecker (*Melanerpes carolinus*); the two seem not to interbreed, however, in Texas, where they meet in a zone that reaches from the Gulf coast northwards to Oklahoma. Red-breasted and Red-naped Sapsuckers interbreed occasionally, although they are distinctly different in coloration. Their hybridization reflects both close genetic relatedness and the secondary contact after the last glaciation.

Gene flow within species is important when it comes to maintaining genetic diversity. It relies on dispersal, and is compromised when the range of a species is very fragmented. This is the case with the Red-cockaded Woodpecker. In this species, movement between colonies is associated with reduced availability of roosting cavities, and seems to be sufficient for the exchange of genes within populations. Overall genetic diversity is, however, low, and gene flow is about adequate to counterbalance genetic drift. All the same, the population as a whole is highly fragmented, and individual populations have already attained notable genetic differentiation.

Morphological Aspects

The size range of woodpeckers is not especially noteworthy when compared with that of other non-passeriform birds, although extant species vary from as little as about 7 g in the case of the tiny piculets up to about 570 g in the largest species, such as the Great Slaty Woodpecker (*Mulleripicus pulverulentus*) and the Ivory-billed Woodpecker. This wide range of sizes permits woodpeckers to live in many different habitat types, and segregation by size may also be an important factor for the co-existence of sympatric species (see Habitat).

The typical picid's morphology features many distinct characteristics, all of which reflect the fundamental habits of these birds of excavating wood, removing bark, and probing deeply into crevices and bore holes, among other things, as well as climbing on vertical surfaces. They include a strong, mostly straight bill, a reinforced skull, a perching foot modified for climbing, and a stiffened tail. The tongue of woodpeckers has undergone many important modifications, rendering it one of the most remarkable anatomical structures to be found among birds.

The Magellanic Woodpecker is just about the largest picid in South America, where it is confined to the Andes of south Chile and adjacent parts of south-west Argentina. In this rather inhospitable climate, it flourishes in the mature forests of southern beech (Nothofagus) and cypress (Cupressus) that grow in the foothills of the Andes Mountains. Washed by heavy rains from clouds that develop over the Pacific Ocean, these forests gather luxuriant coats of mosses and lichens, in which the Magellanic Woodpecker probes for adult beetles and grubs. Despite its large size, it is able to cling skilfully, almost in the manner of a tit (Paridae), to the thinnest of branches. This imposing woodpecker, which can be seen from sea-level up to the timber-line, generally requires big trees, such as this Araucaria, in addition to which it appears to favour areas with an undergrowth of bamboo. It sometimes strays from its preferred habitat into more open woodland, and will also visit disturbed forest, but it seems to be far more at home in relatively quiet tracts of forest.

[Campephilus magellanicus, Conguillo National Park, southern Chile. Photo: Günter Ziesler]

Nest sanitation is especially important for birds which rear their young inside holes. There is, however, considerable variation among, and even within, species as to which sex contributes the more to this task. This female Northern Flicker leaving the nest-hole is carrying a faecal sac mixed with other material from the cavity floor. Like the Golden-fronted (Melanerpes aurifrons) and Grey-faced Woodpeckers (Picus canus), among others, Northern Flickers, especially females, cease removing debris during the last few days before fledging. Other picids, such as the Great Spotted Woodpecker (Dendrocopos major), continue to clean out the cavity until the very end of the nestling period.

[Colaptes auratus, USA.
Photo: J. R. Woodward/ Vireo]

Crop damage by picids remains a problem of varying importance in several parts of the world. In the Neotropics, serious damage to sugar cane and cacao pods has been blamed on such species as the Cream-coloured, Blond-crested, Lineated and Robust Woodpeckers, which are said to perforate the pods and to return later to feed on the insects that have been attracted to them. It is far more likely, however, that the woodpeckers attack pods which are already infested with insects; observations revealed this to be the case when woodpeckers attacked *Cassia* pods in Asia, and the same probably applies in most other instances of such behaviour. In Europe, the Syrian Woodpecker not only attacks ripe apricots and prunes in order to reach the kernels, but also takes the flesh of certain citrus fruits, cherries (*Prunus*) and other fruit crops. This picid is also very fond of almonds and other nuts, and is capable of inflicting appreciable damage in commercial plantations of these. Moreover, in parts of the Middle East, it even sabotages the polyethylene pipes used for irrigation in orchards.

Another type of damage is sometimes caused by White-backed Woodpeckers in Japan, where individuals of the rare subspecies *owstoni*, in their search for wood-boring beetle larvae, not infrequently hammer into the bed logs used for mushroom-growing.

Much has been written over the years concerning the use by woodpeckers of artificial wooden substrates in which to excavate their holes. This behaviour seems to be most prevalent in the New World, particularly in North and Central America, where species as diverse as the Red-headed and Golden-fronted Woodpeckers, the Ladder-backed Woodpecker, the Northern Flicker and the Pileated Woodpecker are among the most frequent users of utility poles. The extent to which, through their actions, they do any real damage to these artificial structures is debatable. There are certainly some instances in which poles have been sufficiently weakened that they break off at the site where they have been hollowed out, this being caused mainly

by strong winds. In regions where poles are used more extensively by woodpeckers, as in parts of the Midwest, replacements made of cement and fibreglass have been erected, and attempts to protect wooden poles have included the use of wire or plastic mesh; in some cases, ropes have been hung from utility poles in an effort to simulate snakes. All of these measures, however, have met with limited success. Among other methods used to prevent woodpecker damage to utility poles in the USA, the most successful is probably the spraying of the wood with non-toxic repellent. Poles are frequently impregnated with creosote, but this generally results in reduced breeding success for any woodpeckers which use them, as the eggs and young die; if the creosote becomes "diluted" over the years, however, nesting success usually improves.

Similar utilization of poles, especially telephone poles, occurs also in the West Indies, where the Hispaniolan, Jamaican and Guadeloupe Woodpeckers excavate at least occasionally in such sites. Woodpeckers dig holes in wooden utility poles in Europe, too, although the habit is less common there. On the other hand, they can cause serious damage in parts of that continent by excavating into the styrofoam material used to insulate houses. The culprit in almost every case is the widespread and common Great Spotted Woodpecker, which hammers along the corners of houses and occasionally under the eaves, and easily drills through the thin outer insulating layer of resin and sand, enabling it to build its hole in the styrofoam itself in a very short time; such holes, incidentally, are apparently used only for roosting. It is probable that this behaviour is prompted by the hollow sound which the picid hears when "testing" the substrate.

An even more amazing event, and one which caught the headlines of the news media, occurred in June 1995, at the Kennedy Space Center in Florida, USA. Not long before the space shuttle *Discovery* was due to be launched, it was discovered that some 200 holes had been made in the rusty-brown foam insulation cov-

After about 25 days of life, the time has come when this young Eurasian Green Woodpecker must leave behind the relative security of the nest-cavity, and venture outside. Inevitably, this is often a clumsy process, the juvenile flapping to a nearby branch or to the ground in order to recover from its exertions. The heavily streaked and spotted plumage that characterizes the juvenile of this species is clearly evident in these photographs. The adults of many members of the family provide much less food for their young during the day or two before the end of the nestling period, this presumably acting to encourage the chicks to leave the cavity. All nestmates leave within an hour or two of one another, and they remain in the vicinity of the nest for a while before moving a short distance to suitable feeding areas. The Eurasian Green Woodpecker is one of several picids in which the fledged brood is often divided between the two adults, each one individually accompanying one or more of the offspring. It is worth noting that nest success is higher among the Picidae than among many comparable avian families, most woodpecker species typically fledging at least one young from 70-100% of nests. Total failure is, therefore, comparatively rare. The majority of losses occur at the egg stage or when the nestlings are small.

[*Picus viridis viridis*, Plaine de La Crau, France. Photos: Guy Bortolato/ Bios]

One factor behind the success of the woodpeckers is that closely related species can exploit different resources. Nowhere is this better illustrated than in the Amazon rainforest, where the two Celeus species depicted, the Cream-coloured Woodpecker and the Ringed Woodpecker, live side-by-side. The Cream-coloured Woodpecker, one of the most brightly plumaged of the family, is found in swampy areas, along the edges of rivers and forest pools. The slightly larger Ringed Woodpecker also lives in the rainforest, but it much prefers tall trees in tall forest, where it is a far more elusive species. The fact that these two close relatives are able to co-exist in the same areas says much about the abundance of food in such habitats, where both species take fruits and seeds, as well as ants. The Cream-coloured Woodpecker, incidentally, is one of many picids which exhibit a wide degree of individual variation, as well as a number of intermediate populations which are difficult to assign to a particular subspecies. The male shown here, with extensive brown colour on the wings, has an appearance much closer to that of the race tectricialis, which intergrades with the nominate race in the area in which the photograph was taken; moreover, the nominate race is so variable that it is hardly practicable to attempt a subspecific identification.

[Above: *Celeus flavus*, Serra dos Carajás, Pará, north-east Brazil. Photo: Luiz Claudio Marigo.

Below: *Celeus torquatus torquatus*, Las Claritas, Bolívar, south-east Venezuela. Photo: Bernard Van Elegem]

A few woodpeckers are equally at home in coastal scrub and mangrove as in inland forest. The Streak-breasted Woodpecker, for example, inhabits broadleaved evergreen forest in the southern parts of Myanmar and adjacent Thailand, but in the south of its small range, which reaches only to the central Thai-Malay Peninsula, it is perhaps more likely to be found in coastal habitats. This female is foraging for ants on a lateral branch above the mud of a mangrove forest. Interestingly, the closely related Laced Woodpecker (Picus vittatus), which is sometimes considered conspecific, also nests and feeds in these same coastal habitats, even where the ranges of the two overlap, in Tenasserim and western Thailand.

[Picus viridanus, Krabi Bay, south Thailand. Photo: Bernard Van Elegem]

different from the insertion points usually found in birds. They sheath the long hyoid bones that provide the necessary stiffness of the total structure. These bones are elongated and thin towards the posterior end and, hence, are flexible. The degree of flexibility of the tongue is modulated by muscle action, so that, when the special tongue muscles contract, the structure becomes stiff. The long bones are wound around the back of the skull; they meet in the frontal region, or, in species with a very long tongue, they enter the bill at the nostril cavity. In some species, the hyoids do not enter the nostrils but are, instead, wound around the right eye. Among the American woodpeckers, this latter condition is incipient in the White-headed Woodpecker and fully developed in the Hairy Woodpecker. It is shown also by the two *Hemicircus* species of southern Asia, one of which, the Heart-spotted Woodpecker, exhibits the development of the condition most spectacularly. Not only do all of these species probe extensively, but they are also strong excavators. The adaptations for the latter activity leave no room for an extension of the hyoid horns and their muscles into the bill, hence this unique solution. In various picid species, the tongue has become shorter as a secondary adaptation. Examples of this are the sapsuckers and the White Woodpecker (*Melanerpes candidus*) of America.

Members of the subfamily Picinae, the true woodpeckers, have the tip of the tongue equipped with a few to many backward-pointing barbs. The number and the particular shape of these are rather variable among species, and reflect their functions. They are arranged in rows of single, loosely spaced barbs, as in, for example, the Neotropical *Piculus* and the Eurasian *Picus*, or in dense to brush-like rows, as in, for instance, *Campephilus*, some *Melanerpes*, *Sphyrapicus* and the Asian Rufous-bellied Woodpecker (*Dendrocopos hyperythrus*). In some cases, the barbs are grouped in clusters of three to five, a condition exhibited by species of *Picumnus*, *Campethera*, *Dendropicos*, *Dendrocopos* and *Veniliornis*, among others. They may occur along the whole tip of the tongue or be concentrated at the extreme tip. Examples of picids with barbs mainly at the very tip of the tongue include the Neotropical Golden-olive Woodpecker (*Piculus rubiginosus*) and, in Europe, the Middle Spotted Woodpecker (*Dendrocopos medius*) when compared with its more widespread congener the Great Spotted Woodpecker. The barbs become thinner and shorter in those species

which carry out much of their foraging on the ground. For these picids, the tongue functions more as an adhesive stick than as a spear, and its tip is also rounded rather than pointed.

In the head of a woodpecker, three particular types of gland can be found. The maxillary gland is usually relatively large, and is characteristic of the family. It is situated in the floor of the orbit and is easily confused with the nasal gland, located nearby. This latter gland is close to the nasal cavity in most picids. In the wrynecks and the piculets it enters the orbital region, which is reminiscent of the condition found in passerines. The largest gland, however, is the mandibular gland, without doubt the most characteristic feature of the picid glandular system. Its size may be reduced in some species, as a secondary specialization in the more habitual excavators. By contrast, species which secure their prey by using the tongue as a glue-stick possess large glands.

A particularly large oil-gland has been found in the Chestnut-coloured Woodpecker of Central America, although why this species should possess a bigger gland than do other picids is not certain. A similarly unexplained phenomenon involves two congeneric picids from the southern parts of Asia, the Heart-spotted and the Grey-and-buff Woodpeckers, on both of which a peculiar resin-like substance is not uncommonly present in the plumage of the back. Rather surprisingly, it has not been possible so far to trace the origin of this substance back to specific glands or, indeed, to any other source, and its provenance remains a mystery. Possibly associated with this is the fact that woodpeckers give off a characteristic strong, resinous odour. It has been suggested that this is connected with their food, although H. Sick maintained that the odour originated from the plumage, perhaps from oils produced by the uropygial gland, or even from the feathers themselves. Certain species, such as the Blond-crested Woodpecker and some populations of the Chestnut Woodpecker, seem to emit a more intense odour, but there seems to be no obvious explanation of why this should be so.

The legs of woodpeckers are short, with strong feet and powerful, curved claws. The tarsus and the toes are covered with well-developed, overlapping scales. The picid foot derives from the yoke arrangement, or the zygodactyl foot, found in many perching birds such as the parrots (Psittacidae), the cuckoos (Cuculidae) and the puffbirds, and in the more closely related barbets. When woodpeckers climb, however, the arrangement

Many picids, apart from those tropical forest species that feed almost exclusively on ants and termites, take advantage of human-provisioned food. This behaviour is most frequent in Europe and North America, bringing a splash of colour and pleasure to garden birdwatchers. As these Black-cheeked Woodpeckers illustrate, however, picids across the world will accept the offerings. Sharing the fleshy fruit on a makeshift birdtable are a Clay-coloured Thrush (Turdus grayi) and a female Scarlet-rumped Tanager (Ramphocelus passerinii).Woodpeckers have learned to hang upside-down if necessary, and to sip sugar water from hummingbird (Trochilidae) feeders.

[Melanerpes pucherani, near Lake Arenal, Costa Rica. Photo: Rolf E. Kunz]

seen in 1999 in the Pearl River Wildlife Management Center, in Louisiana, could not be found in follow-up surveys. As is so often the case, the primary cause of this picid's extinction in the USA is destruction and fragmentation of its forest habitat. Even by the 1940's it had been reduced to a very small number of individuals, and forests have continued to be degraded and destroyed since then. In his superbly evocative writings, J. T. Tanner, who was, until his death in 1991, the leading authority on this species, described a forest wilderness that was "almost primeval", a virgin swamp-forest with many huge trees and an incredible diversity of wildlife. This was the Singer Tract in Louisiana, where Tanner and his guide, J. Kuhn, studied some of the last remaining pairs of Ivory-bills in a habitat which can only be imagined today. Even there, however, where eight species of picid lived, this beautiful woodpecker had disappeared by the mid 1940's.

The fate of the Ivory-billed Woodpecker's slightly smaller-billed Cuban subspecies, *bairdii*, is no better. By the early twentieth century, much of the island's forest cover had gone and the woodpecker was confined to the surviving tracts of forest of Cuban pine (*Pinus cubensis*) in the east. In 1948, a population was discovered in the Cuchillas de Moa Mountains, where six territories of this species were located in 1956; in that year, a total of eight pairs and one juvenile was present in the eastern mountains of Cuba. Unfortunately, political upheaval prevented further study there, and plans for the establishment of reserves were unfulfilled. When research resumed, in 1985, the only possible evidence of the species was the distinctive feeding marks left by the woodpecker, which uses a particular foraging technique in which it scales bark from dead trees. Much of the region's forest had been removed. Further expeditions in April 1986 located one bird at Ojito de Agua and a pair seen repeatedly at Cabezada del Yarey, but by 1991 only a single bird appeared to be left, and in 1992 and 1993, intensive fieldwork in east Cuba failed to locate any Ivory-billed Woodpeckers. It was also discovered that bark could be removed from the pine trees by heavy rain, so that bark-scaled trees could not be interpreted as a sign of the woodpecker's presence.

Yet again, habitat loss appears to be the reason for the disappearance of the Ivory-billed Woodpecker from its Cuban refuge. Almost no old-growth forest remains that is sufficiently extensive and intact to support the species. The single exception is an area of apparently undisturbed pine forest high in the Sierra Maestra, south-west of the species' original range in eastern Cuba. It is, therefore, of great interest that this woodpecker's presence was reported there in 1998, although no confirmatory evidence has since come to light.

The third and last picid having a conservation status of Critical has a far less high profile than the previous two *Campephilus* ivory-bills. This is the Okinawa Woodpecker, which is found only on the island of that name in the Japanese island chain of Nansei-shoto. This picine woodpecker, although occasionally seen in coastal regions, is restricted as a breeding species to the subtropical evergreen forest lying along the mountain ridges in the central mountain chain of Yambaru, in the northern part of the island. Originally more widespread, it has lost much of its habitat and now breeds mainly in the area between the two mountain peaks of Nishime-take and Iyu-take. The breeding population here is extremely small, and in the early 1990's was estimated at a maximum of 70-80 individuals; the total population does not exceed 584 birds, and could even be below 150. As long ago as the 1930's the Okinawa Woodpecker was thought to be close to extinction.

This little-known woodpecker's decline can be attributed primarily to deforestation. It requires forest that is 30 years or more of age, and which contains tall trees with a diameter of at least 20 cm. Such habitat has long since been removed from the lower slopes, and logging has made inroads into the upper parts of the Yambaru. With the pressure on existing suitable habitat unceasing, principally as a result of dam-construction, agricultural development and the building of golf courses, along with the road-building associated with these, the rate of removal of old forest remains significant. Furthermore, the Okinawa Woodpecker's severely restricted range and extremely small population render it vulnerable to disease and to natural disasters such as typhoons.

This picid is present in small protected areas on each of the two mountains at the extremes of its breeding range, as well as in the protected area of Mount Yonaha. In north-eastern Okinawa, it has been found to occur at an estimated density of 12·1 birds per km² in the US Forces Northern Training Area, which offers some hope for its future survival. One is compelled, however, to conclude that, despite the fact that the

Okinawa Woodpecker enjoys legal protection in Japan, and notwithstanding the fact that Yambaru was designated as a national park in 1996, further action is needed if it is to be saved from extinction. Conservation organizations have already purchased some sites where the species is known to be present. In particular, there is an urgent need also for the establishment along the island's central ridge of special protected areas which include all mature forest with an age of 40 years or more, and for the prohibiting of logging in forest that is more than 25 years old. Further conservation measures proposed include the planting of forest "corridors" to connect forest fragments, and the provision of nestboxes in young secondary forest. The institution of a conservation programme, using the Okinawa Woodpecker and the Endangered Okinawa Rail (*Gallirallus okinawae*) as examples by which to inform the public, is a further suggestion deserving of serious consideration.

While thought not to be at quite such high risk as the preceding three species, Fernandina's Flicker is, nevertheless, considered to be seriously threatened and is listed as Endangered. It is found only in Cuba, where its population is extremely small and fragmented. Although the woodpecker seems never to have been very common there, it was formerly widespread on the island. During the course of the twentieth century, however, habitat loss has reduced it to a few localized and small populations in the three provinces of Pinar del Río, in the west, and Matanzas and Camagüey in the central portion of the island. The species may also still survive in several other provinces, and a recent record from a new locality, La Platica in Sierra Maestra, in south-east Cuba, suggests that there could be small, as yet undiscovered populations elsewhere. By far the largest population is at Zapata Swamp, in Matanzas, where there may be 120 pairs, and where, uniquely, loose colonies are occasionally encountered. Over the island as a whole, however, the flicker's numbers have declined, and the maximum total population in the year 2000 has been estimated at no more than 400 pairs, probably only 300 and quite possibly even fewer than that.

Rather open woodland and pasture with palms appears to be this flicker's preferred habitat, but it can also be found in denser woodland. It is closely associated with palm trees, especially the palm *Saval parviflora*, which it utilizes for nesting. Both dead and live palms are accepted, and it has been suggested that these trees are chosen because they are often invaded by fungus, making the wood softer and more suitable for excavation. These trees are used also by the Cuban Amazon (*Amazona leucocephala*), a near-threatened parrot, and the two species often nest in the same individual palm.

Clearance of forest for agricultural purposes, as well as logging, have been at least partly responsible for this woodpecker's decline, and continue to be so, but there are other factors which may be just as important. In the Caribbean, hurricanes can have a major and devastating effect on dead palms, which are quite incapable of withstanding the blast of such mighty winds. In addition, bird-trappers seeking young parrots frequently push over down dead palms in order to collect the nestlings, irrespective of whether or not there is a flicker's nest in the same tree. The result is that the flicker loses not only its brood of young, but also a good nest-site. Competition with other hole-nesting birds, including, especially, the Northern Flicker and two other woodpeckers, adds to the pressure. A further potential problem is nest predation by the West Indian Woodpecker, but the significance of this has not really been assessed.

Although the whole of the Zapata Swamp is a reserve, the available resources for ensuring its effective protection are totally inadequate. In spite of the Cuban government's sterling efforts to secure the country's wildlife, including the creation of many reserves, funding this work has proved to be very difficult. Among the conservation measures proposed with the aim of safeguarding the future for Fernandina's Flicker, that of producing posters and displaying them in villages in areas where the species still exists seems to be the most promising. It should certainly raise awareness of the plight of this rare woodpecker. Additional measures that have been suggested are the implementation of a nestbox scheme in the vicinity of known nesting areas, and a census of all current and former sites where the flicker is known to have bred in order to determine its exact range and status. Detailed study of its feeding and nesting requirements may also help to explain just why the species has declined as it has.

Five of the remaining seven globally threatened picid taxa, all of which are classified as Vulnerable, are found in the New World. In North America, the Red-cockaded Woodpecker is particularly well known as it has been intensively studied in the last

Woodpeckers have a strong relationship with people, adapting to take advantage of gardens, houses and farming. If humans have assisted populations of some species, they are also largely responsible, through forest destruction, for the fact that eleven picid species are globally threatened, and a further dozen listed as Near-threatened. Two are almost certainly extinct, and there is a high risk of several others going the same way in the next hundred years. The Red-necked Woodpecker, shown here, is not yet at risk but, since thousands of hectares of its Amazon rainforest home are cleared every year, it could well become so.

[*Campephilus rubricollis olallae*, Aguiarnópolis, Tocantins, Brazil. Photo: Robson Silva e Silva]

An arid desert is not, at first sight, the most obvious habitat for a woodpecker, but a small number of picids have adapted to living in areas that many bird species would find too inhospitable. The diminutive Ladder-backed Woodpecker of the south-west United States is one such species, being a typical inhabitant of very arid country and deserts. Its southern races, which live in northern Central America south to Nicaragua, are more likely to be found in dry pine-oak (Pinus-Quercus) woodland, but do occur locally in clearings in humid forest; more surprisingly, this rather shy species also lives in mangroves in El Salvador and Honduras. The dominant plants in the desert habitat are cacti, which provide a nest-site for Ladder-backed Woodpeckers, as well as two sources of food: the fruit of the cactus, and a variety of small insects and their larvae. These woodpeckers also forage among yuccas (Yucca), as well as in low scrub and occasionally on the ground.

[Picoides scalaris cactophilus, Rio Grande Valley, Texas, USA. Photo: Tom Vezo]

to deal better with well-armed insects such as ants, and it is interesting to note that the Picidae share this dermal characteristic with the honeyguides, which are regularly subjected to the risk of bites and stings by Hymenoptera.

Only a few picids have body parts that are bare of feathers. Extensive areas of bare orbital skin occur in *Sasia* piculets and in some true woodpeckers, the latter being mainly melanerpines. They consist primarily of bare eyerings, which can be orange-yellowish to blackish, and which are duller and different in colour on juveniles. Often accentuated by striking plumage coloration, this bright orbital-skin colour adds to the striking facial patterns found among many melanerpine woodpeckers. The orbital rings of other species are narrow and exhibit a wide range of colours, from red in the case of some piculets to greenish and bluish in picine woodpeckers. Iris colour varies among species. In addition, it differs between juveniles and adults, changing for example from grey to whitish in some species, such as some melanerpines, and from brown to crimson in Great Spotted Woodpeckers.

The typical body feathers of woodpeckers in essence do not differ from those of other birds. A unique feature of the woodpeckers, however, is the curved or scimitar shape of the basal cells of the barbules of the contour feathers. The afterfeathers are variable in length, with a very short aftershaft. Picids are generally naked upon hatching and, moreover, they do not develop natal downs; instead, they grow a plumage of contour feathers resembling the ones found on the adults. As with other birds, the feathers are arranged in well-defined tracts of growth, the whole arrangement being referred to as pterylosis. A featherless area along the crest of the head and circular bare areas on the temples are features characteristic of woodpeckers.

Within the Picidae, the coloration of the plumage varies moderately among species and genera. Black and brown, white, red and green are the dominant colours. In most cases, the more conspicuous colours are seen on the head and neck, where sexual badges and specific juvenile colour patterns are concentrated.

Plumage colours may be adaptations to habitat characteristics, governed by intraspecific communication, or the result of social mimicry. They may be conservative in nature and be best explained in terms of a phylogenetic origin, or they may signal that the species in question is unpalatable to potential predators.

Tests of the latter hypothesis, using Great Spotted Woodpeckers, failed to corroborate it. Adaptation to habitat characteristics, whereby the bird achieves camouflage through the matching of its plumage with the background, is probably widespread, although corresponding quantitative data are lacking. The most convincing example of a cryptic pattern is certainly that of the two wrynecks. Dull and brown colours are found in species that occur deep in the shade of the forest understorey, as typified by the Bay Woodpecker in the Malay Peninsula and the Greater Sundas, and they may also be prevalent among picids that spend much time on brown-coloured bark or similarly brown substrates such as ant nests, as do various species of *Celeus*. Bright colours and stark contrasts are least conspicuous in the upper forest strata, and in open woodland. The various black-and-white patterns found for instance in the *Dendrocopos* and *Picoides* pied woodpeckers, and which are also rather common among the melanerpines, may serve as appropriate examples. Woodpeckers which frequently descend to the ground, on the other hand, are generally less brightly coloured, having the head not strongly marked, and the plumage generally dominated by brown, grey or greenish colours. In many cases, these largely terrestrial picids are barred, and have a pale, white or bright yellowish, rump that is conspicuous when the bird takes off. These birds, when seen from above, are perfectly camouflaged against their background, as demonstrated supremely by a Eurasian Green Woodpecker foraging on a grassy meadow.

Several instances exist of species of different genera showing parallel variation wherever they occur sympatrically. This is best illustrated by the case of the *Chrysocolaptes* and *Dinopium* flamebacks. Both genera contain red-backed and golden-tailed forms, and sympatric subspecies of these two different genera have the same colour of the back. All subspecies of the Black-rumped Flameback (*Dinopium benghalense*) and the Common Flameback that are sympatric with the more widespread of the two *Chrysocolaptes*, the Greater Flameback, possess the red rump of the latter. The black-rumped subspecies of the former are not sympatric with red-rumped Greater Flamebacks. The large *Dryocopus* and *Campephilus* woodpeckers, which are structurally well separated from each other and yet often strikingly similar in plumage pattern, are perhaps another example of social mimicry. There have been two different hypotheses put forward

One of only three woodpeckers that can truly be described as terrestrial, the Andean Flicker is common in the grasslands of the Andean puna, *where it thrives at altitudes of up to 5000 m. These wary birds also venture into the humid shrubland of the* páramo, *feeding in broken, rolling country. The long bill, constituting 15% of the total length, is used to obtain larvae from deep beneath the soil surface. Andean Flickers even nest on the ground, where they dig a metre-long tunnel in an earth bank, although natural holes in rocky cliffs are also utilized. They often excavate roost-holes in the walls of abandoned native houses.*

[*Colaptes rupicola rupicola*, Lauca National Park, north Chile. Photo: Andres Hinojosa Morya]

very few records are from just three sites, but it appears to be not uncommon locally. It lives in semi-deciduous forest and adjacent tall *caatinga* on hillsides, at up to 1000 m, and potentially suitable habitat has been greatly reduced through agricultural expansion, grazing and burning. In some areas, removal of forest has been virtually complete, while the remaining habitat is under threat from the construction of holiday homes. Both piculets occur also in degraded scrub or edge, the Tawny Piculet regularly so. The latter is present in five protected areas, at one of which, the Pedra Talhada Biological Reserve in Alagoas, reforestation with indigenous trees is an encouraging step that has been supported by local people, and guard patrols ensure that illegal actions do not occur. The Chapada do Araripe in south Ceará is apparently another important site for this species. Although the Ochraceous Piculet occasionally forages in degraded edge habitat with exotic bamboo and abandoned orchards, this is probably unusual. One of this piculet's known localities, in the Serra do Baturité, was granted protection in 1991, but with possibly limited success in safeguarding the species' remaining habitat there, although some local hotels in the region have had more success in this respect. For the effective conservation of both piculets, further survey work aimed at assessing their distribution, status and ecology is required, along with the proper protection of all appropriate sites.

Only two globally threatened picids are found in the Old World. The Arabian Woodpecker, with a small and probably declining population of fewer than 10,000 individuals, is at best rather uncommon and in some parts of its range is decidedly rare, with densities varying from 0·1 to 1·0 adults per square kilometre. Its woodland habitat on the western edge of the Arabian Peninsula has become highly fragmented following centuries of human colonization and its associated activities. Clearance for agriculture and building, as well as cutting for firewood, is a continuing process, and the result is often the removal of the large trees which this woodpecker prefers for its nest-sites. This is sometimes compounded by the effects of heavy grazing, which can prevent the regeneration of trees. Although many wooded areas in this part of the world have long been protected from over-exploitation, primarily as a source of fodder in times of drought, the traditional management of them has been largely abandoned in more recent decades as it has become easier to obtain supplies of animal feed. The Arabian Woodpecker occurs in at least two officially protected areas. The designation of additional such sites, the encouragement of non-intensive, traditional methods of woodland management, and the raising of the profile of this Vulnerable species in its Arabian homelands would all help to secure its future survival.

The final one of the eleven globally threatened woodpecker taxa is the distinctive Sulu Islands subspecies *ramsayi* of the Philippine Woodpecker. With a very small range, currently estimated at only 1760 km² and decreasing, this picid gives genuine cause for concern; it is currently listed as Vulnerable. Its range originally covered eight islands in the Sulu Archipelago, between the Philippine island of Mindanao and north-east Borneo, but it appears now to be confined to perhaps just one, Tawitawi, and even there its continued presence has been confirmed at only three localities. From having been widespread and abundant in the first half of the twentieth century, this small woodpecker has become scarce, with a severely restricted range. It inhabits forest edge and clearings, mangroves and cultivations, but is sometimes found also in primary forest; its true habitat preferences are, however, unclear. The cause of this woodpecker's rapid decline is the familiar one of habitat destruction, which in this case has been extremely extensive and, on some islands, more or less complete. Even in its remaining stronghold of Tawitawi, the forest that is left is highly degraded and fragmented, and there are plans to replace the final surviving patches with commercial plantations of oil palms (*Elaeis guineensis*). With uncontrolled logging of the little remaining forest in the mountains almost certain to lead to expanding human settlement, and the attendant conversion to agriculture of any forest still left, the prospects for *ramsayi* do not appear at all good. Despite initiatives to raise awareness of the importance of conserving wildlife and biodiversity on Tawitawi, no formally protected areas exist anywhere in the Sulu chain. Moreover, military activity and other human problems in the region conspire to make conservation efforts a very difficult and dangerous operation. Organized campaigns and surveys are urgently needed if this picid, which would perhaps be better classified as Endangered, is to survive the constant and increasing pressure placed upon it. Even though it appears to tolerate degraded habitats, there is no doubt that its total numbers have continued to fall at a rapid rate. The fact that some recent authors have regarded *ramsayi* as a distinct species, under the name of "Sulu Woodpecker", could aid conservationists in their attempts to gain protected status for any sites that support populations of this distinctive brown-backed picid.

In addition to the eleven globally threatened taxa discussed above, there are twelve near-threatened species which should not be ignored. Seven of these are found in the Neotropics, including the Caribbean. The Rusty-necked Piculet (*Picumnus fuscus*) is confined to *várzea* forest straddling the border between north-east Bolivia and Brazil, while the Mottled Piculet is found mostly in lowland evergreen and mixed forest in south-east Brazil and adjacent parts of Uruguay and Argentina. The former may be not uncommon, but increasing human settlement along the largely uninhabited banks of the Guaporé river could become a threat. The Mottled Piculet's habitat has for years been subject to clearance for agricultural and other purposes, and is currently suffering even more from the effects of urbanization; in Argentina, the few areas of forest known to harbour this species would be flooded if permission is granted to build a proposed dam on the Río Uruguay.

Among the Picinae, the poorly known Choco Woodpecker (*Veniliornis chocoensis*) of west Colombia and north-west Ecuador has already lost more than a third of its habitat of lowland evergreen forest, and the rate of deforestation is increasing alarmingly; in the absence of controls on forest clearance and human activities, the conservation status of this picid could well become Vulnerable. Much the same applies to the Guayaquil Woodpecker (*Campephilus gayaquilensis*) living in the same general region, but extending southwards to north-west Peru, where it requires dry deciduous and humid forests in the lowlands and up

Only 22% or less of the earth's original forest remains intact. Of the 902 threatened bird species which depend on forest habitats, 93% occur entirely in the tropics, and 82% in moist forest. This is thus an important habitat for a range of species, including the little-known Yellow-browed Woodpecker, an apparently shy species of east-central South America. This attractive woodpecker inhabits humid forest, much of which has already been cleared by bulldozers or destroyed by uncontrolled fires, in both cases with the aim of agricultural expansion. This species is commoner in south-east Brazil, where montane forest has suffered less, but this situation could easily change. Hence, it is accorded Near-threatened status.

[*Piculus aurulentus*, Ponta Grossa, Paraná, Brazil. Photo: Haroldo Palo Jr]

The Knysna Woodpecker is a restricted-range species, present in the South African Forests Endemic Bird Area. It occurs only along a narrow zone of the south-facing coast and, although locally common, it is generally rather sparsely distributed. By the end of the nineteenth century, building development and sugar-cane farming had already reduced the total area of its bush habitat, and hence its range, and the losses have continued since then. The global population of this unobtrusive woodpecker is estimated at no more than 1500-5000 individuals, all of these now contained in an area of some 50,000 km². It appears that perhaps more than half of these nest in nature reserves, a land-use proving to be increasingly important to the world's rarest birds. The Knysna Woodpecker is considered a Near-threatened species. So long as sufficient of its forest habitat can be preserved and effectively protected, it should be possible for this species to survive.

[Campethera notata, Eastern Cape, South Africa. Photo: Warwick Tarboton]

Woodpeckers have a well-organized daily routine. Unless there are chicks in the nest which need to be fed, the level of activity is reduced in the middle of the day. At this time the birds generally rest, as this female Chilean Flicker appears to be doing in the dry scrub of southern South America. Some individuals may doze, fluffing up the plumage and creating a more huddled appearance. A resting woodpecker may intermittently stretch its gape, commonly referred to as "yawning", or remove unwanted items from its bill by vigorously shaking its head. The woodpecker usually remains in the open during the daytime, but roost-holes are sometimes used during this midday rest.

[Colaptes pitius, Puerto Natales, Chile. Photo: Isabel Martínez & Andy Elliot]

also do females of the far more widespread Old World Lesser Spotted Woodpecker. Otherwise, males of the pied species, with the exception of the Downy and Red-cockaded Woodpeckers, are slightly heavier than females, and also have a longer bill but, often, a proportionally shorter tail. Sexual size differences are weakly developed in the colaptine woodpeckers. In the Campephilini and the Picini tribes, the general pattern is that males are slightly heavier, longer-billed and proportionally short-tailed when compared with females. Of course, some variation exists among species in the extent of this dimorphism.

Of particular interest is the way in which sexual morphological differences relate to ecological differences between the sexes. This is discussed in more detail below (see Habitat).

The coloration of young woodpeckers is usually distinct from that of the adults, and this has given rise to many speculative theories. These centre mainly on the question of whether the great diversity of colour patterns found on nestling and juvenile woodpeckers comprises "primitive" or "advanced" character states. A functional explanation would seem possible, but corresponding experimental studies have not been carried out. There are several species the juveniles of which show more red on the head than do the adults. This condition is found in the well-studied Great Spotted Woodpecker and its allies, among them the Syrian Woodpecker, the immature of which in addition possesses a more or less conspicuous red breastband which the adults lack. Juveniles of both sexes of these species have the forecrown red, whereas the red sexual badge of adult males is located at the nape. A similar age-dependent condition is presented by the Maroon Woodpecker of southern Myanmar to Sumatra and Borneo. Rather intriguingly, the reverse pattern is found in the Afrotropical *Campethera* picids, the juvenile males of which have the badge only on the hindcrown or nape, while the adult males have the entire crown red or yellow. There are some other cases in which the position of the juvenile marking differs from that of the adult: the immature Red-cockaded Woodpecker, for instance, has a red patch in the centre of the crown. The juvenile coloration of some species, such as many Colaptini and some Melanerpini, Picini and *Dryocopus*, more or less matches that of the adult. In the Black Woodpecker, for example, the sexual differences appear when the nestling is ten days old, although some individuals, probably females, do not show any red at this stage.

In fact, the extent of the red on juveniles of many species, as typified by the Great Spotted Woodpecker, varies within and among nests, and what seem to be sexual differences are already visible in these early stages. Unfortunately, however, no study based on large sample sizes has yet shown whether these apparent sexual differences agree with the actual sex of all the individuals involved.

The juvenile plumage of the wrynecks does not exhibit any conspicuous marks that could serve as signals. The young of these two Old World species differ, however, in having a barred underside, a pattern that is replaced by arrowhead marks in the adult plumage.

The embryonic development of woodpeckers is shorter than that of most other birds of comparable size, while the juvenile development is slower. Wrynecks and woodpeckers are naked on hatching. The pads or flaps on the base of the lower jaw extend over the edge of the bill, and are almost completely reduced upon fledging. They are certainly organs that help in the transfer of food from the parents to the nestlings in the darkness of the hole (see Breeding). The outer edge of the "heel" of the newly hatched wryneck or woodpecker bears wart-like swellings that are shed in the early phase of the nestling's development. Feathers can be seen to develop under the skin on about the sixth day, and they break through the skin three days later.

When discussing the development of the larger flight-feathers, it is necessary to consider this in connection with the peculiar moult of the Picidae. The extent of the juvenile moult varies among species. Piculets of the genus *Picumnus* shed only the feathers of the crown after they have left the nest. *Sasia* species, on the other hand, moult the feathers of the underside, too, upon leaving the nest. All piculets, however, renew their plumage in a full first moult after they have bred for the first time. Conversely, young wrynecks and true woodpeckers replace the primaries, the tail feathers and the rest of the plumage, but do not renew the secondaries and primary coverts until later. The outer primary of juveniles is longer and wider than that of adults; in addition, the tail is shorter and is different in shape, because the feathers adjacent to the central pair remain shorter. Juveniles commence their moult with the primaries. The innermost, first primary is replaced first, and the moult then proceeds outwards; only when the sixth or seventh primary has been shed does the moult of the contour feathers begin. This moult is completed before the new outer primary has developed fully. In some species, the juvenile begins the moult when still in the nest, and some time before leaving it, which means that the first primaries are grown and then dropped without having ever been used. In these cases, therefore, the two innermost primaries remain small and thin. This pattern is developed to the greatest extreme in the Eurasian Three-toed Woodpecker, the chicks of which replace the five to seven innermost primaries before they leave the nest-hole. This is probably adaptive, since northern and montane species living in cool-temperate areas have to complete the moult before the end of the short summer season, so that they are then able to disperse or migrate. Tropical woodpeckers, in contrast to those of more temperate areas, have the innermost primary only somewhat reduced.

Tropical species lead a more sedentary life than do temperate ones, and their moult can therefore be spread over a long period. The variation in juvenile moult patterns within the genus *Picus* may serve as an instructive example. The tropical Laced Woodpecker (*Picus vittatus*) in South-east Asia has only the innermost primary reduced, whereas, in the temperate Eurasian Green Woodpecker and, even more so, in northern subspecies of the Grey-faced Woodpecker, the two innermost feathers are greatly reduced and measure only one-third or less of the corresponding adult feathers. Similar variation occurs among the pied woodpeckers. As already mentioned, the strongest reduction is found in the Eurasian Three-toed Woodpecker. Compared with that species, the juvenile innermost primaries are less reduced in the Great Spotted Woodpecker, and they are comparatively even less so in the closely related, generally more southern Syrian and Fulvous-breasted Woodpeckers. Melanerpine woodpeckers, incidentally, do not begin to shed their juvenile primaries until after they have left the nest.

Adult moult is tied in with the breeding cycle and occurs after the nesting season. Neither the wrynecks nor the true woodpeckers moult the eleven secondaries during the first moult. For those species for which data are available, there are two moult centres in the secondaries, located respectively at the first and the eighth secondary. In the genus *Colaptes*, for example, after three or four feathers have been moulted from the eighth secondary outwards on either side, moult starts at the first secondary and progresses inwards. Some deviations from the normal pattern of wing moult do, however, occur. Migratory Red-headed Woodpeckers in North America arrest the wing moult immediately after it has begun, and continue it once they arrive in the wintering areas. The related Lewis's Woodpecker completes the moult of its wings and tail early, but it does not complete the body moult until late autumn or early winter. In similar fashion, the sapsuckers terminate their juvenile moult very late in the season, such that they do not acquire adult plumage until as late as February. Of particular interest is the wing moult of the Andean Flicker, which is very variable and protracted, and therefore does not interfere greatly with its capacity for flight. This strategy is presumably crucial when one considers this open-country species' habitat utilization and vertical migration. Migratory populations of species which are partial migrants may also adapt the moult strategy to fit their behaviour. For example, large numbers of Great Spotted Woodpeckers, primarily juveniles, periodically leave the northern parts of Europe after the breeding season. Studies in Norway have shown that these migrating individuals frequently show a reduced intensity of wing and tail moult compared with non-migrants; in addition, the primary moult is sometimes arrested, just as happens with Red-headed Woodpeckers in America.

The specialized function of the picid tail requires some adaptive changes in the moult sequence, too. Species with a stiff tail that is heavily used in arboreal climbing replace the central pair of rectrices last of all. The moult begins at the second-innermost feathers and continues outwards, although some species of *Celeus* and *Dendropicos* may start the tail moult at the third-innermost pair of feathers. In analogy with the moult of the inner primaries, these feathers initially remain short on juveniles, causing the juvenile tail to have a graduated shape, as can be seen on, for example, young Black Woodpeckers and Eurasian Three-toed Woodpeckers. The tiny outermost rectrix may be shed before

the fourth. In the wrynecks and at least some individuals of the Cardinal Woodpecker, the tail is moulted in a reversed sequence, beginning with the outer feathers, and this is also the case with some picine species. From what is known of the Picumninae, the tail moult of these tiny woodpeckers does not appear to follow any regular pattern.

Habitat

The various adaptations of woodpeckers, manifest in their morphology, locomotion, and foraging and nesting habits, have developed over the course of the evolution of these birds towards a life in trees. The forests and woodlands of the world, with the exception of those of Australasia, are therefore the prime home of the family. A few picids have evolved partly ground-living habits, but they still nest in trees and live in wooded habitats. Woodpeckers which frequently feed on the ground are found among the African Campetherini, the flickers and the Picini. Even fewer species are completely terrestrial, and only three could really be so described. These are the aptly named Ground Woodpecker of South Africa, the Andean Flicker living in the mountains of that name, and the Campo Flicker of the *pampas* and savannas of South America. The vast majority of woodpeckers are, however, tied to wooded habitats, these ranging from dense tropical and boreal forests to lighter woodlands and to sparsely timbered semi-deserts. Trees offer food, protection, signalling posts and nesting sites. Numerous studies have shown that, for many species, a minimal amount of dead wood is required for a habitat to be suitable.

Tropical rainforest harbours the greatest numbers of woodpeckers. In this respect, the forests of South-east Asia and South America are the most diverse and, in both regions, as many as 13 species can be found living sympatrically within an area of about 100 ha or less. This may seem surprising when one considers the fact that woodpeckers are already highly specialized in ways that are to a greater or lesser degree similar for all species, so that it may be difficult for them to partition the habitat by developing further specializations.

As this Northern Flicker illustrates, woodpeckers use the bill to preen their body feathers and to clean the feet. A more difficult manoeuvre involves stretching a leg and foot to tend to the head, neck and bill, as this requires that the bird temporarily releases its grip on the vertical surface. Woodpeckers also maintain their plumage in prime condition by shaking the body and wings, by rubbing the face and other areas on tree bark, and by using the bill to apply preen oil to their feathers. This fatty substance, produced by the uropygial gland, is worked into the plumage with the bill, which the woodpecker then wipes clean on twigs or branches.

[*Colaptes auratus auratus*, Illinois, USA. Photo: R. & S. Day/VIREO]

seems not to be under immediate threat. On the contrary, it has extended its range westwards since the 1980's and has colonized many parts of the continent; the fact that its expansion has not reached Britain may be due simply to the absence there of the woodpecker's staple food of *Camponotus* ants. This species is important for the wellbeing of many other forms of wildlife (see Breeding), as it provides nest-sites for, among others, Eurasian Jackdaws (*Corvus monedula*) and Stock Doves (*Columba oenas*), several bat species, and dormice. Its future in Europe can be regarded as secure, provided that mature forest with sufficient nest trees remains available.

Still in Europe, a species of great concern is the Middle Spotted Woodpecker, since it has suffered from forest-dieback insofar as this has also affected oaks. Old oak forests have become a rare natural habitat for several reasons, and preserving them is the main management measure that can be taken, while the protection of species-rich riverine forest is also important. Locally, this species is threatened because of the loss of old orchards. One of Europe's largest picids, the often overlooked White-backed Woodpecker, depends on large montane forests that are little influenced by forestry; in eastern Europe, however, this is a lowland species, and it is mainly these populations that are threatened by severe habitat loss. At the eastern extreme of this woodpecker's world range, the subspecies *owstoni*, confined to the island of Amami in south Japan, inhabits montane evergreen forest, where its small population is considered to be at risk. Another pied species, the Lesser Spotted Woodpecker, has suffered greatly from the loss of riverine forest in many parts of central Europe, although it has, in contrast, increased in the Netherlands and expanded its range in Denmark. Its populations are difficult to monitor, but this species does not seem to be likely to become seriously endangered in the near future.

Competition from other cavity-nesting birds, which take over woodpecker nest-sites, has already been referred to earlier in this section. This pressure can sometimes be heavy enough to place the members of the Picidae at a disadvantage. In those areas from where there are sufficient data, the most serious hole competitor is almost certainly the Common Starling, which has been introduced in many regions, including North America, where it can sometimes usurp a significant proportion of the new cavities made by local woodpeckers (see Breeding). In such situations, and in others where the number of sites suitable for excavation is limited, the provision of artificial snags consisting of hard cylinders filled with styrofoam or polystyrene cylinders

Knowledge of the ecology of threatened picids varies considerably. The best-studied of all is North America's Red-cockaded Woodpecker, once found across southeastern USA but now scattered in small and diminishing populations. It requires mature open pine (Pinus) forest with a particular structure, produced by regular lightning-induced fires. This site-faithful social picid has not adapted well to the era of commercial forestry, and its conservation status is now Vulnerable. Modern harvesting leaves few of the old, tall trees that the birds need, and forestry companies appear unwilling to implement recovery plans.

[Picoides borealis, Talladega National Forest, Alabama, USA. Photo: Stephen G. Maka/ DRK]

range and the requirement for more or less closed forest with a very specific tree-species composition and general ecology. Yet even these species may be tolerant of human activities, so long as they do not change the quality of the habitat. Red-cockaded Woodpeckers, for instance, become tolerant of loud noise, and groups are known to survive on golf courses, on interstate rights-of-way, and in suburbs.

In Europe, woodpeckers are affected by human activities to varying degrees. None of the ten species is threatened, but some of them have suffered losses. The Eurasian Wryneck is a species which originally profited from human activities, as open woodland and orchards are very suitable habitats for it. Nowadays, however, these habitats are continually being destroyed, mainly because of the increasingly intensive and industrial methods of modern agriculture and forestry, which leave no room for old orchards and mixed hardwood forest. Lack of suitable nest-sites is another cause for concern, and the still heavy use of insecticides takes its toll, too. Other reasons for the severe decline of the species in central Europe may be climatic changes, or may lie in the African wintering grounds. Much less clear-cut is the status in Europe of the globally widespread Grey-faced Woodpecker; it has declined in many parts in its European range, while in others it has apparently increased. The precise habitat requirements of this species, which occupies deciduous forest, are still not fully understood, but natural, large and mature deciduous forest at middle elevations seems to hold the main source populations. As the two preceding species, the Eurasian Green Woodpecker requires meadows with plenty of ants, a habitat that is threatened by eutrophication, the use of pesticides, and a regime of either too much or too little cutting; the species has declined in many areas and is potentially at risk, despite its apparent abundance in some parts of the continent. The Black Woodpecker, despite its large size,

Adequate monitoring is crucial if limited resources are to be directed to the most threatened species. The little-studied Helmeted Woodpecker, classified as Vulnerable chiefly because its primary-forest habitat has been extensively cleared and fragmented, may not be so rare as was previously feared. It is a quiet and unobtrusive species, difficult to locate, but individuals and pairs have recently been found in secondary habitats and in degraded forest, as well as in regions from which the species had not been reported for up to 50 years.

[Dryocopus galeatus, Puerto Península, Misiones, Argentina. Photo: Juan Mazar Barnett]

The Fernandina's Flicker, while never abundant in Cuba, is now restricted to a handful of areas on the island, with a total population of fewer than 400 pairs. It is not known precisely what has caused the rapid decline, but, as with most woodpeckers, logging and the clearance of natural forests for agriculture have taken their toll. The birds favour palm trees, either in open country or in primary forest, perhaps because they are often invaded by fungus, making the wood softer and more suitable for excavation. With numbers so low and populations so widely scattered, the fortunes of every breeding pair can influence the trend in status. Hurricanes, such as those that hit Cuba in 1996 and 2001, can devastate localized populations, and are capable of extirpating several of them. It will be some time before the effects of the latest hurricane become apparent. Moreover, since these flickers often nest in the same palms as Cuban Amazons (Amazona leucocephala), they not infrequently lose their broods to trappers, who topple palm trees in order to collect the young parrots; the flicker's nest is destroyed in the process, and the breeding site is lost forever. Whichever factors have reduced this picid's status from that of a widespread species to its current one of Endangered, the focus of conservation effort is now on Zapata Swamp, a nature reserve which holds almost a third of the remaining population. Even here, however, despite efforts to provide protection, it is proving difficult to police the area effectively.

[Colaptes fernandinae, Zapata Swamp, Cuba. Photo: Doug Wechsler/ BBC]

Many birdwatchers dream of finding an Ivory-billed Woodpecker in the dense bottomland woods of Louisiana, or in the montane pinewoods of Cuba. It is not just its huge size or its sad history that make this picid so famous, for this is a species that had its own public-relations champion. The vivid narrative and photographs of James T. Tanner, who studied some of the last breeding pairs in the USA, evoke wonder of both the bird and its wild forest habitat: "A dramatic reason for the variety in the shape of the forest was age, and its follower, death. Big trees gradually lost their vigor until damage suffered from insects and disease outweighed the yearly growth; then they gradually died, from the top down, until only a rotten trunk stood alone. In so dying, they supplied food for woodpeckers, bare branches for flycatchers to perch upon, and finally let the sun thru to the ground to nurture the bushes, vines and new saplings." Its need for large dead trees hosting wood-boring beetle larvae was the Ivory-bill's undoing; logging and forest clearance ensured that, within a decade, the birds had gone from the Singer Tract of Louisiana, where these photos of birds engaged in breeding were taken during the 1930's. The species survived longer in Cuba, where it was last seen in 1991. How sad that such an enigmatic bird should be lost from the world; and how much sadder that, without urgent action, so many other forest species could easily follow it. The official conservation status of the Ivory-billed Woodpecker is Critical; so, perhaps it is not yet extinct. Following an unconfirmed 1999 report of a pair in Pearl River Wildlife Management Center, in Louisiana, a major expedition in early 2002 may tell us whether this guarded optimism is justified.

[Campephilus principalis principalis, Singer Tract, near Tallulah, Louisiana. Photos (digitally coloured for HBW): James T. Tanner]

The world's rarest extant picid, the Critically Endangered Okinawa Woodpecker, inhabits the evergreen forest of the Yambaru Mountains, on the tiny Japanese island of Okinawa. As few as 150 individuals remain, in an area of just 20 km × 30 km. Yet again, deforestation and the developments that follow are the cause of this species' demise. As the lower tree-line advances uphill, ahead of logging, construction, agriculture and the building of golf courses, this reddish-brown picid's numbers have been reduced to a point where disease or typhoons could strike the final blow. Is this a bird which, living in one of the world's richest countries, could yet be saved?

[Sapheopipo noguchii, Okinawa, Japan. Photo: Masakazu Kudaka]

may represent an important measure in managing woodpecker populations. Although these artificial sites have not always produced the hoped-for results, success has often been achieved; further research and refinements should help to make them even more attractive to woodpeckers as nesting sites.

Because many of the Picidae consume large quantities of ants (see Food and Feeding), there is a potential risk of their being subject to secondary poisoning as a result of the spraying with insecticides of important commercial forests. This possibility has not yet been investigated in any detail, but needs to be borne in mind. Correspondingly, woodpeckers which forage in orchards are perhaps vulnerable to the effects of herbicides and pesticides.

Other possible hazards, also alluded to above, include storms, which can destroy large areas of woodland habitat, and fires. In the late 1990's, for example, a major fire which swept through the forest and scrub of the Andean foothills in central Chile effectively destroyed over 6000 ha of the habitat, which was already suffering the effects of a prolonged drought. This region, which forms part of the Central Chile Endemic Bird Area, is at the northern edge of the range of the Magellanic Woodpecker, an uncommon species which is becoming increasingly scarce.

On the whole, woodpeckers are not persecuted by man. On the eastern seaboard of the USA large numbers of migrating Northern Flickers were once killed by gunners in New Jersey and at Cape May, but this practice has, fortunately, now ceased. Nevertheless, the picids can be a nuisance in some areas, where they are therefore considered pests (see Relationship with Man). In parts of the USA, for example, commercial crops are sometimes attacked by some of the frugivorous and nucivorous melanerpines, and both Red-headed and Lewis's Woodpeckers may be shot as a result of such depredations. In early colonial America, the former of those two was considered a major agricultural pest in orchards and cornfields; a bounty of twopence was paid for each head of that species, and one report tells of over 100 shot from a single cherry tree in one day. Nowadays, this kind of persecution occurs on a far lower scale than was the case in the past, and it seems unlikely to have an adverse effect on the species' total population. Similarly, the damage inflicted by Syrian Woodpeckers on commercial orchards and polyethylene irrigation pipes in parts of the Middle East resulted in large numbers of this woodpecker being shot, but it

had already expanded its range northwards into south-east and central Europe and appears to be thriving in that part of the world. While individual woodpeckers which irritate people by drumming and excavating on houses and other buildings, or which damage utility poles, are still shot on occasion, such actions are generally very localized and do not normally lead to any serious conservation problems.

In summary, it can be said that the Picidae as a family are reasonably secure. Although the two biggest woodpeckers have almost certainly become extinct since about 1990, it is probably fair to add that sufficient knowledge is available to ensure that the vast majority of the remaining 214 species can be conserved. Much remains to be learnt about the ecology and biology of many of them, especially the tiny Neotropical piculets, but at the beginning of the twenty-first century, more than at any other time in man's history, conservationists are aware of the importance of protecting the varied habitats of these and all other wild inhabitants of our shared planet. So long as the political will exists, and the human population does not multiply beyond control, nor engage in large-scale habitat-destroying warfare, there are grounds for cautious optimism.

General Bibliography

Avise & Aquadro (1987), Beecher (1953), Blackburn et al. (1998), Blume & Tiefenbach (1997), Bock (1992, 1994, 1999), Bock & Miller (1959), Brodkorb (1971), Burt (1930), Burton (1984), Chapin (1921), Cracraft (1981), Delamain (1937), Dodenhoff et al. (2001), Donatelli (1991, 1996, 1998), Gerasimov & Dzerzhinsky (1998), Goodge (1972), Goodwin (1968), Ishida (1990b), Jackson (1976b), Johnson (2000), Kilham (1959b), Kirby (1980), Krassowsky (1936), Lanyon & Zink (1987), Laurent (1947), Laybourne et al. (1994), Lowe (1946), Madon (1930, 1936), May et al. (1979), Mayr (1998, 2001), Miller (1955a), Moore et al. (1999), Olson (1983), Peters, D.S. (1988), Peters, J.L. (1948), Popp & Ficken (1991), Raikow & Cracraft (1983), Reynolds & Lima (1994), Selander (1966), Short (1970b, 1971c, 1971d, 1971e, 1972b, 1973d, 1979, 1980, 1982b, 1985a, 1985b), Short & Horne (1988), Shufeldt (1900), Sibley (1957, 1996), Sibley & Ahlquist (1990), Sibley & Monroe (1990, 1993), Sibley et al. (1988), Sielmann (1959), Simpson & Cracraft (1981), Skutch (1985d), Swierczewski (1977), Swierczewski & Raikow (1981), Tennant (1991), Test (1942), Vaurie (1959a, 1959b, 1959c, 1959d), Villeneuve (1936), Voous (1947), Winkler & Short (1978), Winkler et al. (1995), Yom-Tov & Ar (1993).

ssp *himalayana*

ssp *torquilla*

1

ssp *ruficollis*

ssp *aequatorialis*
variants

2

ssp *pulchricollis*

form "*thorbeckei*"

typical

PLATE 22

inches		3
cm		8

PLATE 22

Family PICIDAE (WOODPECKERS)
SPECIES ACCOUNTS

Subfamily JYNGINAE

Genus *JYNX* Linnaeus, 1758

1. Eurasian Wryneck

Jynx torquilla

French: Torcol fourmilier   **German**: Wendehals   **Spanish**: Torcecuello Euroasiático
Other common names: (Northern) Wryneck

Taxonomy. *Jynx Torquilla* Linnaeus, 1758, Europe = Sweden.
Forms a superspecies with *J. ruficollis*. Several additional races described from Asia, but geographical variation largely clinal, also somewhat random, and individual variation notable, with much overlap in characters, and all are considered better lumped with nominate race: birds breeding from Ural Mts to R Yenisey named as *sarudnyi* on basis of paler plumage with fewer markings below, and others farther E and in China as race *chinensis* on basis of more barred plumage, but both populations contain individuals closely resembling or identical to W birds; Japanese birds described as *japonica*, more barred and with more rufous in plumage, but some are identical to W (including European) breeders. Four subspecies recognized.
Subspecies and Distribution.
J. t. torquilla Linnaeus, 1758 - most of Eurasia, except parts of S; winters in Africa and S Asia.
J. t. tschusii Kleinschmidt, 1907 - Corsica, Sardinia, Italy and E Adriatic coast; winters in Africa.
J. t. mauretanica Rothschild, 1909 - NW Africa.
J. t. himalayana Vaurie, 1959 - NW Himalayas (N Pakistan E to Himachal Pradesh); winters to S, at lower altitudes.

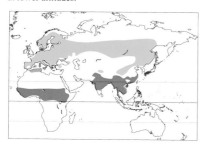

Descriptive notes. 16-17 cm; c. 30-50 g. Small, aberrant, long-tailed woodpecker with short, pointed bill very narrow across nostrils. Both sexes have forehead to hindneck pale grey, speckled darker, finely barred black and rufous, with tiny white feather tips (white spots and black bars usually more distinct on crown); narrow creamy stripe from nostril to below eye; thin creamy supercilium, broad rufous-mottled black band from eye through upper ear-coverts and irregularly down neck side; buff to cinnamon-buff stripe from bill base to lower ear-coverts and neck side, usually finely barred dark; upperparts pale grey, finely dark-speck-

led and with narrow dark shaft streaks, feathers sometimes with black, rufous and whitish marks at tips; central mantle black, edged rufous, this pattern often continuing as irregular band up to crown centre; outer scapulars black, large pale buffish spot at tip; wing-coverts and tertials brownish-buff, speckled grey and rufous-buff, thin black shaft streaks, black subterminal bars, creamy tips; primaries and secondaries dark brown with rufous-buff spot-bars; tail with usually 4-5 (variable) irregular, thin black bars often bordered by grey and buff bands; chin whitish, throat and upper breast buff or cinnamon-buff, all narrowly vermiculated black, often incomplete dark malar stripe; rest of underparts whitish with variable cream or buff suffusion, narrow dark bars on breast, arrowhead marks on lower underparts (extent of markings variable, belly often plain); underwing barred grey and white, coverts buff with black bars; bill dark horn-brown; iris brown to red-brown; legs brownish to grey-green, occasionally tinged yellow or pink. Differs from *J. ruficollis* in lack of rufous on throat and breast, more barred than streaked flanks. Juvenile like adult, but duller, darker, more barred (less streaked) above, more clearly barred below, fewer but more pronounced tail bars, outer primary much longer. Race *tschusii* is darker than nominate, has dark patch on upperparts more prominent, markings below heavier, shorter wings more rounded; *mauretanica* similar but slightly smaller, paler below; *himalayana* is much more strongly barred below, including belly. VOICE. Song slightly ascending series of 8-15 "kwia" notes, sometimes raucous, similar to call of small falcon (*Falco*), by single bird or both of pair simultaneously; low, guttural notes during close contacts between mates; long wavering series of "tak" notes in alarm; hissing notes by nestlings in defence.
Habitat. Open forest, clearings, woodland with low undergrowth, wooded pasture, and unimproved meadowland with scattered trees, so long as dry and sunlit, and grass areas not too well developed; avoids damper vegetation and higher mountains. Prefers open riparian forest, and lighter parts of more closed mixed or deciduous broadleaf forest and forest edge; also copses, avenues, plantations, parks, orchards, larger gardens, non-intensive farmland; locally, also pure stands of pine (*Pinus*) or larch (*Larix*). In non-breeding season, open dry woodland, bushy grassland and gardens, in S Asia typically in scrub, thickets, also in canopy of forest and in cultivations; overwinterers in S Europe found mostly in coastal wetlands and *maquis*. Migrants also in treeless open habitats, including desert. Mostly lowlands to c. 1000 m, occasionally higher, in Europe to 1600 m in Alps and Caucasus; in Himalayas, breeds at 1500-3300 m; non-breeders to 1800 m in SE Asia.
Food and Feeding. Diet mostly ants, mainly larvae and pupae; other insects include e.g. small beetles, aphids (Aphididae), Lepidoptera, dipteran flies, bugs (Hemiptera). Some spiders taken, also woodlice (Isopoda); occasionally molluscs, frog tadpoles (*Rana*), bird eggs; rarely, plant matter (berries). In Europe, the ant genera *Lasius* and *Tetramorium* especially important; in studies of 7 broods in 2 areas of Switzerland, using photography at nest, *Lasius*, *Formica*, *Tetramorium*, *Tapinoma* and *Myrmica* were brought to nestlings, and ants recorded in 95% of feeds. On non-breeding grounds, genera *Crematogaster* and *Camponotus* are typical prey. Forages mainly on the ground, occasionally in trees. Procures prey from crevices or from the surface; uses bill to open anthills. Hops on ground and along horizontal or sloping branches.
Breeding. Lays in May-Jun; in S of range, second clutch sometimes laid in Jun, rarely Jul, occasionally third brood attempted. Territorial; home range large at start of breeding season, shrinking considerably after pairing; sings on exposed perch or from prospective nest-hole. On meeting, partners display by head-swinging with ruffled head feathers; courtship feeding may extend into

incubation period. Nest-site selected by both sexes, in natural cavity, in old hole of another woodpecker, or in artificial nestbox, at height of 1-15 m; occasionally in building in China; cavity cleaned out over several days, removes any eggs or chicks of other hole-nester. Clutch 7-12 eggs, sometimes far fewer, but clutches of 18-23 eggs are product of more than one female; incubation by both adults, average period c. 11-12 days; nestlings fed by both parents, respond to intruders with characteristic snake-like head movements and hissing, fledge after 20-22 days, independent 1-2 weeks later. Breeding success good; fledging rate over 70%; productivity 3-4 young per pair. First breeds at 1 year. Longevity generally 2-10 years.

Movements. Largely migratory. European and W Asian populations move to W, C & E Africa, E populations to mainly N & C Indian Subcontinent and SE Asia; migrates mainly at night, can cover 600 km in 8 days. Leaves Europe in late summer, sometimes as early as Jul; some Scandinavian birds wander through Britain; otherwise, passage on broad front through C Europe mid-Aug to end Sept, crossing Alps, and then Iberia or the Balkans, reaching African winter quarters from late Aug and early Sept; birds from E Europe and W Asia probably move through Turkey and Arabian Peninsula, with peak in Caucasus mid-Aug, in C Anatolia end Sept or early Oct; present in E Africa Oct-Apr. Returns N begins Jan-Mar, reaching C European breeding grounds early Apr, Russia and Mongolia late Apr to early May, and N Europe by mid-May. Some individuals of nominate race winter in Mediterranean region and in SE Iran; Mediterranean race *tschusii* and N African *mauretanica* migrate short distances, or make only altitudinal movements. In E Asia, migrants pass through Korea in Sept, and in Apr-May; non-breeders present early Sept to end Apr in N India, Oct-Apr in Myanmar. Straggles occasionally to W Alaska.

Status and Conservation. Not globally threatened. European population estimated at c. 382,000 pairs, of which most in E, including c. 158,000 in Russia; 45,000 in Spain, probably 5000-10,000 in Sweden, c. 4000 in Finland. Densities vary widely, in Europe decreasing from E to W & S and with preference for continental climate over maritime one, e.g. 1 pair/2·5 km² in Russia and Belarus but less than 1 pair/50 km² in Denmark, Netherlands, Greece and Portugal; in E Europe, densities in optimal habitats can be high, with inter-nest distances of only 40-50 m, even 20 m. In NW Himalayas, scarce to locally common; uncommon in N Pakistan, frequent in Kashmir. In W & C Europe, long-term decline since mid-19th century, with considerable reduction in range and numbers during 20th century; disappeared from N France and from parts of Belgium, Netherlands and Germany after 1960's; rapid decline in Britain, where almost extinct by 1990's; numbers in Finland and Sweden decreased by over 50% in latter decades of 20th century. Decline possibly initiated by climatic changes, with increase in rainfall during breeding season; since 1950's, various other factors, including loss of important habitats such as orchards and unimproved meadows, replacement of hardwoods with conifers, and intensive farming practices accompanied by large-scale pesticide and herbicide usage, are likely major causes of acceleration of the decline; reduction of ant populations almost certainly a further significant factor.

Bibliography. Ali (1996), Ali & Ripley (1983), Arnhem (1960), Axelsson *et al*. (1997), Bannerman (1953), Barlow *et al*. (1997), Beaman & Madge (1998), van den Berk (1990), Berndt & Winkel (1987), Berndt & Wolfgang (1979), Bitz & Rohe (1992), Borgstrom (1980), Brazil (1991), Cheke & Walsh (1996), Chiba (1969), Colston & Curry-Lindahl (1986), Cortés & Domínguez (1994, 1997), Cramp (1985), Cunningham-van Someren (1977), Deignan (1945), Dementiev *et al*. (1966), Demey *et al*. (2000), Demongin (1993), Desfayes (1969), Diaz (1997), Díaz *et al*. (1996), Dowsett & Dowsett-Lemaire (1993), Dowsett & Forbes-Watson (1993), Eck & Geidel (1974), Epple (1992), Étchécopar & Hüe (1964, 1978), Farinello *et al*. (1994), Fraticelli & Wirz (1991), Freitag (1996, 1998, 2000), Fry *et al*. (1988), Glutz von Blotzheim & Bauer (1980), Goodman *et al*. (1989), Goy (1994), Greig-Smith (1977a), Grimmett *et al*. (1998), Hagemeijer & Blair (1997), Hald-Mortensen (1971), Harrison (1999), Heath *et al*. (2000), Hedenstrom & Lindstrom (1990), Heimer (1992), Hölzinger (1992a, 1992b), Hüe & Étchécopar (1970), Jackson (1967), Joebges *et al*. (1998), Kasparek (1989), Klaver (1964), König (1961), Krištín (1992), Langslow (1977), Ledant *et al*. (1981), Löhrl (1978), MacKinnon & Phillipps (2000), Mackworth-Praed & Grant (1970), Mikusinski (2001), Mikusinski & Angelstam (1997, 1998), Murai & Higuchi (1991), Olioso & Orsini (1999), Orsini (1997), Paz (1987), Pearson & Turner (1986), Purroy (1997), Ravkin *et al*. (1988), Roberts (1991), Rogacheva (1992), Ruge (1971a), Sauvage *et al*. (1998), Scebba & Lövei (1985), Scherner (1989), Scherzinger (1989), Shirihai (1996), Simms (1994), Snow (1978), Snow & Perrins (1998), Stevenson & Webster (1992), Struwe (1992), Sutter (1941), Svensson *et al*. (1999), Terhivuo (1976, 1977, 1983), Tobalske & Tobalske (1999), Tomialojc (1994), Winkel (1992), Young *et al*. (1993), Zhao Zhengjie (1995).

2. Rufous-necked Wryneck
Jynx ruficollis

French: Torcol à gorge rousse **German**: Rotkehl-Wendehals **Spanish**: Torcecuello Africano
Other common names: Rufous-breasted/Red-breasted Wryneck, Rufous-throated/Red-throated Wryneck, African Wryneck

Taxonomy. *Jynx ruficollis* Wagler, 1830, Uitenhage, eastern Cape Province, South Africa.
Forms a superspecies with *J. torquilla*. Cameroon birds formerly separated as race *thorbeckei* on basis of more completely barred throat, but this feature occurs also in E populations of *pulchricollis*. Birds from N Angola sometimes separated as race *pectoralis*, but indistinguishable from nominate; proposed race *cosensi* (Kenya, Tanzania) now considered synonymous with nominate. Three subspecies recognized.

Subspecies and Distribution.
J. r. aequatorialis Rüppell, 1842 - Ethiopia.
J. r. pulchricollis Hartlaub, 1884 - SE Nigeria and Cameroon to NW Zaire, S Sudan and NW Uganda.
J. r. ruficollis Wagler, 1830 - SE Gabon to SW & E Uganda, SW Kenya and extreme N Tanzania, and S to N & E Angola (S to Cuanza Norte and Malanje, E to Moxico), NW Zambia and E South Africa.

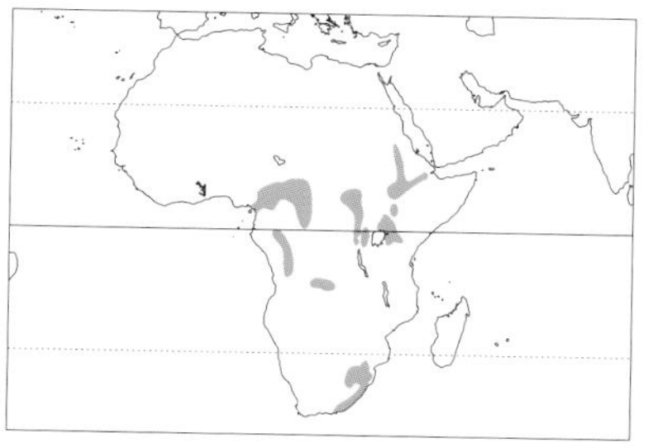

Descriptive notes. 19 cm; male 52-59 g, female 46-52 g. Small, aberrant, long-tailed woodpecker with short, pointed bill. Both sexes have lores and ear-coverts barred buff-white and brown, malar area whitish with brown vermiculations; forehead to uppertail-coverts, including scapulars, wing-coverts and tertials, grey-brown, variably marked with black shaft streaks/bars and subterminal spots, wing-coverts with white tips; irregular central black stripe from crown centre to mantle; crown sides, rump, uppertail-coverts, wing-coverts and tertials usually very finely vermiculated; flight-feathers dark brown, barred light rusty to rufous-white; uppertail brownish-grey with prominent white-bordered black bars; chin to upper breast rufous-chestnut (extent of colour somewhat variable), central throat occasionally barred (e.g. in Kenya); rest of underparts whitish with brown shaft streaks, flanks and lower belly to vent tinged buffy, lower flanks also barred, undertail-coverts barred; underwing barred brown and pale rufous-buff; bill brownish-grey, darker tip; iris brown; legs olive-green to brownish. Differs from *J. ruficollis* in larger size, rufous breast or throat, more streaked and less barred belly, much longer outer primary. Juvenile darker with more barring above, most of underparts finely barred, rufous colour duller and less extensive. Races differ mainly in tone of upperparts and in amount and darkness of rufous below, but much variation: *aequatorialis* has rufous reaching lower breast, and often upper flanks, also extensive rufous-buff on lower flanks to lower belly and undertail-coverts, ventral streaking less prominent, sometimes some barring on throat; *pulchricollis* is less grey-brown above, more rufous-tinged, throat to breast chestnut rather than rufous, throat more strongly barred and sometimes without rufous, flanks washed rusty, chestnut on lower belly to undertail-coverts. Voice. Sings from dead tree, loud, high "kwik-kwik-kwik-kwik-kwik-kwik, kwee kwee kwee" or "week-week-week-week" series by male, lower-pitched "uit-uit-uit-uit-uit" by female; also low, guttural "peegh-peegh-peegh"; long series of "krok" notes in display; quiet "klik" calls in alarm.

Habitat. Inhabits wooded grassland, open forest and forest edge, as well as open areas with trees. Widespread in drier acacia (*Acacia*) savanna and open bush, especially in wooded gorges on hillsides and along streams; occurs in miombo woodland, also in denser *Cryptosepalum* woodland in E Angola; also found in plantations, gardens, and stands of exotic trees in urban areas. Occurs from 600 m up to 3000 m, in Kenya mostly 1400-2500 m; recorded up to 1550 m in S Africa.

Food and Feeding. Mainly ants and their pupae and eggs; also some other small arthropods. Gleans items from the bark of dead branches of trees, also from larger bushes; also forages frequently on ground, where it hops about with tail raised.

Breeding. Apr in Gabon; in Angola, adult in breeding condition in Aug, juvenile seen in Sept; breeds Aug-Dec in South Africa; often two broods reared in a season, but sometimes even three or four. Courtship feeding by male sometimes continues into incubation period. Nest situated in disused hole of barbet (Capitonidae) or woodpecker, or in natural crevice in trunk or bough of tree; sometimes uses artificial nestbox, hollow fence post, or hole under eaves of a house. Clutch 3 or 4 eggs, with exceptional extremes 1-6; both sexes incubate, period 12-15 days; both care for chicks, which give snake-like head movements and hissing sounds in response to intruders; fledging period 25-26 days. One pair was recorded raising three successive broods, with 14-24 days between fledging of one brood and laying of next clutch. Nests regularly parasitized by honeyguides (Indicatoridae).

Movements. Largely resident, but dispersive, and perhaps somewhat nomadic. Movements not well understood; records outside known breeding areas, particularly in E (including Mozambique), may represent post-breeding dispersal or, possibly, short-distance migration. At least partially migratory in S parts of range; migrants pass through NE South Africa in Feb and Mar; some S African birds migrate as far N as E Zaire. Often colonizes an area for a period and then vanishes, only to reappear several years later; also breeds, at least occasionally, in regions outside normal, disjunct breeding areas.

Status and Conservation. Not globally threatened. Locally common, but often irregular in occurrence. Not uncommon in Angola; uncommon in Ethiopia; uncommon in Kenya; locally common in South Africa, where appears to have expanded considerably due to introduction of alien trees to many grassland areas which formerly lacked trees. Shows a rather disjunct breeding range, and presence in many areas is rather erratic; breeds at least occasionally in regions outside normal range; pairs are usually widely scattered, and there are considerable annual fluctuations in numbers, making assessment of population size difficult. Occurs in many protected areas throughout range.

Bibliography. Bannerman (1953), Bennun & Njoroge (1996), Benson (1981), Benson & Benson (1977), Benson *et al*. (1971), Bowen (1983), Brown & Britton (1980), Cheeseman & Sclater (1935), Clancey (1987), Dean (2000), Demey *et al*. (2000), Desfayes (1969), Dowsett (1982, 1989b), Dowsett & Dowsett-Lemaire (1993), Dowsett & Forbes-Watson (1993), Elgood *et al*. (1994), Farnsworth *et al*. (2000), Friedmann (1930a), Fry *et al*. (1988), Ginn *et al*. (1989), Harrison *et al*. (1997), Hustler *et al*. (1992), Lewis & Pomeroy (1989), Lippens & Wille (1976), Louette (1981b), Mackworth-Praed & Grant (1957, 1962, 1970), Maclean (1993), Newman (1996), Nikolaus (1987), Pinto (1983), Sargeant (1993), Short (1980, 1985b), Short & Bock (1972), Short *et al*. (1990), Sinclair (1987), Sinclair & Davidson (1995), Sinclair & Hockey (1996), Sinclair & Whyte (1991), Sinclair *et al*. (1993), Snow (1978), Storer & Dalquest (1967), Tarboton (1976, 2001), Urban & Brown (1971), Zimmerman *et al*. (1996).

with yellow
forehead
♂

ssp *innominatus*

♀

with rufous
forehead
♂

3

ssp *chinensis*

♀

ssp *aurifrons*

♀

ssp *borbae*

♂

♂

ssp *transfasciatus*

♂

ssp *wallacii*

♂

ssp *lafresnayi*

♀

6

ssp *punctifrons*

ssp *taczanowskii*

♂

PLATE 23

inches   2
cm   5

5

♀

♂

♀

8

ssp *exilis*

♂

7

ssp *undulatus*

♂

♀

ssp *buffoni*

♂

ssp *squamulatus*

♀

ssp *obsoletus*

♂

♀

ssp *sclateri*

♂

9

ssp *parvistriatus*

♂

10

♂

ssp *apurensis*

♂

ssp *rohli*

♂

ssp *lovejoyi*

♂

Subfamily PICUMNINAE
Tribe PICUMNINI
Genus *PICUMNUS* Temminck, 1825

3. Speckled Piculet

Picumnus innominatus

French: Picumne tacheté   **German**: Tüpfelzwergspecht   **Spanish**: Carpinterito Moteado
Other common names: Spotted Piculet(!)

Taxonomy. *Picumnus innominatus* Burton, 1836, Sikkim.
Despite enormous geographical separation, present species appears to be closely related to congeners (see page 300). Proposed races *simlaensis* (NW Himalayas) and *avunculorum* (SW India) now considered synonymous with, respectively, nominate and race *malayorum*. Three subspecies currently recognized.
Subspecies and Distribution.
P. i. innominatus Burton, 1836 - NE Afghanistan, N Pakistan and Kashmir E through N India and Nepal to SE Tibet and Assam.
P. i. malayorum Hartert, 1912 - peninsular and NE India (except Assam) E to SW China (S Yunnan), S to Indochina, Sumatra and N Borneo.
P. i. chinensis (Hargitt, 1881) - C, E & S China (S from Sichuan and S Jiangsu).

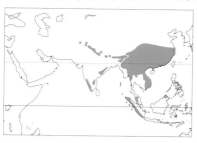

Descriptive notes. 10 cm; 9-13·2 g. Male has rufous-orange to yellow forehead barred or spotted black, yellowish-white lores; broad black stripe from eye backwards, bordered by white stripes, black malar stripe with white feather fringes; olive-green crown, bright olive-green upperparts; upperwing and coverts brownish-black with greenish or yellow-green edges; black uppertail, inner webs of central feather pair and subterminal patches of outer 2 pairs white; dull white chin and throat, yellowish lower throat usually with few black spots; remaining underparts white to pale yellowish-white with black spots, flanks more barred, belly and central undertail-coverts usually unmarked; underwing grey, coverts tinged yellow and spotted black; bill short, culmen slightly curved, black or bluish-black; iris brown, blue-grey orbital skin; legs blue-grey. Female as male, but forehead olive-green. Juvenile as female, but plumage duller, bill paler. Race *malayorum* is slightly smaller and duller, with darker, greyer crown, heavier spotting below; *chinensis* is slightly larger, with cinnamon-brown crown and upper mantle, black facial markings brown-tinged, whiter lores, coarser markings below. Voice. High "ti-ti-ti-ti-ti" by male as advertising or territorial call; frequently a high-pitched squeaky "sik-sik-sik"; occasional sharp "tsick" or "tsit"; drums loudly.
Habitat. Deciduous and mixed deciduous forest, evergreen tropical montane forest, also open second growth, particularly where bamboo present. Mostly in foothills or lower hills, locally higher or lower: 900-1830 m in Nepal and Sikkim, up to 2400 m in NE India and to 3000 m in NW Himalayas; c. 900-1400 m in Peninsular Malaysia; down to 100 m, and even to sea-level, in Sumatra and Borneo.
Food and Feeding. Diet consists of insects and their larvae, especially ants, but also geometrid caterpillars, weevils (Curculionidae) and longhorn beetles (Cerambycidae); also takes spiders and their eggs. Hunts singly or in pairs; often present in mixed-species flocks, though in general only outside breeding season. Forages in undergrowth, on trunk and branches of small trees, and in bushes, vines and bamboo; frequently hangs upside-down, and moves along thin vertical twigs; often concentrates on one spot for several minutes, pecking and hammering vigorously; presence often revealed by loud persistent tapping. Also hovers to catch prey, or pursues flushed prey to take it on the wing.
Breeding. Jan-May. Male displays by circling around mate and pursuing her around branch. Nest excavated by both sexes, at 1-5 m, occasionally as low as 0·3 m, in dead branch or small tree, or bamboo, occasionally in palm fronds; hole entrance c. 2·5 cm across. Clutch 2-4 eggs; both parents incubate, period 11 days; both also feed nestlings, which fledge after 11 days; young disperse soon after leaving nest.
Movements. Resident.
Status and Conservation. Not globally threatened. Common or fairly common throughout much of range; generally uncommon in peninsular India; uncommon in China. Has been considered local and very rare in most of NW part of range, but recent observations in N Pakistan suggest small population at low density in Margalla Hills and other sightings there indicate that species is probably uncommon to scarce, and possibly overlooked. Status in Borneo uncertain; specimens known only from N Sabah, but this species may possibly be present elsewhere. Occurs in several protected areas within its range, including Thattakad Bird Sanctuary in Kerala and Namdapha National Park in Arunachal Pradesh (India), and Nam Nao and Doi Inthanon National Parks (Thailand).
Bibliography. Ali (1969, 1996), Ali & Ripley (1983), Ali *et al.* (1996), Andrew (1992), Bangs & Van Tyne (1931), Benstead *et al.* (1997), Betts (1934), Champion-Jones (1938), Chasen & Hoogerwerf (1941), Deignan (1945), Eames & Robson (1992), Étchécopar & Hüe (1978), Gandy *et al.* (1998), Grimmett *et al.* (1998), Harvey (1990), Hüe & Étchécopar (1970), Inskipp & Inskipp (1991), Jeyarajasingam & Pearson (1999), Law (1948), Lekagul & Round (1991), Leven (1998), Li Yanjuan (1962), Ludlow (1937, 1944), MacKinnon & Phillipps (1993, 2000), Madoc (1976), van Marle & Voous (1988), Medway & Wells (1976), Osmaston (1902), Paludan (1959), Raja *et al.* (1999), Riley (1938), Ripley (1982), Roberts (1991), Robson (2000), Shankar Raman (2001), Short (1973d), Smythies (1986, 1999), Stepanyan (1995), Storrs-Fox (1937), Tymstra *et al.* (1997), Vowles & Vowles (1997), Wells (1985, 1999), Zhao Zhengjie (1995).

4. Bar-breasted Piculet

Picumnus aurifrons

French: Picumne barré   **German**: Goldstirn-Zwergspecht   **Spanish**: Carpinterito del Amazonas
Other common names: Gold-fronted/Golden-fronted Piculet (yellow-crowned races)

Taxonomy. *Picumnus aurifrons* Pelzeln, 1870, Engenho do Gama, Caiçara and Salto do Girao, west-central Brazil.
May be more closely related to *P. fuscus*. Races *juruanus* and *borbae*, with red forehead streaks, sometimes treated as forming a separate species "*P. borbae*", although from a biogeographical standpoint there are major objections. Seven subspecies currently recognized.
Subspecies and Distribution.
P. a. flavifrons Hargitt, 1889 - NE Peru and W Brazil (along R Solimões).
P. a. juruanus Gyldenstolpe, 1941 - E Peru to W Brazil (upper R Juruá).
P. a. purusianus Todd, 1946 - W Brazil (upper R Purus).
P. a. wallacii Hargitt, 1889 - middle and lower R Purus E to lower R Madeira.
P. a. borbae Pelzeln, 1870 - lower R Madeira E to lower R Tapajós.
P. a. transfasciatus Hellmayr & Gyldenstolpe, 1937 - R Tapajós E to R Tocantins.
P. a. aurifrons Pelzeln, 1870 - N Mato Grosso from upper R Madeira E to upper R Tapajós.

Descriptive notes. 7·5 cm; 8-10 g, male 9·2 g, female 8·6 g. Male has top of head black, yellow streaks mostly on forehead, remainder spotted white; buff lores, grey-brown cheeks and ear-coverts, whitish line behind eye; olive-green upperparts, somewhat browner wing-coverts and tertials with paler greenish edgings; brownish-black primaries and secondaries, edged greenish-yellow; black uppertail, central feather pair with yellowish-white inner webs, outer 2 pairs with whitish subterminal patch; whitish chin and throat weakly barred dark at sides; remaining underparts pale yellowish-white, breast barred brown, breast sides and upper belly with arrowhead-shaped streaks, belly and flanks broadly streaked brown; underwing-coverts yellowish; bill short, grey to blue-grey, iris brown, orbital skin grey; legs greyish. Differs from similar *P. lafresnayi* in yellow forehead streaks, unbarred back, streaked belly. Female has entire forehead and crown spotted white. Juvenile duller brown, crown browner and streaked (not spotted), markings below less heavy, streaks extending up to lower breast. Race *purusianus* is darker above, breast more heavily barred black; *flavifrons* similar but faintly barred above, breast barring less heavy, belly strongly spotted; *wallacii* is obscurely barred above, paler below, breast bars fainter, belly more spotted; *transfasciatus* has heavily barred upperparts, strongly barred breast; *borbae* has red forehead streaks, yellower tertial edges, yellower belly, stronger blacker breast bars; *juruanus* also has reddish-orange forehead streaks, but far weaker breast barring. Voice. Call "tsirrrit-tsit-tsit", resembling that of hummingbird (Trochilidae).
Habitat. Inhabits humid tropical *terra firme* forest, and also seasonally inundated *várzea* forest; found mainly at edges and in clearings, and also in second growth. Recorded from lowlands up to 1100 m.
Food and Feeding. Virtually unknown; presumably insects. Seems to prefer the upper canopy for foraging.
Breeding. Season presumably Jun-Nov. No other information.
Movements. Apparently resident.
Status and Conservation. Not globally threatened. Very poorly known. Appears to be at best uncommon, but possibly overlooked. Occurs in Manu National Park and Tambopata Reserve, both in Peru.
Bibliography. Angehr & Aucca (1997), Clements & Shany (2001), Donahue (1994), Dubs (1992), Meyer de Schauensee (1982), Olrog (1968), Oren & Parker (1997), Remsen & Traylor (1989), Ruschi (1979), Sick (1993), da Silva (1996), da Silva *et al.* (1990), Snethlage (1914), Stotz, Fitzpatrick *et al.* (1996), Stotz, Lanyon *et al.* (1997), Terborgh *et al.* (1984), Wheatley (1994).

5. Orinoco Piculet

Picumnus pumilus

French: Picumne de l'Orénoque   **Spanish**: Carpinterito del Orinoco
German: Orinokozwergspecht

Taxonomy. *Picumnus pumilus* Cabanis and Heine, 1863, no locality.
Forms a superspecies with *P. lafresnayi*. Often considered conspecific, but no evidence of interbreeding where ranges overlap slightly in SE Colombia; probably separated ecologically. Monotypic.
Distribution. E Colombia, S Venezuela (S Amazonas) and NW Brazil (R Uaupés E to R Jaú).

Descriptive notes. 9 cm; 9-10 g. Male has dark brown cap with small yellow forecrown spots, whiter spots on rest of crown; pale buff lores, blackish ear-coverts with variable white spots, white line behind eye; brownish-green upperparts; wing-coverts and tertials sometimes browner, with yellowish-green edgings; primaries and secondaries brown, edged and tipped greenish; black uppertail, central feather pair with white inner webs, outer 3 pairs with white subterminal patch; pale yellowish to buff-white underparts barred dark brown, belly centre usually unbarred; underwing grey-brown, dark-barred yellower coverts; bill short, culmen slightly curved, blackish with paler base; iris brown to grey-brown, orbital skin grey to blue-grey; legs grey. Differs from *P. lafresnayi* in slightly smaller size, yellow rather

On following pages: 6. Lafresnaye's Piculet (*Picumnus lafresnayi*); 7. Golden-spangled Piculet (*Picumnus exilis*); 8. Black-spotted Piculet (*Picumnus nigropunctatus*); 9. Ecuadorian Piculet (*Picumnus sclateri*); 10. Scaled Piculet (*Picumnus squamulatus*).

than red forehead streaks, darker unbarred upperparts, darker ear-coverts. Female has white forecrown spots. Juvenile greener above, forehead and crown streaked or spotted buff, less prominently marked below. VOICE. Undescribed.
Habitat. Humid forest; recorded from edge of gallery forest and in dense thickets. Lowlands to 300 m, locally to 500 m.
Food and Feeding. No information; presumably ants and similar small insects. Forages from lower levels up to the canopy.
Breeding. Not recorded; season likely to be Nov-Dec.
Movements. Presumably resident.
Status and Conservation. Not globally threatened. Restricted-range species: present in Orinoco-Negro White-sand Forests EBA. Poorly known and probably uncommon. Present in Jaú National Park, in Brazil.
Bibliography. Hilty & Brown (1986), Meyer de Schauensee (1982), Olrog (1968), Rodner *et al.* (2000), Ruschi (1979), Sick (1993), Stattersfield *et al.* (1998), Stotz *et al.* (1996).

6. Lafresnaye's Piculet

Picumnus lafresnayi

French: Picumne de Lafresnaye **Spanish**: Carpinterito de Lafresnaye
German: Lafresnayezwergspecht

Taxonomy. *Picumnus Lafresnayi* Malherbe, 1862, Ecuador.
Forms a superspecies with *P. pumilus*; these two are sometimes considered conspecific, but their ranges overlap slightly in SE Colombia apparently without interbreeding. Four subspecies recognized.
Subspecies and Distribution.
P. l. lafresnayi Malherbe, 1862 - SE Colombia, E Ecuador and N Peru.
P. l. pusillus Pinto, 1936 - NC Brazil on middle R Amazon E to R Negro.
P. l. taczanowskii Domaniewski, 1925 - NE & NC Peru (S to Huánuco).
P. l. punctifrons Taczanowski, 1886 - E Peru.

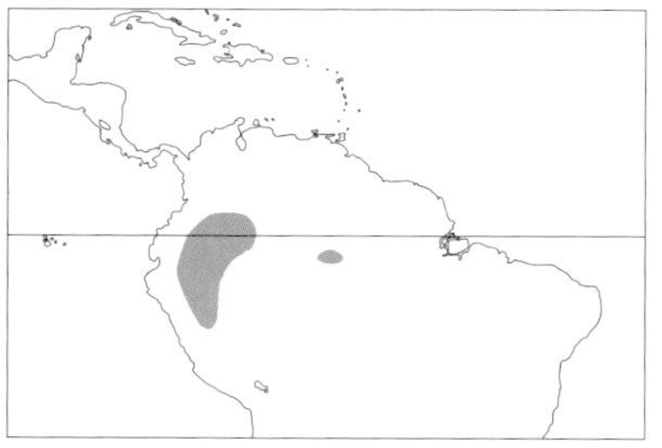

Descriptive notes. 9-10 cm; 9-10 g. Male has dark olive-brown cap with red forecrown spots, whitish spots on rest of crown and nape; pale buff lores, whitish feather edges forming pale stripe behind eye, greyish-buff ear-coverts streaked or spotted brown; dark green or brownish-green upperparts barred yellowish-green; upperwing and its coverts greenish-brown with yellower edgings, primaries browner; uppertail blackish, central feather pair with broad white stripe on inner webs, outer 3 pairs with large area of white towards tip; buffish-white chin and throat with narrow black feather edges; rest of underparts pale yellowish-white with broad black bars, bars broadest on lower areas, occasionally broken in belly centre; underwing brownish with dark-barred yellowish-white coverts; bill short, culmen curved, black with grey base; iris brown to brown-grey, orbital skin greyish; legs grey. Differs from *P. pumilus* in larger size, barred and brighter upperparts, red forehead spots, paler ear-coverts. Female has white forecrown spots. Juvenile duller, with greener upperparts, less evenly barred below. Races other than nominate differ in having yellow-orange forecrown spots, and less heavily barred upperparts: *punctifrons* has slightly larger bill, darker ear-coverts, narrower bars below; *taczanowskii* has blacker crown, and broader, more irregular dark barring below; *pusillus* has upperparts slightly rufous-tinged, narrow dark bars below, centre of belly more or less unbarred. VOICE. Largely silent, but occasional high-pitched "tseeyt, tsit".
Habitat. Inhabits heavily forested, very humid country, preferring secondary growth, forest edges and clearings. Occurs in lowlands and foothills up to 1400 m; occasionally found up to 1800 m in Ecuador.
Food and Feeding. Termites; presumably also other small invertebrates. Forages in lower and middle strata. Gleaning is the only feeding technique recorded. Often accompanies mixed-species feeding flocks.
Breeding. Few records available suggest nesting in Jul-Nov. One nest was in hole c. 3 m up in a shrub, and contained 2 eggs; both sexes care for the brood, and once an additional full-grown female observed to roost with the eggs; incubation and fledging periods undocumented.
Movements. Presumably resident.
Status and Conservation. Not globally threatened. Uncommon to fairly common in Ecuador; regularly recorded on Baeza-Tena and Loreto roads. Considered rare in Peru.
Bibliography. Balchin & Toyne (1998), Bloch *et al.* (1991), Clements & Shany (2001), Hilty & Brown (1986), Peres & Whittaker (1991), Ridgely & Greenfield (2001), Ridgely *et al.* (1998), Rodner *et al.* (2000), Salaman *et al.* (1999), Sick (1993), Stotz *et al.* (1996), Wheatley (1994), Williams & Tobias (1994), Zimmer (1930).

7. Golden-spangled Piculet

Picumnus exilis

French: Picumne de Buffon **Spanish**: Carpinterito Telegrafista
German: Goldschuppen-Zwergspecht

Taxonomy. *Picus exilis* M. H. K. Lichtenstein, 1823, São Paulo; error = Bahia.
May be more closely related to *P. fuscus*. Formerly treated by many authors as conspecific with *P. nigropunctatus*, which was included as a synonym of the form "*salvini*"; latter, described from "Bogotá" skins with no type locality, had earlier been lumped as a race of present species; all pre-1990's taxonomic conclusions were, however, based on totally inadequate material, with very few study skins available, and recent research using series of specimens has shown "*salvini*" to be almost certainly a synonym of *P. squamulatus obsoletus*. Six subspecies recognized.
Subspecies and Distribution.
P. e. undulatus Hargitt, 1889 - extreme E Colombia (NE Guainía), SE Venezuela, N Brazil (Roraima) and W Guyana.
P. e. clarus J. T. Zimmer & Phelps, Sr., 1946 - E Venezuela in E Bolívar and S Delta Amacuro.
P. e. buffoni Lafresnaye, 1845 - E Guyana E to NC Brazil (Amapá).
P. e. alegriae Hellmayr, 1929 - coastal NE Pará and NW Maranhão (NC Brazil).
P. e. pernambucensis J. T. Zimmer, 1947 - coasts of Pernambuco and Alagoas (NE Brazil).
P. e. exilis (M. H. K. Lichtenstein, 1823) - coastal Bahia S to Espírito Santo (EC Brazil).

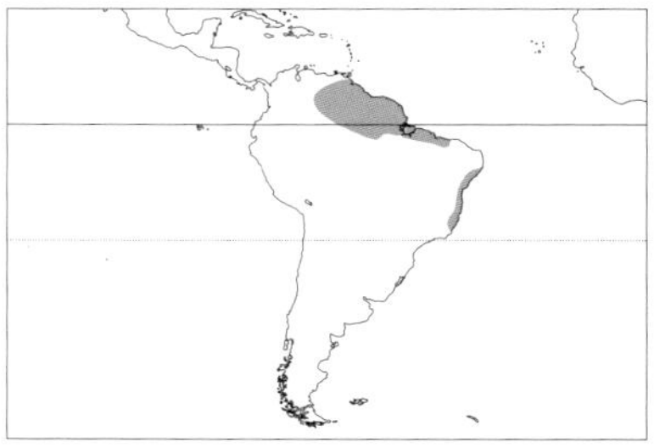

Descriptive notes. 9-10 cm; 8·5-10 g. Male has black forehead to hindneck, feathers of forecrown tipped red, those of mid-crown to hindneck tipped white; buffish-white lores, white line behind eye; yellowish-white cheeks and ear-coverts with dark feather edges; olive-green upperparts with darker feather centres, broad yellow-green edgings; wing-coverts olive-green, narrowly edged white, with black-edged white tips; brownish-green flight-feathers edged yellow-green, tertials broadly edged and with black submarginal lines; dark brown uppertail, central feather pair with broad white stripe on inner webs, outer 3 pairs with large white subterminal mark on outer webs; pale yellowish-white malar, chin and throat, barred blackish; rest of underparts pale yellowish, barred blackish, bars broken and more spot-like on belly; brown and white underwing with whitish coverts; bill short, pointed, culmen curved, black upper mandible, silvery-based lower mandible; iris yellow to dark brown, orbital skin greyish; legs greyish, sometimes tinged green or blue. Differs from *P. nigropunctatus* in yellower upperparts, yellower underparts with bars rather than spots. Female has entire top of head white-spotted. Juvenile duller, crown olive or greyish with off-white streaking, markings above and below more diffuse and irregular. Race *undulatus* is slightly larger, more olive-brown to yellowish-olive with large blackish feather centres above, wing-coverts less obviously pale-tipped, paler and broadly dark-barred below; *clarus* is slightly yellower above and has broken narrower barring below than previous; *buffoni* has distinctive black-bordered white spots at feather tips above; *alegriae* is rather dull, more olive above, whiter below; *pernambucensis* has more olive upperparts, more evenly barred underparts. VOICE. Described as "tsilit, tsirrrr".
Habitat. Rainforest and cloudforest, second growth, disturbed forest; also dense growth with bamboo along rivers, mangroves; also open woodland and savanna edge in the sandy belt. Lowlands, to 1900 m in areas with tepuis.
Food and Feeding. Ants are the only kind of food documented. Species forages inconspicuously, alone or in pairs; also joins mixed-species flocks. Pecks and hammers on small branches in lower strata of forest, at 1-5 m; moves about in manner similar to that of a tit (Paridae), often hanging on thin twigs.
Breeding. Dec-Mar in Venezuela and Surinam. Nest excavated in branch or stump with soft wood. No other information available.
Movements. Presumably resident.
Status and Conservation. Not globally threatened. A very poorly known species; no data available on numbers; possibly at best uncommon. Occurs in Parque Estadual da Pedra Talhada in Brazil, and in Imataca Forest Reserve and El Dorado in Venezuela. Since this piculet is often found in more open habitats, including disturbed forest, human activities may possibly lead to its range being expanded.
Bibliography. Chapman (1931), Cohn-Haft *et al.* (1997), Haverschmidt & Mees (1994), Hilty & Brown (1986), Meyer de Schauensee & Phelps (1978), Parker & Goerck (1997), Pinto & Camargo (1961), Reynaud (1998), Rodner *et al.* (2000), Ruschi (1979), Sick (1993), Snyder (1966), Stotz *et al.* (1996), Thiollay & Jullien (1998), Tostain *et al.* (1992), Wheatley (1994).

8. Black-spotted Piculet

Picumnus nigropunctatus

French: Picumne maculé **Spanish**: Carpinterito Punteado
German: Schwarzflecken-Zwergspecht
Other common names: Black-dotted Piculet

Taxonomy. *Picumnus nigropunctatus* J. T. Zimmer & Phelps, Sr., 1950, Araguaimujo Mission, Orinoco Delta, Venezuela.
Sometimes treated as conspecific with *P. spilogaster*, but vocalizations differ. Although initially described as a full species, was later lumped in *P. exilis* as a synonym of form "*salvini*"; however, latter shown by recent research to be almost certainly a synonym of the taxon *P. squamulatus obsoletus*, from which present species differs significantly in plumage details. Further research needed on relationships. Monotypic.
Distribution. NE Venezuela, from N & E Sucre to NE Monagas and Delta Amacuro (S to R Orinoco).

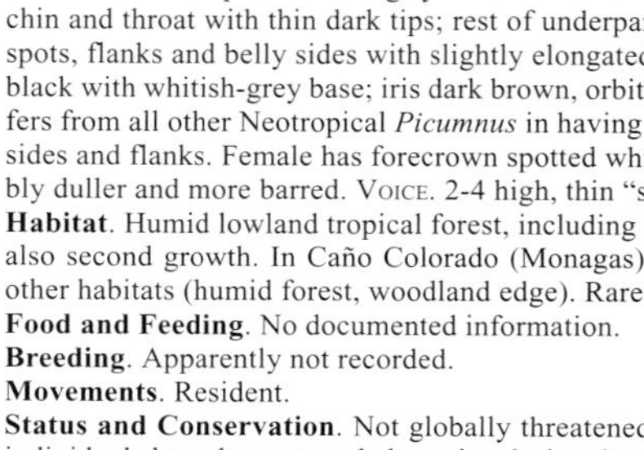

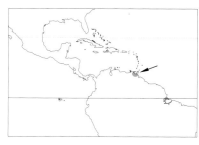

Descriptive notes. 9 cm. Male has top of head black, forecrown feathers tipped scarlet-red, rest spotted white; buff-white lower forehead and lores, whitish line behind eye; buffish ear-coverts broadly dark-edged; brownish upperparts with greenish-yellow edgings, mantle feathers with oval-shaped dark brown centre and usually whitish subterminal spot, uppertail-coverts yellower; darker brown wings, coverts with paler edges tending towards white or with indistinct white subterminal spots, secondaries and tertials broadly edged yellow to whitish; black uppertail, central feather pair with broad white or yellow-white stripe on inner webs, outer 2 pairs with large yellowish-white stripe across outer webs; yellowish-white malar, chin and throat with thin dark tips; rest of underparts straw-yellow, breast with broad large black spots, flanks and belly sides with slightly elongated spots; underwing brownish, coverts buff; bill black with whitish-grey base; iris dark brown, orbital ring dark blue-grey; legs greenish-grey. Differs from all other Neotropical *Picumnus* in having large black spots on breast, as well as on belly sides and flanks. Female has forecrown spotted white. Juvenile apparently undescribed, presumably duller and more barred. VOICE. 2-4 high, thin "seeet" notes, rather halting and well separated.
Habitat. Humid lowland tropical forest, including *várzea* and *terra firme*, mainly at forest edges; also second growth. In Caño Colorado (Monagas), common at forest borders and present in all other habitats (humid forest, woodland edge). Rarely occurs much above sea-level.
Food and Feeding. No documented information.
Breeding. Apparently not recorded.
Movements. Resident.
Status and Conservation. Not globally threatened. Common at Caño Colorado, where up to 15 individuals have been recorded per day during dry season.
Bibliography. Boesman (1995), Meyer de Schauensee (1982), Meyer de Schauensee & Phelps (1978), Olrog (1968), Rodner *et al.* (2000).

9. Ecuadorian Piculet

Picumnus sclateri

French: Picumne de Sclater   **German**: Braunohr-Zwergspecht   **Spanish**: Carpinterito Ecuatoriano

Taxonomy. *Picumnus sclateri* Taczanowski, 1877, Lechugal, Peru.
Three subspecies recognized.
Subspecies and Distribution.
P. s. parvistriatus Chapman, 1921 - W Ecuador from Manabí S to Guayas.
P. s. sclateri Taczanowski, 1877 - SW Ecuador (El Oro, Loja) and extreme NW Peru.
P. s. porcullae Bond, 1954 - NW Peru from C Piura S to N Lambayeque.

Descriptive notes. 8-9 cm; 9-12·4 g. Male has black forehead to hindneck, feathers of central forehead to about mid-crown narrowly tipped yellow, remainder tipped white; white lores, short white line behind eye; dark ear-coverts streaked white; upperparts dark brownish with darker barring, wing-coverts edged and tipped paler, edges broadest and whitest on tertials; dark grey-brown uppertail, central feather pair with broad white stripe on inner webs, outer 3 pairs with much white subterminally; underparts whitish, chin and throat barred blackish, breast more broadly barred, flanks and belly broadly streaked blackish; underwing whitish, coverts barred grey; bill short, culmen curved, black with greyer base; iris brown; legs grey. Female has entirely white-spotted top of head. Juvenile duller, forehead and crown with off-white streaks or spots, markings below more diffuse. Race *parvistriatus* is much paler, pale brownish-grey above, secondaries and tertials broadly white-edged, bars below narrow and greyer, sparser streaks much thinner and greyish; *porcullae* has chin and throat bars even broader and blacker than nominate, very broad black bars on breast, very broad black streaks on flanks and belly. Voice. High-pitched "tseee-tsuit", also single or double "tseeet".
Habitat. Dry deciduous forest, and arid areas with cacti and low thorny scrub; also in more humid lower montane forest in SW Ecuador (Loja). From lowlands to 1400 m, locally to 1900 m, rarely to 2100 m; in Ecuador, mostly below 800 m but locally to 1700 m.
Food and Feeding. No information on diet; probably similar to that of *P. olivaceus*. Forages at lower levels of habitat.
Breeding. Nests from Jun in Peru and from Jul in Ecuador, to Sept. No other information.
Movements. Presumably resident.
Status and Conservation. Not globally threatened. Restricted-range species: present in Tumbesian Region EBA. Uncommon in Ecuador, where occurs in Machalilla National Park. Uncommon in Peru.
Bibliography. Becker & López (1997), Best & Clarke (1991), Bloch *et al.* (1991), Butler (1979), Clements & Shany (2001), Meyer de Schauensee (1982), Olrog (1968), Parker *et al.* (1982), Pople *et al.* (1997), Ridgely & Greenfield (2001), Ridgely *et al.* (1998), Rodner *et al.* (2000), Stattersfield *et al.* (1998), Stotz *et al.* (1996), Taylor (1995), Wheatley (1994), Williams & Tobias (1994).

10. Scaled Piculet

Picumnus squamulatus

French: Picumne squamulé   **German**: Schuppenzwergspecht   **Spanish**: Carpinterito Escamoso

Taxonomy. *Picumnus squamulatus* Lafresnaye, 1854, Colombia.
Race *lovejoyi* possibly not sufficiently distinct to warrant acceptance. Race *obsoletus* almost certainly includes the form previously known as "*P. exilis salvini*", described from "Bogotá" skins with no type locality. Five subspecies currently recognized.
Subspecies and Distribution.
P. s. rohli J. T. Zimmer & Phelps, Sr., 1944 - N Colombia (Santa Marta Mts S to about Boyacá) and N Venezuela (Zulia E to W Sucre and Monagas).
P. s. lovejoyi Phelps, Jr. & Aveledo, 1987 - extreme NW Venezuela (NW Zulia).
P. s. apurensis Phelps, Jr. & Aveledo, 1987 - NC Venezuela in Apure, Guárico and Anzoátegui (R Zuata and R Pariaguán).
P. s. obsoletus Allen, 1892 - extreme NE Venezuela (E Sucre).
P. s. squamulatus Lafresnaye, 1854 - NE & C Colombia (Arauca S to Huila and NE Meta).

Descriptive notes. 8-9·2 cm; 7-12 g. Male has black forehead to nape, feathers of forecrown narrowly tipped red, those of rest of crown tipped white; whitish lores and thin line behind eye, brown ear-coverts tipped white; hindneck brownish-black, spotted white; upperparts olive-brown and scaly-looking, with paler feather centres and narrow black borders, wing-coverts browner with black fringes; flight-feathers brown, secondaries and tertials with broad yellowish edges; uppertail brownish-black, central feather pair with broad white stripe on inner webs, outer 2 pairs with white subterminal stripe; malar, chin and throat white with narrow grey-brown feather tips; rest of underparts whitish with prominent scaly markings, dark brown to black feather margins becoming paler and narrower on belly and undertail-coverts; underwing brownish with white coverts; bill short, culmen curved, grey, paler on lower mandible, blackish tip; iris brown; legs grey to olive-grey. Female has forecrown spots white. Juvenile darker above, often with darker feather centres, more diffusely and irregularly patterned below. Race *rohli* has forecrown spots of male sometimes yellow or orange, hindcrown paler, upperparts brighter, underparts with narrower scaly markings, belly tinged brownish-yellow; *lovejoyi* is similar, but male forecrown spots always yellow instead of red, greyer upperparts; *obsoletus* is tinged yellow-green above, yellowish-white below with finer paler scallop markings and small dark wedge-shaped streaks in feather centres; *apurensis* is whiter-looking below, scaly markings narrow and indistinct. Voice. Rather high-pitched squeaky "chi-chi-ch'e'chi", becoming trill-like at end.
Habitat. Inhabits gallery forest, forest edge, second growth, and deciduous woodland; also found in open terrain and in farmland with scattered trees, xerophytic areas, and pastures. Occurs from lowlands up to 1900 m.
Food and Feeding. Small insects. Forages singly or in pairs, in dense scrub, tangled undergrowth and small trees. Investigates thin branches and twigs.
Breeding. Birds in breeding condition in Jan and Oct in Colombia; nesting in Apr-Jun and Sept in Venezuela. Displays include wing-spreading and "synchronized" movements. No other information.
Movements. Presumably resident.
Status and Conservation. Not globally threatened. No data on population sizes. Possibly not uncommon, and may perhaps be overlooked owing to inconspicuous behaviour. Occurs in Henri Pittier and Cueva de los Guácharos National Parks (Venezuela).
Bibliography. Friedmann & Smith (1950), Hilty & Brown (1986), Meyer de Schauensee (1982), Meyer de Schauensee & Phelps (1978), Olrog (1968), Phelps & Aveledo (1987), Rodner *et al.* (2000), Salaman *et al.* (1999), Stotz *et al.* (1996), Verea & Solórzano (1998), Verea *et al.* (1999), Wetmore (1939), Wheatley (1994), Zimmer & Phelps (1944).

ssp *spilogaster*

♀

♂

11

♂

ssp *orinocensis*

♀

12

♂

♀

13

♂

♀

14

♂

♀

15

♂

♀

ssp *cirratus*

♂

ssp *thamnophiloides*

♂

ssp *pilcomayensis*

♂

16

♂

ssp *tucumanus*

ssp *macconnelli*

♂

♀

17

♂

♀

18

♂

♀

ssp *albosquamatus*

19

♂

ssp *guttifer*

♀

20

♂

♀

ssp *rufiventris*

♂

21

♂

ssp *brunneifrons*

PLATE 24

inches 3

cm 8

11. White-bellied Piculet

Picumnus spilogaster

French: Picumne à ventre blanc   **Spanish**: Carpinterito Ventriblanco
German: Weißbauch-Zwergspecht
Other common names: Sundevall's Piculet; Para Piculet (*pallidus*)

Taxonomy. *Picumnus spilogaster*, Sundevall, 1866, the Guianas.
Sometimes considered to include *P. nigropunctatus*, but the two are vocally different. Race *pallidus* sometimes considered a separate species, or treated as a race of *P. minutissimus*, but appears very close morphologically to other forms of present species. Form previously listed as "*P. leucogaster*", described from R Cauamé (Roraima), is a synonym of nominate *spilogaster*, further sampling having shown complete gradation towards typical *spilogaster*; possibly represents a link between nominate and *orinocensis*, showing some intermediate features. Three subspecies currently recognized.

Subspecies and Distribution.
P. s. orinocensis J. T. Zimmer & Phelps, Sr., 1950 - C Venezuela, from SE Apure E along R Meta and R Orinoco to Delta Amacuro.
P. s. spilogaster Sundevall, 1866 - N parts of the Guianas, and N Brazil (Roraima).
P. s. pallidus Snethlage, 1924 - NE Brazil in E Pará (Belém area).

Descriptive notes. c. 9 cm; 13-14 g. Male has top of head black, crown with broad red feather tips forming fairly solid patch, hindcrown to nape spotted white; buffish lores, dark brown ear-coverts vermiculated white; neck sides white, finely barred black; dull olive-brown hindneck and upperparts diffusely barred pale greyish, wing-coverts olive-brown with narrow pale edges; brown flight-feathers edged light buffish, edges broadest and brightest on secondaries and tertials; uppertail dark brown, central feather pair with broad white stripe on inner webs, outer 2 pairs with white stripe on outer webs except tips; malar, chin and throat whitish, barred blackish; upper breast washed pale yellowish-buff with fairly broad, sometimes broken, black bars, lower breast to belly cream-white with sparse broad black spots, flanks occasionally barred; underwing grey-brown, coverts white; bill short, culmen slightly curved, slate-grey with black tip; iris brown; legs greenish-grey. Differs from *P. minutissimus* in smaller size, less marked upperparts, barred and spotted (not scaled) underparts, dark eyes. Female lacks red on head. Juvenile has crown sooty-brown, buffish spots restricted to hindneck, more buffish underparts, is generally more barred both above and below. Race *orinocensis* is slightly smaller, usually unmarked below or occasionally with trace of vermiculation on flanks, slightly more white in tail; race *pallidus* resembles nominate, but slightly smaller, tail proportionately shorter. VOICE. Song a high-pitched thin trill c. 3 seconds long, c. 25-35 notes on slightly descending scale.
Habitat. Inhabits rainforest, gallery forest and deciduous forest, clearings, forest edge, and also mangroves; also found in open woodland and thickets. Occurs from lowlands up to 100 m.
Food and Feeding. Diet unrecorded. Observed singly and in pairs, but no documented information on foraging behaviour.
Breeding. Probably Sept-Nov. No information on nest or breeding biology.
Movements. Apparently resident.
Status and Conservation. Not globally threatened. Poorly known, and no data available on numbers. Locally not uncommon in *llanos* of Venezuela.
Bibliography. Hilty (1999), Meyer de Schauensee & Phelps (1978), Reynaud (1998), Rodner *et al.* (2000), Ruschi (1979), Sick (1993), Stotz *et al.* (1996), Tostain *et al.* (1992), Wheatley (1994).

12. Guianan Piculet

Picumnus minutissimus

French: Picumne de Cayenne   **German**: Däumlingsspecht   **Spanish**: Carpinterito de Guayana
Other common names: Arrowhead Piculet

Taxonomy. *Picus minutissimus* Pallas, 1782, Cayenne.
Sometimes considered to include race *pallidus* of *P. spilogaster*. Monotypic.
Distribution. Coastal lowlands from Guyana E to French Guiana.

Descriptive notes. 9-10 cm; 11-16 g. Male has top of head black, crown with broad red feather tips forming solid patch, rest spotted white; buff-white lores, short white line behind eye, dark brown cheeks and ear-coverts with white feather fringes; rear neck side white, barred or spotted black; upperparts olive-brown, feathers with blackish wedge-shaped centre, very thin black bar at tip, and pale subterminal spot or diffuse bar; plainer rump obscurely dark-barred, uppertail-coverts sometimes barred pale and dark; wing-coverts olive-brown with paler edgings; flight-feathers brown, secondaries and tertials broadly edged buffish-white on outer webs; uppertail brownish-black, central feather pair with broad white stripe along inner webs, outer 2 pairs with angled white stripe on outer webs; malar, chin and throat white, narrowly barred black; rest of underparts white, tinged brownish-buff on belly and lower flanks, all with brownish-black feather fringes creating distinctive scaly pattern; underwing grey-brown, coverts mottled brown and white; bill short, stout, culmen curved, dark grey with pale base of lower mandible; iris yellow to deep red or red-brown, orbital skin greyish; legs green-grey. Distinguished from *P. spilogaster* and *P. cirratus* by upperpart markings, brownish belly, entirely scaly underparts. Female lacks red on head, has slightly shorter bill, slightly longer wing and tail. Juvenile has unspotted dark brown

---

crown, browner upperparts barred blackish, duller underparts less clearly patterned. VOICE. Series of c. 14 thin notes, "it-it-it-it...", or "kee kee kee", reminiscent of Old World *Dendrocopos minor*; loud twitter in aggressive attacks.
Habitat. Wide variety of habitats, including secondary forest, plantations, mangroves, riverine and lakeside vegetation, up to montane forest.
Food and Feeding. Ants and small beetles (Bostrichidae) recorded as forming part of diet. Forages in shrubs and trees in manner of a tit (Paridae), hanging from small branches and twigs; hammers on branches.
Breeding. Season Mar-Dec. Nest-hole excavated mostly by male, high up (e.g. 8 m) in tree; during breeding, other birds, even bigger ones, are attacked in vicinity of nest. Clutch 2-3 eggs; incubation by both sexes, period 12-14 days; both adults also feed the young and remove faeces; fledging c. 28 days; parents and young stay together for at least a further 2 months, and adults often accompanied in roost-hole by a third individual (presumably from previous brood) until next breeding attempt.
Movements. Resident.
Status and Conservation. Not globally threatened. No details available on population sizes. Species is considered common in Surinam, and probably also common in rest of range.
Bibliography. Haverschmidt (1951), Haverschmidt & Mees (1994), Meyer de Schauensee (1982), Motta-Júnior (1990), Olrog (1968), Rodner *et al.* (2000), Snyder (1966), Stotz *et al.* (1996), Tostain *et al.* (1992), Wheatley (1994), Willis & Oniki (1990).

13. Spotted Piculet

Picumnus pygmaeus

French: Picumne ocellé   **German**: Fleckenzwergspecht   **Spanish**: Carpinterito Ocelado

Taxonomy. *Picus pygmaeus* M. H. K. Lichtenstein, 1823, Brazil = Bahia.
Monotypic.
Distribution. E Brazil, from C Maranhão and Piauí E to Pernambuco, and S to NE Goiás and extreme N Minas Gerais.

Descriptive notes. 10 cm. Distinctive with dark plumage spotted with white. Male has top of head black, forecrown with broad red feather tips forming solid patch, rest of crown and nape spotted white; buff-white lores, often white crescent above eye, dark brown cheeks and ear-coverts variably spotted white; moustachial region and neck sides broadly barred white; dark brown upperparts with prominent black-based whitish tips on mantle, scapulars and back, rump paler; wing-coverts edged paler, broadly tipped white; flight-feathers darker brown, secondaries and tertials broadly edged and tipped light buff or cinnamon-buff; uppertail blackish, central feather pair with broad white stripe along inner webs, outer 2 pairs with white subterminal area; chin and throat variable, black with large white spots or mainly white with black scale-like markings; rest of underparts darkish brown to medium or light brown, usually tinged rufous, often paler on belly, with large white spots each with contrasting black mark at base and tip, spots usually larger on flanks; underwing pale brownish, coverts whitish; undertail as uppertail, but paler; bill short, culmen very slightly curved, black with blue-grey base; iris deep brown; legs grey. Female lacks red on head. Juvenile is duller, more diffusely patterned, markings below tending towards bars. VOICE. Distinctive, very high-pitched, squeaky "tsirrrrr, tsi, tsi, tsi".
Habitat. Dry and open woodland and dense shrubs (*caatinga*), at up to 750 m.
Food and Feeding. No information available.
Breeding. No definite information. Season possibly Nov-Feb, possibly also Jul.
Movements. Presumably resident.
Status and Conservation. Not globally threatened. A poorly known species. No information on numbers. Probably uncommon, or overlooked.
Bibliography. Meyer de Schauensee (1982), Olrog (1968), Pinto & Camargo (1961), Ruschi (1979), Sargeant & Wall (1996), Sick (1993), Stotz *et al.* (1996), Tobias *et al.* (1993), Wheatley (1994), Willis (1992).

14. Speckle-chested Piculet

Picumnus steindachneri

French: Picumne perlé   **German**: Perlenbrust-Zwergspecht   **Spanish**: Carpinterito Perlado

Taxonomy. *Picumnus steindachneri* Taczanowski, 1882, Chirimoto, Peru.
Monotypic.
Distribution. Andes of NW Peru in SE Amazonas and NW San Martín (region of R Huallaga and its tributaries).

Descriptive notes. 10 cm; 9-11 g. Very distinctive piculet. Male has top of head black, feathers of forecrown broadly tipped red, rest of crown and hindneck spotted white; creamy lores and nasal tufts; sides of head and neck white with black bars; grey-brown upperparts with obscure paler greyish feather fringes and darker submarginal borders, producing slightly scalloped pattern; brown wings and wing-coverts edged and tipped pale grey to off-white, edges broadest on secondaries and tertials; uppertail blackish, central feather pair with white stripe along inner webs, outer 2 pairs with white subterminal area; white chin and throat with narrow black fringes; black breast with large drop-shaped white spots, white belly to undertail-

---

coverts broadly barred black; underwing pale brown, coverts white; bill short, almost straight, black, with blue-grey base and most of lower mandible; iris brown; legs grey. Female lacks red on crown. Juvenile not described; presumably duller and less clearly patterned than adults. VOICE. High-pitched trill, lasting several seconds; fledged young beg noisily.
Habitat. Inhabits humid tropical and subtropical montane forest with many epiphytes and tall second growth; observed also in newer second growth (2·5 m tall) in cultivated terrain, and in bamboo stands mixed with other plants. Mainly found between 1150 m and 1800 m, but regularly up to c. 2300 m, and locally perhaps up to 2500 m; occasionally occurs at lower altitudes, down to c. 900 m.
Food and Feeding. No data available on diet. Forages singly, in pairs or in small family groups; also joins mixed-species flocks, moving with them through canopy and second growth. Forages low down in dense shrubbery, and to 10-12 m up at the end of thin twigs and on vines; hammers loudly.
Breeding. No information available.
Movements. Resident.
Status and Conservation. VULNERABLE. Restricted-range species: present in Ecuador-Peru East Andes EBA. Tiny range covers c. 7000 km², within which it has been recorded at no more than 5 localities, and is probably extinct at one of those (Mendoza, in SE Amazonas). No accurate data on numbers; population estimated at fewer than 10,000 individuals, and declining. Occurs in Alto Mayo Protected Forest, where locally quite common, e.g. at Abra Patricia. Primary threat is habitat loss and degradation: logging has occurred in area since at least 1930; deforestation for coca plantations a threat in 1980's, but commercial production seems now to have ceased. Continuing increase in human population and incursion has led to heavy disturbance of forest, including both clear-cutting and selective logging, and in SE of species' range forest is now confined to highest slopes; large areas have been converted to agriculture, especially coffee plantations, and pastures; even in Alto Mayo Protected Forest, designated in 1986 to protect R Alto Mayo watershed for agricultural sustainability, forest clearance has continued unchecked. Media interviews and discussions with local leaders have been utilized to inform people of urgent need to protect region's forests. Co-operation with local agricultural bodies recommended as a further tool to promote conservation. In addition, surveys are needed in order to establish this species' true population size and ecological requirements, as well as its precise distribution.
Bibliography. Begazo *et al.* (2001), Clements & Shany (2001), Collar *et al.* (1994), Hornbuckle (1999), Meyer de Schauensee (1982), Olrog (1968), Parker *et al.* (1982), Stattersfield & Capper (2000), Stattersfield *et al.* (1998), Stotz *et al.* (1996), Wheatley (1994).

15. Varzea Piculet

Picumnus varzeae

French: Picumne des varzéas **German**: Varzeazwergspecht **Spanish**: Carpinterito de las Várzeas

Taxonomy. *Picumnus varzeae* Snethlage, 1912, Fazenda Paraiso, near Faro, Pará, Brazil.
Apparently hybridizes occasionally with *P. cirratus*. Monotypic.
Distribution. Amazonian Brazil, between lower R Madeira in E Amazonas and Obidos in extreme NW Pará, including the river islands.

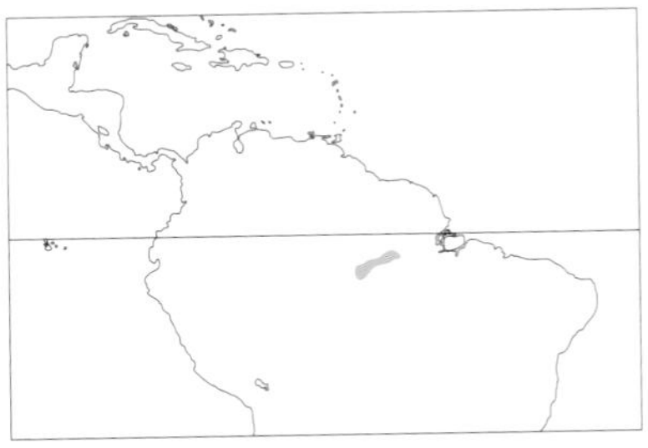

Descriptive notes. 8-9 cm. Male has black forehead and crown, all but lowermost forehead with broad red feather tips forming solid patch; hindcrown and nape black, spotted white; white lores speckled black; sides of head and neck dark brown, feathers tipped black and obscurely vermiculated or spotted whitish; hindneck and upperparts dark olive-brown to greenish-brown, sometimes with a few faint black bars; dark brown upperwing and wing-coverts narrowly edged and tipped paler, edges broader and brighter on secondaries and tertials; uppertail dark brown, central feather pair with white stripe along inner webs, outer 2 pairs with narrow white subterminal area; chin and throat black-brown, finely spotted or barred white; rest of underparts variable in colour and markings, generally brown or greenish-brown with rows of broadly white-tipped black feathers; underwing pale brownish, coverts barred white; bill short, culmen slightly curved, black with blue-grey base, sometimes dull yellowish base of lower mandible; iris brown; legs grey. Female has entire top of head black with white spots. Juvenile more barred below. VOICE. Not documented.
Habitat. Lowland *várzea* with dense undergrowth.
Food and Feeding. No information.
Breeding. Season possibly Jun-Dec. No other information.
Movements. Presumably resident.
Status and Conservation. Not globally threatened. Restricted-range species: present in Amazon Flooded Forests EBA. Little-known species. No information available on numbers or on relative densities. Small range may suggest a rather small total population, but no known threats currently exist. Data required on this species' ecology and breeding biology.
Bibliography. Meyer de Schauensee (1982), Olrog (1968), Ruschi (1979), Sick (1993), Stattersfield *et al.* (1998), Stotz *et al.* (1996), Wheatley (1994).

16. White-barred Piculet

Picumnus cirratus

French: Picumne frangé **German**: Zebrazwergspecht **Spanish**: Carpinterito Variable
Other common names: Pilcomayo Piculet (SW races)

Taxonomy. *Picumnus cirratus* Temminck, 1825, Brazil and Paraguay.
Forms a superspecies with *P. dorbignyanus* and *P. temminckii*, and sometimes treated as conspecific with one or the other, or both; hybridizes frequently with latter in SE Brazil (São Paulo and Paraná), also occasionally with former in Bolivia. Also interbreeds to limited extent with *P. albosquamatus* and apparently with *P. varzeae*. SW races *thamnophiloides*, *tucumanus* and *pilcomayensis* intergrade in N Argentina, and sometimes considered together to form a separate species, but last of those also intergrades with nominate race in E Paraguay. Also, N races *confusus* and *macconnelli* possibly form a distinct species. Further study needed to clarify relationships of this entire complex of taxa. Six subspecies currently recognized.
Subspecies and Distribution.
P. c. confusus Kinnear, 1927 - SW Guyana, extreme N Brazil (E Roraima) and French Guiana.
P. c. macconnelli Sharpe, 1901 - E Amazon region of NE Brazil (W to lower R Tapajós).
P. c. thamnophiloides Bond & Meyer de Schauensee, 1942 - SE Bolivia (Chuquisaca) S along Andes to NW Argentina (N Salta).
P. c. tucumanus Hartert, 1909 - N Argentina (W Salta S to La Rioja).
P. c. pilcomayensis Hargitt, 1891 - SE Bolivia (S Santa Cruz, E Tarija) and Paraguay S to N Argentina (S to Santiago del Estero, N Buenos Aires and N Corrientes).
P. c. cirratus Temminck, 1825 - SE Brazil (from N Minas Gerais and Espírito Santo S to Paraná), S Mato Grosso and E Paraguay.

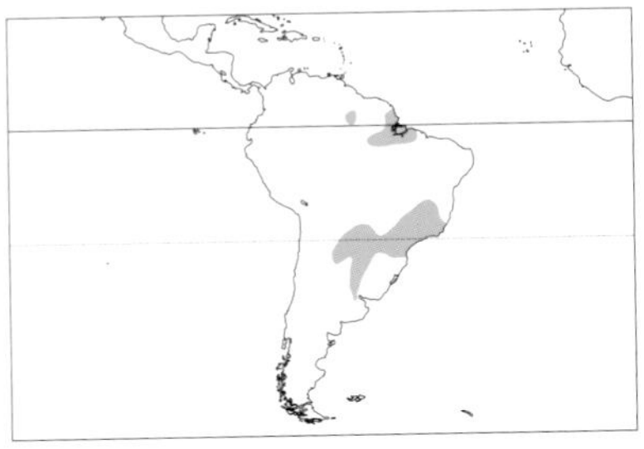

Descriptive notes. 10 cm; 6·8-12 g. Male has black forehead to nape, crown feathers with broad red tips often forming fairly solid patch, remainder spotted white; white to buffish nasal tufts; dark buff-brown cheeks and ear-coverts faintly barred blackish, bordered above by white stripe behind eye; buff moustachial area and neck sides barred blackish; dull brownish upperparts sometimes faintly barred, brown wing-coverts narrowly edged buffish; flight-feathers dark brown, secondaries and tertials edged buffish-white; uppertail dark brown, central feather pair with white stripe along inner webs, outer 2 or 3 pairs with diagonal white subterminal area; chin and throat white to pale buff, barred blackish; rest of underparts white, belly and flanks tinged buff, all fully barred black; underwing pale brown, coverts paler; bill fairly short, culmen slightly curved, black with distinctly paler base of lower mandible; iris dark chestnut-brown, orbital skin blue-grey; legs grey. Differs from *P. dorbignyanus* in browner upperparts, barred rather than scaly underparts; from *P. temminckii* in lack of cinnamon-buff tones above and below. Female lacks red tips on crown feathers. Juvenile duller and darker, lacks white crown spots, tends to show more obvious barring above and heavier barring below. Race *confusus* has darker ear-coverts lacking white upper border, brown upperparts with pale mantle bars, very narrow pale wing edgings, well-barred throat; *macconnelli* is similar above but unbarred, has deep brown ear-coverts sometimes white-spotted, heavier broader bars on moustachial area, throat and breast; *thamnophiloides* is greyish above, less marked below, throat and upper breast with few dark bars, flanks with variable arrowheads or Y-marks, belly almost plain; *tucumanus* has grey-brown upperparts more distinctly barred, buffier throat and breast more obscurely barred, more widely spaced black bars below, male has red restricted to forecrown, often reduced white crown spots; *pilcomayensis* is also greyish above, has narrower black and white barring below, barring sometimes broken, male has reduced red on crown. VOICE. High descending or long and wavering "tsirrrr" used apparently for long-range communication; also "tsirit, tsick"; drums a loud staccato on small dead stub.
Habitat. Frequents tall bushes and gallery forest of savannas, as well as open woodland and edges, transitional forest and scrub. Present from lowlands up into mountains, occurring at up to 2100 m.
Food and Feeding. Small insects, including ants; also insect larvae and eggs, especially of wood-boring beetles; possibly also sap, obtained by wounding the tip of a twig. Generally hunts singly, sometimes with mixed-species flocks; rather tame. Forages at low and middle heights, mainly in undergrowth. Seen mostly at tips of branches and on twigs, often clinging to the underside; also gathers food from vines, small trees and bamboo. Main feeding technique is vigorous and audible hammering, whereby it excavates small holes in the substrate. Actions typical of piculets; sometimes moves downwards like a nuthatch (*Sitta*). Flies considerable distances between foraging sites.
Breeding. Jul-Dec in N, Sept-Mar in S. Nest-hole excavated by both sexes, at varying height but often low down, in slender stub or narrow stem, but also recorded in broader trunk 22·5 cm wide; circular or oval entrance with dimensions 2-3·7 cm, long hole 10-20 cm deep, internal diameter 5-6·3 cm. Launches pecking attacks on opponents, but without hitting. Clutch 2-4 eggs; no information on incubation and fledging periods.
Movements. Probably resident.
Status and Conservation. Not globally threatened. Fairly common locally; locally common in Argentina; probably common in some places, but no detailed data on numbers or densities. Occurs in Itatiaia National Park, Serra do Cipo National Park, Rio Doce State Park, Nova Lombardia Biological Reserve and Sooretama Biological Reserve, in Brazil; in El Rey National Park and Calilegua National Park in Argentina; and in Ybicuí National Park in Paraguay. No known threats to population as a whole; locally threatened by continuing deterioration of remnant forest habitat, e.g. in N Buenos Aires (Argentina).
Bibliography. Alves *et al.* (1997), dos Anjos & Schuchmann (1997), Belton (1984), Bodrati *et al*, (2001), Brooks *et al.* (1993), Buzzetti (2000), Canevari *et al.* (1991), Capper *et al.* (2000), Contreras (1983), Contreras *et al.* (1990), Dubs (1992), Ferreira de Vasconcelos & Melo-Júnior (2001), Figueiredo & Lo (2000), Figueiredo *et al.* (2000), Fjeldså & Mayer (1996), Friedmann (1927), Giraudo *et al.* (1993), Goerck (1999), Hayes (1995), López (1997), Maldonado-Coelho & Marini (2000), Melo-Júnior (2001a), Parker & Goerck (1997), de la Peña (1994), Remsen & Traylor (1989), do Rosário (1996), Schmitt *et al.* (1997), Scott & Brooke (1985), Short (1975), Sick (1993), da Silva *et al.* (1997), Silveira (1998), Snyder (1966), Stotz *et al.* (1996), Tobias *et al.* (1993), Tostain *et al.* (1992), Wetmore (1926).

17. Ocellated Piculet

Picumnus dorbignyanus

French: Picumne d'Orbigny **German**: Orbignyzwergspecht **Spanish**: Carpinterito Boliviano

Taxonomy. *Picumnus d'Orbignyanus* Lafresnaye, 1845; no locality = Bolivia.
Forms a superspecies with *P. cirratus* and *P. temminckii*, and sometimes treated as conspecific with former, or with both. Interbreeds with former and with *P. albosquamatus*. Apparently as the result of a perpetuated error, species name has almost universally been misspelt "*dorbygnianus*", but in original description scientific name incorporated d'Orbigny's name correctly spelt, so rectification is required. Two subspecies recognized.
Subspecies and Distribution.
P. d. jelskii Taczanowski, 1882 - Andes of E Peru.
P. d. dorbignyanus Lafresnaye, 1845 - C Bolivia (La Paz, Cochabamba, W Santa Cruz) and extreme NW Argentina (Jujuy, Salta).
Descriptive notes. 10 cm. Relatively pale-looking. Male has top of head black, crown feathers tipped red, hindcrown and nape spotted white; buffish-white lores and nasal tufts; buff-brown cheeks and ear-coverts streaked whitish, bordered above by short white stripe behind eye; buffy-white neck sides with darker streaking; hindneck pale grey-brown; upperparts grey-brown, usually some

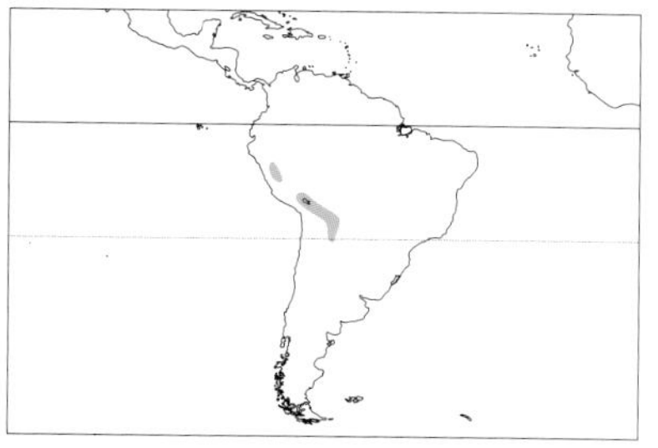

feathers with pale tip and blackish subterminal bar, wing-coverts narrowly edged paler; dark brown flight-feathers prominently edged and tipped buffish-white; uppertail blackish, central feather pair with broad white stripe on inner webs, outer 2 pairs with diagonal white subterminal area; malar, chin and throat whitish, faintly buff-tinged, with dark feather edges sometimes giving throat scaly appearance; rest of underparts white, belly buffish, breast and flank feathers with black centres or shaft streaks and thin dark edges, belly unmarked or with some faint narrow bars; underwing pale grey-brown, coverts whitish; bill fairly short, culmen barely curved, black with grey base; iris brown, orbital skin greyish; legs greyish. Female lacks red feather tips on crown. Juvenile duller and slightly darker than adult, diffusely barred above and below. Race *jelskii* has shorter tail than nominate, markings below generally more restricted to broad black shaft streaks on breast, finer streaking on flanks, fewer dark spots on belly. VOICE. High-pitched trill, similar to that of *P. cirratus*.

Habitat. Humid tropical and subtropical montane and submontane forest with many epiphytes; also tall bushes in transitional forest in Argentina. Between 900 m and 2500 m; 1100-2200 m in Peru.

Food and Feeding. No details available on diet. Usually observed singly or in pairs; often accompanies mixed-species flocks. Commonly hangs upside-down on twigs and branches like a nuthatch (*Sitta*).

Breeding. No definite information; probably breeds before Dec.

Movements. Presumably resident; possibly some vertical movements.

Status and Conservation. Not globally threatened. Uncommon and local in Peru, but quite common in some places (e.g. between Aguas Calientes and Mandor Valley); probably uncommon to rare in rest of range. Occurs in Machu Picchu Historical Sanctuary in Peru.

Bibliography. Blendinger (1998), Canevari *et al.* (1991), Chebez (1994), Chebez *et al.* (1999), Clements & Shany (2001), Fjeldså & Mayer (1996), Mazar Barnett & Pearman (2001), Narosky & Yzurieta (1993), Olrog (1958), Parker *et al.* (1982), Schmitt *et al.* (1997), Short (1975), Stotz *et al.* (1996), Walker (2001), Wheatley (1994), Zimmer (1930).

18. Ochre-collared Piculet

Picumnus temminckii

French: Picumne de Temminck **Spanish**: Carpinterito Cuellicanela
German: Temminckzwergspecht

Taxonomy. *Picumnus Temminckii* Lafresnaye, 1845, Paraguay.
Forms a superspecies with *P. cirratus* and *P. dorbignyanus*, and sometimes treated as conspecific with former, or alternatively with both. Hybridizes frequently with nominate race of former, producing many intermediate individuals; also occasionally interbreeds with race *guttifer* of *P. albosquamatus*. Monotypic.

Distribution. E Paraguay, NE Argentina (Misiones) and SE Brazil (São Paulo S to Rio Grande do Sul).

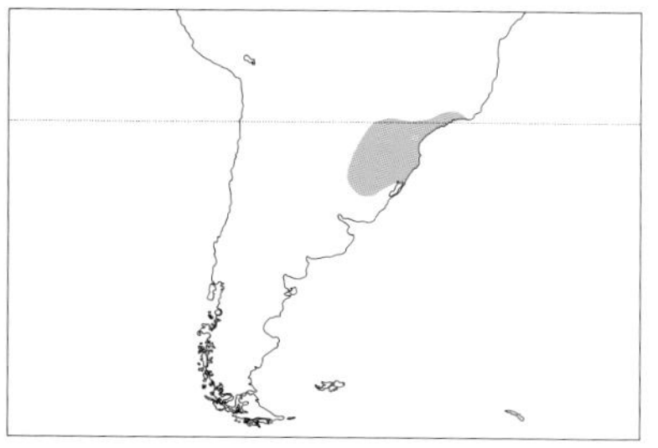

Descriptive notes. 9-10 cm; 10-12·5 g. Male has top of head black, feathers of forecrown tipped red, hindcrown and nape finely spotted white; buff-white lower forehead, lores and nasal tufts; rich buff-brown cheeks and ear-coverts bordered above by bright buff-white or white line behind eye; broad cinnamon-buff hindneck-collar, often brighter at junction with nape; brown upperparts plain or very faintly barred paler, brown wing-coverts edged buff; flight-feathers dark brown, narrowly edged buff; uppertail blackish, central feather pair with white stripe on inner webs, outer 2 pairs with diagonal white subterminal area; malar, chin and throat pale buffish-white, feathers narrowly tipped blackish; rest of underparts whitish, becoming strongly buff on flanks and lower belly, all with bold but rather narrow black bars; underwing light brown, coverts whitish; bill short, culmen slightly curved, black with greyish base; iris brown, orbital skin greyish; legs greyish. Female lacks red on crown. Juvenile darker and duller than adult, heavier but more diffuse barring below. VOICE. High-pitched whistle, "tsirrrr, si-si-si..."; drums loudly in short bursts of strokes, similar to drumming of *P. nebulosus* but slower.

Habitat. Inhabits tall scrub and *tacuarales* of humid forest, and forest edge.

Food and Feeding. Very little known. Diet includes ants (*Myrmelachista*) and insect larvae. Forages at low levels, usually on slender stalks, also on thin, hollow branches.

Breeding. No definite data; presumably nests in Oct-Mar.

Movements. Apparently resident.

Status and Conservation. Not globally threatened. No data available on numbers; fairly common, at least locally, e.g. at Urugua-i Provincial Park in Misiones (N Argentina). Occurs in neighbouring Iguaçú and Iguazú National Parks (Brazil/Argentina).

Bibliography. Aleixo & Galetti (1997), dos Anjos (2001), dos Anjos & Schuchmann (1997), dos Anjos *et al.* (1997), Belton (1984), Bencke & Kindel (1999), Canevari *et al.* (1991), Guix *et al.* (1992), Hayes (1995), Hinkelmann & Fiebig (2001), Krügel & dos Anjos (2000), Lencioni-Neto (1995), Lowen *et al.* (1995), Madroño, Clay, Robbins *et al.* (1997), Mazar Barnett & Pearman (2001), Mendonça-Lima *et al.* (2001), Narosky & Yzurieta (1993), Parker & Goerck (1997), de la Peña (1994), Ruschi (1979), Saibene *et al.* (1996), Sick (1993), Soares & dos Anjos (1999), Stotz *et al.* (1996), Tobias *et al.* (1993).

19. White-wedged Piculet

Picumnus albosquamatus

French: Picumne noir et blanc **Spanish**: Carpinterito Albiescamoso
German: Weißschuppen-Zwergspecht
Other common names: Guttate Piculet (*guttifer*); Blackish Piculet ("*P. asterias*")

Taxonomy. *Picumnus albosquamatus* d'Orbigny, 1840, Río Tamanipaya, Yungas, Bolivia.
Hybridizes with *P. dorbignyanus*, also to limited extent with *P. cirratus*, and occasionally with *P. temminckii*. Race *guttifer* formerly considered a separate species, but appears to intergrade with nominate in W Mato Grosso; these mixed populations probably account for the form previously listed as race *P. a. corumbanus*. Forms described as species "*P. asterias*", known only from single type specimen, and "*P. sagittatus*" are indistinguishable from variable race *guttifer*, and are thus synonymized with it. Two subspecies currently recognized.

Subspecies and Distribution.
P. a. guttifer Sundevall, 1866 - E & C Brazil, from S Pará and S Maranhão S to S & E Mato Grosso and W São Paulo.
P. a. albosquamatus d'Orbigny, 1840 - NC & E Bolivia and SW Brazil (in SW Mato Grosso), and adjacent N Paraguay.

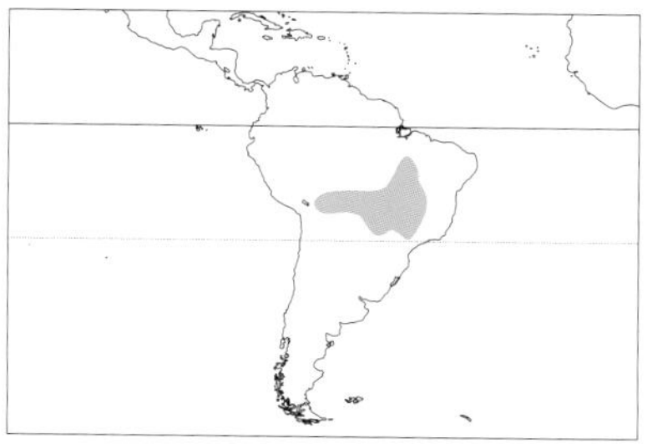

Descriptive notes. 10-11 cm; 9-11 g. Male has top of head black, forecrown feathers broadly tipped red, hindcrown and crown sides to nape finely spotted white; buffish-white nasal tufts and lores bordered by black line across lower forehead; whitish side of head to hindneck strongly tinged brown, with black feather margins, white line behind eye; upperparts warm brown to greyish-brown, often some feathers with variable pale tips; brown wing-coverts broadly pale-edged; flight-feathers dark brown, secondaries and tertials with broad buffish-white edges on outer webs; uppertail dark brown, central feather pair with broad white stripe on inner webs, outer 2 pairs with broad diagonal white subterminal area; white malar, chin and throat with black borders to feathers, appearing scaly; rest of underparts whitish, variably washed pale buff, breast with narrow black feather borders giving scalloped effect, flanks almost unmarked or with subterminal black wedges, belly plain or slightly streaked; underwing pale brown, coverts whitish; longish bill pointed, culmen barely curved, blackish with paler base of lower mandible; iris brown, orbital skin greyish; legs grey to green-grey. Female lacks red on head. Juvenile duller, less contrastingly patterned than adults, more barred appearance. Race *guttifer* is bigger than nominate, with plumage variable: typically darker, has more contrasting dark brown ear-coverts, distinct pale spots on wing-covert tips, often more black-centred pale-edged feathers above, black shaft streaks and broader black feather borders on throat and breast (can appear largely black), warm buff lower underparts with broad black wedges, male with more red on crown. VOICE. Descending "si-si-si...".

Habitat. Occupies denser parts of open, moderately dry savanna woodland (*cerrado*), and also gallery forest. Present in lowlands and foothills, locally occurring up to 2100 m.

Food and Feeding. No information.

Breeding. Juveniles collected from end May to Dec in Bolivia, and Jun-Dec in Mato Grosso. One nest-hole c. 3 cm wide being excavated 1·5 m up in fence post in Sept, Pantanal. No further information.

Movements. Presumably resident.

Status and Conservation. Not globally threatened. No precise data on population sizes, but locally not uncommon in N Pantanal, around Poconé. Occurs in Brasília, Pantanal do Mato Grosso and Chapada dos Guimarães National Parks (Brazil).

Bibliography. Aleixo (1997), dos Anjos (2001), Brace *et al.* (1997), Cândido (2000), Contreras *et al.* (1993), Dubs (1992), Hayes (1995), Lencioni-Neto (1995), Marini *et al.* (1997), Meyer de Schauensee (1982), Olrog (1968), Oniki & Willis (1999), Perry *et al.* (1997), Piratelli *et al.* (2000), Ruschi (1979), Sick (1993), da Silva (1996), Stager (1961a), Stotz *et al.* (1996), Tubelis & Tomás (1999), Willis & Oniki (1991).

20. Rusty-necked Piculet

Picumnus fuscus

French: Picumne à nuque rousse **Spanish**: Carpinterito Cuellirrufo
German: Rostnacken-Zwergspecht
Other common names: Natterer's Piculet

Taxonomy. *Picumnus fuscus* Pelzeln, 1870, Rio Guaporé, Mato Grosso, Brazil.
Although generally considered to be related to the "*P. cirratus* complex" or to *P. rufiventris*, may possibly be closer to *P. aurifrons* or *P. exilis*. Monotypic.

Distribution. R Guaporé drainage in NE Bolivia (Beni) and WC Brazil (extreme W Mato Grosso).

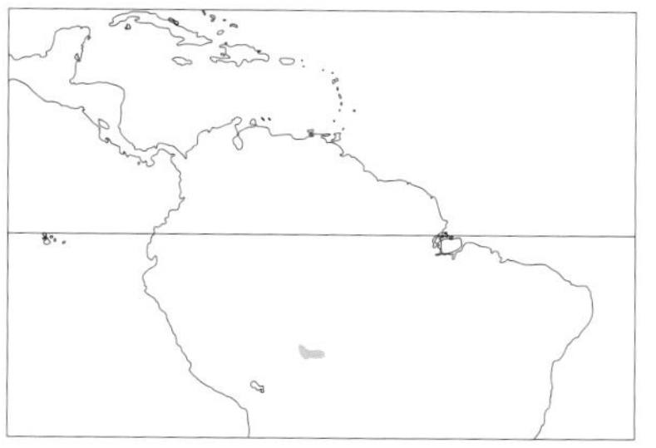

Descriptive notes. 10 cm. Distinctive piculet with unique head pattern. Male has top of head blackish, feathers of hindcrown broadly tipped reddish-orange; buffish lores, sides of lower forehead and nasal tufts; buffish-brown cheeks and ear-coverts tinged rufous, broken pale stripe behind eye; hindneck and neck side rusty-buff to buff-brown; upperparts brown to brownish-green, scapulars often tinged rufous; upperwing dark brown, wing-coverts with paler borders, secondaries and tertials edged yellowish-buff; uppertail dark brown, central feather pair with broad white stripe on inner webs, outer 2 pairs with narrower diagonal white bar; buff malar region usually faintly dark-barred, buff-brown chin and throat occasionally with trace of fine barring; rest of underparts pale buffish, breast sides and flanks tinged cinnamon or light rusty, either unmarked or with faint vestigial barring on flanks and, occasionally, breast and belly; underwing pale brown, coverts rufous-buff; bill short, culmen slightly curved, black with paler base; iris brown, orbital skin greyish; legs greyish-brown. Female lacks reddish feather tips on head. Juvenile apparently undescribed. VOICE. Not documented.

Habitat. Lowland riverine forest (*várzea*).

Food and Feeding. Not documented.

Breeding. No information.

Movements. Presumably resident.

Status and Conservation. Not globally threatened. Currently considered Near-threatened. No details on numbers; possibly not uncommon, but is restricted to a particular habitat type (*várzea*) within a very small range. Occurs in Noel Kempff Mercado National Park in Bolivia. Appears to be reasonably secure, but increasing human settlement along the currently largely uninhabited banks of the R Guaporé could become a threat. Little is known of the species' ecology and breeding biology; research required.

Bibliography. Dubs (1992), Mazar Barnett & Kirwan (2000), Parker & Rocha (1991), Remsen & Traylor (1989), Ruschi (1979), Sick (1993), Stattersfield & Capper (2000), Stattersfield *et al.* (1998), Stotz *et al.* (1996), Wheatley (1994).

21. Rufous-breasted Piculet

Picumnus rufiventris

French: Picumne à ventre roux   **Spanish**: Carpinterito Ventrirrufo
German: Rotbauch-Zwergspecht

Taxonomy. *Asthenurus rufiventris* Bonaparte, 1838, western Brazil near border with Peru.
Three subspecies recognized.

Subspecies and Distribution.

P. r. rufiventris (Bonaparte, 1838) - E slope of Andes from C & S Colombia (N Meta S to SE Nariño, Putumayo and Amazonas) to E Ecuador, NE Peru and W Amazonian Brazil.

P. r. grandis Carriker, 1930 - CE Peru (W to Huánuco and Junín) and neighbouring SW Amazonian Brazil.

P. r. brunneifrons Stager, 1968 - NW & C Bolivia (Pando, Beni, Cochabamba).

Descriptive notes. 9-11 cm; 12-16 g, 21 g (*grandis*). Male has black forehead to nape, crown feathers tipped red, rest spotted white to buff, most prominently on nape; white lores and nasal tufts variably tipped black; rest of head and hindneck rufous to cinnamon-rufous, ear-coverts often darker; dark green upperparts usually tinged rufous, especially on rump; dark brown upperwing, wing-coverts edged and tipped greenish, secondaries and tertials edged cinnamon on inner webs and rusty on outer webs and tips; uppertail dark brown, central feather pair with pale cinnamon stripe on inner webs, outer 2 pairs with cinnamon stripe on outer webs; entire underparts plain rufous; underwing brown, coverts rufous; bill comparatively long, straight, blackish with slightly paler base of lower mandible; iris brown, orbital skin greyish-blue; legs grey. Differs from similar *P. cinnamomeus* in dark forehead, red (not yellow) on crown, darker orbital ring, greener upperparts. Female has entire top of head spotted white. Juvenile is grey-tinged above, less rufous on hindneck,

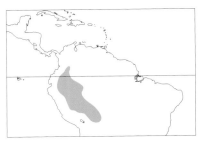

has breast and flanks grey, belly sometimes grey-barred. Race *grandis* is bigger than nominate, has upperparts tinged yellowish, underparts paler, black cap ending higher on nape, male with more red on crown; *brunneifrons* is intermediate in size, has plumage similar to previous but darker, upperparts with stronger rufous-chestnut suffusion. VOICE. Quiet; occasional high thin "tseeyt-tseeyt-tsit", notes dropping in pitch.

Habitat. Humid forest in thick understorey of forest edge, also in second growth, including overgrown clearings, and vegetation along watercourses; also locally in tangled clearings and edges inside *terra firme* and *várzea* forest; typically found in stands of bamboo. Mostly at lower elevations up to 400 m; locally higher, to 900 m, in Peru; in Ecuador mostly below 1100 m, in some places to 1500 m.

Food and Feeding. Diet not documented. Usually occurs singly or in pairs; often in mixed-species flocks. Forages in dense lower strata, 1-7 m above the ground; hops about, taps on dead and live twigs.

Breeding. Season Jan-Mar in Peru and Bolivia, probably later in Ecuador. No other information.

Movements. Presumably resident.

Status and Conservation. Not globally threatened. Fairly common in Colombia; rare to locally uncommon in Peru. Probably overlooked owing to inconspicuous behaviour; may be more common than believed. Occurs in Amacayacu National Park (Colombia); also present in Manu National Park and Tambopata Reserve (Peru).

Bibliography. Angehr & Aucca (1997), Brace *et al.* (1997), Butler (1979), Clements & Shany (2001), Donahue (1994), Guilherme (2001), Hilty & Brown (1986), Kratter (1997), Munn (1985), Norton (1965), Parker *et al.* (1982), Remsen & Traylor (1989), Remsen *et al.* (1986), Ridgely & Greenfield (2001), Ridgely *et al.* (1998), Robinson & Terborgh (1997), Rodner *et al.* (2000), Ruschi (1979), Sick (1993), Stotz *et al.* (1996), Terborgh *et al.* (1984).

PLATE 25 ➤

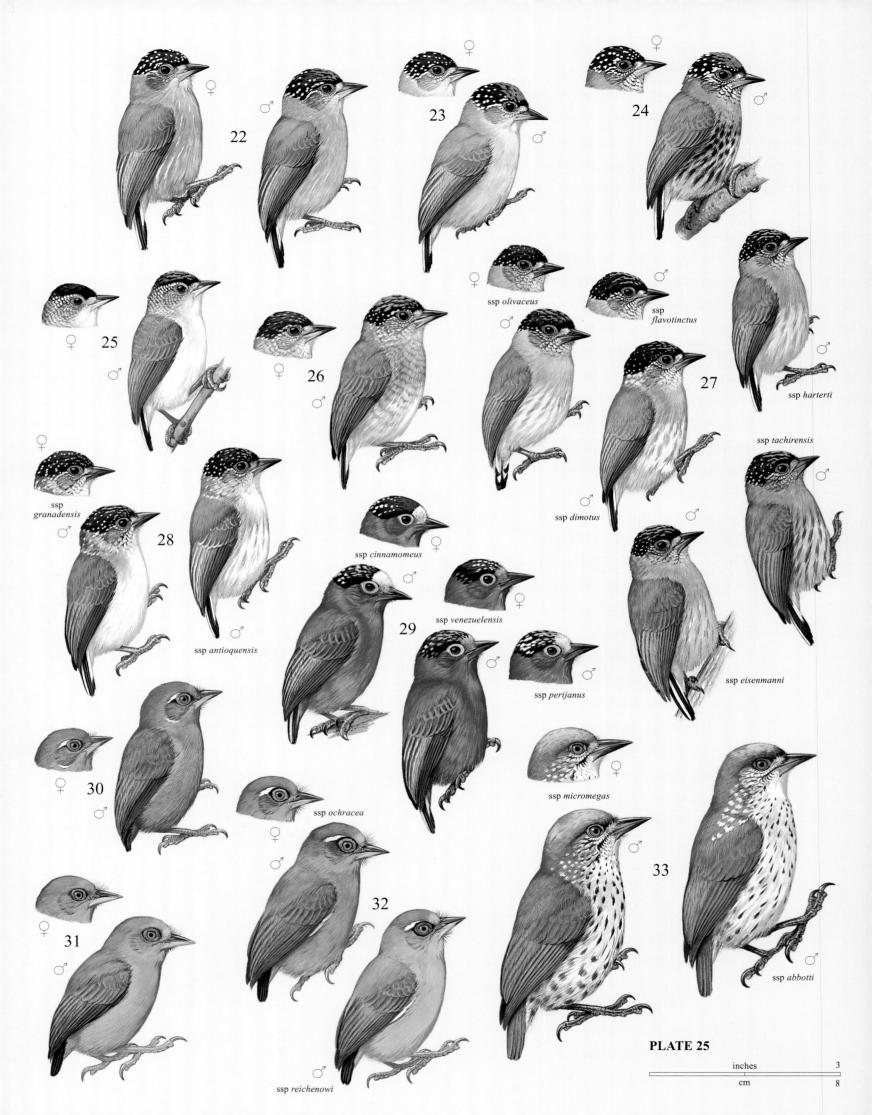

22

23

24

♀

♀

♂

♂

♀

♂

ssp *olivaceus*

ssp *flavotinctus*

♀

25

♂

26

♀

♂

♀

♂

ssp *dimotus*

ssp *harterti*

ssp *tachirensis*

ssp *granadensis*

♂

28

♂

ssp *antioquensis*

ssp *cinnamomeus*

♀

♂

29

ssp *venezuelensis*

♀

♂

ssp *perijanus*

ssp *eisenmanni*

30

♂

♀

ssp *micromegas*

♂

ssp *ochracea*

♀

31

♂

♀

♂

32

♂

33

ssp *abbotti*

PLATE 25

ssp *reichenowi*

♂

inches 3

cm 8

22. Tawny Piculet

Picumnus fulvescens

French: Picumne fauve **German**: Fahlzwergspecht **Spanish**: Carpinterito Canela

Taxonomy. *Picumnus fulvescens* Stager, 1961, Garanhuns, south-eastern Pernambuco, Brazil.
Probably related to *P. limae*, and sometimes even regarded as conspecific, but may perhaps be closer to *P. nebulosus*. Form *saturatus*, described from Paraíba and previously listed as a race of *P. limae*, is now considered a junior synonym of *fulvescens* (see page 302), which has priority by merely one day. Monotypic.
Distribution. NE Brazil, from E Piauí through S Ceará to Paraíba, Pernambuco and Alagoas.

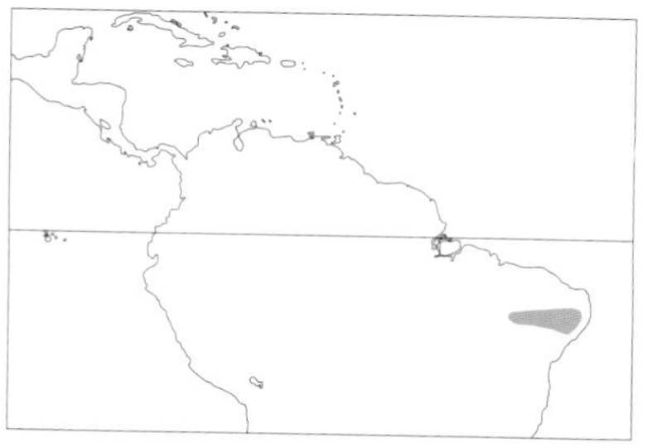

Descriptive notes. 10 cm. Male has top of head black, crown feathers broadly tipped red and forming almost solid patch, rest spotted white; white or buffish-white lores, nasal tufts and upper moustachial region, whitish line behind eye, dark brown ear-coverts obscurely pale-streaked; rusty-buff hindneck and neck sides; upperparts unmarked brown to rufous-brown or tinged yellowish-brown, uppertail-coverts paler, dark brown upperwing and wing-coverts narrowly edged and tipped paler; uppertail brownish-black, central feather pair with broad white stripe on inner webs, outer 2 pairs with diagonal white subterminal area; chin and throat variably whitish to buff or buffish-brown; rest of underparts light yellow-brown to rufous or rusty, breast with indistinct whitish shaft streaks, streaks broader and more cinnamon-toned on flanks and belly; underwing pale brown, coverts yellowish-brown to rusty; bill short, pointed, culmen slightly curved, black with pale grey base; iris dark brown, orbital ring greyish; legs grey. Female has entire top of head spotted white; underparts may be more heavily streaked on average. Juvenile undescribed. Voice. Call a descending series of "driée driée driée...".
Habitat. Inhabits deciduous, semi-deciduous and secondary stands in the Atlantic forest; also found in degraded secondary scrub, and edges; to lesser extent also *caatinga*. Recorded from lowlands up to c. 950 m.
Food and Feeding. No information.
Breeding. Undocumented.
Movements. Presumably resident.
Status and Conservation. VULNERABLE. Restricted-range species: present in North-east Brazilian Caatinga EBA and Atlantic slope of Alagoas and Pernambuco EBA. Scarce. Known range covers only 470 km² in 5 states; has been recorded from no more than 10 localities, and has probably already disappeared from some of those. Most of its habitat in the Atlantic forest has been destroyed, mainly through logging and conversion to commercial plantations and pasture; the little remaining is fragmented, greatly threatened by fires and also subject to continuing exploitation, with new roads being built in 1999. Distribution in *caatinga* little known, but expansion of agriculture, along with burning and grazing, has also destroyed much suitable habitat there. Recorded in five protected areas: at one of these, Pedra Talhada Biological Reserve (Alagoas), reafforestation with indigenous trees has been supported by local inhabitants, and area is patrolled by official guards to prevent illegal activities; other sites with formal protection are Serra da Capivara National Park, Serra Negra Biological Reserve, Tapacurá Ecological Station and Araripe National Forest. Chapada do Araripe, in S Ceará, seems to be another important site for the species. Regular occurrence of species in degraded scrub and edge habitat may indicate potential adaptability. Recommendations include survey work to establish its exact distribution, status and ecology, and effective protection of all sites where it occurs.
Bibliography. Bañuelos-Irusta *et al.* (2000a, 2000b), Collar *et al.* (1994), Forrester (1993), Lima (2001), do Nascimento (2000), do Nascimento *et al.* (2000), Olrog (1968), Pinto & Camargo (1961), Ruschi (1979), Sick (1993), Stager (1961b), Stattersfield & Capper (2000), Stattersfield *et al.* (1998), Stotz *et al.* (1996), Teixeira (1990), Wheatley (1994).

23. Ochraceous Piculet

Picumnus limae

French: Picumne ocré **German**: Ockerzwergspecht **Spanish**: Carpinterito de Ceará

Taxonomy. *Picumnus limae* Snethlage, 1924, Serra de Maranguape, Ceará, Brazil.
Probably related to *P. fulvescens*, and sometimes regarded as conspecific. Form *saturatus*, described from Paraíba and previously listed as a race of present species, is now considered a junior synonym of *P. fulvescens* (see page 302). Monotypic.
Distribution. NC Ceará in NE Brazil.

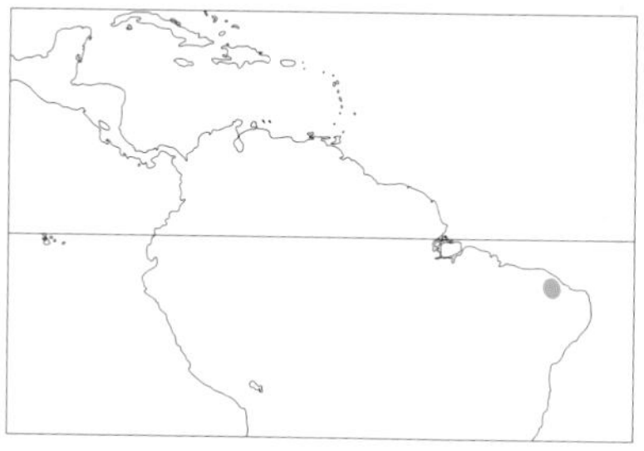

Descriptive notes. 10 cm. Male has top of head black, crown with broad red feather tips forming almost solid patch, rest spotted white; white lores and nasal tufts, white line behind eye, pale rusty-brown ear-coverts; greyish-brown hindneck and upperparts with yellowish-rusty wash, dark brown upperwing and wing-coverts edged and tipped pale to buffish; secondaries and tertials more broadly pale-edged; uppertail dark brown, central feather pair with broad white or buff-white stripe on inner webs, outer 2 pairs with diagonal white subterminal area; neck side, malar, chin and entire underparts white, with buff or pale yellow tinge especially on lower underparts, occasionally faint fine barring in malar and chin region, sometimes very faint trace of bars on belly and flanks; underwing pale brown, coverts whitish; bill short, culmen curved, blackish with greyish-horn base of lower mandible; iris deep brown, orbital skin greyish; legs blue-grey. Female has entire top of head spotted white. Juvenile apparently undescribed. Voice. High-pitched "sirr-sirr-sirr", recalling hummingbird (Trochilidae).
Habitat. Semi-deciduous forest and adjacent tall *caatinga* on hillsides, at up to 1000 m; also forages occasionally in degraded scrub or edge with exotic bamboo and abandoned orchards, but this thought probably unusual.
Food and Feeding. No information.
Breeding. No details known.
Movements. Presumably resident.
Status and Conservation. VULNERABLE. Has tiny range, within which it is known from only three sites: Serra do Ibiapaba, Serra do Baturité and Serra do Arataruai. Fairly common locally, but very few recent records. Potentially suitable habitat has been greatly reduced through agricultural expansion, grazing and burning, with forest virtually completely destroyed in some areas; in Serra do Baturité, for example, clearance for coffee plantations since early 1970's has resulted in loss of 99% of original forest habitat. Remaining habitat is also under threat from construction of holiday homes, as well as fires. A protected area was established in the Serra do Baturité in 1991, but whether this has led to surviving forest being preserved is unclear; some areas of habitat are protected by hotel-owners in the region. Preferred habitats are not typical of the *caatinga* dry zone inhabited by this species, suggesting that it is dependent on specific habitat types. Investigation of the species' precise distribution, status, habitat requirements and general ecology is urgently needed, together with full protection of all sites where it is found.
Bibliography. Collar *et al.* (1994), Lima (2001), Meyer de Schauensee (1982), Pinto & Camargo (1961), Ruschi (1979), Sargeant & Wall (1996), Sick (1993), Stattersfield & Capper (2000), Stattersfield *et al.* (1998), Stotz *et al.* (1996), Teixeira (1990), Wheatley (1994), Willis (1992).

24. Mottled Piculet

Picumnus nebulosus

French: Picumne strié **German**: Braunbrust-Zwergspecht **Spanish**: Carpinterito Uruguayo

Taxonomy. *Picumnus nebulosus* Sundevall, 1866, southern Brazil.
Possibly related to *P. fulvescens*. Monotypic.
Distribution. SE Brazil (Paraná S to Rio Grande do Sul), marginally NE Argentina (E Corrientes), and Uruguay (except W & SW).

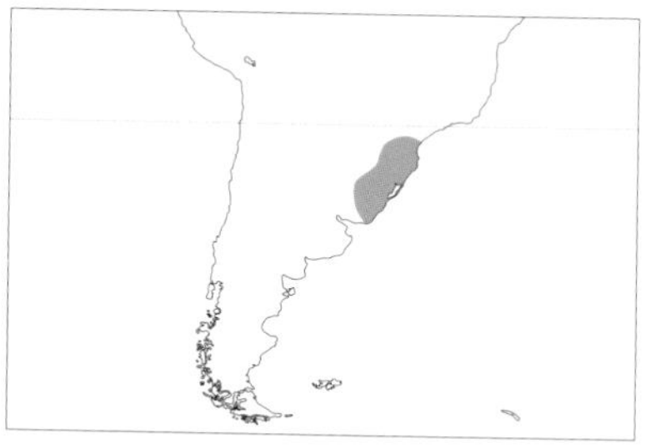

Descriptive notes. 10-11 cm; 11-12 g. Male has black forehead to nape, feathers of upper forehead and crown with broad red tips often forming patch, crown sides and nape tipped white; white lores; rather dark olive-brown cheeks and lower ear-coverts, large but irregular white area on upper ear-coverts; neck side buffy olive-brown; warm olive-brown hindneck and upperparts tinged buff or rusty on back and scapulars; dark brown to blackish upperwing and wing-coverts with broad pale margins, broadest and palest on secondaries and tertials; uppertail black, central feather pair with white stripe on inner webs, outer 3 pairs with white streak on outer webs; malar, chin and throat white, thinly barred black; rusty buffish-brown breast sometimes with faint dark streaks, paler buff belly and usually richer buff flanks, with broad blackish streaks, spots or U-shaped bars from lower breast to flanks; underwing pale brownish, coverts rusty-buff; bill short, straight, slightly chisel-tipped, black with grey base of lower mandible; iris brown, orbital skin greyish; legs grey. Female has entire top of black head spotted white. Juvenile duller than adults, dull brown crown streaked pale buffish. Voice. Humming "tsewrewt, si-si-si"; series of weak single squeaks by juvenile as contact with parent; drums loudly on bamboo, short pauses between bursts of 2-4 strokes, sound resembling that of some frogs (*Strombus*).
Habitat. Inhabits forest, mostly lowland evergreen forest and mixed *Araucaria* forest with dense understorey, also forest edge, gallery woodland; often in areas with bamboo. Occurs from lowlands up to 1100 m; in SE Brazil, recently recorded at 1400 m in Jun in Santa Catarina.
Food and Feeding. Diet not documented. Hunts singly; joins mixed-species flocks. Forages at low levels on slender woody stems, particularly dead bamboo, also in dense scrub, including roadside scrub; also to at least 7-8 m above ground, working along thin branches.
Breeding. Season Oct-Dec. No other information.
Movements. Mainly resident; some altitudinal movements may occur.
Status and Conservation. Not globally threatened. Currently considered Near-threatened. Generally local and uncommon; more common in S part of Brazilian range; very few recent records from Argentina. Occurs in Aparados da Serra National Park in Brazil. Has for many years suffered from habitat loss and degradation, with lowland forest in species' range cleared for agricultural and other purposes, including mining; most serious of current threats are urbanization, industrialization, continuing expansion of agriculture, and human colonization accompanied by further road-building. The few areas of remaining forest known to harbour this species in Argentina would be flooded if proposed Garabí dam is built on the R Uruguay.
Bibliography. dos Anjos (1999), dos Anjos & Schuchmann (1997), dos Anjos *et al.* (1997), Belton (1984), Bencke & Kindel (1999), Canevari *et al.* (1991), Chebez (1994), Chebez *et al.* (1999), Meyer de Schauensee (1982), Naka *et al.* (2000), Narosky & Yzurieta (1993), Olrog (1968), Parker & Goerck (1997), de la Peña (1994), do Rosário (1996), Ruschi (1979), Sick (1993), Stattersfield & Capper (2000), Stotz *et al.* (1996), Tobias *et al.* (1993).

25. Plain-breasted Piculet

Picumnus castelnau

French: Picumne de Castelnau **German**: Gelbbauch-Zwergspecht **Spanish**: Carpinterito Blancuzco

Taxonomy. *Picumnus castelnau* Malherbe, 1862, Sarayacu, Ecuador.
Possibly close to *P. subtilis*, with which may occasionally hybridize. Monotypic.

On following pages: 26. Fine-barred Piculet (*Picumnus subtilis*); 27. Olivaceous Piculet (*Picumnus olivaceus*); 28. Greyish Piculet (*Picumnus granadensis*); 29. Chestnut Piculet (*Picumnus cinnamomeus*); 30. African Piculet (*Sasia africana*); 31. Rufous Piculet (*Sasia abnormis*); 32. White-browed Piculet (*Sasia ochracea*); 33. Antillean Piculet (*Nesoctites micromegas*).

Distribution. SE Colombia (SE Amazonas) and S in E Peru to Pucallpa, on R Ucayali; old specimens supposedly from E Ecuador considered to have originated from elsewhere.

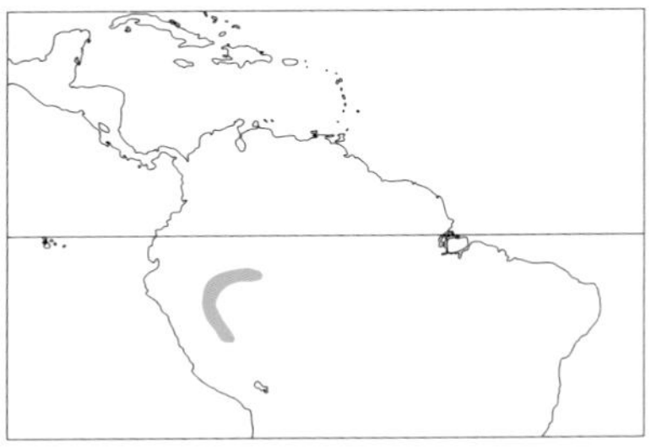

Descriptive notes. 8-9 cm; 11-12 g. Male has black forehead to nape, central crown with broad red feather tips, lower nape finely vermiculated whitish; buffish-white lores and nasal tufts, whitish streak above eye; brown ear-coverts vermiculated grey and whitish; olive-brown rear superciliary area, hindneck and neck sides barred or vermiculated buff-grey; dark greyish-olive upperparts sometimes indistinctly barred paler, wing-coverts edged and tipped yellow-green; dark brown flight-feathers edged paler, tertials more broadly margined brighter yellow; uppertail dark brown, white stripe on inner webs of central feather pair and on outer 3 pairs; moustachial and malar area, chin and throat pale yellowish-white, moustache sometimes faintly barred near bill; rest of underparts white, lightly washed yellowish, breast sides, belly and flanks occasionally with some almost invisible darker bars; underwing grey-brown, coverts white; short bill pointed, culmen curved, black with pale blue-grey to whitish base of lower mandible; iris dark brown, orbital ring buff-grey; legs greyish. Distinguished from *P. subtilis* by redder crown tips, lack of white nape spots, paler unbarred underparts. Female has unmarked black crown. Juvenile like adult female, but duller, with stronger hint of barring above, faint barring below. VOICE. Very high-pitched, thin trill, "té'é'e'e'e'e'e", dropping in pitch and amplitude at end.
Habitat. Swamp-forest, *várzea* forest, and forest edge near water; especially favours well-developed second growth dominated by *Cecropia* and *Mimosa*. Lowlands to 900 m.
Food and Feeding. Diet not recorded. Hunts solitarily or in pairs; regularly joins mixed-species flocks in Peru, more rarely so in Colombia. Forages in lower parts of the canopy and down to understorey; taps on dead branches, often spending lengthy time at favoured spots.
Breeding. Female feeding fledgling in mid-Jun in Colombia; season probably May-Jul. No further details available.
Movements. Presumably resident.
Status and Conservation. Not globally threatened. Comparatively rare overall, though possibly commoner than it appears to be, as it is rather inconspicuous. Generally uncommon and local in Peru, but locally not uncommon near Iquitos, around Explornapo and Explorama Lodges. Occurs in Amacayacu National Park in Colombia.
Bibliography. Butler (1979), Clements & Shany (2001), Hilty & Brown (1986), Meyer de Schauensee (1982), Olrog (1968), Parker *et al.* (1982), Remsen (1977), Ridgely & Greenfield (2001), Rodner *et al.* (2000), Stotz *et al.* (1996), Wheatley (1994).

26. Fine-barred Piculet

Picumnus subtilis

French: Picumne de Cuzco **German**: Cuzcozwergspecht **Spanish**: Carpinterito de Cuzco
Other common names: Marcapata/Stager's Piculet

Taxonomy. *Picumnus subtilis* Stager, 1968, Hacienda Villacarmen, Cuzco, south-eastern Peru.
Possibly close to *P. castelnau*, with which may occasionally hybridize. Monotypic.
Distribution. E Peru, from R Ucayali in Loreto S to Cuzco (Marcapata).

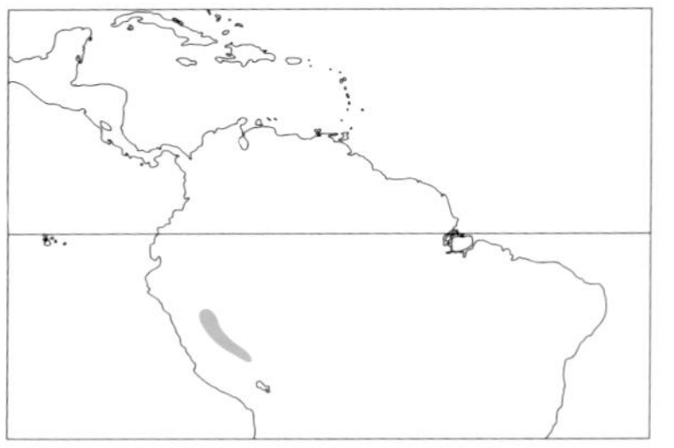

Descriptive notes. 10 cm; 10-11 g. Male has black forehead to nape, feathers of upper forehead and crown tipped orange-red, crown sides and nape spotted white; pale buff-white lores and nasal tufts; brownish-olive ear-coverts barred whitish; pale olive-buff neck sides vermiculated darker; yellowish-green hindneck and upperparts with obscure olive barring, dark olive-brown wing-coverts edged yellow-green; dark brown flight-feathers narrowly margined yellowish-green, outer webs of secondaries with broader pale edges; uppertail dark brown, central feather pair with broad white stripe on inner webs, outer 2 pairs with narrower white subterminal area; pale buffish malar barred olive, pale greyish-buff chin and throat occasionally finely olive-barred; breast light olive-grey with fine olive barring or vermiculation, belly and flanks paler yellow to buff-grey with bars usually less distinct (or absent on belly); underwing pale brownish, coverts largely white; bill short, culmen curved, black with blue-grey base of lower mandible; iris brown, orbital skin greyish; legs olive, tinged green. Female has black crown with white spots. Juvenile more heavily barred than adults, but barring below more diffuse. VOICE. Apparently not described.
Habitat. Humid tropical forests. From lowlands to Andean foothills at 1000 m.
Food and Feeding. No information.
Breeding. No definite information; season probably Apr-Jul.
Movements. Presumably resident.
Status and Conservation. Not globally threatened. Restricted-range species: present in South-east Peruvian Lowlands EBA. Rare and little known. Occurs at Amazonia Lodge. Formerly considered Near-threatened, this species' conservation status may merit further reassessment.
Bibliography. Clements & Shany (2001), Collar *et al.* (1994), Parker *et al.* (1982), Schifter (2000), Stager (1968), Stattersfield *et al.* (1998), Stotz *et al.* (1996), Wheatley (1994).

27. Olivaceous Piculet

Picumnus olivaceus

French: Picumne olivâtre **German**: Olivrücken-Zwergspecht **Spanish**: Carpinterito Oliváceo

Taxonomy. *Picumnus olivaceus* Lafresnaye, 1845, Bogotá, Colombia.
Forms a superspecies with *P. granadensis*, and possibly conspecific. Proposed race *panamensis* (E Panama to extreme NW Colombia) considered insufficiently distinct from *flavotinctus*, and *malleolus* (N Colombia from N Sucre S to upper R Sinú and S Bolívar) not distinguishable from nominate. In past, race *eisenmanni* was referred to as race "*perijanus*", but this name is preoccupied by a race of *P. cinnamomeus*. Six subspecies currently recognized.
Subspecies and Distribution.
P. o. dimotus Bangs, 1903 - E Guatemala, N Honduras and E Nicaragua.
P. o. flavotinctus Ridgway, 1889 - Costa Rica, Panama and extreme NW Colombia (N Chocó).
P. o. eisenmanni Phelps, Jr. & Aveledo, 1966 - Sierra de Perijá in extreme NW Venezuela, possibly also in adjacent N Colombia.
P. o. olivaceus Lafresnaye, 1845 - W Colombia from N Sucre (Serranía de San Jacinto) S to upper R Sinú and S Bolívar, S in C Andes to lower Cauca Valley and in E Andes to Huila.
P. o. tachirensis Phelps, Sr. & Gilliard, 1941 - E slope of E Andes in NC Colombia (Norte de Santander) and adjacent SW Venezuela (SW Táchira).
P. o. harterti Hellmayr, 1909 - SW Colombia (SW Nariño) and W Ecuador; recently recorded in NW Peru (Tumbes).

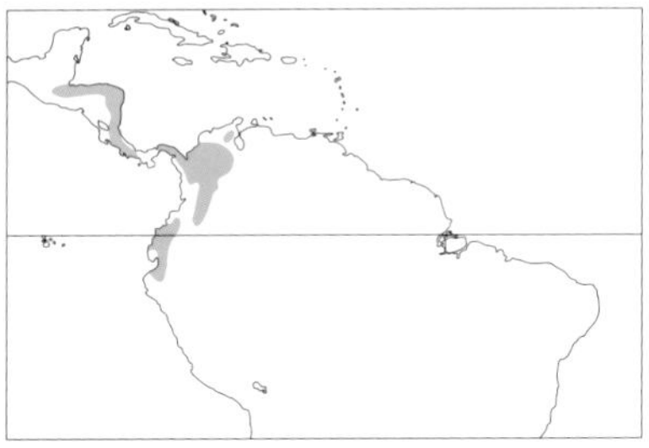

Descriptive notes. 8·5-10 cm; 10-15 g. Male has black forehead to nape, feathers of upper forehead and crown tipped red, hindcrown and nape spotted white; whitish lores; brown cheeks and ear-coverts, feathers below and behind eye tipped white; neck sides light yellowish-brown; olive-brown upperparts tinged yellow, wing-coverts narrowly edged yellowish; dark brown flight-feathers with prominent yellow to yellow-green edges; uppertail brown, central feather pair with pale buff or yellowish stripe on inner webs, outer 2 pairs with diagonal stripe; malar, chin and throat buff to yellowish-white, narrow dark feather edges producing scaly pattern; breast yellowish-brown, lower underparts paler buffish-white to dull yellowish, belly and, especially, flanks with broad brownish streaks but variable; underwing brownish-grey, coverts whitish; bill short, culmen slightly curved, black with greyer base of lower mandible; iris dark brown, orbital skin grey to blue-grey; legs grey, often tinged blue or green. Distinguished from *P. granadensis* by paler yellower upperparts, darker underparts, red crown spots of male. Female has entire top of head dotted white. Juvenile duller and browner than adults, sometimes paler and more heavily streaked below. Races differ relatively little from nominate: *dimotus* greener-tinged above, paler below, breast more olive, male crown tips yellow-orange; *flavotinctus* dark olive to olive-green above, more olive-toned below, male crown tips yellow; *eisenmanni* distinctly yellowish above, more yellow in wings, pale yellowish-olive breast, yellow belly, male crown tips orange to yellow; *tachirensis* green-tinged above, male crown tips orange to yellow; *harterti* rather small, generally darker olive, male crown tips yellow to golden. VOICE. Fine, rapid twitter or trill, soft and clear by partner arriving at hole, shrill and insect-like in self-announcement, suggesting song of Yellow-faced Grassquit (*Tiaris olivacea*) or Worm-eating Warbler (*Helmitheros vermivorus*); sharp sibilant "sst, ssip-ssip" or "peep", sometimes repeated, e.g. by fledglings responding to parents' trills; nestlings utter continuous buzz.
Habitat. Wide variety of habitats, including borders of humid rainforest and cloudforest (apparently avoiding mature stands), also drier forest, semi-open and open woodland, overgrown shrubby clearings, second growth, and cultivated land at dense forest edge with many creepers; also shady plantations and gardens. Most frequent in lowlands and foothills, but occurs also at higher elevations: to 500 m in Guatemala to Honduras; to 1400 m in Costa Rica; mostly below 1200 m in Panama but to 1600 m on Pacific slope (Chiriquí); 800-2300 m in Venezuela; to 1800 m, rarely to 2500 m, in Colombia; mainly below 900 m in Ecuador. Replaced by *P. granadensis* in W Andes.
Food and Feeding. Primarily ants (e.g. *Camponotus*, *Pseudomyrmex*, *Crematogaster*) and termites, including larvae and pupae; also beetles, and cockroach (Blattodea) eggs. Hunts singly, in pairs, or in family groups of 4-5 birds; frequently joins mixed-species flocks. Forages mainly at lower and middle heights in undergrowth, open thickets and low tangles, occasionally also in treetops; creeps up and down, often perches crosswise, many movements recall a nuthatch (*Sitta*) or xenops (*Xenops*); investigates thin branches, fine twigs and vines, apparently avoiding trunks and large limbs of tall trees. Drills tiny holes by very rapid hammering in thin branches to reach ant nests; extracts ant brood and gleans the adults. Also gleans insects from dead twigs and vines; pecks in petioles of large leaves, including fallen ones and those caught up in vines or branches, and extracts grubs.
Breeding. Dec-May in Costa Rica and Panama, and Feb-Sept in Colombia; often double-brooded. Nest excavated by both sexes at 0·9-9 m, mostly below 2 m, in slender stub with very soft wood, or in rotting post near thicket; circular entrance 2·2-2·5 cm in diameter, cavity 5-6 cm at widest point, 9-10 cm deep; excavation takes c. 1-4 weeks, but sometimes only 4-5 days. Clutch 2 or 3 eggs, but usually no more than 2 young reared; both parents sleep in nest before egg-laying and also during incubation; both also incubate, male apparently taking greater share, period 13-14 days; chicks fed by both parents, sometimes more by male; in one study, hourly feeding rate per chick was 1·3 at 7 days, 4·5 at 14 days, 1·6 at 22 days; young leave nest after 24-25 days; fledglings roost with both parents in nest for 4-16 weeks, remaining during incubation of second brood, at least until hatching.
Movements. Resident.
Status and Conservation. Not globally threatened. Fairly common to uncommon in Guatemala to Honduras; uncommon to fairly common in Costa Rica; uncommon and rather local in Panama, but more widespread and numerous in E; uncommon in Colombia; uncommon to fairly common in Ecuador. Occurs in several protected areas, e.g. Corcovado National Park (Costa Rica) and Río Palenque Science Centre (Ecuador).
Bibliography. Anon. (1998b), Becker & López (1997), Clements & Shany (2001), Fjeldså & Krabbe (1990), Haffer (1975), Hilty (1997), Hilty & Brown (1986), Howell & Webb (1995), Land (1970), Meyer de Schauensee & Phelps (1978), Monroe (1968), Otvos (1967), Parker *et al.* (1995), Ridgely & Greenfield (2001), Ridgely & Gwynne (1989), Robbins *et al.* (1985), Rodner *et al.* (2000), Skutch (1948b, 1969a, 1998), Slud (1964), Stiles (1985), Stiles & Skutch (1989), Stotz *et al.* (1996), Wetmore (1968a).

28. Greyish Piculet

Picumnus granadensis

French: Picumne gris **German**: Braunrücken-Zwergspecht **Spanish**: Carpinterito Colombiano

Taxonomy. *Picumnus granadensis* Lafresnaye, 1847, Cali, Colombia.
Forms a superspecies with *P. olivaceus*, and possibly conspecific. Two subspecies recognized.
Subspecies and Distribution.
P. g. antioquensis Chapman, 1915 - W Andes in NW Colombia, from Antioquia S, on W slope, to upper R San Juan.
P. g. granadensis Lafresnaye, 1847 - C Cauca Valley S to upper Patía Valley.
Descriptive notes. 9-10 cm; 12-13 g. Male has black forehead to nape, crown feathers finely tipped yellow, rest tipped white; white lores; chestnut-brown ear-coverts sometimes with few white streaks;

grey-brown neck sides often with some white spots or streaks; greyish-brown hindneck and upperparts often tinged olive, dark brown upperwing and wing-coverts edged yellowish-green; uppertail dark brown, central feather pair with broad white stripe on inner webs, outer 2 pairs with diagonal subterminal white stripe; cheeks, malar, chin and throat off-white with narrow blackish feather tips; grey-brown of neck sides extending slightly onto breast sides, rest of underparts dull white, sometimes very fine greyish streaks on flanks; underwing pale brownish, coverts grey and white; bill short, culmen curved, black; iris brown, orbital skin grey-blue; legs grey, tinged blue or green. Differs from *P. olivaceus* in less olive tone above, much paler underparts, smaller and yellow crown tips of male. Female has white-spotted crown. Juvenile duller, darker than adults, greyish and streaked below. Race *antioquensis* has greyer upperparts, more obvious grey streaking on belly and flanks. Voice. Calls infrequently, a high-pitched weak trill on one pitch.

Habitat. Edges of dry to moderately humid forest, second growth, scrub and woodland, at 800-2100 m, possibly down to 600 m in N of range. Replaces *P. olivaceus* in W Andes.

Food and Feeding. No details; presumably similar to *P. olivaceus*.

Breeding. Season apparently Jan to about Jun. No other information.

Movements. Resident.

Status and Conservation. Not globally threatened. Restricted-range species: present in Colombian Inter-Andean Valleys EBA. No data on numbers; uncommon.

Bibliography. Fjeldså & Krabbe (1990), Hilty & Brown (1986), Meyer de Schauensee (1982), Miller (1963), Olrog (1968), Rodner *et al.* (2000), Stattersfield *et al.* (1998), Stotz *et al.* (1996), Vélez & Velázquez (1998), Wheatley (1994).

29. Chestnut Piculet

Picumnus cinnamomeus

French: Picumne cannelle   **German:** Zimtzwergspecht   **Spanish:** Carpinterito Castaño

Taxonomy. *Picumnus cinnamomeus* Wagler, 1829, Cartagena, north Colombia.
Four subspecies recognized.

Subspecies and Distribution.
P. c. cinnamomeus Wagler, 1829 - coastal N Colombia, S locally to lower Cauca Valley (R Nechí) and lower Magdalena Valley.
P. c. persaturatus Haffer, 1961 - Serranía de San Jerónimo, in Bolívar (NC Colombia).
P. c. perijanus J. T. Zimmer & Phelps, Sr., 1944 - N shores of L Maracaibo (NW Venezuela).
P. c. venezuelensis Cory, 1913 - S & E shores of L Maracaibo (W Venezuela).

Descriptive notes. 9-10 cm. Very distinctive piculet. Male has pale creamy forehead, lores and nasal tufts, black crown to nape, crown feathers tipped yellow, nape feathers tipped white; rest of body plumage deep rufous to rusty-brown, rump and belly a shade paler; upperwing and wing-coverts dark brown, edged and tipped cinnamon to rufous; uppertail brownish-black, central feather pair with broad pale cinnamon stripe on inner webs, outer 2 pairs with stripe on outer webs; underwing grey-brown, coverts rufous; bill short, stout, culmen slightly curved, blackish; iris brown, orbital skin yellow; legs grey. Female lacks yellow on crown, white spots confined to hindcrown and nape. Juvenile apparently undescribed. Race *persaturatus* is darker, more chestnut, than nominate, has brighter wing edgings, more obscurely patterned tail, female crown fully white-spotted; *perijanus* is similar to previous, but not quite so dark, female with crown much more heavily spotted; *venezuelensis* is as dark as first, has cinnamon-tawny forehead, female crown spotted white but nape unspotted. Voice. Apparently undescribed.

Habitat. Wide range of habitats, from rainforest, humid coffee plantations, and deciduous forest, to open terrain with scattered trees, borders of dry forest, and arid and semi-arid scrub; also mangroves in Colombia; particularly favours thorny woodland. From sea-level to 100 m in Venezuela, to 300 m in Colombia.

Food and Feeding. Diet apparently not documented; probably takes ants and other small insects. Observed singly, in pairs, sometimes in small family groups; joins mixed-species groups. Tends to forage in dense thickets and vine tangles; forages at virtually all levels. Very active, not shy; hops through thickets, creeps like a nuthatch (*Sitta*) over trunks and branches.

Breeding. Laying in Dec and juvenile seen in Mar in Colombia. No other details documented.

Movements. Resident.

Status and Conservation. Not globally threatened. Restricted-range species: present in Caribbean Colombia and Venezuela EBA. Common in Colombia; probably common locally in Venezuela, but few records. Considering that this species is not so inconspicuous as most other piculets, it is rather poorly known.

Bibliography. Haffer (1975), Hilty & Brown (1986), Meyer de Schauensee (1982), Meyer de Schauensee & Phelps (1978), Olrog (1968), Rodner *et al.* (2000), Stattersfield *et al.* (1998), Stotz *et al.* (1996), Wheatley (1994), Zimmer & Phelps (1944).

Genus *SASIA* Hodgson, 1836

30. African Piculet

Sasia africana

French: Picumne de Verreaux   **German:** Graubauch-Mausspecht   **Spanish:** Carpinterito Africano

Other common names: Pygmy Wood Piculet, Pygmy Woodpecker(!)

Taxonomy. *Sasia africana* J. Verreaux and E. Verreaux, 1855, Gabon.
Sometimes placed in monotypic genus *Verreauxia*, but appears close to *S. abnormis* and *S. ochracea*. Monotypic.

Distribution. S Cameroon and SW Central African Republic E to SW Uganda (Bwamba Forest), S to NW Angola (S to Cuanza Norte, N Lunda Norte) and SC & SW Zaire; a few isolated records in recent decades from Liberia, Ivory Coast and Ghana indicate existence of a small population in forests of Upper Guinea.

Descriptive notes. 9-10 cm; 7·5-10·5 g. The only African piculet. Male has chestnut to rufous forehead, olive-green to greyish-olive crown to hindneck; blackish lores, thin blackish stripe behind eye bordered above by short white line; rest of head rather dark grey, often streaked darker on ear-coverts, which have white crescent at lower rear border; entire upperparts dark green, tinged yellow, uppertail-coverts duller; wing-coverts, secondaries and tertials sometimes slightly darker, but with brighter yellow fringes; brownish-black primaries with whitish on inner webs, narrowly edged and tipped yellow on outer webs; extremely short tail with 8 (not 10) brownish-black feathers edged olive-greenish, rest of underparts darkish grey with slight to strong olive tinge, belly often paler; underwing mostly whitish; bill short, culmen curved, black with paler lower mandible; iris red, orbital skin light red to pale purple-red or pinkish-purple; legs reddish to purple-red. Female slightly longer-winged, lacks chestnut on forehead. Juvenile has rufous feather tips on head, especially ear-coverts, and on throat, belly and flanks, grey and buffy tones admixed in mantle and back, brown iris. Voice. Weak high trill, "ti-ti-ti-ti-ti-ti".

Habitat. Inhabits humid forest, mainly in ecotone between primary and secondary growth, also gallery forest; prefers old second growth to open primary forest. Occurs from lowlands to c. 700 m, locally up to 1000 m.

Food and Feeding. Principal food made up of wood-boring beetle larvae; also consumes adult beetles and other insects, but appears not to take ants. Commonly encountered in pairs or trios; occasionally joins mixed-species flocks. Forages mainly in lower storeys; constantly on the move, hops and flies rapidly through dense vegetation. Forages in bushes, also clings to stems of larger herbaceous plants and grass. Hammers vigorously into the substrate, splitting it open to get at prey.

Breeding. Laying dates span Jun-Feb; juvenile collected in Mar in Angola. Nest excavated 1-5 m above ground in narrow branch, entrance 2 cm across, cavity dimensions c. 4 × 5 cm. Clutch usually 2 eggs; both parents incubate eggs and tend brood, periods unknown.

Movements. Essentially resident. Several records from Upper Guinea, including two from Liberia, one from Ivory Coast, two from Ghana, and possibly one from Nigeria, have been suggested as pointing to abnormal long-distance dispersal, but much more likely to refer to small, sparse populations.

Status and Conservation. Not globally threatened. Locally common, e.g. in parts of Gabon; common in Bwamba Forest in Uganda; not uncommon in Angola. Occurs at Mount Kupé and in Korup National Park in Cameroon. Although this species has been considered generally uncommon, its habits make it likely to be overlooked; in much of range, it seems to be reasonably common in secondary forest. No immediate threats known.

Bibliography. Bannerman (1953), Bowden (2001), Christy & Clarke (1994), Dean (2000), Delacour (1951a), Demey & Fishpool (1991, 1994), Dowsett (1989b), Dowsett & Dowsett-Lemaire (1993, 1997), Dowsett & Forbes-Watson (1993), Dowsett-Lemaire & Dowsett (1999, 2000), Dowsett-Lemaire *et al.* (1993), Fjeldså & Jensen (1990), Fry *et al.* (1988), Gatter (1988), Germain & Cornet (1994), Grimes (1987), Lippens & Wille (1976), Louette (1981b), Macdonald & Taylor (1977), Mackworth-Praed & Grant (1962, 1970), Pinto (1983), Rand *et al.* (1959), Sargeant (1993), Short (1971d, 1980, 1985b), Snow (1978), Thiollay (1985b).

31. Rufous Piculet

Sasia abnormis

French: Picumne roux   **German:** Malaienmausspecht   **Spanish:** Carpinterito Malayo

Taxonomy. *Picumnus abnormis* Temminck, 1825, Java.
Two subspecies recognized.

Subspecies and Distribution.
S. a. abnormis (Temminck, 1825) - S Myanmar (Tenasserim) and adjacent SW Thailand, S to Sumatra (including Belitung I), Borneo and W & C Java.
S. a. magnirostris Hartert, 1901 - Nias I, off NW Sumatra.

Descriptive notes. 9 cm; 7·2-12 g. Male has yellow forehead, sometimes with rufous admixed, yellowish-olive crown to hindneck; remainder of head and neck rufous to orange-rufous, generally darker on ear-coverts; upperparts yellowish-olive, rump partly or wholly rufous, uppertail-coverts black; olive-brown wing-coverts, secondaries and tertials edged yellow; primaries brown, inner webs edged rufous, outer webs sometimes edged dark rufous; uppertail (10 feathers) very short, black, edged dull olive; entire underparts rufous, flanks usually washed yellow; underwing whitish, with pale rufous or cinnamon primary patch; relatively long bill curved on culmen, grey to brown with yellow lower mandible; iris red to orange-rufous, orbital skin dark red to purplish; legs dull yellow to orange, only 3 toes. Distinguished from *S. ochracea* by lack of white rear supercilium, more olive upperparts without rufous tones, yellow lower mandible. Female has slightly larger bill, wing and tail, all-rufous forehead. Juvenile darker than adults, has head and underparts mostly slate-brown, mantle washed slate-grey, all-dark bill, brown iris. Race *magnirostris* differs from nominate only in having longer, deeper bill. Voice. Single sharp "tsit" or "tic", usually repeated; high-pitched rapid "kih-kih-kih-kih-kih" or "kik-ik-ik-ik-ik-ik" by territorial male; alarm "kip, kip, kip"; drums loudly, a fast rattle slowing to paired beats, rolls c. 1-1·5 seconds in duration.

Habitat. Secondary forest with old decaying trees, swamp-forest, to lesser extent primary forest; much prefers dense second growth, particularly bamboo stands, and other low dense vegetation. Often found near water. Lowlands and hills to 800 m, to 1370 m in Malay Peninsula.
Food and Feeding. Ants and their larvae, and small bark beetles (Scolytidae); soft insects and their larvae; also spiders. Hunts singly, or in family parties of 3-5 individuals; often joins mixed-species flocks. Forages at low and middle levels, generally no higher than 5 m above ground; moves very rapidly through dense vegetation, often flies longer distances from one spot to another rather than proceeding steadily from tree to tree. Inspects bamboo, thin trunks, dead branches, vines, shrubs and saplings, also feeds among grasses in the understorey. Often perches crosswise, and moves upwards in short flights. Foraging techniques include persistent quiet pecking, and gleaning; reaches ants in bamboo stems by excavating small holes, then inserting the long tongue to obtain prey.
Breeding. May-Aug; from Feb in Borneo. Nest excavated low down in dead branch, sapling or bamboo stem; 2 nest-holes in Peninsular Malaysia were less than 1 m from ground, entrance less than 2·5 cm wide. Clutch usually 2 eggs, possibly sometimes 3; incubation and fledging periods unrecorded; young remain with parents for some time after leaving nest. Maximum recorded longevity at least 7 years 2 months.
Movements. Resident. In ringing studies in Malaysia, two females retrapped after several years only 800 m from ringing site.
Status and Conservation. Not globally threatened. Fairly common to common in Myanmar, Thailand, Sumatra and Borneo; common in Peninsular Malaysia, but absent from Singapore. Occurs in several protected areas within its range, including Khao Nor Chuchi Non-hunting Area (Thailand), Taman Negara National Park and Panti Forest Reserve (Malaysia), and Way Kambas National Park (Sumatra). Difficult to observe, and possibly overlooked. Appears reasonably adaptable, and preference for secondary habitats suggests that it is not likely to be threatened in near future.
Bibliography. Andrew (1992), Baker (1919), van Balen (1999), Bromley (1952), Delacour (1951a), Duckworth & Kelsh (1988), Duckworth *et al.* (1997), Hellebrekers & Hoogerwerf (1967), Holmes (1994), Jeyarajasingam & Pearson (1999), Lekagul & Round (1991), MacKinnon (1988), MacKinnon & Phillipps (1993), Madoc (1976), van Marle & Voous (1988), Medway & Wells (1976), Riley (1938), Robinson (1928), Robson (2000), Short (1973d), Smythies (1986, 1999), Vowles & Vowles (1997), Wells (1985, 1999), Wilkinson, Dutson & Sheldon (1991), Wong (1985).

32. **White-browed Piculet**
Sasia ochracea

French: Picumne à sourcils blancs **German**: Rötelmausspecht **Spanish**: Carpinterito Cejiblanco
Other common names: Himalayan Rufous Piculet (*ochracea*); Burmese Rufous Piculet (*reichenowi*)

Taxonomy. *Sasia ochracea* Hodgson, 1836, Nepal.
Race *hasbroucki*, described from S Myanmar and S Thailand, is synonymous with *reichenowi*. Birds from S Assam, Bangladesh and SW Myanmar sometimes separated as race *querulivox* on basis of paler coloration, but this matched by individuals from SE Asia. Three subspecies recognized.
Subspecies and Distribution.
S. o. ochracea Hodgson, 1836 - N India (N Uttar Pradesh) and C Nepal E to N & C Thailand and Vietnam.
S. o. kinneari Stresemann, 1929 - extreme N Vietnam (Tonkin) and adjacent S China (Yunnan, Guangxi).
S. o. reichenowi Hesse, 1911 - S Myanmar (Tenasserim) and SW Thailand S to Isthmus of Kra.

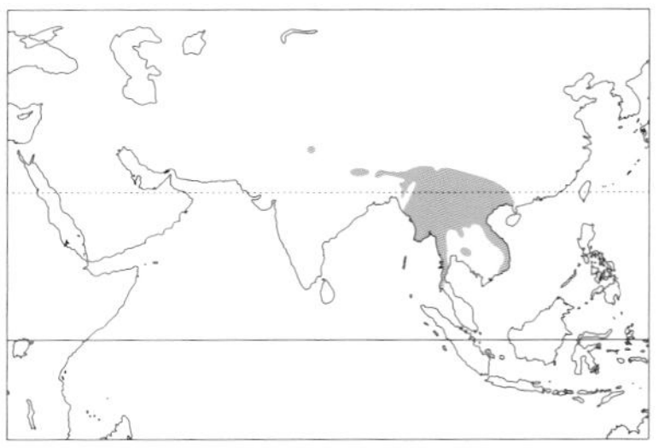

Descriptive notes. 9-10 cm; 8·3-11·8g. Male has rufous to orange-rufous forehead and forecrown, with bright golden-yellow patch in centre of forehead; rest of crown to hindneck olive-green, variably tinged rufous; white stripe behind eye; rufous to cinnamon-rufous lores, cheeks and sides of neck, darker ear-coverts; upperparts green with variable element of rufous, rump (sometimes also mantle and back) mainly rufous, uppertail-coverts blackish; brown upperwing and wing-coverts edged and tipped green to yellow-green, primaries edged buffish on inner webs; uppertail (10 feathers) very short, brownish-black, feathers narrowly edged greenish; entire underparts varying from deep rufous to lighter rufous, sometimes hint of yellowish on breast and flanks; underwing mostly buffish-white; bill shortish, culmen curved, black upper mandible, grey lower mandible; iris red, orbital skin pinkish-red; legs orange or yellow-orange, only 3 toes. Distinguished from *S. abnormis* by white stripe behind eye, rufous tones above, darker lower mandible. Female has entirely rufous forehead, often paler orbital skin. Juvenile is greener, less rufous-tinged, above, has variably strong element of grey or green below. Race *reichenowi* generally paler, has blackish bare orbital skin, often black-tipped feathers on lores, more rufous above; race *kinneari* has darker plumage. Voice. Short sharp "chi" or "tsick"; fast high-pitched trill starting with call, "chi-rrrrrrrra" or "ti-i-i-i-i-i", by territorial male, both perched and in flight; series of weak squeaks during close contact in courtship; loud, rapid tinny drumming, often on bamboo, also loud tapping.
Habitat. Dense low vegetation in broadleaved evergreen and mixed deciduous forest, also dense second growth and mixed scrub; strong preference for bamboo; often near water. To 1850 m in SE Asia; 250-2130 m in N Indian Subcontinent, and recorded to 2600 m.
Food and Feeding. Ants and their brood, small bark beetles (Scolytidae), spiders. Occurs singly, in pairs or in small groups of 4 or 5; joins mixed-species flocks. Forages at low levels, moving rapidly through dense vegetation near ground; climbs bamboo, shrub stems and vines; also forages at times on the ground, hopping among leaf litter. Feeding techniques include frequent pecking; not known to excavate for wood-dwelling larvae.
Breeding. Mar-Jun in Indian Subcontinent, Apr-Jul in SE Asia. Courting male hops around crouched female, repeatedly flying above her and dropping down again, with squeaking calls. Nest excavated at low level, c. 50 cm, just below a node in dead bamboo, or in small branch or tree stem; entrance hole 1·3-2·5 cm across. Clutch 2-4 eggs; no data on incubation and fledging periods.
Movements. Resident.
Status and Conservation. Not globally threatened. Fairly common to common in SE Asia, but rare in Malay Peninsula and rare in China; uncommon in Nepal, generally uncommon in India but locally fairly common in E Himalayas, and frequent in Bhutan; local and uncommon in NE & S Bangladesh. Occurs in Kaziranga and Namdapha National Parks (India), Chitwan National Park (Nepal), Doi Inthanon, Nam Nao and Kaeng Krachan National Parks (Thailand), and Nam Bai Cat Tien National Park (Vietnam). As with other piculets, its unobtrusive behaviour makes it likely to be overlooked. Is able to exploit regrowth and disturbed forest, and does not appear to be under any threat at present.
Bibliography. Ali & Ripley (1983), Ali *et al.* (1996), Baker (1919), Bangs & Van Tyne (1931), Biswas (1961a), Deignan (1945), Delacour (1951a), Delacour & Jabouille (1940), Duckworth *et al.* (1999), Eames & Robson (1992), Étchécopar & Hüe (1978), Evans & Timmins (1998), Grimmett *et al.* (1998, 2000), Harvey (1990), Inskipp & Inskipp (1991), Inskipp *et al.* (1999), Lekagul & Round (1991), Ludlow (1937, 1944), MacKinnon & Phillipps (2000), Ripley (1982), Robson (2000), Shankar Raman (2001), Shrestha (2000), Smythies (1986), Stepanyan (1995), Wells (1985, 1999), Zhao Zhengjie (1995).

Tribe NESOCTITINI
Genus *NESOCTITES* Hargitt, 1890

33. **Antillean Piculet**
Nesoctites micromegas

French: Picumne des Antilles **German**: Hüpfspecht **Spanish**: Carpinterito Antillano

Taxonomy. *Picumnus micromegas* Sundevall, 1866, Brazil; error = Hispaniola.
No obvious close relatives. Two subspecies recognized.
Subspecies and Distribution.
N. m. micromegas (Sundevall, 1866) - Hispaniola.
N. m. abbotti Wetmore, 1928 - Gonâve I, off W Hispaniola.

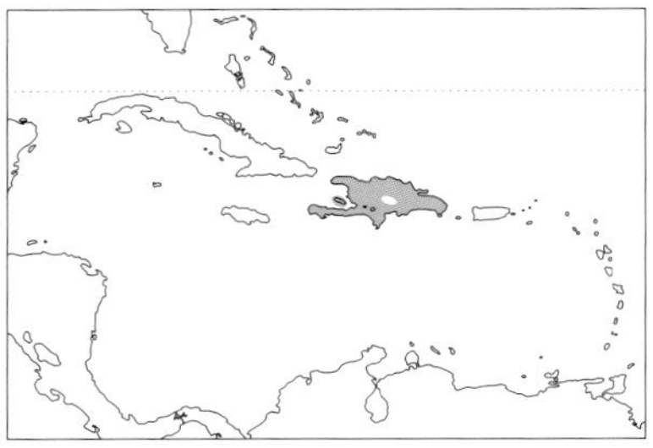

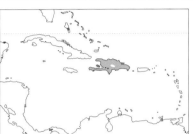

Descriptive notes. 14-16 cm; 26-33 g. Unmistakable; the largest piculet, roughly twice the size of any other. Male has yellowish-green forehead, crown sides and hindneck, lemon-yellow crown to nape with patch of orange-red to dull red in centre of hindcrown, sometimes a few white spots on nape; buff-white lores and nasal tufts; dull whitish ear-coverts barred olive, more uniform olive-grey neck sides with variable white spots; white moustachial region spotted or barred greyish-olive; dull olive-green to yellow-green upperparts faintly tinged rusty-bronze, wing-coverts and tertials edged and tipped brighter paler greenish; brown primaries and secondaries edged yellow-green; uppertail brownish-olive, suffused bronze; white chin and throat faintly tinged yellow, with few small dark spots or bars; rest of underparts pale yellowish-white, breast sometimes deeper yellow, all with variably broad dark streaks; underwing greyish-olive; bill short, culmen curved, and narrow and flattened between nostrils, blackish; iris brown to red-brown or red, orbital skin dark grey; legs dark green-grey. Female is larger than male, lacks red on hindcrown. Juvenile duller, both sexes with crown pattern as adult female but yellow colour less bright, belly obscurely barred rather than streaked; may become bare-crowned for short period, but soon acquires adult feathers. Race *abbotti* is paler, with greyer upperparts, sometimes white spots extending to mantle side, plainer white throat, less heavy streaks below, both sexes with less yellow on crown. Voice. Single mechanical "pit" and "pew" notes in alarm; loud, rapid, musical whistling "kuk-ki-ki-ki-ke-ku-kuk", sometimes associated with alarm call, as long-distance signal between pair-members, also in territorial encounters; short series of weak "wiii" notes in close proximity to conspecific; continuous noisy "yeh-yeh-yeh-yeh" chatter during fights; not known to drum.
Habitat. Humid to dry primary and secondary forest, also mixed pine (*Pinus*) and broadleaved forest, and especially mixed desert scrub and thorn-forest in semi-arid regions; also mangroves and, locally or more rarely, orchards and dense cultivation and plantations. Favours dense undergrowth. Both in lowlands and in mountains, occurring up to 1800 m in Sierra de Bahoruco; in pine-forest zone prefers elevations below 300 m.
Food and Feeding. Mainly insects, especially ants and small beetles; also other arthropods; also eats relatively large amounts of fruit. Occurs singly or in pairs, partners keeping loose contact. Forages mainly in understorey below 8 m, flitting rapidly through vegetation; often perches and moves in passerine-like manner, zigzagging through entangled vegetation; also moves up to the crown, from where it departs in fast direct flight to another feeding site, which may be some distance away. Forages on vines, small branches and twigs, stalks of herbaceous plants, and leaf clusters, much less commonly on trunks. Feeds mainly by gleaning; also makes occasional weak pecks, often directed laterally; also probes in fruits and flowers, and in leaf or pine-needle clusters.
Breeding. Mar-Jul. Nest excavated at below 5 m in stub, small tree, palm or fence post. Territorial; aggressive calling bouts and jerky head-swinging displays directed at rivals. Clutch 2-4 eggs; incubation and fledging periods not documented.
Movements. Resident.
Status and Conservation. Not globally threatened. Restricted-range species: present in Hispaniola EBA. Common in most of range, but less numerous in W (Haiti); has been reported as fairly common on Gonâve I, although destruction of habitat has been a serious problem on this island. Habitat destruction generally considered a potential threat, particularly in Haiti; much forest has been lost since 1970's. Hunting possibly also a problem. Occurs in several protected areas, e.g. Sierra de Bahoruco and Este National Parks (Dominican Republic). Environmental matters are generally given scant attention in the region, especially by decision-makers, and programmes are required aimed at encouraging local human populations to safeguard their natural resources. Lack of adequate laws to protect wildlife, and to safeguard habitats, could become a major problem unless addressed as a matter of urgency.
Bibliography. Anon. (1998b), Bernstein (1964, 1965), Bond (1928, 1985), Cruz (1974a), Dod (1972, 1987, 1992), Faaborg (1985), Laybourne *et al.* (1994), Olson (1978), Poinar *et al.* (1985), Raffaele *et al.* (1998), Short (1974d), Stattersfield *et al.* (1998), Stotz *et al.* (1996), Wetmore & Swales (1931), Wunderle & Latta (1996).

PLATE 26 ➤

34

35

♀

♂

36

♀

♂

37

♂

38

♂
ssp *formicivorus*

♀

39

♂
ssp *flavigula*

♀

♀
ssp *angustifrons*
♂

♂
ssp *bairdi*

♀

♂
variants

40

♀

♂

ssp *chrysauchen*

♂

♀

41

♀
ssp *pulcher*
♂

♀
black-headed
morph

42

♂

♂

43

with yellow
throat

♀

♂

♂

with
white throat

44

♂

♀

45

♂

46

♀
yellow-tufted
morph

♀

♀
ssp *chrysogenys*
♂

47

♂
ssp *flavinuchus*

PLATE 26

inches   4

cm   10

Subfamily PICINAE
Tribe MELANERPINI
Genus *MELANERPES* Swainson, 1832

34. **White Woodpecker**
Melanerpes candidus

French: Pic dominicain **German**: Weißspecht **Spanish**: Carpintero Blanco

Taxonomy. *Picus candidus* Otto, 1796, Cayenne.
Distinctive; sometimes placed in monotypic genus *Leuconerpes*, but shows many morphological similarities to typical *Melanerpes*. Monotypic.
Distribution. Lower Amazon (W to R Madeira), and from extreme SE Peru (Pampas del Heath), S Mato Grosso and NE Brazil (N Maranhão) S to E Bolivia, N Argentina (S to Córdoba, N Buenos Aires) and W & S Uruguay.

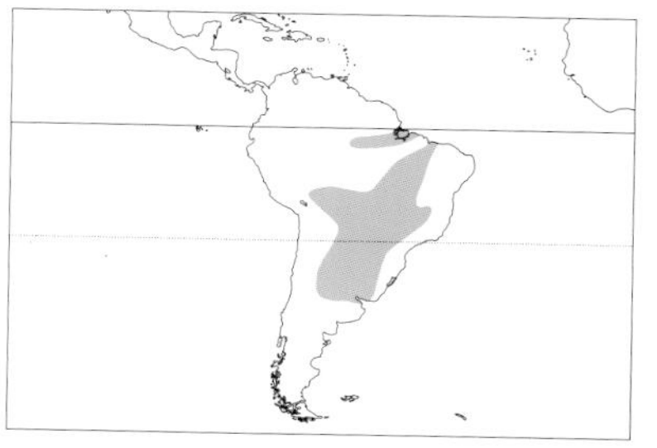

Descriptive notes. 24-29 cm; 98-136 g. Smallish to medium-sized, very distinctive woodpecker. Male has almost entire head and underparts white to creamy-white, occasionally slightly buff-tinged (and often becoming stained brownish); dusky to blackish loral line, narrow black stripe from lower rear of eye curving down to mantle; pale lemon-yellow lower hindneck; black mantle to upper back, wing-coverts and tertials, slightly glossed blue, white lower back to uppertail-coverts; flight-feathers brownish-black; uppertail brownish-black, some white at base, usually a few white spots in distal part of outer feathers; yellow patch in centre of lower belly of variable extent (occasionally reaching lower breast); underwing grey-brown, coverts black; longish bill slightly chisel-tipped, culmen curved, moderately broad across nostrils, black, paler (even greenish or whitish) at base; iris white to pale bluish-white or yellow, very broad orbital ring golden-yellow; legs olive to grey-green or brownish. Female lacks yellow on hindneck. Juvenile has dark areas browner, less glossy, white areas more buff-tinged, yellow on belly duller, iris grey, orbital ring possibly bluish; young male with yellow extending from hindneck or nape up to crown, female with broken band of yellow in nape area. Voice. Common call when perched "ghirreh" or "kreer"; very distinctive "kirr-kirr-kirr" or "cree-cree-cree-creek" in flight, recalling a tern (*Sterna*).
Habitat. Principally dry subtropical forest, woodland and open wooded areas, savannas with scattered trees, and dry scrub areas; often at forest edge and in cultivated areas, where it inhabits palm groves and orchards. Not uncommonly seen in stands of *Eucalyptus*, and recorded in other exotic trees (*Salix*, *Populus*) in Argentina. Mainly lowlands, locally to c. 2200 m.
Food and Feeding. Predominantly fruits, also seeds and honey; in addition, insects, including wild bees and wasps and their larvae. Also recorded feeding on meat hung up to dry. Usually observed in small groups of c. 5-8; sometimes accompanies *Colaptes* species. Often visits more open places; may fly long distances across open country in relatively straight (non-undulating) flight, pausing to forage on any trees encountered. Arboreal, foraging mostly by pecking and gleaning. Opens nests of hymenopterans to take their brood and honey. Occasionally catches insects on the wing.
Breeding. Season Sept-Nov. Possibly social breeder, but details insufficiently known. Nest not described; apparently able to use holes among rocks. Display flights occur during breeding season. Clutch 3-4 eggs; incubation by both parents, period unrecorded; fledging period 36 days in captivity.
Movements. Apparently resident. Recent records in coastal Rio Grande do Sul possibly only of wandering individuals, but might represent expansion of breeding range.
Status and Conservation. Not globally threatened. No data on numbers and density; probably not uncommon. Rare in Peru. Occurs in several protected areas, such as Serra da Canastra and Das Emas National Parks and Sooretama Biological Reserve (Brazil). Appears to have expanded its range in S since early 1990's. Causes some damage locally in commercial fruit plantations, e.g. of oranges, and is sometimes persecuted as a result. Trapped for cage-bird trade in and around Buenos Aires (Argentina).
Bibliography. Aleixo & Galetti (1997), dos Anjos & Schuchmann (1997), Belton (1984), Bodrati (2001), Brace *et al.* (1997), Brooks *et al.* (1993), de Bustamante (1997), Buzzetti (2000), Canevari *et al.* (1991), Capper *et al.* (2000), Chebez *et al.* (1999), Clements & Shany (2001), Contreras (1983), Contreras *et al.* (1990), Davis (1993), Dubs (1992), Figueiredo & Lo (2000), Figueiredo *et al.* (2000), Fjeldså & Krabbe (1990), Graham *et al.* (1980), Lando & Haene (1996), López (1997), Macklin (1937), Maurício & Dias (2000), Melo-Júnior (2001a), Navas & Bó (1993), Parker & Goerck (1997), de la Peña (1994), Pereyra (1950), do Rosário (1996), Scott & Brooke (1985), Short (1975, 1985b), Sick (1993), da Silva *et al.* (1997), Stotz *et al.* (1996), Stradi & Hudon (1998), Stradi *et al.* (1998), Tobias *et al.* (1993), Wetmore (1926).

35. **Lewis's Woodpecker**
Melanerpes lewis

French: Pic de Lewis **German**: Blutgesichtsspecht **Spanish**: Carpintero de Lewis

Taxonomy. *Picus Lewis* G. R. Gray, 1849, no locality = Montana, USA.
Rather distinctive; sometimes placed in monotypic genus *Asyndesmus*, but shows many similarities to typical *Melanerpes*. Monotypic.
Distribution. Coastal ranges and foothills of Rocky Mts from S British Columbia S to Arizona and New Mexico, E to South Dakota, Wyoming and SE Colorado; in winter mostly in S parts of range.

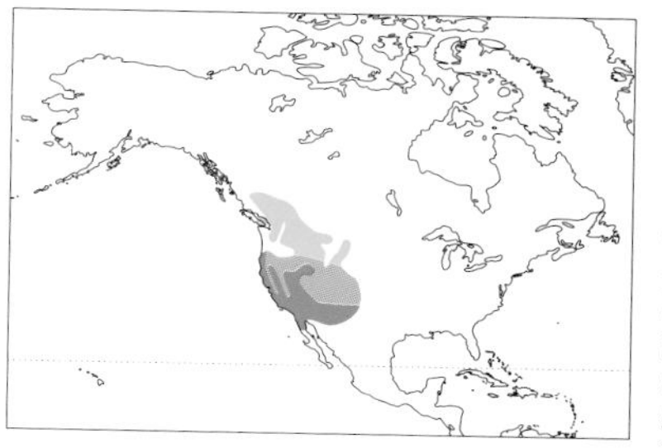

Descriptive notes. c. 26-29 cm; 85-138 g. Small to medium-sized woodpecker, unmistakable; flies with slow beats in straight line, not undulating, appears very dark. Both sexes have green-glossed black head, deep crimson-red feathers with black bases on lower forehead, lores, around eye and on cheeks, brownish-black chin and throat; black-based silver-grey feathers on rear neck sides usually forming collar around hindneck, also continuing broadly across breast; blackish upperparts, including wings and uppertail, strongly glossed green, normally more blue-green on flight-feathers; secondaries occasionally with small white tips, rarely outer tail narrowly edged white; belly silver-pink, becoming greenish-black on lower flanks and undertail-coverts; underwing and undertail blackish-brown; longish bill almost pointed, culmen slightly curved, fairly broad across nostrils, slaty-grey to blackish; iris dark red-dish-brown; legs bluish to blue-black. Juvenile is drabber, less glossy than adult, has browner head and neck, no or minimal red on face, no silvery collar, dull red belly variably barred whitish and brown, eyes brown; has prolonged moult, sometimes not fully until autumn or early winter. Voice. Series of short, rather loud and harsh "churr" calls, usually 3-8 in quick succession, by male during breeding season, each call about half as long as equivalent call of *M. erythrocephalus*; throughout year, "Chatter-calls" comprising rapidly descending series of short squeaks, most frequently in encounters of any kind; in alarm, single "yick" notes by male, double "yick-ick" by female. Drumming infrequent, restricted to courtship period, a weak roll followed by 3 or 4 taps.
Habitat. Breeds in open habitats with some dead trees with decayed wood for nesting, and with rich food sources: primarily open pine forest, especially of ponderosa pine (*Pinus ponderosa*), but logged or burned forest as well as open riparian woodland with cottonwoods (*Populus*) also important; occasionally oak (*Quercus*) woodland, orchards, even farmland with suitable trees. In areas of contact with *M. erythrocephalus*, more on cultivated land and at edges, whereas latter prefers riverine woodland and clearings. In winter, most commonly oak woodland and commercial orchards (e.g. almond, walnut, pecan); areas with good supply of corn also favoured. From sea-level to 2000 m, to 2800 m in Arizona.
Food and Feeding. In spring and summer, various insects, especially ants and other Hymenoptera, also beetles, Orthoptera (mainly Tettigoniidae); also fruits (e.g. cherries) and berries. In winter, mostly acorns and nuts obtained from stores laid up in autumn; if latter type of crop in ample supply, as in almond plantations or exceptionally in corn silos, may do without stores. Probably the most specialized of all woodpeckers in flycatching; spends much time scanning surroundings from prominent perch; approaches prey in crow-like flight, with elaborate manoeuvres leading to final capture; glides back to perch. Over 10% of flycatching performed in continuous flights lasting several minutes, when several insects may be taken. Also takes insects on ground or in low brush, showing considerable agility when moving among outer branches. Also gleans, probes, taps lightly, chips off small pieces of bark; most frequently searches visually for prey. In autumn, harvests acorns and nuts, shells nuts in several anvils; stores food in natural crevices, occasionally after widening cracks; tends stores by moving individual items around, to inhibit fungal growth. When superabundant, insects, such as swarming carpenter ants (*Camponotus*), are also stored in cracks near nest, and later fed to young. Individual food caches defended vigorously; competition for stored mast is intense, main competitor *M. formicivorus*.
Breeding. Apr-Sept, mostly May-Jul; breeds 1-3 weeks later in S of range or at low altitudes than in N or uplands. Apparently monogamous, with lifelong pair-bond. Nest 1·5-5·2 m up in cottonwood, conifer, oak or other tree, most (c. 75%) in dead stub, or occasionally in electricity pole; entrance diameter 5-7·5 cm, cavity depth 22·8-76·2 cm; may use same nest in consecutive years, or male selects winter roost as nest-site; only infrequently excavates new nest-hole, and then prefers to adapt natural hollow or flicker (*Colaptes*) hole; male defends immediate nest vicinity from intruders. Displaying male exposes pink feathers of flanks and belly; perches on horizontal limb, wings extended, head lowered, silvery feathers of throat and upper breast fluffed; also glides around nest tree with wings held at high angle, alighting at nest entrance. Clutch 4-9 eggs, usually 6-7, increasing from S to N; incubation period c. 14 days, nestling period 4-5 weeks; parents seem to contribute equally to feeding and brooding, but male alone spends the night in nest and possibly removes faecal sacs more often; fledged young remain near nest with adults for at least 10 days, sometimes each parent accompanies part of the brood; post-breeding flocks in autumn or early winter, within which relationship between adults and their offspring is not certain. Success variable: in Colorado, 60·2% of nests in agricultural plains with cottonwood produced at least 1 fledgling, but only 29·4% in cottonwood-oak woodland in foothills; in Idaho, success greater in burned pine forest than in cottonwood forest. First breeds probably at 1 year.
Movements. Mostly migratory. Because of marked seasonal changes in diet, has to move variable distances to non-breeding grounds that provide acorns or nuts; populations of Idaho, Wyoming and Montana migrate longer distances, c. 50% of population in SE Colorado may be resident throughout year. Migrants generally winter within S part of breeding range (S from SW Oregon, C Utah and C Colorado), also locally S to NW Baja California, W & C Arizona and S New Mexico, more rarely to N Mexico (S to Sonora and Chihuahua); non-breeding distribution heavily dependent on weather conditions and distribution of acorn crops. Migration sometimes spectacular, with more than 2000 birds in small groups and loose flocks passing a single point in 1 hour; before arrival at wintering grounds, nomadic flocks may exploit habitats in mountains or visit orchards. Arrives on winter grounds in late Sept and first half Oct, staying until late Apr; sometimes in large flocks in winter. Spring return less nomadic than autumn migration, and therefore takes less time.
Status and Conservation. Not globally threatened. Locally common to uncommon or rare. No figures for total population size; estimated 700-1200 breeding birds in British Columbia in 1990. Maximum density in Pacific Northwest (Blue Mts) c. 16 pairs/ha, but probably wide annual and local variation dependent on food supply. Global population thought possibly to have decreased by c. 60% since 1960's; reduction in breeding range recorded in British Columbia, NW Washington, Oregon, California. Habitat degradation and loss, especially of open ponderosa pine forest and cottonwoods, considered major factors in decline, at least locally, and loss of oakwoods in wintering range may also be important; nest-site competition not thought to be an important problem for

On following pages: 36. Guadeloupe Woodpecker (*Melanerpes herminieri*); 37. Puerto Rican Woodpecker (*Melanerpes portoricensis*); 38. Red-headed Woodpecker (*Melanerpes erythrocephalus*); 39. Acorn Woodpecker (*Melanerpes formicivorus*); 40. Black-cheeked Woodpecker (*Melanerpes pucherani*); 41. Golden-naped Woodpecker (*Melanerpes chrysauchen*); 42. Yellow-tufted Woodpecker (*Melanerpes cruentatus*); 43. Yellow-fronted Woodpecker (*Melanerpes flavifrons*); 44. White-fronted Woodpecker (*Melanerpes cactorum*); 45. Hispaniolan Woodpecker (*Melanerpes striatus*); 46. Jamaican Woodpecker (*Melanerpes radiolatus*); 47. Golden-cheeked Woodpecker (*Melanerpes chrysogenys*).

this species. Sometimes shot because of its habit of foraging in commercial orchards, but human persecution relatively minimal and local.

Bibliography. Adams (1941a), Anderson & Linder (1997), Baicich & Harrison (1997), Baldwin & Schneider (1963), Bent (1939), Block & Brennan (1987), Bock (1968, 1970), Bock *et al.* (1971), Campbell *et al.* (1990), Constantz (1974), Currier (1928), Farrand (1992), Galen (1989), Garrett (1999), Gates (1981), Hadow (1973), Hatch & L'Arrivée (1981), Howell & Webb (1995), Janos (1991), Johnsgard (1979), Kaufman (1996), Koehler (1981), Koenig (1986, 1987), Linder (1994), Linder & Anderson (1998), Michael (1926), Price *et al.* (1995), Root (1988), Saab & Dudley (1998), Saab & Vierling (2001), Sherwood (1927), Short (1985b), Siddle & Davidson (1991), Small (1994), Smith (1941), Snow (1941), Sorensen (1986), Sousa (1983a), Spring (1965), Stradi & Hudon (1998), Stradi *et al.* (1998), Tashiro-Vierling (1994), Tate (1981), Tate & Tate (1982), Tobalske (1996, 1997), Tyler (1979), Vierling (1997, 1998), Weber (1980), Wilbur (1987).

36. Guadeloupe Woodpecker

Melanerpes herminieri

French: Pic de la Guadeloupe **German**: Guadeloupespecht **Spanish**: Carpintero de la Guadalupe

Taxonomy. *Picus Herminieri* Lesson, 1830, North America; error = Guadeloupe.
Sometimes placed in a monotypic genus *Linneopicus*, but shows many similarities to typical *Melanerpes*. Monotypic.

Distribution. Guadeloupe (Lesser Antilles).

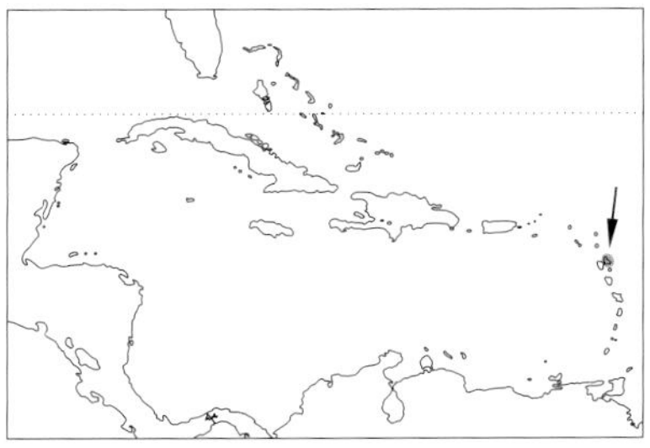

Descriptive notes. c. 24 cm; male 86-97 g, female 69-78 g. Rather small, distinctive woodpecker, appearing all black in the field. Male has head and upperparts, including wings and tail, black with blue gloss; tail feathers and inner parts of flight-feathers more brownish-black, unglossed; sooty-black underparts, dull red tips of feathers from throat to belly, blackish-brown flanks and undertail-coverts; long bill somewhat pointed, culmen slightly curved, narrow across nostrils, blackish; iris deep brown; legs blue-black. Female as male, but slightly smaller, bill up to 20% shorter. Juvenile is duller, less glossy, browner, underparts suffused dull orange-red. Voice. Main call a single or repeated "kwa", female higher-pitched; series of variable "wa-wa-wa" or "kakakakaka" calls when excited, in various contexts; loud "ch-arrgh", also in series of 3-8 notes, apparently to maintain contact; "tratratratra" by adult arriving for change-over at nest. Drums in relatively slow rolls, mean duration 1·3 seconds at 11 strikes per second, may contain an initial beat or beats out of rhythm; short, weak series in mutual tapping at or in cavity.

Habitat. Occurs in all available forest types within range. Prefers humid semi-deciduous forest and evergreen forest, but also uses swamp-forest and mangroves; occurs also near plantations with larger trees. Present from sea-level up to c. 1000 m; most common on wooded hills at elevations of 100-700 m.

Food and Feeding. Diet includes termites (Isoptera), ants, insect larvae, myriapods and other arthropods; also many seeds and fruits when available, especially those of *Clusia*; in one study, 16 species of fruit recorded eaten. Reported also to take ripening cacao pods. Female observed eating shell of white crab (*Cardisoma guanhumi*). Nestling diet better known: one study found orthopterans most common (44% of items), followed by larvae of beetles and Diptera (20%), the tree-frog *Eleutherodactylus martinicensis* (11%), adult beetles (Curculionidae, Cerambycidae, Scarabaeidae), caterpillars, Gastropoda, beetle and dipteran pupae, millipedes (Diplopoda); also unidentified spider; chicks also fed fruits and seeds. Forages mostly in canopy, male more often on trunks and larger branches, female more on smaller branches; visits treetops to obtain fruits. Does not remain long at one spot when foraging, but regularly revisits clusters of fruits and fruit-bearing trees. Main techniques are pecking, probing and gleaning; clings upside-down when obtaining fruits, or perches on or beside larger ones. Bigger prey such as tree-frogs, cockroaches (Blattodea) or large orthopterans usually placed in anvil for treatment; crab shell also recorded being treated in anvil. Smaller fruits swallowed whole; larger ones may be carried to tree and secured in crack or under bark, before flesh removed.

Breeding. Jan-Aug, mostly from Apr. Monogamous; solitary. Nest 2-20 m up in dead coconut palm (*Cocos nucifera*), rarely in live one, occasionally in other tree or in utility pole, excavation completed in c. 10 days; mean dimensions of entrance hole 6·2 cm high and 5·7 cm across, with tunnel 4·6 cm, cavity depth 31·9 cm, cavity diameter 12·1 cm; sometimes reused in successive years; territorial. Clutch up to 5 eggs, laid at daily intervals, but no more than 3 young reared; incubation by both parents, period 14-16 days; both also feed chicks, c. 1 food delivery every 12-12·5 minutes; nestling period 33-37 days; fledglings, which often still retain egg-tooth, stay with parents for several months, sometimes until next breeding season. Success generally low: at 22 nests, 100 eggs produced 10 fledglings. First breeds probably at 1 year.

Movements. Resident; juveniles disperse short distances. Recorded once on Antigua, c. 80 km N of Guadeloupe, but probably blown there by hurricane or tropical storm.

Status and Conservation. Not globally threatened. Currently considered Near-threatened. Restricted-range species: present in Lesser Antilles EBA. Estimated population 10,330 pairs, of which 7920 on W half of island (Basse-Terre) and 2410 on E half (Grande-Terre). On Basse-Terre, average territory size in semi-deciduous forest on igneous soil 2 ha in N and 5 ha in S, in evergreen forest 2·3 ha; on Grande-Terre, average territory size in semi-deciduous forest on clay soil 2·5 ha in N and 11 ha in S, in swamp-forest 3·3 ha and in mangrove-forest 3·0 ha. Has adapted to all forest types, which should make it less vulnerable. A major adverse factor is hurricanes, which can have a serious impact through destroying habitat and, particularly, nesting sites. In addition, road-building and other human activities have already led to loss of much habitat on the island. Although the species is not at present endangered, continuing deforestation, especially on Grande-Terre, could become a significant threat; even within the National Park of Guadeloupe, on Basse-Terre, felling is permitted for the tourism industry. Main conservation priority is effective protection of all non-fragmented forest areas with dead trees and palms for nesting. Assessment of possible effects of biocides on the local environment and on the species' ecology is also required. Potential threat posed by introduced rats (*Rattus*) also needs investigation. Although this woodpecker has long been protected on the island, it is considered a bad omen by hunting parties and is still sometimes shot.

Bibliography. Anon. (1998b), Benito-Espinal & Hautcastel (1988), Bond (1985), Cruz (1974a), Faaborg (1985), Feldmann & Villard (1993), Feldmann *et al.* (1998), Raffaele *et al.* (1998), Short (1974d, 1985b), Stattersfield & Capper (2000), Stotz *et al.* (1996), Villard (1995, 1997, 1999a, 1999b, 2000, 2001), Villard & Pavis (1998), Villard & Peacock (1999), Villard & Pradel (1998), Villard & Rousteau (1998).

37. Puerto Rican Woodpecker

Melanerpes portoricensis

French: Pic de Porto Rico **German**: Scharlachbrustspecht **Spanish**: Carpintero Puertorriqueño

Taxonomy. *Picus portoricensis* Daudin, 1803, Puerto Rico.
Monotypic.

Distribution. Puerto Rico and nearby Vieques I (Greater Antilles).

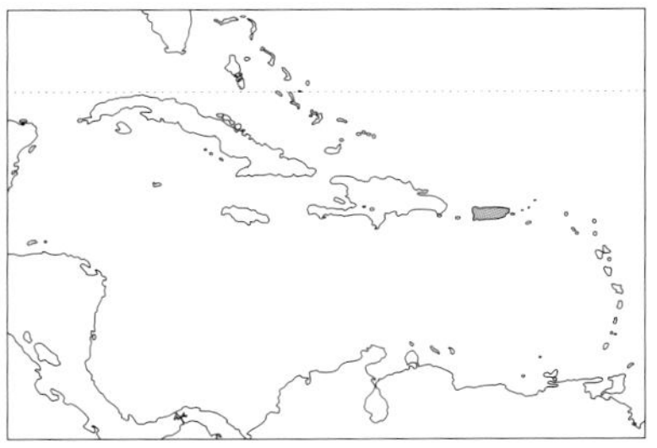

Descriptive notes. c. 22 cm; 45-72 g. Small, distinctive woodpecker. Male has white forehead, lores and narrow circle of feathers around eye, tinged buffish on forehead; blue-glossed black crown to hindneck, ear-coverts and narrow line beneath eye, bright red moustachial region, chin and throat; most of upperparts, including wing-coverts, glossy blue-black, lower back to uppertail-coverts white; brownish-black flight-feathers slightly glossed blue on edges, with variable amount of white at bases of inner webs of tertials, secondaries sometimes narrowly tipped white; uppertail glossy blue-black, outer feathers occasionally tipped white; bright red breast with blue-black of neck extending onto breast side (occasionally black-based feathers across entire breast), red continuing down central belly, pale buffish-brown sides and flanks, pale brownish undertail-coverts; underwing brown, coverts black and white; longish bill slightly chisel-tipped, culmen curved, fairly broad across nostrils, blackish; iris dark brown; legs greyish. Female is smaller and c. 16% shorter-billed than male, has chin, throat and often moustachial region largely brown, red of belly usually narrower and sometimes orange-yellow; plumage occasionally much as male. Juvenile less glossy, and with red below less extensive and more orange-tinged, male usually with a few red feather tips on crown. Voice. Wide variety of calls, most commonly "wek, wek, wek-wek-wek-wek-wek" or similar, increasing in volume and speed; also harsh sounds, e.g. rolling "gurrr-gurrr"; also "kuk" notes like those of domestic hen, and "mew" notes. Drums weakly and infrequently.

Habitat. Wooded areas, ranging from mangrove-swamps and coconut plantations on coast to montane forest; also shaded coffee plantations, less frequently in secondary forest. Appears to be most numerous in hills and lower mountains.

Food and Feeding. Animal food principally wood-boring beetle larvae, ants and earwigs (Dermaptera), also grasshoppers, bugs, occasionally frogs and lizards. Vegetable matter constitutes about one-third of diet, comprises seeds and fruits from various palms, trees (*Ficus*) and shrubs, and possibly bark. Forages singly, in pairs or in small family groups of up to 5 birds; sometimes loose groups of up to 10 individuals in non-breeding season. Forages mainly on trunks and branches. Sexes differ in foraging strata and techniques: male tends to forage in lower and middle parts of trees and uses more pecking and probing, female more frequently in middle layers and in canopy and prefers gleaning. Sexual differences most pronounced in harsh conditions of the dry season: respective percentages of gleaning and pecking/hammering 54% and 31% for females, compared with 27% and 45% for males.

Breeding. Nest-building from Jan, laying mostly in Apr-May. Solitary; possibly occasionally colonial. Nest excavated in dead stump, usually high in tree, especially coconut (*Cocos nucifera*), sometimes in pole; territory defended. Clutch up to 4 eggs; incubation and fledging periods not documented; at one nest watched for 5·25 hours, total of 20 food deliveries to chicks shared equally by male and female, 1 delivery every 16 minutes; both parents continue to feed young for 2 weeks after fledging, and family-members stay together for longer period. Nesting success variable, 77% in 1999 but as low as 8% in 1998.

Movements. Resident.

Status and Conservation. Not globally threatened. Restricted-range species: present in Puerto Rico and the Virgin Islands EBA. Common and widespread on Puerto Rico; rare on Vieques. No data on population size. Not surprisingly, found to be much more common in areas with good availability of nesting and foraging sites (e.g. coffee plantations) than in other areas (e.g. second growth). Huge annual variation in breeding success possibly due partly to ectoparasite infestation; *Philornis* parasite found on 11 of 23 individuals in 1998, but on none in 1999. No data on any other potential threats; hurricanes probably pose the most serious danger.

Bibliography. Anon. (1998b), Biaggi (1983), Bond (1985), Bowdish (1904), Cruz (1974a), Faaborg (1985), Leck (1972), Muiznieks & Collazo (1999), Raffaele (1989), Raffaele *et al.* (1998), Short (1985b), Stattersfield *et al.* (1998), Stotz *et al.* (1996), Villard (1999a, 2001), Wallace (1969, 1974a, 1974b).

38. Red-headed Woodpecker

Melanerpes erythrocephalus

French: Pic à tête rouge **German**: Rotkopfspecht **Spanish**: Carpintero Cabecirrojo

Taxonomy. *Picus erythrocephalus* Linnaeus, 1758, America = South Carolina.
Possibly closer to *M. portoricensis* and *M. herminieri* than to *M. formicivorus*. Slightly longer-winged (more migratory) populations of W Great Plains S & W to C Colorado sometimes separated as race *caurinus*, supposedly also with slightly deeper yellow wash below; tone of underparts, however, varies greatly among all populations, and subspecific division considered unwarranted. Monotypic.

Distribution. Breeds in extreme S Canada from S Manitoba (L Winnipeg) E to New Brunswick, and in C & E USA from Montana (E of Rocky Mts) across to Atlantic coast, S to C Colorado, C New Mexico, Gulf of Mexico and Florida.

Descriptive notes. c. 24 cm; 56-97 g. Rather small woodpecker with distinctive plumage pattern. Both sexes have head, neck and throat to upper breast red, rarely some admixed orange or yellow feathers; glossy blue-black mantle, upper back and wing-coverts, white lower back to uppertail-coverts often with indistinct black shaft streaks; brown primaries and outer secondaries, white inner secondaries and tertials with indistinct black shaft streaks and occasionally hint of barring; uppertail blackish-brown with faint blue gloss, outer feathers narrowly tipped white, outermost edged white; black line across upper breast; rest of underparts white, with dull yellowish to reddish wash of variable intensity and extent; white or creamy undertail-coverts, often with indistinct shaft streaks; underwing as above, but coverts black and white; long bill chisel-tipped, culmen slightly curved, broad across nostrils and at base, bluish-grey, paler towards base; iris brown; legs olive-grey. Female slightly smaller than male. Juvenile has similar pattern, but colours brown and white, usually some dull red on nape or around eye, mantle to back barred, white secondaries partly barred, throat

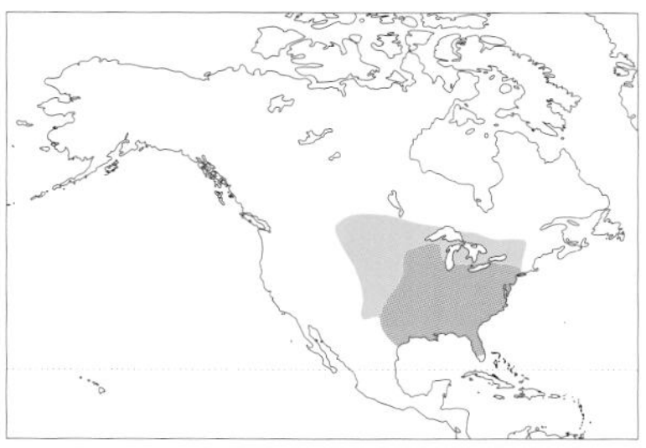

streaked, upper breast barred, rest of underparts variably streaked; acquires adult plumage in gradual moult through autumn and winter, most with much red on head, blue-black back and largely unstreaked below by Dec (some already fully adult by late Sept/Oct), but barring on secondaries may still be evident in May. VOICE. Many, variable calls: aggressive "quirr" in fast series of 5-7 notes, given throughout year, most frequently prior to intraspecific encounters or copulation; in breeding season very rapid series of "churr" or "kweer", or with higher-pitched initial note, "kwi-urr", probably as announcement and as contact between pair-members, sometimes by 2 birds simultaneously; also quieter variants in close encounters, become chattering "er-er" or "er-r-r-r" during copulation; "chee-chee" from nestlings. Drumrolls in breeding season weak and short, c. 20-25 strokes per second; mutual tapping, with 1 bird inside hole and the other at entrance, is typical.

Habitat. Mature lowland forest with dead trees for nesting, open areas for flycatching, and relatively open understorey allowing access to ground; open deciduous woodland, especially with beech (*Fagus*) or oak (*Quercus*); also riparian forest, pine (*Pinus*) forest, various types of wooded savanna, orchards and agricultural land, including in villages and suburbs; attracted to wooded swamps. In E prefers old woodlots with some undergrowth as in e.g. suburbs and agricultural areas, while farther S favours clearings with some tall stumps; in SE USA, pine scrub, mixed pine and hardwood forest, urban environments, pine-oak savanna, also nests in longleaf pine (*Pinus palustris*) forest. Preference for tall mature forest pronounced in post-breeding season. Also forages in open country, e.g. upland meadows and short-grass areas, such as pastures or golf courses, with scattered deciduous trees or groves; visits burned areas and clearings. Usually in habitats that are less dense and with less undergrowth than those frequented by *M. carolinus*; where occurring with *M. lewis*, is found more in riverine woodland and in clearings, whereas latter tends to prefer agricultural areas and edges.

Food and Feeding. About two-thirds of diet is made up of animal matter in spring; seeds and other plant material predominant food in winter. One of the most omnivorous picids: very wide range of prey, including earthworms, lizards, mice, nestlings of hole-nesting and open-nesting birds, eggs, grasshoppers, crickets, beetles and their larvae, caterpillars, adult Lepidoptera, wasps, honeybees (*Apis mellifera*), other arthropods; great variety of fruits, both wild and cultivated, e.g. mulberries (*Morus*), cherries, grapes, apples; also bark, and takes tree sap; in winter, mostly acorns, various types of nut, corn. Generally, flying insects more important than wood-boring larvae, which scarcely figure in diet. Forages singly or in pairs. Visits both live and dead trees, preferring higher levels (12-18 m) and medium-sized limbs (5-30 cm in diameter), may cling to smaller twigs in manner of tit (Paridae); regularly descends to ground; hops on ground and on horizontal branches. Often makes aerial sorties from perch for flying insects. In breeding season, main foraging techniques are hawking insects and gleaning, with some occasional pecks during arboreal foraging; pecking more important during winter. Obtains young of hole-nesting birds by widening hole entrance. Larger animal prey are pounced on and worked with blows of the bill. Places larger insects in crevices or cavities as interim stores. During years with good mast crops, spends most of active time in early autumn harvesting acorns, beechmast, corn and nuts; stores these in pre-existing cracks and bark crevices, breaks items into pieces if too big to fit; sometimes seals stores with wood chips. Defends stores against all intruders, including other woodpeckers; from Sept onwards establishes winter territory, size 0·04-2·0 ha. Dominant over other members of bark-foraging guild, including *M. carolinus*, generally causing them to shift habitat or foraging stratum.

Breeding. Apr-Sept, mainly May-Jun; from Feb in S; up to 50% of pairs raise 2 broods. Monogamous, solitary; occasional trios of male and 2 females reported, but possible polygyny unconfirmed. Nest-hole excavated mostly by male, work takes c. 2 weeks (but up to 50 days recorded); at variable height (2-25 m, in Arkansas mainly 7-12·5 m) in dead tree or dead part of tree, typically in barkless trunk, stump or branch, occasionally in live trunk; sometimes uses natural hole, or hole in building or other artificial structure (e.g. pump, pole), occasionally nestbox; territory size in Florida 3·1-8·5 ha. Courtship displays include horizontal posture with head and neck forward, plumage sleeked, also mutual "hide and seek" and chasing. Clutch usually 4-7 eggs, rarely 3-10; incubation by both parents, only male at night, period 12-14 days; both also tend nestlings, female providing c. 75% of feeds after day 12; fledging period 24-27 days, sometimes up to 31 days; young fed by parents for c. 25 days after leaving nest, then chased away. Success in rearing at least 1 fledgling c. 78%; snakes a major nest predator. First breeds at 1 year. Recorded longevity at least 9 years 11 months.

Movements. N populations migrate S more or less regularly; NW populations particularly migratory. Non-breeding distribution greatly dependent on abundance of mast; in most years, N limits from S & E Minnesota and SC Wisconsin across to extreme S Ontario, and W limits E Kansas and Oklahoma. Also somewhat nomadic in winter throughout range. Autumn dispersal and migration from Aug to Nov, singly and in small groups; return from winter quarters from late Feb, mostly in Mar, often large numbers along shores of Great Lakes. Migration mostly diurnal. Records outside range not infrequent, especially in W USA, more rarely in W Canada; single vagrant recorded in Bermuda.

Status and Conservation. Not globally threatened. Fairly common. Breeding numbers fluctuate, probably greatest in seasons following high productivity of mast. Recorded breeding densities of pairs/40 ha 2·3 in SE USA, up to 6-7 in Oklahoma. Was very common in 19th century, but thereafter decreased; possible causes were loss of some prey species (Orthoptera), also habitat loss; expansion of introduced Common Starling (*Sturnus vulgaris*), a probable nest competitor, may also have been relevant, although studies suggest that present species usually wins such encounters. Destruction of American chestnut (*Castanea dentata*) and American elm (*Ulmus americana*) by fungal disease led to population increase in mid-20th century, e.g. in Illinois c. 24-64 pairs/40 ha after death of elms but only 5 pairs before. Currently appears to be declining over most of range, especially in Florida and in Great Lakes Plain; considered fastest-declining hole-nester in Florida; decline of 2·2% annually in E USA since 1966. Habitat degradation resulting from removal of dead trees and branches in urban areas, and clear-cutting and agricultural development in rural areas, largely responsible for reduction in numbers of this woodpecker; collisions with motor vehicles may also be a contributing factor. Formerly considered a serious pest by farmers and was shot in large numbers, e.g. over 100 shot at a single tree in 1 day; was also shot because thought to do considerable damage to utility poles. Current levels of such persucution only minimal.

Bibliography. Atkins (1989), Bancroft (1983, 1984), Becker (1982), Belson (1998), Belson & Small (1998), Bent (1939), Bock *et al.* (1971), Brackbill (1969b), Campbell *et al.* (1990), Conner (1973, 1975, 1976), Conner & Adkisson (1977), Conner, Jones & Jones (1994), Cyr (1995a), Doherty *et al.* (1996), Friederici (1994), Gamboa & Brown (1976), Garrett (1999), Graber (1979), Grant (1966), Howard (1980), Husak (1997d), Ingold (1987, 1989a, 1989b, 1989c, 1990, 1991, 1994a, 1994b), Ingold & Densmore (1992), Jackson (1970c, 1976c), Jackson & Jackson (1994), Jones (1988), Kilham (1958b, 1958c, 1959a, 1959c, 1977a, 1977b, 1978, 1983), Koenig (1987), Lochmiller (1977), Lungstrom (1949), MacRoberts (1975), McNair (1996), Moskovits (1978), Nichols & Jackson (1987), Peck & James (1983), Petit *et al.* (1985), Reller (1972), Rogers *et al.* (1979), Roth (1978), Rumsey (1968, 1970), Schaffer (1997), Schwab & Monnie (1959), Sedgwick & Knopf (1990), Selander & Giller (1959), Shackelford & Conner (1997), Shadick (1980), Shaw (1951), Short (1985b), Smith, D.R. & Layne (1986), Smith, K.G. (1986a, 1986b), Smith, K.G. & Scarlett (1987), Smith, K.G. *et al.* (2000), Southern (1960), Spring (1965), Toland & Elder (1984), Venables & Collopy (1989), Volman *et al.* (1997), Wander & Brady (1980), Wiedenfeld *et al.* (1992), Williams (1975), Williams & Batzli (1979a), Willson (1970), Wood & Eichholz (1986), Woods (1984), Zusi & Marshall (1970).

39. Acorn Woodpecker

Melanerpes formicivorus

French: Pic glandivore **German**: Eichelspecht **Spanish**: Carpintero Bellotero

Taxonomy. *Picus formicivorus* Swainson, 1827, Temiscáltepec, Mexico.

Geographical variation clinal, and some races rather poorly defined. Proposed race *martirensis* (N Baja California) considered indistinguishable from *bairdi*. Race *lineatus* doubtfully distinct from *albeolus*. Seven subspecies currently recognized.

Subspecies and Distribution.

M. f. bairdi Ridgway, 1881 - NW Oregon S to N Baja California.

M. f. formicivorus (Swainson, 1827) - Arizona, New Mexico and W Texas S to SE Mexico (W of Chiapas).

M. f. angustifrons Baird, 1870 - extreme S Baja California.

M. f. albeolus Todd, 1910 - SE Mexico (E Chiapas, probably also Tabasco and Campeche), NE Guatemala and Belize.

M. f. lineatus (Dickey & van Rossem, 1927) - Chiapas E to Guatemala and N Nicaragua.

M. f. striatipectus Ridgway, 1874 - Nicaragua to W Panama.

M. f. flavigula (Malherbe, 1849) - Colombia (W & C Andes and W slope of E Andes).

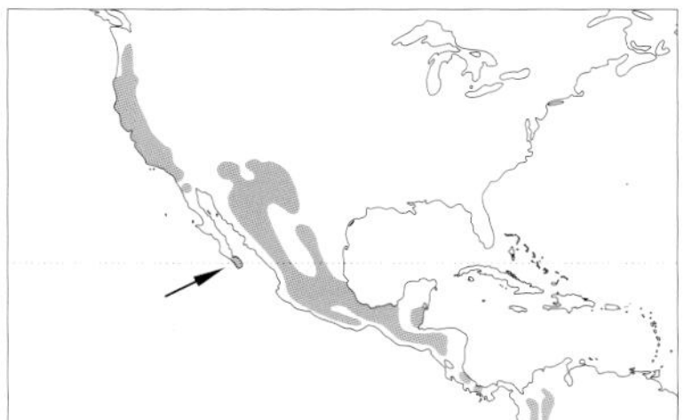

Descriptive notes. c. 23 cm; 65-90 g. Rather small, distinctively patterned woodpecker. Male has white forehead and lores, red crown to nape, black chin, pale yellowish cheeks and throat; area around eye and entire ear-coverts, rear and side of neck, mantle and upper back glossy black, lower back to uppertail-coverts white; upperwing black or brownish-black, primaries with white at bases, wing-coverts glossed purplish or greenish; uppertail black or brownish-black, sometimes white shaft streaks at base, occasionally white tips and subterminal spots on outer feathers; black extends from neck across upper breast, where variable white streaks and spots (usually also a few red feather tips in centre); rest of underparts white, lower breast with variable black streaking, flanks also streaked, undertail-coverts with black streaks or tear-shaped spots; underwing as above but duller, coverts with white streaks; moderately long bill slightly chisel-tipped, culmen curved, broad across nostrils, black; iris white to yellow-white or pinkish-white, orbital skin grey, sometimes brown or blackish; legs grey to greenish-grey. Female has red on head restricted to hindcrown, bill c. 10% shorter than male's. Juvenile browner and less glossy above, central crown orangey (may be less extensive on female), tail often with more white barring on outer feathers, more prominent white shaft streaks on central rectrices, buff-tinged underparts with less contrasting markings on upper breast, some barring across flank streaks, heavily streaked undertail-coverts, eyes initially brown, becoming greyish before turning white. Races differ only moderately in plumage, to lesser extent in size: *bairdi* is slightly larger than other races, with long stout bill, moderately yellow throat, breastband well demarcated and little streaked, less streaking below; *angustifrons* is smallest, with relatively long bill, reduced white on forehead, yellower throat, more heavily streaked below and with more white in breastband, female with red extending farther forward on crown; *albeolus* is very like nominate, but throat palest of all races, underparts with reduced streaking; *lineatus* is like previous, but has slightly yellower throat, white primary patch larger and unbarred, breastband fully streaked; *striatipectus* has throat very yellow, white primary patch narrower and often with some black bars; *flavigula* has rump and uppertail-coverts feathers tipped and edged black, throat very yellow, underparts most heavily streaked of all races, male with red confined to nape, female with no red on head, juveniles of both sexes with fully red crown and nape. VOICE. Rather noisy, with nasal whinnying, laughing or rattling calls: most common is "whaaka-whaaka" or "wa-ka", usually repeated, as greeting and during territorial disputes, at full intensity terminated by rasp, "wa-ka, wa-ka, wa-ka, trtrtr"; repeated "karrit-cut" or "rack-up, rack-up" or varied to rolling "r-r-r-rack-up" in bowing displays, also in presence of predator; in general alarm, vibrating "karrit" calls; more intimate "hick a ick a ick" chatters between group-members in close contact; chatters when attacked by other group-member; also "urrk" notes (not loud) and "garrick" notes in various contexts; also "squee-trtr" by fledgling when fed by adult. Drums with 2-20 evenly spaced taps, mostly in intraspecific territorial encounters.

Habitat. Oak (*Quercus*) woodland, and mixed woodland of pine (*Pinus*) and oak; also Douglas fir (*Pseudotsuga*), redwood (*Sequoia sempervirens*) and hardwood stands where some oaks also present. Mostly in interior and at edges of forest, sometimes in adjacent second growth; also visits clearings and pastures with scattered trees. Migrating birds also sometimes in open areas, e.g. open grassland, desert. Occurs primarily in uplands and associated valleys: above 750 m in USA, but down to sea-level in California; at 500-3000 m in Mexico, locally lower on Caribbean slope; from 1200 m up to tree-line in tropical Central America, straying down to 900 m; on both slopes of Andes between 1400 m and 3300 m in Colombia.

Food and Feeding. Acorns; also other vegetable matter, including other seeds (e.g. of pine), oak catkins, berries and other fruits, sap, nectar. Drinks sugar water from feeders. Insects also important, especially flying ants and other Hymenoptera, Coleoptera, Lepidoptera, Diptera, eaten throughout year. Readily eats other birds' eggs, and occasionally takes lizards. Acorns (mostly dried, but green ones also taken) make up c. 50-60% of diet of N populations, and are basic energy source in winter; S populations less dependent on acorns. Nestling food mainly insects (hymenopterans, beetles, hemipterans, homopterans, caterpillars, dipterans); older broods also fed acorns and fruits. Forages singly and in groups, mostly in or near canopy, rarely descending to ground. Acorns picked directly from trees, sometimes several together by breaking off twig, occasionally from ground; usually placed in anvil (crack or crevice in horizontal limb) for treatment, before being swallowed piecemeal. Sap especially important in spring and mid-summer (e.g. Feb-Mar and Jul-Aug in California), obtained by drilling holes 3-19 mm deep and 5-15 mm wide into live oaks; holes exploited by all group-members. Expert fly-catcher, frequently sallys from treetop or post, especially towards dusk, catching 1 insect on each flight; this foraging method most important in spring (Apr-May), often involves the whole group. Also probes (including into epiphytes) and gleans for insects;

occasionally descends to ground to feed on ants. Many groups store acorns in autumn, but this varies geographically (rare among S populations). Acorns stored whole or piecemeal in crevices in bark or wood, including man-made wooden structures, or amid epiphytes in tropics, or often in specially made holes covering large areas of a tree (oak, pine or other) and densely spaced (c. 28 mm nearest-neighbour distances); such "granaries" can contain up to 40,000-50,000 holes, excavated over many years; stores are constantly tended. Other nuts and seeds similarly stored when available; some animal prey stored in appropriate places. Food stores and anvils, as well as sap trees and favourite hawking perches, vigorously defended.

Breeding. In USA, Mar-Jul and less often also Aug-Nov in C California, mostly May-early Sept in New Mexico, from Jun in Arizona; Apr-Aug in Central America; May-Jun, occasionally to Sept, in Colombia; not all groups breed in any one year; sometimes 2 or even 3 broods in a season, at 2-month intervals. Some populations monogamous, especially in Arizona and in S of range; others co-operative and polygynous, or polygynandrous in groups usually of 1-4 (sometimes up to 7) reproducing related males and 1 breeding female, or with 2 or 3 breeding females (usually sisters of first) in c. 20% of groups, and up to 10 helpers (group's offspring of previous years); joint nesting of females more likely as population size increases. Nest-hole excavated 2·3-21 m up in dead, usually well-decayed tree; if new nest made, all group-members participate in task, which may take up to 3 months; internal diameter c. 15 cm, depth 22-70 cm; hole often reused for many years; mean territory size in California 6 ha, hole defended vigorously, in groups females very aggressive, destroy rivals' eggs but unable to prevent laying in nest by subordinate females. Clutch (including multiple-female layings) 4-6 eggs, average 5·06, clutch size increasing with latitude; incubation by both parents, minimal contribution by any helpers present, period 11-12 days; chicks brooded and fed by all group-members, female helpers contributing greater effort than males, feeding rate variable depending on e.g. group size; fledging period 30-32 days; fledglings fed by parents, or group-members, for several weeks, may then disperse, females earlier than males, and form temporary breeding pairs, or remain in parental territory for at least 1 year; in groups, juveniles in high-quality territories tend to stay on and become helpers, many broodmates stay together for entire life and share mates. Success variable: about two-thirds of eggs hatch, of which two-thirds produce fledglings; in a study in California, groups with stored acorns still available started breeding earlier, had larger clutches and fledged more than 5 times as many young as groups without stores; jointly nesting females raise c. 35% fewer offspring per year than females which nest singly, but lifetime reproductive success about equal since females sharing nest with another have marginally better survival. First breeds at 1 or 2 years, some not until 6 years. Recorded longevity at least 16 years for males, at least 15 years for females.

Movements. Mostly resident; occasional wandering, sometimes on large scale, in response to food shortage. Juveniles disperse short distances, females farther than males. In SE Arizona (near Huachuca Mts) and adjacent Mexican mountains apparently wholly migratory in most years; presumed to move S into oak forests of Sierra Madre, in N & W Mexico. Occurs regularly outside normal range; recorded N to British Columbia (Canada) and NE to North Dakota.

Status and Conservation. Not globally threatened. Common in most of range; common to fairly common in Mexico and Central America; local in Colombia. Often the most abundant woodpecker within its range in USA. Occurs in many protected areas and relatively undisturbed areas throughout its range. Numbers vary locally according to abundance and fruiting of oaks; thus, populations limited largely by that factor, and also by availability of storage sites. Was formerly killed for its feathers and for food. Since second half of 20th century, however, habitat loss and degradation are far greater threats; conversion of oak and pine-oak forest to agricultural use has led to substantial loss of habitat; species may have declined considerably in SW USA, Mexico and possibly elsewhere as a result of overgrazing of montane, riparian and pine-oak habitats; however, surveys in early 1990's indicate numbers of present species to be on increase. Competition for holes from introduced Common Starlings (*Sturnus vulgaris*) may be a limiting factor. Sometimes shot, both legally and illegally, to prevent damage to nut and fruit crops. Nevertheless, remains very common in most areas and adapts well to human presence, readily utilizing man-made structures for roost-holes and food-storing. Preservation of its preferred woodland habitats, with sufficient old snags and dead branches, should ensure its future.

Bibliography. Adams (1941b), Baicich & Harrison (1997), Benitez (1993), Bennun & Read (1988), Bent (1939), Binford (1989), Bock & Bock (1974a), Brewer & McCann (1985), Burgess (1983), Burgess *et al.* (1982), Callegari (1966), Chao (1997), Chinchilla (1991), Cully (1987), Dickinson *et al.* (1995), Dillingham & Vroman (1997), Fajer *et al.* (1987), Fjeldså & Krabbe (1990), Gutiérrez & Koenig (1978), Hannon, Mumme, Koenig & Pitelka (1985), Hannon, Mumme, Koenig, Spon & Pitelka (1987), Hayes *et al.* (1992), Henshaw (1921), Hilty & Brown (1986), Hitchcock & Houston (1994), Hooge (1989, 1991), Hooge *et al.* (1999), Howell & Webb (1995), Jamieson (1999), Jehl (1979), Jobanek (1994), Joste, Koenig *et al.* (1982), Joste, Ligon & Stacey (1985), Kattan (1988), Kattan & Murcia (1985), Koenig (1978, 1980a, 1980b, 1981a, 1981b, 1987, 1990, 1991), Koenig & Haydock (1999), Koenig & Heck (1988), Koenig & Mumme (1987), Koenig & Pitelka (1979, 1981), Koenig & Stacey (1990), Koenig & Williams (1979), Koenig, Hannon *et al.* (1988), Koenig, Haydock & Stanback (1998), Koenig, Hooge *et al.* (2000), Koenig, Mumme & Pitelka (1983, 1984), Koenig, Mumme, Stanback & Pitelka (1995), Koenig, Stacey *et al.* (1995), Koenig, Stanback & Haydock (1999), Koenig, Stanback, Hooge & Mumme (1991), Leach (1925), Levey & Cipollini (1999), Ligon & Stacey (1996), MacRoberts (1970, 1974), MacRoberts & MacRoberts (1976), Michael (1926), Miller (1955c), Mumme (1984), Mumme & de Queiroz (1985), Mumme, Koenig & Pitelka (1983a, 1983b, 1983c, 1988, 1990), Mumme, Koenig, Zink & Marten (1985), Peyton (1917), du Plessis *et al.* (1994), Pratini (1989), Ritter (1921, 1922, 1929, 1938), Roberts (1976, 1979), Seveyka (1996), Short (1985b), Shuford (1985), Skutch (1969a), Spray & MacRoberts (1975), Spring (1965), Stacey (1978, 1979a, 1979b, 1979c, 1981), Stacey & Bock (1978), Stacey & Edwards (1983), Stacey & Jansma (1977), Stacey & Koenig (1984), Stacey & Ligon (1987), Stacey & Taper (1992), Stanback (1988, 1989, 1991, 1994, 1998), Stanback *et al.* (1994), Stark *et al.* (1998), Stiles (1985), Swearingen (1977), Todd (1979), Trail (1980), Troetschler (1974, 1976), Walker (1952), Weathers *et al.* (1990), Wong (1989), Yaeger (1994).

40. Black-cheeked Woodpecker
Melanerpes pucherani

French: Pic de Pucheran **German**: Schläfenfleckspecht **Spanish**: Carpintero Centroamericano
Other common names: Pucheran's Woodpecker

Taxonomy. *Zebrapicus Pucherani* Malherbe, 1849, Tobago; error = Colombia.
Sometimes placed in a separate genus *Tripsurus*, along with *M. chrysauchen*, *M. cruentatus* and *M. flavifrons*. Forms a superspecies with first of those, or both sometimes included in the superspecies represented by last two. N populations sometimes separated as race *perileucus*, with supposed tendency towards stronger white barring on upperparts and wings, but much overlap occurs with S populations and racial separation considered not sustainable. Monotypic.

Distribution. S Mexico (Veracruz, Chiapas) S to W Colombia and W Ecuador (S to El Oro; may also occur in W Loja).

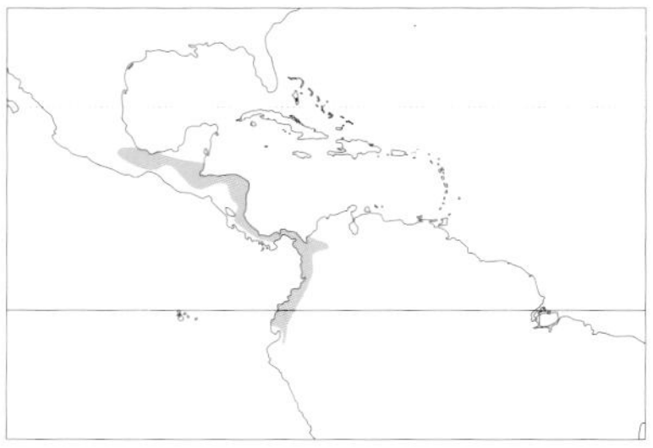

Descriptive notes. c. 17-19 cm; 42-68 g. Male has golden-yellow forehead, red crown and nape, variable amount of black at side of forecrown (and often some white feathers at front edge); white line behind and slightly higher than eye, black around eye and through ear-coverts down to neck side and hindneck; whitish lores, cheeks, chin and upper throat; black mantle and upper back barred white, black scapulars unbarred or partly barred, white lower back to uppertail-coverts tinged pale buff, occasionally faintly barred or streaked blackish; wing-coverts black, greaters and some medians spotted white; flight-feathers black or brownish-black, narrowly tipped white when fresh, all but outer webs of outer primaries barred white (bars broadest on tertials); uppertail black, central feathers variably barred white, sometimes indication of bars on outer feathers; lower throat and breast olive-buff, tinged grey, feathers initially tipped yellowish; rest of underparts buffish-white, red on centre of belly, with strong arrowhead barring; underwing barred dark and white; undertail yellow-brown; longish bill almost pointed, culmen curved, broad across nostrils, black, usually paler base of lower mandible; iris brown, orbital skin brown to greyish; legs greenish-grey or olive. Female is somewhat smaller than male, has forecrown white to buffy-white, black border extending backwards and then across hindcrown, red confined to nape. Juvenile is duller, browner with more diffuse barring above, has duller barring below, red of belly paler and less extensive, male with orangey-red on nape and red on crown, female with far less red (and often barred) on crown. VOICE. Commonest call a series of c. 4 short rattling trills on same pitch, "churrr, churrr, churrr, churrr" or "cherrr", higher-pitched than *M. rubricapillus*, less nasal than *M. aurifrons*; also longer smoother rattle, and loud full-toned "krrrr"; also higher-pitched piercing "chirriree" or "keereereek" recalling Boat-billed Flycatcher (*Megarhynchus pitangua*). Drumming infrequent, by both sexes.

Habitat. Humid and wet evergreen forest, forest borders, scattered tall trees in clearings, and old secondary growth and abandoned plantations; enters gardens, sometimes far from forest. Replaces *M. rubricapillus* in more wooded areas. Lowlands and foothills, to 700-900 m, occasionally 1200 m; locally to 1500 m in Ecuador.

Food and Feeding. Spiders, termites, beetles, grubs, ants, caterpillars, and aerial insects. Also eats large quantities of plant material, including fruits, berries, seeds of large bromeliads (may even be fed to nestlings), arils and catkins of *Cecropia*; drinks nectar from large flowers of balsa and kapok trees. Forages singly or in pairs, occasionally in larger family parties; 12 or more individuals may gather at fruiting trees; joins mixed-species flocks. Forages mostly in upper and middle levels inside forest. Most frequently probes crevices and cracks in bark, bases of epiphytes, also pecks and hammers dead wood. Gleans insects from trunks, branches and lianas, often searches epiphytes for animal prey and seeds; plucks fruits regularly; sallies for aerial insects. Moves actively, and peers; reaches for prey, also clings with great agility on underside of branches and twigs.

Breeding. Mar-Jul. Nest-hole 4-30 m up in dead trunk (including of palm) or branch, in one case cavity 35 cm deep, entrance hole 10 × 8 cm; used by male also as roost-hole, at least sometimes joined by female. Clutch 2-4 eggs; incubation by both sexes, period 14 days; in captivity fledging period c. 3 weeks, fledglings may return to nest to roost, adults may start second brood and still tolerate young of previous one, even in relatively small aviary.

Movements. Resident.

Status and Conservation. Not globally threatened. Common to fairly common throughout range. Occurs in several protected areas, including Tikal National Park (Guatemala), Braulio Carrillo and Cahuita National Parks and Guayabo National Monument (Costa Rica), Los Katíos National Park (Colombia), and Río Palenque Science Centre and Tinalandia Reserve (Ecuador). Numbers decline with extensive deforestation.

Bibliography. Anon. (1998b), Binford (1989), Bloch *et al.* (1991), England (2000), Friedmann *et al.* (1957), González-García (1993), Hilty & Brown (1986), Howell, S.N.G. & Webb (1995), Howell, T.R. (1957), Land (1970), Marín & Schmitt (1991), Moermond (1985), Monroe (1968), Otvos (1967), Paynter (1957), Ridgely & Greenfield (2001), Ridgely & Gwynne (1989), Robbins *et al.* (1985), Salaman (1994), Selander & Giller (1963), Short (1985b), Skutch (1969a), Slud (1964), Smithe (1966), Stiles (1985), Stiles & Skutch (1989), Stotz *et al.* (1996), Wetmore (1968a), Wilbur (1987), Willis (1980).

41. Golden-naped Woodpecker
Melanerpes chrysauchen

French: Pic masqué **German**: Buntkopfspecht **Spanish**: Carpintero Nuquigualdo
Other common names: Beautiful Woodpecker (*pulcher*)

Taxonomy. *Melanerpes chrysauchen* Salvin, 1870, Chiriquí, Panama.
Sometimes placed in a separate genus *Tripsurus*, along with *M. pucherani*, *M. cruentatus* and *M. flavifrons*. Forms a superspecies with first of those, or both sometimes included in the superspecies represented by last two. Distinctive race *pulcher* geographically isolated, sometimes treated as separate species. Two subspecies recognized.

Subspecies and Distribution.
M. c. chrysauchen Salvin, 1870 - SW Costa Rica to W Panama.
M. c. pulcher P. L. Sclater, 1870 - NC Colombia (Magdalena Valley).

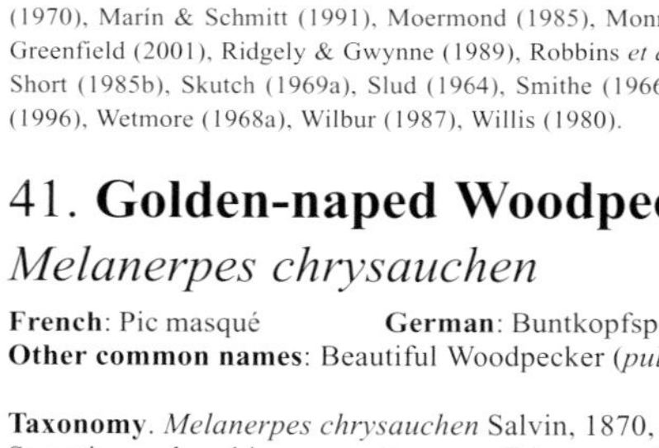

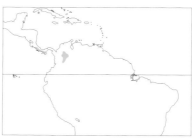

Descriptive notes. c. 17-18 cm; 45-68 g. Male has golden-yellow forehead, occasionally tinged orange, red crown (often some olive-yellow feather bases visible), golden-yellow hindcrown to hindneck; short black-streaked white line just behind eye; black narrowly around eye, across ear-coverts and down neck side; lores, moustachial region, chin and upper throat white, strongly tinged grey-buff at rear and on throat; mantle and scapulars blue-glossed black, narrow white panel down mantle centre, white back to uppertail-coverts often tinged pale buffish; blue-black wing-coverts; brownish-black (blacker towards bases) flight-feathers tipped white when fresh, inner webs with short white bars; uppertail black, outer feathers often with 1 or 2 white bars or spots; lower throat to upper belly olive-buff, washed grey, central belly orange-red, rest of underparts pale buffish-white with broad black arrowhead barring; underwing brownish, coverts blackish, barred white, marginal coverts white; undertail brownish-black; longish bill almost pointed, culmen curved, fairly broad across nostrils, black with paler base; iris brown;

legs grey, sometimes tinged green or brown. Female is slightly smaller, shorter-billed than male, has forehead and forecrown golden-yellow, central crown black (occasionally a few red feather tips), hindcrown to hindneck golden-yellow. Juvenile duller, black areas browner, yellow of forehead paler and less extensive, barring below duller and less contrasting, belly patch smaller and more orange, both sexes with red-tipped feathers on crown, less extensive on female. Race *pulcher* has white on mantle partly or sometimes fully barred black, forehead patch paler buffish or creamy-white and extending to forecrown, barring below extending across upper belly, male with red of crown continuing to upper nape, golden lower nape and hindneck, female with black central crown, red hindcrown, golden nape and hindneck. VOICE. Resonant "churr"; loud, rattling or laughing short trill rapidly repeated 3-5 times on same pitch; also several short rattles; nestlings utter squeaking buzz. Both sexes drum occasionally.

Habitat. Humid areas with dense tall rainforest, including edges of clearings, forest edge and plantations enclosed by forest; increasingly extending into semi-open areas with scattered trees as forests shrink. Replaces *M. pucherani* in drier areas in Colombia. From lowlands to 1200 m, locally to 1500 m; from 400 m to 1500 m in Colombia.

Food and Feeding. Wood-boring beetles and their larvae, winged termites, also other insects. Takes much fruit: *Cecropia*, figs (*Ficus*), arillate seeds, bananas, oranges, palm fruits; takes fruits from artificial feeders. Forages in pairs or family parties of 3-6 individuals throughout year. Prefers canopy and middle levels of humid forest. Constantly pecks and hammers into decaying trunks and branches. Frequently captures insects on the wing, showing great skill; ascends above treetops to catch these, especially on wet evenings.

Breeding. Mar-Jun; rarely, 2 broods in a season. Displays with deep bows accompanied by "churr" calls. Nest-hole excavated by both sexes, 5-30 m up, usually in massive dead trunk, excavation can be completed in 2 weeks. Clutch 3 or 4 eggs, but usually 2 or 3 young fledge; both sexes incubate, in long sessions, both sleep together in nest, incubation period c. 12 days; chicks fed by both parents, apparently more by male, fledging 33-34 days; fledglings cared for by parents for up to 3 months, roost with them in hole until next breeding season; when 2 broods, a juvenile from first brood may also incubate and feed second brood, and roost in same nest.

Movements. Resident.

Status and Conservation. Not globally threatened. Restricted-range species: present in South Central American Pacific Slope EBA and Nechí Lowlands EBA. Rather scarce and local thoughout range. In Pacific lowlands of Costa Rica, occurs in Caracara Biological Reserve, in Manuel Antonio National Park and in Corcovado National Park.

Bibliography. Anon. (1998b), Heisler (1994), Hilty & Brown (1986), Ridgely & Gwynne (1989), Selander & Giller (1963), Short (1985b), Skutch (1948a, 1969a), Slud (1964), Stattersfield *et al.* (1998), Stiles (1985), Stiles & Skutch (1989), Stotz *et al.* (1996), Wetmore (1968a).

42. Yellow-tufted Woodpecker
Melanerpes cruentatus

French: Pic à chevron d'or **German**: Gelbbrauenspecht **Spanish**: Carpintero Azulado
Other common names: Red-fronted Woodpecker ("*M. rubrifrons*")

Taxonomy. *Picus cruentatus* Boddaert, 1783, Cayenne.
Sometimes placed in a separate genus *Tripsurus*, along with *M. pucherani*, *M. chrysauchen* and *M. flavifrons*. Forms a superspecies with last of those, sometimes also including first two. Black-headed morph (mostly in S & SE Venezuela, the Guianas and Amazonian Brazil, where it predominates) was formerly considered a separate species, "*M. rubrifrons*", but interbreeds freely with yellow-tufted morph wherever the two co-occur; hence, there are no grounds even for subspecific division. Population in W & S of range (Colombia to Venezuela and W Brazil, and S of there) described as race *extensus*, on basis of difference in tone and extent of red on belly; this character, however, varies greatly among all populations, and racial separation considered untenable. Monotypic.

Distribution. E Colombia and S & SE Venezuela E to the Guianas and NE Brazil (E to Maranhão), S to E Ecuador, E Peru, N & E Bolivia and Mato Grosso.

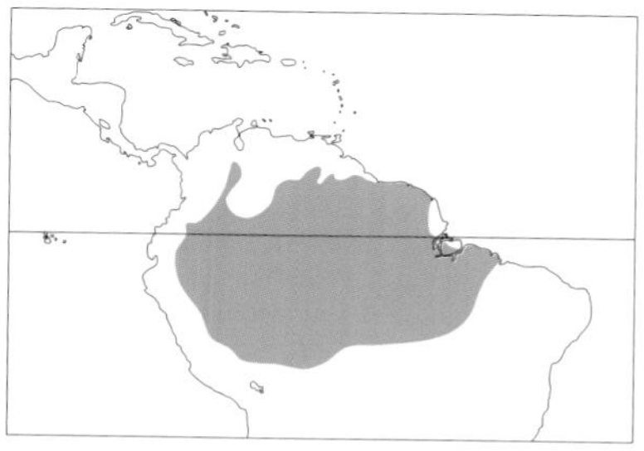

Descriptive notes. c. 19 cm; 48-64 g. Small, dark-looking woodpecker with broad pale eyering, occurring in two morphs. Male of black-headed morph has red, often round-shaped patch on central crown; rest of head and neck down to breast, and most of upperparts, including wing-coverts, blue-glossed black; lower back to uppertail-coverts white, often with hint of black barring, black shaft streaks on uppertail-coverts; flight-feathers blackish, slightly glossy, short white bars on inner webs (on primaries, restricted to bases); uppertail bluish-black, central feather pair usually with white spots on inner webs, outer feathers occasionally tipped white; red on belly centre extending as wedge to lower breast, but depth of colour and its extent considerably variable individually; lower breast sides to sides of belly and undertail-coverts white or pale yellowish-white with bold black arrowhead barring; underwing barred black and white, margins browner; undertail brownish-black; long bill almost pointed, culmen curved, rather broad across nostrils, black; iris pale yellow, very broad orbital skin whitish to pale yellow; legs grey to pinky-grey. Male of yellow-tufted morph differs in having white (often yellow-tinged) supercilium from just in front of eye back to lower nape, golden-yellow or sometimes orangey lower nape and hindneck, red on crown usually more extensive and less rounded in shape. Intermediates between the 2 morphs have restricted or broken supercilium, less yellow on hindneck. Female is slightly shorter-billed than male, lacks red on crown, yellow-tufted female often with less golden-yellow on head. Juvenile duller than adult, black areas much browner, underparts greyer with barring more obscure, belly patch more orange-coloured, both sexes with red in crown centre; juvenile yellow-tufted morph has reduced white and yellow head markings. VOICE. Noisy, with various loud, hoarse calls like those of *M. formicivorus*: single "chowp" notes, and double "r-r-r-aack-up", "trrr-eh" or "churr-dówp" notes; also nine-syllable "ih-ih-ih-ih…" or "treh-treh-treh…", slowing towards end; more rasping variants during display, frequent "kat-sup, kat-sup" calls in bowing ceremony when two birds meet.

Habitat. Rainforest, secondary growth, forest edge, and burnt-over clearings with isolated trees; sometimes near houses and even in towns. Tall dead trees seem to be important element of habitat. Sea-level to 1350 m, mostly below 1200 m; locally to 1500 m (e.g. in Ecuador).

Food and Feeding. Insects (ants and others) and large quantities of fruits (berries) are main constituents of diet; other arthropods, e.g. spiders and chilopods, also taken. Forages mostly in groups of 3-5 birds, sometimes up to 12 or more. Forages in upper parts of tall, dead trees. Main technique is gleaning from surface of trunks and branches and from twigs and leaves of canopy; also probes; flycatching common in evening hours.

Breeding. Mainly Jun-Aug in E Peru E to the Guianas, from Mar in Colombia, to Sept along R Negro; Mar-Jun in Bolivia and Amazonian Basin to Ecuador; Dec-Feb in SE Peru and Mato Grosso. Communal breeder, with adult helpers; single adult may attend to 3 nests, but other details not known. Various displays include bowing. Nest excavated in dead tree or tall dead stump; sometimes several nests found in fairly close proximity. Clutch size and incubation and fledging periods not documented; nestlings apparently tended by entire social unit, and an adult may feed at several nests; fledglings accompanied by individual or by group.

Movements. Resident.

Status and Conservation. Not globally threatened. Generally common and conspicuous; fairly adaptable. Common in Colombia, Ecuador and Peru. Occurs in numerous protected areas, including Amacayacu National Park (Colombia), Canaima National Park, Imataca Forest Reserve and El Dorado (Venezuela), Cuyabeno Reserve (Ecuador) and Manu National Park (Peru).

Bibliography. Allen (1995), Balchin & Toyne (1998), Bloch *et al.* (1991), Brace *et al.* (1997), Canaday & Jost (1999), Clements & Shany (2001), Cohn-Haft *et al.* (1997), Donahue (1994), Flores *et al.* (2001), Friedmann (1948), Guilherme (2001), Haverschmidt & Mees (1994), Hilty & Brown (1986), Meyer de Schauensee & Phelps (1978), Oniki & Willis (1999), Oren & Parker (1997), Parker *et al.* (1982), Perry *et al.* (1997), Remsen & Traylor (1989), Ridgely & Greenfield (2001), Robinson (1997), Robinson & Terborgh (1997), Short (1985b), Sick (1993), da Silva (1996), Snyder (1966), Stotz, Fitzpatrick *et al.* (1996), Stotz, Lanyon *et al.* (1997), Terborgh *et al.* (1984), Tostain *et al.* (1992), Willis & Oniki (1990).

43. Yellow-fronted Woodpecker
Melanerpes flavifrons

French: Pic à front jaune **German**: Goldmaskenspecht **Spanish**: Carpintero Arcoiris

Taxonomy. *Picus flavifrons* Vieillot, 1818, Brazil.
Sometimes placed in a separate genus *Tripsurus*, along with *M. pucherani*, *M. chrysauchen* and *M. cruentatus*. Forms a superspecies with last of those, sometimes also including first two. Birds from E & S of range, generally much darker below than NW populations, are sometimes separated as race *rubriventris*, but considerable variation exists throughout entire range; recognition of geographical races considered unwarranted. Monotypic.

Distribution. E & SE Brazil from Bahia and Goiás S to SE Mato Grosso and Rio Grande do Sul, E Paraguay and NE Argentina (Misiones).

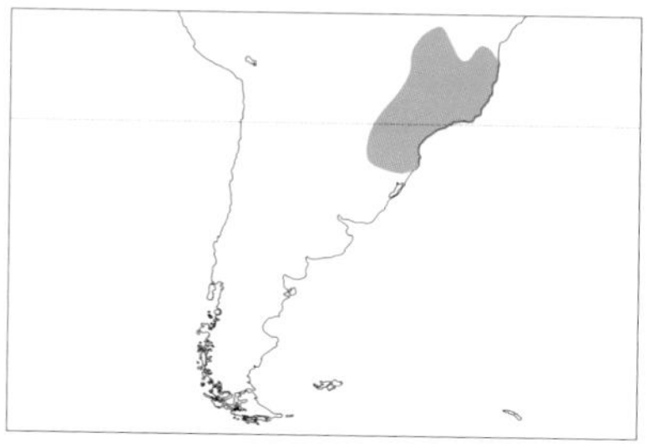

Descriptive notes. c. 17 cm; 49-64 g. Male has golden-yellow forehead and forecrown with white feather bases, red central crown to hindneck; glossy blue-black lores, area around eye, and ear-coverts down neck side to mantle; pale yellow to deep golden-yellow cheeks, chin and throat, sometimes to upper breast; blue-black mantle, central feathers with white on one web and black on other (pattern of broad white streaks), white back to uppertail-coverts usually with few black spots (rarely, hint of bars), black shaft streaks on uppertail-coverts; glossy blue-black wing-coverts; black to brownish-black flight-feathers glossed blue on edges, white bars on inner webs of secondaries and patches on tertials; uppertail black, central feather pair often with 1 or 2 white bars on inner webs, outer feathers tipped white when fresh; pale grey to yellowy olive-grey lower neck sides and breast, orange to crimson-red belly highly variable in intensity and extent of red, whitish flanks to undertail-coverts (often tinged olive or buff-yellow) with black barring; NW populations generally much paler below than coastal ones, with throat yellowish, breast whitish-grey, belly more orange, but considerable variation throughout entire range; underwing brownish, barred white; undertail brown, outer feathers often olive-brown; long bill chisel-tipped, culmen barely curved, fairly broad across nostrils, black; iris blackish to blue-black, broad orbital skin whitish to orange-yellow; legs olive, tinged green or brown. Female is slightly smaller, shorter-billed than male, has crown to hindneck blue-black. Juvenile duller, black areas browner, less glossy, belly patch smaller and more orange, eyes brown, male with red on crown and hindcrown, female generally only on mid-crown. VOICE. Noisy, with strident "kikiki", "tsilidit"; also flight calls sounding like "benedito"; series of "chlit" notes when meeting perched conspecific; also "tweewetwee tweewetwee…" apparently in aggression, and "eeeuk eeeuk". Drums, usually on tall trees.

Habitat. Humid forest; also secondary vegetation, such as cane fields, palm groves, orchards; recorded in partly burnt forest. Sea-level to 1800 m.

Food and Feeding. Takes many fruits, berries and seeds; also insects; captives fed sugar water and mealworms. Nestlings fed fruits, especially of *Virola*, also insects, including larger ones such as katydids and dragonflies (Odonata). Stores seeds; caches fruit and insects near nest. Observed in groups; probes in crevices, but details of foraging methods not recorded. Anvils used for breaking up larger food items.

Breeding. Jan-May in most of range, to Jun in SE Brazil; recorded in Nov in Espírito Santo. Co-operative breeder, up to 4 males and 2 females seen to attend single brood; solitary or in loose colonies. Display with head-waving and head-weaving. One nest was 28 m up in trunk of tall dead tree, attended by 1 male and 3 females, male fed chicks less often than females, 2 females (possibly young helpers) seemed to feed less than the other, feeding often interrupted by bouts of display or arrival of toucans (Ramphastidae), faecal sacs removed frequently, male roosted with young at night; incubation and fledging periods unrecorded; fledglings return to nest to roost. Toucans probably usurp nest-holes and prey on nestlings.

Movements. Resident.

Status and Conservation. Not globally threatened. No information on numbers. Occurs in neighbouring Iguaçú and Iguazú National Parks (Brazil/Argentina), Rio Doce State Park and Carlos Botelho State Park (Brazil), and Urugua-í Provincial Park (Argentina). Ability to exploit secondary habitats may indicate some adaptability, but lack of information on ecology and breeding makes it difficult to assess any possible threats. In SE Brazil (São Paulo), this species plays an important role in the reproduction of the Plain Parakeet (*Brotogeris tirica*) and the Maroon-bellied Parakeet (*Pyrrhura frontalis*), both of which use its abandoned holes as nesting sites.

Bibliography. Aleixo & Galetti (1997), dos Anjos (2001), dos Anjos & Schuchmann (1997), dos Anjos *et al.* (1997), Belton (1984), Brooks *et al.* (1993), Buzzetti (2000), Canevari *et al.* (1991), Capper *et al.* (2000), Descourtilz (1983), Dubs (1992), Figueiredo & Lo (2000), Goerck (1999), Guix, Martín & Mañosa (1999), Guix, Tabánez *et al.* (1992), Hayes (1995), Lowen *et al.* (1995), Machado & Rodrigues (2000), Oniki & Willis (1998), de la Peña (1994), Pereyra (1950), do Rosário (1996), Scott & Brooke (1985), Short (1985b), Sick (1993), da Silva (1996), Soares & dos Anjos (1999), Stager (1961a), Stotz *et al.* (1996), Tobias *et al.* (1993), Yamashita & Lo (1995).

44. White-fronted Woodpecker

Melanerpes cactorum

French: Pic des cactus **German**: Kaktusspecht **Spanish**: Carpintero de los Cardones

Taxonomy. *Picus cactorum* d'Orbigny, 1840, near Chaluani and Chilon, Mizqué, Bolivia.
Despite some variation in throat colour (from all white to all yellow), differences not sufficiently constant geographically to warrant recognition of any races. Monotypic.
Distribution. SE Peru (Puno), C & SE Bolivia (S from Cochabamba and Santa Cruz) and SW Brazil (SW Mato Grosso) S to W Paraguay and N Argentina (S to La Rioja, San Luis and Entre Ríos, E to to W Corrientes).

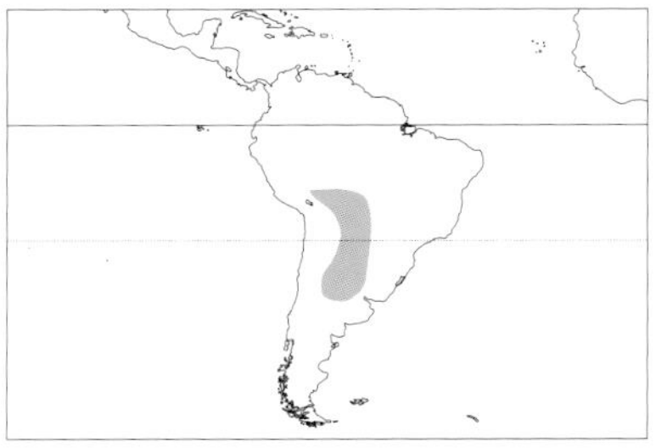

Descriptive notes. c. 16-18 cm; 29-53 g. Male has white forehead and forecrown, lores, moustachial region and lower ear-coverts; small partly concealed patch of red near front of central crown (sometimes totally concealed); otherwise blue-black from central crown to hindcrown, narrowly around eye and back through upper ear-coverts, continuing down neck side to mantle; white nape faintly tinged buff or yellow, pure white on hindneck; chin and throat white (mostly in S), or partly yellow, or entirely yellow or golden (mostly in Bolivia and W Argentina); glossy blue-black mantle and scapulars, broad white or buff-white streaks down mantle centre (feathers with one web white, other black), white back to uppertail-coverts barred or spotted black; black wing-coverts glossed blue, greaters spotted and tipped white, medians with black-spotted white distal half; flight-feathers blackish, primaries browner, white bars on both webs of secondaries and tertials and on bases of primaries; uppertail black, tipped white (when fresh), all feathers barred white; buff below, belly paler and greyer, lower flanks and undertail-coverts barred; underwing brown, barred white, coverts whiter and unbarred; undertail brownish-black, barred white; relatively short bill almost straight, slightly chisel-tipped, broad across nostrils, black or grey-black; iris brown to red-brown; legs slate-coloured. Female smaller, shorter-billed than male, lacks red spot on crown. Juvenile browner, less glossy above, more barred below, both sexes with some orange-red on crown centre. VOICE. Loud "weep-weep" and "wee-beep", resembling call of *Sphyrapicus varius*; faster renditions when displaying. Short, weak drumrolls near hole early in breeding season.
Habitat. Dry forest; frequents forest edge, savanna, gallery forest, bush country (Chaco), montane scrub; associates with cacti (*Cereus*). Also found in palm groves with trees. From lowlands to 1700 m, locally to 2500 m in Bolivia.
Food and Feeding. Diet includes insects and fruits; ants apparently important, beetles also recorded. Some food cached. During cold dry season (Jun-Sept), regularly drills holes in e.g. mesquite (*Prosopis*) to take exuding sap; in one study in Argentina, sap-feeding comprised 16-83% of observations of foraging in Jun-Jul. Usually in groups of 3-5 birds. Forages on palms, trunks and branches; gleans and probes.
Breeding. Sept-Dec. Co-operative breeder in groups of up to 5 or more birds; possibly loosely colonial. Bowing displays observed, with much calling. Nest excavated in dead tree, palm or cactus. No other information.
Movements. Probably some seasonal movements.
Status and Conservation. Not globally threatened. Reasonably common in much of range; locally very common in Argentina; rare in Peru. Occurs in Chancaní and Monte de las Barrancas Reserves (Argentina). Probably secure, but conservation status difficult to assess in absence of data.
Bibliography. Blendinger (1999), Canevari *et al*. (1991), Chebez *et al*. (1999), Clements & Shany (2001), Contreras (1980a), Contreras *et al*. (1990), Fjeldså & Krabbe (1990), Friedmann (1927), Genise *et al*. (1993), Hayes (1995), Lago-Paiva & Willis (1994), López (1997), Mazar Barnett & Pearman (2001), Miserendino (1998), Narosky & Yzurieta (1993), Nellar (1993), Nores *et al*. (1983), Paiva & Willis (1994), Parker *et al*. (1982), de la Peña (1994, 1997), Remsen & Traylor (1989), Remsen *et al*. (1986), Schmitt *et al*. (1997), Short (1975, 1985b), Stotz *et al*. (1996), Strussmann (1998), Wetmore (1926), Yamashita & Lo (1995).

45. Hispaniolan Woodpecker

Melanerpes striatus

French: Pic d'Hispaniola **German**: Haitispecht **Spanish**: Carpintero de la Española

Taxonomy. *Picas* [sic] *striatus* P. L. S. Müller, 1776, Santo Domingo, southern Dominican Republic. Monotypic.
Distribution. Hispaniola and nearby Beata I.

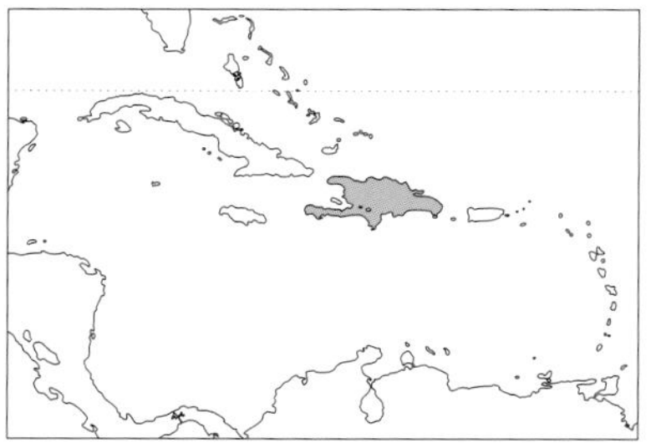

Descriptive notes. c. 20-24 cm; male 83-92 g, female 65-75 g. Small woodpecker with marked sexual size dimorphism. Male has bright red forecrown to upper hindneck, feathers with black bases; rest of head, including forehead and superciliary area, pale buffish-white to greyish, ear-coverts often greyer, chin and throat more olive-buff; lower hindneck broadly striped black and whitish; black upperparts and tertials broadly barred greenish-yellow to golden, bars whiter in worn plumage; yellow or greenish-yellow rump, red-tipped feathers on lower rump, often with faint blackish bars; red uppertail-coverts with black bases; brownish-black primaries and secondaries broadly barred yellowish, bars whiter on primaries; uppertail brownish-black, outer feathers edged whitish; dark reddish-buff below, washed grey, tinged olive on upper breast and belly, occasionally a few red-tipped feathers on belly and/or darker streaks on lower flanks, latter rarely with obscure thin bars; underwing barred brown and white, coverts plain olive; undertail brownish, outer feathers washed yellow; long bill straight, broad, dark grey, blacker tip; iris white to pale yellowish; legs greenish-grey. Female is smaller, less bulky, bill up to c. 21% shorter than male's, has black crown often white-speckled at sides. Juvenile much as adult, but red of nape and tail-coverts more orangey and less extensive, both sexes with white-spotted black crown with few red tips. VOICE. Highly variable: long series of up to 23 notes in long-distance communication; commonly several connected "waa" notes during encounters, when also aggressive "wup", more defensive "ta" and "ta-a" calls; also 3-5 distinct notes combined in short "bdddt" call. Instrumental signals near hole; drumming infrequent to rare.
Habitat. Wooded swamps, mangroves, coastal scrub and semi-arid country in lowlands to humid forest in mountains; also pine (*Pinus*) woodland, and trees and palms in and around villages and towns; most numerous in cultivated areas with trees and palms, especially in hilly areas.
Food and Feeding. Various insects, especially beetles, Lepidoptera, ants (both adults and pupae), also spiders, scorpions (Scorpiones); lizards (*Anolis*) also recorded. Also fruits, including commercially grown crops (oranges, cacao pods), and seeds, including corn, readily taken; vegetable matter, including tree sap, seems especially important. Occurs in pairs or, often, in groups; particularly large aggregations at fruiting trees. Forages above ground at all levels, mainly 7-20 m, on trees, bushes, vines, poles and cacti. Often hangs upside-down, on twigs and pine cones, and reaches for fruits. Main feeding techniques are pecking, probing and gleaning; also takes insects by hawking; probably excavates sap wells. Probes in crevices and holes, most often in dead substrates; also probes at bromeliads and other large epiphytes, and fruits (to obtain seeds or insects). Females glean c. 1·5 times as much as males, and probe much less frequently (0·6%, compared with 34% for males; difference may be reversed if other types of probing included); males use hammering or pecking twice as much as females. Pecks less forcefully than e.g. *M. aurifrons*. Larger items placed in anvil for treatment.
Breeding. Breeds in all months, predominantly Feb-Jul. Both solitary and colonial; often loose colonies of 3-20 nests in 1-3 trees, up to 26 recorded in single tree, highest holes apparently occupied by dominant individuals; possibly several helpers but further study needed. Displays include bowing and lateral swinging, gliding with raised wings; courtship feeding recorded. Nest excavated by both sexes, mainly by male, at 2-11 m in dead tree, live or dead palm, cactus, stub, or telephone pole; mean dimensions of entrance 9·7 cm high, 7·9 cm wide; nest-site and prominent perches defended. Clutch 4-6 eggs; incubation and fledging periods apparently not documented; in one study, 4 nestlings fed 15 times by male and 17 times by female in 3·6 hours, average 1 feed every 6·8 minutes; nestlings fed mostly by regurgitation; fledglings fed by parents near nest for at least several days.
Movements. Resident.
Status and Conservation. Not globally threatened. Restricted-range species: present in Hispaniola EBA. Common and widespread throughout range. Although this species is currently secure, continuing habitat loss and degradation, and increasing urbanization, could become threats unless adequate legislation is put in place to protect important habitats. Lack of general environmental awareness also a problem. This woodpecker's predilection for fruits and seeds can bring it into conflict with farming interests; sometimes persecuted locally for attacking commercial crops.
Bibliography. Albaine & Grullón (1981), Anon. (1998b), Ashmole (1967), Bernstein (1964, 1965), Bond (1928, 1985), Cruz (1974a), Delacour & Legendre (1925), Dod (1973, 1977, 1987, 1992), Faaborg (1985), Grullón (1976), Latta & Wunderle (1996), Olson (1972), Raffaele *et al*. (1998), Rimmer *et al*. (1998), Samedy *et al*. (1986), Selander & Giller (1963), Short (1970b, 1974d, 1985b), Stotz *et al*. (1996), Villard (1999a, 2001), Wallace (1969, 1974a), Wetmore & Swales (1931), Wiley & Ottenwalder (1990).

46. Jamaican Woodpecker

Melanerpes radiolatus

French: Pic de la Jamaïque **German**: Jamaikaspecht **Spanish**: Carpintero Jamaicano

Taxonomy. *Picus radiolatus* Wagler, 1827, Jamaica.
Sometimes combined with other barred congeners in a separate genus *Centurus*. Monotypic.
Distribution. Jamaica.

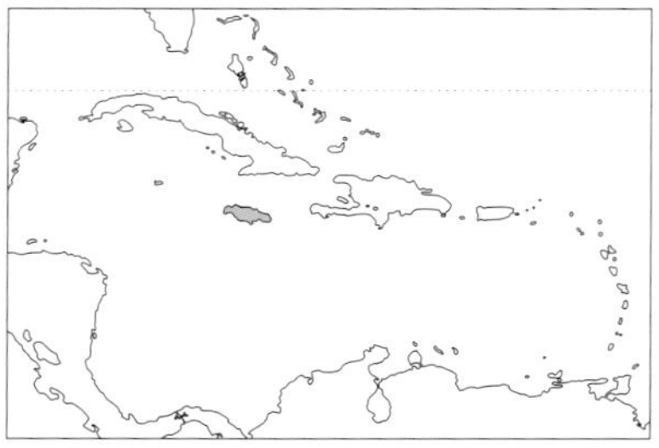

Descriptive notes. c. 24-26 cm; 92-131 g. Male has whitish to buff forehead, red forecrown to hindneck, yellowish lores; rest of head, including superciliary area, and chin to uppermost breast white, rear ear-coverts tinged greyish or olive; upperparts, including wing-coverts and tertials, black with thin white to green-tinged white bars, broadest on rump and uppertail-coverts; black flight-feathers, browner on primaries, all but outer primaries with narrow white bars on both webs (broader on inner webs); uppertail black, central feather pair finely barred white on inner (rarely, also outer) webs, outer pair with small white spots or bars on outer (and sometimes inner) webs; olive-grey to olive-buff below, feathers tipped greenish when fresh, central belly diffusely yellow to reddish, lower flanks to undertail-coverts black with white to olive-white bars; underwing brownish-black, barred white; undertail brownish-black, outer feathers tinged olive; long bill more or less pointed, culmen curved, fairly broad across nostrils, black; iris red, orbital skin grey to brown; legs slaty-black. Female is less bulky than male, has crown grey to dark grey, sometimes buff-tinged or partly black. Juvenile duller than adult, greyer below with yellower belly patch, more diffuse flank bars, brown eyes, both sexes with red on crown, less on female. VOICE. Most frequently a loud "kaaa", sometimes repeated 2 or 3 times; single "kao" calls in mild alarm; very loud "kaaaah" apparently as territorial advertisement; "wee-cha weecha" in intraspecific encounters; also "krirr, krirr" and more intimate "whirr-whirr" during breeding season. Loud drumming, by both sexes, mutual tapping near nest-hole.
Habitat. Variety of wooded habitats, including mangroves, wooded pastures, lowland copses, citrus groves, coconut plantations, shaded coffee plantations, gardens, also dry and wet limestone forest, mistforest, lower montane rainforest. At highest densities in secondary mesophytic forest. From sea-level to mountains.
Food and Feeding. Animal prey mostly insects (Orthoptera, Lepidoptera, Coleoptera, also ants), mainly of surface-dwelling species, majority of items 1-10 mm in size; also snails, occasionally lizards (*Anolis*). Vegetable content comprises almost half of all food eaten; includes much fruit, especially of *Cecropia* and *Ficus*, also of *Daphnopsis*. Hunts singly or in pairs. Forages mostly at mid-crown level; visits lower and upper canopy, and vines. Seeks food on trees, particularly in bromeliads and other epiphytes; rarely searches on trunks more than c. 10 cm in diameter. Predominant techniques are snatching (for fruit) and probing, followed by pecking (c. 15%), gleaning, and aerial feeding; no clear differences between sexes in foraging behaviour. Reported to peck at sugar canes to extract juice. Larger items broken up in anvil, before being swallowed or fed to chicks.
Breeding. Dec-Aug, sometimes in other months; laying Jan to early Jul; sometimes 2 or even 3 broods in a season. Monogamous; solitary. Nest excavated at 5-15 m in trunk or branch of dead tree or dead branch of live tree, or in utility pole, male doing two-thirds of work; mean dimensions of entrance hole 7·2 cm high, 6·8 cm wide; radius of 40 m around nest defended, but no interspecific aggression recorded, and even potential nest-hole competitors not attacked. Clutch 3-5 eggs, laid at

daily intervals; incubation by both sexes, only male at night, period 13 days; chicks brooded equally by both sexes, fed at average of 10·3 visits per hour, peak feeding during days 10-20 of nestling period, male feeding slightly more than female; in one observation totalling 6·4 hours, however, male fed 38 times, female 68 times, average 1 feed per 3·6 minutes; fledging period c. 1 month; fledglings accompanied by parents for at least 1 further month. Reproductive success adversely affected by usurpation of nest-hole by Common Starlings (*Sturnus vulgaris*).

Movements. Resident.

Status and Conservation. Not globally threatened. Restricted-range species: present in Jamaica EBA. Very common throughout the island. No data on population size. Home ranges of pairs overlap; highest recorded densities 0·91 individuals/ha, in secondary mesophytic forest. Main potential threat is habitat loss; although many forest areas are protected, enforcement of laws is often non-existent. Programmes to provide the human population with reliable information on environmental matters would help considerably in the conservation of this and other species in Jamaica.

Bibliography. Anon. (1998b), Bond (1985), Cruz (1973, 1974b, 1977, 1997), Faaborg (1985), Golding (1991, 1993), Johnston (1970), Lewis (1950), Machado (1972), Perkins (1943, 1970), Raffaele *et al.* (1998), Ritchie (1918), Salmon (1972, 1990, 1991), Selander & Giller (1963), Short (1985b), Spence (1975, 1976), Stotz *et al.* (1996), Verley (1974), Villard (1999a, 1999c, 2001), Walker (1976), Wallace (1969, 1974a).

47. Golden-cheeked Woodpecker

Melanerpes chrysogenys

French: Pic élégant   **German**: Goldwangenspecht   **Spanish**: Carpintero Cariamarillo
Other common names: Gold-cheeked Woodpecker

Taxonomy. *Picus chrysogenys* Vigors, 1839, no locality; probably Mazatlan, in Sinaloa, or San Blas or Tepic, in Nayarit, western Mexico.
Sometimes combined with other barred congeners in a separate genus *Centurus*. Variation clinal; population in interior (Morelos, adjacent Michoacán) often separated as race *morelensis*, tending to be paler with less yellow and orange than *flavinuchus*, but considerable overlap exists with latter in plumage characteristics. Two subspecies recognized.

Subspecies and Distribution.
M. c. chrysogenys (Vigors, 1839) - W Mexico from S Sinaloa to Nayarit.
M. c. flavinuchus (Ridgway, 1911) - Jalisco E to SW Puebla and SE along coast to E Oaxaca.

Descriptive notes. 19-22 cm; 55-88 g. Male has whitish forehead with golden-yellow at base of bill, red crown (usually becoming more golden-orange on nape), bright yellow-gold hindneck; broad black area encircling eye; deep golden-yellow band from lower lores to ear-coverts, broad buffish to yellow-

buff area below this; golden-buff chin and throat; black upperparts barred white, rump and uppertail-coverts more black-barred white; black wing-coverts with large white spots and tips; black secondaries and tertials barred white; black primaries thinly edged and tipped white (when fresh), bases barred white and forming patch about half-way along; uppertail black, central feather pair broadly barred white, third pair sometimes with a few bars, fourth with half-bars, outer pair fully white-barred; grey-brown to brownish-buff underparts strongly washed olive-yellow (yellowish feather tips), central belly with variably sized yellowish-orange patch, lower parts becoming paler and greyer, flanks to undertail-coverts with dark bars; underwing brown, barred white, white patch on primaries; longish bill barely chisel-tipped, culmen curved, rather broad across nostrils, black; iris reddish to orange-brown, orbital skin blackish; legs green-grey. Female is slightly shorter-billed than male, has crown greyish-buff, often with some darker feathers, nape orange-red. Juvenile is browner or greyer above with less contrasting bars, paler and greyer below with strong yellow suffusion, obscure bars in lower regions, both sexes with red on crown, female less red and often much black in crown. Race *flavinuchus* is slightly larger and duller, greyer below, has less yellow on face, more yellow instead of red on hindneck. VOICE. Many churring calls and short series of notes, e.g. nasal "ki-di-dik", more explosive than call of *M. uropygialis*; loud, nasal "cheek-oo, cheek-oo, cheek-oo, keh-i-heh-ek", softer "keh-i-heh" or "kuh-uh-uh".

Habitat. Mesic to xeric forest and edge, forest patches, open areas with scattered trees and plantations. Restricted to Pacific slope and plain, from sea-level to c. 1500 m.

Food and Feeding. Insects, including adults and larvae of beetles, ants; also various fruits and seeds. Forages singly and in pairs, at middle and upper levels, on trees. Feeding techniques are gleaning, probing and pecking. No further details available.

Breeding. May-Jul. Nest-hole in tree or cactus. Clutch size and other aspects of breeding undescribed.

Movements. Resident.

Status and Conservation. Not globally threatened. Common to fairly common; widespread within range, recorded at numerous sites. A little-known species. Research required on its ecology and breeding biology. No known threats.

Bibliography. Anon. (1998b), Binford (1989), Friedmann *et al.* (1957), Howell & Webb (1995), Hutto (1980, 1992), Peterson & Navarro-Sigüenza (2000), Schaldach (1963), Selander & Giller (1963), Short (1985b), Stotz *et al.* (1996).

♀

48

♂

ssp *pygmaeus*

♀

♂

ssp *tysoni*
♂

49

♂

ssp *rubricomus*

♀

ssp *rubricapillus*

♂

form "*terricolor*"
♂

50

♂

ssp *paraguanae*

♀

51

♂

form "*perplexus*"
♂

♀

typical
♂

52

♀

ssp *superciliaris*

♂

53

ssp *blakei*
♀

♂

ssp *aurifrons*

♀

ssp *dubius*
♂

♂

♀

ssp *polygrammus*

ssp *caymanensis*
♂

♂

ssp *santacruzi*
♂

54

ssp *leei*

♂

55

♀

♂

PLATE 27

inches   4
cm   10

48. Grey-breasted Woodpecker

Melanerpes hypopolius

French: Pic alezan **German**: Graukehlspecht **Spanish**: Carpintero Pechigris
Other common names: Balsas Woodpecker

Taxonomy. *Picus hypopolius* Wagler, 1829, Tehuacán and Tecuapán, Puebla, Mexico.
Sometimes combined with other barred congeners in a separate genus *Centurus*. Possibly closer to *M. lewis*, *M. formicivorus* and *M. erythrocephalus*. Formerly considered conspecific with *M. uropygialis*. Monotypic.
Distribution. Interior of SW Mexico from N Guerrero and Morelos E to EC Oaxaca.

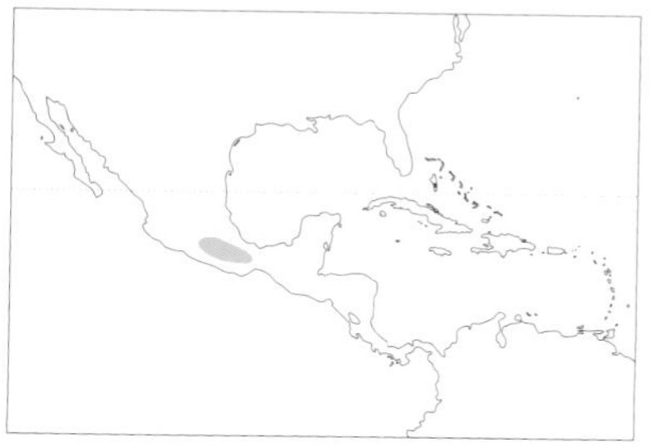

Descriptive notes. c. 19-21 cm; 46-54 g. Male has white to buffish-white forehead, red patch on central crown, narrow area of black around eye, a few red feathers beneath eye and sometimes also in moustachial region (red occasionally absent); rest of head and neck to upper mantle pale buff-brown to grey-brown, rear ear-coverts often slightly darker, malar usually paler or whitish; black upperparts and wing-coverts barred white to buffish-white, white rump and uppertail-coverts with black spots, streaks or bars; black flight-feathers broadly barred white, primaries also tipped and edged white and with white bars sometimes forming patch near base; uppertail black, tipped white (fresh), central feather pair with large white spots on inner webs, outer pair barred white on outer webs; grey-brown below, becoming paler with variable black arrowhead bars on lower underparts; underwing brown, barred white, white patch at base of primaries; fairly long bill slightly chisel-tipped, culmen curved, fairly broad across nostrils, blackish with paler lower mandible; iris reddish to brown, orbital skin grey to whitish; legs grey. Distinguished from *M. uropygialis* by smaller size, somewhat greyer plumage, red beneath eye, stronger white bars above. Female resembles male, but lacks red on crown. Juvenile is duller, browner and greyer, barring less contrasting, both sexes with dark red on crown. Voice. Variable calls include nasal "yek-a yek-a", e.g. during interactions; series of usually 4 dry rattling "chi-i-i-ir" churrs; nasal "chuck" repeated 2-4 times, often by female near nest; voice generally lower-pitched and harsher than that of *M. aurifrons*. Drums loudly, mostly when intruder present.
Habitat. Xeric areas with scattered trees, shrubs, or large cacti, also agricultural areas; extends into riverside groves, but avoids these if *M. chrysogenys* present. Hills, between 900 m and 2100 m.
Food and Feeding. Fruits, including those of *Ziziphus* and cacti (e.g. *Opuntia*); also insects, including termites (Isoptera), cicadas (Cicadidae). Some food stored. Generally observed in groups of 3-10 individuals. Forages at various levels, descends to ground. Flycatching frequent; sallies from top of cactus, mostly upwards but also in downward swoops, with skilful aerial manoeuvres. Also probes in cactus flowers, bromeliads; gleaning and digging apparently rare. Uses anvils, both natural cracks and excavated ones.
Breeding. Breeds from late Apr to Jul. Co-operative, colonial breeder; at one site, 3 nests with 5 males and 3 females present. Nest-hole built in tree or, frequently, at 3-6 m in cactus. Clutch size and incubation and fledging periods not recorded; in one study, peak of brood-feeding in early afternoon, up to 40 feeds per hour, males provided more frequent feeds than did females; fledglings spent most of time concealed within cacti.
Movements. Resident.
Status and Conservation. Not globally threatened. Restricted-range species: present in Balsas Region and Interior Oaxaca EBA. Common to fairly common throughout range; uncommon in some places (e.g. C Oaxaca). A very poorly known species. Study needed to determine its ecology and breeding biology. No known threats.
Bibliography. Anon. (1998b), Binford (1989), Friedmann *et al.* (1957), Hendricks *et al.* (1990), Howell & Webb (1995), Hunn *et al.* (2001), Leonard (2000), Peterson & Navarro-Sigüenza (2000), Rowley (1984), Selander & Giller (1963), Short (1985b), Stattersfield *et al.* (1998), Stotz *et al.* (1996).

49. Yucatan Woodpecker

Melanerpes pygmaeus

French: Pic de Yucatan **German**: Yucatanspecht **Spanish**: Carpintero Yucateco
Other common names: Red-vented Woodpecker

Taxonomy. *Centurus rubriventris pygmæus* Ridgway, 1885, Cozumel Island, Mexico.
Sometimes combined with other barred congeners in a separate genus *Centurus*. Forms a superspecies with *M. rubricapillus*, and sometimes treated as conspecific, but geographical isolation, combined with minor morphological differences, supports allospecies treatment. Three subspecies recognized.
Subspecies and Distribution.
M. p. rubricomus J. L. Peters, 1948 - Yucatán Peninsula S to C Belize.
M. p. pygmaeus (Ridgway, 1885) - Cozumel I (off E Yucatán Peninsula).
M. p. tysoni (Bond, 1936) - Guanaja I (off N Honduras).

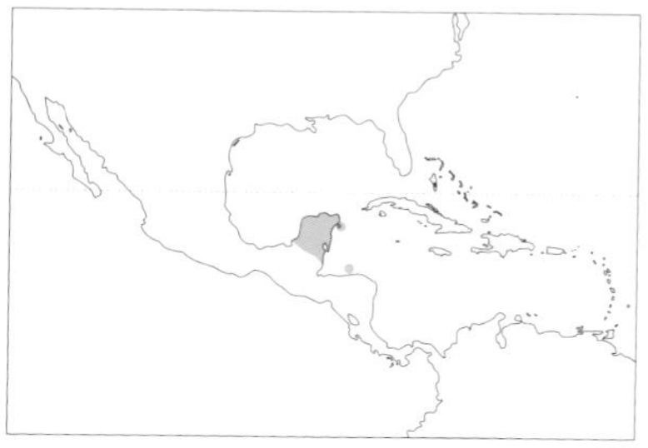

Descriptive notes. c. 16-18 cm; 35-43 g. Male has golden to golden-orange lower forehead, lores, front of moustachial region and chin, buffish-white upper forehead, forecrown and supercilium, bright red central crown to hindneck; rest of head and throat buff-brown, tinged grey; black mantle, scapulars and back narrowly barred whitish, white lower back to uppertail-coverts rarely with a few black streaks or bars; black upperwing and wing-coverts narrowly barred white, browner primaries tipped white (when fresh) with bars restricted to bases; uppertail black, outer feathers barred or spotted white on outer webs; buffish-brown below, variably sized red patch in centre of belly, flanks to undertail-coverts variably barred black; underwing brown, barred white; long bill almost pointed, culmen curved, broad across nostrils, blackish; iris red to brown; legs grey. Distinguished from very similar *M. rubricapillus* by darker underparts more barred on flanks, more extensive golden coloration on face, longer tail. Female is slightly shorter-billed than male, has red on head restricted to nape and hindneck often duller. Juvenile duller, barring above less contrasting, belly patch paler, head pattern less well defined, male with red crown to hindneck, female with blackish crown often barred and occasionally with traces of red. Race *rubricomus* is slightly larger than nominate, paler, has flanks less barred; *tysoni* is larger-billed, has forehead less golden or orange, less golden-yellow on face, usually more white in tail, red on head of male usually broken by buff-brown at rear. Voice. Soft rolling "churr, pyurr-r-r", also dry laugh e.g "chuh-uh-uh-uh-uh-uh" or "keh heh heh-heh heh-heh heh-heh"; vocalizations generally softer and less nasal than those of *M. aurifrons*.
Habitat. Deciduous forest, edge, clearings, second growth, coastal scrub. Generally at lower elevations than those used by *M. aurifrons*.
Food and Feeding. Diet not documented. Forages at lower levels than sympatric congeners. In other aspects, probably very similar to *M. rubricapillus*.
Breeding. Breeds Apr-May. No other details available.
Movements. Resident.
Status and Conservation. Not globally threatened. Fairly common to common within relatively small range. Occurs in Dr Alfredo Barrera M. Botanical Garden, Quintana Roo. Very poorly known. Research required to establish its ecology and breeding biology. No current known threats.
Bibliography. Anon. (1998b), England (2000), Friedmann *et al.* (1957), Gómez de Silva (1998), Howell & Webb (1995), Klaas (1968), Monroe (1968), Paynter (1955), Selander & Giller (1963), Stotz *et al.* (1996).

50. Red-crowned Woodpecker

Melanerpes rubricapillus

French: Pic à couronne rouge **German**: Rotkappenspecht **Spanish**: Carpintero Coronirrojo
Other common names: Little Red-headed Woodpecker; Wagler's Woodpecker (Panama)

Taxonomy. *Centurus rubricapillus* Cabanis, 1862, Barranquilla, Colombia.
Sometimes combined with other barred congeners in a separate genus *Centurus*. Forms a superspecies with *M. pygmaeus*, and sometimes treated as conspecific, but geographical isolation, combined with minor morphological differences, supports allospecies treatment. Hybridizes with *M. hoffmannii* in C Costa Rica. Rather variable; population of SW Costa Rica described as race *costaricensis*, but now considered indistinguishable from nominate; relatively large and dark birds from Margarita I, NE Venezuela and Tobago named as race *terricolor*, but identical individuals occur in other parts of species' range. In addition, race *paraguanae* may be invalid, as some individuals in E parts of range exhibit similar characteristics. Name "*wagleri*", originally applied to birds from Panama, is junior synonym of *rubricapillus*. Four subspecies recognized.
Subspecies and Distribution.
M. r. rubricapillus (Cabanis, 1862) - SW Costa Rica E to N & C Colombia, Venezuela (except S), Tobago, W Guyana and coastal Surinam.
M. r. subfuscus Wetmore, 1957 - Coiba I (SW Panama).
M. r. seductus Bangs, 1901 - San Miguel I (SE Panama).
M. r. paraguanae (Gilliard, 1940) - Paraguaná Peninsula (NW Venezuela).

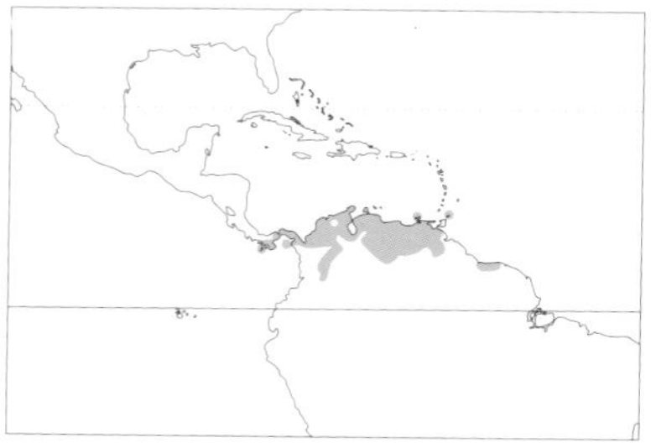

Descriptive notes. c. 16-18·5 cm; 40-65 g. Male has pale yellow nasal tufts and lower forehead, whitish upper forehead, bright red crown becoming more orange-red on nape and hindneck (some with grey-brown nape); rest of head greyish-buff, lores, side of forecrown and chin paler, rarely with faint yellow on chin, lores and malar region; black mantle, scapulars and back barred white, white lower back to uppertail-coverts; black upperwing and wing-coverts barred white, browner primaries tipped white (when fresh) with bars only at bases and forming white patch; uppertail black, central feather pair white with black spots at tip, outer pair barred white on outer webs; variable below, typically buffish-grey to grey-buff, sometimes darker, washed olive or yellowish (when fresh), paler in lower regions, central belly diffusely reddish to orange-red, lower flanks to undertail-coverts barred black; underwing brown, barred white, white patch at base of primaries; undertail brownish-black, outer feathers washed yellow, markings as above; longish bill slightly chisel-tipped, culmen curved, fairly broad across nostrils, blackish; iris red to brown, orbital skin grey-brown; legs grey. Differs from *M. pygmaeus* in patterning of face and underparts, and in shorter tail; from *M. hoffmannii* in smaller size, darker coloration, reddish (not golden) nape and belly patch. Female has slightly shorter bill than male, crown pale grey-buff to whitish, nape and hindneck reddish to orange-red. Juvenile duller and browner, nape and hindneck paler or yellowish, bars above less contrasting, underparts often slightly streaked, belly patch paler and usually mottled, male with red on crown duller, female with dark crown often barred and occasionally with some reddish tips. Race *subfuscus* is marginally smaller than nominate, typically much darker below, breast and sides deep grey-brown; *seductus* is shorter-winged, has breast a shade darker, female has more red on nape; *paraguanae* is longer-tailed, has paler yellow on forehead, buff-brown nape, yellower hindneck, white bars above broader, belly patch more golden-yellow, female with nape and hindneck pale orange-brown. Voice. Typical calls often wavering and protracted with abrupt terminal note, e.g. "churr, churr, krr-r-r-r", also various other calls, e.g. "wícka, wícka" in display, similar to those of *M. carolinus* and *M. hoffmannii*; chattering calls like those of Boat-billed Flycatcher (*Megarhynchus pitangua*). Both sexes drum during breeding season, rolls slower than in *M. carolinus*; mutual tapping at nest-hole.
Habitat. Deciduous forest, edge, clearings, second growth, coastal scrub, plantations, gardens, also mangroves. Replaced by *M. pucherani* in more wooded areas. Lowlands to 1700 m; to 1900 m in N Venezuela.
Food and Feeding. Diet includes ants, beetles, grubs, Orthoptera, other small insects, also spiders; wood-boring larvae of minor importance. Also eats many fruits and berries, including papayas (*Carica*), cashews and bananas; visits balsa flowers for nectar. Generally less dependent on arthropods than e.g. *M. hoffmannii*. Observed frequently in pairs. Forages at various heights, with preference for middle

On following pages: 51. Gila Woodpecker (*Melanerpes uropygialis*); 52. Red-bellied Woodpecker (*Melanerpes carolinus*); 53. West Indian Woodpecker (*Melanerpes superciliaris*); 54. Golden-fronted Woodpecker (*Melanerpes aurifrons*); 55. Hoffmann's Woodpecker (*Melanerpes hoffmannii*).

and lower levels. Feeding techniques include hammering into bark, probing, gleaning from trunks, branches and foliage, and reaching for fruits; pierces the skin of larger fruits to obtain contents. Readily takes fruit from feeders. Larger items are secured in crevice and processed by pecking.
Breeding. Feb-Jul in Costa Rica and Panama, May-Jun in Colombia, May-Nov in Venezuela and Mar-Jul on Tobago; sometimes double-brooded. Monogamous, in pairs throughout year; solitary breeder. Nest-hole excavated by both sexes, 3-23 m up in slender dead tree or branch, or in large cactus or sometimes fence post, or may use roost-hole of male; territorial, but nest-hole often lost in competition with *M. chrysauchen* and tityras (*Tityra*). Clutch 3-4 eggs, but usually only 2 young reared; incubation 10 days, by both sexes, only male at night; chicks fed and brooded by both parents, fledging period 31-33 days; fledglings cared for by parents for c. 1 month.
Movements. Resident.
Status and Conservation. Not globally threatened. A common and conspicuous woodpecker, widespread within its range. Common to abundant in Costa Rica and Panama; common in Colombia; common in Venezuela and on Tobago. Occurs in Manuel Antonio and Corcovado National Parks (Costa Rica), and Henri Pittier and Morrocoy National Parks (Venezuela). May benefit from forest clearance; numbers tend to increase in areas where thinning and clearance creates more open woodland. Is considered a nuisance locally in plantations and gardens because of its fruit-eating habits.
Bibliography. Anon. (1998b), Blake (1958), Bond *et al.* (1989), Friedmann & Smith (1950), Goossen (1989), Haverschmidt & Mees (1994), Heisler (1994), Herklots (1961), Hilty & Brown (1986), Kilham (1972c), Meyer de Schauensee & Phelps (1978), Olson (1997), Otvos (1967), Ridgely & Gwynne (1989), Selander & Giller (1963), Short (1985b), Skutch (1969a), Slud (1964), Stiles (1985), Stiles & Skutch (1989), Stotz *et al.* (1996), Varty *et al.* (1986), Verea *et al.* (2000), Villard (1999a), Wetmore (1939, 1957, 1968a).

51. Gila Woodpecker

Melanerpes uropygialis

French: Pic des saguaros **German**: Gilaspecht **Spanish**: Carpintero del Gila

Taxonomy. *Centurus uropygialis* Baird, 1854, Bill Williams Fork of Colorado River, Arizona, USA.
Sometimes combined with other barred congeners in a separate genus *Centurus*. Formerly considered conspecific with *M. hypopolius*. Interbreeds to limited extent with *M. aurifrons* in SW Mexico. Geographical races poorly differentiated owing to rather marked degree of individual variation; dark birds from S Sonora, SW Chihuahua and N Sinaloa often separated as race *fuscescens*, but probably better treated as part of nominate or, since many appear indistinguishable from *cardonensis*, should perhaps be merged with latter; further study needed. In addition, described races *albescens* (from S Nevada and SE California to NW Sonora), *tiburonensis* (from Tiburon I, off W Sonora) and *sulfuriventer* (from S of range, S from Sinaloa and Zacatecas) fall within range of variation of nominate, with which they are therefore synonymized. Three subspecies recognized.
Subspecies and Distribution.
M. u. uropygialis (Baird, 1854) - SE California (Imperial Valley, lower Colorado Valley) and extreme S Nevada E to extreme SW New Mexico, and S in W Mexico to Jalisco and Aguascalientes.
M. u. cardonensis (Grinnell, 1927) - N & C Baja California.
M. u. brewsteri (Ridgway, 1911) - S Baja California (S from San Ignacio).

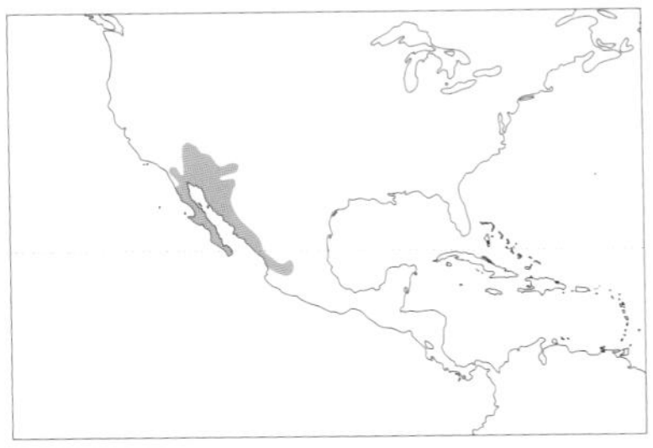

Descriptive notes. 21·5-24 cm; 51-81 g. Male has small red patch in centre of forecrown, buffish (rarely, pale yellow) nasal tufts, usually whitish-buff forehead and upper lores and occasionally also chin, sometimes yellow-tinged hindneck; rest of head typically pale grey-brown, variably paler or darker, this colour extending to uppermost mantle and over most of underparts; black upperparts barred white (or bars grey-buff on uppermost mantle), rump mainly white with narrow black bars, uppertail-coverts white with narrow black bars; black wing-coverts, tertials and secondaries barred white, brownish-black primaries tipped white (when fresh) and with white bars at bases forming patch; uppertail black, tipped white when fresh, central feather pair barred white on inner webs and often with white streak near shaft on outer webs, outer feathers barred white, fourth pair white-barred on tip of inner webs and edge of outer webs; yellow to golden-yellow patch on central belly, lower underparts paler with arrowhead bars; white underwing-coverts barred black; long bill barely chisel-tipped, culmen curved, fairly broad across nostrils, blackish; iris deep red; legs blue-grey to grey. Differs from *M. hypopolius* in larger size, no red beneath eye. Female is smaller, less bulky, shorter-billed than male, lacks red on crown. Juvenile duller, has white bars above more buff-tinged, flank bars more diffuse, belly patch paler, throat often faintly streaked or barred, crown usually dark-barred, male with some red on crown. Races vary mainly in darkness of head and underparts and width of black bars above, but much individual variation: *brewsteri* is very like nominate, but smaller, has longer bill, on average narrower barring above, more numerous black markings on rump; *cardonensis* typically has darker head and underparts, heavier black barring above, but sometimes less dark. VOICE. Noisy, with wide range of variable calls; rolling vibrato "chürr üh-rr" often in short series, notes varying in length, 0·18-0·38 seconds, as contact between pair-members and as territorial advertisement, most frequently by male; more rasping versions, e.g. "rruhk-rruhk", when more agitated; raucous laugh, "geet geet geet geet geet"; high squeaky "kee-u kee-u kee-u"; series of sharp "pip pip" in alarm, more often by female. Both sexes drum occasionally, female even less so, long regular rolls, especially in pre-nesting period.
Habitat. Arid habitats with large cacti or scattered trees, including deserts; also mesic habitats such as riparian woodland, subtropical forest, plantations; also occurs around habitations, and visits gardens. Lowlands to c. 1000 m; to 1600 m in far S of range.
Food and Feeding. Essentially omnivorous. Animal food includes insects of various kinds, especially ants, beetles, Orthoptera, termites (Isoptera), cicadids, Lepidoptera, Hemiptera, also larvae; also eggs and chicks of other birds, occasionally earthworms and lizards. Wide range of non-animal food, particularly fruits of cacti, especially saguaro cactus (*Carnegiea gigantea*), and berries, mainly of *Lycium* and mistletoes (*Phoradendron*); also seeds, including corn and acorns, latter occasionally stored, and nuts; honey and sugar water taken from feeders, and observed to feed young with pieces of bark or seeds soaked in syrup. Accepts household scraps of all kinds. Hunts singly or in pairs. Forages at all levels, from treetops, cacti and bushes to the ground. Very versatile in its foraging techniques, uses gleaning, reaching, probing and pecking; also taps on trees.
Breeding. Apr-Aug; often 2 or 3 broods in a season. Monogamous, in pairs throughout year; solitary nester. Nest-hole excavated by both sexes, at 1-10 m in cactus, tree or palm, when in living cactus used only after drying out; entrance often not circular, average c. 5·7 cm high and 6·3 cm wide, mean cavity depth 27·8 cm; hole reused for several years; territorial, aggressively defends radius of 40-50 m around nest-hole. Clutch 2-7 eggs, mostly 3-5, later clutches smaller; both sexes incubate, period c. 13 days; both also feed young, in one study hourly feeding rate of male c. 8 and of female 12; fledging period c. 4 weeks; fledglings fed by parents for lengthy period, family group remaining in territory until juveniles disperse or are driven away prior to subsequent breeding attempt; at least occasionally, young from first brood remain with parents during rearing of second brood. Recorded longevity at least 7 years 9 months.
Movements. Resident; occasionally wanders short distances N or NW in California (as far W as Los Angeles area). In non-breeding season, some local movements to areas where food sources abundant.
Status and Conservation. Not globally threatened. Common to fairly common in all suitable habitats in its range. A mid-1980's study in Tucson (Arizona) gave densities of 29 birds/km² in urban areas with plenty of native vegetation, 16 birds/km² in urban areas with high percentage of exotic vegetation, 9 birds/km² in natural desert, and 5 birds/km² in urban parks and cemeteries with exotic vegetation; native vegetation a highly important factor, but urbanized areas had higher densities of this species than did areas without houses. Population in USA stable or declining; estimated numbers in riparian habitats in Arizona c. 650 birds in 1976, then 600 in 1983, and 561 in 1986. Significant recent decline in SE California possibly associated with clearing of woodlands, possibly also a result of competition for nest-sites from introduced Common Starling (*Sturnus vulgaris*); further increase in starling numbers might seriously threaten the woodpecker's future survival in some places. Holes produced by this picid provide quarters for many other bird species, as well as mammals and reptiles, which also compete with it for nest-sites. This woodpecker is likely to be important seed disperser of saguaro cactus. Main conservation priorities are ensuring protection of native vegetation in its habitat, and keeping a check on starling populations.
Bibliography. Antevs (1948), Baicich & Harrison (1997), Bent (1939), Braun (1969), Brenowitz (1978a, 1978b), Brush *et al.* (1990), Christensen (1971), Cornett (1986), Edwards & Schnell (2000), Friedmann *et al.* (1957), Howell & Webb (1995), Hunter (1984), Hutto (1980, 1992), Inouye *et al.* (1981), Kaufman (1996), Kemlage *et al.* (1981), Kerpez (1986), Kerpez & Smith (1990a, 1990b), Koenig (1986, 1987), Korol & Hutto (1984), Larsen (1987), Larson (1996), MacRoberts & MacRoberts (1985), Martindale & Lamm (1984), McAuliffe & Hendricks (1988), Price *et al.* (1995), Root (1988), van Rossem (1942), Selander & Giller (1963), Short (1985b), Small (1994), Speich & Radke (1975), Wilbur (1987).

52. Red-bellied Woodpecker

Melanerpes carolinus

French: Pic à ventre roux **German**: Carolinaspecht **Spanish**: Carpintero de Carolina

Taxonomy. *Picus carolinus* Linnaeus, 1758, North America = South Carolina.
Sometimes combined with other barred congeners in a separate genus *Centurus*. Forms a superspecies with *M. superciliaris*. Interbreeds to limited extent with *M. aurifrons* in S USA (Texas). Individual variation considerable, but considered not sufficiently correlated to any geographical pattern to warrant recognition of races; examination of extensive series of specimens indicates that width of white bars above varies clinally, increasing from E to W. Described race *zebra* from W of range indistinguishable. Birds from S Florida described as race *perplexus*, being slightly smaller and tending to show more white on upperparts, paler red on lower forehead and less white in tail, possibly sufficiently distinct to be separated; birds from E & C Texas described as race *harpaceus*, with greyer cheeks and throat, perhaps also warrant subspecific status; further study required. Monotypic.
Distribution. SE North America from SE North Dakota, C Minnesota and N Wisconsin E to extreme S Ontario and S Massachusetts, and S through E USA (W along valleys of R Missouri and R Platte to C South Dakota and extreme NE Colorado) to coastal SC Texas and Florida.

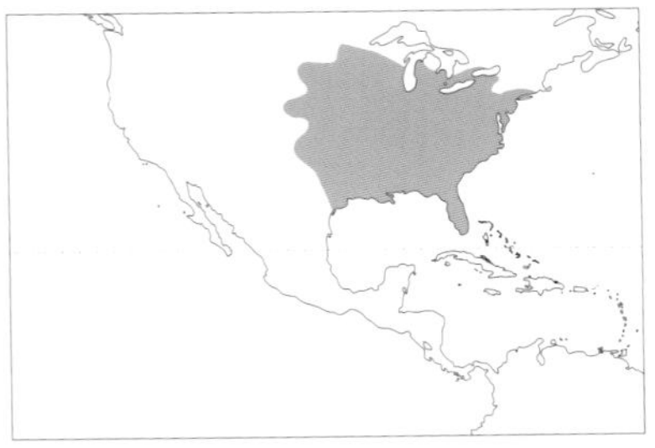

Descriptive notes. c. 24 cm; 56-91 g. Male has pinkish to reddish-orange lower forehead, bright red upper forehead and crown to hindneck and uppermost mantle (rarely, nape or hindneck more orange or, exceptionally, yellowish), occasionally some grey feathering across central upper forehead; rest of head, including chin and throat, and short supercilium, grey to whitish-grey, with variably strong orange or pinkish tinge from lores to cheeks and chin; black upperparts barred white, white rump with variable black streaks and bars, white uppertail-coverts sometimes with a few indistinct black streaks or U-shaped markings; black wing-coverts, secondaries and tertials with white bars or spots, black primaries with large area of white at base forming patch; uppertail black, central feather pair with white on inner webs, outer pair barred black and white on outer webs; all flight-feathers and rectrices tipped white in fresh plumage; pale grey below, breast tinged olive, buffish or pink, central belly pale red or pink (sometimes orange) and bordered by diffuse yellowish wash, lower flanks to undertail-coverts with black V-shaped markings; underwing grey, white primary patch, coverts barred grey and white; long bill slightly chisel-tipped, culmen curved, fairly broad across nostrils, black; iris deep red to red-brown; legs grey to green-grey. Differs from *M. superciliaris* in smaller size, shorter bill, redder upper forehead, less buff underparts. Female is somewhat smaller than male, has upper forehead and crown grey (occasionally small red central patch), normally less extensive reddish colour on cheeks, less reddish suffusion below, often smaller or paler belly patch. Juvenile has barring above less contrasting than on adult, is darker below with variable streaking on breast and usually more extensive but diffuse barring in lower regions, belly patch often indistinct, has brown eyes, male with smaller paler red patch on crown and nape than adult, crown mostly grey with black bars (occasionally, entirely blackish), female with even less red on nape but small area of red on crown. VOICE. Highly vocal; calls include vibrato "churr" calls, singly or in series of up to 4 notes, as contact, also in association with other vocalizations and drumming; long series of harsh, low-pitched notes, "cha-aa-ah", typically in territorial conflict; highly variable "chip" or "chup" as single notes or sometimes in series up to 8 seconds long, in alarm or agitation; "chee-wuk" or "wuck-ah", also in long series, in close-contact aggression; quiet "grr" notes in more intimate contacts. Drums in weak rolls, steady rhythm, sometimes a single introductory strike separated by longer interval from following ones; mutual tapping at nest-hole.
Habitat. Mesic habitats with dead trees, including swampy woods, open deciduous or mixed coniferous woodland with very large trees, and pecan (*Carya*) groves, also heavy woods of oak (*Quercus*) and elm (*Ulmus*) along rivers and creek bottoms; also longleaf pine (*Pinus palustris*) savanna in E Texas; also shade trees and dead trees in residential areas. Both foraging and nesting habitats tend to be denser with more developed understorey than those used by sympatric woodpeckers, e.g. *M. erythrocephalus*. From sea-level to 600 m, locally to 900 m.
Food and Feeding. More or less omnivorous. Animal food mostly arthropods, especially beetles, ants, Orthoptera, Hemiptera, flies, caterpillars, other larvae including some wood-boring ones, also spiders; bigger animal items are tree-frogs, *Anolis* lizards, and bird eggs and nestlings. Great variety of fruits (e.g. apples, peaches, oranges) taken, and berries from many different plants, including

poison-ivy (*Toxicodendron radicans*), hawthorn (*Crataegus*) and others. Seeds and nuts major food in winter; stores acorns, pine seeds, nuts of pecan, hazel (*Corylus*) and beech (*Fagus*); corn important locally. Also takes sap from tree wounds or from wells made by sapsuckers (*Sphyrapicus*); drinks nectar from blossoms. Wide range of items accepted at feeders. In study of diet over all months, plant material constituted 69% of diet and animal food 31%; by season, plant material 82% in winter, 44% in late spring, 60% in summer, 83% in autumn. In C Illinois, winter diet 94% vegetable matter, 6% animal. Usually forages solitarily. Prefers upper storeys of live and dead deciduous trees, particularly oaks, favouring branches 10-30 cm in diameter; dead substrates constitute a third to more than half of those visited, but relative use of these dependent on local availability. Surface probing is most frequent technique, with some pecking and hammering; gleaning is main foraging method during breeding season; also uses aerial flycatching on occasion, but far less than *M. erythrocephalus*. Sexual differences in foraging not always marked; most pronounced in winter, when males more often search trunks for arthropod food. Stores mast in autumn through to early winter, single food items usually cached in crevices; insects and fruit also occasionally cached.
Breeding. Late Mar to Aug; occasionally 2 or 3 broods in a season in S. Monogamous, 1 report of possible polygyny; solitary. Nest excavated by male, helped by female towards end of work, at 2-18 m in usually dead tree, or dead branch of live tree, or in fence post or pole, mean size of entrance hole 5·7 cm tall, 5·9 cm wide, cavity depth 22-32 cm; usually new cavity dug each season, but sometimes male's roost-hole used. Female often initiates copulation by mounting male, even after eggs laid. Clutch 2-8 eggs, usually 4-6, laid at 1-day intervals; both parents incubate, only male at night, period 12 days; both also feed chicks, combined rate up to 45 feeds per hour; both sexes brood chicks, female more during day, only male overnight; faeces removed throughout almost entire nestling period; fledging period c. 22-27 days; fledged brood usually divided between parents, and accompanied for up to 6 weeks, occasionally longer; period of dependence shorter, 2-3 weeks, if another brood attempted. Few data on breeding success; in Kansas, 55% of eggs laid produced fledglings; nest contents preyed on by *M. erythrocephalus*, *Dryocopus pileatus* and Common Starling (*Sturnus vulgaris*), and by snakes (*Elaphe*). In captivity, first breeding at 1 year. Recorded longevity in wild 12 years 1 month.
Movements. Mostly resident; at least during severe winters, however, N populations may withdraw to S. Generally, tends to concentrate in favourable areas in winter, when sometimes more common in places where rare or absent in summer. Recorded irregularly outside normal range, N to S Saskatchewan, C Ontario, S Quebec and Nova Scotia, W to Idaho and E New Mexico.
Status and Conservation. Not globally threatened. Common in most of range; the commonest picid in S of range. Densities in preferred habitats can reach almost 1 bird/ha. In Texas, one of the most numerous bird species in combined forest habitats (bottomland hardwood, mixed pine-hardwood, long pine savanna); one of most abundant species in Mississippi Valley and floodplain. Significant increase recorded in N since mid-1960's. Was formerly shot as a pest in commercial orchards and pecan plantations; nowadays considered only a minor nuisance and generally tolerated. Adaptable, and able to flourish in most types of woodland, including in urban areas; not shy of humans. Suffers competition for nest-sites from other woodpeckers, especially the more dominant *M. erythrocephalus*, also with Common Starling, but population size seems essentially unaffected by this. No known threats.
Bibliography. Arndt (1995), Baicich & Harrison (1997), Baker & Payne (1993), Barnett *et al*. (1983), Bent (1939), Boone (1963), Brackbill (1969a), Breitwisch (1977), Burleigh & Lowery (1944), Cartwright (1942), Cicero & Johnson (1995), Conner (1974, 1975), Conner & Saenz (1996), Conner, Jones & Jones (1994), Crumb (1984), Deviney (1957), Dunn (1984), Duyck & McNair (1991), Fales (1977b), Ferguson (1977), Gamboa & Brown (1976), Gardella (1997), Garrett (1999), Gerber (1986), Haas (1987), Hatch & L'Arrivée (1981), Hauser (1959), Hess (1992), Hickman (1970), Ingold (1989a, 1989b, 1989c, 1990, 1991, 1994a, 1994b), Ingold & Densmore (1992), Ingold & Jackson (1986), Jackson (1975, 1976c, 1997b), Jackson & Davis (1998), Johnsgard (1979), Jones (1988), Kilham (1958a, 1961b, 1963, 1977a, 1983), Koenig (1987), Loftin (1981), Maddux (1989), McGrath (1988), McGuire (1932), Meyers (1978), Moulton & Lowell (1991), Mueller (1971), Neal *et al*. (1992), Neill & Harper (1990), Nero (1959), Owens & Owens (1992), Peck & James (1983), Petit *et al*. (1985), Reller (1972), Rines (1998), Roach (1975), Robinson (1977), Rodgers (1990), Saul (1983), Saul & Wassmer (1983), Selander & Giller (1959, 1963), Shackelford & Conner (1997), Shackelford *et al*. (2000), Skadsen (1983), Smith, G.A. & Jackson (1994), Smith, J.I. (1987), Smith, L.M. (1971), Spring (1965), Stickel (1962, 1963a, 1963b, 1964, 1965a, 1965b), Sullivan (1992), Sutton (1984), Swallow *et al*. (1988), Thompson (1994), Towles (1989), Trail (1991), Volman *et al*. (1997), Wallace (1969, 1974a), Watt (1980), Wilkins (1996), Wilkins & Ritchison (1999), Williams (1975), Williams & Batzli (1979a), Willson (1970), Woods (1984), Woolfenden (1975), Zusi & Marshall (1970).

53. West Indian Woodpecker
Melanerpes superciliaris

French: Pic à sourcils noirs **German**: Bahamaspecht **Spanish**: Carpintero Antillano
Other common names: Great/West Indian Red-bellied Woodpecker; Bahama Woodpecker (*nyeanus*, *blakei*); Cayman Woodpecker (*caymanensis*); Cuban Red-bellied Woodpecker (*superciliaris*)

Taxonomy. *Picus superciliaris* Temminck, 1827, Cuba.
Sometimes combined with other barred congeners in a separate genus *Centurus*. Forms a superspecies with *M. carolinus*. Birds on Grand Bahama sometimes separated as race *bahamensis*: on average marginally shorter-billed, slightly darker below and tending to show slightly more black behind eye, but otherwise identical to San Salvador race *nyeanus*, which is itself somewhat variable, so the two are more appropriately lumped. Race *caymanensis* formerly considered a separate species. Five subspecies currently recognized.
Subspecies and Distribution.
M. s. nyeanus (Ridgway, 1886) - Grand Bahama and San Salvador (N & E Bahamas).
M. s. blakei (Ridgway, 1886) - Great Abaco (N Bahamas).
M. s. superciliaris (Temminck, 1827) - Cuba, Cantiles Keys and associated keys.
M. s. murceus (Bangs, 1910) - I of Pines, Cayo Largo and Cayo Real.
M. s. caymanensis (Cory, 1886) - Grand Cayman.

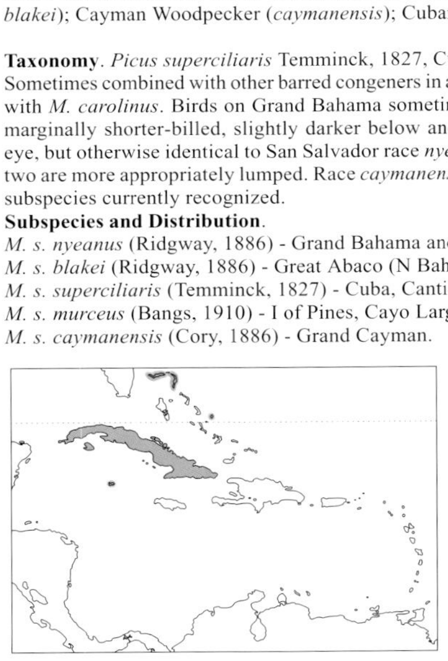

Descriptive notes. c. 27-32 cm; 83-126 g (*superciliaris*), 63-81 g (*caymanensis*). Male has red nasal tufts, white to buffish-white forehead and sides of forecrown, red crown, nape and hindneck; narrow black area from just in front of eye backwards along side of mid- crown; pale grey to whitish head side, chin and throat, tinged buffy or yellow-brown; buffish-white upperparts (whiter when worn) barred black, rump with fewer and narrower bars, white uppertail-coverts with narrow black horseshoe markings; largely white wing-coverts narrowly barred black; black secondaries and tertials barred white, black primaries tipped white (when fresh) and with white at bases forming patch; uppertail black, central feather pair with very broad white bars on inner webs and white at base of outer webs, outer pair barred white on outer webs; greyish below, breast strongly tinged buffy-brown, paler olive-yellow on lower breast, with central belly red to orange-red, flanks and undertail-coverts whitish with black arrowhead barring; underwing greyish, coverts barred black and white; undertail somewhat paler than above, greyish on outer tail; noticeably long bill only slightly chisel-tipped, culmen curved, fairly broad across nostrils, black; iris red-brown; legs olive-grey. Female is slightly (12%) shorter-billed, less bulky than male, has whitish forehead and crown, blackish rear crown joining black area behind eye. Juvenile similar to adult but less contrastingly patterned, often has red tinge above, larger but more diffuse red area below, both sexes with red crown, on female mixed with black feathering. Races differ mainly in size, also in plumage coloration and pattern: *murceus* resembles nominate, but averages smaller in bill, wing and, particularly, tail measurements; *nyeanus* is much smaller than nominate, rather variable in plumage, has only small amount of black behind eye or none at all, markings on uppertail-covert more bar-like, underparts slightly greenish-tinged; *blakei* averages somewhat bigger and darker than previous, has pale bars above narrower and often tinged greenish-buff on mantle, generally greyer and darker face and underparts, less and paler red on nasal tufts, more black around and behind eye; *caymanensis* is size of previous or smaller, with shorter wing, has dark barring above much narrower, pale bars on back often strongly buffish, more evenly barred tail with white extending to outer webs of central rectrices, less regular uppertail-covert markings, no black around and behind eye, red of nasal tufts much paler and restricted, female with greyish (not black) hindcrown. Voice. Typical "churr" call a loud "krrru", or repeated as "krrruu-krrru-krru-krru", slightly higher-pitched than that of *M. carolinus*; also "waa" notes as *M. striatus*; also "key-ou", and continuous "ke-ke-ke-ke-ke" series.
Habitat. Various types of wooded area, especially dry forest, including edges; also coastal forest, palms, scrub, and edges of swampland; often around human habitations on Abaco and Grand Cayman. On Grand Cayman, occurs in all forest types, and is fairly common in mangrove forest, but possibly visits limestone forest only outside breeding season. Appears to favour open forest or bushy country with scattered royal palms (*Roystonea regia*) in Cuba, where probably partly excluded from many other habitats by competition from more aggressive *Xiphidiopicus percussus*. Sea-level to c. 900 m.
Food and Feeding. Arthropods, including beetles, orthopterans, cockroaches (Blattodea) and others, and spiders. Occasionally small vertebrates taken, e.g. tree-frogs (*Hyla*) and geckos (*Sphaerodactylus*). Also fruit, including *Carica*, *Ficus*. In study on Grand Cayman, 56% of diet was insects, especially grasshoppers (Acrididae), and spiders, with the rest made up of fruit. Forages singly or in pairs. Forages at all levels, also descends to the ground. Pecks and probes in coarse bark on trunks or in dead branches, also in dry leaves at base of bromeliads; much of time spent in gleaning arthropods, and taking small fruits; shows great skill and agility in obtaining fruits at tips of small branches. On Grand Cayman, males foraged higher on trees and used pecking, while females more often hunted lower down by gleaning; fruit consumed in 38% of foraging time, with pecking recorded for 13% of time. Large items are broken in anvil before being swallowed or fed to chicks.
Breeding. Jan-Aug; possibly 2 broods. Nest excavated by both sexes, at 4-14 m, on average c. 7 m, in dead tree, live or dead palm (especially *Roystonea regia* in Cuba), or utility pole, occasionally in cactus; cavity depth 35-38 cm, mean size of entrance hole 8·8 cm high, 7·1 cm wide; territorial, radius of 20 m around hole defended. Clutch 2-6 eggs, usually 4-5; incubation period 12 days; fledging period not documented; both parents feed chicks, mean 13·5 deliveries per hour in one study; at another nest watched for 3·3 hours, male delivered 15 feeds and female 20, a rate of 1 feed every 5·6 minutes; young accompanied by parents for c. 10 days after leaving nest.
Movements. Resident.
Status and Conservation. Not globally threatened. Common and widespread in Cuba and on I of Pines and offshore cays; common on Great Abaco; fairly common on Grand Cayman. Race *nyeanus* is uncommon to scarce on San Salvador and probably extinct on Grand Bahama; surviving population considered to be threatened by continued loss of habitat. In most of range (but not islands occupied by *nyeanus*), abandoned holes of this species are taken over by Cuban Amazon (*Amazona leucocephala*) for nesting.
Bibliography. Anon. (1998b), Barbour (1943), Bond (1985), Bradley (2000), Cruz (1974a), Cruz & Johnston (1984), Delacour & Legendre (1925), Emlen (1977), Faaborg (1985), Félix (1965), Garcia (1989, 1993, 1994), Garrido (1985), Garrido & Kirkconnell (2000), Hernández (1999), Jiménez (1997), King (1978/79), Kirkconnell (1992, 2000a), Miller, J.R. (1978), Paulson (1966), Raffaele *et al*. (1998), Short (1985b), Stotz *et al*. (1996), Todd & Worthington (1911), Torres (1988), Villard (1999a, 2001), White (1998), Willimont (1990), Willimont *et al*. (1991).

54. Golden-fronted Woodpecker
Melanerpes aurifrons

French: Pic à front doré **German**: Goldstirnspecht **Spanish**: Carpintero Frentidorado
Other common names: Gold-fronted Woodpecker

Taxonomy. *Picus Aurifrons* Wagler, 1829, Hidalgo, Mexico.
Sometimes combined with other barred congeners in a separate genus *Centurus*. Forms a superspecies with *M. hoffmannii*, and sometimes regarded as conspecific. Hybridizes with latter in S Honduras (R Pespire), with *M. carolinus* in S USA (Texas) and infrequently with *M. uropygialis* in SW Mexico. Geographical variation complex, and strong clinal variation in many plumage characters, making delimitation of races very difficult; in addition, mainland races, themselves variable to greater or lesser extent, intergrade, producing many populations with intermediate characters; *grateloupensis* possibly no more than an intergrade population. Subspecific treatment has varied greatly in the past, and some authors have recognized only 9 or fewer races; conversely, others have grouped races to form up to 4 separate species; further study needed. Paler birds from C Texas S to W Mexican Plateau described as race *incanescens*, but considered better merged with nominate; others from interior Chiapas described as race *frontalis*, tending towards nominate, but better treated as part of *polygrammus*. Twelve subspecies recognized.
Subspecies and Distribution.
M. a. aurifrons (Wagler, 1829) - S USA from NW Texas and SW Oklahoma S across Mexican Plateau to Jalisco, NW San Luis Potosí and Hidalgo.
M. a. grateloupensis (Lesson, 1839) - C San Luis Potosí and SW Tamaulipas to E Puebla and C Veracruz.
M. a. veraecrucis Nelson, 1900 - Atlantic slope from S Veracruz to NE Guatemala.
M. a. dubius (Cabot, 1844) - Yucatán Peninsula S to NE Guatemala and Belize.
M. a. polygrammus (Cabanis, 1862) - Pacific slope from SW Oaxaca E through interior Chiapas.
M. a. santacruzi (Bonaparte, 1838) - SE Chiapas E to El Salvador, SW Honduras and NC Nicaragua.
M. a. hughlandi Dickerman, 1987 - upper R Negro and upper Motagua Valley in Guatemala.
M. a. pauper (Ridgway, 1888) - coastal N Honduras.
M. a. leei (Ridgway, 1885) - Cozumel I (off NE Yucatán Peninsula).
M. a. turneffensis Russell, 1963 - Turneffe Is (off Belize).
M. a. insulanus (Bond, 1936) - Utila I (off N Honduras).
M. a. canescens (Salvin, 1889) - Roatán I and Barbaretta I (E of Utila).

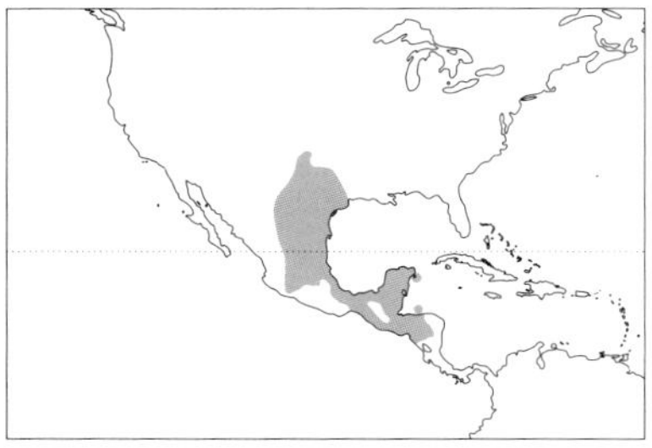

Descriptive notes. c. 22-26 cm; male 73-99 g, female 63-90 g. Male of nominate race has yellow (rarely, orange-gold) nasal tufts, small red patch on centre of crown (very occasionally extending to nape), golden-orange (occasionally yellow) nape, becoming more orange-yellow on lower hindneck and often uppermost mantle; rest of head pale grey, darkest on hindcrown, palest on forehead and chin (rarely, faint yellowish wash); upperparts, including wing-coverts, evenly barred black and white, white rump and uppertail-coverts rarely with dark shaft streaks; flight-feathers black, secondaries and tertials barred white, outer primaries tipped white (when fresh) and with white at bases forming patch; uppertail black, tipped white (when fresh), outermost feathers barred white on outer webs, sometimes also at tip of inner webs; entire underparts pale grey to whitish, central lower belly with narrow diffuse area of yellow (occasionally more golden-yellow), lower flanks and undertail-coverts barred blackish, often indistinctly on flanks; underwing greyish, coverts and inner wing barred, white primary patch; undertail often tinged buffish at sides; medium-long to long bill slightly chisel-tipped, culmen barely curved, fairly broad across nostrils, black to grey-black; iris deep red or red-brown, orbital skin grey to grey-brown; legs grey, usually tinged greenish. Differs from *M. hoffmannii* in larger size, more orange nape, somewhat paler underparts. Female is somewhat smaller than male, has pale grey crown without red (rarely, some red feathers), often yellower nape and hindneck than male. Juvenile duller than adult, markings less contrasting, dark bars above broader, dusky bars on forehead, streaked breast, paler belly patch, brown eyes, male with reddish crown patch smaller than adult's, female crown without red or with few scattered red tips (rarely, more red, almost as male) and nape and hindneck paler. Races differ from nominate mainly in head pattern, width of pale bars above, tail pattern, darkness of underparts, but very variable: *grateloupensis* is highly variable, some very like nominate, nasal tufts sometimes red, pale bars above tend to be rather narrow, male crown often all red; *veraecrucis* is rather small and dark, has red nasal tufts, nape and belly patch, pale bars above narrower, little or no white in tail; *dubius* as previous but longer-billed, pale bars above very narrow, underparts more grey-buff, red belly patch sometimes with diffuse golden border, white primary patch smaller, male with red crown to hindneck, female with nape and hindneck more orange-red; *polygrammus* has nasal tufts yellow or tinged orange, pale bars above broader than on previous, underparts somewhat paler, belly patch golden-yellow, central rectrices barred white on inner webs, male with orange-red crown grading into yellower nape and hindneck (sometimes broken at upper nape), female with whitish to grey crown and nape, orange-yellow hindneck; *santacruzi* has short bill, short tail, nasal tufts yellow or yellow-orange, pale bars above tinged yellow-brown in fresh plumage, central rectrices usually with some white, rather dark buff-grey below, belly patch more golden-orange or orange-yellow, male with entire crown red, nape orange-red, female generally with pale upper nape; *hughlandi* resembles previous, but longer-winged, has pale bars above broader, no yellow wash; *pauper* is like previous, but much shorter-winged, pale bars above normally very narrow; *leei* is long-billed, long-tailed, dark, has red nasal tufts, pale bars above very narrow and brown-tinged, white rump and tail-coverts dark-barred, little or no white in tail, brownish below, dark red belly patch, male with entire crown to hindneck red, sometimes meeting red of nasal tufts; *turneffensis* resembles previous, but red colours more orangey, pale bars above slightly broader, underparts paler; *insulanus* is rather large, long-tailed, has yellow-orange nasal tufts, white supercilium, little or no white in tail, male crown all red, hindneck orange-red; *canescens* has very long bill, red nasal tufts, hindneck and belly, very pale face and underparts, pale bars above fairly narrow, white spots on inner primaries, male crown all red. Voice. Tremulous rolling "pwurr-rr-rr", slightly shorter and higher than that of *M. carolinus*, as contact and advertisement, also "kek-kek-kek-kek" as warning, and other nasal and rolled calls; repertoire as for *M. carolinus*, but calls generally louder, harsher. Drumming occasional, almost always by male, series of single short rolls preceded or followed by 1-4 taps; mutual tapping.

Habitat. Typically, arid or semi-arid country with sparse to tall second-growth woodland; also mesic areas. In USA, xeric vegetation dominated by mesquite (*Prosopis*), also riparian cottonwood (*Populus*), mixed oak (*Quercus*) woodland, and juniper (*Juniperus*) country, also in pecan (*Carya*) groves and in open areas on floodplains; small numbers in areas of live oaks (*Q. fusiformis*), elms (*Ulmus*) and other mesic types in residential districts, especially where adjacent to stands of mesquite, deciduous oak and/or juniper. Enters suburban areas and urban parks. In Mexico and Central America, also arid tropical scrub with paloverde (*Cercidium praecox*), mesquite and cacti, and short-tree tropical deciduous forest with dense thorny understorey; also tropical evergreen forest with open canopy in SE. From sea-level to 2500 m.

Food and Feeding. Rather catholic in diet. Wide variety of insects and their larvae, including those of wood-boring beetles, ants, and grasshoppers, Lepidoptera, Homoptera, mantids, phasmids; also spiders; possibly also bird eggs, and once seen to kill lizard (*Sceloporus*). Consumes large amounts of fruits, berries, nuts (e.g. pecan) and various seeds, particularly acorns and corn, also mesquite. Visits feeders. Hunts singly or in pairs, sometimes in family groups; occasionally joins mixed-species flocks on ground. Most foraging is on medium-sized to large branches and on trunks. Gleaning and searching (50%), pecking and hammering (28%), and probing in crevices and holes (13%) constitute most important feeding techniques; also some flycatching, ground-feeding, and picking of fruits. Slight sexual differences in foraging behaviour recorded in Texas: in autumn males pecked more and gleaned less than females, which resorted more to ground-feeding; in late winter, however, males pecked less frequently than females and fed more on ground, visiting small twigs rarely. Occasionally stores food (seeds, nuts, fruits) in crevices and holes in early winter. Attacks other bird species at fruit trees or near seed stores.

Breeding. Late Mar to Jul in Texas, from Jan in S Mexico (Chiapas), and Feb-Aug in Guatemala; sometimes 2 broods, in Central America even rarely 3. Monogamous; solitary. Nest excavated by both sexes, completed in less than 2 weeks, at 2-9 m, sometimes lower or higher, in large branch or trunk or live or dead tree, or often at top of telephone pole, or in fence post, mean cavity depth 31·6 cm, and entrance hole 5·5 cm high, 4·9 cm wide; nest-hole often reused; nestbox, or male's roost-hole occasionally used; territory large, 14·4-23·3 ha in WC Texas. Clutch 4-5 eggs, occasionally up to 7, average 4·75, clutch size increasing somewhat with latitude; incubation by both parents, only male during the night, period 12-14 days; both also brood and feed chicks, deliver insects and berries carried in bill; fledging period c. 30 days; juveniles accompanied by parents for several weeks, sometimes until autumn. Annual success in WC Texas 1-4 young per successful pair; nests sometimes preyed on by rat snakes (*Elaphe*). First breeding at 1 year. Recorded longevity 5 years 8 months.

Movements. Resident; occasionally wanders N, E or W of normal range.

Status and Conservation. Not globally threatened. Common to fairly common throughout its range, locally very common. Local abundance varies annually; breeding surveys in a study area in S Texas found 3·65 territories/ha during 1973 to 1978 but 1·04 territories/ha in 1994 to 1996. Expanded N and W in 20th century; first recorded in Oklahoma in 1954. Population size and range in large parts of Texas and Oklahoma appear to have increased since 1960; species has benefited from proliferation of mesquite on rangeland. Was formerly persecuted in S USA for its habit of nesting in utility poles and fence posts, as a result of which it sufferered significant decline during 1930-1950; current levels of persecution considered minimal, and unlikely to have adverse effect on total population. Habitat alteration, especially removal of mesquite in S USA brushlands, can reduce availability of nesting and foraging sites. Nevertheless, this woodpecker seems adaptable, able to flourish in human-altered environments, and has successfully colonized urban parks. No real threats known.

Bibliography. Anon. (1998b), Baicich & Harrison (1997), Bent (1939), Calvo & Blake (1998), Corcuera & Butterfield (1999), Dearborn (1907), Dennis (1964, 1967), Dickerman (1987), Friedmann *et al.* (1957), García *et al.* (2001), Garrett (1999), Gerber (1986), Howell & Webb (1995), Husak (1995, 1996, 1997a, 1997b, 1997c, 1997d, 1999, 2000), Husak & Maxwell (1998), Johnsgard (1979), Kaufman (1996), Klaas (1968), Koenig (1986, 1987), Kujawa (1984), Lowery & Dalquest (1951), Lynch (1992), Martin & Kroll (1975), Monroe (1968), Paynter (1955), Price *et al.* (1995), Root (1988), Rowley (1984), Selander & Giller (1959, 1963), Short (1985b), Skutch (1969a), Smith (1987), Stotz *et al.* (1996), Urban (1959), Wallace (1969, 1974a), Wetmore (1948).

55. Hoffmann's Woodpecker

Melanerpes hoffmannii

French: Pic de Hoffmann **German**: Hoffmannspecht **Spanish**: Carpintero de Hoffmann

Taxonomy. *Centurus Hoffmannii* Cabanis, 1862, Costa Rica.

Sometimes combined with other barred congeners in a separate genus *Centurus*. Forms a superspecies with *M. aurifrons*, and sometimes regarded as conspecific. Hybridizes with latter in S Honduras (R Pespire) and with *M. rubricapillus* in C Costa Rica, producing numerous individuals with intermediate appearance (e.g. majority between Tárcoles and Quepos, in Costa Rica, have orange hindneck and belly). Monotypic.

Distribution. Pacific slope from S Honduras and Nicaragua S to Costa Rica (S to Quepos, and on Caribbean slope to Turrialba).

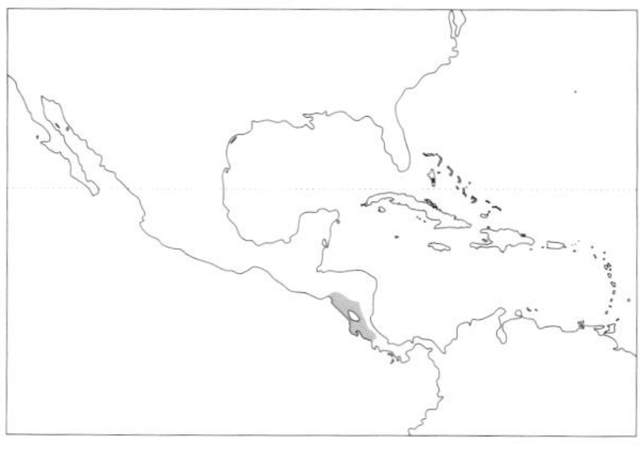

Descriptive notes. c. 19-21 cm; 62-84 g. Male has pale golden-yellow nasal tufts, red crown patch, golden-yellow to orange-yellow nape and hindneck sometimes with few scattered red tips, becoming paler on uppermost mantle; rest of head very pale grey-buff to brownish-grey, this colour frequently continuing over hindcrown, whiter at front of face, often pale yellow feather tips in loral area; black upperparts barred white, white rump and uppertail-coverts occasionally with few black spots or bars; black wing-coverts usually with fewer white bars than back, broad on greaters; secondaries and tertials similarly barred, white bars broadest on tertials; black primaries tipped white (when fresh), outer feathers broadly barred white at base of inner webs, may form small patch; uppertail black, central feather pair white on inner webs with black half-bars, outer webs with white at base, outermost pair narrowly barred white on outer webs; pale greyish below, breast slightly olive-tinged, central belly diffusely golden-orange or orange-gold, flanks and undertail-coverts often yellow-washed, ventral region with blackish arrowhead bars; underwing dark brownish, barred white; undertail as above, sides browner; fairly long bill minimally chisel-tipped, culmen slightly curved, rather broad across nostrils, black; iris red or red-brown, orbital skin brownish; legs grey. Female is slightly smaller, shorter-billed than male, nasal tufts often paler, lacks red on head, having crown and nape pale. Juvenile duller and darker, has barring above less sharp, underparts more olive, belly patch paler, lower underparts (and sometimes breast) mottled dark, eyes brown, head pattern as respective adult, female occasionally with trace of red on crown. Voice. Most common are loud to soft "churr" calls, like those of *M. aurifrons*; hard metallic rattle in short bursts; prolonged nasal rattle or splutter, wavering in pitch; querulous, grating "woick-a-woick-a-woick-a" or "wit wit wit" in excitement. Also drums.

Habitat. Xeric to mesic open and semi-open country. Typically, deciduous forest, light woodland, second growth, shade trees in coffee plantations, gardens, also scattered trees in pastures; often near human habitation. Avoids dense wet forest, but may invade when forest cut. Occurs from sea-level up to 200 m in Honduras; mostly at 600-2150 m in Costa Rica, though also occurs at lower altitudes in N.

Food and Feeding. Insects, particularly ants, beetles, lepidopterans, and their larvae. Eats many fruits, including figs (*Ficus*), also *Cecropia* catkins, and arils. Takes nectar of balsa (*Ochroma*), African tulip tree (*Spathodea*), and other large flowers. Forages singly or in pairs. Largely arboreal, but often descends to low level on stumps and posts. Pecks and hammers wood, flakes off pieces of bark, probes; clings head downward to obtain berries, reaching with stretched neck.

Breeding. Feb-Jul; often 2 broods. Monogamous, in pairs throughout year; solitary nester. Often conspicuous encounters between pairs before breeding season; displays include bobbing entire body, with calling and wing-spreading. Nest-hole 1·5-9 m up in dead trunk or branch, sometimes only 1 m up in fence post. Clutch 2-3 eggs; incubation and fledging periods not documented, probably similar to *M. aurifrons*. Frequently mobs pygmy-owls (*Glaucidium*), indicating possible hole competition or nest predation by latter.

Movements. Resident.

Status and Conservation. Not globally threatened. Fairly common to common in N of range; common to locally very common in Costa Rica. Occurs in Santa Rosa, Palo Verde and Barra Honda National Parks (Costa Rica). Adaptable, able to utilize human-altered habitats. Has expanded its range in Costa Rica since 1960; as it prefers open and semi-open terrain with scattered trees, it benefits from clearance or thinning of forest. No known threats.

Bibliography. Anon. (1998b), Cooper (1997), Howell & Webb (1995), Monroe (1968), Orians & Paulson (1969), Otvos (1967), Selander & Giller (1963), Short (1985b), Slud (1964, 1980), Stiles (1985), Stiles & Skutch (1989), Stotz *et al.* (1996), Young *et al.* (1998).

PLATE 28 ➤

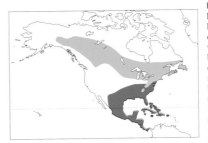

PLATE 28

inches 4
cm 10

PLATE 28

Genus *SPHYRAPICUS* Baird, 1858

56. Yellow-bellied Sapsucker

Sphyrapicus varius

French: Pic maculé   **German**: Gelbbauch-Saftlecker   **Spanish**: Chupasavia Norteño
Other common names: Common Sapsucker

Taxonomy. *Picus varius* Linnaeus, 1766, North America = South Carolina.
Forms a superspecies with *S. nuchalis* and *S. ruber*; sometimes treated as conspecific with former, and in past also with latter; hybridizes to limited extent with former in SW Canada (Alberta), more rarely with latter where ranges overlap. Birds from S Appalachian Mountains sometimes separated as race *appalachiensis* on basis of slightly darker plumage and marginally smaller size, but considerable overlap with N populations; subspecific recognition considered unwarranted. Monotypic.
Distribution. S Yukon, SW Northwest Territories and NE British Columbia E to NC Ontario, S Labrador and Newfoundland, and S to C Alberta, E South Dakota, N Iowa and Appalachians (S to SW North Carolina). Winters SE USA (S from about S Kansas, S Ohio and Connecticut) S to Panama.
Descriptive notes. c. 19-21 cm; 41-62 g, mean 50.3 g. Male has bright red (exceptionally, yellow) forehead and crown bordered black, broader black across hindcrown, white stripe from above eye broadening at rear and nape (nape rarely with trace of red) and down hindneck side, narrow black band down hindneck, broad black band through ear-coverts and down neck side bordered below by white stripe from nasal tufts to neck side and down to breast side; red chin and throat bordered

black; white mantle to rump with heavy, irregular black bars, black outer scapulars, white lower rump and uppertail-coverts with black outer webs; black wing-coverts with large white panel on medians and central greaters; black flight-feathers tipped white, white spots on both webs forming bar-like pattern, innermost tertials white with black bars; uppertail black, central feather pair with white inner webs (few black bars or spots) and sometimes some white at tips of outer webs, outer 2 or 3 pairs often with white marks near tips, outermost also with thin white edge on outer web; underparts below breast pale yellow, whiter in lower region, breast side to lateral undertail-coverts with narrow blackish arrowheads and usually shaft streaks; underwing barred greyish and white, coverts mostly dusky; in fresh autumn plumage, white parts tinged yellow or buffish, black breast patch and markings below partly obscured by broad yellowish fringes; relatively short bill straight, chisel-tipped, broad across nostrils, slaty-grey to blackish; iris deep brown; legs blue-grey to green-grey. Distinguished from extremely similar *S. nuchalis* by lack of red nape patch, less red on throat, more white in wings; from *S. ruber* by patterns of head and breast. Female differs from male in having white chin and throat, usually paler red forehead and crown sometimes mixed with black, or red restricted to patches on forehead, or occasionally top of head all black or with few buff spots. Juvenile very different, mainly dark olive-brown, head striped buff, crown streaked, above barred and mottled blackish and pale, throat whitish, breast scaly, central belly pale yellowish-white, tail more extensively barred, male sometimes with some red on throat; protracted moult to adult plumage, not completed until spring. VOICE. Nasal, cat-like, single or grouped squeals, "neaaah", "owee-owee", "wee-wee-wee-wee" or "kweeurk", at start of breeding, as long-distance signal; soft mew in alarm, louder and hoarser with increasing excitement; "weetik-weetik" calls in aggression; "juk-juk-juk" during encounters; soft "mjuk" notes, e.g. when pair-members meet at nest; incessant chatter by nestlings. Drumrolls very distinctive with well-separated taps at end, sometimes also at beginning, "tap-tap-trrrrrrrrr-ta-ta-tat–tat—tat", by both sexes; ritual tapping at lower rim of nest-hole.

Habitat. When breeding, inhabits deciduous and mixed coniferous forests; presence of aspen (*Populus*) important for nesting, birch (*Betula*) and hickory (*Carya*) also important tree species in habitat; generally up to c. 2000 m. In winter, mostly forest, including montane forest, but usually not pure conifer stands; also forest edge, open woodland and semi-open habitats; visits larger trees in pastures, clearings and suburban areas; occasionally found in coastal palm groves; in wintering zones occurs from sea-level up to c. 3200 m, locally up to 3500 m, but mainly 900-3000 m.

Food and Feeding. Arthopods, especially beetles and their larvae, ants and their brood, also Lepidoptera, and dragonflies (Odonata); also large quantities of tree sap; fruit and nuts also taken, and in spring buds. Berries occasionally taken, even fed to nestlings in times of food shortage. Insects comprise almost half of diet during nesting season; sap and phloem make up main food in late summer and autumn, and important also at other times; fruits taken mostly in Oct-Feb. Observed to place fruits, nuts or acorns in crevices, but uncertain whether this behaviour involves anvil use or food-storing. Forages singly; sometimes small groups on migration; will join mixed flocks of insectivores in winter. In spring, prefers to forage on live branches in lower canopy; descends to ground to take carpenter ants (*Crematogaster*). Digs in dead or dying wood, flakes off bark to expose ants and their brood. Hangs on outermost tips of twigs when reaching for buds. Flycatching also important at times; sallies from exposed perch, returning to the same or another perch. Sap and phloem are sought at all levels, on trunk as well as in crown of trees. Numerous tree species utilized, both deciduous (especially *Populus*, *Salix*, *Betula*, *Acer*, *Carya*, *Alnus*) and coniferous (mainly *Pinus*, *Picea*, *Abies*); in N Michigan preferentially selected paper birch (*Betula papyrifera*), red maple (*Acer rubrum*), juneberry (*Amelanchier*) and bigtooth aspen (*Populus grandidentata*). In late summer and autumn, drills shallow holes arranged in vertical columns, in horizontal bands, or on twigs in spiralling bands; in spring, uses old sap wells or other sources of sap on bruised parts of trees. Sap wells exploited by a wide variety of other birds, as well as numerous insects and mammals.

Breeding. Apr-Jul. Monogamous; solitary. Nest excavated mostly by male, taking c. 15-28 days, some further excavation by both sexes after chicks hatch; at 2-20 m, mostly 3-14 m, in live tree, especially *Populus* or *Betula*, usually one with rotten heartwood; nest-hole very occasionally reused; territorial. Flutter-aerial displays, also perched displays with bill-pointing, wing-spreading, bobbing. Clutch 4-7 eggs, average 4·93, clutch size increases from S to N; incubation by both sexes, period 12-13 days; both also take about equal share in feeding chicks, male carries out most of the nest sanitation; young leave nest after 25-29 days, fully independent after c. 2 weeks. Nest preyed on by snakes. First breeding at 1 year.

Movements. Migratory, winters well S of breeding range. Leaves breeding areas from late Aug, sometimes not until Oct-Nov; a few may remain in N parts. Winter range from S & SE USA to Central America (S to Costa Rica, more rarely to W Panama), including all of West Indies; in Mexico mainly E & S from E Chihuahua and S Sinaloa. Females migrate farther S than males. N migration from Mar, arrival at breeding grounds from late Apr to May; males return earlier than females. Most passage is through C & E parts of North America, but numerous records also from W; vagrants recorded in Netherlands Antilles, and three times in British Is.

Status and Conservation. Not globally threatened. Fairly common to common throughout range; reasonably common, but often inconspicuous, on non-breeding grounds. Has disappeared from some former breeding grounds in south of range; precise reasons uncertain. No known threats, but fairly specific habitat requirements, including presence of suitable trees for sap-feeding, need to be borne in mind; preservation of older large trees for nesting important. Within the ecosystem, plays an important role in providing other organisms with a rich resource in the form of sap.

Bibliography. Baicich & Harrison (1997), Baldwin (1960), Bent (1939), Bond (1957), Bradley (2000), Browning (1977), Bull (1981), Campbell *et al.* (1990), Cicero & Johnson (1994, 1995), Conner & Kroll (1979), Cruz (1974a), Cyr (1995b), DeGraaf & Rappole (1995), Downer (1968), Dunn (1978), Eberhardt (1994, 1997, 2000), Ellison (1992), Emlen (1977), Gamboa & Brown (1976), Garrett (1999), Garrido & Kirkconnell (2000), Harestad & Keisker (1989), Hart (1977), Holmes & Sherry (2001), Howell, S.N.G. & Webb (1995), Howell, T.R. (1952, 1953), Inouye (1976), Jiménez (1997), Johnsgard (1979), Johnson, N.K. & Johnson (1985), Johnson, N.K. & Zink (1983), Johnson, R.A. (1947), Kilham (1956, 1962a, 1962c, 1964, 1971, 1977c, 1977d, 1979b, 1983), Koenig (1987), Kreisel (1974), Lawrence (1966), Mayr & Short (1970), McGuire (1932), Monroe (1968), Moulton & Lowell (1991), Murphy (1981), Peck & James (1983), Perkins (1943), Petit *et al.* (1985), Rissler (1995), Rudolph *et al.* (1991), Shackelford & Conner (1997), Short (1969a), Short & Morony (1970), Slud (1964), Small (2000), Spring (1965), Stradi & Hudon (1998), Stradi *et al.* (1998), Sutherland *et al.* (1982), Tate (1973), Townsend (1932), Trombino (2000), Welsh & Capen (1987, 1992), Wiedenfeld *et al.* (1992), Williams, J.B. (1975, 1980b), Woods (1984), Zusi & Marshall (1970).

57. Red-naped Sapsucker

Sphyrapicus nuchalis

French: Pic à nuque rouge **German**: Rotnacken-Saftlecker **Spanish**: Chupasavia Nuquirrojo

Taxonomy. *Sphyrapicus varius* var. *nuchalis* Baird, 1858, southern Rocky Mountains = Mimbres River, New Mexico, USA.

Forms a superspecies with *S. varius* and *S. ruber*; sometimes treated as conspecific with former, and in past also with latter; hybridizes occasionally with former in SW Canada (Alberta), more frequently with latter in various areas; has interbred rarely with *S. thyroideus*. Monotypic.

Distribution. Rocky Mountains from SE British Columbia and SW & SE Alberta E to W South Dakota, and S, discontinuously, to SE California, E Arizona and NE & S New Mexico; in winter from S California, Arizona and W Texas S to SC Mexico.

Descriptive notes. c. 19-21 cm; 36-61 g, mean 52·4 g. Male has bright red forehead and crown, black band on hindcrown, red nape, black band down hindneck, narrow white stripe from eye to nape side and down hindneck side, black band from eye through ear-coverts (sometimes dull red) to neck side, white stripe from nasal tufts back to neck side and down to breast side; red chin, throat and malar, black band below; black upperparts, broad row of white bars each side of mantle and back (white less obvious in worn summer plumage), white lower rump to uppertail-coverts, white panel on wing-coverts; black flight-feathers tipped white, variably barred white; uppertail black, central feather pair with white inner webs barred black, outer pair with thin white edge on outer web; underparts below breast pale yellow, belly to vent whiter, blackish arrowheads and usually shaft streaks from breast side to lateral undertail-coverts; underwing barred greyish and white; in fresh autumn plumage, white parts tinged yellow or buffish, black breast patch and markings below

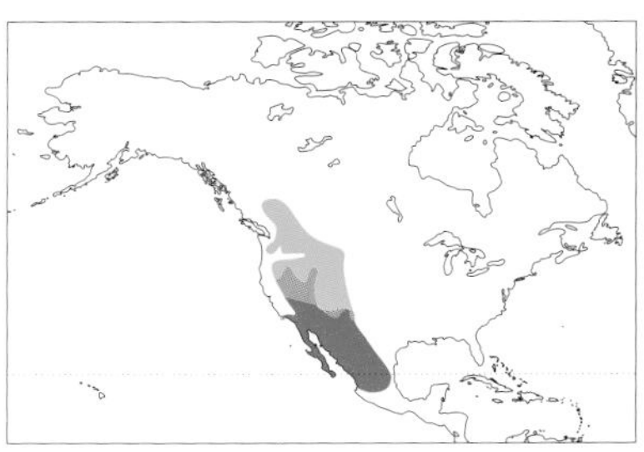

partly obscured by broad yellowish fringes; comparatively short bill straight, chisel-tipped, broad across nostrils, black to dark slaty; iris deep brown; legs greyish. Distinguished from extremely similar *S. varius* by red nape, more extensive red on throat, narrower white bands on head, less white above; from *S. ruber* mainly by head pattern. Female differs mainly in having white chin and upper throat, but variable, sometimes virtually identical to male; occasionally has white (not red) nape. Juvenile very different, dark blackish-olive, buff supercilium, above blackish with pale spots, throat buff, breast black-brown, belly greyish, flanks well barred; more as adult by autumn (from Oct), but not fully so until Jan. Voice. Mewing "meeah", lower-pitched than that of *S. varius*, also more vibrant shorter versions in flight; squealing series, mainly by male in early breeding season, individual notes shorter and delivered at faster rate than by *S. thyroideus*; low calls during change-over at nest. Drumroll as initial burst, followed by irregular slower burst of 2-3 strokes, 8-9 rolls per minute, by both sexes.

Habitat. Deciduous forest containing aspen (*Populus tremuloides*), or in pure aspen stands; also coniferous forest, e.g. with Douglas fir (*Pseudotsuga menziesii*), larch (*Larix*), spruce (*Picea*) or fir (*Abies*), particularly if aspen present; in montane habitats to 2900 m. Where sympatric with *S. thyroideus* in Colorado, favours areas near deciduous or mixed coniferous forest, whereas latter prefers sites adjoining open ponderosa pine (*Pinus ponderosa*) forest. Non-breeding habitats include forest and forest edge, also mixed oak (*Quercus*) and juniper (*Juniperus*) woodland, mixed pine-oak and pure oak woodland, in mountains to 1700 m; in Mexican winter quarters from sea-level to 2500 m.

Food and Feeding. Arthropods, tree sap; diet presumably similar to that of *S. varius*. Ants (*Camponotus*) apparently important as nestling food. Relies greatly on conifer sap during spring. Forages singly, sometimes small groups on migration. In spring mostly in lower canopy, where excavates in dead wood, flakes off bark. Sap holes used throughout year; exploits various conifers and deciduous trees and bushes on breeding grounds; oaks preferred in winter quarters.

Breeding. May-Aug. Monogamous, male and female may reunite in consecutive seasons; solitary. Nest excavated at 1-25 m in tree, e.g. aspen, paper birch (*Betula papyrifera*) or larch, preferably with some dead parts; several holes may be initiated, and one started in previous season is often selected, but old holes also reused; territorial, attacks *S. thyroideus* and other picids, e.g. *Picoides villosus*, in vicinity of nest. Clutch 3-7 eggs, usually 4-6; incubation by both sexes, period c. 13 days; nestlings fed by both parents, male takes greater share in nest sanitation; female helper once observed feeding nestlings of hybrid pair; fledging period 25-28 days; young quickly become independent, both they and adults soon leave nest area. Productivity 1-6 young reared per nest, mean c. 3 chicks fledging.

Movements. Migratory. Leaves breeding areas mostly in Sept, moving relatively short distances. Winter range from S Nevada, Arizona, SW New Mexico and W Texas S to S Baja California and NW Mexico (E to SW Nuevo León, S to Jalisco); some individuals occasionally reach Guatemala and Honduras. Females tend to migrate farther than males. Return passage from Mar, often not until Apr, arrival on breeding grounds Apr-May. Recorded on passage in W California, and E to Louisiana.

Status and Conservation. Not globally threatened. Fairly common in breeding range; fairly common in Mexican non-breeding range; few data. No known threats; protection and appropriate management of its habitats would appear to be sufficient to secure its future. At least locally important as a provider of holes for other birds; in 3019 ha of forest reserve in NW Montana, all nests of Mountain Chickadee (*Poecile gambeli*) and almost 50% of Red-breasted Nuthatch (*Sitta canadensis*) nests were found in old holes made by this species.

Bibliography. Anon. (1998b), Baicich & Harrison (1997), Bent (1939), Bock & Larson (1986), Campbell *et al.* (1990), Cicero & Johnson (1994, 1995), Crockett & Hadow (1975), Daily (1993), DeGraaf & Rappole (1995), Ehrlich & Daily (1988), Hadow (1977), Howell, S.N.G. & Webb (1995), Howell, T.R. (1952), Johnson & Johnson (1985), Johnson & Zink (1983), Kaufman (1996), Keisker (1986), Koenig (1986, 1987), Lockwood & Shackelford (1998), Mayr & Short (1970), McClelland & McClelland (2000), Price *et al.* (1995), Rojas *et al.* (2001), Saab & Dudley (1998), Schepps *et al.* (1999), Scott *et al.* (1976), Short (1969a), Short & Morony (1970), Small, A. (1994), Small, B. (2000), Smith (1982), Tobalske (1992, 1996), Trombino (1998, 2000), Weisser (1973), Wiedenfeld *et al.* (1992).

58. Red-breasted Sapsucker

Sphyrapicus ruber

French: Pic à poitrine rouge **German**: Feuerkopf-Saftlecker **Spanish**: Chupasavia Pechirrojo

Taxonomy. *Picus ruber* J. F. Gmelin, 1788, Cayenne; error = Nootka Sound, British Columbia, Canada.

Forms a superspecies with *S. varius* and *S. nuchalis*, and in the past sometimes treated as conspecific; hybridizes with both, but especially latter, wherever ranges overlap. Races intergrade, fully so in extreme S Oregon. Two subspecies recognized.

Subspecies and Distribution.

S. r. ruber (J. F. Gmelin, 1788) - S Alaska S to W Oregon.

S. r. daggetti Grinnell, 1901 - SW Oregon N & E California and W Nevada.

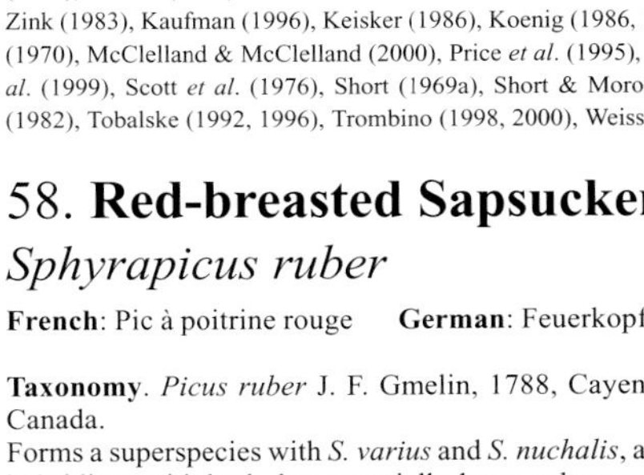

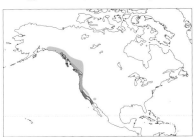

Descriptive notes. 20-22 cm; 40-55 g. Both sexes have bright red head, neck and breast, brightest in spring, some black feather bases visible when very worn (summer), white nasal tufts and front of lores, black spot in front of eye; black upperparts, rows of buffish-white to golden spots on mantle to upper rump, white lower rump and uppertail-coverts with black on outer webs of feathers, white panel on median and greater wing-coverts; black flight-feathers tipped white, narrowly barred white; uppertail black, central feather pair with white bars on inner webs, outermost with narrow white edge on outer web; pale yellow to yellowish-white belly, white lower ventral region, irregular arrowhead markings most prominent on

On following pages: 59. Williamson's Sapsucker (*Sphyrapicus thyroideus*); 60. Cuban Green Woodpecker (*Xiphidiopicus percussus*).

flanks; underwing barred grey and white, coverts more uniform; shortish bill straight, chisel-tipped, broad across nostrils, black; iris deep brown; legs grey to green-grey. Juvenile has similar pattern, but different colours: red replaced by dark brown with red wash, rump barred, underparts grey-brown and extensively barred except central belly; identical to adult by late summer or early autumn. Race *daggetti* marginally smaller, red duller, has white of lores continuing as moustachial stripe of variable length, pale markings above whiter and more like bars, red on breast less extensive, belly paler. VOICE. Mewing, rather drawn-out "meeah", quiet "puc" or "pwuc" notes, also other call types; voice much as that of *S. varius*. Drumroll as initial burst, followed by irregular, slower burst of 2-3 strokes, by both sexes.

Habitat. Mixed deciduous and coniferous forest and forest edge, particularly associations of aspen (*Populus tremuloides*) and ponderosa pine (*Pinus ponderosa*); coastal populations inhabit humid forest dominated by conifers. At up to 2900 m during breeding season; 500-3000 m in winter quarters.

Food and Feeding. Arthropods and sap; presumably, nuts and fruits also taken. Insects, especially ants, comprise an important nestling food. Diet and foraging habits similar to those of *S. varius* and *S. nuchalis*. Forages singly, sometimes in small groups; may join *S. thyroideus* on migration. Mostly in lower canopy; excavates in dead wood, flakes off bark. Sap holes apparently utilized throughout year.

Breeding. Apr-Jul. Monogamous; solitary. Nest usually high up in tree, conifer apparently preferred. Clutch 4-7 eggs; incubation 14-15 days; both parents feed chicks, possibly exceptionally with 1 helper; also, male *S. thyroideus* once seen helping pair of present species, fed nestlings less frequently than did parents; fledging period probably c. 28-30 days.

Movements. Resident and short-distance migrant. Less migratory than congeners; nominate race more or less sedentary, or withdraws only short distance from extreme N parts. In non-breeding season occurs S to N Baja California, sometimes slightly farther S to about 29°N. Remains in winter quarters Oct-Mar, return to breeding grounds beginning Apr. Occasional migrants recorded W to C Texas.

Status and Conservation. Not globally threatened. Reasonably common throughout most of its range; race *daggetti* fairly common in Sierra Nevada; no detailed information on numbers. Outside breeding season, uncommon to rare in Baja California but possibly overlooked. No obvious threats.

Bibliography. Anon. (1998b), Baicich & Harrison (1997), Bent (1939), Campbell *et al.* (1990), Cicero & Johnson (1994, 1995), Howell, S.N.G. & Webb (1995), Howell, T.R. (1952), Johnson, E.V. (2000), Johnson, N.K. & Johnson (1985), Johnson, N.K. & Zink (1983), Kaufman (1996), Koenig (1986, 1987), Lockwood & Shackelford (1998), Mayr & Short (1970), Price *et al.* (1995), Scott *et al.* (1976), Short (1969a), Short & Morony (1970), Shuford (1985), Small, A. (1994), Small, B. (2000), Stark *et al.* (1998), Steventon *et al.* (1998), Trombino (1998, 2000), Weisser (1973), Wiedenfeld *et al.* (1992).

59. Williamson's Sapsucker

Sphyrapicus thyroideus

French: Pic de Williamson   **German**: Kiefernsaftlecker   **Spanish**: Chupasavia Oscuro

Taxonomy. *Picus thyroideus* Cassin, 1851, Georgetown, Eldorado County, California, USA.
Has hybridized rarely with *S. nuchalis*. Two subspecies recognized.

Subspecies and Distribution.
S. t. thyroideus (Cassin, 1851) - S British Columbia S through Cascade Range and Sierra Nevada to N Baja California (San Pedro Mártir Mts).
S. t. nataliae (Malherbe, 1854) - SE British Columbia S through Rockies to Arizona and New Mexico; winters in S of range and S to SC Mexico.

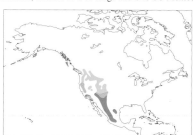

Descriptive notes. c. 21-23 cm; 44-64 g. Male has white nasal tufts, lores and long moustachial stripe, white stripe from above eye curving down on nape side, red chin and upper throat; rest of head and neck, breast and most of upperparts glossy blue-black, gloss strongest on head, mantle and scapulars; white rump and uppertail-coverts with black on outer webs of feathers; large white panel across median and greater wing-coverts; black flight-feathers, small white spots on inner webs of primaries and secondaries, primaries also small white spots on outer webs, tertials narrowly tipped white; uppertail black, sometimes a few white bars or streaks on central feathers; bright yellow lower breast to lower belly, white breast sides down to undertail-coverts with broad black streaks or arrowheads; underwing barred dark grey and white, coverts more uniform; shortish bill straight, chisel-tipped, broad across nostrils, black; iris deep brown to dark chestnut; legs grey. Female very different, head rather variable, brownish to buffish, usually streaked darker, buff moustachial area, dark-streaked or blackish submoustachial, generally yellowish-brown throat centre, sometimes buff with blackish chin (rarely, very small area of red), upperparts barred black-brown and buff to white, white rump and uppertail-coverts, dark brown wings barred buff to white, brownish-black tail barred buff-white on central and outer feathers; barred black and buff to white below, breast often solidly black (especially when worn), pale yellow lower breast to lower belly unmarked, some have brighter yellow belly, more solid black on breast, more streaked pattern at sides. Juvenile male like adult but duller, no gloss, has more barring on wings and tail, often a few small white spots on upperparts, generally some white on hindneck and nape sides often meeting to form pale patch, also white throat, paler yellow belly; juvenile female like adult but duller, browner, more heavily barred, head and throat often streaked or barred, fully barred breast (no impression of black patch), unmarked area of belly smaller and paler yellow to whitish; both sexes much as adult by early autumn. Race *nataliae* has longer, broader, deeper bill. VOICE. Single explosive, pulsating calls distinctive; also low-pitched guttural "k-k'-r-r-r"; squealing series, slower with shorter elements than *S. nuchalis*; low, nasal calls in close encounters between pair-members; whinnying chorus by nestlings when fed, also constant chattering in nest. Drumming distinctive, roll begins with a burst, followed by several rhythmic groups of 2-4 strokes that are slower than in congeners, c. 5 rolls per minute.

Habitat. Mixed montane forest dominated by spruce (*Picea*), firs (*Abies*) and pines (*Pinus*); also mixed stands of aspen (*Populus tremuloides*) and fir. Typical trees in habitat are ponderosa pine (*Pinus ponderosa*) and Douglas fir (*Pseudotsuga menziesii*), also larch (*Larix*), other pines. Prefers bottom of drainages rather than slopes and ridges. Breeds at 1500-3200 m, in extreme N at 850-1300 m. In Colorado, found at sites adjoining open ponderosa pine forest, while *S. nuchalis* more in areas near deciduous or mixed coniferous forest. Winters in humid to mesic habitats, especially mixed pine and oak (*Quercus*) and mixed oak-juniper (*Juniperus*) woodland, at up to 1830 m in

Arizona and at 1000-3500 m in Mexico. Observed also in various lower-lying habitats, including scrub and desert, on migration.

Food and Feeding. Diet consists of insects, including ants, beetles, larvae, dipterans, Homoptera; also sap; nestlings fed mostly wood ants (*Formica*) and carpenter ants (*Crematogaster*). In non-breeding season tree sap and phloem, also many fruits, and berries; in S Arizona, wintering females took large quantities of madrone (*Arbutus*) berries. Forages singly, on migration in small groups. Hunts from crown down to low levels. Insects taken mostly by gleaning, but other techniques used are bark-scaling, probing and pecking; also hawks aerial insects. Some sexual differences apparent: females forage more on oaks, and on trunks; males prefer pines, and glean more on limbs and on the ground. Sap taken from various tree species, including lodgepole pine (*Pinus contorta*), alpine hemlock (*Tsuga*), red fir (*Abies magnifica*), white fir (*A. concolor*), Jeffrey pine (*P. jeffreyi*) and aspen.

Breeding. Mid-Apr to Jul; peak of laying in first week Jun. Monogamous; solitary. Nest-hole drilled at 0·8-26 m in snag, or in live tree with rotten core, most commonly quaking aspen, also conifer (e.g. larch), exceptionally in utility pole; mean depth of cavity c. 27 cm; territory 4-9 ha, inter-nest distance 175-375 m. Flutter-aerial displays, particularly when approaching mate on the wing, also perched displays with bill-pointing, swinging, bobbing. Clutch 3-7 eggs, most commonly 4-6; both sexes incubate, only male at night, period 12-14 days; chicks fed and brooded by both parents, also fed sometimes by unmated males but these chased off; male carries out most of nest sanitation; initial feeding rate low, rises to 1 feed every 3 minutes in third week, drops again 3-4 days prior to fledging; nestling period 31-32 days; young fed by parents for further 1-2 days, siblings may remain together for 1-3 weeks. Number of nests producing at least 1 fledgling 89·4% to 100% in Arizona; nests preyed on by squirrels (*Tamiasciurus*), weasels (*Mustela*) and snakes. First breeding at 1 year.

Movements. Largely resident; but some migratory movements, and also post-breeding dispersal to lower elevations. Leaves British Columbia in early Sept, some not until mid-Oct; E race *nataliae* more migratory than nominate, moves S to N Mexico, some to as far as Jalisco and Michoacán, in flocks of up to c. 12 individuals; females probably migrate farther S than males. Return passage from Mar or earlier; arrival on breeding grounds mid-Mar to Apr in Oregon, mid-Apr in British Columbia, from early Apr in Colorado; males earlier than females. Casual records E of range, E to Minnesota, Illinois, Louisiana, mostly in spring.

Status and Conservation. Not globally threatened. Fairly common in USA; fairly common breeder in N Baja California. No information on total numbers; density 1 pair/40 ha in California, 4·1 pairs/40 ha in N Colorado, 1 pair/17 ha in S Colorado. Has decreased in USA since early 1980's; 60% decline reported in Pacific Northwest between 1984 to 1993. Locally considered a sensitive species, with rather specialized habitat requirements; needs relatively soft trees for excavation. Tolerant of habitat disturbance, but requires high density of dead wood. Preservation of groups of large dead trees, as well as of large sap trees (conifers), important for this species' survival.

Bibliography. Baicich & Harrison (1997), Baldwin (1960), Bent (1939), Bock & Larson (1986), Bull (1981), Campbell *et al.* (1990), Cicero & Johnson (1994), Conway & Martin (1993), Crockett (1975), Crockett & Hadow (1975), Crockett & Hansley (1977), DeGraaf & Rappole (1995), Dobbs *et al.* (1997), Hadow (1977), Howell & Webb (1995), Hutto (1992, 1998), Johnson & Zink (1983), Kaufman (1996), Koenig (1986, 1987), Kratter (1991), Michael (1935), Pinel (1993), Price *et al.* (1995), Raitt (1959), Remsen (1991), Root (1988), Russell (1947), Schepps *et al.* (1999), Short & Morony (1970), Small (1994), Smith (1982), Sousa (1983b), Stallcup (1968), Stark *et al.* (1998), Swarth (1917), Trombino (2000), Wilbur (1987), Wilson & Rea (1976), Zusi & Marshall (1970).

Genus *XIPHIDIOPICUS*   Bonaparte, 1854

60. Cuban Green Woodpecker

Xiphidiopicus percussus

French: Pic poignardé   **German**: Blutfleckspecht   **Spanish**: Carpintero Tajá
Other common names: Cuban Woodpecker

Taxonomy. *Picus percussus* Temminck, 1826, Cuba.
Distinctive, with no very close relatives. Four additional races have been named, but species exhibits considerable variation in size and coloration throughout range, and much overlap in characters among different populations; thus, described races *monticola* (E Cuba) and *cocoensis* (Cayo Coco and nearby cays) are regarded as synonyms of nominate race, and *gloriae* (Cantiles Keys) and *marthae* (Cayo Caballones) as synonyms of *insulaepinorum*. Two subspecies currently recognized.

Subspecies and Distribution.
X. p. percussus (Temminck, 1826) - Cuba, including archipelagos of Sabana and Camagüey.
X. p. insulaepinorum Bangs, 1910 - I of Pines, Cantiles Keys and Archipiélago Jardines de la Reina (Cayo Caballones).

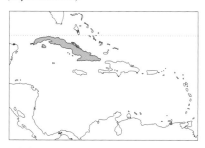

Descriptive notes. c. 21-25 cm; 48-97 g, male c. 20% heavier than female. Male has red crown to nape, short crest and hindneck, some black feather bases usually visible (especially on forecrown), blackish stripe from behind eye and down rear neck side; white forehead and rest of face; black chin; feathers of throat and centre of upper breast broadly tipped red, forming red patch; green upperparts variably tinged yellow or grey, rump yellower and usually with some pale and dark bars and dark shaft streaks, paler uppertail-coverts barred dark; dark brown primaries and secondaries broadly barred white, bars tinged green on outer webs of secondaries; uppertail dark brown, centre washed buff-grey or pearl-grey, pale brown bars on c. 3 outer feathers, occasionally on all feathers; yellow below, breast streaked blackish, belly sometimes orange-tinged, flanks and lower underparts whitish (often washed pale green) with heavy black bars; underwing barred brown and whitish, coverts tinged greenish; brown undertail barred at sides; short bill straight, slightly chisel-tipped, fairly broad across nostrils, bluish-black; iris brown, orbital skin grey; legs greenish to greyish-olive. Female is significantly smaller than male, shorter-billed, has most of crown black with very fine white streaks, more extensive barring below. Juvenile duller, more barred, has narrow dark bars above heavier on rump, sometimes hint of red on mantle, fully barred tail, more barred and streaked below, throat more brownish-black, smaller belly patch often orange or orange-red; both sexes have adult-like head pattern but more black on forecrown, female soon acquiring white-streaked black crown. Race *insulaepinorum* is on average smaller, paler, with smaller red throat patch, paler yellow belly, also fully barred tail. VOICE. Short harsh "jorr" or "gwurr" in short series is commonest call; also higher "eh-eh-eh"; mewing or squealing "ta-há", like call of *Sphyrapicus varius*.

Habitat. Inhabits forest and woodland of most types, including mangroves and open woodland with palms; visits patches of cultivation and areas of habitation only rarely. Occurs from lowlands to mountains.

Food and Feeding. Diet consists of insects, reportedly of relatively large size. Also observed preying on eggs at nests of egrets (*Egretta*, *Bubulcus*) built in mangroves. Usually forages in pairs, but sometimes in parties of three to five individuals. Forages from low levels up to the canopy, on trunks and branches, and among vines and creepers. Pecks in crevices and beneath bark on dead wood, also gleans.

Breeding. Feb-Aug, possibly peak in May-Jun. Nest-hole 4-5 m up in palm, or in live or dead tree, apparently at times in nest of arboreal termites; territorial, attacks *Melanerpes superciliaris* in vicinity of nest. Clutch 3-4 eggs; incubation and fledging periods not documented; both parents feed chicks about equally.

Movements. Resident. Recorded rarely on Hispaniola after storms.

Status and Conservation. Not globally threatened. Common and widespread within range. Probably more numerous than *M. superciliaris*; is able to exploit wide variety of wooded habitats at all elevations. No known threats.

Bibliography. Alayón *et al.* (1986), Allen (1961), Anon. (1998b), Arredondo (1984), Barbour (1943), Berovides *et al.* (1982), Bond (1985), Cruz (1974a), Denis *et al.* (1999), Faaborg (1985), Garrido (1971, 1978), Garrido & Kirkconnell (2000), González-Alonso *et al.* (1992), Hernández (1999), Kirkconnell (2000b), Kirkconnell, Alayón *et al.* (1989), Kirkconnell, Garrido *et al.* (1992), Melián (2000), Posada & Kirkconnell (1993), Raffaele *et al.* (1998), Read (1914), Regalado (1977), Seth-Smith (1912), Stotz *et al.* (1996), Wallace (2001).

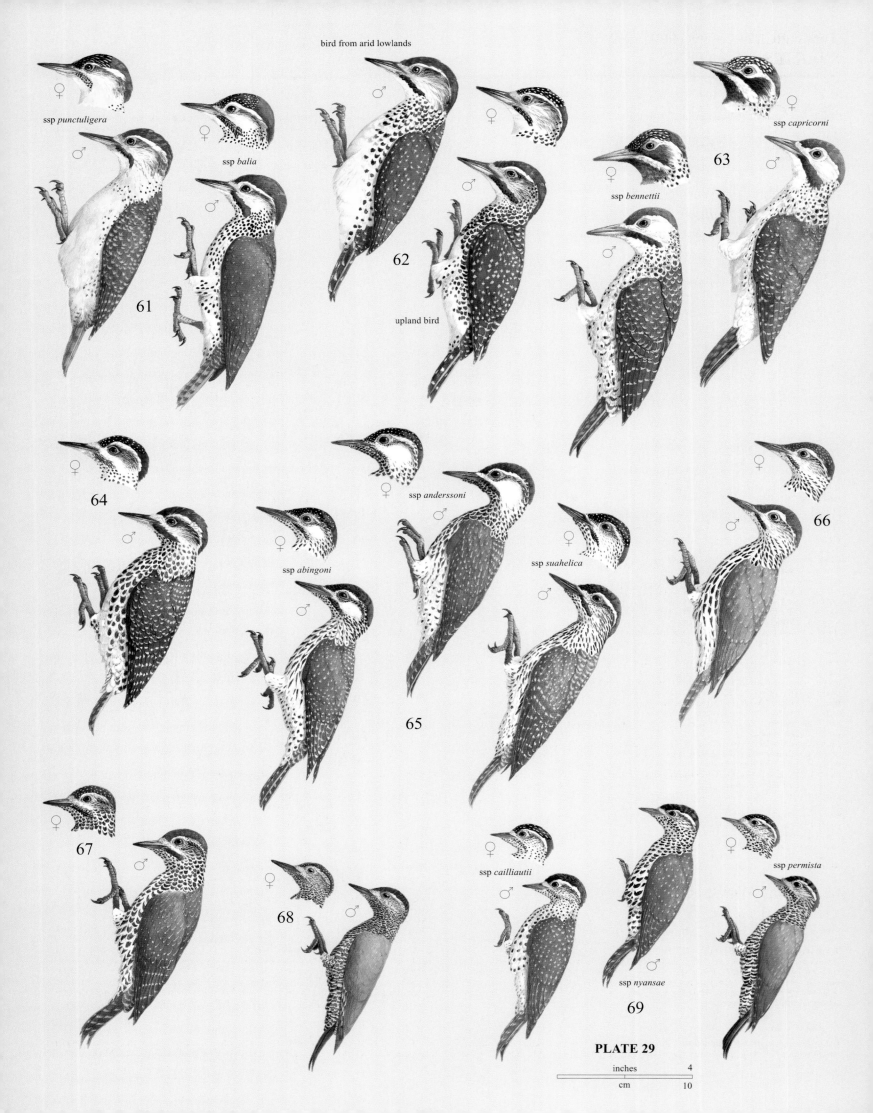

bird from arid lowlands

ssp *punctuligera*

♀

♂

ssp *balia*

♀

61

♂

♂

62

upland bird

♂

♀

♂

ssp *bennettii*

♀

♂

ssp *capricorni*

63

♀

♂

64

♀

♂

ssp *anderssoni*

♀

♂

ssp *abingoni*

♂

65

♀

♂

ssp *suahelica*

♂

66

♀

♂

67

♀

♂

68

♀

♂

ssp *cailliautii*

♀

♂

ssp *nyansae*

69

♂

ssp *permista*

♀

♂

PLATE 29

inches   4

cm   10

Tribe CAMPETHERINI

Genus *CAMPETHERA* G. R. Gray, 1841

61. **Fine-spotted Woodpecker**

Campethera punctuligera

French: Pic à taches noires **German**: Pünktchenspecht **Spanish**: Pito Salpicado

Taxonomy. *Picus punctuligerus* Wagler, 1827, Senegambia.
Forms a superspecies with *C. nubica*, *C. bennettii* and *C. scriptoricauda*, and all sometimes considered conspecific. Races intergrade in Sudan and NE Zaire. Described race *batesi* (N Cameroon) synonymized with nominate. Two subspecies recognized.

Subspecies and Distribution.
C. p. punctuligera (Wagler, 1827) - SW Mauritania (c. 60 km N of Rosso) and Senegambia E to SW Sudan and S to C Ivory Coast (Lamto), Ghana (Mole), S Nigeria (Abeokuta), C Cameroon (Mt Zoro and Mbakaou) and NE Zaire (upper Uele Valley).
C. p. balia (Heuglin, 1871) - S Sudan to extreme NE Zaire.

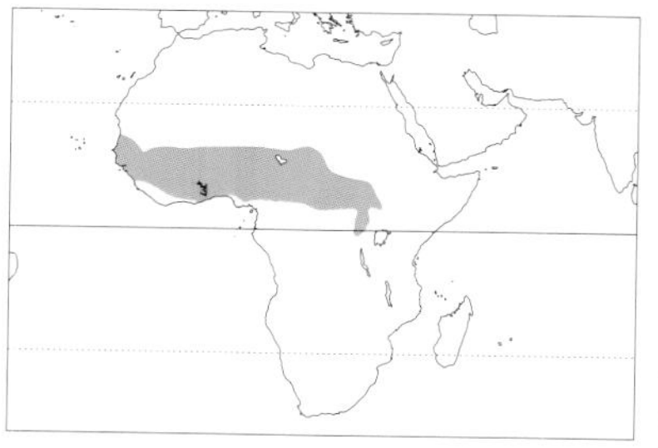

Descriptive notes. c. 22 cm; 56-74 g. Male has red forehead to nape, crown feathers with small grey bases, white supercilium faintly streaked at rear, blackish rear eyestripe, whitish ear-coverts, red malar stripe spotted black, white chin occasionally with fine black spots; buffy-white neck sides and throat spotted black; green or yellow-green upperparts, feathers tipped yellow, yellowish-white of shafts extending to feather webs to form variable number of bars; rump narrowly barred; brown flight-feathers barred yellowish-white or white; uppertail barred brown and yellow, prominent yellow shafts; underparts yellowish-white, whiter on belly and lower flanks, delicate small black spots on breast sometimes extending to flanks, where may be more bar-like; underwing pale yellow-white, barred dark; bill medium-long, culmen slightly decurved, broad base, narrower across nostrils, slate-grey, tip black; iris pinkish-red to violet, orbital skin grey; legs greenish-grey. Differs from *C. nubica* in whiter face, and by having spotting on underparts less extensive, with much smaller spots. Female has black forehead and forecrown with heavy white streaking, malar area spotted black and white. Juvenile as female, but darker, more olive, above, with darker barring, more buffish below, brownish or bluish-tinged (less green) legs, brownish-grey eyes, both sexes with unstreaked black forehead and forecrown, blacker eyestripe, more prominent black malar. Race *balia* is slightly smaller, has less yellow in upperparts, whiter underparts with larger spots over more extensive area; female's black forehead and forecrown distinctly spotted (not streaked) white. Voice. Repeated "kweeyer" or "peer", like call of *Jynx torquilla* or Common Kestrel (*Falco tinnunculus*); more complex "wik-wik-whew-wee-yeu, wee-yweu" as contact between partners; soft "nyaa, nyaa, nyaa" or "tik-tik-tik-tik" calls during encounters.

Habitat. Wooded savanna, and acacia (*Acacia*) grassland with scattered or widely scattered trees and patches of bare ground; often around oil palms (*Elaeis guineensis*); also enters closed forest. Lowlands.

Food and Feeding. Ants and their larvae, as well as termites (Isoptera), form bulk of diet, including that of nestlings. Commonly in pairs or family parties of up to 4 birds; sometimes joins mixed-species flocks. Forages in trees and bushes, often in oil palms; often searches base of trees, and descends to the ground to feed. Frequently visits termite mounds.

Breeding. Season Jun-Aug in Senegambia, Apr-May in Sierra Leone, from Feb in Nigeria; Nov to early Apr or to Jun in Zaire. Nest excavated in tree or in termite mound. Clutch 2-3 eggs; incubation and fledging periods not recorded; juveniles stay with parents for a long time after leaving nest, but precise figures lacking.

Movements. Resident; possibly some local seasonal movements in Senegambia.

Status and Conservation. Not globally threatened. Generally considered to be common or at least locally common. Widespread and common in Senegambia; not uncommon in Sierra Leone; common and widespread in Nigeria. Occurs in numerous protected areas, e.g. Saloum Delta and Niokola Koba National Parks (Senegal), Comoé National Park (Ivory Coast), W National Park (Niger), Bénoué National Park (Cameroon), and Bamingui-Bangoran National Park (Central African Republic).

Bibliography. Bannerman (1953), Barlow *et al.* (1997), de Bie & Morgan (1989), Carroll (1988), Cave & Macdonald (1955), Cheke & Walsh (1996), Dowsett & Dowsett-Lemaire (1993, 2000), Dowsett & Forbes-Watson (1993), Elgood *et al.* (1994), Fry *et al.* (1988), Gee (1984), Green (1983, 1990), Giraudoux *et al.* (1988), Grimes (1987), King (2000), Koster & Grettenberger (1983), Lamarche (1980), Mackworth-Praed & Grant (1957, 1970), Nikolaus (2000), Pedersen (2000), Rodwell (1996), Salewski (2000), Scholte *et al.* (1999), Short (1973c, 1980, 1985b), Short & Horne (1988b), Snow (1978), Tarboton (1997), Thiollay (1985a).

62. **Nubian Woodpecker**

Campethera nubica

French: Pic de Nubie **German**: Nubierspecht **Spanish**: Pito de Nubia

Taxonomy. *Picus Nubicus* Boddaert, 1783, Nubia, north Sudan.
Forms a superspecies with *C. punctuligera*, *C. bennettii* and *C. scriptoricauda*, and sometimes all considered conspecific. Identity of birds in E Rwanda uncertain; they probably belong either to *C. bennettii* or to nominate race of present species. Races poorly differentiated, and they intergrade; delimitation uncertain, complicated by apparent habitat-conditioned variation of nominate. Two subspecies currently recognized.

Subspecies and Distribution.
C. n. nubica (Boddaert, 1783) - WC & NE Sudan, Ethiopia and NW & SW Somalia, S to NE Zaire (Beni, Rutshuru Plain), adjacent W Uganda, Kenya and C & SW Tanzania (Morogoro and Rukwa Valley); possibly this taxon in E Rwanda.
C. n. pallida (Sharpe, 1902) - E & S Somalia and coastal Kenya.

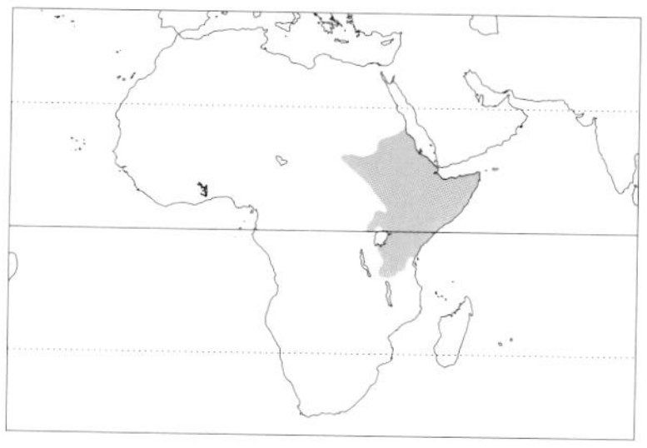

Descriptive notes. c. 23 cm; 46-71 g. Male has red forehead to nape, white supercilium, streaky black stripe from just in front of eye to rear crown side, white ear-coverts streaked dark at rear, red malar stripe spotted with black; white neck sides and hindneck heavily spotted black; buffish-white chin occasionally slightly spotted black (e.g. in Ethiopia), whitish throat spotted black; upperparts olive-brown, barred white and yellow, white on mantle, back and wing-coverts more as spots, rump more regularly barred; dark brown flight-feathers barred yellow or whitish; uppertail barred brown and yellow; underparts pale buff-white or yellowish-white, large black spots on breast and upper flanks, sometimes more as bars on lower flanks, small spots on undertail-coverts; underwing barred yellow and brown, sometimes plain yellowish; undertail as above, brown bars duller; medium-length bill fairly straight, broad base, broad across nostrils, grey to dark horn or sometimes blackish, tip black; iris red to pinkish, orbital skin grey; legs grey, tinged olive. In higher-lying areas throughout range, occurs in a darker form, darker above and with heavier spotting below. Distinguished from very similar *C. scriptoricauda* by less regular barring above. Female has forehead, forecrown and malar black with white spots. Juvenile generally darker than adult, more heavily marked below, breast often more streaked, streaks often extending to throat and chin, eyes greyish or grey-brown, both sexes with black forehead and crown either spotted or unspotted, white-spotted malar. Race *pallida* is on average slightly smaller than nominate, paler above, less strongly spotted below. Voice. Loud, shrill, metallic, accelerating "weee-weee-weee...kweek", dying away at end, as contact between partners; various low "kwick" and "kweek" notes in close encounters. Drums occasionally.

Habitat. Drier bushland, bushy grassland, riverine woodland, and open woodland; occurs in *Euphorbia-Acacia* woodland, open acacia savanna, also in areas with extensive growth of elephant grass (*Pennisetum*). From sea-level to 2300 m; to 1800 m in Ethiopia, to c. 2000 m in Somalia, to 1530 m in SW Uganda (Ruwenzori Range).

Food and Feeding. Diet almost entirely ants; also termites (Isoptera), other insects; also spiders. Observed mainly singly, but pair-members keep vocal contact. Forages on trunks and limbs of trees; occasionally descends to ground. Spends much time investigating cracks in bark, stubs and similar sites; foraging techniques include gleaning and pecking.

Breeding. Nov-Mar in Ethiopia; Jan-Feb, and eggs found also end Jun and mid-Nov, in Somalia; Jun-Jul in Uganda; from Feb in Zaire; in E Africa, during or shortly after main rainy season or in the small rains; possibly sometimes 2 broods in a season, e.g. in Somalia. New hole excavated every season, mainly by male, in rotten stump, fence post, or trunk of tree or palm, usually where natural cavities already present; territory large. Clutch 2-5 eggs, usually 2 or 3; incubation by both sexes, male roosting in nest at night, period not documented; both parents feed chicks, nestling period unrecorded; adults accompany young sex for sex in post-fledging period. Nests parasitized by Lesser and Scaly-throated Honeyguides (*Indicator minor*, *I. variegatus*).

Movements. Resident.

Status and Conservation. Not globally threatened. Common to very common and patchily distributed throughout Somalia; fairly common and widespread in E Africa; race *pallida* uncommon in coastal Kenya. Occurs in Awash National Park (Ethiopia), Murchison Falls National Park (Uganda), Samburu Reserve (Kenya) and Serengeti and Arusha National Parks (Tanzania).

Bibliography. Archer & Godman (1937-1961), Ash & Miskell (1983, 1998), Britton (1980), Brown & Britton (1980), Carroll (1988), Cave & Macdonald (1955), Cheesman & Sclater (1935), Dowsett & Dowsett-Lemaire (1993), Dowsett & Forbes-Watson (1993), Friedmann (1930a), Fry *et al.* (1988), Lewis & Pomeroy (1989), Lippens & Wille (1976), Mackworth-Praed & Grant (1957, 1970), Nikolaus (1987), Schels & Lavoyer (1987), Short (1973c, 1980, 1985b), Short & Horne (1988b), Short *et al.* (1990), Smith (1957), Snow (1978), Stevenson & Fanshawe (2001), Tarboton (1997), Urban & Brown (1971), Vande weghe (1992), Wilson & Wilson (1992), Zimmerman *et al.* (1996), Zinner (2001).

63. **Bennett's Woodpecker**

Campethera bennettii

French: Pic de Bennett **German**: Bennettspecht **Spanish**: Pito de Bennett

Taxonomy. *Chrysoptilus Bennettii* A. Smith, 1836, western Transvaal.
Forms a superspecies with *C. punctuligera*, *C. nubica* and *C. scriptoricauda*; sometimes treated as conspecific with last-mentioned, or with all three. Identity of birds in E Rwanda uncertain; they probably belong either to *C. nubica* or to nominate race of present species. Proposed race *uniamwesica* (Angola E to L Victoria and S to C Zambia) synonymized with nominate. Two subspecies currently recognized.

Subspecies and Distribution.
C. b. bennettii (A. Smith, 1836) - WC Angola E to SE Zaire and Rwanda, possibly also Uganda (Merama Hills), and to W & S Tanzania, S to W Malawi, NE South Africa and S Mozambique; possibly this taxon in E Rwanda.
C. b. capricorni Strickland, 1853 - S Angola, SW Zambia, and adjacent N Namibia and N Botswana.

Descriptive notes. c. 24 cm; 61-84 g. Male has red forehead, crown and nape, forehead with small grey feather bases, broad red malar stripe with scattered black feather bases; neck side spotted black; rest of head side, including superciliary area, and chin and throat white, occasionally traces of brown on ear-coverts and throat, or throat yellow-buff; upperparts and wing-coverts barred olive-brown, yellow and white, coverts usually more spotted and pale-fringed; rump and uppertail-coverts similarly barred, but in arid zones often very pale and unbarred; brown flight-feathers edged greenish, yellowish-white bars on inner webs; uppertail variably dull to bright yellow, narrower brown bars; underparts pale yellowish-white, breast often tinged golden-buff and with bold, round to elongated dark spots, spots usually more bar-like on flanks; white undertail-

On following pages: 64. Reichenow's Woodpecker (*Campethera scriptoricauda*); 65. Golden-tailed Woodpecker (*Campethera abingoni*); 66. Mombasa Woodpecker (*Campethera mombassica*); 67. Knysna Woodpecker (*Campethera notata*); 68. Little Green Woodpecker (*Campethera maculosa*); 69. Green-backed Woodpecker (*Campethera cailliautii*).

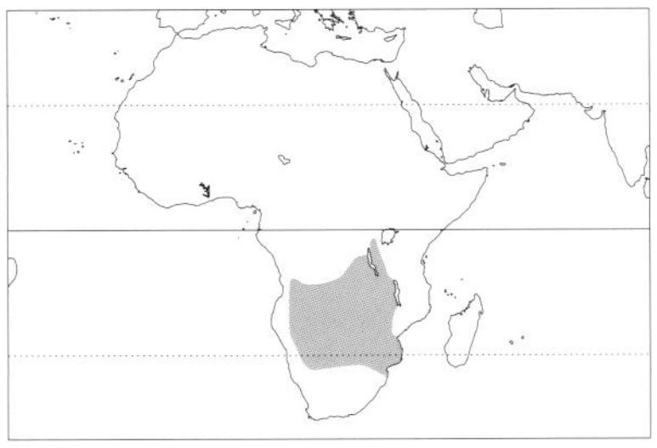

coverts often spotted or barred; underwing as above or paler; undertail yellowish, often tipped black; medium-length bill pointed, culmen moderately curved, narrow between nostrils, slaty-grey, paler near base; iris red, orbital skin grey; legs bluish-green to grey-green. Differs from *C. nubica* mainly in whiter face, less distinct patterning above. Female differs in having white-spotted black forehead and crown, white malar with black flecks, and brown to blackish-brown colour from bill to ear-coverts and chin and throat; ear-coverts and throat darker in W of range, becoming paler to E. Juvenile has black head top, is somewhat darker and more spotted (less barred) above, more coarsely spotted below, eyes dark brown, male with blackish malar, few or no crown spots, female with white-spotted crown and at least indication of adult's brown head markings. Race *capricorni* is slightly larger than nominate, has paler, whitish, rump and uppertail-coverts, generally deeper yellow underparts with fewer or, sometimes, no spots; female has, on average, heavier white spotting on forehead and crown and much blacker ear-coverts and throat, but some are similar to darkest-throated nominate. VOICE. Most frequent are "chuur" notes, and long series varying from "wi-wi-wi-wi" or "kee-kee-kee" to "ddrahh, ddrahh, ddray-ay, ddray-ay, dray-ay"; during encounters, high-pitched repeated "wirrit" or "whirrwhirrwhirrwhir-it-whir-it-whir-it-wrrrrrrrrr" chatter, and "wicka"-type calls. Drums softly, infrequently.

Habitat. Well-developed mature woodland and bush country. Typically, miombo (*Brachystegia*) and gusu (*Baikiaea*) woodland; in dry *Acacia* woodland, mainly in taller parts. Appears to replace *C. abingoni* in *Brachystegia* woodland on sandy soils and in less diverse closed woodland e.g. in parts of Zimbabwe, although the two occur together in many other areas, especially in valley woodland. Up to 1600 m in E Africa.

Food and Feeding. Primarily ants, and termites (Isoptera) and their eggs; occasionally other insects and larvae. Rather social, regularly in pairs or family parties of c. 3-5 birds; frequently accompanies glossy-starlings (*Lamprotornis*) when foraging. Highly terrestrial, commonly searches grassy sites or bare ground with patches of short grass, hops clumsily; ground-feeding accounts for 70-85% of foraging effort. Arboreal feeding mostly on trunks and larger branches of trees; main techniques are gleaning, and probing in cracks.

Breeding. Aug-Feb; peak in Oct- Nov in S. Hole excavated by both sexes, at 2-10 m in dead tree or in dead section of live tree, old hole often reused; hole made by other species of woodpecker, or natural cavity, also used; cavity depth 13-20 cm. Clutch 2-5 eggs, usually 3; both parents incubate, period 15-18 days; both also feed chicks, nestling period not documented; young remain with parents until start of next breeding attempt.

Movements. Resident; some short-distance post-breeding movement from arid areas to more favourable ones.

Status and Conservation. Not globally threatened. Everywhere variable in abundance, and with patchy distribution; locally common, in some places rare; absent from large parts of general range.

Bibliography. Benson & Benson (1977), Benson *et al.* (1971), Brewster (1991), Britton (1980), Brown (1993), Dean (2000), Dowsett & Dowsett-Lemaire (1993), Dowsett & Forbes-Watson (1993), Fry *et al.* (1988), Ginn *et al.* (1989), Harrison *et al.* (1997), Harwin (1972), Hines (1995, 1996), Irwin (1978), Leonard (1998b), Lippens & Wille (1976), Mackworth-Praed & Grant (1957, 1962, 1970), Maclean (1993), Penry (1994), Pinto (1983), Schouteden (1966), Short (1971a, 1973c, 1980, 1985b), Short & Horne (1988b), Short *et al.* (1990), Snow (1978), Stevenson & Fanshawe (2001), Tarboton (1997, 2001), Tarboton *et al.* (1987), Vande weghe (1992).

64. **Reichenow's Woodpecker**

Campethera scriptoricauda

French: Pic de Reichenow **German**: Reichenowspecht **Spanish**: Pito de Tanzania
Other common names: Speckle-throated/Tanzanian Woodpecker

Taxonomy. *Dendromus scriptoricauda* Reichenow, 1896, no locality = Bumi, Tanzania.
Forms a superspecies with *C. punctuligera*, *C. nubica* and *C. bennettii*; frequently treated as conspecific with *C. bennettii*, and sometimes with all three. Monotypic.

Distribution. Inland E & S Tanzania S to S Malawi (S to Nsanje area) and C Mozambique; recorded also at base of Mt Kilimanjaro, in N Tanzania.

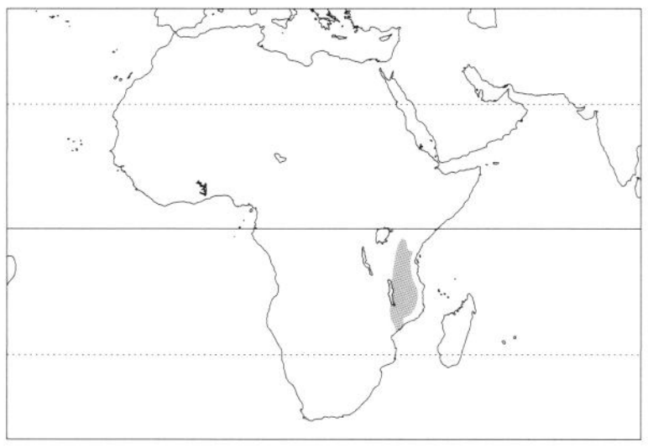

Descriptive notes. c. 22 cm. Male has red forehead to nape, forehead with small grey feather bases, white supercilium, dark stripe behind eye, dark-streaked ear-coverts, red malar stripe with scattered black feather bases; white neck side, chin and throat all spotted black; upperparts barred dark olive, yellow and white, wing-coverts more spotted; brown flight-feathers barred yellowish-white on inner webs; uppertail barred yellow and brown; underparts pale yellowish-white with large rounded dark spots, ventral region usually plainer; underwing as above or paler; medium-length bill slightly curved, narrow between nostrils, slaty-grey, lower mandible mostly pale yellow or yellow-green; iris red, orbital skin grey; legs bluish-green to grey-green. Differs from very similar *C. bennettii* in slightly smaller size, shorter wing, dark eyestripe and ear-coverts, black-spotted chin and throat, larger spots below, yellow lower mandible. Female differs from male in pale-spotted black forehead and crown, white moustachial area, streaky black malar. Juvenile resembles female, but more spotted above, spots below more diffuse. VOICE. Frequent "churr" notes and chattering series, very like those of *C. bennettii*.

Habitat. Open woodland, savanna and thorn-scrub; occurs in open miombo (*Brachystegia*) woodland with grassy ground layer in S of range.

Food and Feeding. Mainly ants and their larvae. In pairs or family parties. Largely terrestrial, seeking food in grassy areas; hops clumsily on ground. In trees feeds mostly on trunks and larger branches, by gleaning and probing.

Breeding. Oct-Nov in Malawi. Nest-hole excavated in dead tree or palm trunk. Clutch 3 eggs; no other details, but likely to be much as for *C. bennettii*.

Movements. Apparently resident.

Status and Conservation. Not globally threatened. Reasonably common. Occurs in Mikumi National Park, in Tanzania. True status masked by confusion over taxonomic position; further research required, especially in areas where its range meets that of *C. bennettii*.

Bibliography. Archer & Godman (1937-1961), Britton (1980), Dowsett & Dowsett-Lemaire (1993), Fry *et al.* (1988), Ginn *et al.* (1989), Hockey (1996), Mackworth-Praed & Grant (1962), Maclean (1993), Newman (1996), Short (1973c, 1980), Short & Horne (1988b), Sinclair (1987), Sinclair & Hockey (1996), Stevenson & Fanshawe (2001), Zimmerman *et al.* (1996).

65. **Golden-tailed Woodpecker**

Campethera abingoni

French: Pic à queue dorée **German**: Goldschwanzspecht **Spanish**: Pito Colidorado

Taxonomy. *Chrysoptilus Abingoni* A. Smith, 1836, district of Zeerust, western Transvaal, South Africa.
Forms a superspecies with *C. mombassica* and *C. notata*. Often treated as conspecific with former, but differs in plumage and vocalizations; apparent hybrids between *C. mombassica* and race *suahelica* of present species recorded from EC Tanzania and from just S of Mt Kilimanjaro; further studies needed. Proposed race *tessmanni* (Central African Republic) not distinguishable from *chrysura*; nor *annectens* (lower Congo and C Angola to Rwanda and Malawi) from nominate. In past, type locality of species erroneously listed as Durban, Natal; with rectification, hitherto accepted name *smithii* becomes junior synonym of nominate. Six subspecies currently recognized.

Subspecies and Distribution.
C. a. chrysura (Swainson, 1837) - Senegambia and N Guinea, and recently recorded in NE Ivory Coast; also Central African Republic, S Sudan, NE Zaire and W Uganda.
C. a. abingoni (A. Smith, 1836) - lower R Congo and W Zaire E to W Tanzania, and S to NE Namibia, NW Zambia, Zimbabwe and N Transvaal.
C. a. kavirondensis van Someren, 1926 - E Rwanda, NW & NC Tanzania and SW Kenya.
C. a. suahelica (Reichenow, 1902) - N Tanzania (Arusha, Moshi, N Pare Mts) to E Zimbabwe, Mozambique and N Swaziland.
C. a. anderssoni (Roberts 1936) - SW Angola, Namibia (except NE) and SW Botswana to N Cape Province and SW Transvaal.
C. a. constricta Clancey, 1965 - S Swaziland, extreme S Mozambique and Natal.

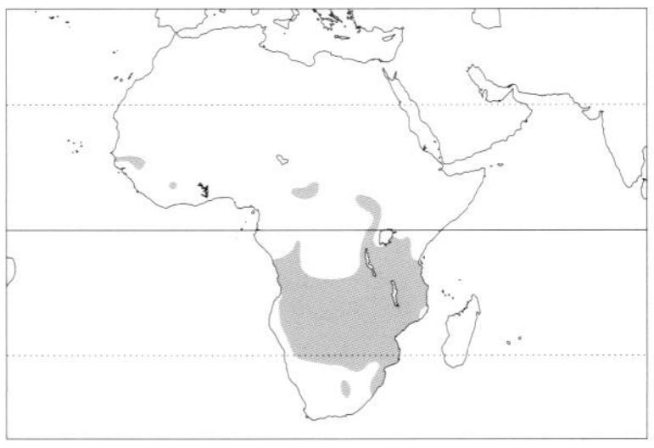

Descriptive notes. 20-23 cm; 51-58 g (race *chrysura*), 61-83 g (*abingoni*, *suahelica*). Male has red forehead to nape, feathers with greyish-black bases, white lores, thin white supercilium with dark upper border, thin black-streaked white line below eye, dark stripe behind eye, white or whitish ear-coverts, narrow red malar with dark feather bases, white neck sides streaked blackish, whitish chin and throat heavily spotted black; olive-brown upperparts narrowly barred pale yellow-white and greenish-yellow, pale bars broader on rump and uppertail-coverts, wing-coverts spotted and tipped yellowish; brown flight-feathers barred whitish, bars broader on inner webs; uppertail brown, barred yellowish-white, bars sometimes obscured by overall yellow wash; white underparts tinged yellow on breast and flanks, heavy blackish streaking on breast, spots on flanks and belly; underwing as above, but paler; undertail yellow-brown, obscurely pale-barred; moderately long bill broad-based, culmen slightly curved, slaty-black, base of lower mandible often tinged green; iris usually reddish but variable from hazel to blackish, orbital skin grey; legs dark greenish with olive or grey tinge. Differs from *C. mombassica* in darker appearance, barred upperparts. Female differs from male in having black forehead and crown with fine white spots, blackish malar. Juvenile as adult female, but less yellow above with spots and streaks instead of bars, more heavily streaked below, flanks and belly more barred, eyes brown or brownish-grey. Races differ mainly in tone of upperparts and in strength of markings below: *chrysura* is smaller than nominate, greener above, ear-coverts streaked, blacker on throat and breast; *kavirondensis* has pale barring above broader, ear-coverts streaked, underparts more narrowly streaked; *suahelica* as previous but yellower-toned above; *constricta* is very like previous, but greener above; *anderssoni* resembles nominate, but greyer above, rump pale, markings below heavier, throat and breast almost wholly black. VOICE. Call loud and distinctive, single plaintive "dreee-aw" or "weeea", often by male; series of 2-12 "yaooaak-yaaaaaak" notes as long-distance call; more aggressive "weet-wit-wit" and "kyek" notes; intimate "pew-pew-pew". Drums in slow rolls 1·5 seconds long.

Habitat. Almost all kinds of woodland and forest edge. Occurs in coastal forest, evergreen forest and thickets, riparian forest, and in savanna with dense *Acacia* bush; also recorded in rich miombo (*Brachystegia*) woodland and montane forest, but in such habitats it keeps mostly to the edge. Some preference for vicinity of rivers in more open regions, but always in areas of dense trees and thickets. Occasionally visits parks, large gardens and exotic trees; also visits rather isolated trees for foraging. Generally replaced by *C. bennettii* in *Brachystegia* woodland, but sometimes occurs there. Occurs from sea-level up to 2000 m in E Africa; up to 1500 m in Malawi, to 1800 m in Zimbabwe, and to c. 1400 m in Natal.

Food and Feeding. Insects and their larvae, mainly arboreal ants; also millipedes (Diplopoda). Generally singly or in pairs; often associates with *Dendropicos fuscescens*. Forages mainly at middle and lower levels; explores larger branches and twigs, often moving along underside. Predominant techniques are probing and gleaning; also hammers forcefully on dead trunks or branches affected by wood-boring larvae, using this method more frequently than do congeners. Often flies rather long distances between foraging sites.

Breeding. Fledgling fed by adult in Jun in the Gambia; otherwise Aug-Dec. Nest-hole drilled into tree at height of 1-5 m; occupies relatively large territory, 10-15 ha. Clutch 2-5 eggs, usually 2 or 3; incubation by both sexes, only male at night, period c. 13 days; both parents also brood chicks, and feed them by regurgitation; nestling period 22-25 days. Nests parasitized by honeyguides (*Indicator*).

Movements. Resident.

Status and Conservation. Not globally threatened. Locally common; common in Angola; uncommon and local in Kenya and Tanzania; rare in W Africa. Common in Akagera National Park (Rwanda); occurs in Masai Mara Reserve (Kenya), Arusha National Park (Tanzania) and Liwonde National Park (Malawi). Common in Caprivi Strip (Namibia); common in South Africa, where present in numerous protected areas, e.g. Kruger National Park, Mkuzi Game Reserve and Umlalazi Nature Reserve. Recorded in Ivory Coast for first time in 1995, where present in Comoé National Park.

Bibliography. Anon. (1998a), Baillie (1983), Bannerman (1953), Barlow *et al.* (1997), Benson *et al.* (1971), Brown (1993), Cave & Macdonald (1955), Clancey (1965, 1984e, 1988b), Dean (2000), Dowsett & Dowsett-

Lemaire (1993, 2000), Dowsett & Forbes-Watson (1993), Evans *et al.* (1994), Falk & Salewski (1999), Fry *et al.* (1988), Ginn *et al.* (1989), Gore (1990), Greig-Smith (1976), Grimes (1987), Harrison *et al.* (1997), Hines (1995), Irwin (1978, 1981), King (2000), Lewis & Pomeroy (1989), Mackworth-Praed & Grant (1957, 1962, 1970), Maclean (1993), Parker (1994), Penry (1994), Pinto (1983), Salewski (2000), Sauvage & Rodwell (1998), Short (1980, 1985b), Short & Horne (1988b), Short *et al.* (1990), Snow (1978), Tarboton (1980, 1997, 2001), Zimmerman *et al.* (1996).

66. Mombasa Woodpecker

Campethera mombassica

French: Pic de Mombasa **German**: Mombasaspecht **Spanish**: Pito de Mombasa

Taxonomy. *Picus (Campothera)* [sic] *mombassicus* Fischer and Reichenow, 1884, Mombasa.
Forms a superspecies with *C. abingoni* and *C. notata*. Often treated as conspecific with former, but differs in plumage and vocalizations; apparent hybrid individuals with appearance intermediate between *C. abingoni suahelica* and present species recorded from EC Tanzania and from just S of Mt Kilimanjaro; further study required. Monotypic.
Distribution. S Somalia, coastal Kenya (including R Tana inland to Garissa) and NE Tanzania (S to about Dar es Salaam, W to W Usambara Mts, possibly also at E Mt Kilimanjaro).

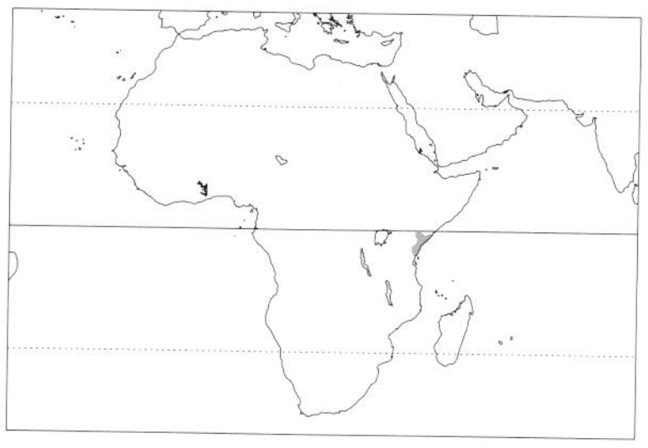

Descriptive notes. c. 22 cm; 50-71 g. Male has olive-green forehead and crown feathers with broad red tips, red nape, buffish lores, short white supercilium, whitish sides of head and neck with black streaks, short red malar stripe streaked black; whitish chin and throat, sometimes with few dark streaks or spots; bright golden-green upperparts with fine yellowish-white spots and shaft streaks; brown flight-feathers with some spots; uppertail golden-green to olive-brown, outer feathers faintly barred; white or buffy-white below, breast and flanks tinged yellowish, fairly broad blackish streaks narrower on flanks and belly; underwing as above, coverts paler; undertail brownish, suffused yellow; medium-length bill broad-based, culmen slightly decurved, slate-grey, distinct green tone on lower mandible; iris dark reddish, orbital skin grey; legs greenish to olive or olive-grey. Distinguished from similar *C. abingoni* by much brighter upperparts with small dots, not bars, paler throat, olive-green bases of crown feathers, different vocalizations. Female differs in having dark olive-green forehead and crown with small yellow-buff spots, olive-grey malar with black and white streaks and spots. Juvenile resembles female, but duller, more spotted above, more heavily streaked below, sometimes some bars on lower underparts, eyes more brownish or greyish. Voice. Accelerating series ending with short "yuk", distinctly different from *C. abingoni*, initial notes less buzzing; intimate calls include grating "drrrrdddt". Very rarely, if ever, drums.
Habitat. Coastal forest and woodland.
Food and Feeding. Mostly ants and their larvae. Usually found singly; joins mixed feeding parties. Forages at middle and lower levels, in large and small trees, often within cover of foliage. Main techniques are probing and gleaning; sometimes hammers on dead branches.
Breeding. Season Dec-Feb. Nest-hole in tree; no other information.
Movements. Resident.
Status and Conservation. Not globally threatened. Uncommon or rare in Somalia, where few recent records; possibly overlooked among much commoner *C. nubica*. Locally fairly common in Kenya and Tanzania. Occurs in several protected areas, e.g. Shimba Hills National Park and Arabuko-Sokoke Forest (Kenya) and Pugu Forest Reserve (Tanzania). Although not officially considered at risk, this species' limited range means that any degradation or erosion of its coastal woodland habitat could lead to a potentially serious decline in its population.
Bibliography. Ash & Miskell (1983, 1998), Bennun & Njoroge (1999), Clancey (1988b), Cordeiro & Githiru (1998), Dowsett & Dowsett-Lemaire (1993), Dowsett & Forbes-Watson (1993), Evans, Hague *et al.* (1994), Evans, Tye *et al.* (1997), Fanshaw (1994), Fry *et al.* (1988), Lewis & Pomeroy (1989), Moreau (1935), Seddon *et al.* (1996), Short (1980), Short & Horne (1988b), Short *et al.* (1990), Snow (1978), Stevenson & Fanshawe (2001), Tarboton (1997), Waiyaki & Bennun (2000), Williams (1997), Zimmerman *et al.* (1996).

67. Knysna Woodpecker

Campethera notata

French: Pic tigré **German**: Knysnaspecht **Spanish**: Pito de Knysna

Taxonomy. *Picus notatus* M. H. K. Lichtenstein, 1823, southern South Africa.
Forms a superspecies with *C. abingoni* and *C. mombassica*. Variation in plumage darkness and markings rather large, but based on individual rather than geographical differences, so that no races are recognizable. Monotypic.
Distribution. S South Africa, from Swellendam region E to extreme S Natal.

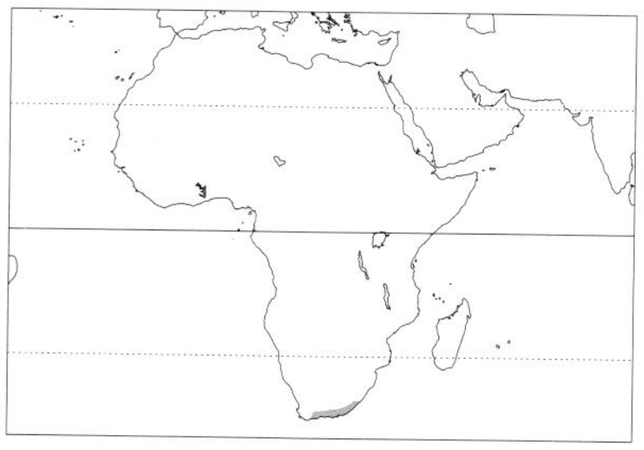

Descriptive notes. 20-22 cm; 62 g. Male has red forehead to nape, feathers of forehead with extensive dark olive-brown bases, buffish-white lores, narrow white supercilium with dark spotting, red malar stripe sometimes obscured by heavy white and black spotting on feather bases; buffish-white sides of head heavily spotted and streaked dark, whitish neck sides with prominent black spots; whitish chin and throat heavily spotted black, especially on throat; pale-spotted olive hindneck; green or yellow-green upperparts with fine pale yellow spots (rarely, form broken bars), mantle very occasionally with slight trace of red, rump and uppertail-coverts finely barred whitish; scapulars and upperwing-coverts with small pale spots often streak-like; dark brown flight-feathers edged green, barred white, bars broader on inner webs; uppertail yellowish-olive, narrowly barred yellowish; whitish below, breast buffish-tinged, large dark brown spots on breast and flanks, narrower streaks on belly and undertail-coverts; underwing as above but paler; undertail washed yellow, barring obscured; longish bill narrow, culmen slightly curved, dark slate-grey, tip black; iris reddish, orbital skin grey; legs green-grey. Distinguished from *C. abingoni* by darker appearance, greener upperparts spotted, not barred, heavily spotted face, neck and underparts. Female has forehead and crown olive-brown with fine pale yellowish to white spots, malar spotted black and white with no red. Juvenile resembles female, but upperparts greener, less yellow, with fewer spots, larger spots and barring below. Voice. Common call an almost whistled "wliee" or "peeeah", weaker but shriller than that of *C. abingoni*; triple-note "weee-we-wi" series, and "kra kra kree-kree-kree-kree kra kra", between croaking and whistling; nestling calls likened to puffing engine.
Habitat. Inhabits light forest, evergreen forest, and dense bush; also riparian woodland and bush; found also at large trees in comparatively open country, and in *Euphorbia* scrub. Occasionally enters gardens.
Food and Feeding. Mainly ants and their brood, also wood-boring beetles and their larvae. Occurs singly or in pairs, also in small family parties; occasionally accompanies mixed-species flocks. Forages at medium levels in trees, often dead ones, both on branches and on trunks; movements quick, perches crosswise at times. Frequently pecks and probes among lichens.
Breeding. Aug-Nov. Nest excavated by both sexes, in dead trunk or branch of tree. Clutch 2-4 eggs; incubation period probably 12 days; both parents feed chicks, by regurgitation, and both also tend to nest sanitation; nestling period 3-4 weeks.
Movements. Resident.
Status and Conservation. Not globally threatened. Currently considered Near-threatened. Restricted-range species: present in South African Forests EBA. Locally common; unobtrusive. Appears to be thinly dispersed within its small coastal range, where suitable sites for hole-excavating are often sparsely scattered. Total range covers c. 50,000 km², within which this species' population is thought to be between 1500 and 5000 individuals; c. 30-60% of these probably live in protected reserves, e.g. known to be present in Oribi Gorge Nature Reserve (South Africa). By early 20th century, clearance of habitat, both forest and bush, for settlements and agriculture had reduced its range, and much more habitat has been lost since then. With the remaining population so small, and habitat loss likely to continue, regular monitoring is required in order to assess whether any conservation action becomes necessary in the future.
Bibliography. Brooke (1984), Clancey (1958a, 1988b, 1992), Dowsett & Dowsett-Lemaire (1993), Dowsett & Forbes-Watson (1993), Fry *et al.* (1988), Furlong (2000), Ginn *et al.* (1989), Harrison *et al.* (1997), Hockey (1996), Hockey *et al.* (1989), Mackworth-Praed & Grant (1962), Maclean (1993), Martin & Martin (1993, 1996), Newman (1996), Nichols (1983a, 1983b), Schmidt (1961), Schultz (1991), Short (1980, 1985b), Short & Horne (1988b), Sigfried (1992), Sinclair (1987), Sinclair & Davidson (1995), Sinclair & Hockey (1996), Sinclair *et al.* (1993), Skead (1964), Snow (1978), Stattersfield & Capper (2000), Tarboton (1997, 2001).

68. Little Green Woodpecker

Campethera maculosa

French: Pic barré **German**: Goldmantelspecht **Spanish**: Pito de Guinea
Other common names: (African) Golden-backed Woodpecker

Taxonomy. *Picus maculosus* Valenciennes, 1826, Senegal.
Forms a superspecies with *C. cailliautii*. Hybridizes rarely with latter in Ghana. Monotypic.
Distribution. Senegal and W Guinea-Bissau E in coastal zone to C Ghana (Aburi region); extends inland to Mt Nimba (Liberia).

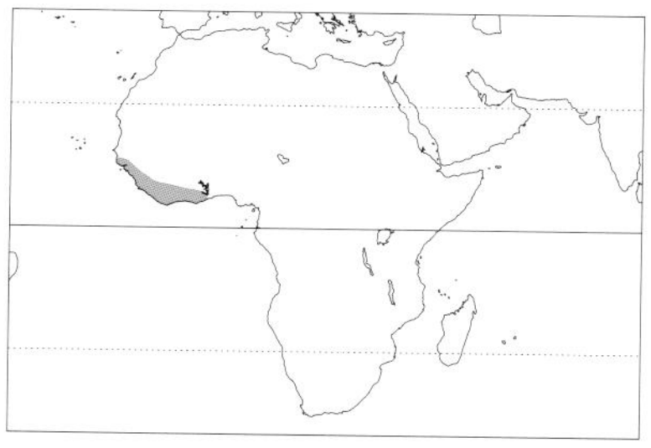

Descriptive notes. c. 16 cm; 54 g. Fairly distinctive, small-bodied woodpecker. Male has olive-blackish forehead and crown with small red feather tips, red nape rather poorly defined; rest of head, neck, chin and throat buff with dense brown spotting; upperparts bright yellowish-green to bronze-green, occasionally a few whitish spots on mantle, sometimes slight traces of red, rump faintly barred; brown flight-feathers with pale buffish bars, broadest on inner webs; uppertail blackish, indistinct yellow shafts, green outer feathers; underparts buffish, greenish-white below breast, and all heavily barred deep olive; underwing-coverts pale yellowish-white, sometimes with few indistinct bars; undertail blackish, tinged yellow; short bill relatively broad-based, fairly broad across nostrils, dark olive-green to blackish, lower mandible with bluish or olive tint; iris brown or pinkish-brown, orbital skin greyish; legs olive-grey or greenish. Female lacks red on head, has forehead and crown olive-black and nape deep olive, all spotted with buff, also greater tendency towards some spotting on upperparts. Juvenile is much as adult, but greener, less bronzy above, usually some paler streaks on back, generally paler and less buff below with barring less even, eyes dark brown. Voice. Common call regular series of 3-4 ascending "teeay" notes, faster than in *C. cailliautii*; also repeated "teerweet" in aggression.
Habitat. Most forest types, mainly at edges. Inhabits edges of primary and secondary forest, clearings with second growth and dead trees, and forest-shrub mosaic; also open forest fringing rivers. Occurs in all lowland forests in Sierra Leone, also in gallery forest, open woodland, degraded forest, and in small hillside trees, even in mangroves; also in farmland in Liberia. Ventures into open country where lots of trees are present. Occurs from lowlands up to mountain ridges above 1000 m; up to 1200 m in Liberia.
Food and Feeding. Known to feed on ants, primarily of genus *Crematogaster*. Usually encountered singly or in pairs, sometimes in mixed-species parties. Forages from canopy down to lower levels, occasionally low in shrub layer, mostly at 5-25 m; at times descends to ground. Uses branches of 2-20 cm in diameter; often perches upright across branches. Main feeding techniques are gleaning and pecking.
Breeding. Recorded in Aug in Senegal (1 record); Dec and Feb in Sierra Leone; in Liberia, nest-excavation seen in May and Oct, adults feeding nestlings in early Aug. Nest excavated in tree, or in arboreal nest of ants or termites (Isoptera). No other information.
Movements. Presumably resident.
Status and Conservation. Not globally threatened. Not uncommon in Sierra Leone; not uncommon in Liberia; very few records from Senegal, all since late 1960's. Relatively little known, and possibly overlooked in some areas. Occurs in Gola Forests Reserves (Sierra Leone), and Taï Forest National Park and Yapo Forest Reserve (Ivory Coast). Probably best studied in Liberia, where densities of 2-3 pairs/km² found in forest edges, clearings and farmland; total Liberian population estimated at c. 50,000 pairs. Appears to benefit from logging and clearance of forest, at least temporarily, since it favours more open habitats.
Bibliography. Allport *et al.* (1989), Bannerman (1953), Barlow *et al.* (1997), Cheke & Walsh (1996), Colston & Curry-Lindahl (1986), Dowsett & Dowsett-Lemaire (1993), Dowsett & Forbes-Watson (1993), Fry *et al.* (1988), Gartshore *et al.* (1995), Gatter (1997), Grimes (1987), Halleux (1994), Lamarche (1980), Mackworth-Praed & Grant (1970), Short (1980, 1985b), Snow (1978), Tarboton (1997), Thiollay (1985a, 1985b).

69. Green-backed Woodpecker

Campethera cailliautii

French: Pic de Cailliaut **German**: Tüpfelspecht **Spanish**: Pito de Cailliaud
Other common names: Little Spotted Woodpecker

Taxonomy. *Chrysopicos Cailliautii* Malherbe,1849, Mombasa.
Forms a superspecies with *C. maculosa*. Has hybridized rarely with latter in Ghana. Distinctive race *permista* often thought to be separate species, but interbreeds freely with *nyansae* in Angola and Zaire. Proposed race *togoensis* (Ghana E to S Nigeria) regarded as synonymous with *permista*; and *kaffensis* (SW Ethiopia) with *nyansae*; *fuelleborni* (sometimes misspelt *fulleborni*), from W Tanzania to Zambia, is also synonymized with *nyansae*. Orange-naped form "*quadrosi*", known only from the Mozambique type specimen, is considered to be an aberrant form of *loveridgei*. Four subspecies recognized.

Subspecies and Distribution.
C. c. permista (Reichenow, 1876) - E Ghana E to extreme SW Sudan, SW Uganda, and S to N Angola and C Zaire.
C. c. nyansae (Neumann, 1900) - SW Ethiopia, SW Kenya and NW Tanzania through E Zaire to N Zambia and NE Angola.
C. c. loveridgei Hartert, 1920 - C Tanzania (Kilosa area) S to extreme E Zimbabwe (Mt Zelinda) and Mozambique (S to R Limpopo).
C. c. cailliautii (Malherbe, 1849) - coastal zone from S Somalia (lower R Jubba and Boni Forest) S to NE Tanzania, including Zanzibar I.

Descriptive notes. c. 16 cm; 34-57 g. Male has black forehead and crown feathers tipped red, red nape, buffish lores, white supercilium, buffish-white sides of head to chin and upper throat all densely spotted with black, yellow-buff neck sides and hindneck heavily spotted black; bright green upperparts with small, neat yellowish-white spots, rump and uppertail-coverts yellower and faintly barred; brown flight-feathers edged yellow-green on outer webs, barred whitish; uppertail greenish-brown, sides barred yellow; pale yellow below, belly whiter, with regular dark brown spots, spots smaller on belly and flanks; underwing-coverts pale yellowish, spotted blackish; undertail brownish; short bill broad-based, grey or blackish, tip dark; iris reddish to brownish, orbital skin greyish-white; legs grey to olive-grey or green. Female differs in having black forehead and crown with white spots. Juvenile duller and greener above than adult, forehead and crown as female but spots finer and whiter, red on nape reduced or lacking, eyes more brown or even greyish. Race *loveridgei* is slightly bigger than nominate, yellower above, with spots forming more bar-like pattern, tail greener, spots below less regular; *nyansae* is slightly longer-winged than previous, greener, less yellow, above with markings often in form of narrow streaks, more heavily spotted below with spots tending to form bars, also bill broader across nostrils; *permista* distinctive, with greyer face, unmarked green upperparts, completely dark-barred underparts (some in S Nigeria are paler below with narrower barring), bill also broad across nostrils. VOICE. Thin, plaintive "hee" or "hlieee", repeated c. 4-12 times at regular intervals; grating "grrrr" or "dddn" calls in encounters, including aerial ones; also "tew-a", "wik-a" and variations, sometimes faster in long series; "aaaa" or "aa-aa" in intimate contacts. Drumrolls short, soft.

Habitat. Wide range of habitats, from forest to thornbush savanna; often near water in dry country. Occupies e.g. rich miombo (*Brachystegia*) woodland and mahobohobo (*Uapaca*) woodland in S parts of range; elsewhere, edges of lowland or other evergreen forest, woodland, wooded grassland, locally palm groves. Strongly associated with riparian forest in Malawi. Enters gardens. To 1750 m in Malawi and most of E Africa, but found at up to 2100 m in SW Uganda; to 1000 m in Zimbabwe, locally to 1200 m.

Food and Feeding. Diet consists largely of arboreal formicid ants and termites (Isoptera). Observed singly or in pairs. Forages high in the canopy; also in thickets and denser patches of vegetation, where easily overlooked. Visits live and dead sections of trees, also ant and termite nests. Gleaning seems to be the principal foraging technique; also pecks. Observed attacking seed pods in search of insects.

Breeding. Feb-Aug in Angola; Sept-Nov in E and probably Mar-Sept in Zaire, with egg-laying associated with rainy seasons. Nest excavated in tree or palm. Clutch 2-3 eggs, occasionally 4; both sexes incubate, and both feed nestlings probably by regurgitation; incubation and fledging periods not documented.

Movements. Resident; some short-distance wandering.

Status and Conservation. Not globally threatened. Generally localized and uncommon. Rare in Somalia, where very few records; uncommon and local in E Africa, possibly more common in some places, but distribution discontinuous. Fairly widespread and not uncommon in S parts of range. Possibly overlooked owing to its unobtrusive behaviour, may possibly be more common than it appears. Race *permista* uncommon to locally not uncommon in Nigeria, common in Angola, locally common in Cameroon and Gabon. Present in numerous protected areas throughout extensive range, e.g. Bamingui-Bangoran National Park (Central African Republic), Impenetrable Forest National Park (Uganda), Masai Mara Reserve (Kenya), Pugu Forest Reserve (Tanzania), Ruvuvu National Park (Burundi) and Akarega National Park (Rwanda).

Bibliography. Anon. (1998c), Ash & Miskell (1983, 1998), Bannerman (1953), Benson & Benson (1977), Chapin (1952), Cheke & Walsh (1996), Christy & Clarke (1994), Clancey (1971b, 1980a), Davies & Boon (1999), Dean (2000), Dowsett (1972b, 1989b), Dowsett & Dowsett-Lemaire (1991, 1993, 1997), Dowsett & Forbes-Watson (1993), Dowsett-Lemaire & Dowsett (1999, 2000), Elgood *et al.* (1994), Evans *et al.* (1994), Fry *et al.* (1988), Ginn *et al.* (1989), Harrison *et al.* (1997), Irwin (1981), Lewis & Pomeroy (1989), Lippens & Wille (1976), Louette (1981b), Mackworth-Praed & Grant (1957, 1962, 1970), Maclean (1993), Moreau (1935), Newman (1996), Nikolaus (1987), Pakenham (1979), Pinto (1983), Prigogine (1987), Sargeant (1993), Schouteden (1966), Short (1980, 1985b), Short & Horne (1988b), Short *et al.* (1990), Sinclair (1987), Sinclair & Hockey (1996), Sinclair *et al.* (1993), Snow (1978), Solomon (1998), Sørensen *et al.* (1996), Stuart & Turner (1980), Tarboton (1997), Thiollay (1985b), Urban & Brown (1971), Vande weghe (1992), Vernon *et al.* (1989), Wilkinson & Beecroft (1988), Zimmerman *et al.* (1996).

PLATE 30 ➤

ssp *hausburgi* ♂

ssp *tullbergi* ♀

♂

71

ssp *poensis* ♂

ssp *herberti* ♂

ssp *nivosa* ♂

♀

70

ssp *taeniolaema* ♂

♀

ssp *caroli* ♀

♂

72

ssp *arizela* ♂

74

♀

♂

ssp *olivaceus* ♂

♀

73

75

♂

ssp *prometheus* ♂

77

♀

♀

ssp *lafresnayi* ♂

ssp *hemprichii* ♂

76

♀

♂

ssp *hartlaubii* ♂

ssp *fuscescens* ♀

PLATE 30

inches 3

cm 8

70. Tullberg's Woodpecker
Campethera tullbergi

French: Pic de Tullberg **German**: Kehlbindenspecht **Spanish**: Pito de Tullberg
Other common names: Fine-banded Woodpecker (*taeniolaema*/*hausburgi*)

Taxonomy. *Campothera* [sic] *Tullbergi* Sjöstedt, 1892, Cameroon.
Distinctive E African races *taeniolaema* and *hausburgi* were formerly considered to form a separate species, and wide geographical separation suggests this might be more appropriate; close structural similarity, however, supports conspecific treatment. Proposed races *bansoensis* and *wellsi* (Banso Mts, W Cameroon) and *insularis* (Bioko) are indistinguishable from nominate; *barakae* (mountains of E Zaire) inseparable from *taeniolaema*. Three subspecies currently recognized.
Subspecies and Distribution.
C. t. tullbergi Sjöstedt, 1892 - SE Nigeria (Obudu Plateau), W Cameroon and Bioko I (Fernando Póo).
C. t. taeniolaema Reichenow & Neumann, 1895 - extreme E Zaire and SW & E Uganda to W Kenyan highlands, S to W Rwanda, Burundi and extreme W Tanzania (Mt Mahari).
C. t. hausburgi Sharpe, 1900 - Kenya E of Rift Valley, also extreme N Tanzania (Loliondo).

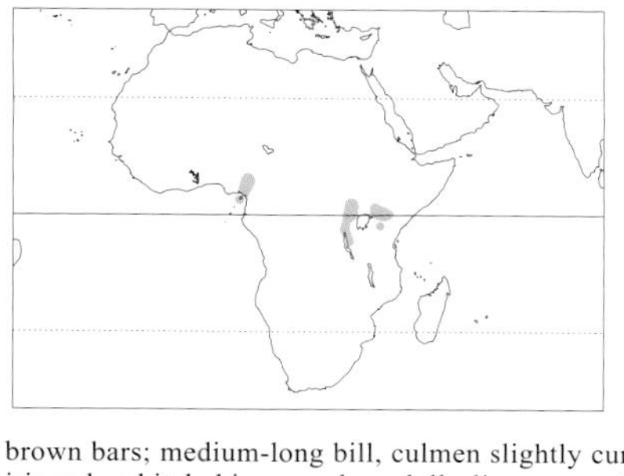

Descriptive notes. c. 18-20 cm; 43-66 g. Male has black-based forehead and crown feathers broadly tipped red, red nape; rest of head whitish with dense fine black spots, neck sides tinged green and more barred; upperparts green, lesser wing-coverts tipped red; brown flight-feathers edged yellow-green on outer webs, inner webs barred yellowish; uppertail dark brown, feathers green-edged; entire underparts pale greenish-yellow, chin to breast with fine black spots, upper flanks and belly with large black spots, lower region with black arrowheads; underwing-coverts yellowish; undertail yellowish-green, sometimes faint brown bars; medium-long bill, culmen slightly curved, fairly narrow across nostrils, dark grey; iris red, orbital skin grey; legs dull olive-green. Female differs in having forehead and crown feathers black with white spots. Juvenile has greyer upperparts variably pale-spotted, heavier markings below, brown eyes, both sexes with finely spotted olive-black forehead and crown, males soon acquiring red tips. Races are slightly smaller and shorter-billed than nominate, lack red on wing-coverts, have barred face and underparts: *taeniolaema* has yellowish-olive upperparts, rump sometimes barred paler, pale greenish-yellow underparts closely barred black, female with reddish feathers on upper lores (rarely absent); *hausburgi* has brighter yellow-green upperparts, stronger yellow-green ground colour below with narrower bars more widely spaced, bars occasionally broken. Voice. Series of "kweek" calls.
Habitat. Moist mountain forest at 900-3000 m. Appears to prefer ravines and edges, but also visits dead trees away from main forest cover.
Food and Feeding. Mainly ants; also caterpillars. Occurs singly or in pairs; joins mixed-species flocks. Forages in the canopy, where it probes into epiphytes (moss, lichens). Seems also to be attracted to trees killed by fire.
Breeding. Laying probably Oct-Nov; bird in post-breeding moult in Apr in Cameroon. Nest excavated in tree. No information on clutch size and on incubation and fledging periods. Nests parasitized by Greater and Scaly-throated Honeyguides (*Indicator indicator*, *I. variegatus*).
Movements. Resident.
Status and Conservation. Not globally threatened. Locally fairly common; not uncommon in limited range in Nigeria. A little-known woodpecker; difficult to observe, as it generally forages at high levels in forest. Occurs in Impenetrable Forest National Park (Uganda); locally quite common in Kenyan mountain forests, and present in several protected areas, e.g. Mt Elgon, Mt Kenya and Aberdares National Parks; also in Kibira National Park (Burundi) and Nyungwe Forest Reserve (Rwanda).
Bibliography. Ash & Sharland (1986), Bannerman (1953), Bennun & Njoroge (1999), Bowden (2001), Bowden & Andrew (1994), Britton (1980), Brown & Britton (1980), Dowsett (1989a, 1990), Dowsett & Dowsett-Lemaire (1993), Dowsett & Forbes-Watson (1993), Elgood *et al.* (1994), Fotso (2001), Friedmann (1930a), Fry *et al.* (1988), Gaugris *et al.* (1981), Lewis & Pomeroy (1989), Lippens & Wille (1976), Louette (1981b), Mackworth-Praed & Grant (1957, 1970), Pérez del Val (1996), Pérez del Val *et al.* (1994), Short (1980, 1985b), Short *et al.* (1990), Snow (1978), Stevenson & Fanshawe (2001), Tarboton (1997), Taylor & Taylor (1988), Zimmerman *et al.* (1996).

71. Buff-spotted Woodpecker
Campethera nivosa

French: Pic tacheté **German**: Termitenspecht **Spanish**: Pito Nevado

Taxonomy. *Dendromus nivosus* Swainson, 1837, West Africa.
Race *maxima*, known only from 2 specimens from N Ivory Coast, doubtfully valid, possibly only larger form of nominate. Latter intergrades with race *herberti*, the resultant intermediates formerly known as race *efulenensis*; *yalensis* (W Kenya) synonymized with *herberti*. Four subspecies recognized.
Subspecies and Distribution.
C. n. nivosa (Swainson, 1837) - Senegambia E to Cameroon and W Zaire and S to NW Angola and NW Zambia.
C. n. maxima Traylor, 1970 - N Ivory Coast.
C. n. poensis Alexander, 1903 - Bioko I (Fernando Póo).
C. n. herberti (Alexander, 1908) - S Central African Republic and extreme SW Sudan (Bangangai Forest) to W Kenya (Kakamega and S Nandi Forests) and S to SC & E Zaire.
Descriptive notes. c. 14-16 cm; 30-49 g. Male has dark green-olive to blackish-olive forehead and crown, red nape; rest of head whitish to pale yellow-buff, heavily streaked olive, sometimes trace of pale supercilium behind eye; bronze-green upperparts, very occasionally with some pale spots; brown flight-feathers edged green, barred yellow-green on inner webs, pale spots on outer webs; uppertail blackish-brown; dark olive-green below, buff-white spots from throat to lower breast, tending towards bars on flanks and lower underparts; underwing yellowish; undertail blackish-

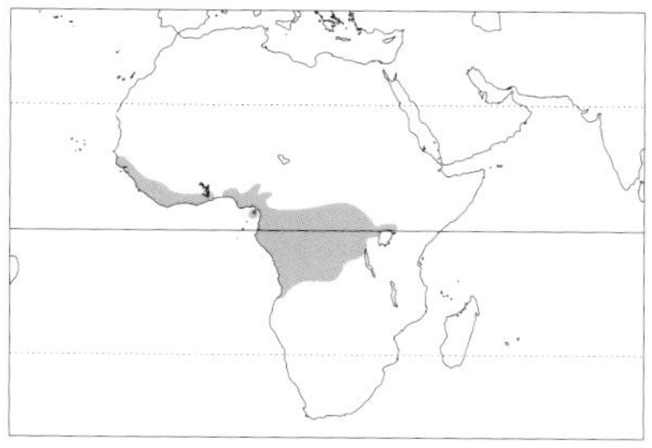

brown, yellowish outer feathers; short bill, culmen slightly curved, narrow across nostrils, slaty-black, blue-grey to greenish-grey base; iris reddish-brown to red, orbital skin dull olive; legs olive to greenish. Female has nape blackish-olive, not red. Juvenile less bronze-tinged above, browner below with spots tending towards bars, eyes brown, both sexes with forehead to nape greyish-olive without red. Race *poensis* differs from nominate in somewhat yellower tail and uppertail-coverts, more bar-like breast markings, whiter belly; *herberti* is slightly smaller, greener and less bronzy above, tail greener, yellower below, breast spots bigger, belly broadly pale-barred; *maxima* differs from nominate only in size, being c. 10% larger. Voice. Calls "preeeew", and "dee-dee-dee" trills; repeated "te-te-te-te-te" series during encounters.
Habitat. Primary and dense secondary lowland and montane forest, at up to c. 1800 m, mostly to 950 m; on Bioko up to 400 m. Also in gallery forest, *Gmelina* woodland, and forest patches interspersed with shrubland and grassland; also mangroves, swamp-forest; visits gardens; in Bioko, shaded cacao plantations. Habitat requirements similar to those of larger and longer-billed *C. caroli*, but more adaptable.
Food and Feeding. Main food black ants (*Crematogaster*) and termites (Isoptera). Singly or in pairs; joins mixed-species flocks. Forages quietly in lower storey, but also up to forest canopy; moves rapidly, and often perches crosswise. Inspects smaller branches, vines and trunks, feeding by gleaning and pecking; can spend long periods exploiting arboreal termite and ant nests.
Breeding. Season Nov-Jun; Jan-Mar in Sierra Leone; eggs in Apr in Nigeria; probably breeds in Nov-Jan and Mar-Jun in Cameroon, in Oct-Mar in Angola, in Jan-May in Zaire, and in Dec-Mar in Uganda and Kenya. Displays with wing-spreading and head- and body-swinging. Nest-hole excavated in arboreal nest of ants or termites, occasionally in tree itself. Clutch 2 eggs; no information on incubation and fledging periods. Most likely brood parasite is Spotted Honeyguide (*Indicator maculatus*).
Movements. Resident.
Status and Conservation. Not globally threatened. Common in most of range; not uncommon in Nigeria and Angola; uncommon in Kenya. Common in Liberia, densities 13 pairs/km² in logged forest, 8 pairs/km² in unlogged forest, estimated population as many as 280,000 pairs. Occurs in several protected areas, e.g. Abuko Nature Reserve (Gambia), and Korup National Park (Cameroon). Quiet and unobtrusive, easy to overlook, and possibly occurs more widely than currently known.
Bibliography. Allport *et al.* (1989), Amadon (1953), Ash & Sharland (1986), Bannerman (1953), Barlow *et al.* (1997), Bowden (2001), Cawkell (1965), Cheke & Walsh (1996), Cheke *et al.* (1986), Christy & Clarke (1994), Colston & Curry-Lindahl (1986), Dean (2000), Dowsett (1989b, 1990), Dowsett & Dowsett-Lemaire (1993, 1997), Dowsett & Forbes-Watson (1993), Dowsett-Lemaire & Dowsett (1999, 2000), Elgood *et al.* (1994), Friedmann (1966), Fry *et al.* (1988), Gartshore *et al.* (1995), Gatter (1988, 1997), Germain & Cornet (1994), Gore (1990), Jensen & Kirkeby (1980), Lewis & Pomeroy (1989), Lippens & Wille (1976), Louette (1981b), Mackworth-Praed & Grant (1957, 1962, 1970), Morel & Morel (1990), Nikolaus (1987, 2000), Pérez del Val (1996), Pérez del Val *et al.* (1994), Pinto (1983), Rand (1951), Sargeant (1993), Short (1980, 1985b), Short *et al.* (1990), Snow (1978), Tarboton (1997), Taylor & Macdonald (1978), Thiollay (1985b), Wacher (1993), Wilkinson & Beecroft (1988), Zimmerman (1972), Zimmerman *et al.* (1996).

72. Brown-eared Woodpecker
Campethera caroli

French: Pic à oreillons bruns **German**: Braunohrspecht **Spanish**: Pito Orejipardo

Taxonomy. *Chloropicus Caroli* Malherbe, 1852, Gabon.
Proposed race *budongoensis* (Uganda and W Kenya) inseparable from nominate. Two subspecies recognized.
Subspecies and Distribution.
C. c. arizela (Oberholser, 1899) - Guinea-Bissau and Sierra Leone to Ghana.
C. c. caroli (Malherbe, 1852) - Benin and Nigeria (rare), and Cameroon E to SW Sudan, Uganda (except NE) and W Kenya (Kakamega), and S to NW Angola, S Zaire and NW Zambia, W Burundi and NW Tanzania (Bukoba).

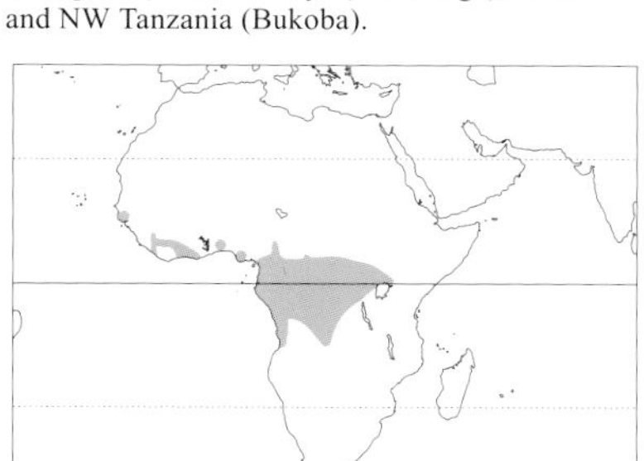

Descriptive notes. c. 18 cm; 50-68 g. Male has olive to blackish-olive forehead to nape, feathers tipped red on hindcrown, broad red tips on nape; olive-streaked buffish supercilium from eye curving around rear ear-coverts, sometimes obscured by green algal staining; brown ear-coverts; green upperparts strongly tinged bronze, mantle occasionally with indistinct yellow spots, rump and uppertail-coverts often with whitish spots; brown flight-feathers edged green, barred paler, bars on inner webs often forming pale patch; uppertail blackish, edged green, outer feathers spotted or barred greenish; throat, neck sides and entire underparts olive to dull green below, heavily spotted buffish-white, spots tending towards bars in lower region; underwing yellowish-white; undertail yellowish-black; longish bill fairly narrow across nostrils, grey-black, base tinged olive or greenish; iris reddish to brown, bare orbital skin greyish to olive; legs greyish to olive-yellow. Female lacks red on crown and nape. Juvenile greener above, lacking bronze tinge, has brown ear-coverts tinged pinkish, chin pale-streaked, breast spots larger and whiter, belly and flanks more barred, eyes brown. Race *arizela* is less bronzy, more deep olive, above than nominate, less heavily spotted below. Voice. Common call a slurred "kwaa-kwaa-kwaa"; also sharp "prrrriiirrii", high-pitched "trrrèè" and fast "ttrrrmmmmmmmup-trrrup".
Habitat. Lowland primary forest, dense secondary growth, forest-shrub-grassland mosaic, and plantations; also, less commonly, in riverine gallery forest. Mainly lowlands; to 1500 m in Liberia, to 1800 m in Kenya.
Food and Feeding. Primarily ants; also other insects, and larvae. Shy and inconspicuous; often in mixed-species flocks. Searches dead branches in the canopy and lower down in forest, mainly

On following pages: 73. Ground Woodpecker (*Geocolaptes olivaceus*); 74. Little Grey Woodpecker (*Dendropicos elachus*); 75. Speckle-breasted Woodpecker (*Dendropicos poecilolaemus*); 76. Abyssinian Woodpecker (*Dendropicos abyssinicus*); 77. Cardinal Woodpecker (*Dendropicos fuscescens*).

below 15 m; inspects trunks, vines and saplings. Main techniques are probing, gleaning and pecking.
Breeding. Few data. Season Dec-Jun in Sierra Leone and Liberia; Aug-Feb in Zaire; nest building in Nov in Gabon. Nest at low to medium height, 3-7 m, in tree or dead stump; clutch 2-3 eggs.
Movements. Resident.
Status and Conservation. Not globally threatened. Generally uncommon, though locally common, e.g. in Sierra Leone and Gabon. Reasonably common in Liberia, with densities of 3-6 pairs/km², and estimated population of 100,000 pairs. Rare in Nigeria. Not uncommon in Angola. Occurs in Korup National Park (Cameroon), La Lopé National Park (Gabon) and Kibale Forest National Park (Uganda).
Bibliography. Allport *et al.* (1989), Ash (1990), Ash & Sharland (1986), Aspinwall & Beel (1998), Bannerman (1953), Britton (1980), Colston & Curry-Lindahl (1986), Dean (2000), Dowsett (1973, 1979b, 1989b), Dowsett & Dowsett-Lemaire (1991, 1993, 1997), Dowsett & Forbes-Watson (1993), Dowsett-Lemaire & Dowsett (1999, 2000), Elgood *et al.* (1994), Fry *et al.* (1988), Gartshore *et al.* (1995), Gatter (1988, 1997), Germain & Cornet (1994), Grimes (1987), Heigham (1976), Leonard & Van Daele (1999), Lewis & Pomeroy (1989), Lippens & Wille (1976), Louette (1981b), Mackworth-Praed & Grant (1957, 1962, 1970), Nikolaus (1987), Pinto (1983), Short (1980, 1985b), Short *et al.* (1990), Snow (1978), Sørensen *et al.* (1996), Tarboton (1997), Thiollay (1985b), Zimmerman (1972), Zimmerman *et al.* (1996).

Genus *GEOCOLAPTES* Swainson, 1832

73. Ground Woodpecker
Geocolaptes olivaceus

French: Pic laboureur **German**: Erdspecht **Spanish**: Pito Terrestre
Other common names: African Ground Woodpecker

Taxonomy. *Picus olivaceus* J. F. Gmelin, 1788, Cape of Good Hope.
No close relatives. Two subspecies recognized.
Subspecies and Distribution.
G. o. olivaceus (J. F. Gmelin, 1788) - W & SC Cape Province.
G. o. prometheus Clancey, 1952 - S Cape Province NE to N Transvaal and W Swaziland.

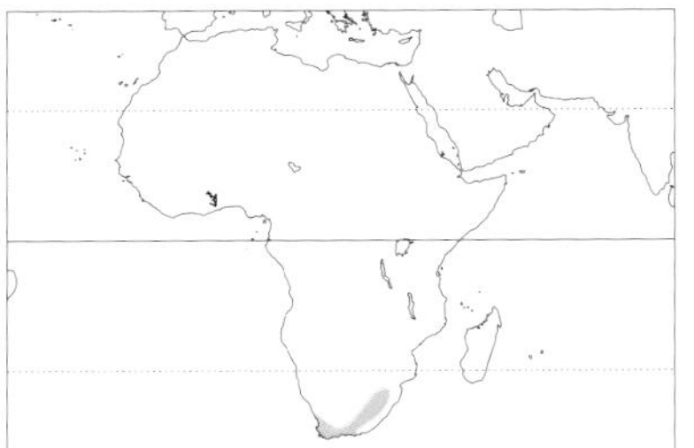

Descriptive notes. 22-30 cm; 105-134 g. Male has brownish-grey forehead and crown, browner nape often with slight trace of red, grey sides of head and neck, dark grey malar with fine red feather tips (red visible only at close range); white chin and throat; upperparts grey-ish-brown to dull green-brown, in fresh plumage with pale feather tips forming small spots and hint of barring; red rump, white-barred brown uppertail-coverts; wing-coverts spotted or barred pale; dark brown flight-feathers all barred whitish, tertials also tinged greenish; uppertail brown, prominent narrow whitish bars; whitish breast feathers broadly tipped pinkish-red with some pale streaks, belly deeper crimson with pale bases, flanks barred grey-brown and whitish, bars often extending to undertail-coverts; underwing brown and yellowish-white; undertail light brown, barred yellowish-white; long bill pointed, culmen curved, very narrow between nostrils, black, greyer base; iris pink to golden, whiter near pupil; legs grey. Female is very like male, but lacks red malar tips. Juvenile has adult pattern but duller, usually some red on nape, paler and more light pinkish below, eyes all white. Race *prometheus* is much paler, especially below; upland populations tend to be darker overall. Voice. Loud, harsh "peer, peer, peer" or "pee-aa-r-g-h" screams when flushed; loud series of up to 5 "ree-chick, ree-chick" notes, as contact and territorial call; also falcon-like "krrrreee" when joining group; "chew-kee" calls when displaying.
Habitat. Open rocky terrain in uplands, including grassy boulder-strewn slopes and hillsides, open grassland with rocky ridges, mountain slopes, barren or eroded areas; recorded also around reedy marshes. Also roadsides in lowlands in SW of range. To c. 2100 m, in Natal from 1200 m upwards; rarely recorded as low as 600 m, but descends to sea-level in SW of range.
Food and Feeding. Highly specialized on ants, ant broods and alates; termites (Isoptera), beetles and other insects, and mites (Acari) also taken. Ants of 8 genera comprise 95% of food taken, and include *Camponotus*, *Anoplolepis*, *Acantholepis*, *Tetramorium*, *Crematogaster*, *Pheidole*; total of c. 60 ant species has been recorded in diet. Termites regularly eaten, but form only 1·25% of total food intake; other arthropods probably taken accidentally. Usually in pairs or small parties of c. 6 birds, groups occupying area of 21-70 ha; groups appear to know exact locations of ant nests within their home range, spend at most 3 days in a particular place. Perches upright on large boulders, flies from one rocky outcrop to the next. Forages mostly on ground, occasionally on dead trees; moves on ground primarily by hopping, also walks on more level terrain. Explores any fault, crevice or hole, including interfaces between stones and the soil; makes single inquisitive pecks, sweeps away debris with the bill. Penetrates soil with heavy pecks when an ant colony detected; then feeds in characteristic posture, head down and beak deeply implanted in ground, continuous activity of tongue indicated by jerky tail movements. Wood-dwelling ants (*Crematogaster*) obtained by probing into dead wood. Surface gleaning only a minor feeding technique used. Forages mostly in morning hours, with secondary peak of activity in late afternoon; during these periods large quantities of ants consumed, digested slowly; even during cooler season (Mar-Aug), requires only c. 35% of total daylight hours to procure sufficient food.
Breeding. Aug-Sept in Cape Province and Transvaal; Aug-Dec, mainly Oct-Nov, in Natal. In pairs or trios, copulations occurring during excavation phase of cycle; pre-copulation display by male in upright stance with spread wings. Nest dug mainly by male, in bank, often in road cutting, or in vertical wall of donga, or among rocks; tunnel usually c. 1 m long, range 50-120 cm, 7·5 cm in diameter, ending in enlarged nest-chamber 15 cm in diameter; same nest may be used over several seasons, and also serves as roost. Clutch 2-5 eggs, usually 3; both parents incubate, sometimes possibly with 1 or more helpers; chicks fed by both parents and helper; incubation and fledging periods apparently not documented; juveniles stay with parents until the next breeding season.
Movements. Resident.
Status and Conservation. Not globally threatened. Common in most of range. Its use of essentially unthreatened, often remote, habitats implies that species is probably secure in most areas. Few historical data available; no evidence of any significant decline in range or numbers. Occurs in several protected areas, e.g. Giant's Castle and Suikerbosrand Reserves.
Bibliography. Barnes (1999), Brooke (1984), Brown & Barnes (1984), Clancey (1952, 1988a, 1992), Dowsett & Dowsett-Lemaire (1993), Dowsett & Forbes-Watson (1993), Earlé (1986), Every (1974), Fry *et al.* (1988), Ginn *et al.* (1989), Harrison *et al.* (1997), Hockey (1996), Hockey *et al.* (1989), Mackworth-Praed & Grant (1962), Maclean (1993), Newman (1996), Oatley (1995), Oatley *et al.* (1989), Short (1971e, 1980, 1985b), Sinclair (1987), Sinclair & Davidson (1995), Sinclair & Hockey (1996), Sinclair *et al.* (1993), Tarboton (1997, 2001), Tarboton, Allan *et al.* (1993), Tarboton, Kemp & Kemp (1987).

Genus *DENDROPICOS* Malherbe, 1849

74. Little Grey Woodpecker
Dendropicos elachus

French: Pic gris **German**: Wüstenspecht **Spanish**: Pito Saheliano
Other common names: Least (Grey) Woodpecker

Taxonomy. *Dendropicos elachus* Oberholser, 1919, Senegal and coast of Guinea.
Monotypic.
Distribution. SW Mauritania, Senegambia, and in narrow belt from C Mali E to C Chad and WC Sudan and S to NE Nigeria (to Aliya) and extreme N Cameroon (S to around Maroua); possible presence between Senegambia and C Mali requires confirmation.

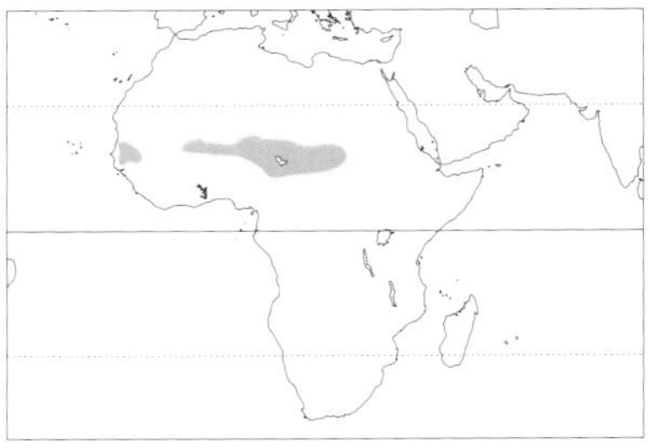

Descriptive notes. 12-14 cm; 17-21 g. Male has pale grey-brown forehead to mid-crown, dull red hindcrown and nape, white supercilium from behind eye to rear of ear-coverts, pale brown-grey lores, ear-coverts and sides of neck, whitish stripe from lower lores below ear-coverts, thin dark brown malar stripe; head markings fade rapidly, leaving plain-faced appearance; white chin and throat faintly streaked brown in fresh plumage; greyish-brown upperparts barred white, rump and uppertail-coverts red; brown wing-coverts barred off-white, tipped white; brown flight-feathers barred whitish; uppertail brown, barred off-white; whitish below, breast spotted or sometimes vaguely barred brown, smaller rather faint spots on belly; underwing whitish, spotted brown; all plumage colours fade very quickly, very pale when worn; relatively long bill proportionately broad, grey, paler base, whitish base of lower mandible; iris brown; legs greenish-grey. Female as male, but entire crown and nape with more brown. Juvenile duller. Voice. Common call a grating rattle, "skree-eek-eee-eee-eeee-ee-eee-eeek", often repeated; also softer "tee-tee-tee-..."; low whirring "wi-i-i-i-i" to "ch-ch-ch-ch" in interactions; also louder rattling series of "wi" or "wik" notes.
Habitat. Lightly wooded steppe and semi-desert, scattered trees in dry streambeds and wadis. Lowalnds; to 1600 m in Niger.
Food and Feeding. Poorly known. Diet insect larvae. Forages in trees, such as *Balanites* and acacias (*Acacia*), by pecking and hammering.
Breeding. Breeds Jan-Feb in Senegal and Mali, Mar-May in Niger, about Oct in Chad. Nest in dead branch of acacia. No other information.
Movements. Resident.
Status and Conservation. Not globally threatened. Rare and little-known species. Sparsely distributed throughout its range. Rare in Senegal, occurs in N at Richard Toll; no recent records from Gambia. Uncommon in Nigeria. Total population likely to be small. Research needed on its ecology and breeding biology. Present in several protected areas, e.g. Djoudj National Park (Senegal), Aïr et Ténére National Park (Niger), Waza National Park (Cameroon) and Ouadi Rimé-Ouadi Achim Reserve (Chad).
Bibliography. Bannerman (1953), Barlow *et al.* (1997), Cave & Macdonald (1955), Cawkell (1965), Dowsett & Dowsett-Lemaire (1993), Dowsett & Forbes-Watson (1993), Elgood *et al.* (1994), Fairon (1975), Fry *et al.* (1988), Gee (1984), Giraudoux *et al.* (1988), Gore (1990), Lamarche (1980, 1988), Louette (1981b), Mackworth-Praed & Grant (1957, 1970), Morel & Morel (1990), Newby (1980, 1987), Nikolaus (1987), Sauvage & Rodwell (1998), Scholte *et al.* (1999), Short (1980, 1985b), Short & Horne (1988b), Snow (1978), Tarboton (1997).

75. Speckle-breasted Woodpecker
Dendropicos poecilolaemus

French: Pic à poitrine tachetée **German**: Tropfenspecht **Spanish**: Pito Cuellipinto
Other common names: Uganda Spotted Woodpecker

Taxonomy. *Dendropicus* [sic] *poecilolaemus* Reichenow, 1893, Sconga, west of Lake Albert, Zaire.
Monotypic.
Distribution. Extreme S Nigeria (Serti) and C Cameroon E to NW Zaire and N Congo, and S Sudan, W & C Uganda and W Kenya (Nandi and Kabarnet); probably also in intervening parts of Central African Republic and N Zaire, but confirmation required.

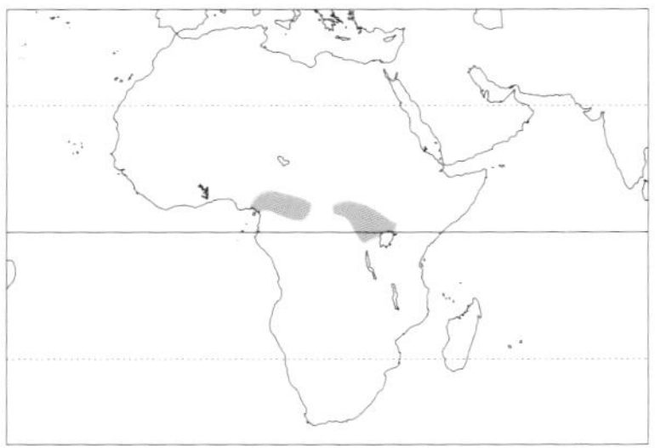

Descriptive notes. c. 15 cm; 25-30 g. Male has brown forehead to mid-crown, red hindcrown and nape, white ear-coverts and neck sides streaked brown, brown-streaked malar stripe better defined along lower edge; white chin and throat sometimes lightly spotted grey; yellow-green upperparts, sometimes faint dark barring on mantle; faint bars on rump and uppertail-coverts, which also have red tips in fresh plumage (soon wear off); brown wing-coverts spotted and tipped dull yellow; brown flight-feathers edged yellow-ish-green, barred yellowish-white; uppertail brown, sometimes faint dull green bars; pale greenish-yellow underparts usually suffused grey, scattered dark spots on breast and hint of bars on flanks, variable, sometimes breast narrowly barred, broader pale grey flank bars, faint belly streaking; underwing barred brown and yellowish-white; undertail yellowish-brown; fairly long bill broad across nostrils, dark grey or brownish-grey, sometimes blue-grey, culmen and base paler; iris red, sometimes brown; legs greenish to olive or olive-grey. Female has nape black, not red, blackish barring above more distinct than on male. Juvenile greyer than adult, lacking yellow tone, has mantle indistinctly barred black, underparts greyish-white with less obvious markings, eyes brown, both sexes with red on crown, more restricted on female, black nape and rear crown sides. Voice. Dry "che che che che che".

Habitat. Forest edge and clearings, especially those bordering cultivations with trees; also upland savanna with forest, and riverine forest. To 2100 m in W of range; found at 700-2100 m in E.

Food and Feeding. Diet comprises beetle larvae, caterpillars, ants. Occurs singly or in pairs. Forages on dead trees; often visits isolated trees, even ventures into areas of elephant grass (*Pennisetum*). Uses pecking and hammering.

Breeding. Season May-Sept in Zaire; Mar-Sept and Nov-Jan in Uganda. Nest excavated in tree. No other information.

Movements. Resident.

Status and Conservation. Not globally threatened. Locally common. Uncommon and local in Kenya. Rather poorly known. Research needed on its breeding biology.

Bibliography. Bannerman (1953), Britton (1980), Brown & Britton (1980), Carroll (1988), Cave & Macdonald (1955), Dowsett & Dowsett-Lemaire (1993), Dowsett & Forbes-Watson (1993), Elgood *et al.* (1994), Fry *et al.* (1988), Germain & Cornet (1994), Green (1990), Hall (1977), Lewis & Pomeroy (1989), Lippens & Wille (1976), Louette (1981b), Mackworth-Praed & Grant (1957, 1970), Nikolaus (1987), Pedersen (2000), Quantrill & Quantrill (1998), Short (1980, 1985b), Short & Horne (1988b), Short *et al.* (1990), Snow (1978), Stevenson & Fanshawe (2001), Tarboton (1997), Zimmerman *et al.* (1996).

76. **Abyssinian Woodpecker**

Dendropicos abyssinicus

French: Pic d'Abyssinie **German**: Wacholderspecht **Spanish**: Pito Abisinio
Other common names: Gold-mantled/(Abyssinian/African) Golden-backed Woodpecker

Taxonomy. *Picus Abyssinicus* Stanley, 1814, Ethiopia.
Sometimes regarded as forming a superspecies with *D. fuscescens*. Monotypic.

Distribution. Ethiopian Highlands, from upper R Anseber in Eritrea E to Harar region and S to Alata.

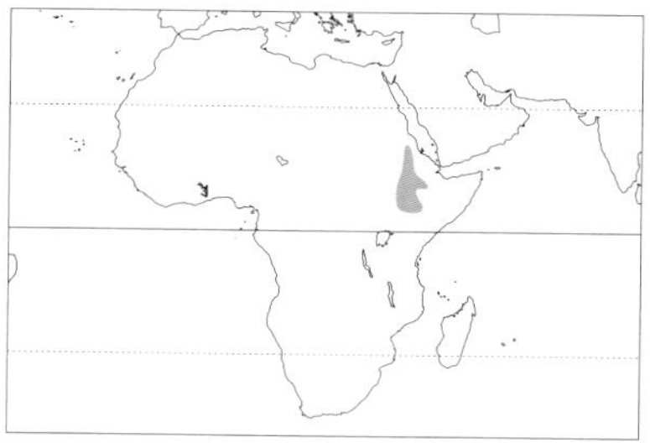

Descriptive notes. c. 16 cm; 23-26 g. Male has brown forehead and forecrown, red hindcrown and nape, brown band through ear-coverts to neck side, broad brown malar stripe; rest of face white, chin and throat streaked brown; greenish-brown mantle, back, scapulars and inner wing-coverts with broad yellowish-golden tips, occasionally some reddish-green tips, brown bases, appearing quite mottled when worn; red rump and uppertail-coverts; brown outer wing-coverts broadly tipped white; dark brown flight-feathers edged yellowish, barred white, bars broadest but duller on tertials; uppertail brown, narrowly barred white; underparts white, tinged yellow, streaked blackish-brown, streaks broadest on breast and flanks; underwing-coverts off-white, barred and streaked brown; undertail yellowish-brown, obscurely pale-barred; longish bill fairly broad, dark grey, paler towards base; iris brown to reddish; legs lead-grey. Female has brown hindcrown merging into dark nape. Juvenile greener, less golden above, rump paler red, whiter and heavily streaked below, indication of barring on belly, both sexes with red crown, slightly smaller on female, black nape. Voice. Not recorded.

Habitat. Mostly juniper (*Juniperus*) woods and *Hagenia* forest, also areas of *Euphorbia*, mostly between 1600 m and 3000 m, occasionally higher; has been found also in wooded savanna, including at slightly lower elevations. Largely separated by altitude from *D. fuscescens*.

Food and Feeding. Diet not recorded. Forages on trees, by probing into mosses.

Breeding. Season probably Dec-May. No other information.

Movements. Resident.

Status and Conservation. Not globally threatened. Uncommon. Occurs in Bale Mountains National Park, Ethiopia. A little-known species; research is required to determine its ecology and breeding biology. Has probably suffered some contraction of its range in recent decades as a result of habitat destruction, as increasingly large areas of native woodland have been converted to eucalyptus (*Eucalyptus*) plantations. This species' conservation status possibly merits reassessment; research and monitoring desirable, but very difficult in the region because of nature of terrain and unstable political situation.

Bibliography. Ash & Gullick (1989), Cheesman & Sclater (1935), Dowsett & Dowsett-Lemaire (1993), Dowsett & Forbes-Watson (1993), Francis & Shirihai (1999), Fry *et al.* (1988), Mackworth-Praed & Grant (1957), Ryan (2001), Shirihai & Francis (1999), Short (1980, 1985b), Short & Horne (1988b), Smith (1957), Snow (1978), Tarboton (1997), Tilahun *et al.* (1996), Urban (1980), Urban & Brown (1971), Zinner (2001).

77. **Cardinal Woodpecker**

Dendropicos fuscescens

French: Pic cardinal **German**: Kardinalspecht **Spanish**: Pito Cardenal

Taxonomy. *Picus fuscescens* Vieillot, 1818, Swellendam district, Cape Province, South Africa.
Sometimes regarded as forming a superspecies with *D. abyssinicus*. Races often treated as comprising three geographical groups: NE "*hemprichii* group", also including *massaicus*; W & C "*lafresnayi* group", also including *sharpii* and *lepidus*; and S "*fuscescens* group", which also contains *intermedius*, *centralis* and *hartlaubii*. Races intergrade to variable extent, also interbreed, especially in E & S. Numerous other described races are all considered insufficiently differentiated to warrant recognition: *cosensi*, known from single type specimen (Senegal), is merged with *lafresnayi*, and *camerunensis* (Cameroon) with *sharpii*; *chyulu* (Chyulu Hills, in S Kenya) is synonymized with *hartlaubii*; *loandae* (N Angola to W Zaire) is synonymized with *centralis*, as are *camacupae* (Angolan plateau E to Malawi), *stresemanni* (N Namibia) and *capriviensis* (SW Zambia to N Botswana); *harei* (S Namibia) and *orangensis* (Orange River Basin in E South Africa) are lumped with nominate; and *transvaalensis* (S Zimbabwe and NE Transvaal), *noomei* (coastal S Mozambique and NE Natal) and *natalensis* (lowland E Transvaal and Natal) are regarded as synonyms of *intermedius*. Nine subspecies recognized.

Subspecies and Distribution.
D. f. lafresnayi Malherbe, 1849 - Senegambia E to Nigeria.
D. f. sharpii Oustalet, 1879 - Cameroon and Central African Republic E to S Sudan, S to N Angola and W Zaire.
D. f. lepidus (Cabanis & Heine, 1863) - E Zaire, and highlands of Ethiopia, Uganda, W & C Kenya, Rwanda and NW Tanzania.
D. f. massaicus Neumann, 1900 - S Ethiopia at middle elevations, and W Kenya and C Tanzania at lower altitudes.
D. f. hemprichii (Ehrenberg, 1833) - Ethiopia (lower elevations), Somalia, and N & E Kenya.
D. f. centralis Neumann, 1900 - E Angola E to W Tanzania, S to N Namibia and Zambia.
D. f. hartlaubii Malherbe, 1849 - from Kenya-Tanzania border S to extreme E Zambia, Malawi and C Mozambique (R Zambezi).
D. f. fuscescens (Vieillot, 1818) - NC Namibia, Botswana, and most of South Africa E to S Transvaal and W Natal.
D. f. intermedius Roberts, 1924 - C Mozambique (R Zambezi) S to Transvaal and Natal.

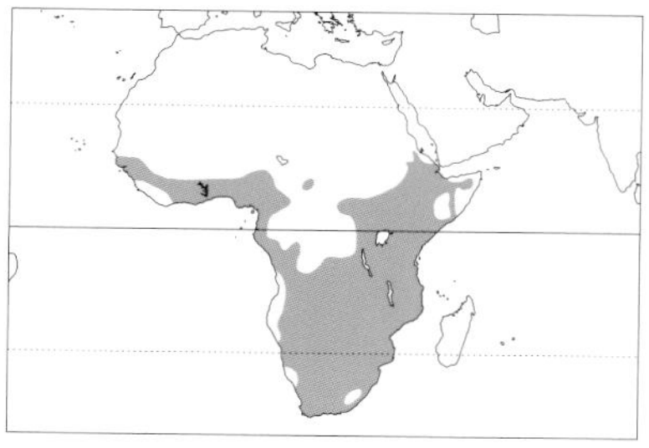

Descriptive notes. 14-16 cm; 20-31 g (*lepidus*), 29-37 g (*fuscescens*). Male has brownish forehead to mid-crown, red hindcrown to hindneck, broad white supercilium behind eye extending around rear of ear-coverts, buffish or white lores, off-white or grey-white cheeks and ear-coverts very finely and inconspicuously streaked dark; broad brownish-black malar stripe expanding on lower neck sides; white chin and throat sometimes finely spotted or streaked brown; upperparts dark brown with white to pale olive-white bars, rump and uppertail-coverts yellower, latter tipped light reddish; blackish-brown wing-coverts strongly spotted white or yellowish-white, flight-feathers barred whitish; uppertail brown, barred yellow-white, pale shafts; white below, often tinged yellow-buff when fresh, breast and sides broadly streaked brownish-black, lower flanks, belly and undertail-coverts more barred; underwing greyish-black, coverts white; undertail barred; entire plumage duller when worn, less olive or yellow tinge in pale areas, can appear very black and white; longish bill broad, blackish, sometimes with blue or brown tones, lower mandible paler; iris red to red-brown; legs greenish-grey to green-brown. Female differs in having darker brown forehead merging into black rear crown and nape. Juvenile duller, greyer, less contrastingly patterned, has eyes brown or grey-brown, both sexes with red patch in centre of crown, somewhat smaller on female, black nape and hindneck. Races vary mostly in upperpart coloration and degree of barring, less so in size, W & C group of races small, green and less barred above, NE group smallest and palest, S group biggest and most barred: *lafresnayi* is green above with obscure bars, yellowish below with fine dark streaks, female has darker face; *sharpii* similar, but streaks below broader; *lepidus* is larger than last two, unbarred above (female somewhat more barred in Kenyan highlands), pale below with streaks very narrow; *massaicus* is fully barred above, tinged yellow above and below, but more contrasted than previous, birds at higher elevations larger and darker; *hemprichii* is slightly smaller than previous, paler, has narrower dark barring above; *centralis* is browner, less black, above than nominate, barring more yellow, yellower below with streaks finer, less barring on belly; *hartlaubii* is smaller, especially coastal populations, than previous, bars above olive-brown and pale yellowish-olive, yellow with olive-brown streaks below; *intermedius* has bars above more olive-black and yellowish-white, streaks below narrower. Voice. Shrill chittering "kweek-eek-eek-ik-ik" by both sexes; "creek, creek, creek" and "kweek-a, kweek-a" in aggression; repeated "kee-kee-kee-kee" from nestlings. Drumming rapid, not very loud.

Habitat. Variety of open and dense woodland, wooded grassland and bushland; absent only from moist mountain forest. Inhabits riparian fringing forest, edges of lowland forest, and montane forest in highlands (where drier); occurs in, for example, *Euphorbia-Acacia* woodland in Ethiopia, and *Brachystegia* woodland, especially if not disturbed by human activities, in Zambia. Also in arid scrub (*hemprichii*). Also found in mangroves in W Africa, and in plantations, orchards, parks and gardens. Race *lepidus* more an inhabitant of forest than are other races. Avoids thick forest and treeless areas in Somalia. From lowlands to middle and higher elevations; common at c. 1800 m in Ethiopia; to 1800 m in Zimbabwe, to 2100 m in Malawi, to 2600 m in E Africa, even to 3500 m in Zaire.

Food and Feeding. Insects and their larvae, particularly beetles; also caterpillars. Termites (Isoptera), grasshoppers (Orthoptera) and fruits also recorded eaten. Usually hunts singly or in pairs; commonly joins mixed feeding flocks. Moves quickly through habitat, giving frequent contact calls. Forages mostly at lower levels, but also at higher levels in outer canopy, and down to ground; in trees, bushes, creepers, preferring smaller branches and twigs; hangs from smallest twigs; visits reeds and even dry stalks of cultivated maize, also seed pods (e.g. of *Swartzia madagascariensis*). Main techniques are pecking and probing, also hammering. Sometimes accompanied by *Campethera abingoni*, which pecks less and does not exploit very small twigs. Subordinate to *D. namaquus* when the two meet.

Breeding. Season about Feb-Jul in W Africa, nest in Dec in Sierra Leone; Jun-Nov in Angola; nest with chicks in mid-late Mar in N Somalia; breeds throughout year in E Africa, with wide local variation, no clear association with rainy or dry seasons; Apr-Jan, but mostly Aug-Oct, in S Africa. Nest-hole excavated by both sexes, duration c. 2 weeks, at 1·5-18 m in dead trunk or branch of tree; cavity depth 15 cm or more. Clutch 2 or 3 eggs, rarely 1 or 5; incubation by both parents, from first egg, male sometimes feeding female at nest, incubation period 10-13 days; both also feed chicks, nestling period c. 27 days; fledged brood divided between parents, sex for sex, accompanied by them for 8-10 weeks. Nests parasitized by Scaly-throated Honeyguide (*Indicator variegatus*), probably also by Greater Honeyguide (*I. indicator*).

Movements. Resident.

Status and Conservation. Not globally threatened. Common and widespread throughout almost entire range; Africa's most widespread woodpecker, occurring in most of continent S of Sahara; commonest woodpecker in E & S Africa, also in many other areas. Occurs in numerous national parks, e.g. Comoé (Ivory Coast), Bénoué (Cameroon), Awash (Ethiopia), Murchison Falls (Uganda), Amboseli and Tsavos (Kenya), Serengeti and Mikumi (Tanzania), and Kruger (South Africa).

Bibliography. Allport *et al.* (1989), Archer & Godman (1937-1961), Ash & Miskell (1998), Attwell (1952), Bannerman (1953), Barlow *et al.* (1997), Benson & Benson (1977), Benson *et al.* (1971), Brown (1993), Cave & Macdonald (1955), Cheke & Walsh (1996), Christy & Clarke (1994), Dean (1974b, 2000), Dowsett (1990), Dowsett & Dowsett-Lemaire (1991, 1993), Dowsett & Forbes-Watson (1993), Elgood *et al.* (1994), Evans *et al.* (1994), Friedmann (1930a), Fry *et al.* (1988), Germain & Cornet (1994), Ginn *et al.* (1989), Gore (1990), Graaf (1992), Greig-Smith (1976), Harrison *et al.* (1997), King (2000), Lewis & Pomeroy (1989), Mackworth-Praed & Grant (1957, 1962, 1970), Maclean (1993), Nikolaus (2000), Pakenham (1979), Penry (1994), Pinto (1983), Ripley & Heinrich (1969), Roberts (1924), Sauvage & Rodwell (1998), Short (1980, 1985b), Short & Horne (1988b), Snow (1978), Spottiswoode (1994), Tarboton (1980, 1997, 2001), Tarboton *et al.* (1987), Underhill & Underhill (1992b), Vernon (1980), Willows (1989), Wilson & Wilson (1992), Zimmerman (1972), Zimmerman *et al.* (1996).

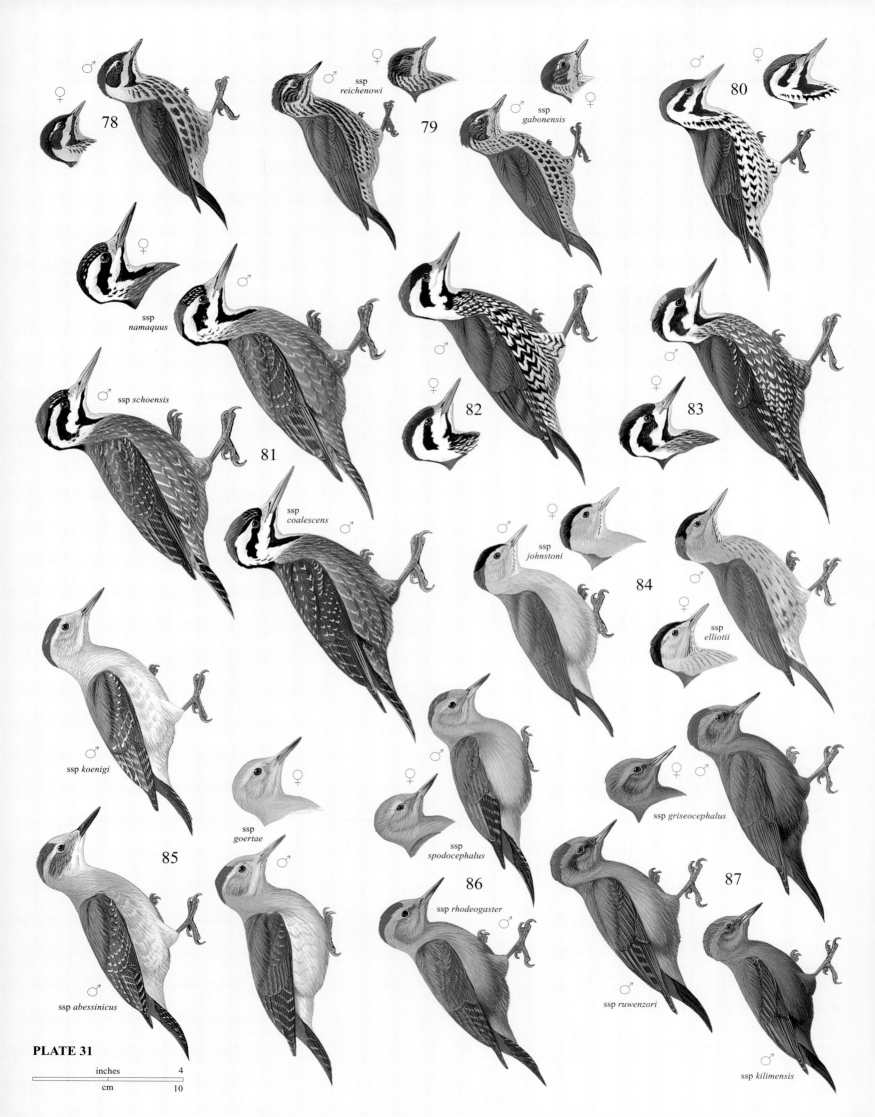

♀ ♂ 78

ssp *reichenowi* ♂ 79

♂ ssp *gabonensis* ♀

♂ 80 ♀

♀ ssp *namaquus*

82 ♀

83 ♀

♂ ssp *schoensis*

81

ssp *coalescens* ♂

♂ ♀ ssp *johnstoni*

84

♂ ssp *elliotii* ♀

♂ ssp *koenigi*

ssp *goertae* ♀

ssp *spodocephalus* ♀

♀ ♂ ssp *griseocephalus*

85

♂ ssp *rhodeogaster*

86

ssp *abessinicus* ♂

ssp *ruwenzori* ♂

87

ssp *kilimensis* ♂

PLATE 31

inches 4

cm 10

78. Melancholy Woodpecker

Dendropicos lugubris

French: Pic à raies noires **German**: Düsterspecht **Spanish**: Pito Lúgubre

Taxonomy. *Dendropicus lugubris* Hartlaub, 1857, Aguapim, Ghana.
Forms a superspecies with *D. gabonensis*; sometimes treated as conspecific, a view supported by the fact that race *reichenowi* of latter in Nigeria and Cameroon is somewhat intermediate between present species and nominate *D. g. gabonensis*; indeed, *reichenowi* was formerly considered to belong instead to present species. Monotypic.
Distribution. Sierra Leone to SE Ghana, S Nigeria and SW Cameroon.

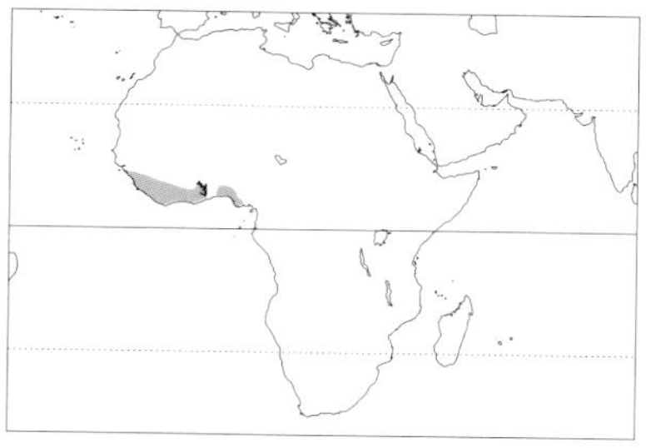

Descriptive notes. c. 17-18 cm. Male has olive-brown forehead and crown, red nape, thin white supercilium, brown ear-coverts, white neck sides and broad white cheekstripe, broad brown malar stripe; white chin and throat, often with some dark spots or streaks; entire upperparts bronze-green, occasionally paler feather tips forming very indistinct bars; brown flight-feathers edged greenish-bronze, barred or spotted white on inner webs; uppertail black; underparts pale greenish-yellow, feathers with broad dark brown centres, streaks continuing to vent; underwing pale yellowish-white, spotted brown; undertail grey-black; shortish bill fairly broad across nostrils, greyish to blackish, paler base and lower mandible; iris red to red-brown; legs greenish, tinged brown, olive or yellow. Distinguished from *D. gabonensis* by head pattern, broader dark markings below, more bronzy upperparts, blacker tail. Female has nape blackish, not red. Juvenile duller, lacking bronze tone above, has eyes brown, both sexes with black nape, small red patch on hindcrown. Voice. Common call a drawn-out buzzing note, as that of *D. gabonensis*; also fast rattle, "bdddddddddddd-d-it" or "br-r-r-r-r-r-ip"; also "rrek-rrek-rrek-rrak-rrak" and low "pit" or "pa-bit" during encounters. Drums fairly loudly.
Habitat. Open forest, second growth, forest edge, clearings, also *Gmelina* woodland; also gallery forest, swamp-forest, exotic plantations and gardens in W Africa. From lowlands to c. 1200 m; ascends above 1300 m in Liberia, possibly also elsewhere.
Food and Feeding. Insects, including ants, beetle larvae. Usually in pairs or family parties; often joins mixed-species foraging flocks. Forages mainly in canopy, sometimes descending to understorey; prefers smaller horizontal branches. Probes, gleans; appears to use pecking and hammering to only minimal extent.
Breeding. Oct-Mar in Sierra Leone; nestlings found in Mar and Apr in Liberia. Nest-hole at 15-30 m in dead tree branch or dead part of trunk. No other information.
Movements. Resident.
Status and Conservation. Not globally threatened. Rather uncommon throughout relatively small range. Common in Sierra Leone. Locally not uncommon to common in Liberia, where estimated 50,000 pairs. Occurs in Gola Forests Reserves (Sierra Leone) and Taï Forest National Park and IIRSDA Research Station (Ivory Coast). Not a well-known species; further research on its ecology and breeding biology is desirable.
Bibliography. Allport *et al*. (1989), Bannerman (1953), Cheke & Walsh (1996), Colston & Curry-Lindahl (1986), Dowsett & Dowsett-Lemaire (1993), Dowsett & Forbes-Watson (1993), Fry *et al*. (1988), Gartshore *et al*. (1995), Gatter (1997), Grimes (1987), Mackworth-Praed & Grant (1970), Rand (1951), Salewski (2000), Short (1980), Tarboton (1997), Thiollay (1985a), Waltert *et al*. (1999), Wheatley (1995).

79. Gabon Woodpecker

Dendropicos gabonensis

French: Pic du Gabon **German**: Gabunspecht **Spanish**: Pito del Gabón

Taxonomy. *Dendrobates Gabonensis* J. Verreaux and E. Verreaux, 1851, Gabon.
Forms a superspecies with *D. lugubris*; sometimes treated as conspecific, a view supported by the fact that race *reichenowi* is somewhat intermediate between that species and nominate *gabonensis*; indeed, *reichenowi* was formerly considered to belong instead to *D. lugubris*. Two subspecies recognized.
Subspecies and Distribution.
D. g. reichenowi Sjöstedt, 1893 - S Nigeria and SW Cameroon.
D. g. gabonensis (J. Verreaux & E. Verreaux, 1851) - S Cameroon (except SW) and SW Central African Republic S to N Angola (Cabinda), and E across N & C Zaire (E to W slope of Ruwenzoris, S to W Kasai) to extreme W Uganda.

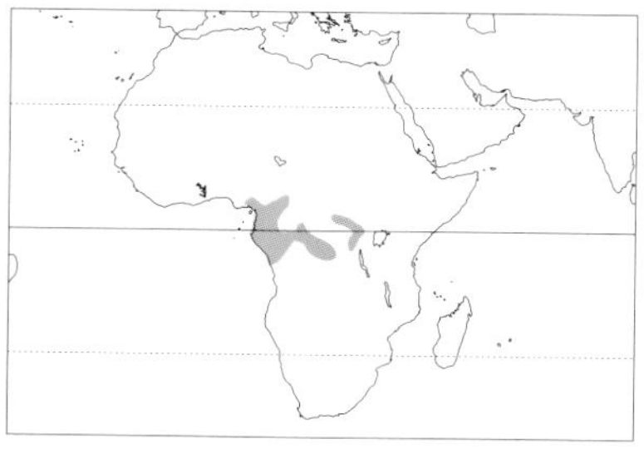

Descriptive notes. c. 16-17 cm; 24-30 g. Male has olive-brown forehead and forecrown, rarely with pale streaks, red hindcrown and nape, indistinct dark-streaked white supercilium, heavily brown-streaked ear-coverts bordered below by dark-streaked buffish cheekstripe, thin brown malar stripe; buffish-green neck sides streaked dark; whitish chin and throat spotted or streaked brown; entire upperparts green, mantle and rump rarely with faint barring; brown flight-feathers edged green, bars on inner webs; uppertail olive, edged greenish-brown, tipped dark, occasionally hint of pale green bars; pale yellowish below, breast with fairly narrow short spot-like streaks, becoming broader spots on lower underparts, bars on lower flanks; underwing yellow-white, spotted brown; undertail yellow-green; rather short bill fairly broad across nostrils, dark grey to blackish, paler base and lower mandible; iris red to red-brown; legs brown-green to yellow-green. Differs from *D. lugubris* in greener upperparts, greener tail, dark-patterned neck sides, narrower markings below. Female lacks red on head, has blackish-brown crown and nape. Juvenile duller, above greener, with brown eyes, both sexes with red patch on central crown, black nape. Race *reichenowi* differs from nominate in brighter coloration, stronger brown malar, darker tail, broader streaks below, male with slightly less red on hindcrown and female generally darker about crown. Voice. Common call a single buzzing "zh-dzeeeep", or fast repeated "dzhaah, dzhaah, dzheep" and variations.
Habitat. Inhabits forest edge, tall second growth, and edges of cultivation, generally at altitudes below 1400 m; apparently avoids open savanna-type habitats and riverine forest, as well as denser woodland.
Food and Feeding. Insects, mainly ants, and insect larvae, especially wood-boring ones. Mostly in pairs. Feeds in canopy and understorey. Forages by probing and gleaning; also pecks, and prises off pieces of bark or wood.
Breeding. Specimens with slightly enlarged gonads in Oct, and male excavating nest-hole in mid-Oct, in Nigeria; birds in breeding condition in Sept-Oct in Cameroon and Zaire; Jun in Uganda. Nest-hole in tree; no other information.
Movements. Resident.
Status and Conservation. Not globally threatened. Uncommon to locally common. Uncommon in Nigeria; locally quite common in Gabon. Present in several protected areas, e.g. Korup National Park (Cameroon) and La Lopé National Park (Gabon). Poorly known; further study required to determine its exact distribution, as well as its ecology and breeding habits.
Bibliography. Bannerman (1953), Bowden (2001), Britton (1980), Christy & Clarke (1994), Dean (2000), Dowsett (1989b), Dowsett & Dowsett-Lemaire (1991, 1993), Dowsett & Forbes-Watson (1993), Dowsett-Lemaire & Dowsett (1999, 2000), Elgood *et al*. (1994), Fry *et al*. (1988), Lippens & Wille (1976), Louette (1981b), Mackworth-Praed & Grant (1970), Sargeant (1993), Short (1980, 1985b), Snow (1978), Stevenson & Fanshawe (2001), Tarboton (1997), Thiollay (1985b).

80. Stierling's Woodpecker

Dendropicos stierlingi

French: Pic de Stierling **German**: Stierlingspecht **Spanish**: Pito de Stierling

Taxonomy. *Dendropicos stierlingi* Reichenow, 1901, Songea, Tanzania.
Relationships uncertain. Monotypic.
Distribution. S Tanzania (Songea, Lindi), N Mozambique and adjacent SW Malawi; possibly also E Zambia.

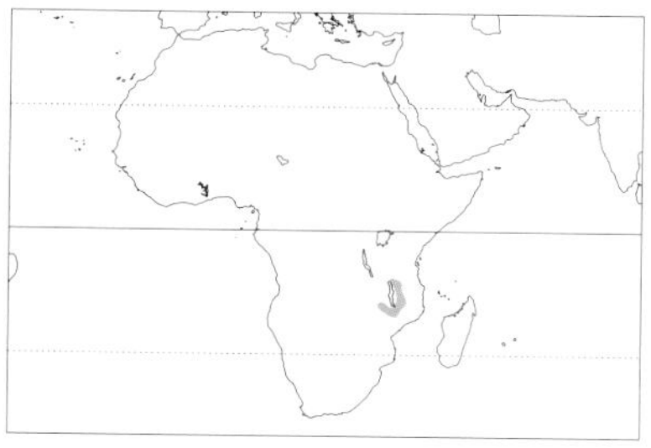

Descriptive notes. c. 17-18 cm; 25-31 g. Male has blackish-brown forehead and forecrown, in fresh plumage with narrow pale feather edges, red hindcrown and nape, white neck side and face with blackish-brown ear-coverts, broad blackish-brown malar stripe expanding on neck side and down to breast side; white chin and upper throat; black hindneck and uppermost mantle; rest of upperparts olive-brown, slightly paler tips when fresh, uppertail-coverts faintly pale-barred, occasionally reddish tips in fresh plumage; brown flight-feathers and outer wing-coverts edged olive, remiges barred white on inner webs; uppertail brown, tip yellow; lower throat chequered white and dark brown, rest of underparts scaly-looking, white with dark brown bars and shaft streaks; underwing white, spotted brown; undertail yellowish-brown; long bill fairly broad, slate-grey, paler base of lower mandible; iris red to red-brown; legs olive to grey-green. Female lacks red on head, has faintly pale-streaked brown crown, blacker nape. Juvenile duller, markings below more irregular, has brown eyes, both sexes with red in centre of crown. Voice. Common call somewhat wavering "pi-di-di, da-da-di, da-da-da-da, da-da", as territorial and long-distance communication; also soft single or repeated "pik" notes, sometimes in short bursts; "bdddt" notes in aggression; irregular "weep" series also recorded. Drumming loud, rapid, c. 5 rolls per minute.
Habitat. Inhabits rich miombo (*Brachystegia*) woodland, from lowlands up to 1500 m.
Food and Feeding. Diet includes insects and their larvae; occasionally centipedes (Chilopoda). Occurs singly or in pairs; associates loosely with mixed-species flocks. Forages in middle to upper levels of forest; may spend considerable time at one site. Investigates large to medium-sized branches, less frequently twigs. Main foraging technique consists of powerful pecking; can excavate deeply into bark; also probes in bark. During rainy season hawks alate termites (Isoptera), in rather clumsy fashion.
Breeding. Season probably Jul-Oct; nestlings in Aug in Malawi, juvenile observed in Nov in Tanzania; juvenile also reported in Mar in NW Mozambique. Nest-hole in tree; nest in Malawi contained 2 chicks. No other data.
Movements. Resident.
Status and Conservation. Not globally threatened. Not uncommon in most parts of small range, but rather localized. A generally little-known species, with few published observations. Exact status requires further investigation. Information required also on its breeding biology.
Bibliography. Benson & Benson (1977), Britton (1980), Dowsett & Dowsett-Lemaire (1993), Dowsett & Forbes-Watson (1993), Fry *et al*. (1988), Johnston-Stewart (1988), Johnston-Stewart & Heigham (1982), Mackworth-Praed & Grant (1957, 1962), Newman *et al*. (1992), Short (1980, 1985b), Short & Horne (1981), Short *et al*. (1990), Snow (1978), Stevenson & Fanshawe (2001), Tarboton (1997).

81. Bearded Woodpecker

Dendropicos namaquus

French: Pic barbu **German**: Namaspecht **Spanish**: Pito Namaqua

Taxonomy. *Picus Namaquus* A. A. H. Lichtenstein, 1793, Damaraland, Namibia.
Often placed in a separate genus *Thripias* along with *D. pyrrhogaster* and *D. xantholophus*. Races knwon to intergrade. Proposed races *saturatus* (W Central African Republic) and *decipiens* (SW Uganda and S Kenya S to C Tanzania) inseparable from nominate. Three subspecies currently recognized.

On following pages: 82. Fire-bellied Woodpecker (*Dendropicos pyrrhogaster*); 83. Golden-crowned Woodpecker (*Dendropicos xantholophus*); 84. Elliot's Woodpecker (*Dendropicos elliotii*); 85. Grey Woodpecker (*Dendropicos goertae*); 86. Grey-headed Woodpecker (*Dendropicos spodocephalus*); 87. Olive Woodpecker (*Dendropicos griseocephalus*).

Subspecies and Distribution.
D. n. namaquus (A. A. H. Lichtenstein, 1793) - W Central African Republic E to S Sudan, Uganda and W & S Kenya, and from W & S Angola across to SE Zaire and Tanzania, S to W & C Namibia, Botswana, N South Africa and N & C Mozambique.
D. n. schoensis (Rüppell, 1842) - Ethiopia, NW & S Somalia and N Kenya.
D. n. coalescens (Clancey, 1958) - C & S Mozambique and E South Africa.

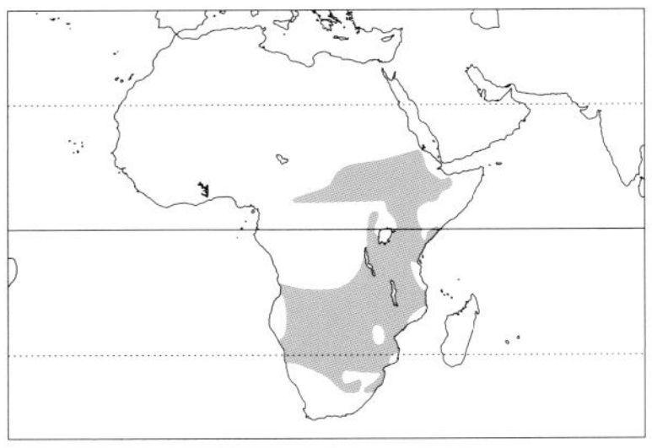

Descriptive notes. 24-27 cm; 61-89 g. Male has black forehead and forecrown with small white spots, red hindcrown sometimes with yellowish at fore edge, black nape and hindneck; whitish lores, short black stripe in front of eye; broad white supercilium curving behind black ear-coverts, broad white band from bill base backwards, dark streaks on neck side; black malar stripe broadening on throat side; white chin and throat sometimes with few dark streaks or bars; uppermost mantle black, rest of upperparts yellowish-brown with thin pale bars, rump paler, grey-brown uppertail-coverts tipped yellow (or reddish); brown wing-coverts pale-fringed, spotted white; brown flight-feathers heavily barred whitish on both webs; uppertail brownish, barred whitish, prominent yellow shafts; underparts olive-grey, browner in lower parts, all barred whitish; underwing barred blackish and grey-white; undertail dull yellowish-brown, barred paler; very long bill broad, grey-black, paler base of lower mandible; iris reddish-brown or red; legs grey, often tinged olive or green. Female resembles male, but bill slightly shorter, no red on head. Juvenile tinged green and more diffusely barred above than adult, has eyes greyer or browner, both sexes with red crown patch mixed with black and usually heavily white-spotted, red sometimes extending to nape. Race *schoensis* is shorter-winged than nominate, browner above, sometimes with black bar between rear ear-coverts and malar, markings below more as spots or arrowheads; *coalescens* is darker, olive-brown with broken barring above, often red-tipped tail-coverts, darker grey below, bars on breast incomplete. Voice. Common call an accelerating rattle series of 5-15 "wik" notes, similar to song of Grey-headed Kingfisher (*Halcyon leucocephala*); chattering "wickwickwickwickwick-wick-wick" series; also "chip chip chip"; loud nasal scream also recorded; piping cackle by nestlings. Drums loudly, each roll followed by 4 regular taps, "trrrrrrr-tap-tap-tap-tap", longer rolls than those of *D. pyrrhogaster*.
Habitat. Open woodland with large trees. Favours wooded dry savanna, especially with mopane (*Colophospermum*), also edges of riparian fringing forest, and taller *Acacia* on alluvium soils; occurs regularly in miombo (*Brachystegia*) woodland, *Euphorbia-Acacia* woodland, and bushland. Least numerous in richer woodland, and avoids moist mountain slopes. In Somalia, associated with tall trees bordering seasonal rivers and groups of larger trees in grasslands in N, and lowland riverine forest in more open areas in S. Ranges from sea-level to at least 2600 m, locally to 3000 m; to 1800 m in Ethiopia; mostly at 900-1350 m in N Somalia.
Food and Feeding. Diet consists of insects and their larvae, particularly wood-boring beetles and their larvae, caterpillars and ants; also takes spiders. Will pursue geckos or small lizards, and then feeds them to young. Seen mostly singly and in pairs. Forages at all levels, from ground up to canopy. Foraging ranges large, and may cover lengthy distances between foraging localities; spends long periods at a single site. Forages on dead trees, preferentially larger ones, often high on trunk, and on larger and smaller branches. Females apparently prefer smaller trees and smaller branches than those exploited by males. Excavates with vigorous pecking and hammering; also probes, and gleans to some extent.
Breeding. Probably Jun-Oct in Angola; Apr/May-Jun in Ethiopia; laying recorded in late Sept in N Somalia; Apr-Oct in Kenya, Jun-Nov in Tanzania, Jun-Jul in Malawi, and Jun-Dec in Zimbabwe and Zambia; May-Nov in South Africa, mostly May-Aug. Nest-hole excavated at 2-20 m in dead part of tree, rather large entrance 7·5 cm high, 5·5 cm wide; may be reused several times; territory large. Clutch 2-4 eggs, usually 3; both parents incubate, period 13 days; both provide equally for chicks, nestling period c. 27 days.
Movements. Resident.
Status and Conservation. Not globally threatened. Widespread and fairly common, but often very local; seldom numerous. Not uncommon in Angola; fairly common in Ethiopia; uncommon in Somalia; uncommon to fairly common and local in Kenya; locally common in Namibia. Occurs in numerous protected areas, e.g. Awash National Park (Ethiopia), Lake Nakuru and Samburu National Parks (Kenya), Serengeti and Mikumi National Parks (Tanzania), Etosha National Park (Namibia) and Mkuzi Game Reserve (South Africa). Apparent scarcity in some areas is possibly due to the fact that it occupies large home ranges.
Bibliography. Ash & Miskell (1983, 1998), Benson & Benson (1977), Benson *et al.* (1971), Brown, C.J. (1993), Brown, L.H. & Britton (1980), Carroll (1988), Clancey (1958b, 1989a), Davey (1994), Dean (2000), Dowsett & Dowsett-Lemaire (1993), Dowsett & Forbes-Watson (1993), Farnsworth *et al.* (2000), Fry *et al.* (1988), Ginn *et al.* (1989), Harrison *et al.* (1997), Hines (1995), Irwin (1981), Lewis & Pomeroy (1989), Lippens & Wille (1976), Mackworth-Praed & Grant (1957, 1962), Maclean (1993), Nikolaus (1987), Oatley (2001), Penry (1994), Pinto (1983), Pringle (1991), Short (1980, 1985b), Short & Horne (1988b), Short *et al.* (1990), Skead (1967), Snow (1978), Tarboton (1970, 1997, 2001), Tarboton *et al.* (1987), Urban & Brown (1971), Zimmerman *et al.* (1996).

82. Fire-bellied Woodpecker
Dendropicos pyrrhogaster

French: Pic à ventre de feu **German**: Rotbauchspecht **Spanish**: Pito Ventrirrojo

Taxonomy. *Picus (Chloropicus) Pyrrhogaster* Malherbe,1845, South Africa; error = Sierra Leone.
Often placed in a separate genus *Thripias* along with *D. namaquus* and *D. xantholophus*. Forms a superspecies with latter. Monotypic.
Distribution. Sierra Leone and S Guinea E to S Nigeria (Niger Delta) and SW Cameroon.
Descriptive notes. c. 24 cm; 63-74 g. Male has brownish-black forehead, red crown to nape, rarely buffish-yellow in crown centre, black feather bases more obvious in worn plumage; white lores, black ear-coverts curving down at rear; neck side and rest of face white, with black malar stripe continuing to breast side; white chin and throat; bronze-green mantle, scapulars and back, often some indistinct bars and red tips to feathers when fresh; red rump and uppertail-coverts with black feather bases; brownish bronze-green wing-coverts narrowly fringed paler, few pale spots on medians; brown flight-feathers narrowly edged paler, inner webs with broad white bars, outerwebs with narrow yellow-white bars; uppertail olive-black; broad red band centrally from breast to vent, broad black streaks on upper breast sides, rest of underparts off-white with heavy arrowhead barring; underwing whitish; undertail dull yellow-green; long bill broad, dark grey,

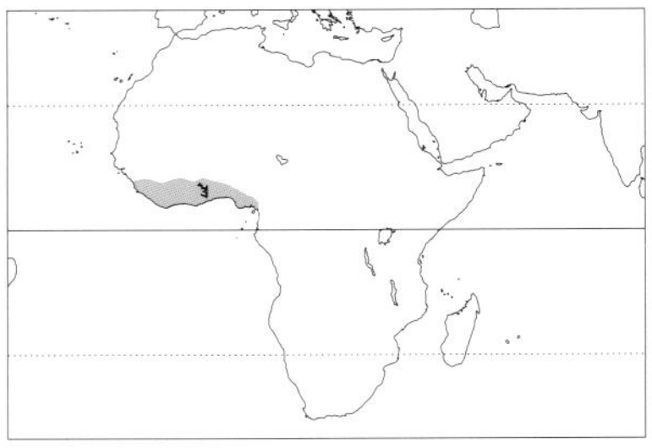

paler lower mandible; iris brown to red; legs green to grey-green. Female has slightly shorter bill, relatively longer tail than male, no red on head. Juvenile duller, less bronzy above, black areas of plumage browner, red areas duller and less extensive, eyes brown, both sexes with red on crown, on female red mixed with brown. Voice. Sharp "wip"; "wip-wi-di-di-di-dit" as long-distance call. Drums often in loud accelerating rolls weakening towards end, rolls shorter than those of *D. namaquus* and *D. xantholophus*.
Habitat. Inhabits primary and secondary forest in lowlands and on lower slopes. Prefers the vicinity of large trees, and not uncommon at edges and clearings with fire-killed trees; also visits tall trees, often dead ones, along rivers or in isolated forest patches, and forest-grassland mosaic.
Food and Feeding. Diet consists of insects, larvae of beetles and white ants. Often forages in pairs; will join mixed-species flocks. Forages in upper levels of trees, at 10-40 m; may descend to fallen logs. Inspects branches mostly of 5-30 cm in diameter. Excavates in search of food by means of pecking and hammering.
Breeding. Nov-Feb in Sierra Leone; Nov-Mar, also nestlings once in Jul, in Liberia; breeds Oct-Mar, possibly from Aug/Sept, in Nigeria. Nest-hole excavated at 20-30 m or higher in tree, often in dead branch. No information on clutch size and incubation and nestling periods.
Movements. Resident.
Status and Conservation. Not globally threatened. Generally common. Not uncommon in Sierra Leone; not uncommon in Liberia, where densities of more than 3 pairs/km², estimated population 60,000 pairs; common in Nigeria. Benefits from practice of forest clearance whereby largest trees are left standing, to die naturally; this species' preference for big trees means that resultant habitat provides ideal conditions, although only temporarily. Present in several protected areas, e.g. Gola Forests Reserves (Sierra Leone), Taï Forest National Park (Ivory Coast) and Korup National Park (Cameroon).
Bibliography. Allport *et al.* (1989), Ash & Sharland (1986), Bannerman (1953), Cheke & Walsh (1996), Cheke *et al.* (1986), Colston & Curry-Lindahl (1986), Dowsett & Dowsett-Lemaire (1993), Dowsett & Forbes-Watson (1993), Elgood *et al.* (1994), Farmer (1979), Fry *et al.* (1988), Gartshore *et al.* (1995), Gatter (1988, 1997), Grimes (1987), Hopkins (1998), Louette (1981b), Mackworth-Praed & Grant (1970), Ntiamoa-Baidu, Asamoah *et al.* (2000), Ntiamoa-Baidu, Owusu *et al.* (2000), Rand (1951), Salewski (2000), Short (1980, 1985b), Short & Horne (1988b), Snow (1978), Sørensen *et al.* (1996), Thiollay (1985a, 1985b), Waltert *et al.* (1999).

83. Golden-crowned Woodpecker
Dendropicos xantholophus

French: Pic à couronne d'or **German**: Scheitelfleckspecht **Spanish**: Pito Coronado
Other common names: Yellow-crested Woodpecker

Taxonomy. *Dendropicus* [sic] *xantholophus* Hargitt, 1883, Gabon.
Often placed in a separate genus *Thripias* along with *D. namaquus* and *D. pyrrhogaster*. Forms a superspecies with latter. Monotypic.
Distribution. SW Cameroon E to S Sudan, W & C Uganda and extreme W Kenya, and S to NW Angola and SW & SC Zaire; unconfirmed sight records from Nigeria thought to be unreliable.

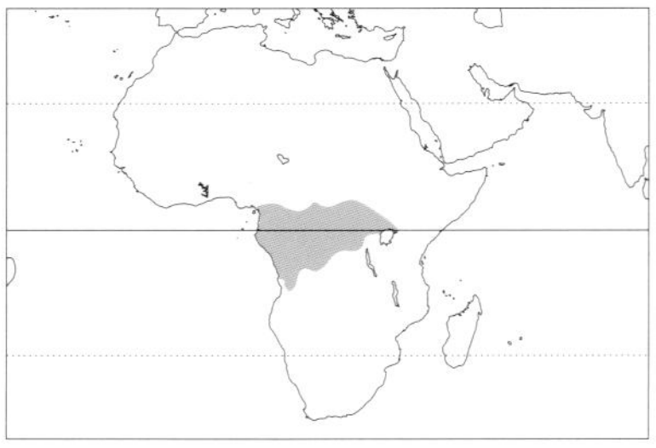

Descriptive notes. c. 25 cm; 50-73 g. Male has brown forehead merging into blackish crown, crown feathers with few white speckles, broad yellow tips, black nape and hindneck; white lores, broad black band from just before eye through ear-coverts and down to side of neck; rest of neck and face white, black malar stripe broadening on side of throat; white chin and throat, lower throat tinged olive and with row of black spots; uppermost mantle black, rest of upperparts olive-brown, mantle sometimes with few faint paler bars, rump and uppertail-coverts with narrow yellow tips; olive wing-coverts with variable number of pale tips and subterminal spots; brownish-black flight-feathers narrowly edged and tipped green, barred white on both webs; uppertail black; greenish-olive below, breast with white spots, flanks to belly and undertail-coverts barred whitish; underwing off-white; undertail dull blackish; bill long and broad, dark grey to black, paler cutting edges, paler lower mandible; iris red to brown; legs green to olive or brownish. Female is slightly shorter-billed than male, has no yellow on crown. Juvenile duller and greener above, greyer and more barred below, has eyes less red, both sexes with hindcrown feathers tipped yellow, less on female. Voice. Single "dit" and "dit-it" notes to fast bursts of purring "ddditrrrrrr" and grating "grrrrrr"; also very fast "dddit, graa" and "a-wik a-wik" during encounters. Both sexes drum, rolls accelerating, weakening towards end, longer than rolls of *D. pyrrhogaster*.
Habitat. Mainly areas with large trees in lowland forest, forest edge, also in nearby thick secondary growth, occasionally densely wooded areas and cultivated plantations (e.g. coffee, cocoa); visits isolated large trees outside forest. Lowlands to c. 1700 m; to 2150 m in E.
Food and Feeding. Diet largely of wood-boring beetles and their larvae; also takes other insects (ants), and spiders. Mostly singly or in pairs. Forages in middle and upper storeys; pecks strongly and hammers or removes bark. Also takes prey on the wing.
Breeding. Probably Oct-Mar in Cameroon, and Jan-Apr and Sept elsewhere in W; Jun-Sept in Angola; Sept-Mar in Uganda and Kenya. Nest-hole excavated by both sexes, at up to 17 m in dead tree or dead section of tree. No other information available.
Movements. Resident.
Status and Conservation. Not globally threatened. Common forest woodpecker. Considered common in Angola; uncommon in Kenya. Rather poorly known, but appears to be under no threat. Present in several protected areas, e.g. Korup and Mount Kupé National Parks (Cameroon), Kakmenga Nature Reserve (Kenya) and Nyungwe Forest Reserve (Rwanda).
Bibliography. Bannerman (1953), Bowden (2001), Britton (1980), Brown & Britton (1980), Carroll (1988), Cave & Macdonald (1955), Christy & Clarke (1994), Dean (2000), Dowsett & Dowsett-Lemaire (1993), Dowsett & Forbes-Watson (1993), Dowsett-Lemaire & Dowsett (2000), Elgood *et al.* (1994), Fry *et al.* (1988), Lippens & Wille (1976), Louette (1981b), Mackworth-Praed & Grant (1957, 1962), Nikolaus (1987), Pedersen (2000), Pinto

(1983), Short (1971b, 1971d, 1980, 1985b), Short & Horne (1988b), Short *et al.* (1990), Snow (1978), Stevenson & Fanshawe (2001), Tarboton (1997), Thiollay (1985b), Zimmerman (1972), Zimmerman *et al.* (1996).

84. Elliot's Woodpecker

Dendropicos elliotii

French: Pic d'Elliot **German**: Elliotspecht **Spanish**: Pito de Elliot
Other common names: Johnston's Woodpecker (*johnstoni*)

Taxonomy. *Polipicus Elliotii* Cassin, 1863, Muni River, Gabon.
Sometimes placed in a separate genus *Mesopicos* along with *D. goertae*, *D. spodocephalus* and *D. griseocephalus*; in past, sometimes separated alone in genus *Polipicus*. Race *johnstoni* regarded by some authors as a separate species, but interbreeds with nominate in Cameroon; apparent intermediates between these two races on Mt Kupé have been separated by some authors as race *kupeensis* but probably best considered a hybrid population. Other named races are *schultzei* (Bioko I) and *sordidatus* (Oku district, in Bamenda Highlands of Cameroon), both of which seem indistinguishable from *johnstoni*. Angolan birds formerly split as race *gabela* or *angolensis* but they differ from nominate barely, if at all. Two subspecies currently recognized.
Subspecies and Distribution.
D. e. johnstoni (Shelley, 1887) - highlands of SE Nigeria, SW Cameroon and Bioko I.
D. e. elliotii (Cassin, 1863) - lowland SW Cameroon and SW Central African Republic discontinuously to Gabon and W Angola (Cuanza Norte S to Benguela), and E across W, SC & NE Zaire to SW & E Uganda (Kibale S to Bwindi Forest, also Mt Elgon).

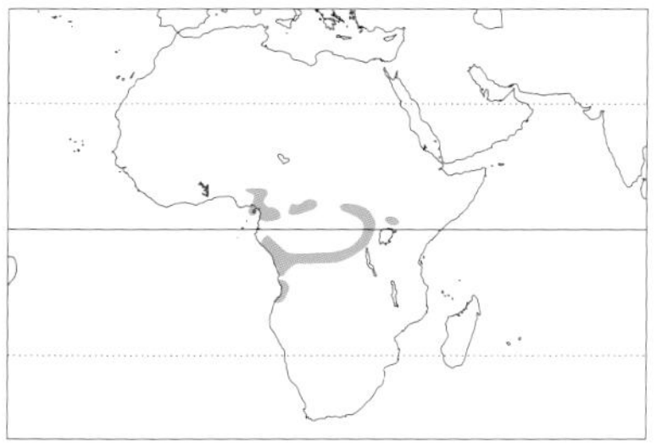

Descriptive notes. c. 20-22 cm; 32-40 g. Male has black forehead and forecrown, red hindcrown and nape, reddish-buff lores; crown sides and rest of head buff, rear ear-coverts and neck sides tinged greenish, very thin dark malar line; white chin and throat narrowly streaked olive; entire upperparts plain green with bronze or brownish tinge; brown flight-feathers broadly edged bronzy-green on outer webs, white on inner webs; uppertail brown, feathers edged green, outer rectrices occasionally barred buff at base; pale yellowish to yellow-brown below with broadly brown or olive streaks, often becoming bars on flanks and belly; underwing yellowish-white; undertail yellow-brown; bill longish, broad, greyish to black, often tipped yellowish, paler lower mandible; iris red-brown to red; legs grey or green, tinged olive or brown. Female has forehead to nape entirely black. Juvenile duller overall, more streaked below, with browner eyes, male with red on crown, female red on rear crown. Race *johnstoni* has greenish-yellow underparts with streaking very fine and sparse, or even lacking. Voice. Shrill "bwe-bwe" notes and series reported; voice apparently similar to that of *D. goertae*. Weak drumrolls.
Habitat. Dense primary forest, also secondary forest with tall trees. In moist, gloomy, mossy montane forest at up to 2320 m in NE of range; elsewhere, nominate race found from upland areas down to lowlands. Race *johnstoni* restricted to montane areas.
Food and Feeding. Larvae of beetles, also other insects. Occurs singly or in pairs; joins mixed-species flocks, occasionally with other woodpecker species. Forages at all levels of forest, including understorey. Moves rapidly, not staying for long at a single site. Pecks powerfully, and probes into epiphytes (mosses) on branches and on very large leaves.
Breeding. Birds in breeding condition in Sept in Angola, in Oct-Nov in Cameroon; young birds seen in Dec and Jan on Bioko. One nest-hole in Cameroon was 8 m up a tree. No further information available.
Movements. Resident.
Status and Conservation. Not globally threatened. Generally uncommon. Race *johnstoni* not uncommon throughout range, in Nigeria and Cameroon and also on Bioko. Nominate is uncommon in Angola; uncommon to rare in Uganda. Within its range species has a very patchy distribution; range may perhaps be more extensive than currently known. Research needed to determine details of this species' breeding habits and biology. Occurs in several protected areas, e.g. Gashaka-Gumti Reserve (Nigeria), Korup and Mount Kupé National Parks (Cameroon), Impenetrable Forest and Kibale Forest National Parks (Uganda), Nyungwe Forest Reserve (Rwanda) and Kibira National Park (Burundi).
Bibliography. Ash *et al.* (1989), Bannerman (1953), Bowden (2001), Britton (1980), Carroll (1988), Dean (2000), Demey *et al.* (2000), Dowsett (1989a, 1989b, 1990), Dowsett & Dowsett-Lemaire (1993, 1997), Dowsett & Forbes-Watson (1993), Dowsett-Lemaire & Dowsett (1998, 1999, 2000), Elgood *et al.* (1994), Fotso (2001), Fry *et al.* (1988), Green (1990), Larison *et al.* (2000), Lippens & Wille (1976), Louette (1981b), Mackworth-Praed & Grant (1957, 1962, 1970), Pedersen (2000), Pérez del Val (1996), Pérez del Val *et al.* (1994), Pinto (1983), Short (1980, 1985b), Short *et al.* (1990), Snow (1978), Stevenson & Fanshawe (2001), Tarboton (1997).

85. Grey Woodpecker

Dendropicos goertae

French: Pic goertan **German**: Graubrustspecht **Spanish**: Pito Gris Occidental
Other common names: African Grey Woodpecker

Taxonomy. *Picus Goertae* P. L. S. Müller, 1776, Senegal.
Often placed with *D. spodocephalus* and *D. griseocephalus* in a separate genus *Mesopicos*, sometimes also including *D. elliotii*; forms a superspecies with the first two, hybridizing with them where ranges meet; often treated as conspecific with *D. spodocephalus*. Races intergrade. Proposed races *agmen* (tree-savanna belt from Gambia S to Liberia and across to EC Sudan), *centralis* (savanna from Cameroon to SW Sudan and W Kenya) and *oreites* (highlands of C Cameroon) all considered inseparable from nominate. Four subspecies currently recognized.
Subspecies and Distribution.
D. g. koenigi (Neumann, 1903) - Sahel zone from EC Mali E to W & S Sudan.
D. g. goertae (P. L. S. Müller, 1776) - SW Mauritania and Senegambia E to S Sudan and W & C Kenya, and S to NE Zaire, Rwanda and NW Tanzania.
D. g. abessinicus (Reichenow, 1900) - E Sudan and N & W Ethiopia.
D. g. meridionalis Louette & Prigogine, 1982 - S Gabon to NW Angola (Cabinda, possibly S to Malanje), and SC Zaire.
Descriptive notes. c. 20 cm; 40·5-52·5 g. Male has grey forehead and forecrown, red hindcrown and nape sometimes with grey feather bases showing on hindcrown; rest of head grey, on ear-

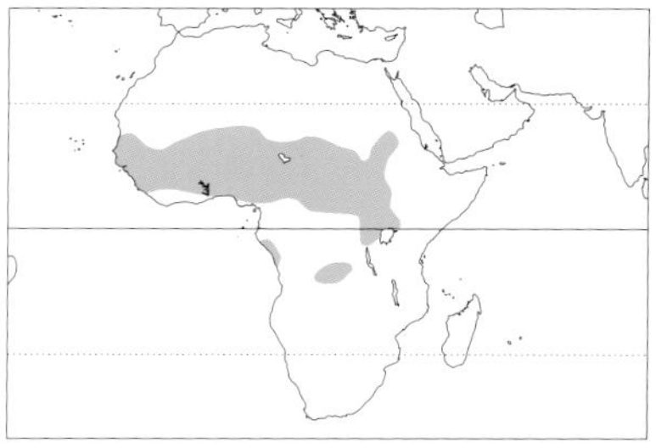

coverts sometimes darker, hindneck and sides of neck often tinged buffish to olive, obscure whitish supercilium behind eye, faint whitish malar stripe extending to lores and base of forehead; pale grey chin and throat; upperparts bronze-green to olive-green or brownish-green, red rump and uppertail-coverts; wing-coverts edged and tipped paler, hint of pale bars; brown flight-feathers barred pale, bars strongest on inner webs; uppertail brown, pale bars not quite meeting in centre; pale grey below, normally faintly tinged pale yellow, flanks with variable but usually weak white and yellowish-white bars, belly with small yellow or orange-yellow central patch (rarely mixed with red); underwing barred black and white; undertail brown, obscurely barred pale, suffused yellow; longish bill straight, broad, slaty-grey to black, paler lower mandible; iris red to brown; legs greenish-grey, suffused chalky, with whitish joints. Distinguished from *D. spodocephalus* mainly by much smaller orange, not red, belly patch, more barred wings and tail; from *D. griseocephalus* also by paler coloration. Female has slightly shorter bill than male, no red on head. Juvenile duller above than adult, lacking bronze tinge, has red of rump paler, more obvious pale facial markings, grey-brown eyes, more barring below, smaller paler belly patch, both sexes with red in crown centre, more extensive on male. Race *koenigi* is noticeably paler than nominate, has pale bars and spots on lower back and wings, somewhat stronger pale facial markings, yellow belly patch small but more often lacking; *abessinicus* has pale supercilium, whiter malar, darker face, red belly patch; *meridionalis* resembles nominate, but browner above, no yellowish tinge below. Voice. Series of 20-30 "wik" notes as long-distance call; irregular series of "week" or "weeka" during interactions; also "pew" and "pit-it". Drums rarely.
Habitat. Inhabits woodland, wooded grassland and pasture, riverine woodland, thickets with larger trees, forest edges, gardens, cultivations with trees; shows strong liking for palms. Also found in mangroves in W of range.
Food and Feeding. Ants, termites (Isoptera), beetle larvae, other insects; also observed hunting crabs among aerial roots of mangroves, and taking nuts of oil palm (*Elaeis guineensis*). Seen in pairs or family groups. Forages mostly at medium levels, on live and dead trees, on larger branches and trunks; also descends to ground. Moves rapidly. Main technique pecking, excavating for prey. Some insects taken on the wing.
Breeding. Dec-Jun in W of range, from Oct in Sierra Leone, Jan-Mar in Nigeria, Dec-Feb and Jul-Sept in Zaire, and Feb-Jul and Sept-Nov in E Africa. Nest excavated by both sexes, at 0·3-20 m in dead tree or dead section of tree, or dead palm, once in telegraph pole; cavity depth 25-30 cm. Clutch 2-4 eggs; no further information.
Movements. Mostly resident. Some movement in non-breeding season; recorded in Mauritania at Atar, well N of breeding range, also isolated records from S Nigeria and Ghana coast.
Status and Conservation. Not globally threatened. Fairly common to common, and widespread. Commonest woodpecker in Senegambia; common in Sierra Leone. Uncommon in Liberia, estimated population 2000 pairs. Uncommon in Angola; fairly common in Kenya. Occurs in several protected areas, including W National Park (Niger), Bénoué National Park (Cameroon) and Serengeti National Park (Tanzania).
Bibliography. Bannerman (1953), Barlow *et al.* (1997), Britton (1980), Brown & Britton (1980), Carroll (1988), Cave & Macdonald (1955), Cheesman & Sclater (1935), Cheke & Walsh (1996), Dean (2000), Dowsett (1989b), Dowsett & Dowsett-Lemaire (1993), Dowsett & Forbes-Watson (1993), Fry *et al.* (1988), Gaugris *et al.* (1981), Gee (1984), Giraudoux *et al.* (1988), Gore (1990), Green (1996), Grimes (1987), Jensen & Kirkeby (1980), Lamarche (1988), Lewis & Pomeroy (1989), Lippens & Wille (1976), Louette (1981b), Louette & Prigogine (1982), Mackworth-Praed & Grant (1957, 1962, 1970), Moore (1980), Morel & Morel (1990), Newby (1987), Nikolaus (1987, 2000), Pinto (1983), Prigogine & Louette (1983), Rodwell *et al.* (1996), Sauvage & Rodwell (1998), Schmidl (1982), Short (1980, 1985b), Short & Horne (1988b), Short *et al.* (1990), Snow (1978), Tarboton (1997), Urban & Brown (1971), Vande weghe (1981), Wilkinson & Beecroft (1988), Zimmerman *et al.* (1996).

86. Grey-headed Woodpecker

Dendropicos spodocephalus

French: Pic spodocéphale **German**: Graukopfspecht **Spanish**: Pito Gris Oriental
Other common names: Eastern Grey Woodpecker

Taxonomy. *Dendrobates spodocephalus* Bonaparte, 1850, West Africa; error = Shewa, southern Ethiopia.
Often placed with *D. goertae* and *D. griseocephalus* in a separate genus *Mesopicos*, sometimes also including *D. elliotii*; forms a superspecies with the first two, hybridizing with them where ranges meet; often treated as conspecific with *D. goertae*. Two subspecies recognized.
Subspecies and Distribution.
D. s. spodocephalus (Bonaparte, 1850) - E Sudan and W & C Ethiopian Highlands.
D. s. rhodeogaster (Fischer & Reichenow, 1884) - highlands of C & SW Kenya and NC Tanzania.

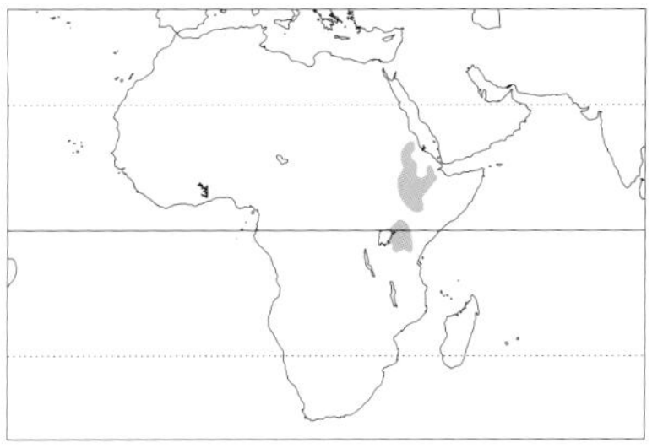

Descriptive notes. 20 cm; 43-52 g. Male has red hindcrown and nape, sometimes some grey feather bases visible when worn; entire rest of head grey, including forehead, forecrown and hindneck, ear-coverts sometimes slightly darker; upperparts green, rump and uppertail-coverts red; dark brown flight-feathers edged yellowish-green on outer webs, broadly on tertials, whitish bars on inner webs of primaries and secondaries; uppertail dark brown, outer feathers barred white on outer webs; grey below, red patch from central belly to vent, sometimes to undertail-coverts; underwing barred blackish and white; undertail brown, outer feathers barred yellowish; fairly long bill straight, broad, slaty-grey to black, paler lower mandible; iris red to brown; legs light greenish-grey, joints white. Differs from *D. goertae* in brighter upperparts, more uniform grey head and underparts, larger and red belly patch, less barred tail; from *D. griseocephalus* mainly in paler general coloration. Female has slightly shorter bill than male, no red on head. Juvenile duller, with red of rump paler, indication of barring below, smaller red belly patch, grey-brown eyes, both sexes with red in crown centre, more extensive on male. Race *rhodeogaster* resembles nominate, but has bright yellow feather tips on upperparts, darker underparts. VOICE. Series of "wik" notes, also irregular series of "weeka" in interactions, very like *D. goertae*. Drums rarely.

Habitat. Moist forest, forest edge, and riverine forest, in highlands, up to at least 3300 m.

Food and Feeding. Diet includes Geophilidae centipedes, lepidopteran pupae and larvae. Found singly or in pairs at middle levels and on ground. Pecks at trees; hawks insects opportunistically.

Breeding. Season Aug-Apr in Ethiopia; breeds in most months in Kenya and N Tanzania, peak in Apr-May and Jul-Oct. Nest-hole in tree; no other details, presumably as for *D. goertae*.

Movements. Resident.

Status and Conservation. Not globally threatened. Generally quite common within its limited range. Quite common in Kenya. Present in several protected areas, e.g. Mt Kenya, Lake Nakuru and Amboseli National Parks (Kenya) and Ngurdoto Crater National Park (Tanzania).

Bibliography. Britton (1980), Cheesman & Sclater (1935), Friedmann (1930a), Fry *et al.* (1988), Mackworth-Praed & Grant (1957), Prigogine & Louette (1983), Short & Horne (1988b), Short *et al.* (1990), Urban & Brown (1971), Wheatley (1995).

87. **Olive Woodpecker**

Dendropicos griseocephalus

French: Pic olive   **German**: Goldrückenspecht   **Spanish**: Pito Oliváceo

Taxonomy. *Picus griseocephalus* Boddaert, 1783, Cape of Good Hope.

Often placed with *D. goertae* and *D. spodocephalus* in a separate genus *Mesopicos*, sometimes also including *D. elliotii*; forms a superspecies with the first two, interbreeding where ranges meet. Proposed race *persimilis* (Angola to N Malawi) inseparable from *ruwenzori*. Three subspecies currently recognized.

Subspecies and Distribution.

D. g. ruwenzori (Sharpe, 1902) - Angolan highlands, and E Zaire and SW Uganda (Ruwenzoris and Impenetrable Forest), S to NC & NE Namibia, SC Zambia and N Malawi.

D. g. kilimensis (Neumann, 1926) - Tanzanian highlands: Mt Kilimanjaro, Mt Meru, and mountains of N Pare, Usambara, Uluguru and Udzungwa.

D. g. griseocephalus (Boddaert, 1783) - extreme S Mozambique (Lebombo Mts) and E & S South Africa (E Natal to S Cape Province).

Descriptive notes. 20 cm; 33-51 g. Male has red hindcrown and nape feathers often with some fine black subterminal bars, grey bases often evident in worn plumage; rest of head, including forehead, forecrown, hindneck, chin and throat, darkish grey; dull olive-green upperparts tinged bronze (brighter in N & E of range); red rump and uppertail-coverts, latter sometimes showing dark bases; wing-coverts edged paler bronze-green; dark brown flight-feathers sometimes with pale spots on inner webs, with olive-green edges sometimes reddish-tinged; uppertail blackish-brown or black, feathers edged olive; bronze-olive below, breast with distinct golden tinge, belly and undertail-coverts much greyer, sometimes very small red patch on belly, occasionally obscure whitish bars on flanks; underwing pale brownish; undertail brownish, yellow tinge to outer feathers; longish bill straight, broad, grey to blackish, lower mandible paler and tinged green or blue; iris brown; legs grey to greyish-olive or olive-grey. Distinguished from *D. goertae* and *D. spodocephalus* by much darker general coloration, unbarred tail, golden breast. Female has shorter bill than male, entirely grey head without red. Juvenile duller, greener above, greyer below, paler red on rump, usually barred below, red belly patch paler if present, both sexes with black-barred red in crown centre, red more extensive on male. Race *ruwenzori* is brighter than nominate, has yellower or more golden tinge above, golden or yellow-olive breast, flight-feathers more clearly barred, red belly patch sometimes fairly extensive; *kilimensis* averages smaller than other races, has less yellow in upperparts, greyer underparts, always lacks red on belly, can have red eyes. VOICE. Long, slightly nasal trilled whistle

of 3-4 notes, "whee-whee-whee"; "pep" to "pep-pep-pep" conversational notes within groups; soft "tick" alarm, sometimes followed by contracted trill, "chi-r-r-r--re"; "tweet" on take-off, "wat-chew" in flight; repeated "wer chick" with head movements; also quiet "kiwi-kiwi-kiwi" between two birds at close distance; soft, high-pitched "kee-kee-kee-kee-kee" twitter by nestlings. Drums in soft, fast rolls.

Habitat. Forest, evergreen thickets and dense woodland, and forest fringing watercourses, in uplands; usually in more open parts, as in *Hagenia* forest. Shows some preference for forest patches rather than continuous closed forest. More common inland in evergreen forest; less in thick coastal bush, but the only picid species likely to be found in that habitat type in South Africa. Occurs at altitudes of between 450 m and 3700 m; usually higher up and in denser forest than *D. spodocephalus* on Mt Kilimanjaro (Tanzania); low-level records may involve stragglers.

Food and Feeding. Insects and their larvae, particularly ants, beetles (Scarabaeidae). Occurs singly or in pairs, often in parties of up to 6; frequently joins mixed-species feeding flocks. Strictly arboreal, forages on upper trunks and on branches, preferring small trees and small branches in larger trees. Moves quickly through a tree, often shifting sideways or backwards. Forages at 1-24 m; preferred heights between 10 m and 15 m, modal height 12 m. Pecks with lateral blows, excavating for large larvae; probes frequently among mosses, gleans from bark.

Breeding. Possibly Apr-Jun in Tanzania; breeds Feb-Sept in Zaire, Jul-Sept in Malawi, May-Jul in Zambia, Sept in Natal and Zululand, and Oct-Nov in the Cape; Jun in Angola; sometimes 2 broods in a season. Male helpers present at some nests. Head-swinging displays with calling. Nest-hole excavated mostly by male, at 1·5-18 m in dead trunk or dead branch, sometimes on underside of horizontal branch; territory small. Clutch usually 2 or 3 eggs; both sexes incubate, period 15-17 days; both also feed chicks and tend to nest sanitation, possibly with one or two helpers, female may feed brood more frequently but often with smaller amounts, and collects food close to nest, whereas male makes longer foraging trips; partners roost together in nest during egg and nestling stages; fledging period c. 26 days; often only one young reared successfully, cared for by parents for further 3 months or more, during which family roosts together in nest, or male alone accompanies young; if two juveniles reared, parents accompany one each. Nests parasitized by Scaly-throated Honeyguide (*Indicator variegatus*).

Movements. Resident; possibly some local short-distance or vertical movements.

Status and Conservation. Not globally threatened. Variably common to uncommon in most of range, but local to scarce in Tanzania; uncommon in Angola; generally common in South Africa. Densities vary from 2·2 pairs/10 ha in forest patches to 0·2-0·3 pairs/10 ha in more continuous forest. Present in several protected areas, e.g. Impenetrable Forest National Park (Uganda), Kahuzi-Biega National Park (Zaire), Nyungwe Forest Reserve (Rwanda), Kibira National Park (Burundi) and Oribi Gorge Nature Reserve and Langeberg, Hlabeni, Balgoan and Ngoye Forest Reserves (South Africa).

Bibliography. Benson & Benson (1977), Benson *et al.* (1971), Britton (1980), Brown & Britton (1980), Clancey (1992), Dean (2000), Dowsett (1990), Dowsett & Dowsett-Lemaire (1993), Dowsett & Forbes-Watson (1993), Dowsett-Lemaire (1983c), Earlé (1989), Fry *et al.* (1988), Ginn *et al.* (1989), Harrison *et al.* (1997), Holland (1997), Irwin (1981), Leonard (1998a), Lippens & Wille (1976), Liversidge (1959), Mackworth-Praed & Grant (1957, 1962, 1970), Maclean (1993), Pinto (1983), Richardson (1989), Short (1980, 1985b), Short & Horne (1988b), Short *et al.* (1990), Sigfried (1989), Snow (1978), Tarboton (1997, 2001), Tarboton *et al.* (1987), Van der Merwe (1986), Vande weghe (1981), Zimmerman *et al.* (1996).

PLATE 32 ➤

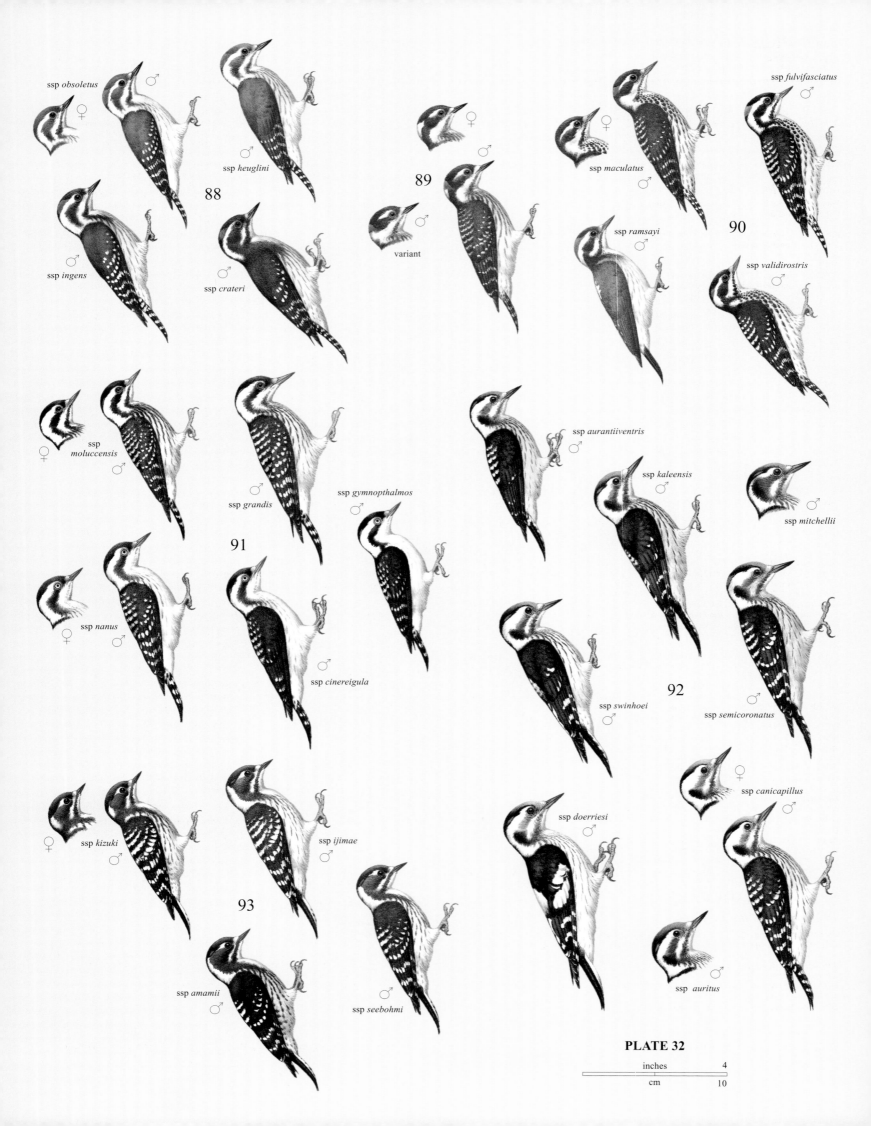

ssp *obsoletus* ♀

♂

ssp *heuglini*

♂

ssp *ingens*

♂

ssp *crateri*

88

89

♀

♂

variant

ssp *maculatus* ♀

ssp *fulvifasciatus* ♂

ssp *ramsayi*

90

ssp *validirostris* ♂

♀

ssp *moluccensis*

♂

ssp *grandis*

♂

ssp *gymnopthalmos*

♂

91

ssp *aurantiiventris*

♂

ssp *kaleensis*

♂

ssp *mitchellii* ♂

♀

ssp *nanus*

ssp *cinereigula*

♂

ssp *swinhoei*

♂

92

ssp *semicoronatus*

♀

ssp *kizuki*

♂

ssp *ijimae*

♂

♀

ssp *canicapillus*

ssp *doerriesi* ♂

93

ssp *amamii* ♂

ssp *seebohmi*

♂

ssp *auritus* ♂

PLATE 32

inches 4

cm 10

Genus *DENDROCOPOS* Koch, 1816

88. Brown-backed Woodpecker

Dendrocopos obsoletus

French: Pic à dos brun **German**: Braunrückenspecht **Spanish**: Pico Dorsipardo
Other common names: Lesser White-spotted Woodpecker

Taxonomy. *Picus obsoletus* Wagler, 1829, Senegambia.
Genus sometimes merged into *Picoides*. Species has also been included with other African species in *Dendropicos*, but probably more closely related to Asian *D. temminckii*, *D. maculatus* and *D. moluccensis*. S Ethiopian birds described as a separate race *nigricans*, but considered indistinguishable from *ingens*. Four subspecies recognized.
Subspecies and Distribution.
D. o. obsoletus (Wagler, 1829) - Senegambia E to W Sudan and Uganda (E to Teso), S to C Sierra Leone, S Cameroon and NE Zaire.
D. o. heuglini (Neumann, 1904) - E Sudan, N Ethiopia and Eritrea.
D. o. ingens (Hartert, 1900) - WC & S Ethiopia, NE Uganda, W & C Kenya and extreme N Tanzania (Loliondo).
D. o. crateri (W. L. Sclater & Moreau, 1935) - N Tanzania from Crater Highlands S to Nou Forest.

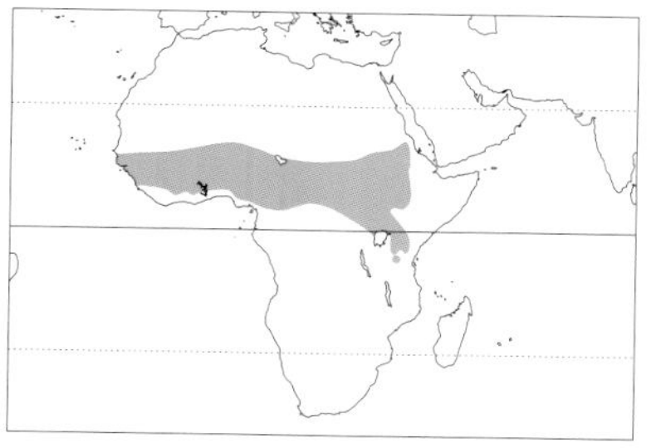

Descriptive notes. c. 13-16 cm; 18-25 g. Male has pale brown forehead becoming darker on crown, red hindcrown and nape; white supercilium from behind eye, extending as stripe behind ear-coverts and down neck side to breast; brown ear-coverts, white cheekstripe, dark brown malar stripe expanding on upper breast side; white chin and throat sometimes with small dark spots; dull brown hindneck and upperparts, white rump and uppertail-coverts streaked brown; wing-coverts tipped white (amount of spotting variable); dark brown flight-feathers barred white; uppertail brown, barred white; whitish below, breast often washed buff-brown and lightly streaked brown (streaks occasionally almost absent); longish bill straight, chisel-tipped, blackish, paler lower mandible; iris red-brown; legs grey, often tinged green. Female has on average shorter bill than male, hindcrown and nape brown, not red. Juvenile somewhat darker above than adult, plumage tinged greyish, eyes brown, usually some barring below, both sexes with red on hindcrown, more extensive on male. Race *heuglini* is larger than nominate, has much-reduced or no spotting on wing-coverts, heavier streaking below; *ingens* resembles previous, but darker above, especially on crown, has spotted wing-coverts; *crateri* is larger and darker than others, has upperparts almost black, very broad and dark streaks below meeting to form patch on breast. Voice. Single clicking calls; weak high-pitched trill; also longer or shorter series of "kweek-week". Drums.
Habitat. Inhabits drier areas, favouring scrubby terrain, wooded grassland, edges of cultivation, *Combretum* woodland and *Hagenia* forest; commonly occupies *Lophira* woodland in Sierra Leone; also open savanna with scattered trees. Occurs quite regularly in suburban gardens. Found in highlands to 2300 m, locally to 3000 m (Mt Kenya), but also down to sea-level; more in lowlands in W Africa.
Food and Feeding. Lepidopteran and coleopteran larvae, and various adult insects; also fruits recorded. Usually singly or in pairs; often joins mixed-species flocks. Forages on thin trunks and branches of trees, frequently on saplings; uses gleaning and pecking.
Breeding. Dec-Jun in W of range, Jan-Apr and Aug in E. Nest-hole excavated by both sexes, at 2-7 m in tree or stub, often isolated one. Clutch 2 eggs; both parents incubate and both feed chicks; incubation and fledging periods not recorded.
Movements. Apparently resident. Individuals recorded in SE Kenya (E to Shimba Hills and Mombasa area) and NE Tanzania (near Arusha) presumably wanderers.
Status and Conservation. Not globally threatened. Rather local and generally uncommon. Widespread in Senegal; locally frequent to common in Gambia; not uncommon in Sierra Leone; local and uncommon in Kenya and Tanzania. Occurs in a number of protected areas throughout its range, including Niokola Koba National Park (Senegal), Comoé National Park (Ivory Coast), Bénoué National Park (Cameroon) and several parks and reserves in E Africa. Probably reasonably secure; no known threats.
Bibliography. Bannerman (1953), Barlow *et al*. (1997), Brown & Britton (1980), Carroll (1988), Cave & Macdonald (1955), Cheesman & Sclater (1935), Cheke & Walsh (1996), Demey *et al*. (2000), Dowsett & Dowsett-Lemaire (1993), Dowsett & Forbes-Watson (1993), Elgood *et al*. (1994), Fry *et al*. (1988), Giraudoux *et al*. (1988), Gore (1990), Green (1990), Greig-Smith (1977b), Grimes (1987), Jensen & Kirkeby (1980), King (2000), Lewis & Pomeroy (1989), Lippens & Wille (1976), Louette (1981b), Mackworth-Praed & Grant (1957, 1970), Morel & Morel (1990), Nikolaus (2000), Ouellet (1977a), Rodwell (1996), Salewski (2000), Sauvage & Rodwell (1998), Short (1971d, 1980, 1985b), Short *et al*. (1990), Smith (1957), Snow (1978), Tarboton (1997), Urban & Brown (1971), Wilkinson & Beecroft (1988), Winkler & Short (1978), Zimmerman *et al*. (1996).

89. Sulawesi Woodpecker

Dendrocopos temminckii

French: Pic de Temminck **German**: Temminckspecht **Spanish**: Pico de Célebes
Other common names: Celebes/Sulawesi Pygmy Woodpecker, Temminck's (Pygmy) Woodpecker

Taxonomy. *Picus Temminckii* Malherbe, 1849, Sulawesi.
Genus sometimes merged into *Picoides*. Forms a superspecies with *D. maculatus*. Populations in S and uplands tend to be somewhat larger than those in N and lowlands, but no grounds for racial subdivision. Monotypic.
Distribution. Sulawesi, including Togian Is and Buton.

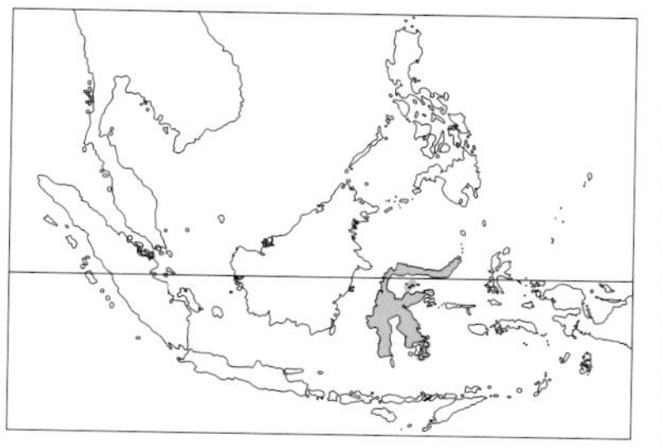

Descriptive notes. 13-14 cm. Male has buff-brown lower forehead, dark brown upper forehead and crown with grey feather bases, in worn plumage appearing streaked; narrow red napeband (red often lacking on central nape); narrow white supercilium from front edge of eye to nape side, dark brown ear-coverts (grey-streaked when worn); broad white cheekband expanding on neck side, often extending to central hindneck; brown malar stripe thinly barred white; dull, pale greyish-brown chin and throat, sometimes extensively marked with off-white; olive-brown upperparts sometimes tinged green, barred very pale brownish-white; whitish rump barred dark brown, occasionally pale yellowish-white or unbarred; uppertail-coverts barred brown and white; dark brown wing-coverts and tertials with faint olive tinge, coverts tipped white, tertials barred white; darker brown primaries and secondaries barred white on both webs; uppertail brown, buffish or buff-white bars of variable width; pale buffish-olive to yellowish-grey below, broadly streaked brown or olive-brown, lower underparts paler and more narrowly streaked; undertail paler than above, usually with slight yellowish wash; longish bill pointed, culmen slightly curved, black, greyer base of lower mandible; iris red to light brown; legs olive-green. Female has no red on nape. Juvenile browner, with barring above and streaking below less prominent. Voice. Sharp "tirr-tirr"; also rapid, thin "geegeegeegeegeegeegee". Drums.
Habitat. Wooded areas, including secondary forest, riparian woodland, orange and coffee plantations in cultivated lowlands, large trees along roadsides, and gardens; also in deforested hills and at edges of primary montane forest, at up to 2300 m.
Food and Feeding. Details of diet not known; thought to be similar to that of *D. maculatus*. Spends most of its time high up in treetops.
Breeding. Drumming and copulations recorded in Aug; probably breeds also early in year. Nest-hole in dead tree, preferentially rain-tree (*Pithecolobium*) but also e.g. mango (*Mangifera indica*), or in dead branch. No other information.
Movements. Resident and sedentary.
Status and Conservation. Not globally threatened. Not uncommon within its range. Occurs in Lore Lindu, Dumoga-Bone and Rawa Aopa National Parks, and Manembonembo and Tangkoko Nature Reserves; common in Gunung Ambang Nature Reserve in NE Sulawesi. Seems to be fairly adaptable.
Bibliography. Andrew (1992), Bororing *et al*. (2000), Catterall (1997), Coates & Bishop (1997), Ekstrom *et al*. (1998), Fraser & Henson (1996), Holmes & Phillipps (1996), Inskipp *et al*. (1996), Ouellet (1977a), Riley & Mole (2001), Rozendaal (1989), Wardill (1995), Watling (1983), Wheatley (1996), White (1977), White & Bruce (1986), Winkler & Short (1978).

90. Philippine Woodpecker

Dendrocopos maculatus

French: Pic des Philippines **German**: Scopolispecht **Spanish**: Pico Filipino
Other common names: Pygmy Woodpecker(!), Philippine Pygmy Woodpecker; Sulu Woodpecker (*ramsayi*)

Taxonomy. *Picus maculatus* Scopoli, 1786, Antigua, Panay, Philippines.
Genus sometimes merged into *Picoides*. Forms a superspecies with *D. temminckii*. Distinctive race *ramsayi* may be a separate species, perhaps even derived from *D. temminckii*, on basis of plumage and vocal differences; further study needed. Other named races are *menagei* (Sibuyan), *leytensis* (Samar, Calicoan, Leyte, Bohol), *apo* (Mt Apo, on Mindanao) and *siasiensis* (Siasi I, in Sulus), all considered insufficiently distinct. Four subspecies recognized.
Subspecies and Distribution.
D. m. validirostris (Blyth, 1849) - Luzon, Lubang, Marinduque, Mindoro and Catanduanes.
D. m. maculatus (Scopoli, 1786) - Sibuyan, Panay, Gigantes, Guimaras, Negros and Cebu.
D. m. fulvifasciatus (Hargitt, 1881) - Samar, Calicoan, Leyte, Bohol, Dinagat, Mindanao and Basilan.
D. m. ramsayi (Hargitt, 1881) - Sulu Is.

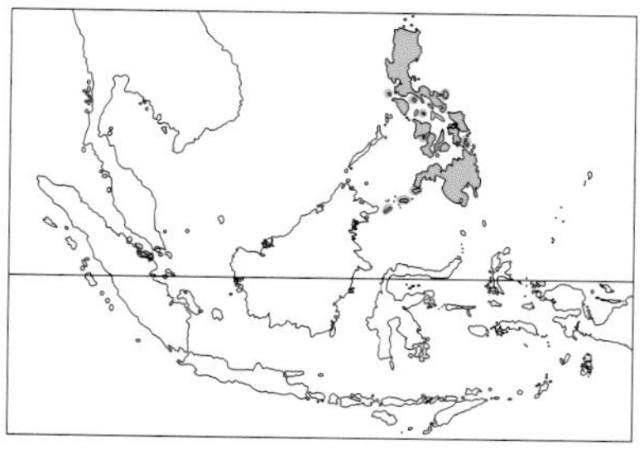

Descriptive notes. 13-14 cm; 22-30 g. Male has dark brown forehead to hindcrown, blacker at sides, small red patch at side of hindcrown (sometimes extending across rear nape); white supercilium from rear of eye to nape side, blackish-brown ear-coverts back to hindneck; buffish-brown upper lores, white lower lores and broad band through cheek to lower neck side; dark brown malar stripe variably spotted or streaked white; white chin, greyer throat and uppermost breast, brown spotting on lower throat and throat sides; dark brown hindneck and upperparts, white bars on lower mantle, scapulars and back, whiter rump with a few dark spots or bars; white uppertail-coverts broadly streaked dark; brown upperwing darker on primaries and secondaries, coverts narrowly tipped white, flight-feathers narrowly barred white; uppertail dark brown, barred white; underparts below throat pale buffish-white, breast washed yellow-buff and with dark brown spots, belly and flanks streaked, whitish undertail-coverts broadly streaked dark; fairly long bill slightly chisel-tipped, culmen barely curved, dark grey, paler base; iris brown to brownish-red; legs brownish to olive-brown. Female has slightly longer bill, wing and tail than male, lacks red on hindcrown. Juvenile much as adult, but browner with heavier pale barring above, markings below less sharp. Race *validirostris* is shorter-tailed than nominate, darker above, has rump more barred (often fully so), white supercilium usually continuing behind ear-coverts, male with red reduced to small line on hindcrown side; *fulvifasciatus* is still darker than previous, almost black above, has pale bars tinged buff, rump unmarked white, more white behind ear-coverts (often meeting white of supercilium), stronger buff wash below; *ramsayi* highly distinctive, browner and unbarred above, broad, irregular white streaks on back, rump mostly white, pale wing markings reduced to small bars on inner webs of flight-feathers, hardly streaked below and few or no spots,

On following pages: 91. Brown-capped Woodpecker (*Dendrocopos moluccensis*); 92. Grey-capped Woodpecker (*Dendrocopos canicapillus*); 93. Pygmy Woodpecker (*Dendrocopos kizuki*).

instead a brownish breastband with yellow or golden lower border, male with red over entire nape and along rear crown side. VOICE. Slightly descending stuttered series, "pilt-pilt-pilt-pilt-pilt", c. 2-2·5 seconds long, irregularly repeated; *ramsayi* apparently a slightly lower "kikikikikikiki", rising at start; also single "pit", more commonly "pitit"; single "chrrit" notes apparently as long-distance signals. Drums.

Habitat. Light to dense primary and secondary forest to cloudforest, mature mixed plantations, forest edge, and woods along rivers, also grassy clearings with scattered trees; typically, in areas with many dead, often rather small, trees. Forages out into recently burned clearings where dead trees present. Also mangroves in Sulu Is (*ramsayi*). From sea-level, but mostly above 500 m, to 1350 m, locally to 2500 m.

Food and Feeding. Insects, mostly ants, also grubs and other larvae. Singly, in pairs, or in small family parties of up to 5 birds; often joins mixed-species flocks with tits (Paridae), nuthatches (*Sitta*) and other small birds. Forages mostly in upper levels, above 9 m, on twigs and smaller branches, also on trunks; dead trees or trees with dead branches clearly favoured. Pecks and hammers, and gleans from bark and foliage.

Breeding. Season Feb-Aug; nestlings found in Feb. Nest-hole in tree; no other information.

Movements. Resident.

Status and Conservation. Not globally threatened. Race *ramsayi* Vulnerable. Generally common, and the most abundant woodpecker within its range; appears resonably adaptable, but little is known of its breeding biology and requirements. Further study needed. Sulu race *ramsayi*, currently listed as Vulnerable but perhaps better classified as Endangered, is known to survive for certain only on Tawitawi, and at only three sites there, with greatly restricted range of at most 1760 km² and decreasing; despite apparent tolerance of degraded habitats, its numbers have continued to decline rapidly; was widespread and abundant on eight islands in Sulu Archipelago in first half of 20th century, since when extensive or complete destruction of habitat on most islands has resulted in its total disappearance from all but one; even the few remaining forest patches on Tawitawi are highly degraded, and further threatened by uncontrolled logging and plans for conversion to commercial plantations of oil palms (*Elaeis guineensis*). Despite initiatives to raise awareness of importance of conservation in the region, and especially on Tawitawi, no formally protected areas exist anywhere in Sulu chain; campaigns and surveys urgently needed, but political problems make all conservation efforts difficult and dangerous. It seems likely that *ramsayi* will end up being generally treated as a distinct species, and this could, theoretically, be of help in gaining protection of the handful of sites known to harbour this woodpecker.

Bibliography. Alcalá & Sanguila (1969), Brooks, Dutson *et al.* (1996), Brooks, Evans *et al.* (1992), Collar *et al.* (1999), Danielsen *et al.* (1994), Delacour & Mayr (1946), Dickinson *et al.* (1991), Dutson, Allen & Brooks (1996), Dutson, Evans *et al.* (1992), Evans *et al.* (1993), Gilliard (1950), Goodman & Gonzales (1990), Hachisuka (1931-1935), Inskipp *et al.* (1996), Lambert (1993), McGregor (1904, 1905, 1909-1910), Mearns (1909), Ouellet (1977a), Pardo & Gogorza y González (1997), Parkes (1958, 1971), duPont (1971), duPont & Rabor (1973), Potter (1953), Rabor (1977), Rand & Rabor (1960), Salomonsen (1953), Stattersfield & Capper (2000), Winkler & Short (1978).

91. Brown-capped Woodpecker

Dendrocopos moluccensis

French: Pic nain **German**: Braunscheitelspecht **Spanish**: Pico Crestipardo

Other common names: Brown-capped Pygmy Woodpecker; Sunda/Malaysian Woodpecker/Pygmy Woodpecker (nominate group); Indian Pygmy Woodpecker (*nanus* group); Ceylon/Sri Lanka Pygmy Woodpecker (*gymnopthalmos*)

Taxonomy. *Picus moluccensis* J. F. Gmelin, 1788, Moluccas; error = Malacca.

Genus sometimes merged into *Picoides*. Closest to *D. temminckii* and *D. maculatus*. Indian Subcontinent races often treated as forming a separate species on grounds of shared morphological differences from E races. Alternatively, race *nanus* has sometimes been considered conspecific with *D. canicapillus*, but the two are sympatric in Nepal without interbreeding. Birds in E peninsular India described as race *hardwickii*, and those from Alor (E Lesser Sundas) as *excelsior*, but in both cases differences are a result of clinal variation. Five subspecies recognized.

Subspecies and Distribution.

D. m. nanus (Vigors, 1832) - N and peninsular India (except SW) and S Nepal E to Bangladesh.
D. m. cinereigula (Malherbe, 1849) - SW India in Kerala and W Tamil Nadu.
D. m. gymnopthalmos (Blyth, 1849) - Sri Lanka.
D. m. moluccensis (J. F. Gmelin, 1788) - W & S Peninsular Malaysia S to Greater Sundas, including Riau Archipelago, Bangka and Belitung.
D. m. grandis (Hargitt, 1882) - Lesser Sundas, from Lombok E to Alor.

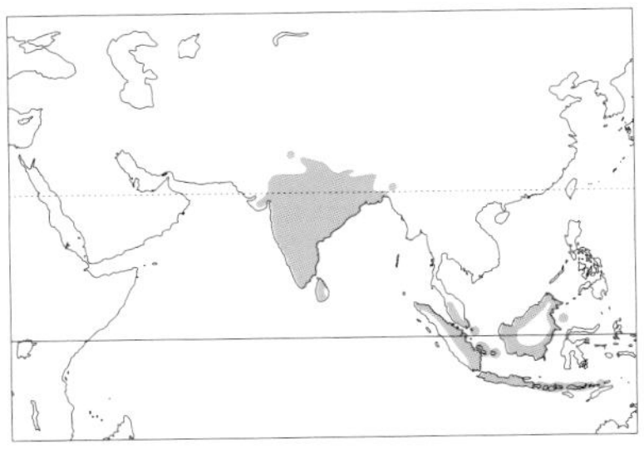

Descriptive notes. 13 cm; 13-17 g (*nanus* group), 15-18 g (*moluccensis* group). Male has blackish-brown forehead to hindneck, small red line at side of hindcrown, broad blackish-brown band through ear-coverts and down neck side, prominent dark malar stripe continuing to breast side; rest of head white; blackish-brown upperparts barred white, white rump and uppertail-coverts spotted and barred blackish, wing-coverts with white spots at tips, flight-feathers with white spots forming bars; uppertail blackish-brown, central feathers with white spots, outers barred white; whitish underparts browner on breast, heavily dark-streaked; underwing and undertail barred brown and white; shortish bill rather straight, slightly chisel-tipped, grey, pale inner half; iris light brown; legs greyish. Differs from *D. canicapillus* mainly in smaller size, darker forehead, more solid facial markings, broader streaks below. Female lacks red on hindcrown. Juvenile like adult but browner, duller, less contrastingly patterned, male with orange to red on nape more extensive than on adult. Race *grandis* is bigger and longer-tailed than nominate, has malar usually white-streaked, rump generally less barred, pale wingbars broader, underparts often washed yellow-buff and more finely streaked, tends to become larger and less heavily streaked from W to E; *nanus* is browner, crown sometimes tinged yellowish, lacks dark malar, has white eyes, bare red orbital ring, more elongated wing-covert spots, whitish underparts washed very pale buff with little or no streaking; *cinereigula* is darker than previous, especially on crown, has less white in wing, streaks below very fine (can appear unstreaked); *gymnopthalmos* is small, even darker, more sooty-black, above, with blackish crown, underparts unstreaked. VOICE. Common call a fast trilled "kikikikikiki" or "trrrrr-i-i" or "clickr-r-r". Drums, c. 7 rolls per minute.

Habitat. Light deciduous forest, secondary forest, bamboo, trees near cultivation, also tall trees near villages, old plantations, sometimes parks and gardens; also coastal scrub and mangroves, and *Casuarina* trees, especially in E of range. Mainly semi-evergreen forest and lower montane forest in Lesser Sundas. Mostly in lowlands, up to 1200 m in SW India and Sri Lanka; to 2200 m in Lesser Sundas.

Food and Feeding. Insects, particularly ants and other hymenopterans, beetles and their larvae, caterpillars; fruits, berries and flower nectar also taken. Usually solitary, also in pairs and family parties; joins mixed-species flocks. Moves slowly over dead trees or dead parts of trees when foraging for ants and other insects; prefers smaller branches and twigs high up in trees, also forages on thin stems of shrubs close to ground. Gleaning from surface seems to be the commonest feeding method; also probes under surface layers of bark; sometimes hammers feverishly and loudly, but in most cases delivers only few pecks.

Breeding. Jan-Jul, mainly Mar-Apr, in Indian Subcontinent, in Sri Lanka also Oct-Dec when conditions favourable; Mar-Aug in Peninsular Malaysia, and Apr-Jul, also Oct, in Sundas. Nest-hole excavated at 2-14 m, mostly 4-10 m, in small dead branch, often on underside; entrance diameter c. 3·3 cm. Clutch 2-3 eggs, occasionally 4; details of incubation and fledging periods not known.

Movements. Resident.

Status and Conservation. Not globally threatened. Locally fairly common in Indian Subcontinent; status in Bangladesh uncertain, probably rare resident. Uncommon to locally common in Peninsular Malaysia and Greater and Lesser Sundas. Occurs in numerous protected areas, e.g. Keoladeo Ghana and Ranthambore National Parks (India), Sigiriya Sanctuary and Kelani River and Bodhinagala Forest Reserves (Sri Lanka), Bako National Park (Malaysia), Sungei Buloh Nature Park (Singapore), Way Kambas National Park (Sumatra), Baluran National Park (Java) and Bali Barat National Park (Bali). Increases in numbers in some areas where forests are opened up; appears to be fairly adaptable.

Bibliography. Ali (1996), Ali & Ripley (1983), Andrew (1992), van Balen & Prentice (1978), Betts (1934), Chasen (1937), Chasen & Hoogerwerf (1941), Coates & Bishop (1997), Davison (1997), Duckworth & Kelsh (1988), Grimmett *et al.* (1998), Hails & Jarvis (1987), Harrison (1999), Harvey (1990), Henry (1998), Hoffmann (1999), Holmes (1996, 1997), Holmes & van Balen (1996), Holmes & Burton (1987), Inskipp, C. (1989), Inskipp, C. & Inskipp (1991), Inskipp, T. *et al.* (1996), Jeyarajasingam & Pearson (1999), Lamsfuss (1998), MacKinnon (1988), MacKinnon & Phillipps (1993), Madoc (1976), van Marle & Voous (1988), Medway & Wells (1976), Mees (1986), Mukherjee (1995), Nash & Nash (1988), Parrott & Andrew (1996), Phillips (1978), Rensch (1931), Ripley (1950c, 1982), Roberts (1991), Robson (2000), Santharam (1998c, 1999a), Sargeant (1997), Short (1973d), Smythies (1999), Spittle (1952), Thompson *et al.* (1993), Vowles & Vowles (1997), Wells (1990, 1999), White & Bruce (1986), Winkler & Short (1978).

92. Grey-capped Woodpecker

Dendrocopos canicapillus

French: Pic à coiffe grise **German**: Grauscheitelspecht **Spanish**: Pico Crestigrís

Other common names: Grey-headed Woodpecker(!), Pygmy Woodpecker(!), Grey-crowned Woodpecker(!); Taiwan/Formosan Woodpecker ("*wattersi*")

Taxonomy. *Picus canicapillus* Blyth, 1845, Ramree Island, Arakan, Myanmar.

Genus sometimes merged into *Picoides*. Most closely related to *D. kizuki* and sometimes thought to form a superspecies with it, although ranges of the two overlap rather extensively in mainland E Asia; more distantly related to *D. temminckii*, *D. maculatus* and *D. moluccensis*. Has at times been considered conspecific with race *nanus* of *D. moluccensis*, in which case name *nanus* has priority; however, the two are sympatric in Nepal without interbreeding. Mainland races intergrade. Taiwan population originally named as a separate species, "*D. wattersi*", but specimen shown to be juvenile of present species; name subsequently synonymized with *kaleensis*. Other named races include *szetschuanensis* (C China), *nagamichii* (E China), *omissus* (SW China), *obscurus* (SE Yunnan) and *tonkinensis* (Tonkin), all considered either to represent intergrades between populations or to fall within range of variation of adjacent races. Eleven subspecies recognized.

Subspecies and Distribution.

D. c. mitchellii (Malherbe, 1849) - N Pakistan E to Nepal.
D. c. semicoronatus (Malherbe, 1849) - extreme E Nepal E to W Assam.
D. c. canicapillus (Blyth, 1845) - E Assam, Bangladesh, C & S Myanmar, most of Thailand and Laos.
D. c. delacouri (Meyer de Schauensee, 1938) - SE Thailand, Cambodia and Cochinchina.
D. c. auritus (Eyton, 1845) - S Thailand and Peninsular Malaysia.
D. c. volzi (Stresemann, 1920) - Riau Archipelago and Sumatra, including Nias I.
D. c. aurantiiventris (Salvadori, 1868) - Borneo.
D. c. doerriesi (Hargitt, 1881) - E Siberia (Ussuriland), E Manchuria and Korea.
D. c. scintilliceps (Swinhoe, 1863) - E & C China from Liaoning S to Sichuan and Zhejiang.
D. c. kaleensis (Swinhoe, 1863) - W & S Sichuan E to Fujian and Taiwan, and S to N Myanmar and N Indochina.
D. c. swinhoei (Hartert, 1910) - Hainan.

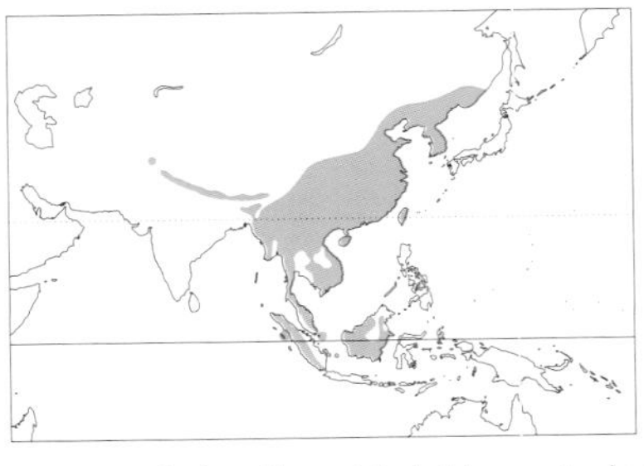

Descriptive notes. 14-16 cm; 20-27 g (*mitchellii*), 21-32 g (*semicoronatus*, *scintilliceps*). Male has grey forehead and crown, black crown sides, hindcrown and nape, small red streak on nape side, buffish nasal tufts; white face with grey-brown band through lower ear-coverts, darker at rear and continuing down neck side, narrow brownish malar stripe; whitish chin and throat; black upperparts tinged brown, barred white, wing-coverts with variable amount of white at tips; black flight-feathers tipped white, white spots forming bars on inner wing; uppertail black, central feathers barred or spotted white, outer 2 or 3 pairs barred whitish; whitish below, breast strongly tinged brownish, dark brown streaks most pronounced on breast; fairly long bill almost straight, barely chisel-tipped, blackish, paler base and lower mandible; iris red-brown to grey-brown, orbital skin grey; legs greyish to olive-grey. Female lacks red on crown. Juvenile is darker above than adult, with crown blackish, darker below with heavier streaking and often hint of barring, male with orange-red on nape and rear crown sides often more extensive than on adult. Races vary in both plumage and size: *semicoronatus* has buffish cheekband, strong yellow-brown to buff or even orangey tinge below, differs from all others races in that male has red extending across nape; *mitchellii* is very like previous, but red on male restricted to narrow lateral nape streak, often more extensive brown on face; *delacouri* resembles nominate, but larger, with broader dark streaking below; *auritus* has head pattern clearly defined, is slightly shorter-tailed, with plumage blacker, less brown-toned, grey-brown breastband, central rectrices barred on some, plain on others; *volzi* has less white in wings, orangey to orange-gold underparts; *aurantiiventris* is smallest race, resembles previous but has longer bill, shorter tail, often more pronounced malar; *doerriesi* is largest race, distinctive, has mantle and upper back black, lower back and rump white, uppertail-coverts black, wing-coverts with much white forming patches, wingbars broad, pale underparts with streaks rather narrow; *scintilliceps* is similar to previous but slightly smaller, with upper back barred white, less white in wings, darker and more heavily streaked below; *kaleensis* is like previous but more streaked below; *swinhoei* is slightly smaller than previous, whiter below with narrower streaking, has more white in wings. VOICE. Short, soft "cheep" or "pic" or "tzit"; doubled "chip-chip", second note shorter and lower-pitched; also "tit-tit-erh-r-r-r-h", "pic-chirru-chirru-chihihihi" or "click-r-r-r", and irregular squeaking series, "kweek-kweek-kweek". Drumming sounds muted.

Habitat. Inhabits a great variety of forests and woodlands. Oak (*Quercus*), deciduous and mixed forest in N parts of range. In Nepal and E to SE Asia, occurs in closed as well as more open forest, including sal (*Shorea*) forest, deciduous and open evergreen woodland, second growth, scrub and gardens, but avoids very dense forest; also in *Casuarina* forest and mangroves in coastal SE Asia. Frequents lowland forest, montane forest and pine (*Pinus*) forest, and found also at jungle clearings, in Greater Sundas. Lowlands to 400 m in Nepal, less commonly to 1350 m, and to 1700 m, occasionally 2000 m, elsewhere in Himalayas; to 1830 m in SE Asia; mainly lowlands up to 1680 m in Borneo, and in Sumatra found mostly at 1000-2800 m; to 2000 m in China.

Food and Feeding. Diet includes caterpillars, homopterans, small beetles, insect pupae, grubs, Diptera, ants, and fruits; seeds (grass) and other plant matter (e.g. carmine cherries) of some importance in winter. Solitary, in pairs, or in small family groups. Forages in crowns of tall trees, also at edges of bushes and saplings; seeks out dead twigs or stubs, but most foraging is on outer twigs and branches. Frequently perches crosswise, and hangs on twigs and leaf clusters, often upside-down. Does not peck and hammer at one spot for very long; undertakes much gleaning; occasionally removes a piece of bark or lichen and probes into crevices and at base of leaves. Even flutters to catch less accessible items.

Breeding. Apr-Jul in Indian Subcontinent and Dec-Apr in SE Asia; somewhat later in N parts of range. Display with crest-raising, bill-directing, and slow body-swinging and tail-spreading. Nest excavated by both sexes, at 2·5-15 m, mostly 5-10 m, in tree branch, particularly on underside. Clutch 3-5 eggs in S of range, 6-8 in N; incubation by both sexes, period 12-13 days; both also feed chicks, nestling period c. 21 days.

Movements. Largely resident. Minor post-breeding movements down to lowlands in N parts of range. Probably only a breeding visitor to Pakistan.

Status and Conservation. Not globally threatened. Locally common to fairly common in much of range. Rare and very local in Pakistan; in Nepal, rare in W and more common in E; locally fairly common in India and Bhutan; local and not common in Bangladesh, but status uncertain; common throughout most of SE Asia; fairly widespread but uncommon in China, including Hainan; rare and local in NE of range. Occurs in several protected areas, e.g. Corbett National Park (India) and Chitwan National Park (Nepal).

Bibliography. Ali & Ripley (1983), Ali *et al.* (1996), Andrew (1992), Baker (1919), Bangs & Van Tyne (1931), Biswas (1950), Bucknill & Chasen (1990), Chasen & Hoogerwerf (1941), Davison (1997), Deignan (1945), Dementiev *et al.* (1966), Duckworth & Kelsh (1988), Eames & Robson (1992), Étchécopar & Hüe (1978), Friedmann (1997), Greenway (1943), Grimmett *et al.* (1998), Harvey (1990), Holmes (1996, 1997), Holmes & Burton (1987), Inskipp, C. (1989), Inskipp, C. & Inskipp (1991), Inskipp, T. *et al.* (1996), Jeyarajasingam & Pearson (1999), King & Rappole (2001), Knystautas (1993), Lekagul & Round (1991), Ludlow (1937), MacKinnon (1988), MacKinnon & Phillipps (1993, 2000), Madoc (1976), van Marle & Voous (1988), Medway & Wells (1976), Meyer de Schauensee & Ripley (1940), Ouellet (1977a), Riley (1938), Ripley (1982), Roberts (1991), Robson (2000), Sargeant (1997), Severinghaus & Blackshaw (1976), Short (1973d), Smythies (1986, 1999), Stepanyan (1995), Thompson *et al.* (1993), Tsai Hangyeh (1985), Verheugt *et al.* (1993), Vowles & Vowles (1997), Wells (1985, 1999), Winkler & Short (1978), Won Pyongoh (1993), Zhao Zhengjie (1995), Zhou Shie *et al.* (1980).

93. Pygmy Woodpecker

Dendrocopos kizuki

French: Pic kisuki   **German:** Kizukispecht   **Spanish:** Pico Kizuki
Other common names: Japanese Pygmy/Spotted Woodpecker, Japanese Woodpecker(!)

Taxonomy. *Picus kizuki* Temminck, 1835, Kyushu.
Genus sometimes merged into *Picoides*. Has been thought to form a superspecies with *D. canicapillus*, although their ranges overlap rather extensively in NE Asia. Varies clinally, becoming smaller and darker from N to S. Described mainland races *permutatus* (Sidemi, in Ussuriland), *wilderi* (NE Hebei) and *acutirostris* (E Korea), and island races *kurilensis* (Kuril Is), *nippon* (Honshu), *shikokuensis*

(S Honshu and Shikoku), *matsudairai* (Izu Is), *kotataki* (Oki and Tsushima), *nigrescens* (Okinawa) and *orii* (Iriomote in S Ryukyus), all considered insufficiently distinct. Four subspecies recognized.

Subspecies and Distribution.
D. k. ijimae (Takatsukasa, 1922) - SE Siberia (S Ussuriland) and Sakhalin S to NE Korea, N Japan (Hokkaido) and S Kuril Is.
D. k. seebohmi (Hargitt, 1884) - Korea (except NE), Quelpart I (Cheju-do) and Honshu.
D. k. kizuki (Temminck, 1835) - NE China (S to Shandong), and S Japan including Tsushima, Shikoku, Kyushu, Izu Is, and S Ryukyu Is (S to Iriomote).
D. k. amamii (Kuroda, 1922) - Amami and Tokunoshima in N Ryukyus.

Descriptive notes. 13-15 cm; 18-26 g. Male has grey-brown forehead and crown, darker hindcrown and hindneck, small red patch at nape side (often concealed by overlying feathers) with white patch behind, short white supercilium behind eye, brown ear-coverts and band on neck side continuing to breast side; whitish lores and moustachial stripe, grey-brown malar stripe, white chin and throat; dark brown upperparts darker rearwards and on wing-coverts, all barred white, brownish-black flight-feathers barred white; uppertail blackish, outer feathers white with dark bars near tips; white below, breast and sides washed pale brown, heavily streaked dark brown, undertail-coverts lightly barred; short bill straight, slightly chisel-tipped, grey-black, paler base; iris brown to red-brown; legs grey. Differs from *D. canicapillus* in smaller size, browner coloration, less white on head. Female has slightly longer wing, bill and tail than male, lacks red on nape side. Juvenile has greyer below than adult, throat streaked and spotted, male with small red patch in crown centre. Race *ijimae* is larger, has white band down neck side, often longer white supercilium, also less streaking below, no bars on vent; *seebohmi* is smaller and darker than previous, has less white above, heavier streaks below; *amamii* is blacker above, has rich buff-brown on flanks, barred undertail-coverts. VOICE. Distinctive, buzzing "kzz, kzz" notes, also single "khit" or "khit-khit-khit". Drums weakly, very short rolls in rapid succession.

Habitat. Ranges from lowland woods to subalpine mixed coniferous forest, and from subtropical evergreen to N boreal forests with firs (*Abies*) and birches (*Betula*); broadleaved deciduous and mixed forest in riverine lowlands in Ussuri region. Besides coniferous woodland, occupies light stands of pine (*Pinus densiflora*) in Japan and dense montane coniferous forest in Korea. Also in parks and gardens, even in major cities, especially in Japan. Sea-level to 1300 m on mainland, and to c. 2100 m in Japan.

Food and Feeding. Mainly arthropods: insects and their pupae, caterpillars, weevils (Curculionidae), aphids, small ants of genera *Lasius* and *Formica*, and spiders. Some berries (*Rhus*) taken; exceptionally, small lizards. Met with singly, in pairs or in family parties; frequently in mixed-species flocks with tits (Paridae) and nuthatches (*Sitta*). Hammers and excavates bark of thin trunks and twigs, also visits stronger herbaceous plants; during breeding season, predominant foraging method is gleaning in the canopy.

Breeding. Late Apr to end May in Amur-Ussuri region; in Japan, from late May or early Jun in N and from Mar in S. Monogamous and solitary, but helping by a third adult once recorded. Nest dug into soft, rotten stump at height of 2-10 m, mostly below 7 m; active nests sometimes attacked by conspecifics when available sites in short supply. Clutch 5-7 eggs, exceptionally 9 recorded; incubation period 12-14 days; fledging period c. 3 weeks.

Movements. Mostly resident; minor altitudinal movements to lowlands take place in winter in N parts of range.

Status and Conservation. Not globally threatened. Fairly common; in Japan the commonest woodpecker. Rarer in S parts of range; generally uncommon in Siberia and China. Adaptable species, able to live in relatively close proximity to humans; colonization of urbanized environments indicates that it is unlikely to become threatened in the near future, although lack of suitable nest-sites in city parks could be a problem. Present in Kirishima-Yaku and Sarak-San National Parks (Japan).

Bibliography. Austin (1948), Brazil (1991), Dementiev *et al.* (1966), Étchécopar & Hüe (1978), Friedmann (1997), Ham Kyuhwang (1982), Higuchi (1980), Inskipp *et al.* (1996), Ishida (1994), Kiyosu (1936), Knystautas (1993), MacKinnon & Phillipps (2000), Nakamura *et al.* (1995), Sugiyama & Akatsuka (1999), Winkler & Short (1978), Won Pyongoh (1993), Yamagami (1992), Yoon Mooboo (1992), Zhao Zhengjie (1995).

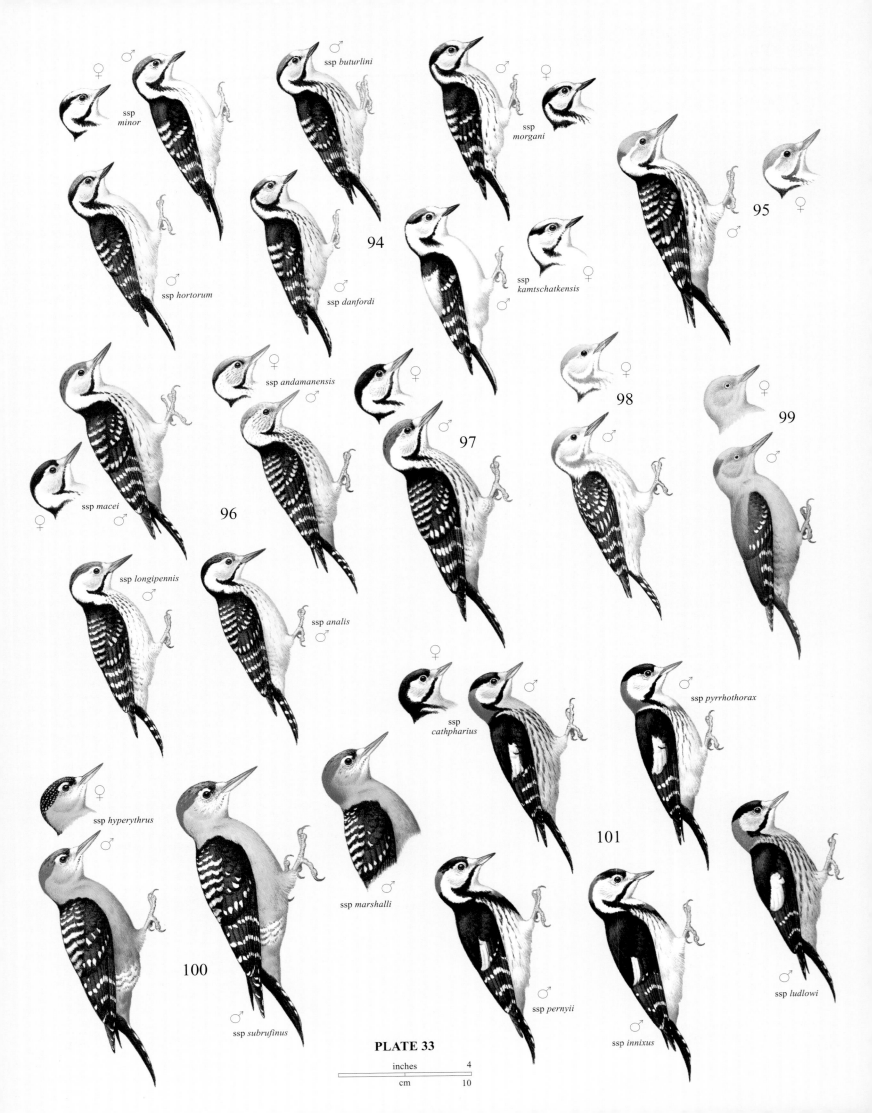

ssp *minor*

ssp *buturlini*

ssp *morgani*

ssp *hortorum*

94

ssp *danfordi*

ssp *kamtschatkensis*

95

ssp *macei*

ssp *andamanensis*

97

98

99

96

ssp *longipennis*

ssp *analis*

ssp *cathpharius*

ssp *pyrrhothorax*

ssp *hyperythrus*

ssp *marshalli*

101

100

ssp *subrufinus*

ssp *pernyii*

ssp *innixus*

ssp *ludlowi*

PLATE 33

inches   4

cm   10

94. Lesser Spotted Woodpecker

Dendrocopos minor

French: Pic épeichette **German**: Kleinspecht **Spanish**: Pico Menor
Other common names: Lesser Pied Woodpecker

Taxonomy. *Picus minor* Linnaeus, 1758, Sweden.
Genus sometimes merged into *Picoides*. Related to *D. canicapillus* and *D. kizuki*. Recent genetic data suggest also a link to North American "*Picoides pubescens* group". Races intergrade extensively over species' huge range, with many intermediate populations; numerous additional races have been described, but often on rather weak grounds, and differences are often part of a clinal variation. Named races not accepted include *hispaniae* (Spain), *jordansi* (C European mountains), *serbicus* (Montenegro), *wagneri* (Romania), *hyrcanus* (N Iran), *mongolicus* (SW Siberia to Mongolia), *nojidoensis* (NE Korea) and *immaculatus* (Kamchatka). Eleven subspecies recognized.
Subspecies and Distribution.
D. m. minor (Linnaeus, 1758) - N Europe from Scandinavia E to Ural Mts.
D. m. kamtschatkensis (Malherbe, 1861) - Urals E to R Anadyr and Kamchatka.
D. m. amurensis (Buturlin, 1908) - lower R Amur and Sakhalin S to NE Korea and N Japan (Hokkaido).
D. m. comminutus Hartert, 1907 - SC & S Britain.
D. m. hortorum (C. L. Brehm, 1831) - France E to Poland and S to Switzerland, Hungary and N Romania.
D. m. buturlini (Hartert, 1912) - Iberia, S France and Italy E to Romania, Bulgaria and N Greece.
D. m. ledouci (Malherbe, 1855) - N Africa (NE Algeria, NW Tunisia).
D. m. danfordi (Hargitt, 1883) - Greece and Turkey.
D. m. colchicus (Buturlin, 1908) - Caucasus and Transcaucasia.
D. m. quadrifasciatus (Radde, 1884) - Lenkoran region of SE Transcaucasia.
D. m. morgani Zarudny & Loudon, 1904 - NW Iran and Zagros Mts.

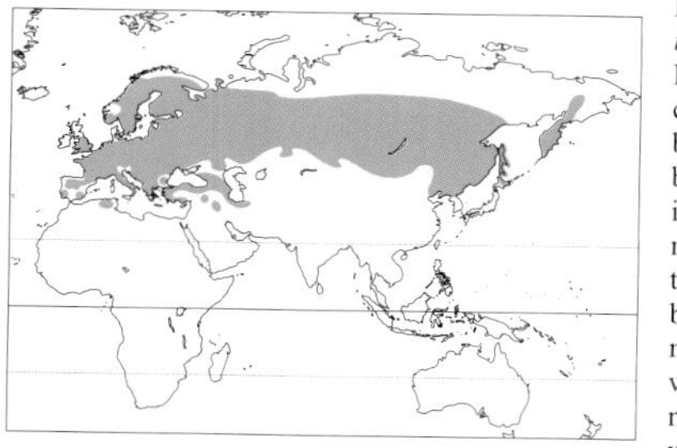

Descriptive notes. 14-16 cm; 16-25 g (*hortorum*), 18-22 g (*comminutus*), 19-26 g (*minor*). Male has buff-tinged white forehead and lores, crimson-red crown (usually some pale feather bases showing) bordered by narrow black lines, black nape and hindneck; rest of head, including chin and throat, white or whitish, with black malar stripe expanding on neck side and extending irregularly down to upper breast side; black upperparts, broad white bars on lower mantle and lower scapulars to upper rump, wing-coverts with broad white spots or bars near tips; black flight-feathers broadly barred white; uppertail black, outer feathers white with 2 or 3 dark bars near tip; white underparts with slight buff tinge, breast sides and flanks with thin black streaks, undertail-coverts usually spotted black; short bill chisel-tipped, dark grey to blackish, paler base of lower mandible; iris red-brown or brownish; legs greenish-grey. Female lacks red on head, has white or buffish-white forecrown, black crown sides and hindcrown. Juvenile duller than adult, black areas tinged brown, pale forehead patch obscured by darker tips, heavier but duller and less defined streaks below, male with greyish-mottled pinkish-red forecrown, female with pale forecrown obscured by dark tips and usually a few reddish tips. Races differ in size, plumage darkness and pattern, but variation often clinal and many intermediates: *kamtschatkensis* is largest, long-winged, has proportionately longer bill than nominate, much more white above, almost unmarked white outer tail, few or no streaks below; *amurensis* is very like nominate, but narrower white bars above, slightly greyer and usually more streaked below; *hortorum* has slightly less white on back than nominate, outer rectrices more barred, buff or light brown face and underparts, throat sometimes tinged pink, flanks more heavily streaked; *buturlini* is darker than previous, more heavily streaked below; *comminutus* resembles previous, but slightly smaller, with much fainter streaks below; *ledouci* is also dark, but pale areas of head to breast somewhat darker buff-brown, often heavier streaking below, may show some black behind ear-coverts, usually has all-black bill; *danfordi* is similarly dark below, sometimes brown-tinged, has black band from hindcrown around rear ear-coverts; *colchicus* is like previous, but has more white above, black band behind ear-coverts sometimes broken; *quadrifasciatus* is small, short-billed, has less white above, sometimes hint of black band joining malar with nape, outer rectrices heavily barred black, pale areas buff-brown, flanks heavily dark-streaked and sometimes barred; *morgani* is distinctive, has very long and narrow bill, broad black band behind ear-coverts, buff face, deep buffish-brown upper breast (and sometimes chin and throat) contrasting with white rest of underparts, very sharp black streaks on breast and flanks. Voice. Commonest is series of notes, "gee-geegeegee" or longer; single "gig" and various other calls rarely heard. Both sexes drum, characteristic long high-pitched rolls at 14-19 per minute, often interspersed with call series at height of courtship.
Habitat. Temperate and boreal deciduous woodland in lowlands. Open forest with softwood deciduous trees in vicinity of lakes or rivers are preferred; also forest edge, and in parks, orchards and gardens. Requires good number of thin snags, as in old stands or in riparian woodland. Restricted to cork-oak forest, especially with *Quercus suber*, in N Africa. Lowlands and foothills to 850 m, locally to 1260 m, in Europe; at higher elevations in Asia, to 1400-2000 m in Caucasus, 1700 m in Altai Mts, and 1400 m in Mongolia; to 1300 m in N Africa.
Food and Feeding. Small insects comprise main bulk of diet. In summer, mostly caterpillars, aphids, ants, beetles, and other surface-dwelling arthropods, including Diptera and spiders; even small snails (*Discus*) taken. In winter, wood-boring larvae (e.g. Buprestidae, Cerambycidae, Curculionidae) and those living under the bark (e.g. Scolytidae, Ipidae) become important. Ants more important in S parts of range. Eats very little vegetable matter, but occasionally takes fruit and berries, and seeds at feeders. Generally forages singly; may join mixed flocks, especially with tits (Paridae), outside breeding season. Forages quietly in upper stratum or in dense vegetation. Prefers to seek food from (vertical) twigs 1-3 cm in diameter in the canopy, rarely on the trunk or base of large trees; descends to lower levels mainly to visit bushes and plant stalks, latter including particularly reed (*Phragmites*), occasionally corn. Foraging techniques include gleaning, hammering, pecking series to dislodge large pieces of bark, and probing; gleaning predominates when foraging for nestling food. Also makes aerial sallies for insects, and visits sap holes made by other woodpecker species.
Breeding. Laying Apr to mid-May, to Jun in N. Generally monogamous, pair-bond may extend over several years; also, study in S Sweden found almost 10% of females polyandrous, c. 3% of males polygynous. Courtship from Feb, most conspicuous displays wing-spreading and tail-spreading, characteristic flutter-aerial display, and gliding flight with wings held well above back. Nest-hole excavated by both sexes, male often taking greater share, work lasting 2-4 weeks, sometimes as few as 6 days; at 0·4-20 m, usually below 8 m, in soft wood of dead or decaying trunk, stump or underside of a branch, hole entrance 3-3·5 cm, cavity depth 10-18 cm; nestbox used rarely; territory often small. Clutch 5-6 eggs, rarely 3 or up to 9; incubation by both sexes, male often doing more, period 10-12 days; chicks fed by both parents, fledging period 18-21 days, rarely up to 23 days; juveniles cared for by parents for a further 1-2 weeks. Success variable; in study in S Sweden, 34% of breeding attempts failed to produce fledglings, and polyandrous females c. 40% more successful than monogamous ones. First breeding at 1 year.
Movements. Resident in most of range. N populations partly migratory; movements often eruptive in nature, in parallel with movements of *D. major*. Autumn migration mainly late Aug to Nov; N European birds may reach C Europe and Black Sea.
Status and Conservation. Not globally threatened. Fairly common to scarce in most of range; nowhere very common; scarce in N Africa. European population estimated at c. 195,000-240,000 pairs, of which 40,000-60,000 in Belarus, c. 30,000-50,000 in Germany, 20,000-40,000 in Poland, 20,000-30,000 in Hungary. Densities generally low, e.g. 2-3 pairs/100 ha in primeval deciduous forest in Poland, and elsewhere in Europe only 0·06-1·6 pairs/km². Appears to have declined in many parts of Europe, largely as a result of loss of deciduous habitats, especially riverine forest and old orchards, which were previously used extensively. Responds negatively to forest fragmentation and admixture of conifers. Main conservation measure required is to ensure that adequate suitable habitat remains for this species.
Bibliography. Alatalo (1978), Artíguez & Franco (1997), Beaman & Madge (1998), Blagosklonov (1968), Brazil (1991), Costantini & Melletti (1992), Cramp (1985), Delacour (1951a), Dementiev *et al.* (1966), Dentesani (1989, 1990), Díaz (1997), Díaz *et al.* (1996), Étchécopar & Hüe (1964, 1978), Fellenberg & Pfennig (1980), Friedmann (1997), Fry *et al.* (1988), Gerasimov & Ozaki (2000), Hagemeijer & Blair (1997), Hågvar & Hågvar (1989), Hågvar *et al.* (1990), Harris (1999), Heath *et al.* (2000), Hogstad (1978), Hüe (1949-1950), Hüe & Étchécopar (1970), Kawada (1980), Kilham (1979b), Ledant *et al.* (1981), Lenz (1997, 1998), Lobkov (1999), MacKinnon & Phillipps (2000), Marchant *et al.* (1990), Mauersberger *et al.* (1982), Melde (1994), Mikusinski (2001), Mikusinski & Angelstam (1997, 1998), Mulhauser, Kaiser & Claude (2000), Mulhauser, Kaiser & Junod (2001), Nilsson *et al.* (1992), Olsson (1998), Olsson *et al.* (1992), Pavlík (1994), Pfennig (1988), Purroy (1997), Radermacher (1970, 1980), Richardson (1948), Rogacheva (1992), Romero (1994), Schlegel & Schlegel (1971), Schmid (1993), Snow & Perrins (1998), Spitznagel (1990), Svensson *et al.* (1999), Tobalske & Tobalske (1999), Väisänen & Koskimies (1989), Wesolowski & Tomialojc (1986), Wiktander (1998), Wiktander, Nilsson, I.N. *et al.* (1992), Wiktander, Nilsson, S.G. *et al.* (1994), Wiktander, Olsson & Nilsson (2000, 2001a, 2001b), Winkler (1971b), Winkler & Short (1978), Yamauchi *et al.* (1997), Zhao Zhengjie (1995).

95. Brown-fronted Woodpecker

Dendrocopos auriceps

French: Pic à tête jaune **German**: Braunstirnspecht **Spanish**: Pico Frentipardo
Other common names: Brown-fronted Pied Woodpecker

Taxonomy. *Picus auriceps* Vigors, 1831, Himalayas.
Genus sometimes merged into *Picoides*. Size decreases clinally from W to E, but no grounds for naming of geographical races. Some variation in the nape colour of females, but few details; further study required. Monotypic.
Distribution. N Baluchistan, and W Himalayas from NE Afghanistan (Nuristan) E to N India and E Nepal.

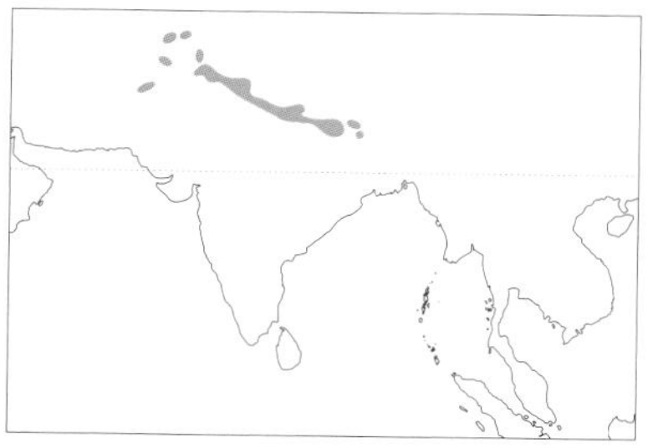

Descriptive notes. 19-20 cm; 37-50 g. Male has dull brown to yellow-brown forehead and forecrown, yellower mid-crown, orange-red nape patch, black hindneck; rest of head white, grey-brown feather tips forming darker patch on ear-coverts, narrow brown-grey malar stripe becoming broader and black at rear, continuing to upper breast side; white chin and throat tinged brown or grey; black upperparts barred white on mantle and back, wing-coverts broadly tipped white; brownish-black flight-feathers barred white; uppertail black, outer feathers barred white; white below, lower breast and flanks tinged yellow, becoming pink or orange on central belly and undertail-coverts, broad black streaks on breast becoming paler and narrower on lower underparts, belly sometimes plain; medium-long bill slightly chisel-tipped, culmen barely curved, slate-grey to bluish, paler base of lower mandible; iris red-brown to red; legs grey-green to slate-grey. Distinguished from *D. macei* by shorter bill, yellow crown, and heavier streaking on whiter underparts; from *D. mahrattensis* also by slightly larger size, duller crown colour, darker malar, and red undertail-coverts. Female differs from male in head pattern, has crown duller yellow, occasionally with hint of orange, sometimes greener, this colour continuing to nape, also duller red eyes. Juvenile duller than adult, with browner ear-coverts, is greyer below with paler pink vent, both sexes with crown as adult female's or sometimes streaked, male with trace of red in hindcrown, female with orange or yellow. Voice. Call "chick" or "peek", more squeaky than that of *D. himalayensis*, resembling call of *D. hyperythrus*; also "chitter-chitter-chitter-r-r-rh" or "cheek-cheek-cheek-rrrr", recalling a kingfisher (Alcedinidae). Drums frequently in breeding season.
Habitat. Coniferous and pine-oak forest, and montane dry deciduous forest; also park-like woodland and secondary growth. In Pakistan mainly in subtropical pine belt (*Pinus roxburghii*, *P. longifolia*), but also visits *P. gerardiana* forest and cedar (*Cedrus*) stands. Breeds to at least 2100 m in Afghanistan; at 900-1800 m in Pakistan, with few to 3000 m; 1000-2400 m, less commonly to 2950 m, in Nepal. Generally replaced by *D. himalayensis* at higher altitudes.
Food and Feeding. Insects and their larvae, mainly lepidopteran caterpillars, grubs. Commonly takes vegetable matter, including fruits, berries and pine seeds; possibly sap. Forages singly or in pairs; often joins mixed flocks of tits (Paridae) and minivets (*Pericrocotus*). Foraging mostly confined to trees and bushes, rarely visits ground. Main techniques gleaning and probing; also hammers.

On following pages: 96. Fulvous-breasted Woodpecker (*Dendrocopos macei*); 97. Stripe-breasted Woodpecker (*Dendrocopos atratus*); 98. Yellow-crowned Woodpecker (*Dendrocopos mahrattensis*); 99. Arabian Woodpecker (*Dendrocopos dorae*); 100. Rufous-bellied Woodpecker (*Dendrocopos hyperythrus*); 101. Crimson-breasted Woodpecker (*Dendrocopos cathpharius*).

Breeding. Season Apr-Jul. Nest-hole excavated at 2-12 m, mostly below 8 m, in dead trunk or in underside of large branch of pine, Himalayan elm (*Ulmus wallichiana*) or other tall tree. Clutch 3-5 eggs, usually 4; incubation and fledging periods not recorded; chicks fed by both parents.
Movements. Descends to lower altitudes in winter.
Status and Conservation. Not globally threatened. Locally common throughout range. No known threats. Research required to determine details of its breeding.
Bibliography. Ali & Ripley (1983), Bates & Lowther (1952), Biswas (1961a), Christison (1942), Delacour (1951a), Diesselhorst (1968), Fulton (1904), Grimmett *et al.* (1998, 2000), Hüe & Étchécopar (1970), Inskipp, C. (1989), Inskipp, C. & Inskipp (1991), Inskipp, T. *et al.* (1996), Kazmierczak (2000), Mason & Lefroy (1912), Mohan (1997), Proud (1958), Raja *et al.* (1999), Rand & Fleming (1956), Ripley (1982), Roberts (1991), Shrestha (2000), Whitehead (1911), Winkler & Short (1978).

96. Fulvous-breasted Woodpecker

Dendrocopos macei

French: Pic de Macé **German**: Isabellbrustspecht **Spanish**: Pico de Macé
Other common names: Fulvous-breasted/Spotted-breasted Pied Woodpecker, Streak-bellied Woodpecker

Taxonomy. *Picus Macei* Vieillot, 1818, Bengal.
Genus sometimes merged into *Picoides*. Forms a superspecies with *D. atratus*. E races *analis*, *longipennis* and *andamanensis* have sometimes been treated as forming a separate species. Birds from W Javan hills described as race *montis*, but inseparable from *analis*. Five subspecies recognized.
Subspecies and Distribution.
D. m. westermani (Blyth, 1870) - N Pakistan (Margalla Hills), NW India (Himachal Pradesh) and W Nepal.
D. m. macei (Vieillot, 1818) - C Nepal E to N Myanmar, and S in E peninsular India to Orissa and NE Andhra Pradesh.
D. m. andamanensis (Blyth, 1859) - Andaman Is.
D. m. longipennis Hesse, 1912 - S Myanmar, NW, W & C Thailand, and C Laos and Annam S to Cambodia and Cochinchina.
D. m. analis (Bonaparte, 1850) - Java and Bali; probably also S Sumatra.

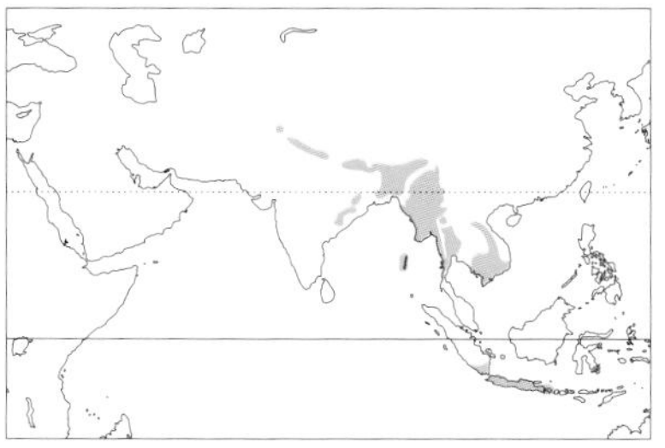

Descriptive notes. 18-19 cm; 23-38 g (*macei*). Male has buffish lower forehead, red upper forehead to nape with black feather bases showing, white lores, face and sides of neck tinged pale buffish, especially on ear-coverts, black malar stripe expanding at rear and continuing just on to upper breast side; very pale buffish-white chin and throat; black hindneck and upperparts, broad white bars from mantle to upper rump, wing-coverts broadly tipped white; black flight-feathers barred white; uppertail black, outer 1 or 2 feather pairs barred white; light buffish-brown below, breast occasionally tinged reddish, belly and flanks sometimes browner, breast sides and flanks streaked blackish, lower flanks and belly sometimes barred, central lower belly to undertail-coverts unmarked red; long bill straight, chisel-tipped, blackish-grey, paler base; iris red-brown, orbital skin grey; legs grey-green to greenish-slate. Distinguished from *D. auriceps* by much longer bill, fully red crown, darker underparts with less heavy streaking; from *D. atratus* by slightly smaller size, less heavy streaking below. Female has entire top of head black. Juvenile duller above and below than adult, has only small area of pink (not red) on undertail-coverts, both sexes with some red in crown centre, much less on female. Race *westermani* has longer bill, wing and tail than nominate, slightly darker throat contrasting less with breast; *analis* has black nape, buff-brown ear-coverts, fully barred tail, white throat, paler yellow-buff tinge below, breast with small blackish spots, reduced markings on belly and flanks, pale pink undertail-coverts; *longipennis* as previous, but paler below with markings more prominent, broader spots and streaks on breast forming necklace, thin bars on flanks, deeper red-pink undertail-coverts; *andamanensis* distinctive, has pale bill, black-streaked face, fully barred tail, white throat, large rounded or heart-shaped spots on breast, barred upper belly and flanks, female with brown, not black, crown. Voice. Call "tchick", sharper than that of *D. canicapillus*, less sharp and less loud than *D. atratus*, given singly or in series; also "pik-pik" or "chik-it-chik-it"; rattle comprising call note and a series of slightly lower "pit" notes, terminating with call note, slower than similar vocalization of *D. canicapillus*. Drums in weak, short rolls.
Habitat. In S Asian lowlands and foothills prefers open forest, edge, secondary forest, open country with scattered trees, plantations and gardens; also found in bamboo stands, and in scattered trees and larger bushes along dry riverbeds. In Himalayas, occurs in tall deciduous stands, especially mixed *Bombax-Ficus* woods; also tropical dry deciduous scrub in Pakistan. Generally found below 1200 m in SE Asia, and mostly below 600 m; present up to 2800 m in Himalayas and Greater Sundas.
Food and Feeding. Ants, a variety of other insects, larvae (usually large ones), also small scorpions (Scorpiones); berries and fruits also taken. Occurs singly or in pairs, or in family parties, also in mixed-species flocks. Favours tall trees, including isolated ones in open areas near forest. Forages on trunks and larger branches, also well up under the crown and among crown foliage on small branches and large twigs; rarely at lower levels (except in Andamans), or on the ground when seeking ants. Feeding techniques include gleaning, probing and strong pecks and hammering; also prises off bark.
Breeding. Jan-May, sometimes to Jun, in Indian Subcontinent; Dec-Mar, less commonly to Jun, in SE Asia; mostly between Apr and Oct, rarely Jan, in Java. Display with crest-raising, swinging movements, and others, also fluttering aerial display. Nest-hole excavated by both sexes, at 1-3 m, sometimes higher, in branch (often on underside) of free-standing tree, or in bamboo, or in fence post or palm stub in open ground at edge of forest. Clutch 2-5 eggs, usually 3; incubation and brood-feeding by both parents, respective periods not documented.
Movements. Resident.
Status and Conservation. Not globally threatened. Local and rare in Pakistan, but possibly more common than believed; common to frequent in Nepal, common in India and Bangladesh, uncommon in Bhutan; uncommon to fairly common in Myanmar and SE Asia; fairly common in Java and Bali. Occurs in several protected areas, e.g. Corbett, Dibru Saikhowa and Kaziranga National Parks (India), Doi Inthanon National Park (Thailand), Baluran National Park (Java) and Bali Barat National Park (Bali).
Bibliography. Ali & Ripley (1983), Ali *et al.* (1996), Andrew (1992), van Balen (1999), Barker *et al.* (1999), Biswas (1961a), Deignan (1945), Delacour (1951a, 1951b), Duckworth *et al.* (1999), Fleming & Traylor (1968), George (1968), Grimmett *et al.* (1998), Harvey (1990), Hesse (1912), Inskipp, C. (1989), Inskipp, C. & Inskipp (1991), Inskipp, T. *et al.* (1996), King & Rappole (2001), Lekagul & Round (1991), MacKinnon (1988), MacKinnon & Phillipps (1993, 2000), van Marle & Voous (1988), Mees (1996), Proud (1952, 1958), Rattray (1905), Riley (1938), Ripley (1982), Roberts (1991, 1996), Robson (2000), Sargeant (1997), Short (1973d), Smythies (1986), Stresemann (1921a), Tykader (1984), Tymstra *et al.* (1997), Wexler (1996), White & Bruce (1986), Winkler & Short (1978), Yoganand & Davidar (2000).

97. Stripe-breasted Woodpecker

Dendrocopos atratus

French: Pic à poitrine rayée **German**: Streifenbrustspecht **Spanish**: Pico Estriado
Other common names: Stripe-breasted Pied Woodpecker

Taxonomy. *Dryobates atratus* Blyth, 1849, Tenasserim.
Genus sometimes merged into *Picoides*. Forms a superspecies with *D. macei*. Birds from Vietnam have sometimes been separated as race *vietnamensis*, but available evidence suggests they are not clearly distinguishable; further study required. Monotypic.
Distribution. NE Indian hills (Meghalaya, Manipur, Mizoram), and possibly also C & SE Bangladesh, to W, S & E Myanmar and SW China (W & S Yunnan), and S to W & C Thailand, Cambodia, S Laos and SC Annam.

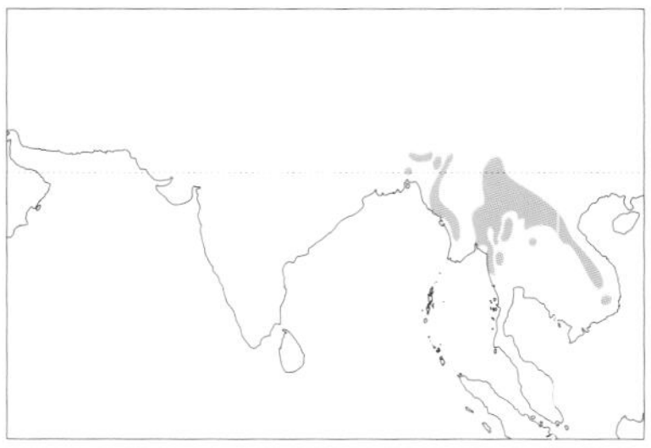

Descriptive notes. 21-22 cm; 42-52 g. Male has whitish nasal tufts beneath dark lower forehead, bright red upper forehead to nape (rarely, some admixed yellow) with usually some black streaks, black hindneck; rest of head and neck white, usually with a few thin black streaks, black malar stripe expanding on side of neck and extending to upper breast side, whitish throat lightly streaked dark; upperparts black, broad white bars from lower mantle to upper rump, wing-coverts with large white subterminal spots (much smaller on lesser coverts); black flight-feathers barred white; uppertail black, white bars on outer 2, sometimes 3, feather pairs; pale greyish-yellow below, belly yellower, very broad long black streaks over entire area down to lower belly (occasionally absent on central belly), lower flanks slightly barred, undertail-coverts tipped bright red; long bill straight, chisel-tipped, horn-brown to dark grey or sometimes greenish, paler base; iris brown to brown-red; legs grey, often tinged blue or greenish. Differs from *D. macei* mainly in larger size, stronger bill, much heavier markings below. Female lacks red on head, has crown and nape entirely black. Juvenile duller than adult, greyer below with broader but more obscure streaks, vent more orangey, male with dark red on crown, female with a few red-tipped feathers in mid-crown. Voice. Explosive "tchick", and whinnying rattle call. Probably drums.
Habitat. Open oak (*Quercus*) and pine (*Pinus*) woodland in hill evergreen forest; pine forest preferred, but edges of open broadleaved forest also occupied. Also occurs in cultivated areas and in clearings with scattered trees. Between 800 m and 2200 m, occasionally higher; to 1500 m in NE Indian hills.
Food and Feeding. Insects, particularly beetle larvae and ants. Seen singly, in pairs or in family parties. Forages mostly at middle to upper levels, but sometimes at lower levels. Pecking and hammering seem to be rather important feeding modes.
Breeding. Mar-May in India and Apr-May in Myanmar; Feb-May elsewhere. Nest-hole excavated at up to 4 m in stump, or much higher, to 20 m, in tree. Clutch 4-5 eggs. No information on incubation and fledging periods; few data, but one record of fledglings accompanied by parents for at least 10 days.
Movements. None recorded.
Status and Conservation. Not globally threatened. Status in India uncertain, but appears to be uncommon; in Bangladesh, possibly rare to scarce, but no recent information. Rare in China (Yunnan). Fairly common but rather local in SE Asia. Occurs in Doi Inthanon and Nam Nao National Parks (Thailand).
Bibliography. Ali & Ripley (1983), Chazee (1994), Deignan (1945), Delacour (1951a), Delacour & Jabouille (1940), Duckworth *et al.* (1999), Evans & Timmins (1998), Grimmett *et al.* (1998), Inskipp, C. *et al.* (1999), Inskipp, T. *et al.* (1996), Kazmierczak (2000), Khan (1982), Lekagul & Round (1991), MacKinnon & Phillipps (2000), Riley (1938), Ripley (1982), Robson (2000), Smythies (1986), Winkler & Short (1978), Zhao Zhengjie (1995), Zusi & Marshall (1970).

98. Yellow-crowned Woodpecker

Dendrocopos mahrattensis

French: Pic mahratte **German**: Gelbscheitelspecht **Spanish**: Pico Mahratta
Other common names: Yellow-fronted/Mahratta Woodpecker/Pied Woodpecker

Taxonomy. *Picus Mahrattensis* Latham, 1801, Mahratta country, south-west India.
Genus sometimes merged into *Picoides*. Most closely related to the *D. macei* superspecies. Variation mostly clinal, and named races *aurocristatus* (N Myanmar) and *koelzi* (NW Sri Lanka) are thus unacceptable. Two subspecies recognized.
Subspecies and Distribution.
D. m. pallescens Biswas, 1951 - E Pakistan (E of R Indus) and N & NW India.
D. m. mahrattensis (Latham, 1801) - most of India E to Assam, Sri Lanka, and W, C & S Myanmar, E Cambodia, S Laos and S Annam; formerly also WC Thailand (extinct).
Descriptive notes. 17-18 cm; 28-46 g. Male has golden-yellow forehead and forecrown, becoming red on hindcrown and nape, dark brown hindneck; white sides of head tinged or streaked brownish below eye and on ear-coverts; rich brown rear malar stripe continuing upwards behind ear-coverts and down on to upper breast side; white chin and throat sometimes tinged brown; blackish-brown or black upperparts, feathers broadly edged white near tips, rump largely white; white uppertail-coverts with black central wedge; wing-coverts tipped white, flight-feathers barred white; uppertail dark brown-black, fully barred white; whitish below, streaked brown or blackish, streaks often lacking or indistinct in breast centre but broad on breast sides and upper flanks, belly centre orange-red; long bill fairly straight, slightly chisel-tipped, slate-grey to horn, paler base of lower mandible; iris brown to red-brown; legs blue-grey. Distinguished from similar *D. auriceps* by less barred upperparts, fainter incomplete malar, fully barred tail, orange belly patch, and white undertail-coverts. Female has yellowish crown with no red or with just few red tips, brownish nape. Juvenile duller than adult, more brownish above, with streaks below more dif-

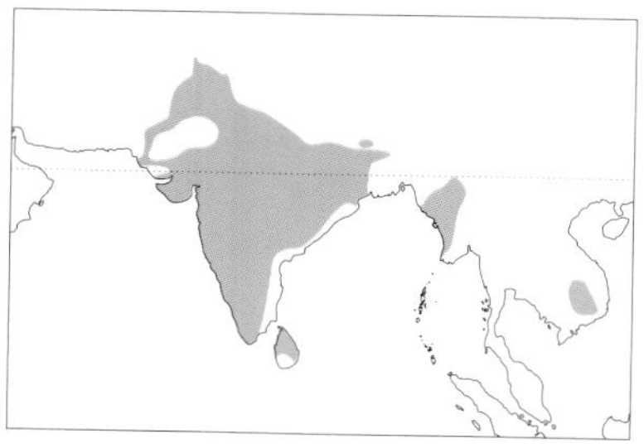

fuse, belly pinker, eyes brown, bill usually paler, male with some orange-red on crown and often nape, female with a few orange-red feathers in central crown. Race *pallescens* is paler than nominate, has paler head markings, larger white markings above, rump sometimes completely white, streaks below very light brown. VOICE. Feeble "peek" or sharp "click, click", also "click-r-r-r-r", "kik-kik-kik-r-r-r-r-h". Drums.

Habitat. Dry to very dry open woodland and desert scrub, including deciduous woodland, second growth, riverine forest, wild olive (*Olea cuspidata*) woodland, plantations, and trees bordering roadsides or watercourses; also found in cultivations and gardens. Visits remnant semi-evergreen patches near coast in W India. Shows distinct preference for the abundant big *Euphorbia antiquorum* trees in dry districts of Sri Lanka. Below 1000 m in most of range; only occasionally higher, to 1700 m in Nepal, to 2000 m in S India.

Food and Feeding. Bark-dwelling insects, also fruits and nectar. In particular, caterpillars (Geometridae), grubs (Elateridae, Curculionidae, Buprestidae) and dragonflies (Odonata) reported. Forages singly or in pairs, members of which keep in loose vocal contact; also joins mixed-species flocks. Stays mostly in crown of trees and on trunks, comes down to the ground rarely; regularly clings upside-down. Excavates bark and dead wood for insect larvae; observed pecking holes in dry pods of *Cassia fistula* to extract insect larvae.

Breeding. Feb-Jul, also Dec, in Indian Subcontinent; Feb-Apr in SE Asia. Nest-hole excavated at 1-10 m in dead section of live tree, often on underside of a sloping branch; usurpation of hole by *Dinopium benghalense* recorded. Clutch 3 eggs; both parents incubate and both feed chicks; incubation period 13 days, fledging period not documented; fledglings may stay with parents until onset of next breeding cycle.

Movements. None recorded.

Status and Conservation. Not globally threatened. Frequent in Pakistan, locally common in India, uncommon in Nepal, common in SE Sri Lanka; no recent records from Bangladesh; rare to uncommon in SE Asia. Occurs in several protected areas, e.g. Keoladeo Ghana, Ranthambore and Mudumalai National Parks and Peechi-Vazhani Wildlife Sanctuary (India) and Uda Walawe, Yala and Bundala National Parks (Sri Lanka).

Bibliography. Ali (1996), Ali & Ripley (1983), Betts (1934), Biswas (1951), Delacour (1951a), Delacour & Jabouille (1940), Duckworth *et al.* (1999), Eates (1937), Gokula & Vijayan (1997), Grimmett *et al.* (1998, 2000), Harrison (1999), Harvey (1990), Henry (1998), Inskipp, C. (1989), Inskipp, C. & Inskipp (1991), Inskipp, T. *et al.* (1996), Javed & Rahmani (1998), Kalsi (1998), Kazmierczak (2000), King & Rappole (2001), Lainer (1999), Lamsfuss (1998), Lekagul & Round (1991), Mason & Lefroy (1912), Morioka & Sakane (1981), Mukherjee (1995), Phillips (1978), Ripley (1982), Roberts (1991), Robson (2000), Round (1988), Santharam (1998a, 1998b, 1998c), Shrestha (2000), Smythies (1986), Thewlis *et al.* (1998), Whitehead (1911), Winkler & Short (1978).

99. **Arabian Woodpecker**

Dendrocopos dorae

French: Pic d'Arabie **German**: Araberspecht **Spanish**: Pico Árabe

Taxonomy. *Desertipicus doræ* Bates and Kinnear, 1935, Ukadh, Taif-Mecca road, Arabia.
Genus sometimes merged into *Picoides*. Relationships unclear; thought most likely to be related to *D. mahrattensis* and the *D. macei* superspecies. Monotypic.

Distribution. SW Arabian Peninsula, in narrow band from just N of Mecca S to W South Yemen.

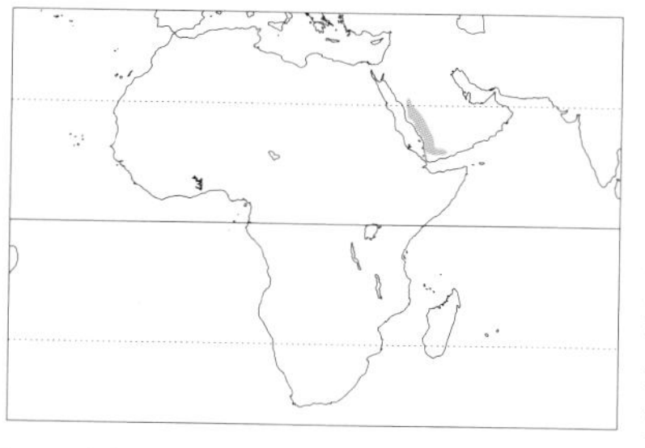

Descriptive notes. 18 cm; 19-20 g. Male has crimson-red hindcrown and nape, olive-grey to brown hindneck; rest of head variably brownish to light grey-brown or dark brown, paler streaks on ear-coverts and sometimes above eye, often paler in malar region and sometimes behind ear-coverts; whitish to pale brownish chin and throat; upperparts brown to olive-brown or grey-brown, often tinged golden, rump and uppertail-coverts darker; wings blackish, coverts (except lessers) tipped white, flight-feathers barred white; uppertail blackish, outer rectrices barred white, second-outer with few white bars; pale olive-brown to greyish-brown below, red or orange-red patch on central belly, flanks and lower belly faintly barred brown and white, browner undertail-coverts spotted or barred white; fairly long bill almost straight, chisel-tipped, broad across nostrils, slate-grey to horn, usually paler base of lower mandible; iris whitish or grey-brown; legs grey. Female lacks red on head, tends to be somewhat duller, with less prominent red on belly. Juvenile much as adult, but greyer with some streaking below, belly more pink than red, male with orange-red patch on crown. VOICE. Common vocalization "pweek pit-pit-pit-pit-pit-pit-pit-ptptpt". Occasionally drums, feebly.

Habitat. Inhabits riparian woodland dominated by *Cordia abyssinica*, well-mixed and dense stands of predominantly *Juniperus*, *Olea* and *Nuxia* on mountain slopes; also uses pure stands of *Acacia origena*, and scattered acacias (predominantly *A. iraquensis*) in flat desert areas; also palm and fig groves with adjacent acacias at base of escarpments. Breeds mainly in valleys, on slopes and in highlands at altitudes of 1200-2400 m; occurs from sea-level up to 3000 m outside breeding season.

Food and Feeding. Larvae of wood-boring insects, fig wasps, and aphids and other winged insects recorded as adult and nestling food. Ants living in base of acacias possibly important. Tree sap important in winter; may take fruits as well. Usually singly or in pairs. Forages commonly in crown of trees, mostly *Acacia*, on medium to thin branches and twigs, frequently along underside; also descends to ground. Hammers, probes, and occasionally flakes off bark; gleaning is predominant foraging technique in nesting season.

Breeding. Mar-May, occasionally from Feb; possibly in Nov in Yemen. Nest excavated mostly at 0·5-6 m up tree trunk or limb in live or dead wood, or at up to 9 m and rarely even 25 m in stump of palm tree. Clutch 3 eggs; incubation by both parents, for period of 11 days; both adults also feed chicks, fledging period c. 22 days; young birds remain in nesting area for at least two months after fledging.

Movements. Some seasonal altitudinal movements apparent; found down to lowlands in winter, and in summer at least part of population moves c. 350 m farther upslope.

Status and Conservation. VULNERABLE. Generally rather uncommon, locally rare. Occurs in Asir National Park and Rayah Reserve (Saudi Arabia). Population small, estimated at fewer than 10,000 individuals, and probably declining. Densities vary from 0·1 to 1·0 adults/km². Following centuries of human colonization and associated activities, this species' woodland habitat has become highly fragmented. Continuing clearance for agriculture and building, and for firewood, oftens result in removal of large trees required by this woodpecker for its nest-sites; heavy grazing can prevent the regeneration of trees. Although many wooded areas in W Arabia have long been protected from overexploitation, to ensure a source of fodder during drought, traditional management was largely abandoned in latter part of 20th century as it became easier to obtain alternative supplies of feed. Effective conservation measures proposed include designation of additional protected areas, the encouragement of non-intensive, traditional methods of woodland management, and the raising of the profile of this species in its Arabian homeland.

Bibliography. Brooks *et al.* (1987), Cornwallis & Porter (1982), Everett (1987), Hansbro & Sargeant (2000), Hollom *et al.* (1988), Jennings, M.C. (1995), Lees-Smith (1986), Newton & Newton (1996), Porter, Christensen & Schiermacker-Hansen (1996), Porter, Martins *et al.* (1996), Rands *et al.* (1987), Stagg (1985), Stanton (1997), Stattersfield & Capper (2000), Varisco *et al.* (1992), Winkler & Short (1978), Winkler *et al.* (1996).

100. **Rufous-bellied Woodpecker**

Dendrocopos hyperythrus

French: Pic à ventre fauve **German**: Braunkehlspecht **Spanish**: Pico Ventrirrufo
Other common names: Rufous-bellied Pied Woodpecker/Sapsucker

Taxonomy. *Picus hyperythrus* Vigors, 1831, eastern Himalayas.
Genus sometimes merged into *Picoides*. Relationships within genus somewhat obscure; most likely related to S Asian *D. macei* superspecies and *D. cathpharius*. Variation, particularly in tone of underparts, is considerable, but largely individual. Four subspecies recognized.

Subspecies and Distribution.
D. h. marshalli (Hartert, 1912) - NE Pakistan, Kashmir and N India.
D. h. hyperythrus (Vigors, 1831) - Nepal E to SE Tibet and W & SW China (Sichuan, Yunnan), S to Bangladesh, C Myanmar and NW Thailand.
D. h. annamensis (Kloss, 1925) - E Thailand, Cambodia and S Vietnam.
D. h. subrufinus (Cabanis & Heine, 1863) - Manchuria and Ussuriland; winters S China.

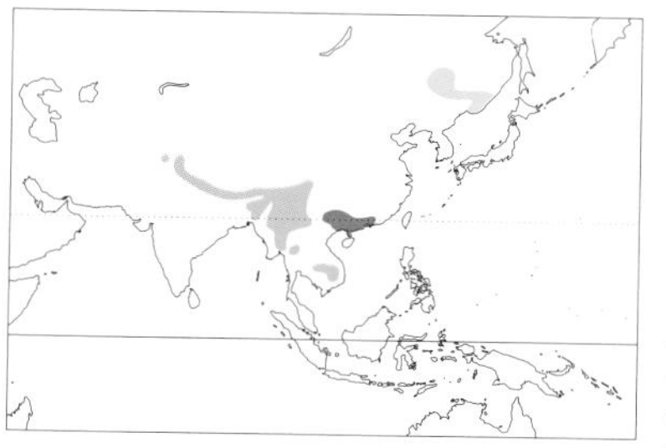

Descriptive notes. 20-25 cm; 40-53 g (*hyperythrus*, *annamensis*), 53-74 g (*marshalli*, *subrufinus*). Male has bright red forehead to nape (in W populations, red often continues behind ear-coverts), nape sometimes tinged orange, often a few black feather bases showing on crown; white lores, forecheeks and thin line over and just behind eye, a few greyish marks in loral area; whitish malar region with dusky streaks; rest of head rufous-chestnut; entire upperparts black, mantle to upper rump barred white, bars broadest on upper back, wing-coverts and flight-feathers with white spots forming bars; uppertail black, outer 2 feather pairs barred white; rufous-chestnut continues over underparts, but for pinkish-red lower belly and undertail-coverts, narrow band of black and white bars on lower belly sides and flanks; long bill almost straight, chisel-tipped, black or blackish, lower mandible pale yellow or greener; iris red-brown to pale reddish or deep brown; legs olive to greenish-grey or slaty. Female has black forehead to hindneck with white spots, occasionally a few red feather tips. Juvenile has white-spotted black crown, streaked head, heavily streaked throat, upperparts more spotted than barred, browner wings, brownish underparts barred black and white, paler pinkish vent, darker brown eyes, male with many orange-red tips on crown, female with fewer; adult plumage acquired gradually, traces of juvenile plumage still evident in winter. Race *marshalli* is larger than nominate, red on head of male extends over entire nape, hindneck and rear part of sides of neck; *subrufinus* is on average largest, and paler, more rufous-buff, below; *annamensis* resembles previous, but is somewhat smaller, with relatively long bill. VOICE. Call "chit-chit-chit-r-r-r-r-h"; fast "ptikitititititit" in alarm. Both sexes drum in breeding season, rolls fading towards end.

Habitat. Broadleaved forest and mixed and coniferous forest. In Pakistan, prefers deciduous forest with Himalayan poplar (*Populus ciliata*) and false dogwood (*Cornus macrophylla*); farther E, found in evergreen montane forest and cloudforest, in oak (*Quercus*), chestnut (*Castanopsis*), silver fir (*Abies*) and pine (*Pinus*) forests, in mixed forest and in rhododendron. Occurs in oak and alder (*Alnus*) stands in N Myanmar, and open woodland of oak, pine and dry dipterocarp trees elsewhere in SE Asia. Occurs at 1500-2000 m in Pakistan, and 2100-4100 m in Nepal and Sikkim; in NW Myanmar most common at 2000-2800 m, and in other parts of SE Asia ranges between 500 m and 1200 m; to 4300 m in China.

Food and Feeding. Insects, and vegetable matter. Ants can constitute more than 60% of diet; beetles (Carabidae), Orthoptera, Lepidoptera and caterpillars, and other small insects also recorded. Feeds on sap in spring. Often singly; may associate with flocks of small insectivorous birds outside breeding season. Forages on tree trunks in the canopy; probes frequently, also hammers and gleans. Sometimes catches prey on the wing. Creates sap wells by drilling dense rows of 8-10 small holes girdling trunks of various tree species.

Breeding. Apr-May in Nepal and India; Mar-May in SE Asia. Nest a typical woodpecker hole excavated at 5-6 m in trunk of tree. Clutch 4 or 5 eggs; incubation and fledging periods not documented; both sexes care for chicks.

Movements. NE populations (*subrufinus*) migratory, passing through C China in May and again in Aug-Sept, and wintering in S & SE China; vagrant in Korea (last record 1933). Altitudinal movements in Tibet, moving down to 1500 m after breeding; possibly some similar movements in Nepal, down to 2000 m outside breeding season.

Status and Conservation. Not globally threatened. Rather uncommon to scarce in most of range. Possibly locally more common in N India and Nepal, common in Bhutan; no recent records from Bangladesh. Uncommon to scarce in China and Ussuriland. Has disappeared from some parts of range since 1960's; in Pakistan, loss of deciduous trees through cutting for animal forage has resulted in some forests becoming dominated by coniferous stands, unsuitable for this species.

Bibliography. Ali & Ripley (1983), Ali *et al.* (1996), Deignan (1945), Delacour (1951a, 1951b), Diesselhorst (1968), Eames (1995), Étchécopar & Hüe (1978), Grimmett *et al.* (1998), Harvey (1990), Inskipp, C. (1989), Inskipp, C. & Inskipp (1991), Inskipp, T. *et al.* (1996), Knystautas (1993), Koelz (1952), Lekagul & Round (1991), Ludlow (1937), MacKinnon & Phillipps (2000), Osmaston (1916), Proud (1958), Riley (1938), Ripley (1982, 1991), Roberts (1991, 1996), Robson (2000), Shrestha (2000), Smythies (1986), Tymstra *et al.* (1997), Vaurie (1972), Winkler & Short (1978), Won Pyongoh (1993), Zhao Zhengjie (1995), Zusi & Marshall (1970).

101. **Crimson-breasted Woodpecker**

Dendrocopos cathpharius

French: Pic à plastron rouge   **German**: Rotbrustspecht   **Spanish**: Pico Pechirrojo
Other common names: (Small) Crimson-breasted Pied Woodpecker, Lesser Pied Woodpecker

Taxonomy. *Picus (Dendrocopus)* [sic] *cathpharius* Blyth, 1843, Darjeeling.
Genus sometimes merged into *Picoides*. Most closely related to *D. darjellensis*, and probably more distantly to the *D. macei* superspecies. Six subspecies recognized.
Subspecies and Distribution.
D. c. cathpharius (Blyth, 1843) - WC Nepal E to Arunachal Pradesh.
D. c. ludlowi Vaurie, 1959 - SE Tibet (S Tsangpo Valley).
D. c. pyrrhothorax (Hume, 1881) - NE India S of R Brahmaputra (Meghalaya, Nagaland, Manipur, Mizoram) and W Myanmar (W of R Chindwin).
D. c. pernyii (J. Verreaux, 1867) - WC & SW China (SW Gansu, N & E Sichuan, NW Yunnan).
D. c. innixus (Bangs & J. L. Peters, 1928) - C China (S Shaanxi, Hubei).
D. c. tenebrosus (Rothschild, 1926) - N, C & E Myanmar, C & S Yunnan, NW Thailand, N Laos and W Tonkin.
Descriptive notes. 17-19 cm; 23-35 g. Male has buffish-white forehead with indistinct dark central line, black crown, red nape, hindneck and rear part of sides of neck; white lores and side of head, ear-coverts with faint buff tinge and sometimes very faint dark streaks; black malar stripe joining black patch on side of neck and extending down to breast side; white chin, pale buff throat; black upperparts and wings, inner wing-coverts mainly white, flight-feathers with small white spots forming narrow bars; uppertail black, outer 3 feather pairs barred whitish; pale buffish below, more yellowish on belly and flanks, small ill-defined patch of orange-red in breast centre (red can be lacking), breast broadly streaked black, streaks thinner from lower breast and mid-flanks, undertail-coverts streaked black and broadly tipped orange-red; relatively short bill grey to blue-grey, lower mandible very pale grey to whitish; iris brown to red-brown, orbital skin slate-grey or paler; legs dull grey to grey-green. Female has red on head replaced by black. Juvenile much as adult but darker and duller below, no red on breast, red of vent much paler or absent, male with orange-red from mid-crown to nape, female with smaller area of orange-red. Race *ludlowi* is slightly bigger than nomi-

nate, has more red on breast; *pyrrhothorax* is much paler on face and below, less streaked below, with prominent red patch on breast, redder undertail-coverts; *pernyii* is larger, has red on head restricted to nape, less white in wing, red breast patch bordered by broad black band, redder undertail-coverts; *innixus* resembles previous, but much paler below, black breastband narrower, lower underparts unstreaked or nearly so; *tenebrosus* is similar to last but smaller, has slightly more black on breast, much heavier streaking. VOICE. Loud monotonous "chip" or "tchick"; also very short, fast descending rattle. Drums.

Habitat. Broadleaved evergreen and deciduous forest with oaks (*Quercus*), rhododendron and chestnut (*Castanopsis*), at higher elevations. At 700-3000 m, occasionally to 3900 m, but mostly 1200-2800 m; occurs above 1400 m in Thailand, and is most common above 1500 m in Nepal.
Food and Feeding. Insects and their larvae; nectar. Usually found singly. Often forages in lower parts of trees and on bushes; prefers dead trees. Frequently hammers.
Breeding. Apr-May in W of range. Nest-hole in tree, but no details known. Clutch 2-4 eggs. No other information.
Movements. Some altitudinal movement seem possible, but no details available.
Status and Conservation. Not globally threatened. Generally uncommon throughout range. Frequent in Nepal, Bhutan and NE India; rare in China; scarce to uncommon elsewhere. Relatively poorly known; research required to determine details of its ecology and breeding. Present in Jiuzhaigou Reserve (China).
Bibliography. Ali & Ripley (1983), Ali *et al*. (1996), Bishop (1999b), Choudhury (2001), Deignan (1945), Delacour (1951a), Delacour & Jabouille (1940), Duckworth *et al*. (1999), Étchécopar & Hüe (1978), Grimmett *et al*. (1998, 2000), Inskipp, C. (1989), Inskipp, C. & Inskipp (1991), Inskipp, C. *et al*. (1999), Inskipp, T. *et al*. (1996), Lekagul & Round (1991), MacKinnon & Phillipps (2000), Ripley (1982), Robson (2000), Robson *et al*. (1998), Round (1988), Short (1973d), Shrestha (2000), Smythies (1986), Thewlis *et al*. (1998), Tymstra *et al*. (1997), Vaurie (1972), Winkler & Short (1978), Zhao Zhengjie (1995).

PLATE 34 ➤

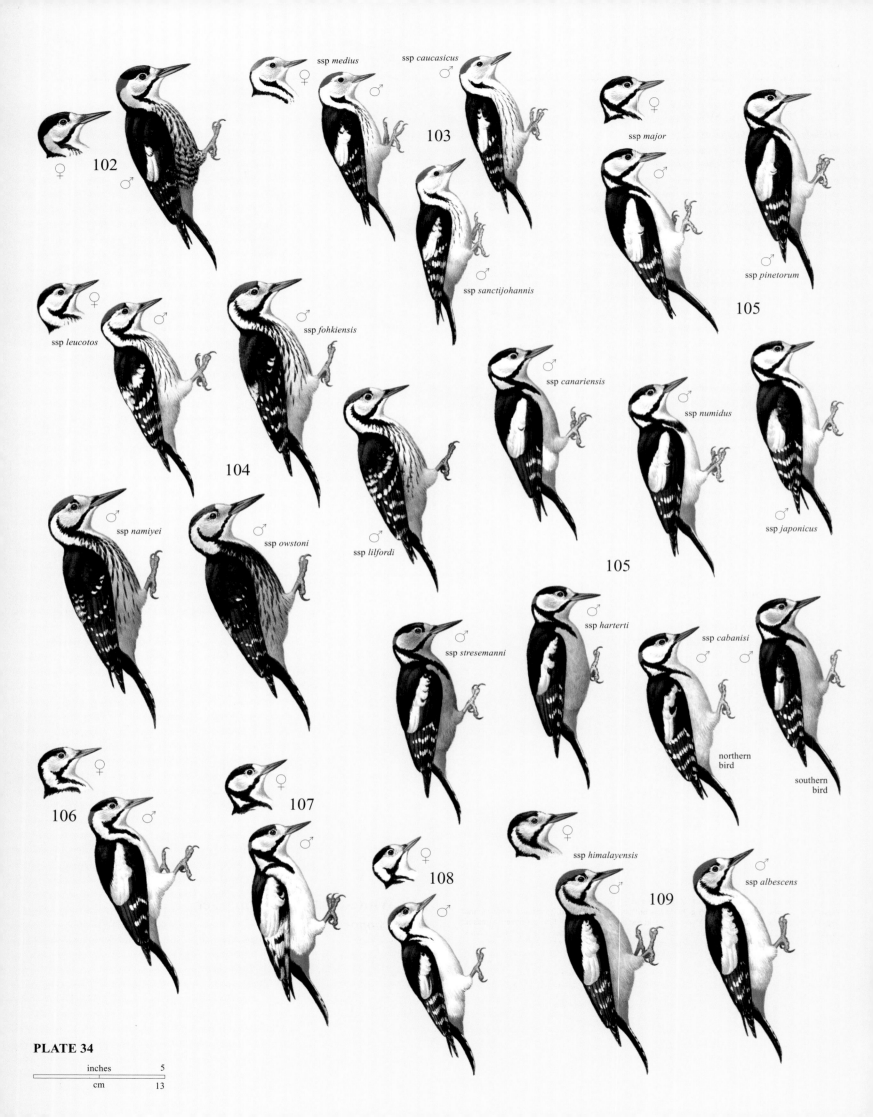

ssp *medius* ♂

ssp *caucasicus* ♂

103

ssp *sanctijohannis* ♂

♀

102 ♂

ssp *major* ♀

♂

ssp *pinetorum*

105

ssp *leucotos* ♀

♂ ssp *fohkiensis*

ssp *canariensis* ♂

ssp *numidus* ♂

104

♂ ssp *lilfordi*

ssp *japonicus* ♂

ssp *namiyei* ♂

♂ ssp *owstoni*

105

ssp *stresemanni* ♂

ssp *harterti* ♂

ssp *cabanisi* ♂

northern
bird

southern
bird

106 ♂

107 ♀

108 ♀

ssp *himalayensis* ♀

♂

109

ssp *albescens* ♂

♂

♂

PLATE 34

inches   5
cm   13

102. **Darjeeling Woodpecker**

Dendrocopos darjellensis

French: Pic de Darjiling **German**: Darjeelingspecht **Spanish**: Pico de Darjeeling
Other common names: Darjeeling Pied Woodpecker, Brown-throated Woodpecker

Taxonomy. *Picus (Dendrocopus)* [sic] *darjellensis* Blyth, 1845, Darjeeling and Nepal.
Genus sometimes merged into *Picoides*. Related to *D. cathpharius*; other possible relationships require clarification. NE populations average slightly smaller; birds from W China thus described as race *desmursi*, but variation is clinal in nature. Monotypic.
Distribution. WC Nepal and S & SE Tibet E to hills of NE India, N & W Myanmar, W & SW China (S Sichuan, W Yunnan) and N Vietnam (NW Tonkin).

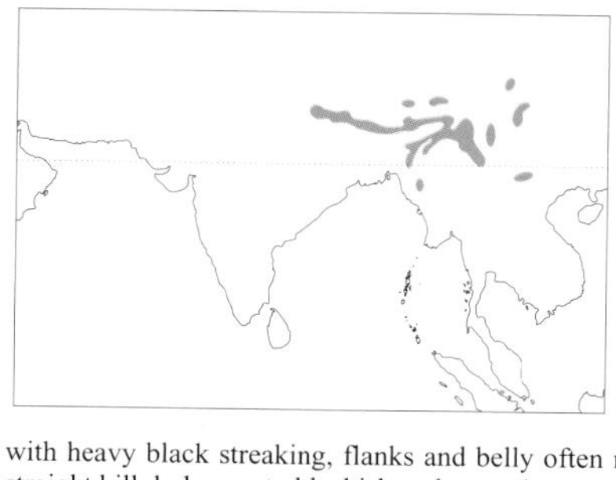

Descriptive notes. 25 cm; 61-87 g. Male has whitish lower forehead, black upper forehead and crown, narrow red nape patch, black hindneck; white lores, white sides of head tinged buff (sometimes strongly), golden-yellow to deep orange-buff sides of neck; black malar stripe extending to lower rear ear-coverts and down to sides of upper breast; black upperparts, wings sometimes browner, inner coverts largely white, flight-feathers narrowly barred white; uppertail black, outer 1-3 feather pairs barred white to pale buff; chin to upper breast brownish-buff to buff-brown, paler on lower breast, more yellow on flanks and belly, breast sides and lower breast with heavy black streaking, flanks and belly often more barred, undertail-coverts pinkish-red; long straight bill dark grey to blackish, pale grey lower mandible with greener or ivory-coloured base; iris red to red-brown, orbital skin slaty-grey; legs grey-green. Female has red of nape replaced by black. Juvenile as adult, but lacks golden patch on neck, is duller below with streaked throat, more barred belly and flanks, duller paler red on undertail-coverts, eyes dark brown, male with dull red crown, female usually with small red central patch or red tips but red may be lacking. Voice. Single "tsik" calls, as fast series in alarm; also trill-like rattle. Drums frequently in breeding season.
Habitat. High-elevation forest, cloudforest with moss-covered trees, open woodland; also evergreen and coniferous forest, and rhododendron woods. Rarely below 1500 m in SE Asia; mainly 2500-3500 m in Nepal, to almost 4000 m in Sikkim, Tibet and China.
Food and Feeding. Larvae of wood-boring insects; also adults, larvae and pupae of other insects. Usually forages singly or in pairs, which keep loose contact; will also join mixed-species flocks. Exploits all levels of habitat, visiting fallen logs, tree trunks and canopy. Mossy and dead surfaces carefully inspected, debris removed. Forceful pecking is rather common technique, and also uses gleaning and probing.
Breeding. Apr-May in W of range, sometimes to Jun; first nestlings in May. Moderate crest-raising is only visual display so far described. Nest-hole excavated at 1-2 m in tree. Clutch 2-4 eggs; incubation and fledging periods not documented; chicks fed by both parents.
Movements. Not well known; some altitudinal movements in Tibet and China, but some may remain at high elevations even in non-breeding season.
Status and Conservation. Not globally threatened. Fairly common in Nepal, locally fairly common in India, common in Bhutan; uncommon in Tibet and China; uncommon in Myanmar and Tonkin. Rather poorly known species, appears to be sparsely distributed throughout range. More study required on its ecology and breeding behaviour.
Bibliography. Ali & Ripley (1983), Ali *et al.* (1996), Choudhury (2001), Delacour & Jabouille (1940), Diesselhorst (1968), Étchécopar & Hüe (1978), Grimmett *et al.* (1998, 2000), Inskipp, C. (1989), Inskipp, C. & Inskipp (1991, 1993, 1998), Inskipp, C. *et al.* (1999), Inskipp, T. *et al.* (1996), Kazmierczak (2000), Ludlow (1937), MacKinnon & Phillipps (2000), Martens & Eck (1995), Ripley (1982), Robson (2000), Short (1973d), Shrestha (2000), Smythies (1986), Stanford & Mayr (1941), Stevens (1925), Tymstra *et al.* (1997), Vaurie (1972), Winkler & Short (1978), Zhao Zhengjie (1995).

103. **Middle Spotted Woodpecker**

Dendrocopos medius

French: Pic mar **German**: Mittelspecht **Spanish**: Pico Mediano

Taxonomy. *Picus medius* Linnaeus, 1758, Sweden.
Genus sometimes merged into *Picoides*. Superficial similarity to *D. leucotos* may suggest possible relationship, although this not supported by available genetic data; may be related to *D. macei* superspecies, but little evidence; more study required. Variation is largely clinal, e.g. nominate race becoming darker with flank streaking more pronounced towards S, and races rather poorly differentiated; other named races are *lilianae* (NW Spain), *splendidior* (SE Europe to Greece and Turkey) and *laubmanni* (S Transcaucasia), all regarded as unacceptable. Four subspecies recognized.
Subspecies and Distribution.
D. m. medius (Linnaeus, 1758) - NW Spain and France NE to S Sweden (recently extinct), Estonia, W Russia and Ukraine, and SE to Italy and the Balkans.
D. m. caucasicus (Bianchi, 1904) - N Turkey, Caucasus and Transcaucasia; probably this race in NW Iran.
D. m. anatoliae (Hartert, 1912) - W & S Asia Minor.
D. m. sanctijohannis (Blanford, 1873) - Zagros Mts in SW Iran.

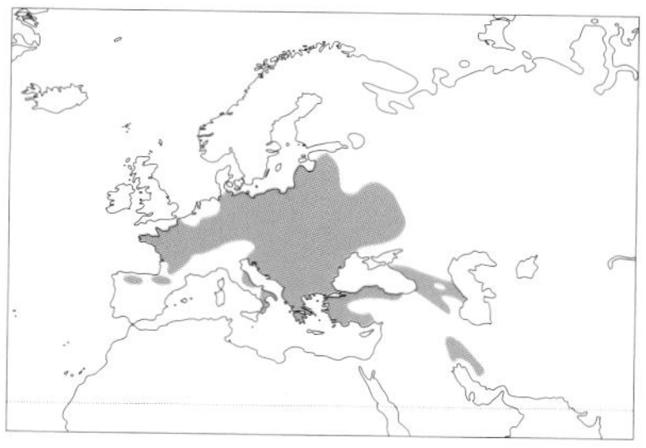

Descriptive notes. 20-22 cm; 50-85 g. Male has buffish-white forehead, crimson-red crown and nape (feathers long, narrow), narrow black hindneck; rest of head and neck white, ear-coverts streaked or mottled greyish, faint buff or pale greyish malar stripe, and large black patch on side of neck which curves up in narrow stripe behind ear-coverts (occasionally almost to nape) and down on to side of upper breast; dull black mantle and inner scapulars to uppertail-coverts, mainly white outer scapulars and inner wing-coverts with some black at base; black flight-feathers with large white spots forming 4-6 broken bars; uppertail black, outer 2 rectrices with white tips and outer webs, latter with 2-3 dark bars; white below, breast and flanks strongly tinged yellow-buff, becoming pinkish on upper belly and lower flanks, darker pink vent and undertail-coverts, long black streaks on sides of breast and flanks usually well defined; medium-length bill rather pointed, lead-grey or darker, paler base of lower mandible; iris red-brown or red; legs lead-grey, sometimes tinged greenish. Female is like male, some almost identical, but often red of crown paler, becoming browner to golden at rear, pale areas of head more buff. Juvenile duller than adult, especially on head (crown feathers shorter, less narrow), has brownish tips in pale areas of body, some brown in white wing patch, is greyer below, pink area paler and smaller, streaking more diffuse and usually hint of thin bars on flanks, eyes often grey-brown, male with grey-mottled red crown becoming blackish with red tips on nape, female with smaller area of duller red, hindcrown mostly black. Race *caucasicus* is brighter below than nominate, belly more golden-yellow, pink of ventral region less extensive but redder, breast sides and flanks more heavily streaked, outer rectrices more strongly and symmetrically barred; *anatoliae* is very similar to previous but marginally smaller, perhaps with heavier markings below, paler vent; *sanctijohannis* has much whiter head and underparts, yellow restricted to band across lower belly, deeper pink-red vent and undertail-coverts. Voice. Most frequent vocalization is rattle call "kíg-gag-gag-gag-gag-gag", most commonly with 3 or 4 elements; long-drawn, loud nasal "gwaaag" series territorially in spring, unmistakable. Instrumental signals include loud tapping at nest-hole, rarely drumming.
Habitat. Restricted to mature deciduous forest; prefers mixed oak (*Quercus*) and hornbeam (*Carpinus*) in primeval forest. Original habitat in C Europe probably floodplain-forest and hillsides covered with mature oak or beech (*Fagus sylvatica*), but nowadays depends on presence of oaks in large parts of range; old open orchards bordering deciduous woodland also used, but of dwindling importance. Occupies beech, mixed oak-beech and oak forest in S, and beech forest in NE Anatolia and Caucasus. Generally below 600 m, locally to 700 m or more (900 m); 300-1700 m in Italy; reaches 2300 m in SW Iran.
Food and Feeding. Bark-dwelling arthropods, caterpillars, dipterans, aphids, also plant material; no wood-boring larvae. Small beetles and ants predominate in adult food; nestlings fed with caterpillars, bugs, lice, beetles, hymenopterans and dipterans, as well as arachnids. Plant material taken mainly in winter, but fruits (cherries, plums, grapes) sometimes eaten during breeding season and even fed to nestlings; in winter, nuts (acorns, hazel nuts, walnuts, beech, rarely seeds of conifers) of some importance. Forages mostly singly; may join mixed-species flocks with tits (Paridae) and other woodpecker species. Explores most levels of trees; rarely descends to the ground. Seasonal differences in parts of tree preferred for foraging: in winter larger branches of lower crown, as well as trunks, are searched, trunks becoming most important in late winter and early spring, whereas in late spring use of the crown increases. About a third of foraging, particularly by males, is on dead wood. Probing and gleaning are most frequent techniques; usually does not hammer persistently; flycatches to some extent. Use of anvils not very frequent and not well developed. Ringing of trees and sap-sucking is common in early spring. Slight foraging differences between sexes outside breeding season probably due to dominance of males.
Breeding. Mid-Apr to beginning of May. Conspicuous crest-raising display, near hole also flutter-aerial display. Nest excavated by both sexes, taking 8-20 days, at up to 20 m, mostly 5-10 m, in trunk or in larger branch of deciduous tree, mainly in dead or decaying wood; cavity depth c. 35 cm; old hole frequently reused. Clutch 4-8 eggs, usually 5-6; incubation by both sexes, period 11-14 days; both also contribute to nest sanitation and feed chicks, nestling period 20-26 days; fledglings accompanied by parents for 8-11 days. First breeding at 1 year.
Movements. Resident; short-distance dispersal may lead individuals outside breeding range.
Status and Conservation. Not globally threatened. Fairly common to common, but often rather local. European population estimated at 62,000-78,440 pairs, with additional 1000-10,000 in European Russia and similar number in Turkey; main strongholds in Germany (9000-13,000), Poland (c. 11,000), Croatia (9000) and Belarus (7000). Densities in C Europe 0·3-2·4 pairs/10 ha, but 1 pair/10 ha in most oak woodlands; average 0·6 pairs/10 ha in area of 122 km² (with 7920 ha of woodland) in SW Germany. Has increased and expanded in NC Europe; first 20th-century record in Estonia in 1990; returned as breeder to Netherlands in 1997 (10 pairs), having not bred there since 1962. On other hand, strong decline and local extinctions in many parts of range; last bred S Sweden in 1980. Exact figures, however, rarely available. Most sensitive to habitat deterioration through forestry practices (loss of old-age hardwood stands) and forest fragmentation. Climatic changes and adverse weather also influence populations locally.
Bibliography. Ahlén *et al.* (1978), Arambarri & Rodríguez (1996), Beaman & Madge (1998), Bauer & Berthold (1997), van den Berg & Bosman (1999), Bergmanis & Strazds (1993), Bezzel (1985), Blagosklonov (1968), Blume (1968), Bühlmann & Pasinelli (1996), Cairenius (1996), Christie (1990), Christie & Winkler (1994), Cramp (1985), Cuisin (2000), Cuisin & Maly (1999), Dejaegere (1993), Dejaegere & Vandevenne (1993), Dementiev *et al.* (1966), Díaz (1997), Díaz *et al.* (1996), Fauvel, Balandras & Carré (1995), Fauvel, Carré & Lallement (2001), Feindt (1956), Feindt & Reblin (1959), Ferry (1962), Friedmann (1997), Gebauer *et al.* (1984, 1992), Glutz von Blotzheim & Bauer (1980), Gorman (2000), Günther (1993), Hagemeijer & Blair (1997), Heath & Evans (2000), Heath *et al.* (2000), Heinze (1994), Hinterkreuser (1998), Hochebner (1993), Hüe & Étchécopar (1970), Jenni (1981, 1983), Kilham (1979b), Knysh (1999), Kossenko & Kaygorodova (1998), Lenz (1997), Letourneau (1998), Liesen (1996), Michalek (1998), Miech (1986), Mikusinski (2001), Mikusinski & Angelstam (1997, 1998), Mulhauser, Kaiser & Claude (2000), Mulhauser, Kaiser & Junod (2001), Müller (1982), Pasinelli (1993, 1998, 1999, 2000a, 2000b), Pasinelli & Hegelbach (1997), Pavlík (1994), Perthuis (1996), Pettersson (1983, 1984, 1985), Purroy (1997), Purroy *et al.* (1984), Radermacher (1970), Romero (1990), Ruge (1971b, 1993), Schmitz (1993), Schubert (1978), Snow & Perrins (1998), Spitznagel (1993), Südbeck & Gall (1993), Svensson *et al.* (1999), Tobalske & Tobalske (1999), Tombal (1993a, 1993b, 1993c, 1993d), Villard (1991), Villard *et al.* (1987), Wesolowski & Tomialojc (1986), Winkler & Short (1978).

104. **White-backed Woodpecker**

Dendrocopos leucotos

French: Pic à dos blanc **German**: Weißrückenspecht **Spanish**: Pico Dorsiblanco
Other common names: Owston's Woodpecker (*owstoni*)

Taxonomy. *Picus leucotos* Bechstein, 1803, Silesia, south Poland.
Genus sometimes merged into *Picoides*. No very close relatives within genus; has hybridized rarely with *D. major*, and probably closest to that superspecies; similarity to *D. medius* may suggest relatedness, but this not borne out by available genetic data. Subspecific differentiation largely a

On following pages: 105. Great Spotted Woodpecker (*Dendrocopos major*); 106. Syrian Woodpecker (*Dendrocopos syriacus*); 107. White-winged Woodpecker (*Dendrocopos leucopterus*); 108. Sind Woodpecker (*Dendrocopos assimilis*); 109. Himalayan Woodpecker (*Dendrocopos himalayensis*).

result of vast range that includes many isolated and island populations, some of which are highly distinctive and possibly merit status of full species; SW race *lilfordi* possibly also a distinct species, separated by altitude and ecology from parapatric nominate race. Other described races are *uralensis* (W Siberia), *voznesenskii* (E Siberia and Kamchatka), *saghalinensis* (Sakhalin), *ussuriensis* (Ussuriland and NE China), *sinicus* (Korea) and *quelpartensis* (Quelpart I), all considered inadequately differentiated or representing intergrades. Ten subspecies recognized.

Subspecies and Distribution.

D. l. leucotos (Bechstein, 1803) - W Norway, Sweden, Finland and Poland S in Europe to E Switzerland, Austria, N Serbia and Carpathian Mts, and E through S *taiga* to Kamchatka, Sakhalin, NE China and Korea.

D. l. lilfordi (Sharpe & Dresser, 1871) - Pyrenees, C Italy, the Balkans and Peloponnese, Turkey (N Anatolia, Taurus Mts), Caucasus and Transcaucasia.

D. l. subcirris (Stejneger, 1886) - Hokkaido (N Japan).

D. l. stejnegeri (Kuroda, 1921) - N Honshu (NC Japan).

D. l. namiyei (Stejneger, 1886) - S Honshu, Shikoku, Kyushu and Quelpart I (Cheju-do).

D. l. takahashii (Kuroda & Mori, 1920) - Dagelet I (Ullung do), off E Korea.

D. l. owstoni (Ogawa, 1905) - Amami-oshima (N Ryukyu Is).

D. l. tangi Cheng Tschsin, 1956 - C China (Sichuan).

D. l. fohkiensis (Buturlin, 1908) - SE China (Fujian).

D. l. insularis (Gould, 1863) - Taiwan.

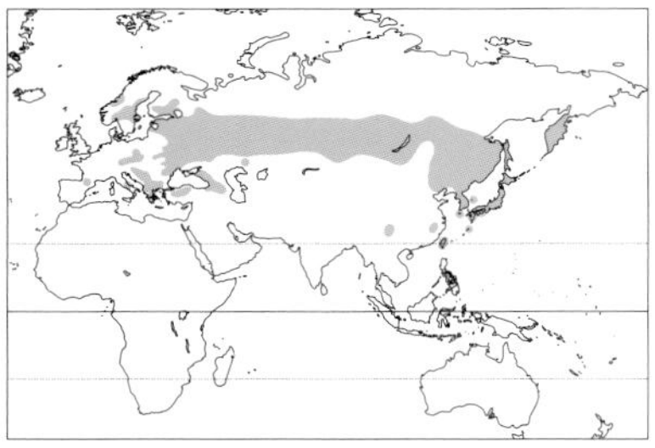

Descriptive notes. 23-28 cm; 99-112 g (Europe, Russia), 92-158 g (China), 115 g (*lilfordi*). Male has white forehead and lores tinged grey or buff, red forecrown to upper nape (often some black feather bases visible), black lower nape and band down central hindneck; white face and rear part of side of neck, often pale buffish area behind eye, and with black malar stripe meeting fairly large black patch on side of neck that extends up behind ear-coverts (not reaching nape) and down on to side of breast; white chin and throat; slightly glossy black mantle and most of scapulars, white back and rump extending partly on to lower scapulars (some dark feather bases usually visible), black uppertail-coverts; black wings, greater coverts tipped white, flight-feathers including tertials with broad white spots forming prominent bars; uppertail black centrally, third pair tipped white, outers white with 3-4 narrow black bars; white to pale creamy below, black streaks from breast to flanks and belly sides, reddish-pink belly to undertail-coverts (and often lower flanks); long bill chisel-tipped, dark slate-grey; iris red-brown or red; legs grey. Female has entire top of head black. Juvenile duller and browner than adult, pale areas tinged grey or buff, markings below more diffuse, red area on vent smaller and paler, both sexes with red or orange-red on crown, reduced on female, usually mixed with black. Races vary mainly in coloration and markings, also in size: *lilfordi* is darker than nominate, rump mostly black, back barred black, red below more extensive; *subcirris* differs little from nominate, has buff tinge to face, more black on neck and breast, ventral region paler, pinker; *stejnegeri* is slightly smaller and darker than previous, rump partly barred, darker and more streaked below, pink on ventral area more extensive; *namiyei* as last but buffer face, fully barred back and rump, little white in wing, side of breast broadly black with heavy streaking below, darker pink ventral region; *takahashii* resembles previous, but wing and bill shorter, more white above, face and underparts much paler; *owstoni* is distinctive, largest and darkest of all, black above, very little white in wings and tail, face and throat pale buff, very dark below, breast mainly black with broad streaks below, dark pink-red lower breast to undertail-coverts; *fohkiensis* is nearly as dark as previous, but smaller, with some white on back, paler below with less black on breast; *tangi* very like last, but bigger, less black below; *insularis* is smallest, rather similar to previous, but more white on back, more extensive pink below. Voice. Soft low "gig"; series of "kyig gyig" notes in alarm; also "gig gig kwerrrr", and "gaee" calls interspersed with drumming. Drumrolls long, moderately fast, slightly accelerating.

Habitat. Old-growth and overmature but relatively open deciduous and mixed forest with high proportion of dead trees and fallen timber, favouring stands older than 80 years; often on steep slopes or near water. In primeval E European forest, prefers swampy woods with ash (*Fraxinus*) and alder (*Alnus*) and stands of oak (*Quercus*) and hornbeam (*Carpinus*); occasionally in coniferous stands. In light, sunny mixed forest (beech-oak, beech-fir, maple-spruce and similar) little affected by management in C Europe and Pyrenees. Closely associated with mature montane forest dominated by *Abies cephalonica* on the Peloponnes. Deciduous forest, particularly birch (*Betula*), mixed light coniferous forest, and willows (*Salix*) along floodplains in Siberia. Japanese populations depend to great extent on natural beech forest. Requires large continuous areas of suitable habitat; enters burned areas and those devastated by insect plagues. Lowlands in E Europe and N Asia; at 400-1850 m in Pyrenees and Alps; between 860 m and 1740 m on the Peloponnes; from sea-level to montane forest in Japan.

Food and Feeding. Specializes on large wood-boring insect larvae, mainly cerambycid (*Aromia*, *Necydalis*, *Rhagium*, *Saperda*, *Strangalia*) and buprestid coleopterans, and Lepidoptera (*Cossus*, *Lamellocossus*); also takes other insects, including adult beetles, ants and their larvae. Some plant material consumed, including wild cherries and prunes, berries (*Rhus*); acorns and hazel nuts taken in summer. Singly, occasionally in pairs. Most foraging is on dead trees, least so in late spring and summer. Both sexes prefer the trunk as a foraging site. Techniques include stripping off bark, hammering holes through bark, and hammering on already exposed wood. Males hammer more strongly and more persistently than females, more often visit live and taller trees, and forage on larger branches. Foraging techniques change seasonally, with gleaning most common in post-breeding season, then comprising about a quarter of all techniques used; occasionally hunts aerial prey.

Breeding. Laying from late Apr, but significant courtship from Feb; season extends to May or Jun, is c. 2 weeks earlier than other woodpeckers in same habitat. Display with bill-pointing, relatively slow lateral swinging, and flutter-aerial display. Both sexes work for 2-4 weeks on excavating nest, at up to 20 m in soft wood of a dead or decaying trunk, stump or branch, or in utility pole; hole entrance c. 5·5-7 cm high, 4·7-6·4 cm wide, cavity depth 25-37 cm. Clutch 3-5 eggs; both parents incubate eggs and feed chicks, female's share often less; incubation period 14-16 days, occasionally only 12; fledging period 27-28 days. Breeding success 2·4 fledglings per nest in a 10-year study in Norway.

Movements. Generally resident; some local movements. A few individuals seem to be carried along with eruptive movements of *D. major*; sometimes relatively large numbers undertake longer migrations, e.g. at least 100 juveniles together with considerably larger numbers of *Picoides tridactylus* seen along coasts of Finland in autumn 1993. A degree of dismigration occurs among N Asian populations after breeding.

Status and Conservation. Not globally threatened. Seems to be at best uncommon in most of its range, and in many parts rare or extremely rare, but may be commonest woodpecker in parts of Siberia. Population in Europe and W Russia estimated at c. 67,000 pairs, mostly in E parts, including 17,000 in Romania and 8000 in Belarus. Maximum densities in optimal habitat 1 pair/km² in N & C Europe, 2 pairs/km² in Italy, but elsewhere usually much lower. Pairs require large home range, e.g. 50-100 ha in Sweden, 100 ha in Poland, 75-150 ha in Norway; 0·3-0·77 pairs/100 ha in SW France (Pyrenees). Numbers have decreased in many parts of Europe; massive decline in Fennoscandia, from 1000 pairs in early 1950's to only 30-40 pairs in late 1990's; only 3 isolated populations remain in Sweden. More stable in SE & E Europe; has extended range in Slovenia, and first bred in Switzerland in 1999. Often overlooked because of its secretive habits and very large territories. Since mid-20th century has become endangered wherever forest management is intense, leading to reduction of dead stems or introduction of conifers; reduction in population size is accompanied by loss of genetic diversity. Race *owstoni*, confined to old mature evergreen broadleaved forest in hills of Amami-oshima, is rare; *insularis* fairly common on Taiwan; status of other island populations uncertain. Everywhere, this species' survival is dependent on preservation of reasonably large areas of unmanaged deciduous forest.

Bibliography. Ahlén & Andersson (1976), Ahlén *et al.* (1978), Andersson & Hamilton (1972), Anon. (1998e), Aulén (1979, 1988, 1990), Aulén & Lundberg (1991), Beaman & Madge (1998), Bergmanis & Strazds (1993), Bernoni (1994, 1995), Bezzel (1985), Blagosklonov (1968), Brazil (1991), Bühler (2001), Carlson (1998), Carlson & Stenberg (1995), Chiba (1969), Christie & Winkler (1994), Costantini & Melletti (1992), Costantini *et al.* (1993, 1995), Cramp (1985), Dementiev (1934), Dementiev *et al.* (1966), Dernfalk (1983), Díaz (1997), Díaz *et al.* (1996), Ellegren *et al.* (1999), Ern (1959), Étchécopar & Hüe (1978), Fernández & Azkona (1996), Fernández *et al.* (1994), Franz (1937), Friedmann (1997), Glutz von Blotzheim & Bauer (1980), Gorman (2000), Grangé (1991, 1993, 2001), Hachisuka & Udagawa (1953), Hagemeijer & Blair (1997), Hågvar & Hågvar (1989), Hågvar *et al.* (1990), Hainard & Burnier (1958), Håland & Toft (1983), Heath *et al.* (2000), Higuchi (1980), Hogstad (1978), Hogstad & Stenberg (1994, 1997), Hölzinger (1970), Hüe & Étchécopar (1970), Ishida (1989, 1990a), Ishida *et al.* (1994), Kilham (1979b), King (1978/79), Leconte (1999), Lenz (1997), MacKinnon & Phillipps (2000), Matsuoka (1979a), Merikallio (1958), Mikusinski (2001), Mikusinski & Angelstam (1997, 1998), Nuorteva *et al.* (1981), Pavlik (1996), Pechacek (1994a, 1996), Pechacek & Krištín (1993), Petrov & Rudkovski (1985), Purroy (1972, 1997), Rogacheva (1992), Ruge & Weber (1974b), Scherzinger (1982), Schubert (1969), Senosian (1977), Snow & Perrins (1998), Spiridinov (1984), Stenberg (1990), Stenberg & Hogstad (1992), Svensson *et al.* (1999), Thiollay (1963), Tomialojc (2000), Tsai Hangyeh (1985), Ueta & Yamaguchi (1997), Virkkala *et al.* (1993), Wesolowski (1995a, 1995b), Wesolowski & Tomialojc (1986), Winkler & Short (1978), Zhao Zhengjie (1995).

105. **Great Spotted Woodpecker**

Dendrocopos major

French: Pic épeiche **German**: Buntspecht **Spanish**: Pico Picapinos
Other common names: Greater Pied Woodpecker

Taxonomy. *Picus major* Linnaeus, 1758, Sweden.

Genus sometimes merged into *Picoides*. Forms a superspecies with *D. syriacus*, *D. leucopterus*, *D. assimilis* and *D. himalayensis*. Hybridizes rarely with first two, and named race *tianshanicus* from C Tien Shan considered to refer to offspring of mixed pairs of present species and *D. leucopterus*; has also interbred with more distantly related *D. leucotos*. Variation over vast range is largely clinal, with races intergrading extensively and many intermediate populations. Many additional named races thus not certainly identifiable, and considered unacceptable: *anglicus* (Britain), *italiae* (Pyrenees E to Switzerland and Italy), *parroti* (Corsica), *lynesi* (Atlas Mts in Morocco), *candidus* (S Russia, Romania, Bulgaria), *paphlagoniae* (N Turkey), *tenuirostris* (Crimea, Caucasus, Transcaucasia), *tscherskii* (Ussuriland and Sakhalin), *hondoensis* (N & C Honshu and smaller islands), *beicki* (Gansu, in W China), *mandarinus* (S & SE China) and *hainanus* (Hainan I). Fourteen subspecies recognized.

Subspecies and Distribution.

D. m. major (Linnaeus, 1758) - Scandinavia and W Siberia E to Urals and S to N Poland and N Ukraine.

D. m. brevirostris (Reichenbach, 1854) - from W Siberia E to lower R Amur, Manchuria and Sea of Okhotsk, and S to C Tien Shan and Mongolia.

D. m. kamtschaticus (Dybowski, 1883) - Kamchatka and N Okhotsk coast.

D. m. pinetorum (C. L. Brehm, 1831) - Britain, France and C Europe E to R Volga and S to Italy, Balkans, Turkey, S Ukraine and Caucasus.

D. m. hispanus (Schlüter, 1908) - Iberia.

D. m. harterti Arrigoni, 1902 - Sardinia and Corsica.

D. m. canariensis (König, 1889) - Tenerife, in Canary Is.

D. m. thanneri le Roi, 1911 - Gran Canaria.

D. m. mauritanus (C. L. Brehm, 1855) - Morocco.

D. m. numidus (Malherbe, 1843) - N Algeria and Tunisia.

D. m. poelzami (Bogdanov, 1879) - S Caspian region and Transcaspia.

D. m. japonicus (Seebohm, 1883) - C & E Manchuria to Sakhalin and Kuril Is, and S to Korea and Japan (Hokkaido, Honshu, Tsushima).

D. m. cabanisi (Malherbe, 1854) - S Manchuria S to E Myanmar, N Laos, N Vietnam (NW Tonkin), SE China and Hainan.

D. m. stresemanni (Rensch, 1924) - C China (E Qinghai, Gansu, Shaanxi, Sichuan) S to SE Tibet, NE India, W & N Myanmar and Yunnan.

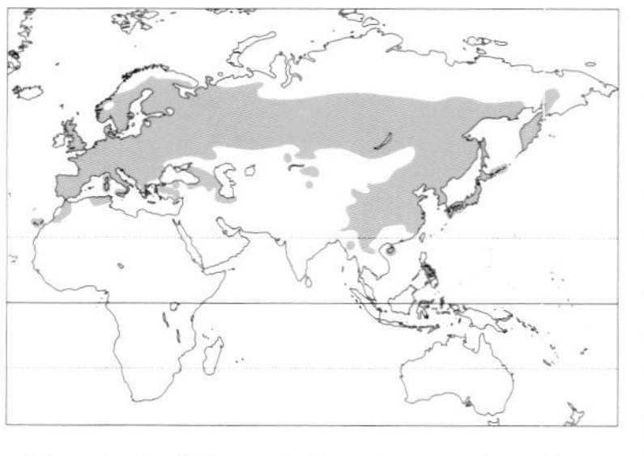

Descriptive notes. 20-24 cm; 70-98 g (*major*), 68-93 g (*pinetorum*), 66-98 g (*cabanisi*). Male has black nasal tufts, white to buffish forehead, blue-glossed black crown, bright crimson-red nape, black hindneck with large white patch on each side; white to creamy lores and side of head bordered below by black stripe from nape to base of lower mandible, black broadening in centre and extending to side of breast; bluish-black upperparts, often greyish feather bases visible on rump, white outer scapulars; innermost greater and median wing-coverts white, joining with outer scapulars to form large white patch; black or brownish-black flight-feathers with up to 6 white spots forming prominent bars, some white in primary coverts; uppertail black, off-white bars at tips of rectrices increasing in size from second-innermost outwards, two outermost pairs mostly white with 2 or 3 black bars; generally white, pale greyish-white or buff-white below, bright scarlet vent and undertail-coverts; strong bill short to moderately long, chisel-tipped, blackish-grey, lead-grey or slate-grey, paler base of lower mandible; iris deep red or reddish-brown; legs slate-grey, tinged olive or brown. Distinguished from *D. syriacus* by black behind ear-coverts, more white in outer tail, redder vent, smaller red nape patch; from *D. leucopterus* by less white in wing, less extensive red on vent. Female lacks red on nape. Juvenile less glossy, more brown-tinged above, bases of white scapulars often with black barring, malar less sharply defined, post-auricular bar narrower and sometimes not extending to nape, dirtier underparts often with dusky streaks, flanks sometimes barred, ventral area pink or occasionally even buff or whitish, rarely some pinkish colour on breast, eyes browner, male with red crown narrowly edged black, red usually less extensive on female. Races differ both in size and in plumage, as well as in length and shape of bill, generally N populations bigger, with shorter, heavier bill, whiter below: *brevirostris* is very like nominate but slightly bigger, plumage very fluffy, perhaps whiter below, vent deeper red; *kamtschaticus* similar but even whiter, white wing patch bigger, outer tail all white; *pinetorum* is smaller, has longer, narrower bill, light buffish underparts; *hispanus* resembles previous but darker; *harterti* like last but bigger, dark grey-brown below, darker red vent; *canariensis* as previous but not quite so dark, has contrasting whitish flanks, more orangey vent; *thanneri* is paler than last, with white from flanks up to breast; *mauritanus* is rather pale below, often with red in breast centre, size and darkness increasing clinally with altitude; *numidus* distinctive, larger than previous, has black breastband with red feather tips, red of vent often extending to belly; *poelzami* is rather small, with proportionately long bill, very brown below; *japonicus* is blacker above, has less white on scapulars, more white on flight-feathers; *cabanisi* is even blacker above, has buff-brown head and underparts, darkest in S, paler pink vent, often some red on breast; *stresemanni* resembles previous but even darker below, again darkest in S. VOICE. Single sharp "kix", in alarm sometimes in rapid series; wooden "krrarraarr" of varying length and introduced by "kix"; series of "gwig" notes in courtship season, especially during flutter-aerial display. Both sexes drum, male much more frequently, from winter until fledging period, rolls rather short, slightly accelerating.

Habitat. All kinds of woodland and forest, from pure broadleaved forest to unmixed stands of conifers; also common in copses, tree avenues, parks, gardens. Inhabits olive and poplar (*Populus*) plantations and up to cedar (*Cedrus*), pine (*Pinus*), pine-oak and cork oak (*Quercus suber*) woods in N Africa; found in alder (*Alnus*) and rhododendron in N Myanmar; common in deciduous, mixed or coniferous woods, and parks in Japan. Occurs from sea-level to the timber-line in Europe, where breeding recorded at over 2000 m; in N Africa, to 1000 m in Tunisia, 2200 m in Morocco; to 2500 m in C Asian mountains; *cabanisi* occupies forest above 1800 m in SE Asia; at up to 2300 m in N Myanmar and Japan.

Food and Feeding. Very varied diet, with clear seasonal changes in more seasonal habitats. Animal food consists mainly of larvae of wood-boring beetles (Cerambycidae, Scolytidae, Buprestidae), Lepidoptera (Cossidae, Sesiidae) and Hymenoptera (Siricidae); adult beetles (Curculionidae, Chrysomelidae, Carabidae), hymenopterans, hemipterans, homopterans (e.g. Aphidina, Coccoidea), spiders and many other arthropods also consumed. Ants can form substantial part of diet, and include genera *Lasius*, *Formica*, also *Camponotus* and *Dolichoderus*. Also takes crustaceans and mussels, carrion (small mammals), and obtains suet and other food, including household scraps, at feeders. Notorious for taking eggs and young of other hole-nesting birds; also raids open nests and nest pouches. Plant material rich in fat, mostly in form of coniferous seeds and various nuts (e.g. hazel, walnut, beech, hornbeam), and acorns (particularly in Caucasus), become more important as winter food towards N of range; seeds usually contribute c. 30% but often up to 80% of energy intake in winter. Other vegetable matter includes buds and, of major importance locally and seasonally, tree sap, and possibly nectar; wide array of berries and fruit also regularly eaten, and even fed to nestlings. Forages singly, also in pairs with members keeping in loose contact. Makes use of all strata, mainly tree crowns in winter, may resort more frequently to lower trunk in summer; in canopy visits branches and small twigs. Climbs quickly, mostly straight up, but often backwards and downwards; in crown prefers to climb rather than to use wings. Clings to twigs and leaf clusters in manner of tits (Paridae); occasionally hovers briefly, and sallies for aerial prey. Pecking and hammering are commonest techniques, especially outside breeding season; pries, tears and pecks off pieces of bark; gleaning and probing more important at times of high food availability. Generally rather opportunistic, and seasonal and local differences marked; sexual differences minimal. Drilling of sap holes and sap-sucking very common. Uses anvils to work on unwieldy arthropod prey, fruits and, most importantly of all, pine, spruce (*Picea*) or larch (*Larix*) cones, and nuts; single main anvil, with 1000s of processed cones, and several ancillary anvils maintained.

Breeding. Laying from mid-Apr to Jun, later in far N and at higher altitude, but courtship commences in Dec. Monogamous, but polyandry also recorded in Japan. Flutter-aerial display mostly by male flying away from partner, shallow wingbeats, fully spread tail turned upwards, with call series; on landing, may demonstrate prospective nest-hole. Usually a new hole excavated annually, by both sexes, mostly by male, at 0·3-26 m, usually below 8 m (but in primeval forest in Poland average 12 m), in dead or live tree of wide variety of species, occasionally in utility pole; hole entrance 5-6 cm across, cavity depth 25-35 cm; occasionally in nestbox, rarely old hole reused. Clutch 4-8 eggs, normally 5-7; incubation by both sexes, period 10-12 days; both also feed chicks and attend to nest sanitation, fledging period 20-23 days; fledged brood divided between parents, fed by them for 10 days, remain near nest for further 5-10 days. First breeding at 1 year. Recorded longevity in wild 9 years.

Movements. Largely resident and dispersive; N populations also subject to eruptive migration. Juvenile dispersal often over 100 km, and up to c. 600 km. In N Europe, periodic eruptive movements triggered by poor crop of pine or spruce seeds, begin in late Jul; small groups and loose flocks migrate S & W, and occasionally large numbers involved, e.g. 2240 through Pape, in Latvia, during Aug-Oct 1999, and sizeable flocks recorded in N Britain in autumn 2001; individuals may stray more than 3000 km, some reaching oceanic islands. Similar movements in Far East, but less well studied; stragglers found even on remote islands. Also, populations in mountain areas descend to valleys in winter.

Status and Conservation. Not globally threatened. In many parts of range by far the commonest woodpecker; less common locally, and rare in SE Asia. In Europe estimated population c. 3,300,000-4,480,000 pairs, with further 1,000,000-10,000,000 in European part of Russia; largest numbers in Germany (500,000-900,000 pairs), Belarus (c. 600,000) and France (over 300,000). Densities vary from 0.1 pairs/10 ha to 6·6 pairs/10 ha, highest in mature alluvial forest. Increase in extent of forested area, with greater proportion of dead wood, has resulted in stable or slightly increasing numbers in many regions in Europe. On other hand, harsh winters can cause significant mortality, and fragmentation of habitat can pose problems locally; Canary Is races *canariensis* and *thanneri* are currently probably the most vulnerable, especially the former, which may be at some risk because of human exploitation of Canarian pine forest. Nevertheless, species is generally highly adaptable in much of its range, capable of existing in very close proximity to man, and able to colonize wide variety of wooded habitats.

Bibliography. Alatalo (1978), Anon. (1972, 1973), Aschoff (1967), Bardin (1986), Bauer & Berthold (1997), Bavoux (1987), Beaman & Madge (1998), Berger *et al.* (1992), Bezzel (1985), Blagosklonov (1968), Blume (1961, 1968), Brazil (1991), de Bruyn *et al.* (1972), Cabanne (1948), Camerini & Quadrelli (1991), Chauvin-Muckensturm (1973, 1980), Chiba (1969), Conrads & Mensendiek (1973, 1980), Cramp (1985), Dawson (2001), Dementiev (1935), Dementiev *et al.* (1966), Díaz (1997), Díaz *et al.* (1996), Étchécopar & Hüe (1964, 1978), Flousek *et al.* (1993), Fraile (1984), Friedmann (1997), Fry *et al.* (1988), Gebauer (1984), Glutz von Blotzheim & Bauer (1980), Gorman (2000), Groppali & Pedrazzani (1996), Günther & Hellmann (1998), Hagemeijer & Blair (1997), Hågvar & Hågvar (1989), Hågvar *et al.* (1990), Ham Kyuhwang (1982), Harrison (1951), Heath & Evans (2000), Heath *et al.* (2000), Heim de Balsac (1936), Heim de Balsac & Mayaud (1962), Hernández (1989), Higuchi (1980), Hodgetts (1943), Hogstad (1971a, 1971b, 1978), Hüe & Étchécopar (1970), Jenni (1981, 1983), Jin RuiLan & Yin YaNing (1988), Kawada (1980), Kilham (1979b), Kostyushin (1995), Kotaka (1998), Kovalev (1993, 1996, 1999), Kroneisl-Rucner (1957), László (1988), Lenz (1997), Lobkov (1999), Löhrl (1972), MacKinnon & Phillipps (2000), Marchant *et al.* (1990), Matsuoka (1983, 1986), Mauersberger *et al.* (1982), Melde (1994), Merikallio (1958), Michalek (1998), Michalek & Winkler (1997a, 1997b), Miech (1986), Mikusinski (2001), Mikusinski & Angelstam (1997, 1998), Moreau (1969), Muckensturm (1971), Mulhauser, Kaiser & Claude (2000), Mulhauser, Kaiser & Junod (2001), Murai & Higuchi (1991), Nakamura *et al.* (1995), Nyholm (1968), Osborne (1983), Osiejuk (1994), Pavlík (1994), Pechacek (1992, 1995, 1996), Pechacek & Krištín (1993), Pflumm (1979), Pulliainen (1963), Purroy (1997), Radermacher (1970), Ree (1974), Robson (2000), Rogacheva (1992), Ruge (1973), Smith (1997), Smythies (1986), Snow & Perrins (1998), Sparks (1995), Spitznagel (1993), Stanford & Mayr (1941), Stradi & Hudon (1998), Stradi *et al.* (1998), Svensson *et al.* (1999), Tobalske & Tobalske (1999), Voous (1947), Wesolowski & Tomialojc (1986), Willeneger & Ravussin (1995), Winkler (1979b), Winkler & Short (1978), Witt (1988), Yamauchi *et al.* (1997), Zhao Zhengjie (1995).

106. **Syrian Woodpecker**

Dendrocopos syriacus

French: Pic syriaque **German**: Blutspecht **Spanish**: Pico Sirio

Taxonomy. *Picus syriacus* Ehrenberg, 1833, Mount Lebanon.
Genus sometimes merged into *Picoides*. Forms a superspecies with *D. major*, *D. leucopterus*, *D. assimilis* and *D. himalayensis*; has hybridized rarely with first and third of those. Some geographical variation, e.g. smaller birds in N Iran and Transcaucasia named as race *transcaucasicus*, often with more white in outer tail, while latter population and also those from Asia Minor tend to be darker below, but overlap in characters exists between these and other populations; similarly, *balcanicus* (E Balkans) with dark flank marks and supposedly larger *milleri* (S Iran) matched by individuals from elsewhere in range; subdivision into geographical races seems unwarranted. Monotypic.

Distribution. Austria, Czech Republic, Poland and S Belarus E to W & S Ukraine and SW Russia, and S to Balkans, Turkey, Levant countries, extreme NE Egypt (NE Sinai), N Iraq, Transcaucasia, and to N, W & S Iran.

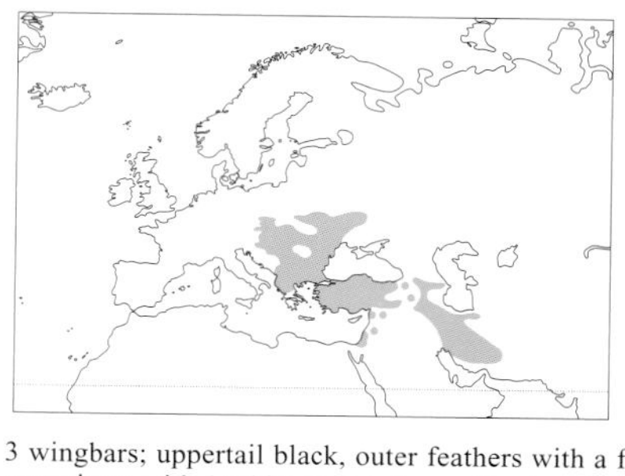

Descriptive notes. 23 cm; 55-63 g (Iran), 70-82 g (C Europe). Male has buffy nasal tufts and lower forehead, white to creamy upper forehead, black crown (rarely, a few scattered red feathers), red central hindcrown and nape, black hindneck; rest of head white, including thin line above eye, with black malar stripe expanding a little upwards on side of neck and continuing down to side of upper breast; dull black upperparts, white outer scapulars and innermost greater coverts, also some white median coverts, remaining wing-coverts black but outer primary coverts mostly white; black flight-feathers with large white spots forming 3 wingbars; uppertail black, outer feathers with a few white spots or white tip, next-inner rectrix sometimes with 1 white spot or bar; white to pale creamy below, becoming pinkish-red on lower belly to undertail-coverts, often faint dusky streaks or bars on lower flanks; rather long bill almost straight, chisel-tipped, dark grey to slaty-blue, paler base of lower mandible; iris red-brown, sometimes deep red; legs slate-grey with blue, brown or olive tinge. Distinguished from *D. major* by more white on head, including more extensively pale forehead, less white in tail, larger red nape patch, duller black upperparts, pinker (less red) vent, pale nasal tufts; from *D. assimilis* by black crown, stronger malar and stripe on side of breast, less white in tail. Female resembles male, but lacks red on nape. Juvenile slightly duller than adult, but often some pinkish feathers across upper breast (rarely, complete band), flanks usually with obvious streaks and bars, sometimes reaching breast side, both sexes with black-bordered red crown, black nape. VOICE. Commonest call a single "kewg" (better rendered as "püg", or "puc" pronounced as in French *duc*), sometimes in rapid series when alarmed at nest; also loud "kweg-kweg kririririrrr"; loud series of distinct "kweek" notes characteristic during courtship. Drumming, mainly by male, in accelerating rolls up to twice as long as those of *D. major*.

Habitat. Open country with wooded areas. Often in plantations of all kinds, including olive, pecan (*Carya*) and avocado in S, and vineyards in C Europe, where also in roadside trees, groups of trees, mainly near habitations, also forest edge, parks and gardens. Inhabits oak (*Quercus*) woodland and light montane forest in SE; also breeds in coniferous forest at lower levels in Turkey. Lowlands to 700 m in C Europe; to 1000 m in Bulgaria and C Anatolia; reaches 2700 m in S Iran.

Food and Feeding. Animal food and a relatively large amount of plant material. Beetles and their larvae, ants, lepidopterous larvae (even hairy ones) and pupae; spiders; also various aerial insects. Nuts and seeds eaten both in summer and in winter, include almonds, walnuts, pecans, hazel nuts, apricot stones, acorns, pine seeds, sunflower seeds, pistachios and similar; ripe fruits (e.g. apricots and prunes) taken to get at the seeds. Takes the flesh of cherries, mulberries, raspberries and other fruits, which may also be fed to nestlings. Sap sometimes taken. Forages singly and in pairs. Uses all levels, from ground to canopy, but almost half of all foraging takes place in lower strata. Hops on the ground, and moves swiftly during arboreal feeding. Marked seasonal changes, from foraging more in crown in winter to opportunistic habitat use during nesting season. Especially in summer, gleaning and probing most common foraging activities, and commonly takes prey on the wing. Anvils used frequently to process large insects (beetles), fruits and nuts. Covers relatively large distances between feeding sites, and between them and the nest.

Breeding. Lays from mid- Apr to May, rarely to Jun. Lateral swinging displays and aerial chasing. Nest-hole excavated by both sexes, mostly by male, at 1-6 m in trunk or large branch of tree, with wide variety of species used, less often in utility pole or similar structure; hole diameter averages 3·5 cm, cavity depth 20 cm; old nest sometimes reused. Clutch 3-7 eggs, usually 4 (Israel) or 5 (Hungary); incubation by both sexes, period 9-11 days; both also feed chicks and share nest sanitation, nestling period c. 20-24 days; juveniles accompanied by parents for 2 weeks.

Movements. Resident and dispersive. Long distances covered during dispersal, but no seasonal movements have been documented.

Status and Conservation. Not globally threatened. Common in most parts of range. European population estimated at c. 170,000 pairs, including 80,000 or more in Romania and at least 30,000 in Bulgaria; Turkish population 10,000-100,000 pairs, probably nearer lower end of that range. Densities much lower than those of *D. major*; highest in orchards and vineyards, where 0·5-1 pair/100 ha. Considerable range extension since late 19th century; formerly restricted to E Mediterranean, it spread via Balkans to C Europe, also E to Ukraine; had colonized almost whole of Hungary by late 1950's after first recorded there in 1937; rather rapid expansion to N & W in Poland since c. 1980. Range expansion probably fostered by agricultural development and other human activities.

Some local declines in SE Europe (Greece, Albania) since c. 1985. Causes some damage in commercial plantations, especially of almond, also pecks holes in irrigation pipes in parts of Middle East; was formerly persecuted locally as a pest, and sometimes large numbers shot, but generally tolerated in more recent times.

Bibliography. Adamian & Klem (1999), Barnea (1985), Bauer, K.M. (1952, 1953), Bauer, H.G. & Berthold (1997), Beaman & Madge (1998), Bezzel (1985), Cramp (1985), Degan & Popovici (1973), Dementiev *et al.* (1966), Desfayes & Praz (1978), Dornbusch (1968), Friedmann (1997), Glutz von Blotzheim & Bauer (1980), Goodman *et al.* (1989), Gorman (1996, 1997a, 1997b, 1998a, 1999a, 1999b, 2000), Hagemeijer & Blair (1997), Handrinos & Akriotis (1997), Heath & Evans (2000), Heath *et al.* (2000), Hollom *et al.* (1988), Hüe & Étchécopar (1970), Keve (1960, 1963), Klitin *et al.* (1994), Kren (2000), Kroneisl-Rucner (1957), Lenz (1997), Lorek & Durczynska (1992), Marissova (1965), Mikusinski (2001), Mikusinski & Angelstam (1997), Moran (1977), Munteanu (1968), Paz (1987), Ruge (1969b, 1970), Saari & Mikusinski (1996), Shirihai (1996), Skakuj & Stawarczyk (1994), Snow & Perrins (1998), Stefanovic (1958-1959), Szlivka (1957, 1960), Tomialojc (1990), Walasz & Mielczarek (1992), Winkler (1968, 1971a, 1972, 1973), Winkler & Short (1978).

107. White-winged Woodpecker

Dendrocopos leucopterus

French: Pic à ailes blanches **German**: Weißflügelspecht **Spanish**: Pico Aliblanco
Other common names: White-winged Pied/White-winged Spotted Woodpecker

Taxonomy. *Picus* (*Dendrocopus*) [sic] *leucopterus* Salvadori, 1870, Yarkand, Kashgaria, in extreme west China.
Genus sometimes merged into *Picoides*. Forms a superspecies with *D. major*, *D. syriacus*, *D. assimilis* and *D. himalayensis*; has hybridized very occasionally with first of those. Birds of the Turkestan uplands, described as race *leptorhynchus*, tend to be less white, but difference minor and not constant, and racial separation regarded as unwarranted; named races *albipennis* (SE Turkmenia), *jaxartensis* (lower R Syr Darya) and *korejevi* (SW Alatau Mts) likewise insufficiently differentiated. Monotypic.
Distribution. W shore of Aral Sea E to S Kazakhstan, N Kyrgyzstan (N to S tip of L Balkhash) and W China (N Xinjiang to Karamay and Lop Nur), and S to SW Turkmenia (possibly also extreme NE Iran) and NE Afghanistan in W and Chinese Turkestan S to edge of Kunlun Shan in E.

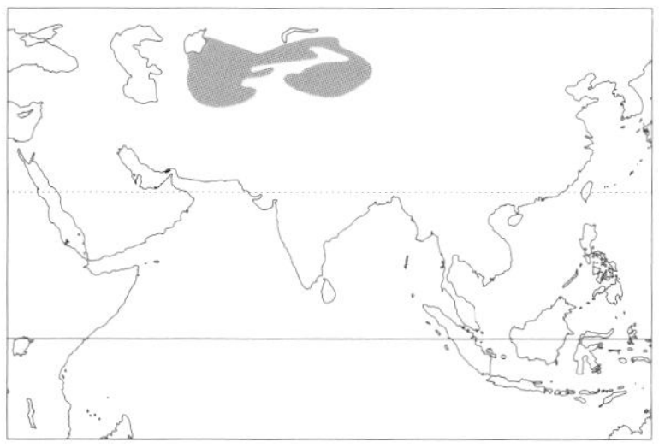

Descriptive notes. 22-23 cm; 67 g. Male has white forehead, black crown, red nape, black hindneck; thin white line above eye, white cheeks and ear-coverts (often stained); black malar stripe curving up behind ear-coverts to upper nape, broadening on side of neck, extending down to breast and back to join side of mantle, isolating large white patch on rear part of side of neck; black upperparts, wing with large white area on scapulars and inner wing-coverts, very broad white bars on primaries and secondaries, white edges of outer webs of tertials, white marginal coverts; black uppertail, broad white bars towards tips of outer 2 or 3 feather pairs; white below, sometimes with faint grey or buff tinge or staining, vent and undertail-coverts red to pinkish-red, in fresh plumage pink feather tips extending centrally up to lower breast; medium-long bill straight, slightly chisel-tipped, greyish-black, paler base of lower mandible; iris deep red, red-brown or brown; legs dull blackish or dark grey. Distinguished from all congeners by much more extensive white in wings. Female lacks red on nape. Juvenile duller than adult, more brown-black above, buffish below, often more white in wings and tail but occasionally scapulars finely barred black, ventral area pink rather than red, sometimes black streaks on side of breast, male with red crown mixed with black and white feathers, black nape, female with usually variable amount of red in forecrown. Voice. Common call "kewk" or "kig"; also rattling calls. Drums.
Habitat. Riparian woodland with poplars (*Populus*) and other softwoods, willows (*Salix*), saxaul (*Haloxylon ammodendron*) scrub in deserts, frequently orchards and gardens. Also found in broadleaved montane forest, often containing hazel (*Corylus*) and fruit trees or mixed with fir (*Abies*) or juniper (*Juniperus*), and in juniper stands. Generally at low elevations, locally to 1050 m; above 1800 m, to 2500 m, on N slopes of Kunlun Shan.
Food and Feeding. No reliable information.
Breeding. Egg-laying from late Mar to Apr. Nest-hole at 1-5 m in softwood tree (e.g. poplar, willow), also recorded in slope of sandhill. Clutch 4-6 eggs, occasionally 7; no information on incubation and fledging periods.
Movements. Some nomadic movements outside breeding season, but essentially non-migratory.
Status and Conservation. Not globally threatened. Previously considered Near-threatened. Appears to be common within its range. Little-known species; further study required, especially of its ecology.

Bibliography. Collar *et al.* (1994), Dementiev *et al.* (1966), Étchécopar & Hüe (1978), Friedmann (1997), Hollom *et al.* (1988), Hüe & Étchécopar (1970), Inskipp *et al.* (1996), Knystautas (1993), MacKinnon & Phillipps (2000), Porter, Christensen & Schiermacker-Hansen (1996), Wheatley (1996), Winkler & Short (1978), Zhao Zhengjie (1995).

108. Sind Woodpecker

Dendrocopos assimilis

French: Pic du Sind **German**: Tamariskenspecht **Spanish**: Pico del Sind
Other common names: Sind Pied Woodpecker

Taxonomy. *Picus assimilis* Blyth, 1849, Rawalpindi, Punjab.
Genus sometimes merged into *Picoides*. Forms a superspecies with *D. major*, *D. syriacus*, *D. leucopterus* and *D. himalayensis*; hybridizes rarely with second of those. Monotypic.
Distribution. SE Iran and Pakistan (Baluchistan, Sind and Punjab).
Descriptive notes. 20-22 cm; 42-64 g. Male has red crown and nape usually with some black or grey feather bases visible, black hindneck; rest of head and neck white, usually stained buffish on forehead and lores, sometimes dusky area in centre of ear-coverts, with narrow black malar stripe from bill to just behind lower ear-coverts, joined to black stripe that continues back to upper mantle and narrowly forwards to uppermost part at side of breast; blue-glossed black upperparts, large area of white on mostly inner wing-coverts and reaching to outermost scapulars; brownish-black flight-feathers broadly barred white; uppertail black, outer 2 feather pairs with broad white bars (rarely, much reduced or almost absent); white below, occasionally very faint grey or buffy tinge, flanks with minimal black streaking barely visible, pink in centre of lower breast and belly, red undertail-coverts; longish bill almost straight, slate-grey, paler lower mandible; iris red-brown to brown; legs grey to blue-grey. Differs from *D. syriacus* in smaller size, red crown, black stripe from side of neck to mantle, shorter

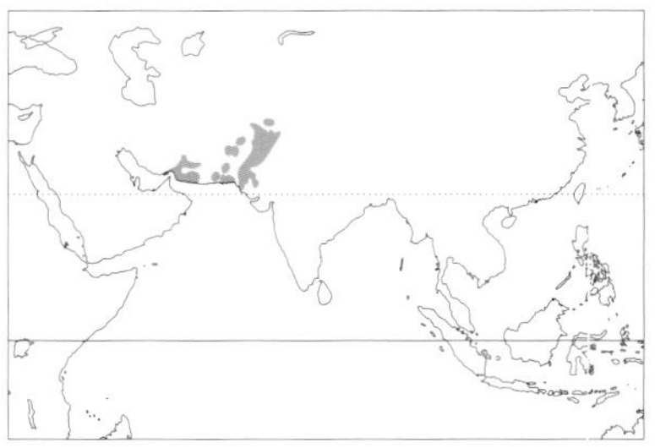

black stripe on to breast. Female has entire crown and nape black. Juvenile duller than adult, with black areas browner, white areas buff-tinged, undertail-coverts pink rather than red, both sexes with red patch in crown centre, smaller on female. Voice. Single "ptik" call; weak "chir-rir-rirrh-rirrh", also "wicka, toi-whit toi-whit toi-whit". Both sexes drum.
Habitat. Riverine forest, thorn-scrub, and desert wadis with scattered acacias (*Acacia*) and other thorny trees, and euphorbias; also roadside trees and irrigated plantations, e.g. of mulberry (*Morus*); also palm stands and gardens. Inhabits stands of wild olives (*Olea cuspidata*), *Pistacia integerrima* and ash (*Fraxinus excelsior*) in hilly country. Mainly in lowlands, but in Pakistan ascends to 1600 m in Salt Range and perhaps to 2200 m in Baluchistan.
Food and Feeding. Ants, especially *Camponotus*, and larvae of wood-boring beetles. Usually forages singly. Explores branches and twigs of *Acacia*, *Pistacia* and other trees, as well as euphorbias and fence posts; often near ground and on fallen trees. Techniques are hammering and probing.
Breeding. Season Mar-Apr. Nest-hole excavated by both sexes, sometimes rather low, c. 1-4 m from ground, in trunk or dead branch, often of tamarisk (*Tamarix*). Clutch 3-4 eggs; incubation by both sexes, period 15-16 days; no other information.
Movements. Resident. No movements recorded, but 19th-century record from NW India possibly a result of long-distance dispersal.
Status and Conservation. Not globally threatened. Widespread and locally common. Rather rare in lower Sind, commoner in upper Sind and Punjab. Appears fairly adaptable, using several man-made habitats, e.g. plantations alongside roads and canals. Present in Khirthar National Park (Pakistan).

Bibliography. Ali & Ripley (1983), Barker *et al.* (1999), Christison (1942), Christison & Ticehurst (1943), Grimmett *et al.* (1998), Hollom *et al.* (1988), Hüe & Étchécopar (1970), Inskipp *et al.* (1996), Porter, Christensen & Schiermacker-Hansen (1996), Ripley (1982), Roberts (1991), Wheatley (1996), Whitehead (1911), Winkler & Short (1978).

109. Himalayan Woodpecker

Dendrocopos himalayensis

French: Pic de l'Himalaya **German**: Himalajaspecht **Spanish**: Pico del Himalaya
Other common names: Himalayan Pied Woodpecker

Taxonomy. *Picus himalayensis* Jardine and Selby, 1835, Mussoorie, near Dehra Dun, northern India.
Genus sometimes merged into *Picoides*. Forms a superspecies with *D. major*, *D. syriacus*, *D. leucopterus* and *D. assimilis*. Races intergrade in N India. Two subspecies recognized.
Subspecies and Distribution.
D. h. albescens (Stuart Baker, 1926) - NE Afghanistan (Safed Koh) and N Pakistan to Himachal Pradesh.
D. h. himalayensis (Jardine & Selby, 1835) - E Himachal Pradesh E to W Nepal.

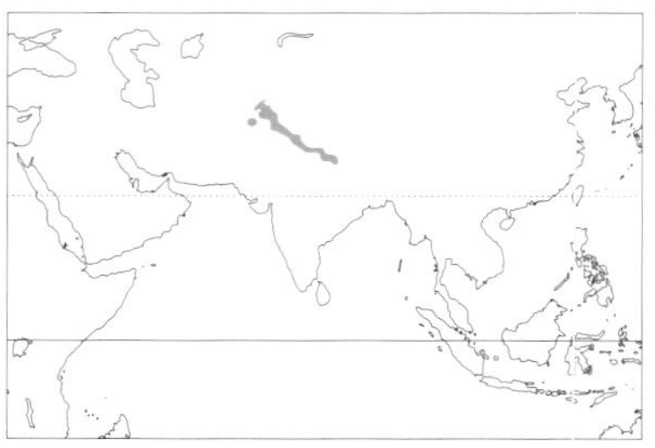

Descriptive notes. 23-25 cm; 57-85 g. Male has pale buff-white forehead, crimson-red crown to upper nape usually with some black or grey feather bases showing (especially forecrown and crown sides), black hindneck; white lores, superciliary area, cheeks and ear-coverts tinged buff; variable black patch behind eye, often isolated and prominent, sometimes meeting crown, frequently absent; complete black malar stripe expanding on side of neck, joining black stripe that continues slightly down on to side of upper breast and up behind ear-coverts (where often broken) to meet side of hindcrown; rear part of side of neck white to light buffish; entire upperparts black, inner wing-coverts with much white, flight-feathers barred white; uppertail black, outer 2 feathers largely white with black at base and few black bars at tip, adjacent ones with white bars at tip, but amount of white in outer tail variable, sometimes more black barring; pale buff or greyish-brown below, breast often sullied yellowish-brown, yellower on belly, red on lower belly and undertail-coverts, occasionally hint of streaks or bars on lower flanks; moderately long bill almost straight, chisel-tipped, blackish to dark grey, often paler lower mandible; iris red-brown; legs grey to dull green or green-brown. Female has black crown to nape. Juvenile duller than adult, black areas browner, ventral area pink, not red, and not reaching belly, some streaks on upper flanks and bars on lower flanks, both sexes with white spots on forecrown and orange-red patch in crown centre, smaller on female. Race *albescens* is paler than nominate, with forehead white, underparts pale greyish-white, narrower white tailbars. Voice. Single "kit", much like that of *D. major*; also rapid high "chissik-chissik", and fast "tri" series possibly as long-distance call. Short drumrolls.
Habitat. Rather dense, dry to wet, extensive coniferous forest, also oak (*Quercus*) and rhododendron mountain forest, locally in smaller patches of mixed pine (*Pinus*) and juniper (*Juniperus*). Between 1970 m and 3200 m, regionally up to tree-line; also down to 1500 m in Pakistan. Generally replaces *D. auriceps* at higher altitudes.
Food and Feeding. Insects and their larvae, other arthropods; also plant matter, possibly including sap. Takes wood-boring beetle larvae, weevils (Curculionidae), caterpillars and spiders; acorns (*Quercus dilatata*) and seeds of pines (*Pinus wallichiana*, *P. longifolia*) important food in winter. Forages singly or in pairs; occasionally joins mixed-species flocks of tits (Paridae) and warblers (Sylviidae). Arboreal feeder, rarely descends to ground. Techniques include pecking, probing, hammering, gleaning. Anvils used for processing pine cones.
Breeding. Laying in second half Apr and first half May. Aerial pursuits near nest. Nest-hole excavated by both sexes, mostly by male, at 1·5-15 m, mostly below 12 m, in usually dead part of trunk or large branch of tree, with local preference for deciduous (e.g. *Prunus cornuta*); entrance hole 5 cm in diameter. Clutch 3-5 eggs; both sexes incubate, period c. 2 weeks; both also feed nestlings, fledging period c. 3 weeks.
Movements. Largely resident; some local movement to lower hills may occur in winter.
Status and Conservation. Not globally threatened. Common in Pakistan; fairly common in India and Nepal; the commonest woodpecker in most of its range. No known threats, and seems unlikely to suffer any significant habitat loss in immediate future.

Bibliography. Ali (1979), Ali & Ripley (1983), Bates & Lowther (1952), Fleming & Traylor (1961), Grimmett *et al.* (1998, 2000), Hüe & Étchécopar (1970), Inskipp, C. (1989), Inskipp, C. & Inskipp (1991), Inskipp, T. *et al.* (1996), Kazmierczak (2000), Löhrl & Thielcke (1969), Macdonald & Henderson (1977), Martens & Eck (1995), Osmaston (1916), Raja *et al.* (1999), Ripley (1982), Roberts (1991), Shrestha (2000), Whitehead (1911), Winkler & Short (1978).

PLATE 35 ➤

PLATE 35

inches 5

cm 13

variant

110

ssp *mixtus*

ssp *berlepschi*

ssp *cancellatus*

111

112

ssp *scalaris*

ssp *cactophilus*

ssp *sinaloensis*

ssp *pubescens*

115

113

ssp *parvus*

ssp *eremicus*

114

ssp *gairdnerii*

ssp *leucurus*

ssp *stricklandi*

ssp *harrisi*

ssp *icastus*

ssp *piger*

ssp *sanctorum*

116

ssp *villosus*

117

ssp *arizonae*

ssp *septentrionalis*

ssp *picoideus*

118

Genus *PICOIDES* Lacépède, 1799

110. Striped Woodpecker
Picoides lignarius

French: Pic bûcheron **German**: Strichelkopfspecht **Spanish**: Pico Bataraz Grande

Taxonomy. *Picus Lignarius* Molina, 1782, Chile.
Forms a superspecies with *P. mixtus*; they seem to be genetically close and may be conspecific, but possible overlap of breeding ranges not well documented. Related more distantly to other American congeners. Birds of isolated N population slightly smaller than those of Patagonia, with other morphological, plumage and genetic differences, probably representing a separate taxon, for which the name *puncticeps* is available; further study currently in progress. Monotypic.
Distribution. WC & S Bolivia (La Paz, Cochabamba, Santa Cruz southwards) S to N Argentina (Salta); Andean foothills and lowlands in C & S Chile (Bío-Bío to Magallanes) and SW Argentina (Neuquén to Santa Cruz).

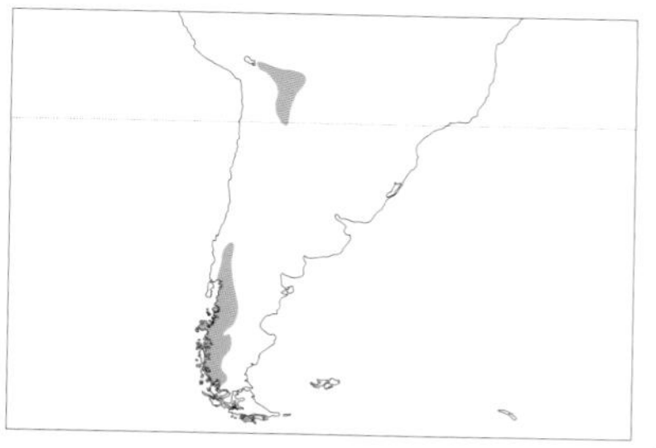

Descriptive notes. 15-16 cm; 35-39 g. Male has black forehead and crown, crown with variable amount of streaking or spotting, red to orange-red nape or red sometimes restricted to nape side, blackish hindneck; dark brownish-black ear-coverts faintly spotted white; white from supercilium continuing behind ear-coverts to join broad white line from lores; blackish malar stripe mixed with white feathering, heavily white-streaked near bill; whitish chin, throat finely streaked or spotted black; dark brownish-black upperparts narrowly barred (S population) or scalloped (N population) white to pale brownish-white, wing-coverts with large white spots, flight-feathers barred white; uppertail dark brownish-black, all feathers narrowly barred white or buff-white; white below, often tinged yellow or buff, and heavily and coarsely streaked blackish (streaks much finer in N population), streaks finer on belly, bars on lower flanks and undertail-coverts; longish bill (shorter in N) virtually straight, black, paler base and lower mandible; iris deep brown; legs grey or grey-brown. Distinguished from extremely similar *P. mixtus* by marginally larger size, slightly darker appearance, narrower white bars above, heavier markings below. Female lacks red on nape, usually has no white crown spots. Juvenile duller and browner than adult, more irregularly barred above, with heavier streaks and bars below, male with entire crown red, female with small red crown patch. Voice. Loud "peek"; also trill as long-distance call, lower and less harsh than that of *P. mixtus*.
Habitat. Humid to transitional forest. *Nothofagus* forest, *Podocarpus* forest, *Polylepis* woodland; open forest and edge of dense forest, open stunted forest, and interior of tall wet forest with water-courses in N; dry areas with scattered trees and cacti. Also found in pastures with shade trees, plantations and orchards; enters gardens. Occurs at 1600-4000 m in Bolivia; to 1800 m in Chile and Argentina.
Food and Feeding. Diet unrecorded; presumably includes surface-dwelling insects and wood-boring larvae. Forages solitarily; occasionally joins mixed-species feeding flocks. Main techniques are gleaning and probing; also pecks and hammers.
Breeding. Probably in Jun-Sept in Bolivia; from Oct in N to Jan in S in Chile and Argentina. Nest-hole excavated in tree or cactus. Clutch 3-5 eggs; no information on incubation and fledging periods.
Movements. Resident; some altitudinal movements. Populations breeding farthest S said to migrate N as far as WC Argentina (La Rioja, Cordoba) after breeding; recent research suggests, however, that this assertion probably based on misidentified specimens and confusion of scientific names.
Status and Conservation. Not globally threatened. No information on numbers; probably fairly common. Occurs in Cerro La Campana, Nahuelbuta and Vicente Pérez Rosales National Parks (Chile). A poorly known species; requires study.
Bibliography. Araya & Chester (1993), Canevari *et al.* (1991), Chebez *et al.* (1999), Cofré (1999), Fjeldså & Krabbe (1990), Flores & Capriles (1998), Grigera *et al.* (1996), Herzog *et al.* (1997), Johnson (1967), Mazar Barnett (2001a, 2001b), Mazar Barnett & Pearman (2001), Mazar Barnett *et al.* (1998), Narosky & Yzurieta (1993), de la Peña (1994), Remsen & Traylor (1989), Schmitt *et al.* (1997), Short (1970c, 1985b), Stotz *et al.* (1996), Vuilleumier (1985), Winkler & Short (1978).

111. Chequered Woodpecker
Picoides mixtus

French: Pic varié **German**: Streifenschwanzspecht **Spanish**: Pico Bataraz Chico
Other common names: Checked Woodpecker

Taxonomy. *Picus mixtus* Boddaert, 1783, Buenos Aires, Argentina.
Forms a superspecies with *P. lignarius*; they seem to be genetically close and may be conspecific, but possible overlap of breeding ranges not well documented. Races intergrade, and *malleator* and *berlepschi* may be more appropriately lumped into nominate. Four subspecies tentatively recognized.
Subspecies and Distribution.
P. m. cancellatus (Wagler, 1829) - extreme E Bolivia (Huanchaca Mts) to E Brazil (W Piauí S to S Mato Grosso, W Minas Gerais and Rio Grande do Sul), NE Paraguay and W Uruguay.
P. m. malleator (Wetmore, 1922) - Chaco region of SE Bolivia, Paraguay and N Argentina.
P. m. berlepschi (Hellmayr, 1915) - C & E Argentina from San Luis and Córdoba S to Neuquén, Río Negro and S Buenos Aires.
P. m. mixtus (Boddaert, 1783) - R Paraná and Buenos Aires (except S).
Descriptive notes. 14 cm; 29·8-37 g. Male has blackish-brown forehead and crown faintly streaked white or buffish-white, occasionally some crown feathers tipped red, nape red or orange-red but this

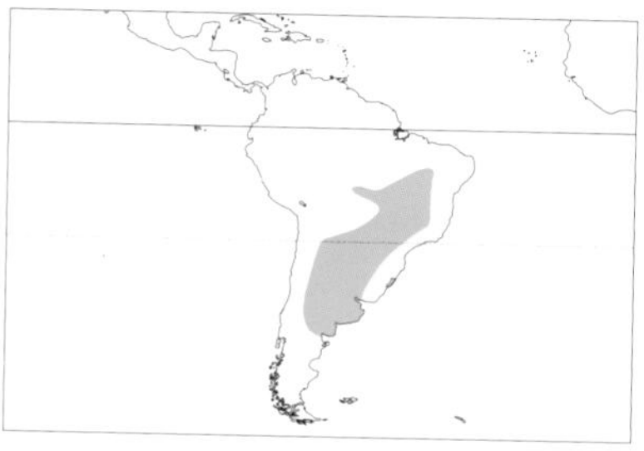

colour often restricted to nape sides, blackish-brown hindneck; dark brown ear-coverts; white from supercilium continuing behind ear-coverts to join broad white line from lores; thin weak malar stripe of dark brown streaks and spots; white chin, throat faintly streaked brown; blackish-brown upperparts barred whitish or brownish-white, bars more irregular or spot-like on mantle; deep brown wings barred white, bars more as spots on wing-coverts; uppertail brownish-black, all feathers narrowly but distinctly barred white; white below, tinged pale yellow or buff, breast and flanks streaked dark brown, lower belly and flanks sometimes with hint of barring; whitish undertail-coverts with fine brown spot-like streaks; longish bill straight, slightly chisel-tipped, black, paler base and lower mandible; iris deep brown to reddish; legs pale greyish. Differs from extremely similar *P. lignarius* in slightly smaller size, slightly paler appearance, broader white bars above, less heavy markings below. Female lacks red on nape and pale streaks on crown, occasionally has slight streaking on forehead. Juvenile duller and darker than adult, with barring above usually broken, dull white and more heavily streaked and barred below, both sexes with red on crown (not nape), red area smaller on female. Race *cancellatus* is rather distinctive, much browner, less black, with crown distinctly browner, white bars above broader than dark ones, much whiter below with far fewer and smaller streaks; *berlepschi* resembles nominate, but bill tends to be longer, brown areas somewhat darker, dark ear-covert patch bigger, ground colour of underparts cleaner white; *malleator* is like previous, but generally more heavily streaked below, usually some bars on flanks. Voice. Single "peek"; also trilling "ti-ti-ti-ti-ti..." as long-distance call, and "we-we-we...". Drums.
Habitat. Inhabits various types of rather humid open woodland and riparian growth; also savanna woodland, and open *cerrado* woodland; in S of range, *berlepschi* occurs in arid bush country with spiny mesquite (*Prosopis*) species. Generally found in lowlands; recorded up to 610 m in Bolivia.
Food and Feeding. Insects, seeds. Forages singly or in pairs. Most common foraging substrates are twigs and small branches of bushes and trees. Main techniques are gleaning and probing; also pecks weakly.
Breeding. Sept-Nov. Nest excavated by both sexes, at 3-6 m in tree or palm. Clutch 4 eggs; no information on incubation and fledging periods.
Movements. Insufficiently known. Some post-breeding movement in S; Mato Grosso birds leave in May, and return in Jan.
Status and Conservation. Not globally threatened. No data on numbers. Probably quite common, but appears to be very local, for reasons not understood. Present in Serra do Cipó, Chapada dos Guimarães and Brasília National Parks (Brazil) and also Chancaní Provincial Park and Ribera Norte Reserve (Argentina).
Bibliography. Belton (1984), Brooks, D.M. (1997), Brooks, T.M. *et al.* (1993), Canevari *et al.* (1991), Chebez *et al.* (1999), Contreras (1980b), Contreras *et al.* (1990), Dubs (1992), Fjeldså & Krabbe (1990), Gore & Gepp (1978), Hayes (1995), Klimaitis & Moschione (1987), López (1997), López de Casenave *et al.* (1998), Marelli (1919), Mazar Barnett (2001a), Mazar Barnett & Pearman (2001), Mazar Barnett & Kirwan (2001), Melo-Júnior (2001a), Miserendino (1998), Narosky & di Giacomo (1993), Nellar (1993), Nores *et al.* (1983), de la Peña (1994), Praderi (2000), Remsen & Traylor (1989), Short (1970c, 1975, 1985b), Sick (1993), Souza (1999), Stotz *et al.* (1996), Tubelis (2000), Tubelis & Cavalcanti (2001), Wetmore (1926), Willis & Oniki (1990), Winkler & Short (1978).

112. Nuttall's Woodpecker
Picoides nuttallii

French: Pic de Nuttall **German**: Nuttallspecht **Spanish**: Pico de Nuttall

Taxonomy. *Picus Nuttalii* [sic] Gambel, 1843, Los Angeles County, California.
Forms a superspecies with *P. scalaris*, both being closely related to *P. pubescens*. Hybridizes occasionally with both. Monotypic.
Distribution. N California S (mainly W of desert areas) to NW Baja California.

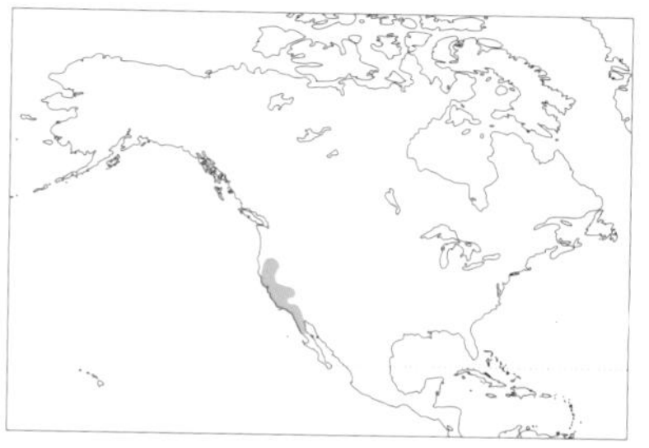

Descriptive notes. 19 cm; 28-47 g. Male has black forehead and forecrown contrasting strongly with white nasal tufts, forecrown well streaked with white, red hindcrown and nape normally with a few white spots, black hindneck; black ear-coverts bordered above by white supercilium which curves down on to rear neck side, bordered below by white stripe backwards from lores; thin black malar stripe expands on neck sides into large patch, this joining with rear ear-coverts and also extending back to mantle side; white chin and throat; black upperparts, lower mantle to upper rump broadly barred white, wing-coverts spotted white, flight-feathers narrowly barred white; uppertail black, white outer feathers often with 1 or 2 black spots, next 2 inner feathers barred black and white at tips; white below, lightly tinged cream-buff, breast side spotted, flanks, lower belly and undertail-coverts more barred; fairly long bill straight, chisel-tipped, blackish-grey to dull greyish-horn, paler base and lower mandible; iris deep brown; legs greyish or grey-olive, sometimes dark horn. Differs from *P. scalaris* mainly in having less red on head, more black on head and neck side, whiter underparts. Female has forehead to nape black, occasionally with some white spots on fore and rear areas, rarely entire head top white-streaked. Juvenile duller and less contrastingly patterned than adult, with more extensive pale (but greyer) areas above, dull buff to greyish below with more diffuse spots and more obvious bar marks, male with white-speckled red on crown centre, female with smaller and more broken red patch. Voice. Double "pitit" or single "pit" calls, sometimes followed by a rapid low rattle, "itititititit"; also "kweek", "tew-tew-tew" and other calls. Both sexes drum, with rolls relatively long, averaging 1·06 seconds.

On following pages: 113. Ladder-backed Woodpecker (*Picoides scalaris*); 114. Downy Woodpecker (*Picoides pubescens*); 115. Red-cockaded Woodpecker (*Picoides borealis*); 116. Strickland's Woodpecker (*Picoides stricklandi*); 117. Hairy Woodpecker (*Picoides villosus*); 118. White-headed Woodpecker (*Picoides albolarvatus*).

Habitat. Arid to mesic woodland. Primarily open oak (*Quercus*) woodland, also riparian woodland, chaparral; more rarely conifer forest; suburbs. From sea-level to 1250 m, locally to 1700 m, rarely 2000 m.
Food and Feeding. Mainly insects and other arthropods: predominantly beetles (mainly Cerambycidae, Elateridae), also hemipterans, caterpillars, ants; also termites (Isoptera), millipedes (Diplopoda), Diptera, Neuroptera, spiders. Berries, seeds, acorns and nuts play a lesser role in diet; also visits sap wells made by *Sphyrapicus*. Forages singly. Most foraging is in oaks and other trees (e.g. *Populus*, *Salix*) with dense foliage; also in mesquite (*Prosopis*) and yuccas (*Yucca*); occasionally on ground. Common feeding techniques gleaning and probing, also tapping; excavates only rarely, and flycatches occasionally. Seasonal and sexual differences more or less well expressed; males forage at lower levels, on larger branches, and tap more than do females.
Breeding. Season starts in Feb, egg-laying mostly in Apr-May, rarely to Jun. New nest-hole excavated each year, mostly by male, at 1-14 m (average 5 m) in dead tree stub or branch, or in fence post; hole entrance averages 5 cm across, cavity depth 28 cm. Clutch 3-6 eggs, usually 4 or 5; both sexes incubate, period recorded for only 1 nest, 14 days; both also feed chicks, rate of 6·3 feeds per hour in first week, 7·2 per hour thereafter; nestling period 15 days; fledglings remain with parents for c. 2 weeks. First breeding probably at 1 year.
Movements. Resident; some altitudinal movement. Casual records outside breeding range in California, and to N & W (S Oregon, and possibly Arizona), related to post-breeding dispersal.
Status and Conservation. Not globally threatened. Restricted-range species: present in California EBA. Fairly common to common. Total population roughly estimated at c. 100,000-200,000 individuals, though numbers possibly rather lower; density of 20·1 pairs/km² in one study in San Bernardino County. No obvious trends detected. Relatively poorly known for a North American species; research required on its breeding biology.
Bibliography. Anon. (1998b), Baicich & Harrison (1997), Bent (1939), Block (1991), Browning & Cross (1994), Dodenhoff *et al*. (2001), Howell & Webb (1995), Jenkins (1979), Johnson (2000), Kaufman (1996), Koenig (1986, 1987), Lowther (2000), Manolis (1987), Miller & Bock (1972), Price *et al*. (1995), Root (1988), Short (1965c, 1969a, 1971c), Small (1994), Stark *et al*. (1998), Stotz *et al*. (1996), Unitt (1986), Wilbur (1987), Winkler & Short (1978), Zusi & Marshall (1970).

113. **Ladder-backed Woodpecker**
Picoides scalaris

French: Pic arlequin **German**: Texasspecht **Spanish**: Pico Mexicano

Taxonomy. *Picus scalaris* Wagler, 1829, central Veracruz, Mexico.
Forms a superspecies with *P. nuttallii*, with which it occasionally hybridizes; also closely related to *P. pubescens*. Has possibly interbred also with *P. villosus*. Considerable individual and some clinal variation; described races *centrophilus* (W Mexico), *azelus* (S Mexico), *symplectus* (SE Colorado and W Oklahoma S to NE Mexico), *giraudi* (EC Mexico), *ridgwayi* (SE Veracruz) and *percus* (Chiapas) regarded as indistinguishable. Eight subspecies recognized.
Subspecies and Distribution.
P. s. cactophilus (Oberholser, 1911) - SW USA, from SE California, S Nevada, SW Utah, SE Colorado, W Oklahoma and W Texas, S to NE Baja California and S in C Mexico to Michoacán and Puebla.
P. s. eremicus (Oberholser, 1911) - N Baja California.
P. s. lucasanus (Baird, 1859) - S Baja California.
P. s. sinaloensis (Ridgway, 1887) - coastal W Mexico from S Sonora S to Guerrero, SW Puebla and C Oaxaca.
P. s. graysoni (Baird, 1874) - Tres Marías Is, off W Mexico.
P. s. scalaris (Wagler, 1829) - Veracruz and Chiapas.
P. s. parvus (Cabot, 1845) - N Yucatán Peninsula, including Cozumel I and Holbox I.
P. s. leucoptilurus (Oberholser, 1911) - Belize, Guatemala and El Salvador to NE Nicaragua.

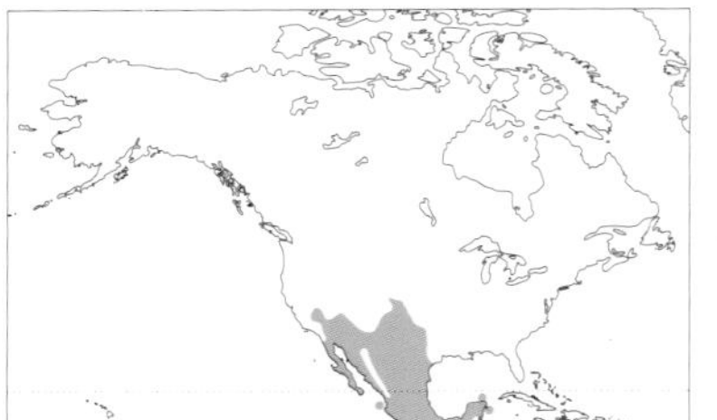

Descriptive notes. 18 cm; 21-48 g, mostly 25-41 g. Male has buffish forehead, black forecrown with broad red feather tips, red central crown to nape, narrowly black hindneck; broad white supercilium from above eye, continuing as wide band down rear neck side to upper breast side; broad black eyestripe across upper ear-coverts, bordered below by white band from lower lores; narrow black malar stripe streaked white near bill, at rear bending up to meet black eyestripe and usually continuing down a little towards upper breast; white chin and throat washed buffish; black upperparts barred white from lower mantle to upper rump, wing-coverts spotted with white, flight-feathers white-barred; uppertail black, outer 2 feathers barred white, adjacent pair barred at tip; pale buffish-white below, breast sides (sometimes also centre) and upper flanks finely streaked dark, lower flanks and undertail-coverts with spot-like bars; long bill rather straight, chisel-tipped, blackish to dark brown-grey or grey, paler base and lower mandible; iris brown to red-brown, sometimes dull red; legs greyish-olive. Distinguished from *P. nuttallii* by having more red on crown, less black on head and neck, more numerous pale bars above and on outer tail, more buffy underparts with smaller dark streaks. Female has crown to nape black, sometimes with a few white spots on forecrown. Juvenile duller than adult, barring above diffuse, generally more buff below with heavy dull brown streaks and more barring, both sexes with white spots on forecrown, red patch in crown centre, patch usually smaller on female. Race *cactophilus* is larger than nominate, has blacker forecrown, complete black malar, white bars on upper mantle, variably broader pale bars on back, paler underparts with spots rather than streaks, sometimes all-white outer rectrix; *eremicus* is larger, longer-tailed and longer-billed than previous, has thinner pale bars above, darker face and underparts, stronger dark bars on lower underparts; *lucasanus* is smaller and whiter than last, with white bars above broader, underparts paler; *graysoni* resembles previous, but slightly smaller and shorter-tailed, and more buff (less grey-brown) below with thinner streaks on breast side; *sinaloensis* is medium-sized, usually with malar interrupted towards bill, has dark face and underparts, latter streaked rather than spotted; *parvus* is smaller and darker than nominate, has black forehead, more black in malar, broader black bars above, spotted rather than streaked below, belly more obviously barred; *leucoptilurus* is smallest, just smaller than previous, with more white in upperparts, darker and buffier below with little spotting on breast, relatively indistinct barring on lower belly. Voice. Single "peek", often repeated in alarm; accelerating series e.g. "cheekeekeekeekeekikk", dropping in pitch at end. Drums infrequently, rolls short and fast.
Habitat. Very arid country and deserts; open to semi-open woodland and woods along (seasonally dry) rivers, with deciduous trees or cacti; also pine (*Pinus*) woods and pine mixed with oak (*Quercus*) in Central America. Also locally in clearings of humid forest, and in mangroves in El Salvador and Honduras. From lowlands to 2300 m in USA; at 1500-2100 m, rarely to 2600 m, in NE Mexico, and to 3000 m in Baja California; to 1800 m in Guatemala.
Food and Feeding. Mainly insects, some other arthropods. Larvae and adults of beetles; also caterpillars, ants and hemipterans. Also takes fruit. Forages singly, occasionally in pairs. Seeks food on trunks and branches of broadleaved and coniferous trees, mesquite (*Prosopis*), bushes, yuccas (*Yucca*) and cacti; rarely on ground. Foraging generally varies with location and season. Sexes differ in use of plant species, females spending more time in bushes and mesquite; females also utilize smaller branches and twigs more, and excavate less. Surface-oriented techniques, i.e. gleaning, probing, removing of bark or debris, predominant; excavating is uncommon.
Breeding. Laying recorded Mar-Jul, normally Apr-Jun. Flutter-aerial display and other typical displays. Nest excavated at c. 1-9 m in dead part of tree, stub, often in yucca, agave (*Agave*), sometimes large cactus, or in fence post or utility pole; entrance hole c. 4 cm across, cavity depth 18-36 cm. Clutch 2-7 eggs, usually 3-5, clutches smaller in S; both sexes incubate eggs and feed young; incubation and fledging periods not recorded. First breeding probably at 1 year. Longevity in wild 4·5 years.
Movements. Resident and sedentary.
Status and Conservation. Not globally threatened. Fairly common in USA; common to fairly common in Mexico. Estimated density 1·15 birds/40 ha in one study area in S California. Long-term decline since 1960's in Texas. Preference for very arid habitats makes this species less likely to come into contact with humans; locally, could suffer some degradation or loss of habitat through livestock grazing.
Bibliography. Anon. (1998b), Arnold (1984), Austin (1976), Baicich & Harrison (1997), Bent (1939), Binford (1989), Brush (1983), Brush *et al*. (1990), Corcuera & Butterfield (1999), Dennis (1964, 1967), Friedmann *et al*. (1957), García *et al*. (2001), Heilfurth (1938), Howell & Webb (1992, 1995), Hutto (1992), Johnsgard (1979), Johnson (2000), Kaufman (1996), Koenig (1986, 1987), Komar *et al*. (1997), Lowther (2001), Manolis (1987), Miller (1955b), Monroe (1968), Oberholser (1911), Price *et al*. (1995), Root (1988), van Rossem (1942), Russell (1964), Schaldach (1963), Short (1968, 1971c, 1985b), Small (1994), Spofford (1977), Stark *et al*. (1998), Stotz *et al*. (1996), Urban (1959), Wilbur (1987), Wilson & Ceballos-Lascuráin (1993), Winkler & Short (1978), Winternitz (1998).

114. **Downy Woodpecker**
Picoides pubescens

French: Pic mineur **German**: Dunenspecht **Spanish**: Pico Pubescente

Taxonomy. *Picus pubescens* Linnaeus, 1766, South Carolina, USA.
Most closely related to *P. nuttallii* and *P. scalaris*, and has hybridized with former. DNA analyses also indicate possible relationship with *Dendrocopos minor* of Old World; further study required. Nominate race and *medianus* intergrade widely in C USA. Clinal variation in size, decreasing from N to S. Additional named races *nelsoni* (Alaska to Alberta) and *microleucus* (Newfoundland) considered unacceptable. Six subspecies recognized.
Subspecies and Distribution.
P. p. medianus (Swainson, 1832) - C Alaska and Canada (E of Rockies, from S Mackenzie and Alberta) E to S Quebec and Newfoundland, and S in USA to Nebraska and Virginia.
P. p. glacialis (Grinnell, 1910) - SE Alaskan coast.
P. p. gairdnerii (Audubon, 1839) - W British Columbia S along coast to NW California.
P. p. leucurus (Hartlaub, 1852) - Rocky Mts from SE Alaska S to NE California, Arizona and New Mexico.
P. p. turati (Malherbe, 1861) - inland Washington and Oregon, and California (except NW & NE).
P. p. pubescens (Linnaeus, 1766) - Kansas E to North Carolina and S to E Texas and Florida.

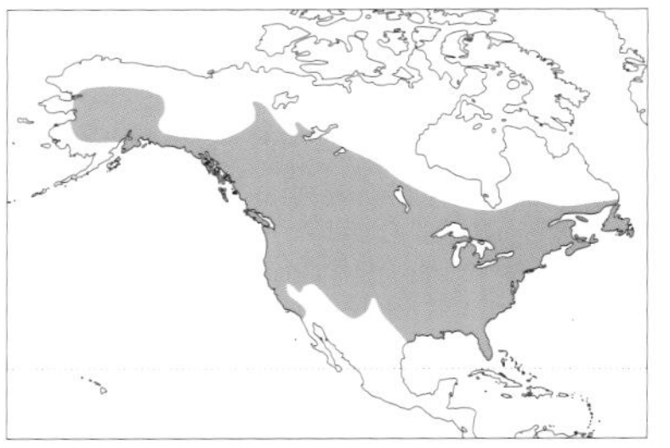

Descriptive notes. 15-17 cm; 20·7-32·2 g, mean 27·0 g. Male has whitish nasal tufts, black forehead to hindcrown, red nape, narrowly black hindneck; white supercilium from above eye, broadening at rear to meet nape; black ear-covert patch extending up to lower nape; white lores and broad cheekband, becoming broad white patch on rear neck side, bordered below by black malar stripe (often broken near bill) which continues back to mantle side; white chin and throat; black upperparts except for white central panel from mid-mantle to lower back, wing-coverts with large white subterminal spots, flight-feathers with spots on outer webs and bars on inner webs; uppertail black, all but central feather pair with white at tip, white increasing in extent outwards, outer pair mostly white with variable but often prominent black bars; white to greyish-white below, undertail-coverts sometimes with faint streaks or spots; short bill almost straight, slightly chisel-tipped, dark grey or blackish, paler base and lower mandible; iris deep brown or red-brown; legs olive-grey or grey. Differs from *P. villosus* in clearly smaller size, much smaller and shorter bill, black-barred outer tail, malar not extending to breast side. Female has nape black or white-streaked black. Juvenile has black areas browner, white of back streaked darker, greyish or buffish underparts finely streaked on breast and flanks, variably barred on lower flanks, greyish or olive eyes, male with red feather tips on crown (but not nape) and variable white spotting on forecrown, female with crown brownish-black and either unmarked or lightly or heavily streaked pale. Races differ mainly in size, amount of white in wings, and tone of underparts: *medianus* is larger and paler than nominate; *leucurus* is largest and whitest, with few or no white wing-covert spots, little black in outer tail, pure white below with undertail-coverts unstreaked; *glacialis* is very like previous but more pale buffish-white below, with more dark bars in outer tail; *gairdnerii* has wing-coverts largely unspotted, outer tail strongly barred, is darkest below, brownish-grey to buff; *turati* is smaller than previous, with slightly paler, pale buffish-grey, underparts. Voice. Single "pik" notes, sometimes at high rates in alarm; characteristic series of notes, dropping in pitch at end, "peet-peet-peet-peet-peet-pit-pit-pitpit". Drums in short rolls.
Habitat. Deciduous and mixed forest, woodland, second growth, parks and gardens, including in suburban and urban areas. Partial to riverine woodland in SW & S parts of range; prefers moist aspen (*Populus tremula*) and willow (*Salix*) stands in coniferous zone. From sea-level to hills; 1860-2750 m in SW mountains.
Food and Feeding. Mainly insects, some vegetable matter. Wood-boring larvae an important component; beetles and ants each form about a third of the diet; other animal items include bugs (Hemiptera), plant lice, Diptera, caterpillars, grasshoppers (Acrididae), spiders and myriapods. Bark beetles (*Scolytus*), spiders, ants and moths fed to nestlings. Various types of berries taken when available; seeds and nuts become more important in winter. Forages singly or in pairs; commonly joins mixed-species flocks, especially with tits (Paridae). Visits garden feeders, especially in winter. Foraging rather flexible, and substrate use changes with season, supply, and competition. Live

wood usually selected, but occasionally species shifts completely to dead trees, including fire-killed ones. Generally, limbs of small diameter (less than 25 cm) are preferred, and foraging may take place at all heights in a tree, with some emphasis on lower canopy; also descends to fallen logs. Larger trees and those with more furrowed bark are favoured in winter. Male concentrates more on upper levels, maintaining this segregation through supplanting attacks on female. Pecking is commonest technique, followed by hammering and probing; bark and wood are not deeply excavated; also, some flycatching in summer. Commonly removes bark, and on dead trees in particular this may amount to more than half of foraging activity.

Breeding. Egg-laying in Apr-May in Florida, in May-Jul in British Columbia; may rear more than 1 brood within a season. Flutter-aerial displays mainly by male; nape feathers erected during courtship. Nest-excavation completed within 13-20 days, hole in dead tree or in dead part of tree, often located just beneath broken-off top of a stub, or in fence post or utility pole. Clutch 3-7 eggs, usually 4 or 5, mean 4·81, clutch size tending to increase with latitude (to 7 eggs in British Columbia); male and female share all breeding duties, incubation, brooding, feeding, nest sanitation, female often reducing her effort towards end of nestling period; incubation period 12 days, nestling period 20-23 days; fledglings accompanied by parents for up to 3 weeks.

Movements. Resident in most of range. N and montane populations partially migratory or disperse over longer distances, some individuals moving as far as 1200 km away from breeding grounds; stragglers recorded S to NW Mexico.

Status and Conservation. Not globally threatened. Common to very common; the commonest woodpecker in many parts of range. Populations generally stable, with some local increases; adaptable, able to exploit human-altered habitats. Benefits from opening-up of forest and creation of second-growth habitats.

Bibliography. Askins (1983), Baldwin (1960), Ball & Avise (1992), Bent (1939), Blake (1981), Blom (2000), Bock & Lepthien (1975), Brazier (1989), Brenner *et al.* (1992), Browning (1995, 1997), Campbell *et al.* (1990), Confer & Paicos (1985), Confer *et al.* (1986), Conner (1973, 1975, 1977, 1979, 1980, 1981), Conner & Adkisson (1977), Conner & Crawford (1974), Conner & Saenz (1996), Conner, Hooper *et al.* (1975), Conner, Jones & Jones (1994), Conner, Miller & Adkisson (1976), Cyr (1995c), Davis, G.L. (1973), Davis, W.E. (1995), Delacour (1951a), Dodenhoff *et al.* (2001), Dolby & Grubb (1998, 1999), Ellison (1992), Ferguson (1977), Gamboa & Brown (1976), Gardella (1997), Garrett (1999), George (1972), Grubb (1982, 1989), Hadow (1976), Harestad & Keisker (1989), Hawkins & Ritchison (1996), Holmes & Sherry (2001), Howell (1943), Jackman (1974), Jackson (1970a, 1970d, 1994b), Jackson & Hoover (1975), James (1970), Jones (1988), Kilham (1961a, 1962b, 1970, 1972b, 1974a, 1974b, 1974d, 1979b, 1983), Kisiel (1972), Koenig (1987), Koplin (1969, 1972), Kreisel & Stein (1999), Laskey (1966), Lawrence (1966), Liknes & Swanson (1996), Lima (1983, 1984), Martin & Li (1992), Matthysen *et al.* (1991), Mecum & Abrahamson (1994), Moeller & Thogerson (1978), Moulton & Lowell (1991), Ouellet (1977b, 1997), Peck & James (1983), Peters (1982), Peters & Grubb (1983), Peterson & Grubb (1983), Petit, Grubb *et al.* (1988), Petit, Petit *et al.* (1985), Richardson (1942), Ritchison (1999), Romary (1990), Saab & Dudley (1998), Schepps *et al.* (1999), Schlichter (1978), Schroeder (1983), Schwab & Monnie (1959), Setterington *et al.* (2000), Shackelford & Conner (1997), Shanley & Shanley (1978), Short (1969a, 1971c), Smith, K.G. (1986c), Smith, L.M. (1971, 1973), Snyder (1923), Spring (1965), Staebler (1949), Stark *et al.* (1998), Sullivan (1984a, 1984b, 1985a, 1985b), Swallow *et al.* (1988), Tiebout (1986), Tobalske (1996), Townsend (1932), Travis (1977), Unitt (1986), Volman *et al.* (1997), Waite & Grubb (1988), Waldbauer *et al.* (1970), Welsh & Capen (1987, 1992), Wiedenfeld *et al.* (1992), Williams, J.B. (1975, 1980a), Williams, J.B. & Batzli (1979a, 1979b, 1979c), Willson (1970), Winkler & Leisler (1985), Winkler & Short (1978), Wood & Wood (1973), Woods (1984), Yunich (1988).

115. **Red-cockaded Woodpecker**

Picoides borealis

French: Pic à face blanche **German**: Kokardenspecht **Spanish**: Pico de Florida

Taxonomy. *Picus borealis* Vieillot, 1807, Mount Pleasant, South Carolina, USA.
Basal relationships with *P. stricklandi*, *P. villosus* and *P. albolarvatus*. Birds from C & S Florida named as race *hylonomus* on basis of smaller size, but unacceptable, since size decreases clinally from N to S. Monotypic.

Distribution. Patchily in SE USA, from SE Oklahoma and E Texas E to Atlantic coast: extends N to Kentucky and S Virginia, S to C Louisiana, S Mississippi and C Florida.

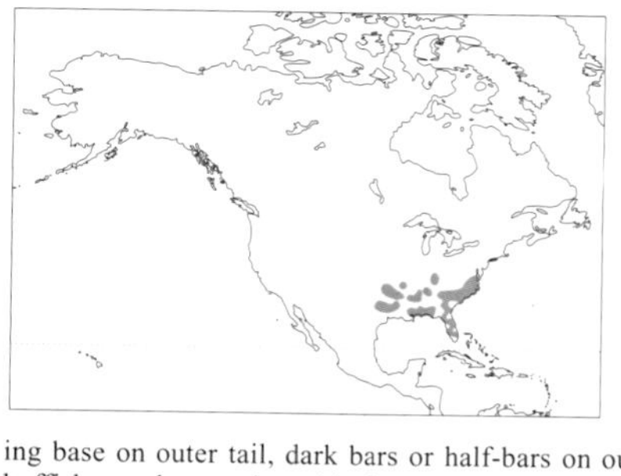

Descriptive notes. 22 cm; 40-55 g, male on average 1·5 g heavier than female. Male has whitish nasal tufts, black forehead to hindneck, short white stripe behind eye, small red spot at side of nape (hardly visible in field), black lores, and broad black malar stripe broadening on neck side and extending slightly to upper breast side; rest of head white, ear-coverts sometimes faintly tinged grey or buff; black upperparts barred white from central mantle to upper rump, wing-coverts with white subterminal spots, flight-feathers barred white; uppertail black, white at tips increasing in extent from second or third pair outwards, reaching base on outer tail, dark bars or half-bars on outer 2 feathers; white underparts often sullied buffish or pale grey, large black spots and streaks on breast side, becoming smaller or narrower on flanks, sometimes thin bars on lower flanks and undertail-coverts; fairly long bill chisel-tipped, culmen slightly curved, blackish-grey; iris dark brown; legs olive-grey. Female lacks red spot at nape side. Juvenile duller and browner above than adult, with dusky cheek patch, duller and more diffusely marked below, male also with dull reddish crown centre. VOICE. Commonest call in human presence and alarm a distinctive "shrrit" or "sklit", singly or in groups or series, depending on context; much rarer is preamble of call-like notes followed by up to 30 notes that are shorter and lower-pitched versions of call, also in shorter and more variable form by fledged young; groups rather vocal, frequently a wide range of twittering calls and chortles varying from low and short to clear "wic-a wic-a" notes, may be combined with call notes; low soft notes in intimate contacts, especially at nest or roost; nestling calls change considerably during course of chick development. Drumming infrequent, by both sexes, not particularly loud.

Habitat. Adapted to open mature pine (*Pinus*) forest and forests of pine mixed with oak (*Quercus*), requiring open pine stands with a park-like structure for nesting. Also uses adjacent stands of cypress (*Taxodium*), cornfields and orchards for foraging. Dependent on a few species belonging to the "longleaf pine savanna" of the SE USA: primarily longleaf pine (*P. palustris*), slash pine (*P. elliottii*), shortleaf pine (*P. echinata*), also loblolly pine (*P. taeda*), pitch pine (*P. rigida*) and pond pine (*P. serotina*), all of which meet the species' particular nest-site requirements. Old-growth forest very important as a high-quality foraging habitat. Restricted to Atlantic coastal plain and hills below 500 m.

Food and Feeding. Diet mainly insects, their larvae, and other arthropods; some plant material. Ants, particularly eggs, larvae, pupae, also adults of arboreal *Crematogaster*, are most important, forming up to 80% of diet (annual average c. 50%), followed by adults and larvae of wood-boring beetles (*Dendroctonus frontalis*, *Ips*, 15%); other insect larvae, Hemiptera, wood roaches (Blattodea), termites (Isoptera), other beetles, dipterans, hymenopterans, moths, damselflies (Zygoptera), spiders, scorpions (Scorpiones), centipedes (Chilopoda), and millipedes (Diplopoda) also recorded as food. Male's diet contains higher proportion of ants. Nestling food mainly spiders, ants, beetles and their larvae, centipedes, as well as carpenter-bees (Xylocopidae) and miscellaneous other arthropods and larvae. Fruits (e.g. cherries) and berries of various species (e.g. *Vaccinium*, *Myrica*) taken to some extent, even fed to nestlings; pine seeds taken mainly in winter; other plant food includes nuts (*Carya*). Females observed to cache bone fragments during egg-laying period. Roams through territory singly, in pairs or in groups; accompanies mixed-species foraging flocks in winter. Pines are main tree species utilized (90% of foraging), with larger (older) ones preferred, but hardwood and other trees and orchards also exploited; cornfields entered when infested with earworms (*Heliothis*). Live and dead trees visited about equally, although local differences seem to exist, with live and only recently dead pines preferred in some places. Most foraging is on tree trunks; males, which feed more often on limbs, frequently move along underside of branches. Clear sexual differences, most pronounced in Jan-Mar: males use mainly upper trunk and branches, females tend to feed on lower trunk, sexes overlap greatly in use of mid-trunk; consequently, sexes differ in foraging height by c. 3-7 m. Food frequently obtained by removing bark, achieved by grasping pieces with the bill, by prying it off, and often by grabbing bark with both feet and making short flying leap or by scratching with both feet; exposed prey then gleaned. Scaled trees give away species' presence. Also probes crevices and needle and cone clusters; males, in particular, sometimes peck to excavate decayed wood. Occasionally makes aerial sallies to catch flying insects.

Breeding. Lays in late Apr; rarely, 2 broods. In pairs; a third of these have helpers, 70-95% of which are males, generally offspring from previous broods; once established, such breeding units are sedentary, or at least breeding male; when male dies or when forced out by group-members or intruders, female may break away from unit. Nest-hole excavated mostly 10-13 m above ground in mature pine, entrance 5·7-7·1 cm wide with slightly upward-inclined tunnel up to 6 cm long in sapwood, nest-chamber excavated in rotten heartwood and at least 17-18 cm deep with diameter 9-10 cm; nest is breeding male's roost; nest-site highly distinctive, with sap flowing from holes drilled around entrance and much bark removed from trunk. Clutch 2-5 eggs, usually 3 or 4; incubation begins with last or next to last egg, shared by both members of pair about equally during day, sometimes a helper also incubates, breeding male stays in nest overnight, incubation period 10-11 days, occasionally to 13 days; chick hatches blind and naked, with bright pink skin, by 4th or 5th day feather sheaths become visible, eyes open c. 10th day, nestlings stay at bottom of hole for 15 days; both parents feed nestlings, male helpers contribute as much to nest sanitation, brooding and brood-feeding as do parents, fledging weight of 42-45 g (males tend to be heavier) reached c. 3-4 days before leaving nest; nestling period 26-29 days, sometimes shorter (22 days); male and any helpers continue to feed young for 2-6 months. Usually 2 chicks reared.

Movements. Resident and sedentary. Stragglers recorded N to Ohio.

Status and Conservation. VULNERABLE. Uncommon to rare, and extremely local. Adapted to open mature pine and pine-oak forests, which form a unique ecosystem in SE USA that is found primarily on federal and state lands. Estimated population in 2000 no more than 10,000 mature adults, concentrated in c. 30 sub-populations, largest in Carolinas and N Florida. Recently became extinct in Maryland, imminent extinction seems likely in Tennessee, few remain in Kentucky, and populations continue to decline elsewhere. Strict habitat requirements led to dramatic decline in numbers in 20th century, with reduction by at least 23% during 1980's alone; decline caused primarily by extreme fragmentation of habitats resulting in concentrations of breeding groups. A clan of 3 or 4 birds requires c. 58-91 ha of suitable habitat for its survival; genetically healthy populations possibly require more than 25,000 ha. Habitat fragmentation, clear-cutting and mid-storey encroachment of hardwood are major causes of the decline of this species, which also suffers locally from devastating effects of hurricanes; irregular shelterwood-cutting seems to be less detrimental. Dense hardwood mid-storey is generally detrimental, but there seem to be regional differences in negative effects of hardwood admixture; up to 52% non-pine species have been registered in Kentucky habitats. Numerous conservation strategies have been employed in recent decades, some more successful than others, some having had adverse effects. Since start of habitat management in 1988, infestations of nesting trees by southern pine beetle (*Dendroctonus frontalis*) have increased; beetles infest nest-holes and kill trees used for nesting. Management should ensure sufficient number of mature trees for replacement holes, and old trees for foraging. Optimum habitats assume their typical structure through frequent fires, to which the pines are well adapted; prescribed fires (best during Mar-Apr) to control woody mid-storey vegetation are the most commonly used management tool to restore the pine-grassland communities that are important for this species; such measures need to be properly regulated.

Bibliography. Allen *et al.* (1993), Anon. (1985), Baker (1971a, 1971b, 1981), Baker *et al.* (1980), Beckett (1971, 1974), Bent (1939), Blue (1985), Bonnie (1997), Bowman *et al.* (1999), Bradshaw (1990), Burnside (1983), Carrie *et al.* (1998), Carter, J.H. (1974), Carter, J.H. *et al.* (1983a, 1983b), Collar & Andrew (1988), Collar, Crosby & Stattersfield (1994), Collar, Gonzaga *et al.* (1992), Conner (1975, 2001), Conner & Locke (1982), Conner & O'Halloran (1987), Conner & Rudolph (1989, 1991, 1995a, 1995b), Conner, Rudolph & Bonner (1995), Conner, Rudolph, Saenz & Coulson (1997), Conner, Rudolph, Saenz & Schaefer (1994, 1996, 1997), Conner, Rudolph, Schaefer & Saenz (1997), Conner, Rudolph, Schaefer, Saenz & Shackleford (1999), Conner, Rudolph & Walters (2001), Conner, Saenz *et al.* (1998), Conner, Snow & O'Halloran (1991), Copeyon *et al.* (1991), Costa & Escaño (1989), Costa & Kennedy (1994), Crosby (1971a, 1971b), Crowder (1998), Daniels, S.J. (1997, 2000), Daniels, S.J. & Walters (1999, 2000), Davenport *et al.* (2000), DeLotelle & Epting (1988, 1992), DeLotelle, Epting & Newman (1987), DeLotelle, Newman & Jerauld (1983), Dennis (1971), Doerr *et al.* (1989), Doster & James (1998), Eddleman & Clawson (1987), Engstrom & Mikusinski (1998), Engstrom & Sanders (1997), Engstrom *et al.* (1996), Escaño (1995), Ferral (1997), Field & Williams (1985), Franzreb (1994, 1997, 1999), Gaines *et al.* (1995), Gowarty & Lennartz (1985), Hagan & Reed (1988), Haig, Belthoff & Allen (1993a, 1993b), Haig, Walters & Plissner (1994), Hanula & Franzreb (1995), Hanula, Franzreb & Pepper (2000), Hanula, Lipscomb *et al.* (2000), Harlow (1983), Harlow & Lennartz (1977, 1983), Hernández (1992), Hess & James (1998), Hooper, R.G. (1982, 1983, 1988), Hooper, R.G. & Harlow (1986), Hooper, R.G. & Lennartz (1981, 1983, 1995), Hooper, R.G., Krusac & Carlson (1991), Hooper, R.G., Lennartz & Muse (1991), Hooper, R.G., Niles *et al.* (1982), Hooper, R.G., Robinson & Jackson (1980), Hopkins & Lynn (1971), Hovis (1982, 1996), Hovis & Labisky (1985), Jackson (1971, 1974, 1976a, 1977a, 1977b, 1978a, 1978b, 1978c, 1979, 1983a, 1983b, 1986, 1987, 1990b, 1994a), Jackson & Jackson (1986), Jackson, Baker *et al.* (1979), Jackson, Lennartz & Hooper (1979), James, D.A. & Neal (1989), James, F.C. (1991, 1995), James, F.C. *et al.* (1997), Jerauld *et al.* (1983), Jones & Ott (1973), Kalisz & Boettcher (1991), Kappes (1993, 1997), Kelly *et al.* (1993, 1994), Khan & Walters (1998, 2000), Khan *et al.* (1999), Kilham (1979b), King (1978/79), Koenig (1987), LaBranche (1992), LaBranche & Walters (1994), LaBranche *et al.* (1994), Lape (1990), Laves (1992), Laves & Loeb (1999), Lennartz (1983), Lennartz & Harlow (1979), Lennartz & Henry (1985), Lennartz, Hooper & Harlow (1987), Lennartz, Knight *et al.* (1983), Ligon (1968b, 1970, 1971), Ligon *et al.* (1986), Locke (1980), Locke *et al.* (1983), Manor (1991), McConnell (1999), McFarlane (1992), Mengel & Jackson (1977), Miller, G.L. (1978), Mitchell, J.H. *et al.* (1991), Mitchell, L.R. *et al.* (1999), Montague (1995),

Morse (1972), Murphy (1982), Neal (1992), Neal, Douglas *et al.* (1993), Neal, Montague & James (1992), Nesbitt *et al.* (1981), Odum *et al.* (1982), Patterson & Robertson (1981), Phillips *et al.* (1998), Pizzoni-Ardemani (1990), Porter & Labisky (1986), Ramey (1980), Reed (1990), Reed & Walters (1996), Reed, Doerr & Walters (1988), Reed, Walters *et al.* (1993), Repasky (1984), Repasky & Doerr (1991), Richardson & Smith (1992), Richardson *et al.* (1999), Rossell & Britcher (1994), Rossell & Gorsira (1996), Rudolph & Conner (1991, 1994, 1995), Rudolph, Conner, Carrie & Schaefer (1992), Rudolph, Conner & Schaefer (1991, 1995), Rudolph, Conner & Turner (1990), Rudolph, Kyle & Conner (1990), Saenz *et al.* (1998), Schaefer (1996), Seagle *et al.* (1987), Shackelford & Conner (1997), Sherrill & Case (1980), Skorupa (1979), Skorupa & McFarlane (1976), Sparks *et al.* (1999), Stangel (1991), Stangel *et al.* (1992), Stattersfield & Capper (2000), Steirly (1957), Walters (1990, 1991), Walters, Copeyon & Carter (1992), Walters, Doerr & Carter (1988, 1992), Walters, Hansen *et al.* (1988), Watson *et al.* (1995), Wigley *et al.* (1999), Winkler & Short (1978), Wood, D.A. (1977, 1983a, 1983b), Wood, D.R. *et al.* (2000), Yezerinac (1999), Zwicker (1995), Zwicker & Walters (1999).

116. **Strickland's Woodpecker**

Picoides stricklandi

French: Pic de Strickland **German**: Stricklandspecht **Spanish**: Pico de Strickland
Other common names: Brown-backed Woodpecker(!); Arizona Woodpecker (*arizonae*/*fraterculus*)

Taxonomy. *Picus (Leuconotopicus) Stricklandi* Malherbe, 1845, Mount Orizaba massif, Veracruz, Mexico.
Closest to *P. borealis*, *P. villosus* and *P. albolarvatus*. Races *arizonae* and *fraterculus* originally treated as together forming a separate species, *P. arizonae*, subsequently lumped into present species, but recently resplit by several authors: distinctive morphological differences suggest that separation into two species is perhaps tenable, although vocalizations apparently very similar, plumage differences perhaps clinal in nature, and ecological requirements of the two groups overlap; further research needed. Birds from SE Sinaloa E to W Zacatecas and S to S Jalisco separated as race *websteri*, but apparently only an intermediate form between *arizonae* and *fraterculus*; also, birds from C Mexico (E Michoacán to Distrito Federal) named as race *aztecus*, being less heavily marked below than nominate, but this character apparent only in very fresh plumage and also subject to clinal variation, degree of streaking increasing towards E. Three subspecies recognized.
Subspecies and Distribution.
P. s. arizonae (Hargitt, 1886) - SE Arizona, extreme SW New Mexico, and Mexico in Sierra Madre Occidental (S to NE Sinaloa and neighbouring parts of Durango).
P. s. fraterculus (Ridgway, 1887) - S Sinaloa and adjacent Durango S to Michoacán.
P. s. stricklandi (Malherbe, 1845) - E Mexico, from E Michoacán E to WC Veracruz and Puebla.

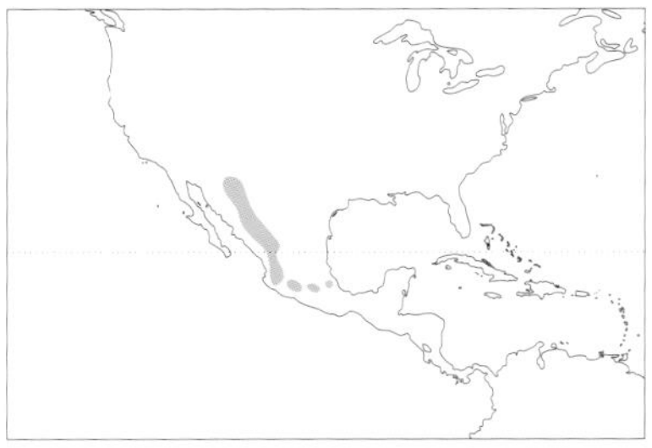

Descriptive notes. 18-20 cm; 34-51 g. Male has buff nasal tufts, blackish-brown forehead and crown, red nape, blackish-brown hindneck; white stripe behind eye; dark brown upper lores and ear-coverts, white cheekband broadening behind ear-coverts and continuing down rear neck side; blackish malar stripe broadening on neck side, extending to uppermost breast side; white chin and throat variably spotted; blackish-brown upperparts barred greyish from back to rump, flight-feathers with small white spots forming indistinct bars on inner webs, small spots on outer webs of primaries; uppertail dark black-brown, outer 2 or 3 feather pairs barred white; whitish below, breast heavily marked with blackish spots, more barred on flanks and lower underparts; longish bill straight, chisel-tipped, blackish, paler base and lower mandible; iris dark brown; legs greenish-grey. Female has nape black-brown, not red. Juvenile duller than adult, has less white on neck side and tail, is darker below with heavier markings and much barring, both sexes with orange-red on crown, usually restricted to hindcrown on female. Races differ from nominate in much paler upperparts without barring, clearly longer bill: *arizonae* has all dark parts of head and upperparts medium to darkish brown, rather than blackish-brown, mantle to rump usually unmarked but occasionally with hint or more of pale bars, often more obvious white in outer tail; *fraterculus* is very similar, but slightly smaller and darker. Voice. Single "peep"; distinctive rattle, "peep chree-chree-chree-chree-chree". Both sexes, mainly male, loud longish rolls; signal-tapping at prospective nest-site.
Habitat. In N of range (Arizona) and W Mexico, mixed subtropical pine-oak (*Pinus*-*Quercus*) woodland, also riparian woodland with sycamore (*Platanus*) and walnut (*Juglans*); almost entirely pine woods in SE; at 1200-2400 m. In C & E Mexico, nominate race inhabits temperate coniferous forest in higher mountains of C volcanic belt, in woods dominated by pines, mixed with firs (*Abies*), oaks, cypresses (*Cupressus*) and alders (*Alnus*), at 2500-4100 m (Veracruz, Puebla).
Food and Feeding. Insects, mainly beetle larvae, and some fruits and seeds (acorns). Forages mainly on pines; less selective during breeding season. Usually singly; joins mixed-species feeding flocks. Forages mostly from middle to low levels, on trunks, branches and twigs; female more on twigs, especially in breeding season. Trunk-foraging clearly predominates during early spring, at which time pecking and hammering (to excavate or to remove bark, which is also removed with feet) are most common techniques, followed by probing, gleaning and flycatching. Surface-feeding more common in summer.
Breeding. Mainly from Apr-May. Displays include head-swinging, wing-spreading and flutter-aerial display. Nest excavated at 2·4-15 m, mostly at about 3-6 m, in dead tree or dead part of tree, or in agave (*Agave*) stem; hole entrance 5-5·7 cm across, cavity depth 30-38 cm. Clutch 2-4 eggs; both sexes incubate, period uncertain, 14 days or probably fewer; both also feed chicks, male more than female, fledging period 24-27 days; juveniles accompanied and fed by parents for 2-3 weeks. Fledging success averaged 1·8 at five nests in Arizona; youngest chick often starves.
Movements. Resident. Periodic downslope movements after breeding recorded in SE Arizona, possibly in response to food shortage.
Status and Conservation. Not globally threatened. Generally uncommon throughout range, though locally quite common. Densities low: 4 pairs/40 ha in oak-juniper-pine woodland and 1 pair/40 ha in oak woodland in SE Arizona; 1-5 pairs/1·6 km in linear censuses in pine-oak woodland in SW USA and NE Mexico; in Huachuca Mts (SE Arizona), more than 1 bird/10 ha recorded in riparian habitats in both summer and winter. Populations possibly threatened locally because of habitat fragmentation and loss; heavy grazing may have important local effects.
Bibliography. Anon. (1998b), Bent (1939), Corcuera & Butterfield (1999), Davis (1965), Howell & Webb (1995), Hutto (1992), Kaufman (1996), Koenig (1986, 1987), Ligon (1968a, 1968b), Manolis (1987), Marshall (1957a, 1957b), Moore (1946), Morris & Buffa (1996), Peterson & Navarro-Sigüenza (2000), Price *et al.* (1995), Root (1988), Schaldach (1963), Spofford (1977), Stotz *et al.* (1996), Wilson & Ceballos-Lascuráin (1993), Winkler (1979a), Winkler & Short (1978).

117. **Hairy Woodpecker**

Picoides villosus

French: Pic chevelu **German**: Haarspecht **Spanish**: Pico Velloso

Taxonomy. *Picus villosus* Linnaeus, 1766, New Jersey, USA.
Related to *P. stricklandi* and *P. albolarvatus*, with which it forms a relatively closely related cluster of species that is linked with *P. borealis*. May have interbred with *P. scalaris*. Molecular-genetic analysis suggests very close relationship to *Veniliornis fumigatus*, perhaps to extent that the two could justifiably be treated as congeneric; further study needed. Spectacular variation in size, coloration and plumage pattern is largely clinal in nature, associated with temperature and moisture, with races intergrading in many areas. A large number of races have been described, of which many are unsustainable: *monticola* (Rocky Mts from British Columbia to New Mexico), *leucothorectis* (mountains of SW USA), *scrippsae* (N Baja California), *intermedius* (E Mexico), *parvulus* (N El Salvador to N & W Honduras), *fumeus* (highlands of S Honduras and N Nicaragua), *extimus* (highlands of Costa Rica and Panama). Fourteen subspecies currently recognized.
Subspecies and Distribution.
P. v. septentrionalis (Nuttall, 1840) - from tree-line in Alaska E across S Canada to Ontario, and S to SC British Columbia, Colorado, N New Mexico, Montana and North Dakota.
P. v. villosus (Linnaeus, 1766) - from E North Dakota E to S Quebec and Nova Scotia, and S to E Colorado, C Texas, Missouri (Ozark Plateau) and N Virginia.
P. v. terraenovae (Batchelder, 1908) - Newfoundland.
P. v. sitkensis (Swarth, 1911) - coast of SE Alaska and N British Columbia.
P. v. picoideus (Osgood, 1901) - Queen Charlotte Is, off British Columbia.
P. v. harrisi (Audubon, 1838) - coastal region from S British Columbia to NW California.
P. v. audubonii (Swainson, 1832) - from E Texas, S Illinois and SE Virginia S to Gulf coast.
P. v. hyloscopus (Cabanis & Heine, 1863) - W California S to N Baja California.
P. v. orius (Oberholser, 1911) - Cascade Mts in British Columbia S through C Oregon to SE California, C Arizona, New Mexico and extreme W Texas.
P. v. icastus (Oberholser, 1911) - SE Arizona and SW New Mexico S in W Mexico to Jalisco.
P. v. jardinii (Malherbe, 1845) - C Mexico from San Luis Potosí, Tamaulipas and Veracruz to Jalisco, Guerrero and Oaxaca.
P. v. sanctorum (Nelson, 1897) - S Mexico (Chiapas) and Guatemala SE to W Panama.
P. v. piger (G. M. Allen, 1905) - N Bahamas (Grand Bahama, Abaco, Mores).
P. v. maynardi (Ridgway, 1887) - S Bahamas (Andros, New Providence).

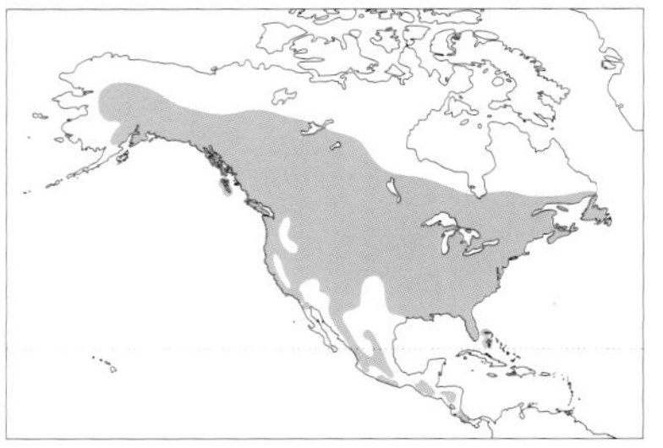

Descriptive notes. 16·5-26 cm; 59-80 g (*villosus*), 72-80 g (*picoideus*), 42 g (*sanctorum*). Male has white nasal tufts, black forehead and crown, narrow red to orange-red nape patch, black hindneck; white supercilium from above eye to nape; small black area in front of eye and broad black band through ear-coverts to nape; white lores, wide white band below eye and ear-coverts and broadly down rear neck side; black malar stripe usually partly obscured by white near bill, expanding on neck side and continuing back to mantle and down to upper breast side; white chin and throat; black sides of mantle and back, contrasting broad white central panel from mid-mantle to lower back, black rump and uppertail-coverts; black wings, coverts with large white subterminal spots, flight-feathers barred white; uppertail black centrally, white tips on rest of feathers, with extent of white increasing outwards so that outermost feathers are all white; white with very slight grey tinge below, rarely with a few streaks on breast side below malar extension or faint streaks on flanks; long bill chisel-tipped, culmen slightly curved, dark grey to blackish, paler base and lower mandible; iris deep brown or red-brown; legs grey or blue-grey, sometimes darker or green-tinged. Differs from *P. pubescens* in larger size, distinctly longer more powerful bill, unbarred white outer tail, black band from neck side to upper breast. Female has nape black or mixed black and white. Juvenile duller than adult, black areas browner, underparts somewhat darker with at least some streaks or bars, some bars on outer tail, greyer eyes, white eyering, male with orangey or red patch on crown, normally much smaller on female. Races differ considerably in size, plumage coloration and pattern, largest and palest in N and in cold dry climates, white in wing reduced in W and S: *septentrionalis* is largest and whitest, large-billed, much white on head; *terraenovae* is greyer and buff-tinged below with fine flank streaks, has narrower white face stripes, narrower dark-streaked white back panel, less white in wing, often some bars on outer tail, juvenile buff below with well-streaked breast side, barred flanks; *audubonii* is smaller and darker than nominate, has greyish-buff underparts; *picoideus* has buff-brown face and underparts, pale of back barred dark, little white in wing, obvious streaking on flanks, barred outer tail; *sitkensis* is large, buffish below, has more white in wing than previous; *harrisi* is smaller than previous, with longer bill, pale parts of plumage grey-brown, white in wing very much reduced; *hyloscopus* is a trifle smaller than last, paler, more buff (less grey-brown) below, with whitish suffusion; *orius* is bigger than previous, relatively longer-billed, paler below; *icastus* has shorter wing and tail than last, much shorter bill, no pale wing-covert spots, darker buffer underparts; *jardinii* is smaller than previous, has pale head markings narrow, much darker (deep buff-brown) underparts with few streaks on breast side; *sanctorum* is even smaller, on average smallest of all races, with supercilium very narrow, darker below, sometimes pale flanks (especially in Nicaragua), streaks on breast side variable; *piger* also very small, with back slightly dark-streaked, white wing-covert spots, usually 1-2 dark bars in outer tail, has brownish throat, paler breast, dusky flanks streaked and barred; *maynardi* differs from previous in unstreaked back, plain white outer tail, paler unmarked underparts with buff tinge on breast. Voice. Rather high-pitched "keek"; calls of Panama birds higher-pitched and more subdued than in N, perhaps harsher in W North America than in E; also "keek kit-kit-kit-kit-kit-kt" series. Both sexes drum, producing short rolls tending to slow down towards end; taps at nest.
Habitat. Wide range of forest types and woodlands, especially with pines (*Pinus*). In NW USA found in mixed forest with Douglas fir (*Pseudotsuga*) and western hemlock (*Tsuga heterophylla*), preferring former species for foraging; in W USA also in open juniper (*Juniperus*) woodland; in riparian forest in plains; virtually all types of forest in E North America. Mainly pine woods in Bahamas. Restricted to highlands in Mexico and Guatemala, in pine-oak forest and in oak and other broadleaved forest, cypress (*Cupressus*) stands, and second growth. In Costa Rica and Panama occurs in wet, epiphyte-laden highland forest up to stunted forest at timber-line, and in neighbouring clearings and semi-open areas; main abundance centred in oak forest of higher elevations. Also visits gardens, but less frequently than e.g. *P. pubescens*. In N parts of range occurs from sea-level to 2900 m in W mountains; usually above 2000 m in Arizona; recorded at 1200-

3700 m in Mexico, 900-2900 m in Guatemala; from 1200 m but mostly 1500-3400 m in Costa Rica and Panama.

Food and Feeding. Largely animal food; c. 50% of this made up by larvae of wood-boring beetles (especially cerambycids and buprestids, but also curculionids, scolytids, siricids and others), remainder consisting of caterpillars (even hairy ones) and other arthropods, e.g. spiders, millipedes (Diplopoda). Diet also includes fruits and seeds, mostly coniferous, particularly in winter; sap taken at *Sphyrapicus* wells. S races seem to take more fruit and berries than do N ones, may even feed young with figs (*Ficus*); wild raspberries and blackberries and hardy fruits, such as cornel (*Cornus*) berries, and acorns eaten in summer, Virginia creeper (*Parthenocissus*) berries and apples in winter. Forages usually singly or in pairs; occasionally joins mixed flocks; may concentrate locally in areas where forest fires have occurred. Live and large trees generally visited more often, except during winter, although often forages on dead branches. Mean foraging height shifts seasonally, higher in winter; snags without branches more frequently visited in winter. Parts of trees below crown and without limbs are favoured foraging substrate. Visits Joshua trees (*Yucca brevifolia*) in California, and in Central America also utilizes bamboo (*Chusquea*), old stalks of giant thistle and stems of soft shrubs such as *Senecio*. Descends to ground, most frequently in early spring. Pecking and hammering are characteristic foraging techniques, by which bark is removed or funnel-shaped holes drilled into bark; also probes, and pries or tears off bark. Seasonal changes in foraging methods involve mainly increase in probing from winter to spring and parallel addition to the repertoire of gleaning and searching; pecking and hammering, very important in winter, are somewhat reduced in spring, but excavating by vigorous hammering and pecking comprise major foraging activities in all seasons. Male uses more subsurface-feeding than female.

Breeding. Season varies relatively little; nests found in Apr-Jun in British Columbia and Ontario, end Mar to Jun (peak Apr-May) in California, in Mar-Jul in Bahamas, and in Feb-Apr in Costa Rica; pair-formation starts 2-3 months before nesting. During courtship male erects red parts of nape feathering and spreads tail fully; flutter-aerial display, often with calls, in breeding period. Nest-excavation takes 17-24 days, nest-hole usually in live tree but in a dead section or in wood afflicted with fungal heart-rot, or in utility pole or fence post; sometimes in palm in Bahamas; may usurp hole of other woodpecker and enlarge it if necessary. Clutch 2-5 eggs, mean 3·93 in main part of range, decreasing to S, c. 3 eggs in Costa Rica; both sexes incubate and both feed nestlings, incubation period 14 days, nestling period 28-30 days; fledglings divided between parents, accompanied by adult for at least 2 weeks. First breeds probably at 1 year.

Movements. Resident in most of range. Some seasonal movements performed by populations farthest N, and highland populations move downslope in winter. Recorded as a vagrant in Puerto Rico (Mona I).

Status and Conservation. Not globally threatened. Fairly common in most of range; fairly common in Bahamas; rather common in Mexico. Rather widespread in much of range, especially where more adaptable in terms of habitat selection. Possibly subject to some threat locally through loss or degradation of habitat.

Bibliography. Askins (1983), Baldwin (1960), Beal (1895), Bent (1939), Binford (1989), Blackford (1955), Blake, E.R. (1965), Blake, H.E. (1981), Blom (2000), Bock & Lepthien (1975), Bonta (1997), Bull (1981), Campbell *et al.* (1990), Chambers (1979), Confer *et al.* (1992), Conner (1973, 1975, 1977, 1979, 1980, 1981), Conner & Adkisson (1977), Conner & Crawford (1974), Conner & Saenz (1996), Conner *et al.* (1976), Cruz (1974a), Cyr (1995d), Davis (1973), Delacour (1951a), Dodenhoff *et al.* (2001), Ellison (1992), Emlen (1977), Fales (1977a), Gamboa & Brown (1976), George (1972), Harestad & Keisker (1989), Harris, M.A. (1982), Holmes & Sherry (2001), Howell & Webb (1995), Jackman (1974), Jackson (1970b, 1992a), Jackson & Hoover (1975), Jenkins (1906), Kaufman (1993), Kilham (1960, 1965, 1966b, 1968, 1969, 1974d, 1979b, 1983), Kisiel (1972), Koenig (1986, 1987), Koplin (1969), Kreisel & Stein (1999), Land (1970), Lawrence (1966), Lehnhausen & Murphy (1985), Lundquist & Manuwal (1990), Martin & Li (1992), Maxson & Maxson (1981), Miller *et al.* (1999), Monroe (1968), Morrison & With (1987), Moulton & Lowell (1991), Murphy & Lehnhausen (1998), Otvos (1967), Ouellet (1977b, 1997), Owre (1978), Peck & James (1983), Petit, Grubb *et al.* (1988), Petit, Petit *et al.* (1985), Saab & Dudley (1998), Sassi (1939), Schepps *et al.* (1999), Selander (1965), Setterington *et al.* (2000), Shackelford & Conner (1997), Shelley (1933), Short (1971c, 1985b), Skutch (1955, 1969a), Slud (1964), Smith (1971), Snyder (1923), Sousa (1987), Spring (1965), Staebler (1949), Stallcup (1969), Stark *et al.* (1998), Steventon *et al.* (1998), Stiles (1985), Stiles & Skutch (1989), Stradi & Hudon (1998), Stradi *et al.* (1998), Swallow *et al.* (1988), Taylor (1996), Thurber *et al.* (1987), Tobalske (1996), Villard & Beninger (1993), Volman *et al.* (1997), Waldbauer *et al.* (1970), Weikel & Hayes (1999), Welsh & Capen (1987, 1992), Wetmore (1968a), Winkler & Short (1978), Woods (1984), Yunich (1988), Zusi & Marshall (1970).

118. White-headed Woodpecker
Picoides albolarvatus

French: Pic à tête blanche   **German**: Weißkopfspecht   **Spanish**: Pico Cabeciblanco

Taxonomy. *Leuconerpes albolarvatus* Cassin, 1850, Oregon Canyon, California.
Closest to *P. borealis*, *P. stricklandi* and *P. villosus*. Races rather poorly differentiated, with variation possibly clinal. Two subspecies recognized.

Subspecies and Distribution.
P. a. albolarvatus (Cassin, 1850) - SC British Columbia S, discontinuously in mountains, to Washington, W Idaho, Oregon, California (S in Coast Ranges to NW Colusa, and along Sierra Nevada in E), and extreme W Nevada.
P. a. gravirostris (Grinnell, 1902) - SW California (mountains around Los Angeles and San Diego).

Descriptive notes. 24 cm; 50-79 g, mostly 52-68 g. Male has white forehead, crown, lores, side of head, and chin to upper breast, usually faint buff tinge on forehead, greyish tinge on crown; very thin dark line behind eye often obscured, red nape; hindneck, rear neck side, entire upperparts and underparts below breast black, upperparts, wing-coverts and breast slightly blue-glossed, most of primaries with white bases, on some extending almost to tip on outer web, central primaries with 2 or 3 small white spots near tip of outer web; black tail; sometimes isolated white feather edges visible on underparts; longish bill slightly curved, chisel-tipped, dark grey; iris deep brownish-red or dull red; legs greyish-olive to grey. Female has nape black, not red. Juvenile much browner than adult, white wing patch somewhat larger but with dark barring, sometimes obscure paler barring on belly, male with orange-red patch from crown centre to nape, female with red restricted to hindcrown or, rarely, absent. Race *gravirostris* differs from nominate only in significantly longer tail and longer bill. VOICE. Call "peek-it" or "pee-dink", often trisyllabic; also "kit-kit-kit-kit-kit" varying in length. Both sexes drum, long rolls; rhythmic tapping at nest-hole.

Habitat. Tall, open mixed coniferous forest in mountains, particularly with ponderosa pine (*Pinus ponderosa*), sugar pine (*P. lambertiana*), lodgepole pine (*P. contorta*), white fir (*Abies concolor*), incense cedar (*Calocedrus decurrens*), also Douglas fir (*Pseudotsuga menziesii*); habitats of S race *gravirostris* characterized by similar conifer species, also by presence of Coulter pine (*P. coulteri*) and Jeffrey Pine (*P. jeffreyi*). Mainly below 700 in far N; at 850-1600 m in Washington and Oregon; 1000-2750 m in California (Sierra Nevada), exceptionally to 3200 m, *gravirostris* mainly at 1500-2300 m.

Food and Feeding. Animal food mostly insects and their larvae, especially ants, beetles, also scale insects (Homoptera); pine seeds regularly taken from cones, and pine sap also taken. Accepts suet at feeders. Mostly singly or in pairs. Forages mainly on lower trunk of large conifers, also on large branches and among needle clusters; clings acrobatically to cones; also descends to ground. Searches non-coniferous trees less frequently. Favoured stratum shifts moderately with season, foraging in crown becoming more frequent in early summer. Sexual differences in foraging most pronounced in S of range: females feed more on trunks, males more on cones, particularly the huge ones of Coulter pine. Foraging techniques include removal of bark, probing and pecking; hammers rarely. Occasionally sallies after aerial insects.

Breeding. May-Jul; from Apr in S. Flutter-aerial display by male during courtship. Nest excavated by both partners, duration 3-4 weeks, mostly at height of 2-4 m (rarely even up to 32 m), in snag, sloping log, stump, or live tree with soft centre caused by heart-rot, and majority of sites in conifer; sometimes in fence post; hole diameter averages c. 4·6 cm, cavity depth 20-25 cm. Clutch usually 4-5 eggs, but 3-7 recorded; incubation by both sexes, period 14 days; both parents brood and feed chicks, remove faecal material, nestling period c. 26 days; fledglings divided between parents, accompanied for several weeks. In Oregon, 83-87·5% of nests produced at least 1 fledgling.

Movements. Some downslope movement and wandering after breeding season. Recorded outside normal range on several occasions, including rare small-scale influxes on Pacific coast, e.g. 19 individuals in coastal California in 1987/88 winter. Vagrants recorded E to NW Wyoming.

Status and Conservation. Not globally threatened. Uncommon to rare in N of range; fairly common to common elsewhere. Occurs in low densities: estimates include 0·5 birds/40·5 ha in managed mixed coniferous forest and 1 bird/40·5 ha in old-growth coniferous in NE Oregon; 0·18-1·06 birds/40 ha in C & SC Oregon; somewhat higher in California, average 2·3 birds/40 ha in Sierra Nevada during 1948 to 1978, with later estimates ranging from maximum of 1·2 birds/40 ha (early 1980's) to locally 3·0-5·5 birds/40 ha (W Sierra Nevada, 1988-1992). Home range in C Oregon 67-163 ha in continuous habitat and 57-445 ha in fragmented habitat; respective figures in SC Oregon 172-324 ha and 171-704 ha. Total population seems unlikely to be very high. Probably stable or increasing generally since late 1960's; declines reported locally owing to degradation or fragmentation of habitat, as in Oregon and Idaho; loss of large trees of ponderosa pine considered greatest threat to species in Oregon. Relatively tolerant of forest disturbance so long as suitable snags and stumps remain; also tolerates close short-term presence of humans.

Bibliography. Anon. (1998b), Bent (1939), Blair & Servheen (1993), Bull (1981), Campbell *et al.* (1990), Cooper (1969), Dixon (1995a, 1995b), Dodenhoff *et al.* (2001), Duncan (1933), Frederick & Moore (1991), Garrett *et al.* (1996), Grinnell (1902), Hilkevitch (1974), Jackman (1974), Johnson (2000), Kaufman (1996), Koch *et al.* (1970), Koenig (1986, 1987), Ligon (1973), Manolis (1987), Milne & Hejl (1989), Morrison & With (1987), Price *et al.* (1995), Robinson (1957), Root (1988), Saab & Dudley (1998), Small (1994), Stark *et al.* (1998), Weber & Cannings (1976), Winkler & Short (1978).

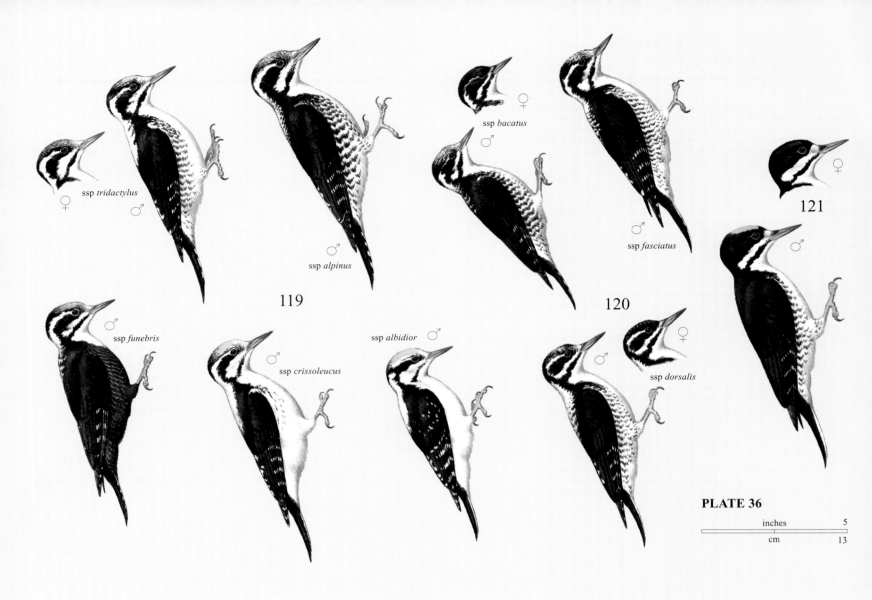

ssp *tridactylus*

♀

♂

ssp *alpinus*

119

♂

ssp *funebris*

ssp *crissoleucus*

ssp *albidior* ♂

ssp *bacatus*

♂

♀

ssp *fasciatus*

120

121

♀

♀

ssp *dorsalis*

♂

PLATE 36

inches   5
cm   13

PLATE 36

Family PICIDAE (WOODPECKERS)
SPECIES ACCOUNTS

119. Eurasian Three-toed Woodpecker
Picoides tridactylus

French: Pic tridactyle   **German**: Dreizehenspecht   **Spanish**: Pico Tridáctilo Euroasiático
Other common names: Three-toed Woodpecker (with *P. dorsalis*)

Taxonomy. *Picus tridactylus* Linnaeus, 1758, Sweden.
Forms a superspecies with *P. dorsalis*, and commonly treated as conspecific; genetic evidence, however, coupled with geographical isolation and differences in plumage, indicate that the two are probably better considered separate species. Closely related also to *P. arcticus*, but links with other American congeners apparently not strong. Currently accepted races designated according to coloration, but variation is clinal, birds becoming darker and larger from N to S; revision based on genetic and biogeographical grounds required. Birds from Sakhalin, described as race *sakhalinensis*, appear indistinguishable from nominate; named races *tianschanicus* (Tien Shan), *kurodai* (Korea) and *inouyei* (EC Hokkaido) barely differ from European *alpinus*, thus regarded as better merged with that taxon. Five subspecies recognized.
Subspecies and Distribution.
P. t. tridactylus (Linnaeus, 1758) - N Europe E across S *taiga* to Altai Mts, N Mongolia, Manchuria, Ussuriland and Sakhalin.
P. t. crissoleucus (Reichenbach, 1854) - N *taiga* from Urals E to Sea of Okhotsk.
P. t. albidior Stejneger, 1885 - Kamchatka.
P. t. alpinus C. L. Brehm, 1831 - mountains of C, S & SE Europe, Tien Shan, NE Korea and N Japan (Hokkaido).
P. t. funebris J. Verreaux, 1870 - SW China to Tibet.
Descriptive notes. 20-24 cm; male 65-74 g, female 54-66 g (*tridactylus*), 46-76 g (other races). Male has long nasal tufts mixed black and white, black forehead mottled whitish, brass-yellow or pale lemon-yellow central forecrown usually with some black and white feather bases showing through; glossy black crown sides, hindcrown and band down central hindneck, crown usually with some white streaks; white supercilium from rear of eye broadening backwards, extending as band down rear neck side to meet white of mantle; glossy black from in front of and just below eye, through ear-coverts and down neck side, bordered by broad white cheekband; deep black malar stripe, obscured by white tips near bill, extending back to broad area of black on neck side that continues irregularly down to upper breast side; white chin and throat; white central mantle, inner-

most scapulars, back and rump, a few dull black spots or bars at margins, dull brownish-black mantle side, remaining scapulars and uppertail-coverts; dull brownish-black wings, outer flight-feathers with variably sized white spots largest on inner webs, including those of tertials, forming prominent barred pattern; uppertail black, tips of outer 3 feather pairs with increasing amount of black-barred white; white below, faintly tinged cream-buff in fresh plumage, breast side streaked black, flanks and undertail-coverts variably barred; longish bill straight, chisel-tipped, very broad across nostrils, slaty-grey, darker tip, paler base of lower mandible; iris deep red or brown-red; legs slate-grey, only 3 toes. Differs from *P. dorsalis* mainly in larger size, more white on forehead, broader white head stripes, black bars in outer tail. Female has forehead and crown black with variable amount of white spots and streaks. Juvenile duller, browner, than adult, with white of back less extensive and sometimes barred, underparts duller and buffer with heavier but diffuse markings, eyes paler, male with dull yellow forecrown patch smaller than on adult, patch probably reduced or sometimes absent on female. Races differ mostly in amount of white in plumage, E ones also on average slightly larger and longer-billed: *crissoleucus* has plumage more fluffy than nominate, more white on head, back and flight-feathers, less black in outer tail, very few or no markings below; *albidior* is even whiter, with pure white outer tail and underparts, much white in wings, including spots on coverts; *alpinus* is darker overall, with white of back narrower and barred or spotted black, dark underside pale-barred with narrow central white band, outer tail more broadly barred black, juvenile mostly dark above and below with pale restricted to throat, spots on mantle and mottling on underparts; *funebris* is considerably darker, black above with narrow area of white or a few pale bars, thin white bars on outer tail and flight-feathers, pale buffish throat contrasting with finely pale-barred black underparts. VOICE. Single "kip", in series when alarmed; short, "kri-kri-kri-kri-kri". Both sexes drum, rolls slightly accelerating at very end.
Habitat. Mature boreal and montane mixed conifer forests. Spruce (*Picea*) and fir (*Abies*) forest typical habitat in N Europe; in E European natural forest, territories are in wettest parts of ash-alder (*Fraxinus-Alnus*), coniferous and oak-hornbeam (*Quercus-Carpinus*) stands; primarily in *taiga* of

larch (*Larix*) in Siberia. Forest with a good proportion of insect-infested dead trees and fallen timber, and often dense and shady, are favoured. Outside breeding season, also in more open areas or brush. Will concentrate locally in windfall areas, also takes advantage of forest areas damaged by insect plagues or pollution. Mainly lowlands at higher latitudes; from 650 m and to over 1900 m in European Alps; at 3300-4000 m in SE Tibet.
Food and Feeding. Larvae and pupae of beetles living beneath bark form bulk of diet, and also important as nestling food; other insect larvae (hymenopterans) and imagines also taken, also spiders. Insects prone to occur in heavy infestations, e.g. *Polygraphus* and *Ips*, particularly frequent items. Apart from sap, vegetable matter (e.g. berries, spruce seeds) taken only occasionally. Forages singly; local concentrations in areas of food abundance, especially in areas of insect plagues. Prefers trunks of dead trees and stubs, foraging mostly at heights of 1-3 m, occasionally on ground. On average, males forage slightly lower than females, mainly on trunks, and prefer large trees; females forage slightly higher up and have a greater niche breadth, also using relatively thin trees and branches, and more frequently live trees (in summer). Both sexes forage lower in winter. Pecking, hammering and, especially, stripping-off of bark are predominant foraging techniques; gleaning and probing less common. Conspicuous sap wells drilled into a wide range of tree species, mainly conifers, locally lime (*Tilia*), trees becoming covered with sap holes from base of trunk up into crown; this habit seems to be particularly common in subalpine zone.
Breeding. Laying from mid-May, up to 2 weeks earlier in S Europe. Courtship from second half of Mar; flutter-aerial display, bill-pointing, head-swinging with crest erect. Nest-hole excavated in dead tree, or in dead section of live tree with heart-rot, with spruce and other conifers preferred, hole diameter averages 4·7 cm, cavity depth 30·5 cm; usually a new nest made each year. Clutch 3 or 4 eggs in Alps, 3-6 (rarely 7) with mean 4·1 in Scandinavia; both sexes share all nest duties; incubation period 11-14 days, nestling period 22-26 days; fledglings accompanied by parents for up to c. 1 month. Average young produced per nest 1·7 in Switzerland; dormice (*Eliomys*) possibly significant nest predators. First breeding probably at 1 year.
Movements. Mountain populations (Alps, Tien Shan, Altai) sedentary; N Eurasian populations perform eruptive migrations at long intervals. In Scandinavia, most juveniles move out of nesting area and appear far outside breeding areas; Siberian populations (*crissoleucus*) regularly migrate greater distances.
Status and Conservation. Not globally threatened. Fairly common, locally common, but numbers vary annually; rather scarce in many parts of range. Estimated W European population in 1990's c. 51,370-65,340 pairs, with further 10,000-100,000 pairs in European part of Russia, combined total probably c. 90,000 pairs; largest known concentrations in Finland (15,000-20,000) and Belarus (9000-14,000), with 10,000-25,000 in Scandinavia. Densities vary depending on habitat quality; in Finland, 10 pairs/km^2 in partially burned old-growth forest but 0·03-1·2 pairs in other habitats; lower densities in S European mountains, e.g. 1 pair/42-200 ha (mean 108 ha) in Switzerland, and all pairs requiring home range of at least 100 ha. Has expanded since 1980's in C Europe, but declines also noted in some areas (e.g. Czech Republic); evidence of reduction in numbers in N Europe. No data on Asian populations, but said to be locally common in China; occurs in Jiuzhaigou Reserve, in China. Conservation requires preservation of sufficient areas of habitat with plenty of old and dead or dying trees.
Bibliography. Alekseev & Martyanov (1986), Ali & Ripley (1983), Amcoff & Eriksson (1996), Austin & Kuroda (1953), Baciocchi & Baumgart (2001), Beaman & Madge (1998), Bergmanis & Strazds (1993), Bezzel (1985), Blagosklonov (1968), Brazil (1991), Bürkli *et al.* (1975), Chabloz & Wegmüller (1994), Cramp (1985), Delacour (1951a), Dementiev *et al.* (1966), Derleth *et al.* (2000), Desmet (1999), Étchécopar & Hüe (1978), Fayt (1999), Friedmann (1997), Gardenfors (1978), Géroudet (1987), Hagemeijer & Blair (1997), Hågvar & Hågvar (1989), Hågvar *et al.* (1990), Heath & Evans (2000), Heath *et al.* (2000), Hess (1983), Hogstad (1970, 1971a, 1976a, 1976b, 1977, 1978, 1983, 1991, 1993), King (1978/79), Kropil & Kornan (1991), Lanz (1950), Liberek & Baumann (1990), Linkola (1967), Lobkov (1999), MacKinnon & Phillipps (2000), Mauersberger *et al.* (1982), Mikusinski (2001), Mikusinski & Angelstam (1997), Nyholm (1968), Pechacek (1992, 1994b, 1996, 1998), Pechacek & Krištín (1993, 1996), Rogacheva (1992), Ruge (1968, 1969a, 1971c, 1973, 1974, 1975), Ruge & Weber (1974a), Scherzinger (1972, 1982), Snow & Perrins (1998), Sollien *et al.* (1978, 1982a, 1982b, 1982c), Stradi & Hudon (1998), Stradi *et al.* (1998), Svensson *et al.* (1999), Thibault de Maisières (1940), Ullman (1995), Väisänen *et al.* (1986), Wabakken (1973), Wegmüller & Chabloz (1992), Wesolowski & Tomialojc (1986), Winkler & Short (1978), Zhao Zhengjie (1995), Zink *et al.* (1995), Zusi & Marshall (1970).

120. American Three-toed Woodpecker
Picoides dorsalis

French: Pic à dos rayé **German**: Fichtenspecht **Spanish**: Pico Tridáctilo Americano
Other common names: White-backed Three-toed Woodpecker; Three-toed Woodpecker (with *P. tridactylus*)

Taxonomy. *Picoides dorsalis* Baird, 1858, Laramie Peak, Wyoming.
Forms a superspecies with *P. tridactylus*, and commonly treated as conspecific; genetic evidence, however, coupled with geographical isolation and differences in plumage, indicate that the two are probably better considered separate species. Closely related also to *P. arcticus*, but probably less so to other congeners. Races intergrade. Labrador birds named as separate race *labradorius*, supposedly larger and darker with more barred flanks than *bacatus*, but differences thought not to be constant or significant, and new taxon subsequently abandoned by describer. Three subspecies recognized.
Subspecies and Distribution.
P. d. fasciatus Baird, 1870 - NW & C Alaska E to NW Canada (E to NW & C Mackenzie and N Saskatchewan) and S to Oregon, N Idaho and W Montana.
P. d. bacatus Bangs, 1900 - N Manitoba and N Ontario E to N Quebec, Labrador and Newfoundland, S to Great Lakes, NE New York, N New Hampshire and NE Maine.
P. d. dorsalis Baird, 1858 - Rocky Mts from Montana to EC Nevada, Arizona and NW New Mexico.
Descriptive notes. 21-23 cm; male 50-64·5 g, female 47-59 g (*fasciatus*). Male has black forehead and fore lores mottled whitish, brass-yellow or pale lemon-yellow central forecrown usually with some black and white feather bases showing, glossy black crown sides, hindcrown and band down to central hindneck, crown usually streaked white; narrow white supercilium from rear of eye, extending as mottled line behind ear-coverts; glossy black area in front of and just below eye, through ear-coverts, black band down neck side, narrow white cheekband from lores, black malar stripe extending back to black band on neck side, continuing irregularly down to upper breast side; white chin and throat; white lower hindneck to back, brownish-black at sides, with few (variable) dark bars, black rump and uppertail-coverts; dull brownish-black wings, flight-feathers with variably sized white spots forming barred pattern; uppertail black, outer feathers white towards tips and sometimes with few black bars; white underparts, barred black on sides and undertail-coverts, variable streaks on sides of breast and belly; longish bill straight, chisel-tipped, very broad across nostrils, grey, darker tip; iris deep red-brown; legs slate-grey, only 3 toes. Differs from *P. tridactylus* mainly in smaller size, slightly shorter bill, less white on head; from *P. arcticus* in smaller size,

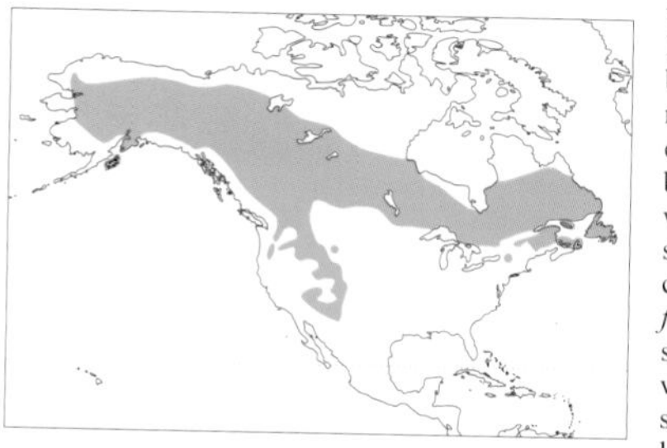

white on back, more white on head. Female lacks yellow on crown, has forehead and crown black with few white spots and streaks. Juvenile duller than adult, with white of back less extensive and sometimes barred, washed buff below with brown spots, grey-brown eyes, male with dull yellow forecrown patch, female with smaller patch or, rarely, none. Races differ chiefly in size and in amount of white on back: *fasciatus* averages smaller than nominate, with shorter bill, more white spots on forehead, white back with numerous thin black bars, body sides strongly barred; *bacatus* is smallest, has less white on head, supercilium broken or absent, sometimes completely black forehead, back mostly black with few small bars or spots, female with crown all black or with just a few white speckles. Voice. Single high-pitched "kip" or "pwik"; short "kliklikliklikli" rattle. Both sexes drum, rolls slow, faster at end, 2 per minute, similar to *P. arcticus* but only half as long and slower.
Habitat. Mature boreal and montane conifer forests; usually in denser forest than that preferred by *P. arcticus*. Spruce (*Picea*) preferred generally, but in W forests containing fir (*Abies*) or lodgepole pine (*Pinus contorta*) also occupied. Not normally found in ponderosa pine (*Pinus ponderosa*) or Douglas fir (*Pseudotsuga menziesii*), but has bred in old stands dominated by latter species and lodgepole pine in British Columbia. Often in swampy areas in E of range. Requires plenty of insect-infested dead trees and fallen timber; disturbed forest frequently occupied or visited. Also in more open areas outside the breeding season, even in urban areas during irruptions. Local concentrations form in burned sites or windfall areas, and in forest damaged by insect plagues or pollution. From 1300 m to 2700 m, locally 3350 m, in W; at 360-1250 m in E.
Food and Feeding. Chiefly larvae and pupae of bark beetles (Scolytidae); present species is an important predator of spruce bark beetle (*Dendroctonus obesus*). Also larvae of wood-boring beetles (mainly Cerambycidae); smaller quantities of ants, larvae of hymenopterans, lepidopterans, other insects, and spiders. Minimal vegetable matter; small berries eaten rarely; some sap-drinking in spring, but this behaviour apparently less common than in *P. tridactylus*, possibly because of greater competition from other Nearctic woodpeckers (*Sphyrapicus*, other *Picoides*). Forages singly or in pairs; sometimes small groups outside breeding season, mostly at local food abundances. Largely arboreal, rarely descends to ground. Prefers upper sections of trunks of dead trees and stubs. Bark-scaling is the predominant foraging technique, used especially on fire-killed trees, to expose beetles and their larvae; also pecks; occasionally drills sap wells, these being small and shallow.
Breeding. Laying from mid-May to end Jun, occasionally to early Jul, but courtship activities start in second half Mar. Nest-hole excavated by both sexes, at c. 2-10 m, mostly in dead tree, less often in section of live tree with heart-rot, spruce and other conifers preferred, but non-coniferous species (*Populus*, *Betula*, *Alnus*) also used; entrance diameter 3·8-4·5 cm, cavity depth c. 24-30 cm. Clutch 3-5 eggs, usually 4; both sexes incubate, period 11-14 days; both also brood and feed chicks, male possibly feeding more than female; fledging period undocumented, probably c. 24 days; fledglings apparently divided between parents. Success in producing at least 1 young 79·2% in Montana and Idaho. Longevity in wild at least 6 years.
Movements. Largely resident, but often shifts to lower altitudes or moves short distances after breeding. E populations make periodic eruptive migrations, occasionally appear S of breeding range in winter; casual records S to Nebraska, S Wisconsin and Pennsylvania; movements less marked than those of *P. arcticus*.
Status and Conservation. Not globally threatened. Not very common; numbers vary over years, but species can become locally common during insect outbreaks. Occurs in low densities, highest in burned or otherwise disturbed forest; c. 1 bird/4·05 ha in burned coniferous forest in SE Montana; in a Colorado conifer forest, 0·25 individuals/ha before burn but 1·20/ha 2 years after fire. Susceptible to habitat loss, forest degradation and fragmentation. Owing to this species' low population sizes, dependence on snags, preference for burned forest, and preference for large stands of old-growth conifer that are vulnerable to commercial cutting, there should be some concern for its survival in managed forests.
Bibliography. Anon. (1998b), Baldwin (1960), Bangs (1900), Beal (1895), Bent (1939), Blackford (1955), Bock & Bock (1974b), Campbell *et al.* (1990), Cyr (1995e), Cyr & Alvo (1996), Eckert, C.D. (1997), Eckert, K. (1981), Ellison (1992), Gibbon (1966), Goggans (1989b), Goggans *et al.* (1988), Gunn & Hagan (2000), Harris, B. (1987), Harris, M.A. (1982), Hobson & Schieck (1999), Hooper, D.F. (1988), Hoyt (2000), Kaufman (1996), Koenig (1987), Koplin (1969), Kreisel & Stein (1999), Lehnhausen & Murphy (1985), Leonard (2001), Murphy & Lehnhausen (1998), Oatman (1985), Peck (1999), Peck & James (1983), Peterson (1988), Price *et al.* (1995), Root (1988), Scott (1993), Shanahan (1993), Short (1974a), Smith (1992), Spring (1965), Stallcup (1962), Steffen (1981), Thiel (1978), Toone (1993), Trochet *et al.* (1988), Versaw (1998), Villard (1994), West & Speirs (1959), Winkler & Short (1978), Yunich (1985), Zink *et al.* (1995).

121. Black-backed Woodpecker
Picoides arcticus

French: Pic à dos noir **German**: Schwarzrückenspecht **Spanish**: Pico Ártico
Other common names: Arctic (Three-toed) Woodpecker, Black-backed Three-toed Woodpecker

Taxonomy. *Picus (Apternus) arcticus* Swainson, 1832, near the sources of the Athabasca River, eastern slope of the Rockies.
Closely related to *P. tridactylus* and *P. dorsalis*. Monotypic.
Distribution. W & C Alaska E through C Canada (N to area W of Great Bear Lake, C Manitoba and N Ontario) to S Labrador and Newfoundland, and S, discontinuously in W, to California and W Nevada (Sierra Nevada), Wyoming, SC Saskatchewan and NE Minnesota, and in E to N Michigan, SE Ontario, New York and Nova Scotia.
Descriptive notes. 23-25 cm; 61-88 g. Male has white rear part of nasal tufts, yellow to golden-yellow forecrown, white lores and band running back below ear-coverts to neck side, above black submoustachial line; sometimes also a very fine pale line behind eye; white chin and throat; rest of head and entire upperparts deep blue-glossed black, rarely a few pale tips on rump feathers; black wings, coverts glossed blue and occasionally with a few small white spots, primaries and usually also secondaries with small white spots forming narrow bars; black tail with white at tip of third rectrix, white increasing in extent outwards to almost all-white outer tail; white below, lower regions washed greyish, black of upper mantle extending down to breast side and breaking up into bars, which become very regular on flanks and belly sides; longish bill straight, chisel-tipped, slate-grey, paler lower mandible where sometimes horn-coloured at base; iris red-brown to brown; legs dark grey or slaty, only 3 toes. Distinguished from *P. dorsalis* by bigger size, stronger bill, entirely black back, blue gloss, less white on head. Female has entire crown black. Juvenile duller and browner than adult, with more white in wing, markings below less regular and more diffuse, eyes

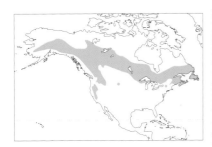

paler, male with some yellow or orange-yellow on crown, female usually with a few small yellow spots or no yellow. Voice. Very distinctive short, high-pitched double click; peculiar, long grating snarl, varying in pitch in course of delivery, changing from fast series of clicks into fast rasping snarl to accelerate at end. Drumming rolls tend to accelerate at end.

Habitat. N and montane coniferous forest. Burned and windfall areas and those afflicted by outbreaks of forest pests particularly favoured. Compared with *P. dorsalis*, tends to occur in somewhat less dense habitats and not particularly tied to spruce (*Picea*), but frequents wider range of coniferous habitats; found regularly in pine forest, mainly of jack pine (*Pinus banksiana*) and lodgepole pine (*P. contorta*), and in other conifer types, e.g. larch (*Larix*), fir (*Abies*), typically those which occur also at lower elevations. In particular, enters forest of Douglas fir (*Pseudotsuga menziesii*) and ponderosa pine (*P. ponderosa*) in areas of overlap with its sibling species. During irruptions, occurs in all kinds of wooded habitats, including parks and urban areas. Restricted to mountains in W part of range, at 1200-2400 m in S Oregon, above 1350 m in Montana, and at 1200-3100 m in California; from sea-level to 1300 m in E.

Food and Feeding. Largely wood-boring beetle larvae, particularly the large grubs of white-spotted sawyer (*Monochamus scutellatus*), an insect confined to burned forest, and bark-dwelling scolytids (*Pissodes*); larvae of mountain pine beetle (*Dendroctonus ponderosae*) also important component of diet. Other insects also taken, as well as spiders and centipedes (Chilopoda). Some fruits and seeds, and occasionally pieces of phloem, eaten occasionally. Mostly singly or in pairs. Forages mostly on lower sections of large-diameter trunks, to some extent also on large limbs, and on fallen timber; where available, fire-killed trees (e.g. *Pinus strobus*) strongly preferred. Generally, about half to two-thirds of trees visited are dead, and pines seem to be selected as feeding stations even when not the dominant tree species. Predominant techniques, especially in winter, are pecking, including blows which remove pieces of bark and other forms of scaling; also hammering, whereby deep excavations made into wood of dead trees; these foraging modes important throughout year, although gleaning and probing increase during breeding period. Flycatching is rare.

Breeding. Laying from end Apr, mostly mid-May to mid Jun. Courtship includes flutter-aerial display, raising of crown feathers. Nest excavated by both sexes, mean height above ground varying from 5 m to 11 m, in dead tree or in live one with heart-rot, often conifer but wide range of species recorded; occasionally in telephone pole, or old cavity from previous years reused; hole diameter averaged 4·4 cm and cavity depth 21 cm in one study, but can be up to 41 cm deep; exposed wood around entrance renders nest rather conspicuous. Clutch 2-6 eggs, usually 3 or 4; both sexes incubate, period not accurately documented; both parents brood and provide for young, nestling period 21-25 days; fledglings divided between parents. Of 33 nests in W Idaho, 87% produced at least 1 young; 100% success in burned forest in Wyoming; flying squirrels (*Glaucomys*) a major nest predator in some areas.

Movements. Resident; subject to irregular dismigration and eruptive movements, possibly caused by regional population increase due to very favourable conditions (e.g. outbreaks of spruce budworm, or following fires). Largest irruption in autumn 1974, over 460 individuals reported; such movements range S to S Ontario and New York, and occasionally recorded somewhat outside breeding range; rare visitors reach as far S as Iowa, C Illinois, W Virginia and Delaware.

Status and Conservation. Not globally threatened. Generally uncommon. Responds positively to fire, which increases availability of snags and foraging habitat; 0·25 birds/ha along perimeter of newly burned area in Alaska, the highest ever recorded density for this species. Significant declines noted during 1980's and 1990's in spruce-hardwood forest. Numbers can increase markedly when conditions favourable, making assessment of population sizes difficult to interpret. Main conservation focus should be on ensuring continued availability of suitable habitat; importance for this species of fire-damaged forest, and retention of snags and fallen trees, needs to be understood.

Bibliography. Beal (1895), Bent (1939), Blackford (1955), Bock & Bock (1974b), Bull (1981), Campbell *et al.* (1990), Crumb (1988), Cyr (1995f), Delacour (1951a), Dixon & Saab (2000), Eckstein (1983), Ellison (1992), Erskine (1959), Goggans (1989a), Goggans *et al.* (1988), Haig (1980), Harris, M.A. (1982), Hobson & Schieck (1999), Hutto (1995, 1998), Johnson (1984), Kaufman (1996), Kilham (1966a, 1983), Koenig (1986, 1987), Kreisel & Stein (1999), Lehnhausen & Murphy (1985), Lisi (1988), Mayfield (1958), McMichael & Wilcove (1977), Murphy & Lehnhausen (1998), Peck (1999), Peck & James (1983), Price *et al.* (1995), Raphael (1981), Root (1988), Saab & Dudley (1998), Setterington *et al.* (2000), Short (1974a), Small (1994), Spring (1965), Stark *et al.* (1998), Steffen (1981), Taylor (1958), Thompson *et al.* (1999), Van Tyne (1926), Villard, M.A. & Schieck (1997), Villard, P. (1994), Villard, P. & Beninger (1993), Weinhagen (1998), West & Speirs (1959), Wickman (1965), Winkler & Short (1978), Yunich (1985).

PLATE 37 ➤

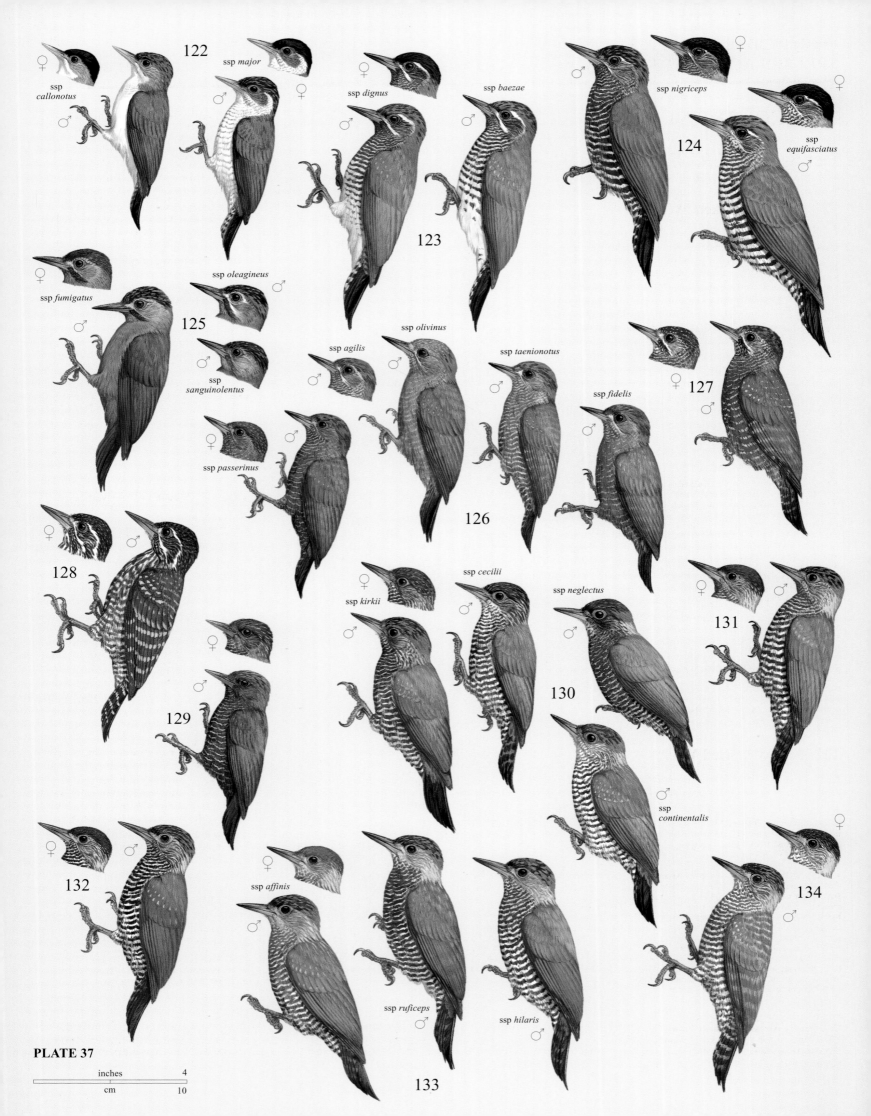

ssp *callonotus* ♀ ♂

122

ssp *major* ♀ ♂

ssp *dignus* ♀ ♂

ssp *baezae* ♂

123

ssp *nigriceps* ♂

124

♀ ssp *equifasciatus* ♂

ssp *fumigatus* ♀ ♂

125

ssp *oleagineus* ♂

ssp *sanguinolentus* ♂

ssp *agilis* ♂

ssp *olivinus* ♂

ssp *taenionotus* ♂

ssp *fidelis* ♂

♀ 127 ♂

ssp *passerinus* ♀ ♂

126

128 ♀ ♂

129 ♀ ♂

ssp *kirkii* ♀ ♂

ssp *cecilii* ♂

ssp *neglectus* ♂

130

131 ♀ ♂

ssp *continentalis* ♂

132 ♀ ♂

ssp *affinis* ♀ ♂

ssp *ruficeps* ♂

ssp *hilaris* ♂

133

134 ♀ ♂

PLATE 37

inches 4

cm 10

Tribe COLAPTINI

Genus *VENILIORNIS* Bonaparte, 1854

122. **Scarlet-backed Woodpecker**
Veniliornis callonotus

French: Pic rubin   **German**: Scharlachrückenspecht   **Spanish**: Carpintero Escarlata

Taxonomy. *Picus callonotus* Waterhouse, 1841, Guayaquil, Ecuador.
Race *major* intergrades freely with nominate in SW Ecuador, where many individuals have intermediate appearance. Two subspecies recognized.
Subspecies and Distribution.
V. c. callonotus (Waterhouse, 1841) - SW Colombia (Nariño) and W Ecuador (S to Guayas and coastal El Oro).
V. c. major (Berlepsch & Taczanowski, 1884) - SW Ecuador (El Oro, Loja) and NW Peru.

Descriptive notes. c. 13 cm; 23-33 g. Male has black feathers of forehead to nape extensively tipped red, greyish-brown ear-coverts; rest of face, including very thin line below eye, white, often dirtier or even brown on rear neck side, sometimes with hint of a thin dark malar line; brownish-scarlet upperparts, usually some brown feather bases showing through (more when worn); dark brown or blackish-brown flight-feathers, redder on secondaries and tertials; uppertail blackish-brown, central feather pair blacker, outer feathers whitish-yellow and barred black; white below with very light (variable) pale buff wash, sometimes faintly vermiculated darker; fairly long, broad bill, culmen straight or slightly curved, yellowish, usually darker base and sometimes tip; iris deep brown, occasionally deep red or tinged bluish; legs greenish-grey. Female has forehead to nape wholly black, often some white feathers at rear. Juvenile is heavily mottled with olive or greyish above, more green, head pattern more diffuse, male with small red feather tips on forecrown. Race *major* differs from nominate in darker ear-coverts with pale band behind and below, on average more dark vermiculations below. VOICE. Commonest call a rattle, 1-2 seconds long; also sharp "ki-dik", sometimes in short fast series.
Habitat. Arid scrub with scattered trees and cacti, dry deciduous forest, semi-humid forest and edges, and dense growth along watercourses; also partially cleared areas. Lowlands to 1000 m, locally to 1400 m and 1800 m (Loja) in Ecuador; to 1500 m in Peru.
Food and Feeding. Details of diet not recorded. Often in pairs. Forages at various levels in trees, often on smaller branches and very thin twigs.
Breeding. No information. Season most likely Jan-Jul.
Movements. Apparently resident.
Status and Conservation. Not globally threatened. Reported to be very local in SW Colombia; fairly common in Ecuador and also in Peru. Occurs in Río Palenque Science Centre and Cerro Blanco Protected Reserve (Ecuador) and Tumbes National Reserve (Peru). Extension of range apparent in Ecuador since late 1970's; has spread into more humid areas, presumably as a result of deforestation.
Bibliography. Allen (1998), Becker & López (1997), Best & Clarke (1991), Bloch *et al.* (1991), Butler (1979), Clements & Shany (2001), Hilty & Brown (1986), Kirwan & Marlow (1996), López & Gastezzi (2000), Meyer de Schauensee (1982), Olrog (1968), Parker *et al.* (1982), Pople *et al.* (1997), Ridgely & Greenfield (2001), Ridgely *et al.* (1998), Rodner *et al.* (2000), Short (1985b), Stotz *et al.* (1996), Williams & Tobias (1994), Zimmer (1942).

123. **Yellow-vented Woodpecker**
Veniliornis dignus

French: Pic à ventre jaune   **German**: Gelbbauchspecht   **Spanish**: Carpintero Ventriamarillo

Taxonomy. *Chloronerpes dignus* P. L. Sclater and Salvin, 1877, Antioquia, Colombia.
Races rather weakly differentiated. Venezuelan birds described as race *abdominalis*, but considered inseparable from nominate. Three subspecies recognized.
Subspecies and Distribution.
V. d. dignus (P. L. Sclater & Salvin, 1877) - extreme SW Venezuela S in Andes to W slope in N Ecuador.
V. d. baezae Chapman, 1923 - E slope of Andes in Ecuador.
V. d. valdizani (Berlepsch & Stolzmann, 1894) - E slope of Andes in Peru.
Descriptive notes. c. 16-17 cm; 35-40 g (*dignus*), 46 g (*valdizani*). Male has greenish-buff lower forehead, deep crimson crown to nape, rear neck sides and upper mantle, some black feather bases showing through especially on crown; blackish-olive ear-coverts bordered above by whitish stripe behind eye, below by thin white moustachial stripe; blackish chin vermiculated or spotted whitish; dark yellow-green lower mantle to back tinged bronze, lower mantle with red tips or edges, rump and uppertail-coverts barred pale and dark olive; brownish-olive wings, median and sometimes lesser coverts with pale yellow (often red-edged) spots, browner flight-feathers with small pale bars on inner webs; uppertail blackish, suffused yellow, outer 2 feather pairs barred pale; greenish-white below, becoming yellow on belly and flanks, with heavy olive-blackish bars from throat to upper flanks; underwing barred brown and yellow-white; medium-long

bill straight, broad across nostrils, blackish, paler base; iris brown to red-brown; legs dark olive-grey. Female has blackish top of head. Juvenile duller and less yellow, above, both sexes with some red tips on crown feathers. Races differ in bill length and in extent of barring below: *baezae* has shorter bill than nominate, dark bars below tend to be blacker and more marked on flanks; *valdizani* has longer bill than nominate, bars on rump more obscure. VOICE. Fast, weak, high-pitched nasal rattle heard infrequently.

Habitat. Inhabits humid montane forest, especially cloudforest, and forest edge; occurs rarely outside primary forest, for instance in abandoned coffee plantations. Found at lower altitudes than *V. nigriceps*. Mostly found at 1200-2700 m, rarely down to 700 m; 1400-2600 m in Ecuador; 700-2700 m in Peru.
Food and Feeding. Diet not recorded. Usually singly or in pairs, and unobtrusive; occasionally joins mixed foraging parties. Forages in middle level of trees up to the canopy. Hammers frequently, with weak blows; spends long periods at single spot high up on tree trunk, on limbs and smaller branches.
Breeding. Very little information suggests breeding season Mar-Aug.
Movements. Resident.
Status and Conservation. Not globally threatened. Uncommon in most of range; rare in Peru. Possibly quite widespread but at very low densities. Occurs in Río Ñambí Nature Reserve, in Colombia. First records on W slope of Andes in N Ecuador in late 1980's may indicate possible range extension, but more likely that species had been overlooked previously.
Bibliography. Butler (1979), Clements & Shany (2001), Davies *et al.* (1994), Donegan & Dávalos (1999), Hilty & Brown (1986), Meyer de Schauensee (1982), Meyer de Schauensee & Phelps (1978), Miller (1963), Olrog (1968), Parker *et al.* (1982), Ridgely & Gaulin (1980), Ridgely & Greenfield (2001), Ridgely *et al.* (1998), Salaman (1994), Salaman *et al.* (1999), Short (1985b), Stotz *et al.* (1996), Vélez & Velázquez (1998), Wetmore (1968b), Zimmer (1942).

124. **Bar-bellied Woodpecker**
Veniliornis nigriceps

French: Pic à ventre barré   **German**: Bindenbauchspecht   **Spanish**: Carpintero Ventribarrado

Taxonomy. *Picus nigriceps* d'Orbigny, 1840, Palca Grande, Ayupaya, Bolivia.
Race *pectoralis* poorly differentiated. Three subspecies recognized.
Subspecies and Distribution.
V. n. equifasciatus Chapman, 1912 - Andes from N Colombia to Ecuador.
V. n. pectoralis (Berlepsch & Stolzmann, 1902) - Andes of Peru.
V. n. nigriceps (d'Orbigny, 1840) - C Bolivia (Cochabamba, W Santa Cruz).

Descriptive notes. 17-20 cm; 39-46 g (*pectoralis*). Male has red forehead to hindneck with black feather bases visible; very narrow short pale supercilium, dark olive-brown ear-coverts finely streaked pale, very thin pale moustachial line; dark olive neck side barred whitish, feathers variably tipped golden; blackish-olive chin and throat barred pale; dark olive upperparts tinged bronze, often a few dull red feather tips on mantle, with obscure paler spots or bars on rump and uppertail-coverts; olive-brown wings, feathers edged and tipped bronze-olive; uppertail blackish, outer 2 feather pairs barred pale; underwing barred brown and buffish-white below, tinged olive, with very broad dark olive bars; longish bill straight, broad across nostrils, dark grey to blue-grey, paler lower mandible; iris deep red to brown; legs grey to olive-grey. Distinguished from very similar *V. frontalis* chiefly by larger size, no white spots on forehead or upperparts, less barred tail. Female resembles male, but has forehead to nape black or with a few red feather edges, hindneck golden. Juvenile duller and greener than adult, has more barring in tail, both sexes with red crown patch, female's smaller. Race *equifasciatus* has pale and dark bars below about equal in width, upperwing-coverts sometimes with very narrow pale central streaks, female with blackish crown tinged olive; *pectoralis* is very like nominate, possibly darker below with pale bars very narrow. VOICE. Occasional soft "chik", and high descending "kzzrr"; song up to c. 25 high-pitched "kee" notes, rising before dropping at end, heard infrequently.
Habitat. Humid and wet montane forest, forest edge, stunted forest at tree-line and on mountain ridges, occasionally above tree-line in patches of *Polylepis* woodland. Prefers stands with dense undergrowth, especially of bamboo (*Chusquea*). Present at 2000-3600 m, mostly above 2600 m; locally to 4000 m in Ecuador.
Food and Feeding. Diet not recorded. Usually seen singly, sometimes in pairs, very unobtrusive; regularly in mixed-species flocks. Forages at all levels, from canopy down to near ground. Pecks at bark, removes bark, and probes among mosses on horizontal branches.
Breeding. Breeds Feb-Mar in Ecuador and Apr-May in Bolivia; specimens from Peru with enlarged testes in August. No other information.
Movements. Resident; whether any altitudinal movement occurs is not recorded.
Status and Conservation. Not globally threatened. Uncommon in Colombia; uncommon generally in Peru; rare to uncommon in Ecuador. Occurs in Podocarpus National Park (Ecuador) and fairly common in Machu Picchu Historical Sanctuary (Peru). Recorded at Abra Málaga and along Cuzco-Manu road in Peru; in Bolivia at Comarapa and Tambo, and at Sorata. A very poorly known species. Possibly overlooked owing to its unobtrusive habits, but likely to occur at very low densities in humid montane forest.

On following pages: 125. Smoky-brown Woodpecker (*Veniliornis fumigatus*); 126. Little Woodpecker (*Veniliornis passerinus*); 127. Dot-fronted Woodpecker (*Veniliornis frontalis*); 128. White-spotted Woodpecker (*Veniliornis spilogaster*); 129. Blood-coloured Woodpecker (*Veniliornis sanguineus*); 130. Red-rumped Woodpecker (*Veniliornis kirkii*); 131. Choco Woodpecker (*Veniliornis chocoensis*); 132. Golden-collared Woodpecker (*Veniliornis cassini*); 133. Red-stained Woodpecker (*Veniliornis affinis*); 134. Yellow-eared Woodpecker (*Veniliornis maculifrons*).

Bibliography. Bloch *et al.* (1991), Butler (1979), Clements & Shany (2001), Cresswell, Hughes *et al.* (1999), Cresswell, Mellanby *et al.* (1999), Davies *et al.* (1994), Fjeldså & Krabbe (1990), Hilty & Brown (1986), Meyer de Schauensee (1982), Olrog (1968), Parker, Parker & Plenge (1982), Parker, Schulenberg *et al.* (1985), Poulsen (1996), Remsen (1985), Remsen & Traylor (1989), Remsen *et al.* (1986), Ridgely & Greenfield (2001), Ridgely *et al.* (1998), Short (1985b), Stotz *et al.* (1996), Vélez & Velázquez (1998), Walker (2001), Williams & Tobias (1994), Zimmer (1930, 1942).

125. Smoky-brown Woodpecker

Veniliornis fumigatus

French: Pic enfumé **German**: Rußspecht **Spanish**: Carpintero Ahumado
Other common names: Brown Woodpecker

Taxonomy. *Picus fumigatus* d'Orbigny, 1840, Yungas, Bolivia.
Relationships uncertain; molecular-genetic analysis suggests very close relationship to *Picoides villosus*, perhaps to extent that the two could justifiably be treated as congeneric; further study needed. Races intergrade to some extent; birds from SW Ecuador may be intermediate between nominate and race *obscuratus*. N Colombian (Santa Marta) birds previously separated as race *exsul*, those of NE Venezuelan mountains as *tectricialis*, and those of C Colombia and Ecuador as *aureus*, but all appear insufficiently different to warrant recognition. Five subspecies currently recognized.
Subspecies and Distribution.
V. f. oleagineus (Reichenbach, 1854) - E Mexico.
V. f. sanguinolentus (P. L. Sclater, 1859) - C & S Mexico to W Panama.
V. f. reichenbachi (Cabanis & Heine, 1863) - N & NE Venezuela.
V. f. fumigatus (d'Orbigny, 1840) - E Panama and Colombia S through Ecuador and E Peru to W Bolivia and NW Argentina (Jujuy).
V. f. obscuratus Chapman, 1927 - SW Ecuador (El Oro and W Loja) to NW Peru (Huancabamba and bend of R Marañón).

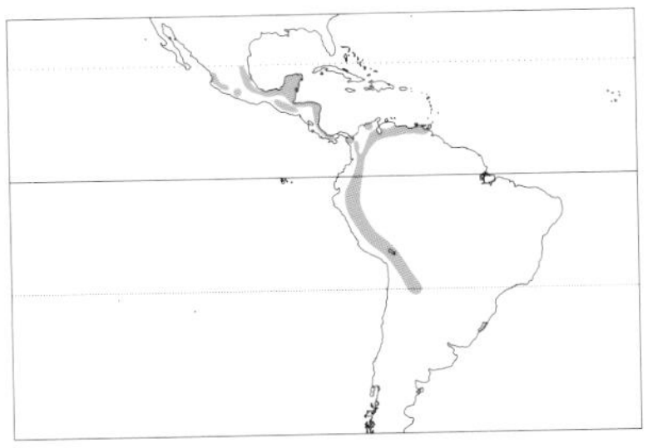

Descriptive notes. 18 cm; 31-40 g (*sanguinolentus*), 36-42 g (*oleagineus*), 35-50 g (*reichenbachi*). Male has red forehead to nape, forehead and crown with dark feather bases showing; rest of head and neck olive-brown, ear-coverts paler, whitish lores and thin line above eye, dark malar stripe with very thin whitish line above; brown to olive-brown upperparts, mantle tinged red or with some golden to orange feather edges when fresh, rump and uppertail-coverts duller brown; dark brown wings, coverts tinged greenish and often with some red edges, flight-feathers barred pale on inner webs; uppertail blackish-brown, outer feathers paler brown; olive-brown below, uniform or with paler lower region, latter occasionally with faint darker bars; underwing barred whitish and brown; rather long bill straight, broad across nostrils, blackish, paler lower mandible; iris deep brown to red-brown; legs greyish. Female has forehead to nape olive-tinged dark brown, occasionally with a few white speckles. Juvenile similar to adult but duller, more sooty-brown, lacking bright tinges above, with some white bars on inner webs of secondaries, male with dull red crown patch sometimes reaching to nape, on female normally restricted to forecrown. Races differ mainly in plumage tone and wing length: *oleagineus* is longer-winged than most, has much white around eyes; *sanguinolentus* is smaller, shorter-winged, richer brown than previous, has pale ear-coverts, no obvious whitish around eye; *reichenbachi* resembles previous, but slightly longer-winged, and duller brown; *obscuratus* has longest wing, is similar to previous but with darker, more grey-brown, plumage. VOICE. Short "wick", "chuk", "pwik" or "quip", softer and more slurred than similar note of *Picoides villosus*; rattle fast, high-pitched and piping "keer-keer-keer-keer" or hard, rolling, gravelly "zur-zur-zur-zur", at higher intensity as "tchk, tchk zr-r-r-r uh kuh-kuh-kuh-kuh"; squeaky, sucking "wick-a wick-a" or "tsewink tsewink" in interactions. Drums in very rapid, protracted tattoos.
Habitat. Humid and wet forest, cloudforest, dry montane woodland with *Eugenia*, alder (*Alnus*) woodland, occasionally above tree-line in patches of *Polylepis* growth. Oak (*Quercus*) forest in Mexico. In lowlands, forest edge and clearings, also along wooded streams, in shady and tall second growth, in thickets, lighter woodland and woodland borders with dense understorey, and coffee plantations. Occurs from almost sea-level up to 1500 m in Mexico; in lowlands up to 750 m, locally to 1850 m, through Central America; at 800-2700 m in Venezuela; mostly 1200-2800 m in Colombia and Peru, occasionally as low as 600 m, or higher, up to at least 4000 m in Peru (Cordillera Blanca); 600-2400 m in Ecuador, mostly at 1000-1800 m, but recorded to 2700 m; 1200-2500 m in Argentina.
Food and Feeding. Small wood-boring beetles and their larvae comprise bulk of diet, occasionally supplemented with fruits. In pairs throughout year, but often forages singly, or in family groups of 4-6 birds after breeding; often joins mixed-species flocks. Forages high in broken canopy or lower at edges and in undergrowth; often in vine tangles or on slender branches and among foliage, mostly at middle and low levels. Also visits isolated trees. Moves along branches with many sideward lunges. Pecks and hammers industriously on variety of substrates, from thin stems to large branches and vines. Probing infrequent; gleaning seems rarely to be used.
Breeding. Feb-Jun in Central America, Feb-Mar in N Venezuela, and Oct-Apr in Colombia. Nest-hole dug by both sexes, 1·5-8 m up in dead limb or tree trunk or in fence post. Clutch 4 eggs; no data on incubation and fledging periods.
Movements. Resident.
Status and Conservation. Not globally threatened. Fairly common to common in Central America, perhaps somewhat less common farther S; uncommon to fairly common in Ecuador, fairly common in Peru, locally frequent in Argentina. Occurs in numerous protected areas, including Braulio Carrillo National Park and Monteverde Biological Reserve (Costa Rica), Henri Pittier National Park (Venezuela), Río Ñambí Nature Reserve (Colombia), Protected Forest of Alto Mayo (Peru) and Calilegua National Park (Argentina). Probably reasonably secure.
Bibliography. Best & Clarke (1991), Binford (1989), Blendinger (1998), Bloch *et al.* (1991), Canevari *et al.* (1991), Clements & Shany (2001), Davies *et al.* (1994), Fjeldså & Krabbe (1990), Friedmann *et al.* (1957), Hernández *et al.* (1995), Hilty (1997), Hilty & Brown (1986), Howell & Webb (1995), Koepcke (1961), Mazar Barnett *et al.* (1998), Meyer de Schauensee & Phelps (1978), Miller (1963), Monroe (1968), Parker, Parker & Plenge (1982), Parker, Schulenberg *et al.* (1985), de la Peña (1994), Remsen *et al.* (1986), Ridgely & Greenfield (2001), Ridgely & Gwynne (1989), Rojas *et al.* (2001), Salaman (1994), Schaldach (1963), Short (1985b), Slud (1964), Stiles (1985), Stotz *et al.* (1996), Thurber *et al.* (1987), Wetmore (1968a), Zimmer (1930, 1942).

126. Little Woodpecker

Veniliornis passerinus

French: Pic passerin **German**: Sperlingsspecht **Spanish**: Carpintero Chico

Taxonomy. *Picus passerinus* Linnaeus, 1766, Dominica; error = Cayenne.
Forms a superspecies with *V. frontalis*; the two sometimes hybridize, and have occasionally been considered conspecific. Races tend to intergrade. Birds from extreme W French Guiana described as race *saturatus* and those from E Brazil (N Goiás, W Bahia) as *transfluvialis*, but appear to be no more than intergrades. Nine subspecies recognized.
Subspecies and Distribution.
V. p. modestus J. T. Zimmer, 1942 - NE Venezuela.
V. p. fidelis (Hargitt, 1889) - W Venezuela to E Colombia.
V. p. passerinus (Linnaeus, 1766) - the Guianas and NE Brazil.
V. p. diversus J. T. Zimmer, 1942 - N Brazil.
V. p. agilis (Cabanis & Heine, 1863) - E Ecuador E to W Brazil and S to N Bolivia.
V. p. insignis J. T. Zimmer, 1942 - WC Brazil.
V. p. tapajozensis Gyldenstolpe, 1941 - C Brazil.
V. p. taenionotus (Reichenbach, 1854) - E Brazil.
V. p. olivinus (Natterer & Malherbe, 1845) - S Bolivia, S Brazil, Paraguay and NW & NE Argentina.

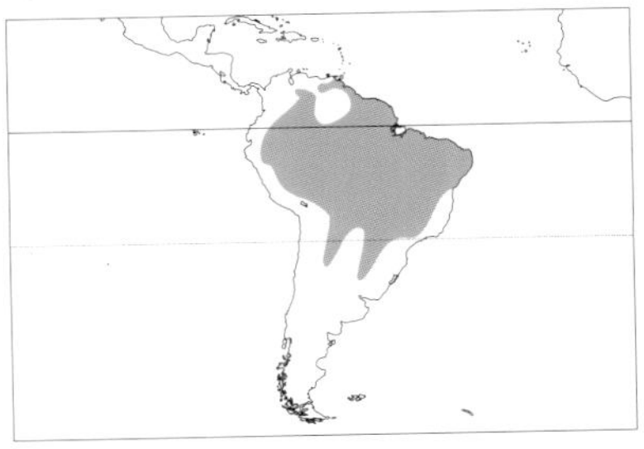

Descriptive notes. c. 14-15 cm; 24-37 g. Male has greyish forehead, red forecrown to hindneck with dark feather bases showing; rest of head dark brownish-olive, neck sides with paler feather tips, chin and throat barred pale; bronzy olive-green above sometimes with a few red feather tips, with variable obscure paler barring very indistinct, most evident on rump, median wing-coverts usually with small subterminal spots; brown flight-feathers edged green, broadly on secondaries and tertials, narrow whitish bars on inner webs of primaries and secondaries; uppertail dark brown, outer feathers usually with some thin pale bars; dark olive underparts entirely barred buffish-white, underwing barred olive-brown and pale; fairly long bill straight, broad across nostrils, blackish, paler lower mandible; iris deep brown; legs dark grey. Distinguished from *V. frontalis* by smaller size, lack of pale facial stripes, lack of obvious spots and bars above, less barred tail. Female lacks red on head, has forehead to nape greyish olive-brown, usually with indistinct pale spots. Juvenile resembles adult but duller, less bronzy, with bars below less regular, eyes paler, both sexes with dull red crown patch, smaller on female. Races differ mainly in presence of facial stripes, extent of red on male's head, tone of upperparts and amount of spotting in wing-coverts, nature of barring below, and size: *modestus* has fairly prominent whitish moustachial line, obvious pale wing-coverts spots, grey-brown underparts with breast barring irregular; *fidelis* has pale supercilium, much more marked whitish moustachial line, larger wing-covert spots, breastbars broken or scallop-shaped, tail usually unbarred; *diversus* has only faint indication of facial stripes or none at all, wing-coverts sometimes with very narrow pale shaft streaks, bars below broad, male with red only from central crown to hindneck; *agilis* has well-developed supercilium and moustachial stripes; *insignis* is smallest, has no pale facial stripes, no wing-covert spots, pale bars below broad, red on male as previous; *tapajozensis* is tinged yellower above with some red spots, red of male's head extending to forecrown; *taenionotus* is even yellower above, often with scattered red tips and stronger hint of barring, has larger wing-covert spots, pale bars below noticeably broad, red of male's head extending to forehead; *olivinus* is largest, usually has short pale supercilium (often absent), thin whitish moustachial (often partly lacking), male with red restricted to hindcrown and nape. VOICE. High-pitched "ki, ki, ki, ki" or "wi-wi-wi-wi-wi-wi-wi", apparently as long-distance call; also "wicka" or series of "wik-wik-wik" in encounters. Drums.
Habitat. Rather versatile, generally preferring edges and clearings, and second growth. Occurs at edges of humid forest, including cloudforest, *várzea* forest, riparian forest, also gallery forest with bamboo bordering swampy lagoons and rivers; also deciduous woodland, mangroves, second growth, transitional forest, densely wooded savanna, shrub-forest (*caatinga*), also lightly wooded habitats, including savanna with scattered trees. Occasionally visits gardens. To 850 m in N Venezuela and 1200 m in Colombia; to 1300 m but mostly below 700 m in Ecuador, to 900 m in Peru and to 400 m farther S.
Food and Feeding. Ants, termites (Isoptera), beetles and their larvae, and various other insects. Found singly, in pairs or in small groups; joins mixed-species flocks. Forages from low in undergrowth, preferentially on bamboo, to upper levels in trees; often in semi-open sites. Techniques include vigorous pecking and hammering on bark, branches and limbs, around bamboo nodes, and on saplings; small holes drilled by hammering.
Breeding. Sept-Dec in French Guiana and Oct-Mar in Argentina; copulation observed in Feb in Colombia. Displays include wing-spreading, head-swinging, tail-spreading. Nest excavated possibly by male only, at 5-13 m in stub, palm or bamboo. Details of clutch size and incubation and fledging periods not documented; observations suggest that possibly male alone tends brood.
Movements. Resident.
Status and Conservation. Not globally threatened. Uncommon to fairly common in Ecuador; fairly common in Peru. Appears generally to be not uncommon. Occurs in Serra do Cipó and Chapada dos Guimarães National Parks (Brazil) and Podocarpus National Park (Ecuador). An adaptable species, able to exploit a variety of wooded habitats.
Bibliography. Allen (1995), Brace *et al.* (1997), Canevari *et al.* (1991), Clements & Shany (2001), Contreras *et al.* (1990), Ferreira de Vasconcelos & Melo-Júnior (2001), Guix *et al.* (1999), Hayes (1995), Hilty & Brown (1986), Lima & Aleixo (2000), Maldonado-Coelho & Marini (2000), Marini (2001), Marini *et al.* (1997), Melo-Júnior (2001a), Meyer de Schauensee & Phelps (1978), Munn (1985), Oniki & Willis (1999), Parker *et al.* (1982), de la Peña (1994), Pinto & Camargo (1961), Piratelli *et al.* (2000), Remsen & Traylor (1989), Ridgely & Greenfield (2001), Robinson (1997), Robinson & Terborgh (1997), Short (1975), Sick (1993), da Silva *et al.* (1997), Snyder (1966), Stotz, Fitzpatrick *et al.* (1996), Stotz, Lanyon *et al.* (1997), Straube & Bornschein (1995), Terborgh *et al.* (1984), Thiollay & Jullien (1998), Tostain *et al.* (1992), Tubelis & Tomás (1999), Wetmore (1926), Zimmer (1942).

127. Dot-fronted Woodpecker

Veniliornis frontalis

French: Pic étoilé **German**: Perlstirnspecht **Spanish**: Carpintero de las Yungas

Taxonomy. *Cloronerpes* [sic] (*Campias*) *frontalis* Cabanis, 1883, Tucumán, Argentina. Forms a superspecies with *V. passerinus*; the two sometimes hybridize, and have occasionally been considered conspecific. Monotypic.
Distribution. Andes from Bolivia (Cochabamba, W Santa Cruz) S to NW Argentina (S to Tucumán).

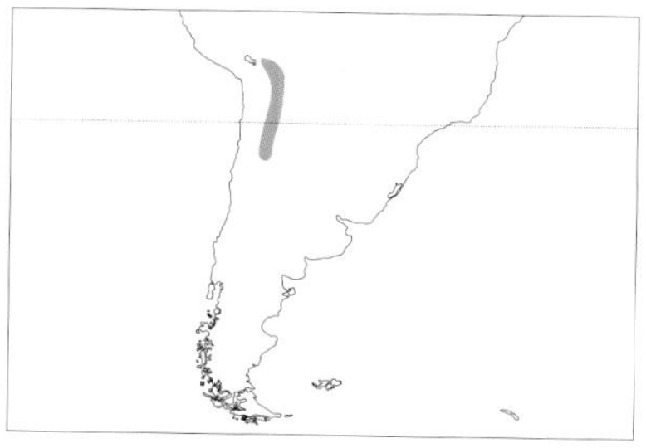

Descriptive notes. c. 16 cm; 30-40 g. Male has olive to grey-brown forehead heavily spotted with white, red forecrown to nape with extensive dark grey feather bases showing through, yellowish-olive hindneck; long thin white supercilium, thin white line from lores, one or both often partly obscured by darker spots; rest of head olive-brown, ear-coverts streaked buffish, neck side and chin barred pale; yellowish-olive upperparts barred and streaked pale and with golden feather tips (markings much less obvious in worn plumage), median wing-coverts and outer scapulars with pale wedge-shaped spots, greater coverts with narrow pale central streaks; brown flight-feathers broadly edged yellow-green, narrowly pale-barred on inner webs; uppertail dark brown with thin whitish bars (bars less distinct on central feathers), all suffused yellow; olive-grey underparts all narrowly barred whitish, underwing barred dusky and pale; fairly long bill straight, broad across nostrils, slate-grey to blackish, paler lower mandible; iris dark brown; legs dark grey. Differs from *V. passerinus* in larger size, facial stripes (also present in some races of latter), stronger markings above, barred tail. Female has crown to nape olive-brown with white spots. Juvenile duller and greyer than adult, both sexes with red crown patch, smaller on female. Voice. Similar to that of *V. spilogaster*: makes series of 8-10 "juíc!" or "jíc!" calls, or a rather harsh "wík!". Also utters similar cries as isolated individual calls.
Habitat. Dry montane woodland and transitional and humid forest of Andean slopes; to 2000 m, generally lower.
Food and Feeding. Diet not described. Often forages at low levels, near ground, on trunks and smaller branches.
Breeding. Very few data. Active nest in mid-Nov in Argentina; juveniles recorded in Sept and Oct. Single known nest c. 8 m above ground in cavity in dead tree; male apparently incubating. No other information.
Movements. Some downslope movements occur outside breeding season.
Status and Conservation. Not globally threatened. Generally rather uncommon. In Argentina, occurs in El Rey National Park and fairly common in Calilegua National Park. Very poorly known species; research required on its ecology and reproduction.
Bibliography. Babarskas *et al*. (1995), Blake & Rougès (1997), Canevari *et al*. (1991), Chebez *et al*. (1999), Contreras (1983), Di Giacomo & López (2000), Fjeldså & Mayer (1996), Malizia (2001), Malizia *et al*. (1998), Mazar Barnett & Pearman (2001), Meyer de Schauensee (1982), Narosky & Yzurieta (1993), Nores *et al*. (2000), Olrog (1968), de la Peña (1994), Remsen & Traylor (1989), Short (1985b), Stotz *et al*. (1996), Wetmore (1926).

128. White-spotted Woodpecker
Veniliornis spilogaster

French: Pic aspergé **German**: Perlbauchspecht **Spanish**: Carpintero Manchado

Taxonomy. *Picus Spilogaster* Wagler, 1827, Brazil and Paraguay.
Monotypic.
Distribution. SE Brazil (S from Minas Gerais) S to adjacent SE Paraguay, NE Argentina (Misiones, E Corrientes) and Uruguay.

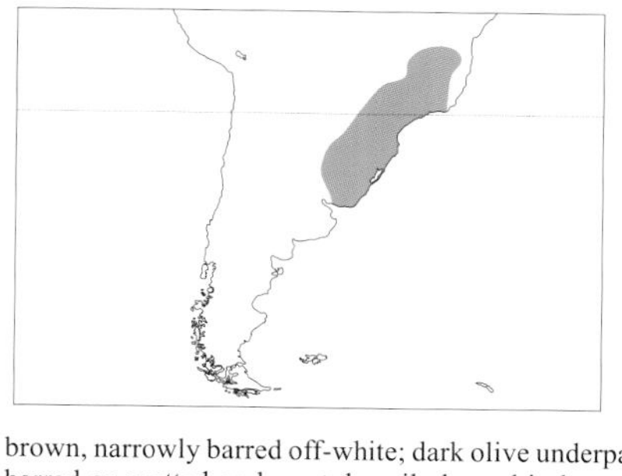

Descriptive notes. 16-19·5 cm; 35-45 g. Distinctive small woodpecker. Male has buffy to olive lower forehead, blackish-brown crown very narrowly streaked dark red when fresh (plainer in worn plumage), olive-green hindneck; brownish ear-coverts patterned with white, bordered above by thin white supercilium, below by thin white moustachial stripe; pale chin and side of neck striped dark olive-brown; olive-green upperparts with pale yellowish to white feather edges forming bars, sometimes becoming spots on rump, dark olive wing-coverts tipped whitish, dark brown flight-feathers barred whitish; uppertail dark brown, narrowly barred off-white; dark olive underparts heavily streaked yellowish-white on throat, barred or spotted on breast, heavily barred in lower regions, underwing barred brown and white; rather short to longish bill straight, broad across nostrils, blackish-grey, paler base, often yellowish base of lower mandible; iris deep chestnut-brown; legs olive or olive-grey. Female has noticeably shorter bill than male, crown olive-brown and finely spotted white. Juvenile much as adult, but bars above less obvious and less regular. Voice. Single "pic" notes in mild alarm; also great variety of other distinctive calls, e.g. sharp "cheékit" and "ti-rra-rra", "reh-reh-reh-reh" and similar, or "cheékit ch che che che che che"; variable high-pitched, almost whistled chittering by nestlings. Gentle tapping signal in groups of 2-4, with pauses and single taps, also described.
Habitat. Various types of forest and woodland, from humid lowland forest, riverine forest and isolated forest patches to open and very open woodland and open parkland with low and spiny trees.
Food and Feeding. Beetle larvae and other insects; berries also taken. Observed foraging on tree trunks, saplings and fence posts; pecks, and hammers vigorously to excavate bark. Also plucks berries.
Breeding. Apparently breeds in Aug-Oct, or to Nov. Nest-holes excavated low down, once at 2·2 m, in stub, the chamber occupying most of the heartwood. No information on clutch size or on incubation and fledging periods.
Movements. Resident.
Status and Conservation. Not globally threatened. Common; locally very common. Occurs in Itatiaia National Park and Aparados da Serra National Park (Brazil) Ybicuí National Park (Paraguay) and Iguazú National Park (Argentina). Fairly adaptable, able to use a variety of wooded habitats.
Bibliography. Aleixo & Galetti (1997), dos Anjos (2001), dos Anjos & Schuchmann (1997), dos Anjos *et al*. (1997), Belton (1984), Bencke & Kindel (1999), Brooks *et al*. (1993), Buzzetti (2000), Canevari *et al*. (1991), Capper *et al*. (2000), Figueiredo & Lo (2000), Figueiredo *et al*. (2000), Goerck (1999), Guix, Martín & Mañosa (1999), Guix, Tabánez *et al*. (1992), Hayes (1995), Hayes & Scharf (1995a), Lowen *et al*. (1995), Machado & Rodrigues (2000), Madroño, Clay, Robbins *et al*. (1997), Madroño, Robbins & Zyskowski (1997), Meyer de Schauensee (1982), Olrog (1968), Parker & Goerck (1997), de la Peña (1994, 1997), do Rosário (1996), Short (1985b), Sick (1993), Soares & dos Anjos (1999), Stotz *et al*. (1996), Tobias *et al*. (1993), Wetmore (1926).

129. Blood-coloured Woodpecker
Veniliornis sanguineus

French: Pic rougeâtre **German**: Blutrückenspecht **Spanish**: Carpintero Sanguíneo

Taxonomy. *Picus sanguineus* A. A. H. Lichtenstein, 1793, Guyana.
Monotypic.
Distribution. Coastal lowlands of the Guianas.

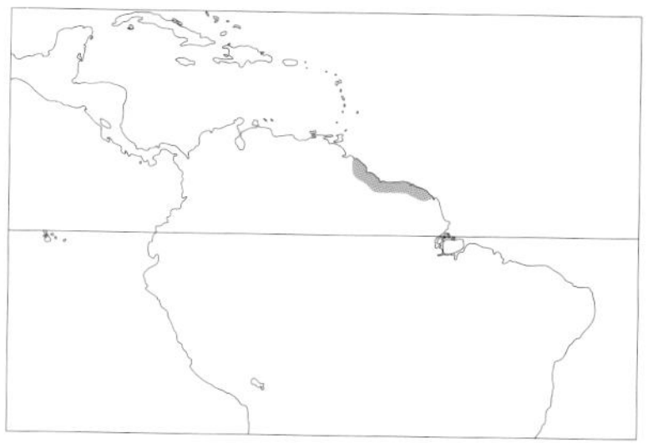

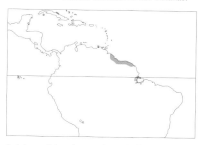

Descriptive notes. c. 13 cm; 23-30 g. Male has brown forehead faintly spotted white, crimson-red crown to hindneck with brown feather bases and centres usually fairly visible; brown superciliary area, ear-coverts and neck side, ear-coverts usually very finely streaked whitish; chin, throat and malar region barred dark and pale brown; upperparts dark crimson-red with extensive greenish-brown feather bases, dark brown wing-coverts broadly edged and tipped crimson, medians with a few tiny white spots; dark brown flight-feathers, primaries edged greenish-brown, secondaries and tertials broadly edged crimson; uppertail dark brown; dark brownish underparts barred off-white, bars broader on belly, underwing entirely barred brown and whitish; in worn plumage red areas duller and much browner, underparts even more boldly barred; relatively long bill straight, broad across nostrils, dark grey, paler tip; iris dark red-brown; legs blackish. Female as male, but has crown brown with fine white feather tips. Juvenile as adult, but duller and browner, feathering looser, usually larger pale wing-covert spots. Voice. Common call single "keek" notes; fast series of c. 16 "wih" notes also given; nestlings produce rattling noise. Both sexes drum.
Habitat. Mangroves, swampy forest, also coffee plantations; lowlands.
Food and Feeding. Ants, beetles (Cerambycidae), caterpillars. Usually singly or in pairs. Forages in trees and shrubs of various kinds.
Breeding. Recorded in Feb-Mar and May-Nov in Surinam. Hole excavated by both sexes, working for up to 2 months, low down (e.g. 1·4 m) in stump or larger branch. Partners may copulate before entering joint roost. Clutch 1 or 2 eggs, sometimes 3; both parents incubate; nestlings apparently fed with single food items, by both sexes, male accounting for slightly larger share; incubation and fledging periods not documented; pair-members roost together, and may share roost with another individual, presumably young of previous brood, until next brood initiated.
Movements. Resident.
Status and Conservation. Not globally threatened. Reasonably common. Fairly widespread in its range, but restricted to lowlands of the Guianas. No information on numbers, but probably secure; loss of habitat could become a threat, although no indication of this occurring in the short term.
Bibliography. Haverschmidt (1953), Haverschmidt & Mees (1994), Meyer de Schauensee (1982), Olrog (1968), Rodner *et al*. (2000), Short (1985b), Snyder (1966), Stotz *et al*. (1996), Tostain *et al*. (1992), Wheatley (1994).

130. Red-rumped Woodpecker
Veniliornis kirkii

French: Pic à croupion rouge **German**: Blutbürzelspecht **Spanish**: Carpintero Culirrojo
Other common names: Kirk's Woodpecker

Taxonomy. *Picus* (*Chloropicus*) *Kirkii* Malherbe, 1845, Tobago.
Forms a superspecies with *V. chocoensis*, *V. cassini*, *V. affinis* and *V. maculifrons*. Five subspecies recognized.
Subspecies and Distribution.
V. k. neglectus Bangs, 1901 - SW Costa Rica and W Panama, including Coiba I.
V. k. cecilii (Malherbe, 1849) - E Panama and W Colombia S to W Ecuador and extreme NW Peru (Pacific slope S to Lambayeque).
V. k. continentalis Hellmayr, 1906 - W & N Venezuela.
V. k. kirkii (Malherbe, 1845) - Trinidad and Tobago and NE Venezuela.
V. k. monticola Hellmayr, 1918 - Mt Roraima and Cerro Uei-tepui, in SE Venezuela.

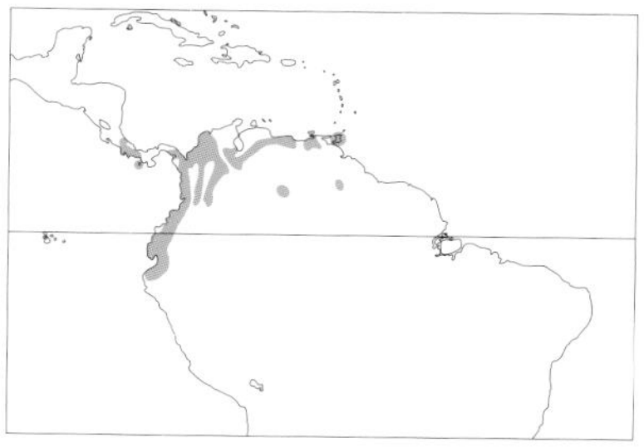

Descriptive notes. c. 15-16 cm; 30-42 g. Male has buffish forehead, lores and superciliary area, dusky brown or dark grey crown and nape with red feather tips, golden-yellow lower nape to upper neck side; olive-brown ear-coverts with whitish shaft streaks, whitish chin and throat barred dark olive; golden olive-brown upperparts with paler yellow shaft streaks (often obscure), sometimes some red feather edges and tips, rump and uppertail-coverts bright crimson-red; wing-coverts with pale buff wedge-shaped spots, reddish tips, mostly on medians; dark brown flight-feathers broadly edged greenish-olive, broadest on secondaries and tertials, pale bars on inner webs of primaries and secondaries; uppertail dark brown, paler outer feathers barred pale buff; entirely barred olive-brown and whitish below, pale bars becoming broader in belly region, underwing barred dark brown and whitish; longish bill straight, broad across nostrils, blackish, paler lower mandible; iris dark brown to red-brown, occasionally paler orbital ring; legs dark greyish, tinged green to blue. Differs from *V. chocoensis* in red rump, less yellow nape, less patterned face, narrower pale bars below. Female lacks red on head, has crown dark brown with green tinges. Juvenile resembles adult, but both sexes have red tips on crown, female less extensively. Race *monticola* is large as nominate or larger, with heavy blackish barring below; *continentalis* is smaller, with more yellow on nape, and pale bars below broader; *cecilii* is smaller than previous, with paler chin and upper throat less patterned, wing-coverts less spotted, tail more barred; *neglectus* is usually brighter above and darker below than last, tending to lack spots on wing-coverts. Voice.

Nasal "keer", decreasing in intensity, softer than similar note of *Piculus simplex*, recalling kiskadee (*Pitangus*) or even *Piculus rubiginosus*; mewing "wih" or "kwee" in shorter or longer ventriloquial series of up to 16 notes, becoming louder at end, sometimes with weak throaty "yuk" or "yk" added; also repeated "kee-yik kee-yik". Drumming rapid, noisy, often prolonged.
Habitat. Variety of lowland and foothill habitats, from wet forest, adjacent second growth and overgrown clearings, edge of mangroves, to gallery forest, xerophytic areas, dry deciduous forest, tall open woodland, savanna, coconut (*Cocos nucifera*) plantations, cemeteries. Tends to favour rather open habitats. To 900 m in Panama; to 1000 m in W Venezuela, and to 1500-1750 m in tepuis S of R Orinoco; to c. 1200 m in Ecuador but below 300 m in NW (N Esmeraldas); to 1500 m in Peru.
Food and Feeding. Larvae and adults of small to medium-sized wood-boring beetles and other insects. Usually forages singly or in pairs, or in small groups; joins mixed-species flocks. Mainly in mid-levels and canopy of forest, coming lower only in adjacent second growth and clearings; visits trees at forest borders, but rarely ventures outside forest; inconspicuous. Forages on trunks to smaller branches, often among thick foliage. Pecking and hammering are frequently used techniques; hammers steadily.
Breeding. Dec-Feb, possibly Mar, in Panama and in Trinidad and Tobago, and Feb-Mar in N Venezuela; Jul in Ecuador; also, birds in breeding condition in Jan and Sept in Colombia and Ecuador. Nest-hole 3-8 m up in living tree or palm, even slender one, often at edge of forest; hole diameter 5 cm, cavity depth 35 cm. Clutch 2-3 eggs. No other information.
Movements. Resident.
Status and Conservation. Not globally threatened. Fairly common to uncommon. Uncommon to locally fairly common in Ecuador, where widespread in N lowlands; apparently no recent records from SW (Loja). Fairly common at Campo Verde (Peru). Occurs in Salamanca National Park (Colombia), Henri Pittier National Park (Venezuela), Tinalandia Natural Reserve (Ecuador) and Tumbes National Reserve (Peru). Generally inconspicuous, possibly overlooked, but presence often revealed by sound of its frequent pecking and hammering.
Bibliography. Anon. (1998b), Becker & López (1997), Bond *et al.* (1989), Clements & Shany (2001), Friedmann & Smith (1950), Hayes & Samad (1998), Herklots (1961), Hilty & Brown (1986), Marín & Carrión (1991), Meyer de Schauensee (1982), Meyer de Schauensee & Phelps (1978), Olrog (1968), Parker *et al.* (1982), Pople *et al.* (1997), Ridgely & Greenfield (2001), Ridgely & Gwynne (1989), Robbins *et al.* (1985), Short (1985b), Slud (1964), Snow (1985), Stiles (1985), Stiles & Skutch (1989), Stotz *et al.* (1996), Verea & Solórzano (1998), Verea *et al.* (2000), Wetmore (1939, 1957, 1968a).

131. Choco Woodpecker

Veniliornis chocoensis

French: Pic du Choco **German**: Chokospecht **Spanish**: Carpintero del Chocó

Taxonomy. *Veniliornis chocoensis* Todd, 1919, Malagita, Chocó, Colombia.
Forms a superspecies with *V. kirkii*, *V. cassini*, *V. affinis* and *V. maculifrons*. Has often been treated as conspecific with second or third of those, but differs in plumage details, in size and in habitat preferences, apparently also vocally, and is separated from both by Andes chain. Monotypic.
Distribution. W Colombia (W Antioquia S to Nariño) and NW Ecuador (S to NW Pichincha).

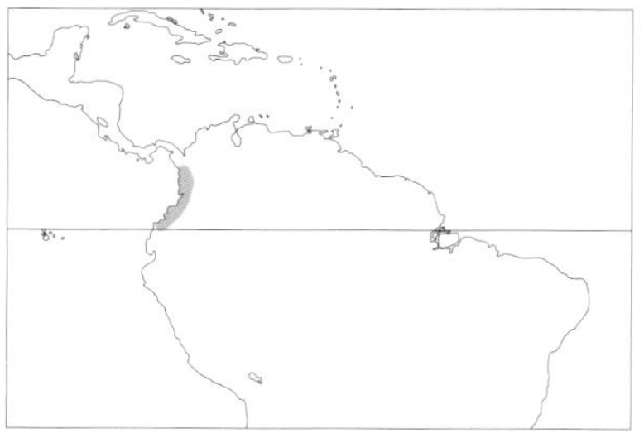

Descriptive notes. 15-16 cm; c. 30 g. Male has buffish forehead, blackish crown with broad red feather tips, dull golden nape and upper neck side; brownish-buff lores and side of head, obscurely streaked darker at rear, often some pale tips (can appear variegated); pale buffish chin and upper throat spotted or barred darker, sometimes almost fully dark; bronzy golden-green above, mantle and scapulars often suffused red, obscure pale yellow shaft streaks, rump and uppertail-coverts barred olive and yellowish; wing-coverts with small, obscure pale yellow spots, mostly on medians; dark brown flight-feathers edged olive-yellow, barred buffish, tertials sometimes tinged red; uppertail dark brown, barred yellowish, bars most pronounced on outer tail; underparts barred olive and whitish-buff, underwing barred pale and dark; rather short bill straight or slightly curved, broad across nostrils, dark, paler lower mandible; iris red-brown to brown; legs dark olive, tinged grey or green. Distinguished from very similar *V. cassini* by slightly brighter upperparts, dark bars below less blackish; from *V. affinis* by generally somewhat smaller size, slightly darker coloration, and less red on upperparts. Female differs from male in having crown dark olive-brown, becoming yellow-streaked on nape. Juvenile as adult but looser-plumaged, with streaked face side, both sexes with red-tipped crown feathers, on female confined mostly to central area. VOICE. Details apparently not documented, but said to differ to some extent from *V. cassini* and *V. affinis*.
Habitat. Humid to very wet forest and forest edge in foothills, less in lowlands; recorded at up to 1000 m, mostly below 700 m. Generally prefers wetter forest than e.g. *V. affinis*.
Food and Feeding. Details not known; diet presumably as for *V. affinis*. Pair seen foraging with mixed-species party in primary forest in Jul and Jan in SW Colombia (Nariño).
Breeding. No information.
Movements. Presumably resident.
Status and Conservation. Not globally threatened. Considered Near-threatened. Restricted-range species: present in Chocó EBA. Little-known species which seems to be rare throughout its small range. Rare in Colombia; rare to uncommon and local in Ecuador, with most records in Esmeraldas. Occurs in El Pangán Reserve in Nariño, Colombia; occurs in 2 protected areas in Ecuador, in Cotocachi-Cayapas Ecological Reserve and at Bilsa. Habitat loss and degradation are the most serious threats. Large-scale logging concessions, accompanied by human settlement following road construction, have already resulted in more than 40% of Chocó forest being lost or severely degraded; forest destruction continuing at accelerating rate, and most severe in altitudinal range occupied by this species. Mining activities, coca and palm cultivation and livestock grazing combine to intensify the pressure caused by intensive logging. Without appropriate measures to conserve its habitats, this species' conservation status could become Vulnerable.
Bibliography. Ridgely & Greenfield (2001), Ridgely *et al.* (1998), Rodner *et al.* (2000), Short (1974c), Stattersfield & Capper (2000), Stattersfield *et al.* (1998), Strewe (2000b), Taylor (1995).

132. Golden-collared Woodpecker

Veniliornis cassini

French: Pic de Cassin **German**: Goldnackenspecht **Spanish**: Carpintero Cebra

Taxonomy. *Mesopicus cassini* Malherbe, 1862, Cayenne.
Forms a superspecies with *V. kirkii*, *V. chocoensis*, *V. affinis* and *V. maculifrons*. Often considered conspecific with second, but differs in details of plumage, in habitat preferences, apparently also in voice, and is geographically isolated by Andes. Has also been regarded as possibly conspecific with third of those species, with which may overlap slightly in range; further study needed. Monotypic.
Distribution. E & SE Venezuela (Bolívar, Amazonas), the Guianas, and NE Brazil N of Amazon (E Roraima and lower R Negro to Amapá).

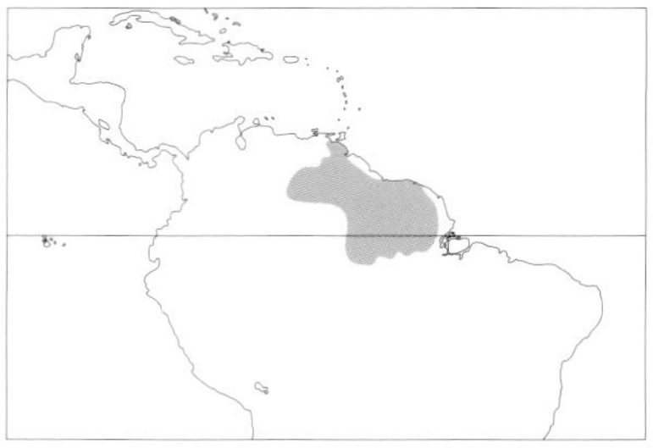

Descriptive notes. c. 16 cm; 24-38 g. Male has buffish lower forehead and lores, greyish-black upper forehead and crown with narrow red feather tips, larger tips on upper nape, golden-yellow lower nape to neck side and rearmost superciliary area; buffish-white ear-coverts finely streaked darker; whitish chin lightly barred or spotted dark; yellowish-green upperparts slightly bronzey, rump sometimes obscurely barred yellowish, median wing-coverts (and some greaters) with pale buff subterminal spots, sometimes also basal spots; dark brown flight-feathers edged greenish, broadly on inner secondaries and tertials, white bars on inner webs of primaries and secondaries; uppertail dark brown, obscurely barred paler, outer 2 feather pairs with clearer whitish notches; throat and underparts white to pale buffish-white, barred black to brownish-black, bars narrower in lower regions; underwing barred dark brown and white; undertail as above, but bars more obvious; rather long bill straight, fairly broad across nostrils, dark grey, paler tip and cutting edges; iris dark brown to red-brown; legs olive to dark grey or blackish, sometimes tinged blue. Differs from *V. affinis* in lack of red tones above, brighter yellow nape, more contrasting barring below. Female has crown green-tinged brown, whitish-yellow spots at rear merging with golden-yellow of nape. Juvenile greener, less yellow, above than adult, duller nape, darker face, wing-coverts more streaked, both sexes with some red on crown. VOICE. Very similar to that of *V. affinis*: a series of 33-35 nasal "khir" notes, rising in frequency. Generally rather silent.
Habitat. Rainforest, clearings, open terrain with trees, shrubbery; lowlands to 1500 m.
Food and Feeding. Beetles (Cerambycidae) recorded. generally solitary, often foraging in treetops. Also joins mixed-species feeding flocks.
Breeding. No information available.
Movements. Presumably resident.
Status and Conservation. Not globally threatened. A very poorly known canopy-dwelling woodpecker; possibly not uncommon, but difficult to observe. Not uncommon in Canaima National Park and Imataca Forest Reserve and El Dorado (Venezuela); observed at Manaus (Brazil). Research required to determine its ecology and breeding biology.
Bibliography. Cohn-Haft *et al.* (1997), Haverschmidt & Mees (1994), Meyer de Schauensee (1982), Meyer de Schauensee & Phelps (1978), Olrog (1968), Reynaud (1998), Ruschi (1979), Sargeant (1994), Short (1974c, 1985b), Sick (1993), Snyder (1966), Stotz *et al.* (1996), Thiollay & Jullien (1998), Tostain *et al.* (1992).

133. Red-stained Woodpecker

Veniliornis affinis

French: Pic affin **German**: Blutflügelspecht **Spanish**: Carpintero Teñido

Taxonomy. *Picus affinis* Swainson, 1821, Bahia, Brazil.
Forms a superspecies with *V. kirkii*, *V. chocoensis*, *V. cassini* and *V. maculifrons*. Has often been treated as conspecific with second, but differences exist in plumage, habitat choice and, reputedly, vocalizations. Sometimes believed to be conspecific with third of those species; study needed of circumstances in apparent small range of overlap. Races intergrade to large extent; specimen from E Colombia described as a separate race, "*caquetanus*", but considered to represent subadult of *orenocensis*. Four subspecies recognized.
Subspecies and Distribution.
V. a. orenocensis Berlepsch & Hartert, 1902 - SE Colombia, S Venezuela and N Brazil.
V. a. hilaris (Cabanis & Heine, 1863) - E Ecuador, E Peru and W Brazil S to N Bolivia and W Mato Grosso.
V. a. ruficeps (Spix, 1824) - C & NE Brazil S to Mato Grosso.
V. a. affinis (Swainson, 1821) - E Brazil (Alagoas and E Bahia).

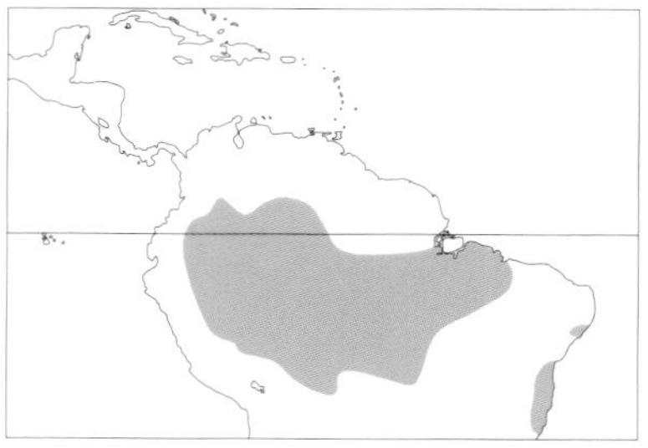

Descriptive notes. c. 15-18 cm; 32-44 g. Male has cinnamon-buff lower forehead and lores, black upper forehead and crown with feathers broadly tipped red, becoming golden-yellow on nape and hindneck and slightly on to feather edges of upper neck side; dark buffish ear-coverts streaked olive, buffish chin and malar region; yellowish-green upperparts with variable red suffusion, pale yellow shaft streaks, rump and uppertail-coverts variably barred; wing-coverts with yellowish subterminal spots, reddish tips; dark brown flight-feathers broadly edged green, broadest on tertials, barred buffish-white on primaries and secondaries; uppertail dark brown, barred yellowish, central pair often plain; light cinnamon-buff below, whiter on lower underparts, all barred dark olive-brown, dark bars more widely spaced on belly and flanks; underwing barred dark brown and whitish; longish bill straight, broad across nostrils, blackish, paler lower mandible; iris brown to red-brown; legs olive-grey to green-grey. Female has crown dark olive-brown, golden-yellow streaks on hindcrown merging with golden nape. Juvenile as adult, but face darker, more streaked, both sexes with red on crown, on female generally restricted to central area. Race *orenocensis* is greener, less yellow, above, shaft streaks much fainter, usually less red tinge; *hilaris* is larger than previous, more bronzy or yellow above, has prominent broad red tips on wing-coverts; *ruficeps* is same size as last, but wing-covert markings much larger, pale shaft streaks on upperparts often more obvious. VOICE. Series of up to c. 10-14 high-pitched nasal "ghi" or "kih" notes given infrequently.
Habitat. Tall rainforest; less common in forest edge, second growth and scrub; in humid lowland *terra firme* forest, to lesser extent in *várzea* forest, in Ecuador and Peru. Occasionally forages out into riparian forest and woodland, also visits trees in clearings. Occurs at 100-500 m in Venezuela;

to 500 m on E slope and 1000 m on Pacific slope in Colombian Andes; to 850 m but mostly 600 m in Ecuador; to 1300 m in Peru.

Food and Feeding. Arthropods; also fond of fruit. Forages singly, only occasionally in pairs; regular in mixed-species flocks. Foraging strata mostly high, from canopy down to middle levels; sometimes to lower levels, especially at forest edge. Accompanies army-ant processions to obtain flushed arthropods.

Breeding. Presumed to be Jan-Sept. No information.

Movements. Apparently resident.

Status and Conservation. Not globally threatened. Uncommon to locally fairly common in Ecuador; uncommon in Peru. Occurs in Manu National Park (Peru), Murici Reserve, Sooretama Biological Reserve, Parque Estadual da Pedra Talhada and Rio Cristalino Private Reserve (Brazil). Very poorly known. Possibly not uncommon but overlooked.

Bibliography. Allen (1995), Balchin & Toyne (1998), Borges *et al.* (2001), Brace *et al.* (1997), Clements & Shany (2001), Donahue (1994), Friedmann (1948), Hilty & Brown (1986), Meyer de Schauensee & Phelps (1978), Munn (1985), Oren & Parker (1997), Parker & Goerck (1997), Parker *et al.* (1982), Peres & Whittaker (1991), Remsen *et al.* (1986), Ridgely & Greenfield (2001), Robinson & Terborgh (1997), Sargeant (1994), Short (1974c, 1985b), Sick (1993), da Silva (1996), Smith (1983), Stotz, Fitzpatrick *et al.* (1996), Stotz, Lanyon *et al.* (1997), Terborgh *et al.* (1984), Tobias *et al.* (1993), Zimmer (1930, 1942).

134. Yellow-eared Woodpecker
Veniliornis maculifrons

French: Pic à oreilles d'or **German**: Goldohrspecht **Spanish**: Carpintero Orejigualdo

Taxonomy. *Picus maculifrons* Spix, 1824, Rio de Janeiro, Brazil.
Forms a superspecies with *V. kirkii*, *V. chocoensis*, *V. cassini* and *V. affinis*. Monotypic.

Distribution. E Brazil from SE Bahia S to Rio de Janeiro.

Descriptive notes. c. 15 cm. Male has brown forehead and crown feathers, tipped whitish on forehead, streaked white and tipped red on forecrown (red lost when worn), becoming largely red on hindcrown, pale golden-yellow nape and neck side; thin pale supercilium from rear upper edge of eye barely visible; olive-brown ear-coverts streaked whitish; whitish chin and malar region spotted or barred olive, usually very thin white moustachial line; yellowish-green upperparts sometimes

slightly bronzey, with yellow spots or bars, rump more distinctly barred, median wing-coverts with faint streaks or spots; darkish brown flight-feathers barred pale yellow to white; uppertail dark brown, barred paler; off-white underparts all narrowly barred olive, dark bars broader on breast and flanks, underwing barred brown and white; undertail as above, but barring stronger; long bill straight, quite broad across nostrils, blackish, paler base; iris deep brown to reddish; legs olive or grey. Distinguished from similar *V. affinis* by darker forehead and no red tinges. Female differs from male in having crown olive with pale spots, golden tips on hindcrown merging with yellow nape. Juvenile duller and more barred above than adult, with duller yellow nape, barring below more irregular and coarser, crown possibly with some red at front but insufficient details available. VOICE. Long series of vibrating sonorous "ew" notes, rising and then falling; different call reported in breeding season, but no details. Drums.

Habitat. Secondary forest and parks in lowlands and hills.

Food and Feeding. No information available.

Breeding. No information. Presumably breeds in Sept-Oct.

Movements. Probably resident.

Status and Conservation. Not globally threatened. Restricted-range species: present in Atlantic Forest Lowlands EBA. A very little-known woodpecker, but appears to be common in at least S part of range. Occurs in Serra dos Órgãos National Park, in Nova Lombardia Biological Reserve, and in Sooretama Biological Reserve. Research and field studies required to determine its ecology and breeding biology. Attempts to determine and subsequently monitor this species' population in this unique Brazilian habitat would appear to be desirable.

Bibliography. Alves *et al.* (1997), Buzzetti (2000), Mallet-Rodrigues *et al.* (1997), Mazar Barnett & Kirwan (2001), Meyer de Schauensee (1982), Olrog (1968), Parker & Goerck (1997), Ruschi (1979), Sargeant & Wall (1996), Scott & Brooke (1985), Short (1985b), Sick (1993), da Silva (1996), Souza (1999), Stattersfield *et al.* (1998), Stotz *et al.* (1996), Tobias *et al.* (1993), Venturini *et al.* (2001).

PLATE 38

Genus *PICULUS* Spix, 1824

135. Rufous-winged Woodpecker
Piculus simplex

French: Pic à ailes rousses   **German**: Zimtflügelspecht   **Spanish**: Carpintero Alirrufo

Taxonomy. *Chloronerpes simplex* Salvin, 1870, Bugaba, Chiriquí, Panama.
May form a superspecies with *P. callopterus*, *P. litae* and *P. leucolaemus*; all four have often been treated as conspecific. Proposed race *allophyeus*, from Honduras, known from only two specimens; further study needed. Monotypic.
Distribution. E Honduras S to Costa Rica and W Panama (W Chiriquí, W Bocas del Toro, Atlantic slope of Veraguas).
Descriptive notes. c. 18 cm; 51-55 g. Male has red forehead to hindneck, red lores, very broad red malar band; brownish-green ear-coverts, sometimes some red feather tips towards eye; pale brownish-green chin; bronze-green upperparts, including wing-coverts and tertials; flight-feathers mostly cinnamon-rufous, dark olive-brown outer webs and bars on inner webs; uppertail blackish, often an element of cinnamon-rufous in outer feathers; olive-green throat and upper breast, feathers of upper breast with pale buffish-yellow subterminal spots or wedges and darker tips, pale yellow-buff lower

breast to undertail-coverts barred dark olive; underwing-coverts cinnamon-rufous; fairly short bill slightly curved on culmen, relatively narrow across nostrils, blackish, paler grey lower mandible; iris pale bluish or yellowish to white; legs olive to greyish. Distinguished from *P. callopterus* by pale eyes, lack of pale stripe above malar. Female differs from male in having head mostly plain brownish-olive, red confined to nape and hindneck. Juvenile duller, greyer and greener, with throat to breast mottled or spotted buffish-green, barring below uneven, often a very short narrow yellowish-white stripe above malar, male with red only on rear crown to hindneck. VOICE. Loud, sharp, nasal "deeeah", more drawn out and higher than note of *P. rubiginosus*; loud, emphatic series of slightly nasal downslurred "heew" notes. Drums in long bursts.
Habitat. Canopy and edge of humid forest, sometimes large trees in adjacent semi-open terrain. Lowlands and foothills, locally to 750 m on Caribbean slope, to 900 m on Pacific slope.
Food and Feeding. Ants, beetles and their larvae. Occurs singly, less often in pairs; occasionally accompanies mixed-species flocks. Forages high in trees, but also at or below middle levels; prefers forest interior rather than edge. Pecks into mossy and rotting branches, lianas, and dead wood trapped in vine tangles; taps incessantly and irregularly.

Breeding. Feb-May. Nest-hole excavated 2·5-5 m up in recently dead tree or rotten stub. Clutch 2-4 eggs; no other information.
Movements. Resident.
Status and Conservation. Not globally threatened. Uncommon to fairly common. Occurs in Braulio Carrillo National Park and Guayabo National Monument, in Costa Rica.
Bibliography. Anon. (1998b), Blake & Loiselle (2000, 2001), Monroe (1968), Ridgely & Gwynne (1989), Skutch (1981), Slud (1960, 1964), Stiles (1985), Stiles & Skutch (1989), Stotz *et al.* (1996), Wetmore (1968a), Young *et al.* (1998).

136. Stripe-cheeked Woodpecker
Piculus callopterus

French: Pic bridé   **German**: Panamaspecht   **Spanish**: Carpintero Panameño

Taxonomy. *Chloronerpes callopterus* Lawrence, 1862, Lion Hill, Canal Zone, Panama.
May form a superspecies with *P. simplex*, *P. litae* and *P. leucolaemus*, and all four often treated as conspecific. Monotypic.
Distribution. WC to E Panama: Veraguas, and Caribbean slope of Canal Zone to Darién.

Descriptive notes. c. 17 cm. Male has red forehead to hindneck, greenish-yellow lores and side of head, short narrow yellowish-white stripe from lores to lower edge of ear-coverts, broad red malar band back to neck side; pale greenish chin; bronze-green upperparts, including wing-coverts and tertials; mostly cinnamon-rufous flight-feathers, dark olive-brown outer webs and bars on inner webs; uppertail blackish, often some cinnamon-rufous on outer feathers; greenish-olive throat and upper breast, pale yellowish spots on breast tending to form bar-like pattern, rest of underparts pale yellow with greenish-olive barring; underwing-coverts with some cinnamon-rufous; fairly short bill, culmen slightly curved, rather narrow across nostrils, blackish, paler lower mandible; iris red-brown to dark brown; legs olive-grey. Differs from *P. simplex* in dark eyes, yellow cheekstripe, more barred pattern on breast. Female has red on head restricted to rear. Juvenile duller than adult, more irregularly barred below, with mottled or barred upper breast, males without red moustache and crown. VOICE. No documented information; said to differ from that of *P. simplex*.
Habitat. Humid forest and forest borders in foothills on Caribbean slope, between 300 m and 900 m.
Food and Feeding. Small ants are only food items on record. Usually found singly or in pairs, also with mixed-species flocks. Forages on lower or middle parts of trees; pecks steadily.
Breeding. No relevant information available.
Movements. Presumed resident.
Status and Conservation. Not globally threatened. Restricted-range species: present in Central American Caribbean Slope EBA and Darién Lowlands EBA. Uncommon and local. Poorly known species; research required on its breeding behaviour and other details.
Bibliography. Anon. (1998b), Ridgely & Gwynne (1989), Robbins *et al.* (1985), Stattersfield *et al.* (1998), Wetmore (1968a).

137. Lita Woodpecker
Piculus litae

French: Pic de Lita   **German**: Litaspecht   **Spanish**: Carpintero de Lita

Taxonomy. *Chloronerpes litæ* Rothschild, 1901, Lita, Ecuador.
May form a superspecies with *P. simplex*, *P. callopterus* and *P. leucolaemus*, and all four have often been treated as conspecific. Frequently lumped with *P. leucolaemus*, but differs significantly in plumage details; possibly not even closely related. Includes SW Colombian birds formerly thought to represent an undescribed race of *P. flavigula*. Monotypic.
Distribution. W Colombia (Pacific slope of N Andes, middle Magdalena Valley) S to NW Ecuador (S to NW Pichincha).

Descriptive notes. c. 17-18 cm. Male has red forehead to hindneck, golden-yellow lores to ear-coverts and neck side, broad red malar with thin olive-yellow stripe below; dusky olive chin and throat with small white spots, appearing blackish in field; olive-yellow to bronze-green upperparts, including wing-coverts and tertials, yellower feather tips in fresh plumage, rump slightly darker; dark brown flight-feathers tipped black, outer webs edged olive, pale cinnamon-rufous area on inner webs; uppertail blackish, feathers edged greenish; whitish below with black wedge-shaped bars, coverts paler; shortish bill pointed, culmen slightly curved, broad across nostrils, light bluish, black tip; iris dark brown; legs dark slate-blue.
Distinguished from similar *P. leucolaemus* by smaller size, darker red on crown, more yellow on head, darker chin and throat. Female differs from male in having entire head yellow apart from red nape and malar. Juvenile duller and greener than adult, without red malar or head top, less yellow on head side, streaked throat. VOICE. Hissing "shreeyr" or "peessh", very like that of *P. leucolaemus* and *P. flavigula*.
Habitat. Humid and wet forest, also forest edges and mature second growth; in lowlands and foothills, to c. 800 m.
Food and Feeding. No details of diet; presumably insects and larvae. Forages singly, occasionally in pairs, in subcanopy and middle levels of forest.
Breeding. Very little information. Single observation, in Aug, of male excavating two holes 8 m and 10 m up large dead tree, with female in attendance; another possible nest in Jul.
Movements. Presumed resident.

Status and Conservation. Not globally threatened. Restricted-range species: present in Chocó EBA. Uncommon to locally common. Occurs in El Pangán Reserve (Colombia). Very poorly known; easily overlooked as it tends to remain in forest subcanopy; additional research and field study required. Extensive deforestation has occurred in range, and appears to be continuing unabated. In view of this, and the very small range, species should perhaps be considered Near-threatened.
Bibliography. Ridgely & Greenfield (2001), Ridgely *et al.* (1998), Rodner *et al.* (2000), Salaman (1994), Stattersfield *et al.* (1998).

138. White-throated Woodpecker
Piculus leucolaemus

French: Pic à gorge blanche   **German**: Weißkehlspecht   **Spanish**: Carpintero Gorgiblanco
Other common names: Rufous-winged Woodpecker(!)

Taxonomy. *Picus leucolaemus* Natterer and Malherbe, 1845, Brazil.
May form a superspecies with *P. simplex*, *P. callopterus* and *P. litae*; all four have often been treated as conspecific. Present species frequently lumped with *P. litae*, but differs significantly in plumage and possibly not even closely related. Depth of plumage coloration varies slightly, but with no obvious geographical pattern. Monotypic.
Distribution. S Colombia (Serranía de Churumbelos, in E Cauca) and E Ecuador E to W & C Amazonian Brazil and S to SE Peru and N Bolivia.

Descriptive notes. c. 19-20 cm; 69 g. Male has bright red forehead to hindneck, yellowish-green ear-coverts bordered below by golden-yellow band from bill base to rear neck side, broad red malar region; white chin and throat; bronze-green upperparts, wing-coverts and tertials, feathers tipped and edged yellow when fresh; dark brown flight-feathers, pale cinnamon-rufous on inner webs; uppertail blackish, edged greenish; yellowish-green upper breast with paler feather centres and darker tips, lower breast to undertail-coverts white with olive bars, underwing-coverts cinnamon; fairly short bill pointed, culmen slightly curved, broad across nostrils, blackish to grey; iris dark brown to red-brown; legs dark olive to blackish. Distinguished from similar *P. litae* by slightly bigger size, less yellow on head, all-white chin and throat. Female has red on head restricted to small nape patch. Juvenile greener than adult, without male's red malar and crown. VOICE. Harsh sibilant "piissh" or "shreeyr", heard infrequently.
Habitat. Tall, humid *terra firme* forest and lowland *várzea* forest along rivers; recorded at edge of primary forest and in second growth in Colombia. Lowlands and foothills, to 1000 m in Ecuador and to 1400 m in Peru.
Food and Feeding. Diet not recorded; presumably insects and their larvae. Usually forages singly, occasionally in pairs; will join mixed flocks. Forages in canopy down to mid-levels. Probes, flakes off bark.
Breeding. No information.
Movements. Presumed resident.
Status and Conservation. Not globally threatened. Rare to locally uncommon in Ecuador; recent records from only seven sites. Uncommon in Peru; occurs in Manu National Park and surrounding area. First recorded in Colombia in 1998; possibly overlooked previously. A poorly known species. Uncertainty over its taxonomic position has made assessment of any past records very difficult.
Bibliography. Allen (1995), Angehr & Aucca (1997), Balchin & Toyne (1998), Brace *et al.* (1997), Butler (1979), Clements & Shany (2001), Donahue (1994), Dubs (1992), Hilty (1997), Hilty & Brown (1986), Hornbuckle (1999), Mazar Barnett & Kirwan (1999), Meyer de Schauensee (1982), Olrog (1968), Parker *et al.* (1982), Perry *et al.* (1997), Remsen & Traylor (1989), Ridgely & Greenfield (2001), Ridgely *et al.* (1998), Robinson & Terborgh (1997), Sick (1993), da Silva (1996), Stotz *et al.* (1996), Terborgh *et al.* (1984), Willis & Oniki (1990).

139. Yellow-throated Woodpecker
Piculus flavigula

French: Pic à gorge jaune   **German**: Gelbkehlspecht   **Spanish**: Carpintero Gorgigualdo

Taxonomy. *Picus flavigula* Boddaert, 1783, Cayenne.
E race *erythropis*, with distinctive plumage and different habitat preferences, possibly a separate species. Race *magnus* intergrades with nominate in NE Brazil. Birds from SW Colombia, previously thought to represent an undescribed race of present species, have now been reidentified as *P. litae*. Three subspecies recognized.
Subspecies and Distribution.
P. f. flavigula (Boddaert, 1783) - Extreme E Colombia, S Venezuela and the Guianas, S to N Amazonia.
P. f. magnus (Cherrie & Reichenberger, 1921) - SE Colombia, NE Ecuador and Amazonian Brazil S to E Peru, NE Bolivia and Mato Grosso.
P. f. erythropis (Vieillot, 1818) - E Brazil in Pernambuco and from Bahia to São Paulo.

Descriptive notes. 19-20 cm; 44-63 g (*flavigula*). Male has bright red forehead to nape with dark feather bases, yellowish-green lores, short red malar band; rest of head, including chin and throat, bright golden-yellow; entire upperparts yellowish-green, brighter on mantle and back, occasionally a few paler spots on rump; brownish-black flight-feathers, inner webs with cinnamon patches; uppertail black, edged greenish; green below, breast with whitish feather centres and dark tips, pattern more barred or scaly on belly and undertail-coverts; underwing with paler coverts somewhat barred; shortish bill pointed, culmen slightly curved, narrow across nostrils, black, paler base; iris brown; legs dark green-grey. Female lacks red on crown and malar,

---

On following page: 140. Golden-green Woodpecker (*Piculus chrysochloros*); 141. Yellow-browed Woodpecker (*Piculus aurulentus*).

having these areas more golden to yellow with green tips. Juvenile duller and greener above than adult, less yellow on head, darker and less marked below but still yellow throat, male sometimes with some red on crown, female with crown entirely green. Race *magnus* has malar area golden-yellow in both sexes; *erythropis* is smaller than others, distinctive, male with red extending variably over neck side and from malar over chin and throat, female with golden-yellow forecrown, malar and throat, throat usually with red markings, both with entire underparts more barred than spotted or scaly. VOICE. Far-carrying hissing "queea" or "shaa, gheh" or "shreeyr", sometimes doubled, given at infrequent intervals; rattle-type call "kee" in series 6-8 seconds long, slowing towards end.

Habitat. Tall, humid *terra firme* forest and seasonally inundated *várzea* forest along rivers; also forest edge. Also drier forest types (*caatinga*) in E Brazil. Lowlands; below 300 m in Ecuador, to 500 m in Peru.

Food and Feeding. Mainly ants (*Camponotus*, *Pheidole*, *Crematogaster*) recorded in diet. Met with singly, in well-separated pairs, or in mixed-species flocks. Forages at middle levels in subcanopy up to treetops, on limbs, branches and trunks. More vigorous feeding techniques, such as pecking and hammering, seem to be commonest; flakes off pieces of bark, also probes.

Breeding. Probably breeds in Nov in Colombia and Venezuela; May-Jul in the Guianas, and Aug-Dec in Brazil to Bolivia. Hole built in stub, apparently not very high up, rarely to 15 m. Clutch size and incubation and fledging periods not documented.

Movements. Resident.

Status and Conservation. Not globally threatened. Rather common throughout most of range; rare to uncommon in Ecuador and Peru. Occurs in Canaima National Park and Imataca Forest Reserve and El Dorado (Venezuela), Cuyabeno Reserve (Ecuador) and Serra dos Órgãos National Park, Rio Cristalino Private Reserve and Sooretama Biological Reserve (Brazil).

Bibliography. Aleixo (1997), Aleixo & Galetti (1997), Allen (1995), Buzzetti (2000), Clements & Shany (2001), Cohn-Haft *et al.* (1997), Donahue (1994), Ferreira de Vasconcelos & Melo-Júnior (2001), Figueiredo & Lo (2000), Friedmann (1948), Goerck (1999), Guix *et al.* (1999), Haverschmidt & Mees (1994), Hilty & Brown (1986), Meyer de Schauensee & Phelps (1978), Oren & Parker (1997), Parker & Goerck (1997), Parker *et al.* (1982), Remsen & Traylor (1989), Ridgely & Greenfield (2001), Scott & Brooke (1985), Sick (1993), da Silva (1996), Snyder (1966), Stotz, Fitzpatrick *et al.* (1996), Stotz, Lanyon *et al.* (1997), Thiollay & Jullien (1998), Tostain *et al.* (1992).

140. Golden-green Woodpecker

Piculus chrysochloros

French: Pic vert-doré **German**: Bronzespecht **Spanish**: Carpintero Verdiamarillo

Taxonomy. *Picus chrysochloros* Vieillot, 1818, Paraguay and Brazil.

Forms a superspecies with *P. aurulentus*. Specific name sometimes misspelt as *chrysochlorus*. Racial differentiation partly obscured by considerable individual variation; birds in S Colombia (Putumayo) and NE Ecuador lacking red malar stripe may possibly represent a new, as yet unnamed race; further study needed, possibly also taxonomic revision. Nine subspecies recognized.

Subspecies and Distribution.

P. c. aurosus (Nelson, 1912) - E Panama.
P. c. xanthochlorus (P. L. Sclater & Salvin, 1875) - N Colombia and NW Venezuela.
P. c. capistratus (Malherbe, 1862) - SE Colombia and NW Brazil E to Surinam.
P. c. guianensis Todd, 1937 - French Guiana.
P. c. paraensis (Snethlage, 1907) - NE Brazil.
P. c. laemostictus Todd, 1937 - NW Brazil.
P. c. hypochryseus Todd, 1937 - W Brazil S to N Bolivia.
P. c. chrysochloros (Vieillot, 1818) - C & S Brazil S to E Bolivia, W Paraguay and N Argentina (Formosa S to Santa Fe).
P. c. polyzonus (Valenciennes, 1826) - SE Brazil (Espírito Santo, Rio de Janeiro).

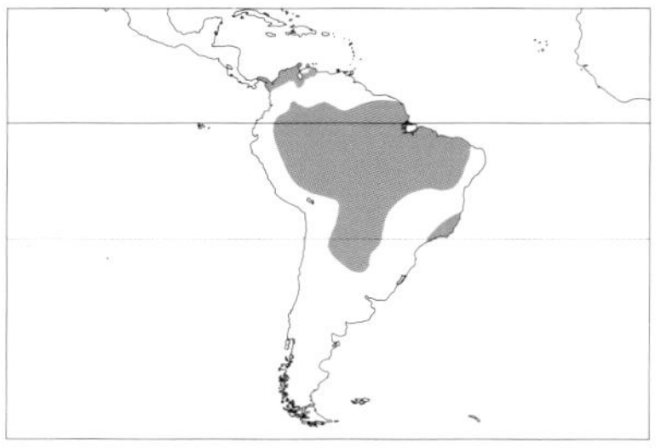

Descriptive notes. 18-21 cm (*chrysochloros*), 26-27 cm (*capistratus*, *polyzonus*); 55 g (*chrysochloros*), 62-91 g (*capistratus*). Male has red forehead to nape, olive-green lores, area around eye, ear-coverts and rear neck side, pale yellow stripe from lower lores to hindneck, short red malar band bordered below by olive-green stripe; yellow chin and upper throat; olive-green upperparts, darker olive-brown wings; uppertail dark olive-brown; pale yellow-buff underparts entirely barred olive-brown, underwing largely cinnamon; longish bill slightly curved, broad across nostrils, dark grey to blackish, paler base; iris white or bluish-white; legs greyish-green. Differs from *P. aurulentus* in yellower underparts, lack of yellow stripe behind eye. Female lacks red on head, has forehead to nape olive, malar olive-brown. Juvenile much as respective adult, but duller, less regularly marked, darker eyes. Races differ greatly in size and plumage: *aurosus* is small, very yellow in tone, golden-yellow throat, yellow ground colour below, female with yellow crown; *xanthochlorus* is similar to previous, but generally duller in colour; *capistratus* is very large, darker, more olive-green, with less red in malar, barred throat, whitish to pale greenish-white ground colour below; *guianensis* resembles last, but usually has unbarred throat; *paraensis* is intermediate in size, has deeper golden or cinnamon-buff cheekstripe and throat, and often entire ground colour of underparts, male with green (not red) malar, female with greenish-yellow crown; *laemostictus* is quite big, rather dark, less yellow, with plain whitish throat; *hypochryseus* is very like previous, perhaps slightly larger; *polyzonus* is large, with pale yellow cheekstripe, unmarked pale yellow throat, yellow ground colour below, sometimes barred pale primary coverts. VOICE. Shrill sibilant "shreer", sometimes doubled, uttered infrequently.

Habitat. Humid *terra firme* and *várzea* forest, rainforest, also deciduous forest, patches of wood in savanna and in xerophytic vegetation; also visits forest edge, tall trees in clearings and pastures, often near water or marshy ground. Lowlands; to 450 m in NW Venezuela and at 100-650 m in S; to 500 m in Colombia; mostly below 300 m but locally to 600 m in Ecuador, and to 650 m in Peru.

Food and Feeding. Ants (*Camponotus*) and termites (Isoptera) recorded. Forages singly, in pairs, or in mixed-species flocks. Forages rather high in subcanopy of forest interior, sometimes lower; ventures to edge or into open or semi-open. Gleaning seems to be commonest feeding technique; also pecks, and excavates to obtain subsurface prey, with intensive use of the tongue.

Breeding. Records from Colombia suggest breeding in Feb-Mar; in Sept in Argentina. Nest-hole in tree or in arboreal nest of insects. No data on clutch size and incubation and fledging periods.

Movements. Resident.

Status and Conservation. Not globally threatened. Status uncertain, possibly not uncommon in much of range. Rare to uncommon and local in Ecuador; uncommon in Peru. Occurs in several protected areas, including Tayrona National Park (Colombia), Cuyabeno Reserve (Ecuador) and Rio Cristalino Private Reserve (Brazil). Despite large range, this species is not particularly well known. Further research required on its taxonomy, which may possibly indicate that some populations should be regarded as separate species; in that case, status of these would need to be established.

Bibliography. Allen (1995), Brace *et al.* (1997), Canevari *et al.* (1991), Clements & Shany (2001), Cohn-Haft *et al.* (1997), Contreras *et al.* (1990), Donahue (1994), Friedmann (1948), Haverschmidt & Mees (1994), Hayes (1995), Hilty & Brown (1986), Meyer de Schauensee & Phelps (1978), Munn (1985), Oren & Parker (1997), Parker & Goerck (1997), de la Peña (1994), Remsen & Traylor (1989), Ridgely & Greenfield (2001), Ridgely & Gwynne (1989), Robinson & Terborgh (1997), Scott & Brooke (1985), Short (1974b, 1975), Sick (1993), Snyder (1966), Stotz, Fitzpatrick *et al.* (1996), Stotz, Lanyon *et al.* (1997), Terborgh *et al.* (1984), Thiollay & Jullien (1998), Tostain *et al.* (1992), Wetmore (1926, 1968a).

141. Yellow-browed Woodpecker

Piculus aurulentus

French: Pic à bandeaux **German**: Weißbrauenspecht **Spanish**: Carpintero Cejigualdo
Other common names: White-browed Woodpecker

Taxonomy. *Picus aurulentus* Temminck, 1821, Paraguay and Brazil.

Forms a superspecies with *P. chrysochloros*. Monotypic.

Distribution. SE Brazil (São Paulo, E Minas Gerais and W Espírito Santo S to Rio Grande do Sul), E Paraguay and NE Argentina (Misiones, NE Corrientes).

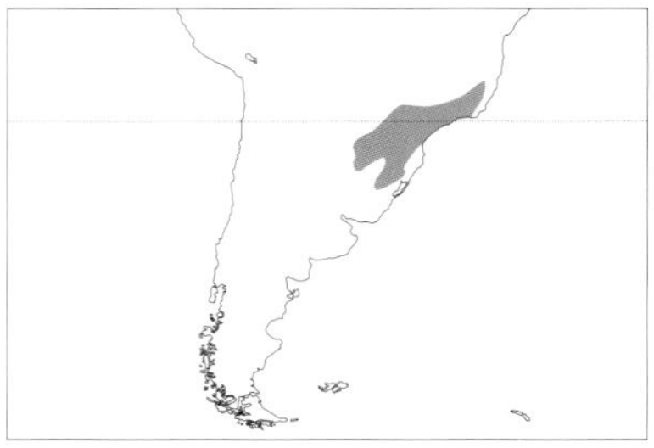

Descriptive notes. 21-22 cm; 22-68 g. Male has bright red forehead to nape with very thin olive border, narrow pale yellowish-white supercilium from eye to nape side; dark olive-green area around eye, ear-coverts and rear neck side, pale yellow band from lores to neck side, red malar stripe becoming green at rear; pale golden chin and throat, often some red on side of chin; olive-green hindneck and upperparts, including tertials, sometimes with faint bronze tinge; dark brown flight-feathers edged greenish, dark-barred cinnamon-rufous patch on inner webs; uppertail blackish; whitish underparts densely and broadly barred dark olive, cinnamon-rufous underwing mostly barred black; medium-length bill slightly curved on culmen, fairly broad across nostrils, blackish-grey, paler base of lower mandible; iris chestnut-brown, orbital ring dark grey; legs greenish-grey. Distinguished from *P. chrysochloros* by pale supercilium, whiter underparts with broader dark bars. Female differs from male in having forehead and crown olive, occasionally with golden tips, and only little red in malar. Juvenile much as respective adult, but duller, with coarser barring. VOICE. Single, sharp loud note, and descending series of plaintive "eeeww" notes. Drums in rapid, regular rolls.

Habitat. Humid montane forest, forest edge, and dense second growth and woodland; also humid lowland forest. Present at 750-2000 m in Brazil, though generally lower in Paraguay and Argentina.

Food and Feeding. Ants and their larvae and eggs. Singly or in pairs. Forages in middle tiers, by gleaning and pecking.

Breeding. Sept in Argentina. Nest high up, to 7 m, in tree. No other information.

Movements. Presumably resident.

Status and Conservation. Not globally threatened. Considered Near-threatened. Rather uncommon; apparently shy in nature, and not often seen. Apparent extension towards S in Rio Grande do Sul recorded in 1994 and 1995, possibly overlooked previously. Occurs in Serra dos Órgãos and Itatiaia National Parks and Serra do Mar State Park (Brazil). Much of this species' forest habitat has already been lost, and surviving patches continue to be destroyed by clearance and uncontrolled fires; montane forest in SE Brazil appears to have remained more intact, providing a relatively safe refuge, but this situation could easily change for the worse. Further field studies required to determine more about this woodpecker's requirements, and monitoring of the population is desirable.

Bibliography. dos Anjos (2001), dos Anjos & Schuchmann (1997), dos Anjos *et al.* (1997), Belton (1984), Bencke & Kindel (1999), Brooks *et al.* (1993), Buzzetti (2000), Canevari *et al.* (1991), Efe *et al.* (2000), Ferreira de Vasconcelos & Melo-Júnior (2001), Figueiredo & Lo (2000), Goerck (1999), Guix *et al.* (1999), Hayes (1995), Lowen, Bartrina *et al.* (1996), Lowen, Clay *et al.* (1995), Madroño, Clay & Hostettler (1997), Madroño, Clay, Robbins *et al.* (1997), Maurício & Dias (1998), Meyer de Schauensee (1982), Olrog (1968), Pacheco *et al.* (1996), Parker & Goerck (1997), de la Peña (1994), do Rosário (1996), Saibene *et al.* (1996), Scott & Brooke (1985), Short (1985b), Sick (1993), Stattersfield & Capper (2000), Stotz *et al.* (1996), Tobias *et al.* (1993).

PLATE 39 ➤

142

♀

♂

ssp *rubiginosus*
♀

ssp *aeruginosus*
♀

♂

143

ssp *paraquensis* ♂

ssp *buenavistae* ♀

ssp *guianae* ♂

ssp *yucatanensis* ♂

ssp *chrysogaster* ♂

ssp *viridissimus* ♂

ssp *gularis* ♀

♂

ssp *rubripileus* ♀

ssp *tucumanus* ♂

ssp *rivolii* ♀

♂

144

♂

ssp *atriceps* ♀

♀

145

ssp *atricollis* ♂

ssp *peruvianus* ♂

ssp *brevirostris* ♂

ssp *melanolaimus* ♀

♂

ssp *punctigula* ♀

146

♂

ssp *guttatus* ♂

♀

ssp *ujhelyii* ♂

ssp *leucofrenatus* ♂

147

ssp *nattereri* ♂

ssp *melanochloros* ♂

PLATE 39

inches 5

cm 13

142. **Grey-crowned Woodpecker**
Piculus auricularis

French: Pic à tête grise **German**: Graukappenspecht **Spanish**: Carpintero Cabecigrís

Taxonomy. *Chloronerpes auricularis* Salvin and Godman, 1889, Xautipa, Sierra Madre del Sur, Guerrero, Mexico.
Forms a superspecies with *P. rubiginosus*, and sometimes considered conspecific. Greyer birds from SE Sonora, named as race *sonoriensis*, unacceptable, based on worn specimens. Monotypic.
Distribution. Pacific slope of W Mexico, from S Sonora to Oaxaca.

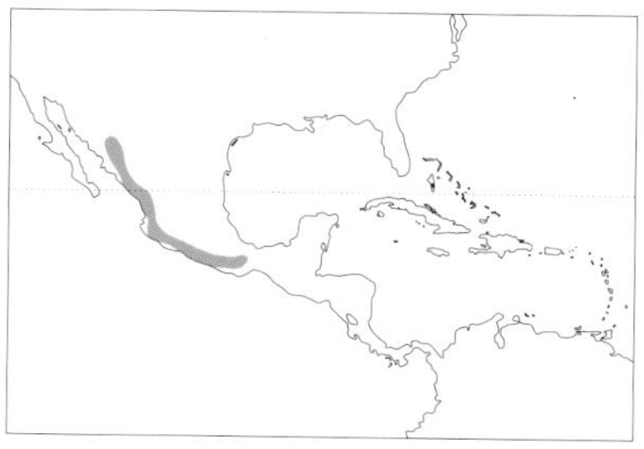

Descriptive notes. c. 16-17 cm; 52-68 g. Male has grey to green-grey forehead to nape, often red at crown and nape sides, buff lores, area around eye and ear-coverts, red malar stripe, sometimes also small red patch on lores; olive neck side and hindneck barred paler; chin and throat streaked or barred olive and white; green to greyish-green upperparts, greyer when worn, faintly barred, wing-coverts tinged deep golden-bronze; darker flight-feathers with greenish-yellow area on inner webs; uppertail brown, feathers edged greenish; pale cream-white to yellowish below with broad dark olive bars, densest on breast, pale yellowish underwing, yellow undertail; medium-length bill straight, narrow, blackish; iris hazel-brown; legs green-grey. Distinguished from *P. rubiginosus* by smaller size, no red on nape. Female differs in having malar barred olive and whitish, not red. Juvenile duller than adult, with less regular barring, male with grey in malar. Voice. Single explosive "kee-ah", mewing "growh"; also rapid shrill rattle, similar to that of *P. rubiginosus*.
Habitat. Humid to mesic forests and forest edge; locally also highland pine-oak (*Pinus-Quercus*) forest and tropical deciduous oak forest. Lowlands to foothills, mostly from 900 m to 2400 m.
Food and Feeding. Little information. Diet includes berries; forages from high levels down to low ones.
Breeding. No data. Probably similar to *P. rubiginosus*.
Movements. Resident.
Status and Conservation. Not globally threatened. Fairly common to common. Very poorly known species; requires field research to determine various aspects of its behaviour. No known threats, but little information.
Bibliography. Anon. (1998b), Baptista (1978), Binford (1989), Friedmann *et al.* (1957), Hernández *et al.* (1995), Howell & Webb (1995), Hutto (1980, 1992), Peterson & Navarro-Sigüenza (2000), Schaldach (1963), Short (1985b), Stotz *et al.* (1996).

143. **Golden-olive Woodpecker**
Piculus rubiginosus

French: Pic or-olive **German**: Olivmantelspecht **Spanish**: Carpintero Oliváceo
Other common names: Green Woodpecker(!), Blue-headed Woodpecker; Bronze-winged Woodpecker (*aeruginosus* group)

Taxonomy. *Picus rubiginosus* Swainson, 1820, Caracas, Venezuela.
Forms a superspecies with *P. auricularis*, and sometimes regarded as conspecific. N races *aeruginosus* and *yucatanensis* possibly represent a distinct species, apparently differing in vocalizations. Considerable individual variation in coloration and pattern, making defining and delimitation of races difficult; those listed best regarded as a tentative general guide, requiring clarification through further research. Additional named races include *maximus* (E & C Pacific highlands of SE Mexico and Guatemala), *differens* (Pacific slope of Guatemala), *uropygialis* (mountains of Costa Rica and W Panama), and in Colombia *pacificus* (W Andes), *michaelis* (SE Nariño), *palmitae* (W slope of E Andes in N) and *nuchalis* (E slope of Andes near Ecuador border), all of which fall within range of variation of other races. Nineteen subspecies recognized.
Subspecies and Distribution.
P. r. aeruginosus (Malherbe, 1862) - E Mexico (Tamaulipas to Veracruz).
P. r. yucatanensis (Cabot, 1844) - S Mexico (from Oaxaca) S to W Panama.
P. r. alleni (Bangs, 1902) - N Colombia (Santa Marta area).
P. r. meridensis (Ridgway, 1911) - NW Venezuela.
P. r. rubiginosus (Swainson, 1820) - NC & NE Venezuela.
P. r. tobagensis (Ridgway, 1911) - Tobago.
P. r. trinitatis (Ridgway, 1911) - Trinidad.
P. r. deltanus Alvedo & Ginés, 1953 - Delta Amacuro in NE Venezuela.
P. r. paraquensis Phelps, Sr. & Phelps, Jr., 1947 - mountains of SC Venezuela.
P. r. viridissimus Chapman, 1939 - Auyán tepui in SE Venezuela.
P. r. guianae (Hellmayr, 1918) - E Venezuela and adjacent Guyana.
P. r. nigriceps Blake, 1941 - Acarai Mts of S Guyana and adjacent S Surinam.
P. r. gularis (Hargitt, 1889) - W & C Andes in Colombia.
P. r. rubripileus (Salvadori & Festa, 1900) - SW Colombia, W Ecuador and NW Peru.
P. r. buenavistae (Chapman, 1915) - E Andes in Colombia and E Ecuador.
P. r. coloratus (Chapman, 1923) - extreme SE Ecuador and NC Peru.
P. r. chrysogaster (Berlepsch & Stolzmann, 1902) - C Peru.
P. r. canipileus (d'Orbigny, 1840) - C & SE Bolivia.
P. r. tucumanus (Cabanis, 1883) - S Bolivia to NW Argentina (S to Tucumán).
Descriptive notes. c. 18-23 cm; 51-68 g (*trinitatis*), 51-72 g (*meridensis*), 69-82 g (*aeruginosus*), 74-84 g (*gularis*), 77-88 g (*rubripileus*), 78-86 g (*yucatanensis*). Male has dark slate-grey forehead and crown with narrow red border, red nape, pale buff to whitish lores, area around eye and ear-coverts, broad red malar stripe expanding slightly at rear; neck side barred yellow-buff and olive; pale buffish-white chin and upper throat heavily streaked blackish; green upperparts and tertials with slight bronze tinge, rump and uppertail-coverts paler with dark olive barring; dark brownish-olive flight-feathers edged green, yellowish on shafts extending slightly on to inner webs of primaries; uppertail brown; pale buffish-yellow underparts entirely barred blackish-olive, bars closest on breast; underwing largely

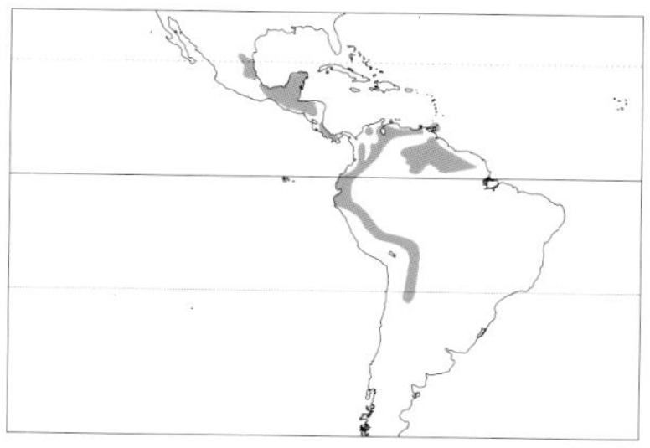

yellow; medium-length bill broad, culmen curved, slaty to black; iris deep dull red; legs grey to olive-grey. Female lacks red on crown side and malar, has latter streaked like throat. Juvenile much as respective adult but much duller, with pattern less regular. Races differ greatly in size, also in plumage tone, strength of barring below, throat colour, and amount of red on male's crown, but much variation: *aeruginosus* is larger than nominate, proportionately long-tailed, has distinctly green back, bronze-edged green wings, less barred rump, blackish breast with pale scallop-like markings rather than bars, male with less red on side of crown, female with narrower U-shaped red band; *yucatanensis* is similar to last, but more red on side of crown, coarsely barred breast less dark, variable, tends to be slightly larger and greener in highlands than in lowlands, and lowland populations decrease in size from N to S; *alleni* is large, bronze-gold with some red tinges above, has rump more or less unbarred, white-spotted black throat, narrow blackish breast bars, male with moderate red on crown; *tobagensis* resembles last, but breast bars less black, more green, and broader; *trinitatis* is much smaller than previous, with less heavy bill; *deltanus* is small, with greener back, larger white throat spots; *paraquensis* is large, has strong bronze tinge to back, very dark crown with much-reduced red, some females with no red in crown; *viridissimus* is very large, bright yellow-green on back, breast has whitish ground colour, very black broad barring, male with much less red on head; *guianae* is smaller than previous, with back more bronzy, very fine pale spots on black throat, moderate red in crown; *nigriceps* resembles last, but bronze tinge more or less lacking; *buenavistae* is very large, has back bronzy with reddish tinge, well-barred rump, bars below olive-green; *meridensis* is somewhat smaller than last, with less bronzy back; *gularis* is rather large, has black throat finely spotted white (rarely, no spots), rather pale underparts, male with forehead to nape entirely red, female with slightly less red; *rubripileus* as previous but smaller, with breast bars blacker; *coloratus* has bright yellow belly with barred flanks, is only slightly bronzy above; *chrysogaster* has yellow belly unbarred, back very bronzy with red tinge, male usually with much red on crown; *canipileus* is similar to last, but belly weakly barred; *tucumanus* is large, with thin bill, duller green back less bronzy, whiter underparts, blackish barring. Voice. Loud, clear "dree" repeated c. 6 times in 2-3 seconds, higher-pitched and faster than that of *Melanerpes*, as long-distance call; also single sharp "deeeeh", "geep" or "keeah"; also "churr", "choo-úr" (first note longer than second); liquid "woick-woick-woick" or "utzia-deek" in interactions; low whirring notes in intimate contacts; race *aeruginosus* sharp "kyown" singly or in short series, also sharp "weeyk" or "wheeir" in series of 10 notes per 4-6 seconds, also short low chatter.
Habitat. Wide range of habitats occupied, both humid and dry. Rainforest and cloudforest, dry cloudforest, heavy epiphyte-laden forest, and their edges, also adjacent clearings and semi-open parts with scattered trees, and second growth; also oak-pine (*Quercus-Pinus*) woodland, dry deciduous oak forest, riparian thickets, mangroves; commonly associated also with trees bordering fields and coffee plantations with shade trees, as well as with clearings with scattered trees in mountainous terrain. In Mexico, race *aeruginosus* occurs in lowlands and foothills with cottonwoods (*Populus*), mesquite (*Prosopis*) and cacti. From near sea-level and foothills to highlands; to 2100 m in Mexico; from 750 m, rarely 400 m, to 2150 m in Central America; 350-2100 m in Venezuela, but to 2800 m in N & NW and down to sea-level in Orinoco Delta; 900-3100 m in Colombia, and to 2300 m in Ecuador, Peru and Bolivia; at 1000-2500 m in Argentina.
Food and Feeding. Ants, termites (Isoptera), beetles and their wood-boring larvae; rarely, fruits and berries. Generally singly, or in pairs with partners maintaining loose contact; also in mixed-species groups. Forages in interior of forest, but most frequently seen in more open places near tall forest; often sits quietly on horizontal perch in top of a tree. Forages at middle levels to upper canopy; also descends lower, but seems not to feed on the ground. Explores limbs, branches and vines, and tree trunks; usually on large trees, also on low stubs and fence posts along hedgerows and edges. Moves slowly when working up a tree. Commonest techniques are pecking, hammering (live soft bark, soft green wood), pecking with probing, surface probing, prying into crevices; gleaning plays a minor role. In particular, probes among vines, dense foliage, or into clusters of epiphytes or on mossy branches; tears apart bromeliads to reach food items. Opens cocoa pods to obtain insects inside.
Breeding. Jan-May from Mexico to Colombia and Trinidad; recorded in Oct in Guyana and Ecuador. Hole excavated 1·2-18 m up in dead or live stub or tree, or in palm. Clutch 2-4 eggs; both sexes incubate, in long stints, period not documented; nestlings fed at long intervals, by regurgitation, male apparently making greater contribution; nestling period c. 24 days.
Movements. Resident.
Status and Conservation. Not globally threatened. Common throughout most of range; common to fairly common in Central America; fairly common on Pacific slope in Ecuador and Peru, less common on E side. Occurs in many protected areas in range, including El Triunfo and Ría Lagartos Biosphere Reserves (Mexico), Tikal National Park (Guatemala), Guayabo National Monument and Monteverde Biological Reserve (Costa Rica), La Planada, Río Ñambí and El Pangán Reserves (Colombia), Henri Pittier, Macarao and Cueva de los Guácharos National Parks (Venezuela), Tinalandia Reserve (Ecuador), Asa Wright Nature Centre (Trinidad), Machu Picchu Historical Sanctuary (Peru), and El Rey and Calilegua National Parks (Argentina). This widespread species' ability to live in a wide variety of wooded habitats suggests that its future is secure.
Bibliography. Balchin & Toyne (1998), Baptista (1978), Barrowclough *et al.* (1995), Binford (1989), Bloch *et al.* (1991), Bond *et al.* (1989), Canevari *et al.* (1991), Chapman (1931), Clements & Shany (2001), Fjeldså & Krabbe (1990), Haverschmidt & Mees (1994), Heisler (1994), Herklots (1961), Hernández *et al.* (1995), Hilty (1997), Hilty & Brown (1986), Howell & Webb (1995), Ibáñez (2000), Krabbe *et al.* (1996), Meyer de Schauensee & Phelps (1978), Miller (1963), Monroe (1968), Nores *et al.* (2000), de la Peña (1994), Pople *et al.* (1997), Ridgely & Greenfield (2001), Ridgely & Gwynne (1989), Rowley (1984), Salaman (1994), Schmitt *et al.* (1997), Short (1985b), Sick (1993), Skutch (1956, 1969a), Slud (1964), Snyder (1966), Stiles (1985), Stotz *et al.* (1996), Sutton (1953), Thiollay & Jullien (1998), Tostain *et al.* (1992), Walker (2001), Wetmore (1968a).

144. **Crimson-mantled Woodpecker**
Piculus rivolii

French: Pic de Rivoli **German**: Rotmantelspecht **Spanish**: Carpintero Candela

Taxonomy. *Picus Rivolii* Boissonneau, 1840, no locality = near Bogotá, Colombia.

On following pages: 145. Black-necked Woodpecker (*Colaptes atricollis*); 146. Spot-breasted Woodpecker (*Colaptes punctigula*); 147. Green-barred Woodpecker (*Colaptes melanochloros*).

Races rather poorly differentiated except for *atriceps*. Five subspecies recognized.
Subspecies and Distribution.
P. r. rivolii (Boissonneau, 1840) - NW Venezuela (Sierra de Perijá) S in Andes to EC Colombia.
P. r. meridae (Chapman, 1923) - W Venezuela (Mérida, Táchira).
P. r. quindiuna (Chapman, 1923) - Andes of NC Colombia.
P. r. brevirostris (Taczanowski, 1875) - SW Colombia S to C Peru.
P. r. atriceps (P. L. Sclater & Salvin, 1876) - SE Peru and W & C Bolivia.

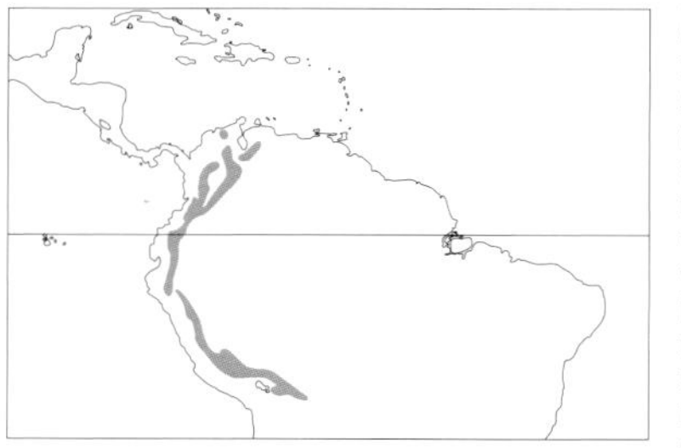

Descriptive notes. 22-28 cm; 85-97 g (*brevirostris*), 100-112 g (*rivolii*). Male has black forehead to hindcrown feathers broadly tipped red, bright red nape, hindneck and lower neck side; pale yellowish lores, area around eyes and ear-coverts, black malar feathers broadly tipped red; black chin and upper throat speckled with white; red upperparts with olive feather bases variably visible, lower back olive and often black-barred, rump and uppertail-coverts black narrowly fringed whitish; wing-coverts mainly red, olive bases and inner webs; dark brown flight-feathers edged olive, outer edges of secondaries dark red; uppertail black; lower throat and breast black with whitish and red feather edges, appearing scalloped, belly to undertail-coverts golden or golden-buff, usually a few black bar-like spots on upper flanks (sometimes extending farther down); underwing with at least some yellow; undertail blackish, yellow at base; in worn plumage, when brighter feather tips lost, plumage blacker on crown, more olive on upperparts, solidly black on throat and breast; shortish to fairly long bill broad-based, culmen curved, blackish; iris red-brown to brown; legs grey or brown-grey. Female lacks red on malar and crown, which are instead solid black. Juvenile duller than adult, mottled blackish, olive and dull red above, with breast all blackish, belly more brownish-buff, male with a few narrow red tips on crown. Race *meridae* is very like nominate, but bill shorter, wing on average longer; *quindiuna* also much as nominate, but female has some red in crown; *brevirostris* has more black on forehead of male, paler yellow belly, more spots on flanks; *atriceps* is distinctive, with noticeably shorter bill, both sexes have black forehead and crown, olive-tinged ear-coverts, darker more bronzy-olive upperparts, little or no red in flight-feathers, paler ground colour below, breast feathers with no red tips, bar-like spotting tends to reach farther down on flanks. Voice. Sharp, upward-inflected "kawíp" or "kre-ép", sometimes in short series, and loud rolling "chrrr-rr-r-r", like *Colaptes*; also "kick-kick-kick-kick-kick-kick-kick" and fast repeated "wik" as long-distance calls; does not call often. Both sexes drum, described as slow, or as fast short bursts.
Habitat. Tall humid and wet montane forests, especially mossy and epiphyte-rich rainforest and cloudforest, also forest edge, clearings with some trees, dry cloudforest; also dwarf forest at timber-line, venturing into adjacent *páramo* as well. Occurs at 950-3700 m in Venezuela, 1800-3200 m in Colombia, mostly 1900-3300 m in Ecuador, and to 3700 m in Peru; locally in smaller numbers down to 700 m.
Food and Feeding. Ants and their brood, beetle larvae, occasional spiders and millipedes (Diplopoda); some fruit also consumed. Forages alone, in pairs or in family groups, and often joins mixed-species flocks; quiet and inconspicuous, moves slowly. Forages at practically all levels, mostly high; intermittently descends to ground to search for ants, or to feed at *Puya* and *Espletia* flowers. Inspects surfaces of thicker branches overgrown with moss and epiphytes, pays particular attention to bases of epiphytes and leaves. Often feeds in open, also in dense vegetation. Probes, gleans and pecks; hammering not a typical technique.
Breeding. Recorded in Feb-Mar in Colombia and Jun-Nov in Peru. No other details documented.
Movements. Resident. Presumably altitudinal movements may occur sometimes.
Status and Conservation. Not globally threatened. Fairly common. Uncommon to fairly common and widespread in Ecuador; fairly common in Peru. Unobtrusive behaviour suggests that it is perhaps overlooked. Occurs in Pasochoa Forest Reserve and Podocarpus National Park (Ecuador) and Machu Picchu Historical Sanctuary (Peru); observed along Pico Humboldt Trail (Venezuela). Ability to survive in partially deforested areas and its rather frequent occurrence at trees in more open areas suggests that it is unlikely to become threatened in the near future.
Bibliography. Angehr & Aucca (1997), Bloch *et al*. (1991), Butler (1979), Clements & Shany (2001), Cresswell, Hughes *et al*. (1999), Cresswell, Mellanby *et al*. (1999), Davies *et al*. (1994), Fjeldså & Krabbe (1990), Hilty & Brown (1986), Hornbuckle (1999), Kirwan & Marlow (1996), Meyer de Schauensee & Phelps (1978), Moynihan (1979), Parker, Parker & Plenge (1982), Parker, Schulenberg *et al*. (1985), Poulsen (1996), Remsen (1985), Remsen & Traylor (1989), Ridgely & Gaulin (1980), Ridgely & Greenfield (2001), Ridgely *et al*. (1998), Salaman (1994), Short (1985b), Stotz *et al*. (1996), Varty *et al*. (1986), Vélez & Velázquez (1998), Walker (2001), Williams & Tobias (1994), Zimmer (1930).

Genus *COLAPTES* Vigors, 1826

145. **Black-necked Woodpecker**
Colaptes atricollis

French: Pic à cou noir **German**: Graustirnspecht **Spanish**: Carpintero Peruano
Other common names: Black-necked Flicker

Taxonomy. *Chrysopicos atricollis* Malherbe, 1850, Peru.
Sometimes placed with *C. punctigula* and C. *melanochloros* in a separate genus *Chrysoptilus*, the so-called "forest flickers". Two subspecies recognized.
Subspecies and Distribution.
C. a. atricollis (Malherbe, 1850) - W slope of Peruvian Andes from La Libertad and Ancash S to W Arequipa.
C. a. peruvianus (Reichenbach, 1854) - Marañón Valley S on E slope to W Huánuco.
Descriptive notes. 26-27 cm; 73-90 g (*atricollis*). Male has dark grey forehead to hindcrown, feathers tipped red on forehead and crown side, occasionally over entire crown, red hindcrown and upper nape; yellowish-white lores and line above eye, ear-coverts similar but often tinged buffish-olive; olive-grey neck side barred black; red malar band with black feather bases; black chin, throat and upper breast; hindneck and upperparts, including wing-coverts and tertials, bronze-green with narrow blackish bars, rump and uppertail-coverts paler and with paler bars; dark brown

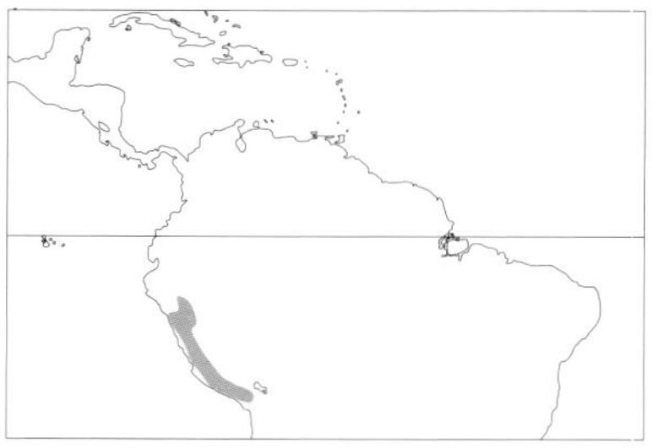

flight-feathers barred yellowish, olive-yellow shafts often forming paler panel; uppertail dark brown, central feathers and outer web of outermost barred pale; underparts below breast pale yellow with black bars, more as arrowhead marks on flanks and undertail-coverts, belly more weakly marked; underwing yellow, primary coverts barred darker; undertail brown, yellower at base, barred whitish-yellow; medium-long bill pointed, culmen curved, narrow across nostrils, black, paler base; iris brown or chestnut-brown; legs green-grey. Female lacks red on forehead and crown side, has malar region blackish, not red. Juvenile duller and darker-faced than adult, but top of head often wholly red with dark bars, more diffusely barred above and below, malar mixed red and black or, perhaps only female, all black. Race *peruvianus* differs from nominate in smaller size, shorter bill, paler and more barred upperparts, pale-edged wing-coverts, paler and less barred below. Voice. Short repeated "peah" and "chypp", mainly in alarm; loud clear "wic" in long series, similar to but not so long as that of *C. auratus*.
Habitat. Arid to semi-arid areas in dry cloudforest, montane scrub with large cacti, desert scrub, and wooded areas; also in riparian vegetation, irrigated areas, orchards, plantations and gardens. Locally above main tree-line into *Polylepis* woodland. At 500-2800 m, occasionally to 3400 m on W Andean slopes, to 4000 m in Cordillera Blanca (Ancash); at 1700-4300 m around Marañón Valley.
Food and Feeding. Ants and their larvae and pupae. Usually singly or in pairs. Essentially arboreal, but also forages near or on ground, often among bushes. Recorded techniques are gleaning and probing, including into soil, and occasional pecking.
Breeding. Probably Jun-Jul, and Sept (Marañón Valley). Nest-hole excavated in tree or telephone pole (*atricollis*), or in large cactus (*peruvianus*). No other details available.
Movements. Resident. Presumably some altitudinal movements may sometimes occur.
Status and Conservation. Not globally threatened. Uncommon generally; locally somewhat more common. A little-known scrubland woodpecker restricted to Peruvian Andes. Observed regularly at c. 2500 m along Santa Eulalia road, above Lima, and recorded along Trujillo-Chiclayo Circuit in NW and on dry slopes above Balsas.
Bibliography. Clements & Shany (2001), Fjeldså & Krabbe (1990), González & Málaga (1997), Johnson (1972), Koepcke (1961, 1970), Meyer de Schauensee (1982), Olrog (1968), Parker *et al*. (1982), Stotz *et al*. (1996), Zimmer (1930).

146. **Spot-breasted Woodpecker**
Colaptes punctigula

French: Pic de Cayenne **German**: Tüpfelbrustspecht **Spanish**: Carpintero Moteado
Other common names: Spot-breasted Flicker

Taxonomy. *Picus punctigula* Boddaert, 1783, Cayenne.
Sometimes placed in a separate genus *Chrysoptilus* with the other "forest flickers" *C. atricollis* and *C. melanochloros*. May form a superspecies with latter. Other named races are *lutescens* (E Darién), not reliably distinct from *ujhelyii*; "*notatus*" (Colombia), known only from unique type, possibly an aberrant *punctipectus*; and *speciosus* (E Peru) and *rubidipectus* (NE Brazil N of Amazon), both considered indistinguishable from *guttatus*. Six subspecies recognized.
Subspecies and Distribution.
C. p. striatigularis (Chapman, 1914) - WC Colombia.
C. p. ujhelyii (Madarász, 1912) - E Panama (E Darién) and N Colombia.
C. p. zuliae (Cory, 1915) - NW Venezuela.
C. p. punctipectus (Cabanis & Heine, 1863) - E Colombia and most of Venezuela (except NW).
C. p. punctigula (Boddaert, 1783) - the Guianas.
C. p. guttatus (Spix, 1824) - Amazonia from E Ecuador and E Peru E to NE Brazil (Pará), S to NW Bolivia and N Mato Grosso.

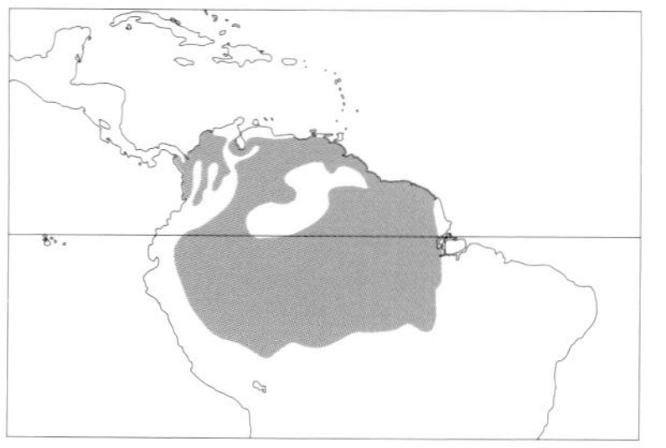

Descriptive notes. c. 18-21 cm; 50-70 g (*punctigula*), 75-79 g (*guttatus* from upper Amazonia). Male has black forehead and forecrown, red hindcrown and nape (exceptionally, red extends forwards along crown side, even over entire crown); white lores, area above and below eye and ear-coverts, red malar stripe with black feather bases; black chin and throat spotted white; upperparts, including wing-coverts and tertials, bronze-green with brownish-black bars, rump paler and less barred; brown flight-feathers indistinctly barred paler, yellow shafts often forming panel; uppertail brown, outer feathers strongly barred green to yellow, central pair sometimes also with weak bars; dull yellow-olive below, upper breast often tinged reddish, becoming paler on belly, breast with fine black spots, flanks more sparsely spotted, yellowish undertail-coverts spotted black; underwing pale yellowish; undertail yellow-brown, barred brown; short bill pointed, culmen curved, narrow across nostrils, blackish; iris rufous-brown; legs greenish-grey to yellow-tinged. Distinguished from *C. melanochloros* by much smaller size, less green appearance, less barred and variegated upperparts and wings. Female lacks red malar, always has red restricted to rear crown and nape. Juvenile as adult, but duller and greener above, duller below with larger spots, male with some red in malar. Races differ from nominate in larger size, plumage tones and markings: *striatigularis* has throat very white with few black streaks, strong reddish tinge on rump and breast, spotting below fairly heavy; *ujhelyii* has throat as previous, is very bright, with red to orange on breast, barring above much reduced, male's crown sometimes almost entirely red; *zuliae* is almost as small as nominate, dull above, with relatively little black on throat, breast spots sparse; *punctipectus* is greener above, lacking bronzy tone, dull below with spots fewer and small, throat generally black with large white spots; *guttatus* has rump less contrasting, throat black with large white spots, very olive on breast, relatively heavy spotting below, variable. Voice. Rather high-pitched weak and nasal "wha" or "kah" or "keeh" in series of 8-12 notes, first and second slightly lower; "peek" notes in series when alarmed; whistled "whew" during courtship or in agonistic encounters; also series of "ta-wick" or "week-a" associated with visual displays, likewise or in response to calls of other individuals typically fast series of "wick" notes sometimes commencing with "ka-wick" elements; low soft "pee-ya" calls at intimate meetings, e.g. during change-over at nest.

Habitat. Wide array of wooded and open habitats: occurs in rainforest, deciduous and gallery forest, *várzea* forest, riparian woodland, second growth, open woodland, mangroves, swamp edges, *llanos*, forest edge, open terrain with large trees, scrub, clearings, moriche palm groves, coffee plantations, other cultivations with sufficient trees, palm savanna. Commonly prefers sparsely wooded regions, generally not a typical forest species. Primarily in humid lowlands; to 600 m in Venezuela, to 1500 m in Colombia, to 1200 m and locally 1600 m in Ecuador, and to 900 m in Peru.

Food and Feeding. Ants and their brood. Lives in pairs or family groups. Arboreal foraging takes place at medium heights and lower; also descends to ground among scattered trees to forage at anthills. In trees, gleaning, probing and occasional light pecking predominant techniques. On ground, probes into soil and sweeps away litter.

Breeding. Oct-May in Colombia, Jun-Aug in the Guianas, Apr-Oct in Amazonian Basin, and Feb-Sept in Peru. In close encounters, displays with head-swinging and head-bobbing, and spread tail. Nest-hole excavated by both sexes in live or dead tree, sometimes in fence post. No information on clutch size or on incubation and fledging periods.

Movements. Resident.

Status and Conservation. Not globally threatened. Rare in Panama; fairly common in rest of range. Occurs in Laguna de Sonso Reserve (Colombia) and in Manu National Park (Peru). Adaptable species; its preference for more open woodland means that it does not suffer too much from effects of clearance. Indeed, appears to have increased in some regions as a result of deforestation; in Ecuador, has spread upwards on Andean slopes following creation of clearings. No known threats.

Bibliography. Allen (1995), Anon. (1998b), Borges *et al.* (2001), Clements & Shany (2001), Donahue (1994), Fjeldså & Mayer (1996), Friedmann (1948), Friedmann & Smith (1950, 1955), Guilherme (2001), Haverschmidt & Mees (1994), Hilty & Brown (1986), Meyer de Schauensee & Phelps (1978), Remsen & Traylor (1989), Remsen *et al.* (1986), Ridgely & Greenfield (2001), Ridgely & Gwynne (1989), Robinson (1997), Robinson & Terborgh (1997), Short (1985b), Sick (1993), da Silva *et al.* (1990), Snyder (1966), Stotz *et al.* (1996), Strewe (2000a), Terborgh *et al.* (1984), Tostain *et al.* (1992), Vélez & Velázquez (1998), Wetmore (1968a).

147. Green-barred Woodpecker

Colaptes melanochloros

French: Pic vert et noir   **German**: Grünbindenspecht   **Spanish**: Carpintero Real
Other common names: Green-barred Flicker; Golden-breasted Woodpecker (*melanolaimus* group)

Taxonomy. *Picus melanochloros* J. F. Gmelin, 1788, Cayenne; error = Rio de Janeiro, Brazil.
Sometimes placed in a separate genus *Chrysoptilus* with the other "forest flickers" *C. atricollis* and *C. punctigula*. May form a superspecies with latter. Partly terrestrial group of S races inhabiting *pampas* and Chaco woodland sometimes regarded as forming a separate species comprising the taxa *melanolaimus*, *nigroviridis* and *leucofrenatus*, distinct from the more arboreal nominate race and *nattereri*. The last two intergrade widely, the others to a lesser extent, and the two groups interbreed along the R Paraná and R Uruguay. Additional named races *mariae* (Marajó I, NE Brazil), *fluvilumbis* (Bahia), *perplexus* (E Argentina) and *patagonicus* (WC Argentina) are all considered insufficiently differentiated to warrant recognition. Five subspecies recognized.

Subspecies and Distribution.
C. m. nattereri (Malherbe, 1845) - NE & SC Brazil S to E Bolivia (Santa Cruz).
C. m. melanochloros (J. F. Gmelin, 1788) - S & SE Brazil, SE Paraguay, NE Argentina (E Formosa, Misiones) and Uruguay.
C. m. melanolaimus (Malherbe, 1857) - arid upland valleys in C & S Bolivia.
C. m. nigroviridis (C. H. B. Grant, 1911) - S Bolivia, W Paraguay, N & E Argentina (S to Córdoba and Buenos Aires) and W Uruguay.
C. m. leucofrenatus Leybold, 1873 - NW & WC Argentina (S to Neuquén, W Río Negro).

Descriptive notes. c. 27-30 cm; 104-150 g (smaller races), 154-178 g (*leucofrenatus*). Male has black forehead and forecrown, red hindcrown and nape, whitish lores, cheeks and ear-coverts, ear-coverts strongly tinged olive; red malar stripe with black feather bases; whitish-green chin and throat streaked black; upperparts, including wing-coverts and tertials, yellowish-green, barred dark brown, rump paler and less barred, uppertail-coverts buff with black bars; greenish-brown flight-

feathers narrowly barred paler, olive shafts; uppertail black, at least outer feathers barred pale; pale green below, usually darker and brighter on breast, with prominent black spots, often tending towards bars on flanks, spots becoming smaller or absent on belly; yellowish-white underwing, primary coverts sometimes spotted; black undertail barred yellowish; fairly long bill pointed, culmen curved, narrow across nostrils, black; iris brown to chestnut-brown; legs grey, usually tinged greenish or yellow. Female has proportionately longer tail than male, has malar mostly black with white streaks, without red. Juvenile duller than adult, with broader barring above, markings below more bar-like. Races differ in size and colour tones, S group living in *pampas* and Chaco being bigger and browner: *nattereri* resembles nominate, but smaller, shorter-billed, more yellow, spots below often very small or streak-like; *melanolaimus* is longer-billed, fairly green in tone, with rump less marked, tail less barred, golden tinge on breast but whiter below, black patch on throat side; *nigroviridis* is like previous, but tends to more greenish coloration above, tail strongly barred, less golden on breast, less black on throat side, spots below larger; *leucofrenatus* is large, browner above, even golden-brown, with white rump, whitish bars and edges, breast golden to orange, flanks strongly barred, large spots or arrowhead marks below. VOICE. Call "kwiek-kwik-kwik", similar to that of *C. campestris*; also "peah" or screechy "wheéo", and "krrew", "pikwarrr"; "peek" as alarm, also given singly; also "ta-wick" or "ker wick" and variations, much as those of *C. auratus* or perhaps slightly sharper, and long series. Both sexes drum, rolls slower than those of *C. auratus*.

Habitat. Variety of habitats, from lowland forest to Andean desert scrub. Nominate race inhabits subtropical humid forest and transitional forest, especially when mixed with bamboo. Race *melanolaimus* generally in woodland, savanna, open country and arid bushland; *nattereri* in savanna and *caatinga*. Lowlands and foothills; to 3000 m in Bolivia (*melanolaimus*).

Food and Feeding. Almost exclusively ants and their brood; genera *Camponotus*, *Crematogaster*, *Paracryptocerus* and others identified. Spiders also recorded. Cactus fruits and berries taken, also sap. Mostly singly, sometimes in pairs; joins groups of the larger and more wary *C. campestris* to feed on ants on ground. Forages regularly in lower and middle sections of trees and palms, in low bushes, and bamboo; hops through crown of trees, also hangs on underside of branches. Probing and gleaning are main techniques in trees. Breaks through surface with a few pecks; if prey detected, considerable time may be spent in removing it with tongue. Also forages on ground, especially "*melanolaimus* group"; progresses in long bounds or moves in short hops.

Breeding. From Aug-Sept to Jan in S; earlier in N. Display with wing flicks, spread tail, swinging and bobbing head-and-body movements; calls for prolonged periods from top of tree or palm. Nest-hole made in dead tree or dead stump, palm, cactus, or telephone pole, at height of 2-6 m. Clutch 4 eggs; both parents incubate, and both also feed chicks, by regurgitation; incubation and fledging periods not documented.

Movements. At least partly migratory in extreme S and in Córdoba highlands of C Argentina; some move N to Gran Chaco region (e.g. Santiago del Estero) after breeding.

Status and Conservation. Not globally threatened. Common in most of range. Occurs in numerous protected areas, including Itatiaia, Serra do Cipó and Brasília National Parks (Brazil), Ybicuí National Park (Paraguay), Iguazú National Park and Urugua-í, La Araucaria and Chancaní Provincial Parks (Argentina). Recorded regularly on Montevideo-Chuy-Minas Circuit (Uruguay). No known threats.

Bibliography. Aleixo & Galetti (1997), dos Anjos & Schuchmann (1997), Belton (1984), Bencke & Kindel (1999), Brooks *et al.* (1993), Buzzetti (2000), Cândido (2000), Canevari *et al.* (1991), Capper *et al.* (2000), Contreras *et al.* (1990), Dubs (1992), Figueiredo & Lo (2000), Figueiredo *et al.* (2000), Fjeldså & Mayer (1996), Francisco & Galetti (2001), Goerck (1999), Hayes (1995), Hayes *et al.* (1990), Herzog *et al.* (1997), Klimaitis & Moschione (1987), López (1997), Marini (2001), Miserendino (1998), Narosky & di Giacomo (1993), Parker & Goerck (1997), de la Peña (1994, 1995), Pereyra (1950), Pinto & Camargo (1961), Piratelli *et al.* (2000), Remsen & Traylor (1989), do Rosário (1996), Schmitt *et al.* (1997), Scott & Brooke (1985), Short (1969b, 1974b, 1975, 1985b), Sick (1993), Soares & dos Anjos (1999), Stager (1961a), Stotz *et al.* (1996), Stradi & Hudon (1998), Tobias *et al.* (1993), Traylor (1951c), Tubelis & Tomás (1999), Wetmore (1926).

ssp *auratus* ♂

♀ ♂

ssp *mexicanoides* ♂

ssp *chrysocaulosus* ♂   ♀

ssp *gundlachi* ♂

148

ssp *cafer* ♂   ♀

ssp *nanus*

ssp *collaris* ♂   ♀

♂

ssp *chrysoides* ♂   ♀

149

ssp *tenebrosus* ♂

ssp *mearnsi* ♂

150   ♀   ♂

151   ♂

♀

ssp *campestris* ♂

ssp *campestroides*

153

ssp *rupicola* ♀   ♂

ssp *puna* ♀   ♂

ssp *cinereicapillus* ♂

152

PLATE 40

inches   5

cm   13

148. Northern Flicker

Colaptes auratus

French: Pic flamboyant **German**: Goldspecht **Spanish**: Carpintero Escapulario
Other common names: Common Flicker; Yellow-shafted Flicker (*auratus* group); Red-shafted Flicker (*cafer* group); Cuban Flicker (*chrysocaulosus* group); Guatemalan Flicker (*mexicanoides* group)

Taxonomy. *Cuculus auratus* Linnaeus, 1758, South Carolina.

Forms a superspecies with *C. chrysoides*; sometimes treated as conspecific but, although SW populations not significantly different genetically from that species, hybridization is very limited (in C & S Arizona), with moderate ecological separation too, and the two are better regarded as allospecies. Races commonly divided into four geographical groups, each considered a separate species in the past: "*auratus* group" (which includes *luteus*) in N & E North America, with yellow flight-feather shafts; "*cafer* group" (also including *collaris*, *mexicanus*, *nanus* and extinct *rufipileus*) in W North America and Mexico, with red shafts; "*mexicanoides* group" in highlands from S Mexico to Nicaragua; and geographically isolated "*chrysocaulosus* group" (with *gundlachi*) in Cuba and Grand Cayman. First two groups interbreed in extensive and long since stable hybrid zone from Alaska through the Great Plains, where relatively few individuals are typical of one form or the other, and non-assortative mating is common. Relationships among groups and individual races complex, poorly understood; also, considerable individual variation occurs, and races interbreed wherever they meet; further research and revision needed. Additional described races, considered to represent intergrades or otherwise inadequately differentiated, include *borealis* (NW to NC North America), *sedentarius* (Santa Cruz I, California), *martirensis* (San Pedro Mártir Mts, in NW Baja California) and *pinicolus* (highlands of El Salvador to N Nicaragua). Race *rufipileus* (Guadalupe I, off W Baja California) is extinct. Nine extant subspecies recognized.

Subspecies and Distribution.

C. a. luteus Bangs, 1898 - C Alaska E across Canada to S Labrador and Newfoundland, and S to Montana and NE USA.

C. a. auratus (Linnaeus, 1758) - SE USA.

C. a. cafer (J. F. Gmelin, 1788) - S Alaska and British Columbia S to N California.

C. a. collaris Vigors, 1829 - SW USA S to NW Baja California and W Mexico (S to about Durango).

C. a. mexicanus Swainson, 1827 - Durango E across Mexican Plateau to San Luis Potosí and S to Oaxaca.

C. a. nanus Griscom, 1934 - W Texas S to NE Mexico.

C. a. mexicanoides Lafresnaye, 1844 - highlands from S Mexico (Chiapas) to Nicaragua.

C. a. chrysocaulosus Gundlach, 1858 - Cuba.

C. a. gundlachi Cory, 1886 - Grand Cayman I.

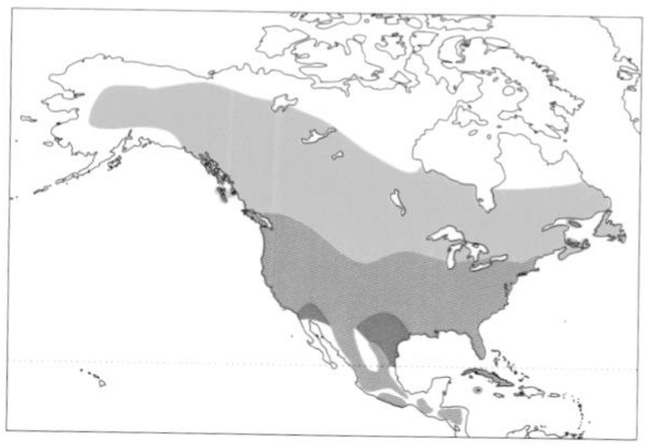

Descriptive notes. c. 30-35 cm; 106-164 g (*auratus*), 121-167 g (*collaris*), 105-126 g (*nanus*), 88 g (*gundlachi*). Male has grey forehead to hindneck and rear neck side, patch of deep red on lower nape extending to side of nape (forming V shape), black malar stripe; rest of head and down to upper breast cinnamon, usually darker around eye, often more greyish on rear ear-coverts; brown upperparts barred blackish, rump unbarred white (occasionally variable black marks), uppertail-coverts white with black subterminal marks; dark brown flight-feathers narrowly barred pale brown, shafts yellow; uppertail blackish-brown, initially tipped and edged buffy, outermost feather with hint of pale bars on outer web, centre of shafts yellow; broad black crescent across centre of breast; rest of underparts white with pale buffish-yellow wash, rounded black spots becoming more crescentic on flanks, more bar-like or wedge-shaped on undertail-coverts; yellowish underwing, darker tip and trailing edge, spots or bars on primary coverts; undertail yellow, tip black; fairly long bill pointed, culmen curved, narrow across nostrils, black or slaty; iris deep brown; legs grey, tinged green. Distinguished from *C. chrysoides* by larger size, head pattern, yellow shafts. Female is slightly smaller than male, lacks black malar, has breast crescent slightly less deep. Juvenile as adult, but often more greyish colour on head, crown sometimes barred, usually black loral patch, dark bars above much broader, tail-coverts with more black, breast crescent smaller, spots larger, underwing duller yellow, male usually with dull red on crown and less distinct black malar, female head even less marked. Races differ considerably in size, plumage coloration and markings: *luteus* resembles nominate but somewhat larger; *cafer* has grey face and throat to breast, red malar, no red nape patch, salmon-pink shafts, underwing and undertail, female sometimes with cinnamon malar; *collaris* is like previous but paler, female with moderate rufous malar; *mexicanus* is smaller and browner than last; *nanus* is smaller still, and greyer; extinct *rufipileus* had short wing and tail, rather long bill, rufous crown; *mexicanoides* is large, bright, with rusty forehead to hindneck, grey face and breast, male's red malar mixed with black, above strongly barred buff, grey-brown and blackish, breast patch deeper and less crescent-shaped, spots below often larger, shafts and undersurfaces of wings and tail orange-red, female with pale cinnamon-brown malar finely streaked darker; *chrysocaulosus* has proportionately longer tail, head pattern as nominate, upperparts more olive above, even occasionally tinged reddish, rump more heavily barred, tail more barred, breast crescent deeper, spots below broader, yellow of shafts and undersurfaces more golden; *gundlachi* is very like previous but smaller, shorter-tailed, with smaller red nape patch. Voice. Common call a descending "peah" or "klee-yer"; typical is a long series of up to c. 70 "whit" notes, given throughout breeding season to autumn; "wicka" and variants, e.g. "ew-i", "cha-week-a", "wee-cha", "wik-up" and suchlike, varying in intensity, during aggressive encounters or courtship; soft "wee-tew" when approaching mate, or "wa-wa-wa" in flight or when mildly disturbed; low hissing by young nestlings, louder and variable later. Drumrolls not very loud, slower than similar rolls of *Picoides villosus*, but uniform rhythm.

Habitat. Broad range of habitats giving access to open ground; mainly open areas and forest edge. Primarily open forest, younger (2-6 years) clear-cuts, burnt areas, farmland, pastures and residential areas in main part of range; parkland with e.g. aspen (*Populus*) and lodgepole pine (*Pinus contorta*), ponderosa pine (*P. ponderosa*) forest, alpine meadow edge, riparian woodland and forest edge are typical habitats in N; occurs in woodland along streams in the Great Plains, and in W common in quaking aspen (*Populus tremuloides*) stands. Inhabits the oak (*Quercus*) and pine-oak zone in Mexico; also second growth in cloudforest belt in Guatemala and Honduras. Also mangroves in Caribbean region. Wide variety of habitats used in winter, too; in temperate zone, denser habitats visited at that season than at other seasons. Breeds from sea-level to 2100 m in N; at 750-3300 m, occasionally to 4000 m, in Mexico; occurs from c. 600 m, mostly above 900 m, to 3200 m in Guatemala and Honduras.

Food and Feeding. Chiefly ants and their brood, also other insects, spiders, occasionally molluscs and crustaceans; fruits, berries and seeds also important, especially in winter. Ants form up to c. 75% of diet, sometimes more, and include especially *Formica*, *Lasius*, *Camponotus*, *Myrmica*, *Crematogaster*, but at least 6 other genera commonly recorded. Other insects include termites (Isoptera), caterpillars, beetles and their larvae, wasps, Orthoptera, aphids. Fruits and berries of wide variety of plants taken, e.g. several species of *Rhus* and especially poison ivy (*R. radicans*), dogwood (*Cornus florida*), hackberry (*Celtis occidentalis*), cherries (*Prunus*), black gum (*Nyssa*), *Rubus*, *Ribes* and many others, as well as seeds, acorns and other kinds of nut-like crops. Visits feeders. Forages singly, in pairs or in family groups; also in flocks of up to c. 15 birds during migration. Feeds commonly on the ground, on lawns, road shoulders, forest floor and similar sites; trees and bushes also visited for harvesting fruits and other plant matter; more arboreal in Cuba (*chrysocaulosus*) and Grand Cayman (*gundlachi*). On ground progresses by hopping; sweeps away litter, digs into ant nests with the bill; berries also collected on ground. In arboreal foraging, dead trees or broken ends of dead branches are important sites (about 75% of observed cases); moves in manner of tit (Paridae) among the twigs, frequently perches crosswise. Main techniques gleaning and probing; most prey secured with the tongue. Also catches insects on the wing.

Breeding. Apr-Jul; from Jun in N and from Feb-Mar in S; rarely, 2 broods reared in a season. Monogamous, apparently pairs for life. Displays characterized by steep upward-pointing of bill with tail-spreading, bill describing circles or figures-of-eight, bobbing movements with wings raised, also tail spread and twisted to reveal underside. Nest excavated by both sexes, taking 5-20 days, male about twice as active as female, in dead tree or in dead part of live tree, usually close to distal end of a stub, at variable height, often below 3 m but to 27 m, mostly c. 6-12 m in forests; average entrance diameter 7-9 cm, cavity depth 33-40 cm; very often, however, old cavity selected, or wide variety of other sites (e.g. fence post, utility pole, clothesline pole, marine breakwater pilings, soft cliff, haystack or suitable structure on building), or old burrow of other bird, or nestbox used; territory vigorously defended. Clutch 3-12 eggs, mostly 4-9, average of 411 clutches was 6·5 eggs, larger clutches of up to 17 eggs probably product of more than 1 female; both sexes incubate, male taking greater share, period 11-12 days; chicks fed by regurgitation, male seeming to feed at higher rate than female, feeding and nest sanitation reduced towards end of nestling period; fledging period 25-28 days; young remain with parents for variable period, fed by them for up to c. 15-20 days. Hatching success 1-10 chicks, mostly 5-7, on average 1·1 fewer than eggs produced; holes often usurped by Common Starlings (*Sturnus vulgaris*). First breeding at 1 year, some females not until 2 years. Maximum recorded longevity 9 years 2 months.

Movements. Resident in C & S of range. Canadian populations migratory, as indeed are many of those breeding N of California, Oklahoma and Georgia; autumn migration begins towards end Aug and lasts to late Oct or Nov, with peak in Sept; migrates by day, in sometimes large flocks, low over ground. Winter concentrations in USA from SW states through Texas to Florida; *auratus* group winters S to N Mexico (Sonora E to Tamaulipas), where present Oct-Mar. N populations arrive back on breeding grounds from early Mar to May.

Status and Conservation. Not globally threatened. Common throughout most of range, locally very common to abundant in Canada and USA; common to fairly common in Mexico. In Caribbean, fairly common on Grand Cayman (*gundlachi*); generally uncommon and local in Cuba, where more arboreal race *chrysocaulosus* is decreasing, chiefly as a result of deforestation. Breeding densities very variable, locally as high as 4·8 pairs/10 ha in North America; 1-8 pairs/40 ha in oak and conifer woodland. Decline recorded in Canada and USA, with reduction of 52% in *auratus* group and 19% in *cafer* group since mid-1960's. Likely cause of decline is loss of suitable nest-sites following removal of snags and dead tree limbs; competition with other hole-nesters, including other woodpeckers and introduced Common Starlings, also probably significant, at least locally. In early part of 20th century, migrants shot in large numbers, particularly on E coast at Cape May (New Jersey), with hundreds killed in a single morning; such practices now illegal, and probably only very few shot. Nevertheless, can cause problems in the human environment, mainly through excavating in unusual places; a notorious instance, in 1995, involved two individuals which excavated c. 200 holes in the insulation of fuel tanks of the Space Shuttle on its launch pad at the Kennedy Space Centre, resulting in costs totalling more than US$1,000,000. Race *rufipileus* of Guadalupe I extinct: last record in 1906, when remaining population estimated at c. 40 birds (this total perhaps included 12 birds collected during this same visit); extinction almost certainly due to habitat destruction by goats, compounded by predation by cats.

Bibliography. Anderson (1971), Baker (1975), Baldwin (1960), Barbour (1943), Beck (1971), Bent (1939), Berman *et al.* (1998), Blockstein & Fall (1986), Blomme (1983), Bock (1971), Bower (1993, 1995), Brackbill (1955, 1957), Bradley (2000), Bull (1981), Burkett (1989), Burns (1900), Campbell *et al.* (1990), Conner (1973, 1975, 1977), Conner & Adkisson (1977), Conner & Crawford (1974), Conner *et al.* (1976), Cruz (1974a), Cruz & Johnston (1979), Cyr (1995g), DeBenedictis (1997), Dennis (1969), Duncan (1990), Duyck & McNair (1991), Ellison (1992), Erskine (1962), Faaborg (1985), Fletcher & Moore (1992), Gamboa & Brown (1976), Ganier & Jackson (1976), García *et al.* (2001), Garrett (1999), Garrido & Kirkconnell (2000), Gifford (1987), Grudzien & Moore (1986), Grudzien *et al.* (1987), Gullion (1949), Harestad & Keisker (1989), Harris, M.A. (1982), Hartup & Natarajan (1996), Hayes & Hayes (1983), Hendricks (1996), Howe *et al.* (1987), Howell & Webb (1995), Ingold (1994a, 1994b, 1996, 1998), Ingold & Densmore (1992), Ingold & Weise (1985), Inouye (1976), Jackman (1974), Jackson (1970e, 1997a), Janssen (1981), Johnson, C.A. (1934), Johnson, E.V. (1998), Johnson, N.K. (1969), Johnston (1970), Kemlage *et al.* (1981), Kerpez (1986), Kerpez & Smith (1990a, 1990b), Kilham (1959f, 1973a, 1983), Koenig (1984a, 1984b, 1987), Konrad (1998), Laskey (1966), Lawrence (1966), McGillivray & Biermann (1987), Meyer (1981), Moore (1987, 1994, 1995), Moore & Buchanan (1985), Moore & Koenig (1986), Moore & Price (1993), Moore *et al.* (1991), Moulton & Lowell (1991), Murphy (1981), Neff (1928), Noble (1936), Olsen (1978), Peslak (1990), Petit *et al.* (1985), Phillips (1887), Potter (1970), Rowley (1966, 1984), Saab & Dudley (1998), Schaldach (1963), Schemnitz (1964), Sedgwick & Knopf (1990), Self (1980), Shackelford & Conner (1997), Shelley (1935), Sherman (1910), Shields (1988), Short (1965a, 1965b, 1967, 1971e, 1985b), Skutch (1969a), Smith (1971), Spring (1965), Stark *et al.* (1998), Stradi & Hudon (1998), Stradi *et al.* (1998), Swallow *et al.* (1988), Test (1945, 1969), Thayer & Bangs (1908), Tobalske (1996), Wagner & Miller (1986), Welsh & Capen (1987, 1992), Weston (1999), Wiebe (2000, 2001), Wiebe & Swift (2001), Wiedenfeld *et al.* (1992), Woods (1984).

149. Gilded Flicker

Colaptes chrysoides

French: Pic chrysoïde **German**: Wüstengoldspecht **Spanish**: Carpintero de California

On following pages: 150. Fernandina's Flicker (*Colaptes fernandinae*); 151. Chilean Flicker (*Colaptes pitius*); 152. Andean Flicker (*Colaptes rupicola*); 153. Campo Flicker (*Colaptes campestris*).

Taxonomy. *Geopicus* (*Colaptes*) *chrysoides*, Malherbe, 1852, Cape San Lucas, Baja California.
Forms a superspecies with *C. auratus*. Genetically is not significantly divergent from SW "*cafer* group" of that species, and treated as conspecific by some authors, but separated to a reasonable extent by habitat preferences, with limited hybridization; considered better treated as allospecies. Races intergrade clinally. Four subspecies recognized.
Subspecies and Distribution.
C. c. brunnescens Anthony, 1895 - N & C Baja California.
C. c. chrysoides (Malherbe, 1852) - S Baja California.
C. c. mearnsi Ridgway, 1911 - extreme SE California (Colorado Valley) and S & C Arizona S in desert to NW Mexico (N Sonora).
C. c. tenebrosus van Rossem, 1930 - N Sonora to N Sinaloa.

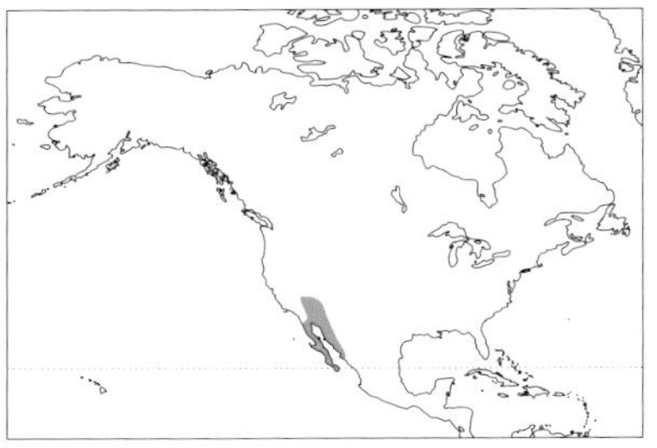

Descriptive notes. c. 26-30 cm; 92-129 g (*mearnsi*). Male has rusty to rufous-yellow forehead to hindneck, red malar, rest of head down to upper breast grey; pale brownish upperparts heavily barred blackish, rump white, uppertail-coverts white with black bars, median wing-coverts tipped white; dark brown flight-feathers narrowly barred pale brown, yellow shafts; uppertail blackish-brown, outermost feather with faint pale lines on outer web, shafts yellow; broad, deep black breast crescent, otherwise white below with rounded black spots, these becoming more crescent-shaped on flanks, more bar-like on undertail-coverts; yellow underwing, darker tip and trailing edge; undertail yellow, broad black tip; medium-long bill pointed, culmen slightly curved, narrow across nostrils, dark grey to black; iris deep brown; legs grey. Female lacks red malar, may have faint pale rusty mark. Juvenile has broader dark bars above, smaller breast crescent, bigger spots below, duller yellow on underwing, male usually with red tinge on crown and malar, female head plainer. Races differ little from nominate: *brunnescens* is browner above, moderately barred; *mearnsi* is largest, rather pale; *tenebrosus* is smaller, darker, heavily barred. VOICE. Descending "peah" or "klee-yer", long series of "whit" notes in spring to autumn, "wicka" and variants, also other vocalizations, all much as for *C. auratus* but voice on average slightly higher. Drumrolls soft.
Habitat. Arid scrub and desert with large cacti and yucca (*Yucca*) plants, and dry riverine woodland with cottonwoods (*Populus*) and willows (*Salix*); from sea-level to 250 m in Baja California, to about 900 m farther E.
Food and Feeding. Ants and their brood, and other insects. Also fruits, e.g. of cactus, and berries; also nuts, including pecan (*Carya*) and walnut (*Juglans*). Forages singly or in pairs, frequently on ground. Visits feeders. Main techniques probing and gleaning.
Breeding. Laying Feb-Jun. Nest most frequently excavated in large cactus, particularly saguaro cactus (*Carnegiea gigantea*), at 3-12 m, less commonly in cottonwood or willow tree or in stub at 1·5-8 m; entrance hole averages c. 7 cm tall, c. 8·5 cm across, mean cavity depth 36-38 cm. Clutch usually 3-5 eggs; incubation c. 11 days; fledging period c. 24-25 days.
Movements. Resident; wanderers recorded N to SW Utah.
Status and Conservation. Not globally threatened. Common. Stable or increasing in USA, with average increase of 8% annually since 1968. In Mexico, conversion of cactus deserts to irrigated farmland has probably resulted in a decline in this species' numbers, but no data available. Strong competition for nest-sites likely from introduced Common Starlings (*Sturnus vulgaris*), which have successfully conquered the arid habitats of the SW; one study, however, reported that this woodpecker suffered far less in this respect than did *Melanerpes uropygialis*. Occasional conflict with man possible, as it can cause some damage in commercial plantations of pecans and walnuts.
Bibliography. Anon. (1998b), Baicich & Harrison (1997), Bent (1939), Braun (1969), Brush *et al.* (1990), DeBenedictis (1997), Friedmann *et al.* (1957), Howell & Webb (1995), Hunter (1984), Johnson (1969), Kaufman (1996), Koenig (1984a), McAuliffe & Hendricks (1988), Price *et al.* (1995), Root (1988), Small (1994), Test (1945), Zwartjes & Nordell (1998).

150. Fernandina's Flicker
Colaptes fernandinae

French: Pic de Fernandina **German**: Kubaspecht **Spanish**: Carpintero Churroso
Other common names: Cuban Flicker/Woodpecker

Taxonomy. *Colaptes Fernandinæ* Vigors, 1827, near Habana, Cuba.
Formerly separated in monotypic genus *Nesoceleus*. Monotypic.
Distribution. Cuba (distribution now very patchy).

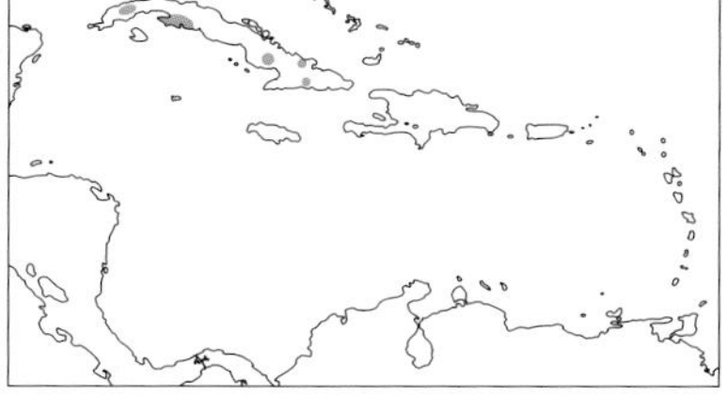

Descriptive notes. c. 30 cm. Male has buff-cinnamon forehead to nape finely streaked black, occasionally hint of red on nape; whitish-buff lores and narrow line above and below eye, buffish-yellow ear-coverts more cinnamon at rear; black malar stripe, sometimes mixed with red; whitish chin and throat heavily streaked black, black spots on lower throat and throat sides; pale yellow to buffish-yellow upperparts, including wing-coverts and tertials, densely barred blackish-brown, rump and uppertail-coverts paler with bars narrower; dark brown flight-feathers narrowly barred yellow-buff; uppertail brownish-black, all feathers narrowly barred buff-yellow; pale yellowish-buff below with dark brown bars, markings weaker on belly; yellow underwing rather obscurely barred, yellow undertail; long bill pointed, curved, narrow across nostrils, black; iris deep brown; legs dark grey. Female differs from male in having black malar heavily streaked white, never any hint of red on nape. Juvenile duller and browner, with less barring above, broader markings below. VOICE. Loud "pic" series, slower and lower-pitched than *C. auratus*; also typical "wicka" series, loud, nasal "ch-ch-ch" during breeding.
Habitat. Prefers rather open woodland and pasture with palms, in both dry and wetter habitats; occurs to lesser extent also in denser woodland. Closely associated with palm trees, especially *Saval parviflora*.
Food and Feeding. Insects, worms, grubs, seeds. Forages singly, also in pairs when breeding. Often feeds on ground, more so than local race *chrysocaulosus* of *C. auratus*; visits lawns and dusty tracks. Probes into the soil and under leaves.

Breeding. Mar-Jun. Solitary; locally (Zapata Swamp, in Matanzas) loosely colonial. Frequent aerial chases in courtship. Nest excavated at relatively low height, c. 3-6 m, in dead or live palm, especially *Saval parviflora*, or dead tree, entrance hole averages c. 9 cm across, c. 8·5 cm tall, cavity depth 60 cm; old hole, even of another species, quite often reused. Clutch 3-5 eggs; incubation period c. 18 days; fledging period c. 22 days.
Movements. Resident.
Status and Conservation. ENDANGERED. Population extremely small and fragmented; maximum total estimated at 400 pairs, probably only 300, possibly even fewer. By far largest population is at Zapata Swamp, in Matanzas, where perhaps 120 pairs (occasionally in loose colonies).Was formerly widespread in Cuba, although seems never to have been very common. Declined during 20th century, and now restricted to a few small localized populations in three provinces: Pinar del Río in W Cuba, and Matanzas and Camagüey in C part of island. May still survive in several other provinces; recent record from a new locality in SE Cuba (La Platica, in Sierra Maestra) suggests that small, undiscovered populations could exist elsewhere. Extensive habitat loss resulting from clearance of forest for agricultural purposes, as well as logging, at least partly responsible for its decline, and continue to be so, but other factors may be important. Dead palms are often shared for nesting with the Near-threatened Cuban Amazon (*Amazona leucocephala*), and are frequently pushed over by bird-trappers in order to collect parrot nestlings; the flicker then loses both its own brood of young and a good nest-site. Hurricanes, too, can have a devastating effect on dead palms. Additional pressure comes from competition with other hole-nesting birds, especially *C. auratus*, *Melanerpes superciliaris* and *Xiphidiopicus percussus*; a further potential problem is nest predation by *M. superciliaris*, although significance of this has not been assessed. Despite efforts of Cuban government to safeguard the country's wildlife, including creation of many reserves, funding has proved very difficult; Zapata Swamp an important reserve, but resources for ensuring its effective protection are totally inadequate. Conservation measures proposed include the displaying of posters in villages in areas where the species still exists, aimed at raising awareness of the plight of this rare woodpecker. Additional measures are implementation of a nestbox scheme in known nesting areas, and census of all current and former sites where it is known to have bred in order to determine its exact range and status. Detailed study of its feeding and nesting requirements also considered desirable.
Bibliography. Anon. (1998b), Barbour (1943), Bond (1985), Collar & Andrew (1988), Collar, Crosby & Stattersfield (1994), Collar, Gonzaga *et al.* (1992), Cruz (1974a), Faaborg (1985), Garcia (1992, 1993), García & González (1985), Garrido (1985), Garrido & Kirkconnell (2000), Gotto (1997), Melián (2000), Mitchell (1998), Mitchell & Wells (1997), Mitchell *et al.* (2000), Raffaele *et al.* (1998), Rompré *et al.* (1999), Rutten (1934), Salmon (1974), Seth-Smith (1912), Short (1965b, 1971e), Stattersfield & Capper (2000), Stotz *et al.* (1996), Suárez & Arredondo (1997), Wallace (2001).

151. Chilean Flicker
Colaptes pitius

French: Pic du Chili **German**: Bänderspecht **Spanish**: Carpintero Pitío

Taxonomy. *Picus Pitius* Molina, 1782, Chile.
Birds in S Argentina named as race *cachinnans* on basis of proportionately shorter tail, but differences are insignificant. Monotypic.
Distribution. C & S Chile (Coquimbo S to C Magellanes) and adjacent SW Argentina (Neuquén S to W Santa Cruz).

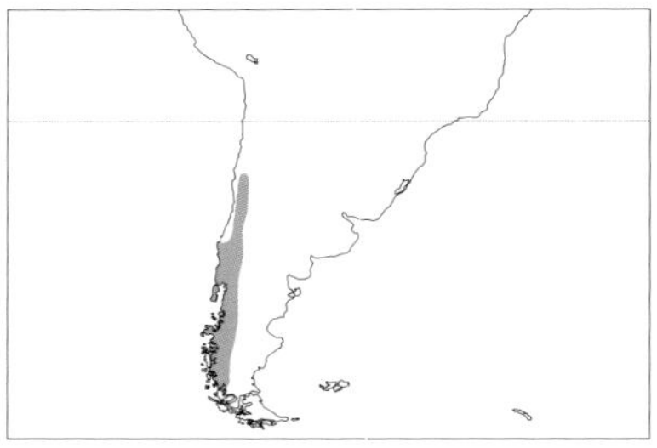

Descriptive notes. c. 30 cm; 100-163 g. Male has dark slate-grey forehead to nape, blacker at sides, nape rarely with hint of red; buffish lores, area around eye and ear-coverts, buffish malar region finely spotted black or black and red; buffish-white chin and throat, spotted black on lower throat; upperparts, including wing-coverts and tertials, blackish-brown with narrow white to buff-white bars, in worn plumage much browner with pale bars mostly lost; rump unmarked white or with few black spots; dark brown flight-feathers, primaries notched whitish with pale shafts, secondaries narrowly barred whitish-buff; uppertail brown-black, outer and central feather pairs narrowly barred white; whitish below, broadly barred blackish-brown, bars tending to merge on breast, belly with smaller markings or plain; underwing yellowish, darker tip, some bars on primary coverts; undertail yellowish, obscurely barred; fairly long bill pointed, culmen curved, narrow across nostrils, black; iris yellowish; legs grey or green-grey. Female lacks black or red in malar, never shows any red on nape. Juvenile as adult, but crown blacker with narrow buff tips, more broadly barred above, more spotted below, eyes brown. VOICE. Distinct repeated "piteéu"; whistled variable "kwee", singly or in series, louder and more raucous than note of *C. rupicola*; long "wic wic wic" series, higher-pitched and less clear than corresponding notes of *C. auratus*; "week-a, week-a" during encounters similarly higher.
Habitat. Inhabits woodland and open wooded country, including open areas within *Nothofagus* forest, forest edge, riparian woodland, tree plantations, and various types of scrubby vegetation, typically with scattered bushes. Ranges from 600 m to over 1000 m; sometimes down to sea-level, at least in winter.
Food and Feeding. Almost exclusively ants and their brood; other items, such as scorpions (Scorpiones) and grubs, occasionally taken. Roves about in noisy family groups, easily detected. Forages mainly on ground, but never far from trees. Hops on ground, where feeds by poking, sweeping away debris, and digging into soil; also investigates fallen logs and stumps. Rarely forages in trees, and then rather unenthusiastically; flies into trees when alarmed, and may then peck in agitated manner.
Breeding. Reported in Oct-Dec. Known displays are head-swinging, bobbing with tail-spreading. Nest excavated in dead tree or stub, or in bank; apparently highly territorial. Clutch 4-6 eggs; no information on incubation and fledging periods.
Movements. Resident; possibly nomadic to some extent.
Status and Conservation. Not globally threatened. Generally rather common, though few data available. Occurs in Cerro La Campana, Nahuelbuta and Vicente Pérez Rosales National Parks (Chile); recorded from Calafate (Argentina), and also at L Peñuelas and Puerto Natales (Chile). No known threats.
Bibliography. Araya & Chester (1993), Canevari *et al.* (1991), Chebez *et al.* (1999), Cofré (1999), Fjeldså & Krabbe (1990), Johnson (1967), Mazar Barnett & Pearman (2001), Meyer de Schauensee (1982), Narosky & Yzurieta (1993), Olrog (1968), de la Peña (1994), Pereyra (1950), Stotz *et al.* (1996), Vuilleumier (1985), Wetmore (1926).

152. Andean Flicker

Colaptes rupicola

French: Pic des rochers **German**: Andenspecht **Spanish**: Carpintero Andino

Taxonomy. *Colaptes rupicola* d'Orbigny, 1840, no locality = Sicasica, La Paz, Bolivia.
Races interbreed in Peru. Three subspecies recognized.

Subspecies and Distribution.
C. r. cinereicapillus Reichenbach, 1854 - extreme S Ecuador (SE Loja) and N Peru (Piura, Amazonas).
C. r. puna Cabanis, 1883 - C & S Peru.
C. r. rupicola d'Orbigny, 1840 - W, C & S Bolivia, N Chile (Tarapacá) and NW Argentina (Jujuy S to Catamarca).

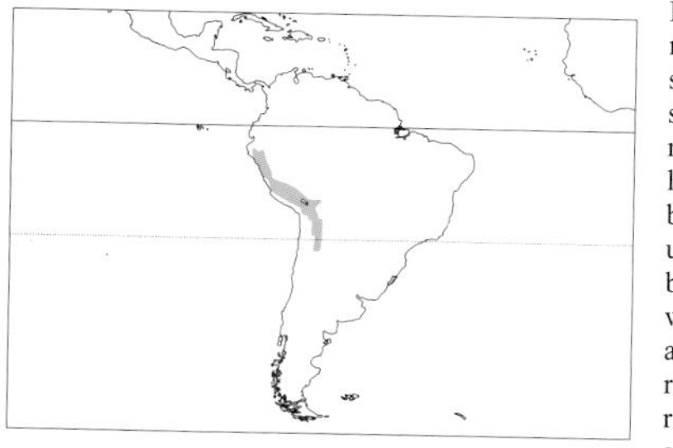

Descriptive notes. c. 32 cm; 142-204 g, female c. 5% lighter than male. Male has dark slate-grey forehead to hindneck, blacker at side, sometimes trace of red on hindneck, thin black malar stripe tipped red, rest of face including line above eye, neck side, chin and throat pale buffish-white, slightly darker on ear-coverts; upperparts, including wing-coverts and tertials, barred with brown, light brown and buffish-white, rump plain buffish-white (occasionally a few bars), uppertail-coverts white with narrow dark bars; dark brown flight-feathers narrowly barred pale buff; uppertail black, outer and central feathers thinly barred; whitish below, breast washed variable orange-buff and with blackish spots or small chevrons, marks sometimes extending to neck side and flanks; undertail-coverts occasionally with short bars; underwing pale buff-yellow, darker tip and trailing edge, a few spots on primary coverts; undertail often yellowish at sides; extremely long bill pointed, culmen curved, narrow across nostrils but broad-based, black; iris pale lemon-yellow; legs yellowish-grey to greyish-pink. Female lacks red in black malar, never has any red on hindneck. Juvenile duller than adult, with indistinct, narrow buff tips on rear crown, markings below more bar-like and often extending to flanks and belly, eyes reddish-brown, male usually with some red on nape. Race *puna* is similar to nominate but darker above, often also below, with larger breast markings, tail usually less barred, legs dull greenish, both sexes with dark red patch on hindneck, female's malar often indistinct; *cinereicapillus* is largest, distinctive, face and underparts deep cinnamon, breast with thin bars, throat partly grey, tailbars irregular, no red on nape, legs more orange-yellow. Voice. Loud whistled "tew-tew-tew", very like call of Greater Yellowlegs (*Tringa melanoleuca*); single or grouped "peek" or "kek" presumed location call and alarm (apparently shorter and higher-pitched in *cinereicapillus*), often with interspersed "cloit" or "quoi-ik-ik" in encounters (*puna*); also clear descending trill, "brrrridip", c. 2·5 seconds long with up to c 70 elements (tends to be shorter, higher, slower in *puna*), often from rock, presumably long-distance communication; low "peea" when meeting conspecific; louder "kwa-kwa-kwa, wee-a, wee-a" or "kway-áp" calls in display.

Habitat. Open country and forest edge at high elevations; broken, rolling country favoured over flat land. Inhabits stony steppes and gorges, montane scrub, *Polylepis* woodland; common in grassland of Andean *puna*, less common in humid grass-shrub of *páramo*. Between 2000 m and 5000 m throughout *puna* zone; reports at or below 2900 m, exceptionally down to 800 m, possibly foraging parties of non-breeders.

Food and Feeding. Insects, including large lepidopteran and coleopteran larvae. Beetles (Scarabeidae, Melolonthinae, Rutelinae) and noctuid moths recorded as components of diet. Gregarious: 8-10 individuals may be seen foraging together, moving considerable distances as a group; group of at least 21 birds seen feeding actively in *puna* of NE Peru. Foraging decidedly terrestrial; occasional pecks on arboreal perch indicate excitement and alertness, rather than true feeding. Preferred foraging grounds are grassy areas around rocky outcrops and other vantage points, such as cliff, rock, building, road cutting or riverbank; trees, where present, used as lookouts; feeding areas can be far from nesting grounds or roosts, and may be at lower altitudes. Starts a ground-foraging bout from vantage point, and returns to it immediately after feeding, or at slightest sign of danger. Food is sought at bases of tussocks; brushes away earth, pebbles and debris; probes into soil with remarkably long bill, digs up ground to obtain larvae hidden at depth of 5 cm or more. Feeding area is scoured evenly, searching not restricted to certain areas such as anthills. Walks on ground; in steep, rocky or densely grass-covered terrain, also hops.

Breeding. Season probably Sept-Nov in C Peru, and Jan-Mar elsewhere; possibly breeds also at other times of year; cold and snowfall in wet season of great influence in determining timing of nesting. Chiefly colonial, in groups of up to 10 or many more pairs, inter-nest distance sometimes only 50 cm. Displays include raising head to vertical position and then lowering it, wing-flicking, head-swinging with bobbing, tail-spreading. Nest-burrow dug in earth bank, cliff or rocky terrain, a horizontal or slightly upward-sloping entrance tunnel c. 1-1·5 m long, ending in nest-chamber 30 cm wide; nest-hole often excavated in native building, especially abandoned one (30-60 holes made in single hut over time, mostly for roosting), rarely in tree (*Polylepis*). Clutch size not documented, but 2-4 nestlings recorded; both parents feed chicks, also remove faeces; no information on incubation and fledging periods.

Movements. Probably some seasonal movements, with cold temperatures or snow forcing birds to retreat from high altitude to somewhat lower elevations.

Status and Conservation. Not globally threatened. Common to fairly common; locally very common. Noisy and conspicuous, difficult to overlook where present. Only recently recorded in Ecuador, where is uncommon and local. Occurs in Machu Picchu Historical Sanctuary (Peru), Sajama National Park (Bolivia), Lauca National Park (Chile) and Los Cardones National Park (Argentina). No known threats.

Bibliography. Araya & Chester (1993), Canevari *et al*. (1991), Cicero & Johnson (1995), Clements & Shany (2001), Dorst (1956, 1963), Fjeldså & Krabbe (1990), Flores & Capriles (1998), Johnson (1967), Kent *et al*. (1999), Koepcke (1970), Narosky & Yzurieta (1993), Parker, Parker & Plenge (1982), Parker, Schulenberg *et al*. (1985), de la Peña (1994), Remsen & Traylor (1989), Remsen *et al*. (1986), Ridgely & Greenfield (2001), Rocha & Peñaranda (1995), Short (1985b), Stotz *et al*. (1996), Walker (2001), Zimmer (1930).

153. Campo Flicker

Colaptes campestris

French: Pic champêtre **German**: Feldspecht **Spanish**: Carpintero Campestre
Other common names: Campos Flicker; Field Flicker (*campestroides*)

Taxonomy. *Picus campestris* Vieillot, 1818, Paraguay.
Race *campestroides* often considered a separate species, but hybridizes with nominate in Paraguay, and probably occasionally elsewhere, and the two appear to intergrade. Birds from NE Brazil, described as race *chrysosternus*, considered indistinguishable from nominate. Two subspecies recognized.

Subspecies and Distribution.
C. c. campestris (Vieillot, 1818) - S Surinam and NC Brazil (near Santarem); E Brazil (Maranhão S to Santa Catarina), N & E Bolivia (Beni, Santa Cruz) and C Paraguay.
C. c. campestroides (Malherbe, 1849) - C & S Paraguay, SE Brazil (Rio Grande do Sul) and Uruguay to NE & E Argentina (S to E Río Negro).

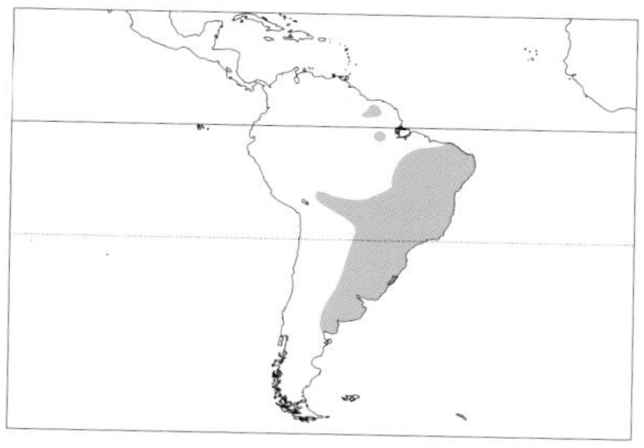

Descriptive notes. c. 28-31 cm; 145-192 g, female up to c. 15 g lighter than male (*campestroides*); c. 155 g (*campestris*). Male has black forehead to nape, buffish-white lores and area around eye, more golden-buff on ear-coverts, neck and upper breast; black malar region with red and buff feather tips, black chin and throat, chin often flecked white; upperparts, including wing-coverts and tertials, dark brown with narrow light brown and whitish bars, pale bars broader on scapulars and coverts, white rump variably (occasionally heavily) spotted or barred dark, uppertail-coverts barred brown and white; dark brown flight-feathers thinly barred buffish-white; uppertail brown-black, narrow buff bars on outer webs, also on inner webs of central feathers; underparts below breast white, tinged pale yellow, with narrow dark barring, underparts frequently soiled through ground-feeding habits; underwing yellowish, darker tip and trailing edge, some spots on primary coverts; undertail as above, pale bars more obscure; longish bill pointed, culmen curved, narrow across nostrils but broad-based, black; iris chestnut to red-brown; legs green-grey or pink-tinged. Female has malar area whitish and black, without red tips. Juvenile duller than adult, dark bars broader, golden-buff areas paler and less extensive. Race *campestroides* differs from nominate mainly in white to buff-white chin and throat, thus malar more conspicuous, also often more narrowly barred below, belly almost plain. Voice. Loud double or triple whistle, notes run together more than in corresponding vocalization of *C. rupicola*, heard infrequently; "week" or "keep" series as location call; wavering "wewwwew", "gwik", "ewuh", and "pya" or "kyow"; also wavering "we-a, kwih" or "kya-wi" notes, like low versions of "wicka" calls of *C. auratus*; fast series of "wick" (slightly higher-pitched in *campestroides*) in close contacts; also long or short series of fairly clear "oo" and "ee" notes.

Habitat. Savanna and other grassland, *campos*, farmland, edges. Sub-arid scrub (*caatinga*), forest clearings and woodland edge, and tree plantations in open areas, in N of range. S race *campestroides* typically inhabits open pampas, at forest edge and in clearings, and is a characteristic bird of open level country. Secondary habitats include overgrazed land, and undeveloped areas along major highways. Locations with termite (Isoptera) nests, fence posts, trees and similar structures suitable for nesting are favoured. Lowlands, to 600 m in Argentina.

Food and Feeding. Predominantly ants and termites, and their brood; more than 2000 ants found in 1 stomach. Adult beetles, Orthoptera, and nestlings also taken. Often in small groups; loose parties of up to 8 individuals seen foraging together, or concentrated at an anthill, sometimes joined by *C. melanochloros*. Forages almost exclusively on the ground, among stones, at decaying fallen logs, and on roads; also visits termite mounds or anthills and other prominent structures, such as isolated trees, utility or fence poles, cacti and rocks. Regularly perches on wires. Walks when searching for food, hops to cover long distances; also hops to ascend termite hills and similar structures. Opens the large mounds of terrestrial termites; sometimes breaks into nests of Rufous Hornero (*Furnarius rufus*) to reach the nestlings. Known to hammer large holes, up to 7 cm in diameter, into buildings, but uncertain whether this behaviour designed to create roost-sites or for securing food.

Breeding. Jan-Apr in Surinam and Aug-Nov in Argentina. Availability of nest-sites probably a crucial factor in social behaviour; groups of 3 or 4 birds seen more commonly than pairs or solitary individuals during breeding season, but relationships within such groups not well known; sometimes in loose colonies, e.g. 5-6 nests/100 m along lines of trees. Displays with fluttering or spreading of wings to reveal bright yellow shafts; head-swinging not very conspicuous. Nest excavated at up to 12 m in tree trunk or dead stump, or in telephone pole or large fence post where available, or occasionally in nest of arboreal termites (*Constrictotermes cypergaster*); in mound of terrestrial termites (*Cornitermes cumulans*) and in banks in treeless country. Clutch 4-5 eggs; incubation by both partners; incubation and fledging periods not documented; family-members stay together for an extended period.

Movements. Resident; possibly wanders to some extent.

Status and Conservation. Not globally threatened. Generally common; locally very common. Occurs in several protected areas, e.g. Beni Biosphere Reserve (Bolivia), Monte Pascoal, Aparados da Serra and Serra do Cipó National Parks, Rio Doce State Park and Sooretama Biological Reserve (Brazil), and Iguazú National Park and Costanera Sur Ecological Reserve (Argentina). Benefits from deforestation; clearance of forest for road-building creates new areas of habitat for this open-country species, enabling it to expand its range; can now be observed in clearings in subtropical moist forest, and on so-called wasteland bordering major highways.

Bibliography. Aleixo & Galetti (1997), dos Anjos & Schuchmann (1997), Belton (1984), Bencke & Kindel (1999), Brace *et al*. (1997), Buzzetti (2000), Canevari *et al*. (1991), Capper *et al*. (2000), Castro (1991), Contreras *et al*. (1990), Dubs (1992), Ferreira de Vasconcelos & Melo-Júnior (2001), Figueiredo & Lo (2000), Figueiredo *et al*. (2000), Fjeldså & Krabbe (1990), Friedmann (1927), Haverschmidt & Mees (1994), Hayes (1995), Klimaitis & Moschione (1987), López (1997), Madroño, Robbins & Zyskowski (1997), Marini (2001), Marini *et al*. (1997), Melo-Júnior (2001a), Parker & Goerck (1997), de la Peña (1994, 1996), Pinto & Camargo (1961), Raw (1997), Remsen & Traylor (1989), do Rosário (1996), Scott & Brooke (1985), Short (1969b, 1975, 1985b), Sick (1993), da Silva *et al*. (1997), Stager (1961a), Stotz *et al*. (1996), Stradi & Hudon (1998), Stradi *et al*. (1998), Tobias *et al*. (1993), Tubelis & Tomás (1999), Venturini *et al*. (2001).

ssp *brachyurus* ♂ ♀

ssp *jerdonii* ♂

ssp *squamigularis* ♂

ssp *badiosus* ♂

154

ssp *holroydi* ♂

ssp *fokiensis* ♂

ssp *loricatus* ♀ ♂

ssp *diversus* ♂

155

ssp *innotatus* ♂

ssp *grammicus* ♀ ♂

156

ssp *latifasciatus* ♀ ♂

Venezuelan bird ♂

Brazilian bird ♀

ssp *undatus* ♂

157

ssp *multifasciatus* ♂

ssp *amacurensis* ♂

PLATE 41

inches   4

cm   10

Genus *CELEUS* Boie, 1831

154. **Rufous Woodpecker**

Celeus brachyurus

French: Pic brun **German**: Rötelspecht **Spanish**: Carpintero Rufo
Other common names: Brown Woodpecker

Taxonomy. *Picus brachyurus* Vieillot, 1818, Java.
Sometimes placed in a monospecific genus *Micropternus*. Taxonomic position uncertain; not very closely related to other, Neotropical species of present genus, and possibly closer to genus *Picus*; further study required. Considerable individual variation rendering racial delimitation difficult; proposed races *badius* (Sumatra) and *celaenephis* (Nias I) inseparable from continental *squamigularis*. Nine subspecies recognized.
Subspecies and Distribution.
C. b. humei (Kloss, 1918) - N India (Himachal Pradesh) E to to W Nepal.
C. b. jerdonii (Malherbe, 1849) - W India (S from S Gujarat) S to Sri Lanka.
C. b. phaioceps (Blyth, 1845) - C Nepal and E India E to SE Tibet, Myanmar and S China (W & S Yunnan) and S to S Thailand.
C. b. fokiensis (Swinhoe, 1863) - S & SE China and N Vietnam.
C. b. holroydi (Swinhoe, 1870) - Hainan.
C. b. annamensis (Delacour & Jabouille, 1924) - Laos, Cambodia and S Vietnam.
C. b. squamigularis (Sundevall, 1866) - S peninsular Thailand S to Sumatra, including offshore islands of Bangka, Belitung and Nias.
C. b. brachyurus (Vieillot, 1818) - Java.
C. b. badiosus (Bonaparte, 1850) - Borneo and N Natuna Is.

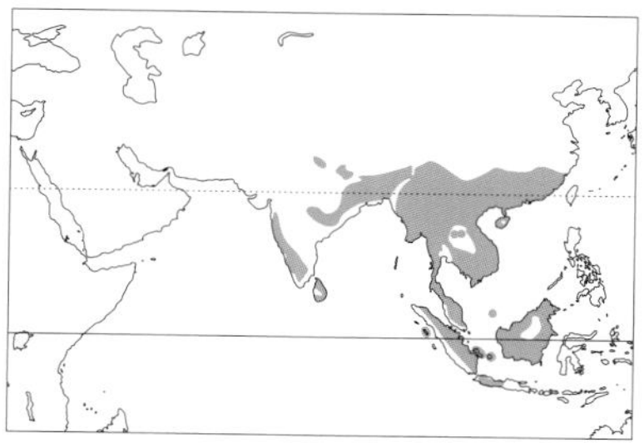

Descriptive notes. c. 25 cm; 55-84 g (*squamigularis*, *badiosus*), 82-107 g (*jerdonii*), 92-114 g (*phaioceps*). Male has dark brown forehead to nape and short crest, broad red feather tips beneath eye back to front of ear-coverts, dark throat with buff feather tips; rest of head and body plumage dark rufous to chestnut, upperparts very narrowly barred black, flanks to undertail-coverts with widely spaced thin black bars, belly sometimes with thin broken bars; wings similar to upperparts; tail also narrowly dark-barred, broader black tips; underwing rufous, barred black; short bill, culmen slightly curved, rather narrow-based, dark grey, blacker tip; iris reddish to brown, narrow orbital skin grey; legs blue-grey or bluish-green to brown. Female lacks red on side of head. Juvenile as adult, variably barred, often less heavily, or sometimes with bars extending to breast. Races highly variable, including individually, in ground colour of plumage, some much paler than others: *humei* is large, pale, with greyish head, streaked throat; *jerdonii* is smaller and more rufous than previous, with paler head, scaly throat markings; *phaioceps* is large, rather dark rufous, with brownish head; *squamigularis* is fairly small, generally much paler than previous, with heavily streaked throat, belly strongly barred with arrowheads (barring less extensive in Sumatran population); *badiosus* has long bill, contrasting black tail narrowly barred rufous, unbarred back, little or no barring on belly, throat feathers black-based with chestnut tips and buff edges; *fokiensis* is distinctive, with creamy head streaked black on crown, heavily black-streaked throat, broad black bars above, sooty-brown and little streaked below, greyer or browner breast, proportionately longest tail; *annamensis* resembles previous, but slightly smaller, head darker; *holroydi* is smaller than previous, very dark chestnut all over, with narrow bars above, throat streaked brown, flanks barred black. VOICE. Highly vocal: series of 3 nasal "kweep" or "keenk" notes delivered in less than 1 second (sometimes pause before final note), reminiscent of calls of Common Myna (*Acridotheres tristis*); in encounters 4 or 5 "kweek" notes, some perhaps similar to variable "whi-chi" in same context; slightly falling accelerating series 2 seconds long of up to 16 notes, may be repeated several times, probably as territorial announcement and contact between pair-members. Drumming highly distinctive, single roll 1·5-5 seconds long, slows gradually to halt like stalling motorcycle engine, "bdddd-d-d–d—dt", rolls 2-3 minutes apart, delivered commonly, often on bamboo, by both sexes.
Habitat. Primary forest and secondary forest, both evergreen and deciduous. Open forest, secondary growth, forest edge and scrub preferred; habitats include sal (*Shorea*) forest, and has strong liking for bamboo jungle, at least locally. May also visit reedbeds and mangroves. Mostly well away from human habitations in some areas; may be found in plantations, palm groves and gardens in others, e.g. in Sumatra. Resident from plains up to 610 m in Sri Lanka, to 1530 m in Nepal; to 1450 m in China and SE Asia, but mostly below 1000 m in Thailand and Malay Peninsula; to 1740 m in Borneo.
Food and Feeding. Chiefly ants and their brood, particularly of genus *Crematogaster*, but also *Pheidole* and *Oecophylla*; also termites (Isoptera), other insects. Vegetable matter taken occasionally, includes fruits (e.g. *Ficus*), nectar, sap. Often in pairs; sometimes with mixed-species flocks. Forages at all levels, including high canopy of tall forest, and occasionally on ground; densely vegetated sites generally preferred, but more open ones also visited at times. May perch crosswise on twigs. Searches vines, trunks, branches, twigs, bamboo; on ground, observed to seek food in small termite mounds or anthills, even in cow-pats; also explores rotting logs. Chief feeding techniques are gleaning and probing, with occasional weak and barely audible blow. Pecks at *Crematogaster* nests from a perch close by; clings at nest, tears it apart, gleans ants that swarm out, also picking them from its plumage and feet. Also observed to puncture banana stems to feed on the oozing sap. Very active, almost constantly on the move, remains at a site only if abundant food source, e.g. ants, present.
Breeding. Apr-Jun in Nepal, Sikkim and N Myanmar, Feb-Jun in S India and Sri Lanka, Jan-Apr in Thailand and Malaysia, May-Jun in Sumatra, and in Apr and Sept in Java. Displays include tail-spreading, head-swinging and body-swinging. Nest-hole, dug by both sexes, is in active arboreal nest of ants, mostly of genus *Crematogaster* but sometimes others (e.g. *Plagiolepis*), usually high up on tree trunk, occasionally lower (c. 3 m) around fork in sapling; less often, hole excavated in tree or stub. Clutch 2-3 eggs, up to 7 recorded rarely (China), clutch size increasing S to N; both sexes incubate, period 12-14 days; both also feed chicks, by regurgitation, fledging period not documented.
Movements. Resident.
Status and Conservation. Not globally threatened. Locally common in India, uncommon in Nepal, scarce in Sri Lanka; common in China; fairly common to common throughout SE Asia and Greater Sundas. Occurs in many protected areas throughout its extensive range, e.g. Corbett, Periyar and Kaziranga National Parks (India) and Cuc Phuong National Park (Vietnam). Although habitat loss could possibly limit or reduce its populations, this woodpecker readily accepts more open forest and a variety of secondary habitats, so long as plenty of nests of arboreal ants are available.
Bibliography. Ali (1996), Ali & Ripley (1983), Ali *et al.* (1996), Andrew (1992), Baker (1919), van Balen (1999), Bangs & Van Tyne (1931), Betts (1934), Biswas (1961b), Bucknill & Chasen (1990), Deignan (1945), Duckworth & Kelsh (1988), Eames & Robson (1992), Edgar (1933), Étchécopar & Hüe (1978), Grimmett *et al.* (1998), Hails & Jarvis (1987), Harrison (1999), Harvey (1990), Henry (1998), Hoffmann (1998), Inskipp, C. & Inskipp (1991), Inskipp, T. *et al.* (1996), Jeyarajasingam & Pearson (1999), Lainer (1999), Lamsfuss (1998), Lekagul & Round (1991), Ludlow (1937, 1944), MacKinnon (1988), MacKinnon & Phillipps (1993, 2000), van Marle & Voous (1988), McClure (1998), Medway & Wells (1976), Mees (1986), Meyer de Schauensee & Ripley (1940), Phillips (1978), Proud (1958), Riley (1938), Ripley (1982), Robinson & Kloss (1921-1924), Robson (2000), Santharam (1997, 1998c), Sargeant (1997), Short (1973d, 1985b), Smythies (1986, 1999), Stepanyan (1995), Taylor (1961), Vowles & Vowles (1997), Wells (1985, 1999), Wilkinson, Dutson & Sheldon (1991), Wilson (1898), Zacharias & Gaston (1999), Zhao Zhengjie (1995).

155. **Cinnamon Woodpecker**

Celeus loricatus

French: Pic cannelle **German**: Rotkehlspecht **Spanish**: Carpintero Canelo

Taxonomy. *Meiglyptes loricatus* Reichenbach, 1854, Peru.
Possibly not very closely related to others of genus. Wide individual variation, making racial delimitation difficult; birds from C Magdalena Valley, in Colombia, described as race *degener*, but differences from *innotatus* considered insignificant. Designated type locality of Peru falls outwith known range of species, and may require revision. Four subspecies recognized.
Subspecies and Distribution.
C. l. diversus Ridgway, 1914 - E Nicaragua S to W Panama.
C. l. mentalis Cassin, 1860 - Panama and NW Colombia.
C. l. innotatus Todd, 1917 - N Colombia.
C. l. loricatus (Reichenbach, 1854) - W Colombia to SW Ecuador (S to Guayas).

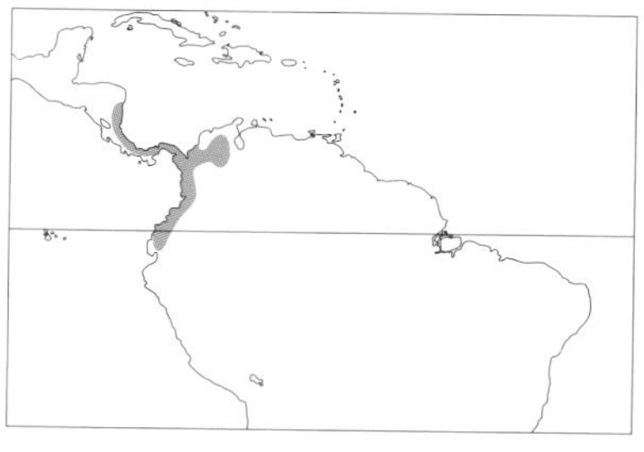

Descriptive notes. c. 19-23 cm; 74-83 g. Male has rufous head and bushy crest, crown streaked black, red-tipped black chin, throat and malar area, sometimes also a few red tips around eye; upperparts, including wing-coverts and tertials, dark rufous, rump paler, all narrowly barred black; blackish flight-feathers with very broad rufous bars; uppertail black, very broadly barred buff to whitish; upper breast light rufous with black edges and tips, rest of underparts paler buff, with striking bold black markings on breast, arrowhead bars on flanks and belly to undertail-coverts; rufous underwing barred black on flight-feathers; medium-long bill almost pointed, culmen slightly curved, narrow across nostrils, greyish to yellowish; iris red; legs grey. Female lacks red on throat, head rather uniformly rufous. Juvenile much as adult but dusky-mottled on throat, less regularly marked below, male with red on face. Races differ mainly in amount of barring: *diversus* is largest, more cinnamon-tinged than nominate, has large red tips on throat, narrower black bars above, more widely spaced narower bars below, yellower bill; *mentalis* is smaller than previous, paler below, with less barring above and below; *innotatus* resembles previous, but even less marked, very weakly barred or even unbarred above, may lack crown streaks, plain below but for a few breast spots. VOICE. Accelerating series of 3-5 fast ringing notes, descending in pitch and amplitude, e.g. "peee-peew-peu-pu", sometimes introduced with "chuweéoo"; sharp, descending rolling chatter when agitated; also hard "chikikikirík", squeaky "tititit-toò", and "chweé-titit". Drumrolls rather slow, short.
Habitat. Inhabits humid and wet forest, rarely in drier areas; occasionally visits forest edge, nearby semi-open areas, old second growth, and clearings. Occurs in lowlands and foothills, from sea-level up to 760 m in Costa Rica and Panama, up to 1500 m in Colombia; to 800 m in Ecuador.
Food and Feeding. Ants and termites; also fruit, e.g. ripening bananas. Usually forages singly or in pairs; only occasionally joins mixed-species flocks. Active in or near canopy in forest interior; also at lower levels, particularly in open areas. Generally visits trunks, often thin ones, and twigs and branchlets; often clings to seedlings and bushes in undergrowth. Pecks frequently, and gleans to some extent; observed to peck into swollen nodes of laurel (*Cordia alliodra*) twigs and *Cecropia* trunks to reach ants, and into tunnels for termites.
Breeding. Mar-May in Costa Rica and Jan-Apr in Colombia. Hole excavated by both sexes, at 6-9 m in soft wood of living or recently dead tree. Clutch size and incubation and fledging periods apparently not described.
Movements. Resident.
Status and Conservation. Not globally threatened. Generally uncommon, but locally fairly common. Normally inconspicuous, more often heard than seen. Occurs in a number of protected areas throughout range, e.g. Braulio Carrillo National Park and Finca La Selva (Costa Rica), Los Katíos National Park, Río Ñambí Nature Reserve and El Pangán Reserve (Colombia), and Manglares-Churute Ecological Reserve (Ecuador). Recorded at several sites in W Panama (e.g. El Copé and Santa Fe).
Bibliography. Anon. (1998b), Blake & Loiselle (2000, 2001), Butler (1979), Cooper (1997), Gillespie (2001), Haffer (1974, 1975), Hilty (1997), Hilty & Brown (1986), Meyer de Schauensee (1982), Olrog (1968), Pople *et al.* (1997), Ridgely & Greenfield (2001), Ridgely & Gwynne (1989), Ridgely *et al.* (1998), Robbins *et al.* (1985), Salaman (1994), Slud (1960, 1964), Stiles (1985), Stiles & Skutch (1989), Stiles *et al.* (1999), Stotz *et al.* (1996), Wetmore (1968a).

On following page: 156. Scaly-breasted Woodpecker (*Celeus grammicus*); 157. Waved Woodpecker (*Celeus undatus*).

156. Scaly-breasted Woodpecker

Celeus grammicus

French: Pic de Verreaux   **German**: Gelbflankenspecht   **Spanish**: Carpintero Rojizo
Other common names: Scale-breasted Woodpecker

Taxonomy. *Picus grammicus* Natterer and Malherbe, 1845, Marabitanas, upper Rio Negro, Brazil. Forms a superspecies with *C. undatus*. Proposed race *undulatus*, described from R Mocho (R Caura area, SC Venezuela), is known only from type locality; now included within nominate. Four subspecies recognized.
Subspecies and Distribution.
C. g. grammicus (Natterer & Malherbe, 1845) - SE Colombia and S Venezuela S to NE Peru and W Brazil; also French Guiana (Nouragues area).
C. g. verreauxii (Malherbe, 1858) - E Ecuador and adjacent NE Peru.
C. g. subcervinus Todd, 1937 - Brazil, S of R Amazon, E to lower R Tapajós and S to N Mato Grosso.
C. g. latifasciatus Seilern, 1936 - SE Peru and SW Brazil (upper R Madeira) S to N Bolivia (Beni).

Descriptive notes. c. 23-26 cm; 63-75 g (*grammicus*), 77-82 g (*verreauxii*), 75-87 g (*latifasciatus*). Male has rufous-chestnut forehead to pointed crest usually streaked black (streaking variable), broad red patch on cheeks and malar region extending to front part of ear-coverts, rest of plumage mostly rufous-chestnut; neck side barred black, upperparts narrowly barred black, rump pale greenish-yellow to yellow-buff, very occasionally with some red-tipped feathers; rufous-chestnut uppertail-coverts occasionally slightly barred; blackish flight-feathers narrowly edged rufous, bases paler greenish-yellow; uppertail brownblack, feathers edged chestnut, base sometimes wholly chestnut; flanks paler rufous-chestnut to yellowish-buff; breast with black bars or arrowhead marks, narrower on lower breast, sparse spots on belly; underwing dull brown, paler yellowish coverts and flight-feather bases; undertail brown or yellow-brown, cinnamon base; shortish bill slightly chisel-tipped, culmen curved, narrow across nostrils, greenish to yellow-green or ivory; iris red; legs dark greenish-grey to grey. Differs from *C. undatus* in much darker head, unbarred tail, darker underparts. Female has red of face replaced by rufous-chestnut. Juvenile as adult, but head darker with some blackish areas, usually paler upperparts more broadly barred, male with some red in malar. Race *verreauxii* resembles nominate, but less barred below; *subcervinus* has rump and flanks more cinnamon to buff, lacking yellow tone; *latifasciatus* is distinctive, pale cinnamon-coloured above with yellow or buffish feather bases visible, very pale rump, mantle broadly barred, much paler ground colour below. VOICE. Common call a loud, abrupt, slightly nasal whistle, "curry-kuuu" or "doit-gua" or "kuwee? kuuu", clearly enunciated; very loud and metallic "pring-pring!" notes, in series of up to 4, also heard.
Habitat. Inhabits rainforest, humid *terra firme* and *várzea* forests, forest edge, second growth, and savanna with scattered trees. Ranges from 100 m up to 900 m, locally up to 1140 m; to c. 500 m in Ecuador.
Food and Feeding. Ants and fruit. Sometimes in groups of 3 or 4 birds, probably family parties; frequently associates with mixed-species groups. Forages inconspicuously in middle to upper levels, on trunks and larger limbs, also on vines. Pecks rapidly; probes and gleans at bark surface.
Breeding. Feb-Apr in Venezuela, possibly somewhat later in Brazil. No other information available.
Movements. Presumably resident.
Status and Conservation. Not globally threatened. Rather uncommon to common; uncommon in Peru; uncommon to fairly comon in Ecuador. Inconspicuous and not often seen. Occurs at La Selva (Ecuador), Tambopata and Alpahuayo-Mishana Reserves (Peru) and Rio Cristalino Private Reserve (Brazil). Study required on its ecology and breeding biology.
Bibliography. Allen (1995), Borges *et al*. (2001), Clements & Shany (2001), Cohn-Haft *et al*. (1997), Donahue (1994), Friedmann (1948), Haffer (1974), Hilty & Brown (1986), Meyer de Schauensee (1982), Meyer de Schauensee

& Phelps (1978), Olrog (1968), Oren & Parker (1997), Parker *et al*. (1982), Peres & Whittaker (1991), Remsen & Traylor (1989), Ridgely & Greenfield (2001), Robinson & Terborgh (1997), Sick (1993), da Silva (1996), Stotz, Fitzpatrick *et al*. (1996), Stotz, Lanyon *et al*. (1997), Terborgh *et al*. (1984), Tostain *et al*. (1992).

157. Waved Woodpecker

Celeus undatus

French: Pic ondé   **German**: Olivbürzelspecht   **Spanish**: Carpintero Ondoso

Taxonomy. *Picus undatus* Linnaeus, 1766, Surinam.
Forms a superspecies with *C. grammicus*. Three subspecies recognized.
Subspecies and Distribution.
C. u. undatus (Linnaeus, 1766) - E Venezuela (E Sucre S to E Bolivar), the Guianas, and NE Brazil N of Amazon (W from middle and lower R Negro).
C. u. amacurensis Phelps, Sr. & Phelps, Jr., 1950 - Delta Amacuro (NE Venezuela).
C. u. multifasciatus (Natterer & Malherbe, 1845) - NE Brazil S of Amazon, from C Pará E to lower R Tocantins and NW Maranhão border.

Descriptive notes. c. 23-24 cm; male 61-73 g, female 58-68 g. Male has broad red band from upper bill back to front edge of ear-coverts; rest of head light chestnut-rufous, crown and crest often paler and sometimes barred, rear earcoverts and neck side finely spotted or streaked; chin and throat cinnamon-buff with black spots or bars; entire upperparts, including wing-coverts and tertials, rufous-chestnut, usually paler or yellower on rump, all broadly barred black; black flight-feathers with cinnamon-rufous bars; black uppertail with variable number of rufous bars, sometimes none; rufous below, paler in lower regions, breast with irregular wavy bars, variable (breast feathers sometimes black with narrow pale edges, all black when abraded), belly and flanks with more regular bars or arrowheads; underwing cinnamon, barred bases of flight-feathers; undertail as above but duller, sometimes tinged yellowish; shortish bill almost pointed, culmen curved, fairly narrow across nostrils, dull yellow to yellow-green; iris red-brown to red; legs green-grey. Considerable variation in intensity of black barring: Brazilian populations of nominate tend to show heavier black barring, with upper breast appearing almost solid black. Female lacks red on head, and generally more heavily barred. Juvenile duller than adult, less barred above. Race *amacurensis* is darker, more chestnut, than nominate, with head same colour as upperparts (not paler), rump more cinnamon-rufous (not yellow), crown unmarked, all bars narrower; *multifasciatus* is somewhat bigger than others, proportionately shorter-tailed, paler, more buffy, with head streaked (not barred), tail often unbarred, paler below, has blackish bill with paler lower mandible. VOICE. Loud "wit-koa", very like corresponding call of *C. grammicus*; soft, whispered "kowahair", rising in pitch, also described. Both sexes drum.
Habitat. Most frequent in dense rainforest, at up to 500 m; occasionally in more open terrain of savanna regions, at forest edge, and near rivers.
Food and Feeding. Ants and termites; occasionally seeds. Forages inconspicuously in treetops; sometimes joins mixed-species feeding flocks.
Breeding. Season from end of May to Aug in the Guianas; possibly in earlier part of that period in SE of range. Nest in dead or live tree at 4-30 m. No other information.
Movements. Resident.
Status and Conservation. Not globally threatened. Uncommon. Occurs in Canaima National Park and Imataca Forest Reserve and El Dorado (Venezuela). Observed at Mana, in French Guiana. Poorly known woodpecker, unobtrusive and not often seen. Research on its ecology and breeding biology desirable, and censuses required to determine its population status, but fieldwork not easy in areas inhabited by this species.
Bibliography. Cohn-Haft *et al*. (1997), Haffer (1974), Haverschmidt & Mees (1994), Meyer de Schauensee (1982), Meyer de Schauensee & Phelps (1978), O'Brien (1979), Olrog (1968), Ruschi (1979), Sick (1993), Snyder (1966), Stotz *et al*. (1996), Thiollay & Jullien (1998), Tostain *et al*. (1992), Wheatley (1994).

PLATE 42 ➤

158

♀ ♂

ssp elegans

♀ ♂

ssp leotaudi

ssp hellmayri

♂

159

♀

160

♀ ♂

ssp jumanus

♀ ♂

ssp citreopygius

♂

♂

ssp intercedens

161

♂ ♀

ssp flavus

162

♀ ♂

ssp flavescens

♂ ochraceus

♂

ssp subflavus

♂ ♀

ssp torquatus

164

♀

ssp spectabilis

♀ ♂

163

♀

ssp obrieni

♂

ssp occidentalis

♂

ssp tinnunculus

♂

PLATE 42

♂

ssp exsul

inches   5

cm   13

158. **Chestnut-coloured Woodpecker**

Celeus castaneus

French: Pic roux **German**: Kastanienspecht **Spanish**: Carpintero Castaño
Other common names: Chestnut Woodpecker(!)

Taxonomy. *Picus castaneus* Wagler, 1829, no locality = Veracruz, Mexico.
Possibly forms a superspecies with *C. elegans*, *C. lugubris* and *C. flavescens*. Monotypic.
Distribution. E Mexico (from S Veracruz, N Oaxaca) S to W Panama.

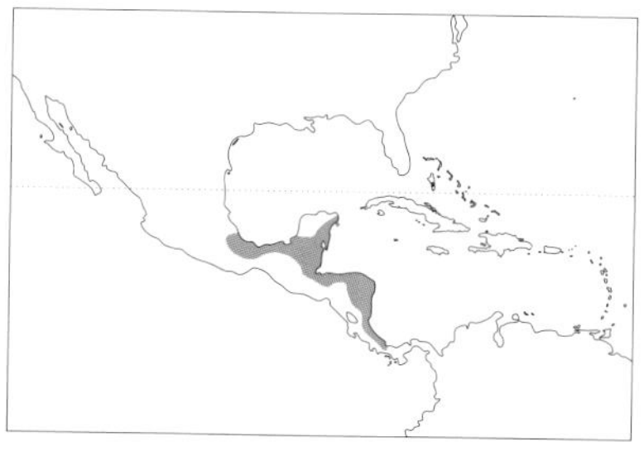

Descriptive notes. c. 23-25 cm; 80-105 g. Male has broad red band from bill base back to lower cheeks, red feather tips around eye, and sometimes along crown side; rest of head ochraceous-buff to cinnamon-buff, crest more golden; upperparts, including wing-coverts and tertials, chestnut or rufous-chestnut, rump yellower, mantle, back and wing-coverts with variable number of widely spaced broken black bars, uppertail-coverts usually spotted or barred black; dark rufous-brown flight-feathers, blacker tips, rarely with sparse spots or bars on secondaries; uppertail blackish, base often dark rufous-chestnut; dark rufous-chestnut below, golden-buff on inner flanks (feather bases), all with black chevrons or more regular bars, markings narrower on belly; underwing-coverts yellowish, cinnamon bases to dark-tipped flight-feathers; rather short bill slightly chisel-tipped, culmen curved, fairly narrow across nostrils, pale greenish to pale ivory-yellow, often blue-green base; iris chestnut to brown, orbital ring grey or blackish; legs dark olive to grey. Female lacks red on head. Juvenile duller than adult, often dark bars on face, less barred on belly. Voice. Sibilant descending whistle, "peew" or "kheeu", often followed by 2-10 sharp nasal "wet" notes; regular series of "howp" notes, often with terminal "r'rrp"; also single low "kwar"; series of sharp "wik-kew" in excitement. Drumroll c. 1·5 seconds, shorter and softer than that of e.g. *Melanerpes pucherani*.
Habitat. Prefers dense humid evergreen and semi-deciduous forest, tall second growth; also forest edge, and densely foliaged trees with epiphytes in semi-open areas, occasionally mangroves. Lowlands, also entering foothills, to 500 m, locally to 750 m, rarely 1000 m.
Food and Feeding. Mainly ants and termites (Isoptera), and other insects; some fruit, and arillate seeds (e.g. *Stemmadenia*), possibly also cultivated crops (cacao). Usually singly or in pairs; occasionally with mixed-species flocks. Forages mainly in canopy and subcanopy, down to middle levels along edges. Explores trees with dense foliage and epiphytes in semi-open, more often on trunks and larger limbs than *C. loricatus*. Sometimes clings to foliage, and moves sideways along a twig; able to obtain fruits hanging from distal ends of branches. Pecks into tunnels and hard nests of arboreal termites, and in *Cecropia* trunks; also pries off bark flakes, eating prey thus uncovered. Pecking and probing are most frequent foraging techniques, followed by hammering; gleans rarely.
Breeding. Mar-Jun, sometimes Aug, in N of range; Feb-Jul in Costa Rica and Panama. Nest excavated by both sexes, 4-21 m up in soft wood of living or recently dead tree, sometimes much lower (e.g. 0·9 m) in palm. Clutch 3 or 4 eggs (Belize). No other information.
Movements. Some seasonal movements; wanders into coastal scrub and mangrove in winter.
Status and Conservation. Not globally threatened. Fairly common to common in Mexico, less common farther S. Occurs in several protected areas, including Finca La Selva (Costa Rica). Alleged to cause some damage in commercial cacao plantations.
Bibliography. Angehr (2001), Anon. (1998b), Binford (1989), Blake & Loiselle (2000, 2001), Cooper (1999), Dearborn (1907), England (2000), Friedmann *et al*. (1957), Gillespie (2001), González-Garcia (1993), Howell & Webb (1995), Kilham (1979a), Land (1970), Paynter (1955), Ridgely & Gwynne (1989), Short (1972a, 1975, 1985b), Slud (1960, 1964), Smithe (1966), Stiles (1985), Stiles & Skutch (1989), Stotz *et al*. (1996), Vallely & Whitman (1997), Wetmore (1968a).

159. **Chestnut Woodpecker**

Celeus elegans

French: Pic mordoré **German**: Fahlkopfspecht **Spanish**: Carpintero Elegante
Other common names: Elegant Woodpecker, Pale-crowned Crested Woodpecker; Russet-crested/Rufous-crested Woodpecker (*elegans* group); Chestnut-crested Woodpecker (*jumanus* group); Yellow-crested Woodpecker (*leotaudi*)

Taxonomy. *Picus elegans* P. L. S. Müller, 1776, Cayenne.
Possibly forms a superspecies with *C. castaneus*, *C. lugubris* and *C. flavescens*. Dark-crowned, short-crested races *jumanus* and *citreopygius* sometimes considered to form a separate species. Birds from upper R Branco, in N Brazil, described as race *approximans*, but appear inseparable from nominate; proposed race *saturatus* (N Bolivia) indistinguishable from *jumanus*. Form "*C. immaculatus*", known only from type specimen, supposedly from Panama, appears to be an aberrant form of nominate race of present species with erroneous locality data. Six subspecies recognized.
Subspecies and Distribution.
C. e. hellmayri Berlepsch, 1908 - E Venezuela, Guyana and most of Surinam.
C. e. leotaudi Hellmayr, 1906 - Trinidad.
C. e. deltanus Phelps, Sr. & Phelps, Jr., 1950 - Delta Amacuro (NE Venezuela).
C. e. elegans (P. L. S. Müller, 1776) - E Surinam, French Guiana, and N Brazil N of Amazon (Roraima to Amapá).
C. e. jumanus (Spix, 1824) - E Colombia and S Venezuela (Amazonas, S Bolívar) through W & C Brazil (N of Amazon E to R Negro and S of Amazon E to Maranhão, and S to Rondônia and Mato Grosso) to N Bolivia.
C. e. citreopygius P. L. Sclater & Salvin, 1868 - E Ecuador and E Peru.
Descriptive notes. c. 26-32 cm; 138-168 g (*hellmayri*), 112-146 g (*jumanus*), 93-139 g (*leotaudi*). Male has buffish-cream forehead, crown and long crest, broad red malar area and cheek; rest of head and neck, chin and throat deep chestnut-brown; deep rufous-chestnut upperparts occasionally

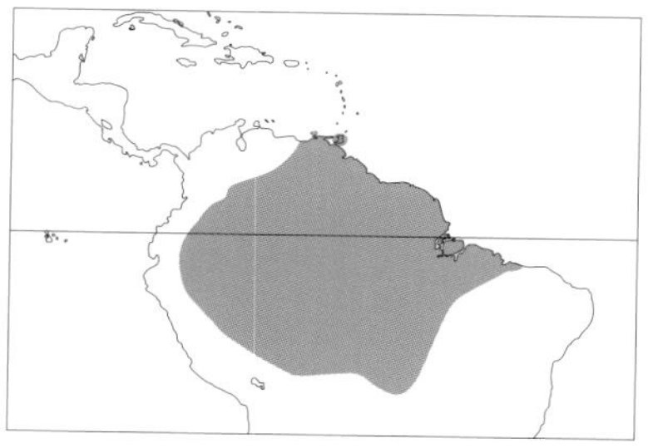

with faint black bars, rarely with yellow feather bases showing through, cream-buff rump occasionally with some red-tipped feathers, uppertail-coverts as rump or sometimes with rufous tips; wing-coverts with small white spots or thin shaft streaks, creamy area on alula; secondaries barred brown on inner webs, and sometimes on outer, blackish-brown outer primaries usually with rufous bars at base of inner webs; uppertail blackish, rufous on outermost (concealed) feather; dark chestnut-brown below, belly and vent sometimes paler, flanks paler creamy cinnamon-buff and often obscurely barred; underwing mainly cream-buff or pale cinnamon, browner flight-feathers, usually some barring; short bill slightly chisel-tipped, culmen curved, fairly narrow across nostrils, ivory to yellow or greenish-yellow, darker tip; iris red-brown to red, orbital ring blue; legs olive to dark grey. Female lacks red moustache. Juvenile much as adult, but dull blackish on face, usually mottled darker below, male soon acquires red feathers in malar, also sometimes on forehead and around eyes. Race *hellmayri* differs from nominate in somewhat darker plumage, darker crown, more spots on wing-coverts, spots on scapulars, more barred primaries; *deltanus* is even darker on crown; *leotaudi* is much smaller than nominate, paler and brighter, with tawny crown, yellower rump; *jumanus* is darker overall than preceding races, also has shorter crest, rufous tips on back and wing-coverts, no white spots, more rufous tertials and secondaries, buffish thighs; *citreopygius* is also short-crested but blacker, less rufous, than previous, with contrasting red cheekband. Voice. Descending "wewa ew-ew-ew-ew-ew-ew" or sarcastic-sounding "har-hahaha" as territorial call, and rattling screeches, e.g. "whick-frrr" or grating "wháa-jer", occasionally rapidly repeated several times; also "wick-wick-wick-wick-wick", mellow "gwarrr", nasal "kyeenh". Both sexes drum, frequently and loudly in breeding season, double rap as "dop-dop".
Habitat. Variety of tall dense and light forests, including humid *terra firme*, gallery and *várzea* forests, and forest edge; also occupies secondary habitats, such as cocoa plantations. Lowlands, from sea-level to 1000 m in Venezuela, to 500 m in Colombia and to 1100 m in Peru; mostly below 500 m but recorded at 700 m in Ecuador.
Food and Feeding. Ants and termites (Isoptera); also dipteran larvae. Fruits (e.g. *Cecropia*, citrus and introduced mango) and berries also taken, sometimes in large quantities. Alone or in pairs, or in loose groups of up to 5 birds, frequently with mixed-species flocks. Forages inconspicuously, mainly at low to medium heights, from understorey up to subcanopy; moves along larger limbs and trunks. Techniques include gleaning from bark, hammering into arboreal termitaria. Hangs upside-down to reach for fruit.
Breeding. Apr-May in Trinidad and French Guiana; specimens with enlarged gonads in Jan-Feb in S Venezuela and NW Brazil. Nest-cavity in dead tree or stub; clutch 3 eggs. No other information available.
Movements. Resident.
Status and Conservation. Not globally threatened. Relatively common; very common in NE Venezuela; uncommon to locally fairly common in Ecuador and Peru. Occurs in several protected areas, e.g. Imataca Forest Reserve and El Dorado (Venezuela), Asa Wright Nature Centre (Trinidad), and Cuyabeno Reserve (Ecuador). Observed at Emerald Towers (Guyana), around Iquitos (Peru), and in area of Manaus (Brazil). Generally less unobtrusive than most congeners, and therefore better known.
Bibliography. Bond *et al*. (1989), Brace *et al*. (1997), Clements & Shany (2001), Cohn-Haft *et al*. (1997), Donahue (1994), Friedmann (1948), Gilliard (1941), González (1998), Haverschmidt & Mees (1994), Herklots (1961), Hilty & Brown (1986), Meyer de Schauensee & Phelps (1978), Oren & Parker (1997), Peres & Whittaker (1991), Remsen & Traylor (1989), Ridgely & Greenfield (2001), Robinson (1997), Robinson & Terborgh (1997), Short (1972a, 1975), Sick (1993), Snyder (1966), Stotz, Fitzpatrick *et al*. (1996), Stotz, Lanyon *et al*. (1997), Terborgh *et al*. (1984), Thiollay & Jullien (1998), Tostain *et al*. (1992), Willis & Oniki (1990).

160. **Pale-crested Woodpecker**

Celeus lugubris

French: Pic à tête pâle **German**: Blassschopfspecht **Spanish**: Carpintero Lúgubre

Taxonomy. *Celeopicus lugubris* Malherbe, 1851, Mato Grosso, Brazil.
Possibly forms a superspecies with *C. castaneus*, *C. elegans* and *C. flavescens*. Sometimes treated as conspecific with last of these. Has apparently hybridized, rarely, with *C. elegans*. Proposed race *roosevelti* (W Mato Grosso) regarded as synonymous with nominate. Two subspecies currently recognized.
Subspecies and Distribution.
C. l. lugubris (Malherbe, 1851) - E Bolivia and WC Brazil (W Mato Grosso).
C. l. kerri Hargitt, 1891 - Paraguay (except extreme E) and WC Brazil (S Mato Grosso) to NE Argentina (E Formosa, Corrientes).

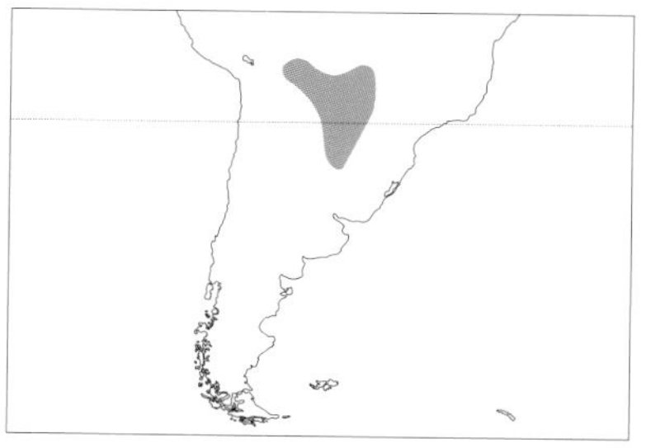

Descriptive notes. c. 23-24 cm; 115-130 g (*lugubris*), 134-157 g (*kerri*). Distinctive. Male has brown lores, broad red malar and cheek-band, red occasionally continuing to forehead and around eyes; rest of head and long pointed crest, also chin and throat, pale blond to buffish, sometimes tinged cinnamon, often some brown feathering on neck side; upperparts dark rufous-black with narrow whitish to pale cinnamon-buff bars, lower back and rump blond to cream-buff or sometimes with cinnamon tinge; longest uppertail-coverts rufous with black subterminal bars; blackish wing-coverts edged whitish to pale buff; blackish-brown flight-feathers barred rufous on basal half, tertials fully barred rufous; uppertail black, concealed outer feathers rufous with black spots; neck and underparts dark sooty-rufous, usually a few brighter rufous feather edges, more creamy and rufous on rear inner flanks, creamy thighs variably barred

On following pages: 161. Blond-crested Woodpecker (*Celeus flavescens*); 162. Cream-coloured Woodpecker (*Celeus flavus*); 163. Rufous-headed Woodpecker (*Celeus spectabilis*); 164. Ringed Woodpecker (*Celeus torquatus*).

dark; black undertail-coverts with rufous bars; brown underwing barred pale buff or cinnamon, axillaries and coverts creamy; fairly long bill slightly chisel-tipped, culmen curved, rather narrow across nostrils, greyish to horn-coloured, paler lower mandible; iris dark red to red-brown, orbital ring blue-grey; legs grey. Distinguished from *C. flavescens* by somewhat paler general coloration, pale rump and tail-coverts, rufous instead of white wingbars. Female lacks red on face, has cheeks barred or scaly brown. Juvenile resembles adult, but has large blackish areas on head, barring above irregular. Race *kerri* is slightly larger and darker than nominate. VOICE. Call "wee-wee-week". Drums weakly.

Habitat. Semi-deciduous forest, *cerrado* woodland and dry Chaco woodland; frequently seen in areas with palms. Lowlands.

Food and Feeding. Ants and their brood, including those of the genera *Camponotus*, *Crematogaster*, *Dolichoderus* and others. Utilizes the middle stratum. Forages by probing, gleaning and pecking; excavated dead wood to gain access to tunnels of ants, which are obtained with the sticky tongue.

Breeding. Sept-Nov, or later in S. Nest-hole excavated in tree or dug into arboreal nest of ants or termites, at 4-10 m. No other information.

Movements. Resident.

Status and Conservation. Not globally threatened. Generally fairly common throughout much of range. Occurs in several protected areas, e.g. Das Emas and Chapada dos Guimarães National Parks (Brazil) and Pilcomayo National Park (Argentina). Not well known; research required to ascertain more about its ecology and breeding behaviour.

Bibliography. Brace *et al.* (1997), Canevari *et al.* (1991), Chebez *et al.* (1999), Contreras *et al.* (1990), Davis (1993), Dubs (1992), Flores *et al.* (2001), Hayes (1995), Hayes & Scharf (1995a, 1995b), López (1997), Mazar Barnett & Pearman (2001), Meyer de Schauensee (1982), Miserendino (1998), Narosky & Yzurieta (1993), Olrog (1968), Oniki & Willis (1999), de la Peña (1994), Remsen & Traylor (1989), Ruschi (1979), Short (1972a, 1975), Sick (1993), Stotz *et al.* (1996), Wetmore (1926), Willis & Oniki (1990).

161. Blond-crested Woodpecker

Celeus flavescens

French: Pic ocré **German**: Blondschopfspecht **Spanish**: Carpintero Amarillento

Taxonomy. *Picus flavescens* J. F. Gmelin, 1788, Rio de Janeiro, Brazil.

Possibly forms a superspecies with *C. castaneus*, *C. elegans* and *C. lugubris*. Sometimes treated as conspecific with last of these. Nominate and race *ochraceus* appear to intergrade in CE Brazil (SW Bahia to Espírito Santo), where intermediate race *intercedens* seems to be absent. Three subspecies recognized.

Subspecies and Distribution.

C. f. ochraceus (Spix, 1824) - E Brazil, from W Pará (S of Amazon) to Atlantic coast and S to E Bahia and Espírito Santo.

C. f. intercedens Hellmayr, 1908 - W Bahia to Goiás and Minas Gerais.

C. f. flavescens (J. F. Gmelin, 1788) - CE & SE Brazil (S Bahia to Rio Grande do Sul) to E Paraguay and NE Argentina (Misiones).

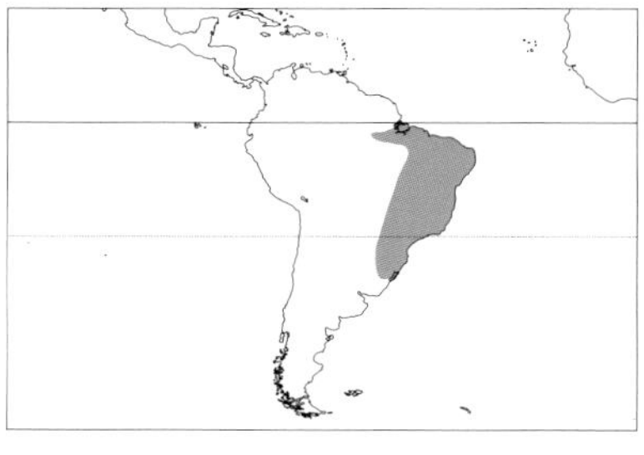

Descriptive notes. c. 25-30 cm; 110-165 g (*flavescens*). Distinctive, striking woodpecker. Male has broad red malar and cheekband, red sometimes spreading beneath eye, occasionally some red on lower forehead; rest of head, including long pointed crest, together with chin, throat and upper neck, pale creamy-buff to yellowish-white, sometimes a few dark spots on lores, often black streaks or feather centres on foreneck side; black mantle to upper back and scapulars narrowly barred white, lower back to uppertail-coverts buffish-white to pale yellow, tail-coverts sometimes with black barring; black wing-coverts edged and barred white; black flight-feathers narrowly barred white, tertials with white tips and diagonal bars; uppertail black, concealed outer feathers edged or barred whitish; lower neck and underparts black, often hint of paler barring on flanks and undertail-coverts, pale yellow to buffish thighs streaked or spotted black; underwing-coverts buffish; medium-long bill almost pointed, culmen curved, fairly narrow across nostrils, horn-coloured or blue-grey to black, paler lower mandible; iris red or red-brown, orbital ring blue-grey; legs blue-grey. Female has red of malar replaced by black streaks. Juvenile duller than adult, more black around face. Race *ochraceus* is smaller than nominate, less bulky, with less black, head more buffy or cinnamon-tinged, sometimes much black around eye, upperparts more cinnamon-buff with variable black spots and heart-shaped markings, flight-feather bars broader and more cinnamon-buff, underparts more sooty and often with buff-cinnamon edges, flanks usually with much cinnamon to buff, juveniles head sometimes mostly brownish-black; *intercedens* is intermediate in size and plumage, pale areas whitish to buff-white, black below, sometimes some rufous in flight-feathers. VOICE. Resonant "tsew tsew tsew-tsew", "wee-wee-week", or well-spaced series of "wheep" notes; also aggressive "tttrrr", raucous "wicket wicket". Drums weakly.

Habitat. Humid forest, also savanna and *caatinga*; found at forest edge, in gallery forest, and in orchards. Lowlands.

Food and Feeding. Arboreal ants (*Dolichoderus*, *Crematogaster*), also *Camponotus* ants, and termites (Isoptera) are important part of diet; fruits and berries regularly eaten. Generally seen in pairs or small family groups. Mainly arboreal, but also descends to ground to search for insects. Forages on slender branches, with gleaning, probing; also with pecking and hammering, particularly on dead branches.

Breeding. Apr-Jun in E Brazil and Oct-Nov in Argentina. Nest-hole in arboreal nest of ants. No other information available.

Movements. Resident.

Status and Conservation. Not globally threatened. Generally not uncommon. Another very little-known woodpecker. Occurs in several protected areas, e.g. Serra da Canastra and Iguaçú National Parks, Rio Doce State Park and Sooretama Biological Reserve (Brazil) and Iguazú National Park (Argentina).

Bibliography. Aleixo & Galetti (1997), dos Anjos (2001), dos Anjos & Schuchmann (1997), dos Anjos *et al.* (1997), Belton (1984), Bencke & Kindel (1999), Brooks *et al.* (1993), Buzzetti (2000), Canevari *et al.* (1991), Capper *et al.* (2000), Chebez *et al.* (1999), Dubs (1992), Figueiredo & Lo (2000), Figueiredo *et al.* (2000), Goerck (1999), Guix *et al.* (1999), Hayes (1995), Madroño, Clay, Robbins *et al.* (1997), Madroño, Robbins & Zyskowski (1997), Meyer de Schauensee (1982), Mikich (1997), Navas & Bó (1988), Olrog (1968), Pacheco & Parrini (2000), Parker & Goerck (1997), de la Peña (1994), Pinto & Camargo (1961), do Rosário (1996), Ruschi (1979), Scott & Brooke (1985), Short (1972a, 1975, 1985b), Sick (1993), Silveira (1998), Soares & dos Anjos (1999), Stager (1961a), Stotz *et al.* (1996), Tobias *et al.* (1993).

162. Cream-coloured Woodpecker

Celeus flavus

French: Pic jaune **German**: Strohspecht **Spanish**: Carpintero Amarillo

Taxonomy. *Picus flavus* P. L. S. Müller, 1776, Cayenne.

Races intergrade extensively, producing many intermediates, and in much of range many individuals impossible to assign to a particular race; geographical limits given are therefore somewhat arbitrary. Races *peruvianus* and *tectricialis* perhaps better merged with nominate. Birds from NE Amazonian Brazil named as race *inornatus*, but inseparable from nominate. Four subspecies recognized.

Subspecies and Distribution.

C. f. flavus (P. L. S. Müller, 1776) - E Colombia, SW & NE Venezuela and the Guianas S to E Ecuador, W Brazil (S to Mato Grosso) and N Bolivia (Beni).

C. f. peruvianus (Cory, 1919) - E Peru.

C. f. tectricialis (Hellmayr, 1922) - Maranhão (NE Brazil).

C. f. subflavus P. L. Sclater & Salvin, 1877 - E Brazil in Alagoas and S on coast from Bahia to Espírito Santo.

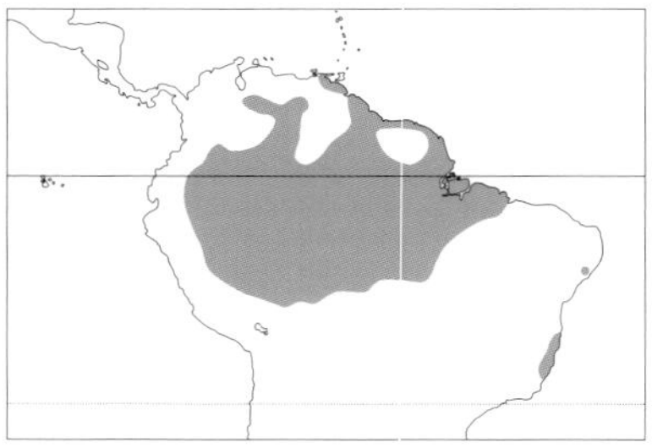

Descriptive notes. c. 24-26 cm; 95-131 g (*flavus*), c. 200 g (*subflavus*). Unmistakable; pale yellowish with long crest, black tail, dark wings. Male has bright red malar stripe, sometimes pale-streaked; most of plumage otherwise pale creamy-yellow to buffish or sulphur-yellow, occasionally cinnamon-white, sometimes a few brown feathers or bases visible on head and back (plumage frequently soiled and discoloured, and can acquire browner tone as darker bases appear through abrasion); wing-coverts variable, usually with brown bases, sometimes all brown or rufous-brown, flight-feathers usually brown with rufous-chestnut inner webs and edges of outer webs, tertials usually as back, sometimes darker, rarely with 1 or more dark bars, uppertail blackish-brown, concealed outer feather occasionally with pale bars; underwing brownish, coverts and axillaries creamy-buff; bill slightly chisel-tipped, culmen curved, rather narrow across nostrils, yellowish; iris red or red-brown; legs dark grey to green-grey. Female lacks red on malar. Juvenile as adult, usually somewhat more buff or cinnamon-buff, often with some barring on tertials, male soon acquires red tips in malar. Race *peruvianus* is slightly bigger than nominate, rufous in wings typically replaced mostly or entirely by brown; *tectricialis* is similar in size to nominate, but wing-coverts with much brown, flight-feathers with much less rufous; *subflavus* is largest, feathers of mantle and breast have broad brown bases and centres, no rufous in wings. VOICE. Distinctive high-pitched laugh, "wutchuk kee-hoo-hoo-hoo", "pueer, pueer, purr, paw" or similar, with final note lower in pitch; also "kiu-kiu-kiu-kiu", or "whéejah", sometimes repeated, during encounters involving several birds; calls higher-pitched and not so rasping as those of *C. elegans*.

Habitat. Humid forest, often near water. Frequents rainforest, such as *várzea* and swamp-forest, forest borders, occasionally gallery forest, mangroves, deciduous woodland, open woodland and second growth; also occurs in other secondary habitats, such as cacao plantations. Lowlands to 700 m, mostly below 400 m.

Food and Feeding. Ants (*Crematogaster*) and termites (Isoptera); also eats fruits and seeds. Forages singly, but mostly in pairs or in groups of 3 or 4; not shy. Forages in lower and middle parts of trees, also in canopy; spends much time breaking into nests of arboreal ants and termites. Descends to the ground at times. Not infrequently in open.

Breeding. Apr-Jun in Colombia, possibly somewhat earlier in Venezuela. Nest and other details apparently not documented.

Movements. Resident.

Status and Conservation. Not globally threatened. Generally rather uncommon; very common in NE Venezuela; uncommon in Ecuador and Peru; possibly common locally in Brazil. Occurs in Imataca Forest Reserve and El Dorado (Venezuela), Amacayacu National Park (Colombia), Tambopata Reserve (Peru) and Noel Kempff Mercado National Park (Bolivia). Research required on its breeding biology.

Bibliography. Allen (1995), Brace *et al.* (1997), Clements & Shany (2001), Cohn-Haft *et al.* (1997), Donahue (1994), Friedmann (1948), Guilherme (2001), Haverschmidt & Mees (1994), Hilty & Brown (1986), Meyer de Schauensee & Phelps (1978), Oren & Parker (1997), Parker & Goerck (1997), Parker *et al.* (1982), Peres & Whittaker (1991), Remsen & Traylor (1989), Ridgely & Greenfield (2001), Robinson & Terborgh (1997), Scott & Brooke (1985), Sick (1993), da Silva (1996), Snyder (1966), Stotz, Fitzpatrick *et al.* (1996), Stotz, Lanyon *et al.* (1997), Terborgh *et al.* (1984), Tostain *et al.* (1992), Traylor (1958).

163. Rufous-headed Woodpecker

Celeus spectabilis

French: Pic à tête rousse **German**: Zimtkopfspecht **Spanish**: Carpintero Cabecirrufo

Other common names: Caatinga Woodpecker (*obrieni*)

Taxonomy. *Celeus spectabilis* P. L. Sclater and Salvin, 1880, Sarayacu, Ecuador.

Isolated race *obrieni*, known from only single, female specimen, differs significantly in plumage, and data on habitat indicate major distinction from other races; possibly a separate species, but no further information available. Three subspecies recognized.

Subspecies and Distribution.

C. s. spectabilis P. L. Sclater & Salvin, 1880 - E Ecuador and NE Peru.

C. s. exsul Bond & Meyer de Schauensee, 1941 - SE Peru, extreme W Brazil (W Acre) and N Bolivia (Beni, N Cochabamba).

C. s. obrieni Short, 1973 - E Brazil (W Piauí).

Descriptive notes. c. 26-28 cm; 111 g (*exsul*). Male has rufous-chestnut head and bushy crest, red malar patch, yellow to cream-buff patch on lower neck side and down side of breast, large area of dull red from above ear-coverts into crest; lower throat to breast black; hindneck to upper back and scapulars creamy-buff to pale cinnamon-yellow with very broad black bars, lower back to uppertail-coverts yellow-buff to cinnamon-buff, occasionally with a few black streaks; black wing-coverts

edged and narrowly barred cream-buff; brownish-black primaries with rufous at base, inner primaries becoming more rufous, secondaries and tertials wholly rufous-chestnut with black tips, shorter tertials usually barred black; uppertail black, concealed outer feather sometimes pale-barred; breast side and rest of underparts cream-buff to pale cinnamon-buff, black of breast breaking up into heavy bars, more as chevrons on flanks and lower underparts; underwing rufous-cinnamon, coverts black-barred cinnamon-buff; bill chisel-tipped, culmen slightly curved, relatively broad across nostrils, pale yellowish or greyish-ivory; iris deep red-brown; legs olive-green to greyish. Female lacks red on head, but may show trace in crest. Juvenile as adult, but much blackish colour around front of head, more red in crown area, bill darker. Race *exsul* resembles nominate, but underpart barring very variable with individual, ranging almost to extremes of other two races, though most commonly less barred below than nominate, with heart-shaped or chevron markings below black breast patch, a few spots on belly and bars on flanks; female *obrieni* (male unknown) is smaller, almost unmarked above (a few bars on mantle), wing-coverts creamy-buff with only small central marks, tertials creamy-buff with irregular black spots, belly unmarked, underwing-coverts unbarred, small outer rectrix pale buffish with black markings. VOICE. Loud squealing "skweeah" followed by bubbling "kluh-kluh-kluh-kluh-kluh". Drums on hollow bamboo.

Habitat. Inhabits humid tropical forest, especially along rivers and on river islands. Regularly found in bamboo (*Chusquea*, *Guadua*) thickets in Peru, and also strongly associated with bamboo in W Brazil; in Ecuador, favours areas with *Cecropia* trees and cane (*Gynerium*) understorey, as well as *Heliconia*. Occurs in lowlands, up to c. 300 m. Sole specimen of *obrieni* was apparently collected from very different habitat: dry *cerrado* mixed with arid scrub with stunted thorny trees (*caatinga*).

Food and Feeding. Contents of diet not recorded to date, although probably feeds on ants, among other items. Forages singly or in pairs, from dense undergrowth up to middle and upper levels of forest. Also descends to ground to work over fallen logs. Probes on trunks and branches, e.g. of *Cecropia*; pecks rather forcefully, and more frequently than most of its congeners, except possibly *C. torquatus*. Observed pecking at horizontal bamboo stems, at heights of 3-10 m, in W Brazil.

Breeding. Rather little information available. In Peru, male and female with enlarged gonads collected in Jun, two females in breeding condition taken in Aug. Only two nests found to date, both in SE Peru: one in Jun, 2·8 m up in dead snag with broken-off top, in area of *Guadua* spiny bamboo, hole a vertical oval 12 cm × 10 cm, entrance tunnel sloping upwards, cavity 24 cm deep, incubation suspected but pre-hatch predation thought likely; the other at 1·75 m in a *Cavanillesia* tree with *Heliconia* and *Guadua* understorey, situated in hole 15 cm × 9·3 cm, containing one chick, which was fed solely by male.

Movements. Resident.

Status and Conservation. Not globally threatened. Rare generally; appears to be not uncommon in W Brazil. In SE Peru, 3-4 territories located in c. 150 ha of bamboo habitats surveyed. Regularly recorded in Manu Wildlife Center and Tambopata Research Center (Peru). Rediscovered in Ecuador, at Sacha Lodge, in 1994, after absence of records since 1965; subsequently observed in that country at La Selva, near Pompeya, at Yuturi and at Kapawi Lodge. Very poorly known species; field study and surveys required to determine its true status, as well as its ecology and breeding habits. Race *obrieni* from E Brazil has not been observed in the wild since the holotype was collected, in 1926; fieldwork in 1980 failed to relocate it, and it has to be assumed either that the taxon is extinct or that it represents a highly aberrant form of another species. In view of this species' apparently strict habitat requirements and its low density and general scarcity, it probably merits the conservation status of Near-threatened.

Bibliography. Allen (1995), Angehr & Aucca (1997), Brace *et al.* (1997), Butler (1979), Clements & Shany (2001), Donahue (1994), Kratter (1997, 1998), Lloyd (2000), Meyer de Schauensee (1982), Olrog (1968), Parker *et al.* (1982), Remsen & Traylor (1989), Ridgely & Greenfield (2001), Ridgely *et al.* (1998), Rodner *et al.* (2000), Short (1973b, 1985b), Sick (1993), Stotz *et al.* (1996), Taylor (1995), Terborgh *et al.* (1984), Traylor (1958), Whittaker & Oren (1999).

164. Ringed Woodpecker

Celeus torquatus

French: Pic à cravate noir   **German**: Schwarzbrustspecht   **Spanish**: Carpintero Pechinegro

Taxonomy. *Picus torquatus* Boddaert, 1783, Cayenne.
Named race *angustus* (R Tapajós, Brazil) regarded as synonymous with *occidentalis*, which intergrades with nominate. Three subspecies recognized.

Subspecies and Distribution.
C. t. occidentalis (Hargitt, 1889) - NE Ecuador, SE Colombia and W & C Amazonian Brazil E to S Venezuela, and S to E Peru, N Bolivia and Mato Grosso.
C. t. torquatus (Boddaert, 1783) - E Venezuela and the Guianas S to Pará in NE Brazil.
C. t. tinnunculus (Wagler, 1829) - E Brazil (SE Bahia, Espírito Santo).

Descriptive notes. c. 26-28 cm; 107-124 g (*torquatus*), c. 134 g (*occidentalis*). Male has broad red band from malar region to lower edge of ear-coverts; rest of head, including bushy crest, hindneck, chin and upper throat pale rufous-tinged cinnamon, occasionally hint of reddish on forehead and side of crest; black lower throat, black line from rear malar joining black of breast and upper mantle; lower mantle to uppertail-coverts, including wing-coverts and tertials, rufous-brown, sometimes a few black feathers in lower mantle, usually black subterminal bars or V-shaped marks on coverts and 1 or 2 (or more) bars on tertials; flight-feathers barred black and rufous, rufous more extensive on secondaries; uppertail rufous, narrowly barred black, broader black tip; lower breast to vent plain cinnamon-buff; underwing cinnamon-buff, faint barring on primaries; long bill almost straight, chisel-tipped, relatively broad across nostrils, grey to yellowish-grey or dull olive-brown; iris red to red-brown or brown; legs dark grey. Female lacks red on head. Juvenile as adult, but much black on front of head, more barred. Race *occidentalis* has darker head more cinnamon-tinged, more barred above, but variable, bars sometimes rather weak, lower breast to undertail-coverts much whiter and barred; *tinnunculus* is like previous, but head paler, upperparts brighter rufous and more heavily barred, outer tail feathers mostly black, more strongly barred below and on underwing. VOICE. Series of 3-5 loud whistled "kleee", "kuu" or "deeee" notes, evenly pitched.

Habitat. Tall humid forest, including rainforest, *terra firme* forest, *várzea* forest, gallery forest; also tall second growth and clearings. Mostly in lowlands, from 100 m to 500 m; to 725 m in Peru.

Food and Feeding. Ants and seeds recorded in diet. Singly or in pairs, or in loose groups of up to 5 birds; frequently associated with mixed-species flocks in some areas (in N of range), less often in others (e.g. Ecuador). Forages inconspicuously, mainly at low to medium heights, from understorey to subcanopy; apparently confined more to middle and upper levels in W of range. Moves along larger limbs and trunks. Feeding techniques include gleaning from bark, and hammering into arboreal termitaria.

Breeding. No details known.

Movements. Resident.

Status and Conservation. Not globally threatened. Uncommon to rare; uncommon in Venezuela; scarce to uncommon or rare in Ecuador; fairly common but local in Peru. Isolated race *tinnunculus*, restricted to forest remnants of E Brazil in Bahia and Espírito Santo, is regarded as endangered. Observed at Emerald Towers and at Timberhead (Guyana). In Brazil, present in Rio Cristalino Private Reserve. In Peru, occurs in Tambopata Reserve and Manu National Park, is regularly seen in Iquitos region, and recorded at Lago Sandoval. In Ecuador, most numerous in lowlands well E of Andes, being absent from areas closer to the mountains. A very poorly known species; in need of research on its diet and feeding, and on its breeding requirements and biology.

Bibliography. Allen (1995), Boesman (1995), Butler (1979), Clements & Shany (2001), Cohn-Haft *et al.* (1997), Donahue (1994), Dubs (1992), Haverschmidt & Mees (1994), Hilty & Brown (1986), Meyer de Schauensee & Phelps (1978), Oren (1992), Parker *et al.* (1982), Peres & Whittaker (1991), Remsen & Traylor (1989), Ridgely & Greenfield (2001), Ridgely *et al.* (1998), Sharpe *et al.* (2001), Short (1985b), Sick (1993), da Silva (1996), Snyder (1966), Stotz, Fitzpatrick *et al.* (1996), Stotz, Lanyon *et al.* (1997), Teixeira *et al.* (1988), Terborgh *et al.* (1984), Thiollay & Jullien (1998), Tostain *et al.* (1992).

165

ssp *pileatus* ♀

ssp *abieticola* ♂

166

ssp *scapularis* ♂

ssp *lineatus* ♀

167

ssp *erythrops* ♂

ssp *fuscipennis* ♂

168 ♂

without scapular line

ssp *javensis* ♀ ♂

ssp *hodgsonii* ♂

169

ssp *confusus* ♂

ssp *parvus*

ssp *pectoralis* ♂

170 ♀ ♂

ssp *philippinensis* ♂

ssp *richardsi* ♀

171 ♂ ♀

PLATE 43

inches 7

cm 18

Tribe CAMPEPHILINI

Genus *DRYOCOPUS* Boie, 1826

165. **Helmeted Woodpecker**

Dryocopus galeatus

French: Pic casqué **German**: Wellenohrspecht **Spanish**: Picamaderos Caricanelo

Taxonomy. *Picus galeatus* Temminck, 1822, Brazil.
Monotyic.
Distribution. E Paraguay, NE Argentina (Misiones) and SE Brazil (São Paulo, Paraná and Santa Catarina; probably extinct in Rio Grande do Sul).

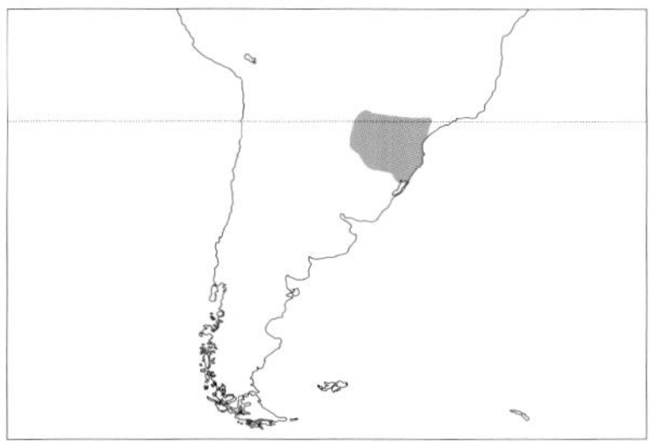

Descriptive notes. c. 27-28 cm; 124 g. Male has red head and long crest, sometimes with buff or black feather bases showing through, forehead, lores and ear-coverts more cinnamon, ear-coverts thinly dark-streaked or barred; black neck, white stripe from lower rear edge of ear-coverts down neck side to upper breast side; rusty-cinnamon chin and throat, lower throat usually barred dark; black to brownish-black mantle, scapulars and upper back, cream-buff lower back to uppertail-coverts (latter very long) often tinged pale cinnamon, sometimes a few darker bars on middle back, occasionally also rump; wings brownish-black, inner flight-feathers with cinnamon bases; uppertail black; blackish upper breast barred cinnamon, whitish to cinnamon-buff central breast to undertail-coverts entirely barred black; underwing grey-brown, cinnamon coverts and inner wing, coverts variably barred black; fairly long bill slightly chisel-tipped, culmen curved, rather broad across nostrils, grey to blue-grey, paler ivory-coloured tip; iris brown; legs dark grey. Female has slightly smaller bill than male, somewhat longer wings and tail, less red on face. Juvenile little known; browner, less black, than adult, with less red on crown, grey ear-coverts, more extensively barred. Voice. Loud ringing series of 3-12 "keer" notes, shorter and slower than that of *D. lineatus*, probably associated with territorial behaviour; less loud, mournful "tu-hu-u-u-u-u-u" series, of which "kee-doo-doo-doo-doo-doo" probably a variant, as contact between pair-members; soft "chic" notes; intimate calls between partners "che-che-che". Drumming soft, pattern uniform, roll 1·5 seconds long.
Habitat. Tall lowland and montane forest. Primary forest, disturbed and even logged (primary) forest, so long as not severely affected; recorded also in gallery forest and small patches of degraded forest, usually near large tracts of intact forest. Association with bamboo probably accidental. In lowland valleys, and in cloudforest to c. 800 m.
Food and Feeding. Feeds on beetle larvae living beneath bark. Mostly found singly or in pairs. Forages in middle storey at 14-15 m in forest interior; also lower, down to 2-5 m, at forest edge. Searches branches of a broad range of sizes (2-30 cm in diameter), including those covered with mosses and lichens. Obtains prey by removing bark, often combined with pecking, probing beneath bark, and some gleaning; hammers only occasionally, with little persistence, and does not make large cavities.
Breeding. Nests found in Sept-Oct; season probably to Feb. Nest seems to be surprisingly low down, at 2-3 m, in tree. No further details known.
Movements. Resident.
Status and Conservation. VULNERABLE. Total population estimated at no more than 10,000 individuals. Known from only a small area of at most 24,000 km²; probably extinct in Rio Grande do Sul, where formerly occurred in the coastal NE. Occurs in numerous protected areas throughout its range: in Paraguay, in Estancia San Antonio Private Nature Reserve, Mbaracayú Forest Nature Reserve, Itabó Private Reserve, San Rafael National Park, Caaguazú National Park, Golondrina Private Reserve, and Cerro Corá National Park; in Brazil, Intervales State Park, Ilha do Cardoso State Park, and Iguaçu National Park; and in Argentina, Iguazú National Park (4 pairs located), Esmeralda Provincial Reserve, Urugua-í Provincial Park, Caa Porá Private Reserve, Moconá Provincial Park, and Campo San Juan Protected Reserve. Legally protected in Brazil. Preferred habitats have suffered extensive clearance, fragmentation and degradation over many decades, and it seems reasonable to assume that this picid has declined quite significantly since the 1950's. Nevertheless, it may have been under-recorded in recent years, since it is not easy to locate except during the brief period of the year when it calls. Intensive searches have revealed its presence in both lowland and montane forest, also in selectively logged areas, gallery forest, and even in small patches of degraded forest. Numerous sightings since mid-1980's, including a pair in 1998 in Brazilian state of Santa Catarina, where the species had not been seen since 1946. These encouraging reports suggest that this woodpecker is not so scarce as was previously believed, but continuing forest destruction remains a serious threat. Further studies required, aimed at clarifying its distribution and status.
Bibliography. Anon. (1995c, 1998f), Belton (1984), Blendinger (1998), Brooks *et al.* (1993), Canevari *et al.* (1991), Chebez (1986, 1994, 1995), Chebez *et al.* (1999), Collar & Andrew (1988), Collar, Crosby & Stattersfield (1994), Collar, Gonzaga *et al.* (1992), Gliesch (1930), Guix *et al.* (1999), Hayes (1995), King (1978/79), Knox & Walters (1994), Lowen, Bartrina *et al.* (1996), Lowen, Clay *et al.* (1995), Lucero & Alabarce (1980), Madroño & Esquivel (1995), Madroño, Clay & Hostettler (1997), Naka *et al.* (2000), Navas & Bó (1993), Parker & Goerck (1997), Paynter (1985, 1989), Paynter & Traylor (1991), de la Peña (1994), Pinto (1938b), Pinto & Camargo (1955), Short (1985b), Shuker (1993), Sick (1985, 1993), Stattersfield & Capper (2000), Storer (1989), Stotz *et al.* (1996), Willis (1987), Willis & Oniki (1993).

166. **Pileated Woodpecker**

Dryocopus pileatus

French: Grand Pic **German**: Helmspecht **Spanish**: Picamaderos Norteamericano

Taxonomy. *Picus pileatus* Linnaeus, 1758, America = South Carolina.
Forms a superspecies with *D. lineatus* and *D. schulzi*. Little geographical variation, mostly clinal: proposed races *picinus* (British Columbia) and *floridanus* (Florida) considered not to differ significantly from, respectively, *abieticola* and nominate. Two subspecies recognized.
Subspecies and Distribution.
D. p. abieticola (Bangs, 1898) - S British Columbia E across S Canada to Nova Scotia, S to NW & CE California, C Idaho, W Montana, C Saskatchewan, SE Iowa and about Virginia.
D. p. pileatus (Linnaeus, 1758) - SE USA, from approximately Illinois E to Virginia and S to SE Texas and Florida.

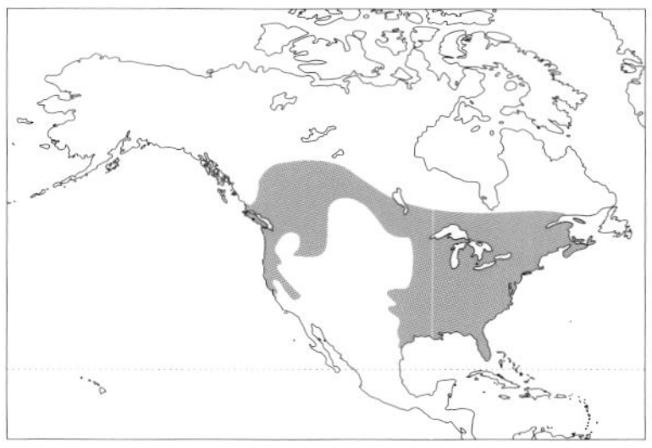

Descriptive notes. 40-48 cm; 250-340 g (*abieticola*). Large. Male has buffish nasal tufts, bright red forehead, crown and long crest, narrow white stripe behind eye, black band from upper lores through eye to nape side, white band from base of upper mandible back to rear neck side and continuing broadly down side of neck to upper flank; dark red malar stripe black at rear, joining with black of foreneck; white chin and upper throat, sometimes with greyish streaks; upperparts and wings black, small white tips on outer primaries, larger area of white at bases of primaries and outer secondaries, alula and primary coverts variably edged white; uppertail black, initially with small white tips; apart from white upper flanks, grey-black to blackish below, narrowly barred grey on lower flanks, sometimes also on belly; underwing white, primary coverts barred blackish, broad black tip and trailing edge; in worn plumage, black areas become browner; medium-length bill broad, chisel-tipped, culmen slightly curved, slate-grey, blackish tip; iris pale yellow, orbital skin greyish-olive; legs dark blue-grey to blackish. Female is slightly smaller, shorter-billed than male, has forehead and forecrown black, sometimes with some brown-buff tips and often also some red tips, malar fully black. Juvenile duller, more sooty, than adult, throat greyish or grey-streaked, eyes blue-grey, male with orange-red tips on forehead, crown and small crest, faint red tips in malar, female with grey-brown forehead to crown sides and no red in malar. Race *abieticola* is slightly bigger than nominate, has longer bill, some birds in extreme W also with grey throat. Voice. Single or repeated "wuk", "cuk" or "cac" notes, particularly in flight, as e.g. contact between pair-members, when approaching roosting area, and in series when alarmed, also in fast series; higher-pitched calls given on landing; mewing calls associated with sexual activities; various repeated "waak", "woick woick" and "wok" notes during encounters, also associated with visual displays; low-pitched "waaa", sometimes in irregular series, as intimate call; squeaking to churring calls by young. Drumrolls distinctive, loud, with full timbre, accelerate at end, usually 1-2 seconds long, 1-2 per minute; loud taps from inside nest when partner approaches; double raps in context of copulation and hole demonstration.
Habitat. Coniferous and deciduous forest, and mixed forest, from rather open deciduous to dense mature coniferous stands. Mature and extensive stands favoured. Occurs also in second growth having some large trees and at least 5 years old; enters suburbs and parks. Data from Oregon and elsewhere suggest that stands over 70 years old, and often close to water, preferred for nesting, and that riparian woodland and stands older than 40 years preferred for foraging. Juniper (*Juniperus*) woodland and pure pine monocultures are avoided. From sea-level to above 1500 m in E mountains, to c. 2300 m in W.
Food and Feeding. Mainly ants, principally carpenter ants (*Camponotus*), but *Crematogaster* and *Formica* also recorded; beetle larvae also taken throughout year. Also other insects, including termites (Isoptera). Fruits, e.g. cherries, dogwood (*Cornus*), wild grapes (*Vitis*) and similar, and berries, e.g. holly (*Ilex*), various *Rhus* species, *Smilax*, hackberry (*Cletis*) and others, also eaten, as well as nuts (e.g. acorn, pecan). Importance of fruits varies locally, and can comprise almost a third of diet. Fruits and suet accepted at feeders. Mostly singly; paired birds keep loose contact. Not very shy. Feeds at all levels, including on ground, where it works over fallen logs or attacks anthills. Dead wood preferred for foraging. Pecking and hammering comprise 60-95% of foraging activities in non-breeding season; often hammers for long periods at one spot. Scaling of bark also a very important technique. Probing and, less so, gleaning are minor foraging methods, used most in breeding season and then comprising almost 20% of foraging activities. Plucks fruit from very thin branches.
Breeding. Laying from Apr in S, May-Jun in N and at higher altitudes; courtship from Feb. Displays include crest-raising, wing-spreading, also head-swinging with bobbing and head-raising, also flutter-aerial display. Usually new nest excavated each year, by both sexes, taking 3-6 weeks, at 4-30 m (mostly 6-12 m) in main trunk of dead tree, or old living tree, with breast-height diameter 33-91 cm (usually exceeding 40 cm), frequently conifer but also deciduous (e.g. *Quercus*, *Acer*, *Ulmus*); sometimes in utility pole; hole dimensions 11-12 cm tall, 7·5-9 cm wide, cavity depth c. 30-45 cm; territory defended by both sexes. Clutch 1-6 eggs, usually 2-4, average 3·8, larger clutch sizes in N populations; incubation by both sexes, period c. 15-16 days, only male incubating at night; both parents feed chicks, by regurgitation, both also brood them and share in nest sanitation, male broods more than female, partners take about equal share of feeding duties; fledging period 24-28 days, sometimes up to 31 days in S; fledged brood accompanied by both parents or divided between them, fed for several months, family group remaining intact until Sept or later. Mean brood size at fledging 2·0 young in Montana, 2·26 in Oregon, 2·14 in Louisiana; 83% of nests produced at least 1 young in Oregon. First breeds at 1 year. Recorded longevity in wild over 9 years.
Movements. Chiefly resident. Possibly some short-distance movement or wandering; in montane areas may move to lower elevations after breeding.
Status and Conservation. Not globally threatened. Not very common, and generally rather local. Estimates of density in first half of 20th century include 1 pair/67 ha in Florida and 1 pair/43-260 ha in Louisiana; approximate estimates in 1980's and 1990's range from 0·4-4·1 territories/100 ha in Missouri to 1 pair/160-220 ha in California and 1 pair/356 ha in Oregon. Large home ranges, c. 480 ha post-breeding, but can overlap by up to 30%. Predation can have significant adverse effect on populations; habitat alteration can eliminate nesting and foraging areas. Suffered greatly in 19th century during period of extensive land clearance, but has regained much of its former range from c. 1920 onwards. Has increased in most of range since mid-1960's. Although a legally protected species, it is sometimes persecuted for its occasional habit of excavating on buildings.
Bibliography. Aubrey & Raley (1992, 1994), Baicich & Harrison (1997), Beckwith & Bull (1985), Bent (1939), Bonar (1994, 2000), Brown (1978), Bull (1974, 1978, 1981, 1987), Bull & Holthausen (1993), Bull & Jackson (1995), Bull & Meslow (1977, 1988), Bull & Snider (1993), Bull, Beckwith & Holthausen (1992), Bull, Holthausen

On following pages: 167. Lineated Woodpecker (*Dryocopus lineatus*); 168. Black-bodied Woodpecker (*Dryocopus schulzi*); 169. White-bellied Woodpecker (*Dryocopus javensis*); 170. Andaman Woodpecker (*Dryocopus hodgei*); 171. Black Woodpecker (*Dryocopus martius*).

& Henjum (1990, 1992), Campbell *et al.* (1990), Carter, W.A. (1974), Conner (1973, 1975, 1977, 1979, 1980, 1981, 1982), Conner & Adkisson (1977), Conner & Saenz (1996), Conner, Jones & Jones (1994), Conner, Miller & Adkisson (1976), Conway (1957), Cooper *et al.* (1995), Cyr (1995h), Ellison (1992), Flemming *et al.* (1999), Garrett (1999), Giefer (1978), Harestad & Keisker (1989), Harris, B. (1995), Harris, R.D. (1982), Hendricks (1996), Hoyt, J.S.Y. (1940, 1944, 1948), Hoyt, J.S.Y. & Hoyt (1951), Hoyt, S.F. (1952, 1953, 1957), Humphrey (1946), Jackman (1974), Jones (1988), Kaplan (1986), Kilham (1959d, 1959e, 1973b, 1974c, 1975, 1976, 1979b, 1979c, 1983), Koenig (1987), Kreisel & Stein (1999), Lochmiller (1977), Loftin (1981), Mannan (1984), Maxson & Maxson (1981), McClelland (1979), McClelland & McClelland (1999), McVoy (1978), Mellen (1987), Mellen *et al.* (1992), Menten (1994), Millar (1992), Moulton & Lowell (1991), Nero & Copland (1997), Nichols (1994), Nolan (1959), Oberman (1989, 1995), Peck & James (1983), Pfitzenmeyer (1956), Renken (1988), Renken & Wiggers (1989, 1993), Rounds (1958), Rumsey (1968, 1970), Saab & Dudley (1998), Saenz *et al.* (1998), Savignac *et al.* (2000), Schardien & Jackson (1978), Schemnitz (1964), Shackelford & Conner (1997), Short (1965d, 1985b), Spring (1965), Stark *et al.* (1998), Stradi & Hudon (1998), Stradi *et al.* (1998), Swallow *et al.* (1988), Tobalske (1996), Truslow (1967), Wedgwood (1988), Welsh & Capen (1992), Wilson & Bull (1977), Wood & Eichholz (1986), Woods (1984).

167. **Lineated Woodpecker**

Dryocopus lineatus

French: Pic ouentou **German**: Linienspecht **Spanish**: Picamaderos Listado
Other common names: Black-mantled Woodpecker (*erythrops*)

Taxonomy. *Picus lineatus* Linnaeus, 1766, Cayenne.
Forms a superspecies with *D. pileatus* and *D. schulzi*. Interbreeds with latter. Large degree of individual variation exists among all populations. Race *erythrops*, previously regarded as a separate species, is perhaps only a variable morph. Additional described races are *obsoletus* (Sonora), *petersi* (Tamaulipas), *mesorhynchus* (Costa Rica), *nuperus* (Santa Marta, in N Colombia), *improcerus* (Bahia, in E Brazil) and *fulcitus* (Chaco, in Argentina), all considered insufficiently differentiated to be accepted. Five subspecies recognized.
Subspecies and Distribution.
D. l. scapularis (Vigors, 1829) - W Mexico (S from Sonora).
D. l. similis (Lesson, 1847) - E & S Mexico S to NW Costa Rica.
D. l. lineatus (Linnaeus, 1766) - E & S Costa Rica to W Colombia and E to Trinidad, the Guianas and NE & E Brazil (Maranhão, Bahia), S to E Peru, N Paraguay and São Paulo.
D. l. fuscipennis P. L. Sclater, 1860 - W Ecuador and NW Peru.
D. l. erythrops (Valenciennes, 1826) - E Paraguay, N & NE Argentina (E Salta, Misiones, Corrientes) and SE Brazil (Espírito Santo and São Paulo S to Rio Grande do Sul).

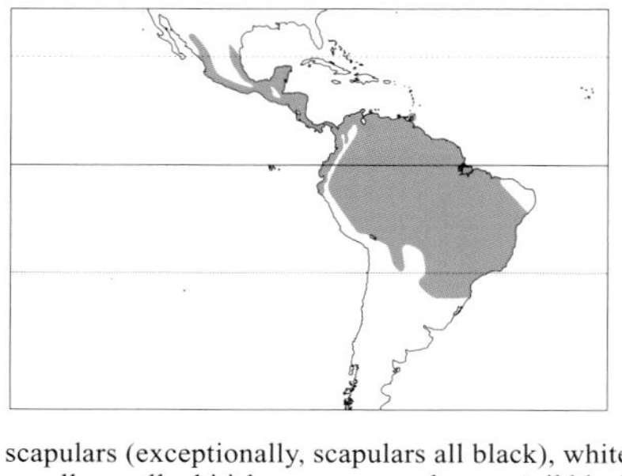

Descriptive notes. c. 30-36 cm; male 204-217 g, female 186-213 g (*lineatus*), 150-164 g (*similis*), male 182-264 g (*erythrops*). Male has bright red forehead, crown and crest, often some dark grey feather bases visible, blackish area from upper lores back across ear-coverts to hindneck (rarely, very thin white line behind eye), white stripe from yellowish loral area to lower rear border of ear-coverts and down neck side, black malar stripe with much red in fore part, expanding at rear and joining with black of breast; white chin and throat with variable, often heavy, black streaking; black hindneck and upperparts, white outer webs of outer scapulars (exceptionally, scapulars all black), white area on bases of inner webs of flight-feathers, usually small whitish area on carpal; uppertail black; black breast, black occasionally extending to belly, greyish-buff to whitish belly, flanks and undertail-coverts variably barred brownish-black, in N of range more buff and bars more irregular; underwing blackish, coverts and bases of flight-feathers white or pale buff, sometimes small black patch on primary coverts; in worn plumage, all black areas browner, feather bases more visible; long bill chisel-tipped, culmen slightly curved, broad across nostrils, grey to grey-black, paler lower mandible, usually dark tip; iris white to pale orange, orbital skin brown; legs grey, tinged green, blue or yellow, sometimes olive. Differs from *D. schulzi* mainly in barred underparts, pale eyes. Female is somewhat smaller than male, has forehead, forecrown and malar all black. Juvenile duller than adult, black areas browner, breast more extensively dark, barring below more obscure and less regular, flight-feathers with obvious white tips, eyes brown, head pattern as that of respective adult or, rarely, crown more yellow than red, male with less red in malar. Race *scapularis* is smaller than nominate, but slight size increase clinally to N, lacks white stripe from lores to neck side, bill pale; *similis* is larger than previous, ground colour of underparts buff; *erythrops* is larger than S nominate, dark-billed, occurs in 2 forms, S birds lack white scapular lines, N birds may or may not have these markings, exceptionally only partial white on scapulars, population in Iguazú area of N Misiones (Argentina) often with much rufous in ground coloration below; *fuscipennis* is smaller than nominate, dark-billed, distinctly brown, upperparts deep brown, breast sooty, belly to undertail-coverts buffish with obscure brown barring, wing and tail shafts pale, undertail glossed yellow-brown on outer feathers. Voice. Call note a loud sharp "pik"; rattle as "kip-whurrr", "pik-urrr-r-r", "ik-rrrr", "cuchrrrrrrrr", or "k'rroo"; common call loud, explosive, far-carrying "wicwic-wicwicwic", "wuk wuk wuk", "kyah-yik-yik-yik", or "weep weep weep weep", up to c. 30 notes, dying at end; also unwoodpecker-like "wer wer wer". Both sexes drum, loudly, making 5-8 slow taps followed by long accelerating tattoo.
Habitat. Humid, transitional and moderately dry areas; generally avoids xerophytic areas or marshes, but frequents mangroves. Occasionally found in dense forest or tall rainforest, but more open areas preferred generally; especially numerous around new clearings and at forest edge. Enters pine (*Pinus*) forest and gallery forest in drier areas, as well as thorn-scrub. Also occurs in shaded gardens, moriche groves (Venezuela), on trees in pastures and cultivations, and particularly in second growth with sufficiently large trees (e.g. fast-growing *Cecropia*). Lowlands, foothills, and even higher, to 1200-2100 m.
Food and Feeding. Known to consume beetles and their wood-boring larvae, ants (*Crematogaster*, *Camponotus*, *Azteca*) and their brood, caterpillars, orthopteran egg cases; also takes fruit and seeds (*Heliconia*). Often in pairs, also in family groups of 4-6 birds; single individuals may join mixed-species flocks, e.g. with antwrens (*Myrmotherula*). Active and noisy; easily alarmed. Forages at all heights; also descends to ground, where tosses aside leaves in search of food. Readily visits isolated trees in open areas. Forages on trunks and large limbs, occasionally also on telephone poles; males prefer larger branches than those used by females. Hammering and pecking deeply and persistently into both live and rotting wood predominate among feeding techniques; probing into excavations also common. Particularly adept in securing ants and their brood in *Cecropia*. Frequently pries up and scales pieces of bark from dead trunks and branches. Visits well-foliated parts of the crown in search of fruits, even on very thin twigs. May feed at one spot for 10-15 minutes, then fly long distance to another.
Breeding. Mar-Apr in Panama, Apr-May in Belize, and Feb-Apr in Trinidad and Surinam; birds in breeding condition in Jan-Feb in Colombia; season Jul-Nov in S. Remains paired throughout year. Display with crest-raising. Nest excavated in dead tree or top of stub of small girth (18-23 cm), sometimes up to 27 m up in very tall tree, sometimes rather low down, to c. 2 m; toucans (Ramphastidae) are important hole competitors. Clutch 2-3 eggs; incubation and fledging periods not documented; chicks fed by both parents, by regurgitation.
Movements. Resident.
Status and Conservation. Not globally threatened. Fairly common to common, and widespread, throughout most of range; uncommon to fairly common in Ecuador and Peru. Occurs in numerous protected areas throughout its extensive range, e.g. Santa Rosa National Park (Costa Rica), Guatapo National Park (Venezuela), Asa Wright Nature Centre (Trinidad) and Serra do Cipó National Park (Brazil). Preference for open habitats means that it benefits from clearance of forest; survives well in degraded areas. No known threats.
Bibliography. dos Anjos & Schuchmann (1997), Belton (1984), Binford (1989), Brooks, D.M. (2000), Brooks, T.M. *et al.* (1993), Buzzetti (2000), Canevari *et al.* (1991), Capper, Clay, Madroño, Mazar Barnett, Burfield *et al.* (2001), Capper, Esquivel *et al.* (2000), Clements & Shany (2001), Cohn-Haft *et al.* (1997), Contreras *et al.* (1990), Figueiredo & Lo (2000), Goerck (1999), Guix *et al.* (1999), Haverschmidt & Mees (1994), Hayes (1995), Hayes & Samad (1998), Heisler (1994), Herklots (1961), Hernández *et al.* (1995), Hilty (1997), Hilty & Brown (1986), Howell & Webb (1995), Kilham & O'Brien (1979), Marini (2001), Maurício & Dias (1998), Mayr & Short (1970), Melo-Júnior (2001a), Meyer de Schauensee & Phelps (1978), Monroe (1968), Parker & Goerck (1997), de la Peña (1994), Pople *et al.* (1997), Ridgely & Greenfield (2001), Ridgely & Gwynne (1989), Robinson (1997), Robinson & Terborgh (1997), Rowley (1966, 1984), Short (1975), Sick (1993), Skutch (1969a), Slud (1964), Stager (1961a), Stiles (1985), Stotz *et al.* (1997), Tostain *et al.* (1992), Wetmore (1968a), Willis (1980).

168. **Black-bodied Woodpecker**

Dryocopus schulzi

French: Pic lucifer **German**: Schwarzbauchspecht **Spanish**: Picamaderos Chaqueño
Other common names: White-shouldered Woodpecker ("*shiptoni*"); Chaco Woodpecker ("*major*")

Taxonomy. *Phloeotomus Schulzi* Cabanis, 1883, Tucumán, Argentina.
Forms a superspecies with *D. pileatus* and *D. lineatus*. Hybridizes with latter. Forms described as "*D. shiptoni*" and "*D. major*" are only variants or colour morphs. White scapular line more prevalent among N birds, and S birds average minimally smaller than others, but differences insufficient to justify subspecific separation. Monotypic.
Distribution. S Bolivia (Santa Cruz, Tarija), C Paraguay and S to NC Argentina (S to Córdoba and San Luis).

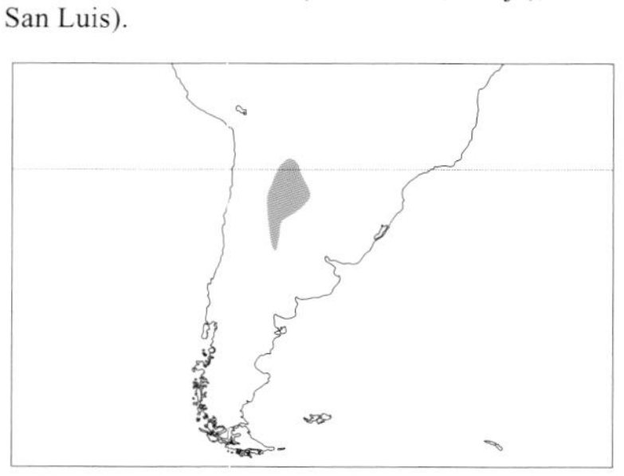

Descriptive notes. 29-30 cm. Male has yellowish-buff nasal tufts, bright red forehead to nape and long crest, sometimes some white feather bases showing through, grey ear-coverts often spotted white, usually very thin white supercilium behind eye (more or less invisible in field), white stripe from lores back through ear-coverts expanding just before nape, continuing down neck side; red malar stripe becoming black at rear, joining with black of breast; white to greyish-white chin and upper throat occasionally with very fine brown to blackish streaks (streaks rarely visible); hindneck and entire upperparts black, scapulars all black (most of S population) or with white on outer webs meeting white of neckstripe (most of N population, some S birds), or with partial white forming broken line (a few throughout range); black wings, white at bases of flight-feathers, sometimes whitish area at margin of carpal region; uppertail black, white shafts, sometimes white feather tips when fresh; black to brownish-black below, often very narrow obscure yellowish barring on lower flanks and belly (rarely, barring reaching upper flanks, even across entire belly); underwing blackish, axillaries and coverts whitish, primary coverts with irregular large black patch, variable, patch can be almost absent; in worn plumage, black areas browner, pale or dark feather bases more obvious on head and other areas; long bill straight, slightly chisel-tipped, broad across nostrils, pale ivory-white, darker culmen and base; iris deep brown to red-brown, orbital skin grey to blackish; legs dark grey. Female has slightly shorter bill than male, malar lacking red, lower forehead blackish, sometimes white specks in forecrown, but red often extends well down forehead. Juvenile duller and browner than adult, more flank barring, forecrown often with white spots, head pattern as respective adult. Voice. Common call a loud "wic wic wic wic wic", slower and generally shorter than that of *D. lineatus*; harsh rattle, "ti-chrr", heard much less frequently; descending "kirrrrrr" repeated when disturbed near nest. Drums like *D. lineatus*, possibly slightly shorter rolls.
Habitat. Xeric woodland and savanna of the Chaco with *Lithrea*, *Celtis*, acacias, carob (*Prosopis*) and cacti, and transitional habitats to mesic montane forest with alder (*Alnus*) and *Tipuana*. More humid Chaco areas possibly of marginal importance. Occurs up to 1500 m in foothills of Andes, in EC Bolivia and NW Argentina.
Food and Feeding. Diet not described. Forages singly or in pairs, occasionally in family groups of 5-6 birds, apparently on trunks and main limbs. Techniques include pecking, hammering and probing.
Breeding. Oct-Dec, possibly Mar. Nest-hole built in dead tree or utility pole; one in Argentina (Córdoba), in Dec, was c. 4 m above ground in dead limb of *Schinopsis haenkeana*, entrance hole 8 cm wide and 6 cm high, cavity depth c. 40 cm, contained 2 well-grown chicks. No other information.
Movements. Resident.
Status and Conservation. Not globally threatened. Currently considered Near-threatened. Generally rare. Has declined in many areas, and seems to have been reduced to two main populations, one in Argentine provinces of Córdoba and San Luis, the other in C Paraguayan Chaco. Apparently few survive elsewhere, where expansion of agriculture and cattle-raising has resulted in extensive clearance of woodland, and the planting of exotic trees. Details of this woodpecker's habitat preferences are not yet fully understood; further research required.
Bibliography. Brooks (1997), Canevari *et al.* (1991), Chebez (1994), Chebez *et al.* (1999), Contreras *et al.* (1990), Degan & Popovici (1973), Hayes (1995), Heredia *et al.* (1999), Madroño (1995), Madroño & Pearman (1992), Mazar Barnett & Pearman (2001), Narosky & Yzurieta (1993), Nellar (1993), Nellar & Fraga (1999), Nores *et al.* (1983), de la Peña (1994), Remsen & Traylor (1989), Remsen *et al.* (1986), Short (1975, 1985b), Stattersfield & Capper (2000), Stotz *et al.* (1996).

169. White-bellied Woodpecker

Dryocopus javensis

French: Pic à ventre blanche **German**: Weißbauchspecht **Spanish**: Picamaderos Ventriblanco
Other common names: Great Black/White-bellied Black Woodpecker; Indian Great Black Woodpecker (*hodgsonii*)

Taxonomy. *Picus Javensis* Horsfield, 1821, Java.
Forms a superspecies with *D. hodgei*, and sometimes considered conspecific. Proposed race *buettikoferi* (Nias I) appears indistinguishable from nominate; *esthloterus* (N Luzon, in Philippines), supposedly with thinner bill and less white on head, is not safely separable from *confusus*. Race *philippinensis* frequently misspelt "*philippensis*". Fourteen subspecies recognized.
Subspecies and Distribution.
D. j. hodgsonii (Jerdon, 1840) - peninsular India in Western Ghats, S Madhya Pradesh, and Orissa to N Andhra Pradesh.
D. j. forresti Rothschild, 1922 - montane N Myanmar and adjacent SW China (SW Sichuan, NW & S Yunnan).
D. j. richardsi Tristram, 1879 - Korea; extinct on Tsushima I (Japan).
D. j. feddeni (Blyth, 1863) - Myanmar (except N), most of Thailand, and Indochina.
D. j. javensis (Horsfield, 1821) - S Thailand S to Sumatra and Nias I, Java, Bali, and Borneo and associated islands, including N Natunas.
D. j. parvus (Richmond, 1902) - Simeulue I (off NW Sumatra).
D. j. confusus (Stresemann, 1913) - Luzon (N Philippines).
D. j. mindorensis (Steere, 1890) - Mindoro.
D. j. hargitti (Sharpe, 1884) - Palawan.
D. j. philippinensis (Steere, 1890) - Panay, Masbate, Guimaras, Negros.
D. j. cebuensis Kennedy, 1987 - Cebu (probably extinct).
D. j. pectoralis (Tweeddale, 1878) - Samar, Calicoan, Leyte, Panaon, Bohol.
D. j. multilunatus (McGregor, 1907) - Basilan, Dinagat, Mindanao.
D. j. suluensis (W. Blasius, 1890) - Sulu Is.

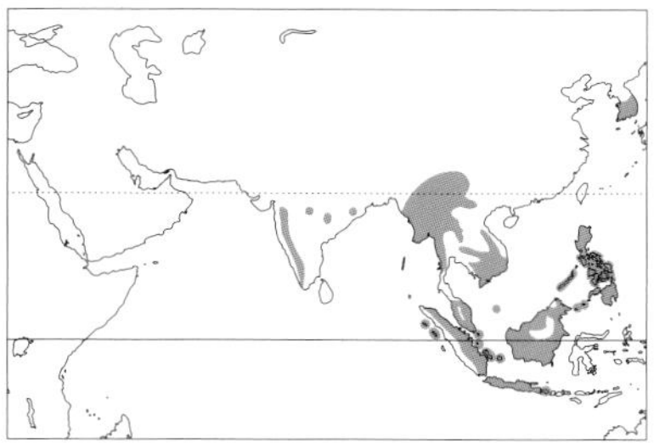

Descriptive notes. 40-48 cm; 197-347 g. Large to very large woodpecker. Male has deep red forehead to nape and crest, fairly broad red malar stripe; rest of head, entire upperparts, including wings and tail, and chin to lower breast black, white streaks on ear-coverts (especially at rear), neck side and chin to throat, primaries tipped white when fresh, small patch of cream-white at bases of inner webs; belly creamy, occasionally narrow creamy bars on lower breast side, usually black bars on flanks and ventral area, black undertail-coverts; underwing grey-black, coverts creamy, black carpal patch; undertail greyish; long bill broad-based, chisel-tipped, culmen curved, black to grey-black, sometimes pale greenish lower mandible; iris yellow, orbital skin grey; legs dark grey or blue-grey. Female is slightly less bulky than male, has forehead and forecrown black, malar area black with white streaking. Juvenile duller, browner, throat paler, often trace of white on rump, eyes grey, male with red forehead and crown mottled with black and white, only little red in malar. Races differ from nominate in size and plumage, most having white on rump: *hodgsonii* has larger all-blackish bill, shorter wing and tail, white rump; *forresti* is quite big, with proportionately short tail, has rump white, throat mainly black; *richardsi* is very large, with long bill, white rump, much white at primary bases, male's malar somewhat narrow, female distinctive with head entirely black; *feddeni* is smaller than nominate, with orange-red head colour, white rump, much white on primary bases, usually white-tipped primaries; *parvus* is smallest of all races, has black rump, very dark red on crown, hint of buff barring on ear-coverts, throat and breast; *hargitti* has large white rump, crown colour more orange-red, red malar more extensive, flanks and lower underparts black, pale thighs, base of lower mandible pale greenish-yellow or horn; *mindorensis* is like previous but much smaller, with less white on rump, usually white-tipped primaries, bill wholly blackish; *confusus* is like last but longer-billed, with very little or no white on rump, sometimes black throat with few white spots, sometimes pale lower mandible, male with more extensive red malar; *philippinensis* is larger than previous, has narrow white rump, pale lower mandible, some have black throat with sparse white spots, male with red of malar invading throat and face; *multilunatus* is similar to last but no white on rump, has white streaking on neck sides and ear-coverts, buffish barring on breast, usually white-tipped primaries; *cebuensis* is smaller and shorter-billed than last, has small white patch on lower back; *pectoralis* is fairly distinctive, has black-streaked white throat and rear ear-coverts, pale bars or streaks over breast, more heavily barred flanks, sometimes dark spots on belly, occasionally hint of white on rump; *suluensis* is small, with no white on rump or, rarely, very small patch, normally pale lower mandible. Voice. Loud single "kiyow", "kyah", "kiauk" or "keer" call note, slightly lower-pitched and more explosive than similar call of *D. martius*; long calls "kek-ek-ek-ek-ek" or "kiau kiau kiau kiau kiau", 3-4 notes per second, some series over 5 seconds long, both in flight and when perched; low "ch-wi" notes between pair-members. Both sexes drum, loud accelerating rolls, slower at beginning than those of *D. martius*, less than 2 seconds long, c. 3 rolls per minute; a low fast tapping at nest.
Habitat. Various types of evergreen and deciduous forest, locally also pine (*Pinus*) forest; closed primary forest, forest edge, dry dipterocarp forest, mixed bamboo stands, light secondary forest with large trees. Wet primary forest with many dead and rotting trees often preferred, but readily occupies selectively logged and degraded forest; sometimes forages up to c. 200 m from forest, also appears near cultivations, gardens. In Japan (Tsushima), occurred in dense mature coniferous forest mixed with oaks (*Quercus*) and camphors. Lowlands to 1200 m in India; to 1000 m in most parts of SE Asia and in Greater Sundas, generally below 600 m in Thailand, but above 1400 m and up to 3600 m in NE Myanmar, NW Tonkin and Yunnan; to 1600 m in Philippines, locally (N Luzon) to 2500 m.
Food and Feeding. Diet comprises large ants and their brood, termites (Isoptera), beetles and their (large) wood-boring larvae, also other insects, e.g. bees, and Myriapoda. Fruits (e.g. *Cornus*, *Macaranga*, *Olea*) also taken. Usually solitary or in pairs, and groups of 4-6 birds sometimes observed. Forages from lower to upper strata, in tall trees, on small dead stubs, on fallen timber, and on ground, searching among the litter; prefers dead trees, or dead parts of trees. Pecks and hammers, and commonly strips bark; also probes, and pries off pieces of bark and wood; removes large pieces of bark before digging big pits up to 20 cm long and 8 cm deep into the wood. Will spend up to one hour or more at a single favoured feeding site.
Breeding. Jan-Mar in India, Feb-May in Myanmar, late Mar to early May in Korea, Dec-Mar in Peninsular Malaysia, Apr-May and Aug-Sept in Greater Sundas, and Mar-May in Philippines. Displays poorly known, include moderate crest-raising. Nest-hole excavated by both sexes, 4-24 m up in tall stump or tall old or half-dead tree, cavity depth up to 60 cm; male demonstrates intended nest with long series of regular taps. Clutch 2 eggs, in N sometimes 3 or 4 eggs; both parents incubate, period 14 days; both also feed chicks, by regurgitation, female possibly feeding more than male; nestlings fledge after 26 days, accompanied by adults for variable period.
Movements. Resident.
Status and Conservation. Not globally threatened. Race *richardsi* CITES I. Local and uncommon throughout range; uncommon to rare and very local in India, most frequent in N part of Western Ghats; uncommon in China; scarce in peninsular Thailand; believed extinct in Singapore but observed at two different sites in 1993, the first since 1988; still reasonably common on Simeulue (*parvus*); scarce to rare in Java and Bali; fairly common to uncommon in Philippines, apparently extinct on Cebu (*cebuensis*). Race *richardsi* rare and endangered in Korea, extinct in Japan (Tsushima). Occurs in many protected areas, such as Panti Forest Reserve (Malaysia), Doi Inthanon National Park (Thailand), Nam Bai Cat Tien National Park (Vietnam), Way Kambas National Park (Sumatra), and Aas Purwo National Park (Java). Occurs at rather low densities; radius of home range c. 2 km. Habitat loss could pose a threat to this species in the longer term.
Bibliography. Abdulali (1941), Ali (1951b, 1996), Ali & Ripley (1983), Andrew (1992), Austin (1948), van Balen (1999), Betts (1934), Bharos (1992), Brazil (1991), Brooks *et al.* (1995), Bucknill & Chasen (1990), Champion-Jones (1938), Danielsen *et al.* (1994), Deignan (1945), Delacour & Mayr (1946), Dickinson *et al.* (1991), Duckworth & Kelsh (1988), Dutson *et al.* (1996), Eames & Robson (1992), Étchécopar & Hüe (1978), Evans *et al.* (1993), Gilliard (1950), Goes (1999), Goodman & Gonzales (1990), Grantham (2000), Greenway (1967), Grimmett *et al.* (1998), Ham Kyuhwang (1982), Ham Kyuhwang & Won Pyongoh (1980, 1982), Higuchi (1980), Hutchinson (1950), Inskipp *et al.* (1996), Jeyarajasingam & Pearson (1999), Kennedy (1987), King, D.I. & Rappole (2001), King, W.B. (1978/79), Kinloch (1923), Knox & Walters (1994), Lekagul & Round (1991), Lim Kim Seng (1992), MacKinnon (1988), MacKinnon & Phillipps (1993, 2000), van Marle & Voous (1988), McGregor (1905), Medway & Wells (1976), Mees (1986), Morris (1939), Neelakantan (1976), Parkes (1960a, 1971), Peterson *et al.* (1995), duPont (1971), Rajathurai (1996), Rand & Rabor (1960), Riley (1938), Ripley (1982), Robson (2000), Santharam (1999b), Sargeant (1997), Short (1973d, 1985b), Smythies (1986, 1999), Sonobe & Izawa (1987), Stresemann (1913), Thewlis *et al.* (1998), Vowles & Vowles (1997), Wang Sung (1998), Wells (1985, 1999), Wilkinson, Dutson & Sheldon (1991), Wolfe (1950), Won Pyongoh (1963, 1967, 1993), Wong (1985), Zhao Zhengjie (1995).

170. Andaman Woodpecker

Dryocopus hodgei

French: Pic des Andaman **German**: Andamanenspecht **Spanish**: Picamaderos de Andamán
Other common names: Andaman Black Woodpecker

Taxonomy. *Mulleripicus Hodgei* Blyth, 1860, Andaman Islands.
Forms a superspecies with *D. javensis*, and sometimes treated as conspecific. Monotypic.
Distribution. Andaman Is.

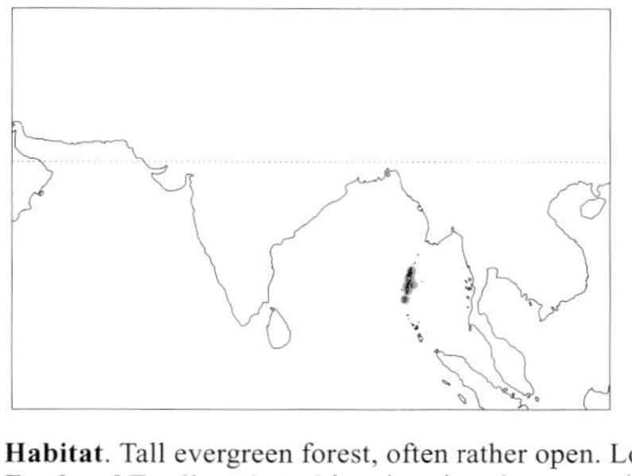

Descriptive notes. 38 cm; 156-225 g. Male has crimson forehead, crown and crest and malar area; rest of head, and upperparts, including wings and tail, greyish-black to sooty-black; entire underparts sooty-black; bill blackish; iris pale yellow, orbital skin greyish; legs slaty. Female has red only on hindcrown and crest. Juvenile as adult but duller, browner, eyes grey, male with black and white mixed in red crown feathers, much less red in malar. Voice. Loud chattering "kuk kuk kuk" terminating with whistled "kui", also loud sharp "kik, kik, kik"; calls differ from those of *D. javensis*. Drumming loud, far-carrying.
Habitat. Tall evergreen forest, often rather open. Lowlands.
Food and Feeding. Ants. Lives in pairs; also occurs in loose family parties. Forages mainly on trunks of large trees or on main (dead) branches; descends to ground to hunt for ants. Hammers powerfully.
Breeding. Jan-Mar. Nest-hole built 6-14 m up in trunk of dead tree or in large branch; 2 eggs; no other details.
Movements. Resident.
Status and Conservation. Not globally threatened. Currently considered Near-threatened. Restricted-range species: present in Andaman Islands EBA. Although still common in evergreen forest where large trees remain, recent rapid expansion of human population on the larger islands of Andamans has brought problems. Logging and conversion of forest to agricultural and grazing land likely to become a serious threat. Conservation recommendations include monitoring of the woodpecker's numbers and, if necessary, implementation of measures to prevent further loss of forest habitat.
Bibliography. Andreev *et al.* (2001), Collar *et al.* (1994), Curson (1989), Davidar *et al.* (1997), Grimmett *et al.* (1998), Inskipp *et al.* (1996), Sankaran & Vijayan (1993), Stattersfield & Capper (2000), Stattersfield *et al.* (1998), Wheatley (1996).

171. Black Woodpecker

Dryocopus martius

French: Pic noir **German**: Schwarzspecht **Spanish**: Picamaderos Negro
Other common names: Great Black Woodpecker

Taxonomy. *Picus martius* Linnaeus, 1758, Europe = Sweden.
Size varies clinally, decreasing from N to S and, in Asia, from E to W; birds from S Europe E to Transcaucasia sometimes separated as race *pinetorum* (slightly smaller than N breeders) and those from E Asia as *reichenowi* (on average larger than W Asian populations), but much overlap occurs in measurements, and racial separation not warranted. Two subspecies recognized.
Subspecies and Distribution.
D. m. martius (Linnaeus, 1758) - Europe from Spain, France and Scandinavia (N to Arctic Circle), S to Balkans and N Turkey, and E in broad belt across Asian *taiga* (S to Altai Mts, N Mongolia) to Kamchatka, Sakhalin and Japan (Hokkaido, extreme N Honshu), NE China and Korea; also Caucasus and N Iran.
D. m. khamensis (Buturlin, 1908) - SW China and Tibet (Qinghai S to NW Yunnan).
Descriptive notes. 45-55 cm; 250-370 g. Very large. Male has red central forehead to hindcrown, a few grey feather bases sometimes showing through; rest of plumage black, head and upperparts (especially wing-coverts) glossed dark blue, primaries tinged dark brown, underparts slightly duller and often tinged grey; in worn plumage duller, distinctly grey-tinged below, and red on head mixed

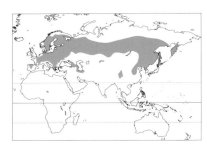

with dark grey; long bill chisel-tipped, very broad-based, culmen slightly curved, pale ivory-white to pale horn, culmen and tip bluish to blackish; iris whitish or yellowish-white, sometimes pale cream-grey; legs dark greyish to blue-grey. Female has forehead and forecrown glossy black, red only on hindcrown, bill shorter than male's. Juvenile duller, more sooty-black, often with paler (dark grey) throat, red on head duller or paler with larger dark feather bases, male with less red than adult. Race *khamensis* differs from nominate in blacker and more glossy plumage. VOICE. Loud "krry-krry-krry" in flight, "ke-yaa" on landing and when perched; before and during breeding, long series of 10-20 more melodious notes, "kwee kweekweekweekweekwek-wikwik"; "kiyák" as alarm or in aggression; intimate calls shorter "kyah", or "rirrirrrirr". Drumroll long, sometimes over 3 seconds, c. 14 (female) to 17 (male) strokes, rate c. 4 rolls per minute, males drum more frequently; loud rhythmic tapping at nest, by both sexes.

Habitat. All types of mature forest, so long as not extremely dense and gloomy; also forest edge. Spruce (*Picea*) and pine (*Pinus*) forests with larch (*Larix*), birch (*Betula*), aspen (*Populus*) and alder (*Alnus*) occupied in Scandinavia and Siberia; all habitat types in primeval Polish forests; in C Europe occurs in all types of not over-dense deciduous, mixed or coniferous forest, from riparian woodland to subalpine forest. In Japan occurs in open boreal mixed or coniferous forest at 100-1000 m, rarely in lowlands. Requires decaying trees and stumps for foraging, and tall timber for nests and roosts. Outside breeding season also in open areas such as forest clear-cuts, even on outskirts of cities. Mostly lowlands to 2000 m: usually below 1200 m but also up to timber-line in European Alps and in Caucasus; to 1700-2000 m in Asia, but to 2400 m in China.

Food and Feeding. Mainly ants (*Camponotus*, *Formica*, *Lasius*) and their brood; at least locally, may switch from *Camponotus* in winter to *Lasius* in spring. Wood-boring beetles and bark beetles and their larvae (e.g. Cerambycidae, Elateridae) also taken; also various other arthropods, and occasionally snails. Reported to break into beehives. Fruits and berries eaten only rarely. Mostly solitary, partners keeping in loose contact. Foraging is concentrated at lower levels on tree trunks, mostly below 3 m, and at bases of trees, and on ground. Both live trees and dead ones are visited; climbs straight on tree trunks and larger branches; very rarely perches crosswise. On ground, moves with a few clumsy hops. Chisels deep elongated rectangular holes into trunks to reach food items in burrows deep inside; bark removed by tangential blows, or pried off in large pieces. Drinking from sap wells recorded, also the drilling of wells. Seems to be well aware of location of ant nests in its territory, is able to locate them even under deep snow.

Breeding. Laying mid-Mar to mid-May, but sexual activities may begin in mid-Jan; long period of pair-formation, during which final location of nest decided upon. Nest-excavation takes 10-15 days, site in tall tree, in most cases (c. 75%) living one, either coniferous or deciduous, at height of 3-27 m, mostly 5-10 m (mean height of 102 nests in Norway was 8·0 m), entrance a vertical oval, average dimensions 13 cm × 8·5 cm, cavity depth up to c. 60 cm; often (up to 50% of nestings) old hole reused, or telephone pole used; active nests at least 900 m apart. Clutch 2-6 eggs, usually 3-5, average clutch size ranging from c. 4·8 eggs in Sweden to 3·3 eggs in S Germany, and earlier clutches tend to be larger; incubation by both sexes, only male at night, period 12-14 days; both parents also brood chicks, for c. 8 days, and both feed them, by regurgitation; fledging period 24-31 days, usually 27-28 days; juveniles fed for up to 1 month, generally by male parent. Fledging success averaged 2·7 in Germany, 4·4 in Finland; martens (*Martes*) are major nest predators.

Movements. Resident in most areas, and even N populations only partially migratory; juvenile dispersal more pronounced. Scandinavian populations migrate in Sept or earlier, early migrants or dispersing birds recorded in Aug and early Sept in C Europe; some movements also in winter; movements of between 500 km and 1000 km recorded. Vertical winter movements take place in some mountainous regions.

Status and Conservation. Not globally threatened. Locally common in some W parts of range, but more uncommon in E. Estimated population of c. 316,000 pairs in European Russia and c. 233,000 pairs in rest of Europe in late 1990's, of which 60,000 in Belarus and 50,000 in Germany. Densities usually low, e.g. 1 pair/300-1000 ha in C Europe. Stable or increasing in W; during 20th century range extended in W Europe and EC European lowlands, and since c. 1970 has colonized large areas where formerly absent. Has also spread recently in Japan, with extension from Hokkaido S to other parts of country. A key species in many forests, as it creates holes for wide variety of other hole-nesters.

Bibliography. Alatalo (1978), Arisawa (1991), Aschoff (1967), Beaman & Madge (1998), Blagosklonov (1968), Blume (1956, 1961, 1981, 1996), Borgstrom (1989), Brazil (1991), Burow (1970), Callegari (1955), Christensen (1984, 1995a, 1995b), Christensen & Sorensen (1986), Clarenbach (1998), Cramp (1985), Cuisin (1967, 1967-1968, 1972, 1975, 1976, 1977, 1980, 1981, 1983, 1985, 1988, 1990, 1992, 1997, 1998), Dementiev (1939), Dementiev *et al.* (1966), Diaz (1997), Díaz *et al.* (1996), Diener (1996), Érard (1962), Étchécopar & Hüe (1978), Eygenraam (1947), Fernández & Azkona (1996), Ferry *et al.* (1957), Fitter (1992), Garoche & Sohier (1992), Gatter (1977, 1981), Gentilin (1967), Gorman (1998b), Grebe (1998), Guichard (1961), Haessler (1989), Hagemeijer & Blair (1997), Hågvar & Hågvar (1989), Hågvar *et al.* (1990), Haila & Jarvinen (1977), Hansen (1984, 1987, 1989), Haribal & Ganguli-Lachungpa (1991), Hasse (1961), Heath *et al.* (2000), Hüe & Étchécopar (1970), Ishigaki *et al.* (1987), Iso & Fujimaki (1990), Ivanchev (1995), Järvinen *et al.* (1977), Johansen (1989a, 1989b), Johnsson (1993), Johnsson *et al.* (1993), Kojima & Arikawa (1983), Kojima & Matsuoka (1985), Kuhlke (1985), Labidoire (1992), Lang & Rost (1990a, 1990b), Lange (1995, 1996), Liu Huanjin & Shen Shouyi (1988), Lucker (1992), MacKinnon & Phillipps (2000), Majewski & Rolstad (1993), Matsumoto (1987), Matsuoka & Kojima (1979a), Mauersberger *et al.* (1982), Mayaud (1950), Melde (1994), Merikallio (1958), Mikusinski (1995, 1997, 2001), Mikusinski & Angelstam (1997, 1998), Mosansky (1986), Mouillard (1946), Mueller (1998), Mulhauser, Kaiser & Claude (2000), Mulhauser, Kaiser & Junod (2001), Müller (1977), Nilsson, Johnsson & Tjernberg (1991, 1993a, 1993b), Nilsson, Olsson *et al.* (1992), Ogasawara & Izumi (1977, 1978), de Pardieu (1937), Pavlík (1994), Pechacek (1992, 1995, 1996), Pechacek & Krištin (1993), Prodon (1991), Purroy (1997), Radermacher (1970), Ravussin & Sermet (1975), Rivière (1990), Rogacheva (1992), Rolstad & Rolstad (2000), Rolstad, Majewski & Rolstad (1998), Rolstad, Rolstad & Saeteren (2000), Rost *et al.* (1992), Roze (1987), Rudat *et al.* (1979), Ruge & Bretzendorfer (1981), Sautereau & Courtillot (1961), Short (1985b), Snow & Perrins (1998), Sollien *et al.* (1977), Striegler *et al.* (1982), Svensson *et al.* (1999), Tjernberg *et al.* (1993), Tobalske & Tobalske (1999), Villarán (1999), Voous (1961), Wesolowski & Tomialojc (1986), Zhao Zhengjie (1995).

PLATE 44 ➤

ssp *pollens*

♂

♀

172

173

ssp *haematogaster*

♀

♂

ssp *splendens*

♀ ssp *rubricollis*

♂

174

♂ ssp *trachelopyrus*

♂

ssp *peruvianus*

♀ ssp *guatemalensis*

♂

175

♀

♂

176

♀

ssp *melanoleucos*

♂

177

♀

♂

178

♂ ssp *malherbii*

♂ ssp *nelsoni*

♀

♂

179

♀

♂

180

♀

181

♂

ssp *principalis*

♂ ssp *bairdii*

♀

♂

182

PLATE 44

inches   7

cm   18

Genus *CAMPEPHILUS* G. R. Gray, 1840

172. **Powerful Woodpecker**

Campephilus pollens

French: Pic puissant   **German**: Zimtbindenspecht   **Spanish**: Picamaderos Poderoso

Taxonomy. *Picus pollens* Bonaparte, 1845, Colombia.
Formerly placed in genus *Phloeoceastes* with seven other species, all of which are now lumped into *Campephilus*. Two subspecies recognized.
Subspecies and Distribution.
C. p. pollens (Bonaparte, 1845) - Andes from NC Colombia and SW Venezuela (Táchira) S to Ecuador.
C. p. peruvianus (Cory, 1915) - Peru (S to Pasco).

Descriptive notes. c. 32 cm. Male has bright red forehead to crest, sometimes some black and white of feather bases visible, white band from lores to lower rear edge of ear-coverts continuing down side of neck to side of upper breast; rest of head, including chin and throat, black; black hindneck, mantle, scapulars and upper back, narrow white stripes on sides of mantle (often some cinnamon markings) more or less meeting at top of lower back and often joining with neck stripes; white lower back and rump, edges with a few dark-barred cinnamon-buff feathers, black uppertail-coverts; upperwing black, primaries narrowly tipped
white, white spots or bars on inner webs of secondaries and all but outermost primaries; uppertail black, very occasionally white spots towards tips of outer feathers, only 10 feathers (not 12); black central breast, cinnamon-buff lower breast to undertail-coverts with black bars or chevrons, latter less pronounced on belly; underwing blackish, barred white, coverts white; long bill chisel-tipped, culmen slightly curved, broad across nostrils, black; iris white to pinkish-white; legs dark grey. Female has red areas of head replaced with black. Juvenile duller and browner than adult, more barring on back, duller and greyer with broader barring below, crest feathers longer, head pattern as respective adult. Race *peruvianus* differs from nominate in having lower back and rump cinnamon-buff and often strongly barred, often narrow cinnamon-buff bars on uppertail-coverts. Voice. Commonest call nasal "kyaaah" or "peeyáw", often repeated; fast "kikikikikawh", mostly in flight; descending "kikikiki-keh-keh-kah-kah" in excitement. Loud instrumental signal a brief double rap.
Habitat. Inhabits mature montane forest, humid and wet forest, cloudforest, and forest borders; also occurs in secondary forest, and open forest. Recorded between 900 m and 3750 m, mainly at 1700-2600 m.
Food and Feeding. Details of diet not documented. Often in pairs. Forages in interior of forest, at all levels, predominantly on trunks and large limbs.
Breeding. Season apparently Apr-Aug. Nest situated in tree or telegraph pole, high up, e.g. at 7 m. No other information.
Movements. Resident.
Status and Conservation. Not globally threatened. Local in Colombia; rare to uncommon and local in Ecuador; rare in Peru. Occurs in Cueva de los Guácharos National Park and La Planada Nature Reserve (Colombia) and also in Podocarpus National Park (Ecuador). Not often seen; appears to require very large home range.
Bibliography. Allen (1998), Bloch *et al.* (1991), Butler (1979), Clements & Shany (2001), Davies *et al.* (1994), Donegan & Dávalos (1999), Fjeldså & Krabbe (1990), Hilty (1985), Hilty & Brown (1986), Hornbuckle (1999), Kirwan & Marlow (1996), Meyer de Schauensee (1982), Meyer de Schauensee & Phelps (1978), Olrog (1968), Parker, Parker & Plenge (1982), Parker, Schulenberg *et al.* (1985), Poulsen (1996), Ridgely & Greenfield (2001), Ridgely *et al.* (1998), Salaman (1994), Salaman *et al.* (1999), Stotz *et al.* (1996), Vélez & Velázquez (1998), Williams & Tobias (1994).

173. **Crimson-bellied Woodpecker**

Campephilus haematogaster

French: Pic superbe   **German**: Blutbauchspecht   **Spanish**: Picamaderos Ventrirrojo
Other common names: Splendid Woodpecker (*splendens*)

Taxonomy. *Picus haematogaster* Tschudi, 1844, Peru.
Formerly placed in genus *Phloeoceastes* with seven other species, all of which are now lumped into *Campephilus*. Race *splendens*, sometimes regarded as a separate species, appears to differ vocally; further study needed. Two subspecies currently recognized.
Subspecies and Distribution.
C. h. splendens Hargitt, 1889 - Panama to W Ecuador.
C. h. haematogaster (Tschudi, 1844) - E Colombia to E Peru.
Descriptive notes. 33-34 cm; 225-250 g. Male has buffish nasal tufts, thin buff supercilium behind eye, broad buff cheekband, black line from upper bill to mid crown side, black upper ear-coverts, black chin to foreneck; rest of head red, hindneck and entire underparts red; mantle, scapulars and upper back black to brownish-black, lower back and rump deep red, uppertail-coverts black; upperwing black or brownish-black, primaries narrowly tipped pale when fresh, large white to buff-white spots on inner webs of secondaries and all but outermost primaries; uppertail black; underwing blackish, barred pale, coverts white; in worn plumage, red areas duller, black feather bases visible on crown and below, black areas of plumage browner; long bill almost straight, chisel-tipped, broad across nostrils, grey-black to black; iris red-brown, orbital skin black; legs brownish-black. Female differs from male in having buffish-white cheekband con-

tinuing broadly down neck side to upper breast side. Juvenile duller than adult, black areas browner, less red below, has forehead more sooty-coloured, sexes differ as for adults. Race *splendens* has larger black feather bases than nominate, especially on head, red tips on throat and foreneck, back narrowly barred, feathers of underparts black-based with barred central part. Voice. Call a loud "stk! st-kr-r-r-r-r-r-r", c. 2 seconds long, drumroll fast series of 3-4 loud raps; race *splendens* a loud "stk", drum a strong double rap like that of *C. rubricollis*.
Habitat. Humid and wet forest, montane forest, and edges; most often inside tall forest, such as semi-open *várzea* forest. From lowlands to 1600 m in Panama; 800-1700 m in Ecuador; 900-2200 m in Peru.
Food and Feeding. Large adult beetles, and very large larvae of wood-boring beetles. Often in pairs. Forages at low levels, usually close to ground, in dense forest, especially on trunks of big trees; visits slightly higher levels in more open habitats. Hammers, probes in crevices. Where sympatric with *C. gayaquilensis*, separated ecologically by preference for lower levels.
Breeding. Mar-May in Panama, and Sept-Apr in Colombia and Ecuador. No other information.
Movements. Resident.
Status and Conservation. Not globally threatened. Generally rather rare in Panama, though perhaps somewhat more numerous in E; locally quite numerous in Colombia; rare to locally uncommon in Ecuador; rare in Peru. Occurs in El Pangán Reserve (Colombia), and in Machu Picchu Historical Sanctuary (Peru). Recorded at El Placer (Ecuador), and at Tingo María and Abra Patricia (Peru).
Bibliography. Anon. (1998b), Balchin & Toyne (1998), Butler (1979), Clements & Shany (2001), Davies *et al.* (1994), Hilty (1997), Hilty & Brown (1986), Hornbuckle (1999), Meyer de Schauensee (1982), Olrog (1968), Parker, Parker & Plenge (1982), Parker, Schulenberg *et al.* (1985), Ridgely & Greenfield (2001), Ridgely & Gwynne (1989), Ridgely *et al.* (1998), Robbins *et al.* (1985), Salaman (1994), Stotz *et al.* (1996), Walker (2001), Wetmore (1968a), Williams & Tobias (1994).

174. **Red-necked Woodpecker**

Campephilus rubricollis

French: Pic à cou rouge   **German**: Rothalsspecht   **Spanish**: Picamaderos Cuellirrojo

Taxonomy. *Picus rubricollis* Boddaert, 1783, Cayenne.
Formerly placed in genus *Phloeoceastes* with seven other species, all of which are now lumped into *Campephilus*. Race *trachelopyrus* intergrades with nominate in SW of range. Three subspecies recognized.
Subspecies and Distribution.
C. r. rubricollis (Boddaert, 1783) - E Colombia and E Ecuador to Venezuela, the Guianas and N Brazil (N of Amazon).
C. r. trachelopyrus (Malherbe, 1857) - NE Peru and W Brazil (S of Amazon) S to WC Bolivia (La Paz).
C. r. olallae (Gyldenstolpe, 1945) - Brazil S of Amazon, from R Madeira E to Pará and Maranhão, and S to C Bolivia (Cochabamba) and N Mato Grosso.

Descriptive notes. 30-32 cm; 178-239 g. Male has small oval spot of black and white on lower rear ear-coverts; rest of head, crest and neck to uppermost mantle bright red, feathers of neck and side of head black-based and with cinnamon bar below red tip (some barring usually visible when worn); upperparts black to brownish-black, upperwing black, bases of primaries with extensive rufous on inner webs and shafts, primaries very occasionally (fresh plumage) with very small pale rufous to whitish tips; uppertail black; rufous to rufous-cinnamon below, feathers of upper and occasionally lower breast with red tips; underwing
rufous, coverts darker, blackish tip and trailing edge; long bill almost straight, chisel-tipped, broad across nostrils, pale ivory to greyish or pale yellow; iris yellowish-white; legs blackish-grey or olive. Female lacks ear-covert spot, instead has black-bordered broad whitish malar stripe from base of bill to lower ear-coverts. Juvenile duller than adult, more brownish-black and orange-red, male with whitish malar, usually some red tips, some black feathering on foreneck, female like adult but with black extending to forehead. Race *trachelopyrus* is larger than nominate, darker, more chestnut, below, with red tips extending to lower breast or to belly, rufous in wing on both webs; *olallae* is slightly smaller than previous, and brighter. Voice. Explosive nasal "ngkah-ngkah", "kiahh", and "querra-querra", similar to calls of *C. melanoleucos*. Drumming a loud double rap, "tó-ro".
Habitat. Rainforest, *terra firme* and *várzea* forests, cloudforest, forest edge, light second growth, semi-open woodland on sand, and riverine woodland in savanna regions. Mainly lowlands, usually to 600 m, locally (S Venezuela, NW Brazil) to 1800 m, even 2400 m (La Paz, Bolivia).
Food and Feeding. Large larvae of beetles and moths (Pyralidae). In pairs or small family parties. Forages actively from middle to upper levels, on trunks and limbs of tall trees; often visits lower storey and canopy.
Breeding. Jan-May in N part of range, Nov in Ecuador, and Sept in Peru. Nest situated in live or dead trunk; has oval-shaped entrance; only one chick recorded at any particular nest. No other information available.
Movements. Resident.
Status and Conservation. Not globally threatened. Often the commonest large woodpecker within its range. Rare to uncommon and seemingly local in Ecuador; fairly common in Peru. Occurs in several protected areas, e.g. Canaima National Park, and Imataca Forest Reserve and El Dorado (Venezuela), Amacayacu National Park (Colombia), Cuyabeno Reserve (Ecuador), Tambopata Re-

---

On following pages: 175. Robust Woodpecker (*Campephilus robustus*); 176. Pale-billed Woodpecker (*Campephilus guatemalensis*); 177. Crimson-crested Woodpecker (*Campephilus melanoleucos*); 178. Guayaquil Woodpecker (*Campephilus gayaquilensis*); 179. Cream-backed Woodpecker (*Campephilus leucopogon*); 180. Magellanic Woodpecker (*Campephilus magellanicus*); 181. Imperial Woodpecker (*Campephilus imperialis*); 182. Ivory-billed Woodpecker (*Campephilus principalis*).

serve (Peru) and Rio Cristalino Private Reserve (Brazil). Research required to investigate its breeding behaviour.
Bibliography. Allen (1995), Brace *et al.* (1997), Clements & Shany (2001), Cohn-Haft *et al.* (1997), Donahue (1994), Dubs (1992), Fjeldså & Krabbe (1990), Flores *et al.* (2001), González (1998), Haverschmidt & Mees (1994), Hilty & Brown (1986), Meyer de Schauensee & Phelps (1978), Oren & Parker (1997), Peres & Whittaker (1991), Perry *et al.* (1997), Remsen & Traylor (1989), Ridgely & Greenfield (2001), Robinson & Terborgh (1997), Short (1985b), Sick (1993), da Silva (1996), Snyder (1966), Stager (1961a), Stotz, Fitzpatrick *et al.* (1996), Stotz, Lanyon *et al.* (1997), Terborgh *et al.* (1984), Thiollay & Jullien (1998), Tostain *et al.* (1992), Traylor (1958), Willard *et al.* (1991).

175. Robust Woodpecker

Campephilus robustus

French: Pic robuste **German**: Scharlachkopfspecht **Spanish**: Picamaderos Robusto

Taxonomy. *Picus robustus* M. H. K. Lichtenstein, 1819, Brazil.
Formerly placed in genus *Phloeoceastes* with seven other species, all of which are now lumped into *Campephilus*. Size of present species increases slightly from N to S, but insufficient to warrant separation of any geographical races. Monotypic.
Distribution. E Brazil (S from S Bahia and E Goiás) S to E Paraguay, NE Argentina (Misiones, Corrientes) and Rio Grande do Sul.

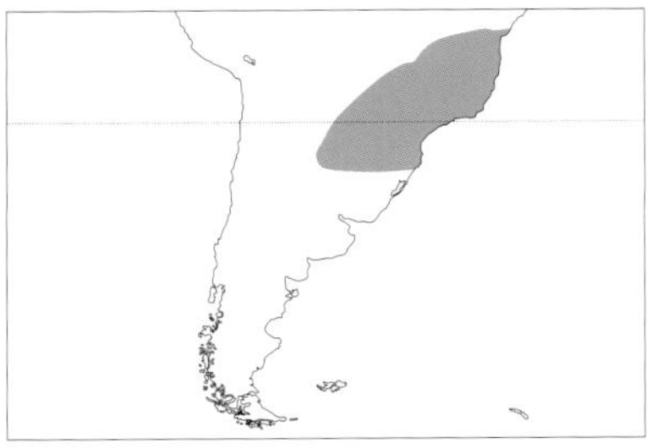

Descriptive notes. 32-37 cm; 230-294 g. Large, distinctive woodpecker. Male has small oval black and white spot on lower rear ear-coverts; rest of head, small crest, and neck to uppermost breast bright red, often some black and buff of feather bases visible, especially on neck and side of head (more obvious when plumage worn); whitish upperparts tinged pale buff or cinnamon, a few blackish bars on upper mantle and often at sides; black upperwing, coverts and scapulars, small rusty-buff spots on inner webs of flight-feathers; uppertail black; underparts from breast buff to whitish-buff, barred black, bars narrower or occasionally absent on belly; underwing blackish-brown, rufous-buff coverts and spots on flight-feathers; long bill almost straight, chisel-tipped, broad across nostrils, horn-coloured; iris white to yellow-white; legs dark grey. Female lacks ear-covert spot, has black-margined whitish malar stripe, blackish chin. Juvenile duller than adult, browner, with less contrasting barring below, undertail-coverts usually unbarred, upperparts generally whiter, head pattern as adult female, male with red tips in malar area. Voice. Call "kee" or "kew", both when perched and in flight; also "psó-ko po-po-po-po-rrat" series. Drumming a double tap, "to-plóp" or "thump-ump", 1-3 per minute.
Habitat. Humid forest, araucaria forest; occurs in disturbed forest only if large trees present. Lowlands to 1000 m, in hills to 2200 m.
Food and Feeding. Beetles, apparently also wood-boring larvae; berries sometimes taken. Singly, or in pairs or family parties; rarely joins mixed-species flocks. Forages at all levels, with slight preference for middle storey; only rarely on ground. Prefers larger trees, dead or living; visits mainly trunks and base of branches. Pecks and hammers vigorously; hammering may, rarely, create large excavations. Also probes, and removes bark.
Breeding. Two records, from Oct and Jan, of birds excavating holes 3·5-4·5 m up dead trees in forest clearings. Only known display is wing-spreading. No further information available.
Movements. Resident.
Status and Conservation. Not globally threatened. Not uncommon in S of range. Occurs in Caaguazú National Park and Estancia San Antonio Private Nature Reserve (Paraguay), and in neighbouring Iguaçú and Iguazú National Parks (Brazil/Argentina). Has possibly extended range in SE Brazil, where recent sightings in Rio Grande do Sul much farther S than previous records. Poorly known; requires research on its ecology and breeding.
Bibliography. Aleixo & Galetti (1997), dos Anjos & Schuchmann (1997), dos Anjos *et al.* (1997), Belton (1984), Brooks *et al.* (1993), Buzzetti (2000), Cândido (2000), Canevari *et al.* (1991), Descourtilz (1983), Dubs (1992), Hayes (1995), Hayes & Scharf (1995a, 1995b), Lowen *et al.* (1995), Madroño, Clay, Robbins *et al.* (1997), Madroño, Robbins & Zyskowski (1997), Maurício & Dias (1998), Meyer de Schauensee (1982), Olrog (1968), Parker & Goerck (1997), de la Peña (1994), Pereyra (1950), Pichorim *et al.* (2000), do Rosário (1996), Saibene *et al.* (1996), Sargeant & Wall (1996), Sick (1993), da Silva (1996), Silveira (1998), Stotz *et al.* (1996), Tobias *et al.* (1993), Urben-Filho *et al.* (2000), Willis (1989).

176. Pale-billed Woodpecker

Campephilus guatemalensis

French: Pic à bec clair **German**: Königspecht **Spanish**: Picamaderos Piquiclaro
Other common names: Flint-billed Woodpecker

Taxonomy. *Picus guatemalensis* Hartlaub, 1844, Guatemala.
Formerly placed in genus *Phloeoceastes* with seven other species, all of which are now lumped into *Campephilus*. Forms a superspecies with *C. melanoleucos* and *C. gayaquilensis*. Birds from Sonora described as race *dorsofasciatus*, on basis of more barred rump, but this character matched by individuals of *nelsoni*. Three subspecies recognized.
Subspecies and Distribution.
C. g. nelsoni (Ridgway, 1911) - W Mexico, from S Sonora S to Oaxaca.
C. g. regius Reichenbach, 1854 - E Mexico, from Tamaulipas S to Veracruz.
C. g. guatemalensis (Hartlaub, 1844) - Veracruz to W Panama.
Descriptive notes. 31-38 cm; 205-244 g (*guatemalensis*), 263-282 g (*regius*). Male has entire head and short bushy crest red, usually slightly darker on rear ear-coverts, often some black and white of feather bases showing through when worn; black neck, upper breast and upperparts, white stripe on neck side continuing along side of mantle to centre of back, occasionally some paler bars on lower back, rump and uppertail-coverts; upperwing black to brownish-black, whitish bases to flight-feathers, in fresh plumage white tips to primaries; uppertail black; underparts below breast buffish-white, flanks and belly tinged pale greenish, all barred blackish-brown; underwing whitish or pale yellowish, blacker tip and trailing edge; undertail brown to yellow-brown, paler at base; long bill straight, chisel-tipped, broad across nostrils, ivory-coloured, base tinged blue-grey; iris pale yellow, orbital skin greyish; legs greenish-grey to grey-brown. Female differs from male in having black forehead, crown and centre of crest, black chin and throat. Juvenile duller and browner above than adult,

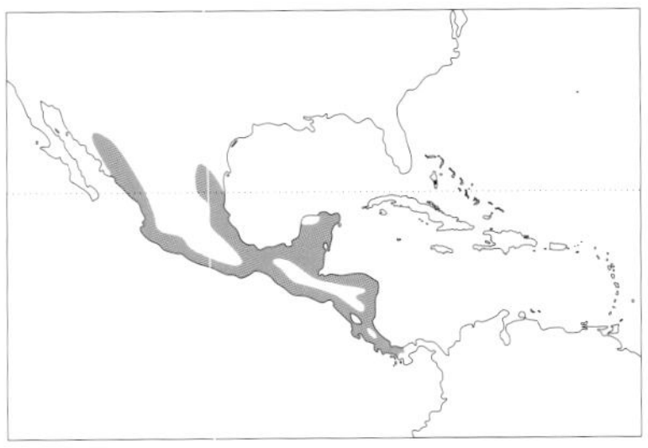

browner with more obscure barring below, with bill dark, eyes grey to brown, head pattern as female but more orange, head side more dark reddish-brown, male soon like adult. Race *nelsoni* is on average slightly smaller than nominate, browner above, less buff-tinged below, with greater tendency towards barring on rump, especially in N of range; *regius* is larger and longer-billed than nominate. Voice. Loud bleating "kint", similar to that of *C. principalis*; loud nasal rattle, "ka ka ka ka ka kay, nyuck, nyuck"; whining or moaning sounds, or low "keeu keeu keeu keeu", in intimate contacts. Instrumental signal of 2 powerful taps in quick succession, second stroke not so loud; roll of c. 7 strokes also reported.
Habitat. Humid and dry forest and edge, clearings with scattered trees, also tall second growth, plantations and mangroves. In lower parts of pine-oak (*Pinus-Quercus*) woodland in N parts of range. Tall rainforest occupied in areas where *Dryocopus lineatus* is absent. Although basically a forest bird, it often forages in cleared areas. Lowlands and foothills to 2000 m in Mexico and Guatemala; to 1000 m in N Costa Rica, and to 1200 m and locally 1500 m on S Pacific slope of Costa Rica and in Panama.
Food and Feeding. Insects, mostly larvae of wood-boring beetles (frequently Cerambycidae), scarabaeid larvae and ant larvae, comprise more than 70% of diet; some fruit also taken. Singly or in pairs. Forages at all heights, but middle to fairly high levels preferred; comes lower at edges, clearings, or in second growth. Trunks and larger branches favoured, but small twigs also investigated. Digs deeply into decaying trunks with hammering and pecking, removes large flakes and splinters, also probes into such excavations; removes bark from dead wood; other feeding techniques uncommon.
Breeding. Jan-May in Mexico and N Central America, and Aug-Dec farther S. Paired throughout year. Crest-raising display. Nest a deep cavity, excavated by both sexes, 4-15 m up in large trunk. Clutch 2 eggs; incubation by both sexes, in long bouts, period not documented; both also feed chicks, directly rather than by regurgitation; fledging period not recorded.
Movements. Resident; possibly some local movements.
Status and Conservation. Not globally threatened. Fairly common to common; widespread in suitable habitats. Locally common in wholly or partly forested areas, but infrequent in extensively deforested regions. Occurs in many protected areas, notably in Costa Rica, where present in Corcovado, Santa Rosa, Manuel Antonio, Cahuita, Barra Honda and Braulio Carrillo National Parks, Carara Biological Reserve, Guayabo National Monument, and Finca La Selva; also present in Tikal National Park (Guatemala). Seems to be fairly adaptable; accepts more open forest.
Bibliography. Anon. (1998b), Binford (1989), Blake & Loiselle (2000, 2001), Dearborn (1907), England (2000), Friedmann *et al.* (1957), González-García (1993), Heisler (1994), Hernández *et al.* (1995), Howell, S.N.G. & Webb (1995), Howell, T.R. (1957), Hutto (1992), Kilham (1977e, 1977f, 1983), Land (1970), Miller (1995), Moermond (1985), Monroe (1968), Otvos (1967), Paynter (1955), Ridgely & Gwynne (1989), Schaldach (1963), Short (1985b), Skutch (1969a), Slud (1964), Smithe (1966), Stiles (1985), Stiles & Skutch (1989), Stotz *et al.* (1996), Throp (1957), Thurber *et al.* (1987), Wauer (1998), Wetmore (1968a), Wilbur (1987).

177. Crimson-crested Woodpecker

Campephilus melanoleucos

French: Pic de Malherbe **German**: Schwarzkehlspecht **Spanish**: Picamaderos Barbinegro
Other common names: Black-and-white Woodpecker; Malherbe's Woodpecker (*malherbii*)

Taxonomy. *Picus melanoleucos* J. F. Gmelin, 1788, Surinam.
Formerly placed in genus *Phloeoceastes* with seven other species, all of which are now lumped into *Campephilus*. Forms a superspecies with *C. guatemalensis* and *C. gayaquilensis*. Possibly conspecific with latter. Races intergrade quite extensively; birds from S half of range formerly grouped together as race *albirostris*. Three subspecies recognized.
Subspecies and Distribution.
C. m. malherbii G. R. Gray, 1845 - W Panama E to N & C Colombia.
C. m. melanoleucos (J. F. Gmelin, 1788) - E of Andes, from Colombia E to Trinidad and NE Brazil, S to Bolivia, Paraguay, N & NE Argentina and Mato Grosso.
C. m. cearae (Cory, 1915) - E & S Brazil.

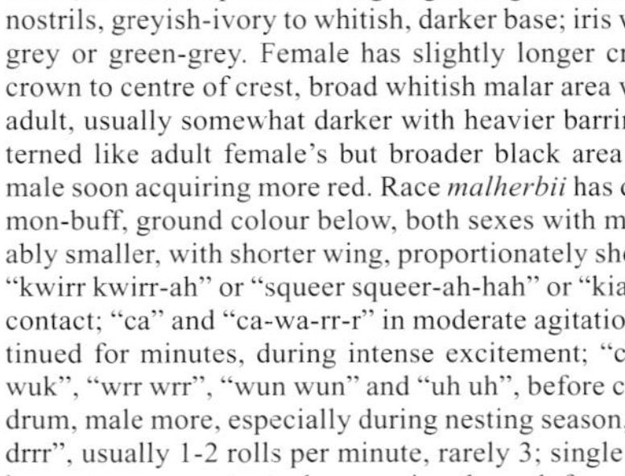

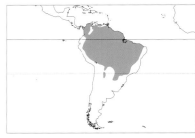

Descriptive notes. 33-38 cm; 181-284 g. Large woodpecker. Male has cream-buff feathering around base of bill, narrow black line across lower forehead, small oval area of black and white at lower rear ear-coverts; rest of head and crest red, throat black; neck to upper breast and upperparts black, white stripe down neck and side of mantle to centre of back, often with a few black spots or bars on back; upperwing black, primaries with small white tips when fresh, small area of white at bases of inner webs; uppertail black; lower breast to undertail-coverts pale buffish-white, sometimes tinged green, barred blackish-brown; underwing white, blackish tip and trailing edge; long bill chisel-tipped, culmen slightly curved, broad across nostrils, greyish-ivory to whitish, darker base; iris white to pale yellowish, orbital skin greyish; legs grey or green-grey. Female has slightly longer crest than male, also black central forehead and crown to centre of crest, broad whitish malar area with black borders. Juvenile browner above than adult, usually somewhat darker with heavier barring below, both sexes with pinkish-red head patterned like adult female's but broader black area across lower ear-coverts, whitish supercilium, male soon acquiring more red. Race *malherbii* has dark grey to brown-grey bill, darker, more cinnamon-buff, ground colour below, both sexes with more extensive red around eyes; *cearae* is noticeably smaller, with shorter wing, proportionately shorter tail. Voice. Main call likened to tree-frog's, "kwirr kwirr-ah" or "squeer squeer-ah-hah" or "kiarhh rai-ai-ai-ai", when perched or on landing, as contact; "ca" and "ca-wa-rr-r" in moderate agitation; shrill piping "put put puttas", sometimes continued for minutes, during intense excitement; "chiz-ik" in display; low intimate notes as "wuk wuk", "wrr wrr", "wun wun" and "uh uh", before copulation and at change-over at nest. Both sexes drum, male more, especially during nesting season, strong blow followed by 2-4 weak strokes, "da-drrr", usually 1-2 rolls per minute, rarely 3; single "torrrrr" roll given throughout day, presumably by partners as contact when moving through forest.

Habitat. Very wide range of habitats: cloudforest, rainforest, *terra firme* and *várzea* forest, gallery forest and deciduous forest, also rather open woodland in savanna. Occurs in second growth, clearings, forest edge, semi-open country, plantations, palm groves, pastures, and swampy areas; sometimes at single trees well away from forest. Presence of big dead trees probably important element in habitat. Occurs in lowlands, up to 900 m in Panama; in Venezuela, up to 2000 m in N and to 950 m in S; up to 1350 m, but mostly around 900 m, in Ecuador; up to 1500 m in Peru; up to 2500 m, locally 3100 m, elsewhere in Andes.
Food and Feeding. Chiefly larvae of large (e.g. 4 cm) wood-boring beetles, also hard-shelled insects, ants, termites (Isoptera); takes pyralid caterpillars, also smaller insects, and berries (Loranthaceae). In pairs or small groups; pair-members usually within 15 m of each other, often much closer. Forages at heights varying from 6 m to 25 m, mostly at intermediate levels, on tall, dead tree trunks in forest, or on isolated trees a considerable distance from forest or woodland. Moves from one tree to the next, rather than making long flights from one profitable tree to another; explores many parts of tree in quick succession. Moves along underside of dead limbs high up in crown; frequently hangs upside-down on relatively thin branches. Versatile feeder, with strong preference for wood-boring techniques. Uncovers prey with few powerful blows against bark or surface layers of wood; light taps probably more exploratory. Excavates on well-rotted stubs, cavities 10 cm or more in depth created; combines pecking with sideways blows to dislodge pieces of loose bark; also probes natural cavities or clumps of epiphytes.
Breeding. Mainly Nov-Jan in Panama, from end of rainy season to beginning of dry; Dec-May in Colombia, Apr-Jul in N Venezuela, Dec-Mar in the Guianas; Jul in N & NW Brazil, May-Dec elsewhere; mostly May-Oct in S, and Sept-Nov in Argentina. Displays with crest-raising, head-swinging, simultaneous calling. Nest-hole excavated by both sexes, high up in stub, preferably of large diameter (45-50 cm), entrance hole oval in shape; araçaris (*Pteroglossus*) important hole competitors; territory relatively small. Clutch 2-3 eggs, occasionally 4; both sexes incubate, stints lasting over 30 minutes, period not recorded; both also brood and feed chicks, nestling period not documented; young remain with parents almost until following breeding season.
Movements. Resident.
Status and Conservation. Not globally threatened. Fairly common in much of range; uncommon in some regions, e.g. Trinidad. Occurs in numerous protected areas throughout exensive range, e.g. Henri Pittier, Ciénaga de Catatumbo, Canaima and Morrocoy National Parks (Venezuela), Cuyabeno Reserve (Ecuador), Manu National Park and Alpahuayo-Mishana Reserve (Peru) and Rio Cristalino Private Reserve (Brazil). Acceptance of more open habitats suggests that it is unlikely to become threatened in immediate future.
Bibliography. dos Anjos & Schuchmann (1997), Brace *et al.* (1997), Canaday & Jost (1999), Canevari *et al.* (1991), Capper, Clay, Madroño & Mazar Barnett (2001), Chebez (1994), Clements & Shany (2001), ffrench (1991), Figueiredo & Lo (2000), Fjeldså & Krabbe (1990), Haverschmidt & Mees (1994), Hayes (1995), Herklots (1961), Hilty (1997), Hilty & Brown (1986), Kilham (1972a, 1983), Marini (2001), Meyer de Schauensee & Phelps (1978), Oren & Parker (1997), de la Peña (1994), Pinto & Camargo (1961), Piratelli *et al.* (2000), Ridgely & Greenfield (2001), Ridgely & Gwynne (1989), Robbins *et al.* (1985), Robinson (1997), Robinson & Terborgh (1997), Short (1975, 1985b), Sick (1993), Snyder (1966), Stotz, Fitzpatrick *et al.* (1996), Stotz, Lanyon *et al.* (1997), Terborgh *et al.* (1984), Tostain *et al.* (1992), Wetmore (1939, 1968a), Willis (1980).

178. Guayaquil Woodpecker
Campephilus gayaquilensis

French: Pic de Guayaquil **German**: Guayaquilspecht **Spanish**: Picamaderos de Guayaquil

Taxonomy. *Picus Gayaquilensis* Lesson, 1845, Guayaquil, Ecuador.
Formerly placed in genus *Phloeoceastes* with seven other species, all of which are now lumped into *Campephilus*. Forms a superspecies with *C. guatemalensis* and *C. melanoleucos*. May be conspecific with latter. Monotypic.
Distribution. W slope of Andes and adjacent lowlands, from SW Colombia (SW Cauca) S to NW Peru (S to Cajamarca).

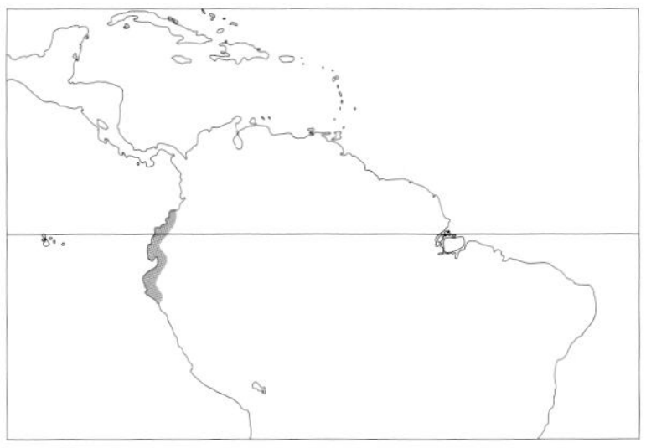

Descriptive notes. 32-34 cm; 230-253 g. Large woodpecker. Male has small black and white oval spot on rear lower ear-coverts; rest of head and crest red, sometimes black and buff of feather bases showing through; black chin and throat sometimes with red feather tips at side; neck to upper breast, mantle, scapulars and upper back black, white stripe down side of neck and mantle to centre of back; lower back to uppertail-coverts variably barred pale whitish-buff and blackish, central part of back and rump sometimes all blackish; upperwing brownish-black to black, flight-feathers browner with small cinnamon or buff patch on inner webs; uppertail dark brown to black-brown; whitish-buff to pale cinnamon-buff lower breast to undertail-coverts barred brownish-black, bars narrower on lower underparts; underwing white, pale cinnamon at bases of primaries, brown tip and trailing edge; long bill chisel-tipped, culmen slightly curved, broad across nostrils, greyish, paler lower mandible; iris pale yellow; legs grey-brown to greenish-grey. Differs from *C. melanoleucos* mainly in lacking pale area around bill base. Female has broad creamy malar stripe joining with white neck stripe, black patch at lower rear ear-coverts, fully black chin and throat. Juvenile as adult but normally less barred rump and underparts, male head pattern much as adult female but some red tips in white malar, female with black band through crown centre and dark cheekband back to hindneck, patch of white on rear side of head. Voice. Rather similar to *C. melanoleucos*. Commonest call is a liquid, rolling "kwi-kwi-kwe-rrrrrr", often given upon alighting on a tree trunk; when excited, "kwik-kwik-kwikerrr" and "kik-kwiddit" notes, and variations on this theme for long periods. Drumming a loud, far-carrying double rap.
Habitat. Humid to dry deciduous forest, forest edge, and tall second growth. Recorded up to 800 m, occasionally up to 1500 m in Ecuador and Peru. Replaces *C. melanoleucos* to W of Andes.
Food and Feeding. Details of diet not documented; probably similar to *C. melanoleucos*. Often in pairs. Forages on dead branches in canopy and in emergent trees; easily detected by its loud hammering. Where sympatric with *C. haematogaster*, separated ecologically by preference for lower levels.
Breeding. Season Oct and May. No details known.
Movements. Resident.
Status and Conservation. Not globally threatened. Currently considered Near-threatened. Uncommon to locally fairly common in Ecuador; uncommon in Peru. In Ecuador, occurs in Río Palenque Science Centre, Tinalandia Natural Reserve and Cerro Blanco Protected Forest; substantial population in Machalilla National Park. In Peru, recorded in Tumbes National Reserve and Cerros de Amotape National Park. Occurs naturally at low densities. The dry deciduous and humid forests inhabited by this woodpecker have suffered extensive clearance; remaining forest extremely fragmented, with very few and very small patches, but appears to survive well in disturbed patchy forest. Further habitat loss, however, could easily lead to its becoming threatened.
Bibliography. Allen (1998), Becker & López (1997), Best & Clarke (1991), Bloch *et al.* (1991), Butler (1979), Clements & Shany (2001), Hilty & Brown (1986), Kirwan & Marlow (1996), Meyer de Schauensee (1982), Olrog (1968), Parker *et al.* (1982), Pople *et al.* (1997), Ridgely & Greenfield (2001), Ridgely *et al.* (1998), Rodner *et al.* (2000), Salaman (1994), Short (1985b), Stattersfield & Capper (2000), Stotz *et al.* (1996), Williams, M.D. (1980), Williams, R.S.R. & Tobias (1994).

179. Cream-backed Woodpecker
Campephilus leucopogon

French: Pic à dos crème **German**: Weißmantelspecht **Spanish**: Picamaderos Dorsiblanco

Taxonomy. *Picus leucopogon* Valenciennes, 1826, Brazil.
Formerly placed in genus *Phloeoceastes* with seven other species, all of which are now lumped into *Campephilus*. Monotypic.
Distribution. NC Bolivia (Cochabamba, Santa Cruz) and W & C Paraguay to NC Argentina (S to La Rioja, Córdoba, Entre Ríos, Corrientes), N Uruguay and SE Brazil (W Rio Grande do Sul).

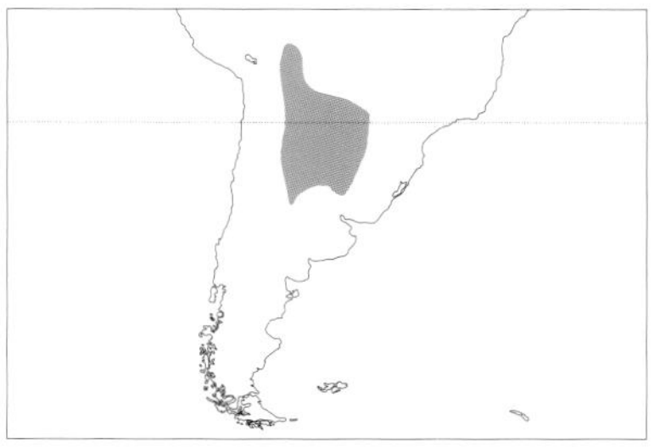

Descriptive notes. 28-30 cm; 203-281 g. Rather large, with short tail. Male has small oval spot of black and white at lower rear ear-coverts; rest of head and crest red, red tips extending variable distance down foreneck (latter all black when worn); whitish mantle feathers tipped pale cinnamon-buff, lower back to uppertail-coverts black, sometimes a few black-barred buff feathers in centre of back; upperwing black, flight-feathers with large area of pale cinnamon towards bases of inner webs; uppertail black; entirely black below; underwing black, pale cinnamon at bases of flight-feathers, narrow whitish to pale cinnamon-buff on leading coverts; long bill straight, chisel-tipped, very broad across nostrils, ivory-coloured; iris pale yellow; legs grey. Female has longer crest than male, also black from forehead through crown to central part of crest, black around eyes and along lower ear-coverts, creamy cheekband bordered by black, black upper chin, all-black neck. Juvenile has red of head more orangey and less extensive, male similar to adult female but red on crown to crest, red feathers in white cheekband, more black on chin, female with red restricted to rear crown side and underside of crest. Voice. Call "pi-ow" or "kwee-yaw", sometimes repeated; whirring notes during close encounters between partners. Drums a double rap.
Habitat. Xeric woodlands of Chaco; occurs in savanna, pastures with copses, groves, woodland and transitional forest, at up to 2500 m.
Food and Feeding. Larvae of beetles. Generally solitary outside breeding season. Forages in tall trees, isolated trees in open areas; descends to fallen logs. Forages mainly by powerful hammering; pecking and probing less frequent.
Breeding. Mainly in Sept, also Oct-Nov. Nest-hole built at 6-8 m in tree or palm; entrance described as "droplet-shaped". No data on clutch size and incubation and fledging periods; both adults feed nestlings.
Movements. Resident.
Status and Conservation. Not globally threatened. Poorly known; probably not common. Occurs in El Rey and Calilegua National Parks and Chancaní Provincial Park (Argentina).
Bibliography. Belton (1984), Brooks, D.M. (1997), Brooks, T.M. *et al.* (1993), Canevari *et al.* (1991), Contreras (1983), Contreras *et al.* (1990), Dubs (1983, 1992), Fjeldså & Mayer (1996), Hayes (1995), Krabbe *et al.* (1996), López (1997), López de Casenave *et al.* (1998), Mazar Barnett & Pearman (2001), Meyer de Schauensee (1982), Miserendino (1998), Nellar (1993), Nores *et al.* (1983), Olrog (1968), de la Peña (1994, 1997), Remsen & Traylor (1989), Remsen *et al.* (1986), Schmitt *et al.* (1997), Short (1975), Sick (1993), Stotz *et al.* (1996), Stradi & Hudon (1998), Stradi *et al.* (1998), Tubelis & Tomás (1999), Wetmore (1926).

180. Magellanic Woodpecker
Campephilus magellanicus

French: Pic de Magellan **German**: Magellanspecht **Spanish**: Picamaderos de Magallanes

Taxonomy. *Picus Magellanicus* P. P. King, 1828, Straits of Magellan.
Monotypic.
Distribution. Andes of S Chile, from Curico to SW Isla Grande (Tierra del Fuego), and in forested parts of adjacent SW Argentina.

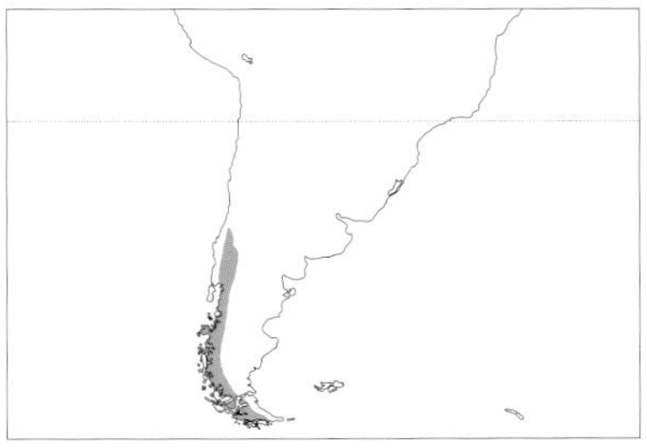

Descriptive notes. 36-38 cm; male 312-363 g, female 276-312 g. Large, distinctive woodpecker. Male has entire head and long crest red, normally some black and white bars of feather bases visible (particularly on ear-coverts, crown and throat); rest of plumage glossy black to brown-black, browner on underparts; white on bases of inner webs of primaries, more broadly on inner webs of tertials, primaries also with small white tips, usually narrow area of white in alula region; uppertail-coverts, exceptionally also rump, with white shaft streaks, white extending rarely to webs; in worn plumage duller and less glossy, with black and white bases of head feathers more obvious, white-based feathers of flanks and belly often show, white primary tips lost; long bill chisel-tipped, culmen slightly curved, broad across nostrils, blue-grey to blackish-grey; iris yellow, more golden outer ring, orbital ring grey; legs dark grey. Female is somewhat smaller and shorter-billed than male, has narrow crest longer than male's, black head with red restricted to area around bill. Juvenile much as female but browner, without gloss, smaller crest, male with scattered pale red tips on head. Voice. Most common calls explosive, nasal, of 2 notes, "pi-caá" to "keé-yew"; also more gargling "weerr-weeeerrr"; also 1-3 "toot" notes, not so nasal as calls of *C. imperialis* and *C. principalis*; also a loud long "cray-cra-cra-cra-cra-cra". Instrumental signal loud single or double blows.

Habitat. Mature *Nothofagus* forest and *Nothofagus-Cupressus* forest, often with bamboo undergrowth; visits disturbed forest and more open woodland. Sea-level to timber-line, at about 2000 m.
Food and Feeding. Grubs and adult beetles. Singly, in pairs, or in groups of 3-4. Forages at all heights, from ground, on fallen logs, to main trunks and the outer twigs of crown. Both dead and live trees, or parts of trees, are visited. Moves swiftly within a tree, and will cling almost in manner of a tit (Paridae); moves frequently from one tree to another. Pecks and probes; sustained powerful hammering less common. Bark sometimes removed, and deep excavations also created. Possible strong ecological dimorphism; further study needed.
Breeding. Oct-Jan. Crest-raising a common display. Nest-hole excavated at 5-15 m above ground, in large tree with dead parts, entrance hole circular to drop-shaped; inter-nest distance c. 2 km. Clutch 1-4 eggs; no information on incubation and fledging periods.
Movements. Resident.
Status and Conservation. Not globally threatened. Not uncommon; perhaps locally common; probably decreasing. Occurs in several protected areas, e.g. Nahuelbuta, Vicente Pérez Rosales, Torres del Paine and Puyehué National Parks (Chile); fairly common in Tierra del Fuego National Park (Argentina). Only potentially competing picid within its range is the much smaller and less numerous *Picoides lignarius*. Temperate forest in N of range in Chile was recently destroyed by fire, causing significant loss of habitat.
Bibliography. Anon. (1999), Araya & Chester (1993), Canevari *et al.* (1991), Chebez *et al.* (1999), Clark (1986), Cofré (1999), Fjeldså & Krabbe (1990), Grigera *et al.* (1996), Hackenberg (1989), Humphrey *et al.* (1970), Johnson (1967), Mazar Barnett & Pearman (2001), Meyer de Schauensee (1982), Narosky & Yzurieta (1993), Olrog (1968), de la Peña (1994), Pereyra (1950), Short (1970a, 1985b), Stotz *et al.* (1996), Vuilleumier (1985).

181. Imperial Woodpecker
Campephilus imperialis

French: Pic impérial **German**: Kaiserspecht **Spanish**: Picamaderos Imperial

Taxonomy. *Picus imperialis* Gould, 1832, "California" = Jalisco, Mexico.
Forms a superspecies with *C. principalis*. Monotypic.
Distribution. W Mexico in Sierra Madre Occidental, from W Sonora and Chihuahua S to Jalisco and Michoacán (probably extinct).

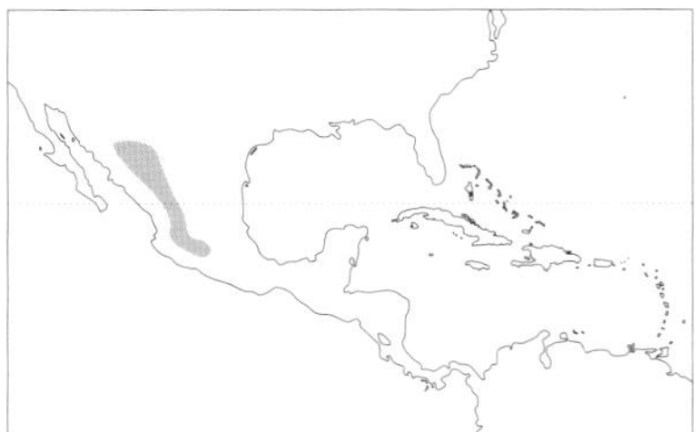

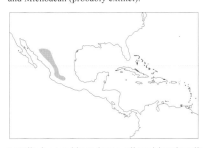

Descriptive notes. c. 56-60 cm. World's largest woodpecker; huge, with pointed crest. Male has side of crown back to underside of crest and nape red, feathers with white bases; rest of head and neck, also upperparts, underparts and tail, black, with blue gloss on head, neck and upperparts, narrow white line down each side of mantle; upperwing black, coverts glossed blue, inner primaries tipped white, secondaries and tertials all white apart from black bases; underwing as above, but lesser and median coverts and primary coverts also white, with a few black spots or bars; very long bill chisel-tipped, culmen slightly curved, broad across nostrils, ivory-white to ivory-yellow; iris pale yellow; legs grey. Distinguished from *C. principalis* by larger size, no white stripes on neck. Female as male, but no red on head, even longer crest curving strongly upwards and forwards. Juvenile duller, browner, than adult, unglossed, with white tips to all flight-feathers, somewhat less white in secondaries, eyes greyish, both sexes initially without red on head and with very long crest, red soon appearing on rear of male's head. Voice. Calls sounding like toy trumpet.
Habitat. Found in oak-pine (*Quercus-Pinus*) forest belt of mountains, in extensive park-like stands of large pines (*Pinus*) containing many dead trees. Recorded from 1670 m up to 3050 m, but mostly above 1900 m.
Food and Feeding. Presumably large beetle larvae (Cerambycidae). In pairs and in family groups of 3-4 birds, occasionally larger groups. Main foraging technique is scaling bark from dead trees, and excavating deeply; same tree sometimes revisited over prolonged period of time. Occasional clinging upside-down, and foraging on underside of branches.
Breeding. Laying Feb-Jun. Nest-hole excavated high up in trunk of dead tree. Clutch generally 2 eggs (1-4). No other relevant information. Groups seem to roost in neighbouring holes. Apparent nest competitors are large parrots.
Movements. Resident; probably rather nomadic within habitat.
Status and Conservation. CRITICAL. CITES I. Restricted-range species: present in Sierra Madre Occidental and Trans-Mexican Range EBA. Probably extinct. No confirmed reports since 1958, when it was seen in the state of Durango. A number of claimed sightings include several post-1965 reports; in particular, a solitary female alleged to have been seen in N Sonora in 1993, a pair in C Durango in same year, and a single male c. 20 km from latter site two years later. Were any still left, however, remaining habitat is so fragmented that they would have little chance of continued survival; none seen during a year-long survey of pine forests of NW Mexico in 1994 and 1995. Seems never to have been particularly common, with estimated maximum population of no more than c. 8000 individuals; indiscriminate shooting and habitat destruction over many decades have led to its almost certain recent extermination. A single pair would probably need an area of at least 25 km² in order to forage and to breed successfully; moreover, since food (large larvae) probably available only for restricted periods, and at different times in different parts of forest, it is likely that small groups need to wander widely to be able to exploit these resources; a group of c. 8 birds could require at least 98 km² of continuous old-growth forest, and such extensive stands no longer exist. In fact, there is now no continuous area of old-growth forest remaining anywhere in the Sierra Madre Occidental that is large enough to support a single breeding pair of this picid. Centuries of hunting, for sport and because parts of this bird were thought to have useful medicinal properties, followed by the complete degradation and destruction of the habitat, have ensured that the species' dwindling numbers continued to fall to unsustainable levels. No reserve has ever been established with the aim of protecting this unique woodpecker, and it is now too late.
Bibliography. Anon. (1996b, 1998b), Baicich & Harrison (1997), Collar & Andrew (1988), Collar, Crosby & Stattersfield (1994), Collar, Gonzaga *et al.* (1992), Fleming & Baker (1963), Friedmann *et al.* (1957), Howell & Webb (1995), King (1978/79), Knox & Walters (1994), Lammertink (1996), Marshall (1957a), Miller *et al.* (1957), Nelson (1898), Peterson & Navarro-Sigüenza (2000), Plimpton (1977), van Rossem (1945), Short (1985b), Smith (1908), Stattersfield & Capper (2000), Stotz *et al.* (1996), Tanner (1964), Wege & Long (1995).

182. Ivory-billed Woodpecker
Campephilus principalis

French: Pic à bec ivoire **German**: Elfenbeinspecht **Spanish**: Picamaderos Picomarfil
Other common names: Northern Ivory-billed Woodpecker (*principalis*); Cuban Ivory-billed Woodpecker (*bairdii*)

Taxonomy. *Picus principalis* Linnaeus, 1758, South Carolina, USA.
Forms a superspecies with *C. imperialis*. Race *bairdii* considered possibly a separate species by some. Two subspecies recognized.
Subspecies and Distribution.
C. p. principalis (Linnaeus, 1758) - SE USA (probably extinct).
C. p. bairdii Cassin, 1863 - Cuba (probably extinct).

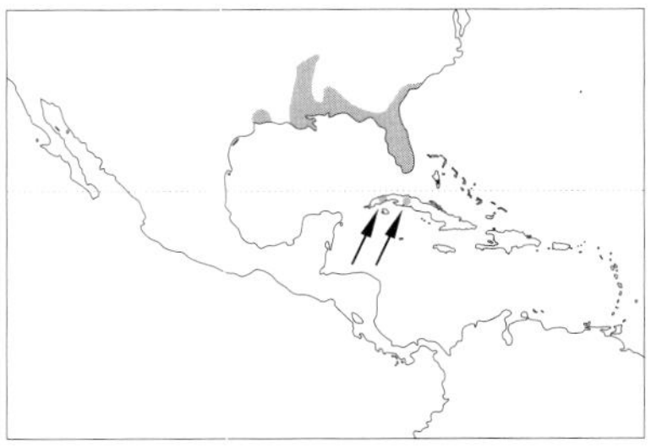

Descriptive notes. 48-53 cm; c. 450-570 g. Extremely large, distinctive woodpecker. Male has side of crown back to underside of crest, rear of head and nape red, with paler feather bases; rest of head and neck black, white stripes from lower edge of rear ear-coverts and down neck sides and along mantle sides meeting in centre of back; rest of upperparts black, glossed blue; upperwing black, coverts glossed blue, inner primaries tipped white, secondaries and tertials all white apart from black bases; uppertail black, occasionally some white spots in outer tail; underparts black to brownish-black, sometimes vague pale barring on flanks; underwing as above, but lesser and median coverts and primary coverts also white, usually a few black spots or bars on primary coverts; long bill chisel-tipped, slightly curved on culmen, broad across nostrils, ivory-white to creamy; iris white to creamy; legs grey. Female is slightly smaller than male, has somewhat longer crest sometimes slightly upcurved, no red on head. Juvenile browner, less glossy than adult, crest shorter, white tips to all primaries but less white on underwing, eyes brown, head pattern of both sexes as adult female, male gradually acquiring red over 3 months. Race *bairdii* differs from nominate in slightly shorter and narrower bill, and white neckstripe extending a little farther forwards along lower edge of ear-coverts. Voice. Common note when alarmed "kent" or "hant", timbre like clarinet or toy trumpet, repeated up to 6 times; low conversational notes between pair-members; nestlings initially utter weak buzz, later a louder chirp. Instrumental signal of single or double raps; tapping at or inside nest.
Habitat. Heavy forest in often inaccessible hardwood and cypress swamps; originally, probably mainly pine (*Pinus*) forest with many dead trees. Lowland forest and mountain forest in Cuba, more recently in pine (*P. cubensis*) forest. Presence of many dead trees, especially fire-killed ones, imporant.
Food and Feeding. Chiefly large larvae of wood-boring beetles (Cerambycidae, Buprestidae, Scolytidae, Elateridae, Eucnemidae), which also fed to young; fruits, berries and nuts also taken. Forages at low to upper levels; rarely, if ever, on ground. Dead trees, e.g. fire-killed pines, or dead parts of live trees, favoured feeding sites. Removal of bark from dead trees with blows of bill a very common feeding technique; deep pits also produced, similar in size to those made by *Dryocopus pileatus*. From a few minutes to up to half an hour spent at a single site.
Breeding. Jan-Apr in USA; Mar-Jun in Cuba, with peak in Apr. Displays with crest-raising, possibly also head-swinging. Nest excavated in large dead or dying tree, occasionally in palm in Cuba, at 8-15 m, entrance hole more or less vertically oval or drop-shaped, minimum of 8·9 cm in diameter, height 14·6 cm, rarely 17 cm, width up to 12 cm. Clutch 2-4 eggs; incubation by both sexes, only male at night, period c. 20 days; both also feed chicks, directly, male apparently does most of brooding and nest sanitation; fledging period c. 35 days; young regularly fed by parents for at least 2 months after fledging, remain much longer in parental territory.
Movements. Resident.
Status and Conservation. CRITICAL. Probably extinct. Last confirmed records in USA in 1950's, although possibly still survived there in 1970's. Since then, intermittent reports from SE parts of country always found to refer to superficially similar but much smaller *Dryocopus pileatus*. Pair said to have been seen in 1999 in Pearl River Wildlife Management Center, Louisiana, but not found in follow-up surveys; further surveys under way in early 2002. Was once widely distributed in SE USA, from Oklahoma and Missouri across to North Carolina and S to Texas and Florida, prime habitat being tall lowland swamp-forest. Occurred at low densities, maximum in USA 0·006 pairs/10ha, with 1 pair requiring at least 16 km² of suitable habitat. Destruction and fragmentation of its habitat caused massive decline in numbers; even by 1940's the species had been reduced to a very small number of individuals, and forests have continued to be destroyed since then. Interactions with *Dryocopus pileatus* may also have been detrimental to declining populations. Similarly, much of the forest inhabitated by race *bairdii* in Cuba had gone by start of 20th century, and it was confined to a few surviving tracts of Cuban pine forest in E of island. In 1948, a population was discovered in the Cuchillas de Moa Mts, and 6 territories were located there in 1956, in which year 8 pairs and 1 juvenile were found in E Cuba; political problems prevented further field research until 1985, by when much of the region's forest had been removed, and the species was not seen. Further expeditions in 1986 located 1 bird at Ojito de Agua and a pair at Cabezada del Yarey; by 1991 only a single bird appeared to be left; in 1992 and 1993, intensive fieldwork in E Cuba failed to locate any individuals. With insufficient old-growth forest remaining in the ranges of both races, it seems highly unlikely that this woodpecker still survives. The only realistic hope seems to lie in an area of apparently undisturbed pine forest high in the Sierra Maestra (SE of original range in E Cuba); indeed, the species was reported there in 1998, but with no subsequent confirmation.
Bibliography. Agey & Heinzmann (1971), Aguilera (1986), Alayón & Estrada (1986), Alayón & Garrido (1991), Allen & Kellogg (1937), Anon. (1986), Baicich & Harrison (1997), Bailey (1939), Barbour (1943), Bent (1939), Collar & Andrew (1988), Collar, Crosby & Stattersfield (1994), Collar, Gonzaga *et al.* (1992), Cottam & Knappen (1939), Cruz (1974a), Dennis (1948a, 1948b, 1979), Ehrlich *et al.* (1992), Estrada & Alayón (1986a, 1986b), Faaborg (1985), Fergenbauer-Kimmel (1986), Garrido (1985), Garrido & Kirkconnell (2000), Greenway (1967), Hardy (1978), Heinrich & Welch (1983), Jackson (1988, 1990a, 1991a, 1991b, 1992b, 1996), Kaufman (1996), Kilham (1983), King (1978/79), Knox & Walters (1994), Lamb (1957, 1958), Lammertink (1992, 1995), Lammertink & Estrada (1993, 1995), Lapham (1985), Loftin (1994), McNeely (1992), Murphy & Farrand (1979), Peña *et al.* (1999), Raffaele *et al.* (1998), Regalado (1975), Reynard (1987), Short (1983, 1985b, 1985c, 1988), Short & Horne (1986b, 1987a, 1990b), Shuker (1993), Shull (1985), Stattersfield & Capper (2000), Tanner (1941, 1942, 2001), Varona (1980), Wood & Eichholz (1986).

PLATE 45 ➤

ssp *miniaceus* ♀

♂

ssp *niasensis*

ssp *chlorolophus* ♀

♂

ssp *chlorolophus*

♂ ssp *citrinocristatus*

♀ ssp *citrinocristatus*

ssp *wellsi* ♂

183

ssp *perlutus* ♂

ssp *malaccensis* ♂

184

ssp *chlorigaster* ♀

♂

♂ ssp *vanheysti*

ssp *puniceus* ♂

♀

ssp *flavinucha* ♀

♂ ssp *flavinucha*

♂ ssp *wrayi*

185

ssp *observandus* ♂

ssp *soligae* ♂

186

ssp *mystacalis* ♂

ssp *korinchi* ♀

♂ ssp *ricketti*

ssp *humii* ♀

♂

ssp *mentalis*

♀

189

187

♂

188

♀

♀

190

♂

PLATE 45

inches 5

cm 13

Tribe PICINI

Genus *PICUS* Linnaeus, 1758

183. **Banded Woodpecker**

Picus miniaceus

French: Pic minium **German**: Mennigspecht **Spanish**: Pito Miniado
Other common names: Banded Red Woodpecker

Taxonomy. *Picus miniaceus* Pennant, 1769, highlands of Java.
Species name sometimes misspelt *mineaceus*, and in past *miniatus*, but original spelling is *miniaceus*. Proposed race *dayak* (Landak, Borneo) inseparable from *malaccensis*. Four subspecies recognized.
Subspecies and Distribution.
P. m. perlutus (Kloss, 1918) - S Myanmar (S Tenasserim) and peninsular Thailand.
P. m. malaccensis Latham, 1790 - Peninsular Malaysia, Sumatra (including Bangka and Belitung) and Borneo.
P. m. niasensis (Büttikofer, 1897) - Nias I (off NW Sumatra).
P. m. miniaceus Pennant, 1769 - Java.

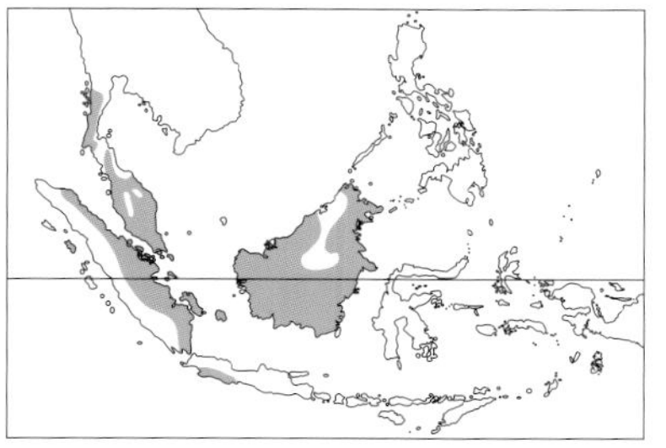

Descriptive notes. 23-26 cm; 79-102 g. Male has reddish-brown forehead, dull red crown to nape, thin elongated crest feathers yellow at tips; sides of head and neck dark brown, reddish feather tips; brown chin and throat usually tipped rufous; dull red above, mantle and back barred dull buff, rump yellow, uppertail-coverts olive-brown with buff barring; wing-coverts dull red; flight-feathers brown, extensively dull olive-red on outer webs of primary bases, secondaries and tertials, barred buffish on outer webs and base of inner webs of primaries and inner webs of secondaries; uppertail blackish; rufous-brown upper breast with faint barring, pale speckles, whitish-buff to pale rufous rest of underparts narrowly barred dark brown; brown underwing barred buff; in worn plumage, red areas browner, pale barring on upperparts less obvious; shortish bill slightly chisel-tipped, curved on culmen, fairly broad across nostrils, very broad at base, dark grey, paler lower mandible; iris dark chestnut to red; legs green-grey. Female is slightly smaller than male, with proportionately longer tail, face and throat browner with few red tips, pale buffish speckling. Juvenile duller than adult, more obscure barring below, male with red on crown and nape, female red only on hindcrown. Race *perlutus* is dull greenish-olive above, has more extensive yellow on crest, less patterned breast, on average shorter bill; *malaccensis* is very like previous, but dark bars below broader; *niasensis* is slightly smaller than last, brighter, with red mantle feathers, red extending to upper breast. VOICE. Single "keek"; mournful descending "kwee" or "peew" in series of up to 7, as territorial call; "kwi-wi-ta-wi-kwi" series during encounters.
Habitat. Mainly dense primary (dipterocarp) evergreen forest; also secondary growth, forest edge and open woods, including rubber plantations, gardens and mangroves at lower altitudes. Lowlands to montane habitats, usually below 900 m but occasionally to 1200 m in SE Asia; to 1500 m in Java, and to 1400 m, possibly 1700 m, in Borneo.
Food and Feeding. Ants and their eggs and larvae. Singly or in pairs, unobtrusive; partners may feed close together. Forages at all levels. Searches for food among vines and dense branches, on large-diameter trunks, particularly of dead trees, and on fallen logs; visits branches, decayed stubs and bases of epiphytes in canopy. Main techniques are light tapping, also probing and gleaning. Movements slow and deliberate; may pause to scan surroundings. Considerable periods spent in exploiting single sites.
Breeding. Nov-Sept. Both sexes excavate nest-hole, in decayed tree or in dead or rotten part of live tree. Displays include crest-raising, swinging movements of head and body; gliding and floating flight interspersed with weak fluttering, by male in presence of female. Clutch 2 or 3 eggs; incubation and fledging periods not documented; both parents feed chicks. Often only 1 young fledges.
Movements. Resident.
Status and Conservation. Not globally threatened. Uncommon to fairly common; rather uncommon in N of range; more frequent in S, common in Peninsular Malaysia and Singapore; rare in Java.
Bibliography. Andrew (1992), van Balen (1999), Bucknill & Chasen (1990), Chasen (1937), Duckworth & Kelsh (1988), Dupond (1942), Dymond (1994), Edgar (1933), Grantham (2000), Hails & Jarvis (1987), Hellebrekers & Hoogerwerf (1967), Holmes (1994), Inskipp *et al.* (1996), Jepson & Brinkman (1993), Jeyarajasingam & Pearson (1999), Lekagul & Round (1991), MacKinnon (1988), MacKinnon & Phillipps (1993), Madoc (1976), van Marle & Voous (1988), Medway & Wells (1976), Mees (1986), Nash & Nash (1985), Robinson & Kloss (1919a), Robson (2000), Sargeant (1997), Short (1973d), Smythies (1986, 1999), Vowles & Vowles (1997), Wells (1985, 1990, 1999), Wong (1985).

184. **Lesser Yellownape**

Picus chlorolophus

French: Pic à huppe jaune **German**: Gelbhaubenspecht **Spanish**: Pito Crestigualdo
Other common names: Lesser/Small Yellow-naped Woodpecker; Ceylon Yellow-naped Woodpecker (*wellsi*)

Taxonomy. *Picus chlorolophus* Vieillot, 1818, Bengal.
Forms a superspecies with *P. puniceus*, which is separated altitudinally in small area of range overlap. Considerable variation, both individual and geographical, and races also intergrade; proposed races *chlorolophoides* (N Thailand), *laotianus* (Laos) and *krempfi* (Cochinchina) considered not acceptable. Nine subspecies recognized.
Subspecies and Distribution.
P. c. simlae Meinertzhagen, 1924 - N India (Himachal Pradesh) E to W Nepal.
P. c. chlorigaster Jerdon, 1844 - peninsular India.
P. c. wellsi Meinertzhagen, 1924 - Sri Lanka.
P. c. chlorolophus Vieillot, 1818 - E Nepal E to Myanmar and N Vietnam.
P. c. annamensis Meinertzhagen, 1924 - SE Thailand to S Vietnam.
P. c. citrinocristatus (Rickett, 1901) - N Vietnam (Tonkin) and SE China (Fujian).
P. c. longipennis (Hartert, 1910) - Hainan I.
P. c. rodgeri (Hartert & Butler, 1898) - W Malaysian highlands.
P. c. vanheysti (Robinson & Kloss, 1919) - Sumatran highlands.

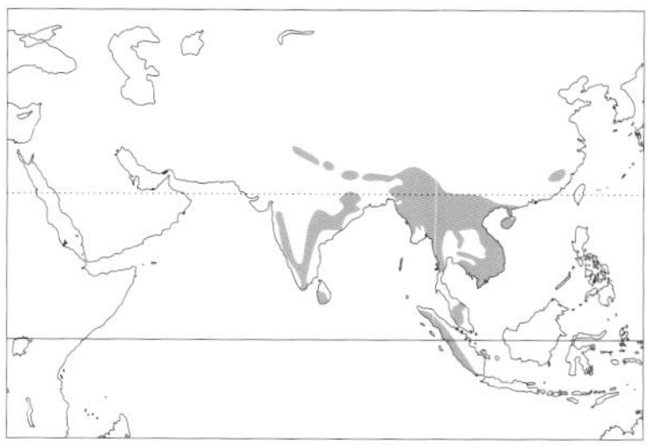

Descriptive notes. 25-28 cm; 57-74 g (*chlorigaster*), 74-83 g (*simlae*). Male has green forehead and crown bordered with red feather tips, golden-yellow or orangey on crest and hindneck; olive-green ear-coverts and neck side, usually small area of white just behind upper corner of eye; upper lores black, lower lores to below lower edge of ear-coverts white, streaked olive; red malar stripe with some olive-green feather bases usually showing; olive to greyish chin and throat variably marked with white streaks or bars, throat pattern very variable, sometimes mainly whitish but can be all dark; green upperparts tinged golden-yellow, rump often brighter; outer webs of secondaries and of inner primaries rufous, edged green (rufous more prominent when wings worn), rest of primaries and inner webs of secondaries dark brown with white bar-like spots; uppertail blackish, outer feathers washed green; lower throat and breast grey-green to dark green, belly to undertail-coverts off-white with slightly diffuse olive to olive-grey or brownish-olive chevrons; underwing brownish, olive coverts, barred whitish; fairly long bill almost straight, chisel-tipped, broad across nostrils, blackish-grey, paler, yellower base of lower mandible; iris red-brown to dark red, orbital skin greyish; legs grey-green. Female is slightly smaller than male, lacks red in malar, has red of crown confined to small patch at rear sides. Juvenile duller above, more barred on breast, with less red on crown than respective adult. Races differ mainly in tone of upperparts, pattern of underparts, and size: *simlae* is largest, with longer wings and longer tail than nominate, greener, less yellow, above, nape less golden; *annamensis* is smaller than nominate, darker green above, with more red on crown, whiter lower underparts, barring reaching to lower breast but more obscure on belly and flanks; *chlorigaster* is smaller than previous races, lacks white on face, has more red but less yellow on head, is darker green above with more red on wings, dull olive-green below with pale bar-like spotting on flanks and belly, pale spots on breast; *wellsi* is somewhat darker than last, with even more red on crown, wings with slightly more rufous, reduced pale markings below; *rodgeri* resembles previous but not quite so dark above, has prominent pale cheekstripe, less red on crown, slight golden tinge on crest, more bars below; *vanheysti* resembles last, but somewhat yellower above, greener, less grey, below; *citrinocristatus* lacks red malar, has upperparts only slightly yellow-tinged, underparts sooty-grey with paler bars on flanks, brighter lemon-yellow nape; *longipennis* is slightly smaller than previous, with stronger green tinge below, flanks more barred. VOICE. Loud, mournful, "pée-a" or "péee-ui", also short "chak"; up to 10 "kwee" notes in slow, slightly descending series; low chuckling noises in close intersexual confrontations. Drums occasionally.
Habitat. Evergreen forest and moist deciduous forest, dry forest, woodland, bamboo, scrub, plantations, and well-wooded gardens. Habitats most diverse in India, especially where no other congeners occur. From lowlands and foothills to 1800 m; to c. 2100 m in Sikkim and Nepal (common only to 1750 m); above 900 m in Peninsular Malaysia; 800-1400 m in Sumatra. Replaces *P. puniceus* at higher altitudes.
Food and Feeding. Ants, including *Crematogaster*, also beetles and their larvae (including dung beetles); other insect larvae. Also takes berries and nectar. Forages singly, in pairs, or in small family groups; regularly joins mixed-species flocks, particularly with babblers (Timaliidae), drongos (Dicruridae) and other insectivores, or other woodpeckers. Forages in smaller trees, in undergrowth, often on fallen logs and dead trees in windthrow areas. Seems usually to prefer trunks and larger branches, but also moves along thin branches to reach arboreal nests of ants, or to probe at flowers. Forages commonly on ground, even seeks insects in dung pats. Gleaning and probing are the main foraging techniques; excavating with pecking and hammering infrequent. Movements are slow, except when accompanying other species. Can spend much time at a single site.
Breeding. Feb-Jul, mainly Mar-May. Crest-raising in display. Nest excavated by both sexes in (partly) dead trunk or branch, at 1·5-20 m, mostly below 5 m. Usually 3-4 eggs (2-5), clutches smaller in S; both sexes incubate, and both feed chicks, by regurgitation; incubation and fledging periods unknown.
Movements. Resident. Possible dispersal; recorded as rare vagrant in NE Pakistan.
Status and Conservation. Not globally threatened. Common to fairly common, or locally common, throughout most of range; common in SE Asia; uncommon in China. Occurs in numerous protected areas in all parts of range. Adaptable; able to thrive in secondary habitats.
Bibliography. Ali (1996), Ali & Ripley (1983), Ali *et al.* (1996), Andrew (1992), Bangs & Van Tyne (1931), Betts (1934), Biswas (1961a), Bromley (1952), Chasen & Hoogerwerf (1941), Chazee (1994), Deignan (1945), Delacour (1951b), Eames & Robson (1992), Étchécopar & Hüe (1978), Evans & Timmins (1998), Goes (1999), Grimmett *et al.* (1998), Harrison (1999), Harvey (1990), Henry (1998), Inskipp, C. & Inskipp (1991), Inskipp, T. *et al.* (1996), Jeyarajasingam & Pearson (1999), King & Rappole (2001), Kloss (1931), Lamsfuss (1998), Lekagul & Round (1991), Ludlow (1937, 1944), MacKinnon & Phillipps (1993, 2000), Madoc (1976), van Marle & Voous (1988), Medway & Wells (1976), Meyer de Schauensee & Ripley (1940), Parrott & Andrew (1996), Phillips (1978), Proud (1958), Rand & Fleming (1957), Riley (1938), Ripley (1982), Roberts (1991), Robson (2000), Santharam (1997, 1998c), Shankar Raman (2001), Short (1973d), Smythies (1986), Stepanyan (1995), Wells (1999), Zhao Zhengjie (1995).

185. **Crimson-winged Woodpecker**

Picus puniceus

French: Pic grenadin **German**: Rotflügelspecht **Spanish**: Pito Alirrojo
Other common names: Crimson-winged Yellownape

Taxonomy. *Picus puniceus* Horsfield, 1821, Java.
Forms superspecies with *P. chlorolophus*; separated altitudinally in small area of overlap. Proposed race *continentis* (Malay Peninsula) merely averages slightly larger. Three subspecies recognized.
Subspecies and Distribution.
P. p. observandus (Hartert, 1896) - S Myanmar (S Tenasserim) and peninsular Thailand S to Sumatra (including Bangka) and Borneo.
P. p. soligae Meyer de Schauensee & Ripley, 1940 - Nias I (off NW Sumatra).
P. p. puniceus Horsfield, 1821 - Java.
Descriptive notes. c. 25 cm; 66-96 g. Male has dark red forehead to hindcrown, often dark olive feather bases showing through, elongated crest of red feathers, yellow under crest and down hindneck;

On following pages: 186. Greater Yellownape (*Picus flavinucha*); 187. Chequer-throated Woodpecker (*Picus mentalis*); 188. Streak-breasted Woodpecker (*Picus viridanus*); 189. Laced Woodpecker (*Picus vittatus*); 190. Streak-throated Woodpecker (*Picus xanthopygaeus*).

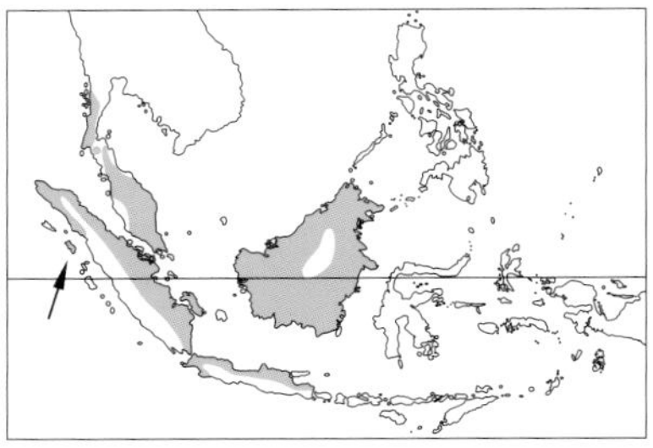

black lores, short red malar stripe, brownish throat; rest of head olive-green; upperparts green, rump somewhat paler, wing-coverts crimson-red, red often extending partly onto scapulars; green tertials crimson-red on outer webs; primaries and secondaries blackish-brown, outer webs of secondaries and basal edges of primaries crimson-red, well-spaced pale yellowish spots on inner webs of all feathers and on outer webs of most primaries; uppertail brownish-black; dark olive to olive-green below, flanks with some pale buffish spots or small chevrons; underwing brown, barred pale yellowish on coverts and bases of flight-feathers; longish bill almost straight, chisel-tipped, broad across nostrils, dark brown or grey-brown, contrasting yellowish lower mandible; iris red to red-brown, orbital ring blue to blue-grey; legs dark greenish to olive. Female lacks red malar. Juvenile duller than adult, with more extensive markings below, red of head normally confined to rear and side of crown, male with at least some red tips in malar. Other races smaller and paler than nominate: *observandus* is yellowish-green above, with more yellow in crest, bright yellow rump, olive-green throat; *soligae* is even yellower above, greyer below, with red of crown extending farther on to crest, often more bars on flanks. Voice. Distinctive "peé-bee", second syllable a little lower and shorter, sometimes extended to "peé-dee-dee-dee"; single short "peep" heard occasionally; 5-7 or low-pitched "peep" notes, c. 2 per second, in encounters; low "wee-eek" series at close encounters. Drums weakly, short bursts less than 1 second long.

Habitat. Evergreen primary and secondary forest with scattered tall trees, forest edge, secondary growth, and plantations. Occasionally visits coastal scrub and gardens in Sumatra and Java. Lowlands, to c. 900 m; below 600 m in Thailand; to c. 1300 m in Peninsular Malaysia (Fraser's Hill); perhaps to 1500 m in Borneo. Generally replaced by *P. chlorolophus* at higher elevations.

Food and Feeding. Mainly ants and termites (Isoptera), including their eggs and grubs. Forages singly, but mainly in pairs, partners keeping contact at moderate distances; regularly joins mixed-species flocks. Favours tall trees, particularly emergent forest trees, even those in lower second growth or free-standing. Forages mainly in canopy, on trunks and major branches. Explores bark, especially where lichens present, and crevices; hammers in short bursts, frequently in hard live wood, and probes, gleans, and removes pieces of bark. Moves rather systematically, rarely spending much time at a single spot.

Breeding. Feb-May; Jun in Borneo, and Sept in C Java. Conspicuous crest-raising display, with upward bill-pointing. Nest-hole is high up, to 18 m above ground, in tree. Clutch 2 or 3 eggs; no information on incubation and fledging periods.

Movements. Resident.

Status and Conservation. Not globally threatened. Common to fairly common throughout range; one of the most frequently encountered woodpeckers in Malaysian rainforest; extinct in Singapore. Occurs in Taman Negara National Park (Peninsular Malaysia), Way Kambas National Park (Sumatra), Gunung Gede-Pangrango National Park (Java) and Mount Kinabalu National Park (Borneo).

Bibliography. Andrew (1985, 1992), Bucknill & Chasen (1990), Castelletta *et al.* (2000), Chasen & Hoogerwerf (1941), Duckworth & Kelsh (1988), Ford & Davison (1995), Grantham (2000), Hellebrekers & Hoogerwerf (1967), Holmes (1994, 1996), Inskipp *et al.* (1996), Jeyarajasingam & Pearson (1999), Kloss (1931), Lekagul & Round (1991), MacKinnon (1988), MacKinnon & Phillipps (1993), van Marle & Voous (1988), McClure (1998), Medway & Wells (1976), Mees (1986), Meyer de Schauensee & Ripley (1940), Nash & Nash (1985), Riley (1938), Robinson & Kloss (1924a), Robson (2000), Short (1973d), Smythies (1986, 1999), Vowles & Vowles (1997), Wells (1985, 1999), Wilkinson, Dutson & Sheldon (1991), Wong (1985).

186. Greater Yellownape

Picus flavinucha

French: Pic à nuque jaune **German**: Gelbnackenspecht **Spanish**: Pito Nuquigualdo
Other common names: Greater/Large Yellow-naped Woodpecker

Taxonomy. *Picus flavinucha* Gould, 1834, Himalayas and lower regions of India.

Forms a superspecies with *P. mentalis*, which is separated altitudinally in small area of range overlap. Much individual variation in plumage tone and markings, with races intergrading, and clinal decrease in size from N to S. Birds from extreme NW of range, on average longer-winged and generally with less yellow tinge to upperparts, have been separated as race *kumaonensis*, but differences probably insufficient to warrant subspecific status. Proposed races *archon* (N Vietnam) and *lylei* (N & W Thailand) barely distinguishable, and features fall within range of individual variation of other races. Seven subspecies recognized.

Subspecies and Distribution.

P. f. flavinucha Gould, 1834 - N & E India (from N Uttar Pradesh, Orissa) E to Myanmar, S China (S Sichuan, Yunnan) and N Vietnam.

P. f. ricketti (Styan, 1898) - Tonkin area of N Vietnam, and E to SE China (Fujian).

P. f. pierrei Oustalet, 1889 - SE Thailand to S Vietnam.

P. f. styani (Ogilvie-Grant, 1899) - Hainan I.

P. f. wrayi (Sharpe, 1888) - Malayan highlands.

P. f. mystacalis (Salvadori, 1879) - N Sumatra.

P. f. korinchi (Chasen, 1940) - SW Sumatra.

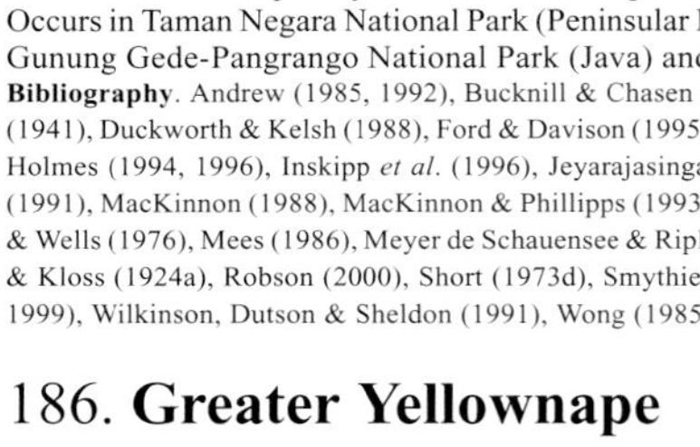

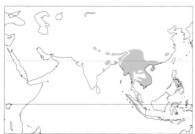

Descriptive notes. c. 33-34 cm; 153-198 g. Male has olive-green forehead and crown, feathers tipped rufous-brown when fresh, tips of elongated hindcrown feathers and nape bright golden-yellow, this colour continuing down hindneck; dark olive-green lores and ear-coverts, blacker rear neck side; bright yellow chin and throat, lower throat feathers blackish with white edges; bright yellowish-green upperparts, tertials sometimes with rufous barring on inner webs; primaries and secondaries dark green, outer primaries blackish-brown, all broadly barred rufous on both webs; uppertail blackish; upper breast olive-black, rest of underparts greenish-grey; underwing brownish, barred paler; undertail blackish-brown, outer feathers washed greenish; long bill slightly chisel-tipped, variably curved culmen, fairly broad across nostrils, broad at base, dark grey; iris brownish-red or reddish, orbital ring grey to greenish or blue-grey; legs green-grey or grey. Female is less bulky, shorter-billed than male, yellow of chin and throat replaced by rufous-brown. Juvenile duller than adult, crest less golden, greyer below, eyes brown, male with buff-yellow throat occasionally spotted dark, rufous colour in malar, sometimes some red feather tips in crown, female as adult but less rufous on throat. Other races differ from nominate in being darker green above, males with much-reduced yellow on throat: *styani* has crest pale yellow, reddish bars extend to wingtips; *ricketti* is slightly longer-winged and darker-billed than previous, reddish primary bars more extensive; *pierrei* is slightly yellower above than previous races, with less extensive barring on primaries; *mystacalis* has breast more extensively dark green, barring on wing reduced, lacks black and white markings on lower throat; *korinchi* resembles previous, but darker green above, paler on belly, wing barring duller and browner; *wrayi* is rather small and dark, male has pale yellow malar. Voice. Variety of "keep" notes, including disyllabic "chup-chup" or "ke-eep", also rather variable (often loud) "kiyaep", "kyew" or "kyaa" calls, some wavering, all sometimes in series; very long accelerating series, "kwee-kwee-kwee-kwee-kwee-kwee-kwee-kwee-kwi-kwi-kwi-kwi-wi-wi-w i-wik", similar to that of *P. viridis*, exchanged between pair-members, also as territorial announcement. Drums infrequently, rolls weak and rapid.

Habitat. Various types of forest, open evergreen and deciduous forests with tall trees, oak (*Quercus*) and sal (*Shorea*) forests, mixed forest, pine (*Pinus*) forest, and secondary growth; sometimes near edges or on single dead trees in clearings. Retreats to forest patches in cultivated areas. Lowlands and at higher elevations; to 2750 m in SE Asia and India; most common at 300-1500 m in Nepal; above 900 m and to 2000 m in Peninsular Malaysia; above 800 m in Sumatra.

Food and Feeding. Animal food mainly ants and termites (Isoptera), and large insect larvae, particularly of wood-boring beetles (Cerambycidae); unusual items include centipedes (Chilopoda) and frogs, and may take nestlings of other hole-nesting species. Berries and seeds also taken. Shy and restless, occurs in pairs and in family groups of 4 to 5; commonly with various species of drongo (*Dicrurus*), babbler (Timaliidae) or bulbul (Pycnonotidae). Prefers to forage on trunks and branches of small to large trees, but exploits all levels of forest; seldom, if ever, visits ground. Moves rapidly on smaller branches, and perches crosswise. All foraging techniques directed to the surface; gleaning, reaching, sweeping away debris, and probing, are common; excavating, or even single pecks, rare.

Breeding. Mar-Jun in Indian Subcontinent, from Feb in SE Asia, and Apr-May in Sumatra. Crest-raising, in intense display combined with head-lifting with bill upwards. Nest-hole excavated by both sexes, at 2-6 m, rarely to 15 m, in tree; cavity depth c. 20 cm. Clutch 2-4 eggs; incubation by both parents, both also share brood-feeding; incubation and fledging periods apparently not documented; fledglings accompanied by parents for a while.

Movements. Resident.

Status and Conservation. Not globally threatened. Common or fairly common throughout its range; common in SE Asia; rare in China. Occurs in many protected areas, e.g. Chitwan National Park (Nepal), Khao Yai National Park (Thailand) and Kerinci-Seblat National Park (Sumatra). No known threats.

Bibliography. Ali & Ripley (1983), Ali *et al.* (1996), Andrew (1992), Baker (1919), Bangs & Van Tyne (1931), Bates (1952), Biddulph (1954), Deignan (1945), Delacour (1951b), Eames (1995), Eames & Robson (1992), Étchécopar & Hüe (1978), Evans & Timmins (1998), Grimmett *et al.* (1998), Harvey (1990), Hussain *et al.* (1977), Inskipp, C. & Inskipp (1991), Inskipp, T. *et al.* (1996), Jeyarajasingam & Pearson (1999), Lekagul & Round (1991), Ludlow (1937, 1944), MacKinnon & Phillipps (1993, 2000), Madoc (1976), van Marle & Voous (1988), Medway & Wells (1976), Meyer de Schauensee & Ripley (1940), Riley (1938), Ripley (1950b, 1982), Robson (2000), Robson *et al.* (1993a), Shankar Raman (2001), Short (1973d), Smythies (1986), Stepanyan (1995), Wells (1999), Zhao Zhengjie (1995).

187. Chequer-throated Woodpecker

Picus mentalis

French: Pic gorgeret **German**: Tropfenkehlspecht **Spanish**: Pito Gargantilla
Other common names: Chequer-throated Yellownape, Banded Red Woodpecker

Taxonomy. *Picus mentalis* Temminck, 1825, Java.

Forms a superspecies with *P. flavinucha*, from which it is largely separated by altitude in small area of overlap. Birds of E & S Borneo formerly separated as race *saba*. Two subspecies recognized.

Subspecies and Distribution.

P. m. humii (Hargitt, 1889) - S Myanmar (S Tenasserim) and S peninsular Thailand to Sumatra (including Bangka) and Borneo.

P. m. mentalis Temminck, 1825 - W Java.

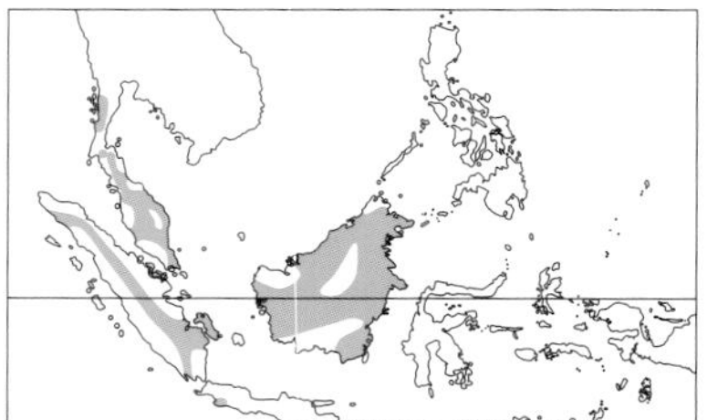

Descriptive notes. 26-28 cm; 88-113 g. Male has dark green to olive forehead and crown, sometimes rufous feather tips at side, elongated nape feathers chestnut and yellow, yellow hindneck; dark green ear-coverts, tipped rufous when fresh, blackish chin and throat spotted with white; rufous-chestnut from neck side to breast; dark green upperparts, bright reddish-chestnut greater and median wing-coverts narrowly margined green when fresh; flight-feathers blackish-brown, outer webs of secondaries and inner primaries reddish-chestnut, all with rufous spots on both webs; uppertail blackish; underparts below breast green; underwing brown, coverts greener, barred cinnamon-rufous; fairly long bill chisel-tipped, culmen curved, rather broad across nostrils, dark grey; iris red to red-brown or brown, orbital ring olive to olive-grey; legs olive to grey. Female is shorter-billed than male, has chestnut over chin and throat. Juvenile as adult, but less red in wings, entire underparts rufous-chestnut, may show trace of red on nape. Race *humii* smaller than nominate, brighter, tinged yellow above, with more yellow on crest, has white throat streaked olive-green. Voice. Single "kyick" calls, sometimes followed by series of longer "kwee" or "kyew" notes, which can also be given singly; long fast series of "wi" notes. Drums in rather short bursts, with strike rate slightly faster than that of *P. canus*, much faster than *P. puniceus*.

Habitat. Primary evergreen forest or moss forest, especially wetter parts; prefers areas with dense understorey and large trees, e.g. dipterocarps. Also overgrown clearings, dense forest edge, occasionally mangroves; rarely, ventures into dense tall secondary growth, or scrub or cultivated land. Lowlands and mountains, to 1220 m; to 1700 m in Greater Sundas.

Food and Feeding. Ants, termites (Isoptera), larvae, beetles, Orthoptera, cockroaches (Blattodea), and other insects; occasionally berries. Mostly singly, occasionally in pairs; not infrequently in mixed-species flocks. Forages in lower and middle storeys, at 3-15 m, thus most frequently seen in lower canopy and in higher parts of understorey. Visits trunks of smaller trees, low branches, decaying stubs with epiphytes, and vines. Most frequent feeding techniques are gleaning and probing; will also pry off obstacles, occasionally peck; less frequently excavates, with intense hammering. May cling upside-down, and often flutters to reach prey items. Moves very rapidly through habitat, on rather erratic path.

Breeding. Mar-Aug; Mar in W Java, and Feb-June in Borneo. Nest excavated 5-6 m up in dead stub. Clutch 2 or 3 eggs; no information on incubation and fledging periods.

Movements. Resident. Single record from E Java; significance unclear.

Status and Conservation. Not globally threatened. Uncommon to locally common; extinct in Singapore; rare in Java, now restricted to W, where very small numbers remain. Occurs in Khao Nor

Chuchi Reserve (Thailand), Taman Negara National Park (Peninsular Malaysia), Way Kambas National Park (Sumatra) and Mount Kinabalu National Park (Borneo).

Bibliography. Andrew (1985, 1992), van Balen (1999), Bucknill & Chasen (1990), Castelletta *et al.* (2000), Duckworth & Kelsh (1988), Duckworth *et al.* (1997), Grantham (2000), Hellebrekers & Hoogerwerf (1967), Inskipp *et al.* (1996), Jepson & Brinkman (1993), Jeyarajasingam & Pearson (1999), Kloss (1931), Lekagul & Round (1991), MacKinnon (1988), MacKinnon & Phillipps (1993), van Marle & Voous (1988), Medway & Wells (1976), Mees (1986), Meyer de Schauensee & Ripley (1940), Robinson & Kloss (1924a), Robson (2000), Sargeant (1997), Short (1973d), Smythies (1986, 1999), Vowles & Vowles (1997), Wells (1985, 1999), Wilkinson, Dutson & Sheldon (1991), Wong (1985).

188. Streak-breasted Woodpecker

Picus viridanus

French: Pic verdâtre **German**: Burmagrünspecht **Spanish**: Pito Verdoso
Other common names: Burmese/Small/Little Scaly-bellied (Green) Woodpecker

Taxonomy. *Picus viridanus* Blyth, 1843, Arakan, Myanmar.
Forms a superspecies with *P. vittatus*. Has often been considered conspecific, but appears to be separated by habitat, although some possible overlap in this respect; further study needed. Birds from Thai-Malay Peninsula described as race *weberi*, being slightly smaller and darker, but differences insignificant and probably due to clinal variation. Monotypic.
Distribution. SW & SE Myanmar and SW Thailand S to extreme NW Peninsular Malaysia.

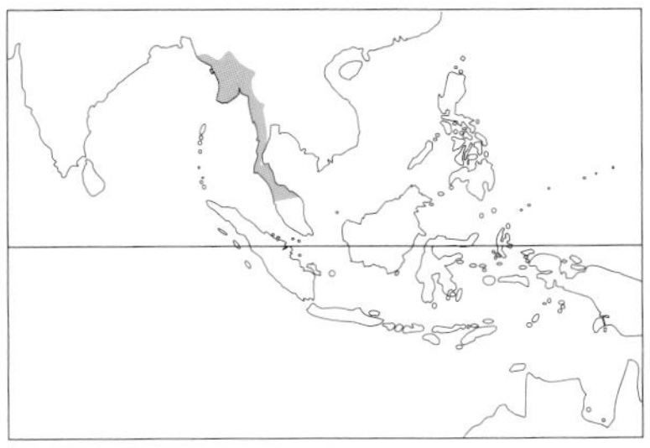

Descriptive notes. 30-33 cm; c. 90-120 g. Male has red forehead to nape and slight crest, black base of forehead, upper lores and narrow line bordering crown; thin white supercilium back to nape; lower lores and ear-coverts off-white to greyish, ear-coverts streaked dark; white-streaked black malar stripe, pale brown chin and throat, throat usually with tinged green or olive and variably streaked white; bronzy yellow-green hindneck and neck sides; bronze-green upperparts, dull yellow-green rump, olive-green uppertail-coverts; blackish-brown flight-feathers, bronze-green on outer webs of secondaries, narrow pale buff-white bars on inner webs of all feathers, also on outer webs of primaries; uppertail blackish, poorly defined brownish bars; olive-green below, paler towards rear, with whitish or buff feather edges, tips and central streak producing bold scaly pattern; whitish undertail-coverts streaked dark olive; underwing brownish, barred whitish, coverts white with olive barring; longish bill fairly broad-based, slightly chisel-tipped, dirty yellowish, lower mandible paler, blackish culmen and tip; iris reddish-brown to red; legs grey-green. Distinguished from *P. vittatus* by darker throat, duller breast, more bronzy upperparts. Female is slightly shorter-billed than male, has entire forehead to nape black. Juvenile duller than adult, more diffusely marked below, often with stronger tail barring, male with orange-red on crown. VOICE. Explosive "kirrr"; "tcheu-tcheu-tcheu-tcheu" series.
Habitat. Broadleaved evergreen forest, mangroves, coastal scrub. Lowlands.
Food and Feeding. Ants. Commonly forages on the ground; also on moss-covered trees and boulders.
Breeding. Feb-Apr. Nest-hole excavated in tree. Clutch 4 eggs. No other information.
Movements. Resident.
Status and Conservation. Not globally threatened. Uncommon, locally fairly common; possibly overlooked. Occurs in Kaeng Krachan National Park and Khao Nor Chuchi Reserve(Thailand). Has a very small range, within which it appears to have fairly strict habitat requirements. Could be adversely affected by increased forest destruction. Research required on its ecology and breeding biology; taxonomic study also desirable.

Bibliography. Baker (1919), Deignan (1955), Inskipp *et al.* (1996), Jeyarajasingam & Pearson (1999), Kloss (1926), Lekagul & Round (1991), Riley (1938), Robson (2000), Smythies (1986), Wells (1999), Wheatley (1996).

189. Laced Woodpecker

Picus vittatus

French: Pic médiastin **German**: Netzbauchspecht **Spanish**: Pito Colinegro
Other common names: Laced Green Woodpecker, Small Scaly-bellied (Green) Woodpecker

Taxonomy. *Picus vittatus* Vieillot, 1818, Java.
Forms a superspecies with *P. viridanus*. Sometimes considered conspecific, but may be separated by habitat, although some possible overlap in this respect; further study needed. S & E populations tend to have more bronze tinge on upperparts, and rump colour tends more towards orange in E, but much individual variation, and racial separation unwarranted. Proposed races *eisenhoferi* (N Thailand), *connectens* (Langkawi I, off NW Peninsular Malaysia) and *limitans* (Kangean I) considered unacceptable. Monotypic.
Distribution. E Myanmar E to extreme SC China (S Yunnan) and N Vietnam (N Annam), and S to S Thailand, Cochinchina, W & S Peninsular Malaysia, E Sumatra (including Lingga Archipelago), Java, Bali and Kangean Is.

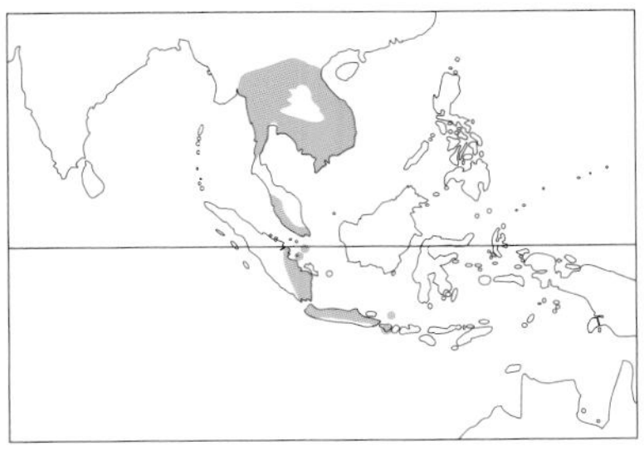

Descriptive notes. 30-33 cm; 94-132 g. Male has red forehead to crown and short crest, bordered by thin black line; narrow white eyering and short supercilium; pale greyish to buffish ear-coverts often tinged bluish, faintly streaked brown; lower lores buffy or whitish, extending into diffuse pale cheekstripe; black malar area usually with a few small white streaks or spots; plain whitish-buff to pale yellow-green or yellow chin and throat; hindneck, neck side and upperparts yellow-green, rump more yellowish; blackish-brown flight-feathers, outer webs of secondaries bronze-green, narrow pale buff-white bars on inner webs of all feathers, also on outer webs of primaries; uppertail blackish, usually a few thin pale bars on outer feathers, sometimes also central feathers; breast buffish-yellow or olive-buff, lower breast to vent buffy to greenish-white with scaly pattern of olive-green submarginal markings on both webs; underwing-coverts yellow-white, barred brown; undertail as above but paler, outer feathers often tinged dull yellow; longish bill fairly broad-based, somewhat chisel-tipped, curved culmen, blackish, lower mandible dull yellow with darker tip; iris red-brown or red; legs grey-green. Distinguished from *P. viridanus* by paler throat, yellow breast, more distinct black malar stripe, less bronzy upperparts. Female is slightly shorter-billed than male, has forehead to nape black. Juvenile duller, with underpart markings more diffuse, usually some streaking on throat, tail more clearly barred, male with orange-red crown. VOICE. Call "keep" or "kee-ip"; long series of "kew" notes as territorial call, very like *P. canus* but lower-pitched, shorter, delivered in faster succession; loud or low "wick, a-wick, a-wick" series in close encounters. Drums in short steady rolls.
Habitat. Deciduous forest, evergreen forest, secondary growth, bamboo, plantations, and village and suburban gardens; rather open coastal forest and scrub, including casuarinas, mangroves and coconut plantations. Where overlaps with *P. viridanus* in W & SW Thailand, mainly restricted to mangroves, drier deciduous woodland and coastal scrub, rarely in gardens. From sea-level to 200 m in Greater Sundas, to 1500 m in SE Asia.
Food and Feeding. Beetles and flies. Occurs singly or in pairs, partners keeping in close contact. Forages on ground, on fallen trees, as well as in bamboo and trees. In trees prefers the trunk or larger branches, staying low in mangroves; prefers the bases of fronds in palms; on bamboo, pays particular attention to nodes. Techniques include vertical and lateral pecking, probing; on the ground, sweeps away debris, and probes into soil or, in mangroves, mud.
Breeding. Feb-Jul; in Jan, Apr and Sept in Java. Crest-raising a common display; swinging movements also occur. Nest-hole excavated at 0·5-9 m in tree. Clutch 3 or 4 eggs; no further details available.
Movements. Resident.
Status and Conservation. Not globally threatened. Locally common; uncommon in Singapore; rare in Java. Occurs in several protected areas, e.g. Kaeng Krachan National Park (Thailand), Kuala Selangor Reserve (Malaysia), Nam Bai Cat Tien National Park (Vietnam), Sungei Buloh Nature Park (Singapore) and Aas Purwo National Park (Java). Has declined greatly in Sumatra due to loss of habitat.

Bibliography. Andrew (1992), Baker (1919), van Balen (1999), Bucknill & Chasen (1990), Chasen (1935), Deignan (1945, 1955), Eames & Robson (1992), Edgar (1933), Grantham (2000), Grimmett *et al.* (1998), Hails & Jarvis (1987), Harvey (1990), Holmes (1996), Inskipp *et al.* (1996), Jeyarajasingam & Pearson (1999), Kloss (1926), Lekagul & Round (1991), MacKinnon (1988), MacKinnon & Phillipps (1993, 2000), Madoc (1976), van Marle & Voous (1988), McClure (1998), Medway & Wells (1976), Mees (1996), Meyer de Schauensee & Ripley (1940), Paynter (1970), Riley (1938), Robinson & Kloss (1919a), Robson (2000), Robson *et al.* (1993a), Sargeant (1997), Short (1973d), Smythies (1986), Stepanyan (1995), Stresemann (1921a), Van Tyne & Koelz (1936), Wells (1990, 1999), Zhao Zhengjie (1995).

190. Streak-throated Woodpecker

Picus xanthopygaeus

French: Pic striolé **German**: Hindugrünspecht **Spanish**: Pito Culigualdo
Other common names: Little Scaly-bellied (Green) Woodpecker

Taxonomy. *Brachylophus xanthopygæus* J. E. Gray and G. R. Gray, 1846, Himalayas and central India.
Species name sometimes erroneously given as *P. myrmecophoneus*, a junior synonym. Monotypic.
Distribution. N and peninsular India and lower foothills of Himalayas in S Nepal E to Myanmar and S China (W Yunnan), and S to Sri Lanka, SW Thailand; also Cambodia, S Laos and Cochinchina.

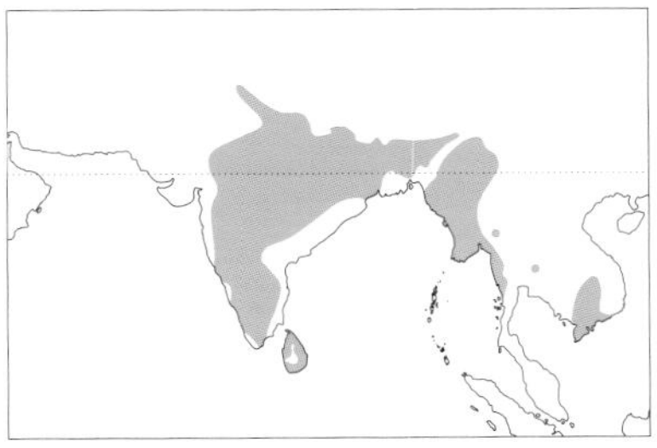

Descriptive notes. 30 cm; 83-111 g. Male has red forehead to hindcrown and crest with variable amount of black at borders, thin white supercilium, greyish ear-coverts streaked brownish, narrow white cheekstripe, blackish malar stripe greatly obscured by pale whitish tips and edges; whitish chin and throat with variable fine dark brown or olive streaks; hindneck and upperparts yellowish-green, rump and most of uppertail-coverts bright yellow (sometimes some orangey feathers admixed); dark green wing-coverts and tertials, tertials sometimes with few white bars at base; brownish-black flight-feathers, outer webs of secondaries dark green, white bars on inner webs of secondaries and both webs of primaries; uppertail blackish, narrowly barred brown; whitish to pale buff-white below, tinged green on breast, feathers with broad olive edges and tips and occasionally shaft streaks, forming distinct scaly pattern, sometimes more diffuse on lower belly; whitish undertail-coverts with dark arrowheads; underwing brownish, coverts paler, all barred white; undertail dark brown, washed dull yellow, variable dull yellow-brown bars; longish bill broad-based, slightly chisel-tipped, slightly curved culmen, dark brown or grey-brown, dull yellow base of lower mandible; iris white or pale pinkish, darker outer area; legs grey-green. Distinguished from very similar *P. viridanus* by pale eyes, more obvious pale cheekstripe, streaked throat, more streaky breast, slightly paler ground colour and less scaly appearance below. Female has forehead to nape black with greyish streaking. Juvenile less yellow-tinged above, grey feather bases creating more variegated appearance, less scaly-looking below, male with less red on head than adult. VOICE. Sharp single "queemp" and drumming the only acoustic signals reported.
Habitat. Open deciduous forest, dry dipterocarp forest, also semi-evergreen, sal (*Shorea*) and mixed bamboo forests; occurs also in secondary growth, sparsely wooded park-like country, teak and particularly rubber plantations, and tea estates. Avoids dense forest. Lowlands and lower hills, to 500 m; to 450 m, rarely over 900 m, in Nepal, but reported at up to 1700 m in Himalayan foothills; to 1500 m in Sri Lanka.
Food and Feeding. Ants, termites (Isoptera) and other small insect larvae; flower nectar and seeds also taken. Generally solitary. Forages frequently on ground, and may climb over boulders. Little known.
Breeding. Jan-May in India, Apr-Sept in Sri Lanka, and Mar-May in SE Asia. Nest-hole excavated by both sexes, sometimes very low (0·6 m) but usually at c. 4-8 m, in tree trunk or large branch, cavity c. 30 cm deep. Clutch 3-5 eggs; both parents feed chicks; no information on incubation and fledging periods.
Movements. Resident.
Status and Conservation. Not globally threatened. Fairly common in much of Indian Subcontinent, but rare and local in Bhutan, Bangladesh and Sri Lanka; uncommon to scarce in Myanmar and Thailand, very rare in Yunnan; few recent records from Indochina, where current status uncertain. Occurs in several protected areas, e.g. Corbett, Kaziranga and Mudumalai National Parks (India) and Chitwan National Park (Nepal). Poorly known; research needed to determine true status.

Bibliography. Ali (1969, 1996), Ali & Ripley (1983), Barua & Sharma (1999), Biswas (1961a), Delacour & Jabouille (1940), Duckworth *et al.* (1999), Evans & Timmins (1998), Grimmett *et al.* (1998, 2000), Harrison (1999), Harvey (1990), Henry (1998), Hoffmann (1998), Inskipp, C. & Inskipp (1991), Inskipp, T. *et al.* (1996), Kazmierczak (2000), Lamsfuss (1998), Lekagul & Round (1991), MacKinnon & Phillipps (2000), Mohan (1997), Mukherjee (1995), Phillips (1978), Prasad & Madhusudan (1993), Riley (1938), Ripley (1982), Robson (2000), Round (1988), Santharam (1998c), Shrestha (2000), Thewlis *et al.* (1998), Zhao Zhengjie (1995).

ssp *squamatus*

♂

♀

191

ssp *flavirostris*
♂

northern birds

♀

♂

192

southern bird
♂

ssp *sharpei*

♀

♂

ssp *innominatus*
♂

ssp *viridis*

♀

193

194
♀   ♂

ssp
vaillantii
♀

ssp *canus*

♀

ssp
jessoensis
♂

ssp *erythropygius*

♀

ssp *nigrigenis*

♀

♂

195

ssp *guerini*   ♀

ssp
hessei

♀

196

white-lined
form

♂

♂

ssp
robinsoni
♀

♀

ssp
sanguiniceps

ssp *dedemi*
♀   ♂

PLATE 46

inches   5

cm   13

191. **Scaly-bellied Woodpecker**

Picus squamatus

French: Pic écaillé **German**: Schuppengrünspecht **Spanish**: Pito Escamoso
Other common names: Common/Large Scaly-bellied Woodpecker, Scaly-bellied Green Woodpecker, Great Scaly Woodpecker

Taxonomy. *Picus squamatus* Vigors, 1831, Simla-Almora district, western Himalayas.
Two subspecies recognized.
Subspecies and Distribution.
P. s. flavirostris (Menzbier, 1886) - Afghanistan (except NE) and W Pakistan.
P. s. squamatus Vigors, 1831 - NE Afghanistan E to Darjeeling.

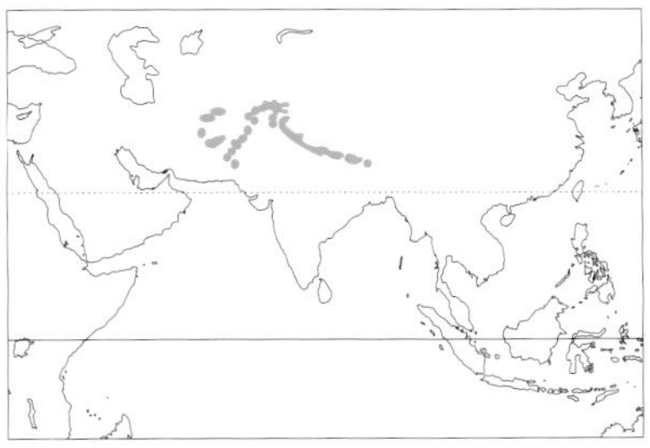

Descriptive notes. c. 35 cm; 156-194 g. Male has red forehead, crown and nape, usually some dark feather bases showing through (especially when worn), more orangey in narrow wedge down hindneck; black upper lores and narrow line along crown side, white supercilium from above eye to side of nape, narrow black eyestripe; lower lores yellowish-white, cheeks and ear-coverts olive-grey, greener or yellower on neck side; black malar stripe streaked whitish; olive chin, throat and breast, variably grey-tinged; green upperparts, yellow on rump and uppertail-coverts, latter with green bases; flight-feathers and primary coverts blackish-brown, secondaries and tertials with green outer (and part of inner) webs, all barred whitish; uppertail dark brown, barred buff-white, strong green suffusion on outer feathers; lower breast and belly greyish-white, tinged greenish, feathers with broad black submarginal lines producing strong scaly appearance, usually also thin black shaft streaks; underwing barred brown and white, coverts yellowish; undertail as above but paler, yellowish barring; in worn plumage, upperparts much greyer, duller yellow rump, breast greyer, markings below even more contrasting; long bill almost straight, slightly chisel-tipped, fairly broad across nostrils, pale horn-yellow to yellowish-grey, usually darker tip; iris pinkish-red, paler outer ring; legs greenish-grey to olive. Female is shorter-billed than male, perhaps duller green, has forehead to nape black with grey streaks. Juvenile greyer than adult, blotchy grey and dull green above, black hindneck, entire underparts with scaly pattern but markings less contrasting, eyes brownish, male with much black in red of crown. Race *flavirostris* is much paler than nominate, yellower above with more obvious barring on wings, and has whiter throat, pale olive-buff breast, yellowish belly to vent; scaling narrower and less contrasting. VOICE. Main call, also in flight, a melodious vibrating "klee-guh kleeguh" or "kuik-kuik-kuik", rapidly repeated 3-8 times, as advertisement; also, short high-pitched "kik", more rarely a single nasal "cheenk" or "peer"; laughing calls similar to those of *P. viridis*; soft notes in close encounters between two individuals; squeaky "chissuh-chissuh" in greater excitement; nestlings give loud wheezing "chuff-chuff". Drums regularly in breeding season.
Habitat. Coniferous and mixed coniferous forest, and forests with temperate deciduous trees, e.g. oaks (*Quercus*) and ash (*Fraxinus*). Adaptable, found in juniper (*Juniperus*) scrub-forest, coniferous forest (*Abies spectabilis*, *Picea smithiana*), pine (*Pinus*) forest, subtropical dry deciduous forest, also in arid areas wherever tamarisk (*Tamarix*) scrub, groves, orchards or plantations provide foraging and nesting sites; also inhabits large clearings in burned forest with plenty of dead and decaying trees. Restricted to riparian woodland dominated by poplars (*Populus*) in NW of range. Frequently in orchards in winter. From 1500 m to 3700 m, locally down to 600 m, on Himalayan slopes; wanders above timber-line outside breeding season.
Food and Feeding. Predominantly ants and termites (Isoptera), also larvae of wood-boring insects; berries also taken in winter. Forages singly or in pairs, or in family groups. Forages by pecking and hammering on trees; regularly descends to ground, also inspects rocks. Moves on the ground by hopping.
Breeding. Laying late Apr to early Jun, mainly early to late May. Nest excavated by both sexes, in tree of wide range of species, including e.g. holm oak (*Quercus ilex*), pistachio (*Pistacia*), apricot, tamarisk, at 2-6 m or higher (to 15 m), or may be low down, even close to ground (30 cm), or in exposed roots in a riverbank; circular entrance hole 6 cm wide, cavity depth 30 cm; many holes sometimes started before final selection made, which may be hole from a previous year. Clutch 4-6 eggs; both sexes incubate, period 17 days; chicks fed by regurgitation, fully feathered and come to hole entrance after 2 weeks; juveniles accompanied by parents for some days after fledging.
Movements. Some individuals of Himalayan populations move to lower altitudes in winter.
Status and Conservation. Not globally threatened. Common to fairly common, but rather local. Formerly extended west into Transcaspia, but no recent records; apparently extinct W of Afghanistan. Appears to be adaptable. No obvious threats.
Bibliography. Ali & Ripley (1983), Bates & Lowther (1952), Borodin (1984), Christison (1941), Dementiev (1952), Dementiev *et al.* (1966), Grimmett *et al.* (1998, 2000), Hollom *et al.* (1988), Holmes (1986), Hüe & Étchécopar (1970), Inskipp, C. & Inskipp (1991), Inskipp, T. *et al.* (1996), Kazmierczak (2000), Löhrl & Thielcke (1969), MacKinnon & Phillipps (2000), Mathews (1941), Porter, Christensen & Schiermacker-Hansen (1996), Raja *et al.* (1999), Ripley (1982), Roberts (1991), Short (1973d), Shrestha (2000), Storrs-Fox (1943), Stradi & Hudon (1998), Stradi *et al.* (1998), Waite (1948).

192. **Japanese Woodpecker**

Picus awokera

French: Pic awokéra **German**: Japangrünspecht **Spanish**: Pito Japonés
Other common names: Japanese Green Woodpecker, Wavy-bellied Woodpecker

Taxonomy. *Picus awokera* Temminck, 1826, Honshu.
Three races often recognized: large and pale *awokera* (Honshu and nearby islands), smaller and darker *horii* (Shikoku, Kyushu, Tsushima) and smallest and darkest *takatsukasae* (Tanegashima, Yakushima). These, however, simply reflect a cline of decreasing size and increasing plumage darkness from N to S, and division into geographical races seems unjustified. Monotypic.
Distribution. Japan, from Honshu S to Shikoku, Kyushu, Yakushima and Tanegashima, and including offshore islands of Tobishima, Awashima, Sado and Tsushima.

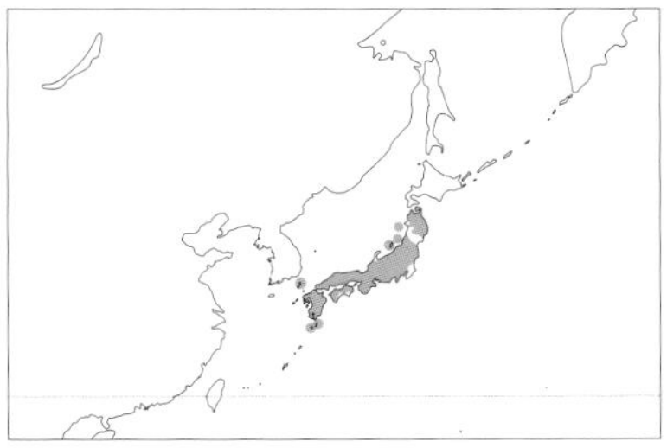

Descriptive notes. c. 29-30 cm; 120-138 g. Male has blackish lower forehead and lores to below eye, red from mid-forehead to nape, variable amount of black and grey feathers (especially in nape area); black malar stripe with extensive red in centre; rest of head and neck side grey, often tinged greenish when fresh, chin white to greyish-white; hindneck greyish-green; upperparts grey-green to olive-green, rump and central uppertail-coverts broadly tipped yellow, outer tail-coverts green; wing-coverts and tertials edged and tipped bronze-yellow; flight-feathers blackish-brown, outer webs of secondaries and inner primaries greenish, white bars on inner webs of all feathers, also on outer webs of outer primaries; uppertail brown, central feathers edged green, indistinct broad yellow-brown bars; throat white, often tinged greyish, sometimes some blackish in centre of throat, breast greyish-white or pale buffish-green, belly paler, lower breast downwards with broad dark brown vermiculated barring, bars tinged greenish-olive on flanks; whitish underwing barred brown, blackish bars on coverts; fairly long bill broad-based, pointed with slightly curved culmen, overall yellowish with blackish culmen and tip; iris red; legs pale grey, tinged green or blue. Southern populations smaller and darker than northern ones. Female is slightly smaller than male, with shorter bill, has crown grey with black streaks or bars in centre, sometimes black patch, usually small red patch on nape, less red in malar. Juvenile much as adult but duller, greyer above, barring below coarser, especially on breast. VOICE. Loud "piyo" call, also "ket, ket". Drums in quite fast rolls which are fairly long.
Habitat. Fairly open mixed forest in N, and evergreen forest in S; rarely in mature conifer plantations. Has recently become more common in parks and gardens. Commonest at 300-1400 m; occasionally somewhat higher in mountains, to c. 2000 m, particularly in primitive *Cryptomeris* forest on Yakushima; also descends to lowlands.
Food and Feeding. Chief component of diet is ants (*Lasius*, *Formica*, *Camponotus*, *Crematogaster*); other arthropods taken include Hemiptera, beetles and their larvae, and spiders. Also eats fruits, berries and seeds (*Sorbus*, *Rhus*, *Ilex*). Forages mainly at middle levels, at 2-10 m, on substrates ranging from larger branches to slender twigs; seasonal shifts in foraging preferences occur, with lower levels visited in Jan-May. Compared with *P. canus*, seems to forage little on ground (c. 20% of observations in winter). Gleaning and pecking are commonest techniques, followed by probing, and sap-drinking (winter, early spring).
Breeding. Apr-Jun. Nest-hole in tree at 2-4 m; also excavates holes in telephone poles (possibly only roosts). Clutch 7 or 8 eggs; no other information.
Movements. Moves to lower habitats in severe winters.
Status and Conservation. Not globally threatened. A fairly common inhabitant of hill areas and low mountains in Japan. Habit of digging holes in telephone poles can cause some problems locally, but not considered serious. Occurs in Kirishima-Yaku National Park.
Bibliography. Austin & Kuroda (1953), Brazil (1991), Chiba (1969), Fujii (1993), Higuchi (1980), Inskipp *et al.* (1996), Kazama (1980), King (1978/79), Nakamura *et al.* (1995), Wheatley (1996).

193. **Eurasian Green Woodpecker**

Picus viridis

French: Pic vert **German**: Grünspecht **Spanish**: Pito Real
Other common names: (European) Green Woodpecker; Levaillant's/Algerian (Green) Woodpecker, North African Green Woodpecker (*vaillantii*); Iberian Woodpecker (*sharpei*)

Taxonomy. *Picus viridis* Linnaeus, 1758, Europe = Sweden.
Has hybridized with *P. canus* in C Europe. Distinctive N African race *vaillantii* is often treated as a full species on basis of plumage differences and possibly ecological differences, but Iberian form *sharpei*, also sometimes suggested as a separate species, effectively represents an intermediate bridge between it and nominate; further study needed. Race *karelini* intergrades with nominate. Other proposed races are *pluvius* (Britain), *frondium* (C Europe), *pronus* (Italy), *dofleini* (Macedonia), *romaniae* (Romania) and *saundersi* (Caucasus), all of which exhibit insignificant differences which come within range of variation of other races. Additional named form *bampurensis*, known only from type locality in R Bampur Basin in SE Iran (where species no longer survives), said to have particularly well-marked tailbars and heavy barring over entire lower underparts; validity and possible survival of this isolated form requires further investigation. Five subspecies recognized.
Subspecies and Distribution.
P. v. viridis Linnaeus, 1758 - Europe from Britain and S Scandinavia E to W Russia, S to France, N Balkans and Black Sea.
P. v. sharpei (Saunders, 1872) - Pyrenees and Iberia.
P. v. karelini J. F. Brandt, 1841 - Italy E to Bulgaria, Asia Minor, Caucasus, N Iran and SW Turkmenia.
P. v. vaillantii (Malherbe, 1847) - NW Morocco to NW Tunisia.
P. v. innominatus (Zarudny & Loudon, 1905) - SW Iran (Zagros Mts).

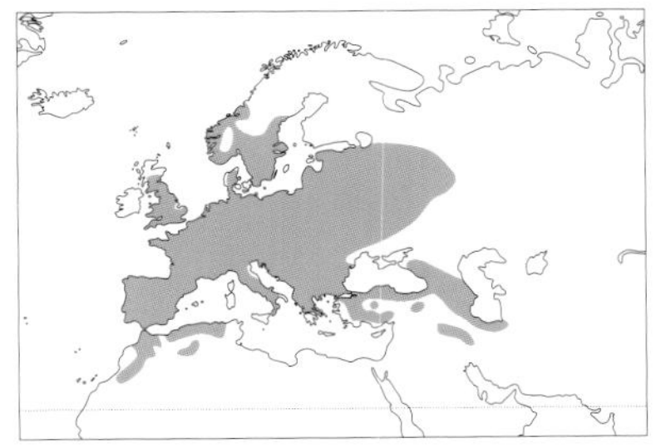

Descriptive notes. 31-33 cm; 138-250 g (*viridis*). Male has bright red forehead to nape, usually some grey feather bases visible, especially on crown; black nasal tufts, lores and broad area around eye back to central crown side, continuing over malar region, latter with broad red stripe in centre; rear ear-coverts pale green, paler feather bases showing through, darker on neck side; chin and upper throat greyish-white, often tinged light green; hindneck and upperparts bright yellow-green, rump and uppertail-coverts bright yellow, latter with green bases usually visible, wing-coverts and tertials sometimes tinged golden or bronzy; primaries and their coverts blackish, inner feathers edged green, white spots on both webs forming bars, secondaries golden-green on outer webs, blackish with white half-bars on inner webs; uppertail blackish, feathers edged green, faintly barred pale on central feather pair, sometimes indistinctly on others; yellow-green below, paler and more yellowish in lower regions, with fairly indistinct dark

On following pages: 194. Red-collared Woodpecker (*Picus rabieri*); 195. Black-headed Woodpecker (*Picus erythropygius*); 196. Grey-faced Woodpecker (*Picus canus*).

chevrons or bars from lower flanks to undertail-coverts; underwing barred grey and white, coverts tinged yellow or green; undertail as above, outer feathers paler and more clearly barred; when worn, plumage greener and less yellow above, greyer below, flank barring more obvious, grey bases of crown feathers more extensive; long bill slightly chisel-tipped, culmen slightly curved, broad across nostrils, dark grey or blackish, paler base of lower mandible; iris white to pinkish or with pinkish outer ring; legs olive-grey. Female lacks red in moustache, flank bars may reach farther up. Juvenile distinctive, much duller, more olive, eyes duller or greyer, upperparts with whitish spots and bars, duller yellow rump barred, pale greenish underparts with dark spotting on breast and barred lower region, head spotted and streaked with grey bases in red forehead to nape, black areas duller, wings and tail more barred, male usually with narrow red tips in malar. Race *karelini* is slightly smaller and duller than nominate, less yellow, more grey; *innominatus* resembles previous, but head side and underparts very pale, almost whitish, upperparts less green, often small paler spots on mantle and scapulars, bars on wings and tail more prominent, juvenile even more strongly spotted and barred; *sharpei* is rather short-billed, resembles previous apart from facial pattern, with dusky area around eye, ear-coverts similarly greyish, thin whitish line above malar (more obvious on female), male malar almost all red with minimal black border, little or no barring below, juvenile less heavily patterned; *vaillantii* is distinctive, closest to last but slightly shorter-billed, with fairly strong barring in ventral region, both sexes with all-black malar bordered above by well-marked white line, area around eyes and through ear-coverts grey-green, female with blackish-grey crown, red restricted to nape and side of hindcrown, juvenile less heavily barred and spotted than in other races. Voice. Most calls are "kyack" or "kewk" and variations, singly or as regular or loose series; more explosive, single or repeated "kyik" in agonistic contexts; distinctive laughing, somewhat accelerating "klew-klew-klew-klew-klew-klew", decreasing loudness, in breeding season; calls of *vaillantii* thinner, more whistling, and series less regular; nestlings noisier than those of *P. canus*, with "rak-ak-âk" in presence of feeding adults. Only rarely drums, in weak and irregular bouts; drumming more frequent in N Africa (*vaillantii*).

Habitat. Great variety of semi-open habitats; confined to larger open sections or clearings in extensively wooded areas. Forest edge, copses, parks, orchards and residential areas, usually near mature deciduous trees, but often associated with conifers in mountains and in N; requires higher proportion of deciduous trees than does *P. canus*. N Africa race *vaillantii* occurs in openings and clearings of oak (*Quercus faginea*, *Q. suber*) and cedar (*Cedrus*) forests, also in pine (*Pinus*) forest. From coastal areas and lowlands to subalpine forest; to 1500 m in E Alps, to 2100 m in W Alps, and to 3000 m in Caucasus; 950-2100 m in N Africa, also lower in Morocco.

Food and Feeding. Predominantly ants, chiefly meadow-dwelling species of genera *Formica* (winter) and *Lasius* (spring to autumn); generally, larger ant species preferred. Various other insects also taken, also earthworms and snails; occasionally catches reptiles. Sometimes eats fruits (apples, pears, cherries, grapes), berries, rarely seeds. Lives solitarily, in pairs, and in family groups. Forages mostly on ground. Uses bill to sweep away moss, dead leaves, other debris, or snow; pecks funnel-shaped holes up to 12 cm deep in ground, and procures prey with action of the very long tongue; such holes may be exploited in lengthy and repeated visits. When snow cover heavy, can dig tunnels almost 1m long to reach prey. Forages also on trunks and branches, as well as on buildings and rocks, by gleaning and probing. Takes sap on ringed trees, but not recorded to drill sap wells. Moves only short distances on ground.

Breeding. Laying from early Apr, locally Mar, to Jun; calling commences much earlier, in Dec. Male feeds female during courtship, e.g. prior to copulation. Nest excavated often at 2-10 m, sometimes to 12 m, in dead or soft living wood in unbroken tree (e.g. *Populus* favoured in Norway), work taking 2-4 weeks; entrance hole circular with diamter c. 6·4 cm, or vertically oval and 7·5 cm × 5·0 cm. Clutch usually 5-8 eggs, but 4-11 recorded; both sexes incubate, only male during the night, period 14-17 days; chicks fed by regurgitation, by both parents, fledge after 23-27 days; brood divided between parents, accompanaied for 3-7 weeks.

Movements. Essentially resident; some local winter movements. Continental European populations disperse on average shorter distances than do *P. canus*, although extreme instances of up to 170 km recorded.

Status and Conservation. Not globally threatened. Common to very common throughout much of its range, but local in some parts (e.g. Turkey). Population estimates in 1980's and 1990's include 10,000-100,000 pairs (probably c.31,500) in European Russia and a further 450,000-1,360,000 pairs (probably c. 670,000) in rest of Europe; highest numbers in France, where c. 300,000 pairs. Densities not very high: maximum in France c. 0·6 pairs/km², but in parts of N only 0·02 pairs/km². Most populations stable or increasing, and this species has, for example, spread N into Scotland since 1950's. On the other hand, declines recorded in several European countries in recent decades: 20-30% reduction in Sweden, and since 1960's has declined by 50-75% in Netherlands. Main problems are intensification of agriculture and forestry, and conversion of pasture to arable land, which considerably reduces ant populations. Harsh winter weather can also cause major mortality, effects of which may last for years. Race *vaillantii* is fairly common in Tunisia and Algeria, local in Morocco; appears to have decreased in numbers, but slight expansion in Morocco.

Bibliography. Adamian & Klem (1999), Barreau & Rocher (1992), Beaman & Madge (1998), Blagosklonov (1968), Blume (1955, 1961, 1981, 1996), Blume *et al.* (1957), Chartier (1993), Chatfield (1970), Choffat (1995), Christen (1994), Cramp (1985), Cuisin (1999b), Dementiev *et al.* (1966), Díaz *et al.* (1996), Étchécopar & Hüe (1964), Fry *et al.* (1988), Glue & Boswell (1994), Gorman (1997a, 1999a), Groppali & Priano (1993), Hagemeijer & Blair (1997), Hågvar & Hågvar (1989), Hågvar *et al.* (1990), Handrinos & Akriotis (1997), Havelka & Ruge (1993), Heath & Evans (2000), Heath *et al.* (2000), Horstkotte (1973), Hüe & Étchécopar (1970), Jourdain (1936), Keßler (1986), Knistautas & Lyutkus (1981), Labitte (1953), Ledant *et al.* (1981), Löhrl (1977), Marchant *et al.* (1990), Melde (1994), Merikallio (1958), Mikusinski (2001), Mikusinski & Angelstam (1997, 1998), Mulhauser, Kaiser & Claude (2000), Mulhauser, Kaiser & Junod (2001), Nilsson *et al.* (1992), Osiek & Hustings (1994), Pechacek (1992, 1995, 1996), Pechacek & Krištín (1993), Purroy (1997), Radermacher (1970), Radford (1997), Rolstad *et al.* (2000), Ruedi (1983), Salomonsen (1947), Schandy (1981), Schmid (1993), Schneider (1979), Sermet (1983), Snow & Perrins (1998), Soler *et al.* (1982), Sovago (1954), Sparks (1995), Stenberg (1978), Stradi & Hudon (1998), Stradi *et al.* (1998), Südbeck (1991), Svensson *et al.* (1999), Tobalske & Tobalske (1999), Tomec & Kilimann (1998).

194. **Red-collared Woodpecker**

Picus rabieri

French: Pic de Rabier **German**: Halsbandspecht **Spanish**: Pito Vietnamita
Other common names: Rabier's Woodpecker

Taxonomy. *Gecinus Rabieri* Oustalet, 1898, Tonkin.
Monotypic.

Distribution. SC China (extreme S Yunnan), Laos and Vietnam (W & E Tonkin, N & C Annam); single report from Cambodia.

Descriptive notes. c. 30 cm. Male has whitish line above eye, olive-grey lores and ear-coverts, pale greenish-buff chin and throat often streaked white, sometimes some red feather tips; rest of head,

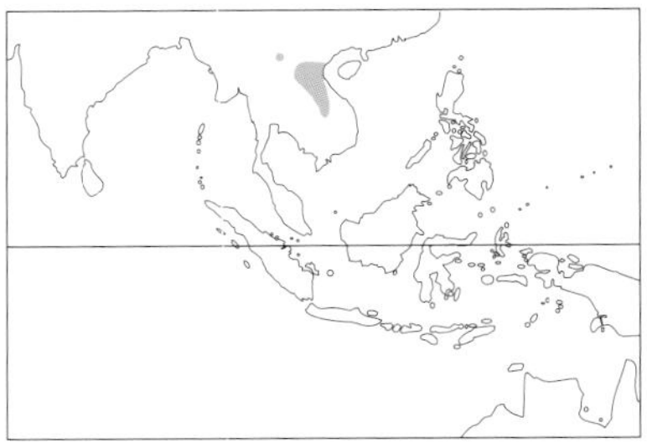

also neck and upper breast, red; upperparts green, rump slightly paler, tail-coverts with dark shaft streaks, wing-coverts and tertials with bronze tinge (sometimes also tinged red); flight-feathers blackish-brown, outer webs of secondaries bronze-green or tinged reddish, broad white bars on inner webs of all feathers, narrower white spots or bars on outer webs of primaries; uppertail blackish, central feathers edged green; lower breast and upper belly green, slightly paler than upperparts, feathers of flanks and lower belly olive-green with off-white shaft streaks and paler green edges and tips, producing scaly pattern; undertail-coverts olive-grey, edged and tipped olive-green; underwing whitish, barred greyish-brown; undertail blackish, tinged green-yellow, especially on outer feathers, central feathers sometimes with narrow paler bars; fairly long bill broad-based, slightly chisel-tipped with curved culmen, overall blackish with paler base; iris reddish-brown or pinkish-brown; legs yellow-green or greenish-grey. Female has blackish forehead and crown, also less red in facial area, may also have less obvious red collar. Juvenile male resembles adult female, but duller above, greyer below, with orange-red on head and upper breast, crown mixed with black feathers. Voice. Not described. Drums in fast irregular rolls of medium length.

Habitat. Broadleaved evergreen and semi-evergreen forest, also secondary growth; occurs also in tall mixed deciduous forest, and even in logged and disturbed forest with some large trees remaining. Lowlands to 700 m, very rarely to 1050 m.

Food and Feeding. Ants probably form main bulk of diet. Occurs singly, in pairs, or in family parties; regularly accompanies mixed-species flocks, e.g. with laughingthrushes (*Garrulax*) and other woodpeckers. Often forages low down on trees, and frequently on ground.

Breeding. May-Jun. No other details known.

Movements. Resident.

Status and Conservation. Not globally threatened. Currently considered Near-threatened. Scarce to uncommon; locally more common (Laos). Occurs in Bach Ma and Cuc Phuong National Parks (Vietnam). First recorded in Cambodia in 2001. Has a very small known range, within which the continued degradation and destruction of lowland forest gives cause for concern. This species occurs in tall mixed deciduous forest in some places, and seems able to survive in logged and disturbed forest if some large trees remain; some evidence suggests that, locally, it may prefer the latter habitats. Even so, this is a very poorly known woodpecker, and research is needed to ascertain its precise habitat requirements, particularly in terms of nesting.

Bibliography. Andreev *et al.* (2001), Campey (1996), Cheng Tsohsin (1987), Collar & Andrew (1988), Collar *et al.* (1994), Delacour & Jabouille (1940), Duckworth (1996), Duckworth, Evans & Timmins (1993), Duckworth, Salter & Khounboline (1999), Duckworth, Timmins & Cozza (1993), Eames (1996), Evans & Timmins (1998), Inskipp *et al.* (1996), MacKinnon & Phillipps (2000), Meyer de Schauensee (1984), Robson (1989, 2000), Robson *et al.* (1993a), Stattersfield & Capper (2000), Thewlis *et al.* (1998), Timmins *et al.* (1993), Tobias *et al.* (1998), Zhao Zhengjie (1995).

195. **Black-headed Woodpecker**

Picus erythropygius

French: Pic à tête noire **German**: Rotbürzelspecht **Spanish**: Pito Cabecinegro

Taxonomy. *Gecinus erythropygius* Elliot, 1865, Cochinchina.
Races intergrade. Two subspecies recognized.

Subspecies and Distribution.
P. e. nigrigenis (Hume, 1874) - C & E Myanmar (S to N Tenasserim) and NW & W Thailand.
P. e. erythropygius (Elliot, 1865) - NE Thailand and Indochina.

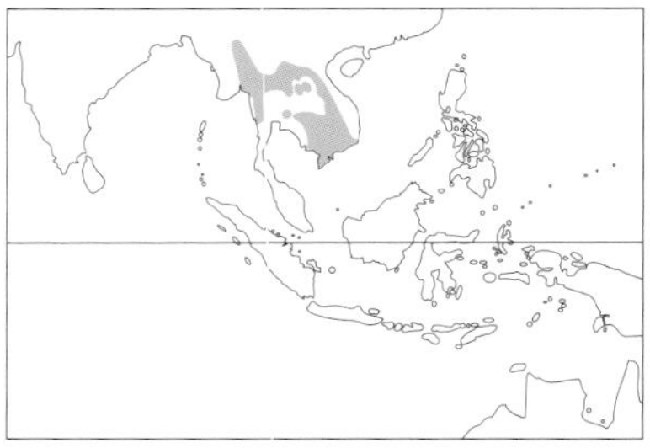

Descriptive notes. 33 cm; 100-135 g. Male has black forehead, lores and cheeks to nape, red patch in centre of crown and sometimes down to eye; a few (both sexes and both races) have a thin whitish line from eye over ear-coverts; neck side, chin and throat to upper breast bright yellow, often tinged olive on upper breast; yellow-green mantle and back, bright red lower back and rump to central uppertail-coverts, tail-coverts otherwise olive-green with indistinct black shaft streaks; wing-coverts darker green, less tinged yellow; primary coverts and flight-feathers blackish, latter with 5 or 6 broad white bars; uppertail blackish, central feathers edged green with obscure pale bars near base; lower breast brownish-white with faint chevrons, paler and whitish with heavier dark chevrons on flanks and belly; white undertail-coverts heavily barred dark brown; underwing whitish, blackish bars across flight-feathers; rather narrow pointed bill, slightly curved culmen, greyish-horn to yellow, darker tip; iris whitish to lemon-yellow, narrow orbital ring slate-grey; legs pale grey to grey-green. Female has crown entirely black. Juvenile less yellow above than adult, throat paler, upper breast buff, markings below more diffuse, male with some red feather tips on central crown. Race *nigrigenis* is very like nominate, but has blackish bill, male perhaps with more red in crown. Voice. Distinctive undulating yelping laugh "ka-tek-a-tek-a-tek-a-tek" or "cha-cha-cha, cha-cha-cha", rapidly repeated, stress on first note in each series.

Habitat. Deciduous forest, especially dry dipterocarp, also pine (*Pinus*) forest. Recorded up to 1000 m, but generally commoner below 600 m.

Food and Feeding. Termites (Isoptera), also ants and other invertebrates. Usually in small, noisy groups of 2-6 birds, often associated with jays or treepies (Corvidae). Forages in canopy and in understorey; seems also to descend to lower levels, e.g. to stumps and the ground. Active and restless, constantly on the move through forest.

Breeding. Feb-Jun. Nest-hole in tree; clutch 3-4 eggs. No other information.

Movements. Resident.

Status and Conservation. Not globally threatened. Generally scarce to uncommon; locally more common. Occurs in Doi Inthanon National Park (Thailand).

Bibliography. Baker (1919), Chazee (1994), Deignan (1945), Delacour & Jabouille (1940), Duckworth *et al.* (1999), Eames & Ericson (1996), Evans, G.H. (1905), Evans, T.D. & Timmins (1998), King & Rappole (2001), Lekagul & Round (1991), Riley (1938), Robson (2000), Smythies (1986), Thewlis *et al.* (1998).

196. Grey-faced Woodpecker
Picus canus

French: Pic cendré **German**: Grauspecht **Spanish**: Pito Cano
Other common names: Grey-headed Woodpecker(!), Grey-headed Green Woodpecker, Ashy Woodpecker(!); Black-naped (Green) Woodpecker (*sobrinus*, *sanguiniceps*)

Taxonomy. *Picus canus* J. F. Gmelin, 1788, Norway.
Has hybridized with *P. viridis* in C Europe. Races often divided into two main groups, the N "*canus* group" of two taxa and S & E "*guerini* group" of seven taxa, with two other isolated forms in the highlands of Peninsular Malaysia and Sumatra. Races intergrade in many areas. Several other races have been described throughout species' vast range, but differ in only very minor, insignificant characters; thus, named races *perspicuus* (Bulgaria), *biedermanni* (Altai Mts), *zimmermanni* (NE China), *perpallidus* (Manchuria, Ussuriland, Korea), *setschuanus* (Sichuan) and *gyldenstolpei* (NE Indian Subcontinent) do not warrant separation. Eleven subspecies currently recognized.
Subspecies and Distribution.
P. c. canus J. F. Gmelin, 1788 - Europe (from S Scandinavia and France) E to W Siberia.
P. c. jessoensis Stejneger, 1886 - E Siberia to Sakhalin and N Japan (Hokkaido), S to NE China and Korea.
P. c. sanguiniceps Stuart Baker, 1926 - NE Pakistan, N India and extreme W Nepal.
P. c. hessei Gyldenstolpe, 1916 - Nepal E to Myanmar, extreme S China (S Yunnan) and most of Thailand to Vietnam.
P. c. guerini (Malherbe, 1849) - NC China S to C Sichuan.
P. c. kogo (Bianchi, 1906) - C China, from Qinghai E to Shanxi and S to Sichuan.
P. c. sordidior (Rippon, 1906) - SE Tibet E to W Sichuan, S to NE Myanmar and Yunnan.
P. c. sobrinus J. L. Peters, 1948 - NE Vietnam and SE China (Guangxi E to Fujian).
P. c. tancolo (Gould, 1863) - Taiwan and Hainan.
P. c. robinsoni (Ogilvie-Grant, 1906) - mountains of C Peninsular Malaysia (Gunung Tahan and Cameron Highlands).
P. c. dedemi (van Oort, 1911) - highlands of Sumatra.

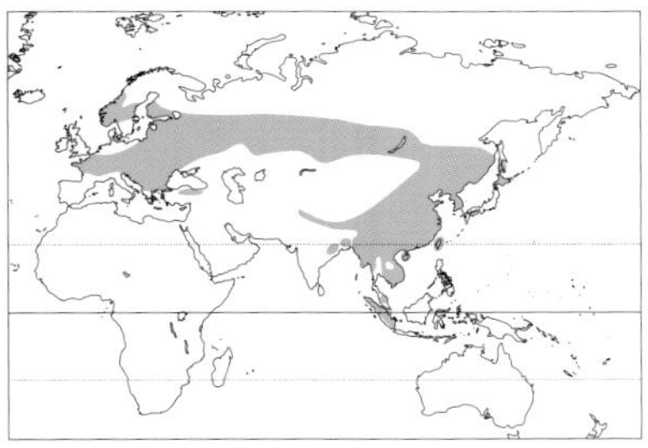

Descriptive notes. 26-33 cm; 125-165 g (*canus*), 110-206 g (*jessoensis*), 143-165 g (*sanguiniceps*), 137 g (female *hessei*). Male has red upper forehead and forecrown (often yellowish at rear), crown usually with very fine black streaks, short pale line over eye, narrow black malar stripe often mottled grey at rear; rest of head and neck ash-grey, slightly tinged greenish when fresh, darker on nape and neck; chin and throat pale grey-white, tinged buff or olive; olive-green upperparts, yellowish or greenish-yellow on rump and uppertail-coverts, latter with olive-green feather bases, wing-coverts occasionally with slight bronze or yellowish tinge; primaries greyish-black to brownish-black, small whitish spots on outer webs, sometimes also on some inner webs, secondaries greyish-black with dull olive-green outer webs, outer feathers often with paler spots; uppertail greenish-brown, obscure paler bars; pale grey below, lower flanks and belly with slight tinge of pale olive-green when fresh, occasionally obscure darker chevrons on lowermost underparts; underwing greyish, heavily barred; undertail blackish, tipped greenish-grey, a few obscure paler bars; fairly long bill slightly chisel-tipped, rather broad-based, culmen moderately curved, blackish-brown to grey-black, usually with olive tinge; iris pinkish to bluish-white, or deep carmine-red with admixed white; legs olive-grey to yellowish-olive. Female on average slightly smaller than male, proportionately shorter bill, head lacking red, has forehead and forecrown pale grey with narrow black shaft streaks, occasionally a few scattered red tips on forehead, black malar weaker and often incomplete. Juvenile duller than adult, greyer above with slight scaly appearance, rump more greenish, some indistinct bars on wing, malar more diffuse and mottled, inconspicuous darker barring below, eyes red-brown, male with small orange-red crown patch. Races highly variable, some highly distinctive: *jessoensis* is variable, generally slightly paler and greyer, less green, than nominate, in fresh plumage can be almost indistinguishable; *guerini* is greenish above and below, with black nape, female with pale-streaked black crown; *sobrinus* has golden tint above, is greener, less grey, below; *tancolo* is smaller than last, has deep green upperparts, very green underparts, greyer face; *kogo* is larger than previous, much paler green, female with black nape and pale-streaked black crown, a few greyish-green on head top; *sordidior* is same size as last, dark; *hessei* is even darker than previous, dark golden-green above, deeper green below, tail darker and less barred, crown and nape deep black, male with more extensive red on crown; *sanguiniceps* is largest race, plumage as previous but less golden or bronzy above, male with even more extensive red on crown; *robinsoni* is small, very dark green above and below, but paler throat, yellow-green rump, crown and nape black, male with red forecrown, female crown slightly streaked; *dedemi* is smallest and darkest, highly distinctive, deep brownish-red above, brighter red rump, unbarred blackish tail, reddish-brown with some admixed grey and greenish below, blackish undertail-coverts, crown and nape unstreaked black, male with small red forecrown patch, juveniles more blackish above and below. Voice. Single "kik" calls; descending sequence of 5-20 clearly separated mournful "kiu" or "pew" notes, female's series usually shorter, more raucous, possibly also racial differences in number of syllables, series also softer and less descending in Himalayan birds than in C European ones; low "dyook dyook" series between partners at close distances; low to moderately loud "kyak kyak kyak" in agonistic situations; "wíte-wíte.." during body-swinging displays; "keek, kak kak kak kak" calls common outside breeding season. Drums regularly pre-breeding, rolls longer than those of *P. vittatus* but rhythm slightly slower, in Europe 19-40 strokes at rate of c. 20 per second.
Habitat. Great diversity of habitats occupied over wide range. Various types of temperate and moist subtropical forest, woodland, second growth with evergreen, deciduous and coniferous trees; trees can be dense, but some open ground required; occurs in parks, including larger ones in urban areas, but visits open country only when woodland nearby. In Europe, open country with many copses, in not over-dense forest, floodplain-forest, parks, orchards, gardens; associated mostly with deciduous trees, but locally in pine-oak (*Pinus-Quercus*) woodland, or more open coniferous montane forest with larch (*Larix*); broad overlap in habitat with *P. viridis*, but more in forest interior. Avoids pure coniferous *taiga* in C Siberia, preferring broadleaved forest. Open alder (*Alnus*) or oak forest in Nepal and N Myanmar, and open deciduous and coniferous country in Tibet and W China. Race *hessei* in Myanmar and Thailand prefers deciduous forest and drier and more open parts of teak forest, rather than evergreen; in highlands of S Annam (Vietnam), shows a liking for native pine forest. Other habitats in Asia include bamboo groves mixed with second growth. Considerable altitudinal range, from lowlands to mountains: lowlands and hills in Europe, to 1700 m, non-breeders to 2000 m; to 2200 m in Indian Subcontinent, but to 2600 m in Nepal (more common below 2000 m); to 2300 m in N Myanmar and China; c 900-1830 m in Peninsular Malaysia, and to 2000 m in Sumatra.
Food and Feeding. Appears to have more varied diet than that of *P. viridis*. Chiefly ants (*Myrmica*, *Lasius*), termites (Isoptera) and their brood, which often make up more than 90% of stomach contents; also other insects (e.g. Coleoptera larvae), and spiders; also nest contents of other birds. Fruits (e.g. apple, pear, cherries, camphor), berries, seeds (e.g. *Rhus*), nuts and acorns also consumed, and nectar taken. Regularly visits feeders. Usually solitary outside breeding season, otherwise in pairs or small family parties; in tropical areas (e.g. Thailand), will associate with mixed bird flocks of other terrestrial foragers. Regularly feeds on ground; probes into soil, pushing and digging with the bill, using the tongue to lick up prey. Funnel-shaped holes dug into ground, used repeatedly as sources of ants. Arboreal foraging with single pecks, some excavation in decaying wood at low levels, and intensive use of the tongue at crevices and sites of decayed wood. Also licks from sap wells, but seems not to ring trees itself. Simple anvils used occasionally. Moves on ground with heavy hops; otherwise, more lively and agile than *P. viridis*, flies even short distances within a tree.
Breeding. Lays from end Apr to early Jun. During courtship, landing with fluttering wingbeats associated with presence of partner and a nest-hole; occasional courtship feeding by male. Nest-hole excavated in 9-20 days or more, at 0·2-24 m, commonly between 1·5 m and 8 m, in dead wood or soft living wood, or in fungus-afflicted hard wood, most often in deciduous tree of variety of species; entrance hole a vertical oval c. 6 cm × 5·5 cm, cavity depth c. 28 cm. Clutch 4-10 eggs, clutch size varies geographically, generally 4-5 in Himalayas, 7-9 in C Europe; both sexes incubate, male during night, male also seems to incubate more than female during day, period 14-17 days; chicks fed by regurgitation, by both parents equally, helping by a second female known to have occurred; fledging period 23-27 days; young accompanied by parents for some time afterwards.
Movements. Essentially non-migratory. Some local post-breeding movements to more favourable, usually lower-lying, wintering grounds, e.g. riparian woodland, human habitations. Normally disperses farther than *P. viridis* in Europe; some nomadic winter movements occur among N Asian populations, also in connection with irregular movements of *Dendrocopos major* in Scandinavia.
Status and Conservation. Not globally threatened. Reasonably common, if rather local, throughout most of range. Locally common in Europe and much of Asia; widespread but generally uncommon in China; common or locally common in N Indian Subcontinent, but rare in Pakistan; fairly common to scarce in SE Asia, but rare to very rare in Peninsular Malaysia and Sumatra. Estimated population in European Russia c. 31,600 pairs; c. 94,000 pairs in rest of Europe, including 35,000 in Romania and 20,000 in Germany. Density in C Europe c. 0·1 pairs/km², locally up to 10 pairs/km². Has decreased in some areas, e.g. Romania, probably as a result of intensification of forestry methods. Few relevant data from other parts of range, but appears to be fairly stable.
Bibliography. Ahlén & Andersson (1976), Alatalo (1978), Ali & Ripley (1983), Ali *et al.* (1996), Anon. (1975), Baker (1919), Beaman & Madge (1998), van den Berg (1988), Bergmanis & Strazds (1993), Biswas (1961a), Blankert & de Heer (1982), Blume (1965, 1981, 1996), Blume & Jung (1959), Brazil (1991), Bussmann (1944), Christen (1994), Conrads (1964), Conrads & Herrmann (1963), Cramp (1985), Cuisin (1999a), Deignan (1945), Dementiev *et al.* (1966), Du Hengqin (1987), Eames & Robson (1992), Edenius *et al.* (1999), Ehrenroth (1973), Erdmann (1974), Étchécopar & Hüe (1978), Fleming & Traylor (1961), Greenway (1940), Grimmett *et al.* (1998), Guichard (1948), Hagemeijer & Blair (1997), Hågvar & Hågvar (1989), Hågvar *et al.* (1990), Haila & Jarvinen (1977), Ham Kyuhwang (1982), Harvey (1990), Hazevoet (1984), Heath *et al.* (2000), Higuchi (1980), Higuchi & Koike (1978), Inskipp & Inskipp (1991), Jeyarajasingam & Pearson (1999), Laurent (1941-1945), Lekagul & Round (1991), Liu Yikang & Wang Jinghua (1984), Löhrl (1977), Ludlow (1944), MacKinnon & Phillipps (1993, 2000), Majumdar (1979), van Marle & Voous (1988), Matsuoka (1976, 1979b), Matsuoka & Kojima (1979b, 1985), Medway & Wells (1976), Melde (1994), Merikallio (1958), Mikusinski (2001), Mikusinski & Angelstam (1997, 1998), Mulhauser, Kaiser & Claude (2000), Mulhauser, Kaiser & Junod (2001), Pavlik (1994), Pedrini (1984), Proud (1958), Radermacher (1970), Rand & Fleming (1957), Ree (1984), Roberts (1991), Rogacheva (1992), Rolstad & Rolstad (1995), Ruge (1982), Salomonsen (1947), Scherzinger (1982), Schmid (1993), Short (1973d), Smythies (1986), Snow & Perrins (1998), Spitznagel (1993), Storrs-Fox (1943), Südbeck (1991, 1993), Südbeck & Meinecke (1992), Svensson *et al.* (1999), Tobalske & Tobalske (1999), Tsai Hangyeh (1985), Vitkauskas & Raudonikis (1989), Wabakken (1973), Wells (1999), Won Pyongoh & Koo Taehoe (1986), Zhao Zhengjie (1995).

PLATE 47

inches 4

cm 10

197

♀

♂

♂ ssp *shorii*

198

ssp *anguste* ♀

199

♀ ssp *everetti*

♂

ssp *montanus* ♂

ssp *lucidus* ♀

♂

♀

ssp *haematribon*

201

♀ ssp *rufopunctatus* ♂

ssp *erythrocephalus* ♀

ssp *xanthocephalus* ♂

♂ ssp *javanense* ♀

ssp *benghalense* ♀

ssp *intermedium* ♂

ssp *psarodes* ♀

♂

200

ssp *puncticolle* ♂

ssp *stricklandi* ♀

201

♀ ssp *strictus*

♂

ssp *guttacristatus* ♀

♀

♂

202

Genus *DINOPIUM* Rafinesque, 1814

197. **Olive-backed Woodpecker**

Dinopium rafflesii

French: Pic oriflamme **German**: Olivrückenspecht **Spanish**: Pito Dorsioliva
Other common names: Olive-backed Three-toed Woodpecker, Raffles's Woodpecker

Taxonomy. *Picus Rafflesii* Vigors and Horsfield, 1830, no locality = Sumatra.
Individual variation considerable, and races poorly marked, differing only in size; described race *peninsulare* (Malacca) considered synonymous with nominate. Two subspecies recognized.
Subspecies and Distribution.
D. r. rafflesii (Vigors & Horsfield, 1830) - S Myanmar (S Tennaserim) and peninsular Thailand S to Sumatra, including Bangka.
D. r. dulitense Delacour, 1946 - Borneo.

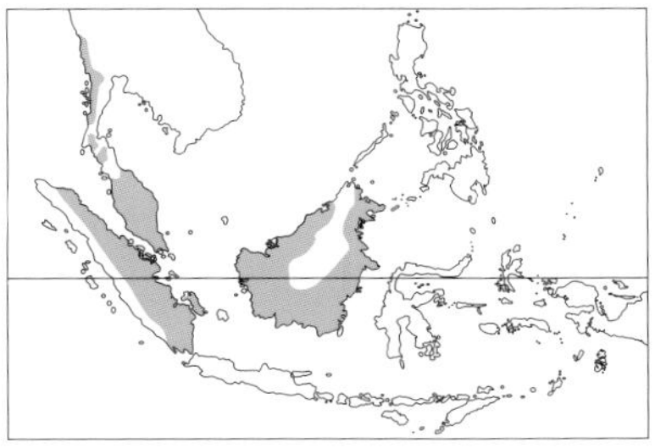

Descriptive notes. c. 26-28 cm; 87-119 g (*rafflesii*), 76-84 g (*dulitense*). Male has red forehead, crown and crest, black and white stripes on side of head and down side of neck, buffy-yellow lores, cinnamon to yellowish or rusty malar area (sometimes red feather tips); chin and upper throat buffish-cinnamon, yellowish or rusty-yellow; hindneck and uppermost mantle black, rest of upperparts dark olive-green with bronzy or yellowish feather tips, rump and uppertail-coverts occasionally with orange tips (rarely, dull reddish), bronzy or yellowish olive-green wing-coverts; brownish-black flight-feathers, yellow-green outer webs of secondaries, inner webs with white spots; uppertail black; olive to greyish-olive below, often with rusty staining, flanks usually with white spots, sometimes absent; underwing dark brownish, spotted white; fairly long bill chisel-tipped, culmen slightly curved, narrow across nostrils, grey to blackish; iris dark red-brown; legs blue-grey or grey, only 3 toes. Female has red on head replaced by black, forehead and crown often more olive, crest slightly smaller than male's. Juvenile duller, greyer, male with crown blackish or dark olive, red only on crest or also a few scattered spots on forehead, females as adult but crown more olive. Race *dulitense* is smaller than nominate. Voice. Single "chak" note; also rapid series of loud notes in 2 versions, slow "chakchakchak-chak", 6-34 notes, varies in rate and pitch, sometimes single notes appended, given when pair-members interact, and faster, more regular, with 10-50 notes, probably as territorial call; low "ch-wee, ch-wee, ch-wee" calls during encounters and sometimes associated with head-swinging; soft, even trilling "ti-i-i-i-i", and squeaky "tiririt" also described. Not known to drum, but incubating birds tap in soft regular bursts of 10-12 strokes.
Habitat. Dense, wet evergreen forest, including swamp-forest, mangroves; avoids secondary growth and clearings. Mainly lowlands and hills, to 1200 m; locally to 1600 m in Borneo.
Food and Feeding. Ants, termites (Isoptera), and especially ant pupae. Singly and in pairs. Forages at low and middle heights, below 10 m, on fallen logs, at bases of trees and saplings, and to tops of lower saplings and snags; also on branches of lower crown. Rarely, ventures outside forest to visit dead stumps. Main technique is gleaning; pecks occasionally, more frequently than *D. javanense*. Moves slowly and continuously, pausing only briefly.
Breeding. Mar-May; apparently Oct in Borneo. Displays include crest-raising, bowing movements, head-swinging; courtship feeding by male. Nest excavated by both sexes, at 4·5-9 m up in tree, even in live wood. Clutch size not recorded; both sexes incubate. No other information.
Movements. Resident.
Status and Conservation. Not globally threatened. Currently considered Near-threatened. Scarce to uncommon throughout its range; perhaps somewhat commoner in parts of Borneo; extinct in Singapore. Occurs in several protected areas, e.g. Kaeng Krachan National Park (Thailand) and Gunung Mulu National Park, Batu Punggul Forest Reserve, and Danum Valley Conservation Area (Borneo). Within this species' range, huge areas of lowland forest have already been destroyed; although it appears to remain in reasonable numbers in the higher parts, additional habitat loss could easily pose a major threat.
Bibliography. Andreev *et al*. (2001), Andrew (1992), Baker (1919), van Balen (1999), Bucknill & Chasen (1990), Castelletta *et al*. (2000), Danielsen & Heegaard (1995), Delacour (1951a), Duckworth & Kelsh (1988), Duckworth *et al*. (1997), Dupond (1942), Inskipp *et al*. (1996), Jepson & Brinkman (1993), Jeyarajasingam & Pearson (1999), Lekagul & Round (1991), MacKinnon & Phillipps (1993), van Marle & Voous (1988), Medway & Wells (1976), Mees (1986), Riley (1938), Robinson & Kloss (1924a), Robson (2000), Short (1973d), Smythies (1986, 1999), Stattersfield & Capper (2000), Vowles & Vowles (1997), Wells (1985, 1999), Wilkinson, Dutson & Sheldon (1991), Wilkinson, Dutson, Sheldon, Darjono & Noor (1991), Wong (1985).

198. **Himalayan Flameback**

Dinopium shorii

French: Pic de Shore **German**: Himalaya-Feuerrückenspecht **Spanish**: Pito de Shore
Other common names: Himalayan Goldenback, Himalayan/Three-toed Golden-backed Woodpecker

Taxonomy. *Picus Shorii* Vigors, 1832, Himalayas.
Forms a superspecies with *D. javanense*. Races weakly differentiated. Two subspecies recognized.
Subspecies and Distribution.
D. s. shorii (Vigors, 1832) - N India (Haryana) E through lowlands and S foothills of Himalayas to Nagaland and N Bangladesh; possibly still in peninsular hills (Eastern Ghats).
D. s. anguste Ripley, 1950 -W Myanmar.
Descriptive notes. 30-32 cm; 101 g. Male has yellowish-red forehead, redder on crown and crest, narrowly bordered black; broad black and white bands on side of head and neck, pale reddish malar stripe outlined in black, becoming all black at rear and continuing down to side of breast; whitish

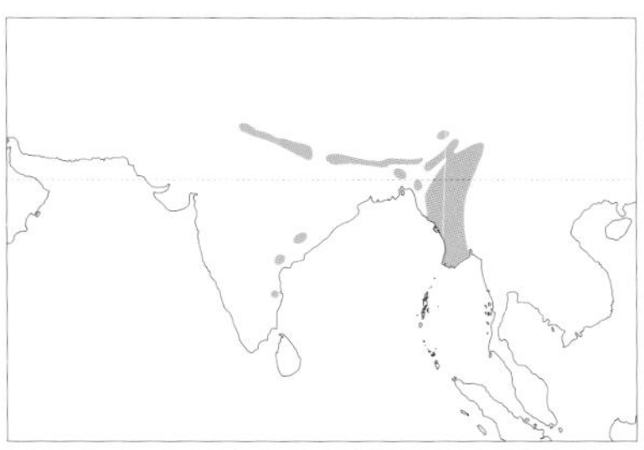

chin, thin buff-brown central line broadening through centre of throat and expanding over upper breast, where bordered with black spots; hindneck and upper mantle black; lower mantle, scapulars and upper back olive-green with yellower or golden feather tips, strongly red on edges and tips; lower back to rump bright red, uppertail-coverts blackish olive-brown with some red tips; wing-coverts with a hint of red; flight-feathers blackish-brown, yellow-olive outer webs of secondaries, inner webs spotted white; uppertail black; white below, feathers with brownish-black edges and black tips creating scaly pattern; underwing brown, spotted white; undertail brownish-black, outer feathers tinged yellow-olive; longish bill almost pointed, curved culmen, narrow across nostrils, blackish; iris red to brownish, possibly sometimes gold or crimson; legs green-grey or brownish-green, 3 toes. Female has blackish crown and crest with narrow white streaks, pale malar with black outline. Juvenile browner than adult, markings below more obscure, male with forehead and crown brownish-buff and streaked paler, red only on crest, female with brown crown and crest with broad pale streaks. Race *anguste* has bill, wing and tail a little smaller than nominate, possible tendency for slightly less red on back, female has crown streaks much finer than nominate and hindcrown almost unstreaked. Voice. Rapid tinny "klak-klak-klak-klak-klak", slower and not so loud as that of *Chrysocolaptes lucidus*.
Habitat. Mature deciduous and semi-evergreen forest; in deciduous forest in Nepal, preferring primary lowland forest with *Ficus* and *Bombax*. Lowlands and foothills, up to c. 700 m, locally to 1220 m; below 300 m in Nepal.
Food and Feeding. Poorly known. No details of diet. Associates with mixed-species flocks; also with *Chrysocolaptes lucidus* where the two occur together.
Breeding. Mar-May; nest-hole excavated in tree; clutch 2-3 eggs. No other information.
Movements. Resident.
Status and Conservation. Not globally threatened. Fairly common locally; rare in Bangladesh; uncommon in Myanmar. Occurs in several protected areas, e.g. Corbett National Park (India) and Chitwan National Park (Nepal). Very poorly known species; requires field research. Could be seriously affected by deforestation.
Bibliography. Abdulali & Hussain (1973), Ali & Ripley (1983), Ali *et al*. (1996), Barua & Sharma (1999), Biswas (1961a), Choudhury (2001), Delacour (1951a), Grimmett *et al*. (1998, 2000), Harvey (1990), Inskipp, C. & Inskipp (1991, 1993), Inskipp, C. *et al*. (1999), Inskipp, T. *et al*. (1996), Javed & Rahmani (1998), Kazmierczak (2000), MacKinnon & Phillipps (2000), Ripley (1950a, 1982), Robson (2000), Shrestha (2000), Smythies (1986), Waite (1938).

199. **Common Flameback**

Dinopium javanense

French: Pic à dos rouge **German**: Feuerrückenspecht **Spanish**: Pito Culirrojo
Other common names: Common Golden-back, Common Golden-backed Woodpecker, Golden-backed Three-toed Woodpecker; Indian Flameback (*malabaricum*)

Taxonomy. *Picus javanensis* Ljungh, 1797, Java.
Forms a superspecies with *D. shorii*. Proposed race *borneonense* (Borneo except NE) considered inseparable from nominate. Six subspecies recognized.
Subspecies and Distribution.
D. j. malabaricum Whistler & Kinnear, 1934 - W India.
D. j. intermedium (Blyth, 1845) - Bangladesh and Assam to C & E Myanmar, SC China (SW Yunnan) and N Vietnam, and S to Thailand (except peninsular) and Cochinchina.
D. j. everetti (Tweeddale, 1878) - W & C Philippines (Balabac, Palawan and Calamian Is).
D. j. javanense (Ljungh, 1797) - peninsular Thailand S to Sumatra, including Riau Archipelago, W Java and Borneo.
D. j. raveni Riley, 1927 - NE Borneo and offshore islets.
D. j. exsul (Hartert, 1901) - E Java and Bali.

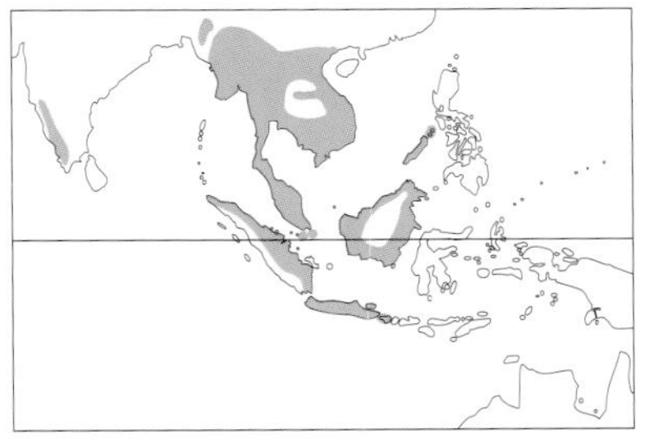

Descriptive notes. 28-30 cm; 67-90 g (*javanense*), 85-98 g (*everetti*), 79-100 g (*intermedium*). Male has brownish-red forehead and upper lores, red crown and crest, crown narrowly edged black; white supercilium from above eye to nape side, black stripe from eye to hindneck, broad white cheekstripe from lores continuing down side of neck to side of breast; thin black moustachial line, broader at rear, then continuing down to upper breast; buffish chin and throat, central line of small black spots from bill base generally somewhat broader and more numerous on lower throat; hindneck and upper mantle black; rest of upperparts mostly olive with strong golden suffusion, yellow feather tips, sometimes also hint of orange or red, lower back and rump bright red; uppertail-coverts blackish-brown, occasionally tinged olive; outer webs of secondaries and tertials olive-yellow, rest of flight-feathers blackish-brown, white spots on inner webs; uppertail black; white below, feathers irregularly edged and tipped black, markings heaviest on breast, less prominent and more bar-like on lower underparts; underwing brown, spotted white; undertail brownish-black, outer feathers tinged yellowish; shortish bill pointed, curved on culmen, narrow across nostrils, blackish to dark grey-brown, paler base; iris red-brown or brown, orbital skin black; legs grey or brown, usually tinged greenish, 3 toes. Female has crown and crest black with white streaks. Juvenile very like adult, but breast more blackish-brown with white spots, lower underparts more obscurely barred, eyes greyer, male with black forehead and crown, red crest, female with pale crown streaks more spot-like. Other races differ little from nominate, only one being distinctive: *intermedium* is very like nominate but bigger, with whiter throat; *malabaricum* is on average slightly smaller than last, has back and wings less golden-yellow, more olive; *exsul* has underparts strongly but irregularly barred, female with narrow orange to red napeband; *raveni* is

On following pages: 200. Black-rumped Flameback (*Dinopium benghalense*); 201. Greater Flameback (*Chrysocolaptes lucidus*); 202. White-naped Woodpecker (*Chrysocolaptes festivus*).

slightly more buff and less black below, throat more broadly spotted, female tending to have crown streaks very narrow; *everetti* is distinctive, has pale reddish or buff-brown colour from throat to upper breast, throat spots more extensive, more barred pattern below, males with red of crown extending to side of head, dark eyestripe broader, red tips in malar, female with red on nape and crest, very small streaks on crown or none. VOICE. Variable series of notes, "kowp-owp-owp-owp", in flight; single or double "kow" when perched; "wicka"-like calls with display during encounters; rattle a harsh prolonged "churrrrrrrr", or "ka-di-di-di-di-di-di", faster than that of *D. rafflesii*. Drums more softly than *Chrysocolaptes lucidus*.

Habitat. Moist secondary and open forest, open deciduous woodland, scrub, and mangroves; also in teak forest and, at higher elevations, in pine (*Pinus*) forest. Favours penang and coconut groves, cultivation, gardens, parkland, and golf courses. Generally found in lowlands, but up to 1000 m in Greater Sundas, to 1530 m in Myanmar, and to 1700 m in India.

Food and Feeding. Ants, insect larvae; also small scorpions (Scorpiones), cockroaches (Blattodea), other insects. In pairs, or in mixed-species flocks. Forages at all levels, with preference for lower parts of trees, but also inspects crown branches and all other parts of trees and palms. Main techniques are gleaning, sideways reaching, and probing; occasionally pecks, as when removing loose bark. Climbs quickly and erratically, with occasional brief pauses. Observed to hawk flying insects. Sometimes moves long distances between foraging sites.

Breeding. Jan-Jun, mostly Feb-Apr, in India; Jan-Oct in SE Asia, mostly Jun in Thailand, to Jul in Peninsular Malaysia; Apr-Jul and Nov-Dec in Borneo; Mar-Apr in Philippines. Displays include crest-raising, bowing movements, head-swinging; male courtship-feeds female. Nest-hole excavated at 1·4-10 m, mostly below 5 m, in tree or stump, often usually in fruit tree or coconut palm, in open area. Clutch 2 or 3 eggs; no information on incubation and fledging periods. Maximum recorded longevity 10 years, 6 months.

Movements. Resident.

Status and Conservation. Not globally threatened. Locally fairly common in India; local in Bangladesh; uncommon to common in SE Asia; uncommon in Philippines. Occurs in many protected areas in all parts of its range, e.g. Baluran, Mudumalai, Periyar and Kaziranga National Parks (India), Khao Yai National Park (Thailand), Nam Bai Cat Tien National Park (Vietnam), Bako National Park (Malaysia), Sungei Buloh Nature Reserve (Singapore), Way Kambas National Park (Sumatra) and St Paul's Subterranean River National Park (Palawan, Philippines). Could be adversely affected by habitat destruction, but preference for more open woodland is an advantage; accepts human-altered landscapes.

Bibliography. Ali (1996), Ali & Ripley (1983), Andrew (1992), Baker (1919), van Balen (1999), Bangs & Van Tyne (1931), Betts (1934), Bucknill & Chasen (1990), Champion-Jones (1938), Chasen (1935), Deignan (1945), Delacour (1951a), Dickinson *et al.* (1991), Edgar (1933), Grimmett *et al.* (1998), Hails & Jarvis (1987), Harrison (1958), Harvey (1990), Inskipp *et al.* (1996), Jeyarajasingam & Pearson (1999), King & Rappole (2001), Lainer (1999), Lekagul & Round (1991), MacKinnon (1988), MacKinnon & Phillipps (1993, 2000), Madoc (1976), van Marle & Voous (1988), McClure (1998), Medway & Wells (1976), Mees (1996), Meyer de Schauensee & Ripley (1940), Noske (1991), Parrott & Andrew (1996), duPont (1971), Riley (1938), Ripley (1982), Robinson & Kloss (1924b), Robson (2000), Sargeant (1997), Short (1973d), Smythies (1986, 1999), Spittle (1949, 1952), Stepanyan (1995), Vowles & Vowles (1997), Wells (1999), Zacharias & Gaston (1999), Zhao Zhengjie (1995).

200. Black-rumped Flameback

Dinopium benghalense

French: Pic du Bengale **German**: Orangespecht **Spanish**: Pito Bengalí

Other common names: Lesser Flameback/Goldenback, Lesser/Black-rumped Golden-backed Woodpecker; Ceylon Golden-backed Woodpecker (*psarodes*)

Taxonomy. *Picus benghalensis* Linnaeus, 1758, Bengal.

S Sri Lankan race sometimes referred to as *erithronothos* (or, erroneously, as *erithronothon*), but *psarodes* has priority. Clinal decrease in size and variation in colour from N to S, and considerable individual variation, together with intergrading of populations, all combine to make racial delimitation difficult; indeed, W Indian birds sometimes separated as race *tehminae* and those in N Sri Lanka as *jaffnense*, but both probably more appropriately included in *puncticolle*. Four subspecies currently recognized.

Subspecies and Distribution.

D. b. dilutum (Blyth, 1849) - Pakistan.

D. b. benghalense (Linnaeus, 1758) - NW & N India E to Assam and SW Myanmar.

D. b. puncticolle (Malherbe, 1845) - C India S to N Sri Lanka.

D. b. psarodes (A. A. H. Lichtenstein, 1793) - Sri Lanka (except N).

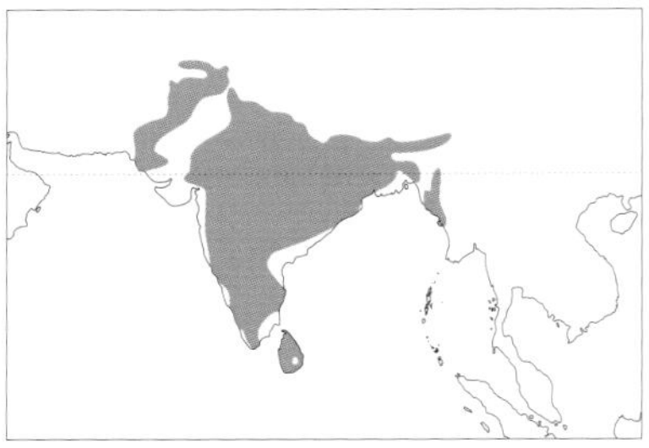

Descriptive notes. 26-29 cm; 86-133 g. Male has black forehead and crown with red feather tips, red crest; white supercilium, white-streaked black band from eye through ear-coverts, white cheekband meeting supercilium at rear, continuing down side of neck to side of upper breast; chin and throat black, broadly streaked white; hindneck and upper mantle black; lower mantle, scapulars and upper back golden-yellow, lower back to uppertail-coverts black; wing-coverts golden-olive, outer medians and most of lessers black with white subterminal spots, inner greaters often with white central streak; flight-feathers brownish-black, outer webs of tertials and secondaries golden-olive, primaries and inner webs of secondaries and tertials with well-spaced white spots; uppertail black; white to buffish-white below, feathers broadly edged and tipped black on breast, more narrowly on lower underparts, sometimes more bar-like on belly and undertail-coverts; underwing brown, coverts white with black barring; in worn plumage, forehead and crown mostly black, often olive feather bases visible on back; longish bill almost pointed, culmen curved, fairly narrow across nostrils, blackish; iris red-brown to crimson, orbital skin green to grey; legs grey-green. Female has forehead and forecrown black with small white spots. Juvenile duller than adult, black areas browner, underparts greyer and more obscurely marked, male with narrower red tips and sometimes white spots on crown, female with few or no crown spots. Race *dilutum* is generally paler golden-yellow above, whiter below; *puncticolle* has back and wings more orange-yellow, throat spotted rather than streaked, lower underparts more creamy, variable, sometimes olive wash on rump and wing-coverts, wing-covert spots smaller or lacking (especially in W & SW India); *psarodes* is distinctive, has back and wings deep crimson-red, often red tips on rump and tail-coverts, also more black on crown, black eye-stripe extending to hindneck, often more black on throat and underparts, proportionately longer tail. VOICE. Single strident "kierk"; repeated "kyi-kyi-kyi", from perch or in flight; high-pitched squeaks by excited birds in encounters. Drums in weak bouts lasting 2-3 seconds.

Habitat. All types of moist to dry woodland, mostly deciduous; open woodland and light forest, groves around villages, old wooded gardens, tree plantations along roads and canals, open country with trees. Found in *Borassus* palms and coconut (*Cocos nucifera*) plantations, as well as rubber plantations in S India. Avoids heavy forest and arid regions. Lowlands, to 1200 m; in coastal areas in N Sri Lanka; locally to 1700 m in India.

Food and Feeding. Chiefly ants, e.g. *Camponotus* and *Meranoplus*, and including larvae and pupae of the fierce red ant *Oecophylla smaragdina*. Spiders, caterpillars, also weevils (Curculionidae) and other beetles, taken occasionally. Fruits (e.g. mango) and nectar not uncommon constituents of the diet. Often in pairs and with mixed-species flocks. Forages at all levels in trees; clings to underside of horizontal branches, moves backwards occasionally. Breaks into leaf-nests of *Oecophylla smaragdina*; also descends to the ground to feed at ant nests.

Breeding. Mainly Mar-Apr, in S India also in Jul-Aug, and in Dec-Sept, depending on conditions, in Sri Lanka; sometimes 2 broods in a season in S. Crest-raising by male, which also observed to feed insects to female. Nest-hole excavated by both sexes, often low, down to 1·5 m, but sometimes to 15 m, in tree with soft or hard wood (e.g. acacia, tamarisk, mango), or in palm; entrance hole c. 8 cm in diameter. Clutch 2 or 3 eggs; incubation by both parents, period 17-19 days; both also feed chicks, by regurgitation; fledging period c. 3 weeks.

Movements. Resident.

Status and Conservation. Not globally threatened. Common to locally common throughout range; one of the commonest and most widespread woodpeckers in Indian Subcontinent. Occurs in numerous protected areas, e.g. Chitwan National Park (Nepal), Corbett, Bharatpur, Ranthambore, Mudumalai, Periyar and Kaziranga National Parks (India) and Bellanwila-Attidiya Sanctuary (Sri Lanka). Seems unlikely to be at risk in the immediate future.

Bibliography. Alagar (1992), Ali (1996), Ali & Ripley (1983), Balasubramanian (1992), Betts (1934), Chakravarthy (1988), Champion-Jones (1938), Gokula & Vijayan (1997), Grimmett *et al.* (1998, 2000), Harrison (1999), Harvey (1990), Henry (1998), Himmatsinhji (1980), Inskipp, C. & Inskipp (1991), Inskipp, T. *et al.* (1996), Javed & Rahmani (1998), Jha (1999), Jones *et al.* (1998), Kalsi (1998), Kazmierczak (2000), Khacher (1989), Lainer (1999), Lamsfuss (1998), Mason & Lefroy (1912), Mohan (1997), Mukherjee (1995), Neelakantan (1962), Phillips (1978), Rajan (1992), Ripley (1982), Roberts (1991), Robson (2000), Santharam (1998a, 1998c), Shrestha (2000), Smythies (1986), Van Tyne & Koelz (1936), Vijayaraghavan (1957).

Genus *CHRYSOCOLAPTES* Blyth, 1843

201. Greater Flameback

Chrysocolaptes lucidus

French: Pic sultan **German**: Sultanspecht **Spanish**: Pito Sultán

Other common names: Greater Goldenback, Greater/Large Golden-backed Woodpecker; Crimson-backed Woodpecker (*guttacristatus*)

Taxonomy. *Picus lucidus* Scopoli, 1786, Mindanao, Philippines.

Exhibits considerable individual variation and, in particular, extreme geographical variation in plumage, especially in E of range; appreciable size variation also exists, being largest in N & W. Race *guttacristatus* has sometimes been treated as separate species, as also has *strictus*. Further research may reveal that some of the more distinctive taxa, especially those isolated on islands, have evolved into full species, but present knowledge insufficient to enable accurate assessment; DNA analysis and detailed study of vocalizations and ecology required. Proposed races *sultaneus* (N India, Nepal), *grandis* (Polillo, in Philippines) and *maculiceps* (Basilan, in Philippines) considered too poorly differentiated to warrant recognition. Thirteen subspecies recognized.

Subspecies and Distribution.

C. l. socialis Koelz, 1939 - W coast of India.

C. l. guttacristatus (Tickell, 1833) - NW India and Nepal E to S China (Yunnan) and S to Thailand and Indochina.

C. l. stricklandi (E. L. Layard, 1854) - Sri Lanka.

C. l. chersonesus Kloss, 1918 - Peninsular Malaysia S to Sumatra and W Java.

C. l. andrewsi Amadon, 1943 - NE Borneo (from around Sandakan to Sebatik I).

C. l. strictus (Horsfield, 1821) - E Java.

C. l. kangeanensis Hoogerwerf, 1963 - coastal E Java, Bali and Kangean Is.

C. l. haematribon (Wagler, 1827) - N Philippines (Luzon, Polillo, Marinduque and Catanduanes).

C. l. erythrocephalus Sharpe, 1877 - Balabac, Palawan and Calamian Group.

C. l. xanthocephalus Walden & E. L. Layard, 1872 - Ticao, Masbate, Panay, Guimaras and Negros.

C. l. rufopunctatus Hargitt, 1889 - Samar, Biliran, Leyte, Calicoan, Bohol and Panaon.

C. l. lucidus (Scopoli, 1786) - Basilan and W Mindanao (Zamboanga Peninsula).

C. l. montanus Ogilvie-Grant, 1905 - Mindanao (except W) and Samal.

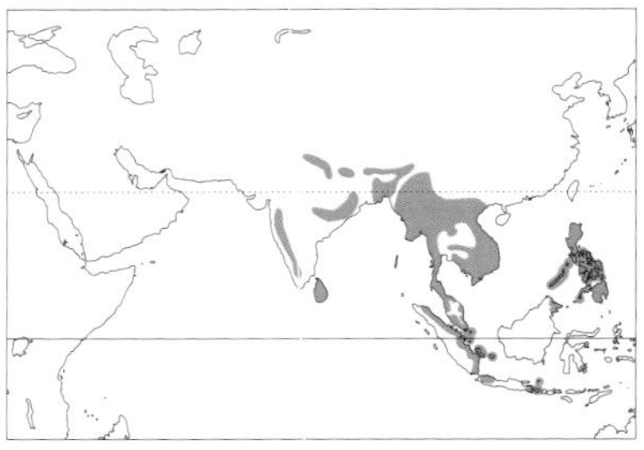

Descriptive notes. c. 28-34 cm; 150-233 g (*guttacristatus*), 110-145 g (*haematribon*), 125-164 g (*rufopunctatus*), 127 g (*lucidus*). Male has deep crimson forehead, crown and crest, reddish-buff face, neck and upper breast with broad black feather edges; upperparts and wings deep crimson-red, rump bright red; flight-feathers blackish, outer webs of secondaries olive-gold to reddish, all with white spots on inner webs; uppertail black; underparts light golden with broad black feather edges; long bill slightly chisel-tipped, straight, broad across nostrils, blackish; iris bright red, orbital ring purplish; legs green-brown. Female has crown and crest dark olive-brown to reddish-black with dark golden spots. Juvenile is duller than adult, more olive-tinged, more obscurely marked below, has brown eyes, male with less red in crest. Races differ considerably in plumage, those from India to Indonesia mostly having golden-green to olive or bronzy back and wings, black and white bands on face and neck, white underparts with black scalloping, male with bright red crown and crest, those in Philippines highly variable, iris red in Philippine races, pale in all other races: *guttacristatus* is largest race, has forehead, crown and crest red, broad black and white bands on face, golden-olive or golden-green back and wings, bright crimson-red rump, white to buff-white underparts with feathers edged and tipped black, black strongest on throat and breast, pale creamy eyes, female has similar head pattern to male, but crest black with white spotting; *socialis* is slightly smaller than previous, back and wings more olive, less golden, red of rump extending farther up back; *stricklandi* is smaller than last, back and wing-coverts entirely dark red, more black on head and neck side, much narrower white supercilium, bill and eyes very pale; *chersonesus* has olive back and wings, broad black markings below, broad white supercilium; *andrewsi* is larger than previous, dark markings below distinctly browner, less black, flanks more barred; *strictus* is small, has back and wings yellow-green, red of rump duller with hint of spots or bars, pale areas of head and breast buffish, female with crown and crest golden to orange-gold; *kangeanensis* is smaller than last, with redder rump, reduced black facial markings, dark markings below narrower and browner, female crown and crest golden-yellow; *erythrocephalus* has back and wings golden-green with traces of red (all other Philippine races red-backed), red of rump extending well up back, neck with fairly narrow black and white stripes, pale bill and legs, male with entire head and crest red, black spot on ear-coverts, thin dark malar, female has head darker with pale golden crown spots; *montanus* is like nominate but slightly smaller, with more gold or yellow in upperparts, dark markings below browner, less black; *rufopunctatus* has back and wings dark red, reddish-buff face, belly strongly patterned dark, male usually with black-bordered pale red malar, female crown and crest dark brown with reddish-buff spots; *xanthocephalus* is small, highly distinctive, with back and wings dark red, crown and crest red, head, neck and entire underparts golden-yellow, dark markings restricted to neck and upper breast, usually thin blackish malar, bill and legs pale, female with entire head yellow, often tinged orange on crest; *haematribon* has dark red back and wings often tinged olive, belly buffish with grey-brown barring obscure, male with much black on face and neck, female head dark with prominent white spots from forehead to crest. VOICE. Single "kik" calls occasionally; more often short or longer series of highly variable "kowk-kowk", "ke-dew-kow" or single "kow" notes, especially in flight; rapid insect-like series, monotonous or varying in speed and pitch, e.g. "di-di-di-di-di-di-di", "tibittititititit" or "kilkilkitkitkit", sometimes rather long, both on the wing and when perched, possibly some variation at subspecific level; "t-wuit-wuit" series during close encounters. Drums loudly, rolls are c. 2 seconds long, accelerating and weakening.

Habitat. Open deciduous and evergreen forest, secondary forest, edge of primary forest, riparian woodland in open country, old plantations. Mangroves in Peninsular Malaysia, Sumatra and Borneo. More humid areas preferred. Mature lowland forest with big trees and mixed *Bombax-Ficus* are main habitats in Nepal. In Philippines, found in primary forest, mature secondary forest, lighter secondary forest with dense understorey, dense riparian vegetation, also near cultivations and close to human settlements. Found at all elevations, to over 2100 m, in Sri Lanka; to 920 m in Nepal; in India, to 1600 m in N and to 1800 m in S; below 1200 m in SE Asia; from lowlands to 1500 m in Philippines.

Food and Feeding. Large caterpillars, larvae of wood-boring beetles, pupae, ants and other insects; also takes nectar. In pairs and in family parties; associates also with other woodpecker species, e.g. *Dryocopus javensis*. Forages almost exclusively on big trees and snags, including somewhat isolated ones in the open; sometimes descends to ground. Prefers trunks and larger branches. Pecking and hammering to excavate wood are commonest foraging techniques; large pieces of bark removed with powerful lateral blows, and probing for prey follows. Pecking and probing also used to uncover subsurface prey among epiphytes. Movements rapid; tree searched from base of trunk to canopy, though much time is spent at a single site when substrate excavated. Gleans rarely; occasional flycatching, e.g. for swarming termites (Isoptera). Will move long distances, including over open areas, from one tree to the next.

Breeding. Mar-May in N India, Dec-Mar in S; in Sri Lanka Aug-Apr, mainly Dec-Jan; from Dec in SE Asia; Jul-Nov in Greater Sundas, and Feb-Aug in Philippines. Nest-hole excavated by both sexes, work sometimes taking 4 weeks, at 2-20 m in tree of variety of types, often in soft live wood (although heart of trunk may be rotten); entrance a vertical oval in shape. Clutch 2 eggs in S areas, 4-5 in N; incubation by both parents, period 14-15 days; chicks fed by both parents, which carry food in tip of the bill, fledging period 24-26 days; young stay with parents for some weeks, possibly until start of next breeding season.

Movements. Resident.

Status and Conservation. Not globally threatened. Common, or at least locally common, throughout much of range; local in Peninsular Malaysia; rare in China; only few recent records from Java (in E) and Bali; fairly common in Philippines. Occurs in numerous protected areas in many countries. Not likely to become threatened overall, but could be at risk to some extent in some areas; continued habitat destruction in Greater Sundas and Philippines, for example, may eventually result in populations falling to levels at which survival becomes difficult. Taxonomic revision urgently required, particularly as it may call for recognition of several species within this complex, and some of these could well prove to be threatened.

Bibliography. Ali & Ripley (1983), Ali *et al.* (1996), Andrew (1992), Bangs & Van Tyne (1931), Betts (1934), Biswas (1961a), Bucknill & Chasen (1990), Chasen (1931, 1935), Danielsen *et al.* (1994), Deignan (1945), Delacour & Mayr (1946), Dickinson *et al.* (1991), Eames & Robson (1992), Evans *et al.* (1993), Frith & Frith (1978), Gilliard (1950), Gonzales (1983), Goodman & Gonzales (1990), Grimmett *et al.* (1998), Hachisuka (1930), Harrison (1999), Harvey (1990), Hellebrekers & Hoogerwerf (1967), Henry (1998), Holmes (1997), Hoogerwerf (1949, 1963), Inskipp, C. & Inskipp (1991), Inskipp, T. *et al.* (1996), Jeyarajasingam & Pearson (1999), Kloss (1918), Lamsfuss (1998), Lekagul & Round (1991), MacKinnon (1988), MacKinnon & Phillipps (1993, 2000), van Marle & Voous (1988), McClure (1998), Medway & Wells (1976), Mees (1986, 1996), Meyer de Schauensee (1957), Morioka & Sakane (1981), Noske (1991), Parkes (1960b), Phillips (1978), duPont (1971), Rabor (1977), Rand & Rabor (1960), Riley (1938), Ripley (1950c, 1982), Robinson (1917), Robson (2000), Salomonsen (1952, 1953), Santharam (1998c), Sargeant (1997), Short (1973d), Smythies (1986, 1999), Stepanyan (1995), Stresemann (1921a, 1921b), Wells (1999), Winkler *et al.* (1994), Zhao Zhengjie (1995).

202. **White-naped Woodpecker**

Chrysocolaptes festivus

French: Pic de Goa   **German**: Goldschulterspecht   **Spanish**: Pito Dorsiblanco
Other common names: Black-rumped Woodpecker, Black-backed Woodpecker(!), Black-backed Yellow Woodpecker

Taxonomy. *Picus festivus* Boddaert, 1783, Goa, India.
Two subspecies recognized.
Subspecies and Distribution.
C. f. festivus (Boddaert, 1783) - SW Nepal and most of India (except E coast).
C. f. tantus Ripley, 1946 - N & S Sri Lanka.

Descriptive notes. c. 29 cm; 213 g. Male has white forehead spotted brown, red crown and crest narrowly bordered black, broad white supercilium back to side of nape and sometimes meeting white of hindneck, broad black band through ear-coverts and down side of neck to side of upper breast, bordered below by white stripe from lores; white malar area enclosed by 2 thin black lines; white chin and throat with narrow black central line; white hindneck and mantle, black scapulars and back to uppertail-coverts, rump occasionally showing some yellowish feather edges; wing-coverts mostly olive-green with golden-yellow suffusion, golden tips and edges (occasionally tinged red); flight-feathers brownish-black, olive-yellow outer webs of secondaries and tertials, white spots on (usually) both webs; uppertail black; underparts white, black throatstripe breaking into streaks on foreneck and breast, narrower streaks on lower underparts; undertail-coverts often more barred; underwing dark grey, spotted white; very long bill almost straight, chisel-tipped, broad across nostrils, blackish; iris red to orange; legs green-grey. Female has crown and crest yellow, usually some brown at front and side. Juvenile as adult but duller, black areas browner, can show some red in rump, eyes brown, male with yellow crown with orange-red tips, female crown as adult but some orange in nape area. Race *tantus* is slightly smaller than nominate, has blackish forehead, broader black gular stripe, broader black streaks below. VOICE. Laughing rattle, "kwirri-rr-rr-rr-rr", like corresponding call of *C. lucidus* but weaker. Drums.

Habitat. Open deciduous woodland and scrub; also cultivations with scattered trees. Plantations around villages in the dry zone in Sri Lanka. Lowlands and foothills, to c. 1000 m.

Food and Feeding. Ants, and larvae of wood-boring insects; also seeds, seemingly indicating ingestion of fruits. Feeds singly or in pairs; sometimes family parties. Forages in lower strata, on tree trunks; occasionally on ground, especially at bare patches. Pecking and hammering seem to be major feeding techniques.

Breeding. Season varies regionally, generally Nov-Mar; in Sri Lanka, also in Aug-Sept. A new nest-hole excavated each year, by both sexes, at 2-7 m in tree or palm stump; entrance pear-shaped. Clutch usually only 1 egg, rarely 2 or 3; incubation by both parents, both also feeding chicks; incubation and fledging periods not documented; young accompanied by parents for a long time after fledging.

Movements. Resident.

Status and Conservation. Not globally threatened. Uncommon in Nepal; widespread and locally fairly common in India; scarce and local in Sri Lanka. Occurs in several protected areas, e.g. Corbett, Ranthambore, Rajiv Gandhi (Nagarhole) and Mudumalai National Parks (India) and Yala National Park (Sri Lanka).

Bibliography. Abdulali (1985), Ali (1996), Ali & Ripley (1983), Betts (1934), Daniels, R.J.R. (1997), Fleming & Traylor (1968), Gokula & Vijayan (1997), Grimmett *et al.* (1998, 2000), Harrison (1999), Henry (1998), Hoffmann (1998), Inskipp, C. & Inskipp (1991), Inskipp, T. *et al.* (1996), Kazmierczak (2000), Kirkpatrick (1960), Lamsfuss (1998), Neelakantan (1958), Phillips (1978), Ripley (1982), Shrestha (2000), Tirimanne (1978).

ssp *viridanus* ♂ 203

ssp *grantia* ♀

♀

♂ 204

♀ 205

♀

♂ 206

ssp *cameroni* ♂

♂ 207
ssp *sinensis* ♂

♂
♀
ssp *pyrrhotis* ♀

208

♂

♀
ssp *tristis*
♂

ssp *concretus*

209

♀

♂ 211

♀

ssp *grammithorax* ♂

210

♂ 212
ssp *sordidus*

213
♂

PLATE 48

inches 3
cm 8

Genus *GECINULUS* Blyth, 1845

203. **Pale-headed Woodpecker**
Gecinulus grantia

French: Pic grantia   **German**: Blassscheitel-Bambusspecht   **Spanish**: Pito del Bambú Norteño
Other common names: Bamboo Woodpecker (when lumped with *G. viridis*)

Taxonomy. *Picus (Chrysonotus) Grantia* McClelland, 1840, Assam.
Forms a superspecies with *G. viridis*, and the two are sometimes treated as conspecific. Three subspecies recognized.
Subspecies and Distribution.
G. g. grantia (McClelland, 1840) - E Nepal E to N, C & S Myanmar and S China (W Yunnan).
G. g. indochinensis Delacour, 1927 - SW Yunnan, NW Thailand, Laos and Vietnam.
G. g. viridanus Slater, 1897 - SE China (N Guangdong, Fujian).

Descriptive notes. 25-27 cm; 68-85 g. Male has greenish-yellow crown to nape and crest, central patch of red-tipped pinkish feathers reaching to upper nape; rest of head and neck buff-green to pale olive-brown, tinged yellow, darker and more olive on chin and throat; upper mantle dark olive, rest of upperparts, and secondaries and tertials, dull brownish-crimson; brown primaries narrowly edged dull red on outer webs, with broad buff bars; uppertail blackish-brown, edged reddish, variable broad buff barring; dark olive or brownish-olive below, sometimes browner in lower region; underwing brownish with faint barring, coverts mottled grey and whitish; undertail as above, with dull yellow-green cast; fairly long bill chisel-tipped, culmen slightly curved, broad across nostrils, pale horn-yellow to whitish or pale ivory, grey or greenish base; iris red or reddish-brown; legs olive-green, 3 toes. Female has forehead to nape yellow-green, yellower at rear. Juvenile resembles female but darker, upperparts dark brown, underparts very dark brown to grey-brown. Races differ mainly in colour of upperparts and crown pattern: *indochinensis* is duller red above than nominate, greyer and less yellow on side of head, more sooty-brown, less olive, below, has dull buffish wingbars continuing over secondaries, male with crown patch more pinkish, less crimson; *viridanus* is bigger, with proportionately longer tail, shorter bill, even less red than previous, more olive above and grey-brown below, male's crown patch dull pink. VOICE. Nasal "chaik-chaik-chaik-chaik" or "kwéek kwek-kwek", 4-5 times in succession, accelerating and becoming lower towards end; loud castanet-like rattles, "kereki kereki kereki kereki", when agitated; also series of "kwee-kwee" notes. Drums, fast steady rolls of medium length.
Habitat. Inhabits evergreen forest, semi-deciduous forest, secondary mixed bamboo forest, secondary forest and scrub; bamboo is particularly favoured. Occurs up to 1200 m, but usually found below 1000 m.
Food and Feeding. Mainly ants, larvae of beetles, and other insects. Often in pairs or small family parties. Forages mainly in lower levels, on trunks of smaller trees, and particularly on large bamboo. Rarely visits canopy, fallen logs or ground.
Breeding. Mar-May. Nest-cavity excavated 1-6 m up in dead tree, rotten stump or bamboo. Clutch 3 eggs. No other information.
Movements. Resident.
Status and Conservation. Not globally threatened. Very rare in Nepal, only few records (from E), where not discovered until 1974; uncommon in India and Bhutan; rare, perhaps extinct, in Bangladesh, only 1 recent record; rare to uncommon in SE Asia; uncommon in China. Occurs in Manas Wildlife Sanctuary in Bhutan, and in Nam Bai Cat Tien National Park, in Vietnam. Habitat loss could become a problem for this species, which appears to be dependent on certain environmental features, especially bamboo.
Bibliography. Ali & Ripley (1983), Ali *et al.* (1996), Bangs & Van Tyne (1931), Choudhury (2001), Delacour (1951b), Delacour & Jabouille (1940), Duckworth *et al.* (1999), Eames & Robson (1992), Étchécopar & Hüe (1978), Evans & Timmins (1998), Grimmett *et al.* (1998, 2000), Harvey (1990), Inskipp, C. & Inskipp (1991), Inskipp, C. *et al.* (1999), Inskipp, T. *et al.* (1996), Kazmierczak (2000), King *et al.* (2001), Lekagul & Round (1991), MacKinnon & Phillipps (2000), Ripley (1982), Robson (2000), Robson *et al.* (1993a), Round (1988), Shrestha (2000), Smythies (1986), Stepanyan (1995), Thewlis *et al.* (1998), Thompson *et al.* (1993), Zhao Zhengjie (1995).

204. **Bamboo Woodpecker**
Gecinulus viridis

French: Pic des bambous   **German**: Rotscheitel-Bambusspecht   **Spanish**: Pito del Bambú Sureño

Taxonomy. *Gecinulus viridis* Blyth, 1862, Toungou, south Myanmar.
Forms a superspecies with *G. grantia*, and the two are sometimes treated as conspecific. Birds from Peninsular Malaysia, tending to be a shade darker, with narrower wingbars, females also with more uniform crown and nape, are sometimes separated as race *robinsoni*; some individuals from northern populations, however, show similar variation, and recognition of geographical races seems unwarranted. Monotypic.
Distribution. S & SE Myanmar, Thailand (except C) and N Laos, S to Tenasserim and Peninsular Malaysia.
Descriptive notes. c. 25-26 cm. Male has red crown to nape, rest of head buff-brown, tinged yellow, more golden-green on rear crown side and neck side, darker and browner on chin; upperparts, including wing-coverts and tertials, dull yellowish-green with strong bronzy cast, rump and uppertail-coverts with dark crimson feather tips; primaries and secondaries dark brown, narrowly edged greenish on outer webs, rather ill-defined pale bars (sometimes stronger on primaries); uppertail blackish-brown,

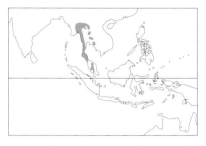

edged greenish; dark olive-brown below, very slightly paler in lowermost region; underwing brownish, faint barring, coverts mottled grey and whitish; undertail brown, dull yellowish cast; fairly long bill chisel-tipped, straight or culmen slightly curved, broad across nostrils, pale yellow to whitish, grey or greenish base; iris dark red or red-brown; legs olive-green, 3 toes. Female has crown dull greenish-yellow. Juvenile resemble adult female but darker, browner above, very dark and often grey-tinged below. VOICE. Single "bik" calls occasionally; most common is a dry rattle, changing in loudness and pitch, not in speed; also loud clear "keép-kee-kee-kee-kee-kee-kee", c. 3 notes per second; "kweek-week-week-week-week", "wee-a-wee-a-wee" or similar during encounters. Drums in loud bursts lasting c. 1 second.
Habitat. Evergreen and deciduous forest with extensive clusters of large bamboo. Lowlands in N of range, 600-1400 m farther S.
Food and Feeding. Ants. Feeds singly or in pairs, mainly at lower levels; only occasionally descends to ground. Forages mainly on live or dead bamboo; gleans, and probes into fractures, crevices, cracks and holes. Pecking is light, not sustained for long, producing very small round holes just above nodes of stalks; moves between nodes by gliding along the smooth surface while clasping around the stalk. Movements slow and deliberate, searches substrate carefully.
Breeding. Apr-May. Nest excavated at up to 5 m in bamboo, above a node, cavity c. 25 cm deep. No other details known.
Movements. Resident.
Status and Conservation. Not globally threatened. Generally uncommon and local, depending on habitat availability; discontinuous distribution. Occurs in Nam Nao and Kaeng Krachan National Parks and Khao Nor Chuchi Reserve (Thailand). This species' specialized habitat requirements could make it vulnerable to extensive changes in the environment. Habitat loss could become a major problem for this woodpecker.
Bibliography. Deignan (1945), Delacour & Jabouille (1940), Duckworth (1996), Duckworth *et al.* (1999), Inskipp *et al.* (1996), Jeyarajasingam & Pearson (1999), Lekagul & Round (1991), Lewin (1954), Medway & Wells (1976), Riley (1938), Robinson & Kloss (1921-1924), Robson (2000), Round (1988), Short (1973d), Wells (1985, 1999).

Genus *SAPHEOPIPO* Hargitt, 1890

205. **Okinawa Woodpecker**
Sapheopipo noguchii

French: Pic d'Okinawa   **German**: Okinawaspecht   **Spanish**: Pito de Okinawa
Other common names: Pryer's Woodpecker

Taxonomy. *Picus noguchii* Seebohm, 1887, Okinawa, Ryukyu Islands.
Monotypic.
Distribution. Okinawa, in S Ryukyus.

Descriptive notes. 31-35 cm. Male has forehead to nape red with blackish feather bases visible, pale buffish-brown nasal tufts, lores and line above eye, darker and browner ear-coverts and neck side with deep brown streaking, suggestion of darker stripe in malar region; chin to upper breast paler grey-brown, hint of whitish coloration; hindneck and upperparts rich dark brown, dull red feather tips, these most obvious on rump and uppertail-coverts; upperwing very dark brown, flight-feathers edged reddish, small white bar-like spots on outer primaries and on inner webs of inner primaries and secondaries; uppertail blackish-brown; dark brown below, feathers tipped dull red, more extensively reddish (larger tips) on belly and flanks, almost entirely deep red on undertail-coverts; underwing brown, flight-feathers barred whitish; undertail brown, paler sides; long bill strongly chisel-tipped, slightly curved on culmen, broad across nostrils, pale yellow, greener base; iris deep red-brown or brown; legs dark slaty. Female is slightly shorter-winged, shorter-billed, has forehead to nape blackish-brown, sometimes some paler feather bases showing. Juvenile duller and greyer than adult, red tips absent or much reduced, male with less red on head top. VOICE. Long irregular series of clear whistled notes, "kwe kwe kwe" or "pwip pwip", rather similar to calls of *Picus viridis* or *P. awokera*; also common are several "kup" notes, "kyu-kyu", or "kyu-kyu-kup" calls; single "whit" notes when disturbed; nestlings have 2 distinct types of note, "kyaa" and "pip". Drumrolls vary greatly in length, from c. 0·5 seconds to more than 1 second, accelerating, rhythm slightly slower than those of *Picus canus*, c. 3 rolls per minute.
Habitat. Occupies undisturbed, mature subtropical evergreen broadleaf forest in C mountain range of Yambaru; occasionally seen in secondary forest outside main range. On hilltops with large trees, down to forest edge along clearings or roads. Areas with soft, decaying wood preferred; conifers appear to be avoided.
Food and Feeding. Large arthropods, beetle larvae (e.g. Cerambycidae), moths, spiders, centipedes; observed feeding gecko to nestlings. Fruits, berries and seeds (*Rhus*, *Rubus*), acorns and other nuts (*Pasania*, *Machilus*) also important in diet. Forages chiefly near the ground, mostly below 5 m, where it searches tree trunks, bamboo and fallen logs; also in canopy, especially when

feeding on fruits. Prefers very soft and rotten wood. Pecking and hammering very important techniques; makes deep excavations, about 4 cm in length, on larger trunks, branches and stumps; smaller fallen branches hacked to pieces. Some of the forceful foraging methods resemble digging rather than excavating; creates smaller holes in harder live wood and bamboo. Also, frequently forages with probing, and sweeping aside litter.

Breeding. Laying from late Feb to May, typically in Mar-Apr; nestlings present up to Jun. Nest-hole excavated in large old tree at least 20 cm in diameter, often a hollow *Castanopsis cuspidata*, at 3-9 m, frequently on underside of a large sloping branch; entrance hole ovate; nests often reused. Clutch size not recorded; 1-3 chicks raised per brood.

Movements. Resident.

Status and Conservation. CRITICAL. Restricted-range species: present in Nansei Shoto EBA. Extremely small breeding population estimated at a maximum of 70-80 individuals in early 1990's, and total numbers, including non-breeders, thought not to exceed 584 individuals, and possibly fewer than 150. As long ago as 1930's was thought to be close to extinction. Breeding now restricted to subtropical evergreen forest along ridges in C mountain chain of Yamburu, mainly between the peaks of Nishime-take and Iyu-take. Formerly more widespread, but has lost much of its habitat during the past century. Decline attributed primarily to deforestation; requires forest 30 years or more of age, with tall trees at least 20 cm in diameter, all of which has long since been destroyed on the lower slopes. Logging operations have also penetrated upper parts of Yamburu. With constant and increasing pressure on existing habitat, associated with dam-construction, agricultural development and building of golf courses, as well as associated road-building, old forest continues to be destroyed. In addition, with its tiny range and extremely small population, this species is vulnerable to disease, and to natural disasters such as typhoons. Occurs in small protected areas on each of the mountains at extremes of range, as well as in protected area of Mt Yonaha; in NE Okinawa, estimated density of 12·1 birds/km² in the US Forces Northern Training Area offers some hope for its future survival. Although this picid is legally protected in Japan, and Yambaru was designated as a national park in 1996, further action is still needed. Conservationists have already purchased some sites known to be inhabited by the species; special protected areas need to be established to include all mature forest with an age of 40 years or more, logging in forest over 25 years of age should be prohibited. Further measures proposed include planting of forest "corridors" to connect forest fragments, and provision of nestboxes in secondary forest. A conservation programme, using this woodpecker and the Endangered Okinawa Rail (*Gallirallus okinawae*) as examples, has been suggested as a means of informing public opinion.

Bibliography. Andreev *et al.* (2001), Azama (1995), Azama & Shimabukuro (1984), Azama, Shimabukuro & Takehara (1990), Azama, Shimabukuro, Takehara, Harato & Tamaki (1992), Brazil (1985, 1991), Bruce (1975), Collar (1987), Collar & Andrew (1988), Collar *et al.* (1994), Greenway (1967), Hachisuka & Udagawa (1953), Ichida (1997), Ikehara (1975, 1988), Ikehara *et al.* (1976), Inskipp *et al.* (1996), Ishida (1989), Ito *et al.* (2000), King (1978/79), Kinjo (1992), Knox & Walters (1994), Miyagi (1989), Nackejima (1973), Ogasawara & Ikehara (1977), Short (1973a), Sonobe (1982), Stattersfield & Capper (2000), Yamashina (1941).

Genus *BLYTHIPICUS* Bonaparte, 1854

206. Maroon Woodpecker

Blythipicus rubiginosus

French: Pic poephyroïde **German**: Maronenspecht **Spanish**: Pito Herrumbroso

Taxonomy. *Hemicircus rubiginosus* Swainson, 1837, western Africa; error = Malacca.
Birds from Sumatra and Borneo described as race *parvus*, on average slightly smaller than N ones, but overlap considerable, and minor variations in plumage considered insufficient to warrant racial separation. Monotypic.

Distribution. S Myanmar (S Tenasserim) and SW Thailand S to Sumatra and Borneo.

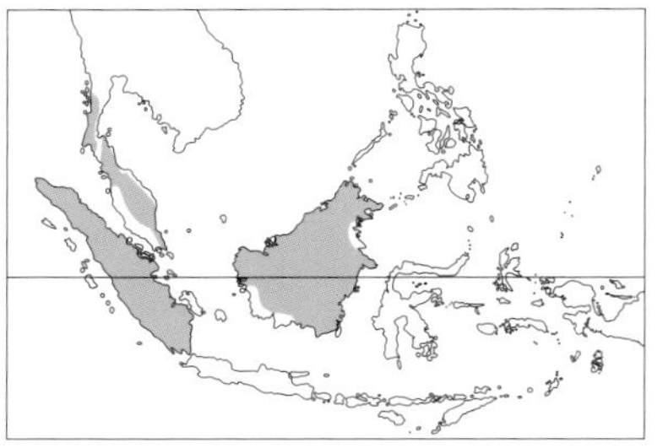

Descriptive notes. 23 cm; 64-92 g. Male has dull olive-brown head, paler feather tips on forehead, crimson tips on side of nape, often also of hindcrown and occasionally in malar region; upperparts brown with dull reddish-chestnut suffusion, a few obscure bars near bases of feathers, bars more numerous on rump and tail-coverts; wing-coverts dull brownish-red, often a few indistinct pale chevrons towards tips; flight-feathers dark brown, edged and tipped dull reddish, indistinct narrow buffish bars; uppertail dark brown, faintly barred slightly paler; throat dull brown, darker sooty-brown to blackish remaining underparts, sometimes a few reddish-tipped feathers on breast; underwing dull brown; long bill straight, chisel-tipped, broad across nostrils, pale yellow to yellowish-white or deeper yellow, dark greenish base; iris deep red or brownish-red, orbital skin blue; legs grey to blackish. Female has shorter bill, lacks crimson on head, often having dull reddish tinge on hindcrown and nape, sometimes barring on flight-feathers more prominent. Juvenile much as adult, but upperparts dull orangey rather than dull red, eyes brown, more red on crown, male with redder nape than adult. Voice. Metallic "pit", "pyick" or "kyuk" notes; sometimes double "kik kik" or "chikick", second syllable markedly higher in pitch; also, wavering sequence of 6-14 higher-pitched call-note elements, "kik-kik-kik-kik-kik-kik", slowing a little; loud descending series of 7-11 or more longer "chai" notes.

Habitat. Understorey of primary and secondary evergreen forest, second growth, bamboo, and rubber plantations; favours primary forest with dense undergrowth, as e.g. along small watercourses. Mainly lowlands; to 900 m in Thailand, to 1800 m elsewhere in SE Asia, and to 2200 m in Sumatra and Borneo.

Food and Feeding. Beetle larvae and other insect larvae form bulk of diet. Feeds singly or in pairs. Forages in very low strata, usually below 6 m, moving along ground, climbing only a few metres up trees. Forages on live trees, rotten snags, and fallen decaying logs of all sizes. Hammers with bill into rotten wood, breaking it into pieces. Moss or other debris removed from trunk, and medium-sized pits 2-3 cm deep, to 7 cm long, are rapidly excavated.

Breeding. Dec-May in Malaysia, and nests found in Jan in uplands of Borneo; season probably extends to Aug. Crest-raising and wing-flicking are only displays described. Nest-site may be at edge of dense forest. No other information.

Movements. Resident.

Status and Conservation. Not globally threatened. Common in Thailand, common in Peninsular Malaysia, and common in Sumatra and Borneo. Occurs in several protected areas, including Khao Nor Chuchi Reserve (Thailand), Taman Negara National Park (Peninsular Malaysia), Kerinci-Seblat and Way Kambas National Parks (Sumatra) and Gunung Mulu and Mount Kinabalu National Parks and Danum Valley Conservation Area (Borneo). Could be vulnerable to extensive logging.

Bibliography. Andrew (1992), Bucknill & Chasen (1990), Castelletta *et al.* (2000), Chasen & Hoogerwerf (1941), Davison (1992), Duckworth & Kelsh (1988), Duckworth *et al.* (1997), Gibson-Hill (1949b), Jeyarajasingam & Pearson (1999), Lekagul & Round (1991), MacKinnon & Phillipps (1993), van Marle & Voous (1988), Medway & Wells (1976), Meyer de Schauensee & Ripley (1940), Pope (1997), Riley (1938), Robinson & Kloss (1918), Robson (2000), Short (1973d), Smythies (1986, 1999), Vowles & Vowles (1997), Wells (1985, 1999), Wilkinson, Dutson & Sheldon (1991), Wong (1985).

207. Bay Woodpecker

Blythipicus pyrrhotis

French: Pic à oreillons rouge **German**: Rotohrspecht **Spanish**: Pito Orejirrojo
Other common names: Red-eared Bay/Red-eared Rufous Woodpecker

Taxonomy. *Picus Pyrrhotis* Hodgson, 1837, Nepal.
Races intergrade in Vietnam. Population in Sichuan possibly a separate race; further study needed. Five subspecies recognized.

Subspecies and Distribution.
B. p. pyrrhotis (Hodgson, 1837) - Nepal E to SC China (S Sichuan, Yunnan), Laos and N Vietnam.
B. p. sinensis (Rickett, 1897) - SE China (Guizhou and Guangxi E to Fujian).
B. p. annamensis Kinnear, 1926 - highlands of S Vietnam.
B. p. hainanus (Ogilvie-Grant, 1899) - Hainan.
B. p. cameroni Robinson, 1928 - Peninsular Malaysia.

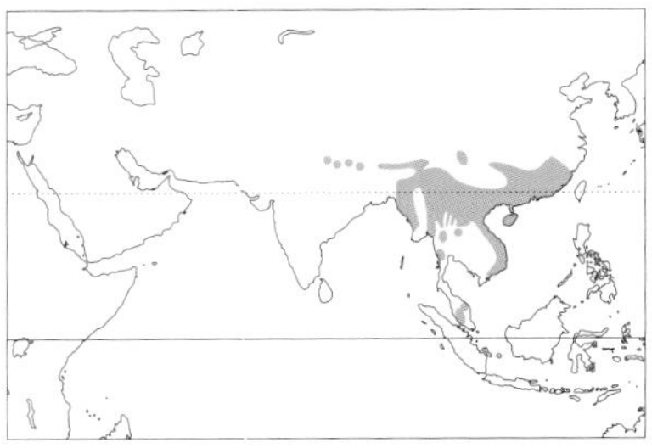

Descriptive notes. 30 cm; 126-170 g (*pyrrhotis*), 100-102 g (*cameroni*). Male has dull brown crown, short crest and nape with variable rufous or buff streaking, pale brownish-buff forehead, lores, chin and throat, slightly darker ear-coverts with pale streaks; side of neck bright crimson; upperparts dark brown to blackish with narrow dark rufous bars, very fine pale shaft streaks, pattern prominent in worn plumage (often obscured when fresh), rufous and blackish bars on uppertail-coverts; upperwing barred rufous and black; uppertail rufous, widely spaced narrow blackish bars, bars occasionally lacking; dark brown below with rusty tinge, usually inconspicuous narrow rusty bars on lower belly and lower flanks, deep rufous undertail-coverts barred black; long bill chisel-tipped, very broad-based, pale yellow or greenish-yellow, greyish-green base; iris red-brown, orbital skin blue; legs greyish-black with faint yellowish tinge. Female has shorter bill than male, pale head without red. Juvenile duller and darker below than adult, faintly rufous bars, more prominently barred above, head darker with prominent pale streaks, male with dull red on nape. Race *sinensis* is paler than nominate, often with narrow buff streaks on breast, bars on upperparts more cinnamon-rufous; *annamensis* is much darker below than last, almost blackish, usually without bars, much more rufous, less cinnamon, above, male with less red on head; *hainanus* is small, short-billed, browner, less sooty, below than previous; *cameroni* is very dark, male with little red on head. Voice. Long, dry rattle of up to 30 "pit" elements, faster than rattles of *B. rubiginosus*, change in tempo and pitch giving undulating quality, "dit-d-d-di-di-di--di-dit-d-d-di-di-di"; series of up to 24 long "kwaa" elements at c. 4 per second (slower than similar call of *B. rubiginosus*), dropping down scale, elements and intervals shorter at end; somewhat slower version of 9-13 "pee" notes, descending and accelerating, as contact between partners, probably also as territorial announcement, audible over great distances.

Habitat. Evergreen and mixed deciduous forest, and mixed bamboo forest, as found, for instance, in heavily wooded ravines; always in dense growth. Generally from 600 m to 2200 m; most common between 1500 m and 2500 m in Nepal, but also in valley bottoms; to 2750 m in Myanmar, and above 1000 m in Peninsular Malaysia; occasionally down to foothills in Thailand, even to 50 m in Vietnam (N Annam).

Food and Feeding. Diet consists of termites (Isoptera), ants, large larvae of wood-boring beetles, also various other insects; occasional berries. Normally singly; partners maintain only loose acoustic contact, do not forage close to each other. Most foraging (more than 50% of activities) concentrated within 3-4 m of ground, on trunks, rotting snags, logs, and on saplings, vines and bamboo, rarely ventures into periphery of tree crown; compared with *B. rubiginosus*, however, is less confined to lower strata of forest, extends more into middle storeys. Digs big holes into soft, rotten wood, probes into crevices; removes moss and other epiphytes to glean prey hidden beneath. Occasionally sallies to capture aerial prey.

Breeding. Mar-Jun. Only described displays are crest-raising and wing-flicking when calling. Nest-hole is low down, at 1-4 m, excavated by both sexes, in live or dead wood. Clutch 2 or 3 eggs, occasionally 4; parents share incubation and brood-feeding; incubation and fledging periods not documented.

Movements. Records outside breeding season at elevations down to 50 m indicate some vertical movements.

Status and Conservation. Not globally threatened. Generally uncommon, though locally common in parts of SE Asia; uncommon in China. Perhaps frequently overlooked as a result of its skulking habits, and because it frequents thick undergrowth, and it may in fact be more widespread than currently realized. Occurs in several protected areas, e.g. Namdapha and Dibru Saikhowa National Parks (India), Doi Inthanon and Kaeng Krachan National Parks (Thailand) and Wolong Reserve (China).

Bibliography. Ali & Ripley (1983), Ali *et al.* (1996), Bangs & Van Tyne (1931), Barua & Sharma (1999), Deignan (1945), Delacour (1951b), Duckworth & Hedges (1998), Eames (1995), Eames & Robson (1992), Edge (1993), Étchécopar & Hüe (1978), Evans & Timmins (1998), Grimmett *et al.* (1998), Harvey (1990), Hill (2001), Inskipp, C. (1989), Inskipp, C. & Inskipp (1991, 1993), Inskipp, T. *et al.* (1996), Jeyarajasingam & Pearson (1999), Lekagul & Round (1991), MacKinnon & Phillipps (2000), Madoc (1976), McClure (1964a), Medway & Wells (1976), Osmaston (1902), Riley (1938), Ripley (1982), Robson (2000), Robson *et al.* (1993a), Shankar Raman (2001), Short (1973d), Shrestha (2000), Smythies (1986), Stepanyan (1995), Tymstra *et al.* (1997), Wells (1999), Zhao Zhengjie (1995).

Genus *REINWARDTIPICUS* Bonaparte, 1854

208. **Orange-backed Woodpecker**

Reinwardtipicus validus

French: Pic vigoureux **German**: Reinwardtspecht **Spanish**: Pito Dorsinaranja

Taxonomy. *Picus validus* Temminck, 1825, Java.
In past, commonly placed in *Chrysocolaptes*. Races weakly differentiated, with much overlap in features. Two subspecies recognized.
Subspecies and Distribution.
R. v. xanthopygius (Finsch, 1905) - extreme S Thailand S to Sumatra and Borneo, including Riau Archipelago, Bangka I and N Natuna Is.
R. v. validus (Temminck, 1825) - Java.

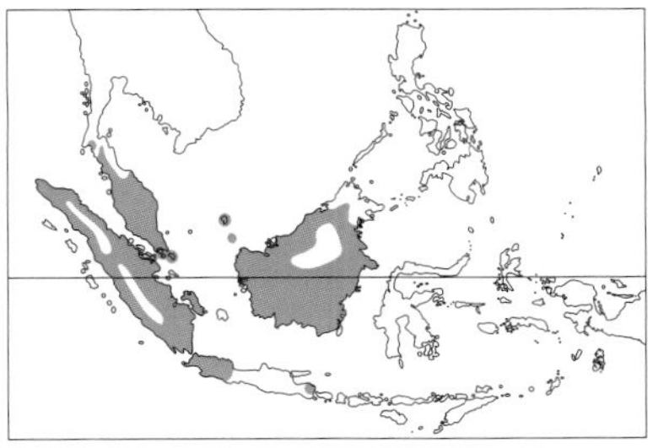

Descriptive notes. 30 cm; 155-185 g. Male has red forehead, crown and short crest bordered pale orange, orange-brown side of head, darker and browner towards rear; chin and malar area golden-brown; lower nape and hindneck white, bordered brownish-grey, mantle and back feathers extensively tipped yellow to orange, rump deeper orange to red with yellow-olive suffusion, variable brownish barring; uppertail-coverts dark brown to dull orange; scapulars and wing-coverts black-brown; flight-feathers blackish, 3-5 broad rufous-chestnut bars across all feathers, spots on primary coverts; uppertail very dark brown; side of neck, foreneck and most of underbody brown, broad deep red feather tips creating red appearance, narrowly edged yellowish on flanks and lower regions, ventral area grey-brown, dark brown on undertail-coverts and undertail; underwing barred brownish or cinnamon, coverts sometimes paler buffish and barred brown; long bill slightly curved, broad-based, distinct chisel tip, light brown, yellowish lower mandible; iris brownish to orange-red; legs brownish to grey. Female has forehead to nape and crest dark brown, side of head grey-brown, hindneck and upperparts white or off-white, rump brownish, narrow band on side of neck tinged rufous, foreneck and underparts dark grey-brown with obscure paler barring on flanks and belly. Juvenile much as female, but young male usually has some red on crown and often hint of yellow-orange on rump. Race *xanthopygius* usually has less red on rump of male than nominate (but much overlap between races), no brown barring on back and rump. Voice. Various loud, ringing calls, e.g. "pit", singly or in loose irregular series; slow regular "kit kit kit kit kit-it" series of c. 9 elements, terminating with double call rising sharply; other, higher-pitched, more irregular series may commence with lower note; much faster series of "pit" notes as rattle call; loud rapid "wheet-wheet-wheet-wheet-wheow" or "polleet, polleet" and excited "toweetit-toweetit, cha-cha" also described. Drums weakly, bursts very short.
Habitat. Primary or secondary evergreen rainforest, coastal vegetation, mature plantations; also along forest edge, and in clear-cuts with single dead trees. Lowlands, extending uncommonly to hilly country throughout range; below 1000 m in Thailand and Peninsular Malaysia, where most common below 700 m; in lowlands, occasionally in montane habitats to 2200 m, in Java; common in lowland forests of Borneo, where has also been found to 2000 m.
Food and Feeding. Beetle larvae, termites (Isoptera), caterpillars, ants and other insects. Lives in pairs and family parties. Forages in very low (rarely) and middle strata, and in canopy as well. Attacks rotting logs on the ground, also dead stumps, tree trunks and larger branches; even visits thin vines. Pecks and hammers with loud blows to excavate substrate, sometimes spends minutes to excavate at a single site. Often removes bark with lateral strokes, or quickly opens holes in bark. Moves rapidly along trunk and branches. Trees, stumps and logs searched systematically; tends not to move great distances between foraging locations.
Breeding. Jan-Sept; insufficient data on regional differences; in N Borneo (Sabah) nest with young in late Mar, another nest being built in Apr. Displays include crest-raising, bill-directing, wing-flicks, wing-spreading and swinging head movements, associated with many vocalizations. Nest-hole excavated c. 5 m up in dead tree. Clutch 1 or 2 eggs; incubation and fledging periods not documented; fledglings fed by parents directly, not by regurgitation.
Movements. Resident.
Status and Conservation. Not globally threatened. Uncommon or scarce in most of its range; rare in Java, but commoner in Sumatra and Borneo. Occurs in Khao Nor Chuchi Reserve (Thailand), Taman Negara National Park (Peninsular Malaysia), Gunung Leuser and Way Kambas National Parks (Sumatra), Gunung Gede-Pangrango National Park (Java) and Mount Kinabalu National Park (Borneo).
Bibliography. Andrew (1985, 1992), van Balen (1999), Bucknill & Chasen (1990), Castelletta *et al.* (2000), Duckworth & Kelsh (1988), Duckworth *et al.* (1997), Fogden (1970), Ford & Davison (1995), Holmes (1996), Hutchinson (1950), Inskipp *et al.* (1996), Jepson & Brinkman (1993), Jeyarajasingam & Pearson (1999), Lekagul & Round (1991), MacKinnon (1988), MacKinnon & Phillipps (1993), van Marle & Voous (1988), Medway & Wells (1976), Nash & Nash (1986, 1988), Pearson (1975a), Riley (1938), Robson (2000), Sargeant (1997), Short (1973d), Smythies (1999), Vowles & Vowles (1997), Wells (1985, 1999), Wilkinson, Dutson & Sheldon (1991).

Tribe MEIGLYPTINI

Genus *MEIGLYPTES* Swainson, 1837

209. **Buff-rumped Woodpecker**

Meiglyptes tristis

French: Pic strihup **German**: Braunbürzelspecht **Spanish**: Pito Triste
Other common names: Fulvous-rumped (Barred) Woodpecker

Taxonomy. *Picus tristis* Horsfield, 1821, Java.
Named races *micropterus* (Borneo) and *microterus* (Nias I) considered synonymous with *grammithorax*. Two subspecies recognized.
Subspecies and Distribution.
M. t. grammithorax (Malherbe, 1862) - S Myanmar (S Tenasserim) and peninsular Thailand S to Sumatra, including islands of Nias and Bangka, N Natunas, and Borneo (including Banggi I and islands off NE coast).
M. t. tristis (Horsfield, 1821) - Java.

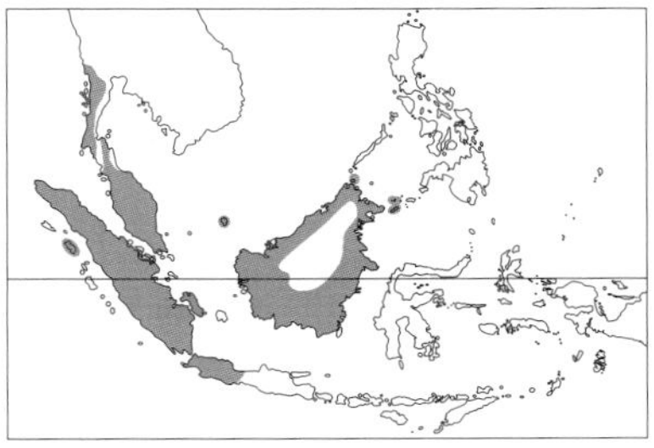

Descriptive notes. 17-18 cm; 31-50 g. Distinctive small, short-tailed woodpecker. Male has short red malar patch; rest of head, crest and neck to upper breast greyish-brown with narrow paler vermiculations, these are usually less pronounced or lacking in fore area, pale buff eyering, lores and area around bill base; upperparts barred blackish and white, rump creamy; upperwing black with white bars, broadest on covert tips and on inner webs of flight-feathers; uppertail black, thin whitish barring; lower breast and rest of underparts blackish, some white on flanks, sometimes a few bars; underwing blackish, buffish-white coverts; undertail brown, narrowly barred buff; longish bill narrow-based, rather pointed, culmen curved, black; iris deep brown; legs grey to greenish. Female lacks red malar. Juvenile as adult, but dark areas duller, more brownish, bars usually broader. Race *grammithorax* has much more buff plumage, and entire underparts closely barred. Voice. Single "pit" or "chit", also as double click or in loose series, from mildly excited birds or in flight; also much longer "pee", apparently as alarm; "wicka" calls in encounters between sexes recall similar vocalizations of American *Colaptes*; soft rattle, "drrrrrrrr", as long-distance communication, is higher-pitched than corresponding vocalization of *M. tukki*, can last over 2 seconds, has wavering quality (rises in pitch around middle). Drumming weak, 18 to over 40 beats at rate of 15 per second, faster at beginning, slower later, roll lasts for 1·5-3 seconds.
Habitat. Primary and secondary forests; found in rather open coastal habitats as well as in inland forest. Most common at forest edges, around clearings, in areas of second growth within forest, and in second growth. Also frequents mature rubber stands, and orchards. From lowlands to 600 m in Thailand, to 800 m in Peninsular Malaysia; to 1100 m in other parts of mainland SE Asia.
Food and Feeding. Ants, other insects. Often in pairs, members of which keep more or less in close contact; may join mixed-species flocks. Forages in canopy of tall trees, on twigs and distal ends of branches, and in saplings and smaller trees; feeding sites often several trees apart. Gleaning with occasional probing the commonest techniques, with food items gathered from bark and from tips and leaves of tiny twigs; rarely pecks, and then weakly. Moves rapidly, and frequently perches crosswise or hangs upside-down.
Breeding. Season not well known, Mar-Apr, probably to Jul. Both sexes display with head-swinging. Nest-hole excavated by both sexes, can be low, below 2 m, or higher up, 8-15 m, and in live tree or dead stump. Clutch 2 eggs; no details on incubation and fledging periods.
Movements. Resident.
Status and Conservation. Not globally threatened. Common to fairly common in most of range; however, extinct in Singapore. Nominate race of Java is rare, possibly extinct, with no recent records. Occurs in several protected areas, e.g. Khao Nor Chuchi Reserve (Thailand), Panti Forest Reserve (Peninsular Malaysia), Way Kambas National Park (Sumatra) and Danum Valley Conservation Area (Borneo).
Bibliography. Andrew (1992), van Balen (1999), Bucknill & Chasen (1990), Castelletta *et al.* (2000), Chasen & Hoogerwerf (1941), Duckworth & Kelsh (1988), Duckworth *et al.* (1997), Dymond (1994), Ford & Davison (1995), Hellebrekers & Hoogerwerf (1967), Holmes (1994), Jeyarajasingam & Pearson (1999), Lekagul & Round (1991), MacKinnon (1988), MacKinnon & Phillipps (1993), van Marle & Voous (1988), Medway & Wells (1976), Mees (1986), Meyer de Schauensee & Ripley (1940), Nash, A.D. & Nash (1985), Nash, S.V. & Nash (1988), Riley (1938), Robinson & Kloss (1924a), Robson (2000), Sargeant (1997), Short (1973d), Smythies (1986, 1999), Stresemann (1921a), Vowles & Vowles (1997), Wells (1985, 1999), Wilkinson, Dutson & Sheldon (1991).

210. **Black-and-buff Woodpecker**

Meiglyptes jugularis

French: Pic à jugulaire **German**: Dommelspecht **Spanish**: Pito Blanquinegro

Taxonomy. *Picus (Meiglyptes) jugularis* Blyth, 1845, Arakan and Tenasserim, Myanmar.
Monotypic.
Distribution. SW, S & E Myanmar, including Tenasserim, much of Thailand (except C), and Indochina except Tonkin.

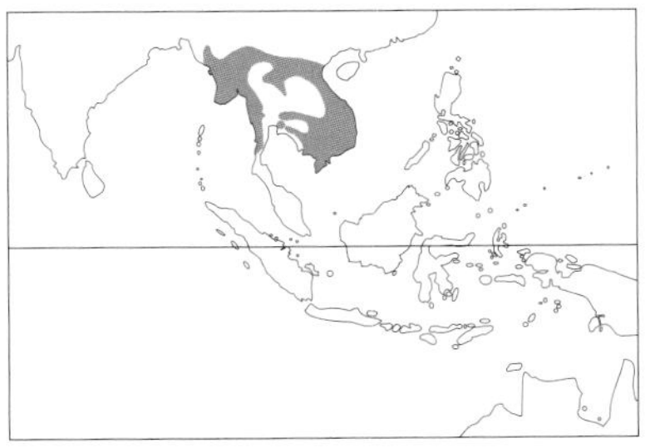

Descriptive notes. c. 22 cm; 50-57 g. Small, short-tailed woodpecker. Male has short malar stripe of dark red feather tips, often appearing barred red and black, lores mainly buff, often with black barring; rest of head black, narrowly barred pale buff, hindcrown and nape feathers plain black and elongated to form long crest; hindneck and side of neck creamy; upperparts black, mantle sometimes with a few pale bars, rump white to buffish-white, inner scapulars black, outers mainly white to pale cream-buff; upperwing mostly black, coverts tipped creamy, flight-feathers with thin white to buff bars, broader on inner webs, white to pale cream-buff tertials with prominent broad dark bars on distal parts, variable; uppertail black; throat black, variably barred buff, can appear chequered; rest of underparts black to brown-black, sometimes 2 or 3 whitish bars on lower flanks, rarely also on belly; underwing dusky, black tip and whitish bars, coverts creamy; fairly long bill narrow-based, slightly chisel-tipped, culmen strongly curved, black, often slightly paler base of lower mandible; iris brown; legs grey-green or grey-blue. Female lacks red in malar, which instead is barred black and buff. Juvenile as adult but duller, head more clearly barred. Voice. Nasal "ki-yew", and series as "tititi-wéek week week".
Habitat. Evergreen forest; often shows distinct preference for more open areas, such as edges and clearings, also bamboo; often seems to avoid dense forest. Lowlands, in forested areas to 900 m, occasionally 1000 m.

Food and Feeding. Ants, other insects. Feeds singly or in pairs; not noted in association with other species. Often hangs upside-down on small leafy twigs and branches in lower and middle storeys. Habits not well known, but appear to be similar to those of *M. tristis* and *Hemicircus canente*.
Breeding. Mar-Jun. No other information.
Movements. Resident.
Status and Conservation. Not globally threatened. Uncommon to locally fairly common. Occurs in Khao Yai and Kaeng Krachan National Parks and Khao Nor Chuchi Reserve (Thailand), and in Nam Bai Cat Tien National Park (Vietnam). Poorly known. Research required to determine its feeding ecology and breeding biology.
Bibliography. Deignan (1945), Delacour & Jabouille (1940), Duckworth *et al.* (1999), Eames & Ericson (1996), Eames & Robson (1992), Evans & Timmins (1998), Lekagul & Round (1991), Riley (1938), Robson (2000), Robson *et al.* (1993a), Smythies (1986), Stepanyan (1995), Wheatley (1996).

211. Buff-necked Woodpecker

Meiglyptes tukki

French: Pic tukki **German**: Tukkispecht **Spanish**: Pito Tukki
Other common names: Buff-necked Barred Woodpecker

Taxonomy. *Picus tukki* Lesson, 1839, Sumatra.
N Natunas population, sometimes separated as race *azaleus*, may show more obscure barring, but much variation and separation not warranted; similarly, described race *calceuticus* (Banyak Is, off NW Sumatra) appears indistinguishable from nominate. Five subspecies recognized.
Subspecies and Distribution.
M. t. tukki (Lesson, 1839) - S Myanmar (S Tenasserim) and peninsular Thailand S to Sumatra, nearby Banyak Is, Bangka, N Natunas and N Borneo.
M. t. infuscatus Salvadori, 1887 - Nias I (off NW Sumatra).
M. t. batu Meyer de Schauensee & Ripley, 1940 - Batu Is (off NW Sumatra).
M. t. pulonis Chasen & Kloss, 1929 - Banggi I (off N Borneo).
M. t. percnerpes Oberholser, 1924 - S Borneo.

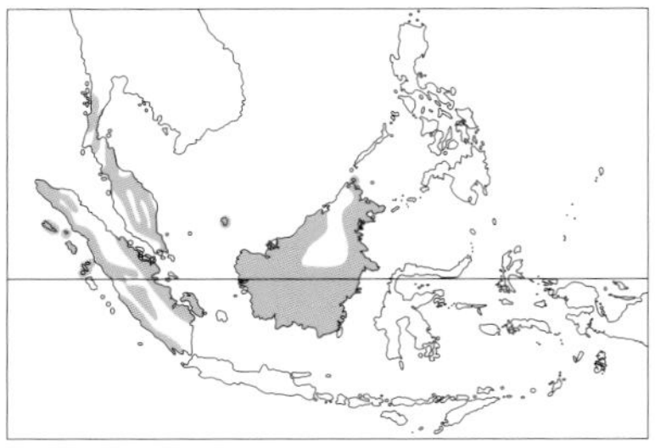

Descriptive notes. c. 21 cm; 43-64 g. Male has red malar patch barred black and buffy at rear, large buffish-white or yellowish-buff patch from lower edge of rear ear-coverts to rear throat side; rest of head, including short crest, dark grey-brown or olive-brown, forehead often slightly paler or, rarely, with hint of red, sometimes somewhat darker indistinct eyestripe; chin and throat barred blackish-brown and buff; entire upperparts and uppertail dull dark olive-brown, all narrowly barred buff, wing-coverts occasionally edged dull red; flight-feathers dark brown, narrowly barred buff, bars broader and paler (whitish) on inner webs; lower throat and upper breast blackish-brown, sometimes obscured by barring; rest of underparts brown, narrowly barred buff, bars slightly broader on flanks, often only vague on belly centre; underwing brown, pale coverts and bases of flight-feathers; moderately long bill fairly narrow-based, pointed, culmen strongly curved, black, paler lower mandible; iris deep crimson, red-brown or brown; legs grey-green to grey-brown. Female lacks red in malar region. Juvenile has pale bars broader, dark throat patch less well defined, male with reddish malar, sometimes red tips to forehead and, less often, crown feathers. Race *percnerpes* is strongly barred, browner, without olive tinges, often with more rusty or reddish tone than nominate; *batu* has blackish crown, more contrasting blackish breast patch; *pulonis* is much longer-billed than others, also browner than nominate, less olive, with paler throat; *infuscatus* is slightly shorter-winged than others, also barring weak, pale bars tending to be obscured, dark crown. Voice. Single "pee" calls like those of *M. tristis*, also series of "dwit" or "ki-ti" and "wick-wick-wick-wick" during encounters; commonest vocalization is high-pitched trill, "kirr-r-r", lower in pitch, longer and slower than that of *M. tristis*. Both sexes drum, single roll may last less than 1 second or over 3 seconds and contain from c. 12 to almost 60 beats, initial section of longer bouts and shorter bouts delivered at faster rate than the final one.
Habitat. Primary and tall secondary evergreen and semi-evergreen forest with dense undergrowth and rotting stumps; also peatswamp-forest. Less often at forest edges and clearings than *M. tristis*. Lowlands; generally below 600 m, occasionally to 1200 m, in mainland SE Asia; reaches 1000 m in Greater Sundas.
Food and Feeding. Ants and termites (Isoptera). Feeds singly, in small groups, or in pairs, partners sometimes staying in close contact, even feeding side by side; regularly joins mixed-species flocks. Generally forages in middle and lower strata of forest, often comes down into low bushes and saplings, visiting overgrown gulleys and similar; altogether, exploits more diverse sites than does *M. tristis*. Higher strata visited mainly when with other birds. Forages on branch tips and leaf buds in crown of tall trees, also visits larger branches and trunks and decayed logs of the understorey. Predominant foraging technique is gleaning; some probing, pecking and working at dead wood. Movements rapid; in most cases, spends only little time at a single spot or tree.
Breeding. Feb-Jul; May-Jun in Peninsular Malaysia; young found in early Jun in Borneo. Head-swinging displays. Nest built in rotten wood in live tree, or low in tree stump, at 1·5-5 m. Clutch 2 eggs; chicks fed by both parents, apparently by regurgitation; no details of incubation and fledging periods. Recorded longevity 5 years, 3 months.
Movements. Resident.
Status and Conservation. Not globally threatened. Currently considered Near-threatened. Uncommon to fairly common in continental range; perhaps commoner elsewhere. Occurs in Taman Negara National Park (Peninsular Malaysia) and Kerinci-Seblat and Way Kambas National Parks (Sumatra); fairly common in Danum Valley Conservation Area (Borneo). Within this species' range, massive destruction of lowland forest has already taken place, especially in the Sundas, where primary forest is likely to have disappeared by 2010; significant habitat loss also a major problem in Thailand and Peninsular Malaysia. Although it appears to have a reasonable population in the higher parts of its range, and can also be found in secondary growth, extension of deforestation to more elevated parts of the region could quickly place this woodpecker, as well as many other wildlife species, at considerable risk.
Bibliography. Andreev *et al.* (2001), Andrew (1992), Bucknill & Chasen (1990), Castelletta *et al.* (2000), Chasen (1937), Chasen & Hoogerwerf (1941), Duckworth & Kelsh (1988), Duckworth *et al.* (1997), Dymond (1994), Holmes (1994, 1996), Inskipp *et al.* (1996), Jepson & Brinkman (1993), Jeyarajasingam & Pearson (1999), Lekagul & Round (1991), MacKinnon (1988), MacKinnon & Phillipps (1993), van Marle & Voous (1988), Medway & Wells (1976), Mees (1986), Nash & Nash (1988), Riley (1938), Robinson & Kloss (1924a), Robson (2000), Short (1973d), Smythies (1986, 1999), Stattersfield & Capper (2000), Vowles & Vowles (1997), Wells (1985, 1999), Wilkinson, Dutson & Sheldon (1991), Wong (1985).

Genus *HEMICIRCUS* Swainson, 1837

212. Grey-and-buff Woodpecker

Hemicircus concretus

French: Pic trapu **German**: Kurzschwanzspecht **Spanish**: Pito Colicorto
Other common names: Grey-breasted Woodpecker(!)

Taxonomy. *Picus concretus* Temminck, 1821, Java.
Sumatra and Borneo populations named as race *coccometopus*, but insufficiently different from *sordidus* to warrant separation. Two subspecies recognized.
Subspecies and Distribution.
H. c. sordidus (Eyton, 1845) - S Myanmar (S Tenasserim) and peninsular Thailand S to Sumatra (including N Mentawai I and Bangka I), and Borneo.
H. c. concretus (Temminck, 1821) - W & C Java.

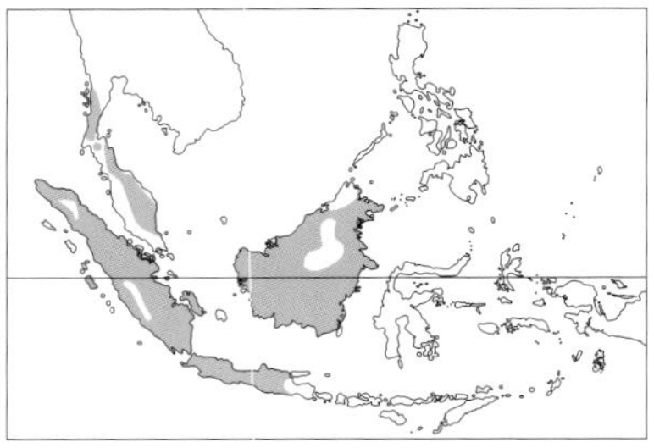

Descriptive notes. 13-14 cm; 27-32 g. Very small and compact woodpecker, with slender neck, large head and extremely short, rounded tail. Male has red forehead, crown and crest; rest of head and neck dark grey, apart from whitish hindneck and thin pale line on malar area and down side of neck; upperparts dark brownish-black, feathers broadly edged and tipped buffish-white to white, rump whitish (normally stained buff by glandular secretion), black uppertail-coverts tipped white; tertials black with whitish edges and tips, or whitish with large black heart-shaped spots; flight-feathers black, inner webs of primaries edged buffish-white, secondaries with a few whitish bars; uppertail black, sometimes paler bars on outer feathers; grey of head and neck extends over underparts, blacker in lower region, variably barred buffish on flanks and undertail-coverts; underwing blackish, buff patch at base of primaries, coverts buffish or barred black and white; longish bill straight, chisel-tipped, rather broad base, greyish-black; iris red-brown; legs dark brown. Female has shorter bill than male, has top of head dark grey, not red. Juvenile has broader and more rufous edges and tips above, underparts more heavily barred with pale rufous-buff, top of head cinnamon-rufous with narrow black tips, male with orange-red crest, female with less red. Race *sordidus* is slightly smaller and paler grey than nominate, has rear of crest grey, not red; juvenile has buff crown. Voice. Sharp "chick", "pit" or "tsip", slightly higher-pitched and louder than calls of *Meiglyptes tristis*; similar but longer "peew", "ki-oo", "ki-yow", or "kee-yew" notes, barely distinguishable from corresponding calls of *H. canente*, during encounters; vibrating "chitterr" in agonistic situations and during aerial chases. Drums weakly.
Habitat. Evergreen forest, especially evergreen secondary forest, forest edge, also gardens and plantations; seems to favour habitat with bamboo. To 1100 m in SE Asia, up to 1500 m in Borneo.
Food and Feeding. Insects; fruits, such as lime and mistletoe (*Loranthus*), also recorded in diet. Singly, in pairs, sometimes in groups (up to 10 individuals observed together); also joins mixed-species flocks. Forages in treetops, among twigs and leaves, as well as on trunks and branches; attracted to trees projecting above the rest of the vegetation, even when isolated in open area. Occasionally in bushes. Main foraging technique is gleaning; frequently pecks, too, more so than *Meiglyptes*; also pries off bark, and probes. Usually moves rapidly in dense foliage of the canopy, flits between twigs, branches and leaf clusters; hops, twists, peers under leaves, clings like tit (Paridae) to twigs and fruits. When moving along trunks, darts about in all directions, can move almost straight downwards, head first. Possible sexual differences in foraging in terms of micro-habitat selection and relative use of foraging techniques, but insufficiently documented. Flies long distances, including over open areas, between feeding sites.
Breeding. Dec-Jul; apparently Apr-Jul in Peninsular Malaysia, and May-Jun in Java. Crest-raising is commonest display. Nest-hole excavated in tree, at heights between 9 m and 30 m. No other information.
Movements. Resident.
Status and Conservation. Not globally threatened. Uncommon throughout most of range; locally common in Sumatra, possibly also Borneo; extinct Singapore. Occurs in Khao Nor Chuchi Reserve (Thailand) and Way Kambas National Park (Sumatra). Poorly known; requires field study.
Bibliography. Andrew (1992), van Balen (1999), van Balen & Prentice (1978), Bucknill & Chasen (1990), Castelletta *et al.* (2000), Duckworth & Kelsh (1988), Duckworth *et al.* (1997), Ford & Davison (1995), Grantham (2000), Hellebrekers & Hoogerwerf (1967), Holmes (1994), Inskipp *et al.* (1996), Jensen & Bahr (2000), Jeyarajasingam & Pearson (1999), Lekagul & Round (1991), MacKinnon (1988), MacKinnon & Phillipps (1993), van Marle & Voous (1988), Medway & Wells (1976), Mees (1986), Meyer de Schauensee & Ripley (1940), Nash, A.D. & Nash (1985), Nash, S.V. & Nash (1988), Riley (1938), Robinson & Kloss (1924a), Robson (2000), Sargeant (1997), Short (1973d), Smythies (1986, 1999), Stresemann (1921a), Vowles & Vowles (1997), Wells (1985, 1990, 1999), Wilkinson, Dutson & Sheldon (1991).

213. Heart-spotted Woodpecker

Hemicircus canente

French: Pic canente **German**: Rundschwanzspecht **Spanish**: Pito de Corazones

Taxonomy. *Picus canente* Lesson, 1830, Pegu, Myanmar.
Clinal increase in size from SW to NE India, but differences negligible; individual variation fairly marked, but no significant geographical pattern; as a result, proposed race *cordatus* (W India) is unsustainable. Monotypic.
Distribution. W & NE peninsular India, Bangladesh; and from SW, S & E Myanmar, and S Annam, S to S Thailand, Cambodia, and Cochinchina.
Descriptive notes. 15-16 cm; 37-50 g. Very small, compact wodpecker with thin neck, large head with prominent crest, and strikingly short and rounded tail. Male has black head and hindneck,

very small white spots or speckles on fore-head and forecrown; throat and side of neck white, tinged buff or cream, olive-grey or buffish-grey on lower throat and breast; upperparts except rump black, sometimes some white bars on back or uppertail-coverts, rump white or off-white (special gland pro-duces secretion causing buff staining); inner scapulars black, outer scapulars, tertials, lesser and median coverts and variable number of inner greater coverts white to buffish-white with large, black heart-shaped marks, remain-ing coverts black with thin white edges and tips; flight-feathers black, narrowly edged white on inner webs; uppertail black; belly and undertail-coverts black (sometimes very nar-rowly barred), rarely entire underparts, including breast, black; underwing blackish, white cov-erts and base of primaries; long bill relatively slender but broad-based, with chisel tip, dark brown to blackish; iris brown to dull red-brown; legs brown, or tinged greenish. Female has shorter bill and shorter wing than male, and also differs in having white or buffish-white forehead and forecrown. Juvenile similar to adult female, but pale areas more buffy, less white, forehead often partly barred black, usually darker below, including throat, but always at least some white on side of neck. VOICE. Squeaky nasal "ki-yew", "chirrick" or "ch-yew", emphasis on second syllable, repeated several times, very like corresponding call of *H. concretus*; also, high-pitched "kee-kee-kee-kee" and long-drawn grating "chur-r"; "su-sie" notes in display. Drums weakly, infrequently.

Habitat. Moist and dense deciduous and evergreen forests, at forest edge, in secondary forest, bamboo, and open deciduous forest; particularly fond of bamboo and coffee plantations (and teak) in W of range, and shows similar liking for bamboo in Cochinchina. Lowlands, from plains up to 900 m and 1000 m in SE Asia, to 1300 m in India.

Food and Feeding. Ants, termites (Isoptera), larvae, and other insects comprise bulk of diet. Usu-ally singly or in pairs, or in mixed-species parties. Forages on twigs in canopy, also on trunks and higher dead branches; gleans, pecks and hammers. Often perches crosswise on twig; moves rapidly along twigs and branches. Observed pecking holes in dry pods of *Cassia fistula* to extract insect larvae. Significant morphological differences between the sexes suggest differences in foraging behaviour, but no quantitative data exist.

Breeding. Nov-Apr. Displays with bowing or bobbing movements and associated vocalizations. Tiny nest-hole excavated in dead branch, occasionally fence post, usually low down, 1-4 m, but occasionally much higher, to 12 m or more. Clutch 3 eggs, less commonly 2; no other information.

Movements. Resident.

Status and Conservation. Not globally threatened. Sparsely distributed in India, locally more fre-quent; no recent records from Bangladesh, last recorded in 1984, possibly extinct; fairly common in SE Asia. Occurs in numerous protected areas, e.g. Indira Gandhi and Periyar National Parks and Thunakadavu Reserve (India), Khao Yai, Nam Nao and Kaeng Krachan National Parks (Thailand) and Nam Bai Cat Tien National Park (Vietnam).

Bibliography. Ali (1951a, 1996), Ali & Ripley (1983), Betts (1934), Bock & Short (1971), Champion-Jones (1938), Chazee (1994), Deignan (1945), Delacour & Jabouille (1940), Eames (1995), Eames & Robson (1992), Evans & Timmins (1998), Goes (1999), Gokula & Vijayan (1997), Grimmett *et al*. (1998), Harvey (1990), Inglis (1931), Kannan (1998), Kazmierczak (2000), Lainer (1999), Lekagul & Round (1991), Meyer de Schauensee (1946b), Riley (1938), Ripley (1982), Robson (2000), Robson *et al*. (1993a), Santharam (1998b, 1998c), Short (1973d), Smythies (1986), Stepanyan (1995), Thompson *et al*. (1993), Wells (1999).

214

215

216
♂

PLATE 49

inches   4
cm   10

PLATE 49

Genus *MULLERIPICUS*   Bonaparte, 1854

214. Ashy Woodpecker
Mulleripicus fulvus

French: Pic fauve   **German**: Celebesspecht   **Spanish**: Picatroncos de Célebes
Other common names: Fulvous/Celebes Woodpecker

Taxonomy. *Picus fulvus* Quoy and Gaimard, 1830, Sulawesi.
Two subspecies recognized.
Subspecies and Distribution.
M. f. fulvus (Quoy and Gaimard, 1830) - N Sulawesi, including islands of Manterawu and Lembeh, and archipelagos of Banggai and Togian.
M. f. wallacei Tweeddale, 1877 - S Sulawesi, including Muna I and Buton I.
Descriptive notes. c. 40 cm. Large, long-tailed woodpecker. Male has dark red on forehead, lores, cheeks and malar area, red usually to central crown and front of ear-coverts, but often more re-

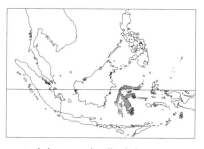

stricted at rear, sometimes a few dark feather bases visible, e.g. forming dark line on lores; dark grey rear head and hindneck, and paler grey-buff chin, throat and foreneck, all with very small whitish spots; upperparts dark grey-brown to blackish-slate, a little paler on tail-coverts, a shade darker on wings, occasionally some pale spots or shaft streaks (especially on tail-coverts); uppertail dark grey-brown to blackish-grey; rich buff to creamy yellowish-brown below, rather greyer on breast, often washed yellow-grey on flanks (underparts frequently stained dark reddish or ochre by foraging activities); underwing pale brownish-grey to dark grey; undertail pale brown to grey, washed yellow; long bill slightly chisel-tipped, culmen curved, narrow across nostrils, black; iris pale yellow, orbital skin grey, or tinged bluish. Female has red of head replaced by dark grey, all but forehead very finely spotted pale. Juvenile much as adult but duller, more spotted, with red on face, male with less than adult, red on female even less. Race *wallacei* has slightly longer wing and longer tail than nominate, but shorter bill, plumage perhaps a shade paler, red on head of male brighter and far more extensive.

VOICE. Laughing rapid "hew-hew-hew-hew-hew-hew" or "tuk tuk tuk", muffled, not loud. Drums in breeding season.
Habitat. Inhabits primary and secondary forest; prefers closed forest, but seen regularly in forest patches on the Lanowulu savanna. Rarely close to habitation. From lowlands to mountains, up to 2200 m.
Food and Feeding. Termites (Isoptera), caterpillars; presumably also other arthropods. In pairs, or family groups of up to 5 birds. Most commonly seen foraging on tree trunks. Indirect evidence indicates at least occasional ground-foraging; probably breaks into termite mounds.
Breeding. A few observations and evidence from specimens indicate nesting in Mar-Aug. Nest-hole excavated in dead tree or in dead part of live tree; one hole watched during excavation was c. 12 m above ground, entrance facing away from morning sun, male did 75% of work. Clutch 2-3 eggs; other details not known.
Movements. Probably resident.
Status and Conservation. Not globally threatened. Not uncommon. Occurs in Manembonembo, Gunung Ambang and Tangkoko Nature Reserves, Dumoga-Bone, Lore Lindu and Rawa Aopa National Parks. In Gunung Ambang, common at L Iloloi. Seems to be reasonably common, and unlikely to become threatened in near future, as long as habitat is conserved.
Bibliography. Andrew (1992), Andrew & Holmes (1990), Baltzer (1990), Catterall (1997), Coates & Bishop (1997), Ekstrom *et al*. (1998), Holmes & Phillipps (1996), Inskipp *et al*. (1996), Riley & Mole (2001), Rozendaal (1989), Wardill (1995), Watling (1983), Wheatley (1996), White & Bruce (1986).

215. Sooty Woodpecker
Mulleripicus funebris

French: Pic en deuil **German**: Philippinenspecht **Spanish**: Picatroncos Filipino
Other common names: Tweeddale's Woodpecker (*fuliginosus*)

Taxonomy. *Picus funebris* Valenciennes, 1826, Philippines.
In past, race *fuliginosus* was considered a separate species. Races *mayri* and *parkesi* differ little from nominate, and might be better synonymized. Four subspecies currently recognized.
Subspecies and Distribution.
M. f. mayri Gilliard, 1949 - N Luzon.
M. f. funebris (Valenciennes, 1826) - C & S Luzon, Marinduque and Catanduanes.
M. f. parkesi Manuel, 1957 - Polillo Is.
M. f. fuliginosus Tweeddale, 1877 - Samar, Leyte and Mindanao.

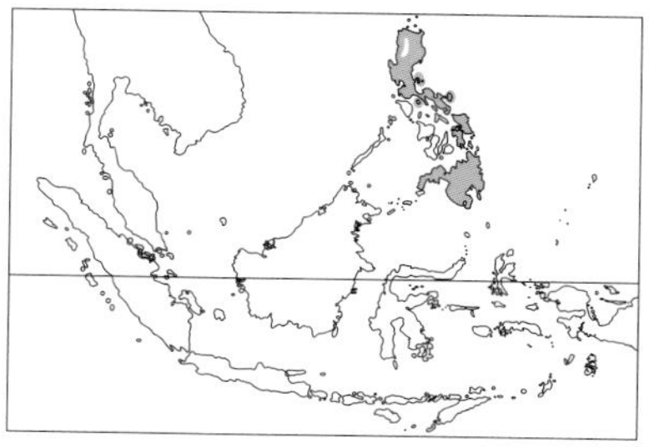

Descriptive notes. 30 cm; 139-183 g. Male has dark red forehead and forecrown, lores, cheeks, malar region and front of ear-coverts, usually some black feather bases showing, sometimes red not extending far on to crown; rest of head and neck black, sometimes slightly greyish on throat, finely speckled with white (spots sometimes lacking); entire upperparts, including wings and tail, blue-glossed black; underparts slightly paler, more sooty-black, unglossed, rarely a few small pale spots on breast; in worn plumage, browner and less glossy, fewer or no spots, black feather bases more visible on face; longish bill almost pointed, culmen curved, narrow across nostrils, blackish, pale horn-yellow at side; iris pale yellow; legs brownish-grey. Female has entire head blackish with fine white spots, spots sometimes few or absent. Juvenile as adult, but duller and browner, without gloss, pale spots bigger but less sharp, male with red face like adult. Race *mayri* tends to have longer bill and longer tail than nominate, but considerable overlap in measurements, bill yellowish-grey or ivory-yellow with grey base; *parkesi* is very like nominate, perhaps on average slightly larger, red on male's head not reaching to forecrown; *fuliginosus* has shorter tail, differs from others in greyer, less black, coloration, more slate-grey than black above, greyer below, male with red restricted to broad malar band (occasionally traces elsewhere on head), bill relatively short and deep. VOICE. Distinctive trill, "chil-lel-lel-lel-lel-lel", c. 1 second long, repeated at irregular intervals, sometimes every 5-10 seconds.
Habitat. Evergreen forest, secondary forest, forest edge, and near cultivations; also montane oak (*Quercus*) and pine (*Pinus*) forest above 300 m, to 1000 m, occasionally or locally to c. 1350 m.
Food and Feeding. No information on diet. Usually singly or in pairs, members of which maintain frequent vocal contact. Forages in upper storeys, above 20 m, in tall trees, both live ones and partly or fully dead ones; also descends to understorey, on tree trunks and large limbs.
Breeding. Specimens with enlarged gonads in Mar, and recently fledged juvenile seen in May; season reported as Mar-May in N (Luzon, Polillo) and Apr-Aug in S (Samar, Leyte). Nest and eggs not described.
Movements. Probably resident.
Status and Conservation. Not globally threatened. Uncommon to locally fairly common. Occurs in Quezon National Park (Luzon). Very poorly known; inconspicuous in its forest habitat and may be overlooked. Field studies urgently needed, in order to determine details of its diet and feeding ecology, as well as its nesting behaviour.
Bibliography. Danielsen *et al*. (1994), Delacour & Mayr (1945), Dickinson *et al*. (1991), Dupond (1942), Gilliard (1949b, 1950), Gonzales (1983), Goodman & Gonzales (1990), Manuel (1957), McGregor (1909-1910), Pardo & Gogorza y González (1997), duPont (1971), Rand & Rabor (1960), Wheatley (1996).

216. Great Slaty Woodpecker
Mulleripicus pulverulentus

French: Pic meunier **German**: Puderspecht **Spanish**: Picatroncos Pizarroso
Other common names: Himalayan Great Slaty Woodpecker (*harterti*)

Taxonomy. *Picus pulverulentus* Temminck, 1826, Java and Sumatra.
Geographical variation not well marked, and individual variation makes racial delimitation difficult; size varies only slightly and inconstantly throughout range. Populations from NW (Nepal to N Assam) described as race *mohun* on basis of darker coloration, especially below, but some birds from Myanmar and Thailand appear identical. Races intergrade in peninsular Thailand, intermediates from which previously separated as race *celadinus*. Two subspecies recognized.
Subspecies and Distribution.
M. p. harterti Hesse, 1911 - N India (Himachal Pradesh) E through Himalayan foothills to N Myanmar and S China (S Yunnan), S to S Thailand and Indochina.
M. p. pulverulentus (Temminck, 1826) - peninsular Thailand S to E Sumatra and Riau Archipelago, W Java, Borneo and N Natunas, and W Philippines (Balabac, Palawan).

Descriptive notes. c. 50 cm; 360-563 g. Very large, the biggest Old World woodpecker, with very long bill, long neck and long tail. Male has pale red cheek patch, creamy to yellow-buff chin and throat, feathers of lower throat tipped pale red; rest of head and upperparts slate-grey with variable amount of small whitish feather tips (small pale spots often most prominent on ear-coverts and hindneck); wings and tail darker blackish-grey, very narrowly edged and tipped blue-grey; slate-grey below, slightly paler than upperparts, small pale streak-like spots on upper breast, becoming paler grey on lower belly; very long, strong bill chisel-tipped, blackish on culmen and tip, yellowish on lower mandible and base of upper mandible; iris brown, orbital skin grey; legs blue-grey or greenish-grey. Female lacks red on cheeks and red tips on lower throat. Juvenile duller, browner, particularly above, chin and throat whiter, generally more spotted below, male with red malar larger than on adult, sometimes some red on crown. Race *harterti* is paler, less blackish. VOICE. Loud whinnying cackle of 2-5 (most commonly 4) notes, "woikwoikwoikwoik", initial note often slightly higher-pitched, final one distinctly lower, shorter version with consecutive notes dropping more in pitch, frequently in flight; single "dwot" calls, variable, perched or in flight; low soft mewing notes by partners at very close contacts; "ta-whit" or "dew-it" in more agonistic situations (with head-swinging). Drumming not certainly reported.
Habitat. Primary semi-open moist deciduous and tropical evergreen forests, adjacent secondary forest, clearings with scattered tall trees; also similar, almost park-like, woodland. Dipterocarp and teak forests preferred in some areas; mature sal (*Shorea*) forest, swamp-forest and tall mangroves. Most frequent in lowlands and lower hills below 600 m, but also occurs in montane habitats up to 1100 m (foothills of Himalayas), occasionally to 2000 m.
Food and Feeding. Predominantly ants; also other insects, such as larvae of wood-boring beetles. Small fruits possibly eaten at times. Usually in pairs, and regularly in noisy family parties of 4-6 birds, sometimes more (12), roaming through forest; sometimes associates with other woodpeckers, such as *Dryocopus javensis* and *Chrysocolaptes lucidus* when foraging. Forages mainly in tall trees, including solitary ones in open areas; flies long distances to reach these (thus, home range very extensive); sometimes visits smaller trees and saplings at low levels, not infrequently close to ground. Climbs trunks and larger branches slowly, pausing frequently at crevices and other depressions and cracks in bark; may perch crosswise in crown, even on small branches. Gleaning is the most frequent technique, and the long neck and bill assist it in reaching a long way out. Other foraging techniques include probing, pecking, prying-off of bark; also hammering with powerful loud blows to excavate wood. Does not remain long at one spot to peck or hammer. Relatively nimble when foraging among branches, but climbs almost in "slow motion".
Breeding. Mar-May in W and Mar-Aug in SE Asia. Displays include strange-looking head-swinging, head appearing to lag behind body in its swinging movement; during chases, wings extended widely, tail also spread. Nest-hole excavated by both sexes, although male does most of the work, very high up (range 9-45 m) in tree, in large trunk or branch, entrance hole c. 10 cm across; old nest occasionally reused, probably only when new one usurped. Clutch 2-4 eggs; both sexes incubate, and both feed chicks; incubation and fledging periods not known; fledged young remain with parents for some time, probably until next breeding cycle commences.
Movements. Resident.
Status and Conservation. Not globally threatened. Uncommon in N Indian Subcontinent, and possibly extinct in Bangladesh, where no recent records; uncommon to fairly common, but often rather local, in SE Asia, extinct in Singapore; rare in S China; exceedingly rare in Sumatra and Java, and not likely to survive, but somewhat more common in Borneo; uncommon and decreasing in Philippines. Although generally uncommon or rare throughout its range, can be conspicuously noisy where present; not likely to be overlooked. Occurs in many protected areas, e.g. Corbett and Namdapha National Parks (India), Khao Yai and Nam Nao National Parks (Thailand), Nam Bai Cat Tien National Park (Vietnam), Taman Negara National Park and Panti Forest Reserve (Peninsular Malaysia), Aas Purwo National Park (Java), Danum Valley Conservation Area (Borneo) and St Paul's Subterranean River National Park (Palawan, Philippines). Extensive habitat destruction seems likely to have led to the demise of this magnificent woodpecker in Sumatra, and there seems little chance that it can fare much better in Java. Densities are naturally low, since it lives in large home ranges; it should be secure in the mainland parts of its current range, so long as reasonably large tracts of habitat remain intact.
Bibliography. Ali & Ripley (1983), Ali *et al*. (1996), Andrew (1992), van Balen (1999), Bangs & Van Tyne (1931), Bucknill & Chasen (1990), Castelletta *et al*. (2000), Deignan (1945), Dickinson *et al*. (1991), Dodsworth (1911), Duckworth & Kelsh (1988), Duckworth *et al*. (1997), Eames & Robson (1992), Goes (1999), Grimmett *et al*. (1998), Harvey (1990), Holmes (1973), Inskipp, C. (1989), Inskipp, C. & Inskipp (1991), Inskipp, T. *et al*. (1996), Jeyarajasingam & Pearson (1999), Khacher (1976), Lekagul & Round (1991), MacKinnon (1988), MacKinnon & Phillipps (1993, 2000), Madoc (1976), van Marle & Voous (1988), Medway & Wells (1976), Nash & Nash (1988), duPont (1971), Rajathurai (1996), Rand & Fleming (1957), Riley (1938), Ripley (1950a, 1982), Robinson (1917), Robson (2000), Round (1988), Sargeant (1997), Shankar Raman (2001), Short (1973d), Smythies (1986, 1999), Stepanyan (1995), Stresemann (1921a), Vowles & Vowles (1997), Wells (1985, 1999), Wilkinson, Dutson & Sheldon (1991), Zhao Zhengjie (1995).

REFERENCES

REFERENCES OF SCIENTIFIC DESCRIPTIONS

Alexander (1901). *Bull. Brit. Orn. Club* **12**: 11.
Alexander (1903). *Bull. Brit. Orn. Club* **13**: 33.
Alexander (1908). *Bull. Brit. Orn. Club* **21**: 89; **23**: 15.
Allen, G.M. (1905). *Auk* **22**: 124.
Allen, J.A. (1892). *Bull. Amer. Mus. Nat. Hist.* **4**: 55.
Alvedo & Ginés (1953). *Nov. Cient. Contrib. Ocas. Mus. Hist. Nat. La Salle, Ser. Zool.* **10**: 4.
Amadon (1943). *Ibis* **85**: 332.
Anthony (1895). *Auk* **12**: 347.
Arrigoni (1902). *Avicula* **6**: 103.
Audubon (1833). *Birds Amer.* **2**: pl. 185.
Audubon (1838). *Birds Amer.* **4**: pl. 417.
Audubon (1839). *Orn. Biogr.* **5**: 317.
Baird (1854). *Proc. Acad. Nat. Sci. Philadelphia* **7**: 120.
Baird (1858). *Rep. Expl. Surv. R.R. Pac.* **9**.
Baird (1859). *Proc. Acad. Nat. Sci. Philadelphia* **11**: 302.
Baird (1870). *Cooper's Orn. Cal.* **1**: 385, 405.
Baird (1874). In: Baird, Brewer & Ridgway, *Hist. North Amer. Birds* **2**: 501, 517.
Bangs (1898). *Auk* **15**: 176-177. [*Colaptes auratus luteus, Dryocopus pileatus abieticola*]
Bangs (1898). *Proc. Biol. Soc. Washington* **12**: 133, 173. [*Galbula ruficauda pallens, Aulacorhynchus prasinus lautus*]
Bangs (1900). *Auk* **17**: 136.
Bangs (1901). *Auk* **18**: 26. [*Melanerpes rubricapillus seductus*]
Bangs (1901). *Proc. New Engl. Zoöl. Club* **2**: 99. [*Veniliornis kirkii neglectus*]
Bangs (1902). *Proc. New Engl. Zoöl. Club* **3**: 83.
Bangs (1903). *Bull. Mus. Comp. Zool.* **39**: 146.
Bangs (1910). *Proc. Biol. Soc. Washington* **23**: 173.
Bangs & Barbour (1922). *Bull. Mus. Comp. Zool.* **65**: 200.
Bangs & Peters, J.L. (1928). *Bull. Mus. Comp. Zool.* **68**: 334.
Bannerman (1923). *Bull. Brit. Orn. Club* **43**: 161.
Bannerman (1928). *Bull. Brit. Orn. Club* **49**: 20.
Batchelder (1908). *Proc. New Engl. Zoöl. Club* **4**: 37.
Bates (1909). *Bull. Brit. Orn. Club* **25**: 26.
Bates & Kinnear (1935). *Bull. Brit. Orn. Club* **55**: 156.
Bechstein (1803). *Orn. Taschenbuch Deutschland* **1**: 66.
Bechstein (1811). *Allgem. Ueb. Vög.* **4**: 64.
Benson (1948). *Bull. Brit. Orn. Club* **68**: 144.
Benson (1964). *Arnoldia* **1**: 1-4.
Berlepsch (1908). *Nov. Zool.* **15**: 272.
Berlepsch & Hartert (1902). *Nov. Zool.* **9**: 93.
Berlepsch & Stolzmann (1894). *Ibis* **Ser. 6, no. 6**: 401.
Berlepsch & Stolzmann (1902). *Proc. Zool. Soc. London* **1902**: 32-33.
Berlepsch & Taczanowski (1884). *Proc. Zool. Soc. London* **1883**: 571.
Bianchi (1904). *Ann. Mus. Zool. Acad. Imp. Sci. St. Pétersb.* **9**: 4.
Bianchi (1906). *Bull. Brit. Orn. Club* **16**: 69.
Biswas (1951). *Amer. Mus. Novit.* **1500**: 8.
Blake (1941). *Field Mus. Nat. Hist. Publ., Zool. Ser.* **24**: 228, 230.
Blanford (1873). *Ibis* **Ser. 3, no. 3**: 226.
Blasius, W. (1890). *J. Orn.* **38**: 140.
Blundell & Lovat (1899). *Bull. Brit. Orn. Club* **10**: 21.
Blyth (1842). *J. Asiatic Soc. Bengal* **11**: 116, 167.
Blyth (1843). *J. Asiatic Soc. Bengal* **12**: 1000, 1004, 1006.
Blyth (1845). *J. Asiatic Soc. Bengal* **14**: 192-193, 195-197.
Blyth (1847). *J. Asiatic Soc. Bengal* **16**: 465.
Blyth (1849). *Cat. Birds Mus. Asiatic Soc. Bengal*: 56, 64. [*Dendrocopos maculatus validirostris, Dinopium benghalense dilutum*]
Blyth (1849). *J. Asiatic Soc. Bengal* **18**: 803-804. [*Dendrocopos moluccensis gymnopthalmos, Dendrocopos atratus, Dendrocopos assimilis*]
Blyth (1859). *J. Asiatic Soc. Bengal* **28**: 412.
Blyth (1860). *J. Asiatic Soc. Bengal* **29**: 105.
Blyth (1862). *J. Asiatic Soc. Bengal* **31**: 341.
Blyth (1863). *J. Asiatic Soc. Bengal* **32**: 75.
Blyth (1870). *Ibis* **Ser. 2, no. 6**: 163.
Bocage (1869). *Proc. Zool. Soc. London* **1869**: 436.
Bocage (1877). *J. Sci. Math. Phys. e Nat., Acad. Real Sci. Lisboa* **6**: 63.
Boddaert (1783). *Table Planches Enlum.*
Bogdanov (1879). *Verh. Ges. Kasan* **8**: 121.
Boie (1826). *Isis von Oken* **18/19**: col. 977.
Boie (1831). *Isis von Oken* **24**: col. 542.
Boissonneau (1840). *Rev. Zool.*: 36, 70.
Bonaparte (1838). *Proc. Zool. Soc. London* **1838**: 116, 120.
Bonaparte (1845). *Atti Sesta Riun. Sci. Ital.*: 406.
Bonaparte (1850). *Consp. Av.* **1**.
Bonaparte (1854). *Ateneo Italiano* **2**: 122, 124-126, 129.
Bond (1936). *Proc. Acad. Nat. Sci. Philadelphia* **88**: 360-361.

Bond (1954). *Proc. Acad. Nat. Sci. Philadelphia* **106**: 56-57.
Bond & Meyer de Schauensee (1940). *Notulae Naturae* **50**: 1.
Bond & Meyer de Schauensee (1941). *Notulae Naturae* **93**: 4.
Bond & Meyer de Schauensee (1942). *Notulae Naturae* **105**: 1.
Boulton (1931). *Ann. Carnegie Mus.* **21**: 44, 46.
Brandt, J.F. (1841). *Bull. Sci. Acad. Imp. Sci. St. Pétersbourg* **9**: col. 12.
Brehm, C.L. (1831). *Handb. Naturg. Vög. Deutschl.*: 187, 192, 194.
Brehm, C.L. (1855). *Vogelfang*: 69.
Brisson (1760). *Orn.* **1**: 42; **4**: 86, 91-92.
Bryant, W.E. (1887). *Bull. Calif. Acad. Sci.* **2**: 450.
Buller (1887). *Birds New Zealand* **1**: 25.
Burton (1836). *Proc. Zool. Soc. London* **1836**: 154.
Büttikofer (1897). *Notes Leyden Mus.* **18**: 169.
Buturlin (1908). *Ann. Mus. Zool. Acad. Imp. Sci. St. Pétersb.* **13**: 229, 235, 243, 249.
Cabanis (1851). In: Ersch & Gruber, *Allg. Encycl. Wiss. Künste, sec. 1* **52**: 308.
Cabanis (1861). *Sitzungsb. Ges. Naturf. Freunde Berlin.*
Cabanis (1862). *J. Orn.* **10**.
Cabanis (1878). *J. Orn.* **26**: 205-206, 239-241.
Cabanis (1880). *J. Orn.* **28**: 351.
Cabanis (1883). *J. Orn.* **31**: 98, 102-103, 110.
Cabanis (1889). *J. Orn.* **39**: 331.
Cabanis & Heine (1863). *Mus. Hein., Th. 4* **1**: 139, 143, 146-149; **2**.
Cabot (1844). *Proc. Boston Soc. Nat. Hist.* **1**: 164.
Cabot (1845). *Boston J. Nat. Hist.* **5**: 92.
Carriker (1930). *Proc. Acad. Nat. Sci. Philadelphia* **82**: 367.
Carriker (1933). *Proc. Acad. Nat. Sci. Philadelphia* **85**: 5.
Cassin (1850). *Proc. Acad. Nat. Sci. Philadelphia* **5**: 106.
Cassin (1851). *Proc. Acad. Nat. Sci. Philadelphia* **5**: 154, 349.
Cassin (1855). *Proc. Acad. Nat. Sci. Philadelphia* **7**: 324, 440.
Cassin (1856). *Proc. Acad. Nat. Sci. Philadelphia* **8**: 156-157.
Cassin (1857). *Proc. Acad. Nat. Sci. Philadelphia* **9**: 214.
Cassin (1860). *Proc. Acad. Nat. Sci. Philadelphia* **12**: 134, 137.
Cassin (1863). *Proc. Acad. Nat. Sci. Philadelphia* **15**: 197, 322.
Cassin (1867). *Proc. Acad. Nat. Sci. Philadelphia* **19**: 112.
Cassin (1868). *Proc. Acad. Nat. Sci. Philadelphia* **19**: 114.
Chapin (1932). *Amer. Mus. Novit.* **570**: 5.
Chapin (1958). *Bull. Brit. Orn. Club* **78**: 46.
Chapman (1912). *Bull. Amer. Mus. Nat. Hist.* **31**: 144.
Chapman (1914). *Bull. Amer. Mus. Nat. Hist.* **33**: 195, 608-609, 611.
Chapman (1915). *Bull. Amer. Mus. Nat. Hist.* **34**: 385-386, 639-640.
Chapman (1917). *Bull. Amer. Mus. Nat. Hist.* **36**: 338.
Chapman (1921). *Amer. Mus. Novit.* **2**: 1-2; **18**: 6.
Chapman (1923). *Amer. Mus. Novit.* **96**: 5-6, 8.
Chapman (1927). *Amer. Mus. Novit.* **250**: 1.
Chapman (1928). *Amer. Mus. Novit.* **332**: 7-8; **335**: 3, 6, 8, 15.
Chapman (1929). *Amer. Mus. Novit.* **380**: 16.
Chapman (1931). *Amer. Mus. Novit.* **450**: 1.
Chapman (1939). *Amer. Mus. Novit.* **1051**: 8.
Chasen (1940). *Treubia* **17**: 261.
Chasen & Kloss (1929). *J. Orn.* **2**: 110, 112.
Cheng Tsohsin (1956). *Acta Zool. Sinica* **8(2)**: 133-142.
Cherrie (1916). *Bull. Amer. Mus. Nat. Hist.* **35**: 391, 394.
Cherrie & Reichenbeger (1921). *Amer. Mus. Novit.* **27**: 4.
Clancey (1952). *J. Sci. Soc. Univ. Natal* **8**: 2.
Clancey (1956). *Durban Mus. Novit.* **4**: 249-250.
Clancey (1958). *Bull. Brit. Orn. Club* **78**: 42-43.
Clancey (1965). *Bull. Brit. Orn. Club* **85**: 65.
Clancey (1977). *Durban Mus. Novit.* **11**: 251-252.
Clarke, S.R. (1920). *Bull. Brit. Orn. Club* **41**: 50.
Cory (1886). *Auk* **3**: 498-499, 502.
Cory (1913). *Field Mus. Nat. Hist. Publ., Orn. Ser.* **1**: 287-288.
Cory (1915). *Field Mus. Nat. Hist. Publ., Orn. Ser.* **1**: 305-307.
Cory (1919). *Field Mus. Nat. Hist. Publ., Zool. Ser.* **13**: 457.
Cretzschmar (1826). In: Rüppell's *Atlas, Vög.*: 30, 41.
Cuvier (1816). *Règne Animal* **1**: 420, 428.
Cuvier (1829). *Règne Animal, nouv. ed.* **1**: 458.
Dalmas (1900). *Bull. Zool. Soc. France* **25**: 177.
Daudin (1803). *Ann. Mus. Hist. Nat.* **2**: 286.
Deignan (1939). *J. Washington Acad. Sci.* **29**: 177.
Deignan (1956). *Proc. Biol. Soc. Washington* **69**: 207-208.
Deignan (1960). *Bull. Brit. Orn. Club* **80**: 121.
Delacour (1927). *Bull. Brit. Orn. Club* **47**: 153-154.
Delacour (1946). *Zoologica* **31**: 2.
Delacour & Jabouille (1924). *Bull. Brit. Orn. Club* **45**: 31.

Des Murs (1845). *Rev. Zool.*: 207.
Deville (1849). *Rev. et Mag. Zool.* **1**: 55-56.
Deville & Des Murs (1849). *Rev. et Mag. Zool.* **1**: 161, 171.
Dickerman (1987). *West. Found. Vertebrate Zool.* **3**: 1-6.
Dickey & van Rossem (1927). *Proc. Biol. Soc. Washington* **40**: 1.
Dickey & van Rossem (1930). *Ibis* **Ser. 12, no. 6**: 50, 53.
Dole (1878). *Hawaiian Alm. Ann.* **1879**: 49, 54.
Domaniewski (1925). *Ann. Zool. Mus. Polon. Hist. Nat.* **4**: 297.
Du Bus de Gisignies (1847). *Bull. Acad. Roy. Sci. Belg.* **14**: 107.
Dumont (1816). *Dict. Sci. Nat. (éd. Levrault)* **4**: 50, 52, 54, 56.
Dybowski (1883). *Bull. Soc. Zool. France* **8**: 368.
Dziadosz & Parkes (1984). *Proc. Biol. Soc. Washington* **97**: 789.
Ehrenberg (1833). *Symb. Phys., Aves*.
Elliot (1865). *Nouv. Arch. Mus. Hist. Nat.* **1**: 76.
Erlanger (1901). *Orn. Monatsber.* **9**: 182.
Eyton (1845). *Ann. and Mag. Nat. Hist.* **16**: 229.
de Filippi (1853). *Rev. et Mag. Zool.* **5**: 290-291.
Finsch (1905). *Notes Leyden Mus.* **26**: 34.
Fischer & Reichenow (1884). *J. Orn.* **32**: 179-180, 262.
Forster, J.R. (1844). *Descr. Anim.*: 265.
Franklin (1831). *Proc. Comm. Zool. Soc. London* **1**: 121.
Fraser (1841). *Proc. Zool. Soc. London* **1841**: 61.
Fraser (1843). *Proc. Zool. Soc. London* **1843**: 3.
Frohawk (1892). *Ann. and Mag. Nat. Hist.* **9**: 247.
Gambel (1843). *Proc. Acad. Nat. Sci. Philadelphia* **1**: 259.
Geoffroy Saint-Hilaire, I. (1851). *Ann. Sci. Nat. Zool.* **Ser. 3, no. 14**: 209.
Gilliard (1940). *Amer. Mus. Novit.* **1071**: 7.
Gilliard (1949). *Auk* **66**: 277, 279-280.
Gloger (1827). *Froriep's Notizen* **16**: col. 277.
Gmelin, J.F. (1788). *Syst. Nat.* **1(1)**.
Gmelin, J.F. (1789). *Syst. Nat.* **1(2)**.
Goeldi (1904). *Verz. Neuen Thiere Pflanz.* **7**(Suppl.): 3.
Goffin (1863). *Mus. Pays-Bas* **1**: 15.
Gould (1832). *Proc. Comm. Zool. Soc. London* **2**: 140.
Gould (1833). *Proc. Zool. Soc. London* **1833**: 69-70.
Gould (1834). *Proc. Zool. Soc. London* **1834**: 78, 119-120.
Gould (1835). *Proc. Zool. Soc. London* **1835**: 49, 147.
Gould (1836). *Proc. Zool. Soc. London* **1836**: 19, 73, 157.
Gould (1837). *Icones Avium* **1**: pl. 7. [*Selenidera*]
Gould (1837). *Proc. Zool. Soc. London* **1837**: 80-81. [*Hypnelus bicinctus, Chelidoptera*]
Gould (1837). *Synop. Birds Australia* **1**: pl. 11. [*Heteralocha acutirostris*]
Gould (1843). *Proc. Zool. Soc. London* **1843**: 15.
Gould (1844). *Proc. Zool. Soc. London* **1844**: 147.
Gould (1846). *Proc. Zool. Soc. London* **1846**: 68-69.
Gould (1851). *Proc. Zool. Soc. London* **1851**: 93.
Gould (1854). *Monogr. Ramphastidae, 2nd ed.*: pls. 3, 21, 30. [*Pteroglossus azara mariae, Pteroglossus torquatus sanguineus, Ramphastos sulfuratus brevicarinatus*]
Gould (1854). *Proc. Zool. Soc. London* **1854**: 45. [*Aulacorhynchus prasinus caeruleogularis*]
Gould (1855). *Proc. Zool. Soc. London* **1855**: 166.
Gould (1858). *Proc. Zool. Soc. London* **1858**: 149.
Gould (1861). *Proc. Zool. Soc. London* **1860**: 381.
Gould (1863). *Proc. Zool. Soc. London* **1862**: 283.
Gould (1866). *Proc. Zool. Soc. London* **1866**: 24.
Gould (1868). *Proc. Zool. Soc. London* **1868**: 219.
Gould (1874). *Ann. and Mag. Nat. Hist.* **14**: 183-184.
Grant, C.H.B. (1911). *Ibis* **Ser. 9, no. 5**: 321.
Grant, C.H.B. (1915). *Bull. Brit. Orn. Club* **35**: 100.
Grant, C.H.B. & Mackworth-Praed (1938). *Bull. Brit. Orn. Club* **58**: 65.
Graves (1986). *Proc. Biol. Soc. Washington* **99(1)**: 61-64.
Gray, G.R. (1840). *List Gen. Birds*: 54.
Gray, G.R. (1841). *List Gen. Birds*: 13, 70.
Gray, G.R. (1842). *List Gen. Birds*: 12.
Gray, G.R. (1843). *Trav. New Zealand* **2**: 197.
Gray, G.R. (1845). *Gen. Birds* **2**: 436.
Gray, G.R. (1846). *Gen. Birds* **1**: 74, pl. 26; **2**: pl. 106.
Gray, G.R. (1847). *Gen. Birds* **2**: pl. 113.
Gray, G.R. (1849). *Gen. Birds* **3**: 22.
Gray, G.R. (1859). *Cat. Birds Trop. Isl. Pac. Ocean*: 9.
Gray, J.E. (1831). *Zool. Misc.*: 33.
Gray, J.E. & Gray, G.R. (1846). *Cat. Spec. Mammals Birds Nepal Thibet*: 117.
Grinnell (1901). *Condor* **3**: 12.
Grinnell (1902). *Condor* **4**: 89.
Grinnell (1910). *Univ. Calif. Publ. Zool.* **5**: 390.
Grinnell (1927). *Condor* **29**: 168.
Griscom (1929). *Bull. Mus. Comp. Zool.* **69**: 163.
Griscom (1934). *Bull. Mus. Comp. Zool.* **75**: 381.
Griscom & Greenway (1937). *Bull. Mus. Comp. Zool.* **81**: 431.
Grote (1927). *Orn. Monatsber.* **35**: 144.
Grote (1934). *Orn. Monatsber.* **42**: 86.
Gundlach (1858). *Ann. Lyceum Nat. Hist. New York* **6**: 273.
Gyldenstolpe (1916). *Orn. Monatsber.* **24**: 28.
Gyldenstolpe (1941). *Ark. Zool.* **33A(6)**: 15; **33B(12)**: 7-8. [*Semnornis ramphastinus caucae, Picumnus aurifrons juruanus, Veniliornis passerinus tapajoensis*]
Gyldenstolpe (1941). *Ark. Zool. (2nd Ser.)* **2(1)**: 14, 114. [*Eubucco richardsoni purusianus*]
Gyldenstolpe (1945). *Kungl. Svenska Vet.-Akad. nya Handl.* **22**: 127.
Haffer (1961). *Noved. Colomb.* **1**: 6.
Hahn & Küster (1823). *Voeg. Asien, Afrika, Amerika Neuholland* **14**: pl. 2.
Hargitt (1881). *Ibis* **Ser. 4, no. 5**: 228, 398, 598.
Hargitt (1882). *Ibis* **Ser. 4, no. 6**: 45.
Hargitt (1883). *Ibis* **Ser. 5, no. 1**: 172, 173.
Hargitt (1884). *Ibis* **Ser. 5, no. 2**: 100.
Hargitt (1886). *Ibis* **Ser. 5, no. 4**: 115.
Hargitt (1889). *Ibis* **Ser. 6, no. 1**: 58-59, 229-231, 354.
Hargitt (1890). *Cat. Birds Brit. Mus.* **18**: 6, 8.
Hargitt (1891). *Ibis* **Ser. 6, no. 3**: 605-606.
Hargitt (1893). *Bull. Brit. Orn. Club* **3**: 3.
Harrison & Hartley (1934). *Bull. Brit. Orn. Club* **54**: 151.
Hartert (1896). *Nov. Zool.* **3**: 542.
Hartert (1900). *Nov. Zool.* **7**: 33.

Hartert (1901). *Nov. Zool.* **8**: 51.
Hartert (1907). *Birds of the British Isles*: 22.
Hartert (1909). *Nov. Zool.* **16**: 229.
Hartert (1910). *Nov. Zool.* **17**: 221-222.
Hartert (1912). *Vögel Pal. Fauna* **2**: 921, 924, 926, 937.
Hartert (1920). *Bull. Brit. Orn. Club* **40**: 139.
Hartert (1924). *Nov. Zool.* **31**: 23.
Hartert & Butler (1898). *Nov. Zool.* **5**: 508.
Hartlaub (1844). *Rev. Zool.*: 214.
Hartlaub (1852). *Naumannia* **2**: 55.
Hartlaub (1854). *J. Orn.* **2**: 410.
Hartlaub (1857). *Syst. Orn. West-Afr.*: 171, 175, 178.
Hartlaub (1883). *Abh. Naturwiss. Ver. Bremen* **8**: 208.
Hartlaub (1884). *Ibis* **Ser. 5, no. 2**: 28.
Hartlaub (1886). *Ibis* **Ser. 5, no. 4**: 106.
Hartlaub & Finsch (1871). *Proc. Zool. Soc. London* **1871**: 25.
Hellmayr (1906). *Nov. Zool.* **13**: 39.
Hellmayr (1907). *Bull. Brit. Orn. Club* **19**: 55.
Hellmayr (1908). *Nov. Zool.* **15**: 82.
Hellmayr (1909). *Bull. Brit. Orn. Club* **23**: 67; **25**: 20.
Hellmayr (1915). *Verh. Orn. Ges. Bayern* **12**: 212.
Hellmayr (1918). *Verh. Orn. Ges. Bayern* **13**: 314-315.
Hellmayr (1921). *Anz. Orn. Ges. Bayern* **5**: 42.
Hellmayr (1922). *Anz. Orn. Ges. Bayern* **6**: 46.
Hellmayr (1929). *Field Mus. Nat. Hist. Publ., Zool. Ser.* **12**: 419.
Hellmayr & Gyldenstolpe (1937). *Ark. Zool.* **29B(6)**: 1.
Hermann (1783). *Tab. Affin. Anim.*: 217.
Hesse (1911). *Orn. Monatsber.* **19**: 181-182.
Hesse (1912). *Orn. Monatsber.* **20**: 82.
Heuglin (1861). *Ibis* **Ser. 3, no. 3**: 124, 126.
Heuglin (1862). *J. Orn.* **10**: 37.
Heuglin (1864). *J. Orn.* **12**: 266.
Heuglin (1871). *Orn. Nord-Ost. Afr.* **1**: 810.
Hodgson (1836). *J. Asiatic Soc. Bengal* **5**: 778.
Hodgson (1837). *J. Asiatic Soc. Bengal* **6**: 108.
Hombron & Jacquinot (1841). *Ann. Sci. Nat. Zool.* **16**: 320.
Hoogerwerf (1963). *Bull. Brit. Orn. Club* **83**: 113.
Horsfield (1821). *Trans. Linn. Soc. London* **13(1)**: 175-177, 181.
Hume (1870). *Ibis* **Ser. 3, no. 1**: 528.
Hume (1874). *Proc. Asiatic Soc. Bengal* **5**: 106. [*Picus erythropygius nigrigenis*]
Hume (1874). *Stray Feathers* **2**: 442. [*Megalaima incognita*]
Hume (1877). *Stray Feathers* **5**: 108.
Hume (1881). *Stray Feathers* **10**: 150.
Hutton (1872). *Ibis* **Ser. 3, no. 2**: 247.
Hutton (1891). *New Zealand J. Sci.* **1(6)**: 2476.
Illiger (1811). *Prodromus Syst. Mammalium Avium*: 202.
Jardine (1855). *New Philos. J.* **2**: 404.
Jardine & Fraser (1852). In: *Jardine's Contr. Orn.*: 155.
Jardine & Selby (1835). *Ill. Orn.* **3**: pl. 116.
Jensen & Stuart (1982). *Bull. Brit. Orn. Club* **102**: 96.
Jerdon (1840). *Madras J. Lit. Sci.* **11**: 215.
Jerdon (1844). *Madras J. Lit. Sci.* **13**: 139.
Kennedy (1987). *Proc. Biol. Soc. Washington* **100**: 40-43.
King, P. P. (1828). *Zool. J.* **3**: 430.
Kinnear (1926). *Bull. Brit. Orn. Club* **46**: 72.
Kinnear (1927). *Bull. Brit. Orn. Club* **47**: 112.
Kittlitz (1830). *Mém. Acad. Imp. Sci. St. Pétersb.* **1**: 244-245.
Kittlitz (1832). *Kupfer. Nat. Vög.* **1**: 5; **2**: 12.
Kleinschmidt (1907). *Falco*: 103.
Kloss (1918). *Ibis* **Ser. 10, no. 6**: 101, 109-110, 113.
Kloss (1925). *Bull. Brit. Orn. Club* **46**: 7.
Kloss & Chasen (1927). *Bull. Brit. Orn. Club* **48**: 46.
Koch (1816). *Syst. Baier. Zool.* **1**: xxvii, 72.
Koelz (1939). *Proc. Biol. Soc. Washington* **52**: 78.
König (1889). *J. Orn.* **37**: 263.
Kuroda (1917). *Tori* **1**: 1.
Kuroda (1921). *Auk* **38**: 579.
Kuroda (1922). *Ibis* **Ser. 11, no. 4**: 87.
Kuroda & Mori (1920). *Tori* **2**: 266.
Lacépède (1799). *Tableaux Ois.*: 7.
Lafresnaye (1841). *Rev. Zool.*: 241.
Lafresnaye (1844). *Dict. Univ. Hist. Nat.* **2**: 463. [*Pogoniulus*]
Lafresnaye (1844). *Rev. Zool.*: 42. [*Colaptes auratus mexicanoides*]
Lafresnaye (1845). *Rev. Zool.*: 6-7, 179.
Lafresnaye (1847). *Rev. Zool.*: 78-79.
Lafresnaye (1850). *Rev. et Mag. Zool.* **2**: 215.
Lafresnaye (1854). *Rev. et Mag. Zool.* **6**: 208.
Latham (1790). *Index Orn.* **1**; **2**: 866.
Latham (1801). *Index Orn.* (Suppl.): 31.
Lawrence (1861). *Ann. Lyceum Nat. Hist. New York* **7**: 300.
Lawrence (1862). *Ann. Lyceum Nat. Hist. New York* **7**: 476.
Lawrence (1877). *Ann. New York Acad. Sci.* **1**: 50.
Layard, E.L. (1854). *Ann. and Mag. Nat. Hist.* **13**: 449.
Layard, E.L. (1871). *Ibis* **Ser. 3, no. 1**: 226.
Leach (1815). *Zool. Misc.* **2**: 104.
Lesson (1830). *Cent. Zool.*: 215. [*Hemicircus canente*]
Lesson (1830). *Traité d'Orn.* **2**: 155; **3**: 164-165, 173, 228, 234-235. [*Jacamaralcyon, Jacamerops, Megalaima australis duvaucelii, Capito niger punctatus, Ramphastos sulfuratus, Indicator variegatus, Melanerpes herminieri*]
Lesson (1839). *Rev. Zool.*: 41, 137-138, 167.
Lesson (1845). *Écho du Monde Savant* **12**: 920.
Lesson (1847). *Descr. Mamm. et Ois. réc. découv.*: 204.
Leybold (1873). *Leopoldina* **8**: 53.
Lichtenstein, A.A.H. (1793). *Cat. Rer. Nat. Rar.* 17-18.
Lichtenstein, M.H.K. (1819). *Verz. ausgestop. Säug. Vög.*: 9.
Lichtenstein, M.H.K. (1823). *Verz. Doubl. Zool. Mus. Berlin*: 7, 11-12.
Linnaeus (1758). *Syst. Nat.* **10**.
Linnaeus (1766). *Syst. Nat.* **12**.
Linnaeus (1771). *Mantissa*: 524.

Ljungh (1797). *Kungl. Vet.-Akad. nya Handl.* **18**: 134.
Louette (1981). *Rev. Zool. Afr.* **95**: 131-135.
Louette & Prigogine (1982). *Rev. Zool. Afr.* **96**: 473.
Madarász (1912). *Orn. Monatsber.* **20**: 97.
Malherbe (1843). *Mém. Acad. Roy. Metz* **24**: 242.
Malherbe (1845). *Mém. Soc. Roy. Sci. Liége* **2**: 66. [*Colaptes melanochloros nattereri*]
Malherbe (1845). *Rev. Zool.*: 373-374, 399-400, 404. [*Dendropicos pyrrhogaster, Picoides stricklandi, Picoides villosus jardinii, Veniliornis kirkii, Dinopium benghalense puncticolle*]
Malherbe (1847). *Mém. Acad. Roy. Metz* **28**: 130.
Malherbe (1849). *Bull. Soc. Hist. Nat. Moselle*: 22. [*Dendrocopos canicapillus mitchelli, Dendrocopos canicapillus semicoronatus*]
Malherbe (1849). *Mém. Acad. Natl. Metz* **30**: 316, 338. [*Dendropicos*]
Malherbe (1849). *Rev. et Mag. Zool.* **1**. [*Melanerpes formicivorus flavigula, Melanerpes pucherani, Campethera cailliautii, Dendropicos fuscescens lafresnayi, Dendropicos fuscescens hartlaubii, Dendrocopos temminckii, Dendrocopos moluccensis cinereigula, Veniliornis kirkii cecilii, Colaptes campestris campestroides, Celeus brachyurus jerdonii, Picus canus guerini*]
Malherbe (1850). *Rev. et Mag. Zool.* **2**: 156.
Malherbe (1851). *Bull. Soc. Hist. Nat. Moselle*: 77.
Malherbe (1852). *Rev. et Mag. Zool.* **4**: 550, 553.
Malherbe (1854). *J. Orn.* **2**: 171-172.
Malherbe (1855). *Bull. Soc. Hist. Nat. Moselle*: 22.
Malherbe (1857). *Bull. Soc. Hist. Nat. Moselle*: 1, 11.
Malherbe (1858). *Rev. et Mag. Zool.* **10**: 8.
Malherbe (1861). *Monogr. Picidées* **1**: 115, 125.
Malherbe (1862). *Monogr. Picidées* **2**.
Manuel (1957). *Phil. J. Sci.* **86**: 4.
Marshall, C.H.T. & Marshall, G.F.L. (1870). *Proc. Zool. Soc. London* **1870**: 118.
Mathews (1912). *Nov. Zool.* **18**: 451.
Mayr (1941). *Ibis* **Ser. 14, no. 5**: 489.
McClelland (1840). *Proc. Zool. Soc. London* **1839**: 165.
McGregor (1907). *Phil. J. Sci.* **2**: 285.
Mees (1968). *Gerfaut* **58**: 101-107.
Meinertzhagen (1924). *Bull. Brit. Orn. Club* **44**: 54, 56-57.
Menzbier (1886). *Bull. Soc. Imp. Nat. Moscou* **62**: 439.
Merrem (1786). *Av. Rar. Icon. Descr.* **1**: 7.
Meyer de Schauensee (1929). *Proc. Acad. Nat. Sci. Philadelphia* **81**: 521.
Meyer de Schauensee (1938). *Proc. Acad. Nat. Sci. Philadelphia* **90**: 110.
Meyer de Schauensee (1945). *Proc. Acad. Nat. Sci. Philadelphia* **97**: 13-16.
Meyer de Schauensee & Ripley (1940). *Proc. Acad. Nat. Sci. Philadelphia* **91**: 405-406.
Milne-Edwards (1867). *Ann. Sci. Nat. Zool.* **Ser. 5, no. 8**: 151.
Milne-Edwards (1874). *Ann. Sci. Nat. Zool.* **Ser. 5, no. 19**: 10, 13-15.
Molina (1782). *Sagg. Stor. Nat. Chili*: 236, 343.
Monard (1934). *Arq. Mus. Bocage* **5**: 55.
Müller, P.L.S. (1776). *Natursyst.* (Suppl.): 82-83, 88-89, 91-92, 94.
Müller, S. (1835). *Tijdschr. Natuurl. Gesch. Phys.* **2**: 339, 341.
Natterer (1837). *Proc. Zool. Soc. London* **1837**: 44.
Natterer (1842). In: *Monogr. Ramphastidae* **3**: pl. 7.
Natterer & Malherbe (1845). *Mém. Soc. Roy. Sci. Liége* **2**: 67-69.
Nelson (1897). *Auk* **14**: 50.
Nelson (1900). *Auk* **17**: 259.
Nelson (1912). *Smiths. Misc. Coll.* **56(37)**: 1; **60(3)**: 3-4.
Neumann (1900). *J. Orn.* **48**: 195, 204, 206.
Neumann (1903). *Bull. Brit. Orn. Club* **14**: 16. [*Lybius undatus salvadorii*]
Neumann (1903). *Orn. Monatsber.* **11**: 59, 181. [*Lybius undatus thiogaster, Dendropicos goertae koenigi*]
Neumann (1904). *J. Orn.* **52**: 402.
Neumann (1908). *Bull. Brit. Orn. Club* **21**: 43, 47; **23**: 30.
Neumann (1926). *Orn. Monatsber.* **34**: 80.
Newton, A. (1872). *Ibis* **Ser. 3, no. 2**: 33.
Newton, A. (1894). *Proc. Zool. Soc. London* **1893**: 690.
Novaes (1991). *Bull. Brit. Orn. Club* **111**: 187-188.
Nuttall (1840). *Man. Orn. US & Canada, 2nd ed.*: 684.
O'Neill, Lane, Kratter, Capparella & Joo (2000). *Auk* **117(3)**: 569-577.
Oberholser (1899). *Proc. US Natl. Mus.* **22**: 29.
Oberholser (1905). *Proc. US Natl. Mus.* **28**: 869.
Oberholser (1911). *Proc. US Natl. Mus.* **40**: 597; **41**: 140-141, 146.
Oberholser (1912). *Smiths. Misc. Coll.* **60(7)**: 6.
Oberholser (1919). *Proc. Biol. Soc. Washington* **32**: 8.
Oberholser (1924). *J. Washington Acad. Sci.* **14**: 301.
Ogawa (1905). *Annot. Zool. Japon* **5**: 203.
Ogilvie-Grant (1899). *Ibis* **Ser. 7, no. 5**: 585.
Ogilvie-Grant (1904). *Bull. Brit. Orn. Club* **15**: 29.
Ogilvie-Grant (1905). *Bull. Brit. Orn. Club* **16**: 16.
Ogilvie-Grant (1906). *Bull. Brit. Orn. Club* **19**: 11.
Ogilvie-Grant (1907). *Bull. Brit. Orn. Club* **19**: 42, 107.
Olson (1973). *Smithsonian Contrib. Zool.* **152**: 7.
van Oort (1911). *Notes Leyden Mus.* **34**: 59.
d'Orbigny (1840). *Voy. Am. Mérid.* **50**: pl. 64; **51**: pls. 62-63, 65-66.
Osgood (1901). *No. Am. Fauna* **21**: 44.
Otto (1796). *Buffon's Naturg. Vögel* **23**: 191.
Oustalet (1879). *Nouv. Arch. Mus. Hist. Nat.* **2**: 62.
Oustalet (1889). *Naturaliste* **11**: 44-45.
Oustalet (1898). *Bull. Mus. Hist. Nat. Paris* **4**: 12.
Owen (1866). *Ibis* **Ser. 2, no. 2**: 168.
Owen (1870). *Trans. Zool. Soc. London* **7**: 123.
Owen (1883). *Trans. Zool Soc. London* **11**: 257.
Pallas (1782). *Neue Nord. Beytr.* **3**: 2, 5.
Pallas (1811). *Zoographia Russo-Asiat.* **2**: 305.
Parkes (1970). *Bull. Brit. Orn. Club* **90**: 155.
Parrot (1907). *Abh. K. Bay. Akad. Wiss. München, Math.-Phys. Kl.* **22**: 169.
Peale (1848). *US Expl. Exped.* **8**: 147.
Pelzeln (1856). *Sitzungsb. K. Akad. Wiss. Wien, Math.-naturwiss. Kl.* **20**: 500.
Pelzeln (1870). *Orn. Bras. Abth.* **3**: 241-242.
Pennant (1769). *Indian Zool.*: 4.
Peters, J.L. (1948). *Check-list of the Birds of the World*. Vol. 6.
Peters, W.K.H. (1854). *Ber. K. Preuss. Akad. Wiss. Berlin*: 134.
Phelps, Jr. & Aveledo (1966). *Amer. Mus. Novit.* **2270**: 3.
Phelps, Jr. & Aveledo (1987). *Bol. Soc. Venez. Cienc. Nat.* **41(144)**: 12, 17.
Phelps, Sr. & Gilliard (1941). *Amer. Mus. Novit.* **1153**: 1.
Phelps, Sr. & Phelps, Jr. (1947). *Bol. Soc. Venez. Cienc. Nat.* **11(71)**: 62.
Phelps, Sr. & Phelps, Jr. (1950). *Proc. Biol. Soc. Washington* **63**: 115-118.
Phillips, E.L. (1897). *Bull. Brit. Orn. Club* **6**: 47.
Pinto (1936). *Rev. Mus. Paulista* **20**: 234.
Prévost & Des Murs (1850). *Voy. Abyssinie* **6**: 133.
Quoy & Gaimard (1830). *Voy. 'Astrolabe', Zool.* **1**: 228, 242.
Radde (1884). *Orn. Caucasica*: 315.
Rafinesque (1814). *Principes Fondamentaux de Somiologie*: 2.
Rand (1948). *Fieldiana Zool.* **31**: 202.
Rand & Traylor (1959). *Fieldiana Zool.* **39**: 270.
Ranzani (1821). *Elem. Zool.* **3(2)**: 157, 159.
Reichenbach (1854). *Handb. Spec. Orn. Scansoriae Picinae.*
Reichenow (1876). *J. Orn.* **24**: 97.
Reichenow (1877). *J. Orn.* **25**: 110.
Reichenow (1879). *Orn. Centralbl.* **4**: 114.
Reichenow (1880). *Orn. Centralbl.* **5**: 181.
Reichenow (1887). *J. Orn.* **35**: 59-60.
Reichenow (1891). *J. Orn.* **39**: 149.
Reichenow (1892). *J. Orn.* **40**: 25, 181. [*Pogoniulus coryphaeus, Lybius rubrifacies*]
Reichenow (1892). *Sitzungsb. Deutsche Orn. Ges.* [*Trachyphonus purpuratus togoensis*]
Reichenow (1893). *Orn. Monatsber.* **1**: 30.
Reichenow (1896). *Orn. Monatsber.* **4**: 131.
Reichenow (1898). In: *Werther's mittl. Hochl. nordl. Deutsch-Ost.-Afr.*: 273. [*Lybius torquatus congicus*]
Reichenow (1898). *Orn. Monatsber.* **6**: 22. [*Melignomon, Melignomon zenkeri*]
Reichenow (1900). *Orn. Monatsber.* **8**: 58.
Reichenow (1901). *Orn. Monatsber.* **9**: 166.
Reichenow (1902). *Vög. Afr.* **2**: 175.
Reichenow (1910). *Orn. Monatsber.* **18**: 160.
Reichenow (1915). *Orn. Monatsber.* **23**: 90.
Reichenow (1921). *J. Orn.* **69**: 46.
Reichenow & Neumann (1895). *Orn. Monatsber.* **3**: 73.
Rensch (1924). *Abh. Ber. Mus. Dresden* **16**: 38.
Rensch (1928). *Orn. Monatsber.* **36**: 80.
Richmond (1900). *Auk* **17**: 179.
Richmond (1902). *Proc. Biol. Soc. Washington* **15**: 189.
Rickett (1897). *Bull. Brit. Orn. Club* **6**: 1.
Rickett (1901). *Bull. Brit. Orn. Club* **11**: 46.
Ridgway (1874). *Hist. No. Am. Birds* **2**: 561.
Ridgway (1876). *Bull. US Geol. Geogr. Surv. Terr.* **2(2)**: 191.
Ridgway (1881). *Bull. US Natl. Mus.* **21**: 85.
Ridgway (1885). *Proc. Biol. Soc. Washington* **3**: 22. [*Melanerpes aurifrons leei*]
Ridgway (1885). *Proc. US Natl. Mus.* **8**: 576. [*Melanerpes pygmaeus*]
Ridgway (1886). *Auk* **3**: 336-337. [*Melanerpes superciliaris nyeanus, Melanerpes superciliaris blakei*]
Ridgway (1886). *Proc. US Natl. Mus.* **9**: 93. [*Aulacorhynchus prasinus dimidiatus*]
Ridgway (1887). *Man. No. Am. Birds*: 282, 285-286.
Ridgway (1888). *Proc. US Natl. Mus.* **10**: 582.
Ridgway (1889). *Proc. US Natl. Mus.* **11**: 543.
Ridgway (1911). *Proc. Biol. Soc. Washington* **24**: 32-34.
Ridgway (1912). *Proc. Biol. Soc. Washington* **25**: 88-89.
Ridgway (1914). *Bull. US Natl. Mus.* **50(6)**: 140, 145, 382.
Riley (1927). *Proc. Biol. Soc. Washington* **40**: 139.
Ripley (1946). *Spolia Zeylanica* **24**: 214.
Ripley (1950). *Proc. Biol. Soc. Washington* **63**: 102-103.
Rippon (1906). *Bull. Brit. Orn. Club* **19**: 32.
Roberts (1924). *Ann. Transvaal Mus.* **10**: 83.
Roberts (1928). *Ann. Transvaal Mus.* **12**: 308.
Roberts (1932). *Ann. Transvaal Mus.* **15**: 26.
Roberts (1936). *Ann. Transvaal Mus.* **18**: 255.
Robinson (1915). *Ibis* **Ser. 10, no. 3**: 738.
Robinson (1928). *Bull. Brit. Orn. Club* **48**: 57.
Robinson & Kloss (1919). *Ibis* **Ser. 11, no. 1**: 428. [*Megalaima franklinii auricularis, Megalaima oorti annamensis*]
Robinson & Kloss (1919). *J. Str. Branch Roy. As. Soc.* **80**: 97. [*Picus chlorolophus vanheysti*]
le Roi (1911). *Orn. Monatsber.* **19**: 81.
van Rossem (1930). *Trans. San Diego Nat. Hist. Soc.* **6**: 171.
Rothschild (1892). *Ann. and Mag. Nat. Hist.* **Ser. 6, no. 10**: 111-112.
Rothschild (1893). *Bull. Brit. Orn. Club* **1**: 24, 41.
Rothschild (1894). *Bull. Brit. Orn. Club* **4**: 10.
Rothschild (1901). *Bull. Brit. Orn. Club* **11**: 70.
Rothschild (1903). *Bull. Brit. Orn. Club* **13**: 78.
Rothschild (1909). *Bull. Brit. Orn. Club* **23**: 103.
Rothschild (1922). *Bull. Brit. Orn. Club* **43**: 9.
Rothschild (1926). *Nov. Zool.* **33**: 240.
Rüppell (1837). *Neue Wirbelth. Vög.*: 52, 61.
Rüppell (1842). *Mus. Senckenb.* **3**: 120-121.
Russell (1963). *Occas. Pap. Mus. Zool. La. St. Univ.* **25**: 1-3.
Salvadori (1868). *Atti R. Accad. Sci. Torino* **3**: 524.
Salvadori (1870). *Atti R. Accad. Sci. Torino* **6**: 129.
Salvadori (1879). *Ann. Mus. Civ. Genova* **14**: 182.
Salvadori (1887). *Ann. Mus. Civ. Genova* **24**: 531.
Salvadori & Festa (1900). *Boll. Mus. Zool. Anat. Comp. Univ. Torino* **15**: 14, 22.
Salvin (1870). *Proc. Zool. Soc. London* **1870**: 212-213.
Salvin (1876). *Ibis* **Ser. 3, no. 6**: 494.
Salvin (1889). *Ibis* **Ser. 6, no. 1**: 370.
Salvin (1897). *Bull. Brit. Orn. Club* **7**: 16.
Salvin & Godman (1882). *Ibis* **Ser. 4, no. 6**: 83.
Salvin & Godman (1889). *Ibis* **Ser. 6, no. 1**: 381.
Sassi (1911). *J. Orn.* **59**: 181.
Sassi (1932). *Orn. Monatsber.* **40**: 121.
Saunders (1872). *Proc. Zool. Soc. London* **1872**: 153.
Schlegel (1863). *Mus. Pays-Bas* **1**: 72.
Schlegel (1865). *Nederlandsch Tijdschrift Dierkunde* **3**: 190.
Schlüter (1908). *Falco* **4**: 11.
Sclater, P.L. (1853). In: *Jardine's Contr. Orn.*: 61.
Sclater, P.L. (1854). *Ann. and Mag. Nat. Hist.* **13**: 479. [*Nonnula frontalis*]
Sclater, P.L. (1854). *Proc. Zool. Soc. London* **1854**: 122-124. [*Nystalus radiatus, Nystalus maculatus striatipectus, Malacoptila fulvogularis, Nonnula*]
Sclater, P.L. (1855). *Proc. Zool. Soc. London* **1855**: 14-15, 110, 193-194.
Sclater, P.L. (1856). *Proc. Zool. Soc. London* **1856**: 193-194.
Sclater, P.L. (1858). *Proc. Zool. Soc. London* **1858**: 267.

Sclater, P.L. (1859). *Proc. Zool. Soc. London* **1859**: 60.
Sclater, P.L. (1860). *Proc. Zool. Soc. London* **1860**: 286, 296.
Sclater, P.L. (1862). *Cat. Am. Birds*: 275. [*Chelidoptera tenebrosa brasiliensis*]
Sclater, P.L. (1862). *Proc. Zool. Soc. London* **1862**: 86. [*Malacoptila panamensis poliopis*]
Sclater, P.L. (1864). *Ibis* **Ser. 1, no. 6**: 371.
Sclater, P.L. (1870). *Proc. Zool. Soc. London* **1870**: 330.
Sclater, P.L. (1878). *Proc. Zool. Soc. London* **1878**: 140.
Sclater, P.L. (1881). *Ibis* **Ser. 4, no. 5**: 600. [*Nonnula brunnea*]
Sclater, P.L. (1881). *Proc. Zool. Soc. London* **1881**: 776-778. [*Micromonacha*, *Nonnula rubecula cineracea*, *Hapaloptila*]
Sclater, P.L. (1891). *Cat. Birds Brit. Mus.* **19**: 171.
Sclater, P.L. & Salvin (1868). *Proc. Zool. Soc. London* **1867**: 758; **1868**: 327.
Sclater, P.L. & Salvin (1869). *Proc. Zool. Soc. London* **1869**: 253.
Sclater, P.L. & Salvin (1875). *Proc. Zool. Soc. London* **1875**: 237.
Sclater, P.L. & Salvin (1876). *Proc. Zool. Soc. London* **1876**: 254.
Sclater, P.L. & Salvin (1877). *Proc. Zool. Soc. London* **1877**: 20-21.
Sclater, P.L. & Salvin (1879). *Proc. Zool. Soc. London* **1879**: 535.
Sclater, P.L. & Salvin (1880). *Proc. Zool. Soc. London* **1880**: 161.
Sclater, W.L. (1927). *Bull. Brit. Orn. Club* **47**: 85.
Sclater, W.L. (1930). *Bull. Brit. Orn. Club* **51**: 16.
Sclater, W.L. & Moreau (1935). *Bull. Brit. Orn. Club* **56**: 15.
Scopoli (1786). *Deliciae Florae Faunae Insubricae* **2**: 89, 93.
Seebohm (1883). *Ibis* **Ser. 5, no. 1**: 24.
Seebohm (1887). *Ibis* **Ser. 5, no. 5**: 178.
Seilern (1913). *Verh. Orn. Ges. Bayern* **11**: 276.
Seilern (1936). *Ann. k. k. naturh. Hofsmus. Wien* **47**: 36.
Sélys Longchamps (1848). *Rev. Zool.*: 292.
Sharpe (1877). *Trans. Linn. Soc. London* **1**: 315.
Sharpe (1884). *Ibis* **Ser. 5, no. 2**: 317.
Sharpe (1888). *Ibis* **Ser. 5, no. 6**: 393. [*Megalaima pulcherrima*]
Sharpe (1888). *Proc. Zool. Soc. London* **1888**: 279. [*Picus flavinucha wrayi*]
Sharpe (1889). *Ann. and Mag. Nat. Hist.* **3**: 424.
Sharpe (1891). *Ibis* **Ser. 6, no. 3**: 122.
Sharpe (1892). *Ibis* **Ser. 6, no. 4**: 310, 324, 441.
Sharpe (1897). *Bull. Brit. Orn. Club* **7**: 7.
Sharpe (1898). *Bull. Brit. Orn. Club* **7**: 36.
Sharpe (1900). *Bull. Brit. Orn. Club* **10**: 36.
Sharpe (1901). *Bull. Brit. Orn. Club* **12**: 4.
Sharpe (1902). *Bull. Brit. Orn. Club* **12**: 80; **13**: 8. [*Indicator conirostris ussheri*, *Dendropicos griseocephalus ruwenzori*]
Sharpe (1902). *Ibis* **Ser. 8, no. 2**: 638. [*Campethera nubica pallida*]
Sharpe (1906). *Bull. Brit. Orn. Club* **16**: 86.
Sharpe & Dresser (1871). *Ann. and Mag. Nat. Hist* **8**: 436.
Shaw (1790). In: White's *J. Voy. New South Wales*: 235.
Shaw (1798). *Nat. Misc.* **10**: pl. 393.
Shelley (1880). *Ibis* **Ser. 4, no. 4**: 334. [*Stactolaema olivacea*]
Shelley (1880). *Proc. Zool. Soc. London* **1879**: 680. [*Tricholaema leucomelas affinis*]
Shelley (1881). *Ibis* **Ser. 4, no. 5**: 117.
Shelley (1887). *Proc. Zool. Soc. London* **1887**: 122.
Shelley (1889). *Ibis* **Ser. 6, no. 1**: 476-477.
Shelley (1891). *Cat. Birds Brit. Mus.* **19**: 88, 97, 108.
Shelley (1893). *Ibis* **Ser. 6, no. 5**: 10-11.
Shelley (1894). *Ibis* **Ser. 6, no. 6**: 8.
Shelley (1895). *Bull. Brit. Orn. Club* **5**: 3.
Shelley (1899). *Bull. Brit. Orn. Club* **8**: 35.
Short (1973). *Wilson Bull.* **85**: 465-467.
Sjöstedt (1892). *J. Orn.* **40**: 313.
Sjöstedt (1893). *Orn. Monatsber.* **1**: 138.
Slater (1879). *Philos. Trans.* **168**: 427.
Slater (1897). *Ibis* **Ser. 7, no. 3**: 176.
Smith, A. (1836). *Rep. Exped. Central Africa*: 53.
Snethlage (1907). *Orn. Monatsber* **15**: 163, 195.
Snethlage (1912). *Orn. Monatsber.* **20**: 154.
Snethlage (1924). *J. Orn.* **72**: 448-449.
van Someren (1926). *Bull. Brit. Orn. Club* **47**: 70.
Sousa (1886). *J. Sci. Math. Phys. e Nat., Acad. Real Sci. Lisboa* **11**: 158.
Sparrman (1777). *Philos. Trans.* **67**: 43.
Sparrman (1787). *Mus. Carlsonianum* **2**: 45.
Sparrman (1798). *Vetensk.-Acad. Handl.* **19**: 305.
Spix (1824). *Av. Bras.* **1**.
Stager (1961). *Contrib. Sci. Los Angeles Co. Mus.* **46**: 1.
Stager (1968). *Contrib. Sci. Los Angeles Co. Mus.* **143**: 1-2; **153**: 1.
Stanley (1814). In: Salt's *Voyage in Abyssinia*: pl. 56.
Steere (1890). *List Birds Mammals Steere Exped.*: 8.
Stejneger (1885). *Bull. US Natl. Mus.* **29**: 321, 338, 342.
Stejneger (1886). *Proc. US Natl. Mus.* **9**: 106, 113, 116.
Stejneger (1887). *Amer. Nat.* **21**: 583.
Stephens (1815). In *Shaw's Gen. Zool.* **9(1)**: 131, 140.
Stolzmann (1926). *Ann. Zool. Mus. Polon. Hist. Nat.* **5**: 214.
Stresemann (1913). *Nov. Zool.* **20**: 317-318.
Stresemann (1920). *Verh. Orn. Ges. Bayern* **14**: 288.
Stresemann (1929). *J. Orn.* **77**: 335-336.
Strickland (1850). In: *Jardine's Contr. Orn.*: 47.
Strickland (1853). In: *Jardine's Contr. Orn.*: 155.
Stuart Baker (1926). *Bull. Brit. Orn. Club* **46**: 70; **47**: 43.
Sturm (1841). *Monogr. Ramphastidae* **2**: pls. 2, 16.
Styan (1898). *Bull. Brit. Orn. Club* **7**: 40.
Sundevall (1850). *Oefv. Kongl. Vet.-Akad. Forh.* **7**: 109.
Sundevall (1866). *Consp. Av. Picinarum*: 89, 95, 100-101, 103.
Swainson (1820). *Quart. J. Sci. Lit. Arts* **9**: 267. [*Aulacorhynchus sulcatus*]
Swainson (1820). *Zool. Illustr.* **1**: pl. 14. [*Piculus rubiginosus*]
Swainson (1821). *Zool. Illustr.* **2**: pl. 72, 78.
Swainson (1822). *Zool. Illustr.* **2**: pl. 90.
Swainson (1823). *Zool. Illustr.* **3**: pl. 168.
Swainson (1827). *Philos. Mag. (New Ser.)* **1**: 439-440.
Swainson (1832). In: Swainson & Richardson, *Fauna Bor. Am.* **2**: 306, 308, 313, 315-316.
Swainson (1837). *Birds W. Afr.* **2**: 150, 158, 162. [*Campethera abingoni chrysura*, *Campethera nivosa*, *Blythipicus rubiginosus*]
Swainson (1837). *Classif. Birds* **2**: 306, 309. [*Meiglyptes*, *Hemicircus*]
Swainson (1838). *Anim. in Menag.*: 329.
Swarth (1911). *Univ. Calif. Publ. Zool.* **7**: 315.
Swinhoe (1863). *Ibis* **Ser. 1, no. 5**: 96, 390. [*Dendrocopos canicapillus scintilliceps*, *Dendrocopos canicapillus kaleensis*]
Swinhoe (1863). *Proc. Zool. Soc. London* **1863**: 87. [*Celeus brachyurus fokiensis*]
Swinhoe (1870). *Ann. and Mag. Nat. Hist.* **6**: 348. [*Megalaima virens marshallorum*]
Swinhoe (1870). *Ibis* **Ser. 3, no. 1**: 95-96. [*Megalaima oorti faber*, *Celeus brachyurus holroydi*]
Taczanowski (1875). *Proc. Zool. Soc. London* **1874**: 546.
Taczanowski (1877). *Proc. Zool. Soc. London* **1877**: 327.
Taczanowski (1882). *Proc. Zool. Soc. London* **1882**: 40-41.
Taczanowski (1886). *Orn. Pérou* **3**: 65.
Taczanowski & Berlepsch (1885). *Proc. Zool. Soc. London* **1885**: 107.
Takatsukasa (1922). *Dobuts. Zasshi* **34**: 292.
Temminck (1821). *Planches Color* **10**: wrapper p. [4] of pl. 59; **15**: pls. 89-90.
Temminck (1822). *Planches Color* **29**: pl. 171.
Temminck (1823). *Planches Color* **34**.
Temminck (1824). *Planches Color* **48**: pl. 285; **53**: pl. 315.
Temminck (1825). *Planches Color* **62**: pl. 371; **64**: pls. 378, 402; **65**: pl. 384.
Temminck (1826). *Planches Color* **66**: pls. 389-390, 424; **99**: pl. 585.
Temminck (1827). *Planches Color* **73**: 433.
Temminck (1830). *Planches Color* **83**: pl. 490.
Temminck (1831). *Planches Color* **88**: pls. 522, 524, 527.
Temminck (1832). *Planches Color* **90**: pl. 536; **91**: pl. 542.
Temminck (1835). *Planches Color* **99**: pl. 585.
Tickell (1833). *J. Asiatic Soc. Bengal* **2**: 578.
Todd (1910). *Proc. Biol. Soc. Washington* **23**: 153.
Todd (1917). *Proc. Biol. Soc. Washington* **30**: 5.
Todd (1919). *Proc. Biol. Soc. Washington* **32**: 116.
Todd (1925). *Proc. Biol. Soc. Washington* **38**: 111.
Todd (1932). *Proc. Biol. Soc. Washington* **45**: 217.
Todd (1937). *Ann. Carnegie Mus.* **25**: 247-250, 252.
Todd (1943). *Ann. Carnegie Mus.* **30**: 2, 6, 9-10, 15.
Todd (1946). *Ann. Carnegie Mus.* **30**: 317.
Todd & Carriker (1922). *Ann. Carnegie Mus.* **14**: 228.
Traylor (1970). *Bull. Brit. Orn. Club* **90**: 78-80.
Tristram (1879). *Proc. Zool. Soc. London* **1879**: 386.
Tschudi (1844). *Archiv Naturgeschichte* **10**: 300-302.
Tweeddale (1877). *Ann. and Mag. Nat. Hist.* **20**: 533-534.
Tweeddale (1878). *Proc. Zool. Soc. London* **1878**: 340, 612.
Valenciennes (1826). *Dict. Sci. Nat. (éd. Levrault)* **40**: 170, 173, 178-179.
Vaurie (1959). *Amer. Mus. Novit.* **1946**: 23; **1963**: 9.
Verreaux, J. (1866). *Rev. et Mag. Zool.* **18**: 355.
Verreaux, J. (1867). *Rev. et Mag. Zool.* **19**: 271.
Verreaux, J. (1868). *Nouv. Arch. Mus. Hist. Nat.* **4**: 87.
Verreaux, J. (1870). *Nouv. Arch. Mus. Hist. Nat.* **6**: 33.
Verreaux, J. & Verreaux, E. (1851). *Rev. et Mag. Zool.* **3**: 260, 262-263, 513.
Verreaux, J. & Verreaux, E. (1855). *J. Orn.* **3**: 101-102. [*Pogoniulus scolopaceus flavisquamatus*, *Tricholaema*, *Tricholaema hirsuta flavipunctata*]
Verreaux, J. & Verreaux, E. (1855). *Rev. et Mag. Zool.* **7**: 217. [*Sasia africana*]
Vieillot (1807). *Ois. Am.* **2**: 66.
Vieillot (1816). *Analyse*: 27. [*Monasa*, *Capito*]
Vieillot (1816). *Nouv. Dict. Hist. Nat.* **3**: 239; **4**: 500. [*Nystalus chacuru*, *Megalaima lineata*]
Vieillot (1817). *Nouv. Dict. Hist. Nat.* **16**: 444-445.
Vieillot (1818). *Nouv. Dict. Hist. Nat.* **26**.
Vieillot (1819). *Nouv. Dict. Hist. Nat.* **34**: 282-283.
Vigors (1826). *Trans. Linn. Soc. London* **14**: 457. [*Colaptes*]
Vigors (1826). *Zool. J.* **2**: 466, 481. [*Pteroglossus bitorquatus*, *Ramphastos vitellinus ariel*]
Vigors (1827). *Zool. J.* **3**: 445.
Vigors (1829). *Zool. J.* **4**: 354.
Vigors (1831). *Proc. Comm. Zool. Soc. London* **1**: 8, 23, 44.
Vigors (1832). *Proc. Comm. Zool. Soc. London* **1**: 172, 175.
Vigors (1839). In: *Zool. Beechey's Voy. Pacific & Behring's Strait*: 24.
Vigors & Horsfield (1830). In: Lady Sophia Raffles' *Mem. Life and Public Services Sir T. S. Raffles*: 669.
Vincent (1934). *Bull. Brit. Orn. Club* **54**: 176.
Wagler (1827). *Systema Avium*.
Wagler (1829). *Isis von Oken* **22**: cols. 510-512, 514-516, 646.
Wagler (1830). *Nat. Syst. Amphibien*: 118.
Wagler (1832). *Isis von Oken* **25**: col. 280.
Walden (1870). *Ann. and Mag. Nat. Hist.* **5**: 219.
Walden (1875). *Ann. and Mag. Nat. Hist.* **15**: 400.
Walden & Layard, E.L. (1872). *Ibis* **Ser. 3, no. 2**: 99.
Waterhouse (1839). *Proc. Zool. Soc. London* **1839**: 111.
Waterhouse (1841). *Proc. Zool. Soc. London* **1841**: 182.
Wetmore (1922). *J. Washington Acad. Sci.* **12**: 326.
Wetmore (1928). *Proc. Biol. Soc. Washington* **41**: 167.
Wetmore (1939). *Smiths. Misc. Coll.* **98(4)**: 1.
Wetmore (1953). *Smiths. Misc. Coll.* **122(8)**: 3.
Wetmore (1957). *Smiths. Misc. Coll.* **134(9)**: 50-51.
Whistler & Kinnear (1934). *J. Bombay Nat. Hist. Soc.* **37**: 294.
White, C.M.N. (1945). *Bull. Brit. Orn. Club* **65**: 18.
Wilson (1888). *Proc. Zool. Soc. London* **1888**: 218.
Winker, K. (2000). *Orn. Neotropical* **11**: 253-257.
Zarudny & Loudon (1904). *Orn. Jahrb.* **15**: 227.
Zarudny & Loudon (1905). *Orn. Monatsber.* **13**: 49.
Zedlitz (1910). *Orn. Monatsber.* **18**: 57.
Zedlitz (1915). *J. Orn.* **63**: 12.
Zimmer, J.T. (1931). *Amer. Mus. Novit.* **500**: 3.
Zimmer, J.T. (1942). *Amer. Mus. Novit.* **1159**: 2-3.
Zimmer, J.T. (1947). *Proc. Biol. Soc. Washington* **60**: 99-100.
Zimmer, J.T. & Phelps, Sr. (1944). *Amer. Mus. Novit.* **1270**: 5-6.
Zimmer, J.T. & Phelps, Sr. (1946). *Amer. Mus. Novit.* **1312**: 6.
Zimmer, J.T. & Phelps, Sr. (1947). *Amer. Mus. Novit.* **1338**: 3.
Zimmer, J.T. & Phelps, Sr. (1950). *Amer. Mus. Novit* **1455**: 4, 6.

GENERAL LIST OF REFERENCES

Abdulali, H. (1941). The Great Black Woodpecker in the neighbourhood of Bombay. *J. Bombay Nat. Hist. Soc.* **42(4)**: 933-934.

Abdulali, H. (1974). A catalogue of the birds in the collection of the Bombay Natural History Society - 16. *J. Bombay Nat. Hist. Soc.* **71(3)**: 244-265.

Abdulali, H. (1985). On the juvenile plumage of female *Chrysocolaptes festivus* (Boddaert) and other nesting notes near Bombay. *J. Bombay Nat. Hist. Soc.* **82(1)**: 202-203.

Abdulali, H. & Hussain, S.A. (1973). On the occurrence of Golden-backed Three-toed Woodpecker *Dinopium shorii* (Vigors) south of the Himalayan range. *J. Bombay Nat. Hist. Soc.* **70(1)**: 200-201.

Abell, A.G.W. (1992). Black-collared Barbet *Lybius torquatus* sighting in Maseru, Lesotho. *Mirafra* **9(3&4)**: 65.

Adamian, M.S. & Klem, D. (1999). *Handbook of the Birds of Armenia.* American University of Armenia, Oakland & Yerevan.

Adams, L. (1941a). Lewis Woodpecker migration. *Condor* **43(2)**: 119.

Adams, L. (1941b). Aberrant mating activities of the California Woodpecker. *Condor* **43(6)**: 268-269.

Adams, N.J. & Slotow, R.H. (1999). *Proceedings of the XXII International Ornithological Congress, Durban 1998.* BirdLife South Africa, Johannesburg.

Agey, H.N. & Heinzmann, G.M. (1971). The Ivory-billed Woodpecker found in central Florida. *Florida Nat.* **44**: 46-47, 64.

Aguilera, A.R. (1986). El Carpintero Real se salva en Cuba. *Ahora* **89**: 5.

Aguirre, A.C. & Aldrighi, A.D. (1983). *Catálogo das Aves do Museu da Fauna.* Part 1. Delegacia Estadual do Estado do Rio de Janeiro, Instituto Brasileiro de Desenvolvimento Florestal, Rio de Janeiro.

Ahlén, I. & Andersson, Å. (1976). Graspett *Picus canus* och Vitryggig Hackspett *Dendrocopos leucotos* i Sverige 1973. [Grey-headed Woodpecker *Picus canus* and White-backed Woodpecker *Dendrocopus leucotos* in Sweden in 1973.] *Vår Fågelvärld* **35(1)**: 21-25. In Swedish with English summary.

Ahlén, I., Andersson, Å., Aulén, G. & Petersson, B. (1978). Vitryggig hackspett och mellanspet - två hotade arters ekologi. *Anser* **3**(Suppl.): 5-11.

Alagar, R.S. (1992). Unusual foraging site of Golden-backed Woodpecker *Dinopium benghalense* (Linn.). *J. Bombay Nat. Hist. Soc.* **89(3)**: 374.

Alatalo, R. (1978). Resource partitioning in Finnish Woodpeckers. *Ornis Fenn.* **55(2)**: 49-59. In English with Finnish summary.

Alayón, G. & Estrada, R. (1986). El Carpintero Real (*Campephilus principalis* Cassin: Piciformes: Picidae) - estado de conservación en Cuba. Page 140 in: *Resúmenes de la Quinta Conferencia Científica sobre Ciencias Naturales y Biología, 24-26 Febrero 1986.* Universidad de la Habana, La Habana. 215 pp.

Alayón, G. & Garrido, O.H. (1991). Current status of the Ivory-billed Woodpecker (*Campephilus principalis*) in Cuba. *Pitirre* **4(2)**: 11. (Abstract).

Alayón, G., Kirkconnell, A., Llanes, A. & Posada, R.M. (1986). Observaciones conductales en un nido del Carpintero Verde (*Xiphidiopicus percussus percussus* Temminck; Aves: Piciformes: Picidae). Page 139 in: *Resúmenes de la Quinta Conferencia Científica sobre Ciencias Naturales y Biología, 24-26 Febrero 1986.* Universidad de la Habana, La Habana. 215 pp.

Albaine, J.R. & Grullón, G. (1981). *Introducción al Estudio del Régimen Alimenticio del Pájaro Carpintero (*Melanerpes striatus V.) en la República Dominicana.* Cuadernos de la Universidad Central del Este **5**. San Pedro de Macorís, Dominican Republic. 19 pp.

Albrecht, H. & Wickler, W. (1968). Freiland Beobachtungen zur "Bergrüssungszeremonie" des Schmuckbartvogels *Trachyphonus d'arnaudii* [sic] (Prévost U. Des Murs). *J. Orn.* **109**: 225-263.

Alcalá, A.C. & Sanguila, W.M. (1969). The birds of small islands off the eastern coast of Panay. *Silliman J.* **16**: 375-383.

Aleixo, A. (1997). Composition of mixed-species bird flocks and abundance of flocking species in a semideciduous forest of southeastern Brazil. *Ararajuba* **5(1)**: 11-18.

Aleixo, A. & Galetti, M. (1997). The conservation of the avifauna in a lowland Atlantic forest in south-east Brazil. *Bird Conserv. Int.* **7(3)**: 235-261.

Aleixo, A., Whitney, B.M. & Oren, D.C. (2000). Range extensions of birds in southeastern Amazonia. *Wilson Bull.* **112(1)**: 137-142.

Alekseev, V.N. & Martyanov, V.N. (1986). [Breeding record of the Three-toed Woodpecker (*Picoides tridactylus*) in Moscow region]. *Ornitologiya* **21**: 126. In Russian.

Ali, S. (1951a). The Heart-spotted Woodpecker *Hemicircus canente*. *J. Bombay Nat. Hist. Soc.* **49(4)**: 786-787.

Ali, S. (1951b). Discovery of the so-named "Malabar" Black Woodpecker *Dryocopus javensis hodgsoni* (Jerdon) in Bastar (east Madhya Pradesh). *J. Bombay Nat. Hist. Soc.* **49(4)**: 787-788.

Ali, S. (1962). *The Birds of Sikkim.* Oxford University Press, Madras, India.

Ali, S. (1969). *Birds of Kerala.* Oxford University Press, Madras, India.

Ali, S. (1977). *Field Guide to the Birds of the Eastern Himalayas.* Oxford University Press, Delhi.

Ali, S. (1979). *Indian Hill Birds.* Oxford University Press, Delhi.

Ali, S. (1996). *The Book of Indian Birds.* 12th revised and enlarged centenary edition. Bombay Natural History Society, Bombay.

Ali, S. & Ripley, S.D. (1983). *Handbook of the Birds of India and Pakistan.* Vol. 4. 2nd edition. Oxford University Press, Delhi.

Ali, S., Biswas, B. & Ripley, S.D. (1996). *The Birds of Bhutan.* Zoological Survey of India Occasional Paper **136**, Calcutta.

Allen, A.A. & Kellogg, P.P. (1937). Recent observations on the Ivory-billed Woodpecker. *Auk* **54(2)**: 164-184.

Allen, D.H., Franzreb, K.E. & Escaño, R.E.F. (1993). Efficacy of translocation strategies for Red-cockaded Woodpeckers. *Wildl. Soc. Bull.* **21(2)**: 155-159.

Allen, F.G.H. (1953). Further notes on birds nesting at Fraser's Hill. *Malay. Nat. J.* **8**: 16-22.

Allen, R.P. (1961). *Birds of the Caribbean.* Viking Press, New York.

Allen, S. (1995). *A Birder's Guide to Explorer's Inn.* Published privately.

Allen, S. (1998). *A Birder's Guide to Mindo, Ecuador.* Published privately.

Allin, E.K. & Edgar, A.T. (1948). Notes on the nesting of some birds of the Malayan mountains. *Malay. Nat. J.* **3**: 51-57.

Allport, G. (1991). The status and conservation of threatened birds in the Upper Guinea Forest. *Bird Conserv. Int.* **1**: 53-74.

Allport, G., Ausden, M., Hayman, P.V., Robertson, P. & Wood, P. (1989). *The Conservation of the Birds of Gola Forest, Sierra Leone.* ICBP Study Report **38**, Cambridge.

Álvarez del Toro, M. (1980). *Las Aves de Chiapas.* Universidad Autónoma de Chiapas, Tuxtla Gutiérrez, Chiapas, Mexico.

Álvarez-López, H. (1987). *Introducción a las Aves de Colombia.* 2nd edition. Biblioteca Banco Popular, Textos Universitarios, Cali.

Álvarez-López, H. (1989). Colombia in focus. *World Birdwatch* **11(3)**: 9.

Alves, M.A.S., da Silva, J.M.C., Van Sluys, M., Bergallo, H.G. & da Rocha, C.F.D. (2000). *A Ornitologia no Brasil: Pesquisa Atual e Perspectivas.* Universidade do Estado do Rio de Janeiro, Rio de Janeiro.

Alves, V.S., Mallet-Rodrigues, F. & de Noronha, M.L.M. (1997). O uso do tartaro emetico no estudo da alimentação das aves silvestres Brasileiras. Page 75 in: Marini (1997). (Abstract).

Amadon, D. (1953). Avian systematics and evolution in the Gulf of Guinea, the J. G. Correira collection. *Bull. Amer. Mus. Nat. Hist.* **100(3)**: 393-452.

Amadon, D. & Short, L.L. (1992). Taxonomy of lower categories - suggested guidelines. Pp. 11-38 in: Monk (1992).

Amcoff, M. & Eriksson, P. (1996). Forekomst av tretaig hackspett *Picoides tridactylus* pa bestands-och landskapsniva. [Occurrence of Three-toed Woodpecker *Picoides tridactylus* at the scales of forest stand and landscape]. *Ornis Svecica* **6(3)**: 101-119. In Swedish with English summary.

Anderson, B.W. (1971). Man's influence on hybridization in two avian species in South Dakota. *Condor* **73(3)**: 342-347.

Anderson, J.A.R., Jermy, A.C. & Cranbrook, E. (1982). *Gunung Mulu National Park, Sarawak - A Management and Development Plan.* Appendix VI. Birds. Royal Geographic Society, London.

Anderson, S.H. & Linder, K.A. (1997). Behavior of nesting Lewis' Woodpeckers in the Laramie Range, southeastern Wyoming. *Intermt. J. Sci.* **3(2/3)**: 55-61.

Andersson, Å. & Hamilton, G. (1972). Vitryggiga hackspetten *Dendrocopos leucotos* i Östergötland. *Vår Fågelvärld* **31**: 257-262.

de Andrade, M.A. (1992). *Aves Silvestres: Minas Gerais.* CIPA, Belo Horizonte, Brazil.

Andreev, A.V., Chan, S., Crosby, M.J., Subramanya, S. & Tobias, J.A. eds. (2001). *Threatened Birds of Asia: the BirdLife International Red Data Book.* BirdLife International, Cambridge, UK.

Andrew, P. (1985). An annotated checklist of the birds of the Cibodas–Gunung Gede Nature Reserve. *Kukila* **2(1)**: 10-28.

Andrew, P. (1992). *The Birds of Indonesia. A Checklist (Peter's Sequence).* Kukila Checklist **1**. Indonesian Ornithological Society, Jakarta.

Andrew, P. & Holmes, D.A. (1990). Sulawesi bird report. *Kukila* **5(1)**: 4-26.

Angehr, G. (1995). El Chorogo, Burica Península, Chiriquí. *Tucan* **21(9)**: 8-10.

Angehr, G. (2001). The field editor's report. *Tucan* **27(5)**: 1-2.

Angehr, G. & Aucca, C. (1997). *Birds: Biodiversity Assessment in the Lower Urubamba Region.* SPDP & Smithsonian Institute of Conservation Biology, Washington, D.C.

dos Anjos, L. (1999). Análise preliminar das manifestações sonoras e do habitat de *Picumnus nebulosus* Sundevall (Aves, Picidae). *Rev. Bras. Zool.* **16(2)**: 433-439.

dos Anjos, L. (2001). Bird communities in five Atlantic forest fragments in southern Brazil. *Orn. Neotropical* **12(1)**: 11-27.

dos Anjos, L. & Schuchmann, K.L. (1997). Biogeographical affinities of the avifauna of the Tibagi River Basin, Paraná drainage system, southern Brazil. *Ecotropica* **3(1)**: 43-65.

dos Anjos, L., Schuchmann, K.L. & Berndt, R. (1997). Avifaunal composition, species richness, and status in the Tibagi River Basin, Paraná State, southern Brazil. *Orn. Neotropical* **8(2)**: 145-173.

Anon. (1972). Extermination of harmful insects by the Great Spotted Woodpecker *Dendrocopos major*. *Animal Utilization and Control* **5**: 32.

Anon. (1973). Extermination of longicorn beetles by Great Spotted Woodpeckers *Dendrocopos major*. *Forestry Tech. Newsl.* **7**: 14-15.

Anon. (1975). The Black-naped Green Woodpecker, *Picus canus*, in Yunan and Guizhou Province. *Selection of the Research Work of Yunnan Institute of Zoology* **5**: 23-25.

Anon. (1985). *Red-cockaded Woodpecker Recovery Plan.* US Fish & Wildlife Service, Atlanta, Georgia.

Anon. (1986). Ivory-billed Woodpecker found in Cuba. *World Birdwatch* **8(2)**: 1-2.

Anon. (1995a). *A Birdlist of Bolivia.* 4th edition. Asociación Armonía, Santa Cruz de la Sierra, Bolivia.

Anon. (1995b). Neotropical News. Hope for Helmeted Woodpecker in Misiones, Argentina. *Cotinga* **3**: 9.

Anon. (1996a). *1996 IUCN Red List of Threatened Animals.* IUCN, Gland, Switzerland.

Anon. (1996b). World round-up. Imperial Woodpecker extinct? *World Birdwatch* **18(1)**: 2.

Anon. (1997). International zoo news. News in brief: Ohrada Zoo. *Int. Zoo News* **44(2)**: 126.

Anon. (1998a). 1997 species records. Pp. 59-139 in: Leonard & Peters (1998).

Anon. (1998b). *The A.O.U. Check-list of North American Birds.* 7th edition. American Ornithologists' Union, Washington, D.C.

Anon. (1998c). Bird of the month. Little Spotted Woodpecker. *Zambian Orn. Soc. Newsl.* **28(3)**: 3-4.

Anon. (1998d). Bird of the month. Golden-rumped Tinkerbird. *Zambian Orn. Soc. Newsl.* **28(11)**: 3-4.

Anon. (1998e). Woodpecker as umbrella species. *Oryx* **32(4)**: 251.

Anon. (1998f). Projeto: "Aves ameaçadas de extinção do estado de São Paulo". *Bol. Soc. Antioqueña Orn.* **13**: 28-32.

Anon. (1999). World round-up. Fire sweeps through San Fernando, Chile. *World Birdwatch* **21(1)**: 4.

Anon. (2000). The birds of Indonesia, *Kukila* Checklist No. 1: additions, corrections and notes. Part 2. *Kukila* **11**: 3-12.

Anon. (2001). Taxonomic round-up. A new colourful barbet from the eastern Andes of Peru. *Cotinga* **15**: 5.
Antas, P.T.Z. & Cavalcanti, R.B. (1988). *Aves Comums do Planalto Central*. Editora Universidade de Brasília, Brasília.
Antevs, A. (1948). Behavior of the Gila Woodpecker, Ruby-crowned Kinglet, and Broad-tailed Hummingbird. *Condor* **50(2)**: 91-92.
Anzenberger, G. (1974). Über das Auftreten der geschlechtsspezifischen Duettelemente in der Gesangsentwicklung des Schmuckbartvogels *Trachyphonus d'arnaudii*. *Z. Tierpsychol.* **34**: 395-397.
Aparicio, K.M. (1996). Informaciones del Programa AIA. *Tucan* **22(9)**: 6.
Arambarri, R. & Rodríguez, A.F. (1996). Distribución y estima poblacional del Pico Mediano (*Dendrocopos medius*) en Álava. [Distribution and population estimates of Middle Spotted Woodpecker (*Dendrocopos medius*) in Álava]. *Ardeola* **43(2)**: 221-223.
Araya, B. & Chester, S. (1993). *The Birds of Chile. A Field Guide*. LATOUR, Santiago.
Archer, A.L. & Glen, R.M. (1969). Observations on the behaviour of two species of honey-guides *Indicator variegatus* (Lesson) and *Indicator exilis* (Cassin). *Contrib. Sci. Los Angeles Co. Mus.* **160**: 1-6.
Archer, G.F. & Godman, E.M. (1937-1961). *The Birds of British Somaliland and the Gulf of Aden*. Vols. 1-2. Gurney & Jackson, London. Vols. 3-4. Oliver & Boyd, Edinburgh & London.
Argel-de-Oliveira, M.M. (1992). Comportamento alimentar de aves em *Trichilia micrantha* Benth. (Meliaceae) na Serra dos Carajás, Pará. *Bol. Mus. Paraense Emilio Goeldi (Zool.)* **8(2)**: 305-313.
Arisawa, H. (1991). [Breeding nest density and the characteristics of nest tree of Black Woodpecker, *Dryocopus martius martius*]. *Bull. Tokyo Univ. For.* **84**: 21-37. In Japanese with English summary.
Arndt, R.G. (1995). Red-bellied Woodpecker, *Melanerpes carolinus*, predation on adult green anole, *Anolis carolinensis*. *Florida Scientist* **58(3)**: 249-251.
Arnhem, R. (1960). À propos d'une triple couvaison normale chez le Torcol, *Jynx torquilla* L. *Gerfaut* **50**: 1-10.
Arnold, K.A. (1984). *Checklist of the Birds of Texas*. Texas Ornithological Society, Austin, Texas.
Arredondo, O. (1984). Sinopsis de las aves halladas en depósitos fosilíferos pleisto-holocénicos de Cuba. *Rep. Invest. Inst. Zool. Acad. Cienc. Cuba* **17**: 1-35.
Artíguez, G. & Franco, J. (1997). Primeros datos sobre la distribución y tamaño de población del Pico Menor (*Dendrocopos minor*) en Bizkaia (N de España). Pp. 255-260 in: Manrique, J., Sánchez, A., Suárez, F. & Yanes, M. eds. (1997). *Actas de las XII Jornadas Ornitológicas Españolas*. Instituto de Estudios Almerienses, Almería, Spain.
Aschoff, J. (1967). Circadian rhythms in birds. Pp. 81-105 in: Snow, D.W. ed. (1967). *Proceedings of the XIV International Ornithological Congress, Oxford, July 1966*. Blackwell Scientific Publications, Oxford.
Ash, J.S. (1990). Additions to the avifauna of Nigeria, with notes on distributional changes and breeding. *Malimbus* **11(2)**: 104-116.
Ash, J.S. & Gullick, T.M. (1989). The present situation regarding the endemic breeding birds of Ethiopia. *Scopus* **13**: 90-96.
Ash, J.S. & Miskell, J.E. (1983). *Birds of Somalia: their Habitat, Status and Distribution*. Scopus Special Supplement **1**, Nairobi. 97 pp.
Ash, J.S. & Miskell, J.E. (1998). *Birds of Somalia*. Pica Press, Nr. Robertsbridge, UK.
Ash, J.S. & Sharland, R.E. (1986). *Nigeria Assessment of Bird Conservation Priorities*. ICBP Study Report **11**. ICBP & Nigerian Conservation Foundation, Cambridge.
Ash, J.S., Dowsett, R.J. & Dowsett-Lemaire, F. (1989). New ornithological distribution records from eastern Nigeria. *Tauraco Res. Rep.* **1**: 13-27.
Ashmole, N.P. (1967). Sexual dimorphism and colonial breeding in the woodpecker *Centurus striatus*. *Amer. Naturalist* **101**: 353-356.
Askins, R.A. (1983). Foraging ecology of temperate-zone and tropical woodpeckers. *Ecology* **64**: 945-956.
Aspinwall, D.R. (1973). Spotted-flanked Barbet *Tricholaema lacrymosum*: a species new to Zambia. *Bull. Zambian Orn. Soc.* **5**: 32.
Aspinwall, D.R. & Beel, C. (1998). *A Field Guide to Zambian Birds not Found in Southern Africa*. Zambian Ornithological Society, Lusaka.
Athanas, N. & Davis, J. (2000). Notes on the nest and breeding behavior of White-faced Nunbird (*Hapaloptila castanea*). MS.
Atkins, A. (1989). Bizarre nocturnal behavior of Red-headed Woodpecker. *Oriole* **52(2/3)**: 46.
Atkins, J.D. (1985). Moustached Green Tinkerbird *Pogoniulus leucomystax* on Soche Mountain. (With comments by D.B. Hanmer). *Nyala* **11(1)**: 27-28.
Attwell, G.D. (1952). The breeding of the Cardinal Woodpecker at Gatooma, Southern Rhodesia. *Ostrich* **23**: 88-91.
Aubrey, K.B. & Raley, C.M. (1992). *Landscape-level Responses of Pileated Woodpeckers to Forest Management and Fragmentation: a Pilot Study*. Progress report for the Pacific Northwest Research Station, Olympia, Washington.
Aubrey, K.B. & Raley, C.M. (1994). Landscape- and stand-level studies of Pileated Woodpeckers: design constraints and stand-level results. *Northwest Science* **68(2)**: 113.
Aulén, G. (1979). En hybrid mellan större - och vitryggig hackspett i Uppsala. *Fåglar i Uppsala* **6**: 27-32.
Aulén, G. (1988). *Ecology and Distribution History of the White-backed Woodpecker* Dendrocopos leucotos *in Sweden*. Report **14**. Department of Wildlife Ecology, Swedish University of Agricultural Sciences, Uppsala, Sweden.
Aulén, G. (1990). Research and conservation of the White-backed Woodpecker *Dendrocopos leucotos* in Sweden - experiences from a 15 years period. In: *Report to the 20th ICBP Conference in Hamilton, New Zealand, November 1990*. SOF, Stockholm.
Aulén, G. & Lundberg, A. (1991). Sexual dimorphism and patterns of territory use by the White-backed Woodpecker *Dendrocopos leucotos*. *Ornis Scand.* **22**: 60-64.
Austin, G.T. (1976). Sexual and seasonal differences in foraging of Ladder-backed Woodpeckers. *Condor* **78(3)**: 317-323.
Austin, O.L. (1948). *The Birds of Korea*. Bulletin of the Museum of Comparative Zoology **101**, Cambridge, Massachusetts. 301 pp.
Austin, O.L. & Kuroda, N. (1953). *The Birds of Japan. Their Status and Distribution*. Bulletin of the Museum of Comparative Zoology **109**, Cambridge, Massachusetts. 361 pp.
Avise, J.C. & Aquadro, C.F. (1987). Malate dehydrogenase isozymes provide a phylogenetic marker for the Piciformes (woodpeckers and allies). *Auk* **104(2)**: 324-328.
Axelsson, C., Nomm, M., Carlsson, H. & Carlsson, L. (1997). Projekt Goktyta *Jynx torquilla*: biotopval och hackningsframgang. [Project Wryneck *Jynx torquilla*: habitat selection and breeding success]. *Ornis Svecica* **7(1)**: 35-36. In Swedish with English summary.
Azama, Y. (1995). [The status and conservation recommendations to *Sapheopipo noguchii*]. Pp. 4-5 in: *Proceedings of the Annual Meeting of the Ornithological Society of Japan*. In Japanese.
Azama, Y. & Shimabukuro, N. (1984). Notes on the feeding rate of young of Noguchigera, *Sapheopipo noguchii* (Seebohm). *Biol. Mag. Okinawa* **22**: 79-90.
Azama, Y., Shimabukuro, T. & Takehara, K. (1990). [Habitat survey of Okinawa Woodpecker around Mount Terukubi-san and Binoki Dam]. Pp. 110-124 in: *Habitat and Environmental Survey on Special Birds III. Interim Report*. Naha, Division of Nature Conservation, Okinawa Prefecture, Japan. In Japanese.
Azama, Y., Shimabukuro, T., Takehara, K., Harato, T. & Tamaki, K. (1992). [Habitat survey of the Okinawa Woodpecker in the US practising ground in northern Okinawa]. Pp. 123-137 in: *Habitat and Environmental Survey on Special Birds V. Interim Report*. Naha, Division of Nature Conservation, Okinawa Prefecture, Japan. In Japanese.
Azara, F. de (1802-1805). *Apuntamientos para la Historia Natural de los Páxaros del Paragüay y Río de la Plata*. Vol. 3. Viuda de Ibarra, Madrid.
Babarskas, M., Veiga, J.O. & Filiberto, F.C. (1995). *Inventario de Aves del Parque Nacional El Rey, Salta, Argentina*. Monografía Especial **6**. Literature of Latin America, Buenos Aires.
Baciocchi, S. & Baumgart, P. (2001). Altercation entre un Chevêchette d'Europe *Glaucidium passerinum* et un Pic tridactyle *Picoides tridactylus*. *Nos Oiseaux* **48(1)**: 33-34. In French with English summary.
Baez, S., Fjeldså, J., Krabbe, N., Morales, P., Navarrete, H., Poulsen, B.O., Resl, R., Schjellerup, I., Skov, F., Ståhl, B. & Øllgaard, B. (1997). *Oyacachi – People and Biodiversity*. DIVA Technical Report **2**. Center for Research on Cultural and Biological Diversity of Andean Rainforests, Rønde, Denmark.
Baicich, P.J. & Harrison, C.J.O. (1997). *A Guide to the Nests, Eggs, and Nestlings of North American Birds*. Academic Press, San Diego, California.
Bailey, A.M. (1939). Ivory-billed Woodpecker's beak in an Indian grave in Colorado. *Condor* **41(4)**: 164.
Baillie, V.W. (1983). Breeding note: Golden-tailed Woodpecker *Campethera abingoni*. *Bull. Zambian Orn. Soc.* **13/15**: 137-139.
Baird, D.A. (1979). Twenty-eight additions to Archer & Godman's *Birds of British Somaliland and the Gulf of Aden*. *Bull. Brit. Orn. Club* **99(1)**: 6-9.
Baker, E.C.S. (1919). Some notes on Oriental woodpeckers and barbets. *Ibis* **Ser. 11, no. 2**: 181-222.
Baker, E.C.S. (1934a). *Fauna of British India. Birds*. 2nd edition. Vols. 3-4. Taylor & Francis, London.
Baker, E.C.S. (1934b). *The Nidification of Birds of the Indian Empire*. Vol. 3. Taylor & Francis, London.
Baker, J.L. & Payne, R.L. (1993). Nest usurpation of a starling nest by a pair of Red-bellied Woodpeckers. *Florida Field Nat.* **21(2)**: 33-34.
Baker, J.N. (1975). Egg-carrying by a Common Flicker. *Auk* **92(3)**: 614-615.
Baker, W.W. (1971a). Progress report on life history studies of the Red-cockaded Woodpecker at Tall Timber Research Station. Pp. 44-59 in: Thompson (1971).
Baker, W.W. (1971b). Observations on the food habits of the Red-cockaded Woodpecker. Pp. 100-107 in: Thompson (1971).
Baker, W.W. (1981). The distribution, status and future of the Red-cockaded Woodpecker in Georgia. Pp. 82-87 in: Odom, R.R. & Guthrie, J.W. eds. (1981). *Proceedings of the Nongame and Endangered Wildlife Symposium*. Technical Bulletin **WL-5**. Georgia Department of Natural Resources, Game and Fish Division.
Baker, W.W., Thompson, R.L. & Engstrom, R.T. (1980). The distribution and status of Red-cockaded Woodpecker colonies in Florida: 1969-1978. *Florida Field Nat.* **8(2)**: 41-45.
Balachandran, S. (1999). Moult in some birds of Palni Hills, Western Ghats. *J. Bombay Nat. Hist. Soc.* **96(1)**: 48-54.
Balança, G. & de Visscher, M. (1997). Composition et évolution saisonnière d'un peuplement d'oiseaux au nord du Burkina Faso (nord-Yatenga). *Malimbus* **19(2)**: 68-94.
Balasubramanian, P. (1992). Southern Golden-backed Woodpecker *Dinopium benghalense* feeding on the nectar of banana tree *Musa paradisiaca*. *J. Bombay Nat. Hist. Soc.* **89(2)**: 254.
Balchin, C.S. & Toyne, E.P. (1998). The avifauna and conservation status of the Río Nangaritza Valley, southern Ecuador. *Bird Conserv. Int.* **8(3)**: 237-253.
Baldwin, P.H. (1960). Overwintering of woodpeckers in bark beetle-infested spruce-fir forests of Colorado. Pp. 71-84 in: Bergman, G., Donner, K.O. & Haartman, L. eds. (1960). *Proceedings of the XII International Ornithological Congress, Helsinki, 1958*. Tilgmannin Kirjapaino, Helsinki.
Baldwin, P.H. & Schneider, R.W. (1963). Flight in relation to form of wing in the Lewis' Woodpecker. *J. Colo. Wyo. Acad. Sci.* **5**: 58-59.
van Balen, S. (1997). Faunistic notes from Kayan Mentarang with new records for Kalimantan. *Kukila* **9**: 108-113.
van Balen, S. (1999). *Birds on Fragmented Islands. Persistence in the Forests of Java and Bali*. PhD thesis, Wageningen University.
van Balen, S. & Prentice, C. (1978). Birds of the Negara River basin, South Kalimantan, Indonesia. *Kukila* **9**: 81-107.
Ball, R.M. & Avise, J.C. (1992). Mitochondrial DNA phylogeographic differentiation among avian populations and the evolutionary significance of subspecies. *Auk* **109(3)**: 626-636.
Ballmann, P. (1983). A new species of fossil barbet (Aves: Piciformes) from the late Miocene of the Nördlinger Ries (southern Germany). *J. Vertebr. Paleontol.* **3**: 43-48.
Baltzer, M.C. (1990). A report on the wetland avifauna of South Sulawesi. *Kukila* **5(1)**: 27-55.
Bancroft, J. (1983). Red-headed Woodpecker. *Blue Jay* **41(3)**: 164-165.
Bancroft, J. (1984). Red-headed Woodpecker predation. *Blue Jay* **42(4)**: 209-210.
Bangs, O. (1900). A review of the three-toed woodpeckers of North America. *Auk* **17**: 126-142.
Bangs, O. & Barbour, T. (1922). Birds from Darién. *Bull. Mus. Comp. Zool.* **65(6)**: 191-229.
Bangs, O. & Penard, T.E. (1918). Notes on a collection of Surinam birds. *Bull. Mus. Comp. Zool.* **62**: 25-93.
Bangs, O. & Van Tyne, J. (1931). *Birds of the Kelley-Roosevelts Expedition to French Indo-China*. Publications of the Field Musem of Natural History (Zoological Series). **290, pt. 18(3)**. 86 pp.
Bannerman, D.A. (1933). *The Birds of Tropical West Africa with Special Reference to those of The Gambia, Sierra Leone, the Gold Coast, and Nigeria*. Vol. 3. Crown Agents for the Colonies, London.
Bannerman, D.A. (1953). *The Birds of West and Equatorial Africa*. Vols. 1-2. Oliver & Boyd, Edinburgh.
Bañuelos-Irusta, J., da Silveira, A.G. & Varela-Freire, A.A. (2000a). Levantamento da ornitofauna e considerações ecológicas na Estação Ecológica do Seridó, Serra Negra do Norte, Rio Grande do Norte. Pp. 246-247 in: Straube *et al.* (2000).
Bañuelos-Irusta, J., da Silveira, A.G. & Varela-Freire, A.A. (2000b). Lista provisória das aves do Estado de Rio Grande do Norte. Pp. 247-248 in: Straube *et al.* (2000).
Baptista, L.F. (1978). A revision of the Mexican *Piculus* (Picidae) complex. *Wilson Bull.* **90(2)**: 159-181.
Baranga, J. & Kalina, J. (1991). Nesting association between Narrow-tailed Starling *Poeoptera lugubris* and Grey-throated Barbet *Gymnobucco bonapartei*. *Scopus* **15**: 59-61.
Barbour, D. (1973). Greater Honeyguide parasitizing Swallow-tailed Bee-eater. *Ostrich* **44**: 79.
Barbour, T. (1943). *Cuban Ornithology*. Memoirs of the Nuttall Ornithological Club **9**, Cambridge, Massachusetts. 144 pp.
Bardin, A.V. (1986). The effect of Great Spotted Woodpecker predation on breeding success of Willow Tit and Crested Tit. *Ekologiya* **6**: 77-79.
Barker, C., Bean, N., Davidson, P., Drijvers, R. & Showler, D. (1999). Some recent records of birds around Islamabad, Pakistan. *Forktail* **15**: 96-97.
Barker, F.K. & Lanyon, S.M. (1996). *A Hypothesis of Intrafamilial Relationships in the Toucans and New World Barbets (Ramphastidae) Based upon Variation in Cytochrome b*. Abstract **137**. American Ornithologists' Union & Raptor Research Foundation, Boise, Idaho.
Barlow, C., Wacher, T. & Disley, T. (1997). *A Field Guide to the Birds of The Gambia and Senegal*. Pica Press, Nr. Robertsbridge, UK.
Barnard, P. (1998). Variability in the mating systems of parasitic birds. Pp. 339-353 in: Rothstein, S.I. & Robinson, S.K. eds. (1998). *Parasitic Birds and their Hosts. Studies in Coevolution*. Oxford University Press, Oxford.
Barnea, A. (1985). The Syrian Woodpecker. *Tzufit* **3**: 9-40.
Barnes, K.N. (1999). Birding Africa's basement - the Cape to the Kalahari. *Bull. African Bird Club* **6(2)**: 121-132.
Barnes, K.N. ed. (2000). *The Eskom Red Data Book of Birds of South Africa, Lesotho and Swaziland*. BirdLife South Africa, Johannesburg.
Barnes, R., Batrina, L., Butchart, S.H.M., Clay, R.P., Esquivel, E.Z., Etcheverry, N.I., Lowen, J.C. & Vincent, J. (1993). *Bird Surveys and Conservation in the Paraguayan Atlantic Forest*. BirdLife Study Report **57**. BirdLife International, Cambridge.
Barnes, V. & Phelps, W.H. (1940). Las aves de la Península de Paraguana. *Bol. Soc. Venez. Cienc. Nat.* **46**: 269-301.
Barreau, D. & Rocher, A. (1992). Un biotope inhabituel pour le Pic vert *Picus viridis levaillantii*: la palmeraie de Marrakech (Maroc). *Alauda* **60(1)**: 49.
Barrowclough, G.F., Escalante, P., Aveledo, R. & Pérez, L.A. (1995). An annotated list of the birds of the Cerro Tamacuarí region, Serranía de Tapirapecó, Federal Territory of Amazonas, Venezuela. *Bull. Brit. Orn. Club* **115(4)**: 211-219.
Bartmann, W. (1975). Ein Bruterfolg bei Rotkopfbartvögeln (*Eubucco bourcierii* Lafr.). [A successful breeding of *Eubucco bourcierii*]. *Zool. Garten* **45(4/6)**: 385-392.

Barua, M. & Sharma, P. (1999). Birds of Kaziranga National Park, India. *Forktail* **15**: 47-60.

Bates, G.L. (1909). Field-notes on the birds of southern Kamerun, West Africa. *Ibis* **Ser. 9, no. 3**: 1-74.

Bates, G.L. (1930). *Handbook of the Birds of West Africa*. John Bale, Sons & Danielsson, London.

Bates, J.M., Garvin, M.C., Schmitt, D.C. & Schmitt, C.G. (1989). Notes on bird distribution in northeastern Dpto. Santa Cruz, Bolivia, with 15 species new to Bolivia. *Bull. Brit. Orn. Club* **109(4)**: 236-244.

Bates, J.M., Parker, T.A., Capparella, A.P. & Davis, T.J. (1992). Observations on the campo, cerrado and forest avifaunas of eastern Dpto. Santa Cruz, Bolivia, including 21 species new to the country. *Bull. Brit. Orn. Club* **112(2)**: 86-98.

Bates, R.S.P. (1952). Possible association between the Large Yellow-naped Woodpecker *Picus flavinucha* and the Large Racket-tailed Drongo *Dissemurus paradiseus*. *J. Bombay Nat. Hist. Soc.* **50(4)**: 941-942.

Bates, R.S.P. & Lowther, E.H.N. (1952). *Breeding Birds of Kashmir*. Oxford University Press, Bombay.

Bauer, H.G. & Berthold, P. (1997). *Due Brutvögel Mitteleuropas: Bestand und Gefährdung*. 2nd edition. AULA-Verlag, Wiesbaden, Germany.

Bauer, K.M. (1952). Der Blutspecht (*Dryobates syriacus*) Brutvogel in Österreich. *J. Orn.* **93**: 104-111.

Bauer, K.M. (1953). Weitere Ausbreitung des Blutspechts (*Dendrocopos syriacus*) in Österreich. *J. Orn.* **94**: 300-303.

Bavoux, C. (1987). Fidélité des conjoints chez le Pic épeiche *Dendrocopos major*. *Oiseau et RFO* **57**: 49-52.

Beal, F.E.L. (1895). Preliminary report on the food of woodpeckers. *Bull. Div. Orn. Mammol. US Dept. Agr.* **7**: 7-33.

Beaman, M. & Madge, S. (1998). *The Handbook of Bird Identification for Europe and the Western Palearctic*. Christopher Helm, London.

Beck, C.E. (1971). Fairing in hybrid flicker populations in eastern Colorado. *Auk* **88(4)**: 921-924.

Becker, C.D. & López, B. (1997). Conservation value of a *Garua* forest in the dry season: a bird survey in Reserva Ecológica de Loma Alta, Ecuador. *Cotinga* **8**: 66-74.

Becker, C.N. (1982). Red-headed Woodpecker removes House Sparrow from a nest box. *Audubon Bull.* **201**: 37-38.

Becker, D., Agreda, A., Richter, A. & Rodríguez, O. (2000). Interesting bird records from the Colonche Hills, western Ecuador. *Cotinga* **13**: 55-58.

Beckett, T.A. (1971). A summary of Red-cockaded Woodpecker observations in South Carolina. Pp. 87-95 in: Thompson (1971).

Beckett, T.A. (1974). Habitat acreage requirements of the Red-cockaded Woodpecker. *EBBA News* **37**: 3-7.

Beckwith, R.C. & Bull, E.L. (1985). Scat analysis of the arthropod component of Pileated Woodpecker diet. *Murrelet* **66(3)**: 90-92.

Beddard, F.B. (1898). *The Structure and Classification of Birds*. Longmans-Green, London.

Beebe, W. (1909). An ornithological reconnaissance of northeastern Venezuela. *Zoologica* **1**: 67-114.

Beebe, W. (1916). Notes on the birds of Pará, Brazil. *Sci. Contrib. New York Zool. Soc.* **2**: 53-106.

Beebe, W., Hartley, G.I. & Howes, P.G. (1917). *Tropical Wild Life in British Guiana*. Vol. 1. New York Zoological Society, New York.

Beecher, W.J. (1953). Feeding adaptations and systematics in the avian order Piciformes. *J. Washington Acad. Sci.* **43**: 293-299.

Beel, C. (1997). Bird of the month. Scaly-throated Honeyguide. *Zambian Orn. Soc. Newsl.* **27(8-9)**: 35-36.

Begazo, A.J. & Valqui, T. (1998). Birds of Pacaya-Samiria National Reserve with a new population (*Myrmotherula longicauda*) and new record for Peru (*Hylophilus semicinereus*). *Bull. Brit. Orn. Club* **118(3)**: 159-166.

Begazo, A.J., Valqui, T., Sokol, M. & Langlois, E. (2001). Notes on some birds from central and northern Peru. *Cotinga* **15**: 81-87. In English with Spanish summary.

van Beirs, M. (1997). Black-billed Barbet *Lybius guifsobalito* new to Cameroon and West Africa. *Malimbus* **19(1)**: 32.

Belcher, C.F. (1930). *The Birds of Nyasaland*. Technical Press, Ludgate Hill, UK.

Belfort, H., Campolina, C., Rodríguez, M. & García, Q.S. (2000). O tucanuçu (*Ramphastos toco*) (Ramphastidae) como agente dispersor da copaíba (*Copaifera langsdorffii*) (Leguminoseae, Caesalpinoidea). Pp. 143-144 in: Straube *et al.* (2000). (Abstract).

Bell, B.D., Cossee, R.O., Flux, J.E.C., Heather, B.C., Hitchmough, R.A., Robertson, C.J.R. & Williams, M.J. eds. (1991). *Acta XX Congressus Internationalis Ornithologici*. Vols. 1-4. New Zealand Ornithological Congress Trust Board, Wellington.

Belson, M.S. (1998). *Red-headed Woodpecker (*Melanerpes erythrocephalus*) Use of Habitat at Wekiwa Springs State Park, Florida*. MSc thesis, University of Central Florida, Orlando, Florida.

Belson, M.S. & Small, P.E. (1998). Uncommon behaviors of Red-headed Woodpeckers in central Florida. *Florida Field Nat.* **26(2)**: 44-45.

Belton, W. (1984). *Birds of Rio Grande do Sul, Brazil*. Part 1. Rheidae through Furnariidae. Bulletin of the American Museum of Natural History **178(4)**, New York. 267 pp.

Belton, W. (1994). *Aves do Rio Grande do Sul*. Editora da Universidade do Vale do Rio dos Sinos, Rio dos Sinos.

Beltrán, J.W. (1994). *Natural History of the Plate-billed Mountain Toucan* Andigena laminirostris *in Colombia*. Center for Study of Tropical Birds, Miscellaneous Publications **2**. 91 pp.

Bencke, G.A. & Kindel, A. (1999). Bird counts along an altitudinal gradient of Atlantic forest in northeastern Rio Grande do Sul, Brazil. *Ararajuba* **7(2)**: 91-107.

Benítez, H. (1993). Geographic variation in coloration and morphology of the Acorn Woodpecker. *Condor* **95(1)**: 63-71.

Benito-Espinal, E. & Hautcastel, P. (1988). Les oiseaux menacés de Guadeloupe et de Martinique. Pp. 37-60 in: Thibault, J.C. & Guyot, I. eds. (1988). *Livre Rouge des Oiseaux Menacés des Régions Françaises d'Outre-Mer*. ICBP Monograph **5**, Saint-Claude, France.

Bennett, G.F., Caines, J.R. & Whiteway, M.A. (1986). Avian Haemoproteidae. The haemoproteids of the avian families Apodidae (swifts), Bucconidae (puffbirds), and Indicatoridae (honeyguides). *Can. J. Zool.* **64(3)**: 766-770. In English with French summary.

Bennun, L. (1991). Courtship feeding in Yellow-rumped Tinker-birds *Pogoniulus bilineatus*. *Scopus* **15**: 64.

Bennun, L. ed. (1992). *Proceedings of the VII Pan-African Ornithological Congress, Nairobi, 1988*.

Bennun, L. & Njoroge, P. eds. (1996). Birds to watch in East Africa: a preliminary red data list. *Centre Biodiversity Res. Rep.: Orn.* **23**: 1-16.

Bennun, L. & Njoroge, P. (1999). *Important Bird Areas in Kenya*. Nature Kenya, Nairobi.

Bennun, L. & Read, A.F. (1988). Joint nesting in the Acorn Woodpecker. *Trends Ecol. Evol.* **3(12)**: 319.

Benson, C.W. (1946). Notes on the birds of southern Abyssinia. *Ibis* **88(1)**: 25-48.

Benson, C.W. (1948). A new race of barbet from south-western Tanganyika Territory and northern Nyasaland. *Bull. Brit. Orn. Club* **68**: 144-145.

Benson, C.W. (1964). A further revision of the races of Whyte's Barbet *Buccanodon whytii* Shelley. *Arnoldia* **1**: 1-4.

Benson, C.W. (1981). Migrants in the afrotropical region south of the equator. *Ostrich* **53**: 31-49.

Benson, C.W. & Benson, F.M. (1975). Studies of some Malawi birds. *Arnoldia* **7(32)**: 1-27.

Benson, C.W. & Benson, F.M. (1977). *The Birds of Malawi*. Monfort Press, Limbe.

Benson, C.W. & Irwin, M.P.S. (1965a). A new species of tinker-barbet from Northern Rhodesia. *Bull. Brit. Orn. Club* **85(1)**: 5-9.

Benson, C.W. & Irwin, M.P.S. (1965b). The birds of *Cryptosepalum* forests, Zambia. *Arnoldia, Rhodesia* **1(28)**: 1-12.

Benson, C.W. & White, C.M.N. (1957). *Check-list of the Birds of Northern Rhodesia*. Government Printer, Lusaka, Zambia.

Benson, C.W., Brooke, R.K., Dowsett, R.J. & Irwin, M.P.S. (1971). *The Birds of Zambia*. Collins, London.

Benstead, P.J., Bean, N.J., Showler, D.A. & Whittington, P.A. (1997). Recent sightings of Speckled Piculet (*Picumnus innominatus* Burton) in Pakistan. *J. Bombay Nat. Hist. Soc.* **94(3)**: 568-569.

Bent, A.C. (1939). *Life Histories of North American Woodpeckers. Order Piciformes*. US National Museum Bulletin **174**. Smithsonian Institution, Washington, D.C. 334 pp. (Reprinted by Dover Publications, New York, 1964).

van den Berg, A.B. (1988). Grey-headed Woodpecker, *Picus canus*, in north-eastern Turkey. *Zool. Middle East* **2**: 12-15.

van den Berg, A.B. & Bosman, C.A.W. (1999). *Rare Birds of the Netherlands. With Complete List of All Species. Zeldzame Vogels van Nederland. Met Vermelding van alle Soorten*. Pica Press, Nr. Robertsbridge, UK. In English and Dutch.

Berger, B., Buechele, S., Foeger, M. & Dallinger, R. (1992). Embryonic metabolism in altricial birds: *Tyto alba* (Strigiformes) and *Dendrocopos major* (Piciformes). Page 50 in: *Proc. Soc. Exp. Biol. Meeting, Cambridge, 1992*. (Abstract).

Bergmanis, M. & Strazds, M. (1993). Rare woodpecker species in Latvia. *Ring* **15(1-2)**: 255-266.

van den Berk, V. (1990). The rapid movement of a Turkish-ringed Wryneck to Beirut, Lebanon. *Bull. Orn. Soc. Middle East* **24**: 15-17.

Berlepsch, H. von (1889). Systematisches Verzeichness der von Herrn Gustav Garlepp in Brasilien und Nord-Peru im Gebiete das oberen amazonas gesammelten Vogelbälge. *J. Orn.* **87**: 289-321.

Berlepsch, H. von (1908). On the birds of Cayenne. *Novit. Zool.* **15**: 103, 164, 261-324.

Berlepsch, H. von & Hartert, E. (1902). *On the Birds of the Orinoco Region*. Novitates Zoologicae **9**. 134 pp.

Berlepsch, H. von & Stolzmann, J. (1906). Rapport sur les nouvelles collections ornithologiques faites au Perou para M. Jean Kalinowski. *Ornis* **13**: 63-133.

Berlioz, J. (1936). Étude critique des Capitonidés de la région orientale. *Oiseau et RFO* **6**: 28-56.

Berlioz, J. (1937). Étude critique des Capitonidés de la région neotropicale. *Oiseau et RFO* **7**: 223-239.

Berlioz, J. (1954). Note sur un specimen d'*Hapaloptila castanea* (Verr.). *Oiseau et RFO* **24**: 141-153.

Berman, S., Addesa, J., Hannigan, R., Restivo, V. & Rodrigues, J. (1998). Intraspecific variation in the hindlimb musculature of the Northern Flicker. *Condor* **100(3)**: 574-579.

Bernardes, A.T., Machado, A.B.M. & Rylands, A.B. (1990). *Fauna Brasileira Ameaçada de Extinção*. Fundação Biodiversitas para a Conservação da Diversidade Biológica, Belo Horizonte.

Berndt, R. & Winkel, W. (1987). [Breeding season re-captures of Wrynecks (*Jynx torquilla*) in south-east lower Saxony]. *Vogelwelt* **108(2)**: 58-60. In German with English summary.

Berndt, R. & Wolfgang, W. (1979). Zur Populationsentwicklung von Blaumeise (*Parus caeruleus*), Kleiber (*Sitta europaea*), Gartenrotschwanz (*Phoenicurus phoenicurus*) und Wendehals (*Jynx torquilla*) in mitteleuropaeischen Untersuchungsgebieten von 1927 bis 1978. [On population dynamics in the Blue Tit (*Parus caeruleus*), Nuthatch (*Sitta europaea*), Redstart (*Phoenicurus phoenicurus*) and Wryneck (*Jynx torquilla*) in central European study areas from 1927 to 1978]. *Vogelwelt* **100(1/2)**: 55-69. In German with English summary.

Bernoni, M. (1994). [The White-backed Woodpecker in the Abruzzo National Park]. *Contrib. Sci. Conoscenza Parco Nazionale d'Abruzzo* **46**: 231-238. In Italian with English summary.

Bernoni, M. (1995). Densità della popolazione di Picchio dorsobianco *Picoides leucotos lilfordi* nel Parco Nazionale d'Abruzzo. *Avocetta* **19(1)**: 130.

Bernstein, L. (1964). *Fossil Birds from the Dominican Republic*. MSc thesis, University of Florida, Gainesville, Florida.

Bernstein, L. (1965). Fossil birds from the Dominican Republic. *Quart. J. Florida Acad. Sci.* **28(3)**: 271-284.

Berovides, V., González, H.J. & Ibarra, M.E. (1982). Evaluación ecológica de las comunidades de aves del área protegida de Najasa (Camagüey). [Ecological assessment of the avian communities of the protected area of Najasa (Camagüey)]. *Poeyana* **239**: 1-14.

Berruti, A., McIntosh, B. & Walter, R. (1995). Parasitism of the Blue Swallow *Hirundo atrocaerulea* by the Greater Honeyguide *Indicator indicator*. *Ostrich* **66**: 94.

Berry, R.J. & Coffey, B. (1976). Breeding the Sulphur-breasted Toucan, *Ramphastos s. sulfuratus*, at Houston Zoo. *Int. Zoo Yb.* **16**: 108-110.

Berwick, E.J.H. (1952a). Notes on some birds in Kelantan and Trengganu. *Malay. Nat. J.* **7**: 10-14.

Berwick, E.J.H. (1952b). Bird notes from Kelantan. *Bull. Raffles Mus., Singapore* **24**: 183-198.

Best, B.J. & Clarke, C.T. eds. (1991). *The Threatened Birds of the Sozoranga Region, Southwest Ecuador*. ICBP Study Report **44**, Cambridge.

Best, B.J., Clarke, C.T., Checker, M., Broom, A.L., Thewlis, R.M., Duckworth, W. & McNab, A. (1993). Distributional records, natural history notes, and conservation of some poorly known birds from southwestern Ecuador and northwestern Peru. *Bull. Brit. Orn. Club* **113**: 108-119, 234-255.

Best, B.J., Heijnen, T. & Williams, R.S.R. (1997). *A Guide to Bird-watching in Ecuador and the Galápagos Islands*. Biosphere Publications Ltd, Otley, UK.

Betts, F.N. (1934). South Indian woodpeckers. *J. Bombay Nat. Hist. Soc.* **37(1)**: 197-203.

Bezzel, E. (1985). *Kompendium der Vögel Mitteleuropas. Nonpasseriformes*. AULA-Verlag, Wiesbaden, Germany.

Bharos, A.M.K. (1992). Occurrence of the Indian Great Black Woodpecker *Dryocopus javensis* (Horsfield). *J. Bombay Nat. Hist. Soc.* **89(2)**: 255.

Bharos, A.M.K. (1997). Unusual feeding pattern and diet of Crimson-breasted Barbet (*Megalaima haemacephala*). *J. Bombay Nat. Hist. Soc.* **94(2)**: 411.

Bhunya, S.P. & Sultana, T. (1983). C-banded somatic chromosomes of *Megalaima zeylanica caniceps* (Franklin) (Capitonidae, Piciformes, Aves). A case of pericentric inversion. *Cytologia* **48**: 215-220.

Biaggi, V. (1983). *Las Aves de Puerto Rico*. Editorial de la Universidad de Puerto Rico, Río Piedras, Puerto Rico.

Biddulph, C.H. (1954). Possible association between the Large Yellow-naped Woodpecker and the Large Racket-tailed Drongo. *J. Bombay Nat. Hist. Soc.* **52(1)**: 209.

de Bie, S. & Morgan, N. (1989). Les oiseaux de la reserve de la Biosphere "Boucle du Baoule", Mali. *Malimbus* **11**: 41-60.

Bierregaard, R.O. (1988). Morphological data from understory birds in Terra Firme forest in the central Amazonian basin. *Rev. Bras. Biol.* **48(2)**: 169-178.

Binford, L.C. (1989). *A Distributional Survey of the Birds of the Mexican State of Oaxaca*. Ornithological Monographs **43**. American Ornithologists' Union, Washington, D.C. 418 pp.

Bingham, P. (1999). Nesting Black-collared Barbets. *Zambian Orn. Soc. Newsl.* **29(3)**: 4-5.

Bishop, K.D. (1999a). Preliminary notes on some birds in Bhutan. *Forktail* **15**: 87-91.

Bishop, K.D. (1999b). The road between Ura and Limithang in eastern Bhutan. *Bull. Oriental Bird Club* **29**: 44-47.

Biswas, B. (1947). Notes on a collection of birds from the Darrang District, Assam. *Rec. Indian Mus.* **45**: 225-244.

Biswas, B. (1950). On the taxonomy of some Asiatic pygmy woodpeckers. *Proc. Zool. Soc. Bengal* **3(1)**: 1-37.

Biswas, B. (1951). Revision of Indian birds. *Amer. Mus. Novit.* **1500**: 1-42.

Biswas, B. (1961a). The birds of Nepal. Part 3. *J. Bombay Nat. Hist. Soc.* **58(1)**: 100-134.

Biswas, B. (1961b). The birds of Nepal. Part 4. *J. Bombay Nat. Hist. Soc.* **58(2)**: 441-474.

Bitz, A. & Rohe, W. (1992). Der Einfluss der Witterung auf den Nahrungseintrag des Wendehalses (*Jynx torquilla*). *Beitr. Landespfl. Rheinland-Pfalz* **15**: 575-591.

Blackburn, T.M., Gaston, K.J. & Lawton, J.H. (1998). Patterns in the geographic ranges of the world's woodpeckers. *Ibis* **140(4)**: 626-638.

Blackford, J.L. (1955). Woodpecker concentration in burned forest. *Condor* **57(1)**: 28-30.

Blagosklonov, K.N. (1968). [Nesting trees of woodpeckers in different forest types]. *Ornitologiya* **9**: 95-102. In Russian.

Blair, G.S. & Servheen, G. (1993). *Species Conservation Plan for the White-headed Woodpecker (*Picoides albolarvatus*)*. US Department of Agriculture, Forest Service and Idaho Department of Fish and Game.

Blake, E.R. (1941). Two new birds from British Guiana. *Field Mus. Nat. Hist. (Zool. Ser.)* **24**: 227-232.

Blake, E.R. (1950). Birds of the Acary Mountains, southern British Guiana. *Fieldiana Zool.* **32(7)**: 419-474.

Blake, E.R. (1958). Birds of Volcán de Chiriquí, Panama. *Fieldiana Zool.* **36(5)**: 499-577.

Blake, E.R. (1961). Notes on a collection of birds from southeastern Colombia. *Fieldiana Zool.* **44(4)**: 25-44.

Blake, E.R. (1962). Birds of the Sierra Macarena, eastern Colombia. *Fieldiana Zool.* **44(11)**: 69-112.
Blake, E.R. (1963). The birds of southern Surinam. *Ardea* **51**: 53-72.
Blake, E.R. (1965). *Birds of Mexico. A Guide for Field Identification*. University of Chicago Press, Chicago & London.
Blake, H.E. (1981). Subspecific identification of Hairy and Downy Woodpeckers in Colorado. *Colorado Field Orn. J.* **15(4)**: 98-101.
Blake, J.G. (2001). Bird assemblages in second-growth and old-growth forests, Costa Rica: perspectives from mist nets and point counts. *Auk* **118(2)**: 304-326.
Blake, J.G. & Loiselle, B.A. (2000). Diversity of birds along an elevational gradient in the Cordillera Central, Costa Rica. *Auk* **117(3)**: 663-686.
Blake, J.G. & Loiselle, B.A. (2001). Bird assemblages in second-growth and old-growth forests, Costa Rica: perspectives from mist nets and point counts. *Auk* **118(2)**: 304-326.
Blake, J.G. & Rougès, M. (1997). Variation in capture rates of understory birds in El Rey National Park, northwestern Argentina. *Orn. Neotropical* **8(2)**: 185-193.
Blankert, J.J. & de Heer, P. (1982). Voorkomen van Grijskopspecht in Nederland. [Occurrence of Grey-headed Woodpecker in the Netherlands]. *Dutch Birding* **4(1)**: 18-19. In Dutch with English summary.
Blendinger, P.G. (1998). Registros de aves poco frecuentes en la Argentina y sector antártico argentino. *Nuestras Aves* **38**: 5-8.
Blendinger, P.G. (1999). Facilitation of sap-feeding birds by the White-fronted Woodpecker in the Monte desert, Argentina. *Condor* **101(2)**: 402-407.
Bloch, H., Poulsen, M.K., Rahbek, C. & Rasmussen, J.F. (1991). *A Survey of the Montane Forest Avifauna of the Loja Province, Southern Ecuador*. ICBP Study Report **49**, Cambridge.
Block, W.M. (1991). Foraging ecology of Nuttall's Woodpecker. *Auk* **108(2)**: 303-317.
Block, W.M. & Brennan, L.A. (1987). Characteristics of Lewis' Woodpecker habitat on the Modoc Plateau, California. *Western Birds* **18(4)**: 209-212.
Blockstein, D.E. & Fall, B.A. (1986). A heavy migration of Northern Flickers on the lower North Shore. *Loon* **58(1)**: 11-13.
Blom, E.A.T. (2000). Hairy & Downy Woodpeckers. *Bird Watcher's Digest* **22(4)**: 48-51.
Blomme, C. (1983). Egg-carrying behaviour observed in Northern Flicker. *Ontario Field Biol.* **37(1)**: 34-35.
Blue, R.J. (1985). *Home Range and Territory of Red-cockaded Woodpeckers Utilizing Residential Habitat in North Carolina*. MSc thesis, North Carolina State University, Raleigh, North Carolina.
Blume, D. (1955). Über einige Verhaltensweisen des Grünspechtes in der Fortpflanzungszeit (*Picus viridis pluvius* und *Picus viridis viridis*). *Vogelwelt* **76**: 193-210.
Blume, D. (1956). Verhaltensstudien an Schwarzspechten (*Dryocopus martius*). *Vogelwelt* **77**: 129-151.
Blume, D. (1961). *Über die Lebensweise Einiger Spechtarten (*Dendrocopos major, Picus viridis, Dryocopus martius*)*. Journal für Ornithologie **102**. 116 pp.
Blume, D. (1965). Ergänzende Mitteilungen zu Aktivitätsbeginn und - ende bei einigen Spechtarten unter Berücksichtigung des Grauspechtes (*Picus canus*). *Vogelwelt* **86**: 33-42.
Blume, D. (1968). *Die Buntspechte (Gattung* Dendrocopos*)*. A. Ziemsen Verlag, Wittenberg Lutherstadt.
Blume, D. (1981). *Schwartzspecht, Grünspecht, Grauspecht*. Neue Brehm-Bücherei **300**, Ziemsen, Germany.
Blume, D. (1996). *Schwarzspecht, Grauspecht, Grünspecht*. Dryocopus martius, Picus canus, Picus viridis. Die Neue Brehm-Buecherei Überarb. Auflage, Spektrum Akademischer Verlag, Heidelberg. 111 pp.
Blume, D. & Jung, G. (1959). Beobachtungen an Grauspechten (*Picus canus*) im Hessischen Hinterland. *Vogelwelt* **80**: 65-74.
Blume, D. & Tiefenbach, J. (1997). *Die Buntspechte Gattung* Picoides. Die Neue Brehm-Bücherei, Westarp Wissenschaften, Magdeburg.
Blume, D., Jung, G., Keutzer, W. & Werner, K.H. (1957). Verhaltensstudien an Grünspechten (*Picus viridis*). *Vogelwelt* **78**: 41-48.
Bock, C.E. (1968). *The Ecology and Behavior of the Lewis' Woodpecker*. PhD thesis, University of California, Berkeley, California.
Bock, C.E. (1970). *The Ecology and Behavior of the Lewis' Woodpecker (*Asyndesmus lewis*)*. University of California Publications in Zoology **92**. 101 pp.
Bock, C.E. (1971). Pairing in hybrid flicker populations in eastern Colorado. *Auk* **88(4)**: 921-924.
Bock, C.E. & Bock, J.H. (1974a). Geographical ecology of the Acorn Woodpecker: diversity versus abundance of resources. *Amer. Naturalist* **108**: 694-698.
Bock, C.E. & Bock, J.H. (1974b). On the geographical ecology and evolution of the three-toed woodpeckers, *Picoides tridactylus* and *P. arcticus*. *Amer. Midl. Nat.* **92(2)**: 397-405.
Bock, C.E. & Larson, D.L. (1986). Winter habitats of sapsuckers in southeastern Arizona. *Condor* **88(2)**: 246-247.
Bock, C.E. & Lepthien, L.W. (1975). A Christmas count analysis of woodpecker abundance in the United States. *Wilson Bull.* **87(3)**: 355-366.
Bock, C.E., Hadow, H.H. & Somers, P. (1971). Relations between Lewis' and Red-headed Woodpeckers in southeastern Colorado. *Wilson Bull.* **83(3)**: 237-248.
Bock, W.J. (1992). Methodology in avian macrosystematics. Pp. 53-72 in: Monk (1992).
Bock, W.J. (1994). *History and Nomenclature of Avian Family-group Names*. Bulletin of the American Museum of Natural History **222**, New York. 281 pp.
Bock, W.J. (1999). Functional and evolutionary morphology of woodpeckers. Proceedings of the XXII International Ornithological Congress, Durban 1998. *Ostrich* **70(1)**: 23-31.
Bock, W.J. & Miller, W. De W. (1959). The scansorial foot of the woodpeckers, with comments on the evolution of perching and climbing feet in birds. *Amer. Mus. Novit.* **1931**: 1-45.
Bock, W.J. & Short, L.L. (1971). "Resin secretion" in *Hemicircus* (Picidae). *Ibis* **113(2)**: 234-236.
Bodrati, A. (2001). Notas sobre aves infrecuentes o poco conocidas para la provincia de Buenos Aires, Argentina. *Nuestras Aves* **41**: 13-17.
Bodrati, A., Bodrati, G. & Fernández, H. (2001). Notas sobre la avifauna del norte de la provincia de Buenos Aires, Argentina. *Nuestras Aves* **41**: 17-21.
Boesman, P. (1995). Caño Colorado: a lowland tropical forest in north-east Venezuela. *Cotinga* **3**: 31-34.
Boesman, P. (1998). Some new information on the distribution of Venezuelan birds. *Cotinga* **9**: 27-39.
Bohmke, B.W. & Macek, M. (1994). St. Louis Zoo husbandry and reproduction of the Brown-breasted Barbet (*Lybius melanopterus*). *AFA Watchbird* **21(6)**: 4-7.
Boinski, S. (1992). Monkeys with inflated sex. *Nat. Hist.* **101**: 42-49.
Bomfim, R. & Reis, I. (1996). Avifauna associada a um reflorestamento de eucalipto no município de Antônio Dias, Minas Gerais. [Bird species associated to an *Eucalyptus* plantation in the county of Antônio Dias, Minas Gerais]. *Ararajuba* **4(1)**: 15-22. In Portuguese with English summary.
Bonar, R.L. (1994). Habitat ecology of the Pileated Woodpecker in Alberta. *Alberta Nat.* **24(1)**: 13-15.
Bonar, R.L. (2000). Availability of Pileated Woodpecker cavities and use by other species. *J. Wildl. Manage.* **64(1)**: 52-59.
Bond, J. (1928). The distribution and habits of the birds of the Republic of Haiti. *Proc. Acad. Nat. Sci. Philadelphia* **80**: 483-521.
Bond, J. (1954). Notes on Peruvian Piciformes. *Proc. Acad. Nat. Sci. Philadelphia* **106**: 45-61.
Bond, J. (1985). *Birds of the West Indies*. 5th edition. Collins, London.
Bond, J. & Meyer de Schauensee, R. (1940). On some birds from southern Colombia. *Proc. Acad. Nat. Sci. Philadelphia* **92**: 153-169.
Bond, J. & Meyer de Schauensee, R. (1943). The birds of Bolivia. Part II. *Proc. Acad. Nat. Sci. Philadelphia* **95**: 167-221.
Bond, J. & Meyer de Schauensee, R. (1944). *Results of the Fifth George Vanderbilt Expedition (1941)*. Academy of Natural Sciences of Philadelphia Monographs **6**. 49 pp.
Bond, R., Convey, P., Sharpe, C. & Varey, A. (1989). Cambridge Columbus zoological expedition to Venezuela 1988. Unpublished report for the Cambridge Expeditions Committee, University of Cambridge, Cambridge, UK.
Bond, R.M. (1957). A second record of the Yellow-bellied Sapsucker from St. Croix, Virgin Islands. *Condor* **59(3)**: 211-212.
Bonnie, R. (1997). Strategies for conservation of the endangered Red-cockaded Woodpecker on private lands. *Endangered Species Update* **14(7&8)**: 45-47.
Bonta, M. (1997). Hairy Woodpeckers. *Bird Watcher's Digest* **20(2)**: 28-35.
Boone, G.C. (1963). *Ecology of the Red-bellied Woodpecker in Kansas*. MSc thesis, University of Kansas, Manhattan, Kansas.
Borges, S.H. (1994). Listagem e novos registros de aves para a região de Boa Vista, Roraima, Brasil. *Bol. Mus. Paraense Emilio Goeldi (Zool.)* **10(2)**: 191-202.
Borges, S.H. & Guilherme, E. (2000). Comunidade de aves em um fragmento florestal urbano em Manaus, Amazonas, Brasil. *Ararajuba* **8(1)**: 17-23.
Borges, S.H., Cohn-Haft, M., Pereira, A.M., Magalli, L., Pacheco, J.F. & Whittaker, A. (2001). Birds of Jaú National Park, Brazilian Amazon: species check-list, biogeography and conservation. *Orn. Neotropical* **12(2)**: 109-140.
Borgstrom, E. (1980). [Wryneck, *Jynx torquilla*, brings strange objects into its nest]. *Vår Fågelvärld* **39(2)**: 101-102. In Swedish with English summary.
Borgstrom, E. (1989). [Unusual nesting sites of Black Woodpecker, *Dryocopus martius*, and Redwing, *Turdus iliacus*]. *Vår Fågelvärld* **48(2)**: 91-92. In Swedish with English summary.
Borodin, A.M. ed. (1984). [*The Red Data Book of the USSR: Rare and Endangered Species of Animals and Plants*]. Vol. 1. Animals. 2nd. edition. Lesnaya Promyshlennost, Moskow. In Russian.
Bororing, R.F., Hunowu, I., Hunowu, Y., Maneasa, E., Mole, J., Nusalawo, M.H., Talangamin, F.S. & Wangko, M.F. (2000). Birds of the Manembonembo Nature Reserve, North Sulawesi, Indonesia. *Kukila* **11**: 58-72.
Borrero, J.I. (1959). Notas aclaratorias sobre *Pteroglossus didymus* Sclater. *Lozania* **11**: 15-23.
Borrero, J.I. (1960). Notas sobre aves de la Amazonia y Orinoquia colombianas. *Caldasia* **8(39)**: 485-514.
Borrero, J.I. (1962). Notas sobre aves de la Amazonia (Caqueta). *Acta Biol. Colombiana* **1(1)**: 77-97.
Bouet, G. (1961). *Oiseaux de l'Afrique Tropicale*. Part 2. Faune de l'Union Française XVII, Paris.
Bourne, G.R. (1974). The Red-billed Toucan in Guyana. *Living Bird* **15**: 99-126.
Bowden, C.G.R. (2001). The birds of Mount Kupe, southwest Cameroon. *Malimbus* **23(1)**: 13-44.
Bowden, C.G.R. & Andrew, S.M. (1994). Mount Kupe and its birds. *Bull. African Bird Club* **1(1)**: 13-18.
Bowden, C.G.R., Hayman, P.V., Martins, R.P., Robertson, P.A., Mudd, S.H. & Woodcock, M.W. (1995). The *Melignomon* honeyguides: A review of recent range extensions and some remarks on their identification, with a description of the song of Zenker's Honeyguide. *Bull. African Bird Club* **2(1)**: 32-38.
Bowdish, B.S. (1904). An abnormal bill of *Melanerpes portoricensis*. *Auk* **21(1)**: 53-55.
Bowen, P.S.J. (1983). The Red-breasted Wryneck *Jynx ruficollis* in Zambia. *Bull. Zambian Orn. Soc.* **13/15**: 35-41.
Bower, A. (1993). Fledging flickers. *Jack-Pine Warbler* **70(6)**: 10-11.
Bower, A. (1995). Northern Flickers nest successfully in a nest box in Michigan. *Sialia* **17(1)**: 7-11.
Bowland, A.E. (1988). Helpers at the nest of Black-collared Barbets *Lybius torquatus*. *Naturalist* **33(1)**: 3-7.
Bowman, R., Leonard, D.L., Backus, L.K. & Maines, A.R. (1999). Interspecific interactions with foraging Red-cockaded Woodpeckers in south-central Florida. *Wilson Bull.* **111(3)**: 346-353.
Brabourne, Lord & Chubb, C.L. (1912a). *The Birds of South America*. Part 1. R.H. Porter, London.
Brabourne, Lord & Chubb, C.L. (1912b). Notes on Guiana birds. *Ann. Mag. Nat. Hist. (Ser. 8)* **10**: 261-262.
Brace, R.C. & Hornbuckle, J. (1998). Distributional records of and identification notes on birds of the Beni Biological Station, Beni, Bolivia. *Bull. Brit. Orn. Club* **118(1)**: 36-47.
Brace, R.C., Hornbuckle, J. & Pearce-Higgins, J.W. (1997). The avifauna of the Beni Biological Station, Bolivia. *Bird Conserv. Int.* **7(2)**: 117-159.
Brackbill, H. (1955). Possible function of the Flicker's black breast crescent. *Auk* **72(2)**: 205.
Brackbill, H. (1957). Observations on a wintering Flicker. *Bird-Banding* **28**: 40-41.
Brackbill, H. (1969a). Red-bellied Woodpecker taking bird's eggs. *Bird-Banding* **40**: 323-324.
Brackbill, H. (1969b). Reverse mounting by the Red-headed Woodpecker. *Bird-Banding* **40**: 255-256.
Bradley, P.E. (2000). *The Birds of the Cayman Islands. An Annotated Check-list*. BOU Check-list **19**. British Ornithologists' Union, Tring, UK.
Bradshaw, D.S. (1990). *Habitat Quality and Seasonal Foraging Patterns of the Red-cockaded Woodpecker (*Picoides borealis*) in Southeastern Virginia*. MSc thesis, William and Mary College, Williamsburg, Virginia.
Braun, E.J. (1969). *Metabolism and Water Balance of the Gila Woodpecker and Gilded Flicker in the Sonoran Desert*. PhD dissertation, University of Arizona, Tucson, Arizona.
Braun, M.J., Finch, D.W., Robbins, M.B. & Schmidt, B.K. (2000). *A Field Checklist of the Birds of Guyana*. Smithsonian Institution, Washington, D.C.
Brazier, F.H. (1989). Erratic flight of a Downy Woodpecker. *Blue Jay* **47(2)**: 109-111.
Brazil, M.A. (1985). The endemic birds of the Nansei Shoto. Pp. 11-35 in: *Conservation of the Nansei Shoto, 2*. World Wildlife Fund Japan, Tokyo.
Brazil, M.A. (1991). *The Birds of Japan*. Christopher Helm, London.
Brehm, W.W. (1969). Breeding the Green-billed Toucan *Ramphastos dicolorus* at the Walsrode Bird Park. *Int. Zoo Yb.* **9**: 134-135.
Breitwisch, R.J. (1977). *The Ecology and Behavior of the Red-bellied Woodpecker,* Centurus carolinus *(Linnaeus; Aves: Picidae), in South Florida*. MSc thesis, University of Miami, Coral Gables, Florida.
Brenner, F.J., Brant E.F. & Laferrierre, D. (1992). Habitat use and differential foraging behavior in the Downy Woodpecker (*Picoides pubescens*). *J. Pennsylvania Acad. Sci.* **66(1)**: 15-17.
Brenowitz, G.L. (1978a). Gila Woodpecker agonistic behavior. *Auk* **95(1)**: 49-58.
Brenowitz, G.L. (1978b). An analysis of Gila Woodpecker vocalizations. *Wilson Bull.* **90(3)**: 451-455.
Bretagnolle, F. (1993). An annotated checklist of birds of north-eastern Central African Republic. *Malimbus* **15**: 6-16.
Brewer, R. & McCann, M.T. (1985). Spacing in Acorn Woodpeckers. *Ecology* **66(1)**: 307-308.
Brewster, C.A. (1991). Birds of the Gumare area, northwest Botswana. *Babbler* **17**: 34-35.
Brightsmith, D.J. (1999). *The Roles of Predation and Competition in Nest Niche Differentiation: Evidence from Termitarium Nesting Parrots and Trogons*. PhD dissertation, Duke University, Durham, North Carolina.
Britton, P.L. ed. (1980). *Birds of East Africa. Their Habitat, Status and Distribution*. East African Natural History Society, Nairobi.
Britton, P.L. & Britton, H.A. (1971). Black-billed Barbet and Chestnut-fronted Shrike breeding in Kenya. *Bull. East Afr. Nat. Hist. Soc.* **1971**: 126-127.
Brodkorb, P. (1939a). New subspecies of birds from the district of Soconusco, Chiapas. *Occas. Pap. Mus. Zool. Univ. Mich.* **401**: 1-7.
Brodkorb, P. (1939b). Two undescribed South American barbets. *Proc. Biol. Soc. Washington* **52**: 135-136.
Brodkorb, P. (1943). Birds from the gulf lowlands of southern Mexico. *Misc. Publ. Univ. Mich. Mus. Zool.* **55**: 1-90.
Brodkorb, P. (1970). An Eocene puffbird from Wyoming. *Univ. Wyoming Contrib. Geol.* **9(1)**: 13-15.
Brodkorb, P. (1971). Catalogue of fossil birds: part 4 (Columbiformes through Piciformes). *Bull. Florida State Mus. Biol. Sci.* **15(4)**: 163-266.
Brom, T.G. (1990). Villi and the phyly of Wetmore's order Piciformes (Aves). *Zool. J. Linn. Soc.* **98**: 63-72.
Bromley, E.H. (1949). Notes on the birds of some parts of Kedah. *Bull. Raffles Mus., Singapore* **19**: 120-132.
Bromley, E.H. (1952). A note on birds seen at Maxwell's Hill, Perak, April 1950 and February 1951. *Bull. Raffles Mus., Singapore* **24**: 199-218.
Bronaugh, W.M. (1984). *Prey Selection, Handling, and Strike Distance in Four Neotropical Insectivorous Birds*. MSc thesis, Pennsylvania State University, Pennsylvania.
Brooke, R.K. (1964). Avian observations on a journey across central Africa and additional information on some of the species seen. *Ostrich* **35**: 277-292.

Brooke, R.K. (1970). The White-headed Barbet in Angola. *Bull. Brit. Orn. Club* **90(6)**: 161-162.
Brooke, R.K. (1984). *South African Red Data Book - Birds*. South African National Scientific Programmes Report **97**. Council for Scientific and Industrial Research, Pretoria.
Brooks, D.J., Evans, M.I., Martins, R.P. & Porter, R.F. (1987). The status of birds in north Yemen and the records of OSME Expedition in autumn 1985. *Sandgrouse* **9**: 4-66.
Brooks, D.M. (1997). Avian seasonality at a locality in the central Paraguayan Chaco. *Hornero* **14(4)**: 193-203.
Brooks, D.M. (2000). New distributional records for birds in the Paraguayan Chaco. *Cotinga* **13**: 77-78.
Brooks, T.M., Barnes, R., Bartrina, L., Butchart, S.H.M., Clay, R.P., Esquivel, E.Z., Etcheverry, N.I., Lowen, J.C. & Vincent, J.P. (1993). *Bird Surveys and Conservation in the Paraguayan Atlantic Forest: Project CANOPY '92 Final Report*. BirdLife Study Report **57**. BirdLife International, Cambridge.
Brooks, T.M., Dutson, G.C.L., King, B. & Magsalay, P.M. (1996). An annotated checklist of the forest birds of Rajah Sikatuna National Park, Bohol, Philippines. *Forktail* **11**: 121-134.
Brooks, T.M., Evans, T.D., Dutson, G.C.L., Anderson, G.Q.A., Asane, D.C., Timmins, R.J. & Toledo, A.G. (1992). The conservation status of the birds of Negros, Philippines. *Bird Conserv. Int.* **2(4)**: 273-302.
Brooks, T.M., Lens, L., Barnes, J., Barnes, R., Kihuria, J.K. & Wilder, C. (1998). The conservation status of the forest birds of the Taita Hills, Kenya. *Bird Conserv. Int.* **8(2)**: 119-139.
Brooks, T.M., Magsalay, P.M., Dutson, G.C.L. & Allen, R. (1995). Forest loss, extinction and last hope for birds on Cebu. *Bull. Oriental Bird Club* **21**: 24-27.
Brosset, A. (1964). Les oiseaux de Pacaritambo (ouest de l'Équateur). *Oiseau et RFO* **34**: 1-24, 112-135.
Brosset, A. (1981). Observation de l'Indicateur parasite *Prodotiscus insignis* nourissant un jeune de son espèce. *Oiseau et RFO* **51**: 59-61.
Brosset, A. & Érard, C. (1986). *Les Oiseaux des Régions Forestières du Nord-est du Gabon. Écologie et Comportement des Espèces*. Vol. 1. Société Nationale du Protection de la Nature, Paris.
Brown, C.J. (1993). The birds of Owambo, Namibia. *Madoqua* **18(2)**: 147-161.
Brown, C.J. & Barnes, P.R. (1984). Birds of the Natal Alpine Belt. *Lammergeyer* **33**: 1-13.
Brown, L.H. & Britton, P.L. (1980). *The Breeding Seasons of East African Birds*. East Africa Natural History Society, Nairobi.
Brown, L.N. (1978). Fall foraging of Pileated Woodpeckers on *Magnolia grandiflora* seeds. *Florida Field Nat.* **6(1)**: 18-19.
Brown, N. (1998). Out of control: fires and forestry in Indonesia. *Trends Ecol. Evol.* **13**: 41.
Browning, M.R. (1977). Interbreeding members of the *Sphyrapicus varius* group (Aves: Picidae) in Oregon. *Bull. South. Calif. Acad. Sci.* **76**: 38-41.
Browning, M.R. (1995). Do Downy Woodpeckers migrate? *J. Field Orn.* **66(1)**: 12-21.
Browning, M.R. (1997). Taxonomy of *Picoides pubescens* (Downy Woodpecker) from the Pacific Northwest. Pp. 25-33 in: Dickerman (1997).
Browning, M.R. & Cross, S.P. (1994). Third specimen of Nuttall's Woodpecker (*Picoides nuttallii*) in Oregon from Jackson County and comments of earlier records. *Oregon Birds* **20(4)**: 119-120.
Bruce, M.D. (1975). Okinawa bird notes. *Bull. Brit. Orn. Club* **95(4)**: 154-157.
Brush, A.H. (1967). Additional observations on the structure of unusual feather tips. *Wilson Bull.* **79(3)**: 322-327.
Brush, T. (1983). First nesting of a new world woodpecker in tamarisk (*Tamarix chinensis*). *Southwest. Nat.* **28(1)**: 113.
Brush, T., Anderson, B.W. & Ohmart, R.D. (1990). Habitat use by cavity-nesting birds of desert riparian woodland. Pp. 191-198 in: Krausman, P.R. & Smith, N.S. eds. (1990). *Managing Wildlife in the Southwest*. Arizona Chapter of the Wildlife Society, Phoenix, Arizona.
de Bruyn, G.J., Goosen-deRoo, L., Hubregtse-van den Berg, A.I.M. & Feijen, H.R. (1972). Predation of ants by woodpeckers. *Ekol. Polska* **20(9)**: 83-91.
Brydon, A. (1995). Intra-specific aggression in Pale-mandibled Araçari *Petroglossus erythropygius*. *Cotinga* **3**: 55.
Buckley, P.A., Foster, M.S., Morton, E.S., Ridgely, R.S. & Buckley, F.G. eds. (1985). *Neotropical Ornithology*. Ornithological Monograph **36**. American Ornithologists' Union, Washington, D.C.
Bucknill, J.A.S. & Chasen, F.N. (1990). *Birds of Singapore and South-east Asia*. Tynron Press, Thornhill, UK.
Bühl, K. (1982). Red-breasted Toucans flourish in Phoenix. *AFA Watchbird* **9**: 26-30.
Bühler, P. (1993). Interaktionen zwischen Tukanen (Ramphastidae, Aves) und Fruchtenden Palmen (*Oenocarpus bacaba*, Arecoideae). Pp. 89-102 in: Barthlott, W., Neumann, C.M., Schmidt-Loske, K. & Schuchmann, K.L. eds. (1993). *Animal-Plant Interactions in Tropical Environments*. Museum Alexander Koenig, Bonn, Germany.
Bühler, P. (1995a). Grösse, Form und Färbung des Tukanschnabels - Grundlage für den evolutiven Erfolg der Ramphastidae? [Size, form and colouration of the ramphastid bill as basis of the evolutionary success of the toucans]. *J. Orn.* **136(2)**: 187-193.
Bühler, P. (1995b). Tukane-optimierte Steinfruchtfresser. Pp. 171-184 in: Kull, U., Ramm, E. & Reiner, R. eds. (1995). *Evolution und Optimierung*. Wissenschaftliche Verlagsgesellschaft, Stuttgart, Germany.
Bühler, P. (1996). Die neotropischen Tukane (Ramphastidae) als Model einer ökomorphologischen Evolutionsanalyse. *Ökol. Vögel* **18**: 127-162.
Bühler, P. (1997). The visual peculiarities of the toucan's bill and their principal biological role (Ramphastidae, Aves). Pp. 305-310 in: Ulrich, H. ed. (1997). *Tropical Biodiversity and Systematics*. Proceedings of the International Symposium on Biodiversity and Systematics in Tropical Ecosystems, Bonn, 1994. Zoologisches Forschungsinstitut und Museum Alexander Koenig, Bonn, Germany.
Bühler, U. (2001). Brutvorkommen des Weissrückenspechts *Dendrocopos leucotos* in Nordbünden. *Orn. Beob.* **98**: 1-11.
Bühlmann, J. & Pasinelli, G. (1996). [Do forest management and weather influence the breeding density of the Middle Spotted Woodpecker *Dendrocopos medius*?] *Orn. Beob.* **93**: 267-276. In German with English summary.
Bull, E.L. (1974). *Habitat Utilization of the Pileated Woodpecker, Blue Mountains, Oregon*. MSc thesis, Oregon State University, Corvallis, Oregon.
Bull, E.L. (1978). Roosting activities of a male Pileated Woodpecker. *Murrelet* **59(1)**: 35-36.
Bull, E.L. (1981). *Resource Partitioning among Woodpeckers in Northeastern Oregon*. PhD dissertation, University of Idaho, Moscow, Idaho.
Bull, E.L. (1987). Ecology of the Pileated Woodpecker in northeastern Oregon. *J. Wildl. Manage.* **51(2)**: 472-481.
Bull, E.L. & Holthausen, R.S. (1993). Habitat use and management of Pileated Woodpeckers in northeastern Oregon. *J. Wildl. Manage.* **57(2)**: 335-345.
Bull, E.L. & Jackson, J.A. (1995). Pileated Woodpecker (*Dryocopus pileatus*). No. **148** in: Poole, A.F. & Gill, F.B. eds. (1995). *The Birds of North America*. Vol. 4. Academy of Natural Sciences & American Ornithologists' Union, Philadelphia & Washington, D.C.
Bull, E.L. & Meslow, E.C. (1977). Habitat requirements of the Pileated Woodpecker in northeastern Oregon. *J. Forestry* **75(6)**: 335-337.
Bull, E.L. & Meslow, E.C. (1988). *Breeding Biology of the Pileated Woodpecker - Management Implications*. Research note **PNW-RN-474**. US Department of Agriculture, Forest Service, Portland, Oregon.
Bull, E.L. & Snider, M. (1993). Master carpenter. Species profile: Pileated Woodpecker (*Dryocopus pileatus*). *Wildbird* **7(2)**: 41-43.
Bull, E.L., Beckwith, R.C. & Holthausen, R.S. (1992). Arthropod diet of Pileated Woodpeckers in northeastern Oregon. *Northwestern Naturalist* **73(2)**: 42-45.
Bull, E.L., Holthausen, R.S. & Henjum, M.G. (1990). *Techniques for Monitoring Pileated Woodpeckers*. General Techniques Report **PNW-GTR-269**. US Department of Agriculture, Forest Service, Pacific Northwest Research Station, Portland, Oregon.
Bull, E.L., Holthausen, R.S. & Henjum, M.G. (1992). Roost trees used by Pileated Woodpeckers in northeastern Oregon. *J. Wildl. Manage.* **56(4)**: 786-793.
Büngener, W. (1990). Bartvögel. *Gefiederte Welt* **114**: 238-240.
Burgess, J.W. (1983). Reply to a comment by R.L. Mumme *et al. Ecology* **64(5)**: 1307-1308.
Burgess, J.W., Roulston, D. & Shaw, E. (1982). Territorial aggregation: an ecological spacing strategy in Acorn Woodpeckers. *Ecology* **63(2)**: 575-578.
Burkett, E.W. (1989). *Differential Roles of Sexes in Breeding Northern Flickers (*Colaptes auratus*)*. PhD dissertation, University of Wisconsin, Milwaukee, Wisconsin.
Bürkli, W., Juon, M. & Ruge, K. (1975). Zur Biologie des Dreisehenspechtes *Picoides tridactylus*. 5. Beobachtungen zur Fütterungszeit und zur Grösse des Aktionsgebietes. [On the biology of the Three-toed Woodpecker *Picoides tridactylus*. 5. Observations upon post-fledging care and home range]. *Orn. Beob.* **72(1)**: 23-28. In German with English summary.
Burleigh, T.D. & Lowery, G.H. (1944). *Geographical Variation in the Red-bellied Woodpecker in the Southeastern United States*. Occasional Papers of the Museum of Zoology Louisiana State University **17**. Louisiana State University, Baton Rouge, Louisiana.
Burmeister, H. (1856). *Systematische Uebersicht der Thiere Brasiliens*. Part 2. Vögel. Georg Reimer, Berlin.
Burns, F.L. (1900). *Monograph of the Flicker*. Wilson Bulletin **7**. 81 pp.
Burnside, F.L. (1983). The status and distribution of the Red-cockaded Woodpecker in Arkansas. *Amer. Birds* **37**: 142-145.
Burow, E. (1970). Zum Biotop des Schwarzspechtes (*Dryocopus martius*) und der Uferschwalben (*Riparia riparia*) in den 70er Jahren. *Orn. Mitt.* **22(10)**: 203-204.
Burt, W.H. (1930). Adaptive modifications in the woodpeckers. *Univ. Calif. Publ. Zool.* **32(8)**: 455-524.
Burton, P.J.K. (1973). Non-passerine bird weights from Panama and Colombia. *Bull. Brit. Orn. Club* **93(3)**: 116-118.
Burton, P.J.K. (1976). Feeding behavior in the Paradise Jacamar and the Swallow-wing. *Living Bird* **15**: 223-238.
Burton, P.J.K. (1984). *Anatomy and Evolution of the Feeding Apparatus in the Avian Orders Coraciiformes and Piciformes*. Bulletin of the British Museum (Natural History) **47(6)**, London. 113 pp.
Bussmann, J. (1944). Beitrag zur Kenntnis der Brutbiologie des Grauspechts (*Picus c. canus* Gm.). *Arch. Suisses Orn.* **2**: 105-136.
de Bustamante, P.F.S. (1997). Predaçao do ninho de *Synoeca* sp. (Insecta: Hymenoptera: Vespidae) por *Melanerpes candidus* (Piciformes: Picidae) em Vicosa, Minas Gerais. Page 105 in: Marini (1997). (Abstract).
Butler, T.Y. (1979). *The Birds of Ecuador and the Galapagos Archipelago*. The Ramphastos Agency, Portsmouth, New Hampshire.
Buzzetti, D.R.C. (2000). Distribuição altitudinal de aves em Angra dos Reis e Parati, sul do Estado do Rio de Janeiro, Brasil. Pp. 131-148 in: Alves *et al.* (2000).
Cabanis, J. & Heine, F. (1850-1851). *Museum Heineanum. Verzeichniss der Ornithologischen Sammlung. Part I. Die Singvögel*. R. Frantz, Halberstadt.
Cabanne, F. (1948). Sur un tambourinage de Pic épeiche *Dryobates major pinetorum* (Br.) particulièrement précoce. *Alauda* **16**: 217-220.
Cabot, J., Castroviejo, J. & Urios, V. (1988). Cuatro especies nuevas para Bolivia. [Four bird species new for Bolivia]. *Doñana Acta Vertebrata* **15(2)**: 235-238.
Cadena, C.D., Álvarez, M., Parra, J.L., Jiménez, I., Mejía, C.A., Santamaría, M., Franco, A.M., Botero, C.A., Mejía, G.D., Umaña, A.M., Calixto, A., Aldana, J. & Londoño, G.A. (2000). The birds of CIEM, Tinigua National Park, Colombia: an overview of 13 years of ornithological research. *Cotinga* **13**: 46-54.
Cairenius, S. (1996). Tammitikka - uhanalainen eurooppalainen. The Middle Spotted Woodpecker - an endangered European. *Alula* **2(3)**: 126-129. In Finnish and English.
Caldwell, H.R. & Caldwell, J.C. (1931). *South China Birds*. Hester May Vanderburgh, Shanghai.
Callaghan, E. (1999). Breeding the Bearded Barbet. *Avicult. Mag.* **105(2)**: 49-53.
Callegari, E. (1955). Observations on a Black Woodpecker in captivity: its perception of food trough layers of wood. *Avicult. Mag.* **61**: 168-172.
Callegari, E. (1966). Breeding of the Acorn Woodpecker. *Avicult. Mag.* **72**: 79-83.
Calvo, L. & Blake, J. (1998). Bird diversity and abundance on two different shade coffee plantations in Guatemala. *Bird Conserv. Int.* **8(3)**: 297-308.
Camargo, H.F. de A. (1967). Sôbre as racas geográficas brasileiras de "*Ramphastos vitellinus*" Lichtenstein, 1823. *Hornero* **10**: 335-338.
Camerini, G. & Quadrelli, G. (1991). [Predation of Great Spotted Woodpecker, *Picoides major*, upon the caterpillars of corn borer, *Ostrinia nubilalis*]. *Riv. ital. Orn.* **61(1-2)**: 43-47. In Italian with English summary.
Campbell, B. & Lack, E. eds. (1985). *A Dictionary of Birds*. T. & A.D. Poyser, Calton, UK.
Campbell, R.W., Dawe, N.K., McTaggart-Cowan, I., Cooper, J.M., Kaiser, G.W. & McNall, C.E. (1990). *The Birds of British Columbia*. Vol. 2. Nonpasserines. Diurnal Birds of Prey through Woodpeckers. UBC Press, Vancouver.
Campey, R. (1996). Out of the ashes. *Birdwatch* **49**: 34-36.
Canaday, C. (1996). Loss of insectivorous birds along a gradient of human impact in Amazonia. *Biol. Conserv.* **77(1)**: 63-77.
Canaday, C. & Jost, L. (1999). *Aves Comunes de la Amazonía: 50 Especies Fáciles de Observar*. Parques Nacionales y Conservación Ambiental **8**. CECIA, Quito.
Cândido, J.F. (2000). The edge effect in a forest bird community in Rio Claro, São Paulo State, Brazil. *Ararajuba* **8(1)**: 9-16.
Canevari, M., Canevari, P., Carrizo, G.R., Harris, G., Mata, J.R. & Straneck, R.J. (1991). *Nueva Guía de las Aves Argentinas*. Vols. 1-2. Fundación Acindar, Buenos Aires.
Capper, D.R., Clay, R.P., Madroño, A. & Mazar Barnett, J. (2001). New information on the distribution of twenty-two bird species in Paraguay. *Ararajuba* **9(1)**: 57-59.
Capper, D.R., Clay, R.P., Madroño, A., Mazar Barnett, J., Burfield, E.J., Esquivel, E.Z., Kennedy, C.P., Perrens, M. & Pople, R.G. (2001). First records, noteworthy observations and new distributional data for birds in Paraguay. *Bull. Brit. Orn. Club* **121(1)**: 23-37.
Capper, D.R., Esquivel, E.Z., Pople, R.G., Burfield, I.J., Clay, R.P., Kennedy, C.P. & Mazar Barnett, J. (2000). Surveys and recommendations for the management of Aguará Ñu in the Reserva Natural del Bosque Mbaracayú, eastern Paraguay. Unpublished report.
Cardiff, S.W. (1983). Three new bird species from Peru, with other distributional records from northern Departamento de Loreto. *Gerfaut* **73**: 185-192.
Carlson, A. (1998). Territory quality and feather growth in the White-backed Woodpecker *Dendrocopos leucotos*. *J. Avian Biol.* **29**: 205-207.
Carlson, A. & Aulén, G. eds. (1990). *Conservation and Management of Woodpecker Populations*. Swedish University of Agricultural Sciences Department of Wildlife Ecology Report **17**. Uppsala, Sweden.
Carlson, A. & Stenberg, I. (1995). *Vitryggig Hackspett (*Dendrocopos leucotos*) Biotopval och Sårbarhetsanalys*. Report **27**. Department of Wildlife Ecology, Swedish University of Agricultural Sciences, Uppsala, Sweden.
Carrie, N.R., Moore, K.R., Stephens, S.A. & Keith, E.L. (1998). Influence of cavity availability on Red-cockaded Woodpecker group size. *Wilson Bull.* **110(1)**: 93-99.
Carriker, M.A. (1910). *An Annotated List of the Birds of Costa Rica, Including Cocos Island*. Annals of the Carnegie Museum **6**. 657 pp.
Carriker, M.A. (1933). Descriptions of new birds from Peru, with notes on other little-known species. *Proc. Acad. Nat. Sci. Philadelphia* **85**: 1-38.
Carriker, M.A. (1935). Descriptions of new birds from Bolivia, with notes on other little-known species. *Proc. Acad. Nat. Sci. Philadelphia* **87**: 313-359.
Carriker, M.A. (1955). Notes on the occurrence and distribution of certain species of Colombian birds. *Noved. Colombianas* **2**: 48-64.
Carroll, R.W. (1988). Birds of the Central African Republic. *Malimbus* **10(2)**: 177-200.
Carter, C. (1978a). Eastern Least Honeyguide (*Indicator meliphilus*) at Ndola. *Bull. Zambian Orn. Soc.* **10**: 30-31.

Carter, C. (1978b). Responses of Little Bee-eaters to a Black-throated Honeyguide entering their nest hole. *Scopus* **2(1)**: 23.

Carter, C., Shepherd, D. & Shepherd, R. (1984). The nest and eggs of the Black-backed Barbet *Lybius minor*. *Bull. Brit. Orn. Club* **104(1)**: 8-9.

Carter, J.H. (1974). *Habitat Utilization and Population Status of the Red-cockaded Woodpecker in South-central North Carolina*. MSc thesis, North Carolina State University, Raleigh, North Carolina.

Carter, J.H., Stamps, R.T. & Doerr, P.D. (1983a). Red-cockaded Woodpecker distribution in North Carolina. Pp. 20-23 in: Wood (1983c).

Carter, J.H., Stamps, R.T. & Doerr, P.D. (1983b). Status of the Red-cockaded Woodpecker in the North Carolina Sandhills. Pp. 24-29 in: Wood (1983c).

Carter, W.A. (1974). Pileated Woodpeckers desert nest after encounter with black rat snake. *Bull. Okla. Orn. Soc.* **7**: 6-8.

Cartwright, B.W. (1942). Red-bellied Woodpecker in Manitoba. *Can. Field Nat.* **56**: 45-46.

Cassin, J. (1867). A study of the Ramphastidae. *Proc. Acad. Nat. Sci. Philadelphia* **19**: 100-124.

Castelletta, M., Sodhi, N.S. & Subaraj, R. (2000). Heavy extinctions of forest avifauna in Singapore: lessons for biodiversity conservation in Southeast Asia. *Conserv. Biol.* **14(6)**: 1870-1880.

Castro, S.I.R. (1991). Comportamento e ecologia do *Colaptes campestris* Vieillot, 1818 (Aves, Picidae). Pp. 8-9 in: Oren, D.C. & da Silva, J.M.C. (1991). *I Congresso Brasileiro de Ornitologia*. (Abstract).

Catterall, M. (1997). *Results of the 1996 Bird Survey of Buton Island, Sulawesi, Indonesia*. Ecosurveys, Spilsby, UK.

Cavalcanti, R.B. (2000). Modelagem e monitoramento de estrutura da avifauna em ambientes fragmentados: exemplos do cerrado. Pp. 17-24 in: Alves *et al.* (2000).

Cavalcanti, R.B. & Marini, M.Â. (1993). Body masses of birds of the Cerrado Region, Brazil. *Bull. Brit. Orn. Club* **113**: 209-212.

Cave, F.O. & Macdonald, J.D. (1955). *Birds of the Sudan: their Identification and Distribution*. Oliver & Boyd, Edinburgh & London.

Cawkell, E.M. (1965). Notes on Gambian birds. *Ibis* **107**: 535-540.

Celliers, A. (1994). [Lesser Honeyguide (476)]. *Promerops* **212**: 9-10. In Afrikaans.

Chabloz, V. & Wegmüller, P. (1994). Nidification du Pic tridactyle (*Picoides tridactylus*) dans le Jura Vaudois (Suisse). *Nos Oiseaux* **42(5)**: 261-266.

Chai, P. (1986a). Field observations and feeding experiments on the response of Rufous-tailed Jacamars (*Galbula ruficauda*) to free-flying butterflies in a tropical rainforest. *Biol. J. Linn. Soc.* **29(3)**: 161–189.

Chai, P. (1986b). Signals which communicate unpalatability in butterflies learned by their specialized avian predator in a Neotropical rain forest. *Int. Congr. Ecol.* **4**: 113. (Abstract).

Chai, P. (1987). *Patterns of Prey Selection by an Insectivorous Bird on Butterflies in a Tropical Rainforest*. PhD dissertation, University of Texas, Austin, Texas.

Chai, P. (1988). Wing coloration of free-flying Neotropical butterflies as a signal learned by a specialized avian predator. *Biotropica* **20(1)**: 20–30.

Chai, P. (1990). Relationships between visual characteristics of rainforest butterflies and response of a specialized insectivorous bird. Pp. 31–60 in: Wicksten, E. (1990). *Adaptive Coloration in Invertebrates*. Texas A & M University Press, College Station, Texas.

Chai, P. (1996). Butterfly visual characteristics and ontogeny of responses to butterflies by a specialized tropical bird. *Biol. J. Linn. Soc.* **59(1)**: 37-67.

Chai, P. & Srygley, R.B. (1990). Predation and the flight, morphology, and temperature of Neotropical rainforest butterflies. *Amer. Naturalist* **135(6)**: 748–765.

Chakravarthy, A.K. (1988). Predation of Golden-backed Woodpecker, *Dinopium benghalense* (Linn.), on cardamom shoot-and-fruit borer, *Dichocrocis punctiferalis* (Guene). *J. Bombay Nat. Hist. Soc.* **85(2)**: 427-428.

Chakravarthy, A.K. & Purna Chandra Tejasvi, K.P. (1992). *Birds of Hill Region of Karnataka: an Introduction*. Navbharath Enterprises, Bangalore, India.

Chambers, J.A. (1979). Unusual feeding behavior of a Hairy Woodpecker. *Bird-Banding* **50(4)**: 365.

Champion-Jones, R.N. (1938). Drumming of woodpeckers. *J. Bombay Nat. Hist. Soc.* **40(1)**: 122-124.

Chandler, A.C. (1916). *A Study of the Structure of Feathers with Reference to their Taxonomic Significance*. University of California Publications in Zoology **13**. 204 pp.

Chao, L. (1997). Evolution of polyandry in a communal breeding system. *Behav. Ecol.* **8(6)**: 668-674.

Chapin, J.P. (1921). The abbreviated inner primaries of nestling woodpeckers. *Auk* **38(4)**: 531-552.

Chapin, J.P. (1939). *The Birds of the Belgian Congo*. Part 2. Bulletin of the American Museum of Natural History **75**, New York. 632 pp.

Chapin, J.P. (1952). *Campethera cailliautii* and *permista* are conspecific. *Ibis* **94**: 535-536.

Chapin, J.P. (1954). *The Birds of the Belgian Congo*. Part 4. Bulletin of the American Museum of Natural History **75B**, New York. 846 pp.

Chapin, J.P. (1958). A new honey-guide from the Kivu District, Belgian Congo. *Bull. Brit. Orn. Club* **78**: 46-48.

Chapin, J.P. (1962). Sibling species of small African honeyguides. *Ibis* **104**: 40-44.

Chapin, J.P., Chapin, R.T., Short, L.L. & Horne, J.F.M. (1987). Notes on the diet of the Least Honeyguide *Indicator exilis* in eastern Zaire. *Bull. Brit. Orn. Club* **107(1)**: 32-35.

Chapman, F.M. (1914a). Descriptions of a new genus and species of birds from Venezuela. *Bull. Amer. Mus. Nat. Hist.* **33**: 193-197.

Chapman, F.M. (1914b). Diagnoses of apparently new Colombian birds. III. *Bull. Amer. Mus. Nat. Hist.* **33**: 603-637.

Chapman, F.M. (1917). *The Distribution of Bird-life in Colombia: a Contribution to a Biological Survey of South America*. Bulletin of the American Museum of Natural History **36**, New York. 729 pp.

Chapman, F.M. (1921a). Description of apparently new birds from Bolivia, Brazil, and Venezuela. *Amer. Mus. Novit.* **2**: 1-8.

Chapman, F.M. (1921b). *The Distribution of Bird-life in the Urubamba Valley of Peru*. Smithsonian Institution Bulletin **117**. 138 pp.

Chapman, F.M. (1926). *The Distribution of Bird-life in Ecuador: a Contribution to a Study of the Origin of Andean Bird-life*. Bulletin of the American Museum of Natural History **55**, New York. 784 pp.

Chapman, F.M. (1928a). Descriptions of new birds from eastern Ecuador and eastern Peru. *Amer. Mus. Novit.* **332**: 1-12.

Chapman, F.M. (1928b). Mutation in *Capito auratus*. *Amer. Mus. Novit.* **335**: 1-21.

Chapman, F.M. (1929). Descriptions of new birds from Mt. Duida, Venezuela. *Amer. Mus. Novit.* **380**: 1-27.

Chapman, F.M. (1931). *The Upper Zonal Bird-life of Mts. Roraima and Duida*. Bulletin of the American Museum of Natural History **63(1)**, New York. 135 pp.

Chappuis, C. (1981). Illustration sonore des problèmes bioacoustiques posés par les oiseaux de la zone éthiopienne. Disque No. 12. *Alauda* **49**: 35-58.

Chartier, A. (1993). [Green Woodpecker against starling]. *Cormoran* **8(3)**: 235-236. In French.

Chasen, F.N. (1931). Birds from Bintang Island in the Rhio Archipelago. *Bull. Raffles Mus., Singapore* **5**: 114-120.

Chasen, F.N. (1934). Noteworthy records of birds from Perak. *Bull. Raffles Mus., Singapore* **9**: 89-91.

Chasen, F.N. (1935). *A Handlist of Malaysian Birds. A Systematic List of Birds of the Malaya Peninsula, Sumatra, Borneo and Java, Including the Adjacent Small Islands*. Bulletin of the Raffles Museum, Singapore **11**.

Chasen, F.N. (1937). The birds of Billiton Island. *Treubia* **16**: 205-238.

Chasen, F.N. (1939). *The Birds of the Malay Peninsula*. Vol. 4. The Birds of the Low Country Jungle and Scrub. H.F. & G. Witherby, London.

Chasen, F.N. & Hoogerwerf, A. (1941). *The Birds of the Netherlands Indian Mt Leuser Expedition 1937 to North Sumatra*. Treubia **18**(Supplement). 125 pp.

Chatfield, D.G.P. (1970). Abnormally plumaged Green Woodpecker. *British Birds* **63(10)**: 429.

Chauvin-Muckensturm, B. (1973). Solution brusque d'un problème nouveau chez le Pic épeiche. *Rev. Comp. Animal* **7**: 163-168.

Chauvin-Muckensturm, B. (1980). Une manipulation complexe chez le Pic épeiche *Dendrocopos major*. *C. R. Acad. Sci. Paris* **291**: 489-492.

Chazee, L. (1994). *Oiseaux du Laos. Identification, Distribution et Chasse*. Published privately, Vientiane.

Chebez, J.C. (1986). Nuestras aves amenazadas. 13. Carpintero Cara Canela (*Dryocopus galeatus*). *Nuestras Aves* **4(10)**: 16-18.

Chebez, J.C. (1994). *Los Que se Van. Especies Argentinas en Peligro*. Albatros, Buenos Aires.

Chebez, J.C. (1995). Nuevos datos sobre *Dryocopus galeatus* (Piciformes: Picidae) en la Argentina. *Hornero* **14**: 54-57.

Chebez, J.C., Rey, N.R., Barbaskas, M. & Di Giacomo, A.G. (1999). *Las Aves de los Parques Nacionales de la Argentina*. Literature of Latin America, Buenos Aires.

Cheesman, R.E. & Sclater, W.L. (1935). On a collection of birds from north-western Abyssinia. Part II. *Ibis* Ser. 13, no. 5: 297-329.

Cheke, R.A. & Walsh, J.F. (1996). *The Birds of Togo. An Annotated Check-list*. BOU Check-list **14**. British Ornithologists' Union, Tring, UK.

Cheke, R.A., Walsh, J.F. & Sowah, S.A. (1986). Records of birds seen in the Republic of Togo during 1984-1986. *Malimbus* **8(2)**: 51-72.

Cheng Tsohsin ed. (1964). *China's Economic Fauna: Birds*. English translation by Office of Technical Services, Joint Publications Research Service, Washington, D.C.

Cheng Tsohsin (1987). *A Synopsis of the Avifauna of China*. Science Press, Beijing, China.

Cherrie, G.K. (1916). *A Contribution to the Ornithology of the Orinoco Region*. Museum of the Brooklyn Institute of Arts and Sciences Bulletin **2(6)**. 242 pp.

Cherrie, G.K. & Reichenberger, E.M.B. (1921). Descriptions of proposed new birds from Brazil, Paraguay, and Argentina. *Amer. Mus. Novit.* **27**: 1-6.

Chiba, S. (1969). Stomach analysis of Japanese woodpeckers. *Misc. Yamashina Inst. Orn.* **5**: 487-505.

Chinchilla, F.A. (1991). [First report on acorn storage by *Melanerpes formicivorus* (Aves, Picidae) in Costa Rica]. *Brenesia* **35**: 123-124. In Spanish.

Chittenden, H., Coley, D. & Coley, V. (1998). Woodward's Barbet, a unique forest specialist. *Afr. Wildl.* **52(2)**: 18-21.

Chiweshe, N.C. & Dale, J. (2000). A merry-go-round story of a Greater Honeyguide. *Honeyguide* **46(2)**: 167-169.

Choffat, P. (1995). Curieux comportement d'un Pic vert (*Picus viridis*). *Nos Oiseaux* **43(4)**: 245.

Choudhury, A. (2001). Some bird records from Nagaland, north-east India. *Forktail* **17**: 91-103.

Christen, W. (1994). [Number of Green and Grey-headed Woodpeckers *Picus viridis* and *Picus canus* north of Solothurn (Switzerland), 1980 to 1993]. *Orn. Beob.* **91(1)**: 49-51. In German with English summary.

Christensen, H. (1984). Der Schwarzspecht *Dryocopus martius* auf der Jütländischen Halbinsel. [The Black Woodpecker *Dryocopus martius* on Jutland Peninsula]. *Ann. Zool. Fennici* **21(3)**: 403-404. In German with English summary.

Christensen, H. (1995a). Bestandsentwicklung und Verwandtschaftsbeziehungen in einer kleinen Population von Schwarzspechten (*Dryocopus martius*) im deutsch-daenischen Grenzraum. *Corax* **16(2)**: 196-198.

Christensen, H. (1995b). Neue Fernfunde des Schwarzspechts (*Dryocopus martius*) im deutsch-daenischen Grenzraum. *Corax* **16(2)**: 198-199.

Christensen, H. & Sorensen, B.R. (1986). [Initial results of a banding study of *Dryocopus martius* in Jutland (Denmark/Schleswig-Holstein), with a review of sightings outside the range in Europe]. *Corax* **12(1)**: 54-57. In German.

Christensen, L.L. (1971). *Seasonal Variation in Differential Niche Utilization by the Sexes in the Gila Woodpecker*. MSc thesis, University of Arizona, Tucson, Arizona.

Christie, D.A. (1990). Mystery photographs. 158. Middle Spotted Woodpecker. *British Birds* **83**: 395-396.

Christie, D.A. & Winkler, H. (1994). White-backed and Middle Spotted Woodpeckers. *Birding World* **7**: 283-285.

Christison, A.F.P. (1941). Notes on the birds of Chagai. *Ibis* Ser. 14, no. 4: 531-536.

Christison, A.F.P. (1942). Some additional notes on the distribution of the avifauna of northern Baluchistan. *J. Bombay Nat. Hist. Soc.* **43(3)**: 478-487.

Christison, A.F.P. & Ticehurst, C.B. (1943). Some additional notes on the distribution of the avifauna of northern Baluchistan. *J. Bombay Nat. Hist. Soc.* **43**: 478-487.

Christy, P. & Clarke, W. (1994). *Guide des Oiseaux de la Réserve de la Lopé*. ECOFAC Gabon, Libreville.

Chrostowski, T. (1921). On some rare or little known species of south-Brasilian birds. *An. Zool. Mus. Polonici Hist. Nat.* **1(1)**: 31-40.

Chubb, C.L. (1910). The birds of Paraguay. *Ibis* Ser. 9, no. 4: 53-78.

Chubb, C.L. (1916). *The Birds of British Guiana*. Vol. 1. Bernard Quaritch, London.

Cicero, C. & Johnson, N.K. (1994). Mitochondrial DNA divergence at the cytochrome-b locus in sapsuckers. Page 351 in: Dittami (1994).

Cicero, C. & Johnson, N.K. (1995). Speciation in sapsuckers (*Sphyrapicus*). Part 3. Mitochondrial DNA sequence divergence at the cytochrome-b locus. *Auk* **112(3)**: 547-563.

Clancey, P.A. (1952). Geographical variation in the Ground Woodpecker *Geocolaptes olivaceus* (Gmelin), a unique South African avian endemism. *J. Sci. Soc. Univ. Natal* **8**: 3-7.

Clancey, P.A. (1956). Miscellaneous taxonomic notes on African birds. VII. The South African races of the Black-collared Barbet *Lybius torquatus* (Dumont). *Durban Mus. Novit.* **4**: 273-280.

Clancey, P.A. (1958a). Geographical variation in the Knysna Woodpecker *Campethera notata* (Lichtenstein). *Bull. Brit. Orn. Club* **78(2)**: 31-35.

Clancey, P.A. (1958b). The South African races of the Bearded Woodpecker *Thripias namaquus* (Lichtenstein). *Bull. Brit. Orn. Club* **78(2)**: 35-43.

Clancey, P.A. (1958c). The barbets and woodpeckers of Natal and Zululand. *Condenser* **1958**(Dec.): 47-51.

Clancey, P.A. (1964). *The Birds of Natal and Zululand*. Oliver & Boyd, Edinburgh & London.

Clancey, P.A. (1965). On the type locality of *Campethera abingoni abingoni* (Smith), 1836. *Bull. Brit. Orn. Club* **85(4)**: 64-65.

Clancey, P.A. (1971a). A handlist of the birds of southern Moçambique. *Inst. Invest. Científica Moçambique* (Ser. A) **10**: 145-302.

Clancey, P.A. (1971b). On the South African race of the Little Spotted Woodpecker. *Ostrich* **42**: 119-122.

Clancey, P.A. (1971c). Miscellaneous taxonomic notes on African birds. XXXII. A name for an undescribed race of *Pogoniulus bilineatus* (Sundevall) from Malawi. *Durban Mus. Novit.* **9**: 44-46.

Clancey, P.A. (1971d). Miscellaneous taxonomic notes on African birds. XXXII. On variation in *Viridibucco leucomystax* (Sharpe). *Durban Mus. Novit.* **9**: 46-47.

Clancey, P.A. (1974a). The characters and range of *Pogoniulus chrysoconus extoni* (Layard), 1871. *Bull. Brit. Orn. Club* **94(4)**: 139-141.

Clancey, P.A. (1974b). Miscellaneous taxonomic notes on African birds. XXXIX. Subspeciation in *Trachyphonus vaillantii* Ranzani, 1821. *Durban Mus. Novit.* **10**: 87-95.

Clancey, P.A. (1975). Miscellaneous taxonomic notes on African birds. XLIII. Subspeciation in the Sharpbilled or Wahlberg's Honeyguide *Prodotiscus regulus* Sundevall. *Durban Mus. Novit.* **11**: 9-15.

Clancey, P.A. (1977a). Miscellaneous taxonomic notes on African birds. XLVII. The characters and range limits of the nominates subspecies of *Indicator minor* Stephens. *Durban Mus. Novit.* **11**: 181-187.

Clancey, P.A. (1977b). Miscellaneous taxonomic notes on African birds. XLVIII. On southern African *Indicator variegatus* Lesson. *Durban Mus. Novit.* **11**: 213-215.

Clancey, P.A. (1977c). Miscellaneous taxonomic notes on African birds. XLVIII. A further subspecies of *Indicator exilis* (Cassin). *Durban Mus. Novit.* **11**: 215-217.

Clancey, P.A. (1977d). Miscellaneous taxonomic notes on African birds. XLIX. On the status of *Lybius zombae* Shelley, 1893. *Durban Mus. Novit.* **11**: 228-229.

Clancey, P.A. (1977e). Miscellaneous taxonomic notes on African birds. L. A name for *Lybius zombae* auct., nec Shelley, 1893. *Durban Mus. Novit.* **11**: 251-252.
Clancey, P.A. (1979a). Miscellaneous taxonomic notes on African birds. LIII. On the generic status of the Green Barbet. *Durban Mus. Novit.* **12**: 6-7.
Clancey, P.A. (1979b). Miscellaneous taxonomic notes on African birds. LIII. The subspecies of the Scaly-throated Honeyguide *Indicator variegatus* Lesson. *Durban Mus. Novit.* **12**: 11-15.
Clancey, P.A. (1979c). Miscellaneous taxonomic notes on African birds. LV. A new isolated subspecies of Woodwards' Barbet *Cryptolybia woodwardi* (Shelley) from south-eastern Tanzania. *Durban Mus. Novit.* **12**: 50-52.
Clancey, P.A. (1980a). Miscellaneous taxonomic notes on African birds. LVIII. The status of *Campethera loveridgei* Hartert, 1920. *Durban Mus. Novit.* **12(13)**: 156-157.
Clancey, P.A. ed. (1980b). *SAOS Checklist of Southern African Birds*. Southern African Ornithological Society, Johannesburg.
Clancey, P.A. (1984a). Miscellaneous taxonomic notes on African birds. LXIV. The *Lybius torquatus* (Dumont) races of East Africa. *Durban Mus. Novit.* **13**: 174-175.
Clancey, P.A. (1984b). Miscellaneous taxonomic notes on African birds. LXIV. The validity of *Lybius diadematus mustus* (Friedmann), 1929. *Durban Mus. Novit.* **13**: 175-177.
Clancey, P.A. (1984c). Miscellaneous taxonomic notes on African birds. LXIV. Variation in *Pogoniulus atroflavus* (Sparrman), 1798, of forested Upper and Lower Guinea. *Durban Mus. Novit.* **13**: 177-178.
Clancey, P.A. (1984d). Miscellaneous taxonomic notes on African birds. LXIV. Subspeciation in *Pogoniulus simplex* (Fisher and Reichenow), 1888, of tropical eastern Africa. *Durban Mus. Novit.* **13**: 179-180.
Clancey, P.A. (1984e). Miscellaneous taxonomic notes on African birds. LXIV. On East African *Campethera abingoni* (Smith). *Durban Mus. Novit.* **13**: 180-182.
Clancey, P.A. (1985a). On the East African races of the Scaly-throated Honeyguide. *Honeyguide* **31**: 101-103.
Clancey, P.A. (1985b). *The Rare Birds of Southern Africa*. Winchester Press, Johannesburg.
Clancey, P.A. (1985c). On the littoral populations of the Golden-rumped Tinker Barbet. *Honeyguide* **31**: 166-167.
Clancey, P.A. (1987). On the Red-throated Wryneck *Jynx ruficollis* Wagler, 1830, in East Africa. *Bull. Brit. Orn. Club* **107(3)**: 107-112.
Clancey, P.A. (1988a). Variation in the Ground Woodpecker *Geocolaptes olivaceus*. *Bull. Brit. Orn. Club* **108(2)**: 93-98.
Clancey, P.A. (1988b). Relationships in the *Campethera notata*, *C. abingoni* and *C. (a.) mombassica* complex of the Afrotropics. *Bull. Brit. Orn. Club* **108(4)**: 169-172.
Clancey, P.A. (1989a). Bearded Woodpecker. *Bee-eater* **40(3)**: 43-44.
Clancey, P.A. (1989b). The taxonomy of the Green Barbets (Aves: Lybiidae) of the Eastern Afrotropics. *Bonn. zool. Beitr.* **40(1)**: 11-18.
Clancey, P.A. (1992). Subspeciation, clines and contact zones in the southern Afrotropical avifauna. Pp. 73-86 in: Monk (1992).
Clancey, P.A. (1993). The type-locality of the Crested Barbet. *Ostrich* **64(1)**: 43.
Clancey, P.A. (1995). The taxonomy of the *Stactolaema anchietae* biogeographical unit of southern savanna woodland barbets. *Honeyguide* **41**: 131-135.
Clancey, P.A. (1996). *The Birds of Southern Mozambique*. African Bird Book Publishing, Westville, South Africa.
Clarenbach, G. (1998). 8 Jahre Schwarzspechtbeobachtungen in der Haard. *Charadrius* **34(3-4)**: 159-164.
Clark, C. (1986). *Aves de Tierra del Fuego y Cabo de Hornos. Guía de Campo*. Literature of Latin America, Buenos Aires.
Clarke, G. (1985). Bird observations from northwest Somalia. *Scopus* **9**: 24-42.
Clements, J.F. & Shany, N. (2001). *A Field Guide to the Birds of Peru*. Ibis Publishing Company & Lynx Edicions, Temecula, California & Barcelona.
Coates, B.J. & Bishop, K.D. (1997). *A Guide to the Birds of Wallacea. Sulawesi, The Moluccas and Lesser Sunda Islands, Indonesia*. Dove Publications, Alderley, Australia.
Cocker, M. (2000). African birds in traditional magico-medicinal use - a preliminary survey. *Bull. African Bird Club* **7(1)**: 60-66.
Cofré, H.L. (1999). Patrones de rareza de las aves del bosque templado de Chile: implicancias para su conservación. *Bol. Chileno Orn.* **6**: 8-16. In Spanish with English summary.
Cohn-Haft, M., Whittaker, A. & Stouffer, P.C. (1997). A new look at the "species-poor" central Amazon: the avifauna north of Manaus, Brazil. Pp. 205-235 in: Remsen (1997).
Colebrook-Robjent, J.F.R. (1984). A nest of the Double-toothed Barbet *Lybius bidentatus* parasitized by a honeyguide in Uganda. *Bull. Brit. Orn. Club* **104(4)**: 123-124.
Colebrook-Robjent, J.F.R. & Stjernstedt, R. (1976). Chaplin's Barbet *Lybius chaplini*: first description of eggs, a new host record for the Lesser Honeyguide *Indicator minor*. *Bull. Brit. Orn. Club* **96(3)**: 109-111.
Collar, N.J. (1987). Rising sun, falling trees. *World Birdwatch* **9(1)**: 6-7.
Collar, N.J. (1997). Taxonomy and conservation: chicken and egg. *Bull. Brit. Orn. Club* **117**: 122-136.
Collar, N.J. & Andrew, P. (1988). *Birds to Watch. The ICBP World Checklist of Threatened Birds*. ICBP Technical Publication **8**, Cambridge.
Collar, N.J. & Stuart, S.N. (1985). *Threatened Birds of Africa and Related Islands*. The ICBP/IUCN Red Data Book. Part 1. 3rd edition. ICBP & IUCN, Cambridge.
Collar, N.J., Crosby, M.J. & Stattersfield, A.J. (1994). *Birds to Watch 2: the World List of Threatened Birds*. BirdLife Conservation Series **4**. BirdLife International, Cambridge.
Collar, N.J., Gonzaga, L.P., Krabbe, N., Madroño, A., Naranjo, L.G., Parker, T.A. & Wege, D.C. (1992). *Threatened Birds of the Americas. The ICBP/IUCN Red Data Book*. Part 2. 3rd edition. ICBP, Cambridge.
Collar, N.J., Mallari, N.A.D. & Tabaranza, B.R. (1999). *Threatened Birds of the Philippines*. The Haribon Foundation / BirdLife International Red Data Book. Bookmark, Makati City.
Collar, N.J., Wege, D.C. & Long, A.J. (1997). Patterns and causes of endangerment in the New World avifauna. Pp. 237–260 in: Remsen (1997).
Colston, P.R. (1981). A newly described species of *Melignomon* (Indicatoridae) from Liberia, West Africa. *Bull. Brit. Orn. Club* **101(2)**: 289-291.
Colston, P.R. & Curry-Lindahl, K. (1986). *The Birds of Mount Nimba, Liberia*. British Museum (Natural History), London.
Confer, J.L. & Paicos, P. (1985). Downy Woodpecker predation at goldenrod galls. *J. Field Orn.* **56(1)**: 56-64.
Confer, J.L., Confer, K. & Seeholzer, B. (1992). An early Hairy Woodpecker fledgling. *Kingbird* **42(4)**: 224.
Confer, J.L., Hibbard, C.J. & Ebbets, D. (1986). Downy Woodpecker reward rates from goldenrod gall insects. *Kingbird* **36(4)**: 188-192.
Conner, R.N. (1973). *Woodpecker Utilization of Cut and Uncut Woodlands*. MSc thesis, Virginia Polytechnic Institute and State University, Blacksburg, Virginia.
Conner, R.N. (1974). Red-bellied Woodpecker predation on nestling Carolina Chickadees. *Auk* **91(4)**: 836.
Conner, R.N. (1975). Orientation of entrances to woodpecker nest cavities. *Auk* **92(2)**: 371-374.
Conner, R.N. (1976). Nesting habitat for Red-headed Woodpeckers in southwestern Virginia. *Bird-Banding* **47(1)**: 40-43.
Conner, R.N. (1977). The effect of tree hardness on woodpecker nest entrance orientation. *Auk* **94(2)**: 369-370.
Conner, R.N. (1979). Seasonal changes in woodpecker foraging methods: strategies for winter survival. Pp. 95-105 in: Dickson, J.G., Conner, R.N., Fleet, R.R., Kroll, J.C. & Jackson, J.A. eds. (1979). *The Role of Insectivorous Birds in Forest Ecosystems*. Academic Press, New York.
Conner, R.N. (1980). Bill and body size in three syntopic woodpeckers. *Raven* **51(1)**: 7-11.
Conner, R.N. (1981). Seasonal changes in woodpecker foraging patterns. *Auk* **98(3)**: 562-570.
Conner, R.N. (1982). Pileated Woodpecker feeds on horned passalus colony. *Bull. Texas Orn. Soc.* **15**: 15-16.
Conner, R.N. (2001). A Red-cockaded Woodpecker group with two simultaneous nest trees. *Wilson Bull.* **113(1)**: 101-104.
Conner, R.N. & Adkisson, C.S. (1977). Principal component analysis of woodpecker nesting habitat. *Wilson Bull.* **89(1)**: 122-129.
Conner, R.N. & Crawford, H.S. (1974). Woodpecker foraging in Appalachian clearcuts. *J. For.* **72(9)**: 564-566.
Conner, R.N. & Kroll, J.C. (1979). Food-storing by Yellow-bellied Sapsuckers. *Auk* **96**: 195.
Conner, R.N. & Locke, B.A. (1982). Fungi and Red-cockaded Woodpecker cavity trees. *Wilson Bull.* **94(1)**: 64-70.
Conner, R.N. & O'Halloran, K.A. (1987). Cavity tree selection by Red-cockaded Woodpeckers as related to growth dynamics of southern pines. *Wilson Bull.* **99(3)**: 398-412.
Conner, R.N. & Rudolph, D.C. (1989). *Red-cockaded Woodpecker Colony Status and Trends on the Angelina, Davy Crockett and Sabine National Forests*. Research Paper **SO-250**. US Department of Agriculture, Forest Service, Southern Forest Experiment Station, New Orleans, Louisiana. 15 pp.
Conner, R.N. & Rudolph, D.C. (1991). Forest habitat loss, fragmentation, and Red-cockaded Woodpecker populations. *Wilson Bull.* **103(3)**: 446-457.
Conner, R.N. & Rudolph, D.C. (1995a). Losses of Red-cockaded Woodpeckers cavity trees to southern pine beetles. *Wilson Bull.* **107(1)**: 81-92.
Conner, R.N. & Rudolph, D.C. (1995b). Excavation dynamics and use patterns of Red-cockaded Woodpecker cavities: relationships with cooperative breeding. Pp. 343-352 in: Kulhavy *et al.* (1995).
Conner, R.N. & Saenz, D. (1996). Woodpecker excavation and use of cavities in polystyrene snags. *Wilson Bull.* **108(3)**: 449-456.
Conner, R.N., Hooper, R.G., Crawford, H.S. & Mosby, H.S. (1975). Woodpecker nesting habitat in cut and uncut woodlands in Virginia. *J. Wildl. Manage.* **39**: 144-150.
Conner, R.N., Jones, S.D. & Jones, G.D. (1994). Snag condition and woodpecker foraging ecology in a bottomland hardwood forest. *Wilson Bull.* **106(2)**: 242-257.
Conner, R.N., Miller, O.K. & Adkisson, C.S. (1976). Woodpecker dependence on trees infected by fungal heart rots. *Wilson Bull.* **88(4)**: 575-581.
Conner, R.N., Rudolph, D.C. & Bonner, L.H. (1995). Red-cockaded Woodpecker population trends and management on Texas national forests. *J. Field Orn.* **66(1)**: 140-151. In English with Spanish summary.
Conner, R.N., Rudolph, D.C., Saenz, D. & Coulson, R.N. (1997). The Red-cockaded Woodpecker's role in the southern pine ecosystem, population trends and relationships with southern pine beetles. *Texas J. Sci.* **49(3)**(Suppl.): 139-154.
Conner, R.N., Rudolph, D.C., Saenz, D. & Schaefer, R.R. (1994). Heartwood, sapwood, and fungal decay associated with Red-cockaded Woodpecker cavity trees. *J. Wildl. Manage.* **58(4)**: 728-734.
Conner, R.N., Rudolph, D.C., Saenz, D. & Schaefer, R.R. (1996). Red-cockaded Woodpecker nesting success, forest structure, and southern flying squirrels in Texas. *Wilson Bull.* **108(4)**: 697-711.
Conner, R.N., Rudolph, D.C., Saenz, D. & Schaefer, R.R. (1997). Species using Red-cockaded Woodpecker cavities in eastern Texas. *Bull. Texas Orn. Soc.* **30**: 11-16.
Conner, R.N., Rudolph, D.C., Schaefer, R.R. & Saenz, D. (1997). Long-distance dispersal of Red-cockaded Woodpeckers in Texas. *Wilson Bull.* **109(1)**: 157-160.
Conner, R.N., Rudolph, D.C., Schaefer, R.R., Saenz, D. & Shackelford, C.E. (1999). Relationships among Red-cockaded Woodpecker group density, nestling provisioning rates, and habitat. *Wilson Bull.* **111(4)**: 494-498.
Conner, R.N., Rudolph, D.C. & Walters, J.R. (2001). *The Red-cockaded Woodpecker: Surviving in a Fire-Maintained Ecosystem*. University of Texas Press, Austin & London.
Conner, R.N., Saenz, D., Rudolph, D.C., Ross, W.G. & Kulhavy, D.L. (1998). Red-cockaded Woodpecker nest-cavity selection: relationships with cavity age and resin production. *Auk* **115(2)**: 447-454.
Conner, R.N., Snow, A.E. & O'Halloran, A. (1991). Red-cockaded Woodpecker use of seed-tree/shelterwood cuts in eastern Texas. *Wildl. Soc. Bull.* **19(1)**: 67-73.
Conrads, K. (1964). Über das "Drohschwenken" und einige Rufe beim Grünspecht (*Picus canus*). *J. Orn.* **105**: 182-185.
Conrads, K. & Herrmann, A. (1963). Beobachtungen beim Grauspecht (*Picus canus* Gmelin) in der Brutzeit. *J. Orn.* **104**: 205-248.
Conrads, K. & Mensendiek, H. (1973). Beobachtungen an Fichtensapfenschmieden des Buntspechts (*Dendrocopos major*) im NSG "Donoper Teich" bei Detenold. *Bericht Naturwiss, Verains Bielefeld* **21**: 97-117.
Conrads, K. & Mensendiek, H. (1980). Zum Konsum von Fichtensamen durch den Buntspecht (*Dendrocopos major*) im Winterhalbjahr. *Orn. Mitt.* **32**: 204-207.
Constantz, G.D. (1974). Robbing of breeding Lewis' Woodpecker food stores. *Auk* **91(1)**: 171.
Contino, F. (1980). *Aves del Noroeste de Argentina*. Universidad Nacional de Salta, Salta, Argentina.
Contreras, J.R. (1980a). Sobre un ave nueva para la provincia de Mendoza y otra poco conocida. [On a new bird for the province of Mendoza and another little known species]. *Hist. Nat., Mendoza* **1(5)**: 26-28. In Spanish with English summary.
Contreras, J.R. (1980b). Avifauna mendocina. III. El Carpintero Chico *Picoides mixtus* en Mendoza: subespecie presente y comentarios biogeográficos (Picidae). [Avifauna mendocina. III. The Checkered Woodpecker *Picoides mixtus* in Mendoza: subspecies and biogeographic comments]. *Hist. Nat., Mendoza* **1(13)**: 85-90. In Spanish with English summary.
Contreras, J.R. (1983). Notas sobre el peso de aves argentinas. Part 1. *Hist. Nat., Mendoza* **3(1)**: 16.
Contreras, J.R., Berry, L.M., Contreras, A.O., Bertonatti, C.C. & Utges, E.E. (1990). *Atlas Ornitogeográfico de la Provincia del Chaco - República Argentina*. Vol. 1. No Passeriformes. Cuadernos Técnicos "Félix de Azara" **1**.
Contreras, J.R., Pérez, N. & Colman, A. (1993). [On *Picumnus albosquamatus* Lafresnaye, 1844, and its presence in the avifauna of Paraguay (Picidae: Picumninae)]. *Not. Faun.* **44**: 1-3. In Spanish with English summary.
Conway, C.J. & Martin, T.E. (1993). Habitat suitability for Williamson's Sapsuckers in mixed-conifer forests. *J. Wildl. Manage.* **57**: 322-328.
Conway, W.G. (1957). Pileated Woodpecker king of the woods. *Animal Kingdom* **60**: 52-58.
Cooper, D.S. (1997). Birds of the Río Negro Jaguar Preserve, Colonia Libertad, Costa Rica. *Cotinga* **8**: 17-22.
Cooper, D.S. (1999). Notes on the birds of Isla Popa, western Bocas del Toro, Panama. *Cotinga* **11**: 23-26.
Cooper, H.D., Raley, C.M. & Aubrey, K.B. (1995). A noose trap for capturing Pileated Woodpeckers. *Wildl. Soc. Bull.* **23**: 208-211.
Cooper, J. & Groves, J.U. (1969). Abnormal behaviour of Black-collared Barbet. *Ostrich* **40**: 22.
Cooper, J.K. (1969). First breeding record of the White-headed Woodpecker for Canada. *Can. Field-Nat.* **83**: 276-277.
Copeyon, C.K., Walters, J.R. & Carter, J.H. (1991). Induction of Red-cockaded Woodpecker group formation by artificial cavity construction. *J. Wildl. Manage.* **55(4)**: 549-556.
Corcuera, P. & Butterfield, J.E.L. (1999). Bird communities of dry forests and oak woodland of western Mexico. *Ibis* **141(2)**: 240-255.
Cordeiro, N.J. (1989). Observations on some nesting habits of three birds in Moshi, Tanzania. *Bull. East Afr. Nat. Hist. Soc.* **19(1)**: 3-4.
Cordeiro, N.J. & Githiru, M. (1998). Avifauna of the *Brachylaena* woodlands in the Usambara lowlands. *Bull. African Bird Club* **5(1)**: 13-16.
Cornett, J.W. (1986). Gila Woodpecker nesting in northern Baja California. *Western Birds* **17(3)**: 139-140.
Cornwallis, L. & Porter, R.F. (1982). Spring observations on the birds of North Yemen. *Sandgrouse* **4**: 1-36.
Cortés, J.A. & Domínguez, M.A. (1994). Método de detección del Torcecuello (*Jynx torquilla*) durante la época de reproducción. *Apus* **4**: 4-5.
Cortés, J.A. & Domínguez, M.A. (1997). Distribución y caracterización del hábitat del Torcecuello (*Jynx torquilla*) en la provincia de Málaga. Datos preliminares. Pp. 39-45 in: Manrique, J., Sánchez, A., Suárez, F. & Yanes, M. eds. (1997). *Actas de las XII Jornadas Ornitológicas Españolas*. Instituto de Estudios Almerienses, Almería, Spain.
Cory, C.B. (1919). *Catalogue of Birds of the Americas*. Publications of the Field Museum of Natural History, Zoological Series **13(2)**. 608 pp.

Costa, R. & Escaño, R.E.F. (1989). *Red-cockaded Woodpecker: Status and Management in the Southern Region in 1986*. Technical Publication **R8-TP 12**. US Department of Agriculture, Forest Service, Atlanta, Georgia.
Costa, R. & Kennedy, E. (1994). Red-cockaded Woodpecker translocations 1989-1994: state-of-our-knowledge. Pp. 74-81 in: *Proc. Assoc. Zool. Parks Aquariums Annu. Conf., 1994*.
Costantini, C. & Melletti, M. (1992). [The White-backed Woodpecker, *Picoides leucotos lilfordi*, and the Lesser Spotted Woodpecker, *Picoides minor*, in the beechwoods of the Simbruini and Ernici mountains (central Italy)]. *Riv. ital. Orn.* **62(3-4)**: 164-170. In Italian with English summary.
Costantini, C., Melletti, M. & Papi, R. (1993). [Preliminary observations on the reproductive biology of the White-backed Woodpecker *Picoides leucotos lilfordi* in central Italy]. *Avocetta* **17(1)**: 81-83. In Italian with English summary.
Costantini, C., Melletti, M. & Papi, R. (1995). Tecniche di alimentazione e nicchia di foraggiamento del Picchio dorsobianco *Picoides leucotos lilfordi* in Italia centrale: dati preliminari. *Avocetta* **19(1)**: 138.
Cottam, C. & Knappen, P. (1939). Food of some uncommon North American birds. *Auk* **56(2)**: 138-169.
Cottrell, C.B. (1998). A recent record of human guiding behaviour by the Greater Honeyguide near Harare. *Honeyguide* **44(4)**: 208-211.
Cottrell, G.W. (1968). *The Genera of Puffbirds (Bucconidae)*. Breviora **285**.
Cracraft, J. (1968). The lacrimal-ectethmoid bone complex in birds: a single character analysis. *Amer. Midl. Nat.* **80(2)**: 316–359.
Cracraft, J. (1981). Toward a phylogenetic classification of the recent birds of the world (class Aves). *Auk* **98(4)**: 681-714.
Cracraft, J. (1985). Historical biogeography and patterns of differentiation within the South American avifauna: areas of endemism. Pp. 49-84 in: Buckley *et al*. (1985).
Cracraft, J. & Prum, R.O. (1988). Patterns and processes of diversification: speciation and historical congruence in some Neotropical birds. *Evolution* **42**: 603-620.
Cramp, S. ed. (1985). *The Birds of the Western Palearctic*. Vol. 4. Terns to Woodpeckers. Oxford University Press, Oxford.
Cresswell, W., Hughes, M., Mellanby, R., Bright, S., Catry, P., Chaves, J., Freile, J., Gabela, A., Martineau, H., Macleod, R., McPhee, F., Anderson, N., Holt, S., Barabas, S., Chapel, C. & Sánchez, T. (1999). Densities and habitat preferences of Andean cloud-forest birds in pristine and degraded habitats in north-eastern Ecuador. *Bird Conserv. Int.* **9(2)**: 129-145.
Cresswell, W., Mellanby, R., Bright, S., Catry, P., Chaves, J., Freile, J., Gabela, A., Hughes, M., Martineau, H., MacLeod, R., McPhee, F., Anderson, N., Holt, S., Barabas, S., Chapel, C. & Sánchez, T. (1999). Birds of the Guandera Biological Reserve, Carchi Province, north-east Ecuador. *Cotinga* **11**: 55-63.
Crockett, A.B. (1975). *Ecology and Behavior of the Williamson's Sapsucker in Colorado*. PhD thesis, University of Colorado, Boulder, Colorado.
Crockett, A.B. & Hadow, H.H. (1975). Nest site selection by Williamson and Red-naped Sapsuckers. *Condor* **77(3)**: 365-368.
Crockett, A.B. & Hansley, P.L. (1977). Coition, nesting, and postfledging behavior of Williamson's Sapsucker in Colorado. *Living Bird* **16**: 7-19.
Cronin, R. & Sherman, P.W. (1977). A resource-based mating system: the Orange-rumped Honeyguide, *Indicator xanthonotus*. *Living Bird* **15**: 5-37.
Crosby, G.T. (1971a). Home range characteristics of the Red-cockaded Woodpecker in north-central Florida. Pp. 60-70 in: Thompson (1971).
Crosby, G.T. (1971b). *Ecology of the Red-cockaded Woodpecker in the Nesting Season*. MSc thesis, University of Florida, Gainesville, Florida.
Crowder, G.M. (1998). Impacts of translocation on nesting success of Red-cockaded Woodpeckers *Picoides borealis*, USA. *Endangered Species Update* **16**: 6-7.
Crumb, D.W. (1984). Late nesting of a Red-bellied Woodpecker. *Kingbird* **34(4)**: 231.
Crumb, D.W. (1988). Late nesting of Black-backed Woodpecker. *Kingbird* **38(4)**: 248-249.
Cruz, A. (1973). *Ecology and Behavior of the Jamaican Woodpecker*. PhD thesis, University of Florida, Gainesville, Florida.
Cruz, A. (1974a). Distribution, probable evolution, and fossil record of West Indian woodpeckers (family Picidae). *Caribb. J. Sci.* **14(3)**: 183-188.
Cruz, A. (1974b). Ecology and behavior of the Jamaican Woodpecker. *Gosse Bird Club Broadsheet* **23**: 3-5.
Cruz, A. (1977). Ecology and behavior of the Jamaican Woodpecker. *Bull. Florida State Mus. Biol. Sci.* **22(4)**: 149-204.
Cruz, A. (1997). Interference competition between Jamaican Woodpeckers and European Starlings for nest cavities in Jamaica. *Pitirre* **10(2)**: 70-71.
Cruz, A. & Johnston, D.W. (1979). Occurrence and feeding ecology of the Common Flicker on Grand Cayman Island. *Condor* **81(4)**: 370-375.
Cruz, A. & Johnston, D.W. (1984). Ecology of the West Indian Red-bellied Woodpecker on Grand Cayman: distribution and foraging. *Wilson Bull.* **96(3)**: 366-379.
Cuisin, M. (1967). [The activity of the Black Woodpecker (*Dryocopus martius*) in the forest]. *Rev. Forest. Franc.* **1**: 1-12. In French.
Cuisin, M. (1967-1968). Essai d'une monographie du Pic noir (*Dryocopus martius* L.). *Oiseau et RFO* **37**: 163-192, 285-315; **38**: 20-52.
Cuisin, M. (1972). Notes sur l'écologie du Pic noir (*Dryocopus martius*). *Oiseau et RFO* **42**: 28-34.
Cuisin, M. (1975). Observations sur le Pic noir (*Dryocopus martius*) dans le département de l'Aube. [Observations on the Black Woodpecker *Dryocopus martius* in Aube Department]. *Oiseau et RFO* **45(3)**: 197-206. In French with English summary.
Cuisin, M. (1976). Note sur le plumage d'un Pic noir *Dryocopus martius* (L.). [Note on the plumage of the Black Woodpecker *Dryocopus martius*]. *Oiseau et RFO* **46(1)**: 63-67. In French with English summary.
Cuisin, M. (1977). Le Pic noir (*Dryocopus martius*) en forêt. Bilan des observations sur son régime alimentaire et nouvelles donées sur son activité de charpentier. [The Black Woodpecker and the forest]. *Oiseau et RFO* **47(2)**: 159-165. In French with English summary.
Cuisin, M. (1980). Nouvelles données sur la répartition du Pic noir (*Dryocopus martius*) (L.) en France et comparaison avec la situation dans d'autres pays. *Oiseau et RFO* **50**: 23-32.
Cuisin, M. (1981). Note sur le nid et les jeunes du Pic noir (*Dryocopus martius* L.). [Note on the nesting and young of the Black Woodpecker, *Dryocopus martius* L.]. *Oiseau et RFO* **51(4)**: 287-295. In French with English summary.
Cuisin, M. (1983). [Note on some adaptations of the Black Woodpecker (*Dryocopus martius* L.) and its ecological niche in two biocenoses]. *Oiseau et RFO* **53(1)**: 63-77. In French with English summary.
Cuisin, M. (1985). Range-expansion of the Black Woodpecker in western Europe. *British Birds* **78(4)**: 184-187.
Cuisin, M. (1988). Le Pic noir (*Dryocopus martius* L.) dans les biocénoses forestières. *Oiseau et RFO* **58**: 173-276.
Cuisin, M. (1990). La répartition du Pic noir *Dryocopus martius* (L.) en France. *Oiseau et RFO* **60**: 1-9.
Cuisin, M. (1992). Longévité remarquable d'un nid de Pic noir (*Dryocopus martius*, L.) dans les Vosges. *Ciconia* **16(2)**: 113-116.
Cuisin, M. (1997). L'évolution des nids du Pic noir *Dryocopus martius* (L.). *Alauda* **65(2)**: 198-199. In French with English summary.
Cuisin, M. (1998). L'expansion du Pic noir *Dryocopus martius* (L.) en France n'a pas encore pris fin. *Alauda* **66(2)**: 131-134. In French with English summary.
Cuisin, M. (1999a). Pic cendré *Picus canus*. Pp. 412-413 in: Rocamora & Yeatman-Berthelot (1999).
Cuisin, M. (1999b). Pic vert *Picus viridis*. Pp. 414-415 in: Rocamora & Yeatman-Berthelot (1999).
Cuisin, M. (2000). Note sur le chant du Pic mar *Dendrocopos* (= *Picoides*) *medius*. *Alauda* **68(2)**: 151-153. In French with English summary.
Cuisin, M. & Maly, L. (1999). Pic mar *Dendrocopos medius*. Pp. 416-417 in: Rocamora & Yeatman-Berthelot (1999).
Cully, J.F. (1987). Autumnal breeding Acorn Woodpeckers in southern New Mexico. *Southwest. Nat.* **32(3)**: 399.
Cunningham-van Someren, G.R. (1970). On *Prodotiscus insignis* (Cassin) parasitising *Zosterops abyssinica* Guérin. *Bull. Brit. Orn. Club* **90**: 129-131.
Cunningham-van Someren, G.R. (1972). A Honey-buzzard *Pernis apivorus* at Kiambu. *Bull. East Afr. Nat. Hist. Soc.* **2**: 155-156.
Cunningham-van Someren, G.R. (1977). The European Wryneck *Jynx torquilla* in East Africa. *Scopus* **1(2)**: 54.
Curio, E. (1978a). Brutreifalter und Bruteinsatz beim Rotstirnbartvögel (*Tricholaema l. leucomelan*). *J. Orn.* **119**: 330-331.
Curio, E. (1978b). Scheinpaarungen eines Paar von Rotstirnbartvogel *Tricholaema l. leucomelan*. *J. Orn.* **119**: 331-333.
Currier, E.S. (1928). Lewis' Woodpeckers nesting in colonies. *Condor* **30**: 356.
Curson, J. (1989). Birdwatching areas. South Andaman Island. *Bull. Oriental Bird Club* **10**: 28-31.
Curson, J. & Lowen, J. (2000). Neotropical News. Ecuador. Jatun Sacha threatened by road. *Cotinga* **13**: 7.
Curzon, M. & Curzon, N. (1996). Breeding the Yellow-fronted Tinkerbird. *Avicult. Mag.* **102(1)**: 36-38.
Cyr, A. (1995a). Répartition saisonnière et spatio-temporelle du Pic à tête rouge (*Melanerpes erythrocephalus*) pour le Québec méridional de 1969 à 1989. Pp. 392-393 in: Cyr & Larivée (1995).
Cyr, A. (1995b). Répartition saisonnière et spatio-temporelle du Pic maculé (*Sphyrapicus varius*) pour le Québec méridional de 1969 à 1989. Pp. 394-395 in: Cyr & Larivée (1995).
Cyr, A. (1995c). Répartition saisonnière et spatio-temporelle du Pic mineur (*Picoides pubescens*) pour le Québec méridional de 1969 à 1989. Pp. 396-397 in: Cyr & Larivée (1995).
Cyr, A. (1995d). Répartition saisonnière et spatio-temporelle du Pic chevelu (*Picoides villosus*) pour le Québec méridional de 1969 à 1989. Pp. 398-399 in: Cyr & Larivée (1995).
Cyr, A. (1995e). Répartition saisonnière et spatio-temporelle du Pic tridactyle (*Picoides tridactylus*) pour le Québec méridional de 1969 à 1989. Pp. 400-401 in: Cyr & Larivée (1995).
Cyr, A. (1995f). Répartition saisonnière et spatio-temporelle du Pic à dos noir (*Picoides arcticus*) pour le Québec méridional de 1969 à 1989. Pp. 402-403 in: Cyr & Larivée (1995).
Cyr, A. (1995g). Répartition saisonnière et spatio-temporelle du Pic flamboyant (*Colaptes auratus*) pour le Québec méridional de 1969 à 1989. Pp. 404-405 in: Cyr & Larivée (1995).
Cyr, A. (1995h). Répartition saisonnière et spatio-temporelle du Grand Pic (*Dryocopus pileatus*) pour le Québec méridional de 1969 à 1989. Pp. 406-407 in: Cyr & Larivée (1995).
Cyr, A. & Alvo, R. (1996). Three-toed Woodpecker. Pp. 652-655 in: Gauthier, J. & Aubry, Y. eds. (1996). *The Breeding Birds of Québec: Atlas of the Breeding Birds of Southern Québec*. Association Québecoise des Groupes d'Ornitologues, Province of Québec Society for the Protection of Birds, Canada Wildlife Service & Environment Canada, Québec Region, Montréal.
Cyr, A. & Larivée, J. eds. (1995). *Atlas Saisonnier des Oiseaux du Québec*. Presses de l'Université de Sherbrooke & Societé Ornithologique de l'Estrie, Sherbrooke.
Cyrus, D. (1988). Observations on the parasitism of Black-collared Barbets *Lybius torquatus* by the Lesser Honeyguide *Indicator minor* at Lake St. Lucia Forest Station. *Ostrich* **59(3)**: 138-139.
Daily, G.C. (1993). Heartwood decay and vertical distribution of Red-naped Sapsucker nest cavities. *Wilson Bull.* **105**: 674-679.
Daniels, R.J.R. (1997). *A Field Guide to the Birds of Southwestern India*. Oxford University Press, Delhi.
Daniels, S.J. (1997). *Female Dispersal and Inbreeding in the Red-cockaded Woodpecker*. MSc thesis, Virginia Polytechnic Institute and State University, Blacksburg, Virginia.
Daniels, S.J. (2000). Inbreeding depression and its effects on natal dispersal in Red-cockaded Woodpeckers. *Condor*. **102(3)**: 482-491.
Daniels, S.J. & Walters, J.R. (1999). Inbreeding depression and its effects on natal dispersal in wild birds. Pp. 2492-2498 in: Adams & Slotow (1999).
Daniels, S.J. & Walters, J.R. (2000). Between-year breeding dispersal in Red-cockaded Woodpeckers: multiple causes and estimated cost. *Ecology* **81(9)**: 2473-2484.
Danielsen, F. & Heegaard, M. (1995). The birds of Bukit Tigapuluh, southern Riau, Sumatra. *Kukila* **7(2)**: 99-120.
Danielsen, F., Balete, D.S., Christensen, T.D., Heegaard, M., Jakobsen, O.F., Jensen, A., Lund, T. & Poulsen, M.K. (1994). *Conservation of Biological Diversity in the Sierra Madre Mountains of Isabela and Southern Cagayan Province, the Philippines*. Department of Environment and Natural Resources, BirdLife International & Danish Ornithological Society, Manila & Copenhagen.
Darlington, P.J. (1931). Notes on the birds of the Rio Frio (near Santa Marta), Magdalena, Colombia. *Bull. Mus. Comp. Zool., Harvard* **71**: 349-421.
Davenport, D.E., Lancia, R.A., Walters, J.R. & Doerr, P.D. (2000). Red-cockaded Woodpeckers: a relationship between reproductive fitness and habitat in the North Carolina sandhills. *Wildl. Soc. Bull.* **28(2)**: 426-434.
Davey, P. (1994). Woodpeckers feeding immature honeyguide. *Scopus* **18**: 61.
Davidar, P., Yoganand, T.R.K., Ganesh, T. & Joshi, N. (1997). An assessment of common and rare forest bird species of the Andaman Islands. *Forktail* **12**: 99-105.
Davies, C.W.N., Barnes, R., Butchart, S.H.M., Fernández, M. & Seddon, N. (1994). *The Conservation Status of the Cordillera de Colán. A Report Based on Bird and Mammal Surveys in 1994*. Published privately.
Davies, C.W.N., Barnes, R., Butchart, S.H.M., Fernández, M. & Seddon, N. (1997). The conservation status of birds on the Cordillera de Colán, Peru. *Bird Conserv. Int.* **7(2)**: 181-195.
Davies, G.B. & Boon, R. (1999). Little Spotted Woodpecker using arboreal ant nest for breeding in central Mozambique. *Honeyguide* **45**: 143.
Davis, G.L. (1973). Hairy Woodpecker feeding immature Downy Woodpecker. *Kingbird* **23**: 189.
Davis, J. (1965). Natural history, variation, and distribution of the Strickland's Woodpecker. *Auk* **82(4)**: 537-590.
Davis, L.I. (1972). *A Field Guide to the Birds of Mexico and Central America*. University of Texas Press, Austin & London.
Davis, S.E. (1993). Seasonal status, relative abundance, and behavior of the birds of Concepción, Departamento Santa Cruz, Bolivia. *Fieldiana Zool. (New Ser.)* **71**: 1-33.
Davis, T.J. (1986). Distribution and natural history of some birds from the departments of San Martín and Amazonas, northern Peru. *Condor* **88(1)**: 50-56.
Davis, W.E. (1995). Downy Woodpecker and White-breasted Nuthatch use "vice" to open sunflower seeds: is this an example of tool use? *Bird Obs.* **23(6)**: 339-342.
Davison, G.W.H. (1992). *Birds of Mount Kinabalu. Borneo*. Natural History Publications (Borneo) Sdn. Bhd. & Koktas Sabah Berhad, Kota Kinabalu & Ranau, Indonesia.
Davison, G.W.H. (1997). Bird observations in the Muratus Mountains, Kalimantan Selatan. *Kukila* **9**: 114-121.
Dawson, R. (2001). Great Spotted Woodpecker bathing in leaf clusters after rain. *British Birds* **94(3)**: 145.
Day, D. (1981). Golden-rumped Tinkerbird. *Witwatersrand Bird Club News* **113**: 8.
Dean, W.R.J. (1974a). Breeding and distributional notes on some Angolan birds. *Durban Mus. Novit.* **10**: 109-125.
Dean, W.R.J. (1974b). *Dicrurus assimilis* robbing *Dendropicos fuscescens* of food. *Ostrich* **45**: 185.
Dean, W.R.J. (1985). Greater Honeyguides and ratels: how long will the myth continue? Pp. 217-223 in: Bunning, L.J. (1985). *Proceedings of the Birds and Man Symposium, Johannesburg 1983*. The Witwatersrand Bird Club, Johannesburg.
Dean, W.R.J. (2000). *The Birds of Angola. An Annotated Check-list*. BOU Check-list **18**. British Ornithologists' Union, Tring, UK.
Dean, W.R.J., Siegfried, W.R. & Macdonald, I.A.W. (1990). The fallacy, fact, and fate of guiding behavior in the Greater Honeyguide. *Conserv. Biol.* **4(1)**: 99-101.

Dearborn, N. (1907). *Catalogue of a Collection of Birds of Guatemala*. Publications of the Field Museum of Natural History (Ornithological Series) **125, pt. 1(3)**. 69 pp.

DeBenedictis, P.A. (1997). Flicker futures. *Birding* **29(5)**: 420-424.

Dedekind, H. (1997). Barbets and honeyguides. *Lanioturdus* **30(2)**: 9-10.

Dégallier, N., Travassos da Rosa, A.P.A., da Silva, J.M.C., Rodrigues, S.G., Vasconcelos, P.F.C., Travassos da Rosa, J.F.S., Pereira da Silva, G. & Pereira da Silva, R. (1992). As aves como hospedeiras de arbovírus na Amazônia brasileira. *Bol. Mus. Paraense Emílio Goeldi (Zool.)* **8(1)**: 69-101.

Degan, C. & Popovici, N. (1973). Variatii biometrice ale scheletului si ale musculatruii aripilor la citeva specii de pasari din familia Picidelor. [Variations of the skeleton and musculature of the wings of different bird species of the family Picidae]. *Stud. Univ. "Babes-Bolyai" Biol.* **18(1)**: 91-98. In Romanian with Russian and French summary.

DeGraaf, R.M. & Rappole, J.H. (1995). *Neotropical Migratory Birds. Natural History, Distribution and Population Change*. Comstock Publishing Associates, Ithaca & London.

Deignan, H.G. (1941). New bird from the Indo-Chinese sub-region. *Auk* **58**: 396-398.

Deignan, H.G. (1945). *The Birds of Northern Thailand*. US National Museum Bulletin **186**. Smithsonian Institution, Washington, D.C. 616 pp.

Deignan, H.G. (1955). Remarks on *Picus vittatus* Vieillot and some of its allies. *Ibis* **97**: 18-24.

Deignan, H.G. (1956). New races of birds from Laem Thong, the golden Chersonese. *Proc. Biol. Soc. Washington* **69**: 207-214.

Deignan, H.G. (1960). A new race of the Brown Barbet from Thailand. *Bull. Brit. Orn. Club* **80(7)**: 121.

Deignan, H.G. (1963). *Checklist of the Birds of Thailand*. US National Museum Bulletin **226**. Smithsonian Institution, Washington, D.C. 263 pp.

Dejaegere, J.C. (1993). Le Pic mar *Dendrocopos medius* en forêt de Trélon (Nord) en 1993. *Heron* **26(1)**: 36-43.

Dejaegere, J.C. & Vandevenne, I. (1993). Le Pic mar *Dendrocopos medius* en forêt de Trélon (Nord) en 1992. *Heron* **26(1)**: 29-35.

Delacour, J. (1951a). The significance of the number of toes in some woodpeckers and kingfishers. *Auk* **68(1)**: 49-51.

Delacour, J. (1951b). Commentaires, modifications et additions à la liste des oiseaux de l'Indochine Française. *Oiseaux et RFO* **21**: 1-32, 81-119.

Delacour, J. & Jabouille, P. (1931). *Les Oiseaux de l'Indochine Française*. Vol. 2. Exposition Coloniale Internationale, Paris.

Delacour, J. & Jabouille, P. (1940). *Liste des Oiseaux de l'Indochine Française*. Oiseau et RFO **1-2**. 132 pp.

Delacour, J. & Legendre, M. (1925). The woodpeckers. *Avicult. Mag.* **3(8)**: 192-197.

Delacour, J. & Mayr, E. (1945). Notes on the taxonomy of the birds of the Philippines. *Zoologica* **30**: 105-117.

Delacour, J. & Mayr, E. (1946). *Birds of the Philippines*. Macmillan Co., New York.

Delamain, J.M. (1937). Le tambourinage des pics. *Alauda* **9(1)**: 46-63.

Delgado, F.S. (1985). Present situation of the forest birds of Panama. Pp. 77-93 in: Diamond & Lovejoy (1985).

DeLotelle, R.S. & Epting, R.J. (1988). Selection of old trees for cavity excavation by Red-cockaded Woodpeckers. *Wildl. Soc. Bull.* **16(1)**: 48-52.

DeLotelle, R.S. & Epting, R.J. (1992). Reproduction of the Red-cockaded Woodpecker in central Florida. *Wilson Bull.* **104(2)**: 285-294.

DeLotelle, R.S., Epting, R.J. & Newman, J.R. (1987). Habitat use and territory characteristics of Red-cockaded Woodpeckers in central Florida. *Wilson Bull.* **99(2)**: 202-217.

DeLotelle, R.S., Newman, J.R. & Jerauld, A.E. (1983). Habitat use by Red-cockaded Woodpeckers in central Florida. Pp. 59-67 in: Wood (1983c).

Dementiev, G.P. (1934). Sur la distribution géographique de *Dryobates leucotos* (Bechstein) au Caucase. *Alauda* **6(2)**: 313-315.

Dementiev, G.P. (1935). Sur la variabilité géographique de *Dryobates major* (L.). *Alauda* **6(4)**: 428-451.

Dementiev, G.P. (1939). Remarques sur la variabilité géographique du Pic noir *Dryocopus martius* (L.) dans la région paléarctique orientale. *Alauda* **11(1)**: 7-17.

Dementiev, G.P. (1952). *The Birds of Turkmenistan*. Published privately, Ashkabad.

Dementiev, G.P., Gladkov, N.A., Ptushenko, E.S., Spangenberg, E.P. & Sudilovskaya, A.M. (1966). *Birds of the Soviet Union*. Vol. 1. Israel Program for Scientific Translations, Jerusalem.

Demey, R. & Fishpool, L.D.C. (1991). Additions and annotations to the avifauna of Côte d'Ivoire. *Malimbus* **12(2)**: 61-86.

Demey, R. & Fishpool, L.D.C. (1994). The birds of Yapo Forest, Ivory Coast. *Malimbus* **16(2)**: 100-122.

Demey, R., Herroelen, P. & Pedersen, T. (2000). Additions and annotations to the avifauna of Congo-Kinshasa (ex-Zaïre). *Bull. Brit. Orn. Club* **120(3)**: 154-172.

Demongin, L. (1993). [Results of Wryneck enquiry in department of Eure]. *Cormoran* **8(4)**: 299-302, 246. In French with English summary.

Denis, D., Torrella, L., Jiménez, A. & Beovides, K. (1999). Observación de Carpinteros Verdes (*Xiphidiopicus percussus*) depredando huevos de garzas (Aves: Ardeidae). *Pitirre* **12(3)**: 95.

Dennis, J.V. (1948a). A last remnant of Ivory-billed Woodpeckers in Cuba. *Auk* **65(4)**: 497-507.

Dennis, J.V. (1948b). In search of the Cuban Ivory-billed Woodpecker. *Bull. Mass. Audubon Soc.* **32(7)**: 257-259.

Dennis, J.V. (1964). Woodpecker damage to utility poles: with special reference to the role of territory and resonance. *Bird-Banding* **35(4)**: 225-253.

Dennis, J.V. (1967). Damage by Golden-fronted and Ladder-backed Woodpeckers to fence posts and utility poles in South Texas. *Wilson Bull.* **79(1)**: 75-88.

Dennis, J.V. (1969). The Yellow-shafted Flicker (*Colaptes auratus*) on Nantucket Island, Massachusetts. *Bird-Banding* **40(4)**: 290-308.

Dennis, J.V. (1971). Utilization of pure resin by the Red-cockaded Woodpecker and its effectiveness in protecting roosting and nest sites. Pp. 78-86 in: Thompson (1971).

Dennis, J.V. (1979). The Ivory-billed Woodpecker *Campephilus principalis*. *Avicult. Mag.* **85(2)**: 75-84.

Dentesani, B. (1989). Interessante presenza del Picchio rosso minore, *Picoides minor*, in provincia di Udine. *Riv. ital. Orn.* **59(3-4)**: 293-296.

Dentesani, B. (1990). Prima indagine sulla distribuzione del Picchio rosso minore, *Picoides minor*, in provincia di Udine. *Riv. ital. Orn.* **60(3-4)**: 185-189.

Derleth, P., Buetler, R. & Schlaepfer, R. (2000). Le Pic tridactyle (*Picoides tridactylus*): un indicateur de la qualité écologique de l'écosystème forestier du Pays-d'Enhaut (Préalpes suisses). *Schweizerische Zeitschrift fuer Forstwesen* **151(8)**: 282-289.

Dernfalk, C. (1983). Hybrid mellan större hackspett och vitryggig hackspett i Närke. *Fåglar i Närke* **6**: 11-14.

Descourtilz, J.T. (1983). *História Natural das Aves do Brasil. (Ornitologia Brasileira). Notáveis por sua Plumagem, Canto e Hábitos*. Editora Itatiaia Limitada, Belo Horizonte, Brazil.

Desfayes, M. (1969). A possible hybrid *Jynx ruficollis* x *torquilla*. *Bull. Brit. Orn. Club* **89(4)**: 110-112.

Desfayes, M. (1975). Birds from Ethiopia. *Rev. Zool. Afr.* **89(3)**: 505-535.

Desfayes, M. & Praz, J.C. (1978). Notes on habitat and distribution of montane birds in southern Iran. *Bonn. zool. Beitr.* **29**: 18-37.

Desmet, J.F. (1999). Pic tridactyle *Picoides tridactylus*. Pp. 174-175 in: Rocamora & Yeatman-Berthelot (1999).

Deviney, E. (1957). Unusual nesting site of the Red-bellied Woodpecker. *Oriole* **22**: 29.

Dhindsa, M.S. & Sandhu, P.S. (1982). Occurrence of the Northern Green Barbet *Megalaima zeylanica caniceps* (Franklin) at Ludhiana (Punjab). *J. Bombay Nat. Hist. Soc.* **79(2)**: 415.

Dhindsa, M.S., Sandhu, J.S. & Sohi, A.S. (1986). Pesticidal mortality of Crimson-breasted Barbet *Megalaima haemacephala* with a note on its body size. *Bull. Brit. Orn. Club* **106(3)**: 93-96.

Di Giacomo, A.G. & López, B. (2000). Nuevos aportes al conocimiento de la nidificación de algunas aves del noroeste argentino. [New notes on the nesting of some species of northwestern Argentina birds]. *Hornero* **15(2)**: 131-134. In Spanish with English summary.

Diamond, A.W. (1985). Honeyguide. Pp. 288-289 in: Campbell & Lack (1985).

Diamond, A.W. & Lovejoy, T.E. eds. (1985). *Conservation of Tropical Forest Birds*. ICBP Technical Publication **4**, Cambridge.

Diamond, A.W. & Place, A.R. (1988). Wax digestion in Black-throated Honeyguides, *Indicator indicator*. *Ibis* **130(4)**: 558-561.

Díaz, M. (1997). Pájaros carpinteros: excelentes indicadores forestales. *Garcilla* **99**: 8-15.

Díaz, M., Asensio, B. & Tellería, J.L. (1996). *Aves Ibéricas*. Vol 1. No Paseriformes. J.M. Reyero Editor, Madrid.

Dickerman, R.W. (1987). Two new subspecies of birds from Guatemala. *West. Found. Vertebrate Zool.* **3**: 1-6.

Dickerman, R.W. compiler (1997). *The Era of Allan R. Phillips: A Festschrift*. Horizon Communications, Albuquerque, New Mexico.

Dickerman, R.W. & Phelps, W.H. (1982). An annotated list of the birds of Cerro Urutani on the border of Estado Bolívar, Venezuela and Território Roraima, Brazil. *Amer. Mus. Novit.* **2732**: 1-20.

Dickerman, R.W., Cane, W.P., Carter, M.F., Chapman, A. & Schmitt, C.G. (1994). Report on three collections of birds from Liberia. *Bull. Brit. Orn. Club* **114(4)**: 267-278.

Dickey, D.R. & van Rossem, A.J. (1930). Geographic variation in *Aulacorhynchus prasinus* (Gould). *Ibis* **Ser. 12, no. 6**: 48-55.

Dickey, D.R. & van Rossem, A.J. (1938). *The Birds of El Salvador*. Field Museum of Natural History (Zoological Series) **23**. 609 pp.

Dickinson, E.C. (1986). A third race of the Golden-throated Barbet, *Megalaima franklinii*, in Thailand. *Nat. Hist. Bull. Siam Soc.* **34(1)**: 71.

Dickinson, E.C., Kennedy, R.S. & Parkes, K.C. (1991). *The Birds of the Philippines. An Annotated Checklist*. BOU Check-list **12**. British Ornithologists' Union, Tring, UK.

Dickinson, J., Haydock, J., Koenig, W., Stanback, M.T. & Pitelka, F. (1995). Genetic monogamy in single-male groups of Acorn Woodpeckers, *Melanerpes formicivorus*. *Mol. Ecol.* **4**: 765-769.

Diener, U. (1996). Nächtigungsverhalten beim Schwarzspecht *Dryocopus martius*. *Charadrius* **32(3)**: 113-116.

Diesselhorst, G. (1968). Beiträge zur Ökologie der Vögel Zentral- und Ost-Nepals. Pp. 1-47 in: Hellmich, W. ed. (1968). *Khumbu Himalaya*. Vol. 1. Universitätsverlag Wagner, Innsbruck & Munich.

Dilger, W.C. (1953). Duetting in the Crimson-breasted Barbet. *Condor* **55(4)**: 220-221.

Dillingham, C.P. & Vroman, D.P. (1997). Notes on habitat selection and distribution of the Acorn Woodpecker in southwestern Oregon. *Oregon Birds* **23(1)**: 13-14.

Dittami, J. ed. (1994). *Proceedings of the XXI International Ornithological Congress*. Journal für Ornithologie **135(3)**.

Dittami, J., Bock, W., Taborsky, M., van den Elzen, R. & Vogel-Millesi, E. eds. (1994). *Research Notes on Avian Biology 1994: Selected Contributions from the XXI International Ornithological Congress*. Journal für Ornithologie **135**(Supplement).

Dixon, R.D. (1995a). *Density, Nest-site and Roost-site Characteristics, Home-range, Habitat Use, and Behavior of White-headed Woodpeckers: Deschutes and Winema National Forests, Oregon*. Technical Report **93-3-01**. Oregon Department of Fish & Game, Nongame Wildlife Program, Portland, Oregon.

Dixon, R.D. (1995b). *Ecology of White-headed Woodpeckers in the Central Oregon Cascades*. MSc thesis, University of Idaho, Moscow, Idaho.

Dixon, R.D. & Saab, V.A. (2000). Black-backed Woodpecker (*Picoides arcticus*). No. **509** in: Poole, A.F. & Gill, F.B. eds. (2000). *The Birds of North America*. Vol. 13. Academy of Natural Sciences & American Ornithologists' Union, Philadelphia & Washington, D.C.

Dobbs, R.C., Martin, T.E. & Conway, C.J. (1997). Williamson's Sapsucker (*Sphyrapicus thyroideus*). No. **285** in: Poole, A.F. & Gill, F.B. eds. (1997). *The Birds of North America*. Vol. 8. Academy of Natural Sciences & American Ornithologists' Union, Philadelphia & Washington, D.C.

Dod, A.S. (1972). Aves de nuestro país: el Carpintero de la Sierra. Birds of our country: the Antillean Piculet. *Caribe* **16**: 11-A.

Dod, A.S. (1973). Aves de nuestro país: ¿es dañino el Carpintero? *Caribe* **16**: 11-A.

Dod, A.S. (1977). ¿Es dañino nuestro Carpintero? *Terra* **1(2)**: 7-8.

Dod, A.S. (1987). *Aves de la República Dominicana*. 2nd edition. Museo Nacional de Historia Natural, Santo Domingo.

Dod, A.S. (1992). *Endangered and Endemic Birds of the Dominican Republic*. Cypress House, Fort Bragg, California.

Dodenhoff, D.J., Stark, R.D. & Johnson, E.V. (2001). Do woodpecker drums encode information for species recognition? *Condor* **103(1)**: 143-150.

Dodsworth, P.T.L. (1911). Occurrence of *Hemilophus pulverulentus*, (Temm.), the Great Slaty Woodpecker in the neighbourhood of Simla, N.W. Himalayas. *J. Bombay Nat. Hist. Soc.* **21(1)**: 263.

Dodsworth, P.T.L. (1912). Habits, food and nesting of the Great Himalayan Barbet (*Megalaima marshallorum*). *J. Bombay Nat. Hist. Soc.* **21(2)**: 681-684.

Doerr, P.D., Walters, J.R. & Carter, J.H. (1989). Reoccupation of abandoned clusters of cavity trees (colonies) by Red-cockaded Woodpeckers. *Proc. Ann. Conf. Southeastern Assoc. Fish. & Wildl. Agencies* **43**: 326-336.

Doherty, P.F., Grubb, T.C. & Bronson, C.L. (1996). Territories and caching-related behaviors of Red-headed Woodpeckers wintering in a beech grove. *Wilson Bull.* **108(4)**: 740-747.

Dolby, A.S. & Grubb, T.C. (1998). Benefits to satellite members in mixed-species foraging groups: an experimental analysis. *Anim. Behav.* **56(2)**: 501-509.

Dolby, A.S. & Grubb, T.C. (1999). Effects of winter weather on horizontal and vertical use of isolated forest fragments by bark-foraging birds. *Condor* **101(2)**: 408-412.

Donahue, P. (1994). *Birds of Tambopata. A Checklist*. Tambopata Reserve Society, London.

Donatelli, R.J. (1987). *Osteologia e Miologia Cranianas de Galbulidae (Aves, Piciformes) com um Enfoque Filogenético*. MSc thesis, Universidade de São Paulo, São Paulo.

Donatelli, R.J. (1991). *Anatomia Craniana e Aspectos Evolutivos de Picidae (Aves, Piciformes) Neotropicais e Afrotropicais*. PhD thesis, Universidade de São Paulo, São Paulo.

Donatelli, R.J. (1992). Cranial osteology and myology of the jaw apparatus in the Galbulidae (Aves, Piciformes). *Arq. Zool. São Paulo* **32(1)**: 1–32.

Donatelli, R.J. (1996). The jaw apparatus of the Neotropical and of the Afrotropical woodpeckers (Aves: Piciformes). *Arq. Zool. São Paulo* **33(1)**: 1-70.

Donatelli, R.J. (1998). The relationships of Neotropical and of Afrotropical woodpeckers: dispersion or vicariance model? Proceedings of the XXII International Ornithological Congress, Durban 1998. *Ostrich* **69(3&4)**: 399. (Abstract).

Donegan, T.M. & Dávalos, L. (1999). Ornithological observations from Reserva Natural Tambito, Cauca, south-west Colombia. *Cotinga* **12**: 48-55.

Donegan, T.M., Dávalos, L. & Salaman, P.G.W. (1998). An ornithological expedition to Tambito Nature Reserve, Cauca, Colombia, Aug-Sept 1997. Unpublished report.

Donnelly, B.G. (1973). Communal roosting in the Black-collared Barbet. *Honeyguide* **76**: 41.

Dornbusch, M. (1968). Erstbeobachtung des Blutspechts (*Dendrocopos syriacus*) in Deutschland. *J. Orn.* **109**: 128-129.

Dorst, J. (1956). Notes sur la biologie des *Colaptes*, *Colaptes rupicola*, des Hauts Plateaux Peruviens. *Oiseau et RFO* **26**: 118-125.

Dorst, J. (1963). Quelques adaptations écologiques des oiseaux des hautes Andes péruviennes. Pp. 658-665 in: Sibley, C.G. ed. (1963). *Proceedings of the XIII International Ornithological Congress, Ithaca, June 1962*. Vol. 2. American Ornithologists' Union, Baton Rouge, Louisiana.

Doster, R.H. & James, D.A. (1998). Home range size and foraging habitat of Red-cockaded Woodpeckers in the Ouachita Mountains of Arkansas. *Wilson Bull.* **110(1)**: 110-117.

Downer, A. (1968). Unusual bill growth in sapsucker. *Gosse Bird Club Broadsheet* **10**: 13.

Dowsett, R.J. (1969). The call and distribution of the Black-backed Barbet, *Lybius minor*. *Puku* **3**: 222-223.

Dowsett, R.J. (1972a). Eastern Least Honeyguide in Mpika District. *Bull. Zambian Orn. Soc.* **4**: 24.
Dowsett, R.J. (1972b). The type locality of *Campethera cailliautii fuelleborni*. *Bull. Brit. Orn. Club* **92(2)**: 81-82.
Dowsett, R.J. (1973). Brown-eared Woodpeckers (*Campethera caroli*) in Mwinilunga: a species new to Zambia. *Bull. Zambian Orn. Soc.* **5**: 72.
Dowsett, R.J. (1979a). A problem involving the Golden-rumped Tinkerbird (*Pogoniulus bilineatus*). *Bull. Zambian Orn. Soc.* **11(1)**: 30-31.
Dowsett, R.J. (1979b). Recent additions to the Zambian list. *Bull. Brit. Orn. Club* **99(3)**: 94-98.
Dowsett, R.J. (1980). Comments on some ornitholgical type-localities in Zambia. *Zambia Mus. J.* **5**: 7-16.
Dowsett, R.J. (1982). On the supposed occurrence of the Red-breasted Wryneck *Jynx ruficollis* in Malawi. *Nyala* **8(2)**: 101.
Dowsett, R.J. (1985). The conservation of tropical forest birds in central and southern Africa. Pp. 197-212 in: Diamond & Lovejoy (1985).
Dowsett, R.J. ed. (1989a). *A Preliminary Natural History Survey of Mambilla Plateau and some Lowland Forests of Eastern Nigeria*. Tauraco Research Report **1**. Tauraco Press, Ely, UK.
Dowsett, R.J. ed. (1989b). *Enquête Faunistique dans la Forêt du Mayombe et Check-liste des Oiseaux et des Mammifères du Congo*. Tauraco Research Report **2**. Tauraco Press, Liège, Belgium.
Dowsett, R.J. (1989c). The nomenclature of some African barbets of the genus *Tricholaema*. *Bull. Brit. Orn. Club* **109(3)**: 180-181.
Dowsett, R.J. ed. (1990). *Enquête Faunistique et Floristique dans la Forêt de Nyungwe au Rwanda. Survey of the Fauna and Flora of Nyungwe Forest, Rwanda*. Tauraco Research Report **3**. Tauraco Press, Liège, Belgium. In French and English.
Dowsett, R.J. & Dowsett-Lemaire, F. (1980). The systematic status of some Zambian birds. *Gerfaut* **70**: 151-199.
Dowsett, R.J. & Dowsett-Lemaire, F. eds. (1991). *Flore et Faune du Bassin du Kouilou (Congo) et leur Exploitation. Flora and Fauna of the Kouilou Basin (Congo) and their Exploitation*. Tauraco Research Report **4**. Tauraco Press, Liège, Belgium. In French and English.
Dowsett, R.J. & Dowsett-Lemaire, F. (1993). *A Contribution to the Distribution and Taxonomy of Afrotropical and Malagasy Birds*. Tauraco Research Report **5**. Tauraco Press, Liège, Belgium.
Dowsett, R.J. & Dowsett-Lemaire, F. (1997). *Flore et Faune du Parc National d'Odzala, Congo. Flora and Fauna of the Odzala National Park, Congo*. Tauraco Research Report **6**. Tauraco Press, Liège, Belgium. In French and English.
Dowsett, R.J. & Dowsett-Lemaire, F. (2000). New species and amendments to the avifauna of Cameroon. *Bull. Brit. Orn. Club* **120(3)**: 179-185.
Dowsett, R.J. & Forbes-Watson, A.D. (1993). *Checklist of Birds of the Afrotropical and Malagasy Regions*. Vol. 1. Species Limits and Distribution. Tauraco Press, Liège, Belgium.
Dowsett-Lemaire, F. (1983a). Ecological and territorial requirements of montane birds on the Nyika Plateau, south-central Africa. *Gerfaut* **73**: 345-378.
Dowsett-Lemaire, F. (1983b). Scaly-throated Honeyguide *Indicator variegatus* parasitizing Olive Woodpeckers *Dendropicos griseocephalus* in Malawi. *Bull. Brit. Orn. Club* **103(2)**: 71-76.
Dowsett-Lemaire, F. (1983c). Studies of a breeding population of Olive Woodpecker, *Dendropicos griseocephalus*, in montane forests of south-central Africa. *Gerfaut* **73**: 221-237.
Dowsett-Lemaire, F. & Dowsett, R.J. (1987). Vocal responses of Green Barbet populations, and the taxonomic implications. *Ostrich* **58(4)**: 160-163.
Dowsett-Lemaire, F. & Dowsett, R.J. (1998). Further additions to and deletions from the avifauna of Congo-Brazzaville. *Malimbus* **20(1)**: 15-32.
Dowsett-Lemaire, F. & Dowsett, R.J. (1999). Birds of the Parque Nacional de Monte Alen, mainland Equatorial Guinea, with an updating of the country's list. *Alauda* **67(3)**: 179-188.
Dowsett-Lemaire, F. & Dowsett, R.J. (2000). Birds of the Lobéké Faunal Reserve, Cameroon, and its regional importance for conservation. *Bird Conserv. Int.* **10(1)**: 67-87.
Dowsett-Lemaire, F., Dowsett, R.J. & Bulens, P. (1993). Additions and corrections to the avifauna of Congo. *Malimbus* **15(2)**: 68-80.
Dranzoa, C. (1994). Lyre-tailed Honeyguide *Melichneutes robustus* and Grey Ground Thrush *Zoothera princei batesi*: new records for Uganda. *Scopus* **18**: 128-130.
Du Hengqin (1987). [The breeding habits of the Grey-headed Green Woodpecker *Picus canus*]. *Chinese J. Zool.* **5**: 49-50. In Chinese.
Dubs, B. (1983). *Phloeoceastes leucopogon* - brutvogel im Pantanal, Mato Grosso do Sul, Brasilien. [First breeding record for *Phloeoceastes leucopogon* in Pantanal, Mato Grosso do Sul Brazilia]. *J. Orn.* **124(3)**: 294. In German with English summary.
Dubs, B. (1992). *Birds of Southwestern Brazil: Catalogue and Guide to the Birds of the Pantanal of Mato Grosso and its Border Areas*. Betrona Verlag, Küsnacht, Switzerland.
Duckworth, J.W. (1996). Bird and mammal records from the Sangthong District, Vientiane Municipality, Laos in 1996. *Nat. Hist. Bull. Siam Soc.* **44**: 217-242.
Duckworth, J.W. & Hedges, S. (1998). Bird records from Cambodia in 1997, including records of sixteen species new for the country. *Forktail* **14**: 29-36.
Duckworth, J.W. & Kelsh, R. (1988). *A Bird Inventory of Similajau National Park*. ICBP Study Report **31**, Cambridge.
Duckworth, J.W., Evans, T.D. & Timmins, R.J. (1993). *A Wildlife and Habitat Survey of the Xe Piane National Biodiversity Conservation Area*. National Office for Nature Conservation and Watershed Management, Vientiane, Laos.
Duckworth, J.W., Salter, R.E. & Khounboline, K. eds. (1999). *Wildlife in Lao PDR: 1999 Status Report*. IUCN-The World Conservation Union/Wildlife Conservation Society/Centre for Protected Areas and Watershed Management, Vientiane.
Duckworth, J.W., Timmins, R.J. & Cozza, K. (1993). A wildlife and habitat survey of the Phou Xang He proposed protected area. National Office for Nature Conservation and Watershed Management, Vientiane, Laos. Unpublished report.
Duckworth, J.W., Wilkinson, R.J., Tizard, R.J., Kelsh, R.N., Irvin, S.A., Evans, M.I. & Orrell, T.D. (1997). Bird records from Similajau National Park, Sarawak. *Forktail* **12**: 117-154.
Dugand, A. (1947). *Aves del Departamento del Atlántico, Colombia*. Caldasia **4(20)**. 149 pp.
Dugand, A. (1948). Notas ornitológicas colombianas, IV. *Caldasia* **5(21)**: 157-199.
Dugand, A. (1952). Algunas aves del Río Apaporis. *Lozania* **4**: 1-12.
Dugand, A. & Borrero, J.I. (1946). Aves de la ribera colombiana del Amazonas. *Caldasia* **4**: 131-167.
Dugand, A. & Phelps, W.H. (1948). Aves de la ribera colombiana del Río Negro (Frontera de Colombia y Venezuela). *Caldasia* **5(22)**: 225-245.
Duncan, D. (1933). The White-headed Woodpecker in Marin County, California. *Condor* **35(3)**: 123-124.
Duncan, S. (1990). *Auditory Communication in Breeding Northern Flickers (*Colaptes auratus*)*. PhD dissertation, University of Wisconsin, Milwaukee, Wisconsin.
Dunn, J. (1978). The races of the Yellow-bellied Sapsucker. *West. Tanager* **44**: 1-4.
Dunn, M.L. (1984). Red-bellied Woodpecker predation on nestling nuthatches. *Chat* **48(3)**: 74-75.
Dunning, J.B. ed. (1993). *CRC Handbook of Avian Body Masses*. CRC Press, Boca Raton, Florida.
Dupond, C. (1942). *Contribution a l'Étude de la Faune Ornithologique des Iles Philippines et des Indes Orientales Néerlandaises*. Mémoirs du Musée Royal d'Histoire Naturelle de Belgique **23** (2nd Series), Brussel.
Dutson, G.C.L. & Branscombe, J. (1990). *Rainforest Birds in South-west Ghana*. ICBP Study Report **46**, Cambridge.
Dutson, G.C.L., Allen, D. & Brooks, T.M. (1996). Tawi-Tawi - extreme Philippine birding. *Bull. Oriental Bird Club* **24**: 32-35.
Dutson, G.C.L., Evans, T.D., Brooks, T.M., Asane, D.C., Timmins, R.J. & Toledo, A. (1992). Conservation status of birds on Mindoro. *Bird Conserv. Int.* **2(4)**: 303-325.
Duyck, B.E. & McNair, D.B. (1991). Notes on egg-laying, incubation, nestling periods and food brought to the nest by four species of cavity-nesting birds. *Chat* **55(2)**: 21-29.
Dwight, J. & Griscom, L. (1924). Descriptions of new birds from Costa Rica. *Amer. Mus. Novit.* **142**: 1-5.
Dye, S.E. & Morris, A. (1984). Attempted breeding of the Toco Toucan, *Ramphastos toco*, at Penscynor Wildlife Park, Cilfrem, Neath, Wales. *Avicult. Mag.* **90(2)**: 73-75.
Dyer, M. (1975). An unsuccessful attempt by a Greater Honey-guide to parasitise Red-throated Bee-eaters. *Bull. Niger. Orn. Soc.* **11**: 86.
Dyer, M., Gartshore, M.E. & Sharland, R.E. (1986). The birds of Nindam Forest Reserve, Kagoro, Nigeria. *Malimbus* **8(1)**: 2-20.
Dymond, J.N. (1994). A survey of the birds of Nias Island, Sumatra. *Kukila* **7(1)**: 10-27.
Dymond, J.N. (1998). Birds in Vietnam in December 1993 and December 1994. *Forktail* **13**: 7-12.
Dziadosz, V.M. & Parkes, K.C. (1984). Two new Philippine subspecies of the Crimson-breasted Barbet (Aves: Capitonidae). *Proc. Biol. Soc. Washington* **97(4)**: 788-791.
Eames, J.C. (1995). Endemic birds and protected area development on the Da Lat Plateau, Vietnam. *Bird Conserv. Int.* **5(4)**: 491-523.
Eames, J.C. (1996). Ke Go Nature Reserve - the place of wood. *World Birdwatch* **18(1)**: 6-8.
Eames, J.C. & Ericson, P.G.P. (1996). The Björkegren expeditions to French Indochina: a collection of birds from Vietnam and Cambodia. *Nat. Hist. Bull. Siam Soc.* **44**: 75-111.
Eames, J.C. & Robson, C.R. (1992). *Forest Bird Surveys in Vietnam 1991*. BirdLife Study Report **51**. BirdLife International, Cambridge.
Eames, J.C., Lambert, F.R. & Nguyen Cu (1994). A survey of the Annamese Lowlands, Vietnam, and its implications for the conservation of Vietnamese and Imperial Pheasants *Lophura hatinhensis* and *L. imperialis*. *Bird Conserv. Int.* **4(4)**: 343-382.
Earlé, R.A. (1986). Reappraisal of variation in the Ground Woodpecker *Geocolaptes olivaceus* (Gmelin) (Aves: Picidae) with notes on its moult. *Navors. Nas. Mus. Bloemfontein* **5(7)**: 79-92. In English with Afrikaans summary.
Earlé, R.A. (1989). Aspects of the foraging behaviour of some insectivorous birds in three Transvaal indigenous evergreen forests. *Ostrich* **14**(Suppl.): 71-74.
Earlé, R.A. & Grobler, N. (1987). *First Atlas of Bird Distribution in the Orange Free State*. National Museum, Bloemfontein, South Africa.
Earlé, R.A. & Herholdt, J.J. (1987). Notes on a Greater Honeyguide *Indicator indicator* chick raised by Anteating Chats *Myrmecocichla formicivora*. *Bull. Brit. Orn. Club* **107(2)**: 70-73.
Eates, K.R. (1937). A note on the distribution and nidification of the Northern Yellow-fronted Pied Woodpecker *Leiopicus mahrattensis blanfordi* (Blyth) in Sind. *J. Bombay Nat. Hist. Soc.* **39(3)**: 628-631.
Eberhardt, L.S. (1994). Food-tree selection of the Yellow-bellied Sapsucker. Page 172 in: Dittami *et al.* (1994).
Eberhardt, L.S. (1997). A test of an environmental advertisement hypothesis for the function of drumming in Yellow-bellied Sapsuckers. *Condor* **99(3)**: 798-803.
Eberhardt, L.S. (2000). Use and selection of sap trees by Yellow-bellied Sapsuckers. *Auk* **117(1)**: 41-51.
Ebert, D. (1985). Biologie und Haltung einiger Bartvögelarten. *Trochilus* **6**: 110-143.
Ebert, D. (1986). Erfolgreiche Zuecht des Andenbartvogels (*Eubucco bourcierii*). *Trochilus* **7**: 128-132.
Eck, S. & Geidel, B. (1974). Die flügel-schwanz-verhaeltnisse paläarktischer Wendehälse (*Jynx torquilla*) (Aves, Picidae). [The wing-tail of Palearctic Wrynecks (*Jynx torquilla*) (Aves, Picidae)]. *Zool. Abh. Staatl. Mus. Tierk. Dresden* **32(16)**: 257-265. In German with English summary.
Eckelberry, D.R. (1962). The White-eared Puffbird. *Auk* **78(1)**: 1-2.
Eckelberry, D.R. (1964). A note on the toucans of northern Argentina. *Wilson Bull.* **76(1)**: 5.
Eckert, C.D. (1997). High densities of Three-toed Woodpeckers in southwestern Yukon. *Birders J.* **6**: 75.
Eckert, K. (1981). First Minnesota nesting record of Northern Three-toed Woodpecker. *Loon* **53(4)**: 221-223.
Eckstein, R.G. (1983). Nesting Black-backed Three-toed Woodpeckers in Forest County. *Passenger Pigeon* **45(1)**: 16-17.
Eddleman, W.R. & Clawson, R.L. (1987). Population status and habitat conditions for the Red-cockaded Woodpecker in Missouri. *Trans. Missouri Acad. Sci.* **21**: 105-117.
Edenius, L., Brodin, T. & Sunesson, P. (1999). Vinterbeteendet hos gråspetten *Picus canus* i forhallande till sentida populationstrender i Sverige. [Winter behaviour of the Grey-headed Woodpecker *Picus canus* in relation to recent population trends in Sweden]. *Ornis Svecica* **9(1-2)**: 65-74. In Swedish with English summary.
Edgar, A.T. (1933). Notes on the nidification of some Perak birds. *Bull. Raffles Mus., Singapore* **8**: 121-162.
Edge, J.S.R. (1993). Birds new to Hong Kong - Bay Woodpecker in Tai Po Kau: a new species for Hong Kong. *Hong Kong Bird Rep.* **1993**: 121-122. In English with Chinese summary.
Edwards, H.H. & Schnell, G.D. (2000). Gila Woodpecker (*Melanerpes uropygialis*). No. **532** in: Poole, A.F. & Gill, F.B. eds. (2000). *The Birds of North America*. Vol. 14. Academy of Natural Sciences & American Ornithologists' Union, Philadelphia & Washington, D.C.
Efe, M.A., Mohr, L.V., Bugoni, L., Scherer, A. & Scherer, S.B. (2000). Inventário e distribução da avifauna do Parque Saint Hilaire, Viamão, Rio Grande do Sul. Pp. 221-222 in: Straube *et al.* (2000).
Ehrenroth, B. (1973). Gråspettens *Picus canus* uppträdande i Värmland. *Vår Fågelvärld* **32**: 260-268.
Ehrlich, P.R. & Daily, G.C. (1988). Red-naped Sapsucker feeding at willows: possible keystone herbivores. *Amer. Birds* **42**: 357-365.
Ehrlich, P.R., Dobkin, D.S. & Wheye, D. (1992). *Birds in Jeopardy. The Imperiled and Extinct Birds of the United States and Canada, Including Hawaii and Puerto Rico*. Stanford University Press, Stanford, California.
Eisenmann, E.S.B. (1952). Annotated list of birds of Barro Colorado Island, Panama Canal zone. *Smiths. Misc. Coll.* **117(5)**: 1-62.
Eisenmann, E.S.B. (1957). Notes on birds of the province of Bocas del Toro, Panama. *Condor* **59(4)**: 247-262.
Eitniear, J.C. (1982). Toucans of northern Central America. *AFA Watchbird* **9(3)**: 27-29.
Ekstrom, J., Tobias, J.A. & Robinson-Dean, J. (1998). Forests at the edge of Lore Lindu National Park, central Sulawesi. *Bull. Oriental Bird Club* **28**: 37-39.
Elgood, J.H., Heigham, J.B., Moore, A.M., Nason, A.M., Sharland, R.E. & Skinner, N.J. (1994). *The Birds of Nigeria. An Annotated Check-list*. BOU Check-list **4**. British Ornithologists' Union, Tring, UK.
Ellegren, H., Carlson, A. & Stenberg, I. (1999). Genetic structure and variability of White-backed Woodpecker (*Dendrocopos leucotos*) populations in northern Europe. *Hereditas* **130**: 291-299.
Ellison, W.G. (1992). Different drummers: identifying the rhythms of northeastern woodpeckers. *Birding* **24(6)**: 351-355.
Emlen, J.T. (1977). *Land Bird Communities of Grand Bahama Island: the Structure and Dynamics of an Avifauna*. Ornithological Monographs **24**. American Ornithologists' Union, Washington, D.C.
Emmons, L.H. (1990). *Neotropical Rainforest Mammals. A Field Guide*. University of Chicago Press, Chicago, Illinois.
England, M.C. (2000). The Landbird Monitoring Programme at Lamani, Belize: a preliminary assessment. *Cotinga* **13**: 32-43.
England, M.D. (1973a). Breeding the Red-fronted Barbet (*Tricholaema diadematum*). *Avicult. Mag.* **79**: 9-13.
England, M.D. (1973b). Breeding the Red and Yellow Barbet (*Trachyphonus erythrocephalus*). *Avicult. Mag.* **79**: 194-196.
England, M.D. (1976). Breeding the Double-toothed Barbet *Lybius bidentatus*. *Avicult. Mag.* **82(4)**: 191-193.
England, M.D. (1977). Breeding the Spotted-flanked Barbet *Tricholaema lacrymosum*. *Avicult. Mag.* **83(1)**: 1-3.
England, M.D. (1985). Barbets. Pp. 36-37 in: Campbell & Lack (1985).
Engleman, D. (1997). The field editor's report. *Tucan* **23(1)**: 4-5.
Engstrom, R.T. & Mikusinski, G. (1998). Ecological neighborhoods in Red-cockaded Woodpecker populations. *Auk* **115(2)**: 473-478.

Engstrom, R.T. & Sanders, F.J. (1997). Red-cockaded Woodpecker foraging ecology in an old-growth longleaf pine forest. *Wilson Bull.* **109(2)**: 203-217.

Engstrom, R.T., Brennan, L.A., Neel, W.L., Farrar, R.M., Lindeman, S.T., Moses, W.K. & Hermann, S.M. (1996). Silvicultural practices and Red-cockaded Woodpecker management: a reply to Rudolph and Conner. *Wildl. Soc. Bull.* **24(2)**: 334-338.

Epple, W. (1992). Einfuehrung in das Artenschutzsymposium Wendehals. *Beih. Veröff. Naturschutz Landschaftspflege Bad.-Württ.* **66**: 7-18.

Érard, C. (1962). Le Pic noir *Dryocopus martius* poursuit son extension en France. *Alauda* **30(1)**: 66-67.

Érard, C. (1976). Comments on the races of *Lybius melanocephalus* (Cretzschmar) in Ethiopia. *Bull. Brit. Orn. Club* **96**: 107-109.

Erdmann, G. (1974). Vorkommen des Grauspechts (*Picus canus*) in der Leipziger gegend. *Beitr. Vogelkd.* **19(5)**: 329-341.

Ern, H. (1959). Le Pic à dos blanc *Dendrocopos leucotos* dans les Pyrénées. *Alauda* **27(3)**: 230.

Erskine, A.J. (1959). *Picoides arcticus* nesting in the Cariboo, British Columbia. *Can. Field-Nat.* **73**: 205.

Erskine, A.J. (1962). Some new data on introgression in flickers from British Columbia. *Can. Field-Nat.* **76**: 82-87.

Escaño, R.E.F. (1995). Red-cockaded Woodpecker extinction or recovery: summary of status and management on our national forests. Pp. 28-35 in: Kulhavy *et al.* (1995).

Estrada, A.R. & Alayón, G. (1986a). Reporte de expedición: búsqueda de Carpintero Real. *Volante Migratorio* **6**: 15.

Estrada, A.R. & Alayón, G. (1986b). La existencia del Carpintero Real o Pico de Marfil en Cuba es realidad, no un sueño. *Volante Migratorio* **7**: 25-27.

Étchécopar, R.D. & Hüe, F. (1964). *Les Oiseaux du Nord de l'Afrique de la Mer Rouge aux Canaries*. Éditions N. Boubée, Paris.

Étchécopar, R.D. & Hüe, F. (1978). *Les Oiseaux de Chine, de Mongolie et de Corée. Non Passereaux*. Les Éditions du Pacifique, Papeete, Tahiti.

Evans, G.H. (1905). A woodpecker's dilemma. *J. Bombay Nat. Hist. Soc.* **16(3)**: 518-519.

Evans, K. & Coles, D. (1982). Breeding the Crimson-rumped Toucanet *Aulacorhynchus haematopygus* at Padstow Bird Gardens (Cornwall). *Avicult. Mag.* **88(4)**: 193-198.

Evans, T.D. & Anderson, G.Q.A. eds. (1992). *A Wildlife Survey of the East Usambara and Ukaguru Mountains, Tanzania*. ICBP Study Report **53**, Cambridge.

Evans, T.D. & Timmins, R.J. (1998). Records of birds from Laos during January-July 1994. *Forktail* **13**: 69-96.

Evans, T.D., Dutson, G.C.L. & Brooks, T.M. (1993). *Cambridge Philippines Rainforest Project 1991. Final Report*. BirdLife Study Report **54**. BirdLife International, Cambridge.

Evans, T.D., Hague, M., Hipkiss, A., Kiure, J., Makange, A., Perkin, A., Timmins, R. & Watson, L. (1994). *A Biological and Human Impact Survey of the Lowland Forests, East Usambara Mountains, Tanzania*. BirdLife Study Report **59**. BirdLife International, Cambridge.

Evans, T.D., Tye, A., Cordeiro, N.J. & Seddon, N. (1997). Birding in and around the East Usambaras, north-east Tanzania. *Bull. African Bird Club* **4(2)**: 116-129.

Everett, M.J. (1987). The Arabian Woodpecker in North Yemen. *Sandgrouse* **9**: 74-77.

Every, B. (1974). A partial albino Ground Woodpecker. *Ostrich* **45**: 192-193.

Eygenraam, J.A. (1947). Het gedrag van de Zwarte specht, *Dryocopus m. martius* (L.). *Ardea* **35**: 1-44.

Faaborg, J. (1985). Ecological constraints on West Indian bird distributions. Pp. 621-662 in: Buckley *et al.* (1985).

Fabian, D.T. (1981). Sharp-billed Honeyguide. *Witwatersrand Bird Club News* **115**: 14.

Fairon, J. (1975). Contribution à l'ornithologie de l'Aïr (Niger). *Gerfaut* **65**: 107-134.

Fajer, E.D., Schmidt, K.J. & Eschler, J.G. (1987). Acorn Woodpecker predation on Cliff Swallow nests. *Condor* **89(1)**: 177-178.

Fales, J.H. (1977a). Unusual food habit for Hairy Woodpecker. *Maryland Birdlife* **33(3)**: 125-126.

Fales, J.H. (1977b). Notes on behavior of Red-bellied Woodpecker. *Maryland Birdlife* **33(4)**: 150.

Falk, K.H. & Salewski, V. (1999). First records of Golden-tailed Woodpecker *Campethera abingoni* in Ivory Coast. *Bull. African Bird Club* **6(2)**: 101-102.

Fanshaw, J.H. (1994). Birding Arabuko-Sokoke Forest and Kenya's northern coast. *Bull. African Bird Club* **1(2)**: 79-89.

Farinello, F., Maragna, P., Pesente, M. & Sandrini, S. (1994). [Observations of Wryneck, *Jynx torquilla*, in wintering season in the Venetian region (NE Italy)]. *Riv. ital. Orn.* **63(2)**: 219-221. In Italian.

Farmer, R. (1979). Checklist of birds of the Ile-Ife area, Nigeria. *Malimbus* **1(1)**: 56-64.

Farnsworth, S.J., Coomber, R.F., Jones, P., Madge, S.C., Webb, R. & Witherick, M. (2000). Recent observations of some bird species previously considered uncommon or rare in Ethiopia. *Bull. African Bird Club* **7(1)**: 34-46.

Farrand, J. (1992). Moments in history: the oldest Lewis' Woodpecker. *Amer. Birds* **46**: 488-490.

Faust, I. (1969). Breeding the Double-toothed Barbet *Lybius bidentatus* at Frankfurt Zoo. *Int. Zoo Yb.* **8**: 157-158.

Fauvel, B., Balandras, G. & Carré, F. (1995). *Évaluation des Densités de Pics Nicheurs du Massif de la Forêt d'Orient (Aube); Cas Particulier du Pic Mar (*Dendrocopos medius*)*. Parc Naturel Régional de la Forêt d'Orient, Office National des Forêts. LPO Champagne-Ardennes.

Fauvel, B., Carré, F. & Lallement, H. (2001). Écologie du Pic mar *Dendrocopos medius* en Champagne (est France). In French with English summary. *Alauda* **69(1)**: 87-101.

Fayt, P. (1999). Available insect prey in bark patches selected by the Three-toed Woodpecker *Picoides tridactylus* prior to reproduction. *Ornis Fenn.* **76(3)**: 135-140.

Feduccia, A. (1976). *Neanis schucherti* restudied: another Eocene piciform bird. *Smithsonian Contrib. Paleobiol.* **27**: 95-99.

Feduccia, A. (1999). *The Origin and Evolution of Birds*. 2nd edition. Yale University Press, New Haven & London.

Feduccia, A. & Martin, L.D. (1976). The Eocene zygodactyl birds of North America (Aves: Piciformes). *Smithsonian Contrib. Paleobiol.* **27**: 101-110.

Feindt, P. (1956). Zur Psychologie und Stimme des Mittelspechts *Dendrocopos medius medius* (L.). *Natur und Jagd in Niedersachsen* **8**(Suppl.): 99-113.

Feindt, P. & Reblin, K. (1959). Die Brutbiologie des Mittelspechts. *Beitr. Naturkd. Niedersachsens* **12**: 36-48.

Feldmann, P. & Villard, P. (1993). *Oiseaux de Guadeloupe et de Martinique*. Association pour l'Étude et la protection des Vertébrés des Petits Antilles, Guadeloupe. 7 pp.

Feldmann, P., Villard, P. & Barre, N. (1998). Les populations d'oiseaux forestiers de la Basse-Terre en Guadeloupe. Comunidades de aves de Basse-Terre, Guadalupe, Antillas Francesas. [Forest birds community in Basse-Terre, Guadeloupe, F.W.I.]. *Progr. Abstr. Soc. Caribb. Orn. Ann. Meet.* **11**: C9. (Abstract).

Félix, J. (1965). An interesting woodpecker from Cuba. *Avicult. Mag.* **71(1)**: 1-2.

Fellenberg, W. & Pfennig, H.G. (1980). Weitere Mitteilungen zur Brutverbreitung des Kleinspechts (*Picoides minor*) im Sauerland. *Charadrius* **16(4)**: 164-166.

Fergenbauer-Kimmel, A. (1986). Elfenbein-spechte in Kuba gesichtet. *Trochilus* **7(4)**: 137.

Ferguson, H.L. (1977). Displacement of a Red-bellied by a Downy Woodpecker. *Raven* **48(3)**: 66-67.

Fernald, R.D. (1973). A group of barbets. 2. Quantitative measures. *Z. Tierpsychol.* **33**: 341-351.

Fernández, C. & Azkona, P. (1996). Influence of forest structure on the density and distribution of the White-backed Woodpecker *Dendrocopos leucotos* and Black Woodpecker *Dryocopus martius* in Quinto Real (Spanish western Pyrenees). *Bird Study* **43(3)**: 305-313.

Fernández, C., Azkona, P. & Lorente, L. (1994). Corología y caracterización del hábitat del Pico Dorsiblanco (*Dendrocopos leucotos lilfordi*) en el Pirineo occidental español. *Ardeola* **41**: 135-140.

Ferral, D.P. (1997). Long-distance dispersal of Red-cockaded Woodpeckers. *Wilson Bull.* **109(1)**: 154-157.

Ferreira de Vasconcelos, M. & Melo-Júnior, T.A. (2001). An ornithological survey of Serra do Caraça, Minas Gerais, Brazil. *Cotinga* **15**: 21-31. In English with Portuguese summary.

Ferreira de Vasconcelos, M., Maldonado-Coelho, M. & Durães, R. (1999). Notas sobre algumas espécies de aves ameaçadas e pouco conhecidas da porcão meridional da Cadeia do Espinhaço, Minas Gerais. *Melopsittacus* **2(2/4)**: 44-50.

Ferry, C. (1962). Sur l'utilisation du sont chant vocal par le Pic mar *Dendrocopos medius*. *Alauda* **30**: 204-209.

Ferry, C., Deschaintre, A. & Viennot, R. (1957). Un nid de Pic noir en Côte d'Or. *Alauda* **25(3)**: 296-303.

ffrench, R.P. (1991). *A Guide to the Birds of Trinidad and Tobago*. 2nd edition. Cornell University Press, Ithaca, New York.

Field, G.D. (1999). The birds of Sierra Leone. MS.

Field, R. & Williams, B.K. (1985). Age of cavity trees and colony stands selected by Red-cockaded Woodpeckers. *Wildl. Soc. Bull.* **13(1)**: 92-96.

Figueiredo, L.F.A. & Lo, V.K. (2000). Lista das aves do município de São Paulo. *Bol. CEO* **14**: 15-35.

Figueiredo, L.F.A., Gussoni, C.O.A., de Campos, R.P. (2000). Levantamento da avifauna do Parque Estadual Juquery, Franco da Rocha, São Paulo: uma avaliação auto-crítica das técnicas de campo para inventários ornitológicos. *Bol. CEO* **14**: 36-50.

Fishpool, L. (1993). New bird records from Budongo and Kifu forests, Uganda, with an addition to the East African avifauna. *Scopus* **17**: 37-39.

Fishpool, L., Bennun, L., Oyugi, J. & Weeks, P. (1997). Distinctive foraging behaviour by Willcocks' and Least Honeyguides *Indicator willcocksi* and *I. exilis*. *Scopus* **19**: 110-112.

Fitter, R. (1992). From the archives: the Black Woodpecker, a lost British bird. *Birding World* **5(2)**: 75-77.

Fitzpatrick, J.W. & Willard, D.E. (1982). Twenty-one bird species new or little known from the Republic of Colombia. *Bull. Brit. Orn. Club* **102(4)**: 153-158.

Fjeldså, J. (1987). *Birds of Relict Forests in the High Andes of Peru and Bolivia*. Zoological Museum of the University of Copenhagen, Copenhagen, Denmark.

Fjeldså, J. & Jensen, H. (1990). A record of the African Piculet *Sasia africana* from Liberia. *Bull. Brit. Orn. Club* **110(2)**: 62-64.

Fjeldså, J. & Krabbe, N. (1986). Some range extensions and other unusual records of Andean birds. *Bull. Brit. Orn. Club* **106(3)**: 115-124.

Fjeldså, J. & Krabbe, N. (1990). *Birds of the High Andes*. Apollo Books & Zoological Museum, Svendborg & Copenhagen.

Fjeldså, J. & Mayer, S. (1996). *Recent Ornithological Surveys in the Valles Region, Southern Bolivia, and the Possible Role of Valles for the Evolution of the Andean Avifauna*. Technical Report **1**. DIVA, Rønde, Denmark.

Fleming, R.L. (1963). Occurrence of the Orange-rumped Honey Guide (*Indicator xanthonotus xanthonotus*) in Nepal. *Pavo* **1**: 66-67.

Fleming, R.L. & Baker, R.H. (1963). Notes on the birds of Durango, Mexico. *Publ. Mus. Michigan State. Univ. Biol. Series* **2**: 275-303.

Fleming, R.L. & Traylor, M.A. (1961). Notes on Nepal birds. *Fieldiana Zool.* **35(9)**: 447-487.

Fleming, R.L. & Traylor, M.A. (1968). Distributional notes on Nepal birds. *Fieldiana Zool.* **53(3)**: 147-203.

Fleming, R.L., Fleming, R.L. Jr. & Bangdel, L.S. (1976). *Birds of Nepal*. 2nd edition. Avalok Publishers, Kathmandu.

Flemming, S.P., Holloway, G.L., Watts, E.J. & Lawrence, P.S. (1999). Characteristics of foraging trees selected by Pileated Woodpeckers in New Brunswick. *J. Wildl. Manage.* **63(2)**: 461-469.

Fletcher, S.D. & Moore, W.S. (1992). Further analysis of allozyme variation in the Northern Flicker, in comparison with mitochondrial DNA variation. *Condor* **94(4)**: 988-991.

Flores, B., Rumiz, D.I. & Cox, G. (2001). Avifauna del bosque semideciduo Chiquitano (Santa Cruz, Bolivia) antes y después de un aprovechamiento forestal selectivo. *Ararajuba* **9(1)**: 21-31.

Flores, E. & Capriles, C. (1998). Las aves del Parque Nacional Toro Toro, Dpto. Potosí; una lista preliminar comentada. Pp. 23-31 in: Sagot & Guerrero (1998).

Flousek, J., Hudec, K. & Glutz von Blotzheim, U.N. (1993). Inmissionsbedingte Waldschäden und ihr Einfluß auf die Vogelwelt Mitteleuropas. Pp. 11-30 in: Glutz von Blotzheim, U.N. & Bauer, K.M. eds. (1993). *Handbuch der Vögel Mitteleuropas*. Vol. 13/I. AULA-Verlag, Wiesbaden, Germany.

Fogden, M. (1970). *Some Aspects of the Ecology of Bird Populations in Sarawak*. PhD thesis, Oxford University, Oxford.

Fogden, M. (1976). A census of a bird community in a tropical rainforest in Sarawak. *Sarawak Mus. J.* **24**: 251-267.

Fogden, M. (1993). *An Annotated Checklist of the Birds of Monteverde and Peñas Blancas*. Published privately, Monteverde, Costa Rica.

da Fonseca, J.P. (1922). Notas biologicas sobre o *Bucco chacuru* (Vieill.). *Rev. Mus. Paulista* **13**: 793-797.

Forbes-Watson, A.D. (1977). Notes on the field identification of East African honeyguides (Indicatoridae). *Scopus* **1(1)**: 17-20.

Ford, H.A. & Davison, G.W.H. (1995). Forest avifauna of Universiti Kebangsaan Malaysia and some other forest remnants in Selangor, Peninsular Malaysia. *Malay. Nat. J.* **49**: 117-138.

Forrester, B.C. (1993). *Birding Brazil. A Check-list and Site Guide*. Published privately, Rankinston, UK.

Foster, R.B., Carr, J.L. & Forsyth, A.B. eds. (1994). *The Tambopata-Candamo Reserved Zone of Southeastern Perú: a Biologial Assessment*. Rapid Assessment Program Working Papers **6**. Conservation International, Washington, D.C.

Fotso, R.C. (2001). A contribution to the ornithology of Mount Oku forest, Cameroon. *Malimbus* **23(1)**: 1-12.

Fox, E.A.S. (1933). Occurrence of the Blue-throated Barbet (*Cyanops asiatica*) at Murree. *J. Bombay Nat. Hist. Soc.* **36(3)**: 750.

Fraile, B. (1984). Impacto silvícola del Pito Real (*Picus viridis*) y Pico Picapinos (*Dendrocopos major*) sobre choperas de la provincia de León. *Alytes* **2**: 134-143.

Francis, J. & Shirihai, H. (1999). *Ethiopia. In Search of Endemic Birds*. Published privately, London.

Francisco, M.R. & Galetti, M. (2001). Frugivoria e dispersão de sementes de *Rapanea lancifolia* (Myrsinaceae) por aves numa área de cerrado do Estado de São Paulo, sudeste de Brasil. *Ararajuba* **9(1)**: 13-19. In Portuguese with English summary.

Franz, J. (1937). Beobachtungen über das Brutleben des Weißrückenspechts. *Beitr. Fortpflanzungsbiol. Vögel* **13**: 165-174.

Franzreb, K.E. (1994). Intersexual habitat partitioning in the endangered Red-cockaded Woodpecker. Page 175 in: Dittami *et al.* (1994).

Franzreb, K.E. (1997). Success of intensive management of a critically imperiled population of Red-cockaded Woodpeckers in South Carolina. *J. Field Orn.* **68(3)**: 458-470.

Franzreb, K.E. (1999). Factors that influence translocation success in the Red-cockaded Woodpecker. *Wilson Bull.* **111(1)**: 38-45.

Fraser, B.J. & Henson, S.M. (1996). *Survai Jenis-jenis Burung Endemik di Gunung Lompobattang, Sulawesi Selatan. Survey of Endemic Bird Species on Gunung Lompobattang, South Sulawesi*. Technical Memorandum **12**. PHPA/BirdLife International, Bogor, Indonesia. In Indonesian and English.

Fraticelli, F. & Wirz, A. (1991). Evidence of intraspecific nest parasitism in Wryneck *Jynx torquilla*. *Avocetta* **15(1-2)**: 65.

Frederick, G.P. & Moore, T.L. (1991). Distribution and habitat of White-headed Woodpeckers (*Picoides albolarvatus*) in west-central Idaho. Conservation Data Center, Idaho Department of Fish and Game, Boise, Idaho.

Freile, J.F. & Endara, L. (2000). First nesting record of Lanceolated Monklet *Micromonacha lanceolata* and notes on its conservation status. *Cotinga* **14**: 14-16. In English with Spanish summary.

Freitag, A. (1996). Le régime alimentaire du Torcol fourmilier (*Jynx torquilla*) en Valais (Suisse). *Nos Oiseaux* **43**: 497-512.

Freitag, A. (1998). *Analyse de la Disponibilité Spatio-temporelle des Fourmis et des Stratégies de Fourragement du Torcol Fourmilier (*Jynx torquilla *L.)*. PhD thesis, Université de Lausanne, Lausanne, Switzerland.

Freitag, A. (2000). La photographie des nourrissages: une technique originale d'étude du régime alimentaire des jeunes Torcols fourmiliers *Jynx torquilla*. *Alauda* **68(2)**: 81-93. In French with English summary.

Friederici, P. (1994). Flashing red: the arresting Red-headed Woodpecker commands your attention. *Birder's World* **8(5)**: 19-22.
Friedmann, H. (1927). *Notes on some Argentina Birds*. Bulletin of the Museum of Comparative Zoology **68(4)**, Cambridge, Massachusetts. 98 pp.
Friedmann, H. (1930a). *Birds Collected by the Childs Frick Expedition to Ethiopia and Kenya Colony*. Part 1. Non-passerines. US National Museum Bulletin **153**. Smithsonian Institution, Washington, D.C. 156 pp.
Friedmann, H. (1930b). The caudal molt of certain coraciiform, coliiform and piciform birds. *Proc. US Natl. Mus.* **77(7)**: 1-6.
Friedmann, H. (1948). *Birds Collected by the National Geographic Society's Expeditions to Northern Brazil and Southern Venezuela*. Proceedings of the US National Museum **97**. Smithsonian Institution, Washington, D.C. 197 pp.
Friedmann, H. (1954a). Honey-guide: the bird that eats wax. *Natl. Geogr. Mag.* **105(4)**: 551-560.
Friedmann, H. (1954b). A revision of the classification of the honey-guides, Indicatoridae. *Ann. Mus. Congo Tervuren, Zool.* **50**: 21-27.
Friedmann, H. (1955). *The Honey-guides*. US National Museum Bulletin **208**. Smithsonian Institution, Washington, D.C. 292 pp.
Friedmann, H. (1958a). Advances in our knowledge of the honey-guides. *Proc. US Natl. Mus.* **108**: 309-320.
Friedmann, H. (1958b). The status of *Pteroglossus didymus* P. L. Sclater. *Auk* **75**: 93-94.
Friedmann, H. (1963). Morphological data on two sibling species of small honey-guides. *Contrib. Sci. Los Angeles Co. Mus.* **79**: 1-5.
Friedmann, H. (1966). A contribution to the ornithology of Uganda. *Bull. Los Angeles County Mus. Nat. Hist. Sci.* **3**: 1-55.
Friedmann, H. (1968). Zenker's Honey-guide. *J. Orn.* **109**: 276-283.
Friedmann, H. (1969). Phenotypic potential and speciation in *Indicator* and *Prodotiscus*. *Ostrich* **8**(Suppl.): 21-26.
Friedmann, H. (1970). Further information on the breeding biology of honey-guides. *Contrib. Sci. Los Angeles Co. Mus.* **205**: 1-5.
Friedmann, H. (1971). Phenotypic potential and speciation in *Indicator* and *Prodotiscus*. *Ostrich* **8**(Suppl.): 21-26.
Friedmann, H. (1976). The Asian honey-guides. *J. Bombay Nat. Hist. Soc.* **71(3)**: 426-432.
Friedmann, H. (1978a). Results of the Lathrop Central African Republic Expedition 1976, ornithology. *Contrib. Sci. Los Angeles Co. Mus.* **287**: 1-22.
Friedmann, H. (1978b). Current knowledge of the Lyre-tailed Honey-guide, *Melichneutes robustus* Bates, and its implications (Aves, Indicatoridae). *Rev. Zool. Afr.* **92**: 644-656.
Friedmann, H. & Kern, J. (1956). The problem of cerophagy or wax-eating in the honey-guides. *Quart. Rev. Biol.* **31**: 19-30.
Friedmann, H. & Loveridge, A. (1937). *Notes on the Ornithology of Tropical East Africa*. Bulletin of the Museum of Comparative Zoology **81**, Cambridge, Massachusetts. 413 pp.
Friedmann, H. & Smith, F.D. (1950). *A Contribution to the Ornithology of Northeastern Venezuela*. Proceedings of the US National Museum **100**. Smithsonian Institution, Washington, D.C. 128 pp.
Friedmann, H. & Smith, F.D. (1955). *A Further Contribution to the Ornithology of Northeastern Venezuela*. Proceedings of the US National Museum **104**. Smithsonian Institution, Washington, D.C. 60 pp.
Friedmann, H. & Williams, J.G. (1968). Notable records of rare or little known birds from western Uganda. *Rev. Zool. Bot. Afr.* **77(1/2)**: 12-36.
Friedmann, H. & Williams, J.G. (1971). The birds of the lowlands of Bwamba, Togo Province, Uganda. *Contrib. Sci. Los Angeles Co. Mus.* **211**: 1-70.
Friedmann, H., Griscom, L. & Moore, R.T. (1957). *Distributional Check-list of the Birds of Mexico*. Part 2. Cooper Ornithological Society, Berkeley, California.
Friedmann, W.S. (1997). [Ways and regularities of the social evolution in pied woodpeckers (Genera *Dendrocopos* et *Picoides*; Picidae; Aves)]. *Berkut* **6(1-2)**: 52-66. In Russian with English summary.
Frith, C.B. & Frith, D.W. (1978). Field observations on incubation and roosting behaviour of the Greater Golden-backed Woodpecker, *Chrysocolaptes lucidus*, in Thailand. *Nat. Hist. Bull. Siam Soc.* **27**: 169-180.
Fry, C.H. (1970a). Convergence between jacamars and bee-eaters. *Ibis* **112(2)**: 257–259.
Fry, C.H. (1970b). Ecological distribution of birds in north-eastern Mato Grosso State, Brazil. *An. Acad. Bras. Ciênc.* **42**: 275-318.
Fry, C.H. (1974). Vocal mimesis in nestling Greater Honeyguide. *Bull. Brit. Orn. Club* **94(2)**: 58-59.
Fry, C.H. (1977). Relation between mobbing and honey-guiding. *British Birds* **70**: 268-269.
Fry, C.H., Keith, S. & Urban, E.K. (1988). *The Birds of Africa*. Vol. 3. Academic Press, London & San Diego.
Fujii, T. (1993). [Initial roosting time of the Japanese Green Woodpecker *Picus awokera*]. *Strix* **12**: 222-223. In Japanese with English summary.
Fukaya, K. (1985). [Breeding the Toco Toucan]. *Anim. Zoos* **37(12)**: 12-13. In Japanese with English summary.
Fulton, H.T. (1904). Notes on the birds of Chitral. *J. Bombay Nat. Hist. Soc.* **16(1)**: 44-64.
Fürbringer, M. (1888). *Untersuchungen zur Morphologie und Systematik der Vögel, zugleich ein Beitrag zur Anatomie der Stütz- und Bewegungsorgane*. Van Holkema, Amsterdam.
Furlong, R. (2000). Knysna Woodpecker hosts Scaly-throated Honeyguide. *Bee-eater* **50**: 24.
Gaines, G.D., Franzreb, K.E., Allen, D.H., Laves, K.S. & Jarvis, W.L. (1995). Red-cockaded Woodpecker management on the Savannah River Site: a management/research success story. Pp. 81-88 in: Kulhavy *et al.* (1995).
Galen, C. (1989). *A Preliminary Assessment of the Status of the Lewis's Woodpecker in Wasco County, Oregon*. Technical Report **88-3-01**. Oregon Department of Fish & Game, Nongame Wildlife Program, Portland, Oregon.
Galetti, M., Laps, R. & Pizo, M.A. (1998). Frugivory by toucans (Ramphastidae) at two altitudes in the Atlantic forest in Brazil. Proceedings of the XXII International Ornithological Congress, Durban. *Ostrich* **69**: 371.
Gamboa, G.J. & Brown, K.M. (1976). Comparative foraging behavior of six sympatric woodpecker species. *Proc. Iowa Acad. Sci.* **82(3-4)**: 179-181.
Gandy, D.W. (1994). *An Investigation of the Factors Determining the Altitudinal Distribution of the Forest-Dependent Avifauna of the Pacific Slope Andes in Colombia*. BSc dissertation, Anglia Polytechnic University, Cambridge, UK.
Gandy, D.W. (1995). Lanceolated Monklet, *Micromonacha lanceolata*. *Cotinga* **3**: 80.
Gandy, D.W., Durwyn, L. & Thompson, G. (1998). Speckled Piculet *Picumnus innominatus* and Golden-spectacled Flycatcher-warbler, *Seicercus burkii* from Margalla Hills, Pakistan. *J. Bombay Nat. Hist. Soc.* **95(2)**: 345-346.
Ganier, E.J. & Jackson, J.A. (1976). Common Flicker nesting in the ground. *Mississippi Kite* **6(1)**: 8-10.
García, J.A., Badii, M.H., Contreras, A.J., González, J.I. & Guzmán, A. (2001). Estructura de la avifauna asociada a *Yucca treculeana* en un matorral mediano subinerme en General Escobedo, Nuevo León, México. *Cotinga* **16**: 28-35.
García, M.E. (1989). Algunos datos sobre la nidificación del Carpintero Jabado (*Melanerpes superciliaris* Temminck) (Aves: Picidae) en la Ciénaga de Zapata. *Misc. Zool. Acad. Cienc. Cuba* **44**: 2.
García, M.E. (1992). Datos acerca de la reproducción del Carpintero Churroso *Colaptes fernandinae* Vigors (Aves: Picidae) en la Ciénaga de Zapata, Cuba. Pp. 19-20 in: *Comunicaciones Breves de Zoología*. Instituto de Ecología y Sistemática, Academia de Ciencias de Cuba, La Habana.
García, M.E. (1993). Datos sobre la reproducción de *Melanerpes s. superciliaris* y *Colaptes fernandinae* (Aves: Picidae) en la Ciénaga de Zapata. *Pitirre* **6(1)**: 12. (Abstract).
García, M.E. (1994). Aspectos etoecológicos del Carpintero Jabado, *Melanerpes s. superciliaris* (Aves: Picidae). *Cienc. Biol. Acad. Cienc. Cuba* **27**: 171-174.
García, M.E. & González, H. (1985). Nueva localidad para el Carpintero Churroso (*Colaptes fernandinae*) (Aves: Picidae). *Misc. Zool. Acad. Cienc. Cuba* **25**: 4.
Gardella, L. (1997). Red-bellied Woodpecker (*Melanerpes carolinus*) usurping nest of Downy Woodpecker (*Picoides pubescens*). *Alabama Birdlife* **43(1)**: 44-48.
Gardenfors, U. (1978). Hotbeteende av tretaig Hackspett. [Threat behaviour of male Three-toed Woodpeckers, *Picoides tridactylus*]. *Vår Fågelvärld* **37(2)**: 138-140. In Swedish with English summary.
Garoche, J. & Sohier, A. (1992). Nidification du Pic noir (*Dryocopus martius*) dans les Côtes-d'Armor. *Ar Vran* **3**: 3-5.
Garrett, J.D. (1999). Oklahoma's flying hammerheads. *Outdoor Oklahoma* **55(3)**: 16-23.
Garrett, K.L., Raphael, M.G. & Dixon, R.D. (1996). White-headed Woodpecker (*Picoides albolarvatus*). No. **252** in: Poole, A.F. & Gill, F.B. eds. (1996). *The Birds of North America*. Vol. 7. Academy of Natural Sciences & American Ornithologists' Union, Philadelphia & Washington, D.C.
Garrido, O.H. (1971). Variación del género monotípico *Xiphidiopicus* (Aves: Picidae) en Cuba. *Poeyana* **83**: 1-12.
Garrido, O.H. (1978). Nueva subespecie de Carpintero Verde (Aves: Picidae) para Cayo Coco, Cuba. *Inf. Cient.-Téc. Acad. Cienc. Cuba* **67(19)**: 1-6.
Garrido, O.H. (1985). Cuban endangered birds. Pp. 992-999 in: Buckley *et al.* (1985).
Garrido, O.H. & Kirkconnell, A. (2000). *Birds of Cuba*. Christopher Helm, London.
Gartshore, M.E. (1989). *An Avifaunal Survey of Taï National Park, Ivory Coast. 28 January - 11 April 1989*. ICBP Study Report **39**, Cambridge.
Gartshore, M.E., Taylor, P.D. & Francis, I.S. (1995). *Forest Birds in Côte d'Ivoire. A Survey of Taï National Park and other Forests and Forestry Plantations, 1989-1991*. BirdLife International Study Report **58**. BirdLife International, Cambridge.
Gates, D. (1981). Lewis' Woodpeckers in western Nebraska. *Nebr. Bird Rev.* **49(2)**: 33-34.
Gatter, W. (1977). Zug und Jahresperiodik nord- und mitteleuropäischer Schwarzspechte *Dryocopus martius* mit Bemerkungen zum Zug der Gattung *Picus*. [Migration and annual periodicity of north and central European Black Woodpeckers *Dryocopus martius* with remarks on the migration of the genera *Picus*]. *Anz. Orn. Ges. Bayern* **16(2/3)**: 141-152. In German with English summary.
Gatter, W. (1981). Der Schwarzspecht - ein Zugvogel? *Beih. Veröff. Naturschutz Landschaftspflege* **20**: 75-82.
Gatter, W. (1988). The birds of Liberia (West Africa). A preliminary list with status and open questions. *Verh. orn. Ges. Bayern* **24**: 689-723.
Gatter, W. (1997). *Birds of Liberia*. Pica Press, Nr. Robertsbridge, UK.
Gaud, J. & Atyeo, W.T. (1996). *Feather Mites of the World (Acarina, Astigmata). The Supraspecific Taxa*. Annales de Sciences Zoologiques **277(1&2)**. 436 pp.
Gaugris, Y., Prigogine, A. & Vande weghe, J.P. (1981). Additions et corrections à l'avifaune du Burundi. *Gerfaut* **71**: 3-39.
Gebauer, A. (1984). Die Lautentwicklung beim Buntspecht, *Dendrocopos major* (L.). *Mitt. Zool. Mus. Berlin* **60**(Suppl.): 107-127.
Gebauer, A., Kaiser, M. & Wallschläger, D. (1984). Beobachtungen zum Verhalten und zur Lautgebung des Mittelspechts (*Dendrocopos medius*) während der Nestlingszeit. Part 1. Brutbiologische Daten und Verhalten. *Beitr. Vogelkd.* **30**: 115-137.
Gebauer, A., Kaiser, M. & Wallschläger, D. (1992). Beobachtungen zum Verhalten und zur Lautgebung des Mittelspechts (*Dendrocopos medius*) während der Nestlingszeit. Part 2. Das Lautinventar. *Beitr. Vogelkd.* **38**: 175-199.
Gee, J.P. (1984). The birds of Mauritania. *Malimbus* **6(1&2)**: 31-66.
Genise, J.F., Starneck, R.J. & Hazeldine, P.L. (1993). Sapsucking in the White-fronted Woodpecker *Melanerpes cactorum*. *Orn. Neotropical* **4**: 77-82. In English with Spanish summary.
Gentilin, C. (1967). Le Pic noir *Dryocopus martius* nicheur en Saône-et-Loire. *Alauda* **35(2)**: 153-154.
Genz, H.W. (1999). Haltung und Zucht des Furchenschnabelbartvogels. *Gefiederte Welt* **123(7)**: 254-256.
George, P.V. (1968). On the occurrence of the Fulvous-breasted Woodpecker *Dendrocopus macei* (Vieillot) in Sikkim. *J. Bombay Nat. Hist. Soc.* **64(3)**: 559-560.
George, W.G. (1972). Age determination of Hairy and Downy woodpeckers in eastern North America. *Bird-Banding* **43(2)**: 128-135.
Gerasimov, K.B. & Dzerzhinsky, F.Y. (1998). Functional morphology of woodpeckers' jaw apparatus. Proceedings of the XXII International Ornithological Congress, Durban 1998. *Ostrich* **69(3&4)**: 388. (Abstract).
Gerasimov, Y.N. & Ozaki, K. (2000). [Nesting birds of the Anava River]. Pp. 33-42 in: Anon. (2000). *[The Biology and Conservation of the Birds of Kamchatka]*. Vol. 2. Russian Academy of Science, Far Eastern Brunch & Kamchatka Institute of Ecology, Moscow. In Russian with English summary.
Gerber, D.T. (1986). Female Golden-fronted Woodpecker or mutant female Red-bellied Woodpecker? *Amer. Birds* **40(2)**: 203-204.
Germain, M. (1992). Sur quelques données erronées concernant l'avifaune de la Lobaye, République Centrafricaine. *Malimbus* **14(1)**: 1-6.
Germain, M. & Cornet, J.P. (1994). Oiseaux nouveaux pour la République Centrafricaine ou dont les notifications de ce pays sont peu nombreuses. *Malimbus* **16**: 30-51.
de Germiny, G. (1930a). Révision de la famille des Rhamphastidés [sic.]. *L'Oiseaux* **11**: 469-480, 553-556, 589-604.
de Germiny, G. (1930b). Histoire systematique des toucans. *L'Oiseaux* **11**: 655-676.
de Germiny, G. (1937a). Un nouvel hybride de Rhamphastidés [sic]. *L'Oiseaux (Nouv. Sér.)* **7**: 81-84.
de Germiny, G. (1937b). Note sur les toucans du Muséum de Vienne. *L'Oiseaux (Nouv. Sér.)* **7**: 375-376.
Géroudet, P. (1987). A propos du Pic tridactyle dans les forêts jurassiennes. *Nos Oiseaux* **39**: 5-12.
Gibbon, R.S. (1966). Observations on the behavior of nesting Three-toed Woodpeckers, *Picoides tridactylus*, in central New Brunswick. *Can. Field-Nat.* **80(4)**: 223-226.
Gibbons, A. (1992). Rain forest diet: you are what you eat. *Science* **255**: 163.
Gibson-Hill, C.A. (1949a). *An Annotated Checklist of the Birds of Malaya: an Annotated List of the Birds Occurring or Known to Have Occurred in the Territories of the Federation of Malaya and the Colony of Singapore*. Bulletin of the Raffles Museum, Singapore **20**. 299 pp.
Gibson-Hill, C.A. (1949b). A checklist of the birds of Singapore Island. *Bull. Raffles Mus., Singapore* **21**: 132-183.
Giefer, J.M. (1978). Courtship ritual of the Pileated Woodpecker? *Inl. Bird Banding News* **50(3)**: 93.
Gifford, J.L. (1987). Intergrading of Red-shafted and Yellow-shafted races of Northern Flicker in Zion National Park area. *Utah Birds* **3(2)**: 30-31.
Gillespie, T.W. (2001). Application of extinction and conservation theories for forest birds in Nicaragua. *Conserv. Biol.* **15(3)**: 699-709.
Gilliard, E.T. (1941). The birds of Mt. Auyan-Tepui, Venezuela. *Bull. Amer. Mus. Nat. Hist.* **77(9)**: 439-508.
Gilliard, E.T. (1949a). A new puff-bird from Colombia. *Amer. Mus. Novit.* **1438**: 1-3.
Gilliard, E.T. (1949b). Five new birds from the Philippines. *Auk* **66**: 275-280.
Gilliard, E.T. (1950). Notes on a collection of birds from Bataan, Luzon, Philippine Islands. *Bull. Amer. Mus. Nat. Hist.* **94(8)**: 457-504.
Gines, H., Aveledo, R., Pons, A., Yepez, G. & Muñoz-Tebar, R. (1953). Lista y comentario de las aves colectadas en la región. *Mem. Soc. Cienc. Nat. La Salle* **13(35)**: 145-202.
Ginn, P.J., McIlleron, W.G. & Milstein, P. le S. eds. (1989). *The Complete Book of Southern African Birds*. Struik Publishers Ltd, Cape Town.
Giraudo, A.R. & Sironi, M. (1992). Registro de *Pteroglossus castanotis australis* (Cassin, 1867) y de *Baillonius bailloni* (Viellot, 1819) (Aves: Ramphastidae) en el noreste de la provincia de Corrientes, República Argentina. *Not. Faun.* **25**: 1-2.
Giraudo, A.R., Brunello, D. & Broggini, G. (1993). Nidificación del Carpinterito Común (*Picumnus cirratus*) en la provincia de Córdoba. *Nuestras Aves* **28**: 24-25.
Giraudoux, P., Degauquier, R., Jones, P.J., Weigel, J. & Isenmann, P. (1988). Avifaune du Niger: état des connaissances en 1986. *Malimbus* **10(1)**: 1-140.
Glenister, A.G. (1971). *The Birds of the Malay Peninsula*. Oxford University Press, London.

Gliesch, R. (1930). Lista das aves colligidas e observadas no estado do Rio Grande do Sul. *Egatea* **15**: 276-292.
Glue, D.E. & Boswell, T. (1994). Comparative nesting ecology of the three British breeding woodpeckers. *British Birds* **87(6)**: 253-269.
Glutz von Blotzheim, U.N. & Bauer, K.M. eds. (1980). *Handbuch der Vögel Mitteleuropas*. Vol. 9. Columbiformes-Piciformes. Akademische Verlagsgesellschaft, Wiesbaden, Germany.
Goerck, J.M. (1999). Distribution of birds along an elevational gradient in the Atlantic forest of Brazil: implications for the conservation of endemic and endangered species. *Bird Conserv. Int.* **9(3)**: 235-253.
Goes, F. (1999). Notes on selected bird species in Cambodia. *Forktail* **15**: 25-27.
Goggans, R. (1989a). Black-backed Woodpecker *Picoides arcticus*. Pp. 88-89 in : Clark, T.W., Harvey, A.H., Dorn, R.D., Genter, D.L. & Groves, C. eds. (1989). *Rare, Sensitive, and Threatened Species of the Greater Yellowstone Ecosystem*. The Nature Conservancy-Idaho, Idaho, Montana.
Goggans, R. (1989b). Three-toed Woodpecker *Picoides tridactylus*. Pp. 90-91 in : Clark, T.W., Harvey, A.H., Dorn, R.D., Genter, D.L. & Groves, C. eds. (1989). *Rare, Sensitive, and Threatened Species of the Greater Yellowstone Ecosystem*. The Nature Conservancy-Idaho, Idaho, Montana.
Goggans, R., Dixon, R.D. & Seminara, L.C. (1988). *Habitat Use by Three-toed and Black-backed Woodpeckers*. Technical Report **87-3-02**. Oregon Department of Fish & Game, Nongame Wildlife Program, Portland, Oregon.
Gokula, V. & Vijayan, L. (1997). Birds of Mudumalai Wildlife Sanctuary, India. *Forktail* **12**: 107-116.
Golding, P. (1991). Jamaican Woodpecker. *Gosse Bird Club Broadsheet* **56**: 23.
Golding, P. (1993). Jamaican Woodpecker. *Gosse Bird Club Broadsheet* **60**: 32.
Gómez de Silva, H. (1998). Distributional and temporal records of some Mexican birds. *Cotinga* **9**: 16-20.
Gönner, C. (2000). Some observations from PT Limbang Ganeca Forest Concession, east Kalimantan. *Kukila* **11**: 37-46.
Gonzales, P.C. (1983). *Birds of Catanduanes*. Philippine Natural Museum of Zoology Papers **2**, Manila. 125 pp.
González, O.E. (1998). Birds of the lowland forest of Cerros del Sira, central Peru. *Cotinga* **9**: 57-60.
González, O.E. & Málaga, E. (1997). Distribución de aves en el Valle de Majes, Arequipa, Perú. *Orn. Neotropical* **8(1)**: 57-69. In Spanish with English summary.
González-Alonso, H., McNicholl, M.K., Hamel, P.B., Acosta, M., Godinez, E., Hernández, J., Rodríguez, D., Jackson, J.A., Marcos, C., McRae, R.D. & Sirois, J. (1992). A cooperative bird-banding project in Peninsula de Zapata, Cuba, 1988-1989. Pp. 131-142 in: Hagan & Johnston (1992).
González-García, F. (1993). *Avifauna de la Reserva de la Biosfera "Montes Azules", Selva Lacandona, Chiapas, México*. Acta Zoológica Mexicana (Nueva Serie) **55**. 86 pp.
Goodfellow, W. (1902). Results of an ornithological journey through Colombia and Ecuador. Part V. *Ibis* **Ser. 8, no. 2**: 207-233.
Goodge, W.R. (1972). Anatomical evidence for phylogenetic relationships among woodpeckers. *Auk* **89(1)**: 65-85.
Goodman, S.M. & Gonzales, P.C. (1990). The birds of Mt. Isarog National Park, southern Luzon, Philippines, with particular reference to altitudinal distribution. *Fieldiana Zool. (New Ser.)* **60**: 1-38.
Goodman, S.M., Meininger, P.L., Baha el Din, S.M., Hobbs, J.J. & Mullié, W.C. eds. (1989). *The Birds of Egypt*. Oxford University Press, Oxford & New York.
Goodwin, D. (1964). Some aspects of taxonomy and relationships of barbets (Capitonidae). *Ibis* **106**: 198-219.
Goodwin, D. (1965). Some remarks on the new barbet. *Bull. Brit. Orn. Club* **85(1)**: 9-10.
Goodwin, D. (1968). Notes on woodpeckers (Picidae). *Bull. Brit. Mus. (Nat. Hist.) Zool.* **17**: 1-44.
Goodwin, W. (1996). A record of the yellow-headed morph of the Black-collared Barbet. *Honeyguide* **42**: 33.
Goossen, J.P. (1989). Behavior of a Red-crowned Woodpecker at an unusual roost site in Venezuela. *J. Field Orn.* **60(1)**: 36-38. In English with Spanish summary.
Gore, M.E.J. (1968). A check-list of the birds of Sabah, Borneo. *Ibis* **110**: 165-196.
Gore, M.E.J. (1990). *The Birds of The Gambia. An Annotated Check-list*. BOU Check-list **3**. 2nd revised edition. British Ornithologists' Union, London.
Gore, M.E.J. (1994). Bird records from Liberia. *Malimbus* **16**: 74-87.
Gore, M.E.J. & Gepp, A.R.M. (1978). *Las Aves del Uruguay*. Mosca Hnos., Montevideo.
Gorman, G. (1996). Identification du Pic syriaque *Dendrocopos syriacus* et répartition en Europe. *Ornithos* **3**: 178-186.
Gorman, G. (1997a). Get tracking. *Birdwatch* **60**: 25-29.
Gorman, G. (1997b). Balkanspett: på snabb expansion genom Europa. *Vår Fågelvärld* **56(5)**: 18-23.
Gorman, G. (1998a). Syrian Woodpecker using wall crevice as "anvil". *British Birds* **91(9)**: 378.
Gorman, G. (1998b). The spread of Black Woodpecker in Europe - will it reach Britain next? *Birding World* **11(10)**: 390-395.
Gorman, G. (1999a). Pecking order. *Birdwatch* **81**: 26-30.
Gorman, G. (1999b). The identification of the Syrian Woodpecker. *Alula* **5(3)**: 82-88.
Gorman, G. (2000). Black-and-white lookalikes. *Birdwatch* **97**: 26-30.
Gotto, K. (1997). Commitment to conservation. *World Birdwatch* **19(1)**: 17-19.
Gould, J. (1854). *Monograph of the Ramphastidae, or Family of Toucans*. 2nd edition, Published privately, London.
Gowarty, P.A. & Lennartz, M.R. (1985). Sex ratios of nestling and fledging Red-cockaded Woodpeckers (*Picoides borealis*) favor males. *Amer. Naturalist* **126(3)**: 347-353.
Goy, D. (1994). Torcol fourmilier *Jynx torquilla*. Pp. 428-429 in: Yeatman-Berthelot, D. & Jarry, G. eds. (1994). *Nouvel Atlas des Oiseaux Nicheurs de France 1985-1989*. Société Ornithologique de France, Paris.
Graaf, J. (1992). Cardinal Woodpeckers at Velddrif. *Promerops* **205**: 10-11.
Graaf, J. (1996). Lesser Honeyguide at Velddrif. *Promerops* **222**: 12.
Graber, R.G.J. (1979). Red-heads and pin oaks. *Illinois Audubon Bull.* **188**: 35-38.
Graham, G.L., Graves, G.R., Schulenberg, T.S. & O'Neill, J.P. (1980). Seventeen bird species new to Peru from the Pampas de Heath. *Auk* **97(2)**: 366-370.
Grangé, J.L. (1991). Sur le dimorphisme sexuel dans la recherche de nourriture chez le Pic à dos blanc pyrénéen (*Dendrocopos leucotos lilfordi*). *Nos Oiseaux* **41(3)**: 185-194.
Grangé, J.L. (1993). Données préliminaires sur la biologie de reproduction du Pic à dos blanc pyrénéen (*Dendrocopos leucotos lilfordi*) en Béarn. *Nos Oiseaux* **42(1)**: 17-28.
Grangé, J.L. (2001). Le Pic à dos blanc *Dendrocopos leucotos lilfordi* dans les Pyrénées françaises. *Ornithos* **8(1)**: 8-17.
Grant, C.H.B. & Mackworth-Praed, C.W. (1942). On the type locality of *Pogonias minor*. *Bull. Brit. Orn. Club* **62**: 46.
Grant, C.H.B. & Mackworth-Praed, C.W. (1946). Notes on East African birds. *Bull. Brit. Orn. Club* **67**: 10-13.
Grant, J. (1966). The Red-headed Woodpecker near Vernon, British Columbia. *Murrelet* **47**: 45.
Grantham, M.J. (2000). Birds of Alas Purwo National Park, East Java. *Kukila* **11**: 97-121.
Graves, G.R. (1986). Geographic variation in the White-mantled Barbet (*Capito hypoleucus*) of Colombia (Aves: Capitonidae). *Proc. Biol. Soc. Washington* **99(1)**: 61-64.
Grebe, T. (1998). Schwarzspechte in der Haard. *Charadrius* **34(3-4)**: 155-158.
Green, A.A. (1983). The birds of Bamingui-Bangoran National Park, Central African Republic. *Malimbus* **5(1)**: 17-30.
Green, A.A. (1990). The avifauna of the southern sector of the Gashaka-Gumti Game Reserve, Nigeria. *Malimbus* **12(1)**: 31-51.
Green, A.A. (1996). More bird records from Rio del Rey estuary, Cameroon. *Malimbus* **18(2)**: 112-121.
Greenway, J.C. (1940). Oriental forms of *Picus canus*. *Auk* **57(4)**: 550-560.
Greenway, J.C. (1943). Oriental forms of the Pygmy Woodpecker. *Auk* **60(4)**: 564-574.
Greenway, J.C. (1967). *Extinct and Vanishing Birds of the World*. Dover Publications, New York.
Greenway, J.C. (1978). *Type Specimens of Birds in the American Museum of Natural History*. Part 2. Otididae ... Picidae. Bulletin of the American Museum of Natural History **161(1)**, New York. 305 pp.
Greig-Smith, P.W. (1976). The composition and habitat preferences of the avifauna of the Mole National Park, Ghana. *Bull. Niger. Orn. Soc.* **12(42)**: 49-66.
Greig-Smith, P.W. (1977a). Bird migration at Mole National Park, Ghana. *Bull. Niger. Orn. Soc.* **13(43)**: 3-14.
Greig-Smith, P.W. (1977b). Breeding dates of birds in Mole National Park, Ghana. *Bull. Niger. Orn. Soc.* **13(44)**: 89-93.
Grigera, D., Úbeda, C. & Reca, A. (1996). Estado de conservación de las aves del Parque y Reserva Nacional Nahuel Huapi. *Hornero* **14(3)**: 1-13.
Grimes, L.G. (1987). *The Birds of Ghana. An Annotated Check-list*. BOU Check-list **9**. British Ornithologists' Union, London.
Grimmett, R., Inskipp, C. & Inskipp, T. (1998). *Birds of the Indian Subcontinent*. Christopher Helm, London.
Grimmett, R., Inskipp, C. & Inskipp, T. (2000). *Birds of Nepal*. Christopher Helm, London.
Grinnell, J. (1902). The southern White-headed Woodpecker. *Condor* **4(4)**: 89-90.
Griscom, L. (1929). A collection of birds from Cana, Darien. *Bull. Mus. Comp. Zool.* **69(8)**: 149-190.
Griscom, L. (1932). The ornithology of the Caribbean coast of extreme eastern Panama. *Bull. Mus. Comp. Zool.* **72**: 303-372.
Griscom, L. (1935). *The Ornithology of the Republic of Panama*. Bulletin of the Museum of Comparative Zoology **78**, Cambridge, Massachusetts. 122 pp.
Griscom, L. & Greenway, J.C. (1937). Critical notes on new Neotropical birds. *Bull. Mus. Comp. Zool.* **81**: 416-437.
Griscom, L. & Greenway, J.C. (1941). *Birds of Lower Amazonia*. Bulletin of the Museum of Comparative Zoology **88(3)**, Cambridge, Massachusetts. 261 pp.
Groppali, R. & Pedrazzani, R. (1996). Importanza del Picchio rosso maggiore *Picoides major* nella degradazione del legno morto e deperiente in ambiente forestale planiziale. [About the importance of the Red Spotted Woodpecker *Picoides major* for dead or decaying wood degradation in plain forests]. *Atti Soc. Ital. Sci. Nat.* **135(2)**: 374-378. In Italian with English summary.
Groppali, R. & Priano, M. (1993). [Predation on populations of *Formica lagubris* by Green Woodpeckers *Picus viridis* in Appennino Pavese, northern Italy]. *Avocetta* **17(1)**: 61-64. In Italian with English summary.
Grubb, T.C. (1982). Downy Woodpecker sexes select different cavity sites; an experiment using artificial snags. *Wilson Bull.* **94(4)**: 577-579.
Grubb, T.C. (1989). Ptilochronology: feather growth bars as indicators of nutritional status. *Auk* **106(2)**: 314-320.
Grubh, R.B. & Ali, S. (1970). Birds of Goa. *J. Bombay Nat. Hist. Soc.* **73**: 42-53.
Grudzien, T.A. & Moore, W.S. (1986). Genetic differentiation between the Yellow-shafted and Red-shafted subspecies of the Northern Flicker. *Biochem. Syst. Ecol.* **14(4)**: 451-453.
Grudzien, T.A., Moore, W.S., Cook, J.R. & Tagle, D. (1987). Genic population structure and gene flow in the Northern Flicker (*Colaptes auratus*) hybrid zone. *Auk* **104(4)**: 654-664.
Grullón, G. (1976). *Régimen Alimentario del Pájaro Carpintero (*Melanerpes striatus *Verril, 1909) en una Zona de Bosque Seco Subtropical*. MSc thesis, Universidad Autónoma de Santo Domingo, Santo Domingo.
Guichard, G. (1948). Le Pic cendré *Picus c. canus* dans l'Yonne. *Alauda* **16**: 200-204.
Guichard, G. (1961). Sur une extension en Basse-Bourgogne de l'habitat du Pic noir *Dryocopus martius* (L.). *Alauda* **39(1)**: 69-70.
Guilherme, E. (2000). Levantamento preliminar da avifauna do Campus e Parque Zoobotânico da Universidade Federal do Acre, Rio Branco, Acre. Pp. 268-269 in: Straube *et al*. (2000).
Guilherme, E. (2001). Comunidade de aves do Campus e Parque Zoobotânico da Universidade Federal do Acre, Brasil. *Tangara* **1(2)**: 57-73.
Guix, J.C. (1995). *Aspectos da Frugivoria, Disseminação e Predação de Sementes por Vertebrados nas Florestas Nativas do Estado de São Paulo, Sudeste do Brasil*. PhD thesis, Universitat de Barcelona, Barcelona.
Guix, J.C. & Jover, L. (2001). Resource partitioning and interspecific competition among coexisting species of guans and toucans in SE Brazil. *Netherlands J. Zool.* **51(3)**: 285-298.
Guix, J.C. & Ruiz, X. (1995). Toucans and thrushes as potential dispersers of seed-predatory weevil larvae in southeastern Brazil. *Can. J. Zool.* **73(4)**: 745-748.
Guix, J.C., Mañosa, S., Pedrocchi, V., Vargas, M.J. & Souza, F.L. (1997). Census of three frugivorous birds in an Atlantic rainforest area of southeastern Brazil. *Ardeola* **44(2)**: 229-233.
Guix, J.C., Martín, M., Hernández, A. & Souza, F.L. (2000). Conservation status of the Saffron Toucanet (*Baillonius bailloni*, Ramphastidae): a new case of population isolation and depletion in South America. *Grupo Estud. Ecol., Sér. Doc.* **6(2)**: 10-25.
Guix, J.C., Martín, M. & Mañosa, S. (1999). Conservation status of parrot populations in an Atlantic rainforest area of southeastern Brazil. *Biodiversity and Conservation* **8**: 1079-1088.
Guix, J.C., Tabánez, A.A.J., da Silva, A.N., López, C., Martínez, C., Matheu, E., de Souza, F.L., Pisciotta, K.R., Bradbury, N. & Portilho, W.G. (1992). *Viagem de Reconhecimento Científico a algumas Áreas Desconhecidas da Fazenda Intervales, Estado de São Paulo, Durante o Período de 04 a 16 de Outubro de 1991*. Grupo de Estudos Ecológicos Série Documentos **4**, São Paulo.
Gullion, G.W. (1949). A heavily parasitized flicker. *Condor* **51(5)**: 232.
Gunn, J.S. & Hagan, J.M. (2000). Woodpecker abundance and tree use in uneven-aged managed, and unmanaged, forests in northern Maine. *For. Ecol. Manage.* **126**: 1-12.
Günther, E. (1993). "Umgekehrte Begattung" beim Mittelspecht (*Dendrocopos medius*). *Orn. Jber. Mus. Heineanum* **11**: 107-108.
Günther, E. & Hellmann, M. (1998). Die Höhlen des Buntspechtes (*Picoides major*) von Fledermäusen nicht gefragt? *Nyctalus* **6(5)**: 468-470.
Gutiérrez, R.J. & Koenig, W.D. (1978). Characteristics of storage trees used by Acorn Woodpeckers in two California woodlands. *J. Forestry* **76(3)**: 162-164.
Gyldenstolpe, N. (1917). Notes on the heel-pads in certain families of birds. *Arkiv för Zool.* **11**: 1-15.
Gyldenstolpe, N. (1941a). On some new or rare birds chiefly from southwestern Colombia. *Arkiv för Zool.* **33A(6)**: 1-17.
Gyldenstolpe, N. (1941b). Preliminary descriptions of some new birds from the Brazilian Amazonas. *Arkiv för Zool.* **33B(12)**: 1-10.
Gyldenstolpe, N. (1945a). *The Bird Fauna of Rio Juruá in Western Brazil*. Kungl. Svenska Vetenskapsakademiens Handlingar (3rd Series) **22**. 338 pp.
Gyldenstolpe, N. (1945b). *A Contribution to the Ornithology of Northern Bolivia*. Kungl. Svenska Vetenskapsakademiens Handlingar **23(1)**. 300 pp.
Gyldenstolpe, N. (1951). *The Ornithology of the Rio Purús Region in Western Brazil*. Arkiv för Zoologi (Ser. 2) **2**. 320 pp.
Haagner, A.K. (1907). A contribution to our knowledge of the Indicatoridae (honey-guides). *J. South Afr. Orn. Union (Ser. 2)* **1**: 1-5.
Haagner, A.K. (1911). A further note on the mandibular hook of the honey-guide. *J. South Afr. Orn. Union (Ser. 2)* **7**: 79.
Haas, F.C. (1987). Recent range expansion and population increase of the Red-bellied Woodpecker, *Melanerpes carolinus* (Linnaeus) in Pennsylvania. *Pennsylvania Birds* **1**: 107-110.
Hachisuka, M. (1930). Contributions to the birds of the Philippines. No. 2. *Orn. Soc. Japan* **14**(Suppl.): 141-222.
Hachisuka, M. (1931-1935). *The Birds of the Philippine Islands, with Notes on the Mammal Fauna*. Vol. 2. Witherby, London.
Hachisuka, M. & Udagawa, T. (1953). *Contribution to the Ornithology of the Ryukyu Islands*. Quarterly Journal of the Taiwan Museum **6(3-4)**. 139 pp.
Hackenberg, C. (1989). Ornithologische Notizem zum borealen Teil Patagoniens. *Trochilus* **10**: 113-148.
Hackett, S.J. & Lehn, C.A. (1997). Lack of genetic divergence in a genus (*Pteroglossus*) of Neotropical birds: the connection between life-history characteristics and levels of genetic divergence. Pp. 267-279 in: Remsen (1997).

Hadow, H.H. (1973). Winter ecology of migrant and resident Lewis' Woodpeckers in southeastern Colorado. *Condor* **75(2)**: 210-224.
Hadow, H.H. (1976). Growth and development of nesting Downy Woodpeckers. *North Amer. Bird Bander* **1(4)**: 155-164.
Hadow, H.H. (1977). *Audible Communication and its Role in Species Recognition by Red-naped and Williamson's Sapsucker (Piciformes)*. PhD dissertation, University of Colorado, Boulder, Colorado.
Haessler, C. (1989). Rauhfusskauz und Schwarzspecht als Brutnachbarn. *Der Falke* **36(5)**: 151-153.
Haffer, J. (1959). Notas sobre las aves de la región de Uraba. *Lozania* **12**: 1-49.
Haffer, J. (1961). Notas sobre la avifauna de la Península de la Guajira. *Noved. Colombianas* **1(6)**: 374-396.
Haffer, J. (1962). Zum Vorkommen von *Brachygalba salmoni* Sclater & Salvin mit Beschreibung einer neuen Form. *J. Orn.* **103**: 38–46.
Haffer, J. (1967a). On birds from the northern Chocó region, NW Colombia. *Veröff. Zool. Staatssammlung München* **11**: 123-149.
Haffer, J. (1967b). *Speciation in Colombian Forest Birds West of the Andes*. American Museum Novitates **2294**. 57 pp.
Haffer, J. (1968). Über die Flügel-und Schwanzmauser columbianischer Piciformes. *J. Orn.* **109**: 157-171.
Haffer, J. (1969). Speciation in Amazonian forest birds. *Science* **165**: 131-137.
Haffer, J. (1974). *Avian Speciation in Tropical South America. With a Systematic Survey of the Toucans (Ramphastidae) and Jacamars (Galbulidae)*. Publications of the Nuttall Ornithological Club **14**. Cambridge, Massachusetts. 390 pp.
Haffer, J. (1975). *Avifauna of Northwestern Colombia, South America*. Bonner Zoologische Monographien **7**. Zoologisches Forschungsinstitut und Museum Alexander Koenig, Bonn. 182 pp.
Haffer, J. (1978). Distribution of Amazon forest birds. *Bonn. zool. Beitr.* **29**: 38-78.
Haffer, J. (1985). Avian zoogeography of the Neotropical lowlands. Pp. 113-146 in: Buckley *et al.* (1985).
Haffer, J. (1987). Biogeography of Neotropical birds. Pp. 105-150 in: Whitmore, T.C. & Prance, G.T. eds. (1987). *Biogeography and Quaternary History of Tropical America*. Oxford University Press, Oxford.
Haffer, J. (1991). Mosaic distribution patterns of Neotropical forest birds and underlying cyclic disturbance processes. Pp. 83-114 in: Remmert, H. ed. (1991). *Ecological Studies* **85**. Springer-Verlag, Berlin.
Haffer, J. (1993a). On the "river effect" in some forest birds of southern Amazonia. *Bol. Mus. Paraense Emilio Goeldi (Zool.)* **8**: 217-248.
Haffer, J. (1993b). Time's cycle and time's arrow in the history of Amazonia. *Biogeographica* **69**: 15-45.
Haffer, J. (1995). Species versus phyletic lineages. *Cour. Forschungsinst. Senckenb.* **181**: 303-309.
Haffer, J. (1997a). Alternative models of vertebrate speciation in Amazonia: an overview. *Biodiversity and Conservation* **6**: 451-476.
Haffer, J. (1997b). Tukane im neotropischen Regenwald. *Biol. Unserer Zeit* **27**: 263-270.
Haffer, J. (1997c). Contact zones between birds of southern Amazonia. Pp. 281-305 in: Remsen (1997).
Haffer, J. & Borrero, J.I. (1965). On birds from northern Colombia. *Rev. Biol. Trop.* **13(1)**: 29-33.
Hagan, J.M. & Johnston, D.W. eds. (1992). *Ecology and Conservation of Neotropical Migrant Landbirds*. Smithsonian Institution Press, Washington & London.
Hagan, J.M. & Reed, J.M. (1988). Red color bands reduce fledging success in Red-cockaded Woodpeckers. *Auk* **105(3)**: 498-503.
Hagemeijer, W.J.M. & Blair, M.J. eds. (1997). *The EBCC Atlas of European Breeding Birds: their Distribution and Abundance*. T. & A.D. Poyser, London.
Hågvar, S. & Hågvar, G. (1989). The direction of the hole in Norwegian woodpecker nests. *Norw. J. Orn.* **12(2)**: 106-107. In English with Norwegian summary.
Hågvar, S., Hågvar, G. & Monness, E. (1990). Nest site selection in Norwegian woodpeckers. *Holarctic Ecol.* **13(2)**: 156-165.
Haig, S.M. (1980). Black-backed Three-toed Woodpeckers in Forest County. *Passenger Pigeon* **42(4)**: 149-150.
Haig, S.M., Belthoff, J.R. & Allen, D.H. (1993a). Population viability analysis for a small population of Red-cockaded Woodpeckers and an evaluation of enhancement strategies. *Conserv. Biol.* **7(2)**: 289-300.
Haig, S.M., Belthoff, J.R. & Allen, D.H. (1993b). Examination of population structure in Red-cockaded Woodpeckers using DNA profiles. *Evolution* **47(1)**: 185-194.
Haig, S.M., Walters, J.R. & Plissner, J.H. (1994). Genetic evidence for monogamy in the cooperatively breeding Red-cockaded Woodpecker. *Behav. Ecol. Sociobiol.* **34(4)**: 295-303.
Haila, Y. & Jarvinen, O. (1977). Competition and habitat selection in two large woodpeckers. *Ornis Fenn.* **54(2)**: 73-78. In English with Finnish summary.
Hails, C. & Jarvis, F. (1987). *Birds of Singapore*. Times Editions, Singapore.
Hainard, R. & Burnier, J. (1958). Le Pic leuconote *Dendrocopos leucotos* dans les Pyrénées. *Alauda* **26**: 63-65.
Håland, A. & Toft, G.O. (1983). Hvitryggspettens forekomst og habitatvalg på Vestlandet. *Vår Fuglefauna* **6**: 3-14.
Hald-Mortensen, P. (1971). En dag I vendehalseparrets (*Jynx torquilla*) ungefordringsperiode. [One day in the nestling period of the Wryneck (*Jynx torquilla*)]. *Flora Fauna* **77(1)**: 1-12. In Danish with English summary.
Hall, P. (1977). The birds of Serti. *Bull. Niger. Orn. Soc.* **13(43)**: 66-79.
Halleux, D. (1994). Annotated bird list of Macenta Prefecture, Guinea. *Malimbus* **16(1)**: 10-29.
Ham Kyuhwang (1982). [An ecological study on the woodpeckers (Picidae) in Korea]. *Bull. Korean Assoc. Cons. (Nature Ser.)* **4**: 199-217. In Korean with English summary.
Ham Kyuhwang & Won Pyongoh (1980). [Ecological studies of endangered birds and their conservation in Korea. Part 2. Breeding ecology of the Tristram's Woodpecker, *Dryocopus javensis richardsi* in Korea]. *Bull. Korean Assoc. Cons.* **2**: 83-103. In Korean with English summary.
Ham Kyuhwang & Won Pyongoh (1982). Ecology and conservation of the Tristram's Woodpecker, *Dryocopus javensis richardsi* Tristram, in Korea. *J. Yamashina Inst. Orn.* **14**: 254-269.
Handrinos, G. & Akriotis, T. (1997). *The Birds of Greece*. Christopher Helm, London.
Hanmer, D.B. (1997). Measurements and moult in Greater and Lesser Honeyguides from Mozambique and Malawi. *Honeyguide* **43(1)**: 19-37.
Hannon, S.J., Mumme, R.L., Koenig, W.D. & Pitelka, F.A. (1985). Replacement of breeders and within-group conflict in the cooperatively breeding Acorn Woodpecker. *Behav. Ecol. Sociobiol.* **17(4)**: 303-312.
Hannon, S.J., Mumme, R.L., Koenig, W.D., Spon, S. & Pitelka, F.A. (1987). Acorn crop failure, dominance, and a decline in numbers in the cooperatively breeding Acorn Woodpecker. *J. Anim. Ecol.* **56(1)**: 197-207.
Hansbro, P. & Sargeant, D. (2000). Interesting ornithological observations from Yemen in spring 1998. *Sandgrouse* **22(1)**: 71-74.
Hansen, F. (1984). Der Schwarzspecht *Dryocopus martius* als Brutvogel auf der Dänischen Insel Bornholm. [The Black Woodpecker *Dryocopus martius* as a breeding bird on the island of Bornholm, Denmark]. *Ann. Zool. Fennici* **21(3)**: 431-433. In German with English summary.
Hansen, F. (1987). [The immigration of the Black Woodpecker *Dryocopus martius* to the island of Bornholm, and its population development during 25 years]. *Acta Regiae Soc. Sci. Litt. Gothob. Zool.* **14**: 53-59. In German with Swedish and English summary.
Hansen, F. (1989). [Nest hole excavation and reuse of nest holes by the Black Woodpecker on Bornholm, Denmark]. *Dan. Orn. Foren. Tidssk.* **83(3-4)**: 125-129. In Danish with English summary.
Hanula, J.L. & Franzreb, K.E. (1995). Arthropod prey of nestling Red-cockaded Woodpeckers in the upper coastal plain of South Carolina. *Wilson Bull.* **107(3)**: 485-495.
Hanula, J.L., Franzreb, K.E. & Pepper, W.D. (2000). Longleaf pine characteristics associated with arthropods available for Red-cockaded Woodpeckers. *J. Wildl. Manage.* **64(1)**: 60-70.
Hanula, J.L., Lipscomb, D., Franzreb, K.E. & Loeb, S.C. (2000). Diet of nestling Red-cockaded Woodpeckers at three locations. [La dieta de crías de *Picoides borealis* en tres localidades]. *J. Field Orn.* **71(1)**: 126-134. In English with Spanish summary.
Hardy, J.W. (1978). Endangered. Ivory-billed Woodpecker, *Campephilus principalis*. Pp. 10-11 in: Kale, H.W. ed. (1978). *Rare and Endangered Biota of Florida*. Vol. 2. Birds. University Press of Florida, Gainesville, Florida.
Harestad, A.S. & Keisker, D.G. (1989). Nest tree use by primary cavity-nesting birds in south central British Columbia. *Can. J. Zool.* **67(4)**: 1067-1073. In English with French summary.
Haribal, M. & Ganguli-Lachungpa, U. (1991). Black Woodpecker *Dryocopus* sp. in Jaldapara Sanctuary, west Bengal. *J. Bombay Nat. Hist. Soc.* **88(1)**: 112.
Harlow, R.F. (1983). Effects of fidelity to nest cavities on the reproductive success of the Red-cockaded Woodpecker in South Carolina. Pp. 94-96 in: Wood (1983c).
Harlow, R.F. & Lennartz, M.R. (1977). Foods of nestling Red-cockaded Woodpeckers in coastal South Carolina. *Auk* **94(2)**: 376-377.
Harlow, R.F. & Lennartz, M.R. (1983). Interspecific competition for Red-cockaded Woodpecker cavities during the nesting season in South Carolina. Pp. 41-43 in: Wood (1983c).
Harris, B. (1987). Nesting Three-toed Woodpecker. *South Dakota Bird Notes* **39(3)**: 69.
Harris, B. (1995). Pileated Woodpecker's nest in South Dakota. *South Dakota Bird Notes* **47(2)**: 28-31.
Harris, M.A. (1982). *Habitat Use among Woodpeckers in Forest Burns*. MSc thesis, University of Montana, Missoula, Montana.
Harris, R.D. (1982). *The Nesting Ecology of the Pileated Woodpecker in California*. MSc thesis, University of California, Berkeley, California.
Harris, T. (1999). Drum minor. *Birdwatch* **81**: 6-9.
Harrison, C.B. (1958). Strange behaviour of a woodpecker. *Malay. Nat. J.* **12**: 124.
Harrison, J. (1999). *A Field Guide to the Birds of Sri Lanka*. Oxford University Press, Oxford.
Harrison, J.A., Allan, D.G., Underhill, L.G., Herremans, M., Tree, A.J., Parker, V. & Brown, C.J. eds. (1997). *The Atlas of Southern African Birds Including Botswana, Lesotho, Namibia, South Africa, Swaziland and Zimbabwe*. Vol. 1. Non-Passerines. BirdLife South Africa, Johannesburg.
Harrison, J.M. (1951). Some phylogenetic trends in *Garrulus glandarius* (Linnaeus) and *Dendrocopos major* (Linnaeus). Pp. 165-172 in: Hörstadius, S. ed. (1951). *Proceedings of the X Ornithological Congress, Uppsala, June 1950*. Almqvist & Wiksell, Uppsala, Sweden.
Harrisson, T.H. (1950). Bird notes from Borneo. *Bull. Raffles Mus.* **12**: 328-335.
Harrisson, T.H. & Hartley, C.H. (1934). New races from mountain areas in Borneo. *Bull. Brit. Orn. Club* **54**: 148-160.
Hart, P. (1977). Yellow-bellied Sapsucker. *Gosse Bird Club Broadsheet* **28**: 27.
Hartert, E. & Venturi, S. (1909). Notes sur les oiseaux de la Republique Argentine. *Nov. Zool.* **16**: 159-267.
Hartup, B.K. & Natarajan, C. (1996). Glucocorticoid treatment of neurologic trauma in Northern Flickers (*Colaptes auratus*): 61 cases. *J. Wildl. Rehab.* **19(2)**: 10-12.
Harvey, W.G. (1990). *Birds in Bangladesh*. University Press Ltd, Dhaka.
Harwin, R.M. (1972). Aggressive behaviour of *Campethera bennettii*. *Ostrich* **43**: 183-184.
Hasse, H. (1961). Schwartzspecht (*Dryocopus martius*) zerstört Gelege de Schellente (*Bucephala clangula*). *J. Orn.* **102**: 368.
Hatch, H.R. & L'Arrivée, L.P. (1981). Status of the Lewis' and Red-bellied Woodpeckers in Manitoba 1929-1980. *Blue Jay* **39(4)**: 209-216.
Hauser, D.C. (1959). Reverse mounting in Red-bellied Woodpeckers. *Auk* **76**: 361.
Havelka, P. & Ruge, K. (1993). Trends der Populationsentwicklung bei Spechten (Picidae) in der Bundesrepublik Deutschland. *Beih. Veröff. Naturschutz Landschaftspflege Bad. -Württ.* **67**: 33-38.
Haverschmidt, F. (1948). Bird weights from Surinam. *Wilson Bull.* **60(4)**: 230-239.
Haverschmidt, F. (1950). Notes on the Swallow-wing, *Chelidoptera tenebrosa*, in Surinam. *Condor* **52(2)**: 74-77.
Haverschmidt, F. (1951). Notes on the life history of *Picumnus minutissimus* in Surinam. *Ibis* **93(2)**: 196-200.
Haverschmidt, F. (1953). Notes on the life history of the Blood-colored Woodpecker in Surinam. *Auk* **70(1)**: 21-25.
Haverschmidt, F. (1958). Nesting of a jacamar in a termite nest. *Condor* **60(1)**: 71.
Haverschmidt, F. (1960). Some further notes on the nesting of birds in termites' nests. *Emu* **60**: 53–54.
Haverschmidt, F. (1977). Trois nouvelles espèces qui se nourrissent de scorpions. *Oiseau et RFO* **47(2)**: 213-214.
Haverschmidt, F. & Mees, G.F. (1994). *Birds of Suriname*. VACO, Paramaribo.
Hawkins, J.A. & Ritchison, G. (1996). Provisioning of nestlings by male and female Downy Woodpeckers. *Kentucky Warbler* **72(4)**: 79-81.
Hayes, F.E. (1995). *Status, Distribution and Biogeography of the Birds of Paraguay*. Monographs in Field Ornithology **1**. American Birding Association, Albany, New York. 224 pp.
Hayes, F.E. & Hayes, W.K. (1983). Differential selection of carotenoid pigments in a leucistic Northern Flicker. *Maryland Birdlife* **39(3)**: 89-90.
Hayes, F.E. & Samad, I. (1998). Diversity, abundance and seasonality of birds in a Caribbean pine plantation and native broad-leaved forest at Trinidad, West Indies. *Bird Conserv. Int.* **8(1)**: 67-87.
Hayes, F.E. & Scharf, P.A. (1995a). The birds of Parque Nacional Ybycuí, Paraguay. *Cotinga* **4**: 14-19.
Hayes, F.E. & Scharf, P.A. (1995b). The birds of Parque Nacional Cerro Corá, Paraguay. *Cotinga* **4**: 20-24.
Hayes, F.E., Baker, W.S. & Lathrop, E.W. (1992). Food storage by Acorn Woodpeckers at the Santa Rosa Plateau Preserve, Santa Ana mountains, California. *Western Birds* **23(4)**: 165-169.
Hayes, F.E., Goodman, S.M. & López, N.E. (1990). New or noteworthy bird records from the Matogrosense region of Paraguay. *Bull. Brit. Orn. Club* **110(2)**: 94-103.
Hazevoet, C.J. (1984). Vocal behaviour of Grey-headed Woodpecker. *Dutch Birding* **6(4)**: 135-136.
Heath, M.F. & Evans, M.I. eds. (2000). *Important Bird Areas in Europe: Priority Sites for Conservation*. 2 Vols. Northern Europe and Southern Europe. BirdLife Conservation Series **8**. BirdLife International, Cambridge.
Heath, M.F., Borggreve, C. & Peet, N. (2000). *European Bird Populations: Estimates and Trends*. BirdLife Conservation Series **10**. BirdLife International, Cambridge.
Hedenstrom, A. & Lindstrom, A. (1990). High body masses of migrating Wrynecks *Jynx torquilla* in southern Sweden. *Vogelwarte* **35(3)**: 165-168.
Heigham, J.B. (1976). Birds of mid-west Nigeria. *Bull. Niger. Orn. Soc.* **12(42)**: 76-93.
Heilfurth, F. (1938). Beitrag zur Faunistik, Ökologie und Besie-delungsgeschichte der Vogelwelt der Tres-Marías Inseln (Mexico). Pp. 456-475 in: Jourdain, F.C.R. ed. (1938). *Proceedings of the VIII International Ornithological Congress, Oxford, July 1934*. Oxford University Press, Oxford.
Heim de Balsac, H. (1936). Un point du régime alimentaire et de l'éthologie du Pic épeiche. *Alauda* **8(2)**: 263-264.
Heim de Balsac, H. & Mayaud, N. (1962). *Les Oiseaux du Nord-ouest de l'Afrique*. P. Lechevalier, Paris.
Heimer, W. (1992). Zur Bestandsentwicklung des Wendehalses (*Jynx torquilla*) in Hessen. *Beih. Veröff. Naturschutz Landschaftspflege Bad.-Württ.* **66**: 19-22.
Heinrich, G. & Welch, C. (1983). A natural history and current conservation projects to save the Ivory-billed Woodpecker, *Campephilus principalis principalis*. Pp. 224-229 in: *Proc. Amer. Assoc. Zool. Parks Aquariums Ann. Conf., 1983*.
Heinze, J. (1994). Bemerkungen zu den Lautausserungen und zum Verhalten des Mittelspechts (*Dendrocopos medius*). *Limicola* **8**: 298-313.
Heisler, D.A. (1994). Costa Rican woodpecker abundances and habitat use in a fragmented landscape. *Bull. Ecol. Soc. Amer.* **75(2)**(Suppl.): 92. (Abstract).
Hellebrekers, W.P.J. (1942). Revision of the Penard oological collection from Surinam. *Zool. Med.* **24(1-2)**: 240-275.
Hellebrekers, W.P.J. & Hoogerwerf, A. (1967). *A Further Contribution to our Oological Knowledge of the Island of Java (Indonesia)*. Zoologische Verhandelingen **88**. Rijksmuseum van Natuurlijke Historie, Leiden. 164 pp.
Hellmayr, C.E. (1907a). Another contribution to the ornithology of the lower Amazons. *Novit. Zool.* **14**: 1-39.

Hellmayr, C.E. (1907b). On a collection of birds from Teffé, Rio Solimoes, Brazil. *Novit. Zool.* **14**: 40-91.
Hellmayr, C.E. (1910). *The Birds of the Rio Madeira*. Novitates Zoologicae **17**. 172 pp.
Hellmayr, C.E. (1911). *A Contribution to the Ornithology of Western Colombia*. Proceedings of the Zoological Society of London **79**. 130 pp.
Hellmayr, C.E. (1913). Critical notes on the types of little-known species of Neotropical birds, 2. *Novit. Zool.* **20**: 227-256.
Hellmayr, C.E. (1929). *A Contribution to the Ornithology of Northeastern Brazil*. Publications of the Field Museum of Natural History (Zoological Series) **255, pt. 12(18)**. 367 pp.
Hellmayr, C.E. (1933). Qu'est-ce que le *Ramphastos osculans* Gould? *Oiseau (New Ser.)* **3**: 244-251.
Hellmayr, C.E. & Seilern, J. von (1912). *Beiträge zur Ornithologie von Venezuela*. Archiv für Naturgeschichte Series A **78**. 133 pp.
Helsens, T. (1996). New information on birds in Ghana, April 1991 to October 1993. *Malimbus* **18(1)**: 1-9.
Hendricks, P. (1996). Ingestion of snow and ice by Pileated Woodpeckers and Northern Flickers. *Northwestern Naturalist* **77(1)**: 20-21.
Hendricks, P., McAuliffe, J.R. & Valiente-Banuet, A. (1990). On communal roosting and associated winter social behavior of Gray-breasted Woodpeckers. *Condor* **92(1)**: 254-255.
Henriques, L.M.P. & Oren, D.C. (1997). The avifauna of Marajo, Caviana and Mexiana islands, Amazon River Estuary, Brazil. *Rev. Bras. Biol.* **57(3)**: 357-382.
Henry, G.M. (1998). *A Guide to the Birds of Sri Lanka*. 3rd edition. Oxford University Press, Delhi.
Henshaw, H.W. (1921). Storage of acorns by the California Woodpecker. *Condor* **23(4)**: 109-118.
Heredia, J., Klavins, J. & Nieto, P. (1999). Primera descripción de la nidificación del Carpintero Negro *Dryocopus schulzi*. *Nuestras Aves* **40**: 3.
Herholdt, J.J. & Earlé, R.A. (1986). Ashy Tit and Pied Barbets roosting in a sandbank. *Ostrich* **57(1)**: 64.
Herholdt, J.J. & Earlé, R.A. (1987). The occurrence of the Crested Barbet, Steelblue Widowfinch and White-fronted Bee-eater in the Orange Free State: a possible range extension? *Mirafra* **4(3)**: 51-59.
Herklots, G.A.C. (1954). *Hong Kong Birds*. South China Morning Post Ltd, Hong Kong.
Herklots, G.A.C. (1961). *The Birds of Trinidad and Tobago*. Collins, London.
Hernández, B.E., Peterson, A.T., Navarro, A.G. & Escalante, P. (1995). Bird faunas of the humid montane forests of Mesoamerica: biogeographic patterns and priorities for conservation. *Bird Conserv. Int.* **5(2/3)**: 251-277.
Hernández, D. (1999). Listado de la avifauna de Ceja de Francisco, Sierra de los Órganos, Pinar del Río, Cuba. *Pitirre* **12(1)**: 4-7.
Hernández, E. (1989). [A new population of the Great Spotted Woodpecker (*Picoides major canariensis*) on Tenerife, Canary Islands]. *Alauda* **57(3)**: 221-222. In French.
Hernández, E.J. (1992). *A Habitat Suitability Index Model for the Red-cockaded Woodpecker*. MSc thesis, Colorado State University, Boulder, Colorado.
Herzog, S.K., Fjeldså, J., Kessler, M. & Balderrama, J.A. (1999). Ornithological surveys in the Cordillera Cocapata, Dpto. Cochabamba, Bolivia, a transition zone between humid and dry intermontane Andean habitats. *Bull. Brit. Orn. Club* **119(3)**: 162-177.
Herzog, S.K., Kessler, M., Maijer, S. & Hohnwald, S. (1997). Distributional notes on birds of Andean dry forests in Bolivia. *Bull. Brit. Orn. Club* **117(3)**: 223-235.
Hess, C.A. & James, F.C. (1998). Diet of the Red-cockaded Woodpecker in the Apalachicola National Forest. *J. Wildl. Manage.* **62(2)**: 509-517.
Hess, P. (1992). The Red-bellied Woodpecker tumbled in 1990 on southeastern Pennsylvania Christmas bird counts. *Pennsylvania Birds* **6(1)**: 15-17.
Hess, R. (1983). Verbreitung, Siedlungsdichte und Habitat des Dreizehenspechts, *Picoides tridactylus alpinus* im Kanton Schwyz. [Distribution, density and habitat of the Three-toed Woodpecker *Picoides tridactylus alpinus* in the Kanton Schwyz]. *Orn. Beob.* **80(3)**: 153-182. In German with English summary.
Hesse, E. (1912). Kritische Untersuchungen über Piciden auf Grund einer Revision des im K. Zool. Mus. Berlin befindlichen Spechtmaterials. *Mitt. Zool. Mus. Berlin* **6**: 133-261.
Heuglin, M.T. von (1861). XI. On new or little-known birds of north-eastern Africa. (Part III. The barbets, Capitonidae). *Ibis* **Ser. 1, no. 3**: 121-128.
Hickman, G.C. (1970). Egg transport recorded for the Red-bellied Woodpecker. *Wilson Bull.* **82(4)**: 463.
Higuchi, H. (1980). Colonization and coexistence of woodpeckers in the Japanese islands. *Misc. Rep. Yamashina Inst. Orn.* **12**: 139-156.
Higuchi, H. & Koike, S. (1978). Distributional records of woodpeckers in the Japanese islands and their neighbouring islands. *Tori* **27**: 27-36.
Hilkevitch, A.N. (1974). *Sexual Differences in Foraging Behavior among White-headed Woodpeckers*. MSc thesis, California State University, Long Beach, California.
Hill, M. (2001). Population sizes, status and habitat associations of forest birds in Chu Yang Sin Nature Reserve, Dak Lak Province, Vietnam. *Bird Conserv. Int.* **11(1)**: 49-70.
Hill, R.L. & Greeney, H.F. (2000). Ecuadorian birds: nesting records and egg descriptions from a lowland rainforest. *Avicult. Mag.* **106(2)**: 49-53.
Hilty, S.L. (1977). *Chlorospingus flavovirens* rediscovered, with notes on other Pacific Colombian and Cauca Valley birds. *Auk* **94(1)**: 44-49.
Hilty, S.L. (1985). Distributional changes in the Colombian avifauna: a preliminary blue list. Pp. 1000-1012 in: Buckley *et al.* (1985).
Hilty, S.L. (1997). Seasonal distribution of birds at a cloud forest locality, the Anchicayá Valley, in western Colombia. Pp. 321-344 in: Remsen (1997).
Hilty, S.L. (1999). Three bird species new to Venezuela and notes on the behaviour and distribution of other poorly known species. *Bull. Brit. Orn. Club* **119(4)**: 220-235.
Hilty, S.L. & Brown, W.L. (1986). *A Guide to the Birds of Colombia*. Princeton University Press, Princeton, New Jersey.
Himmatsinhji, M.K. (1980). Unexpected occurrence of the Golden-backed Woodpecker *Dinopium benghalense* (Linnaeus) in Kutch. *J. Bombay Nat. Hist. Soc.* **76(3)**: 514-515.
Hindwood, K.A. (1959). The nesting of birds in the nest of social insects. *Emu* **59**: 1-36.
Hines, C. (1995). Birds of the Gam Resettlement Area. *Lanioturdus* **28**: 26-38.
Hines, C. (1996). Namibia's Caprivi Strip. *Bull. African Bird Club* **3(2)**: 113-128.
Hinkelmann, C. & Fiebig, J. (2001). An early contribution to the avifauna of Paraná, Brazil. The Arkady Fiedler Expedition of 1928/1929. *Bull. Brit. Orn. Club* **121(2)**: 116-127.
Hinterkreuser, M. (1998). Bruten des Mittelspechtes (*Picoides medius*) im Sieg-Bröl-Bereich, südliches Bergisches Land (Rhein-Sieg-Kreis). *Charadrius* **34(3-4)**: 174-178.
Hitchcock, C.L. & Houston, A.I. (1994). The value of a hoard: not just energy. *Behav. Ecol.* **5(2)**: 202-205.
Hobson, K.A. & Schieck, J. (1999). Changes in bird communities in boreal mixedwood forest: harvest and wildfire effects over 30 years. *Ecol. Appl.* **9(3)**: 849-863.
Hochebner, T. (1993). Siedlungsdichte und Lebensraum einer randalpinen Population des Mittelspechts (*Picoides medius*) im niederösterreichischen Alpenvorland. [Breeding density and habitat of a submontane population of Middle Spotted Woodpecker (*Picoides medius*) in the Alpenvorland (Flyschzone) of lower Austria]. *Egretta* **36(1)**: 25-37. In German with English summary.
Hockey, P.A.R. (1996). *Birds of Southern Africa. Checklist and Alternative Names*. 2nd edition. Struik Publishers Ltd, Cape Town.
Hockey, P.A.R. (1997). New birds in Africa. The last 50 years. *Africa. Birds & Birding* **2(1)**: 39-44.
Hockey, P.A.R., Underhill, L.G., Neatherway, M. & Ryan, P.G. (1989). *Atlas of the Birds of the Southwestern Cape*. Cape Bird Club, Cape Town.
Hodgetts, J.W. (1943). Young of Great Spotted Woodpecker fed on nestling bird. *British Birds* **37**: 97.
Hoesch, W. (1957). Über die Auswirkungen der Besiedlung auf den Vogelbest in Südwest-Afrika. *J. Orn.* **98**: 279-281.
Hoffmann, T.W. (1998). *Threatened Birds of Sri Lanka National Red List*. Ceylon Bird Club, Colombo.
Hoffmann, T.W. (1999). The Brown-capped Pygmy Woodpecker *Dendrocopos nanus gymnopthalmos*. *Ceylon Bird Club Notes* **1999**: 99-100.
Höfling, E. (1991). Étude comparative du crâne chez des Ramphastidae (Aves, Piciformes). [Comparative study of the cranium of Ramphastidae (Aves, Piciformes)]. *Bonn. zool. Beitr.* **42(1)**: 55-65.
Höfling, E. (1995). *Anatomia de Cranio e da Cintura e Escapular dos Ramphastidae (Aves: Piciformes) e alguns Grupes Proximos, com Implicações Sistemáticas*. PhD thesis, Universidade de São Paulo, São Paulo.
Höfling, E. (1998). Comparative cranial anatomy of Ramphastidae and Capitonidae. Proceedings of the XXII International Ornithological Congress, Durban. *Ostrich* **69(3&4)**: 389-390.
Höfling, E. & Camargo, H.F. de A. (1993). *Aves no Campus*. Instituto de Biociencias da Universidade de São Paulo, São Paulo.
Höfling, E. & Gasc, J.P. (1984a). Biomécanique du crâne et du bec chez *Ramphastos* (Ramphastidae, Aves). I. *Gegenbaurs Morphol. Jahrbuch* **130**: 124-147.
Höfling, E. & Gasc, J.P. (1984b). Biomécanique du crâne et du bec chez *Ramphastos* (Ramphastidae, Aves). II. *Gegenbaurs Morphol. Jahrbuch* **130**: 235-262.
Höfling, E., Camargo, H.F. de A. & Imperatriz-Fonseca, V.L. (1986). *Aves na Mantiqueira*. ICI Brasil, São Paulo.
Hogstad, O. (1970). On the ecology of the Three-toed Woodpecker *Picoides tridactylus* (L.) outside the breeding season. *Nytt. Mag. Zool.* **18**: 41-50.
Hogstad, O. (1971a). Stratification in winter feeding of the Great Spotted Woodpecker *Dendrocopos major* and the Three-toed Woodpecker *Picoides tridactylus*. *Ornis Scand.* **2(2)**: 143-146.
Hogstad, O. (1971b). Trekker fra flagspetten (*Dendrocopos major*) vinternaering. *Sterna* **10**: 233-241.
Hogstad, O. (1976a). Sexual dimorphism and divergence in winter foraging behaviour of Three-toed Woodpeckers *Picoides tridactylus*. *Ibis* **118(1)**: 41-50.
Hogstad, O. (1976b). Interseksuell deling av forplantningsterritoriet hos Tretaspett. [Intersexual partitioning of the breeding territory of the Three-toed Woodpecker (*Picoides tridactylus*)]. *Sterna* **15(1)**: 5-10. In Norwegian with English summary.
Hogstad, O. (1977). Seasonal change in intersexual niche differentiation of the Three-toed Woodpecker *Picoides tridactylus*. *Ornis Scand.* **8(2)**: 101-111.
Hogstad, O. (1978). Sexual dimorphism in relation to winter foraging and territorial behavior of the Three-toed Woodpecker *Picoides tridactylus* and three *Dendrocopos* species. *Ibis* **120(2)**: 198-203.
Hogstad, O. (1983). Wing length variation and movement pattern of the Three-toed Woodpecker *Picoides tridactylus* in Fennoscandia. *Fauna Norvegica (Ser. C, Cinclus)* **6(2)**: 81-86. In English with Norwegian summary.
Hogstad, O. (1991). The effect of social dominance on foraging by the Three-toed Woodpecker *Picoides tridactylus*. *Ibis* **133(3)**: 271-276.
Hogstad, O. (1993). Why is the Three-toed Woodpecker (*Picoides tridactylus*) more sexually dimorphic than other European woodpeckers? *Baden-Württemberg* **67**: 109-118.
Hogstad, O. & Stenberg, I. (1994). Habitat selection of a viable population of White-backed Woodpeckers *Dendrocopos leucotos*. *Fauna Norvegica (Ser. C, Cinclus)* **17**: 75-94.
Hogstad, O. & Stenberg, I. (1997). Breeding success, nestling diet and parental care in the White-backed Woodpecker *Dendrocopos leucotos*. *J. Orn.* **138**: 25-38.
Holland, G. (1997). Canopy birding: exploring Zululand's forests. *Africa. Birds & Birding* **2(3)**: 52-59.
Holliday, C.S. & Tait, I.C. (1953). Note on the nidification of *Buccanodon olivacea woodwardi* (Shelley). *Ostrich* **24**: 115-117.
Hollom, P.A.D., Porter, R.F., Christensen, S. & Willis, I. (1988). *Birds of the Middle East and North Africa*. Buteo Books, Vermillion, South Dakota.
Holmes, D.A. (1973). Bird notes from southernmost Thailand, 1972. *Nat. Hist. Bull. Siam Soc.* **25**: 39-66.
Holmes, D.A. (1994). A review of the land birds of the west Sumatran islands. *Kukila* **7(1)**: 28-46.
Holmes, D.A. (1996). Sumatra bird report. *Kukila* **8**: 9-56.
Holmes, D.A. (1997). Kalimantan bird report - 2. *Kukila* **9**: 141-169.
Holmes, D.A. & van Balen, S. (1996). The birds of Tinjil and Deli Islands, West Java. *Kukila* **8**: 117-126.
Holmes, D.A. & Burton, K. (1987). Recent notes on the avifauna of Kalimantan. *Kukila* **3(1-2)**: 2-32.
Holmes, D.A. & Phillipps, K. (1996). *The Birds of Sulawesi*. Oxford University Press, Kuala Lumpur.
Holmes, P.R. (1986). The avifauna of the Suru River Valley, Ladakh. *Forktail* **2**: 21-41.
Holmes, R.T. & Sherry, T.W. (2001). Thirty-year bird population trends in an unfragmented temperate deciduous forest: importance of habitat change. *Auk* **118(3)**: 589-609.
Holsten, B., Braünlich, A. & Huxham, M. (1991). Rondo Forest Reserve, Tanzania: an ornithological note including new records of the East Coast Akalat *Sheppardia gunningi*, the Spotted Ground Thrush *Turdus fischeri*, and the Rondo Green Barbet *Stactolaema olivacea woodwardi*. *Scopus* **14**: 125-128.
Holt, E.G. (1928). An ornithological survey of the Serra do Itatiaya, Brazil. *Bull. Amer. Mus. Nat. Hist.* **58**: 251-326.
Hölzinger, J. (1990). Weissrückenspecht (*Dendrocopos leucotos*, Bechstein, 1803). Brutvogel auf dem Peloponnes. *Kartierung Mediterr. Brutvögel* **4**: 19-22.
Hölzinger, J. (1992a). Brutvorkommen des Wendehalses (*Jynx torquilla*) an seiner südlichen Arealgrenze in Griechenland. [Breeding occurrence of the Wryneck (*Jynx torquilla*) at the southern border of its range in Greece]. *Beih. Veröff. Naturschutz Landschaftspflege Bad. -Württ.* **66**: 43-46.
Hölzinger, J. (1992b). Zur Nestlingsnahrung des Wendehalses (*Jynx torquilla*). *Beih. Veröff. Naturschutz Landschaftspflege Bad. -Württ.* **66**: 47-50.
Hooge, P.N. (1989). *Movement Patterns and Nest Site Selection in the Cooperatively Breeding Acorn Woodpecker* Melanerpes formicivorus. MSc thesis, University of California, Berkeley, California.
Hooge, P.N. (1991). The effects of radio weight and harnesses on time budgets and movements of Acorn Woodpeckers. *J. Field Orn.* **62(2)**: 230-238. In English with Spanish summary.
Hooge, P.N. (1995). *Dispersal Dynamics of the Cooperatively Breeding Acorn Woodpecker*. PhD dissertation, University of California, Berkeley, California.
Hooge, P.N., Stanback, M.T. & Koenig, W.D. (1999). Nest-site selection in the Acorn Woodpecker. *Auk* **116(1)**: 45-54.
Hoogerwerf, A. (1948). Contribution to the knowledge of the distribution of birds on the island of Java, with remarks on some new birds. *Treubia* **19**: 83-137.
Hoogerwerf, A. (1949). *Een Bijdrage tot de Oölogie van het Eiland Java*. Plantentuin van Indonesië, De Kon, Buitenzorg, Netherlands.
Hoogerwerf, A. (1963). The Golden-backed Woodpecker, *Chrysocolaptes lucidus* (Scopoli) in the Kangean Archipelago. *Bull. Brit. Orn. Club* **83(6)**: 112-114.
Hoogerwerf, A. (1969). On the ornithology of the Rhino Sanctuary Udjung Kulon in West Java (Indonesia). *Nat. Hist. Bull. Siam Soc.* **23**: 9-65.
Hooper, D.F. (1988). Boreal Chickadees feeding with Three-toed Woodpeckers. *Blue Jay* **46(2)**: 85.
Hooper, R.G. (1982). Use of dead cavity trees by Red-cockaded Woodpeckers. *Wildl. Soc. Bull.* **10(2)**: 163-164.
Hooper, R.G. (1983). Colony formation by Red-cockaded Woodpeckers: hypothesis and management implications. Pp. 72-77 in: Wood (1983c).
Hooper, R.G. (1988). Longleaf pines used for cavities by Red-cockaded Woodpeckers. *J. Wildl. Manage.* **52(3)**: 392-398.
Hooper, R.G. & Harlow, R.F. (1986). *Foraging Stands Selected by Foraging Red-cockaded Woodpeckers*. Research Paper **SE-259**. US Department of Agriculture, Forest Service.
Hooper, R.G. & Lennartz, M.R. (1981). Foraging behavior of the Red-cockaded Woodpecker in South Carolina. *Auk* **98(2)**: 321-334.
Hooper, R.G. & Lennartz, M.R. (1983). Roosting behavior of Red-cockaded Woodpecker clans with insufficient cavities. *J. Field Orn.* **54(1)**: 72-76.
Hooper, R.G. & Lennartz, M.R. (1995). Short-term response of a high density Red-cockaded Woodpecker population to loss of foraging habitat. Pp. 283-289 in: Kulhavy *et al.* (1995).
Hooper, R.G., Krusac, D.L. & Carlson, D.L. (1991). An increase in a population of Red-cockaded Woodpeckers. *Wildl. Soc. Bull.* **19(3)**: 277-286.

Hooper, R.G., Lennartz, M.R. & Muse, H.D. (1991). Heart rot and cavity tree selection by Red-cockaded Woodpeckers. *J. Wildl. Manage.* **55(2)**: 323-327.

Hooper, R.G., Niles, L.V., Harlow, R.F. & Wood, G.A. (1982). Home ranges of Red-cockaded Woodpeckers in coastal South Carolina. *Auk* **99(4)**: 675-682.

Hooper, R.G., Robinson, A.F. & Jackson, J.A. (1980). *The Red-cockaded Woodpecker: Notes on Life History and Management*. General Report SA-GR9. US Forest Service, Atlanta, Georgia.

Hopkins, M. (1998). Buff-throated Sunbird *Nectarinia adelberti* and Fire-bellied Woodpecker *Dendropicos pyrrhogaster* in Cameroon. *Malimbus* **20(2)**: 124-125.

Hopkins, M.L. & Lynn, T.E. (1971). Some characteristics of Red-cockaded Woodpecker cavity trees and management implications in South Carolina. Pp. 140-169 in: Thompson (1971).

Hornbuckle, J. (1999). The birds of Abra Patricia and the upper río Mayo, San Martín, north Peru. *Cotinga* **12**: 11-28.

Horne, J.F.M. & Short, L.L. (1988). Afrotropical bird vocalisations: a review of current problems. *Bioacoustics* **1/2**: 159-170.

Horstkotte, E. (1973). Untersuchungen zur tagesaktivität des Grünspechtes (*Picus viridis*). [Investigations into the daily activities of the Green Woodpecker *Picus viridis*]. *Orn. Mitt.* **25(8)**: 159-169. In German with English summary.

Houde, P. & Olson, S.L. (1988). Small arboreal nonpasserine birds from the Early Tertiary of western North America. Pp. 2030-2036 in: Ouellet (1988).

Hovis, J.A. (1982). *Population Biology and Habitat Characteristics of the Red-cockaded Woodpecker (Picoides borealis) in Pine Forests of North Florida*. MSc thesis, University of Florida, Gainesville, Florida.

Hovis, J.A. (1996). Red-cockaded Woodpecker, *Picoides borealis*. Pp. 81-102 in: Rodgers *et al.* (1996).

Hovis, J.A. & Labisky, R.F. (1985). Vegetative associations of Red-cockaded Woodpecker colonies in Florida. *Wildl. Soc. Bull.* **13(3)**: 307-314.

Howard, T.E. (1980). Sisyphean behavior in a Red-headed Woodpecker. *Chat* **44(1)**: 17-18.

Howe, H.F. (1977). Bird activity and seed dispersal of a tropical wet forest tree. *Ecology* **58**: 541-550.

Howe, H.F. (1981). Dispersal of a Neotropical nutmeg (*Virola sebifera*) by birds. *Auk* **98(1)**: 88-98.

Howe, H.F. (1983). *Ramphastos swainsonii* (Dios Tede, Toucan de Swainson, Chestnut-mandibled Toucan). Pp. 603-604 in: Janzen (1983).

Howe, S., Kilgore, D.L. & Colby, C. (1987). Respiratory gas concentrations and temperature within the nest cavities of the Northern Flicker (*Colaptes auratus*). *Can. J. Zool.* **65**: 1541-1547.

Howell, A.B. (1943). Starlings and woodpeckers. *Auk* **60(1)**: 90-91.

Howell, S.N.G. & Webb, S. (1992). New and noteworthy bird records from Guatemala and Honduras. *Bull. Brit. Orn. Club* **112(1)**: 42-49.

Howell, S.N.G. & Webb, S. (1995). *A Guide to the Birds of Mexico and Northern Central America*. Oxford University Press, New York.

Howell, T.R. (1952). Natural history and differentiation in Yellow-bellied Sapsucker. *Condor* **54(5)**: 237-282.

Howell, T.R. (1953). Racial and sexual differences in migration in *Sphyrapicus varius*. *Auk* **70(2)**: 118-126.

Howell, T.R. (1957). Birds of a second-growth rain forest area of Nicaragua. *Condor* **59(2)**: 73-111.

Howell, T.R. (1971). An ecological study of the birds of the lowland pine savanna adjacent rain forest in northeastern Nicaragua. *Living Bird* **10**: 185-242.

Hoy, G. (1968). Über Brutbiologie und Eier einiger Vögel aus Nordwest-Argentina. *J. Orn.* **109**: 425-433.

Hoyt, J.S. (2000). *Habitat Associations of Black-backed* Picoides arcticus *and Three-toed* P. tridactylus *Woodpeckers in the Northeastern Boreal Forest of Alberta*. MSc thesis, University of Alberta, Edmonton, Alberta.

Hoyt, J.S.Y. (1940). *A Study of the Pileated Woodpecker* Ceophloeus pileatus *(Linnaeus)*. MSc thesis, Cornell University, Ithaca, New York.

Hoyt, J.S.Y. (1944). Preliminary notes on the development of nestling Pileated Woodpeckers. *Auk* **61(3)**: 376-384.

Hoyt, J.S.Y. (1948). *Further Studies of the Pileated Woodpecker*. PhD dissertation, Cornell University, Ithaca, New York.

Hoyt, J.S.Y. & Hoyt, S.F. (1951). Age records of Pileated Woodpeckers. *Bird-Banding* **22**: 125.

Hoyt, S.F. (1952). An additional age record of a Pileated Woodpecker. *Bird-Banding* **23**: 29.

Hoyt, S.F. (1953). Forehead color of the Pileated Woodpecker (*Dryocopus pileatus*). *Auk* **70(2)**: 209-210.

Hoyt, S.F. (1957). The ecology of the Pileated Woodpecker. *Ecology* **38**: 246-256.

Hüe, F. (1949-1950). Le tambourinage du Pic épeichette *Dendrocopos minor* dans le Midi de la France. *Alauda* **17-18**: 116-117.

Hüe, F. & Étchécopar, R.D. (1970). *Les Oiseaux du Proche et du Moyen Orient de la Méditerranée aux Contreforts de l'Himalaya*. Éditions N. Boubée, Paris.

Hughes, R. (1988). Hand-rearing the Crimson-rumped Toucanet *Aulacorhynchus haematopygus* at Padstow Bird Gardens, Cornwall. *Avicult. Mag.* **94(4)**: 183-189.

Humphrey, P.S. (1946). Observations at the nest of a Pileated Woodpecker. *Migrant* **17**: 43-46.

Humphrey, P.S., Bridge, D., Reynolds, P.W. & Peterson, R.T. (1970). *Birds of Isla Grande (Tierra del Fuego)*. University of Kansas Museum of Natural History, Lawrence, Kansas.

Hunn, E.S., Acuca, D. & Escalante, P. (2001). Birds of San Juan Mixtepec, district of Miahuatlán, Oaxaca, Mexico. *Cotinga* **16**: 14-26. In English with Spanish summary.

Hunter, W.C. (1984). *Status of Nine Bird Species of Special Concern Along the Colorado River*. Wildlife Management Branch Administrative Report CA W-065-R-01. California Department of Fish & Game, Sacramento, California.

Husak, M.S. (1995). Evidence of possible egg predation by Golden-fronted Woodpeckers. *Bull. Texas Orn. Soc.* **28**: 55-56.

Husak, M.S. (1996). Breeding season displays of the Golden-fronted Woodpecker. *Southwest. Nat.* **41**: 441-442.

Husak, M.S. (1997a). *Seasonal Variation in Territorial Behavior of the Golden-fronted Woodpecker*. MSc thesis, Angelo State University, San Angelo, Texas.

Husak, M.S. (1997b). Age of first breeding in the Golden-fronted Woodpecker. *Texas J. Sci.* **49(2)**: 168-169.

Husak, M.S. (1997c). Predation of Golden-fronted Woodpecker nestlings by a Texas rat snake. *Bull. Texas Orn. Soc.* **30**: 17-18.

Husak, M.S. (1997d). Observations of winter territorial interactions between a Red-headed Woodpecker and Golden-fronted Woodpeckers. *Texas J. Sci.* **49(4)**: 348-350.

Husak, M.S. (1999). Observation of survival by a Golden-fronted Woodpecker with an injured tongue. *Bull. Texas Orn. Soc.* **32(1)**: 42-44.

Husak, M.S. (2000). Seasonal variation in territorial behavior of Golden-fronted Woodpeckers in west-central Texas. *Southwest. Nat.* **45(1)**: 30-38.

Husak, M.S. & Maxwell, T.C. (1998). Golden-fronted Woodpecker (*Melanerpes aurifrons*). No. **373** in: Poole, A.F. & Gill, F.B. eds. (1998). *The Birds of North America*. Vol. 10. Academy of Natural Sciences & American Ornithologists' Union, Philadelphia & Washington, D.C.

Hussain, S.A. (1978). Orange-rumped Honeyguide (*Indicator xanthonotus*) in the Garhwal Himalayas. *J. Bombay Nat. Hist. Soc.* **75(2)**: 487-488.

Hussain, S.A. (1988). A comparative look at the Himalayan Orange-rumped Honeyguide *Indicator xanthonotus* and its congenerics in Africa. Page 10 in: *Abstracts of the VII Pan-African Ornithological Congress, Nairobi, 1988*.

Hussain, S.A. & Ali, S. (1979). Beehive predation by wasps (Genus *Vespa*) and its possible benefits to honeyguides (Indicatoridae) in Bhutan. *J. Bombay Nat. Hist. Soc.* **76**: 157-159.

Hussain, S.A. & Ali, S. (1983). Some notes on the ecology and status of the Orange-rumped Honeyguide *Indicator xanthonotus* in the Himalayas. *J. Bombay Nat. Hist. Soc.* **80(3)**: 564-574.

Hussain, S.A., Panday, J.D. & Shekar, P.B. (1977). Extension of range of the Large Yellow-naped Woodpecker *Picus flavinucha* (Gould). *J. Bombay Nat. Hist. Soc.* **73(2)**: 394.

Hustler, K., Tree, A.J. & Irwin, M.P.S. (1992). Fourth report of the OAZ Rarities Committee. *Honeyguide* **38**: 113-118.

Hutchinson, G. (1950). Woodpeckers in Johore. *Malay. Nat. J.* **5**: 36-37.

Hutto, R.L. (1980). Winter habitat distribution of migratory land birds in western Mexico, with special reference to small foliage-gleaning insectivores. Pp. 181-203 in: Keast, A. & Morton, E.S. eds. (1980). *Migrant Birds in the Neotropics: Ecology, Behavior, Distribution, and Conservation*. Smithsonian Institution Press, Washington, D.C.

Hutto, R.L. (1992). Habitat distributions of migratory landbird species in western Mexico. Pp. 221-239 in: Hagan & Johnston (1992).

Hutto, R.L. (1995). Composition of bird communities following stand-replacement fires in northern Rocky Mountain (USA) conifer forests. *Conserv. Biol.* **9**: 1041-1058.

Hutto, R.L. (1998). Using landbirds as an indicator species group. Pp. 75-92 in: Marzluff, J.M. & Sallabanks, R. eds. (1998). *Avian Conservation: Research and Management*. Island Press, Washington, D.C. & Covelo, California.

Ibáñez, G. (2000). Nuevos registros de aves para la costa este del estado de Yucatán, México. *Cotinga* **14**: 52-56. In Spanish with English summary.

Ichida, N. (1997). Sites to save: Yambaru, Japan. *World Birdwatch* **19(4)**: 6-7.

Ihering, H. von (1900). *Catalogo Critico-comparativo dos Ninhos e Ovos dos Aves do Brasil*. Revista do Museu Paulista **4**. Universidade de São Paulo, São Paulo. 110 pp.

Ihering, H. von & Ihering, R. von (1907). *As Aves do Brazil. Catálogo da Fauna Brasileira*. Vol 1. Museu Paulista, São Paulo.

Ikehara, S. (1975). Noguchigera (*Sapheopipo noguchii*). *The Prompt Record of a Fact Finding Research. Part 1*. Educational Committee of Okinawa Prefecture, Naha, Japan.

Ikehara, S. (1988). [Interim report to the bird survey at Mount Yonaha-dake, northern Okinawa Island]. Pp. 63-76 in: *Habitat and Environmental Survey on Special Birds III. Interim Report*. Division of Nature Conservation, Okinawa Prefecture, Naha, Japan. In Japanese.

Ikehara, S., Abe, T., Shimojana, M., Yonashiro, Y. & Miyagi, S. (1976). Nest site of Noguchigera or Okinawa Woodpecker, *Sapheopipo noguchii*. *Biol. Mag. Okinawa* **14**: 55-60.

Inglis, C.M. (1931). The nesting of the Malabar Heart-spotted Woodpecker *Hemicircus canente cordatus* in Travancore. *J. Bombay Nat. Hist. Soc.* **35(1)**: 207-208.

Ingold, D.J. (1987). Documented double-broodedness in Red-headed Woodpeckers. *J. Field Orn.* **58(2)**: 234-235. In English with Spanish summary.

Ingold, D.J. (1989a). *Nesting Phenology and Competition for Nest Sites among Red-headed and Red-bellied Woodpeckers and European Starlings in East-central Mississippi*. PhD dissertation, Mississippi State University, Mississippi.

Ingold, D.J. (1989b). Nesting phenology and competition for nest sites among Red-headed and Red-bellied Woodpeckers and European Starlings. *Auk* **106(2)**: 209-217.

Ingold, D.J. (1989c). Woodpecker and European Starling competition for nest sites. *Sialia* **11(1)**: 3-6.

Ingold, D.J. (1990). Simultaneous use of nest trees by breeding Red-headed and Red-bellied Woodpeckers and European Starlings. *Condor* **92(1)**: 252-253.

Ingold, D.J. (1991). Nest-site fidelity in Red-headed and Red-bellied Woodpeckers. *Wilson Bull.* **103(1)**: 118-122.

Ingold, D.J. (1994a). Nest site characteristics of Red-bellied and Red-headed Woodpeckers and Northern Flickers in east-central Ohio. *Ohio J. Sci.* **94**: 2-7.

Ingold, D.J. (1994b). Influence of nest-site competition between European Starlings and woodpeckers. *Wilson Bull.* **106(2)**: 227-241.

Ingold, D.J. (1996). Delayed nesting decreases reproductive success in Northern Flickers: implications for competition with European Starlings. *J. Field Orn.* **67(2)**: 321-326.

Ingold, D.J. (1998). The influence of starlings on flicker reproduction when both naturally excavated cavities and artificial nest boxes are available. *Wilson Bull.* **110(2)**: 218-225.

Ingold, D.J. & Densmore, R.J. (1992). Competition between European Starlings and native woodpeckers for nest cavities in Ohio. *Sialia* **14(2)**: 43-48, 54.

Ingold, D.J. & Jackson, J.A. (1986). An unusual Red-bellied Woodpecker nest. *Miss. Kite* **16(1)**: 17-18.

Ingold, J.L. & Weise, C.M. (1985). Observations on feather color variation in a presumed Common Flicker intergrade. *J. Field Orn.* **56(4)**: 403-405.

Inouye, D.W. (1976). Nonrandom orientation of entrance holes to woodpecker nests in aspen trees. *Condor* **78(1)**: 101-102.

Inouye, R.S., Huntley, N.J. & Inouye, D.W. (1981). Non-random orientation of Gila Woodpecker nest entrances in saguaro cacti. *Condor* **83(1)**: 88-89.

Inskipp, C. (1989). *Nepal's Forest Birds: their Status and Conservation*. ICBP Monograph **4**, Cambridge.

Inskipp, C. & Inskipp, T. (1991). *Birds of Nepal*. Christopher Helm, London.

Inskipp, C. & Inskipp, T. (1993). Birds recorded during a visit to Bhutan in spring 1993. *Forktail* **9**: 121-143.

Inskipp, C. & Inskipp, T. (1998). Birds of Sagarmatha National Park. *Ibisbill* **1**: 3-34.

Inskipp, C., Inskipp, T. & Grimmett, R. (1999). *Birds of Bhutan*. Christopher Helm, London.

Inskipp, T., Lindsey, N. & Duckworth, W. (1996). *An Annotated Checklist of the Birds of the Oriental Region*. Oriental Bird Club, Sandy, UK.

Irwin, M.P.S. (1978). Distribution, overlap and ecological replacement in Bennett's Woodpecker *Campethera bennettii* and the Golden-tailed Woodpecker *Campethera abingoni* in Rhodesia. *Honeyguide* **93**: 21-28.

Irwin, M.P.S. (1981). *The Birds of Zimbabwe*. Quest, Salisbury.

Irwin, M.P.S. (1996). More on yellow-headed Black-collared Barbets. *Honeyguide* **42**: 122.

Irwin, M.P.S. (1998). Whyte's Barbet eating millipede. *Honeyguide* **44**: 30-31.

Irwin, M.P.S. & Benson, C.W. (1967). Notes on the birds of Zambia, Part III. *Arnoldia, Rhodesia* **3(4)**: 1-30.

Isack, H.A. (1987). *The Biology of the Greater Honeyguide* Indicator indicator *with Emphasis on the Guiding Behaviour*. PhD thesis, Oxford University, Oxford.

Isack, H.A. (1988a). The Greater Honeyguide's dilemma. Pp. 2768-2780 in: Ouellet (1988).

Isack, H.A. (1988b). Territorial behavior of the Greater Honeyguide *Indicator indicator*. Page 11 in: *Abstracts of the VII Pan-African Ornithological Congress, Nairobi, 1988*.

Isack, H.A. (1998). Co-evolution of man, bird, bee and impending death of a unique symbiosis. Proceedings of the XXII International Ornithological Congress, Durban 1998. *Ostrich* **69(1&2)**: 74. (Abstract).

Isack, H.A. (1999). The role of culture, traditions and local knowledge in co-operative honey-hunting between man and honeyguide: a case study of Boran community of northern Kenya. Pp. 1351-1357 in: Adams & Slotow (1999).

Isack, H.A. & Reyer, H.U. (1989). Honeyguides and honey gatherers: interspecific communication in a symbiotic relationship. *Science* **243**: 1344-1346.

Ishida, K. (1989). The protection of and research strategy for the populations of *Dendrocopos leucotos owstoni* and *Sapheopipo noguchii*. *Strix* **8**: 249-260.

Ishida, K. (1990a). The status of woodpeckers in Japan. Pp. 13-20 in: Carlson & Aulén (1990).

Ishida, K. (1990b). Woodpecker activities and forest structure, with regard to recording techniques for conservation research. Pp. 103-115 in: Carlson & Aulén (1990).

Ishida, K. (1994). Japanese Pygmy Woodpecker is distributed also on small islands and city parks, has packed and wide vegetation habitat use, strong pair bond and female dominated sexual dimorphism. Page 240 in: Dittami *et al.* (1994).

Ishida, K., Ueta, M. & Kanai, Y. (1994). The estimated population and distribution of White-backed Woodpeckers on Amami Island. Pp. 69-74 in: *Survey of the Status and Habitat Conditions of Threatened Species, 1993*. Environment Agency, Tokyo.

Ishigaki, K., Kusumato, Y, Ichinose, K. & Saitoh, T. (1987). [Reproductive and morphological description on a family of Black Woodpecker]. *Res. Bull. Coll. Exp. For. Hokkaido Univ.* **41(1)**: 225-230. In Japanese with English summary.

Iso, K. & Fujimaki, Y. (1990). [Breeding habitats and nest tree characteristics of *Dryocopus martius* in central Hokkaido]. *Jap. J. Orn.* **38(4)**: 157-165. In Japanese with English summary.

Ito, Y., Miyagi, K. & Ota, H. (2000). Imminent extinction crisis among the endemic species of the forests of Yanbaru, Okinawa, Japan. *Oryx* **34**: 305-316.

Ivanchev, V.P. (1995). [Nest-site selection, nest-hole construction, and excavation behaviour of the Black Woodpecker *Dryocopus martius* in the Oka Nature Reserve]. *Russ. J. Orn.* **4(3/4)**: 97-102. In Russian with English summary.

Iwinski, D. & Iwinski, B. (1984). Too many toucans. *AFA Watchbird* **11**: 18-20.

Jackman, S.M. (1974). *Woodpeckers of the Pacific Northwest: their Characteristics and their Role in the Forests*. MSc thesis, Oregon State University, Corvallis, Oregon.

Jackson, F.J. & Sclater, W.L. (1938). *The Birds of Kenya Colony and the Uganda Protectorate*. 3 Vols. Gurney & Jackson, London.

Jackson, J.A. (1970a). A quantitative study of the foraging ecology of Downy Woodpeckers. *Ecology* **51**: 318-323.

Jackson, J.A. (1970b). *Character Variation in the Hairy Woodpecker (*Dendrocopos villosus*)*. PhD dissertation, University of Kansas, Lawrence, Kansas.

Jackson, J.A. (1970c). Observations at a nest of the Red-headed Woodpecker. Pp. 3-10 in: *Annual Report of the University of Kansas Museum of Natural History (1968-1969)*.

Jackson, J.A. (1970d). Some aspects of the population ecology of Downy Woodpeckers in relation to a feeding station. *Iowa Bird Life* **40**: 27-34.

Jackson, J.A. (1970e). Predation of a black rat snake on Yellow-shafted Flicker nestlings. *Wilson Bull.* **82(3)**: 329-330.

Jackson, J.A. (1971). The evolution, taxonomy, distribution, past populations and current status of the Red-cockaded Woodpecker. Pp. 4-29 in: Thompson (1971).

Jackson, J.A. (1974). Gray rat snakes versus Red-cockaded Woodpeckers: predator-prey adaptions. *Auk* **91(2)**: 342-347.

Jackson, J.A. (1975). Red-bellied Woodpecker with broken beak excavates cavity. *Inl. Bird Banding News* **47**: 222-223.

Jackson, J.A. (1976a). Rights-of-way management for an endangered species: the Red-cockaded Woodpecker. Pp. 247-252 in: *Proceedings of the Symposium on Environmental Concerns in Rights-of-way Management*. Mississippi State University, Mississippi.

Jackson, J.A. (1976b). How to determine the status of a woodpecker nest. *Living Bird* **15**: 205-221.

Jackson, J.A. (1976c). A comparison of some aspects of the breeding ecology of Red-headed and Red-bellied Woodpeckers in Kansas. *Condor* **78(1)**: 67-76.

Jackson, J.A. (1977a). Red-cockaded Woodpeckers and pine red heart disease. *Auk* **94(1)**: 160-163.

Jackson, J.A. (1977b). Determination of the status of Red-cockaded Woodpecker colonies. *J. Wildl. Manage.* **41(3)**: 448-452.

Jackson, J.A. (1978a). Analysis of the distribution and population status of the Red-cockaded Woodpecker. Pp. 101-111 in: Odom, R.R. & Landers, L. eds. (1978). *Proceedings of the Nongame and Endangered Wildlife Symposium*. Technical Bulletin **WL-4**. Georgia Department of Natural Resources, Game and Fish Division.

Jackson, J.A. (1978b). Predation by a gray rat snake on Red-cockaded Woodpecker nestlings. *Bird-Banding* **49**: 187-188.

Jackson, J.A. (1978c). Competition for cavities and Red-cockaded Woodpecker management. Pp. 103-112 in: Temple, S.A. ed. (1978). *Endangered Birds: Management Techniques for Threatened Species*. University of Wisconsin Press, Madison, Wisconsin.

Jackson, J.A. (1979). Age characteristics of Red-cockaded Woodpeckers. *Bird-Banding* **50(1)**: 23-29.

Jackson, J.A. (1983a). Morphological and behavioral development of post-fledging Red-cockaded Woodpeckers. Pp. 30-37 in: Wood (1983c).

Jackson, J.A. (1983b). Commensal feeding of Brown-headed Nuthatches with Red-cockaded Woodpeckers. Page 101 in: Wood (1983c).

Jackson, J.A. (1986). Biopolitics, management of federal land, and the conservation of the Red-cockaded Woodpecker. *Amer. Birds* **40(5)**: 1162-1168.

Jackson, J.A. (1987). The Red-cockaded Woodpecker. Pp. 479-493 in: *Audubon Wildlife Report 1987*. The National Audubon Society, New York.

Jackson, J.A. (1988). The history of Ivory-billed Woodpeckers in Mississippi. *Miss. Kite* **18(1)**: 3-10.

Jackson, J.A. (1990a). Habitat conditions in the vicinity of Ivory-billed Woodpecker sightings in eastern Cuba. *Pitirre* **3(3)**: 7. (Abstract).

Jackson, J.A. (1990b). Intercolony movements of Red-cockaded Woodpeckers in South Carolina. *J. Field Orn.* **61(2)**: 149-155. In English with Spanish summary.

Jackson, J.A. (1991a). The history of the Ivory-billed Woodpecker in Cuba. *Pitirre* **4(3)**: 6. (Abstract).

Jackson, J.A. (1991b). Will-o'-the-wisp. *Living Bird Quarterly* **10(1)**: 29-32.

Jackson, J.A. (1992a). The Hairy Woodpecker in the Bahamas. *Pitirre* **5(3)**: 12. (Abstract).

Jackson, J.A. (1992b). Morphological variation in the Ivory-billed Woodpecker. *Mississippi Acad. Sci. J.* **37(1)**: 65. (Abstract).

Jackson, J.A. (1994a). Red-cockaded Woodpecker (*Picoides borealis*). No. **85** in: Poole, A.F. & Gill, F.B. eds. (1994). *The Birds of North America*. Vol. 3. Academy of Natural Sciences & American Ornithologists' Union, Philadelphia & Washington, D.C.

Jackson, J.A. (1994b). Up with Downies. *Birder's World* **8(1)**: 12-16.

Jackson, J.A. (1996). Ivory-billed Woodpecker, *Campephilus principalis*. Pp. 103-112 in: Rodgers *et al.* (1996).

Jackson, J.A. (1997a). A hankerin' to hammer. *Birder's World* **11(2)**: 16-21.

Jackson, J.A. (1997b). Backyard survivor. *Birder's World* **11(5)**: 18-22.

Jackson, J.A. & Davis, W.E. (1998). Range expansion of the Red-bellied Woodpecker. *Bird Obs.* **26(1)**: 4-12.

Jackson, J.A. & Hoover, E.E. (1975). A potentially harmful effect of suet on woodpeckers. *Bird-Banding* **46(2)**: 131-134.

Jackson, J.A. & Jackson, B.J.S. (1986). Why do Red-cockaded Woodpeckers need old trees? *Wildl. Soc. Bull.* **14(3)**: 318-322.

Jackson, J.A. & Jackson, B.J.S. (1994). Kleptoparasitism of an American Robin by a Red-headed Woodpecker. *Miss. Kite* **24**: 21-22.

Jackson, J.A., Baker, W.W., Carter, V., Cherry, T. & Hopkins, M.L. (1979). *Recovery Plan for the Red-cockaded Woodpecker*. US Fish & Wildlife Service, Atlanta, Georgia.

Jackson, J.A., Lennartz, M.R. & Hooper, R.G. (1979). Tree age and cavity initiation by Red-cockaded Woodpeckers. *J. Forestry* **77(2)**: 102-103.

Jackson, M.C.A. (1967). Occurrence of the Wryneck *Jynx torquilla* Linnaeus in Kerala State, south India. *J. Bombay Nat. Hist. Soc.* **64(2)**: 367-368.

Jacobs, M.D. & Walker, J.S. (1999). Density estimates of birds inhabiting fragments of cloud forest in southern Ecuador. *Bird Conserv. Int.* **9(1)**: 73-79.

Jahn, O., Robbins, M.B., Mena, P., Coopmans, P., Ridgely, R.S. & Schuchmann, K.L. (2000). Status, ecology and vocalizations of the Five-coloured Barbet *Capito quinticolor* in Ecuador, with notes on the Orange-fronted Barbet *C. squamatus*. *Bull. Brit. Orn. Club* **120(1)**: 16-22.

James, D.A. & Neal, J.C. (1989). *Update of the Status of the Red-Cockaded Woodpecker in Arkansas*. Final report **AR E-001**. Arkansas Game & Fish Commission, Little Rock, Arkansas.

James, F.C. (1970). Geographic size variation in birds and its relationships to climate. *Ecology* **51**: 365-390.

James, F.C. (1991). Signs of trouble in the largest remaining population of Red-cockaded Woodpeckers. *Auk* **108(2)**: 419-423.

James, F.C. (1995). The status of the Red-cockaded Woodpecker in 1990 and the prospect for recovery. Pp. 439-451 in: Kulhavy *et al.* (1995).

James, F.C., Hess, C.A. & Kufrin, D. (1997). Species-centered environmental analysis: indirect effects of fire history on Red-cockaded Woodpeckers. *Ecol. Appl.* **7(1)**: 118-129.

Jamieson, I.G. (1999). Reproductive skew models and inter-species variation in adjustment of individual clutch sizes in joint-nesting birds. Pp. 2894-2909 in: Adams & Slotow (1999).

Janos, M. (1991). An instance of food caching in a Lewis' Woodpecker (*Melanerpes lewis*). *Colorado Field Orn. J.* **25(2)**: 43-44.

Janssen, R.B. (1981). A hybrid Red-shafted x Yellow-shafted Flicker. *Loon* **53(2)**: 117-118.

Janzen, D.H. ed. (1983). *Costa Rican Natural History*. University of Chicago Press, Chicago, Illinois.

Järvinen, O., Kuusela, K. & Väisänen, R.A. (1977). Metsien rakenteen muutoksen vaikutus pesimälinnustoomme viimeisten 30 vuoden aikana. [Effects of modern forestry on the numbers of breeding birds in Finland in 1945-1975]. *Silva Fenn.* **11**: 284-294. In Finnish with English summary.

Javed, S. & Rahmani, A.R. (1998). Conservation of the avifauna of Dudwa National Park, India. *Forktail* **14**: 55-64.

Jayson, E.A. & Mathew, D.N. (2000). Diversity and species-abundance distribution of birds in the tropical forests of Silent Valley, Kerala. *J. Bombay Nat. Hist. Soc.* **97(3)**: 390-399.

Jehl, J.R. (1979). Pine cones as granaries for Acorn Woodpeckers. *Western Birds* **10(4)**: 219-220.

Jenkins, D.V. & de Silva, G.S. (1978). An annotated check-list of the birds of the Mount Kinabalu National Park, Sabah, Malaysia. Pp. 347-402 in: Dingley, E.R. ed. (1978). *Kinabalu, Summit of Borneo*. Monograph of Sabah Society, Sabah.

Jenkins, H.O. (1906). Variation in the Hairy Woodpecker (*Dryobates villosus* and subspecies). *Auk* **23(2)**: 161-171.

Jenkins, J.M. (1979). Foraging behavior of male and female Nuttall Woodpeckers. *Auk* **96(2)**: 418-420.

Jenni, L. (1981). Das Skelettmuskelsystem des Halses von Buntspecht und Mittelspecht *Dendrocopos major* und *medius*. *J. Orn.* **122**: 37-63.

Jenni, L. (1983). Habitatnutzung, Nahrungserwerb und Nahrung von Mittel- und Buntspecht (*Dendrocopos medius* und *D. major*) sowie Bemerkungen zur Verbreitungsgeschichte des Mittelspechts. *Orn. Beob.* **80**: 29-57.

Jennings, J. (1977). Emerald Toucanet. *AFA Watchbird* **4**: 16-17.

Jennings, J. (1979). First captive breeding of the Ariel Toucan. *AFA Watchbird* **6**: 14-16.

Jennings, J. (1981). First captive breeding of the Emerald Toucanet. *AFA Watchbird* **8(1)**: 22-24.

Jennings, J. (1985a). A possible first breeding of the Red-billed Toucan. *AFA Watchbird* **12**: 32-33.

Jennings, J. (1985b). The first captive breeding of the Spot-billed Toucanet. *AFA Watchbird* **12**: 36-38.

Jennings, J. (1986). Ramphastids in the rain forest. *AFA Watchbird* **13**: 26-29.

Jennings, J. (1991). First breeding of the Swainson's (Chestnut-mandibled) Toucan (*Ramphastos swainsonii*). *AFA Watchbird* **18(4)**: 35-36.

Jennings, J. (1993a). Breeding toucans in captivity. Pp. 58-68 in: *Proceedings of the Annual Conference of the American Federation of Aviculture, 1993*.

Jennings, J. (1993b). First breeding of the Guyana Toucanet. *AFA Watchbird* **20(1)**: 40-41.

Jennings, J. (1993c). The Ariel Toucan - beyond the first generation. *AFA Watchbird* **20(2)**: 27-28.

Jennings, J. (1995a). Spot Billed Toucanets: a multi generational breeding success. *Avicult. Soc. Am. Bull.* **24(7)**: 2-5.

Jennings, J. (1995b). Breeding toucanets - the easy toucan. *Bird Breeder* **67(10)**: 22-29.

Jennings, J. (1996). The Collared Aracari. *AFA Watchbird* **23**: 56-57.

Jennings, J. (1998). Chestnut-mandibled Toucan: the second generation. *AFA Watchbird* **25(2)**: 4-5.

Jennings, M.C. (1995). *An Interim Atlas of the Breeding Birds of Arabia*. National Commission for Wildlife Conservation and Atlas of the Breeding Birds of Arabia Project, Riyadh, Saudi Arabia.

Jensen, F.P. & Stuart, S.N. (1982). New subspecies of forest birds from Tanzania. *Bull. Brit. Orn. Club* **102**: 95-99.

Jensen, J.V. & Kirkeby, J. (1980). *The Birds of The Gambia. An Annotated Checklist and Guide to Localities in The Gambia*. Aros Nature Guides, Århus.

Jensen, S.B. & Bahr, N. (2000). Grey-and-buff Woodpecker *Hemicircus concretus* - notes on juvenile plumages. *Bull. Oriental Bird Club* **32**: 13.

Jepson, P. & Brinkman, J.J. (1993). Notes on a mixed woodpecker flock at Bukit Barisan Selatan National Park, Lampung, Sumatra. *Kukila* **6(2)**: 135.

Jerauld, A.E., DeLotelle, R.S. & Newman, J.R. (1983). Restricted Red-cockaded Woodpecker clan movement during reproduction. Pp. 97-98 in: Wood (1983c).

Jeyarajasingam, A. & Pearson, A. (1999). *A Field Guide to the Birds of West Malaysia and Singapore*. Oxford University Press, Oxford.

Jha, A. (1999). Competition between Jungle Myna *Acridotheres fuscus* and Lesser Golden-backed Woodpecker *Dinopium benghalense* for a nest hole. *J. Bombay Nat. Hist. Soc.* **98(1)**: 115.

Jiménez, O. (1997). Seis nuevos registros de aves fósiles en Cuba. *Pitirre* **10(2)**: 49.

Jin Ruilan & Yin Yaning (1988). Survey on the control of wood worm in the hawthorn by Great Spotted Woodpeckers *Picoides major*. *Forest Science and Technology of Shanxi* **3**: 24-26.

Jobanek, G.A. (1994). Some thoughts on Acorn Woodpeckers in Oregon. *Oregon Birds* **20(4)**: 124-127.

Joebges, M., von-Selle, R. & Wegge, J. (1998). Zum Vorkommen und Bestand des Wendehalses (*Jynx torquilla*) in Nordrhein-Westfalen. Unter besonderer Berücksichtigung der Situation auf dem Truppenuebungsplatz "Senne". *Charadrius* **34(3-4)**: 126-135. In German with English summary.

Johansen, B.T. (1989a). [Population, territory size and breeding success of Black Woodpeckers *Dryocopus martius* in Tisvilde Hegn, North Zealand, 1977-1986]. *Dan. Orn. Foren. Tidssk.* **83(3-4)**: 113-118. In Danish with English summary.

Johansen, B.T. (1989b). [Nest trees and nest holes of Black Woodpeckers in North Zealand, 1977-1986]. *Dan. Orn. Foren. Tidssk.* **83(3-4)**: 119-124. In Danish with English summary.

Johnsgard, P.A. (1979). *Birds of the Great Plains. Breeding Species and Distribution*. University of Nebraska Press, Lincoln & London.

Johnsgard, P.A. (1997). *The Avian Brood Parasites*. Oxford University Press, Oxford.

Johnson, A.W. (1967). *The Birds of Chile and Adjacent Regions of Argentina, Bolivia and Peru*. Vol. 2. Platt Establecimientos Gráficos, Buenos Aires.

Johnson, A.W. (1972). *Supplement to the Birds of Chile and Adjacent Regions of Argentina, Bolivia and Peru*. Platt Establecimientos Gráficos, Buenos Aires.

Johnson, C.A. (1934). The chronicle of a Flicker's courtship. *Auk* **51(4)**: 477-481.

Johnson, D.H. (1984). Details of a Black-backed Woodpecker nest tree and nest cavity, lake of the woods county. *Loon* **56(4)**: 275-276.

Johnson, D.N. ed. (1980). *Proceedings of the IV Pan-African Ornithological Congress*. Southern African Ornithological Society, Johannesburg.

Johnson, E.V. (1998). Flicker destroys vacant Cliff Swallow nests. *Western Birds* **29(2)**: 121-122.

Johnson, E.V. (2000). Woodpecker drumming. *Bird Watcher's Digest* **22(3)**: 68-75.

Johnson, N.K. (1969). Review: three papers on variation in flickers (*Colaptes*) by Lester L. Short, Jr. *Wilson Bull.* **81(2)**: 225-230.

Johnson, N.K. & Johnson, C.B. (1985). Speciation in sapsuckers (*Sphyrapicus*). Part 2. Sympatry, hybridization, and mate preference in *S. ruber daggetti* and *S. nuchalis*. *Auk* **102(1)**: 1-15.

Johnson, N.K. & Zink, R.M. (1983). Speciation in sapsuckers (*Sphyrapicus*). Part 1. Genetic differentiation. *Auk* **100(4)**: 871-884.

Johnson, R.A. (1947). Role of male Yellow-bellied Sapsucker in the care of the young. *Auk* **64**: 621-623.

Johnson, R.R., Haight, L.T. & Ligon, J.D. (1999). Strickland's Woodpecker (*Picoides stricklandi*). No. **474** in: Poole, A.F. & Gill, F.B. eds. (1999). *The Birds of North America*. Vol. 12. Academy of Natural Sciences & American Ornithologists' Union, Philadelphia & Washington, D.C.

Johnsson, K. (1993). *The Black Woodpecker* Dryocopus martius *as a Keystone Species in Forest*. PhD thesis, Swedish University of Agricultural Sciences, Uppsala, Sweden.

Johnsson, K., Nilsson, S.G. & Tjernberg, M. (1993). Characteristics and utilization of old Black Woodpecker *Dryocopus martius* holes by hole-nesting species. *Ibis* **135(4)**: 410-416.

Johnston, D.W. (1970). Niche relationships in some West Indian woodpeckers. *Amer. Phil. Soc. Yb.* **1970**: 322-324.

Johnston, D.W. (1988). A morphological atlas of the avian uropygial gland. *Bull. Brit. Mus. (Nat. Hist.) Zool.* **54**: 199-259.

Johnston-Stewart, N.G.B. (1988). Stierling's Woodpecker in Malawi. *Nyala* **13(1/2)**: 82-83.

Johnston-Stewart, N.G.B. & Heigham, J.B. (1982). *Bridging the Bird Gap. A Field Guide to the 64 Species in Malawi not Described in Robert's Birds of South Africa*. Published privately, Malawi.
Jones, G.D. (1988). *Woodpecker Foraging Behavior and Resource Partitioning in an Eastern Texas Bottomland Hardwood Forest*. MSc thesis, Stephen F. Austin State University, Nacogdoches, Texas.
Jones, H.K. & Ott, F.T. (1973). Some characteristics of Red-cockaded Woodpecker cavity trees in Georgia. *Oriole* **38(4)**: 33-39.
Jones, J.P.G., Ferry, C.D., Isherwood, C.E., Knight, C.G., Kumara, C.L. & Weerakoon, K. (1998). *A Conservation Review of Three Wet Zone Forests in South-west Sri Lanka*. CSB Conservation Publications, Cambridge.
Joste, N.E., Koenig, W.D., Mumme, R.L. & Pitelka, F.A. (1982). Intragroup dynamics of a cooperative breeder: an analysis of reproductive roles in the Acorn Woodpecker. *Behav. Ecol. Sociobiol.* **11(3)**: 195-201.
Joste, N.E., Ligon, J.D. & Stacey, P.B. (1985). Shared paternity in the Acorn Woodpecker (*Melanerpes formicivorus*). *Behav. Ecol. Sociobiol.* **17(1)**: 39-41.
Jourdain, F.C.R. (1936). On the winter habits of the Green Woodpecker (*Picus viridis virescens*). *Proc. Zool. Soc. London* **1936**: 251-256.
Jubb, R.A. (1966). Red-billed Wood Hoopoe and a Greater Honey-guide. *Bokmakierie* **18**: 66-67.
Jubb, R.A. (1968). Red-billed Wood Hoopoe and a Greater Honey-guide. *Bokmakierie* **20**: 18-19.
Kalas, K. (1973). A group of barbets. 1. Some ethological observations. *Z. Tierpsychol.* **33(3/4)**: 335-340.
Kalisz, P.J. & Boettcher, S.E. (1991). Active and abandoned Red-cockaded Woodpecker habitat in Kentucky. *J. Wildl. Manage.* **55**: 146-154.
Kalsi, R.S. (1998). Birds of Kalesar Wildlife Sanctuary, Haryana, India. *Forktail* **13**: 29-32.
Kannan, R. (1998). Avifauna of the Animalai Hills (Western Ghats) of southern India. *J. Bombay Nat. Hist. Soc.* **95(2)**: 193-214.
Kantak, G.E. (1979). Observations on some fruit-eating birds in Mexico. *Auk* **96(1)**: 183-186.
Kaplan, J. (1986). Interactions between a Sharp-shinned Hawk and a Pileated Wooodpecker. *Connecticut Warbler* **6(3)**: 34-35.
Kappes, J.J. (1993). *Interspecific Interactions Associated with Red-cockaded Woodpecker Cavities at a North Florida Site*. MSc thesis, University of Florida, Gainesville, Florida.
Kappes, J.J. (1997). Defining cavity-associated interactions between Red-cockaded Woodpeckers and other cavity-dependent species: interspecific competition or cavity kleptoparasitism? *Auk* **114(4)**: 778-780.
Karr, J.R., Robinson, S., Blake, J.G. & Bierregaard, R.O. (1990). Birds of four Neotropical forests. Pp. 237-269 in: *Four Neotropical Rainforests*. Yale University Press, New Haven, Connecticut.
Kasparek, M. (1989). [On passage and on breeding distribution of the Wryneck (*Jynx torquilla*) in Turkey]. *Ecol. Birds* **11(2)**: 251-256. In German with English summary.
Kattan, G. (1988). Food habits and social organization of Acorn Woodpeckers in Colombia. *Condor* **90(1)**: 100-106.
Kattan, G. & Murcia, C. (1985). Hummingbird association with Acorn Woodpecker sap trees in Colombia. *Condor* **87(4)**: 542-543.
Kaufman, K. (1993). Identifying the Hairy Woodpecker. *Amer. Birds* **47(2)**: 311-314.
Kaufman, K. (1996). *Lives of North American Birds*. Houghton Mifflin Company, Boston & New York.
Kaul, D. & Ansari, H.A. (1981). Chromosomal polymorphism in a natural population of the Northern Green Barbet, *Megalaima zeylanica caniceps* (Franklin) (Piciformes: Aves). *Genetica* **54(3)**: 241-245.
Kavkova, R. & Kralickova, J. (1997). Prvni uspesny odchov Arasari Rasnateho (*Pteroglossus beauharnaesii*) v Zoo Ohrada. [The first successful breeding of Curl-crested Aracari (*Pteroglossus beauharnaesii*) at the Ohrada Zoo]. *Gazella* **24**: 197-202. In Czech.
Kawada, M. (1980). Breeding biology of the *Dendrocopos major japonicus* and *D. minor* in Obihiro, Hokkaido. *Misc. Rep. Yamashina Inst. Orn.* **12**: 106-128.
Kazama, T. (1980). Telephone pole breakage caused by Green Woodpeckers *Picus awokera*. *J. Yamashina Inst. Orn.* **12**: 225-226.
Kazmierczak, K. (2000). *A Field Guide to the Birds of the Indian Subcontinent*. Pica Press, Nr. Robertsbridge, UK.
Keisker, D.G. (1986). *Nest Tree Selection by Primary Cavity Nesting Birds in South-central British Columbia*. MSc thesis, Simon Fraser University, Burnaby, Canada.
Keith, S. & Twomey, A. (1968). New distributional records of some East African birds. *Ibis* **110**: 537-548.
Kelly, J.F., Pletschet, S.M. & Leslie, D.M. (1993). Habitat associations of Red-cockaded Woodpecker cavity trees in an old-growth forest of Oklahoma. *J. Wildl. Manage.* **57**: 122-128.
Kelly, J.F., Pletschet, S.M. & Leslie, D.M. (1994). Decline of the Red-cockaded Woodpecker (*Picoides borealis*) in southeastern Oklahoma. *Amer. Midl. Nat.* **132(2)**: 275-283.
Kemlage, T.F., Stark, G.A. & Bowen, D.E. (1981). Heights of woodpeckers' nest hole entrances into saguaro cacti. *Trans. Kansas Acad. Sci.* **84(1)**: 172. (Abstract).
Kennedy, E.T., Costa, R. & Smathers, W.M. (1996). Economic incentives: new directions for Red-cockaded Woodpecker habitat conservation. *J. Forestry* **94**: 22-26.
Kennedy, R.S. (1987). New subspecies of *Dryocopus javensis* (Aves: Picidae) and *Ficedula hyperythra* (Aves: Muscicapidae) from the Philippines. *Proc. Biol. Soc. Washington* **100(1)**: 40-43.
Kent, A.M., Webber, T. & Steadman, D.W. (1999). Distribution, relative abundance, and prehistory of birds on the Taraco Peninsula, Bolivian altiplano. *Orn. Neotropical* **10(2)**: 151-178.
Kerpez, T.A. (1986). *Competition Between European Starlings and Native Woodpeckers for Nest Cavities in Saguaros*. MSc thesis, University of Arizona, Tucson, Arizona.
Kerpez, T.A. & Smith, N.S. (1990a). Competition between European Starlings and native woodpeckers for nest cavities in saguaros. *Auk* **107(2)**: 367-375.
Kerpez, T.A. & Smith, N.S. (1990b). Nest-site selection and nest-cavity characteristics of Gila Woodpeckers and Northern Flickers. *Condor* **92(1)**: 193-198.
Keßler, A. (1986). Zur aktuellen Bestandssituation des Gründspechts (*Picus viridis*) nebst ergänzenden Angaben zur Brutverbreitung im Oldenburgischen. *Jahresber. Orn. Arbeitsgem. Oldenb.* **10**: 23-27.
Keve, A. (1960). Der Blutspecht (*Dendrocopos syriacus* Hempr. & Ehrenb.) in Ungarn. *Vertebrata Hungarica* **2**: 243-260.
Keve, A. (1963). Peculiarities of range expansion of three European bird species. Pp. 1124-1127 in: Sibley, C.G. ed. (1963). *Proceedings of the XIII International Ornithological Congress, Ithaca, June 1962*. Vol. 2. American Ornithologists' Union, Baton Rouge, Louisiana.
Khacher, L.J. (1976). Westernmost record of the Great Slaty Woodpecker *Mulleripicus pulverulentus* in Himachal Pradesh. *J. Bombay Nat. Hist. Soc.* **73(1)**: 216.
Khacher, L.J. (1989). An interesting colour phase of the Lesser Golden-backed Woodpecker *Dinopium benghalense*. *J. Bombay Nat. Hist. Soc.* **86(1)**: 97.
Khan, M.A.R. (1982). *Wildlife of Bangladesh: a Checklist*. University of Dhaka, Dhaka, Bangladesh.
Khan, M.Z. & Walters, J.R. (1998). Is helping a beneficial learning experience for Red-cockaded Woodpecker (*Picoides borealis*) helpers? *Behav. Ecol. Sociobiol.* **41(2)**: 69-73.
Khan, M.Z. & Walters, J.R. (2000). An analysis of reciprocal exchange of helping behavior in the Red-cockaded Woodpecker (*Picoides borealis*). *Behav. Ecol. Sociobiol.* **47(6)**: 376-381.
Khan, M.Z., Walters, J.R., McNabb, F.M.A. & Sharp, P.J. (1999). Testosterone and prolactin concentrations in the cooperatively breeding Red-cockaded Woodpecker (*Picoides borealis*). *Amer. Zool.* **39(5)**: 112A. (Abstract).
Kilham, L. (1956). Winter feeding on sap by sapsucker. *Auk* **73(3)**: 451-452.
Kilham, L. (1958a). Pair formation, mutual tapping and nest hole selection of Red-bellied Woodpeckers. *Auk* **75(3)**: 318-329.
Kilham, L. (1958b). Sealed-in winter stores of Red-headed Woodpeckers. *Wilson Bull.* **70(2)**: 107-113.
Kilham, L. (1958c). Territorial behavior of wintering Red-headed Woodpeckers. *Wilson Bull.* **70(4)**: 347-358.
Kilham, L. (1959a). Mutual tapping of the Red-headed Woodpecker. *Auk* **76(2)**: 235-236.
Kilham, L. (1959b). Head-scratching and wing-stretching of woodpeckers. *Auk* **76(4)**: 527-528.
Kilham, L. (1959c). Bark-eating of Red-headed Woodpeckers. *Condor* **61(5)**: 371-373.
Kilham, L. (1959d). Behavior and methods of communication of Pileated Woodpeckers. *Condor* **61(6)**: 377-387.
Kilham, L. (1959e). Pilot black snake and nesting Pileated Woodpeckers. *Wilson Bull.* **71(2)**: 191.
Kilham, L. (1959f). Early reproductive behavior of Flickers. *Wilson Bull.* **71(4)**: 323-336.
Kilham, L. (1960). Courtship and territorial behavior of Hairy Woodpeckers. *Auk* **77(3)**: 259-270.
Kilham, L. (1961a). Downy Woodpeckers scaling bark on diseased elms. *Wilson Bull.* **73(1)**: 89.
Kilham, L. (1961b). Reproductive behavior of Red-bellied Woodpeckers. *Wilson Bull.* **73(3)**: 237-254.
Kilham, L. (1962a). Breeding behavior of Yellow-bellied Sapsuckers. *Auk* **79(1)**: 31-43.
Kilham, L. (1962b). Reproductive behavior of Downy Woodpeckers. *Condor* **64(2)**: 126-133.
Kilham, L. (1962c). Nest sanitation of Yellow-bellied Sapsuckers. *Wilson Bull.* **74(1)**: 96-97.
Kilham, L. (1963). Food storing of Red-bellied Woodpeckers. *Wilson Bull.* **75(3)**: 227-234.
Kilham, L. (1964). The relations of breeding Yellow-bellied Sapsuckers to wounded birches and other trees. *Auk* **81(4)**: 520-527.
Kilham, L. (1965). Differences in feeding behavior of male and female Hairy Woodpeckers. *Wilson Bull.* **77(2)**: 134-145.
Kilham, L. (1966a). Nesting activities of Black-backed Woodpeckers. *Condor* **68(3)**: 308-310.
Kilham, L. (1966b). Reproductive behavior of Hairy Woodpeckers. Part 1. Pair formation and courtship. *Wilson Bull.* **78(3)**: 251-265.
Kilham, L. (1968). Reproductive behavior of Hairy Woodpeckers. Part 2. Nesting and habitat. *Wilson Bull.* **80(3)**: 286-305.
Kilham, L. (1969). Reproductive behavior of Hairy Woodpeckers. Part 3. Agonistic behavior in relation to courtship and territory. *Wilson Bull.* **81(2)**: 169-183.
Kilham, L. (1970). Feeding behavior of Downy Woodpeckers. Part 1. Preference for paper birches and sexual differences. *Auk* **87(3)**: 544-556.
Kilham, L. (1971). Reproductive behavior of Yellow-bellied Sapsuckers. Part 1. Preference for nesting in *Fomes*-infected aspens and nest hole interrelations with flying squirrels, raccoons, and other animals. *Wilson Bull.* **83(2)**: 159-171.
Kilham, L. (1972a). Habits of the Crimson-crested Woodpecker in Panama. *Wilson Bull.* **84(1)**: 28-47.
Kilham, L. (1972b). Retention of egg in a wild Downy Woodpecker. *Wilson Bull.* **84(4)**: 493-494.
Kilham, L. (1972c). Shortness of tail in Red-crowned Woodpeckers and their habit of entering roost holes backward. *Condor* **74(2)**: 202-204.
Kilham, L. (1973a). Colonial-type nesting in Yellow-shafted Flickers as related to staggering of nest times. *Bird-Banding* **44(4)**: 317-318.
Kilham, L. (1973b). Unusual attack of intruding male on a nesting pair of Pileated Woodpeckers. *Condor* **75(3)**: 349-350.
Kilham, L. (1974a). Copulatory behavior of Downy Woodpeckers. *Wilson Bull.* **86(1)**: 23-34.
Kilham, L. (1974b). Early breeding season behavior of Downy Woodpeckers. *Wilson Bull.* **86(4)**: 407-418.
Kilham, L. (1974c). Loud vocalizations by Pileated Woodpeckers on approach to roosts or nest holes. *Auk* **91(3)**: 634-636.
Kilham, L. (1974d). Play in Hairy, Downy, and other woodpeckers. *Wilson Bull.* **86(1)**: 35-42.
Kilham, L. (1975). Dirt-bathing by a Pileated Woodpecker. *Bird-Banding* **46**: 251-252.
Kilham, L. (1976). Winter foraging and associated behavior of Pileated Woodpeckers in Georgia and Florida. *Auk* **93(1)**: 15-24.
Kilham, L. (1977a). Nest site differences between Red-headed and Red-bellied Woodpeckers in South Carolina. *Wilson Bull.* **89(1)**: 164-165.
Kilham, L. (1977b). Early breeding season behavior of Red-headed Woodpeckers. *Auk* **94(2)**: 231-239.
Kilham, L. (1977c). Nesting behavior of Yellow-bellied Sapsuckers. *Wilson Bull.* **89(2)**: 310-324.
Kilham, L. (1977d). Altruism in nesting Yellow-bellied Sapsucker. *Auk* **94(3)**: 613-614.
Kilham, L. (1977e). Nesting behavior of Pale-billed Woodpeckers in Guatemala. *Auk* **94(4)**: 773-774.
Kilham, L. (1977f). Pale-billed Woodpeckers robbed of nest hole by Collared Araçaris. *Auk* **94(4)**: 774-775.
Kilham, L. (1978). Sexual similarity of Red-headed Woodpeckers and possible explanations based on fall territorial behavior. *Wilson Bull.* **90(2)**: 285.
Kilham, L. (1979a). Chestnut-colored Woodpeckers feeding as a pair on ants. *Wilson Bull.* **91(1)**: 149-150.
Kilham, L. (1979b). Three-week vs. four-week nestling periods in *Picoides* and other woodpeckers. *Wilson Bull.* **91(2)**: 335-338.
Kilham, L. (1979c). Courtship and the pair-bond of Pileated Woodpeckers. *Auk* **96(3)**: 587-594.
Kilham, L. (1983). *Life History Studies of Woodpeckers of Eastern North America*. Publications of the Nuttall Ornithological Club **20**, Cambridge, Massachusetts. (Reprinted by Dover Publications, New York, 1992).
Kilham, L. & O'Brien, P. (1979). Early breeding behavior of Lineated Woodpeckers. *Condor* **81(3)**: 299-303.
King, B., Buck, H., Ferguson, R., Fisher, T., Goblet, C., Nickel, H. & Suter, W. (2001). Birds recorded during two expeditions to north Myanmar (Burma). *Forktail* **17**: 29-40.
King, D.I. & Rappole, J.H. (2001). Mixed-species bird flocks in dipterocarp forest of north-central Burma (Myanmar). *Ibis* **143(3)**: 380-390.
King, M. (2000). Noteworthy records from Ginak Island, The Gambia. *Malimbus* **22(2)**: 77-85.
King, W.B. ed. (1978/79). *Endangered Birds of the World. The ICBP Bird Red Data Book*. Vol. 2. Aves. 2nd edition. IUCN, Morges, Switzerland.
Kingdon, J. (1977). *East African Mammals*. Vol. 3A. Academic Press, London.
Kinjo, M. (1992). [Okinawa Woodpecker - a rare bird in the forest of Yambaru]. Pp. 140-142 in: *Shokan Asahi Encyclopaedia: Globe of Animals*. Asahi Shimbunsha, Tokyo. In Japanese.
Kinloch, A.P. (1923). The nidification of the Malabar Great Black Woodpecker *Thriponax hodgsoni*. *J. Bombay Nat. Hist. Soc.* **29(2)**: 561.
Kirby, V.C. (1980). An adaptive modification in the ribs of woodpeckers and piculets (Picidae). *Auk* **97(3)**: 521-532.
Kirkconnell, A. (1992). Breeding biology of the West Indian Woodpecker. *Pitirre* **5(3)**: 12. (Abstract).
Kirkconnell, A. (2000a). Notas sobre la ecología reproductiva y otros aspectos de la biología del Carpintero Jabado *Melanerpes superciliaris* en Cuba. *Cotinga* **16**: 72-77. In Spanish with English summary.
Kirkconnell, A. (2000b). Variación morfológica del Carpintero Verde *Xiphidiopicus percussus* en Cuba. *Cotinga* **14**: 94-98. In Spanish with English summary.
Kirkconnell, A., Alayón, G., Posada, R.M. & Llanes, A. (1989). Observaciones conductuales en dos nidos de *Xiphidiopicus percussus percussus* (Aves: Piciformes: Picidae). *Poeyana* **371**: 1-18.
Kirkconnell, A., Garrido, O.H., Posada, R.M. & Cubillas, S.O. (1992). Los grupos tróficos en la avifauna cubana. [Trophic guilds in the Cuban avifauna]. *Poeyana* **415**: 1-21.
Kirkpatrick, K.M. (1960). The Black-backed Woodpecker, *Chrysocolaptes festivus* (Boddaert), in Ganjam, Orissa. *J. Bombay Nat. Hist. Soc.* **57(3)**: 662.
Kirwan, G.M. & Marlow, T. (1996). A review of avifaunal records from Mindo, Pichincha province, north-western Ecuador. *Cotinga* **6**: 47-57.
Kisiel, D.S. (1972). Foraging behavior of *Dendrocopos villosus* and *Dendrocopos pubescens* in eastern New York State. *Condor* **74(4)**: 393-398.
Kiyosu, Y. (1936). [Japanese Pygmy Woodpecker]. *Yacho* **1936**: 778. In Japanese.
Klaas, E.E. (1968). Summer birds from the Yucatán Peninsula, Mexico. *Univ. Kansas Publ. Mus. Nat. Hist.* **17(14)**: 579-611.
Klaver, A. (1964). Over de biologie van de Draaihals (*Jynx torquilla* L.). *Limosa* **37**: 221-231.
Klimaitis, J.F. & Moschione, F.N. (1987). *Aves de la Reserva Integral de Selva Marginal de Punta Lara y sus Alrededores*. Dirección de Servicios Generales del Ministerio, Argentina.
Klitin, A.N., Skilsky, I.V. & Bundzyak, P.V. (1994). Distribution and feeding of the Syrian Woodpecker in the Bukovinian pre-Carpathians and Prut-Dniester interfluve. *Berkut* **3(2)**: 108-111. In English with Russian summary.
Kloss, C.B. (1918). On birds recently collected in Siam. *Ibis* **Ser. 10, no. 6**: 76-114.

Kloss, C.B. (1926). On *Picus vittatus* and some of its allies. *Ibis* **Ser. 12, no. 2**: 684-689.

Kloss, C.B. (1931). An account of the Sumatran birds in the Zoological Museum, Buitenzorg, with description of new nine races. *Treubia* **13**: 299-370.

Knistautas, A. & Lyutkus, A. (1981). [Materials on biology of the Green Woodpecker (*Picus viridis*) in south-eastern Litva]. *Ornitologiya* **16**: 168-169. In Russian.

Knox, A.G. & Walters, M.P. (1994). *Extinct and Endangered Birds in the Collections of the Natural History Museum*. British Ornithologists' Club Occasional Publications **1**. 292 pp.

Knysh, N.P. (1999). [Materials on nesting and feeding of the Middle Spotted Woodpecker in forest-steppe oak forests of Sumy region]. *Berkut* **8(2)**: 192-194. In Russian with English summary.

Knystautas, A. (1993). *Birds of Russia*. Harper Collins Publishers, London.

Koch, R.F., Courchesne, A.E. & Collins, C.T. (1970). Sexual differences in foraging behavior of White-headed Woodpeckers. *Bull. South. Calif. Acad. Sci.* **69**: 60-64.

Koehler, G.M. (1981). Ecological requirements for Lewis Woodpeckers (*Melanerpes lewis*), potential impacts of surface mining on their habitat and recommendations for mitigation. Unpublished report to the US Fish & Wildlife Service.

Koelz, W. (1952). New races of Indian birds. *J. Zool. Soc. India* **4**: 38-46.

Koenig, W.D. (1978). *Ecological and Evolutionary Aspects of Cooperative Breeding in Acorn Woodpeckers of Central Coastal California*. PhD dissertation, University of California, Berkeley, California.

Koenig, W.D. (1980a). Variation and age determination in a population of Acorn Woodpeckers. *J. Field Orn.* **51(1)**: 10-16.

Koenig, W.D. (1980b). *Acorn Storage by Acorn Woodpeckers in an Oak Woodland: an Energetics Analysis*. General Techniques Report **PSW-44**. US Department of Agriculture, Forest Service.

Koenig, W.D. (1981a). Space competition in the Acorn Woodpecker: power struggles in a cooperative breeder. *Anim. Behav.* **29(2)**: 396-409.

Koenig, W.D. (1981b). Reproductive success, group size, and the evolution of cooperative breeding in the Acorn Woodpecker. *Amer. Naturalist* **117(4)**: 421-443.

Koenig, W.D. (1984a). Clutch size of the Gilded Flicker. *Condor* **86(1)**: 89-90.

Koenig, W.D. (1984b). Geographic variation in clutch size in the Northern Flicker (*Colaptes auratus*): support for Ashmole's hypothesis. *Auk* **101(4)**: 698-706.

Koenig, W.D. (1986). Geographical ecology of clutch size variation in North American woodpeckers. *Condor* **88(4)**: 499-504.

Koenig, W.D. (1987). Morphological and dietary correlates of clutch size in North American Woodpeckers. *Auk* **104(4)**: 757-765.

Koenig, W.D. (1990). Opportunity of parentage and nest destruction in polygynandrous Acorn Woodpeckers, *Melanerpes formicivorus*. *Behav. Ecol.* **1(1)**: 55-61.

Koenig, W.D. (1991). The effects of tannins and lipids on digestion of acorns by Acorn Woodpeckers. *Auk* **108(1)**: 79-88.

Koenig, W.D. & Haydock, J. (1999). Oaks, acorns, and the geographical ecology of Acorn Woodpeckers. *J. Biogeogr.* **26(1)**: 159-165.

Koenig, W.D. & Heck, M.K. (1988). Ability of two species of oak woodland birds to subsist on acorns. *Condor* **90(3)**: 705-708.

Koenig, W.D. & Mumme, R.L. (1987). *Population Ecology of the Cooperatively Breeding Acorn Woodpecker*. Princeton University Press, Princeton, New Jersey.

Koenig, W.D. & Pitelka, F.A. (1979). Relatedness and inbreeding avoidance: counterploys in the communally nesting Acorn Woodpecker. *Science* **206**: 1103-1105.

Koenig, W.D. & Pitelka, F.A. (1981). Ecological factors and kin selection in the evolution of cooperative breeding in birds. Pp. 261-280 in: Alexander, R.D. & Tinkle, D.W. (1981). *Natural Selection and Social Behavior: Recent Research and New Theory*. Chiron Press, New York.

Koenig, W.D. & Stacey, P.B. (1990). Acorn Woodpeckers: group-living and food storage under contrasting ecological conditions. Pp. 413-453 in: Stacey, P.B. & Koenig, W.D. eds. (1990). *Cooperative Breeding in Birds: Long-term Studies of Ecology and Behavior*. Cambridge University Press, Cambridge.

Koenig, W.D. & Williams, P.L. (1979). Notes on the status of Acorn Woodpeckers in central Mexico. *Condor* **81(3)**: 317-318.

Koenig, W.D., Hannon, S.J., Mumme, R.L. & Pitelka, F.A. (1988). Parent-offspring conflict in the Acorn Woodpecker. Pp. 1221-1230 in: Ouellet (1988).

Koenig, W.D., Haydock, J. & Stanback, M.T. (1998). Reproductive roles in the cooperatively breeding Acorn Woodpecker: incest avoidance versus reproductive competition. *Amer. Naturalist* **151(3)**: 243-255.

Koenig, W.D., Hooge, P.N., Stanback, M.T. & Haydock, J. (2000). Natal dispersal in the cooperatively breeding Acorn Woodpecker. *Condor* **102(3)**: 492-502.

Koenig, W.D., Mumme, R.L. & Pitelka, F.A. (1983). Female roles in cooperatively breeding Acorn Woodpeckers. Pp. 235-261 in: Wasser, S.K. ed. (1983). *Social Behavior of Female Vertebrates*. Academic Press, New York.

Koenig, W.D., Mumme, R.L. & Pitelka, F.A. (1984). The breeding system of the Acorn Woodpecker in central coastal California. *Z. Tierpsychol.* **65(4)**: 289-308. In English with German summary.

Koenig, W.D., Mumme, R.L., Stanback, M.T. & Pitelka, F.A. (1995). Patterns and consequences of egg destruction among joint-nesting Acorn Woodpeckers. *Anim. Behav.* **50(3)**: 607-621.

Koenig, W.D., Stacey, P.B., Stanback, M.T. & Mumme, R.L. (1995). Acorn Woodpecker (*Melanerpes formicivorus*). No. **194** in: Poole, A.F. & Gill, F.B. eds. (1995). *The Birds of North America*. Vol. 5. Academy of Natural Sciences & American Ornithologists' Union, Philadelphia & Washington, D.C.

Koenig, W.D., Stanback, M.T. & Haydock, J. (1999). Demographic consequences of incest avoidance in the cooperatively breeding Acorn Woodpecker. *Anim. Behav.* **57(6)**: 1287-1293.

Koenig, W.D., Stanback, M.T., Hooge, P.N. & Mumme, R.L. (1991). Distress calls in the Acorn Woodpecker. *Condor* **93(3)**: 637-643.

Koepcke, M. (1961). Birds of the western slope of the Andes of Peru. *Amer. Mus. Novit.* **2028**: 1-31.

Koepcke, M. (1970). *The Birds of the Department of Lima, Peru*. Livingston Publishing Company, Wynneywood, Pennsylvania.

Kojima, K. & Arikawa, H. (1983). Habitat and food habits of the Black Woodpecker *Dryocopus martius* in Hokkaido. *Tori* **32(2/3)**: 109-111.

Kojima, K. & Matsuoka, S. (1985). Studies on the food habits of four sympatric species of woodpeckers. Part 2. Black Woodpecker *Dryocopus martius* from winter to early spring. *Tori* **34(1)**: 1-6.

Komar, O., Rodríguez, W. & Dueñas, C. (1997). Notas sobre las aves de los bosques de manglar en la Bahía de La Unión, y una nueva especie de Carpintero *Picoides scalaris* para El Salvador. *Cotinga* **7**: 16-17. In Spanish with English summary.

König, C. (1961). Beobachtungen an einer Brut des Wendehalses (*Jynx torquilla* L.). *Anz. Orn. Ges. Bayern* **6**: 81-83.

Konrad, P.M. (1998). The variable woodpeckers-species profile: Northern Flicker (*Colaptes auratus*). *Wildbird* **12(2)**: 44-45.

Kopij, G. (1998). Distribution, numbers and habitat preference of the Crested Barbet *Trachyphonus vaillantii* in Bloemfontein. *Mirafra* **15(3/4)**: 35-37.

Koplin, J.R. (1969). The numerical response of woodpeckers to insect prey in a subalpine forest in Colorado. *Condor* **71(4)**: 436-438.

Koplin, J.R. (1972). Measuring predator impact of woodpeckers on spruce beetles. *J. Wildl. Manage.* **36(2)**: 308-320.

Korol, J. & Hutto, R.L. (1984). Factors affecting nest site location in Gila Woodpeckers. *Condor* **86(1)**: 73-78.

Kossenko, S.M. & Kaygorodova, E.Y. (1998). Distribution and reproduction of the Middle Spotted Woodpecker *Dendrocopos medius* in continuous and fragmented habitats. Proceedings of the XXII International Ornithological Congress, Durban 1998. *Ostrich* **69(3&4)**: 445. (Abstract).

Koster, S.H. & Grettenberger, J.H. (1983). A preliminary survey of birds in Park W, Niger. *Malimbus* **5(2)**: 62-72.

Kostyushin, V.A. (1995). [Some aspects of the foraging activity of the Great Spotted Woodpecker in the mature pine forest]. *Berkut* **4(1-2)**: 96-97. In Russian with English summary.

Kotagama, S.W. & Fernando, P. (1994). *A Field Guide to the Birds of Sri Lanka*. Wildlife Heritage Trust of Sri Lanka, Colombo.

Kotaka, N. (1998). Classical polyandry in the Great Spotted Woodpecker *Dendrocopos major*. *Ibis* **140(2)**: 335-336.

Kovalev, V.A. (1993). Ageing of the Great Spotted Woodpecker *Dendrocopos major*. *Russ. J. Orn.* **2(3)**: 393-394.

Kovalev, V.A. (1996). [Postjuvenile moult features of the Great Spotted Woodpecker]. In Russian with English summary. *Berkut* **5(1)**: 39-43.

Kovalev, V.A. (1999). [Post-breeding moult in Great Spotted Woodpeckers]. *Berkut* **8(2)**: 183-191. In Russian with English summary.

Krabbe, N. (1991). *Avifauna of the Temperate Zone of the Ecuadorean Andes*. Zoological Museum of the University of Copenhagen, Denmark.

Krabbe, N., Poulsen, B.O., Frølander, A., Hinojosa, M. & Quiroga, C. (1996). Birds of montane forest fragments in Chuquisaca Department, Bolivia. *Bull. Brit. Orn. Club* **116(4)**: 230-243.

Krabbe, N., Poulsen, B.O., Frølander, A. & Rodríguez, O. (1997). Range extensions of cloud forest birds from the High Andes of Ecuador: new sites for rare or little-recorded species. *Bull. Brit. Orn. Club* **117(4)**: 248-256.

Krassowsky, S.K. (1936). Zur Morphology der Spechtschädel. *Anat. Anz.* **82**: 112-128.

Kratter, A.W. (1991). First nesting record for Williamson's Sapsucker (*Sphyrapicus thyroideus*) in Baja California, Mexico, and comments on the biogeography of the fauna of the Sierra San Pedro Mártir. *Southwest. Nat.* **36**: 247-250.

Kratter, A.W. (1997). Macaws and bamboo specialists. *Birding* **29(5)**: 402-409.

Kratter, A.W. (1998). Nidos de dos especialistas de bambú: *Celeus spectabilis* y *Cercomacra manu*. [The nests of two bamboo specialists: *Celeus spectabilis* and *Cercomacra manu*]. *J. Field Orn.* **69(1)**: 37-44.

Kratter, A.W., Carreño, M.D., Chesser, R.T., O'Neill, J.P. & Sillett, T.S. (1992). Further notes on bird distribution in northeastern Dpto. Santa Cruz, Bolivia, with two species new to Bolivia. *Bull. Brit. Orn. Club* **112**: 143-150.

Kreisel, H. (1974). Zum Ringeln der Baumstämme durch den Saftsaugerspecht, *Sphyrapicus v. varius*, in Kuba. *Beitr. Vogelkd.* **20(1/2)**: 53-66.

Kreisel, K.J. & Stein, S.J. (1999). Bird use of burned and unburned coniferous forests during winter. *Wilson Bull.* **111(2)**: 243-250.

Kren, J. (2000). *Birds of the Czech Republic*. Christopher Helm, London.

Krištín, A. (1992). [Nutrition and nutritional ecology of *Jynx torquilla*]. *Tichodroma* **4**: 101-104. In Slovak with German summary.

Kroneisl-Rucner, R. (1957). Der Blutspecht, *Dendrocopos syriacus*, in Kroatian und die Frage seiner Bastardierung mit dem Buntspecht, *Dendrocopos major*. *Larus* **9-10**: 34-47.

Kropil, R. & Kornan, J. (1991). Beitrag zur Brutbiologie und Ökologie des Dreizehenspechtes (*Picoides tridactylus* L.) in der Slovakei. *Zpravy* **49**: 7-12.

Krügel, M.M. & dos Anjos, L. (2000). Bird communities in forest remnants in the city of Maringá, Paraná State, southern Brazil. *Orn. Neotropical* **11(4)**: 315-330.

Kuhlke, D. (1985). [Stock of holes and brood density of Black Woodpeckers (*Dryocopus martius*), Tengmalm's Owls (*Aegolius funereus*) and Stock-doves (*Columba oenas*)]. *Vogelwelt* **106(3)**: 81-93. In German with English summary.

Kujawa, K.I. (1984). *Foraging Behavior of the Golden-fronted Woodpecker (*Melanerpes aurifrons*) in the San Angelo, Texas Region*. MSc thesis, Angelo State University, San Angelo, Texas.

Kulhavy, D.L., Hooper, R.G. & Costa, R. eds. (1995). *Red-cockaded Woodpecker: Recovery, Ecology and Management*. Stephen F. Austin State University, Nacogdoches, Texas.

Kuroda, N. (1933). *Non-Passeres: Birds of the Island of Java*. Part I. Published privately, Tokyo.

Labidoire, P. (1992). Nouvelle progression du Pic noir (*Dryocopus martius*) vers l'ouest du Limousin. *Epops* **2**: 31-36.

Labitte, A. (1953). Notes sur la biologie du Pic-vert *Picus viridis*. *Alauda* **21(3)**: 165-178.

LaBranche, M.S. (1992). *Asynchronous Hatching, Brood Reduction and Sex Ratio Biases in Red-cockaded Woodpeckers*. PhD dissertation, North Carolina State University, Raleigh, North Carolina.

LaBranche, M.S. & Walters, J.R. (1994). Patterns of mortality in nests of Red-cockaded Woodpeckers in the sandhills of southcentral North Carolina. *Wilson Bull.* **106(2)**: 258-271.

LaBranche, M.S., Walters, J.R. & Laves, K.S. (1994). Double brooding in Red-cockaded Woodpeckers. *Wilson Bull.* **106(2)**: 403-408.

Lago-Paiva, C. & Willis, E.O. (1994). New occurrences of *Melanerpes cactorum* (D'Orbigny, 1840) (Aves, Picidae) in Brazilian territory. *Biotemas* **7**: 110-115.

Lainer, H. (1999). The birds of Goa. Part II. *J. Bombay Nat. Hist. Soc.* **96(3)**: 405-423.

Laman, T.G., Gaither, J.C. & Lukas, D.E. (1996). Rainforest bird biodiversity in Gunung Palung National Park, West Kalimantan, Indonesia. *Tropical Biodiversity* **3**: 281-296.

Lamarche, B. (1980). Liste commentée des oiseaux du Mali. 1ère partie: Non-passereaux. *Malimbus* **2(2)**: 121-158.

Lamarche, B. (1988). *Liste Commentée des Oiseaux de Mauritanie*. Études Sahariennes et Ouest-Africaines **1(4)**. 164 pp.

Lamb, G.R. (1957). *The Ivory-billed Woodpecker in Cuba*. ICBP Pan-American Section Research Report **1**. 17 pp.

Lamb, G.R. (1958). Excerpts from a report on the Ivory-billed Woodpecker (*Campephilus principalis bairdii*) in Cuba. *Bull. ICBP* **7**: 139-144.

Lambert, F.R. (1987). *Forest Fig Phenology and Avian Frugivores in Malaysia*. PhD thesis, University of Aberdeen, Aberdeen, UK.

Lambert, F.R. (1989a). Fig-eating by birds in a Malaysian lowland forest. *J. Trop. Ecol.* **5**: 401-412.

Lambert, F.R. (1989b). Daily ranging behaviour of three tropical forest frugivores. *Forktail* **4**: 107-116.

Lambert, F.R. (1993). Some key sites and significant records of birds in the Philippines and Sabah. *Bird Conserv. Int.* **3**: 281-297.

Lammertink, M. (1992). Search for Ivory-billed Woodpecker in Cuba. *Dutch Birding* **14(5)**: 170-173. In English with Dutch summary.

Lammertink, M. (1995). No more hope for the Ivory-billed Woodpecker *Campephilus principalis*. *Cotinga* **3**: 45-47.

Lammertink, M. (1996). The lost empire of the Imperial Woodpecker. *World Birdwatch* **18(2)**: 8-11.

Lammertink, M. & Estrada, A.R. (1993). Reporte sobre la búsqueda del Carpintero Real (*Campephilus principalis*) en Cuba, febrero-marzo 1993. *Pitirre* **6(3)**: 7. (Abstract).

Lammertink, M. & Estrada, A.R. (1995). Status of the Ivory-billed Woodpecker *Campephilus principalis* in Cuba: almost certainly extinct. *Bird Conserv. Int.* **5(1)**: 53-59.

Lamsfuss, G. (1998). *Die Vögel Sri Lankas. Ein Vogel- und Naturführer*. Max Kasparek Verlag, Heidelberg.

Land, H.C. (1970). *Birds of Guatemala*. Livingston Publishing Company, Wynnewood, Pennsylvania.

Lando, R. & Haene, E. (1996). Carpintero Blanco (*Melanerpes candidus*) en la provincia de Buenos Aires. *Nuestras Aves* **35**: 34-35.

Lane, D.F. (1999). *A Phylogenetic Analysis of the American Barbets Using Plumage and Vocal Characters (Aves; Family Ramphastidae; Subfamily Capitonidae)*. MSc thesis, Louisiana State University, Baton Rouge, Louisiana.

Lane, D.F. (2000). New Neotropical barbet. *World Birdwatch* **22(4)**: 4.

Lane, S.S. (1982). Brown-breasted Barbet (*Lybius melanopterus*) in Liwonde National Park. *Nyala* **8(2)**: 102.

Lang, E. & Rost, R. (1990a). Brutaktivitaet, Bruterfolg und Schutz des Schwarzspechtes *Dryocopus martius*. [Breeding activity, breeding success and conservation of the Black Woodpecker *Dryocopus martius*]. *Vogelwelt* **111(1)**: 28-39. In German with English summary.

Lang, E. & Rost, R. (1990b). Hoehlenoekologie und Schutz des Schwarzspechtes (*Dryocopus martius*). [Hole-ecology and conservation of the Black Woodpecker (*Dryocopus martius*)]. *Vogelwarte* **35(3)**: 177-185. In German with English summary.
Lange, R.B. (1967). Contribuição ao conhecimento da bionomía de Aves. *Ramphastos dicolorus* L. (Ramphastidae), sua nidificação e ovos. *Araucariana, Zool.* **1**: 1-3.
Lange, U. (1995). Habitatstrukturen von Höhlenzentren des Schwarzspechtes (*Dryocopus martius*) im Thüringer Wald und dessen Vorland bei Ilmenau. *Anz. Ver. Thüring. Orn.* **2(3)**: 159-192.
Lange, U. (1996). Brutphänologie, Bruterfolg und Geschlechterverhältnis der Nestlinge beim Schwarzspecht *Dryocopus martius* im Ilm-Kreis (Thüringen). [Breeding phenology, reproductive success and juvenile sex ratio of Black Woodpecker *Dryocopus martius* in the Ilm district, Thuringia]. *Vogelwelt* **117(2)**: 47-56. In German with English summary.
Langslow, D.R. (1977). Weight increases and behaviour of Wrynecks on the Isle of May. *Scottish Birds* **9(5)**: 262-267.
Lantermann, W. (1995). Beiträge zur Biometrie und zum Verhalten des Blutbürzel-Arassaris, *Aulacorhynchus haematopygus* (Gould, 1835) - Volierenbeobachtungen in Ekuador. [Notes on the biometry and behaviour of the Crimson-rumped Toucanet - aviary observations in Ecuador]. *Zool. Garten* **65(3)**: 182-192. In German with English summary.
Lanyon, S.M. & Hall, J.G. (1994). Reexamination of barbet monophyly using mitochondrial-DNA sequence data. *Auk* **111(2)**: 389-397.
Lanyon, S.M. & Zink, R.M. (1987). Genetic variation in piciform birds: monophyly and generic and familiar relationships. *Auk* **104(4)**: 724-732.
Lanz, H. (1950). Vom Dreizehenspecht (*Picoides tridactylus alpinus* Brehm) und seinem Brutleben. *Orn. Beob.* **47**: 137-141.
Lape, J.J. (1990). *Mate Guarding in the Red-cockaded Woodpecker*. MSc thesis, North Carolina State University, Raleigh, North Carolina.
Lapham, H.S. (1985). Ivory-billed Woodpecker news. *Wingtips* **2**: 148-151.
Larison, B., Smith, T.B., Fotso, R. & McNiven, D. (2000). Comparative avian biodiversity of five mountains in northern Cameroon and Bioko. Proceedings of the Ninth Pan-African Ornithological Congress, Accra, Ghana, 1-7 December 1996. *Ostrich* **71(1&2)**: 269-276.
Larsen, C.J. (1987). *A Petition to the State of California Fish and Game Commission: List the Gila Woodpecker (*Melanerpes uropygialis*) as Endangered*. California Department of Fish & Game, Sacramento, California.
Larson, D.L. (1996). Seed dispersal by specialist versus generalist foragers: the plant's perspective. *Oikos* **76(1)**: 113-120.
Laskey, A.R. (1966). The manner of feeding fledgling woodpeckers. *Wilson Bull.* **78(1)**: 64-67.
László, V. (1988). The study of bird species foraging on the bark. *Aquila* **95**: 83-92.
Latta, S.C. & Wunderle, J.M. (1996). The composition and foraging ecology of mixed-species flocks in pine forests of Hispaniola. *Condor* **98(3)**: 595-607.
Laubmann, A. (1930). *Wissenschaftliche Ergebnissenden Deutschen Gran Chaco-Expedition. Vögel*. Strecher und Schröder, Stuttgart.
Laubmann, A. (1939). *Wissenschaftliche Ergebnisseden Deutschen Gran Chaco-Expedition. Vögel. Die Vögel von Paraguay*. Strecher und Schröder, Stuttgart.
Laughlin, R.M. (1952). A nesting of the Double-toothed Kite in Panama. *Condor* **54(3)**: 137-139.
Laurance, W.F. (1998). A crisis in the making: responses of Amazonian forests to land use and climate change. *Trends Ecol. Evol.* **13**: 411-415.
Laurent, G. (1941-1945). Sur le tambourinage du Pic cendré *Picus c. canus*. *Alauda* **13**: 123.
Laurent, G. (1947). Note sur le tambourinage des pics pendant l'automne. *Alauda* **14**: 167-168.
Laves, K.S. (1992). *Establishment of a Viable Population of Red-cockaded Woodpeckers at the Savannah River Site*. Annual report **FY1992**. Technical Information Center Oak Ridge, Tennessee. 13 pp.
Laves, K.S. & Loeb, S.C. (1999). Effects of southern flying squirrels *Glaucomys volans* on Red-cockaded Woodpecker *Picoides borealis* reproductive success. *Anim. Conserv.* **2(4)**: 295-303.
Law, S.C. (1948). Occurrence of the Speckled Piculet *Vivia innominatus* (Burton) in Khulna, Bengal. *J. Bombay Nat. Hist. Soc.* **47(3)**: 548.
Lawrence, L.K. (1966). *A Comparative Life-history Study of Four Species of Woodpeckers*. American Ornithologists' Union Monograph **5**, Washington, D.C. 156 pp.
Laybourne, R.C., Deedrick, D.W. & Hueber, F.M. (1994). Feather in amber is earliest New World fossil of Picidae. *Wilson Bull.* **106(1)**: 18-25.
Leach, F.A. (1925). Communism in the California Woodpecker. *Condor* **27(1)**: 12-19.
Leck, C.F. (1972). Observations of birds at *Cecropia* trees in Puerto Rico. *Wilson Bull.* **84(4)**: 498-500.
Leck, C.F. (1979). Avian extinctions in an isolated tropical wet-forest preserve, Ecuador. *Auk* **96(2)**: 343-352.
Leconte, M. (1999). Pic à dos blanc *Dendrocopos leucotos*. Pp. 262-263 in: Rocamora & Yeatman-Berthelot (1999).
Ledant, J.P., Jacob, J.P., Jacobs, P., Mahler, F., Ochando, B. & Roché, J. (1981). Mise à jour de l'avifaune algérienne. *Gerfaut* **71**: 298-398.
Lees-Smith, D.T. (1986). Composition and origins of the south-west Arabian avifauna: a preliminary analysis. *Sandgrouse* **7**: 71-91.
Legge, W.V. (1983). *A History of the Birds of Ceylon*. 2nd edition. Tisara Prakasakayo Ltd, Dehiwala.
Lehnhausen, W. & Murphy, E. (1985). Woodpecker predation on forest insects in the Rosie Creek Burn. *Proc. Alaska Sci. Conf.* **36**: 69. (Abstract).
Lekagul, B. & Round, P.D. (1991). *A Guide to the Birds of Thailand*. Saha Karn Bhaet, Bangkok.
Lencioni-Neto, F. (1995). Um híbrido entre *Picumnus cirratus temminckii* e *P. albosquamatus guttifer* (Piciformes: Picidae). *Ararajuba* **3**: 68-69. In Portuguese with English summary.
Lennartz, M.R. (1983). *Sociality and Cooperative Breeding of Red-cockaded Woodpeckers,* Picoides borealis. PhD dissertation, Clemson University, Clemson, South Carolina.
Lennartz, M.R. & Harlow, R.F. (1979). The role of parent and helper Red-cockaded Woodpeckers at the nest. *Wilson Bull.* **91(2)**: 331-335.
Lennartz, M.R. & Henry, V.G. (1985). *Endangered Species Recovery Plan: Red-cockaded Woodpecker,* Picoides borealis. US Fish & Wildlife Service, Atlanta, Georgia. 88 pp.
Lennartz, M.R., Hooper, R.G. & Harlow, R.F. (1987). Sociality and cooperative breeding of the Red-cockaded Woodpecker, *Picoides borealis*. *Behav. Ecol. Sociobiol.* **20(2)**: 77-88.
Lennartz, M.R., Knight, H.A., McClure, J.P. & Rudis, V.A. (1983). Status of Red-cockaded Woodpecker nesting habitat in the South. Pp. 13-19 in: Wood (1983c).
Lenz, R. (1997). Die bekanntesten Buntspechte. *Gefiederte Welt* **121(12)**: 432-433.
Lenz, R. (1998). Über den Zwerg unter unseren Spechten - den Kleinspecht. *Gefiederte Welt* **122(1)**: 32-33.
Leo, M., Ortiz, E.G. & Rodríguez, L. (1988). *Results of 1988 Field Work: Faunal Inventory, Río Abiseo National Park, Peru*. Asociación Peruana para la Conservación de la Naturaleza, Lima.
Leonard, D.L. (2000). Breeding and life history observations of the Gray-breasted Woodpecker (*Melanerpes hypopolius*). *Orn. Neotropical* **11(4)**: 341-348.
Leonard, D.L. (2001). Three-toed Woodpecker (*Picoides tridactylus*). No. **588** in: Poole, A.F. & Gill, F.B. eds. (2001). *The Birds of North America*. Vol. 15. Academy of Natural Sciences & American Ornithologists' Union, Philadelphia & Washington, D.C.
Leonard, P.M. (1998a). Forest birds in Western Zambezi District. Pp. 12-22 in: Leonard & Peters (1998).
Leonard, P.M. (1998b). Notes on afrotropical bird movements and seasonality near Kafue. Pp. 23-45 in: Leonard & Peters (1998).
Leonard, P.M. & Peters, W. eds. (1998). *Zambia Bird Report 1997*. Zambian Ornithological Society, Lusaka.
Leonard, P.M. & Van Daele, P. (1999). Mwinilunga's marginal forests. Pp. 1-11 in: Leonard, P.M. & Peters, W. eds. (1999). *Zambia Bird Report 1998*. Zambian Ornithological Society, Lusaka.
Leonard, P.M., Beel, C. & Van Daele, P. (2001). 1999 species records. Pp. 100-199 in: Leonard, P.M., Beel, C. & Van Daele, P. eds. (2001). *Zambia Bird Report 1999*. Zambian Ornithological Society, Lusaka.
Letourneau, C. (1998). Enquête Pic mar en Île-de-France: résultats de 1998. *L'Épeichette* **48**: 29-41.
Leven, M.R. (1998). Speckled Piculet at Ma On Shan: the first record for Hong Kong. *Hong Kong Bird Rep.* **1998**: 128-131.
Levey, D.J. & Cipollini, M.L. (1999). Effects of plant secondary metabolites on diet choice and digestion. Pp. 2208-2220 in: Adams & Slotow (1999).
Levey, D.J. & Stiles, F.G. (1994). Birds: ecology, behavior, and taxonomic affinities. Pp. 217–228 in: McDade *et al.* (1994).
Lewin, H.G.D. (1954). A nest of the Bamboo Green Woodpecker. *Malay. Nat. J.* **9**: 16-18.
Lewis, A.D. (1982). Notes on Levaillant's Barbet. *Bull. East Afr. Nat. Hist. Soc.* **1982**: 41-43.
Lewis, A.D. (1984). Notes on the ranges of three species in northern and eastern Kenya. *Scopus* **8**: 27-28.
Lewis, A.D. & Pomeroy, D.E. (1989). *A Bird Atlas of Kenya*. A.A. Balkema, Rotterdam.
Lewis, C.B. (1950). Woodpecker damage to oranges. *Nat. Hist. Notes Nat. Hist. Soc. Jamaica* **4(41)**: 94.
Lewthwaite, R. (1993). Great Barbet eating a lizard. *Hong Kong Bird Rep.* **1993**: 211.
Li Yanjuan (1962). [The Speckled Piculet *Picumnus innominatus* discovered in Henan Province]. *J. Xinxiang Normal College* **4**: 95. In Chinese.
Liberek, M. & Baumann, S. (1990). [New observation of the Northern Three-toed Woodpecker, *Picoides tridactylus*, in Jura, Switzerland]. *Nos Oiseaux* **40(7)**: 432. In French.
Liesen, J. (1996). *Aspekte der Verwendung des Mittelspechtes (*Picoides medius*) als Leitart für die Bewertung Ehemaliger Mittelwaelder*. Natur in Buch und Kunst, Verlag Dieter Prestel, Neunkirchen, Germany. 91 pp.
Ligon, J.D. (1968a). Observations on Strickland's Woodpecker, *Dendrocopos stricklandi*. *Condor* **70(1)**: 83-84.
Ligon, J.D. (1968b). Sexual differences in foraging behavior in two species of *Dendrocopos* woodpeckers. *Auk* **85(2)**: 203-215.
Ligon, J.D. (1970). Behavior and breeding biology of the Red-cockaded Woodpecker. *Auk* **87(2)**: 255-278.
Ligon, J.D. (1971). Some factors influencing numbers of the Red-cockaded Woodpecker. Pp. 30-43 in: Thompson (1971).
Ligon, J.D. (1973). Foraging behavior of the White-headed Woodpecker in Idaho. *Auk* **90(4)**: 862-869.
Ligon, J.D. & Stacey, P.B. (1996). Land use, lag times and the detection of demographic change: the case of the Acorn Woodpecker. *Conserv. Biol.* **10(3)**: 840-846.
Ligon, J.D., Stacey, P.B., Conner, R.N., Bock, C.E. & Adkisson, C.S. (1986). Report of the American Ornithologists' Union Committee for the Conservation of the Red-cockaded Woodpecker. *Auk* **103(4)**: 848-855.
Liknes, E.T. & Swanson, D.L. (1996). Seasonal variation in cold tolerance, basal metabolic rate, and maximal capacity for thermogenesis in White-breasted Nuthatches *Sitta carolinensis* and Downy Woodpeckers *Picoides pubescens*, two unrelated arboreal temperate residents. *J. Avian Biol.* **27(4)**: 279-288.
Lill, A. (1970). Nidification in the Channel-billed Toucan (*Ramphastos vitellinus*) in Trinidad, West Indies. *Condor* **72(2)**: 235-236.
Lim Kim Seng (1992). *Vanishing Birds of Singapore*. The Nature Society (Singapore), Singapore.
Lima, F.C.T. (2001). *Picumnus fulvescens* Stager, 1961, and its synonym *Picumnus limae saturatus* Pinto & Camargo, 1961. MS.
Lima, F.C.T. & Aleixo, A. (2000). Notas sobre algumas aves em ambientes antropizados da cidade de campinas, São Paulo, Brasil. *Bol. CEO* **14**: 2-6.
Lima, S.L. (1983). Downy Woodpecker foraging behavior: foraging by expectation and energy intake rate. *Oecologia* **58(2)**: 232-237.
Lima, S.L. (1984). Downy Woodpecker foraging behavior: efficient sampling in stochastic environments. *Ecology* **65(1)**: 166-174.
Linder, K.A. (1994). *Habitat Utilization and Behavior of Nesting Lewis' Woodpeckers (*Melanerpes lewis*) in the Laramie Range, Southeast Wyoming*. MSc thesis, University of Wyoming, Laramie, Wyoming.
Linder, K.A. & Anderson, S.H. (1998). Nesting habitat of Lewis' Woodpeckers in southeastern Wyoming. *J. Field Orn.* **69(1)**: 109-116.
Linkola, P. (1967). Pohjantikan, *Picoides tridactylus*, pesimisest Kanahaukan, *Accipiter gentilis*, naapuruudessa. *Ornis Fenn.* **44(1)**: 21-24. In Finnish with German summary.
Lippens, L. & Wille, H. (1976). *Les Oiseaux du Zaïre*. Éditions Lannoo, Tielt, Belgium.
Lisi, G. (1988). *A Field Study of Black-backed Woodpeckers in Vermont*. Technical Report **3**. Nongame and Endangered Species Program, Vermont Fish & Wildlife Department, Waterbury, Vermont.
Liu Huanjin & Shen Shouyi (1988). Breeding ecology of the Black Woodpecker *Dryocopus martius* in Pangquangou Natural Reserve (Shanxi Province). *Sichuan J. Zool.* **7(3)**: 21-23.
Liu Yikang & Wang Jinghua (1984). [Study on the breeding and feeding ecology of the Green Woodpecker *Picus canus*]. *Chinese J. Zool.* **5**: 18-21. In Chinese.
Liversidge, R.L. (1959). Tropical mountain birds south of the Zambesi. *Ostrich* **3**(Suppl.): 68-78.
Liversidge, R.L. (1991). *The Birds around Us*. Fontein, Parklands, South Africa.
Lloyd, H. (2000). Nesting behaviour of the Rufous-headed Woodpecker *Celeus spectabilis*. *Bull. Brit. Orn. Club* **120(2)**: 129-133.
Lobkov, E.G. (1999). [Kamchatka as a local center of form generation in birds]. Pp. 5-23 in: *[The Biology and Conservation of the Birds of Kamchatka]*. Vol. 1. Russian Academy of Science, Far Eastern Brunch & Kamchatka Institute of Ecology, Moscow. In Russian with English summary.
Lochmiller, R. (1977). Winter beaver pond usage by Red-headed and Pileated Woodpeckers. *Oriole* **42(4)**: 74-78.
Locke, B.A. (1980). *Colony Site Selection by Red-cockaded Woodpeckers in East Texas*. MSc thesis, Stephen F. Austin State University, Nacogdoches, Texas.
Locke, B.A., Conner, R.N. & Kroll, J.C. (1983). Factors influencing colony site selection by Red-cockaded Woodpeckers. Pp. 46-50 in: Wood (1983c).
Lockwood, G. (1981). Lesser Honeyguide. *Witwatersrand Bird Club News* **115**: 3.
Lockwood, M.W. & Shackelford, C.E. (1998). The occurrence of Red-breasted Sapsucker and suspected hybrids with Red-naped Sapsucker in Texas. *Bull. Texas Orn. Soc.* **31**: 2-6.
Loftin, R.W. (1981). Pileated Woodpecker takes Red-bellied Woodpecker nestling. *Florida Field Nat.* **9(3)**: 41.
Loftin, R.W. (1994). Ivory-billed Woodpeckers in Okefenokee Swamp, 1941-42. *Winging It* **6(8)**: 8-9.
Löhrl, H. (1972). Zum Nahrungserwerb Keim Buntspecht (*Dendrocopos major*). *Anz. Orn. Ges. Bayern* **11**: 248-253.
Löhrl, H. (1977). Zur Nahrungssuche von Grau- und Gruenspecht (*Picus canus*, *P. viridis*) im winterhalbjahr. [Winter-foraging behaviour of Grey-headed and Green Woodpecker (*Picus canus*, *P. viridis*)]. *Vogelwelt* **98(1)**: 15-22. In German with English summary.
Löhrl, H. (1978). Beiträge zur Ethologie und gewichtsentwicklung beim Wendehals *Jynx torquilla*. [Notes on ethology and weight development in the Wryneck *Jynx torquilla*]. *Orn. Beob.* **75(4)**: 193-201. In German with English summary.
Löhrl, H. & Thielcke, G. (1969). Zur Brutbiologie, Ökologie und Systematik einiger Waldvögel Afghanistans. *Bonn. zool. Beitr.* **20**: 85-98.
Longrigg, R. (1993). Lesser Honeyguide. *Promerops* **208**: 14.
López, A., Lynch, J.F. & Mackinnon de Montes, B. (1989). New and noteworthy records of birds from the eastern Yucatán Peninsula. *Wilson Bull.* **101(3)**: 390-409.
López, B. (1997). *Inventario de Aves del Parque Nacional "Río Pilcomayo" Formosa, Argentina*. Monografía Especial **4**. Literature of Latin America, Buenos Aires.
López, B. & Gastezzi, P. (2000). An inventory of the birds of Segua Marsh, Manabí, Ecuador. *Cotinga* **13**: 59-64.
López, B., Salaman, P.G.W., Cowley, T.P., Arango, S. & Renjifo, L.M. (2000). The threatened birds of the río Toche, Cordillera Central, Colombia. *Cotinga* **14**: 17-23.
López de Casenave, J., Pelotto, J.P., Caziani, S.M., Mermoz, M. & Protomastro, J. (1998). Responses of avian assemblages to a natural edge in a Chaco semiarid forest in Argentina. *Auk* **115(2)**: 425-435.
Lorek, G. & Durczynska, J. (1992). Syrian Woodpecker *Dendrocopos syriacus* - new breeding species in Silesia. *Birds of Silesia* **9**: 83-85.

Louette, M. (1981a). A new species of honeyguide from West Africa (Aves, Indicatoridae). *Rev. Zool. Afr.* **95**: 131-135.
Louette, M. (1981b). *The Birds of Cameroon. An Annotated Check-list*. Paleis der Academiën, Brussel.
Louette, M. & Prigogine, A. (1982). An appreciation of the distribution of *Dendropicos goertae* and the description of a new race (Aves: Picidae). *Rev. Zool. Afr.* **96**: 461-492.
Lourenco, W.R. & Dekeyser, P.L. (1976). Deux oiseaux prédateurs de scorpions. [Two avian predators of scorpions]. *Oiseau et RFO* **46(2)**: 167-172. In French with English summary.
Lowe, P.R. (1907). On the birds of Margarita Island, Venezuela. *Ibis* **Ser. 9, no. 4**: 547-570.
Lowe, P.R. (1946). On the systematic position of the woodpeckers (Pici), honey-guides (*Indicator*), hoopoes and others. *Ibis* **88(1)**: 103-127.
Lowen, J.C., Bartrina, L., Clay, R.P. & Tobias, J.A. (1996). *Biological Surveys and Conservation Priorities in Eastern Paraguay: the Final Reports of Projects Canopy '92 and Yacutinga '95*. CSB Conservation Publications, Cambridge.
Lowen, J.C., Clay, R.P., Brooks, T.M., Esquivel, E.Z., Bartrina, L., Barnes, R., Butchart, S.H.M. & Etcheverry, N.I. (1995). Bird conservation in the Paraguayan Atlantic forest. *Cotinga* **4**: 58-64.
Lowery, G.H. & Dalquest, W.W. (1951). *Birds from the State of Veracruz, Mexico*. University of Kansas Publications, Museum of Natural History **3(4)**. University of Kansas, Lawrence, Kansas. 119 pp.
Lowther, P.E. (2000). Nuttall's Woodpecker (*Picoides nuttallii*). No. **555** in: Poole, A.F. & Gill, F.B. eds. (2000). *The Birds of North America*. Vol. 14. Academy of Natural Sciences & American Ornithologists' Union, Philadelphia & Washington, D.C.
Lowther, P.E. (2001). Ladder-backed Woodpecker (*Picoides scalaris*). No. **565** in: Poole, A.F. & Gill, F.B. eds. (2001). *The Birds of North America*. Vol. 15. Academy of Natural Sciences & American Ornithologists' Union, Philadelphia & Washington, D.C.
Lucas, F.A. (1897). The tongues of birds. *Rep. US Natl. Mus.* **1895**: 1001-1019.
Lucero, M.M. & Alabarce, E.A. (1980). Frecuencia de especies e individuos en una parcela de la selva misionera (Aves). *Rev. Mus. Arg. Cienc. Nat. Bernardino Rivadavia Ecol.* **2(7)**: 117-127.
Lucker, L. (1992). [Reactions of two Black Woodpeckers (*Dryocopus martius*) to their exchange of calls and songs]. *Nos Oiseaux* **41(8)**: 491-492. In French.
Lüdicke, M. (1960). Färbung und Hornfluss am Schnabel von *Selenidera maculirostris* (Lichtenstein). Pp. 506-509 in: *Verhandlungen der Deutschen Zoologischen Gesellschaft vom 18. Bis 23. Mai 1959 in Münster/ Westfalen*. Zoologischer Anzeiger **23**(Supplement), Leipzig.
Ludlow, F. (1937). The birds of Bhutan and adjacent territories of Sikkim and Tibet. *Ibis* **Ser. 14, no. 1**: 467-504.
Ludlow, F. (1944). The birds of south-eastern Tibet. *Ibis* **86(3)**: 348-389.
Lundquist, R.W. & Manuwal, D.A. (1990). Seasonal differences in foraging habitat of cavity-nesting birds in the southern Washington Cascades. *Studies in Avian Biology* **13**: 218-225.
Lungstrom, L.G. (1949). *Comparative Microscopic Study of the Proventriculus and Duodenum of the Mourning Dove, Red-headed Woodpecker, and Meadow-lark*. MSc thesis, University of Kansas, Lawrence, Kansas.
Lynch, J.F. (1992). Distribution of overwintering Nearctic migrants in the Yucatan Peninsula, II: use of native and human-modified vegetation. Pp. 178-196 in: Hagan & Johnston (1992).
Lynes, H. (1925). On the birds of north and central Darfur, with notes on the west central Kordofan and north Nuba Provinces of British Sudan. *Ibis* **Ser. 12, no. 1**: 344-416.
Lyons, J. (1999). Brazil's forests: world treasures for bird conservation. *World Birdwatch* **21(2)**: 13-17.
Macdonald, D.W. & Henderson, D.G. (1977). Aspects of the behaviour and ecology of mixed species bird flocks in Kashmir. *Ibis* **119(4)**: 481-493.
Macdonald, I.A.W. (1983). How the Pied Barbet *Lybius leucomelas* invaded the Fynboos of the southwest Cape. *Promerops* **160**: 10-12.
Macdonald, I.A.W. (1984). What can be learnt from the Safring Databank - the case of the Acacia Pied Barbet. *Safring News* **13(1)**: 25-34.
Macdonald, I.A.W. (1986). Range expansion in the Pied Barbet and the spread of alien tree species in southern Africa. *Ostrich* **57(2)**: 75-94.
Macdonald, J.D. (1938). Systematic notes on some African barbets. *Ibis* **Ser. 14, no. 2**: 347-349.
Macdonald, M.A. (1980). Further notes on uncommon forest birds in Ghana. *Bull. Brit. Orn. Club* **100**: 170-172.
Macdonald, M.A. & Taylor, I.R. (1977). Notes on some uncommon forest birds in Ghana. *Bull. Brit. Orn. Club* **97(4)**: 116-120.
MacDonald, M. (1960). *Birds in my Indian Garden*. Jonathan Cape, London.
Machado, C.G. (1999). A composição dos bandos mistos de aves na mata Atlantica da Serra de Paranapiacaba, no sudeste Brasileiro. *Rev. Bras. Biol.* **59(1)**: 75-85.
Machado, C.G. & Rodrigues, N.M.R. (2000). Alteração de altura de forrageamento de espécies de aves quando associadas a bandos mistos. Pp. 231-239 in: Alves *et al.* (2000).
Machado, J.G. (1972). Jamaican Woodpecker. *Gosse Bird Club Broadsheet* **19**: 24.
Machado, R.B. (1996). Avifauna associada a um reflorestamento de eucalipto no município de Antônio Dias, Minas Gerais. *Ararajuba* **4(1)**: 15-22.
Machado, R.B. & Lamas, I.R. (1996). Avifauna associada a um reflorestamento de eucalipto no município de Antônio Dias, Minas Gerais. *Ararajuba* **4(1)**: 15-22.
Machado, R.B., Aguiar, L.M.S., Lamas, I.R. & Corrêa, H.K.M. (1995). Notes on the occurrence of *Jacamaralcyon tridactyla* (Vieillot) (Aves, Piciformes, Galbulidae) in an Atlantic forest fragment, municipality of Antônio Dias (Minas Gerais). *Rev. Bras. Zool.* **12(4)**: 743-746.
MacKinnon, J. (1988). *Field Guide to the Birds of Java and Bali*. Gadjah Mada University Press, Yogyakarta, Indonesia.
MacKinnon, J. & Phillipps, K. (1993). *A Field Guide to the Birds of Borneo, Sumatra, Java and Bali*. Oxford University Press, Oxford.
MacKinnon, J. & Phillipps, K. (2000). *A Field Guide to the Birds of China*. Oxford University Press, Oxford.
Macklin, C.H. (1937). Breeding the White-headed Woodpecker, *Melanerpes candidus*. *Avicult. Mag.* (5th Ser.) **2**: 244-246.
Mackworth-Praed, C.W. & Grant, C.H.B. (1938). On the status of *Trachyphonus margaritatus somalicus* Zedlitz, Orn. Monatsb. 1910, p. 57. Al Dubar, British Somaliland. *Ibis* **Ser. 14, no. 2**: 766-767.
Mackworth-Praed, C.W. & Grant, C.H.B. (1957). *African Handbook of Birds. Series One. Birds of Eastern and North Eastern Africa*. Vol. 1. Longman, London.
Mackworth-Praed, C.W. & Grant, C.H.B. (1962). *African Handbook of Birds. Series Two. Birds of the Southern Third of Africa*. Vol. 1. Longman, London & New York.
Mackworth-Praed, C.W. & Grant, C.H.B. (1970). *African Handbook of Birds. Series Three. Birds of West Central and Western Africa*. Vol. 1. Longman, London & New York.
Maclean, G.L. (1971). Sharp-billed Honeyguide parasitising Neddicky in Natal. *Ostrich* **42**: 75-77.
Maclean, G.L. (1990). *Ornithology for Africa. A Text for Users on the African Continent*. University of Natal Press, Pietermaritzburg, South Africa.
Maclean, G.L. (1993). *Roberts' Birds of Southern Africa*. 6th edition. Trustees of the John Voelcker Bird Book Fund, Cape Town.
Macpherson, D.W.K. (1975). Deliberate guiding by the Greater Honeyguide. *Ostrich* **46**: 186.
Macquarrie, K., Bärtschi, A. & Bärtschi, C. (1992). *Peru's Amazonian Eden: Manu National Park and Biosphere Reserve*. F. O. Patthey Sons, Barcelona, Spain.
MacRoberts, M.H. (1970). Notes on the food habits and food defense of the Acorn Woodpecker. *Condor* **72(2)**: 196-204.
MacRoberts, M.H. (1974). Acorns, woodpeckers, grubs, and scientists. *Pacific Discovery* **27**: 9-15.
MacRoberts, M.H. (1975). Food storage and winter territory in Red-headed Woodpeckers in north-western Louisiana. *Auk* **92(2)**: 382-384.
MacRoberts, M.H. & MacRoberts, B.R. (1976). *Social Organization and Behavior of the Acorn Woodpecker in Central Coastal California*. Ornithological Monographs **21**. American Ornithologists' Union, Washington, D.C. 116 pp.
MacRoberts, M.H. & MacRoberts, B.R. (1985). Gila Woodpecker stores acorns. *Wilson Bull.* **97(4)**: 571.
Maddux, E.H. (1989). Have the Northern Cardinal and the Red-bellied Woodpecker expanded their ranges in Nebraska recently, 1968-1987? *Nebraska Bird Rev.* **57(4)**: 87-92.
Madge, S. (1971). Records of Golden-rumped Tinkerbird on the Copperbelt. *Bull. Zambian Orn. Soc.* **3**: 60-61.
Madge, S. & Cunningham-van Someren, G.R. (1975). Black-throated Honeyguide and Abyssinian Scimitar-bill. *Bull. East Afr. Nat. Hist. Soc.* **1975**: 130-131.
Madoc, G.C. (1976). *An Introduction to Malayan Birds*. Malayan Nature Society, Kuala Lumpur.
Madon, P. (1930). Pics, grimpereaux, sittelles, huppes; leur régime. *Alauda* **2(2)**: 85-121.
Madon, P. (1936). Sur le nourriture des pics. *Alauda* **8(1)**: 119.
Madrid, J.A., Madrid, H.D., Funes, S.H., López, J., Botzoc, R. & Ramos, A. (1991). *Biología de la Reproducción y Comportamiento del Águila Elegante (*Spizaetus ornatus*), en el Parque Nacional de Tikal*. Progress Report IV, Maya Project, The Peregrine Fund, Boise, Idaho.
Madroño, A. (1995). El Chaco Paraguayo: ambientes naturales, sus aves y problemas de conservación. *Cotinga* **4**: 25-29.
Madroño, A. & Esquivel, E.Z. (1995). Reserva Natural del Bosque de Mbaracayú: su importancia en la conservación de aves amenazadas, cuasi-amenazadas y endémicas del Bosque Atlántico. *Cotinga* **4**: 52-57.
Madroño, A. & Pearman, M. (1992). Distribution, status and taxonomy of the near-threatened Black-bodied Woodpecker *Dryocopus schulzi*. *Bird Conserv. Int.* **2**: 253-272.
Madroño, A., Clay, R. & Hostettler, H. (1997). San Rafael National Park, Paraguay. *World Birdwatch* **19(3)**: 6-7.
Madroño, A., Clay, R.P., Robbins, M.B., Rice, N.H., Faucett, R.C. & Lowen, J.C. (1997). An avifaunal survey of the vanishing interior Atlantic forest of San Rafael National Park, Departments Itapúa/Caazapá, Paraguay. *Cotinga* **7**: 45-53.
Madroño, A., Robbins, M.B. & Zyskowski, K. (1997). Contribución al conocimiento ornitológico del Bosque Atlántico Interior del Paraguay: Parque Nacional Caaguazú, Caazapá. *Cotinga* **7**: 54-60.
Mahabal, A. & Lamba, B.S. (1987). *On the Birds of Poona and Vicinity*. Zoological Survey of India Miscellaneous Publication Occasional Paper **94**, Calcutta. 115 pp.
Majewski, P. & Rolstad, J. (1993). The detectability of Black Woodpecker: implications for forest bird censuses. *Ornis Fenn.* **70(4)**: 213-214.
Majumdar, N. (1979). On the occurrence of the Black-naped Green Woodpecker, *Picus canus hessei* Gyldenstolpe (Piciformes: Picidae) in Orissa. *J. Bombay Nat. Hist. Soc.* **75(3)**: 924.
Majumdar, N., Roy, C.S., Ghosal, D.K., Dasgupta, J.M., Basuroy, S. & Datta, B.K. (1992). Aves. Pp. 171-418 in: Ghosh, A.K. ed. (1992). *Fauna of West Bengal*. Part 1. Mammalia, Aves, Wildlife Conservation. Zoological Survey of India, State Fauna Series **3**, Calcutta. 443 pp.
Maldonado-Coelho, M. & Marini, M.A. (2000). Effects of forest fragment size and successional stage on mixed-species bird flocks in southeastern Brazil. *Condor* **102(3)**: 585-594.
Malizia, L.R. (2001). Seasonal fluctuations of birds, fruits, and flowers in a subtropical forest of Argentina. *Condor* **103(1)**: 45-61.
Malizia, L.R., Aragón, R., Chacoff, N.P. & Monmany, A.C. (1998). ¿Son las rutas una barrera para el desplazamiento de las aves? El caso de la Reserva Provincial La Florida (Tucumán, Argentina). [Are roads barriers for bird movements? The case of La Florida Provincial Reserve (Tucumán, Argentina)]. *Hornero* **15(1)**: 10-16. In Spanish with English summary.
Mallet-Rodrigues, F., Alves, V.S. & de Noronha, M.L.M. (1997). O uso do tártaro emético no estudo da alimentação de aves silvestres no estado do Rio de Janeiro. *Ararajuba* **5(2)**: 219-228.
Mannan, R.W. (1984). Summer area requirements of Pileated Woodpeckers in western Oregon. *Wildl. Soc. Bull.* **12(3)**: 265-268.
Manolis, T. (1987). Juvenal plumages of *Picoides* woodpeckers. *North Amer. Bird Bander* **12(3)**: 93.
Manor, P.D. (1991). *Demography of the Red-cockaded Woodpecker in the Sandhills of North Carolina*. MSc thesis, North Carolina State University, Raleigh, North Carolina.
Manson, A.J. (1985). Brown-backed Honeyguide at the Vumba. *Honeyguide* **31**: 172.
Manuel, C.G. (1957). Resident birds of Polillo Islands. *Phil. J. Sci.* **86**: 1-11.
Marchant, J.H., Hudson, R., Carter, S.P. & Whittington, P. (1990). *Population Trends in British Breeding Birds*. British Trust for Ornithology, Tring, UK.
Marelli, C.A. (1919). Sobre el contenido del estómago de algunas aves. *Hornero* **1**: 221-228.
María, H.N. & Olivares, A. (1967). Adiciones a la avifauna colombiana, IV (Apodidae-Picidae). *Hornero* **10**: 403-435.
Marín, M. & Carrión, J.M. (1991). Nests and eggs of some Ecuadorian birds. *Orn. Neotropical* **2**: 44-46.
Marín, M. & Schmitt, N.J. (1991). Nests and eggs of some Costa Rican birds. *Wilson Bull.* **103(3)**: 506-509.
Marín, M., Carrión, J.M. & Sibley, F.C. (1992). New distributional records for Ecuadorian birds. *Orn. Neotropical* **3(1)**: 27-34.
Marini, M.Â. ed. (1997). *VI Congresso Brasileiro de Ornitologia*. Belo Horizonte, Brazil.
Marini, M.Â. (2001). Effects of forest fragmentation on birds of the Cerrado Region, Brazil. *Bird Conserv. Int.* **11(1)**: 13-25.
Marini, M.Â., Motta-Júnior, J.C., Vasconcello, L.A.S. & Cavalcanti, R. (1997). Avian body masses from the Cerrado Region of central Brazil. *Orn. Neotropical* **8(1)**: 93-99.
Marissova, I.V. (1965). [About the Syrian Woodpecker (*Dendrocopos syriacus* Hemp et Ehrent) in the Ukraine]. *Zoologischeskii Zhurnal* **44(11)**: 1735-1737. In Russian.
van Marle, J.G. & Voous, K.H. (1988). *The Birds of Sumatra. An Annotated Check-list*. BOU Check-list **10**. British Ornithologists' Union, Tring, UK.
Marshall, B.E. (1996). More on Whyte's Barbet in Harare. *Honeyguide* **42**: 32.
Marshall, C.H.T. & Marshall, G.F.L. (1871). *A Monograph of the Capitonidae or Scansorial Barbets*. Published privately, London.
Marshall, G.A.K. (1909). Birds as a factor in the production of mimetic resemblances among butterflies. *Trans. Entomol. Soc. London* **3**: 329–339.
Marshall, J.T. (1957a). *Birds of Pine-oak Woodland in Southern Arizona and Adjacent Mexico*. Pacific Coast Avifauna **32**. Cooper Ornithological Society, Berkeley, California. 125 pp.
Marshall, J.T. (1957b). Arizona Woodpecker: *Dendrocopus arizonae*: Pp. 168-169 in: Pough, R.H. ed. (1957). *Audubon Western Bird Guide*. Doubleday & Co. Inc., Garden City, New York.
Martens, J. & Eck, S. (1995). *Towards an Ornithology of the Himalayas: Systematics, Ecology, and Vocalizations of Nepal Birds*. Bonner Zoologische Monographien **38**. Zoologisches Forschungsinstitut und Museum Alexander Koenig, Bonn. 445 pp.
Martin, J.W. & Kroll, J.C. (1975). Hoarding of corn by Golden-fronted Woodpeckers. *Wilson Bull.* **87(4)**: 553.
Martín, M. (2000). Estima de la densidad poblacional de Tucán de Pico Verde (*Ramphastos dicolorus*) en una isla del sureste de Brasil. *Grupo Estud. Ecol., Sér. Doc.* **6(1)**: 1-9.
Martin, R. & Martin, E. (1993). Knysna Woodpeckers at Paarl. *Promerops* **211**: 12.
Martin, R. & Martin, E. (1996). A further record of Knysna Woodpeckers at Paarl. *Promerops* **222**: 14.
Martin, T.E. & Li, P. (1992). Life history traits of open vs. cavity-nesting birds. *Ecology* **73**: 579-592.
Martindale, S.P. (1980). *Foraging Patterns of Nesting Gila Woodpeckers*. PhD dissertation, University of Arizona, Tucson, Arizona.
Martindale, S.P. (1982). Nest defense and central place foraging: a model and experiment. *Behav. Ecol. Sociobiol.* **10(2)**: 85-89.
Martindale, S.P. (1983). Foraging patterns of nesting Gila Woodpeckers. *Ecology* **64(4)**: 888-898.
Martindale, S.P. & Lamm, D. (1984). Sexual dimorphism and parental role switching in Gila Woodpeckers. *Wilson Bull.* **96**: 116-121.
Mason, C.W. & Lefroy, H.M. (1912). *The Food of Birds in India*. Memoirs of the Department of Agriculture in India, Entomological Series **3**. 371 pp.

Mason, V. & Jarvis, F. (1989). *Birds of Bali*. Periplus, Singapore.
Mathews, W.H. (1941). Bird notes from Baltistan. *J. Bombay Nat. Hist. Soc.* **42(3)**: 658-663.
Matsumoto, K. (1987). [Growth and development of the Black Woodpecker *Dryocopus martius* in captivity]. *Jap. J. Orn.* **35(4)**: 155-164. In Japanese with English summary.
Matsuoka, S. (1976). Autolycism in the foraging of the Grey-headed Green Woodpecker (*Picus canus*). *Tori* **25**: 107-108.
Matsuoka, S. (1979a). Ecological significance of the early breeding in White-backed Woodpeckers *Dendrocopos leucotos*. *Tori* **28**: 63-75.
Matsuoka, S. (1979b). Stomach contents of a nestling of Grey-headed Green Woodpecker *Picus canus*. *J. Yamashina Inst. Orn.* **11(2)**: 121-122. In English with Japanese summary.
Matsuoka, S. (1983). Change of iris color with age in Great Spotted Woodpeckers *Dendrocopos major*. *Tori* **32**: 139-143.
Matsuoka, S. (1986). Pellet regurgitation by Great Spotted *Dendrocopos major* and White-backed *D. leucotos* Woodpeckers. *Jap. J. Orn.* **35**: 75-76.
Matsuoka, S. & Kojima, K. (1979a). Contents of fecal droppings collected in a nest of the Black Woodpecker *Dryocopus martius*. *Tori* **28(2/3)**: 97-98. In English with Japanese summary.
Matsuoka, S. & Kojima, K. (1979b). Winter food habits of Grey-headed Green Woodpeckers *Picus canus*. *Tori* **28(4)**: 107-116. In English with Japanese summary.
Matsuoka, S. & Kojima, K. (1985). Studies on the food habits of four sympatric species of woodpeckers. Part 1. Grey-headed Green Woodpecker *Picus canus* in winter. *Tori* **33(4)**: 103-111. In English with Japanese summary.
Matthysen, E., Grubb, T.C. & Cimprich, D. (1991). Social control of sex-specific foraging behaviour in Downy Woodpeckers, *Picoides pubescens*. *Anim. Behav.* **42(3)**: 515-517.
Mauersberger, G., Wagner, S., Wallschläger, D. & Warthold, R. (1982). Neue Daten zur Avifauna Mongolica. *Mitt. Zool. Mus. Berlin* **58(1)**: 11-74.
Maurício, G.N. & Dias, R.A. (1998). Range extensions and new records for forest birds in southern Rio Grande do Sul, Brazil. *Bull. Brit. Orn. Club* **118(1)**: 14-25.
Maurício, G.N. & Dias, R.A. (2000). New distributional information for birds in southern Rio Grande do Sul, Brazil, and the first record of the Rufous Gnateater *Conopophaga lineata* for Uruguay. *Bull. Brit. Orn. Club* **120(4)**: 230-237.
Maxson, S.J. & Maxson, G.A.D. (1981). Commensal foraging between Hairy and Pileated Woodpeckers. *J. Field Orn.* **52(1)**: 62-63.
Maxwell, P.H. (1937). The Collared Puff-bird (*Bucco collaris*). *Avicult. Mag.* **5(2)**: 33-34.
May, P.R.A., Haber, J. & Hirschman, A. (1979). Woodpecker drilling behavior. An endorsement of the rotational theory of impact brain injury. *Arch. Neurol.* **36**: 370-373.
Mayaud, N. (1950). Sur un nid de Pic noir *Dryocopus martius*. *Alauda* **17-18(1)**: 51.
Mayfield, H. (1958). Nesting of the Black-backed Three-toed Woodpecker in Michigan. *Wilson Bull.* **70**: 195-196.
Mayr, E. & Bock, W.J. (1994). Provisional classifications v standard avian sequences: heuristics communication in ornithology. *Ibis* **136(1)**: 12-18.
Mayr, E. & Phelps, W.H. (1967). The origin of the bird fauna of the south Venezuelan highlands. *Bull. Amer. Mus. Nat. Hist.* **136(5)**: 269-328.
Mayr, E. & Short, L.L. (1970). *Species Taxa of North American Birds. A Contribution to Comparative Systematics*. Publications of the Nuttall Ornithological Club **9**, Cambridge, Massachusetts. 127 pp.
Mayr, G. (1998). *"Coraciiforme" und "Piciforme" Kleinvögel aus dem Mittel-Eozän der Grube Messel (Hessen, Deutschland)*. Courier Forschungsinstitut Senckenberg **205**. 102 pp. In German with English summary.
Mayr, G. (2001). The earliest fossil record of a modern-type piciform bird from the late Oligocene of Germany. *J. Orn.* **142(1)**: 2-6.
Mazar Barnett (2001a). Biogeography and taxonomy of the South-American species of *Picoides* (Picidae). Pp. 137-138 in: Straube, F.C. ed. (2001). *Ornitologia sem Fronteiras: Resumos do IX Congresso Brasileiro de Ornitologia, Curitiba, 22 a 27 de Julho de 2001*. (Abstract).
Mazar Barnett (2001b). On the migratory status of the Striped Woodpecker *Picoides lignarius* from Patagonia. MS.
Mazar Barnett, J. & Kirwan, G.M. (1999). Neotropical Notebook. Colombia. *Cotinga* **11**: 102.
Mazar Barnett, J. & Kirwan, G.M. (2000). Neotropical Notebook. Bolivia. *Cotinga* **14**: 106.
Mazar Barnett, J. & Kirwan, G.M. (2001). Neotropical Notebook. Brazil. *Cotinga* **15**: 69-70.
Mazar Barnett, J. & Pearman, M. (2001). *Lista Comentada de las Aves Argentinas. Annotated Checklist of the Birds of Argentina*. Lynx Edicions, Barcelona. In Spanish and English.
Mazar Barnett, J., Clark, R., Bodrati, A., Bodrati, G., Pugnali, G. & della Seta, M. (1998). Natural history notes on some little-known birds in north-west Argentina. *Cotinga* **9**: 64-75.
McAuliffe, J.R. & Hendricks, P. (1988). Determinants of the vertical distributions of woodpecker nest cavities in the saguaro cactus. *Condor* **90(4)**: 791-801.
McClelland, B.R. (1979). The Pileated Woodpecker in forests of the northern Rocky Mountains. Pp. 283-299 in: Dickson, J.G., Conner, R.N., Fleet, R.R., Kroll, J.C. & Jackson, J.A. eds. (1979). *The Role of Insectivorous Birds in Forest Ecosystems*. Academic Press, New York.
McClelland, B.R. & McClelland, P.T. (1999). Pileated Woodpecker nest and roost trees in Montana: links with old-growth and forest "health". *Wildl. Soc. Bull.* **27(3)**: 846-857.
McClelland, B.R. & McClelland, P.T. (2000). Red-naped Sapsucker nest trees in northern Rocky Mountain old-growth forest. *Wilson Bull.* **112(1)**: 44-50.
McClure, H.E. (1964a). Avian bionomics in Malaya. Part 1. The avifauna above 5000 feet altitude on Mount Brinchang, Pahang. *Bird-Banding* **35**: 141-183.
McClure, H.E. (1964b). Know your barbets. *Malay. Nat. J.* **18(1)**: 45-49.
McClure, H.E. (1966). Flowering, fruiting and animals in the canopy of a tropical rain forest. *Malay. Forester* **29**: 182-203.
McClure, H.E. (1974). Some bionomics of the birds of Khao Yai National Park, Thailand. *Nat. Hist. Bull. Siam Soc.* **25(3-4)**: 99-194.
McClure, H.E. (1998). *Migration and Survival of the Birds of Asia*. White Lotus Press, Bangkok.
McClure, H.E. & Bin Othman, H. (1965). Avian bionomics of Malaya. 2. The effect of forest destruction upon a local population. *Bird-Banding* **36**: 242-269.
McConnell, M.J. (1991). Fostering the Green Aracaris. *AFA Watchbird* **18**: 27.
McConnell, W.V. (1999). Red-cockaded Woodpecker cavity excavation in seedtree-shelterwood stands in the Wakulla (Apalachicola National Forest, Florida) sub-population. *Wildl. Soc. Bull.* **27(2)**: 509-513.
McDade, L.A., Bawa, K.S., Hespenheide, H.A. & Hartshorn, G.S. eds. (1994). *La Selva. Ecology and Natural History of a Neotropical Rain Forest*. University of Chicago Press, Chicago & London.
McFarlane, J. (1991). Crested Barbet in the western Cape. *Promerops* **201**: 13-14.
McFarlane, R.W. (1992). *A Stillness in the Pines. The Ecology of the Red-cockaded Woodpecker*. W.W. Norton & Co., New York & London.
McGillivray, W.B. & Biermann, G.C. (1987). Expansion of the zone of hybridization of Northern Flickers in Alberta. *Wilson Bull.* **99(4)**: 690-692.
McGrath, J.E. (1988). Observation of a Red-bellied Woodpecker feeding on a small mammal. *Jack-Pine Warbler* **66(3)**: 116.
McGregor, R.C. (1904). Birds from Benguet province, Luzon, and from the islands of Lubang, Mindoro, Cuyo, and Gagayancillo. *Bull. Philippine Mus.* **3**: 1-16.
McGregor, R.C. (1905). I. Birds from Mindoro and small adjacent islands. II. Notes on three rare Luzon birds. *Department of Interior, Bureau of Government Laboratories* **34**: 1-31.
McGregor, R.C. (1909-1910). *A Manual of Philippine Birds*. Manila Bureau of Sciences **1**. 769 pp.
McGuire, N.M. (1932). A Red-bellied Woodpecker robs a sapsucker. *Wilson Bull.* **44(1)**: 39.
McMichael, D.J. & Wilcove, D.S. (1977). Wintering woodpeckers in an urban environment. *Kingbird* **27(1)**: 3-10.
McNair, D.B. (1996). Late breeding records of a Red-headed Woodpecker and a Summer Tanager in Florida. *Florida Field Nat.* **24(3)**: 78-80.
McNeely, J. (1992). Ivory-billed Woodpecker expedition report. Unpublished report.
McVoy, R.S. (1978). Pileated Woodpecker eating Russian olive fruits. *Prairie Nat.* **10(3)**: 88.
Mearns, E.A. (1909). Additions to the list of Philippine birds, with descriptions of three new and rare species. *Proc. US Natl. Mus.* **36**: 435-447.
Mecum, L.K. & Abrahamson, W. (1994). Downy Woodpecker (*Picoides pubescens*) predation on the goldenrod gallmaker, *Eurosta solidaginis* (Diptera: Tephritidae). *J. Pennsylvania Acad. Sci.* **67**(Suppl.): 186. (Abstract).
Medeiros-Neto, J.J., Arruda, A.A. & Albuquerque, H.N. (1997). Um enfoque etnoecológico sobre o Fura-barreira (*Nystalus maculatus*: Bucconidae) na região do município de Soledade (PB). [An ethnoecological focus on the Spot-backed Puffbird (*Nystalus maculatus*: Bucconidae) in the municipality of Soledad (PB)]. Page 117 in: Marini (1997). (Abstract).
Medina, G. (1955). Sobre la avifauna de "El Paito" y la nidificación de *Galbula ruficauda*. *Bol. Mus. Cienc. Nat. Caracas* **1**: 196–200.
Medway, Lord (1972). The Gunong Benom expedition 1967. Part 6. The distribution and altitudinal zonation of birds and mammals of Gunong Benom. *Bull. Brit. Mus. (Nat. Hist.) Zool.* **23**: 103-154.
Medway, Lord & Wells, D.R. (1976). *The Birds of the Malay Peninsula*. Vol. 5. Conclusions and Survey of Every Species. Witherby & Penerbit University Malaya, London & Kuala Lumpur.
Mees, G.F. (1968). Enige voor de avifauna van Suriname nieuwe Vogelsoorten. *Gerfaut* **58**: 101-107.
Mees, G.F. (1986). *A List of the Birds Recorded from Bangka Island, Indonesia*. Zoologische Verhandelingen **232**. Rijksmuseum van Natuurlijke Historie, Leiden. 176 pp.
Mees, G.F. (1996). *Geographical Variation in Birds of Java*. Publications of the Nuttall Ornithological Club **26**, Cambridge, Massachusetts. 119 pp.
Melde, M. (1994). Zum Verhalten und Vorkommen unserer Spechtarten (Gattungen *Picus*, *Dendrocopos* und *Dryocopus*). *Der Falke* **41(8)**: 258-267.
Melián, L.O. (2000). *Evaluación de las Poblaciones de Carpintero Churroso (*Colaptes fernandinae*) en Territorio del Oriente Cubano. Informe del Proyecto*. Published privately.
Mellen, T.K. (1987). *Home Range and Habitat Use of Pileated Woodpeckers, Western Oregon*. MSc thesis, Oregon State University, Corvallis, Oregon.
Mellen, T.K., Meslow, E.C. & Mannan, R.W. (1992). Summertime home range and habitat use of Pileated Woodpeckers in western Oregon. *J. Wildl. Manage.* **56(1)**: 96-103.
de Mello, F.P. & Mello, M.C. (1998). Ocorrência e registro de nidificação de *Monasa nigrifrons* (Spix) (Aves, Bucconidae) a leste de Mato Grosso do Sul. *Rev. Bras. Zool.* **15(1)**: 191-193.
de Melo, C. & Marini, M.Â. (1999). Comportamento alimentar do *Monasa nigrifrons* (Aves, Bucconidae) em matas do oeste de Minas Gerais, Brasil. *Ararajuba* **7(1)**: 13-15.
Melo-Júnior, T.A. (1996). Registros de algumas aves ameaçadas no estado de Minas Gerais. *Atualidades Orn.* **72**: 13-14.
Melo-Júnior, T.A. (1998). *Jacamaralcyon tridactyla*. Pp. 290-292 in: Machado, A.B.M., da Fonseca, G.A.B., Machado, R.B., Aguiar, L.M.S. & Lins, L.V. eds. (1998). *Livro Vermelho das Espécies Ameaçadas de Extincão da Fauna de Minas Gerais*. Fundação Biodiversitas, Belo Horizonte, Brazil.
Melo-Júnior, T.A. (2000). *Morfometria, Comportamento Alimentar e Social do Cuitelão,* Jacamaralcyon tridactyla *(Galbuliformes, Galbulidae), em Duas Reservas no Estado de Minas Gerais*. MSc thesis, Universidade Estadual Paulista, Rio Claro, São Paulo.
Melo-Júnior, T.A. (2001a). Bird species distribution and conservation in Serra do Cipó, Minas Gerais, Brazil. *Bird Conserv. Int.* **11(3)**: 189-204.
Melo-Júnior, T.A. (2001b). Comportamento reprodutivo do Cuitelão, *Jacamaralcyon tridactyla*, com nova evidência para convergência ecológica entre galbulídeos e meropídeos. Pp. 276-277 in: Straube, F.C. ed. (2001). *Ornitologia sem Fronteiras*. Fundação Boticário, Cuiritiba, Brazil.
Melo-Júnior, T.A. (2001c). Comportamento alimentar do Cuitelão, *Jacamaralcyon tridactyla*, (Galbuliformes, Galbulidae), em duas reservas no estado de Minas Gerais. Pp. 277-278 in: Straube, F.C. ed. (2001). *Ornitologia sem Fronteiras*. Fundação Boticário, Cuiritiba, Brazil.
de Mendonça-Lima, A., Fontana, C.S. & Mähler, J.K.F. (2001). Itens alimentares consumidos por aves no nordeste do Rio Grande do Sul, Brasil. *Tangara* **1(3)**: 115-124.
Ménégaux, A. (1925). Étude d'une collection d'oiseaux. *Rev. Franc. d'Orn.* **17(199)**: 279-297.
Mengel, R.M. & Jackson, J.A. (1977). Geographic variation of the Red-cockaded Woodpecker. *Condor* **79(3)**: 349-355.
Menten, B. (1994). Pileated nest behavior. *Bird Watcher's Digest* **16(4)**: 60-65.
Merikallio, E. (1958). *Finnish Birds: their Distribution and Numbers*. Helsingfors, Helsinki.
van der Merwe, F. (1986). Of Lesser Honeyguides, Olive Woodpeckers and European Starlings. *Promerops* **176**: 8-10.
Messias, C.A., Lainson, R. & Shaw, J. (1990). *Eimeria vitelline* n. sp. (Apicomplexa: Eimeriidae) from the Brazilian Toucan, *Ramphastos vitellinus vitellinus* Lichtenstein (Aves: Piciformes: Ramphastidae). *Mem. Inst. Oswaldo Cruz* **85(2)**: 199-202.
Meyer, E.J.M. (1981). The capture efficiency of flickers preying on larval tiger beetles. *Auk* **98(1)**: 189-191.
Meyer de Schauensee, R. (1934). *Zoological Results of the Third de Schauensee Siamese Expedition*. Part 2. Birds from Siam and the Southern Shan States. Proceedings of the Academy of Natural Sciences of Philadelphia **86**. 116 pp.
Meyer de Schauensee, R. (1945). Notes on Colombian birds. *Proc. Acad. Nat. Sci. Philadelphia* **97**: 1-16.
Meyer de Schauensee, R. (1946a). Colombian zoological survey, part III. Notes on Colombian birds. *Notulae Naturae* **163**: 1-9.
Meyer de Schauensee, R. (1946b). On Siamese birds. *Proc. Acad. Nat. Sci. Philadelphia* **91**: 311-368.
Meyer de Schauensee, R. (1949). *The Birds of the Republic of Colombia. Segunda Entrega, Accipitridae-Picidae*. Caldasia **5**. 264 pp.
Meyer de Schauensee, R. (1950). Colombian zoological survey, part VII. A collection of birds from Bolívar, Colombia. *Proc. Acad. Nat. Sci. Philadelphia* **102**: 111-139.
Meyer de Schauensee, R. (1951). Notes on Ecuadorian birds. *Notulae Naturae* **234**: 1-11.
Meyer de Schauensee, R. (1952). Colombian zoological survey, part X. A collection of birds from southeastern Nariño, Colombia. *Proc. Acad. Nat. Sci. Philadelphia* **104**: 1-33.
Meyer de Schauensee, R. (1957). Notes on Philippine birds. *Not. Nat. (Phila.)* **303**: 1-11.
Meyer de Schauensee, R. (1964). *The Birds of Colombia and Adjacent Areas of South and Central America*. Livingston Publishing Co., Narbeth, Pennsylvania.
Meyer de Schauensee, R. (1966). *The Species of Birds of South America and their Distribution*. Livingston Publishing Co., Narbeth, Pennsylvania.
Meyer de Schauensee, R. (1982). *A Guide to the Birds of South America*. Livingston Publishing Company for the Academy of Natural Sciences of Philadelphia (reprinted with addenda by ICBP Pan-American Section), Wynnewood, Pennsylvania.
Meyer de Schauensee, R. (1984). *The Birds of China*. Oxford University Press, Oxford.
Meyer de Schauensee, R. & Phelps, W.H. (1978). *A Guide to the Birds of Venezuela*. Princeton University Press, Princeton, New Jersey.
Meyer de Schauensee, R. & Ripley, S.D. (1940). *Zoological Results of the George Vanderbilt Sumatran Expedition, 1936-1939*. Part 1. Birds from Atjeh. Proceedings of the Academy of Natural Sciences of Philadelphia **91**.
Meyers, J.M. (1978). Red-bellied Woodpecker status and nesting in the mountains of North Georgia. *Oriole* **43(1)**: 13-14.
Michael, C.W. (1926). Acorn-storing methods of the California and Lewis Woodpeckers. *Condor* **28(2)**: 68-69.
Michael, C.W. (1935). Nesting of the Williamson Sapsucker. *Condor* **37(4)**: 209-210.
Michalek, K. (1998). *Sex Roles in Great Spotted Woodpeckers* Picoides major *and Middle Spotted Woodpeckers* P. medius. PhD thesis, University of Vienna, Vienna.
Michalek, K. & Winkler, H. (1997a). Der Buntspecht - Vogel des Jahres 1997: Hacken und Klettern - ein Leben am Baum. *Der Falke* **44(1)**: 4-9.

Michalek, K. & Winkler, H. (1997b). Sex roles and paternity in the Great Spotted Woodpecker, *Picoides major*. *Adv. Ethol.* **32**: 224.
Michler, I. (1999). Brown-breasted Barbet in Malawi. *Africa. Birds & Birding* **4(4)**: 21.
Miech, P. (1986). Zum Ringeln einiger Spechtarten (Picinae) im Flachland. *Berliner orn. Bericht* **11**: 39-76.
Mierow, D. & Shrestha, T.B. (1978). *Himalayan Flowers and Trees*. Sahayogi Press, Kathmandu.
Mikich, S.B. (1991). Etograma de *Ramphastos toco* em cativeiro (Piciformes: Ramphastidae). *Ararajuba* **2**: 3-17.
Mikich, S.B. (1997). A dieta frugívora de *Celeus flavescens* (Piciformes: Picidae) no P.E. Vila Rica do Espírito Santo, Fenix, PR. Page 140 in: Marini (1997). (Abstract).
Mikusinski, G. (1995). Population trends in Black Woodpecker in relation to changes and characteristics of European forests. *Ecography* **18(4)**: 363-369.
Mikusinski, G. (1997). Spillkrakans fodosok under vintern i mellansvenska brukade skogar. [Winter foraging of the Black Woodpecker *Dryocopus martius* in managed forest in south-central Sweden]. *Ornis Fenn.* **74(4)**: 161-166. In Finnish with English summary.
Mikusinski, G. (2001). Woodpeckers as indicators of forest bird diversity. *Conserv. Biol* **15(1)**: 208-217.
Mikusinski, G. & Angelstam, P. (1997). Bestandssituation europäischer Spechte im Zusammenhang mit anthropogenen Lebensraumveränderungen: ein Überblick. [European woodpeckers and anthropogenic habitat change: a review]. *Vogelwelt* **118(5)**: 277-283.
Mikusinski, G. & Angelstam, P. (1998). Geografía económica, distribución forestal y diversidad de pájaros carpinteros en Europa central. [Economic geography, forest distribution, and woodpecker diversity in central Europe]. *Conserv. Biol.* **12(1)**: 200-208.
Millar, B.R. (1992). *An Ecological Assessment of the Use of Hydro Utility Poles for Nesting by Pileated Woodpeckers in Southeastern Manitoba*. MSc thesis, University of Manitoba, Winnipeg, Manitoba.
Miller, A.H. (1955a). A hybrid woodpecker and its significance in speciation in the genus *Dendrocopos*. *Evolution* **9**: 317-321.
Miller, A.H. (1955b). The avifauna of the Sierra del Carmen of Coahuila, Mexico. *Condor* **57(3)**: 154-178.
Miller, A.H. (1955c). Acorn Woodpecker on Santa Catalina Island, California. *Condor* **57(6)**: 373.
Miller, A.H. (1963). Seasonal activity and ecology of the avifauna of an American equatorial cloud forest. *Univ. Calif. Publ. Zool.* **66(1)**: 1-78.
Miller, A.H. & Bock, C.E. (1972). Natural history of the Nuttall Woodpecker at the Hastings Reservation. *Condor* **74(3)**: 284-294.
Miller, A.H., Friedmann, H., Griscom, L. & Moore, R.T. eds. (1957). *Distributional Check-list of the Birds of Mexico*. Part 2. Pacific Coast Avifauna **33**. Cooper Ornithological Society, Berkeley, California.
Miller, C.M. (1995). *100 Birds of Belize*. American Bird Conservancy, Gallon Jug, Belize.
Miller, E.H., Walters, E.L. & Ouellet, H.R. (1999). Plumage, size, and sexual dimorphism in the Queen Charlotte Islands Hairy Woodpecker. *Condor* **101(1)**: 86-95.
Miller, G.L. (1978). *The Population, Habitat, Behavioral and Foraging Ecology of the Red-cockaded Woodpecker (*Picoides borealis*) in Southeastern Virginia*. MSc thesis, College of William and Mary, Williamsburg, Virginia.
Miller, J.R. (1978). Notes on birds of San Salvador Island (Watling), the Bahamas. *Auk* **95(2)**: 281-287.
Miller, W. De W. (1915). Notes on ptilosis with special reference to the feathering of the wing. *Bull. Amer. Mus. Nat. Hist.* **34**: 129-140.
Miller, W. De W. (1924). Further notes on ptilosis. *Bull. Amer. Mus. Nat. Hist.* **50**: 305-321.
Milne, K.A. & Hejl, S.J. (1989). Nest-site characteristics of White-headed Woodpeckers. *J. Wildl. Manage.* **53(1)**: 50-55.
Milstein, P. le S. (1995). Tinkering around at Mariepskop. *Birding in SA* **47(2)**: 36-39.
Mindell, D.P. & Black, M.L. (1984). Combined-effort hunting by a pair of Chestnut-mandibled Toucans. *Wilson Bull.* **96(2)**: 319-321.
Miserendino, R.S. (1998). Las aves del Izozog y zonas aledañas, Prov. Cordillera, Dpto. Santa Cruz. Pp. 73-82 in: Sagot & Guerrero (1998).
Miskell, J. (1989). Notes on the breeding behaviour of the Red-fronted Tinkerbird, *Pogoniulus pusillus* in Somalia. *Scopus* **13**: 124-125.
Mitchell, A.D. (1998). Red data bird: Fernandina's Flicker *Colaptes fernandinae*. *World Birdwatch* **20(4)**: 20-21.
Mitchell, A.D. & Wells, L. (1997). The threatened birds of Cuba project report. *Cotinga* **7**: 69-71.
Mitchell, A.D., Kirkconnell, A. & Wells, L.J. (2000). Notes on the status and nesting ecology of Fernandina's Flicker *Colaptes fernandinae*. *Bull. Brit. Orn. Club* **120(2)**: 103-112.
Mitchell, J.H., Kulhavy, D.L., Conner, R.N. & Bryant, C.M. (1991). Susceptibility of Red-cockaded Woodpecker colony areas to southern pine beetle infestation in east Texas. *South. J. Appl. For.* **15(3)**: 158-162.
Mitchell, L.R., Carlile, L.D. & Chandler, C.R. (1999). Effects of southern flying squirrels on nest success of Red-cockaded Woodpeckers. *J. Wildl. Manage.* **63(2)**: 538-545.
Mitchell, M.H. (1957). *Observations on Birds of Southeastern Brazil*. University of Toronto Press, Toronto.
Miyagi, K. (1989). Conservation of the Okinawa Rail and Okinawa Woodpecker. Proceedings of the Joint Meeting of the ICBP Asian Section and East Asia Bird Protection Conference, Bangkok, Thailand, April, 1989. Unpublished.
Mlingwa, C.O.F. (2000). Breeding and moult phenology of an avian community in the Pugu Hills, Tanzania. Proceedings of the Ninth Pan-African Ornithological Congress, Accra, Ghana, 1-7 December 1996. *Ostrich* **71(1&2)**: 87-90.
Moeller, R.K. & Thogerson, M.T. (1978). Predation by the Downy Woodpecker on the goldenrod gall fly larva. *Iowa Bird Life* **48(4)**: 131-136.
Moermond, T.C. (1985). Neotropical avian frugivores: patterns of behavior, morphology, and nutrition, with consequences for fruit selection. Pp. 865-897 in: Buckley *et al.* (1985).
Mohan, D. (1997). Birds of New Forest, Dehra Dun, India. *Forktail* **12**: 19-30.
Molesworth, B.D. (1955). A possible nesting association. *Malay. Nat. J.* **9**: 116-118.
Monadjem, A., Passmore, N.I. & Kemp, A.C. (1994). Territorial calls of allopatric and sympatric populations of two species of *Pogoniulus* tinkerbarbet in southern Africa. *Ostrich* **65**: 339-341.
Monk, J.F. ed. (1992). *Avian Systematics and Taxonomy*. Bulletin of the British Ornithologists' Club. Centenary Supplement **112A**.
Monroe, B.L. (1968). *A Distributional Survey of the Birds of Honduras*. Ornithological Monographs **7**. American Ornithologists' Union, Washington, D.C. 458 pp.
Montague, W.G. (1995). Cavity protection techniques for Red-cockaded Woodpeckers. *Proc. Arkansas Acad. Sci.* **49**: 115-120.
de Montes, B.M.V. (1989). *100 Common Birds of the Yucatan Peninsula*. Amigos de Sian Ka'an, A. C., Cancún.
Moore, A. (1980). Some observations on a brood of Grey Woodpeckers in The Gambia. *Malimbus* **2(2)**: 159.
Moore, R.T. (1946). A new woodpecker from Mexico. *Proc. Biol. Soc. Washington* **59**: 103-106.
Moore, W.S. (1987). Random mating in the Northern Flicker hybrid zone: implications for the evolution of bright and contrasting plumage patterns in birds. *Evolution* **41(3)**: 539-546.
Moore, W.S. (1994). The nature of selection in the Northern Flicker hybrid zone. Page 362 in: Dittami (1994).
Moore, W.S. (1995). Northern Flicker (*Colaptes auratus*). No. **166** in: Poole, A.F. & Gill, F.B. eds. (1995). *The Birds of North America*. Vol. 5. Academy of Natural Sciences & American Ornithologists' Union, Philadelphia & Washington, D.C.
Moore, W.S. & Buchanan, D.B. (1985). Stability of the Northern Flicker hybrid zone in historical times: implications for adaptive speciation theory. *Evolution* **39**: 135-151.
Moore, W.S. & Koenig, W.D. (1986). Comparative reproductive success of Yellow-shafted, Red-shafted, and hybrid flickers across a hybrid zone. *Auk* **103(1)**: 42-51.
Moore, W.S. & Price, J.T. (1993). The nature of selection in the Northern Flicker hybrid zone and its implications for speciation theory. Pp. 196-225 in: Harrison, R.G. ed. (1993). *Hybrid Zones and the Evolutionary Process*. Oxford University Press, Oxford.
Moore, W.S., Graham, J.H. & Price, J.T. (1991). Mitochondrial DNA variation in the Northern Flicker (*Colaptes auratus*, Aves). *Mol. Biol. Evol.* **8(3)**: 327-344.
Moore, W.S., Smith, S.M. & Prychitko, T. (1999). Nuclear gene introns versus mitochondrial genes as molecular clocks. Pp. 745-753 in: Adams & Slotow (1999).
Morales, J.E. (1988). Primeros hallazgos de *Pteroglossus aracari* (Linnaeus, 1758) (Aves: Ramphastidae) en Colombia. *Trianea* **2**: 501-504.
Moran, S. (1977). Distribution and characteristics of the damage of the Syrian Woodpecker, *Dendrocopos syriacus* (Hemp & Ehr.) (Aves: Picidae), in polyethylene irrigation pipes in fruit orchards. *Phytoparasitica* **5**: 127-139.
Moreau, G.P.A. (1969). Sur l'utilisation des nichoirs par le Pic épeiche. *Alauda* **37(3)**: 181-187.
Moreau, R.E. (1935). A synecological study in Usambara, Tanganika Territory, with special reference to birds. *J. Ecol.* **23**: 1-43.
Moreau, R.E. & Moreau, W.M. (1937). Biological and other notes on some East African birds. *Ibis* **Ser. 14, no. 1**: 152-174.
Morel, G.J. & Chappuis, C. (1992). Past and future taxonomic research in West Africa. Pp. 217-224 in: Monk (1992).
Morel, G.J. & Morel, M.Y. (1990). *Les Oiseaux de Sénégambie*. Éditions de l'ORSTOM, Paris.
Morioka, H. & Sakane, T. (1981). Notes on the birds of Khumba-Karna Himal, eastern Nepal. *Tori* **29**: 129-146.
Morris, C. & Buffa, J. (1996). Birding Volcán de Fuego, Colima, Mexico. *Winging It* **8(8)**: 1, 4-7.
Morris, R. (1988). Breeding the Pied Barbet at the North Carolina Zoological Park. *AFA Watchbird* **15(2)**: 6-9.
Morris, R.C. (1939). On the occurrence of the Banded Crake *Rallus e. amauroptera* and the Malabar Woodpecker *Macropicus j. hodgsoni* in the Billigirirangan Hills, S. India. *J. Bombay Nat. Hist. Soc.* **40(4)**: 763.
Morrison, M.L. & With, K.A. (1987). Interseasonal and intersexual resource partitioning in the White-headed and Hairy Woodpeckers. *Auk* **104(2)**: 225-233.
Morrone, J.J. (2000). A new regional biogeography of the Amazonian subregion, mainly based on animal taxa. *An. Inst. Biol. Univ. Nac. Aut. Mex. (Ser. Zool.)* **71(2)**: 99-123.
Morse, D.H. (1972). Habitat utilization of the Red-cockaded Woodpecker during the winter. *Auk* **89(2)**: 429-435.
Mosansky, L. (1986). [The occurrence of the Black Woodpecker (*Dryocopus martius* L.) during the nesting period in the East Slovakian lowland]. *Biologia* **41(6)**: 627-629. In Czech with English and Russian summary.
Moskovits, D. (1978). Winter territorial and foraging behavior of Red-headed Woodpeckers in Florida. *Wilson Bull.* **90(4)**: 521-535.
Moskovits, D., Fitzpatrick, J.W. & Willard, D.E. (1985). Lista preliminar das aves da Estação Ecológica de Maracá, Território de Roraima, Brasil, e áreas adjacentes. *Pap. Avuls. Dept. Zool. São Paulo* **36**: 51-68.
Motta-Júnior, J.C. (1990). Estrutura trófica e composição das avifaunas de três hábitats terrestres na região central do estado de São Paulo. *Ararajuba* **1**: 65-71.
Mouillard, B. (1946). Essai sur la distribution du Pic noir *Dryocopus martius* (L.) 1758, dans le nord du Massif Central. *Alauda* **14**: 174-175.
Moulton, C.A. & Lowell, W.A. (1991). Effects of urbanization on foraging strategy of woodpeckers. *Natl. Inst. Urban Wildl. Symp. Ser.* **2**: 67-73.
Moyer, D.C. (1980). On Lesser Honeyguide and Black-collared Barbet. *Zambian Orn. Soc. Newsl.* **10**: 159.
Moynihan, M. (1979). *Geographic Variation in Social Behavior and in Adaptations to Competition among Andean Birds*. Publications of the Nuttall Ornithological Club **18**, Cambridge, Massachusetts.
Muckensturm, B. (1971). Contribution à l'étude de l'utilisation des cavités comme "outils" de contention par le Pic épeiche (*Dendrocopos major*). Part 2. L'ontogénèse de l'utilisation des cavités pour caler les objets manipulés. *Rev. Comp. Animal* **4**: 237-248.
Mueller, H. (1998). Untersuchungen zum Vorkommen des Schwarzspechtes und seiner Folgearten im südlichen Rothaargebirge. *Charadrius* **34(3-4)**: 165-173.
Mueller, H.C. (1971). Sunflower seed carrying by Red-bellied Woodpeckers (*Centurus carolinus*). *Bird-Banding* **42(1)**: 46-47.
Muiznieks, B. & Collazo, J.A. (1999). Some aspects of the ecology of Puerto Rican Woodpeckers (*Melanerpes portoricensis*). *Pitirre* **12(2)**: 59-60.
Mukherjee, A.K. (1952). Taxonomic notes on the Lineated and the Green Barbets of India, with a description of a new race. *Bull. Brit. Orn. Club* **72(3)**: 34-36.
Mukherjee, A.K. (1953). On a collection of birds from the Simlipal Hills, Mayurbhanj District, Orissa. *Rec. Indian Mus.* **50**: 157-172.
Mukherjee, A.K. (1995). *Birds of Arid and Semi-arid Tracts*. Zoological Survey of India Occasional Paper **142**, Calcutta. 318 pp.
Mulhauser, B., Kaiser, N. & Claude, B. (2000). Distribution et état des populations de pics (Picidae) du littoral neuchâtelois (Suisse). *Bull. Soc. Neuchâtel Sci. Nat.* **123**: 81-93.
Mulhauser, B., Kaiser, N. & Junod, P. (2001). Situation et protection des pics (Picidae) dans le canton de Neuchâtel, en relation avec le futur plan d'aménagement forestier cantonal. Pp. 71-79 in: *Actes du 39e Colloque Interrégional d'Ornithologie, Yverdon-les-Bains*. Nos Oiseaux **5**(Supplement).
Müller, W. (1977). Zur Brutverbreitung des Schwarzspechtes *Dryocopus martius* am unteren Niederrhein. *Charadrius* **13(3)**: 71-74.
Müller, W. (1982). Die Besiedlung der Eichenwälder im Kanton Zürich durch den Mittelspecht *Dendrocopos medius*. *Orn. Beob.* **79**: 105-119.
Mumme, R.L. (1984). *Competition and Cooperation in the Communally Breeding Acorn Woodpecker*. PhD thesis, University of California, Berkeley, California.
Mumme, R.L. & de Queiroz, A. (1985). Individual contributions to cooperative behaviour in the Acorn Woodpecker: effects of reproductive status, sex, and group size. *Behaviour* **95(3-4)**: 290-313. In English with German summary.
Mumme, R.L., Koenig, W.D. & Pitelka, F.A. (1983a). Reproductive competition in the communal Acorn Woodpecker: sisters destroy each other's eggs. *Nature* **306**: 583-584.
Mumme, R.L., Koenig, W.D. & Pitelka, F.A. (1983b). Mate guarding in the Acorn Woodpecker: within-group reproductive competition in a cooperative breeder. *Anim. Behav.* **31(4)**: 1094-1106.
Mumme, R.L., Koenig, W.D. & Pitelka, F.A. (1983c). Are Acorn Woodpecker territories aggregated? *Ecology* **64(5)**: 1305-1307.
Mumme, R.L., Koenig, W.D. & Pitelka, F.A. (1988). Costs and benefits of joint nesting in the Acorn Woodpecker. *Amer. Naturalist* **131**: 654-677.
Mumme, R.L., Koenig, W.D. & Pitelka, F.A. (1990). Individual contributions to cooperative nest care in the Acorn Woodpecker. *Condor* **92(2)**: 360-368.
Mumme, R.L., Koenig, W.D., Zink, R.M. & Marten, J.A. (1985). Genetic variation and parentage in a California population of Acorn Woodpeckers. *Auk* **102(2)**: 312-320.
Munn, C.A. (1985). Permanent canopy and understory flocks in Amazonia: species composition and population density. Pp. 683-712 in: Buckley *et al.* (1985).
Munteanu, D. (1968). Syrian Woodpecker (*Dendrocopos syriacus*) in Romania. *Lucrarile* **1**: 351-358.
Murai, M. & Higuchi, H. (1991). [Nesting of Great Spotted Woodpeckers and Wrynecks in artificial cylinders]. *Strix* **10**: 285-290. In Japanese with English summary.
Murphy, E.C. & Lehnhausen, W.A. (1998). Density and foraging ecology of woodpeckers following a stand-replacement fire. *J. Wildl. Manage.* **62(4)**: 1359-1372.
Murphy, G.A. (1982). *Status, Nesting Habitat, Foraging Ecology, and Home Range of the Red-cockaded Woodpecker (*Picoides borealis*) in Kentucky*. MSc thesis, Eastern Kentucky University, Richmond, Kentucky.
Murphy, J.L. & Farrand, J. (1979). Prehistoric occurrence of the Ivory-billed Woodpecker (*Campephilus principalis*), Muskingum County, Ohio. *Ohio J. Sci.* **79(1)**: 22-23.
Murphy, M.T. (1981). Yellow-bellied Sapsucker displaced by Common Flicker. *Loon* **53(3)**: 174.

Murray, K.G. (1988). Avian seed dispersal of three Neotropical gap-dependent plants. *Ecol. Monogr.* **58(4)**: 271-298.
Muthukrishnan, T.S. & Sundarababu, R. (1982). Feeding habits of Coppersmith *Megalaima haemacephala* (Muller). *J. Bombay Nat. Hist. Soc.* **79(1)**: 197-198.
Nackejima, C. (1973). [Habits, breeding behavior, food and conservation of the Pryer's Woodpecker, *Sapheopipo noguchii* (Aves: Picidae)]. *Nature and Animals* **3**: 2-9. In Japanese.
Nadkarni, N.M. & Matelson, T.J. (1989). Bird use of epiphyte resources in Neotropical trees. *Condor* **91(4)**: 891-907.
Naka, L.N., Mazar Barnett, J., Kirwan, G.M., Tobias, J.A. & de Azevedo, M.A.G. (2000). New and noteworthy bird records from Santa Catarina State, Brazil. *Bull. Brit. Orn. Club* **120(4)**: 237-250.
Nakamura, M., Suzuki, Y. & Yui, M. (1995). Artificial wooden boxes for roosting woodpeckers. *Wildl. Soc. Bull.* **23(1)**: 78-79.
Narosky, T. & di Giacomo, A.G. (1993). *Las Aves de la Provincia de Buenos Aires: Distribución y Estatus*. Asociación Ornitológica del Plata, Vázquez Mazzini Editores & Literature of Latin America, Buenos Aires.
Narosky, T. & Yzurieta, D. (1993). *Birds of Argentina and Uruguay - A Field Guide*. Vázquez Mazzini Editores, Buenos Aires.
do Nascimento, J.L.X. (2000). Estudo comparativo da avifauna em duas estações ecológicas da Caatinga: Aiuaba e Seridó. *Melopsittacus* **3(1)**: 12-35.
do Nascimento, J.L.X., do Nascimento, I.L.S. & de Azevedo, S.M. (2000). Aves da Chapada do Araripe (Brasil): biologia e conservação. *Ararajuba* **8(2)**: 115-125.
Nash, A.D. & Nash, S.V. (1985). Breeding notes on some Padang-Sugihan birds. *Kukila* **2(3)**: 59-63.
Nash, S.V. & Nash, A.D. (1986). *The Ecology and Natural History of Birds in the Tanjung Puting National Park, Central Kalimantan, Indonesia*. World Wildlife Fund/IUCN Project 1687, Bogor, Indonesia.
Nash, S.V. & Nash, A.D. (1988). An annotated checklist of the birds of Tanjung Puting National Park, central Kalimantan. *Kukila* **3(3-4)**: 93-116.
Naumburg, E.M.B. (1930). *The Birds of Mato Grosso, Brazil. A Report on the Birds Secured by the Roosevelt-Rondon Expedition*. Bulletin of the American Museum of Natural History **60**, New York. 432 pp.
Navas, J.R. & Bó, N.A. (1988). Aves nuevas o poco conocidas de Misiones, Argentina. II. *Com. Zool. Mus. Hist. Nat. Montevideo* **166(12)**: 1-9.
Navas, J.R. & Bó, N.A. (1993). Aves nuevas o poco conocidas de Misiones, Argentina. V (addenda). *Rev. Mus. Arg. Cienc. Nat. Bernardino Rivadavia* **16(4)**: 37-50.
Ndang'ang'a, K. & Borghesio, L. (1999). Bird records from northern Kenya forests. *Kenya Birds* **7(1&2)**: 62-68.
Neal, J.C. (1992). *Factors Affecting Breeding Success of Red-cockaded Woodpeckers in the Ouachita National Forest, Arkansas*. MSc thesis, University of Arkansas, Fayetteville, Arkansas.
Neal, J.C., Douglas A.J., Montague, W.G. & Johnson, J.E. (1993). Effects of weather and helpers on survival of nestling Red-cockaded Woodpeckers. *Wilson Bull.* **105(4)**: 666-673.
Neal, J.C., Montague, W.G. & James, D.A. (1992). Sequential occupation of cavities by Red-cockaded Woodpeckers and Red-bellied Woodpeckers in the Ouachita National Forest. *Proc. Arkansas Acad. Sci.* **46**: 106-108.
Nee, K. & Guan, L.P. (1993). The avifauna of the north Selangor peat-swamp forest, West Malaysia. *Bird Conserv. Int.* **3**: 169-179.
Neelakantan, K.K. (1958). The Black-backed Woodpecker, *Chrysocolaptes festivus* (Boddaert), in Chittur, Kerala. *J. Bombay Nat. Hist. Soc.* **55(3)**: 559.
Neelakantan, K.K. (1962). Drumming by, and an instance of homo-sexual behaviour in the Lesser Golden-backed Woodpecker *Dinopium benghalense*. *J. Bombay Nat. Hist. Soc.* **59(1)**: 288-290.
Neelakantan, K.K. (1976). A day at a nest of the Great Black Woodpecker *Dryocopus javensis*. *J. Bombay Nat. Hist. Soc.* **72(2)**: 544-548.
Neff, J.A. (1928). *A Study of the Economic Status of the Common Woodpeckers in Relation to Oregon Horticulture*. Free Press Print, Marionville, Missouri.
Neill, A.J. & Harper, R.G. (1990). Red-bellied Woodpecker predation on nestling House Wrens. *Condor* **92(3)**: 789.
Nellar, M.M. (1993). *Aves de la Provincia de San Luis. Lista y Distribución*. Museo Privado de Ciencias Naturales e Investigaciones Ornitológicas "Guillermo E. Hudson", San Luis, Argentina.
Nellar, M.N. & Fraga, R.M. (1999). El Carpintero Negro (*Dryocopus schulzi*) en la Sierra de San Luis, Argentina. *Nuestras Aves* **40**: 22.
Nelson, E.W. (1898). The Imperial Ivory-billed Woodpecker, *Campephilus imperialis* (Gould). *Auk* **15**: 217-223.
Nero, R.W. (1959). Red-bellied Woodpecker at Regina. *Blue Jay* **17**: 95-96.
Nero, R.W. & Copland, H.W.R. (1997). Some interactions between Pileated Woodpeckers and Northern Hawk Owls. *Blue Jay* **55**: 81-84.
Nesbitt, S.A., Harris, B.A., Jerauld, A.E. & Brownsmith, C.B. (1981). *Report of the Investigation of Red-cockaded Woodpeckers in Charlotte County, Florida*. Florida Game and Fresh Water Fish Commission, Tallahassee, Florida.
Neville, S. (1973). Information wanted. Crimson-breasted Barbets. *Newsl. Birdwatchers* **13**: 4-7.
Newby, J.E. (1980). The birds of the Ouadi Rimé - Ouadi Achim Faunal Reserve: a contribution to the study of the Chadian avifauna. Part 2. *Malimbus* **2(1)**: 29-50.
Newby, J.E. (1987). The birds of the Northern Aïr, Niger. *Malimbus* **9(1)**: 4-16.
Newby-Varty, B.V. (1946). Further notes on the birds on Umvukwe Ranch, Banket, S. Rhodesia. *Ostrich* **17**: 343-347.
Newman, J. (1993). Birds. Pp. 61-91 in: Amazon 1992–Final Report: a Cambridge-RHBNC Expedition to Colombia. Unpublished report.
Newman, K. (1996). *Newman's Birds of Southern Africa*. Southern Book Publishers, Halfway House, South Africa.
Newman, K., Johnston-Stewart, N. & Medland, B. (1992). *Birds of Malawi. A Supplement to Newman's Birds of Southern Africa*. Southern Book Publishers, Halfway House, South Africa.
Newton, S.F. & Newton, A.V. (1996). Seasonal changes in the abundance and diversity of birds in threatened juniper forest in the southern Asir mountains, Saudi Arabia. *Bird Conserv. Int.* **6(4)**: 371-392.
Nicéforo, H.M. & Olivares, A. (1967). Adiciones a la avifauna Colombiana. IV. Apodidae-Picidae. *Hornero* **10(4)**: 403-435.
Nichols, G.R. (1983a). An extension of the established range of the Knysna Woodpecker. *Ostrich* **54(3)**: 182.
Nichols, G.R. (1983b). The reappearance of Knysna Woodpecker in Natal. *Bokmakierie* **35(2)**: 44.
Nichols, L.L. & Jackson, A. (1987). Interspecific aggression and the sexual monochromism of Red-headed Woodpeckers. *J. Field Orn.* **58(3)**: 288-290.
Nichols, T.H. (1994). Pileated Woodpecker use of elm trees killed by Dutch Elm Disease in northern Wisconsin. *Passenger Pigeon* **56(1)**: 21-28.
van Niekerk, D.J. (1993). [Crested Barbet (*Trachyphonus vaillantii*)]. *Mirafra* **10(2)**: 27-28. In Afrikaans with English summary.
Nijman, V. & Sözer, R. (1996). *Konservasi Elang Jawa dan Jenis-Jenis Burung Endemik Jawa Lainnya: Daerah Prioritas Kawasan Konservasi di Jawa Tengah. Conservation of the Javan Hawk-eagle and other Endemic Bird Species on Java: Priority Areas for Protection in Central Java*. Technical Memorandum **11**. PHPA/BirdLife International, Bogor, Indonesia. In Indonesian and English.
Nikolaus, G. (1987). *Distribution Atlas of Sudan's Birds with Notes on Habitat and Status*. Bonner Zoologische Monographien **25**. Zoologisches Forschunginstitut und Museum Alexander Koenig, Bonn.
Nikolaus, G. (2000). The birds of the Parc National du Haut Niger, Guinea. *Malimbus* **22(1)**: 1-22.
Nilsson, S.G., Johnsson, K. & Tjernberg, M. (1991). Is avoidance by Black Woodpeckers of old nest holes due to predators? *Anim. Behav.* **41(3)**: 439-441.
Nilsson, S.G., Johnsson, K. & Tjernberg, M. (1993a). Is avoidance by Black Woodpeckers of old nest holes due to predators? Pp. 83-85 in: Report **24**, Department of Wildlife Ecology, Swedish University of Agricultural Sciences, Uppsala, Sweden.
Nilsson, S.G., Johnsson, K. & Tjernberg, M. (1993b). Age, dimensions and loss rates of Black Woodpeckers nesting trees. Pp. 127-144 in: Report **24**, Department of Wildlife Ecology, Swedish University of Agricultural Sciences, Uppsala, Sweden.
Nilsson, S.G., Olsson, O., Svensson, S. & Wiktander, U. (1992). Population trends and fluctuations in Swedish woodpeckers. *Ornis Svecica* **2**: 13-21.
Nitzsch, C.L. (1840). *System der Pterylographie, Herausgegeben von H. Burmeiser*. E. Anton, Halle. 228 pp.
Noble, G.K. (1936). Courtship and sexual selection in the Flicker (*Colaptes auratus luteus*). *Auk* **53**: 269-282.
Nolan, V. (1959). Pileated Woodpecker attacks pilot black snake at tree cavity. *Wilson Bull.* **71(4)**: 381-382.
Nores, M., Salvador, S.A. & Yzurieta, D. (2000). Registros de aves de la selva en Catamarca, Argentina. [Forest bird records in Catamarca, Argentina]. *Hornero* **15(2)**: 111-115. In Spanish with English summary.
Nores, M., Yzurieta, D. & Miatello, R. (1983). *Lista y Distribución de las Aves de Córdoba, Argentina*. Boletín de la Academia Nacional de Ciencias **56(1-2)**. 114 pp.
Norris, K.A. (1950). Some notes on barbets. *Avicult. Mag.* **56**: 135-137.
Norton, D.W. (1965). Notes on some non-passerine birds from eastern Ecuador. *Breviora* **230**: 1-11.
Norton, D.W., Orces, G. & Sutter, E. (1972). Notes on rare and previously unreported birds from Ecuador. *Auk* **89(4)**: 889-894.
Noske, R.A. (1991). Field identification and ecology of the Greater Golden-back *Chrysocolaptes lucidus* in Malaysia. *Forktail* **6**: 72-74.
Novaes, F.C. (1949). Variação nos tucanos Brasileiros do gênero "*Ramphastos*" L. (Ramphastidae, Piciformes). *Rev. Bras. Biol.* **9**: 285-296.
Novaes, F.C. (1957). Contribuição à ornitologia do noroeste de Acre. *Bol. Mus. Paraense Emílio Goeldi (Zool.)* **9**: 1-30.
Novaes, F.C. (1960). Sobre una coleção de aves do Sudeste do estado do Pará. *Arq. Zool. São Paulo* **11**: 133-146.
Novaes, F.C. (1970). Distribuição ecológica e abundância das aves em um trecho da mata do baixo Rio Guama (Estado do Pará). *Bol. Mus. Paraense Emílio Goeldi (Nova Ser.)* **71**: 1-54.
Novaes, F.C. (1976). As aves do Rio Aripuana, Estados de Mato Grosso e Amazonas. *Acta Amazonica* **6**(Suppl.): 61-85.
Novaes, F.C. (1980). Observações sobre a avifauna do alto curso do Rio Paru de Leste, Estado do Pará. *Bol. Mus. Paraense Emílio Goeldi (Nova Ser.)* **100**: 1-58.
Novaes, F.C. (1991). A new subspecies of Grey-cheeked Nunlet *Nonnula ruficapilla* from Brazilian Amazonia. *Bull. Brit. Orn. Club* **111(4)**: 187-188.
Novaes, F.C. (1992). Bird observations in the State of Piauí, Brazil. *Goeldiana Zool.* **17**: 1-5.
Novaes, F.C. & Lima, M.F.C. (1991). Variação geográfica e anotações sobre morfologia e biologia de *Selenidera gouldii* (Piciformes: Ramphastidae). *Ararajuba* **2**: 59-63.
Novaes, F.C. & Lima, M.F.C. (1992a). As aves do Rio Peixoto de Azevedo, Mato Grosso, Brazil. *Rev. Bras. Biol.* **7**: 351-381.
Novaes, F.C. & Lima, M.F.C. (1992b). Aves das campinas, capoeiras e manguezais do leste do Pará. *Bol. Mus. Paraense Emílio Goeldi (Zool.)* **8(2)**: 271-303.
Ntiamoa-Baidu, Y., Asamoah, S.A., Owusu, E.H. & Owusu-Boateng, K. (2000). Avifauna of two upland evergreen forest reserves, the Atewa range and Tano Offin, in Ghana. Proceedings of the Ninth Pan-African Ornithological Congress, Accra, Ghana, 1-7 December 1996. *Ostrich* **71(1&2)**: 277-281.
Ntiamoa-Baidu, Y., Owusu, E.H., Asamoah, S. & Owusu-Boateng, K. (2000). Distribution and abundance of forest birds in Ghana. Proceedings of the Ninth Pan-African Ornithological Congress, Accra, Ghana, 1-7 December 1996. *Ostrich* **71(1&2)**: 262-268.
Nuorteva, M., Patömaki, J. & Saari, L. (1981). Large poplar longhorn, *Saperda carcharias* (L.) as food for White-backed Woodpecker, *Dendrocopos leucotos* (Bechst.). *Silva Fenn.* **15**: 208-221.
Nyholm, E.S. (1968). Notes on the roosting behaviour of the Great Spotted Woodpecker (*Dendrocopos major*) and the Three-toed Woodpecker (*Picoides tridactylus*). *Ornis Fenn.* **45(1)**: 7-9.
Nyirenda, R.G. (1992). Diet of Brown-breasted Barbet. *Nyala* **16(1)**: 28-29.
O'Brien, P. (1979). Breeding activities of Waved Woodpeckers in Surinam. *Wilson Bull.* **91(2)**: 338-344.
O'Neill, J.P. (1969). Distributional notes on the birds of Peru, including twelve species previously unreported from the republic. *Occas. Pap. Mus. Zool. Louisiana State Univ.* **37**: 1-11.
O'Neill, J.P. & Gardner, A.L. (1974). Rediscovery of *Aulacorhynchus prasinus dimidiatus* (Ridgway). *Auk* **91(4)**: 700-704.
O'Neill, J.P. & Pearson, D.L. (1974). Estudio preliminar de las aves de Yarinacocha, Departamento de Loreto, Perú. *Publ. Mus. Hist. Nat. Javier Prado (Ser. A, Zool.)* **25**: 1-13.
O'Neill, J.P., Lane, D.F., Kratter, A.W., Capparella, A.P. & Joo, C.F. (2000). A striking new species of barbet (Capitoninae: *Capito*) from the eastern Andes of Peru. *Auk* **117(3)**: 569-577.
Oatley, T.B. (1968). Observations by W. A. Austen on the breeding biology of the White-eared Barbet, *Buccanodon leucotis* (Sundevall). *Lammergeyer* **8**: 7-14.
Oatley, T.B. (1995). *The Biology and Relationships of the Ground Woodpecker*. PhD thesis, University of the Witwatersrand, Johannesburg.
Oatley, T.B. (2001). Two in the bush... Minziro Forest Reserve, north-west Tanzania. *Africa. Birds & Birding* **6(1)**: 46-53.
Oatley, T.B., Earlé, R.A. & Prins, A.J. (1989). The diet and foraging behaviour of the Ground Woodpecker. *Ostrich* **60(2)**: 75-84.
Oatman, G.F. (1985). Three-toed Woodpecker, *Picoides tridactylus*. Pp. 162-163 in: Laughlin, S.B. & Kibbe, D.P. eds. (1985). *The Atlas of Breeding Birds of Vermont*. University Press of New England, Hanover, New Hampshire.
Oberholser, H.C. (1911). A revision of the forms of the Ladder-backed Woodpecker (*Dryobates scalaris* Wagler). *Proc. US Natl. Mus.* **41**: 139-159.
Oberman, L. (1989). Courtship behavior of a pair of Pileated Woodpeckers. *Maryland Birdlife* **45(2)**: 65-66.
Oberman, L. (1995). Pileated Woodpeckers battle to the death. *Maryland Birdlife* **51(4)**: 158.
Odum, R.R., Rappole, J., Evans, J., Charbonneau, D. & Palmer, D. (1982). Red-cockaded Woodpecker relocation experiment in coastal Georgia. *Wildl. Soc. Bull.* **10(3)**: 197-203.
Ogasawara, K. & Ikehara, Y. (1977). Ecological and behavioural observations of Okinawa Woodpecker *Sapheopipo noguchii*, with notes on conservation. *Misc. Rep. Yamashina Inst. Orn.* **9(2)**: 143-158.
Ogasawara, K. & Izumi, Y. (1977). [Ecological and behavioural observations on Black Woodpecker *Dryocopus m. martius* in *Fagus crenata* forests and its vicinity in Mt. Moriyoshi, Akita Prefecture, northern Honshu, Japan]. *Misc. Rep. Yamashina Inst. Orn.* **9(3)**: 231-243. In Japanese with English summary.
Ogasawara, K. & Izumi, Y. (1978). [Ecological study of Black Woodpecker *Dryocopus martius* in *Fagus crenata* forest on Mt. Moriyoshi]. *Misc. Rep. Yamashina Inst. Orn.* **10(1-2)**: 127-141. In Japanese with English summary.
Olioso, G. & Orsini, P. (1999). Torcol fourmilier *Jynx torquilla*. Pp. 306-307 in: Rocamora & Yeatman-Berthelot (1999).
Olivares, A. (1957). Aves de la costa del Pacífico, Municipio de Guapí, Cauca, Colombia. Part 2. *Caldasia* **8(36)**: 33-93.
Olivares, A. (1962). Aves de la región sur de la Sierra de La Macarena, Meta, Colombia. *Rev. Acad. Colombiana Cienc.* **11(44)**: 305-346.
Olivares, A. (1963). Notas sobre aves de los Andes Orientales en Boyacá. *Bol. Soc. Venez. Cienc. Nat.* **25**: 91-125.
Olivares, A. (1964a). Adiciones a las aves de la Comisaría del Vaupes (Colombia). Part 1. *Rev. Acad. Colombiana Cienc. Exactas, Fisicas y Naturales* **12**: 163-173.
Olivares, A. (1964b). Adiciones a las aves de la Comisaría del Vaupes (Colombia). Part 2. *Caldasia* **9(42)**: 151-184.
Olivares, A. (1967). Seis nuevas aves para Colombia y apuntamiento sobre sesenta especies y subespecies registradas anteriormente. *Caldasia* **10(46)**: 39-58.

Olivares, A. & Romero, H. (1973). Notas sobre la colección ornitológica del Departamento de Biología de la Universidad Industrial de Santander, Bucaramanga, Colombia. Part I. *Rev. Univ. Industrial de Santander* **5**: 43-71.

de Oliveira, R.G. (1985). Mudança na cor da iris em *Ramphastos dicolorus* (Tucano-de-bico-verde) e outras observações. *Sulornis* **6**: 18-21.

Olmos, F. (1993). Birds of Serra da Capivara National Park in the "caatinga" of north-eastern Brazil. *Bird Conserv. Int.* **3(1)**: 21-36.

Olrog, C.C. (1958). Notas ornitológicas sobre la colección del Instituto Miguel Lillo Tucumán. III. *Acta Zool. Lilloana* **15**: 5-19.

Olrog, C.C. (1968). *Las Aves Sudamericanas, una Guía de Campo*. Vol. 1. Universidad Nacional de Tucumán, Tucumán.

Olrog, C.C. (1972). Causal ornithogeography of South America. Pp. 562-573 in: Voous, K.H. *Proceedings of the XV International Ornithological Congress, The Hague, 1970*. E.J. Brill, Leiden.

Olsen, O.V. (1978). Dust-bathing by Common Flickers. *Florida Field Nat.* **6(1)**: 18.

Olson, S.L. (1972). The generic distinction of the Hispaniolan Woodpecker, *Chryserpes striatus* (Aves: Picidae). *Proc. Biol. Soc. Washington* **85(44)**: 499-508.

Olson, S.L. (1978). A paleontological perspective of West Indian birds and mammals. Pp. 99-117 in: Gill, F.B. ed. (1978). *Zoogeography in the Caribbean*. Academy of Natural Sciences of Philadelphia Special Publication **13**, Philadelphia. 128 pp.

Olson, S.L. (1983). Evidence for a polyphyletic origin of the Piciformes. *Auk* **100(1)**: 126-133.

Olson, S.L. (1985). The fossil record of birds. Pp. 79-256 in: Farner, D.S., King, J.R. & Parkes, K.C. eds. (1985). *Avian Biology*. Vol. 8. Academic Press, New York.

Olson, S.L. (1991). Remarks on the fossil record and suprageneric nomenclature of barbets (Aves: Ramphastidae). *Bull. Brit. Orn. Club* **111(4)**: 222-225.

Olson, S.L. (1997). Avian biogeography in the islands of the pacific coast of western Panama. Pp. 69-82 in: Dickerman (1997).

Olson, S.L. & Feduccia, A. (1979). An Old World occurrence of the Eocene avian family Primobucconidae. *Proc. Biol. Soc. Washington* **92(3)**: 494-497.

Olsson, O. (1998). *Through the Eyes of a Woodpecker: Understanding Habitat Selection, Territory Quality and Reproductive Decisions from Individual Behaviour*. PhD thesis, Lund University, Sweden.

Olsson, O., Nilsson, I.N., Nilsson, S.G., Pettersson, B., Stagen, A. & Wiktander, U. (1992). Habitat preferences of the Lesser Spotted Woodpecker *Dendrocopos minor*. *Ornis Fenn.* **69**: 119-125.

Omari, I., Hart, J.A., Butynski, T.M., Birhashirwa, N.R., Upoki, A., M'Keyo, Y., Bengana, F., Bashonga, M. & Bagurubumwe, N. (1999). The Itombwe Massif, Democratic Republic of Congo: biological surveys and conservation, with an emphasis on Grauer's gorilla and birds endemic to the Albertine Rift. *Oryx* **33(4)**: 301-322.

Oniki, Y. (1981). Weights, cloacal temperatures, plumage and molt condition of birds in the State of São Paulo. *Rev. Bras. Biol.* **41(2)**: 451-460.

Oniki, Y. & Emerson, K.C. (1981). A new species of *Picicola* (Mallophaga, Philopteridae) from the Crescent-chested Puffbird, *Malacoptila striata* (Spix) (Piciformes, Bucconidae). *Rev. Bras. Biol.* **41(3)**: 511-513.

Oniki, Y. & Willis, E.O. (1982). Breeding records of birds from Manaus, Brazil. Part II. Apodidae to Furnariidae. *Rev. Bras. Biol.* **42**: 745-752.

Oniki, Y. & Willis, E.O. (1983). A study of breeding birds of the Belém area, Brazil. Part III. Trogonidae to Furnariidae. *Ciênc. Cult.* **35**: 1320-1324.

Oniki, Y. & Willis, E.O. (1998). Nesting of Yellow-fronted Woodpeckers, *Melanerpes flavifrons* (Picidae). *Orn. Neotropical* **9(1)**: 81-85.

Oniki, Y. & Willis, E.O. (1999). Body mass, cloacal temperature, morphometrics, breeding and molt of birds of the Serra das Araras region, Mato Grosso, Brazil. *Ararajuba* **7(1)**: 17-21.

Orejuela, J.E. (1985). Tropical forest birds of Colombia: a survey of problems and a plan for their conservation. Pp. 95-114 in: Diamond & Lovejoy (1985).

Oren, D.C. (1992). *Celeus torquatus pieteroyensi*, a new subspecies of Ringed Woodpecker (Aves, Picidae) from eastern Pará and western Maranhao, Brazil. *Bol. Mus. Paraense Emilio Goeldi (Zool.)* **8(2)**: 385-389. In English with Portuguese summary.

Oren, D.C. & Parker, T.A. (1997). Avifauna of the Tapajós National Park and vicinity, Amazonian Brazil. Pp. 493-525 in: Remsen (1997).

Orians, G.H. & Paulson, D.R. (1969). Notes on Costa Rican birds. *Condor* **71(4)**: 426-431.

Orsini, P. (1997). L'hivernage du Torcol fourmilier *Jynx torquilla* en France continentale. *Ornithos* **4**: 21-27.

Ortiz, F.I. & Carrión, J.M. (1991). *Introducción a las Aves del Ecuador*. FECODES, Quito.

Osborne, P. (1983). The influence of Dutch Elm Disease on bird population trends. *Bird Study* **30**: 27-38.

Osiejuk, T.S. (1994). Sexual dimorphism in foraging behaviour of the Great Spotted Woodpecker *Dendrocopos major* during winters with rich crops of scots pine cones. *Ornis Fenn.* **71**: 144-150.

Osiek, E.R. & Hustings, F. (1994). *Rode Lijst van Bedreigde en Kwetsbare Vogelsoorten in Nederland*. [*Red List of Threatened and Vulnerable Bird Species in The Netherlands*]. Technisch Rapport **12**, Vogelbescherming Nederland, Zeist, The Netherlands. In Dutch with English summary.

Osmaston, A.E. (1916). Curious habits of wood-peckers in the Kumaon hills. *J. Bombay Nat. Hist. Soc.* **24(2)**: 363-366.

Osmaston, B.B. (1902). Curious course taken by the hyoid cornua or tongue muscles in certain woodpeckers. *J. Bombay Nat. Hist. Soc.* **14(3)**: 587-588.

Otvos, I.S. (1967). Observations on the feeding habits of some woodpeckers and woodcreepers in Costa Rica. *Condor* **69(5)**: 522-525.

Ouellet, H.R. (1977a). Relationships of woodpecker genera *Dendrocopos* Koch and *Picoides* Lacépède (Aves: Picidae). *Ardea* **65(3-4)**: 165-183.

Ouellet, H.R. (1977b). *Biosystematics and Ecology of* Picoides villosus *(L.) and* Picoides pubescens *(L.) (Aves: Picidae)*. PhD thesis, McGill University, Montreal, Canada.

Ouellet, H.R. ed. (1988). *Acta XIX Congressus Internationalis Ornithologici, Ottawa, 1986*. Vol. 2. University of Ottawa Press, Ottawa.

Ouellet, H.R. (1997). Comparative foraging ecology of Downy and Hairy Woodpeckers (aves: Picidae). Pp. 113-128 in: Dickerman (1997).

Owens, N. & Owens, S. (1992). Observations on a promiscuous Red-bellied Woodpecker (*Melanerpes carolinus*). *Alabama Birdlife* **39**: 7.

Owre, O.T. (1978). Species of special concern. Southern Hairy Woodpecker, *Picoides villosus auduboni*. Pp. 99-101 in: Kale, H.W. ed. (1978). *Rare and Endangered Biota of Florida*. Vol. 2. Birds. University Press of Florida, Gainesville, Florida.

Pacheco, J.F. & Parrini, R. (2000). Aves do Estado do Rio de Janeiro: região meridional do vale do rio Paraíba do Sul - retificação de limites e complementação dos registros inéditos mais antigos. *Atualidades Orn.* **95**: 12-13.

Pacheco, J.F. & Whitney, B.M. (1995). Range extensions for some birds in northeastern Brazil. *Bull. Brit. Orn. Club* **115(3)**: 157-163.

Pacheco, J.F., Parrini, R., Whitney, B.M., da Fonseca, P.S.M. & Bauer, C. (1996). Novos registros de aves para o estado do Rio de Janeiro: Vale do Paraíba Norte. *Atualidades Orn.* **73**: 6.

Page, L. (1988). Breeding Green Aracaris (*Pteroglossus viridis*) an experience of a novice. *Honeycreeper* **3(1)**: 5-15.

Paiva, C.L. & Willis, E.O. (1994). New occurrences of *Melanerpes cactorum* (d'Orbigny, 1840) (Aves, Picidae) in Brazilian territory. *Biotemas* **7(1-2)**: 110-115.

Pakenham, R.H.W. (1979). *The Birds of Zanzibar and Pemba. An Annotated Check-list*. BOU Check-list **2**. British Ornithologists' Union, London.

Paludan, K. (1959). *On the Birds of Afghanistan*. Vidensk. Medd. Dan. Naturhist. Foren. **122**. 333 pp.

de Pardieu, H. (1937). A propos de la nidification du Pic noir dans le Massif central. *Alauda* **8(3-4)**: 488.

Pardo, R. & Gogorza y González, J. (1997). *Aves de las Islas Filipinas*. Librerías París-Valencia S.L., Valencia, Spain.

Parker, S.A. (1966). *Coracias abyssinica*: an unrecorded host of *Indicator indicator*. *Bull. Brit. Orn. Club* **86**: 81.

Parker, T.A. (1990). La Libertad revisited. *Birding* **22**: 16-22.

Parker, T.A. & Bailey, B. eds. (1991). *A Biological Assessment of the Alto Madidi Region and Adjacent Areas of Northwest Bolivia, May 18-June 15, 1990*. Rapid Assessment Program Working Papers **1**. Conservation International, Washington, D.C.

Parker, T.A. & Carr, J.L. eds. (1992). *Status of Forest Remnants in the Cordillera de la Costa and Adjacent Areas of Southwestern Ecuador*. Rapid Assessment Program Working Papers **2**. Conservation International, Washington, D.C.

Parker, T.A. & Goerck, J.M. (1997). The importance of national parks and biological reserves to bird conservation in the Atlantic Forest region of Brazil. Pp. 527-541 in: Remsen (1997).

Parker, T.A. & Remsen, J.V. (1987). Fifty-two Amazonian bird species new to Bolivia. *Bull. Brit. Orn. Club* **107(3)**: 94-107.

Parker, T.A. & Rocha, O. (1991). Notes on the status and behaviour of the Rusty-necked Piculet *Picumnus fuscus*. *Bull. Brit. Orn. Club* **111(2)**: 91-92.

Parker, T.A., Castillo, U.A., Gell-Mann, M. & Rocha, O.O. (1991). Records of new and unusual birds from northern Bolivia. *Bull. Brit. Orn. Club* **111(3)**: 120-138.

Parker, T.A., Foster, R.B., Emmons, L.H., Freed, P., Forsyth, A.B., Hoffman, B. & Gill, B.D. (1993). *A Biological Assessment of the Kanuku Mountain Region of Southwestern Guyana*. Rapid Assessment Program Working Papers **5**. Conservation International, Washington, D.C.

Parker, T.A., Holst, B.K., Emmons, L.H. & Meyer, J.R. (1994). *A Biological Assessment of the Colombia River Forest Reserve, Toledo District, Belize*. Rapid Assessment Program Working Papers **3**. Conservation International, Washington, D.C.

Parker, T.A., Parker, S.A. & Plenge, M.A. (1982). *An Annotated Checklist of Peruvian Birds*. Buteo Books, Vermillion, South Dakota.

Parker, T.A., Schulenberg, T.S., Graves, G.R. & Braun, M.J. (1985). The avifauna of the Huancabamba region, northern Peru. Pp. 169-197 in: Buckley *et al.* (1985).

Parker, T.A., Schulenberg, T.S., Kessler, M. & Wust, W.H. (1995). Natural history and conservation of the endemic avifauna in north-west Peru. *Bird Conserv. Int.* **5(2/3)**: 201-231.

Parker, V. (1994). *Swaziland Bird Atlas 1985-1991*. Websters, Mbabane, Swaziland.

Parker, V. (1999). *The Atlas of the Birds of Sul do Save, Southern Mozambique*. Avian Demography Unit & Endangered Wildlife Trust, Cape Town & Johannesburg.

Parkes, D.A. (1994). Slender-billed Honeyguide parasitism of Yellow White-eye. *Honeyguide* **40**: 97.

Parkes, K.C. (1958). Nomenclatorial notes on Philippine pygmy woodpeckers. *Bull. Brit. Orn. Club* **78(1)**: 6-7.

Parkes, K.C. (1960a). Notes on Philippine races of *Dryocopus javensis*. *Bull. Brit. Orn. Club* **80(4)**: 59-61.

Parkes, K.C. (1960b). Notes on some non-passerine birds from the Philippines. *Ann. Carnegie Mus.* **35**: 331-340.

Parkes, K.C. (1970). The races of the Rusty-breasted Nunlet (*Nonnula rubecula*). *Bull. Brit. Orn. Club* **90**: 154-157.

Parkes, K.C. (1971). Taxonomic and distributional notes on Philippine Birds. *Nemouria* **4**: 1-67.

Parr, K. (1996). Breeding the Flame-fronted Barbet. *AFA Watchbird* **23**: 30-35.

Parr, M. (2000). New barbet discovered in Peru. *Bird Calls* **4(3)**: 5.

Parrini, R., Raposo, M.A., Pacheco, J.F., Carvalhães, A.M.P., Melo-Júnior, T., Fonseca, P.S.M. & Minns, J.C. (1999). Birds of Chapada Diamantina, Bahia, Brazil. *Cotinga* **11**: 86–95.

Parrott, S. & Andrew, P. (1996). An annotated checklist of the birds of Way Kambas National Park, Sumatra. *Kukila* **8**: 57-85.

Pasinelli, G. (1993). Nachweis eines Helfers bei einer Brut des Mittelspechts *Dendrocopos medius*. *Orn. Beob.* **90**: 303-304.

Pasinelli, G. (1998). Effects of habitat structures on home range size and breeding success of the Middle Spotted Woodpecker *Dendrocopos medius*. Proceedings of the XXII International Ornithological Congress, Durban 1998. *Ostrich* **69(3&4)**: 445. (Abstract).

Pasinelli, G. (1999). *Relations between Habitat Structure, Space Use and Breeding Success of the Middle Spotted Woodpecker* Dendrocopos medius. PhD thesis, University of Zurich.

Pasinelli, G. (2000a). Sexual dimorphism and foraging niche partitioning in the Middle Spotted Woodpecker *Dendrocopos medius*. *Ibis* **142(4)**: 635-644.

Pasinelli, G. (2000b). Oaks *Quercus* sp. and only oaks? Relations between habitat structure and home range size of the Middle Spotted Woodpecker *Dendrocopos medius*. *Biol. Conserv.* **93**: 227-235.

Pasinelli, G. & Hegelbach, J. (1997). Characteristics of trees preferred by foraging Middle Spotted Woodpeckers *Dendrocopos medius* in northern Switzerland. *Ardea* **85**: 203-209.

Paterson, L. (1997). Parent-reared Toco Toucans at Leeds Castle. *Avicult. Mag.* **103(3)**: 97-100.

Patterson, G.A. & Robertson, W.B. (1981). *Distribution and Habitat of the Red-cockaded Woodpecker in Big Cypress National Preserve*. Report **T-613**. National Park Service & South Florida Research Center, Homestead, Florida.

Paulson, D.R. (1966). *New Records of Birds from the Bahama Islands*. Proceedings of the Academy of Natural Sciences of Philadelphia **394**.

Pavlík, Š. (1994). [The habitat preference for woodpeckers in oak tree forests during the breeding period]. *Tichodroma* **7**: 35-42. In Slovak with English summary.

Pavlík, Š. (1996). Habitat distribution of woodpeckers (Aves, Picidae): beech and oak forests. *Biologia* **51**: 213-217.

Payne, R.B. (1967a). *Lybius guifsobalito* occurs in Kenya. *Ostrich* **38**: 283.

Payne, R.B. (1967b). Nest and eggs of *Buccanodon achietae*. *Bull. Brit. Orn. Club* **87(2)**: 34-35.

Payne, R.B. (1971). Duetting and chorus singing in African birds. *Ostrich* **9**(Suppl.): 125-146.

Payne, R.B. (1984). *Sexual Selection, Lek and Arena Behavior, and Sexual Size Dimorphism in Birds*. Ornithological Monographs **33**. American Ornithologists' Union, Washington, D.C.

Payne, R.B. (1986). Bird songs and avian systematics. Pp. 87-126 in: Johnston, R.F. ed. (1986). *Current Ornithology, 1986*. Plenum Publishing Corporation, New York.

Payne, R.B. (1989). Egg size of African honeyguides (Indicatoridae): specialization for brood parasitism? *Tauraco* **1**: 201-210.

Payne, R.B. (1992). Clutch size, laying periodicity behaviour in the honeyguides *Indicator indicator* and *I. minor*. Pp. 537-547 in: Bennun (1992).

Paynter, R.A. (1955). *The Ornithogeography of the Yucatán Peninsula*. Peabody Museum of Natural History Yale University Bulletin **9**, New Haven, Connecticut. 345 pp.

Paynter, R.A. ed. (1957). *Biological Investigations in the Selva Lacandona, Chiapas, Mexico*. Bulletin of the Museum of Comparative Zoology **116(4)**, Cambridge, Massachusetts. 108 pp.

Paynter, R.A. (1970). Species with Malaysian affinities in the Sundarbans, east Pakistan. *Bull. Brit. Orn. Club* **90(5)**: 118-119.

Paynter, R.A. (1985). *Ornithological Gazetteer of Argentina*. Museum of Comparative Zoology, Cambridge, Massachusetts.

Paynter, R.A. (1989). *Ornithological Gazetteer of Paraguay*. 2nd edition. Museum of Comparative Zoology, Cambridge, Massachusetts.

Paynter, R.A. & Traylor, M.A. (1991). *Ornithological Gazetteer of Brazil*. Museum of Comparative Zoology, Cambridge, Massachusetts.

Paz, U. (1987). *The Birds of Israel*. Christopher Helm, Bromley, UK.

Pearce-Higgins, J.W. (2000). The avian community structure of a Bolivian savanna on the edge of the cerrado system. *Hornero* **15(2)**: 77-84.

Pearman, M. (1993a). Some range extensions and five species new to Colombia, with notes on some scarce or little known species. *Bull. Brit. Orn. Club* **113(2)**: 66-75.

Pearman, M. (1993b). The avifauna of the Río Machariapo dry forest, northern La Paz department, Bolivia: a preliminary investigation. *Bird Conserv. Int.* **3(2)**: 105-117.

Pearman, M. (1994a). Neotropical Notebook. Bolivia. *Cotinga* **1**: 27-28.
Pearman, M. (1994b). Neotropical Notebook. Brazil. *Cotinga* **2**: 30.
Pearman, M. (1995). Neotropical Notebook. Peru. *Cotinga* **3**: 62.
Pearson, D.J. (1983). East African bird report 1982. *Scopus* **6**: 109-128.
Pearson, D.J. & Turner, D.A. (1986). The less common Palearctic migrant birds of Uganda. *Scopus* **10**: 61-82.
Pearson, D.L. (1975a). A preliminary survey of the birds of the Kutai Reserve, Kalimantan Timur, Indonesia. *Treubia* **28**: 157-162.
Pearson, D.L. (1975b). Range extensions and new records for bird species in Ecuador, Peru, and Bolivia. *Condor* **77(1)**: 96–99.
Pearson, D.L., Tallman, D. & Tallman, E. (1977). *The Birds of Limoncocha, Napo Province, Ecuador*. Instituto Lingüístico de Verano, Quito.
Pechacek, P. (1992). Anwendungsbeispiel eines Geographischen Informationssytems. Habitatbewertungen der Spechte im Nationalpark Berchtesgaden. *Allgemeine Forst Zeitschrift* **47(15)**: 828-831.
Pechacek, P. (1994a). Habitat use of White-backed Woodpecker *Dendrocopos leucotos*. Page 189 in: Dittami *et al*. (1994).
Pechacek, P. (1994b). Reaktion des Dreizehenspechts auf eine Borkenkäfergradation. *Allgemeine Forst Zeitschrift* **49(12)**: 661.
Pechacek, P. (1995). Habitat use and influence of forest management on the distribution of woodpeckers investigated by a GIS. Pp. 561-565 in: Bissonette, J.A. & Krausman, P.R. eds. (1995). *Integrating People and Wildlife for a Sustainable Future*. Proceedings of the First International Wildlife Management Congress, San José, Costa Rica, 19-25 September 1993. Wildlife Society, Bethesda, Maryland.
Pechacek, P. (1996). Im Spannungsfeld des Artenschutzes im Wald: Spechte und Ameisen. *Allgemeine Forst Zeitschrift* **51(15)**: 852-854.
Pechacek, P. (1998). Home-range size and foraging sites of Three-toed Woodpecker *Picoides tridactylus*: a telemetry study. Proceedings of the XXII International Ornithological Congress, Durban 1998. *Ostrich* **69(3&4)**: 302. (Abstract).
Pechacek, P. & Kristín, A. (1993). Nahrung der Spechte im Nationalpark Berchtesgaden. [Diet of woodpeckers in Berchtesgaden National Park]. *Vogelwelt* **114(4)**: 165-177. In German with English summary.
Pechacek, P. & Kristín, A. (1996). Zur Ernahrung und Nahrungsökologie des Dreizehenspechts *Picoides tridactylus* während der Nestlingsperiode. [Food and foraging ecology of the Three-toed Woodpecker *Picoides tridactylus* during the nestling period]. *Orn. Beob.* **93(3)**: 259-266. In German with English abstract.
Peck, B. (1983). Breeding notes for 1983. *Avicult. Mag.* **89**: 146-151.
Peck, G.K. (1999). *Ontario Nest Records Scheme. Thirtieth Report (1956-1998)*. Royal Ontario Museum, Toronto.
Peck, G.K. & James, R.D. (1983). *Breeding Birds of Ontario: Nidiology and Distribution*. Vol. 1. Nonpasserines. Royal Ontario Museum, Toronto.
Pedersen, T. (2000). *Democratic Republic of Congo: a Bird Checklist*. Published privately.
Pedrini, P. (1984). Nesting of the Grey-headed Woodpecker, *Picus canus*, at high altitude. *Riv. ital. Orn.* **54(3-4)**: 266-267.
Pelzeln, A. von (1867-1871). *Zur Ornithologie Brasiliens. Resultate von Johann Natterers Reisen in den Jahren 1817 bis 1835*. A. Pichlers Witwe & Sohn, Vienna.
Penard, F.B. & Penard, A.P. (1908-1910). *De Vogels van Guyana (Suriname, Cayenne en Demarara)*. N.J. Boon, Amsterdam.
Penrith, E. (2000). Black-collared Barbet nest in Port Elizabeth. *Bee-eater* **50**: 25.
Penry, H. (1976). *Prodotiscus regulus* soliciting *Camaroptera brevicaudata*. *Ostrich* **47**: 136.
Penry, H. (1994). *Bird Atlas of Botswana*. University of Natal Press, Pietermaritzburg, South Africa.
Peña, C.M., Navarro, N. & Fernández, A. (1999). Status actual del Carpintero Real (*Campephilus principalis bairdii*) en Cuba. *Pitirre* **12(3)**: 85-87.
de la Peña, M.R. (1994). *Guía de Aves Argentinas*. Vol. 3. 2nd edition. Columbiformes a Piciformes. Literature of Latin America, Buenos Aires.
de la Peña, M.R. (1995). *Ciclo Reproductivo de las Aves Argentinas*. Part 1. Centro de Publicaciones de la Universidad Nacional del Litoral, Santa Fe.
de la Peña, M.R. (1996). *Ciclo Reproductivo de las Aves Argentinas*. Part 2. Literature of Latin America, Buenos Aires.
de la Peña, M.R. (1997). *Lista y Distribución de las Aves de Santa Fe y Entre Ríos*. Monografía Especial **15**. Literature of Latin America, Buenos Aires.
Peres, C.A. & Whittaker, A. (1991). Annotated checklist of the bird species of the upper Rio Urucu, Amazonas, Brazil. *Bull. Brit. Orn. Club* **111(3)**: 156-171.
Pereyra, J.A. (1950). Avifauna argentina (contribución a la ornitología). *Hornero* **9(2)**: 178-241.
Pérez del Val, J. (1996). *Las Aves de Bioko, Guinea Ecuatorial. Guía de Campo*. Edilesa, León, Spain.
Pérez del Val, J., Fa, J.E., Castroviejo, J. & Purroy, F.J. (1994). Species richness and endemism of birds in Bioko. *Biodiversity and Conservation* **3**: 868-892.
Perkins, L.G. (1943). Nesting habits and other notes on woodpeckers. *Nat. Hist. Notes Nat. Hist. Soc. Jamaica* **2(14)**: 51-52.
Perkins, L.G. (1970). Woodpeckers. *Gosse Bird Club Broadsheet* **15**: 14-16.
Pernalete, J.M. (1989). Breeding the Black-necked Aracari *Pteroglossus aracari* at Barquisimeto Zoo. *Int. Zoo Yb.* **28**: 244-246.
Perry, A., Kessler, M. & Helme, N. (1997). Birds of the central Río Tuichi Valley, with emphasis on dry forest, Parque Nacional Madidi. Dpto. La Paz, Bolivia. Pp. 557-576 in: Remsen (1997).
Perthuis, A. (1996). Oiseau de France: le Pic mar *Dendrocopos medius*. *Ornithos* **3(4)**: 194-195.
Peslak, J. (1990). A woodpecker by any other name. Species profile: Northern Flicker (*Colaptes auratus*). *Wildbird* **4(9)**: 24-29.
Peters, D.S. (1988). Fossil birds from the Oil Shale of Messel (lower middle Eocene, Lutetian). Pp. 2056-2064 in: Ouellet (1988).
Peters, D.S. (1991). Zoogeographical relationships in the Eocene avifauna from Messel (Germany). Pp. 572-577 in: Bell *et al*. (1991).
Peters, J.L. (1948). *Check-list of Birds of the World*. Vol. 6. Museum of Comparative Zoology, Harvard University Press, Cambridge, Massachusetts.
Peters, W.D. (1982). *Control of Sexual Differences in Winter Foraging Behavior of Downy Woodpeckers (*Picoides pubescens*)*. PhD dissertation, Ohio State University, Columbus, Ohio.
Peters, W.D. & Grubb, T.C. (1983). An experimental analysis of sex-specific foraging in the Downy Woodpecker, *Picoides pubescens*. *Ecology* **64(6)**: 1437-1443.
Peterson, A.T. & Navarro-Sigüenza, A.G. (2000). Western Mexico: a significant centre of avian endemism and challenge for conservation action. *Cotinga* **14**: 42-46.
Peterson, A.T., Ingle, N. & Fernández, R. (1995). Notes on the nesting behavior of the White-bellied Woodpecker. *Wilson Bull.* **107(1)**: 182-184.
Peterson, A.W. & Grubb, T.C. (1983). Artificial trees as a cavity substrate for woodpeckers. *J. Wildl. Manage.* **47(3)**: 790-798.
Peterson, J.M.C. (1988). Three-toed Woodpecker, *Picoides tridactylus*. Pp. 236-239 in: Andrle, R.F. & Carroll, J.R. eds. (1988). *The Atlas of Breeding Birds in New York State*. Cornell University Press, Ithaca, New York.
Petit, D.R., Grubb, T.C., Petit, K.E. & Petit, L.J. (1988). Predation on overwintering wood borers by woodpeckers in clear-cut forests. *Wilson Bull.* **100(2)**: 306-309.
Petit, D.R., Petit, K.E., Grubb, T.C. & Reichhardt, L.J. (1985). Habitat and snag selection by woodpeckers in a clear-cut: analysis using artificial snags. *Wilson Bull.* **97(4)**: 525-533.
Petrov, S.Y. & Rudkovsky, V.V. (1985). Avifauna of montane steppes of the Yenisey area of the West Sayan Mountains. *Ornitologiya* **20**: 76-83.
Pettersson, B. (1983). Foraging behaviour of the Middle Spotted Woodpecker *Dendrocopos medius* in Sweden. *Holarctic Ecol.* **6**: 263-269.
Pettersson, B. (1984). *Ecology of an Isolated Population of the Middle Spotted Woodpecker* Dendrocopos medius *(L.), in the Extinction Fase*. Report **11**, Department of Wildlife Ecology, Swedish University of Agricultural Sciences, Uppsala, Sweden.
Pettersson, B. (1985). Extinction of an isolated population of the Middle Spotted Woodpecker *Dendrocopos medius* (L.) in Sweden and its relation to general theories on extinction. *Biol. Conserv.* **32**: 335-353.
Peyton, S. (1917). Large sets of eggs of the California Woodpecker. *Condor* **19(3)**: 103.
Pfennig, H.G. (1988). [Overwintering *Picoides minor* eating *Artemisia vulgaris*]. *Charadrius* **24(1)**: 10-11. In German.
Pfitzenmeyer, H.T. (1956). *Life History and Behavior Patterns of the Pileated Woodpecker Relative to Utility Lines*. MSc thesis, Pennsylvania State University, Pennsylvania.
Pflumm, W. (1979). Beobachtungen zum Bearbeiten von Lärchenzapfen (*Larix decidua*) in einer Schmiede des Buntspechts (*Dendrocopos major*). *J. Orn.* **120**: 64-72.
Phelps, W.H. (1944). Las aves de Perija. *Bol. Soc. Venez. Cienc. Nat.* **56**: 265-338.
Phelps, W.H. & Phelps, W.H. Jr. (1947). Ten new subspecies of birds from Venezuela. *Proc. Biol. Soc. Washington* **60**: 149-164.
Phelps, W.H. & Phelps, W.H. Jr. (1949). Seven new subspecies of birds from Venezuela. *Proc. Biol. Soc. Washington* **62**: 185-196.
Phelps, W.H. & Phelps, W.H. Jr. (1958). *Lista de las Aves de Venezuela con su Distribución*. Vol. 2, Part 1. No Passeriformes. Boletín de la Sociedad Venezolana de Ciencias Naturales **19(90)**. 317 pp.
Phelps, W.H. Jr. & Aveledo, R. (1987). Cinco nuevas subespecies de aves (Rallidae, Trochilidae, Picidae, Furnariidae) y tres extensiones de distribución para Venezuela. *Bol. Soc. Venez. Cienc. Nat.* **41(144)**: 7-26.
Phillips, C.L. (1887). Egg-laying extraordinary in *Colaptes auratus*. *Auk* **4**: 346.
Phillips, L.F., Tomcho, J. & Walters, J.R. (1998). Double-clutching and double-brooding in Red-cockaded Woodpeckers in Florida. *Florida Field Nat.* **26(4)**: 109-113.
Phillips, W.W.A. (1978). *Annotated Checklist of the Birds of Ceylon*. Revised edition. Wildlife & Nature Protection Society of Ceylon & Ceylon Bird Club, Colombo.
Pichorim, M., Uejima, A.M.K. & Gatto, C.A.F.R. (2000). Avifauna de um remanescente florestal do sudoeste do Estado do Paraná. Pp. 212-213 in: Straube *et al*. (2000).
Pinel, H.W. (1993). First verified record of Williamson's Sapsucker for Alberta. *Blue Jay* **51**: 209-210.
Pinto, A.A. da Rosa (1973). The eggs of the White-bellied Barbet *Lybius leucogaster* in Angola. *Ostrich* **44**: 79.
Pinto, A.A. da Rosa (1983). *Ornitologia de Angola*. Vol. 1. Non Passeres. Instituto de Investigação Científica Tropical, Lisboa.
Pinto, O.M. de Oliveira (1932). *Resultados Ornithologicos de uma Excursão pelo Oeste de São Paulo e Sul de Matto Grosso*. Revista do Museu Paulista **17**. Universidade de São Paulo, São Paulo. 138 pp.
Pinto, O.M. de Oliveira (1935). *Aves da Bahia. Notas Criticas e Observações sobre uma Collecção Feita no Reconcavo e na Parte Meridional do Estado*. Revista do Museu Paulista **19**. Universidade de São Paulo, São Paulo. 325 pp.
Pinto, O.M. de Oliveira (1936). *Contribuição á Ornithologia de Goyaz*. Revista do Museu Paulista **20**. Universidade de São Paulo, São Paulo.
Pinto, O.M. de Oliveira (1938a). *Nova Contribuição à Ornithologia Amazonica: Estudo Critico de uma Collecção de Aves do Baixo Solimões e do Alto Rio Negro*. Revista do Museu Paulista **21**. Universidade de São Paulo, São Paulo. 112 pp.
Pinto, O.M. de Oliveira (1938b). *Catalogo das Aves do Brasil e Lista dos Exemplares que as Representam no Museu Paulista*. Revista do Museu Paulista **22**. Universidade de São Paulo, São Paulo.
Pinto, O.M. de Oliveira (1940). Aves de Pernambuco. *Arq. Zool. São Paulo* **1**: 219-282.
Pinto, O.M. de Oliveira (1943). Nova contribuição a ornitologia do Reconcavo (Baia). *Pap. Avuls. Dept. Zool. São Paulo* **3(20)**: 265-284.
Pinto, O.M. de Oliveira (1944a). Sobre as aves do distrito de Monte Alegre, Municipio de Amparo (São Paulo, Brasil). *Pap. Avuls. Dept. Zool. São Paulo* **4(9)**: 117-150.
Pinto, O.M. de Oliveira (1944b). Algumas adendas a avifauna de Monte Alegre. *Pap. Avuls. Dept. Zool. São Paulo* **2(9)**: 135-142.
Pinto, O.M. de Oliveira (1947). *Contribuição a Ornitologia do Baixo Amazonas*. Arquivos de Zoologia do Estado de São Paulo **5**. 172 pp.
Pinto, O.M. de Oliveira (1948). Notas e impressões naturalisticas de una viagem fluvial a Cuiaba. *Bol. Mus. Paraense Emilio Goeldi* **10**: 331-354.
Pinto, O.M. de Oliveira (1952). *Súmula Histórica e Sistemática da Ornitologia de Minas-Gerais*. Arquivos de Zoologia do Estado de São Paulo **8**.
Pinto, O.M. de Oliveira (1953). Sobre a coleção Carlos Estevão de peles, ninhos e ovos das aves de Belém (Pará). *Pap. Avuls. Dept. Zool. São Paulo* **11(13)**: 113-224.
Pinto, O.M. de Oliveira (1966). *Cadernos de Amazônia. Part 8. Estudo Critico a Catalogo Remissivo das Aves do Território Federal de Roraima*. Instituto Nacional de Pesquisas da Amazônia, Manaus.
Pinto, O.M. de Oliveira & Camargo, E.A. (1948). Sobre uma coleção de aves do Rio das Mortes (Estado de Mato Grosso). *Pap. Avuls. Dept. Zool. São Paulo* **8**: 287-336.
Pinto, O.M. de Oliveira & Camargo, E.A. (1952). Nova contribuição à ornitologia do Rio das Mortes. *Pap. Avuls. Dept. Zool. São Paulo* **10**: 213-234.
Pinto, O.M. de Oliveira & Camargo, E.A. (1954). Resultados ornitológicos de uma expedição ao território do Acre pelo Departamento de Zoologia. *Pap. Avuls. Dept. Zool. São Paulo* **11**: 371-418.
Pinto, O.M. de Oliveira & Camargo, E.A. (1955). Lista anotada de aves colecionadas nos limites occidentais do estado do Paraná. *Pap. Avuls. Dept. Zool. São Paulo* **12**: 215-234.
Pinto, O.M. de Oliveira & Camargo, E.A. (1957). Sobre uma coleção de aves da região de Cachimbo (sul do estado do Pará). *Pap. Avuls. Dept. Zool. São Paulo* **13**: 51-69.
Pinto, O.M. de Oliveira & Camargo, E.A. (1961). Resultados ornitologicos de quatro recentes expedições do Departamento de Zoologia ao nordeste do Brasil, com a descrição de seis novas subespecies. *Arq. Zool. São Paulo* **11(9)**: 193-284.
Pinto, R.M., Vicente, J.J. & Noronha, D. (1996). Nematode parasites of Brazilian piciform birds: a general survey with description of *Procyrnea anterovulvata* n. sp. (Habronematoidea, Habronematidae). *Mem. Inst. Oswaldo Cruz* **91(4)**: 479-487.
Piratelli, A.J., de Mello, F.P. & Mello, M.C. (1998). Ocorrencia e registro de nidificação de *Monasa nigrifrons* (Spix) (Aves, Bucconidae) a leste de Mato Grosso de Sul, Brasil. *Rev. Bras. Zool.* **15(1)**: 191-193.
Piratelli, A.J., Pereira, M.R. & Siqueira, M.A.C. (1996). Predation of *Chironius flavolineatus* (Squamata: Colubridae) by *Nystalus maculatus* (Piciformes: Bucconidae). *Ararajuba* **4(2)**: 113.
Piratelli, A.J., Siqueira, M.A.C. & Marcondes-Machado, L.O. (2000). Reprodução e muda de penas em aves de sub-bosque na região leste de Mato Grosso do Sul. *Ararajuba* **8(2)**: 99-107.
Pitman, C.R.S. (1929). The nesting of *Pogoniulus leucolaimae nyanzae* - (Neum.), the Uganda Lemon-rumped Tinker-bird. *Ool. Rec.* **9**: 82-83.
Pizzoni-Ardemani, A. (1990). *Sexual Dimorphism and Geographic Variation in the Red-cockaded Woodpecker (*Picoides borealis*)*. MSc thesis, North Carolina State University, Raleigh, North Carolina.
Place, A.R., Duke, G., Jackson, S. & Roby, D. (1991). The problem of cerophagy - revisited. Page 514 in: Bell *et al*. (1991).
du Plessis, M., Weathers, W.W. & Koenig, W.D. (1994). Energetic benefits of communal roosting by Acorn Woodpeckers during the nonbreeding season. *Condor* **96(3)**: 631-637.
Plimpton, G. (1977). Un gran pedazo de carne. *Audubon* **79(6)**: 10-25.
Plowes, D.C.H. (1948). Nesting of the Greater Honeyguide. *Ostrich* **19**: 171-172.
Poinar, G.O., Warheit, K.I. & Brodzinsky, J. (1985). A fossil feather in Dominican amber. *Int. Res. Comm. Syst. Med. Sci.* **13**: 927.
Poley, D. (1973). Welterszucht von Rotstirnbartvögel *Tricholaema leucomelan* (Bodd.). *Gefiederte Welt* **97**: 121-122.

duPont, J.E. (1971). *Philippine Birds*. Monograph Series **2**. Delaware Museum of Natural History, Greenville, Delaware.
duPont, J.E. & Rabor, D.S. (1973). South Sulu Archipelago birds: an expedition report. *Nemouria* **9**: 1-63.
Poole, C. (1995). Around the Orient. China. First records of Yellow-rumped Honeyguide. *Bull. Oriental Bird Club* **22**: 16.
Pope, N. (1997). Sabah: birding in Borneo. *Birding World* **10(2)**: 62-67.
Pople, R.G., Burfield, I.J., Clay, R.P., Cope, D.R., Kennedy, C.P., López, B., Reyes, J., Warren, B. & Yagual, E. (1997). *Bird Surveys and Conservation Status of Three Sites in Western Ecuador. Final Report of Project Ortalis '96*. CSB Conservation Publications, Cambridge.
Popp, J. & Ficken, M.S. (1991). Comparative analysis of acoustic structure of passerine and woodpecker nestling calls. *Bioacoustics* **3**: 255-274.
Porter, M.L. & Labisky, R.F. (1986). Home range and foraging habitat of Red-cockaded Woodpeckers in northern Florida. *J. Wildl. Manage.* **50(2)**: 239-247.
Porter, R.F., Christensen, S. & Schiermacker-Hansen, P. (1996). *Field Guide to the Birds of the Middle East*. T. & A.D. Poyser, London.
Porter, R.F., Martins, R.P., Shaw, K.D. & Sørensen, U. (1996). The status of non-passerines in southern Yemen and the records of the OSME survey in spring 1993. *Sandgrouse* **17**: 22-53.
Posada, R.M. & Kirkconnell, A. (1993). Aspectos sobre la historia natural del Carpintero Verde (*Xiphidiopicus percussus*). *Pitirre* **6(3)**: 8. (Abstract).
Potter, E.F. (1970). Anting in wild birds, its frequency and probable purpose. *Auk* **87(4)**: 692-713.
Potter, N.S. (1953). The birds of Calicoan, Philippine Islands. *Wilson Bull.* **65(4)**: 252-270.
Poulin, B., Lefebvre, G. & McNeil, R. (1994). Diets of land birds from northeastern Venezuela. *Condor* **96(2)**: 354-367.
Poulsen, B.O. (1996). Species composition, function and home-range of mixed-species bird flocks in a primary cloud forest in Ecuador. *Bull. Brit. Orn. Club* **116(2)**: 67-74.
Poulsen, M. & Wege, D. (1994). Coppery-chested Jacamar *Galbula pastazae*. *Cotinga* **2**: 60–61.
Praderi, R. (2000). Las aves y las distintas zonas botánicas del Uruguay. *Achara* **3(3)**: 25-27.
Prasad, J.N. & Madhusudan, A. (1993). An instance of mating in Little Scaly-bellied Green Woodpecker *Picus myrmecophoneus* Stresemann from Bangalore. *J. Bombay Nat. Hist. Soc.* **90(1)**: 95-96.
Pratini, N.L. (1989). *Acorn Utilization in the Acorn Woodpecker (*Melanerpes formicivorus*)*. MSc thesis, University of California, Davis, California.
Price, J., Droege, S. & Price, A. (1995). *The Summer Atlas of North American Birds*. Academic Press, London.
Prieme, A. & Heegaard, M. (1988). A visit to Gunung Niut in West Kalimantan. *Kukila* **3(3-4)**: 138-140.
Priest, C.D. (1934). *The Birds of Southern Rhodesia*. Vol. 2. William Clowes, London & Beccles.
Priest, C.D. (1948). *Eggs of Birds Breeding in Southern Africa*. Robert Maclehose Company, Glasgow.
Prigogine, A. (1971). *Les Oiseaux de l'Itombwe et de son Hinterland*. Vol. 1. Annales Musée Royal de l'Afrique Centrale Tervuren, Sciences Zoologiques **185**. 298 pp.
Prigogine, A. (1972). Nids et oeufs récoltés au Kivu, Part II. (République du Zaïre). *Rev. Zool. Bot. Afr.* **85**: 203-226.
Prigogine, A. (1977). Le statut de *Pogoniulus leucolaima* (Verreaux). *Gerfaut* **67**: 413-425.
Prigogine, A. (1978). Note sur les petits indicateurs de la Forêt de Kakamega. *Gerfaut* **68**: 87-89.
Prigogine, A. (1980a). Hybridation entre les barbions *Pogoniulus bilineatus* et *Pogoniulus leucolaima* au Rwanda et au Burundi. *Gerfaut* **70**: 73-91.
Prigogine, A. (1980b). Étude de quelques contacts secondaires au Zaïre oriental. *Gerfaut* **70**: 305-384.
Prigogine, A. (1985). Recently recognized bird species in the Afrotropical region - a critical review. Pp. 91-114 in: Schuchmann (1985).
Prigogine, A. (1987). Hybridization between the megasubspecies *cailliautii* and *permista* of the Green-backed Woodpecker, *Campethera cailliautii*. *Gerfaut* **77**: 187-204.
Prigogine, A. & Louette, M. (1983). Contacts secondaires entre les taxons appartenant à la super-espèce *Dendropicos goertae*. *Gerfaut* **73**: 9-83.
Pringle, V. (1991). The Bearded Woodpecker. *Bee-eater* **42(2)**: 25.
Prodon, R. (1991). Erratisme printanier du Pic noir *Dryocopus martius* en zone méditerranéenne. *Alauda* **59(2)**: 113-114.
Proud, D. (1952). Some birds seen on the Gandak-Kosi watershed in March 1951. *J. Bombay Nat. Hist. Soc.* **50**: 355-365.
Proud, D. (1958). Woodpeckers drumming. *J. Bombay Nat. Hist. Soc.* **55(2)**: 350-351.
Prozesky, O.P.M. (1966). A study of the behaviour of the Crested Barbet, *Trachyphonus vaillantii*. *Ostrich* **6**(Suppl.): 171-182.
Prum, R.O. (1988). Phylogenetic interrelationships of the barbets (Aves: Capitonidae) and toucans (Aves: Ramphastidae) based on morphology with comparisons to DNA-DNA hybridization. *Zool. J. Linn. Soc.* **92(4)**: 313-343.
Pulliainen, E. (1963). Observations on the autumnal territorial behavior of the Great Spotted Woodpecker, *Dendrocopos major* (L.). *Ornis Fenn.* **40**: 132-139.
Purroy, F.J. (1972). El Pico Dorsiblanco *Dendrocopos leucotos* del Pirineo. *Ardeola* **20**: 145-158.
Purroy, F.J. (1997). *Atlas de las Aves de España (1975-1995)*. Lynx Edicions, Barcelona.
Purroy, F.J., Álvarez, A. & Pettersson, B. (1984). La población de Pico Mediano *Dendrocopos medius* (L.), de la Cordillera Cantábrica. *Ardeola* **31**: 81-90.
Quantrill, B. & Quantrill, R. (1998). The birds of the Parcours Vita, Yaoundé, Cameroon. *Malimbus* **20(1)**: 1-14.
Rabor, D.S. (1977). *Philippine Birds & Mammals*. University of the Philippines Press, Quezon City.
Radermacher, W. (1970). Beobachtungen an spechten. *Orn. Mitt.* **22(9)**: 179-183.
Radermacher, W. (1980). Hlenbau des Kleinspechts (*Picoides minor*) im Herbst. *Charadrius* **16(4)**: 166-168.
Radford, A.P. (1997). Juvenile Green Woodpecker eating spider's web. *British Birds* **90(9)**: 362-363.
Raffaele, H.A. (1989). *A Guide to the Birds of Puerto Rico and the Virgin Islands*. Princeton University Press, Princeton & London.
Raffaele, H.A., Wiley, J., Garrido, O., Keith, A. & Raffaele, J. (1998). *A Guide to the Birds of the West Indies*. Princeton University, Princeton, New Jersey.
Rahbek, C., Bloch, H., Poulsen, M.K. & Rasmussen, J.F. (1995). The avifauna of the Podocarpus National Park - the "Andean jewel in the crown" of Ecuador's protected areas. *Orn. Neotropical* **6(2)**: 113-120.
Raikow, R.J. & Cracraft, J. (1983). Monophyly of the Piciformes: a reply to Olson. *Auk* **100(1)**: 134-138.
Raitt, R.J. (1959). Rocky Mountain race of the Williamson Sapsucker wintering in California. *Condor* **62(2)**: 142.
Raja, N.A., Davidson, P., Bean, N., Drijvers, R., Showler, D.A. & Barker, C. (1999). The birds of Palas, North-west Frontier Province, Pakistan. *Forktail* **15**: 77-85.
Rajan, S.A. (1992). Unusual foraging site of Golden-backed Woodpecker *Dinopium benghalense* (Linn.). *J. Bombay Nat. Hist. Soc.* **89(3)**: 374.
Rajathurai, S. (1996). The birds of Batam and Bintan Islands, Riau Archipelago. *Kukila* **8**: 86-113.
Ramey, P. (1980). *Seasonal, Sexual, and Geographical Variation in the Foraging Ecology of Red-cockaded Woodpeckers (*Picoides borealis*)*. MSc thesis, Mississippi State University, Starkville, Mississippi.
Rand, A.L. (1948). Five new birds from the Philippines. *Fieldiana Zool.* **31**: 201-205.
Rand, A.L. (1951). *Birds from Liberia. With a Discussion of Barriers between Upper and Lower Guinea Subspecies*. Fieldiana Zoology **32(9)**. 93 pp.
Rand, A.L. & Fleming, R.L. (1956). Two new birds from Nepal. *Fieldiana Zool.* **39**: 1-3.
Rand, A.L. & Fleming, R.L. (1957). *Birds of Nepal*. Fieldiana Zoology **41**. 218 pp.
Rand, A.L. & Rabor, D.S. (1960). *Birds of the Philippine Islands: Siquijor, Mount Malindang, Bohol, and Samar*. Fieldiana Zoology **35(7)**. 117 pp.
Rand, A.L., Friedmann, H. & Traylor, M.A. (1959). *Birds from Gabon and Moyen Congo*. Fieldiana Zoology **41(2)**. 191 pp.
Rands, M.R.W., Rands, G.F. & Porter, R.F. (1987). *Birds in the Yemen Arab Republic*. Report of the Ornithological Society of the Middle East Expedition 1985. ICBP, Cambridge.
Rangel-Salazar, J.L. & Enríquez-Rocha, P.L. (1993). Nest record and dietary items for the Black Hawk-eagle (*Spizaetus tyrannus*) from the Yucatan Peninsula. *J. Raptor Res.* **27**: 121-122.
Ranger, G. (1955). On three species of honey-guide; the Greater (*Indicator indicator*), the Lesser (*Indicator minor*) and the Scaly-throated (*Indicator variegatus*). *Ostrich* **26**: 70-87.
Rankin, R. (1981). Co-operative nesting. *Witwatersrand Bird Club News* **115**: 6.
Raphael, M.G. (1981). Interspecific differences in nesting habitat of sympatric woodpeckers and nuthatches. Pp. 142-151 in: Capen, D.E. (1981). *The Use of Multivariate Statistics in Studies of Wildlife Habitat*. Rocky Mountain Forest and Range Experiment Station, Fort Collins, Colorado.
Rasmussen, J.F., Rahbek, C., Poulsen, B.O., Poulsen, M.K. & Bloch, H. (1996). Distributional records and natural history notes on threatened and little known birds of southern Ecuador. *Bull. Brit. Orn. Club* **116(1)**: 26-46.
Rattray, R.H. (1905). Birds nesting in the Murree Hills and Gullies. Part 1. *J. Bombay Nat. Hist. Soc.* **16(3)**: 421-428.
Ravkin, E.S., Gleich, I.I. & Chernikov, O.A. (1988). [Numbers and distribution of birds in subtaiga forests of central Siberia (the Poyma River basin)]. Pp. 62-77 in: Rogacheva, H.V. (1988). *[Materials on the Fauna of Central Siberia and Adjacent Regions of Mongolia]*. Institute of Evolutionary Morphology and Animal Ecology, USSR Academy of Sciences Publications, Moskow. In Russian with English summary.
Ravussin, P.A. & Sermet, E. (1975). Nidification simultanée du Pic noir *Dryocopus martius* et de la Chouette de Tengmalm *Aegolius funereus* sur le même arbre. *Nos Oiseaux* **33(2)**: 60-63.
Raw, A. (1997). Avian predation on individual Neotropical social wasps (Hymenoptera, *Vespidae*) outside their nests. *Orn. Neotropical* **8(1)**: 89–92.
Read, A.C. (1914). Cuban Green Woodpecker - *Xiphidiopicus*. *Isle Pines News* **6**: 4.
Ree, V. (1974). Mål, vekt og myting hos trekkende flaggspett, *Dendrocopos major* (L.) under invasjonen i 1972. *Fauna* **27**: 39-49.
Ree, V. (1984). Observasjoner av gråspett *Picus canus* i Maridalen in vinterhalvåret. *Vår Fuglefauna* **7**: 209-216.
Reed, J.M. (1990). The dynamics of Red-cockaded Woodpecker rarity and conservation. Pp. 37-56 in: Carlson & Aulén (1990).
Reed, J.M. & Walters, J.R. (1996). Helper effects on variance components of fitness in the cooperatively breeding Red-cockaded Woodpecker. *Auk* **113(3)**: 608-616.
Reed, J.M., Doerr, P.D. & Walters, J.R. (1988). Minimum viable population size of the Red-cockaded Woodpecker. *J. Wildl. Manage.* **52(3)**: 385-391.
Reed, J.M., Walters, J.R., Emigh, T.E. & Seaman, D.E. (1993). Effective population size in Red-cockaded Woodpeckers: population and model differences. *Conserv. Biol.* **7(2)**: 302-308. In English with Spanish summary.
Regalado, P. (1975). El enigma del Carpintero Real. *Forestal* **25**: 10-13.
Regalado, P. (1977). *Xiphidiopicus percussus marthae*, nueva subespecie. *Rev. For.* **33**: 34-37.
Reiser, O. (1905). Bericht über die ornithologische Ausbeute während der von der kaiserliche Akademie der Wissenschaften im Jahre 1903 nach Brasilien entsendeten Expedition. *Anz. Kaiserliche Akad. Wissenschaften, Mathematisch-naturwissenschaftlichen Wien* **41**: 320-324.
Reller, A.W. (1972). Aspects of behavioral ecology of Red-headed and Red-bellied Woodpeckers. *Amer. Midl. Nat.* **88(2)**: 207-290.
Remsen, J.V. (1977). Five bird species new to Colombia. *Auk* **94(2)**: 363.
Remsen, J.V. (1984). Natural history notes on some poorly known Bolivian birds. *Gerfaut* **74**: 163-179.
Remsen, J.V. (1985). Community organization and ecology of birds of high elevation humid forest of the Bolivian Andes. Pp. 733-755 in: Buckley *et al.* (1985).
Remsen, J.V. (1986). Aves de una localidad en la sabana húmeda del norte de Bolivia. [Birds at a wet savanna locality in the north of Bolivia]. *Ecol. Bol. (Rev. Inst. Ecol.)* **8**: 21-35. In Spanish with German and English summary.
Remsen, J.V. (1991). First record of Williamson's Sapsucker from Louisiana. *J. La. Orn.* **2(1)**: 15-17.
Remsen, J.V. ed. (1997). *Studies in Neotropical Ornithology Honoring Ted Parker*. Ornithological Monographs **48**. American Ornithologists' Union, Washington, D.C.
Remsen, J.V. & Parker, T.A. (1983). Contribution of river-created habitats to bird species richness in Amazonia. *Biotropica* **15**: 223-231.
Remsen, J.V. & Parker, T.A. (1984a). Arboreal dead-leaf-searching birds of the neotropics. *Condor* **86(1)**: 36-41.
Remsen, J.V. & Parker, T.A. (1984b). Contribution of river-created habitats to species richness in Amazonia. *Biotropica* **15**: 223-231.
Remsen, J.V. & Traylor, M.A. (1989). *An Annotated List of the Birds of Bolivia*. Buteo Books, Vermillion, South Dakota.
Remsen, J.V., Hyde, M.A. & Chapman, A. (1993). The diets of Neotropical trogons, motmots, barbets and toucans. *Condor* **95(1)**: 178-192.
Remsen, J.V., Traylor, M.A. & Parkes, K.C. (1986). Range extensions of some Bolivian birds, 2 (Columbidae to Rhinocryptidae). *Bull. Brit. Orn. Club* **106(1)**: 22-32.
Renjifo, L.M., Servat, G.P., Goerck, J.M., Loiselle, B.A. & Blake, J.G. (1997). Patterns of species composition and endemism in the northern Neotropics: a case for conservation of montane avifauna. Pp. 577-594 in: Remsen (1997).
Renken, R.B. (1988). *Habitat Characteristics Related to Pileated Woodpecker Densities and Territory Size in Missouri*. PhD dissertation. University of Missouri, Columbia, Missouri.
Renken, R.B. & Wiggers, E.P. (1989). Forest characteristics related to Pileated Woodpecker territory size in Missouri. *Condor* **91(3)**: 642-652.
Renken, R.B. & Wiggers, E.P. (1993). Habitat characteristics related to Pileated Woodpecker densities in Missouri. *Wilson Bull.* **105(1)**: 77-83.
Rensch, B. (1931). Die Vogelwelt von Lombok, Sumbawa and Flores. *Mitt. Zool. Mus. Berlin* **17**: 451-637.
Repasky, R.R. (1984). *Utilization of Home Range and Foraging Substrates by Red-cockaded Woodpeckers*. MSc thesis, North Carolina State University, Raleigh, North Carolina.
Repasky, R.R. & Doerr, P.D. (1991). Home range and substrate use by two family groups of Red-cockaded Woodpeckers in the North Carolina sandhills. *Brimleyana* **17**: 37-52.
Restrepo, C. (1990). *Ecology and Cooperative Breeding in a Frugivorous Bird,* Semnornis ramphastinus. MSc thesis, University of Florida, Gainesville, Florida.
Restrepo, C. & Beltrán, J.W. (1989). *Organización Social y Ecología de* Semnornis ramphastinus *(Aves: Capitonidae)*. Informe Final FEN, Bogotá.
Restrepo, C. & Mondragón, M.L. (1988). *Historia Natural de* Semnornis ramphastinus *(Aves: Capitonidae), una Especie Vulnerable*. Informe Final FEN, Bogotá.
Restrepo, C. & Mondragón, M.L. (1998). Cooperative breeding in the frugivorous Toucan Barbet (*Semnornis ramphastinus*). *Auk* **115(1)**: 4-15.
Reynard, G.B. (1987). The Ivory-billed Woodpecker in Cuba. Pp. 8-10 in: *Proceedings of the Third Southeastern Nongame Endangered Wildlife Symposium*.
Reynaud, P.A. (1998). Changes in understory avifauna along the Sinnamary River (French Guyana, South America). *Orn. Neotropical* **9(1)**: 51-69.
Reynolds, J.F. (1974). Co-operative breeding in Red-and-yellow Barbets. *Bull. East Afr. Nat. Hist. Soc.* **1974**: 144-145.
Reynolds, P.S. & Lima, S. (1994). Direct use of wings by foraging woodpeckers. *Wilson Bull.* **106(2)**: 408-411.
Richardson, D. (1989). Notes on habitat use and feeding behaviour of Olive Woodpeckers in mountain Fynbos near Stellenbosch. *Bokmakierie* **41(1)**: 17-18.
Richardson, D.M. & Smith, D.L. (1992). Hardwood removal in Red-cockaded Woodpecker colonies using a shear V-blade. *Wildl. Soc. Bull.* **20**: 428-433.

Richardson, D.M., Copeland, M. & Bradford, J.W. (1999). Translocation of orphaned Red-cockaded Woodpecker nestlings. [Translocación de pichones huérfanos de *Picoides borealis*]. *J. Field Orn.* **70(3)**: 400-403. In English with Spanish summary.
Richardson, F. (1942). Adaptive modifications for tree-trunk foraging in birds. *Univ. Calif. Publ. Zool.* **46(4)**: 317-368.
Richardson, R.A. (1948). Display behavior of Lesser Spotted Woodpecker in winter. *British Birds* **41**: 311.
Richmond, C.W. (1893). On a collection of birds from eastern Nicaragua and Río Frío, Costa Rica, with notes; and a description of a supposed new trogon. *Proc. US Natl. Mus.* **16**: 479-532.
Ridgely, R.S. & Gaulin, S.J.C. (1980). The birds of Finca Merenberg, Huila Department, Colombia. *Condor* **82(4)**: 378-391.
Ridgely, R.S. & Greenfield, P.J. (2001). *The Birds of Ecuador*. Vols. 1-2. Christopher Helm, London.
Ridgely, R.S. & Gwynne, J.A. (1989). *A Guide to the Birds of Panama with Costa Rica, Nicaragua, and Honduras*. Princeton University Press, Princeton, New Jersey.
Ridgely, R.S., Greenfield, P.J. & Guerrero, M. (1998). *Una Lista Anotada de las Aves del Ecuador Continental. An Annotated List of the Birds of Mainland Ecuador*. CECIA, Quito. In Spanish and English.
Ridgway, R. (1914). *The Birds of North and Middle America*. US National Museum Bulletin **50(6)**. Smithsonian Institution, Washington, D.C. 882 pp.
Riley, C.M. (1986a). Observations on the breeding biology of Emerald Toucanets in Costa Rica. *Wilson Bull.* **98(4)**: 585-588.
Riley, C.M. (1986b). *Foraging Behaviour and Sexual Dimorphism in Emerald Toucanets in Costa Rica*. MSc thesis, University of Arkansas, Fayetteville, Arkansas.
Riley, C.M. & Smith, K.G. (1986). Flower eating by Emerald Toucanets in Costa Rica. *Condor* **88(3)**: 396-397.
Riley, C.M. & Smith, K.G. (1992). Sexual dimorphism and foraging behavior of Emerald Toucanets *Aulacorhynchus prasinus*. *Ornis Scand.* **23(4)**: 459-466.
Riley, J. & Mole, J. (2001). The birds of Gunung Ambang Nature Reserve, North Sulawesi, Indonesia. *Forktail* **17**: 57-66.
Riley, J.H. (1934). One new genus and three new races of birds from the Malay region. *Proc. Biol. Soc. Washington* **47**: 115-118.
Riley, J.H. (1938). *Birds from Siam and the Malay Peninsula in the United States National Museum Collected by Drs. Hugh M. Smith and William L. Abbott*. US National Museum Bulletin **172**. Smithsonian Institution, Wahington D.C. 581 pp.
Rimmer, C.C., Goetz, J.E. & McFarland, K.P. (1998). Bird observations in threatened forest fragments of Sierra de Neiba, Dominican Republic. *Pitirre* **11(2)**: 38-39.
Rines, M.W. (1998). Red-bellied Woodpeckers raising second brood. *Bird Obs.* **26(1)**: 14-15.
Ripley, S.D. (1944). *The Bird Fauna of the West Sumatran Islands*. Bulletin of the Museum of Comparative Zoology **44**, Cambridge, Massachusetts. 124 pp.
Ripley, S.D. (1945). The barbets. *Auk* **62(4)**: 542-563.
Ripley, S.D. (1946). The barbets - errata and addenda. *Auk* **63**: 452.
Ripley, S.D. (1950a). New birds from Nepal and the Indian region. *Proc. Biol. Soc. Washington* **63**: 101-108.
Ripley, S.D. (1950b). Polymorphism in a woodpecker (*Picus flavinucha*). *Evolution* **4(3)**: 276-277.
Ripley, S.D. (1950c). Birds from Nepal 1947-49. *J. Bombay Nat. Hist. Soc.* **49**: 355-417.
Ripley, S.D. (1953). What is *Megalaima robustirostris* (Baker)? *Ibis* **95(3)**: 547-548.
Ripley, S.D. (1982). *A Synopsis of the Birds of India and Pakistan together with those of Nepal, Bhutan, Bangladesh and Sri Lanka*. Bombay Natural History Society, Bombay.
Ripley, S.D. (1991). Comments on sap-sucking by woodpeckers in India. *J. Bombay Nat. Hist. Soc.* **88(1)**: 112-113.
Ripley, S.D. & Heinrich, G.H. (1966). Additions to the avifauna of northern Angola. Part III. *Postilla* **95**: 1-29.
Ripley, S.D. & Heinrich, G.H. (1969). Comments on the avifauna of Tanzania II. *Postilla* **134**: 1-21.
Rissler, L.J. (1995). The influence of Yellow-bellied Sapsuckers on local insect community structure. *Wilson Bull.* **107(4)**: 746-752.
Ritchie, A.H. (1918). Woodpeckers and cocoa. *J. Jamaican Agric. Soc.* **22(3)**: 102-107.
Ritchison, G. (1999). *Wild Bird Guides. Downy Woodpecker*. Stackpole Books, Mechanicsburg, Pennsylvania.
Ritter, W.E. (1921). Acorn-storing by the California Woodpecker. *Condor* **23(1)**: 3-14.
Ritter, W.E. (1922). Further observations on the activities of the California Woodpecker. *Condor* **24(4)**: 109-122.
Ritter, W.E. (1929). The nutritional activities of the California Woodpecker (*Balanosphyra formiscivora*). *Quart. Rev. Biol.* **4**: 455-483.
Ritter, W.E. (1938). *The California Woodpecker and I*. University of California Press, Berkeley, California.
Rivière, J. (1990). [Notes on the Black Woodpecker]. *Cormoran* **37**: 49-51. In French with English summary.
Roach, T.L. (1975). Red-bellied Woodpecker removes young from nest. *Florida Field Nat.* **3(1)**: 19.
Robbins, M.B. & Ridgely, R.S. (1990). The avifauna of an upper tropical cloud forest in southwestern Ecuador. *Proc. Acad. Nat. Sci. Philadelphia* **142**: 59-71.
Robbins, M.B., Parker, T.A. & Allen, S.E. (1985). The avifauna of Cerro Pirre, Darién, eastern Panama. Pp. 198-232 in: Buckley *et al.* (1985).
Robbins, M.B., Ridgely, R.S., Schulenberg, T.S. & Gill, F.B. (1987). The avifauna of the Cordillera de Cutucú, Ecuador, with comparisons to other Andean localities. *Proc. Acad. Nat. Sci. Philadelphia* **139**: 243-259.
Roberts, A. (1924). Classification of South African birds: some additional notes. *Ann. Transvaal Mus.* **10**: 82-85.
Roberts, H.A. (1956). Breeding tactics of the two honey-guides - *Indicator indicator* (Sparrman) and *Indicator minor* (Stephens). *Bull. Brit. Orn. Club* **76**: 114.
Roberts, R.C. (1976). *Ecological Relationships in the Acorn Woodpecker (*Melanerpes formicivorus*)*. PhD dissertation, University of California, Davis, California.
Roberts, R.C. (1979). Habitat and resource relationships in Acorn Woodpeckers. *Condor* **81(1)**: 1-8.
Roberts, T.J. (1991). *The Birds of Pakistan*. Vol. 1. Non-Passeriformes. Oxford University Press, Karachi.
Roberts, T.J. (1996). Twentieth century changes in the avifauna of Pakistan. *J. Bombay Nat. Hist. Soc.* **93(3)**: 374-381.
Robertshaw, D.J. (1987). A possible first captive breeding of the Channel Bill Toucan. *AFA Watchbird* **14**: 8-10.
Robertson, I. (1994). Recent Reports. Cameroon. *Bull. African Bird Club* **1(1)**: 28.
Robertson, I. (1997a). Recent Reports. Uganda. *Bull. African Bird Club* **4(1)**: 51.
Robertson, I. (1997b). Recent Reports. Cameroon. *Bull. African Bird Club* **4(2)**: 142.
Robertson, I. (1998a). Recent Reports. Congo (Brazzaville). *Bull. African Bird Club* **5(1)**: 70.
Robertson, I. (1998b). Recent Reports. Zambia. *Bull. African Bird Club* **5(1)**: 74-75.
Robertson, I. (1998c). Recent Reports. Equatorial Guinea. *Bull. African Bird Club* **5(2)**: 143.
Robinson, G. (1957). Observations of pair relations of White-headed Woodpeckers in winter. *Condor* **59(5)**: 339-340.
Robinson, H.C. (1909). The birds at present known from the mountains of the Malay Peninsula. *J. Fed. Malay States Mus.* **2**: 164-222.
Robinson, H.C. (1911). A list of small collection of mammals and birds from the mountains of Ulu Langat, Selangor. *J. Fed. Malay States Mus.* **4**: 235-241.
Robinson, H.C. (1917). On a collection of birds from Pulau Langkawi and other islands on the north-west coast of the Malay Peninsula. *J. Fed. Malay States Mus.* **7**: 129-191.
Robinson, H.C. (1927). *The Birds of the Malay Peninsula*. Vol. 1. Witherby, London.
Robinson, H.C. (1928). *The Birds of the Malay Peninsula*. Vol. 2. Witherby, London.
Robinson, H.C. & Chasen, F.M. (1939). *The Birds of the Malay Peninsula*. Vol. 4. Witherby, London.
Robinson, H.C. & Kloss, C.B. (1918). *Results of an Expedition to Korinchi Peak, Sumatra. Birds*. Journal of Federated Malay States Museum **8**. 204 pp.
Robinson, H.C. & Kloss, C.B. (1919a). On a collection of birds from N.E. Sumatra. *J. Straits Branch Roy. Asiat. Soc.* **80**: 72-133.
Robinson, H.C. & Kloss, C.B. (1919b). On birds from South America and Cochin China. Part I. Phasianidae-Campephagidae. *Ibis* **Ser. 11, no. 1**: 392-453.
Robinson, H.C. & Kloss, C.B. (1921-1924). *The Birds of South-west and Peninsular Thailand*. Journal of the Natural History Society of Siam **5**. 397 pp.
Robinson, H.C. & Kloss, C.B. (1924a). On a large collection of birds chiefly from West Sumatra made by Mr. E. Jacobson. *J. Fed. Malay States Mus.* **11**: 189-347.
Robinson, H.C. & Kloss, C.B. (1924b). A nominal list of the birds collected in Java. *Treubia* **5**: 267-298.
Robinson, L.J. (1977). The Red-bellied Woodpecker in Massachusetts: a case history of range expansion. *Bird Observer East. Mass.* **5(6)**: 195-197.
Robinson, S.K. (1985). Coloniality in the Yellow-rumped Cacique as a defense against nest predators. *Auk* **102(3)**: 506-519.
Robinson, S.K. (1997). Birds of a Peruvian oxbow lake: populations, resources, predation, and social behavior. Pp. 613-639 in: Remsen (1997).
Robinson, S.K. & Terborgh, J. (1997). Bird community dynamics along primary successional gradients of an Amazonian whitewater river. Pp. 641-672 in: Remsen (1997).
Robinson, W. & Richmond, C.W. (1895). An annotated list of birds observed on the island of Margarita, and at Guanta and Laguayra, Venezuela. *Proc. US Natl. Mus.* **18**: 648-685.
Robson, C.R. (1988). Recent Reports. Thailand. *Bull. Oriental Bird Club* **8**: 35-36.
Robson, C.R. (1989). Birdwatching areas. Omei Shan, Sichuan, China. *Bull. Oriental Bird Club* **9**: 16-21.
Robson, C.R. (1994). From the field. Indonesia. *Bull. Oriental Bird Club* **20**: 57-58.
Robson, C.R. (1996a). From the field. Cambodia. *Bull. Oriental Bird Club* **24**: 60.
Robson, C.R. (1996b). From the field. Indonesia. *Bull. Oriental Bird Club* **24**: 61.
Robson, C.R. (1998). From the field. Malaysia. *Bull. Oriental Bird Club* **28**: 45.
Robson, C.R. (2000). *A Field Guide to the Birds of South-east Asia*. New Holland, London.
Robson, C.R., Buck, H., Farrow, D.S., Fisher, T. & King, B.F. (1998). A birdwatching visit to the Chin Hills, West Burma (Myanmar), with notes from nearby areas. *Forktail* **13**: 109-120.
Robson, C.R., Eames, J.C., Nguyen Cu & Truong Van La (1993a). Further recent records of birds from Viet Nam. *Forktail* **8**: 25-52.
Robson, C.R., Eames, J.C., Nguyen Cu & Truong Van La (1993b). Birds recorded during the third BirdLife/Forest Birds Working Group expedition in Viet Nam. *Forktail* **9**: 89-119.
Robson, C.R., Eames, J.C., Wolstencroft, J.A., Nguyen Cu & Truong Van La (1989). Recent records of birds from Viet Nam. *Forktail* **5**: 71-97.
Rocamora, G. & Yeatman-Berthelot, D. (1999). *Oiseaux Menacés et à Surveiller en France. Listes Rouges et Recherche de Priorités. Populations. Tendances. Menaces. Conservation*. Société d'Études Ornithologiques de France & Ligue pour la Protection des Oiseaux, Paris.
Rocha, O. & Peñaranda, E. (1995). Avifauna de Huaraco: una localidad de la puna semiárida del altiplano central, Departamento de La Paz, Bolivia. *Cotinga* **3**: 17-25. In Spanish with English summary.
Rodewald, P.G., Dejaifve, P.A. & Green, A.A. (1994). The birds of Korup National Park and Korup Project Area, Southwest Province, Cameroon. *Bird Conserv. Int.* **4(1)**: 1-68.
Rodgers, J.A., Kale, H.W. & Smith, H.T. eds. (1996). *Rare and Endangered Biota of Florida*. Vol. 5. Birds. University Press of Florida, Gainesville, Florida.
Rodgers, S.P. (1990). Predation of domestic fowl eggs by Red-bellied Woodpeckers. *Florida Field Nat.* **18(3)**: 57-58.
Rodner, C., Lentino, M. & Restall, R. (2000). *Checklist of the Birds of Northern South America. An Annotated Checklist of the Species and Subspecies of Ecuador, Colombia, Venezuela, Aruba, Curaçao, Bonaire, Trinidad & Tobago, Guyana, Suriname and French Guiana*. Pica Press, Nr. Robertsbridge, UK.
Rodrigues, M., Belfort, H., Campolina, C. & Garcia, Q.S. (2000). O Tucanuçu (*Ramphastos toco*) como agente dispersor de sementes de copaiba. *Melopsittacus* **3(1)**: 6-11.
Rodríguez, J.V. (1982). *Aves del Parque Nacional Natural Los Katios*. INDERENA, USDA, Bogotá.
Rodwell, S.P. (1996). Notes on the distribution and abundance of birds observed in Guinea-Bissau, 21 February to 3 April 1992. *Malimbus* **18(1)**: 25-43.
Rodwell, S.P., Sauvage, A., Rumsey, S.J.R. & Bräunlich, A. (1996). An annotated check-list of birds occurring at the Parc National des Oiseaux du Djoudj in Senegal, 1984-1994. *Malimbus* **18(2)**: 74-111.
Rogacheva, H.V. (1992). *The Birds of Central Siberia*. Husum-Druck und Verlagsgesellschaft, Husum, Germany.
Rogers, D.T., Jackson, J.A., Schardien, B.J. & Rogers, M.S. (1979). Observations at a nest of a partial albino Red-headed Woodpecker. *Auk* **96(1)**: 206-207.
Röhl, E. (1935). Contribución a la ornitología de Venezuela. Monografía de los Ramphastidae o Tucanes. *Bol. Soc. Venezolana Cienc. Nat.* **21**: 24-36.
Rojas, O.R., Sahagún, F.J. & Navarro, A.G. (2001). Additional information on the avifauna of Querétaro, Mexico. *Cotinga* **15**: 48. In English with Spanish summary.
Rolstad, J. & Rolstad, E. (1995). Seasonal patterns in home range and habitat use of the Grey-headed Woodpecker *Picus canus* as influenced by the availability of food. *Ornis Fenn.* **72(1)**: 1-13.
Rolstad, J. & Rolstad, E. (2000). Influence of large snow depths on Black Woodpecker foraging behavior. *Ornis Fenn.* **77(2)**: 65-70.
Rolstad, J., Løken, B. & Rolstad, E. (2000). Habitat selection as a hierarchical spatial process: the Green Woodpecker at the northern edge of its distribution range. *Oecologia* **124(1)**: 116-129.
Rolstad, J., Majewski, P. & Rolstad, E. (1998). Black Woodpecker use of habitats and feeding substrates in a managed Scandinavian forest. *J. Wildl. Manage.* **62(1)**: 11-23.
Rolstad J., Rolstad, E. & Saeteren, O. (2000). Black Woodpecker nest sites: characteristics, selection, and reproductive success. *J. Wildl. Manage.* **64(4)**: 1053-1066.
Romary, C. (1990). *Evaluation of the Habitat Suitability Index Models for the Black-capped Chickadee and Downy Woodpecker*. MSc thesis, Emporia State University, Emporia, Kansas.
Romero, H. (1977). Primer registro de cuatro aves para Colombia. *Lozania* **25(4)**: 1-3.
Romero, H. (1978). Primer registro de doce aves para Colombia. *Lozania* **26**: 1-8.
Romero, J.L. (1990). Localización de algunos ejemplares de Pico Mediano (*Dendrocopos medius*) en el Valle de Arán (Lérida). *Ardeola* **37**: 344-345.
Romero, J.L. (1994). Alimentación de los pollos de Pico Menor *Dendrocopos minor* en un nido de la Vall d'Aran (Lleida, NE de España). *Butll. Grup Català d'Anellament* **11**: 59-62.
Rompré, G., Aubry, Y. & Kirkconnell, A. (1999). Notes on some Cuban birds. *Cotinga* **11**: 31-33.
Root, T. (1988). *Atlas of Wintering North American Birds. An Analysis of Christmas Bird Count Data*. University of Chicago Press, Chicago & London.
do Rosário, L.A. (1996). *As Aves em Santa Catarina. Distribuição Geográfica e Meio Ambiente*. FATMA, Florianópolis, Brazil.
Rosenberg, K.V. (1997). Ecology of dead-leaf-foraging specialists and their contribution to Amazonian bird diversity. Pp. 673-700 in: Remsen (1997).
Ross, G.J.B. (1970). The specific status and distribution of *Pogoniulus pusillus* (Dumont) and *Pogoniulus chrysoconus* (Temminck) in southern Africa. *Ostrich* **41**: 200-204.
Rossell, C.R. & Britcher, J.J. (1994). Evidence of plural breeding by Red-cockaded Woodpeckers. *Wilson Bull.* **106(3)**: 557-559.
Rossell, C.R. & Gorsira, B. (1996). Assessment of condition and availability of active Red-cockaded Woodpecker cavities. *Wildl. Soc. Bull.* **24(1)**: 21-24.
van Rossem, A.J. (1934). A new puff-bird from El Salvador. *Trans. San Diego Soc. Nat. Hist.* **8(2)**: 3-4.
van Rossem, A.J. (1942). Four new woodpeckers from the western United States and Mexico. *Condor* **44(1)**: 22-26.
van Rossem, A.J. (1945). *A Distributional Survey of the Birds of Sonora, Mexico*. Occasional Papers of the Museum of Zoology Louisiana State University **21**. 379 pp.
Rost, R., Lang, E. & Ley, H.W. (1992). Männchen-Überschuß bei Schwarzspechtnestlingen (*Dryocopus martius*)? [Is there a surplus of males in Black Woodpecker nestlings (*Dryocopus martius*)?] *J. Orn.* **133(2)**: 203-208. In German with English summary.

Roth, R.R. (1978). Attacks on Red-headed Woodpeckers by flycatchers. *Wilson Bull.* **90(3)**: 450-451.

Roth, V. & Michalski, D. (1994). Breeding Red-throated Gaudy Barbets. *AFA Watchbird* **21(6)**: 31-32.

Rothschild, M. (1964). An extension of Dr. Lincoln Brower's theory on bird predation and food specifity, together with some observations on bird memory in relation to aposematic colour patterns. *Entomologist* **97**: 73–78.

Rothstein, S.I. & Robinson, S.K. (1998). The evolution and ecology of avian brood parasitism. An overview. Pp. 3-56 in: Rothstein, S.I. & Robinson, S.K. eds. (1998). *Parasitic Birds and their Hosts. Studies in Coevolution*. Oxford University Press, Oxford.

Rougeot, P.C. (1951). Nouvelles observations sur le *Melichneutes robustus* Bates. *Oiseau et RFO* **21**: 127-134.

Rougeot, P.C. (1959). Notes biologiques sur l'Indicateur à queue en lyre: *Melichneutes robustus* Bates. *Ostrich* **3**(Suppl.): 271-273.

Round, P.D. (1988). *Resident Forest Birds in Thailand: their Status and Conservation*. ICBP Monograph **2**, Cambridge.

Rounds, W.D. (1958). Pileated Woodpecker roosting in a barn. *Maine Field Nat.* **13**: 22.

Rowley, J.S. (1966). *Breeding Records of Birds of the Sierra Madre del Sur, Oaxaca, Mexico*. Proceedings of the Western Foundation of Vertebrate Zoology **1(3)**. 97 pp.

Rowley, J.S. (1984). *Breeding Records of Land Birds in Oaxaca, Mexico*. Proceedings of the Western Foundation of Vertebrate Zoology **2(3)**. 147 pp.

Roze, V. (1987). [Tengmalm's Owl and Black Woodpecker inhabiting holes in the same tree]. *Putni Daba* **1**: 98. In Latvian.

Rozendaal, F.G. (1989). Annotated checklist of the birds of the Dumoga-Bone National Park, North Sulawesi. *Kukila* **4(3-4)**: 85-108.

Rudat, V., Kühlke, D., Meyer, W. & Wiesner, J. (1979). Zur Nistökologie von Schwarzspecht (*Dryocopus martius* L.), Rauhfusskauz (*Aegolius funereus* L.) und Hobltaube (*Columba aenas* L.). *Zool. Jb. Syst.* **106**: 295-310.

Rudolph, D.C. & Conner, R.N. (1991). Cavity tree selection by Red-cockaded Woodpeckers in relation to tree age. *Wilson Bull.* **103(3)**: 458-467.

Rudolph, D.C. & Conner, R.N. (1994). Forest fragmentation and Red-cockaded Woodpecker population: an analysis at intermediate scale. *J. Field Orn.* **65(3)**: 365-375. In English with Spanish summary.

Rudolph, D.C. & Conner, R.N. (1995). The impact of southern pine beetle induced mortality on Red-cockaded Woodpecker cavity trees. Pp. 208-213 in: Kulhavy *et al.* (1995).

Rudolph, D.C., Conner, R.N., Carrie, D.K. & Schaefer, R.R. (1992). Experimental reintroduction of Red-cockaded Woodpeckers. *Auk* **109(4)**: 914-916.

Rudolph, D.C., Conner, R.N. & Schaefer, R.R. (1991). Yellow-bellied Sapsuckers feeding at Red-cockaded Woodpecker resin wells. *Wilson Bull.* **103(1)**: 122-123.

Rudolph, D.C., Conner, R.N. & Schaefer, R.R. (1995). Red-cockaded Woodpecker detection of red heart infection. Pp. 338-342 in: Kulhavy *et al.* (1995).

Rudolph, D.C., Conner, R.N. & Turner, J. (1990). Competition for Red-cockaded Woodpecker roost and nest cavities: effects of resin age and entrance diameter. *Wilson Bull.* **102(1)**: 23-36.

Rudolph, D.C., Kyle, H. & Conner, R.N. (1990). Red-cockaded Woodpeckers vs. rat snakes: the effectiveness of the resin barrier. *Wilson Bull.* **102(1)**: 14-22.

Ruedi, M. (1983). Querelle entre deux femelles de Pic vert, *Picus viridis*. *Nos Oiseaux* **37(2)**: 80-81.

Ruge, K. (1968). Zur Biologie des Dreizehenspechts *Picoides tridactylus* L. Part I. [The biology of Three-toed Woodpeckers *Picoides tridactylus* L. Part I]. *Orn. Beob.* **65(3)**: 109-124. In German with English summary.

Ruge, K. (1969a). Zur Biologie des Dreizehenspechts *Picoides tridactylus* L. Part II. [The biology of Three-toed Woodpeckers *Picoides tridactylus* L. Part II]. *Orn. Beob.* **66(2)**: 42-54. In German with English summary.

Ruge, K. (1969b). Beobachtungen am Blutspecht *Dendrocopos syriacus* im Burgenland. *Vogelwelt* **90**: 201-223.

Ruge, K. (1970). Die Lautäusserungen des Blutspechtes, *Dendrocopos syriacus*. *J. Orn.* **11**: 412-419.

Ruge, K. (1971a). Beobachtungen am Wendehals *Jynx torquilla*. *Orn. Beob.* **68**: 9-33.

Ruge, K. (1971b). Beobachtungen am Mittelspecht (*Dendrocopos medius*) im Naturschutzgebiet Favoritepark. *Baden-Württemberg, Veröff. Landess. Naturschutz Landschaft* **39**: 143-155.

Ruge, K. (1971c). Zur Biologie des Dreizehenspechts *Picoides tridactylus* L. Part 3. Beobachtungen während der Brutzeit. *Orn. Beob.* **68**: 256-271.

Ruge, K. (1973). Über das Ringeln der Spechte ausserhalb der subalpinen Nadelwälder. *Orn. Beob.* **70**: 173-179.

Ruge, K. (1974). Zur Biologie des Dreizehenspechts *Picoides tridactylus* L. Part 4. Brutbiologische und Brutökologische daten aus der Schweiz. [On the biology of the Three-toed Woodpecker *Picoides tridactylus*. Part 4. Breeding biology and breeding ecology data for Switzerland]. *Orn. Beob.* **71(5-6)**: 303-311. In German with English summary.

Ruge, K. (1975). Die Lautäusserungen adulter Dreizehenspechte *Picoides tridactylus* und ihre Bedeutung bei der Beurteilung der systematischen Stellung von *Picoides*. [The vocalization of adult Three-toed Woodpeckers *Picoides tridactylus* and its importance in the determination of the systematic position of *Picoides*]. *Orn. Beob.* **72(2)**: 75-82. In German with English summary.

Ruge, K. (1982). *Picus canus* - Grauspecht. Pp. 202-203 in: Schifferli, A., Géroudet, P. & Winkler, R. eds. (1982). *Verbreitungsatlas der Brutvögel der Schweitz*. Schweizerische Vogelwarte, Sempach.

Ruge, K. (1993). Schutz für einheimische Spechtsarten. Folgerungen des Artenschutzsymposiums in Nürtingen. *Beih. Veröff. Naturschutz und Landschaftspflege Bad. -Württ.* **67**: 199-202.

Ruge, K. & Bretzendorfer, F. (1981). Biotopstrukturen und Siedlungsdichte beim Schwartzspecht (*Dryocopus martius*). *Beih. Veröff. Naturschutz Landschaftspflege Bad. -Württ.* **20**: 37-48.

Ruge, K. & Weber, W. (1974a). Brutgebiet des Dreizehenspechts (*Picoides tridactylus*) im Eisenerzer Raum, Steiermark. *Anz. Orn. Ges. Bayern* **13**: 300-304.

Ruge, K. & Weber, W. (1974b). Biotopwahl und Nahrungserwerb beim Weissrückenspecht (*Dendrocopos leucotos*) in den Alpen. *Vogelwelt* **95**: 138-147.

de Ruiter, M. (1997). Breeding the Red-and-yellow Barbet: a success story? *Int. Zoo News* **44(3)**: 144-145.

de Ruiter, M. (1999). Breeding Toco Toucans in The Netherlands. *Int. Zoo News* **46(6)**: 353-355.

Rumsey, R.L. (1968). Capture and care of Pileated and Red-headed Woodpeckers. *Bird-Banding* **39(4)**: 313-316.

Rumsey, R.L. (1970). Woodpecker nest failures in creosoted utility poles. *Auk* **87(2)**: 367-369.

Rumsey, R.L. (1973). *Woodpecker Damage to Wooden Utility Poles*. PhD thesis, Louisiana State University, Baton Rouge, Louisiana.

Rundel, R. (1975). Toucans, tunnelling and reproductive success. *AFA Watchbird* **2(2)**: 1-2.

Ruschi, A. (1979). *Aves do Brasil*. Editora Rios, São Paulo.

Rushforth, D. (1999). Crested Barbet kills Lesser Honeyguide. *Honeyguide* **45**: 142-143.

Russell, S.M. (1964). *A Distributional Study of the Birds of British Honduras*. Ornithological Monographs **1**. 96 pp.

Russell, W.C. (1947). Mountain Chickadees feeding young Williamson's Sapsuckers. *Condor* **49(2)**: 83.

Rutgers, A. & Norris, K.A. eds. (1977). *Encyclopaedia of Aviculture*. Vol. 3. Blandford Press, London.

Rutten, M.G. (1934). Observations on Cuban birds. *Ardea* **23**: 109-126.

Ryan, P. (2001). The world of Abyssinian endemics. *Africa. Birds & Birding* **6(5)**: 38-45.

Saab, V.A. & Dudley, J.G. (1998). *Responses of Cavity-nesting Birds to Stand-replacement Fire and Salvage Logging in Ponderosa Pine / Douglas-fir Forests of Southwestern Idaho*. Research Paper **RMRS-11**. US Forest Service, Boise, Idaho.

Saab, V.A. & Vierling, K.T. (2001). Reproductive success of Lewis's Woodpecker in burned pine and cottonwood riparian forests. *Condor* **103(3)**: 491-501.

Saari, L. & Mikusinski, G. (1996). Tikkojen kannanvaihtelusta lounaissaaristossa. [Population fluctuations of woodpecker species on the Baltic island of Aasla, SW Finland]. *Ornis Fenn.* **73(4)**: 168-178. In Finnish with English summary.

Saenz, D., Conner, R.N., Shackelford, C.E. & Rudolph, D.C. (1998). Pileated Woodpecker damage to Red-cockaded Woodpecker cavity trees in eastern Texas. *Wilson Bull.* **110(3)**: 362-367.

Sagot, F. (1998). Nuevas especies en el país en relación a la Lista de las Aves de Armonía 1995. Pp. 105-112 in: Sagot & Guerrero (1998).

Sagot, F. & Guerrero, J. eds. (1998). *Actas del IV Encuentro Boliviano para la Conservación de las Aves 25 a 27 de Octubre de 1997, Tarija, Bolivia*. Aves y Conservación en Bolivia **1**, Santa Cruz, Bolivia.

Saha, B.C. & Dasgupta, J.M. (1992). *Birds of Goa. Records of the Zoological Survey of India*. Zoological Survey of India Occasional Paper **143**. 56 pp.

Saibene, C.A., Castelino, M.A., Rey, N.R., Herrera, J. & Calo, J. (1996). *Inventario de las Aves del Parque Nacional "Iguazú", Misiones, Argentina*. Literature of Latin America, Buenos Aires.

Salaman, P.G.W. ed. (1994). *Surveys and Conservation of Biodiversity in the Chocó, South-west Colombia*. BirdLife Study Report **61**. BirdLife International, Cambridge.

Salaman, P.G.W., Donegan, T.M. & Cuervo, A.M. (1999). Ornithological surveys in Serranía de los Churumbelos, southern Colombia. *Cotinga* **12**: 29-39.

Salaman, P.G.W., Stiles, F.G., Bohórquez, C.I., Álvarez, R.M., Donegan, T.M., & Cuervo, A.M. (2002). New and noteworthy bird records from the Andean East Slope of Colombia. *Caldasia* **24**.

Salewski, V. (2000). The birds of Comoé National Park, Ivory Coast. *Malimbus* **22(2)**: 55-76.

Salmon, L. (1972). Jamaican Woodpecker. *Gosse Bird Club Broadsheet* **18**: 23.

Salmon, L. (1974). Fernandina's Flicker. *Gosse Bird Club Broadsheet* **22**: 25.

Salmon, L. (1990). Jamaican Woodpecker. *Gosse Bird Club Broadsheet* **55**: 21.

Salmon, L. (1991). Jamaican Woodpecker. *Gosse Bird Club Broadsheet* **57**: 23.

Salomonsen, F. (1947). En hybrid mellem Grønspaette (*Picus v. viridis* L.) og Graaspaete (*Picus c. canus* Gm.). *Vår Fågelvärld* **6**: 141-144.

Salomonsen, F. (1952). Systematic notes on some Philippine birds. *Vidensk. Medd. Dan. Nauturhist. Foren.* **114**: 341-364.

Salomonsen, F. (1953). Miscellaneous notes on Philippine birds. *Vidensk. Medd. Dan. Nauturhist. Foren.* **115**: 205-281.

Salvadori, T. (1895). Viaggio del dott. Alfredo Borelli nella Repubblica Argentina e nel Paraguay. *Bol. Mus. Zool. Anat. Comp. Univ. Torino* **10(208)**: 1-24.

Salvin, O. & Godman, F.D. (1888-1904). *Biología Centrali-Americana. Aves*. Published privately.

Samedy, J.P., Mitchell, G.C., Engeman, R.M., Bornstein, M.S. & Groninger, N.P. (1986). Preharvest corn losses to vertebrate pests in Haiti. *An. Mus. Hist. Nat. Valparaiso* **17**: 129-132.

Sande, E. (2000). Understorey bird species diversity and abundance in three forest types of Semuliki National Park, Uganda. Proceedings of the Ninth Pan-African Ornithological Congress, Accra, Ghana, 1-7 December 1996. *Ostrich* **71(1&2)**: 64-68.

Sankaran, R. & Vijayan, L. (1993). The avifauna of the Andaman and Nicobar Islands: a review and the current scenario. Pp. 255-274 in: Verghese, A., Sridhar, S. & Chakravarthy, A.K. eds. (1993). *Bird Conservation Strategies for the Nineties and Beyond*. Ornithological Society of India, Bangalore.

Santana, C.E. & Milligan, B.G. (1984). Behavior of toucanets, bellbirds, and quetzals feeding on lauraceous fruits. *Biotropica* **16(2)**: 152-154.

Santana, C.E., Moermond, T.C. & Denslow, J.S. (1986). Fruit selection in the Collared Aracari (*Pteroglossus torquatus*) and the Slaty-tailed Trogon (*Trogon massena*): two birds with contrasting foraging modes. *Brenesia* **25-26**: 279-295.

Santharam, V. (1997). Display behaviour in Woodpeckers. *Newsl. Birdwatchers* **37(6)**: 98-99.

Santharam, V. (1998a). Nest usurpation in woodpeckers. *J. Bombay Nat. Hist. Soc.* **95(2)**: 344-345.

Santharam, V. (1998b). Woodpeckers feeding on *Cassia* pods. *J. Bombay Nat. Hist. Soc.* **95(3)**: 505-506.

Santharam, V. (1998c). Drumming frequency in woodpeckers. *J. Bombay Nat. Hist. Soc.* **95(3)**: 506-507.

Santharam, V. (1999a). Apartment nest of the Pygmy Woodpecker *Picoides nanus*. *J. Bombay Nat. Hist. Soc.* **96(1)**: 143.

Santharam, V. (1999b). Frugivory by the Great Black Woodpecker *Dryocopus javensis*. *J. Bombay Nat. Hist. Soc.* **96(2)**: 319.

Sargeant, D.E. (1993). *Gabon. A Birders Guide to Gabon, West Africa*. Published privately, Norfolk, UK.

Sargeant, D.E. (1994). *The Birds of Junglaven, Venezuela*. Published privately, Norfolk, UK.

Sargeant, D.E. (1997). *Java and Bali. A Birder's Guide to Java and Bali*. Published privately, Norfolk, UK.

Sargeant, D.E. & Wall, J. (1996). *Bahia. A Birder's Guide to Bahia, NE Brazil*. Published privately, Norfolk, UK.

Sassi, M. (1939). Die Vögel der Österreichischen Costa-Rica-Expedition (Zweiter Teil). *Temminckia* **4**: 135-222.

Saul, L.J. (1983). Red-bellied Woodpecker responses to accipiters. *Wilson Bull.* **95(3)**: 490-491.

Saul, L.J. & Wassmer, D.A. (1983). Red-bellied Woodpecker roosting outside of cavities. *Florida Field Nat.* **11(3)**: 50-51.

Sautereau, B. & Courtillot, J. (1961). Au nid du Pic noir *Dryocopus martius* dans l'Yonne. *Alauda* **29(1)**: 59-63.

Sauvage, A. & Rodwell, S.P. (1998). Notable observations of birds in Senegal (excluding Parc National des Oiseaux du Djoudj), 1984-1994. *Malimbus* **20(2)**: 75-122.

Sauvage, A., Rumsey, S. & Rodwell, S. (1998). Recurrence of Palearctic birds in the lower Senegal river valley. *Malimbus* **20(1)**: 33-53.

Savignac, C., Desrochers, A. & Huot, J. (2000). Habitat use by Pileated Woodpeckers at two spatial scales in eastern Canada. *Can. J. Zool.* **78(2)**: 219-225.

Scebba, S. & Lövei, G.L. (1985). Winter recurrence, weights and wing lengths of Wrynecks *Jynx torquilla* on a southern Italian island. *Ringing & Migration* **6(2)**: 83-86.

Schaefer, R.R. (1996). *Red-cockaded Woodpecker Reproduction and Provisioning of Nestlings in Relation to Habitat*. MSc thesis, Stephen F. Austin State University, Nacogdoches, Texas.

Schäfer, E. & Phelps, W.H. (1954). *Las Aves del Parque Nacional Henri Pittier (Rancho Grande) y sus Funciones Ecológicas*. Boletín de la Sociedad Venezolana de Ciencias Naturales **16(83)**. 165 pp.

Schaffer, W. (1997). Red-headed Woodpecker: sighting north of Hinton, Alberta. *Alberta Nat.* **27(4)**: 69.

Schaldach, W.J. (1963). *The Avifauna of Colima and Adjacent Jalisco, Mexico*. Proceedings of the Western Foundation of Vertebrate Zoology **1(1)**. 100 pp.

Schandy, T. (1981). Grýnnspett kastet ut Spettmeis. [Green Woodpeckers throw out nuthatches]. *Vår Fuglefauna* **4(3)**: 171. In Norwegian with English summary.

Schardien, B.J. & Jackson, J.A. (1978). Extensive ground foraging by Pileated Woodpeckers in recently burned pine forests. *Miss. Kite* **8(1)**: 7-9.

Schels, C. & Lavoyer, N. (1987). *Balcad Nature Reserve Birds*. Somali Ecological Reserve, Mogadishu.

Schemnitz, S.D. (1964). Nesting association of Pileated Woodpecker and Yellow-shafted Flicker in a utility pole. *Wilson Bull.* **76(1)**: 95.

Schepps, J., Lohr, S. & Martin, T.E. (1999). Does tree hardness influence nest-tree selection by primary cavity nesters? *Auk* **116(3)**: 658-665.

Scherer-Neto, P. (1985). *Lista de Aves do Estado de Paraná*. Prefeitura Municipal de Curitiba, Curitiba, Brazil.

Scherer-Neto, P. & Straube, F.C. (1995). *Aves do Paraná (Historia, Lista Anotada e Bibliografia)*. Published privately, Curitiba, Brazil.

Scherner, E.R. (1989). Wendehals und Populationsbiologie - der "Vogel des Jahres 1988" und die Pflicht zur Forschung. Pp. 24-39 in: *Der Wendehals-Vogel des Jahres 1988*. Seminar Pappenheim Februar 1988, ANL Laufener Seminarbeitraege 3/89.

Scherzinger, W. (1972). Beobachtungen am Dreizehenspecht (*Picoides tridactylus*) im Gebiet des Nationalparks Bayerischer Wald. *Orn. Mitt.* **24(10)**: 207-210.

Scherzinger, W. (1982). *Die Spechte im Nationalpark Bayerischer Wald*. Schriftenreihe des Bayerischen Staatsministeriums für Ernährung Landwirtschaft und Forsten **9**, Passau. 119 pp.

Scherzinger, W. (1989). Der Wendehals (*Jynx torquilla*) - ein Aussenseiter unter den Spechten. Pp. 47-53 in: *Der Wendehals-Vogel des Jahres 1988*. Seminar Pappenheim Februar 1988, ANL Laufener Seminarbeitraege 3/89.

Schifter, H. (1962). Ein seltener Bartvögel aus Südamerika. *Gefiederte Welt* **86**: 47-48.
Schifter, H. (1967). Weitere Angaben über Bartvögel (Capitonidae). *Gefiederte Welt* **91**: 84-87.
Schifter, H. (1996). Vögel aus dem Tiergarten Schönbrunn im Naturhistorische Museum Wien (III). *Zool. Garten* **66**: 13-52.
Schifter, H. (1998). Zur Lebensdauer von Tukanen (Ramphastidae) in Menschenhand. *Zool. Garten* **68(4)**: 261.
Schifter, H. (2000). A further specimen of the Fine-barred Piculet (*Picumnus subtilis*) in the Museum of Natural History, Vienna, Austria. *Orn. Neotropical* **11(3)**: 247-248.
Schlegel, H. (1863). *Revue Méthodique et Critique des Collections Déposées dans cet Établissement*. Muséum d'Histoire Naturelle des Pays-Bas Monograph **15**. Buccones. E.J. Brill, Leiden, The Netherlands.
Schlegel, J. & Schlegel, S. (1971). Beobachtungen der Balz und Kopulation beim Kleinspecht (*Dendrocopos minor*). *Beitr. Vogelkd.* **17**: 251-253.
Schlenker, H. (2000). Notizen zur Haltung von Tukanen und Arassaris in der "Fundación Rescate Fauna Silvestre" in Ecuador. *Gefiederte Welt* **124(4)**: 132-134.
Schlichter, L. (1978). Winter predation by Black-capped Chickadees and Downy Woodpeckers on inhabitants of the goldenrod ball gall. *Can. Field Nat.* **92(1)**: 71-74.
Schmid, H. (1993). Grün-, Grau- und Kleinspecht (*Picus viridis*, *Picus canus*, *Dendrocopos minor*) in der Schweiz: aktuelle Verbreitung und Bestandssituation. [The status of Green, Grey-headed and Lesser Spotted Woodpecker in Switzerland]. *Orn. Beob.* **90(3)**: 201-212. In German with English and French summary.
Schmidl, D. (1982). *The Birds of the Serengeti National Park, Tanzania. An Annotated Check-list*. BOU Check-list **5**. British Ornithologists' Union, London.
Schmidt, R.K. (1961). Knysna Woodpecker *Campethera notata* at Breede River mouth (district of Swellendam). *Ostrich* **32**: 182.
Schmidtuz, C., Güller, R., Di Santo, H., Chévez, R., Tahmazian, R. & Quinteros, A. (2001). Nuevos registros para Misiones (Argentina) de la Viudita Coluda (*Muscipipra vetula*) y el Chacurú Grande (*Notarchus macrorhynchus*). *Nuestras Aves* **41**: 4.
Schmitt, C.G., Schmitt, D.C. & Remsen, J.V. (1997). Birds of the Tambo area, an arid valley in the Bolivian Andes. Pp. 701-716 in: Remsen (1997).
Schmitt, E.C. & Lyvere, P.A. (1980). Breeding of the Red and Yellow Barbet at the Denver zoological gardens. *Avicult. Mag.* **86(3)**: 128-130.
Schmitz, L. (1993). Distribution et habitat du Pic mar (*Dendrocopos medius*) en Belgique. *Aves* **30**: 145-166.
Schneider, W. (1979). Revierkampf beim Grünspecht (*Picus v. viridis*). *Beitr. Vogelkd.* **25(6)**: 364.
Scholte, P., de Kort, S. & van Weerd, M. (1999). The birds of the Waza-Logone Area, Far North Province, Cameroon. *Malimbus* **21(1)**: 16-50.
Schomburgk, R. (1848). *Reisen im Britisch-Guinea in den Jahren 1840-1844*. Vol. 3. Verlagsbuchhandlung von J.J. Weber, Leipzig, Germany.
Schönwetter, M. (1967). *Handbuch der Oologie*. Vol. 1. Nonpasseres. Akademie-Verlag, Berlin.
Schouteden, H. (1962). *La Faune Ornithologique des Districts de la Mongala et de l'Ubangi*. Museé Royal de l'Afrique Centrale, Documentation Zoologique **3**.
Schouteden, H. (1966). *La Faune Ornithologique de Rwanda*. Museé Royal de l'Afrique Centrale, Documentation Zoologique **10**. 130 pp.
Schroeder, D. (1999). Black-spotted Barbet: *Capito niger*. *ASA Avic. Bull.* **28(2)**: 8.
Schroeder, R.L. (1983). *Habitat Suitability Index Models: Downy Woodpecker*. Report **FWS/OBS-82/10.38**. US Fish & Wildlife Service.
Schubart, O., Aguirre, A.C. & Sick, H. (1965). *Contribuição para o Conhecimento da Alimentação das Aves Brasileiras*. Arquivos de Zoologia São Paulo **12**. 154 pp.
Schubert, W. (1969). Neue Beobachtungen zum Vorkommen des Weissrückenspechtes (*Dendrocopos leucotos*) in den Bayerischen Alpen. *Anz. Orn. Ges. Bayern* **8**: 515-517.
Schubert, W. (1978). Verbreitung, Bestandgrosse und Daten zur Brutbiologie des Mittelspechts (*Dendrocopos medius*) im Raumzwischen Stuttgart, Schonbuch und Schwarzwald. *Anz. Orn. Ges. Bayern* **17**: 125-131.
Schuchmann, K.L. ed. (1985). *Proceedings of the International Symposium of African Vertebrates*. Forschungsinstitut und Museum Alexander Koenig, Bonn.
Schulenberg, T.S. & Awbrey, K. (1997). eds. *The Cordillera del Condor Region of Ecuador and Peru: a Biological Assessment*. Rapid Assessment Program Working Papers **7**. Conservation International, Washington, D.C.
Schulenberg, T.S. & Parker, T.A. (1997). Notes on the Yellow-browed Toucanet *Aulacorhynchus hullagae*. Pp. 717-720 in: Remsen (1997).
Schulenberg, T.S. & Remsen, J.V. (1982). Eleven bird species new to Bolivia. *Bull. Brit. Orn. Club* **102(2)**: 52-57.
Schultz, A. (1991). Scaly-throated Honeyguide parasitises Knysna Woodpeckers' nest. *Bee-eater* **42(2)**: 27.
Schürer, U. (1985). Die Zucht des Fischertukans (*Ramphastos sulfuratus*) in Zoologischen Garten Wuppertal. [The breeding of the Sulphur-breasted Toucan (*Ramphastos sulfuratus*) at Wuppertal Zoo]. *Z. Köln. Zoo* **28(2)**: 87-93.
Schürer, U. (1987). Die Zucht des Reisentukans (*Ramphastos toco*) im Zoologischen Garten Wuppertal. [Breeding and rearing of the Toco Toucan (*Ramphastos toco*) in the Wuppertal Zoo]. *Z. Köln. Zoo* **30(3)**: 97-99.
Schütter, F. (2000). Tukane - erfolgreich gehalten und gezüchtet. *Gefiederte Welt* **124(3)**: 78-82.
Schwab, R.G. & Monnie, J.B. (1959). Strife over a nesting site between Downy and Red-headed Woodpeckers. *Wilson Bull.* **71(2)**: 190-191.
Schwartz, P. (1972). On the taxonomic rank of the Yellow-billed Toucanet (*Aulacorhynchus calorhynchus*). *Bol. Soc. Venezolana Cienc. Nat.* **29**: 459-476.
Schwartz, P. (1977). Some clarifications about *Ramphastos "aurantiirostris"*. *Auk* **94(4)**: 775-777.
Sclater, P.L. (1862). *Catalogue of a Collection of American Birds Belonging to Phillip Lutley Sclater*. Trubner, London.
Sclater, P.L. (1879-1882). *A Monograph of the Jacamars and Puff-birds of the Families Galbulidae and Bucconidae*. 4 Vols. R.H. Porter, London.
Sclater, P.L. (1891). Family Bucconidae. Pp. 178-208 in: *Catalogue of the Birds in the British Museum*. Vol. 19. Trustees of the British Museum, London.
Sclater, P.L. & Salvin, O. (1866). Catalogue of birds collected by Mr. E. Bartlett on the River Ucayali, eastern Peru, with notes and descriptions of new species. *Proc. Zool. Soc. London* **1866**: 175-201.
Sclater, P.L. & Salvin, O. (1873). On the birds of eastern Peru with notes on the habits of the birds (by Edward Bartlett). *Proc. Zool. Soc. London* **1873**: 252-311.
Sclater, P.L. & Salvin, O. (1879). On birds collected in Bolivia by Mr. C. Buckley. *Proc. Zool. Soc. London* **1879**: 588-645.
Scott, D.A. & Brooke, M. de L. (1985). The endangered avifauna of southeastern Brazil: a report on the BOU/WWF expeditions of 1980/81 and 1981/82. Pp. 115-139 in: Diamond & Lovejoy (1985).
Scott, D.M., Ankney, C.D. & Jarosch, C.H. (1976). Sapsucker hybridization in British Columbia: changes in 25 years. *Condor* **78(2)**: 253-257.
Scott, O.K. (1993). *A Birder's Guide to Wyoming*. American Birding Association, Colorado Springs, Colorado.
Seagle, S.W., Lancia, R.A., Adams, D.A. & Lennartz, M.R. (1987). A multivariate analysis of rangewide Red-cockaded Woodpecker habitat. *J. Environm. Manage.* **25(1)**: 45-56.
Seddon, N., Capper, D.R., Ekstrom, J.M., Isherwood, I.S., Muna, R., Pople, R.G., Tarimo, E. & Timothy, J. (1996). Project Mount Nilo '95 discoveries in the East Usambara and Nguu Mountains, northern Tanzania. *Bull. African Bird Club* **3(2)**: 91-95.
Sedgwick, J.A. & Knopf, F.L. (1990). Habitat relationships and nest site characteristics of cavity-nesting birds in cottonwood floodplains. *J. Wildl. Manage.* **54(1)**: 112-124.
Seebohm, H. (1895). *Classification of Birds. An Attempt to Diagnose the Subclasses, Orders, Suborders, and some of the Families of Existing Birds*. R.H. Porter, London.
Seibels, R.E. (1979). Breeding the Toco Toucan. *AFA Watchbird* **6**: 30-33.
Seibt, U. & Wickler, W. (1977). Duettieren als Revieranzeige bei Voegeln. [Duetting song as territory display in birds]. *Z. Tierpsychol.* **43(2)**: 180-187. In German with English summary.
Seilern, J. von (1934). Ornithologische Miszellen. *Ann. Naturhist. Mus. Wien* **47**: 33-41.
Selander, R.K. (1965). Sexual dimorphism in relation to foraging behavior in the Hairy Woodpecker. *Wilson Bull.* **77(4)**: 416.
Selander, R.K. (1966). Sexual dimorphism and differential niche utilization in birds. *Condor* **68(2)**: 113-151.
Selander, R.K. & Giller, D.R. (1959). Interspecific relations of woodpeckers in Texas. *Wilson Bull.* **71(2)**: 106-124.
Selander, R.K. & Giller, D.R. (1963). Species limits in the woodpecker genus *Centurus* (Aves). *Bull. Amer. Mus. Nat. Hist.* **124(6)**: 217-273.
Self, T. (1980). On winter food of Common Flicker in central Oklahoma. *Bull. Oklahoma Orn. Soc.* **13(4)**: 29-31.
Senosian, A. (1977). Observaciones del Pico dorsiblanco (*Dendrocopos leucotos*) en el Pirineo Navarro y primera nidificación comprobada en la Península Ibérica. *Ardeola* **24**: 236-242.
Serle, W. (1950). A contribution to the ornithology of the British Cameroons. *Ibis* **92(3)**: 343-376.
Serle, W. (1954). A second contribution to the ornithology of the British Cameroons. *Ibis* **96(1)**: 47-80.
Serle, W. (1957). A contribution to the ornithology of the eastern region of Nigeria. *Ibis* **99(3)**: 371-418; **99(4)**: 628-685.
Serle, W. (1959). Note on the immature plumage of the honey-guide *Melignomon zenkeri* Reichenow. *Bull. Brit. Orn. Club* **79(4)**: 65.
Serle, W. (1964). The lower altitudinal limit of the montane forest birds of the Cameroon Mountain, West Africa. *Bull. Brit. Orn. Club* **84(5)**: 87-91.
Serle, W. (1965). A third contribution to the ornithology of the British Cameroons. *Ibis* **107(1)**: 60-94.
Sermet, E. (1983). Le Pigeon colombin, *Columba oenas*, et le Pic vert, *Picus viridis*, victimes de la martre des pins, *Martes martes*. *Nos Oiseaux* **37(2)**: 79-80.
Seth-Smith, D. (1912). Bird notes from the Zoological Gardens. *Avicult. Mag.* **3(4)**: 124-125.
Seth-Smith, D. (1929). The Fire-tufted Barbet *Psilopogon pyrolophus*. *Avicult. Mag.* **35**: 175.
Setterington, M.A., Thompson, I.D. & Montevecchi, W.A. (2000). Woodpecker abundance and habitat use in mature balsam fir forests in Newfoundland. *J. Wildl. Manage.* **64(2)**: 335-345.
Severinghaus, S.R. & Blackshaw, K.T. (1976). *A New Guide to the Birds of Taiwan*. Mei Ya Publications Inc., Taipei.
Seveyka, J. (1996). Pecking in an arc or a line: what kinematic strategies do woodpeckers employ during excavation? *Amer. Zool.* **36(5)**: 113A. (Abstract).
Shackelford, C.E. & Conner, R.N. (1997). Woodpecker abundance and habitat use in three forest types in eastern Texas. *Wilson Bull.* **109(4)**: 614-629.
Shackelford, C.E., Brown, R.E. & Conner, R.N. (2000). Red-bellied Woodpecker (*Melanerpes carolinus*). No. **500** in: Poole, A.F. & Gill, F.B. eds. (2000). *The Birds of North America*. Vol. 13. Academy of Natural Sciences & American Ornithologists' Union, Philadelphia & Washington, D.C.
Shadick, S.J. (1980). Saskatchewan breeding records for Red Crossbill, Orchard Oriole and Red-headed Woodpecker. *Blue Jay* **38(4)**: 247-249.
Shanahan, D. (1993). Winter roosting behaviour of the Three-toed Woodpecker. *Ontario Birds* **11**: 71-74.
Shankar Raman, T.R. (2001). Effect of slah-and-burn shifting cultivation on rainforest birds in Mizoram, northeast India. *Conserv. Biol.* **15(3)**: 685-698.
Shanley, E. & Shanley, A.F. (1978). Interspecific aggression between a Carolina Chickadee and a Downy Woodpecker. *Bull. Texas Orn. Soc.* **11(1)**: 23-25.
Shannon, P.W. (1991). Breeding biology and captive husbandry of the Plate-billed Mountain Toucan (*Andigena laminirostris*). Pp. 188-195 in: *Proc. Amer. Assoc. Zool. Parks Aquariums Reg. Conf.*
Sharpe, C.J., Ascanio, D. & Rodríguez, G.A. (2001). Further range extensions and noteworthy records for Venezuelan birds. *Bull. Brit. Orn. Club* **121(1)**: 50-62.
Shaw, J.W. (1951). Starlings drive Red-headed Woodpecker from nests. *Migrant* **22**: 43.
Shelley, L.O. (1933). Some notes on the Hairy Woodpecker. *Bird-Banding* **4**: 204-205.
Shelley, L.O. (1935). Flickers attacked by Starlings. *Auk* **52(1)**: 93.
Sherbourne, P. (1996). Breeding the Toucan Barbet at the Tropical Bird Gardens, Rode. *Avicult. Mag.* **102(1)**: 6-7.
Sherman, A.R. (1910). At the sign of the Northern Flicker. *Wilson Bull.* **22**: 133-171.
Sherrill, D.M. & Case, V.M. (1980). Winter home ranges of four clans of Red-cockaded Woodpeckers in the Carolina Sandhills. *Wilson Bull.* **92(3)**: 369-375.
Sherry, T.W. (1983a). *Galbula ruficauda*. Pp. 579-581 in: Janzen (1983).
Sherry, T.W. (1983b). *Monasa morphoeus*. Pp. 587-589 in: Janzen (1983).
Sherry, T.W. & McDade, L.A. (1982). Prey selection and handling in two neotropical hover-gleaning birds. *Ecology* **63(4)**: 1016-1028.
Sherwood, W.E. (1927). Feeding habits of Lewis Woodpecker. *Condor* **29(3)**: 171.
Shields, M.A. (1988). A Red-shafted x Yellow-shafted Flicker intergrade in Carteret County, N.C. *Chat* **52(4)**: 78-79.
Shirihai, H. (1996). *The Birds of Israel*. Academic Press, London.
Shirihai, H. & Francis, J. (1999). Endemic birds of Ethiopia. *Alula* **5(1)**: 2-15.
Short, L.L. (1965a). Hybridization in the flickers (*Colaptes*) of North America. *Bull. Amer. Mus. Nat. Hist.* **129**: 307-428.
Short, L.L. (1965b). Variation in West Indian flickers (Aves, *Colaptes*). *Bull. Florida State Mus.* **10(1)**: 1-42.
Short, L.L. (1965c). Specimens of Nuttall Woodpecker from Oregon. *Condor* **67(3)**: 269-270.
Short, L.L. (1965d). A melanistic Pileated Woodpecker specimen from Georgia. *Wilson Bull.* **77(4)**: 404-405.
Short, L.L. (1967). Variation in Central American flickers. *Wilson Bull.* **79(1)**: 5-21.
Short, L.L. (1968). Variation of Ladder-backed Woodpeckers in southwestern North America. *Proc. Biol. Soc. Washington* **81**: 1-10.
Short, L.L. (1969a). Taxonomic aspects of avian hybridization. *Auk* **86(1)**: 84-105.
Short, L.L. (1969b). Foraging association of Green-barred Flickers and Campo Flickers in Argentina. *Wilson Bull.* **81(4)**: 468-470.
Short, L.L. (1970a). The habits and relationships of the Magellanic Woodpecker. *Wilson Bull.* **82(2)**: 115-129.
Short, L.L. (1970b). Reversed sexual dimorphism in tail length and foraging differences in woodpeckers. *Bird-Banding* **41(2)**: 85-92.
Short, L.L. (1970c). Notes on the habits of some Argentine and Peruvian woodpeckers (Aves, Picidae). *Amer. Mus. Novit.* **2413**: 1-37.
Short, L.L. (1971a). Notes on the habits of Bennett's Woodpecker in Kruger Park. *Ostrich* **42**: 71-72.
Short, L.L. (1971b). Notes on South African woodpeckers. *Ostrich* **42**: 89-98.
Short, L.L. (1971c). *The Systematics and Behavior of some North American Woodpeckers, Genus* Picoides. Bulletin of the American Museum of Natural History **145**. 119 pp.
Short, L.L. (1971d). The affinity of African with Neotropical woodpeckers. *Ostrich* **8**(Suppl.): 35-40.
Short, L.L. (1971e). The evolution of terrestrial woodpeckers. *Amer. Mus. Novit.* **2467**: 1-23.
Short, L.L. (1972a). Relationships among the four species of superspecies *Celeus elegans* (Aves, Picidae). *Amer. Mus. Novit.* **2487**: 1-26.
Short, L.L. (1972b). *Systematics and Behavior of South American Flickers (Aves,* Colaptes*)*. Bulletin of the American Museum of Natural History **149(1)**, New York. 110 pp.
Short, L.L. (1973a). Habits, relationships, and conservation of the Okinawa Woodpecker. *Wilson Bull.* **85(1)**: 5-20.
Short, L.L. (1973b). A new race of *Celeus spectabilis* from eastern Brazil. *Wilson Bull.* **85(4)**: 465-467.
Short, L.L. (1973c). Remarks on the status of *Campethera "scriptoricauda"*, and related species. *Bull. Brit. Orn. Club* **93(2)**: 72-74.
Short, L.L. (1973d). *Habits of Some Asian Woodpeckers (Aves, Picidae)*. Bulletin of the American Museum of Natural History **152(5)**. American Museum of Natural History, New York. 112 pp.
Short, L.L. (1973e). "Woodpecking" by a Red-throated Barbet. *Auk* **90(4)**: 909-910.

Short, L.L. (1974a). Habits and interactions of North American three-toed woodpeckers (*Picoides arcticus* and *tridactylus*). *Amer. Mus. Novit.* **2547**: 1-42.
Short, L.L. (1974b). The Green-barred Flicker and Golden-green Woodpecker of South America. *Living Bird* **12**: 51-54.
Short, L.L. (1974c). Relationship of *Veniliornis "cassini" chocoensis* and *V. "cassini" caquetanus* with *V. affinis*. *Auk* **91(3)**: 631-634.
Short, L.L. (1974d). Habits of three endemic West Indian woodpeckers (Aves, Picidae). *Amer. Mus. Novit.* **2549**: 1-44.
Short, L.L. (1975). *A Zoogeographical Analysis of the South American Chaco Avifauna*. Bulletin of the American Museum of Natural History **154(3)**, New York. 188 pp.
Short, L.L. (1976). Notes on a collection of birds from the Paraguayan Chaco. *Amer. Mus. Novit.* **2597**: 1-16.
Short, L.L. (1979). Burdens of the picid hole-excavating habit. *Wilson Bull.* **91(1)**: 16-28.
Short, L.L. (1980). Speciation in African woodpeckers. Pp. 1-8 in: Johnson (1980).
Short, L.L. (1982a). On the status of *Lybius (minor) macclounii*. *Bull. Brit. Orn. Club* **102(4)**: 142-148.
Short, L.L. (1982b). *Woodpeckers of the World*. Monograph Series **4**. Delaware Museum of Natural History, Greenville, Delaware.
Short, L.L. (1983). Status and conservation of woodpeckers. Page 125 in: Temple, S.A. ed. (1983). *Bird Conservation* **1**. University of Wisconsin Press, Madison, Wisconsin.
Short, L.L. (1985a). Woodpecker. Pp. 659-661 in: Campbell & Lack (1985).
Short, L.L. (1985b). Neotropical-afrotropical barbet and woodpecker radiations: a comparison. Pp. 559-574 in: Buckley *et al.* (1985).
Short, L.L. (1985c). Last chance for the Ivorybill. *Nat. Hist.* **94**: 66-68.
Short, L.L. (1988). Status and conservation of woodpeckers. Pp. 161-163 in: Jackson, J.A. ed. (1988). *Bird Conservation* **3**. University of Wisconsin Press, Madison, Wisconsin.
Short, L.L. & Bock, W.J. (1972). Possible hybrid *Jynx* is an aberrant *Jynx ruficollis*. *Bull. Brit. Orn. Club* **92(1)**: 28-31.
Short, L.L. & Horne, J.F.M. (1979). Vocal displays and some interactions of Kenyan honeyguides (Indicatoridae) with barbets (Capitonidae). *Amer. Mus. Novit.* **2684**: 1-19.
Short, L.L. & Horne, J.F.M. (1980a). Vocal and other behaviour of the Green Barbet in Kenya. *Ostrich* **51(4)**: 219-229.
Short, L.L. & Horne, J.F.M. (1980b). Ground barbets of East Africa. *Living Bird* **18**: 179-186.
Short, L.L. & Horne, J.F.M. (1981). Vocal and other behaviour of Stierling's Woodpecker *Dendropicos stierlingi*. *Scopus* **5(1)**: 5-13.
Short, L.L. & Horne, J.F.M. (1982a). Vocal and other behaviour of Kenyan Black-collared Barbets. *Ibis* **124(1)**: 27-43.
Short, L.L. & Horne, J.F.M. (1982b). "White-tailed" and White-headed Barbet in central western Kenya. *Scopus* **6(2)**: 40-41.
Short, L.L. & Horne, J.F.M. (1983a). The relationships of male Lesser Honeyguides *Indicator minor* with duetting barbet pairs. *Bull. Brit. Orn. Club* **103(1)**: 25-32.
Short, L.L. & Horne, J.F.M. (1983b). A review of duetting, sociality and speciation in some African barbets (Capitonidae). *Condor* **85(3)**: 323-332.
Short, L.L. & Horne, J.F.M. (1984a). Behavioural notes on the White-eared Barbet *Stactolaema leucotis* in Kenya. *Bull. Brit. Orn. Club* **104(2)**: 47-53.
Short, L.L. & Horne, J.F.M. (1984b). Aspects of duetting in some ground barbets. Pp. 729-744 in: Ledger, J.A. ed. (1984). *Proceedings of the V Pan-African Ornithological Congress*. Southern African Ornithological Society, Johannesburg.
Short, L.L. & Horne, J.F.M. (1984c). Nesting and roosting records of piciform birds. *Scopus* **8**: 96.
Short, L.L. & Horne, J.F.M. (1985a). Social behavior and systematics of African barbets (Aves: Capitonidae). Pp. 255-278 in: Schuchmann (1985).
Short, L.L. & Horne, J.F.M. (1985b). Behavioral notes on the nest-parasitic Afrotropical honeyguides (Aves: Indicatoridae). *Amer. Mus. Novit.* **2825**: 1-46.
Short, L.L. & Horne, J.F.M. (1986a). Duetting, sociality and speciation, with reference to barbets (Capitonidae). Page 1040 in: Ilyichev, V.D. & Gavrilov, V.M. eds. (1986). *Proceedings of the XVIII International Ornithological Congress, Moscow 1982*.
Short, L.L. & Horne, J.F.M. (1986b). The Ivorybill still lives. *Nat. Hist.* **95**: 26-28.
Short, L.L. & Horne, J.F.M. (1987a). I saw it! *Int. Wildl.* **17(2)**: 22-23.
Short, L.L. & Horne, J.F.M. (1987b). The gender of the barbet genus *Tricholaema* Verreaux & Verreaux. *Bull. Brit. Orn. Club* **107(2)**: 69.
Short, L.L. & Horne, J.F.M. (1988a). Lesser Honeyguide *Indicator minor* interactions with its barbet hosts. Pp. 65-75 in: Backhurst, G.C. ed. (1988). *Proceedings of the VI Pan-African Ornithological Congress, 1985*. VI PAOC Organizing Committee, Nairobi.
Short, L.L. & Horne, J.F.M. (1988b). Current speciation problems in Afrotropical piciforms. Pp. 2519-2527 in: Ouellet (1988).
Short, L.L. & Horne, J.F.M. (1990a). Behavioural ecology of five sympatric Afrotropical honeyguides. Pp. 319-325 in: van den Elzen, R., Schuchmann, K.L. & Schmidt-Koenig, K. eds. (1990). *Proceedings of International 100 Deutsche Ornithologische Gesellschaft Meeting, Current Topics in Avian Biology, Bonn, 1988*. Verlag der Deutschen Ornithologen-Gesellschaft, Berlin.
Short, L.L. & Horne, J.F.M. (1990b). The Ivory-billed Woodpecker - the costs of specialisation. Pp. 93-98 in: Carlson & Aulén (1990).
Short, L.L. & Horne, J.F.M. (1991). Piciform Afro-Asian zoogeography and speciation. Pp. 468-474 in: Bell *et al.* (1991).
Short, L.L. & Horne, J.F.M. (1992a). Vocalizations and avian systematics. Pp. 233-239 in: Bennun (1992).
Short, L.L. & Horne, J.F.M. (1992b). Bird family profiles. 1: Honeyguides. *Kenya Birds* **1**: 6-7.
Short, L.L. & Horne, J.F.M. (1992c). Honeyguide-host interactions. Pp. 549-552 in: Bennun (1992).
Short, L.L. & Horne, J.F.M. (2001). *Toucans, Barbets and Honeyguides*. Oxford University Press, Oxford.
Short, L.L. & Morony, J.J. (1970). A second hybrid Williamson's x Red-naped Sapsucker and an evolutionary history of sapsuckers. *Condor* **72(3)**: 310-315.
Short, L.L., Horne, J.F.M. & Chapin, J.P. (1987). *Indicator narokensis* (Jackson) is synonym of *Indicator meliphilus* (Oberholser). *Ann. Orn.* **11**: 161-168.
Short, L.L., Horne, J.F.M. & Muringo-Gichuki, C. (1990). *Annotated Check-list of the Birds of East Africa*. Proceedings of the Western Foundation of Vertebrate Zoology **4(3)**. 186 pp.
Short, L.L., Horne, J.F.M. & Vande weghe, J.P. (1983). Aberrantly plumaged barbets. *Scopus* **7(1)**: 10-14.
Shrestha, T.K. (2000). *Birds of Nepal: Field Ecology, Natural History and Conservation*. Published privately, Kathmandu, Nepal.
Shufeldt, R.W. (1900). On the osteology of the woodpeckers. *Proc. Amer. Phil. Soc.* **39**: 578-622.
Shuford, W.D. (1985). Acorn Woodpecker mutilates nestling Red-breasted Sapsuckers. *Wilson Bull.* **97(2)**: 234-236.
Shuker, K. (1993). *The Lost Ark. New and Rediscovered Animals of the 20th Century*. Harper Collins, London.
Shull, A.M. (1985). Endangered and threatened wildlife and plants: review of the status of the Ivory-billed Woodpecker. *US Fish Wildl. Serv. Federal Register* **50**: 14123-14124.
Sibley, C.G. (1956). The aftershaft in jacamars and puff-birds. *Wilson Bull.* **68(3)**: 252-253.
Sibley, C.G. (1957). The abbreviated inner primaries of nestling woodpeckers. *Auk* **74(1)**: 102-103.
Sibley, C.G. (1996). *Birds of the World*. Version 2.0. Thayer Birding Software, Naples, Florida.
Sibley, C.G. & Ahlquist, J.E. (1972). *A Comparative Study of the Egg White Proteins of Non-passerine Birds*. Peabody Museum of Natural History Yale University Bulletin **39**, New Haven, Connecticut. 276 pp.
Sibley, C.G. & Ahlquist, J.E. (1985). The relationships of some groups of African birds, based on comparisons of the genetic material, DNA. Pp. 115-161 in: Schuchmann (1985).
Sibley, C.G. & Ahlquist, J.E. (1990). *Phylogeny and Classification of Birds: a Study in Molecular Evolution*. Yale University Press, New Haven & London.
Sibley, C.G. & Monroe, B.L. (1990). *Distribution and Taxonomy of Birds of the World*. Yale University Press, New Haven & London.
Sibley, C.G. & Monroe, B.L. (1993). *A Supplement to Distribution and Taxonomy of Birds of the World*. Yale University Press, New Haven & London.
Sibley, C.G., Ahlquist, J.E. & Monroe, B.L. (1988). A classification of the living birds of the world based on DNA-DNA hybridization studies. *Auk* **105(3)**: 409-423.
Sick, H. (1958a). On the distribution of Day's Barbet. *Condor* **60(2)**: 139.
Sick, H. (1958b). Resultados de uma excursao ornitologica de Museu Nacional a Brasilia, novo Distrito Federal, Goias, com a descrição de um novo representatante de *Scytalopus* (Rhinocryptidae, Aves). *Bol. Mus. Nac. Zool. (New Ser.)* **185**: 1-41.
Sick, H. (1979). Notes on some Brazilian birds. *Bull. Brit. Orn. Club* **99(4)**: 115-120.
Sick, H. (1985). *Ornitologia Brasileira, uma Introdução*. Editora Universidade de Brasília, Brasília.
Sick, H. (1993). *Birds in Brazil. A Natural History*. Princeton University Press, Princeton, New Jersey.
Sick, H. (1997). *Ornitologia Brasileira*. Nova Fronteira, Rio de Janeiro.
Sick, H. & Pabst, L.F. (1968). As aves do Rio de Janeiro (Guanabara). *Sep. Arqu. Mus. Nac.* **53**: 99-160.
Siddle, C. & Davidson, G. (1991). *Status of the Lewis' Woodpecker (*Melanerpes lewis*) in British Columbia*. Report to the Wildlife Branch of the Ministry of Environment, Victoria, British Columbia.
Sielmann, H. (1959). *My Year with the Woodpeckers*. Barrie & Rockcliffe Ltd, London.
Sigfried, W.R. (1989). Preservation of species in Southern African nature reserves. Pp. 186-201 in: Huntley, B.J. ed. (1989). *Biotic Diversity in Southern Africa*. Oxford University Press, Cape Town.
Sigfried, W.R. (1992). Conservation status of the South African endemic avifauna. *S. Afr. J. Wildl. Res.* **22**: 61-64.
Sill, F.G. & Sosa, F.S. (1996). Beak measurement as a method for sexing Keel-billed Toucans (*Ramphastos sulfuratus*) at Chapultepec Zoo, Mexico City. [Medición del pico como un método de sexado en Tucanes de Pecho Azufrado (*Ramphastos sulfuratus*) en el Zoológico de Chapultepec, Ciudad de México]. Pp. 141-148 in: *Proceedings of the American Association of Zoo Veterinarians Annual Conference, November 3-8, 1996, Puerto Vallarta, Mexico*.
da Silva, J.M.C. (1991). Sistemática e biogeografia da superespécie *Nystalus maculatus* (Piciformes: Bucconidae). *Ararajuba* **2**: 75-79.
da Silva, J.M.C. (1995). Birds of the Cerrado Region, South America. *Steenstrupia* **21**: 69-92.
da Silva, J.M.C. (1996). Distribution of Amazonian and Atlantic birds in gallery forests of the Cerrado Region, South America. *Orn. Neotropical* **7(1)**: 1–18.
da Silva, J.M.C. & Oniki, Y. (1988). Lista preliminar da avifauna da Estação Ecológica Serra das Araras, Mato Grosso, Brasil. *Bol. Mus. Paraense Emilio Goeldi (Zool.)* **4**: 123-143.
da Silva, J.M.C., Lima, M.F.C. & Marceliano, M.L.V. (1990). Pesos de aves de duas localidades na Amazônia Oriental. *Ararajuba* **1**: 99-104.
da Silva, J.M.C., Oren, D.C., Roma, J.C. & Henriques, L.M.P. (1997). Composition and distribution patterns of the avifauna of an Amazonian upland savanna, Amapá, Brazil. Pp. 743-762 in: Remsen (1997).
Silveira, L.F. (1998). The birds of Serra da Canastra National Park and adjacent areas, Minas Gerais, Brazil. *Cotinga* **10**: 55-63.
Silveira, L.F. & Nobre, H. (1998). New records of Three-toed Jacamar *Jacamaralcyon tridactyla* in Minas Gerais, Brazil, with some notes on its biology. *Cotinga* **9**: 47–51.
Simms, E. (1994). The neck twisters. *Birdwatch* **28**: 4-7.
Simpson, B.B. & Haffer, J. (1978). Speciation patterns in the Amazonian forest biota. *Ann. Rev. Ecol. Syst.* **9**: 497-518.
Simpson, S.F. & Cracraft, J. (1981). The phylogenetic relationships of the Piciformes (class Aves). *Auk* **98(3)**: 481-494.
Sinclair, J.C. (1987). *Ian Sinclair's Field Guide to the Birds of Southern Africa*. Collins, London.
Sinclair, J.C. & Davidson, I. (1995). *Southern African Birds. A Photographic Guide*. Struik Publishers Ltd, Cape Town.
Sinclair, J.C. & Hockey, P. (1996). *The Larger Illustrated Guide to Birds of Southern Africa*. Struik Publishers, Cape Town.
Sinclair, J.C. & Whyte, I. (1991). *Field Guide to the Birds of the Kruger National Park*. Struik Publishers, Cape Town.
Sinclair, J.C., Hockey, P. & Tarboton, W. (1993). *Illustrated Guide to the Birds of Southern Africa*. New Holland, London.
Sinclair, J.C., Hockey, P. & Tarboton, W. (1997). *SASOL Birds of Southern Africa*. 2nd edition. Struik Publishers, Cape Town.
Skadsen, D. (1983). Red-bellied Woodpeckers and Cooper's Hawks nesting at Hartford Beach State Park (South Dakota). *South Dakota Bird Notes* **35(1)**: 10.
Skakuj, M. & Stawarczyk, T. (1994). Die Bestimmung des Blutspechts *Dendrocopos syriacus* und seine Ausbreitung in Mitteleuropa. *Limicola* **8**: 5.
Skead, C.J. (1944). Notes on the Red-fronted Tinker Barbet. *Ostrich* **15**: 246.
Skead, C.J. (1945). Timing of the Red-fronted Tinker Bird's call. *Ostrich* **16**: 140-142.
Skead, C.J. (1950). A study of the Black-collared Barbet, *Lybius torquatus*. With notes on its parasitism by the Lesser Honeyguide. *Ostrich* **21**: 84-96.
Skead, C.J. (1951). Notes on honeyguides in southeast Cape Province, South Africa. *Auk* **68(1)**: 52-62.
Skead, C.J. (1964). Birds of the Amatole Forests, King William's Town and Stutterheim, C.P. *Ostrich* **35**: 142-159.
Skead, C.J. (1967). *Ecology of Birds in the Eastern Cape Province*. Ostrich **7**(Supplement). 103 pp.
Skorupa, J.P. (1979). *Foraging Ecology of the Red-cockaded Woodpecker in South Carolina*. MSc thesis, University of California, Davis, California.
Skorupa, J.P. & McFarlane, R.W. (1976). Seasonal variation in foraging territory of Red-cockaded Woodpeckers. *Wilson Bull.* **88(4)**: 662-665.
Skutch, A.F. (1937). Life-history of the Black-chinned Jacamar. *Auk* **54(2)**: 135–146.
Skutch, A.F. (1944a). Life history of the Blue-throated Toucanet. *Wilson Bull.* **56(3)**: 133-151.
Skutch, A.F. (1944b). The life-history of the Prong-billed Barbet. *Auk* **61(1)**: 61-88.
Skutch, A.F. (1948a). Life history of the Golden-naped Woodpecker. *Auk* **65(2)**: 225-260.
Skutch, A.F. (1948b). Life history of the Olivaceous Piculet and related forms. *Ibis* **90(3)**: 433-449.
Skutch, A.F. (1948c). Life history notes on puff-birds. *Wilson Bull.* **60(2)**: 81-97.
Skutch, A.F. (1954). *Life Histories of Central American Birds*. 1. Pacific Coast Avifauna **34**. Cooper Ornithological Society, Berkeley, California. 448 pp.
Skutch, A.F. (1955). The Hairy Woodpecker in Central America. *Wilson Bull.* **67(1)**: 25-32.
Skutch, A.F. (1956). Roosting and nesting of the Golden-olive Woodpecker. *Wilson Bull.* **68(2)**: 118-128.
Skutch, A.F. (1958a). Life history of the White-whiskered Soft-wing *Malacoptila panamensis*. *Ibis* **100(2)**: 209-231.
Skutch, A.F. (1958b). Roosting and nesting of araçari toucans. *Condor* **60(4)**: 201-219.
Skutch, A.F. (1963). Life history of the Rufous-tailed Jacamar *Galbula ruficauda* in Costa Rica. *Ibis* **105(3)**: 354–368.
Skutch, A.F. (1967). *Life Histories of Central American Highland Birds*. Publications of the Nuttall Ornithological Club **7**, Cambridge, Massachusetts. 213 pp.
Skutch, A.F. (1968). The nesting of some Venezuelan birds. *Condor* **70(1)**: 66–82.
Skutch, A.F. (1969a). *Life Histories of Central American Birds*. 3. Pacific Coast Avifauna **35**. Cooper Ornithological Society, Berkeley, California.
Skutch, A.F. (1969b). Nunbirds. *Animal Kingdom* **72**: 8-11.
Skutch, A.F. (1971). Life history of the Keel-billed Toucan. *Auk* **88(2)**: 381-396.
Skutch, A.F. (1972). *Studies of Tropical American Birds*. Publications of the Nuttall Ornithological Club **10**, Cambridge, Massachusetts. 228 pp.
Skutch, A.F. (1980). Arils as food of tropical American birds. *Condor* **82(1)**: 31-42.

Skutch, A.F. (1981). *New Studies of Tropical American Birds*. Publications of the Nuttall Ornithological Club **19**, Cambridge, Massachusetts. 281 pp.
Skutch, A.F. (1983). *Birds of Tropical America*. University of Texas Press, Austin, Texas.
Skutch, A.F. (1985a). Jacamar. Page 311 in: Campbell & Lack (1985).
Skutch, A.F. (1985b). Puffbird. Pp. 488-489 in: Campbell & Lack (1985).
Skutch, A.F. (1985c). Toucan. Pp. 602-604 in: Campbell & Lack (1985).
Skutch, A.F. (1985d). *Life of the Woodpecker*. Ibis Publishing Company, Santa Monica, California.
Skutch, A.F. (1987). *Helpers at Birds' Nests*. University of Iowa Press, Iowa City, Iowa.
Skutch, A.F. (1989). *Birds Asleep*. University of Texas Press, Austin, Texas.
Skutch, A.F. (1998). El carpintero más pequeño. *Bol. Soc. Antioqueña Orn.* **9(16-17)**: 6-17.
Skutch, A.F. (1999). *Trogons, Laughing Falcons, and other Neotropical Birds*. Texas A & M University Press, College Station, Texas.
Slud, P. (1960). *The Birds of Finca "La Selva", Costa Rica: a Tropical Wet Forest Locality*. Bulletin of the American Museum of Natural History **121**, New York. 96 pp.
Slud, P. (1964). *The Birds of Costa Rica. Distribution and Ecology*. Bulletin of the American Museum of Natural History **128**, New York. 430 pp.
Slud, P. (1980). The birds of Hacienda Palo Verde, Guanacaste, Costa Rica. *Smithsonian Contrib. Zool.* **292**: 1-92.
Small, A. (1994). *California Birds: their Status and Distribution*. Ibis Publishing Company, Vista, California.
Small, B. (2000). Sapsucker secrets. *Birder's World* **14(5)**: 88-89.
Smith, A.P. (1908). Destruction of Imperial Woodpeckers. *Condor* **10(2)**: 91.
Smith, C.F. (1941). Lewis Woodpecker migration. *Condor* **43(1)**: 76.
Smith, D.R. & Layne, J.N. (1986). Occurrence of a double brood in Red-headed Woodpeckers in south central Florida. *Florida Field Nat.* **14(4)**: 98-99.
Smith, G.A. & Jackson, J.A. (1994). Red-bellied Woodpecker predation on a green anole. *Miss. Kite* **24**: 7-8.
Smith, J.I. (1987). Evidence of hybridization between Red-bellied and Golden-fronted Woodpeckers. *Condor* **89(2)**: 377-386.
Smith, K.D. (1957). An annotated check list of the birds of Eritrea. *Ibis* **99(1)**: 1-26; **99(2)**: 307-337.
Smith, K.G. (1982). On habitat selection of Williamson's and "Red-naped" Yellow-bellied Sapsuckers. *Southwest. Nat.* **27**: 464-466.
Smith, K.G. (1986a). Winter population dynamics of three species of mast-eating birds in the eastern United States. *Wilson Bull.* **98(3)**: 407-418.
Smith, K.G. (1986b). Winter population dynamics of Blue Jays, Red-headed Woodpeckers, and Northern Mockingbirds in the Ozarks. *Amer. Midl. Nat.* **115(1)**: 52-62.
Smith, K.G. (1986c). Downy Woodpecker feeding on mud-dauber wasp nests. *Southwest. Nat.* **31(1)**: 134.
Smith, K.G. & Scarlett, T. (1987). Mast production and winter populations of Red-headed Woodpeckers and Blue Jays. *J. Wildl. Manage.* **51(2)**: 459-467.
Smith, K.G., Withgott, J.H. & Rodewald, P.G. (2000). Red-headed Woodpecker (*Melanerpes erythrocephalus*). No. **518** in: Poole, A.F. & Gill, F.B. eds. (2000). *The Birds of North America*. Vol. 13. Academy of Natural Sciences & American Ornithologists' Union, Philadelphia & Washington, D.C.
Smith, K.W. (1997). Nest site selection of the Great Spotted Woodpecker *Dendrocopos major* in two oak woods in southern England and its implications for woodland management. *Biol. Conserv.* **80**: 283-288.
Smith, L.M. (1971). *Winter Ecology of Woodpeckers and Nuthatches in Southeastern South Dakota*. PhD thesis, University of South Dakota, Vermillion, South Dakota.
Smith, L.M. (1973). Variation in the horizontal distribution of Downy Woodpeckers. *Iowa Bird Life* **43(1)**: 23-24.
Smith, T.B. (1983). Nest of the Red-stained Woodpecker (*Veniliornis affinis*) from southeastern Peru. *Condor* **85(4)**: 499.
Smith, T.B., Rasmussen, K.K., Whitney, K.D. & Fogiel, M.K. (1996). A preliminary survey of birds from the Lac Lobeke Reserve, south-eastern Cameroon. *Bird Conserv. Int.* **6(2)**: 167-174.
Smith, V.A. (1992). Notes on nesting Three-toed Woodpeckers in northern Utah. *Utah Birds* **8(4)**: 61-65.
Smithe, F.B. (1966). *The Birds of Tikal*. Natural History Press, Garden City, New York.
Smythies, B.E. (1986). *The Birds of Burma*. Nimrod Press Ltd, Liss, UK.
Smythies, B.E. (1999). *Birds of Borneo*. 4th edition revised by G. W. H. Davison. Natural History Publications, Kota Kinabalu.
Sneidern, K. von (1954). Notas sobre algunas aves del Museo de Historia Natural de la Universidad del Cauca, Popayán, Colombia. *Noved. Colombianas* **1**: 3-13.
Sneidern, K. von (1955). Notas ornitológicas sobre la colección del Museo de Historia Natural de la Universidad del Cauca. *Noved. Colombianas* **2**: 35-44.
Snethlage, E. (1908). Sobre uma collecção de aves do Rio Purús. *Bol. Mus. Paraense Emilio Goeldi* **5**: 43-78.
Snethlage, E. (1914). *Catalogo das Aves Amazonicas*. Boletim do Museu Goeldi **8**. Pará, Brazil. 531 pp.
Snethlage, E. (1935). Beiträge zur Brutbiologie brasilianischer Vögel. *J. Orn.* **83(1)**: 1-24; **83(4)**: 532-562.
Snethlage, H. (1927-1928). Meine Reise durch Nordostbrasilien. *J. Orn.* **75**: 453-484; **76**: 503-581, 668-738.
Snow, D.W. ed. (1978). *An Atlas of Speciation in African Non-passerine Birds*. British Museum (Natural History), London.
Snow, D.W. (1979). *Atlas of Speciation in African Non-passerine Birds* - Addenda and corrigenda. *Bull. Brit. Orn. Club* **99(2)**: 66-68.
Snow, D.W. (1981). Tropical frugivorus birds and their food plants: a world survey. *Biotropica* **13**: 1-14.
Snow, D.W. (1985). Affinities and recent history of the avifauna of Trinidad and Tobago. Pp. 238-246 in: Buckley *et al*. (1985).
Snow, D.W. (1997). Should the biological be superseded by the phylogenetic species concept? *Bull. Brit. Orn. Club* **117**: 110-121.
Snow, D.W. & Perrins, C.M. eds. (1998). *The Birds of the Western Palearctic. Concise Edition*. Vol. 1. Non-passerines. Oxford University Press, Oxford & New York.
Snow, R.B. (1941). *A Natural History of the Lewis Woodpecker* Asyndemus lewis *(Gray)*. MSc thesis, University of Utah, Salt Lake City, Utah.
Snyder, D.E. (1966). *The Birds of Guyana*. Peabody Museum, Salem, Massachusetts.
Snyder, L.L. (1923). On the crown markings of juvenile Hairy and Downy Woodpeckers. *Can. Field-Nat.* **37**: 167-168.
Soares, E.S. & dos Anjos, L. (1999). Efeito da fragmentação florestal sobre aves escaladoras de tronco e galho na região de Londrina, norte do estado do Paraná, Brasil. *Orn. Neotropical* **10(1)**: 61-68. In Portuguese with English summary.
Sohtke, H. (1984). Erkenntnisse über die Haltung und Zucht des Haubenbartvogels (*Trachyphonus vaillantii*). [Understanding the maintenance and propagation of Levaillant's Barbet (*Trachyphonus vaillantii*)]. *Gefiederte Welt* **108(7)**: 188-190.
Soler, M., Zúñiga, J.M. & Camacho, I. (1982). Nidificación de *Picus viridis* en taludes de arcilla en ramblas de Guadix (Granada). [Nesting of *Picus viridis* in clay taluses of the watercourses of Guadix (Granada)]. *Doñana Acta Vertebrata* **9**: 195-209. In Spanish with English summary.
Sollien, A., Nesholen, B. & Fosseidengen, J.E. (1977). Neutralism between Tengmalm's Owl and Black Woodpecker. *Fauna* **30**: 195-200.
Sollien, A., Nesholen, B. & Fosseidengen, J.E. (1978). Observasjoner ved et reir av Tretspett *Picoides tridactylus*. [Observations at a nest of Three-toed Woodpecker *Picoides tridactylus*]. *Cinclus* **1(1)**: 58-64. In Norwegian with English summary.
Sollien, A., Nesholen, B. & Fosseidengen, J.E. (1982a). Ungerperioden I et reir av tret spett. [The nestling period at a nest of Three-toed Woodpecker]. *Vår Fuglefauna* **5(3)**: 169-174. In Norwegian with English summary.
Sollien, A., Nesholen, B. & Fosseidengen, J.E. (1982b). Trekk fra tret spettens hekkebiologi. [Aspects of the breeding biology of the Three-toed Woodpecker *Picoides tridactylus*]. *Fauna* **35(3)**: 121-124. In Norwegian with English summary.
Sollien, A., Nesholen, B. & Fosseidengen, J.E. (1982c). Horizontal partition of the breeding territory of the Three-toed Woodpecker *Picoides tridactylus*. *Fauna Norvegica (Ser. C, Cinclus)* **5(2)**: 93-94. In English with Norwegian summary.
Solomon, D. (1998). Another Little Spotted Woodpecker in the Bvumba. *Honeyguide* **44**: 148.
van Someren, V.G.L. (1956). *Days with Birds - Studies of Habits of some East African Species*. Fieldiana Zoology **38**. 520 pp.
van Someren, V.G.L. & Cunningham-van Someren, G.R. (1949). The birds of Bwamba (Bwamba County, Toro District, Uganda). *Uganda J.* **13**: 1-111.
Sonobe, K. ed. (1982). *Field Guide to the Birds of Japan*. Wild Bird Society of Japan, Tokyo.
Sonobe, K. & Izawa, N. eds. (1987). *Endangered Bird Species in the Korean Peninsula*. Museum of Korean Nature & Wild Bird Society of Japan, Tokyo.
Sorensen, E. (1986). A precipitous decline in Lewis' Woodpecker in Salt Lake and Davis Counties. *Utah Birds* **2(3)**: 45-54.
Sørensen, U.G., Bech, J. & Krabble, E. (1996). New and unusual records of birds in Cameroon. *Bull. Brit. Orn. Club* **116(3)**: 145-155.
Sousa, P.J. (1983a). *Habitat Suitability Index Models: Lewis' Woodpecker*. Report **FWS/OBS-82/10.32**. US Fish & Wildlife Service.
Sousa, P.J. (1983b). *Habitat Suitability Index Models: Williamson's Sapsucker*. Report **FWS/OBS-82/10.47**. US Fish & Wildlife Service.
Sousa, P.J. (1987). *Habitat Suitability Index Models: Hairy Woodpecker*. Report **FWS/OBS-82/10.146**. US Fish & Wildlife Service.
Southern, W.E. (1960). Copulatory behavior of the Red-headed Woodpecker. *Auk* **77(2)**: 218-219.
Souza, D.G.S. (1999). Novos registros de espécies de aves no estado da Bahia e sua correlação com os ecossistemas. *Atualidades Orn.* **88**: 6-7.
Sovago, M. (1954). Mating display of *Picus viridis* - Green Woodpecker. *Aquila* **55-58**: 288.
Sparks, G.M.B. (1995). Woodpeckers attacking House Martins' nests. *British Birds* **88(6)**: 297.
Sparks, J.C., Masters, R.E., Engle, D.M., Payton, M.E. & Bukenhofer, G.A. (1999). Influence of fire season and fire behavior on woody plants in Red-cockaded Woodpecker clusters. *Wildl. Soc. Bull.* **27**: 124-133.
Speich, S. & Radke, W.J. (1975). Opportunistic feeding of the Gila Woodpecker. *Wilson Bull.* **87(2)**: 275-276.
Speir, R.P.G. (1990). Sighting of Black-billed Barbet *Lybius guifsobalito* in Tanzania. *Scopus* **14**: 31.
Spence, S. (1975). Jamaican Woodpecker. *Gosse Bird Club Broadsheet* **25**: 23-24.
Spence, S. (1976). Starling usurping woodpecker's nest. *Gosse Bird Club Broadsheet* **27**: 15-16.
Spiridinov, J. (1984). [The southern White-backed Woodpecker *Dendrocopos leucotos lilfordi*]. Pp. 126-127 in: Dakov, M. ed. (1984). *Red Data Book of the People's Republic of Bulgaria*. Bulgarian Academy of Sciences, Sofia. In Bulgarian.
Spittle, R.J. (1949). Nesting habits of some Singapore birds. *Bull. Raffles Mus., Singapore* **21**: 184-204.
Spittle, R.J. (1952). Feeding habits of some Singapore birds. *Malay. Nat. J.* **7**: 23-32.
Spitznagel, A. (1990). The influence of forest and management on woodpecker density and habitat use in floodplain forests of the Upper Rhein Valley. Pp. 117-145 in: Carlson & Aulén (1990).
Spitznagel, A. (1993). Warum sind Spechte schwierig zu erfassende Arten? *Beih. Veröff. Naturschutz Landschaftspflege Bad. -Württ.* **67**: 59-70.
Spofford, S.H. (1977). Poplar leaf-stem gall insects as food for warblers and woodpeckers. *Wilson Bull.* **89(3)**: 485.
Spottiswoode, C. (1994). Lesser Honeyguide parasitising Cardinal Woodpecker. *Promerops* **213**: 9.
Spray, C.J. & MacRoberts, M.H. (1975). Notes on molt and juvenal plumage in the Acorn Woodpecker. *Condor* **77(3)**: 342-344.
Spring, L.W. (1965). Climbing and pecking adaptations in some North American woodpeckers. *Condor* **67(6)**: 457-488.
Stacey, P.B. (1978). *Communal Breeding in the Acorn Woodpecker*. PhD dissertation, University of Colorado, Boulder, Colorado.
Stacey, P.B. (1979a). Kinship, promiscuity, and communal breeding in the Acorn Woodpecker. *Behav. Ecol. Sociobiol.* **6(1)**: 53-66.
Stacey, P.B. (1979b). Habitat saturation and communal breeding in the Acorn Woodpecker. *Anim. Behav.* **27(4)**: 1153-1166.
Stacey, P.B. (1979c). *The Ecology and Evolution of Communal Breeding in the Acorn Woodpecker*. PhD dissertation, University of Colorado, Boulder, Colorado.
Stacey, P.B. (1981). Foraging behavior of the Acorn Woodpecker in Belize, Central America. *Condor* **83(4)**: 336-339.
Stacey, P.B. & Bock, C.E. (1978). Social plasticity in the Acorn Woodpecker. *Science* **202**: 1297-1300.
Stacey, P.B. & Edwards, T.C. (1983). Possible cases of infanticide by immigrant females in a group-breeding bird. *Auk* **100(3)**: 731-733.
Stacey, P.B. & Jansma, R. (1977). Storage of piñon nuts by the Acorn Woodpecker in New Mexico. *Wilson Bull.* **89(1)**: 150-151.
Stacey, P.B. & Koenig, W.D. (1984). Cooperative breeding in the Acorn Woodpecker. *Scientific American* **251(2)**: 114-121.
Stacey, P.B. & Ligon, J.D. (1987). Territory quality and dispersal options in the Acorn Woodpecker, and a challenge to the habitat saturation model of cooperative breeding. *Amer. Naturalist* **130**: 654-676.
Stacey, P.B. & Taper, M. (1992). Environmental variation and persistence of small populations. *Ecol. Appl.* **2(1)**: 18-29.
Stadler, S.G. (1992). Vögel. Pp. 10-16 in: *Jahresbericht des Zoologischen Gartens der Stadt Frankfurt am Main 116-130 für 1974-1991*.
Staebler, A.E. (1949). *A Comparative Life History Study of the Downy and Hairy Woodpeckers (*Dendrocopos pubescens *and* Dendrocopos villosus*)*. PhD thesis, University of Michigan, Ann Arbor, Michigan.
Stager, K.E. (1961a). The Machris Brazilian expedition. Ornithology: Non-Passerines. *Contrib. Sci. Los Angeles Co. Mus.* **41**: 1-27.
Stager, K.E. (1961b). A new bird of the genus *Picumnus* from eastern Brazil. *Contrib. Sci. Los Angeles Co. Mus.* **46**: 1-4.
Stager, K.E. (1967). Avian olfaction. *Amer. Zool.* **7**: 415-419.
Stager, K.E. (1968). A new piculet from southeastern Peru. *Contrib. Sci. Los Angeles Co. Mus.* **153**: 1-4.
Stagg, A. (1985). *Birds of SW Saudi Arabia. An Annotated Check-list*. Published privately, Riyadh, Saudi Arabia.
Stahl, J. (1998). Glatzenbartvögel - Ihre Haltung und Zucht. *Gefiederte Welt* **122(1)**: 20-22.
Stallcup, P.L. (1962). Contents of 103 stomachs of Northern Three-toed Woodpeckers. *J. Colo. Wyo. Acad. Sci.* **5**: 39.
Stallcup, P.L. (1968). Spatio-temporal relationships of nuthatches and woodpeckers in ponderosa pine forests of Colorado. *Ecology* **49**: 831-843.
Stallcup, P.L. (1969). Hairy Woodpeckers feeding on pine seeds. *Auk* **86(1)**: 134-135.
Stanback, M. (1988). Causes, correlates, and consequences of intra-brood dominance hierarchies in the cooperatively breeding Acorn Woodpecker. *Int. Conf. Behav. Ecol.* **2**: 106.
Stanback, M.T. (1989). Observations on food habits and social organization of Acorn Woodpeckers in Costa Rica. *Condor* **91(4)**: 1005-1007.
Stanback, M.T. (1991). *Causes and Consequences of Nestling Size Variation in the Cooperatively Breeding Acorn Woodpecker*. PhD dissertation, University of California, Berkeley, California.
Stanback, M.T. (1994). Dominance within broods of the cooperatively breeding Acorn Woodpecker. *Anim. Behav.* **47(5)**: 1121-1126.
Stanback, M.T. (1998). Getting stuck: a cost of communal cavity roosting. *Wilson Bull.* **110(3)**: 421-423.
Stanback, M.T., Wingfield, J.C. & Koenig, W.D. (1994). Behavioral endocrinology and cooperative breeding. Page 441 in: Dittami (1994).

Stanford, J.K. & Mayr, E. (1941). The Vernay-Cutting expedition to northern Burma. Part 5. *Ibis* **Ser. 4, no. 5**: 479-518.
Stangel, P.W. (1991). *Genetic Variation and Population Structure of the Red-cockaded Woodpecker*. PhD dissertation, University of Georgia, Athens, Geogia.
Stangel, P.W., Lennartz, M.R. & Smith, M.H. (1992). Genetic variation and population structure of Red-cockaded Woodpeckers. *Conserv. Biol.* **6(2)**: 283-292.
Stanton, D. (1997). Al Mahwit: a rich Yemen avifauna. *Sandgrouse* **19(2)**: 92-95.
Stark, R.D., Dodenhoff, D.J. & Johnson, E.V. (1998). A quantitative analysis of woodpecker drumming. *Condor* **100(2)**: 350-356.
Stattersfield, A.J. & Capper, D.R. eds. (2000). *Threatened Birds of the World*. Lynx Edicions & BirdLife International, Barcelona & Cambridge.
Stattersfield, A.J., Crosby, M.J., Long, A.J. & Wege, D.C. (1998). *Endemic Birds Areas of the World. Priorities for Biodiversity Conservation*. BirdLife Conservation Series **7**. BirdLife International, Cambridge.
Stefanovic, A. (1958-1959). Seasonal specialization in the feeding patterns of the Syrian Woodpecker, *Dendrocopos syriacus*, in the Kruševac Area (Zupa). *Larus* **12-13**: 55-64.
Steffen, G.L. (1981). Both species of three-toed woodpeckers observed in the Black Hills. *South Dakota Bird Notes* **33(3)**: 61.
Steinbacher, G. (1935). Funktionell-anatomische Untersuchungen an Vogelfüßen mit Wendezehen und Rückzehen. *J. Orn.* **83**: 214-182.
Steinbacher, J. (1937). Anatomische Untersuchungen über die systematische Stellung der Galbulidae und Bucconidae. *Arch. Naturges.* **6(3)**: 417–515.
Steinbacher, J. (1962). *Beiträge zur Kenntnis der Vögel von Paraguay*. Abhandlungen der Senckenbergischen Naturforschenden Gesellschaft **502**. 106 pp.
Steirly, C.C. (1957). Nesting ecology of the Red-cockaded Woodpecker in Virginia. *Atlantic Naturalist* **12**: 280-292.
Stenberg, I. (1978). Trekk fra Gronnspettens hekkebiologi. [On the biology of the Green Woodpecker]. *Vår Fuglefauna* **1(3/4)**: 152-158. In Norwegian with English summary.
Stenberg, I. (1990). Preliminary results of a study on woodpeckers in Møre og Romsdal county, western Norway. Pp. 67-79 in: Carlson & Aulén (1990).
Stenberg, I. & Hogstad, O. (1992). Habitat use and density of breeding woodpeckers in the 1990s in Møre og Romsdal county, western Norway. *Fauna Norvegica (Ser. C, Cinclus)* **15**: 49-61.
Stenhouse, A. (1993). Crested Barbet - unusual behaviour. *Witwatersrand Bird Club News* **163**: 5.
Stepanyan, L.S. (1995). [*Birds of Vietnam. Based on the Investigations of 1978-1990*]. Nauka, Moscow. In Russian.
Steullet, A.B. & Deautier, E.A. (1946). *Catálogo Sistemático de las Aves de la República Argentina*. Museo de La Plata, La Plata, Argentina.
Stevens, H. (1925). Notes on the birds of the Sikkim Himalayas. Part 6. *J. Bombay Nat. Hist. Soc.* **30**: 664-685.
Stevenson, T. & Fanshawe, J. (2001). *Field Guide to the Birds of East Africa*. T. & A.D. Poyser, London, UK.
Stevenson, T. & Webster, J. (1992). Eurasian Wrynecks *Jynx torquilla* in western Kenya. *Scopus* **15**: 127-128.
Steventon, J.D., MacKenzie, K.L. & Mahon, T.E. (1998). Response of small mammals and birds to partial cutting and clearcutting in northwest British Columbia. *For. Chronicle* **74(5)**: 703-713.
Steyn, P. (1996). *Breeding Birds of Southern Africa*. Fernwood Press, Vlaeberg.
Steyn, P. & Densham, W.D. (1975). Xanthochroism in a Black-collared Barbet. *Lammergeyer* **22**: 51-52.
Steyn, P. & Myburgh, N. (1986). Lesser Honeyguide breeding at Somerset West. *Promerops* **173**: 16.
Steyn, P. & Scott, J. (1974). Blackcollared Barbets evicting a Lesser Honeyguide. *Ostrich* **45**: 143.
Stickel, D.W. (1962). Predation on Red-bellied Woodpecker nestlings by a black rat snake. *Auk* **79(1)**: 118-119.
Stickel, D.W. (1963a). *Natural History of the Red-bellied Woodpecker*. MSc thesis, Southern Illinois University, Carbondale.
Stickel, D.W. (1963b). Interspecific relations among Red-bellied and Hairy Woodpeckers and a flying squirrel. *Wilson Bull.* **75(2)**: 203-204.
Stickel, D.W. (1964). Roosting habits of Red-bellied Woodpeckers. *Wilson Bull.* **76(4)**: 382-383.
Stickel, D.W. (1965a). Territorial and breeding habits of Red-bellied Wodpeckers. *Amer. Midl. Nat.* **74**: 110-118.
Stickel, D.W. (1965b). Wing-stretching of Red-bellied Woodpeckers. *Auk* **82(3)**: 503.
Stiles, F.G. (1983). Checklist of birds. Pp. 530-544 in: Janzen (1983).
Stiles, F.G. (1985). Conservation of forest birds in Costa Rica: problems and perspectives. Pp. 141-168 in: Diamond & Lovejoy (1985).
Stiles, F.G. & Levey, D.J. (1994). Appendix 7. Birds of La Selva and vicinity. Pp. 384–393 in: McDade *et al.* (1994).
Stiles, F.G. & Skutch, A.F. (1989). *A Guide to the Birds of Costa Rica*. Christopher Helm, London.
Stiles, F.G., Rosselli, L. & Bohórquez, C.I. (1999). New and noteworthy records of birds from the middle Magdalena valley of Colombia. *Bull. Brit. Orn. Club* **119(2)**: 113-129.
Storer, R.W. (1989). Notes on Paraguayan birds. *Occas. Pap. Mus. Zool. Univ. Mich.* **719**: 1-21.
Storer, R.W. (1992). The Greater Honeyguide. *Birder's World* **6(5)**: 74-75.
Storer, R.W. & Dalquest, W.W. (1967). Birds from the Save River area of Mozambique. *Occas. Pap. Mus. Zool. Univ. Mich.* **652**: 1-14.
Storrs-Fox, E.A. (1937). Notes on Murree birds. *J. Bombay Nat. Hist. Soc.* **39(2)**: 354-357.
Storrs-Fox, E.A. (1943). Woodpeckers feeding on fruit. *J. Bombay Nat. Hist. Soc.* **44(1)**: 122.
Stotz, D.F. & Bierregaard, R.O. (1989). The birds of the fazendas Porto Alegre, Esteio and Dimona north of Manaus, Amazonas, Brazil. *Rev. Bras. Biol.* **49**: 861-872.
Stotz, D.F., Fitzpatrick, J.W., Parker, T.A. & Moskovits, D.K. (1996). *Neotropical Birds, Ecology and Conservation*. University of Chicago Press, Chicago & London.
Stotz, D.F., Lanyon, S.M., Schulenberg, T.S., Willard, D.E., Peterson, A.T. & Fitzpatrick, J.W. (1997). An avifaunal survey of two tropical forest localities on the middle Rio Jiparaná, Rondônia, Brazil. Pp. 763-781 in: Remsen (1997).
Stradi, R. & Hudon, J. (1998). The complement of yellow and red pigments in true woodpeckers Picinae. Proceedings of the XXII International Ornithological Congress, Durban 1998. *Ostrich* **69(3&4)**: 302. (Abstract).
Stradi, R., Hudon, J., Celentano, G. & Pini, E. (1998). Carotenoids in bird plumage: the complement of yellow and red pigments in true woodpeckers (Picinae). *Comp. Biochem. Physiol.* **120B**: 223-230.
Strange, M. (2000). *A Photographic Guide to the Birds of Southeast Asia Including the Philippines and Borneo*. Periplus, Singapore.
Straube, F.C. & Bornschein, M.R. (1995). New or noteworthy records of birds from northwestern Paraná and adjacent areas (Brazil). *Bull. Brit. Orn. Club* **115(4)**: 219-225.
Straube, F.C., Argel-de-Oliveira, M.M. & Cândido, J.F. (2000). *Ornitologia Brasileira no Século XX. Incluindo os Resumos do VIII Congresso Brasileiro de Ornitologia (Florianópolis, 9 a 14 de Julho de 2000)*. Universidade do Sul de Santa Catarina & Sociedade Brasileira de Ornitologia, Curitiba, Brazil.
Strauch, J.C. (1977). Further bird weights from Panama. *Bull. Brit. Orn. Club* **97(2)**: 61-65.
Stresemann, E. (1913). Die Formen von *Thriponax javensis* (Horsf.). *Novit. Zool.* **20**: 316-321.
Stresemann, E. (1921a). Der Spechte der Insel Sumatra. *Arch. Naturges.* **87**: 62-120.
Stresemann, E. (1921b). Zur Kenntnis eines seltenen sumatranischen Spechtes. *Jaarber. Cl. Ned. Vogelk.* **11**: 32-33.
Stresemann, E. & Stresemann, V. (1966). *Die Mauser der Vögel*. Journal für Ornithologie **107**(Supplement). 439 pp.
Strewe, R. (2000a). New distributional sightings of 28 species of birds from Dpto. Nariño, SW Colombia. *Bull. Brit. Orn. Club* **120(3)**: 189-195.
Strewe, R. (2000b). Las aves y la importancia de la conservación de la Reserva Natural El Pangán, Nariño, en el suroeste de Colombia. *Bol. Soc. Antioqueña Orn.* **11**: 56-65.
Striegler, R., Striegler, U. & Jost, K.D. (1982). Große siedlungsdichte des Schwarzspechtes im Branitzer Park bei Cottbus. *Der Falke* **29(5)**: 164-170.
Strussmann, C. (1998). Presence of the White-fronted Woodpecker *Melanerpes cactorum* (Piciformes: Picidae) in the northern Pantanal, Mato Grosso State, Brazil. *Rev. Biol. Trop.* **46(4)**: 1199. (Abstract).
Struwe, B. (1992). Zum Vorkommen des Wendehalses (*Jynx torquilla*) in Schleswig-Holstein. *Beih. Veröff. Naturschutz Landschaftspflege Bad.-Württ.* **66**: 23-29.
Stuart, C. & Stuart, T. (1999). *Birds of Africa. From Seabirds to Seed-eaters*. Southern Book Publishers, Rivonia, South Africa.
Stuart, S.N. & Jensen, F.P. (1981). Further range extensions and other notable records of forest birds from Tanzania. *Scopus* **5**: 106-115.
Stuart, S.N. & Jensen, F.P. (1986). The status and ecology of montane forest bird species in western Cameroon. Pp 38-105 in: Stuart, S.N. ed. (1986). *Conservation of Cameroon Montane Forests*. ICBP, Cambridge.
Stuart, S.N. & Turner, D.A. (1980). Some range extensions and other notable records of forest birds from eastern and northeastern Tanzania. *Scopus* **4**: 36-41.
Suárez, L. & García, M. (1986). *Extinción de Animales en el Ecuador*. Fundacion Natura, Quito.
Suárez, W. & Arredondo, O. (1997). Nuevas adiciones a la paleornitología cubana. *Pitirre* **10(3)**: 100-102.
Südbeck, P. (1991). [A new hybrid between Green and Grey-headed Woodpecker (*Picus viridis*, *P. canus*)]. *Ecol. Birds* **13(1)**: 89-110. In German with English summary.
Südbeck, P. (1993). Zur Territorialität beim Grauspecht (*Picus canus*). *Beih. Veröff. Naturschutz Landschaftspflege Bad. -Württ.* **67**: 143-156.
Südbeck, P. & Gall, T. (1993). Der Mittelspecht (*Picoides medius*) in Schleswig-Holstein. Erfassungs-Probleme und ihre Konsequenzen fur Bestandsschätzungen. *Corax* **15(3)**: 211-221.
Südbeck, P. & Meinecke, H. (1992). [Grey-headed Woodpecker female helper at the nest]. *J. Orn.* **133(4)**: 443-446. In German with English summary.
Sugathan, R. & Varghese, A.P. (1996). A review of the birds of Thattakad Bird Sanctuary, Kerala. *J. Bombay Nat. Hist. Soc.* **93**: 487-506.
Sugiyama, Y. & Akatsuka, T. (1999). [Struggles for a nest cavity of Japanese Pygmy Woodpecker *Dendrocopos kizuki* at a city park in Nagoya]. *Strix* **17**: 165-172. In Japanese with English summary.
Sujatnika, Jepson, P., Soehartono, T.R., Crosby, M.J. & Mardiastuti, A. (1995). *Melestarikan Keanekaragaman Hayati Indonesia: Pendekatan Daerah Burung Endemik. Conserving Indonesian Biodiversity: the Endemic Bird Area Approach*. PHPA/BirdLife International, Jakarta, Indonesia. In Indonesian and English.
Sullivan, E. (1992). Red-bellied Woodpecker raises two broods in Connecticut. *Connecticut Warbler* **12(1)**: 24-25.
Sullivan, K.A. (1984a). The advantages of social foraging in Downy Woodpeckers. *Anim. Behav.* **32(1)**: 16-22.
Sullivan, K.A. (1984b). Information exploitation by Downy Woodpeckers in mixed-species flocks. *Behaviour* **91(4)**: 294-311. In English with French summary.
Sullivan, K.A. (1985a). Selective alarm calling by Downy Woodpeckers in mixed-species flocks. *Auk* **102(1)**: 184-187.
Sullivan, K.A. (1985b). Vigilance patterns in Downy Woodpeckers. *Anim. Behav.* **33(1)**: 328-330.
Sutherland, G.D., Gass, C.L., Thompson, P.A. & Lertzman, K.P. (1982). Feeding territoriality in migrant Rufous Hummingbirds: defense of Yellow-bellied Sapsucker feeding sites. *Can. J. Zool.* **60**: 2046-2050.
Sutter, E. (1941). Beitrag zur Kenntnis der postembryonalen Entwicklung des Wendehalses (*Jynx torquilla torquilla* L.). *Schweizer Archiv. Orn.* **1**: 481-508.
Sutton, G.M. (1953). Bronzed Woodpecker. *Wilson Bull.* **65(2)**: 65-67.
Sutton, G.M. (1984). The Red-bellied Woodpeckers fail again. *Bull. Okla. Orn. Soc.* **17(1)**: 1-4.
Svensson, S., Svensson, M. & Tjernberg, M. (1999). *Svensk Fågelatlas*. Vår Fågelvärld **31**(Supplement), Stockholm.
Svoboda, F.J. (1988). Toucan tending. *AFA Watchbird* **15(3)**: 36-38.
Swallow, S.K., Howard, R.A. & Gutierrez, R.J. (1988). Snag preference of woodpeckers foraging in a northeastern hardwood forest. *Wilson Bull.* **100(2)**: 236-246.
Swarth, H.S. (1917). Geographical variation in *Sphyrapicus thyroideus*. *Condor* **19(2)**: 62-65.
Swearingen, E.M. (1977). Group size, sex ratio, reproductive success and territory size in Acorn Woodpeckers. *Western Birds* **8(1)**: 21-24.
Swierczewski, E.V. (1977). *The Hindlimb Myology and Phylogenetic Relationship of the Avian Order Piciformes*. PhD dissertation, University of Pittsburgh, Pittsburgh, Pennsylvania.
Swierczewski, E.V. & Raikow, R.J. (1981). Hind limb morphology, phylogeny, and classification of the Piciformes. *Auk* **98(3)**: 466-480.
Szlivka, L. (1957). Von der Biologie des Blutspechtes, *Dendrocopos syriacus* und seinen Beziehungen zu den Staren, *Sturnus vulgaris*. *Larus* **9-10**: 48-70.
Szlivka, L. (1960). Further notes on the Syrian Woodpecker, *Dendrocopos syriacus balcanicus*, from the closer environs of Gunnaroš. *Larus* **14**: 121-134.
Sztolcman, J. (1926). Étude des collections ornithologiques de Parana. *Ann. Zool. Mus. Polonici Hist. Nat.* **5**: 109-196.
Taczanowski, L. (1886). *Ornithologie du Pérou*. Vol. 3. Rennes, Paris.
Takagi, N. & Sasaki, M. (1980). Unexpected karyotypic resemblance between the Burmeister's Seriema, *Chunga burmeisteri* and the Toucan, *Ramphastos toco*. *Chromosome Inf. Serv.* **28**: 10-11.
Tanner, J.T. (1941). Three years with the Ivory-billed Woodpecker, America's rarest bird. *Audubon Magazine* **43(1)**: 5-14.
Tanner, J.T. (1942). *The Ivory-billed Woodpecker*. National Audubon Society Research Report **1**, New York. (Reprinted by Dover Publications, New York, 1966).
Tanner, J.T. (1964). The decline and present status of the Imperial Woodpecker of Mexico. *Auk* **81(1)**: 74-81.
Tanner, J.T. (2001). A forest alive. *Birdwatch* **107**: 18-24.
Tarboton, W.R. (1970). Notes on the Bearded Woodpecker. *Bokmakierie* **22**: 81-84.
Tarboton, W.R. (1976). Aspects of the biology of *Jynx ruficollis*. *Ostrich* **47(2&3)**: 99-112.
Tarboton, W.R. (1980). Avian populations in Transvaal savanna. Pp. 113-124 in: Johnson (1980).
Tarboton, W.R. (1997). Africa's woodpeckers: a guide to their identification. *Africa. Birds & Birding* **2(4)**: 45-49.
Tarboton, W.R. (2001). *A Guide to the Nests and Eggs of Southern African Birds*. Struik Publishers Ltd, Cape Town.
Tarboton, W.R., Allan, W.G., Vernon, C.J., Jenkins, A.R. & Petersen, W. (1993). *Baseline Biological Survey. Fauna and Flora. Lesotho Highlands Water Project, Phase 1A. Birds*. Research report **3**. Avian Demography Unit, University of Cape Town, Cape Town.
Tarboton, W.R., Kemp, M.I. & Kemp, A.C. (1987). *Birds of the Transvaal*. Transvaal Museum, Pretoria.
Tashian, R.E. (1952). Some birds of the Palenque Region of northeastern Chiapas, Mexico. *Auk* **69(1)**: 60-66.
Tashiro-Vierling, K.Y. (1994). *Population Trends and Ecology of the Lewis' Woodpecker (*Melanerpes lewis*) in Southeastern Colorado*. MSc thesis, University of Colorado, Boulder, Colorado.
Tate, J. (1973). Methods and annual sequence of foraging by the Sapsucker. *Auk* **90(4)**: 840-856.
Tate, J. (1981). The blue list for 1981. *Amer. Birds* **35**: 3-10.
Tate, J. & Tate, D.J. (1982). The blue list for 1982. *Amer. Birds* **35**: 126-135.
Taylor, E.M. (1961). Observations on a woodpecker. *Malay. Nat. J.* **15**: 62-63.
Taylor, I.S. & Macdonald, M.A. (1978). The birds of the Bia National Park, Ghana. *Bull. Niger. Orn. Soc.* **14(45)**: 36-41.
Taylor, K. (1995). *A Birders Guide to Ecuador*. Published privately, Victoria, Canada.
Taylor, P.B. (1983). East African nest records scheme. *Scopus* **6**: 129-142.
Taylor, P.B. & Taylor, C.A. (1988). The status, movements and breeding of some birds in the Kikuyu Escarpment Forest, central Kenya highlands. *Tauraco* **1**: 72-89.
Taylor, R.R. (1958). Observations on a Black-backed Three-toed Woodpecker's nest. *Ontario Field Biol.* **12**: 7-9.

Taylor, W.K. (1996). Species of special concern. Hairy Woodpecker, *Picoides villosus*. Pp. 588-594 in: Rodgers *et al.* (1996).
Teixeira, D.M. (1990). Notas sobre algumas aves descritas por Emile Snethlage. *Bol. Mus. Nac. Rio J. Zool.* **337**: 1-6.
Teixeira, D.M., Nacinovic, J.B. & Luigi, G. (1988). Notes on some birds of northeastern Brazil (3). *Bull. Brit. Orn. Club* **108(2)**: 75-79.
Tennant, M. (1991). *Phylogenetic Systematics of the Picinae*. PhD dissertation, Wayne State University, Detroit, Michigan.
Terborgh, J. (1972). Distribution on environmental gradients: theory and a preliminary interpretation of distributional pattern in the avifauna of Cordillera Vilcabamba, Peru. *Ecology* **52**: 23-40.
Terborgh, J. & Winter, B. (1982). Evolutionary circumstances of species with small ranges. Pp. 587-600 in: Prance, G.T. ed. (1982). *Biological Diversification in the Tropics*. Columbia University Press, New York.
Terborgh, J. & Winter, B. (1983). A method of setting parks and reserves with special reference to Colombia and Ecuador. *Biol. Conserv.* **27**: 45-58.
Terborgh, J., Fitzpatrick, J.W. & Emmons, L. (1984). Annotated checklist of bird and mammal species of Cocha Cashu Biological Station, Manu National Park, Peru. *Fieldiana Zool. (New Ser.)* **21**: 1-29.
Terborgh, J., Robinson, S.K., Parker, T.A., Munn, C.A. & Pierpont, N. (1990). Structure and organization of an Amazonian forest bird community. *Ecol. Monogr.* **60**: 213-238.
Terhivuo, J. (1976). Terrestrial snails in the diet of the Wryneck *Jynx torquilla*. *Ornis Fenn.* **53**: 47.
Terhivuo, J. (1977). Occurrence of strange objects in nests of the Wryneck *Jynx torquilla*. *Ornis Fenn.* **54**: 66-72. In English with Finnish summary.
Terhivuo, J. (1983). Why does the Wryneck *Jynx torquilla* bring strange items to the nest? *Ornis Fenn.* **60**: 51-57.
Test, F.H. (1942). The nature of the red, yellow, and orange pigments in woodpeckers of the genus *Colaptes*. *Univ. Calif. Publ. Zool.* **46**: 371-389.
Test, F.H. (1945). Molt in flight feathers of flickers. *Condor* **47(2)**: 63-72.
Test, F.H. (1969). Relation of wing and tail color of the woodpeckers *Colaptes auratus* and *C. cafer* to their food. *Condor* **71(2)**: 206-211.
Thayer, J.E. & Bangs, O. (1908). The present state of the Ornis of Guadaloupe Island. *Condor* **10(3)**: 101-106.
Thewlis, R.M., Duckworth, J.W., Anderson, G.Q.A., Dvorak, M., Evans, T.D., Nemeth, E., Timmins, R.J. & Wilkinson, R.J. (1996). Ornithological records from Laos during October 1992 - August 1993. *Forktail* **11**: 47-100.
Thewlis, R.M., Timmins, R.J., Evans, T.D. & Duckworth, J.W. (1998). *The Conservation Status of Birds in Laos: a Review of Key Species*. Bird Conservation International **8**(Supplement). 159 pp.
Thibault de Maisières, C. (1940). Quelques observations sur le Pic tridactyle, *Picoides tridactylus alpinus* (Brehm), dans les Alpes. *Aquila* **50**: 372-378.
Thiel, R.P. (1978). The distribution of the three-toed woodpeckers in Wisconsin. *Passenger Pigeon* **40(4)**: 477-488.
Thiollay, J.M. (1963). Quelques précisions sur le Pic à dos blanc *Dendrocopos leucotos lilfordi* dans les Pyrénées. *Alauda* **31(1)**: 32-35.
Thiollay, J.M. (1985a). The birds of Ivory Coast: status and distribution. *Malimbus* **7(1)**: 1-59.
Thiollay, J.M. (1985b). The west African forest avifauna: a review. Pp. 171-186 in: Diamond & Lovejoy (1985).
Thiollay, J.M. (1988). Les oiseaux menacés de Guyane. Pp. 61-80 in: Thibault, J.C. & Guyot, I. eds. (1988). *Livre Rouge des Oiseaux Menacés des Régions Françaises d'Outre-Mer*. ICBP Monograph **5**. Saint-Claude, France.
Thiollay, J.M. (1992). Influence of selective logging on bird species diversity in a Guianan rain forest. *Conserv. Biol.* **6**: 47-63.
Thiollay, J.M. (1995). The role of traditional agroforests in the conservation of rain forest bird diversity in Sumatra. *Conserv. Biol.* **9**: 335-353.
Thiollay, J.M. & Jullien, M. (1998). Flocking behaviour of foraging birds in a Neotropical rain forest and the anti-predator defence hypothesis. *Ibis* **140(3)**: 382-394.
Thirkhill, L. (1987). Breeding Red-breasted Toucans. *AFA Watchbird* **13**: 19-24.
Thompson, D.R. (1980). Crimson-rumped Toucanet. *AFA Watchbird* **7(5)**: 28-29.
Thompson, D.R. (1998). Crested or Levaillant's Barbet. *AFA Watchbird* **25(4)**: 42-44.
Thompson, I.D., Hogan, H.A. & Montevecchi, W.A. (1999). Avian communities of mature balsam fir forests in Newfoundland: age-dependence and implications for timber harvesting. *Condor* **101(2)**: 311-323.
Thompson, M.C. (1966). Birds from north Borneo. *Univ. Kansas Publ. Mus. Nat. Hist.* **17**: 377-433.
Thompson, M.C. (1994). Unusual death of a Red-bellied Woodpecker. *Kansas Orn. Soc. Bull.* **45**: 23-24.
Thompson, P.M., Harvey, W.G., Johnson, D.L., Millin, D.J., Rashid, S.M.A., Scott, D.A., Stanford, C. & Woolner, J.D. (1993). Recent notable bird records from Bangladesh. *Forktail* **9**: 12-44.
Thompson, R.L. ed. (1971). *The Ecology and Management of the Red-cockaded Woodpecker*. Bureau of Sport Fisheries & Wildlife & Tall Timbers Research Station, Tallahassee, Florida.
Thomson, M. (1993). Scaly-throated Honeyguide at Redelinghuys. *Promerops* **207**: 14-15.
Thorstrom, R., Ramos, J. & Castillo, J.M. (1991). Breeding biology of the Collared Forest-falcon (*Micrastur semitorquatus*). Pp. 127-131 in: *Progress Report IV, Maya Project*. The Peregrine Fund, Boise, Idaho.
Throp, J.L. (1957). Keeping the Pale-billed Woodpecker. *Avicult. Mag.* **63**: 149-151.
Thurber, W.A., Serrano, J.F., Sermeño, A. & Benítez, M. (1987). *Status of Uncommon and Previously Unreported Birds of El Salvador*. Proceedings of the Western Foundation of Vertebrate Zoology **3(3)**. 184 pp.
Tiebout, H.M. (1986). Downy Woodpecker feeds on insects in a spider's web. *Wilson Bull.* **98(2)**: 319.
Tilahun, S., Edwards, S. & Egziabher, T.B.G. eds. (1996). *Important Bird Areas of Ethiopia. A First Inventory*. Ethiopian Wildlife and Natural History Society, Addis Ababa.
Timmins, R.J., Evans, T.D. & Duckworth, J.W. (1993). *A Wildlife and Habitat Survey of the Dong Hua Sao Proposed Protected Area*. National Office for Nature Conservation & Watershed Management, Vientiane, Laos.
Tirimanne, W. (1978). Bleak future for the Black-backed Woodpecker. *Loris* **14(6)**: 396-397.
Tjernberg, M., Johnson, K. & Nilsson, S.G. (1993). Density variation and breeding success of the Black Woodpecker *Dryocopus martius* in relation to forest fragmentation. *Ornis Fenn.* **70(3)**: 155-162. In English with Swedish summary.
Tobalske, B.W. (1992). Evaluating habitat suitability using relative abundance and fledging success of Red-naped Sapsuckers. *Condor* **94(2)**: 550-553.
Tobalske, B.W. (1996). Scaling of muscle composition, wing morphology, and intermittent flight behavior in woodpeckers. *Auk* **113(1)**: 151-177.
Tobalske, B.W. (1997). Lewis' Woodpecker (*Melanerpes lewis*). No. **284** in: Poole, A.F. & Gill, F.B. eds. (1997). *The Birds of North America*. Vol. 8. Academy of Natural Sciences & American Ornithologists' Union, Philadelphia & Washington, D.C.
Tobalske, C. & Tobalske, B.W. (1999). Using atlas data to model the distribution of woodpecker species in the Jura, France. *Condor* **101(3)**: 472-483.
Tobias, J.A., Catsis, M.C. & Williams, R.S.R. (1993). *Notes on Scarce Birds Observed in Southern and Eastern Brazil: 24 July to 7 September 1993*. Published privately.
Tobias, J.A., Davidson, P. & Robichaud, W. (1998). Nakai-Nam Theun: can development save one of South-east Asia's last wildernesses? *Bull. Oriental Bird Club* **28**: 24-29.
Tobin, J. & Rundel, R.S. (1975). World's first captive breeding of the Plate-billed Mountain Toucan and a few insights. *AFA Watchbird* **11**: 6-7.
Todd, F.S., Gale, N.B. & Thompson, D. (1973). Breeding Crimson-rumped Toucanets at Los Angeles Zoo. *Int. Zoo Yb.* **13**: 117-120.
Todd, W. (1979). Breeding notes on the Acorn Woodpecker *Melanerpes formicivorus* at the Houston Zoological Gardens. *Avicult. Mag.* **85(2)**: 68-74.
Todd, W.E.C. (1919). Descriptions of apparently new Colombian birds. *Proc. Biol. Soc. Washington* **32**: 113-118.
Todd, W.E.C. (1925). Four new birds from Brazil. *Proc. Biol. Soc. Washington* **38**: 111-114.
Todd, W.E.C. (1937). New South American birds. *Ann. Carnegie Mus.* **25**: 243-255.
Todd, W.E.C. (1943a). Studies in the jacamars and puff-birds. *Ann. Carnegie Mus.* **30**: 1-18.
Todd, W.E.C. (1943b). Critical remarks on the toucans. *Proc. Biol. Soc. Washington* **56**: 153-162.
Todd, W.E.C. (1947). Further note on the *Ramphastos ambiguus* of Swainson. *Proc. Biol. Soc. Washington* **60**: 17-18.
Todd, W.E.C. & Carriker, M.A. (1922). *The Birds of the Santa Marta Region of Colombia: a Study in Altitudinal Distribution*. Annals of the Carnegie Museum **14**. 609 pp.
Todd, W.E.C. & Worthington, W.W. (1911). A contribution to the ornithology of the Bahama Islands. *Ann. Carnegie Mus.* **7(3-4)**: 388-464.
Toland, B. & Elder, W.H. (1984). Red-headed Woodpeckers defend occupied American Kestrel nest. *J. Field Orn.* **55(2)**: 250.
Tombal, J.C. (1993a). Historique et état actuel des populations de Pic mar (*Dendrocopos medius*) dans la région Nord-Pas-de-Calais. *Aves* **30(2)**: 232-235.
Tombal, J.C. (1993b). Conditions biogéographiques et écologiques conditionnant la distribution du Pic mar *Dendrocopos medius* dans la région Nord-pas-de-Calais. *Heron* **26(1)**: 5-12.
Tombal, J.C. (1993c). Données historiques sur le Pic mar *Dendrocopos medius* dans la région Nord-pas-de-Calais. *Heron* **26(1)**: 13-20, 21-27.
Tombal, J.C. (1993d). Le Pic mar *Dendrocopos medius* en forêt de Mormal, Nord en 1991, 1992 et 1993. *Heron* **26(1)**: 45-48.
Tomec, M. & Kilimann, N. (1998). Zum Gruenspechtvorkommen (*Picus viridis*) im Ruhrgebiet am Beispiel von Oberhausen/Bottrop und Herne. *Charadrius* **34(3-4)**: 144-154.
Tomialojc, L. (1990). *Ptaki Polski: Rozmieszczenie i Liczebnosc*. [*The Birds of Poland: Their Distribution and Abundance*]. Panstwowe Wydawnictwo Naukowe, Warszawa. In Polish with English summary.
Tomialojc, L. (1994). Wryneck *Jynx torquilla*. Pp. 342-343 in: Tucker, G.M. & Heath, M.F. (1994). *Birds in Europe: their Conservation Status*. BirdLife Conservation Series **3**. BirdLife International, Cambridge.
Tomialojc, L. (2000). Did White-backed Woodpeckers ever breed in Britain? *British Birds* **93(9)**: 453-456.
Toone, R.A. (1993). New locations for Three-toed Woodpecker at the Manti-la Sal National Forest, with comments on survey methods. *Utah Birds* **9(1)**: 1-9.
Tooth, E.E. (1901). Nesting difficulties of the Coppersmith. *J. Bombay Nat. Hist. Soc.* **13**: 713-714.
Torres, A. (1988). Observación de una agresión de Cao Montero (*Corvus nasicus*) a un nido de Carpintero Jabado (*Melanerpes s. superciliaris*). *Garciana* **12**: 4.
Tostain, O. (1980). Contribution à l'ornithologie de la Guyane française. *Oiseau et RFO* **50**: 47-62.
Tostain, O., Dujardin, J.L., Érard, C. & Thiollay, J.M. (1992). *Oiseaux de Guyane*. Société d'Études Ornithologiques, Brunoy, France.
Towles, D.T. (1989). *A Comparative Analysis of the Foraging Behavior of Male and Female Red-bellied Woodpeckers (*Melanerpes carolinus*) in Central Kentucky*. MSc thesis, Eastern Kentucky University, Richmond.
Townsend, C.W. (1932). Are rings of holes in tree bark made by Downy Woodpeckers? *Condor* **34(2)**: 61-65.
Trail, P.W. (1980). Ecological correlates of social organization in a communally breeding bird, the Acorn Woodpecker, *Melanerpes formicivorus*. *Behav. Ecol. Sociobiol.* **7(2)**: 83-92.
Trail, P.W. (1991). Nest predation by a Red-bellied Woodpecker. *Chat* **55(1)**: 6-7.
Travis, J. (1977). Seasonal foraging in a Downy Woodpecker population. *Condor* **79(3)**: 371-375.
Traylor, M.A. (1951a). Notes on some Peruvian birds. *Fieldiana Zool.* **31**: 613-621.
Traylor, M.A. (1951b). Notes on the barbets genus *Eubucco* (Capitonidae) in southern Peru. *Auk* **68(4)**: 508-510.
Traylor, M.A. (1951c). A revision of the woodpeckers *Chrysoptilus melanochloros* and *C. melanolaimus*. *Fieldiana Zool.* **31**: 195-200.
Traylor, M.A. (1952). Notes on birds from the Marcapata Valley, Cuzco, Peru. *Fieldiana Zool.* **34**: 17-23.
Traylor, M.A. (1958). Birds of north-eastern Peru. *Fieldiana Zool.* **35(5)**: 87-141.
Traylor, M.A. (1960). Notes on the birds of Angola, non-passeres. *Publ. Cult. Co. Diamantes Angola* **54**: 129-186.
Traylor, M.A. (1963). *Check-list of Angolan Birds*. Publicações Culturais **61**. Companhia de Diamantes de Angola, Lisboa. 250 pp.
Traylor, M.A. (1965). A collection of birds from Barotseland and Bechuanaland. *Ibis* **107(2)**: 137-172.
Traylor, M.A. & Parelius, D. (1967). A collection of birds from the Ivory Coast. *Fieldiana Zool.* **51**: 91-117.
Trochet, J., Morlan, J. & Roberson, D. (1988). First record of the Three-toed Woodpecker in California. *Western Birds* **19(3)**: 109-115.
Troetschler, R.G. (1974). Ageing Acorn Woodpecker. *Western Bird Bander* **49**: 67-69.
Troetschler, R.G. (1976). Acorn Woodpecker breeding strategy as affected by starling nest-hole competition. *Condor* **78(2)**: 151-165.
Trombino, C. (1998). *Species Interactions in the Hybrid Zone between Red-breasted (*Sphyrapicus ruber*) and Red-naped (*Sphyrapicus nuchalis*) Sapsuckers: Fitness Consequences, Reproductive Character Displacement, and Nest Site Selection*. PhD dissertation, Northern Illinois University, DeKalb, Illinois.
Trombino, C. (2000). Helping behavior within sapsuckers (*Sphyrapicus* spp.). *Wilson Bull.* **112(2)**: 273-275.
Truslow, F.K. (1967). Egg-carrying by the Pileated Woodpecker. *Living Bird* **6**: 227-236.
Tsai Hangyeh (1985). Distribution and status of birds in northern Taiwan. Pp. 163-186 in: Anon. (1985). *The Third East-Asian Bird Protection Conference. Tokyo, Japan 29-31 May 1985*. Wild Bird Society of Japan, Tokyo.
Tubelis, D.P. (2000). Mudanças na abundância de espécies de aves em cerrados *sensu stricto* em função da distância a matas de galeria, na região de Brasília. Pp. 199-200 in: Straube *et al.* (2000).
Tubelis, D.P. & Cavalcanti, R.B. (2001). Community similarity and abundance of bird species in open habitats of a central Brazilian cerrado. *Orn. Neotropical* **12(1)**: 57-73. In English with Portuguese summary.
Tubelis, D.P. & Tomás, W.M. (1999). Distribution of birds in a naturally patchy forest environment in the Pantanal wetland, Brazil. *Ararajuba* **7(2)**: 81-89.
Tucker, J.J. (1975). Host record for the Greater Honeyguide (*Indicator indicator*). *Bull. Zambian Orn. Soc.* **7**: 37.
Tucker, J.J. (1976). Host record for the Greater Honeyguide (*Indicator indicator*). *Bull. Zambian Orn. Soc.* **8**: 29.
Tutt, H.R. (1951). Data on the excavation of the nest hole and feeding of the young of Green Woodpecker (*Picus viridis*). Pp. 555-562 in: Hörstadius, S. ed. (1951). *Proceedings of the X Ornithological Congress, Uppsala, June 1950*. Almqvist & Wiksell, Uppsala, Sweden.
Tykader, B.K. (1984). *Birds of Andaman & Nicobar Islands*. Zoological Survey of India, Calcutta.
Tyler, J.D. (1979). Nest of Lewis' Woodpecker in Cimmarron County, Oklahoma. *Bull. Okla. Orn. Soc.* **12(2)**: 14-15.
Tymstra, R., Connop, S. & Tshering, C. (1997). Some bird observations from central Bhutan, May 1994. *Forktail* **12**: 49-60.
Tyroller, G. (1974). Duett-Entwicklung bei handaufgezogenen Bartvögeln (*Trachyphonus d'arnaudii* [sic] *emini*). *Z. Tierpsychol.* **35**: 102-107.
Ueta, M. & Yamaguchi, Y. (1997). [Habitat preference of Lidth's Jays, White-backed Woodpeckers, and Japanese Wood Pigeons in Anami Island, southern Japan]. *Strix* **15**: 69-74. In Japanese with English summary.
Ullman, M. (1995). Tretåig hackspett. *Vår Fågelvärld* **4**: 31-32.
Underdown, C.E. (1929). A note on *Brachygalba goeringi sclater*. *Auk* **46**: 240.
Underhill, G.D. (1991). Lesser Honeyguide in the southwest Cape. *Promerops* **197**: 16.
Underhill, G.D. & Underhill, L.G. (1992a). First capture dates of Lesser Honeyguides at two localities in the southwestern Cape Province. *Safring News* **21(1)**: 7-10.

Underhill, G.D. & Underhill, L.G. (1992b). Cardinal Woodpecker at Durbanville Nature Reserve. *Promerops* **204**: 9.
Underhill, L.G., Underhill, G.D., Martin, C.G.C. & Fraser, M.W. (1995). Primary moult, wing-length and mass of the Lesser Honeyguide *Indicator minor*. *Bull. Brit. Orn. Club* **115(4)**: 229-234.
Underwood, B.A. (1992). Notes on the Orange-rumped Honeyguide *Indicator xanthonotus* and its association with the Himalayan honey bee *Apis laboriosa*. *J. Bombay Nat. Hist. Soc.* **89(3)**: 290-295.
Unitt, P. (1986). Another hybrid Downy x Nuttall's Woodpecker from San Diego County. *Western Birds* **17(1)**: 43-44.
Urban, E.K. (1959). *Birds from Coahuila, Mexico*. University of Kansas Publications, Museum of Natural History **11(8)**. University of Kansas, Lawrence, Kansas. 74 pp.
Urban, E.K. (1980). *Ethiopia's Endemic Birds*. Ethiopian Tourism Organization, Addis Ababa.
Urban, E.K. & Brown, L.H. (1971). *A Checklist of the Birds of Ethiopia*. Addis Ababa University Press, Addis Ababa.
Urben-Filho, A., Gatto, C.A.F.R. & Straube, F.C. (2000). Avifauna do Parque Estadual do Cerrado, Jaguariaíva, Paraná. Pp. 347-348 in: Straube *et al.* (2000).
Väisänen, R.A. & Koskimies, P. (1989). [Winter birds in Finland in 1988/89: their long-term trends and densities in different habitats]. *Lintumies* **24**: 190-203. In Finnish with English summary.
Väisänen, R.A., Järvinen, O. & Rauhala, P. (1986). How are extensive, human-caused habitat alterations expressed on the scale of local bird populations in boreal forests? *Ornis Scand.* **17**: 282-292.
Vallely, A.C. & Whitman, A.A. (1997). The birds of Hill Bank, northern Belize. *Cotinga* **8**: 39-49.
Valli, E. & Summers, D. (1988). *Honey Hunters of Nepal*. Thames & Hudson Ltd, London.
Van der Merwe, F. (1986). Of Lesser Honeyguide, Olive Woodpeckers and European Starlings. *Promerops* **176**: 8-10.
Van Tyne, J. (1926). An unusual flight of Arctic Three-toed Woodpeckers. *Auk* **43(4)**: 469-474.
Van Tyne, J. (1929). The life history of the toucan *Ramphastos brevicarinatus*. *Misc. Publ. Univ. Mich. Mus. Zool.* **19**: 1-43.
Van Tyne, J. (1935). *The Birds of Northern Petén, Guatemala*. Miscellaneous Publications Museum of Zoology University of Michigan **27**. 50 pp.
Van Tyne, J. & Koelz, W. (1936). Seven new birds from the Punjab. *Occas. Pap. Mus. Zool. Univ. Mich.* **334**: 1-6.
Vande weghe, J.P. (1974). Additions et corrections á l'avifaune de Rwanda. *Rev. Zool. Afr.* **88**: 81-98.
Vande weghe, J.P. (1980). Distribution géographique et eco-climatique de deux formes du Barbion à croupion jaune, *Pogoniulus bilineatus*, au Rwanda et au Burundi. *Gerfaut* **70**: 487-497.
Vande weghe, J.P. (1981). Sympatrie du Pic goertan, *Dendrocopos goertae*, et du Pic olive, *Dendrocopos griseocephalus*, au Rwanda et au Burundi. *Gerfaut* **71**: 41-46.
Vande weghe, J.P. (1992). New records for Uganda and Tanzania along the Rwandan and Burundian borders. *Scopus* **16**: 59-60.
Varisco, D.M., Ross, J.M. & Milroy, A. (1992). *Biological Diversity Assessment of the Republic of Yemen*. ICBP Study Report **52**, Cambridge. 130 pp.
Varona, L.S. (1980). Protection in Cuba. *Oryx* **15(3)**: 282-284.
Varty, N., Adams, J., Espin, P. & Hambler, C. (1986). *An Ornithological Survey of Lake Tota, Colombia, 1982*. ICBP Study Report **12**, Cambridge. 103 pp.
Vaurie, C. (1959a). Systematic notes on Palearctic birds. No. 34. Picidae: the genera *Picus* and *Dryocopus*. *Amer. Mus. Nov.* **1945**: 1-21.
Vaurie, C. (1959b). Systematic notes on Palearctic birds. No. 35. Picidae: the genus *Dendrocopos*. Part I. *Amer. Mus. Nov.* **1946**: 1-29.
Vaurie, C. (1959c). Systematic notes on Palearctic birds. No. 36. Picidae: the genera *Dendrocopos* (Part II) and *Picoides*. *Amer. Mus. Nov.* **1951**: 1-24.
Vaurie, C. (1959d). Systematic notes on Palearctic birds. No. 37. Picidae: the subfamilies Jynginae and Picumninae. *Amer. Mus. Nov.* **1963**: 1-16.
Vaurie, C. (1972). *Tibet and its Birds*. H.F. & G. Witherby Ltd, London.
Vélez, J.H. & Velázquez, J.I. (1998). Aves del municipio de Manizales y áreas adyacentes. *Bol. Soc. Antioqueña Orn.* **9**: 38-60.
Venables, A. & Collopy, M.W. (1989). *Seasonal Foraging and Habitat Requirements of Red-headed Woodpeckers in North-central Florida*. Final Report **GFC-84-006**. Nongame Wildlife Program. Florida Game & Fresh Water Fish Commission, Tallahassee, Florida.
Venturini, A.C., Pacheco, M., de Paz, P.R. & Petronetto do Carmo, L. (2001). Contribução ao conhecimento das aves da região centro Serrana do Espírito Santo: municípios de Santa Maria do Jetibá e Itarana. Part 2. *Atualidades Orn.* **99**: 12.
Verea, C. & Solórzano, A. (1998). La avifauna del sotobosque de una selva decidua tropical en Venezuela. *Orn. Neotropical* **9(2)**: 161–176. In Spanish with English summary.
Verea, C. & Solórzano, A. (2001). La comunidad de aves del sotobosque de un bosque deciduo tropical en Venezuela. *Orn. Neotropical* **12(3)**: 235–253. In Spanish with English summary.
Verea, C., Fernández-Badillo, A. & Solórzano, A. (2000). Variación en la composición de las comunidades de aves de sotobosque de dos bosques en el norte de Venezuela. *Orn. Neotropical* **11(1)**: 65-79. In Spanish with English summary.
Verea, C., Solórzano, A. & Fernández-Badillo, A. (1999). Pesos y distribución de aves del sotobosque del Parque Nacional Henri Pittier al norte de Venezuela. *Orn. Neotropical* **10(2)**: 217-231.
Verheugt, W.J.M., Skov, H. & Danielsen, F. (1993). Notes on the birds of the tidal lowlands and floodplains of South Sumatra Province, Indonesia. *Kukila* **6(2)**: 53-84.
Verheyen, R. (1953). *Oiseaux. Pt. 19. Exploration du Parc National de l'Upemba*. Institut de Parcs Nationale du Congo Belge, Bruxelles.
Verheyen, R. (1955a). Contribution à la systématique des Piciformes basée sur l'anatomie comparée. *Bull. Inst. Roy. Sci. Nat. Belgique* **31(50)**: 1-24.
Verheyen, R. (1955b). Contribution à la systématique des Piciformes basée sur l'anatomie comparée. *Bull. Inst. Roy. Sci. Nat. Belgique* **31(51)**: 1-19.
Verley, D. (1974). Nesting of the Jamaican Woodpecker. *Gosse Bird Club Broadsheet* **23**: 5-7.
Vernon, C.J. (1974). *Prodotiscus regulus* parasitising *Cameroptera brevicaudata*. *Ostrich* **45**: 261.
Vernon, C.J. (1980). Bird parties in central and south Africa. Pp. 313-325 in: Johnson (1980).
Vernon, C.J. (1987a). On the Eastern Green-backed Honeyguide. *Honeyguide* **33**: 6-12.
Vernon, C.J. (1987b). Bill hooks of *Prodotiscus* nestlings. *Ostrich* **58(4)**: 187.
Vernon, C.J., Macdonald, I.A.W. & Dean, W.R.J. (1989). Birds of an isolated tropical lowland rainforest in eastern Zimbabwe. *Ostrich* **14**(Suppl.): 111-122.
Versaw, A.E. (1998). Three-toed Woodpecker. Pp. 264-265 in: Kingery, H.E. ed. (1998). *Colorado Breeding Bird Atlas*. Colorado Bird Atlas Partnership and Colorado Wildlife Division, Denver, Colorado.
Vierling, K.T. (1997). Habitat selection of Lewis's Woodpeckers in southeastern Colorado. *Wilson Bull.* **109(1)**: 121-130.
Vierling, K.T. (1998). Interactions between European Starlings and Lewis's Woodpeckers at nest cavities. *J. Field Orn.* **69(3)**: 376-379.
Vijayaraghavan, B. (1957). Drumming of the Malabar Golden-backed Woodpecker *Brachypternus benghalensis*. *J. Bombay Nat. Hist. Soc.* **54(2)**: 461-462.
Villarán, A. (1999). Contenido estomacal de un ejemplar de Pito Negro *Dryocopus martius* en la Cordillera Cantábrica (Asturias). [Stomach content of a Black Woodpecker *Dryocopus martius* in the Cantabrian Mountains (Asturias)]. *Butll. Grup Català d'Anellament* **16**: 47-52. In Spanish with English summary.
Villard, M.A. & Schieck, J. (1997). Immediate post-fire nesting by Black-backed Woodpeckers, *Picoides arcticus*, in northern Alberta. *Can. Field-Nat.* **111(3)**: 478-479.
Villard, P. (1991). Utilisation de l'espace chez le Pic mar *Dendrocopos medius*: intérêt de la radiotélémétrie. *Oiseau et RFO* **61**: 101-110.
Villard, P. (1994). Foraging behavior of Black-backed and Three-toed Woodpeckers during spring and summer in a Canadian boreal forest. *Can. J. Zool.* **72(1)**: 1957-1959.
Villard, P. (1995). Flux génétique entre populations et fidelité des couples pour une espèce endémique et insulaire, le Pic de Guadeloupe. *Pitirre* **8(3)**: 12. (Abstract).
Villard, P. (1997). Are hurricanes a key factor for the ecology of the Guadeloupe Woodpecker? *Pitirre* **10(3)**: 111. (Abstract).
Villard, P. (1999a). *The Guadeloupe Woodpecker and other Islands* Melanerpes. Société d'Études Ornithologiques de France, Brunoy, France. 136 pp.
Villard, P. (1999b). Vivre sous les tropiques: l'exemple du Pic de la Guadeloupe. *Le Courrier de la Nature* **178**: 24-28.
Villard, P. (1999c). The Jamaican Woodpecker. *BirdLife Jamaica Broadsheet* **(72/73)**: 45.
Villard, P. (2000). Manipulation des proies et diversité du régime alimentaire du Pic de la Guadeloupe *Melanerpes herminieri*. *Alauda* **68(4)**: 257-264.
Villard, P. (2001). Les *Melanerpes* insulaires. *Alauda* **69(1)**: 159-160.
Villard, P. & Beninger, C.W. (1993). Foraging behavior of male Black-backed and Hairy Woodpeckers in a forest burn. *J. Field Orn.* **64(1)**: 71-76.
Villard, P. & Pavis, C. (1998). Diet of nestling Guadeloupe Woodpeckers. *J. Field Orn.* **69(3)**: 415-418.
Villard, P. & Peacock, M. (1999). Structure génétique inter et intra-populationnelle et comportement d'accouplement chez une espèce endémique, le Pic de la Guadeloupe *Melanerpes herminieri*. *Alauda* **67(4)**: 350.
Villard, P. & Pradel, R. (1998). Dynamique des populations du Pic de la Guadeloupe, *Melanerpes herminieri*. Population dynamics of the Guadeloupe Woodpecker, *Melanerpes herminieri*. *Pitirre* **11(2)**: 50. In French and English.
Villard, P. & Rousteau, A. (1998). Habitats, density, population size, and the future of the Guadeloupe Woodpecker (*Melanerpes heminieri*). *Orn. Neotropical* **9(2)**: 121-128.
Villard, P., Ferry, C. & Frochot, B. (1987). Woodpecker densities in old oak-forests and changes from 1960 to 1985. *Acta Oecol.* **8(2)**: 321-322.
Villeneuve, J. (1936). Sur la sève des arbres dans le régime des pics. *Alauda* **8(2)**: 262-263.
Vince, M. (1998). Handrearing the Green Aracari. *AFA Watchbird* **25(2)**: 62-63.
Vincent, A.W. (1946). On the breeding habits of some African birds. *Ibis* **88(3)**: 306-326.
Vincent, J. (1935). The birds of northern Portuguese East Africa. Part VI. *Ibis* **Ser. 13, no. 5**: 1-37.
Viney, C. & Phillipps, K. (1983). *Birds of Hong Kong*. Government Printer, Hong Kong.
Virkkala, R., Alanko, T., Laine, T. & Tiainen, J. (1993). Population contraction of the White-backed Woodpecker *Dendrocopos leucotos* in Finland as a consequence of habitat alteration. *Biol. Conserv.* **66**: 47-53.
Vitkauskas, N. & Raudonikis, L. (1989). [New breeding grounds of the Grey-headed Woodpecker *Picus canus* in Lithuania]. *Acta Orn. Lituanica* **1**: 131-132. In Russian with Lithuanian summary.
Vo Quy & Nguyen Cu (1995). *Checklist of the Birds of Viet Nam*. Centre for Natural Resources & Environmental Studies, Vietnam National University, Hanoi.
Volman, S.F., Grubb, T.C. & Schuett, K.C. (1997). Relative hippocampal volume in relation to food-storing behavior in four species of woodpeckers. *Brain Behav. Evol.* **49(2)**: 110-120.
Voous, K.H. (1947). *On the History of the Distribution of the Genus* Dendrocopos. Limosa **20(1-3)**. 143 pp. In English with Dutch summary.
Voous, K.H. (1961). Birds collected by Carl Lumholtz in eastern and central Borneo. *Nytt. Mag. Zool.* **10**: 127-180.
Voous, K.H. (1961). Geographical variation in the Black Woodpecker. *Bull. Brit. Orn. Club* **81**: 62-66.
Vowles, G.A. & Vowles, R.S. eds. (1997). *An Annotated Checklist of the Birds of Brunei*. Published privately.
de Vries, P.J. (1994). Patterns of butterfly diversity and promising topics in natural history and ecology. Pp. 189–194 in: McDade *et al.* (1994).
Vuilleumier, F. (1985). Forest birds of Patagonia: ecological geography, speciation, endemism, and faunal history. Pp. 255-304 in: Buckley *et al.* (1985).
Vuilleumier, F., LeCroy, M. & Mayr, E. (1992). New species of birds described from 1981 to 1990. Pp. 267-309 in: Monk (1992).
Wabakken, P. (1973). Observasjoner fra Graspett- og Tretaspettreir. [Observations at nests of Grey-headed and Three-toed Woodpeckers]. *Fauna* **26(1)**: 1-6. In Norwegian with English summary.
Wacher, T. (1993). Some new observations of forest birds in The Gambia. *Malimbus* **15(1)**: 24-37.
Wagner, H.O. (1944). Notes on the life history of the Emerald Toucanet. *Wilson Bull.* **56(1)**: 65-76.
Wagner, S.J. & Miller, S.M. (1986). Northern Flicker nesting on the ground. *Chat* **50(1)**: 20-22.
Waite, H.W. (1938). Some interesting records of birds in the Punjab. A correction. *J. Bombay Nat. Hist. Soc.* **40(2)**: 328-329.
Waite, H.W. (1948). The birds of the Punjab Salt range (Pakistan). *J. Bombay Nat. Hist. Soc.* **48(1)**: 97-117.
Waite, T.A. & Grubb, T.C. (1988). Copying of foraging locations in mixed-species flocks of temperate-deciduous woodland birds: an experimental study. *Condor* **90(1)**: 132-140.
Waiyaki, E. & Bennun, L.A. (2000). The avifauna of coastal forests in southern Kenya: status and conservation. Proceedings of the Ninth Pan-African Ornithological Congress, Accra, Ghana, 1-7 December 1996. *Ostrich* **71(1&2)**: 247-256.
Walasz, K. & Mielczarek, P. eds. (1992). *The Atlas of Breeding Birds in Malopolska 1985-1991 (Southeastern Poland)*. Biologica Silesiae, Wroclaw, Poland. In Polish and English.
de Wald, D.D. (1988). Channel-billed Toucans. *AFA Watchbird* **15(1)**: 36-37.
Waldbauer, G.P., Sternburg, J.G., George, W.G. & Scarbrough, A.G. (1970). Hairy and Downy woodpecker attacks on cocoons of urban *Hyalophora cecropia* and other Saturniids (Lepidoptera). *Ann. Entomol. Soc. Amer.* **63(5)**: 1366-1369.
Walker, B. (2001). *Field Guide to the Birds of Machu Picchu*. PROFONANPE & Machu Picchu Program, Lima.
Walker, D. (1976). Jamaican Woodpecker. *Gosse Bird Club Broadsheet* **27**: 19, 21.
Walker, K.M. (1952). Northward extension of range of the Acorn Woodpecker in Oregon. *Condor* **54(5)**: 315.
Wallace, G.E. (2001). Cuba: so close, yet so far. *Birding* **33(2)**: 128-139.
Wallace, R.A. (1969). *Sexual Dimorphism, Niche Utilization, and Social Behavior of Insular Species of Woodpeckers*. PhD thesis, University of Texas, Austin, Texas.
Wallace, R.A. (1974a). Ecological and social implications of sexual dimorphism in five melanerpine woodpeckers. *Condor* **76(3)**: 238-248.
Wallace, R.A. (1974b). Aberrations in the tongue structure of some melanerpine woodpeckers. *Wilson Bull.* **86(1)**: 79-82.
Walters, J.R. (1990). Red-cockaded Woodpeckers: a "primitive" cooperative breeder. Pp. 67-101 in: Stacey, P.B. & Koenig, W.D. eds. (1990). *Cooperative Breeding in Birds. Long-term Studies of Ecology and Behavior*. Cambridge University Press, Cambridge.
Walters, J.R. (1991). Application of ecological principles to the management of endangered species: the case of the Red-cockaded Woodpecker. *Annual Review of Ecology and Systematics* **22**: 505-523.
Walters, J.R., Copeyon, C.K. & Carter, J.H. (1992). Test of the ecological basis of cooperative breeding in Red-cockaded Woodpeckers. *Auk* **109(1)**: 90-97.
Walters, J.R., Doerr, P.D. & Carter, J.H. (1988). The cooperative breeding system of the Red-cockaded Woodpecker. *Ethology* **78(4)**: 275-305.
Walters, J.R., Doerr, P.D. & Carter, J.H. (1992). Delayed dispersal and reproduction as a life-history tactic in cooperative breeders: fitness calculations from Red-cockaded Woodpeckers. *Amer. Naturalist* **139(3)**: 623-643.
Walters, J.R., Hansen, S.K., Carter, J.H., Manor, P.D. & Blue, R.J. (1988). Long-distance dispersal of an adult Red-cockaded Woodpecker. *Wilson Bull.* **100(3)**: 494-496.
Waltert, M., Yaokokore-Beibro, K.H., Mühlenberg, M. & Waitkuwait, W.E. (1999). Preliminary checklist of the birds of the Bossematié area, Ivory Coast. *Malimbus* **21(2)**: 93-109.
Wander, W. & Brady, S.A. (1980). Summer Tanager and Red-headed Woodpecker in the pinelands. *N.J. Audubon* **6(3)**: 34-37.

Wang Sung ed. (1998). *China Red Data Book of Endangered Animals. Aves*. Science Press, Beijing, Hong Kong & New York. In Chinese and English.
Ward, B.S. (1971). Breeding the Black-spotted Barbet at Winged World. *Avicult. Mag.* **77**: 194-195.
Ward, B.S. (1972a). Breeding D'Arnaud's Barbet at Winged World. *Avicult. Mag.* **78**: 52-53.
Ward, B.S. (1972b). Breeding the Toucan Barbet at Winged World. *Avicult. Mag.* **78**: 197-198.
Ward, D. (1986). Vocalizations and associated behaviour of Crested and Black-collared Barbets. *Ostrich* **57(3)**: 129-137.
Ward, D. (1989). The morphology of the syrinx in some southern African barbets (Capitonidae). *Ostrich* **60(1)**: 44-45.
Wardill, J.C. (1995). *The Report of the Ornithological Expedition to the Rawa Aopa Watumohai National Park, South-east Sulawesi, Indonesia. 9th September - 9th November 1995*. Sulawesi '95 Ornithological Expedition & Symbiose Birdwatchers Club, Leeds & Jakarta.
Watling, D. (1983). Ornithological notes from Sulawesi. *Emu* **83**: 247-261.
Watson, J.C., Hooper, R.G., Carlson, D.L., Taylor, W.E. & Milling, T.E. (1995). Restoration of the Red-cockaded Wooodpecker population on the Francis Marion National Forest: three years post Hugo. Pp. 172-182 in: Kulhavy *et al.* (1995).
Watt, D.J. (1980). Red-bellied Woodpecker predation on nestling American Redstarts. *Wilson Bull.* **92(2)**: 249.
Wauer, R.H. (1998). Avian population survey of a Tamaulipan scrub habitat, Tamaulipas, Mexico. *Cotinga* **10**: 13-19.
Weathers, W.W., Koenig, W.D. & Stanback, M.T. (1990). Breeding energetics and thermal ecology of the Acorn Woodpecker in central coastal California. *Condor* **92(2)**: 341-359.
Webb, C.S. (1950). The Plaintive Barbet. *Avicult. Mag.* **56**: 51.
Weber, W.C. (1980). A proposed list of rare and endangered birds species for British Columbia. Pp. 160-182 in: Stace-Smith, R., Johns, L. & Joslin, P. eds. (1980). *Proceedings of the Symposium on Threatened and Endangered Species and Habitats in British Columbia and the Yukon*. British Columbia Ministry of Environment, Victoria.
Weber, W.C. & Cannings, S.R. (1976). The White-headed Woodpecker (*Dendrocopos albolarvatus*) in British Columbia. *Syesis* **9**: 215-220.
Wedgwood, J.A. (1988). Pileated Woodpeckers nest in the Saskatoon district. *Blue Jay* **46(3)**: 142-148.
Wege, D.C. & Long, A.J. (1995). *Key Areas for Threatened Birds in the Neotropics*. BirdLife Conservation Series **5**. BirdLife International, Cambridge.
Wegmüller, P. & Chabloz, V. (1992). Première nidification prouvée du Pic tridactyle *Picoides tridactylus* dans le Jura Vaudois (Suisse). [Proof of the Three-toed Woodpecker *Picoides tridactylus* nesting in the Vaud part of the Swiss Alps]. *Alauda* **61(4)**: 228-230. In French with English summary.
Weikel, J.M. & Hayes, J.P. (1999). The foraging ecology of cavity-nesting birds in young forests of the northern coast range of Oregon. *Condor* **101(1)**: 58-66.
Weinhagen, A.C. (1998). *Nest-site Selection by the Black-backed Woodpecker in Northeastern Vermont*. MSc thesis, University of Vermont, Burlington, Vermont.
Weisser, W. (1973). A mixed pair of sapsuckers in the Sierra Nevada. *Western Birds* **4**: 107-108.
Weldon, P.J. & Rappole, J.H. (1997). A survey of birds odorous or unpalatable to humans: possible indications of chemical defense. *J. Chem. Ecol.* **23(11)**: 2609-2629.
Welford, M.R. (2000). The importance of early successional habitats to rare, restricted-range, and endangered birds in the Ecuadorian Andes. *Bird Conserv. Int.* **10(4)**: 351-359.
Wells, D.R. (1974). Bird report: 1970-1971. *Malay. Nat. J.* **27**: 30-49.
Wells, D.R. (1985). The forest avifauna of western Malesia and its conservation. Pp. 213-232 in: Diamond & Lovejoy (1985).
Wells, D.R. (1990). Malayan bird report: 1986 and 1987. *Malay. Nat. J.* **43**: 172-210.
Wells, D.R. (1999). *The Birds of the Thai-Malay Peninsula*. Vol. 1. Non-passerines. Academic Press, London.
Wells, D.R., Hails, C.J. & Hails, A.J. (1978). *A Study of the Birds of Gunung Mulu National Park, Sarawak, with Special Emphasis on those of Lowland Forest*. Report of the Royal Geographic Society, London.
Welsh, C.E. & Capen, D.E. (1987). Primary cavity-nesting birds and available cavity trees in a northern hardwood forest. *Trans. Northeast Sect. Wildl. Soc.* **44**: 108. (Abstract).
Welsh, C.J.E. & Capen, D.E. (1992). Availability of nesting sites as a limit to woodpecker populations. *For. Ecol. Manage.* **48(1-2)**: 31-41.
Wenny, D.G. & Levey, D.J. (1998). Directed seed dispersal by bellbirds in a tropical cloud forest. *Proc. Natl. Acad. Sci. USA* **95(11)**: 6204-6207.
Wesolowski, T. (1995a). Value of Bialowieza Forest for the conservation of the White-backed Woodpecker *Dendrocopos leucotos* in Poland. *Biol. Conserv.* **71**: 69-75.
Wesolowski, T. (1995b). Ecology and behaviour of White-backed Woodpecker (*Dendrocopos leucotos*) in a primaeval temperate forest (Bialowieza National Park, Poland). *Vogelwarte* **38**: 61-75.
Wesolowski, T. & Tomialojc, L. (1986). The breeding ecology of woodpeckers in a temperate primaeval forest - prelimary data. *Acta Orn., Warszava* **22(1)**: 1-21.
West, J.D. & Speirs, J.M. (1959). The 1956-1957 invasion of Three-toed Woodpeckers. *Wilson Bull.* **71(4)**: 348-363.
West, S. (1976). Observations on the Yellow-eared Toucanet. *Auk* **93(2)**: 381-382.
Weston, S. (1999). Red-shafted/Yellow-shafted Flicker intergrade. *Loon* **71(1)**: 49-50.
Wetmore, A. (1926). *Observations on the Birds of Argentina, Paraguay, Uruguay and Chile*. US National Museum Bulletin **133**. Smithsonian Institution, Washington, D.C. 448 pp.
Wetmore, A. (1939). *Observations on the Birds of Northern Venezuela*. Proceedings of the US National Museum **87**. Smithsonian Institution, Washington, D.C. 87 pp.
Wetmore, A. (1943). *The Birds of Southern Veracruz, Mexico*. Proceedings of the US National Museum **93**. 126 pp.
Wetmore, A. (1948). The Golden-fronted Woodpeckers of Texas and northern Mexico. *Wilson Bull.* **60(3)**: 185-186.
Wetmore, A. (1953). Further additions to the birds of Panama and Colombia. *Smiths. Misc. Coll.* **122(8)**: 1-12.
Wetmore, A. (1957). *The Birds of Isla Coiba, Panamá*. Smithsonian Miscellaneous Collections **134**. Smithsonian Institution, Washington, D.C. 105 pp.
Wetmore, A. (1968a). *The Birds of the Republic of Panama*. Vol. 2. Columbidae (Pigeons) to Picidae (Woodpeckers). Smithsonian Miscellaneous Collections **150**. Smithsonian Institution, Washington, D.C. 605 pp.
Wetmore, A. (1968b). Additions to the list of birds recorded from Colombia. *Wilson Bull.* **80(3)**: 325-326.
Wetmore, A. & Swales, B.H. (1931). *The Birds of Haiti and the Dominican Republic*. US National Museum Bulletin **155**. Smithsonian Institution, Washington, D.C. 483 pp.
Wetmore, A., Pasquier, R.E. & Olson, S.L. (1984). *The Birds of the Republic of Panama*. Vol. 4. Passeriformes: Hirundinidae (swallows) to Fringillidae (finches). Smithsonian Miscellaneous Collections **150**, Smithsonian Institution, Washington, D.C. 670 pp.
Wexler, P. (1996). Breeding the Fulvous-breasted Woodpecker at Birdworld. *Avicult. Mag.* **102(1)**: 18-20.
Wheatley, N. (1994). *Where to Watch Birds in South America*. Christopher Helm, London.
Wheatley, N. (1995). *Where to Watch Birds in Africa*. Christopher Helm, London.
Wheatley, N. (1996). *Where to Watch Birds in Asia*. Christopher Helm, London.
Wheelwright, N.T. (1991). How long do fruit-eating birds stay in the plants where they feed? *Biotropica* **23(1)**: 29-40.
Wheelwright, N.T., Haber, W.A., Murray, K.G. & Guindon, C. (1984). Tropical fruit-eating birds and their food plants: a survey of Costa Rican lower montane forest. *Biotropica* **16(3)**: 173-192.
Whistler, H. (1941). *Popular Handbook of Indian Birds*. 3rd edition. Gurney & Jackson, London.
Whistler, H. (1944). *The Avifaunal Survey of Ceylon, Conducted Jointly by the British and Colombo Museums*. Spolia Zeylanica **23**. 203 pp.
Whistler, H. & Kinnear, N.B. (1935). The Vernay scientific survey of the Eastern Ghats. Part IX. *J. Bombay Nat. Hist. Soc.* **37**: 515-528.
White, A.W. (1998). Birding southern Abaco: a selection from ABA's upcoming birdfinding guide to the Bahama Islands. *Birding* **30(3)**: 196-207.
White, C.M.N. (1953). Systematic and distributional notes on African birds. *Bull. Brit. Orn. Club* **73(7)**: 76-77.
White, C.M.N. (1977). Notes on some non-passerine birds of Wallacea. *Bull. Brit. Orn. Club* **97(3)**: 99-103.
White, C.M.N. & Bruce, M.D. (1986). *The Birds of Wallacea (Sulawesi, The Moluccas & Lesser Sunda Islands, Indonesia). An Annotated Check-list*. BOU Check-list **7**. British Ornithologists' Union, London.
Whitehead, C.H.T. (1911). On the birds of Kohat and the Kurram Valley, northern India. Part 2. *J. Bombay Nat. Hist. Soc.* **20(3)**: 776-799.
Whitmore, T.C. (1990). *An Introduction to Tropical Rain Forests*. Clarendon Press & Oxford University Press, Oxford.
Whittaker, A. (1996). Observations of a group of Red-necked Aracaris (*Pteroglossus bitorquatus*) attacking a vine snake (*Oxybelis fulgidus*) in Rondonia, Brazil. *Orn. Neotropical* **7**: 67-68.
Whittaker, A. & Oren, D.C. (1999). Important ornithological records from the Río Juruá, western Amazonia, including twelve additions to the Brazilian avifauna. *Bull. Brit. Orn. Club* **119(4)**: 235-260.
Whittaker, A., Carvalhaes, A.M.P. & Pacheco, J.F. (1995). Rediscovery of the Chestnut-headed Nunlet *Nonnula amaurocephala* in Amazonian Brazil. *Cotinga* **3**: 48-50.
Wickler, W. (1973). Artunterschiede in Duettgesang zwischen *Trachyphonus d'arnaudii* [sic] *usambiro* und den anderen Unterarten von *T. d'arnaudii* [sic]. *J. Orn.* **114(1)**: 123-128.
Wickler, W. & Uhrig, D. (1969). Bettelrufe, Antwortszeit und Rassenunterschiede im Begrüssungsduett des Schmuckbartvogels *Trachyphonus darnaudii*. *Z. Tierpsychol.* **26**: 651-661.
Wickman, B.E. (1965). Black-backed Three-toed Woodpecker, *Picoides arcticus*, predation on *Monochamus oregonensis* (Coleoptera: Cerambycidae). *Pan-pacific Entomol.* **41**: 162-164.
Wiebe, K.L. (2000). Assortative mating by color in a population of hybrid Northern Flickers. *Auk* **117(2)**: 525-529.
Wiebe, K.L. (2001). Microclimate of tree cavity nests: is it important for reproductive success in Northern Flickers? *Auk* **118(2)**: 412-412.
Wiebe, K.L. & Swift, T.L. (2001). Clutch size relative to nest size in Northern Flickers using tree cavities. *J. Avian Biol.* **32**: 167-173.
Wiedenfeld, D.A., Messick, L.R. & James, F.C. (1992). *Population Trends in 65 Species of North American Birds. 1966 - 1990*. Final Report to National Fish & Wildlife Foundation. US Fish & Wildlife Service & USDA Forest Service.
Wigley, T.B., Sweeney, S.W. & Sweeney, J.R. (1999). Habitat attributes and reproduction of Red-cockaded Woodpeckers in intensively managed forests. *Wildl. Soc. Bull.* **27(3)**: 801-809.
Wijesinghe, D.P. (1994). *Checklist of the Birds of Sri Lanka*. Ceylon Bird Club, Colombo.
Wiktander, U. (1998). *Reproduction and Survival in the Lesser Spotted Woodpecker: Effects of Life History, Mating System and Age*. PhD thesis, Lund University, Sweden.
Wiktander, U., Nilsson, I.N., Nilsson, S.G., Olsson, O., Pettersson, B. & Stagen, A. (1992). Occurrence of the Lesser Spotted Woodpecker *Dendrocopos minor* in relation to area of deciduous forest. *Ornis Fenn.* **69**: 113-118.
Wiktander, U., Nilsson, S.G., Olsson, O. & Stagen, A. (1994). Breeding success of a Lesser Spotted Woodpecker *Dendrocopos minor* population. *Ibis* **136(3)**: 318-322.
Wiktander, U., Olsson, O. & Nilsson, S.G. (2000). Parental care and social mating system in the Lesser Spotted Woodpecker *Dendrocopos minor*. *J. Avian Biol* **31**: 447-456.
Wiktander, U., Olsson, O. & Nilsson, S.G. (2001a). Age and reproduction in Lesser Spotted Woodpeckers (*Dendrocopos minor*). *Auk* **118(3)**: 624-635.
Wiktander, U., Olsson, O. & Nilsson, S.G. (2001b). Annual and seasonal reproductive trends in the Lesser Spotted Woodpecker *Dendrocopos minor*. *Ibis* **143(1)**: 72-82.
Wilbur, S.R. (1987). *Birds of Baja California*. University of California Press, Berkeley & Los Angeles, California.
Wiley, J.W. & Ottenwalder, J.A. (1990). Birds of Islas Beata and Alto Velo, Dominican Republic. *Stud. Neotrop. Fauna Environm.* **25**: 65-88.
Wilkins, H.D. (1996). *The Acoustic Signals of Male and Female Red-bellied Woodpeckers: Description and Causation*. MSc thesis, Eastern Kentucky University, Richmond, Kentucky.
Wilkins, H.D. & Ritchison, G. (1999). Drumming and tapping by Red-bellied Woodpeckers: description and possible causation. *J. Field Orn.* **70**: 578-586.
Wilkinson, R. & Beecroft, R. (1988). *Kagoro Forest Conservation Study*. ICBP Study Report **28**. ICBP & Nigerian Conservation Foundation, Cambridge.
Wilkinson, R. & McLeod, W. (1984). Breeding the Fire-tufted Barbet *Psilopogon pyrolophus* at Chester Zoo. *Avicult. Mag.* **90(4)**: 192-195.
Wilkinson, R. & McLeod, W. (1991). Breeding Channel-billed Toucans at Chester Zoo. *Avicult. Mag.* **97(4)**: 179-184.
Wilkinson, R., Dutson, G. & Sheldon, B. (1991). *The Avifauna of Barito Ulu, Central Borneo, with Additional Notes on the Mammals*. ICBP Study Report **48**, Cambridge.
Wilkinson, R., Dutson, G., Sheldon, B., Darjono & Noor, Y.R. (1991). The avifauna of the Barito Ulu region, central Kalimantan. *Kukila* **5(2)**: 99-116.
Wilkinson, R., Dutson, G., Sheldon, B., Noor, D. & Noor, Y.R. (1991). The avifauna of the Barito Ulu Region, central Kalimantan. *Kukila* **5(2)**: 99-116.
Willard, D.E., Foster, M.S., Barrowclough, G.F., Dickerman, R.W., Cannell, P.F., Coats, S.L., Cracraft, J.L. & O'Neill, J.P. (1991). *The Birds of Cerro de la Neblina, Territorio Federal Amazonas, Venezuela*. Fieldiana Zoology **65**. 80 pp.
Willeneger, L. & Ravussin, P.A. (1995). Une Nichée épeiche (*Dendrocopos major*) nourrie par des Mésanges huppées (*Parus cristatus*). *Nos Oiseaux* **43(3)**: 179-180.
Williams, E. (1997). Birding in the Usambara Mountains, Tanzania. *Bull. African Bird Club* **4(2)** 111-115.
Williams, J.B. (1975). Habitat utilization by four species of woodpeckers in a central Illinois woodland. *Amer. Midl. Nat.* **93(2)**: 354-366.
Williams, J.B. (1980a). Intersexual niche partitioning in Downy Woodpeckers. *Wilson Bull.* **92(4)**: 439-451.
Williams, J.B. (1980b). Foraging by Yellow-bellied Sapsucker in central Illinois during spring migration. *Wilson Bull.* **92(4)**: 519-523.
Williams, J.B. & Batzli, G.O. (1979a). Winter diet of a bark-foraging guild of birds. *Wilson Bull.* **91(1)**: 126-131.
Williams, J.B. & Batzli, G.O. (1979b). Interference competition and niche-shifts in the bark-foraging guild in central Illinois. *Wilson Bull.* **91(3)**: 400-411.
Williams, J.B. & Batzli, G.O. (1979c). Competition among bark-foraging birds in central Illinois: experimental evidence. *Condor* **81(2)**: 122-123.
Williams, J.G. (1951). The birds of Bwamba: some additions. *Uganda J.* **15**: 107-111.
Williams, J.G. (1966). A new race of *Lybius torquatus* from Tanzania. *Bull. Brit. Orn. Club* **86(3)**: 47-48.
Williams, J.G. & Friedmann, H. (1965). The Pygmy Honey-guide *Indicator pumilio* Chapin in East Africa. *Bull. Brit. Orn. Club* **85**: 21-22.
Williams, M.D. (1980). First description of the nest, eggs and nestlings of the Guayaquil Woodpecker (*Campephilus* [*Phloeoceastes gayaquilensis*]). *Wilson Bull.* **92(4)**: 506-508.
Williams, R.S.R. (1995). Neotropical Notebook. Brazil. *Cotinga* **4**: 66-67.
Williams, R.S.R. & Tobias, J.A. eds. (1994). *The Conservation of Southern Ecuador's Threatened Avifauna. Final Report of the Amaluza Projects, 1990-1991*. ICBP Study Report **60**, Cambridge.
Willimont, L.A. (1990). A case of competition between European Starlings and West Indian Woodpeckers on Abaco, Bahamas. *Florida Field Nat.* **18(1)**: 14-15.
Willimont, L.A., Jackson, J.A. & Jackson, B.J.S. (1991). Classical polyandry in the West Indian Woodpecker on Abaco, Bahamas. *Wilson Bull.* **103(1)**: 124-125.
Willis, E.O. (1976). Effects of a cold wave on an Amazonian avifauna in the upper Paraguay drainage, western Mato Grosso, and suggestions on oscine-suboscine relationships. *Acta Amazonica* **6**: 379-394.

Willis, E.O. (1980). Ecological roles of migratory and resident birds on Barro Colorado Island, Panama. Pp. 205-225 in: Keast, A. & Morton, E.S. eds. (1980). *Migrant Birds in the Neotropics: Ecology, Behavior, Distribution, and Conservation*. Smithsonian Institution Press, Washington, D.C.

Willis, E.O. (1982a). *Notharchus* puffbirds (Aves, Bucconidae) as army ant followers. *Ciênc. Cult.* **34(6)**: 777-782.

Willis, E.O. (1982b). Amazonian *Bucco* and *Monasa* (Bucconidae) as army ant followers. *Ciênc. Cult.* **34(6)**: 782-785.

Willis, E.O. (1982c). *Malacoptila* puffbirds (Aves, Bucconidae) as army ant followers. *Ciênc. Cult.* **34(7)**: 924-928.

Willis, E.O. (1983). Toucans (Ramphastidae) and hornbills (Bucerotidae) as ant followers. *Gerfaut* **73**: 239-242.

Willis, E.O. (1987). Redescoberta de *Dryocopus galeatus* (Temminck, 1822) (Aves, Picidae) no Estado de São Paulo. Page 835 in: *Resumos de XXXIX Reunião Anual SBPC*. Brasilia, DF.

Willis, E.O. (1989). Mimicry in bird flocks of cloud forests in southeastern Brazil. *Rev. Bras. Biol.* **49**: 615-619.

Willis, E.O. (1992). Zoogeographical origins of eastern Brazilian birds. *Orn. Neotropical* **3(1)**: 1-15.

Willis, E.O. & Eisenmann, E. (1979). A revised list of birds of Barro Colorado Island, Panama. *Smithsonian Contrib. Zool.* **291**: 1-31.

Willis, E.O. & Oniki, Y. (1990). Levantamento preliminar das aves de inverno em dez áreas do sudoeste de Mato Grosso, Brasil. [Preliminary survey of winter birds of ten localities in southwestern Mato Grosso, Brazil]. *Ararajuba* **1**: 19-38. In Portuguese with English summary.

Willis, E.O. & Oniki, Y. (1991). Avifaunal transects across the open zones of northern Minas Gerais, Brazil. *Ararajuba* **2**: 41-58.

Willis, E.O. & Oniki, Y. (1993). New and reconfirmed birds from the state of São Paulo, Brazil, with notes on disappearing species. *Bull. Brit. Orn. Club* **113(1)**: 23-34.

Willows, N. (1989). Nests in close proximity under artificial conditions. *Bee-eater* **40(3)**: 35.

Willson, M.F. (1970). Foraging behavior of some winter birds of deciduous woods. *Condor* **72(2)**: 169-174.

Wilson, M. & Rea, A.M. (1976). Late Pleistocene Williamson's Sapsucker from Wyoming. *Wilson Bull.* **89(4)**: 622.

Wilson, N. & Bull, E.L. (1977). Ectoparasites found in the nest cavities of Pileated Woodpeckers in Oregon. *Bird-Banding* **48(2)**: 171-173.

Wilson, N. & Wilson, G. (1992). Cardinal attacks Nubian in the Kerio. *Bull. East Afr. Nat. Hist. Soc.* **22(1)**: 9.

Wilson, N.F.T. (1898). The nesting of the Malabar Rufous Woodpecker *Micropternus gularis*. *J. Bombay Nat. Hist. Soc.* **11(4)**: 744-745.

Wilson, R.G. & Ceballos-Lascuráin, H. (1993). *The Birds of Mexico City. An Annotated Checklist and Bird-finding Guide to the Federal District*. BBC Printing & Graphics Ltd, Ontario.

Wingate, J. (1953). The nesting of a pair of Coppersmith Barbets. *Malay. Nat. J.* **8**: 32-34.

Winkel, W. (1992). Der Wendehals (*Jynx torquilla*) als Brutvogel in Nisthöhlen-Untersuchungsgebieten bei Braunschweig. *Beih. Veröff. Naturschutz Landschaftspflege Bad. -Württ.* **66**: 31-41.

Winker, K. (2000). A new subspecies of toucanet (*Aulacorhynchus prasinus*) from Veracruz, Mexico. *Orn. Neotropical* **11**: 253-257.

Winkler, H. (1968). Das Schmiedeverhalten des Blutspechtes (*Dendrocopos syriacus*). *Egretta* **10(2)**: 1-8.

Winkler, H. (1971a). Die artliche Isolation des Blutspechts *Picoides* (*Dendrocopos*) *syriacus*. *Egretta* **14**: 1-20.

Winkler, H. (1971b). Beobachtungen an Kleinspechten *Picoides* (*Dendrocopos*) *minor*. *Egretta* **14**: 21-24.

Winkler, H. (1972). Beiträge zur Ethologie des Blutspechts (*Dendrocopos syriacus*). Das nicht-reproduktive Verhalten. *Z. Tierpsychol.* **31**: 300-325.

Winkler, H. (1973). Nahrungserwerb und Konkurrenz des Blutspechts, *Picoides* (*Dendrocopos*) *syriacus*. [Food acquisition and competition of the Syrian Woodpecker, *Picoides syriacus*]. *Oecologia* **12(2)**: 193-208. In German with English summary.

Winkler, H. (1979a). Foraging ecology of Strickland's Woodpecker in Arizona. *Wilson Bull.* **91(2)**: 244-254.

Winkler, H. (1979b). Bemerkungen zum Maurenspecht, *Picoides major numidus*. [Remarks on *Picoides major numidus*]. *J. Orn.* **120(3)**: 290-298. In German with English summary.

Winkler, H. & Leisler, B. (1985). Morphological aspects of habitat selection in birds. Pp. 415-434 in: Cody, M.L. ed. (1985). *Habitat Selection in Birds*. Academic Press, New York.

Winkler, H. & Short, L.L. (1978). *A Comparative Analysis of Acoustical Signals in Pied Woodpeckers (Aves,* Picoides*)*. American Museum of Natural History **160(1)**. 111 pp.

Winkler, H., Christie, D.A. & Nurney, D. (1994). The colourful world of woodpeckers: an oriental perspective. *Bull. Oriental Bird Club* **19**: 30-33.

Winkler, H., Christie, D.A. & Nurney, D. (1995). *Woodpeckers. A Guide to the Woodpeckers, Piculets and Wrynecks of the World*. Pica Press, Nr. Robertsbridge, UK.

Winkler, H., Newton, A.V. & Newton, S.F. (1996). On the ecology and behaviour of the Arabian Woodpecker *Picoides dorae*. *Zool. Middle East* **12**: 33-45.

Winterbottom, J.M. (1969). Lesser Honeyguide *Indicator minor*: new distributional data: 2. *Ostrich* **40**: 131.

Winternitz, B.L. (1998). Ladder-backed Woodpecker. Pp. 258-259 in: Kingery, H.E. ed. (1998). *Colorado Breeding Bird Atlas*. Colorado Bird Atlas Partnership and Colorado Wildlife Division, Denver, Colorado.

Witt, K. (1988). Anhaltend extreme Brutdichte des Buntspechtes (*Dendrocopos major*) und bevorzugte Brutbaumwahl in einem Berliner Mischwaldpark. *Vogelwelt* **109**: 114-118.

Wolfe, L.R. (1950). Notes on the birds of Korea. *Auk* **67(4)**: 433-455.

Won Pyongoh (1963). The urgent problem of bird protection in Korea with special suggestions for habitat improvement and wildlife management. *Bull. ICBP* **9**: 121-129.

Won Pyongoh (1967). The present status of some threatened and rare birds in Korea, 1962-1966. *Bull. ICBP* **10**: 109-113.

Won Pyongoh (1993). [*A Field Guide to the Birds of Korea*]. Kyo-Hak Publishing Co. Ltd, Seoul. In Korean.

Won Pyongoh & Koo Taehoe (1986). [The reproductive success of the Grey-headed Green Woodpecker, *Picus canus griseoviridis* (Clark)]. *Bull. Inst. Orn., Kyung Hee Univ.* **1**: 57-67. In Korean with English summary.

Wong, M. (1984). Behavioural indication of an African origin for the Malaysian Honeyguide *Indicator archipelagicus*. *Bull. Brit. Orn. Club* **104(2)**: 57-60.

Wong, M. (1985). Understory birds as indicators of regeneration in a patch of selectively logged west Malaysian rainforest. Pp. 249-263 in: Diamond & Lovejoy (1985).

Wong, M. (1986). Trophic organization of understory birds in a Malaysian dipterocarp forest. *Auk* **103(1)**: 100-116.

Wong, M. (1989). The implications of germinating acorns in the granaries of Acorn Woodpeckers in Panama. *Condor* **91(3)**: 724-726.

Wood, D.A. (1977). *Status, Habitat, Home Range, and Notes on the Behavior of the Red-cockaded Woodpecker in Oklahoma*. MSc thesis, Oklahoma State University, Stillwater, Oklahoma.

Wood, D.A. (1983a). Foraging and colony habitat characteristics of the Red-cockaded Woodpecker in Oklahoma. Pp. 51-58 in: Wood (1983c).

Wood, D.A. (1983b). Observations on the behavior and breeding biology of the Red-cockaded Woodpecker in Oklahoma. Pp. 92-94 in: Wood (1983c).

Wood, D.A. ed. (1983c). *Proceedings of the 2nd Red-cockaded Woodpecker Symposium*. State of Florida Game & Fresh Water Fish Commission & US Fish & Wildlife Service, Tallahassee, Florida. 112 pp.

Wood, D.A. & Eichholz, N. (1986). Florida's endangered woodpeckers. *Florida Wildl.* **40(2)**: 20-23.

Wood, D.R., Burger, L., Wesley, J., Vilella, F.J. & Raulston, B.E. (2000). Long-term effects of Red-cockaded Woodpecker cavity-entrance restrictors. *Wildl. Soc. Bull.* **28(1)**: 105-109.

Wood, D.S. & Wood, D.L. (1973). Quantitative iris color change with age in Downy Woodpeckers. *Bird-Banding* **44(2)**: 100-101.

Wood, R.C. (1940). "Drumming" of the Black-throated Honeyguide (*Indicator indicator*). *Ostrich* **11**: 50-51.

Woodbury, C.J. (1998). Two spinal cords in birds: novel insights into early avian evolution. *Proc. Royal Soc. London* **265**: 1721-1729.

Woods, P.E. (1984). Woodpecker bills and their conformance to Hutchinsonian ratios. *Ohio J. Sci.* **84(5)**: 255-258.

Woolfenden, G.E. (1975). Dusting by a Red-bellied Woodpecker. *Florida Field Nat.* **3(2)**: 51.

Worth, C.B. (1938). Nesting of Salvin's Barbet. *Auk* **55(3)**: 535-536.

Wunderle, J.M. & Latta, S.C. (1996). Avian abundance in sun and shade coffee plantations and remnant pine forest in the Cordillera Central, Dominican Republic. *Orn. Neotropical* **7(1)**: 19-34.

Xu Weishu, Zhao Zhengkai, Zheng Guangmei, Yan Changwai & Tan Yaokuang (1996). *A Field Guide to the Birds of China*. Kingfisher Press, Taiwan.

Yaeger, M. (1994). First Colorado record of Acorn Woodpecker. *Colorado Field Orn. J.* **28(4)**: 141-144.

Yahya, H.S.A. (1980). *A Comparative Study of Ecology and Biology of Barbets,* Megalaima *spp. (Capitonidae: Piciformes) with Special Reference to* Megalaima viridis *(Boddaert) and* M. rubricapilla malabarica *(Blyth) at Periyar Tiger Reserve, Kerala*. PhD thesis, University of Bombay, Bombay.

Yahya, H.S.A. (1982). Observation on the feeding behaviour of barbets (*Megalaima* spp.) in coffee estates of South India. *J. Coffee Res.* **12**: 72-76.

Yahya, H.S.A. (1987). Roosting behaviour of barbets. Pp. 101-106 in: Balakrishnan, M. & Alexander, K.K. eds. (1987). *Recent Trends in Ethology in India*. Ethological Society of India, Bangalore, India.

Yahya, H.S.A. (1988). Breeding biology of barbets, *Megalaima* spp. (Capitonidae: Piciformes) at Periyar Tiger Preserve, Kerala. *J. Bombay Nat. Hist. Soc.* **85(3)**: 493-511.

Yahya, H.S.A. (1991). Drinking and bathing behaviour of the Large Green *Megalaima zeylanica* (Gmelin) and Small Green *M. viridis* (Boddaert) Barbets. *J. Bombay Nat. Hist. Soc.* **88**: 454-455.

Yahya, H.S.A. (2000). Food and feeding habits of Indian barbets. *J. Bombay Nat. Hist. Soc.* **97(1)**: 103-116.

Yamagami, N. (1992). [An observation of the Japanese Pygmy Woodpecker *Dendrocopos kizuki* and their helper]. *Strix* **11**: 336-338. In Japanese with English summary.

Yamashina, Y. (1941). On the three endemic birds in the Ryukyu Islands. *Trans. Bio-Geogr. Soc. Japan* **3**: 319-328.

Yamashita, C. & Lo, V.K. (1995). Ninhos cooperativos em *Melanerpes flavifrons* e *M. cactorum* (Piciformes: Picidae). *Ararajuba* **3**: 56-57.

Yamauchi, K., Yamazaki, S. & Fujimaki, Y. (1997). Breeding habitats of *Dendrocopos major* and *D. minor* in urban and rural areas. *Jap. J. Orn.* **46(2)**: 121-131.

Yates, E. (1975). Notes on a White-eared Barbet. *Avicult. Mag.* **81**: 197-199.

Yepez, A.F., Benedetti, F.L. & Phelps, W.H. (1940). Las aves de Margarita. *Bol. Soc. Venez. Cienc. Nat.* **43**: 91-132.

Yezerinac, S.M. (1999). Sex allocation in co-operatively breeding birds. Pp. 467-482 in: Adams & Slotow (1999).

Yoganand, K. & Davidar, P. (2000). Habitat preferences and distributional status of some forest birds in Andaman Islands. *J. Bombay Nat. Hist. Soc.* **97(3)**: 375-380.

Yom-Tov, Y. & Ar, A. (1993). Incubation and fledging durations of woodpeckers. *Condor* **95(2)**: 282-287.

Yoon Mooboo (1992). [*Wild Birds of Korea in Color*]. Kyo-Hak Publishing Co. Ltd, Seoul. In Korean.

Young, B.E., De Rosier, D. & Powell, G.V.N. (1998). Diversity and conservation of understory birds in the Tilarán Mountains, Costa Rica. *Auk* **115(4)**: 998-1016.

Young, H.G., Tonge, S.J. & Wilson, D. (1993). Wryneck on passage roosting in reeds. *British Birds* **86(1)**: 20.

Yunich, R.P. (1985). A review of recent irruptions of the Black-backed Woodpecker and Three-toed Woodpecker in eastern North America. *J. Field Orn.* **56(2)**: 138-152.

Yunich, R.P. (1988). An assessment of the Downy Woodpecker and Hairy Woodpecker on recent New York State Christmas counts. *Kingbird* **38(3)**: 146-158.

Zacharias, V.J. & Gaston, A.J. (1999). The recent distribution of endemic, disjunct and globally uncommon birds in the forests of Kerala State, south-west India. *Bird Conserv. Int.* **9(3)**: 191-225.

Zhao Zhengjie (1995). [*A Handbook of the Birds of China*]. Vol. 1. Non-passerines. Jilin Science & Technology Press, Changchun, China. In Chinese.

Zhou Shie, Sun Mingrong, Ge Qingje, Jin Huali & Sun Chuankai (1980). [Studies on the breeding ecology of the Grey-crowned Pygmy Woodpecker *Dendrocopos canicapillus*]. *Chinese J. Zool.* **3**: 33-35. In Chinese.

van Zijl, G. (1994). Lesser Honeyguide. *Promerops* **212**: 11.

Zimmer, J.T. (1930). *Birds of the Marshall Field Peruvian Expedition, 1922-1923*. Publications of the Field Museum of Natural History (Zoological Series) **282, pt. 17(7)**. 480 pp.

Zimmer, J.T. (1931). Studies of Peruvian birds. 1. New and other birds from Peru, Ecuador and Brazil. *Amer. Mus. Novit.* **500**: 1-23.

Zimmer, J.T. (1942). Studies of Peruvian birds 40. Notes on the genus *Veniliornis*. *Amer. Mus. Novit.* **1159**: 1-12.

Zimmer, J.T. & Mayr, E. (1943). New species of birds described from 1938 to 1941. *Auk* **60(2)**: 249-262.

Zimmer, J.T. & Phelps, W.H. (1944). New species and subspecies of birds from Venezuela. Part 1. *Amer. Mus. Novit.* **1270**: 1-16.

Zimmer, J.T. & Phelps, W.H. (1947). Seven new subspecies of birds from Venezuela and Brazil. *Amer. Mus. Novit.* **1338**: 1-7.

Zimmer, K.J. & Hilty, S.L. (1997). Avifauna of a locality in the upper Orinoco drainage of Amazonas, Venezuela. Pp. 865-885 in: Remsen (1997).

Zimmer, K.J., Parker, D.A., Isler, M.L. & Isler, P.R. (1997). Survey of a southern Amazonian avifauna: the Alta Floresta region, Mato Grosso, Brazil. Pp. 887-918 in: Remsen (1997).

Zimmerman, D.A. (1967). *Agapornis fischeri*, *Lybius guifsobalito*, and *Stiphrornis erythrothorax* in Kenya. *Auk* **84(4)**: 594-595.

Zimmerman, D.A. (1972). *The Avifauna of the Kakamega Forest, Western Kenya, Including a Bird Population Study*. Bulletin of the American Museum of Natural History **149(3)**, New York. 83 pp.

Zimmerman, D.A., Turner, D.A. & Pearson, D.J. (1996). *Birds of Kenya and Northern Tanzania*. Christopher Helm, London.

Zink, R.M., Rohwer, S., Andreev, A.V. & Dittmann, D.L. (1995). Trans-Beringia comparisons of mitochondrial DNA differentiation in birds. *Condor* **97(3)**: 639-649.

Zinner, D. (2001). Ornithological notes from a primate survey in Eritrea. *Bull. African Bird Club* **8(2)**: 95-106.

Zusi, R.L. & Marshall, J.T. (1970). A comparison of Asiatic and North American sapsuckers. *Natur. Hist. Bull. Siam Soc.* **23**: 393-407.

Zwartjes, P.W. & Nordell, S.E. (1998). Patterns of cavity-entrance orientation by Gilded Flickers (*Colaptes chrysoides*) in cardón cactus. *Auk* **115(1)**: 119-126.

Zwicker, S.M. (1995). *Selection of Pines for Foraging and Cavity Excavation by Red-cockaded Woodpeckers*. MSc thesis, North Carolina State University, Raleigh, North Carolina.

Zwicker, S.M. & Walters, J.R. (1999). Selection of pines for foraging by Red-cockaded Woodpeckers. *J. Wildl. Manage.* **63(3)**: 843-852.

van Zyl, A.J. (1987). Crested Barbet trapping techniques. *Safring News* **16(1)**: 25-28.

van Zyl, A.J. (1989). Crested Barbet eats dove egg. *Laniarius* **38**: 6.

van Zyl, A.J. (1994). The influence of the environment on breeding success of a suburban population of Crested Barbets *Trachyphonus vaillantii*. *Ostrich* **65**: 291-296.

INDEX

INDEX